Volkswagen Jetta, Golf, GTI

1999, 2000, 2001, 2002

Service Manual

2.0L gasoline, 1.9L TDI diesel, 2.8L VR6, 1.8L turbo

A4 Platform

RB

Bentley Publishers
Cambridge, Massachusetts

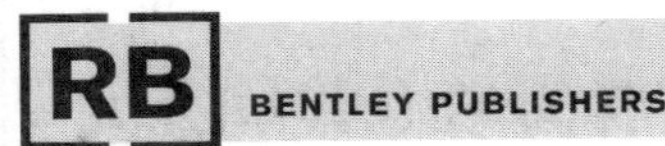

Bentley Publishers, a division of Robert Bentley, Inc.
1734 Massachusetts Avenue
Cambridge, MA 02138 USA
800-423-4595 / 617-547-4170
www.
BentleyPublishers
.com

Information that makes the difference®

Technical Contact Information

We value your feedback. Technical comments and suggestions are helpful to us. Please send your comments and thoughts to Bentley Publishers e-mail:
tech@BentleyPublishers.com

From time to time, updates may be made to this manual. A listing of updates can be found on the web at:
www.BentleyPublishers.com/updates

WARNING—Important Safety Notice

Do not use this manual unless you are familiar with basic automotive repair procedures and safe workshop practices. This manual illustrates the workshop procedures required for most service work; it is not a substitute for full and up-to-date information from the vehicle manufacturer or for proper training as an automotive technician. Note that it is not possible for us to anticipate all of the ways or conditions under which vehicles may be serviced or to provide cautions as to all of the possible hazards that may result.

The vehicle manufacturer will continue to issue service information updates and parts retrofits after the editorial closing of this manual. Some of these updates and retrofits will apply to procedures and specifications in this manual. We regret that we cannot supply updates to purchasers of this manual.

We have endeavored to ensure the accuracy of the information in this manual. Please note, however, that considering the vast quantity and the complexity of the service information involved, we cannot warrant the accuracy or completeness of the information contained in this manual.

FOR THESE REASONS, NEITHER THE PUBLISHER NOR THE AUTHOR MAKES ANY WARRANTIES, EXPRESS OR IMPLIED, THAT THE INFORMATION IN THIS BOOK IS FREE OF ERRORS OR OMISSIONS AND WE EXPRESSLY DISCLAIM THE IMPLIED WARRANTIES OF MERCHANTABILITY AND OF FITNESS FOR A PARTICULAR PURPOSE, EVEN IF THE PUBLISHER OR AUTHOR HAVE BEEN ADVISED OF A PARTICULAR PURPOSE, AND EVEN IF A PARTICULAR PURPOSE IS INDICATED IN THE MANUAL. THE PUBLISHER AND AUTHOR ALSO DISCLAIM ALL LIABILITY FOR DIRECT, INDIRECT, INCIDENTAL OR CONSEQUENTIAL DAMAGES THAT RESULT FROM ANY USE OF THE EXAMPLES, INSTRUCTIONS OR OTHER INFORMATION IN THIS BOOK. IN NO EVENT SHALL OUR LIABILITY WHETHER IN TORT, CONTRACT OR OTHERWISE EXCEED THE COST OF THIS MANUAL.

Your common sense and good judgment are crucial to safe and successful service work. Read procedures through before starting them. Think about whether the condition of your car, your level of mechanical skill, or your level of reading comprehension might result in or contribute in some way to an occurrence which might cause you injury, damage your car, or result in an unsafe repair. If you have doubts for these or other reasons about your ability to perform safe repair work on your car, have the work done at an authorized Volkswagen dealer or other qualified shop.

Part numbers listed in this manual are for identification purposes only, not for ordering. Always check with your authorized Volkswagen dealer to verify part numbers and availability before beginning service work that may require new parts.

Before attempting any work on your Volkswagen, read the warnings and cautions on page vii, and any warning or caution that accompanies a procedure in the service manual. Review the warnings and cautions on page vii each time you prepare to work on your Volkswagen.

Special tools required to perform certain service operations are identified in the manual and are recommended for use. Use of tools other than those recommended in this service manual may be detrimental to the car's safe operation as well as the safety of the person servicing the car.

Copies of this manual may be purchased from authorized Volkswagen dealers, from selected booksellers and automotive accessories and parts dealers, or directly from the publisher by mail.

The publisher encourages comments from the reader of this manual. These communications have been and will be considered in the preparation of this and other manuals. Please write to Robert Bentley, Inc., Publishers at the address listed below.

This manual was prepared, published and distributed by Robert Bentley, Inc., 1734 Massachusetts Avenue, Cambridge, MA 02138. All information in this Manual is based on the latest product information available from Volkswagen at the time of the editorial closing date. Volkswagen has not reviewed and does not vouch for the accuracy or completeness of the technical specifications and work procedures described and given.

Library of Congress Cataloging-in-Publication Data

Volkswagen Jetta, Golf, GTI: 1999, 2000, 2001, 2002 : service manual, 2.0L gasoline,
1.9L TDI diesel, 2.8L VR6, 1.8L turbo : A4 platform
p. cm.
Includes index.
ISBN 0-8376-0388-9 (alk. paper)
1. Jetta automobile--Maintenance and repair--Handbooks, manuals, etc. 2. Golf automobile--Maintenance and repair--Handbooks, manuals, etc. 3. GTI automobile--Maintenance and repair--Handbooks, manuals, etc. I. Robert Bentley, inc.

TL215.J49 V6498 2001
629.28'722--dc21 00-067504

VWoA Inc. Part No. LPV 800 118
Bentley Stock No. VG02

Editorial closing 03/22/01

03 02 01 5 4 3 2 1

The paper used in this publication is acid free and meets the requirements of the National Standard for Information Sciences-Permanence of Paper for Printed Library Materials. ∞

Manufactured in the United States of America

Selected Books and Electronic Editions From Bentley Publishers

Volkswagen

Battle for the Beetle: The Story of the Battle for the Giant VW Factory and the Car that Became an Icon Around the Globe
Karl Ludvigsen ISBN 08376-0071-5

Volkswagen Model Documentation
Joachim Kuch ISBN 0-8376-0078-2

Volkswagen Sport Tuning for Street and Competition
Per Schroeder ISBN 0-8376-0161-4

Volkswagen Beetle: Portrait of a Legend
Edwin Baaske ISBN 0-8376-0162-2

Small Wonder: The Amazing Story of the Volkswagen Beetle
Walter Henry Nelson ISBN 0-8376-0147-9

Jetta, Golf, GTI Service Manual: 1999-2002 2.0L Gasoline, 1.9L TDI Diesel, 2.8L VR6, 1.8L Turbo
Bentley Publishers ISBN 0-8376-0388-9
Volkswagen Part No. LPV 800 118

Jetta, Golf, GTI Official Factory Repair Manual: 1999-2000 2.0L Gasoline, 1.9L TDI Diesel, 2.8L VR6, 1.8L Turbo Electronic Edition CD-ROM
Bentley Publishers ISBN 0-8376-0765-5
VWoA Lit No.: W42 CD-ROM VW A4 00.05

Passat Official Factory Repair Manual 1998-2000 Electronic Edition CD-ROM
Bentley Publishers ISBN 0-8376-0763-9
VWoA Lit No.: W42 CD-ROM VW B5 00.01

New Beetle Official Factory Repair Manual 1998-2000 Electronic Edition CD-ROM
Bentley Publishers ISBN 0-8376-0760-4
VWoA Lit No.: W42 CD-ROM VW NB 99.10

New Beetle Service Manual: 1998-1999 2.0L Gasoline, 1.9L TDI Diesel, 1.8L Turbo
Bentley Publishers ISBN 0-8376-0385-4
Volkswagen Part No. LPV 800 401

Jetta, Golf, GTI, Cabrio Service Manual: 1993–1999, including Jetta$_{III}$ and Golf$_{III}$
Bentley Publishers ISBN 0-8376-0366-8
Volkswagen Part No. LPV 800 116

Eurovan Official Factory Repair Manual: 1992-1999 *Volkswagen of America*
ISBN 0-8376-0335-8
Volkswagen Part No. LPV 800 149

Passat Official Factory Repair Manual 1995-1997 *Volkswagen of America*
ISBN 0-8376-0380-3
Volkswagen Part No. LPV 800 207

Passat Official Factory Repair Manual 1995-1997 Electronic Edition CD-ROM
Bentley Publishers ISBN 0-8376-0762-0
VWoA Lit No.: W42 CD-ROM VW B4 00.01

GTI/Golf/Jetta Service Manual: 1985–1992 Gasoline, Diesel, and Turbo Diesel, including 16V
Bentley Publishers ISBN 0-8376-0342-0
Volkswagen Part No. LPV 800 112

Corrado Official Factory Repair Manual: 1990–1994 *Volkswagen United States*
ISBN 0-8376-0387-0
Volkswagen Part No. LPV 800 300

Corrado Official Factory Repair Manual: 1990–1994 Electronic Edition CD-ROM
Bentley Publishers ISBN 0-8376-0766-3
VWoA Lit No.: W42 CD-ROM VW CR 93.10

Passat Service Official Factory Repair Manual: 1990-1994, 4-cylinder (16V, G60, and diesel), 6-cylinder (VR6) including Wagon and Syncro Electronic Edition CD-ROM *Bentley Publishers* ISBN 0-8376-0768-X
VWoA Lit No.: W42 CD-ROM VWB3 96.01

Passat Service Manual 1990-1993, including GL and Wagon
Bentley Publishers ISBN 0-8376-0378-1
Volkswagen Part No. LPV 800 205

Cabriolet and Scirocco Service Manual: 1985–1993, including 16V
Bentley Publishers ISBN 0-8376-0362-5
Volkswagen Part No. LPV 800 113

Fox Service Manual 1987-1993
Bentley Publishers ISBN 0-8376-0363-3
Volkswagen Part No. LPV 800 504

Vanagon Official Factory Repair Manual: 1980–1991 including Diesel, Syncro, and Camper *Volkswagen of America*
ISBN 0-8376-0336-6
Volkswagen Part No. LPV 800 148

Rabbit, Scirocco, Jetta Service Manual: 1980-1984 Gasoline Models, Including Pickup Truck, Convertible, and GTI
Bentley Publishers ISBN 0-8376-0183-5
Volkswagen Part No. LPV 800 104

Rabbit, Jetta Service Manual: 1977-1984 Diesel Models, Including Pickup Truck and Turbo Diesel
Bentley Publishers ISBN 0-8376-0184-3
Volkswagen Part No. LPV 800 122

Super Beetle, Beetle and Karmann Ghia Official Service Manual Type 1: 1970–1979
Volkswagen of America ISBN 0-8376-0096-0
Volkswagen Part No. LPV 997 109

Station Wagon/Bus Official Service Manual Type 2: 1968–1979 *Volkswagen of America* ISBN 0-8376-0094-4
Volkswagen Part No. LPV 997 288

Fastback and Squareback Official Service Manual Type 3: 1968–1973
Volkswagen of America ISBN 0-8376-0057-X
Volkswagen Part No. LPV 997 383

Beetle and Karmann Ghia Official Service Manual Type 1: 1966–1969
Volkswagen United States ISBN 0-8376-0416-8
Volkswagen Part No. LPV 997 169

Transporter Workshop Manual: 1963-1967, Type 2, including Kombi, Micro Bus, Micro Bus Deluxe, Pickup, Delivery Van, and Ambulance
Volkswagen of America ISBN 0-8376-0391-9
Volkswagen Part No. LPV 800 135

1200 Workshop Manual: 1961-1965, Type 11, 14 and 15, Beetle, Beetle Convertible, Karmann Ghia Coupe, and Karmann Ghia Convertible
Volkswagen of America ISBN 0-8376-0390-0
Volkswagen Part No. LPV 800 121

Workshop Manual: Types 11, 14, and 15 (Beetle & Karmann Ghia): 1958-1960
Volkswagen of America ISBN 0-8376-0392-7
Volkswagen Part No. LPV 800 137

Workshop Manual: Types 11, 14, and 15 (Beetle & Karmann Ghia): 1952-1957
Volkswagen of America ISBN 0-8376-0389-7
Volkswagen Part No. LPV 800 136

Audi

Audi: A History of Progress Chronicle of Audi AG
Audi AG ISBN 0-8376-0384-6

Audi A4/S4 Official Factory Repair Manual 1996-2000 Electronic Edition CD-ROM
Bentley Publishers ISBN 0-8376-0761-2
Audi of America Lit. No.: W42 CD-ROM AUB5 99.12

Audi TT Official Factory Repair Manual MY 2000 Electronic Edition CD-ROM
Audi of America ISBN 0-8376-0758-2
Audi of America Lit. No.: W42 AUDI TT CD-ROM 9.99

Audi 100, A6 Official Factory Repair Manual: 1992–1997, including S4, S6, Quattro and Wagon models *Audi of America*
ISBN 0-8376-0374-9
Audi Part No. LPV 800 702

Audi 80, 90, Coupe Quattro Official Factory Repair Manual: 1988–1992 Electronic Edition CD-ROM
Audi of America ISBN 0-8376-0367-6
Audi of America Lit. No.: W42 CD-ROM AU 80 96.12

Audi 100, 200 Official Factory Repair Manual: 1989-1991, including 100 Quattro, 200 Quattro, Wagon, Turbo and 20-valve
Audi of America ISBN 0-8376-0372-2
Audi Part No. LPV 800 701

Audi 5000S, 5000CS Official Factory Repair Manual: 1984-1988, Gasoline, Turbo, and Turbo Diesel, including Wagon and Quattro
Audi of America ISBN 0-8376-0370-6
Audi Part No. LPV 800 445

Audi 4000S, 4000CS, and Coupe GT Official Factory Repair Manual: 1984-1987, including Quattro and Quattro Turbo
Audi of America ISBN 0-8376-0373-0
Audi Part No. LPV 800 424

Engineering

Bosch Fuel Injection and Engine Management *Charles O. Probst, SAE*
ISBN 0-8376-0300-5

Maximum Boost: Designing, Testing, and Installing Turbocharger Systems
Corky Bell ISBN 0-8376-0160-6

Race Car Aerodynamics *Joseph Katz*
ISBN 0-8376-0142-8

The Scientific Design of Exhaust and Intake Systems
Philip H. Smith and John C. Morrison
ISBN 0-8376-0309-9

www.BentleyPublishers.com

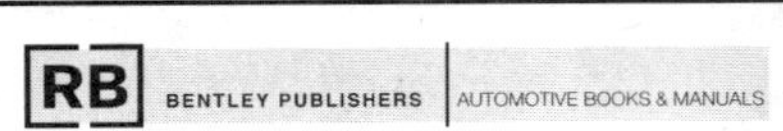

Bentley Publishers has published service manuals and automobile books since 1950. Please write Bentley Publishers at 1734 Massachusetts Avenue, Cambridge, MA 02138, visit our web site at www.BentleyPublishers.com, or call 1-800-423-4595 for a free copy of our complete catalog.

Foreword

Service to Volkswagen owners is a top priority of the Volkswagen organization and has always included the continuing development and introduction of new and expanded services. In line with this purpose, Robert Bentley, Inc., in cooperation with Volkswagen of America, Inc., has introduced this Volkswagen Jetta, Golf, GTI Service Manual.

This manual covers Volkswagen Jettas, Golfs, and GTIs for the model years 1999 through 2002. This manual was created specifically to cover only those models built for sale in the United States and Canada.

For the Volkswagen owner with basic mechanical skills and for independent auto service professionals, this manual includes the specifications and procedures that were available in an authorized Volkswagen dealer service department as this manual went to press. The Volkswagen owner with no intention of working on his or her car will find that owning and referring to this manual will make it possible to be better informed and to more knowledgeably discuss repairs with a professional automotive technician. The aim throughout has been clarity and completeness, with step-by-step procedures and accurate specifications.

The Volkswagen owner intending to do maintenance and repair should have screwdrivers, a set of metric wrenches and sockets, and metric hex wrenches, since these basic hand tools are needed for most of the work described in this manual. Most procedures will also require a torque wrench to ensure that fasteners are tightened properly and in accordance with specifications. In some cases, the text refers to special tools that are recommended or required to accomplish adjustments or repairs. These tools are identified by their Volkswagen special tool number and illustrated. A thorough pre-reading of each procedure is recommended to determine in advance the need for particular tools and for essential replacement parts such as gaskets.

Some of the information in this manual applies only to cars of a particular model year or range of years. For example, "1999 m.y." refers to the 1999 model year. The model year does not necessarily match the calendar year in which the car was manufactured or sold. To be sure of the model year of a particular car, check the vehicle identification number (VIN) on the car. Technical changes made in production within a model year are identified in this manual by listing the VIN for the first car produced with this change.

The VIN is a unique sequence of 17 characters assigned by Volkswagen to identify each individual car. WVWDE21JXYW671801 is an example. Each of the 17 letters and numbers indicates certain facts about the car and its manufacture. VINs used to distinguish information in this manual may refer only to the last eleven digits—the characters 1JXYW671801 in the example above.

Your Volkswagen's VIN can be found on a plate mounted on the top of the instrument panel, on the driver's side where the number can be seen through the windshield. The 10th character is the model year code. The letters "I", "O", "Q" and "U" are not used for model year designation, for example, "X" for 1999 m.y., "Y" for 2000 m.y., "1" for 2001, "2" for 2002 m.y., etc. This manual covers Volkswagen Jettas, Golfs, and GTIs for the model years 1999 through 2002. The table below explains some of the various codes in the VIN numbers of models covered by this manual.

W V W	D	E	2	1 J	X	Y	W	1 2 3 4 5 6
Manufacturer Information	Body	Engine Type	Restraint Type	Body Type	Check Digit	Model Year	Factory	Sequential Chassis No.
3VW-Mexican Passenger car WVW-German passenger car 9BW-Brazilian passenger car	Depends on model year		Depends on type of air-bags and seatbelts	1J-Golf/GTI 9M-Jetta	0-9 or X	X-1999 Y-2000 1-2001 2-2002	M- Puebla, Mexico W- Wolfsburg, E- Emden, H- Hanover, M- Mosel, Germany 4- Curitiba, Brazil	000001-Begin production 999999-End production

We have endeavored to insure the accuracy of the information in this manual. When the vast array of data presented in the manual is taken into account, however, no claim to infallibility can be made. We therefore cannot be responsible for the result of any errors that may have crept into the text. The publisher encourages comments from the readers of this manual with regard to errors, and also, suggestions for improvement in the presentation of the technical material. These communications have been and will be carefully considered in the preparation of this and other manuals. Please write or e-mail to Robert Bentley, Inc., at the address at the beginning of this manual.

Volkswagen offers extensive warranties, especially on components of the fuel delivery and emission control systems. Therefore, before deciding to repair a Volkswagen that may be covered wholly or in part by any warranties issued by Volkswagen of America, Inc., consult your authorized Volkswagen dealer. You may find that the dealer can make the repair either free or at minimum cost. Regardless of its age, or whether it is under warranty, your Volkswagen is both an easy car to service and an easy car to get serviced. So if at any time a repair is needed that you feel is too difficult to do yourself, a trained Volkswagen technician is ready to do the job for you.

Please read these warnings and cautions before proceeding with maintenance and repair work.

WARNING—

- Some repairs may be beyond your capability. If you lack the skills, tools and equipment, or a suitable workplace for any procedure described in this manual, we suggest you leave such repairs to an authorized Volkswagen dealer service department, or other qualified shop.

- Volkswagen is constantly improving its cars. Sometimes these changes, both in parts and specifications, are made applicable to earlier models. Therefore, before starting any major jobs or repairs to components on which passenger safety may depend, consult your authorized Volkswagen dealer about Technical Bulletins that may have been issued since the editorial closing of this manual.

- Do not re-use any fasteners that are worn or deformed in normal use. Many fasteners are designed to be used only once and become unreliable and may fail when used a second time. This includes, but is not limited to, nuts, bolts, washers, self-locking nuts or bolts, circlips and cotter pins. Always replace these fasteners with new parts.

- Never work under a lifted car unless it is solidly supported on stands designed for the purpose. Do not support a car on cinder blocks, hollow tiles or other props that may crumble under continuous load. Never work under a car that is supported solely by a jack. Never work under the car while the engine is running.

- If you are going to work under a car on the ground, make sure that the ground is level. Block the wheels to keep the car from rolling. Disconnect the battery negative (–) terminal (Ground strap) to prevent others from starting the car while you are under it.

- Never run the engine unless the work area is well ventilated. Carbon monoxide kills.

- Finger rings, bracelets and other jewelry should be removed so that they cannot cause electrical shorts, get caught in running machinery, or be crushed by heavy parts.

- Tie long hair behind your head. Do not wear a necktie, a scarf, loose clothing, or a necklace when you work near machine tools or running engines. If your hair, clothing, or jewelry were to get caught in the machinery, severe injury could result.

- Do not attempt to work on your car if you do not feel well. You increase the danger of injury to yourself and others if you are tired, upset or have taken medication or any other substance that may keep you from being fully alert.

- Illuminate your work area adequately but safely. Use a portable safety light for working inside or under the car. Make sure the bulb is enclosed by a wire cage. The hot filament of an accidentally broken bulb can ignite spilled fuel or oil.

- Catch draining fuel, oil, or brake fluid in suitable containers. Do not use food or beverage containers that might mislead someone into drinking from them. Store flammable fluids away from fire hazards. Wipe up spills at once, but do not store the oily rags, which can ignite and burn spontaneously.

- Always observe good workshop practices. Wear goggles when you operate machine tools or work with battery acid. Gloves or other protective clothing should be worn whenever the job requires working with harmful substances.

- Friction materials such as brake or clutch discs may contain asbestos fibers. Do not create dust by grinding, sanding, or by cleaning with compressed air. Avoid breathing asbestos fibers and asbestos dust. Breathing asbestos can cause serious diseases such as asbestosis or cancer, and may result in death.

- Disconnect the battery negative (–) terminal (ground strap) whenever you work on the fuel system or the electrical system. Do not smoke or work near heaters or other fire hazards. Keep an approved fire extinguisher handy.

- Batteries give off explosive hydrogen gas during charging. Keep sparks, lighted matches and open flame away from the top of the battery. If hydrogen gas escaping from the cap vents is ignited, it will ignite gas trapped in the cells and cause the battery to explode.

- Connect and disconnect battery cables, jumper cables or a battery charger only with the ignition switched off, to prevent sparks. Do not disconnect the battery while the engine is running.

- Do not quick-charge the battery (for boost starting) for longer than one minute. Wait at least one minute before boosting the battery a second time.

- Do not allow battery charging voltage to exceed 16.5 volts. If the battery begins producing gas or boiling violently, reduce the charging rate. Boosting a sulfated battery at a high charging rate can cause an explosion.

- The air-conditioning system is filled with chemical refrigerant, which is hazardous. The A/C system should be serviced only by trained technicians using approved refrigerant recovery/recycling equipment, trained in related safety precautions, and familiar with regulations governing the discharging and disposal of automotive chemical refrigerants.

- Do not expose any part of the A/C system to high temperatures such as open flame. Excessive heat will increase system pressure and may cause the system to burst.

- Some aerosol tire inflators are highly flammable. Be extremely cautious when repairing a tire that may have been inflated using an aerosol tire inflator. Keep sparks, open flame or other sources of ignition away from the tire repair area. Inflate and deflate the tire at least four times before breaking the bead from the rim. Completely remove the tire from the rim before attempting any repair.

- Most cars covered by this manual are equipped with a supplemental restraint system (SRS), that automatically deploys an airbag in the event of a frontal impact. The airbag is inflated by an explosive device. Handled improperly or without adequate safeguards, it can be accidently activated and cause serious injury.

- To prevent personal injury or airbag system failure, **only factory trained Volkswagen service technicians** should test, disassemble or service the airbag system.

- Disconnect the power supply before working on the airbag system, or when doing repairs that require removing airbag system components. Disconnect the battery negative (–) terminal and cover the battery.

continued on next page

Please read these warnings and cautions before proceeding with maintenance and repair work.

WARNING (continued) —

- On airbag-equipped cars, never apply stickers or any other type of covering on the steering wheel. Do not let chemical cleaners, oil or grease come into contact with vinyl covering of the airbag unit.

- Never open or otherwise attempt to repair airbag system parts. Always use new parts. Never leave airbag parts or the partially disassembled airbag system unattended.

- Never use a test light to conduct electrical tests on the airbag system. The system must only be tested by trained Volkswagen Service technicians using the Volkswagen VAG 1551/1552 Scan Tool (ST) or an approved equivalent. The airbag unit must never be electrically tested while it is not installed in the car.

- Do not expose the airbag unit to temperatures above 194°F (90°C), even for brief periods. Keep clear of heat sources such as hot plates, soldering irons, heat lamps and welding equipment.

- When driving or riding in an airbag-equipped vehicle, never hold test equipment in your hands or lap while the vehicle is in motion. Objects between you and the airbag can increase the risk of injury in an accident.

- Greases, lubricants and other automotive chemicals contain toxic substances, many of which are absorbed directly through the skin. Read manufacturer's instructions and warnings carefully. Use hand and eye protection. Avoid direct skin contact.

CAUTION—

- If you lack the skills, tools and equipment, or a suitable workshop for any procedure described in this manual, we suggest you leave such repairs to an authorized Volkswagen dealer or other qualified shop. We especially urge you to consult an authorized Volkswagen dealer before beginning repairs on any car that may still be covered wholly or in part by any of the extensive warranties issued by Volkswagen of America.

- Volkswagen offers extensive warranties, especially on components of fuel delivery and emission control systems. Therefore, before deciding to repair a Volkswagen that may still be covered wholly or in part by any warranties issued by Volkswagen United States, Inc., consult your authorized Volkswagen dealer. You may find that he can make the repair for free, or at minimal cost.

- Volkswagen part numbers listed in this manual are for identification purposes only, not for ordering. Always check with your authorized Volkswagen dealer to verify part numbers and availability before beginning service work that may require new parts.

- Before starting a job, make certain that you have all the necessary tools and parts on hand. Read all the instructions thoroughly, do not attempt shortcuts. Use tools appropriate to the work and use only replacement parts meeting Volkswagen specifications. Makeshift tools, parts and procedures will not make good repairs.

- Use pneumatic and electric tools only to loosen threaded parts and fasteners. Never use these tools to tighten fasteners, especially on light alloy parts. Always use a torque wrench to tighten fasteners to the tightening torque specification listed.

- Be mindful of the environment and ecology. Before you drain the crankcase, find out the proper way to dispose of the oil. Do not pour oil onto the ground, down a drain, or into a stream, pond or lake. Consult local ordinances that govern the disposal of wastes.

- On cars equipped with anti-theft radios, make sure you know the correct radio activation code before disconnecting the battery or removing the radio. If the wrong code is entered into the radio when power is restored, that radio may lock up and be rendered inoperable, even if the correct code is then entered.

- Connect and disconnect a battery charger only with the battery charger switched off.

- Do not quick-charge the battery (for boost starting) for longer than one minute. Wait at least one minute before boosting the battery a second time.

- Sealed or "maintenance free" batteries should be slow-charged only, at an amperage rate that is approximately 10% of the battery's ampere-hour (Ah) rating.

- Do not allow battery charging voltage to exceed 16.5 volts. If the battery begins producing gas or boiling violently, reduce the charging rate. Boosting a sulfated battery at a high charging rate can cause an explosion.

0 Maintenance

TABLES

GENERAL

All of the maintenance work described in this repair group is important and should be carried out at the specified time or mileage interval. The Owner's Manual, the Maintenance Record, and the Warranty Booklet originally supplied with the car contain the maintenance schedules that apply to your Volkswagen. Following these schedules will ensure safe and dependable operation. In addition, many of the maintenance procedures are necessary to maintain warranty protection.

> ***NOTE —***
> *Volkswagen is constantly updating their recommended maintenance procedures and requirements. The information contained here may not include updates or revisions made by Volkswagen since publication of the Owner's Manual, the Maintenance Record, and the Warranty Booklet supplied with the car. If there is any doubt about what procedures apply to a specific model or model year, or what intervals should be followed, remember that an authorized Volkswagen dealer has the latest maintenance information.*

> ***CAUTION —***
> *Disconnecting the negative (–) battery cable may erase fault codes and basic settings in the engine management and automatic transmission control modules. Some driveability problems may be noticed until the system re-adapts to operating conditions. OBD II readiness codes, which may be required for emissions testing, may also be erased. Convenience electronics (alarm system, interior light control, power locks, mirrors, and windows) may need to be re-set using a VAG 1551/1552 or equivalent scan tool.*

HOW TO USE THIS MANUAL

The manual is divided into 10 main sections, or partitions:

0 Maintenance
1 Engine
2 Engine Management, Exhaust, and Engine Electrical
3 Clutch, Transmission, and Final Drive
4 Suspension, Brakes, and Steering
5 Body–Assembly
6 Body–Components and Accessories
7 Body–Interior Trim
8 Heating and Air Conditioning
9 Electrical System

0 Maintenance covers the recommended schedules and service procedures needed to do the Volkswagen-specified scheduled maintenance work.

The remaining nine partitions (1 through 9) are repair oriented and are broken down into individual repair groups. Some main partitions begin with a general information group, e.g. **1 General Information.** These general groups are mostly descriptive in nature, covering topics such as theory of operation and troubleshooting. The remainder of the repair groups contain the more involved and more detailed system repair information.

A master listing of the 10 partitions and the corresponding individual repair groups can be found on the inside front cover.

At the end of the manual is a table that describes many of the various Diagnostic Trouble Codes (DTCs) that can be retrieved using a Volkswagen VAG 1551/1552 scan tool or VAS 5051 diagnostic tool. This table also lists the various scan tool codes for generic aftermarket scan tools (P-codes).

Thumb tabs are used on the first page of each repair group page to help locate the groups quickly. Page numbers throughout the manual are organized according to the repair group system. For example, you can expect to find information on engine removal and installation (Repair Group 10) beginning on page 10-1. A comprehensive index can be found on the last pages of the manual.

Warnings, Cautions and Notes

Throughout this manual are many passages with the headings **WARNING**, **CAUTION**, or **NOTE**. These very important headings have different meanings.

> ***WARNING —***
> *The text under this heading warns of unsafe practices that are very likely to cause injury, either by direct threat to the person(s) doing the work or by increased risk of accident or mechanical failure while driving. Warnings are always contained in a box.*

> ***CAUTION —***
> *A caution calls attention to important precautions to be observed during the repair work that will help prevent accidentally damaging the car or its parts. Cautions are always contained in a box.*

> ***NOTE —***
> *A note contains helpful information, tips that will help in doing a better job and completing it more easily.*

Please read every **WARNING**, **CAUTION**, and **NOTE** at the front of the manual and as they appear in repair procedures. They are very important. Read them before you begin any maintenance or repair job.

Some **WARNING**s and **CAUTION**s are repeated wherever they apply. Read them all. Do not skip any. They are important, even to the owner who never intends to work on the car.

Work Safety

Although an automobile presents many hazards, common sense and good equipment can help ensure safety. Many accidents happen because of carelessness. Pay attention and stick to these few important safety rules.

WARNING —

- *Never run the engine in the work area unless it is well-ventilated. The exhaust should be vented to the outside. Carbon Monoxide (CO) is an odorless and colorless gas. Carbon Monoxide (CO) in the exhaust kills.*

- *Remove all neckties, scarfs, loose clothing, and jewelry when working near running engines or power tools. Tuck in shirts. Tie long hair and secure it under a cap. Severe injury can result from these things being caught in rotating parts.*

- *Remove rings, watches, and bracelets. Aside from the dangers of moving parts, metallic jewelry conducts electricity and may cause shorts, sparks, burns, or damage to the electrical system when accidentally contacting the battery or other electrical terminals.*

- *Disconnect the battery negative (–) (GND) cable whenever working on or near the fuel system, airbag system or anything that is electrically powered. Accidental electrical contact may damage the electrical system, cause fire, or result in serious personal injury.*

- *Never work under a lifted car unless it is solidly supported on jack stands that are intended for that purpose. Do not support a car on cinder blocks, bricks, or other objects that may shift or crumble under continuous load. Never work under a car that is supported only by a jack.*

- *The fuel system retains pressure even when the ignition is off. Loosen the fuel lines very slowly to allow the residual pressure to dissipate gradually. Cover fittings with a suitable shop cloth to avoid spraying fuel.*

- *Fuel is highly flammable. When working around fuel, do not smoke or work near fire hazards. Keep an approved fire extinguisher handy. Be aware that water and building heaters may have standing pilot lights.*

- *Illuminate the work area adequately and safely. Use a portable safety light for working inside or under the car. A fluorescent type light is best because it gives off less heat. If using a light with a normal incandescent bulb, use rough service bulbs to avoid breakage. The hot filament of an accidentally broken bulb can ignite spilled fuel or oil.*

- *Keep sparks, lighted matches, and open flame away from the top of the battery. Hydrogen gas emitted by the battery is highly flammable. Any nearby source of ignition may cause the battery to explode.*

- *Never lay tools or parts in the engine compartment or on top of the battery. They may fall and be difficult to retrieve, become caught in belts or other rotating parts, or cause electrical shorts and damage to the electrical system.*

IDENTIFICATION PLATES AND LABELS

Vehicle Identification Number (VIN)

The vehicle year and model can be determined from the VIN or the identification plate. The VIN (Chassis number) is located on the instrument panel on the driver's side and is visible from the outside through the windshield. See Fig. 1.

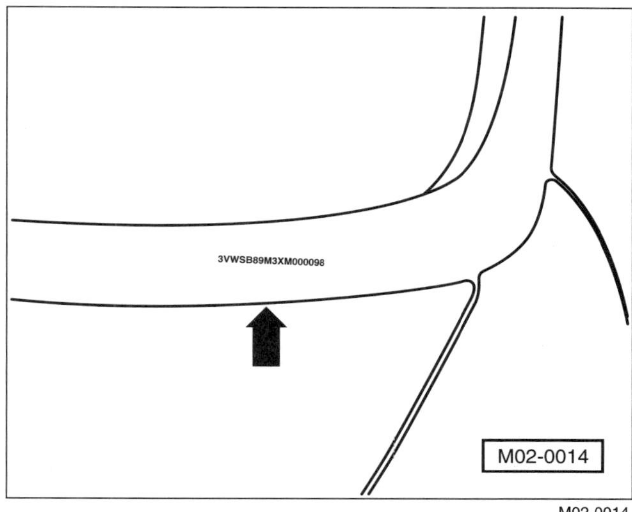

M02-0014

Fig. 1. Vehicle identification number (**arrow**) on instrument panel underneath windshield.

The VIN is also located in the plenum chamber and is visible through an opening in the plenum cover. See Fig. 2.

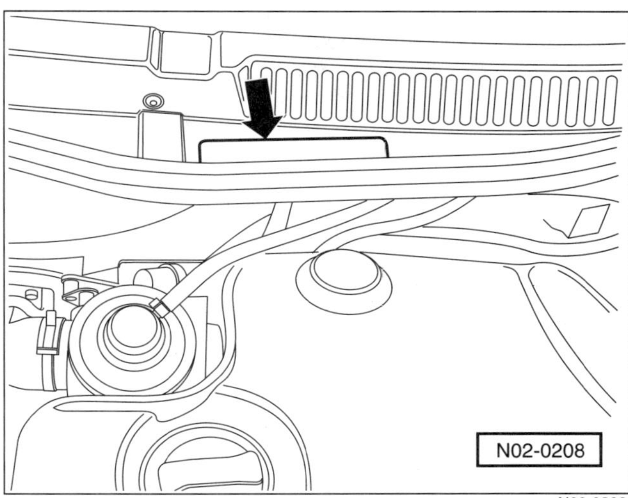

N02-0208

Fig. 2. VIN (**arrow**) located in plenum area.

NOTE —

Additional information on the 17 digit VIN is given in the Foreword on page vi, at the front of the manual.

The vehicle data plate is located in the luggage compartment on the right side of the spare tire recess. See Fig. 3. The data plate contains the following vehicle information:

1. **Production control number**
2. **Vehicle identification number**
3. **Model identification number**
4. **Model explanation/engine output**
5. **Engine and transmission code letters**
6. **Paint number/interior equipment identification number**
7. **Optional equipment identification numbers**

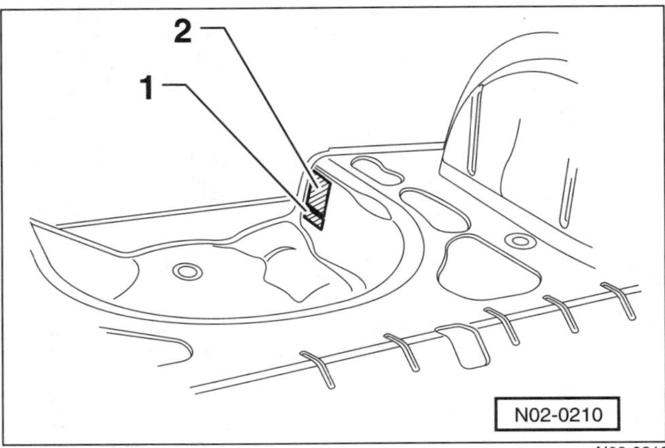

N02-0210

Fig. 3. Vehicle data plate (**2**) in luggage compartment area.

Additional vehicle identification information can also found on a sticker attached to the driver's side door post.

Engine identification

The engines used in vehicles covered by this manual are identified by a three letter code followed by a six digit number such as: AEG 029 452. The engine code and the engine number are located on the engine block.

Engine Codes

- AWD, AWW . . . . 1.8L 4-cylinder turbo gasoline
- ALH . . . . 1.9L 4-cylinder turbo diesel
- AEG, AVH, AZG. . . . . 2.0L 4-cylinder gasoline
- AFP . . . . 2.8L 6-cylinder gasoline

- **4-cylinder** engine code letters and numbers are located at the rear of the cylinder block. This information is stamped into the cylinder block casting near the oil filter flange close to the joint between the engine and transmission. See Fig. 4. or 4a.
- **6-cylinder** engine code is located on the left side of the engine block below the camshaft timing chain tensioner. The code numbers should be visible when looking down between the throttle valve control module and the valve cover. See Fig. 5.

0024320

Fig. 4. Engine code letters and numbers (**arrow**) shown on AEG engine. ALH and AWD engine letters and numbers are similar.

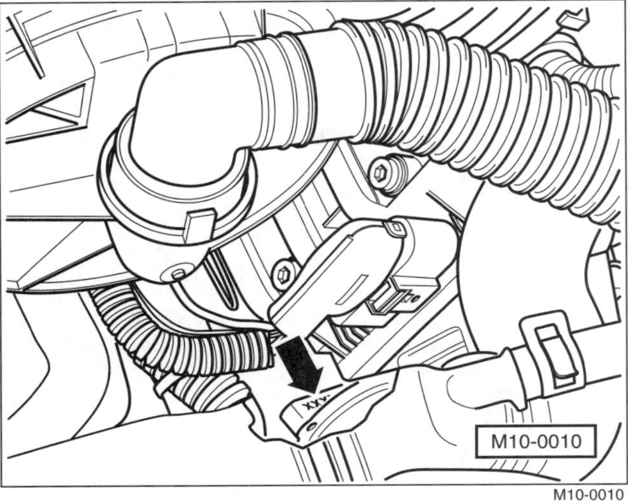

M10-0010

Fig. 4a. Engine code letters and numbers (**arrow**) shown on AVH and AZG engines.

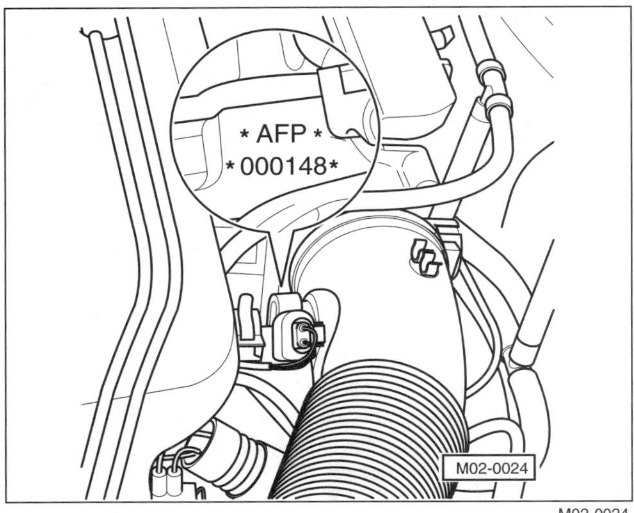

M02-0024

Fig. 5. Engine code for 6-cylinder engine is located the left side of the engine block below the camshaft timing chain tensioner.

- Additionally, the engine codes can often be found on a sticker on the upper section of the toothed belt guard. See Fig. 6.

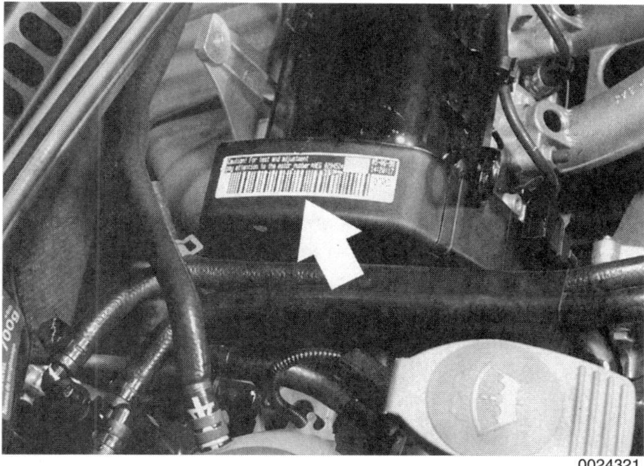

0024321

Fig. 6. Sticker with engine codes (**arrow**) is often attached to upper section of toothed belt guard. AEG engine shown.

Transmission identification

The transmissions used in vehicles covered by this manual are identified by a three letter code followed by a five digit number such as: DQY 17078. The digits indicate the transmission build date and all transmissions built on any given day will have the same number. Two transmissions types are available; a four speed automatic or a five speed manual. For transmission identification see Fig. 7. or Fig. 8. Each transmission type comes in numerous versions, depending on engine type. For a listing of the various transmission codes and specifications see **34 Manual Transmission** or **37 Automatic Transmission**.

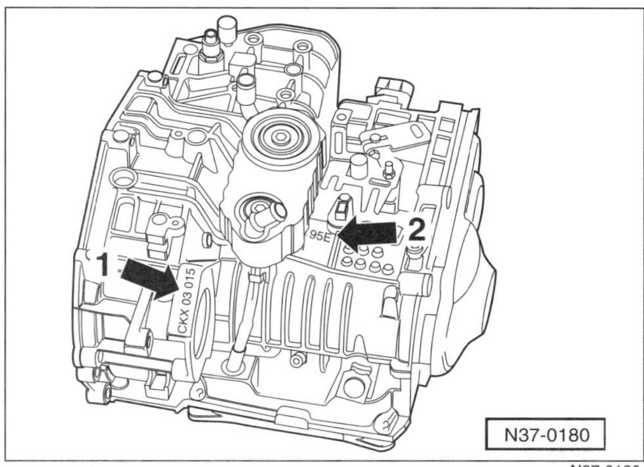

N37-0180

Fig. 7. Transmission code (**arrow 1**) stamped into machined area of case for automatic transmissions. Other numbers (**arrow 2**) may be cast into the case but are not relevant to the code.

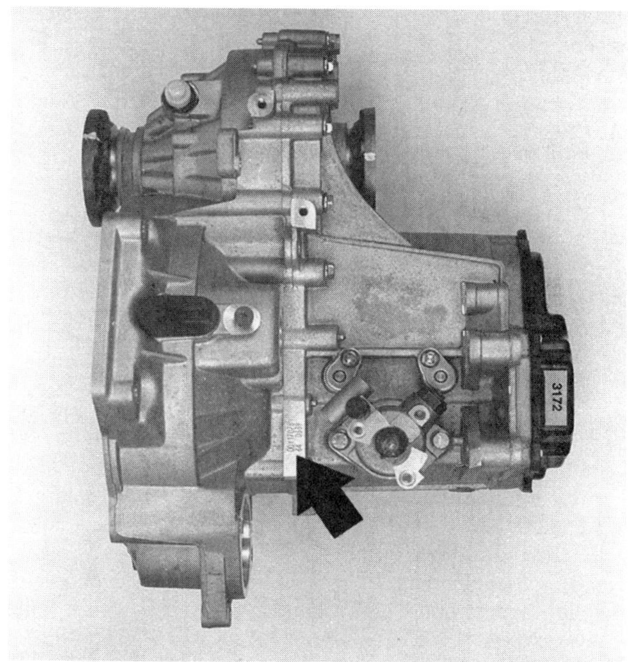

0024322

Fig. 8. Transmission code (**arrow**) stamped into machined area of case for manual transmissions.

TOWING

Emergency towing with commercial equipment

The following information is to be used by commercial tow truck operators who know how to operate their equipment safely. To prevent damage to the vehicle, read and understand all of the following information before proceeding.

> ***WARNING —***
> *Never allow passengers to ride in a towed vehicle for any reason.*

> ***CAUTION —***
> - *The vehicles covered by this manual cannot be towed with conventional sling-type equipment or non-self-loading wheel dollies. Towing with this type of equipment will cause bumper and body panel damage.*
> - *If an automatic transmission vehicle cannot be towed with wheel lift equipment in combination with self-loading wheel dollies, it must be transported with a car carrier (flatbed) to avoid damage to the transmission due to lack of lubrication.*
> - *To reduce the risk of accident and serious personal injury, always stay within manufacturer's rated equipment capacities. Exceeding manufacturer's design specifications is dangerous.*

NOTE —

- *Always follow the manufacturer's recommendations for commercial towing equipment.*
- *Always be thoroughly familiar with specific towing equipment being used.*
- *Always observe all State, Provincial and Local laws regarding such items as warning signals, night illumination, speed, licensing, etc.*

- Whenever possible, tow with the front wheels off the ground.
- The vehicle may be lifted at the rear and moved a short distance to a better position for front wheel lifting.
- If a vehicle with a manual transmission must be towed with the front wheels on the ground, make sure that the transmission oil has not leaked out or been drained.
- If a vehicle is to be towed on its drive wheels, the transmission and differential MUST be operable. Place the transmission in NEUTRAL.
- If any doubt exists about the condition of the transmission or differential, tow the vehicle with the drive wheels lifted, use self-loading wheel dollies or wheel lift equipment.
- Excessive towing speeds and distances may damage both manual and automatic transmissions.
- Move the vehicle only within the recommended speeds and distances.
- During any tow, the raised wheels can contact the road or other ground surfaces, so they need to rotate freely.
- The anti-theft steering column lock is not strong enough to withstand shocks transmitted from the wheels while towing. Before towing, always unlock the steering wheel with the ignition key and secure the steering wheel with a steering wheel clamp which has been specifically designed for towing service.
- To reduce the risk of serious personal injury and vehicle damage, never attempt to rock or pivot the vehicle on jack stands to allow positioning on the dolly.
- Always release the parking brake.
- When the ignition key is not available, DO NOT tow from the rear or serious damage to vehicle systems will result.
- The front of the vehicle must be lifted to prevent damage to the steering column anti-theft lock.
- To reduce the risk of accident and serious injury, never tow any vehicle at a speed in excess of 50 mph for any reason whenever towing with a conventional tow truck, with or without the use of a self-loading wheel dolly.
- Safe operating speeds always depend on weather, road, traffic, visibility, conditions; as well as the condition of the towed vehicle.
- A tow truck is an emergency vehicle to be used to move disabled vehicles to a suitable place of repair. It must not be used for transporting vehicles long distances.
- Towed vehicles should be raised until lifted wheels are a minimum of 6 inches from the ground and there is adequate clearance at opposite end of lifted vehicle.
- Always inspect points of attachment to the disabled vehicle. If they appear to be damaged or deteriorated, select other attachment points at a substantial structural member of the frame.
- Never allow the fuel tank to support any of the vehicle's weight during towing. Before moving the vehicle, carefully secure or remove any loose or protruding parts of damaged vehicles; such as hoods, fenders, trim, etc.
- To avoid serious vehicle damage, never lift or tow any vehicle by attaching towing chains or hooks to shock absorbers, stabilizer bars, or front strut rods.
- Never go under the vehicle while it is lifted by the towing equipment, unless the vehicle is adequately supported by safety stands.
- The safety of the operator and all others in the vicinity of the wrecker or the towed vehicle must be the first consideration at all times during a towing operation.

Vehicle hook-up, front

1. Attach wheel lift equipment to wheels.

2. Attach safety straps to wheels. See Fig. 9.

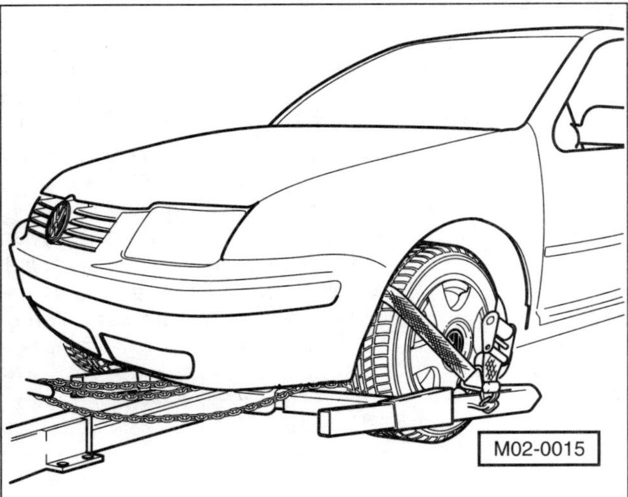

M02-0015

Fig. 9. Jetta shown attached to appropriate towing equipment for front-first towing.

3. Attach safety chains to lower control arms.

NOTE —

- *Always use a safety chain system which is completely independent of the primary lifting and towing attachments.*
- *During installation of safety chains, be careful not to damage lights, bumpers, or painted surfaces.*
- *To prevent damage to brake lines and front driveshaft boots, always position hooks and chains cautiously to prevent damage to these components.*
- *Prior to towing the vehicle, ensure that all attachment points are firmly secured.*
- *Towing clearance: 6-12 inches between tires and ground.*

Vehicle hook-up, rear

CAUTION —

- *Do not tow cars with automatic transmission from the rear.*
- *Do not tow cars with manual transmission from the rear unless transmission is in neutral and ignition is unlocked. Secure steering wheel with a steering wheel clamp which has been specifically designed for towing service.*

1. Attach wheel lift equipment to wheels.
2. Attach safety straps to wheels. See Fig. 10.

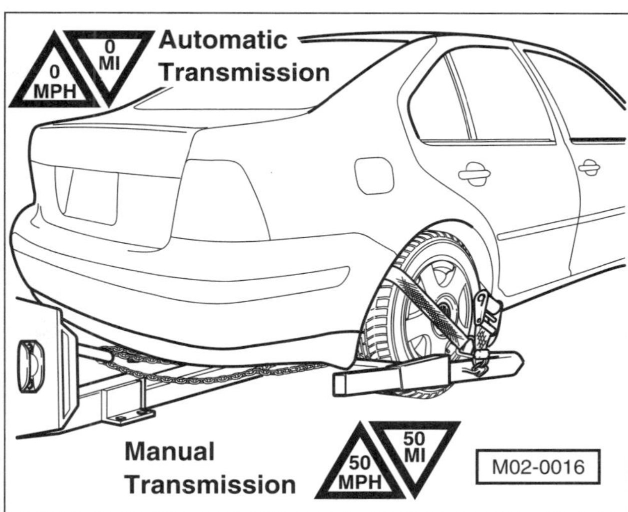

M02-0016

Fig. 10. Jetta shown attached to appropriate towing equipment for rear-first towing on a manual transmission vehicle.

3. Attach safety chains to axle beam.

NOTE —
Observe all notes associated with front vehicle hook-up.

Towing eyes

To be able to pull or be pulled, a towing eye must be threaded into the mount at right front of vehicle. The detachable towing eye is in the vehicle tool kit.

1. Pry cover off forward with flat blade screwdriver. See Fig. 11.

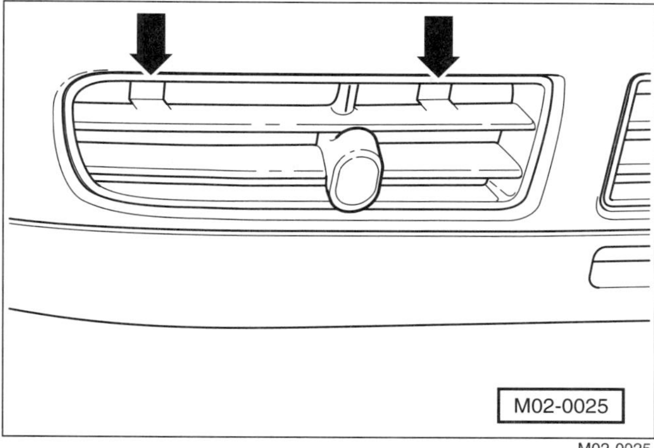

M02-0025

Fig. 11. Pry off towing eye cover at **arrows** from right front section of bumper.

2. Thread towing eye fully into mount and tighten with wheel lug wrench.
3. After use, unscrew towing eye and return to vehicle tool kit.
4. Reinstall cover.

NOTE —
The rear towing eye is welded to the vehicle and is located under rear bumper on right side.

LIFTING VEHICLE

Lifting with hoist or floor jack

The vehicle may be raised for service and repairs by floor jacks and/or hoists. For repairs that require raising the vehicle, proper jacking points must be used. There are four jack points, two on each side of the car, marked by indentations in the lower panel sheet metal just behind the front fender or just in front of rear fender. If using a hoist, similar lift points are just inboard of the aforementioned indentations.

Lifting points

To lift the front of vehicle, place floor jack or hoist at appropriate front lifting point. See Fig. 12.

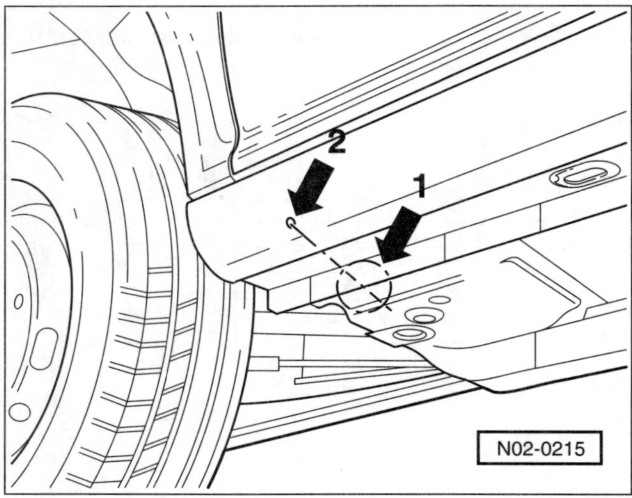

Fig. 12. Front lifting points; position jack pad onto vertical stiffener (**arrow 1**) with center of pad lined up with marking (**arrow 2**).

To lift the rear of vehicle, use appropriate rear lifting points. See Fig. 13.

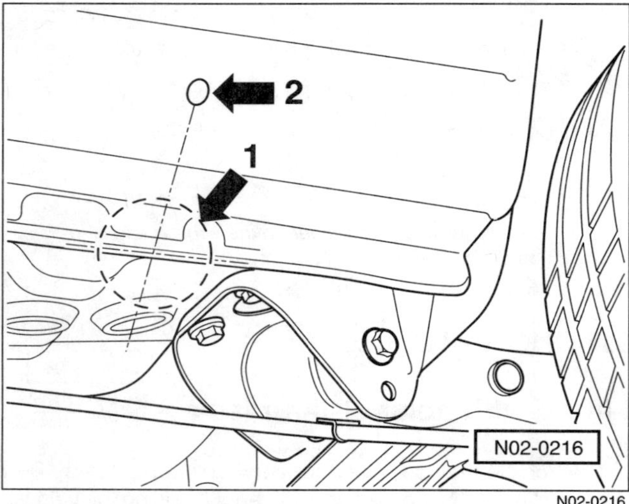

Fig. 13. Rear lifting points; position jack pad onto vertical stiffener (**arrow 1**) with center of pad lined up with marking (**arrow 2**).

> ***CAUTION —***
> *Do not lift vehicle at engine oil pan, transmission, or on front or rear axle as serious damage may result.*

1. Place car on a flat level area with a surface capable of supporting jacks and jackstands, e.g. concrete.
2. Block the wheels to prevent the car from rolling.
3. Place the jack at proper lifting points as shown previously.
4. Operate the jack or hoist and raise the car slowly. If working under the car, support the weight of the car using jack stands.

> ***WARNING —***
> *If work is to be performed under vehicle it must be supported by suitable jack stands.*

> ***CAUTION —***
> - *Vehicle may only be lifted at points indicated in order to avoid damaging vehicle floor pan and to prevent the vehicle from tipping.*
> - *Never start engine and engage a gear with vehicle lifted if any drive wheel has contact with the floor! (There is danger of an accident if this is not observed).*
> - *Before driving on to a vehicle hoist, ensure there is sufficient clearance between low lying vehicle components and the hoist platform.*

Working under the vehicle

When working under any vehicle, the following points should be observed:

1. Disconnect the negative (GND) battery cable so that no one else can start the car. Let others know that you will be under the vehicle.
2. Place at least two jack stands under the car. A jack is a temporary lifting device and should not be used alone to support the car while you are under it. Use positively locking jack stands that are designed for the purpose of supporting a car.
3. If you are using a hoist, be sure that the safety locks are engaged and that the weight of the vehicle is resting on the locks, not the hydraulic system.
4. Lower the car slowly until its weight is fully supported by the jack stands or hoist. Watch to make sure that jack stands do not tip or lean as the car settles on them, and that jack stands and hoist arms are placed solidly and will not move.

> ***WARNING —***
> *Check to make sure vehicle is stable before working under car.*

5. Observe all jacking precautions again when raising the car to remove the jack stands.

ENGINE COMPARTMENT MAINTENANCE

The jobs listed under this heading are the engine compartment maintenance items from the maintenance tables.

Sound absorber panels, removing and installing

1. Remove lower sound absorber panels (belly pans) from below the engine to access lower engine and transmission components. See Fig. 14.

NOTE —
The sound absorber panels shown below are for the ALH diesel engine. For a specific diagram of gasoline engine sound absorber panels, see ***50 Body–Front****.*

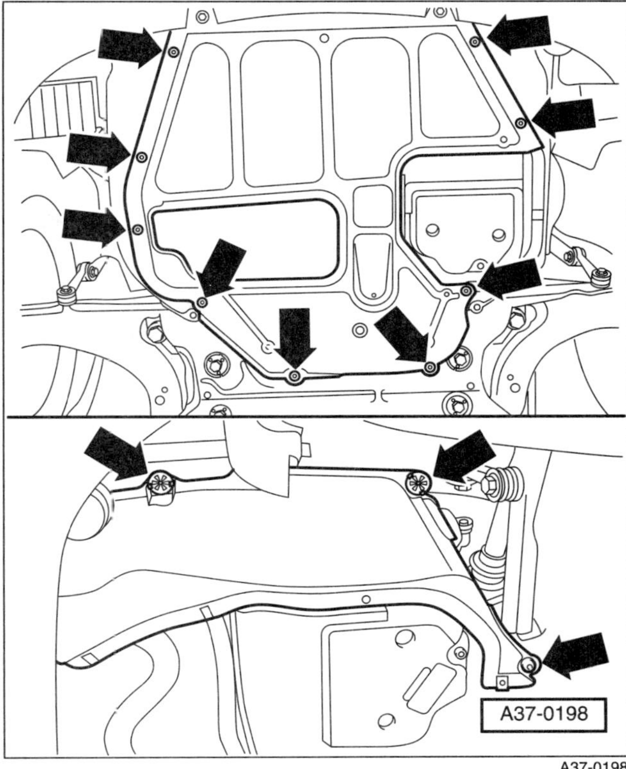

A37-0198

Fig. 14. Remove bolts (**arrows**) and pull sound absorber panels out. ALH engine shown, others similar.

2. Remove upper engine cover.
   - For 2.0L engine, see Fig. 15.

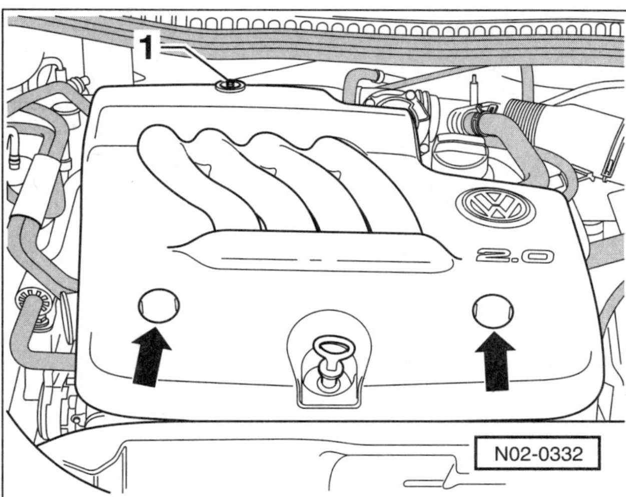

N02-0332

Fig. 15. Remove plastic covers (**arrows**) and mounting nuts underneath. Remove nut (**1**), dipstick and engine cover.

   - For 1.9L engine, see Fig. 16.

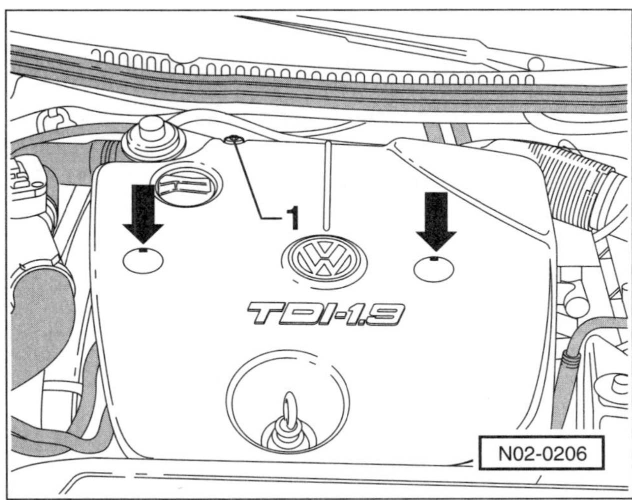

N02-0206

Fig. 16. Remove plastic covers (**arrows**) and mounting nuts underneath. Loosen nut (**1**), remove dipstick and slide off engine cover.

- For 2.8L engine (VR6), remove spark plug wires with VW special tool, T10029, or equivalent see Fig. 17. Label plug wire and place to side.

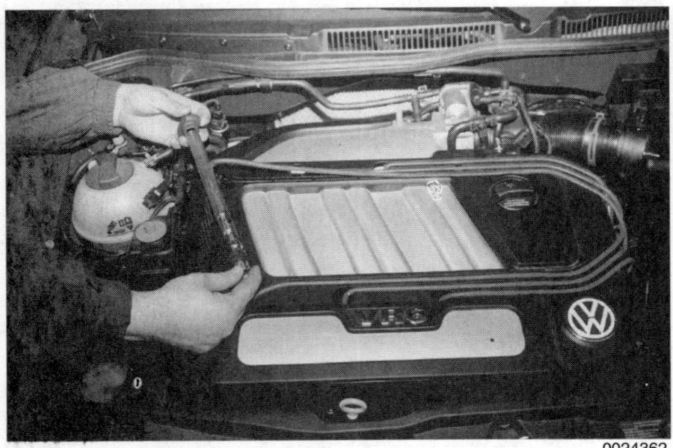

Fig. 17. Remove spark plug connectors with special tool T10029 as shown to avoid damage to spark plug connector. Do not pull on wires.).

- Remove mounting nuts and VR6 engine cover, see Fig. 18.

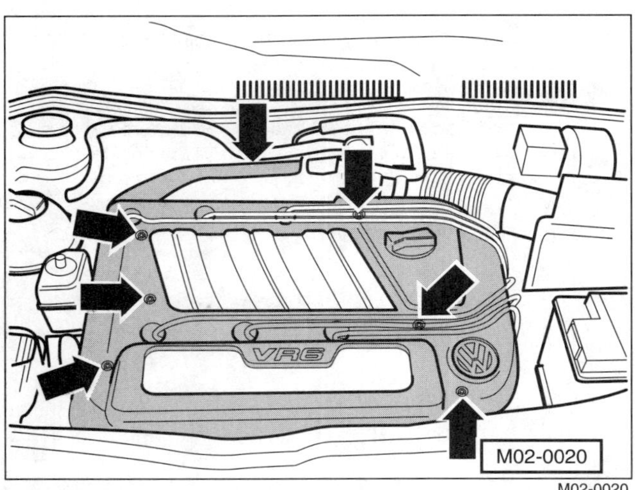

Fig. 18. Remove nuts (**arrows**) and engine cover from AFP VR6 engine. Spark plug wires should be placed out of way before removing cover

- For 1.8L engine, release locking pins for engine cover by turning 90°. Remove engine cover.

Engine oil level, checking

It is normal for your engine to consume a small amount of oil. The rate of consumption will depend on the quality and viscosity of the oil and operating conditions. Make it a habit to check oil level at every fuel filling.

1. After switching ignition OFF, wait at least 3 minutes to allow the oil to flow back into the oil pan.

2. Remove dipstick located in front of intake manifold. Wipe dipstick with a clean cloth and fully re-insert into tube.

3. Remove dipstick again and read oil level. The oil level must be at the top edge of the shaded area but on no account above the maximum level mark. If oil level is below shaded area, fill to top mark. See Fig. 19.

> ***CAUTION —***
> *Risk of damage to the catalytic converter if oil level is too high.*

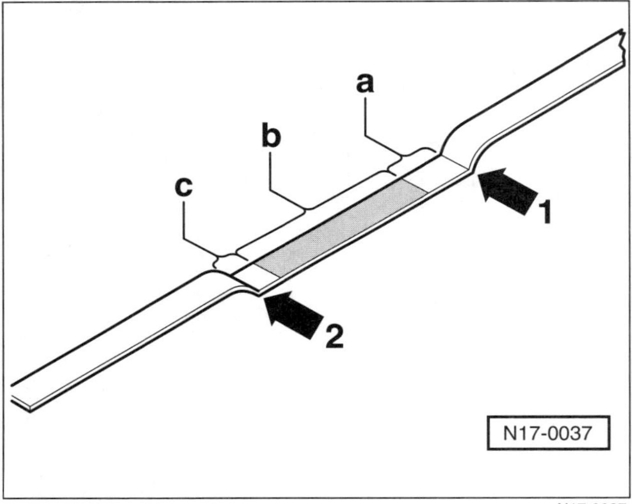

Fig. 19. Oil level in shaded area (**b**) is normal and does not need to be topped up. Oil level must be no higher than **1**. Oil level at **c** or lower must be topped up and rechecked.

Select an oil that conforms to the standards of the American Petroleum Institute (API). A symbol can be found on the oil container with the API rating and viscosity grade. Gasoline engines can use either petroleum or synthetic oils. Volkswagen does, however, recommend that only synthetic oil be used in all TDI diesel engines.

Recommended engine oils

- Gasoline engines . . . . API service rating SJ
- Diesel engines (5W40 or 5W30 synthetic) API service rating CF4 or CG4

Engine oil, changing

1. Warm car to normal operating temperature.

2. Shut off engine and apply parking brake.

3. Raise car and support on jackstands designed for the purpose.

> ***WARNING —***
> *Jack stands should be placed on hard level surface (e.g. concrete).*

4. Remove lower sound absorber panel (belly pan) from beneath engine compartment. Remove drain plug from oil pan and allow oil to drain. See **17 Engine—Lubrication System** for drain plug location.

> ***WARNING —***
> *Hot oil can scald. Wear protective clothing, gloves and eye protection.*

> ***CAUTION —***
> - *Always replace oil-drain plug sealing ring anytime the drain plug is removed.*
> - *Dispose of oil properly at a facility equipped for recycling or storage.*

NOTE —
On 6-cylinder engines an additional oil drain plug is located in oil filter cap. See **Engine oil filter, replacing (6-cylinder engine)**.

5. Replace oil filter. See **Engine oil filter, replacing** for applicable engine.

6. Install oil drain plug with a new seal. Tighten drain plug to proper torque.

Tighting torque

- Oil drain plug to oil pan
  - 4-cylinder .... 30 Nm (22 ft-lb)
  - 6-cylinder .... 40 Nm (30 ft-lb)

7. Fill engine with proper quantity and type of oil. For oil viscosity requirement based on temperature, see Fig. 20. Check dipstick for proper oil level.

Engine oil capacity, with filter change

- 1.8L engine .... 4.35 liters (4.6 qt.)
- 1.9L engine .... 4.5 liters (4.75 qt.)
- 2.0L engine .... 4.0 liters (4.2 qt.)
- 2.8L engine .... 5.8 liters (6.1 qt.)

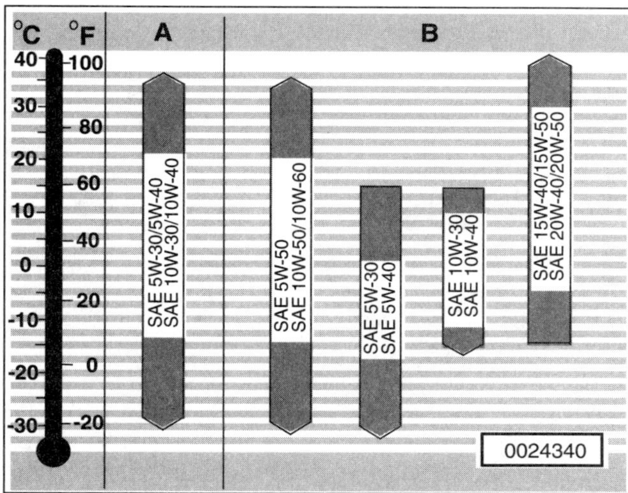

0024340

Fig. 20. Oil viscosity vs. temperature requirements. Section **A** is for high-lubricity multigrade oils. Section **B** is for multigrade only oils.

8. Run engine and check for leaks. Shut off engine and reinstall sound dampening pan. Check oil level after about 3 minutes.

> ***CAUTION —***
> *After changing the engine oil and the oil filter, observe the following at the first engine start:*
> - *The engine must only run at idling speed as long as the oil pressure warning light in the instrument cluster is on. Do not rev the engine! If the engine is revved with the warning light on, the turbocharger on TDI and 1.8L turbo engines could be damaged or fail completely.*
> - *The full oil pressure is not attained until the warning light has gone out. Only then can the engine be revved.*

Engine oil filter, replacing (4-cylinder gasoline engines)

1. Remove lower sound absorber panels as shown earlier.

2. Position drain pan under oil filter to catch spills.

3. Working from under engine, loosen and remove oil filter with oil filter strap or suitable wrench. See Fig. 21.

4. Clean sealing surface on oil filter flange.

5. Lightly lubricate rubber seal with clean oil.

6. Thread on new filter and tighten by hand.

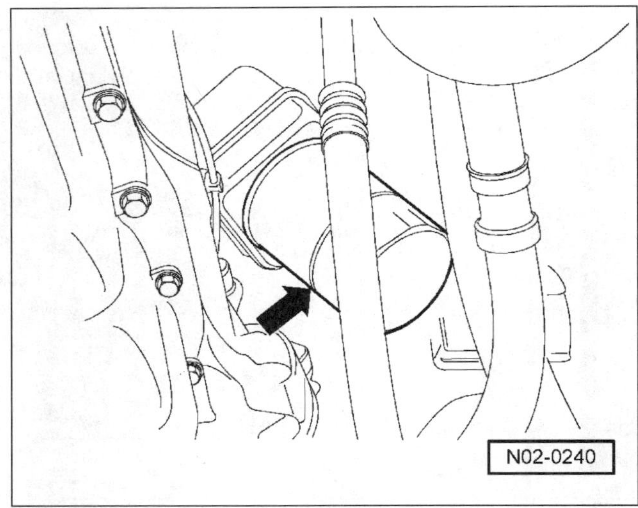

N02-0240

Fig. 21. Oil filter from underneath 4-cylinder gasoline engine.

> ***CAUTION —***
> *Observe all applicable regulations concerning disposal of used oil filters.*

Engine oil filter, replacing (diesel engine)

1. Remove upper sound absorber panel.
2. Working from above the engine, loosen and remove oil filter sealing cap.
3. Pull filter up and out.
4. Install new filter and gaskets. See Fig. 22.

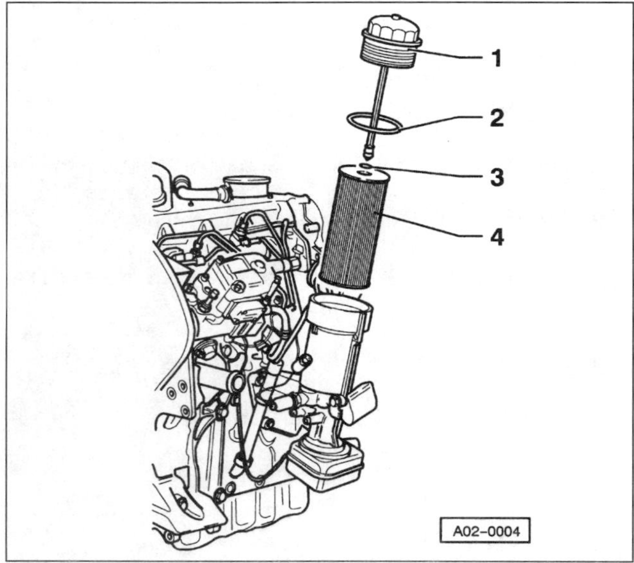

A02-0004

Fig. 22. Diesel oil filter assembly. Install new oil filter (**4**) with new gaskets (**2**) and (**3**). Install sealing cap and torque.

5. Install filter sealing cap.

Tightening torque
- Oil filter sealing cap . . . . 25 Nm (18 ft-lb)

6. Install upper sound absorber panel.

> ***CAUTION —***
> *Observe all applicable regulations concerning disposal of used oil filters.*

Engine oil filter, replacing (6-cylinder engine)

1. Remove oil drain plug in oil filter sealing cap.
2. Remove oil filter cap (lower part of oil filter housing) and install new filter element.

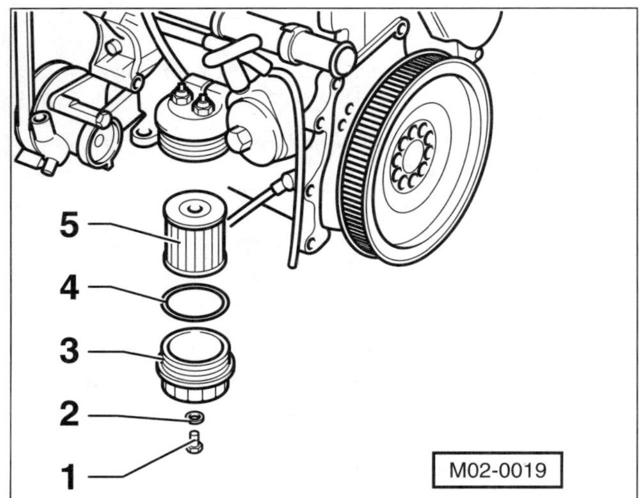

M02-0019

Fig. 23. On VR6 engines, drain oil via drain plug (**1**), remove filter cap (**3**) with oil filter wrench. Replace filter element (**5**) and O-rings (**2** and **4**).

3. Install new rubber O-ring and filter cap.
4. Install oil drain plug with new rubber O-ring.

Tightening torques
- Oil filter sealing cap . . . . 25 Nm (18 ft-lb)
- Oil drain plug . . . . 10 Nm (7 ft-lb)

> ***CAUTION —***
> *Observe all applicable regulations concerning disposal of used oil filters.*

Coolant, checking

Cooling system maintenance consists of maintaining coolant level, checking coolant freezing point, and inspecting hoses. Coolant flushing is not part of Volkswagen's scheduled maintenance.

NOTE —
Volkswagen does not require replacing the coolant as part of routine maintenance. The cooling system has been filled at the factory with a permanent coolant. For coolant system draining and refilling procedures, see **19 Engine-Cooling System.**

WARNING —
- *Hot coolant can scald. Do not work on the cooling system until it has fully cooled.*
- *Use extreme care when draining and disposing of coolant. Coolant is poisonous and lethal. Children and pets are attracted to it because of its sweet smell and taste. See a doctor or veterinarian immediately if any amount is ingested.*

CAUTION —
- *Use only Volkswagen original anti-freeze when filling the cooling system. Use of any other anti-freeze may be harmful to the cooling system. Do not use an anti-freeze containing phosphates.*
- *Never mix green coolant (G11) with red coolant (G12). Mixing can cause serious engine damage.*
- *Do not use tap water in cooling system. Use distilled water only to mix anti-freeze.*

Volkswagen uses only one type of coolant in vehicles covered by this manual. It can be identified by its red color. This coolant/antifreeze is phosphate free and also silicate free. When supplied by Volkswagen, this coolant/antifreeze is known as G12.

The advantages of G12 over earlier types include improvements in corrosion protection, thermal stability, heat transfer/control, hard water tolerance and environmental protection.

CAUTION —
- *G12 (Red Coolant) must NEVER be mixed with ANY other coolant. Engine damage will result!*
- *Contamination of G12 with other colored coolants is identifiable by discoloration (brown, purple, etc.). This mixture causes a foamy deposit to appear in the expansion tank/radiator and MUST be drained immediately.*
- *The cooling system must be completely free of this mixture before refilling with the correct type of coolant/antifreeze.*

A translucent expansion tank, or overflow reservoir, on the left side of the engine compartment provides easy monitoring of coolant level without opening the system. The coolant level should always be checked when engine is cold. The coolant level should be between the maximum and minimum mark on the expansion tank. See Fig. 24.

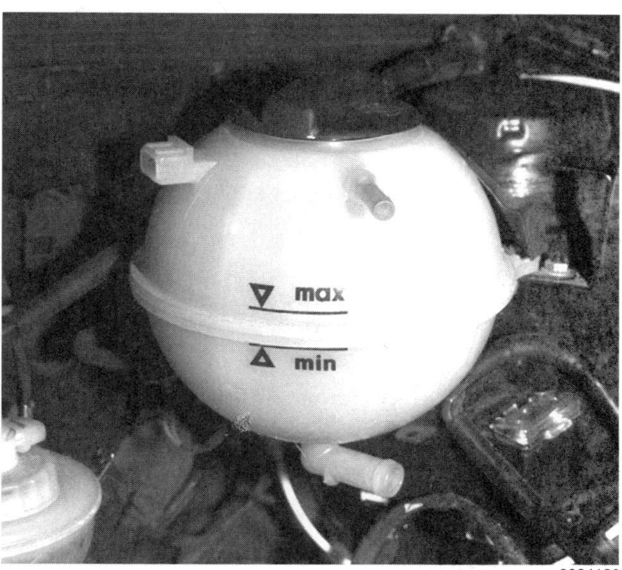

Fig. 24. Coolant level should be between **max** and **min** marks on expansion tank.

Inspect hoses by first checking that all connections are tight and dry. Coolant seepage indicates that either the hose clamp is loose, that the hose is damaged, or that the connection is dirty or corroded. Dried coolant has a chalky appearance. Check hose condition by pinching them. Hoses should be firm and springy. Replace any hose that is cracked, that has become soft and limp, or has been contaminated by oil or diesel fuel. See Fig. 25.

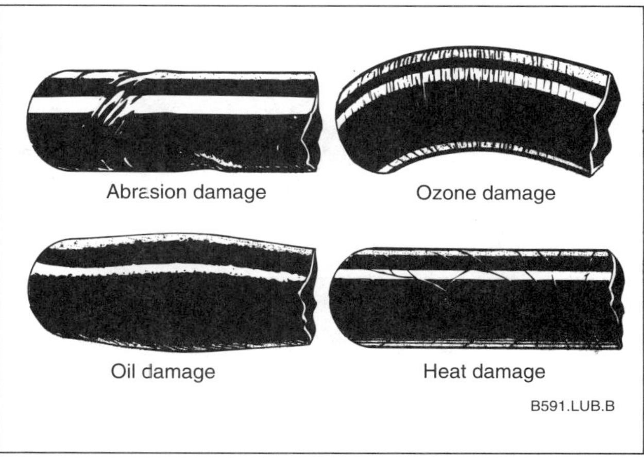

Fig. 25. Examples of damaged coolant hoses. Any of the conditions shown is cause for replacement. (Courtesy of Gates Rubber Inc.)

To check freezing point of the coolant, (and also the boiling point), use a refractometer. With the engine cold, remove cap from expansion tank and draw up some coolant with refractometer siphon. Volkswagen recommends using a 50/50 mixture of anti-freeze and water, which has a freezing point of -35°F (-38°C). If the freezing point is too high, drain a small amount of coolant from the system and add new anti-freeze until proper protection level is obtained. Also see **19 Engine–Cooling System**.

> ***NOTE —***
> *For protection to approx. -40°C (-40°F) the percentage of anti-freeze may be increased up to 60%. The percentage of anti-freeze must not exceed 60%, as higher amounts will decrease frost protection and cooling capacity.*

Brake fluid level, checking

Routine maintenance of the brake system includes maintaining an adequate level of brake fluid in the reservoir, replacing brake fluid every 2 years, checking brake pads for wear, checking hand brake function, and inspecting system for fluid leaks or other damage. See **Under Car Maintenance** for pad inspection and brake system inspection.

> ***WARNING —***
> - *Use only new, previously unopened brake fluid conforming to US Standard FMVSS 116 DOT 4.*
> - *Brake fluid is poisonous. DO NOT ingest brake fluid. Wash thoroughly with soap and water if brake fluid comes into contact with skin.*

> ***CAUTION —***
> - *DO NOT let brake fluid come in contact with paint. Wash immediately with soap and water.*
> - *Brake fluid absorbs moisture from the air and must be stored in an airtight container.*
> - *DO NOT allow brake fluid to exceed the maximum level in the fluid reservoir.*

The brake fluid level will drop slightly as the brakes wear. Check fluid level at brake fluid reservoir, located on driver's side of engine compartment, under air cleaner connecting hose.

Brake fluid	
• Type	FVMSS 116 SAE DOT 4

> ***WARNING —***
> *Do not mix DOT 5 (silicone) brake fluid with DOT 4 brake fluid as severe component corrosion will result. Such corrosion could lead to brake system failure.*

Brake fluid, replacing

Brake fluid readily absorbs moisture from the atmosphere. This moisture can cause brake system corrosion and adversely affect braking performance. Therefore, the old brake should be flushed out of the system and new, fresh fluid added at least every 2 years, regardless of mileage. See **47 Brakes–Hydraulic System** for brake system bleeding procedures and brake fluid replacement.

> ***NOTE —***
> *Vehicles equipped with ABS can be bled using conventional methods.*

Power steering fluid level, checking

There are two methods for checking power steering fluid level.

COLD - When cold checking the power steering fluid level, the engine should not be running and the front wheels should be in the straight ahead position. Use a screwdriver to remove the cap from power steering fluid reservoir. See Fig. 26.

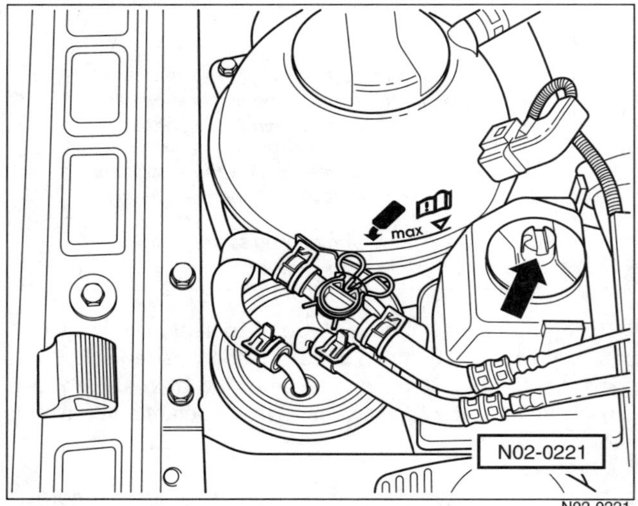

Fig. 26. Power steering fluid reservoir cap (**arrow**) with attached dipstick.

Use a clean shop cloth to wipe the dipstick end and screw the cap back on hand tight only. Remove the dipstick from the fluid reservoir again and check the level on the dipstick. The level should be within ± 2 mm of the **min** mark. See Fig. 27. Adjust the fluid level if required and screw the cap back on hand tight when done.

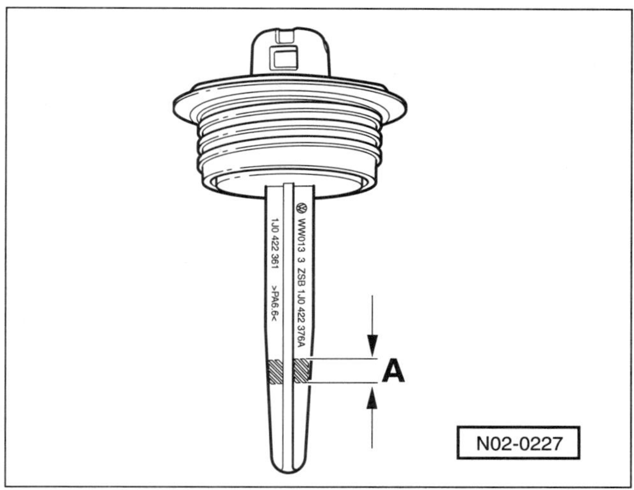

N02-0227

Fig. 27. When checking power steering fluid on cold engine, the level should be within ± 2mm area of MIN marking (**A**).

> ***NOTE —***
> - *If fluid level is above (approx. 2 mm) the MIN mark, some fluid must be extracted.*
> - *If fluid level is more than 2 mm below the MIN mark, the hydraulic system must be checked for leaks. It is not sufficient to top-up with fluid.*

HOT - When hot checking the power steering fluid level, start the engine and let it run until the power steering fluid temperature is above 50°C (122°F). The front wheels should be in the straight ahead position. Use a screwdriver to remove power steering reservoir cap. See Fig. 26. Use a clean shop cloth to wipe the dipstick end and screw the cap back on hand tight only. Remove the dipstick from the fluid reservoir again and check the level on the dipstick. The level should be between the **min** and **max** marks. See Fig. 28. Adjust the fluid level if required and screw the cap back on hand tight when done.

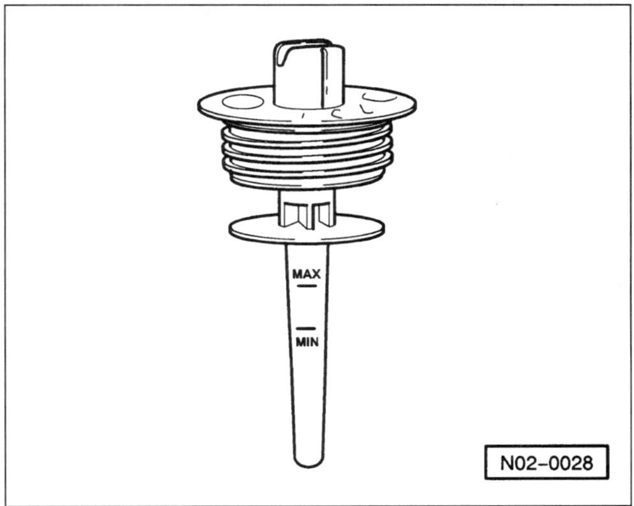

N02-0028

Fig. 28. When checking power steering fluid and engine is hot, fluid should be between **min** and **max** marks.

Power steering fluid
- Type . . . . hydraulic oil (VW part no. G 002 000)

> ***CAUTION —***
> - *Use only Volkswagen hydraulic oil G 002 000 in the power steering system. Do not use ATF or other non-approved types of power steering fluid. If the wrong fluid is used, power steering components may fail.*
> - *Volkswagen part numbers are given for reference only! Always consult your Volkswagen parts department or aftermarket parts specialist for the latest parts information.*

> ***NOTE —***
> - *The power steering system uses a special hydraulic oil and not ATF.*

Fluid leaks

Check the engine compartment for signs of fluid leaks. Fluid leaks attract dust making them easier to spot. Many expensive repairs can be avoided by prompt repair of minor fluid leaks.

Inspect for leaks in engine, cooling, fuel, heating and air conditioning systems. Visually inspect hoses and hose connections for leaks, worn areas, porosity and brittleness.

Fuel filter, draining (diesel engine)

The diesel fuel filter functions to trap water. As water is heavier than diesel fuel, it settles to the bottom of filter and can be drained off.

> ***CAUTION —***
> *Do not allow diesel fuel to contact coolant hoses or other rubber parts. Wipe diesel fuel off hoses immediately and wash with soap and water.*

1. Remove control valve retaining clip. See Fig. 29.

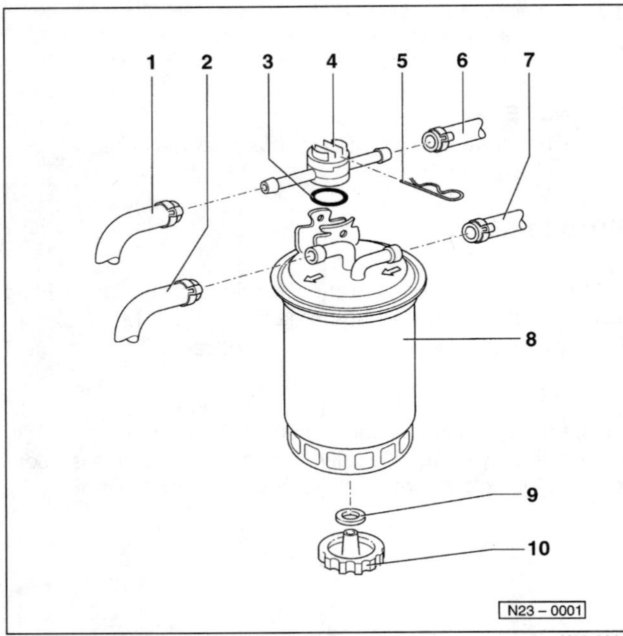

N23-0001

Fig. 29. Diesel fuel filter shown with related components.

The numbered list below applies to Fig. 29.

1. **Fuel return line**
   - From diesel injection pump
2. **Fuel supply line**
   - To diesel injection pump
3. **O-ring**
   - Always replace
4. **Fuel control valve**
   - Recirculates fuel to filter at temperatures below 15°C (59°F)
   - Returns fuel to tank at temperatures above 31°C (88°F)
   - Installed position: arrow points toward fuel tank
5. **Retaining clip**
6. **Fuel return line**
   - To fuel tank
7. **Fuel supply line**
   - From fuel tank
8. **Diesel fuel filter**
   - Fill with diesel fuel before installing
   - Observe fuel flow direction marked on top
9. **Gasket**
10. **Water drain plug**

2. Pull fuel control valve up with fuel lines connected.
3. Loosen water drain plug on bottom of filter and drain out approximately 100cc (1.7 oz.) of fuel/water.
4. Install fuel control valve with a new O-ring.
5. Attach retaining clip and tighten drain plug.
6. Check fuel system for leaks (visual inspection) with the engine running. Raise engine speed several times and let idle. Fuel flow through transparent pipe must be observed.

Fuel filter, replacing (diesel engine)

1. Remove control valve retaining clip. See Fig. 29.
2. Pull fuel control valve up with fuel lines connected.
3. Label and disconnect fuel filter inlet and outlet lines.
4. Unbolt filter bracket from body and remove with filter.
5. Loosen bracket and remove filter.
6. Install new filter.
7. Installation is the reverse of removal, noting the following:
   - Install fuel filter inlet and outlet lines.
   - Install fuel control valve with a new O-ring and attach retaining clip.
8. Check fuel system for leaks (visual inspection) with the engine running. Raise engine speed several times and let idle. Fuel flow through transparent pipe must be observed.

Fuel filter, replacing (gasoline engines)

Volkswagen specifies that the fuel filter used on gasoline engines is designed to last the life of the car. Replacement is only necessary if the filter becomes clogged due to contaminated fuel or failure to keep the fuel tank sealed. If dirt in the fuel filter is suspected, also check the screen on the bottom of the fuel delivery unit for contamination. **See 20 Fuel Storage and Supply.**

Battery service

Under normal operating conditions, the battery is maintenance free. At high outside temperatures, however, it is advisable to check the electrolyte level through the translucent battery housing. The electrolyte level should be just above the battery plates and their separators. The battery plates can be seen once the filler caps are removed. If the electrolyte level is low, replenish it by adding distilled water only. When servicing the battery, observe the following points:

- All cell caps must be equipped with an O-ring seal.
- The electrolyte level on batteries with visible minimum and maximum markings on the outside of the (semi-transparent) battery case is checked by visual inspection.
- The electrolyte level must be above the minimum marking or just reach the maximum marking.
- On batteries where the exterior markings are difficult to recognize (due to installation location, battery case opaqueness or dirt), the cell caps must be removed and individual cell electrolyte levels checked from inside the battery.
- The electrolyte level must align with the internal electrolyte level indicator (lip). This equates to the external "maximum" marking on the battery case.
- Check that battery is securely located and clamping bolt is tight.
- When the electrolyte level is too low and the cell plates are exposed, a loss of battery capacity will result (loss of power). If the cell plates are not completely submerged by electrolyte, (sulfuric acid/water mixture) corrosion will occur on the plates, plate bridges and cell connector. Optimum battery function is not possible under these conditions!
- When electrolyte level is too high, electrolyte (sulfuricacid/water mixture) may leak out and damage the surrounding areas such as the battery tray and engine compartment.
- Only use distilled water to top-up batteries. This prevents electrolyte impurities which cause self-discharging.
- DO NOT overfill the battery.
- Overfilled batteries can boil over.
- Too little electrolyte reduces the service life of the battery.
- Excess electrolyte MUST be extracted using a hydrometer.
- Dispose of electrolyte (sulfuric acid) properly! Waste electrolyte must only be disposed of in appropriate waste disposal sites. Refer to local regulations pertaining to electrolyte disposal.
- Volkswagen recommends that only new generation batteries with central gas venting are to be installed.

For battery testing and service, see **27 Engine Electrical**.

Some batteries have a charge indicator (magic eye) on top that displays electrolyte level and charge condition. See Fig. 30.

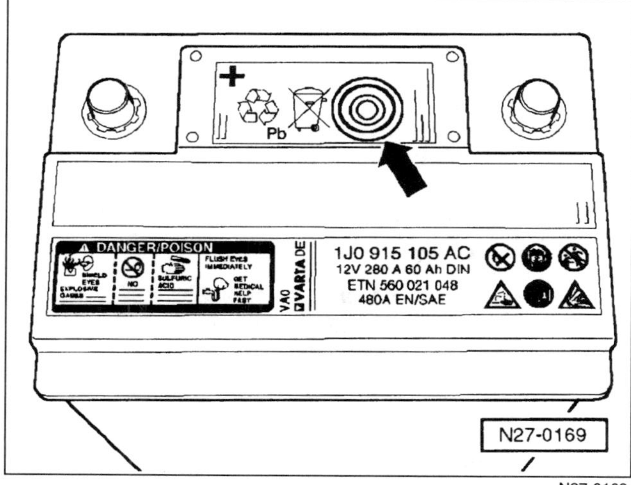

N27-0169

Fig. 30. Battery with charge indicator (**arrow**). If indicator is green, charge and electrolyte level are OK. If indicator is black, there is insufficient or no charge. If indicator is yellow or colorless, the electrolyte level is critically low and should be topped off with distilled water immediately.

NOTE —

- *If the charge indicator on batteries in excess of 5 years old are colorless, do not attempt to top off or recharge battery. Battery must be replaced.*
- *Air bubbles that occur normally during battery charging (even during vehicle operation) may adversely affect charge indicator reading. To obtain an accurate reading, gently tap the charge indicator with a screwdriver handle or rock the vehicle to displace any possible air bubbles that have formed.*
- *For technical reasons, some batteries are equipped with sealing plugs with plastic foil.*

Ribbed V-belt, checking

The ribbed V-belt is self-adjusting and does not require any routine maintenance aside from periodic inspection for wear.

1. Raise vehicle and support safely on jackstands or with hoist, see **Lifting Vehicle**.

2. Remove lower sound absorber panels as described earlier.

3. Turn engine at vibration damper/belt pulley using a socket and wrench. See Fig. 31.

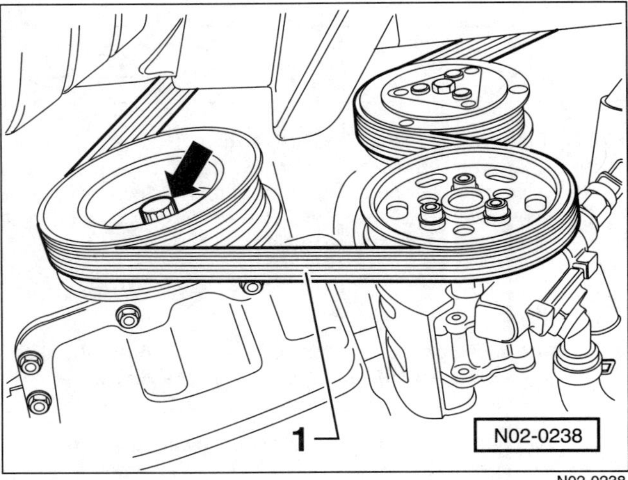

N02-0238

Fig. 31. Check condition of ribbed V-belt by turning engine with 12pt. socket wrench on vibration damper/belt pulley (**arrow**).

4. Check belt condition for the following:
   - Subsurface cracks, core ruptures and cross-sectional breaks
   - Layer separation
   - Fraying of cord strands
   - Flank wear, material condition, fraying, brittleness, glassiness and cracks
   - Traces of oil and grease

NOTE —
It is essential to replace the ribbed belt if it is found to be faulty.

Ribbed V-belt, replacing (4-cylinder gasoline engines)

1. Remove lower sound absorber panel below ribbed V-belt, as described earlier.

2. Mark direction of rotation on ribbed V-belt with chalk or crayon.

3. Swing tension roller off of belt with a wrench and hold. See Fig. 32.

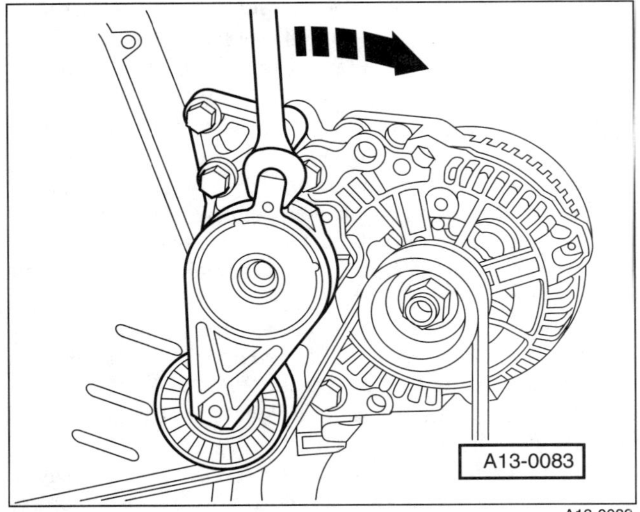

A13-0083

Fig. 32. Using a 15 mm wrench, swing tensioner out of way (**arrow**).

4. Lock tensioner in released position with suitable tool. See Fig. 33.

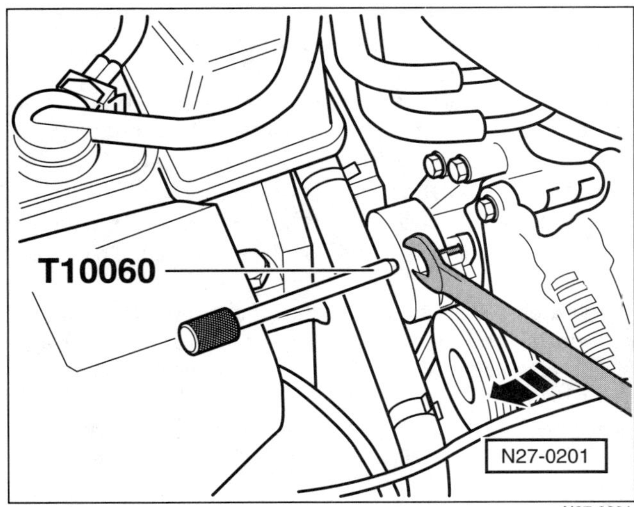

N27-0201

Fig. 33. While holding tensioner, insert holding device (VW T10060 mandrel shown) into tensioner to lock in position.

5. Remove belt.

6. Installation is the reverse of removal. Observe belt routing. See Fig. 34. and Fig. 35.

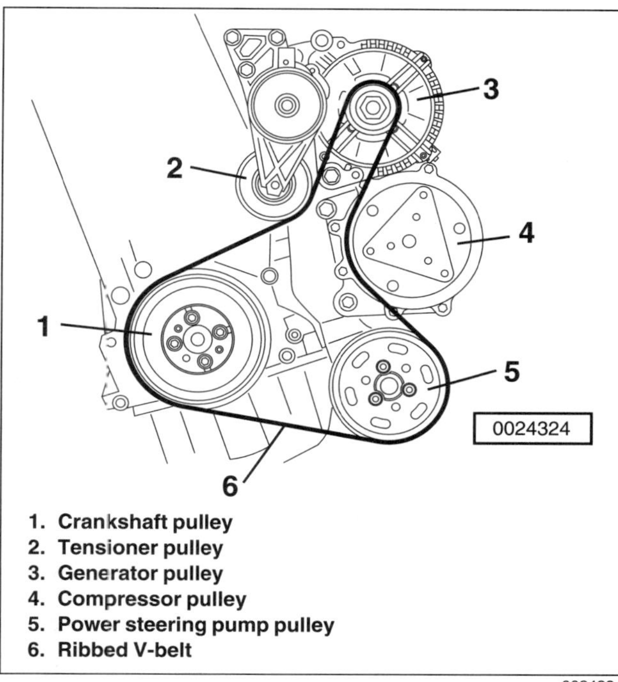

Fig. 34. Ribbed V-belt routing for 4-cylinder gasoline engines with air conditioning.

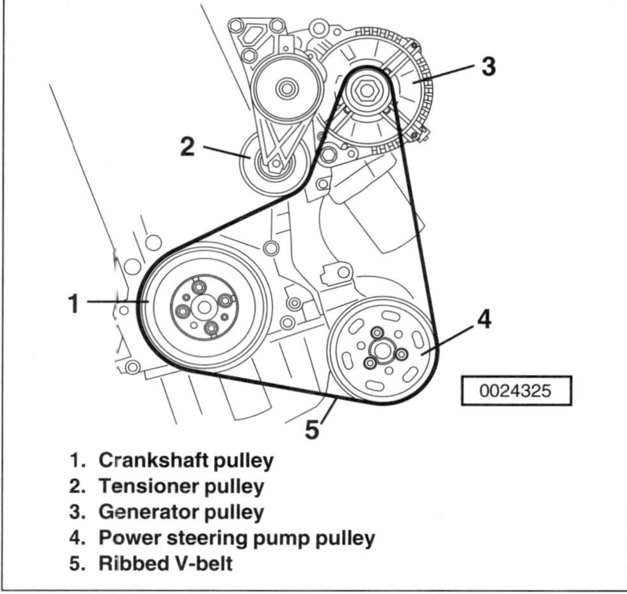

Fig. 35. Ribbed V-belt routing for 4-cylinder gasoline engines without air conditioning.

> ***CAUTION —***
> *Ensure correct seating of ribbed V-belt in pulleys. Failure to seat belt properly will severely damage ribbed V-belt.*

Ribbed V-belt, replacing (diesel engine)

1. Remove right side lower sound absorber panel as given earlier.

2. Remove connecting pipe between intercooler and turbocharger.

3. Mark direction of rotation on ribbed V-belt with chalk or crayon.

4. Swing tension roller off of belt with a wrench and hold while removing belt. See Fig. 36.

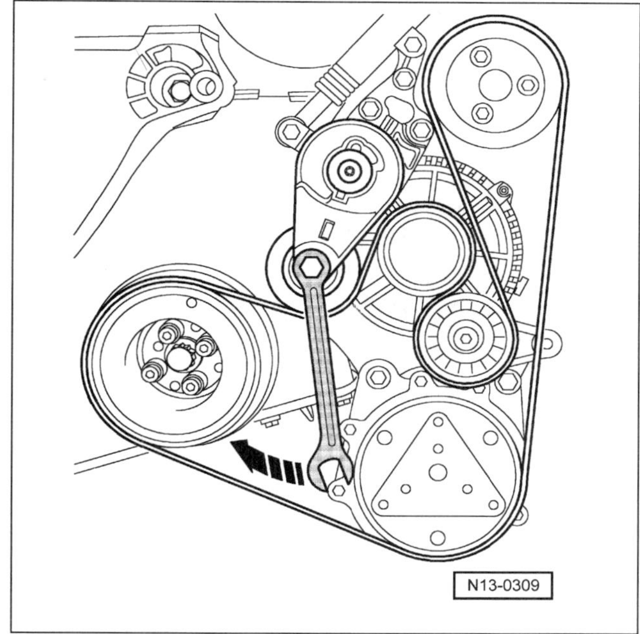

Fig. 36. Using a 15 mm wrench, swing tensioner out of the way (**arrow**) and hold while removing belt from pulleys.

5. Installation is the reverse of removal. Observe belt routing. See Fig. 37. and Fig. 38.

> ***CAUTION —***
> *Ensure correct seating of ribbed V-belt in pulleys. Failure to seat belt properly will severely damage ribbed V-belt very quickly.*

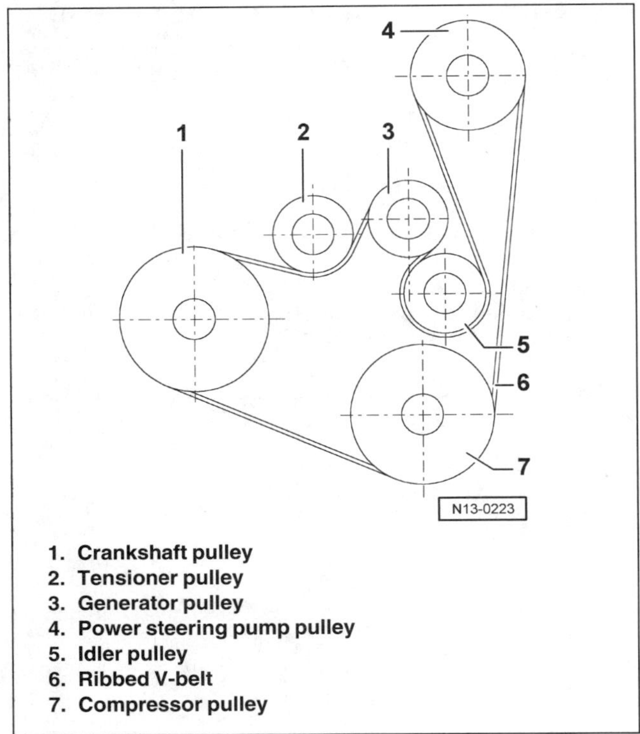

N13-0223

Fig. 37. Ribbed V-belt routing for diesel engines with air conditioning.

> ***NOTE —***
> *On engines with air conditioning, slip belt off of compressor pulley first and install to compressor pulley last.*

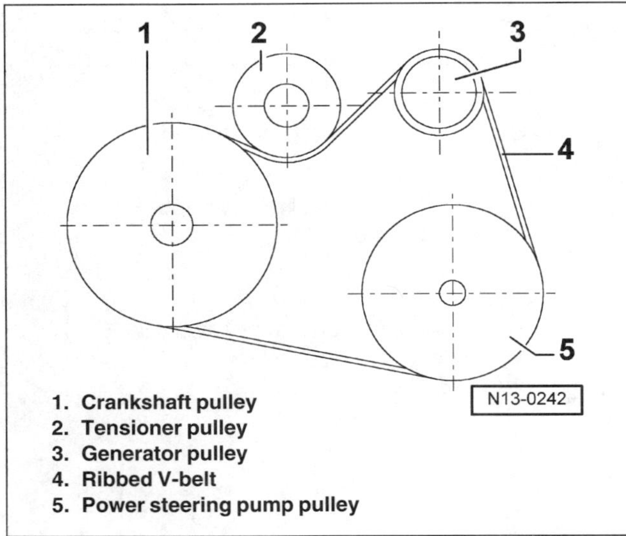

N13-0242

Fig. 38. Ribbed V-belt routing for diesel engines without air conditioning.

> ***NOTE —***
> *On engines without air conditioning, slip belt off of generator pulley first and install to generator pulley last.*

Ribbed V-belt, replacing (6-cylinder engine)

1. Remove upper and lower right sound absorber panels as described earlier.
2. Remove air cleaner housing complete with mass air flow sensor. See **24a Fuel Injection-Motronic**.
3. Temporarily install bolt (M8x80) in threaded hole in belt tensioner and thread bolt in until ribbed V-belt is free of tension. See Fig. 39.

> ***CAUTION —***
> *Do not over tighten bolt. Thread bolt in only until ribbed V-belt can be removed. The tensioner housing may be damaged if the bolt is overtightened.*

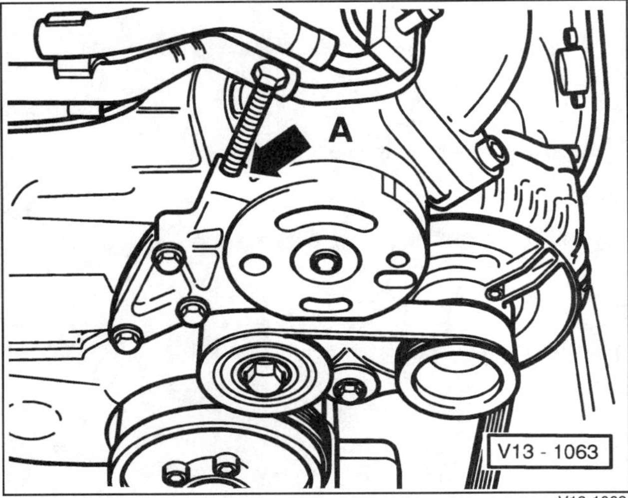

V13-1063

Fig. 39. To relieve poly-ribbed belt tension on 6-cylinder engines, thread M8x80 bolt (**A**) into tensioner until belt is free of tension.

4. If reinstalling the old belt, mark running direction on belt. Remove poly-ribbed belt from pulleys.
5. Install poly-ribbed belt in position. See Fig. 40.
6. Slowly remove M8 bolt from tensioner, making sure belt is correctly seated in pulley grooves.
7. The remainder of installation is the reverse of removal. Start engine and check that belt runs smoothly.

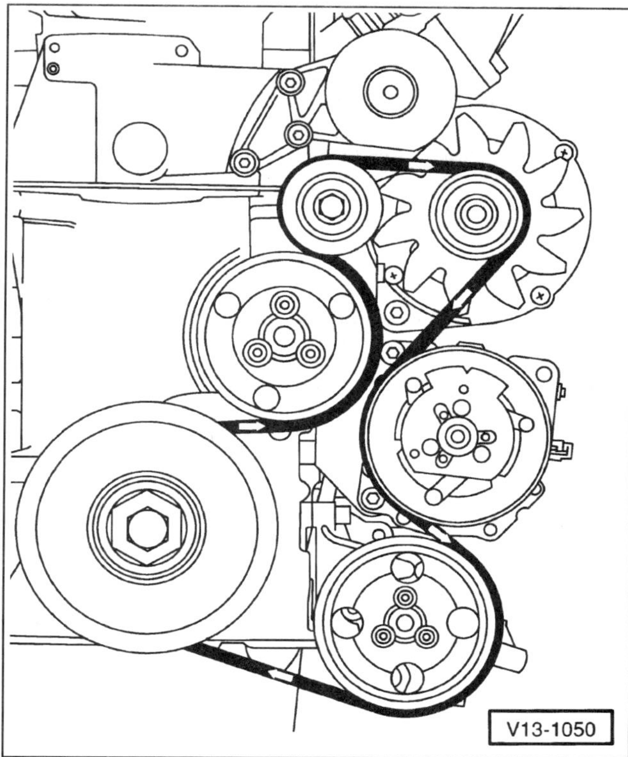

V13-1050

Fig. 40. Poly-ribbed belt routing on 6-cylinder engine. Arrows indicate direction of travel.

Timing belt, checking

The timing belt, also called the camshaft drive belt is a reinforced rubberized toothed belt that drives that camshaft. On diesel engines, the belt also drives the injection pump. The belt is subjected to high temperatures and should be inspected during scheduled maintenance intervals. See **Maintenance Schedules** at the back of this section.

To inspect the toothed belt, the upper section of the toothed belt guard belt must first be removed. Inspect belt for tears, separation of layers, fraying of belt cords, surface cracks, or traces of oil and grease. Replace belt if any faults are found. The belt can also be measured with a Vernier caliper to determine if replacement is necessary. See Fig. 41.

Measured width of timing belt

- Wear limit . . . . 22 mm (0.866 in.)

NOTE —
Volkswagen does not specify a replacement interval for the timing belt on gasoline engines. However, the publisher recommends the belt be replaced at least every 90k miles or 5 years.

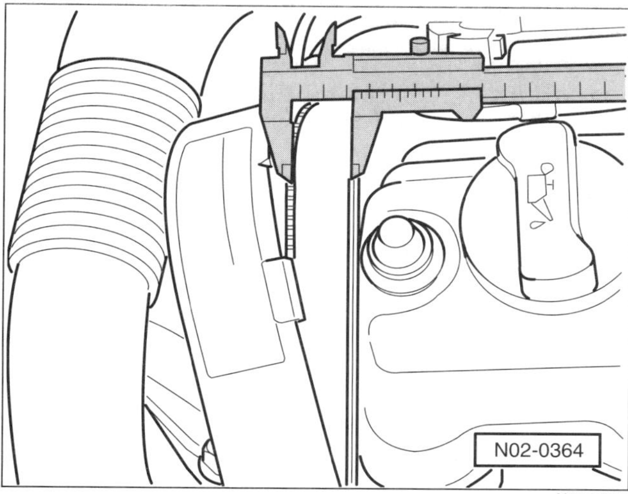

N02-0364

Fig. 41. Release retaining clips and move timing belt upper cover to side. Measure width of belt; wear limit is 22mm (0.866 in.).

Timing belts found on all engines use semi-automatic tensioners that do not generally require adjustments. See **15 Cylinder Head and Valvetrain** for belt and tensioner replacement procedures.

Spark plugs, replacing (gasoline engines)

Spark plugs are generally replaced during scheduled maintenance services. Due to the design of the combustion chambers and shape of the cylinder head, spark plug replacement can easily be accomplished without removal of intake manifold. See Fig. 42.

0024276

Fig. 42. Spark plug wires shown with upper section of intake manifold removed for clarity. Note that spark plugs for cylinders #1 and #2 are angled to the left and that spark plugs for cylinders #3 and #4 are angled to the right. AEG engine shown.

1. Remove the upper sound absorber panel.

NOTE —
For AFP (VR6) engines the spark plug wires must be removed first with special tool T10029, or equivalent before removing the upper sound absorber panel.

2. Remove the spark plug wire from cylinder 1 with a suitable tool such as VW special tool T10029. Do not pull on the wires.

NOTE —
It may be necessary to unplug the injector wire and gently turn the injector in the mounts for access.

3. Remove spark plug with a 5/8 in. (16 mm) spark plug socket and an extension.

4. Check gap on new spark plug and install, re-install injector wire and plug wire.

5. Repeat for each remaining cylinder.

6. Install upper sound absorber panel and spark plug wires.

Tightening torques
- Spark plug to cylinder head
  - 4-cylinder engine .... 30 Nm (22 ft-lb)
  - 6-cylinder engine .... 25 Nm (18 ft-lb)

Specification
- Spark Plugs-Long Life (1.8L engine)
  - Original equipment number 101-000-063-AA
  - Manufacturers number .... NGK PFR 6Q
  - Gap .... 0.80 mm (0.031 in)
- Spark Plugs-Long Life (2.0L engine)
  - Original equipment number 101-000-033-AA
  - Manufacturers number .... NGK BKUR 6 ET-10
  - Gap .... 0.90 to 1.10 mm (0.035 to 0.043 in)
- Spark Plugs-Long Life (2.8L engine)
  - Original equipment number 101-000-035-AA
  - Manufacturers number .... NGK BKR 5 EKUP
  - Gap .... 0.70 mm (0.027 in)

NOTE —
Volkswagen part numbers are given for reference only. Always consult with your Volkswagen parts department or aftermarket parts specialist for the latest parts information.

Air filter element, replacing

The air filter element should generally be replaced as specified in the maintenance tables. Under severe conditions, however, such as driving on dirt or desert roads, or in dusty areas, it is advisable to replace the element more frequently.

1. Disconnect harness connector for mass air flow sensor (MAF).

2. Loosen hose clamp on intake hose and take hose off near mass air flow sensor.

3. Remove air cleaner housing mounting bolts and housing from car. See Fig. 43.

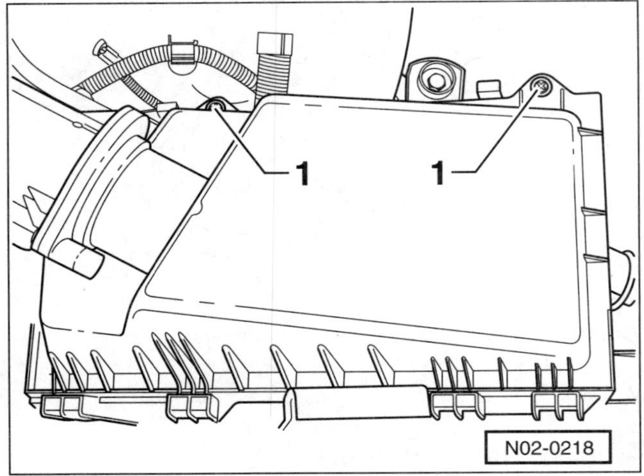

N02-0218

Fig. 43. remove mounting bolts for air cleaner housing (**arrows**). Disconnect MAF sensor harness connector and intake air duct. Remove air cleaner assembly from car.

4. Remove retaining clips/and or screws holding upper and lower sections of air filter housing together.

5. Remove old filter element.

6. Clean filter housing.

7. Install new filter element.

8. Remainder of installation is the reverse of removal.

UNDER CAR MAINTENANCE

Under car maintenance requires that the car be raised on a lift or properly supported on jackstands. Under car maintenance should not be carried out unless proper (safe) lifting equipment is available. See **Lifting Vehicle** for more information on lifting and working under the car.

> ***WARNING —***
> - *Do not work under a car supported solely by a jack. Jack stands must always be used when working under the car.*
> - *Jack stands must be placed on a hard, level surface (e.g. concrete).*

Brake system, visual inspection

Check the brake master cylinder, vacuum brake booster (also hydraulic unit if anti-lock brake system is fitted), brake pressure regulator, and brake calipers for leaks and damage.

- Brake hoses must not be twisted.
- Brake hoses must not touch any part of the vehicle when steering is at full lock.
- Check brake hoses for porosity and deterioration, brake hoses and brake lines for chafing points.
- Check brake connections and attachments for correct seating, leaks and corrosion.
- Any faults found must be repaired.

Brake pads (front and rear), checking

To accurately check the front brake pad thickness, the front wheels should be removed. With the wheel removed, measure the thickness of outer and inner pads. If pad thickness (including backing plate) is 7 mm (0.28 in.) or less, the brake pads should be replaced. See Fig. 44. and Fig. 45.

Brake pad wear limit	
• Minimum width (including backing plate)	7 mm (0.28 in.)

> ***NOTE —***
> - *Before removing the front wheels, mark their position in relation to the brake rotor so the wheel can be reinstalled in the same position.*
> - *When tightening wheel bolts, tighten the bolts in stages using a criss-cross pattern.*

Tightening torque	
• Wheel bolt to wheel hub.	120 Nm (89 ft-lb)

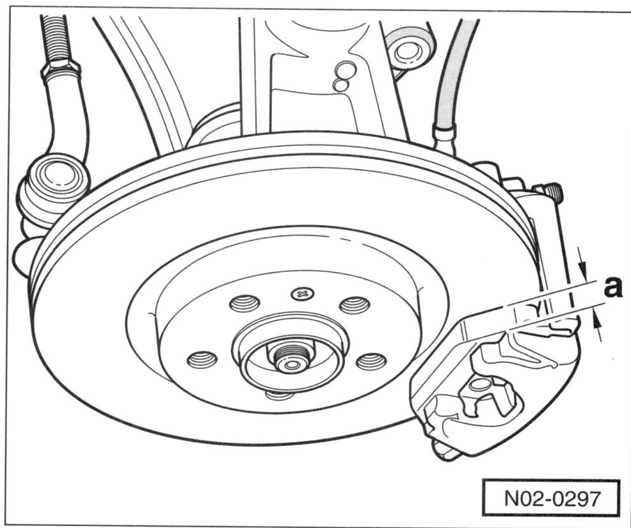

N02-0297

Fig. 44. Front brake pad thickness must be at least 7 mm (0.028 in.) including backing plate as indicated by dimension (**a**).

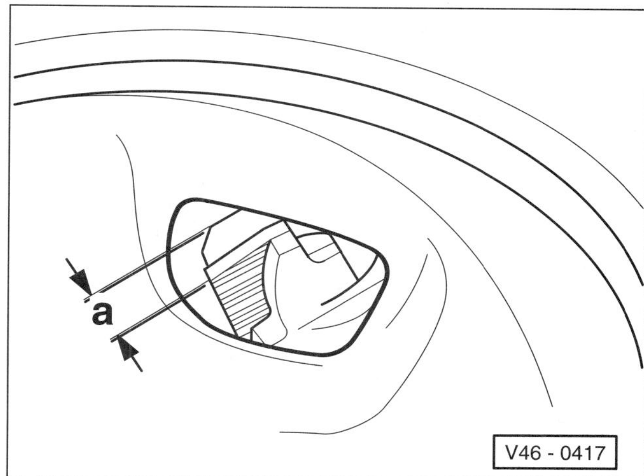

V46-0417

Fig. 45. Rear brake pads can be inspected without removing wheel. Brake pad thickness must be at least 7 mm (0.028 in.) including backing plate as indicated by dimension (**a**). Use flashlight and mirror to inspect if necessary.

Parking brake, adjusting

The parking brake acts on the rear brakes and is self-adjusting to compensate for wear. Adjustment of the parking brake is only necessary if brake components are replaced. See **46 Brakes–Mechanical Components** for parking brake adjustment and service procedures. The parking brake should begin to hold after approximately two clicks of the lever.

Tire service

Tire pressure should be checked on a regular basis. It is best to check pressures when the tires are cold. Refer to the data label on the fuel filler flap for proper inflation pressures. Be sure to also check the spare tire pressure. Check that all tires are the same type and tread pattern. Measure tread depth. If the tread wear has exceeded the minimum specification listed, the tire should be replaced.

Tire tread depth
- Minimum . . . . 1.6 mm (2/32 in.)

> ***CAUTION —***
> *Wheel alignment must be checked after replacing tires to ensure maximum tire life.*

Most tires have tread wear indicators spaced around the tires that will indicate when the tire has reached the wear limit. If the tops of the wear indicators no longer have any tread on them then the tire should be replaced. See Fig. 46.

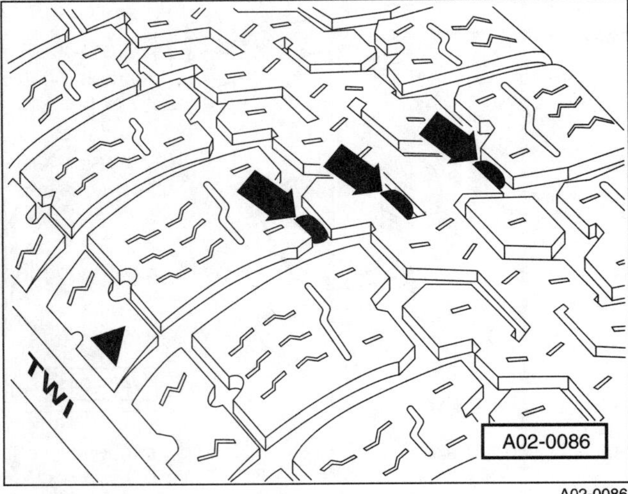

A02-0086

Fig. 46. Tread wear indicators (TWI) (**arrows**); if no tread is visible on top of indicators then the tire should be replaced.

The tires should also be checked for abnormal wear patterns.The tread wear pattern on the front tires is an indication of whether the toe and camber settings need to be checked. "Feathering" on the tread indicates incorrect toe. If the tread is worn on one side, this is usually caused by incorrect camber.

To extended tire life and minimize wear, Volkswagen recommends that the tires be rotated front to rear every 10,000 miles. For more information on tires, see **44 Wheels–Tires, Wheel Alignment**.

Drive axles, checking boots

There are inner and outer CV boots on each front axle shaft. The boots should be regularly inspected for tears, cracks, or deterioration. Once the boot is open to the weather, abrasive road debris can enter the joint and quickly destroy it. If boot replacement is carried out promptly, chances are good that the joint can be saved. See **40 Front Suspension and Drive Axles** for drive boot replacement procedures.

Front suspension components, checking

Check ball joint dust boots for damage and correct seating. Check for play in ball joints. Check inner and outer tie rod end boots for damage and correct seating. Check for play by moving tie rods and wheels. Check attachment of ball joints and tie rod ends. See **40 Front Suspension and Drive Axles** for suspension component replacement.

Transmission, checking for leaks

Inspect the transmission for signs of fluid leakage. Pay particular attention to the axle seals. Repair any leaks found, see **34 Manual Transmission.**

Final drive oil level, checking

On cars with manual transmission, the final drive lubricant shares a common supply with the transmission lubricant. For final drive and transmission fluid level checking, see **Transmission oil level, checking (manual transmission)**.

On cars with automatic transmission, the final drive oil level is checked by removing the speedometer drive gear from the transmission housing and using the drive gear as a dipstick. The car should be on a level surface when making the check.

1. Remove speedometer drive, wipe clean with a cloth and install again.
2. Remove drive and check oil level. See Fig. 47.

> ***NOTE —***
> - *The oil level must between the MIN and MAX markings.*
> - *The amount of oil between the MIN and MAX markings is approximately 0.1 Liter (0.1 qt).*

3. If oil level is too low, add oil in small amounts until proper level is reached.

Specification
- Automatic transmission, final drive lubricant G 052 145 A2 . . . . SAE 75 W90 (Synthetic oil)

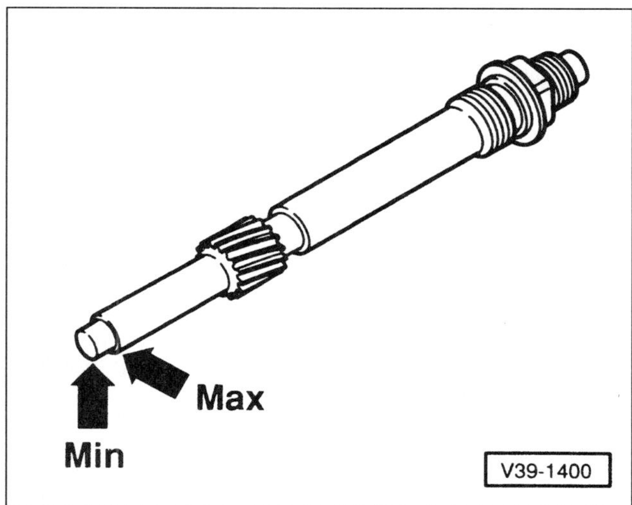

V39-1400

Fig. 47. Automatic transmission speedometer drive doubles as a dipstick. Fluid level should be between **min** and **max** marks.

NOTE —
Volkswagen part numbers are given for reference only! Always consult with your Volkswagen Parts Department or aftermarket parts specialist for the latest parts information.

4. If oil level is too high, suction out excess.

5. When proper level is obtained, install speedometer drive.

Transmission oil level, checking (manual transmission)

1. Remove oil filler plug with 17 mm Allen wrench. See Fig. 48.

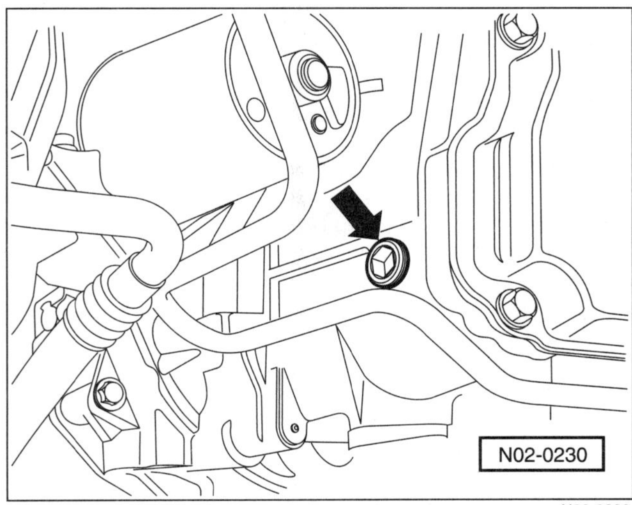

N02-0230

Fig. 48. Manual transmission fill plug (**arrow**).

2. Check oil level.

NOTE —
Oil level must be to lower edge of filler plug hole.

3. If oil level is too low, add oil in small amounts until proper level is reached.

4. Install oil filler plug.

Specification

- Manual transmission lubricant
  G 052 145 A2 . . . . SAE 75 W90 (Synthetic oil)

NOTE —
Volkswagen part numbers are given for reference only! Always consult with your Volkswagen Parts Department or aftermarket parts specialist for the latest parts information.

Transmission fluid (ATF) level, checking and adjusting (automatic transmission)

The 01M automatic transmission does not have a dipstick and the procedure requires measuring and maintaining a specified ATF temperature (which is neither cold nor hot, but in between) during the ATF level checking. Special Volkswagen tools are required for this operation and it is therefore recommended that ATF level checking on 01M transmission be left to an authorized Volkswagen dealer.

Before starting, be sure that the following checking conditions are met:

- Transmission not in limp-home mode, ATF temperature not above approx. 30°C (86° F)
- Vehicle must be level
- Selector lever in “P”
- Center and left sound absorber panels removed

1. Attach container of ATF filler VAG 1924 to vehicle. See Fig. 49.

2. Start engine.

3. Connect suitable scan tool and access Transmission Control Module. If using a Volkswagen supplied VAG 1551/1552, observe the following sequence in the scan tool display window:
   - 1 - Rapid Data
   - Address word 02 - Transmission electronics
   - Advance to Read Measuring Value Blocks - 08
   - Select display group 05
   - Observe display field 1 for transmission temperature (must be below 30°C at start)

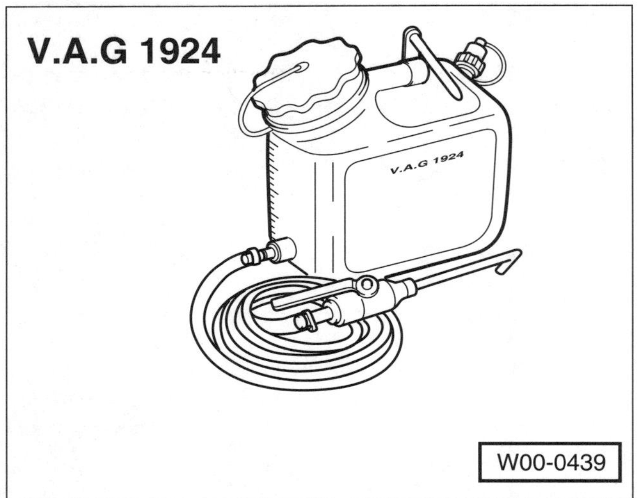

W00-0439

Fig. 49. Volkswagen special tool VAG 1924 used for filling automatic transmissions.

4. Lift vehicle.

5. Place container under transmission.

6. Bring ATF to test temperature.

ATF test temperature
- 35 to 45°C (95 to 113°F)

7. Remove ATF level plug from oil pan. See Fig. 50.

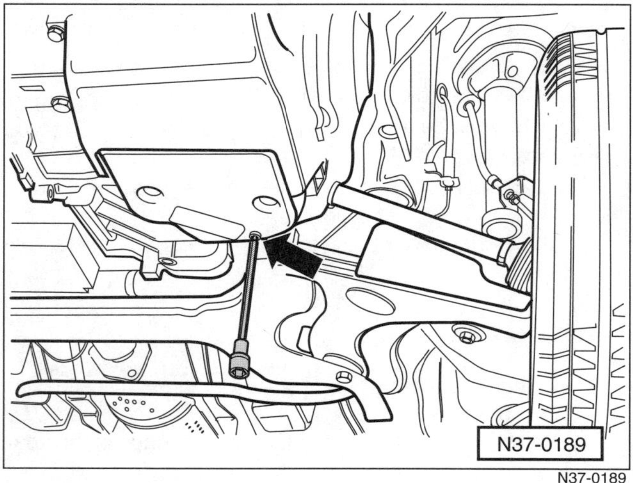

N37-0189

Fig. 50. Remove ATF level plug (**arrow**) in transmission oil pan.

8. If ATF drips out of hole when temperature is between 35°C to 45°C, ATF level is correct and no further action is required. Install new seal on level plug and torque. This completes the ATF check.

Tightening torque
- ATF level plug with new seal. . . . . 15 Nm (11 ft-lb)

9. If no ATF drips out of hole by the time the temperature reaches 45°C (113°F), fill through the filler tube until fluid comes out of the level checking hole. See Fig. 51. and Fig. 52.

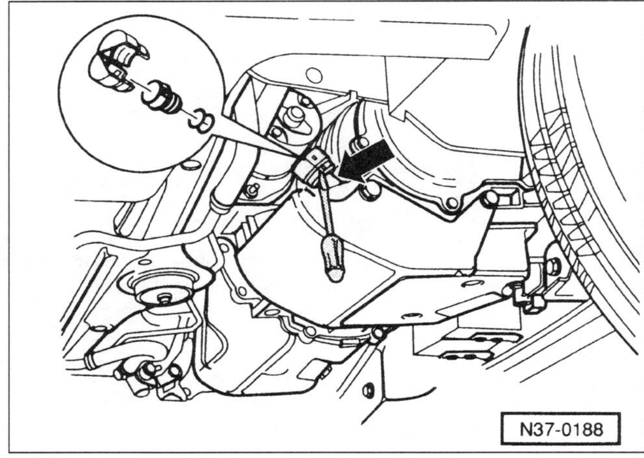

N37-0188

Fig. 51. Pry off plug and seal (**arrow**) with screwdriver. The seal will be destroyed, always replace.

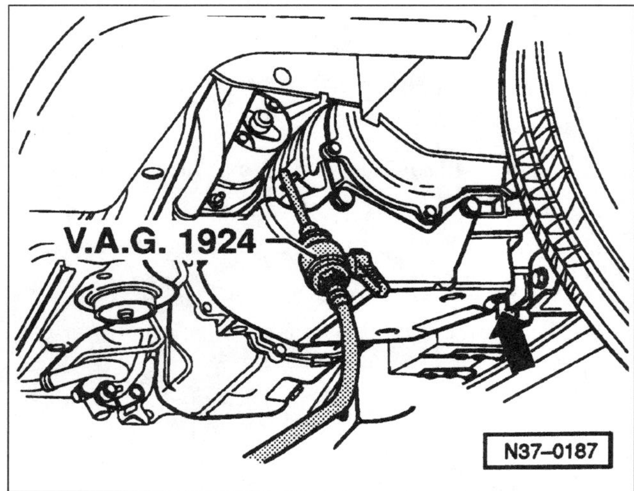

N37-0187

Fig. 52. Special tool VAG 1924 shown inserted into filler tube for automatic transmission filling.

10. Install plug on filler tube and secure with new seal. Install new seal on level plug and torque. This completes the ATF check.

If ATF ran out immediately when plug was removed from level checking hole, transmission was overfilled. Allow fluid to run out until temperature on scan tool is between 35°C and 45°C. Install new seal on level plug and torque. This completes the ATF check.

Transmission fluid (ATF), changing (automatic transmission)

1. Remove center and left sound absorber panels.
2. Place suitable container under transmission.
3. Remove ATF level plug from oil pan. See Fig. 53.

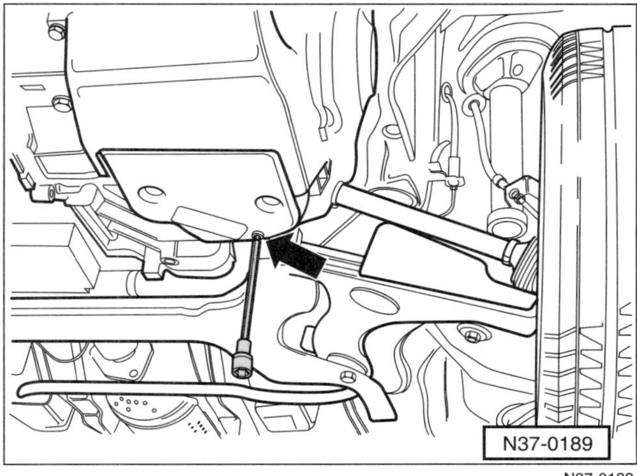

N37-0189

Fig. 53. Remove ATF level plug (**arrow**) and unscrew inner overflow pipe.

4. Remove overflow pipe from within level plug hole. ATF will flow out.
5. Drain ATF.
6. When fluid has drained, install overflow pipe.
7. Install level plug (with old seal) and tighten hand-tight.
8. Fill with 3 liters (3.2 qt.) of ATF through filler line using VAG 1924. See Fig. 52.
9. Start engine and shift through all selector lever positions with the vehicle stationary.
10. Check and top up ATF level as given earlier.

Exhaust system, checking

> ***WARNING —***
> - *The exhaust system operates at extremely high temperatures. Do not touch the exhaust system while the engine is running.*
> - *Allow exhaust system to cool at least one hour before touching.*

Inspect exhaust system for leaks or damage. Inspect exhaust system mounts. Replace faulty, missing or deteriorated parts.

Underbody sealant, checking

When performing the visual inspection for damage to the underbody sealant, also check the underbody, wheel housings and sill panels. Any faults found should be promptly repaired.

BODY AND INTERIOR MAINTENANCE

Body exterior

Automobile finishes are subjected to abuse from industrial fumes, corrosive road salt, acid rain, and other damaging airborn elements. Regular and correct care will contribute to maintaining and preserving the exterior of your Volkswagen.

> ***NOTE —***
> *Proper care may be a condition for upholding the new car warranty, should corrosion damage or paint defects occur.*

The best protection against environmental influences is frequent washing and waxing. How often this is required depends on the environment where the vehicle is used.

Under certain circumstances weekly washing may be necessary. Under other conditions, a monthly washing and waxing may be adequate. Even if a wax solution is used when washing your vehicle, it is advisable to protect the paint with a coat of hard wax at least twice a year. Check the paint for chips and scratches. Paint defects should be touched up soon after they occur to prevent corrosion.

After the winter, the underside of the vehicle should be thoroughly washed.

Exterior plastic and vinyl should be kept clean. Occasionally apply a colorless vinyl or leather preservative. DO NOT wax plastic or vinyl.

Exterior lights, checking

Check operation of headlights (high and low beam), marker lights, taillights, turn signal lights, brake lights, reverse lights and emergency flasher lights. Use a helper when checking lights. See **94 Lights, Accessories–Exterior**.

Interior lights, checking

Check operation of indicator and instrument cluster warning bulbs. Check operation of interior cabin illumination bulbs. See **96 Lights, Accessories-Interior**.

Dust and pollen filter, replacing

All vehicles are equipped with a ventilation air dust and pollen filter. This filter prevents most dust and pollen from entering the passenger compartment. Volkswagen specifies replacement of this filter at regular mileage intervals. **See 80 Heating and Ventilation.**

Airbag unit, visual inspection

All models are fitted with driver's side and passenger's side airbags. In addition, all models are fitted with side airbags built into the front seat backrest..

> ***WARNING —***
> - *The padded airbag covers on the steering wheel and instrument panel must not be covered over or have any objects affixed to them.*
> - *Do not apply any chemical treatment to airbag unit covers. Clean with a dry or water moistened cloth only.*

Inspect padded airbag unit covers on steering wheel and instrument panel and side airbag units for signs of external damage. Check with an authorized Volkswagen dealer if any faults are found.

Inspect seats for covers that may obstruct or hinder proper deployment of side airbag.

> ***WARNING —***
> *Volkswagen of America has issued a directive specifically warning against the installation of aftermarket upholstery on any vehicle equipped with side airbags. The factory-installed upholstery is designed to separate in specific places at specific rates, and in specific directions. Installation of non-factory upholstery including, but not limited to, "beads" and "sheepskins", may cause seat mounted airbags to deploy when they are not supposed to; fail to deploy when they should; or to deploy in some manner other than designed. This is a safety hazard and could result in serious injury or death to occupants of the vehicle.*

Door check straps and hinges, lubrication

The door checks straps and door hinges should be lubricated periodically. Use a lithium grease for the job. Lubricate the hinge securing bolt with lock cylinder spray. It is a good idea to clean the old grease away before applying the new lubricant. See Fig. 54.

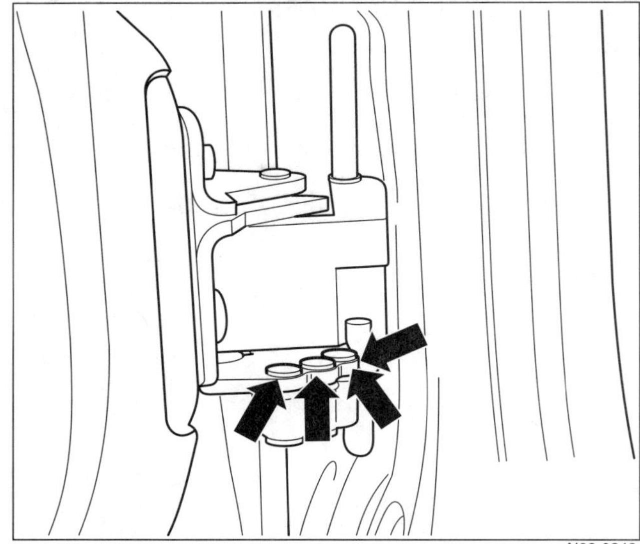

Fig. 54. Lubricate door check strap (**arrow A**) with Volkswagen special grease G 000 400 and securing bolt (**arrow B**) with special lock cylinder lubricant spray G 000 400 01.

Windshield wipers and washers, checking

Inspect windshield wiper blades, front and rear. Replace damaged or deteriorated parts. Check spray pattern of windshield washers, front and rear, adjust as necessary. Fill reservoir for windshield cleaning system. Always add a windshield cleaner to the water (windshield washer antifreeze in winter). See **92 Wipers and Washers**.

In cases where cleaning of the windshield and replacement of the wiper blades or inserts fails to eliminate streaking conditions, a more complete cleaning of the windshield may be needed. Thoroughly clean the outside of the windshield with a non-abrasive cleaner such as Bon Ami® or Soft Scrub® using a soft cloth and water. Rub until windshield is completely clean of all foreign material. Rinse windshield thoroughly.

On board diagnostics (OBD), checking

A final part of Volkswagen's maintenance program specifies checking the On-board Diagnostic (OBD) system memory. The ODB system is integrated into the engine management control module and monitors emissions-related and other electrical components on the car, including the adaptive automatic transmission, the ABS system, and the airbag system. Checking the OBD memory for faults requires special tools and training. Therefore, it is recommended that this job be carried out by an authorized Volkswagen dealer or qualified independent repair shop.

> ***NOTE —***
> *A list of diagnostic trouble codes for generic aftermarket scan tools (P-codes) can be found at the back of this manual.*

QUALITY REVIEW

When you have finished working under the hood and around other areas of the vehicle, it is advisable to take a moment to quality check or review your work. This helps to insure that the operation or repair has been completed properly with all affected systems functioning within normal parameters. These may include the following:

Road test

Upon completion of the maintenance work, the vehicle should be road tested. Check the following systems during the road test:

Automatic transmission shift lock

1. Turn ignition on, but do not start engine. Apply parking brake.
2. With gearshift selector in park attempt to shift into a drive or reverse. Selector lever should not move.
3. Press brake pedal. Selector lever should move into gear.
4. Place gear selector lever in neutral and release brake pedal.
5. Attempt to shift into gear. Selector lever should not move.
6. Press the brake pedal. Selector lever should move into gear.
7. If shift lock does not operate as described, see **37 Automatic Transmission**.

Automatic park/neutral position switch

Apply the parking brake and step on the brake pedal. Place the gear shift selector in park and attempt to start car. Repeat for all gears. The engine should only start in park or neutral. See **37 Automatic Transmission**.

Brake pedal and parking brake

Check pedal and handbrake travel (free play) and operation.

- Travel of brake pedal: max. 1/3 of overall pedal travel
- Travel of parking brake lever: 2 notches (clicks)

Manual gearshift

Check for smooth operation of the transmission and its gearshift.

Steering

Check steering play with vehicle weight on the wheels by turning steering wheel back and forth (wheels in straight ahead position).

- Steering play: zero play with engine running

Kickdown operation

Depress accelerator pedal fully to floor. Depending on vehicle speed and engine speed, upshift is either delayed or the transmission shifts down into the next lower gear.

Air conditioner and heater

Check the full range of the heater and the air conditioner for proper function. Cold or warm air must flow out of the vents.

Additional checks

Perform the following checks in accordance with the vehicle equipment and the road conditions available during the road test:

- Engine performance, idle speed, acceleration, cold and hot starting.
- Clutch operation, smoothness and pedal pressure.
- Brake operation, noise and function of ABS if equipped.
- Cruise control system operation.
- Radio operation, and reception.
- General vehicle handling and dynamics such as pulling to the side, cornering, vibrations in steering wheel and unusual noises.

MAINTENANCE SCHEDULES

The maintenance schedules list all of the routine maintenance specified by Volkswagen, as well as the mileage intervals at which they should be performed.

In addition to the specified mileage intervals, Volkswagen also recommends that services be carried out on the basis of time. For 1999 and 2000 model years, the time interval is generally 6 months after delivery, 12 months after delivery, and every 12 months thereafter.

NOTE —

- *Aside from keeping your Volkswagen in the best possible condition, scheduled maintenance plays a role in maintaining full coverage under Volkswagen's extensive warranties. If in doubt about the terms and conditions of your car's warranty, consult an authorized Volkswagen dealer.*
- *Volkswagen continually updates maintenance schedules to suit changing conditions through the issuance of Maintenance Schedule Service Circulars. If in doubt about any of the requirements for your vehicle, consult an authorized Volkswagen dealer.*
- *The maintenance tables on the following pages contain information for all Volkswagen models available at the time of publication. The information for V6 engines does not apply to vehicles covered by this manual.*

Table a. 1999 model year maintenance schedule

Miles	5	10	15	20	25	30	35	40	45	50	55	60	65	70	75	80	85	90	95	100	105
Kilometers	8	16	24	32	40	48	56	64	72	80	88	96	104	112	120	128	136	144	152	160	168
TDI																					
Engine Oil – change	•	•		•		•		•		•		•		•		•		•		•	
Engine Filter – change	•	•		•		•		•		•		•		•		•		•		•	
Water Sep. – drain	•	•		•		•		•		•		•		•		•		•		•	
Timing Belt – check condition	•	•		•		•		•		•		•		•		•		•		•	
Fuel Filter – replace				•				•				•				•				•	
Timing Belt – replace**												•									
Timing Belt Tensioner – replace***												•									
1.8T																					
Engine Oil – change	•	•	•	•	•	•	•	•	•	•	•	•	•	•	•	•	•	•	•	•	•
Engine Filter – change	•	•	•	•	•	•	•	•	•	•	•	•	•	•	•	•	•	•	•	•	•
V-Belt – replace																•					
Spark Plugs – replace								•								•					
Timing Belt – check condition								•								•					
Timing Belt – replace																					•
Timing Belt Tensioner – replace																					•
2.0																					
Engine Oil – change	•	•		•		•		•		•		•		•		•		•		•	
Engine Filter – change	•	•		•		•		•		•		•		•		•		•		•	
Spark Plugs – replace (all but New Beetle)				•				•				•				•				•	
Spark Plugs – replace (NB)								•								•					
Timing Belt – check condition								•								•					
VR6																					
Engine Oil – change	•	•		•		•		•		•		•		•		•		•		•	
Engine Filter – change	•	•		•		•		•		•		•		•		•		•		•	
Spark Plugs – replace								•								•					
V6																					
Engine Oil – change	•	•	•	•	•	•	•	•	•	•	•	•	•	•	•	•	•	•	•	•	•
Engine Filter – change	•	•	•	•	•	•	•	•	•	•	•	•	•	•	•	•	•	•	•	•	•
Spark Plugs – replace								•								•					
Timing Belt – check condition								•								•					
Timing Belt – replace																					•
Timing Belt Tensioner – replace																					•
All Cars																					
W/W Fluid – check level		•		•		•		•		•		•		•		•		•		•	
Auto-Shift Lock – check		•		•		•		•		•		•		•		•		•		•	
Brake System – check		•		•		•		•		•		•		•		•		•		•	
Wheels – rotate front to rear		•		•		•		•		•		•		•		•		•		•	
Battery – check electrolyte level				•				•				•				•				•	
Dust Pollen Filter – replace				•				•				•				•				•	
Manual Trans. – check for leaks				•				•				•				•				•	
Automatic Trans. – check for leaks				•				•				•				•				•	
Tires/Spare – check condition				•				•				•				•				•	
Drive Shafts – check boots				•				•				•				•				•	
OBD – check DTC memory				•				•				•				•				•	
Door Check Straps – lubricate				•				•				•				•				•	
During Road Test				•				•				•				•				•	
After Road Test				•				•				•				•				•	
Air Cleaner* – replace filter								•								•					
Cooling System – check level				•				•				•				•				•	
V-Belt – check tension/condition								•								•					
Ribbed Belt – check condition								•								•					
Front Axle – check								•								•					
Check ATF and diff. level								•								•					
Headlights – adjust				•				•				•				•				•	

*Every 40,000 miles and 4 years; except Passat and EuroVan, every 2 years **Recommended ***Recommended; replace once only
Brake Fluid – change every 2 years regardless of mileage
Air Bag System – check for function and damage after 4 years, 8 years and every 2 years thereafter

Table b. 2000 model year maintenance schedule

Miles	5	10	15	20	25	30	35	40	45	50	55	60	65	70	75	80	85	90	95	100	105
Kilometers	8	16	24	32	40	48	56	64	72	80	88	96	104	112	120	128	136	144	152	160	168
TDI																					
Engine Oil – change	•	•		•		•		•		•		•		•		•		•		•	
Engine Filter – change	•	•		•		•		•		•		•		•		•		•		•	
Water Sep. – drain	•	•		•		•		•		•		•		•		•		•		•	
Timing Belt – check condition	•	•		•		•		•		•		•		•		•		•		•	
Fuel Filter – replace				•				•				•				•				•	
Timing Belt – replace*								A				M				A					
1.8T																					
Engine Oil – change	•	•	•	•	•	•	•	•	•	•	•	•	•	•	•	•	•	•	•	•	•
Engine Filter – change	•	•	•	•	•	•	•	•	•	•	•	•	•	•	•	•	•	•	•	•	•
Spark Plugs – replace								•								•					
V-Belt – replace																•					
Timing Belt – check condition								•								•					
Timing Belt – replace																					•
Timing Belt Tensioner – replace																					•
2.0																					
Engine Oil – change	•	•		•		•		•		•		•		•		•		•		•	
Engine Filter – change	•	•		•		•		•		•		•		•		•		•		•	
Spark Plugs – replace (Cabrio)				•				•				•				•				•	
Spark Plugs – replace (except Cabrio)								•								•					
Timing Belt – check condition								•								•					
VR6																					
Engine Oil – change	•	•		•		•		•		•		•		•		•		•		•	
Engine Filter – change	•	•		•		•		•		•		•		•		•		•		•	
Spark Plugs – replace								•								•					
V6																					
Engine Oil – change	•	•	•	•	•	•	•	•	•	•	•	•	•	•	•	•	•	•	•	•	•
Engine Filter – change	•	•	•	•	•	•	•	•	•	•	•	•	•	•	•	•	•	•	•	•	•
Spark Plugs – replace								•								•					
Timing Belt – check condition								•								•					
Timing Belt – replace																					•
Timing Belt Tensioner – replace																					•
All Cars																					
W/W Fluid – check level		•		•		•		•		•		•		•		•		•		•	
Auto-Shift Lock – check		•		•		•		•		•		•		•		•		•		•	
Brake System – check		•		•		•		•		•		•		•		•		•		•	
Wheels – rotate front to rear		•		•		•		•		•		•		•		•		•		•	
Air Bag System **		•		•		•		•		•		•		•		•		•		•	
Battery – check electrolyte level				•				•				•				•				•	
Dust Pollen Filter – replace				•				•				•				•				•	
Cooling System – check level				•				•				•				•				•	
Manual Trans. – check for leaks				•				•				•				•				•	
Automatic Trans. – check for leaks				•				•				•				•				•	
Tires/Spare – check condition				•				•				•				•				•	
Drive Shafts – check boots				•				•				•				•				•	
OBD – check DTC memory				•				•				•				•				•	
Door Hinge				•				•				•				•				•	
Headlights – adjust				•				•				•				•				•	
During Road Test				•				•				•				•				•	
After Road Test				•				•				•				•				•	
Air Cleaner*** – replace filter								•								•					
V-Belt – check tension/condition								•								•					
Ribbed Belt – check condition								•								•					
Brake Fluid****								•								•					
Check ATF and diff. level								•								•					
Front Axle (tie rod, etc.)								•								•					

*Recommended **Every 12 months regardless of mileage ***Every 2 years: Cabrio, Passat, EuroVan. Every 4 years: Golf, Jetta, New Beetle
****Replace every 2 years regardless of mileage

Table c. 2001 – 2002 model year maintenance schedule

Miles Kilometers	5 8	10 16	15 24	20 32	25 40	30 48	35 56	40 64	45 72	50 80	55 88	60 96	65 104	70 112	75 120	80 128	85 136	90 144	95 152	100 160	105 168
TDI																					
Engine Oil – change	•	•		•		•		•		•		•		•		•		•		•	
Engine Filter – change	•	•		•		•		•		•		•		•		•		•		•	
Water Sep. – drain	•	•		•		•		•		•		•		•		•		•		•	
Timing Belt – check condition	•	•		•		•		•		•		•		•		•		•		•	
Fuel Filter – replace				•				•				•				•				•	
Timing Belt – replace								A				M				A					
1.8T																					
Engine Oil – change	•	•	•	•	•	•	•	•	•	•	•	•	•	•	•	•	•	•	•	•	•
Engine Filter – change	•	•	•	•	•	•	•	•	•	•	•	•	•	•	•	•	•	•	•	•	•
Spark Plugs – replace								•								•					
V-Belt – replace																•					
Timing Belt – check condition								•								•					
Timing Belt – replace																					•
Timing Belt Tensioner – replace																					•
2.0																					
Engine Oil – change	•	•		•		•		•		•		•		•		•		•		•	
Engine Filter – change	•	•		•		•		•		•		•		•		•		•		•	
Spark Plugs – replace (Cabrio)				•				•				•				•				•	
Spark Plugs – replace (except Cabrio)								•								•					
Timing Belt – check condition								•								•					
VR6																					
Engine Oil – change	•	•		•		•		•		•		•		•		•		•		•	
Engine Filter – change	•	•		•		•		•		•		•		•		•		•		•	
Spark Plugs – replace								•								•					
V6																					
Engine Oil – change	•	•	•	•	•	•	•	•	•	•	•	•	•	•	•	•	•	•	•	•	•
Engine Filter – change	•	•	•	•	•	•	•	•	•	•	•	•	•	•	•	•	•	•	•	•	•
Spark Plugs – replace								•								•					
Timing Belt – check condition								•								•					
Timing Belt Tensioner – replace																					•
Timing Belt – replace																					•
All Cars																					
W/W Fluid – check level		•		•		•		•		•		•		•		•		•		•	
Auto-Shift Lock – check operation		•		•		•		•		•		•		•		•		•		•	
Brake System – check		•		•		•		•		•		•		•		•		•		•	
Wheels – rotate from front to rear		•		•		•		•		•		•		•		•		•		•	
Air Bag System – check function/ damage*		•		•		•		•		•		•		•		•		•		•	
Battery – check electrolyte level		•		•		•		•		•		•		•		•		•		•	
Dust Pollen Filter – replace				•				•				•				•				•	
Cooling System – check level				•				•				•				•				•	
Manual Transmission – for leaks				•				•				•				•				•	
Automatic Transmission – for leaks				•				•				•				•				•	
Tire/Spare Tire – check condition				•				•				•				•				•	
Drive Shafts – check boots				•				•				•				•				•	
OBD – check DTC memory				•				•				•				•				•	
Door Hinge				•				•				•				•				•	
Headlights – check and adjust if necessary				•				•				•				•				•	
Road Test – during				•				•				•				•				•	
Road Test – after				•				•				•				•				•	
Air Cleaner – replace filter**								•								•					
V-Belt – check tension/condition								•								•					
Ribbed Belt – check condition								•								•					
Brake Fluid***								•								•					
Check ATF and diff. level								•								•					
Front Axle (tie rods, etc.)								•								•					

*Check the air bag system every 12 months, regardless of mileage. Check the air bag system at 4 years, 8 years, and then every 2 years (10, 12, 14, etc.)
**Replace the air filter every 2 years or 40,000 miles, whichever occurs first: Cabrio, Passat, EuroVan. Replace the air filter every 4 years or 40,000 miles, whichever occurs first: Golf, Jetta, New Beetle ***Replace the brake fluid every 2 years, regardless of mileage

1 Engine–General

GENERAL

This general information group gives engine application information and general technical data for the engines used in the Volkswagen Jetta, Golf and GTI. Engines are the same for both the United States and Canada.

Much of the engine repair information in **1 Engine** is organized according to engine code. It is therefore important to know the code of the engine installed in your vehicle. For engine code location see **0 Maintenance**.

Engine Codes
- AWD, AWW . . . 1.8L 4-cylinder turbo gasoline, 110 hp
- ALH . . . . . 1.9L 4-cylinder turbo diesel, 90 hp
- AEG, AVH, AZG. . . . 2.0L 4-cylinder gasoline, 115 hp
- AFP . . . . . 2.8L 6-cylinder gasoline, 174 hp

1.8 LITER ENGINE

The 1.8L engine is a further design evolution of the 4-cylinder gasoline turbocharged engine used on previous models of the Volkswagen Passat and New Beetle.

Technical Data - 1.8L Engine
- Type . . . . . 4-cylinder inline, 5 valves/cylinder
- Displacement . . . . .1.8L, 1781 cc (108.7 cubic inches)
- Bore . . . . . 81.0 mm
- Stroke. . . . . 86.4 mm
- Compression Ratio
  - Engine code AWD. 9.5:1
  - Engine code AWW 9.3:1
- Power . . . . . 110 kW (150 HP) @5700 RPM
- Torque
  - Engine code AWD. . .210 Nm (155 ft-lb) @1750 RPM
  - Engine code AWW . 220 Nm (162 ft-lb) @ 1950 RPM
- Fuel requirement . . . . . Gasoline, Premium Unleaded
- Engine Management . . . . Motronic ME7.5, OBD II

1.8L engine design features:

- Cast iron cylinder block, light alloy crossflow cylinder head and aluminum oil pan.
- Crankshaft with 5 main bearings.
- Dual overhead camshafts. Exhaust camshaft driven by toothed belt with tensioning dampener. Intake camshaft driven by self-adjusting chain from the exhaust camshaft.
- Lightweight valvetrain, 5 valves per cylinder.
- Transverse mounting with "Pendulum" type engine mounts.
- Chain-drive internal gear oil pump driven from the front of the crankshaft.
- Coolant pump built into the cylinder block and driven by the toothed camshaft belt.
- Thermostat integral with the cylinder block.
- Turbocharger with intercooler.
- Distributorless ignition with separate coils for each cylinder.
- External engine accessories driven by a single poly-ribbed belt with tensioner.
- Bosch Motronic ME7.5 Multi-point Sequential Fuel Injection (MFI) system with electronic accelerator system.
- Engine code AWW has electronic engine performance control through the use of variable camshaft timing.

1.9 LITER ENGINE

The 1.9L TDI engine is a design evolution of the 4 cylinder diesel engines used on previous models of the Volkswagen Golf and Jetta. Just as in the gas versions, this new engine looks familiar to the older versions, but again there has been significant development. See Fig. 1.

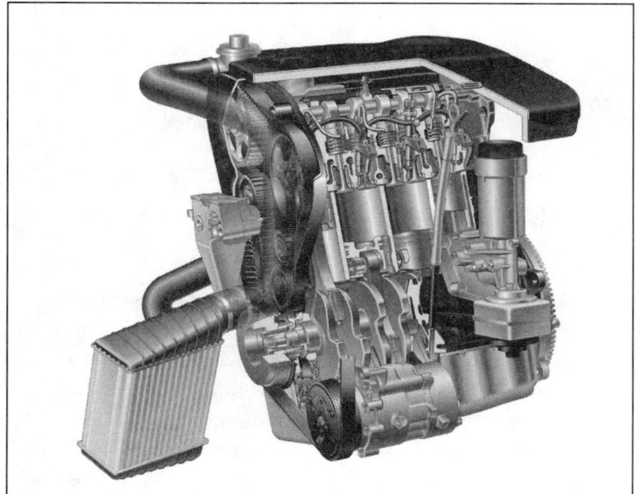

0024307

Fig. 1. 1.9 Liter TDI diesel engine used in Golfs and Jettas.

1.9L engine design features:

- Cast iron cylinder block, light alloy cylinder head and aluminum oil pan and cylinder head cover.
- Piston oil spray nozzles.
- Crankshaft with 5 main bearings.
- Single overhead camshaft driven by a toothed belt with semi-automatic belt tensioner and two guide pulleys.
- Lightweight valvetrain, 2 valves per cylinder.
- Transverse mounting with "Pendulum" type engine mounts.
- Chain-drive internal gear oil pump driven from the front of the crankshaft.
- Camshaft-driven vacuum pump.
- Coolant pump built into the cylinder block and driven by the toothed camshaft belt.
- Thermostat integral with the cylinder block.
- Cartridge-type oil filter.
- External engine accessories driven by a single poly-ribbed belt with tensioner.
- Turbo Direct Injection (TDI) Diesel Fuel Injection.

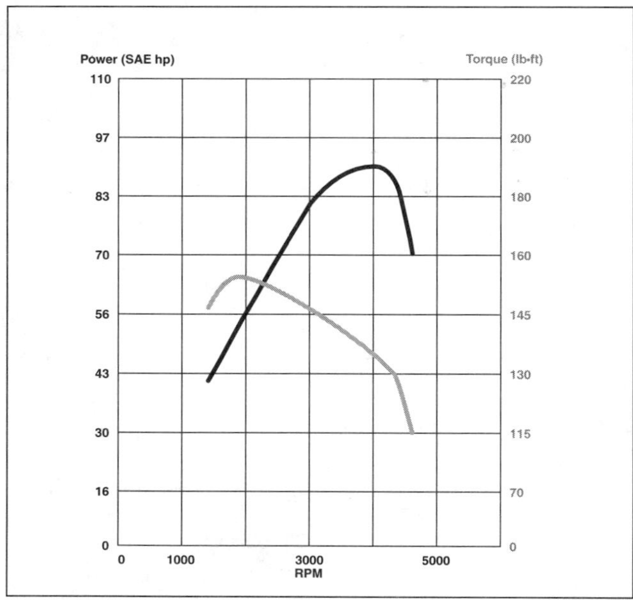

0024306

Fig. 2. Engine performance data of 1.9 Liter TDI engine.

Technical Data - 1.9L Engine

- Type . . . . 4-cylinder inline, 2 valves/cylinder
- Displacement . . . . 1.9L, 1896 cc (115.7 cubic inches)
- Bore . . . . 79.9 mm
- Stroke . . . . 95.5 mm
- Compression Ratio 19.5:1
- Power . . . . 66 kW (90 HP) @4000 RPM
- Fuel requirement . . . . Diesel 45 Cetane
- Engine Management . . . . Turbo Direct Injection (TDI)

2.0 LITER ENGINE

The 2.0 liter engine is a design evolution of the 4-cylinder gasoline engines used on previous models of the Volkswagen Golf and Jetta. And although this new engine looks familiar to the older versions, there has been significant development of the basic 4-cylinder engine for the newest generation of Volkswagens. See Fig. 3.

Fig. 3. 2.0 Liter gas engine used in Jettas, Golfs and GTIs.

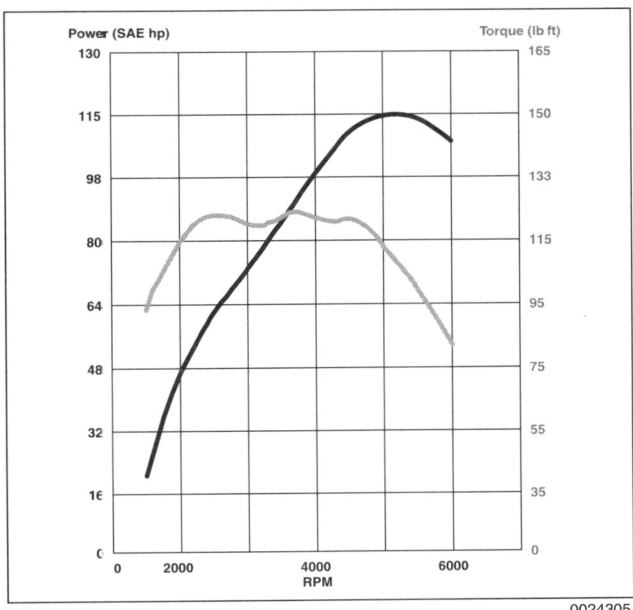

Fig. 4. Engine performance data of 2.0 Liter engine.

Technical Data - 2.0L Engine

- Type . . . . 4-cylinder inline, 2 valves/cylinder
- Displacement . . . . 2.0L, 1984 cc (121.1 cubic inches)
- Bore . . . . 82.5 mm
- Stroke . . . . 92.8 mm
- Compression Ratio 10.0:1
- Power . . . . 85 kW (115 HP) @5200 RPM
- Torque . . . . 165 Nm (122 ft-lb) @2600 RPM
- Fuel requirement . . . . . . Gasoline, Regular Unleaded
- Engine Management
  - Engine code AEG . . . . Motronic M5.9.2
  - Engine code AVH, AZG. . . . . Motronic ME 7.5

2.0L engine design features:

- Cast iron cylinder block, light alloy crossflow cylinder head and aluminum oil pan.
- Crankshaft with 5 main bearings.
- Single overhead camshaft driven by a toothed belt with semi-automatic belt tensioner.
- Lightweight valvetrain, 2 valves per cylinder.
- Transverse mounting with “Pendulum” type engine mounts.
- Chain-drive internal gear oil pump driven from the front of the crankshaft.
- Coolant pump built into the cylinder block and driven by the toothed camshaft belt.
- Thermostat integral with the cylinder block.
- Two-piece aluminum intake manifold.
- Tubular stainless steel exhaust manifold.
- Distributorless ignition.
- External engine accessories driven by a single poly-ribbed belt with tensioner.
- Bosch Motronic M5.9.2 Multi-point Sequential Fuel Injection (MFI) system.

2.8 LITER ENGINE

The 2.8L 6-cylinder, or VR6, engine is used in the 6-cylinder GTI and Jetta GLX models. See Fig. 5.

> **NOTE —**
> *The name VR6 is derived from a combination of Vee (cylinder configuration) and the German word Reihenmotor, which roughly means in-line, or in-line V-6.*

0024131

Fig. 5. Cutaway of VR6 engine.

Technical Data - 2.8L Engine

- Type . . . . 6-cylinder compact inline V-arrangement
- Displacement . . . . 2.8L (2792 cc)
- Bore . . . . 81.0 mm (3.19 in.)
- Stroke . . . . 90.3 mm (3.55 in.)
- V-angle . . . . 15°
- Compression ratio 10:1
- Power . . . . 130kW (174 hp) @ 5,800 rpm
- Torque . . . . 245 Nm (181 ft-lb) @ 3,200 rpm
- Fuel requirement . . . . . Gasoline, Premium Unleaded
- Engine management . . . . Bosch Motronic ME 7.1

The VR6 engine has a unique 15° V-angle between cylinder banks, as compared to the more traditional 60° or 90° angles used in most other V-6 designs. See Fig. 6. This results in a compact engine that can be installed in small spaces, such as in Volkswagen models previously reserved for 4-cylinder engines.

The VR6 engine features a cast iron cylinder block with a one piece light-alloy cylinder head. The overhead camshafts are chain driven and operate two valves per cylinder. The ignition system is distributorless and all fuel and ignition requirements are controlled by the Bosch Motronic Engine Management System.

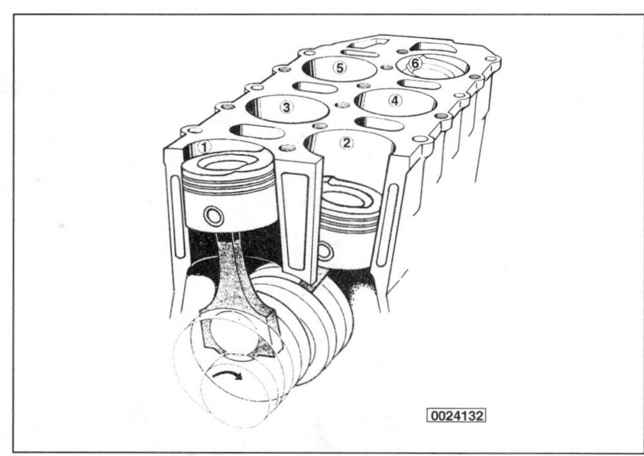

0024132

Fig. 6. VR6 cylinders are staggered along the cylinder block at a15° included angle, resulting in a narrower, more compact engine.

10 Engine–Removing and Installing

GENERAL

The engine and transmission are removed as a unit from below and separated from each other once removed from vehicle.

The operations needed to remove the engine and transmission assembly are generally grouped into two main areas: jobs under the hood and jobs under the vehicle. The steps below follow this general sequence. Most of the operations are simple and straight forward. References to additional repair groups are provided in bold type where additional information may be helpful to complete a step.

Engine Codes
- AWD, AWW . . . . 1.8L 4-cylinder turbo gasoline
- ALH . . . . 1.9L 4-cylinder turbo diesel
- AEG, AVH, AZG. . . . . 2.0L 4-cylinder gasoline
- AFP . . . . 2.8L 6-cylinder gasoline

CAUTION —
Disconnecting the negative (–) battery cable may erase fault codes and basic settings in the engine management and automatic transmission control modules. Some driveability problems may be noticed until the system re-adapts to operating conditions. OBD II readiness codes, which may be required for emissions testing, may also be erased. Convenience electronics (alarm system, interior light control, power locks, mirrors, and windows) may need to be re-set using a VAG 1551/1552 or equivalent scan tool.

NOTE —
- *It will be necessary to cut many wire tie wraps when removing the engine. The tie wraps are installed to prevent the wiring harnesses from chaffing or contacting engine parts. Be sure to make note of all tie wraps removed and install new ones during engine installation.*
- *Most of the hardware used in the vehicles covered by this repair manual is specially coated to prevent corrosion. This coating is known as "dacromet" or "delta tone" and is identified by a green tinted finish. Always use replacement hardware with the same specification.*

ENGINE, REMOVING AND INSTALLING

Engine/transmission assembly, removing

1. Ensure ignition is switched off. Disconnect battery negative (–) terminal and then positive (+) terminal.

   NOTE —
   Be sure to have the anti-theft radio code on hand before disconnecting the battery.

2. On 6-cylinder engines (VR6), pull spark plug boots from plugs with Volkswagen special tool T10029. Remove spark plug wires from engine cover.
3. Remove engine cover.
4. Remove the fuse holder on the top of the battery, the battery and the mounting bracket, see **27 Engine Electrical**.
5. Remove air cleaner assembly and connecting hoses and ducts.
6. On 1.9L diesel engines, remove connecting pipe between turbocharger and intercooler and intercooler and intake manifold complete with the EGR vacuum regulator solenoid valve.
7. On 1.8L turbo engines, remove intake air duct between Mass Air Flow (MAF) sensor and turbocharger. Loosen and disconnect intake air duct (between intercooler and throttle valve control module) at throttle valve control module.
8. Disconnect and label fuel lines.
   - Gas engines: Disconnect fuel supply and return lines. See Fig. 1. Disconnect accelerator cable on 2.0L (code AEG) engines without electronic throttle.
   - Diesel engine: Disconnect fuel supply and return lines at injection pump. See Fig. 2.

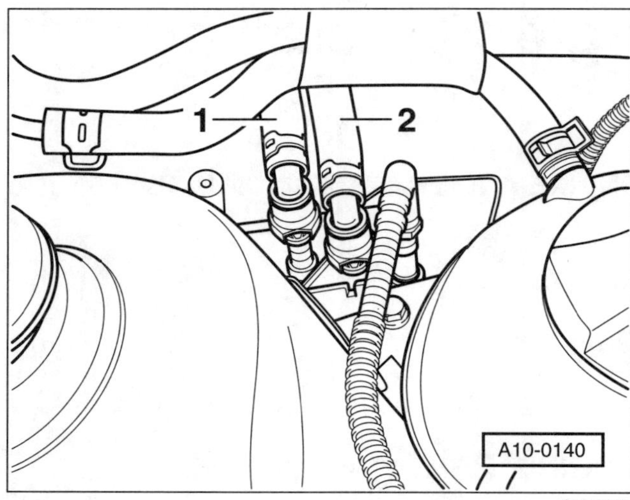

A10-0140

Fig. 1. Fuel line connections on gas engines. Disconnect supply line from tank (**1**) and return line (**2**). Seal off all hoses and fittings.

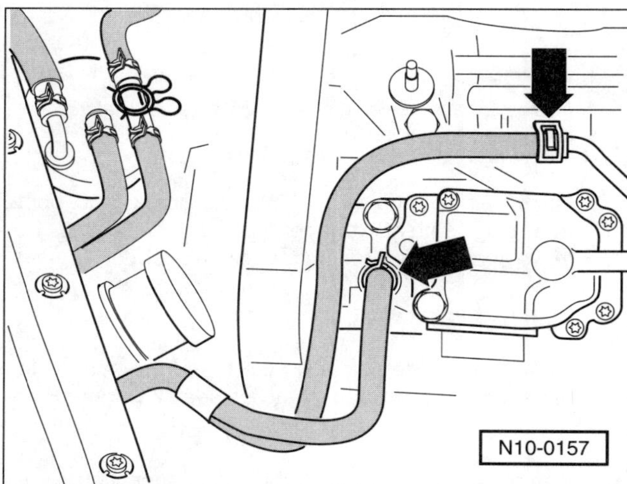

N10-0157

Fig. 2. Fuel line connections at diesel injection pump. Disconnect supply line from tank (**bottom arrow**) and return line (**top arrow**). Seal off all hoses and fittings.

> ***WARNING —***
> *Fuel will be expelled when disconnecting fuel hoses. Wrap a cloth around the fuel line fittings before disconnecting them. Do not smoke or work near heaters or other fire hazards. Have a fire extinguisher handy.*

9. Plug fuel line fittings and open fuel lines to prevent contamination and fuel spillage.

10. Disconnect shift linkage.
    - Manual transmission vehicles: Disconnect cables from selector mechanism and unbolt support bracket, see **34 Manual Transmission**. Unbolt hydraulic clutch slave cylinder and secure to the side with a tie wrap. Do not disconnect the hydraulic line.
    - Automatic transmission vehicles: Disconnect selector cable at selector lever on transmission, see **37 Automatic Transmission**.

> ***CAUTION —***
> *Do not depress the clutch pedal with the slave cylinder removed, damage will result.*

11. Remove lower sound absorber panels below engine.

12. Drain coolant, see **19 Cooling System**.

> ***WARNING —***
> *Hot coolant can scald. Drain the coolant only with engine cold.*

13. Mark running direction and remove ribbed V-belt, see **0 Maintenance**.

14. Remove auxiliary cooling fan on right side of vehicle, if equipped.

15. Disconnect engine coolant hoses to radiator and heater.

16. Remove power steering lines from mounting clamps on cylinder block.

17. Remove power steering pump with its mounting bracket and carefully lay aside with hoses remaining connected, see **48 Steering**.

18. Remove retaining clamp(s) from A/C refrigerant lines. Remove A/C compressor with refrigerant lines still attached, see **87 Air Conditioning**.

19. Attach A/C compressor to lower section of body with a suitable support so that refrigerant lines are not stressed. See Fig. 3.

NOTE —
To prevent damage to the condenser and to the refrigerant lines/hoses, ensure that the lines and hoses are not stretched, kinked or bent.

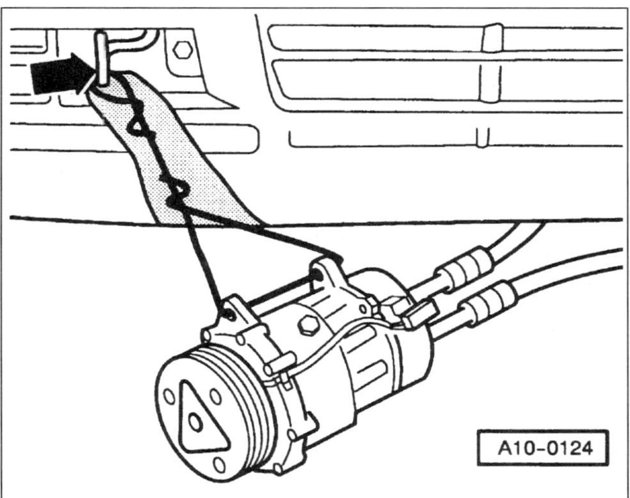

A10-0124

Fig. 3. A/C compressor shown hanging from front of vehicle with a suitable support (**arrow**). Refrigerant lines are still attached.

20. Label and remove all electrical connections on engine, transmission, generator (alternator) and starter.

21. On 2.0L and 2.8L engines, remove upper intake manifold, see **15 Cylinder Head and Valvetrain**.

22. Label and remove all vacuum and breather hoses.

23. Remove front bumper, see **63 Bumpers**.

24. Put lock carrier (radiator support) into service position, see **50 Body–Front**.

25. On gasoline engines, unbolt secondary air injection pump and remove from bracket, see **26 Exhaust System and Emission Controls**.

26. Raise car and support with jack stands or lift. See **0 Maintenance** for proper lifting procedure.

> ***WARNING —***
> *Observe all warnings and cautions associated with lifting vehicle in* **0 Maintenance**.

27. Unbolt and remove pendulum support. See Fig. 4.

28. Remove right side inner CV joint protective cover from engine if equipped.

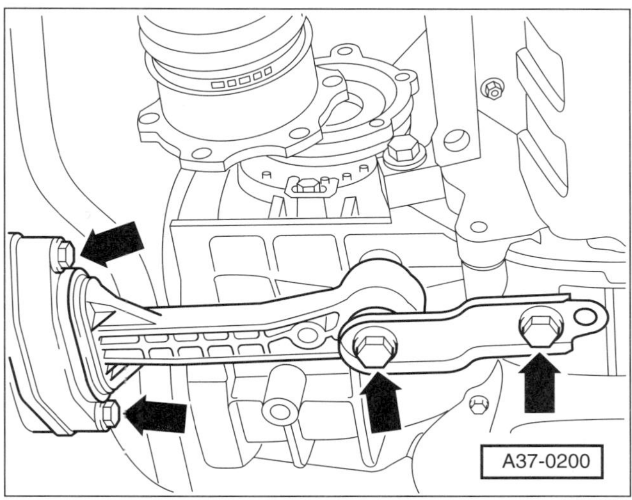

A37-0200

Fig. 4. Pendulum support view from under vehicle. Unbolt at **arrows**.

29. Remove axle nuts from right side outer CV joint and unbolt both inner CV or triple-rotor joints from the transmission. Remove the right side drive axle, see **40 Front Suspension and Drive Axles**. Tie wrap left side axle up and out of way as far as possible taking care not to damage the coating on the axle. On 6-cylinder engines, remove left side drive axle completely.

30. Unbolt front exhaust pipe with catalytic converter from exhaust manifold or turbocharger. Loosen clamp at connection to center muffler and remove front pipe, see **26 Exhaust System/Emission Controls**.

31. For 6-cylinder (2.8L, VR6) engines, the Volkswagen engine support tool 3395, must be modified to fit the bottom of the engine block. See Fig. 5.

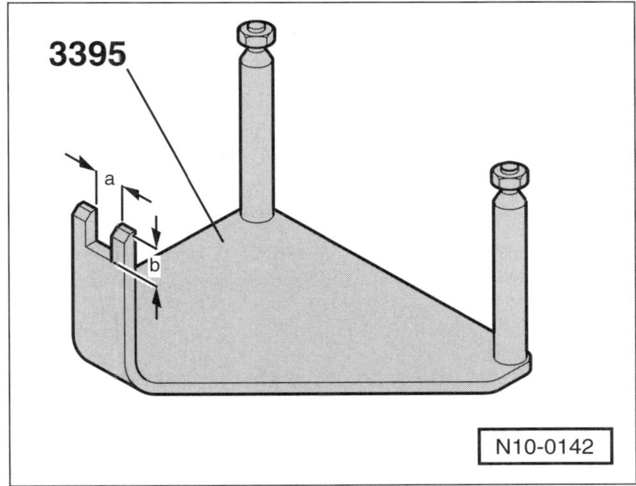

N10-0142

Fig. 5. For 2.8L engines, the slot on VW engine support 3395 must be enlarged to the following dimensions: **a** = 32 mm, **b** = 27 mm.

32. Install a suitable engine supporting device from below, using supporting points. For 4-cylinder engines, see Fig. 6. For 6-cylinder engines, see Fig. 8.

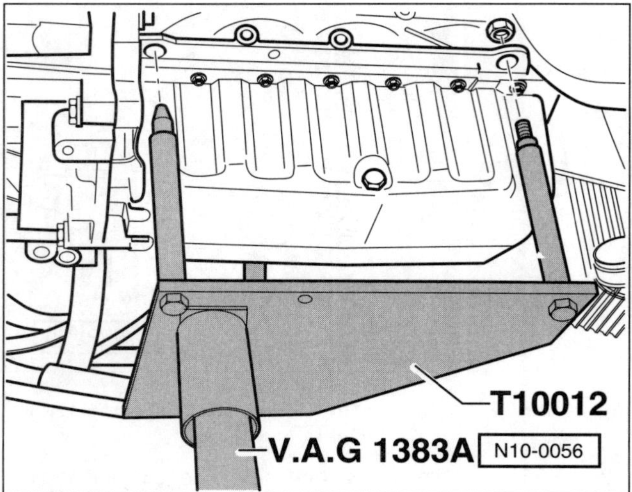

N10-0056

Fig. 6. Engine support tools supplied by Volkswagen shown being installed under 4-cylinder engine. Use of support as shown is necessary for proper weight distribution and safe support and removal.

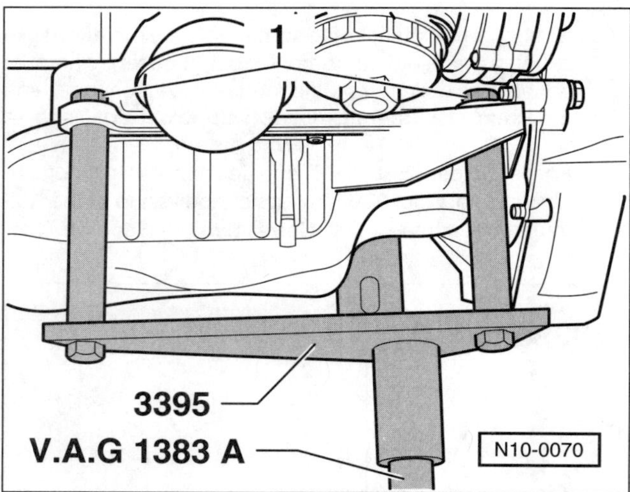

N10-0070

Fig. 7. Engine support tools supplied by Volkswagen shown being installed under 6-cylinder engine. Use of support as shown is necessary for proper weight distribution and safe support and removal.

33. Remove supporting bracket for coolant hose under engine block.

34. Lift supporting device slightly, so that weight of engine and transmission is on supporting device.

35. Unbolt right side engine mount from support on engine. See Fig. 8.

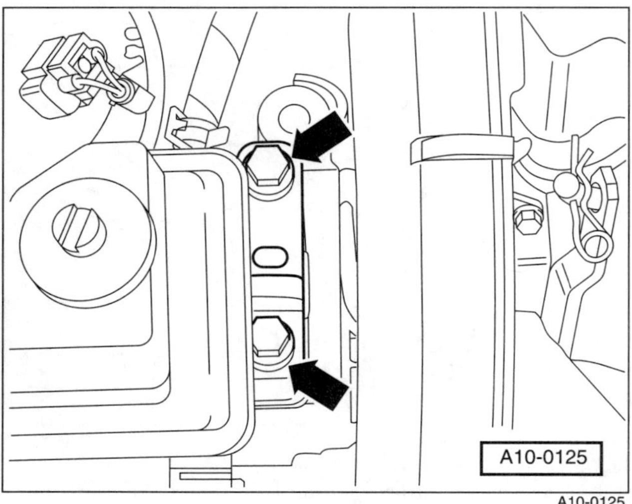

A10-0125

Fig. 8. Top view of right side engine mount. Remove mounting bolts (**arrows**).

36. Unbolt left side transmission mount from support on transmission. See Fig. 9.

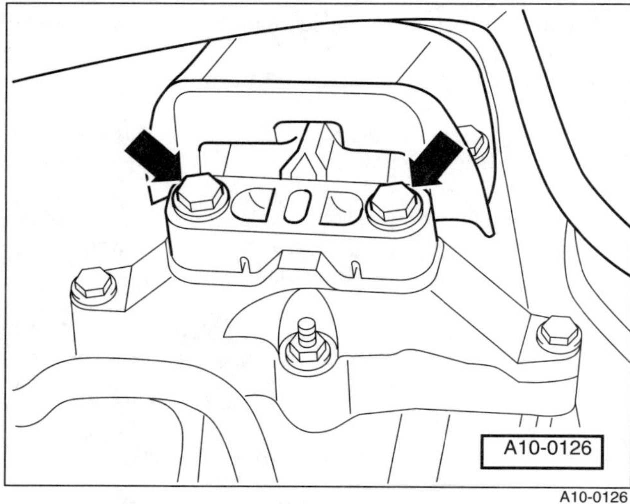

A10-0126

Fig. 9. Remove bolts (**arrows**) from left side transmission mount.

37. Carefully lower engine and transmission assembly out of vehicle using caution to guide assembly past power steering and refrigerant lines.

> ***WARNING —***
> *Before removing the engine and transmission assembly, be sure that the vehicle is properly supported in the rear. Removal of such a large amount of weight from the front can cause an improperly supported vehicle to pivot on the lift and fall to the rear.*

NOTE—
Carefully guide the engine/transmission assembly during the lowering process to prevent damage to it and to the bodywork.

Engine/transmission assembly, installing

1. With engine/transmission assembly on same device as was used for removal, carefully raise assembly up and into position.

2. Guide power steering fluid lines around transmission and the A/C lines around the engine to avoid damage.

3. While raising engine into position on 4-cylinder vehicles, ensure sufficient clearance for drive axle on left side.

4. When engine/transmission assembly is in position, adjust right side engine mount as shown in Fig. 10.

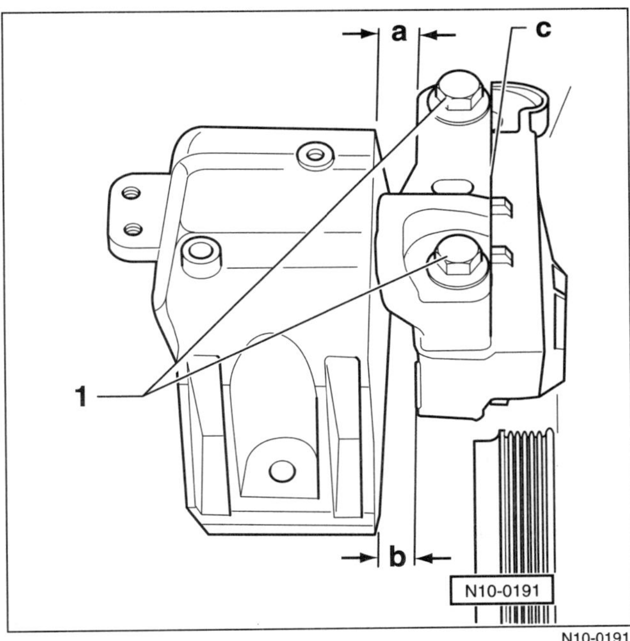

Fig. 10. Right side engine mount is properly positioned when gap **a** is 14 mm and gap **b** is a minimum of 10 mm. Both bolt head (**1**) shoulders must line-up flush with edge **c**.

> ***WARNING—***
> *Do not loosen engine mounting bolts if engine is not fully supported from below.*

5. Make sure left side transmission mount edges are aligned parallel to each other. See Fig. 11.

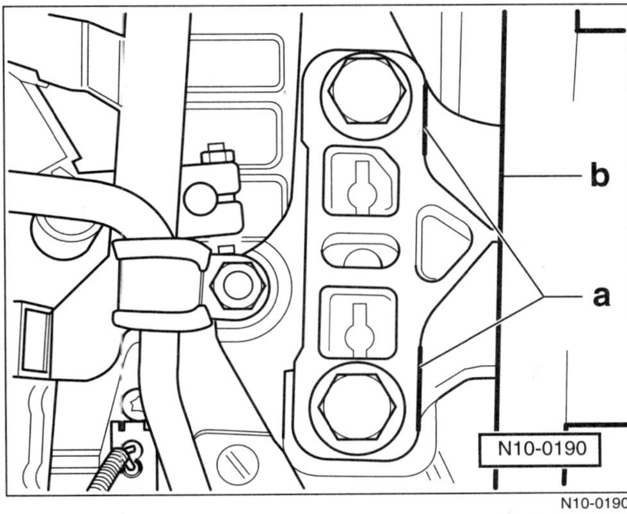

Fig. 11. Ensure that edges **a** and **b** of left side transmission mount are parallel to each other.

6. Install engine, transmission and pendulum mounts with new bolts where indicated and torque to specification, see **Engine and Transmission Mounts**.

7. Install front exhaust pipe with catalytic converter, see **26 Exhaust System/Emission Controls**.

8. On 2.0L and 2.8L engines, install upper intake manifold, see **15 Cylinder Head and Valvetrain**.

9. On 2.8L engines, install left side drive axle, see **40 Front Suspension and Drive Axles**.

10. Attach left side drive shaft to transmission and install right side drive axle and protective cover, see **40 Front Suspension and Drive Axles**.

11. Install A/C compressor and secure A/C lines, see **87 Air Conditioning**.

12. Install power steering pump and lines, see **48 Steering**.

13. Connect shift linkage.
    - Manual transmission vehicles: Connect cables from selector mechanism and attach support bracket. Adjust shift linkage, see **34 Manual Transmission**. Install hydraulic clutch slave cylinder.
    - Automatic transmission vehicles: Connect selector cable and adjust, see **37 Automatic Transmission**.

14. Install secondary air injection pump, and auxiliary fan where equipped.

15. Note running direction and install ribbed V-belt, see **13 Crankshaft/Cylinder Block**.

16. Reinstall fuel supply and return lines.
    - On AEG engines, attach accelerator cable and adjust for full throttle. Have an assistant depress throttle pedal to floor while adjusting throttle cable at manifold to insure that throttle plate is wide open.

17. Install vacuum and breather hoses.

18. Install heater and coolant hoses.

19. Install auxiliary coolant fan, as applicable.

20. Move lock carrier from service position and install front bumper.

21. Refill cooling system with appropriate ratio of distilled water and G12 coolant and check for leaks, see **19 Engine – Cooling System**.

22. Install all remaining electrical connectors and spark plug wires, as applicable. Check for proper routing of wires.

23. Install air cleaner assembly, connecting hoses and ducts. Install bottom portion of air cleaner housing first, then air filter and top half of housing.
    - On diesel engines, install connecting pipe between turbocharger and intercooler and intercooler and intake manifold complete with EGR vacuum regulator solenoid valve.
    - On turbocharged gasoline engines install intake air duct between Mass Air Flow (MAF) sensor and turbocharger. Install intake air duct (between intercooler and throttle valve control module) at throttle valve control module.

24. Install battery mounting bracket, battery and battery fuse holder.

25. Ensure that all removed tie wraps are replaced, and that all electrical wiring and hoses are properly routed and secured.

26. Connect battery cables.

27. Start engine and let it idle. Inspect for oil and coolant leaks. Check for smooth operation of shifter and clutch as required. Road test as required.

28. Shut off engine and install lower sound absorber panel (belly pan) and upper engine cover.

Tightening torques (4-cylinder engines)

- Engine to transmission bolts,
  - M10 bolts . . . . . 40 Nm (30 ft-lb)
  - M12 bolts . . . . . 80 Nm (59 ft-lb)
- Starter to transmission . . . . . 65 Nm (48 ft-lb)
- Triple rotor/CV joint to transmission . . 40 Nm (30 ft-lb)
- Torque converter to drive plate. . . . . . 60 Nm (44 ft-lb)
- Bolts & nuts, not specifically listed
  - M6 . . . . . 10 Nm (7 ft-lb)
  - M7 . . . . . 15 Nm (10 ft-lb)
  - M8 . . . . . 25 Nm (18 ft-lb)
  - M10 . . . . . 40 Nm (30 ft-lb)
  - M12 . . . . . 60 Nm (44 ft-lb)

Tightening torques (6-cylinder engines)

- Assembly support on transmission mount (always replace) . . . . . .60 Nm (44 ft-lb) + 90° (¼ turn)
- Assembly support on engine mount (always replace) . . . . . .60 Nm (44 ft-lb) + 90° (¼ turn)
- Assembly support on body (always replace) . . . . . .60 Nm (44 ft-lb) + 90° (¼ turn)
- Rocker bearing on transmission (always replace) . . . . . .40 Nm (30 ft-lb) + 90° (¼ turn)
- Rocker bearing on assembly carrier (always replace) . . . . . .20 Nm (15 ft-lb) + 90° (¼ turn)
- Bolts & nuts, not specifically listed
  - M6 . . . . . 10 Nm (7 ft-lb)
  - M8 . . . . . 20 Nm (15 ft-lb)
  - M10 . . . . . 45 Nm (33 ft-lb)
  - M12 . . . . . 60 Nm (44 ft-lb)

ENGINE AND TRANSMISSION, MOUNTS

The engine and transmission assembly is suspended on its rotational axis by the engine mount on the right side and the transmission mount on the left side. Engine movement known as torque reaction is limited by the pendulum support mounted in the center underneath. Engine mounts differ slightly depending on transmission type (manual vs. automatic); and engine type, but are all visually similar, see Fig. 12 through 14.

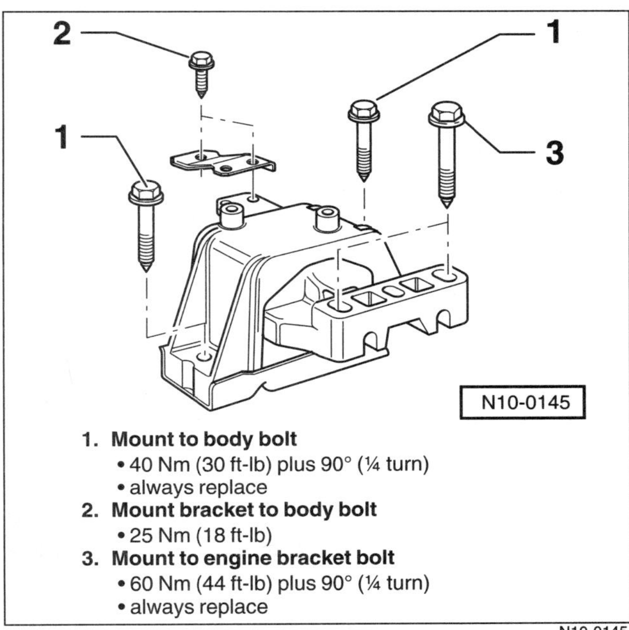

Fig. 12. Right side engine mount.

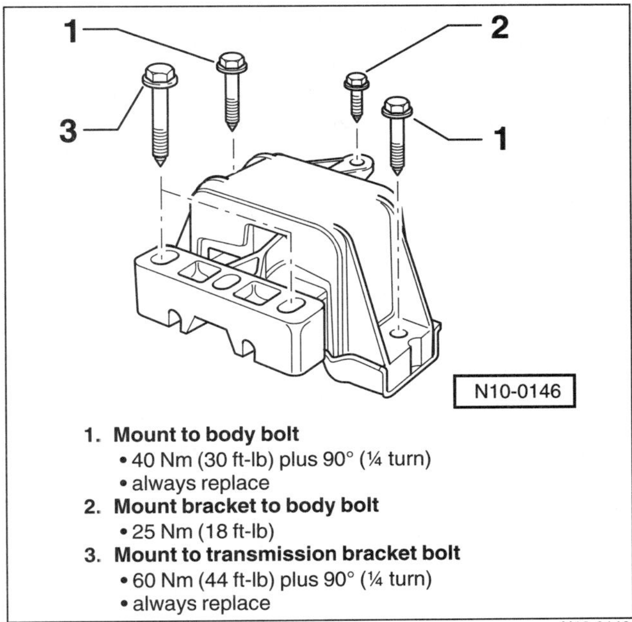

1
2
3
1
N10-0146
1. Mount to body bolt
• 40 Nm (30 ft-lb) plus 90° (¼ turn)
• always replace
2. Mount bracket to body bolt
• 25 Nm (18 ft-lb)
3. Mount to transmission bracket bolt
• 60 Nm (44 ft-lb) plus 90° (¼ turn)
• always replace
N10-0146

Fig. 13. Transmission mount, left side.

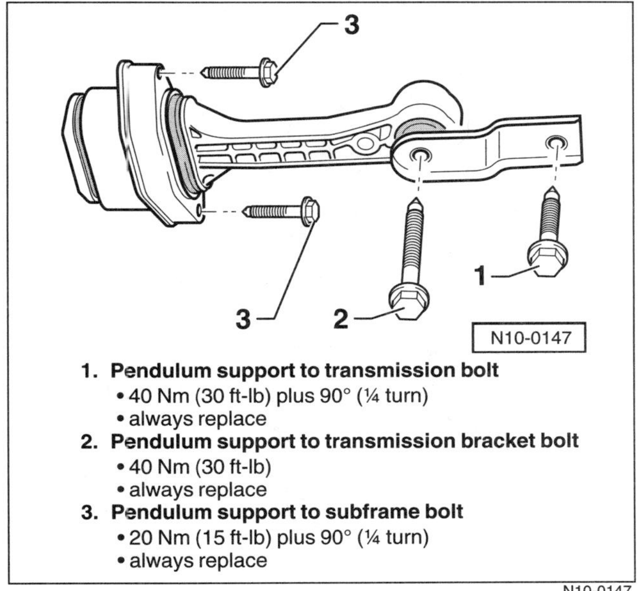

3
1
3
2
N10-0147
1. Pendulum support to transmission bolt
• 40 Nm (30 ft-lb) plus 90° (¼ turn)
• always replace
2. Pendulum support to transmission bracket bolt
• 40 Nm (30 ft-lb)
• always replace
3. Pendulum support to subframe bolt
• 20 Nm (15 ft-lb) plus 90° (¼ turn)
• always replace
N10-0147

Fig. 14. Pendulum support, lower center.

ENGINE/TRANSMISSION, SEPARATING

1. Support engine with device used to remove engine/transmission and rest transmission on work bench.

2. Remove small cover plate from behind right side axle flange if equipped. See Fig. 15.

3. Remove engine oil pan bolts from transmission.

4. Remove nuts from torque converter from engine side of the transmission, if equipped.

5. Remove starter from transmission.

6. Remove bolts holding engine and transmission together.

7. Slide transmission away from engine.

NOTE —

- *On automatic transmissions, the torque converter should come off with transmission. Secure the torque converter to the transmission to prevent damage.*
- *On 4-cylinder engines it may be necessary to remove transmission-to-engine intermediate plate mounted on engine block before mounting engine on engine stand for repairs.*

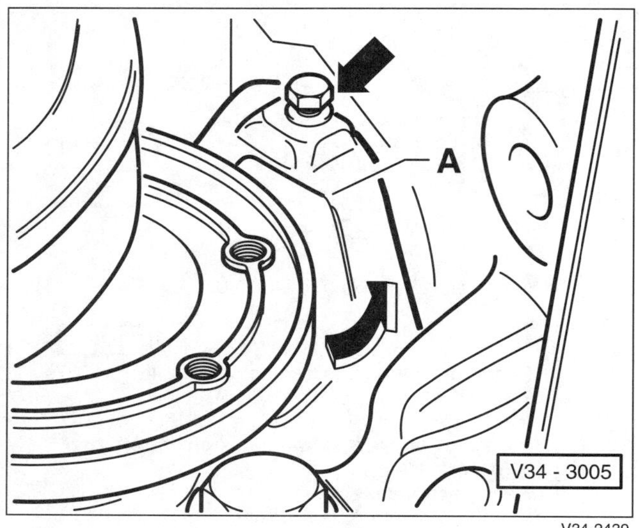

Fig. 15. Remove small cover plate (**A**) near right side drive flange if equipped.

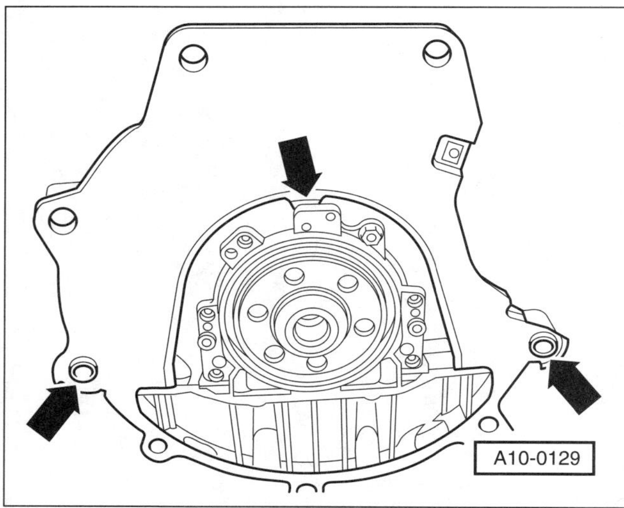

Fig. 16. On 4-cylinder engines, install intermediate plate on sealing flange and slide onto dowel sleeves (**arrows**).

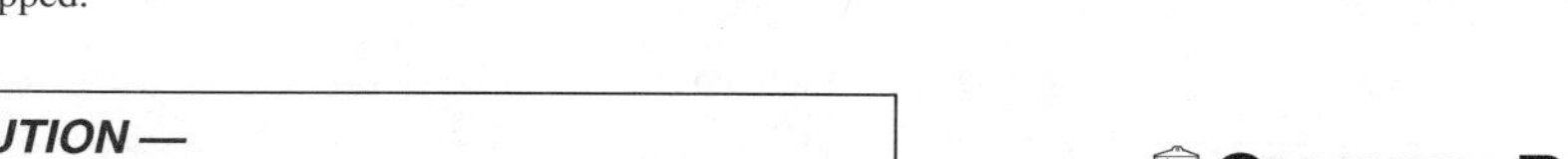

> ***CAUTION —***
>
> - *On cars with automatic transmissions, be sure the drive plate separates cleanly from the torque converter without pulling the torque converter off of its support. Once the engine and transmission are separated, install a suitable bar across the open bell bellhousing to keep the torque converter from falling out.*
>
> - *On cars with manual transmissions, be sure that the weight of the transmission or the engine is never supported on the transmission mainshaft. Clutch or transmission damage could result.*
>
> - *When reattaching transmission to engine, check that centering dowels are installed in engine block. Replace them if they are missing.*
>
> - *Clutch or drive plate damage may result if centering dowels are not installed.*

8. Attaching engine to transmission is the reverse of separating. Observe the following points:
   - Lightly lubricate manual transmission mainshaft with molybdenum disulfide (MoS2) grease.
   - Inspect clutch components, see **30 Clutch**.
   - On automatic transmissions install torque converter to stator support.
   - On 4-cylinder engines install intermediate plate (if previously removed) onto sealing flange and slide onto centering dowel sleeves. See Fig. 16.

QUALITY REVIEW

When you have finished working under the hood and around other areas of the vehicle it is advisable to take a moment to quality check or review your work. This helps to ensure that the operation or repair has been completed properly with all affected systems functioning within normal parameters. This may include the following:

- Make sure that the radiator fan cycles properly and that the coolant level and concentration are correct.
- Ensure that all cable ties and hose clamps that were removed as part of the repair are replaced.
- Check and adjust all other applicable fluid levels.
- Make sure that there are no fluid leaks.
- Make sure there are no air, vacuum or exhaust leaks.
- Make sure that all components involved in the repair are positioned correctly and function properly.
- Male sure all tools, shop cloths, fender covers, and protective tape are removed.
- Clean grease from painted surfaces and steering wheel.

In addition to the above noted points, the ECM and TCM may need to be checked using the Volkswagen supplied VAG 1551 or 1552 scan tool as mentioned at the start of this repair.

13a Crankshaft/Cylinder Block (4-cylinder)

TABLES

GENERAL

This repair group provides the special reconditioning information necessary to repair the Volkswagen 4-cylinder short block. The information contained here is intended to be used as a reconditioning guide for the professional or experienced automotive technician. Many of the operations and specifications listed require precision measuring equipment.

Engine Codes
- AWD, AWW . . . . . 1.8L 4-cylinder turbo gasoline
- ALH . . . . . 1.9L 4-cylinder turbo diesel
- AEG, AVH, AZG . . . . . 2.0L 4-cylinder gasoline

NOTE —
For 6-cylinder crankshaft and cylinder block, see **13b Crankshaft/Cylinder Block (6-cylinder)**.

Cylinder block

The 4-cylinder engine block and related components for the 2.0L engine are shown in Fig. 1.

NOTE —
- *If during engine repairs, metal shavings or large quantities of small metal particles are found in the engine oil, the oil passages in the cylinder block must be thoroughly cleaned out and the oil cooler replaced.*
- *Volkswagen identifies electrical components by a letter and/or a number in the electrical schematics. See* **97 Wiring Diagrams, Fuses and Relays**. *These electrical identifiers are listed in parenthesis as an aid to electrical troubleshooting.*

Cylinder block components

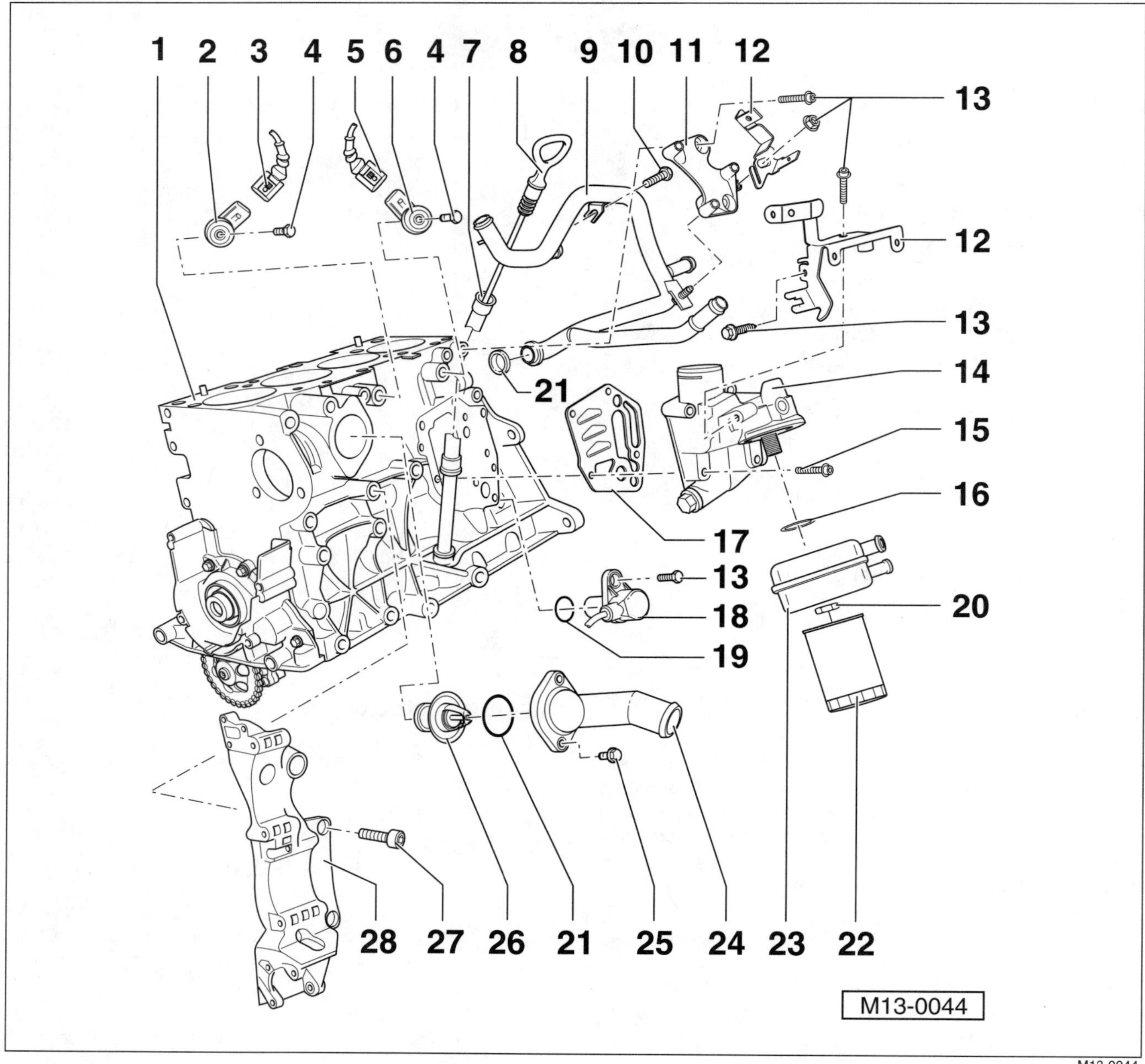

M13-0044

Fig. 1. Cylinder block and related components for 2.0L engine. 1.9L and 1.8L engines are similar.

1. **Cylinder block**
2. **Knock sensor 1 (G61)**
3. **2-pin harness connector**
   - Black
   - For knock sensor 1 (G61)
4. **Bolt**
   - Tighten to 20 Nm (15 ft-lb)
   - Tightening torque influences knock sensor function
5. **2-pin harness connector**
   - Brown
   - For knock sensor 2
6. **Knock sensor 2 (G66)**
7. **Oil dipstick tube**
   - Remove to siphon oil
   - With bracket on lower intake manifold
8. **Dipstick**
   - Oil level must not be above MAX. mark

9. **Coolant pipe**
   - Coolant hose diagram, see **19 Engine–Cooling System**
   - Pipe configuration varies with engine application

10. **Bracket**
    - For ignition coils

11. **Bracket**
    - For engine code AEG only

12. **Bolt**
    - Tighten to 10 Nm (7 ft-lb)

13. **Oil filter bracket**

14. **Bolt**
    - Tighten to 15 Nm (11 ft-lb) + ¼ turn (90°)
    - Always replace

15. **Seal**
    - Always replace
    - Installs on top of oil cooler

16. **O-ring**
    - Always replace

17. **Gasket**
    - Always replace

18. **Engine speed sensor**

19. **Sealing ring**

20. **Nut**
    - Tighten to 25 Nm (18 ft-lb)

21. **Oil filter**
    - Tighten by hand

22. **Oil cooler**
    - Coat contact area to flange, outside the seal, with Volkswagen sealant (part # AMV 188 100 02)

    NOTE —
    Volkswagen part numbers are given for reference only. Always consult with your Volkswagen Parts Department or aftermarket parts specialist for the latest parts information.

23. **Connection**

24. **Bolt**
    - Tighten to 15 Nm (11 ft-lb)

25. **Coolant thermostat**
    - Heat-up in water to check
    - Opening starts approx. 86°C (187°F)
      Ends approx. 102°C (216°F)
    - Opening lift: 7 mm (0.28 in.) minimum

26. **Bolt**
    - Tighten to 45 Nm (33 ft-lb)

27. **Assembly bracket**
    - For ribbed belt tensioning roller, generator and power steering pump
    - For engine without A/C shown
    - For engine with A/C see **87 Air Conditioning**

CYLINDER BLOCK OIL SEALS

The front crankshaft oil seal can be replaced with the engine installed. Replacement of the rear crankshaft oil seal requires that the engine be separated from the transmission. See Fig. 2.

NOTE —
In some instances, individual seals may not be available separately. See an authorized Volkswagen parts dealer, or an aftermarket parts specialist, for the latest in parts information.

Cylinder block oil seals, assembly

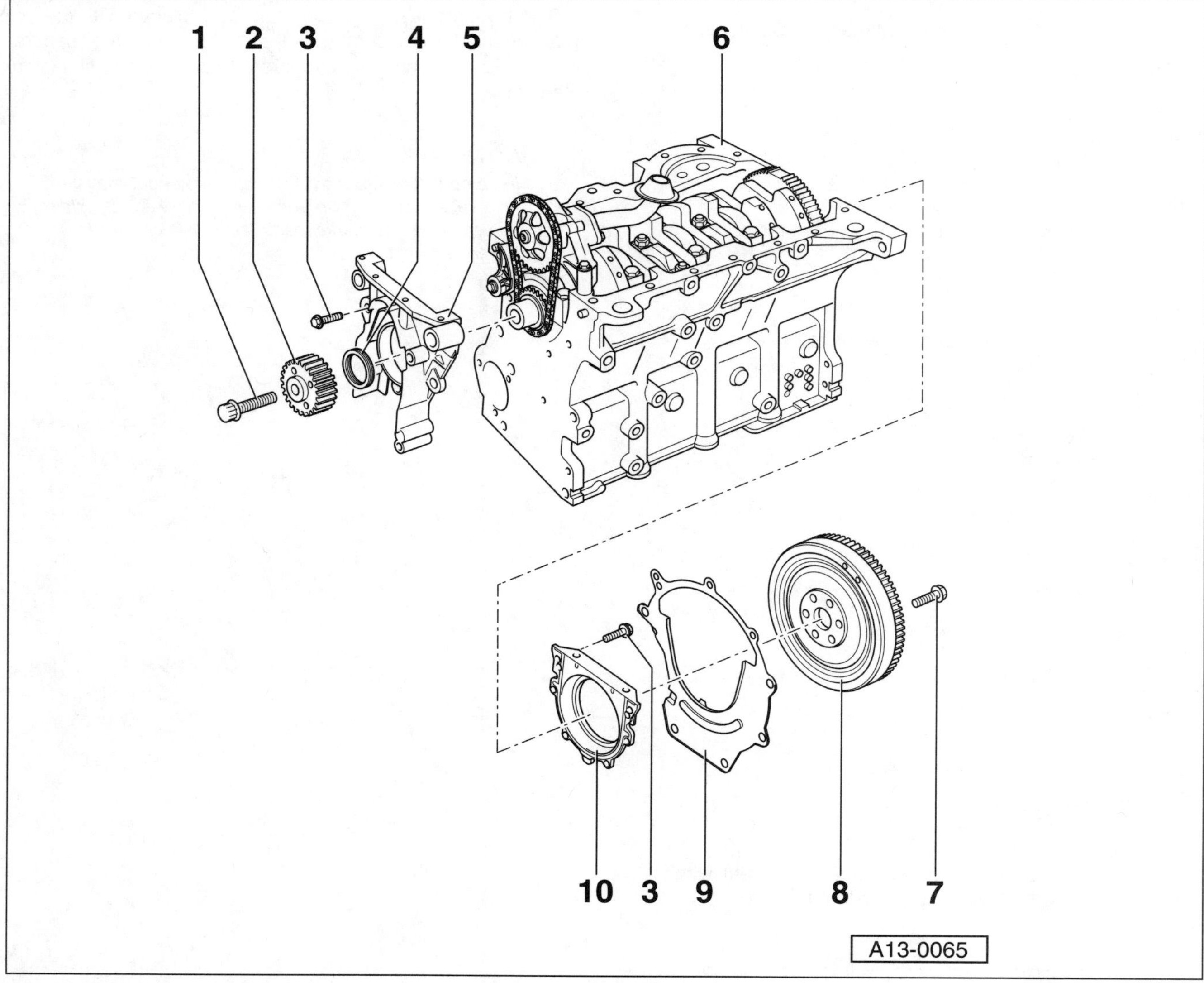

A13-0065

Fig. 2. Exploded view of crankshaft seals in cylinder block. 2.0L engine shown, 1.9L and 1.8L block is identical.

1. **Bolt**
   - Tighten to:
     2.0L and 1.8L: 90 Nm (66 ft-lb) + ¼ turn (90°)
     1.9L: 120 Nm (88 ft-lb) + ¼ turn (90°)
   - Always replace
2. **Crankshaft toothed belt sprocket**
3. **Bolt**
   - Tighten to 15 Nm (11 ft-lb)
4. **Front crankshaft oil seal**
5. **Front oil seal flange**
6. **Engine block**
7. **Bolt**
   - Tighten to 60 Nm (44 ft-lb) + ¼ turn (90°)
   - Always replace
8. **Flywheel/driveplate**
   - Flywheel: remove and install with 3067 counterholder
9. **Intermediate plate**
   - Must be located on dowel sleeves
   - Do not damage or bend when assembling
10. **Rear oil seal flange**
    - May need to replace as complete unit (w/integral oil seal)
    - Only install flange using PTFE sealing ring
    - Lightly oil lip on seal
    - Install new sealing flange with guide sleeve
    - Guide sleeve protects seal during installation

Front crankshaft oil seal, replacing

1. Remove ribbed V-belt, see **0 Maintenance**.

2. Remove camshaft drive belt, see **15 Cylinder Head and Valvetrain**.

3. Hold the crankshaft stationary with a suitable counter-holder and loosen the crankshaft sprocket (hub) center bolt. Remove the bolt and sprocket. See Fig. 3.

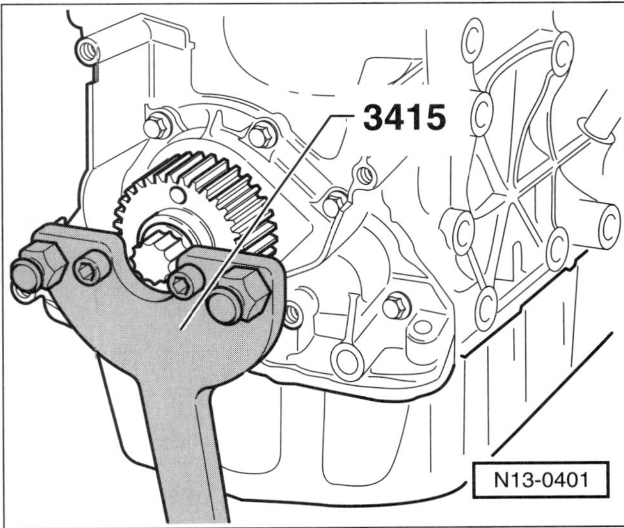

N13-0401

Fig. 3. Counterholder threaded into sprocket to allow removal of center bolt.

4. Reinstall the removed bolt into the crankshaft to prevent damage to the end of the crankshaft when using the seal extractor. Remove the oil seal from the flange using an appropriate seal extractor or by carefully prying it out. See Fig. 4.

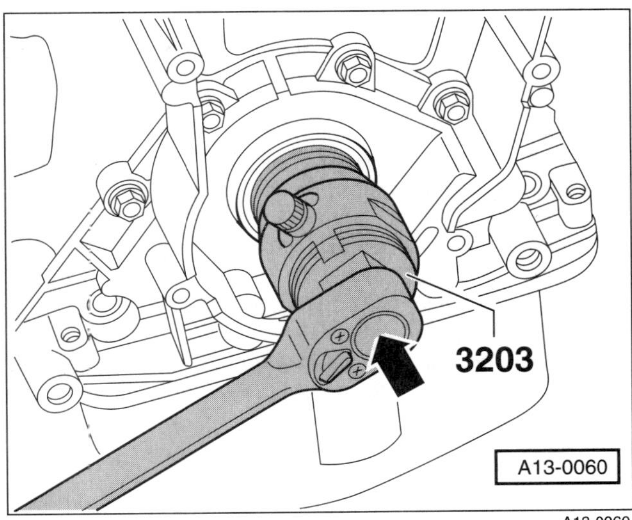

A13-0060

Fig. 4. Seal removal tool threaded into seal. Wrench (**arrow**) is being used to remove crankshaft oil seal.

5. Install new seal, lubricated with clean engine oil, with closed side facing out. Use a guide sleeve to protect seal from sharp edges of the crankshaft as necessary. Carefully press seal into place until it is fully seated. See Fig. 5.

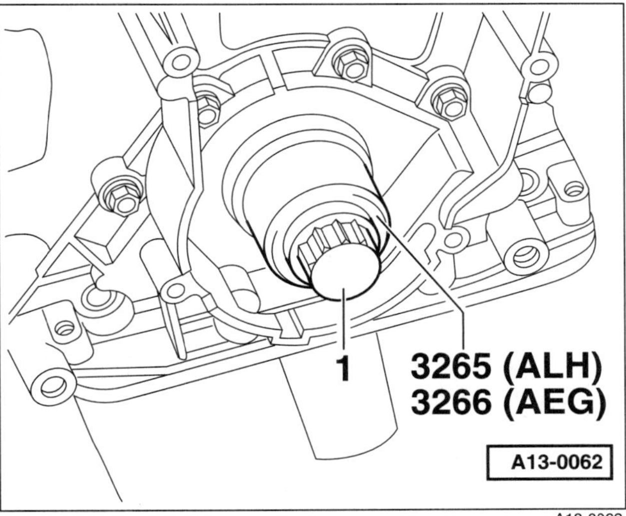

A13-0062

Fig. 5. Front crankshaft oil seal being pressed in using Volkswagen special tools and old crankshaft sprocket bolt (**1**).

6. Align locating key on sprocket with cutout on the end of crankshaft and install sprocket onto the crankshaft with a new bolt. Hold the crankshaft with the counterholder and torque to specification.

7. Install remaining removed components.

> ***CAUTION —***
> *Always replace the crankshaft sprocket bolt. It is a stretch bolt designed to be used only once.*

Tightening torques

- Crankshaft sprocket bolt, 4-cylinder gasoline engine (stretch bolt - always replace)
  - stage I . . . . 90 Nm (66 ft-lb)
  - stage II . . . . additional ¼ turn (90°)
- Crankshaft sprocket bolt, 4-cylinder diesel engine (stretch bolt - always replace)
  - stage I . . . . 120 Nm (88 ft-lb)
  - stage II . . . . additional ¼ turn (90°)

Front oil seal flange, removing and installing

1. Remove crankshaft drive sprocket as described earlier.
2. Drain engine oil and remove oil pan. See **17 Engine–Lubrication System**.
3. Unbolt front oil seal flange from cylinder block and remove. It may be necessary to lightly tap flange with a soft faced mallet to remove it.
4. Thoroughly remove all the old sealant residue from the flange. See Fig. 6.

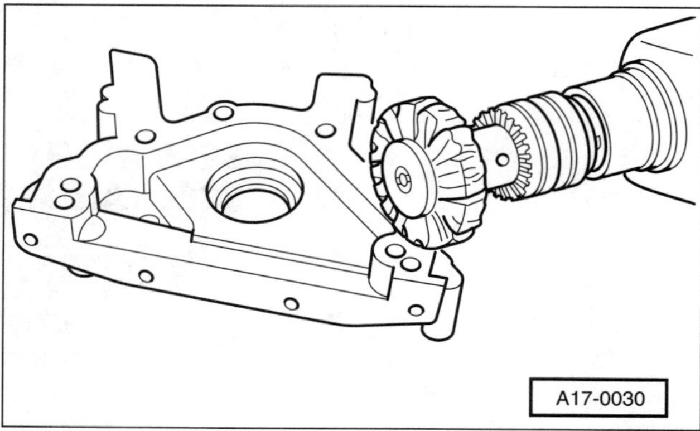

A17-0030

Fig. 6. Old sealant residue being removed with a cleaning pad attached to a drill motor. Use care not to scratch or gouge the aluminum housing.

NOTE —
The front oil seal flange does not use a paper gasket. Special silicone sealant is used instead. Surface must be clean and free from oil and grease before sealant is applied.

5. Apply a 2 to 3 mm (slightly less than 1/8 inch) bead of new sealant to flange as shown in Fig. 6.

NOTE —
Flange must be installed within 5 minutes of applying sealant.

CAUTION —
The sealing compound bead thickness must not be wider than 3 mm (slightly less than 1/8 inch). If this width is exceeded, excess sealing compound will enter the oil pan and could block the oil pump pick-up tube strainer.

6. Use a guide sleeve as necessary to protect the oil seal and install the flange on the guide pins of the cylinder block. Torque the bolts in a staggered pattern.
7. Install the oil pan.

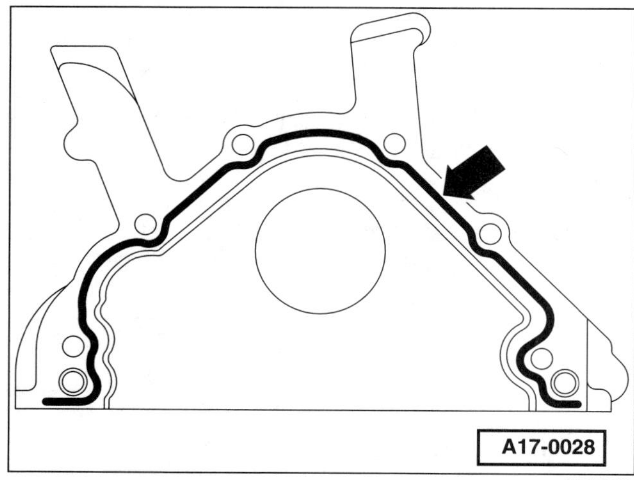

A17-0028

Fig. 7. Apply sealant bead 2 to 3 mm (slightly less than 1/8 inch) wide (**arrow**). Front flange is shown; sealant is applied to the rear seal flange in a similar manner.

8. Install remaining removed components.

Tightening torques

- Front or rear flange to cylinder block (M7) . . . . 15 Nm (11 ft-lb)
- Oil pan to cylinder block (M7) . . . . 15 Nm (11 ft-lb)
- Oil pan to transmission (M10) . . . . . . 45 Nm (33 ft-lb)

Rear crankshaft oil seal, replacing

NOTE —
The rear crankshaft oil seal may not be available separately from the rear crankshaft oil seal flange. See an authorized Volkswagen parts dealer, or an aftermarket parts specialist for the latest in parts information.

1. If engine is still in car, remove transmission as described in **34 Manual Transmission** or **37 Automatic Transmission**, as applicable.
2. If engine and transmission are out of car, separate engine from transmission as described in **10 Engine–Removing and Installing**.
3. Remove flywheel or driveplate as described later.
4. Remove seal from flange by carefully prying it out.
5. Install the new seal, lubricated with clean engine oil, with closed side facing out using a suitable seal installation tool.
6. Install remaining removed components.

Rear oil seal flange, removing and installing

1. If engine is still in car, remove transmission as described in **34 Manual Transmission** or **37 Automatic Transmission**, as applicable.

2. If engine and transmission are out of car, separate engine from transmission as described in **10 Engine– Removing and Installing**.

3. Remove flywheel or drive plate as described later.

4. Drain engine oil and remove oil pan, see **17 Engine–Lubrication System**.

5. Unbolt rear oil seal flange from cylinder block and remove. It may be necessary to lightly tap the flange with a soft faced mallet to remove it.

6. The rear oil seal flange does not use a paper gasket. Special silicone sealant is used instead.

7. Apply a 2 to 3 mm (slightly less than $^1/_8$ inch) bead of new sealant to the flange as shown in Fig. 6.

   NOTE —
   Flange must be installed within 5 minutes of applying sealant.

   > ***CAUTION —***
   > *The sealing compound bead thickness must not be wider than 3 mm (slightly less than $^1/_8$ inch). If this width is exceeded, excess sealing compound will enter the oil pan and could block the oil pump pick-up tube strainer.*

8. Use a guide sleeve as necessary to protect the oil seal and install the flange on the guide pins of the cylinder block. Torque the bolts in a staggered pattern.

9. Install the oil pan, see **17 Engine–Lubrication System**.

10. Install remaining removed components.

FLYWHEEL/DRIVEPLATE

Removal of the flywheel or driveplate requires that the engine be separated from the transmission. Remove the clutch on manual transmission vehicles, see **30 Clutch**.

> ***CAUTION —***
> - *On vehicles with automatic transmissions, special mounting and measuring procedures are required when installing the driveplate.*
> - *The flywheel on manual transmission vehicles and the driveplate on automatic transmission vehicles are mounted to the crankshaft using stretch bolts that are designed to be used only once. Always replace.*

Flywheel/driveplate, removing and installing

1. Attach a suitable holder to the engine and flywheel on manual transmission vehicles or the engine and driveplate on automatic transmission vehicles. See Fig. 8.

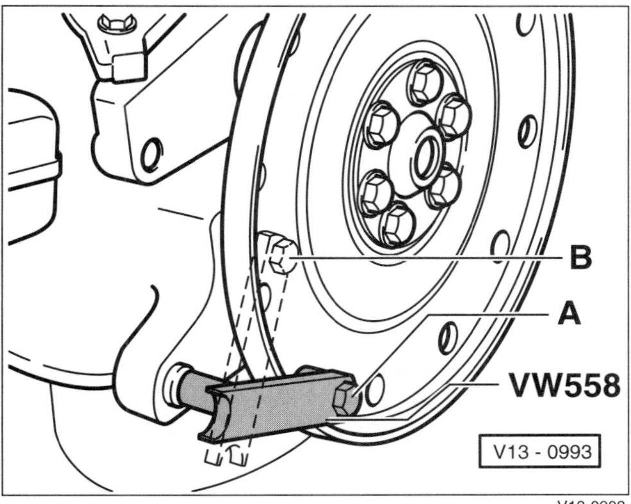

V13-0993

Fig. 8. Driveplate secured with holding fixture VW558. Position **A** is used to loosen and position **B** for tightening. Flywheel is similar.

2. Loosen securing bolts diagonally and remove flywheel or drive plate and any shims.

3. Installation is the reverse of removal observing the following points:
   - Install any removed shims and mount the flywheel or drive plate with new bolts.
   - Check driveplate clearance (as applicable) as described later.
   - Attach the holder and torque diagonally to specifications.

Tightening torques
- Flywheel or driveplate to crankshaft (stretch bolt, always replace)
  - stage I . . . . 30 Nm (22 ft-lb)
  - stage II . . . . 60 Nm (44 ft-lb)
  - stage III . . . . additional ¼ turn (90°)

Driveplate clearance, adjusting (cars with automatic transmission)

Component replacement or other circumstances may necessitate adjustment of the driveplate clearance. Incorrect clearance may result in premature starter wear.

1. Install drive plate with new bolts and backing plate, but without shim(s). See Fig. 9.

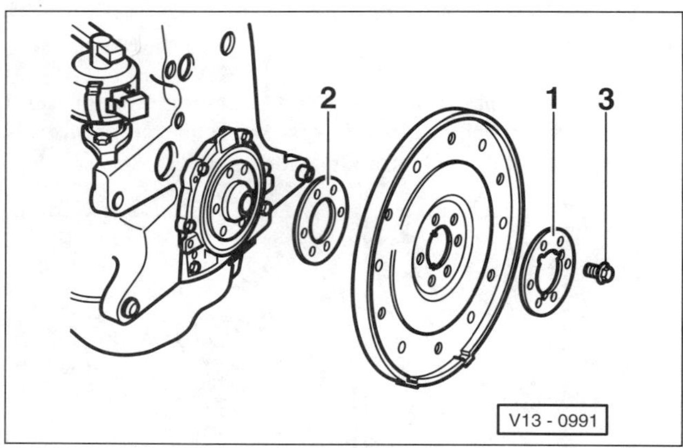

V13-0991

Fig. 9. Automatic transmission driveplate assembly. Shim (**2**) may or may not be present. Backing plate (**1**) is used only with automatic transmission driveplate.

Tightening Torque

- Driveplate checking torque. . . . . 30 Nm (22 ft-lb)

---

2. Measure distance from machined surface on cylinder block to outer edge of driveplate with a suitable measuring tool at three points. Measuring tool must fit through hole in driveplate. See Fig. 10.

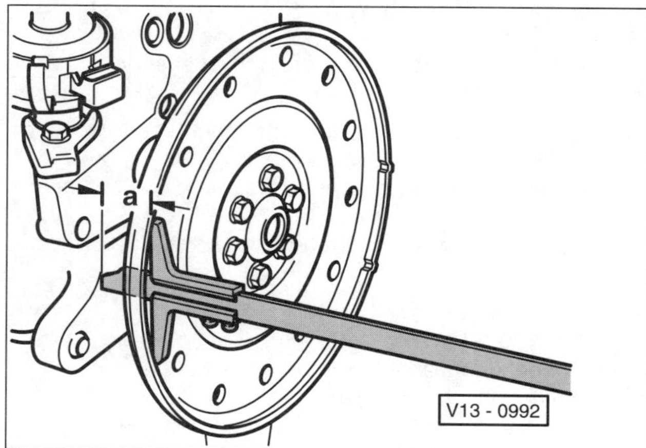

V13-0992

Fig. 10. Measuring tool inserted into hole in drive plate to obtain distance from machined surface of block to outer edge of driveplate, dimension (**a**).

3. Average the three readings to get **dimension a**.

Specification

- Cylinder block to outer edge of driveplate (automatic transmission only), **dimension a**. . . 19.5 mm – 21.1mm (0.77 – 0.83 in.)

---

4. If specification is not obtained, remove driveplate add shim(s) and recheck.

5. When specification is obtained, attach holding fixture and torque to final specification.

Tightening torques

- Flywheel or driveplate to crankshaft (stretch bolt, always replace)
  - stage I . . . . 30 Nm (22 ft-lb)
  - stage II . . . . 60 Nm (44 ft-lb)
  - stage III . . . . additional ¼ turn (90°)

CYLINDER BLOCK INTERNAL COMPONENTS

During engine block disassembly, be sure to mark the position and orientation of all parts as they are removed. This includes connecting rods, rod bearings and caps, piston pins, pistons, main bearings and caps. This ensures that re-used parts are put back in to service in the location where they have been "run-in". Certain cylinder block components such as connecting rod caps and main bearing caps are matched to another part during manufacture and will not fit properly to any other part. Knowing which components came from which location can also be a used to diagnose internal engine problems.

To minimize wear during initial engine start-up, clean engine oil should be used to lubricate all friction surfaces during assembly.

Pistons and Connecting Rods

Pistons, piston pins, piston rings, connecting rods, and bearings should never be interchanged if they are to be reused. Mark cylinder number and installation orientation on pistons, connecting rods and connecting rod bearing caps before removal.

Components of one piston and connecting rod assembly are shown in Fig. 10. Pistons for ALH engines are not all the same. Valve relief pockets machined into the piston crown for cylinders 1 and 2 are the same. Pockets in cylinders 3 and 4 are also the same, but are different from cylinders 1 and 2.

The piston pin should require only a slight push to remove or install. If difficult, heat the piston to approximately 60°C (160°F). Replace the piston and the pin if the fit is excessively loose.

Inspect the connecting rod for any bending, distortion, heat damage or other visual damage. Connecting rod specifications are listed in **Table a**. Connecting rods should always be replaced in complete sets due to weight and dimensional considerations.

NOTE —

- *When checking radial clearance, reuse the old bolt or nut, and lubricate the contact surface of the nut or bolt before tightening. Tighten the nut or bolt only to the 30 Nm (22 ft-lb) specification and not the additional ¼ turn.*
- *If connecting rod radial clearance is excessive, the crankshaft connecting rod journals should be checked. If crankshaft journal diameters are within specifications, recheck radial clearance using new bearing shells.*

Piston and connecting rod, assembly

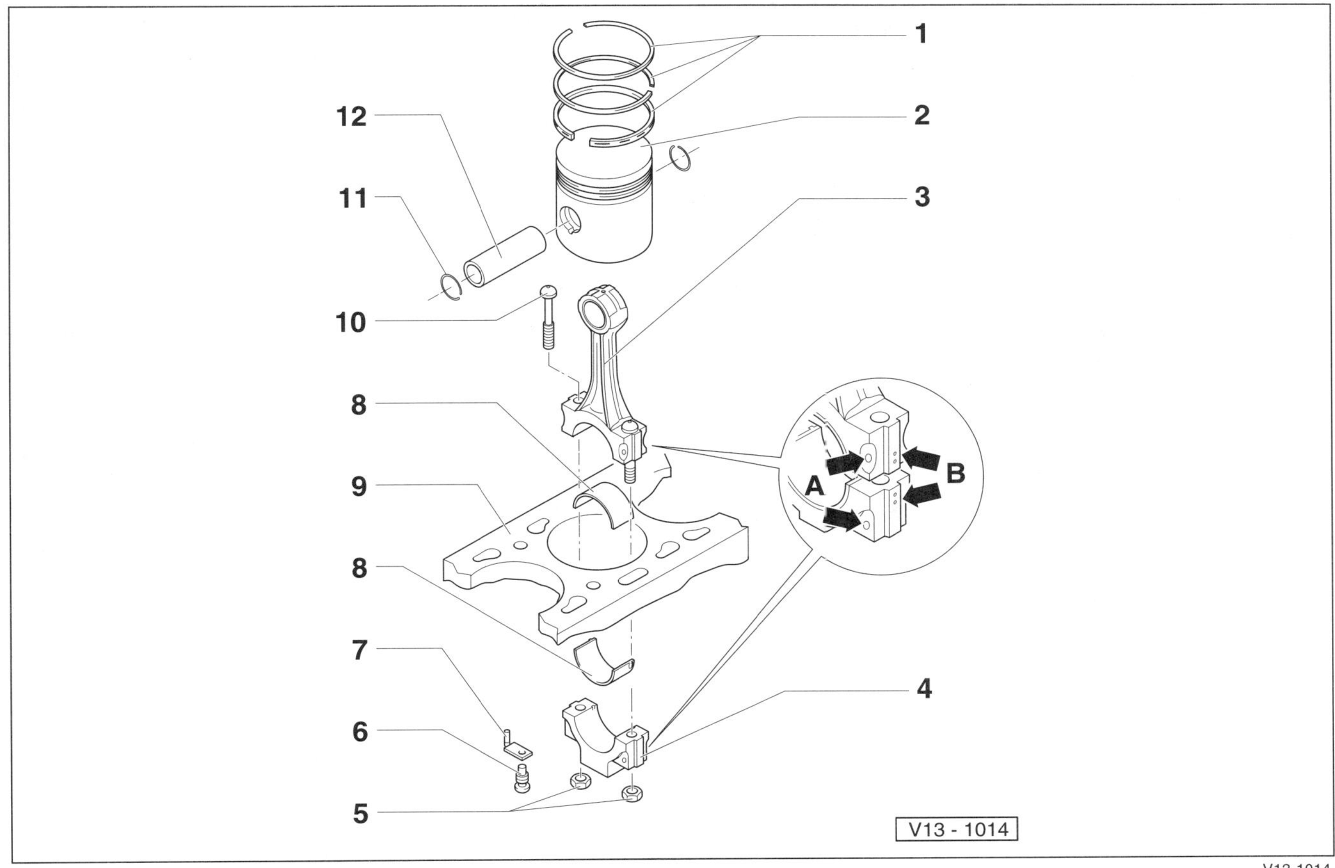

Fig. 11. Exploded view of piston and connecting rod assembly.

1. **Piston ring**
   - Offset gaps by 120°
   - Remove and install using piston ring pliers
   - "TOP" faces piston crown
   - 2-part oil ring
2. **Piston**
   - Mark installation position and cylinder number
   - Arrow on piston crown points to pulley end
   - Install using piston ring clamp
   - Orientation (diesel engine) **see** Ⓐ
3. **Connecting rod**
   - Only replace as a set
   - Mark cylinder number (**B**)
   - Installation position: mark (**A**) faces toward pulley end
4. **Connecting rod bearing cap**
   - Note installation position
5. **Nuts**
   - Tighten to 30 Nm (22 ft-lb) + ¼ turn (90°)
   - Always replace
   - Oil threads and contact surfaces
   - To measure radial clearance tighten to 30 Nm (22 ft-lb), but no further
6. **Pressure relief valve**
   - Tighten to 27 Nm (20 ft-lb)
   - Opening pressure: 2.5 to 3.2 bar (36 to 46 psi)
7. **Oil spray jet**
   - For piston cooling
8. **Bearing shell**
   - Note installation position
   - Do not interchange used bearing shells
   - Ensure retaining lugs fit tightly in recesses
   - Do not rotate crankshaft when checking radial clearance
   - With oil hole for piston pin lubrication
     AWW engine, only upper bearing (large end of rod)
9. **Engine block**
10. **Connecting rod bolt**
    - Tightening torque: 30 Nm + ¼ turn (90°)
    - ALH, AVH, AZG, AWW engines have connecting rod bolt that threads directly into connecting rod (no nut)
      Tightening torque: 30 Nm + ¼ turn (90°)
11. **Circlip**
12. **Piston pin**
    - If difficult to remove, heat piston to 60°C (140°F)
    - Remove and install with VW 222a

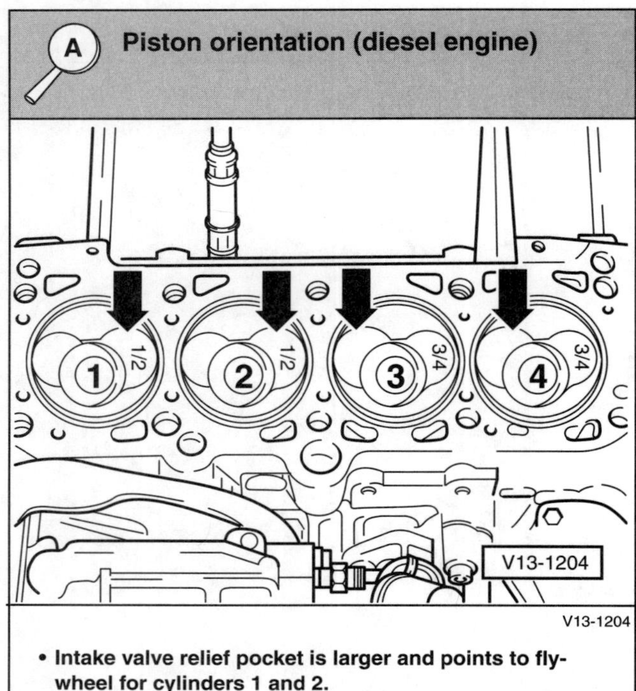

V13-1204

- Intake valve relief pocket is larger and points to flywheel for cylinders 1 and 2.
- Larger valve relief pocket points to belt pulley side for cylinders 3 and 4.
- Pistons are factory marked for proper location.

Piston Rings

Piston ring end gaps are checked with the piston rings inserted evenly approximately 15 mm (5/8 in.) from the bottom of the cylinder. This is because wear in this area of the cylinder is negligible. See Fig. 12. **Table b** lists piston ring end gap specifications.

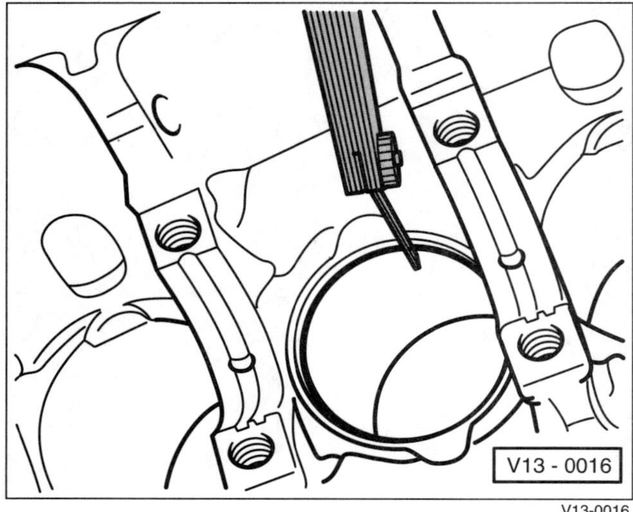

V13-0016

Fig. 12. Piston ring shown inserted into the bottom of the cylinder. Measure gap with a feeler gauge.

Table a. Connecting Rod Specifications

Radial clearance (Plastigage®)	
new (2.0L, 1.9L)	0.01–0.06 mm (0.0004–0.0024 in.)
new (1.8L)	0.01–0.05 mm (0.0004–0.0020 in.)
wear limit	
2.0L, 1.8L engine	0.12 mm (0.0047 in.)
1.9L engine	0.08 mm (0.0031 in.)
Axial (side) clearance	
new (2.0L, 1.9L)	0.05–0.35 mm (0.0020–0.0138 in.)
new (1.8L code AWD)	0.07–0.23 mm (0.0028–0.0091 in.)
new (1.8L code AWW)	0.05–0.31 mm (0.0020–0.0122 in.)
wear limit	
2.0L, 1.9L, 1.8L (code AWW)	0.37 mm (0.0145 in.)
1.8L (code AWD)	0.40 mm (0.0157 in.)
Checking torque	30 Nm (22 ft-lb)
Assembly torque	30 Nm (22 ft-lb) plus ¼ turn (90°)

Table b. Piston Ring End Gaps

	New	Wear limit
Top compression ring		
AEG, AVH, AZG, AWW engines	0.20–0.40 mm (.0079–.0157 in.)	0.8 mm (.0315 in.)
ALH engine	0.20–0.40 mm (.0079–.0157 in.)	1.0 mm (.0394 in.)
AWD engine	0.15–0.40 mm (.0059–.0157 in.)	0.8 mm (.0315 in.)
Bottom compression ring		
AEG, AVH, AZG, AWW engines	0.20–0.40 mm (.0079–.0157 in.)	0.8 mm (.0315 in.)
ALH engine	0.20–0.40 mm (.0079–.0157 in.)	1.0 mm (.0394 in.)
AWD engine	0.15–0.40 mm (.0059–.0157 in.)	0.8 mm (.0315 in.)
Oil scraper ring		
AEG, AVH, AZG, AWW engines	0.25–0.50 mm (.0098–.0197 in.)	0.8 mm (.0315 in.)
ALH, AWD engines	0.25–0.50 mm (.0098–.0197 in.)	1.0 mm (.0394 in.)

Piston ring side clearance (ring to groove clearance) is checked using feeler gauges. Measure each ring in its original groove. See Fig. 13. Piston ring side clearance specifications are listed in **Table c**.

V13 - 0687

V13-0687

Fig. 13. Piston ring side clearance (ring to groove clearance) being measured with a feeler gauge.

NOTE —
Piston ring groove should be thoroughly cleaned before checking ring side clearance.

Table c. Piston Ring Side Clearances

	New	Wear limit
Top compression ring		
AEG, AVH, AZG, AWW engines	0.06–0.09 mm (.0024–.0035 in.)	0.20 mm (.0079 in.)
ALH engine	0.06–0.09 mm (.0024–.0035 in.)	0.25 mm (.0098 in.)
AWD engine	0.02–0.07 mm (.0008–.0027 in.)	0.12 mm (.0047 in.)
Bottom compression ring		
AEG, AVH, AZG, AWW engines	0.06–0.09 mm (.0024–.0035 in.)	0.20 mm (.0079 in.)
ALH engine	0.05–0.08 mm (.0020–.0031 in.)	0.25 mm (.0098 in.)
AWD engine	0.02–0.07 mm (.0008–.0027 in.)	0.12 mm (.0047 in.)
Oil scraper ring		
AEG, AVH, AZG, AWW engines	0.03–0.06 mm (.0012–.0024 in.)	0.15 mm (.0059 in.)
ALH engine	0.03–0.06 mm (.0012–.0024 in.)	0.15 mm (.0059 in.)
AWD engine	0.02–0.06 mm (.0008–.0024 in.)	0.12 mm (.0047 in.)

Specification
- Piston wear–maximum allowable deviation from nominal piston diameter. . . . 0.04 mm (.0016 in.)

Specification
- Cylinder wear–maximum allowable deviation from nominal cylinder bore
  - AEG, AVH, AZG, AWW engines . 0.08 mm (.0031 in.)
  - ALH, AWD engines . . . . 0.10 mm (.0039 in.)

Cylinder bore dimensions

Measure cylinder bores at three places; approximately the top, the middle and the bottom of the piston travel. Make measurements parallel to the crankshaft and at right angles (90°). See Fig. 14.

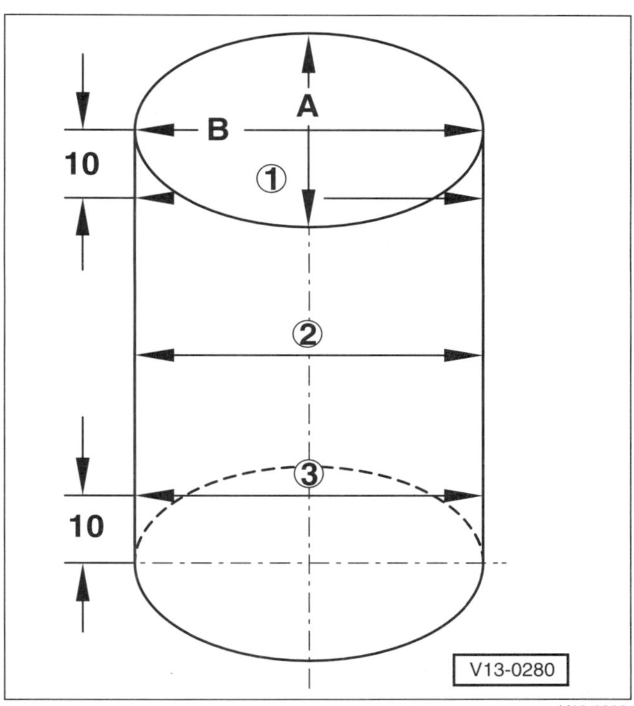

V13-0280

Fig. 14. Measure cylinder bore in directions both perpendicular to the crankshaft (**A**) and parallel to crankshaft (**B**). Make measurements at 3 locations in each cylinder.

CAUTION —
Mounting the bare cylinder block to an engine stand can distort its shape and cause inaccurate cylinder bore measurement. Always check cylinder bores with the block resting unstressed and without mounting brackets on a flat surface.

The top and bottom measurements should be made approximately 10 mm (3/8 in.) from the ends of the cylinder. Measure pistons from the bottom of the piston skirt and at right angles (90°) to the piston pin. See Fig. 15. Nominal piston and cylinder bore diameter specifications are given in **Table d**. Nominal piston diameters are also marked on the piston crowns.

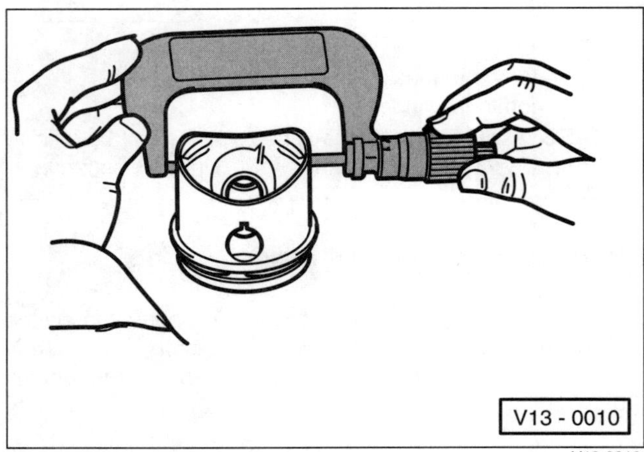

V13-0010

Fig. 15. Check piston diameter approximately 6–10 mm (0.236–0.394 in.) from bottom of skirt at right angle to piston pin. If piston is graphite coated, (dark gray color) allow up to 0.02 mm (0.0008 in.) additional, as the graphite coating will wear away.

Table d. Piston and Cylinder Diameters

Engine code	Piston diameter in mm (in.)	Cylinder bores in mm (in.)
AEG, AVH, AZG		
standard	82.465* (3.2466)	82.51 (3.2484)
1st oversize	82.965* (3.2663)	83.01 (3.2681)
ALH		
standard	79.47 (3.1287)	79.51 (3.1303)
1st oversize	79.72 (3.1386)	79.76 (3.1401)
2nd oversize	79.97 (3.1484)	80.01 (3.1500)
AWD, AWW		
standard	80.95 (3.1870)	81.01 (3.1894)
1st oversize	81.45 (3.2066)	81.51 (3.2090)
* Dimension without graphite coating (thickness 0.02 mm (.0008 in.). The graphite coating wears away.		

Piston Projection at TDC (diesel engine)

Diesel engine pistons protrude slightly out of the block at TDC due to design considerations. The amount of protrusion varies slightly between engines as a result of production tolerance. In order to achieve proper compression ratios, one of three different thickness head gaskets are used to adjust compression height. Piston projection must be measured and adjusted any time components that affect it are replaced. These components include: crankshaft, piston, connecting rod and block. Measure piston height on all 4 cylinders. See Fig. 16.

Select a suitable head gasket based on the highest reading obtained from the available head gaskets listed in **Table e**. The different gaskets are identified by the number of holes punched in an identification tab on the front of the gasket. See Fig. 17.

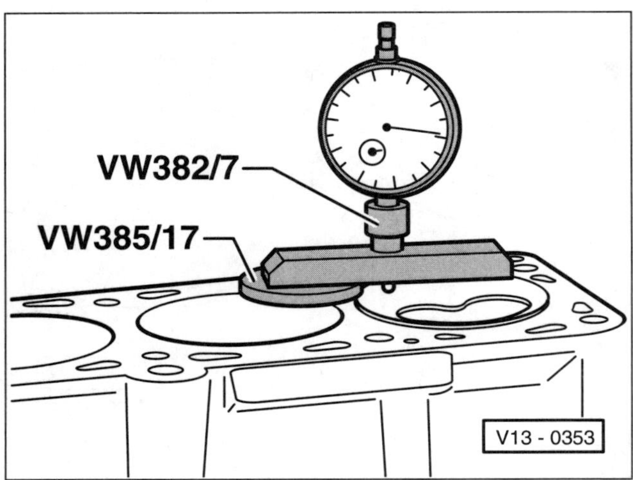

V13-0353

Fig. 16. Piston projection being measured with a dial gauge and suitable adapters.

NOTE —

Cylinder measurements that differ substantially from each other could be an indication of internal engine damage.

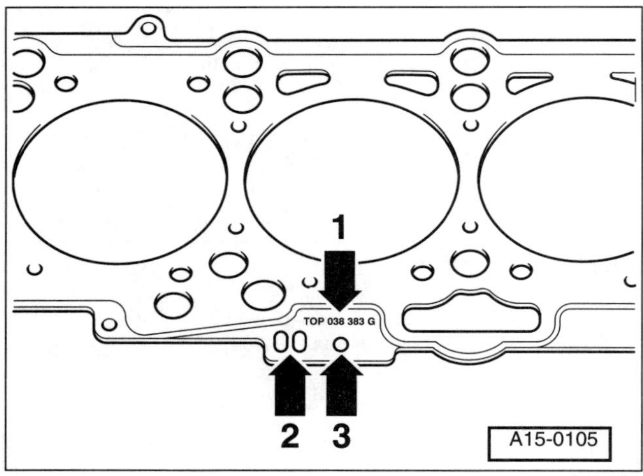

A15-0105

Fig. 17. Diesel cylinder head gasket identification markings: **arrow 1** = part number, **arrow 2** = production information (disregard), **arrow 3** = identification holes.

Table e. Diesel Cylinder Head Gasket Selection

Measured piston projection at TDC	Gasket identification	Thickness
0.91 – 1.00 mm (.0358 – .0394 in.)	1 hole	1.45 mm (.0571 in.)
1.01 – 1.10 mm (.0398 – .0433 in.)	2 holes	1.53 mm (.0602 in.)
1.11 – 1.20 mm (.0437 – .0472 in.)	3 holes	1.61 mm (.0634 in.)

Crankshaft

The crankshaft assemblies and related components for 4-cylinder engines are shown in Fig. 18. and Fig. 19. Observe the installation notes for any components that are to be re-used. The crankshaft mounts a sensor wheel for the engine management system that will only fit on the crankshaft in one position. The sensor wheel on diesel engines uses a dowel pin.

Crankshaft bearing specifications are listed in **Table f** and journal diameters are listed in **Table g**. If a crankshaft must be replaced, a Volkswagen remanufactured crankshaft is available from an authorized Volkswagen Dealer.

> ***CAUTION —***
> *Many of the fasteners used in the cylinder block are stretch bolts that must be replaced once loosened. Review the repair information to identify all bolts and nuts that must be replaced during cylinder block repairs or reconditioning.*

NOTE —

- *On cars with an automatic transmission, see* **Flywheel or Driveplate** *given earlier when reinstalling the driveplate. Special installation procedures apply.*
- *Attach engine to suitable engine stand when disassembling and assembling.*

Table f. Crankshaft Bearing Specifications

Main bearing radial clearance (Plastigage®)	
new parts	
gasoline engines	0.01–0.04 mm (.0004–.0016 in.)
diesel engines	0.03–0.08 mm (.0012–.0031 in.)
wear limit	
gasoline engines	0.15 mm (.0059 in.)
diesel engine	0.17 mm (.0067 in.)
Crankshaft axial play (side clearance)	
new parts	
gasoline engines	0.07–0.23 mm (.0028–.0091 in.)
diesel engines	0.07–0.17 mm (.0028–.0067 in.)
wear limit	
gasoline engines	0.30 mm (.0118 in.)
diesel engine	0.37 mm (.0146 in.)

Table g. Crankshaft Journal Diameters

Journal diameters (nominal)	mm (in.)
Basic dimension	
AEG, AVH, AZG engines	
main	54.00 (2.1260) $^{-0.017\ (0.00067)}_{-0.037\ (0.00146)}$
connecting rod	47.80 (1.8819) $^{-0.022\ (0.00087)}_{-0.042\ (0.00165)}$
ALH, AWD, AWW engines	
main	54.00 (2.1260) $^{-0.022\ (0.00087)}_{-0.042\ (0.00165)}$
connecting rod	47.80 (1.8819) $^{-0.022\ (0.00087)}_{-0.042\ (0.00165)}$
1st undersize (0.25 mm)	
AEG, AVH, AZG engines	
main	53.75 (2.1161) $^{-0.017\ (0.00067)}_{-0.037\ (0.00146)}$
connecting rod	47.55 (1.8720) $^{-0.022\ (0.00087)}_{-0.042\ (0.00165)}$
ALH, AWD, AWW engines	
main	53.75 (2.1161) $^{-0.022\ (0.00087)}_{-0.042\ (0.00165)}$
connecting rod	47.55 (1.8720) $^{-0.022\ (0.00087)}_{-0.042\ (0.00165)}$
2nd undersize (0.50 mm)	
AEG, AVH, AZG engines	
main	53.50 (2.1063) $^{-0.017\ (0.00067)}_{-0.037\ (0.00146)}$
connecting rod	47.30 (1.8622) $^{-0.022\ (0.00087)}_{-0.042\ (0.00165)}$
ALH, AWD, AWW engines	
main	53.50 (2.1063) $^{-0.022\ (0.00087)}_{-0.042\ (0.00165)}$
connecting rod	47.30 (1.8622) $^{-0.022\ (0.00087)}_{-0.042\ (0.00165)}$
3rd undersize (0.75 mm)	
AEG, AVH, AZG engines	
main	53.25 (2.0965) $^{-0.017\ (0.00067)}_{-0.037\ (0.00146)}$
connecting rod	47.05 (1.8524) $^{-0.022\ (0.00087)}_{-0.042\ (0.00165)}$
ALH, AWD, AWW engines	
main	53.25 (2.0965) $^{-0.022\ (0.00087)}_{-0.042\ (0.00165)}$
connecting rod	47.05 (1.8524) $^{-0.022\ (0.00087)}_{-0.042\ (0.00165)}$

Crankshaft assembly (gasoline engines)

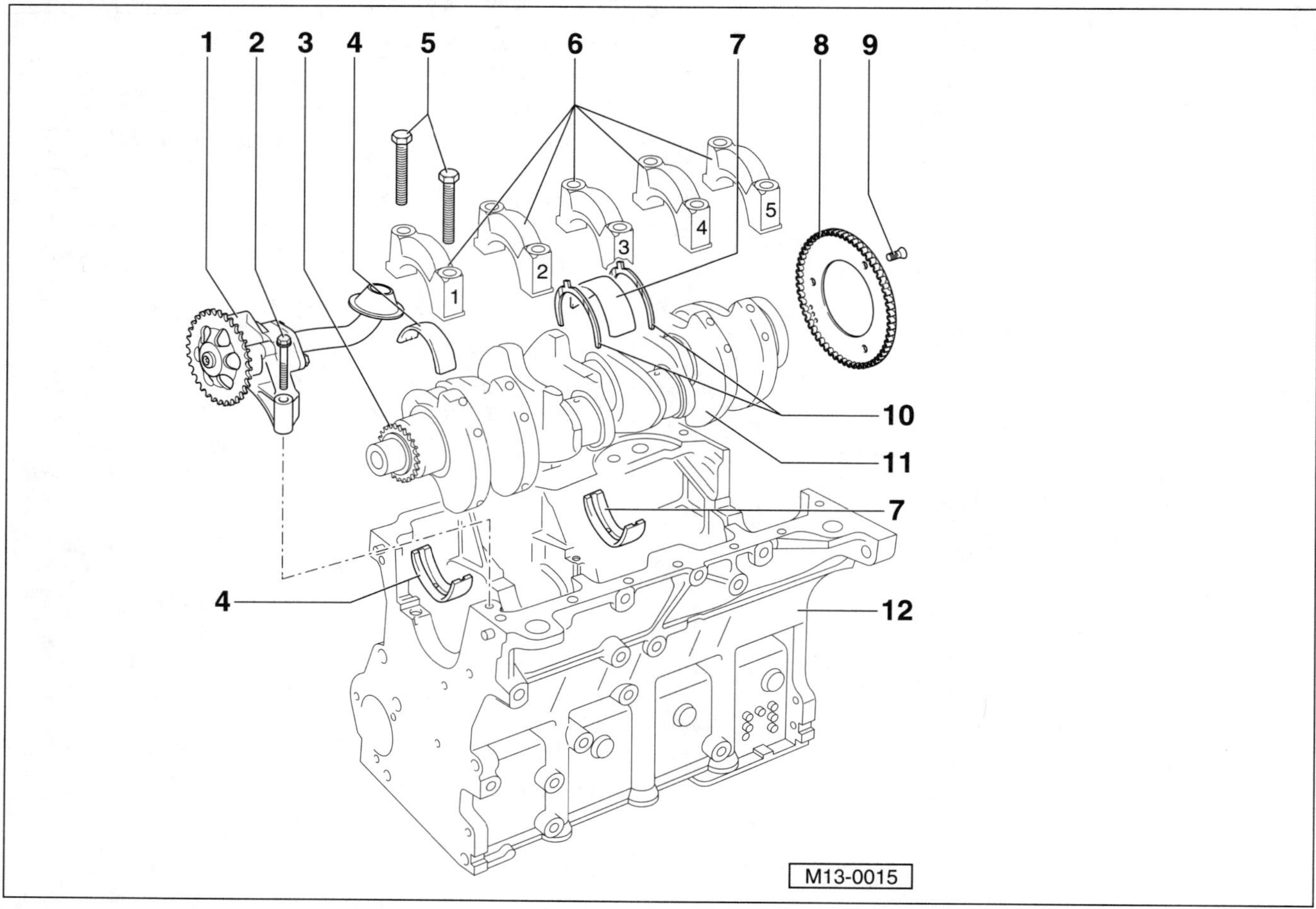

M13-0015

Fig. 18. Exploded view of crankshaft and related components of 4-cylinder gasoline engines.

1. **Oil pump**
   - With 12 bar (174 psi) upper pressure check valve
   - Check that both positioning sleeves are in place
2. **Bolt**
   - Tighten to 15 Nm (11 ft-lb)
3. **Chain sprocket**
   - For oil pump drive
4. **Bearing caps 1, 2, 4 and 5**
   - For bearing cap without oil groove
   - For cylinder block with oil groove
   - Do not interchange used bearing shells (mark)
5. **Bolts**
   - Tighten to 65 Nm (48 ft-lb) + ¼ turn (90°)
   - Always replace
   - Tighten to 65 Nm (48 ft-lb) to measure radial clearance
6. **Bearing cap**
   - Bearing cap 1: pulley end
   - Bearing cap 3: with grooves for thrust washers
   - Bearing shell retaining lugs engine block/bearing cap must be on the same side
7. **Bearing shell 3**
   - For bearing cap without oil groove
   - For cylinder block with oil groove
   - Do not interchange used bearing shells (mark)
8. **Sensor wheel**
   - For engine speed sensor (G28)
   - Can only be installed in one position, holes are offset
9. **Bolt**
   - Tighten to 10 Nm (7 ft-lb) + ¼ turn (90°)
   - Always replace
10. **Thrust washer**
    - For bearing 3 bearing cap
    - Note installation position
11. **Crankshaft**
    - Check radial clearance with Plastigage
    - Do not rotate crankshaft when checking radial clearance

Crankshaft assembly (diesel engine)

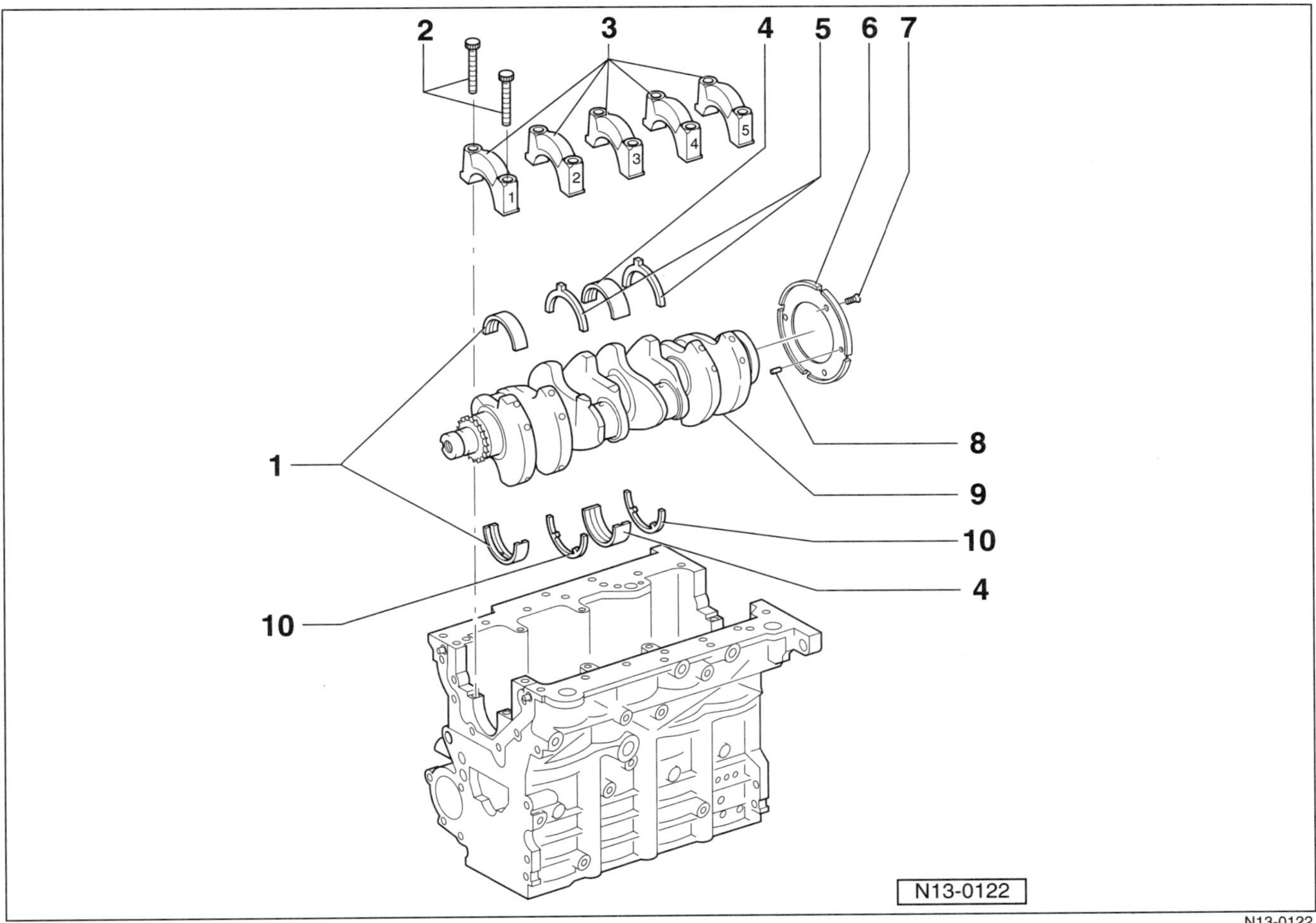

N13-0122

Fig. 19. Exploded view of crankshaft and related components on 4-cylinder diesel engine.

1. **Bearing shells 1, 2, 4 and 5**
   - For bearing caps without oil groove
   - For engine block with oil groove
   - Do not interchange used bearing shells (mark)
2. **Bolt**
   - Tighten to 65 Nm (48 ft-lb) + ¼ turn (90°)
   - Always replace
   - Threaded along complete length
   - Tighten to 65 Nm (48 ft-lb) to measure radial clearance
3. **Bearing cap**
   - Bearing cap 1: pulley end
   - Bearing cap 3 with recesses for thrust washers
   - Bearing shell retaining lugs engine block/bearing cap must be on the same side
4. **Bearing shell 3**
   - Bearing cap without oil groove
   - For engine block with oil groove
   - Do not interchange used bearing shells (mark)
5. **Thrust washer**
   - For bearing cap 3
   - Note installation position
6. **Sensor wheel**
   - For engine speed sensor
7. **Bolt**
   - Tighten to 10 Nm (7 ft-lb) + ¼ turn (90°)
   - Always replace
8. **Dowel pin**
   - For installation position, **see** Ⓐ
9. **Crankshaft**
   - Check radial clearance with Plastigage
   - Do not rotate crankshaft when checking radial clearance
10. **Thrust washer**
    - For engine block, bearing 3
    - Note installation position

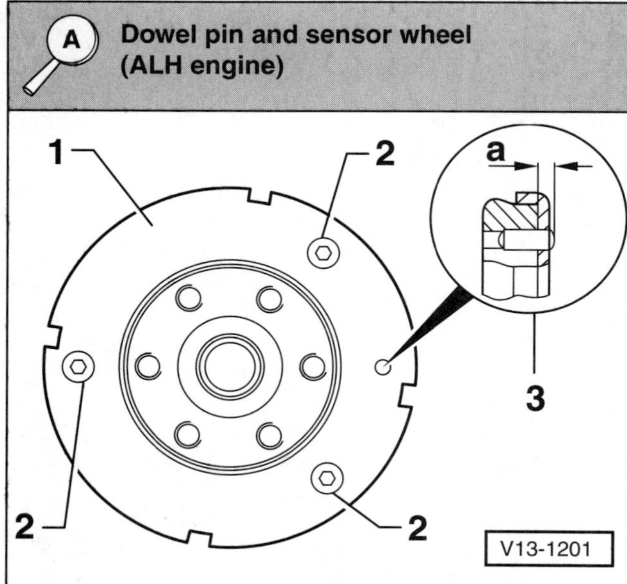

V13-1201

- **ALH engine only.**
- **Sensor wheel (1) mounted on crankshaft with screws (2).**
- **A single dowel pin (3) extends 2.5 – 3.0 mm (.098 – .118 in.) from the flange end, dimension (a).**

QUALITY REVIEW

When you have finished working under the hood and around other areas of the vehicle it is advisable to take a moment to quality check or review your work. This helps to ensure that the operation or repair has been completed properly with all affected systems functioning within normal parameters. This may include the following:

- Make sure that the radiator fan cycles properly and that the coolant level and concentration are correct.
- Ensure that all cable ties and hose clamps that were removed as part of the repair are replaced.
- Check and adjust all other applicable fluid levels.
- Make sure that there are no fluid leaks.
- Make sure that there are no air, vacuum or exhaust leaks.
- Make sure that all components involved in the repair are positioned correctly and function properly.
- Male sure all tools, shop cloths, fender covers, and protective tape are removed.
- Clean grease from painted surfaces and steering wheel.
- Unlock the anti-theft radio and reset the clock.

In addition to the above noted points, the ECM and TCM may need to be checked using the Volkswagen supplied VAG 1551 or 1552 scan tool as mentioned at the start of this repair.

13b Crankshaft/Cylinder Block (6-cylinder)

TABLES

GENERAL

This repair group provides the special reconditioning information necessary to repair the Volkswagen 6-cylinder short block. The information contained here is intended to be used as a reconditioning guide for the professional or experienced automotive technician. Many of the operations and specifications listed require precision measuring equipment.

Engine Codes
• AFP . . . . 2.8L 6-cylinder gasoline

NOTE—
For 4-cylinder crankshaft and cylinder block, see **13a Crankshaft/Cylinder Block (4-cylinder)**.

Cylinder block

The 6-cylinder engine block and related components are shown in Fig. 1.

NOTE—
- *If during engine repairs, metal shavings or large quantities of small metal particles are found in the engine oil, the oil passages in the cylinder block must be thoroughly cleaned and the following components replaced: all oil splash nozzles, oil return barrier, oil cooler, and the oil filter.*
- *Volkswagen identifies electrical components by a letter and/or a number in the electrical schematics. See* **97 Wiring Diagrams, Fuses and Relays**. *These electrical identifiers are listed in parenthesis as an aid to electrical troubleshooting.*

Cylinder block components

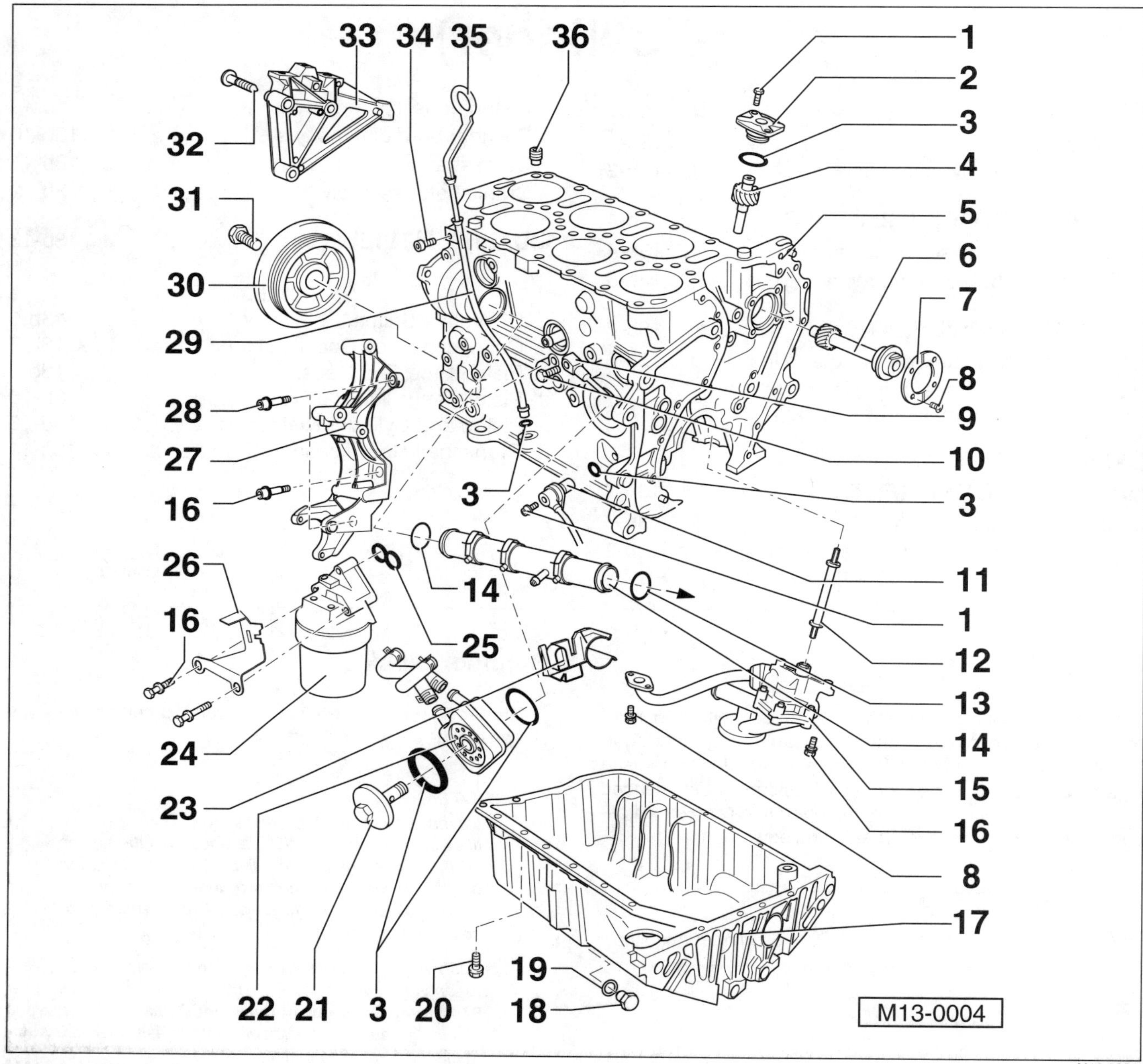

Fig. 1. Cylinder block and related components for 2.8L engine.

1. **Bolt**
   - Tighten to 10 Nm (7 ft-lb)
2. **Oil pump drive cover**
3. **O-ring**
   - Always replace
   - Coat with oil before assembly
4. **Oil pump drive**
5. **Cylinder block**
6. **Intermediate shaft**
7. **Thrust washer**
8. **Bolt**
   - Tighten to 10 Nm (7 ft-lb)
   - Install with "D6" locking compound
9. **Knock sensor 2 (G66)**
10. **Bolt**
    - Tighten to 20 Nm (15 ft-lb)
    - Tightening torque influences function of sensor

11. Engine rpm sensor (G28)

12. Drive shaft
- For oil pump drive

13. O-ring
- Always replace

14. Coolant pipe

15. Oil pump
- Coat oil pressure pipe on engine block and oil pump housing with VW sealant AMV 188 001 02

NOTE —
Volkswagen part numbers are given for reference only. Always consult with your Volkswagen Parts Department or aftermarket parts specialist for the latest parts information.

16. Bolt
- Tighten to 25 Nm (18 ft-lb)

17. Oil pan

18. Oil drain plug
- Tighten to 30 Nm (22 ft-lb)

19. Round gasket
- Always replace

20. Bolt
- Tighten to 15 Nm (11 ft-lb)

21. Oil cooler cover
- Tighten to 25 Nm (18 ft-lb)

22. Oil cooler
- Coat contact surfaces outside oil seal with VW sealant AMV 188 001 02
- Check for adequate clearance with adjacent components
- Replace if metal shavings are found in engine block upon disassembly

23. Bracket

24. Oil filter housing

25. Gasket
- Always replace
- Note installation position
- Coat with oil before installing

26. Bracket
- For valve for two-stage intake pipe switch-over (N156)

27. Compact bracket
- For generator, air conditioning compressor and power steering pump

28. Guide bolt
- Tighten to 25 Nm (18 ft-lb)

29. Guide tube
- For oil dipstick
- Attached to intake pipe-top section with bolt

30. Vibration damper

31. Bolt
- Tighten to 100 Nm plus ¼ turn (90°)
- Always replace
- Use locking bracket 3406 for loosening and tightening, **see** (A)

32. Bolt
- Tighten to 45 Nm (33 ft-lb)

33. Engine bracket

34. Bolt
- Tighten to 10 Nm (7 ft-lb)

35. Oil dipstick
- Oil level must not exceed the max. mark

36. Oil return barrier
- Tighten to 5 Nm (44 in-lb)
- Note installation position
- Clean if severely contaminated
- Replace if metal shavings are found in engine block upon disassembly

(A) Vibration damper, loosening and tightening

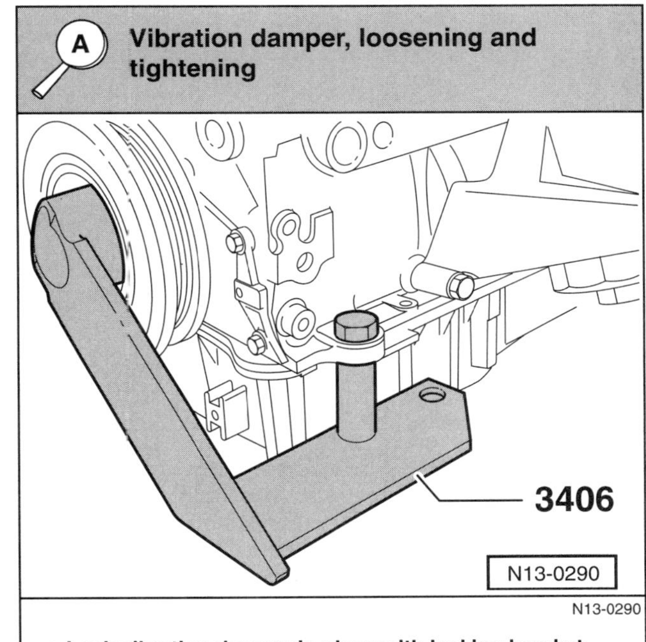

N13-0290

- **Lock vibration damper in place with locking bracket 3406**
- **Always replace vibration damper mounting bolt**

CYLINDER BLOCK OIL SEALS

Cylinder block oil seals, assembly

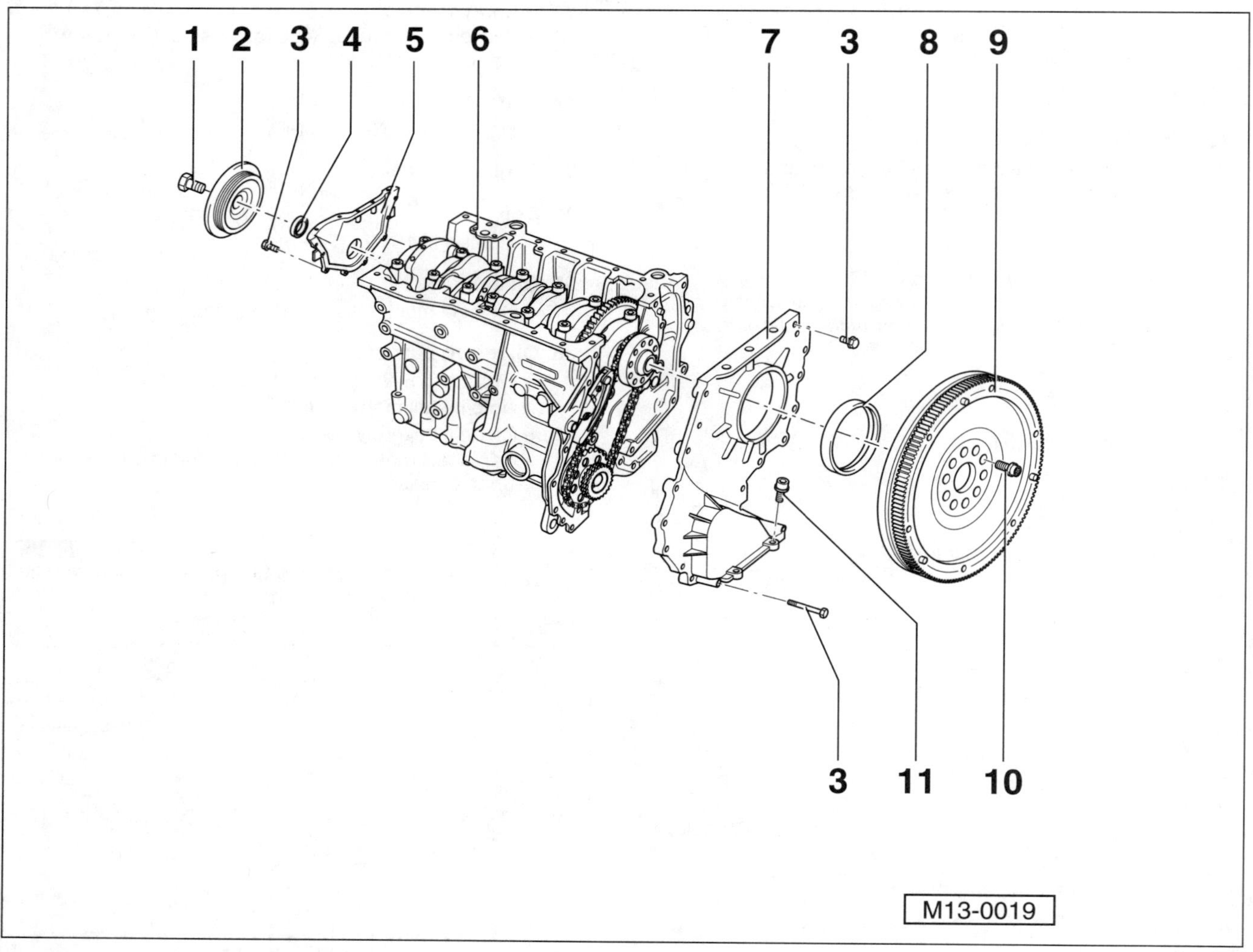

Fig. 2. Exploded view of crankshaft seals in cylinder block.

NOTE —
The engine must be attached to an engine stand with bracket 3269 to carry out assembly work.

1. **Bolt**
   - Tighten to 100 Nm (74 ft-lb) + ¼ turn (90°)
   - Always replace
   - Use locking bracket 3406 to loosen and tighten
2. **Vibration damper**
3. **Bolt**
   - Tighten to 10 Nm (7 ft-lb)
4. **Front crankshaft oil seal**
5. **Front oil seal flange**
   - Coat sealing surface with VW sealant AMV 188 001 02
6. **Cylinder block**
7. **Rear oil seal flange**
   - Coat sealing surface with VW sealant AMV 188 001 02
8. **Rear oil seal**
   - Remove with extractor 2086
   - Lightly coat the sealing lip of the oil seal with oil
   - To install, position with mounting sleeve 2003/2A
   - Pull into stop with 2003/3
9. **Flywheel/driveplate**
   - Remove and install with 3406 locking bracket on vibration damper
10. **Bolt**
    - Tighten to 60 Nm (44 ft-lb) + ¼ turn (90°)
    - Always replace
11. **Bolt**
    - Tighten to 25 Nm (18 ft-lb)

Front crankshaft oil seal, replacing

1. Remove ribbed V-belt, see **0 Maintenance**.

2. Remove the vibration damper by locking it in place with VW special tool 3406 (locking bracket) or equivalent, and loosening mounting bolt. See Fig. 3.

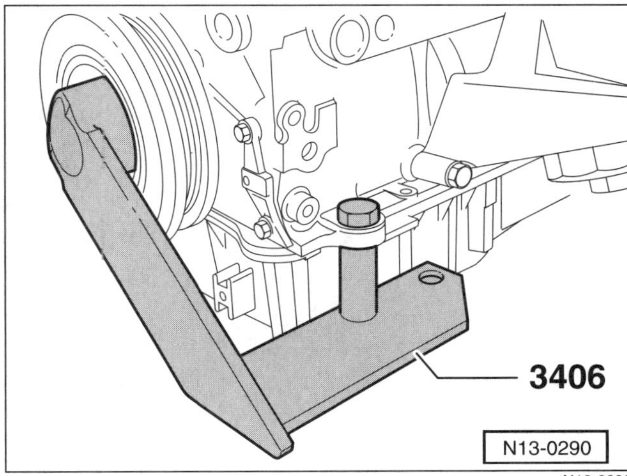

N13-0290

Fig. 3. Locking bracket 3406 attached to vibration damper.

3. Turn the inner section of oil seal extractor (VW special tool 3203) three turns (approx. 4 mm) out from the outer section of the extractor and lock into position with knurled screw. See Fig. 4.

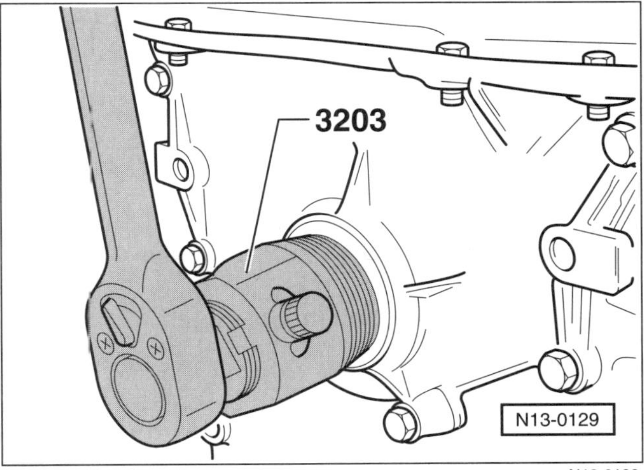

N13-0129

Fig. 4. Seal removal tool (**3202**) threaded into seal. Wrench is being used to remove crankshaft oil seal.

4. Coat the threaded head of oil seal removal tool with oil, set in place and with heavy pressure, screw it as far as possible into the seal.

5. Loosen the knurled screw and turn the inner part against the crankshaft until the seal is removed.

6. Lightly coat the sealing lip of the seal with clean oil.

7. Place a guide sleeve on the crankshaft nose. See Fig. 6.

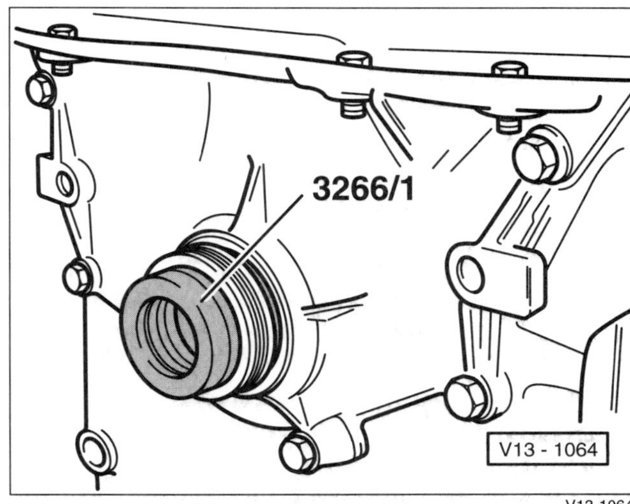

V13-1064

Fig. 5. Place guide sleeve (VW special tool 3266/1 shown) on nose of crankshaft.

8. Press the seal in with a pressure sleeve until it reaches the stop. Use the old mounting bolt from the vibration damper in the pressure sleeve to pull the seal into final installation position. See Fig. 6.

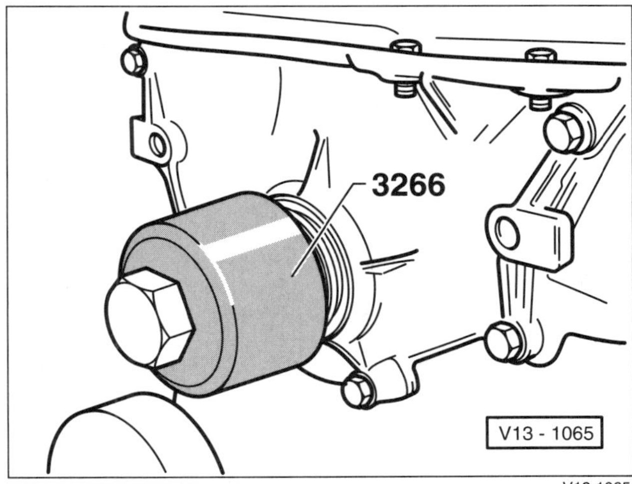

V13-1065

Fig. 6. Front crankshaft oil seal being pressed in using Volkswagen special tools (**3266**) and old vibration damper bolt.

9. Install vibration damper with new mounting bolt and lock in place as shown in Fig. 3. Tighten to final torque.

10. Install remaining removed components.

Tightening torques

- Crankshaft sprocket bolt, (stretch bolt - always replace)
  stage I . . . . 100 Nm (74 ft-lb)
  stage II . . . . additional ¼ turn (90°)

FLYWHEEL/DRIVEPLATE

Removal of the flywheel or driveplate requires that the engine be separated from the transmission. Remove the clutch on manual transmission vehicles, see **30 Clutch**.

> ***CAUTION—***
> - *On vehicles with automatic transmissions, special mounting and measuring procedures are required when installing the driveplate.*
> - *The flywheel on manual transmission vehicles and the driveplate on automatic transmission vehicles are mounted to the crankshaft using stretch bolts that are designed to be used only once. Always replace.*

Flywheel/driveplate, removing and installing

1. Lock the vibration damper in place with VW special tool 3406 (locking bracket) or equivalent, as shown earlier in Fig. 3.

2. Loosen securing bolts diagonally and remove flywheel or drive plate and any shims.

3. Installation is the reverse of removal observing the following points:
   - Install any removed shims and mount the flywheel or drive plate with new bolts.
   - Check driveplate clearance (as applicable) as described later.
   - Attach the holder to the vibration damper and torque the flywheel /driveplate mounting bolts diagonally to specifications.

Tightening torque
- Flywheel or driveplate to crankshaft (stretch bolt, always replace)
  - stage I . . . . 30 Nm (22 ft-lb)
  - stage II . . . . 60 Nm (44 ft-lb)
  - stage III . . . . additional ¼ turn (90°)

Driveplate clearance, adjusting (cars with automatic transmission)

Component replacement or other circumstances may necessitate adjustment of the driveplate clearance. Incorrect clearance may result in premature starter wear.

1. Install drive plate with at least three of the old mounting bolts, but without shim and tighten to checking torque.

Tightening Torque
- Driveplate checking torque. . . . . 30 Nm (22 ft-lb)

2. Measure distance from machined surface on cylinder block to outer edge of driveplate with a suitable measuring tool at three points. Measuring tool must fit through hole in driveplate. See Fig. 7.

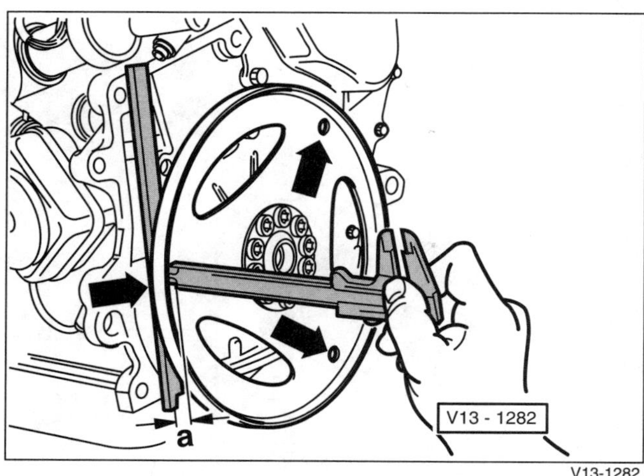

V13-1282

Fig. 7. Insert measuring tool through each hole (**arrows**) in drive plate to obtain distance from machined surface of block to outer edge of driveplate, dimension (**a**).

3. Average the three readings (minus the thickness of the ruler as shown in Fig. 7.) to get **dimension a**.

Specification
- Cylinder block to outer edge of driveplate (automatic transmission only)
  dimension a . . . 15.7 mm – 16.5 mm (0.62 – 0.65 in.)

4. If specification is not obtained, remove driveplate, add appropriate shim and recheck. See **Table a**.

Table a. Driveplate shims

VW part number	Thickness (mm)
021 105 303	0.4
021 105 303 A	0.8
021 105 303 B	1.2
021 105 303 C	1.6
021 105 303 D	2.0
021 105 303 E	2.4

> ***NOTE—***
> *Only one compensating shim of the appropriate thickness may be used. See Fig. 8.*

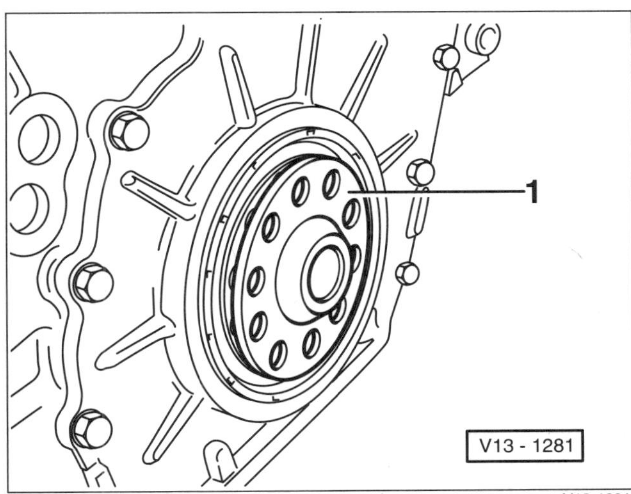

Fig. 8. Use only one compensating shim (**1**) to obtain proper driveplate-to-block clearance.

5. When specification is obtained, use new bolts to attach driveplate and torque to final specification.

Tightening torque

- Driveplate to crankshaft (stretch bolt, always replace)
  - stage I . . . . 30 Nm (22 ft-lb)
  - stage II . . . . 60 Nm (44 ft-lb)
  - stage III . . . . additional ¼ turn (90°)

CYLINDER BLOCK INTERNAL COMPONENTS

During engine block disassembly, be sure to mark the position and orientation of all parts as they are removed. This includes connecting rods, rod bearings and caps, piston pins, pistons, main bearings and caps. This ensures that re-used parts are put back in to service in the location where they have been "run-in". Certain cylinder block components such as connecting rod caps and main bearing caps are matched to another part during manufacture and will not fit properly to any other part. Knowing which components came from which location can also be a used to diagnose internal engine problems.

To minimize wear during initial engine start-up, clean engine oil should be used to lubricate all friction surfaces during assembly.

Pistons and Connecting Rods

Pistons, piston pins, piston rings, connecting rods, and bearings should never be interchanged if they are to be reused. Mark cylinder number and installation orientation on pistons, connecting rods and connecting rod bearing caps before removal. Components of the VR6 piston and connecting rod assembly are shown in Fig. 9.

The piston pin should require only a slight push to remove or install. If difficult, heat the piston to approximately 60°C (160°F). Replace the piston and the pin if the fit is excessively loose.

Inspect the connecting rod for any bending, distortion, heat damage or other visual damage. Connecting rod specifications are listed in **Table b**. Connecting rods should always be replaced in complete sets due to weight and dimensional considerations.

NOTE —

- *When checking radial clearance, reuse the old bolt or nut, and lubricate the contact surface of the nut or bolt before tightening. Tighten the nut or bolt only to the 30 Nm (22 ft-lb) specification and not the additional ¼ turn.*
- *If connecting rod radial clearance is excessive, the crankshaft connecting rod journals should be checked. If crankshaft journal diameters are within specifications, recheck radial clearance using new bearing shells.*

Table b. Connecting Rod Specifications

Radial clearance (Plastigage®)	
new	0.02–0.07 mm (0.0008–0.0028 in.)
wear limit	0.10 mm (0.0039 in.)
Axial (side) clearance	
new	0.05–0.31 mm (0.0020–0.0122 in.)
wear limit	0.40 mm (0.0157 in.)
Checking torque	30 Nm (22 ft-lb)
Assembly torque	30 Nm (22 ft-lb) plus ¼ turn (90°)

Piston and connecting rod, assembly

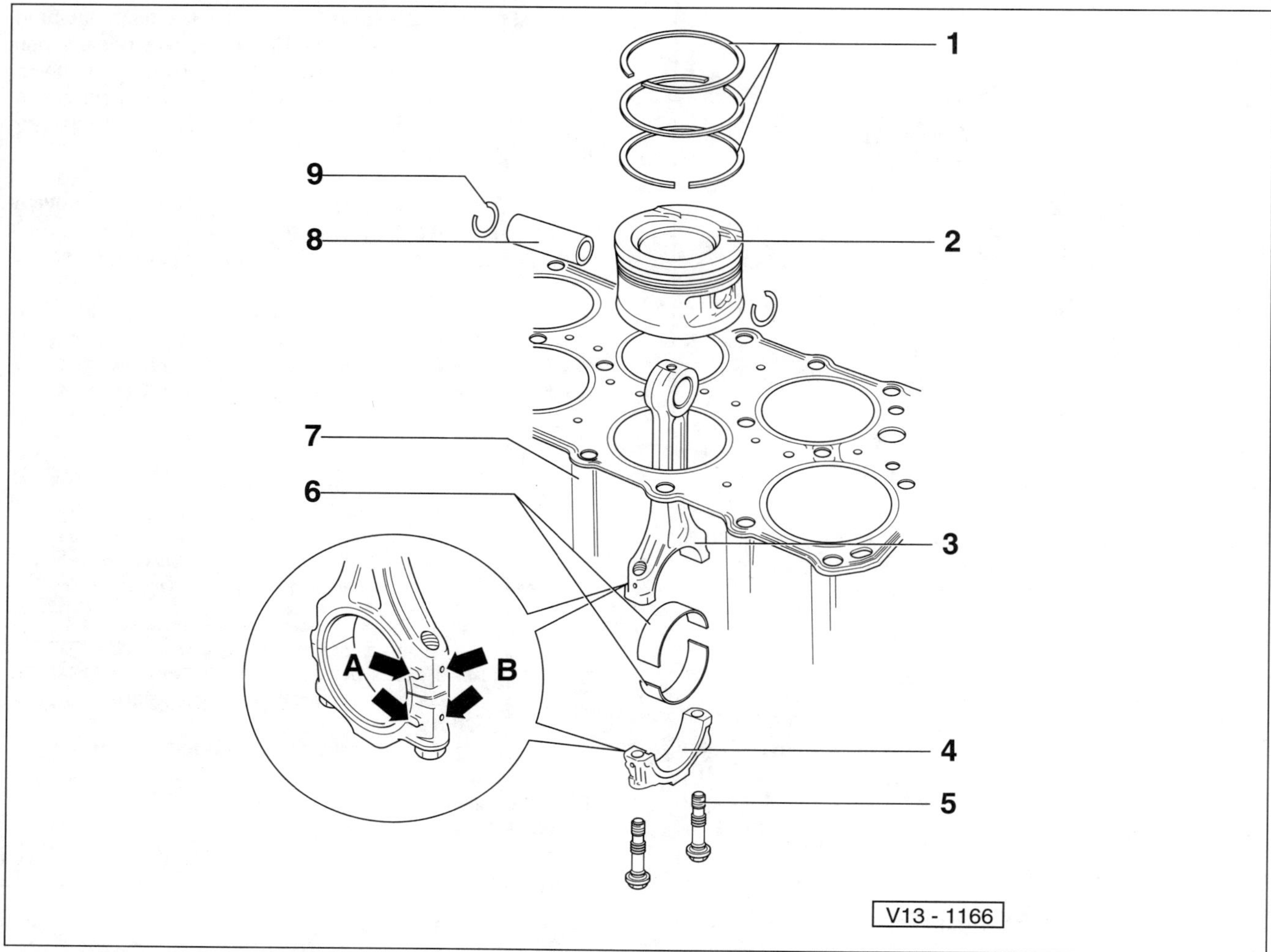

Fig. 9. Exploded view of piston and connecting rod assembly.

1. **Piston ring**
   - Offset gaps by 120°
   - Remove and install using piston ring pliers
   - "TOP" faces piston crown
2. **Piston**
   - Mark installation position and cylinder number
   - Tall side of piston top points toward the middle of the cylinder block
   - Install using piston funnel 3278, **see** Ⓐ
3. **Connecting rod**
   - Only replace as a set
   - Mark cylinder number (**B**)
   - Installation position: mark (**A**) must be positioned on top of each other
4. **Connecting rod bearing cap**
   - Note installation position
5. **Nuts**
   - Tighten to 30 Nm (22 ft-lb) + ¼ turn (90°)
   - Always replace
   - Oil threads and contact surfaces
   - To measure radial clearance tighten to 30 Nm (22 ft-lb), but no further
6. **Bearing shell**
   - Note installation position
   - Do not interchange used bearing shells
   - Ensure retaining lugs fit tightly in recesses
   - Do not rotate crankshaft when checking radial clearance
7. **Engine block**
8. **Piston pins**
   - If difficult to remove, heat piston to 60°C (140°F)
   - Remove and install with VW 222a
9. **Circlip**

Piston installation

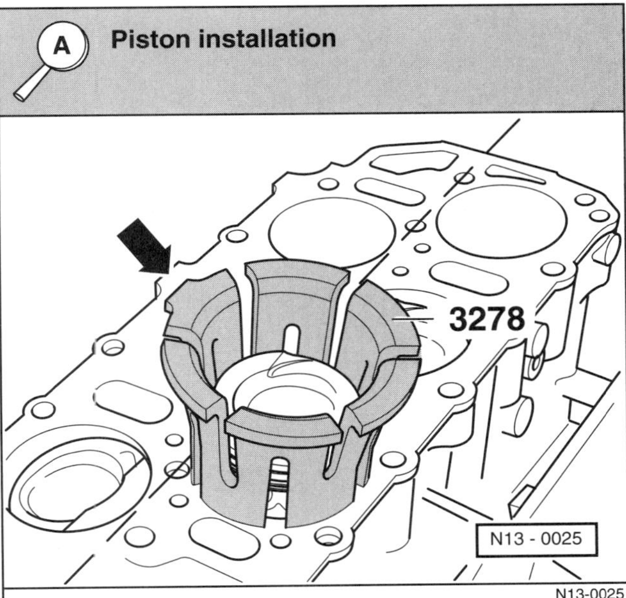

NOTE —

If using a new funnel, guide the piston with oiled piston rings through the funnel twice and, if necessary, remove the resulting shavings. Only then should you install the piston with piston rings into the block.

- **Manually push piston into oiled funnel. The tall side of piston top must point toward funnel spout (arrow).**
- **Hold funnel (with inserted piston) at the upper edge and push piston in with both hands.**
- **Push piston in until it protrudes approx. 15mm (5/8 in.) below bottom edge of funnel.**
- **Start piston in its respective cylinder bore. The funnel spout (arrow) must point toward the middle of the engine block.**
- **Firmly place funnel on cylinder block and push piston in place.**

Piston Rings

Piston ring end gaps are checked with the piston rings inserted evenly approximately 15 mm (5/8 in.) from the bottom of the cylinder. This is because wear in this area of the cylinder is negligible. See Fig. 10. Use a piston without piston rings installed to push ring into cylinder. **Table c** lists piston ring end gap specifications.

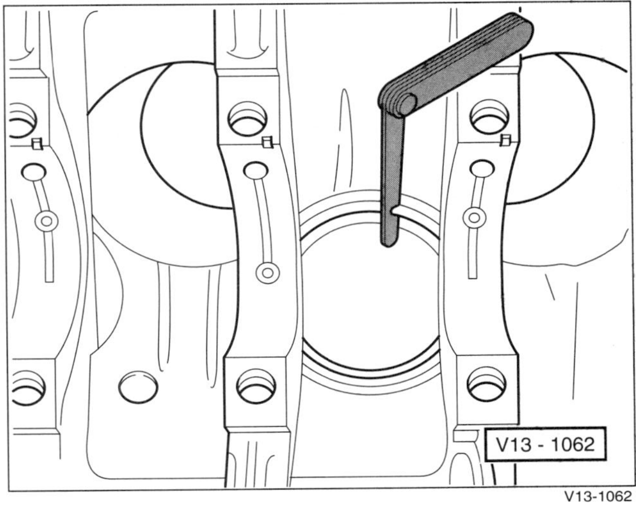

Fig. 10. Piston ring shown inserted into the bottom of the cylinder. Measure gap with a feeler gauge.

Table c. Piston Ring End Gaps

	New	**Wear limit**
Top (compression)	0.20–0.40 mm (.0079–.0157 in.)	1.0 mm (.0394 in.)
Middle (compression)	0.20–0.40 mm (.0079–.0157 in.)	1.0 mm (.0394 in.)
Bottom (oil scraper)	0.25–0.50 mm (.0098–.0197 in.)	1.0 mm (.0394 in.)

Piston ring side clearance (ring to groove clearance) is checked using feeler gauges. Measure each ring in its original groove. See Fig. 11. Piston ring side clearance specifications are listed in **Table d**.

> ***NOTE —***
> *Piston ring groove should be thoroughly cleaned before checking ring side clearance.*

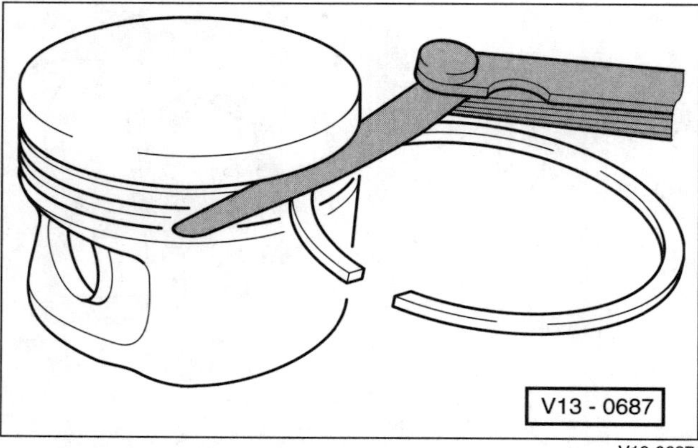

V13-0687

Fig. 11. Piston ring side clearance (ring to groove clearance) being measured with a feeler gauge.

Table d. Piston Ring Side Clearances

	New	Wear limit
Top (compression)	0.04–0.09 mm (.0016–.0035 in.)	0.15 mm (.0059 in.)
Middle (compression)	0.03–0.06 mm (.0012–.0024 in.)	0.15 mm (.0059 in.)
Bottom (oil scraper)	0.02–0.06 mm (.0008–.0024 in.)	0.15 mm (.0059 in.)

Cylinder bore dimensions

Measure cylinder bores at three places; approximately the top, the middle and the bottom of the piston travel. Make measurements parallel to the crankshaft and at right angles (90°). See Fig. 12.

The top and bottom measurements should be made approximately 10 mm (3/8 in.) from the ends of the cylinder. Measure pistons from the bottom of the piston skirt and at right angles (90°) to the piston pin. See Fig. 13. Piston and cylinder bore diameter specifications are given in **Table e**. Piston diameters also should be marked on the piston crowns.

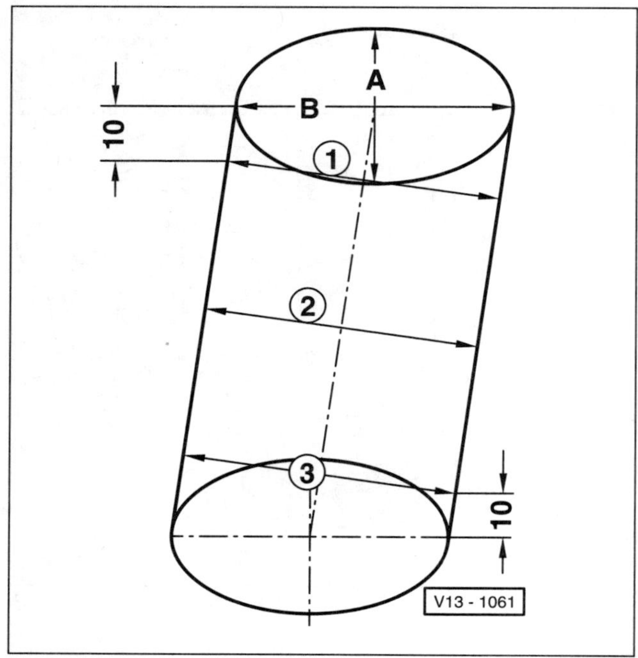

V13-1061

Fig. 12. Measure cylinder bore in directions both perpendicular to the crankshaft (**A**) and parallel to crankshaft (**B**). Make measurements at 3 locations in each cylinder.

> ***CAUTION —***
> *Mounting the bare cylinder block to an engine stand can distort its shape and cause inaccurate cylinder bore measurement. Always check cylinder bores with the block resting unstressed and without mounting brackets on a flat surface.*

Table e. Piston and Cylinder Diameters

2.8L engine	Piston diameter in mm (in.)	Cylinder bores in mm (in.)
standard	80.985 (3.1884)	81.01 (3.1894)
1st oversize	81.485 (3.2081)	81.51 (3.2090)
2nd oversize	81.985 (3.2277)	82.01 (3.2287)

Specification

- Cylinder wear–maximum allowable deviation from nominal cylinder bore . . . . . . 0.08 mm (.0031 in.)

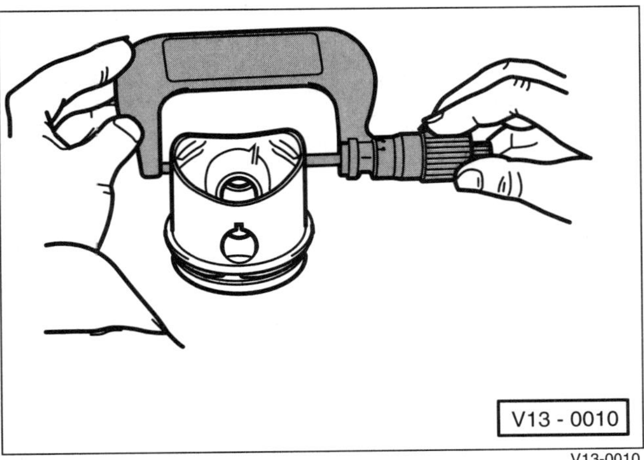

V13-0010

Fig. 13. Check piston diameter approximately 6–10 mm (0.236–0.394 in.) from bottom of skirt at right angle to piston pin. If piston is graphite coated, (dark gray color) allow up to 0.02 mm (0.0008 in.) additional, as the graphite coating will wear away.

Specification

- Piston wear–maximum allowable deviation from nominal piston diameter. . . . 0.04 mm (.0016 in.)

Crankshaft

The crankshaft assemblies and related components are shown in Fig. 14. Observe the installation notes for any components that are to be reused.

Crankshaft specifications are listed in **Table f**. If a crankshaft must be replaced, a Volkswagen remanufactured crankshaft may be available from an authorized Volkswagen Dealer.

> ***CAUTION —***
> *Many of the fasteners used in the cylinder block are stretch bolts that must be replaced once loosened. Review the repair information to identify all bolts and nuts that must be replaced during cylinder block repairs or reconditioning.*

NOTE —

- *On cars with an automatic transmission, see* **Flywheel or Driveplate** *given earlier when reinstalling the driveplate. Special installation procedures apply.*
- *Attach engine to suitable engine stand when disassembling and assembling.*
- *Make sure that prior to removing the crankshaft you have provided a suitable place to put it so that the engine speed sensor wheel does not rest on anything or become damaged.*
- *When replacing bearing shells, use only bearing shells with the same color coding.*

Table f. Crankshaft Specifications

Main bearing radial clearance (Plastigage®)	
new parts	0.02–0.06 mm (.0008–.0024 in.)
wear limit	0.10 mm (.0039 in.)
Crankshaft axial play (side clearance)	
new parts	0.07–0.23 mm (.0028–.0091 in.)
wear limit	0.30 mm (.0118 in.)
Crankshaft measurements	
main bearing	53.958–53.978 mm (2.1243–2.1251 in.)
connecting rod bearing	53.958–53.978 mm (2.1243–2.1251 in.)

Crankshaft assembly

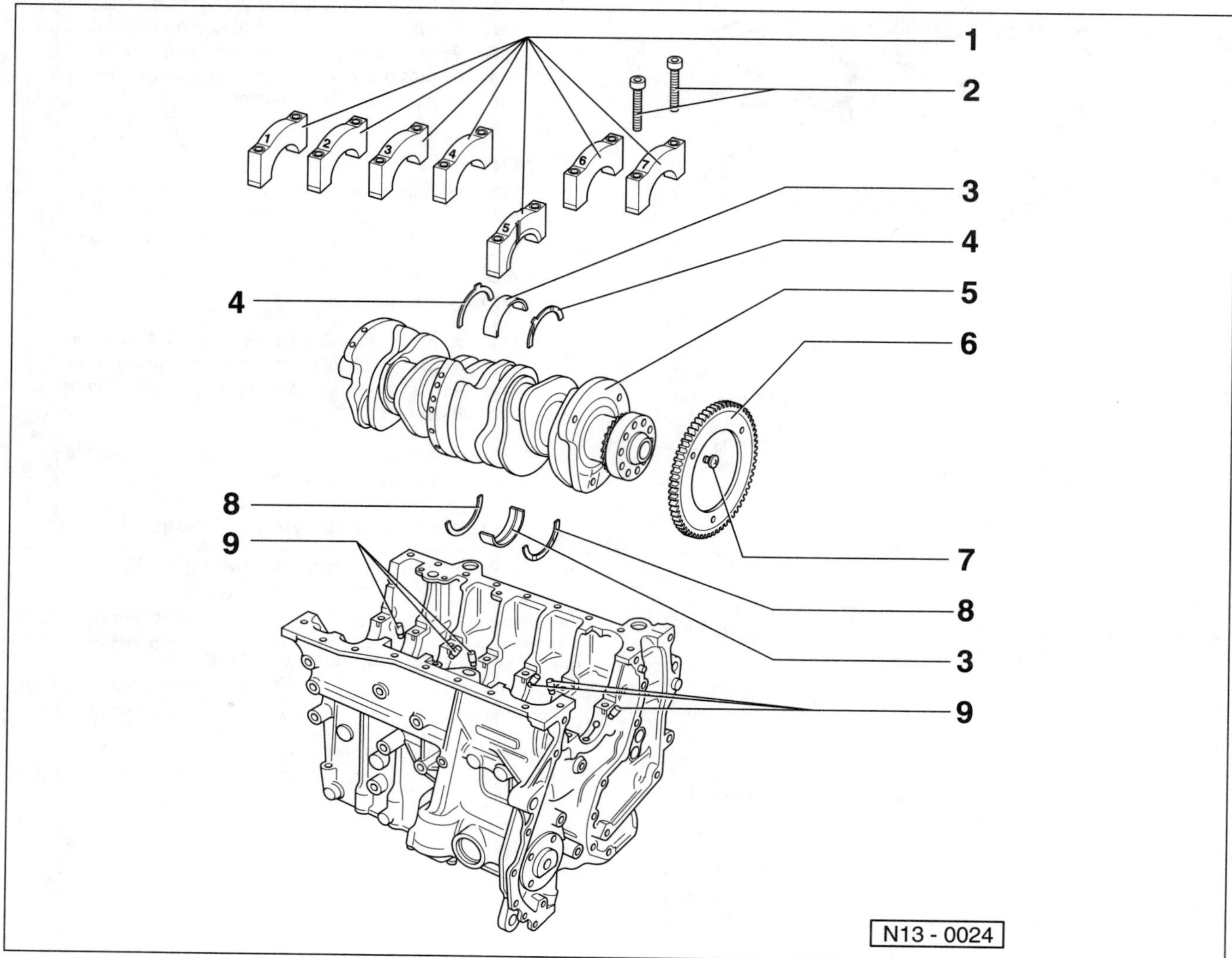

N13-0024

Fig. 14. Crankshaft and related components of 2.8L engine.

1. **Bearing caps**
   - Bearing cap 1: vibration damper side
   - Bearing cap 5 with recesses for thrust bearings
   - Cylinder block to bearing cap bearing shell retaining lips must be placed on top of each other
2. **Bolt**
   - Tighten to 30 Nm (11 ft-lb) + two ¼ turns (180° total)
   - Always replace
3. **Bearing shells 1-7**
   - For bearing caps without oil groove
   - For cylinder block with oil groove
   - Do not interchange used bearing shells (mark)
4. **Thrust bearing**
   - For bearing cap 5
5. **Crankshaft**
   - Finishing not allowable
6. **Engine speed sensor wheel**
   - For engine speed sensor (G28)
   - 58 teeth plus 2 missing for reference point
   - Installing, **see** Ⓐ
7. **Bolt**
   - Tighten to 10 Nm (7 ft-lb) + ¼ turn (90°)
   - Always replace
8. **Thrust washer**
   - For cylinder block, bearing 5
   - Note installation position
9. **Oil spray nozzles**
   - For crankshaft bearings 2-7
   - For piston cooling
   - Opening pressure: 2.0 bar (29 psi)
   - Removing and installing, **see** Ⓑ

A Engine speed sensor wheel, installing

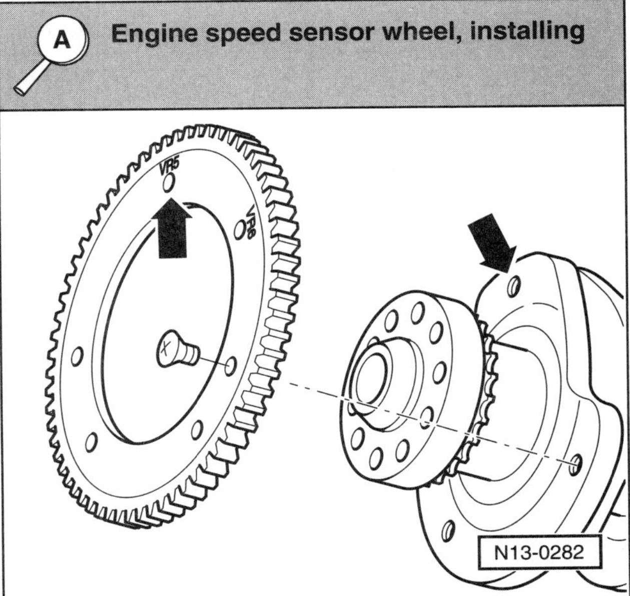

N13-0282

- **Make sure crankshaft connecting surface is free of grease.**
- **Apply a light coat of adhesive (VW 3 D 000 600) to the back of sensor wheel for additional fastening.**
- **Make sure that arrows align as shown.**
- **Ligthly install all mounting screws by hand.**
- **Tighten to 10 Nm plus additional ¼ turn (90°).**

B Oil spray nozzles, removing and installing

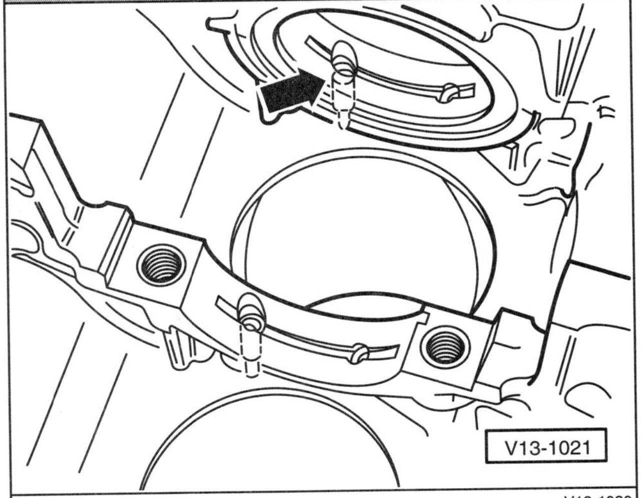

V13-1021

V13-1020

- **Use a 4 mm (5/32 in.) drift from behind to drive nozzles out**
- **Install nozzles using a 6 mm (7/32 in.) drift.**

QUALITY REVIEW

When you have finished working under the hood and around other areas of the vehicle it is advisable to take a moment to quality check or review your work. This helps to ensure that the operation or repair has been completed properly with all affected systems functioning within normal parameters. This may include the following:

- Make sure that the radiator fan cycles properly and that the coolant level and concentration are correct.
- Ensure that all cable ties and hose clamps that were removed as part of the repair are replaced.
- Check and adjust all other applicable fluid levels.
- Make sure that there are no fluid leaks.
- Make sure that there are no air, vacuum or exhaust leaks.
- Make sure that all components involved in the repair are positioned correctly and function properly.
- Male sure all tools, shop cloths, fender covers, and protective tape are removed.
- Clean grease from painted surfaces and steering wheel.
- Unlock the anti-theft radio and reset the clock.

In addition to the above noted points, the ECM and TCM may need to be checked using the Volkswagen supplied VAG 1551 or 1552 scan tool.

15a Cylinder Head and Valvetrain (1.8L Engine)

GENERAL

This section covers cylinder head and valvetrain service and repair work for the 4-cylinder, 5 valve per cylinder, turbocharged 1.8 liter gasoline engine. For information on short block engine rebuilding and internal engine specifications, see **13a Crankshaft/Cylinder Block (4-cylinder)**.

Most of the operations described in this repair group require special equipment and experience. If you lack the skills, tools, or a suitable workplace for servicing or repairing the cylinder head, we suggest that you leave these repairs to an authorized Volkswagen dealer or other qualified shop.

Engine Code
- AWD, AWW . . . . 1.8L 4-cylinder turbo gasoline

The 1.8 liter engine with the AWW engine code uses a camshaft adjuster unit with an electronically operated solenoid to adjust camshaft timing. The engine control module (ECM) will signal the solenoid to adjust camshaft timing based upon engine load and RPM. This allows for variable valve timing, exhaust gas recirculation and cleaner emissions.

DIAGNOSTIC TESTING

The tests that follow can be used to help isolate engine problems, to better understand a problem before starting expensive and extensive repairs, or to just periodically check engine condition.

Compression test

A compression test will tell a lot about the overall condition of the engine without the need for taking it apart. Testing is relatively simple and straightforward.

1. Release locking pins for engine cover by turning 90°. Remove engine cover.
2. Warm-up engine until it is a minimum of 30°C (86°F). Switch off ignition.
3. Disconnect 4-pin harness connectors from all ignition coils. See Fig. 1.
4. Remove all ignition coils.

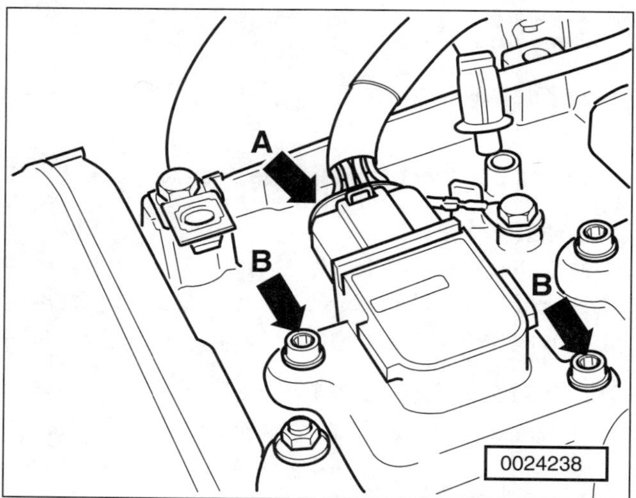

0024238

Fig. 1. Disconnect 4-pin harness connector (**arrow A**) for all 4 ignition coil power output stages. Remove bolts (**arrows B**) to remove each ignition coil.

5. Use compressed air to clear the area around the spark plugs. Remove all spark plugs and lay aside in proper order.

6. Remove fuse #32 for the voltage supply to the injectors.

7. Fit the compression tester into the spark plug hole.

8. Have a helper:
   - depress clutch pedal fully
   - put the transmission in neutral or park
   - depress the accelerator pedal to the floor
   - crank the engine over with the starter motor

NOTE—

Cranking the engine with the ignition system disabled and components disconnected will cause Diagnostic trouble codes (DTCs) to be stored in engine management system memory.

9. Engine should be cranked a minimum of 4 to 5 revolutions.

10. Record readings, release pressure in the gauge and repeat procedure for each cylinder.

11. Compare readings to specification.

Specification

- Compression pressures (1.8L engine)
  new . . . . 10 to 13 bar (147 - 191 psi)
  wear limit. . . . . .7.0 bar (110 psi)
  maximum difference
  between cylinders . . . . 3 bar (44 psi)

---

12. When all cylinders have been checked, reinstall spark plugs and ignition coils, connect harness connectors for coils and install the upper sound absorber panel.

Tightening torques

- Spark plug to cylinder head . . . . 30 Nm (22 ft-lb)
- Ignition coil to cylinder head cover . . . . 10 Nm (7 ft-lb)

Cylinder leakdown test

The most conclusive diagnosis of low compression symptoms requires a cylinder leak-down test. Using a special tester and a supply of compressed air, each cylinder is pressurized. The rate at which the air leaks out of the cylinder, as well as the sound and location of the escaping air can more accurately pinpoint the magnitude and source of the leakage. Any engine compression diagnosis that will require major disassembly should first be confirmed by a cylinder leak-down test. Because this test requires special equipment and experience, it may be desirable to have it performed by a Volkswagen dealer or other qualified repair shop.

CYLINDER HEAD SERVICE

Many cylinder head repairs can be accomplished without removing the cylinder head from the engine. The cylinder head cover (valve cover) gasket, the camshaft, the camshaft oil seal, the valve guide oil seals, the valve springs, and the camshaft followers are all accessible with the cylinder head installed. This heading describes those repairs that can be done with the cylinder head installed.

Fig. 3. shows an exploded view of the internal cylinder head components and Fig. 4. shows the external head components.

NOTE—

Volkswagen identifies electrical components by a letter and/or a number in the electrical schematics. See **97 Wiring Diagrams, Fuses and Relays**. *These electrical identifiers are listed in parenthesis as an aid to electrical troubleshooting.*

Internal cylinder head assembly

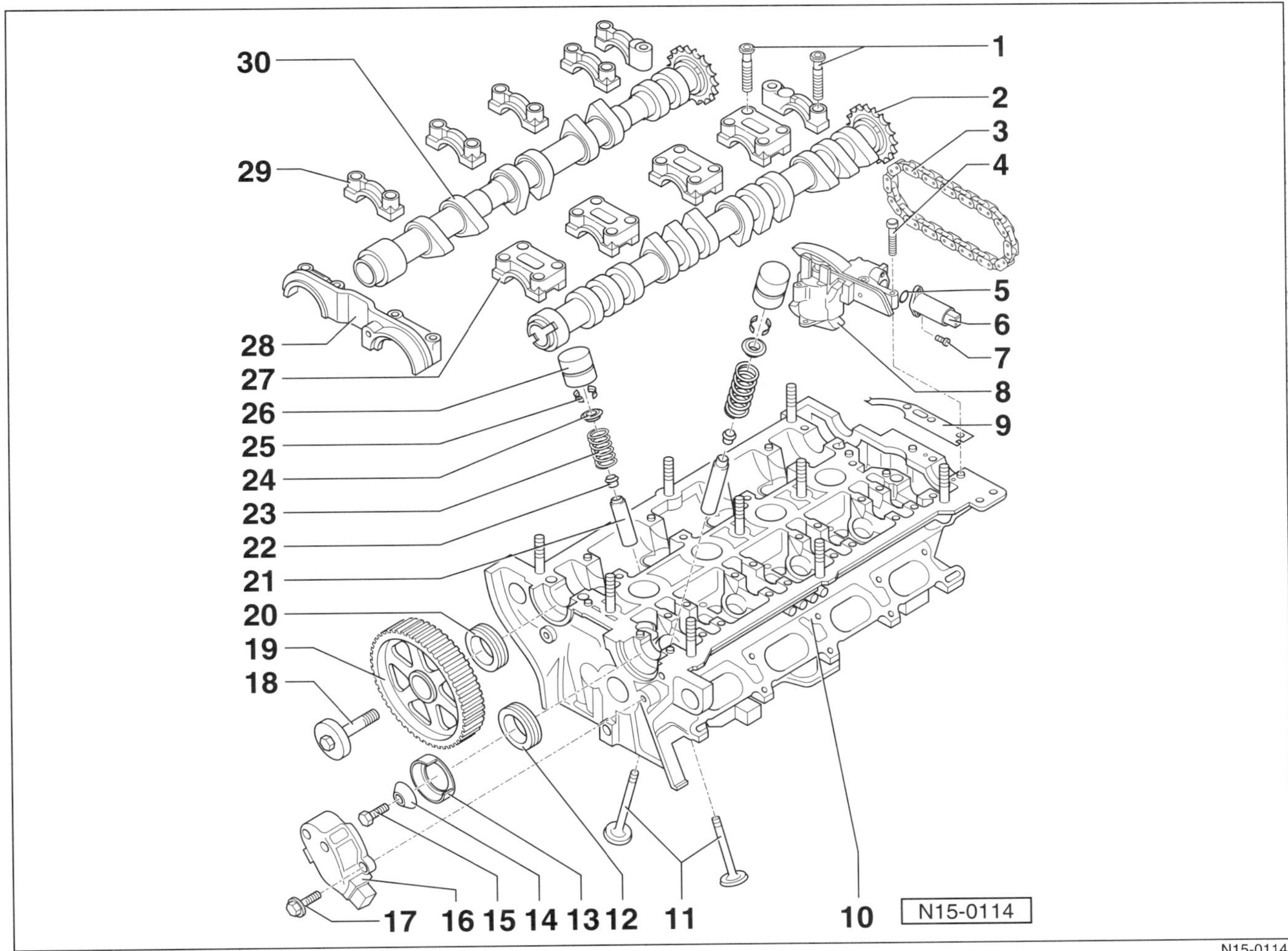

Fig. 2. Exploded view of internal cylinder head components.

1. **Bolt**
   - Tighten to 10 Nm (7 ft-lb)
2. **Camshaft, intake**
   - Chain sprocket is not replaceable
   - Radial clearance checked with plastigage wear limit: 0.1 mm (0.004 in.)
   - Run out: maximum 0.01 mm (0.0004 in.)
3. **Chain, camshaft drive**
   - Clean chain and sprocket and mark direction of rotation with ink or paint mark before removing
4. **Bolt**
   - Tighten to 10 Nm (7 ft-lb)
5. **O-ring**
   - Always replace
   - Only for engine code AWW
6. **Camshaft adjustment valve (N205)**
   - Only for engine code AWW
   - Check resistance between 2 pins on solenoid valve Specification: 10-18Ω at room temperature
7. **Screw**
   - Only for engine code AWW
8. **Tensioner, camshaft drive chain**
   - Compress with 3366 before removing
   - Apply sealant to outer edges before installing
9. **Gasket**
   - Rubber/metal seal
   - Always replace
10. **Cylinder head**
11. **Valves**
    - Quantity: 2 exhaust, 3 intake
    - Sodium filled
    - Do not rework! Only lapping is permitted
12. **Oil seal**

(continued on next page)

Internal cylinder head assembly (continued)

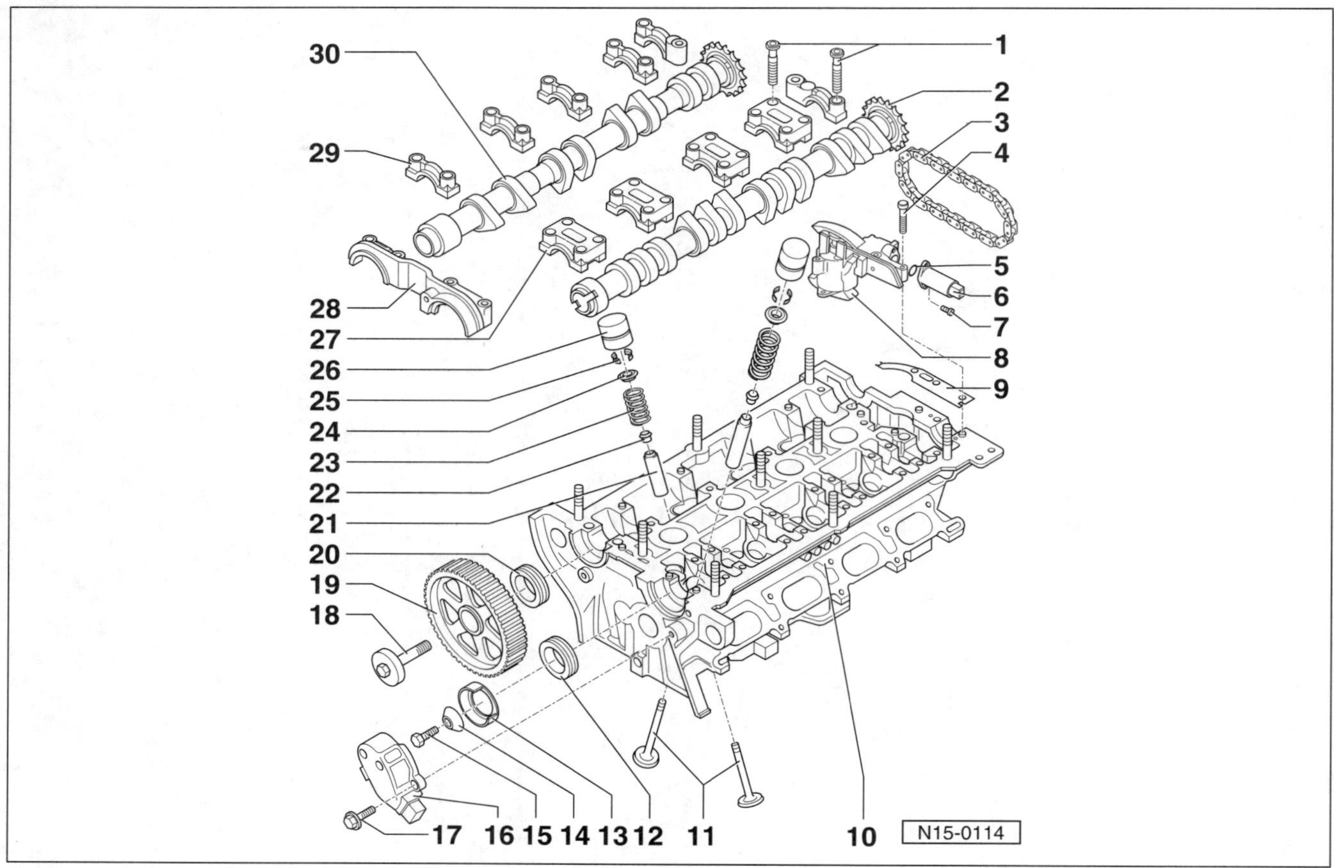

13. Shutter wheel
- For camshaft position sensor
- Note installation position

14. Washer
- Conical shape

15. Bolt
- Tighten to 25 Nm (18 ft-lb)

16. Camshaft position sensor (G40/G163)

17. Bolt
- Tighten to 10 Nm (7 ft-lb)

18. Camshaft sprocket bolt
- Tighten to 65 Nm (48 ft-lb)
- Use 3036 counterholder to loosen and tighten

19. Camshaft sprocket
- Installed position: small web faces outward and cylinder #1 TDC mark is visible

20. Oil seal

21. Valve guide

22. Valve stem seal

23. Valve spring

24. Valve spring retainer

25. Valve keepers

26. Hydraulic lifter
- Do not interchange
- Equipped with hydraulic clearance compensation
- Store with cam contact surface facing downwards
- Before installing check camshaft axial clearance as described later, see **Cylinder Head Components** maximum clearance: 0.20 mm (0.008 in.)
- Oil contact surfaces

27. Bearing cap, intake camshaft
- Note installation position and sequence

28. Bearing cap, double
- Apply sealant to bearing cap/cylinder head mating surface before installing
- Apply sealant to outer edges before installing
- Ensure proper seating on dowel pins

29. Bearing cap, exhaust camshaft
- Note installation position and sequence

30. Camshaft, exhaust
- Radial clearance checked with plastigage wear limit: 0.1 mm (0.004 in.)
- Run out: maximum 0.01 mm (0.0004 in.)

External cylinder head assembly

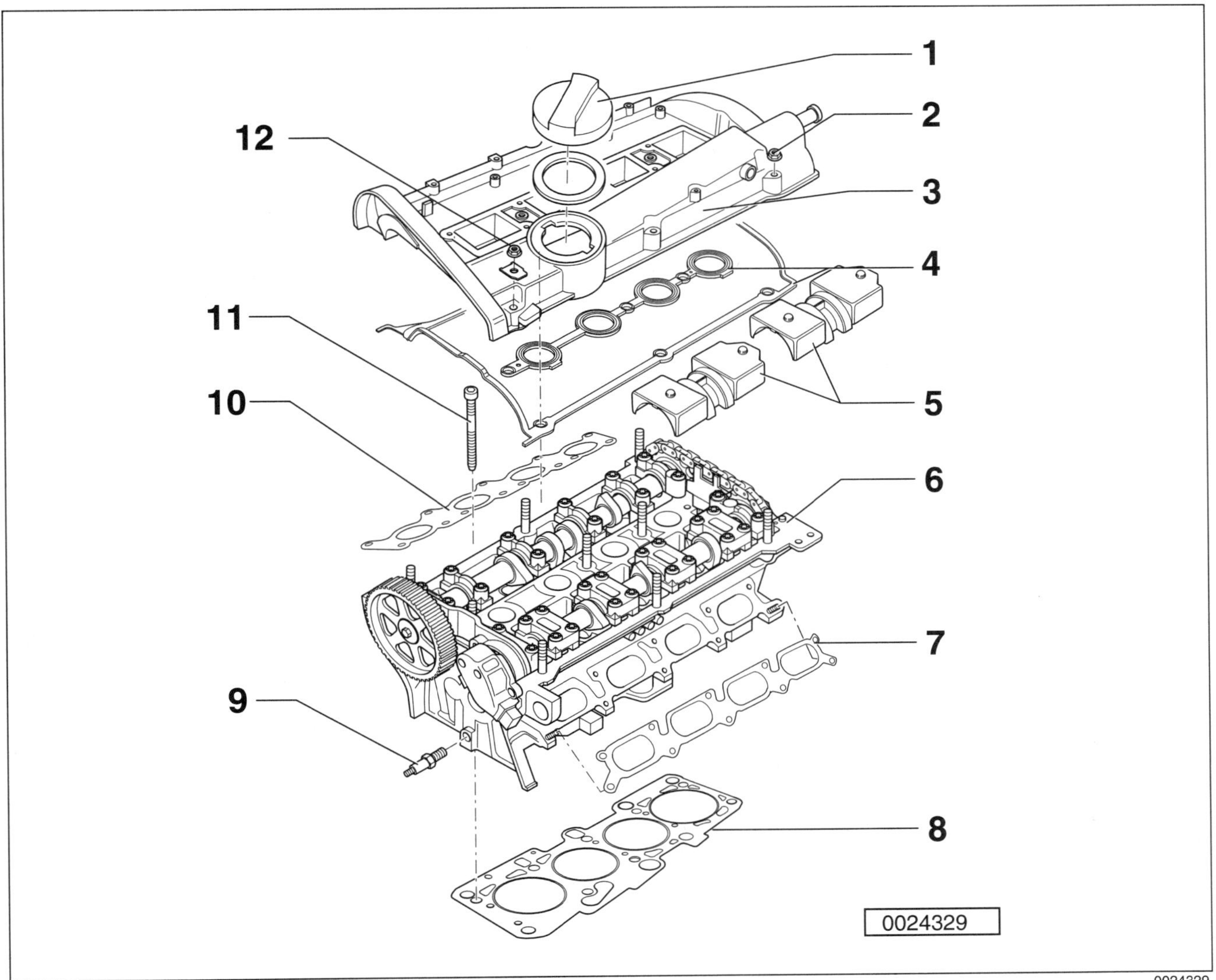

Fig. 3. Exploded view of external cylinder head components.

1. **Cap**
   - Replace gasket if damaged
2. **Bolt**
   - Tighten to 10 Nm (7 ft-lb)
3. **Valve cover**
4. **Gasket, valve cover**
   - Replace if damaged
   - Apply sealant to corner areas at double bearing cap and chain tensioner of before installing
5. **Oil deflector**
6. **Cylinder head**
   - Replace engine coolant if removing head
7. **Gasket, intake manifold**
   - Always replace
8. **Gasket, cylinder head**
   - Always replace
   - Metal construction
   - Installation position: part number must be readable from intake side
9. **Bolt, fitted**
   - Tighten to 25 Nm (18 ft-lbs)
   - Special fitted bolt for toothed belt tensioner
10. **Gasket, exhaust manifold**
    - Always replace
11. **Cylinder head bolt**
    - Always replace
    - Loosen and tighten in sequence only
12. **Bolt**
    - Tighten to 10 Nm (7 ft-lbs)

Cylinder head (valve) cover, removing and installing

1. Remove upper sound absorber panel.
2. Disconnect 4-pin harness connectors from all ignition coils. See Fig. 1.
3. Remove all ignition coils.
4. Remove ground wire terminal from cylinder head (valve) cover.
5. Disconnect crankcase breather valve hoses from cylinder head cover.
6. Remove nuts from cylinder head cover.
7. Lift off cylinder head cover with outer gasket and spark plug well gasket.
8. Installation is reverse of removal noting the following additional points:
   - Use new gaskets where appropriate.
   - Carefully apply a thin coat of sealant to both edges of sealing surfaces between double bearing cap and cylinder head using a small screwdriver or other suitable tool. See Fig. 4.

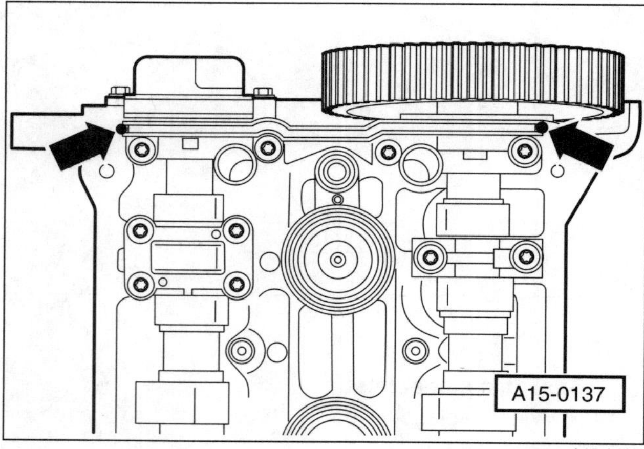

A15-0137

Fig. 4. Carefully apply a thin coat of sealant to both edges of sealing surfaces between double bearing cap and cylinder head (**arrows**) using a small screwdriver or other suitable tool.

   - Carefully apply a thin coat of sealant to both edges of sealing surfaces between camshaft adjuster and cylinder head using a small screwdriver or other suitable tool. See Fig. 5.

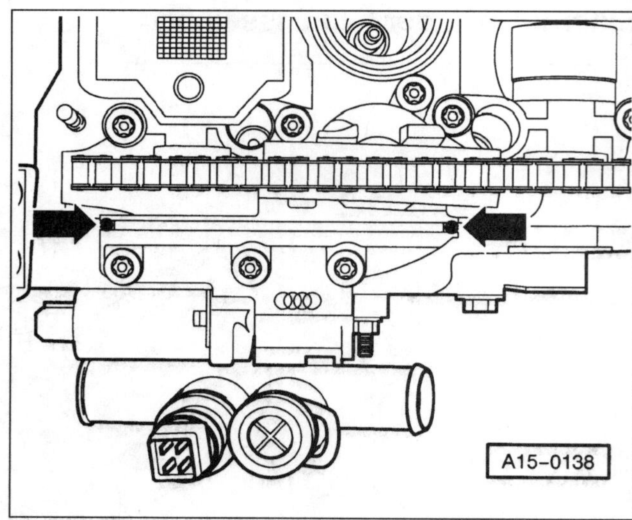

A15-0138

Fig. 5. Carefully apply a thin coat of sealant to both edges of sealing surfaces between camshaft adjuster and cylinder head (**arrows**) using a small screwdriver or other suitable tool.

Tightening torques

- Cylinder head cover to cylinder head . 10 Nm (7 ft-lb)
- Ignition coil to cylinder head cover . . . . 10 Nm (7 ft-lb)
- Ground wire to cylinder head cover . . . 10 Nm (7 ft-lb)

Camshaft oil seal, exhaust cam, replacing

1. Remove upper sound absorber panel and unclip and remove toothed belt guard, upper section.
2. Set engine to TDC for cylinder #1 by turning crankshaft until timing mark on camshaft sprocket aligns with mark on cylinder head (valve) cover. See Fig. 6.
3. Remove cylinder head (valve) cover as given earlier.
4. Release tensioning roller and slide toothed belt off of camshaft sprocket.
5. Turn crankshaft back off of TDC slightly.

NOTE —
Turning the crankshaft away from TDC slightly minimizes the chances of contact between pistons and valves upon re-assembly.

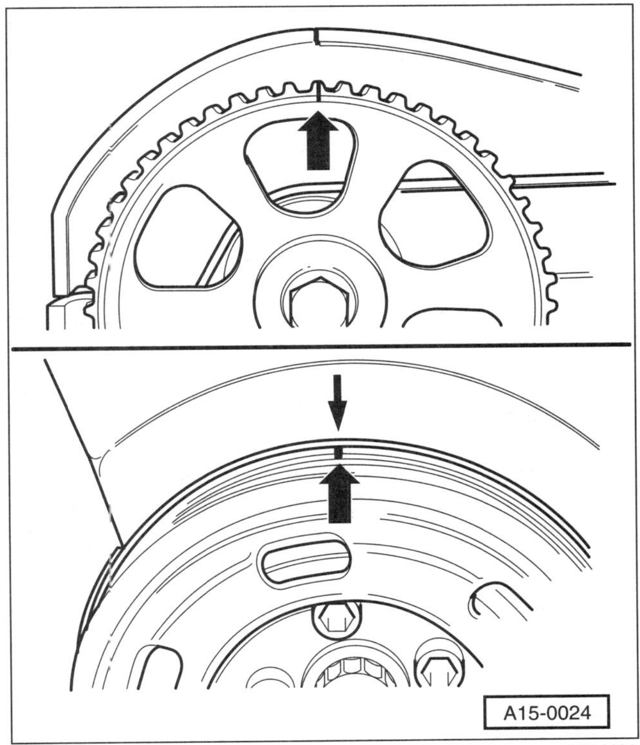

A15-0024

Fig. 6. Line up camshaft sprocket timing mark (**upper arrow**) with notch in cylinder head (valve) cover as shown. Crankshaft timing marks (**lower arrows**) must align.

6. Using a suitable spanner, remove camshaft sprocket bolt. See Fig. 7.

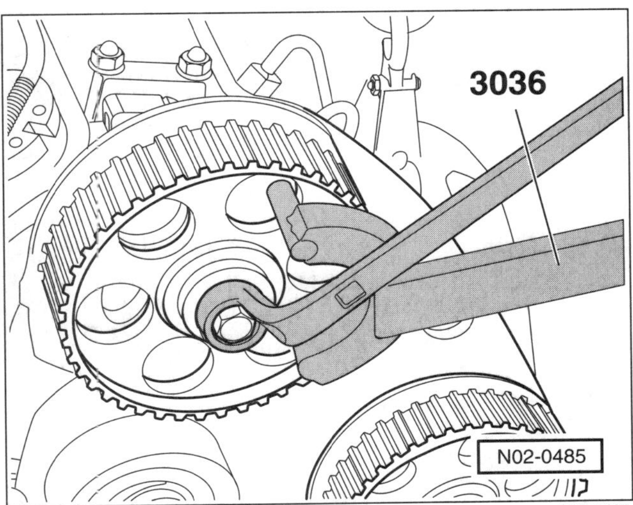

N02-0485

Fig. 7. Volkswagen spanner or counterholder tool shown holding camshaft sprocket to facilitate removal of securing bolt.

7. Remove camshaft drive sprocket and woodruff key.

8. Thread camshaft sprocket bolt back into camshaft by hand until it bottoms in camshaft. See Fig. 8.

NOTE —
Bolt is used to guide seal extractor tool.

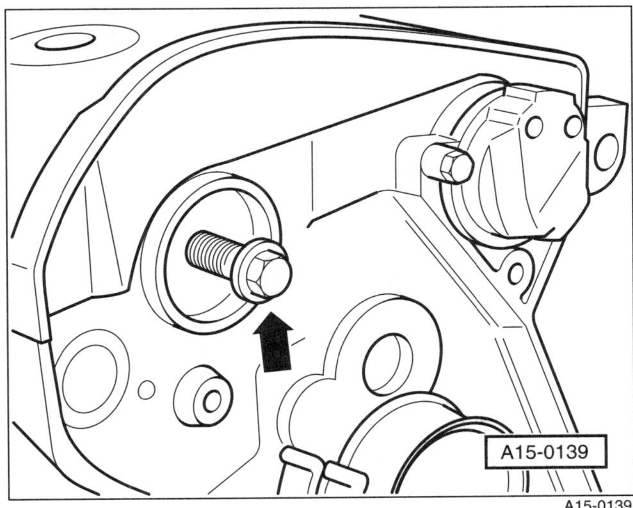

A15-0139

Fig. 8. Camshaft sprocket bolt (**arrow**) shown threaded into camshaft to guide seal extractor.

9. Remove seal using a suitable seal extractor. See Fig. 9.

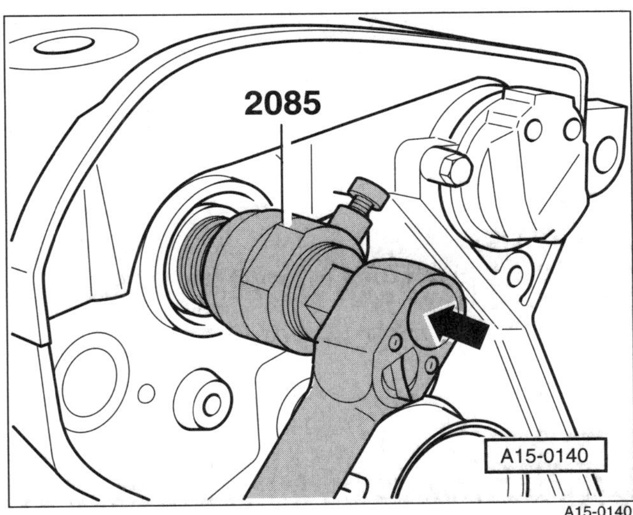

A15-0140

Fig. 9. Volkswagen seal removal tool being used with a ratchet (**arrow**) to remove exhaust camshaft oil seal.

10. Remove camshaft sprocket bolt.

11. Lubricate new seal with clean engine oil.

NOTE —
Volkswagen is gradually introducing a PTFE camshaft oil seal (identifying characteristics: no inner spring, sealing lip wider). The sealing lip of this seal must not be oiled or lubricated. A plain encased seal of older construction (with inner spring) may be replaced with a PTFE oil seal, but not vice versa.

12. Install seal with closed end facing out by sliding over guide sleeve mounted on camshaft pin. See Fig. 10.

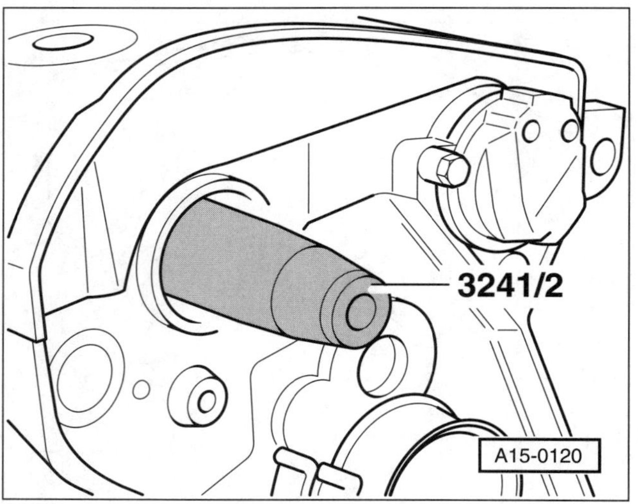

A15-0120
Fig. 10. Slide camshaft oil seal over Volkswagen guide seal 3241/2.

13. Install the new oil seal by pressing seal into bottom of recess using seal installation tools. See Fig. 11.

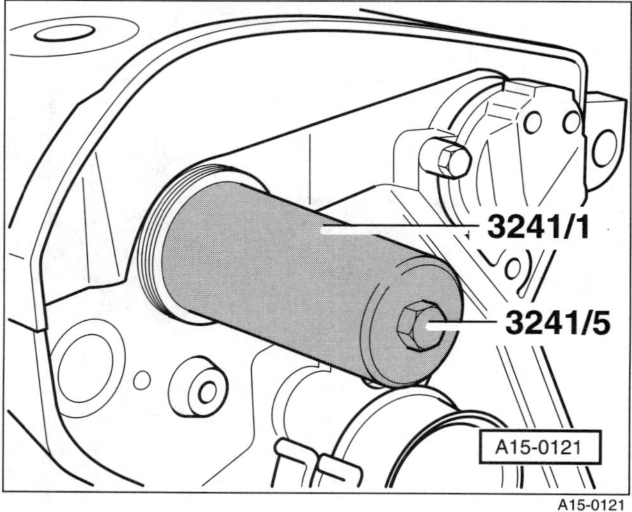

A15-0121
Fig. 11. Volkswagen seal installation tools being used to install exhaust camshaft oil seal. Guide sleeve 3241/2 is under tool 3241/1.

14. Install woodruff key and camshaft sprocket, hold sprocket with a spanner and torque bolt.

Tightening torque
- Camshaft sprocket to camshaft . . . . . 65 Nm (48 ft-lb)

15. Turn crankshaft back to TDC.

16. Install toothed belt and adjust tension, see **Toothed Belt–Camshaft Drive**, given later.

17. Install cylinder head (valve) cover, breather valve hoses and ignition coils.

18. Install toothed belt guard upper section, upper engine cover and any other removed components.

19. Be sure to quality check your work, see **Quality Review** at the end of this repair group.

Camshaft oil seal, intake cam, replacing

The camshaft position sensor is located behind the toothed belt guard, upper section and is driven by the intake camshaft. A seal on the intake camshaft prevents oil leaks into the camshaft position sensor.

1. Remove harness connector from camshaft position sensor. See Fig. 12.

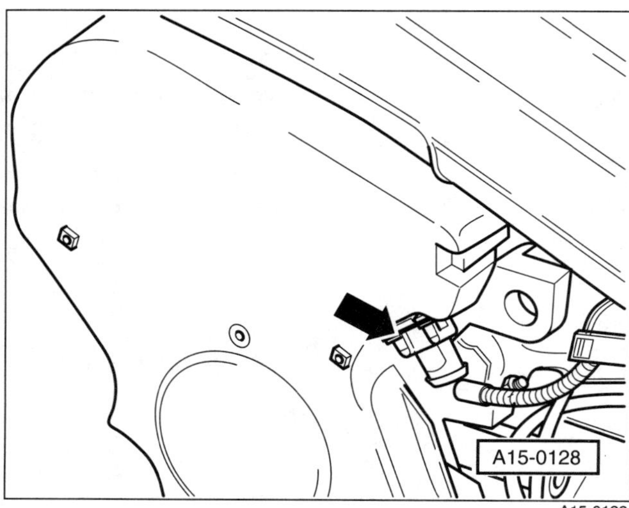

A15-0128
Fig. 12. Disconnect harness connector (**arrow**) from camshaft position sensor.

2. Remove toothed belt guard, upper section.

3. Remove camshaft position sensor.

4. Remove bolt, conical washer and shutter wheel from intake camshaft.

5. Install guide tool into camshaft. See Fig. 13.

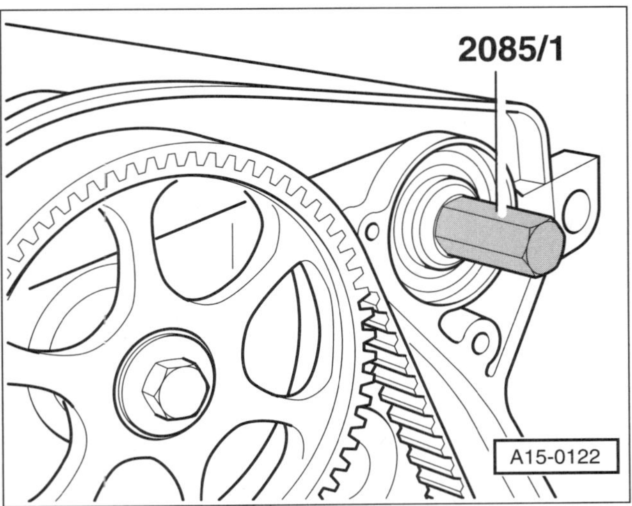

A15-0122

Fig. 13. Guide tool shown installed in intake camshaft. Tool should be used to prevent damage to the end of the camshaft.

6. Remove seal using a suitable seal extractor. See Fig. 14.

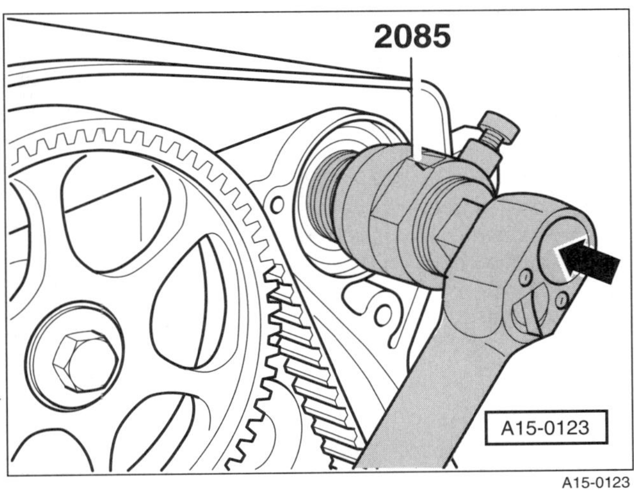

A15-0123

Fig. 14. Volkswagen seal removal tool being used to remove intake camshaft oil seal.

7. Remove guide tool from camshaft.

8. Install the new oil seal. See Fig. 15. Note the following points:

- Lubricate new seal with clean engine oil.
- Install with closed end facing out.
- Use a suitable guide sleeve and installation tool, such as Volkswagen 3241/2.
- Press seal into the bottom of recess.

NOTE —

Volkswagen is gradually introducing a PTFE camshaft oil seal (identifying characteristics: no inner spring, sealing lip wider). The sealing lip of this seal must not be oiled or lubricated. A plain encased seal of older construction (with inner spring) may be replaced with a PTFE oil seal, but not vice versa.

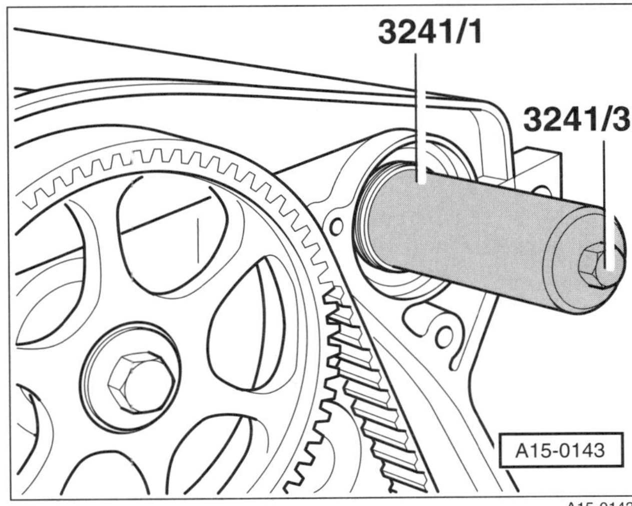

A15-0143

Fig. 15. Volkswagen seal installation tools being used to install intake camshaft oil seal. Guide sleeve 3241/2 is under tool 3241/1.

9. Install shutter wheel, conical washer and bolt.

10. Install camshaft position sensor.

Tightening torque

- Camshaft position sensor to cylinder head . . . . 10 Nm (7 ft-lb)
- Shutter wheel to intake camshaft . . . . 25 Nm (18 ft-lb)

11. Install toothed belt guard, upper section.

12. Install harness connector for camshaft position sensor.

13. Be sure to quality check your work, see **Quality Review** at the end of this repair group.

Camshafts, removing and installing

The intake and exhaust camshafts are removed and installed together with the drive chain and tensioner. This operation can be accomplished with the cylinder head installed. Removing the camshafts allows access to the hydraulic cam followers, the valve springs and the valve stem oil seals.

1. Remove upper sound absorber panel and unclip and remove toothed belt guard, upper section.

2. Set engine to TDC for cylinder #1 by turning crankshaft until timing mark on camshaft sprocket aligns with mark on cylinder head (valve) cover as shown earlier in Fig. 6.
3. Remove cylinder head (valve) cover as given earlier.
4. Release tensioning roller and slide toothed belt off of camshaft sprocket.
5. Turn crankshaft back off of TDC slightly.

NOTE —

Turning the crankshaft away from TDC slightly minimizes the chances of contact between pistons and valves upon re-assembly.

6. Using a suitable spanner, remove the camshaft sprocket bolt as shown earlier in Fig. 7.
7. Remove camshaft drive sprocket.
8. Remove camshaft position sensor, conical washer and shutter wheel.
9. Lift off plastic oil deflector to expose camshafts.
10. Clean drive chain and camshaft sprocket in areas of arrows on bearing caps with a suitable degreaser. Mark installed position of drive chain and camshaft chain sprocket with a permanent marker pen. See Fig. 16.

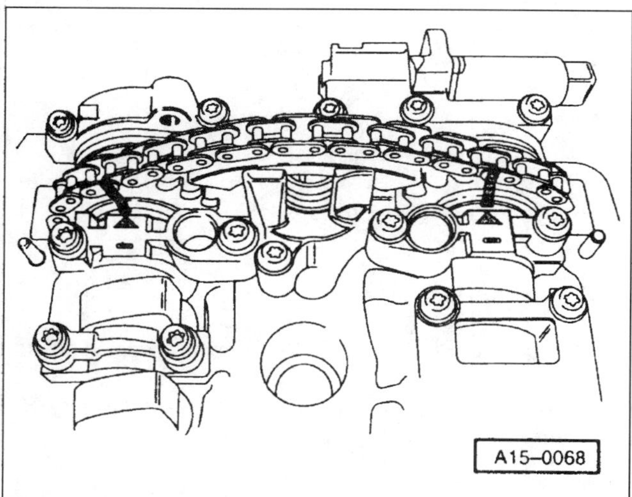

A15-0068

Fig. 16. Mark installed position of drive chain and camshaft sprocket in area of arrows on bearing caps as shown.

NOTE —

- *Do not mark chain with a punch mark, notch or similar.*
- *The distance between both arrows or the permanent marker marks equals 16 rollers on the drive chain.*

11. Compress drive chain tensioner. See Fig. 17.

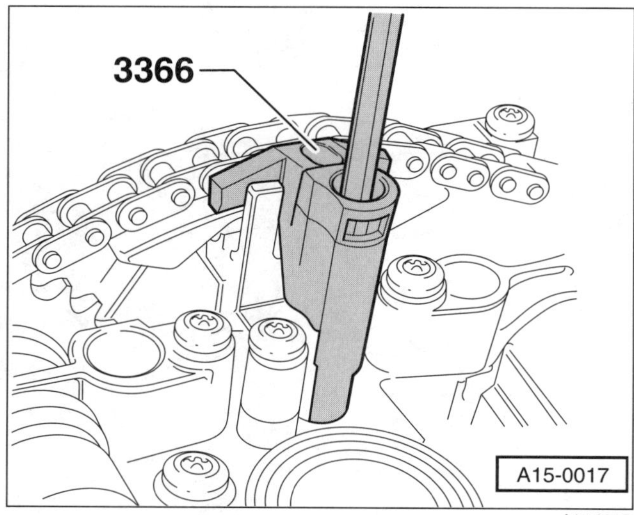

A15-0017

Fig. 17. Chain tensioner compressor tool shown in position. Tool pulls from the bottom and from the top simultaneously.

12. Remove both camshafts together with the tensioner and the chain. See Fig. 18. Use the following sequence:
    - Remove intake camshaft bearing caps 3 and 5.
    - Remove exhaust camshaft bearing caps 3 and 5.
    - Remove double bearing cap at sprocket end.
    - Remove intake and exhaust camshaft bearing caps at chain sprocket end.
    - Remove chain tensioner securing bolts.
    - Remove intake camshaft bearing caps 2 and 4 alternately and evenly.
    - Remove exhaust camshaft bearing caps 2 and 4 alternately and evenly.
    - Remove drive chain tensioner.
    - Remove drive chain tensioner compressor.

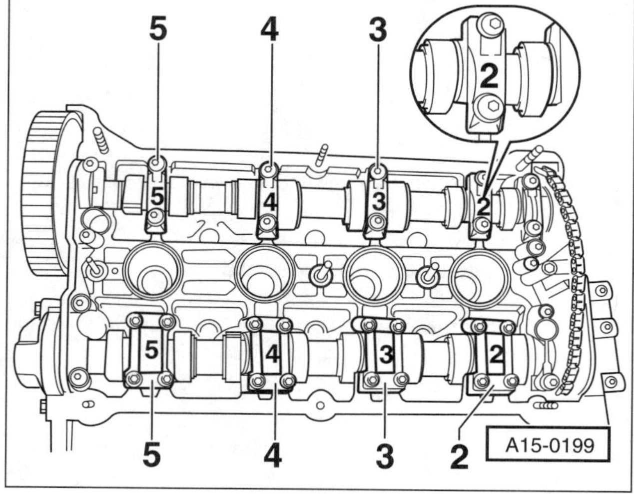

A15-0199

Fig. 18. Camshaft bearing cap identification. Upper camshaft is exhaust and lower camshaft is intake.

NOTE —
Mark each bearing cap before removing. Each cap is machined to each journal and must be reinstalled to that exact location to prevent damage.

13. Lift out both camshafts with drive chain and tensioner and lay aside.

NOTE —
Once removed, the camshafts should be checked for wear and other visible damage as described later under **Cylinder Head Components***.*

14. Replace rubber/metal seal for chain tensioner and lightly coat with sealant. See Fig. 19.

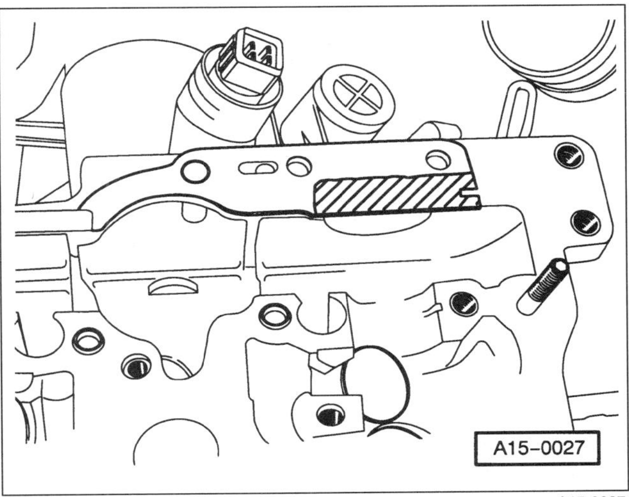

A15-0027

Fig. 19. Lightly coat rubber/metal seal for chain tensioner with sealant on lined area.

15. Install drive chain onto camshaft sprockets.

- Install drive chain with exactly 16 rollers between the notches on the camshafts. See Fig. 20.
- Exhaust camshaft notch is slightly offset to the inside.
- Install compressor onto drive chain tensioner.
- Slide drive chain tensioner into drive chain between camshafts.
- Oil bearing surfaces of cylinder head and both camshafts.
- Install camshafts with drive chain tensioner into cylinder head. Lobes for cylinder number #1 of both camshafts and notches must point up.

NOTE —
When re-using an original drive chain, align marks made prior to removal. In all instances, however, there must be exactly 16 rollers between notches on camshafts.

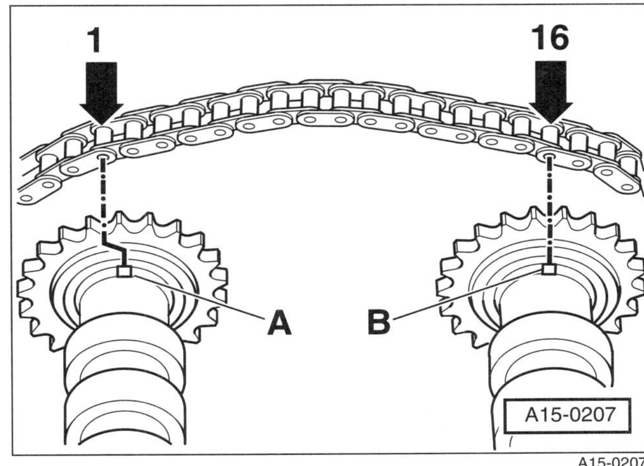

A15-0207

Fig. 20. Install drive chain onto camshafts with exactly 16 rollers between notch on exhaust camshaft (**A**) and intake camshaft (**B**).

16. Install drive chain tensioner over dowel sleeves. Torque to specification.

17. Install bearing caps 2 and 4 for exhaust and intake camshafts over dowel sleeves. Tighten nuts alternately and evenly so that camshafts are drawn down fully and evenly into bearing saddles. Torque to specification.

Tightening torques
- Camshaft bearing cap to cylinder head . . . . 10 Nm (7 ft-lb)
- Drive chain tensioner to cylinder head . . . . 10 Nm (7 ft-lb)

CAUTION —
- *Be sure to install bearing caps correctly. The caps are bored off-center and only fit properly one way. Caps are matched to the cylinder head by the machining process and are not available separately. Broken caps will require the replacement of the cylinder head.*
- *When installed properly, cap markings can be read from intake side of cylinder head.*

18. Install bearing caps over dowel sleeves at chain sprocket ends of both camshafts. Torque to specification.

19. Remove drive chain tensioner compressor.

20. Lightly coat double bearing cap with sealant. Install over dowel sleeves. See Fig. 21. Torque to specification.

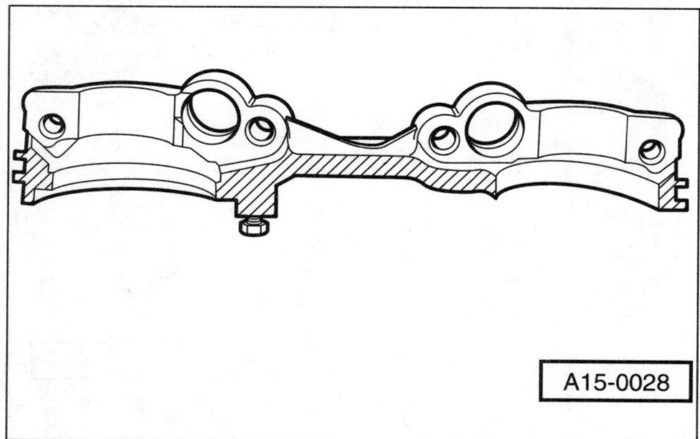

Fig. 21. Lightly coat double bearing cap with sealant on lined area.

21. Install remaining bearing caps. Torque to specification.

Tightening torque
- Camshaft bearing cap to cylinder head . . . . 10 Nm (7 ft-lb)

22. Observe installed position of camshaft drive sprocket.

23. Install camshaft drive sprocket using a suitable spanner as shown earlier. See Fig. 22.

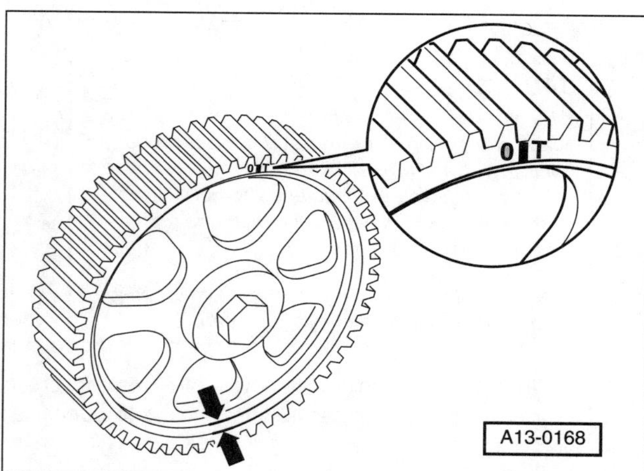

Fig. 22. Install camshaft drive sprocket with beveled edge (**arrows**) and cylinder #1 TDC markings facing outward.

NOTE —
Ensure that camshaft lobes for cylinder #1 are still pointing up.

Tightening torque
- Camshaft sprocket to camshaft . . . . . 65 Nm (48 ft-lb)

24. Re-check position of camshafts. See Fig. 23.

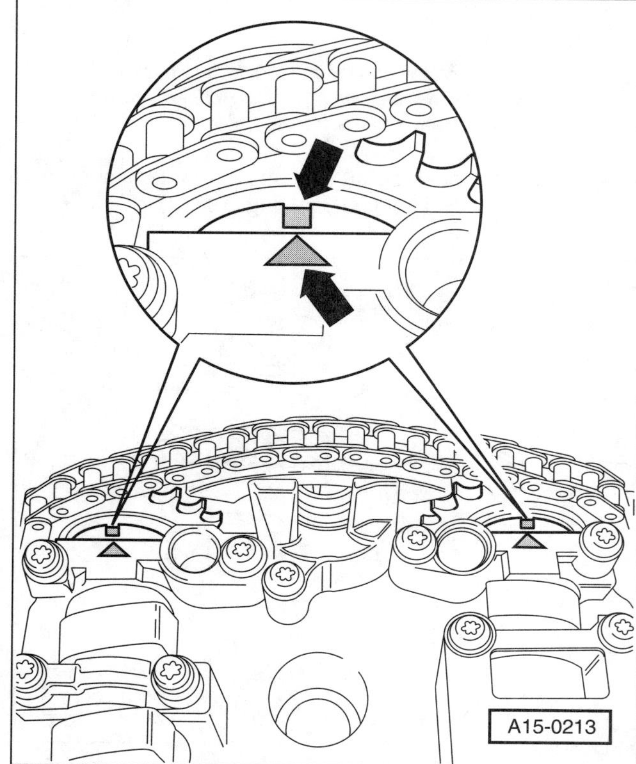

Fig. 23. Position camshafts with drive sprocket so that arrows on bearing caps align with notches on camshafts. There must be exactly 16 chain rollers between notches.

25. Install cylinder head (valve) cover.

26. Install toothed camshaft drive belt and adjust tension, see **Toothed Belt - Camshaft Drive** given later.

27. Install toothed belt guard, upper sound absorber panel and any other removed components.

CAUTION —
After installing the hydraulic cam followers, the engine should not be started for at least 30 minutes. Cam followers must be allowed to bleed down once they are installed. Failure to do so may cause the valves to strike the pistons resulting in serious damage.

28. Be sure to quality check your work, see **Quality Review** at the end of this repair group.

Hydraulic cam followers, checking

The 1.8 liter engine installed in the New Golf and Jettas is equipped with hydraulic cam followers, also known as valve lifters. The cam followers are pumped up by engine oil pressure, expanding as necessary to fill the gap between the valve stem and the camshaft lobe. This occurs continuously and automatically to keep the valve in proper adjustment at all times.

Some valve noise at start-up and during the warm-up period is normal at times due to hydraulic cam followers that have bled down while the engine was not running. Before checking noisy cam followers, check that the engine oil is new and fresh, of the correct weight, and that the level is correct. Allow 2 minutes with a warm engine running at a fast idle for the lubrication system to properly pump up the cam followers.

Cam followers should only be checked when the engine is warm. Run the engine until the radiator fan has switched on at least one time. Increase the engine speed to 2,500 rpm and hold it there for approximately 2 minutes. If the hydraulic cam followers are still noisy, shut the engine off and proceed as follows while the engine is still warm.

1. Remove cylinder head (valve) cover. See **Cylinder head (valve) cover, removing and installing**, given earlier.

2. Turn engine by hand in the running direction until all camshaft lobes of cylinder #1 are pointing approximately up.

NOTE —
Hydraulic cam follower clearance can be checked on any cam follower (lifter) that is not being depressed by the camshaft lobe.

3. Check clearance between cam follower and cam lobe on cylinder #1:
   - Insert a 0.2 mm (0.008 in.) feeler gauge between the camshaft lobe and the follower. If clearance exceeds 0.2 mm (0.008 in.) replace the follower.
   - If clearance is less, or if no clearance is present, lightly depress cam follower with a wooden or plastic wedge and insert a feeler gauge between camshaft lobe and the follower. If clearance exceeds 0.2 mm (0.008 in.), the lifter is faulty and should be replaced. See Fig. 24.

Specification
- Hydraulic cam follower maximum clearance (1.8L engine) . . . . 0.2 mm (0.008 in.)

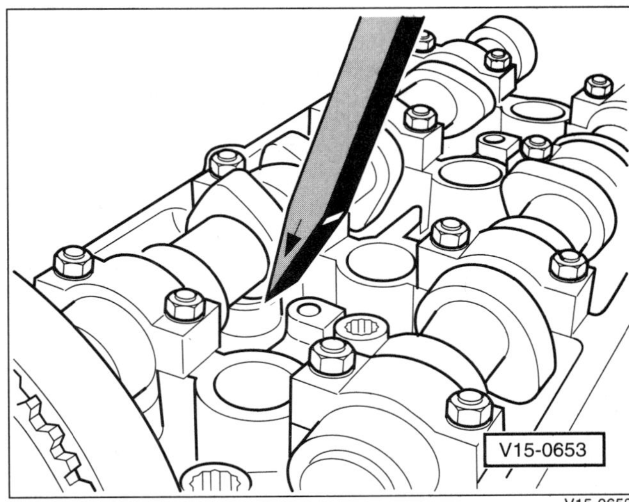

V15-0653

Fig. 24. Hydraulic cam follower shown being pushed down lightly with a plastic wedge.

4. Turn engine by hand and repeat procedure until all cam followers have been checked.

5. Replace a faulty cam follower by removing camshaft as previously described and pulling the follower from the cylinder head. Faulty hydraulic cam followers can be replaced individually but only as a complete assembly.

CAUTION —
After installing new hydraulic cam followers, the engine should not be started for at least 30 minutes. New cam followers are usually at full extended height and must be allowed to bleed down to their proper height once installed. Failure to do so may cause the valves to strike the pistons resulting in serious damage.

NOTE —
Store removed hydraulic cam followers in order on a clean surface with the camshaft contact surface facing down to minimize bleed down. Cover with a clean lint-free shop cloth.

Valve stem oil seals, replacing

The sign of faulty valve stem seals is excessive oil consumption and oil smoke from the exhaust. This is usually most noticeable during periods of high manifold vacuum such as deceleration. If compression and leak-down testing confirm the integrity of the piston rings and the turbocharger shaft seals are good, but the engine consumes oil, it is possible that faulty valve stem seals are present. It should also be noted that worn valve stem seals could be due to worn valve guides and that the worn valve guides are the major cause of the oil consumption. See **Cylinder Head Components** for more information on checking valve guides.

Replacing the valve stem oil seals requires removal of the camshaft, cam followers, and the valve springs. This can be done with the cylinder head installed or removed. In either case, numerous Volkswagen special tools are required to compress the valve springs and remove and install the seals.

Working with the cylinder head installed:

1. Remove cylinder head (valve) cover, camshafts, and hydraulic cam followers as described earlier.

2. Remove spark plugs.

3. Set engine to bottom dead center (BDC) for cylinder #1 by turning crankshaft.

4. Apply a continuous supply of compressed air with a minimum of 6 bar (87 psi) into the first spark plug hole with an adapter. This must be done to hold the valves in place while the springs are removed. Continue with step 7.

> ***CAUTION —***
> *Compressed air supply must be able to maintain at least 6 bar (87 psi) during this repair. If air supply is interrupted while valve spring is removed, valve will fall into the cylinder and may require cylinder head removal to retrieve.*

Working with the cylinder head removed:

5. Secure cylinder head to the workbench. Use care to avoid damage to the head gasket surfaces.

6. Remove camshaft and hydraulic cam followers as described earlier. Continue with step 7.

Working with cylinder head removed or installed:

7. Install appropriate valve spring compressor tools. See Fig. 25. Compress the spring for the first cylinder and remove the spring retainer, both keepers, and the valve spring. If spring will not compress, lightly tap the tool to release the stuck keepers. Use a small magnet to retrieve the keepers.

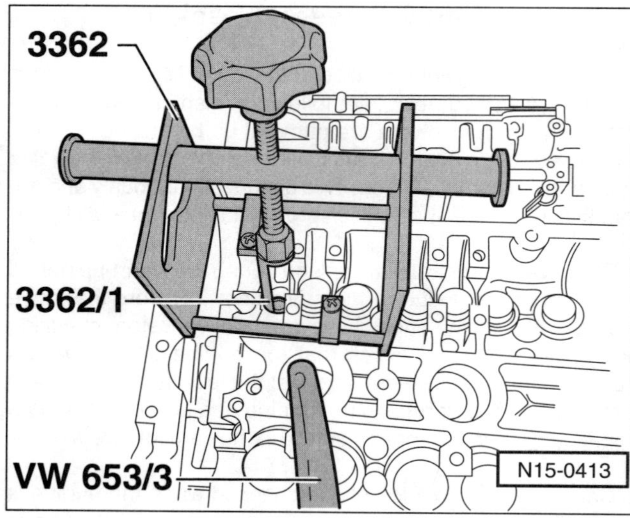

N15-0413

Fig. 25. Valve spring compressor tools being used to compress valve spring for removal of keepers. Note the markings on the tool for the different positions required by the 3 different valve angles. Numbers identify Volkswagen special tools.

> ***NOTE —***
> *Volkswagen valve spring compressor tool 3362 has different positions for compressing the various valves:*
> *outer intake valve - lower position*
> *center intake valve - upper position*
> *exhaust valve - lower position*

8. Remove valve stem seals with special slide hammer tool. See Fig. 26.

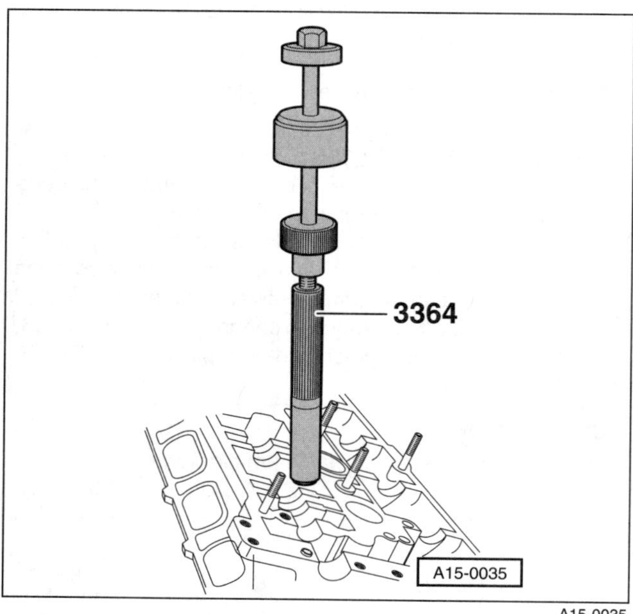

A15-0035

Fig. 26. Valve stem seal removal tool shown in position to remove valve stem seal.

9. Begin installation of new seal by temporarily fitting a protective plastic fitting sleeve over the valve stem. This sleeve is usually included with the new seal set and will prevent damage to the seal due to the sharp edges of the keeper grooves. Lubricate new seal with clean engine oil and fit it to the installation tool. See Fig. 27.

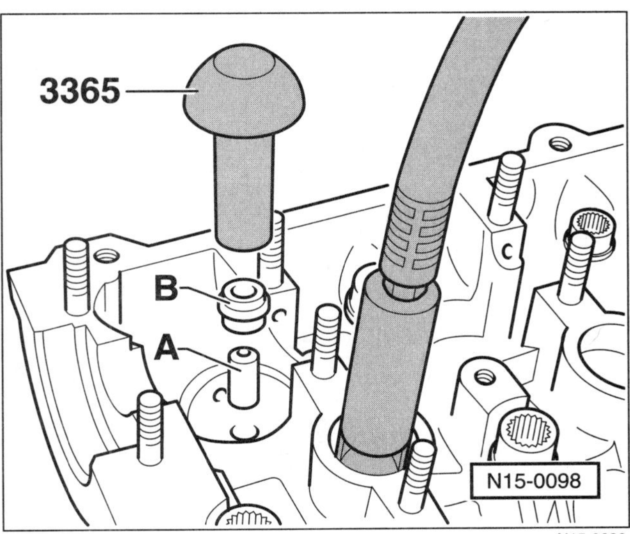

N15-0098

Fig. 27. Plastic fitting sleeve (**A**), shown with valve stem seal (**B**) and plastic installation tool 3365 available from Volkswagen.

10. Push the tool (with seal) down over the valve stem until the seal is fully seated on the guide. Remove the tool and the protective fitting sleeve.

11. Reinstall the valve spring, retainer and keepers.

12. Repeat for the second valve on the cylinder.

13. When all valve seals have been replaced on the first cylinder, transfer the compressed air adapter (if working with cylinder head installed) to the next cylinder and repeat the process until all valve seals have been replaced.

14. Remaining installation is the reverse of removal.

> ***CAUTION —***
> *To prevent cylinder head or camshaft damage, be sure to follow the camshaft installation procedure exactly when tightening the camshaft bearing caps. See* **Camshaft, removing and installing**.

Tightening torque
- Spark plug to cylinder head . . . . 30 Nm (22 ft-lb)

15. Be sure to quality check your work, see **Quality Review** at the end of this repair group.

TOOTHED BELT - CAMSHAFT DRIVE

The camshaft drive belt and its related parts are shown in Fig. 28. Required maintenance involves checking condition and tension every 40,000 miles (60,000 km). Tension adjustment (if needed) should also be carried out at this mileage interval. Replacement is recommended every 105,000 miles (160,000 km). The belt width can also be measured to help determine wear, see **0 Maintenance**. This will help prevent damage to the engine due to belt stretch and the long term effects of heat. The camshaft drive belt is also known as a toothed belt and both terms are used interchangeably.

Drive belts, assembly

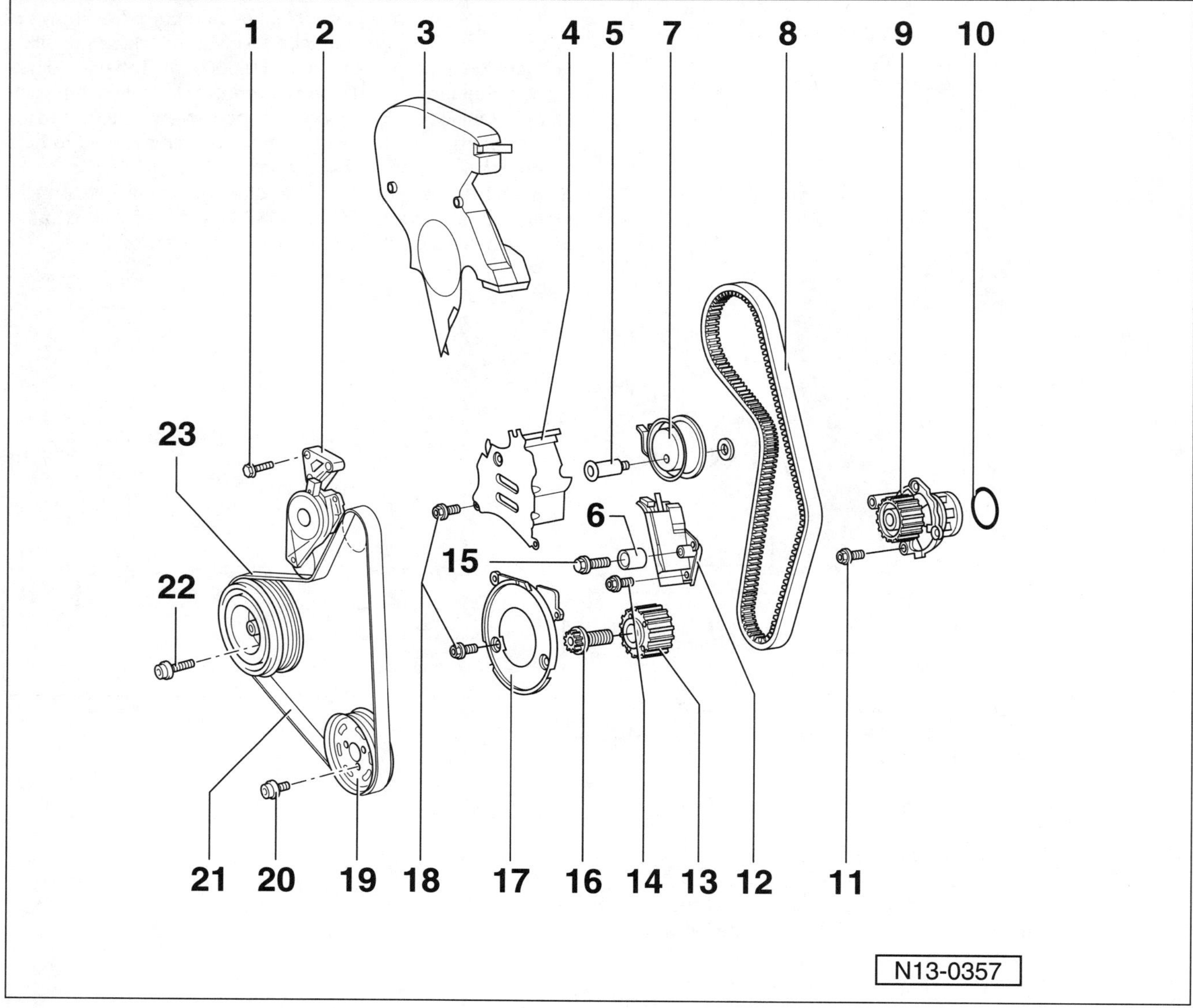

N13-0357

Fig. 28. Exploded view of the ribbed V-belt, the toothed belt and their related components.

1. **Bolt**
   - Tighten to 25 Nm (18 ft-lb)
2. **Tensioner, ribbed V-belt**
   - Loosen ribbed belt by turning with open-end wrench
3. **Toothed belt guard, upper section**
4. **Toothed belt guard, center section**
5. **Bolt, fitted**
   - Tighten to 27 Nm (20 ft-lb)
6. **Idler roller**
7. **Tension roller, toothed belt**
8. **Toothed belt**
   - Mark engine direction of rotation before removing
   - Check for wear
   - Do not kink
9. **Coolant pump**
10. **O-ring**
    - Always replace
11. **Bolt**
    - Tighten to 15 Nm (11 ft-lb)
12. **Tensioning damper, see** Ⓐ

(continued on next page)

13. Toothed belt sprocket (crankshaft)

14. Bolt
- Tighten to 15 Nm (11 ft-lb)

15. Bolt
- Tighten to 20 Nm (15 ft-lb)

16. Bolt
- Tighten to 90 Nm (66 ft-lb) + ¼ turn (90°)
- Always replace
- Threads and shoulder must be free of grease

17. Toothed belt guard, lower section

18. Bolt
- Tighten to 10 Nm (7 ft-lb)

19. Pulley
- For power steering pump

20. Bolt
- Tighten to 25 Nm (18 ft-lb)

21. Ribbed belt
- Mark direction of rotation before removing

22. Bolt
- Tighten to 25 Nm (18 ft-lb)

23. Belt pulley/vibration damper
- Can only be installed in one position, holes are offset
- Note position when installing toothed belt

A . Toothed belt tensioner assembly

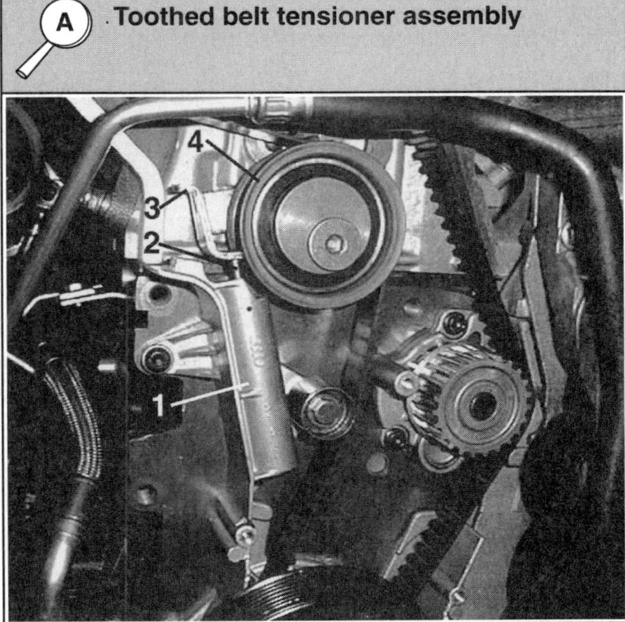

0024330

- **Tension damper (1)**
- **Tension damper piston (2)**
- **Tension damper arm (3)**
- **Tension roller (4)**

Toothed belt for camshaft drive, removing

1. Remove the upper sound absorber panel.
2. Remove the lower sound absorber panel (belly pan).
3. Remove passenger side headlight, see **94 Lights, Accessories–Exterior**.
4. Remove air duct between intercooler and turbocharger. See Fig. 29.

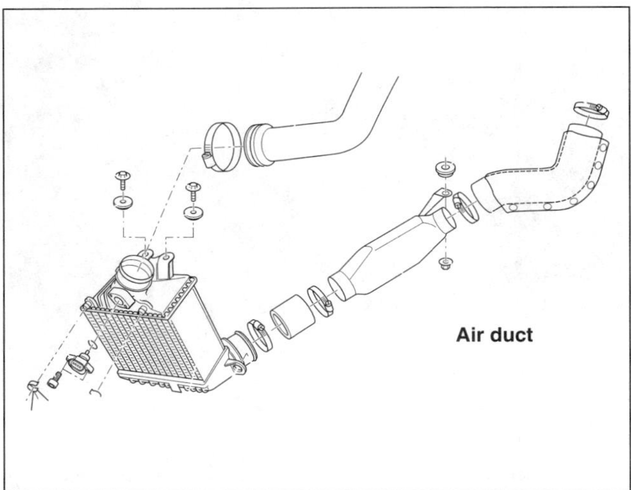

Fig. 29. Remove air duct between turbocharger and intercooler.

5. Remove the ribbed V-belt and tensioner, see **0 Maintenance**.
6. Set engine to TDC for cylinder #1 by turning crankshaft until timing marks line up. See Fig. 30. and Fig. 31.

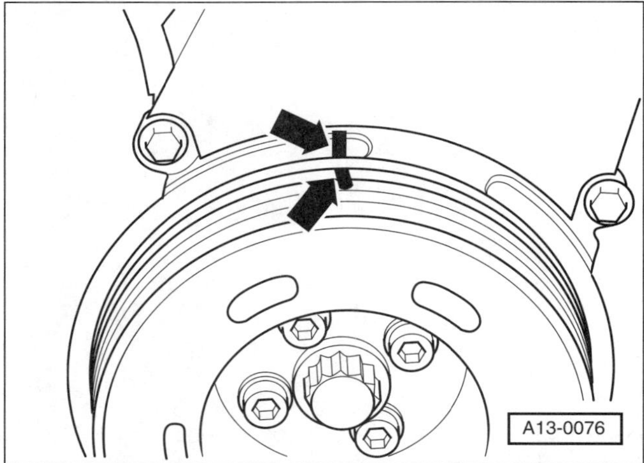

Fig. 30. Mark on belt pulley (**lower arrow**) shown aligned with mark on toothed belt guard, center section (**upper arrow**).

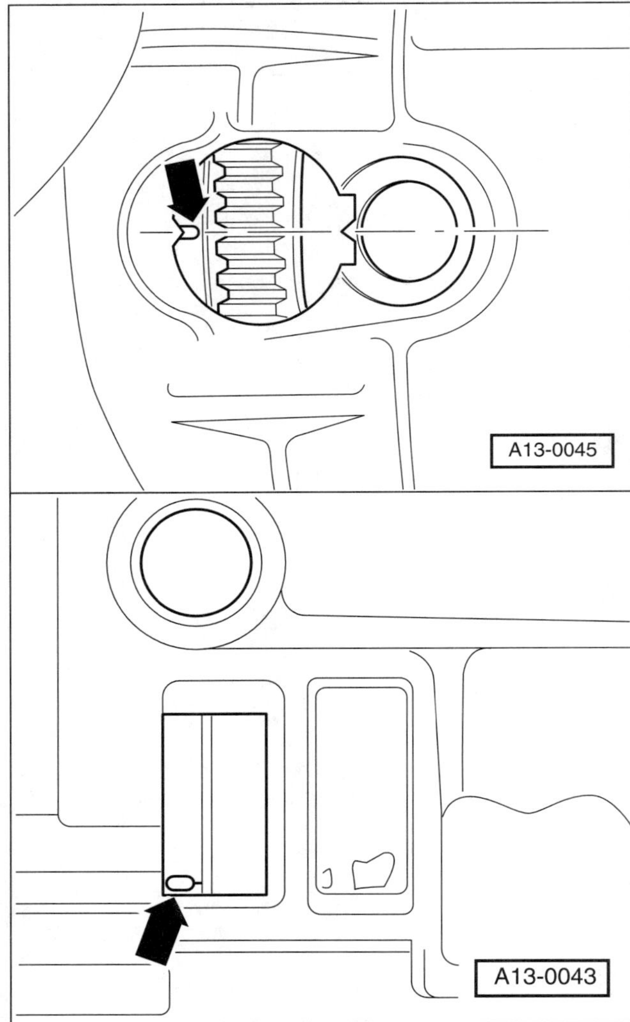

Fig. 31. Mark on flywheel (**upper arrow**) shown aligned with mark on manual transmission case. Mark on torque converter (**lower arrow**) shown aligned with edge of automatic transmission case.

7. Remove coolant expansion without disconnecting hoses and move to the side.
8. Label and remove vacuum hoses from evaporative emission solenoid and throttle control module.
9. Remove toothed belt guard, upper section.
10. Support engine with a suitable fixture that is designed to support the weight of the engine and transmission without damaging the body. See Fig. 32.
11. Lift the supporting device slightly, so that the weight of the engine and transmission is on the supporting device.

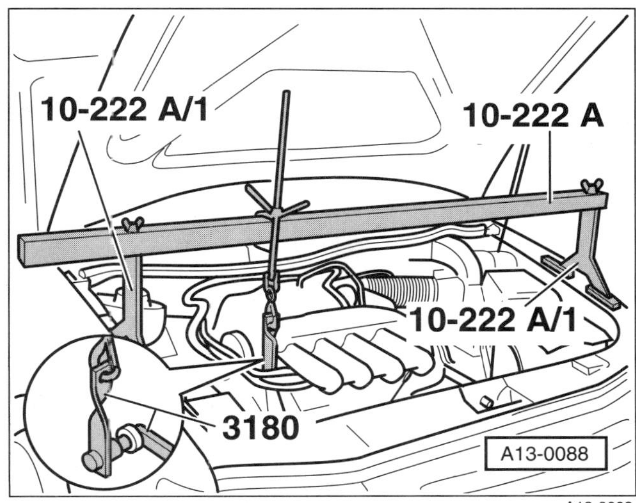

Fig. 32. Volkswagen supplied engine support tools shown attached to the engine.

12. Remove right side engine mount from body and carrier on engine. See Fig. 33.

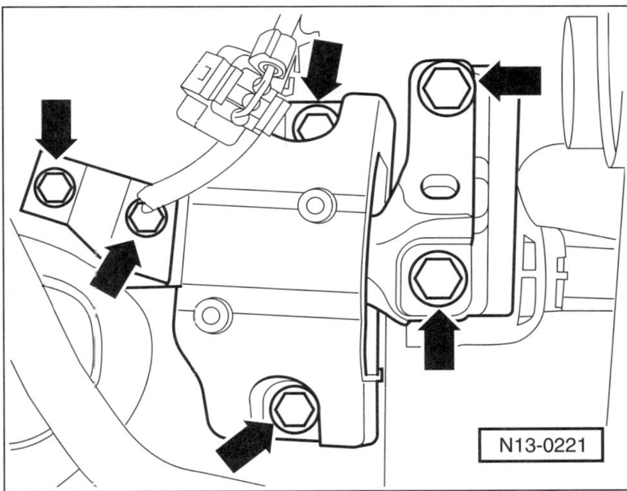

Fig. 33. Right side engine mount assembly as viewed from above. Remove all bolts (**arrows**) to remove assembly.

13. Remove the 4 bolts holding the belt pulley/vibration damper to the toothed belt sprocket and remove the belt pulley.

14. Remove the toothed belt guard, center and lower sections.

15. Remove the right side engine mount bracket from the block. There will not be sufficient room to withdraw the bolts, so the mount and the bolts are all removed at the same time. See Fig. 34.

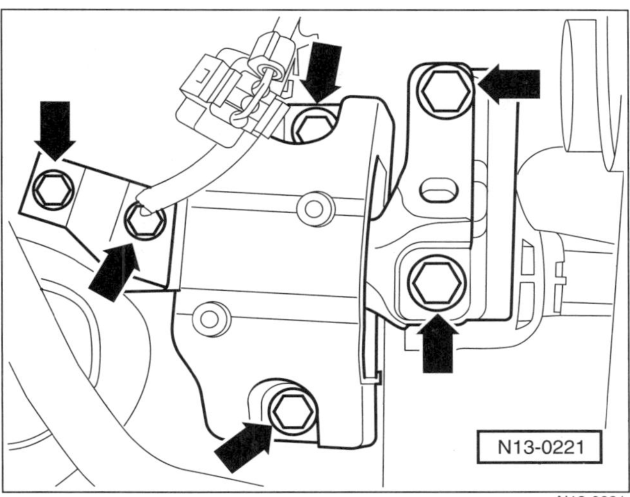

Fig. 34. Completely loosen the bolts (**arrows**) that secure right side engine mount bracket to cylinder block.

NOTE —
When loosening the right side engine mount, raise the engine slightly with the support device.

16. Remove harmonic balancer/belt pulley. See Fig. 35.

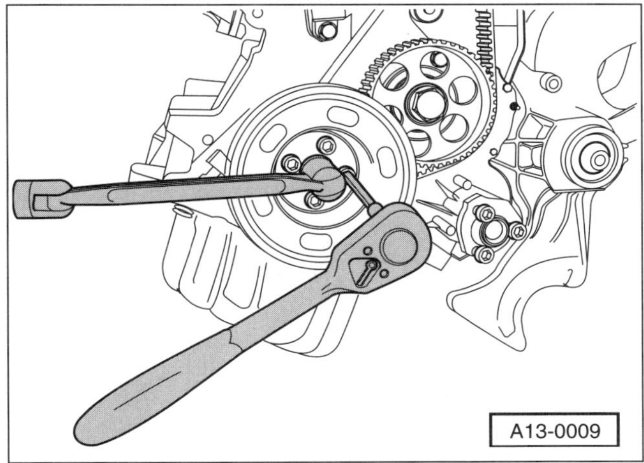

Fig. 35. Loosen outer mounting bolts for harmonic balancer/belt pulley while counter-holding large nut in center.

17. Mark running direction of toothed belt.

18. Release tension on toothed belt and remove belt. Reference the following to Fig. 35.
    - Screw a 5x55 mm threaded stud into toothed belt tensioning damper housing and fit a hex nut and washer to the other end
    - Line up the hole in the tensioning damper housing with the hole in the pressure piston by turning the pressure piston. Use a suitable tool to turn the pressure piston before tightening the nut on the threaded stud
    - Tighten the nut on the threaded stud until the hole in the pressure piston aligns with the hole in the tension damper housing
    - Secure pressure piston in position with a pin inserted through the hole in the tensioning damper housing

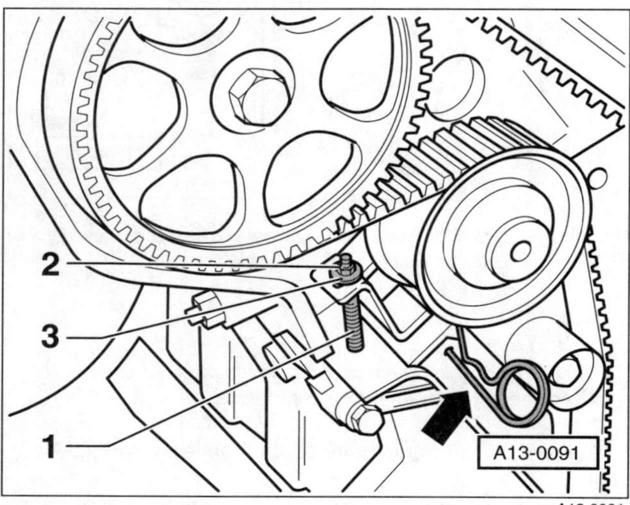

A13-0091

Fig. 36. Release tension of toothed belt roller against belt by threading a 5x55 mm stud (**1**) into tension damper housing. Fit a nut (**2**) and washer (**3**) onto the other end of stud. Line up hole in pressure piston and tension damper housing. Tighten nut (**2**) until holes in pressure piston and tension damper housing align. Insert a pin (**arrow**) to secure in place.

19. Remove toothed belt.

20. Turn crankshaft back off of TDC slightly.

> ***CAUTION —***
> *Due to engine design, care must be used when turning the camshaft with the toothed belt removed. If valves are allowed to open with the piston at TDC, serious internal damage will result.*

Toothed belt for camshaft drive, installing

> ***CAUTION —***
> *Belt tension must not be adjusted on a hot engine. Allow to cool sufficiently before proceeding. Engine temperature must be no hotter than warm to the touch.*

1. Ensure that crankshaft is NOT at TDC.

2. Align the mark on the camshaft with the mark on the toothed belt guard. This brings the camshaft to TDC for cylinder number #1. See Fig. 37.

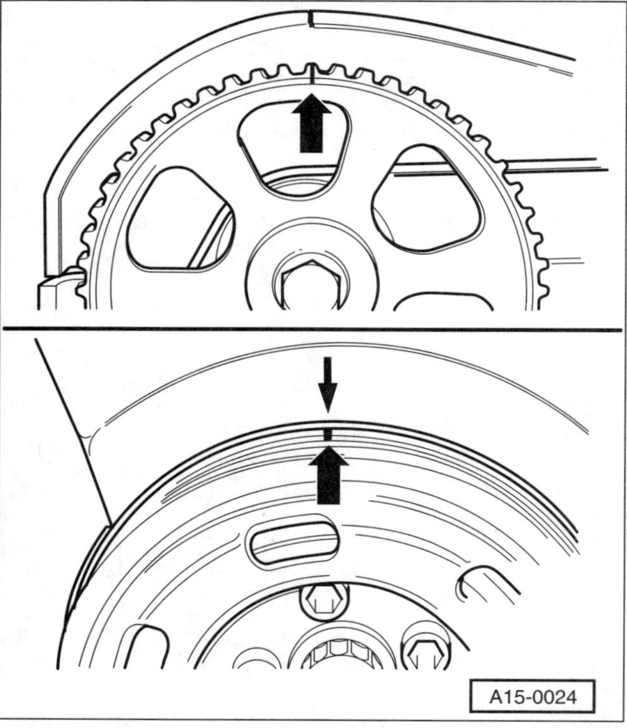

A15-0024

Fig. 37. Line up camshaft sprocket timing mark (**upper arrow**) with notch in cylinder head (valve) cover as shown in upper illustration.

3. Install toothed belt onto the crankshaft drive sprocket.

   NOTE —
   If re-using an old belt, be sure to note running direction marks placed on it before removal.

4. Install bolts into the right side engine mount bracket and install to the cylinder block.

Tightening torques
- Right side engine mount bracket to cylinder block (M10) . . . . 45 Nm (33 ft-lb)

---

5. Install toothed belt guard, lower section.

6. Install the belt pulley/vibration damper to the toothed belt drive sprocket.

Tightening torques

- Vibration dampener/belt pulley to toothed belt drive sprocket (M8) . . . . 25 Nm (18 ft-lb)

---

7. Turn the engine to top dead center (TDC) for cylinder number #1 by aligning mark on belt pulley with the mark on the toothed belt guard.

8. Ensure that camshaft is still at TDC for cylinder number 1.

9. Install the toothed belt onto the tensioner, coolant pump and camshaft drive sprockets and check for correct placement of belt on all sprockets.

10. Tension toothed belt. Reference the following to Fig. 38.
    - Remove securing pin from tensioning damper housing
    - Loosen nut on threaded stud and allow belt tension to tighten
    - Remove threaded stud, nut and washer from tensioning damper housing
    - Ensure that camshaft and crankshaft marks are still at TDC for cylinder number 1
    - Turn engine two full turns in the running direction and confirm that camshaft and crankshaft reference marks still align with the respective points

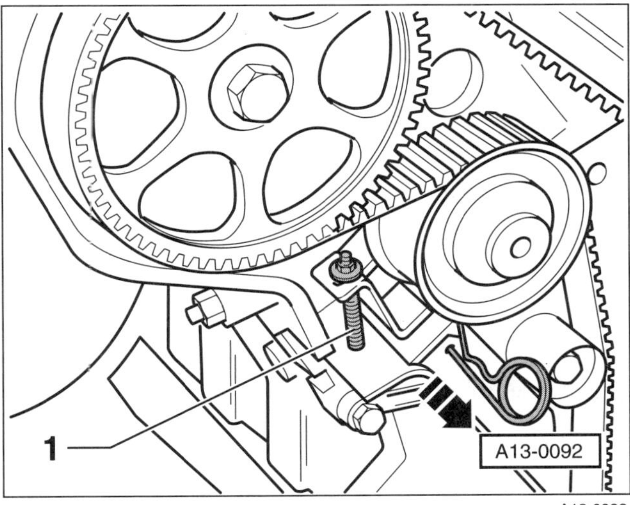

Fig. 38. Release toothed belt roller from tensioning damper housing by removing securing pin (**arrow**) and loosening nut on threaded stud (**1**). Remove nut, washer and stud when all tension is released.

NOTE —
Some movement of the sprockets and their marks is to be expected as belt tension is adjusted. Keep in mind that the smallest possible increment of adjustment is one whole tooth of the belt or sprocket.

11. Install toothed belt guards, center and upper sections.

12. Install right side engine mount using new stretch bolts. See Fig. 39.

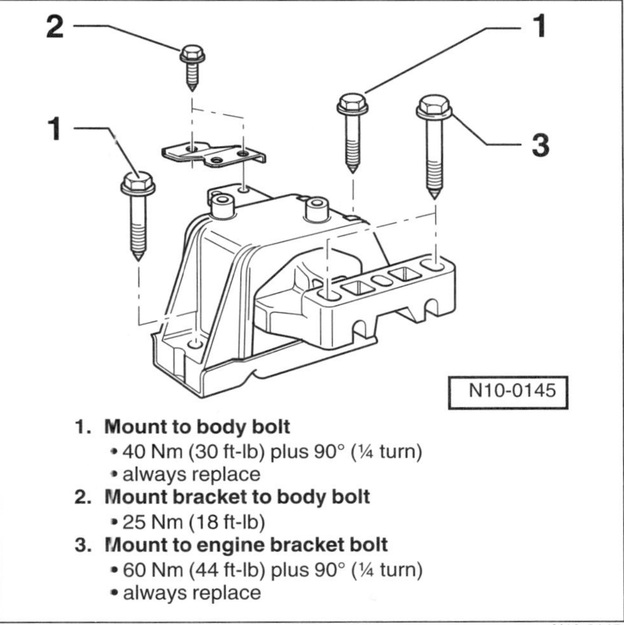

Fig. 39. Right side engine mount.

13. Remove engine support fixture.

14. Install ribbed belt and tensioner.

Tightening torque

- Ribbed belt tensioner to bracket (M8) . . . . 25 Nm (18 ft-lb)

---

15. Install connecting pipe between intercooler and bottom right side of body longmember.

16. Install the lower sound absorber panels (belly pan) and the upper sound absorber panel.

17. Install any remaining parts and quality check your work, see **Quality Review** at the end of this repair group.

CYLINDER HEAD, REMOVING AND INSTALLING

The cylinder head can be removed and installed with the engine in the vehicle. Fig. 2, given earlier, shows a view of the 1.8L cylinder head and related components. Note that the cylinder head bolts are stretch type fasteners and should never be reused. In addition, whenever the cylinder head or the cylinder head gasket is replaced, the coolant must also be replaced, see **19 Engine–Cooling System**.

Cylinder head, removing

> ***WARNING —***
> *Do not start work on a hot engine. Allow to cool sufficiently before proceeding. Engine temperature must be no hotter than warm to the touch. Cylinder head warpage can result due to uneven cooling rates.*

NOTE —

- *Disconnecting the battery cables will erase fault codes and basic settings in the engine management and automatic transmission control unit memories. Some driveability problems may be noticeable until the system re-adapts to operating conditions. OBD II readiness codes, which may be required for emissions testing, may also be erased. See* **24c Fuel Injection – Motronic (1.8L engine)** *for additional information. In most instances proper diagnosis will require the use of a scan tool such as the Volkswagen supplied VAG 1551 or 1552. Use and operation of this tool is outside the scope of this repair manual.*
- *Cylinder head will be removed with the exhaust manifold and the intake manifold still attached.*

1. With ignition switched off, disconnect the battery negative terminal from the battery.

NOTE —
Be sure to have the anti-theft radio code on hand before disconnecting the battery.

2. Remove upper sound absorber panel.
3. Remove the lower sound absorber panels (belly pan).
4. Drain engine coolant, see **19 Engine–Cooling System**.
5. Label and disconnect fuel supply and fuel return lines.

> ***WARNING —***
> *Fuel will be expelled when disconnecting fuel hoses. Wrap a cloth around the fuel line fittings before disconnecting them. Do not smoke or work near heaters or other fire hazards. Have a fire extinguisher handy.*

6. Label and disconnect vacuum connections at cylinder head.
7. Seal off disconnected fuel and vacuum lines to prevent contamination.
8. Unbolt the coolant connection flange from the end of the cylinder head and carefully move aside. The coolant hoses stay connected.
9. Disconnect ignition coil harness connectors and ground wires.
10. Disconnect all other electrical connectors and hoses as necessary and move aside. See Fig. 40.

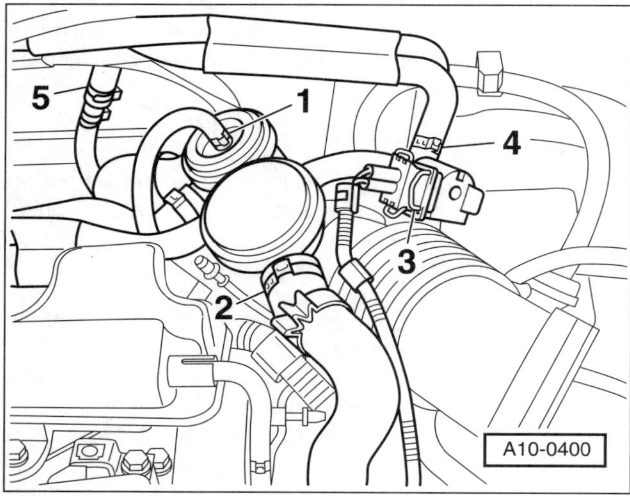

A10-0400

Fig. 40. Detail of connections on turbocharger inlet hose: Over-run shut off valve (**1**), crankcase ventilation valve (**2**), wastegate solenoid electrical (**3**), wastegate solenoid pressure inlet (**4**), wastegate solenoid pressure outlet on bulkhead.

11. Remove intake air hose from connecting pipe to turbocharger inlet.
12. Disconnect hose connecting evaporative emissions canister and turbocharger at bulkhead.
13. Remove retaining clip at turbocharger inlet and remove connecting pipe.
14. Observe position of heat insulation on lower turbocharger outlet pipe and remove.
15. Remove lower turbocharger outlet pipe. See Fig. 41.

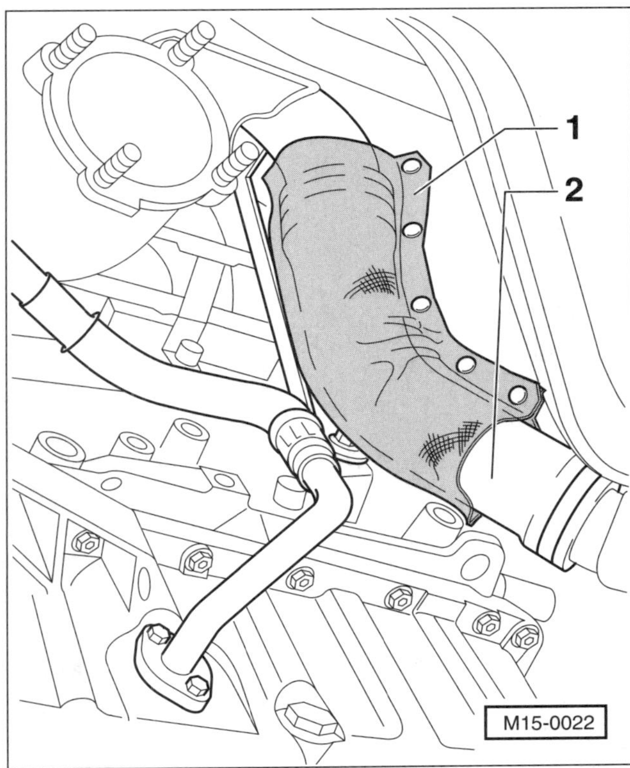

Fig. 41. Underside view of lower turbocharger outlet pipe heat insulation (**1**), and lower outlet pipe (**2**).

16. Loosen securing bolts for turbocharger outlet pipe retaining bracket.

17. Observe position of heat insulation on upper turbocharger outlet pipe and remove.

18. Loosen upper turbocharger outlet pipe clamp.

19. Remove 2 securing bolts for rear cylinder head heat shield and loosen retaining bracket securing bolts. See Fig. 42.

20. Remove upper turbocharger outlet pipe, and rear cylinder head heat shield.

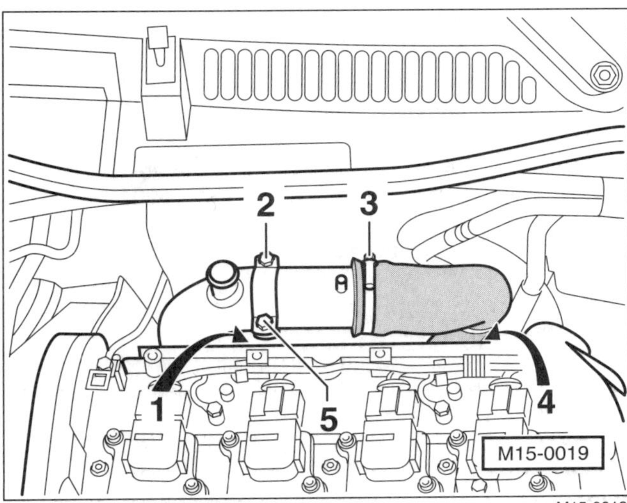

Fig. 42. Upper turbocharger outlet pipe clamp (**3**), rear cylinder head heat shield bolts (**1** & **4**) and retaining bracket bolts (**2** & **5**).

21. Remove turbocharger to exhaust manifold securing bolts. See Fig. 43.

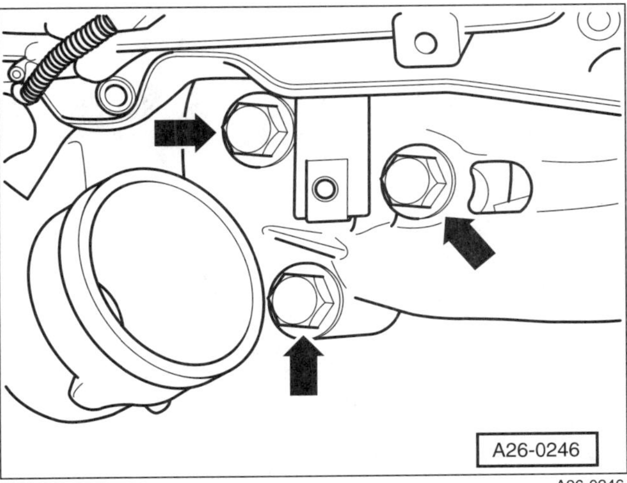

Fig. 43. Remove turbocharger to exhaust manifold securing bolts (**arrows**). Turbocharger remains with vehicle when cylinder head is removed.

22. Remove the ribbed V-belt and tensioner.

23. Remove toothed belt guard, upper section.

24. Set engine to TDC for cylinder #1 by turning crankshaft until timing mark on camshaft sprocket aligns with mark on cylinder head (valve) cover as shown earlier in Fig. 37.

25. Mark running direction of toothed belt.

26. Release tension on toothed belt and remove belt. Reference the following to Fig. 44.
    - Screw a 5x55 mm threaded stud into toothed belt tensioning damper housing and fit a hex nut and washer to the other end.
    - Line up the hole in the tensioning damper housing with the hole in the pressure piston by turning the pressure piston. Use a suitable tool to turn the pressure piston before tightening the nut on the threaded stud.
    - Tighten the nut on the threaded stud until the hole in the pressure piston aligns with the hole in the tension damper housing.
    - Secure pressure piston in position with a pin inserted through the hole in the tensioning damper housing.

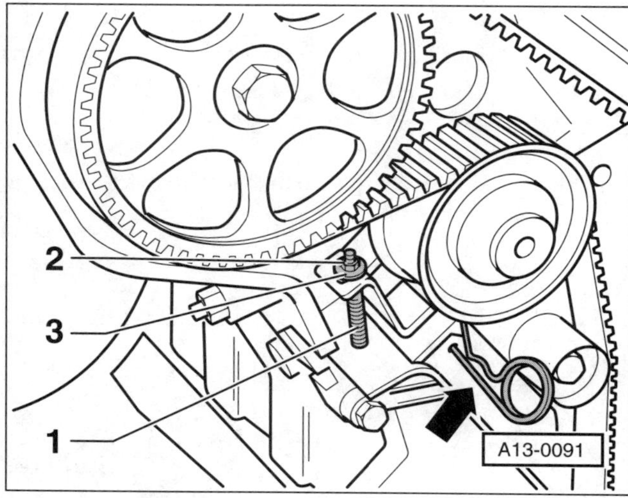

A13-0091

Fig. 44. Release tension of toothed belt roller against belt by threading a 5x55 mm stud (**1**) into tension damper housing. Fit a nut (**2**) and washer (**3**) onto the other end of stud. Line up hole in pressure piston and tension damper housing. Tighten nut (**2**) until holes in pressure piston and tension damper housing align. Insert a pin (**arrow**) to secure in place.

27. Remove toothed belt.

28. Turn crankshaft back off of TDC slightly.

> ***CAUTION —***
> *Due to engine design, care must be used when turning the camshaft with the toothed belt removed. If valves are allowed to open with the piston at TDC, serious internal damage will result.*

29. Loosen nut on threaded stud and remove threaded stud, nut and washer from tensioning damper housing.

30. Remove cylinder head (valve) cover as given earlier.

31. Loosen the socket head bolts slightly in sequence. Do not remove the bolts until all 10 have been loosened. Discard the head bolts. See Fig. 45.

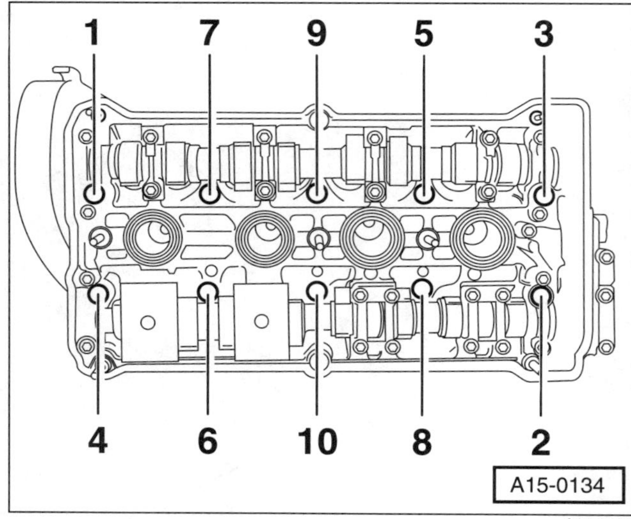

A15-0134

Fig. 45. Loosen the cylinder head bolts in the order shown. Loosen all bolts slightly the first time around, repeat the order, finish loosening and then remove.

32. Carefully lift off cylinder head and place in a clean area. If the head is stuck, use a soft-faced mallet or pry gently with a wooden stick.

> ***CAUTION —***
> *Some of the valves will be open. Use extra care when removing and handling to avoid damage. Place the cylinder head on the bench or table so that the weight of the cylinder head will not rest on the valves.*

Cylinder head, installing

Before proceeding with the installation of the cylinder head, whether an original or a new unit, observe the following important points:

- Check the cylinder head and block for distortion and warpage, see **Cylinder Head Components**, given later in this section.
- Carefully clean the cylinder block and cylinder head sealing surfaces being sure to avoid scratching them during the cleaning process. Do not use metal scrapers or wire brushes.
- When using abrasive paper do not use any grades coarser than 100 grit (such as 80 grit). Lower numbers are coarser.
- If cylinder head will not be reinstalled immediately, take precautions to prevent rust from forming on the cylinder block walls and gasket sealing surfaces.
- When cleaning the old gasket material off of the cylinder block, take precautions to keep the old gasket material and the abrasive particles and dirt out of the cooling and oiling system passages. Place a clean shop cloth over the cylinders to prevent contamination from getting between the cylinder wall and the piston.

- Do not take the new cylinder head gasket out of the packaging until ready to use. Handle the new gasket with extreme care as any damage will lead to leaks.
- There MUST NOT BE any oil or coolant in the head bolt holes in the cylinder block. Any fluids in the holes creates the danger of hydrolock while torquing which could lead to structural damage of the cylinder block. Use thread chasers to remove foreign material as required. Be sure that all 10 bolt holes are clean and dry.
- When all traces of the old gasket material have been removed from the cylinder block and head, carefully remove all traces of metal particles, abrasives and lint. All gasket sealing surfaces and bolt holes must be clean and dry to ensure a proper seal.
- Always use new cylinder head bolts and a new cylinder head gasket.
- Do not use any gasket sealer on the new cylinder head gasket.
- If installing a Volkswagen supplied replacement cylinder head, be sure to inspect for and remove any plastic packaging materials used to protect the head and the open valves.

1. Position the crankshaft so that pistons are NOT at TDC.
2. Loosen turbocharger securing bracket bolts slightly to facilitate cylinder head installation. See Fig. 46.

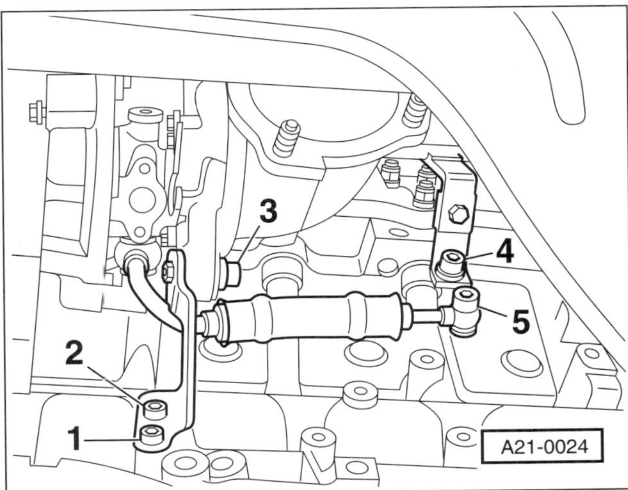

A21-0024

Fig. 46. Loosen turbocharger securing bracket bolts (**1 & 2**) slightly to facilitate cylinder head installation. Remaining bolts (**3, 4 & 5**) do not need to be loosened.

3. Install alignment pins into bolt holes of cylinder block. Use of this tool allows for proper alignment of the head on the block, preventing slippage and damage to the head gasket. See Fig. 47.
4. Install the new cylinder head gasket onto the block with the numbers and letters facing up. Be sure that none of the wiring or any vacuum hoses are caught between the cylinder head and the block.

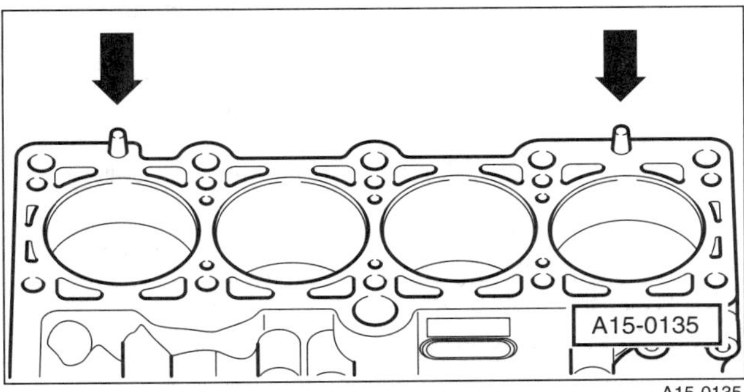

A15-0135

Fig. 47. Volkswagen supplied installation tool 3070 for assembly of cylinder head onto the block.

5. Carefully install the cylinder head onto the block over the alignment pins and screw in 8 of the new head bolts. Tighten the bolts hand-tight only.
6. Remove the alignment pins from the bolt holes with the tool and install the remaining 2 new head bolts. Tighten these bolts hand-tight.
7. Tighten the 10 cylinder head bolts in three stages following the tightening order. See Fig. 48.

Tightening torque

- Cylinder head to cylinder block, 1.8L engine (stretch bolts – always replace)
  - stage I . . . . 40 Nm (30 ft-lb)
  - stage II . . . . additional ¼ turn (90°)
  - stage III . . . . additional ¼ turn (90°)

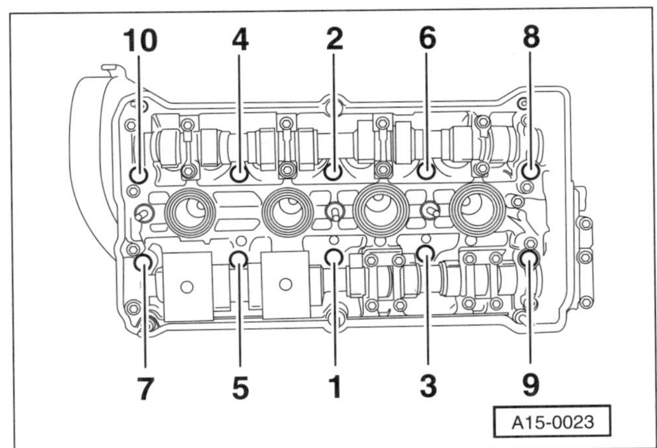

A15-0023

Fig. 48. Tighten the cylinder head bolts in the order shown.

8. Install new gasket and bolts between turbocharger and exhaust manifold.
9. Lubricate the camshafts and followers and install the cylinder head (valve) cover.

10. Install the toothed belt, adjust the tension and the belt timing.

11. Install the toothed belt guard, upper section.

12. Install the ribbed V-belt tensioner and the belt.

13. Install rear cylinder head heat shield and upper turbocharger outlet pipe and heat shield.

14. Install lower turbocharger outlet pipe and heat shield.

15. Install turbocharger inlet connecting pipe.

16. Install hose connecting evaporative emissions canister and turbocharger at bulkhead.

17. Install intake air hose from connecting pipe to turbocharger.

18. Reconnect all disconnected electrical components and connections including ignition coils.

19. Reconnect all coolant flanges and lines.

20. Reconnect all vacuum hoses connections.

21. Reconnect fuel supply and return lines.

22. Refill cooling system with fresh coolant in the appropriate ratio. See **19 Engine–Cooling System.**

> ***CAUTION —***
> - *Use only Volkswagen original coolant when filling the cooling system. Use of any other coolant may be harmful to the cooling system. Do not use coolant containing phosphates.*
> - *Do not use tap water in cooling system. Use distilled water only to mix anti-freeze.*

23. Install the lower sound absorber panels (belly pan).

24. Install the upper sound absorber panel.

25. Reconnect the battery only after all parts/electrical connections have been reinstalled and reconnected.

26. Be sure to quality check your work, see **Quality Review** at the end of this repair group.

Tightening torques

- Cylinder head cover to cylinder head . . 10 Nm (7 ft-lb)
- Ignition coil to cylinder head cover . . . . 10 Nm (7 ft-lb)
- Ground wire to cylinder head cover . . . 10 Nm (7 ft-lb)
- Heat shield to cylinder head . . . . 20 Nm (15 ft-lb)
- Ribbed V-belt tensioner to bracket . . . 25 Nm (18 ft-lb)
- Turbocharger to exhaust manifold (special nuts - always replace) . . . . . . 30 Nm (22 ft-lb)
- Coolant outlet flange to cylinder head . . . . 10 Nm (7 ft-lb)
- Secondary air pump bracket to cylinder block . . . . 25 Nm (18 ft-lb)
- Secondary air pump to support bracket nut . . . . 10 Nm (7 ft-lb)
- Securing bolt for turbocharger connecting pipes . . . . 10 Nm (7 ft-lb)

CYLINDER HEAD COMPONENTS

This section provides the specifications and special information necessary to repair the cylinder head that has been removed from the Volkswagen 1.8L engine. Special service tools and machine shop services are required for most cylinder head repair.

> ***NOTE —***
> - *The information given under this heading assumes that the cylinder head is removed. For cylinder head removal procedures, see* ***Cylinder head, removing*** *given earlier.*
> - *Fig. 2. and Fig. 3., given earlier, show exploded views of the cylinder head and valvetrain assemblies.*

Cylinder head and camshaft

Check the cylinder head for warpage and distortion with an accurate straight edge and a feeler gauge. See Fig. 49.

The cylinder head can be resurfaced as long as the distance from the cylinder head (valve) cover seating surface to the head gasket surface is never less than specified. Measure this distance through a cylinder head bolt hole. See Fig. 50. Machining too much material off of the cylinder head surface will change the compression ratio and will affect engine emissions.

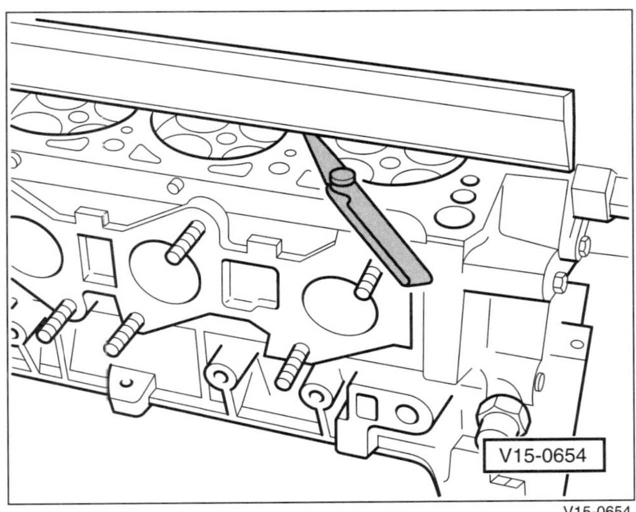

Fig. 49. Cylinder head being checked for distortion with a feeler gauge.

Specification

- Maximum cylinder head distortion/warpage . . . . 0.1 mm (0.004 in.)
- Minimum cylinder dimension (valve cover gasket surface to the head gasket surface) . . . . 139.2 mm (5.48 in.)

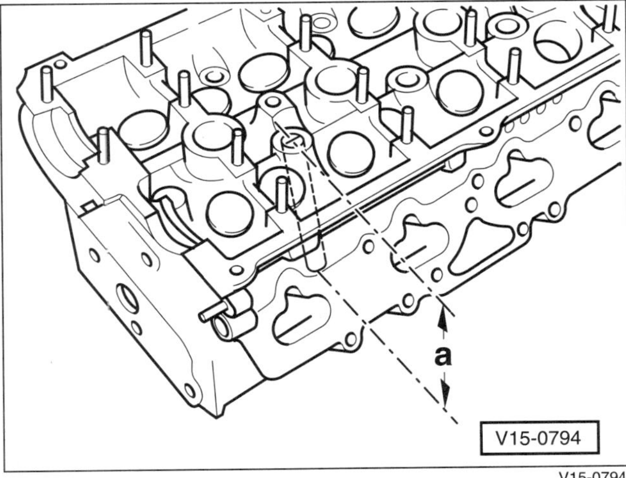

Fig. 50. Resurfacing dimension is measured through the cylinder head bolt holes. It must not be less than 139.2 mm (5.48 in.) after reworking cylinder head sealing surface.

The in and out movement of the camshaft is known as axial play and is measured with the cam followers and drive chain removed and only the first and last bearing caps installed. See Fig. 51.

A dial gauge is set up on the sprocket end of the camshaft and the camshaft axial clearance is checked by moving the camshaft as far as it can go in each direction.

NOTE —
Check camshaft axial clearance with lifters and camshaft timing chain removed and number 2 and 4 bearing caps installed.

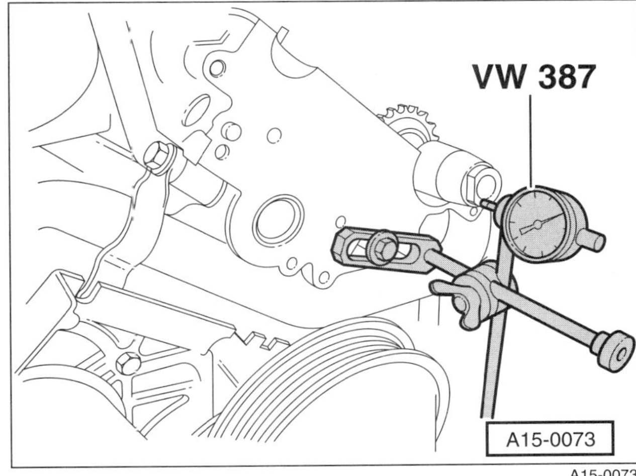

Fig. 51. Dial gauge set up on camshaft to measure axial play (**arrow**).

Specification

- Camshaft axial clearance, maximum . . . . 0.20 mm (0.008 in.)

Valves

Valves should not be re-worked on a machine. Only lapping by hand with valve compound is permitted. Valve dimensions listed in **Table a** apply to the valve shown in Fig. 52.

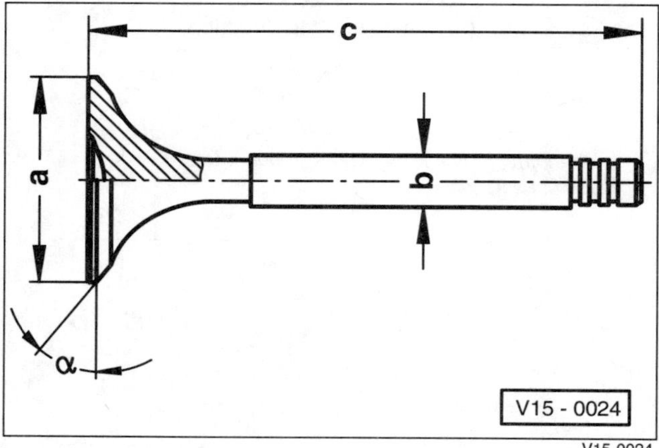

V15-0024

Fig. 52. Intake and exhaust valve dimensions are referenced in **Table a**.

Table a. Valve Dimensions

Engine Code	AWD, AWW
Valve head diameter (**a**) intake exhaust	 26.9 mm (1.059 in.) 29.9 mm (1.177 in.)
Valve stem diameter (**b**) intake exhaust	 5.963 mm (0.235 in.) 5.943 mm (0.234 in.)
Valve length (**c**) intake exhaust	 104.84-105.34 mm (4.128-4.147 in.) 103.64-104.14 mm (4.080-4.100 in.)
Valve face angle (α) intake exhaust	 45° 45°

Valve guides

Special tools and a press are required to replace the valve guides. Check valve guide wear with a new valve. Always use an intake valve in an intake guide and an exhaust valve in an exhaust guide. See Fig. 53. Inspect the valve seats to ensure that the cylinder head can be reconditioned before installing new valve guides. Press out worn original valve guides with Volkswagen special driver tool 3360 from camshaft side of head. Replacement valve guides have a shoulder on the camshaft side to limit the installed depth and must be pressed out from the combustion chamber side.

When installing new valve guides, lubricate with clean engine oil and press in from the camshaft side down to the shoulder. See Fig. 54. The cylinder head should be cold for this operation. Once the shoulder of the valve guide contacts the cylinder head, do not allow the pressure on the guide to exceed 2000 psi (1 ton) otherwise the cylinder head or the guide will be damaged. When the guide has been replaced, ream it to the proper size and continue with the reworking of the valve seats.

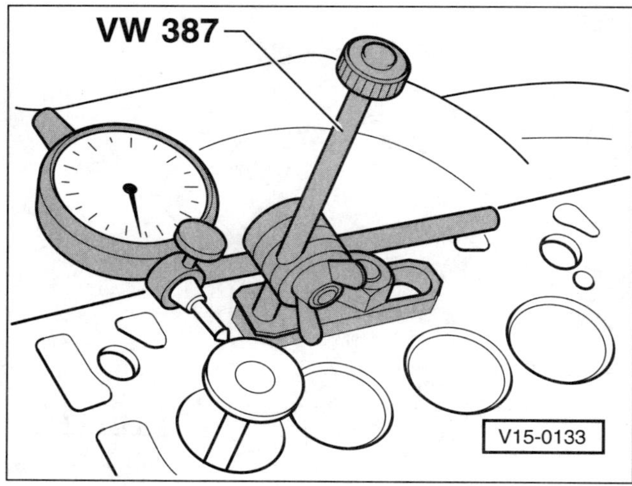

V15-0133

Fig. 53. Valve guide wear being checked with new valve. Insert valve until stem end is flush with end of guide. Rock valve back and forth (**arrow**) to check total travel.

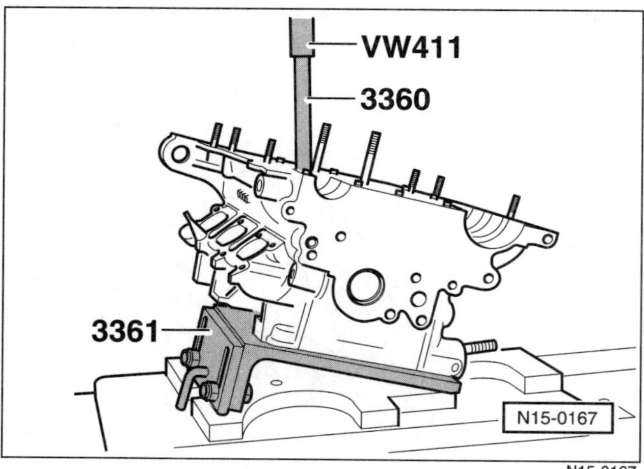

N15-0167

Fig. 54. Special tools for removing valve guides. Exhaust valve angle, 20°; outer intake valve angle, 21.5°; center intake valve angle, 15°.

Specification

- Valve guide (wear limits-maximum play) with new valve
  - intake valve guide . . . . 0.8 mm (0.031 in.)
  - exhaust valve guide. . . . . 0.8 mm (0.031 in.)

NOTE —

Due to the close tolerances found in the valve guides, it is recommended that Volkswagen special tool 3360 be used for removal and installation and special tool 3363 be used to ream the valve guide to size.

Valve seats

When resurfacing valve seats, there is a limit to the amount of material that can be removed to bring the seat back into specification. If too much material is removed, the final assembly will leave too little space for the hydraulic cam follower to function properly. The maximum refacing dimension, that is, the maximum amount of material that can be removed from the valve seat, is calculated from the measurement shown in Fig. 55.

Measure as shown in Fig. 55., and subtract the minimum dimension, as given in **Table b**. The difference is the maximum amount of material that can be removed from the valve seat.

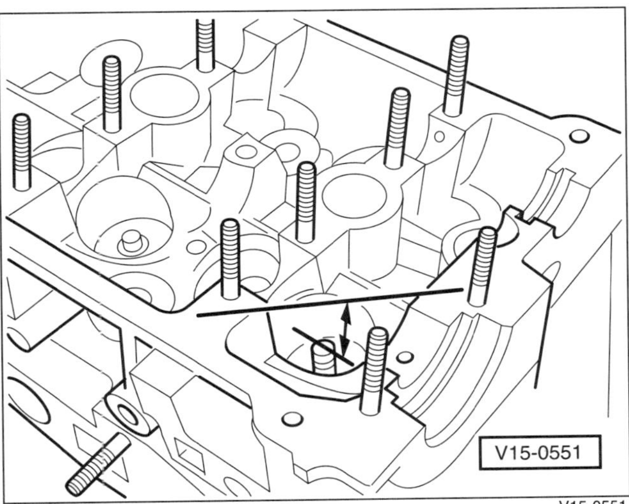

V15-0551

Fig. 55. Distance between top of valve stem and gasket surface of cylinder head is used to calculate maximum valve seat refacing dimensions.

Table b. Minimum Dimensions for Calculating Valve Seat Refacing Dimensions

Engine Code	Intake	Exhaust
AWD, AWW	Outer 34.0 mm (1.339 in.) Center 33.7 mm (1.327 in.)	34.4 mm (1.354in.)

NOTE —
Use care when reworking the exhaust valve seats to avoid changing the shape of the port. This can upset the flow characteristics of the valve.

Table c. Valve Seat Dimensions

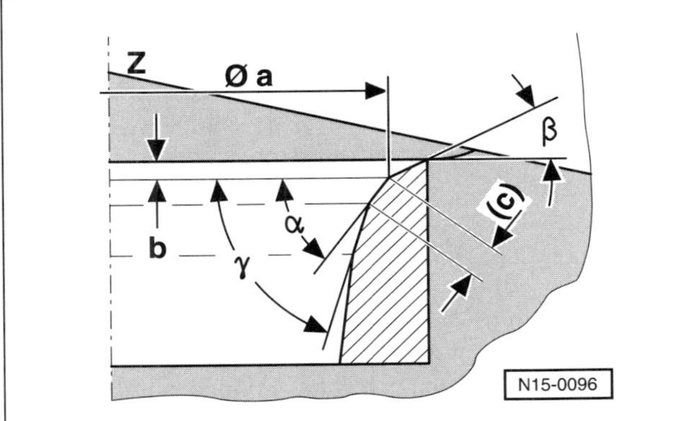

Engine Code: AWD, AWW	Intake	Exhaust
Seat diameter (**a**)	26.2 mm (1.031 in.)	29.0 mm (1.142 in.)
Maximum refacing dimension (**b**)	Calculated See Fig. 55.	Calculated See Fig. 55.
Seat width (**c**)	1.5-1.8 mm (0.059-0.071 in.)	approx. 1.8 mm (0.071 in.)
Valve seat angle (α)	45°	45°
Correction angle, upper (β)	30°	30°
Correction angle, lower (γ)	60°	60°

NOTE —
Z shows cylinder head surface reference.

QUALITY REVIEW

When you have finished working under the hood and around other areas of the vehicle it is advisable to take a moment to quality check or review your work. This helps to ensure that the operation or repair has been completed properly with all affected systems functioning within normal parameters. This may include the following:

- Make sure that the radiator fan cycles properly and that the coolant level and concentration are correct.
- Ensure that all cable ties and hose clamps that were removed as part of the repair are replaced.
- Check and adjust all other applicable fluid levels.
- Make sure that there are no fluid leaks.
- Make sure that there are no air, vacuum or exhaust leaks.
- Make sure that all components involved in the repair are positioned correctly and function properly.
- Male sure all tools, shop cloths, fender covers, and protective tape are removed.
- Clean grease from painted surfaces and steering wheel.
- Unlock the anti-theft radio and reset the clock.

In addition to the above noted points, the ECM and TCM may need to be checked using the Volkswagen supplied VAG 1551 or 1552 scan tool as mentioned at the start of this repair.

15b Cylinder Head and Valvetrain (1.9L Engine)

TABLES

GENERAL

This section covers most cylinder head and valvetrain service and repair work for the 4-cylinder, 2 valve per cylinder, 1.9 liter diesel engine. For information on short block engine rebuilding and internal engine specifications, see **13a Crankshaft/Cylinder Block (4-cylinder)**.

Most of the operations described in this repair group require special equipment and experience. If you lack the skills, tools, or a suitable workplace for servicing or repairing the cylinder head, we suggest that you leave these repairs to an authorized Volkswagen dealer or other qualified shop.

Engine Codes
- ALH . . . . 1.9L 4-cylinder turbo diesel

DIAGNOSTIC TESTING

The tests that follow can be used to help isolate engine problems, to better understand a problem before starting expensive and extensive repairs, or to just periodically check engine condition.

Compression Test

A compression test will tell a lot about the overall condition of the engine without the need for taking it apart. Testing is relatively simple and straightforward.

1. Remove two plastic caps and retaining nuts on upper sound absorber panel. Loosen the rear retaining nut slightly. Remove dipstick, lift cover up slightly and pull forward.

2. Warm-up the engine until it is a minimum of 30°C (86°F).

3. Disconnect harness connector for fuel cut-off valve from diesel injection pump. See Fig. 1.

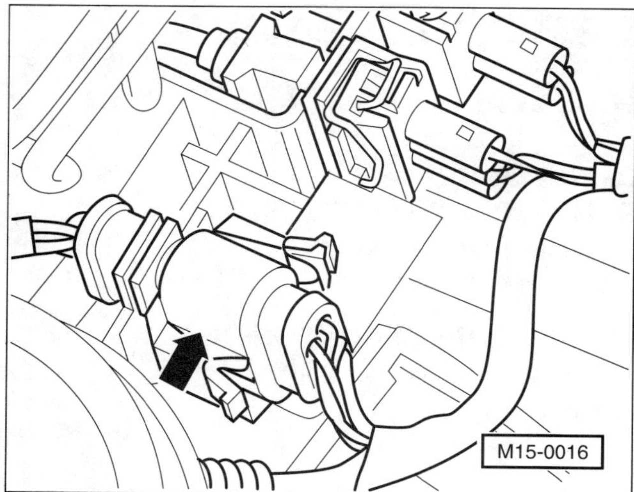

Fig. 1. Disconnect harness connector (**arrow**) for fuel cut off valve on diesel injection pump.

4. Disconnect bus connector from each glow plug by gently pulling up on it. Lay the complete bus connector aside.

5. Use compressed air to clear area around the glow plugs.

6. Using a 10 mm deep socket and swivel or Volkswagen special tool 3220, remove all glow plugs and lay aside in proper order.

7. Install compression tester into glow plug hole.

8. Have a helper:
   - depress clutch pedal fully
   - put the transmission in neutral or park
   - crank the engine over with the starter motor

   NOTE —
   Cranking the engine over with the diesel injection system components disconnected may Diagnostic Trouble Codes (DTCs) to be stored in engine management system memory.

9. Engine should be cranked a minimum of 4 to 5 revolutions.

10. Record readings, release pressure in the gauge and repeat procedure for each cylinder.

11. Compare readings to specification.

Specification
- Compression pressures (ALH engine)
  new . . . . 25 to 31 bar (368 - 456 psi)
  wear limit . . . . 19 bar (279 psi)
  maximum difference
  between cylinders . . . . 5 bar (74 psi)

12. When all cylinders have been checked, reinstall glow plugs and bus connector, connect harness connector for quantity adjuster and fuel cut-off valve. Install the upper engine cover.

Tightening torque
- Glow plug to cylinder head . . . . 15 Nm (11 ft-lb)

Cylinder leakdown test

The most conclusive diagnosis of low compression symptoms requires a cylinder leak-down test. Using a special tester and a supply of compressed air, each cylinder is pressurized. The rate at which the air leaks out of the cylinder, as well as the sound and location of the escaping air can more accurately pinpoint the magnitude and source of the leakage. Any engine compression diagnosis that will require major disassembly should first be confirmed by a cylinder leak-down test. Because this test requires special equipment and experience, it may be desirable to have it performed by a Volkswagen dealer or other qualified repair shop.

CYLINDER HEAD SERVICE

Many cylinder head repairs can be accomplished without removing the cylinder head from the engine. The cylinder head cover (valve cover) gasket, the camshaft, the camshaft oil seal, the valve guide oil seals, the valve springs, and the camshaft followers are all accessible with the cylinder head installed. This heading describes those repairs that can be done with the cylinder head installed.

Fig. 2 shows an exploded view of the internal cylinder head components and Fig. 3 shows the external cylinder head components.

Internal cylinder head assembly

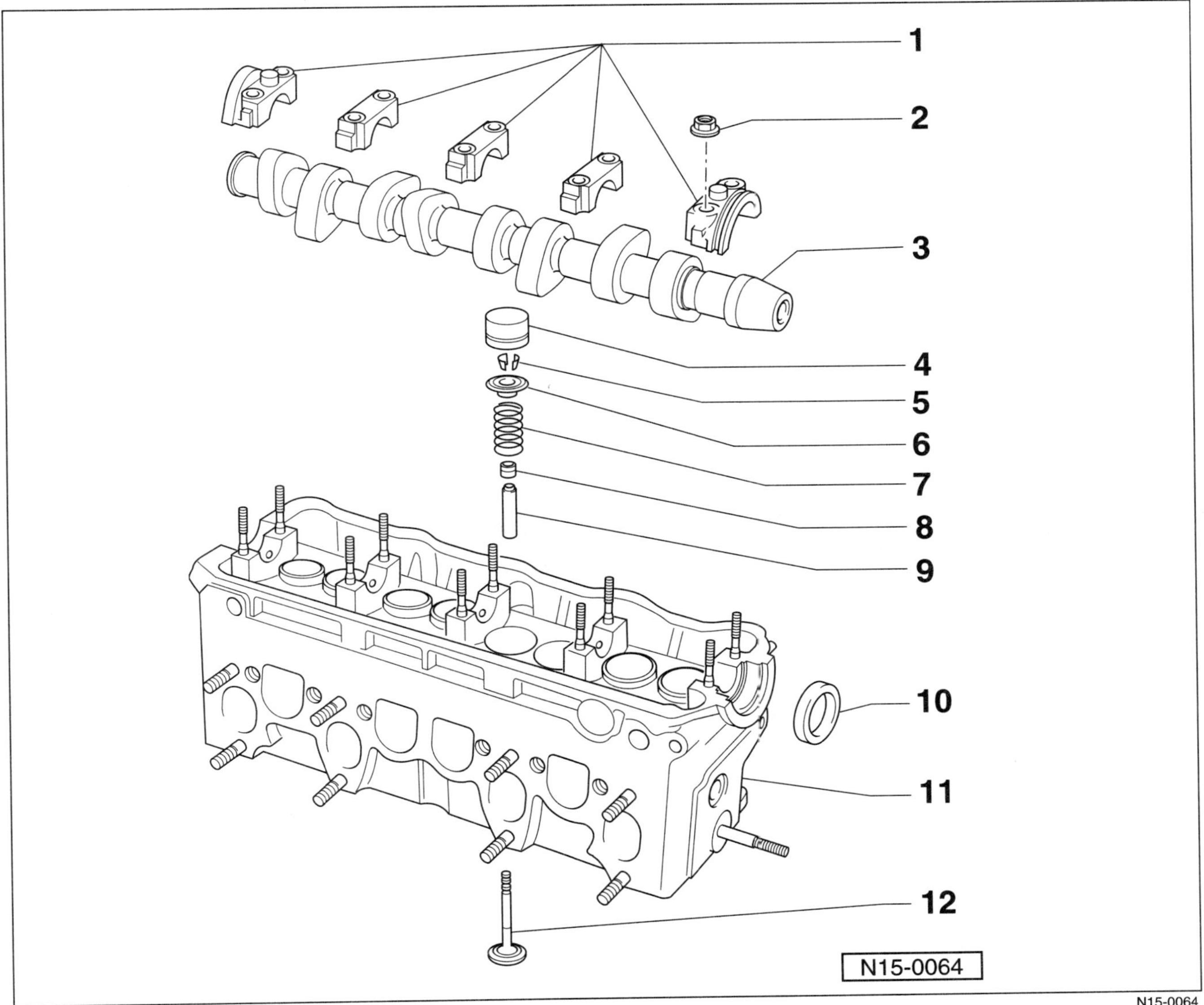

Fig. 2. Exploded view of internal cylinder head components.

1. **Bearing cap**
   - Coat bearing cap #1 lightly with sealant (VW part # AMV 174 004 01)
2. **Nut**
   - Tighten to 20 Nm (15 ft-lb)
3. **Camshaft**
   - Checking radial clearance with plastigage wear limit: 0.11 mm (.0043 in.)
   - Run-out: max. 0.01 mm (.0004 in.)
4. **Hydraulic lifter**
   - Do not interchange
   - Store with cam contact surface facing downwards
   - Before installing, check camshaft axial clearance, see **Cylinder Head Components**
   - Oil contact surfaces
5. **Keepers**
6. **Upper valve spring plate**
7. **Valve spring**
8. **Valve stem seal**
9. **Valve guide**
10. **Oil seal**
    - To remove and install, remove bearing cap
11. **Cylinder head**
12. **Valves**

External cylinder head assembly

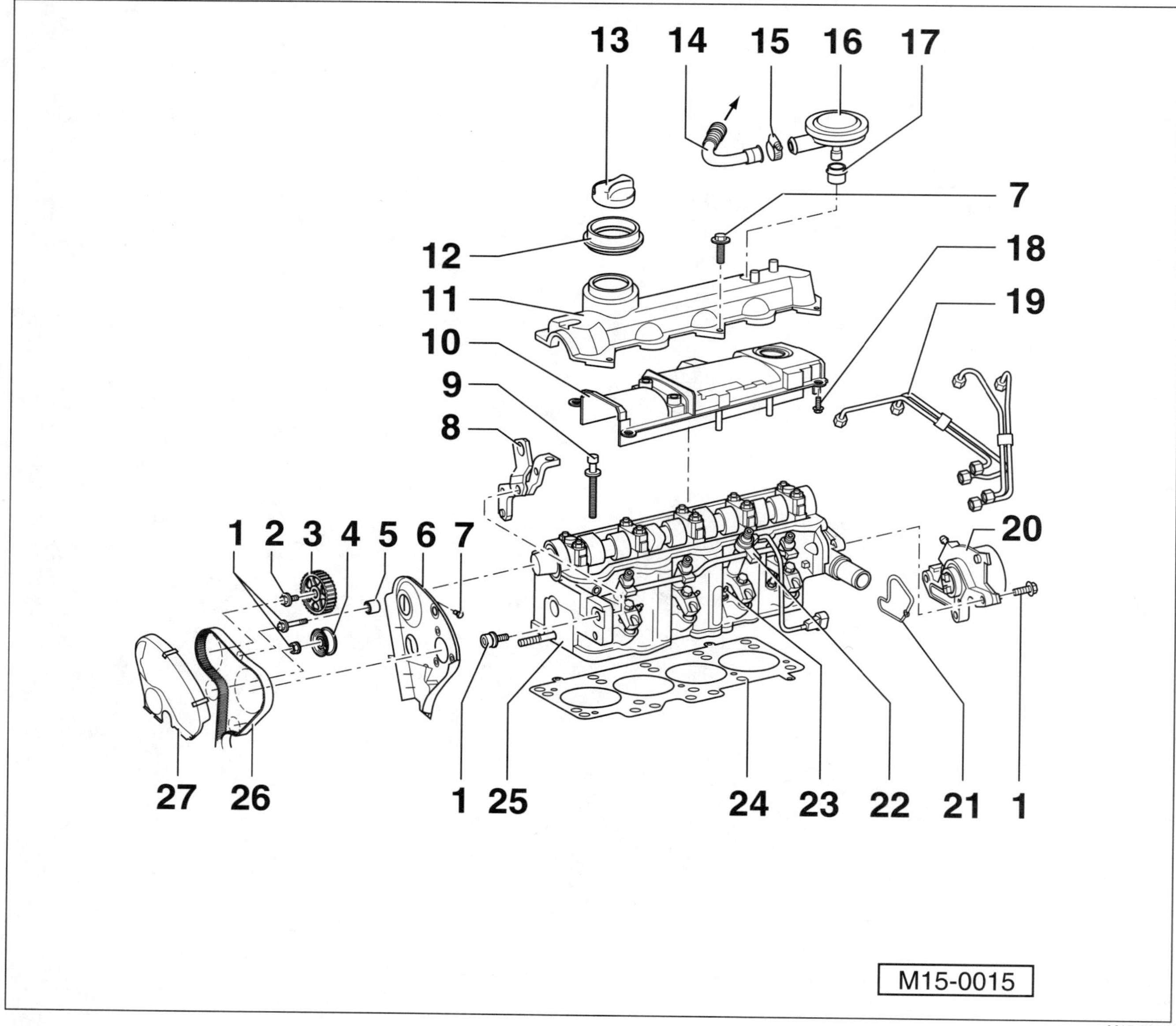

M15-0015

Fig. 3. Exploded view of external cylinder head components.

1. **Nut/Bolt**
   - Tighten to 20 Nm (15 ft-lb)
2. **Bolt**
   - Tighten to 45 Nm (33 ft-lb)
   - To loosen and tighten use counter-holding tool 3036
3. **Camshaft sprocket**
   - Drive off of camshaft taper using hammer and drift through toothed belt guard openings
4. **Tensioning roller (semi-automatic, toothed belt)**
5. **Idler roller**
6. **Toothed belt guard, rear**
7. **Nut**
   - Tighten to 10 Nm (7 ft-lb)
8. **Lifting eye**
9. **Cylinder head bolt**
   - Always replace
   - Note sequence when loosening and tightening, see **Cylinder head, removing and installing**
10. **Oil deflector**

(continued on following page)

11. Valve cover

12. Seal
- Replace if damaged

13. Cap
- Replace seal if damaged

14. Breather pipe

15. Retaining clip

16. Pressure regulating valve
- For positive crankcase ventilation valve

17. Gasket
- Replace if damaged

18. Bolt
- Tighten to 5 Nm (44 in-lb)

19. Fuel injector lines
- Tighten to 25 Nm (18 ft-lb)
- Remove using 3035 offset tubing wrench
- Always remove fuel line cluster as an assembly
- Do not bend, kink or alter shape

20. Vacuum pump
- For brake booster

21. Gasket
- Always replace

22. Fuel injector
- Removing and installing, see **23 Fuel Injection–Diesel (ALH Engine)**

23. Glow plug
- Tighten to 15 Nm (11 ft-lb)
- Checking, see **28 Ignition System–Diesel (ALH Engine)**

24. Cylinder head gasket
- Always replace
- If replaced; also replace entire engine coolant

25. Cylinder head

26. Toothed belt
- Mark direction of engine rotation before removing
- Check for wear
- Do not kink

27. Toothed belt guard, upper section

Cylinder head (valve) cover, removing and installing

> ***NOTE —***
> *The valve cover gasket is vulcanized into the rigid aluminum cover and is not available as a separate part.*

1. Remove the upper engine cover.
2. Remove connecting pipe between the intercooler and the intake hose.
3. Disconnect the breather hose from the breather valve.
4. Remove 4 cylinder head cover securing bolts from the rear and 3 from the front.
5. Lift off cover with attached oil separator and gasket.
6. Installation is the reverse of removal.

Tightening torque
- Cylinder head cover to cylinder head . . . . 10 Nm (7 ft-lb)

Camshaft oil seal, replacing

1. Remove the upper engine cover.
2. Remove connecting pipe between the intercooler and the intake hose.
3. Remove the upper toothed belt guard.
4. Remove cylinder head (valve) cover.
5. Remove brake booster vacuum pump from the end of the cylinder head.

6. Set the engine to TDC for cylinder 1 by turning the crankshaft until the timing mark on the flywheel or torque converter aligns with mark on the transmission case.
    - For manual transmission, see Fig. 4.
    - For automatic transmission, see Fig. 5.

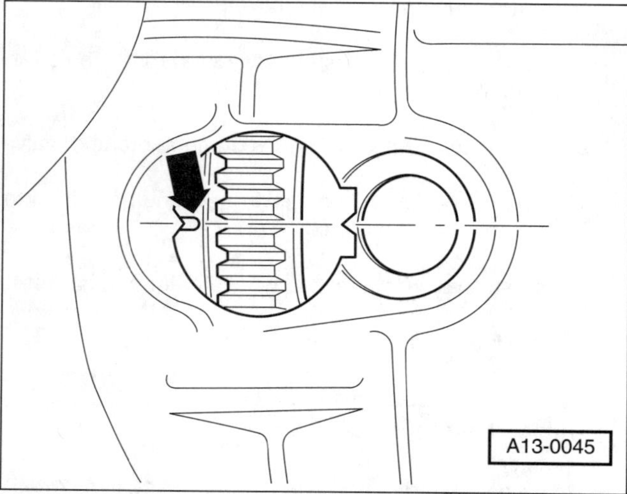

A13-0045

Fig. 4. TDC for manual transmissions: align mark on flywheel (**arrow**) with pointer on transmission case.

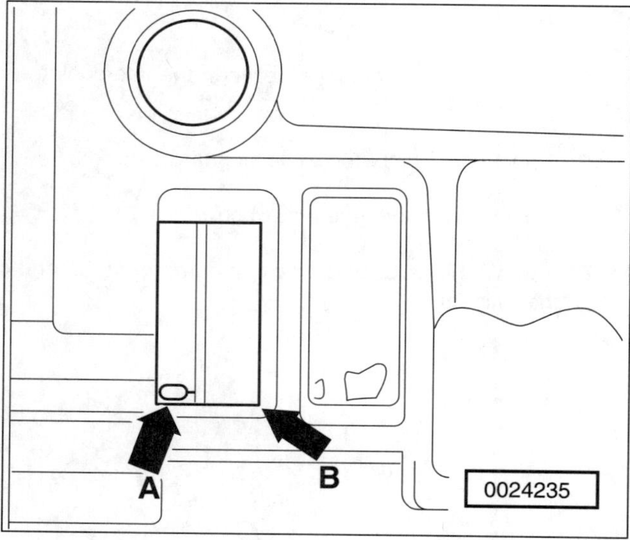

0024235

Fig. 5. TDC for automatic transmissions: align mark on torque converter (**A**) with lower edge of opening in transmission case (**B**).

7. Lock the camshaft at TDC with the setting bar. See Fig. 6.

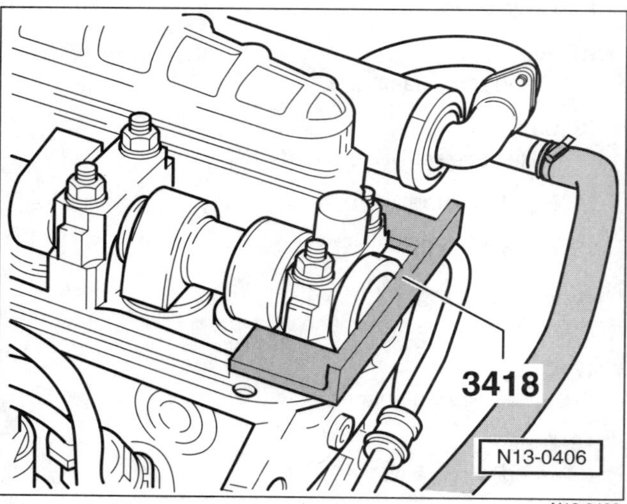

N13-0406

Fig. 6. Volkswagen special tool 3418 shown in position on the vacuum pump end of the camshaft to lock camshaft at TDC.

8. Release the tensioning roller and slip toothed belt off the camshaft sprocket.

9. Loosen camshaft sprocket mounting bolt about 1 turn while counter-holding camshaft sprocket. See Fig. 7.

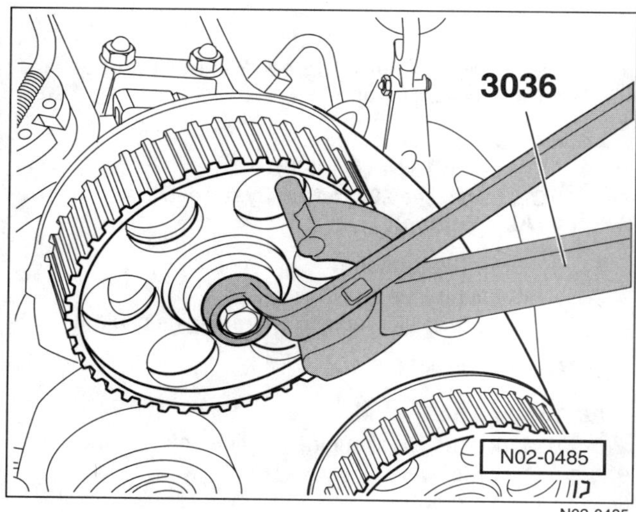

N02-0485

Fig. 7. VW special tool 3036 being used to counter-hold camshaft sprocket while loosening mounting bolt.

> ***CAUTION —***
> *Do not use 3418 setting bar by itself to lock camshaft when loosening camshaft sprocket bolt. Hold camshaft sprocket using 3036 holding tool or equivalent. Possible damage to the camshaft could result if only the setting bar is used to lock camshaft.*

NOTE—
The camshaft end is tapered. Loosening the sprocket will allow the camshaft sprocket to rotate independently of the camshaft. There may be a keyway cut into the end of the camshaft. However, there is no matching keyway cut into the sprocket nor is there a Woodruff key.

10. Release camshaft sprocket from camshaft with two-arm puller. See Fig. 8.

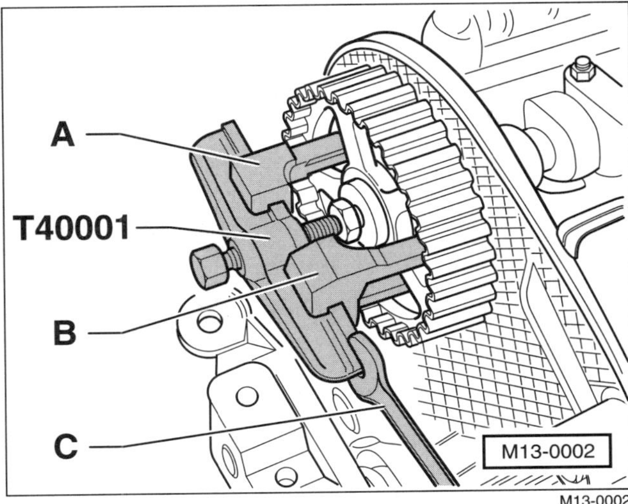

Fig. 8. Release camshaft sprocket with two-arm puller (VW special tool #T40001 shown). Center arms (**A** and **B**) in camshaft sprocket and counter-hold puller using open-end wrench (**C**).

NOTE—
Tapping the camshaft sprocket lightly with a soft mallet may help release the sprocket from the tapered end of the camshaft.

11. Remove the camshaft sprocket mounting bolt and sprocket.

12. Loosen and remove camshaft bearing cap #1.

NOTE—
Bearing cap #1 is closest to the belt end of the camshaft.

13. Slide the seal through the rear toothed belt guard and off the end of the camshaft.

14. Install new seal noting the following points:
    - Lubricate the new seal with clean engine oil.
    - Install with the closed end facing out.
    - Use a suitable installation tool.
    - Press seal into the bottom of the recess.

15. Install bearing cap #1.

Tightening torque
- Camshaft bearing cap to cylinder head . . . . 20 Nm (15 ft-lb)
- Camshaft sprocket to camshaft . . . . . 45 Nm (33 ft-lb)

16. Install camshaft drive belt sprocket.

17. Install toothed belt and adjust tension, see **Toothed Belt–Camshaft Drive**, given later.

18. Install brake booster vacuum pump, cylinder head (valve) cover, and upper toothed belt guard.

Tightening torque
- Vacuum pump to cylinder head . . . . . 20 Nm (15 ft-lb)
- Valve cover to cylinder head. . . . . 10 Nm (7 ft-lb)

19. Install connecting pipe between the intercooler and the intake hose.

20. Check that all components are installed, properly secured, and install upper engine cover.

21. Be sure to quality check your work, see **Quality Review** at the end of this repair group.

Camshaft, removing and installing

The camshaft can be removed and installed with the cylinder head installed. Removing the camshaft allows access to the hydraulic cam followers, the valve springs and the valve stem oil seals.

1. Remove upper sound absorber panel.

2. Remove connecting pipe between intercooler and intake hose.

3. Remove upper toothed belt guard.

4. Remove cylinder head (valve) cover.

5. Remove brake booster vacuum pump from end of the cylinder head.

6. Turn crankshaft to top dead center (TDC) for cylinder 1 as shown earlier, see Fig. 4. or Fig. 5.

7. Lock camshaft with setting bar as shown earlier. See Fig. 6.

8. Release tensioning roller and slide toothed belt off the camshaft sprocket.

9. Slightly turn crankshaft counterclockwise of engine rotation.

10. Loosen camshaft sprocket mounting bolt about 1 turn. Release camshaft sprocket from camshaft with two-arm puller as shown earlier. See Fig. 8.

11. Remove camshaft sprocket mounting bolt and sprocket.

NOTE —
Mark each bearing cap before removing. Each cap is machined to each journal and must be reinstalled to that exact location to prevent damage.

12. Loosen and remove bearing caps from positions 5, 1 and 3 in that order.

NOTE —
Position 1 is closest to the belt end of the camshaft.

13. Loosen the nuts on bearing cap 2 slightly and then loosen the nuts on bearing cap 4 slightly. Loosen the nuts alternately and evenly a little at a time on each of the two bearing caps. Remove the nuts (and washers, if equipped), and remove the bearing caps.

14. Lift out camshaft and lay aside.

NOTE —
Once removed, the camshaft should be checked for wear and other visible damage as described later under **Cylinder Head Components**.

15. Oil the bearing surfaces of the cylinder head and camshaft and install the camshaft into the cylinder head with the lobes for cylinder number 1 pointing up.

16. Install bearing caps 2 and 4. Install nuts (and washers, if equipped) and tighten nuts alternately and evenly so that camshaft is drawn down fully and evenly into bearing saddles. Torque to specification. See Fig. 9.

Tightening torque
- Camshaft bearing cap to cylinder head . . . . 20 Nm (15 ft-lb)

CAUTION —
Be sure to install bearing caps correctly. The caps are bored off-center and only fit properly one way. Caps are matched to the cylinder head by the machining process and are not available separately. Broken caps will require the replacement of the cylinder head. See Fig. 9.

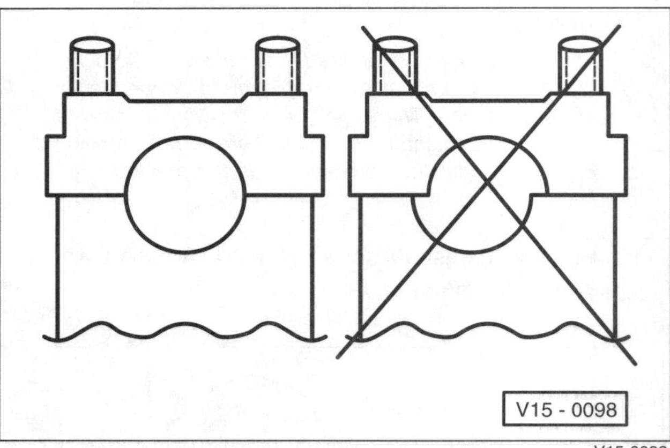

V15-0098

Fig. 9. Bearing caps are bored off-center. If necessary, test install caps without camshaft to confirm installation direction.

17. Install all remaining bearing caps and torque to specification.

18. Install the camshaft drive belt sprocket.

NOTE —
Ensure that camshaft lobes for cylinder #1 are still pointing up.

Tightening torque
- Camshaft sprocket to camshaft . . . . . 45 Nm (33 ft-lb)

19. Install the toothed belt and adjust tension, see **Toothed Belt–Camshaft Drive** given later.

20. Install brake booster vacuum pump, cylinder head (valve) cover, and upper toothed belt guard.

Tightening torque
- Vacuum pump to cylinder head . . . . . 20 Nm (15 ft-lb)
- Valve cover to cylinder head. . . . . 10 Nm (7 ft-lb)

21. Install the connecting pipe between the intercooler and the intake hose.

22. Install upper engine cover.

23. Be sure to quality check your work, see **Quality Review** at the end of this repair group.

Hydraulic cam followers, checking

The 1.9 liter ALH engine is equipped with hydraulic cam followers which are also known as lifters.The cam followers are pumped up by engine oil pressure, expanding as necessary to fill the gap between the valve stem and the camshaft lobe. This occurs continuously and automatically to keep the valve in proper adjustment at all times.

Some valve noise at start-up and during the warm-up period is normal at times due to hydraulic cam followers that have bled down while the engine was not running. Before checking noisy cam followers, check that the engine oil is new and fresh, of the correct weight, and that the level is correct. Allow 2 minutes with a warm engine running at a fast idle for the lubrication system to properly pump up the cam followers.

Cam followers should only be checked when the engine is fully up to operating temperature. Run the engine until the radiator fan has switched on at least one time. Increase the engine speed to 2,500 rpm and hold it there for approximately 2 minutes. If the hydraulic cam followers are still noisy, shut the engine off and proceed as follows while the engine is still warm.

1. Remove the cylinder head (valve) cover. See **Cylinder head (valve) cover, removing and installing**, given earlier.

2. Turn the engine by hand until both camshaft lobes of cylinder #1 are pointing approximately up.

   NOTE —
   Hydraulic cam follower clearance can be checked on any cam follower (lifter) that is not being depressed by the camshaft lobe.

3. Check the clearance between the cam follower and the cam lobe on cylinder #1 by lightly depressing the cam follower with a wooden or plastic wedge and inserting a feeler gauge into the gap. See Fig. 10. If the clearance exceeds the specified limit, the lifter is faulty and should be replaced.

Specification

- Hydraulic cam follower maximum clearance (ALH engine) . . . . 0.2 mm (0.008 in.)

4. Turn engine by hand and repeat procedure until all cam followers have been checked.

5. Replace a faulty cam follower by removing camshaft as previously described and pulling the follower from the cylinder head. Faulty hydraulic cam followers can be replaced individually but only as a complete assembly.

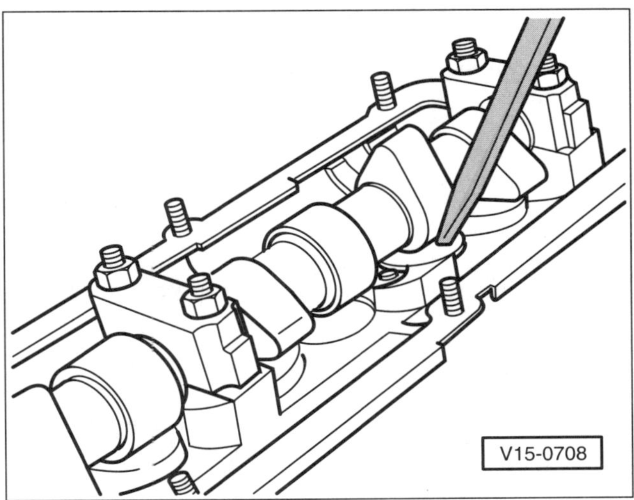

V15-0708

Fig. 10. Hydraulic cam follower shown being pushed down lightly with plastic wedge.

CAUTION —
After installing new cam followers, the engine should not be started for at least 30 minutes. New cam followers are usually at full extended height and must be allowed to bleed down to their proper height once installed. Failure to do so may cause the valves to strike the pistons resulting in serious damage.

NOTE —
Store removed hydraulic cam followers in order on a clean surface with the camshaft contact surface facing down to minimize bleed down. Cover with a clean lint-free shop cloth.

Valve stem oil seals, replacing

The sign of faulty valve stem seals is excessive oil consumption and oil smoke from the exhaust. This is usually most noticeable during periods of high manifold vacuum such as deceleration. If compression and leak-down testing confirm the integrity of the piston rings, but the engine consumes oil, it is likely that faulty valve stem seals are present. It should also be noted that worn valve stem seals could be due to worn valve guides and that the worn valve guides are the major cause of the oil consumption. See **Cylinder Head Components** for more information on checking valve guides.

Replacing the valve stem oil seals requires removal of the camshaft, cam followers, and the valve springs. This can be done with the cylinder head installed or removed. In either case, several Volkswagen special tools are required to compress the valve springs and remove and install the seals.

Working with the cylinder head installed:

1. Remove the cylinder head cover, camshaft, and hydraulic cam followers as described earlier.

2. Turn the crankshaft so that cylinder #1 is at TDC. Continue with step 5.

   NOTE —
   Compressed air is not used as on other engines. When the spring is removed, the valve is properly supported by the piston crown at TDC.

Working with the cylinder head removed:

3. Secure the cylinder head to the workbench. Use care to avoid damage to the head gasket surfaces.

4. Remove the camshaft and hydraulic cam followers as described earlier. Continue with step 5.

Working with cylinder head removed or installed:

5. Install the appropriate valve spring compressor tools. See Fig. 11. Compress the spring for the first cylinder and remove the spring retainer, both keepers, and the valve spring. If spring will not compress, lightly tap the tool to release the stuck keepers. Use a small magnet to retrieve the keepers.

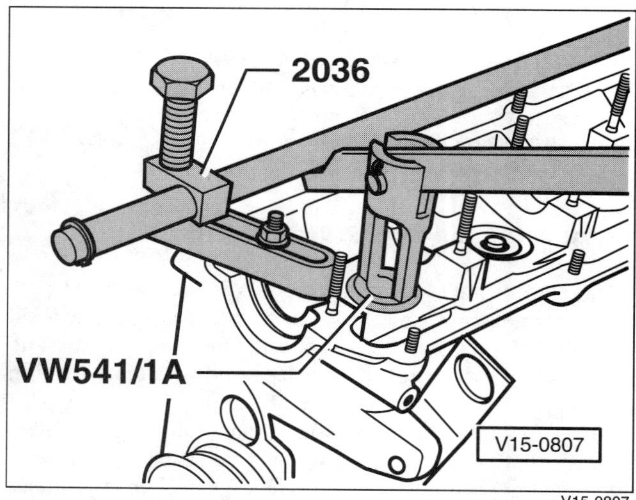

V15-0807

Fig. 11. Valve spring compressor tools being used to compress valve spring for removal of keepers. Numbers identify Volkswagen special tools.

6. Remove the valve stem seals with the special slide hammer tool. See Fig. 12.

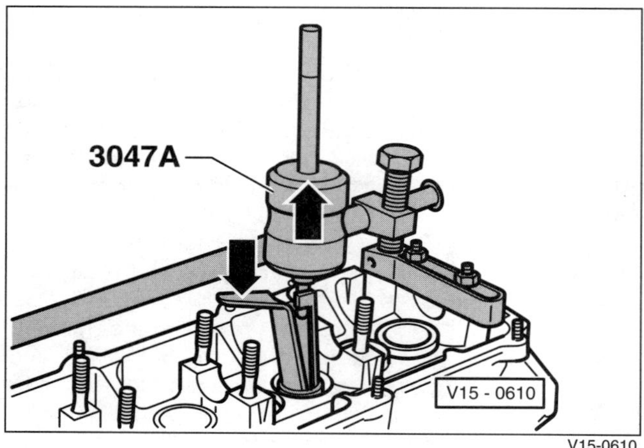

V15-0610

Fig. 12. Valve stem seal removal tool shown in position to remove valve stem seal. Push down on tool (**left arrow**) while sliding hammer up (**right arrow**).

7. Begin installation of new seal by temporarily fitting a protective plastic fitting sleeve over the valve stem. This sleeve is usually included with the new seal set and will prevent damage to the seal due to the sharp edges of the keeper grooves. Lubricate the new seal with clean engine oil and fit it to the installation tool. See Fig. 13.

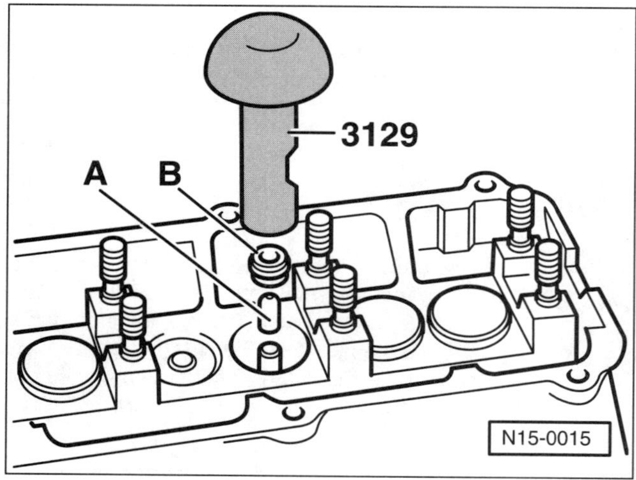

N15-0015

Fig. 13. Plastic fitting sleeve (**A**), shown with valve stem seal (**B**) and plastic installation tool 3129 available from Volkswagen.

8. Push the tool (with seal) down over the valve stem until the seal is fully seated on the guide. Remove the tool and the protective fitting sleeve.

9. Reinstall valve spring, retainer and keepers.

10. Repeat for the second valve on the cylinder.

11. When both valve seals have been replaced on the first cylinder, turn the crankshaft to TDC for the next cylinder (if working with cylinder head installed) and repeat the process until all valve seals have been replaced.

12. Remaining installation is the reverse of removal.

> ***CAUTION —***
> *To prevent cylinder head or camshaft damage, be sure to follow the camshaft installation procedure when tightening the camshaft bearing caps. See* **Camshaft, removing and installing**.

Tightening torque
- Spark plug to cylinder head . . . . 30 Nm (22 ft-lb)

---

13. Be sure to quality check your work, see **Quality Review** at the end of this repair group.

TOOTHED BELT - CAMSHAFT DRIVE

The camshaft drive belt and its related parts are shown in Fig. 14. Required maintenance involves inspection at 5,000, 10,000, 20,000, 30,000, and 50,000 miles. The belt and the tensioner are to be replaced at 40,000 miles on automatic transmission equipped vehicles, and 55,000 miles on manual transmission equipped vehicles. This cycle should then be repeated. This will help prevent damage to the engine due to belt stretch and the long term effects of heat. The camshaft drive belt is known also as a toothed belt and both terms are used interchangeably.

Drive belts, assembly

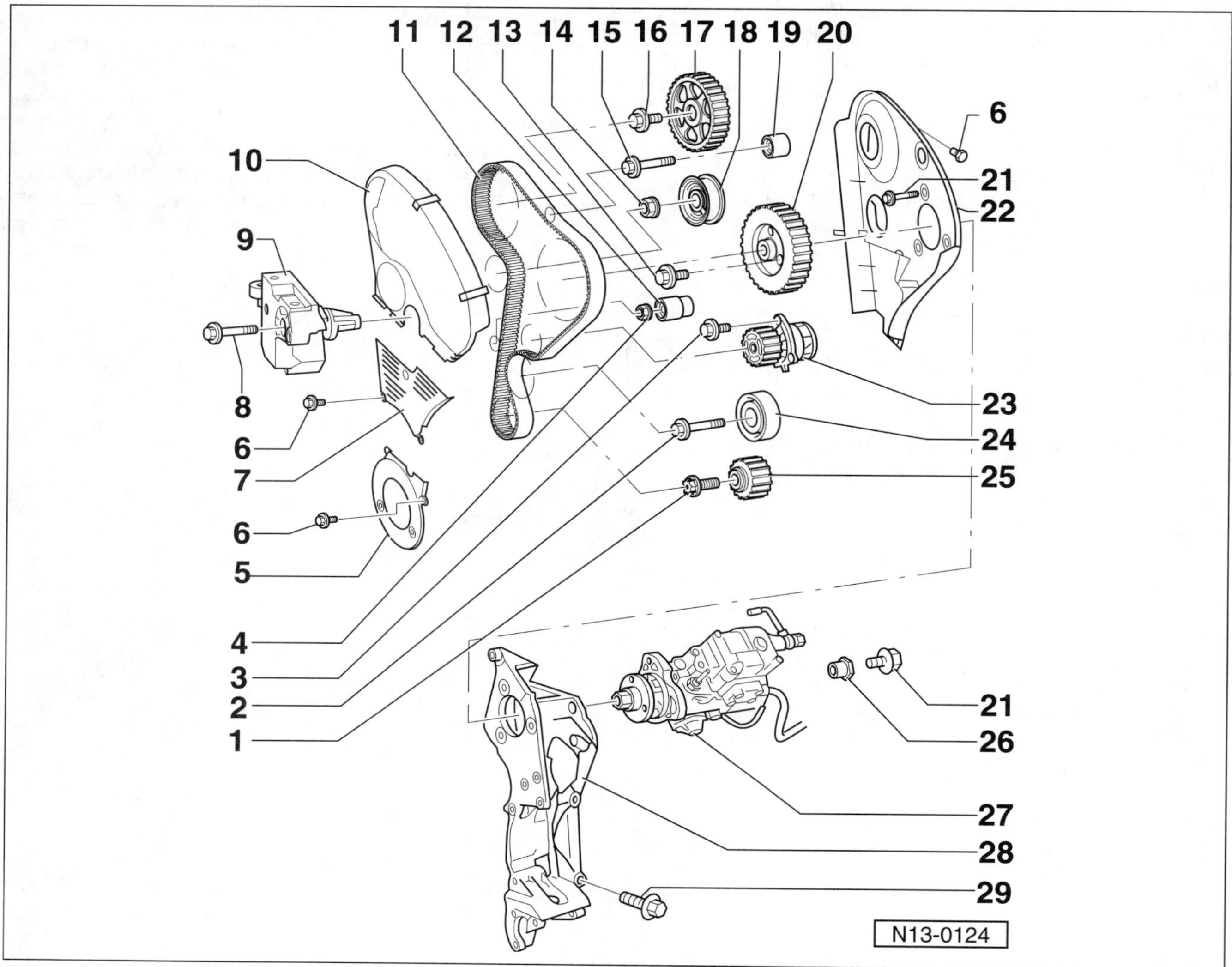

N13-0124

Fig. 14. Exploded view of the toothed belt for the camshaft drive and related components.

1. **Bolt**
   - Always replace
   - Tighten to 120 Nm (88 ft-lb) + ¼ turn (90°)
   - To loosen and tighten, counter-hold with 3415
   - Threads and shoulder must be free of oil and grease
   - The additional quarter turn can be obtained in several stages
2. **Bolt**
   - Always replace
   - Tighten to 40 Nm (30 ft-lb) + ¼ turn (90°)
3. **Bolt**
   - Tighten to 15 Nm (11 ft-lb)
4. **Bolt**
   - Tighten to 22 Nm (16 ft-lb)
5. **Toothed belt guard, lower section**
6. **Bolt**
   - Tighten to 10 Nm (7 ft-lb)
7. **Toothed belt guard, lower section**
8. **Bolt**
   - Tighten to 45 Nm (33 ft-lb)
9. **Right engine bracket**
10. **Toothed belt guard, upper section**
11. **Toothed belt**
    - Mark engine direction of rotation before removing
    - Check for wear
    - Do not kink

(continued on following page)

12. Idler wheel

13. Bolt
- Always replace
- Tighten to 20 Nm (15 ft-lb) + ¼ turn (90°)

14. Bolt
- Tighten to 20 Nm (15 ft-lb)

15. Bolt
- Tighten to 20 Nm (15 ft-lb)
- To loosen and tighten bolt, counter-hold using 3036

16. Bolt
- Tighten to 45 Nm (33 ft-lb)
- To loosen and tighten bolt, counter-hold using 3036

17. Camshaft sprocket
- Release from camshaft using two-arm puller

18. Tensioning roller
- Semi-automatic toothed belt tensioning roller

19. Idler wheel

20. Injection pump sprocket
- Two piece construction

21. Bolt
- Tighten to 30 Nm (22 ft-lb)

22. Toothed belt guard, rear

23. Coolant pump

24. Idler wheel
- Remove before removing coolant pump

25. Crankshaft toothed belt sprocket

26. Bushing

27. Diesel injection pump

28. Assembly bracket
- For diesel injection pump, generator and power steering pump
- For vehicles with A/C

29. Bolt
- Tighten to 45 Nm (33 ft-lb)

Toothed belt for camshaft drive, removing

1. Remove the upper engine cover.
2. Remove the lower sound absorber panel (belly pan).
3. Remove ribbed V-belt and tensioner, see **0 Maintenance**.
4. Remove brake booster vacuum pump from the end of the cylinder head.
5. Remove upper toothed belt guard.
6. Remove cylinder head (valve) cover.
7. Remove connecting pipe between intercooler and intake hose, see **21 Turbocharger and Intercooler**.
8. Turn the engine to top dead center (TDC) for cylinder #1, as shown earlier, see Fig. 5. or Fig. 6. If engine and transmission are separated use alternate procedures shown below. See Fig. 15. or Fig. 16.

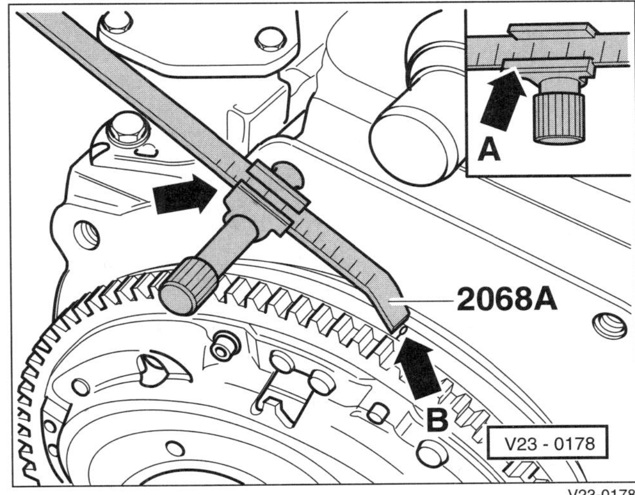

Fig. 15. Alternate procedure for setting TDC for manual transmissions. Install Volkswagen special tool 2068A as shown. Set adjustment to 96 mm (**arrow A,** inset) and align with TDC mark on flywheel (**arrow B**).

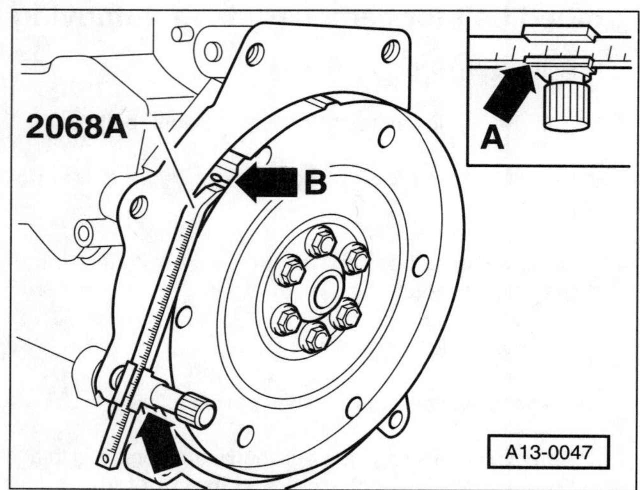

A13-0047

Fig. 16. Alternate procedure for setting TDC for automatic transmissions. Install Volkswagen special tool 2068A as shown. Set adjustment to 30 mm (**arrow A**) and align with TDC mark on driveplate (**arrow B**).

9. Lock camshaft with the setting bar and shim between the gasket surface and both sides of Volkswagen special tool 3418 with equal thickness of feeler gauges. This will insure that the camshaft is at actual TDC. See Fig. 17.

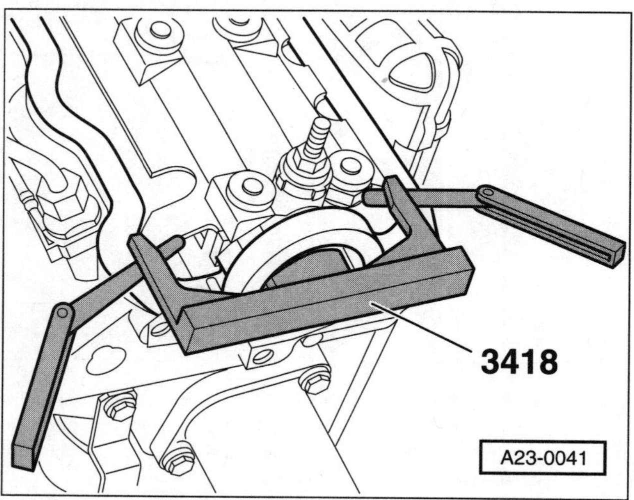

A23-0041

Fig. 17. Lock camshaft with setting bar (VW special tool 3418) and shim between the gasket surface and both sides of setting bar with equal thickness of feeler gauges.

10. Lock the injection pump sprocket with an appropriate locking tool and loosen injection pump sprocket mounting bolts. See Fig. 18.

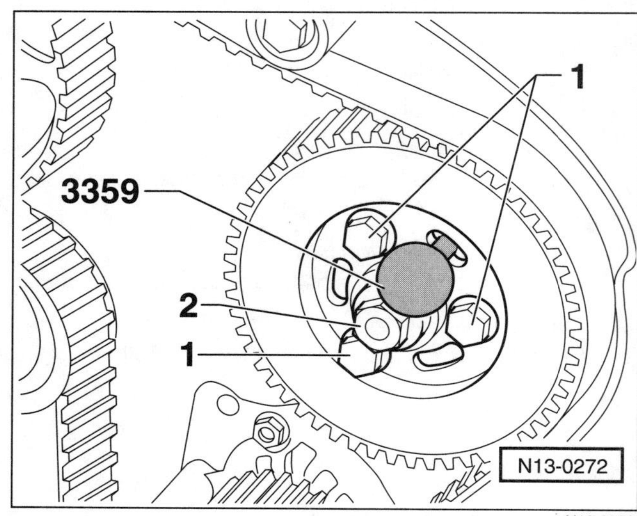

N13-0272

Fig. 18. Volkswagen special tool 3359 installed in injection pump sprocket locking it. Loosen bolts (**1**) only. Do not loosen hub bolt (**2**).

> ***CAUTION —***
> *Do not loosen or remove the hub from the Diesel injection pump. The hub is pressed onto the tapered end of the camshaft and NOT keyed to the pump drive shaft! If removed, it will no longer be correctly indexed to the pump. Correct indexing requires special equipment and training available only at specialized Bosch service centers and is beyond the scope of this manual.*

11. Loosen tensioner for toothed belt.

12. Support the engine with a suitable fixture that is designed to support the weight of the engine and transmission without damaging the body. See Fig. 19.

13. Lift the supporting device slightly, so that the weight of the engine and transmission is on the supporting device.

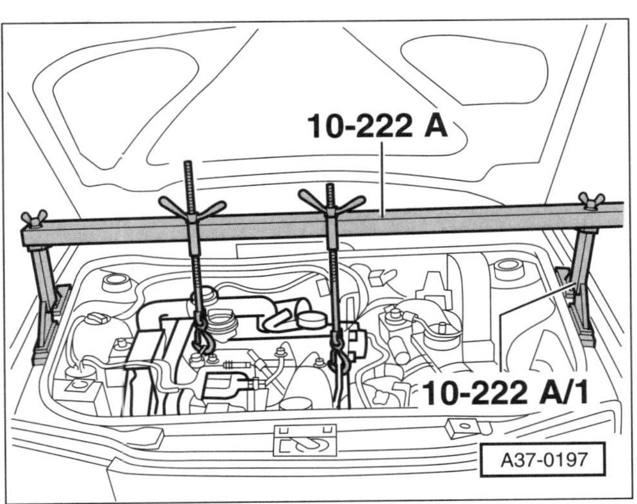

Fig. 19. Volkswagen supplied engine support tools shown attached to the engine.

14. Remove coolant expansion tank (coolant hoses remain attached).

15. Remove power steering fluid reservoir (hoses remain attached).

16. Remove the vibration dampener/belt pulley from the crankshaft.

17. Remove the center and lower toothed belt guards.

18. Unbolt the right side engine mount from the body and the engine support bracket and remove the mount. See Fig. 20.

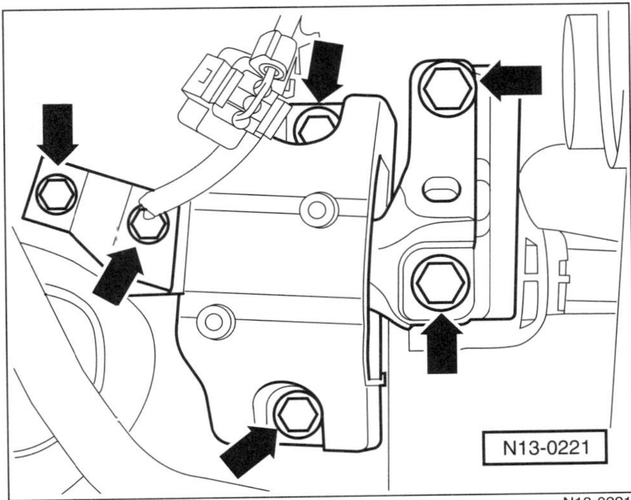

Fig. 20. Remove the bolts (**arrows**) securing the right side engine mount to the body and the engine support bracket.

19. Remove the right side engine support bracket. See Fig. 21.

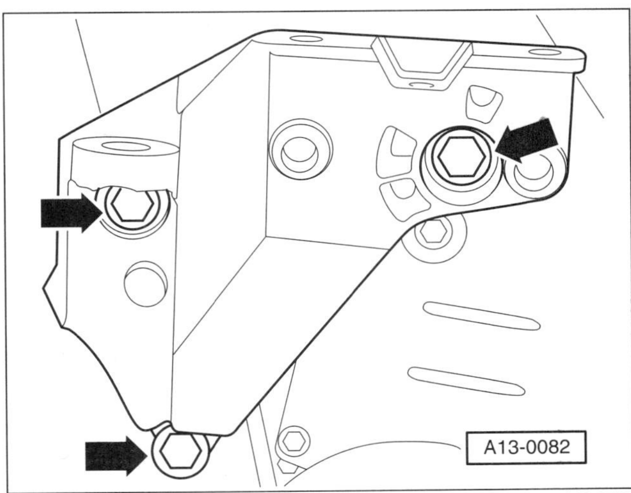

Fig. 21. Remove bolts (**arrows**) for engine mount bracket.

20. Mark the running direction of the toothed belt.

21. Release belt tensioner and remove toothed belt.

Toothed belt for camshaft drive, installing

1. Ensure that the engine is at Top Dead Center (TDC) for cylinder #1. See Fig. 4. or Fig. 5.
   If engine and transmission are separated use alternate procedure to set TDC. See Fig. 15. or Fig. 16.

2. If not previously removed, loosen camshaft sprocket mounting bolt about ½ turn. Hold camshaft sprocket using counter-holding tool. See Fig. 22.

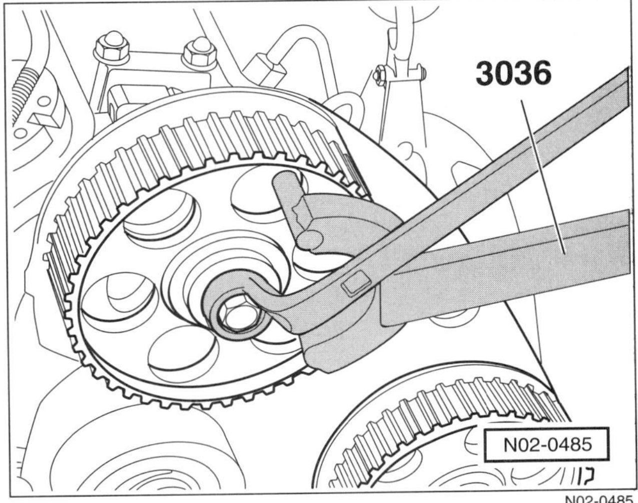

Fig. 22. VW special tool 3036 being used to counter-hold camshaft sprocket while loosening mounting bolt.

3. If not previously removed, remove camshaft sprocket as described earlier with two-arm puller. See Fig. 8.

4. Install new mounting bolts into diesel injection pump sprocket, but do not torque at this time.

5. Install toothed belt (noting directional mark if re-using old belt) on crankshaft toothed belt sprocket, idler wheels, injection pump sprocket and coolant pump.

6. When the belt is properly positioned, slip the camshaft sprocket into the toothed belt and slide onto the camshaft. Install the securing bolt only enough to hold the sprocket in place.

7. Ensure that tab on rear of tensioning roller is positioned into oil galley hole. See Fig. 23.

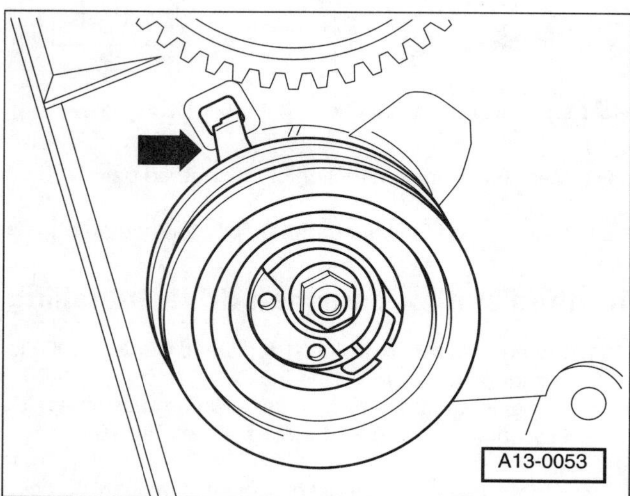

A13-0053

Fig. 23. Positioning tab shown in proper location in oil galley plug (**arrow**).

8. For manual transmission vehicles, tension the toothed belt using a two pin spanner in the holes in the eccentric center section. Belt is tensioned properly when notch and the raised mark are aligned. See Fig. 24.

9. For automatic transmission vehicles, tension the toothed belt using an allen wrench in the eccentric center section. Belt is tensioned properly when notch and raised mark are aligned. See Fig. 25.

NOTE —

If adjusting cam is turned too far and correct tension is exceeded, tension must be fully released, then readjusted.

10. Tighten the lock nut on the toothed belt tensioner.

Tightening torque

- Toothed belt tensioner (M8) . . . . 20 Nm (15 ft-lb)

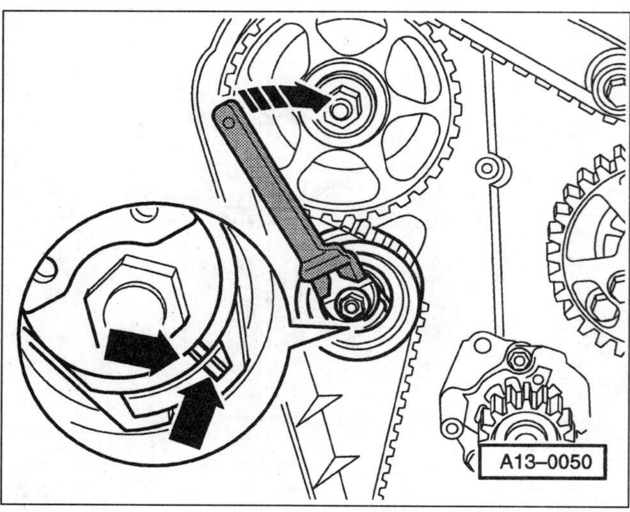

A13-0050

Fig. 24. Two pin spanner wrench shown in position to tension toothed belt on vehicles with manual transmission. Adjustment is correct when notch and raised mark align (**inset arrows**).

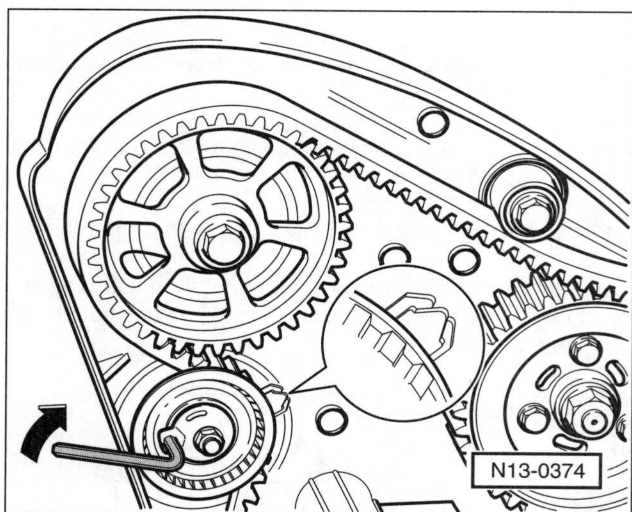

N13-0374

Fig. 25. Allen wrench shown in position to tension toothed belt on vehicles with automatic transmission. Adjustment is correct when notch and pointer align (**inset**).

11. Check toothed belt tensioner by pushing belt with thumb pressure. Tensioner should spring back to original position.

12. Ensure that crankshaft is still at TDC.

13. Tighten camshaft sprocket mounting bolt and remove setting bar and feeler gauges.

Tightening torque

- Camshaft sprocket to camshaft . . . . . 45 Nm (33 ft-lb)

14. Tighten the new injection pump sprocket mounting bolts to stage I only and remove the locking pin.

NOTE —
The injection pump sprocket mounting bolts should only be used one time, since by design they have a reduced shank and are stretch bolts.

15. Turn crankshaft two rotations in the running direction and recheck toothed belt tension.

16. Dynamically check diesel injection pump timing, see **23 Fuel Injection–Diesel (ALH Engine)**. If engine is removed, diesel pump injection timing must be checked and adjusted after engine has been installed.

17. Return engine to TDC for cylinder #1. Install locking pin tool 3359 and tighten injection pump sprocket mounting bolts to final torque (stage II).

Tightening torque
- Injection pump sprocket - always replace
  stage I . . . . 20 Nm (15 ft-lb)
  stage II . . . . additional ¼ turn (90°)

18. Install the center and lower toothed belt guards.

19. Install the vibration dampener/ribbed belt pulley onto the crankshaft.

Tightening torque
- Vibration dampener/ribbed belt pulley to toothed belt drive sprocket (M8) . . . . 25 Nm (18 ft-lb)

20. Insert bolts into right side engine mount bracket and attach bracket to block.

Tightening torque
- Right side engine mount bracket to cylinder block (M10) . . . . 45 Nm (33 ft-lb)

21. Install right side engine mount with new stretch bolts. See Fig. 26.

22. Remove the engine support device.

23. Install coolant expansion tank and power steering reservoir.

Tightening torque
- Coolant expansion tank to body. . . . . . 10 Nm (7 ft-lb)
- Power steering reservoir to bracket . . . 10 Nm (7 ft-lb)

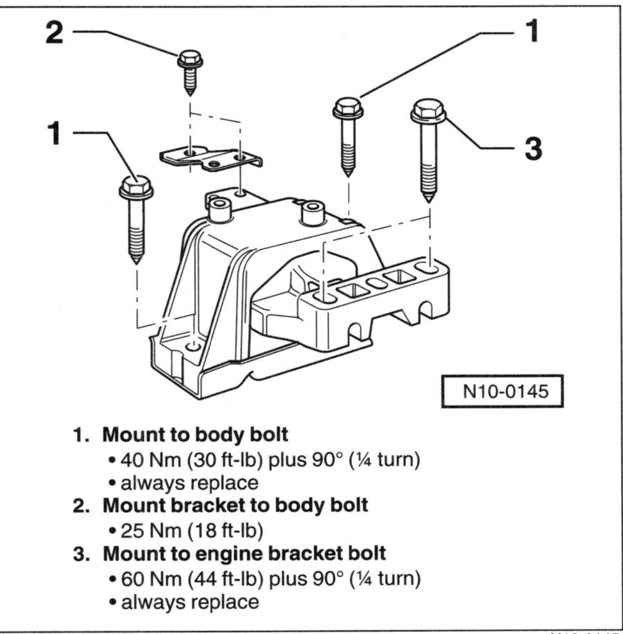

1. **Mount to body bolt**
   - 40 Nm (30 ft-lb) plus 90° (¼ turn)
   - always replace
2. **Mount bracket to body bolt**
   - 25 Nm (18 ft-lb)
3. **Mount to engine bracket bolt**
   - 60 Nm (44 ft-lb) plus 90° (¼ turn)
   - always replace

N10-0145

Fig. 26. Right side engine mount.

24. Install the brake booster vacuum pump and cylinder head (valve) cover.

Tightening torque
- Vacuum pump to cylinder head . . . . . 20 Nm (15 ft-lb)
- Valve cover to cylinder head. . . . . 10 Nm (7 ft-lb)

25. Install ribbed V-belt and tensioner.

Tightening torque
- Ribbed V-belt tensioner (M8) . . . . 25 Nm (18 ft-lb)

26. Install the connecting pipe between the intercooler and the turbocharger and between the intercooler and the intake hose.

27. Install upper toothed belt guard.

28. Start engine and re-check diesel injection pump timing, see **23 Fuel Injection–Diesel (ALH Engine)**.

29. Install lower sound absorber panel (belly pan).

30. Install upper engine cover.

31. Be sure to quality check your work, see **Quality Review** at the end of this repair group.

CYLINDER HEAD, REMOVING AND INSTALLING

The cylinder head can be removed and installed with the engine in the vehicle. Fig. 4, given earlier shows a view of the ALH cylinder head and related components. Note that the cylinder head bolts are stretch type fasteners and should never be reused. In addition, whenever the cylinder head or the cylinder head gasket is replaced, the coolant must also be replaced, see **19 Engine–Cooling System**.

Cylinder head, removing

The cylinder head will be removed with the exhaust manifold, turbo-charger and the intake manifold still attached. The plenum close-out panel at the base of the windshield will be removed to allow easier access to the cylinder head and provide space needed for an engine support.

> ***WARNING —***
> *Do not start work on a hot engine. Allow to cool sufficiently before proceeding. Engine temperature must be no hotter than warm to the touch. Cylinder head warpage can result due to uneven cooling rates.*

NOTE —
Disconnecting the battery cables will erase fault codes and basic settings in the engine management and automatic transmission control unit memories. Some driveability problems may be noticeable until the system re-adapts to operating conditions. OBD II readiness codes, which may be required for emissions testing, may also be erased. See **23 Fuel Injection – Diesel (ALH)** *for additional information. In some instances proper diagnosis will require the use of a scan tool such as the Volkswagen supplied VAG 1551 or 1552. Use and operation of this tool is outside the scope of this repair manual.*

1. With ignition switched off, disconnect the battery negative terminal from the battery.

NOTE —
Be sure to have the anti-theft radio code on hand before disconnecting the battery.

2. Position crankshaft so that pistons are NOT at TDC.
3. Remove upper engine cover.
4. Remove air cleaner assembly and connecting pipe.
5. Remove connecting pipe and hose between the intercooler and intake manifold/EGR solenoid.
6. Remove connecting pipe and hoses between turbocharger and intercooler.
7. Remove lower sound absorber panel (belly pan).
8. Drain engine coolant, see **19 Engine–Cooling System**.
9. Disconnect and label fuel supply and return lines at the fuel filter. See Fig. 27.

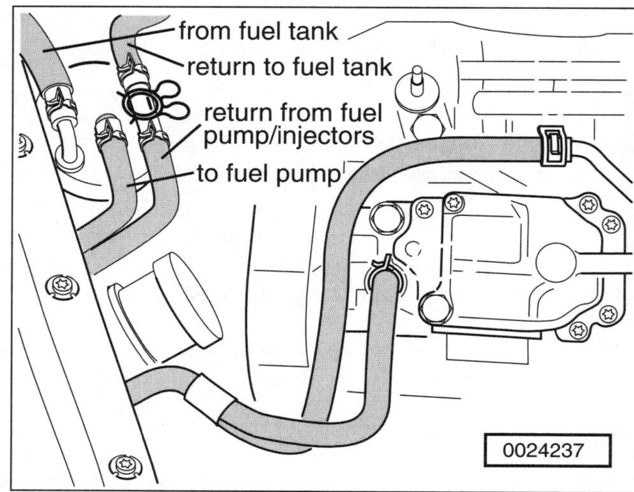

0024237

Fig. 27. Disconnect and label fuel lines at fuel the filter.

> ***WARNING —***
> *Fuel will be expelled when disconnecting fuel hoses. Wrap a cloth around the fuel line fittings before disconnecting them. Do not smoke or work near heaters or other fire hazards. Have a fire extinguisher handy.*

10. Seal off disconnected fuel and vacuum lines to prevent contamination.
11. Remove the fuel filter and bracket.
12. Unbolt front exhaust pipe from the turbo-charger, see **26 Exhaust System and Emission Controls.**

13. Remove the ribbed V-belt and tensioner.
14. Remove both wiper arms and plenum close-out panel at base of windshield, see **92 Wipers and Washers**.
15. Remove the coolant flange from the end of the cylinder head and disconnect the coolant hoses from the EGR cooler.
16. Disconnect breather and vacuum hoses from cylinder head.
17. Disconnect all electrical connectors from cylinder head including the glow plug bus connector.
18. Remove upper toothed belt guard.
19. Remove cylinder head (valve) cover.
20. Remove brake booster vacuum pump.
21. Disconnect oil return line at turbo-charger, see **21 Turbocharger and Intercooler**.
22. Disconnect turbo-charger oil supply line and support bracket.
23. Remove metal fuel injector lines.
    - Remove all four lines together as a set.
    - Use an offset flare nut wrench such as Volkswagen special tool 3035 to loosen the fittings of the injector lines.
    - Take care not to bend the lines or change the shape.
24. Remove the small injector fuel return hoses.
25. Position engine to TDC for cylinder #1 and install setting bar as shown earlier. See Fig. 6.
26. Loosen camshaft sprocket as shown earlier and slip the toothed belt off of the camshaft sprocket. See Fig. 7.
27. Remove toothed belt tensioning roller and camshaft sprocket as shown earlier.
28. Remove upper bolt from rear toothed belt guard.
29. Loosen the socket head bolts slightly in sequence but do not remove until all 10 bolts have been loosened. Discard the head bolts. See Fig. 28.

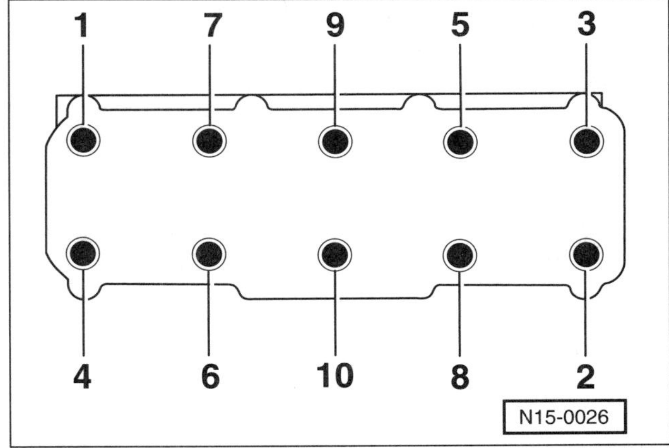

N15-0026

Fig. 28. Loosen the cylinder head bolts in the order shown. Loosen all bolts slightly the first time around, repeat the order, finish loosening and then remove.

30. Carefully lift off cylinder head and place in a clean area. If the head is stuck, use a soft-faced mallet or pry gently with a wooden stick.

> ***CAUTION —***
> *Some of the valves will be open. Use extra care when removing and handling to avoid damage. Place the cylinder head on the bench or table so that the weight of the cylinder head will not rest on the valves.*

Cylinder head, installing

Before proceeding with the installation of the cylinder head, whether an original or a new unit, observe the following important points:

- Check the cylinder head and block for distortion and warpage, see **Cylinder Head Components**, given later in this section.
- Carefully clean the cylinder block and cylinder head sealing surfaces being sure to avoid scratching them during the cleaning process. Do not use metal scrapers or wire brushes.
- When using abrasive paper do not use any grades coarser than 100 grit (such as 80 grit). Lower numbers are coarser.
- If the cylinder head will not be reinstalled immediately, take precautions to prevent rust from forming on the cylinder block walls and gasket sealing surfaces.
- When cleaning the old gasket material off of the cylinder block, take precautions to keep the old gasket material and the used abrasive particles and dirt out of the cooling and oiling system passages. Place a clean shop cloth over the cylinders to prevent contamination from getting between the cylinder wall and the piston.
- Do not take the new cylinder head gasket out of the packaging until ready to use. Handle the new gasket with extreme care as any damage will lead to leaks.
- There MUST NOT BE any oil or coolant in the head bolt holes in the cylinder block. Any fluids in the holes creates the danger of hydrolock while torquing which could lead to structural damage of the cylinder block. Use thread chasers to remove foreign material as required. Be sure that all 10 bolt holes are clean and dry.
- When all traces of the old gasket material have been removed from the cylinder block and head, carefully remove all traces of metal particles, abrasives and lint. All gasket sealing surfaces and bolt holes must be clean and dry to ensure a proper seal.
- Always use a new cylinder head gasket.
- Do not use any gasket sealer on the new cylinder head gasket.
- If installing a Volkswagen supplied replacement cylinder head, be sure to inspect for and remove any plastic packaging materials used to protect the head and the open valves.

1. Position the crankshaft to TDC for cylinder #1 and then turn backwards until all pistons are equally spaced below TDC.

2. Install pins from installation tool into bolt holes of cylinder block. Use of this tool allows for quick and easy alignment of the head on the block. This keeps the head from sliding off of the block and prevents damage to the head gasket. See Fig. 29.

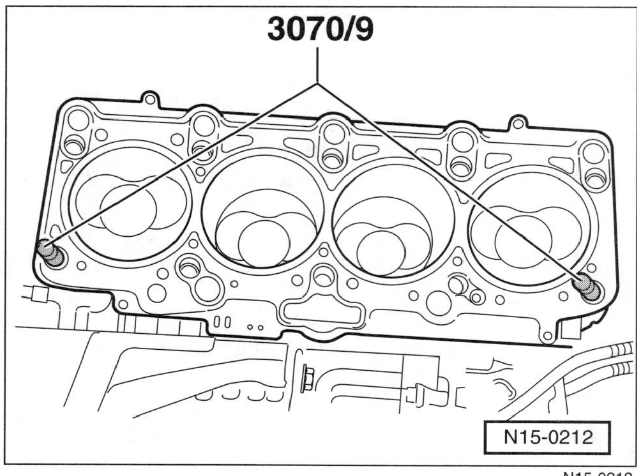

N15-0212

Fig. 29. Volkswagen supplied installation tool for assembly of cylinder head onto the block.

3. Install the new cylinder head gasket onto the block with the numbers and letters facing up. Be sure that none of the wiring or any vacuum hoses are caught between the cylinder head and the block.

4. Carefully install the cylinder head onto the block over the alignment pins and screw in 8 of the new head bolts. Tighten the bolts hand-tight only.

5. Remove the alignment pins from the bolt holes with the tool and install the remaining 2 new head bolts. Tighten these bolts hand-tight.

6. Tighten the 10 cylinder head bolts in three stages following the tightening order. See Fig. 30.

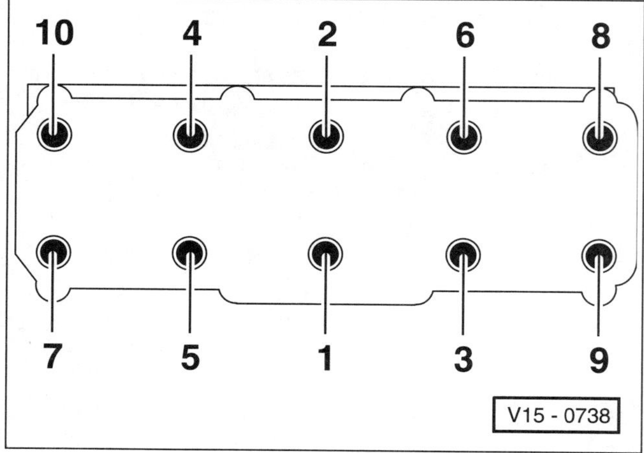

V15-0738

Fig. 30. Tighten the cylinder head bolts in the order shown. The same pattern is used for all four stages of the sequence

Tightening torque

- Cylinder head to cylinder block, engine code ALH (stretch bolt - always replace)
  - stage I . . . . 40 Nm (30 ft-lb)
  - stage II . . . . 60 Nm (44 ft-lb)
  - stage III . . . . additional ¼ turn (90°)
  - stage IV . . . . additional ¼ turn (90°)

7. Ensure that setting bar remains in place on the end of the camshaft as shown earlier. See Fig. 6.

8. Attach the available support hook from the engine support fixture tool to the lifting eye on the cylinder head. Slightly lift this support hook to relieve the tension on the other support hook and remove it along with the adapter.

9. Install upper bolt for the rear toothed belt guard where it is attached to the cylinder head.

10. Position crankshaft at TDC for cylinder #1 by carefully turning in the normal running direction.

11. Install toothed belt, sprocket and tensioner, see **Toothed belt for camshaft drive, installing**, given earlier.

12. Install brake booster vacuum pump.

13. Install cylinder head (valve) cover.

14. Install bolts into right side engine support bracket and attach bracket to block.

15. Install engine mount with new stretch bolts, see **10 Engine–Removing and Installing**.

16. Relieve tension on the engine support bracket hook and remove the fixture.

17. Install metal fuel injector lines and small fuel return hoses.

18. Connect turbo-charger oil lines.

19. Attach front exhaust pipe to the turbo-charger with new nuts.

20. Install lower sound absorber panel (belly pan).

21. Install upper toothed belt guard.

22. Install ribbed V-belt and tensioner.

23. Install plenum close-out panel and the wiper arms.

24. Install coolant flange and hoses to the cylinder head.

25. Install coolant reservoir and refill the cooling system with fresh coolant of the appropriate ratio. See **19 Engine–Cooling System**.

CAUTION —

- *Use only Volkswagen original anti-freeze when filling the cooling system. Use of any other anti-freeze may be harmful to the cooling system. Do not use an anti-freeze containing phosphates.*
- *Do not use tap water in cooling system. Use distilled water only to mix anti-freeze.*

26. Install fuel filter, bracket and fuel hoses.

27. Install breather and vacuum hoses.

28. Install all electrical connectors including glow plug bus.

29. Install connecting pipes between the intercooler, turbo-charger and intake manifold.

30. Install air cleaner assembly and connecting pipe.

31. Install upper sound absorber panel.

32. Reconnect the battery only after all parts have been re-installed and reconnected.

33. Start engine and re-check diesel injection pump timing, see **23 Fuel Injection–Diesel (ALH Engine)**.

34. Be sure to quality check your work, see **Quality Review** at the end of this repair group.

Tightening torques

- Cylinder head cover to cylinder head (M6) . . . . 10 Nm (89 in-lb)
- Cylinder head to cylinder block, engine code ALH (stretch bolt - always replace)
  - stage I . . . . 40 Nm (30 ft-lb)
  - stage II . . . . 60 Nm (44 ft-lb)
  - stage III . . . . additional ¼ turn (90°)
  - stage IV . . . . additional ¼ turn (90°)
- Front exhaust pipe to exhaust manifold (special nuts - always replace)(M8) . . 25 Nm (18 ft-lb)
- Coolant outlet flange to cylinder head (M6) . . . . 10 Nm (7 ft-lb)
- Rear toothed belt guard to cylinder head (M6) . . . . 10 Nm (7 ft-lb)
- Ribbed belt tensioner to bracket (M8) 25 Nm (18 ft-lb)
- Toothed belt tensioner (M8) . . . . 20 Nm (15 ft-lb)
- Fuel injector line flare nut . . . . 25 Nm (18 ft-lb)
- Vacuum pump to cylinder head . . . . . 20 Nm (15 ft-lb)
- Camshaft sprocket to camshaft . . . . . 45 Nm (33 ft-lb)
- Right side engine mount bracket to cylinder block (M10) . . . . 45 Nm (33 ft-lb)

CYLINDER HEAD COMPONENTS

This section provides the specifications and special information necessary to repair the cylinder head that has been removed from the Volkswagen ALH engine. Special service tools and machine shop services are required for most cylinder head repair.

NOTE —

- *The information given under this heading assumes that the cylinder head is removed. For cylinder head removal procedures, see* **Cylinder head, removing** *given earlier.*
- *Fig. 2 and Fig. 3 show exploded views of the cylinder head and valvetrain assemblies.*

Cylinder Head and Camshaft

Check the cylinder head for warpage and distortion with an accurate straight edge and a feeler gauge. See Fig. 31. Resurfacing of the cylinder head is specifically not recommended by Volkswagen. Excessively warped or distorted cylinder heads must be replaced.

Specification

- Maximum cylinder head distortion/warpage . . . . 0.1 mm (0.004 in.)

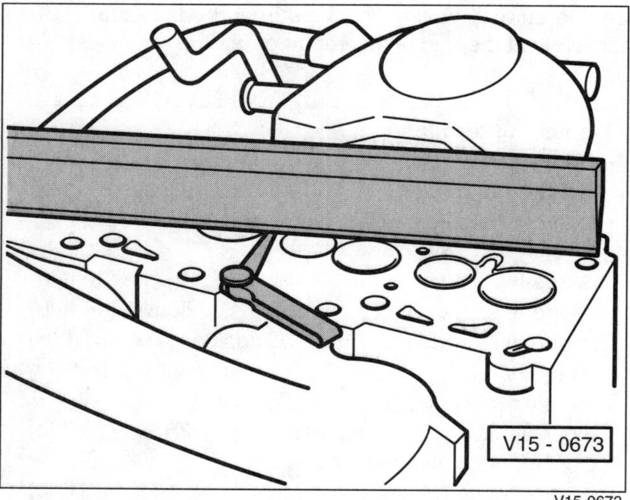

V15-0673

Fig. 31. Cylinder head being checked for distortion with a feeler gauge.

The camshaft for the ALH engines is easily identified by markings cast into it during manufacture. See Fig. 32.

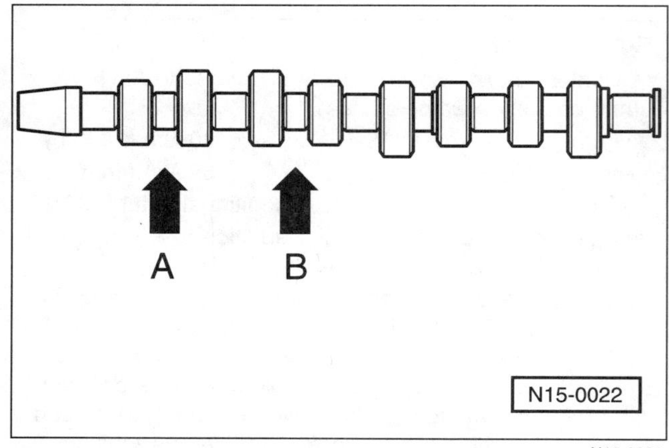

N15-0022

Fig. 32. Camshaft identification marks for ALH engines: **arrow a** identifier is -38K-, and **arrow B** identifier is -DE-.

Specification

- Valve timing at 1 mm valve lift, engine code ALH
  - Intake opens after TDC . . . . 16°
  - Intake closes after BDC. . . . . 25°
  - Exhaust opens before BDC. . . . . 28°
  - Exhaust closes before TDC. . . . . 19°

The in and out movement of the camshaft is known as axial play and is measured with the cam followers removed and only the first and last bearing caps installed.

A dial gauge is set up on the sprocket end of the camshaft and the camshaft clearance is checked by moving the camshaft as far as it can go in each direction. See Fig. 33.

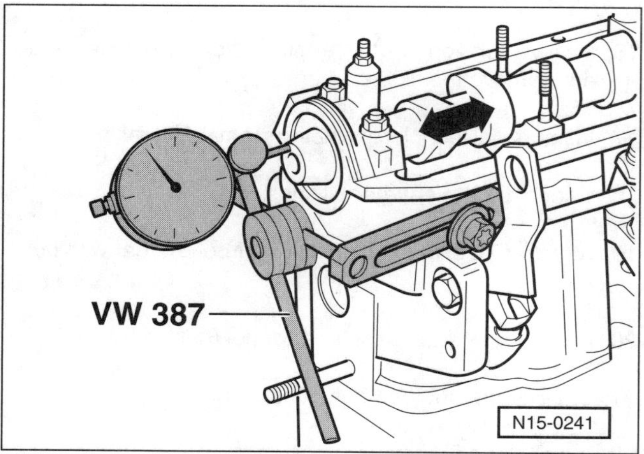

N15-0241

Fig. 33. Dial gauge set up on a camshaft to measure the axial play (**arrow**).

Specification

- Camshaft axial clearance . . . . 0.15 mm (0.006 in.)

Valves

Valves should not be re-worked on a machine. Only lapping by hand with valve compound is permitted. Valve dimensions listed in **Table a** apply to the valve shown in Fig. 34 which is representative of both intake and exhaust valves.

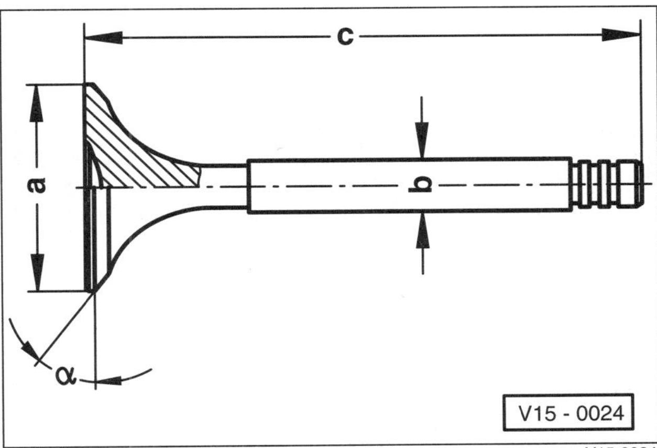

V15-0024

Fig. 34. Valve dimensions are referenced in **Table a**.

Table a. Valve Dimensions

Engine Code	ALH
Valve head diameter (**a**) intake exhaust	 35.95 mm (1.415 in.) 31.45 mm (1.238 in.)
Valve stem diameter (**b**) intake exhaust	 6.963 mm (0.274 in.) 6.943 mm (0.273 in.)
Valve length (**c**) intake exhaust	 96.85 mm (3.813 in.) 96.85 mm (3.813 in.)
Valve face angle (α) intake exhaust	 45° 45°

Valve guides

Special tools and a press are required to replace the valve guides. Check valve guide wear with a new valve. Always use an intake valve in an intake guide and an exhaust valve in an exhaust guide. See Fig. 35. Inspect the valve seats to ensure that the cylinder head can be reconditioned before installing new valve guides. Press out worn original valve guides with Volkswagen special driver tool 3121 from the camshaft side of the head. Replacement valve guides have a shoulder on the camshaft side to limit the installed depth and must be pressed out from the combustion chamber side.

When installing new valve guides, lubricate with clean engine oil and press in from the camshaft side down to the shoulder. The cylinder head must be cold for this operation. Once the shoulder of the valve guide contacts the cylinder head, do not allow the pressure on the guide to exceed 2000 psi (1 ton) otherwise the cylinder head or the guide will be damaged. When the guide has been replaced, ream it to the proper size and continue with the reworking of the valve seats.

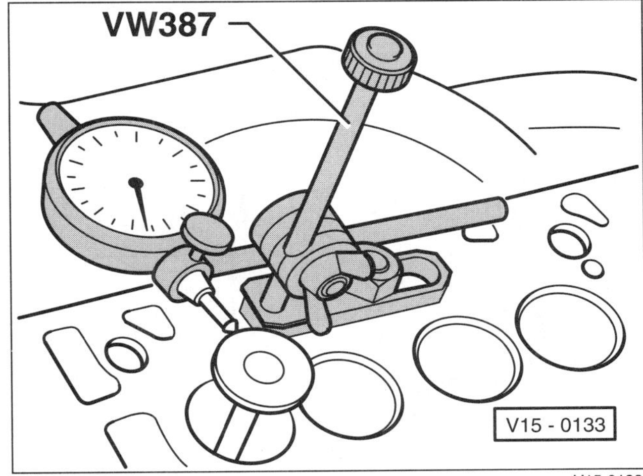

V15-0133

Fig. 35. Valve guide wear being checked with new valve. Insert valve until stem end is flush with end of guide. Rock valve back and forth to check total travel.

Specification

- Valve guide (wear limits-maximum play) with new valve
  intake and exhaust valve guide . . . 1.3 mm (0.051 in.)

> ***NOTE —***
> *Due to the close tolerances found in the valve guides, it is recommended that Volkswagen special tool 3121 be used for removal and installation and special tool 3120 be used to ream the valve guide to size. Be sure to use the appropriate cutting fluid during the reaming operation.*

Valve seats

When resurfacing valve seats, there is a limit to the amount of material that can be removed to bring the seat back into specification. If too much material is removed, the final assembly will leave too little space for the hydraulic cam follower to function properly. The maximum refacing dimension, that is, the maximum amount of material that can be removed from the valve seat, is calculated from the measurement shown in Fig. 36.

Measure dimension **a** in Fig. 36, and subtract the minimum dimension, as given in **Table b**. The difference is the maximum amount of material that can be removed from the valve seat.

Table b. Minimum Dimensions for Calculating Valve Seat Refacing Dimensions

Engine Code	Intake	Exhaust
ALH	35.8 mm (1.409 in.)	36.1 mm (1.421 in.)

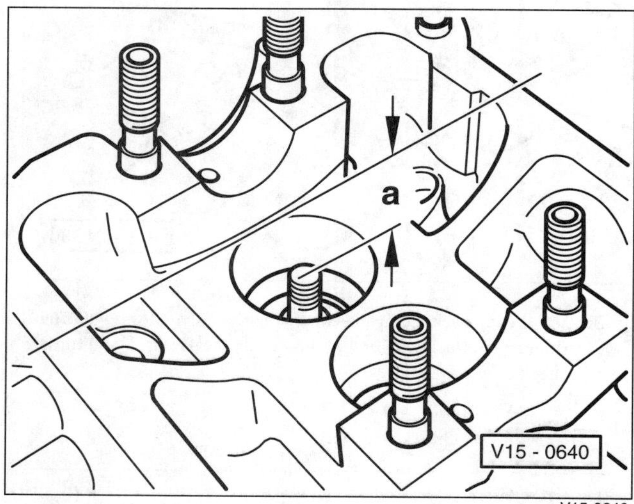

V15-0640

Fig. 36. Dimension (**a**), distance between top of valve stem and gasket surface of cylinder head, is used to calculate maximum valve seat refacing dimensions.

NOTE —
Use care when reworking the exhaust valve seats to avoid changing the shape of the port. The 30° lower valve seat chamfer is necessary to ensure that the intake channel flow characteristics are maintained.

Table c. Valve Seat Dimensions

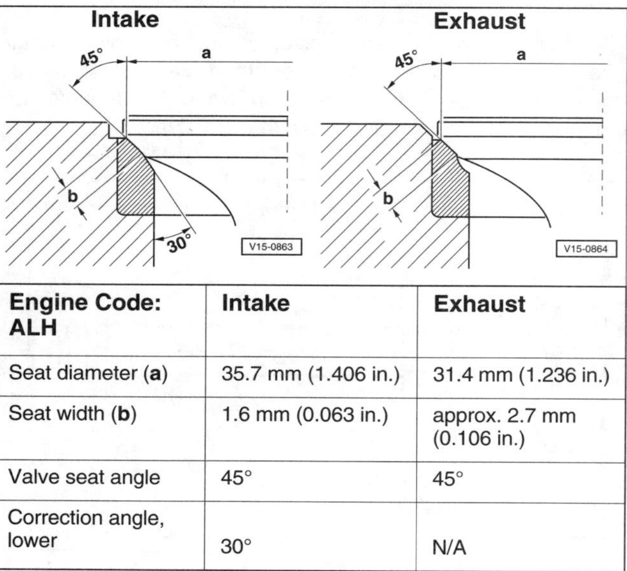

Engine Code: ALH	Intake	Exhaust
Seat diameter (**a**)	35.7 mm (1.406 in.)	31.4 mm (1.236 in.)
Seat width (**b**)	1.6 mm (0.063 in.)	approx. 2.7 mm (0.106 in.)
Valve seat angle	45°	45°
Correction angle, lower	30°	N/A

QUALITY REVIEW

When you have finished working under the hood and around other areas of the vehicle it is advisable to take a moment to quality check or review your work. This helps to ensure that the operation or repair has been completed properly with all affected systems functioning within normal parameters. This may include the following:

- Make sure that the radiator fan cycles properly and that the coolant level and concentration are correct.
- Ensure that all cable ties and hose clamps that were removed as part of the repair are replaced.
- Clean off any diesel fuel that may have spilled onto rubber hoses and belts. It will cause deterioration.
- Check and adjust all other applicable fluid levels.
- Make sure that there are no fluid leaks.
- Make sure that there are no air, vacuum or exhaust leaks.
- Make sure that all components involved in the repair are positioned correctly and function properly.
- Male sure all tools, shop cloths, fender covers, and protective tape are removed.
- Clean grease from painted surfaces and steering wheel.
- Unlock the anti-theft radio and reset the clock.

In addition to the above noted points, the ECM and TCM may need to be checked using the Volkswagen supplied VAG 1551 or 1552 scan tool as mentioned at the start of this repair.

15c Cylinder Head and Valvetrain (2.0L Engine)

GENERAL

This section covers cylinder head and valvetrain service and repair work for the 4-cylinder, 2 valve per cylinder, 2.0 liter gasoline engine. For information on short block engine rebuilding and internal engine specifications, see **13a Crankshaft/Cylinder Block (4-cylinder)**.

Most of the operations described in this repair group require special equipment and experience. If you lack the skills, tools, or a suitable workplace for servicing or repairing the cylinder head, we suggest that you leave these repairs to an authorized Volkswagen dealer or other qualified shop.

Engine Codes
- AEG, AVH, AZG. . . . . 2.0L 4-cylinder gasoline

DIAGNOSTIC TESTING

The tests that follow can be used to help isolate engine problems, to better understand a problem before starting expensive and extensive repairs, or to just periodically check engine condition.

Compression test

A compression test will tell a lot about the overall condition of the engine without the need for taking it apart. Testing is relatively simple and straightforward.

1. Remove two plastic caps and retaining nuts on upper sound absorber panel. Loosen the rear retaining nut slightly. Remove dipstick and lift cover up slightly and pull forward. See Fig. 1.

Fig. 1. Remove dipstick and nuts (**arrows**) to remove engine cover.

2. Replace dipstick and warm-up the engine until it is a minimum of 30°C (86°F).

3. Disconnect spark plug wires from the spark plugs by gently pulling on the boot, do not pull on the wire. Label all wires to avoid confusion during reinstallation.

4. Use compressed air to clear the area around the spark plugs. Remove all spark plugs and lay aside in proper order.

5. Disable ignition system by unplugging 4-pin harness connector from ignition coil power output stage. See Fig. 2.

Fig. 2. Disconnect 4-pin harness connector (**arrow**) for ignition coil power output stage. Secondary air pump removed for clarity. AEG shown, AVH and AZG are similar.

> ***CAUTION —***
> *Failure to disable the ignition system during testing can result in damage to the Motronic ECM or the ignition power output stage due to the high voltage developed in the ignition coil.*

6. Remove fuse 32 for fuel injectors.

7. Fit the compression tester into the spark plug hole.

8. Have a helper:

- depress clutch pedal fully
- put the transmission in neutral or park
- depress the accelerator pedal to the floor
- crank the engine over with the starter motor

NOTE —
Cranking the engine with the ignition system disabled and components disconnected may cause Diagnostic trouble codes (DTCs) to be stored in engine management system memory.

9. Engine should be cranked a minimum of 4 to 5 revolutions.

10. Record readings, release pressure in the gauge and repeat procedure for each cylinder.

11. Compare readings to specification.

Specification
- Compression pressures (2.0L engine)
  - new . . . . 10 to 13 bar (147 - 191 psi)
  - wear limit . . . . .7.5 bar (110 psi)
  - maximum difference between cylinders . . . . 3 bar (44 psi)

When all cylinders have been checked, reinstall spark plugs and wires, connect harness connector for ignition coil power output stage and install the upper engine cover.

Tightening torque
- Spark plug to cylinder head . . . . 30 Nm (22 ft-lb)

Cylinder leakdown test

The most conclusive diagnosis of low compression symptoms requires a cylinder leak-down test. Using a special tester and a supply of compressed air, each cylinder is pressurized. The rate at which the air leaks out of the cylinder, as well as the sound and location of the escaping air can more accurately pinpoint the magnitude and source of the leakage. Any engine compression diagnosis that will require major disassembly should first be confirmed by a cylinder leak-down test. Because this test requires special equipment and experience, it may be desirable to have it performed by a Volkswagen dealer or other qualified repair shop.

CYLINDER HEAD SERVICE

Many cylinder head repairs can be accomplished without removing the cylinder head from the engine. The cylinder head cover (valve cover) gasket, the camshaft, the camshaft oil seal, the valve guide oil seals, the valve springs, and the camshaft followers are all accessible with the cylinder head installed. This heading describes those repairs that can be done with the cylinder head installed.

Fig. 3 shows an exploded view of the internal cylinder head components and Fig. 4 shows the external cylinder head components.

Internal cylinder head assembly

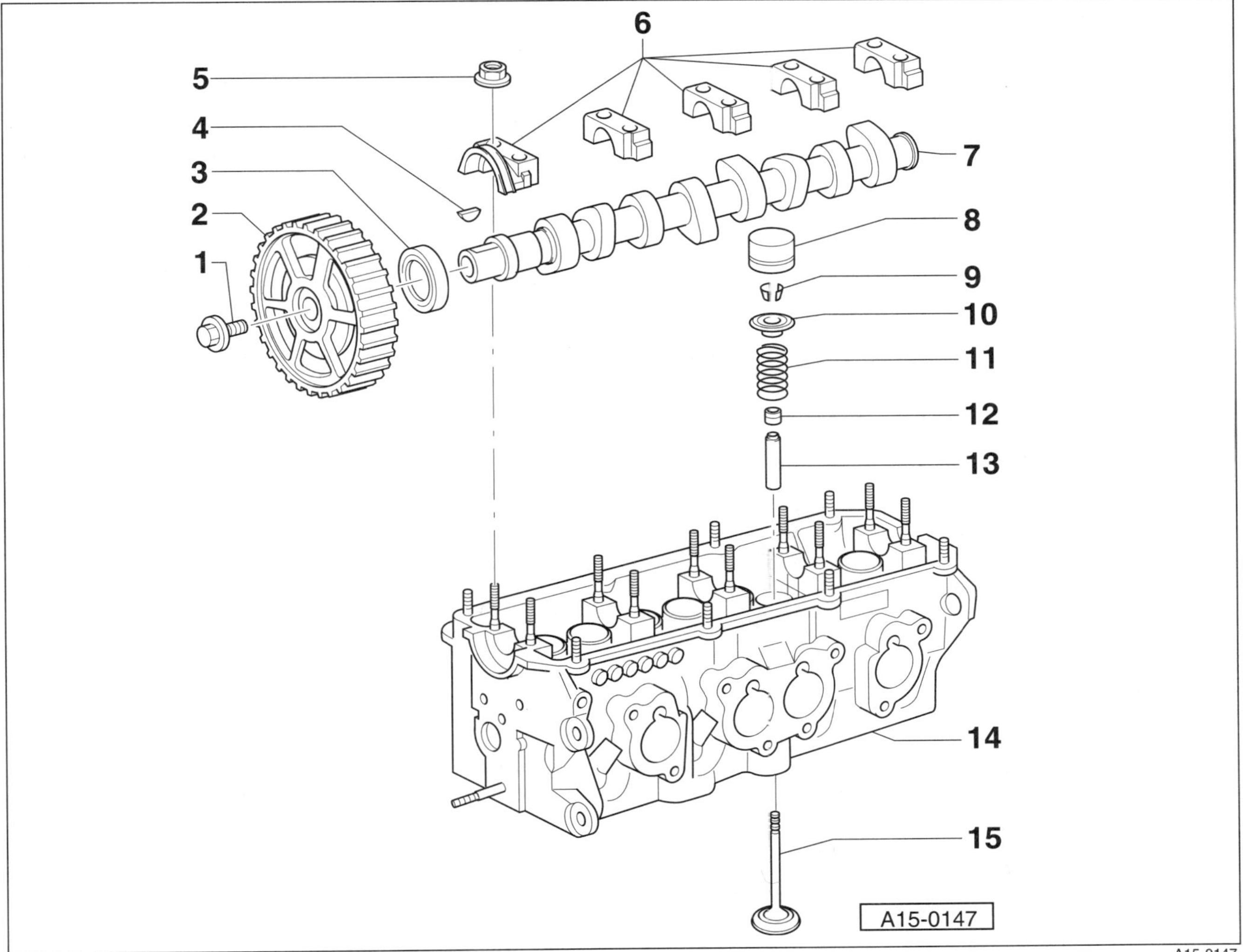

Fig. 3. Exploded view of internal cylinder head components.

1. **Camshaft sprocket bolt**
   - Tighten to 100 Nm (74 ft-lb)
   - Use 3415 counterholder to loosen and tighten
2. **Camshaft sprocket**
3. **Oil seal**
4. **Woodruff key**
   - Ensure tight fit
5. **Bearing cap nut**
   - Tighten to 20 Nm (15 ft-lb)
6. **Bearing cap**
   - Lightly coat bearing cap 1 cylinder head mating surface with VW sealant (part # AVM 174 004 01)
7. **Camshaft**
   - Radial clearance, checking with plastigage Wear limit: 0.1 mm (.004 in.)
   - Run-out, wear limit: 0.05 mm (.002 in.)
8. **Hydraulic lifter**
   - Do not interchange
   - Equipped with hydraulic clearance compensation
   - Store with cam contact surface facing downwards
   - Oil contact surfaces
9. **Keepers**
10. **Valve spring retainer, upper**
11. **Valve spring**
12. **Valve stem seal**
13. **Valve guide**
    - Service version with collar
14. **Cylinder head**
15. **Intake and exhaust valves**
    - Do not rework! Only lapping is permitted

External cylinder head assembly

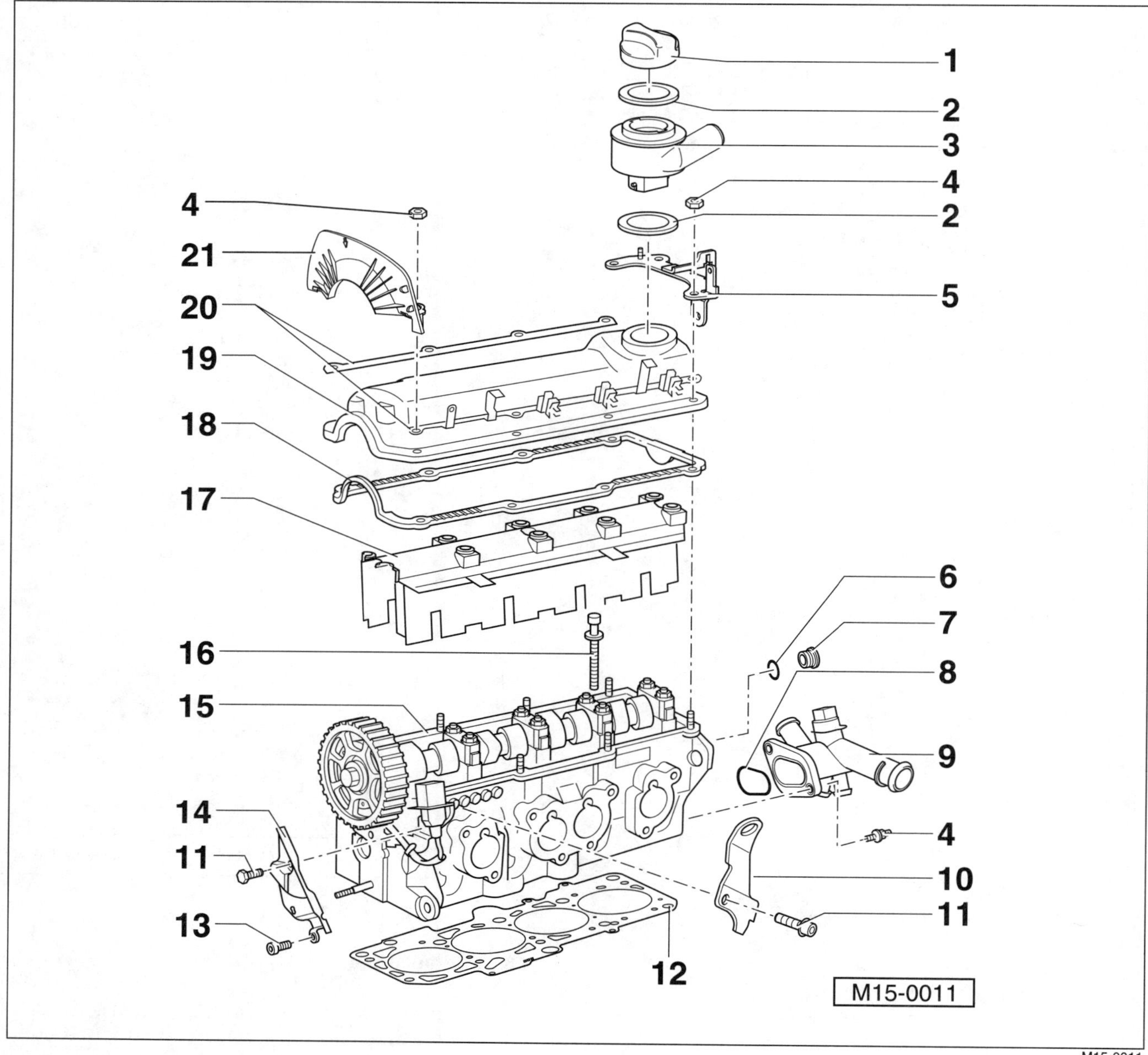

M15-0011

Fig. 4. Exploded view of external cylinder head components.

1. **Cap**
2. **Gasket**
3. **Vent housing**
   - Turn clockwise to remove
4. **Nut**
   - Tighten to 10 Nm (7 ft-lb)
5. **Bracket**
6. **Oil seal**
   - Always replace
7. **Sealing plug**
   - Tighten to 15 Nm (11 ft-lb)
   - Always replace
8. **O-ring**
   - Replace if damaged
9. **Coolant connection flange**
10. **Lifting eye**
11. **Bolt**
    - Tighten to 20 Nm (15 ft-lb)

12. Cylinder head gasket
- Always replace
- Replace engine coolant if replacing gasket

13. Bolt
- Tighten to 15 Nm (11 ft-lb)

14. Toothed belt guard, rear

15. Cylinder head
- Replace engine coolant if removing head

16. Cylinder head bolt
- Always replace

17. Oil deflector

18. Valve cover gasket
- Replace if damaged
- Before installing gasket coat bearing cap 1 cylinder head mating surface with VW sealant (part # AVM 174 004 01)

19. Valve cover

20. Reinforcing strip

21. Upper rear toothed belt (camshaft drive belt) guard

Cylinder head (valve) cover, removing and installing

1. Remove upper sound absorber panel and disconnect intake boot from throttle housing.
2. Disconnect accelerator cable from throttle body.
3. Disconnect all hoses and electrical connectors from upper intake manifold.
4. Remove bolts from warm air deflector plate on the back side of upper intake manifold. See Fig. 5.

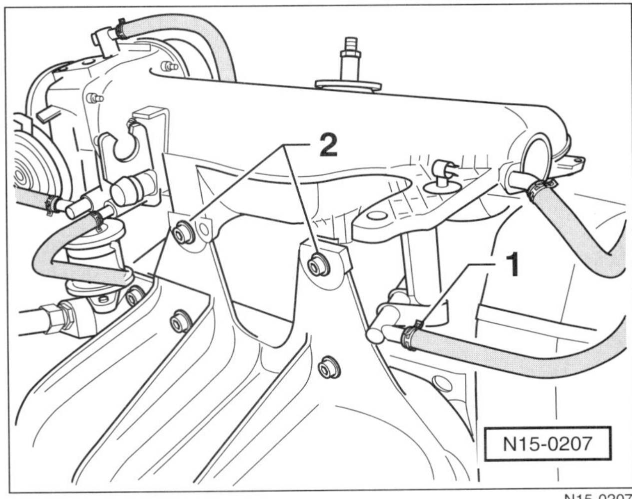

N15-0207

Fig. 5. Rear view of intake manifold showing vent line (**1**) and warm air deflector bolts (**2**).

5. Remove upper intake manifold bolts. Carefully separate upper manifold from lower manifold. Cover open intake runner openings in lower manifold with clean shop rags. See Fig. 6.

0024360

Fig. 6. Remove bolts (**arrows**) that hold upper manifold to lower manifold.

6. Disconnect crankcase breather valve from cylinder head cover.

7. Remove nuts from cylinder head cover.

8. Unclip and remove upper camshaft drive belt cover. Remove small protection cover from back of camshaft drive sprocket.

9. Remove both reinforcing strips from cylinder head cover.

10. Lift off cylinder head cover and gasket.

11. Installation is reverse of removal noting the following additional points:
    - Be sure to remove the shop rags from the lower intake manifold runner openings.
    - Use new gaskets where appropriate.
    - Apply a small amount of sealer to the area where the cylinder head cover gasket and the number one camshaft bearing cap meet.

Tightening Torques

- Cylinder head cover to cylinder head (M6) . . . . 10 Nm (89 in-lb)
- Upper intake manifold to lower manifold (M8) . . . . 20 Nm (15 ft-lb)
- Warm air deflector to upper intake manifold (M8) . . . . 25 Nm (18 ft-lb)

Camshaft oil seal, replacing

1. Remove upper engine cover and unclip and remove toothed belt guard, upper section. See **Toothed belt – Camshaft drive**, given later.

2. Set engine to TDC for cylinder 1 by turning crankshaft until timing mark on camshaft sprocket aligns with mark on toothed belt upper rear guard. See Fig. 7.

3. Release tensioning roller and slide toothed belt off of camshaft sprocket.

4. Turn crankshaft back off of TDC slightly.

5. Using a suitable spanner, remove camshaft sprocket bolt. See Fig. 8.

6. Remove camshaft drive sprocket and woodruff key.

7. Remove seal using a suitable seal extractor. See Fig. 9.

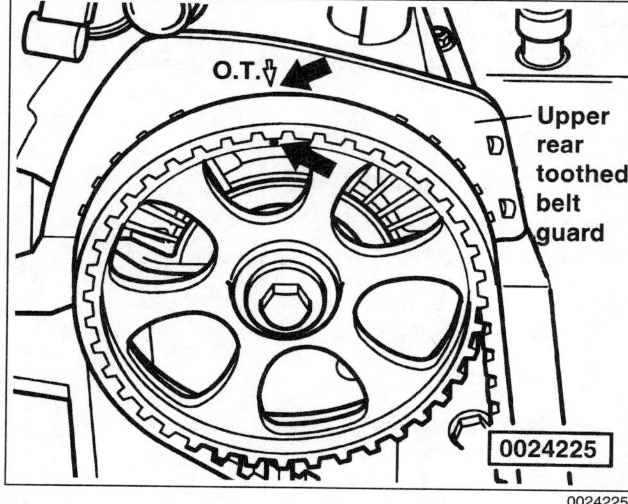

0024225

Fig. 7. Line up camshaft timing marks (**arrows**) as shown.

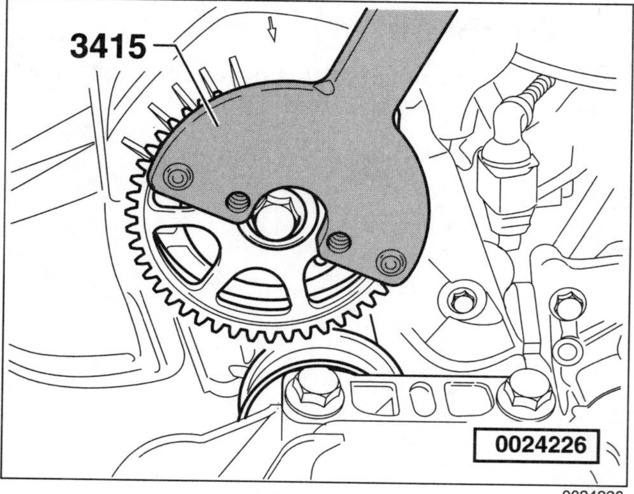

0024226

Fig. 8. Spanner or counterholder tool shown holding camshaft sprocket to facilitate removal of securing bolt.

8. Install the new oil seal noting the following points:
    - Lubricate new seal with clean engine oil.
    - Install with closed end facing out.
    - Use a suitable guide sleeve and installation tool.
    - Press seal into the bottom of recess.

9. Install woodruff key and camshaft sprocket, hold sprocket with a spanner and torque bolt.

Tightening torque

- Camshaft sprocket to camshaft . . . . 100 Nm (74 ft-lb)

---

10. Turn crankshaft back to TDC.

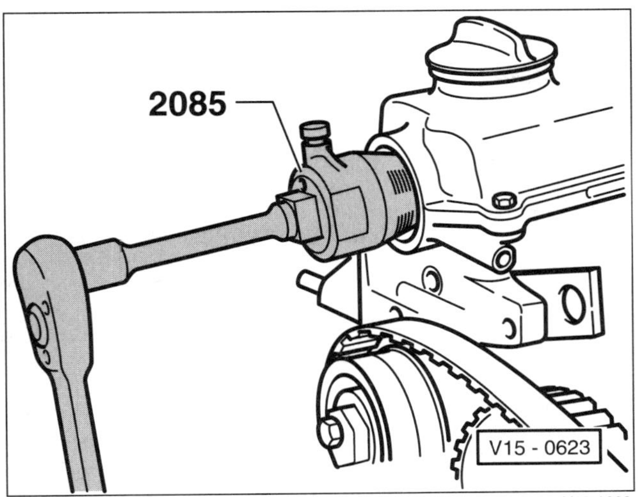

Fig. 9. Volkswagen seal removal tool being used to remove camshaft seal.

11. Install toothed belt and adjust tension, see **Toothed Belt–Camshaft Drive**, given later.

12. Install upper camshaft drive belt cover, upper engine cover and any other removed components.

13. Be sure to quality check your work, see **Quality Review** at the end of this repair group.

Camshaft, removing and installing

The camshaft can be removed and installed with the cylinder head installed. Removing the camshaft allows access to the hydraulic cam followers, the valve springs and the valve stem oil seals.

1. Remove upper engine cover and unclip and remove upper camshaft drive belt cover.

2. Turn engine by hand until timing mark on camshaft sprocket aligns with mark on toothed belt upper rear guard. See Fig. 7.

3. Release tensioning roller and slide toothed belt off of camshaft sprocket.

4. Turn crankshaft back off of TDC slightly.

NOTE —
Turning the crankshaft away from TDC slightly minimizes the chances of contact between pistons and valves upon re-assembly.

5. Using a suitable spanner, remove the camshaft sprocket bolt. See Fig. 8.

6. Remove camshaft drive sprocket and woodruff key.

7. Remove cylinder head (valve) cover and gasket as described previously.

8. Lift off plastic oil deflector to expose camshaft.

9. Loosen and remove the bearing caps from positions 5, 1 and 3 in that order. Position 1 is closest to the belt end of the camshaft.

NOTE —
Mark each bearing cap before removing. Each cap is machined to each journal and must be reinstalled to that exact location to prevent damage.

10. Loosen nuts on bearing cap 2 slightly and then loosen nuts on bearing cap 4 slightly. Loosen nuts alternately and evenly a little at a time on each of the two bearing caps. Remove nuts (and washers, if equipped), and remove bearing caps.

11. Lift out camshaft and lay aside.

NOTE —
Once removed, the camshaft should be checked for wear and other visible damage as described later under **Cylinder Head Components**.

12. Oil bearing surfaces of cylinder head and camshaft and install camshaft into cylinder head with lobes for cylinder number 1 pointing up.

13. Install bearing caps 2 and 4. Install nuts (and washers, if equipped) and tighten them alternatively and evenly so that camshaft is drawn down fully and evenly into bearing saddles. Torque to specification.

Tightening torque
- Camshaft bearing cap to cylinder head . . . . 20 Nm (15 ft-lb)

CAUTION —
Be sure to install bearing caps correctly. The caps are bored off-center and only fit properly one way. Caps are matched to the cylinder head by the machining process and are not available separately. Broken caps will require the replacement of the cylinder head. See Fig. 10.

14. Install bearing cap number 1 with a small amount of sealer (VW part # AMV 174 004 01) on the cylinder head mating surface. Install all remaining bearing caps and torque to specification.

15. Install the plastic oil deflector.

16. Install the camshaft drive sprocket and woodruff key using a suitable spanner as shown earlier. See Fig. 8.

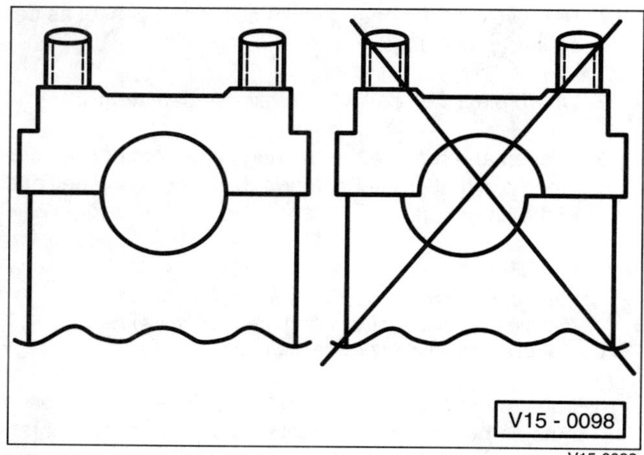

V15-0098

Fig. 10. Bearing caps are bored off-center. If necessary, test install caps without camshaft to confirm installation direction.

> ***NOTE —***
> *Ensure that camshaft lobes for cylinder #1 are still pointing up.*

Tightening torque

- Camshaft sprocket to camshaft . . . . 100 Nm (74 ft-lb)

17. Install cylinder head (valve) cover and rear upper toothed belt guard.

18. Install toothed camshaft drive belt and adjust tension, see **Toothed Belt - Camshaft Drive** given later.

19. Install upper camshaft drive belt cover, upper engine cover and any other removed components.

20. Be sure to quality check your work, see **Quality Review** at the end of this repair group.

Hydraulic cam followers, checking

The 2.0 liter engine installed in the Jetta, Golf and GTI is equipped with hydraulic cam followers which are also known as lifters. The cam followers are pumped up by engine oil pressure, expanding as necessary to fill the gap between the valve stem and the camshaft lobe. This occurs continuously and automatically to keep the valve in proper adjustment at all times.

Some valve noise at start-up and during the warm-up period is normal at times due to hydraulic cam followers that have bled down while the engine was not running. Before checking noisy cam followers, check that the engine oil is new and fresh, of the correct weight, and that the level is correct. Allow 2 minutes with a warm engine running at a fast idle for the lubrication system to properly pump up the cam followers.

Cam followers should only be checked when the engine is warm. Run the engine until the radiator fan has switched on at least one time. Increase the engine speed to 2,500 rpm and hold it there for approximately 2 minutes. If the hydraulic cam followers are still noisy, shut the engine off and proceed as follows while the engine is still warm.

1. Remove cylinder head (valve) cover. See **Cylinder head (valve) cover, removing and installing**, given earlier.

2. Turn engine by hand until both camshaft lobes of cylinder #1 are pointing approximately up.

> ***NOTE —***
> *Hydraulic cam follower clearance can be checked on any cam follower (lifter) that is not being depressed by the camshaft lobe.*

3. Check clearance between cam follower and cam lobe on cylinder #1 by lightly depressing cam follower with a wooden or plastic wedge and inserting a feeler gauge into the gap. See Fig. 11. If clearance exceeds specified limit, the lifter is faulty and should be replaced.

Specification

- Hydraulic cam follower maximum clearance (2.0L engine) . . . . 0.2 mm (0.008 in.)

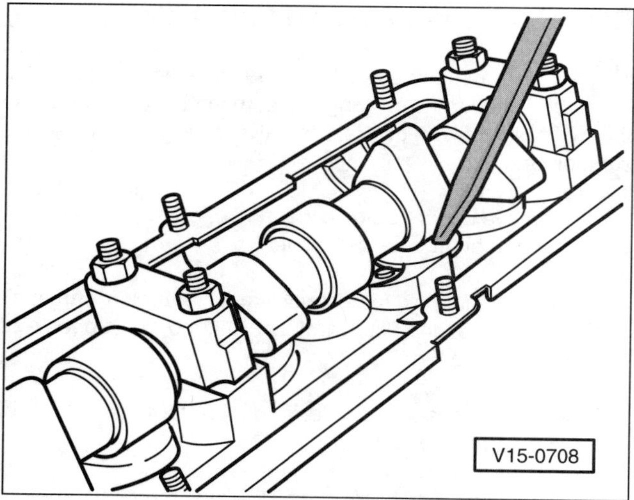

V15-0708

Fig. 11. Hydraulic cam follower shown being pushed down lightly with a plastic wedge.

4. Turn engine by hand and repeat procedure until all cam followers have been checked.

5. Replace a faulty cam follower by removing camshaft as previously described and pulling the follower from the cylinder head. Faulty hydraulic cam followers can be replaced individually but only as a complete assembly.

> **CAUTION —**
> *After installing new cam followers, the engine should not be started for at least 30 minutes. New cam followers are usually at full extended height and must be allowed to bleed down to their proper height once installed. Failure to do so may cause the valves to strike the pistons resulting in serious damage.*

> **NOTE —**
> *Store removed hydraulic cam followers in order on a clean surface with the camshaft contact surface facing down to minimize bleed down. Cover with a clean lint-free shop cloth.*

Valve stem oil seals, replacing

The sign of faulty valve stem seals is excessive oil consumption and oil smoke from the exhaust. This is usually most noticeable during periods of high manifold vacuum such as deceleration. If compression and leak-down testing confirm the integrity of the piston rings, but the engine consumes oil, it is likely that faulty valve stem seals are present. It should also be noted that worn valve stem seals could be due to worn valve guides and that the worn valve guides are the major cause of the oil consumption. See **Cylinder Head Components** for more information on checking valve guides.

Replacing the valve stem oil seals requires removal of the camshaft, cam followers, and the valve springs. This can be done with the cylinder head installed or removed. In either case, several Volkswagen special tools are required to compress the valve springs and remove and install the seals.

Working with the cylinder head installed:

1. Remove cylinder head cover, camshaft, and hydraulic cam followers as described earlier.
2. Remove spark plugs and apply a continuous supply of compressed air with a minimum of 6 bar (87 psi) into the first spark plug hole with an adapter. This must be done to hold the valves in place while the springs are removed. Continue with step 5.

> **CAUTION —**
> *Compressed air supply must be able to maintain at least 6 bar (87 psi) during this repair. If air supply is interrupted while valve spring is removed, valve will fall into the cylinder and may require cylinder head removal to retrieve.*

Working with the cylinder head removed:

3. Secure cylinder head to the workbench. Use care to avoid damage to the head gasket surfaces.
4. Remove camshaft and hydraulic cam followers as described earlier. Continue with step 5.

Working with cylinder head removed or installed:

5. Install appropriate valve spring compressor tools. See Fig. 12. Compress the spring for the first cylinder and remove the spring retainer, both keepers, and the valve spring. If spring will not compress, lightly tap the tool to release the stuck keepers. Use a small magnet to retrieve the keepers.

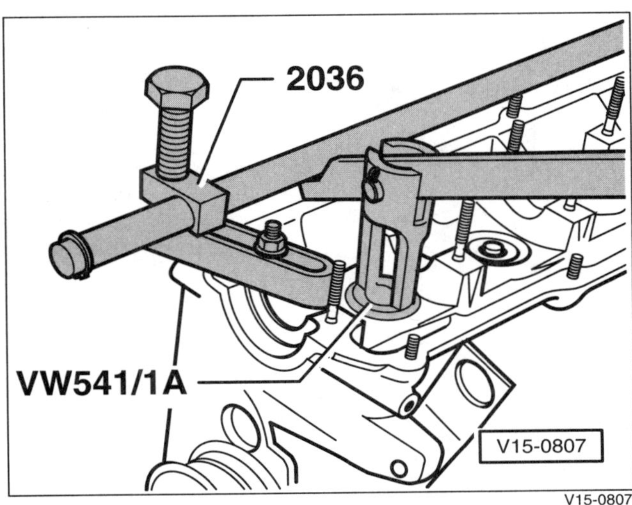

V15-0807

Fig. 12. Valve spring compressor tools being used to compress valve spring for removal of keepers. Numbers identify Volkswagen special tools.

6. Remove valve stem seals with special slide hammer tool. See Fig. 13.

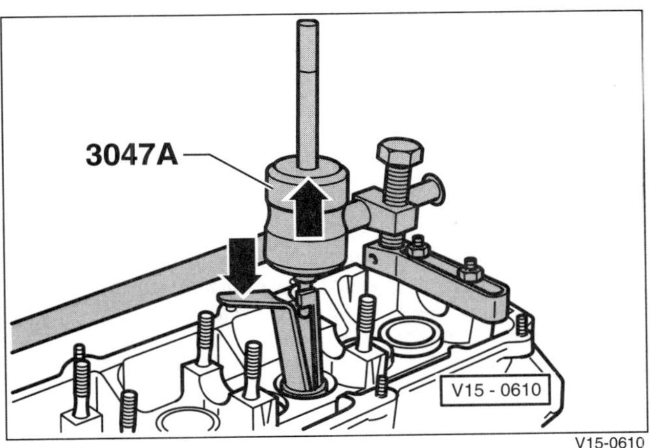

V15-0610

Fig. 13. Valve stem seal removal tool shown in position to remove valve stem seal. Push down on tool (**left arrow**) while sliding hammer up (**right arrow**)

7. Begin installation of new seal by temporarily fitting a protective plastic fitting sleeve over the valve stem. This sleeve is usually included with the new seal set and will prevent damage to the seal due to the sharp edges of the keeper grooves. Lubricate new seal with clean engine oil and fit it to the installation tool. See Fig. 14.

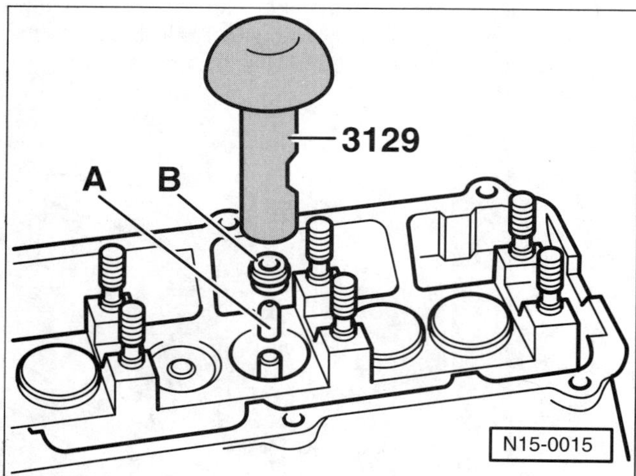

N15-0015

Fig. 14. Plastic fitting sleeve (**A**), shown with valve stem seal (**B**) and plastic installation tool 3129 available from Volkswagen.

8. Push the tool (with seal) down over the valve stem until the seal is fully seated on the guide. Remove the tool and the protective fitting sleeve.

9. Reinstall the valve spring, retainer and keepers.

10. Repeat for the second valve on the cylinder.

11. When both valve seals have been replaced on the first cylinder, transfer the compressed air adapter (if working with cylinder head installed) to the next cylinder and repeat the process until all valve seals have been replaced.

12. Remaining installation is the reverse of removal.

> ***CAUTION —***
> *To prevent cylinder head or camshaft damage, be sure to follow the camshaft installation procedure when tightening the camshaft bearing caps. See* **Camshaft, removing and installing**.

Tightening torque
- Spark plug to cylinder head . . . . 30 Nm (22 ft-lb)

13. Be sure to quality check your work, see **Quality Review** at the end of this repair group.

TOOTHED BELT - CAMSHAFT DRIVE

The camshaft drive belt and its related parts are shown in Fig. 15. Although no maintenance interval is specified, the publisher recommends periodic inspection of the belt, and replacement at 60,000 miles or every 4 years. This will help prevent damage to the engine due to belt stretch and the long term effects of heat. The camshaft drive belt is also known as a toothed belt and both terms are used interchangeably.

The following component list applies to Fig. 15

1. **Bolt**
   - Tighten to 45 Nm (33 ft-lb)
2. **Engine support**
3. **Bolt**
   - Tighten to 25 Nm (18 ft-lb)
4. **Bracket**
5. **Toothed belt guard, upper section**
6. **Toothed belt guard, center section**
7. **Nut**
   - Tighten to 20 Nm (15 ft-lb)
8. **Washer**
9. **Tensioner**
   - Semi-automatic toothed belt tensioning roller
10. **Toothed belt**
    - Mark engine direction of rotation before removing
    - Check for wear
    - Do not kink
11. **Toothed belt guard, rear**
12. **O-ring**
    - Always replace
13. **Coolant pump**
14. **Bolt**
    - Tighten to 15 Nm (11 ft-lb)

Drive belts, assembly

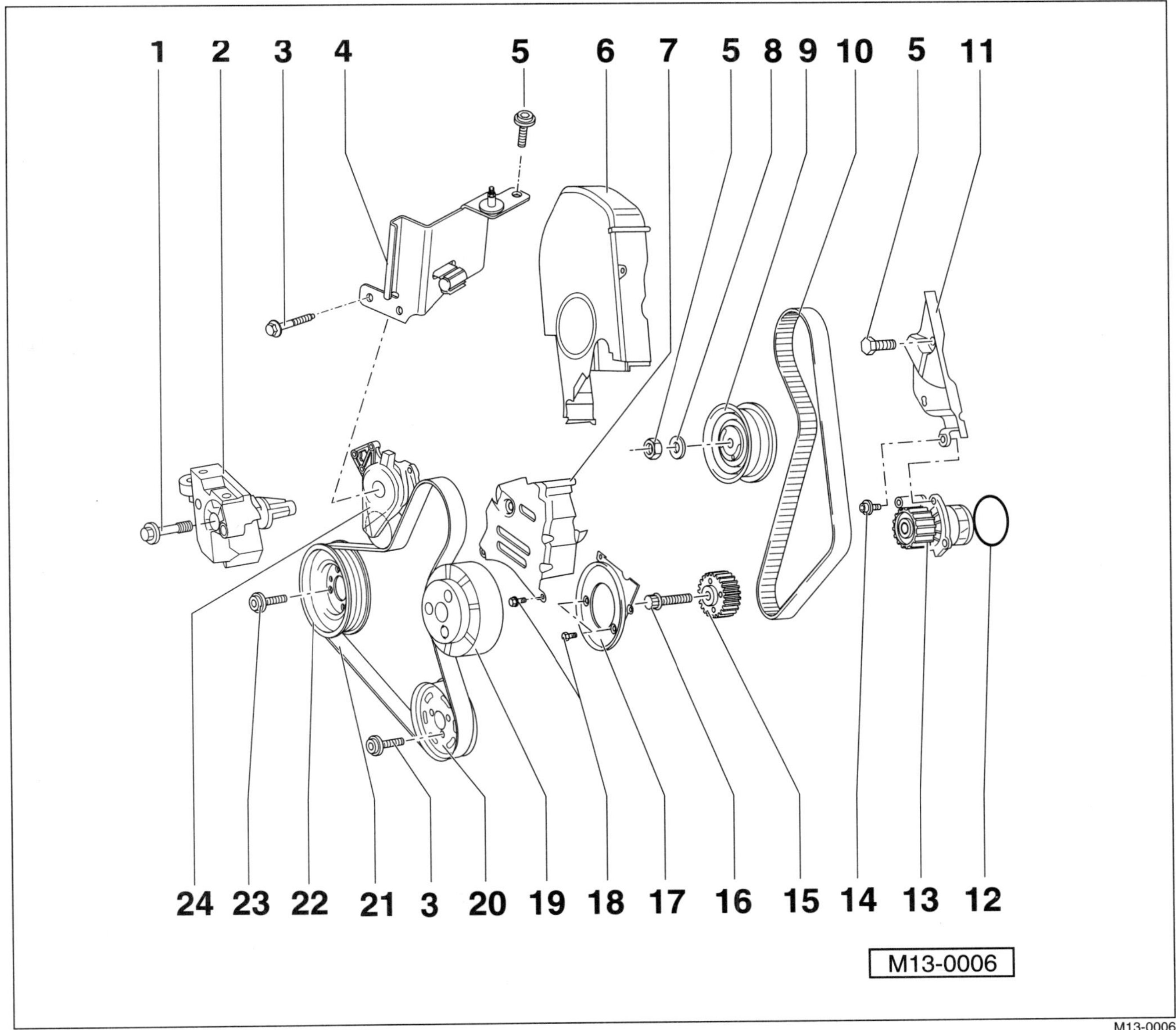

Fig. 15. Exploded view of the ribbed V-belt, the toothed belt and their related components.

15. Toothed belt sprocket (crankshaft)

16. Bolt
- Tighten to 90 Nm (66 ft-lb) + ¼ turn (90°)
- Always replace
- Threads and shoulder must be free of grease

17. Toothed belt guard, lower section

18. Bolt
- Tighten to 10 Nm (7 ft-lb)

19. Pulley
- For power steering pump

20. Ribbed belt
- Mark direction of rotation before removing

21. Belt pulley/vibration damper
- Can only be installed in one position, holes are offset
- Note position when installing toothed belt

22. Ribbed belt, tensioning device
- Loosen ribbed belt by turning with open-ended wrench

Toothed belt for camshaft drive, removing

1. Remove the lower sound absorber panel (belly pan).
2. Remove the upper engine cover.
3. Remove the ribbed V-belt and tensioner.
4. Turn the engine to top dead center, TDC, for cylinder number 1. Use mark on flywheel or torque converter to confirm engine is at TDC. See Fig. 16.

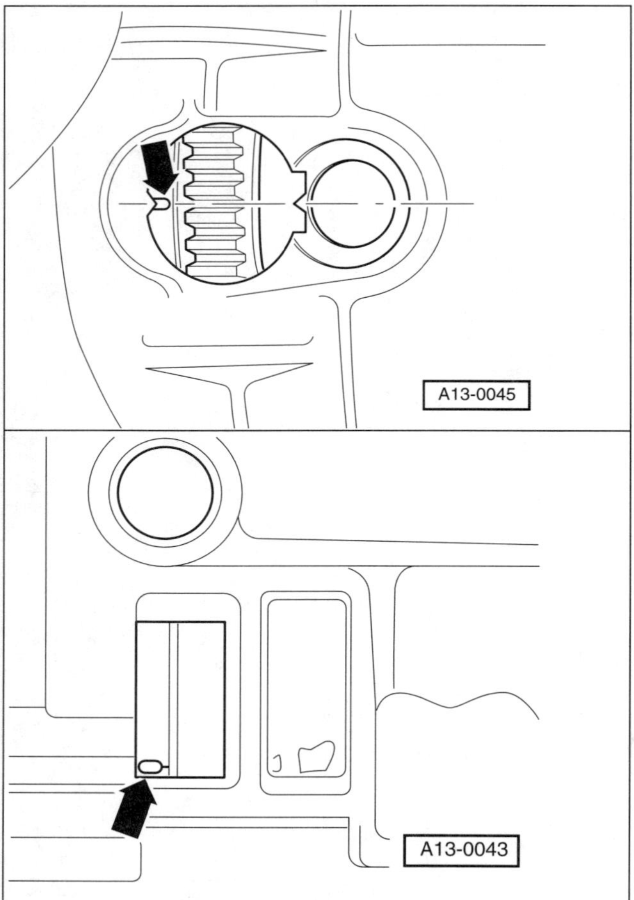

A13-0045, A13-0043

Fig. 16. Mark on flywheel (**upper arrow**) or torque converter (**lower arrow**) shown aligned with mark in transmission inspection hole indicating engine is at TDC.

5. Remove the upper toothed belt cover.
6. Support the engine with a suitable fixture that is designed to support the weight of the engine and transmission without damaging the body. See Fig. 17.
7. Lift the supporting device slightly, so that the weight of the engine and transmission is on the supporting device.

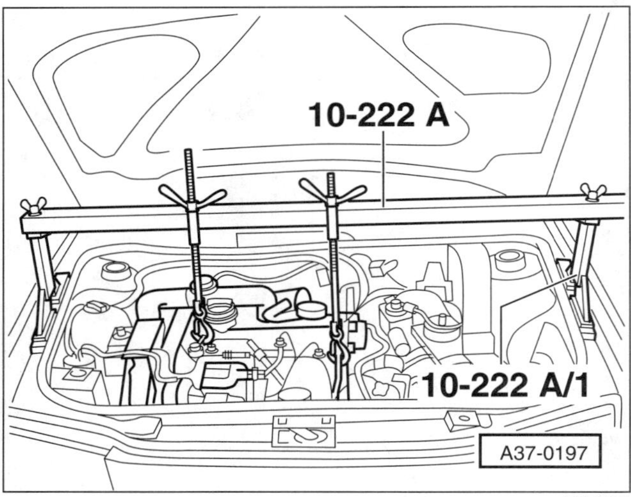

A37-0197

Fig. 17. Volkswagen supplied engine support tools shown attached to the engine.

8. Unbolt reservoirs for coolant and power steering fluids. Leave fluid lines attached to reservoirs and position out of way.
9. Remove right side engine mount from body and carrier on engine. See Fig. 18.

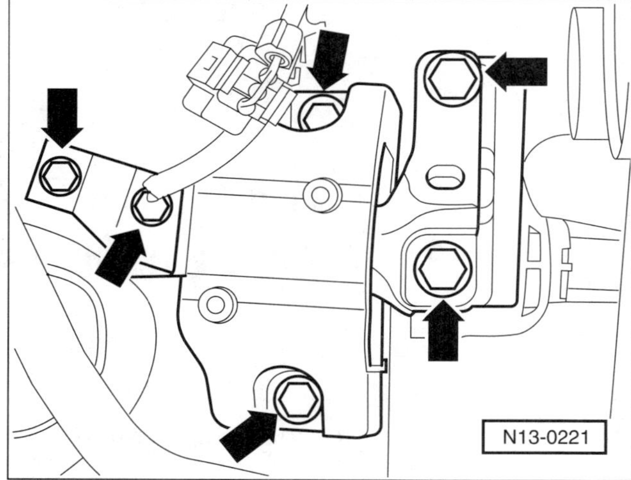

N13-0221

Fig. 18. Right side engine mount (**1**) as viewed from above. Remove the 5 bolts (**arrows**), and loosen body bolt (**arrow A**).

10. Remove the 4 bolts holding the vibration dampener/ ribbed belt pulley to the toothed belt sprocket and remove the belt pulley. See Fig. 19.

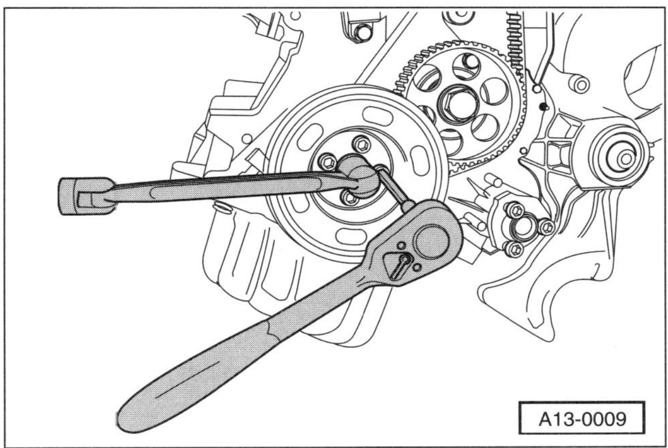

Fig. 19. Remove vibration dampener/belt pulley by counterholding center bolt as shown.

11. Remove the center and lower sections of the toothed belt guard.

12. Remove the right side engine mount bracket from the block. There will not be sufficient room to withdraw the bolts, so the mount and the bolts are all removed at the same time. See Fig. 20.

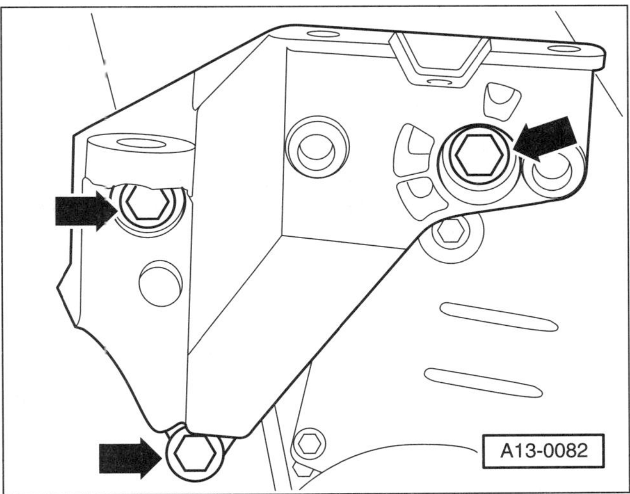

Fig. 20. Completely loosen the 3 long bolts (**arrows**) that secure right side engine mount bracket to cylinder block.

13. Mark running direction of the belt.

14. Loosen the securing nut on the tensioner to release it and remove the belt.

Toothed belt for camshaft drive, installing

1. Align the mark on the camshaft with the mark on the toothed belt guard. This brings the camshaft to TDC for cylinder number 1. See Fig. 21.

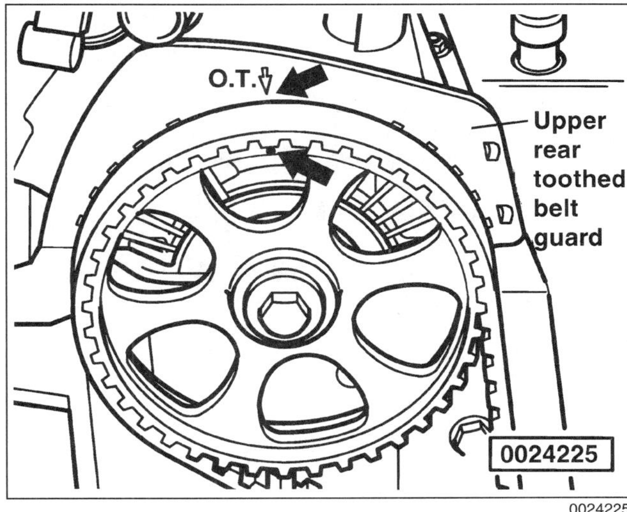

Fig. 21. Line up camshaft timing marks (**arrows**) as shown.

> ***CAUTION —***
> - *Due to engine design, care must be used when turning the camshaft with the toothed belt removed. If valves are allowed to open with the piston at TDC, serious internal damage will result.*
> - *Belt tension must not be adjusted on a hot engine. Allow to cool sufficiently before proceeding. Engine temperature must be no hotter than warm to the touch.*

2. Install toothed belt onto the crankshaft drive sprocket, coolant pump and camshaft drive sprocket.

   NOTE —
   If re-using an old belt, be sure to note running direction marks placed on it before removal.

3. Install bolts into the right side engine mount bracket and install to the cylinder block. See Fig. 20. given earlier.

Tightening torques
- Right side engine mount bracket to cylinder block (M10) . . . . 45 Nm (33 ft-lb)

4. Install the center and lower sections of the toothed belt guard.

5. Install the vibration dampener/ribbed belt pulley to the toothed belt drive sprocket.

Tightening torques
- Vibration dampener/ribbed belt pulley to toothed belt drive sprocket (M8) .... 40 Nm (30 ft-lb)

6. Ensure that crankshaft is at TDC for cylinder 1 by aligning mark on flywheel or torque converter with mark in transmission inspection hole. See Fig. 16. given earlier.

7. Ensure that camshaft is still at TDC for cylinder number 1.

8. Install right side engine mount using new stretch bolts. See Fig. 22.

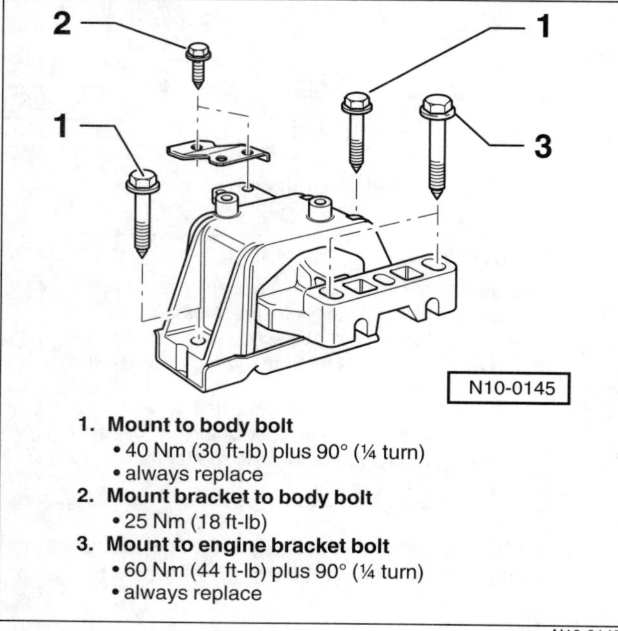

N10-0145

Fig. 22. Right side engine mount.

9. Remove engine support fixture.

10. Install the toothed belt onto the tensioner and check for correct placement of belt on all sprockets. Securing nut should be just tight enough to allow movement of the center section.

11. Ensure that camshaft and crankshaft are still at TDC.

12. Tension the toothed belt by turning the center section eccentric of the tensioner with a 2 pin spanner wrench until the notch and the indictor pointer line up. When marks line up, tighten the securing nut. See Fig. 23.

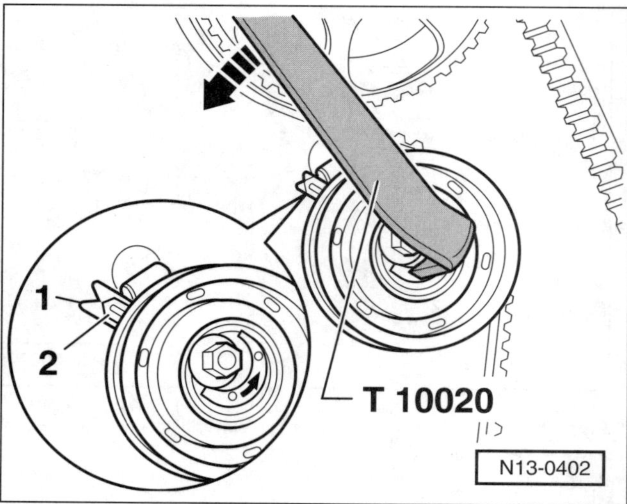

N13-0402

Fig. 23. Move spanner (VW special tool T10020 shown) in direction of **arrow** to align notch (**1**) with pointer (**2**).

Tightening torques
- Toothed belt tensioner (M8) .... 20 Nm (15 ft-lb)

13. Ensure that marks on camshaft sprocket and dampener/pulley still align with their respective TDC marks. If they do not align, repeat until they do.

NOTE —
Some movement of the sprockets and their marks is to be expected as belt tension is adjusted. Keep in mind that the smallest possible increment of adjustment is one whole tooth of the belt or sprocket.

14. With all marks in proper alignment, rotate the crankshaft two revolutions in the running direction and recheck the belt tension marks on the tensioner.

NOTE —
It is important that the last 45° (1/8 turn) of crankshaft rotation is made without interruption.

15. Install toothed belt guard, upper section.

16. Install ribbed belt tensioner and belt.

Tightening torque
- Ribbed belt tensioner to bracket (M8) 25 Nm (18 ft-lb)

17. Install the lower sound absorber panel (belly pan) and the upper engine cover.

18. Install any remaining parts and quality check your work, see **Quality Review** at the end of this repair group.

CYLINDER HEAD, REMOVING AND INSTALLING

The cylinder head can be removed and installed with the engine in the vehicle. Fig. 3 and 4, given earlier, show the 2.0L cylinder head and related components. Note that the cylinder head bolts are stretch type fasteners and should never be re-used. In addition, whenever the cylinder head or the cylinder head gasket is replaced, the coolant must also be replaced, see **19 Engine–Cooling System**.

Cylinder head, removing

> ***WARNING —***
> *Do not start work on a hot engine. Allow to cool sufficiently before proceeding. Engine temperature must be no hotter than warm to the touch. Cylinder head warpage can result due to uneven cooling rates.*

NOTE —

- *Disconnecting the battery cables will erase fault codes and basic settings in the engine management and automatic transmission control unit memories. Some driveability problems may be noticeable until the system re-adapts to operating conditions. OBD II readiness codes, which may be required for emissions testing, may also be erased. See* **24 Fuel Injection – Motronic** *for additional information. In some instances proper diagnosis will require the use of a scan tool such as the Volkswagen supplied VAG 1551 or 1552. Use and operation of this tool is outside the scope of this repair manual.*
- *Cylinder head will be removed with the exhaust manifold and the lower section of the intake manifold still attached.*

1. With ignition switched off, disconnect the battery negative terminal from the battery.

NOTE —
Be sure to have the anti-theft radio code on hand before disconnecting the battery.

2. Position the crankshaft so that pistons are NOT at TDC.
3. Remove the upper engine cover.
4. Remove the lower sound absorber panel (belly pan).
5. Drain engine coolant, see **19 Engine–Cooling System**.
6. Disconnect fuel supply line, fuel return line and vacuum connection for the leak detection pump (LDP). See Fig. 24.

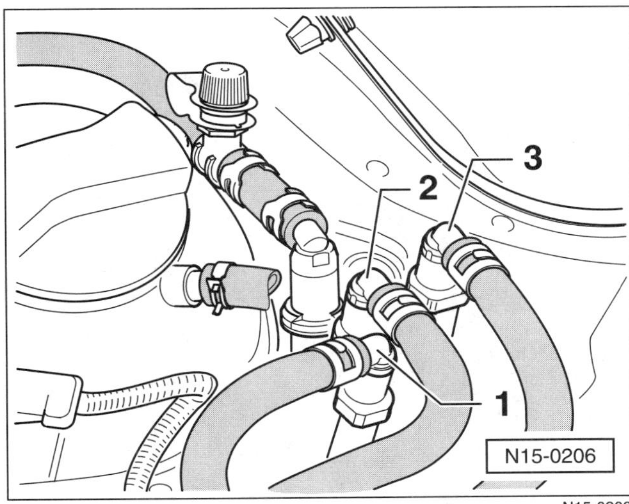

N15-0206

Fig. 24. Separate fuel supply line (**3**), fuel return line (**2**), and vacuum connection (**1**) for leak detection pump (LDP) as shown.

> ***WARNING —***
> *Fuel will be expelled when disconnecting fuel hoses. Wrap a cloth around the fuel line fittings before disconnecting them. Do not smoke or work near heaters or other fire hazards. Have a fire extinguisher handy.*

7. Seal off disconnected fuel and vacuum lines to prevent contamination.
8. Remove air cleaner assembly and connecting hose to throttle housing.
9. Disconnect accelerator cable from the throttle control module linkage and the cable retainers. (AEG engine only)
10. Unplug the wiring harness connector from the throttle control module.
11. Remove the 2 coolant hoses from throttle control module that connect to the reservoir and cylinder head.
12. Disconnect vacuum hose connection for the power brake booster on the back of intake manifold and any remaining connections on the intake manifold.

13. Loosen and remove the bolts holding the upper and lower sections of the intake manifold together. See Fig. 25.

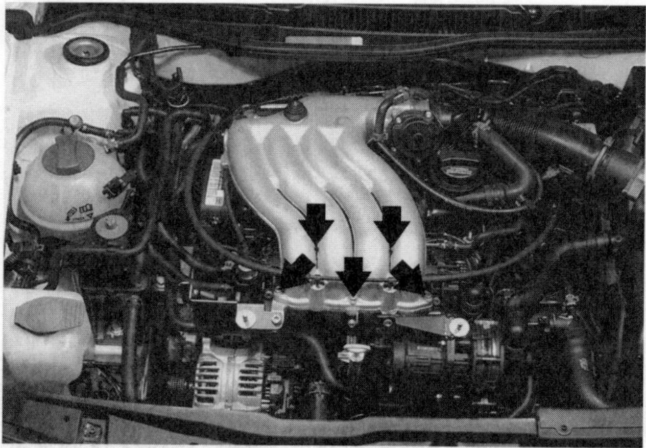

0024360

Fig. 25. Remove bolts (**arrows**) that hold upper manifold to lower manifold.

14. On the rear upper section of the intake manifold, remove vent line and t bolts for warm air deflector plate. See Fig. 26.

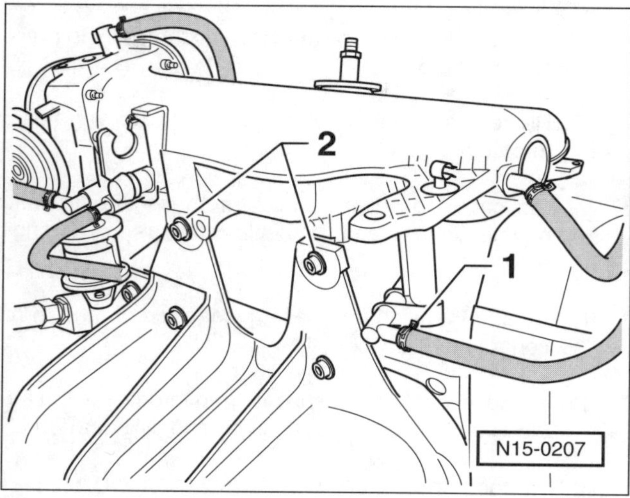

N15-0207

Fig. 26. Rear view of intake manifold showing vent line (**1**) and warm air deflector bolts (**2**).

15. Lift off the upper section of the intake manifold and lay aside. Block off the exposed open ports on the lower section with wide tape or other suitable material. See Fig. 27.

0024229

Fig. 27. Cover intake manifold (**arrow**) holes after removing upper section.

16. Unbolt the coolant connection flange from the end of the cylinder head and carefully move aside. The coolant hoses stay connected. See Fig. 28.

0024361

Fig. 28. Coolant connection flange mounting bolts (**arrows**).

17. Disconnect the intake and pressure hoses from the Secondary Air Injection pump. Unbolt nuts holding pump to bracket and disconnect harness connector. Remove pump. See Fig. 29.

18. Disconnect the following electrical components/connections:

- Fuel Injectors (and unclip the wiring from the holders)
- Camshaft Position Sensor
- Spark Plug Wires

Fig. 29. Disconnect air intake (**A**), pressure hose (**B**), harness connector (**C**) and unbolt nuts (**arrows**) to remove secondary air injection pump from its mounting bracket.

19. Remove the ribbed V-belt from the tensioner and remove the tensioner.
20. Remove the upper toothed belt cover.
21. Release the toothed belt tensioning roller and take the toothed belt off the camshaft sprocket.
22. Remove the upper bolt from the rear toothed belt guard where it is attached to the cylinder head, see Fig. 15 given earlier.
23. Unbolt the front exhaust pipe from the exhaust manifold, see **26 Exhaust System and Emission Controls**.
24. Remove cylinder head (valve) cover as described earlier.
25. Loosen the socket head bolts slightly in sequence. See Fig. 30. Do not remove the bolts until all 10 have been loosened. Discard the head bolts.

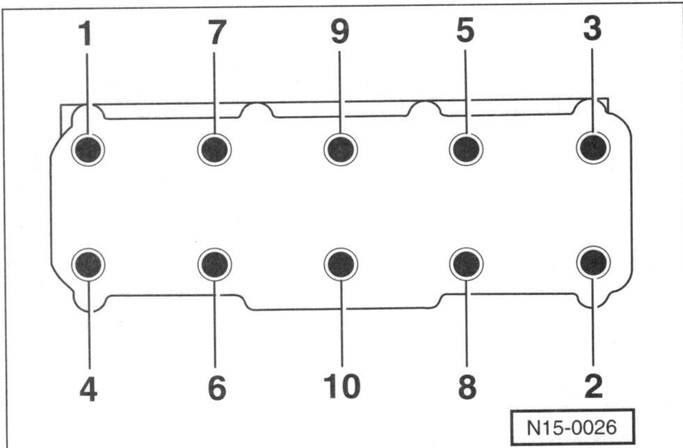

Fig. 30. Loosen the cylinder head bolts in the order shown. Loosen all bolts slightly the first time around, repeat the order, finish loosening and then remove.

26. Carefully lift off cylinder head and place in a clean area. If the head is stuck, use a soft-faced mallet or pry gently with a wooden stick.

> ***CAUTION —***
> *Some of the valves will be open. Use extra care when removing and handling to avoid damage. Place the cylinder head on the bench or table so that the weight of the cylinder head will not rest on the valves.*

Cylinder head, installing

Before proceeding with the installation of the cylinder head, whether an original or a new unit, observe the following important points:

- Check the cylinder head and block for distortion and warpage, see **Cylinder Head Components**, given later in this section.
- Carefully clean the cylinder block and cylinder head sealing surfaces being sure to avoid scratching them during the cleaning process. Do not use metal scrapers or wire brushes.
- When using abrasive paper do not use any grades coarser than 100 grit (such as 80 grit). Lower numbers are coarser.
- If cylinder head will not be reinstalled immediately, take precautions to prevent rust from forming on the cylinder block walls and gasket sealing surfaces.
- When cleaning the old gasket material off of the cylinder block, take precautions to keep the old gasket material and the abrasive particles and dirt out of the cooling and oiling system passages. Place a clean shop cloth over the cylinders to prevent contamination from getting between the cylinder wall and the piston.
- Do not take the new cylinder head gasket out of the packaging until ready to use. Handle the new gasket with extreme care as any damage will lead to leaks.
- There MUST NOT BE any oil or coolant in the head bolt holes in the cylinder block. Any fluids in the holes creates the danger of hydrolock while torquing which could lead to structural damage of the cylinder block. Use thread chasers to remove foreign material as required. Be sure that all 10 bolt holes are clean and dry.
- When all traces of the old gasket material have been removed from the cylinder block and head, carefully remove all traces of metal particles, abrasives and lint. All gasket sealing surfaces and bolt holes must be clean and dry to ensure a proper seal.
- Always use new cylinder head bolts and a new cylinder head gasket.
- Do not use any gasket sealer on the new cylinder head gasket.
- If installing a Volkswagen supplied replacement cylinder head, be sure to inspect for and remove any plastic packaging materials used to protect the head and the open valves.

Cylinder head, installing (continued)

1. Position the crankshaft so that pistons are NOT at TDC.

2. Install alignment pins into bolt holes of cylinder block. Use of this tool allows for proper alignment of the head on the block. preventing slippage and damage to the head gasket. See Fig. 31.

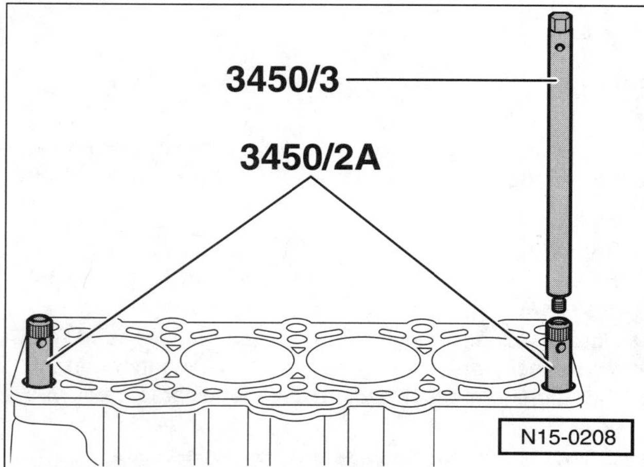

N15-0208

Fig. 31. Volkswagen supplied installation tool for assembly of cylinder head onto the block.

3. Install the new cylinder head gasket onto the block with the numbers and letters facing up. Be sure that none of the wiring or any vacuum hoses are caught between the cylinder head and the block.

4. Carefully install the cylinder head onto the block over the alignment pins and screw in 8 of the new head bolts. Tighten the bolts hand-tight only.

5. Remove the alignment pins from the bolt holes with the tool and install the remaining 2 new head bolts. Tighten these bolts hand-tight.

6. Tighten the 10 cylinder head bolts in three stages following the tightening order. See Fig. 32.

Tightening torque

- Cylinder head to cylinder block (stretch bolt – always replace)
  - stage I . . . . 40 Nm (30 ft-lb)
  - stage II . . . . additional ¼ turn (90°)
  - stage III . . . . additional ¼ turn (90°)

7. Lubricate the camshaft and followers and install the cylinder head (valve) cover.

8. Install the toothed belt, adjust the tension and the belt timing.

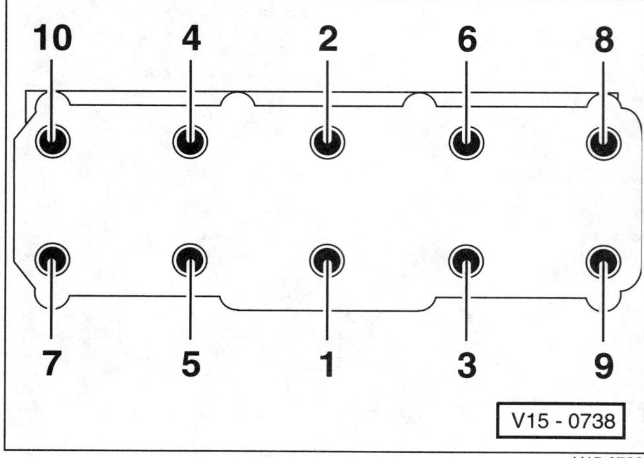

V15-0738

Fig. 32. Tighten the cylinder head bolts in the order shown.

9. Install the upper bolt for the rear toothed belt guard where it is attached to the cylinder head.

10. Install the upper toothed belt cover.

11. Install the ribbed V-belt tensioner and the belt.

12. Remove whatever material was used to seal the exposed lower section of the intake manifold and install the upper section of the intake manifold. Re-attach the vacuum fitting and warm air deflector plate.

13. Reconnect all coolant flanges and lines.

14. Reconnect all vacuum hoses connections.

15. Reconnect fuel supply and return hoses and vacuum hose to leak detection pump.

16. Reconnect accelerator cable and check for smooth operation and full throttle.

17. Reconnect all disconnected electrical components and connections including spark plug wires.

18. Refill cooling system with fresh coolant in the appropriate ratio. See **19 Engine–Cooling System.**

> ***CAUTION —***
> - *Use only Volkswagen original anti-freeze when filling the cooling system. Use of any other anti-freeze may be harmful to the cooling system. Do not use an anti-freeze containing phosphates.*
> - *Do not use tap water in cooling system. Use distilled water only to mix anti-freeze.*

19. Install air cleaner assembly and connecting hoses.

20. Attach the front exhaust pipe to the exhaust manifold with new nuts. See **26 Exhaust System and Emission Controls**.

21. Install the lower sound absorber panel (belly pan).

22. Install the upper engine cover.

23. Reconnect the battery only after all parts/electrical connections have been reinstalled and reconnected.

24. Be sure to quality check your work, see **Quality Review** at the end of this repair group.

Tightening torques

- Cylinder head cover to cylinder head (M6) . . . . 10 Nm (89 in-lb)
- Upper intake manifold bolts to lower manifold (M8) . . . . 20 Nm (15 ft-lb)
- Warm air deflector to upper intake manifold (M8) . . . . 25 Nm (18 ft-lb)
- Cylinder head to cylinder block (stretch bolt - always replace)
  - stage I . . . . 40 Nm (30 ft-lb)
  - stage II . . . . additional ¼ turn (90°)
  - stage III . . . . additional ¼ turn (90°)
- Front exhaust pipe to exhaust manifold (special nuts - always replace)(M10) . 40 Nm (30 ft-lb)
- Coolant outlet flange to cylinder head (M6) . . . . 10 Nm (89 in-lb)
- Rear toothed belt guard to cylinder head (M8) . . . . 20 Nm (15 ft-lb)
- Ribbed belt tensioner to bracket (M8) 25 Nm (18 ft-lb)
- Toothed belt tensioner (M8) . . . . 20 Nm (15 ft-lb)
- Secondary air pump to support bracket nut (M6) . . . . 10 Nm (89 in-lb)

CYLINDER HEAD COMPONENTS

This section provides the specifications and special information necessary to repair the cylinder head that has been removed from the Volkswagen 2.0L engine. Special service tools and machine shop services are required for most cylinder head repair.

NOTE —

- *The information given under this heading assumes that the cylinder head is removed. For cylinder head removal procedures, see* ***Cylinder head, removing*** *given earlier.*
- *Fig. 3 and Fig. 4, given earlier, show exploded views of the cylinder head and valve train assemblies.*

Cylinder Head and Camshaft

Check the cylinder head for warpage and distortion with an accurate straight edge and a feeler gauge. See Fig. 33. The cylinder head can be resurfaced provided that the distance from the valve cover gasket surface to the head gasket surface is never less than specified. See Fig. 34. Resurfacing the cylinder head will require that the valves be set deeper into the seat by the same amount as was removed by the surfacing operation. This can be done by reworking the valve seats. Machining too much material off of this surface will change the compression ratio and will affect engine emissions.

Specification

- Maximum cylinder head distortion/warpage . . . . 0.1 mm (0.004 in.)
- Minimum cylinder dimension (valve cover gasket surface to the head gasket surface) . . . . 132.6 mm (5.22 in.)

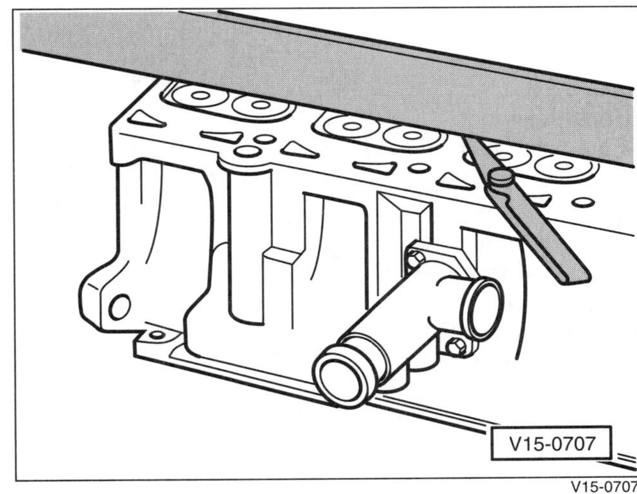

V15-0707

Fig. 33. Cylinder head being checked for distortion with a feeler gauge.

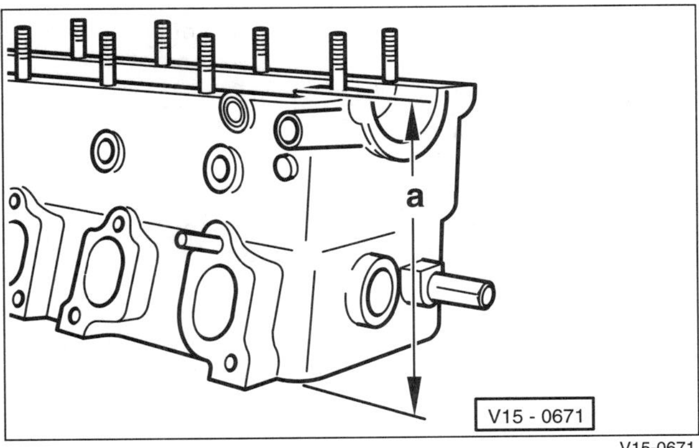

V15-0671

Fig. 34. Dimension (**a**) must not be less than 132.6 mm (5.22 in.) after reworking cylinder head sealing surface.

The camshaft for the 2.0L engine is easily identified by markings cast into it during manufacture. See Fig. 35.

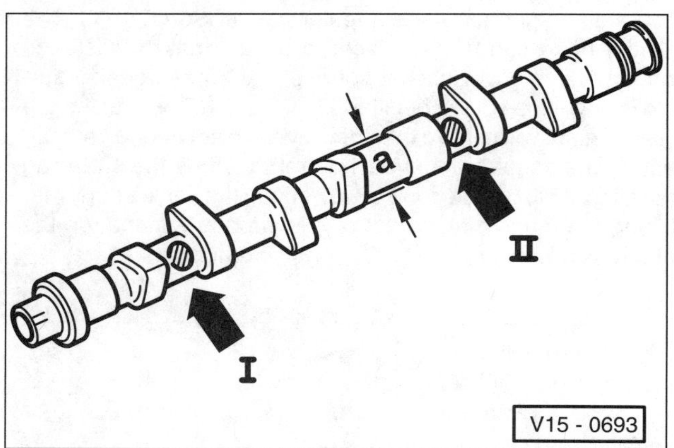

V15-0693

Fig. 35. Camshaft identification marks for 2.0L engines; **a** is the base diameter of 34 mm. For AEG engines, **arrow I** should show the letter -B-, and **arrow II** should show the number -050-. For AVH and AZG engines, **arrow I** should show 50 E/50 P with no apparent marking at **arrow II.**

Specification

- Valve timing at 1 mm valve lift, engine code AEG
  - Intake opens ATDC . . . . 5°
  - Intake closes ABDC . . . . 41°
  - Exhaust opens BBDC . . . . 37°
  - Exhaust closes BTDC . . . . 1°
- Valve timing at 1 mm valve lift, engine code AVH, AZG
  - Intake opens ATDC . . . . 6°, 20'
  - Intake closes ABDC . . . . 42°, 45'
  - Exhaust opens BBDC . . . . 35°, 80'
  - Exhaust closes BTDC . . . . 0°, 45'

The in and out movement of the camshaft is known as axial play and is measured with the cam followers (hydraulic lifters) removed and only the first and last bearing caps installed.

A dial gauge is set up on the sprocket end of the camshaft and the camshaft clearance is checked by moving the camshaft as far as it can go in each direction. See Fig. 36.

Specification

- Camshaft axial clearance . . . . 0.15 mm (0.006 in.)

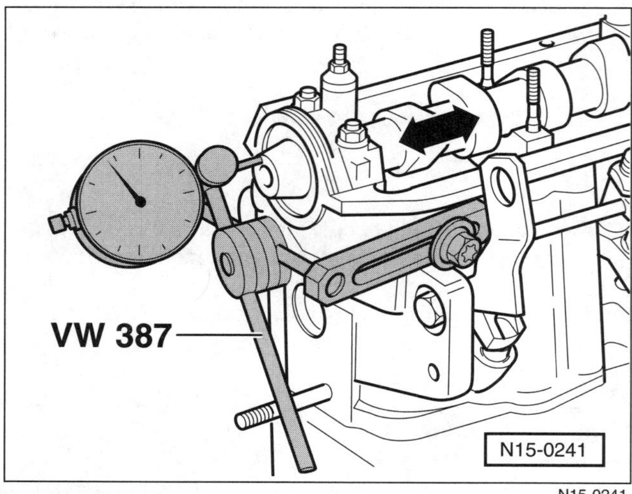

N15-0241

Fig. 36. Dial gauge set up on camshaft to measure axial play (**arrow**).

Valves

Valves should not be re-worked on a machine. Only lapping by hand with valve compound is permitted. Valve dimensions listed in **Table a** apply to the valve shown in Fig. 36.

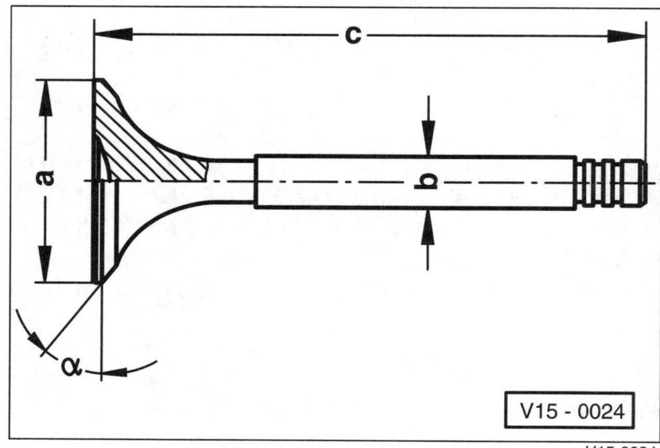

V15-0024

Fig. 37. Valve dimensions are referenced in **Table a**.

Table a. Valve Dimensions

Engine Code	AEG engine	AVH, AZG engine
Valve head diameter (**a**)		
intake	39.5 mm ± 0.15 mm (1.555 in. ± 0.006 in)	39.5 mm ± 0.15 mm (1.555 in. ± 0.006 in)
exhaust	32.9 mm ± 0.15 mm (1.295 in. ± 0.0008 in.)	32.9 mm ± 0.15 mm (1.295 in. ± 0.0008 in.)
Valve stem diameter (**b**)		
intake	6.92 mm ± 0.02 mm (0.272 in. ± 0.0008 in.)	6.98 mm ± 0.007 mm (0.275 in. ± 0.00027 in)
exhaust	6.92 mm ± 0.02 mm (0.272 in. ± 0.0008 in.)	6.965 mm ± 0.007 mm (0.274 in. ± 0.00027 in)
Valve length (**c**)		
intake	91.85 mm (3.616 in.)	91.85 mm (3.616 in.)
exhaust	91.15 mm (3.588 in.)	91.15 mm (3.588 in.)
Valve face angle (α)		
intake	45°	45°
exhaust	45°	45°

Valve guides

Special tools and a press are required to replace the valve guides. Check valve guide wear with a new valve. Always use an intake valve in an intake guide and an exhaust valve in an exhaust guide. See Fig. 38. Inspect the valve seats to ensure that the cylinder head can be reconditioned before installing new valve guides. Press out worn original valve guides with Volkswagen special driver tool 3121 from the camshaft side of the head. Replacement valve guides have a shoulder on the camshaft side to limit the installed depth and must be pressed out from the combustion chamber side.

When installing new valve guides, lubricate with clean engine oil and press in from the camshaft side down to the shoulder. The cylinder head should be cold for this operation. Once the shoulder of the valve guide contacts the cylinder head, do not allow the pressure on the guide to exceed 2000 psi (1 ton) otherwise the cylinder head or the guide will be damaged. When the guide has been replaced, ream it to the proper size and continue with the reworking of the valve seats.

Specification

- Valve guide (wear limits-maximum play) with new valve
  - intake valve guide . . . . 1.0 mm (0.039 in.)
  - exhaust valve guide . . . . 1.3 mm (0.051 in.)

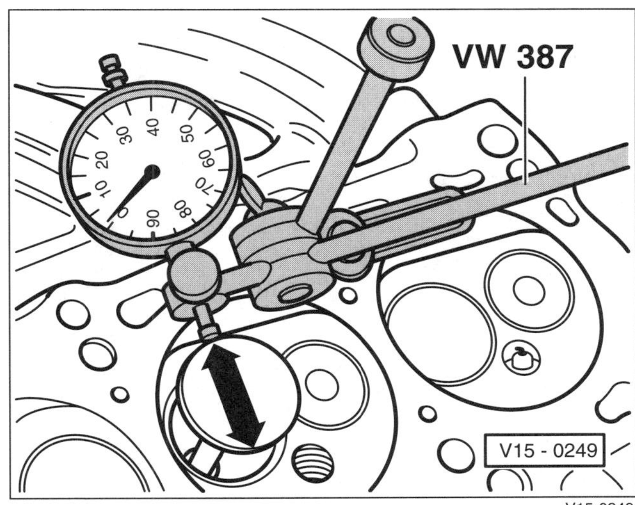

V15-0249

Fig. 38. Valve guide wear being checked with new valve. Insert valve until stem end is flush with end of guide. Rock valve back and forth (**arrow**) to check total travel.

NOTE —

Due to the close tolerances found in the valve guides, it is recommended that Volkswagen special tool 3121 be used for removal and installation and special tool 3120 be used to ream the valve guide to size.

Valve seats

When resurfacing valve seats, there is a limit to the amount of material that can be removed to bring the seat back into specification. If too much material is removed, the final assembly will leave too little space for the hydraulic cam follower to function properly. The maximum refacing dimension, that is, the maximum amount of material that can be removed from the valve seat, is calculated from the measurement shown in Fig. 39.

Measure dimension **a** in Fig. 39, and subtract the minimum dimension, as given in **Table b**. The difference is the maximum amount of material that can be removed from the valve seat.

Table b. Minimum Dimensions for Calculating Valve Seat Refacing Dimensions

Engine Code	Intake	Exhaust
AEG, AVH, AZG	33.8 mm (1.331 in.)	34.1 mm (1.343 in.)

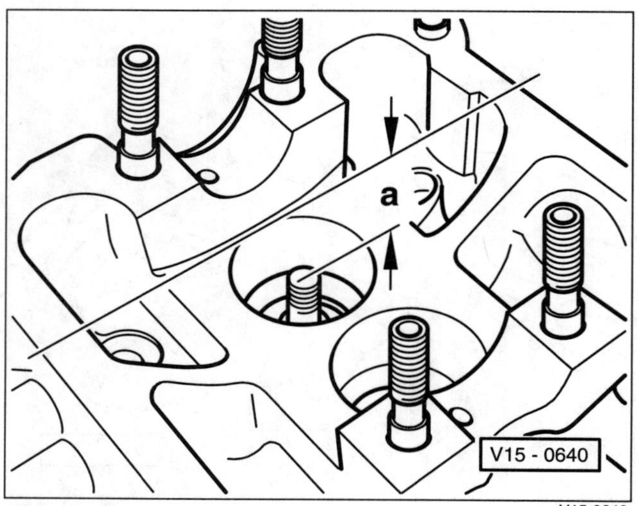

V15-0640

Fig. 39. Dimension (**a**), distance between top of valve stem and gasket surface of cylinder head, is used to calculate maximum valve seat refacing dimensions.

NOTE —
Use care when reworking the exhaust valve seats to avoid changing the shape of the port. This can upset the flow characteristics of the valve.

Table c. Valve Seat Dimensions

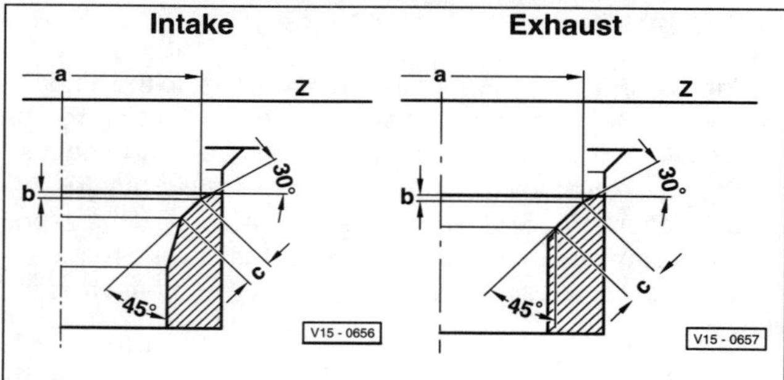

Engine Code: AEG, AVH, AZG	**Intake**	**Exhaust**
Seat diameter (**a**)	39.2 mm (1.543 in.)	32.4 mm (1.276 in.)
Maximum refacing dimension (**b**)	Calculated See Fig. 39.	Calculated See Fig. 39.
Seat width (**c**)	approx. 2.0 mm (0.079 in.)	approx. 2.4 mm (0.094 in.)
Valve seat angle	45°	45°
Correction angle, upper	30°	30°

NOTE —
Z shows cylinder head surface reference.

QUALITY REVIEW

When you have finished working under the hood and around other areas of the vehicle it is advisable to take a moment to quality check or review your work. This helps to ensure that the operation or repair has been completed properly with all affected systems functioning within normal parameters. This may include the following:

- Make sure that the radiator fan cycles properly and that the coolant level and concentration are correct.
- Ensure that all cable ties and hose clamps that were removed as part of the repair are replaced.
- Check and adjust all other applicable fluid levels.
- Make sure that there are no fluid leaks.
- Make sure that there are no air, vacuum or exhaust leaks.
- Make sure that all components involved in the repair are positioned correctly and function properly.
- Male sure all tools, shop cloths, fender covers, and protective tape are removed.
- Clean grease from painted surfaces and steering wheel.
- Unlock the anti-theft radio and reset the clock.

In addition to the above noted points, the Engine Control Module (ECM) and Transmission Control Module (TCM) may need to be checked using the Volkswagen supplied VAG 1551 or 1552 scan tool as mentioned at the start of this repair.

15d Cylinder Head and Valvetrain– (2.8L Engine)

TABLES

GENERAL

This engine section covers cylinder head and valvetrain service and repair work for the 6-cylinder (VR6) 2.8 liter engine. For information on short block engine repair and internal engine specifications, see **13b Crankshaft/Cylinder Block (6-cylinder)**.

Most of the operations described in this repair group require special equipment and experience. If you lack the skills, tools, or a suitable workplace for servicing or repairing the cylinder head, we suggest you leave these repairs to an authorized Volkswagen dealer or other qualified shop.

> ***CAUTION —***
> *Disconnecting the negative (–) battery cable may erase fault codes and basic settings in the engine management and automatic transmission control modules. Some driveability problems may be noticed until the system re-adapts to operating conditions. OBD II readiness codes, which may be required for emissions testing, may also be erased. Convenience electronics (alarm system, interior light control, power locks, mirrors, and windows) may need to be re-set using a VAG 1551/1552 or equivalent scan tool.*

Engine Codes
• AFP . . . . . 2.8L 6-cylinder gasoline

DIAGNOSTIC TESTING

The tests that follow can be used to help isolate engine problems, to better understand a problem before starting expensive repairs, or just to periodically check engine condition.

Compression test

A compression test will tell a lot about the condition of the engine without the need for taking it apart. The test is relatively simple, requiring only a compression tester, a spark plug wire removal tool and a spark plug wrench. For the most accurate test results, the battery should be fully charged and engine should be warm.

> ***NOTE —***
> *Because engine temperature may affect compression, the most accurate results are obtained when the engine is at normal operating temperature.*

1. Warm-up engine until it is a minimum of 30°C (86°F). switch off ignition.

2. Disconnect 2-pin harness connector from crankcase vent heating element on the intake hose between mass air flow sensor and throttle valve control module and remove intake hose.

3. Unplug spark plug wires from spark plugs with Volkswagen special tool T10029 or equivalent.

NOTE —
Volkswagen special tool T10029 is required to remove and install the spark plug connectors to spark plugs without damaging the wires or wire seals.

Fig. 1. Remove spark plug connectors with special tool T10029 as shown to avoid damage to spark plug connector.

4. Unclip spark plug wires from the guides.

5. Remove upper sound absorber panel.

6. Use compressed air to clear the area around the spark plugs. Remove spark plugs and lay aside in proper order.

NOTE —
Due to the limited clearance around the recessed spark plugs, VW special tool no. 3122B is available to easily remove and install the plugs.

7. With ignition off, disable ignition system by disconnecting 5-pin harness connector from coil pack on back of cylinder head. See Fig. 2.

8. Remove fuse #32 for the voltage supply to injectors.

9. Fit compression tester into first spark plug hole.

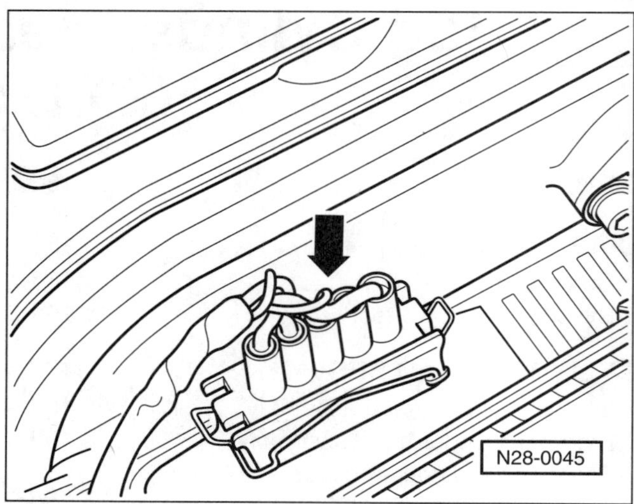

N28-0045

Fig. 2. Disconnect 5-pin harness connector (**arrow**) from ignition coil pack on back of cylinder head.

10. Have a helper:
    - depress clutch pedal fully
    - put transmission in neutral or park
    - depress accelerator pedal to the floor
    - crank engine over with starter motor

NOTE —
Cranking the engine with the ignition system disabled and components disconnected will cause Diagnostic trouble codes (DTCs) to be stored in engine management system memory.

11. Engine should be cranked a minimum of 4 to 5 revolutions.

12. Record readings, release pressure in gauge and repeat procedure for each cylinder.

13. Compare readings to specification.

Specification

- Compression pressures (2.8L engine)
  - new . . . . 10 to 13 bar (147 - 191 psi)
  - wear limit . . . . 7.5 bar (110 psi)
  - maximum difference between cylinders . . . . 3 bar (44 psi)

---

14. When all cylinders have been checked, reinstall spark plugs and connect harness connector for ignition coil pack and install fuse #32. Install upper sound absorber panel and intake hose.

Tightening torque

- Spark plug to cylinder head . . . . 25 Nm (18 ft-lb)

Low compression suggests poorly sealed combustion chambers. Compression pressures which are relatively even but below specifications indicate worn piston rings and/or cylinder walls. Low but erratic values tend to indicate valve leakage. Dramatic differences, such as good values in some cylinders and very low values in one or two cylinders are the sign of a localized failure, such as a burnt valve or a failed cylinder head gasket.

Cylinder leakdown test

The most conclusive diagnosis of low compression symptoms requires a cylinder leak-down test. Using a special tester and a supply of compressed air, each cylinder is pressurized. The rate at which the air leaks out of the cylinder, as well as the sound and location of the escaping air can more accurately pinpoint the magnitude and source of the leakage. Any engine compression diagnosis that will require major disassembly should first be confirmed by a cylinder leak-down test. Because this test requires special equipment and experience, it may be desirable to have it performed by a Volkswagen dealer or other qualified repair shop.

CYLINDER HEAD SERVICE

Many cylinder head repairs can be accomplished without removing the cylinder head from the engine. The cylinder head cover (valve cover) gasket, camshaft, camshaft oil seal, valve guide oil seals, valve springs and cam followers are all accessible with cylinder head installed. This heading describes those repairs that can be done with cylinder head installed.

Fig. 3. shows an exploded view of the internal cylinder head components and Fig. 4. shows the external cylinder head components.

> ***NOTE —***
> *Special alignment tool 3268 is required for most VR6 cylinder head work. This tool is used to accurately set the camshafts at TDC. This plastic tool is relatively inexpensive and should always be used any time camshaft drive chains are removed from camshaft sprockets.*

Internal cylinder head assembly

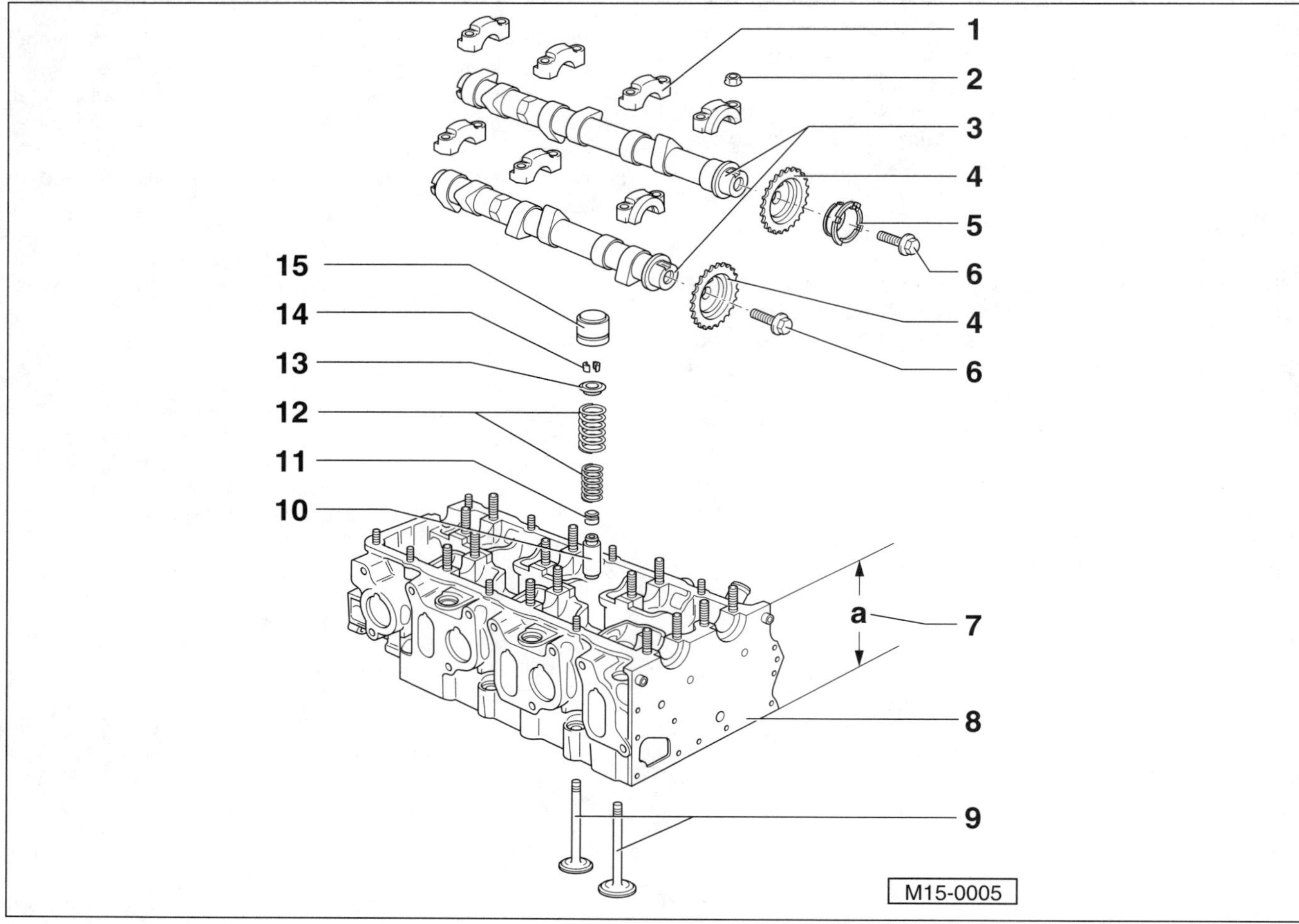

Fig. 3. Exploded view of internal cylinder head components.

1. **Bearing cap**
   - Note installation position and sequence
2. **Nut**
   - Tighten to 20 Nm (15 ft-lb)
3. **Camshafts**
   - Radial clearance checked with Plastigage® wear limit: 0.10 mm (0.004 in)
   - Run out: maximum 0.01 mm (0.0004 in)
4. **Camshaft chain sprockets**
5. **Shutter wheel**
   - For camshaft position sensor
   - Note installation position
   - Contact area between camshaft sprocket and shutter wheel must be clean and dry at installation
6. **Camshaft chain sprocket bolts**
   - Tighten to 100 Nm (74 ft-lb)
   - Note 24 mm hex on camshaft to lock
   - Do not use plastic alignment tool 3268 to lock
   - Lightly oil bolt head contact surface before installing
7. **Cylinder head height**
   - Dimension a: minimum 139.5 mm (5.492 in.)
8. **Cylinder head**
9. **Valves**
   - Do not rework! Only lapping is permitted
10. **Valve guide**
11. **Valve stem seal**
12. **Valve springs, inner and outer**
13. **Valve spring retainer**
14. **Valve keepers**
15. **Hydraulic lifter**
    - Do not interchange
    - Equipped with hydraulic clearance compensation
    - Store with cam contact surface facing downwards
    - Oil contact surfaces

External cylinder head assembly

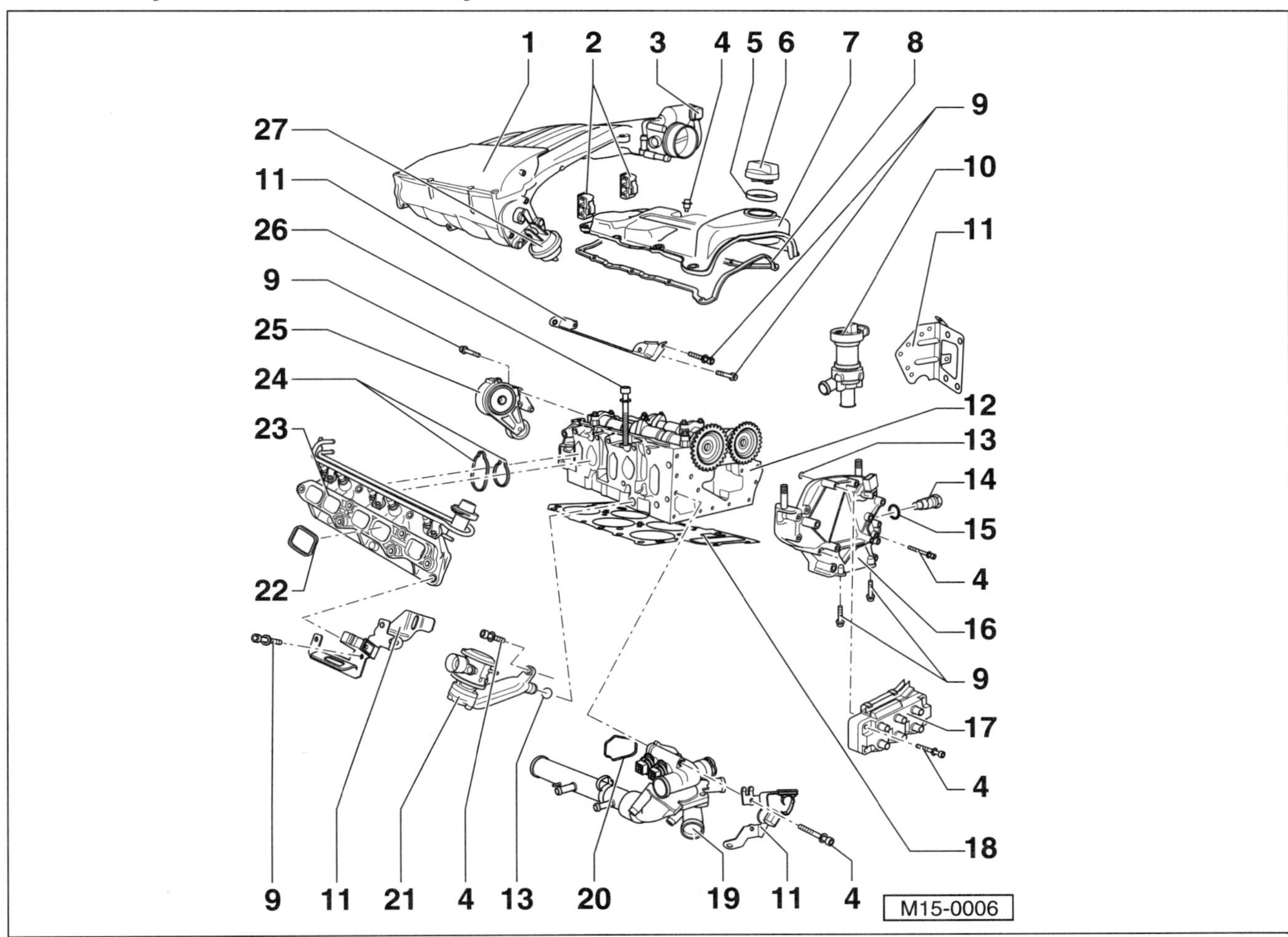

M15-0006

Fig. 4. Exploded view of external cylinder head components.

1. **Intake manifold, upper section**
   - Tighten to lower section first, then tighten to upper section
   - Plastic construction
   - With performance port and rotary valve
2. **Retainer, fuel lines**
3. **Throttle valve control module (J338)**
   - Electronically controlled
   - With Throttle Position Sensor (G88)
   - With Throttle Position Actuator Sensor (G69)
   - Heated by engine coolant
4. **Bolt**
   - Tighten to 10 Nm (7 ft-lb)
5. **Gasket, oil filler cap**
6. **Cap, oil filler**
7. **Cylinder head (valve) cover**
8. **Gasket, cylinder head (valve) cover**
   - Replace if damaged
9. **Bolt**
   - Tighten to 25 Nm (18 ft-lb)
10. **Auxiliary coolant pump (V51)**
11. **Auxiliary coolant pump mounting bracket**
12. **Cylinder head**
    - Replace engine coolant if removing head
13. **O-ring**
    - Always replace
14. **Chain tensioner, upper**
    - Turn engine only with chain tensioner installed
15. **Seal**
    - Always replace
16. **Cover, camshaft sprocket**
    - Can be removed and installed with cylinder head installed
    - Coat sealing surfaces with VW sealant, **see Item 29**
    - If only cover is removed, seal gasket prior to installation, **see** Ⓐ

External cylinder head assembly (continued)

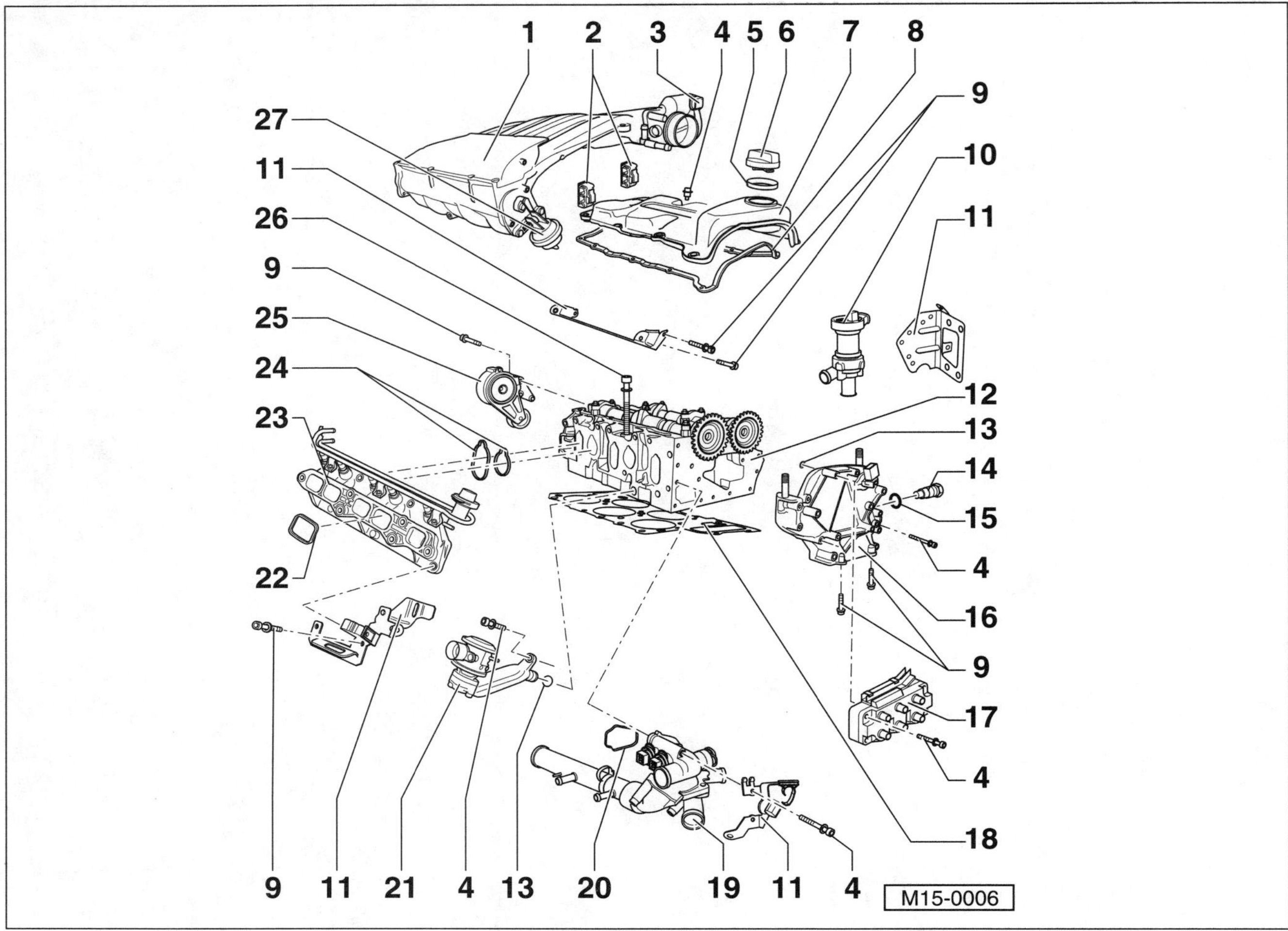

17. Ignition coil pack (N152)

18. Cylinder head gasket
- Always replace
- Metal construction
- Replace engine coolant if removing head

19. Thermostat housing

20. Seal
- Always replace

21. Combi valve
- For secondary air injection system

22. Seal, upper/lower intake manifold
- Replace if damaged

23. Intake manifold, lower section
- Plastic construction

24. Seal, intake manifold/cylinder head
- Replace if damaged

25. Tensioner, ribbed V-belt

26. Cylinder head bolt
- Quantity 20, 3 different lengths
- Stretch bolts, always replace

27. Vacuum actuator, rotary valve

28. Bolts, upper/lower intake manifold
- Tighten to 25 Nm (18 ft-lb)

29. Sealant (not shown)
- Volkswagen recommended sealant for all operations requiring sealant AMV 188 001 02

NOTE —

Volkswagen part numbers are given for reference only! Always consult with your Volkswagen Parts Department or aftermarket parts specialist for the latest parts information.

A Cylinder head gasket, sealing, after removal of upper drive chain cover

V15 - 0821

V15-0821

- **Remove old sealant from the 3 mm bores in the cylinder head gasket and flange (arrows).**
- **Bores may be only partially visible.**
- **Apply sealant to 3 mm bores in the cylinder head gasket and to upper drive chain cover and flange.**

Cylinder head (valve) cover, removing and installing

1. With ignition off, disconnect battery ground strap.
2. Unplug spark plug wires from spark plugs with Volkswagen special tool T10029 or equivalent.

   NOTE —

   Volkswagen special tool T10029 is required to remove and install spark plug connectors without damaging the wires or wire seals.

3. Unclip spark plug wires from guides.
4. Remove upper sound absorber panel.
5. Disconnect 2-pin harness connector from crankcase vent heating element on intake hose between mass air flow sensor and throttle valve control module. Remove intake hose.
6. Disconnect the 6-pin harness connector from the throttle valve control module. See Fig. 5.

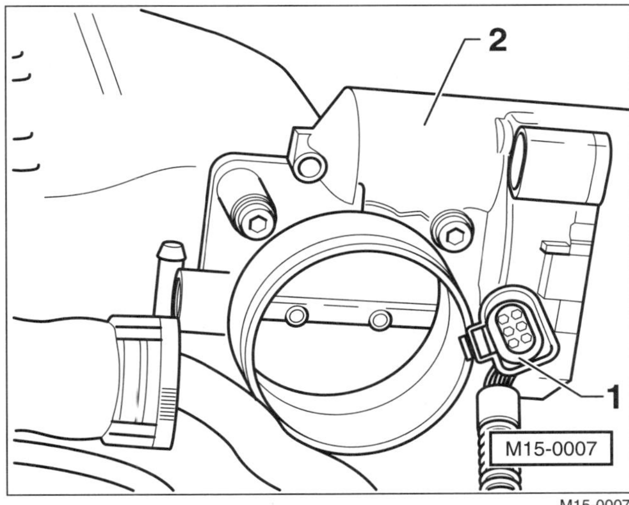

M15-0007

Fig. 5. Harness connector plug (**1**) on throttle valve control module (**2**).

7. Unbolt ground connection at throttle valve control module.
8. Loosen coolant expansion tank cap to release pressure and re-tighten.
9. Remove coolant hoses from throttle valve control module and plug hose ends. See Fig. 6.

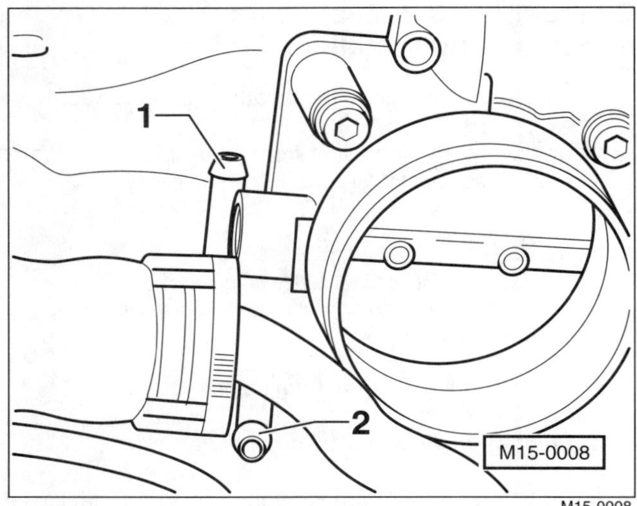

M15-0008

Fig. 6. Coolant connections (**1** & **2**) on throttle valve control module.

10. Unclip fuel lines from guides at cylinder head cover.

11. Label and disconnect vacuum connections on upper section of intake manifold. See Fig. 7.

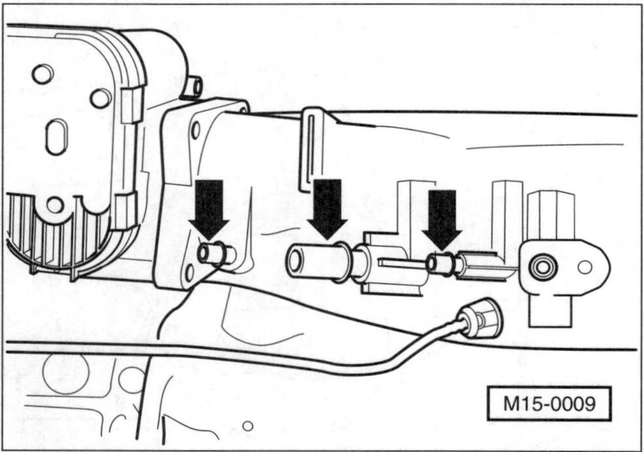

M15-0009

Fig. 7. Vacuum connections (**arrows**) on rear of intake manifold.

12. Unclip secondary air pump inlet hose and remaining lines from guides on upper section of intake manifold.

13. Unbolt dipstick tube from upper section of intake manifold.

14. Remove intake manifold support bolts from upper intake manifold section.

15. Label and disconnect vacuum connections on rotary valve actuator.

16. Disconnect fuel line couplers at fuel rail. See Fig. 8.

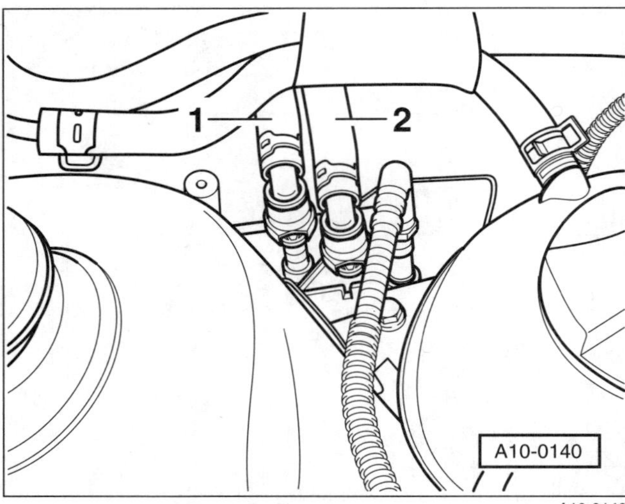

A10-0140

Fig. 8. Disconnect fuel line from fuel pump, marked white (**1**) and fuel return line, marked blue (**2**) at fuel rail. Press coupling tabs together to disconnect.

> ***WARNING —***
>
> *Fuel will be expelled when disconnecting fuel hoses. Wrap a cloth around the fuel line fittings before disconnecting them. Do not smoke or work near heaters or other fire hazards. Have a fire extinguisher handy.*

17. Seal off disconnected fuel and vacuum hoses lines to prevent contamination.

18. Remove lower sound absorber panels (belly pan).

19. Remove front bumper cover and move lock carrier to service position, see **50 Body–Front.**

20. Remove ribbed V-belt.

21. Remove retaining clamps from A/C refrigerant lines. Remove A/C compressor with refrigerant lines still attached, see **87 Air Conditioning**.

NOTE —

To prevent damage to condenser and to refrigerant lines/hoses, ensure that lines and hoses are not stretched, kinked or bent.

22. Remove secondary air injection system combi valve.

23. Remove bolts securing upper intake manifold to lower intake manifold.

24. Cover open intake runners using clean shop rags.

25. Remove upper intake manifold and lay aside taking care to avoid damage to rotary valve actuator.

26. Remove nuts from perimeter of cylinder head cover and lift off cylinder head cover and gasket.

27. Installation is reverse of removal noting the following additional points:
    - Use new gaskets where appropriate.
    - Tighten upper intake manifold to lower intake manifold before tightening upper intake manifold support bolts.
    - Refill coolant as required.
    - Ensure that fuel line couplers are securely attached.

28. Quality check your repair work, see **Quality Review** at the end of this repair group.

Tightening Torques
- Cylinder head cover to cylinder head . 10 Nm (7 ft-lb)
- Upper intake manifold to lower intake manifold . . . . 25 Nm (18 ft-lb)
- Upper intake manifold to supports . . . 25 Nm (18 ft-lb)

Camshafts, removing

The camshafts can be removed with cylinder head installed. Removing camshafts allows access to hydraulic cam followers, valve springs, and valve stem oil seals.

NOTE —
Volkswagen special tool 3268, camshaft ruler, is specified for setting valve timing during camshaft installation. The tool is relatively inexpensive and highly recommended.

1. With ignition off, disconnect battery ground strap.

2. Using a socket wrench on crankshaft vibration damper center bolt, rotate engine clockwise by hand to set #1 cylinder at Top Dead Center (TDC). See Fig. 9.

3. Remove ignition coil pack. See **28 Ignition System**.

4. Remove cylinder head (valve) cover as given earlier.

5. Remove upper drive chain tensioner from camshaft sprocket cover.

6. Disconnect 3-pin harness connector from camshaft position sensor.

7. Remove camshaft sprocket cover from cylinder head together with camshaft position sensor.

NOTE —
*When removing cover, note the two M8 socket-head bolts threaded **up** through the lower cover.*

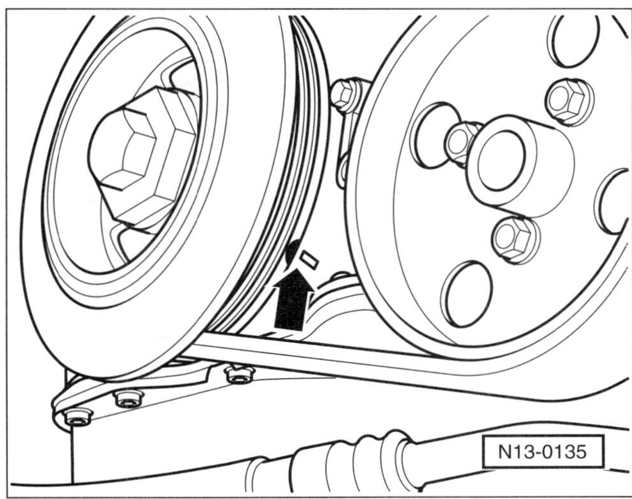

N13-0135

Fig. 9. Timing mark on crankshaft vibration damper aligned with marker on front engine cover.

8. Loosen camshaft sprocket bolts:
    - Hold camshaft only with 24 mm open end wrench on flat area cast between camshaft lobes.
    - Camshaft ruler 3268 will break if in place on end of camshaft.
    - End of camshaft can be broken if metal holder is used to loosen sprocket bolts. See Fig. 10.

CAUTION —
Do not rotate the engine once the camshafts chains are removed from the camshafts. The pistons may contact the open valves.

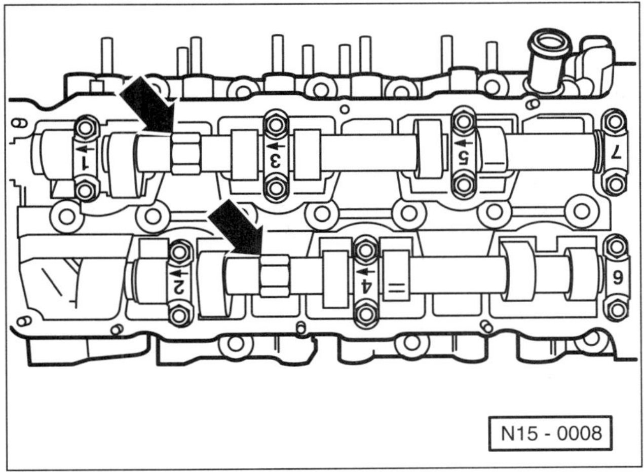

N15-0008

Fig. 10. Counterhold camshaft at 24mm hex flats (**arrows**) when loosening or tightening camshaft sprocket bolt.

9. Remove sprockets from camshafts along with camshaft position sensor shutter wheel on exhaust side camshaft.

10. Tie the double camshaft chain up using stiff wire.

11. Remove the camshaft (exhaust side) for cylinders 1, 3, and 5, as follows:
    - Remove bearing caps 1 and 7.
    - Loosen nuts on caps 3 and 5 alternately and evenly, a little at a time so that valve spring tension is relieved evenly.
    - When all tension is relieved, remove caps.
    - Lift out camshaft and lay aside.

12. Remove the camshaft (intake side) for cylinders 2, 4, and 6, as follows:
    - Remove bearing cap 4.
    - Loosen nuts on caps 2 and 6 alternately and evenly, a little at a time so that valve spring tension is relieved evenly.
    - When all tension is relieved, remove caps.
    - Lift out camshaft and lay aside. See Fig. 11.

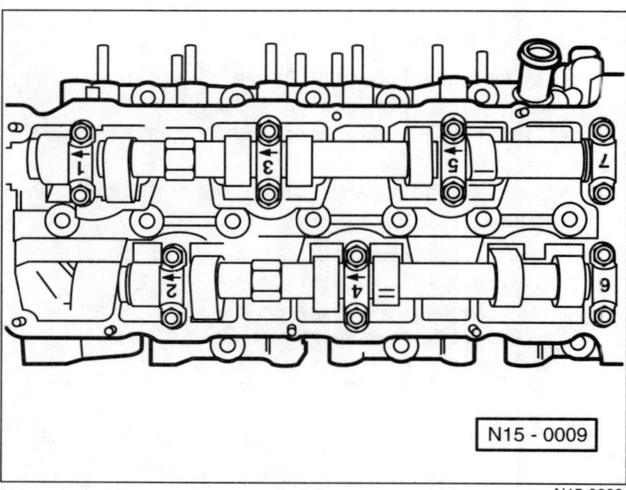

Fig. 11. Cylinder head bearing cap identification.

NOTE —
Once removed, camshafts should be checked for wear and other visible damage as described later under **Cylinder Head Components.**

Camshafts, installing

1. Lubricate contact surfaces of camshafts and then install them into cylinder head so that camshaft sprocket alignment recesses are at top. See Fig. 12.

2. Check that cylinder #1 is at Top Dead Center (TDC) as shown earlier in Fig. 9.

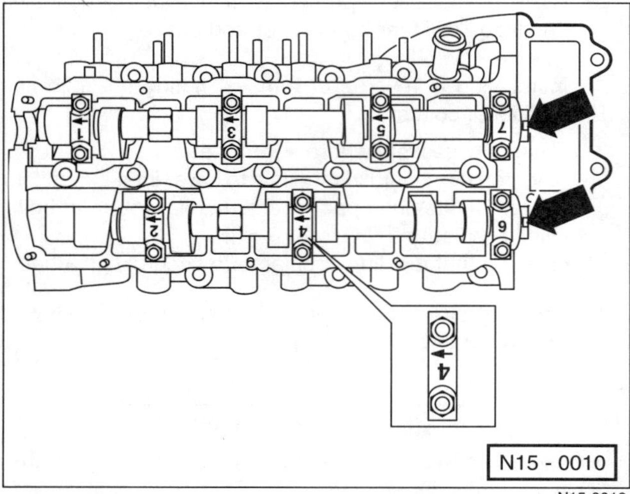

Fig. 12. Install camshafts so that sprocket alignment recesses are facing up (**arrows**). Numbers must be readable from exhaust side and arrows must point towards vibration dampener end of engine (**inset**).

NOTE —
- *To avoid uneven and accelerated wear, bearing caps must be reinstalled in their exact original positions.*
- *During installation, the numbers on camshaft bearing caps must be readable from the exhaust side and arrows must point toward vibration damper end (front) of engine.*

3. Install bearing caps 3 and 5 onto exhaust side camshaft.
    - Tighten nuts on caps 3 and 5 alternately and evenly, a little at a time so that valve spring is tensioned evenly and camshaft is drawn down fully into bearing saddle. Torque to specification.
    - Install bearing caps 1 and 7. Torque to specification.

4. Install bearing caps 2 and 6 onto intake side camshaft.
    - Tighten nuts on caps 2 and 6 alternately and evenly, a little at a time so that valve spring is tensioned evenly and camshaft is drawn down fully into bearing saddle. Torque to specification.
    - Install bearing cap 4. Torque to specification.

Tightening torque
- Camshaft bearing caps to cylinder head . . . . 20 Nm (15 ft-lb)

5. Clean camshaft sprocket cover at sealing surfaces and at cylinder head.

6. Clean sealant from 3 mm bores in cylinder head gasket. See Fig. 4. given earlier.

7. Position camshafts so that Volkswagen special tool 3268 fits into slots in the end of the camshafts. Install 3268 fully into the cutouts. See Fig. 13.

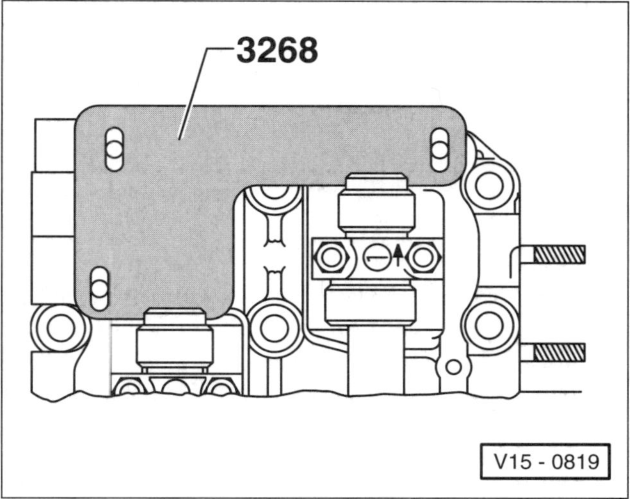

V15-0819

Fig. 13. Volkswagen special tool 3268 aligns camshafts at TDC. Tool engages slots in rear of camshafts.

8. Mount camshaft sprocket to shorter camshaft (cylinders 2, 4, and 6). Install mounting bolt hand-tight. Install chain to sprocket so that there is no slack between intermediate shaft sprocket and cam sprocket.

9. Install the remaining sprocket into chain and onto camshaft so that all chain slack is at tensioner side of chain. Install mounting bolt together with camshaft position sensor shutter wheel. Hand tighten bolt.

> ***CAUTION —***
> *The mating surfaces between the camshaft position sensor wheel and the camshaft sprocket must be dry and free of oil before tightening the center bolt.*

10. Remove camshaft alignment tool from rear of camshafts. Tighten camshaft sprocket mounting bolts. Counterhold camshaft when torquing bolt. See Fig. 10. given earlier.

> ***CAUTION —***
> *Do not tighten the camshaft bolts with the plastic alignment tool installed. It is easily broken.*

Tightening torque

- Camshaft sprockets to camshaft (with bolt contact surface oiled) . . . . 100 Nm (74 ft-lb)

11. Fill 3 mm bores in cylinder head gasket with sealant.

12. Apply sealant to camshaft sprocket cover.

13. Install new O-ring into camshaft sprocket cover insuring proper seating and install cover.

> ***CAUTION —***
> *Be sure to install a new O-ring in the rear of the camshaft sprocket cover. Lightly oil O-ring and install it into cover before installation.*

14. Install all camshaft sprocket cover bolts hand tight. Torque M8 bolts to specification first, torque M6 bolts last.

Tightening torques

- Camshaft sprocket cover to cylinder head or lower drive chain cover
  - M6 . . . . 10 Nm (89 in-lb)
  - M8 . . . . 25 Nm (18 ft-lb)
- Upper camshaft chain tensioner to camshaft sprocket cover. . . . . 30 Nm (22 ft-lb)

15. Install upper chain tensioner using a new seal.

> ***NOTE —***
> *If the tensioner was taken apart, or if the piston has expanded out, it must be bled down. Use a thin wire through opening in tensioner piston. Push wire into piston while apply light pressure. When piston check valve opens, tensioner will collapse. See Fig. 14.*

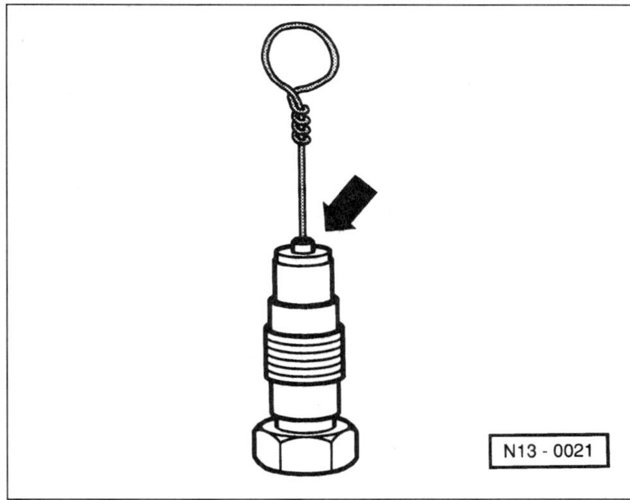

N13-0021

Fig. 14. Bleed tensioner by inserting thin wire (approximately 0.80 mm) into piston hole (**arrow**). Apply pressure to tensioner piston while pushing on wire. When piston check valve opens, piston will move into tensioner body.

16. Turn the engine over by hand in normal engine rotation direction two full revolutions and realign the timing marks shown earlier in Fig. 9.

17. Install Volkswagen tool 3268 to the camshafts. If cam timing is setup correctly, the tool will slide smoothly into camshaft cutouts.

18. Install cylinder head (valve) cover.

19. Remainder of installation is reverse of removal noting the following additional points:
    - Use new gaskets where appropriate.
    - Tighten upper intake manifold to lower intake manifold before tightening upper intake manifold support bolts.
    - Refill coolant as required.
    - Ensure that fuel line couplers are securely attached.

20. Quality check your repair work, see **Quality Review** at the end of this repair group.

> ***CAUTION —***
> *If new hydraulic cam followers were installed, the engine must not be run for at least 30 minutes. New cam followers are at a maximum height and should be allowed to bleed down or the valve heads could contact the pistons on start up.*

Hydraulic cam followers, checking

The VR-6 engine is equipped with hydraulic cam followers also known as valve lifters that automatically maintain proper valve clearance. The cam followers are pumped up by engine oil pressure, expanding as necessary to fill the gap between the valve and the camshaft lobe. This occurs continuously and automatically to keep the valve in proper adjustment at all times.

Some valve noise at start-up is normal at times, due to hydraulic cam followers that have bled down while engine was not running. Before checking noisy cam followers, check to see that engine oil is new and clean and that the level is correct. Allow 2 minutes with a warm engine running at a fast idle for the lubrication system to properly pump up cam followers.

Cam followers should only be checked when engine is warm. Run engine until radiator fan has switched on at least one time. Increase engine speed to 2,500 rpm and hold it there for approximately 2 minutes. If hydraulic cam followers are still noisy, shut engine off and proceed as follows while engine is still warm.

Hydraulic cam followers, checking

1. Remove cylinder head (valve) cover. See **Cylinder head (valve) cover, removing and installing**, given earlier.

2. Turn engine by hand in the running direction until all camshaft lobes of cylinder #1 are pointing approximately up.

> ***NOTE —***
> *Hydraulic cam follower clearance can be checked on any cam follower (lifter) that is not being depressed by the camshaft lobe.*

3. Check clearance between cam follower and cam lobe on cylinder #1:
    - Insert a 0.20 mm (0.008 in.) feeler gauge between camshaft lobe and follower. If clearance exceeds 0.20 mm (0.008 in.) replace follower.
    - If clearance is less, or if no clearance is present, lightly depress cam follower with a wooden or plastic wedge and insert a feeler gauge between camshaft lobe and follower. If clearance exceeds 0.20 mm (0.008 in.), the lifter is faulty and should be replaced. See Fig. 15.

Specification
- Hydraulic cam follower maximum clearance (2.8L engine) . . . . 0.20 mm (0.008 in.)

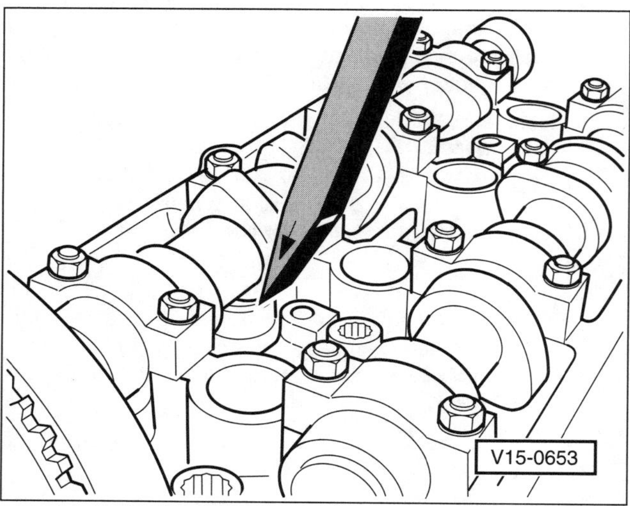

V15-0653
Fig. 15. Hydraulic cam follower shown being pushed down lightly with a plastic wedge.

4. Turn engine by hand and repeat procedure until all cam followers have been checked.

5. Replace a faulty cam follower by removing camshaft as previously described and pulling the follower from cylinder head. Faulty hydraulic cam followers can be replaced individually but only as a complete assembly.

> ***CAUTION —***
> *After installing new cam followers, the engine should not be started for at least 30 minutes. New cam followers are usually at full extended height and must be allowed to bleed down to their proper height once installed. Failure to do so may cause the valves to strike the pistons resulting in serious damage.*

NOTE —
Store removed hydraulic cam followers in order on a clean surface with the camshaft contact surface facing down to minimize bleed down. Cover with a clean lint-free shop cloth.

Valve stem oil seals, replacing

The sign of faulty valve stem seals is excessive oil consumption and oil smoke from the exhaust. This is usually most noticeable during periods of high manifold vacuum such as deceleration. If compression and leak-down testing confirm the integrity of the piston rings, but the engine consumes oil, it is possible that faulty valve stem seals are present. It should also be noted that worn valve stem seals could be due to worn valve guides and that worn valve guides are a major cause of oil consumption. See **Cylinder Head Components** for more information on checking valve guides.

Replacing valve stem oil seals requires removal of camshaft, cam followers, and valve springs. This can be done with cylinder head installed or removed. In either case, numerous Volkswagen special tools are required to compress valve springs and remove and install seals.

Working with cylinder head installed:

1. Remove cylinder head (valve) cover, camshafts, and hydraulic cam followers as described earlier.

2. Remove spark plugs.

3. Set engine to bottom dead center (BDC) for cylinder 1 by turning crankshaft.

4. Apply a continuous supply of compressed air with a minimum of 6 bar (87 psi) into first spark plug hole with an adapter. This must be done to hold valves in place while springs are removed. Continue with step 7.

> ***CAUTION —***
> *Compressed air supply must be able to maintain at least 6 bar (87 psi) during this repair. If air supply is interrupted while valve spring is removed, valve will fall into the cylinder and may require cylinder head removal to retrieve.*

Working with cylinder head removed:

5. Secure cylinder head to workbench. Use care to avoid damage to head gasket surfaces.

6. Remove camshaft and hydraulic cam followers as described earlier. Continue with step 7.

Working with cylinder head removed or installed:

7. Install appropriate valve spring compressor tools. See Fig. 16. Compress the spring for the first cylinder and remove spring retainer, both keepers, and valve spring. If spring will not compress, lightly tap tool to release stuck keepers. Use a small magnet to retrieve keepers.

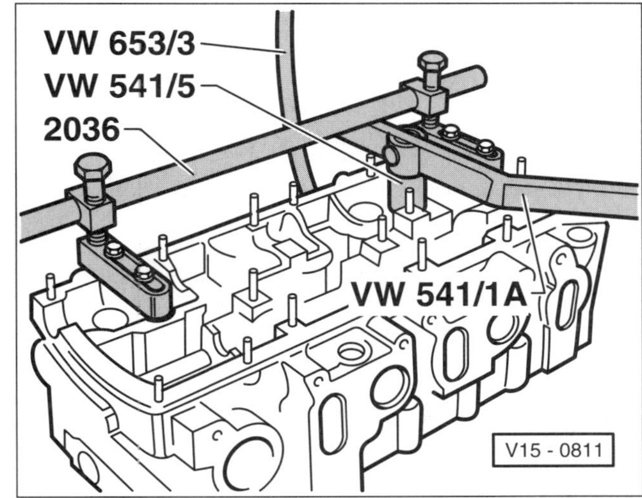

V15-0811

Fig. 16. Valve spring compressor tools being used to compress valve spring for removal of keepers. Numbers identify Volkswagen special tools. VW653/3 is compressed air hose adapter for the spark plug hole.

8. Remove valve stem seals with Volkswagen special slide hammer tool 3047A.

9. Begin installation of new seal by temporarily fitting a protective plastic fitting sleeve over the valve stem. This sleeve is usually included with new seal set and will prevent damage to the seal due to the sharp edges of the keeper grooves. Lubricate new seal with clean engine oil and fit it to installation tool. See Fig. 17.

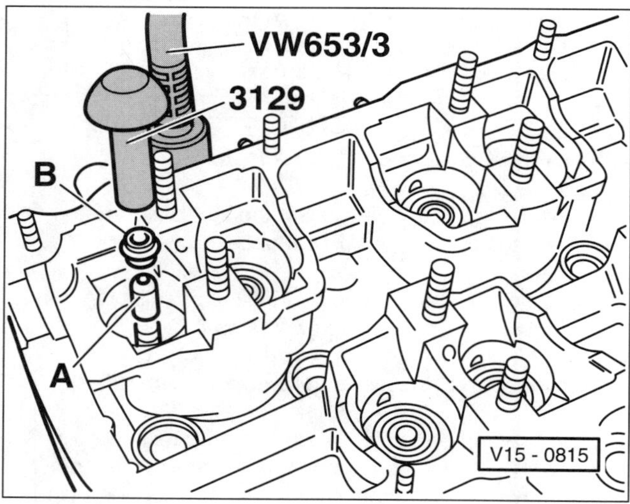

V15-0815

Fig. 17. Plastic fitting sleeve (**A**), shown with valve stem seal (**B**) and plastic installation tool 3129 available from Volkswagen.

10. Push the tool (with seal) down over valve stem until seal is fully seated on the guide. Remove tool and protective fitting sleeve.

11. Reinstall valve spring, retainer and keepers.

12. Repeat for the second valve on the cylinder.

13. When all valve seals have been replaced on the first cylinder, transfer compressed air adapter (if working with cylinder head installed) to the next cylinder and repeat the process until all valve seals have been replaced.

14. Remaining installation is the reverse of removal.

> ***CAUTION —***
> *To prevent cylinder head or camshaft damage, be sure to follow camshaft installation procedure exactly when tightening the camshaft bearing caps. See* **Camshaft, removing and installing**.

Tightening torque
- Spark plug to cylinder head . . . . 25 Nm (18 ft-lb)

---

15. Be sure to quality check your work, see **Quality Review** at the end of this repair group.

CAMSHAFT DRIVE CHAINS

Removal and installation of the camshaft drive chains requires that the transaxle be separated from the engine. Fig. 18. shows an exploded view of the camshaft drive chain assembly and related components.

The numbered list below applies to Fig. 18.

1. **Camshaft sprockets**
2. **Shutter wheel**
   - For camshaft position sensor
   - Note installation position
   - Contact area between camshaft sprocket and shutter wheel must be clean and dry at installation
3. **Camshaft chain sprocket bolts**
   - Tighten to 100 Nm (74 ft-lb)
   - Note 24 mm hex on camshaft to lock
   - Do not use plastic alignment tool 3268 to lock
   - Lightly oil bolt head contact surface before installing
4. **Tensioner guide pivot pin**
   - Tighten to 18 Nm (13 ft-lb)
5. **Seal**
   - Always replace
6. **Chain tensioner, upper**
   - Turn engine only with chain tensioner installed
   - Bleed before installing as required
   - Tighten to 40 Nm (30 ft-lb)
7. **Tensioner guide**
8. **Intermediate shaft sprocket, inner**
9. **Camshaft drive chain, upper (double row)**
   - Mark rotation direction before removal
10. **Intermediate shaft chain sprocket bolt**
    - Tighten to 100 Nm (74 ft-lb)
11. **Intermediate shaft sprocket, outer**
12. **Bolt**
    - Tighten to 10 Nm (89 in-lb)
13. **Chain tensioner, lower**
    - Turn engine only with chain tensioner installed
    - Compress and lock ratchet mechanism with small screwdriver in locking hole before installing
14. **Crankshaft with integral chain sprocket**
    - Beveled (ground) tooth used for TDC timing mark
15. **Camshaft drive chain, lower (single row)**
    - Mark rotation direction before removal
16. **Guide rail, lower**
17. **Locating pin, guide rail (without collar)**
    - Tighten to 10 Nm (7 ft-lb)

Camshaft drive chains, assembly

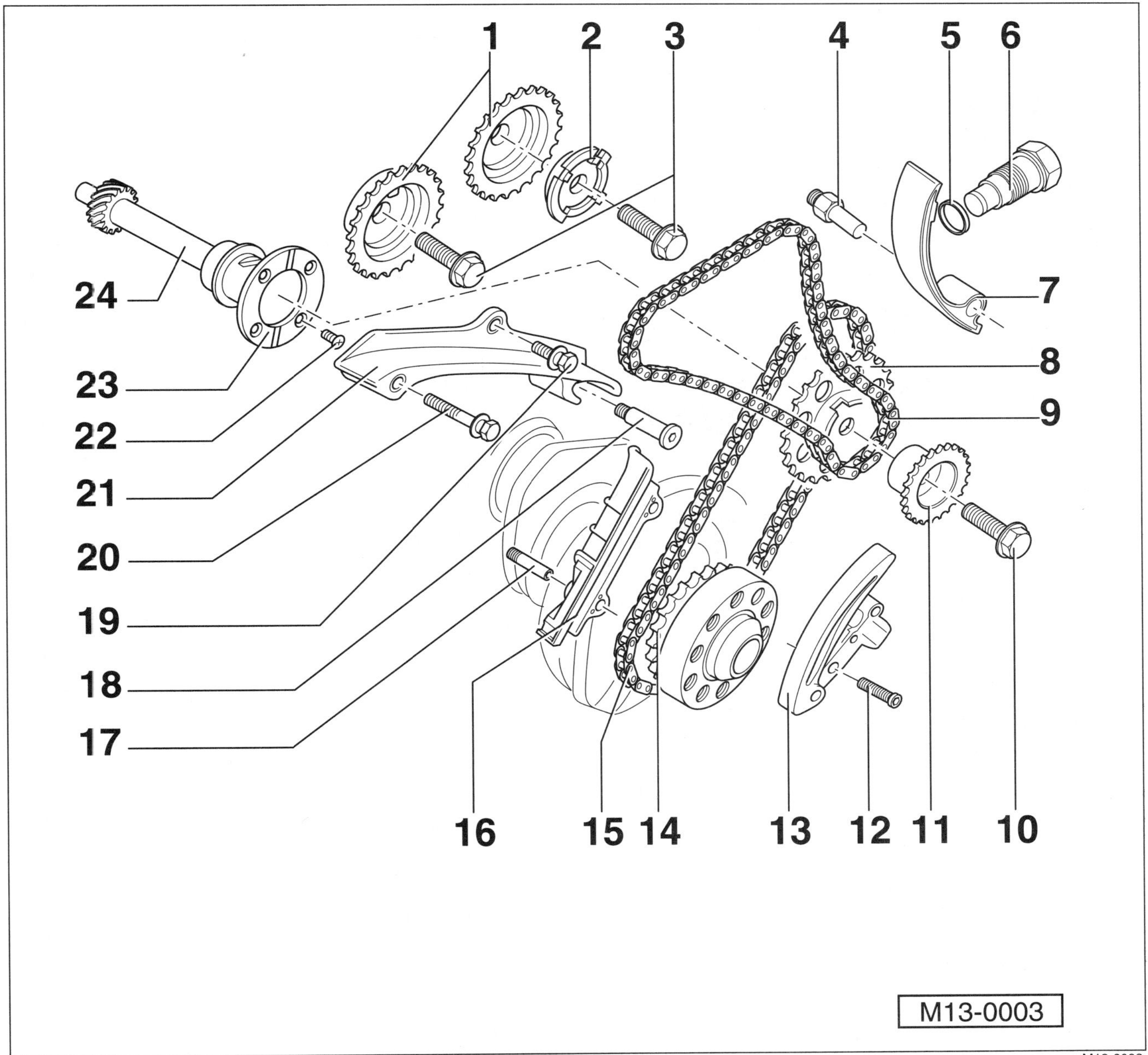

Fig. 18. Camshaft drive chains and related components.

18. Locating pin, upper guide rail (with collar)
- Tighten to 10 Nm (7 ft-lb)

19. Bolt
- Install using locking fluid "D6" or equivalent
- Tighten to 20 Nm (15 ft-lb)

20. Bolt
- Tighten to 20 Nm (15 ft-lb)

21. Guide rail, upper

22. Screw
- Install using locking fluid "D6" or equivalent
- Tighten to 10 Nm (7 ft-lb)

23. Thrust washer
- Secures intermediate shaft

24. Intermediate shaft
- Drives engine oil pump

Valve timing, checking

1. Remove lower sound absorber panels (belly pan).

2. Using a socket wrench on crankshaft vibration damper center bolt, rotate engine clockwise by hand to set the #1 cylinder at Top Dead Center (TDC). See Fig. 19.

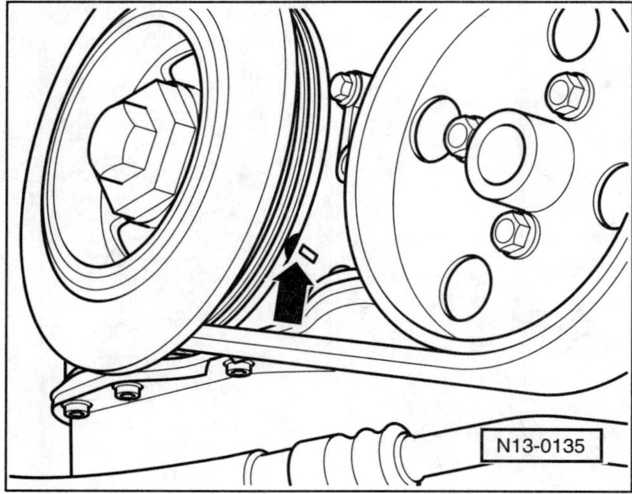

N13-0135

Fig. 19. Timing mark on crankshaft vibration damper aligned with marker on front engine cover.

3. Remove the cylinder head (valve) cover as given earlier.

4. Remove upper drive chain tensioner from camshaft sprocket cover.

5. Remove camshaft sprocket cover together with camshaft position sensor.

6. Position camshafts so that Volkswagen special tool 3268 fits into slots in the end of the camshafts. Install 3268 fully into the cutouts. See Fig. 20.

7. When marks on vibration damper align and camshaft ruler can be fully inserted in camshafts, it will be possible to see a slot on the intermediate shaft sprockets. This indicates that the valve timing is correct. See Fig. 21.

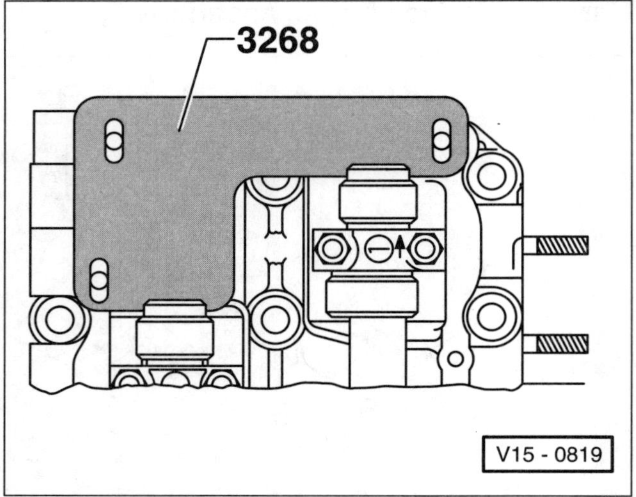

V15-0819

Fig. 20. Volkswagen special tool 3268 aligns camshafts at TDC. Tool engages slots in rear of camshafts.

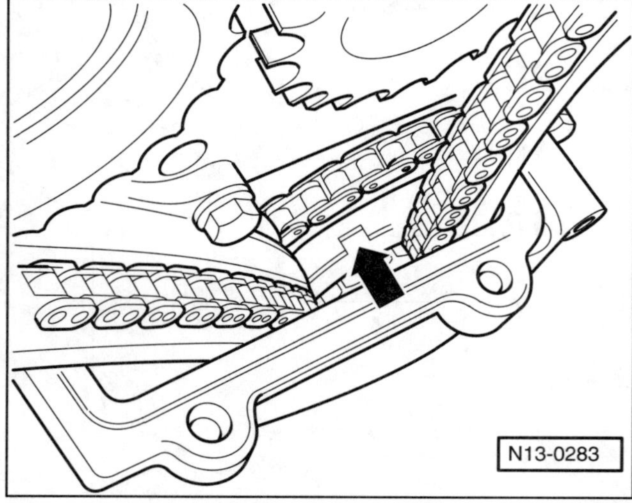

N13-0283

Fig. 21. It will be possible to see a slot (**arrow**) on the intermediate shaft sprockets when valve timing is correct.

8. If valve timing is correct, reinstall all removed components.

9. If valve timing is not correct, proceed with the following steps:

   - Remove camshaft sprockets as described earlier in **Camshafts, removing**.
   - Rotate camshaft until special tool 3268 fits into slots in rear of camshaft. See Fig. 20.
   - Install camshaft drive sprockets.

Camshaft drive chains, removing

1. Depending on the nature of the repair work to be done, proceed with one of the following:
   - Remove engine and transaxle from vehicle and separate transaxle from engine. See **10 Engine, Removing and Installing**.
   - Remove transaxle from engine. With this method, engine remains in vehicle. See **34 Manual Transmission,** or **37 Automatic Transmission** for transmission removal and installation.
2. Using a socket wrench on crankshaft vibration damper center bolt, rotate engine clockwise by hand to set the #1 cylinder at Top Dead Center (TDC). See Fig. 19.
3. Remove cylinder head (valve) cover as given earlier.
4. Remove upper drive chain tensioner from camshaft sprocket cover.
5. Remove camshaft sprocket cover together with camshaft position sensor.

NOTE —
When removing cover, note the two M8 socket-head bolts threaded up through the lower cover and the small O-ring on the rear of cover.

6. Remove flywheel or driveplate. Discard mounting bolts. See **13 Crankshaft/Cylinder Block**.
7. Remove lower drive chain cover from cylinder block and oil pan.

> ***CAUTION —***
> *Use care when removing the lower cover from the oil pan gasket and the cylinder head gasket. If the gaskets are damaged, they will need to be replaced.*

8. Mark engine rotation direction on drive chains. See Fig. 22.
9. Loosen camshaft sprocket bolts:
   - Hold camshaft only with 24 mm open end wrench on flat area cast between camshaft lobes.
   - Camshaft ruler 3268 will break if in place on end of camshaft.
   - End of camshaft can be broken if metal holder is used to loosen sprocket bolts. See Fig. 23.
10. Remove both camshaft sprockets and upper camshaft drive chain.

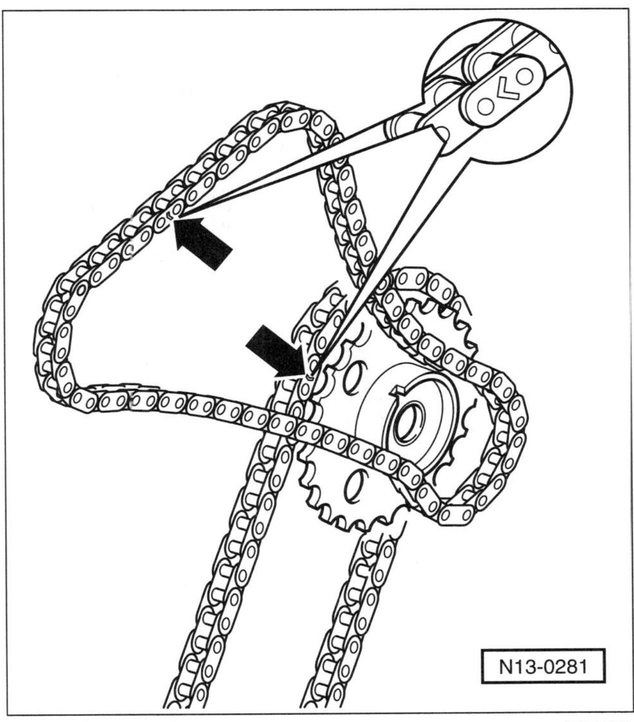

N13-0281

Fig. 22. Before removing drive chains, mark engine rotation direction on chain link (**arrow**).

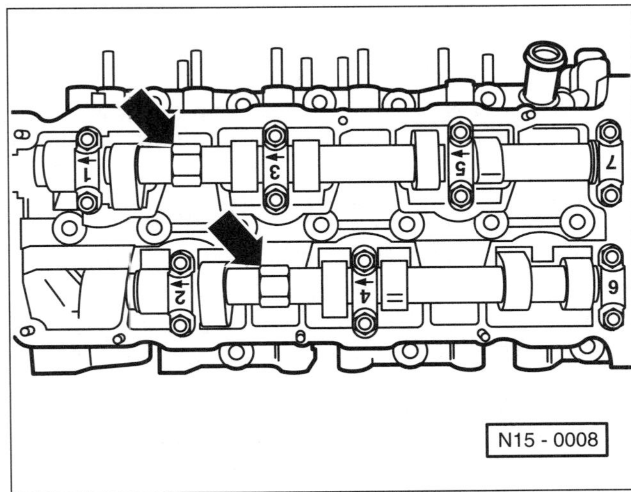

N15-0008

Fig. 23. Counterhold camshaft at 24mm hex flats (**arrows**) when loosening or tightening camshaft sprocket bolt.

11. Temporarily install flywheel or driveplate using three of the old bolts. Lock flywheel or driveplate using a holding tool. See Fig. 24.

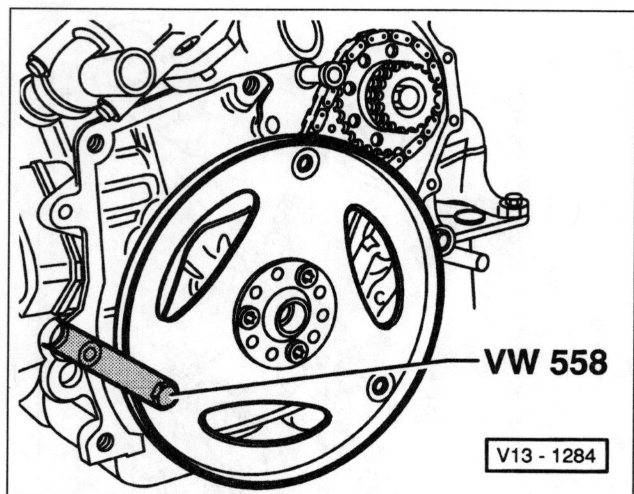

V13-1284

Fig. 24. Installed driveplate shown locked in position using Volkswagen special tool VW558. Lock flywheel in similar manner. Special tool 3406 can also be used on the vibration damper to lock crankshaft.

12. With crankshaft locked, remove intermediate shaft sprocket mounting bolt.

13. Remove lower drive chain tensioner.

14. Remove intermediate shaft sprockets together with lower drive chain and lower guide rail.

15. Remove flywheel or driveplate.

16. Inspect tensioner assemblies and chain guides for wear or damage. Replace any worn or damaged parts.

Camshaft drive chains, installing

1. Set intermediate shaft and crankshaft to TDC. See Fig. 25.
   - Temporarily install the intermediate shaft single-tooth sprocket. Rotate intermediate shaft sprocket so that the mark on the sprocket aligns with the notch on intermediate shaft thrust washer. Remove sprocket.
   - Position crankshaft so the ground-down tooth on sprocket aligns with the main bearing cap joint.

2. If previously removed, install lower guide rail locating pins.

Tightening torque
- Lower guide rail locating pin (w/o collar) to engine block . . . . 10 Nm (7 ft-lb)

3. Install lower guide rail and the intermediate shaft sprocket to the single-row chain, noting rotation direction marks made earlier.

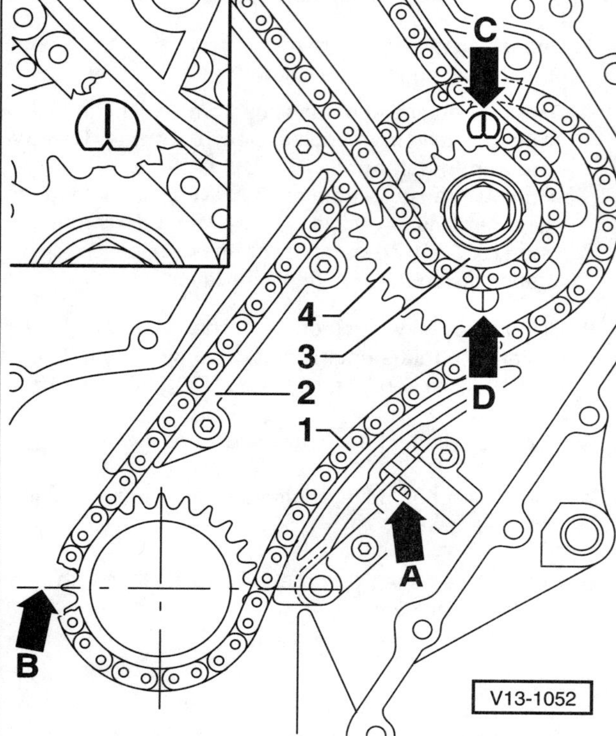

1. **Camshaft drive chain, lower (single row)**
2. **Guide rail, lower**
3. **Intermediate shaft sprocket, outer**
4. **Intermediate shaft sprocket, inner**

A. **Ratchet mechanism locking hole in lower chain tensioner**
   - Release ratchet mechanism with small tool in hole; fully compress tension bar by hand; lock in place with tool

B. **Joint for main bearing cap and cylinder block**
   - Mating surface of main bearing cap and cylinder block aligns with beveled tooth on crankshaft chain sprocket

C. **Alignment mark on intermediate shaft thrust washer**
   - Viewed through pointer hole in inner intermediate shaft sprocket

D. **Alignment mark on intermediate shaft thrust washer**
   - Pointer on inner intermediate shaft sprocket can also point to this mark

V13-1052

Fig. 25. Align beveled (ground) mark on crankshaft chain sprocket with joint for main bearing cap (**B**). Align pointer on inner intermediate shaft sprocket with mark on intermediate shaft thrust washer (**C**). Note that both sprockets are installed on intermediate shaft in this view and one sprocket tooth is cut-away for illustration purposes only (**inset**).

4. Place chain, guide rail and both intermediate shaft sprockets onto engine. Install intermediate shaft sprocket bolt hand tight.

NOTE —
Make sure all chain slack is on the tensioner side of chain and that sprocket positions have not been altered. Make sure intermediate shaft sprockets correctly engage shaft.

5. Compress lower chain tensioner and install. See Fig. 26.
   - Release ratchet mechanism with small tool in hole; fully compress tension bar by hand; lock in place with tool.
   - Install tensioner in compressed condition.
   - Ensure that all chain slack is on the tensioner side and that chain is still properly aligned.
   - Remove tool to release tension bar.

Tightening torque
- Lower chain tensioner to cylinder block . . . . 10 Nm (7 ft-lb)

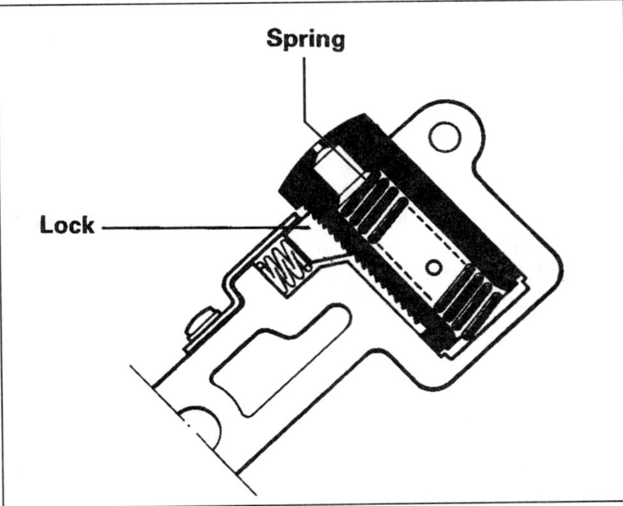

Fig. 26. Use small screwdriver or similar tool to release drive chain tensioner ratchet lock while pushing on tension bar. Wedge tool against lock to prevent movement during installation.

6. Temporarily install flywheel or driveplate using three of the old bolts. Lock flywheel or driveplate using a holding tool as shown earlier in Fig. 24.

7. Tighten intermediate shaft sprocket mounting bolt. Recheck sprocket timing marks.

Tightening torque
- Intermediate shaft sprockets to intermediate shaft. . . . . 100 Nm (74 ft-lb)

8. Position camshafts so that Volkswagen special tool 3268 fits into slots in the end of the camshafts. Install 3268 fully into the cutouts as shown earlier in Fig. 20.

9. If previously removed, install tensioner guide pivot pin and upper guide rail locating pin. Place upper guide rail into position and install the two mounting bolts. Place chain tensioner guide into position on pivot pin.

CAUTION —
Use care when working near the cylinder head gasket. If the gasket is damaged, it should be replaced.

NOTE —
Use Volkswagen locking fluid "D6" or equivalent on the shorter guide rail mounting bolt.

Tightening torques
- Tensioner guide pivot pin to engine block . . . . 18 Nm (13 ft-lb)
- Upper guide rail to engine block locating pin (with collar) . . . . 10 Nm (7 ft-lb)
- Upper guide rail to cylinder head (D6 locking fluid on shorter bolt). . . . . 25 Nm (18 ft-lb)

10. Install the double-row chain onto the intermediate shaft sprocket, noting rotation direction marks made earlier.

11. Mount camshaft sprocket to the shorter camshaft (cylinders 2, 4, and 6). Install mounting bolt hand-tight. Install chain to sprocket so that there is no slack between intermediate shaft sprocket and cam sprocket.

12. Install remaining sprocket into the chain and onto the camshaft so that all chain slack is at tensioner side of chain. Install mounting bolt together with camshaft position sensor shutter wheel. Hand tighten bolt.

CAUTION —
The mating surfaces between the camshaft position sensor wheel and the camshaft sprocket must be dry and free of oil before tightening the center bolt.

13. Remove camshaft alignment tool from the rear of the camshafts. Tighten camshaft sprocket mounting bolts. Counterhold camshaft when torquing bolt. See Fig. 23.

> **CAUTION —**
> *Do not tighten the camshaft bolts with the plastic alignment tool installed. It is easily broken.*

Tightening torque
- Camshaft sprockets to camshaft (with bolt contact surface oiled) . . . . 100 Nm (74 ft-lb)

14. Carefully clean off any old sealer from both sides of head gasket.

15. Remove the temporarily installed flywheel or driveplate.

16. Apply sealant to lower drive chain cover sealing surfaces including head gasket contact surface.

> **CAUTION —**
> *Use care not to damage the crankshaft seal when installing the lower cover. Coat the seal with a light coat of engine oil before installing cover.*

Tightening torque
- Lower drive chain cover to engine block or oil pan (M6). . . . . 10 Nm (7 ft-lb)

17. Fill 3 mm bores in cylinder head gasket with sealant.

18. Apply sealant to camshaft sprocket cover.

19. Install new O-ring into camshaft sprocket cover insuring proper seating and install cover.

> **CAUTION —**
> *Be sure to install a new O-ring to the rear of the cover. Lightly oil O-ring and install it into cover before installation.*

20. Install all camshaft sprocket cover bolts hand tight. Torque M8 bolts to specification first, torque M6 bolts last.

Tightening torques
- Camshaft sprocket cover to cylinder head or lower drive chain cover
  - M6. . . . . 10 Nm (89 in-lb)
  - M8. . . . . 25 Nm (18 ft-lb)
- Upper camshaft chain tensioner to camshaft sprocket cover . . . . 30 Nm (22 ft-lb)

21. Install upper chain tensioner using a new seal.

> ***NOTE —***
> *If the tensioner was taken apart, or if the piston has expanded out, it must be bled down. Use a thin wire through the opening in the tensioner piston. Push the wire into the piston while apply light pressure. When the piston check valve opens, the tensioner will collapse. See Fig. 34. given later.*

22. Turn the engine over by hand in normal engine rotation direction two full revolutions and realign the timing marks shown in Fig. 19.

23. Install Volkswagen tool 3268 to the camshafts. If the chains are setup correctly, tool will slide smoothly into camshaft cutouts.

> **CAUTION —**
> *Do not run the engine if VW special tool no. 3268 does not fit into the camshaft cutouts—the chain assembly may not be installed correctly. If only very minor readjustment of the camshafts allows the tool to slide into place, the assembly is probably setup correctly. If any problems are encountered, reinstall the chains from the beginning of this procedure.*

24. Install cylinder head (valve) cover.

25. Remainder of installation is reverse of removal noting the following additional points:
    - Use new gaskets where appropriate.
    - Tighten upper intake manifold to lower intake manifold before tightening upper intake manifold support bolts.
    - Refill coolant as required.
    - Use new mounting bolts on flywheel or driveplate.
    - Ensure that fuel line couplers are securely attached.

26. Depending on the repair, finish as follows:
    - Attach engine and transaxle and install into vehicle. See **10 Engine, Removing and Installing**.
    - Attach transaxle to engine that remained in vehicle and complete repair. See **34 Manual Transmission,** or **37 Automatic Transmission** for transmission installation.

27. Quality check your repair work, see **Quality Review** at the end of this repair group.

Tightening torques
- Flywheel or driveplate to crankshaft (stretch bolts–**always replace**)
  - stage I . . . . 60 Nm (44 ft-lb)
  - stage II . . . . additional 1/4 turn (90°)

CYLINDER HEAD, REMOVING AND INSTALLING

The cylinder head can be removed and installed with engine in vehicle. Fig. 3. and Fig. 4., given earlier, show views of the APH cylinder head and related components. Note that the cylinder head bolts are stretch type fasteners and should never be reused. In addition, whenever the cylinder head or the cylinder head gasket is replaced, the coolant must also be replaced, see **19 Engine–Cooling System**.

If a failed head gasket or warped head is suspected, a compression test, as described earlier under **Diagnostic Testing,** may aid diagnosis and should be performed before the cylinder head is removed. A failed head gasket may be caused by a warped cylinder head. When replacing a failed head gasket, always check the cylinder head for straightness. See **Cylinder Head Components.**

Cylinder head, removing

> ***WARNING —***
> *Do not start work on a hot engine. Allow to cool sufficiently before proceeding. Engine temperature must be no hotter than warm to the touch. Cylinder head warpage can result due to uneven cooling rates.*

NOTE —

- *Volkswagen special tool 3268, camshaft ruler, is specified for setting valve timing during camshaft installation. The tool is relatively inexpensive and highly recommended.*
- *It is advisable to read the entire procedure through before beginning the job.*
- *Disconnecting the battery cables will erase fault codes and basic settings in the engine management and automatic transmission control unit memories. Some driveability problems may be noticeable until the system re-adapts to operating conditions. OBD II readiness codes, which may be required for emissions testing, may also be erased. See* **24b Fuel Injection – Motronic (2.8L engine)** *for additional information. In most instances proper diagnosis will require the use of a scan tool such as the Volkswagen supplied VAG 1551 or 1552. Use and operation of this tool is outside the scope of this repair manual.*
- *Cylinder head will be removed with the exhaust manifold and the lower intake manifold still attached.*

1. With ignition switched off, disconnect battery negative terminal from the battery.

NOTE —
Be sure to have the anti-theft radio code on hand before disconnecting the battery.

2. Remove the cylinder head (valve) cover as given earlier.
3. Remove lower sound absorber panels (belly pan).
4. Drain engine coolant, see **19 Engine–Cooling System**.
5. Disconnect all coolant hoses from outlets on cylinder head.

> ***WARNING —***
> *Hot coolant can scald. Drain coolant only with the engine cold.*

6. Remove thermostat housing.
7. Remove ignition coil pack and ground strap.
8. Using a socket wrench on the crankshaft vibration damper center bolt, rotate engine clockwise by hand to set #1 cylinder to Top Dead Center (TDC). See Fig. 27.

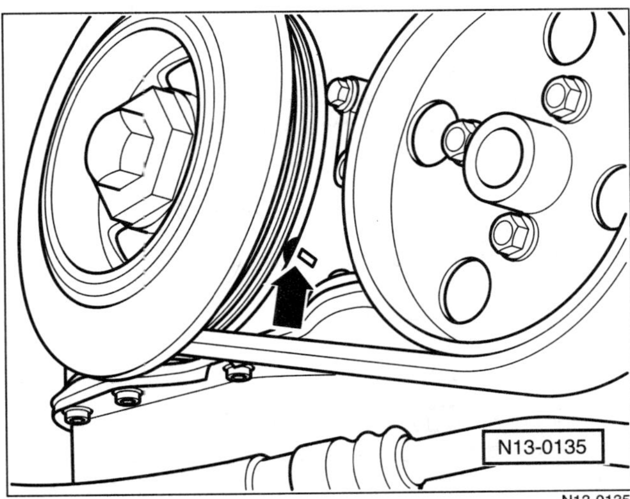

N13-0135

Fig. 27. Timing mark on crankshaft vibration damper aligned with marker on front engine cover.

9. Remove auxiliary coolant pump from mounting bracket with hoses remaining attached.
10. Disconnect 3-wire camshaft position sensor harness connector. See Fig. 28.
11. Remove upper drive chain tensioner from camshaft sprocket cover.
12. Remove camshaft sprocket cover together with camshaft position sensor.

NOTE —
When removing the cover, note the two M8 socket-head bolts threaded up through the lower cover and the small O-ring on the rear of the cover.

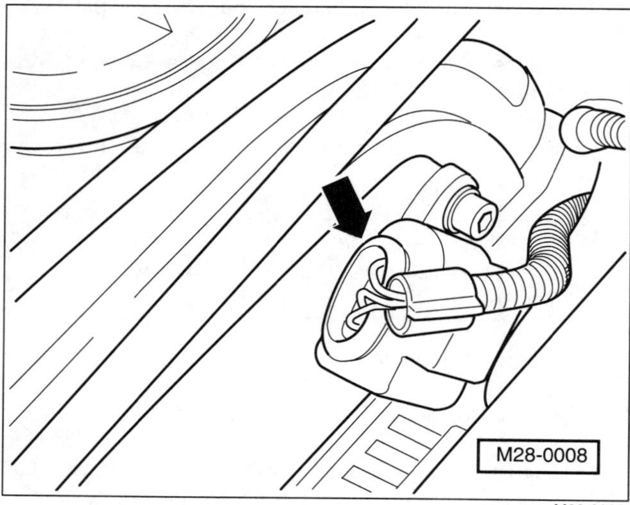

Fig. 28. 3-wire harness connector on camshaft position sensor.

13. Loosen camshaft sprocket bolts:
    - Hold camshaft only with 24 mm open end wrench on flat area cast between camshaft lobes.
    - Camshaft ruler 3268 will break if in place on end of camshaft.
    - End of camshaft can be broken if metal holder is used to loosen sprocket bolts. See Fig. 29.

14. Tie the double camshaft chain up using stiff wire.

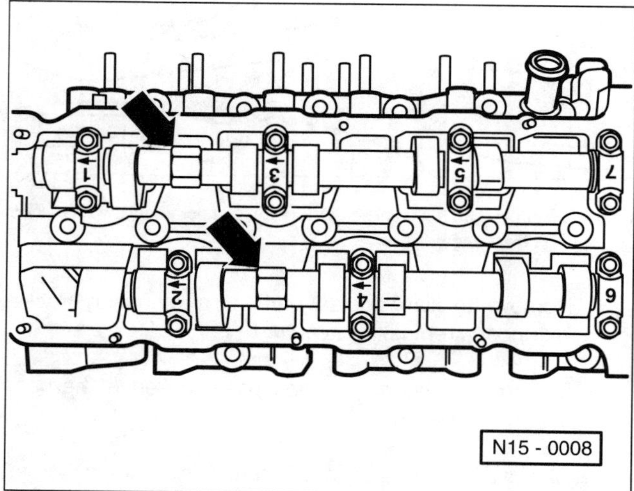

Fig. 29. Counterhold camshaft at 24mm hex flats (**arrows**) when loosening or tightening camshaft sprocket bolt.

15. Remove sprockets from camshafts along with camshaft position sensor shutter wheel on exhaust side camshaft.

16. Remove both upper double camshaft drive chain guide rail bolts and slide guide rail up off of fitted bolt.

17. Disconnect exhaust pipes from exhaust manifolds, see **26 Exhaust System and Emission Controls**.

18. Gradually and evenly loosen the 20 cylinder head bolts, in the loosening sequence. See Fig. 30. Discard bolts.

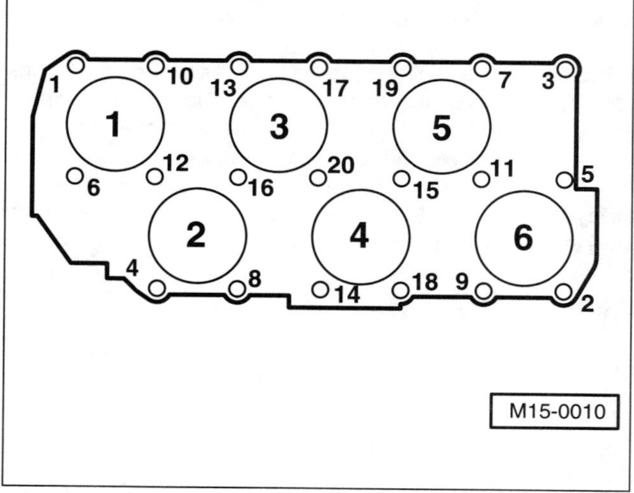

Fig. 30. Cylinder head bolt **loosening** sequence.

19. Carefully lift off cylinder head and place in a clean area. Check to make sure no hoses or wires are interfering with removal. If head is stuck, use a soft-faced mallet or pry gently with a wooden stick.

> ***CAUTION —***
> *Some of the valves will be open. Use extra care when removing and handling to avoid damage. Place the cylinder head on the bench or table so that the weight of the cylinder head will not rest on the valves.*

NOTE —
Cylinder head assembly is heavy. Use of a lifting device is strongly suggested to avoid personal injury and/or damage to cylinder head and vehicle. See Fig. 31.

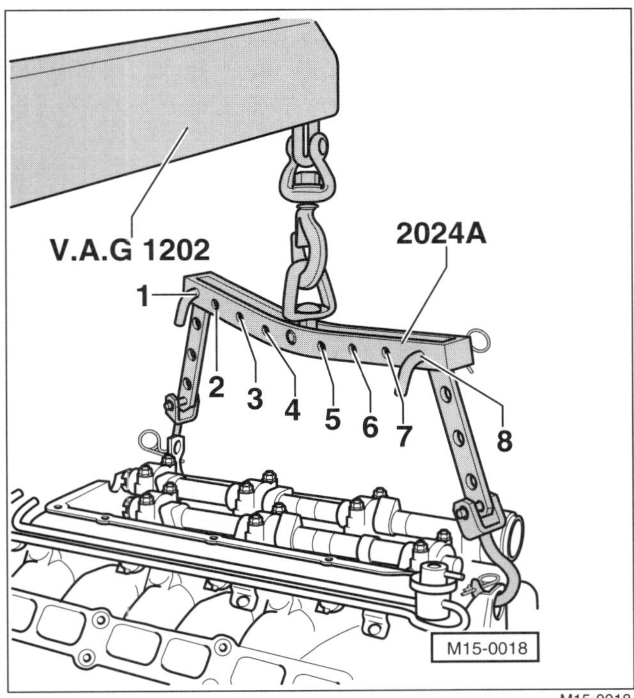

M15-0018

Fig. 31. Cylinder head shown attached to lifting device with Volkswagen special tools.

Cylinder head, installing

Before proceeding with installation of cylinder head, whether an original or a new unit, observe the following important points:

- Check cylinder head and block for distortion and warpage, see **Cylinder Head Components**, given later in this section.
- Carefully clean cylinder block and cylinder head sealing surfaces being sure to avoid scratching them during cleaning process. Do not use metal scrapers or wire brushes.
- When using abrasive paper do not use any grades coarser than 100 grit (such as 80 grit). Lower numbers are coarser.
- If cylinder head will not be reinstalled immediately, take precautions to prevent rust from forming on cylinder block walls and gasket sealing surfaces.
- When cleaning old gasket material off of cylinder block, take precautions to keep old gasket material and abrasive particles and dirt out of the cooling and oiling system passages. Place a clean shop cloth over cylinders to prevent contamination from getting between cylinder wall and piston.
- Do not take new cylinder head gasket out of packaging until ready to use. Handle new gasket with extreme care as any damage will lead to leaks.
- There MUST NOT BE any oil or coolant in the head bolt holes in the cylinder block. Any fluids in the holes creates the danger of hydrolock while torquing which could lead to structural damage of cylinder block. Use thread chasers to remove foreign material as required. Be sure that all 20 bolt holes are clean and dry.
- When all traces of the old gasket material have been removed from cylinder block and head, carefully remove all traces of metal particles, abrasives and lint. All gasket sealing surfaces and bolt holes must be clean and dry to ensure a proper seal.
- Always use new cylinder head bolts and a new cylinder head gasket.
- Do not use any gasket sealer on the new cylinder head gasket except where specifically advised to do so.
- If installing a Volkswagen supplied replacement cylinder head, be sure to inspect for and remove any plastic packaging materials used to protect the head and open valves.

1. Using a socket wrench on crankshaft vibration damper center bolt, rotate engine clockwise by hand to set the #1 cylinder at Top Dead Center (TDC). See Fig. 27.

2. Position camshafts so that Volkswagen special tool 3268 fits into slots in the end of the camshafts. Install 3268 fully into the cutouts. See Fig. 32.

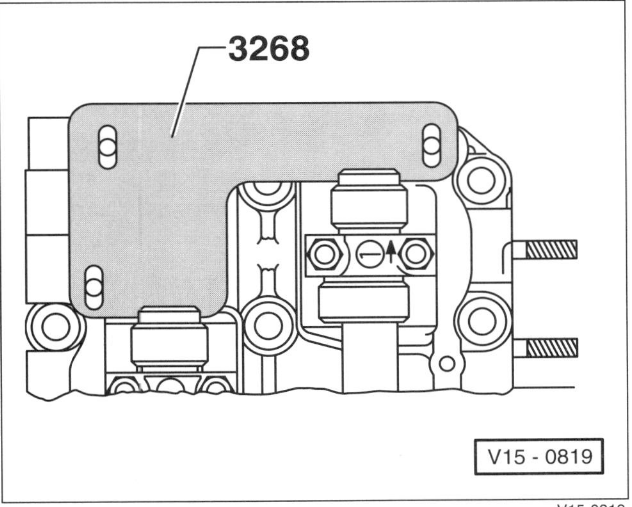

V15-0819

Fig. 32. Volkswagen special tool 3268 aligns camshafts at TDC. Tool engages slots in rear of camshafts.

3. Install new cylinder head gasket onto block over the alignment dowels with numbers and letters facing up. Fill 3 mm bores in cylinder head gasket with sealant.

4. Carefully install cylinder head onto block over the alignment dowels and screw in new head bolts. Tighten the bolts hand-tight only. Be sure that none of the wiring or any vacuum hoses are caught between cylinder head and block.

5. Tighten the 20 cylinder head bolts in three stages following the tightening sequence. See Fig. 33.

> **CAUTION —**
> *Always replace the cylinder head mounting bolts. They are stretch bolts designed to be used only once.*

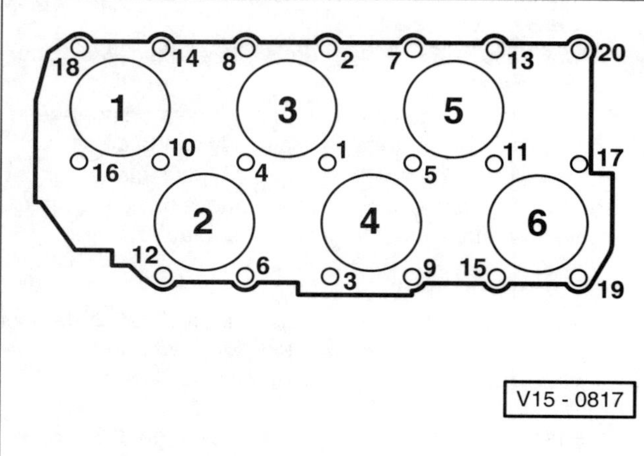

V15-0817

Fig. 33. Cylinder head bolt **tightening** sequence.

Tightening torque

- Cylinder head to cylinder block, 2.8L engine (stretch bolts – always replace)
  - stage I . . . . 50 Nm (37 ft-lb)
  - stage II . . . . additional ¼ turn (90°)
  - stage III . . . . additional ¼ turn (90°)

---

6. Install upper double camshaft drive chain guide rail.

7. Mount camshaft sprocket to the shorter camshaft (cylinders 2, 4, and 6). Install mounting bolt hand-tight. Install chain to sprocket so that there is no slack between intermediate shaft sprocket and cam sprocket.

8. Install remaining sprocket into chain and onto camshaft so that all chain slack is at tensioner side of chain. Install mounting bolt together with camshaft position sensor shutter wheel. Hand tighten the bolt.

> **CAUTION —**
> *The mating surfaces between camshaft position sensor wheel and camshaft sprocket must be dry and free of oil before tightening center bolt.*

9. Remove camshaft alignment tool from the rear of the camshafts. Tighten camshaft sprocket mounting bolts. Counterhold camshaft when torquing the bolt. See Fig. 28. given earlier.

> **CAUTION —**
> *Do not tighten the camshaft bolts with the plastic alignment tool installed. It is easily broken.*

Tightening torque

- Camshaft sprockets to camshaft (with bolt contact surface oiled) . . . . 100 Nm (74 ft-lb)

---

10. Fill 3 mm bores in cylinder head gasket with sealant.

11. Apply sealant to camshaft sprocket cover.

12. Install new O-ring into camshaft sprocket cover insuring proper seating and install cover.

> **CAUTION —**
> *Be sure to install a new O-ring to the rear of the cover. Lightly oil the O-ring and install it into cover before installation.*

13. Install all camshaft sprocket cover bolts hand tight. Torque M8 bolts to specification first, torque M6 bolts last.

Tightening torques

- Camshaft sprocket cover to cylinder head or lower drive chain cover
  - M6 . . . . 10 Nm (89 in-lb)
  - M8 . . . . 25 Nm (18 ft-lb)
- Upper camshaft chain tensioner to camshaft sprocket cover. . . . . 30 Nm (22 ft-lb)

---

14. Install upper chain tensioner using a new seal.

> **NOTE —**
> *If the tensioner was taken apart, or if the piston has expanded out, it must be bled down. Use a thin wire through the opening in tensioner piston. Push wire into piston while applying light pressure. When piston check valve opens, tensioner will collapse. See Fig. 34.*

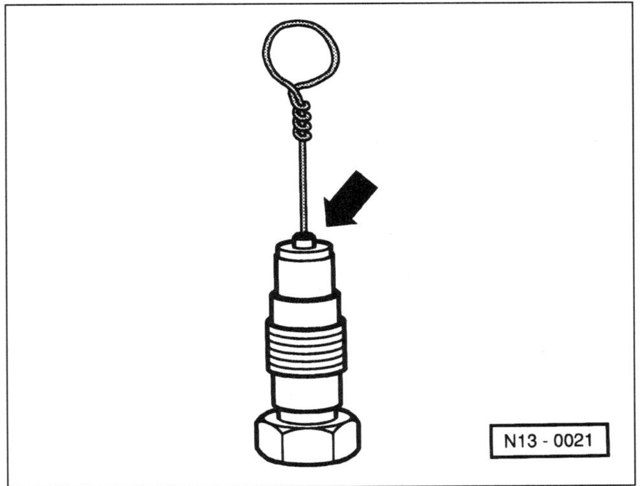

N13-0021

Fig. 34. Bleed tensioner by inserting thin wire (approximately 0.80 mm) into piston hole (**arrow**). Apply pressure to tensioner piston while pushing on wire. When piston check valve opens, piston will move into tensioner body.

15. Turn engine over by hand in normal engine rotation direction two full revolutions and realign timing marks as shown earlier in Fig. 27.

16. Install Volkswagen tool 3268 to camshafts. If cam timing is setup correctly, the tool will slide smoothly into camshaft cutouts.

17. Install cylinder head (valve) cover.

18. Remainder of installation is reverse of removal noting the following additional points:
    - Use new gaskets where appropriate.
    - Tighten upper intake manifold to lower intake manifold before tightening upper intake manifold support bolts.
    - Refill coolant as required.
    - Ensure that fuel line couplers are securely attached.

19. Quality check your repair work, see **Quality Review** at the end of this repair group.

Tightening torques

- Cylinder head cover to cylinder head . . 10 Nm (7 ft-lb)
- Ignition coil to camshaft sprocket cover . . . . 10 Nm (7 ft-lb)
- Ribbed V-belt tensioner to cylinder block . . . . 25 Nm (18 ft-lb)
- Cylinder head to cylinder block, 2.8L engine (stretch bolt - always replace)
  - stage I . . . . 50 Nm (37 ft-lb)
  - stage II . . . . additional ¼ turn (90°)
  - stage III . . . . additional ¼ turn (90°)
- Front exhaust pipe/catalytic converter to exhaust manifold . . . . 40 Nm (30 ft-lb)
- Coolant outlet flange to cylinder head . . . . 10 Nm (7 ft-lb)
- Secondary air pump bracket to cylinder block . . . . 25 Nm (18 ft-lb)
- Secondary air pump to support bracket . . . . 10 Nm (7 ft-lb)
- Camshaft sprocket cover to cylinder head or lower drive chain cover
  - M6 . . . . 10 Nm (89 in-lb)
  - M8 . . . . 25 Nm (18 ft-lb)
- Upper camshaft chain tensioner to camshaft sprocket cover. . . . . 30 Nm (22 ft-lb)

CYLINDER HEAD COMPONENTS

Cylinder head and camshafts

An exploded view of the cylinder head is given in Fig. 3. Cylinder heads with small, fine cracks between valve seats and plug threads are usable provided the cracks are not more than 0.5 mm (0.02 in.) wide, and do not extend into more than the first few spark plug threads. They will not reduce service life of the cylinder head.

If camshafts were removed or if installing a new or remanufactured cylinder head, lubricate the contact surfaces between cam lobes and hydraulic cam followers prior to start-up.

When removing and installing the camshafts, follow the procedure given under **Camshafts, removing** and **Camshafts, installing.** Special procedures and special tools are required for camshaft removal and installation. Incorrect camshaft removal and/or installation will usually result in damaged camshafts, cylinder head or pistons. Always lubricate contact surfaces between cam lobes and hydraulic cam followers prior to start-up.

When replacing cylinder head or cylinder head gasket, always flush out all the old coolant and replace with new coolant. The wil help ensure that any metal shavings and contaminants are removed from engine and cooling system. See **19 Engine–Cooling System** for draining and flushing procedures.

Check cylinder head for warpage and distortion with an accurate straight edge and feeler gauge. See Fig. 35.

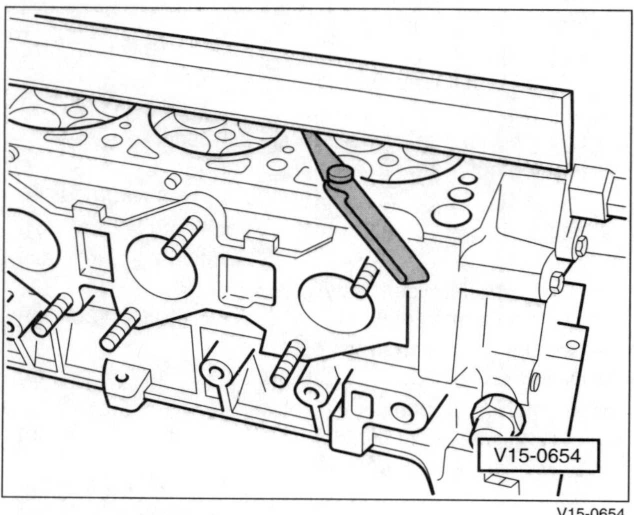

Fig. 35. Cylinder head being checked for distortion with feeler gauge.

Specification

- Maximum cylinder head distortion/warpage . . . . 0.1 mm (0.004 in.)
- Minimum cylinder dimension (valve cover gasket surface to head gasket surface) . . . . 139.5 mm (5.49 in.)

The cylinder head can be resurfaced as long as the distance from cylinder head (valve) cover seating surface to the head gasket surface is never less than specified. Machining too much material off of the cylinder head surface will change the compression ratio and will affect engine emissions.

Camshafts and cam followers

The in and out movement of the camshaft is known as axial play and is measured with the cam followers and drive chain removed and only the first and last bearing caps installed.

A dial gauge is set up on the sprocket end of camshaft and camshaft clearance is checked by moving camshaft as far as it can go in each direction. See Fig. 36.

Do not interchange camshaft bearing caps or cam followers. The arrows on the numbered bearing caps should point towards drive belt end of engine. See Fig. 37.

> ***CAUTION—***
> *After installing new cam followers, the engine should not be started for at least 30 minutes. New cam followers are at full height and must be allowed to bleed down to their proper height. Failure to do this may cause valve or piston damage.*

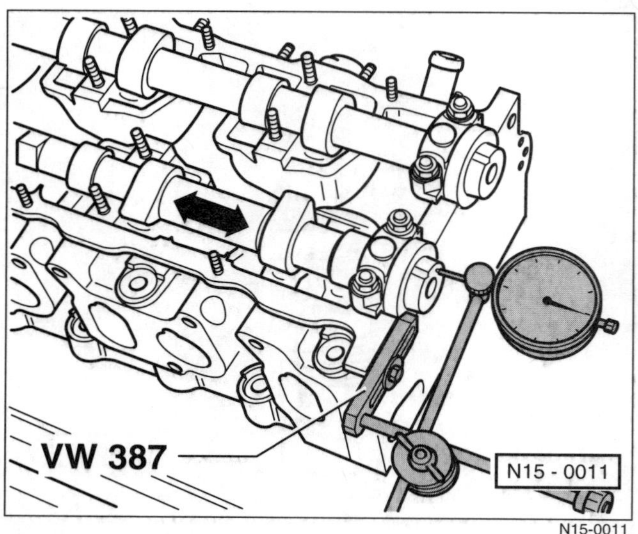

Fig. 36. Dial gauge set up on camshaft to measure axial play (**arrow**).

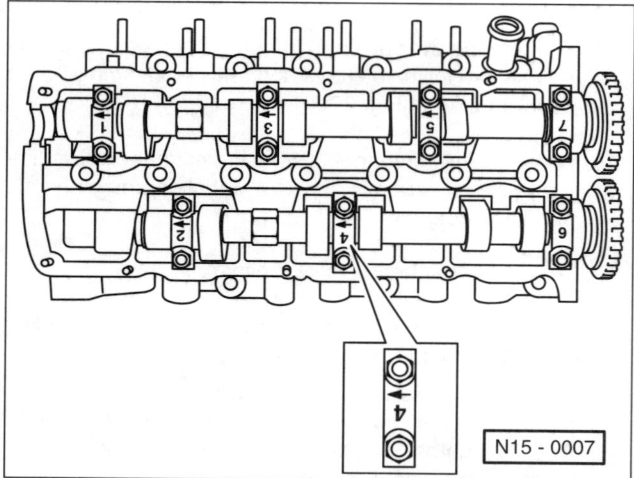

Fig. 37. Arrows on bearing caps face drive belt end of engine. Numbers should be readable from exhaust side of engine.

Valves

Exhaust valves in the VR6 engine are sodium-filled. Intake and exhaust valves must be hand-lapped only. Valve and valve spring specifications are given in **Table a**. When using the table refer to Fig. 38.

> ***WARNING—***
> *Sodium filled valves, when discarded, must be disposed of properly to avoid personal injury. Always wear protective goggles or glasses. By hand, cut off the valve stem near the head of each valve. Use only a hack saw. Do not use a power saw. Sodium reacts violently with water. Do not let water contact valve while cutting. Throw valve parts (no more than 10 valves at a time) into a bucket of water and stand clear. Discard valves when reaction has ceased.*

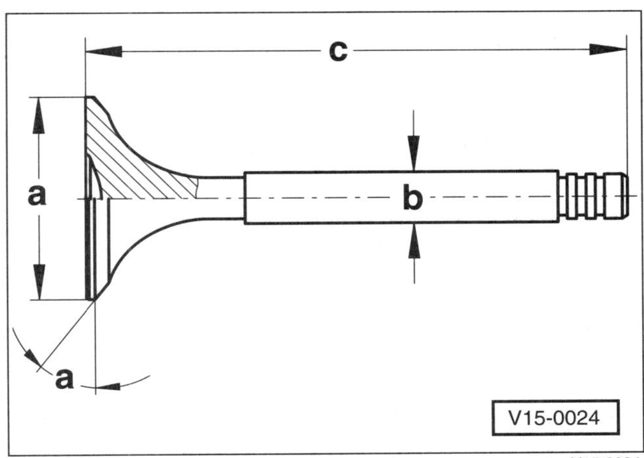

V15-0024

Fig. 38. Intake and exhaust valve dimensions are referenced in **Table a**.

Table a. Valve Dimensions

Engine	2.8L (VR6)
Valve head diameter (**a**) intake exhaust	 39.00 mm (1.5354 in.) 34.20 mm (1.3465 in.)
Valve stem diameter (**b**) intake exhaust	 6.97 mm (0.2744 in.) 6.95 mm (0.2736 in.)
Valve length (**c**) intake exhaust	 105.95 mm (4.1713 in.) 106.95 mm (4.2106 in.
Valve face angle (α) intake exhaust	 45° 45°
Valve margin	N/A

Valve guides

Special tools and a press are required to replace valve guides. Check valve guide wear using new valve. See Fig. 39. Inspect valve seats to ensure that cylinder head can be reconditioned before installing new valve guides.

> ***CAUTION —***
> *When checking valves guides, be sure to use an exhaust valve on the exhaust side and an intake valve on the intake side. Exhaust and intake valve stem diameters are slightly different. See* ***Table b****.*

Specification

- Valve guide wear (with new valve)
  - intake . . . . 1.0 mm (0.039 in.)
  - exhaust . . . . 1.3 mm (0.051 in.)

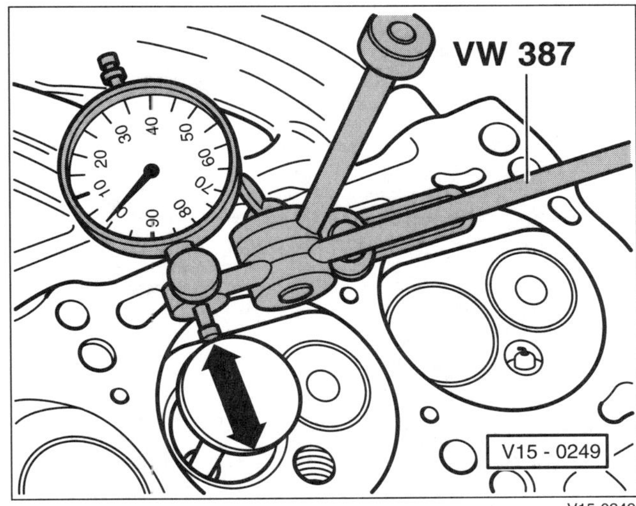

V15-0249

Fig. 39. Valve guide wear being checked with new valve. Insert valve until stem end is flush with end of guide. Rock valve back and forth to check total travel.

Original valve guides (without shoulders) are pressed out from the camshaft side of cylinder head. Cylinder heads with replacement valve guides (with shoulders) are considered unsuitable for further valve guide replacement. Lubricate new valve guides with oil and press them in from the camshaft side until the shoulder is fully seated. See Fig. 40.

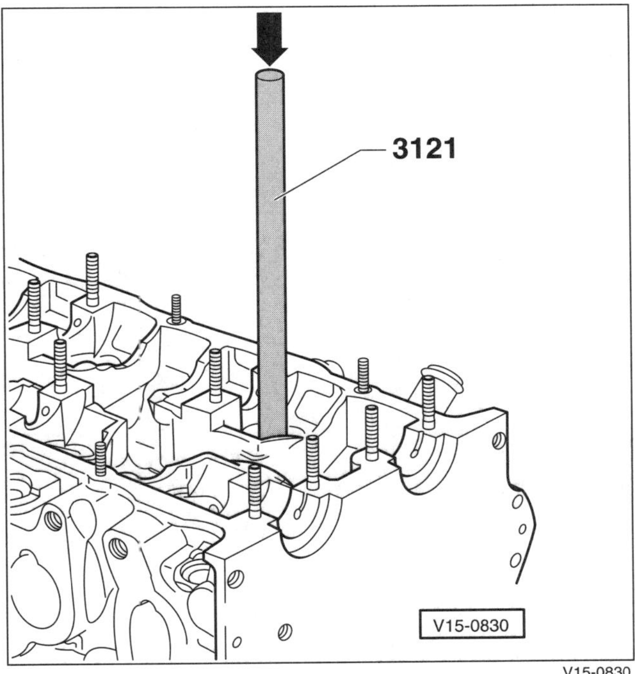

V15-0830

Fig. 40. Valve guide shown being pressed out with Volkswagen special tool 3121 (**arrow**). Cylinder head must be flat during pressing operation.

NOTE —

- *Press old valve guides out using Volkswagen special tool 3121. Use of other press tools may damage the cylinder head or valve guide.*
- *Cylinder head must be positioned flat during pressing operations.*
- *Do not seat shouldered valve guides with more than 1 ton of pressure. Shoulder can break off.*
- *Hand ream new valve guides using Volkswagen special tool 3120 and suitable reaming oil.*

Valve seats

When resurfacing valve seats, there is a limit to the amount of material that can be removed. If too much material is removed, the final assembly will leave too little space for hydraulic cam follower to function correctly. The maximum refacing dimension, that is, the maximum amount of material that can be removed from the valve seat, is calculated from measurement shown in Fig. 41.

Measure dimension (**A**) in Fig. 41., and subtract minimum dimension, as given in **Table b**. The difference is the maximum amount of material that can be removed from valve seat. Valve seat dimensions are given in table **Table c**.

Table b. Minimum Dimensions for Calculating Valve Seat Refacing Dimensions

Engine	Intake	Exhaust
2.8L (VR6)	33.9 (1.335 in.)	34.1 mm (1.343 in.)

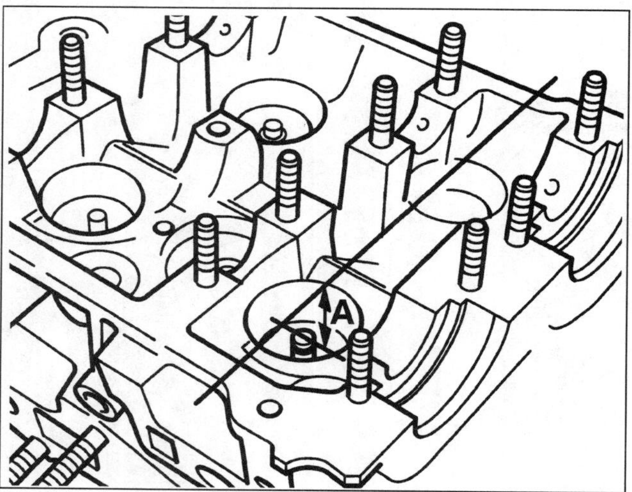

Fig. 41. Dimension **A** (distance between top of valve stem and gasket surface of cylinder head) is used to calculate maximum valve seat refacing dimensions.

Table c. Valve Seat Dimensions

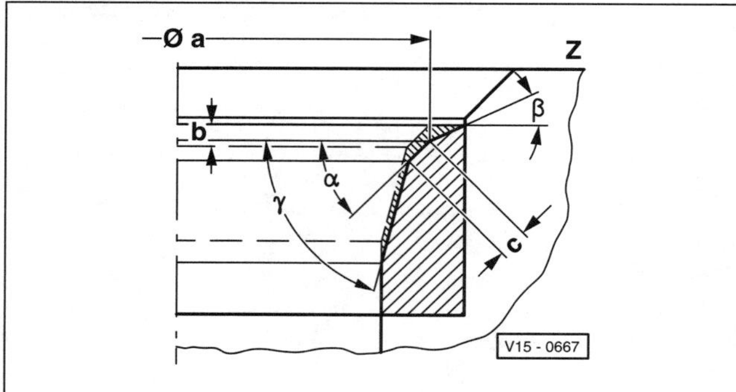

Engine: 2.8L	Intake	Exhaust
Seat diameter (**a**)	38.3 mm (1.508 in.)	33.5 mm (1.319 in.)
Maximum refacing dimension (**b**)	Calculated See Fig. 41.	Calculated See Fig. 41.
Seat width (**c**)	1.4-2.0 mm (0.055-0.079 in.)	2.0-2.5 mm (0.079-0.098 in.)
Valve seat angle (α)	45°	45°
Correction angle, upper (β)	30°	30°
Correction angle, lower (γ)	60°	73°

QUALITY REVIEW

When you have finished working under the hood and around other areas of the vehicle it is advisable to take a moment to quality check or review your work. This helps to ensure that the operation or repair has been completed properly with all affected systems functioning within normal parameters. This may include the following:

- Make sure that the radiator fan cycles properly and that the coolant level and concentration are correct.
- Ensure that all cable ties and hose clamps that were removed as part of the repair are replaced.
- Check and adjust all other applicable fluid levels.
- Make sure that there are no fluid leaks.
- Make sure that there are no air, vacuum or exhaust leaks.
- Make sure that all components involved in the repair are positioned correctly and function properly.
- Male sure all tools, shop cloths, fender covers, and protective tape are removed.
- Clean grease from painted surfaces and steering wheel.
- Unlock the anti-theft radio and reset the clock.

In addition to the above noted points, the ECM and TCM may need to be checked using the Volkswagen supplied VAG 1551 or 1552 scan tool as mentioned at the start of this repair.

17 Engine–Lubrication System

GENERAL

Proper engine lubrication relies on a constant supply of oil, fed to the moving parts under pressure. Pressure is supplied by a gear-type oil pump located inside the engine oil pan. Engine oil returns to the oil pan by way of internal passages in the cylinder block and head. Returned oil collects in the oil pan where it is stored for eventual pickup by the oil pump. Engines with turbo-chargers also have external oil supply and return lines.

Engine Codes

- AWD, AWW . . . . 1.8L 4-cylinder turbo gasoline
- ALH . . . . 1.9L 4-cylinder turbo diesel
- AEG, AVH, AZG. . . . . 2.0L 4-cylinder gasoline
- AFP . . . . 2.8L 6-cylinder gasoline

Oil capacities with filter

- 1.8L . . . . 4.35 liters (4.6 qt.)
- 1.9L . . . . 4.5 liters (4.75 qt.)
- 2.0L . . . . 4.0 liters (4.2 qt.)
- 2.8L . . . . 5.8 liters (6.1 qt.)

NOTE —
• For changing the oil and filter, see **0 Maintenance**.

OIL PRESSURE WARNING SYSTEM

To prevent serious engine damage, a dynamic oil pressure warning system warns the driver of insufficient oil pressure. This system includes a single oil pressure switch, an electric control unit, a warning light and a buzzer. The electronic control unit with buzzer and warning light is integrated into the instrument cluster.

Oil pressure warning system, checking

With the ignition off, the single oil pressure switch is open (no continuity between the terminal connection and the switch body). When the ignition is switched on, but the engine is not started, the oil pressure warning light should come on for approximately 3 seconds and then go out.

When the engine is started and the oil pressure rises, the oil pressure switch should close at the specified pressure completing a circuit to ground. When the engine reaches approximately 1,500 rpm, the electronic control unit checks to see if the ground is complete and if so, the system is functioning normally. If the ground is not complete, the warning light and buzzer are activated. Several small time delays are programmed into the system to prevent accidental warnings due to normal minor fluctuations in pressure.

CAUTION —
If the warning indicators stay on after the engine is started, or while driving, always assume that there is insufficient oil pressure. Check oil level and test oil pressure before proceeding.

A quick-check of the system can be accomplished as follows:

1. Check instrument cluster warning light.
   - Turn key on, but do not start engine.
   - Warning light should come on for about 3 seconds and then go out.
2. Turn key off. Disconnect and ground the wire at oil pressure switch.
3. Turn key on, but do not start engine.
4. Warning light should flash and the buzzer should beep 3 times.

5. Turn key off. Remove oil pressure switch wire from ground but do not re-connect to oil pressure switch.

6. Start engine and let idle.
   - Warning light and buzzer should not come on.

7. Increase engine speed to approx. 1,500-2,000 rpm.
   - Warning light and buzzer should come on after a 2-3 second delay.

If the above tests give results as noted, the oil pressure warning system is functioning within normal parameters. If the above test results deviate from specification, continue by testing the oil pressure and the oil pressure switch, given later.

> ***NOTE—***
> *Since oil temperature can have a considerable influence on oil pressure, it may be advisable to conduct the above noted tests on both a cold and a warmed-up engine.*

Oil pressure and oil pressure switch, testing

It is possible for the oil pressure warning system to be functioning properly and still give an occasional indication of a malfunction. In this case, it is advisable to check the oil pressure switch. This switch is located on the oil filter flange for both gas and diesel engines, see **Oil filter flange assembly**, given later.

The oil pressure switch can be accurately tested by removing it from the oil filter flange and temporarily installing it into an oil pressure tester such as the Volkswagen supplied VAG 1342. See Fig. 1.

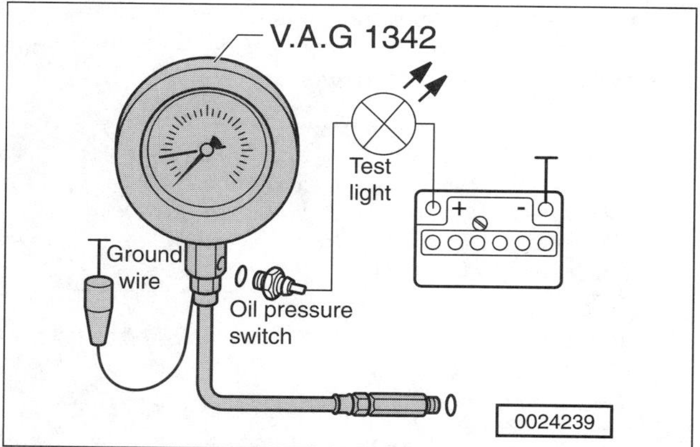

0024239

Fig. 1. Pressure gauge and test light setup for testing oil pressure and oil pressure switch. Oil pressure switch is installed in tester and test light is connected between the switch terminal and battery positive.

1. Disconnect wire from oil pressure switch and leave it unplugged for this test.

2. Remove oil pressure switch and thread it into tester.

3. Thread oil pressure tester hose into hole previously occupied by switch.

4. Connect ground wire from tester to a good ground.

5. Connect a test light from battery positive to oil pressure switch terminal.

6. Start engine and let it warm up.

7. When radiator fan has cycled at least once, accelerate engine until test light comes on and observe pressure gauge. The light must come on at the specified value. If light does not illuminate at specified value, switch is defective and should be replaced.

8. Continue system test by checking oil pressure. With tester still attached, run engine at specified speeds and compare readings on gauge to specification. If specification is not reached, oil pump deficiencies are indicated.

Oil pressure switch closing pressure
- Gasoline engines (1.4 bar). . . . 1.2-1.6 bar (18-24 psi)
- Diesel engine (0.9 bar). . . . . . 0.55-.85 bar (11-15 psi)

> ***NOTE—***
> *Incorrect engine oil viscosity can influence engine oil pressures. Before performing repairs, ensure that engine has a sufficient quantity of fresh oil of correct viscosity.*

Oil pressure at 80°C (176°F)
- Gasoline engines
  - at idle. . . . . minimum 2.0 bar (29 psi)
  - at 2,000 rpm
    - 2.0L and 1.8L . . . . 3.0 to 4.5 bar (44 to 66 psi)
    - 2.8L. above 2.0 bar (29 psi)
  - maximum. .7.0 bar (103 psi)
- Diesel engine
  - at idle. . . . . no factory specification available
  - at 2,000 rpm . . . . minimum 2.5 bar (29 psi)
  - maximum. .7.0 bar (103 psi)

---

9. When testing is completed, remove the test light and tester. Install the oil pressure switch and the wiring.

> ***NOTE—***
> *If an oil pressure switch seal is leaking, a new sealing washer should be installed. The sealing washer is held captive on the switch and must be cut off. New sealing rings are available from authorized Volkswagen parts dealers or aftermarket parts specialists.*

LUBRICATION SYSTEM COMPONENTS

Lubrication system assembly (2.0L and 1.9L engines)

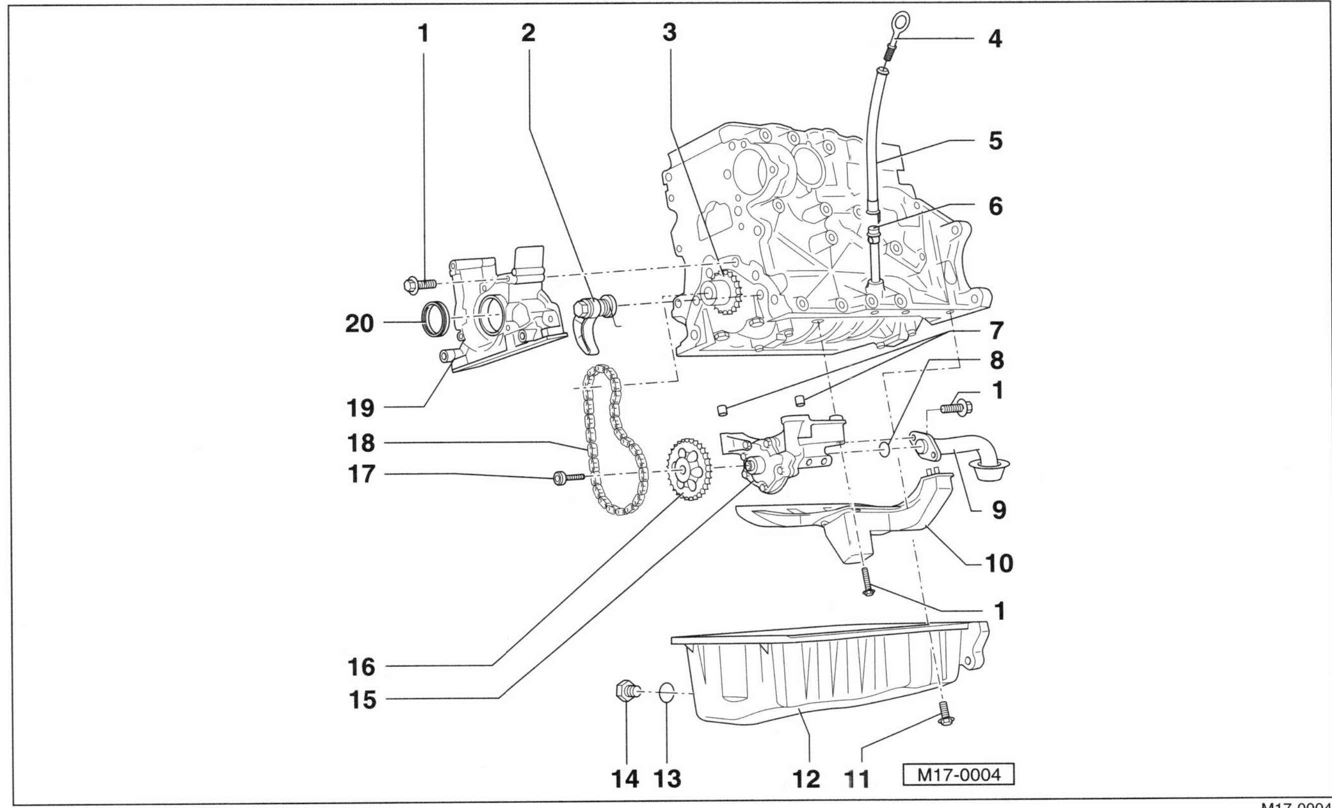

M17-0004

Fig. 2. Lubrication system for 2.0L gasoline and 1.9L diesel engines.

1. **Bolt**
   - Tighten to 15 Nm (11 ft-lb)
2. **Chain tensioner (with tensioning rail)**
   - Tighten to 15 Nm (11 ft-lb)
   - To install, first pretension spring and engage
3. **Chain sprocket**
4. **Oil dipstick**
   - Oil level must NOT be above MAX mark!
5. **Guide**
   - Pull off to extract oil
6. **Guide tube**
7. **Guide sleeves**
   - Check for firm seating
8. **O-ring**
   - Always replace
9. **Suction pipe**
   - Clean strainer if soiled
10. **Baffle plate**
11. **Bolt**
    - Tighten to 15 Nm (11 ft-lb)
12. **Oil pan**
    - Clean oiling surfaces before installing
    - Install with silicone sealant D 176 404 A2
13. **Seal**
    - Always replace
14. **Oil drain plug**
    - Tighten to 30 Nm (22 ft-lb)
15. **Oil pump**
    - 12 bar (174 psi) pressure relief valve
    - Ensure that both centering dowels are installed
    - Replace if any running surfaces or gears are scored
16. **Chain sprocket**
17. **Bolt**
    - Tighten to 25 Nm (18 ft-lb)
18. **Chain**
    - Before removing, mark running direction
19. **Sealing flange, front**
    - Must be seated on dowels
    - Install with silicone sealant D 176 404 A2
20. **Seal**
    - Always replace

Lubrication system assembly (1.8L engine)

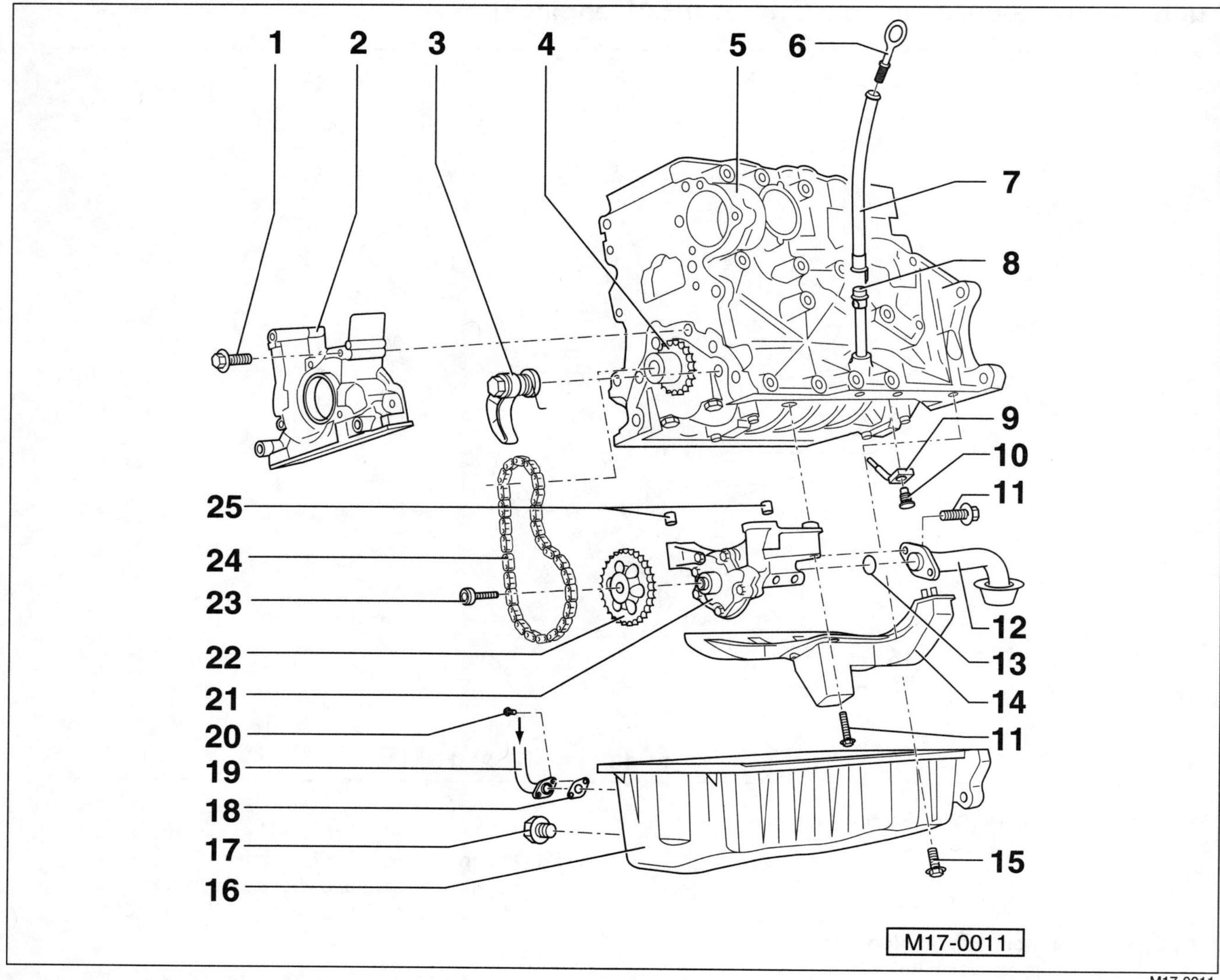

Fig. 3. Cylinder block and lubrication system components for 1.8L engine.

1. **Chain**
2. **Sealing flange**
   - Must be located on dowel sleeves
   - Clean sealing surface before installing
   - Install with silicone sealant D 176 404 A2
3. **Chain tensioner with tensioning track**
   - Tighten to 15 Nm (11 ft-lb)
   - When installing, pre-tighten spring and engage
4. **Chain sprocket for oil pump drive**
5. **Engine block**
6. **Dipstick**
   - Oil level must not exceed max. marking
   - If oil level is in cross-hatched area or below, top off
7. **Guide**
   - Pull off to extract oil
8. **Guide tube**
9. **Oil spray jet**
   - For cooling pistons
10. **Pressure relief valve**
    - Tighten to 27 Nm (20 ft-lb)
    - Opening pressure 1.3 to 1.6 bar
11. **Bolt**
    - Tighten to 15 Nm (11 ft-lb)
12. **Suction pipe**
    - Clean strainer
13. **O-ring**

(continued on following page)

(continued from previous page)

14. Baffle plate

15. Oil pan bolts
- Tighten to 15 Nm (11 ft-lb)

16. Oil pan
- Clean oiling surfaces before installing
- Install with silicone sealant D 176 404 A2

17. Oil drain plug
- Tighten to 30 Nm (22 ft-lb)

18. Gasket
- Always replace

19. Oil return pipe
- From turbocharger

20. Bolt
- Tighten to 10 Nm (7 ft-lb)

21. Oil pump
- 12 bar (174 psi) pressure relief valve
- Ensure that both centering dowels are installed
- Replace if any running surfaces or gears are scored

22. Chain sprocket
- For oil pump
- Check for wear

23. Bolt
- Tighten to 25 Nm (18 ft-lb)

24. Chain
- For oil pump
- Mark direction of rotation before removing

25. Dowel sleeves
- Check for tight fit

Lubrication system assembly (2.8L engine)

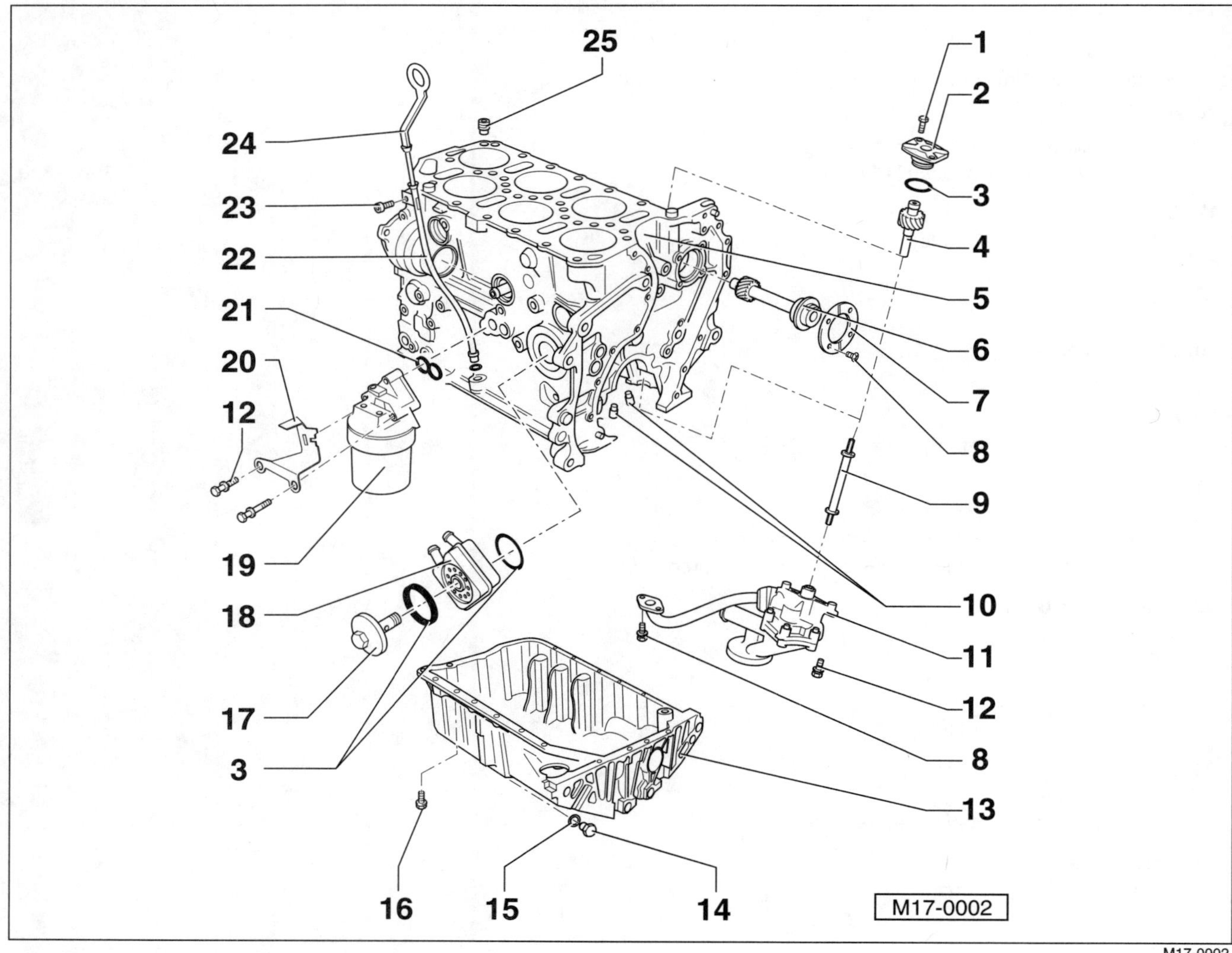

M17-0002

Fig. 4. Lubrication system on 2.8L (VR6) engine.

1. **Bolt**
   - Tighten to 10 Nm (7 ft-lb)
2. **Cover for oil pump drive**
   - Insert with silicone sealer D176 404 A2
3. **O-ring**
   - Always replace
   - Lubricate before assembly
4. **Oil pump drive**
5. **Cylinder block**
6. **Intermediate shaft**
7. **Thrust washer**
8. **Bolt**
   - Tighten to 10 Nm (7 ft-lb)
   - Insert with thread lock "D6"
9. **Drive shaft**
   - For oil pump drive
10. **Spray nozzle**
    - For crankshaft bearings 2-6
    - For piston cooling
    - Opening pressure: 2.0 bar
11. **Oil pump**
    - Coat oil pressure pipe on engine block and oil pump body with sealant (VW part no. AMV 188 001 02)
12. **Bolt**
    - Tighten to 25 Nm (18 ft-lb)
13. **Oil pan**
14. **Oil drain plug**
    - Tighten to 20 Nm (15 ft-lb)

(continued on following page)

(continued from previous page)

15. Sealing ring
- Always replace

16. Bolt
- Tighten to 15 Nm (11 ft-lb)

17. Oil cooler cover
- Tighten to 25 Nm (18 ft-lb)

18. Oil cooler
- Coat all contact surfaces outside the gasket with sealant (VW part no. AMV 188 001 02)

19. Oil filter housing and filter

20. Bracket
- For intake manifold crossover valve (N156)

21. Gasket
- Always replace
- Lubricate before assembly

22. Guide pipe
- For dipstick
- Fastened to top of the intake manifold with bolts

23. Bolt
- Tighten to 5 Nm (44 in-lb)

24. Dipstick
- Do not fill above upper mark

25. Oil return stop
- Tighten to 5 Nm (44 in-lb)
- Clean if very dirty

Oil filter flange assembly (1.8L engine)

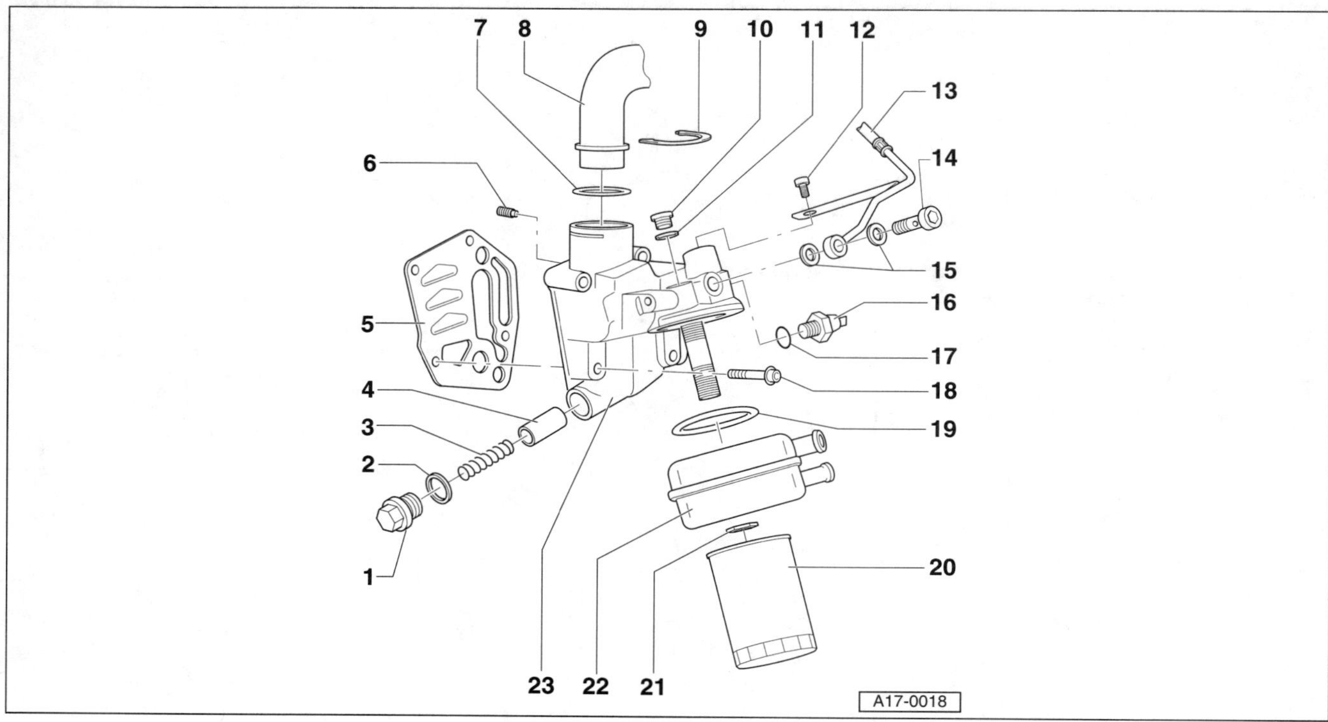

A17-0018

Fig. 5. Oil filter flange with related components for 1.8L engine.

1. **Sealing plug**
   - Tighten to 40 Nm (30 ft-lb)
2. **Seal**
3. **Spring**
   - For pressure relief valve, approx. 4 bar (58 psi)
4. **Piston**
   - For pressure relief valve
5. **Gasket**
   - Always replace
6. **Check valve**
   - Tighten to 8 Nm (71 in-lb)
7. **O-ring**
   - Always replace
   - Install onto sealing cap and shoulder (item 8)
8. **Pipe**
9. **Retaining clip**
10. **Sealing plug**
    - Tighten to 15 Nm (11 ft-lb)
11. **Seal**
12. **Bolt**
    - Tighten to 20 Nm (15 ft-lb)
13. **Oil supply pipe**
    - To turbocharger
14. **Banjo bolt**
    - Tighten to 30 Nm (22 ft-lb)
15. **Gasket**
    - Always replace
16. **Oil pressure switch (1.4 bar)**
    - Tighten to 25 Nm (18 ft-lb)
17. **Seal**
18. **Nut**
    - Tighten to 15 Nm (11 ft-lb) + ¼ turn (90°) further
    - Always replace
19. **Gasket**
    - Always replace
    - Fit into groove on oil cooler
20. **Oil filter**
    - Loosen with strap wrench, hand tighten
21. **Nut**
    - Tighten to 25 Nm (18 ft-lb)
22. **Oil cooler**
    - Installed position: must be turned fully clockwise (viewed from below) until touching its own bracket
23. **Oil filter bracket**
    - With pressure relief valve, approx. 4 bar (58 psi)

Oil filter flange assembly (1.9L engine)

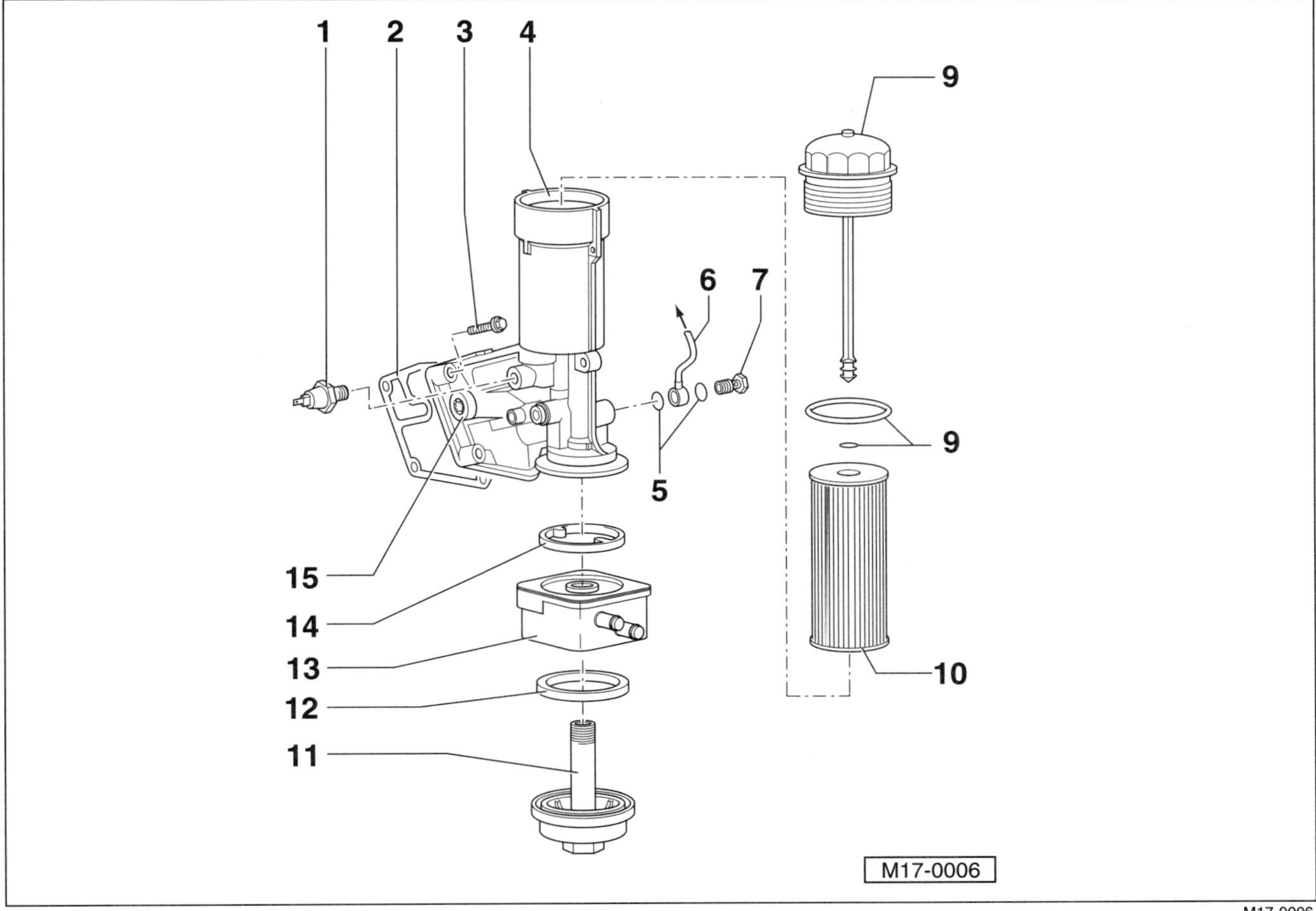

M17-0006

Fig. 6. Oil filter flange with related components for 1.9L engine.

1. **Oil pressure switch (0.7 bar)**
   - Tighten to 25 Nm (18 ft-lb)
   - Brown
2. **Gasket**
   - Always replace
3. **Bolt**
   - Tighten to 15 Nm (11 ft-lb) + ¼ turn (90°) further
   - Always replace
4. **Oil filter bracket**
5. **Seal**
   - Always replace
6. **Oil supply pipe**
   - To turbocharger
7. **Banjo bolt**
   - Tighten to 20 Nm (15 ft-lb)
8. **Sealing cap**
   - Tighten to 25 Nm (18 ft-lb)
   - Loosen and tighten using 3417 oil filter wrench
9. **O-ring**
   - Always replace
10. **Oil filter element**
11. **Sealing plug**
    - Tighten to 25 Nm (18 ft-lb)
12. **Gasket**
    - Always replace
13. **Oil cooler**
    - Installed position: must be turned fully clockwise (viewed from below) until touching its own bracket
14. **Gasket**
    - Always replace
    - Install into oil cooler groove
15. **Sealing plug**
    - Do NOT open

Oil filter flange assembly (2.0L engine)

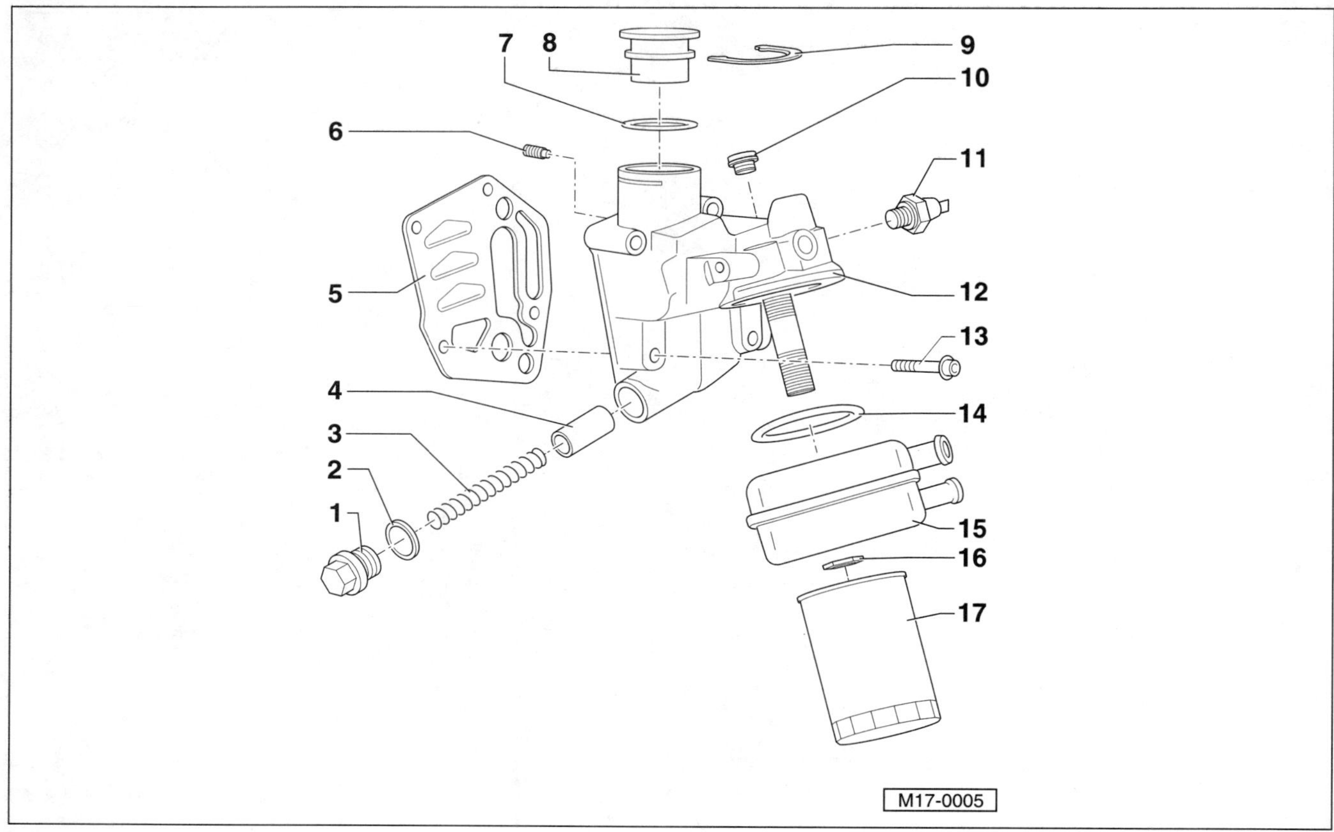

M17-0005

Fig. 7. Oil filter flange with related components for 2.0L engine.

1. **Sealing plug**
   - Tighten to 40 Nm (30 ft-lb)
2. **Seal**
3. **Spring**
   - For pressure relief valve, approx. 4 bar (58 psi)
4. **Piston**
   - For pressure relief valve
5. **Gasket**
   - Always replace
6. **Check valve**
   - Tighten to 8 Nm (71 in-lb)
7. **Seal**
   - Install onto sealing cap and shoulder (item 8)
8. **Sealing cap**
9. **Retaining clip**
10. **Sealing plug**
    - Tighten to 15 Nm (11 ft-lb)
    - Cut off sealing ring and replace if leaking
11. **Oil pressure switch (1.4 bar)**
    - Tighten to 25 Nm (18 ft-lb)
    - Black
    - Cut off sealing ring and replace if leaking
12. **Oil filter flange**
    - With 4 bar (58 psi) relief valve
13. **Nut**
    - Tighten to 15 Nm (11 ft-lb) + ¼ turn (90°) further
    - Always replace
14. **Gasket**
    - Always replace
    - Fit into groove on oil cooler
15. **Oil cooler**
    - Installed position: must be turned fully clockwise (viewed from below) until touching its own bracket
16. **Nut**
    - Tighten to 25 Nm (18 ft-lb)
17. **Oil filter**
    - Loosen with strap wrench
    - Hand tighten
    - Observe installation instructions on oil filter

Oil filter flange assembly (2.8L engine)

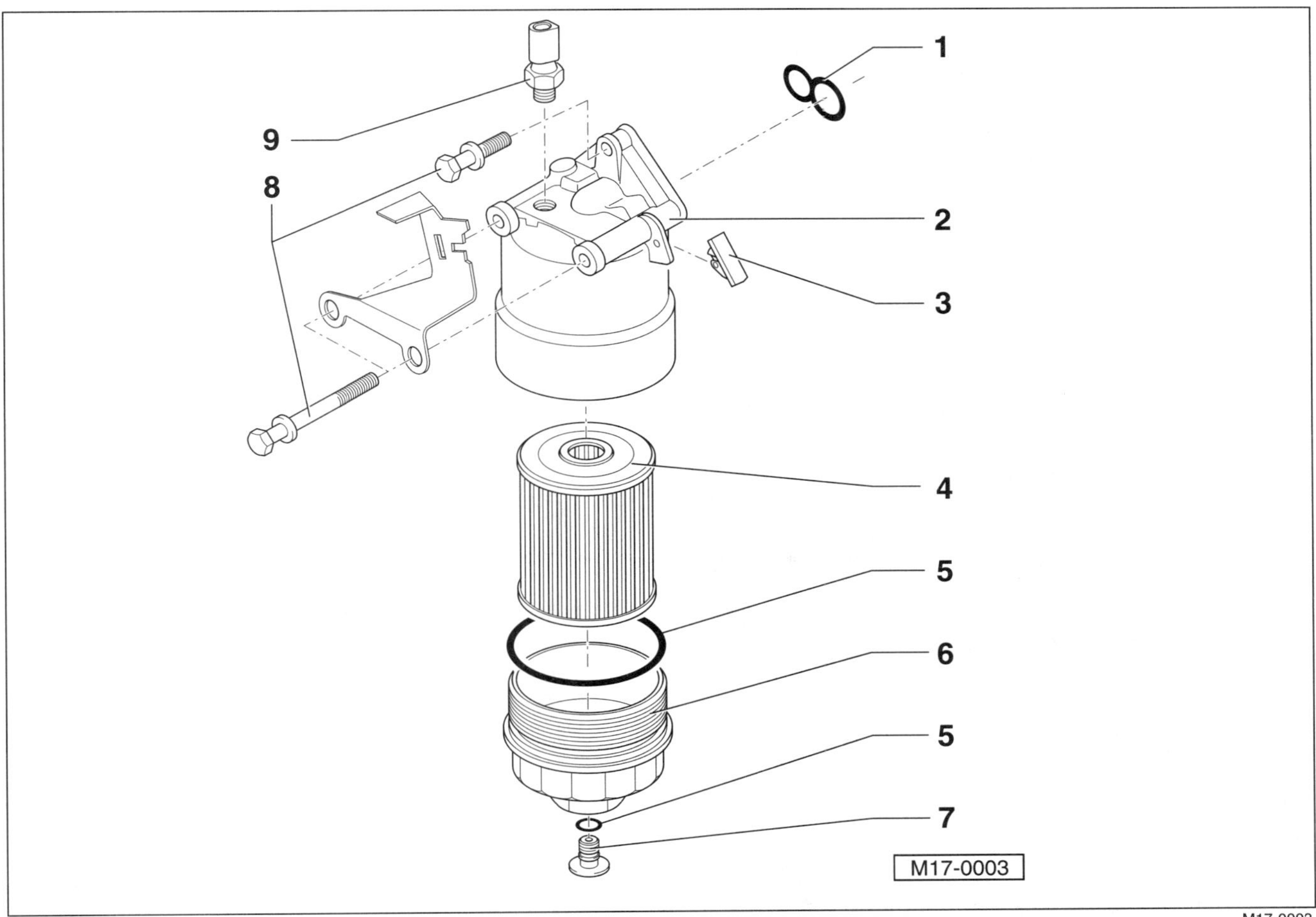

M17-0003

Fig. 8. Oil filter flange with related components for 2.8L engine.

1. **Gasket**
   - Always replace
   - Lubricate with oil before installing
2. **Filter housing**
3. **Stop**
   - For oil cooler
   - Fastened to oil filter housing
4. **Filter cartridge**
   - Maintain regular change intervals
   - With by-pass valve, opening pressure: 2.0 bar
   - Clip into bottom of oil filter before installing
5. **O-ring**
   - Always replace
   - Lubricate with oil before assembly
6. **Bottom of oil filter housing**
   - Empty before disassembling
7. **Oil drain plug**
   - Tighten to 10 Nm (7 ft-lb)
8. **Bolt**
   - 25 Nm (18 ft-lb)
9. **Oil pressure switch (1.4 bar)**
   - Tighten to 25 Nm (18 ft-lb)
   - Black
   - If sealing ring is leaking, cut open and replace

Oil pan, removing

The engine oil pan is a cast aluminum design bolted to both the cylinder block and the transmission. This new design uses silicone sealant instead of a conventional gasket at the joint to the cylinder block.

Oil pan removal is a straight-forward operation.

1. Remove lower sound absorber panel (belly pan).
2. Remove oil drain plug and drain oil into a suitable container.
3. Remove M10 bolts holding the oil pan to the transmission.
4. Remove the M7 bolts holding the oil pan to the cylinder block. See Fig. 9.

Fig. 9. Engine oil pan as viewed from below. Remove bolts at **arrows** to separate oil pan from engine and transmission.

5. Remove oil pan. It may be necessary to free oil pan by tapping it lightly with a rubber hammer.
6. Remove old sealant residue from cylinder block with a flat scraper.
7. Remove old sealant residue from oil pan with a suitable rotating brush/pad. See Fig. 10.

> ***WARNING —***
> *Always wear suitable eye protection when using a rotating brush/pad.*

8. Clean sealing surfaces on oil pan and cylinder block so that there are no traces of oil or grease.

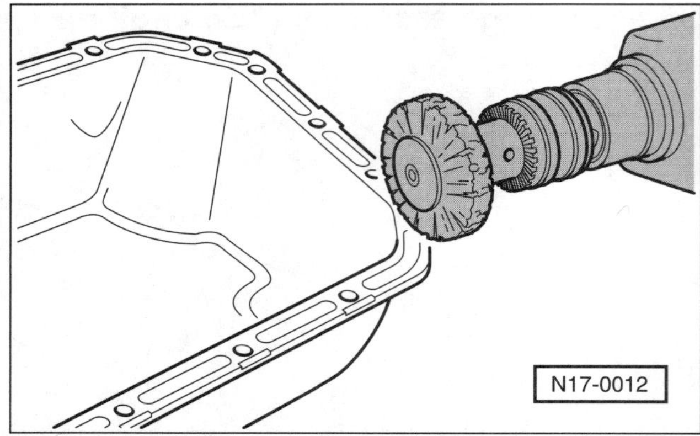

Fig. 10. Old sealant residue being removed with a cleaning pad attached to a drill motor. Use care to avoid scratching aluminum oil pan.

Oil pan, installing

Before installing the oil pan, observe the following points:

- Volkswagen recommends using special silicone sealant D 176 404 A2 on the oil pan and cylinder block.
- The above sealant is date coded. Observe the "Use by date" on the sealant container.
- Oil pan must be installed within 5 minutes of applying sealant.

Allow sealant to cure for 30 minutes before adding engine oil to the pan.

> ***NOTE —***
> *Volkswagen part numbers are given for reference only! Always consult with your Volkswagen Parts Department or aftermarket parts specialist for the latest parts information.*

1. Be sure that the sealing surfaces on the oil pan and cylinder block are clean with no traces of oil or grease.
2. Cut sealant tube nozzle at first mark and apply a 2 to 3 mm (slightly less than 1/8 inch) bead of new sealant to cylinder block sealing surface. Be sure to run bead on inside of bolt holes. See Fig. 11.

> ***CAUTION —***
> *The sealing compound bead thickness must not be wider than 3 mm (slightly less than 1/8 inch). If this width is exceeded, excess sealing compound will enter the oil pan and could block the oil pump pickup tube strainer.*

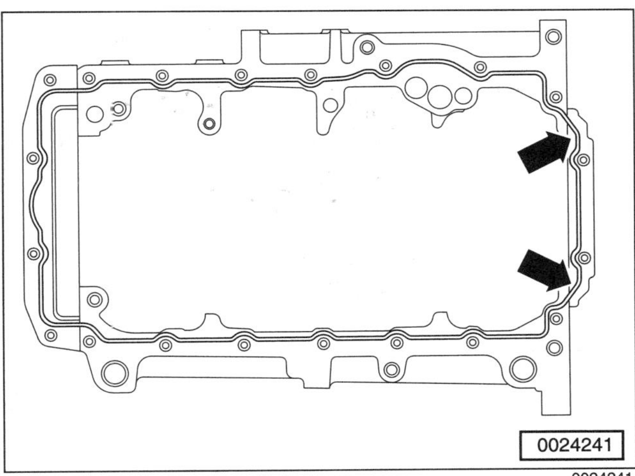

0024241

Fig. 11. Sealant bead (**arrows**) applied to cylinder block. Note how sealant is applied inside of bolt holes. 4 cylinder shown, 6-cylinder is similar.

3. Apply a 2 to 3 mm (slightly less than 1/8 inch) bead of new sealant to oil pan sealing surface. Be sure to run bead on the inside of the bolt holes. See Fig. 12.

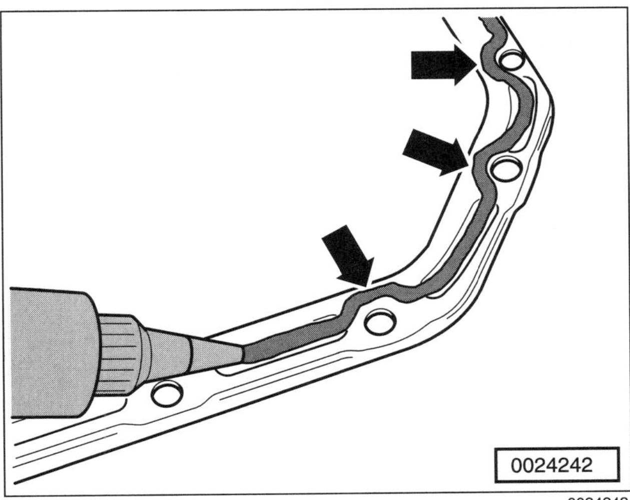

0024242

Fig. 12. Sealant bead (**arrows**) applied to cylinder block. Note how sealant is applied inside of bolt holes.

4. Immediately install oil pan to cylinder block and loosely install M7 bolts diagonally.

NOTE —
If the engine and transmission are separated for this operation, install the oil pan flush with the flywheel edge of the cylinder block.

5. Install and lightly tighten M10 bolts securing oil pan to transmission.

6. Diagonally tighten M7 oil pan bolts further, but not to final torque.

7. Torque M10 bolts securing oil pan to transmission.

8. Diagonally torque M7 bolts securing oil pan to cylinder block.

Tightening torques
- Oil pan to transmission (M10) . . . . . . 45 Nm (33 ft-lb)
- Oil pan to cylinder block (M7). . . . . . . 15 Nm (11 ft-lb)
- Oil drain plug (M14)
  4-cylinder engines. . . . . 30 Nm (22 ft-lb)
  6-cylinder engines. . . . . 20 Nm (15 ft-lb)

9. Install drain plug.

10. Install lower sound absorber panel (belly pan).

11. Wait 30 minutes as prescribed and refill with proper viscosity and quantity of engine oil.

12. Be sure to quality check your work, see **Quality Review** at the end of this repair group.

Oil pump

On 4-cylinder engines the oil pump is located inside the engine oil pan and is bolted to the cylinder block below the front of the crankshaft. The oil pump is driven by a short chain connected directly to the crankshaft rather than by an intermediate shaft as on previous 4-cylinder Volkswagen engines. A spring loaded tensioner takes up any slack in the chain.

There is normally no need to remove and inspect the oil pump unless oil pressure is inadequate. Check the oil pressure as described earlier in **Oil pressure and oil pressure switch, testing**.

There are no serviceable parts inside the oil pump, however the pump can be disassembled and visually inspected for scoring and wear on the gears and running surfaces. If abnormal scoring is found, the pump must be replaced.

Tightening torques (4-cylinder engines)
- Oil pump to cylinder block (M7) . . . . . 15 Nm (11 ft-lb)
- Sprocket to oil pump (M8) . . . . 25 Nm (18 ft-lb)
- Oil pump cover to body (M6) . . . . 10 Nm (7 ft-lb)
- Suction pipe to body (M7) . . . . 15 Nm (11 ft-lb)

On 6-cylinder engines, the oil pump is located inside the engine oil pan and draws engine oil through a pickup tube from near the bottom of the pan. The pump can be removed for inspection of its internal clearances (a potential source of low oil pressure problems) by first removing the oil pan, although internal replacement parts are not available from Volkswagen. An exploded view of the 6-cylinder oil pump is shown in Fig. 13.

Oil pump assembly (2.8L engine)

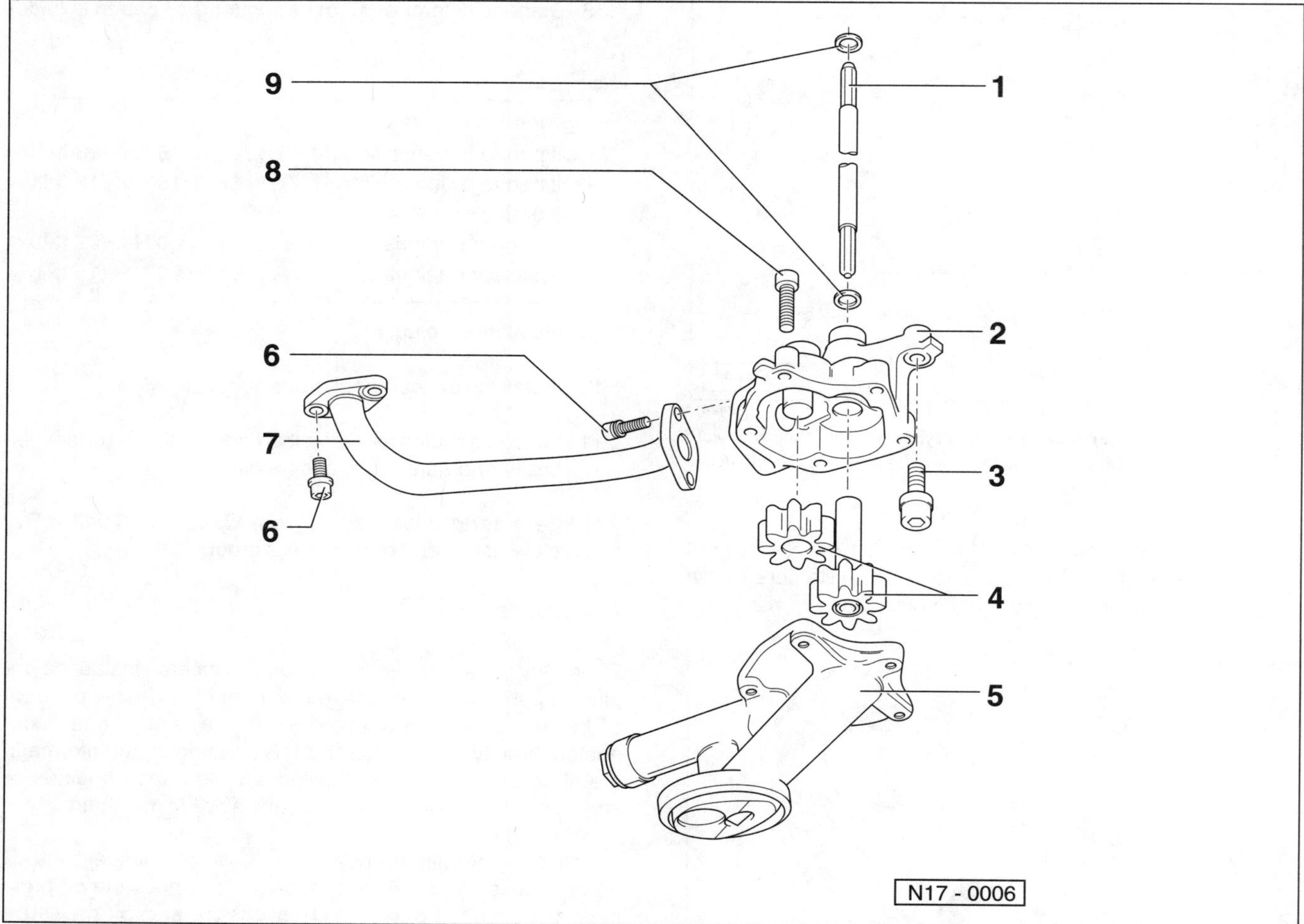

Fig. 13. Oil pump for 2.8L engine.

1. **Drive shaft**
   - For oil pump drive
2. **Oil pump housing**
3. **Bolt**
   - Tighten to 25 Nm (18 ft-lb)
4. **Gears**
   - Checking tooth backlash, **see** Ⓐ
   - Checking end play, **see** Ⓑ
5. **Oil pump cover with pressure relief valve**
   - Opening pressure: 5.3 - 5.7 bar
   - Clean strainer if dirty
6. **Bolt**
   - Always replace
   - Install with thread lock "D6"
7. **Discharge pipe**
   - Coat the engine block and oil pump body mating surfaces with sealant (VW part no. AMV 188 001 02)
8. **Bolt**
   - Tighten to 10 Nm (7 ft-lb)
9. **O-ring**
   - Replace if damaged

A **Oil pump tooth backlash, checking (2.8L engine)**

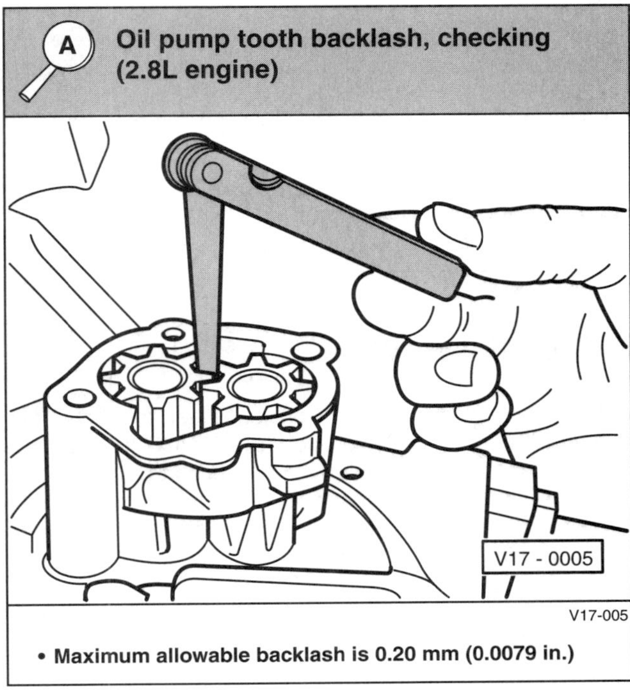

- **Maximum allowable backlash is 0.20 mm (0.0079 in.)**

B **Oil pump gear axial play, checking (2.8L engine)**

- **Use straight edge and feeler gauge as shown.**
- **Wear limit (max. allowable): 0.10 mm (0.0039 in.)**

Oil spray nozzles

Some engines covered by this manual are equipped with oil spray nozzles. The oil spray nozzles atomize a fine mist of engine oil and direct it against the bottom of the piston for additional cooling and lubrication.

On 1.8L engines the oil spray nozzles are attached to the cylinder block at the base of the cylinder bore. The oil spray nozzle is regulated by the valve that secures it to the cylinder block. The valve only opens to allow flow when oil pressure is greater than 2.5 to 3.2 bar (37 to 47 psi). To access the oil spray nozzles, the oil pan must first be removed. See Fig. 14.

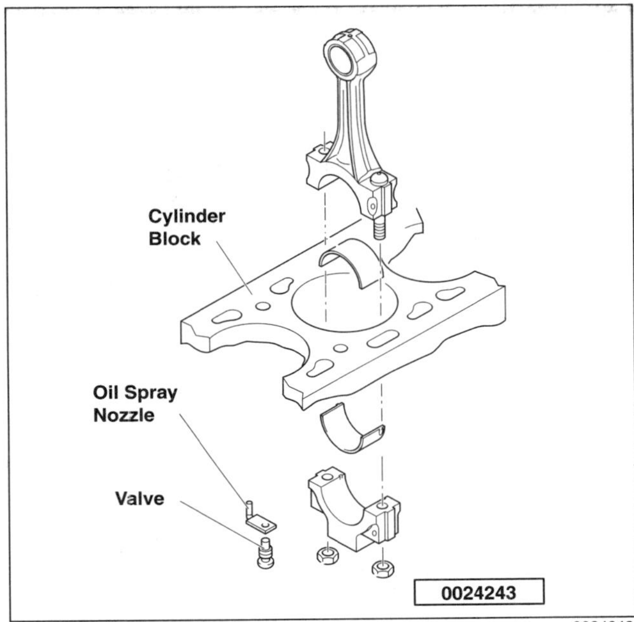

Fig. 14. Oil spray nozzle is secured to the base of the cylinder block by the valve.

> ***CAUTION —***
> *If significant amounts of metal and other abrasive particles (caused by corrosion of the crankshaft, small end bearings, etc.) are discovered in the oil during engine repair work, it will be necessary to replace all spray nozzles, oil filter cartridge, oil cooler and to carefully clean all oil passages to prevent more damage.*

On 2.8L engines, the oil spray nozzles are fitted above the crankshaft main bearing shells in the cylinder block. See Fig. 15. To access the oil spray nozzles on the 2.8L engine, the engine and crankshaft must first be removed.

A 4 mm drift may then be used to press out the spray nozzle toward the engine mount. The spray nozzles can be installed by hand using a 6mm drift. See Fig. 15.

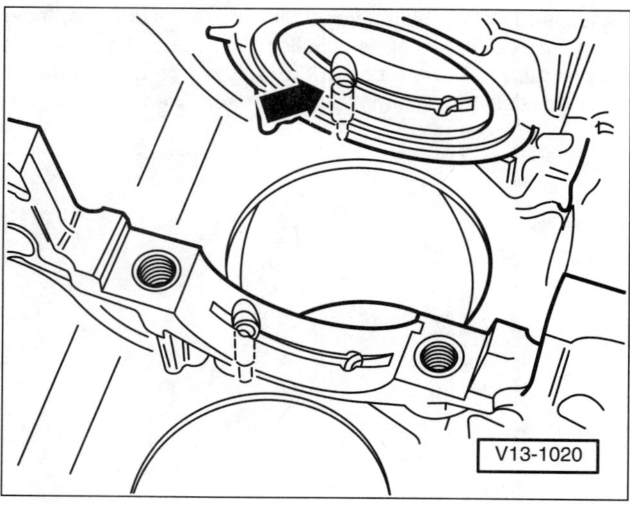

V13-1020

Fig. 15. Oil spray nozzles for each piston are installed above main bearing caps (**arrow**) on 2.8L (VR6) engine.

Oil cooler

The oil cooler is an oil-to-coolant heat exchanger. Engine oil flows through one part of the cooler and gives up heat to the engine coolant flowing through the other part of the cooler. During warm-up, the process is reversed and engine coolant gives up heat to the engine oil because the engine coolant gets warm first. This speeds the warm-up process and gets the engine to operating temperature more quickly. See Fig. 7. through Fig. 5. given earlier for oil cooler location.

NOTE —
- *The oil cooler should be replaced if metal particles or metal shavings are found in the engine oil. The cooler cannot be cleaned.*
- *The cooler is a potential source of leakage between the lubrication system and the cooling system and should be considered whenever such leakage is suspected.*

Remove the cooler only if it needs to be inspected or replaced. Check to see that there is adequate space for the coolant hose connections and that the cooler is properly positioned.

Tightening torque
- Oil cooler sealing cap or nut to filter flange . . . . 25 Nm (18 ft-lb)

QUALITY REVIEW

When you have finished working under the hood and around other areas of the vehicle, it is advisable to take a moment to quality check or review your work. This helps to insure that the operation or repair has been completed properly with all affected systems functioning within normal parameters. These may include the following:

- Ensure that all cable ties and hose clamps that were removed as part of the repair are replaced.
- Check and adjust engine oil and all other applicable fluid levels.
- Make sure that there are no oil leaks.
- Make sure that all components involved in the repair are positioned correctly and function properly.
- Make sure that all tools, shop cloths, fender covers and protective tapes are removed before closing the hood.
- Clean grease and fingerprints from painted surfaces and steering wheel.

19 Engine–Cooling System

TABLES

GENERAL

This section covers repairs and troubleshooting for the engine cooling system. For heater core and related heating and air conditioning components, see **80 Heating and Air Conditioning**. For information on the engine oil cooler, see **17 Engine-Lubrication**. For information on the ATF cooler used on vehicles with automatic transmissions, see **37 Automatic Transmission**.

Engine Codes
- AEG, AVH, AZG . . . . 2.0L 4-cylinder gasoline
- ALH . . . . 1.9L 4-cylinder turbo diesel
- AFP . . . . 2.8L 6-cylinder gasoline
- AWD, AWW . . . . 1.8L 4-cylinder turbo gasoline

Warnings and cautions

The following warnings and cautions should be observed when working on the cooling system.

WARNING —
Hot coolant can scald and result in serious personal injury. Do not work on the cooling system until it has fully cooled.

WARNING —
- *At normal operating temperature the cooling system is pressurized. Allow the system to cool as long as possible before opening, a minimum of an hour, then release the cap slowly to allow safe release of the pressure.*
- *Releasing the cooling system pressure lowers the coolant's boiling point, and the coolant may boil suddenly. Use heavy gloves and wear eye and face protection to guard against scalding.*
- *Use extreme care when working at or near the radiator cooling fans when the engine is hot. The fan can come on at any time, even if the ignition key is switched off.*
- *Use extreme care when draining and disposing of engine coolant. Coolant is poisonous and lethal. Children and pets are attracted to coolant because of its sweet smell and taste. See a doctor or veterinarian immediately if any amount of coolant is ingested.*
- *Disposal of used coolant must be done in conformance with all applicable local, state and federal laws. Do not pour into the ground or down drains or sewers. Contamination of ground water will result.*

> ***CAUTION —***
> *Avoid adding cold water to the cooling system while the engine is hot or overheated. If it is necessary to add coolant to a hot system, do so only with the engine running and the coolant pump operating.*

Coolant, pump and thermostat

Volkswagen uses only one type of antifreeze/coolant in the Golf, Jetta and GTI, regardless of engine type. This antifreeze/coolant is phosphate and silicate free and is identified by its red color. When supplied by Volkswagen, this coolant is known as G12. Due to its special characteristics it should never be mixed with any other type of coolant. See **0 Maintenance** for additional information and cautions.

For best overall performance, the coolant additive proportion must be at least 40%, but not more than 60% to maintain the antifreeze protection and cooling efficiency. Distilled water should always be used due to the various chemicals and minerals usually associated with tap water. Under no circumstances should 100% coolant/antifreeze be used. This will generally result in overheating and poor heater operation due to the poor heat transfer characteristics of pure anti/freeze. For accurate testing of antifreeze/coolant protection, a refractometer such as VW tool CEN5021 should be used, see **Coolant/antifreeze protection, testing**. A 50/50 mixture is generally preferred and will provide freeze protection to -34°F (-37°C).

An impeller-type coolant pump is mounted into cylinder block. The pump is crankshaft-driven by the same toothed belt that drives the camshaft and circulates coolant through the system whenever the engine is running.

The thermostat controls coolant flow through the radiator. When the engine is cold, the thermostat restricts flow through the radiator to allow the engine to reach operating temperature quicker. As the engine heats up, the thermostat opens and coolant circulates through the whole system, including the radiator.

Radiator and cooling fan

A radiator cooling fan assembly provides auxiliary air flow through the radiator. The fan assembly is electrically operated and thermostatically controlled so that it runs only when extra air flow is required to maintain proper coolant temperature.

The radiator is a cross-flow design constructed of an aluminum core and plastic side tanks. A translucent expansion tank, or overflow reservoir, provides for the expansion of the coolant at higher temperatures, easy monitoring of the coolant level and a convenient location for adding coolant.

An electric radiator cooling fan assembly is controlled by a thermoswitch located in the side of the radiator. At higher coolant temperatures, the switch closes to start the cooling fans. Any time the coolant temperature rises to higher than normal levels, the fan will start and continue to run until coolant temperature returns to a normal range. On vehicles with air conditioning, rising refrigerant pressures will also activate the cooling fans.

> ***WARNING —***
> *The electric cooling fans can come on at any time, even if the key is out of the ignition. To avoid personal injury, use extreme caution when working at or near the cooling fan if the engine is hot. As a safety precaution, always disconnect the harness connector from the fan when working around the radiator, fans and associated components.*

Coolant temperature/level warning lights

The Golf, Jetta and GTI are equipped with a conventional coolant temperature gauge. The needle in the gauge will indicate coolant temperature shortly after the ignition is switched on. When the ignition is switched on, the warning light will flash for a few seconds as a functional check. See Fig. 1.

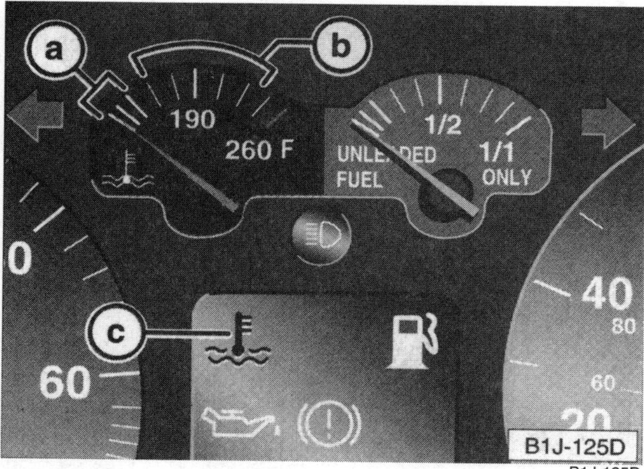

B1J-125D

Fig. 1. Engine coolant temperature gauge with cold engine zone (**a**), normal operating range (**b**) and warning light (**c**).

When the engine is cold the coolant temperature gauge will read in the "a" zone as displayed in Fig. 1. Avoid high engine speeds and heavy throttle when the needle is at the lower end of the dial.

As the engine warms up the gauge will move into the "b" zone as displayed in Fig. 1. If the engine is working hard at high outside temperatures, the needle may move toward the upper end of the scale. This is no cause for immediate concern as long as the coolant temperature warning light does not start flashing. Turning off the air conditioner can help the engine run cooler if it appears to be overheating.

If the warning light flashes when driving, first check the coolant temperature gauge. If the needle is in the normal range, add coolant at the next opportunity. If the needle is in the warning range (upper end of scale) the coolant temperature is too high and the vehicle should be stopped immediately and the engine shut off.

TROUBLESHOOTING

When investigating the cause of overheating or coolant loss, begin with a visual inspection of the system. Check the coolant level and inspect for evidence of coolant leaks.

The system becomes pressurized at normal operating temperatures. Leaks may prevent the system from becoming pressurized and allow the coolant to boil at a lower temperature. If visual evidence is inconclusive, a cooling system pressure test will determine whether the system leaks and may help to indicate the source.

If the cooling system holds pressure, the most probable causes of overheating are an electrical fault with the cooling fans, a faulty thermostat, or poor coolant circulation due to restrictions in the system.

Table a lists overheating and underheating symptoms, their probable causes, and suggested corrective actions. The bold type refers to areas outside of this repair group for suggested repairs.

NOTE —

- *Coolant also circulates through the heater core in the passenger compartment. For problems associated with the heater core and the heating system, see* **80 Heating and Ventilation** *or* **87 Air Conditioning**.
- *Overheating problems may also be caused by an engine fault that leaks hot combustion gases into the cooling system. See* **13 Crankshaft/Cylinder Block** *or* **15 Cylinder Head and Valvetrain** *for additional information concerning the cylinder block and head.*

Table a. Cooling system troubleshooting

Symptom	Probable cause	Corrective action
1. Engine overheats	**a.** Low coolant level	**a.** Fill expansion tank to the MAX mark on a cold engine. Check cooling system for leaks with pressure tester.
	b. Incorrect coolant concentration	**b.** Adjust coolant concentration to a mix of 50% coolant additive and 50% distilled water.
	c. Poor air flow through radiator	**c.** Check for debris (leaves, bugs, etc.) buildup on front of radiator. Clean radiator exterior using compressed air.
	d. Radiator fan not switching on	**d.** Test thermoswitch and fan. Replace faulty parts.
	e. Faulty radiator cap	**e.** Pressure test radiator cap. Replace faulty cap.
	f. Faulty thermostat	**f.** Remove and test thermostat. Replace faulty thermostat.
	g. Coolant pump faulty	**g.** Remove and inspect for spun impeller or pulley hub.
	h. Radiator hose restricted (lower hose may collapse at high engine or highway speeds)	**h.** Check hoses for soft, spongy areas. Replace faulty hoses.
	i. Clogged radiator	**i.** Clean or replace faulty radiator.
	j. Internal engine mechanical fault	**j.** Check internal engine condition, see **15 Cylinder Head and Valvetrain**, for appropriate engine.
2. Temperature gauge reads low, poor heater output	**a.** Incorrect coolant concentration	**a.** Adjust coolant concentration to a mix of 50% coolant additive and 50% distilled water.
	b. Faulty thermostat	**b.** Remove and test thermostat. Replace faulty thermostat.
	c. Radiator fan not switching off	**c.** Test thermoswitch. Replace faulty parts.
3. Temperature gauge reads low, heater output normal	**a.** Faulty instrument cluster or coolant temperature sensor	**a.** Test instrument cluster and sensor. Replace parts as required.
4. Temperature gauge reads normal, poor heater output	**a.** Installed position of heater hoses reversed	**a.** Inspect routing of heater hoses, see **80 Heating and Ventilation**.
	b. Heater hose restriction	**b.** Inspect heater hoses for ply separation and clogging. Replace hoses as required.
	c. Heat core restricted or clogged	**c.** Clean or replace faulty heater core.
	d. Heater or A/C ventilation controls or flaps not operating correctly	**d.** Check operation and adjustment of controls, see **80 Heating and Ventilation**

Diagnostic checks

The following checks and tests should generally be performed prior to any major tear down or repair work. This will help insure that the full extent or nature of the problem is known beforehand and may prevent unneeded repair work.

Coolant/antifreeze concentration, testing

1. Using a refractometer (VW tool CEN5021), take a small amount of coolant and place it onto measuring prism. See Fig. 2.

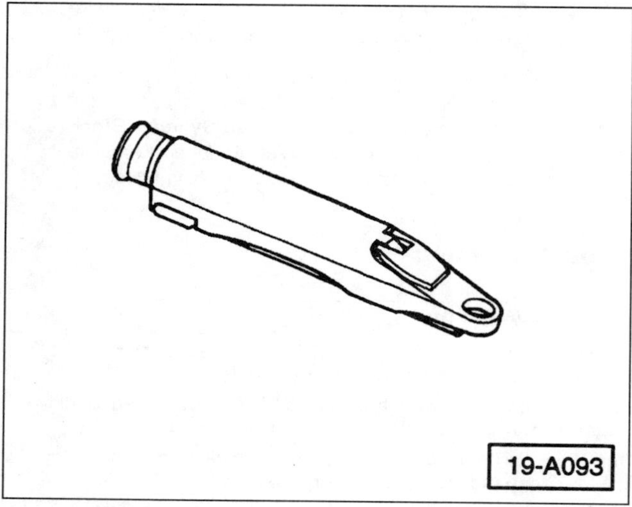

19-A093

Fig. 2. Anti-freeze tester (refractometer), VW special tool CEN5021.

2. Close the cover and hold tester up to a light source.

3. Look into the eyepiece and read the scale for ethylene glycol. The measure point is where the black and white come together. A 50/50 mixture is generally preferred and will provide freeze protection to -34°F (-37°C). See **Coolant, pump and thermostat** given earlier.

4. Rinse the tester clean.

5. Periodically check calibration by placing distilled water onto the prism and closing the cover. The measure point should be at 32°F (0°C) which is the freezing point for pure water. If this reading is not obtained, follow the instructions that came with tester for calibration and adjustment.

Cooling system, pressure testing

A pressure test uses a special tester in place of the cap on the expansion tank to pressurize the system and simulate normal operating conditions. If the system is unable to hold pressure, the engine will overheat more easily and fluid will be lost.

NOTE—
A pressure test also checks for internal leakage. Some of the common sources of internal leakage include a faulty cylinder head gasket, a cracked cylinder head, and a cracked cylinder block.

1. With engine at normal operating temperature, pressure test the system using a cooling system pressure tester with suitable adapters.

2. Observe the gauge reading. If the pressure drops, there is a leak in the system. A rapid drop may indicate a faulty cylinder head gasket if no external leaks can be found. Remove the spark plugs or glow plugs to inspect for coolant in the cylinders.

3. Using the correct tester adapter, test coolant expansion tank cap opening pressure. Compare opening pressure to specification and replace the cap if opening pressure is outside of specification.

NOTE—
It is not unusual for opening pressure to be slightly above specification when pressure is first applied due to slight sticking of the internal valve. Subsequent pressure applications should open the valve within specification, otherwise, replace the cap.

Cooling system test pressures

- Testing pressure (max). . . . . .1.25 bar (18 psi)
- Cap opening pressure . . . . . 1.4 - 1.6 bar (20 - 23 psi)

4. Inspect gasket in expansion tank cap for cuts and damage.

Cooling fans and thermoswitch, testing

Golfs, Jettas, and GTIs use a pair of 2 speed electric cooling fans to pull air across the radiator (and A/C condenser where equipped). A thermo-switch and a fan control module are used to control fan operation. See Fig. 3. The engine will overheat if the electric cooling fans are not operating properly, especially in traffic where speeds are low and there is insufficient natural air flow across the radiator. A/C operation will also be affected and damage to the system could result. In normal operation, the fans will switch on and off according to engine coolant temperature at the radiator thermo-switch or whenever the A/C is on.

WARNING—
Use extreme care when working at or near the radiator cooling fans when the engine is hot. The fan can come on at any time, even if the ignition key is switched off.

Fig. 3. Radiator fan thermo-switch (**A**) and fan control module (**B**) shown from under the left front section of the vehicle. The lower sound absorber panel (belly pan) has been removed. Radiator drain (**C**) is also visible.

NOTE —

If the cooling fans fail to operate normally use the following procedure to help determine where the problem lies.

1. Check fuse #16 (A/C clutch, after-run coolant pump; 10 amp) in the dash fuse box and thermo fuses in the holder on battery cover. See Fig. 4. Replace as necessary. **See 97 Wiring Diagrams, Fuses and Relays** for circuit information.

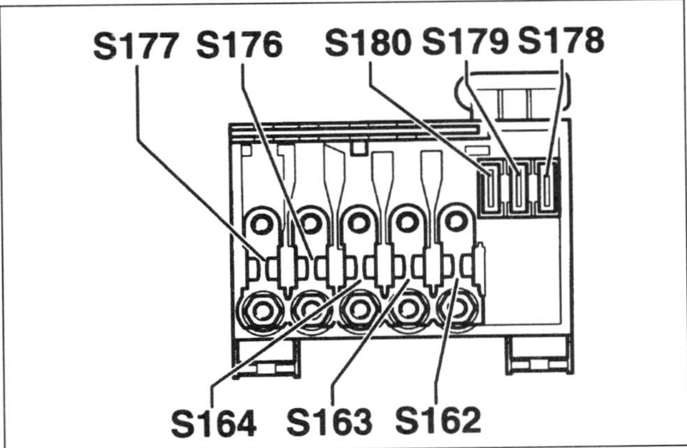

Fig. 4. Fuses on top of battery. Check **S164** (coolant fan control module/coolant fan; 40 amp) and **S180** (coolant fan; 30 amp).

2. Disconnect harness connector from radiator fan thermo-switch on lower left side of radiator.

3. Using a fused jumper wire, bridge terminals 1 and 2 of the connector. See Fig. 5. Both fans should run on the first speed.

4. Using a fused jumper wire, bridge terminals 2 and 3 of the connector. See Fig. 5. Both fans should run on the second speed.

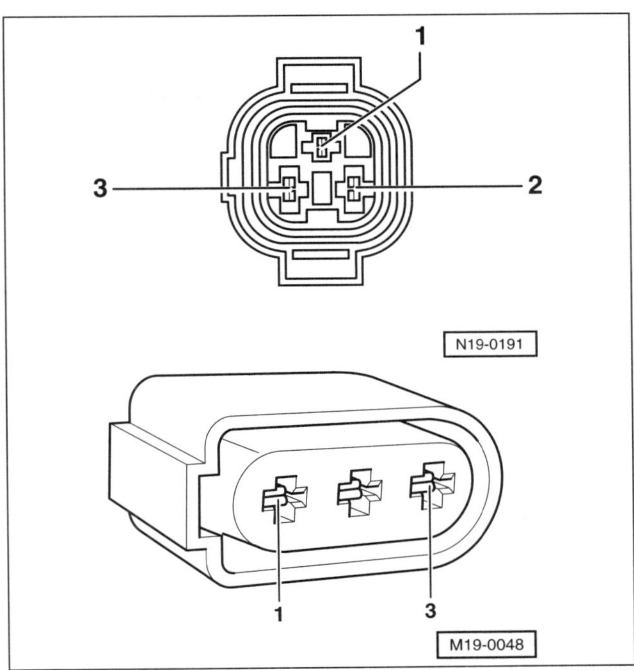

Fig. 5. Jumper terminals 1 and 2 of radiator fan thermo-switch connector to run coolant fans on low speed. Jumper terminals 2 and 3 to run coolant fans on high speed. Early and late connectors shown.

5. If the fans run with the jumpers installed, this indicates the fans are functionng properly and the radiator thermo-switch may be faulty. Switch opening and closing specifications are given below for more accurate testing of the thermo-switch. Drain coolant before replacing a faulty switch.

Radiator fan thermo-switch operating temperatures

- Stage I
  - switch on . . . . .197° - 206°F (92° - 97°C)
  - switch off . . . . .183° - 195°F (84° - 91°C)
- Stage II
  - switch on . . . . .210° - 221°F (99° - 105°C)
  - switch off . . . . .195° - 208°F (91° - 98°C)

Tightening torque

- Thermo-switch to radiator. . . . . 35 Nm (26 ft-lb)

6. If the fans do not run, check for battery voltage at the red wire in the harness connector. No voltage at harness connector indicates a blown fuse or a break in wiring from the fuse. See **97 Wiring Diagrams, Fuses and Relays**.

7. If the fans do not run and voltage is present at the thermo-switch harness connector, reconnect jumper to terminals 1 and 2 of thermo-switch connector.

8. Unplug left side fan motor and plug a suitable test light into terminals 1 and 2 of fan motor harness connector. The light should light.

9. Repeat step 8 for right side fan motor. The light should light.

10. If the light does not come on for steps 8 and 9 check for broken or shorted wiring between the fan control module and the thermo-switch or between the fan control module and the fans. See **97 Wiring Diagrams, Fuses and Relays**. If the wiring is in order, then the fan control module is faulty. If the test light comes on, this indicates that the radiator fan is faulty and should be replaced.

The above tests check first speed fan operation. The second speed can be checked by connecting the jumper to the red wire and red/yellow wire at the thermo-switch harness and a test light to terminals 1 and 3 of the fan harness connectors. As with the first speed, if the light does not come on for steps 8 and 9, check for broken or shorted wiring between the fan control module and the thermo-switch or between the fan control module and the fans. See **97 Wiring Diagrams, Fuses and Relays**. If the wiring is in order, than the fan control module is faulty. If the test light comes on, this indicates that the radiator fan is faulty and should be replaced.

Thermostat, testing

A thermostat that is stuck open will cause the engine to warm up slowly and generally run below normal operating temperature at highway speed. A thermostat that is stuck closed will restrict coolant flow to the radiator and cause overheating.

Accurate testing of the thermostat requires removal and observation while being warmed in a container of hot water. An accurate thermometer is used to note the temperatures at which it begins to open and at which it is fully open.

Specification

- Coolant thermostat operating parameters
  - Opening starts at approx. . . . . 85°C (185°F)
  - Fully open by approx. . . . . 105°C (221°F)
  - Valve travel, min. . . . . 7mm (0.28 in.)

To quickly check if the thermostat is opening and if coolant is circulating through the radiator, allow a cold engine to run at idle and warm up. As the temperature of the coolant rises, carefully feel the heater and expansion tank hoses. They will get hot. Feel the radiator hoses, particularly the lower hose. They will stay relatively cool to the touch. When the thermostat opens, the radiator hoses will quickly get hot and the radiator fan should cycle on shortly thereafter.

> ***CAUTION —***
> *If the engine runs long enough for the warning light in the instrument cluster to indicate an overheat condition, shut down the engine immediately.*

Check the radiator hoses. If they are not hot, then the thermostat has not opened or the radiator is clogged. If the hoses are hot, but the radiator fan did not come on, troubleshoot the radiator fans as per instructions given earlier in this section.

COOLING SYSTEM, DRAINING AND FILLING

> ***CAUTION —***
> *Always use a mixture of genuine Volkswagen coolant/anti-freeze and distilled water to avoid the formation of harmful deposits in the cooling system. Use of coolant/anti-freeze with phosphate compounds or tap water can be harmful to the cooling system.*

When refilling the engine coolant, keep in mind the following points:

- Use only Volkswagen G12 or equivalent phosphate and silicate free coolant/anti-freeze identified by the red color.
- Under no circumstances should G12 be mixed with any other type of coolant/anti-freeze. If the fluid in the expansion tank is brown, mixing with other types has occurred and the system must be flushed and the coolant/anti-freeze changed.
- Under no circumstances should straight coolant/anti-freeze or straight water be used. A 50/50 mix of coolant/anti-freeze to water provides freeze protection to -34°F (-35°C) and boiling protection to 226°F (108°C). The coolant/anti-freeze percentage should always be a minimum of 40% and a maximum of 60%.
- Hoses are secured with spring clamps. If replacement is needed, always replace with spring clamps due to their ability to expand with engine heat and remain tight.
- Most hoses have alignment marks to ensure correct positioning on the appropriate fitting; always line up the marks to ensure stress free installation.

1. Remove lower sound absorber panel (belly pan).

2. With engine fully cold, remove cap from the coolant expansion tank.

3. Position a drain pan under left front part of the radiator.

4. Unscrew drain plug at lower radiator hose fitting and allow coolant to drain. See Fig. 6.

5. On 4-cylinder engines, remove lower hose from oil cooler to drain cylinder block and allow coolant to drain. See Fig. 7.

NOTE —
Dispose of used coolant properly.

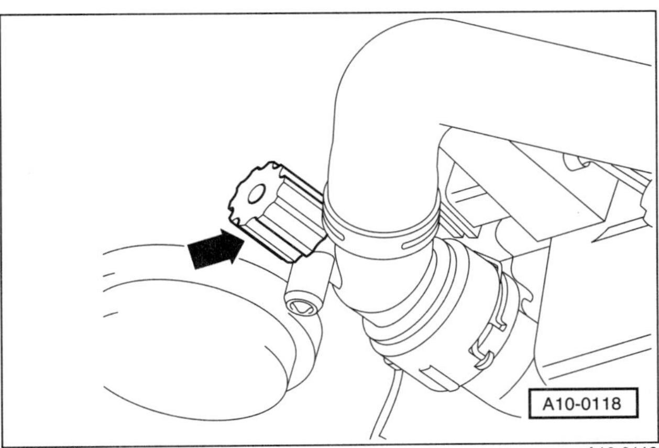

A10-0118

Fig. 6. Drain plug (**arrow**) at lower radiator hose fitting.

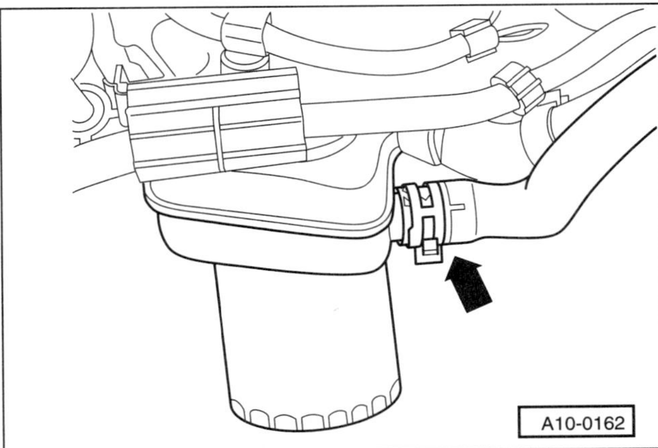

A10-0162

Fig. 7. Remove lower oil cooler hose (**arrow**) to drain coolant from cylinder block of 4-cylinder engines.

6. On 6-cylinder engines, remove upper hose from oil cooler to drain cylinder block and allow coolant to drain. See Fig. 8.

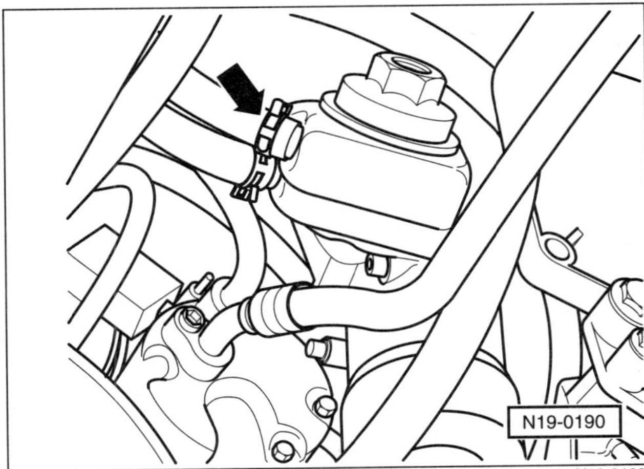

N19-0190

Fig. 8. Remove upper oil cooler hose (**arrow**) to drain coolant from cylinder block of 2.8L engines.

7. Close drain plug on lower radiator hose fitting.

8. Reconnect the lower oil cooler hose.

9. Slowly fill expansion tank with the appropriate mixture of coolant/anti-freeze while allowing the air to escape.

Cooling system capacity

- 1.8L engine. . . . . 5.3 quarts (5.0 liters)
- 1.9L engine. . . . . 6.3 quarts (6.0 liters)
- 2.0L engine. . . . . 5.3 quarts (5.0 liters)
- 2.8L engine. . . . . 9.5 quarts (9.0 liters)

NOTE —

If a cooling system pressure tester is available, connect it to the expansion tank and pressurize the system. This will force the coolant/anti-freeze past the thermostat and into many of the hoses that drained and will speed up the entire process.

10. Install expansion tank cap, start engine and allow to run until the radiator fans cycle at least once.

NOTE —

*If the expansion tank empties completely during warm-up, shut off the engine, carefully remove the expansion tank cap and refill to the **max** marks on the side. Restart the engine and continue until the fans cycle.*

11. Recheck the level in the expansion tank when the engine has cooled. See Fig. 9.

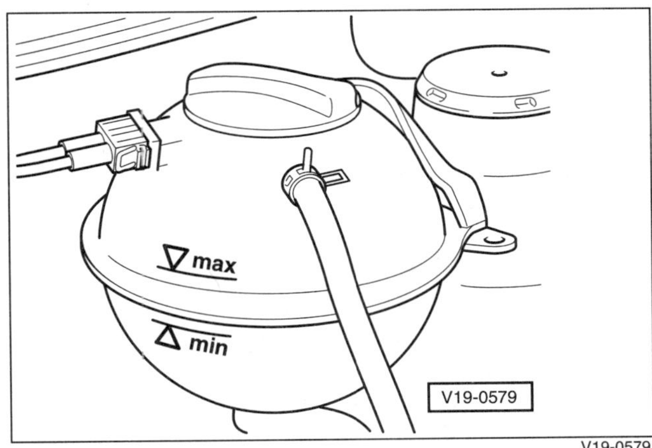

V19-0579

Fig. 9. Coolant/anti-freeze expansion tank showing **min** and **max** marks. 4-cylinder shown, 6-cylinder similar.

NOTE —

*The coolant/anti-freeze level should be at the **max** mark with the engine at operating temperature and between the **min** and **max** marks when cold. The final level is best checked when the cooling system is fully cold.*

COOLING SYSTEM, COMPONENTS

Cooling system, components (1.8L engine)

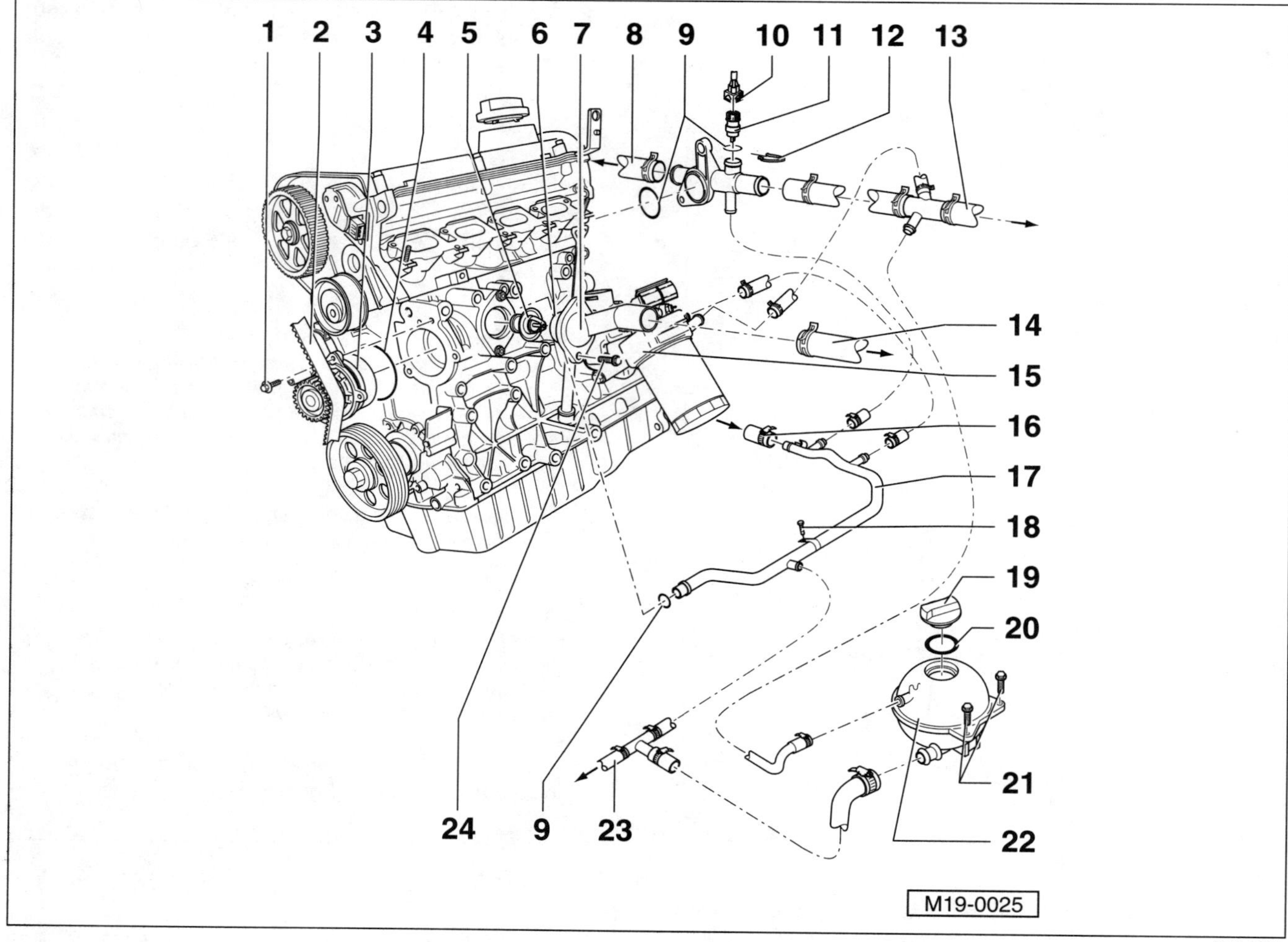

M19-0025

Fig. 10. Coolant pump and related cooling system components on 1.8L engine.

1. **Bolt**
   - Tighten to 15 Nm (11 ft-lb)
2. **Toothed belt**
   - Mark direction of rotation before removing
   - Check for wear
   - Do not kink
3. **Coolant pump**
   - Check pulley for ease of movement
   - If damaged or leaking replace complete assembly
4. **O-ring**
   - Always replace
5. **Coolant thermostat**
   - Checking: heat-up thermostat in water
   - Opening starts at approx. 189°F (87°C)
   - Opening ends at approx. 216°F (102°C)
   - Opening lift: 7 mm minimum
6. **O-ring**
   - Replace if damaged
7. **Flange**
8. **Hose to heat exchanger**
   - For passenger compartment heat
9. **O-ring**
   - Always replace
10. **4-pin harness connector**
    - Wiring cavities 1 and 3 for engine coolant temperature sensor (G62)
11. **Engine coolant temperature sender (G62)**
    - For engine control module
    - With engine coolant temperature warning light sensor (G2)
    - If necessary, release cooling system pressure before removing

(continued from previous page)

12. **Retaining clip**
    - Ensure clip is securely seated
13. **Upper coolant hose**
    - Secured to radiator with retaining clip
14. **Lower coolant hose**
    - From bottom of radiator
    - Secured to radiator with retaining clips
15. **Oil cooler**
16. **Hose from heat exchanger**
17. **Lower coolant pipe**
18. **Bolt**
    - Tighten to 10 Nm (7 ft-lb)
19. **Expansion tank cap**
    - Test pressure: 1.4-1.6 bar (20.3-23.2 psi)
20. **Seal**
    - Replace if damaged
21. **Bolt**
    - Tighten to 10 Nm (7 ft-lb)
22. **Expansion tank**
23. **To turbocharger**
24. **Bolt**
    - Tighten to 15 Nm (11 ft-lb)

NOTE —

Volkswagen identifies electrical components by a letter and/or a number in the electrical schematics. See **97 Wiring Diagrams, Fuses and Relays**. *These electrical identifiers are listed in parenthesis as an aid to electrical troubleshooting.*

Coolant pump, replacing (1.8L engine)

1. Drain coolant as previously described.
2. Remove ribbed V-belt and tensioner, see **0 Maintenance**.
3. Remove upper and center toothed belt guards.
4. Turn the crankshaft to TDC for cylinder 1 and release the toothed belt tensioning roller, see **15a Cylinder Head and Valvetrain (1.8L engine)**. The toothed belt should be left in position on the crankshaft sprocket.
5. Slide toothed belt off coolant pump sprocket.
6. Cover toothed belt with a cloth to prevent contamination from coolant.
7. Remove coolant pump mounting bolts and remove coolant pump.

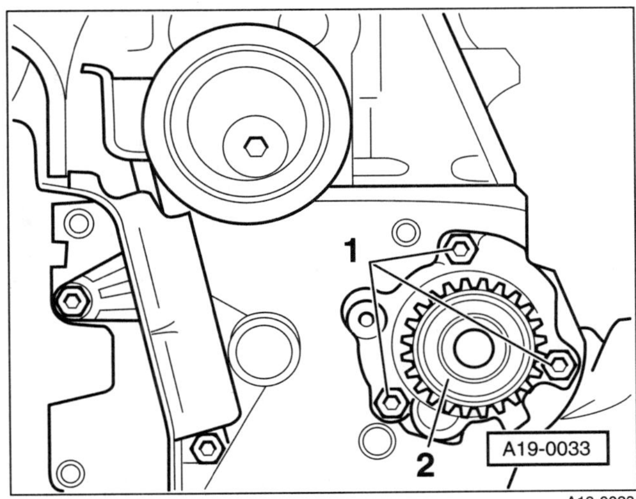

A19-0033

Fig. 11. Coolant pump (**2**) mounting bolts (**1**) on 1.8L engine.

8. Installation is reverse of removal, noting the following:
    - Clean pump mating surface on cylinder block.
    - Always use new O-rings and hardware as indicated.
    - Lubricate O-rings with coolant before installing.

Tightening torque
- Coolant pump to cylinder block . . . . . 15 Nm (11 ft-lb)

9. Fill cooling system as described previously.
10. Start engine and check for leaks.

Cooling system components (1.9L engine)

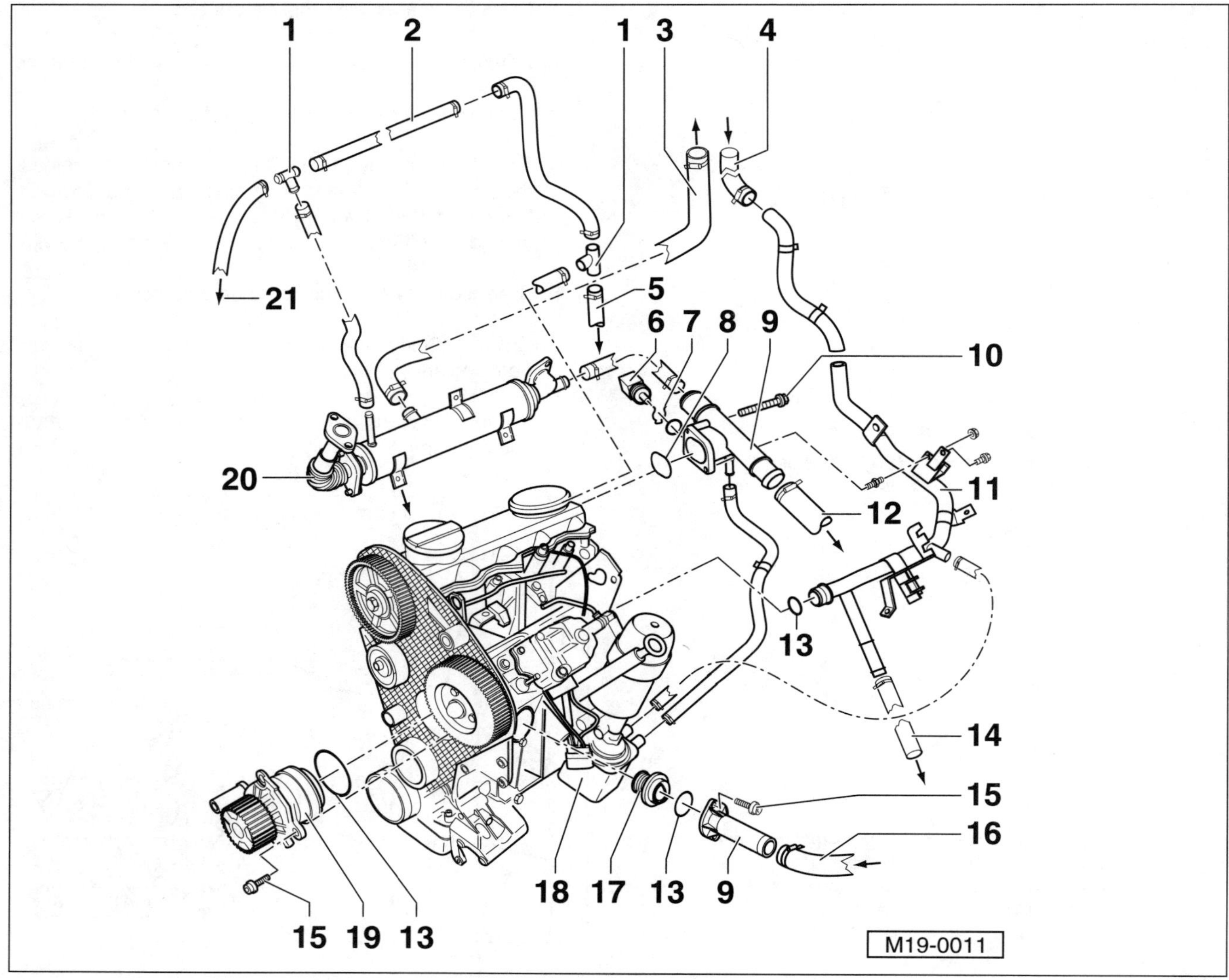

M19-0011

Fig. 12. Coolant pump and related cooling system components on 1.9L diesel engine.

1. **Connector**
2. **Coolant hose, upper**
3. **Hose to heat exchanger**
   - For passenger compartment heat
4. **Hose from heat exchanger**
5. **Hose to upper coolant hose**
6. **Engine coolant temperature sensor (G62)**
   - For engine control module
   - With engine coolant temperature warning light sensor (G2)
   - If necessary, release cooling system pressure before removing
7. **Retaining clip**
   - Check for secure installation
8. **O-ring**
   - Always replace
9. **Connector**
10. **Bolt**
    - Tighten to 10 Nm (7 ft-lb)
11. **Coolant line**
12. **Hose to top of radiator**
13. **O-ring**
    - Always replace

(continued on following page)

(continued from previous page)

14. Hose to expansion tank, lower

15. Bolt
- Tighten to 15 Nm (11 ft-lb)

16. Hose from bottom of radiator

17. Coolant thermostat
- Checking: heat-up thermostat in water
- Opening starts at approx. 185°F (85°C)
- Opening ends at approx. 221°F (105°C)
- Opening lift: 7 mm minimum

18. Oil cooler

19. Coolant pump
- Check pulley for ease of movement
- If damaged and leaking replace complete assembly
- Note installation position, **see** (A)

20. EGR cooler

21. Hose to expansion tank, upper

(A) Coolant pump (1.9L engine)

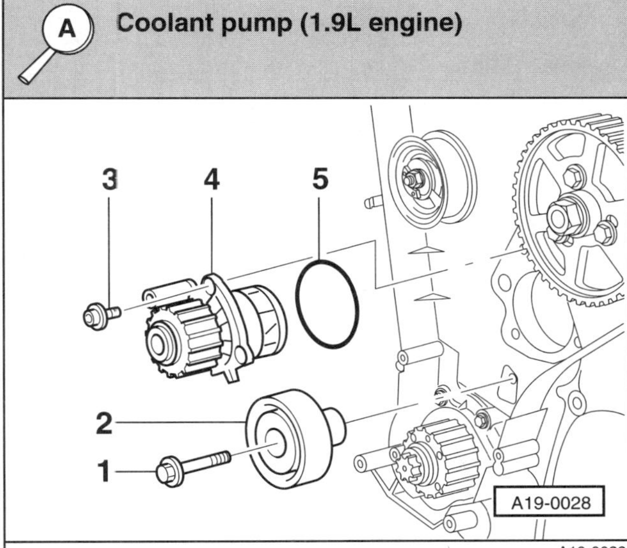

A19-0028

1. **Bolt**
   - Tighten to 40 Nm (30 ft-lb) plus ¼ turn (90°)
   - Always replace
2. **Idler pulley**
3. **Bolt**
   - Tighten to 15 Nm (11 ft-lb)
4. **Coolant pump**
   - Installation position: plug in housing points downward
5. **O-ring seal**

Coolant pump, replacing (1.9L engine)

1. Drain coolant as previously described.
2. Remove ribbed V-belt and tensioner, see **0 Maintenance**.
3. Disconnect fuel supply and return lines at fuel filter.
4. Remove connecting pipe between intercooler and intake manifold.
5. Remove fuel filter and mounting bracket.
6. Remove upper and center toothed belt guards.
7. Turn crankshaft to TDC for cylinder 1 and release toothed belt tensioning roller, see **15b Cylinder Head and Valvetrain (1.9L engine)**. Slide toothed belt off camshaft, injection pump and coolant pump sprockets, but leave it in position on crankshaft sprocket.
8. Remove bolt from idler pulley and work the pulley free from cylinder block. Discard bolt.
9. Cover toothed belt with a cloth to prevent contamination from coolant.
10. Remove coolant pump mounting bolts and carefully lift coolant pump from cylinder block between engine mount support and rear toothed belt guard.
11. Installation is reverse of removal, noting the following:
    - Clean pump mating surface on cylinder block.
    - Always use new O-rings and hardware as indicated.
    - Lubricate O-rings with coolant before installing.
12. Fill cooling system as described previously.
13. Start engine and check for leaks.

Tightening torques

- Coolant pump to cylinder block (M7) . . . . 15 Nm (11 ft-lb)
- Idler pulley bolt, 1.9L engine (M10) (always replace)
  - stage I . . . . 40 Nm (30 ft-lb)
  - stage I . . . . additional ¼ turn (90°)
- Rear toothed belt guard to cylinder block (M8) . . . . 20 Nm (15 ft-lb)

Cooling system components (AEG 2.0L engine)

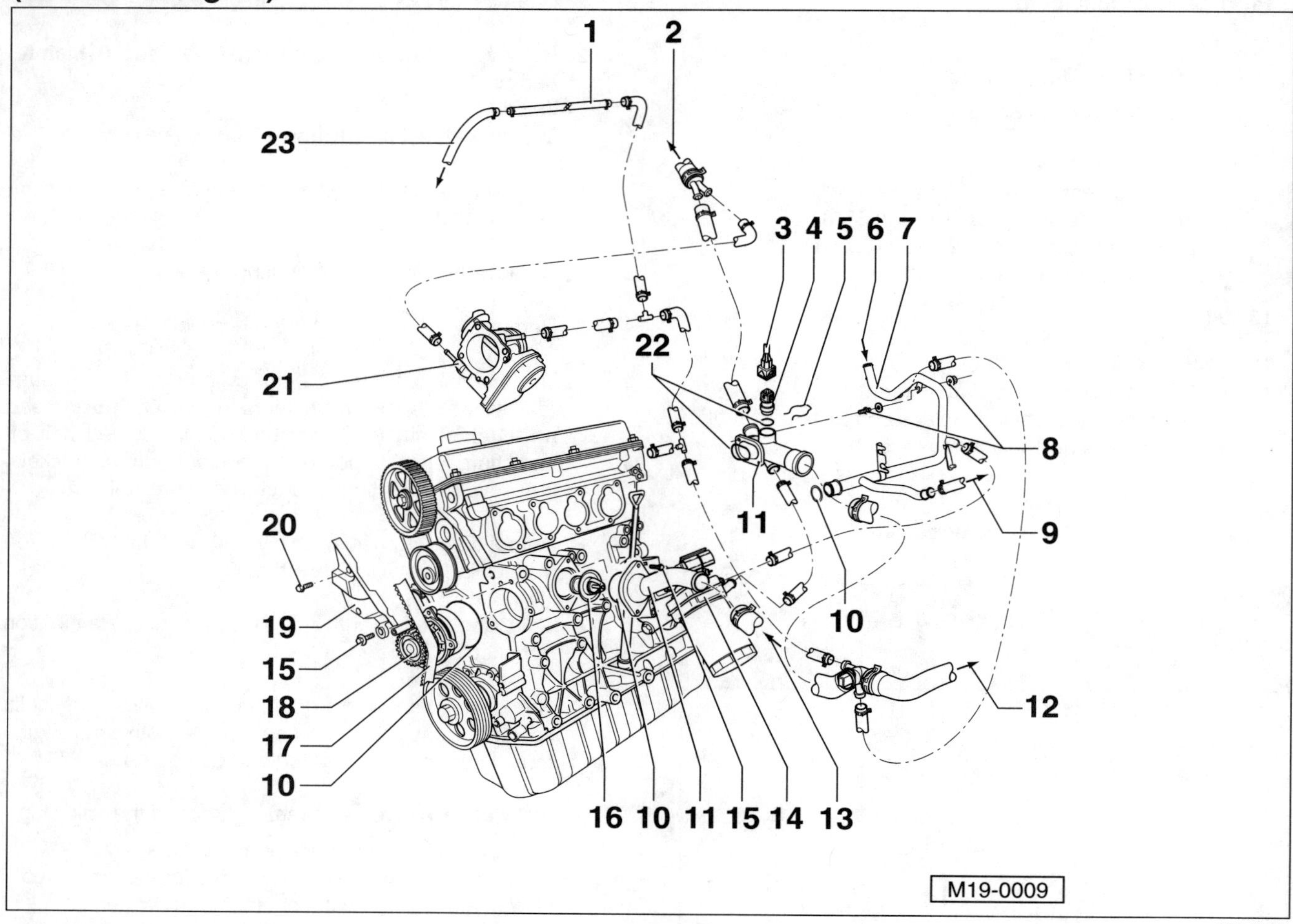

M19-0009

Fig. 13. Coolant pump and related cooling system components on AEG (2.0L) engine.

1. **Coolant pipe, upper**
   - Clipped to engine bulkhead
2. **Hose to heat exchanger**
   - For passenger compartment heat
3. **4-pin harness connector**
   - Wiring cavities 1 and 3 for engine coolant temperature sensor (G62)
   - Terminals 1 and 3: gold plated
4. **Engine coolant temperature sensor (G62)**
   - For engine control module
   - With engine coolant temperature warning light sensor (G2)
   - If necessary, release cooling system pressure before removing
5. **Retaining clip**
   - Check for secure installation
6. **Hose from heat exchanger**
7. **Coolant pipe**
8. **Stepped stud and nut**
   - Tighten to 10 Nm (7 ft-lb)
9. **Hose from expansion tank, lower**
10. **O-ring**
    - Always replace
11. **Coolant flange**
12. **Hose to top of radiator**
13. **Hose from bottom of radiator**
14. **Oil cooler**
15. **Bolt**
    - Tighten to 15 Nm (11 ft-lb)

(continued on following page)

(continued from previous page)

16. Engine coolant thermostat
- Checking: heat-up thermostat in water
- Opening starts at approx. 187°F (86°C)
- Opening ends at approx. 216°F (102°C)
- Opening lift: 7 mm (0.28 in.) minimum

17. Toothed belt
- Mark engine direction of rotation before removing
- Check for wear
- Do not kink

18. Coolant pump
- Check pulley for ease of movement
- If damaged and leaking replace complete assembly
- Note installation position, **see** (A)

19. Toothed belt guard, rear

20. Bolt
- 20 Nm (15 ft-lb)

21. Throttle control module
- Heated by engine coolant

22. O-ring
- Replace if damaged

23. Hose to expansion tank, upper

(A) Coolant pump (2.0L engine)

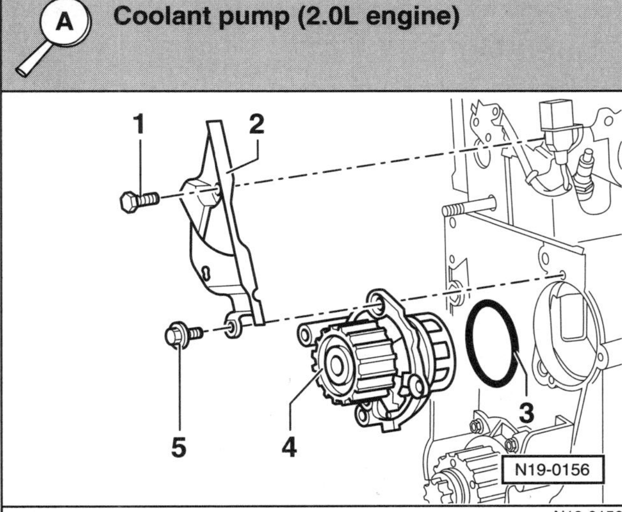

N19-0156

1. **Bolt**
   - Tighten to 20 Nm (15 ft-lb)
2. **Rear toothed belt guard**
3. **O-ring seal**
4. **Coolant pump**
   - Installed position: plug in housing points downward
5. **Bolt**
   - Tighten to 15 Nm (11 ft-lb)

Coolant pump, replacing (2.0L engine)

1. Drain coolant as previously described.
2. Remove ribbed V-belt and tensioner, see **0 Maintenance**.
3. Remove upper and center toothed belt guards.
4. Turn the crankshaft to TDC for cylinder 1 and release the toothed belt tensioning roller, see **15c Cylinder Head and Valvetrain (2.0L engine)**. The toothed belt should be left in position on the crankshaft sprocket.
5. Slide toothed belt off coolant pump sprocket.
6. Remove mounting bolts from rear toothed belt guard.
7. Cover toothed belt with a cloth to prevent contamination from coolant.
8. Remove coolant pump mounting bolts and remove coolant pump.
9. Installation is reverse of removal, noting the following:
   - Clean pump mating surface on cylinder block.
   - Always use new O-rings and hardware as indicated.
   - Lubricate O-rings with coolant before installing.

Tightening torque
- Coolant pump to cylinder block . . . . . 15 Nm (11 ft-lb)
- Rear toothed belt guard to cylinder block . . . . 20 Nm (15 ft-lb)

10. Fill cooling system as described previously.
11. Start engine and check for leaks.

Cooling system components (AVH, AZG 2.0L engines)

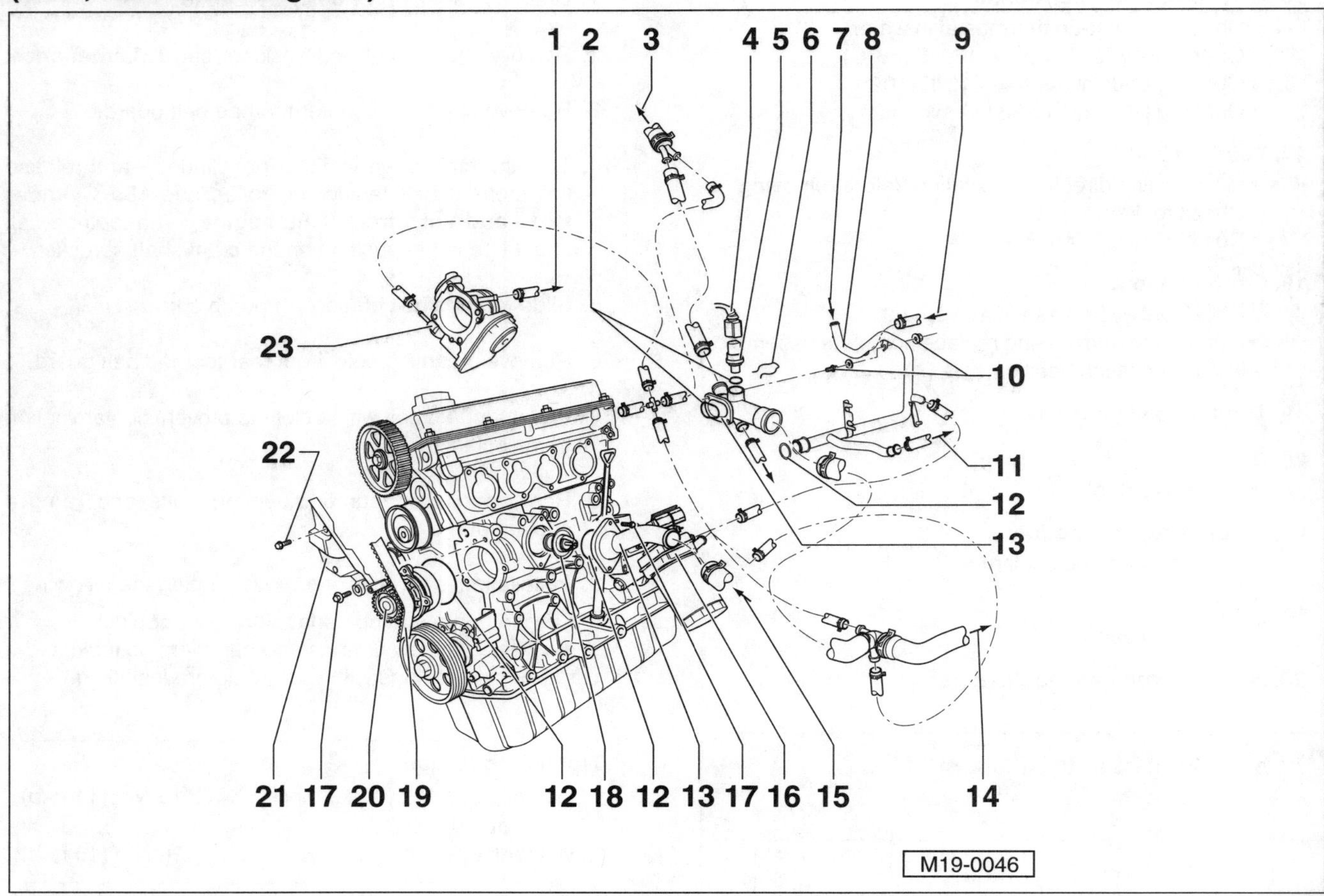

M19-0046

Fig. 14. Coolant pump and related cooling system components on AVH and AZG (2.0L) engines.

1. **Hose to expansion tank, upper**
2. **O-ring**
   - Always replace
3. **Hose to heat exchanger**
   - For passenger compartment heat
4. **4-pin harness connector**
   - Wiring cavities 1 and 3 for engine coolant temperature sensor (G62)
   - Terminals 1 and 3: gold plated
5. **Engine coolant temperature sensor (G62)**
   - For engine control module
   - With engine coolant temperature warning light sensor (G2)
   - If necessary, release cooling system pressure before removing
6. **Retaining clip**
   - Check for secure installation
7. **Hose from heat exchanger**
8. **Coolant pipe**
9. **Hose to transmission cooler**
   - Only for vehicles with automatic transmission
10. **Stepped stud and nut**
    - Tighten to 10 Nm (7 ft-lb)
11. **Hose from expansion tank, lower**
12. **O-ring**
    - Always replace
13. **Coolant flange**
14. **Hose to top of radiator**
15. **Hose from bottom of radiator**
16. **Oil cooler**
17. **Bolt**
    - Tighten to 15 Nm (11 ft-lb)

(continued on following page)

(continued from previous page)

18. Engine coolant thermostat
- Checking: heat-up thermostat in water
- Opening starts at approx. 187°F (86°C)
- Opening ends at approx. 216°F (102°C)
- Opening lift: 7 mm (0.28 in.) minimum

19. Toothed belt
- Mark engine direction of rotation before removing
- Check for wear
- Do not kink

20. Coolant pump
- Check pulley for ease of movement
- If damaged and leaking replace complete assembly
- Note installation position, **see** (A)

21. Toothed belt guard, rear

22. Bolt
- 20 Nm (15 ft-lb)

23. Throttle control module
- Without cable disc for accelerator because of E-gas system
- Heated by engine coolant

(A) Coolant pump (2.0L engine)

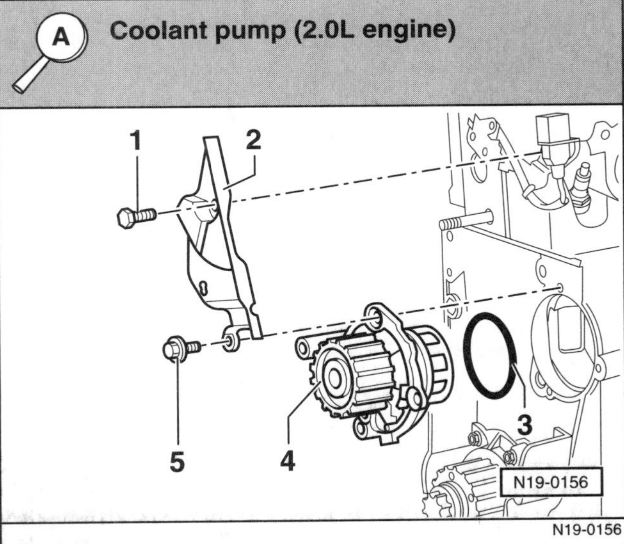

N19-0156

1. **Bolt**
   - Tighten to 20 Nm (15 ft-lb)
2. **Rear toothed belt guard**
3. **O-ring seal**
4. **Coolant pump**
   - Installed position: plug in housing points downward
5. **Bolt**
   - Tighten to 15 Nm (11 ft-lb)

NOTE —

Volkswagen identifies electrical components by a letter and/or a number in the electrical schematics. See **97 Wiring Diagrams, Fuses and Relays**. *These electrical identifiers are listed in parenthesis as an aid to electrical troubleshooting.*

Cooling system components (2.8L engine)

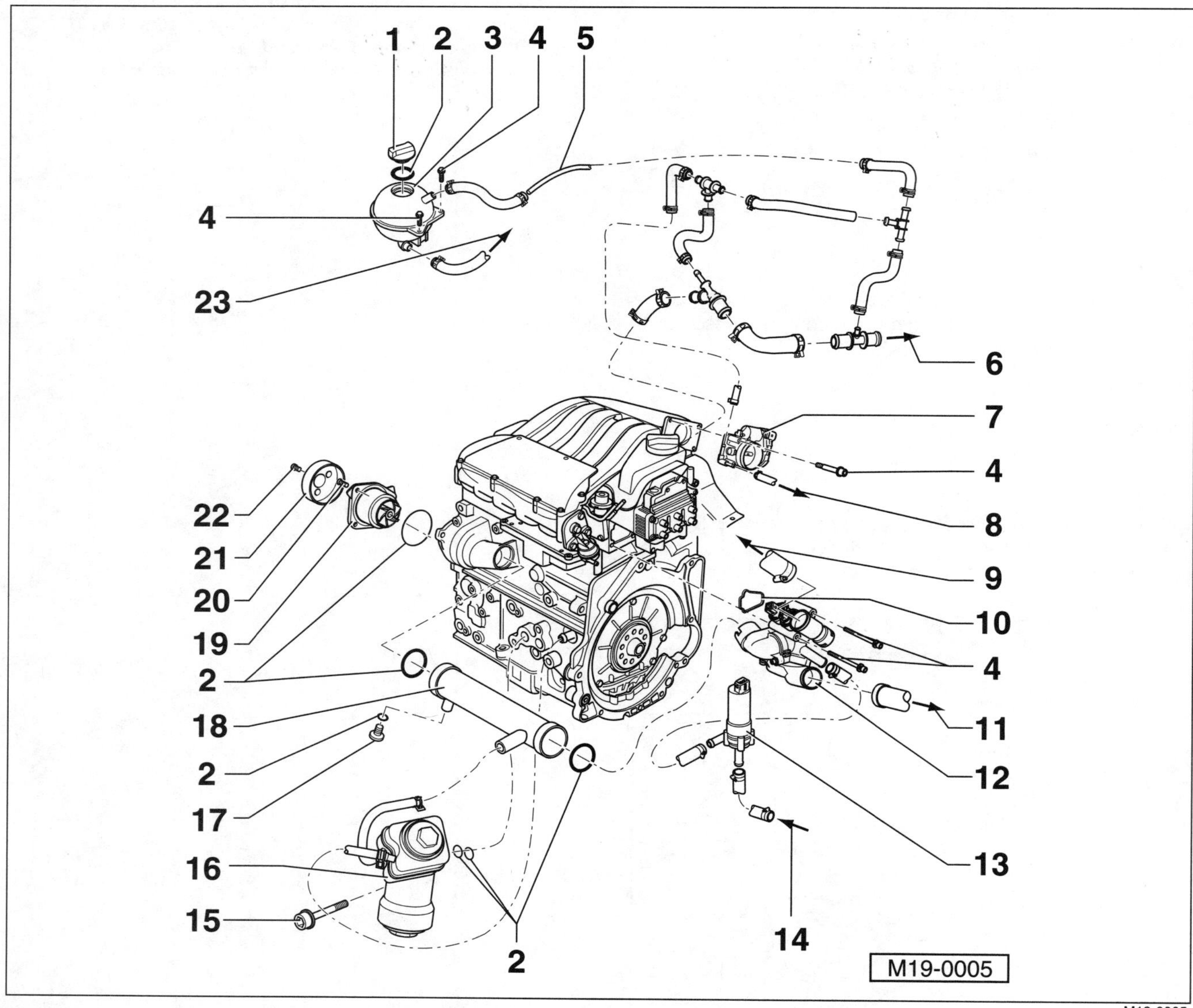

M19-0005

Fig. 15. Cooling system components for 2.8L (VR6) engine.

1. **Pressure cap**
   • Test pressure 1.4-1.6 bar
2. **O-ring**
   • Replace if damaged
3. **Coolant recovery bottle**
4. **Bolt**
   • Tighten to 10 Nm (7 ft-lb)
5. **Upper coolant pipe**
   • Clipped into bulkhead
6. **To heat exchanger**
7. **Throttle valve control unit (J338)**
   • Heated by coolant
8. **To upper coolant hose**
9. **To upper radiator**
10. **Gasket**
    • Always replace
11. **To lower radiator**
12. **Thermostat housing**
13. **Coolant feed pump (V51)**

(continued on following page)

(continued from previous page)

14. From heat exchanger

15. Bolt
- Tighten to 25 Nm (18 ft-lb)

16. Oil cooler
- Coat contact surfaces outside of sealing ring with AMV 188 001 02
- Ensure free movement among surrounding components

17. Screw plug

18. Coolant pipe

19. Coolant pump
- Observe installation position
- Check for smooth running
- Replace complete unit if damaged or leaking

20. Bolt
- Tighten to 15 Nm (11 ft-lb)

21. Pulley
- For coolant pump

22. Bolt
- Tighten to 25 Nm (18 ft-lb)

23. To Y-branch of heat exchanger/coolant feed pump

Coolant pump, replacing (2.8L engine)

1. Drain coolant as previously described.
2. Remove ribbed V-belt and tensioner, see **0 Maintenance**.
3. Using a 2-pin spanner wrench, remove the retaining screws from the coolant pump pulley and remove pulley. See Fig. 16.

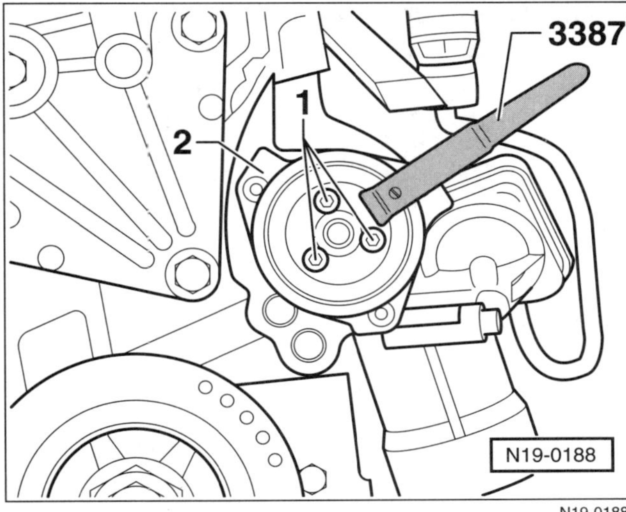

N19-0188

Fig. 16. Counterhold coolant pulley and remove retaining screws (**1**) and pulley.

4. Remove coolant pump retaining screws and coolant pump. See Fig. 17.

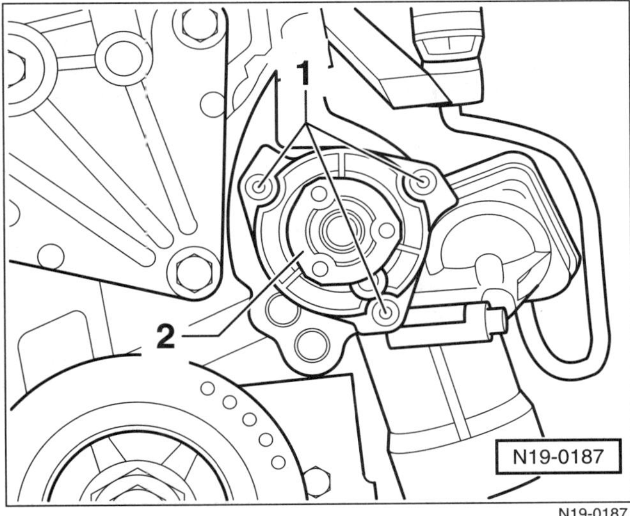

N19-0187

Fig. 17. Remove screws (**1**) and coolant pump (**2**).

5. Assemble in reverse order of removal noting the following points:
   - Moisten new O-ring with coolant.
   - Insert coolant pump into engine block and tighten retaining screws.

Tightening torque
- Coolant pump retaining screws . . . . . 15 Nm (11 ft-lb)

Radiator and cooling fans (1.9L and 2.0L engines)

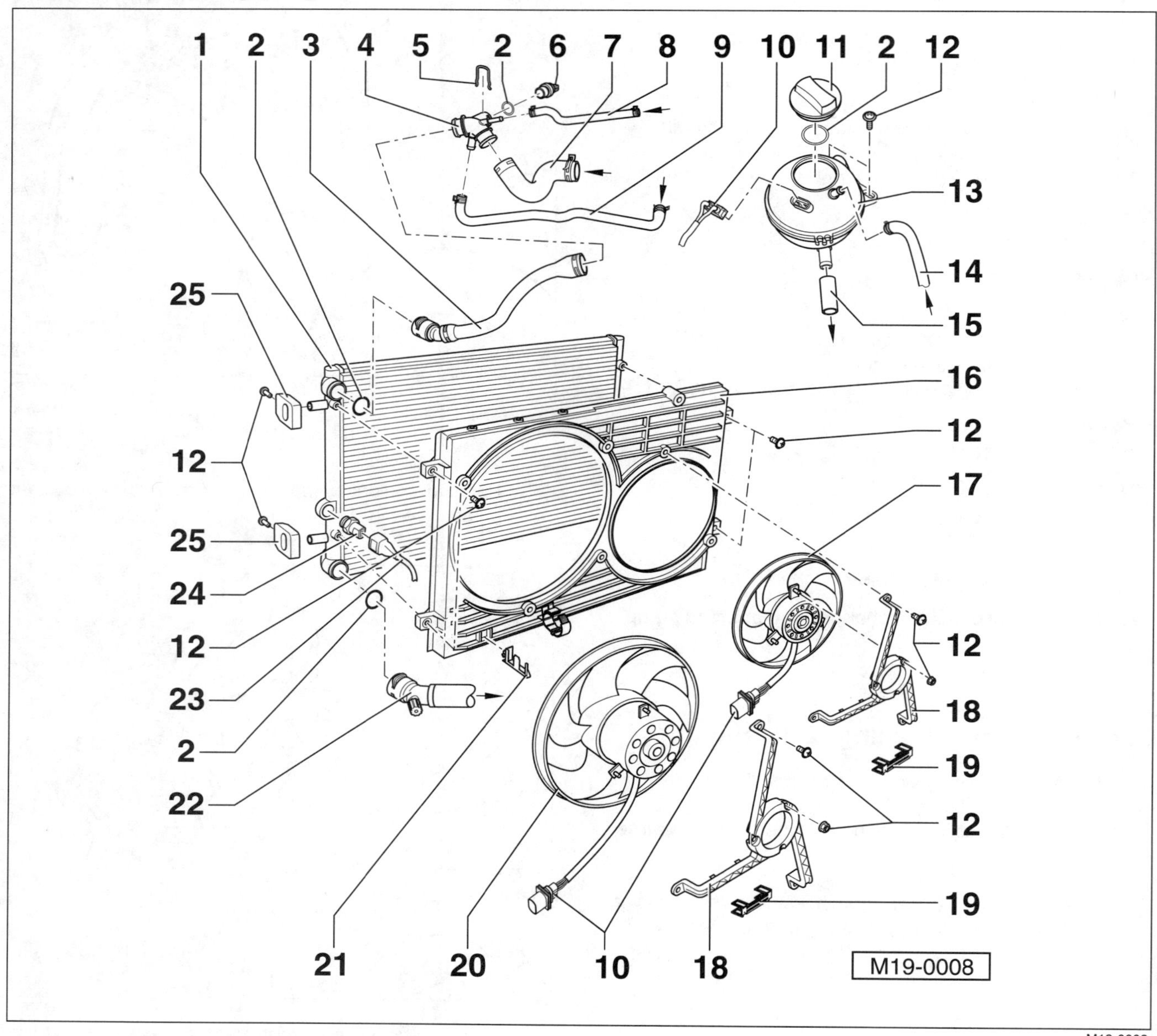

M19-0008

Fig. 18. Radiator and cooling fans for 1.9L and 2.0L engines.

1. **Radiator**
   - If replaced, flush cooling system and use new coolant
2. **O-ring**
   - Always replace
3. **Coolant hose, upper**
   - Attached to radiator with retaining clip
4. **Connector**
5. **Retaining clip**
   - Ensure it is seated securely
6. **A/C cut-out thermal switch (F163)**
   - Vehicles with A/C only
7. **Hose from connector on cylinder head**
8. **Coolant pipe**
9. **Coolant pipe**
10. **Connector**
    - Black, 2-pin
11. **Pressure cap**
    - Test pressure 1.4-1.6 bar

(continued from previous page)

12. Bolt
- Tighten to 10 Nm (7 ft-lb)

13. Expansion tank

14. Hose from throttle control module

15. Hose to coolant pipe

16. Air ducting

17. Radiator fan (V35)
- For vehicles with additional equipment

18. Fan bracket

19. Retaining clip
- Ensure it is seated securely

20. Radiator fan (V7)

21. Bracket
- For radiator fan connector

22. Coolant hose, lower
- Attached to radiator with retaining clip

23. Connector
- Black, 3-pin

24. Thermoswitch (F18)
- Tighten to 35 Nm (26 ft-lb)
- For electric fan

25. Bracket
- For radiator
- Note installation position
- Upper and lower parts may be different

NOTE —
Volkswagen identifies electrical components by a letter and/or a number in the electrical schematics. See **97 Wiring Diagrams, Fuses and Relays**. *These electrical identifiers are listed in parenthesis as an aid to electrical troubleshooting.*

Radiator and cooling fans (1.8L and 2.8L engines)

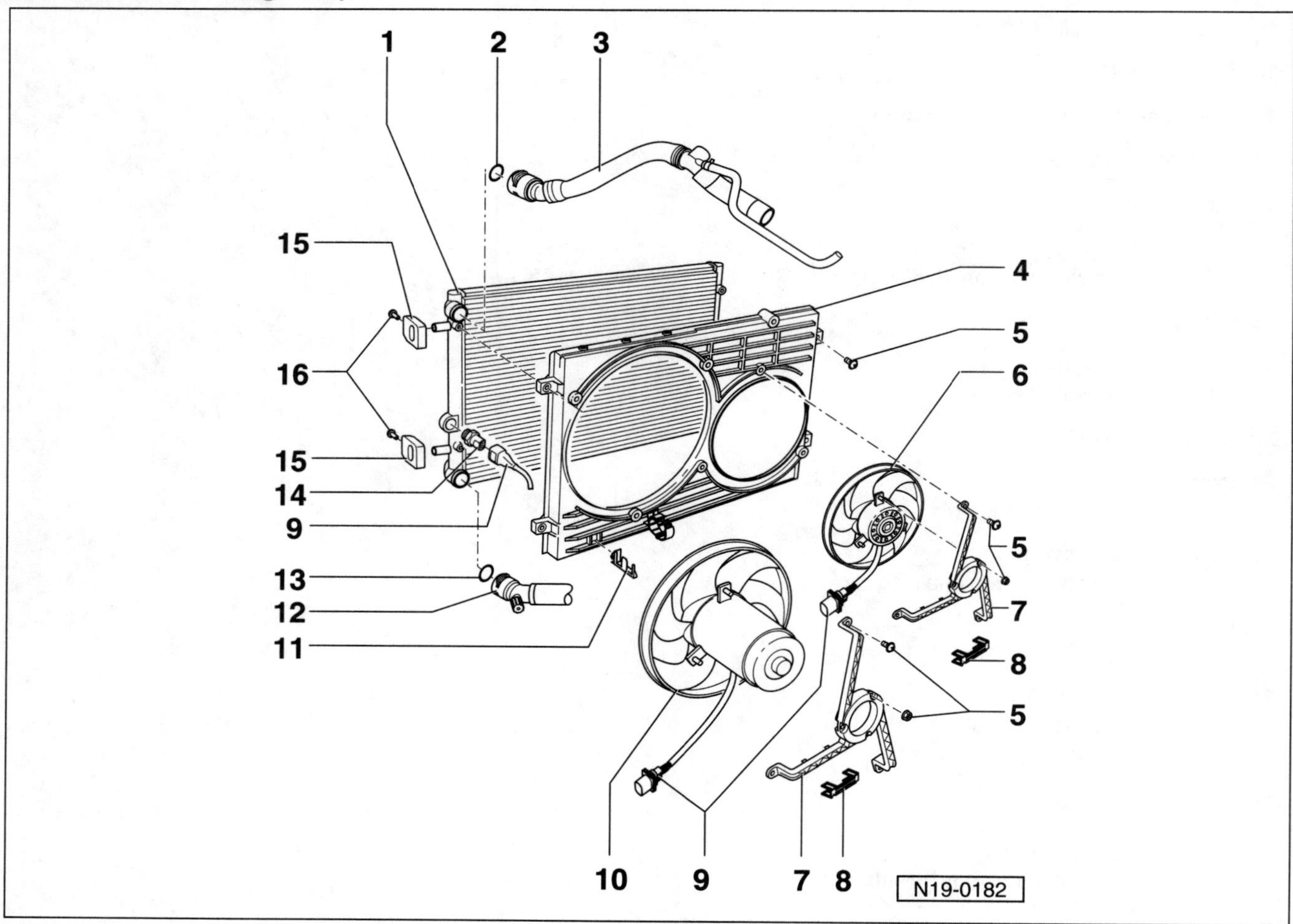

N19-0182

Fig. 19. Radiator and cooling fans for 1.8L and 2.8L engines.

1. **Radiator**
2. **O-ring**
   - Replace if damaged
3. **Upper coolant hose**
   - Fastened to radiator with rapid action hose coupling
   - Ensure tight fit
4. **Air scoop**
5. **Bolt**
   - Tighten to 10 Nm (7 ft-lb)
6. **Coolant fan (V7)**
7. **Fan bracket**
8. **Retaining clamp**
   - Check for tight fit
9. **Connector**
10. **Coolant fan (V35)**
11. **Bracket**
    - For fan connector
12. **Lower coolant hose**
    - Fastened to radiator with rapid action hose coupling
    - Ensure tight fit
13. **O-ring**
    - Always replace
14. **Thermo-switch (F18)**
    - Tighten to 35 Nm (26 ft-lb)
    - For coolant fans
15. **Bracket**
    - For radiator
    - Observe installation position
16. **Bolt**
    - Tighten to 15 Nm (11 ft-lb)

Radiator and cooling fans, removing and installing

The cooling fans provide additional air flow through the radiator. A faulty cooling fan motor or thermoswitch may be the cause of insufficient air flow and overheating.

The Volkswagen Golf, Jetta and GTI models covered by this manual are equipped with dual two-speed radiator fans.

> ***WARNING —***
> *The electric cooling fans can come on at any time, even if the key is out of the ignition. To avoid personal injury, use extreme caution when working at or near the cooling fan if the engine is hot. As a safety precaution, always disconnect the harness connector from the fan when working around the radiator, fans and associated components.*

1. Drain coolant as previously described.

2. Disconnect coolant hoses from radiator.

3. Remove front body section and move lock carrier to service position, see **50 Body-Front**.

4. Disconnect thermo-switch and fan harness connectors.

5. Remove retaining clamps from A/C hoses near condenser.

6. Unbolt A/C condenser from radiator and support condenser with wire or heavy duty tie wraps.

   NOTE —
   Do not discharge the A/C refrigerant. Support the A/C condenser with wire and avoid stretching or kinking the hoses.

7. Remove radiator mounting bolts from both sides and slide radiator slightly to rear. See Fig. 20.

8. Remove radiator and fans together from below.

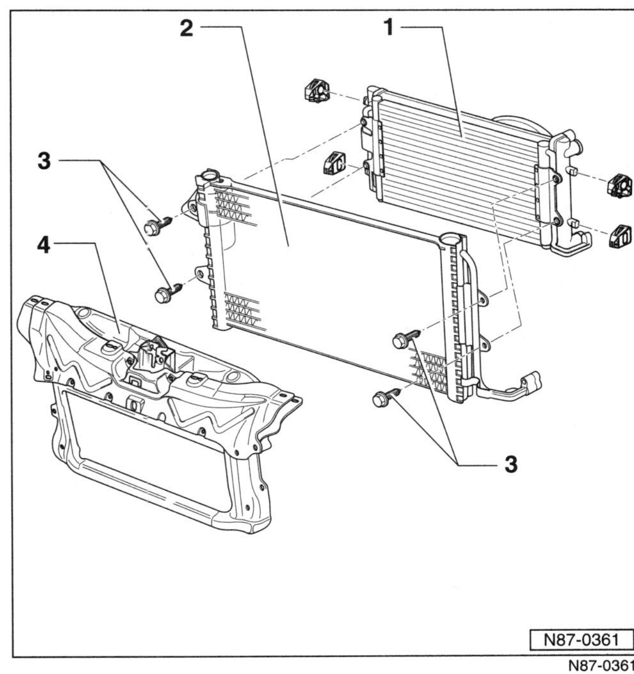

N87-0361

Fig. 20. Radiator (**1**), condenser (**2**), mounting bolts (**3**) and lock carrier (**4**).

9. Installation is the reverse of removal.

Tightening torque
- A/C condenser to radiator . . . . 8 Nm (71 in-lb)

10. Fill the cooling system as described previously. Start engine and check for leaks.

Auxiliary radiator (2.8L engine), removing and installing

Vehicles with the 2.8L (VR6) engine may be equipped with an auxiliary radiator for additional cooling in hot climates.

1. Drain coolant as described earlier.
2. Remove lower right front sound absorption panel, see **50 Body–Front**.
3. Remove right front wheel housing liner, see **66 Body–Exterior Equipment**.
4. Remove auxiliary radiator air scoop, see item 6 in Fig. 22.
5. Remove windshield washer reservoir, see **92 Wipers and Washers**.
6. Pull coolant hoses off auxiliary radiator using pliers (VAG 1921 or equivalent). See Fig. 21.
7. Remove auxiliary radiator upper retaining screws located below right headlight. See Fig. 21.

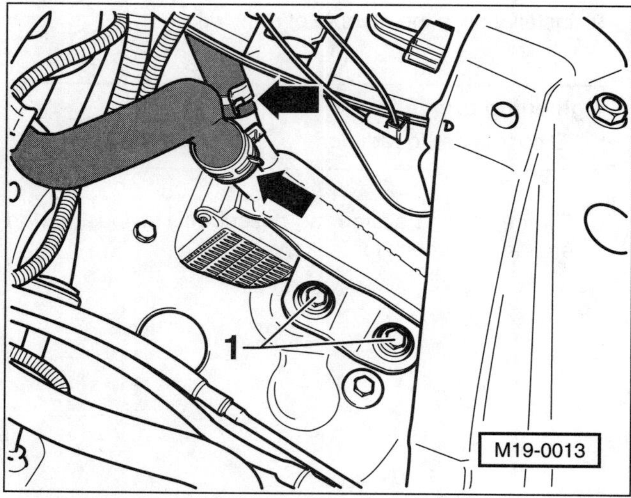

M19-0013

Fig. 21. Remove coolant hoses (**arrows**) and upper retaining screws (**1**) for auxiliary radiator.

8. Remove the lower mounting bolt in the front wheel housing from mounting bracket. See item 5 in Fig. 22.

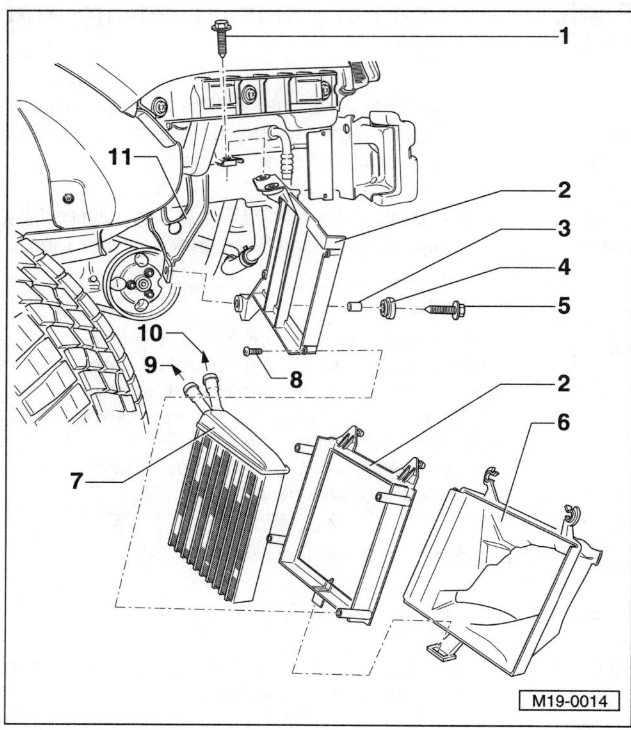

M19-0014

Fig. 22. Auxiliary radiator and related components (2.8L engine).

The following list applies to Fig. 22.

1. **Upper mounting bolts**
   - Tighten to 10 Nm (7 ft-lb)
2. **Retaining frame**
3. **Spacer sleeve**
4. **Rubber disk**
5. **Lower mounting bolt**
   - Tighten to 10 Nm (7 ft-lb)
6. **Air scoop**
   - Clipped onto retaining frame
7. **Auxiliary radiator**
   - Refill with fresh coolant after replacement
8. **Retaining screws**
   - Tighten to 5 Nm (44 in-lb)
9. **To Y-branch of upper coolant hose**
10. **To Y-branch of lower coolant hose**
11. **Bracket**

9. Carefully remove the auxiliary radiator with its attachments from below.
10. Installation is the reverse of removal.

Tightening torque
- Auxiliary radiator mounting bolts ..... 10 Nm (7 ft-lb)

11. Fill the cooling system as described previously. Start engine and check for leaks.

Thermostat, replacing (4-cylinder)

A thermostat mounted in the cylinder block provides primary control of coolant temperature by regulating the flow of coolant to the radiator. The thermostat remains closed when coolant is below the specified temperature allowing the engine to reach operating temperature quickly and providing immediate heat to the passenger compartment. Thermostats for all the 4-cylinder engines covered by this manual operate within the same temperature ranges, but are not interchangeable, see Fig. 23. and Fig. 24.

1. Drain coolant as previously given.
2. Disconnect lower radiator hose from flange on cylinder block.
3. Remove the outlet flange mounting bolts and remove the flange and O-ring seal.
4. Remove the thermostat:
   - 2.0L engines, carefully pull the thermostat out.
   - 1.8L and 1.9L engines, rotate the thermostat ¼ turn, (90°), counterclockwise and pull out.

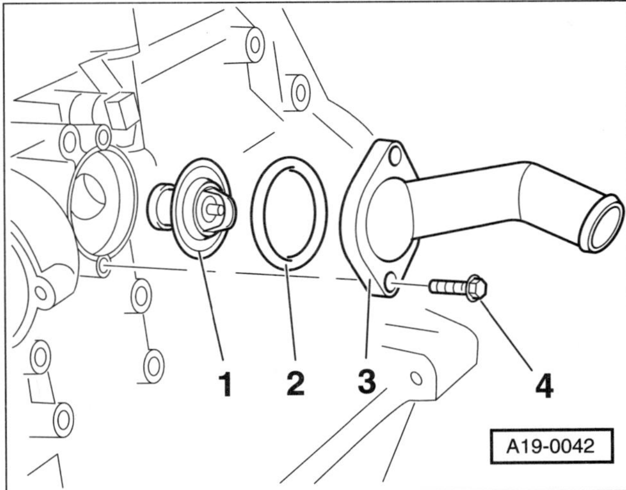

A19-0042

Fig. 23. Thermostat (**1**), O-ring (**2**), flange (**3**) and mounting bolt (**4**) on 4-cylinder gasoline engines.

5. Install thermostat into cylinder block:
   - 2.0L engines, fit thermostat into cylinder block.
   - 1.8L and 1.9L engines, fit thermostat into cylinder block and rotate ¼ turn (90°) clockwise.

NOTE —
On 4-cylinder gasoline engines the support brace on the thermostat must be almost vertical when installed.

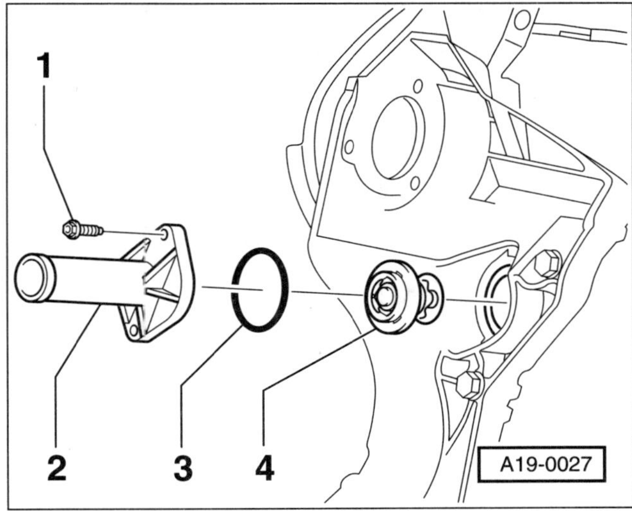

A19-0027

Fig. 24. Mounting bolt (**1**), flange (**2**), O-ring (**3**), and thermostat (**4**) on 1.9L diesel engine.

6. Remaining installation is the reverse of removal noting the following:
   - Clean mating surface on cylinder block before installing outlet flange.
   - Always use new O-rings with coolant before installing.
   - Fill cooling system as described previously.

Tightening torque
- Thermostat flange (4-cylinder engines) . . . . 15 Nm (11 ft-lb)

7. Start engine and check for leaks.

Thermostat (6-cylinder)

The thermostat housing on 6-cylinder engines is located on the rear of the cylinder head. An exploded view of the housing and related components is shown in Fig. 25.

NOTE —
Volkswagen identifies electrical components by a letter and/or a number in the electrical schematics. See ***97 Wiring Diagrams, Fuses and Relays****. These electrical identifiers are listed in parenthesis as an aid to electrical troubleshooting.*

Thermostat assembly (2.8L engine)

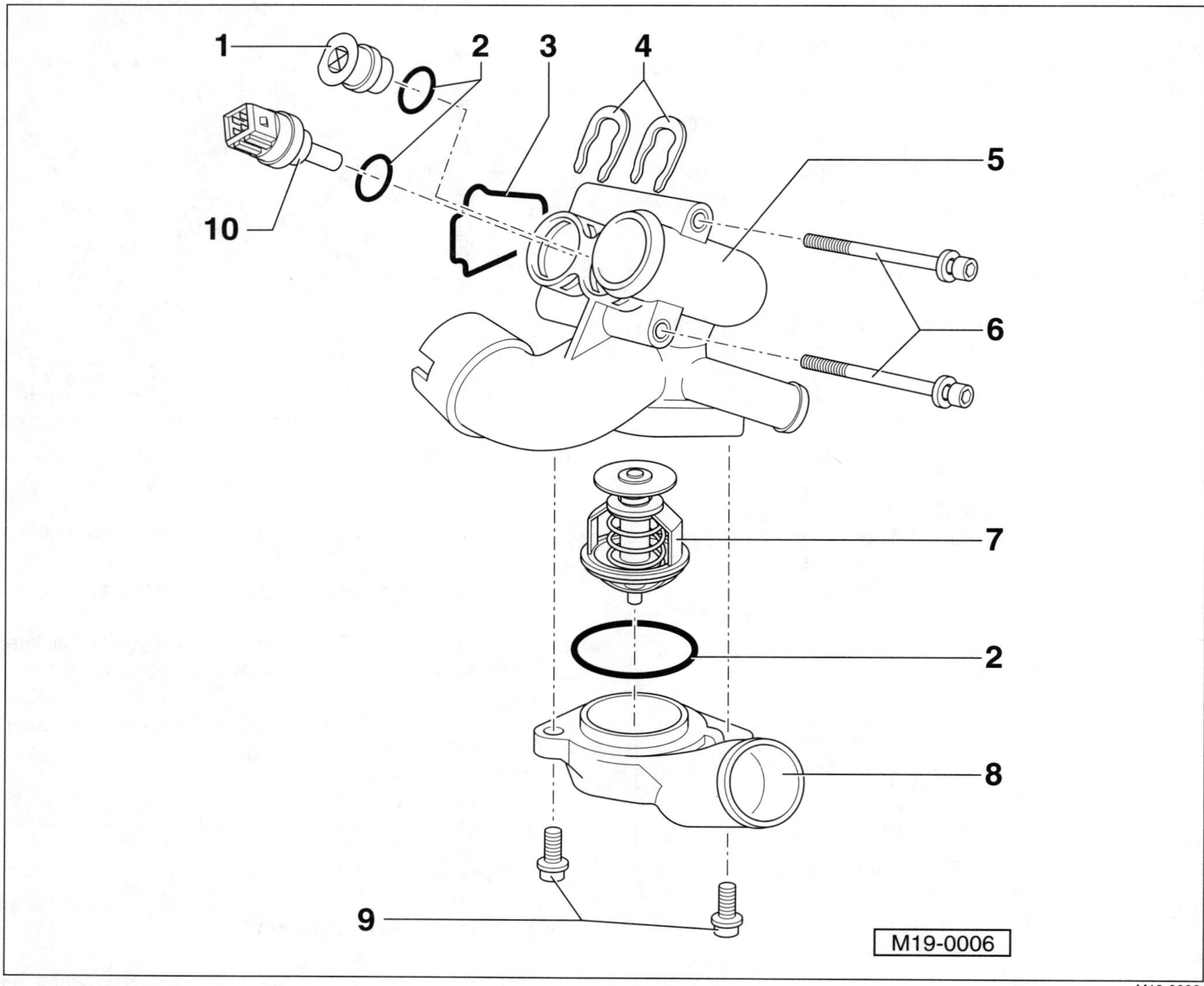

M19-0006

Fig. 25. Thermostat housing and related components on 2.8L (VR6) engine.

1. **Plug**
2. **O-ring**
   - Always replace
3. **Gasket**
   - Always replace
4. **Retaining clamp**
   - Check for tight fit
5. **Thermostat housing**
6. **Bolt**
   - Tighten to 10 Nm (7 ft-lb)
7. **Thermostat**
   - Install with large plate downward
   - Checking: heat controller in water bath
   - Opening starts at approx. 80°C (176°F)
   - Opening ends at approx. 105°C (221°F)
   - Travel at least 7 mm
8. **Connector**
9. **Bolt**
   - Tighten to 10 Nm (7 ft-lb)
10. **Coolant temperature sensor (G62)**
    - With coolant temperature display (G2)
    - For engine control unit
    - Release pressure from cooling system before removing

2 Fuel, Ignition, and Exhaust Systems

GENERAL

This general information group covers application information and system descriptions for the repair groups listed under **2 Fuel, Ignition and Exhaust Systems**.

> ***NOTE —***
> - *For general information on the battery, starter and alternator, see* **27 Engine Electrical Systems**.
> - *For emission control system application information, see* **26 Exhaust System and Emission Controls**.

FUEL SUPPLY

The plastic fuel tank is mounted beneath the rear of the vehicle. On gasoline engines, an electric fuel pump with integral level sensor is submersed in the tank. On diesel engines, only the fuel the level sensor is mounted in the tank, as the engine-mounted diesel injection pump handles fuel delivery to the engine.

This gasoline fuel pump/fuel level sensor assembly is called the fuel delivery unit. An inlet strainer provides course filtration and prevents dirt and debris from entering the fuel system. Built into the fuel delivery unit is a check valve and a relief valve. The check valve is on the outlet side of the pump and holds pressure in the system after the engine is shut off. The relief valve prevents high pressure from damaging the system. The check valve and relief valve are not replaceable.

The fuel tank is designed to prevent overfilling and allow for fuel expansion. The fuel cap contains a valve to prevent a vacuum from forming in the tank.

On all engines, fuel is supplied to the engine and excess fuel is returned to the tank through special plastic fuel lines. In addition, diesel engines with automatic transmissions use a fuel cooler on the supply line to the pump.

FUEL INJECTION

The various types of engine management systems used on the engines covered by this manual are listed below.

Engine Codes
- AEG . . . . 2.0L 4-cylinder gasoline Motronic 5.9.2
- ALH . . . . 1.9L 4-cylinder turbo diesel TDI Diesel Direct Fuel Injection
- AFP . . . . 2.8L 6-cylinder gasoline Motronic ME 7.1
- AWD, AWW . . . . 1.8L 4-cylinder gasoline Motronic ME 7.5
- AVH, AZG. . . . . 2.0L 4-cylinder gasoline Motronic ME 7.5

Motronic 5.9.2 engine management

The AEG (2.0 liter) engine is equipped with an enhanced version of the sophisticated Bosch Motronic engine management system. See Fig. 1. This version (5.9.2) complies with the federal and state government mandated On-Board Diagnostic (OBD) II standards.

Basic fuel metering is determined by engine speed and engine load. The Engine Control Module (ECM) receives engine speed and crankshaft position information from the engine speed and reference sensor, and engine load information from the Mass Air Flow sensor (MAF). The ECM then meters fuel to the engine by sequentially triggering the fuel injectors at a rate proportional to engine speed and load. The length of time the injectors remain open determines fuel quantity.

Motronic 5.9.2 overview

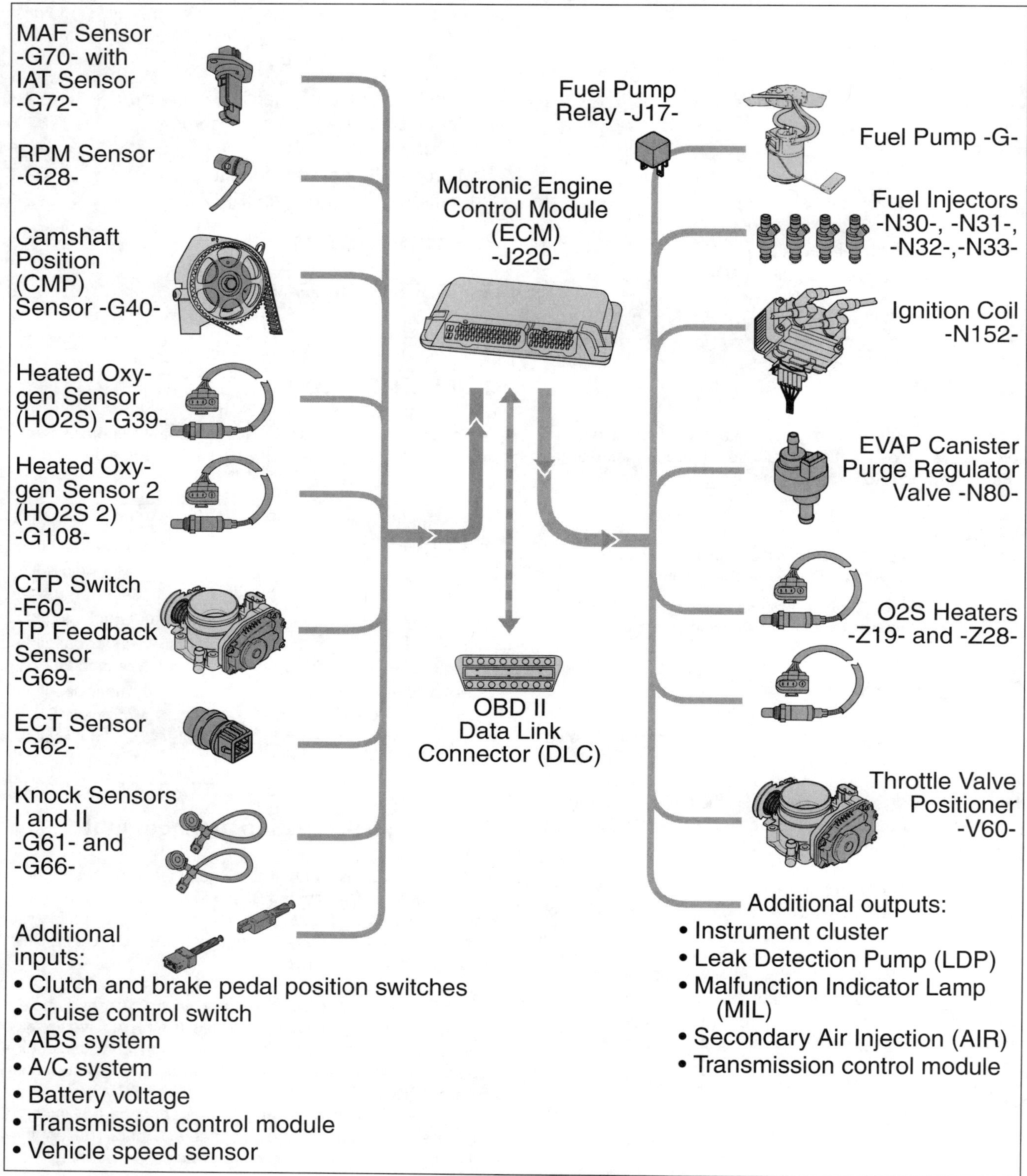

Fig. 1. Bosch Motronic 5.9.2 engine management system. Inputs (**left**) to the ECM are used to control and adapt output signals (**right**) to the individual components. Volkswagen component codes are indicated within dashes (–).

The ECM uses the same information to determine the correct ignition firing point. A small output signal is generated and sent to the Power Output Stages built into the Ignition Coils. The Camshaft Position Sensor (CMP), identifies cylinder number 1 firing position for cylinder-selective injection and ignition knock control. The Engine Coolant Temperature sensor (ECT), supplies engine temperature information to the ECM.

The Throttle Actuator Control Module (TACM), combines 4 functions. Three are used on the input side: the Throttle Position Sensor (TPS), which signals throttle angle; the Closed Throttle Position switch (CTP), which signals fully closed throttle plate; and the Throttle Position Feedback sensor, which signals position of the electric motor used for idle stabilization and cruise control function.

The Pre-Catalyst Heated Oxygen Sensor (HO2S), signals combustion efficiency, and the Post-Catalyst Heated Oxygen Sensor (HO2S), monitors efficiency of the Three-Way Catalytic Converter (TWC).

The Knock Sensors (KS1 and KS2), supply engine knock information for ignition timing regulation and the Intake Air Temperature sensor (IAT), is used for idle stabilization and as a correction factor for ignition timing.

Based on all of the input signals, the ECM precisely controls the following output components:

- Fuel Injectors
- Power Output Stage and Ignition Coil
- Throttle Position Actuator
- Evaporative Canister Purge Valve (EVAP)
- Fuel Pump and Relay

In addition, certain versions have additional outputs controlled by the ECM:

- Secondary Air Pump Relay (AIR); Air Injection Solenoid Control Valve and Secondary Air Injection Pump
- Leak Diagnosis Pump (LDP); and Control Relay

The ECM also controls cruise control functions.

A warning light known as a Malfunction Indicator Lamp (MIL), is located in the instrument cluster and signals the vehicle operator when certain systems have failed. In some instances, it will come on if relatively small malfunctions have been recorded, such as running very low on fuel or leaving off the gas cap. Most malfunctions that occur will cause the light to stay on steadily, but certain very serious situations such as an overheating catalytic converter may cause it to blink.

Because of the Motronic 5.9.2 system is quite complex, proper diagnosis and repair requires the use of a specialized scan tool such as Volkswagen special tool VAG 1551 or VAG 1552. Aftermarket scan tools can also access the ME 5.9.2 system diagnostic trouble codes (known as P-codes). A table is provided at the back of this manual that identifies the various scan tool codes. See **ST Scan Tool Codes**.

In addition to diagnostics, Motronic 5.9.2 systems include the ability to record proper operation of as many as 8 monitored functions. These functional checks are called readiness codes and are set when the proper operating parameters are reached at least one time. These codes are important because some areas with emissions testing check these codes first. If the readiness code is NOT set, the vehicle will not pass the specialized test. Readiness codes may be erased if the battery is disconnected or runs low, if the ECM is disconnected, or if faults or DTCs are erased with a scan tool. Generally speaking, the readiness codes in Volkswagen systems will reset themselves after the vehicle has been started and driven under varying conditions several times. They can also be reset using the scan tool.

Diesel Turbo Direct Injection (TDI)

The 1.9 liter diesel engine is equipped with the Diesel Turbo Direct Injection System that features engine controls that closely resemble those of a gasoline engine. See Fig. 2. The TDI system combines sophisticated computer control of fuel management and emissions with system monitoring and diagnostics. An exhaust driven turbocharger and an intercooler work with a specially designed combustion chamber and cylinder head to produce more efficient combustion and lower fuel consumption. This also results in reduced engine noise and increased power.

In addition, the accelerator pedal is directly connected to the Engine Control Module (ECM) via a potentiometer. This eliminates the need for an accelerator cable and is known as "drive by wire". The ECM also controls all glow plug functions, auxiliary coolant glow plug functions and cruise control.

Basic fuel metering is determined by engine speed and engine load. When the key is switched on and the engine is started, the fuel cut-off valve opens and fuel flows into the injection pump. The ECM receives engine RPM from the engine speed sensor and engine load information from the Throttle Position Sensor (TPS). These signals are modified by the Engine Coolant Temperature sensor (ECT), the Mass Air Flow Sensor (MAF), and the Fuel Temperature Sensor. The ECM then signals the quantity adjuster which allows the proper quantity of fuel to be metered sequentially to the mechanical injectors. The ECM also uses the same information to determine the correct moment of injection which is the ignition firing point. An output signal is generated and sent to the cold start valve at the correct time.

The ECM monitors the operation of the quantity adjuster via a signal received from the modulating piston displacement sensor and makes corrections to the fuel quantity as required.

The ECM monitors the operation of the cold start valve via a signal received from the needle lift sensor attached to injector number 3 and again makes corrections as required.

Diesel Turbo Direct Injection, overview

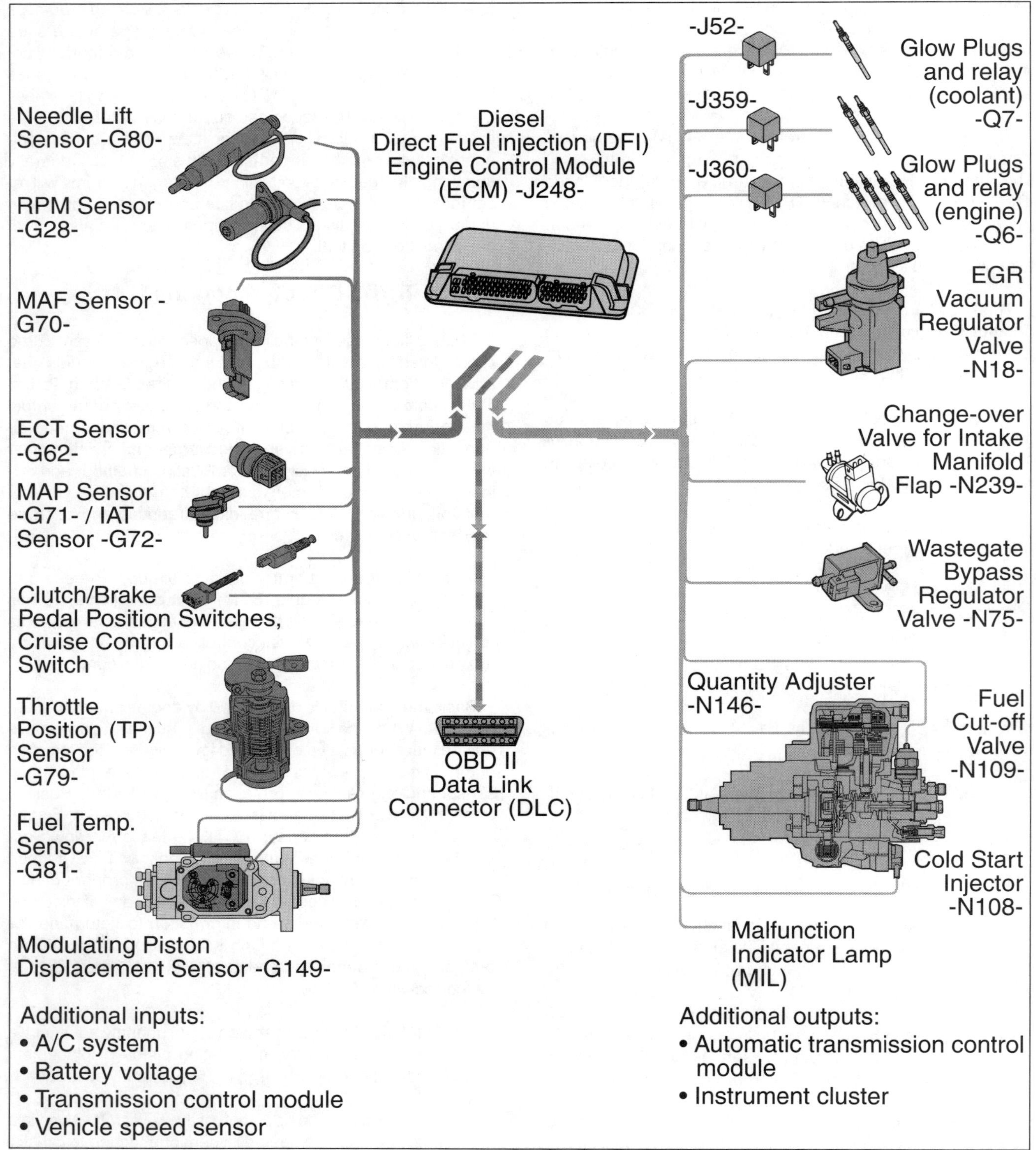

Fig. 2. Diesel Turbo Direct Injection engine management system. Inputs (**left**) to the ECM are used to control and adapt output signals (**right**) to the individual components. Volkswagen component codes are indicated within dashes (–).

Turbocharger boost pressure is regulated by the ECM based on a signal from the Intake Air Temperature sensor (IAT), the Mass Air Flow (MAF) sensor, and an ambient pressure signal from an internal Barometric Pressure Sensor (BARO). The wastegate bypass regulator valve receives output from the ECM and controls a vacuum signal sent to the turbocharger wastegate.

In order to prevent possible damage from simultaneous application of the brake, clutch and accelerator pedals, the brake pedal switch, brake light switch, and clutch pedal switch signal their respective positions to the ECM. These signals are also used by the ECM during in cruise control mode.

Based on all of the input signals, the ECM precisely controls the following output components:

- Quantity Adjuster
- Cold Start Injector
- Fuel Cut-off Valve
- Wastegate Bypass Regulator Valve
- EGR Vacuum Regulator Valve
- Intake Manifold Change-over Valve

In addition, the ECM uses various sensors to control these additional outputs:

- Glow Plugs
- Glow Plug Relay
- Auxiliary Heater Coolant Glow Plugs
- Coolant Glow Plug Relay

When the ECM receives the signal to shut down, a signal is sent to a flap valve mounted in the intake tract. This valve, known as the intake manifold change-over valve, closes and blocks the flow of air to the still-turning engine. Blocking the flow of air during the shut-down cycle reduces the abruptness associated with stopping a diesel engine.

Tailpipe emissions are further reduced by a two-way oxidation-type catalytic converter.

TDI equipped New Beetles have two warning lights in the instrument cluster to advise of system status. The glow plug indicator light operates when the key is first turned on to indicate the need to wait for the glow plugs to pre-heat the combustion chambers. The Malfunction Indicator Lamp (MIL), lights if a failure of a monitored component occurs. In some serious failure modes, both warning indicators can be lit.

Owing to the complex nature, most diagnosis and repair of the TDI system requires the use of specialized scan tools such as Volkswagen special tool VAG 1551 or VAG 1552. Aftermarket scan tools can also access the diagnostic trouble codes (known as P-codes). A table is provided at the back of this manual that identifies the various scan tool codes. See **ST Scan Tool Codes**.

Motronic ME 7 engine management

The 2.8 liter, 1.8 liter, and the AVH and AZG 2.0L engines are equipped with versions of the torque-based Bosch Motronic ME7 engine management systems. See Fig. 3. This system fully complies with the federal and state government mandated On-Board Diagnostic (OBD) II standards.

In previous engine management systems, demands for torque and efficiency are handled by separate sub-systems. The interaction between all of the different subsystems has become increasingly complicated as new demands are placed on the engine management system. These demands can include control of transmission, traction control and vehicle dynamics in addition to enhanced links with existing subsystems.

The Bosch Motronic ME 7 engine management system uses a new internal circuit design to calculate engine torque. The Engine Control Module (ECM) receives all of the relevant signal data from the input sensors and various other sources and computes the required amount of engine torque needed based on pre-established priorities. All torque and efficiency demands are defined as mathematical variables.

The ECM is then able to obtain the calculated engine torque through precise coordination of the following output components:

- Throttle Valve Control Module (throttle angle)
- Wastegate Regulator Solenoid Valve (boost control)
- Fuel Injectors (injection time and fuel cut-off)
- Power Output Stages with Ignition Coils (ignition timing)

Main sensor inputs to the ME 7 ECM (J220) include:

- Mass air flow sensor (G70)
- Speed/reference sensor (G28)
- Camshaft position sensor (G40)
- Pre-Catalyst heated oxygen sensor (G39)
- Post-Catalyst heated oxygen sensor (G108)
- Throttle valve control module (J338) with position sensors (G187) and (G188)
- Intake air temperature sensor (G42)
- Coolant temperature sensors (G2) and (G62)
- Knock sensor, cylinders 1-2, (G61)
- Knock sensor, cylinders 3-4, (G66)
- Accelerator pedal position sensors (G79) and (G185)
- Boost pressure sensor (G31)
- Brake light (F) and pedal switches (F47)
- Clutch pedal switch (F36)
- Leak Detection Pump (V144)

Additional inputs are received from the cruise control switches, transmission control module, vehicle speed sensor, instrument cluster, anti-lock brake system control module, fan control module, airbag control module and air conditioning system.

Motronic ME 7 overview

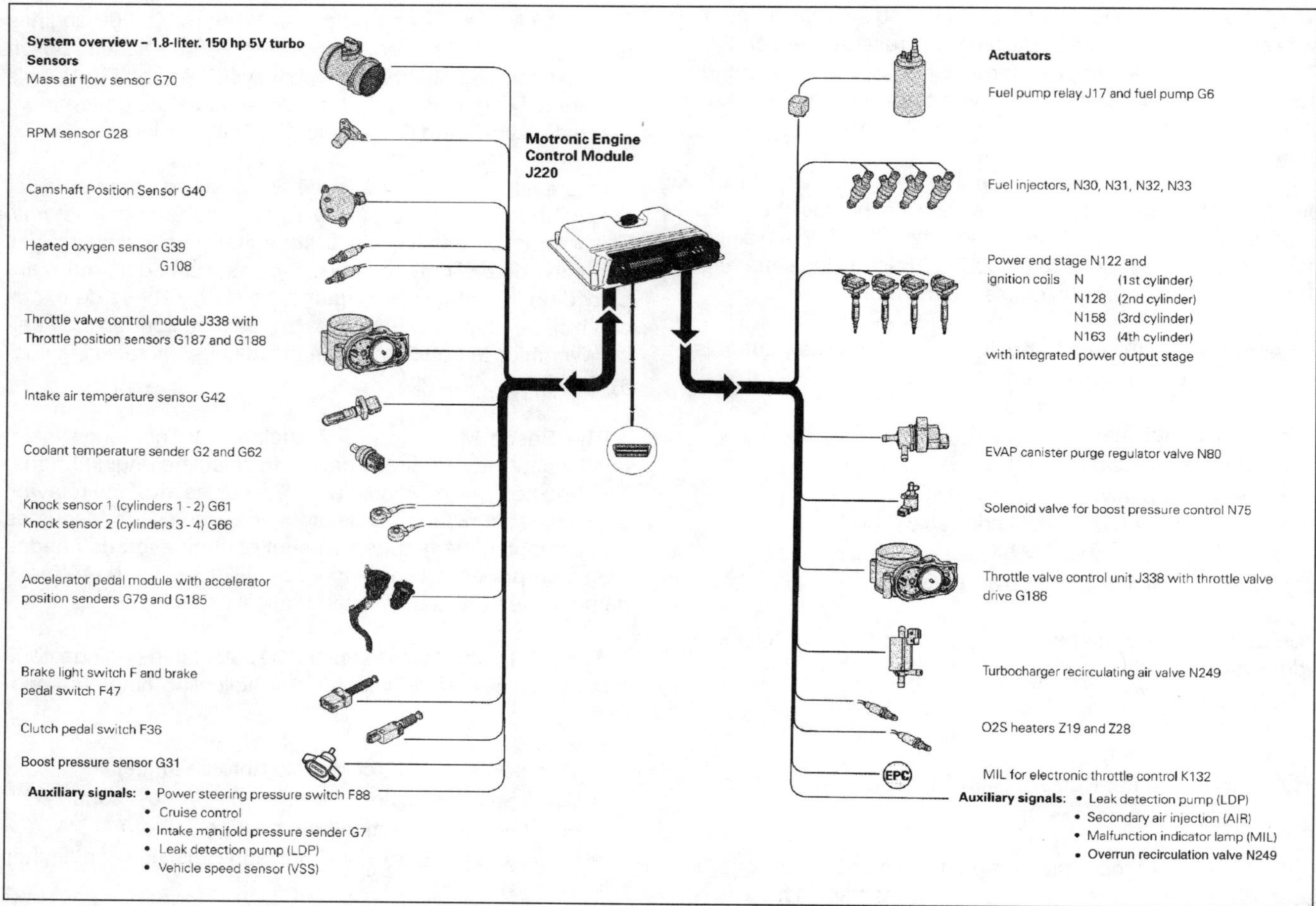

Fig. 3. Bosch Motronic ME 7 engine management system components. Inputs (**left**) to the ECM are used to calculate the required torque. Outputs (**right**) convert demands to torque. Volkswagen component codes are indicated within dashes (–).

Based on the calculations of the torque demand coordinator in the central processor of the ECM, signals are sent to the torque conversion processor for activation of the outputs required to achieve the requested torque.

The primary outputs used to achieve the ECM-requested torque are:

- Throttle valve control module (J338) with throttle valve drive motor (G186)
- Fuel Injectors (N30, N31, N 32, N33)
- Ignition Coil Packs with Power Output Stages (N70, N127, N291, N292)
- Wastegate Regulator Solenoid Valve (N75)

Additional outputs controlled by the ECM include:

- Fuel Pump Relay (J17)
- Evaporative Canister Purge Valve (N80)
- Secondary Air Injection Pump Relay (J299)
- Secondary Air Injection Solenoid Valve (N112)
- Leak Detection Pump (V144)
- Overrun Recirculation Valve (N249)
- Oxygen Sensor Heaters

Motronic ME 7 system structure

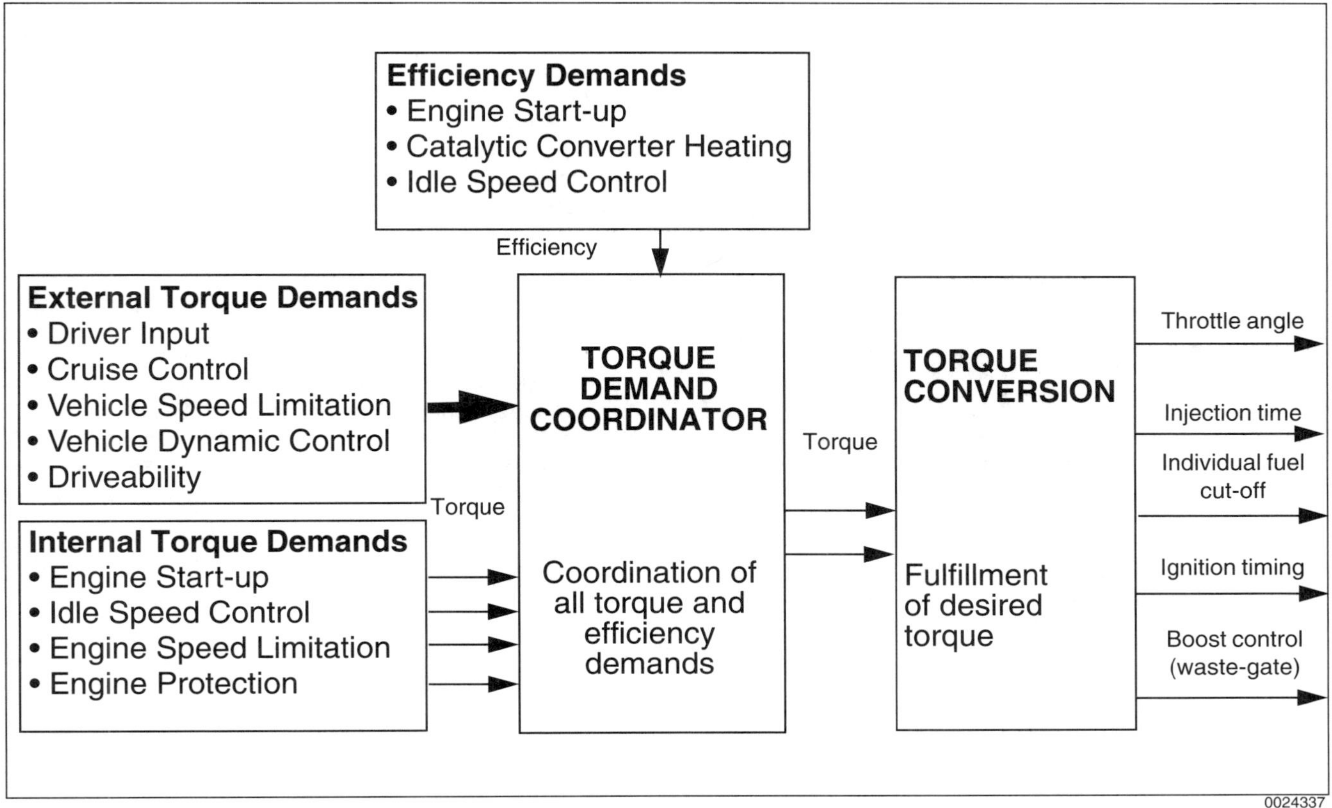

Fig. 4. Schematic representation of Motronic ME 7 torque generation.

A Malfunction Indicator Lamp (MIL), is located in the instrument cluster and signals the vehicle operator when certain emissions-related systems have in some way malfunctioned. In some instances, it will come on if relatively small malfunctions have been recorded, such as running very low on fuel or leaving off the gas cap. Most malfunctions that occur will cause the light to stay on steadily, but certain very serious situations such as an overheating catalytic converter may cause it to blink. An EPC indicator light also located in the instrument cluster will signal the vehicle operator of certain malfunctions within the electronic accelerator pedal system.

Due to the complex nature of the Motronic ME 7 system, proper diagnosis and repair requires the use of a specialized scan tools such as Volkswagen scan tools VAG 1551, VAG 1552 or VAS 5051. Aftermarket scan tools can also access the ME 7 system diagnostic trouble codes (known as P-codes). A table is provided at the back of this manual that identifies the various scan tool codes. See **ST Scan Tool Codes**.

Previous Motronic versions modified basic fuel and ignition maps as required to match the air flow of the mechanical throttle valve. ME 7 systems integrate a mechanically de-coupled accelerator pedal and throttle valve (drive-by-wire) system to allow the ECM processor complete control of engine torque generation as a response to external, internal and efficiency demands. See Fig. 4. Simply stated, the ECM controls all three main combustion requirements: fuel, spark and air, whereas previous systems only controlled fuel and spark.

In addition to diagnostics, Motronic ME 7 systems include the ability to record proper operation of as many as 8 monitored functions. These functional checks are called readiness codes and are set when the proper operating parameters are reached at least one time. These codes are important because some areas with emissions testing check these codes first. If the readiness code is NOT set, the vehicle will not pass the specialized test. Readiness codes may be erased if the battery is disconnected or runs low, if the ECM is disconnected, or if faults or DTCs are erased with a scan tool. Generally speaking, the readiness codes in Volkswagen systems will reset themselves after the vehicle has been started and driven under varying conditions several times. They can also be reset using the scan tool.

Electronic power control (EPC)

The ME 7 engine management system uses electronic controls to operate the throttle valve rather than the usual braided cable. See Fig. 5. Pedal resistance and operation matches cable designs so that the operator is unlikely to differentiate. In the event of a failure with either one of the accelerator pedal position sensors, the other sensor signal would be used in a limited capacity with functions such as cruise control deactivated. If both sensors malfunction, the ECM will limit engine speed to approximately 1200 rpm.

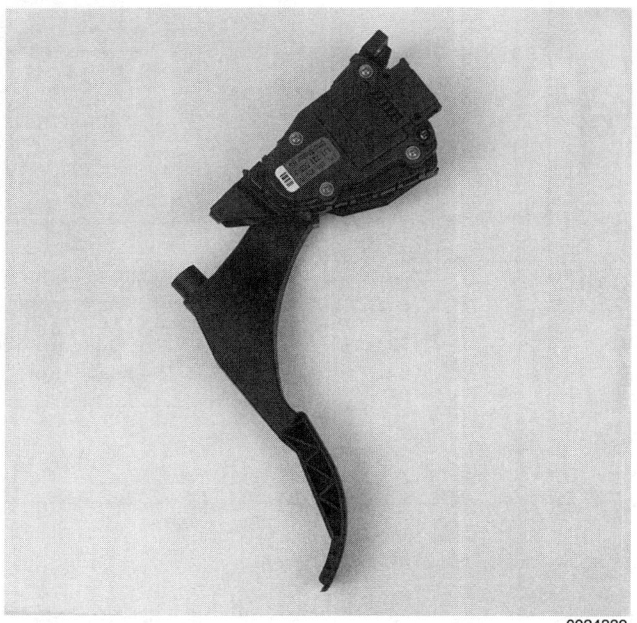

0024339

Fig. 5. Electronic accelerator pedal module with position sensors G79 and G185. Operation is drive-by-wire; there is no mechanical cable connection to the throttle valve.

IGNITION SYSTEM

The ignition function is handled through the fuel injection/engine management system on all engines.

On gasoline engines, the Motronic ECM computes ignition timing based on inputs from the various sensors. Crankshaft position and speed are the main inputs to the ECM used for starting. The other sensors are used to adapt the basic timing map for varying operating conditions. Motronic engines incorporate adaptive knock control to adjust the ignition timing for individual cylinders. See **28 Ignition System** for the appropriate engine for more information.

On diesel engines, the ECM uses the same information that was used to compute the fuel quantity to determine the correct moment of injection. When the fuel is injected into the combustion chamber, heat generated by the high compression ratio causes the fuel to spontaneously burn. This is the ignition firing point. There is no separate ignition system as such. In spite of this high compression ratio, cold engines do not have sufficient heat to burn the fuel. For this reason, glow plugs are used to provide supplementary heat. See **28b Ignition System–Gasoline** for more information.

EMISSION CONTROLS

Gas and diesel engines use different emission controls. Most functions are integral with the engine management systems and are monitored by the On-Board Diagnostic (OBD) system. Most of these functions cannot be isolated. For additional information on those functions, see **26 Exhaust System and Emission Controls,** or **ST Scan Tool Codes** at the back of this manual.

20 Fuel Storage and Supply

GENERAL

This repair group covers the fuel supply portion of the fuel system. For gasoline engines, this includes the components that store and supply fuel under pressure to the fuel injection section of the engine management system. For diesel engines, this includes the components that store and supply fuel to the diesel injection pump. For general system descriptions and overviews, see **2 General Information**.

> ***NOTE —***
> *Fuel filter replacement is covered in* **0 Maintenance**.

Engine Codes
- AWD, AWW . . . . 1.8L 4-cylinder turbo gasoline
- ALH . . . . 1.9L 4-cylinder turbo diesel
- AEG, AVH, AZG . . . . 2.0L 4-cylinder gasoline
- AFP . . . . 2.8L 6-cylinder gasoline

Safety Precautions

Please read and be familiar with the following warnings and cautions before working on the fuel pump, fuel tank or fuel lines.

> ***WARNING —***
> - *Always disconnect the negative (-) battery cable and cover the terminal with an insulated material whenever working on any fuel related component.*
> - *Gasoline and diesel fuel are dangerous to your health. Wear suitable hand and skin protection when working on the fuel system. Do not breath fuel vapors. Always work in a well-ventilated area.*
> - *Fuel and fuel vapors will be present during many of the operations described in this repair group. Do not smoke or create sparks. Be aware of pilot lights in gas operated equipment (heating systems, water heaters, etc.). Have an approved fire extinguisher handy.*
> - *Gasoline fuel supply systems are designed to maintain pressure in the system after the engine is turned off. Fuel will be expelled under pressure as fuel lines are disconnected. This can be a fire hazard, especially if the engine is warm. Always wrap a clean shop rag around any fuel line fitting before loosening or disconnecting it.*
> - *Exercise extreme caution when using spray-type cleaners on a warm engine. Observe all manufacturer recommendations.*

> ***CAUTION —***
> - *Cleanliness is essential when working on any part of the fuel system. Thoroughly clean fuel line unions and hose fittings before disconnecting them. Use only clean tools.*
> - *Use only spring-type clamps on fuel hoses. Do not use screw-type hose clamps, they do not expand and contract with engine heat and will leak.*
> - *Keep removed components clean. Seal or cover them with plastic or paper, especially if the repair cannot be completed immediately. Seal open fuel supply and return lines to prevent contamination.*
> - *When replacing parts, install only new, clean components. Always replace seals and O-rings.*

FUEL PUMP TROUBLESHOOTING (GASOLINE ENGINES)

The fuel supply system is an integral part of the operation of the fuel injection system. Problems such as a no-start condition, hesitation, or stalling may be due to poor fuel delivery. The fuel pump itself is not directly monitored as part of the OBD II system, however, the fuel pump relay is monitored and several Diagnostic Trouble Codes (DTCs) are associated with it. In addition, the fuel injection system will try to adjust for poor fuel delivery and the resultant lean running condition may exceed the system's ability to compensate. This will store DTCs in the system memory. Suspected fuel pump problems should first be investigated with an appropriate scan tool such as the Volkswagen supplied VAG 1551 or 1552. Use of these specialized tools must be in accordance with instructions with the tool by the manufacturer and are outside the scope of this service manual.

There are some preliminary tests that can be used to determine if the fuel pump or its electrical circuits are causing problems. Some of the tests described below require special test equipment such as a fuel pressure gauge and fittings.

The electrical current that operates the fuel pump is controlled by a relay and protected by a 15-amp fuse. This helps to handle the high current load of the pump and also ensures that the pump will not continue to run in the event of an accident or if the engine stalls. If, for any reason, electric power to run the pump is interrupted, the engine will not run.

Begin troubleshooting with a simple check of the fuel pump electrical circuit. The pump should run while cranking the engine with the starter. If necessary, remove the floor cover and access plate in the luggage compartment and listen or feel to verify that the fuel pump is running. If the pump does not run, see **Fuel pump, checking electrical circuit**.

> ***CAUTION —***
> *In cold weather, water in the fuel may freeze in the pump causing the circuit to overload and the fuse to fail. Be sure to check the fuel pump fuse in the dashboard fuse/relay panel. See* **97 Wiring Diagrams, Fuses and Relays** *for fuse locations.*

If the fuel pump runs, begin troubleshooting with a check of the fuel pump delivery rate as described later in this section. The test will indicate whether further tests are necessary. This is especially important on higher mileage cars, where normal pump wear may decrease delivery volume. Also check for correct pump installation and for a clogged or restricted pump inlet screen.

The electric fuel pump operates only when the car is running or being started. Because many of the fuel pump and fuel injection tests require that the pump be operated with the engine off, the fuel pump relay can be temporarily bypassed during testing.

All tests assume that there is sufficient fuel in the tank. If there is any doubt regarding fuel quantity, add more. The fuel gauge may not indicate true fuel level. Avoid running the fuel pump when the tank is empty.

Fuel pump, operating for testing

The procedure below uses a temporary wiring connection to bypass the fuel pump fuse and run the pump directly from the battery by way of the fuse panel connection. The preferred method is to use a remote switch such as Volkswagen special tools VAG 1348/3A and VAG 1348/3-2. See Fig. 1. You can also accomplish the same thing with a homemade fused jumper wire and an in-line switch. See Fig. 2.

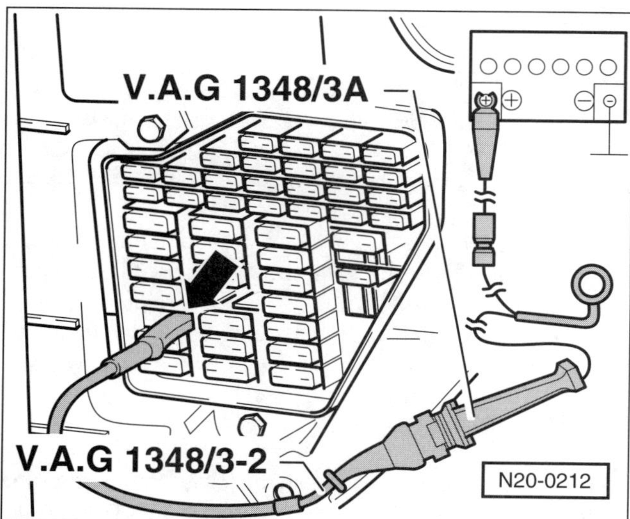

N20-0212

Fig. 1. Fuel pump fuse removed from position 28 of the dashboard fuse panel with one lead of the remote switch in place. Connect the remaining lead to the positive terminal of the battery.

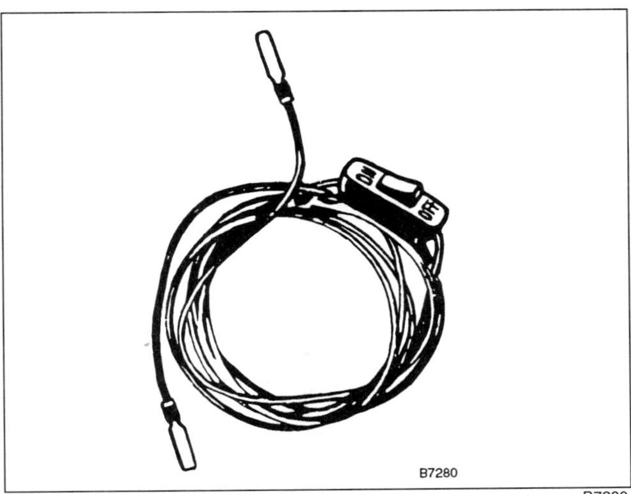

Fig. 2. Homemade jumper wire with flat blade terminals and switch/fuse for running fuel pump.

> ***CAUTION —***
> - *A homemade jumper wire with a switch should be at least 1.5mm metric wire size (14 gauge AWG) and, for safety, include a 15-amp in-line fuse.*
> - *To avoid damaging the fuse panel sockets, the ends of the jumper wires should be flat-blade connectors that are the same size as the fuse blades.*
> - *Connect and disconnect the remote switch or jumper wire only with the switch in the off position.*

1. Remove fuse from position 28 of dashboard fuse panel. See Fig. 3.

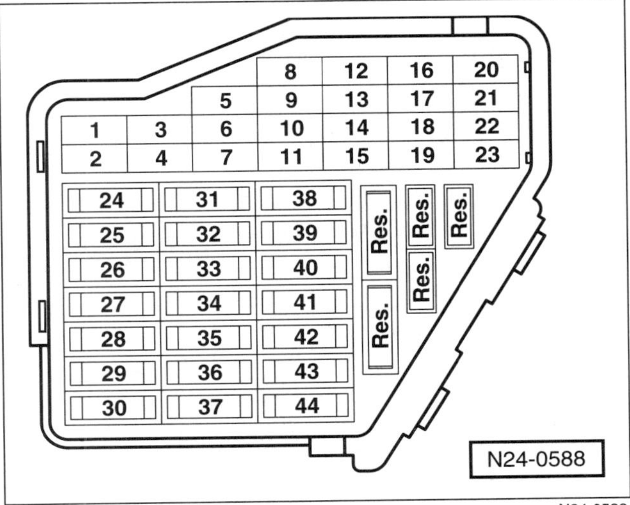

Fig. 3. Dashboard fuse panel showing fuse identification numbers. Be sure to inspect fuse 28 (fuel pump).

2. With the ignition switched off, connect one lead of the fused jumper wire to the rear terminal of the fuse holder number 28.

3. Connect the other lead of the fused jumper to the positive terminal of the battery.

4. Turn the jumper wire switch on to run the pump.
   - If the pump does not run, remove the jumper lead from the rear terminal of fuse holder number 28 and put it in the front terminal.
   - If the pump still does not run, the problem is most likely in the wiring to the pump or the pump itself is faulty. See **Fuel pump, checking electrical circuit**.
   - If the pump runs only with the jumper connected, the relay, the engine control module (ECM), the circuit wiring or fuse 28 is faulty. See **97 Wiring Diagrams, Fuses and Relays**.

Fuel pump, checking electrical circuit

The fuel pump receives power from the fuel pump relay which is energized by the engine control module (ECM). The test given below checks for power at the fuel pump.

1. Check that the battery is fully charged and that fuse 28 is good.

2. Fold down rear seat, pull back floor cover and remove the access plate to the fuel delivery unit.

3. While a helper listens at the fuel pump, turn the ignition key on. The pump may run briefly. If not, turn the key to the start position and crank the engine. If the pump runs, the circuit is probably operating correctly. If the pump does not run, proceed to step 4.

   NOTE —
   Listen carefully for the pump to run, in operation it is barely audible.

4. Remove the fuel pump fuse and run the fuel pump as described in **Fuel pump, operating for testing**.
   - If the pump runs only with the jumper connected, the relay, the engine control module (ECM), the circuit wiring or fuse 28 is faulty. See **97 Wiring Diagrams, Fuses and Relays**.
   - If the pump does not run, leave the jumper connected and go to step 5.

5. Disconnect the 4 pin harness connector from the fuel delivery unit.

6. Check for voltage at the pump harness connector. See Fig. 4.

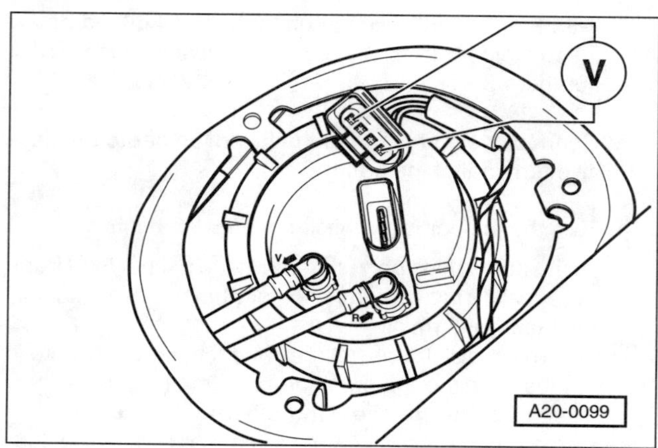

A20-0099

Fig. 4. Voltage supply to fuel pump being checked at outer terminals of connector (terminals 1 and 4).

7. If voltage is not present at connector, check wiring between dashboard fuse panel and fuel pump harness connector. See **97 Wiring Diagrams, Fuses and Relays**.

8. If voltage is present, remove fuel pump and check for open circuits and internal grounds in the delivery unit. If no faults can be found, the fuel pump is probably faulty.

Specification

- Voltage available at fuel pump .... battery voltage minus 2 volts maximum
- Fuel pump amperage (current) draw with engine at idle .... 8 amps maximum

---

Fuel pump, checking delivery rate

The tests given below require an accurate fuel pressure gauge with a shutoff valve and a range of 0-6 bar (approximately 0-100 psi). Volkswagen special tool VAG 1318 with appropriate adapters, or equivalent, can be used to check fuel delivery rate.

1. Connect jumper wire with switch to fuel pump circuit as described earlier in **Fuel pump, operating for testing**.

2. Remove the fuel filler cap from the fuel tank.

3. Working in the engine compartment, disconnect the fuel supply hose from the supply pipe.
   - For 2.0L engines, See Fig. 5.
   - For 1.8L and 2.8L engines. See Fig. 9.

> ***WARNING —***
> *Fire Hazard! Fuel will be expelled under pressure when fuel lines are disconnected. Do not smoke or work near heaters or other fire hazards. Keep a fire extinguisher handy. Cover fuel connections with cloth before disconnecting to prevent excess leakage,*

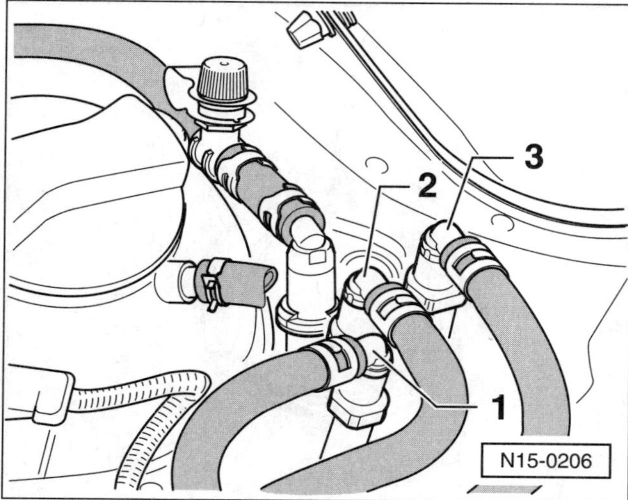

N15-0206

Fig. 5. Separate fuel supply line (**3**) from supply pipe. Fuel may be under pressure; cover connections with a clean shop cloth before disconnecting hoses. Connection (**2**) is fuel return and connection (**1**) is vacuum supply for leak detection pump. 2.0L shown. For 1.8L and 2.8L See Fig. 9.

4. Connect fuel pressure gauge to supply pipe with appropriate adapters. See Fig. 6.

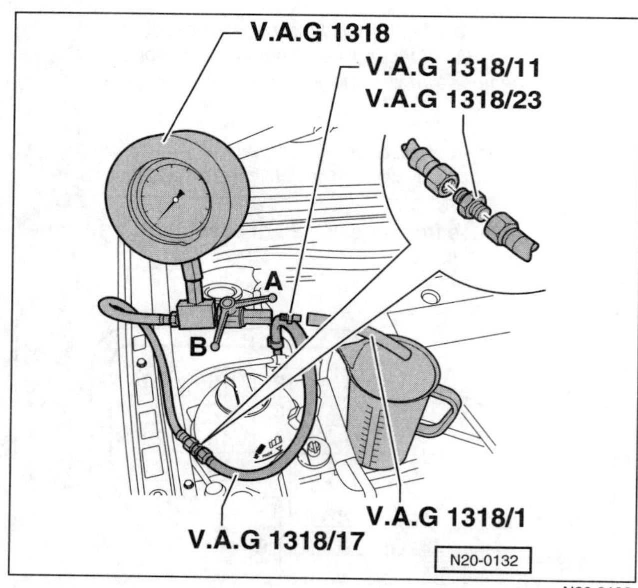

N20-0132

Fig. 6. Volkswagen fuel pressure gauge VAG 1318 and adapters shown connected to fuel supply pipe with valve positioned to regulate fuel flow.

5. Connect one end of a length of hose to valve side of gauge and place other end into a clean, fuel resistant measurement container with at least 1 liter capacity.

6. Open the pressure gauge valve.

7. Operate the fuel pump with the jumper wire switch while slowly closing the valve on the gauge until the pressure reads 3 bar (44 psi).

8. Without moving the valve, shut off fuel pump and empty the measuring container back into the tank.

9. Connect a voltmeter to the battery and record reading.

> ***NOTE —***
> *Fuel pump delivery volume is dependent on the voltage available at pump. For purposes of this test, the factory assumes a 2 volt drop between the battery and pump.*

10. Operate the fuel pump with the jumper wire switch for 30 seconds and note the voltage reading on the meter.

11. Subtract 2 volts from the voltage reading at battery and compare the measured fuel quantity with the graph shown. See Fig. 7.

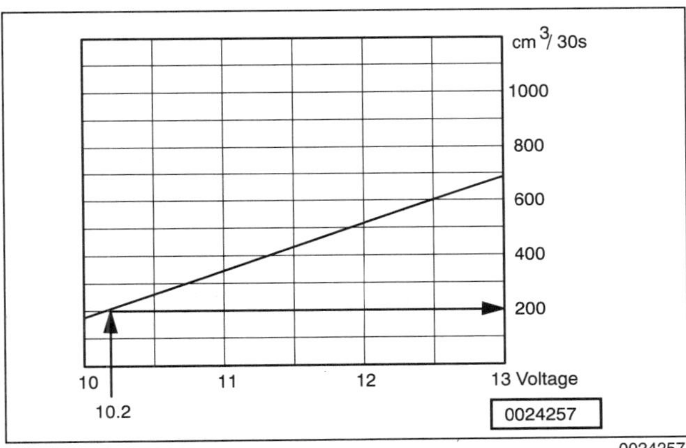

Fig. 7. Fuel delivery graph showing the minimum quantity of fuel to be delivered by the fuel pump in 30 seconds based on calculated voltage at the fuel pump. Fuel quantity must be above the diagonal line.

> ***NOTE —***
> *The line in the graph (Fig. 7.) represents the minimum quantity of fuel at a given voltage. For example, at battery voltage of 12.2 volts the measured volume was 300 cubic centimeters (cm³) after 30 seconds. Subtract 2 volts to get 10.2 volts, locate 10.2 volts on the graph and note that the minimum volume for that voltage is approximately 200 cm³. 300 cm³ is greater than 200 cm³ and is therefore within specification.*

12. If fuel delivery is below specification, check for kinks, blockage or other restrictions in the lines, a blocked or restricted fuel filter or tank strainer, or fuel leakage. If no faults are found, the fuel pump/fuel delivery unit is probably worn or otherwise faulty and should be replaced.

13. When testing is completed, empty measuring container back into tank. Remove pressure gauge and jumper wire switch, connect all fuel lines and check for leaks.

Fuel pump, checking system pressures

Checking fuel pressure is a fundamental part of troubleshooting and diagnosing the Motronic Engine Management System. Fuel pressure has a direct effect on fuel mixture and driveability. Low fuel pressure may set oxygen sensor-related Diagnostic Trouble Codes (DTC) in the Engine Control Module (ECM) as the system attempts to compensate for low pressure. This test will also check the fuel pressure regulator, the fuel pump check valve and the fuel injectors for internal leaks.

Before making the tests described below, make sure the fuel pump is operating correctly and that the fuel pump delivery rate is within specification as given earlier in this section. The tests given below require an accurate fuel pressure gauge with a range of 0-6 bar (approximately 0-100 psi). Volkswagen special tool VAG 1318 with appropriate adapters, or equivalent, can be used to measure fuel pressure.

> ***WARNING —***
> *Fire Hazard! Fuel will be expelled under pressure when fuel lines are disconnected. Do not smoke or work near heaters or other fire hazards. Keep a fire extinguisher handy.*

1. Working in the engine compartment, disconnect the fuel supply hose and catch leaking fuel with a cloth.
   - For 2.0L engine, see Fig. 8.
   - For 1.8L or 2.8L engine, see Fig. 9.

Fig. 8. Fuel supply hose (**arrow**) on fuel rail of 2.0L engine.

2. Connect the fuel pressure gauge between the fuel line and the fuel rail. See Fig. 10. Make sure that if the gauge is equipped with a valve, it is in the open position.

3. Start the engine, let it run at idle speed and make sure that there are no leaks.

> ***NOTE —***
> *If engine does not start, operate the fuel pump with a jumper wire with switch as given earlier in* **Fuel pump, operating for testing**.

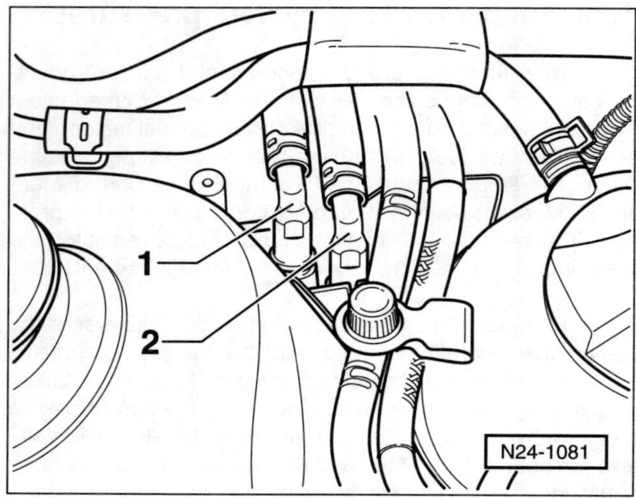

N24-1081

Fig. 9. Fuel supply hose (**1**) for 1.8L and 2.8L engine.

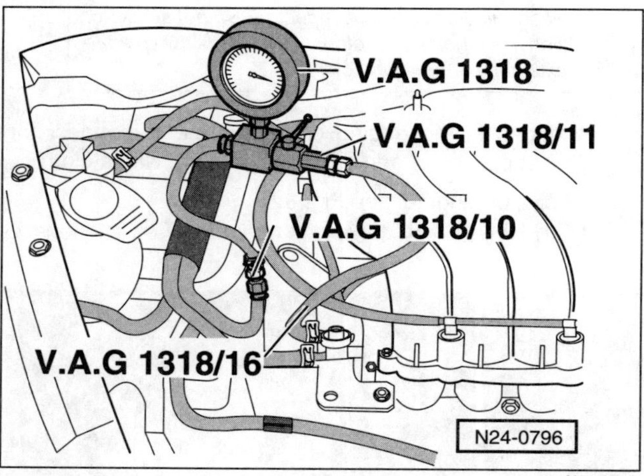

N24-0796

Fig. 10. Volkswagen fuel pressure gauge VAG 1318 with adapters shown installed to measure fuel pressure on 2.0L engine.

4. Observe fuel pressure on gauge with the engine at idle:
   - If system pressure is too high, check for a blocked or restricted fuel line from the fuel pressure regulator. Check the vacuum line to the fuel pressure regulator. If the fuel line has no restrictions and the vacuum line is properly connected, the fuel pressure regulator is probably faulty and should be replaced.
   - If system pressure is too low, check for leaks in the fuel supply lines. Also check for restrictions in the fuel supply lines or a clogged fuel filter. If there are no leaks or restrictions, the fuel pressure regulator is probably faulty and should be replaced.

5. If fuel pressure is OK, disconnect and plug the small vacuum hose on the fuel pressure regulator and check that the fuel pressure increases as specified.

6. If fuel pressure does not increase, check the vacuum hose for kinks, restrictions and proper connections.

Specification
- Fuel pressure at idle. . . . . approx. 2.5 bar (36 psi)
- Fuel pressure (regulator hose disconnected). . . . . approx. 3.0 bar (44 psi)
- Residual pressure (complete system), after 10 minutes . . . . minimum 2.0 bar (29 psi)

7. Switch off engine.

8. Check for leaks and residual pressure by observing pressure drop on gauge after 10 minutes.

9. If pressure drops below specification, restart engine and let idle. While simultaneously closing valve on the pressure gauge, switch off engine.

10. Observe pressure gauge.
    - If pressure drops below 2.5 bar (36 psi), check for leaks in the fuel lines between the gauge and the fuel pump. If no leaks are found, the fuel pump check valve is probably faulty and should be replaced. The check valve is part of the fuel delivery unit which is replaced as a complete unit, see **Fuel delivery unit, removing and installing**.
    - If pressure does not drop, clamp off the return fuel line just past the fuel pressure regulator with a suitable clamp and open the valve. If the pressure drops, check for leaks in the fuel injector rail. If no leaks are found, the fuel injectors are probably leaking. Remove the injector rail and inspect the injectors.
    - If the pressure does not drop when the valve is opened, remove the clamp from the return line and observe the pressure gauge. If it drops, the check valve in the fuel pressure regulator is faulty and the fuel pressure regulator must be replaced.

FUEL PUMP (FUEL DELIVERY UNIT)

The fuel delivery unit is mounted in the top of the tank and retained by a threaded retaining ring. For gasoline engine cars, the fuel delivery unit includes the fuel pump, the fuel gauge sending unit and the fuel pump check valve.

NOTE —
The procedure given below also applies to removing and installing the fuel gauge sensor on diesel engines.

Fuel delivery unit, removing and installing

1. With the ignition switched off, disconnect the negative (-) battery cable.

NOTE —
Be sure to have the anti-theft radio code on hand before disconnecting the battery.

2. Fold rear seat bottom out of way, pull back floor cover and remove the access plate to the fuel delivery unit.

3. Disconnect the 4-pin harness connector from the fuel delivery unit.

4. Disconnect the fuel supply and return lines and wrap with a cloth to prevent fuel spillage. See Fig. 11.

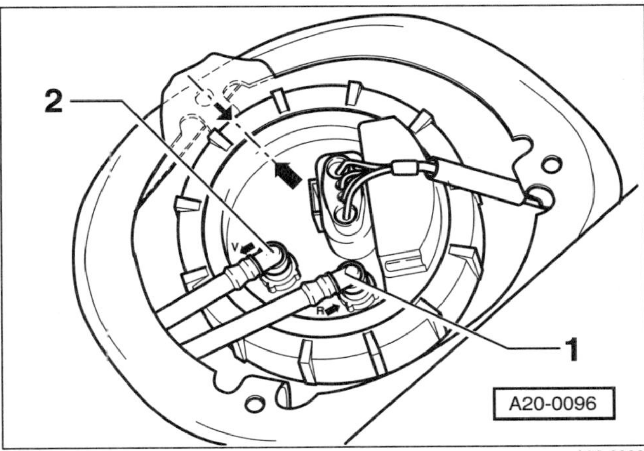

A20-0096

Fig. 11. Fuel pump return line (**1**) is identified with blue markings, fuel supply line (**2**) is identified with black markings. Alignment marks (**arrows**) must match during re-assembly. AEG engine shown, others similar.

> ***WARNING —***
> *Fuel will be discharged and dangerous fuel vapors will be present. Work in a well ventilated area. Do not disconnect wires that could cause sparks. Do not smoke or work near heaters or other fire hazards. Keep a fire extinguisher handy.*

5. Unscrew and remove fuel delivery unit retaining ring. See Fig. 12.

6. Carefully lift fuel delivery unit from tank. Empty fuel delivery unit into a suitable container once it is removed.

7. Installation is reverse of removal noting the following:
   - Inspect and clean intake screen as needed.
   - Do not bend fuel gauge sending unit arm.
   - Inspect fuel tank seal and replace if damaged or distorted. Moisten the seal with fuel when installing.

NOTE —
- *Note the installed position of the fuel delivery unit; marks on the fuel delivery unit must align with marks on the tank as shown in Fig. 11.*
- *Check for leaks before installing access plate.*

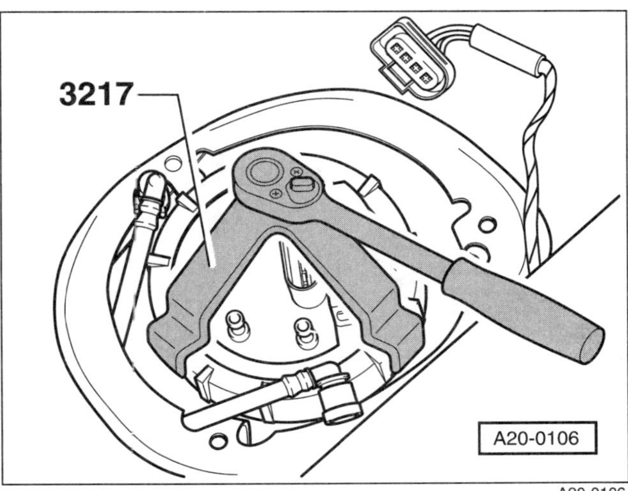

A20-0106

Fig. 12. Volkswagen special tool 3217 shown in position to remove the delivery unit retaining ring.

Fuel gauge sensor, removing and installing

The fuel gauge sensor is part of the fuel delivery unit on gasoline engines and can be replaced as a separate component. On diesel engines the fuel gauge sensor (only) is installed in the top of the fuel tank instead of a fuel delivery unit.

1. Remove the fuel delivery unit as described previously.

2. Release locking tabs and remove electrical sender wires from fuel gauge sensor. See Fig. 13.

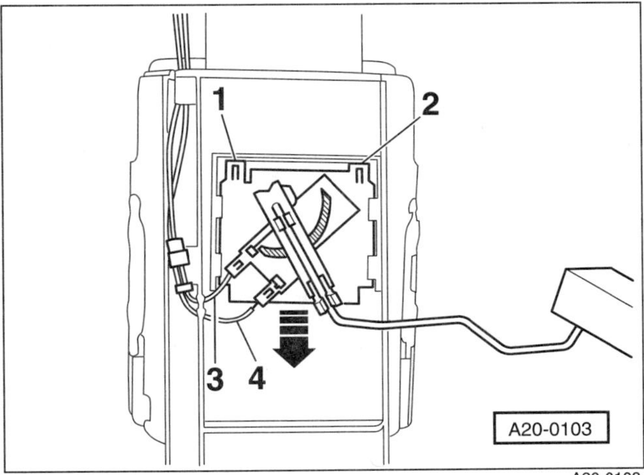

A20-0103

Fig. 13. Remove fuel gauge sensor electrical wires (**3** and **4**), lift retaining tabs (**1** and **2**) and remove in direction of **arrow**.

3. Lift retaining tabs with a screwdriver and remove fuel gauge sensor downward. See Fig. 13.

4. Installation is the reverse of removal.

FUEL TANK AND LINES

Fuel tank assembly (gasoline engines)

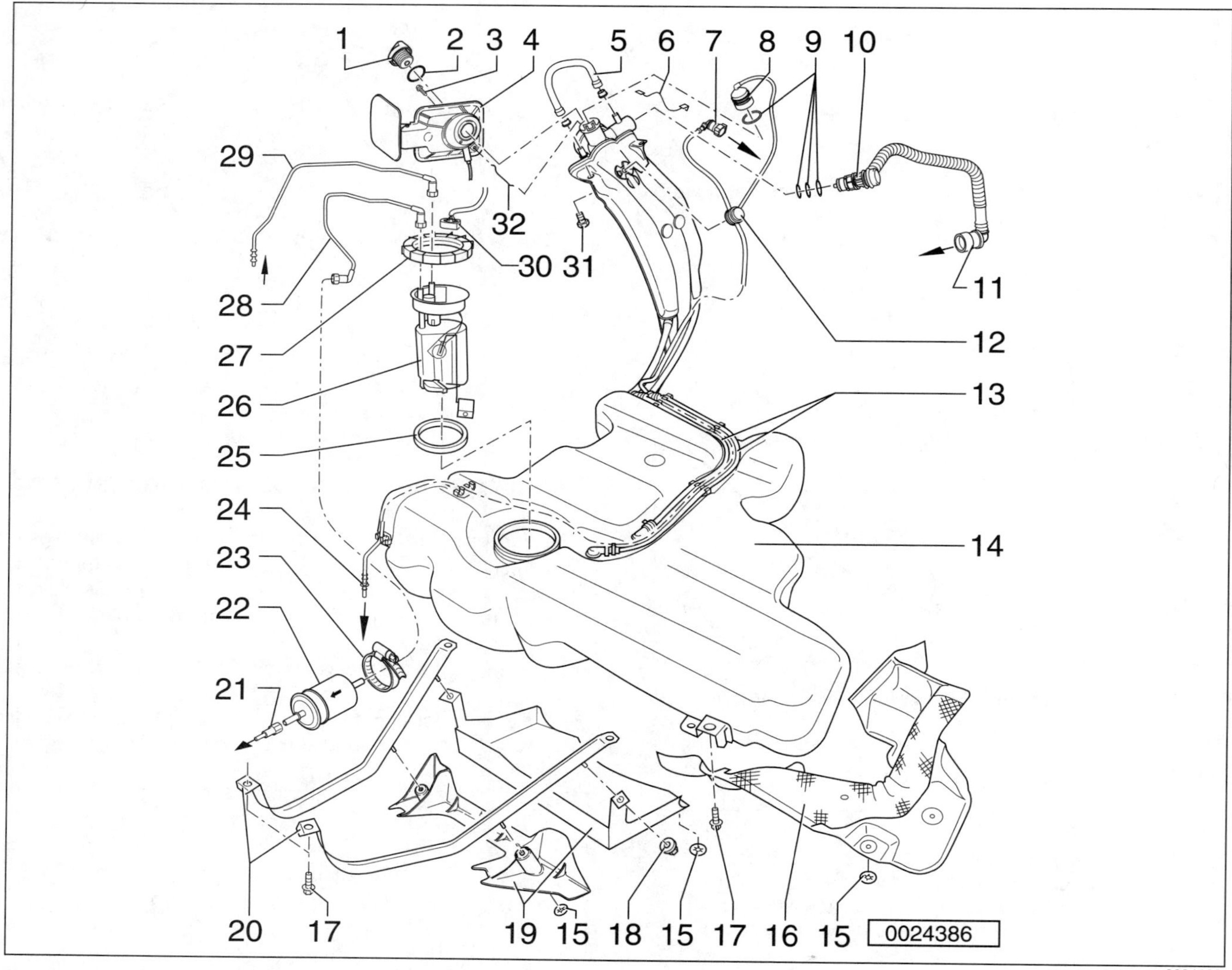

0024386

Fig. 14. Gasoline fuel tank assembly and related components

1. **Fuel tank cap**
   - Secured with retaining strap from m.y. 2000
2. **Seal**
   - Replace if damaged
3. **Bolt**
   - Tighten to 1 Nm (9 in-lb)
4. **Fuel filler door unit**
   - With rubber seal
5. **Vent line (black)**
6. **Ground connection**
7. **Vent line (white)**
   - To activated carbon canister
8. **Gravity/overflow valve**
   - Removing: pull up out of mount
   - Check valve for flow:
     valve vertical: OPEN
     valve tilted 45°: CLOSED
9. **O-ring**
   - Replace if damaged
10. **Change-over valve**
    - Removing: unclip from side of filler neck
    - Before installing, remove fuel tank cap (item 1)
11. **Vent line (black)**
    - Ensure it is securely seated
    - To EVAP canister
12. **Pressure retention valve**
    - For fuel reservoir ventilation
    - Checking **see** (A)

(continued from previous page)

13. Vent line (black)
- Ensure it is securely seated
- Clipped to fuel tank

14. Fuel tank
- Support with engine/transmission jack to remove

15. Clamping washer

16. Heat shield
- For fuel tank

17. Bolt
- Tighten to 25 Nm (18 ft-lb)

18. Self-locking nut
- Tighten to 2 Nm (18 in-lb)

19. Fuel tank cover

20. Mounting straps
- Note differing lengths
- Installed position: attaching points (holes) point in direction of travel

21. Supply line
- Black
- To fuel rail
- Ensure it is securely seated

22. Fuel filter
- Installed position: arrow points in direction of flow

23. Screw clamp

24. Vent line (white)
- Clipped onto top of fuel tank
- With EVAP canister purge regulator valve (N80)
- Ensure it securely seated

25. Sealing ring
- Replace if damaged
- Coat with fuel after installing into fuel tank

26. Fuel delivery unit
- Note installed position on fuel tank
- Clean strainer if soiled

27. Retaining ring
- Tighten to 75 Nm (55 ft-lb)
- Remove and install using 3217 wrench

28. Supply line (black)
- Clipped to side of fuel tank
- Ensure it is securely seated

29. Return line
- Blue or blue markings
- Clipped to side of fuel tank
- Ensure it is securely seated
- From fuel rail

30. Connector
- Black, 4-pin

31. Bolt
- Tighten to 10 Nm (7 ft-lb)

32. Grounding strap
- Not included with replacement tank
- Insert lower end (with bend tab) through hole in ground tab in fuel filler neck. Slide down in until reaching hooked end of strap. Bend ground tab down to secure in fuel filler neck.

WARNING —
If working on a lift or hoist be sure to support the front of the vehicle before removing the fuel tank. The sudden removal of the fuel tank and associated components can unbalance the vehicle sufficiently to cause the vehicle to fall.

CAUTION —
When removing or installing fuel tank, the tank should be as empty as possible for easier handling.

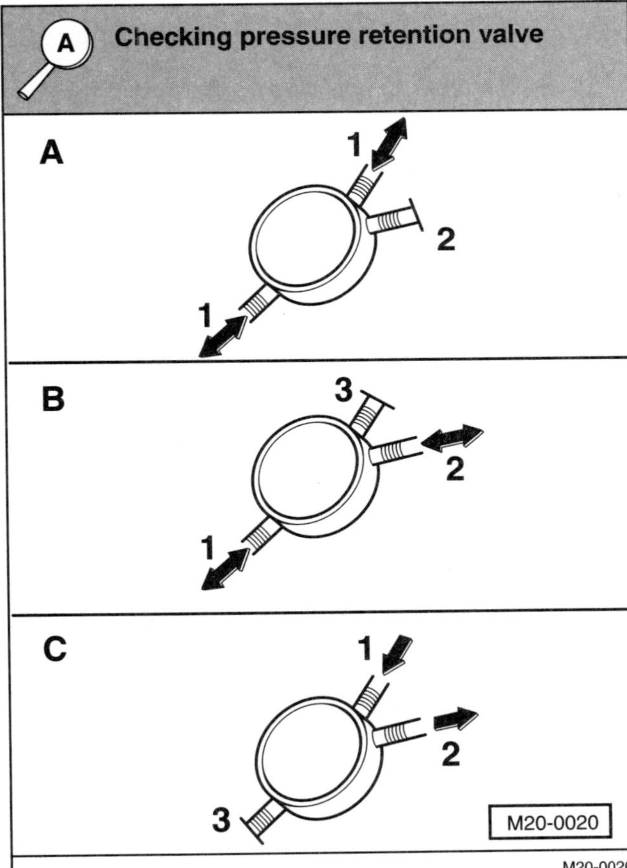

M20-0020

- **Check the valve for flow in various directions:**

A) Orifices 1 and 1, flow in both directions when port 2 is closed

B) Orifices 2 and 1, flow in both directions when port 3 is closed

C) Orifices 1 and 2, flow in one directions when port 3 is closed

- **The valve will close when there is vacuum at opening 1**

Fuel tank assembly (diesel engine)

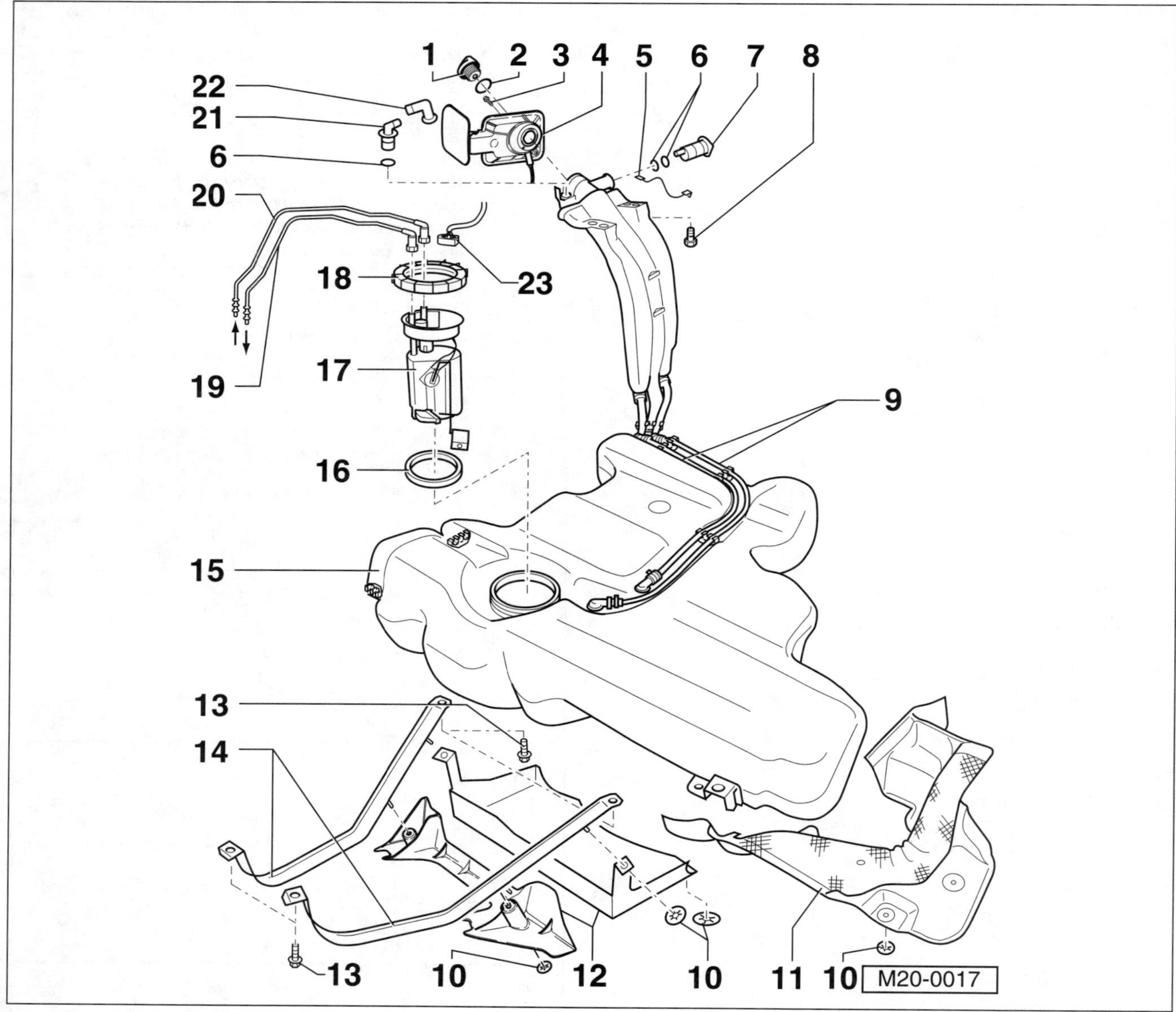

M20-0017

Fig. 15. Diesel fuel tank assembly and related components.

1. **Fuel tank cap**
   - Secured with retaining strap from m.y. 2000
2. **Seal**
   - Replace if damaged
3. **Bolt**
4. **Tank flap unit**
   - With rubber cup
5. **Ground connection**
6. **O-ring**
   - Always replace
7. **Vent valve**
   - To remove: unclip valve from side of filler neck
   - Before installing, remove fuel tank cap (item 1)
8. **Bolt**
   - Tighten to 10 Nm (7 ft-lb)
9. **Vent line (black)**
   - Ensure it is securely seated
   - Clipped to fuel tank
10. **Clamping washer**

(continued from previous page)

11. **Heat shield**
    - For fuel tank
12. **Fuel tank cover**
13. **Bolt**
    - Tighten to 25 Nm (18 ft-lb)
14. **Mounting straps**
    - Note differing lengths
    - Note installation position: locator (hole) must point forward
15. **Fuel tank**
    - Support with engine/transmission jack when removing
16. **Sealing ring**
    - Replace if damaged
    - Moisten with fuel when installing
17. **Fuel gauge sensor**
    - Note installed position on fuel tank
18. **Retaining ring**
    - Remove and install using 3217 wrench
19. **Supply line (black)**
    - To fuel filter
    - Clipped onto fuel tank
    - Ensure it is securely seated
    - To remove from flange, press down on tabs at connection
20. **Return line**
    - Blue or blue markings
    - From fuel filter
    - At connection -R-
    - Clipped onto fuel tank
    - Ensure it is securely seated
    - To remove from flange, press down on tabs at connection
    - Vehicles with automatic transmission are equipped with a fuel cooler, **see** (A)
21. **Gravity overflow valve**
    - To remove, unclip upwards out of support
    - Check valve for flow
      valve vertical: OPEN
      valve tilted 45°: CLOSED
22. **Angled connector**
23. **Electrical connector**
    - Black, 2-pin

WARNING —
If working on a lift or hoist be sure to support the front of the vehicle before removing the fuel tank. The sudden removal of the fuel tank and associated components can unbalance the vehicle sufficiently to cause the vehicle to fall.

CAUTION —
When removing or installing the fuel tank, the tank should be as empty as possible to facilitate easier handling.

(A) Fuel cooler (ALH engine with automatic transmission)

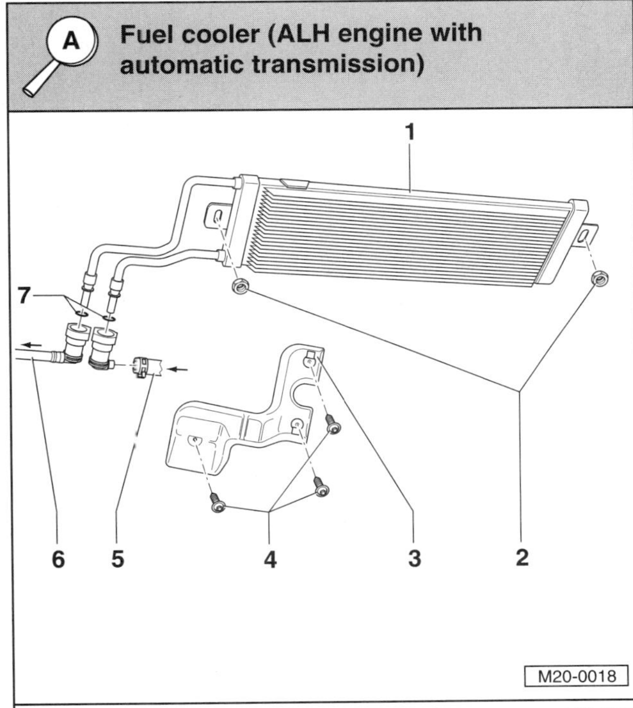

M20-0018

1. **Fuel cooler**
   - Located under vehicle on right side
2. **Nut**
   - Tighten to 20 Nm (15 ft-lb)
3. **Cover**
4. **Bolts**
5. **Return line from fuel filter**
6. **Return line to fuel tank**
7. **O-ring**
   - Always replace

THROTTLE MECHANISM (AEG ENGINE)

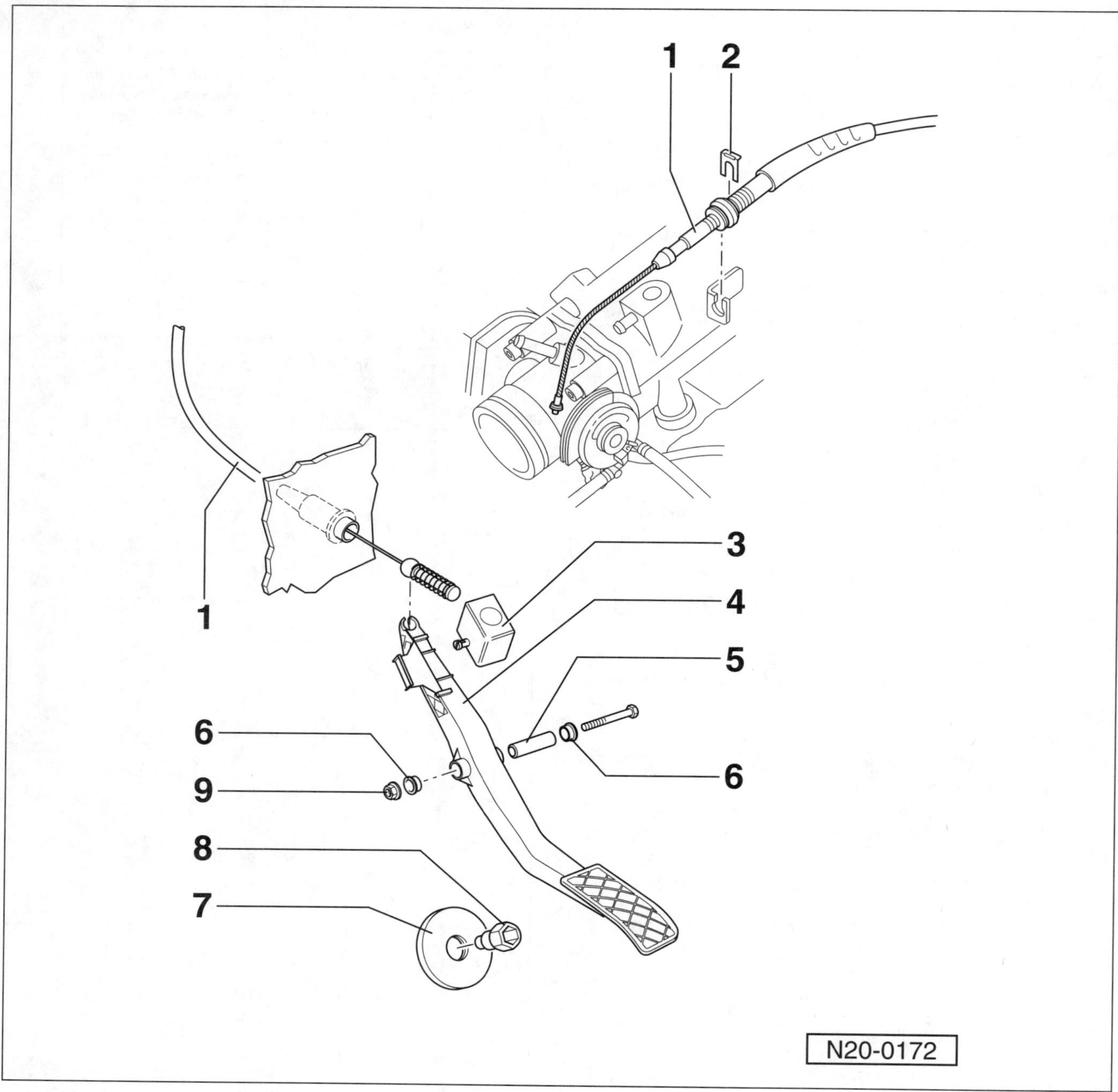

N20-0172

Fig. 16. Throttle mechanism on AEG (2.0L) gas engine.

1. **Throttle cable**
   - Never reuse a damaged cable, replace
2. **Retaining clip**
3. **Balance weight**
4. **Throttle pedal**
5. **Spacer sleeve**
6. **Bushing**
7. **Washer**
8. **Stop bolt**
9. **Bolt**
   - Tighten to 20 Nm (15 ft-lb)

ELECTRONIC POWER CONTROL (EPC)

All the engines covered by this manual, with the exception of the 2.0L AEG engine, use an electronic power control (EPC) system. In the EPC system, the throttle valve is not operated via a cable from the accelerator pedal. There is no mechanical connection between the accelerator pedal and the throttle valve.

The position of the accelerator pedal is communicated to the engine control module via two sensors for accelerator pedal position (changeable resistances; stored in one housing) that are connected with the accelerator pedal. The position of the accelerator pedal (driver's intention/demand) is a main input value for the Engine Control Module (ECM).

Operation of the throttle valve occurs throughout the entire RPM and load range via an electric motor (throttle valve actuator) in the throttle valve control module. The throttle valve is operated by the throttle valve actuator according to the specifications of the ECM.

With the engine at standstill and the ignition switched on, the ECM activates the throttle valve actuator exactly according to the specifications of the accelerator pedal position sensor. This means, if the pedal is depressed halfway, the throttle valve actuator opens the throttle valve to the same degree; the throttle valve is then opened halfway.

With the engine running (under load), the ECM can open and close the throttle valve independently of the accelerator pedal position sensor. In this way, the throttle valve can already be completely open, even though the accelerator pedal has only been depressed half way. This is advantageous since charging losses at the throttle valve can be avoided. Furthermore, it results in significantly better emissions and consumption values under certain load conditions.

It would be wrong to assume that EPC consists of only one or two components. EPC is much more of a system containing all components that contribute to determining, regulating and monitoring the throttle valve position (e.g. accelerator pedal position sensor, throttle valve control module, Electronic Power Control (EPC) warning lamp, Engine Control Module).

EPC warning light

A functional check of the EPC warning lamp can be conducted by first switching on the ignition and noting if the EPC warning lamp comes on. See Fig. 17.

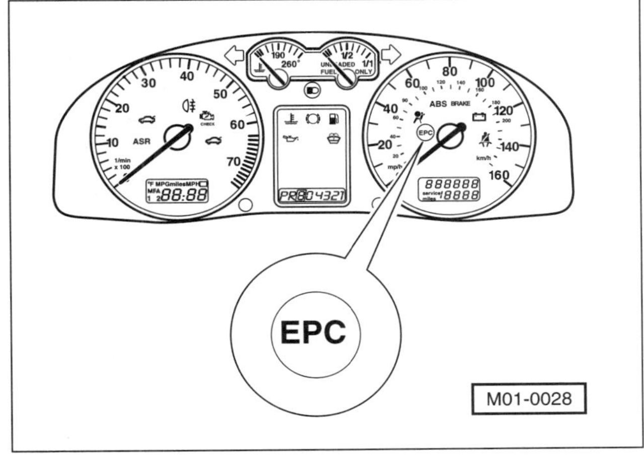

M01-0028

Fig. 17. EPC warning lamp in instrument cluster.

The EPC light should go out once the engine is started and running at idle speed if there are no Diagnostic Trouble Codes (DTCs) relating to the EPC system. Further diagnosis of the EPC warning light involves the use of Volkswagen special tools which is outside the scope of this manual. An assembly view of the electronic throttle pedal is shown in Fig. 18.

EPC pedal components

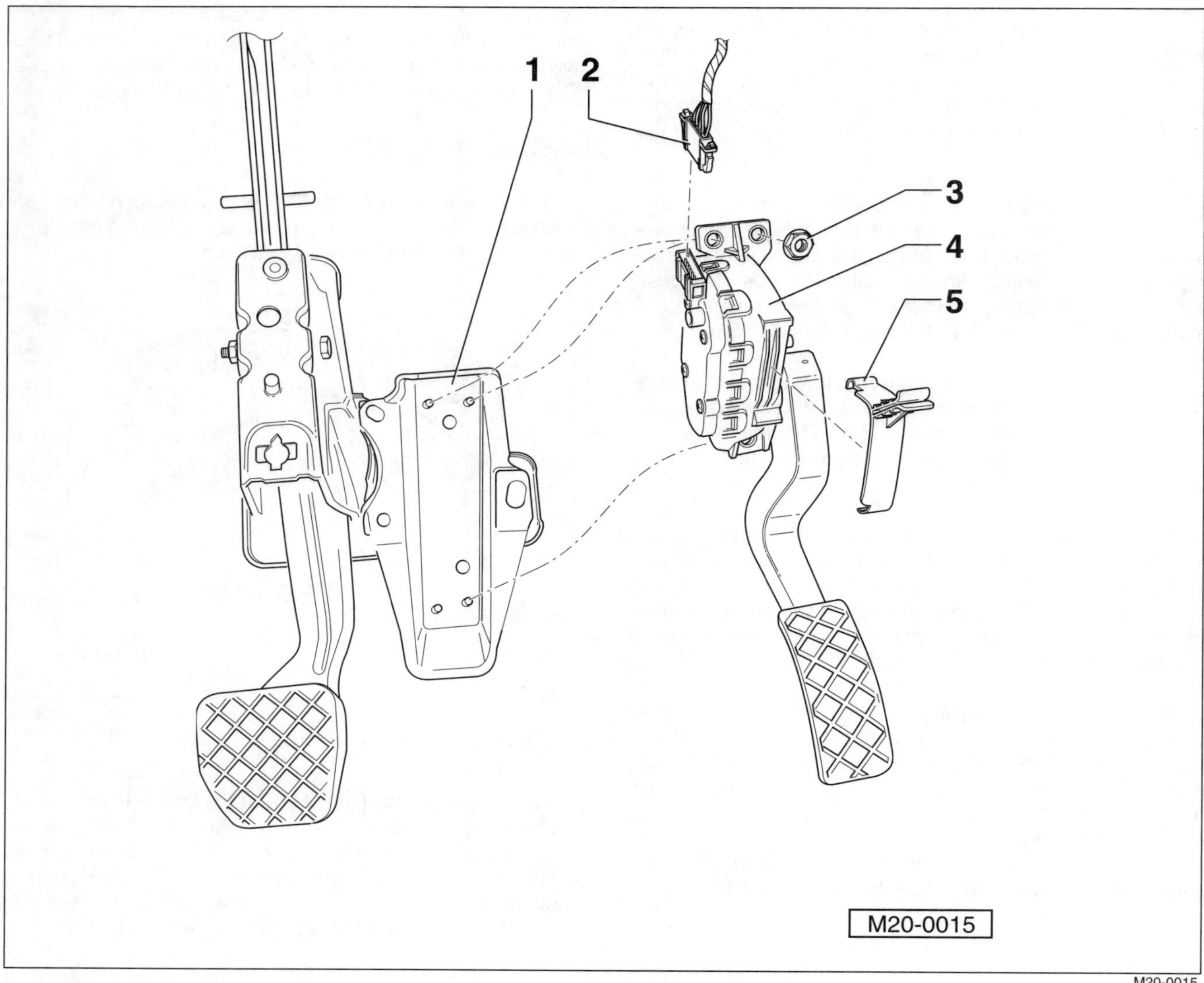

M20-0015

Fig. 18. EPC pedal components used with all engines except for the 2.0L AEG engine.

1. **Pedal bracket**

2. **Connector**
   - For throttle position sensors (G79 and G185)
   - Black, 6-pin
   - Checking supply voltage, **see** Ⓐ

3. **Nut**
   - Tighten to 10 Nm (7 ft-lb)

4. **Accelerator pedal position sensor (G79)**
   - Not adjustable
   - Communicates the driver's intentions to the control module
   - Remove cover in footwell before removing sensor

NOTE —

Volkswagen identifies electrical components by a letter and/or a number in the electrical schematics. See **97 Wiring Diagrams, Fuses and Relays**. *These electrical identifiers are listed in parenthesis as an aid to electrical troubleshooting.*

5. **Bracket**
   - For cover in footwell
   - Clipped on at accelerator pedal position sensor

A **Throttle position sensor, checking supply voltage**

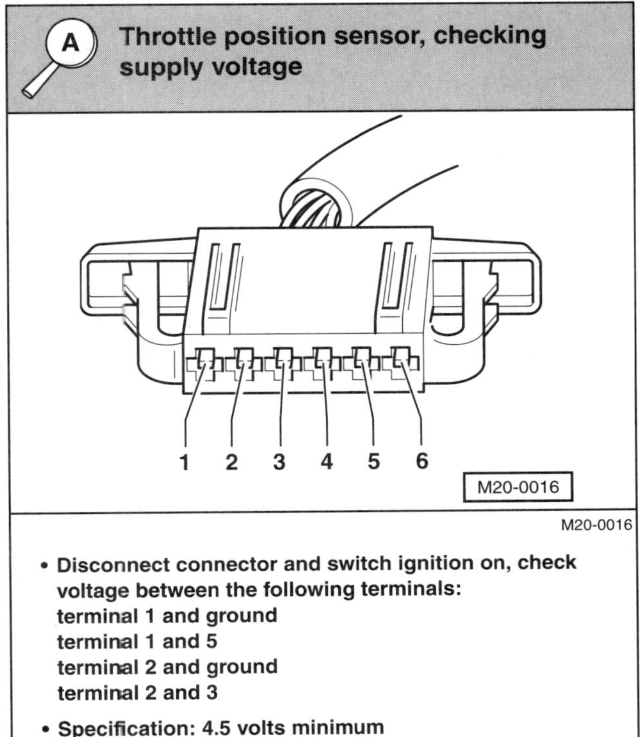

M20-0016

- **Disconnect connector and switch ignition on, check voltage between the following terminals:**
  terminal 1 and ground
  terminal 1 and 5
  terminal 2 and ground
  terminal 2 and 3
- **Specification: 4.5 volts minimum**
- **Switch ignition off before re-connecting**

EVAPORATIVE EMISSIONS (GASOLINE ENGINES)

All Golfs and Jettas with gasoline engines are equipped with evaporative emissions (EVAP) system monitoring. This system includes the On-board Refueling Vapor Recovery (OVRV) system with a Leak Detection Pump (LDP). Overviews of the EVAP systems for the various gasoline engines are shown on this page and the next.

The ORVR system filters fuel vapors through the EVAP canister to prevent these vapors from escaping directly into the atmosphere. The ORVR system is detailed in Fig. 19.

The Engine Control Module (ECM) determines when the appropriate conditions are met and activates the LDP to pump a small amount of air pressure into the fuel tank and lines. The pump runs until a pre-determined pressure or time is reached. If the system does not hold the pressure, a fault or DTC is stored in the ECM memory. The leak various detection systems are shown on page 20-18.

Basic troubleshooting should begin with a visual inspection of the evaporative system hoses and components with particular attention paid to the fuel cap and seal. Further testing will require use of a scan tool such as Volkswagen special tool VAG 1551 or VAG 1552.

EVAP system overview (1.8L engine)

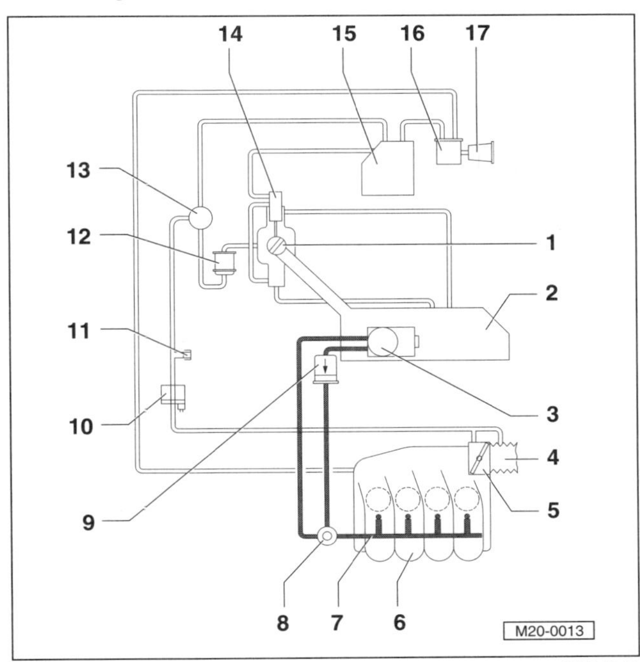

M20-0013

1. **Tank cap unit**
2. **Fuel tank**
3. **Fuel pump**
4. **Intake hose**
5. **Throttle valve control module (J338)**
6. **Intake manifold**
7. **Fuel rail with injectors**
8. **Fuel pressure regulator**
9. **Fuel filter**
   - Arrow points in direction of flow
10. **EVAP canister purge regulator valve (N80)**
    - In right side of engine compartment
    - Arrow points in direction of flow
11. **Test socket**
12. **Gravity/overflow valve**
13. **Check valve**
14. **Change-over valve**
15. **EVAP canister**
    - In right rear wheel housing, mounted on body
16. **Leak detection pump (V144)**
    - On EVAP canister
17. **Air filter for leak detection pump**

EVAP system overview (2.0L engine)

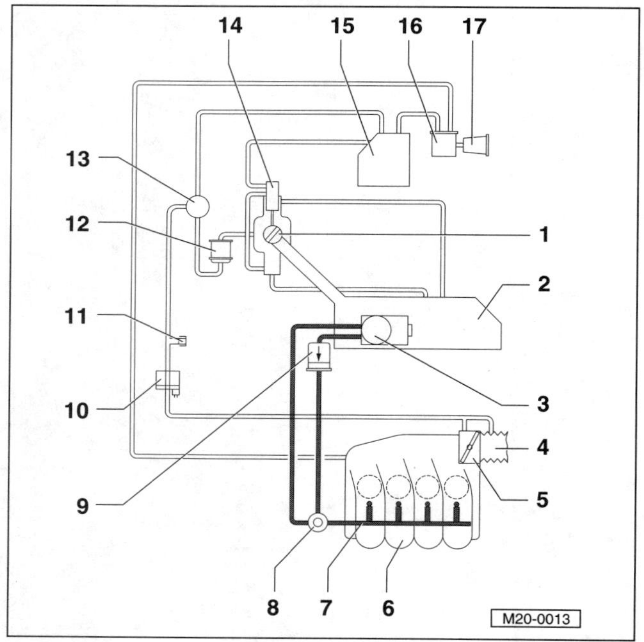

M20-0013

1. **Tank cap unit**
2. **Fuel tank**
3. **Fuel delivery unit**
4. **Throttle control module (J338)**
5. **Intake hose**
6. **Intake manifold upper section**
7. **Fuel rail with injectors**
8. **Fuel pressure regulator**
9. **Fuel filter**
   - Arrow points in direction of flow
10. **EVAP canister purge regulator valve (N80)**
    - In right side of engine compartment
    - Arrow points in direction of flow
11. **Test socket**
12. **Gravity/overflow valve**
13. **Pressure retention valve**
14. **Change-over valve**
15. **EVAP canister**
    - In right rear wheel housing, mounted on body
16. **Leak detection pump (V144)**
    - On EVAP canister
17. **Air filter for leak detection pump**

EVAP system overview (2.8L engine)

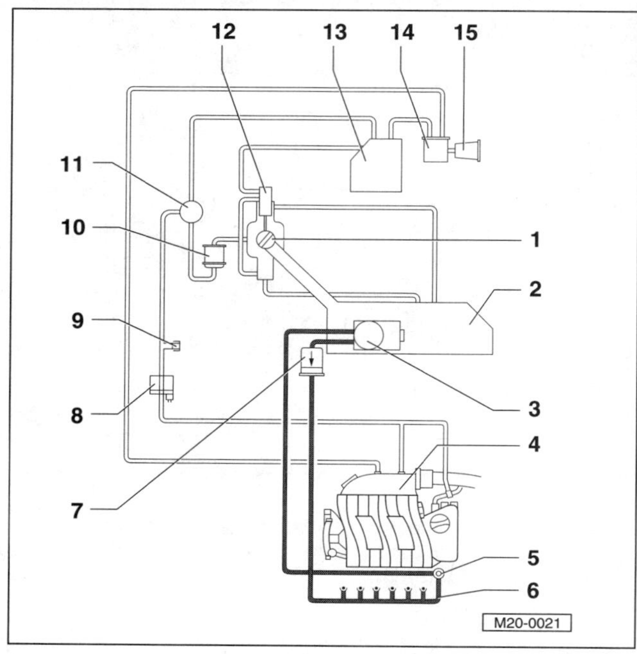

M20-0021

1. **Tank cap unit**
2. **Fuel tank**
3. **Fuel delivery unit**
4. **Upper intake manifold**
5. **Fuel pressure regulator**
6. **Fuel rail with injectors**
7. **Fuel filter**
   - Arrow points in direction of flow
8. **EVAP canister purge regulator valve (N80)**
   - In right side of engine compartment
   - Arrow points in direction of flow
9. **Test socket**
10. **Gravity/overflow valve**
11. **Pressure retention valve**
12. **Change-over valve**
13. **EVAP canister**
    - In right rear wheel housing, mounted on body
14. **Leak detection pump (V144)**
    - On EVAP canister
15. **Air filter for leak detection pump**

On-board refueling vapor recovery system

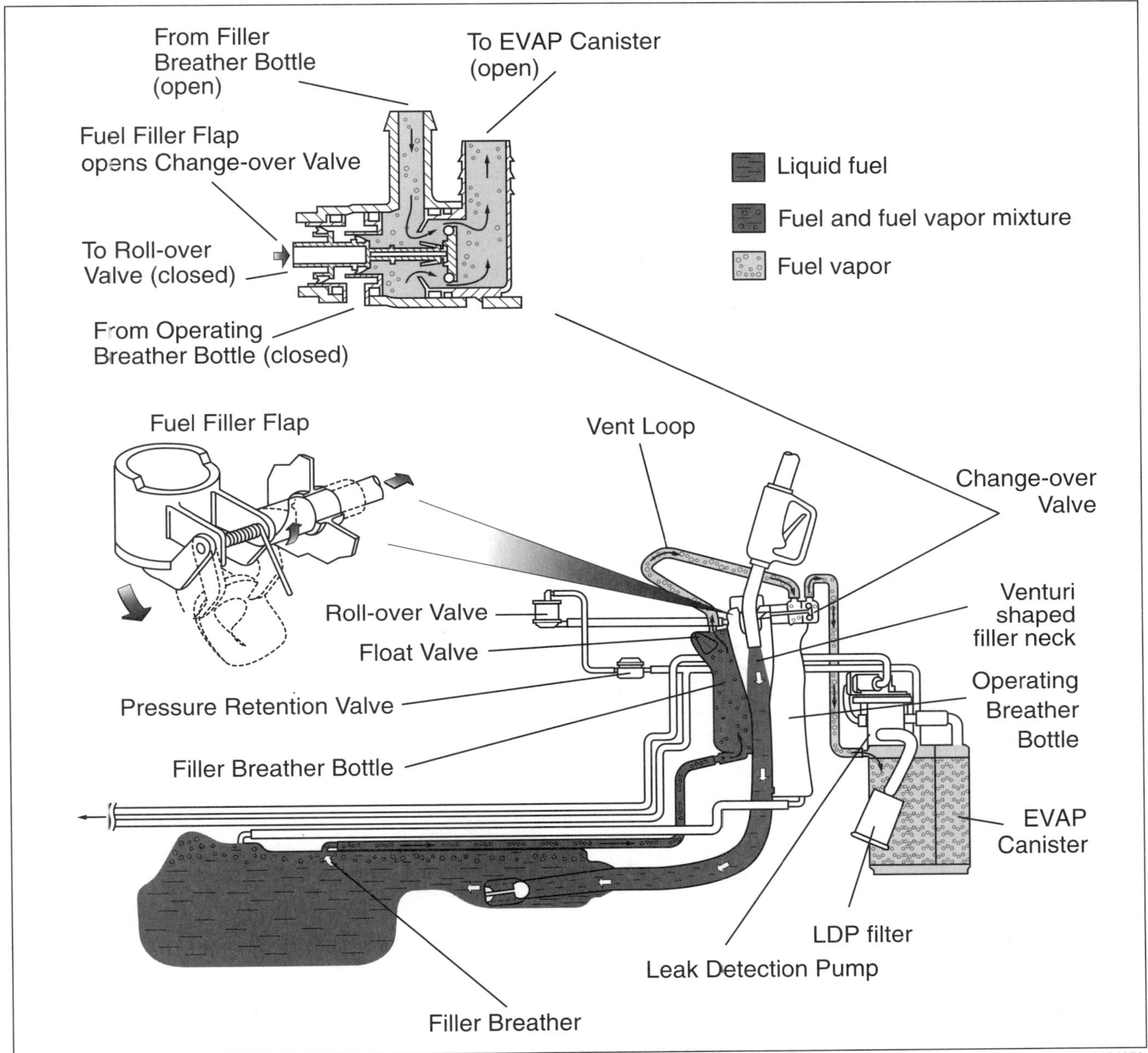

Fig. 19. On-board refueling vapor recovery system located in right rear wheelhousing.

When the vehicle is being refueled, the fuel filler flap is opened when the fuel filler nozzle is inserted. The fuel filler flap operates the change-over valve, closing off the operating breather bottle and the vent to the roll-over valve.

The narrow fuel filler neck creates a "liquid seal" as fuel flows into the tank preventing vapors from escaping out the filler neck. The fuel filler insert, shaped like a venturi also helps keep vapors from escaping.

All vapors vent through the filler breather bottle to the change-over valve and then to the EVAP canister through the large diameter vent loop.

The float valve closes the outlet in the filler breather bottle when the fuel tank is topped off to prevent liquid fuel from entering the EVAP system.

Leak detection system (2.0L and 2.8L)

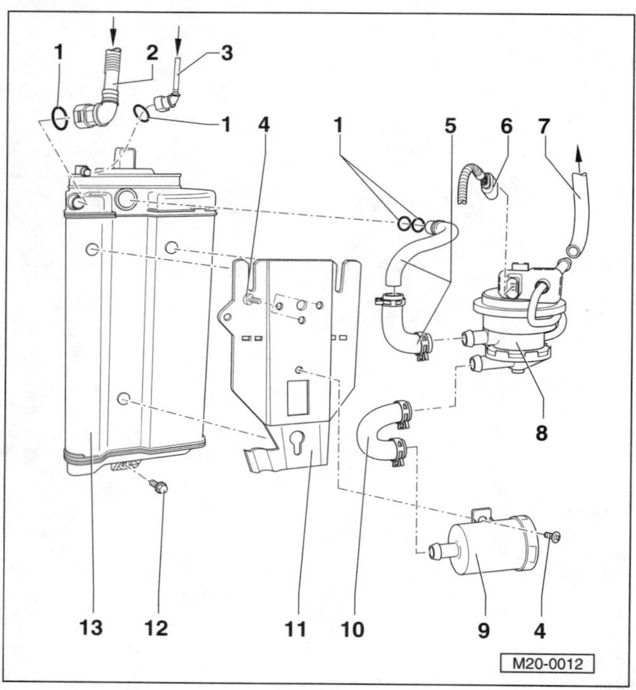

1. **O-ring**
   - Replace if damaged
2. **Vent line (black)**
   - Ensure tight fit
   - From change-over valve on fuel tank
3. **Vent line (white)**
   - Ensure tight fit
   - From pressure retention valve on fuel tank
4. **Retaining screw**
5. **Discharge hose**
   - Ensure tight fit
6. **Connector**
   - Black, 3-pin
7. **Vacuum line**
   - To upper intake manifold
8. **Leak detection pump (V144)**
9. **Air filter**
   - For leak detection pump
10. **Intake hose**
    - Ensure tight fit
11. **Mounting plate**
    - Clipped onto the charcoal canister
12. **Bolt**
    - Tighten to 10 Nm (7 ft-lb)
13. **Activated charcoal canister (EVAP canister)**
    - In right rear wheel housing, fastened to body

Leak detection system (1.8L)

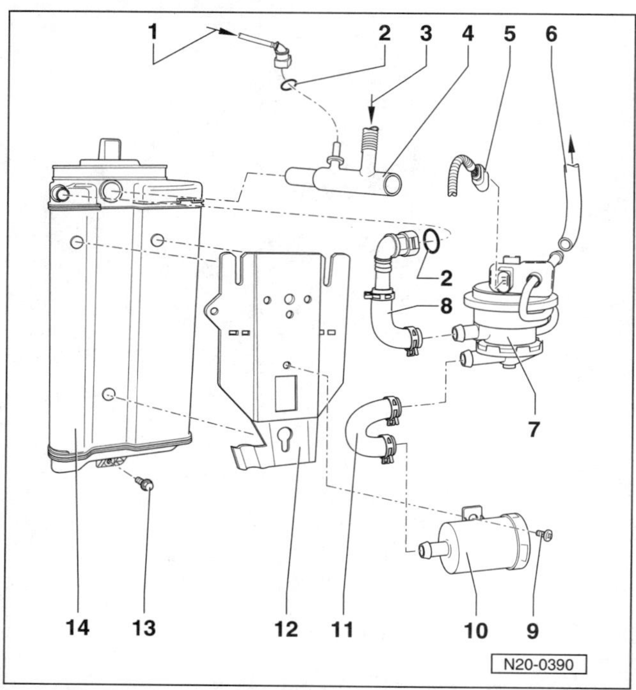

1. **To EVAP canister purge regulator valve (N80)**
2. **O-ring**
   - Replace if damaged
3. **Vent line**
4. **Connector**
5. **Connector**
   - 3-pin
6. **Vacuum line**
   - To throttle valve control module
7. **Leak detection pump (V144)**
   - In rear left wheel housing under wheel housing liner
8. **Discharge hose**
   - Ensure tight fit
9. **Retaining screw**
10. **Air filter**
    - For leak detection pump
11. **Intake hose**
    - Ensure tight fit
12. **Mounting plate**
    - Clipped onto the charcoal canister
13. **Bolt**
    - Tighten to 10 Nm (7 ft-lb)
14. **Activated charcoal canister (EVAP canister)**
    - In right rear wheel housing, fastened to body

21 Turbocharger and Intercooler

GENERAL

This section covers turbocharger and intercooler service and repair for the 1.8L gasoline and 1.9L diesel engines. Turbocharger boost pressure is not adjustable and separate parts for the turbocharger are usually not available from Volkswagen.

> ***WARNING —***
> *The turbocharger and related components operate at very high temperature. Always allow the system to cool or use proper protective clothing to prevent severe burns.*

> ***CAUTION —***
> - *Thoroughly clean all joints, pipe unions and connections, before disconnecting or reconnecting the turbocharger or any of its related components.*
> - *Take measures to prevent dust and dirt contamination. Cover all components with dust-free paper or seal them in plastic bags. Do not use cloth material. Avoid nearby use of compressed air. Do not move the car or work in dusty conditions while the turbocharger is open or removed. Install only clean components. Do not remove components from packaging until just before installation. Avoid use of components that have been stored loose.*

A cutaway view of a typical turbocharger is shown in Fig. 1. The exhaust-driven turbocharger vanes spin at very high speeds and are precisely balanced. The turbocharger is cooled and lubricated by engine oil with additional cooling supplied by a connection to the engine cooling system. Boost pressure is controlled by a mechanical wastegate operated by the Engine Control Module (ECM). When the boost pressure exceeds programmed values, the ECM opens the wastegate to bypass some of the exhaust gases around the turbine.

As the turbocharger compresses the incoming air, it also raises the air temperature. Output from the turbocharger is routed to an air-to-air radiator called an intercooler. The intercooler removes the excess heat allowing for greater boost pressure.

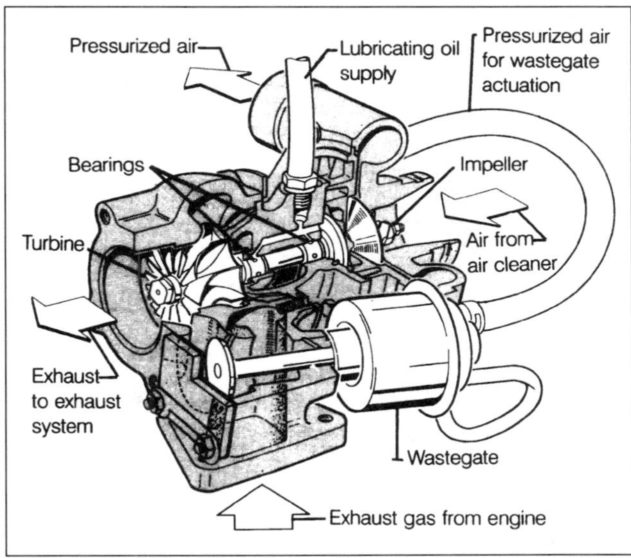

Fig. 1. Cutaway view of representative turbocharger used on AWD engines. The turbocharger unit is not adjustable.

TURBOCHARGER DIAGNOSTICS

Due to the extremely high speeds and temperatures, proper lubrication of the turbocharger is critical. Small oil and coolant passages are drilled into the turbocharger housing and bearings. Seals are placed around the shaft at each end to prevent oil and coolant from entering the compressor and turbine housing. When the turbocharger bearings and seals become worn, the lubricating oil can slip past the seals and into the combustion chamber or exhaust system. The result is blue-gray oil smoke from the tailpipe. When the bearings become severely worn, the turbocharger compressor and turbine impeller may contact the turbocharger housing, making loud screeching or thumping noises.

The major cause of turbocharger bearing and seal failure is "coking", or baking of oil in the turbocharger's oil passages. During operation, the temperature of the turbocharger housing can exceed the boiling point of the oil running through it. However, because oil and coolant are constantly circulating, the turbocharger stays cool enough to prevent oil coking. If the oil or coolant pipes are clogged or if the engine is turned off before the turbocharger has had time to cool down, the oil can quickly turn to coke. When these carbon deposits form, oil flow to the turbocharger is reduced. In addition, this substance is abrasive and can wear the seals, bearing and shafts prematurely.

If engine performance is low, and low boost pressure is suspected, first check for any loose or broken hoses or fittings. Make sure the control line to the wastegate is not blocked, loose, or leaking. Make sure there are no restrictions in the intake air system, such as a dirty air filter element or damage to the intercooler. Check the exhaust system for restrictions such as a damaged catalytic converter or clogged muffler. If no visible faults can be found, check the turbo boost pressure with a scan tool such as Volkswagen supplied VAG 1551 or 1552.

NOTE —

Suspected engine performance problems must first be investigated with an appropriate scan tool such as the Volkswagen supplied VAG 1551 or 1552. Diagnostic Trouble Codes (DTCs) stored in ECM memory must be repaired and the DTCs erased before proceeding. Use of these specialized tools must be in accordance with instructions with the tool by the manufacturer.

Turbo boost pressure, checking

Boost pressure measurements using a conventional pressure gauge on the 1.9L engine are generally not possible due to the lack of an attachment fitting for a gauge. Volkswagen specifies testing with scan tool VAG 1551/ 1552.

Boost pressure on the 1.8L engine can be measured with Volkswagen digital boost pressure gauge VAG1397A or equivalent as follows.

1. For AWD engines, connect boost pressure gauge. See Fig. 2.

2. Observe the following preliminary conditions:
   - Intake and exhaust systems free of leaks and restrictions
   - Engine temperature:
     (1.8L) 60°C (140°) minimum
   - (1.9L) 85°C (185°) minimum
   - Engine compression OK. See **1 Engine**
   - No DTCs in ECM memory

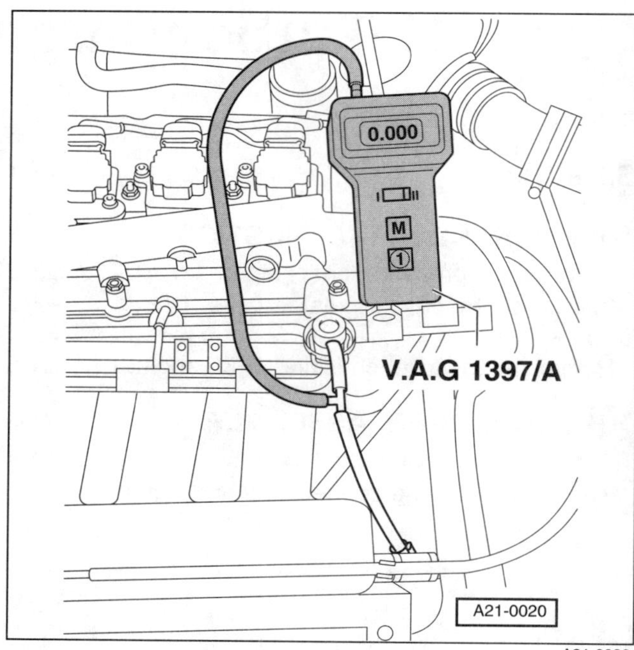

A21-0020

Fig. 2. Pressure gauge VAG 1397A shown connected to vacuum line of fuel pressure regulator on AWD engine.

3. Road test the vehicle under the following conditions:
   - For safety reasons, road test with a helper operating and/or observing the pressure gauge.
   - Road test in an area free from vehicular and pedestrian traffic.
   - Observe all applicable traffic laws.

4. Accelerate at full throttle from approx. 1500 rpm in 3rd gear (manual transmission) or 2nd gear (automatic).

5. Observe and record pressure gauge at specified rpm while accelerating to full throttle.

6. Compare to specification.

Boost pressure (at specified rpm)
- 1.8L engine
  (1800 to 2300 rpm). . . . 1350 to 1650 mbar (absolute)
- 1.9L engine
  (3000 rpm) . . . . 1700 to 2200 mbar (absolute)

NOTE —

Pressure measurements as specified by Volkswagen are given in "absolute' values. This system as used for automotive purposes does not recognize vacuum. The starting point for measurements is 1 atmosphere (1000 mbar). Values commonly referred to as vacuum are simply pressures less than 1 atmosphere.

7. If specified values are not reached or are exceeded, additional testing using an appropriate scan tool will be necessary.

Wastegate by-pass regulator valve, checking

1. Disconnect harness connector from wastegate by-pass regulator valve.

2. Measure resistance between terminals of by-pass regulator valve.
   - 1.8L See Fig. 3.

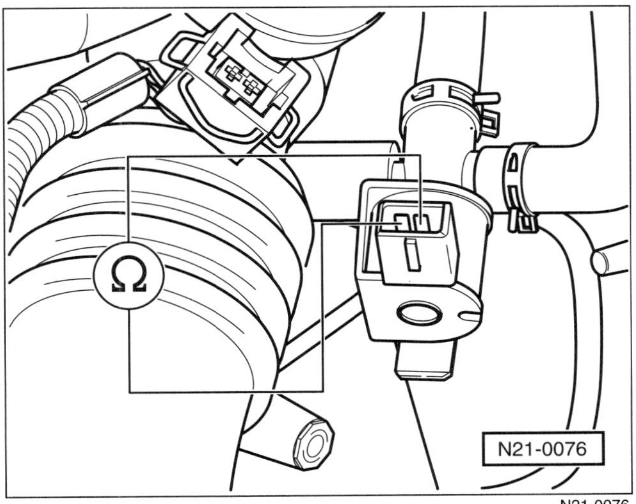

Fig. 3. Measure resistance of wastegate by-pass regulator valve. 1.8L engine shown.

   - 1.9L See Fig. 4.

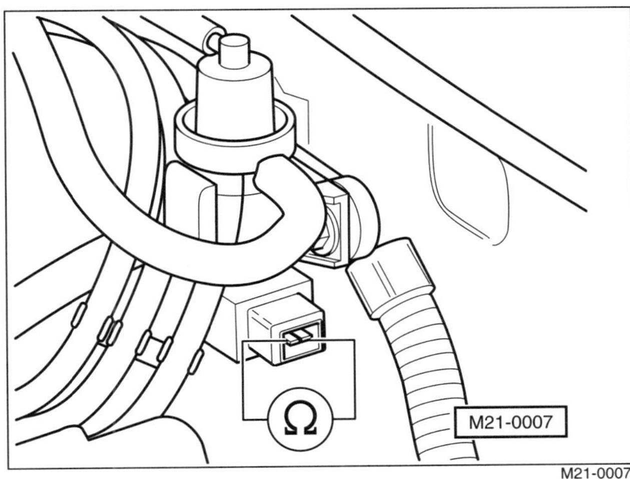

Fig. 4. Measure resistance of wastegate by-pass regulator valve. 1.9L engine shown.

Resistance of wastegate by-pass regulator valve
- 1.8L engine .... 25 to 35 Ω
- 1.9L engine .... 14 to 20 Ω

NOTE —
At room temperature, the resistance value of the wastegate bypass regulator valve should be at the lower end of the range. At normal operating temperature, the resistance should be at the upper end of the range.

Recirculating valve, checking (1.8L engine)

1. Switch ignition off and remove harness connector from recirculating valve for turbocharger. See Fig. 5.

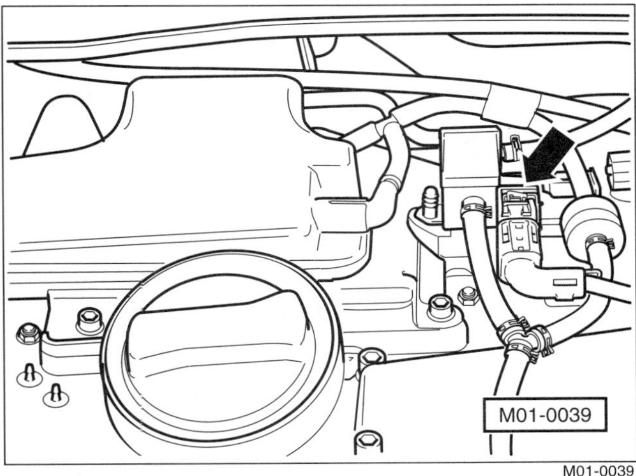

Fig. 5. Pull off connector (**arrow**) and measure resistance between terminals of turbocharger recirculating valve.

2. Measure resistance between terminals on recirculating valve.

Recirculating valve resistance
- 1.8L engine. .... 21 to 24 Ω

3. If the specification is not obtained, replace recirculating valve.

TURBOCHARGER, ASSEMBLY

When replacing the turbocharger, the oil return and supply pipes/lines and coolant return and supply pipes/lines should be removed and thoroughly cleaned using a stiff brush and solvent. If the pipes cannot be completely cleaned, they should be replaced. The engine oil and oil filter should also be changed. If the impeller blades are damaged, inspect the intake connecting pipes and the intercooler for debris and clean or replace as needed. Be sure to check the boost pressure once installation is complete. The various turbocharger components for the 1.8L and 1.9L engines are shown in Fig. 8. through Fig. 6.

Turbocharger assembly (1.8L engine)

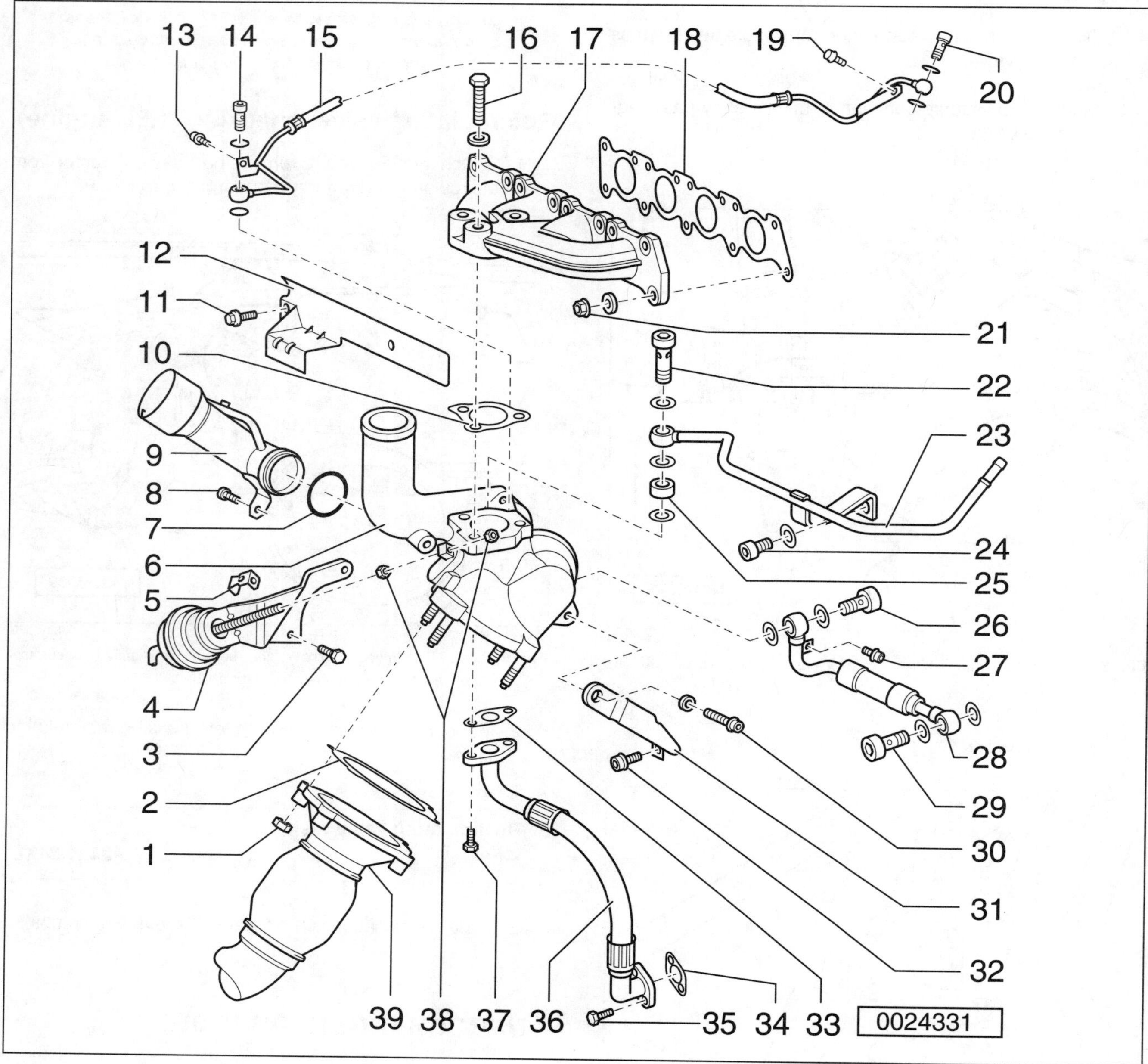

0024331

Fig. 6. Exploded view of turbocharger, exhaust manifold and related components on the 1.8L engine.

1. **Nut**
   - Tighten to 40 Nm (30 ft-lb)
   - Always replace
   - Coat threads with high temperature anti-seize
2. **Gasket**
   - Always replace
3. **Bolt**
   - Do not loosen
   - Tighten to 10 Nm (7 ft-lb)

TURBOCHARGER, ASSEMBLY

4. **Pressure unit (servo) for wastegate**
   - Integral with turbocharger
5. **Clip**
6. **Turbocharger**
   - With integral wastegate and servo
   - Fill with engine oil at connection sleeve before attaching oil supply line
   - Let engine idle for approx. 1 minute after installing engine and do not rev immediately to ensure turbocharger has adequate oil supply

7. **O-ring**
   - Always replace
8. **Bolt**
   - Tighten to 10 Nm (7 ft-lb)
9. **Intake pipe**
   - In from air cleaner
10. **Gasket**
    - Always replace
    - Note installation position
11. **Bolt**
    - Tighten to 20 Nm (15 ft-lb)
12. **Heat shield**
13. **Bolt**
    - Tighten to 10 Nm (7 ft-lb)
14. **Banjo bolt**
    - Tighten to 30 Nm (22 ft-lb)
15. **Oil supply pipe**
    - From oil filter flange
16. **Bolt**
    - Tighten to 30 Nm (22 ft-lb)
    - Always replace
    - Coat threads with high temperature anti-seize
17. **Exhaust manifold**
18. **Gasket**
    - Always replace
    - Note installation position
19. **Bolt**
    - Tighten to 20 Nm (15 ft-lb)
20. **Banjo bolt**
    - Tighten to 30 Nm (22 ft-lb)
21. **Nut**
    - Tighten to 25 Nm (18 ft-lb)
    - Always replace
    - Coat threads with high temperature anti-seize
22. **Banjo bolt**
    - Tighten to 35 Nm (26 ft-lb)
23. **Coolant return pipe**
24. **Bolt**
    - Tighten to 25 Nm (18 ft-lb)
25. **Spacer sleeve**
26. **Banjo bolt**
    - Tighten to 35 Nm (26 ft-lb)
27. **Bolt**
    - Tighten to 10 Nm (7 ft-lb)
28. **Coolant supply pipe**
29. **Banjo bolt**
    - Tighten to 35 Nm (26 ft-lb)
30. **Bolt, special**
    - Tighten to 30 Nm (22 ft-lb)
31. **Support bracket**
    - Between turbocharger and cylinder block
32. **Bolt**
    - Tighten to 25 Nm (18 ft-lb)
33. **Gasket**
    - Always replace
34. **Gasket**
    - Always replace
35. **Bolt**
    - Tighten to 10 Nm (7 ft-lb)
36. **Oil return pipe**
    - To oil pan
37. **Bolt**
    - Tighten to 10 Nm (7 ft-lb)
38. **Nut, adjusting**
    - Do not loosen or alter setting
    - Tighten to 10 Nm (7 ft-lb)
39. **Front exhaust pipe**
40. **Anti-seize compound (not shown)**
    - High temperature
    - Volkswagen recommended anti-seize compound for all operations, G 052 112 A3

NOTE —
Volkswagen part numbers are given for reference only! Always consult with your Volkswagen Parts Department or aftermarket parts specialist for the latest parts information.

Turbocharger hose connections (1.8L engine)

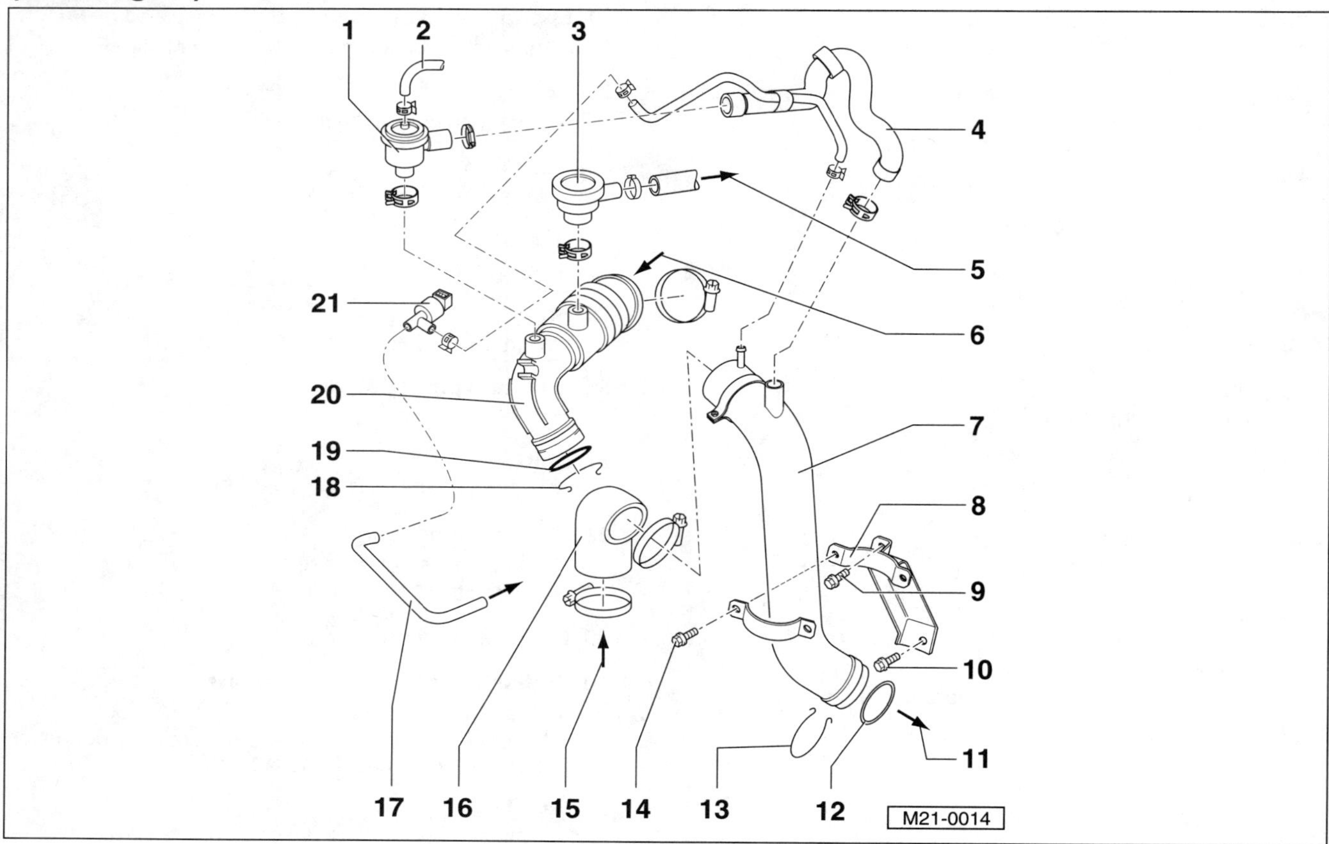

M21-0014

Fig. 7. Turbocharger connecting pipes on 1.8L engine.

1. **Charge pressure by pass valve**
2. **Connecting pipe**
   - To recirculating valve for turbocharger (N249)
3. **Pressure regulation valve for crankcase ventilation**
4. **Connecting pipe**
   - From mechanical recirculating valve to upper air shaft
5. **To crankcase ventilation**
6. **From air filter**
7. **Upper air shaft**
   - Note installation position of heat insulation mat
   - AWD engines have screw-type clamps
   - AWW engines have quick release connectors
8. **Bracket**
9. **Bolt**
   - Tighten to 40 Nm (30 ft-lb)
10. **Bolt**
    - Tighten to 25 Nm (18 ft-lb)
11. **From air filter**
12. **O-ring**
    - Always replace
    - Only on vehicles with AWW engine
13. **Circlip**
    - Always replace
    - Only on vehicles with AWW engine
14. **Bolt**
    - Tighten to 10 Nm (7 ft-lb)
15. **From turbocharger outlet sleeve**
16. **Connecting pipe**
17. **Connecting pipe**
18. **Circlip**
19. **O-ring**
    - Always replace
20. **Intake hose**
    - To intake sleeve of turbocharger
21. **Wastegate bypass regulator valve (N75)**
    - Activated (pulsed) by engine control module

Turbocharger component and hose connections, overview (AWD 1.8L engine)

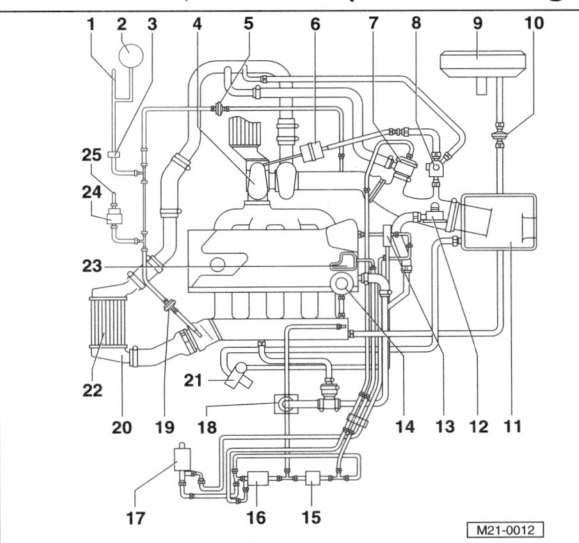

1. **Connecting pipe**
   - From gravity valve connection on fuel tank
2. **Vacuum reservoir**
   - Below right wheel housing liner
3. **Non-return valve**
4. **Turbocharger assembly**
5. **Non-return valve**
6. **Pressure unit**
   - For charge pressure bypass valve
7. **Charge pressure bypass valve**
8. **Wastegate regulator solenoid valve (N75)**
9. **Power brake servo**
10. **Non-return valve for brake booster**
11. **Air cleaner assembly with mass air flow sensor (G70)**
12. **Crankcase pressure regulating (breather) valve**
13. **Combination valve**
    - For secondary air injection system
14. **Fuel pressure regulator**
15. **Non-return valve**
16. **Recirculating valve for turbocharger (N249)**
17. **Secondary air injection solenoid valve (N112)**
18. **Crankcase breather**
19. **Non-return valve**
20. **Charge air pressure sensor (G31)/charge air cooler**
21. **Secondary Air Injection (AIR) pump motor (V101)**
22. **Charge air cooler**
23. **Vacuum reservoir**
24. **Activated charcoal filter solenoid valve 1 (N80)**
25. **Connecting hose to EVAP canister**

Turbocharger component and hose connections, overview (AWW 1.8L engine)

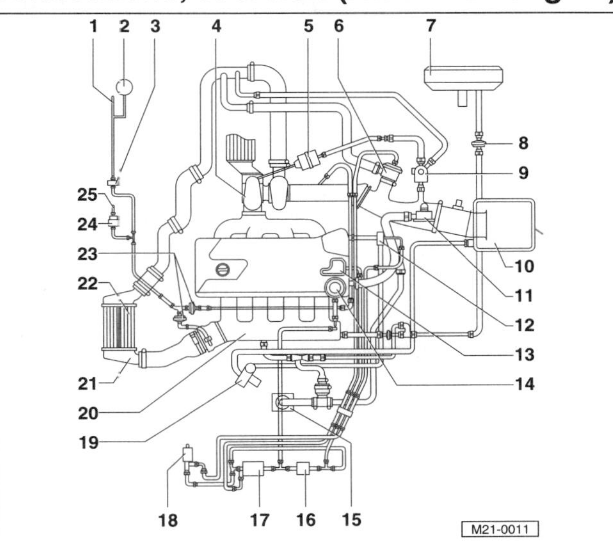

1. **Connecting pipe**
   - From gravity valve connection on fuel tank
2. **Vacuum reservoir**
   - Below right wheel housing liner
3. **Non-return valve**
4. **Turbocharger assembly**
5. **Pressure unit**
   - For charge pressure bypass valve
6. **Charge pressure bypass valve**
7. **Power brake servo**
8. **Non-return valve for brake booster**
9. **Wastegate regulator solenoid valve (N75)**
10. **Air cleaner assembly with mass air flow sensor (G70)**
11. **Crankcase pressure regulating (breather) valve**
12. **Combination valve**
    - For secondary air injection system
13. **Vacuum reservoir**
14. **Fuel pressure regulator**
15. **Crankcase breather**
16. **Non-return valve**
17. **Recirculating valve for turbocharger (N249)**
18. **Secondary air injection solenoid valve (N112)**
19. **Secondary Air Injection (AIR) pump motor (V101)**
20. **Intake pipe**
21. **Charge air pressure sensor (G31)/charge air cooler**
22. **Charge air cooler**
23. **Non-return valve**
24. **Activated charcoal filter solenoid valve 1 (N80)**
25. **Connecting hose to EVAP canister**

Turbocharger assembly (1.9L engine)

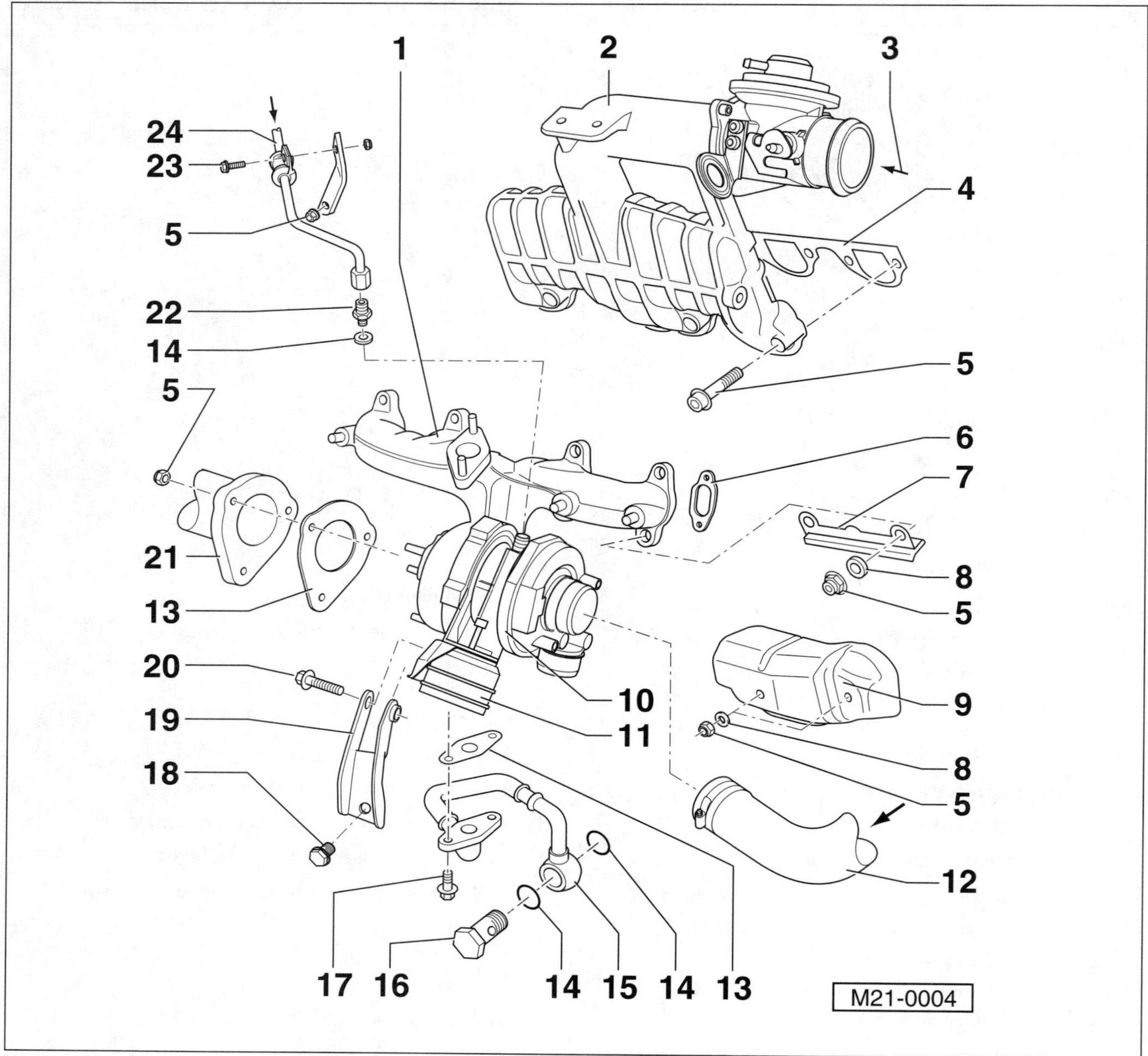

M21-0004

Fig. 8. Exploded view of turbocharger, exhaust manifold and related components on the 1.9L diesel engine.

1. **Exhaust manifold**
   - Integral with turbocharger
2. **Intake manifold**
   - Shown with EGR valve and manifold flap
3. **Air flow in from intercooler**
4. **Gasket**
   - Always replace
   - Coated (beaded) side faces intake manifold
5. **Bolt**
   - Tighten to 25 Nm (18 ft-lb)
6. **Gasket**
   - Always replace
   - Note installation position
7. **Bracket**
   - For heat shield
8. **Washer**

(continued from previous page)

9. Heat shield

10. Turbocharger
- Only replace as complete assembly
- Remove right drive shaft at transmission before removing turbocharger
- Installing:
  fill turbocharger with oil before connecting the oil supply line (item 24)
- After installing, run engine at idle for approx. 1 minute to assure oil supply to turbocharger before increasing engine speed

11. Pressure unit (servo) for wastegate
- Integral part of turbocharger

12. Connecting hose
- Arrow indicates air flow from air cleaner

13. Gasket
- Always replace

14. O-ring
- Always replace

15. Oil return pipe
- To cylinder block

16. Banjo bolt
- Tighten to 40 Nm (30 ft-lb)

17. Bolt
- Tighten to 15 Nm (11 ft-lb)

18. Bolt
- Tighten to 40 Nm (30 ft-lb)

19. Bracket

20. Bolt
- Tighten to 25 Nm (18 ft-lb)

21. Front exhaust pipe

22. Connection

23. Bolt
- Tighten to 10 Nm (7 ft-lb)

24. Oil supply pipe
- From oil filter flange

NOTE —
- *If the turbocharger is being replaced because of excessive exhaust smoke, there will probably be some residual oil in the exhaust upon start-up. Be sure to test drive the car long enough to clear the left over oil from the exhaust system.*
- *Volkswagen identifies electrical components by a letter and/or a number in the electrical schematics. See* **97 Wiring Diagrams, Fuses and Relays**. *These electrical identifiers are listed in parenthesis as an aid to electrical troubleshooting.*

Turbocharger hose connections (1.9L engine)

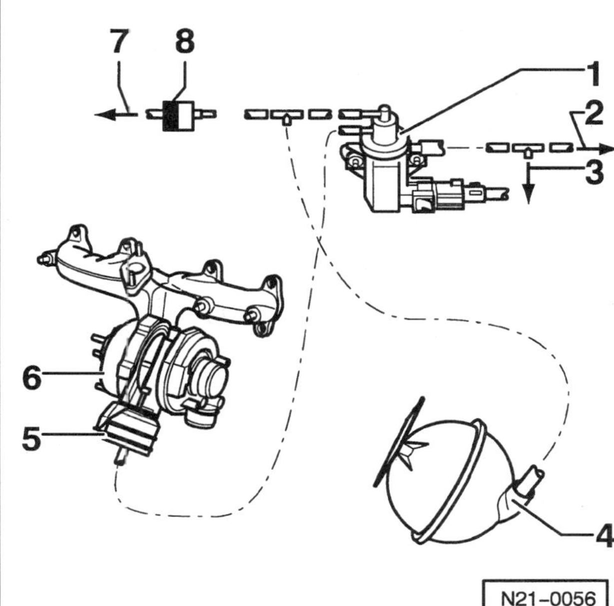

1. **Wastegate regulator valve**
2. **Connection to EGR regulator valve**
3. **Connection to air filter**
4. **Connection to vacuum reservoir/vacuum pump**
5. **Pressure unit (servo) for wastegate**
6. **Exhaust manifold with turbocharger**
7. **Connection to change-over valve for intake manifold**
8. **Check valve**

N21-0056

Fig. 9. Schematic view of hose connections to the turbocharger and wastegate regulator valve for ALH engine.

INTERCOOLER

The intercooler for the 1.8L and 1.9L engines are shown on the following page. The intercooler is used to reduce the temperature of the air compressed by the turbocharger. This cooler air has greater density which reduces Nitrous Oxide (NOS) gases and improves performance.

Intercooler assembly (1.8L engine)

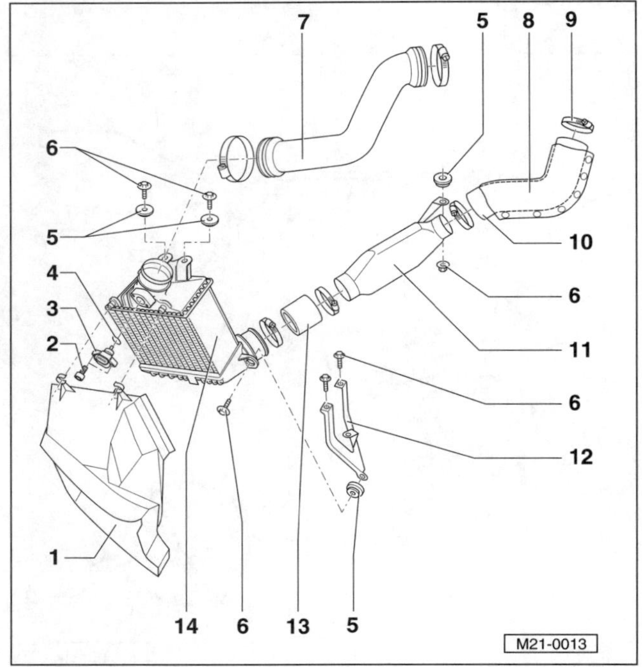

M21-0013

Fig. 10. Intercooler and related components on the 1.8L engine.

1. **Air duct**
   - Clip in at intercooler
2. **Bolt**
   - Tighten to 10 Nm (7 ft-lb)
3. **Charge pressure sender (G31)**
4. **O-ring**
   - Always replace
5. **Rubber grommet**
6. **Bolt**
   - Tighten to 10 Nm (7 ft-lb)
7. **Intake hose**
   - Between intake manifold and intercooler
8. **Heat insulation mat**
9. **Screw-type clip**
   - Only for engine code AWD
   - Engine code AWW has quick release connector
10. **Connecting hose**
11. **Air duct pipe**
12. **Bracket**
13. **Connecting hose**
14. **Intercooler**

Intercooler assembly (1.9L engine)

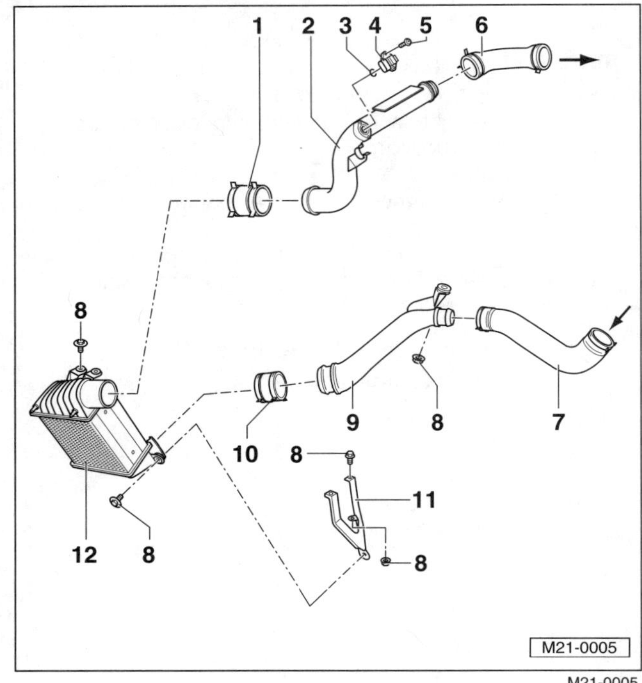

M21-0005

Fig. 11. Intercooler and related components on the 1.9L diesel engine.

1. **Connecting hose**
2. **Connecting pipe**
   - Between intercooler and intake manifold
   - Remove right headlight to remove pipe
3. **O-ring**
   - Always replace
4. **Intake Air Temperature (IAT) sensor (G72)**
5. **Bolt**
   - Tighten to 5 Nm (44 in-lb)
6. **Connecting hose**
   - To intake manifold
7. **Connecting hose**
   - From turbocharger
8. **Bolt**
   - Tighten to 10 Nm (7 ft-lb)
9. **Boost intake air line**
10. **Connecting hose**
11. **Bracket**
12. **Intercooler**

23 Fuel Injection-Diesel (1.9L Engine)

TABLES

23

GENERAL

This repair group covers the diesel fuel injection system for the 1.9 liter Turbo Direct Injection (TDI) diesel engine. Testing on the diesel glow plug system is covered in **28b Ignition System–Diesel (1.9L engine)**.

Most major components of the diesel injection system are shown in Fig. 1.

Fig. 1 does not show the following components:

- Brake pedal switch (F47) and brake light switch (F); located in one housing on brake pedal.
- Throttle position sensor (G79); located in footwell on throttle pedal. In case of malfunction, the scan tool display is Throttle Position Sensor G69
- Clutch pedal switch (F36); located in footwell on clutch pedal.

NOTE—
Volkswagen identifies electrical components by a letter and/or a number in the electrical schematics. See ***97 Wiring Diagrams, Fuses and Relays****. These electrical identifiers are listed as an aid to electrical troubleshooting.*

CAUTION—

- *Repairs and adjustments to the injection pump require specialized equipment, and parts for rebuilding are not generally available. Faulty pumps must be serviced by the manufacturer. Internal problems usually require replacement of the pump.*
- *Adjustments and repairs to the fuel injection system should be made carefully. Cleanliness is especially important. Always clean fuel unions before removing lines*
- *Diesel fuel is damaging to rubber. Wipe off any fuel that spills on hoses, wiring, and rubber steering and suspension parts and wash with soap and water. If coolant hoses have been contaminated with diesel fuel, they must be replaced.*
- *Disconnecting the negative (–) battery cable may erase fault codes and basic settings in the engine management and automatic transmission control modules. Some driveability problems may be noticed until the system re-adapts to operating conditions. OBD II readiness codes, which may be required for emissions testing, may also be erased. Convenience electronics (alarm system, interior light control, power locks, mirrors, and windows) may need to be re-set using a VAG 1551/1552 or equivalent scan tool.*

Diesel injection system, component overview

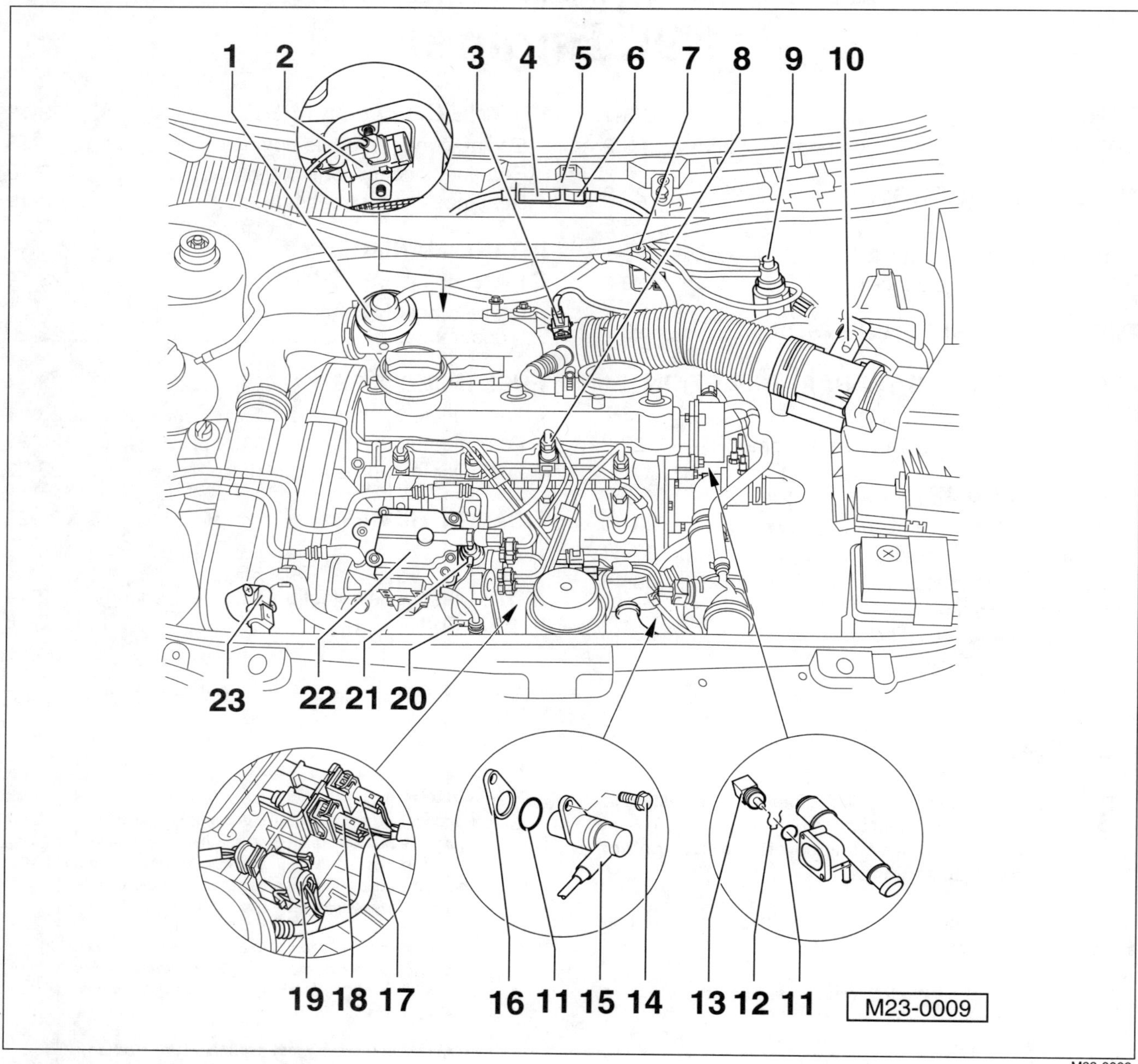

M23-0009

Fig. 1. Major components of diesel injection system.

1. **EGR valve**
2. **Intake manifold change-over valve (N239)**
3. **Positive Crankcase ventilation (PCV) heating element (N79)**
   - Check voltage supply between terminals 1 and 2 of connector with ignition on; specification: at least 11.5V
4. **Connector**
   - Through m.y. 1999: 52 pin
   - From m.y. 2000: 81 pin
   - Only disconnect or connect with ignition switched off
5. **Diesel direct injection system ECM (J248)**
   - With BARO (altitude) sensor (F96)
6. **Connector**
   - Through m.y. 1999: 28 pin
   - From m.y. 2000: 40 pin
   - Only disconnect or connect with ignition switched off
7. **EGR vacuum regulator solenoid valve (N18)**
8. **Injector**
   - For cylinder #3 with needle lift sensor (G80)

(continued from previous page)

9. Wastegate bypass regulator valve (N75)

10. Mass air flow sensor (G70)

11. O-ring

12. Retaining clip

13. Engine coolant temperature sensor (G62)
- Release pressure in cooling system before removing

14. Bolt
- Tighten to 10 Nm (7 ft-lb)

15. Engine speed sensor (G28)

16. Spacer

17. Harness connector
- For needle lift sensor (G80)
- Brown, 2-pin

18. Harness connector
- For engine speed sensor (G28)
- Brown, 2-pin

19. Harness connector
- For fuel temperature sensor (G81)
- For cold start injector (N108)
- For fuel shut-off valve (N109)
- For quantity adjuster (N146)
- For modulating piston displacement sensor (G149)
- Black, 10-pin

20. Cold start injector (N108)

21. Fuel shut-off valve (N109)

22. Injection pump quantity adjuster
- With fuel temperature sensor (G81)
- With quantity adjuster (N146)
- With modulating piston displacement sensor (G149)

23. Manifold absolute pressure sensor (G71) and intake air temperature sensor (G72)

NOTE—
Volkswagen identifies electrical components by a letter and/or a number in the electrical schematics. See **97 Wiring Diagrams, Fuses and Relays**. *These electrical identifiers are listed as an aid to electrical troubleshooting.*

TROUBLESHOOTING

Proper operation of the diesel engine requires a supply of clean fuel under pressure, an unrestricted supply of air, and properly timed fuel delivery. Fuel must be of the proper grade and properly winterized for cold-start and cold-running conditions. Dirt and water can interfere with combustion and will cause problems.

Good compression is especially necessary for the engine to run well. Engine mechanical faults leading to poor compression can cause problems that may seem to be injection related. Engine lubricating oil that leaks past worn piston rings, valve stem seals or turbocharger seals may produce exhaust smoke that also can be mistaken for fuel injection problems.

A faulty glow plug system may contribute to cold starting problems. See **28b Ignition System–Diesel (1.9L engine)**. The battery must have the correct electrical capacity and the starter must be able to turn the engine fast enough (generally at least 150 rpm) to begin compression ignition. See **27 Engine Electrical System**. Insufficient engine power can also be the result of turbocharger or intercooler malfunctions. See **21 Turbocharger and Intercooler**.

Because the diesel engine speed is controlled by the amount of fuel injected and not by the amount of air admitted past a throttle plate, the air intake must be unrestricted. A clogged air filter, faulty turbocharger, or restricted intercooler can lower the air flow and reduce power output.

The injection pump, under the control of the Engine Control Module (ECM), produces the high pressure necessary to open the injectors and spray fuel. Fuel leaks or air in the fuel lines may reduce system pressure. Since power is controlled by the amount of fuel injected, low pressure may cause sluggish performance.

For cold starting, when the compression heat necessary for combustion is dissipated quickly by a cold engine, injection timing is automatically advanced by the ECM to give the fuel more time to burn. At higher rpm, there is less time for fuel to burn, so injection timing is advanced to start the fuel burning sooner. Since the injection pump is driven by the engine and externally mounted, its precise fuel metering and timing can be degraded by such things as a loose timing belt, worn sprocket, or loose mounting bolts. Correct Cetane rating as specified by the vehicle's Owner's Manual will profoundly influence starting and overall performance as well.

Most of the in-depth troubleshooting of this electronically controlled engine management system will require the use of a scan tool such as the Volkswagen supplied VAG 1551 or VAG 1552. However, there are several basic tests that should not be overlooked. **Table a** lists symptoms, their probable causes, and corrective actions. The boldface type refers to other sections in the manual where the repairs are described.

Table a. TDI Diesel Fuel Injection Troubleshooting

Problem	Probable cause	Corrective action
1. Engine does not start	**a.** Cranking speed too low or will not crank	**a.** Repair starting system or charge/replace battery. See **27 Engine Electrical Systems.**
	b. No fuel or wrong fuel in fuel tank	**b.** Verify sufficient fuel of correct type in tank. Add as necessary.
	c. No voltage at fuel cut-off valve on injection pump. Fuel cut-off valve loose or faulty	**c.** Valve should click each time ignition is turned on and off. If not, check for voltage at connector. See **97 Wiring Diagrams, Fuses and Relays.** Replace a faulty solenoid.
	d. No voltage at glow plug bus or glow plug(s) faulty	**d.** The glow plug circuit is activated by the Engine Control Module. See **28b Ignition System–Diesel (1.9L engine)** for glow plug testing and repair information.
	e. Excessive air in fuel system	**e.** Check fuel supply lines from fuel tank for cracks and connections for leaks, especially at and around fuel filter and injection pump inlet.
	f. Injection pump not delivering fuel	**f.** Check for basic fuel delivery to engine. Check for cracked or damaged lines, clogged fuel filter or other fuel supply problems.
	g. Injection timing incorrect	**g.** Adjust injection timing. Requires scan tool VAG 1551/1552.
	h. Faulty injectors	**h.** Test and, if necessary, replace injectors.
	i. Engine mechanical faults	**i.** Test compression. See **15b Cylinder Head and Valvetrain (1.9L engine)**.
	j. Faulty injection pump	**j.** Replace pump.
	k. Fault in engine speed sensor (G28)	**k.** Test sensor at connector.
	l. Fault in ECM or other engine management system component	**l.** Interrogate permanent fault memory. Repair or replace components as required. Requires scan tool VAG 1551/1552.
2. Glow plug warning light not working	**a.** Bulb burned out or malfunction in glow plug relay circuit	**a.** Test and repair as described in **28b Ignition System–Diesel (1.9L engine)**.
3. Idle speed incorrect, rough or irregular	**a.** Accelerator pedal or linkage binding	**a.** Remove driver's side trim panels under dash and inspect pedal and linkage for free movement. Repair as required.
	b. Excessive air in fuel system	**b.** Check fuel supply line from fuel tank for cracks, kinks, or leaks.
	c. Clogged fuel filter, or fuel return line and injector pipes leaking, dirty, kinked, or damaged at connectors	**c.** Inspect and, if necessary, replace lines and hoses, replace fuel filter. See **0 Maintenance**.
	d. Faulty injectors	**d.** Test and, if necessary, replace injector.
	e. Injection timing incorrect	**e.** Adjust injection timing. Requires scan tool VAG 1551/1552.
	f. Engine mechanical faults	**f.** Test compression. See **15b Cylinder Head and Valvetrain (1.9L engine)**.
	g. Faulty injection pump	**g.** Replace pump.
4. Smoky exhaust (black, blue, or white)	**a.** Faulty injectors	**a.** Check and, if necessary, replace injectors.
	b. Injection timing incorrect	**b.** Adjust injection timing. Requires scan tool VAG 1551/1552.
	c. Turbocharger leaking internally	**c.** Inspect and repair, or replace turbocharger.
	d. Engine mechanical faults	**d.** Test compression. See **15b Cylinder Head and Valvetrain (1.9L engine)**.
	e. Faulty injection pump	**e.** Replace pump.
	f. Fault in ECM or other engine management system component	**f.** Interrogate permanent fault memory. Repair or replace components as required. Requires scan tool VAG 1551/1552.

Table a. TDI Diesel Fuel Injection Troubleshooting

Problem	Probable cause	Corrective action
5. Poor power output, slow acceleration or top speed	**a.** Accelerator pedal or linkage binding	**a.** Remove driver's side trim panels under dash and inspect pedal and linkage for free movement. Repair as required.
	b. Air filter dirty or restricted	**b.** Clean or replace air filter. Inspect housing and ducting for debris. See **0 Maintenance**.
	c. Clogged fuel filter; or fuel return line and injection pipes leaking, dirty, kinked, or damaged at connections	**c.** Check for basic fuel delivery to engine. Inspect and, if necessary, replace lines and hoses, replace fuel filter. See **0 Maintenance**.
	d. Excessive air in fuel system	**d.** Check fuel supply line from fuel tank for cracks, kinks, or leaks, especially at and around fuel filter and injection pump inlet.
	e. Faulty injectors	**e.** Check and, if necessary, replace injectors.
	f. Injection timing incorrect	**f.** Adjust injection timing. Requires scan tool VAG 1551/1552.
	g. Engine mechanical faults	**g.** Test compression. See **15b Cylinder Head and Valvetrain (1.9L engine)**.
	h. Faulty injection pump	**h.** Replace pump.
	i. Fault in ECM or other engine management system component	**i.** Interrogate permanent fault memory. Repair or replace components as required. Requires scan tool VAG 1551/1552.
6. Engine runs at a high constant idle and speed does not vary	**a.** Throttle position sensor (G79), malfunctioning	**a.** Interrogate permanent fault memory. Repair or replace components as required. Requires scan tool VAG 1551/1552.
7. Excessive fuel consumption	**a.** Air filter dirty or restricted	**a.** Clean or replace air filter element. Inspect housing and ducting for debris. See **0 Maintenance**.
	b. Fuel leaks	**b.** Check and, if necessary, replace or tighten all pipes, hoses and connections.
	c. Fuel return pipe blocked or restricted	**c.** Check return line for kinks and dents; replace faulty lines. If line is clogged, blow it out with compressed air, then bleed fuel system.
	d. Faulty injectors	**d.** Test and, if necessary, repair or replace injectors.
	e. Injection timing incorrect	**e.** Adjust injection timing. Requires scan tool VAG 1551/1552.
	f. Faulty injection pump	**f.** Replace pump.
	g. Fault in ECM or other engine management system component	**g.** Interrogate permanent fault memory. Repair or replace components as required. Requires scan tool VAG 1551/1552.

Diagnostic quick checks

These tests are used to isolate and diagnose diesel fuel system problems. It is assumed that the glow plug system is functioning within normal parameters and that injection pump timing and valve timing are correct.

> ***NOTE—***
> *Testing and repair information on the diesel glow plug system is covered in* **28b Ignition System–Diesel (1.9L engine).**

Fuel shut-off valve, checking

The diesel engine is stopped by cutting off its fuel supply. This is done by means of an electrical solenoid located on the diesel injection pump and that is closed with power off. An electrical signal from the Engine Control Module (key ON) opens the valve. If the valve is not working, the engine will not start. Conversely, a faulty valve could also allow the engine to continue running after the key is switched off.

1. Turn ignition key on and off without operating the starter. Listen for the valve to operate.
   - The fuel cut-off valve should click open when the key is turned on and click closed when the key is turned off. Do not confuse this sound with continuous sounds coming from other electronic components on the pump.

2. If valve does not operate, check for voltage at harness connector with key on.
   - If voltage is not present, check for wiring faults. See **97 Wiring Diagrams, Fuses and Relays.**
   - If voltage is present, disconnect battery ground (GND) strap from battery negative (–) terminal and proceed with step 3. See the **Caution** at the beginning of this repair group regarding battery disconnection.

> **CAUTION—**
> *Before disconnecting battery cables, be sure to obtain radio anti-theft code.*

3. Clean the area around fuel shut-off valve and remove the valve, spring and plunger. See Fig. 2.

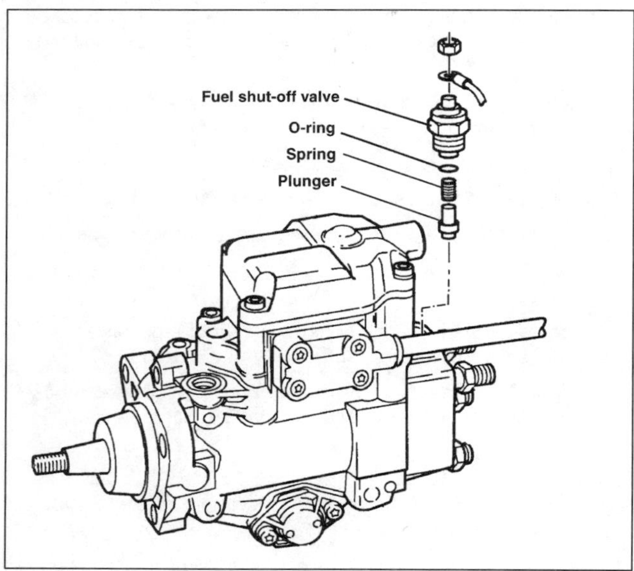

Fig. 2. Fuel shut-off valve removed from injection pump.

> **WARNING—**
> *Fuel will be expelled. Do not smoke or work near heaters or other fire hazards. Have a fire extinguisher handy.*

4. Clean and inspect solenoid plunger and seat. Slide plunger into the valve without spring and check for free movement. If plunger does not move freely, replace valve assembly.

5. Carefully check for dirt and metal particles in valve bore of injection pump. The slightest amount of debris can cause malfunctions.

6. Install fuel cut-off valve using a new O-ring.

7. Reconnect battery negative (–) terminal.

Tightening Torque
- Fuel shut-off valve to injection pump . 40 Nm (30 ft-lb)

8. Be sure to quality check your work, see **Quality Review** at the end of this repair group.

Basic fuel delivery, checking

This test checks if fuel is being delivered to the pump and fuel injectors. Make this test when experiencing hard starting or no-start problems.

1. Check visually for fuel leaks on injector pump and especially around injector line unions.

2. If no leaks are found, clean the fuel union nut for cylinder No. 1 fuel injector pipe at the injector. Slightly loosen the fuel union nut. See Fig. 3.

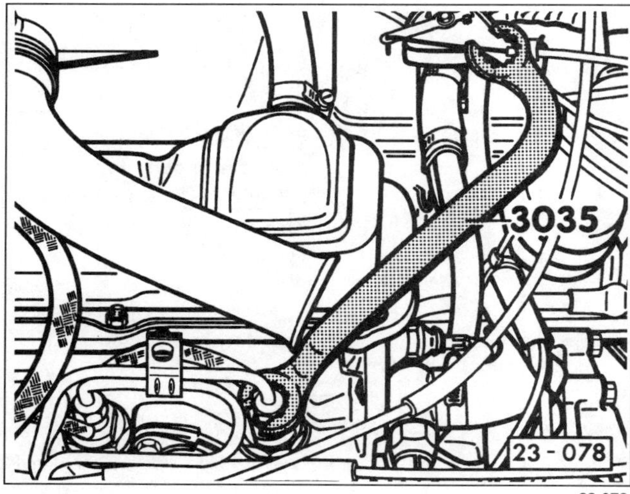

Fig. 3. Flare-nut wrench (Volkswagen special tool 3035) being used to loosen injector union nut for cylinder #4 on an earlier diesel engine version. The same tool is used on TDI diesel engines which are similar.

> **WARNING—**
> - *Loosen the nut only about one-half turn to limit the amount of fuel leakage. The fuel injection system operates at very high pressure. Keep hands and eyes clear. Wear heavy gloves and eye protection. Wrap a cloth around the nut when loosening.*
> - *Fuel will be expelled. Do not smoke or work near heaters or other fire hazards. Have a fire extinguisher handy.*

3. Crank the engine and look for fuel to run out of the loosened union nut at the injector.

> **CAUTION—**
> *Diesel fuel is damaging to rubber. Wipe off any fuel that spills on hoses, wiring, and rubber steering and suspension parts and wash with soap and water. If coolant hoses have been contaminated with diesel fuel, they must be replaced.*

4. If no fuel is observed, the most likely cause is a restriction or air leak in fuel lines between fuel tank and injection pump, or possibly a clogged fuel filter. It is also possible that vehicle has run out of fuel regardless of fuel gauge readings. If vehicle has a semi-transparent plastic fuel pipe on the supply side of diesel injection pump, check for movement of fuel in the line.

NOTE—
A stream of tiny air bubbles moving in the line is normal (unlike previous versions of the diesel engine).

5. If fuel is observed, but engine still fails to start, consult **Table a**, given earlier, for additional troubleshooting checks.

NOTE—
It is not necessary to test for basic fuel delivery on the remaining three cylinders due to the way the TDI system operates.

6. When finished testing, tighten the fuel union nuts and check for leaks. Clean up any spilled fuel.

Tightening torque
- Fuel injector union nut to injector or pump . . . . 25 Nm (18 ft-lb)

7. Be sure to quality check your work, see **Quality Review** at the end of this repair group.

THROTTLE POSITION SENSOR

Fuel quantity is controlled by the Engine Control Module (ECM) in TDI equipped vehicles. There is no accelerator cable connection between the pedal and the engine. The throttle position sensor is part of the electronic accelerator. See Fig. 4. This system is described as electronic throttle control (EPC) in **2 General Information**.

Testing and adjustment of the throttle position sensor requires the use of a scan tool such as VAG 1551 or VAG 1552. Faults related to the throttle position sensor will be stored as diagnostic trouble codes (DTCs) in the ECM. If the fault is severe enough, the ECM will ignore the throttle position sensor completely and run the engine at a constant high idle speed. This should enable the driver to reach the nearest workshop.

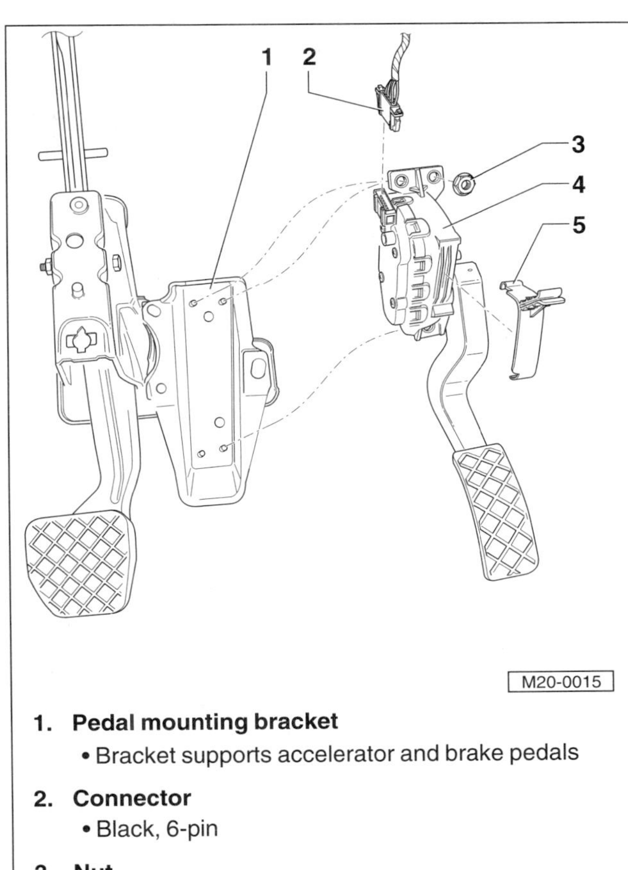

1. **Pedal mounting bracket**
   - Bracket supports accelerator and brake pedals
2. **Connector**
   - Black, 6-pin
3. **Nut**
   - Tighten to 10 Nm (7 ft-lb)
4. **Throttle Position Sensor (G79)**
5. **Bracket**
   - For cover in footwell
   - Clipped to throttle position sensor

M20-0015

Fig. 4. Throttle position sensor, pedal assembly and mounting hardware.

TOOTHED BELT - CAMSHAFT/INJECTION PUMP DRIVE

Any time the camshaft drive belt is removed or installed, camshaft and injection pump timing must be checked and adjusted as required. Special tools are required for setting drive belt tension, camshaft TDC position, and injection pump timing. In addition, a scan tool such as the VAG 1551 or VAG 1552 is required to properly set injection pump timing on this electronically controlled diesel injection system. Fig. 5. shows an exploded view of the camshaft/injection pump drive belt assembly on the 1.9L Turbo Direct Injection diesel engine. See **15b Cylinder Head and Valvetrain (1.9L Engine)** for toothed belt removal and installation.

Toothed belt - camshaft drive, assembly

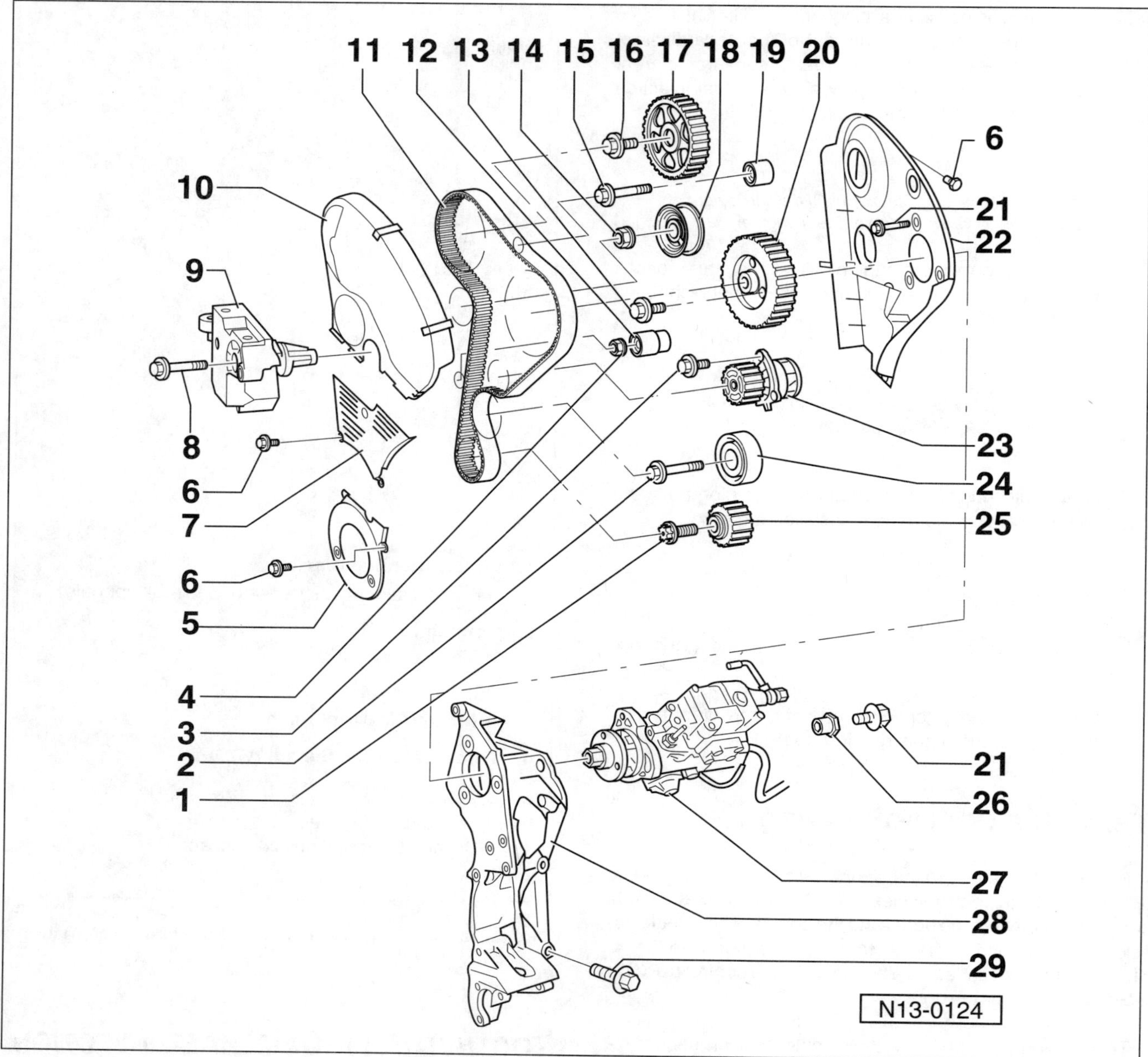

N13-0124

Fig. 5. Toothed belt for camshaft and injection pump drive and related components.

1. **Bolt**
   - Always replace
   - Tighten to 120 Nm (88 ft-lb) + ¼ turn (90°)
   - To loosen and tighten, counter hold with VW special tool 3099, or similar
   - Threads and shoulder must be free of oil and grease
2. **Bolt**
   - Always replace
   - Tighten to 40 Nm (30 ft-lb) + ¼ turn
3. **Bolt**
   - Tighten to 15 Nm (11 ft-lb)
4. **Bolt**
   - Tighten to 22 Nm (16 ft-lb)
5. **Toothed belt guard, lower section**
6. **Bolt**
   - Tighten to 10 Nm (7 ft-lb)

(continued from previous page)

7. **Toothed belt guard, center section**
8. **Bolt**
   - Tighten to 45 Nm (33 ft-lb)
9. **Right engine bracket**
10. **Toothed belt guard, upper section**
11. **Toothed belt**
    - Mark engine direction of rotation before removing
    - Check for wear
    - Do not kink
12. **Idler wheel**
13. **Bolt**
    - Always replace
    - Tighten to 20 Nm (15 ft-lb) + ¼ turn (90°)
14. **Nut**
    - Tighten to 20 Nm (15 ft-lb)
15. **Bolt**
    - Tighten to 20 Nm (15 ft-lb)
16. **Bolt**
    - Tighten to 45 Nm (33 ft-lb)
    - To loosen and tighten, counter hold with VW special tool 3036, or similar
17. **Camshaft sprocket**
    - Remove using T40001, or equivalent two-arm puller
18. **Tensioning roller**
    - Semi-automatic toothed belt tensioning roller
19. **Idler roller**
20. **Injection pump sprocket**
    - Two piece construction
21. **Bolt**
    - Tighten to 30 Nm (22 ft-lb)
22. **Toothed belt guard, rear**
23. **Coolant pump**
24. **Idler wheel pulley**
    - Must be removed before coolant pump
25. **Crankshaft toothed belt sprocket**
26. **Bushing**
27. **Diesel injection pump**
28. **Assembly bracket**
    - For diesel injection pump, generator and power steering pump
    - For A/C compressor if equipped
29. **Bolt**
    - Tighten to 45 Nm (33 ft-lb)

INJECTION PUMP

The diesel fuel injection pump is controlled by the ECM and performs three primary functions:

- It takes the fuel from the tank and pressurizes it to over 3000 psi.
- It precisely times the delivery of fuel to the injectors.
- It accurately meters the quantity of fuel delivered to the injectors.

The pump is driven by the same toothed drive belt that drives the camshaft at 1/2 crankshaft speed. Internal parts are lubricated and cooled by the diesel fuel. No routine maintenance is required or possible because no internal repair parts are available.

Because the Turbo Direct Injection system is fully electronic, the ECM can detect and store most faults associated with the injection pump. These faults are known as DTCs and are held in the ECM memory. Most DTCs will turn on the malfunction indicator light (MIL) and/or the glow plug light, alerting the driver to this condition. In addition, the ECM has diagnostic capabilities that allow an experienced technician with a scan tool to view certain operating parameters of the injection pump and other parts of the system. These must be investigated before a decision is made to replace an injection pump.

Fig. 6. shows the diesel injection pump with related components and mounting hardware.

> ***NOTE—***
> *Volkswagen identifies electrical components by a letter and/or a number in the electrical schematics. See* **97 Wiring Diagrams, Fuses and Relays**. *These electrical identifiers are listed as an aid to electrical troubleshooting.*

Injection pump assembly

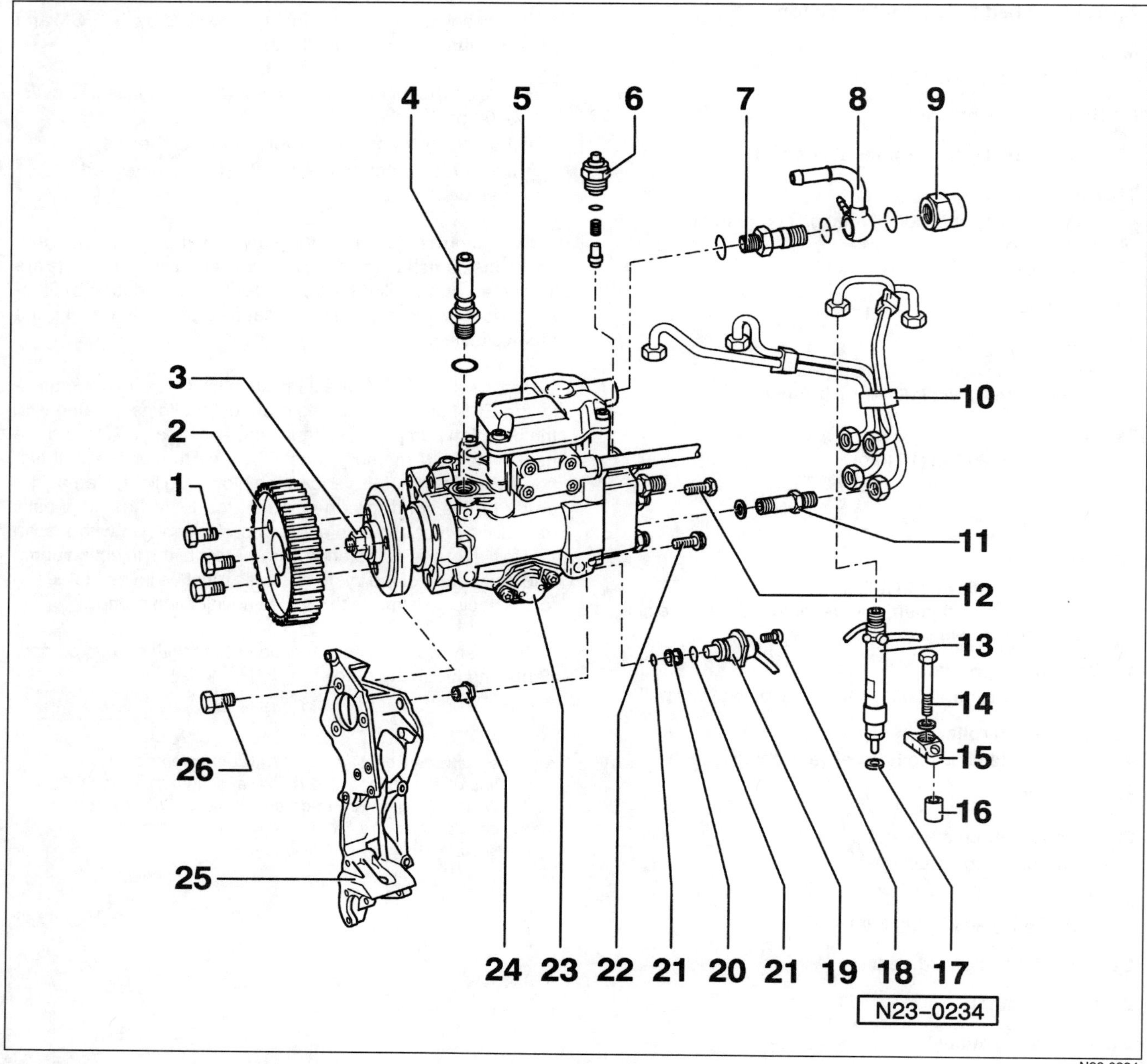

N23-0234

Fig. 6. Diesel injection pump with related fuel system components and mounting parts.

1. **Bolts**
   - Tighten to 20 Nm (15 ft-lb) plus ¼ turn (90°)
   - Always replace
2. **Injection pump sprocket**
3. **Injection pump sprocket nut**
   - Do not loosen for any reason!
4. **Union**
   - Supply line from fuel filter
   - Tighten to 25 Nm (18 ft-lb)
5. **Diesel injection pump**
   - With quantity adjuster (N146)
   - With modulating piston displacement sensor (G149)
   - With Fuel Temperature Sensor (G81)
6. **Fuel shut off valve (N109)**
   - Tighten to 25 Nm (18 ft-lb)
7. **Union**
   - Return line from diesel injection pump

(continued from previous page)

8. **Return line**
   - To control valve on fuel filter
9. **Cap nut**
   - Tighten to 25 Nm (18 ft-lb)
10. **Fuel injector lines**
    - Tighten to 25 Nm (18 ft-lb)
    - Always remove as a complete assembly
    - Do not bend, kink or alter shape
    - Remove and install with VW special tool 3035
11. **Union**
    - To injector lines
    - With check valve
    - Tighten to 45 Nm (33 ft-lb)
12. **Bolt**
    - Tighten to 25 Nm (18 ft-lb)
13. **Fuel injector**
    - Cylinder # 3 with needle lift sensor (G80)
14. **Bolt**
    - Tighten to 20 Nm (15 ft-lb)
15. **Injector retainer**
    - Use special washer only
16. **Injector retainer mounting**
    - Fits into machined hole in cylinder head
17. **Sealing washer**
    - Always replace
18. **Bolt**
    - Bolt
    - Tighten to 10 Nm (7 ft-lb)
19. **Cold Start Injector (N108)**
    - Controls start of injection (timing)
20. **Strainer**
    - Clean as necessary
21. **O-ring**
    - Always replace
22. **Bolt**
    - Tighten to 25 Nm (18 ft-lb)
23. **Timing control cover**
24. **Rear sleeve nut**
25. **Assembly bracket**
    - For injection pump, generator, power steering pump, A/C compressor
    - Shown for vehicles without A/C
26. **Bolt**
    - Tighten to 25 Nm (18 ft-lb)

Injection pump, removing

Removal of the injection pump requires partial removal of the toothed belt driving the camshaft and the injection pump. Special Volkswagen tools including scan tool VAG 1551 or VAG 1552 are required to remove and install the diesel injection pump and properly set it up.

1. Remove upper engine cover.
2. Remove connecting pipes between intercooler and intake hose.
3. Remove fuel supply and return lines at injector pump.

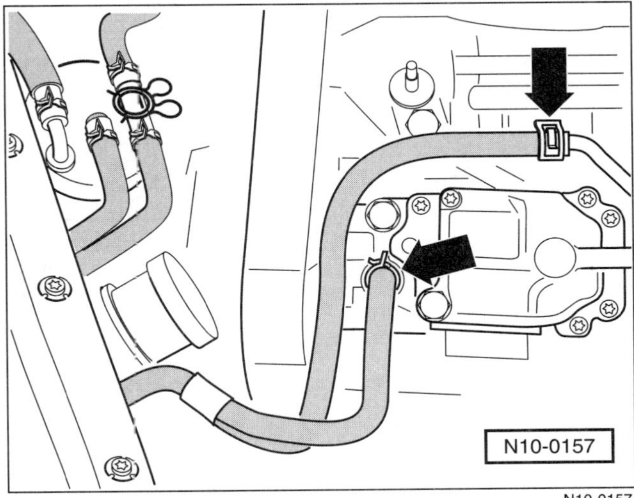

N10-0157

Fig. 7. Disconnect fuel supply (**lower arrow**) and return (**upper arrow**) lines.

4. Remove injector fuel lines as an assembly using a flair nut wrench as shown earlier. See Fig. 3.

> ***WARNING—***
> *Fuel will be expelled. Do not smoke or work near heaters or other fire hazards. Have a fire extinguisher handy.*

NOTE—
Cover all open fuel fittings with a clean cloth to prevent contamination.

5. Remove right side headlight, see **94 Lights, Accessories–Exterior**.
6. Remove connecting hose between intercooler and intake manifold, see **21 Turbocharger and Intercooler**.
7. Remove upper toothed belt guard.
8. Remove vacuum pump from end of cylinder head.
9. Remove cylinder head (valve) cover.

10. Set engine to top dead center (TDC), for cylinder #1 by turning crankshaft until timing mark on flywheel or torque converter aligns with mark on transmission case.
    - Manual transmission equipped vehicles: See Fig. 8.
    - Automatic transmission equipped vehicles: See Fig. 9.

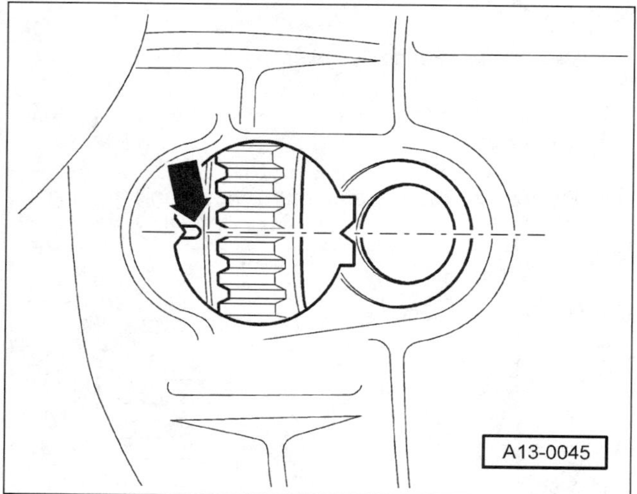

A23-0045

Fig. 8. TDC for manual transmissions: align mark on flywheel (**arrow**) with pointer on transmission case.

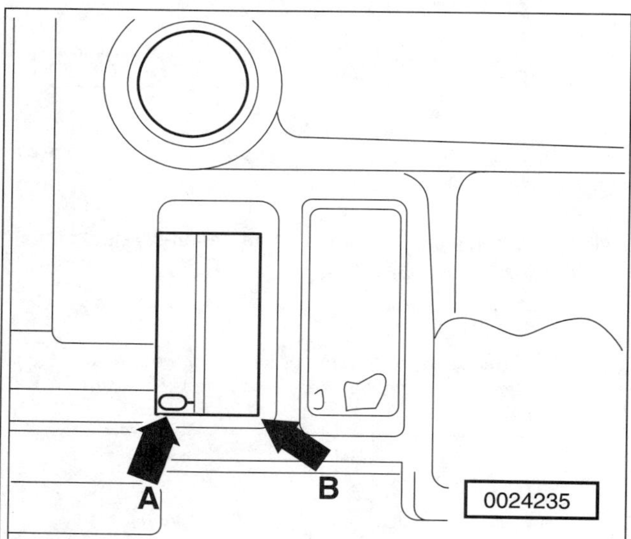

0024235

Fig. 9. TDC for automatic transmissions: align mark on torque converter (**A**) with lower edge of opening in transmission case (**B**).

11. Lock camshaft at TDC with a setting bar such as Volkswagen special tool 3418 and centralize using feeler gauges. See Fig. 10.

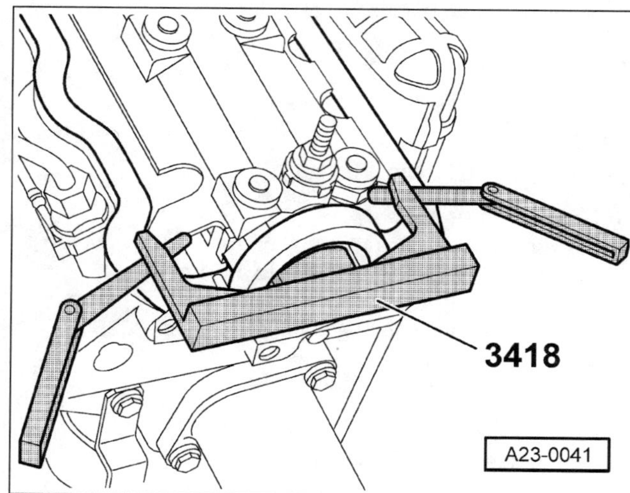

A23-0041

Fig. 10. Volkswagen special tool 3418 shown in position on the vacuum pump end of the camshaft locking it at TDC. Equal thicknesses of feeler gauges are placed under the ends of the tool to ensure exact camshaft TDC.

12. Lock injection pump sprocket with VW special tool 3359 locking pin. Remove injection pump sprocket mounting bolts. See Fig. 11.

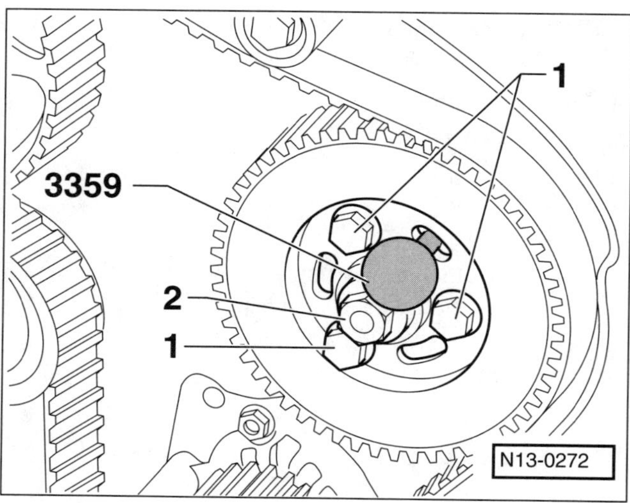

N13-0272

Fig. 11. Lock injection pump sprocket using 3359 locking pin. Remove injection pump sprocket bolts (1), Do not remove hub nut (2).

> ***CAUTION—***
> *Do not loosen the center sprocket nut for any reason. Loosening this nut will allow the sprocket to move on the shaft resulting in altered basic settings which CANNOT be reset with normal workshop equipment.*

13. Release the tensioning roller and slip toothed belt off the camshaft sprocket.

14. Loosen camshaft sprocket mounting bolt about 1 turn while counter-holding camshaft sprocket. See Fig. 12.

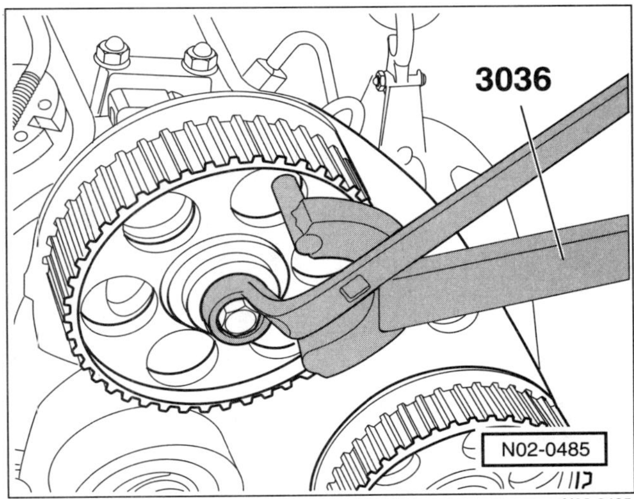

Fig. 12. VW special tool 3036 being used to counter-hold camshaft sprocket while loosening mounting bolt.

> ***CAUTION—***
> *Do not use 3418 setting bar by itself to lock camshaft when loosening camshaft sprocket bolt. Hold camshaft sprocket using 3036 retainer, or equivalent. Possible damage to the camshaft could result if only the setting bar is used to lock camshaft.*

NOTE—
The camshaft end is tapered. Loosening the sprocket will allow the camshaft sprocket to rotate independently of the camshaft. There may be a keyway cut into the end of the camshaft. However, there is no matching keyway cut into the sprocket nor is there a Woodruff key.

15. Release camshaft sprocket from camshaft with two-arm puller. See Fig. 13.

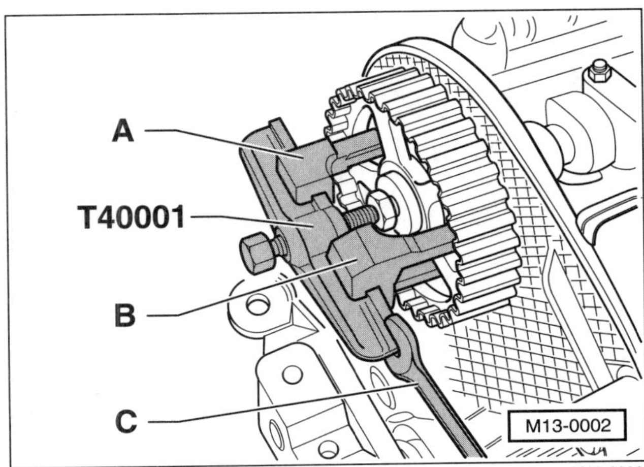

Fig. 13. Release camshaft sprocket with two-arm puller (VW special tool #T40001 shown). Center arms (**A** and **B**) in camshaft sprocket and counter-hold puller using open-end wrench (**C**).

NOTE—
Tapping the camshaft sprocket lightly with a soft mallet may help release the sprocket from the tapered end of the camshaft.

16. Remove camshaft sprocket mounting bolt and sprocket.

17. Disconnect the harness connector for the diesel pump electronics and unclip the connector from the retaining bracket. See Fig. 14.

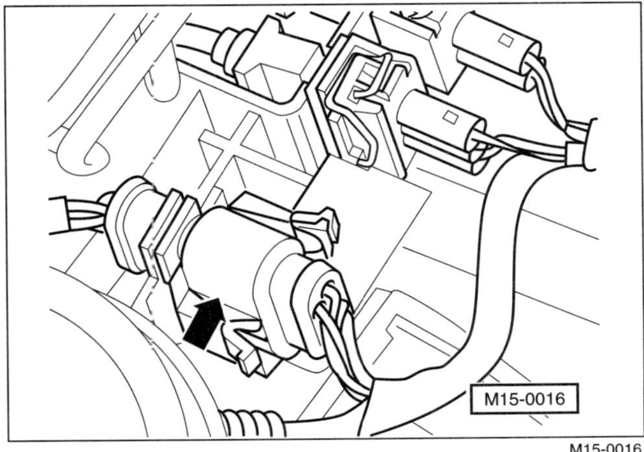

Fig. 14. Harness connector (**arrow**) for diesel pump electronics.

18. Remove front injection pump mounting bolts from assembly bracket. See Fig. 15.

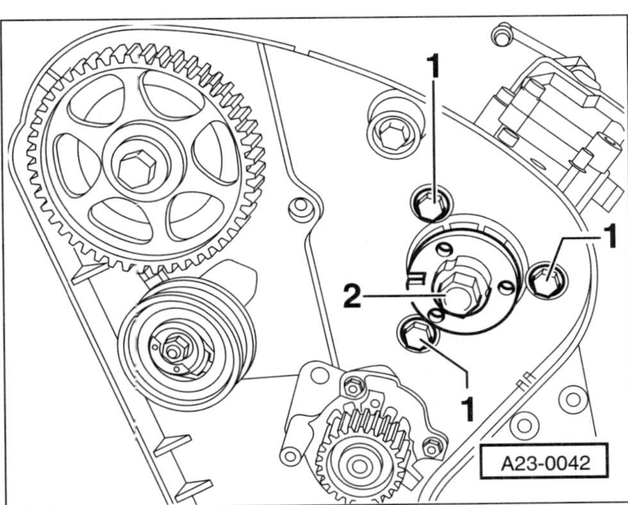

Fig. 15. Front injection pump mounting bolts (**1**). Do not loosen center sprocket nut (**2**).

19. Remove rear injection pump mounting bolt from support bracket. See Fig. 16.

20. Carefully slide pump shaft out of assembly bracket and lift pump out.

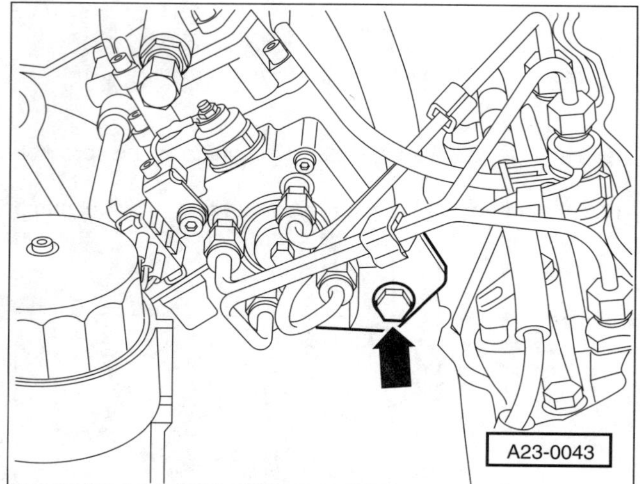

A23-0043

Fig. 16. Rear injection pump mounting bolt (**arrow**) threaded into rear sleeve nut (not visible).

21. If pump will not be immediately reinstalled, take steps to insure that no dirt can get into any of pump openings or injector unions. Store pump so that diesel fuel in the pump will not drain out.

22. Be sure to quality check your work, see **Quality Review** at the end of this repair group.

Injection pump, installing

Before installing a new injection pump or if reusing the original, remove all packaging materials and plugs sealing port openings.

1. Install injection pump into assembly bracket and hand tighten rear injection pump mounting bolt. See Fig. 16.

2. Position pump in assembly bracket. Install and torque front injection pump mounting bolts and torque rear injection pump mounting bolt.

Tightening torque

- Injection pump bolts, front (M8) . . . . . 25 Nm (18 ft-lb)
- Injection pump bolt, rear (M8) . . . . . . 25 Nm (18 ft-lb)

3. Install new bolts into injection pump sprocket and mount sprocket to injection pump hub. Hand tighten only at this time.

4. Position pump sprocket so that bolts are in the middle of the elongated holes

5. Lock injection pump sprocket using Volkswagen special tool 3359. See Fig. 17.

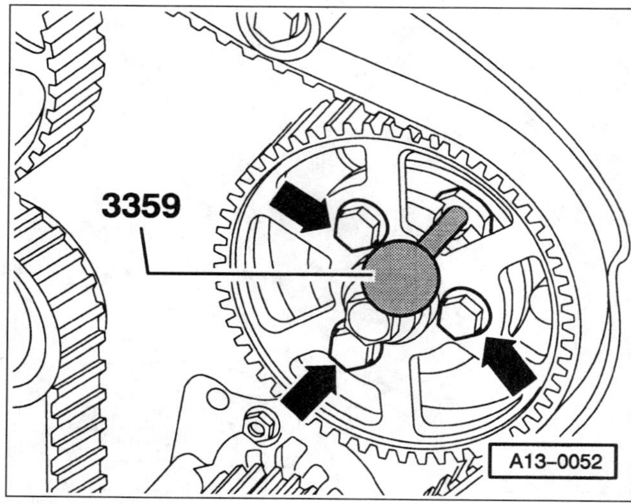

A13-0052

Fig. 17. Injection pump sprocket installed with new bolts (**arrows**) and secured with locking pin 3359.

6. Ensure that crankshaft is at TDC for cylinder #1 as shown earlier. See Fig. 8. See Fig. 9.

7. Ensure that camshaft is locked in position as shown earlier. See Fig. 10.

8. Place toothed belt onto injection pump sprocket and tensioning roller and thread under idler roller. Be sure tensioning roller retaining hook is correctly seated in hole in toothed belt guard and cylinder head. See Fig. 18.

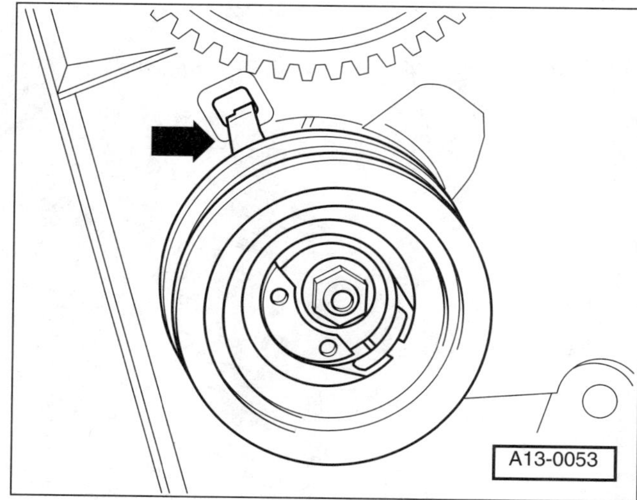

A13-0053

Fig. 18. Tensioning roller retaining lug (**arrow**) shown in proper position through toothed belt guard and into hole in cylinder head.

9. Place camshaft sprocket into toothed belt and slide sprocket onto camshaft. Thread sprocket mounting bolt loosely into camshaft but leave it sufficiently loose to allow sprocket to move.

10. Tension toothed belt using a two-pin spanner in the center holes of the eccentric belt tensioner. Belt is tensioned properly when notch and raised mark are aligned. See Fig. 19.

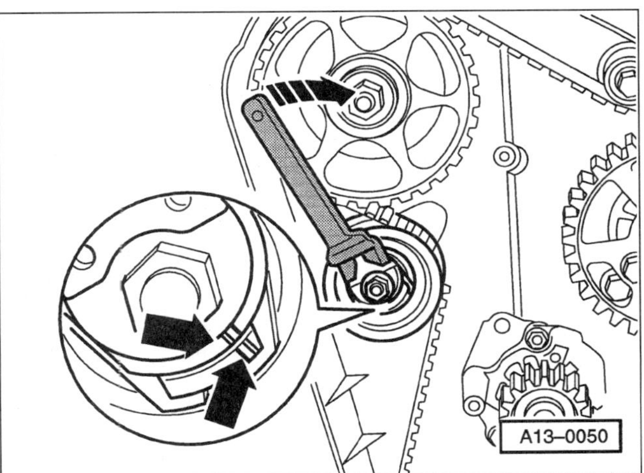

A13-0050

Fig. 19. Two-pin spanner wrench shown in position to tension toothed belt. Adjustment is correct when notch and raised mark align (**inset, arrow**).

> ***NOTE—***
> *On cars equipped with automatic transmissions, a hex wrench is used in the tensioner instead of the two-pin spanner wrench, as shown in Fig. 19.*

11. Tighten lock nut on tensioner while maintaining belt tension.

Tightening torque
- Toothed belt tensioner (M8) . . . . 20 Nm (15 ft-lb)

12. Ensure that crankshaft is still at TDC.
13. Tighten new injection pump sprocket mounting bolts to **stage I** specification only.

> ***NOTE—***
> - *Tighten the new injection pump sprocket mounting bolts to stage I only at this time. Final torque (stage II) will be done after timing has been dynamically checked/adjusted.*
> - *Injection pump sprocket mounting bolts must only be used one time, since by design, they have a reduced shank and are stretch bolts.*

Tightening torque
- Injection pump sprocket bolt - always replace
  - **stage I** . . . . 20 Nm (15 ft-lb)
  - **stage II** . . . . additional ¼ turn (90°)
- Camshaft sprocket bolt . . . . 45 Nm (33 ft-lb)

14. Tighten camshaft sprocket mounting bolt while counter-holding sprocket as shown earlier in Fig. 12.
15. Remove setting bar and feeler gauges from camshaft.
16. Remove locking pin from injection pump sprocket.
17. Turn crankshaft two rotations in the running direction and recheck toothed belt tension.
18. Connect harness connector for diesel pump electronics and slip connector into retaining bracket.
19. Install cylinder head (valve) cover.
20. Install vacuum pump.
21. Install injector fuel line assembly.
22. Install fuel supply line and draw fuel into injection pump with a hand operated vacuum pump. See Fig. 20.

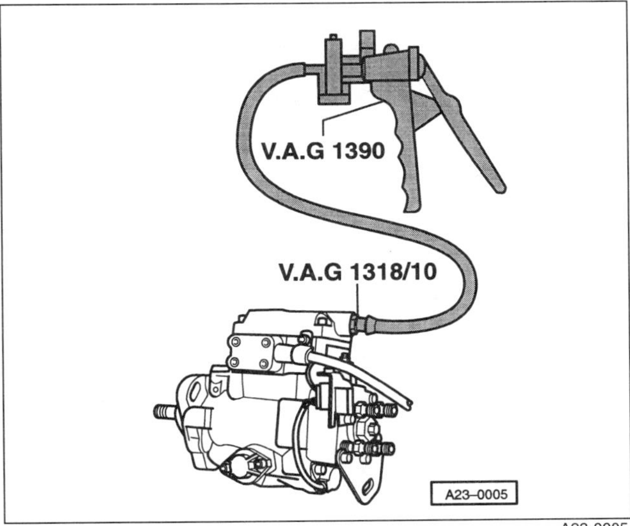

A23-0005

Fig. 20. Plastic hand operated vacuum pump shown connected to diesel injection pump with clear tubing at fuel return port.

> ***CAUTION—***
> *Do not attempt to start engine with a dry diesel injection pump, severe damage can result. Always ensure that pump is full of fuel before cranking engine.*

> ***NOTE—***
> *Do not draw diesel fuel into hand operated vacuum pump made of plastic!*

23. Install fuel return line.
24. Dynamically check diesel injection pump timing as given later in this section.

Injection pump timing, checking and adjusting

Diesel injection pump timing must be set using Volkswagen scan tool VAG 1551, VAG 1552, or equivalent in a mode known as Basic Setting. Injection pump timing is correlated to several factors, including fuel temperature. Failure to properly set injection pump timing will result in hard starting, poor performance, poor fuel economy, excessive noise, smoking and increased emissions. The vehicle may not be drivable.

If timing adjustment is necessary, special adjustment tools and new pump sprocket mounting bolts are required.

The following instructions assume that the individual technician already has a good working knowledge of the operation and use of the VAG 1551 or VAG 1552 scan tool.

1. Connect scan tool to vehicle Data Link Connector (DLC) located in lower left side of the dash panel. The scan tool will be powered up when plugged into the DLC.

2. Start the engine and let it idle.

3. Observe the following sequence in the scan tool display window:

   - 1 – Rapid Data
   - Address Word 01 – Engine Electronics
   - Function 04 – Basic Settings
   - Display Group – 000
   - The display will show 10 fields (groups) of information. See Fig. 21.

System in Basic Setting 000
XX 53 XX XX XX XX XX XX 90 XX

0024190

Fig. 21. Typical VAG 1551/1552 display shows 90 in field 9 and 53 in field 2.

NOTE—
Data is only available in the format shown in Fig. 19 through use of scan tool VAG 1551 or VAG 1552. Scan tools from other manufacturers may provide the same data, but in a different format.

4. Use the graph to find timing value. See Fig. 22. Observe the number in field 9 on the scan tool display. This is a fuel temperature value and is assigned **B** in the table. The timing value must fall within shaded area of the table and is assigned the value **A**. If value is within shaded area, no adjustment is needed. When value is obtained, shut off engine.

   - If this procedure was done for diagnosis purposes, and timing value is within specification, remove scan tool.
   - If this procedure was done as part of injection pump removal and installation, and timing value is not within specification, continue procedure steps.

Example:

- This example assumes the engine is running. Note that the fuel temperature value in the scan tool display window, field 9, is 90. This is value **B**. Look on the table along the B axis until you see 90. Follow the line from 90 up into the shaded area. The shaded area is the range of timing values. Find the center of the shaded area and look to the left for the value on the **A** axis. In this case it is 53. Adjust the pump until the value in the scan tool display field 2 reads 53.

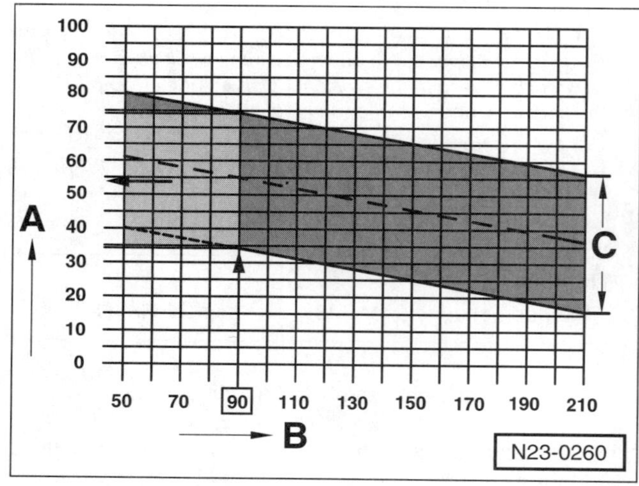

N23-0260

Fig. 22. Graph showing relationship between fuel temperature value **B** and start of injection timing **A**.

5. If timing adjustment is required, access injection pump sprocket. See **Injection pump, removing** given earlier for appropriate steps.

6. Loosen two of the injection pump sprocket mounting bolts. See Fig. 23.

NOTE—
It is permissible to counterhold the pump shaft during loosening (only) using a 22 mm wrench on the center nut. Under no circumstances should the center nut be loosened or used as a counterholder during tightening sequences.

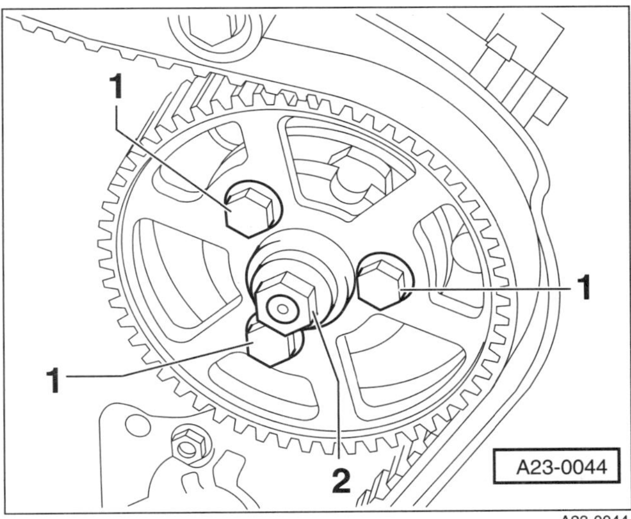

Fig. 23. Remove injection pump sprocket mounting bolts (**1**). Do not loosen center sprocket nut (**2**). Early version sprocket shown, later version is similar.

> ***CAUTION—***
>
> *Do not loosen the center sprocket nut for any reason. Loosening this nut will allow the sprocket to move on the shaft resulting in altered basic settings which CANNOT be reset with normal workshop equipment.*

7. Loosen the third injection pump sprocket mounting bolt only enough to allow movement of the sprocket on the hub. Using a 22mm wrench on the center sprocket nut, move the injection pump shaft to adjust timing. See Fig. 24.

Fig. 24. Injection pump sprocket shown with one mounting bolt removed (**arrow**). Elongated slot for bolt allows sprocket position to vary on the hub.

Specification

- Advance timing (start of injection) . . . . move pump shaft to right (clockwise)
- Retard timing (start of injection) . . . . move pump shaft to left (counter-clockwise)

---

8. Tighten injection pump sprocket bolts to **stage I** specification only, start engine and recheck injection timing value as given earlier using a scan tool. Repeat procedure as necessary to obtain correct injection timing value.

Tightening torque

- Injection pump sprocket bolt - always replace
  - **stage I** . . . . 20 Nm (15 ft-lb)
  - **stage II** . . . . additional ¼ turn (90°)

---

9. When a satisfactory timing value is obtained, remove and replace 3 pump sprocket mounting bolts with new bolts, one at a time. See Fig. 24.

> ***NOTE—***
>
> *If bolts were already replaced as part of injection pump installation and/or replacement, it is not necessary to install new bolts as described in the above step.*

10. Lock injection pump sprocket. See Fig. 25. Tighten all injection pump sprocket mounting bolts to stage I value if not previously done. Tighten injection pump sprocket mounting bolts to **stage II** specification.

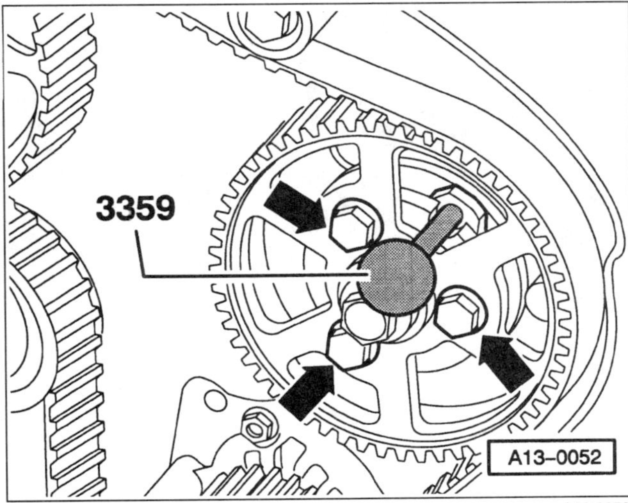

Fig. 25. Injection pump sprocket installed with new bolts (**arrows**) and secured with locking pin 3359.

11. With scan tool still connected, check for any Diagnostic Trouble Codes (DTCs) that may have been set. Repair and erase as required.

12. Disconnect scan tool.

13. Install all remaining fasteners, fuel lines, electrical connectors and components that were removed.

14. Verify that all fuel lines are secure and that there are no leaks.

15. Install upper sound absorber panel.

16. Be sure to quality check your work, see **Quality Review** at the end of this repair group.

ENGINE CONTROL MODULE

Diesel engine management is controlled by an Engine Control Module (ECM). The ECM is located in the air plenum near the base of the windshield in the engine compartment. Access to the ECM requires removal of the windshield wiper arms and the air plenum cover. See Fig. 26.

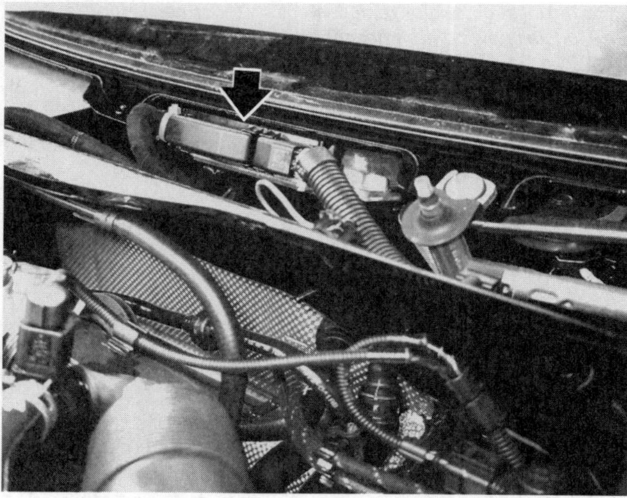

0024273

Fig. 26. Engine Control Module (**arrow**) in the center of the plenum. Motronic ECM shown, TDI ECM is similar.

Engine control module coding

The Engine Control Module must "know" what equipment is installed in the vehicle. This process is known as coding and must be performed whenever the ECM is replaced, as new ECMs are un-coded. If the ECM is moved between vehicles such as might be the case for diagnostic testing, the coding will need to be changed if equipment is different. Coding memory is, however, retained when the battery is disconnected. If a new ECM is installed without being coded, the engine will usually run poorly and the automatic transmission and anti-lock braking system (if equipped) will not function properly. The MIL will be illuminated.

This coding process can only be done with Volkswagen scan tool VAG 1551/1552 or equivalent. The appropriate code is electronically programmed into the ECM according to instructions provided by the scan tool manufacturer. See **Table b**.

Table b. ECM Coding

Coding	Vehicle and Equipment
00001	Golf, Jetta with Automatic Transmission and ABS
00002	Golf, Jetta with Manual Transmission and ABS

Readiness code, checking

Legislation requires that all auto manufacturers build into their engine management systems the ability to check for proper operation of up to 8 functions. These functions are known collectively as the readiness code. For the TDI system on the 1.9L engine, only the exhaust gas recirculation system code is relevant. Most of the time, the readiness code will set itself after the appropriate conditions have been met. These may include a cold or a hot start, operation at a certain load or speed for a certain period of time, or operation at different temperatures. After repairs, it may be advantageous to verify component operation. Setting the readiness code rather than waiting to see if it sets on it's own can confirm a proper repair. The setting procedure is simple and requires the scan tool VAG 1551/1552 to confirm the setting.

1. Connect the scan tool to the vehicle Data Link Connector (DLC) located in the lower left side of the dash panel. The scan tool will be powered up when plugged into the DLC. Start the engine and let it idle. Observe the following sequence in the scan tool display window:
   - 1 – Rapid Data
   - Address Word 01– Engine Electronics
   - Function 08–Measure Value Blocks
   - Display Group 017
   - The display will show four fields of information

> ***CAUTION—***
> *These instructions assume that the technician already has a good working knowledge of the operation and use of the VAG 1551 or VAG 1552 scan tool.*

2. Fig. 27. shows information as it appears on scan tool screen. Disregard information shown as the letter x. These x spaces will have either a 1 or a 0 and do not affect this procedure. The readiness code is the 8 digit number in fields 2 and 4. If scan tool screen displays ones in the indicated fields as shown here, readiness code is not set.

Read Measuring Value Block			17
xxxxxxxx	x111xxxx	xxxxxxxx	1xxxxxxx

0024262

Fig. 27. Display that shows that readiness code is not set.

3. If the scan tool screen displays zeros in the indicated fields, readiness code is set and no further action is required. See Fig. 28.

Read Measuring Value Block			17
xxxxxxxx	x000xxxx	xxxxxxxx	0xxxxxxx

0024263

Fig. 28. Display that shows that readiness code is set and no further action is required.

4. If the readiness code is set, disconnect the scan tool.

5. If readiness code is not set, unplug scan tool and proceed as follows.

Readiness code, setting

1. Start engine and allow to idle for at least 35 seconds.
   - Engine temperature must be over 10° C (50°F)
   - Engine must remain running during test sequence unless directed otherwise.
   - Adhere to test sequence and do not interrupt it.

2. Road test vehicle. When conditions allow, accelerate to 2,000 rpm as indicated on the tachometer.

> ***CAUTION—***
> *Observe all applicable traffic and safety laws while road testing to this procedure. Accelerate only where conditions are appropriate.*

3. At 2,000 rpm, accelerate to wide open throttle (WOT) in 3rd gear for 5 seconds, and allow engine speed to return to 2,200 rpm.

4. At 2,200 rpm, accelerate to WOT in 2nd or 3rd gear for 8 seconds and allow engine to return to idle.

5. When conditions permit, switch off engine, wait at least 10 seconds. Repeat steps 1 through 4.

6. Check readiness code as previously described.
   - If the scan tool screen displays zeros in the indicated fields, readiness code is set and no further action is required. See Fig. 28.
   - If the scan tool screen displays ones in the indicated fields, readiness code is not set. Unplug scan tool and repeat from step 1. If the code does not set after a second attempt, it is likely that there is a malfunction in the system. Consult scan tool directions for additional information on checking for DTCs.

INTAKE MANIFOLD CHANGE-OVER VALVE

The intake manifold change-over valve is a flap valve that closes for approximately 3 seconds when the engine stops, blocking the air to the engine. This reduces the suddenness of the diesel engine shut-down. The valve re-opens once the engine has stopped. See Fig. 29.

Intake manifold change-over valve, assembly

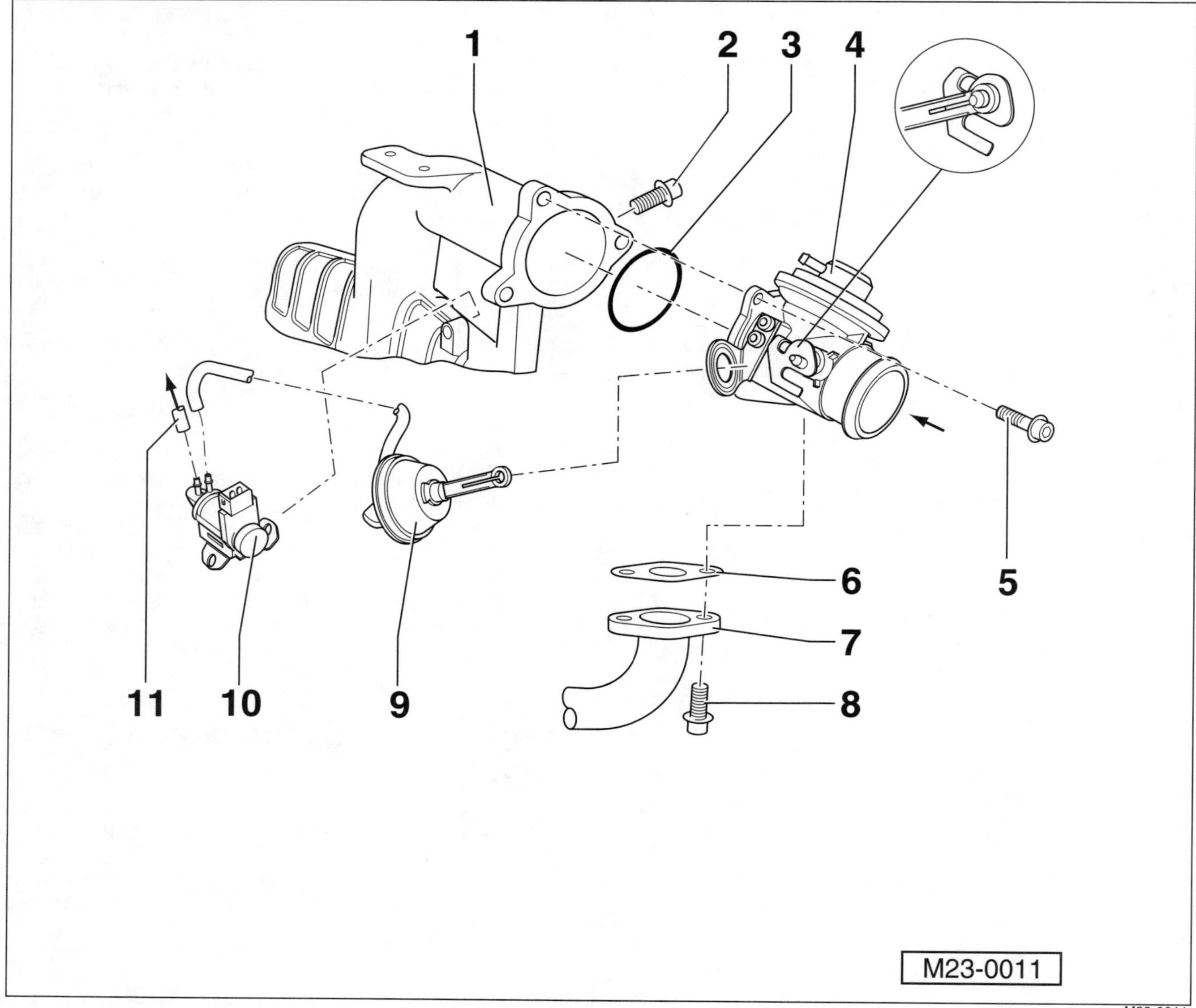

Fig. 29. Intake manifold change-over valve with EGR valve and related components.

1. **Intake manifold**
2. **Bolt**
   - Tighten to 10 Nm (7 ft-lb)
3. **O-ring**
   - Always replace
4. **Connecting flange**
   - With EGR valve
   - With intake manifold change-over valve
   - Check change-over mechanism for intake manifold flap for ease of movement and function
5. **Bolt**
   - Tighten to 10 Nm (7 ft-lb)
6. **Gasket**
   - Always replace
7. **Connecting pipe**
   - From EGR cooler
8. **Bolt**
   - Tighten to 25 Nm (18 ft-lb)
9. **Vacuum servo**
10. **Intake manifold change-over vacuum control valve**
11. **Vacuum supply**
    - From vacuum source

FUEL INJECTORS

The 1.9L TDI diesel engine uses a two-spring injector that enables the fuel to be injected in two stages for "softer" combustion. In addition, the injectors are a 5-hole design that spray fuel from 5 ports in a more lateral direction rather than in a single conical pattern. Injector opening pressures are approximately 220 to 230 bar (3190-3335 psi). All 4 injectors are functionally the same. However, injector for cylinder #3 carries the needle lift sensor (G80). This injector must always be installed in cylinder #3 to prevent erroneous DTCs or performance problems from occurring.

The signs of injector trouble usually appear as misfiring and knocking noises from one or more cylinders, engine overheating, loss of power, smoky black exhaust, and excessive blue smoke during cold starting.

> ***CAUTION—***
> *When working on the injectors, everything must be kept absolutely clean. Clean all pipe unions before disconnecting.*

Fuel injectors, checking

A defective injector (or a weak cylinder) can often be identified by simply "turning it off". This can be done by relieving the fuel pressure so that the injector can not open and inject fuel into the cylinder. Idle speed may not substantially change, however, because the ECM will often be able to compensate for the weak cylinder.

1. Clean area around fuel unions where the fuel pipes meet the injectors.

2. Start engine and let it run at idle.

3. Wrap a cloth around the union nut for cylinder #1 fuel injector at the injector. Slightly loosen the nut. Cylinder #1 is closest to the drive belt. See Fig. 30.
   - If a particular cylinder is defective, the noise or smoke will cease when union nut is loosened.
   - If the problem was roughness, the roughness will be affected very little or not at all because that cylinder was already malfunctioning. Tighten the union nut.

> ***WARNING—***
> - *Loosen the nut only about one half turn to limit the amount of fuel leakage. The fuel injection system operates at very high pressures. Keep hands and eyes clear. Wear heavy duty gloves and eye protection. Wrap a cloth around the nut when loosening. Fuel will be expelled.*
> - *Do not smoke or work near heaters or other fire hazards.*
> - *Have a fire extinguisher handy.*

4. Repeat procedure for other suspected cylinders.

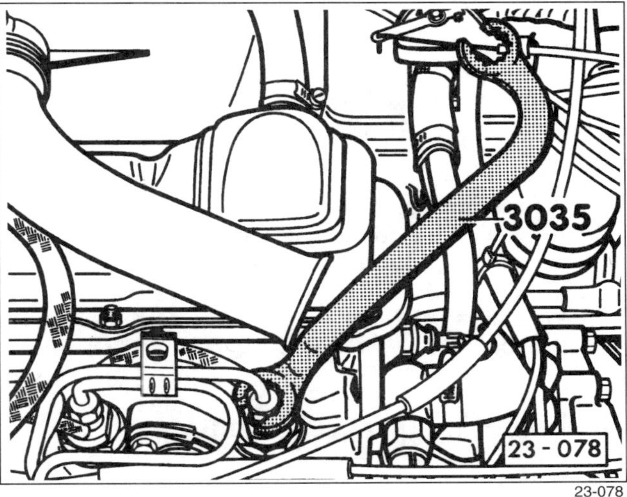

23-078

Fig. 30. Flare-nut wrench (Volkswagen special tool 3035) being used to loosen injector union nut for cylinder 4 on an earlier version diesel engine. The same tool is used on 1.9L diesel engines.

5. When finished, verify that all fuel lines are secure and that there are no fuel leaks. Thoroughly clean any spilled fuel.

> ***CAUTION—***
> *Diesel fuel is damaging to rubber. Wipe off any fuel that spills on hoses, wiring, and rubber steering and suspension parts and wash with soap and water. If coolant hoses are contaminated with diesel fuel, they must be replaced.*

Fuel injectors, replacing

1. Unscrew fuel pipe union nuts at injection pump and injectors. Remove injector fuel pipes as one assembly taking care not to bend them.

2. Remove fuel return hoses from between injectors.

3. Unplug harness connector for the needle lift sensor (G80) on the injector for cylinder #3.

4. Loosen and remove bolt, special washer and hold down clamp for each injector. Lift out injectors.

5. Remove small copper sealing washer from tip of injector or from injector port in head. Discard.

   NOTE—
   The crush-type sealing washers must always be replaced to prevent compression leaks.

6. Install injector with a new copper sealing washer and torque the bolt to specification.

Tightening torque
- Injector line union . . . . 25 Nm (18 ft-lb)
- Injector clamp mounting bolt (M8) . . . 20 Nm (15 ft-lb)

7. Install metal fuel pipes and fuel return hoses. Due to the higher pressures involved, injectors will seldom need to have air bleed from them. Reconnect harness connector to needle lift sensor.

8. When finished, verify that all fuel lines are secure and that there are no fuel leaks.

Fuel injectors, pressure testing

1. Remove injector as described previously.

2. Install fuel injector on pressure tester according to manufacturer's directions. Place a suitable container under injector to catch the spray. See Fig. 31.

> ***WARNING —***
> *When testing fuel injectors, make sure that the high pressure discharge does not contact the hands or any other bare skin. The high pressure spray can be injected directly into the skin causing severe injuries or health complications. Always wear eye protection!*

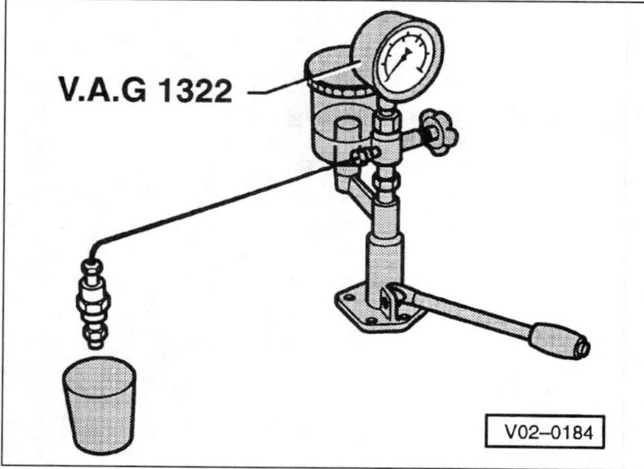

V02-0184

Fig. 31. Injector installed on hand pressure pump. Volkswagen special tool VAG 1322 shown. This tester is designed to work best with mineral spirits. Older version US1111 will also work with suitable fittings.

3. Pump lever to increase pressure. Read opening pressure when spray begins.

Injector Opening Pressure
- New . . . . 220–230 bar (3190–3335 psi)
- Wear limit . . . . 200 bar (2900 psi)

4. Spray should discharge evenly from all 5 ports. See Fig. 32.

> ***WARNING —***
> *Fire hazard! No smoking! Do not have anything in the area that can ignite the spray discharged by the injectors. This includes overhead heating units and hidden sources such as water heaters with standing pilot lights.*

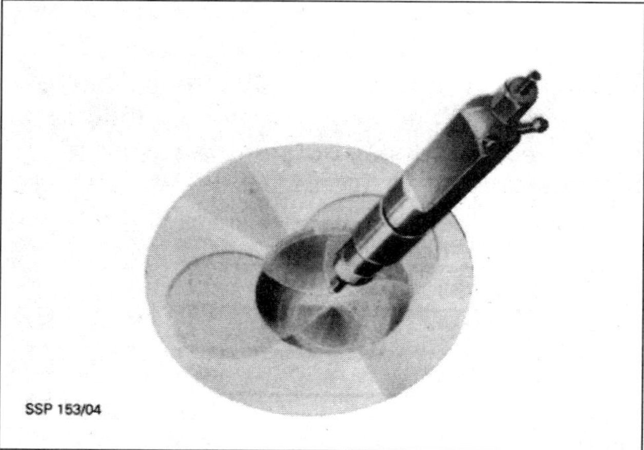

SSP153/04

Fig. 32. TDI fuel injector spray pattern discharging from all 5 ports.

5. Pump lever slowly to a pressure of approximately 150 bar (2175 psi) for 10 seconds. Check for leaks from injector tip. No fuel should leak.

6. If any injector fails to meet opening pressure or leak specifications, it should be replaced. No repairs are possible to the fuel injectors.

QUALITY REVIEW

When you have finished working under the hood and around other areas of the vehicle, it is advisable to take a moment to quality check or review your work. This helps to insure that the operation or repair has been completed properly with all affected systems functioning within normal parameters. These may include the following:

- Make sure that there are no air, fuel, or vacuum leaks.
- Be sure to wipe up any diesel fuel spills, using soap and water as necessary, especially on any rubber or painted surfaces.
- Make sure that all components involved in the repair are positioned correctly and function properly.
- Make sure all tools and shop cloths are removed.
- Road test vehicle to confirm proper engine operation.

24a Fuel Injection–Motronic (1.8L engine)

TABLE

24a

GENERAL

This repair group covers the fuel injection/engine management system for the 1.8 liter turbo gasoline engine. The operation of the Bosch Motronic ME7.5 engine management system is described in **2a Fuel, Ignition and Exhaust Systems.**

Special testing equipment may be necessary for some of the tests and repair procedures given here.

NOTE —

- *1.8L engines are equipped with the Bosch Motronic ME7.5 engine management system which is OBD II compliant. It is recommended that fault diagnosis and troubleshooting be carried out using Volkswagen scan tools VAG 1551, VAG 1552, VAS 5051 or equivalent.*
- *Fuel pump and fuel tank testing and repair along with EVAP information is covered in* **20 Fuel Storage and Supply**.
- *Ignition system testing and repair is covered in* **28a Ignition System–Gasoline.**
- *Related systems such as Exhaust Gas Recirculation (EGR) and catalytic converters are covered in* **26 Exhaust System and Emission Controls**.

The Motronic ME7.5 system combines ignition, fuel injection and electronic accelerator pedal functions into one system managed by a single Engine Control Module (ECM). The system is fully adaptive and features built-in diagnostics that are capable of detecting and storing coded fault information. There are no basic adjustments or settings that can be made to the system without specialized equipment.

CAUTION —

Disconnecting the negative (–) battery cable may erase fault codes and basic settings in the engine management and automatic transmission control modules. Some driveability problems may be noticed until the system re-adapts to operating conditions. OBD II readiness codes, which may be required for emissions testing, may also be erased. Convenience electronics (alarm system, interior light control, power locks, mirrors, and windows) may need to be re-set using a VAG 1551, VAG 1552, VAS 5051 or equivalent scan tool.

Safety precautions

The following warnings and cautions should be adhered to whenever working on the engine management system.

WARNING —

- *Fuel may be discharged during fuel system repairs. Do not smoke or work near heaters or other fire hazards. Have a fire extinguisher handy. Work only in a well-ventilated area.*
- *Wear suitable hand and eye protection when working with gasoline. Prolonged contact with fuel can cause illness and skin disorders.*
- *Fuel hoses in engine compartment must only be secured with spring-type clips. The use of clamp or screw-type clips will damage fuel lines and cause fuel leaks.*

CAUTION —

- *Connect and disconnect wires and test equipment only with the ignition switched off.*
- *Before making any electrical tests that require the engine to be cranked using the starter, disable the ignition system as described in* **28a Ignition System–Gasoline.**
- *Do not use sealants containing silicones. Particles of silicone drawn into the engine will not be burned in the engine and will damage the heated oxygen sensor. Use only sealants and engine chemicals marked as safe for oxygen sensors.*
- *During testing, it is possible for the Engine Control Module to recognize and store a diagnostic trouble code (DTC) that was due solely to the testing procedure. Therefore, after completing repairs, the DTC memory must be checked and erased as necessary with a scan tool such as VAG 1551, VAG 1552, VAS 5051 or equivalent*
- *Cleanliness is essential when working on the fuel system. Thoroughly clean fuel line connections and surrounding areas before loosening. Avoid the use of compressed air. Avoid moving the vehicle. Only install clean components.*

ON BOARD DIAGNOSTICS (OBD)

On Board Diagnostics, found on the Bosch Motronic ME7.5 Engine Management Systems monitor most aspects of engine operation. The current generation OBD II is integrated into all Volkswagen New Beetle gasoline engines. For a description of the system and an overview of operation, see **2a Fuel, Ignition, and Exhaust Systems.**

Because of the large number of operating parameters monitored and the vast quantity of data available, fault diagnosis can only be properly carried out using a suitable scan tool such as Volkswagen special tools VAG 1551, VAG 1552 or VAS 5051 or equivalent. The engine control module or ECM also supports certain limited functions in a government-mandated generic scan tool mode. These functions are standardized for all OBD II compliant vehicles, but are not as comprehensive as those found by using the VAG 1551/1552 or VAS 5051 in the proprietary mode of operation.

During repairs where the battery must be disconnected, consideration must be given to the effect that this will have on the vehicle in general and the engine management system in particular.

- Diagnostic Trouble Codes may be erased.
- Readiness codes may be erased.
- Fault counters that monitor certain functions will be reset to zero.
- Adaptive leaning values will be set to default.

Because the ignition, fuel injection, accelerator system and emission control functions are even more inter-related than on previous Motronic versions, it is difficult, if not impossible to isolate general driveability problems by examining individual components of the system. For this reason, a suitable scan tool must be used for diagnosis if driveability problems occur or if the malfunction indicator light (MIL) or E-Gas System lights (EPC) are illuminated. Access for the scan tool is through the Data Link Connector (DLC) under the lower left side of the instrument panel. See Fig. 1.

Fig. 1. Data Link Connector (DLC), (**arrow**) under left lower side of instrument panel.

Adaptation

The Motronic ME7.5.1 engine management system is adaptive. Idle speed, ignition timing, injection timing and quantity automatically compensate and adapt to changes in the engine due to wear and operating conditions. Minor problems such as mixture changes due to small vacuum leaks can be eliminated. As a result, idle speed, fuel mixture (CO%) and ignition timing are non-adjustable.

NOTE —

Beginning in 1994 (1993 in California) automakers are required by law to apply uniform terminology, words and terms for certain components according to SAE standard J1930. These standardized terms are used throughout this section.

Readiness Codes

Federal and state legislation requires that all auto manufacturers build into their engine management systems the ability to check for proper operation of up to 8 functions. For the ME7.5 engine management system, the exact number depends on the equipment level of each particular vehicle. Most of the time, the readiness code will set itself after the appropriate conditions have been met. These may include a cold or a hot start, operation at a certain load or speed for a certain period of time, or operation at different temperatures. After repairs, it may be advantageous to confirm repairs rather than wait to see if they set on their own. Other than waiting, the only other method of setting the readiness codes on the Motronic ME7.5 system is with a scan tool. This method requires Volkswagen scan tool VAG 1551, VAG 1552, VAS 5051 or an equivalent aftermarket scan tool, and extensive knowledge of its operation and capabilities. Readiness codes are then generated according to instructions provided by the scan tool manufacturer. For the significance of the 8 digit readiness code, see **Table a**

Table a. Readiness code values

Digit position								Diagnostic Function
1	2	3	4	5	6	7	8	
							0	Three Way Catalyst
						0		Catalyst Heating (always 0)
					0			Evaporative Emissions System (Fuel tank vent system)
				0				Secondary Air Injection System
			0					Air Conditioning
		0						Oxygen Sensor
	0							Oxygen Sensor Heater
0								Exhaust Gas Recirculation - EGR (always 0)

The readiness code can be displayed in any of several areas within the ECM's diagnostic memory depending on the individual scan tool. It will always have a format consisting of 8 digits. If the 8 digit code contains characters other than the number 0, such as 10100110, than the readiness code is NOT set. When the code displays all zeros, i.e. 00000000, the readiness code IS set and no further action is required. The specifics of **Table a** apply to the 1.8L engine only. While the format is required to be the same for all engines, certain equipment may not be used on each engine. For example, the 1.8L engine does not use EGR and as such, digit number 8 will always show 0. Other engines that use EGR, such as the 1.9L diesel, will show either a 1 or a 0 as appropriate.

Engine control module coding

The engine control module (ECM) must be supplied with appropriate power sources and grounds to function properly. Also, the engine control module must "know" what equipment is installed in the vehicle. This process is known as coding and must be performed whenever the ECM is replaced as new ECM's are un-coded. If an ECM is moved between vehicles such as might be the case for diagnostic testing, the coding will need to be changed if equipment is different. Coding memory is, however, retained when the battery is disconnected. If a new ECM is installed without being coded, the engine will usually run poorly and the automatic transmission and anti-lock braking system (if equipped) will not function properly. The MIL will be illuminated.

This coding process can only be done with Volkswagen scan tool VAG 1551/1552 or equivalent. The appropriate code is electronically programmed into the ECM according to instructions provided by the scan tool manufacturer. See **Table b**.

Table b. ECM coding

Country/ emissions	Drive type	Transmission	Vehicle type
05 = D3 (european standard)	0 = Front wheel drive only	0 = 5-speed manual (02J)	0 = A class (Jetta, Golf, GTI)
06 = TLEV (transitional low emission vehicle) engine code AWD	5 = Front wheel drive with traction control and data bus	3 = Automatic (01M)	
07 = LEV (low emission vehicle) engine code AWW	6 =All wheel drive without anti-slip regulation (ASR)		

NOTE —

Using the table above, a Golf or Jetta with the engine code AWD, traction control, and a 5-speed manual transmission would need the ECM code 06500.

MOTRONIC ENGINE MANAGEMENT COMPONENTS

Fig. 2 shows an overview of the major underhood components with the upper sound absorber panel removed. Fig. 3 through Fig. 5 show the various other components of the Motronic engine management fuel injection system.

NOTE —

Volkswagen identifies electrical components by a letter and/or a number in the electrical schematics. See **97 Wiring Diagrams, Fuses and Relays**. *These electrical identifiers are listed in parenthesis as an aid to electrical troubleshooting.*

Fuel injection system component locations, overview

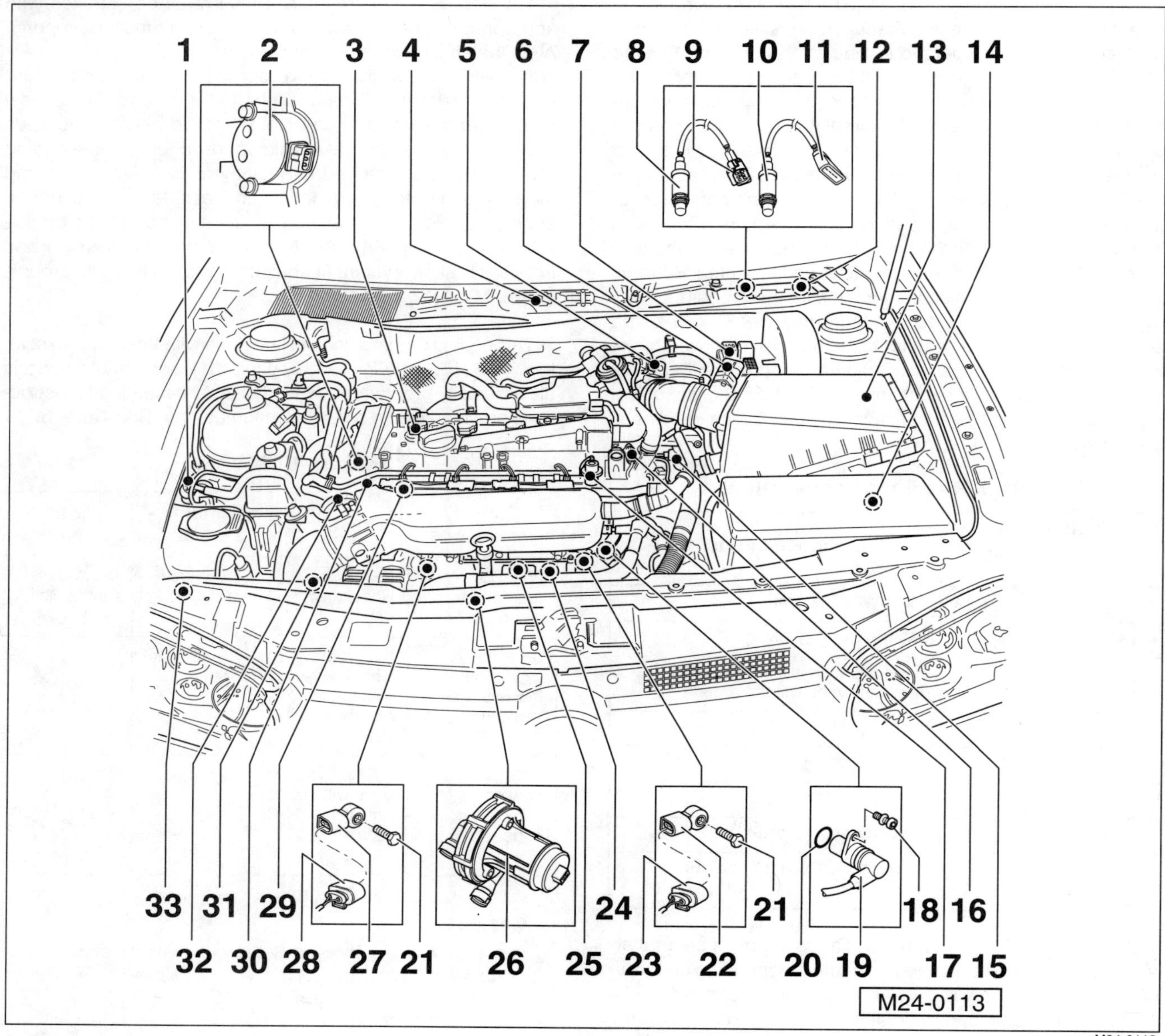

M24-0113

Fig. 2. Motronic ME7.5.1component locations on 1.8L engine.

1. **Activated charcoal filter solenoid valve 1 (N80)**
2. **Hall sender (G163)**
3. **Ignition coil pack (N70, N127, N291, N292)**
   - Separate coil for each cylinder
   - With power output stages
4. **Engine control module**
5. **Charge pressure limitation solenoid valve (N75)**
6. **Mass air flow sensor (G70)**
7. **Secondary air pump relay (J299)**
8. **Heated oxygen sensor (HO2S) (G39)**
   - Before catalyst
9. **Connector**
   - For Oxygen sensor before catalyst and O2S heater
   - Engine code AWD: 4-pin
   - Engine code AWW: 6-pin
10. **Heated oxygen sensor (HO2S) (G130)**
    - After catalyst
11. **4-pin connector**
    - For Oxygen sensor after catalyst and O2S heater

12. **Clutch pedal switch (F36), brake light switch (F) and brake pedal switch**
13. **Air cleaner**
14. **Protective housing**
15. **Engine coolant temperature sensor (G62)**
    - Measuring resistance, **see** Ⓐ
16. **Camshaft adjustment valve 1 (N205)**
    - Engine code AWW only
17. **Fuel pressure regulator**
    - Location: on fuel rail
18. **Screw**
    - Tighten to 10 Nm (7 ft-lb)
19. **Engine speed sensor (G28)**
20. **O-ring**
    - Always replace
21. **Bolt**
    - Tighten to 20 Nm (15 ft-lb)
    - Tightening torque influences function of knock sensor
22. **Knock sensor 2 (G66)**
23. **Knock sensor 2 connector**
    - Engine code AWD: 3-pin
    - AWD engine has both knock sensor connectors (square) and engine rpm sensor connector (grey, oval shaped) mounted together, see Fig. 7. given later
    - Engine code AWW: 2-pin
24. **Divert valve for turbocharger (N249)**
25. **Secondary air injection solenoid valve (N112)**
26. **Secondary air injection pump motor (V101)**
27. **Knock sensor 1 (G61)**
28. **Knock sensor 1 connector**
    - Engine code AWD: 3-pin
    - AWD engine has both knock sensor connectors (square) and engine rpm sensor connector (grey, oval shaped) mounted together, see Fig. 7. given later
    - Engine code AWW: 2-pin
29. **Fuel injectors (N30, N31, N32, N33)**
30. **Intake air temperature sensor (G42)**
31. **Power steering pressure switch (F88)**
32. **Throttle valve control module (J338)**
    - For Electronic Pedal Control, EPC, (E-Gas System)
33. **Charge pressure sender (G31)**

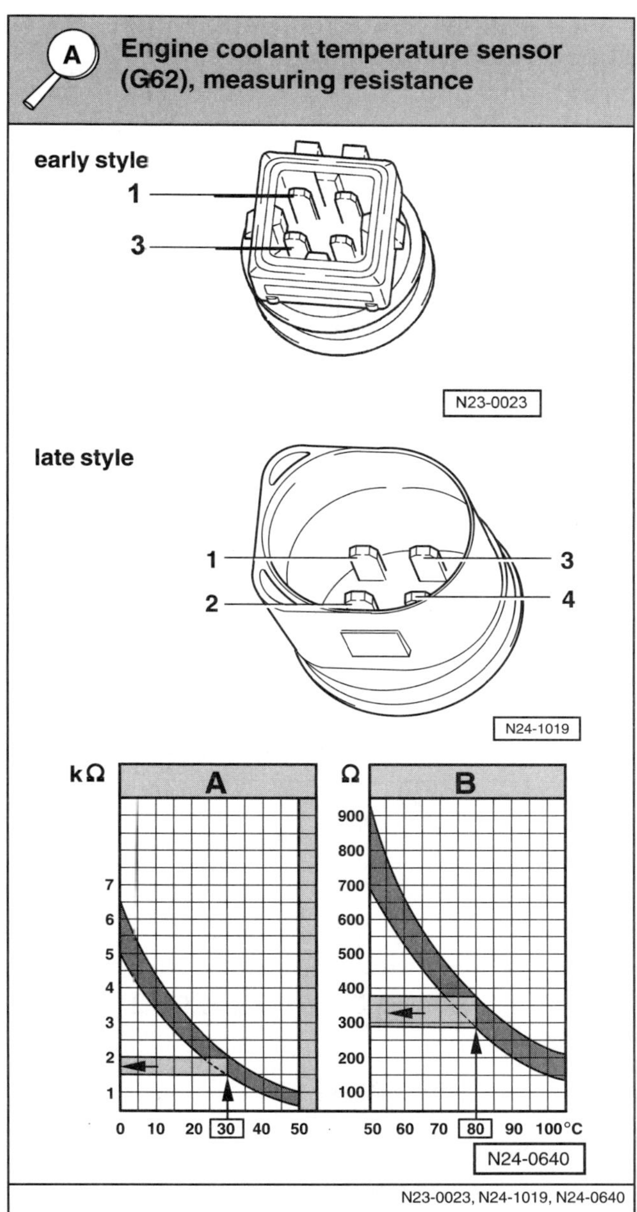

N23-0023, N24-1019, N24-0640

- **Measure resistance at terminals 1 and 3 on early style sensor**
- **Measure resistance at terminals 3 and 4 on later style sensor**
- **Compare reading to graph (bottom):**
  Scale A shows resistance for coolant temperature range 0-50°C (32-122°F)
  Scale B shows resistance for coolant temperature range 50-100°C (122-212°F)
- **Example:**
  30°C corresponds to 1500-2000 Ω
  80°C corresponds to 275-375 Ω

Fuel injection system components, removing and installing

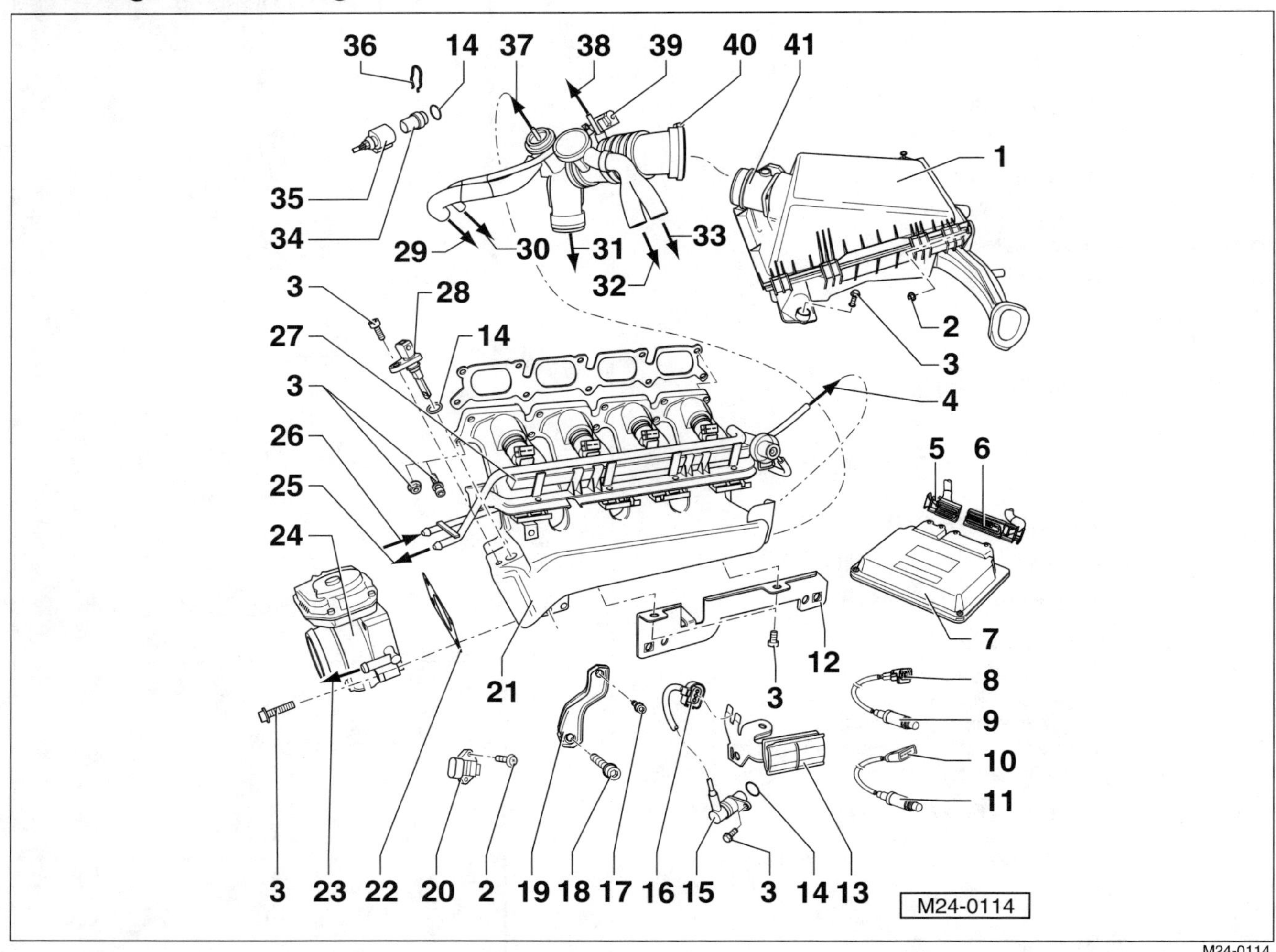

M24-0114

Fig. 3. Motronic ME7.5 system elements and related components.

1. **Air filter assembly**
   - See assembly view on page 47-8
2. **Bolt**
   - Tighten to 10 Nm (7 ft-lb)
3. **Bolt**
   - Tighten to 6 Nm (52 in-lb)
4. **Vacuum connection**
   - To intake manifold
5. **40-pin harness connector (terminals 82 to 121)**
   - Only disconnect or connect with ignition switched OFF
6. **81-pin connector (terminals 1 to 81)**
   - Only disconnect or connect with ignition switched OFF
7. **Engine control module (J220)**
   - Location: in air plenum at forward part of instrument panel near base of the windshield on driver's side
   - Must be matched to throttle valve control module (J338) with a scan tool if replaced
8. **Harness connector**
   - AWD engine: 4-pin
   - AWW engine: 6-pin
   - For pre-catalyst heated oxygen sensor (G39) and oxygen sensor heater (Z19)
   - Right underside of vehicle in plastic shield

(continued from previous page)

9. Oxygen sensor, pre-catalyst (G39)
- Use VW special tool set 3337, or equivalent to remove
- Monitors combustion efficiency
- Location: Threaded into front exhaust pipe
- Tighten to 50 Nm (37 ft-lb)
- Lubricate threads only with high temperature anti-seize (part # G 052 112 A3)
- Do not allow anti-seize compound into the slots on the sensor body

10. 4-pin harness connector
- For post-catalyst heated oxygen sensor (G130) and oxygen sensor heater (Z29)
- Right underside of vehicle in plastic shield

11. Oxygen sensor, post-catalyst (G130)
- Use VW special tool set 3337, or equivalent to remove
- Monitors catalytic converter efficiency
- Location: threaded into rear of catalytic converter
- Tighten to 50 Nm (37 ft-lb)
- Lubricate threads only with high temperature anti-seize (part # G 052 112 A3)
- Do not allow anti-seize compound into the slots on the sensor body

12. Bracket
- For engine speed sensor

13. Bracket
- For engine speed sensor
- AWW engine only

14. O-ring
- Always replace

15. Engine speed sensor (G28)
- See **Engine speed sensor**, given later
- Inductive type sensor

16. 3-pin harness connector
- Grey
- For engine speed sensor

17. Bolt
- Tighten to 20 Nm (15 ft lb)

18. Bolt
- Tighten to 45 Nm (34 ft lb)

19. Support bracket
- Between intake manifold and cylinder block

20. Charge air pressure sensor (G31)
- Location: mounted to intercooler

21. Intake manifold

22. Gasket
- Always replace

23. Connecting hose
- From evaporative emissions (EVAP) canister purge regulator valve (N80)

24. Throttle valve control module (J338)
- For Electronic Power Control, EPC, (E-Gas System)
- Must be matched to Motronic ME7.5.1 engine control module (J220) with a scan tool if replaced

25. Fuel return line
- Secure with spring clips only
- Ensure coupling is securely seated
- To fuel delivery unit in fuel tank

26. Fuel supply line
- Secure with spring clips only
- Ensure coupling is securely seated
- From fuel filter

27. Fuel rail, with fuel injectors (N30-N33) and fuel pressure regulator

28. Intake air temperature sensor (G42)
- Location: mounted in intake manifold just behind throttle valve control module
- Measuring resistance, **see** (A)

29. Connecting hose
- To pipe between turbocharger and intercooler

30. Connecting hose
- To pipe between turbocharger and intercooler

31. To turbocharger

32. From crankcase breather

33. From crankcase breather
- AWW engine only

34. Engine coolant temperature sensor (G62)
- For engine control module
- Combined with coolant temperature gauge sender (G2) for instrument panel warning light

35. 4-pin harness connector
- Black
- For engine coolant temperature sensor (G62/G2)

36. Retaining clip
- Ensure clip is securely seated

37. To turbocharger divert valve (N249)

38. To pressure unit on turbocharger
- From turbocharger to intercooler connecting pipe
- To wastegate regulator solenoid valve (N75)

39. Charge pressure limitation solenoid valve (N75)

40. Intake hose

41. Mass air flow sensor (G70)
- 5-pin harness connector
- Terminal 1 position not used

A **Intake air temperature (IAT) sensor (G42), measuring resistance**

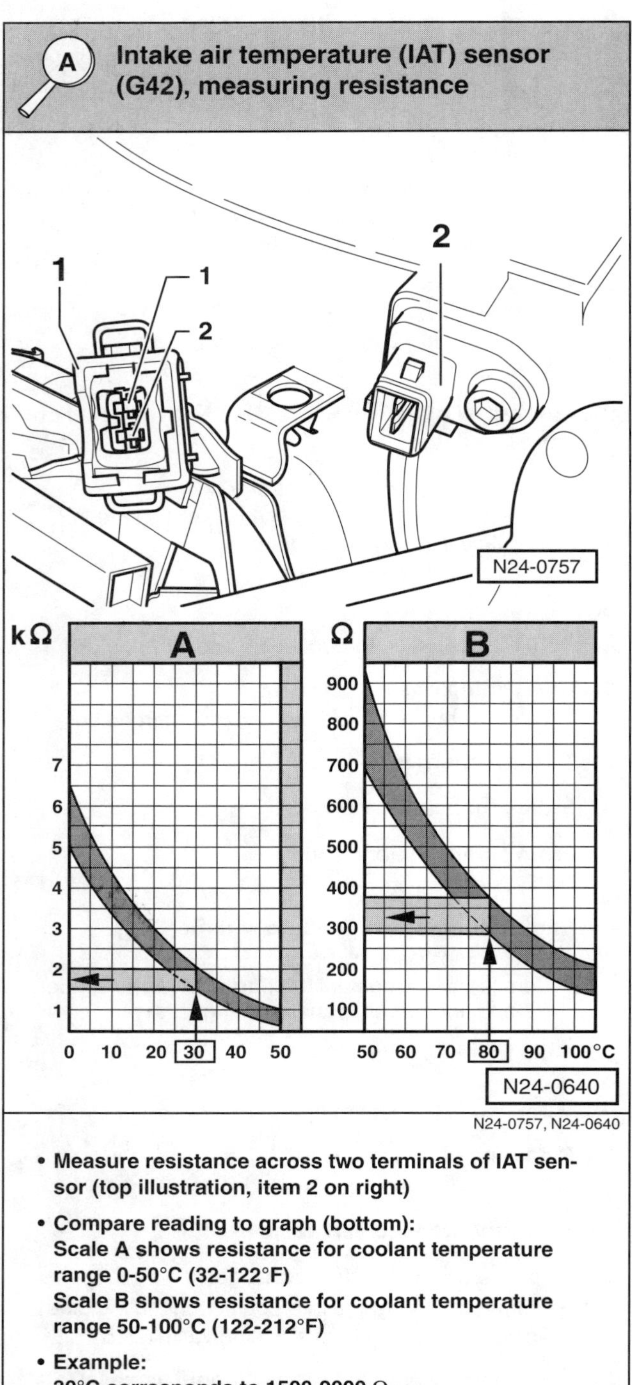

N24-0757, N24-0640

- **Measure resistance across two terminals of IAT sensor (top illustration, item 2 on right)**
- **Compare reading to graph (bottom):**
  Scale A shows resistance for coolant temperature range 0-50°C (32-122°F)
  Scale B shows resistance for coolant temperature range 50-100°C (122-212°F)
- **Example:**
  30°C corresponds to 1500-2000 Ω
  80°C corresponds to 275-375 Ω

Air cleaner assembly

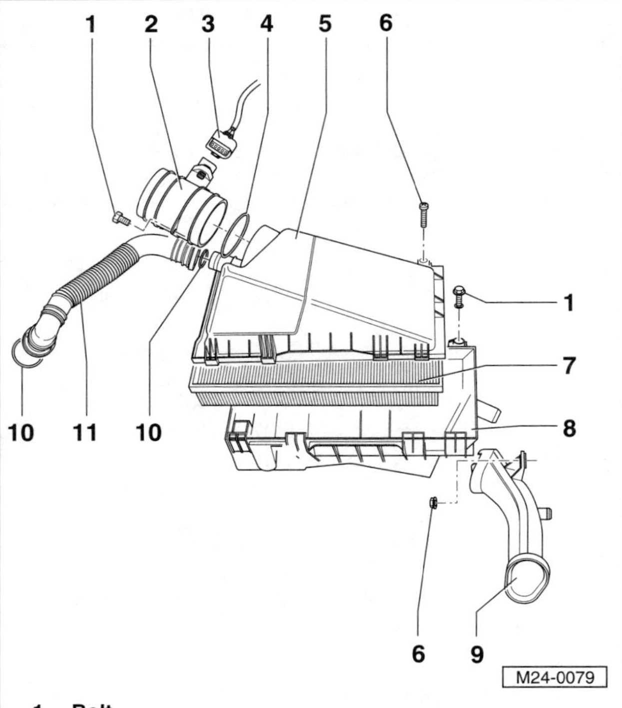

1. **Bolt**
   - Tighten to 10 Nm (7 ft-lb)
2. **Mass air flow sensor (G70)**
   - Terminal 1 position not used
   - All contacts gold plated
3. **5-pin connector**
   - All contacts gold plated
4. **Seal**
   - Replace if damaged
5. **Air cleaner housing, upper section**
6. **Bolt**
   - Tighten to 6 Nm (52 in-lb)
7. **Filter element**
8. **Air cleaner housing, lower section**
9. **Duct, intake air**
10. **O-ring**
    - Replace if damaged
11. **Intake hose**
    - From air cleaner housing upper section to secondary air injection pump intake
    - Ensure hose is seated tightly
    - Press together at front to release

M24-0079

Fig. 4. Air cleaner assembly and related components.

Fuel rail and injector assembly

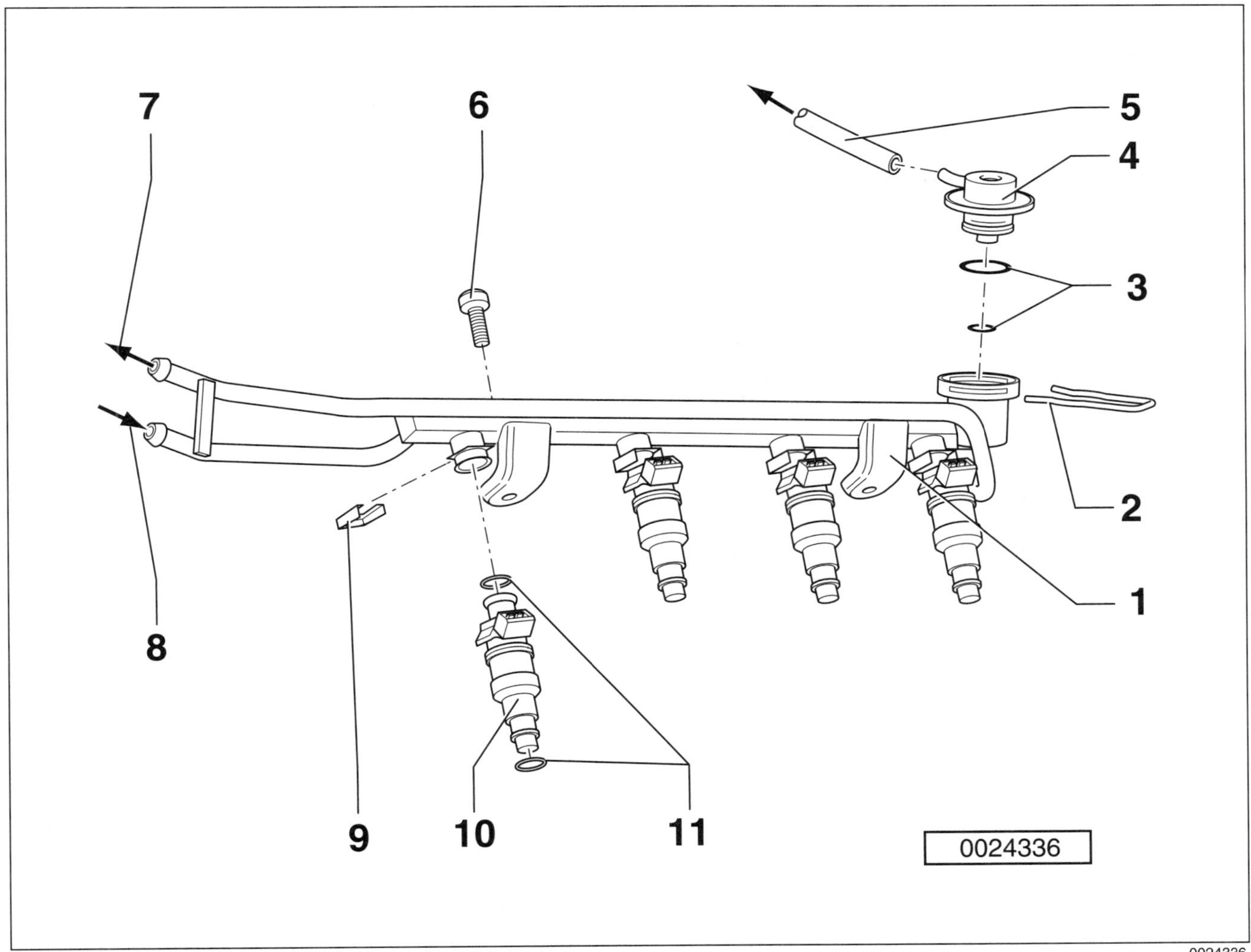

Fig. 5. Fuel rail showing fuel pressure regulator and injectors.

1. **Fuel rail**
2. **Retaining clip**
   - Ensure it is securely seated
3. **O-ring**
   - Replace if damaged
4. **Fuel pressure regulator**
   - Fuel pressure regulator with residual check valve
5. **Connecting hose**
   - To intake manifold
6. **Bolt**
   - Tighten to 10 Nm (7 ft-lb)
7. **Fuel return line/hose**
   - Secure with spring clips only
   - Ensure coupling is securely seated
   - To fuel delivery unit in fuel tank
8. **Fuel supply line/hose**
   - Secure with spring clips only
   - Ensure coupling is securely seated
   - From fuel filter
9. **Retaining clip**
   - Ensure it is securely seated
10. **Fuel injectors (N30, N31, N32, N33)**
    - 2-pin harness connector
11. **O-ring**
    - Always replace
    - Moisten with clean engine oil or fuel before installing

Engine Control Module (ECM)

The engine control module is located in the air plenum near the base of the windshield in the engine compartment. Access to the ECM requires removal of the windshield wiper arms and the air plenum cover. See Fig. 6.

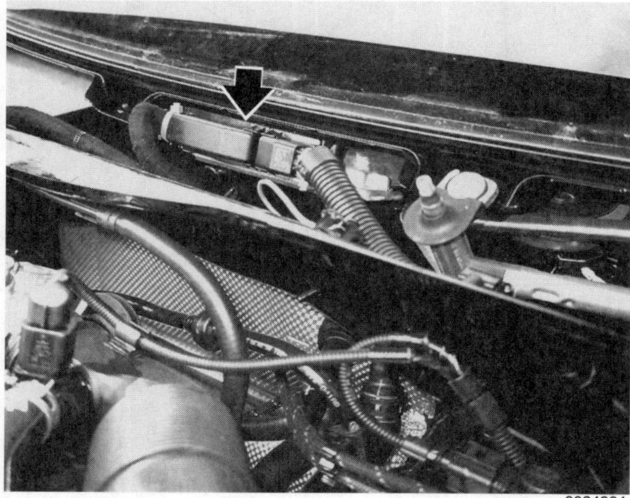

Fig. 6. Engine control module (**arrow**) is accessible from under the hood after removal of the wiper arms and plenum cover as shown.

Engine speed sensor

Operation of the engine management system depends on a wide variety of input sensors. Failure of most of these sensors will allow the engine to continue to run, albeit poorly. One major exception to this is the engine speed sensor (G28). Failure of this sensor will prevent the engine from starting and running and will set a diagnostic trouble code in the ECM.

Note that most diagnostic functions require the use of a scan tool such as the VAG1552, VAG1552, VAS5051 or equivalent, however a quick check can be accomplished as follows:

1. Disconnect the grey 3-pin harness connector from the engine speed sensor plug near the secondary air injection pump.
   - Engine code AWD: See Fig. 7.
   - Engine code AWW: See Fig. 8.
2. Connect an accurate ohmmeter between terminals 2 and 3 on sensor and measure resistance.
3. Measure resistance between terminals 1 and 3, and between terminals 1 and 2 as well. Compare readings to specification.

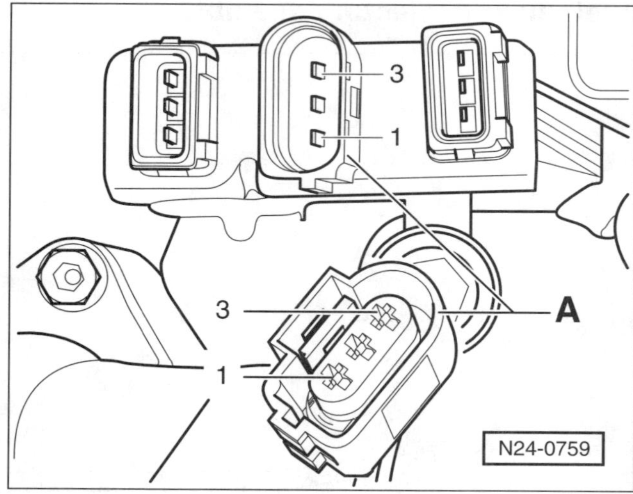

Fig. 7. Engine speed sensor harness connector (**A**), with terminal identification, shown unplugged at multiple harness connector at front of AWD engine. Oxygen sensor connectors are on left and right.

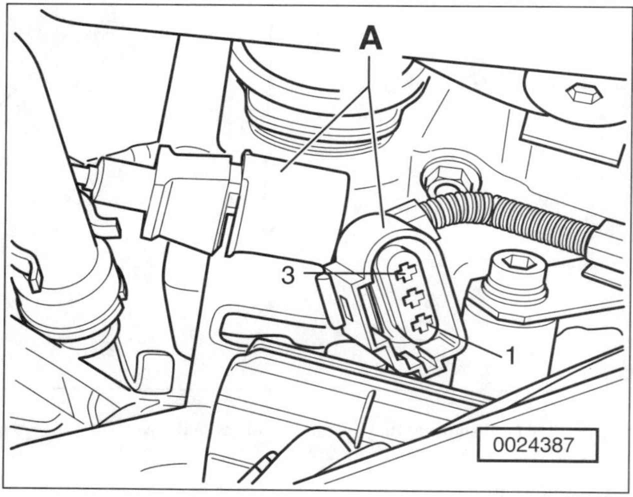

Fig. 8. Engine speed sensor and harness connector (**A**), with terminal identification, shown unplugged at front AWW engine.

Specification

- Engine speed sensor resistance values, (1.8L engine)
  - Between terminals 2 and 3 .... 730 to 1000 Ω
  - Between terminals 1 and 2 .... infinity Ω
  - Between terminals 1 and 3 .... infinity Ω

4. If specification is not obtained, replace engine speed sensor.
5. If specification is obtained, and engine will not start, additional testing with a suitable scan tool will be required.

24b Fuel Injection–Motronic (2.0L engine)

TABLES

GENERAL

This repair group covers the fuel injection/engine management system for the 2.0 liter gasoline engine. The operation of the various Bosch Motronic engine management systems are described in **2 Fuel, Ignition and Exhaust Systems.**

Special testing equipment may be necessary for some of the tests and repair procedures given here.

2.0L Engine management systems
- AEG engine . . . . Motronic 5.9.2
- AVH, AZG engines . . . . Motronic ME 7.5

NOTE —
- *2.0 liter engines are equipped with Bosch Motronic engine management systems which are OBD II compliant. It is recommended that fault diagnosis and troubleshooting be carried out using Volkswagen scan tools VAG 1551/VAG 1552 or equivalent.*
- *Fuel pump and fuel tank testing and repair along with EVAP information is covered in* **20 Fuel Storage and Supply**.
- *Ignition system testing and repair is covered in* **28a Ignition System–Gasoline.**
- *Related systems such as Exhaust Gas Recirculation (EGR) and catalytic converters are covered in* **26 Exhaust System and Emission Controls**.

The Motronic engine management systems combine the ignition and fuel injection functions into one system managed by a single Engine Control Module (ECM). The system is fully adaptive and features built-in diagnostics that are capable of detecting and storing coded fault information. There are no basic adjustments or settings that can be made to the system without specialized equipment.

CAUTION —
Disconnecting the negative (–) battery cable may erase fault codes and basic settings in the engine management and automatic transmission control modules. Some driveability problems may be noticed until the system re-adapts to operating conditions. OBD II readiness codes, which may be required for emissions testing, may also be erased. Convenience electronics (alarm system, interior light control, power locks, mirrors, and windows) may need to be re-set using a VAG 1551/1552 or equivalent scan tool.

Safety precautions

The following warnings and cautions should be adhered to whenever working on the engine management system.

WARNING —
- *Fuel may be discharged during fuel system repairs. Do not smoke or work near heaters or other fire hazards. Have a fire extinguisher handy. Work only in a well-ventilated area.*
- *Wear suitable hand and eye protection when working with gasoline. Prolonged contact with fuel can cause illness and skin disorders.*
- *Fuel hoses in engine compartment must only be secured with spring-type clips. The use of clamp or screw-type clips will damage fuel lines and cause fuel leaks.*

> ***CAUTION —***
> - *Connect and disconnect wires and test equipment only with the ignition switched off.*
> - *Before making any electrical tests that require the engine to be cranked using the starter, disable the ignition system as described in* **28a Ignition System.**
> - *Do not use sealants containing silicones. Particles of silicone drawn into the engine will not be burned in the engine and will damage the heated oxygen sensor. Use only sealants and engine chemicals marked as safe for oxygen sensors.*
> - *During testing, it is possible for the Engine Control Module to recognize and store a diagnostic trouble code (DTC) that was due solely to the testing procedure. Therefore, after completing repairs, the DTC memory must be checked and erased as necessary with a scan tool such as VAG 1551/1552 or equivalent*
> - *Cleanliness is essential when working on the fuel system. Thoroughly clean fuel line connections and surrounding areas before loosening. Avoid the use of compressed air. Avoid moving the vehicle. Only install clean components.*

ON BOARD DIAGNOSTICS (OBD)

On Board Diagnostics, found on the Bosch Motronic Engine Management Systems monitor many aspects of engine operation. The current generation OBD II is integrated into all Volkswagen gasoline engines. For a description of the system and an overview of operation, see **2 Fuel, Ignition, and Exhaust Systems.**

Because of the large number of operating parameters monitored and the vast quantity of data available, fault diagnosis can only be properly carried out using a suitable scan tool such as Volkswagen special tool VAG 1551 or VAG 1552 or equivalent. The engine control module or ECM also supports certain limited functions in a government-mandated generic scan tool mode. These functions are standardized for all OBD II compliant vehicles, but are not as comprehensive as those found by using the VAG 1551/1552 in the original mode of operation.

During repairs where the battery must be disconnected, consideration must be given to the effect that this will have on the vehicle in general and the engine management system in particular.

- Diagnostic Trouble Codes may be erased.
- Readiness codes may be erased.
- Fault counters that monitor certain functions will be reset to zero.
- Adaptive leaning values will be set to default.

Because the ignition, fuel injection, and emission control functions are even more inter-related than on previous Motronic versions, it is difficult, if not impossible to isolate general driveability problems by examining individual components of the system. For this reason, a suitable scan tool must be used for diagnosis if driveability problems occur or if the malfunction indicator light is illuminated. Access for the scan tool is through the Data Link Connector (DLC) under the lower left side of the instrument panel. See Fig. 1.

0024272

Fig. 1. Data Link Connector (DLC), (**arrow**) under left lower side of instrument panel.

The Motronic ME 7.5 system found on vehicles with the 2.0 liter engine having an engine code of AVH or AZG is the latest evolution of the Motronic fuel management system. If these later engines (AVH/AZG) start and run only briefly after troubleshooting with a scan tool and repairing faulty components/systems, it may be the immobilizer that is blocking the engine control module. The diagnostic trouble code (DTC) memory must be checked and if necessary, the control module adapted. For a list of scan tool DTCs, see **ST Scan Tool Codes** at the back of the manual.

Adaptation

The Motronic engine management systems are adaptive. Idle speed, ignition timing, injection timing and quantity automatically compensate and adapt to changes in the engine due to wear and operating conditions. Minor problems such as mixture changes due to small vacuum leaks can be eliminated. As a result, idle speed, fuel mixture (CO%) and ignition timing are non-adjustable.

> ***NOTE —***
> *Beginning in 1994 (1993 in California) automakers are required by law to apply uniform terminology, words and terms for certain components according to SAE standard J1930. These standardized terms are used throughout this section.*

Readiness Codes

Federal and state legislation requires that all auto manufacturers build into their engine management systems the ability to check for proper operation of up to 8 functions. For the Motronic engine management system, the exact number depends on the equipment level of each particular vehicle. Most of the time, the readiness code will set itself after the appropriate conditions have been met. These may include a cold or a hot start, operation at a certain load or speed for a certain period of time, or operation at different temperatures. After repairs, it may be advantageous to confirm repairs rather than wait to see if they set on their own. Other than waiting, the only other method of setting the readiness codes on the Motronic systems is with a scan tool. This method requires Volkswagen scan tool VAG 1551, VAG 1552, or an equivalent aftermarket scan tool, and extensive knowledge of its operation and capabilities. Readiness codes are then generated according to instructions provided by the scan tool manufacturer. For the significance of the 8 digit readiness code, see **Table a**

Table a. Readiness code values

Digit position								Diagnostic Function
1	2	3	4	5	6	7	8	
							0	Three Way Catalyst
						0		Catalyst Heating (always 0)
					0			Evaporative Emissions System (Fuel tank vent system)
				0				Secondary Air Injection System (always 0)
			0					Air Conditioning (no current diagnostic function-always 0)
		0						Oxygen Sensor
	0							Oxygen Sensor Heater
0								Exhaust Gas Recirculation - EGR (always 0)

The readiness code can be displayed in any of several areas within the ECM's diagnostic memory depending on the individual scan tool. It will always have a format consisting of 8 digits. If the 8 digit code contains characters other than the number 0, such as 10100110, than the readiness code is NOT set. When the code displays all zeros, i.e. 00000000, the readiness code IS set and no further action is required.

Engine control module coding

The engine control module (ECM) must be supplied with appropriate power sources and grounds to function properly. Also, the engine control module must "know" what equipment is installed in the vehicle. This process is known as coding and must be performed whenever the ECM is replaced as new ECM's are un-coded. If an ECM is moved between vehicles such as might be the case for diagnostic testing, the coding will need to be changed if equipment is different. Coding memory is, however, retained when the battery is disconnected. If a new ECM is installed without being coded, the engine will usually run poorly and the automatic transmission and anti-lock braking system (if equipped) will not function properly. The MIL will be illuminated.

This coding process can only be done with Volkswagen scan tool VAG 1551/1552 or equivalent. The appropriate code is electronically programmed into the ECM according to instructions provided by the scan tool manufacturer. See **Table b or c**.

Table b. ECM Coding (1999 m.y.)

Coding	Vehicle and Equipment
00000	Cars with Manual Transmission and ABS
00001	Cars with Automatic Transmission and ABS
00040	Cars with Manual Transmission without ABS
00041	Cars with Automatic Transmission without ABS

Table c. ECM Coding (from 2000 m.y.)

Coding	ABS	Air bag	Transmission
00001	No	No	Manual
00011	Yes	No	Manual
00021	No	Yes	Manual
00031	Yes	Yes	Manual
00003	No	No	Automatic
00013	Yes	No	Automatic
00023	No	Yes	Automatic
00033	Yes	Yes	Automatic

NOTE —
The appropriate code is electronically programmed into the ECM according to instructions provided by the scan tool manufacturer.

MOTRONIC ENGINE MANAGEMENT COMPONENTS

Fig. 2 through 5 show the various components of the Motronic engine management fuel injection systems on the 2.0L engine.

NOTE —
Volkswagen identifies electrical components by a letter and/or a number in the electrical schematics. See **97 Wiring Diagrams, Fuses and Relays**. *These electrical identifiers are listed in parenthesis as an aid to electrical troubleshooting.*

Fuel injection system components, overview

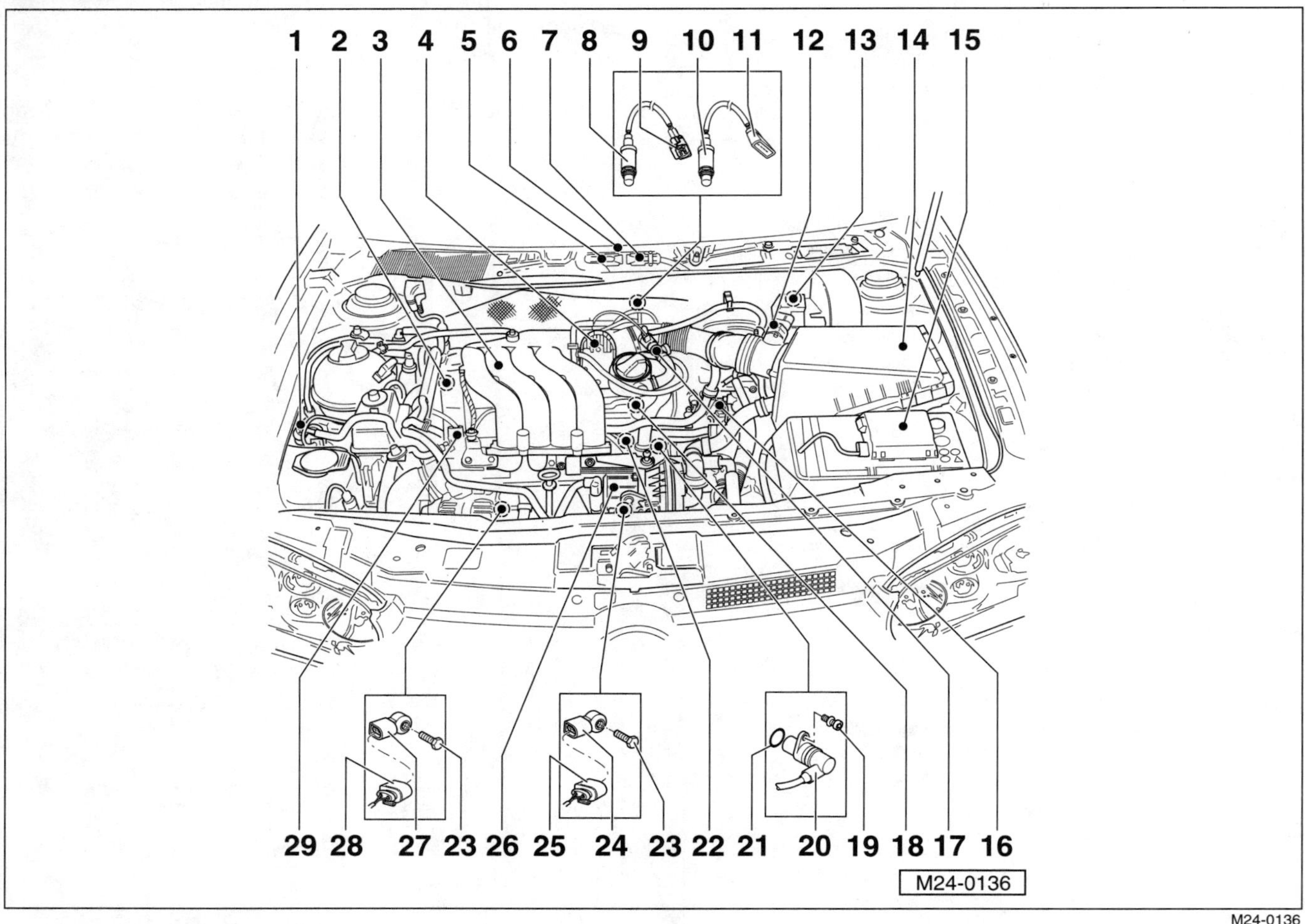

M24-0136

Fig. 2. Fuel injection system component locations on 2.0L engine. AVH, AZG engine shown, AEG is similar.

1. **Evaporative emissions (EVAP) canister purge regulator valve (N80)**
2. **Camshaft position sensor (G40)**
   - Below the upper toothed belt guard
3. **Intake Manifold**
4. **Throttle control module (J338)**
5. **Harness connector**
   - Only disconnect/connect with engine off
   - AEG engine: 52-pin
   - AVH, AZG engines: 81-pin
6. **Engine control module (ECM) (J220)**
7. **Harness connector**
   - Only disconnect/connect with engine off
   - AEG engine: 28-pin
   - AVH, AZG engines: 40-pin
8. **Heated oxygen sensor before catalyst (G39)**
   - Tighten to 50 Nm (37 ft-lb)
   - Located in exhaust manifold
   - When installing, grease threads, do not let grease get into the slots on probe body
   - Remove/install w/VW special tool 3337, or equivalent
   - Oxygen sensor heater voltage via fuel pump relay
9. **Harness connector**
   - Mark connector before disconnecting
   - AEG engine: 4-pin
   - AVH, AZG engines: 6-pin
   - For heated oxygen sensor (G39) before catalytic converter and oxygen sensor heater (Z19)
   - Located on underside of vehicle
10. **Heated oxygen sensor after catalyst (G130)**
    - Tighten to 50 Nm (37 ft-lb)
    - Located in rear of catalytic converter
    - When installing, grease threads, do not let grease get into the slots on probe body
    - Remove/install w/VW special tool 3337, or equivalent
    - Oxygen sensor heater voltage via fuel pump relay

11. 4-pin harness connector
- Mark connector before disconnecting
- For oxygen sensor (G130) behind catalytic converter and heater for Lambda probe (Z29)
- Located at right on underside of vehicle

12. Mass air flow sensor (G70), with intake air temperature sensor (G42)

13. Secondary air injection pump relay (J299)

14. Air cleaner housing

15. Protective housing
- For additional fuses

16. Engine coolant temperature sensor (G62)
- Release pressure in cooling system before removing
- Measuring resistance, **see** (A)

17. Positive crankshaft ventilation (PCV) heating element (N79)

18. Fuel injectors (N30, N31, N32, N33)
- Underneath intake manifold in fuel rail
- Air shrouded

19. Mounting bolt
- Tighten to 10 Nm (7 ft-lb)

20. Engine speed sensor (G28)
- See **Engine Speed Sensor**, given later
- Location: on cylinder block near oil dipstick
- Inductive type sensor

21. O-ring
- Replace if damaged

22. Ignition coil(s) with power output stage
- AEG engine: 1 coil pack (N152)
- AVH, AZG engines: 4 coils (N70, N127, N291, N292)

23. Mounting bolt
- Tighten to 20 Nm (15 ft-lb)
- Tightening torque influences function of knock sensor

24. Knock sensor 2 (G66)

25. Harness connector
- Mark connector before disconnecting
- AEG engine: 3-pin
- AVH, AZG engines: 2-pin

26. Secondary air injection pump motor (V101)

27. Knock sensor 1 (G61)

28. Harness connector
- Mark connector before disconnecting
- AEG engine: 3-pin
- AVH, AZG engines: 2-pin

29. Fuel pressure regulator
- Location: on fuel rail

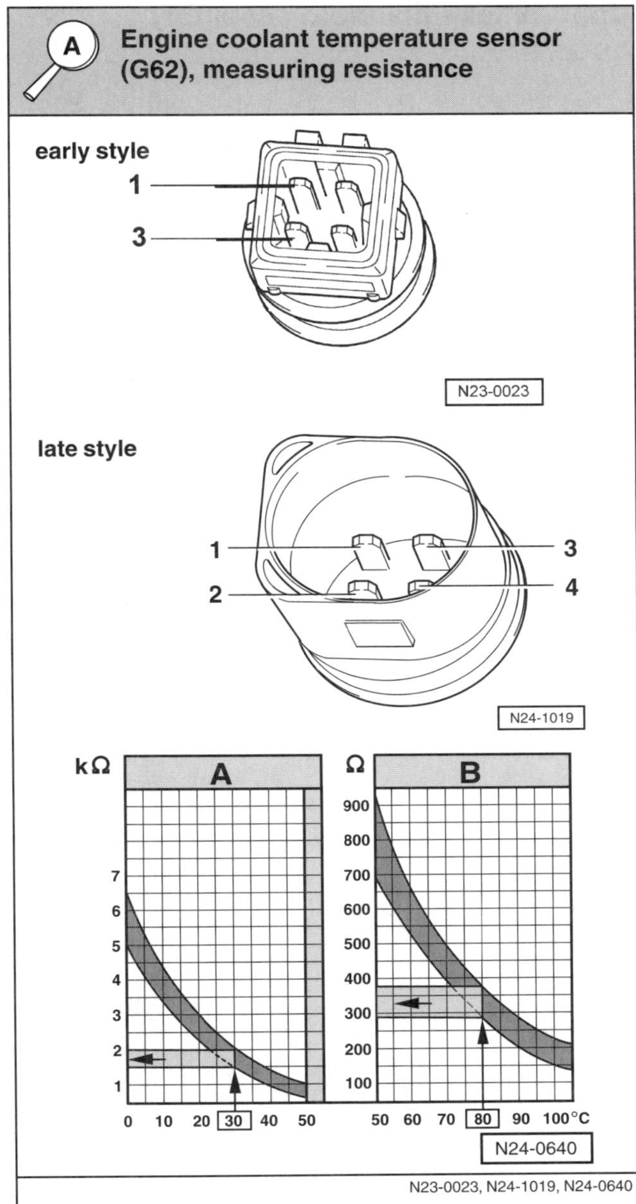

- **Measure resistance at terminals 1 and 3 on early style sensor**
- **Measure resistance at terminals 3 and 4 on later style sensor**
- **Compare reading to graph (bottom):**
  Scale A shows resistance for coolant temperature range 0-50°C (32-122°F)
  Scale B shows resistance for coolant temperature range 50-100°C (122-212°F)
- **Example:**
  30°C corresponds to 1500-2000 Ω
  80°C corresponds to 275-375 Ω

Upper intake manifold assembly

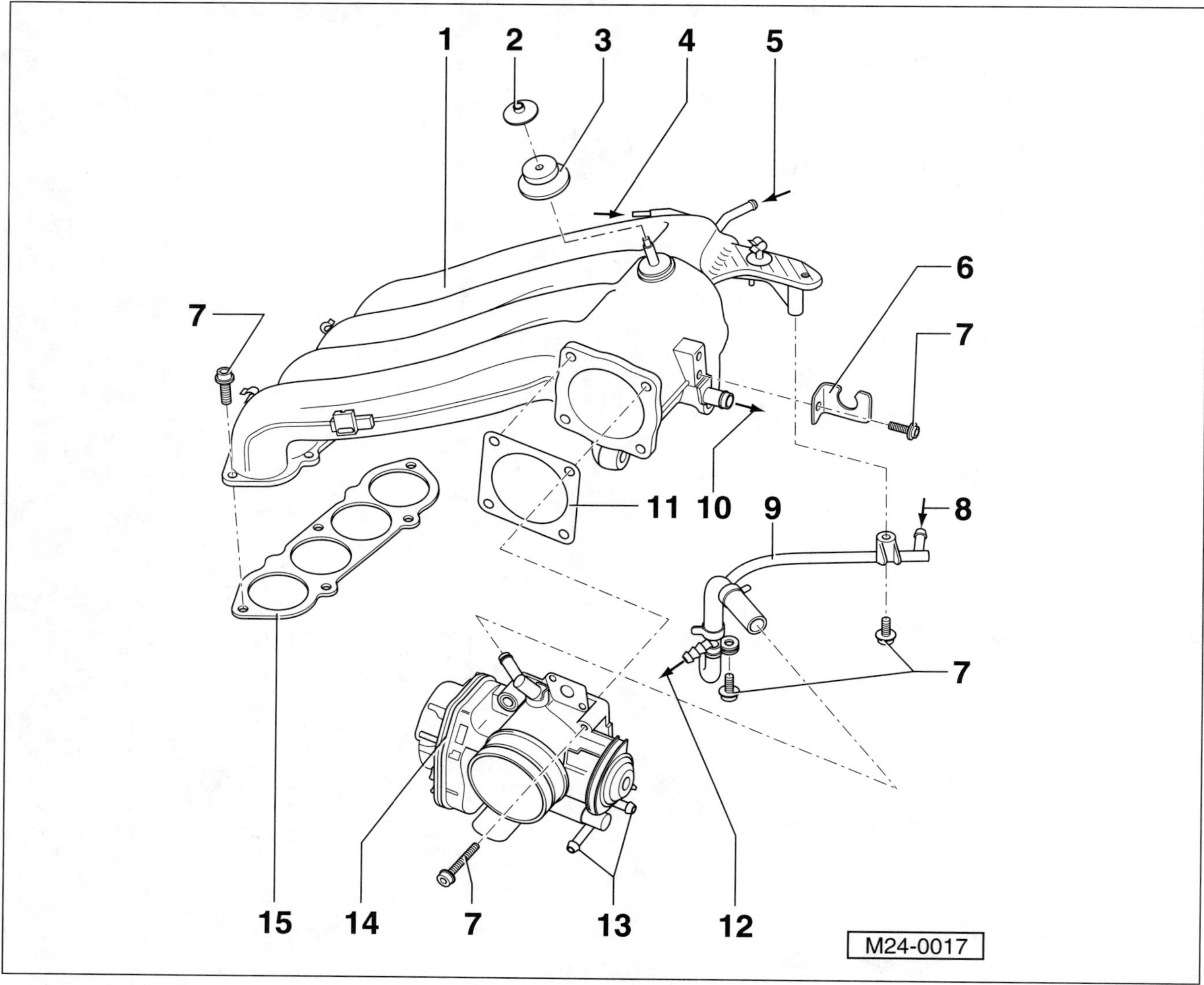

M24-0017

Fig. 3. Motronic system elements and related components.

1. **Intake manifold, upper section**
   - Shown with throttle control module (J338)
2. **Retaining nut**
   - Tighten to 6 Nm (53 in-lb)
3. **Rubber bushing**
   - For engine cover
4. **From fuel pressure regulator**
5. **From leak detection pump**
6. **Support bracket**
   - For accelerator pedal cable
7. **Bolt**
   - Tighten to 10 Nm (7 ft lb)
8. **From EVAP canister purge regulator valve**
9. **Connecting pipe**
10. **To brake servo vacuum pipe**
11. **Gasket**
    - Always replace
12. **To intake hose**
13. **Connections for coolant hoses**
14. **Throttle valve control module**
    - When replacing, adapt ECM using scan tool
15. **Gasket**
    - Always replace

Lower intake manifold assembly

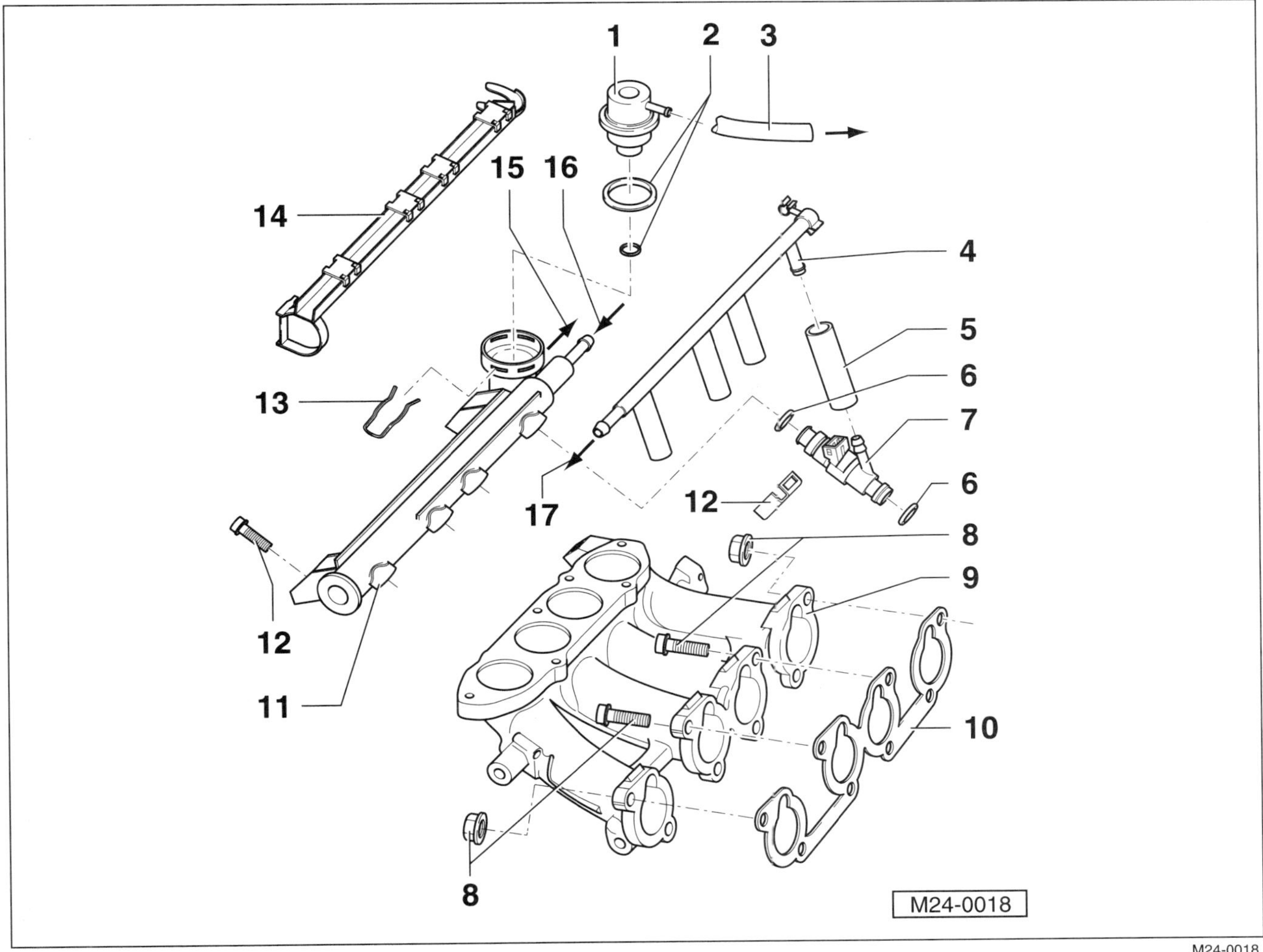

M24-0018

Fig. 4. Lower section of intake manifold and related components.

1. **Fuel pressure regulator**
   - With residual check valve
2. **O-rings**
   - Replace if damaged
3. **Vacuum hose**
   - To upper intake manifold section
4. **Air line**
5. **Air hose**
6. **O-ring**
   - Always replace
   - Moisten with clean engine oil
7. **Fuel injectors (N30, N31, N32, N33)**
8. **Bolt/Nut**
   - Tighten to 20 Nm (15 ft-lb)
9. **Intake manifold, lower section**
10. **Gasket**
    - Always replace
11. **Fuel rail**
    - Ensure it is securely seated
12. **Bolt**
    - Tighten to 10 Nm (7 ft-lb)
13. **Retaining clip**
14. **Cable guide**
15. **Return flow connection**
16. **Supply connection**
17. **To intake hose**

Air cleaner assembly

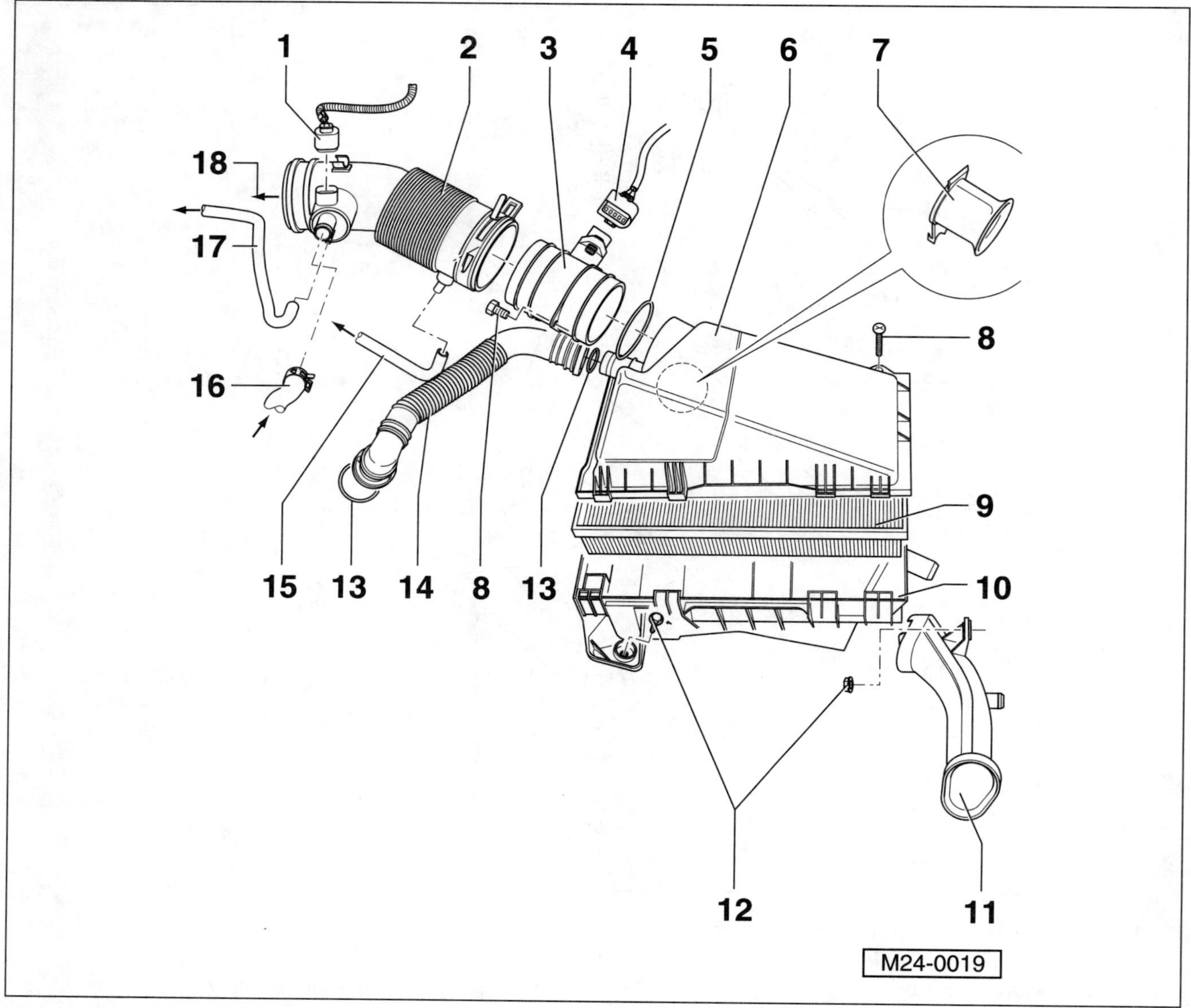

M24-0019

Fig. 5. Air filter assembly shown with element and related components.

1. **Harness connector**
   - Black, 2-pin
   - For PCV heating element
   - Check heating element voltage supply between terminals 1 and 2 with engine running: at least 11.5 V
2. **Intake hose**
   - With PCV heating element for crankcase breather
3. **Mass air flow sensor (G70) with intake air temperature sensor (G42)**
   - Checking intake air temperature sensor resistance, see Ⓐ
4. **Harness connector**
   - Black, 5-pin
5. **Seal**
6. **Air cleaner housing, upper section**
7. **Air duct**
8. **Bolt**
   - Tighten to 6 Nm (53 in-lb)
9. **Filter element**
10. **Air cleaner housing, lower section**
11. **Air duct**
12. **Bolt/nut**
   - Tighten to 10 Nm (7 ft-lb)

13. **O-ring**

14. **Intake hose**
    - Press together at front to release
    - To secondary air injection pump motor

15. **Connecting hose**
    - To air lines for air shrouded injectors

16. **Connecting hose**
    - For crankcase breather
    - From breather housing on cylinder head cover

17. **Connecting hose**
    - From connecting hose on upper intake manifold

18. **To throttle valve control module**

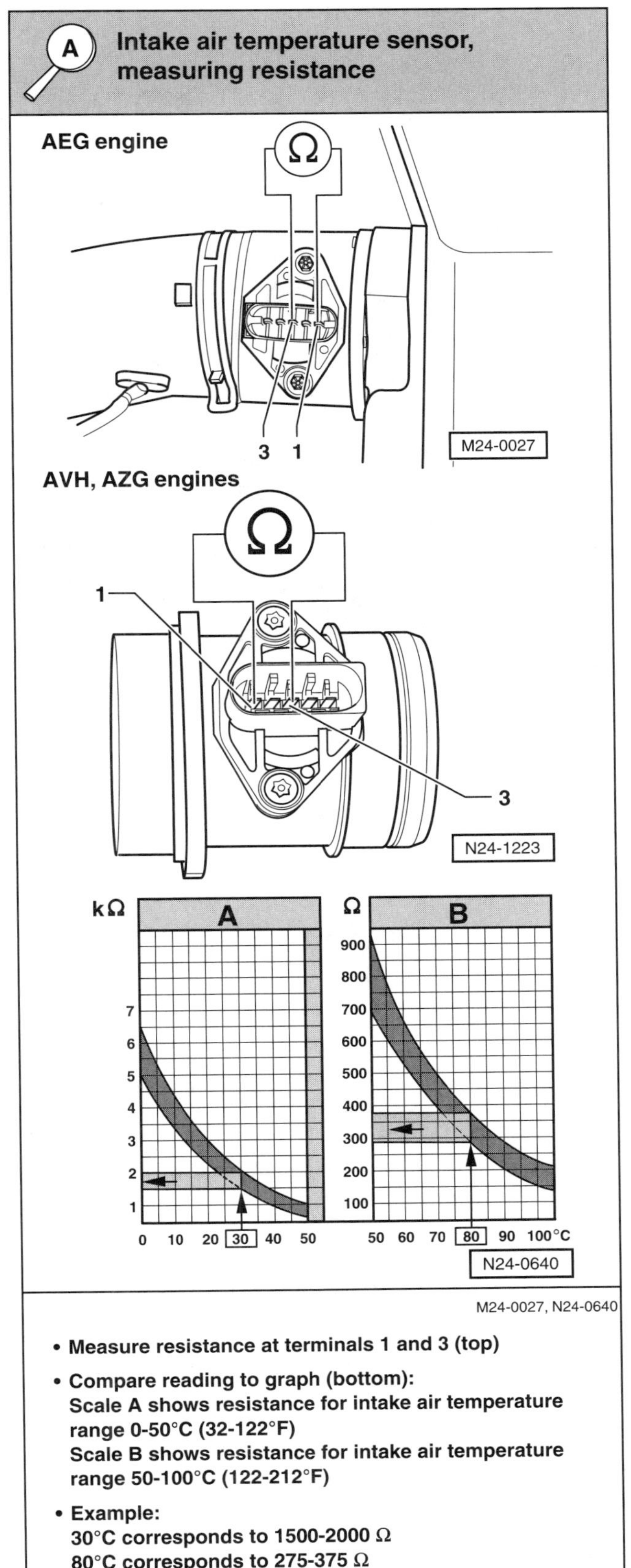

- **Measure resistance at terminals 1 and 3 (top)**
- **Compare reading to graph (bottom):**
  Scale A shows resistance for intake air temperature range 0-50°C (32-122°F)
  Scale B shows resistance for intake air temperature range 50-100°C (122-212°F)
- **Example:**
  30°C corresponds to 1500-2000 Ω
  80°C corresponds to 275-375 Ω

Engine Control Module (ECM)

The ECM is located in the air plenum near the base of the windshield in the engine compartment. Access to the ECM requires removal of the windshield wiper arms and the air plenum cover. See Fig. 6.

0024364

Fig. 6. ECM (**arrow**) at the rear of engine compartment in the center of the plenum (below bottom of windshield).

Engine speed sensor

Operation of the engine management system depends on a wide variety of input sensors. Failure of most of these sensors will allow the engine to continue to run, albeit poorly. One major exception to this is the engine speed sensor (G28). Failure of this sensor will prevent the engine from starting and running and will set a diagnostic trouble code in the ECM.

Note that most diagnostic functions require the use of a scan tool such as the VAG 1552/1552 or equivalent, however a quick check can be accomplished as follows:

1. Disconnect the grey 3-pin harness connector from the engine speed sensor plug near the secondary air injection pump.
   - AEG engine: See Fig. 7.
   - AVH, AZG engines: See Fig. 8.
2. Connect an accurate ohmmeter between terminals 2 and 3 and measure resistance.
3. Measure resistance between terminals 1 and 3, and between terminals 1 and 2.

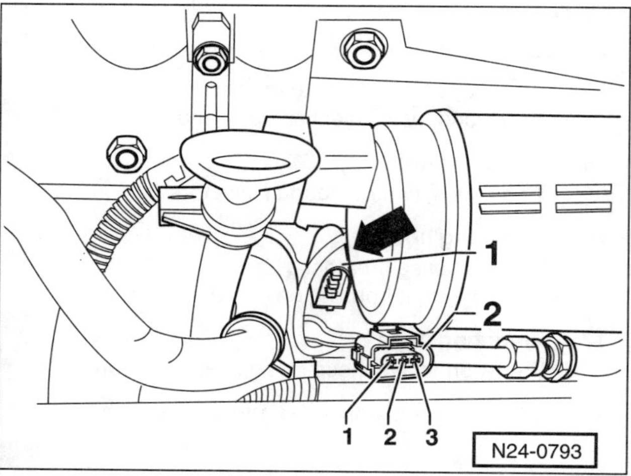

N24-0793

Fig. 7. Engine speed sensor (G28) harness connector (**1**) shown unplugged near secondary air injection pump on AEG engine.

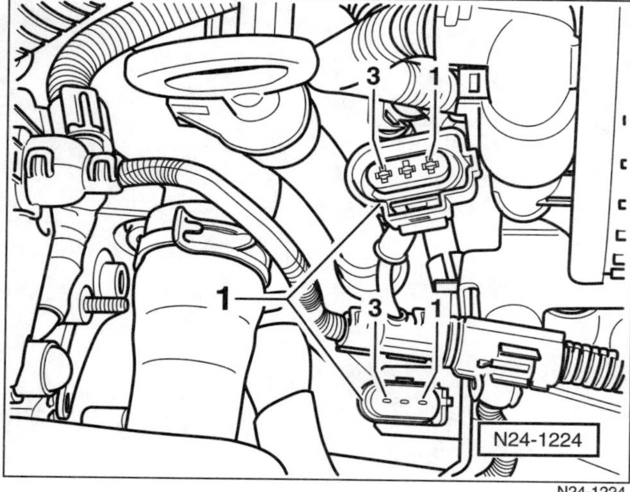

N24-1224

Fig. 8. Engine speed sensor (G28) harness connector (**1**) shown unplugged near secondary air injection pump on AVH/AZG engine.

Specification

- Engine speed sensor resistance values
  - Between terminals 2 and 3
    - AEG engine . . . . 480 to 1000 Ω
    - AVH, AZG engines . . . . 730 to 1000 Ω
  - Between terminals 1 and 2 . . . . infinity Ω
  - Between terminals 1 and 3 . . . . infinity Ω

4. If specification is not obtained, replace engine speed sensor.
5. If specification is obtained, and engine will not start, additional testing with a suitable scan tool will be required.

24c Fuel Injection–Motronic (2.8L engine)

TABLE

24c

GENERAL

This repair group covers the fuel injection/engine management system for the 2.8 liter VR6 gasoline engine. The operation of the Bosch Motronic ME7 engine management system is described in **2 Fuel, Ignition and Exhaust Systems.**

Special testing equipment may be necessary for some of the tests and repair procedures given here.

NOTE —

- *2.8 liter engines are equipped with the Bosch Motronic ME7.1 engine management system which is OBD II compliant. It is recommended that fault diagnosis and troubleshooting be carried out using Volkswagen scan tools VAG 1551, VAG 1552, VAS 5051 or equivalent.*
- *Fuel pump and fuel tank testing and repair along with EVAP information is covered in* **20 Fuel Storage and Supply**.
- *Electronic accelerator system (E-Gas) information is covered in* **20 Fuel Storage and Supply**.
- *Ignition system testing and repair is covered in* **28 Ignition System–Gasoline.**
- *Related systems such as Exhaust Gas Recirculation (EGR) and catalytic converters are covered in* **26 Exhaust System and Emission Controls**.

The Motronic ME7.1 system combines ignition, fuel injection and electronic accelerator pedal functions into one system managed by a single Engine Control Module (ECM). The system is fully adaptive and features built-in diagnostics that are capable of detecting and storing coded fault information.

CAUTION —
Disconnecting the negative (–) battery cable may erase fault codes and basic settings in the engine management and automatic transmission control modules. Some driveability problems may be noticed until the system re-adapts to operating conditions. OBD II readiness codes, which may be required for emissions testing, may also be erased. Convenience electronics (alarm system, interior light control, power locks, mirrors, and windows) may need to be re-set using a VAG 1551, VAG 1552, VAS 5051 or equivalent scan tool.

There are no basic adjustments or settings that can be made to the system without specialized equipment.

Safety precautions

The following warnings and cautions should be adhered to whenever working on the engine management system.

WARNING —

- *Fuel may be discharged during fuel system repairs. Do not smoke or work near heaters or other fire hazards. Have a fire extinguisher handy. Work only in a well-ventilated area.*
- *Wear suitable hand and eye protection when working with gasoline. Prolonged contact with fuel can cause illness and skin disorders.*
- *Fuel hoses in engine compartment must only be secured with spring-type clips. The use of clamp or screw-type clips will damage fuel lines and cause fuel leaks.*

> ***CAUTION —***
> - *Connect and disconnect wires and test equipment only with the ignition switched off.*
> - *Before making any electrical tests that require the engine to be cranked using the starter, disable the ignition system as described in* **28a Ignition System.**
> - *Do not use sealants containing silicones. Particles of silicone drawn into the engine will not be burned in the engine and will damage the heated oxygen sensor. Use only sealants and engine chemicals marked as safe for oxygen sensors.*
> - *During testing, it is possible for the Engine Control Module to recognize and store a diagnostic trouble code (DTC) that was due solely to the testing procedure. Therefore, after completing repairs, the DTC memory must be checked and erased as necessary with a scan tool such as VAG 1551, VAG 1552, VAS 5051 or equivalent*
> - *Cleanliness is essential when working on the fuel system. Thoroughly clean fuel line connections and surrounding areas before loosening. Avoid the use of compressed air. Avoid moving the vehicle. Only install clean components.*

ON BOARD DIAGNOSTICS (OBD)

On Board Diagnostics, found on the Bosch Motronic ME7.1 Engine Management Systems monitor most aspects of engine operation. The current generation OBD II system is integrated into all Volkswagen gasoline engines. For a description of the system and an overview of operation, see **2 Fuel, Ignition, and Exhaust Systems.**

Because of the large number of operating parameters monitored and the vast quantity of data available, fault diagnosis can only be properly carried out using a suitable scan tool such as Volkswagen special tools VAG 1551, VAG 1552 or VAS 5051 or equivalent. The engine control module or ECM also supports certain limited functions in a government-mandated generic scan tool mode. These functions are standardized for all OBD II compliant vehicles, but are not as comprehensive as those found by using the VAG 1551/1552 or VAS 5051 in the proprietary mode of operation.

During repairs where the battery must be disconnected, consideration must be given to the effect that this will have on the vehicle in general and the engine management system in particular.

- Diagnostic Trouble Codes may be erased.
- Readiness codes may be erased.
- Fault counters that monitor certain functions will be reset to zero.
- Adaptive leaning values will be set to default.

Because the ignition, fuel injection, accelerator system and emission control functions are even more inter-related than on previous Motronic versions, it is difficult, if not impossible to isolate general driveability problems by examining individual components of the system. For this reason, a suitable scan tool must be used for diagnosis if driveability problems occur or if the malfunction indicator light (MIL) or E-Gas System lights (EPC) are illuminated. Access for the scan tool is through the Data Link Connector (DLC) under the lower left side of the instrument panel. See Fig. 1.

0024272

Fig. 1. Data Link Connector (DLC), (**arrow**) under left lower side of instrument panel.

Adaptation

The Motronic ME7 engine management system is adaptive. Idle speed, ignition timing, injection timing and quantity automatically compensate and adapt to changes in the engine due to wear and operating conditions. Minor problems such as mixture changes due to small vacuum leaks can be eliminated. As a result, idle speed, fuel mixture (CO%) and ignition timing are non-adjustable.

> ***NOTE —***
> *Beginning in 1994 (1993 in California) automakers are required by law to apply uniform terminology, words and terms for certain components according to SAE standard J1930. These standardized terms are used throughout this section.*

Readiness Codes

Federal and state legislation requires that all auto manufacturers build into their engine management systems the ability to check for proper operation of up to 8 functions. For the ME7.1 engine management system, the exact number depends on the equipment level of each particular vehicle. Most of the time, the readiness code will set itself after the appropriate conditions have been met. These may include a cold or a hot start, operation at a certain load or speed for a certain period of time, or operation at different temperatures. After repairs, it may be advantageous to confirm repairs rather than wait to see if they set on their own. Other than waiting, the only other method of setting the readiness codes on the Motronic ME7.1 system is with a scan tool. This method requires Volkswagen scan tool VAG 1551, VAG 1552, VAS 5051 or an equivalent aftermarket scan tool, and extensive knowledge of its operation and capabilities. Readiness codes are then generated according to instructions provided by the scan tool manufacturer. For the significance of the 8 digit readiness code, see **Table a**

Table a. Readiness code values

Digit position								Diagnostic Function
1	2	3	4	5	6	7	8	
							0	Three Way Catalyst
						0		Catalyst Heating (always 0)
					0			Evaporative Emissions System (Fuel tank vent system)
				0				Secondary Air Injection System
			0					Air Conditioning
		0						Oxygen Sensor
	0							Oxygen Sensor Heater
0								Exhaust Gas Recirculation - EGR (always 0)

The readiness code can be displayed in any of several areas within the ECM's diagnostic memory depending on the individual scan tool. It will always have a format consisting of 8 digits. If the 8 digit code contains characters other than the number 0, such as 10100110, than the readiness code is NOT set. When the code displays all zeros, i.e. 00000000, the readiness code IS set and no further action is required. The specifics of **Table a** apply to the 2.8L engine only. While the format is required to be the same for all engines, certain equipment may not be used on each engine. For example, the 2.8L engine does not use EGR and as such, digit number 8 will always show 0. Other engines that use EGR, such as the 1.9L diesel, will show either a 1 or a 0 as appropriate.

Engine control module coding

The Engine Control Module must "know" what equipment is installed in the vehicle in which it is operating. This process is known as coding and must be performed whenever the ECM is replaced as new ECM's are delivered in an un-coded condition. If the ECM is moved between vehicles such as might be the case for diagnostic testing, the coding will need to be changed if equipment is different. Coding memory is, however, retained when the battery is disconnected. If a new ECM is installed without being coded, the engine will usually run poorly and the automatic transmission (if equipped) will not function properly. The MIL will be illuminated. This coding process can only be done with Volkswagen scan tool VAG 1551, VAG 1552 or equivalent. For individual coding variations, see **Table b**.

Table b.
ECM Coding Variations

Coding	Vehicle and Equipment
00031	2.8L VR6 with Manual Transmission
00033	2.8L VR6 with Automatic Transmission

The appropriate code is electronically programmed into the ECM according to instructions provided by the scan tool manufacturer.

MOTRONIC ENGINE MANAGEMENT COMPONENTS

Fig. 2. shows an overview of the major underhood components with the upper sound absorber panel removed. Fig. 3., Fig. 5. and Fig. 6. show details of the various other components of the Motronic engine management fuel injection system.

NOTE —
Volkswagen identifies electrical components by a letter and/or a number in the electrical schematics. See **97 Wiring Diagrams, Fuses and Relays**. *These electrical identifiers are listed in parenthesis as an aid to electrical troubleshooting.*

Fuel injection system component locations, overview

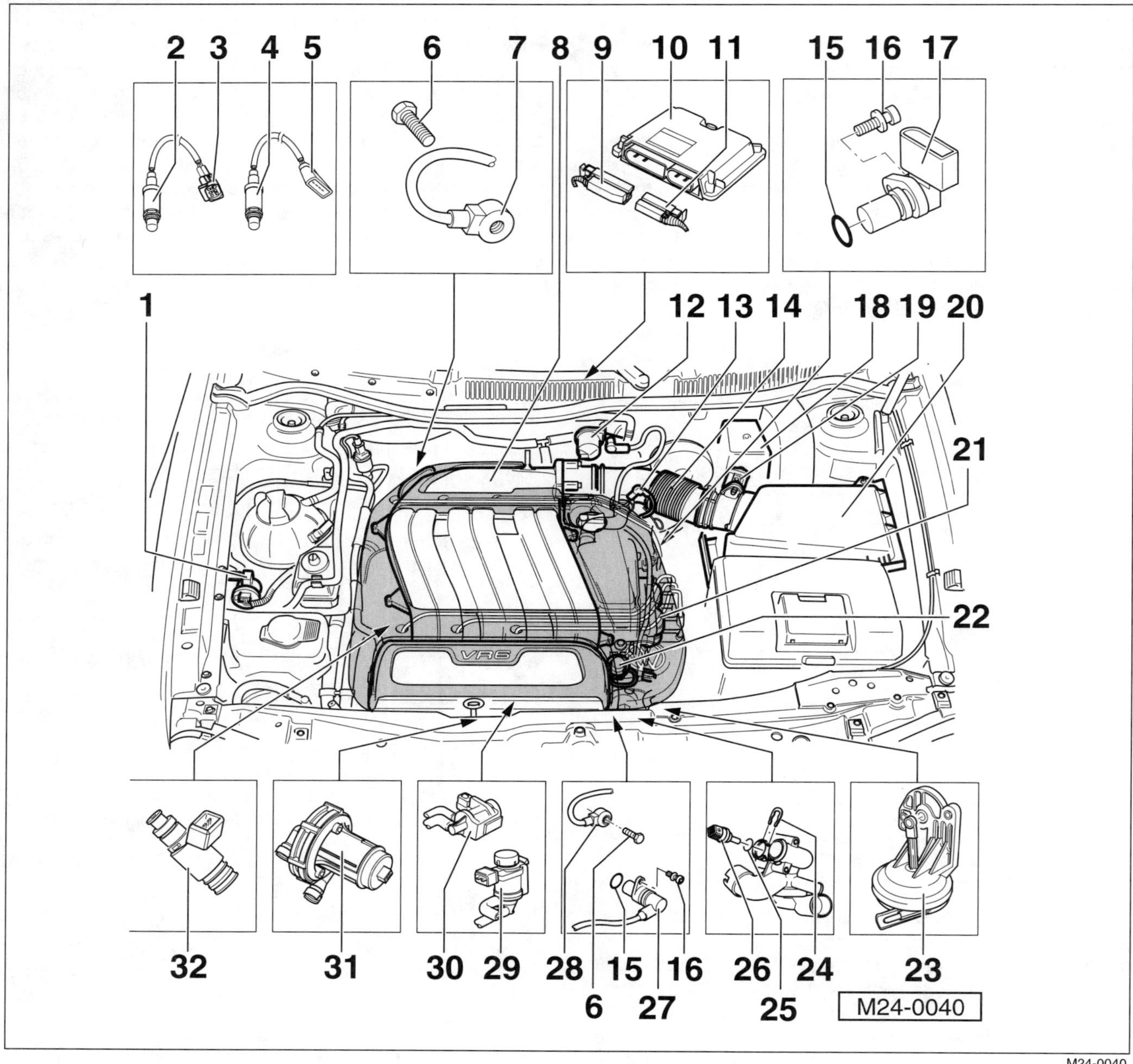

M24-0040

Fig. 2. Motronic ME7.1 underhood component locations on the 2.8L engine.

1. **Evaporative emissions (EVAP) canister purge regulator valve (N80)**
   - Location: Mounted to right side of engine compartment near front strut tower

2. **Heated oxygen sensor (HO2S), pre-catalyst (G39)**
   - Monitors combustion efficiency
   - Location: Threaded into front exhaust pipe ahead of catalytic converter
   - Tighten to 50 Nm (37 ft-lb)
   - Lubricate threads only with high temperature anti-seize
   - Do not allow anti-seize compound into the slots on the sensor body

(continued from previous page)

3. **6-pin harness connector**
   - Black
   - For pre-catalyst heated oxygen sensor (G39) and oxygen sensor heater (Z19)
   - Location: right underside of vehicle in plastic shield
4. **Heated oxygen sensor (HO2S), post-catalyst (G130)**
   - Monitors catalytic converter efficiency
   - Location: threaded into rear of catalytic converter
   - Tighten to 50 Nm (37 ft-lb)
   - Lubricate threads only with high temperature anti-seize
   - Do not allow anti-seize compound into the slots on the sensor body
5. **4-pin harness connector**
   - Black
   - For post-catalyst heated oxygen sensor (G130) and oxygen sensor heater (Z29)
   - Location: right underside of vehicle in plastic shield
6. **Bolt**
   - Tighten to 20 Nm (15 ft-lb)
   - Correct torque is critical for proper operation of knock sensors
7. **Knock sensor 1 (G61)**
   - Location: on rear of cylinder block (exhaust side)
8. **Intake manifold, upper section**
9. **81-pin connector (terminals 1 to 81)**
   - Only disconnect or connect with ignition switched OFF
10. **Motronic ME7.1 engine control module (J220)**
    - Location: in air plenum near base of windshield in the engine compartment
11. **40-pin harness connector (terminals 82 to 121)**
    - Only disconnect or connect with ignition switched OFF
12. **Throttle valve control module (J338)**
    - For Electronic Power Control, EPC, (E-Gas System)
13. **Positive crankcase ventilation (PCV) heating element, N79**
    - Location: in crankcase breather hose
14. **Connecting hose**
    - Between throttle valve control module and mass air flow sensor/air cleaner assembly
15. **O-ring**
    - Always replace
16. **Bolt**
    - Tighten to 10 Nm (7 ft-lb)
17. **Camshaft position sensor (G40)**
    - Location: on rear of cylinder head near ignition coil pack
    - Shutter wheel (rotor) mounted on exhaust side camshaft
18. **Protective cover**
    - For secondary air injection pump relay (J229)
19. **Mass air flow sensor (MAF), (G70) with intake air temperature sensor (IAT), (G42)**
20. **Air filter assembly**
21. **Ignition coil pack (N152)**
    - With power output stages
22. **Fuel pressure regulator**
    - Location: on fuel rail
23. **Vacuum servo**
    - For intake manifold rotary change-over valve
    - For intake manifold change-over to performance port
24. **Retaining clip**
    - Ensure clip is securely seated
25. **O-ring**
    - Replace if damaged
26. **Engine coolant temperature sensor (ECT), (G62)**
    - Blue
    - For engine control module
    - Combined with sensor (G2) for instrument panel warning light
    - Release cooling system pressure before removing
27. **Engine speed sensor (G28)**
    - Location: on front of cylinder block near oil filter
28. **Knock sensor 2 (G66)**
    - Location: on front of cylinder block (intake side)
29. **Secondary air injection (AIR) solenoid valve (N112)**
30. **Intake manifold tuning (IMT) solenoid valve**
31. **Secondary air injection pump motor (V101)**
32. **Fuel injectors (N30, N31, N32, N33, N83, N84)**
33. **Anti-seize compound, (not shown)**
    - High temperature
    - Volkswagen recommended anti-seize compound for all operations, G 052 112 A3

NOTE —

Volkswagen part numbers are given for reference only! Always consult with your Volkswagen Parts Department or aftermarket parts specialist for the latest parts information.

Fuel injection system components, removing and installing

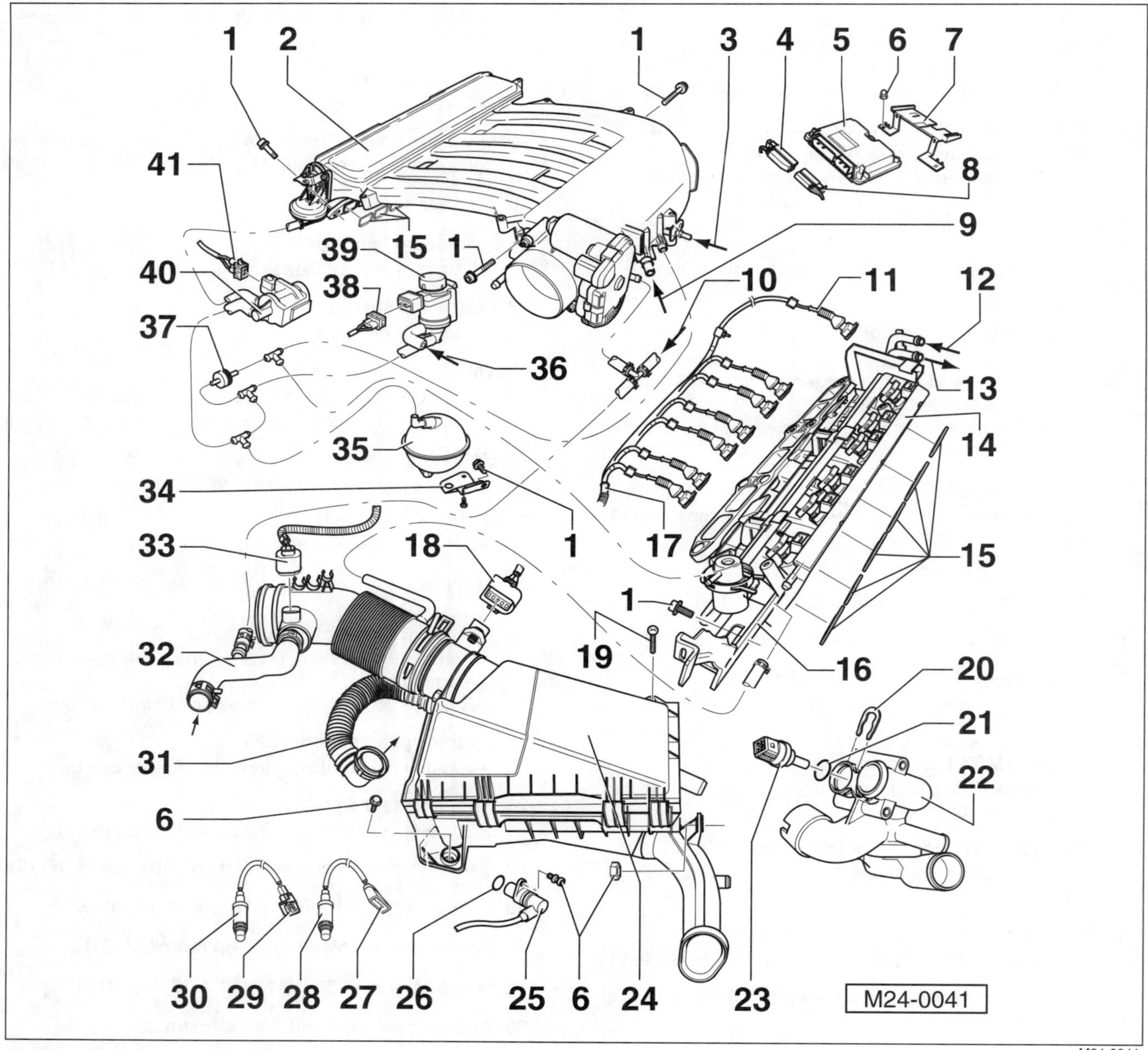

M24-0041

Fig. 3. Motronic ME7.1 system elements and related components.

1. **Bolt**
   - Tighten to 25 Nm (18 ft-lb)
2. **Intake manifold, upper section**
   - Shown with throttle valve control module and intake manifold rotary change-over valve servo
3. **Vacuum connection**
   - To leak detection pump
4. **81-pin connector (terminals 1 to 81)**
   - Only disconnect or connect with ignition switched OFF
5. **Motronic ME7.1 engine control module (ECM), (J220)**
   - Location: in air plenum near base of windshield in the engine compartment
   - Coding required after installation
   - Must be matched to throttle valve control module (J338) with a scan tool if replaced

6. **Bolt**
   - Tighten to 10 Nm (7 ft-lb)

7. **Retaining bracket**
   - For engine control module

8. **40-pin harness connector (terminals 82 to 121)**
   - Only disconnect or connect with ignition switched
   - OFF

9. **Vacuum connection**
   - To power brake servo

10. **Vacuum connection**
    - To evaporative emissions canister purge regulator valve

11. **3-pin harness connector**
    - White
    - For knock sensor 1
    - All contacts gold plated

12. **Fuel supply connection**
    - Secure with spring clips only
    - From fuel filter

13. **Fuel return connection**
    - Secure with spring clips only
    - To fuel delivery unit in fuel tank

14. **Intake manifold, lower section**

15. **Intake manifold seals**
    - 2 different sizes
    - Always replace

16. **Bracket**
    - For secondary air injection pump motor and secondary air inlet valve

17. **Wiring harness**
    - With harness connectors for fuel injectors
    - With harness connector for knock sensor 1

18. **5-pin harness connector**
    - Black
    - For mass air flow sensor with intake air sensor
    - All sensor and harness connectors gold plated

19. **Bolt**
    - Tighten to 6 Nm (53 in-lb)

20. **Retaining clip**
    - Ensure clip is securely seated

21. **O-ring**
    - Replace if damaged

22. **Thermostat housing**

23. **Engine coolant temperature sensor (G62)**
    - Blue
    - 4-pin harness connector
    - For engine control module
    - Combined with sensor (G2) for instrument panel warning light
    - ECT sensor and harness connector contacts1and 3 are gold plated
    - Release cooling system pressure before removing
    - Checking resistance, **see** (A)

24. **Air filter assembly**

25. **Engine speed sensor (G28)**
    - Location: on cylinder block near oil filter
    - Inductive type sensor

26. **O-ring**
    - Always replace

27. **4-pin harness connector**
    - Black
    - For post-catalyst heated oxygen sensor (G130) and oxygen sensor heater (Z29)
    - Location: right underside of vehicle in plastic shield
    - Contacts 3 and 4 are gold plated

28. **Oxygen sensor, post-catalyst (G130)**
    - Monitors catalytic converter efficiency
    - Location: threaded into rear of catalytic converter
    - Tighten to 50 Nm (37 ft-lb)
    - Lubricate threads only with high temperature anti-seize G5
    - Do not allow anti-seize compound into the slots on the sensor body
    - Oxygen sensor heater voltage supplied by fuel pump relay

29. **6-pin harness connector**
    - Black
    - For pre-catalyst heated oxygen sensor (G39) and oxygen sensor heater (Z19)
    - Right underside of vehicle in plastic shield
    - Contacts 1, 2, 5 and 6 are gold plated

30. **Oxygen sensor, pre-catalyst (G39)**
    - Monitors combustion efficiency
    - With additional monitoring sensor
    - Location: Threaded into front exhaust pipe
    - Tighten to 50 Nm (37 ft-lb)
    - Lubricate threads only with high temperature anti-seize G5
    - Do not allow anti-seize compound into the slots on the sensor body
    - Oxygen sensor heater voltage supplied by fuel pump relay

(continued on next page)

Fuel injection system components, removing and installing (continued)

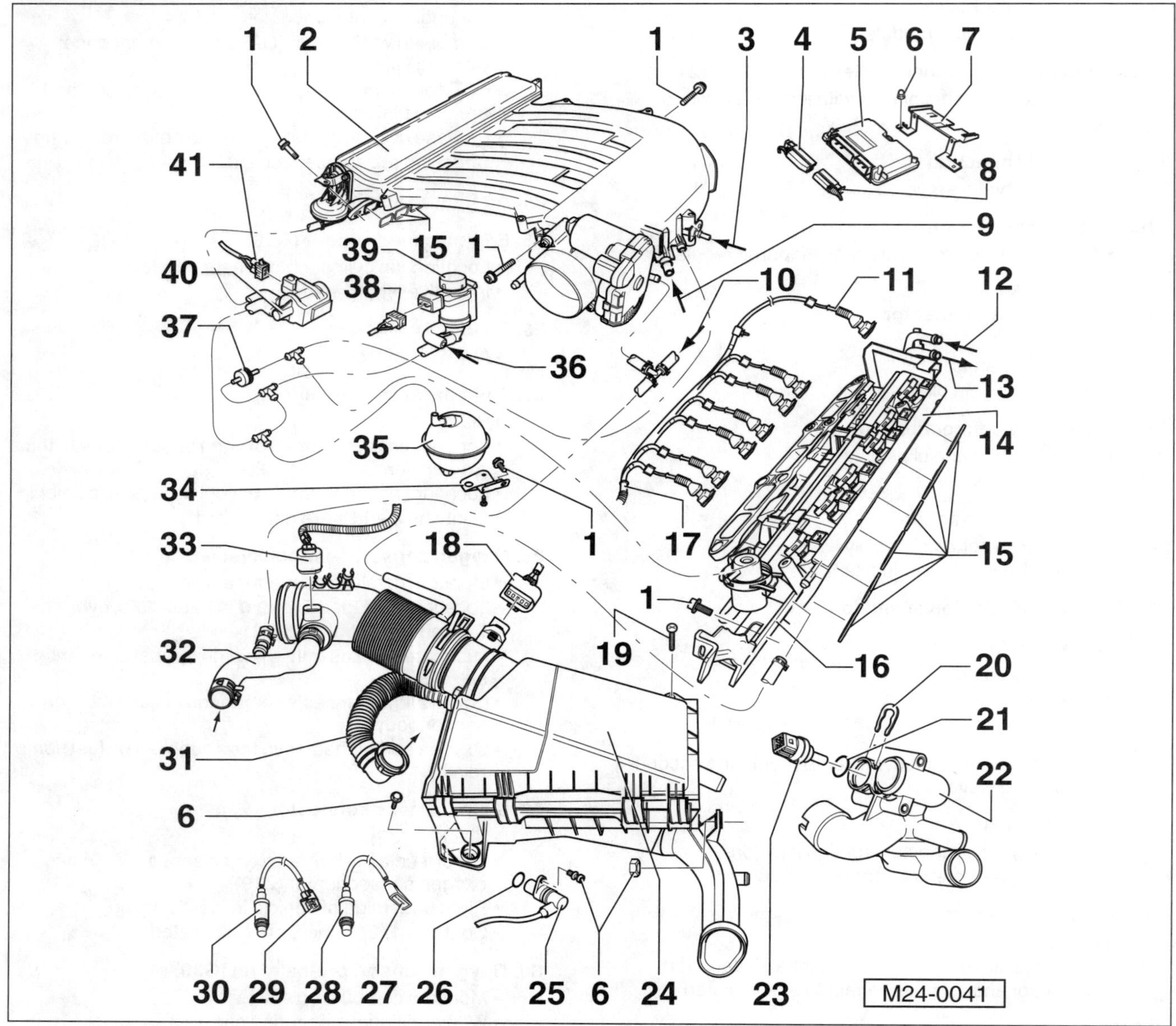

M24-0041

Fig. 4. Motronic ME7.1 system elements and related components.

(continued from previous page)

31. Intake hose
- From air cleaner housing upper section to secondary air injection pump intake
- Ensure hose is seated tightly
- Press together at front to release

32. Connecting hose
- From crankcase breather housing on cylinder head (valve) cover

33. 2-pin harness connector
- Black
- For positive crankcase ventilation (PCV) heating element
- Specified supply voltage with engine running: minimum 11.5 volts

34. Bracket
- Mounted to oil pan

35. Vacuum reservoir
- For intake manifold rotary change-over valve and servo

(continued from previous page)

36. Vacuum connection
- To secondary air injection solenoid valve

37. Check valve
- Black side faces tee connection and vacuum source

38. 2-pin harness connector
- Black
- For secondary air injection solenoid valve

39. Secondary air injection (AIR) solenoid valve (N112)

40. Intake manifold tuning (IMT) solenoid valve

41. 2-pin harness connector
- Black
- For intake manifold tuning solenoid valve

42. Anti-seize compound, (not shown)
- High temperature
- Volkswagen recommended anti-seize compound for all operations, G 052 112 A3

NOTE —

Volkswagen part numbers are given for reference only! Always consult with your Volkswagen Parts Department or aftermarket parts specialist for the latest parts information.

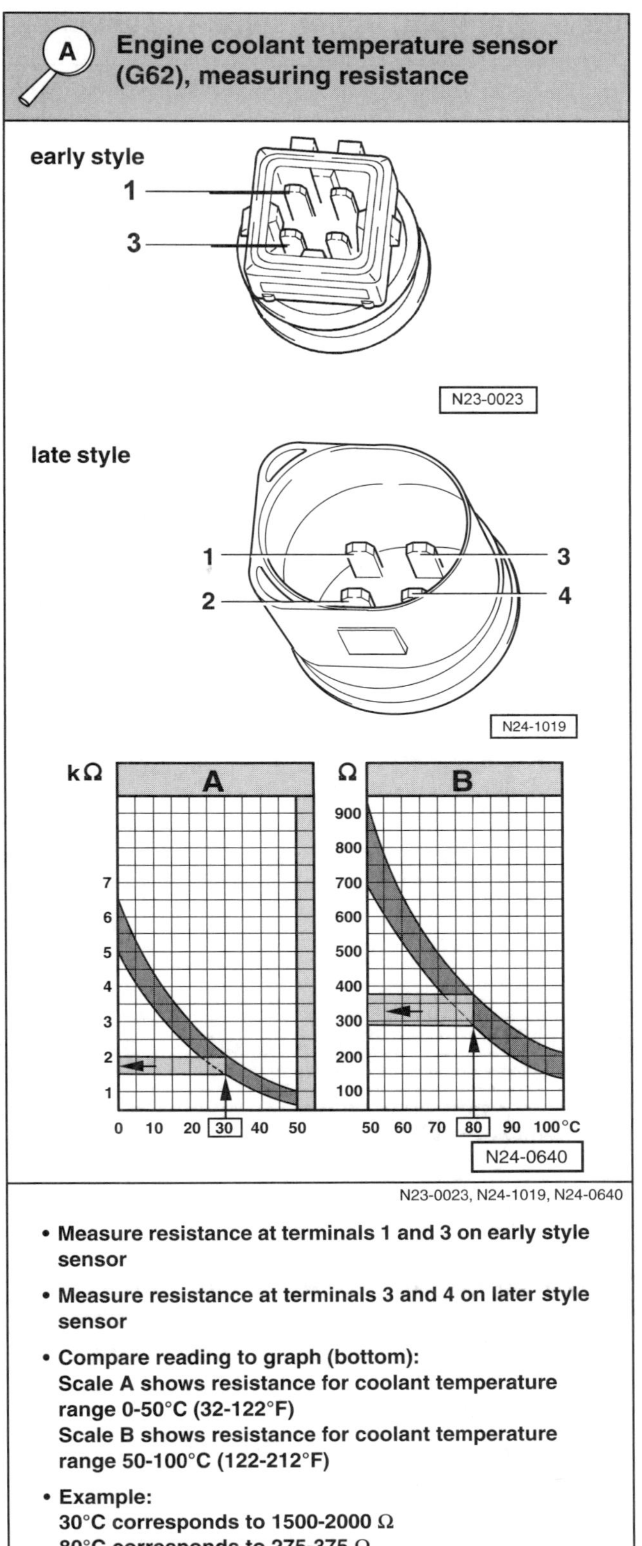

N23-0023, N24-1019, N24-0640

- **Measure resistance at terminals 1 and 3 on early style sensor**
- **Measure resistance at terminals 3 and 4 on later style sensor**
- **Compare reading to graph (bottom):**
  Scale A shows resistance for coolant temperature range 0-50°C (32-122°F)
  Scale B shows resistance for coolant temperature range 50-100°C (122-212°F)
- **Example:**
  30°C corresponds to 1500-2000 Ω
  80°C corresponds to 275-375 Ω

Intake manifold, upper section, assembly

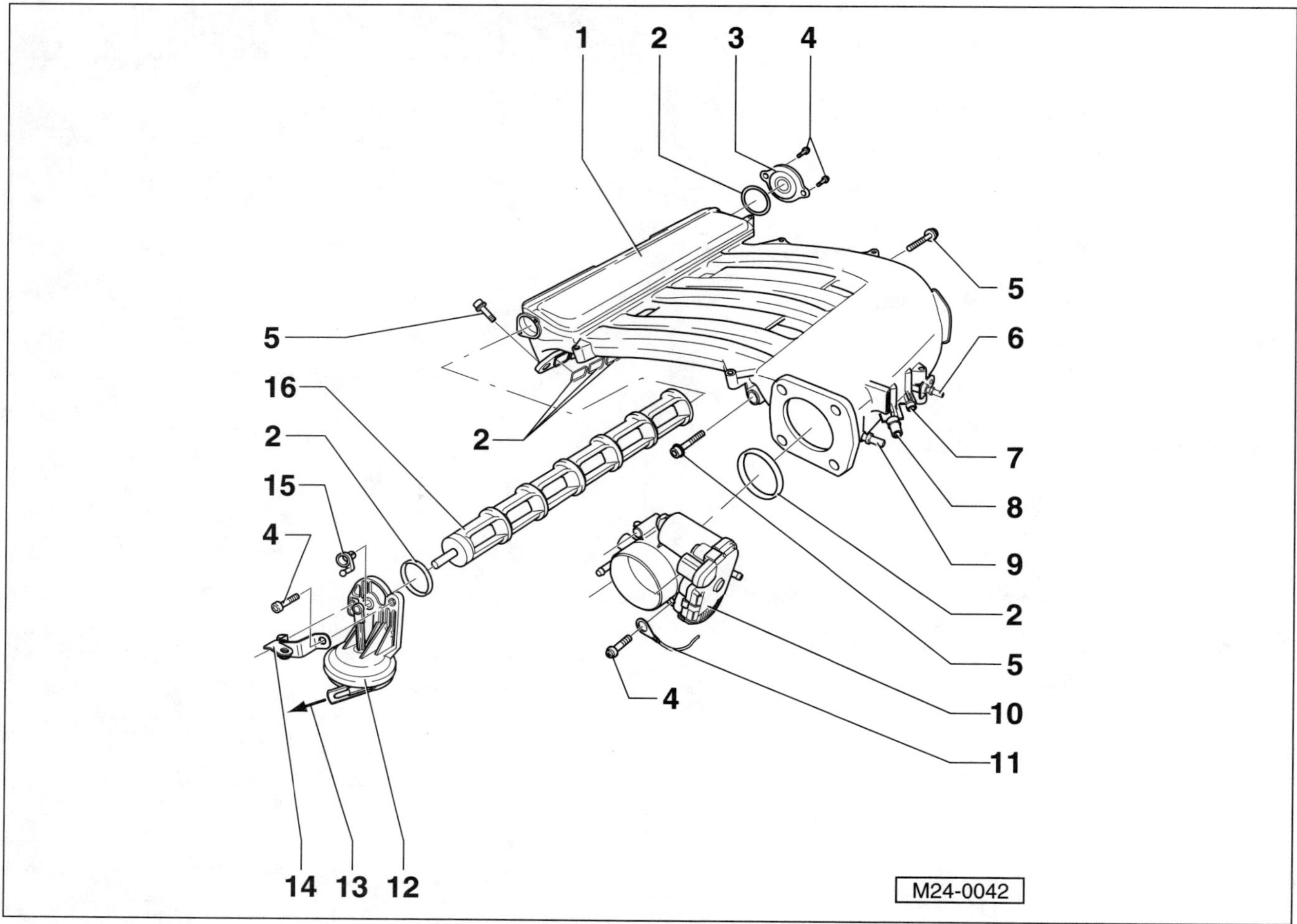

M24-0042

Fig. 5. Upper section of intake manifold shown with rotary change-over valve and related components

1. **Intake manifold, upper section**
2. **O-ring**
   - Always replace
3. **Bearing cap**
4. **Bolt**
   - Tighten to 10 Nm (7 ft-lb)
5. **Bolt**
   - Tighten to 25 Nm (18 ft-lb)
6. **Vacuum connection**
   - To leak detection pump
7. **Vacuum connection**
   - To fuel pressure regulator, t-connectors, check valve related components
8. **Vacuum connection**
   - To power brake servo
9. **Vacuum connection**
   - To EVAP canister purge regulator valve
10. **Throttle valve control module (J338)**
    - For Electronic Power Control, EPC, (E-Gas System)
11. **Ground wire connection**
12. **Vacuum servo**
    - For intake manifold rotary change-over valve
    - For intake manifold change-over to performance port
13. **Vacuum connection**
    - To intake manifold tuning (IMT) solenoid valve
14. **Bracket**
    - For upper sound absorber panel
15. **Operating lever**
    - For intake manifold rotary change-over valve
    - Ensure lever is securely seated at both ends
16. **Intake manifold rotary change-over valve**

Intake manifold, lower section, with fuel rail, assembly

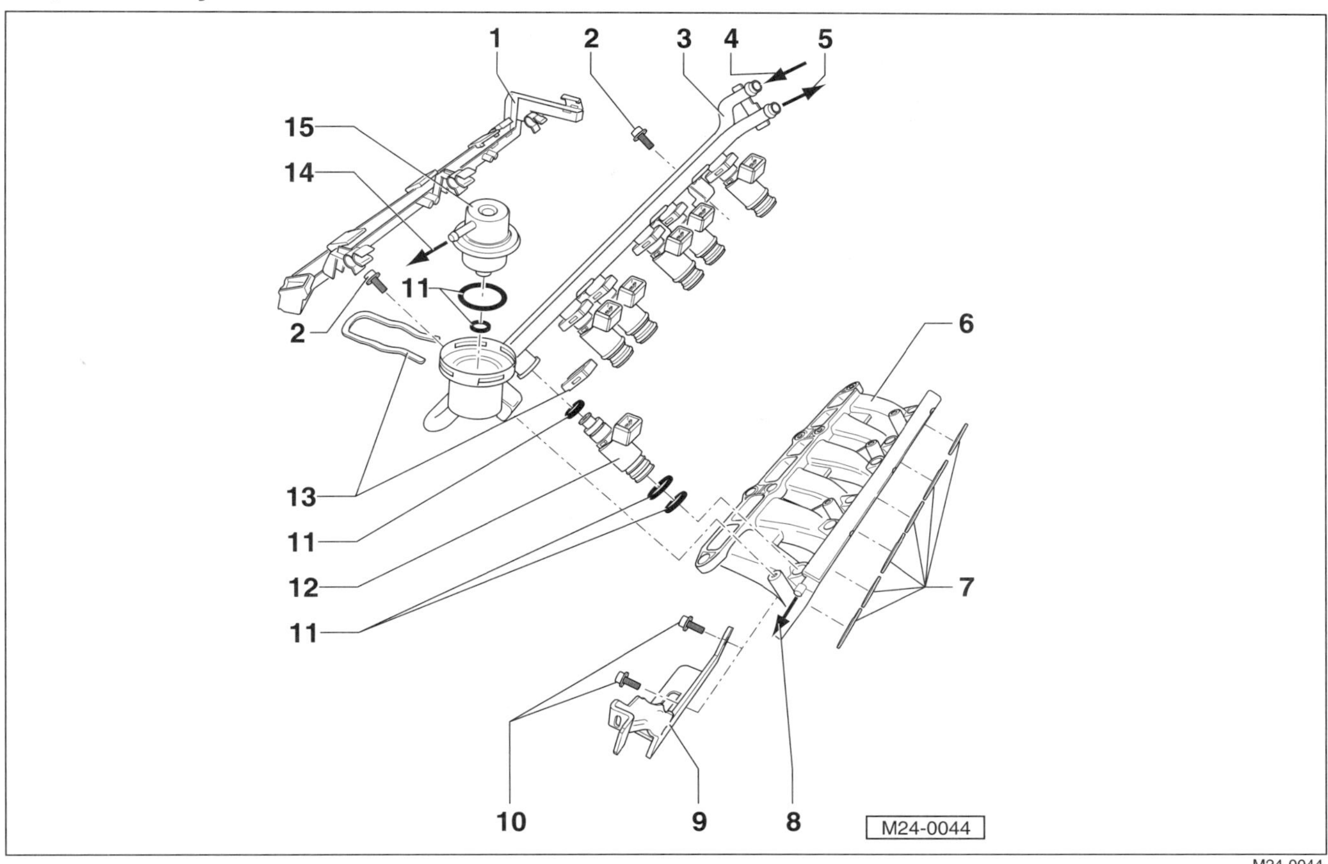

M24-0044

Fig. 6. Lower section of intake manifold shown with fuel rail, injectors and related components.

1. **Wiring harness cable guide**
   - Ensure it is securely clipped into fuel rail
2. **Bolt**
   - Tighten to 10 Nm (7 ft-lb)
3. **Fuel rail**
4. **Fuel supply line/hose**
   - Secure with spring clips only
   - From fuel filter
5. **Fuel return line/hose**
   - Secure with spring clips only
   - To fuel delivery unit in fuel tank
6. **Intake manifold, lower section**
7. **Intake manifold seals**
   - 2 different sizes
   - Always replace
8. **Vacuum connection**
   - To intake hose
   - For air shrouded injectors
9. **Bracket**
   - For secondary air injection pump motor and secondary air inlet valve
10. **Bolt**
    - Tighten to 25 Nm (18 ft-lb)
11. **O-ring**
    - Always replace
    - Moisten with clean engine oil or fuel before installing
12. **Fuel injectors (N30, N31, N32, N33, N83, N84)**
    - 2-pin harness connector
    - Air shrouded to improve fuel atomization
13. **Retaining clip**
    - Ensure it is securely seated
14. **Vacuum connection**
    - To upper section of intake manifold and t-connectors
15. **Fuel pressure regulator**
    - Fuel pressure regulator with residual check valve

Air cleaner assembly

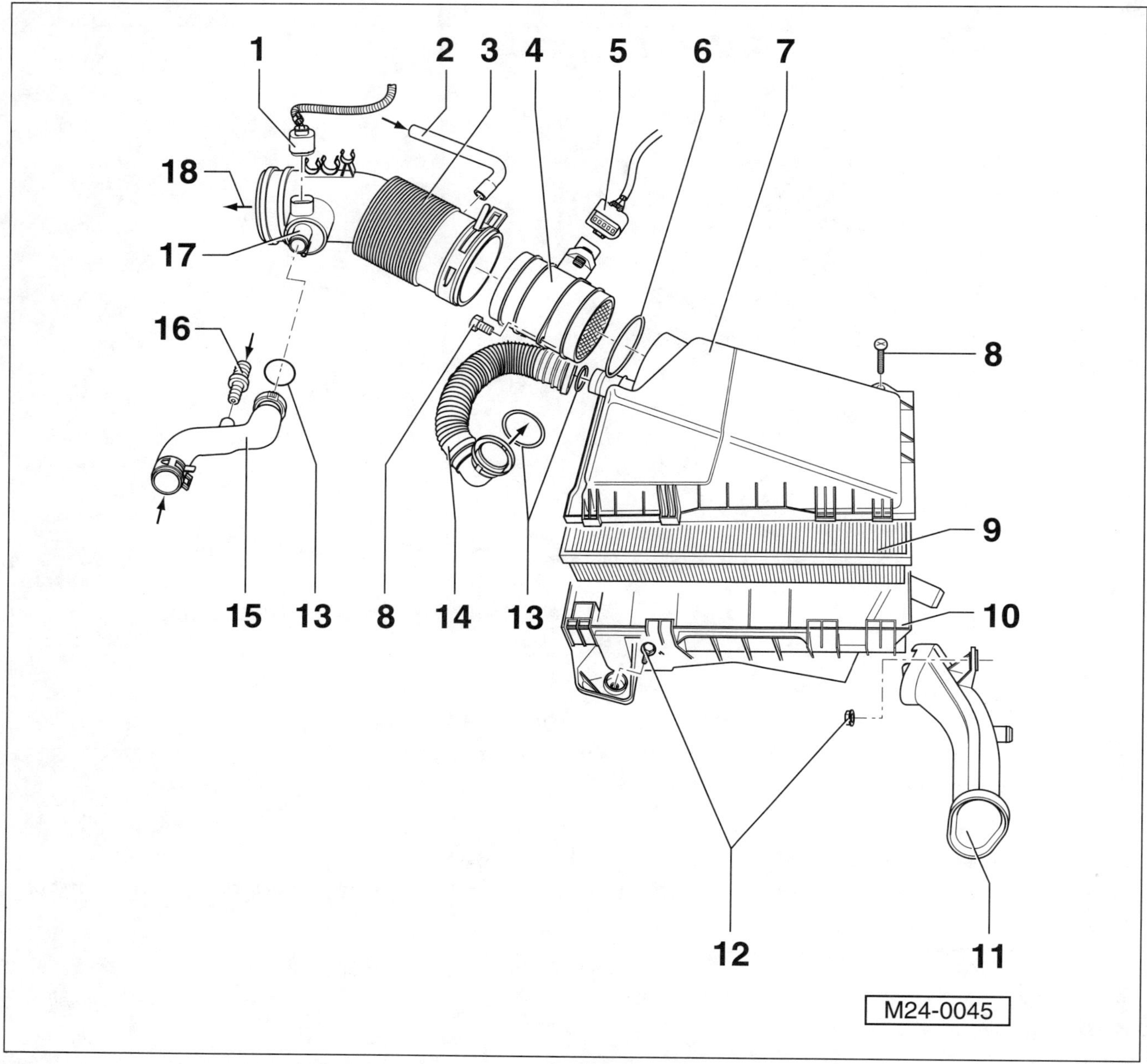

M24-0045

Fig. 7. Air cleaner assembly shown with element and related components.

1. **2-pin harness connector**
   - Black
   - For positive crankcase ventilation (PCV) heating element
   - Specified supply voltage with engine running: minimum 11.5 volts
2. **Connecting hose**
   - To intake manifold, lower section
   - For air shrouded injectors
3. **Connecting hose**
   - Between throttle valve control module and mass air flow sensor/air cleaner assembly
4. **Mass air flow sensor (MAF), (G70) with intake air temperature sensor (IAT), (G42)**
   - All sensor and harness connectors gold plated
   - Checking intake air temperature sensor resistance, **see** Ⓐ

(continued from previous page)

5. **5-pin harness connector**
    - Black
    - For mass air flow sensor with intake air sensor
    - All sensor and harness connectors gold plated
6. **O-ring seal**
    - Replace if damaged
7. **Air cleaner housing, upper section**
8. **Bolt**
    - Tighten to 6 Nm (53 in-lb)
9. **Filter element**
10. **Air cleaner housing, lower section**
11. **Duct, intake air**
12. **Bolt/nut**
    - Tighten to 10 Nm (7 ft-lb)
13. **O-ring**
    - Replace if damaged
14. **Intake hose**
    - From air cleaner housing upper section to secondary air injection pump intake
    - Ensure hose is seated tightly
    - Press together at front to release
15. **Connecting hose**
    - For crankcase breather
    - From breather housing on cylinder head (valve) cover
16. **Connecting fitting**
    - Note installed position
    - From tee connection and evaporative emissions canister purge regulator valve
17. **Positive crankcase ventilation (PCV) heating element (N79)**
    - Location: in crankcase breather hose
18. **Air flow to throttle valve control module**

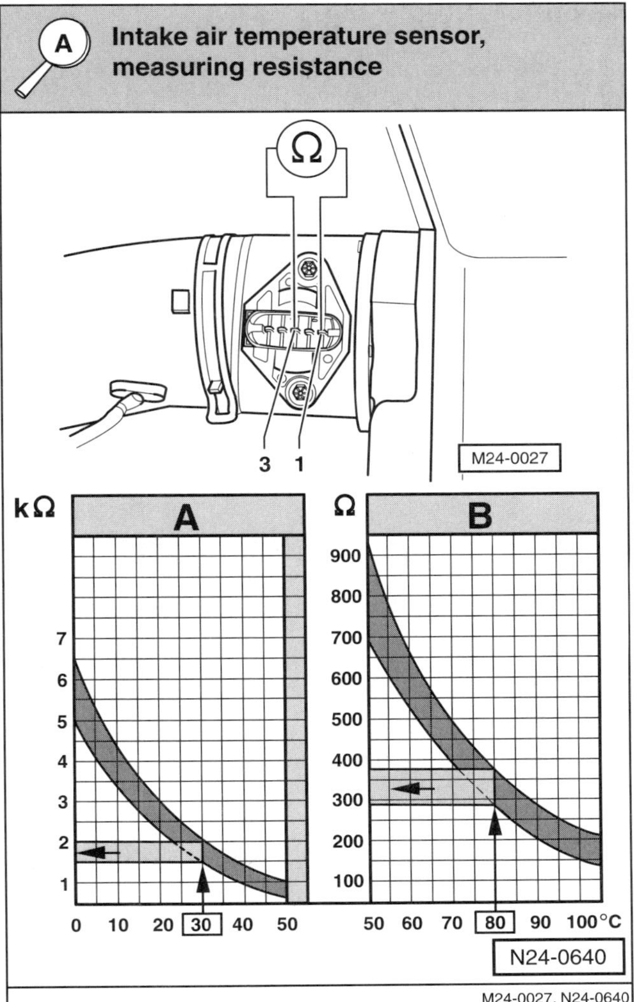

M24-0027, N24-0640

- **Measure resistance at terminals 1 and 3 (top)**
- **Compare reading to graph (bottom):**
  Scale A shows resistance for intake air temperature range 0-50°C (32-122°F)
  Scale B shows resistance for intake air temperature range 50-100°C (122-212°F)
- **Example:**
  30°C corresponds to 1500-2000 Ω
  80°C corresponds to 275-375 Ω

Engine Control Module (ECM)

The engine control module is located in the air plenum near base of windshield in the engine compartment. Access to the ECM requires removal of the windshield wiper arms and the air plenum cover. See Fig. 8.

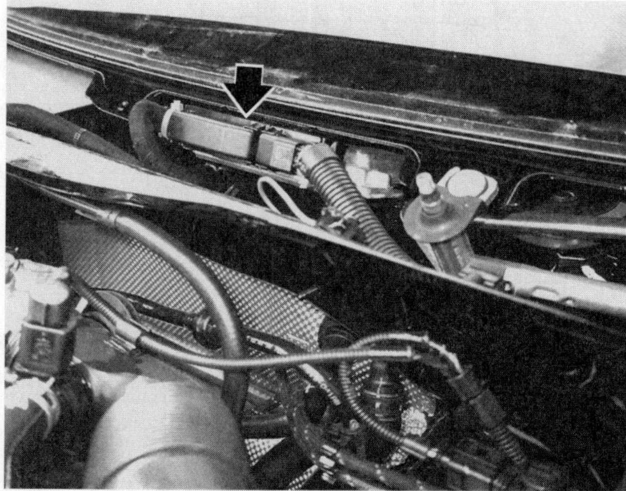

Fig. 8. Engine control module (**arrow**) is accessible from under the hood after removal of the wiper arms and plenum cover as shown.

> ***CAUTION—***
> *Use care when removing wiper arms and air plenum cover.*

Engine speed sensor

Operation of the engine management system depends on a wide variety of input sensors. Failure of most of these sensors will allow the engine to continue to run, albeit poorly. One major exception to this is the engine speed sensor (G28). Failure of this sensor will prevent the engine from starting and running and will set a diagnostic trouble code in the ECM.

Note that most diagnostic functions require the use of a scan tool such as the VAG1552, VAG1552, VAS5051 or equivalent, however a quick check can be accomplished as follows:

1. Disconnect the grey 3-pin harness connector from the engine speed sensor plug near the secondary air injection pump. See Fig. 9.

2. Connect an accurate ohmmeter between terminals 2 and 3 and measure resistance. See Fig. 10.

3. Measure resistance between terminals 1 and 3, and between terminals 1 and 2.

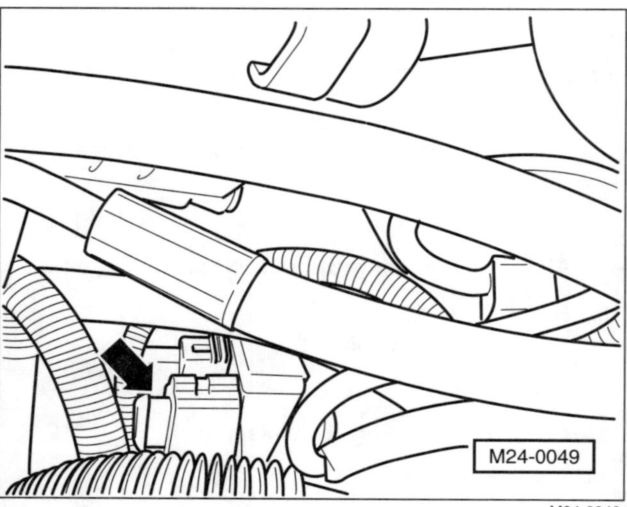

Fig. 9. Engine speed sensor harness connector (**arrow**) shown on front of engine. Harness connector is grey.

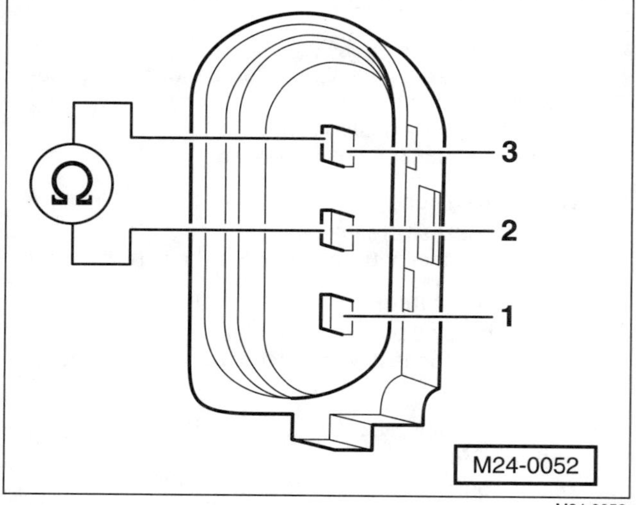

Fig. 10. Terminal arrangement in grey harness connector for engine speed sensor.

Specification

- Engine speed sensor resistance values, (2.8L engine)
  Between terminals 2 and 3 . . . . 480 to 1000 Ω
  Between terminals 1 and 2 . . . . infinity Ω
  Between terminals 1 and 3 . . . . infinity Ω

---

4. If specification is not obtained, replace engine speed sensor.

5. If specification is obtained, and engine will not start, additional testing with a suitable scan tool will be required.

26 Exhaust System and Emission Controls

GENERAL

This repair group covers repair and troubleshooting for the emission control systems and removal and installation of exhaust components.

Engine Codes

- AWD, AWW . . . . 1.8L 4-cylinder turbo gasoline
- ALH . . . . 1.9L 4-cylinder turbo diesel
- AEG, AVH, AZG . . . . 2.0L 4-cylinder gasoline
- AFP . . . . 2.8L 6-cylinder gasoline

NOTE —

- *Oxygen sensor (Lambda) system repair and trouble-shooting is covered in* **23 Fuel Injection–Diesel or 24 Fuel Injection–Gasoline**.
- *All cars have a self-diagnostic program to detect emissions-related problems and store coded fault information in electronic memory. When diagnosing an emissions-related problem it is best to first check for stored fault codes using VAG 1551/1552 or suitable scan tool.*
- *The cars covered by this manual have a vacuum hose routing diagram (sticker) located in the engine compartment which can be helpful when working with vacuum hoses.*

Service precautions

To help guard against personal injury or damage to car components, the following warnings and cautions apply when servicing the exhaust system.

> ***WARNING —***
> - *Exhaust gases are colorless, odorless, and very toxic. Run the engine only in a well-ventilated area. Immediately repair any leaks in the exhaust system or structural damage to the car body that might allow exhaust gases to enter the passenger compartment.*
> - *The exhaust system, catalytic converter and other emission control systems operate at very high temperatures. Allow these components to cool before servicing, or wear protective clothing to prevent burns. Do not use flammable chemicals near a hot catalytic converter.*
> - *Old corroded exhaust system components crumble easily and often have exposed sharp edges. To avoid injury, wear eye protection and heavy gloves when working with such parts.*
> - *Do not work under a lifted car unless it is solidly supported on jack stands designed for that purpose. Never work under a car that is supported solely by a jack.*

> ***CAUTION —***
> *Disconnecting the negative (–) battery cable may erase fault codes and basic settings in the engine management and automatic transmission control modules. Some driveability problems may be noticed until the system re-adapts to operating conditions. OBD II readiness codes, which may be required for emissions testing, may also be erased.*

EXHAUST SYSTEM (ALL ENGINES)

For safe and proper exhaust system operation, all components must be free of holes and all connections must be airtight. Check the system immediately if it becomes noisy or an exhaust odor is detected inside the car.

NOTE —
Excessive exhaust system back pressure can cause driveability problems such as a rough idle or stalling. Back pressure problems are caused by external damage such as crushed or collapsed parts, or internal damage such as a plugged catalytic converter.

Exhaust system replacement

The exhaust systems for the various engines available in the cars covered by this manual are illustrated in several exploded views later in this repair group. Use these illustrations as a guide for removal and installation. Tightening torques and other relevant installation information are given in the component lists.

A liberal application of penetrating oil to cold exhaust system nuts, bolts and slip joints will make removal easier. New fasteners, clamps and rubber mounts are always recommended when replacing exhaust components. Gaskets should be replaced whenever flange joints are disconnected. Use high-temp anti-seize compound on threaded fasteners to extend their service life and make future replacement easier. Some slight smoking and/or odor is normal as new exhaust system parts become hot for the first time.

> ***WARNING —***
> *Inspect the exhaust system heat shields on the car underbody and repair or replace any damaged parts. Heat shields protect the car occupants, undercoating, and various other components from excessive heat. Damaged or missing shields, particularly those above the catalytic converter, will increase interior temperatures and create a fire hazard.*

NOTE —
- *After performing repairs on the exhaust system, ensure that the system is not under stress and that it has sufficient clearance from the body. If necessary, loosen the double clamps and align the muffler and exhaust pipe so sufficient clearance is maintained to the body while the support rings are evenly loaded.*
- *When performing repairs, always replace self-locking nuts.*

Exhaust system, installation details

Fig. 1. through Fig. 4. show various details relevant to installing exhaust components in all cars covered by this manual.

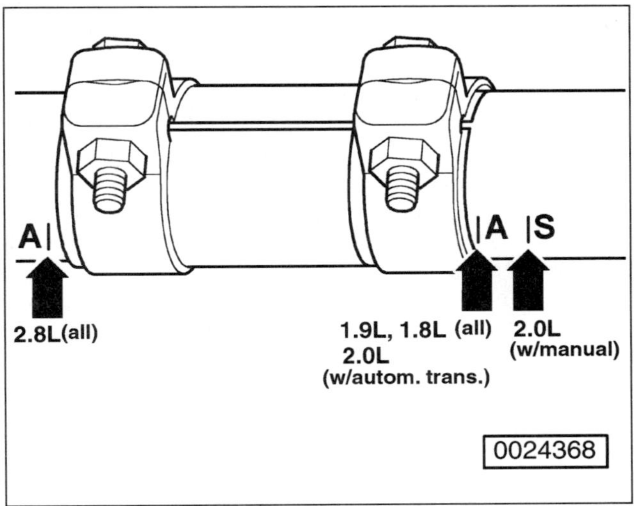

0024368

Fig. 1. Installation position of double clamp that attaches front and rear exhaust sections. Position clamp approx. 5 mm inside of appropriate mark based on engine/transmission.

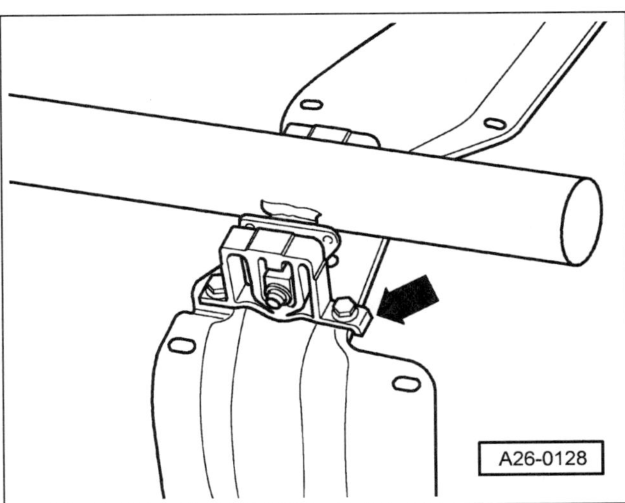

A26-0128

Fig. 2. Exhaust mount located behind double clamp. Ensure that tab (**arrow**) on foot of mount points forward.

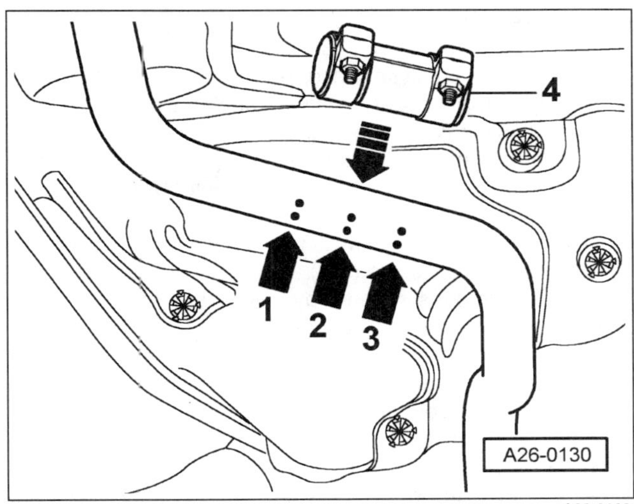

A26-0130

Fig. 3. Exhaust pipe separation point. Cut pipe at right angles at **arrow 2**. Repair clamp (**4**) is then positioned between **arrow 1** and **arrow 3**.

Tightening torque

- Exhaust pipe repair clamp bolts . . . . . 40 Nm (30 ft-lb)

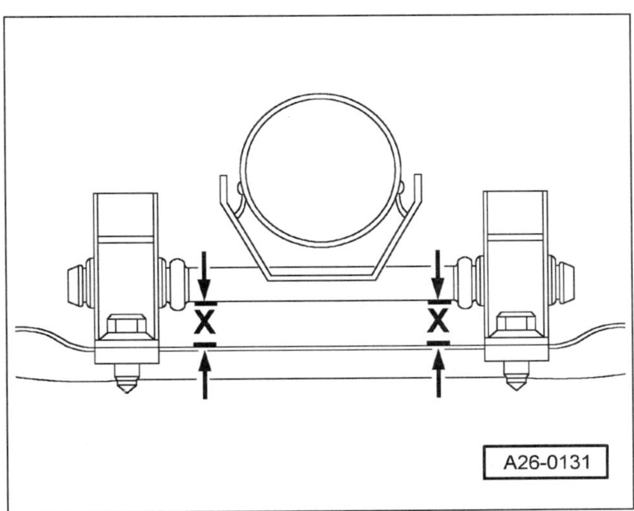

A26-0131

Fig. 4. Ensure that rear muffler is aligned stress free. Mounting pins on exhaust pipe must run parallel with tunnel bridge (dimension **X** should be equal on left and right sides).

Catalytic converter

The three-way catalytic converter used on gasoline engines chemically reduces pollutants in the engine exhaust. A properly operating converter provides a 90-95 percent reduction of the three major exhaust gas pollutants (nitrogen (NO_X), carbon monoxide (CO), and unburned hydrocarbons (HC).

On diesel engines a two-way catalytic converter is used that reduces carbon monoxide (CO) and unburned hydrocarbons (HC). Diesel engines covered by this manual do not use an oxygen sensor to monitor the catalytic converter.

The three-way (gasoline) catalytic converter works correctly only when the air/fuel ratio is kept within a very narrow range. On gasoline powered cars the oxygen sensor provides the feedback for control of the air/fuel mixture. For more information see **24 Fuel Injection–Gasoline**, for the appropriate engine.

The catalytic converter itself does not require any routine maintenance. However, any problem that increases converter temperature beyond its normal operating range (incorrect ignition timing or air/fuel mixture, engine misfire, prolonged idling or extended high engine loads) can damage the converter. Reduced power, stalling, exhaust system rattles and excessive emissions are symptoms that may be caused by a faulty catalytic converter.

Catalytic converters on gasoline powered vehicles covered by this manual use a second heated oxygen sensor to monitor the operation of the catalyst. If the converter fails to properly oxidize the spent combustion gasses, the heated oxygen sensor will detect this malfunction and a fault code (DTC) will be stored in the ECM.

Exhaust leaks anywhere in the system, but especially between the cylinder head and the catalytic converter, can cause running problems, false DTCs or converter failure.

> ***WARNING —***
> *Do not operate the starter for long periods if the engine fails to start. Extended cranking may allow excess fuel to enter the catalytic converter, creating a fire hazard and possibly damaging the converter.*

Accurately testing the function of the catalytic converter requires an infrared exhaust gas analyzer to check the air/fuel mixture adjustment (% CO) at the exhaust system test port upstream of the catalytic converter, and then again at the tailpipe. If the converter is working properly, the tailpipe reading will be lower than the test port reading. If the reading is the same or only slightly less, the converter is probably faulty.

Oxygen sensor, removing and installing

Testing the oxygen sensor requires specialized scan tool equipment. Scan tools are available from Volkswagen and aftermarket suppliers. For a list of the various Diagnostic Trouble Codes (DTCs) applicable to these scan tools, see **ST Scan Tool Codes** at the back of the book.

Removing and installing the oxygen sensor requires a special tool to avoid damaging the sensor. See Fig. 5.

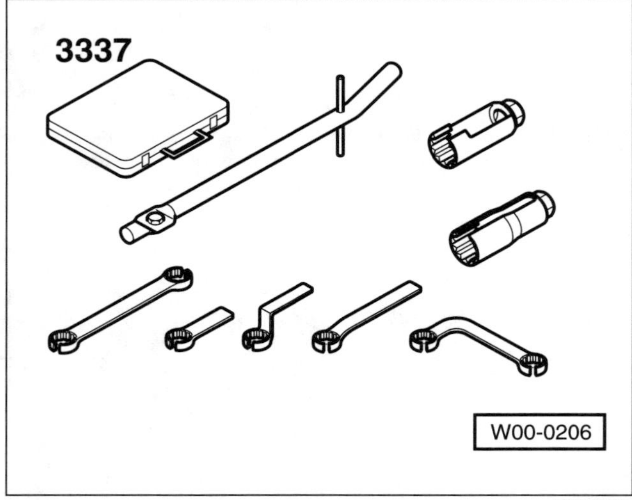

W00-0206

Fig. 5. Volkswagen special tool 3337 wrench kit for removing and installing oxygen sensors.

> ***CAUTION —***
> - *When installing oxygen sensor be sure to use high temperature anti-seize compound that contains no silicone and is marked "safe for oxygen sensors". (VW part # G 052 112 A3)*
> - *Volkswagen part numbers are given for reference only. Always consult with your Volkswagen Parts Department or aftermarket parts specialist for the latest parts information.*
> - *Do not allow anti-seize compound to enter slots on oxygen sensor body.*

EXHAUST SYSTEM (1.8L ENGINE)

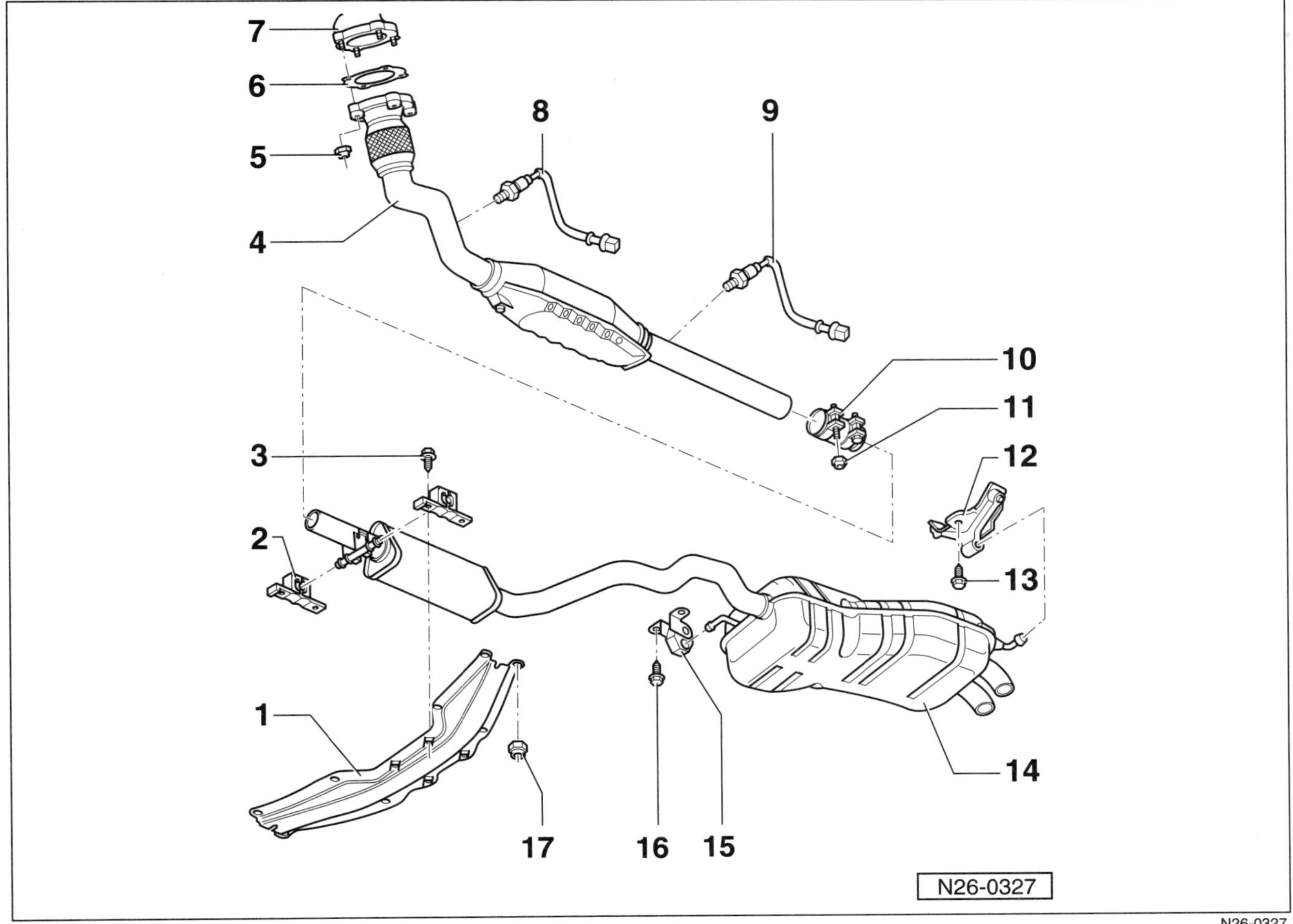

Fig. 6. Front exhaust pipe and catalyst for the 1.8L engine.

1. **Tunnel bridge**
2. **Support ring**
3. **Bolt**
   - Tighten to 25 Nm (18 ft-lb)
4. **Front exhaust pipe with catalyst**
5. **Nut**
   - Tighten to 40 Nm (30 ft-lb)
6. **Gasket**
   - Always replace
7. **Turbocharger**
8. **Oxygen sensor 1 (G39) (pre- catalyst)**
   - Tighten to 50 Nm (37 ft-lb)
   - See **Oxygen sensor, removing and installing**
9. **Oxygen sensor 2 (G130) (post-catalyst)**
   - Tighten to 50 Nm (37 ft-lb)
   - See **Oxygen sensor, removing and installing**
10. **Double clamp**
11. **Nut**
    - Tighten to 40 Nm (30 ft-lb)
12. **Support ring**
13. **Bolt**
    - Tighten to 25 Nm (18 ft-lb)
14. **Center and rear muffler**
    - Center and rear mufflers are installed as one unit but can be obtained individually when replacing
    - Saw through connecting pipe at separation point to replace mufflers individually, see **Exhaust system, installation details** given earlier
    - Install mufflers free of tension
15. **Support ring**
16. **Bolt**
    - Tighten to 25 Nm (18 ft-lb)
17. **Bolt**
    - Tighten to 25 Nm (18 ft-lb)

EXHAUST SYSTEM (1.9L ENGINE)

Front exhaust pipe and catalyst (1.9L engine)

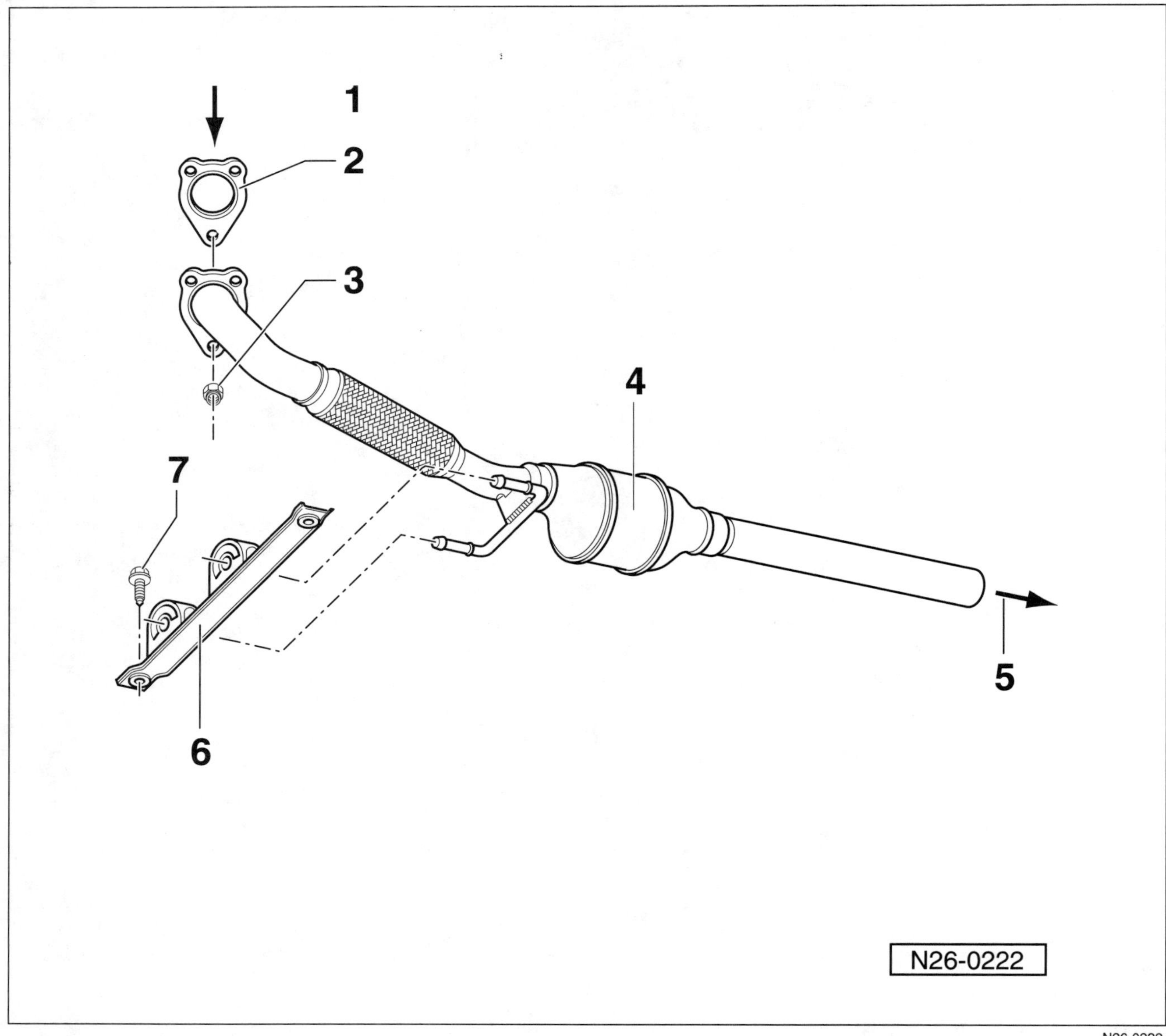

Fig. 7. Front exhaust pipe and catalyst for 1.9L diesel engine.

1. **From turbocharger**
2. **Gasket**
   - Always replace
3. **Nut**
   - Tighten to 25 Nm (18 ft-lb)
4. **Catalyst**
5. **To center muffler**
6. **Front support**
7. **Bolt**
   - Tighten to 25 Nm (18 ft-lb)

Muffler system (1.9L engine)

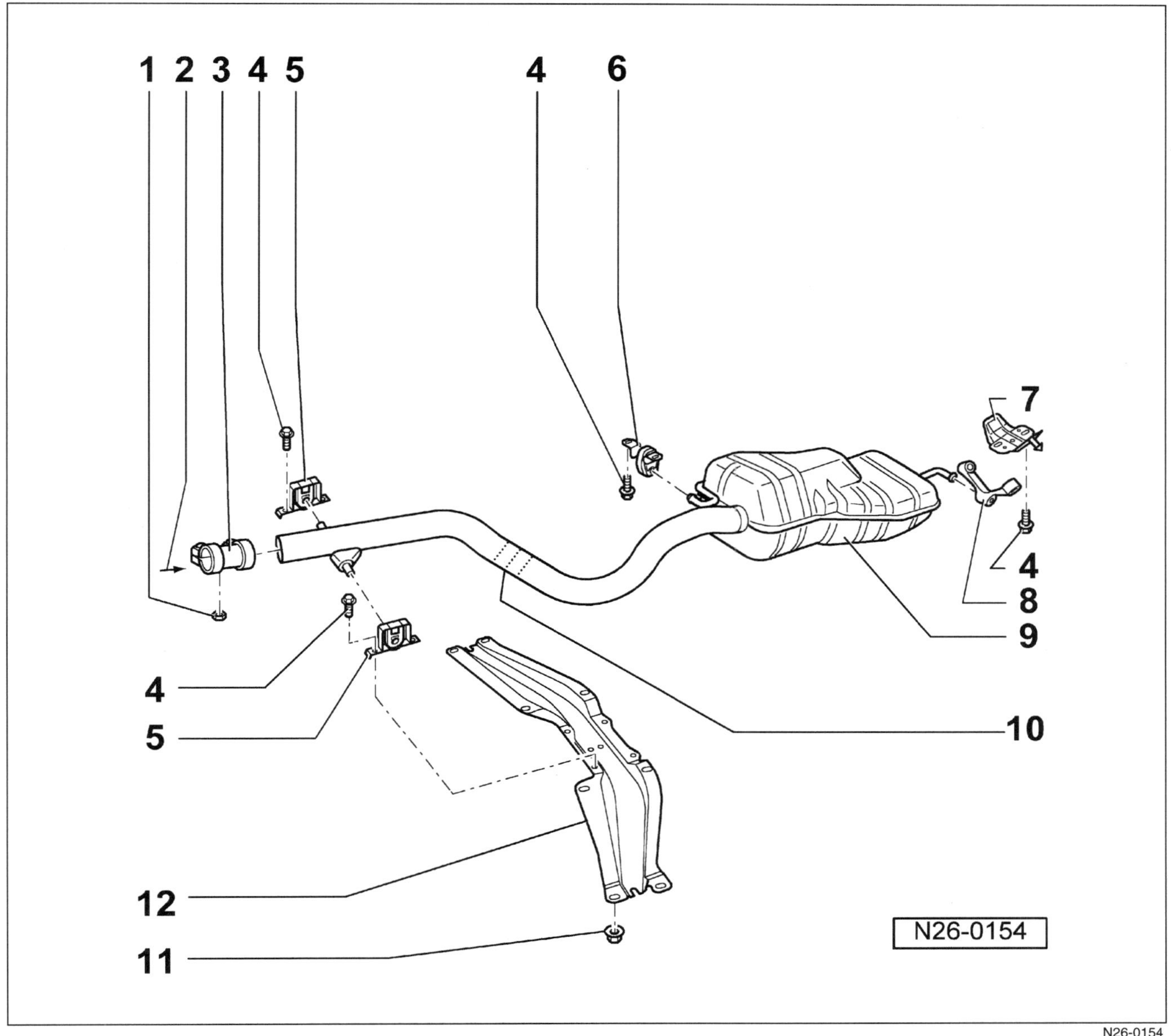

N26-0154

Fig. 8. Muffler and related hardware for 1.9L diesel engine.

1. **Nut**
   - Tighten to 40 Nm (30 ft-lb)
2. **From catalyst**
3. **Double clamp**
4. **Bolt**
   - Tighten to 25 Nm (18 ft-lb)
5. **Mount**
6. **Mount**
7. **Bracket**
8. **Mount**
9. **Rear muffler**
10. **Separation point**
    - Center and rear mufflers are installed as one unit but can be obtained individually when replacing
    - Saw through connecting pipe at separation point to replace mufflers individually
11. **Nut**
    - Tighten to 25 Nm (18 ft-lb)
12. **Tunnel bridge**

EXHAUST SYSTEM (2.0L ENGINE)

Exhaust manifold and catalyst (2.0L engine)

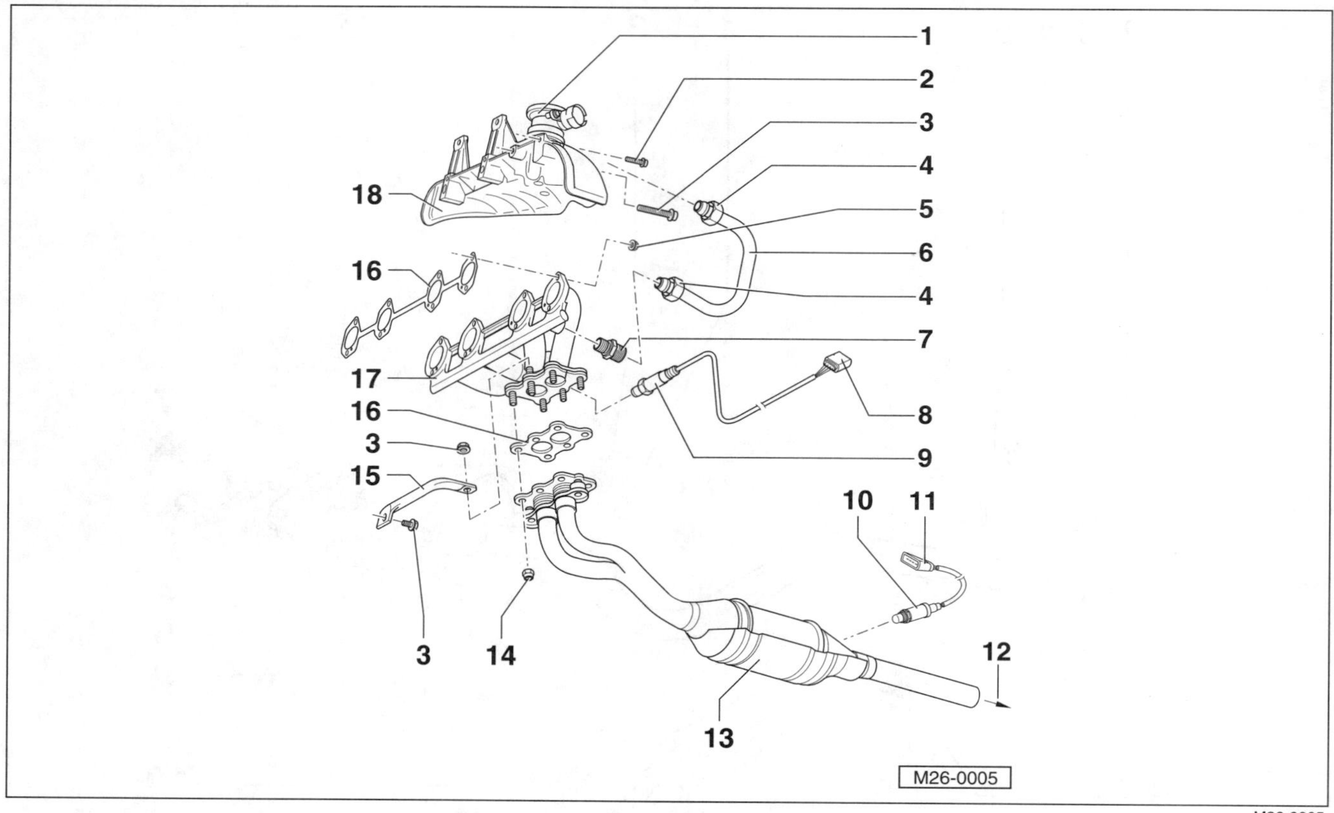

M26-0005

Fig. 9. Exhaust manifold, front exhaust pipe and catalyst for AEG 2.0L engine. AVH, AZG are similar.

1. **Combi-valve**
2. **Bolt**
   - Tighten to 10 Nm (7 ft-lb)
3. **Bolt**
   - Tighten to 25 Nm (18 ft-lb)
4. **Flare nut**
   - Tighten to 30 Nm (22 ft-lb)
5. **Nut**
   - Tighten to 25 Nm (18 ft-lb)
   - Always replace
6. **Connecting pipe for secondary air combi-valve**
7. **Union**
   - Tighten to 35 Nm (26 ft-lb)
8. **Harness connector**
   - For pre-catalyst Oxygen sensor
   - AEG engine: 4-pin
   - AVH/AZG engines: 6-pin
9. **Oxygen sensor 1 (G39) (pre-catalyst)**
   - Tighten to 50 Nm (37 ft-lb)
   - See **Oxygen sensor, removing and installing**
10. **Oxygen sensor 2 (G130) (post-catalyst)**
    - Tighten to 50 Nm (37 ft-lb)
    - See **Oxygen sensor, removing and installing**
11. **4-pin harness connector**
    - For post-catalyst Oxygen sensor
12. **To center muffler**
13. **Front exhaust pipe with catalyst**
    - AEG (shown) has two pipes to manifold
    - AVH, AZG have one pipe to manifold
14. **Nut**
    - Tighten to 40 Nm (30 ft-lb)
    - Always replace
15. **Exhaust manifold support brace**
    - AEG engine only
16. **Gasket**
    - Always replace (AEG shown)
17. **Exhaust manifold**
    - AEG (shown) has dual outlet manifold
    - AVH, AZG has single outlet manifold
18. **Warm air collector plate**

Muffler system (2.0L engine)

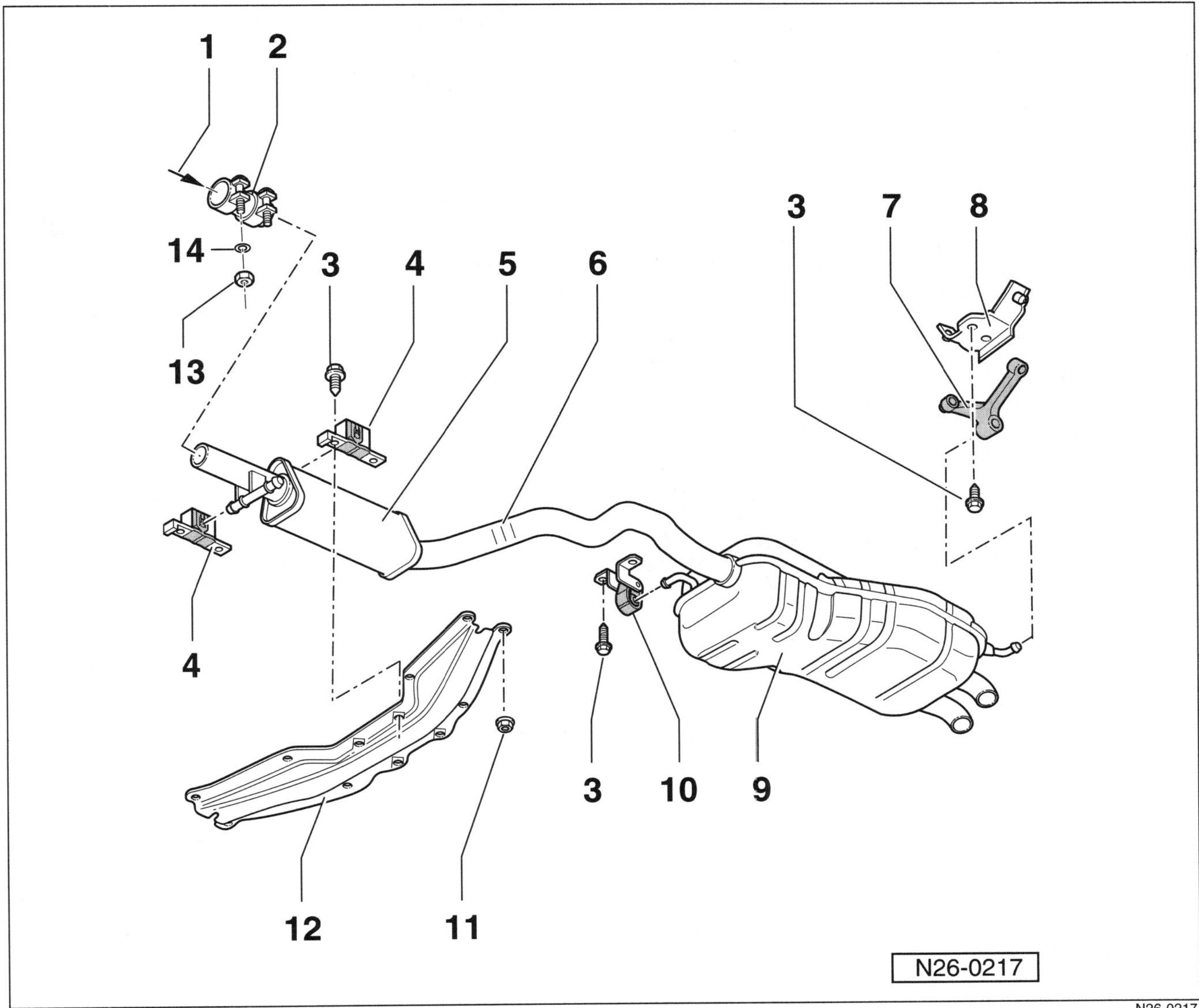

Fig. 10. Muffler system with related hardware for 2.0L engine.

1. **From front catalyst**
2. **Double clamp**
3. **Bolt**
   - Tighten to 25 Nm (18 ft-lb)
4. **Mount**
5. **Center muffler**
6. **Separation point**
   - Center and rear mufflers are installed as one unit but can be obtained individually when replacing
   - Saw through connecting pipe at separation point to replace mufflers individually
7. **Mount**
8. **Bracket**
9. **Rear muffler**
10. **Mount**
11. **Nut**
    - Tighten to 20 Nm (15 ft-lb)
12. **Tunnel bridge**
13. **Nut**
    - Tighten to 40 Nm (30 ft-lb)
14. **Washer**

Exhaust manifold, removing (AEG engine)

NOTE —
For removal of the exhaust manifold on the turbocharged 1.9L and 1.8L engines, see **21 Turbocharger and Intercooler**.

1. Remove engine cover.
2. Remove intake air hose. See Fig. 11.

0024367

Fig. 11. Remove intake air hose (**arrow**).

3. Remove pressure and vacuum hoses from secondary air injection valve (combi-valve). See **Secondary air injection system, components**, given later.

   NOTE —
   The combi-valve is located behind the upper intake manifold.

4. Remove connecting pipe between combi-valve and exhaust manifold. See **Exhaust manifold and catalyst** given earlier.
5. Remove warm air collector plate. See **Exhaust manifold and catalyst** given earlier.
6. Disconnect pre-cat oxygen sensor harness connector.
7. Remove right side inner CV joint protective cover (if installed). See Fig. 12.

0024260

Fig. 12. Remove bolts (**arrows**) for CV joint protective cover.

8. Unbolt right side inner CV joint and secure drive axle with stiff wire.
9. Remove nuts securing front exhaust pipe to exhaust manifold. **Exhaust manifold and catalyst** given earlier.
10. Unbolt exhaust manifold support brace from engine block.
11. Remove exhaust manifold bolts and manifold with support brace still attached.
12. Installation is the reverse of the removal noting the following:
    - Replace all gaskets and self-locking nuts/bolts.
    - **Exhaust manifold and catalyst** given earlier for tightening torques.
    - Use high-temp anti-seize compound on threaded fasteners to extend their service life and make future replacement easier.
13. Be sure to quality check your work, see **Quality Review** at the end of this repair group.

EXHAUST SYSTEM (2.8L ENGINE)

Exhaust manifold and catalyst (2.8L engine)

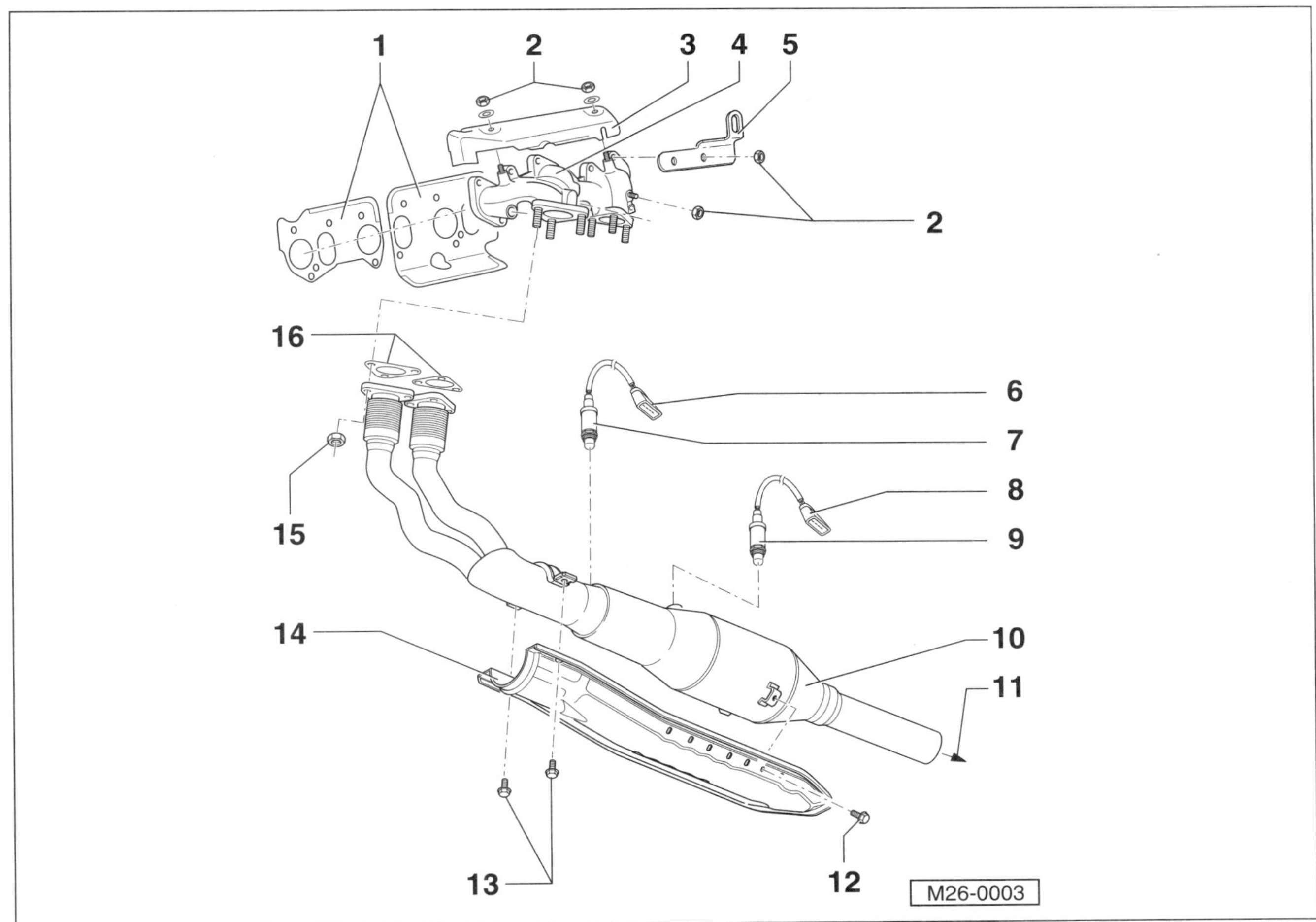

M26-0003

Fig. 13. Manifold, front exhaust pipe with catalyst, and related hardware for 2.8L engine.

1. **Seal**
   - Always replace
2. **Nut**
   - Tighten to 25 Nm (18 ft-lb)
3. **Heat shield**
4. **Exhaust manifold**
   - Two-piece
5. **Hanger shackle**
6. **6-pin connector**
   - Brown
7. **Oxygen sensor 1(G39) (pre-catalyst)**
   - Tighten to 50 Nm (37 ft-lb)
   - See **Oxygen sensor, removing and installing**
8. **Harness connector**
9. **Oxygen sensor 2(G130) (post-catalyst)**
   - Tighten to 50 Nm (37 ft-lb)
   - In catalytic converter
   - See **Oxygen sensor, removing and installing**
10. **Front exhaust pipe with catalytic converter**
11. **To muffler**
12. **Bolt**
    - Tighten to 10 Nm (7 ft-lb)
13. **Bolt**
    - Tighten to 15 Nm (10 ft-lb)
14. **Heat shield**
15. **Nut**
    - Tighten to 40 Nm (30 ft-lb)
16. **Gasket for front exhaust pipe**
    - Always replace

Muffler system (2.8L engine)

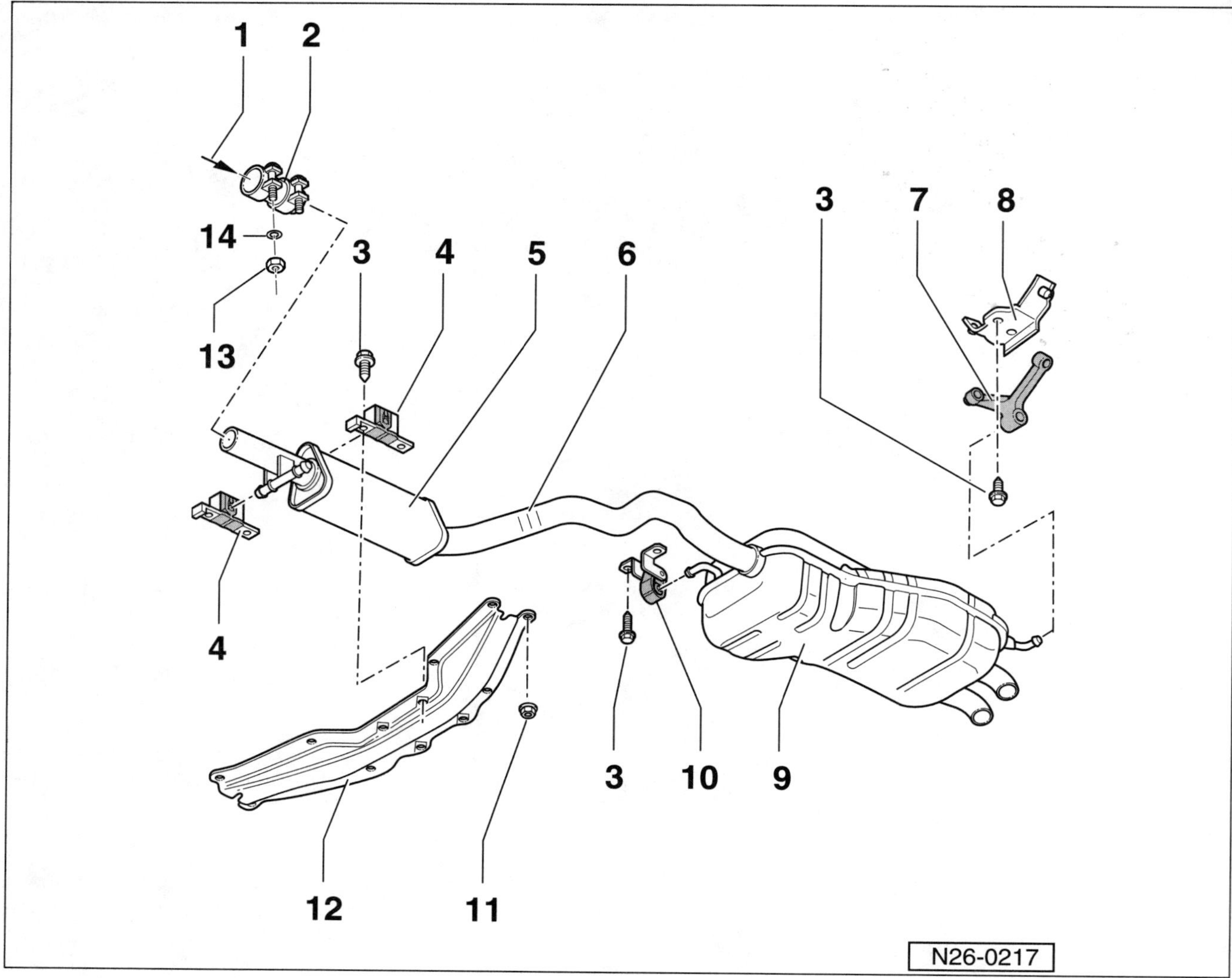

N26-0217

Fig. 14. Muffler system for the 2.8L engine.

1. **From front catalyst**
2. **Double clamp**
3. **Bolt**
   - Tighten to 25 Nm (18 ft-lb)
4. **Mount**
5. **Center muffler**
6. **Separation point**
   - Center and rear mufflers are installed as one unit but can be obtained individually when replacing
   - Saw through connecting pipe at separation point to replace mufflers individually
7. **Mount**
8. **Bracket**
9. **Rear muffler**
10. **Mount**
11. **Nut**
    - Tighten to 20 Nm (15 ft-lb)
12. **Tunnel bridge**
13. **Nut**
    - Tighten to 40 Nm (30 ft-lb)
14. **Washer**

EMISSION CONTROLS (GASOLINE ENGINES)

Positive Crankcase Ventilation (PCV)

The PCV system traps crankcase vapors and routes them back into the intake air stream to be burned.

The system consists simply of a breather hose between the valve cover and the intake air boot. On the 2.0L and 2.8L engines the valve cover contains a flame trap to prevent ignition of the crankcase vapors in the event of a backfire. To prevent icing during cold weather, a heating element is integrated into the breather hose. See Fig. 15.

On the 1.8L turbocharged engine the PCV breather hose has a pressure regulating valve at the intake air boot that prevents turbocharger boost from pressurizing the crankcase.

> ***CAUTION —***
> *Replace PCV hoses only with parts designed for PCV or fuel system service. Conventional vacuum and heater hoses deteriorate rapidly when exposed to oil vapors and combustion gasses.*

0024365

Fig. 15. PCV hose on 2.0L engine (**arrow**). Other engines are similar.

Most crankcase ventilation problems result when the hoses or valves become clogged with oily residues. Restrictions create excessive crankcase pressure that can eventually cause driveability problems. PCV system service is limited to inspecting and cleaning the breather valves, hoses, and replacing faulty parts.

Secondary Air Injection System

The Secondary Air Injection (AIR) system on the 1.8L, 2.0L and 2.8L gasoline engines uses an air pump to inject fresh air behind the exhaust valves for approximately 65 seconds during cold starting.

Specification

- Engine coolant temperature for Secondary Air Injection on initial start-up
  - 1.8L and 2.0L . . . . 5–33°C (41–91°F)
  - 2.8L . . . . 15–35°C (59–95°F)

Also, after each subsequent engine start (up to an 85°C (185°F) max. engine coolant temperature), the secondary air injection system will, after a 20 second delay, switch in for 5 seconds during idle and is then monitored by the system.

The purpose of the AIR system is to reduce exhaust emissions during engine warm-up when the Motronic engine management system is in open loop. The AIR system produces an oxygen rich exhaust gas, causes afterburning and reduces the duration of the catalyst heat-up phase. Activation initiates from the Motronic ECM via the secondary air injection pump relay to the secondary air injection solenoid valve and combi-valve.

The system consists of the electric air pump, the vacuum-operated shut-off valve (combi-valve), the inlet (solenoid) valve, and the related duct work. Exploded views of the AIR system on the various engines covered by this manual are shown on the next few pages.

Secondary air injection pump, testing

1. Disconnect the pressure hose from the outlet on the rear of the secondary air injection (AIR) pump. See the appropriate exploded view of the AIR system for pressure hose identification.

2. With the engine fully warm, start and allow the engine to idle. Approximately 20 seconds after starting, the air pump should run for about five seconds and secondary air should be felt coming from the pump outlet.
   - If the air pump does not run, check the fuse on top of the battery. See Fig. 16.
   - If fuse is OK check the secondary air injection pump relay (J299) using the wiring diagrams in **97 Wiring Diagrams, Fuses and Relays.**

3. If the pump does not run and no wiring faults can be found, check the signal from the ECM to the pump. Disconnect the harness connector from the pump and connect a voltmeter to the connector. Start the engine while checking for voltage 20 seconds after starting.
   - If voltage is present, the pump is most likely faulty and should be replaced.
   - If voltage is not present, check the wiring at the AIR relay and between the ECM and the AIR relay. If no faults are found, the relay or ECM may be faulty.

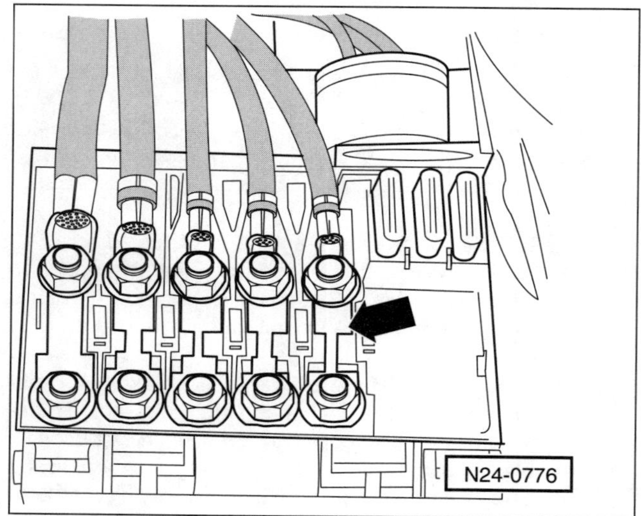

N24-0776

Fig. 16. Fuse (**arrow**) for secondary air pump, located on top of battery.

Secondary air injection solenoid valve, checking

NOTE—

- *Engine oil temperature should be between 5–33°C (41–91°F).*
- *Ensure that secondary air injection pump motor is OK.*
- *2.0L engines with engine code AVH, AZG do not have a secondary air injection valve.*

1. Disconnect the vacuum hose at solenoid valve, or for 1.8L engine, at combination valve. See Fig. 17., Fig. 18., or Fig. 19.

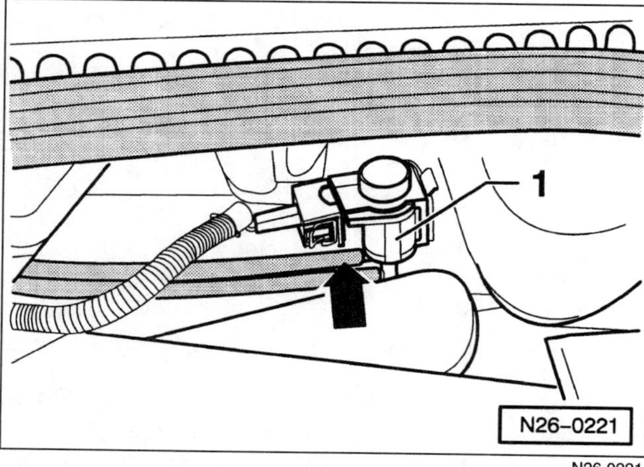

N26-0221

Fig. 17. Disconnect vacuum line (**arrow**) at AIR solenoid valve on 2.0L engine.

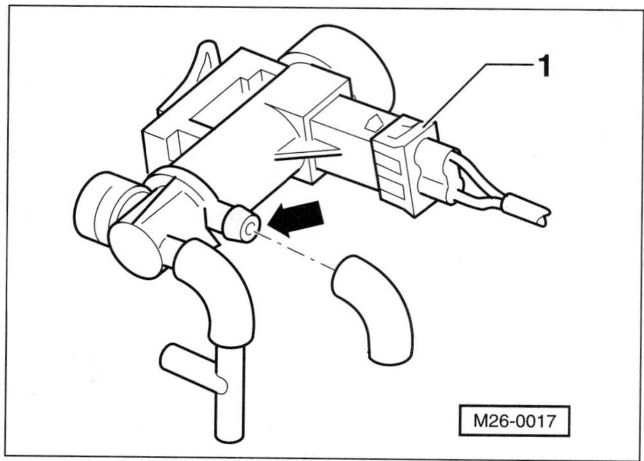

M26-0017

Fig. 18. Disconnect vacuum line (**arrow**) at AIR solenoid valve on 2.8L engine.

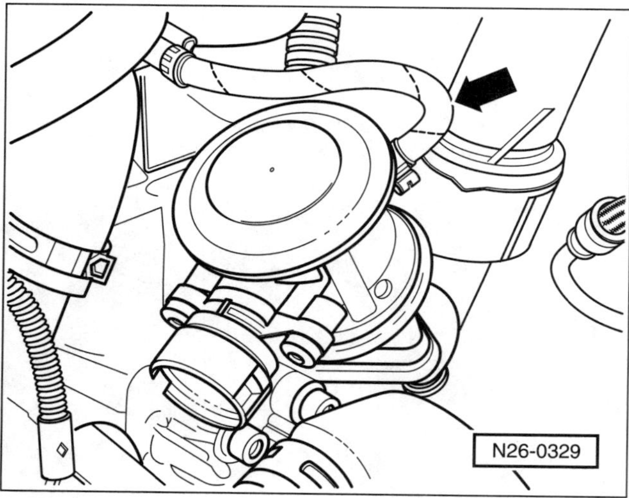

N26-0329

Fig. 19. Disconnect vacuum line (**arrow**) at combination valve on 1.8L engine.

2. Start the engine while checking for vacuum at the hose 20 seconds after starting. If vacuum is present, the valve is functioning correctly.

3. If vacuum is not present, shut off engine and disconnect the harness connector from the solenoid valve and connect a voltmeter to the harness connector. Start the engine while checking for voltage 20 seconds after starting.
   - If voltage is present, the solenoid valve is most likely faulty and should be replaced.
   - If voltage is not present, check the wire between solenoid valve and the ECM. If no faults are found, the ECM may be faulty.

Secondary air injection system, components (1.8L engine)

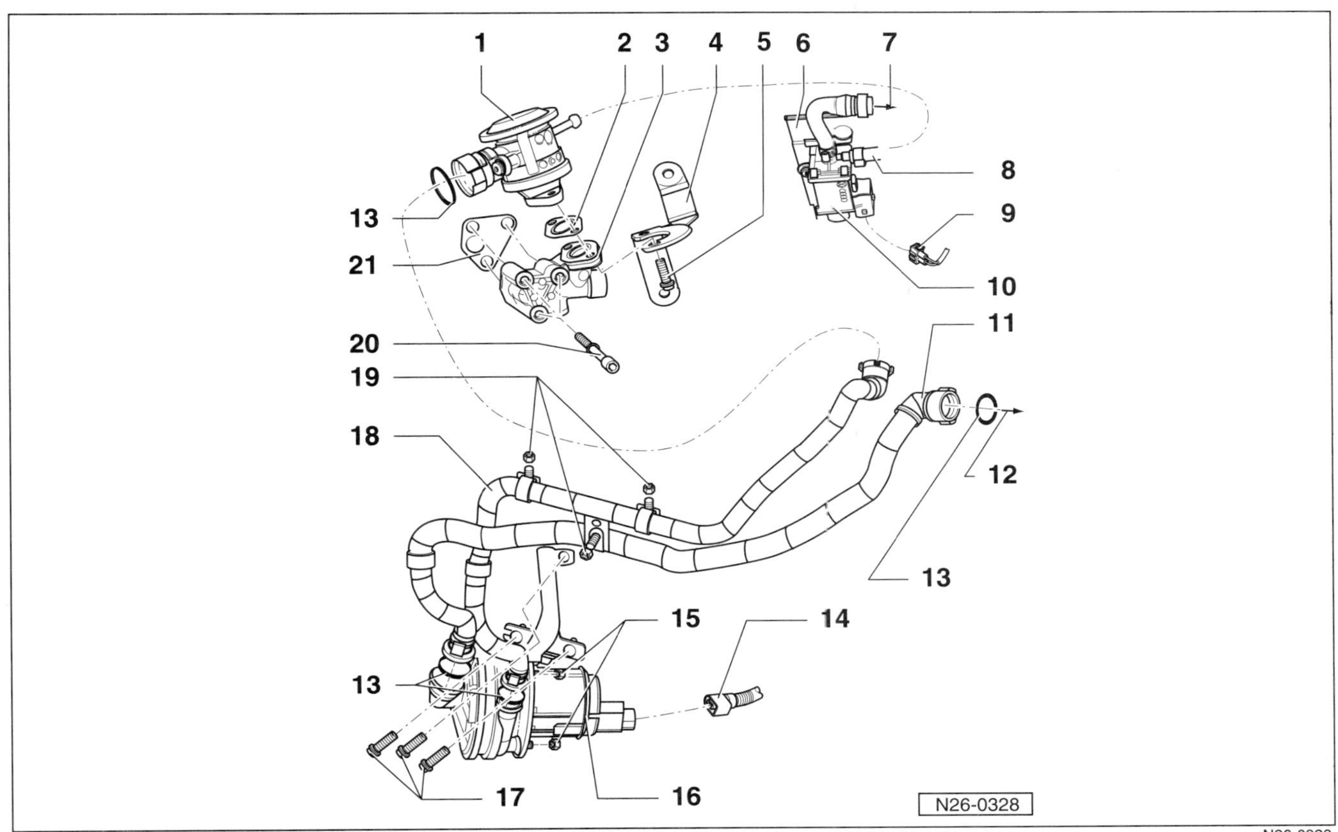

N26-0328

Fig. 20. Components of the secondary air injection system on the 1.8L engine.

1. **Combi-valve**
   - Checking, **see** Ⓐ
2. **Gasket**
   - Always replace
3. **Bracket**
   - Secured at cylinder head
4. **Bracket**
5. **Bolt**
   - Tighten to 10 Nm (7 ft-lb)
6. **Bracket**
   - Secured at intake manifold
7. **To vacuum reservoir**
8. **Vacuum hose**
9. **2-pin harness connector**
10. **Secondary air injection solenoid valve (N112)**
    - Fastened to cylinder head cover
    - resistance: 25-35 Ω
11. **Intake hose**
    - For Secondary Air Injection (AIR) pump
    - Ensure hose is tightly sealed
    - Press together at front to release
12. **To air filter**
13. **O-ring**
    - Replace if damaged
14. **2-pin harness connector**
    - For Secondary Air Injection (AIR) pump
15. **Nut**
    - Tighten to 10 Nm (7 ft-lb)
16. **Secondary air injection pump motor (V101)**
17. **Bolt**
    - Tighten to 10 Nm (7 ft-lb)
18. **Pressure hose**
    - Ensure hose is tightly sealed
    - Press together at front to release
19. **Nut**
    - Tighten to 10 Nm (7 ft-lb)
20. **Bolt**
    - Tighten to 10 Nm (7 ft-lb)
21. **Gasket**
    - Always replace

A Combi-valve, checking (1.8L engine)

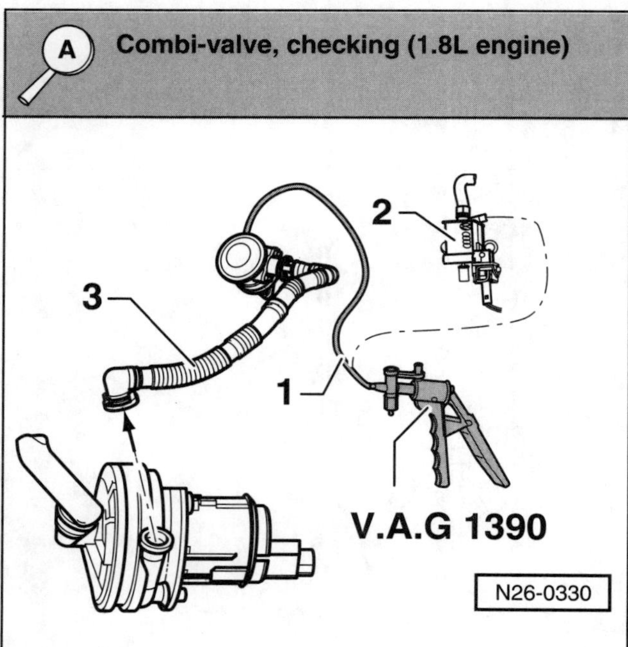

N26-0330

- **Disconnect vacuum hose (1) from AIR solenoid valve (2)**
- **Connect hand vacuum pump (i.e. VAG 1390)**
- **Remove pressure hose (arrow) from pump motor**
- **Blow into pressure hose with slight pressure Do not use compressed air!**
- **Both valves must be closed**
- **Operate hand vacuum pump**
- **Combi valve should open - replace if doesn't open**

Secondary air injection system, components (2.0L engine)

The following list applies to Fig. 21.

1. **2-pin harness connector**
2. **Secondary air injection solenoid valve (N112)**
   - Fastened to cowl panel
   - Only on AEG engine
3. **to Brake booster**
   - Only on AEG engine
4. **Secondary air injection pump motor relay (J299)**
   - In engine compartment left, on fuse/relay panel next to brake master cylinder
   - Relay designation "100"
5. **O-ring**
   - Replace if damaged
6. **Pressure hose**
   - Ensure hose is tightly sealed
   - Press together at front to release
7. **Intake hose**
   - From air filter upper section
8. **Secondary air injection pump motor (V101)**
9. **Nut**
   - Tighten to 10 Nm (7 ft-lb)
10. **Bracket**
    - Attached to lower intake manifold
11. **Harness connector**
12. **Bolt**
    - Tighten to 25 Nm (18 ft-lb)
13. **Lower intake manifold**
14. **To union on exhaust manifold**
15. **Flare nut**
    - Tighten to 30 Nm (22 ft-lb)
16. **Connecting pipe for combi-valve**

(continued on next page)

Secondary air injection system, components (2.0L engine)

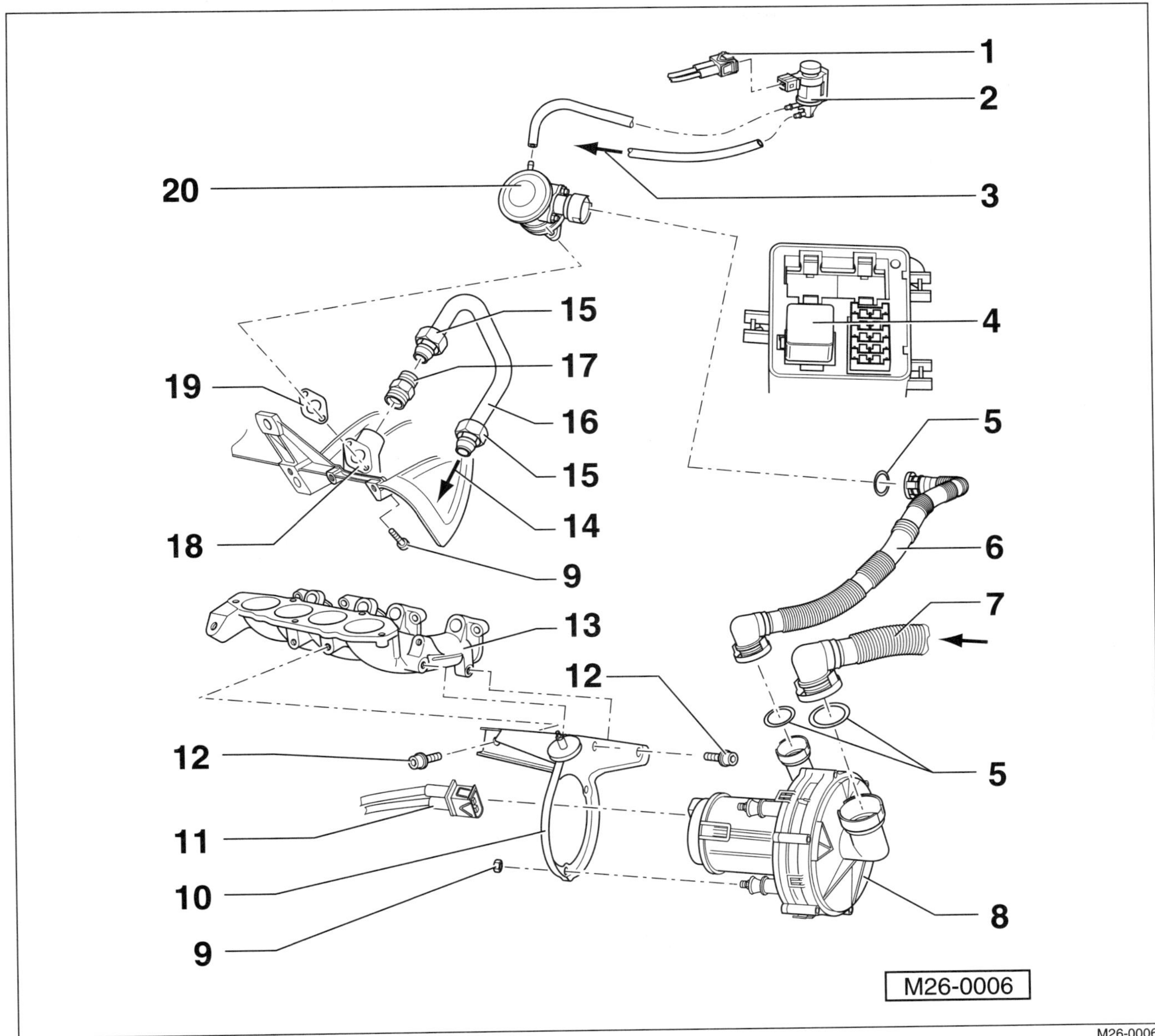

Fig. 21. Components of the secondary air injection system on 2.0L engine. AEG shown, AVH/AZG are similar.

17. Union
- Tighten to 35 Nm (26 ft-lb)

18. Warm air collector plate
- With mount for combi-valve

19. Gasket
- Always replace

20. Combi-valve
- Checking (AEG engine), **see** Ⓐ

A Combi-valve, checking (AEG engine)

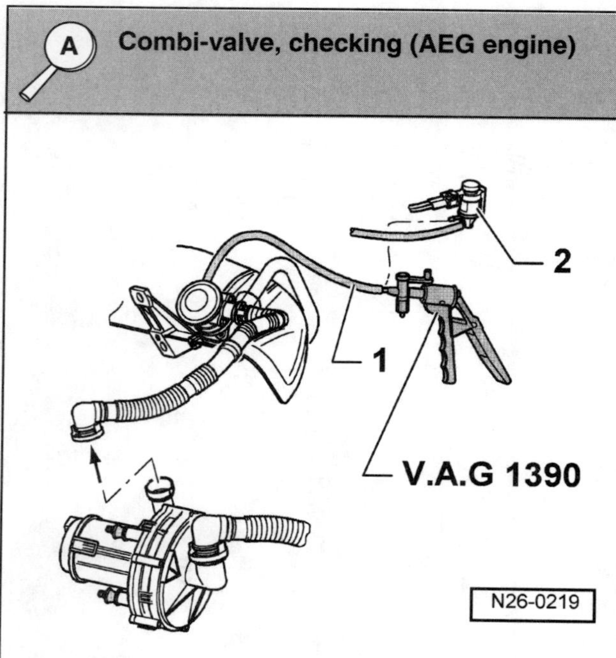

N26-0219

- **Disconnect vacuum hose (1) from AIR solenoid valve (2)**
- **Connect hand vacuum pump (i.e. VAG 1390) to (1)**
- **Remove pressure hose (arrow) from pump motor**
- **Blow into pressure hose with slight pressure**
  Do not use compressed air!
- **Combi-valve must remain closed**
- **Operate hand vacuum pump**
- **Combi-valve should open - replace if doesn't open**

Secondary air injection system, components (2.8L engine)

The numbered list below applies to Fig. 22.

1. **Combi-valve**
   - Checking, **see** (A)
2. **Bolt**
   - Tighten to 10 Nm (7 ft-lb)
3. **O-ring**
   - Always replace
4. **Air duct**
   - In cylinder head
5. **Secondary air injection solenoid valve (N112)**
   - Fastened to cowl panel
6. **To fuel pressure regulator**
7. **To intake manifold**
8. **2-pin harness connector**
9. **Check valve**
   - White terminal points toward the secondary air valve
10. **To vacuum tank**
    - Fastened to the front oil pan
11. **Intake manifold cross-over valve (N156)**
    - Clipped onto the bracket of the oil filter casing
12. **Bracket**
13. **Bolt**
    - Tighten to 25 Nm (18 ft-lb)
14. **Bolt**
    - Tighten to 10 Nm (7 ft-lb)
15. **Bracket**
    - For air pump motor and secondary air valve
16. **To vacuum adjusting screw for intake manifold cross-over valve**
17. **2-pin connector**
18. **Harness connector**
19. **Secondary air injection pump motor (V101)**
    - On the front of engine block
    - For removing and installing, put lock carrier into service position, see **50 Body–Front**
    - Relay is located on left side of engine compartment, in a protective housing next to power brake booster

(continued on next page)

Secondary air injection system, components (2.8L engine)

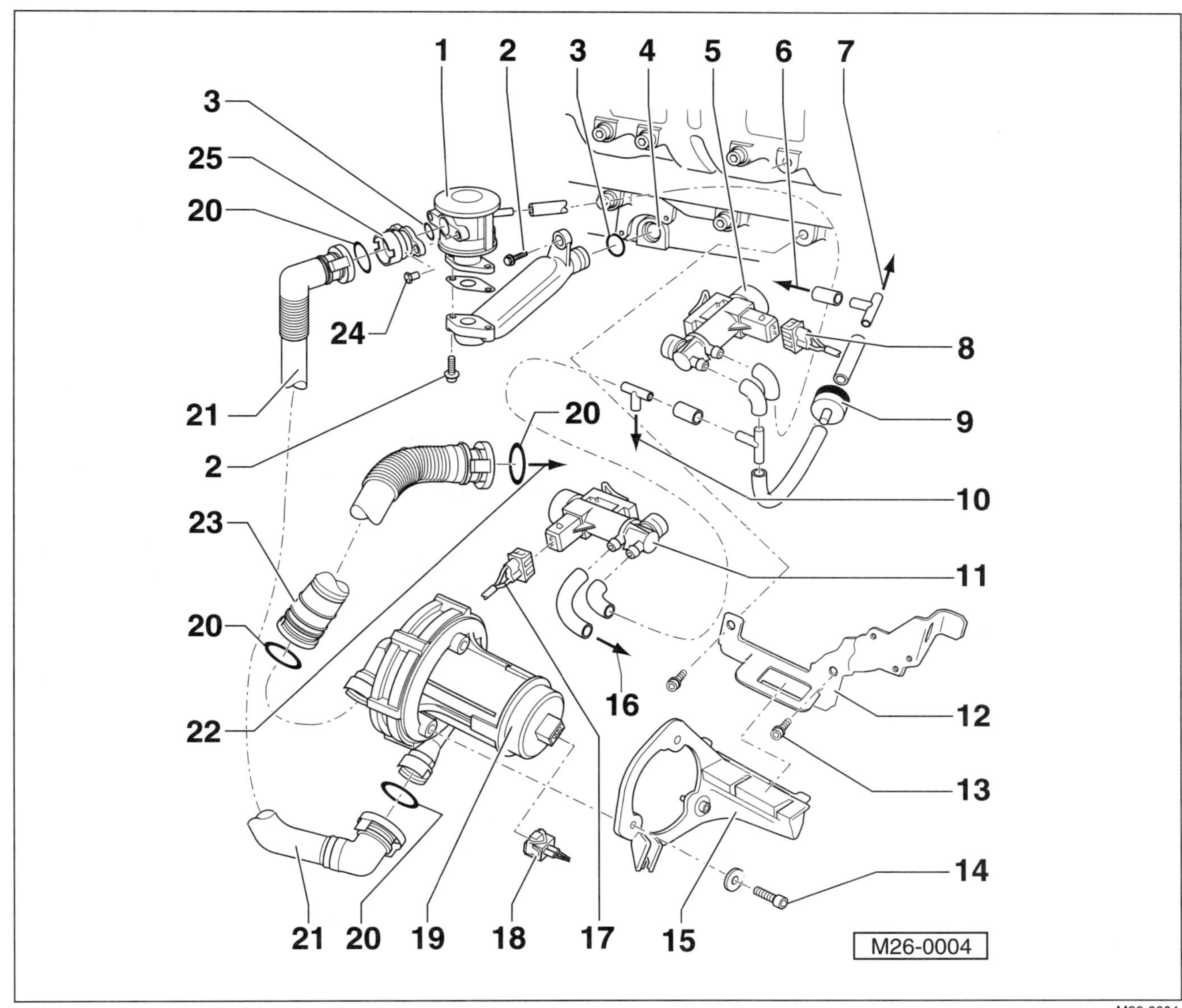

M26-0004

Fig. 22. Components of the secondary air injection system on the 2.8L VR6 engine.

20. O-ring
- Replace if damaged

21. Pressure hose
- Ensure hose is tightly sealed
- Press together at front to release

22. To top of air filter

23. Intake hose
- From air filter upper section

24. Nut
- Tighten to 5 Nm (44 in-lb)

25. Screw connections
- For combi-valve

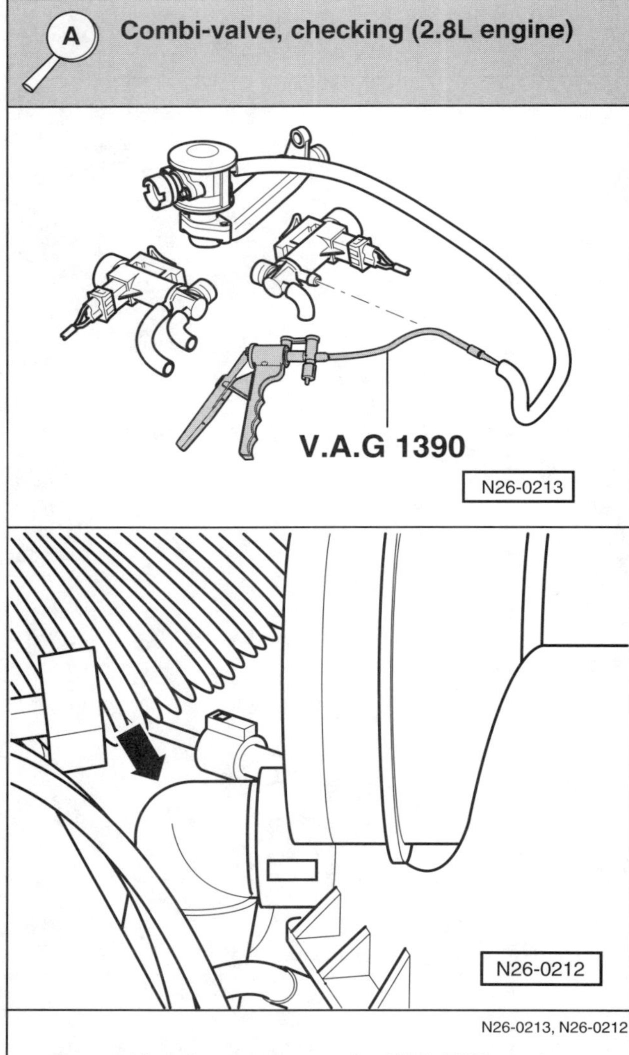

- Connect hand vacuum pump (i.e. VAG 1390) as shown above in upper illustration
- Remove intake hose to the combi-valve on top of the air filter (lower illustration, arrow)
- Blow into pressure hose with slight pressure Do not use compressed air!
- Combi-valve must remain closed
- Operate hand vacuum pump
- Combi-valve should open - replace if doesn't open

EMISSION CONTROLS (DIESEL ENGINE)

Positive Crankcase Ventilation (PCV)

The PCV system traps crankcase vapors and routes them back into the intake air stream to be burned. The system consists simply of a breather hose between the valve cover and the intake air boot. This breather hose has a pressure regulating valve at the intake air boot that prevents turbocharger boost from pressurizing the crankcase. See Fig. 23.

> ***CAUTION —***
> *Replace PCV hoses only with parts designed for PCV or fuel system service. Conventional vacuum and heater hoses deteriorate rapidly when exposed to oil vapors and combustion gasses.*

Fig. 23. PCV hose on ALH engine (**arrow**).

Most crankcase ventilation problems result when the hoses or valves become clogged with oily residues. Restrictions create excessive crankcase pressure that can cause driveability problems. PCV system service is limited to inspecting and cleaning of the breather valves, hoses, and replacing faulty parts.

Exhaust Gas Recirculation (EGR)

The EGR system installed on the 1.9L diesel engine reduces emissions by directing a small quantity of exhaust gases back into the intake manifold to dilute the air/fuel mixture effectively. An EGR cooler reduces the exhaust gas temperature by as much as 122°F. This reduces the amount of oxides of nitrogen (NO_X) pollutants in the exhaust.

The function of the EGR system is managed by the diesel direct injection system Engine Control Module (ECM) via the EGR vacuum regulator solenoid valve. The cone shaped plunger in the mechanical EGR valve ensures that various cross sectional openings are possible at different plunger heights. Every possible valve position is provided via pulsed control from the EGR vacuum regulator solenoid valve.

The EGR system and its various components is shown in Fig. 24.

EGR system, assembly (1.9L engine)

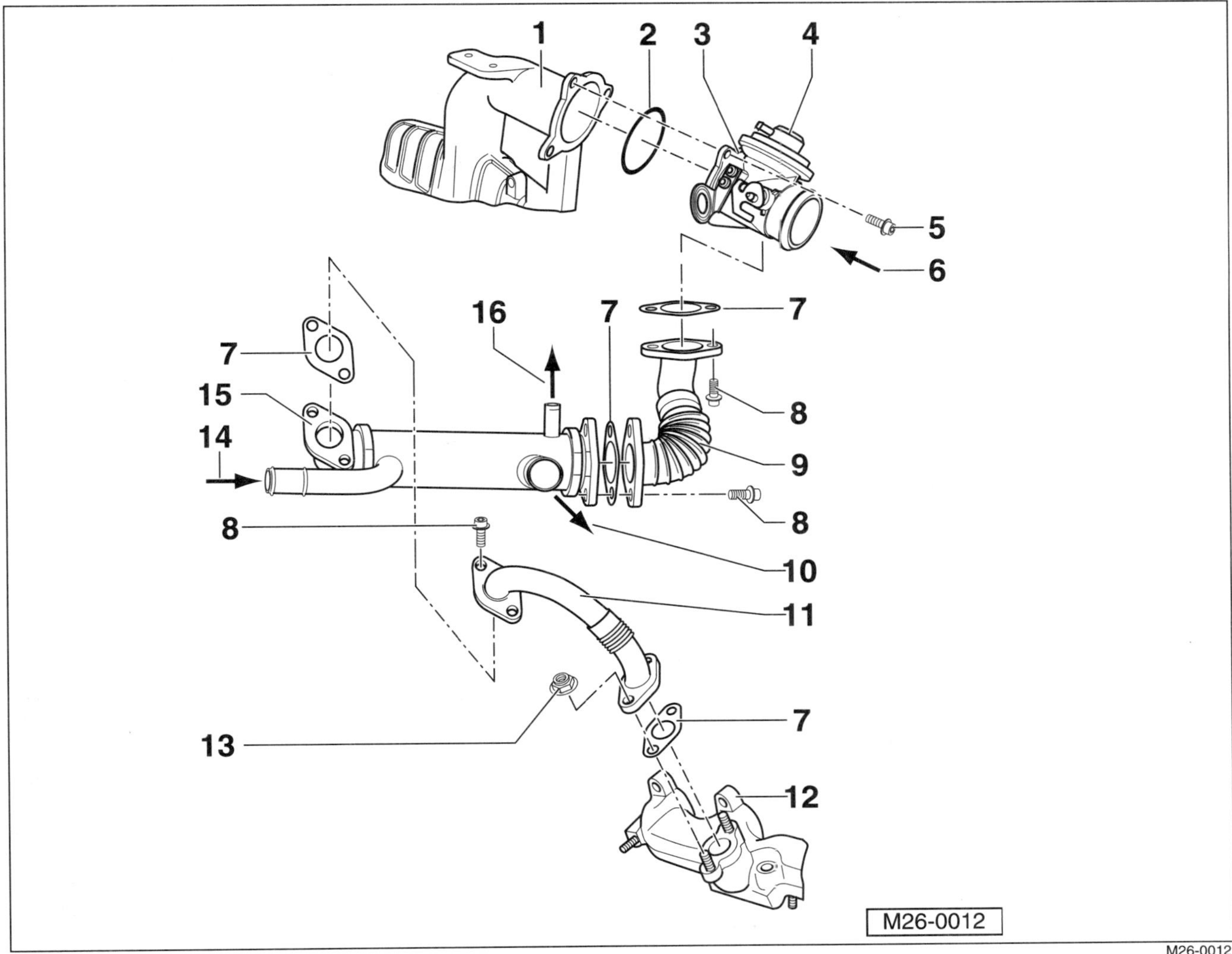

Fig. 24. EGR system on the 1.9L diesel engine.

1. **Intake manifold**
2. **O-ring**
   - Always replace
3. **Intake air connector**
   - With EGR valve and control flap
4. **Exhaust Gas Recirculation (EGR) valve**
   - Can only replace with intake support assembly
   - Vacuum hose connections, **see** Ⓐ
5. **Bolt**
   - Tighten to 10 Nm (7 ft-lb)
6. **Intake air from charge air cooler**
7. **Gasket**
   - Always replace
8. **Bolt**
   - Tighten to 25 Nm (18 ft-lb)
9. **Connecting pipe**
   - EGR cooler to intake support
10. **To heater core**
11. **Connecting pipe**
    - EGR cooler to exhaust elbow
12. **Exhaust manifold**
13. **Nut**
    - Tighten to 25 Nm (18 ft-lb)
14. **Connection**
    - From heater
15. **EGR cooler**
16. **Connection**
    - To coolant expansion tank

A Vacuum hose connections (1.9L engine)

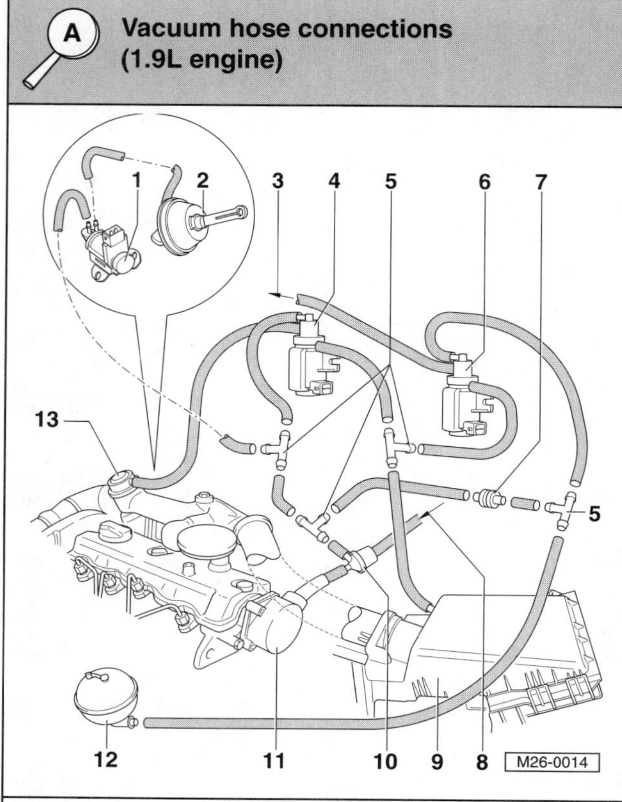

M26-0014

1. **Change-over valve for intake manifold flap (N239)**
2. **Vacuum actuator**
   - Do not bend control rod
3. **Vacuum hose**
   - To vacuum unit for turbocharger boost regulation
4. **EGR vacuum regulator solenoid valve (N18)**
5. **T-connector**
6. **Wastegate bypass regulator valve (N75)**
7. **Check valve**
   - White connection points toward line going to vacuum reservoir
8. **from Brake servo**
9. **Air cleaner**
10. **Check valve**
11. **Vacuum pump**
    - For brake booster
12. **Vacuum reservoir**
    - Mounted with bracket to oil pan
13. **EGR valve**

EGR valve, checking

1. Remove engine cover and disconnect pipe between charge air cooler and intake manifold at manifold.
2. Disconnect vacuum hose from EGR valve.
3. Connect hand vacuum pump, such as VAG 1390 or equivalent, to EGR valve.
4. Operate pump and observe if membrane rod moves. See Fig. 25.

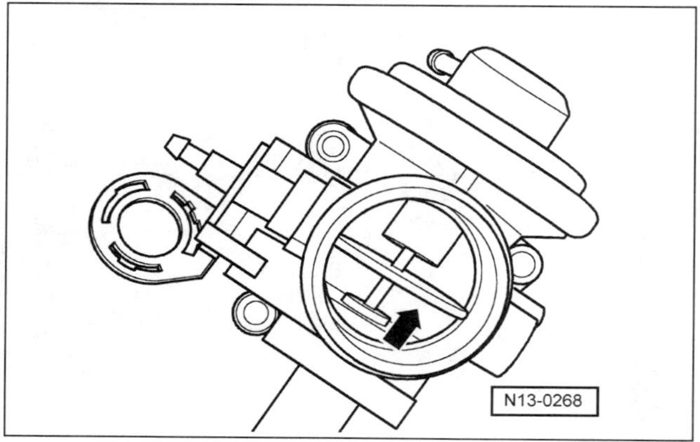

N13-0268

Fig. 25. Membrane rod must move in direction of **arrow** when vacuum is applied to the EGR valve.

5. Disconnect hand vacuum pump hose from EGR valve.
6. Membrane rod must move back to its original position.
7. If the membrane rod did not move then the EGR valve is faulty and should be replaced. If the rod does move correctly then the problem may be with the EGR vacuum regulator solenoid valve. Check the wiring to solenoid valve and check for a duty cycle (on-off) signal at the valve. If no faults can be found, the signal from the ECM may be missing or the valve or ECM may be faulty.

QUALITY REVIEW

When you have finished working under the hood and around other areas of the vehicle, it is advisable to take a moment to quality check or review your work. This helps to insure that the operation or repair has been completed properly with all affected systems functioning within normal parameters. These may include the following:

- Ensure that the exhaust system is not under stress, and that it has sufficient clearance from the body. If necessary, loosen the double clamps and align the muffler and exhaust pipe so sufficient clearance is maintained to the body while the support rings are evenly loaded.
- Confirm that all heat shields are in place.
- Make sure that there are no air, vacuum or exhaust leaks.

27 Engine Electrical

TABLES

GENERAL

This repair group covers battery, starter, and generator troubleshooting and repair.

NOTE —

- *The alternator is identified as generator by the vehicle manufacturer. Car makers must by law use uniform words and terms (nomenclature) to describe certain components and or systems. The uniform word for alternator is generator. Therefore, the component labeled "Generator (GEN)" in the wiring diagrams is the alternator.*
- *Wiring diagrams for the battery, charging system and starter motor are given in* **97 Wiring Diagrams, Fuses and Relays**.

The six-cell, 12-volt lead-acid battery capacity is rated in Ampere/hours (Ah) and cold cranking amps (CCA). The Ah rating is determined by the average amount of current the battery can deliver over time without dropping below a specified voltage. The CCA rating is determined by the battery's ability to deliver starting current at 0°F (–18°C). The battery is installed in the engine compartment, behind the left headlight assembly.

The charging system consists of a belt-driven 14-volt generator and a voltage regulator. The voltage regulator, which is mounted in the generator, also serves as the generator brush holder. The charging system provides the current necessary to keep the battery charged and to operate the vehicle's electrical accessories.

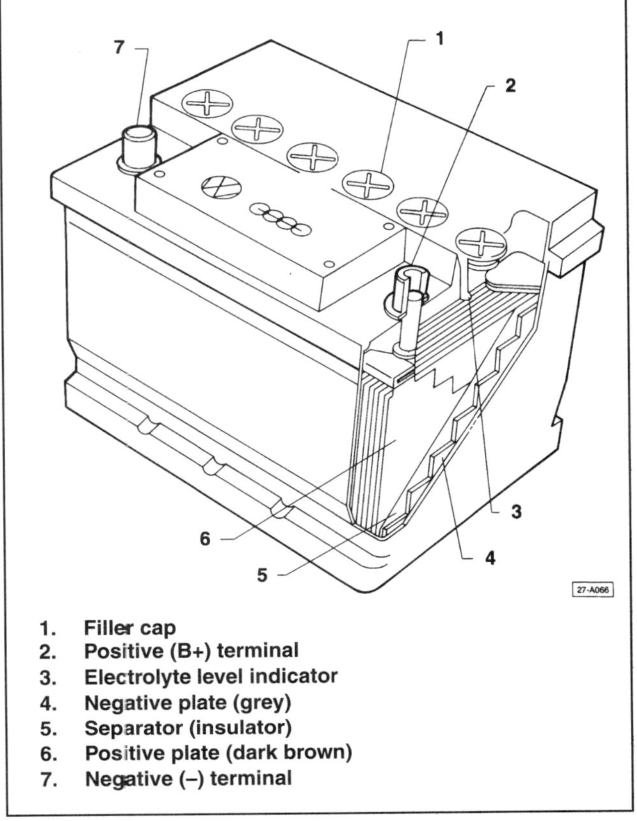

1. **Filler cap**
2. **Positive (B+) terminal**
3. **Electrolyte level indicator**
4. **Negative plate (grey)**
5. **Separator (insulator)**
6. **Positive plate (dark brown)**
7. **Negative (–) terminal**

27-A066

Fig. 1. Battery.

Please read the following warnings and cautions before doing any work on any parts of the engine electrical system.

> ***WARNING —***
> - *Wear goggles, rubber gloves, and a rubber apron when working around batteries and battery acid (electrolyte). Battery acid contains sulfuric acid and can cause skin irritation and burning. If acid is spilled on your skin or clothing, flush the area at once with large quantities of water. If electrolyte gets into your eyes, bathe them with large quantities of clean water for several minutes and call a physician.*
> - *Batteries that are being charged or are fully charged give off explosive hydrogen gas. Keep sparks and open flames away. Do not smoke.*

> ***CAUTION —***
> - *Disconnecting the negative (–) battery cable may erase fault codes and basic settings in the engine management and automatic transmission control modules. Some driveability problems may be noticed until the system re-adapts to operating conditions. OBD II readiness codes, which may be required for emissions testing, may also be erased.Convenience electronics (alarm system, interior light control, power locks, mirrors, and windows) may need to be re-set using a VAG 1551/1552 or equivalent scan tool.*
> - *Do not disconnect the battery cables while the engine is running. The generator will be damaged.*
> - *Never operate the generator with its output terminal (B+ or 30) disconnected and the other terminals connected. Never short, bridge, or ground any terminals of the charging system.*
> - *Always disconnect the negative (–) battery cable when working at or near the generator. Battery voltage is always present at the rear of the generator, even with the ignition key off.*
> - *Always allow a frozen battery to thaw before attempting to recharge it.*
> - *Always disconnect the battery cables during battery charging. This will prevent damage to the generator and any solid-state components. Do not exceed 16.5 volts at the battery.*
> - *Never reverse the battery terminals. Even a momentary wrong connection can damage the generator or electrical components.*
> - *Replace the battery if the case is cracked or leaking. Electrolyte can damage the car. If electrolyte is spilled, clean the area with a solution of baking soda and water.*

BATTERY SERVICE

If the battery discharges when the vehicle is not driven, there may be a constant drain or current draw causing it to discharge when the ignition is off. Depending on the draw and the condition of the battery, a full discharge can happen overnight or it may take a few weeks. Although a small static drain on the battery is normal (for example to operate the clock or radio memory), a large drain such as a relay sticking on or a faulty switch will cause the battery to quickly discharge. Make a static current draw test as the first step when experiencing battery discharge.

If the current draw on the battery is not excessive and the battery still discharges, the condition of the battery should be tested. Battery testing determines the state of battery charge. The most common methods are open-circuit and load voltage testing. Batteries with filler caps can also be tested by checking the specific gravity of the electrolyte. Inexpensive specific gravity testers are available at most auto supply stores.

Some New Beetles are equipped with batteries with a central gas venting system with anti-flash protection. The anti-flash protection consists of a small round fiberglass mat with a diameter of approximately 15 mm and a thickness of 2 mm. Its purpose is to vent gasses that form in the battery. The gasses that form while charging can vent centrally through an opening on the upper side of the battery cover. The anti-flash protection is also installed to prevent ignition of the flammable gasses in the battery.

> ***CAUTION —***
> - *Always use genuine VW battery cell caps. Caps must be fitted with an O-ring seal.*
> - *Before diagnosing electrical problems visually inspect the battery for clean and tight connections at all terminals.*

Electrolyte level, checking

A visual check of the battery electrolyte level is all that is required on batteries with a recognizable minimum and maximum marking. See Fig. 2.

If there are no min. or max. markings on the battery housing, or if the electrolyte level cannot be read, the top plugs must be removed to view the electrolyte level. The level should be the same height as the visible plastic peg.

> ***WARNING —***
> *Always wear protective goggles and clothing when working with battery cells open.*

Top off each battery cell as necessary with distilled water using a battery filling bottle. Use a hydrometer to remove any excess electrolyte. Be sure to install original sealing plug with O-ring.

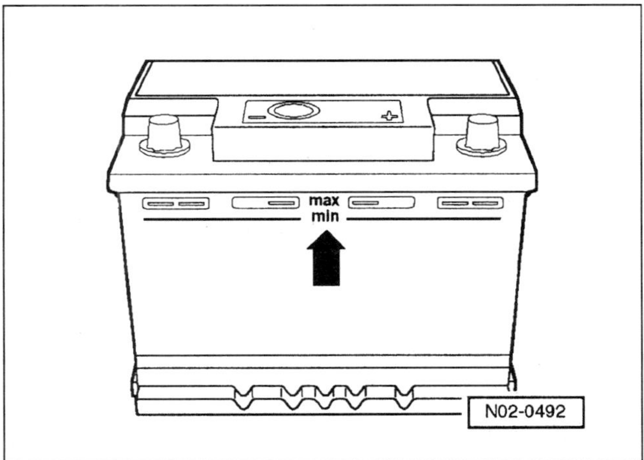

N02-0492

Fig. 2. Electrolyte level should be between **min** and **max** marks on battery.

> ***NOTE —***
> *Use of distilled water to fill battery cells will prevent contamination of battery electrolyte and decrease the likelihood of self discharge.*

Static current draw, checking

1. Make sure the ignition and all electrical accessories are switched off.

2. Disconnect the negative (–) cable from the battery. See the Cautions at the beginning of this repair group regarding battery disconnection.

> ***NOTE —***
> *Be sure to have the anti-theft radio code on hand before disconnecting the battery.*

3. Connect a digital ammeter between the battery negative post and the negative battery cable and measure the current draw. See Fig. 2.

A range of about 0 to 100 milliamps is normal, depending on the number of accessories that need constant power. A current of 500 milliamps (0.5 amp) or more indicates a problem. To determine the circuit or component causing the problem, remove one fuse at a time until the current drops to a normal range. Use the wiring diagrams shown in **97 Wiring Diagrams, Fuses and Relays** to locate wiring or component faults.

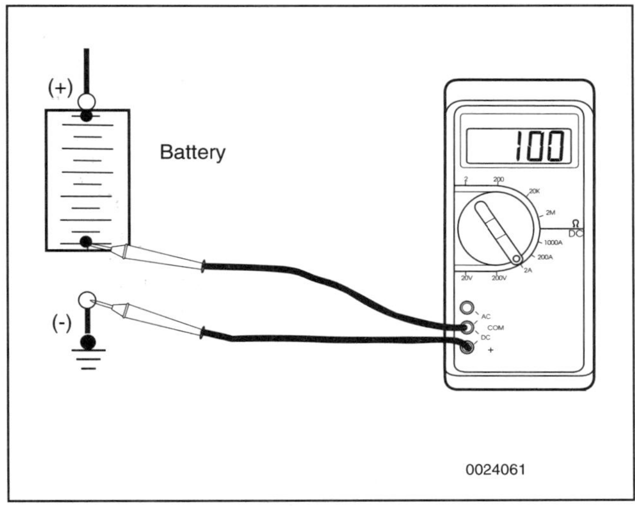

0024061

Fig. 3. Electrical system static current draw being measured.

Open-circuit voltage test

An open-circuit voltage test checks battery voltage by connecting an accurate digital voltmeter to the battery posts after disconnecting the battery ground cable. Before making an open-circuit voltage test on a battery, first load the battery with 15 amps for one minute, for example by turning on the headlights without the engine running. See **Table a** for open-circuit voltage levels and their corresponding percentages of charge.

Table a. Open-Circuit Voltage and Battery Charge

Open-circuit voltage	State of charge
12.6 V or more	Fully charged
12.4 V	75% charged
12.2 V	50% charged
12.0 V	25% charged
11.7 V or less	Fully discharged

The battery is in satisfactory condition if the open-circuit voltage is at least 12.4 volts. If the open-circuit voltage is at this level or above, but the battery still lacks power for starting, make a load voltage test to determine the battery's service condition. If the open-circuit voltage is below 12.4 volts, recharge the battery. If the battery cannot be recharged to at least 75%, it should be replaced.

Specific gravity, checking

Checking the specific gravity of each of the battery's electrolyte cells and doing a load test as described below can provide specific information about the battery's condition.

1. Turn off ignition.

> **WARNING —**
> *Always wear protective goggles and clothing when working with battery cells open.*

2. Remove all battery cell sealing plugs.

3. Check that battery electrolyte temperature is at least 10°C (50°F).

4. Immerse hydrometer in a cell and extract sufficient electrolyte so that float swims free in the electrolyte.

5. Read the specific density and compare to specification.

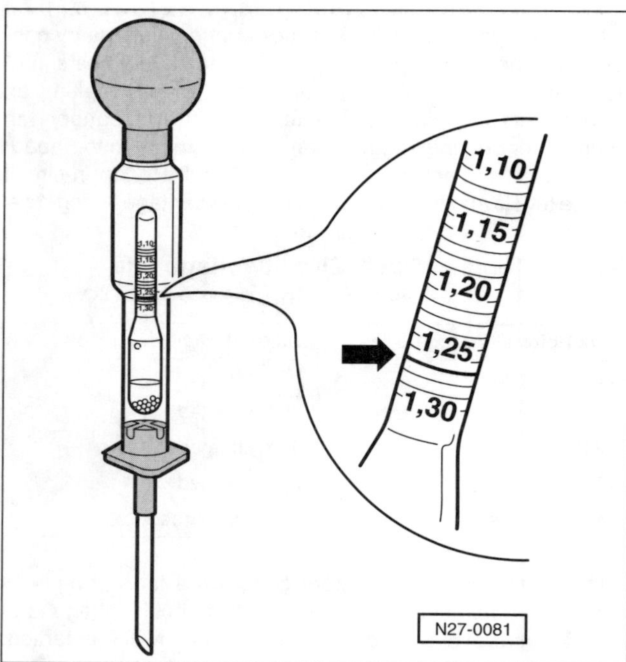

N27-0081

Fig. 4. Checking specific gravity of battery with hydrometer.

Battery charge condition and specific density

- Discharged . . . . 1.15 kg/dm^3
- Half charged. . . . . 1.22 kg/dm^3
- Full charge . . . . 1.28 kg/dm^3

6. The electrolyte density must be at least 1.24 kg/dm^3. If density is insufficient, replace cell caps and charge battery.

7. The specific gravity of the individual battery cells must not differentiate by more than 0.03 kg/dm^3. Replace battery if not within specification.

8. Install cell caps with O-rings and carefully wipe up any spilled electrolyte.

Load voltage testing

A load voltage battery test is made by connecting a specific resistive load to the battery terminals and then measuring the battery's voltage. The test requires a special tester and can generally be performed quickly and inexpensively by an authorized VW dealer or other qualified repair facility.

The battery should be fully charged and at room temperature for the most accurate results. If the equipment is available, disconnect the negative (–) battery cable. Then apply the specified load for 15 seconds and measure the battery's voltage. If the voltage is below that listed, the battery should be replaced. **Table b** lists load current and minimum voltages for original-equipment VW batteries.

> **WARNING —**
> *Always wear protective goggles and clothing when performing a load test.*

Table b. Battery Load Current and Minimum Voltage

Battery Capacity Amp-hour (Ah)	Cold Cranking Amps (CCA)	Load Current (amps)	Minimum voltage (limit value)
36Ah	340	100	10.0
40Ah-49Ah	220	200	9.2
50Ah-60Ah	265-280	200	9.4
61h-80Ah	300-380	300	9.0
81Ah-110Ah	380-500	300	9.5

Battery charging

Discharged batteries can be recharged using a battery charger. Prolonged charging causes gassing that will evaporate the electrolyte to a level that can damage the battery.

Always read and follow the instructions provided by the battery charger's manufacturer. A slow-charging rate (10% of battery capacity) is best to prevent battery damage caused by overheating.

> ***WARNING —***
> - *The gasses given off by the battery during charging are explosive. Do not smoke. Keep open flames away from the top of the battery, and prevent electrical sparks by turning off the battery charger before connecting or disconnecting it.*
> - *Battery cell caps must not be removed while charging.*
> - *Batteries are damaged by quick charging. It should only be used as a last alternative when slow charging is not possible.*
> - *Never quick charge a totally discharged battery.*
> - *Do not allow the battery charging rate to exceed 16.5 volts.*
> - *If the battery begins gassing (boiling) violently when charging, reduce the charging rate immediately.*
> - *Ensure that the battery is charged in a well ventilated area.*
> - *Precision tools must not be kept in the same room where batteries are being charged. Tools may corrode due to chemical reaction.*

Battery, removing and installing

1. Switch ignition off.
2. Disconnect battery ground (GND) strap from battery negative (-) terminal.

> ***CAUTION —***
> *Be sure to have the anti-theft radio code on hand before disconnecting the battery.*

3. Fold the top part of the battery blanket up. Press locking tabs together to remove fuse holder cover. See Fig. 5.

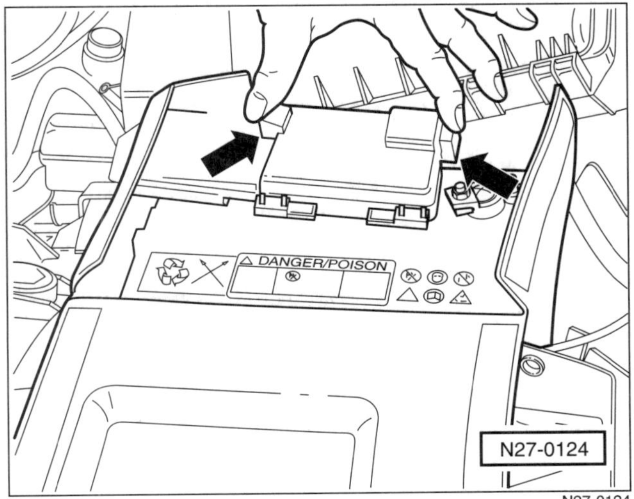

N27-0124

Fig. 5. Press locking tabs (**arrows**) to open hinged fuse cover.

4. Remove hex nuts for positive (+) battery terminal lead and strip fuses on top of battery. See Fig. 6.

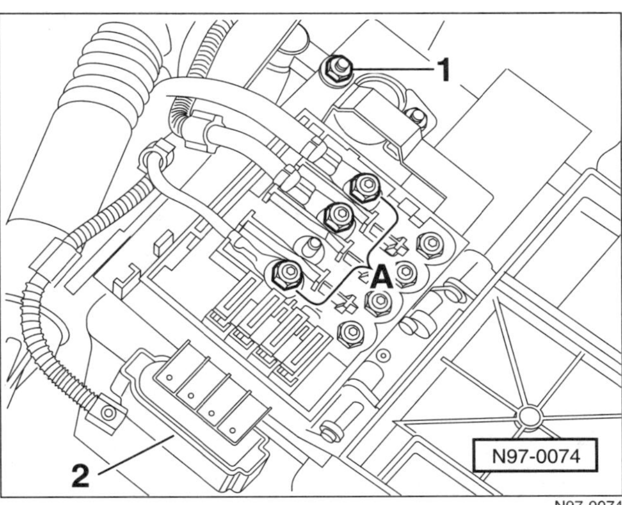

N97-0074

Fig. 6. Remove hex nut for positive battery terminal lead (**arrow**) and nuts (**A**) to disconnect wiring to strip fuses. Pull off harness connector (**2**).

5. Remove harness connector on top of battery as shown in Fig. 6.
6. Unlock fuse holder from top of battery by relieving tension with thumb pressure and using screwdriver to release retaining tab. See Fig. 7.

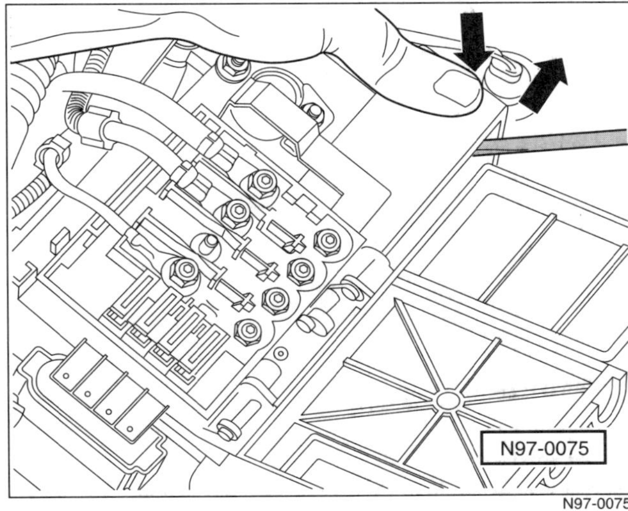

N97-0075

Fig. 7. Relieve tension with thumb pressure and release retaining tab with screwdriver (**arrows**). Remove fuse panel upward.

7. Remove positive (+) battery clamp from battery and position cable out of the way.

8. Remove battery heat insulation jacket (if equipped).

9. Remove battery clamping bracket. See Fig. 8.

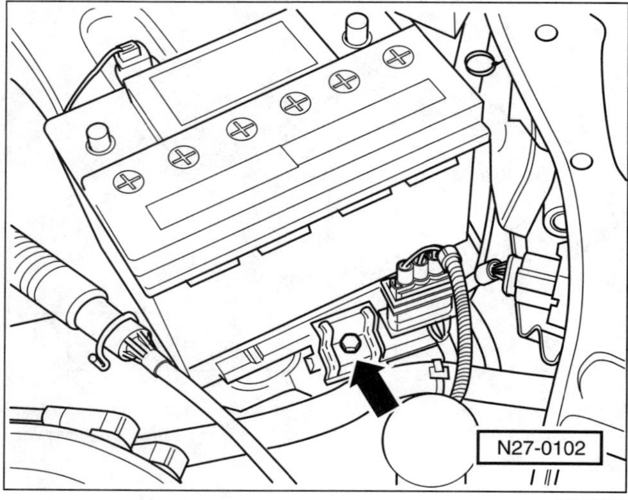

N27-0102

Fig. 8. Remove bolt and battery clamping bracket (**arrow**).

10. Install battery so lug of battery tray engages in battery groove. See Fig. 9.

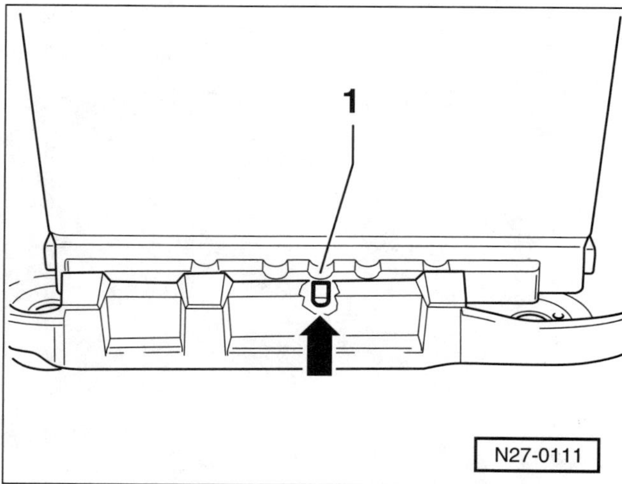

N27-0111

Fig. 9. Install battery so lug (**arrow**) of battery tray lines up in battery foot strip groove (**1**).

11. The battery is correctly installed when the center groove in the battery foot strip aligns with threaded hole in the battery carrier. See Fig. 10.

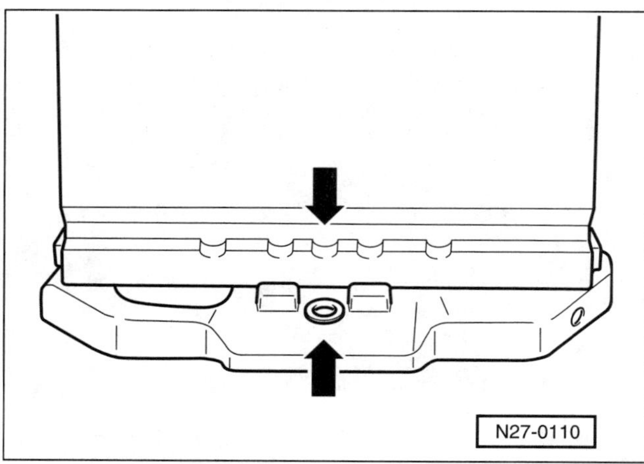

N27-0110

Fig. 10. Correct installation position of battery.

> ***CAUTION —***
> - *To be sure the battery seats securely, only install batteries with a 10.5 mm battery foot strip.*
> - *It must not be possible to move the battery to the left or to the right.*
> - *On batteries with hose for central venting make sure venting hose is not kinked. Only then can battery vent freely.*
> - *On batteries without hose for central venting make sure opening on upper side of battery cover is not blocked.*

12. Install battery clamping bracket and tighten securing bolt.

Tightening torque
- Battery clamping bracket bolt . . . . 22 Nm (16 ft-lb)

13. Remaining installation is the reverse of removal, noting the following points:
    - Be sure the battery is secured properly.
    - Connect all battery positive (+) connections before installing negative (-) battery clamp.

Tightening torque
- Battery terminal clamps . . . . 6 Nm (53 in-lb)

14. Be sure to quality check your work, see **Quality Review** at the end of this repair group.

CHARGING SYSTEM SERVICE

Charging system trouble is indicated by an illuminated generator warning light on the instrument panel, or by an under or overcharged battery.

The generator generates electrical current by electrical induction. When the engine is running, part of the current it produces energizes its electromagnetic field. When starting, some other current must be provided to initially energize the field and begin the current generating process. This current is provided by the battery through the generator warning light in the instrument cluster. If the lamp burns out, the generator will not charge the battery properly.

> ***CAUTION —***
> - *Always disconnect the negative (–) battery cable before servicing the charging system. The large red wire at the rear of the generator comes directly from the battery and is not fuse protected.*
> - *Disconnecting the negative (–) battery cable may erase fault codes and basic settings in the engine management and automatic transmission control modules. Some driveability problems may be noticed until the system re-adapts to operating conditions. OBD II readiness codes, which may be required for emissions testing, may also be erased.*

As a quick-check, measure the voltage across the battery terminal with the key off and then again with the engine running. The battery voltage should be about 12.6 volts with key off and approximately 14.0 volts with the engine running. If the voltage does not increase when the engine is running, there is a fault in the charging system.

> ***NOTE —***
> *The regulated voltage (engine running) should be roughly between 13.8 and 14.5 volts, depending on temperature and operating conditions. If the voltage is much higher than 14.5 volts, the voltage regulator is most likely faulty.*

Charging system, testing

1. Inspect the poly-ribbed drive belt for cracking, glazing or wear. Replace the belt if any faults are found. Check that the belt is not slipping and that the belt tension is correct.

2. Make sure the battery is fully charged and capable of holding a charge. Make sure the battery terminals are clean and tight.

3. Check that the charge warning lamp comes on when the key is on. If the light comes on, proceed to step 4. If the light does not come on, repair any wiring or bulb faults before continuing to test.

> ***NOTE —***
> *The charge warning light must come on when the ignition is switched on or the system may not charge. If any faults are found, see* **97 Wiring Diagrams, Fuses and Relays** *for electrical schematics.*

4. Check for battery voltage between ground and terminal **B+** (large red wire) at the back of the generator. Check that the wire is securely fastened.

5. Turn the ignition key on and check for battery voltage between terminal **D+** and ground. If voltage is not present, check the wiring from the warning light in the instrument cluster.

6. If no faults are found up to this point, have the generator tested with a load tester, such as the Sun VAT40.

> ***NOTE —***
> *If a load test is not possible, an imperfect output test can be done by running the engine at about 2000 rpm and turning on many of the electrical loads such as fans, lights and heated window, wipers, etc. When loaded, the battery should still be 12 volts or higher.*

Generator, removing and installing

> ***NOTE —***
> *The alternator is identified as generator by the vehicle manufacturer. Car makers must by law use uniform words and terms (nomenclature) to describe certain components and or systems. The uniform word for alternator is generator. Therefore, the component labeled "Generator (GEN)" in the wiring diagrams is the alternator.*

1. Disconnect the battery ground (GND) strap from battery negative (-) terminal. See the **Cautions** at the beginning of this repair group regarding battery disconnection.

> ***NOTE —***
> *Be sure to have the anti-theft radio on hand before disconnecting the battery cables.*

2. Mark the running direction on the poly-ribbed drive belt and then remove the belt from the generator pulley. See **0 Maintenance**.

3. Disconnect the wiring from the rear of the generator.

4. Remove the upper and lower generator through-bolts and remove the generator from its bracket.

5. Installation is the reverse of removal. Tightening torques are given in the appropriate generator overview on the following pages.

6. Be sure to quality check your work, see **Quality Review** at the end of this repair group.

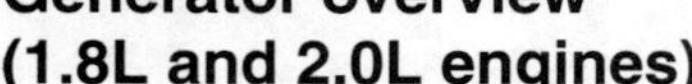

Generator overview (1.8L and 2.0L engines)

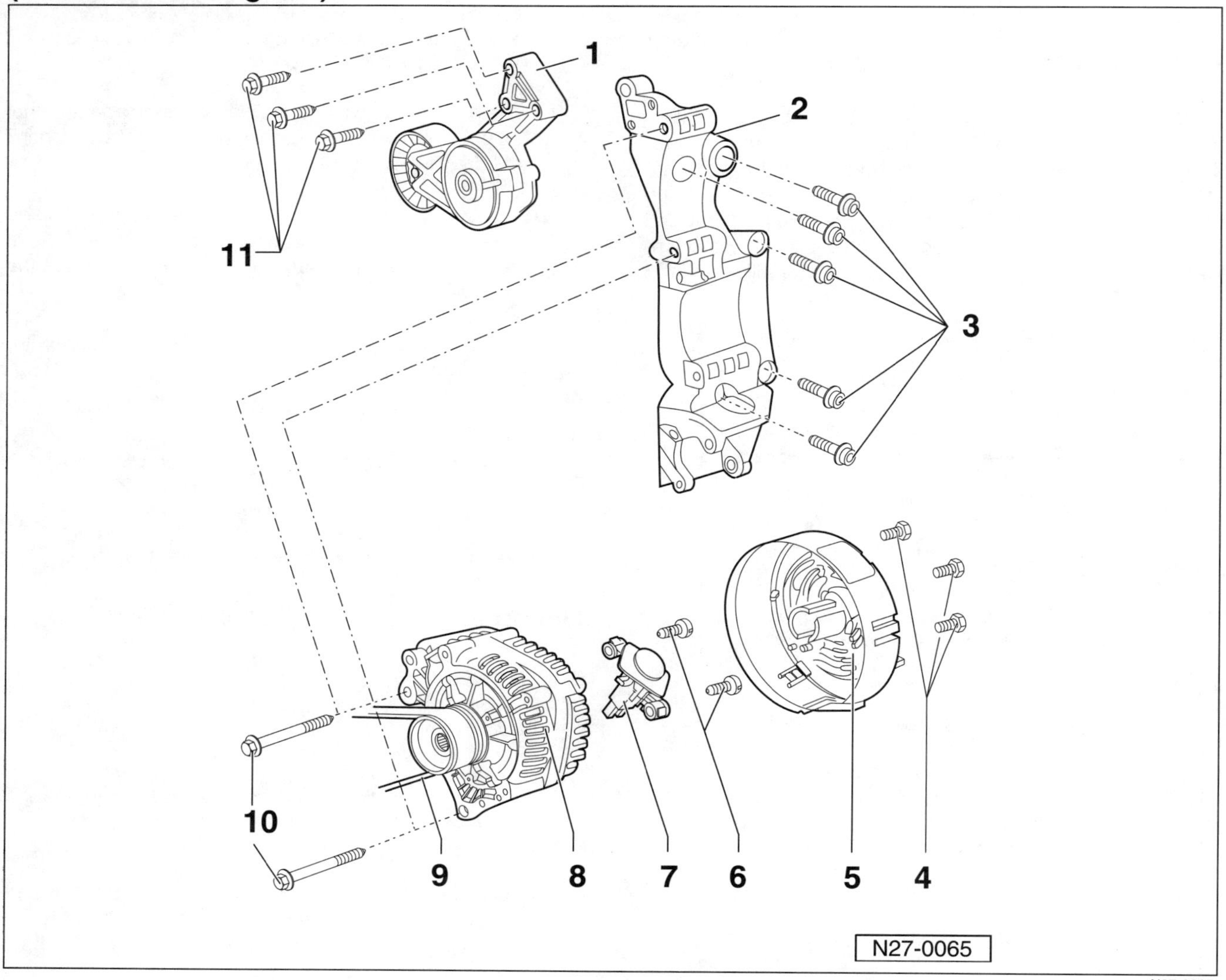

N27-0065

Fig. 11. Generator and bracket on the 1.8L and 2.0L engines.

1. **Tensioning roller**
2. **Bracket**
3. **Socket head bolts**
   - M10 x 45mm
   - Tighten to 45 Nm (33 ft-lb)
4. **Bolts**
   - M3 x 18mm
5. **Protective end cap**
   - Not removable from m.y. 2001
6. **Phillips-head screws**
   - M4 x 25mm
7. **Voltage regulator**
   - To remove and install, remove items 4, 5, 6
   - See **Regulator brushes, checking**
8. **Generator**
   - Tighten nut of B+ wire to generator to 15 Nm (11 ft-lb)
   - Available in 70A, 90A, and 120A
9. **Ribbed belt**
   - Removing and installing, see **0 Maintenance**
10. **Hex bolts**
    - M8 x 85mm
    - Tighten to 25 Nm (18 ft-lb)
11. **Hex bolts**
    - Tighten to 25 Nm (18 ft-lb)

Generator overview (1.9L engine)

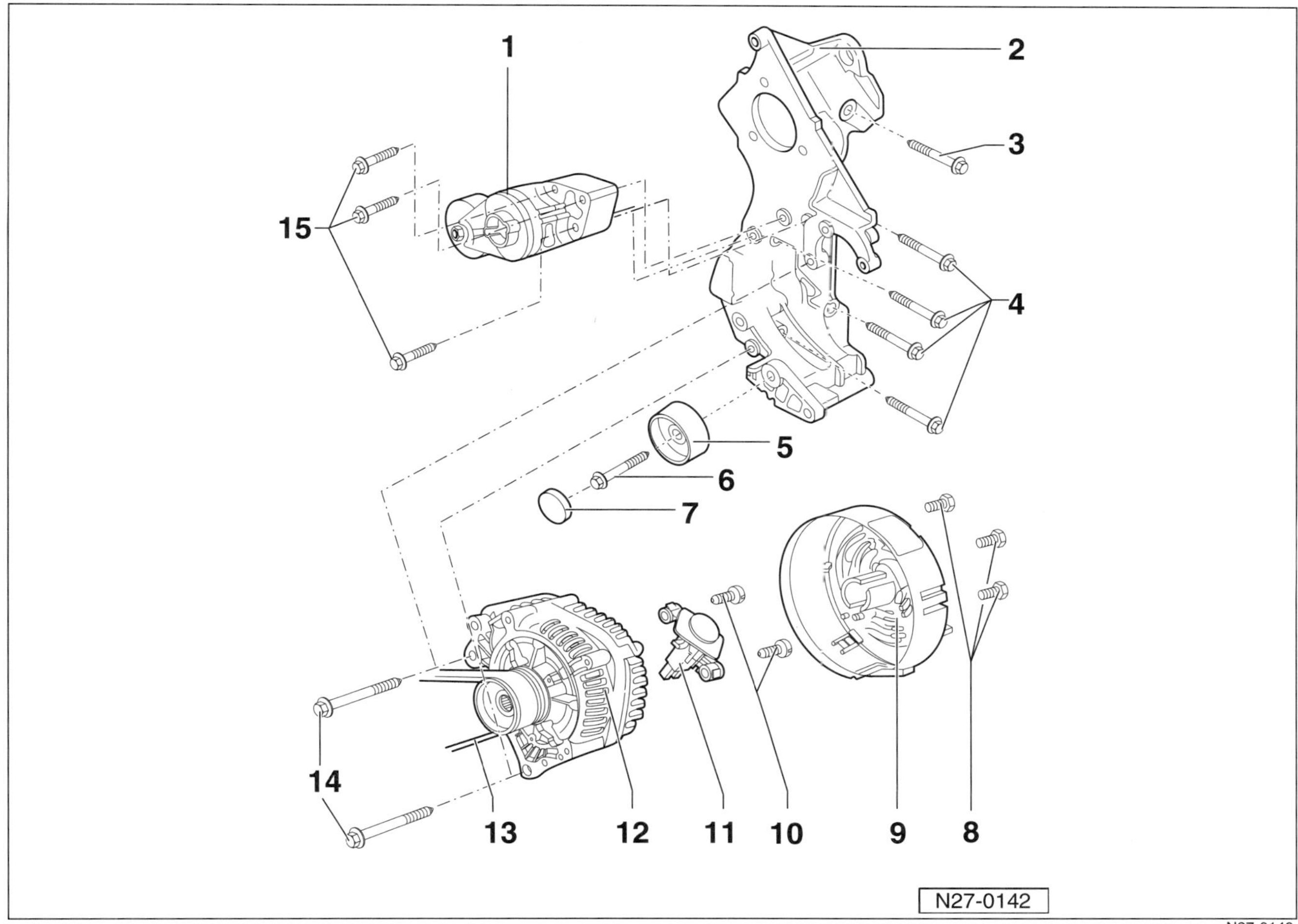

Fig. 12. Generator and bracket for 1.9L engine equipped with power steering and air conditioning.

1. **Tensioning roller**
2. **Bracket**
3. **Bolt**
   - M10 x 45mm
   - Tighten to 45 Nm (33 ft-lb)
4. **Bolts**
   - M10 x 65mm
   - Tighten to 45 Nm (33 ft-lb)
5. **Relay roller**
6. **Bolt**
   - M8 x 50mm
   - Tighten to 25 Nm (18 ft-lb)
7. **Protective cap**
8. **Bolts**
   - M3 x 18mm
9. **Protective end cap**
   - Not removable from m.y. 2001
10. **Phillips-head screws**
    - M4 x 25mm
11. **Voltage regulator**
    - To remove and install, remove items 8, 9, 10
    - See **Regulator brushes, checking**
12. **Generator**
    - Tighten nut of B+ wire to generator to 15 Nm (11 ft-lb)
    - Available in 70A, 90A, and 120A
13. **Ribbed belt**
    - Removing and installing, see **0 Maintenance**
14. **Hex bolts**
    - M8 x 85mm
    - Tighten to 25 Nm (18 ft-lb)
15. **Hex bolts**
    - M8 x 45mm
    - Tighten to 25 Nm (18 ft-lb)

Generator overview (2.8L engine)

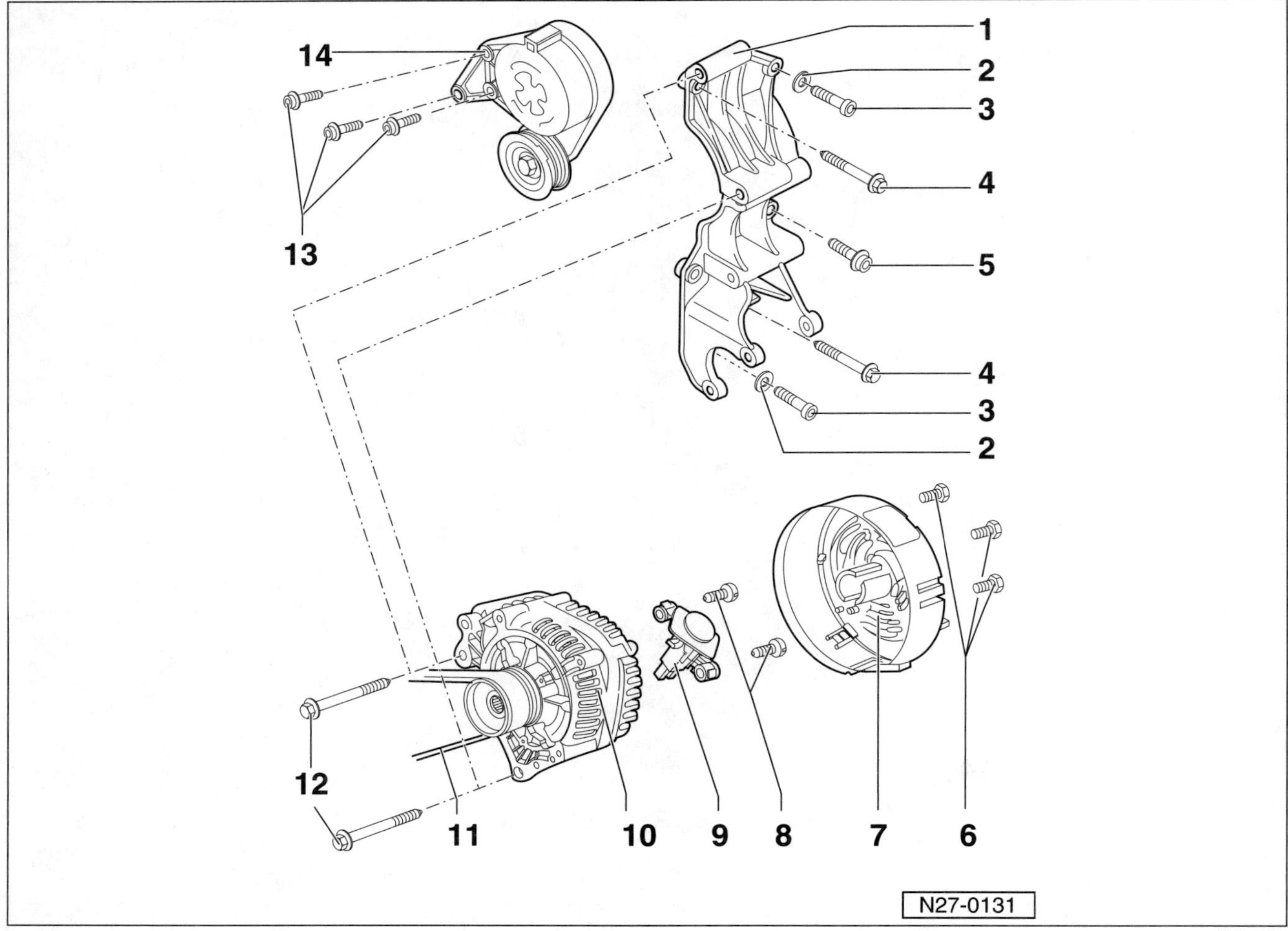

N27-0131

Fig. 13. Generator and bracket for the 2.8L engine.

1. **Bracket**
2. **Washer**
3. **Bolt**
   - M8 x 28mm
   - Tighten to 25 Nm (18 ft-lb)
4. **Bolts**
   - M8 x 85mm
5. **Socket head bolts**
   - M8 x 30mm
   - Tighten to 25 Nm (18 ft-lb)
6. **Bolts**
   - M3 x 18mm
7. **Protective cap**
   - Not removable from m.y. 2001
8. **Phillips-head screws**
   - M4 x 25mm
9. **Voltage regulator**
   - To remove and install, remove items 4, 5, 6
   - See **Regulator brushes, checking**
10. **Generator**
    - Tighten nut of B+ wire to generator to 15 Nm (11 ft-lb)
    - Available in 70A, 90A, and 120A
11. **Ribbed belt**
    - Removing and installing, see **0 Maintenance**
12. **Bolt**
    - M8 x 85mm
    - Tighten to 25 Nm (18 ft-lb)
13. **Socket head bolts**
    - M8 x 30mm
    - Tighten to 25 Nm (18 ft-lb)
14. **Tensioning roller**

Regulator brushes, checking

1999 m.y.

1. On 1999 m.y. generators, as shown in the previous exploded views, remove the screws or bolts securing the protective end cap on the generator. Remove end cap.

2. Remove mounting screws/bolts for voltage regulator and voltage regulator assembly with carbon brushes.

3. Measure the length of the length of the carbon brushes. See Fig. 14.

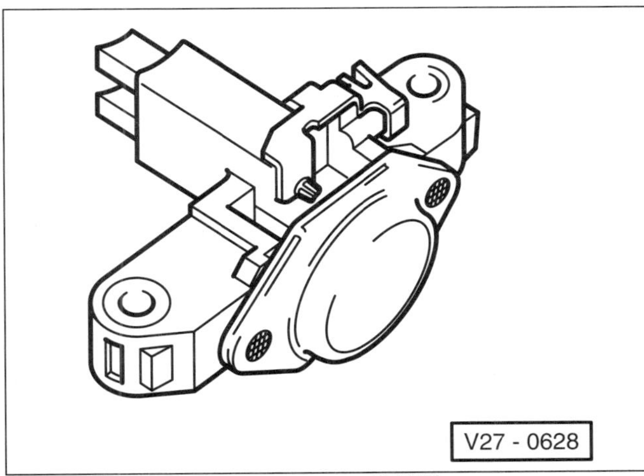

V27-0628

Fig. 14. Voltage regulator with carbon brushes for 1999 m.y.

Voltage regulator brushes (all)

- Length of new brushes. . . . . 12 mm (1.5 in.)
- Wear limit . . . . 5 mm (0.19 in.)
- Tolerance (difference between length of each brush) . . . . + 1 mm (0.03 in.)

2000 m.y.

For model year 2000 compact generators are being implemented with new structures and terminal assignments. They have a modified voltage regulator, and an oval, radially sealed connector mount for the 2-pin harness connector.

1. On 2000 and later m.y. compact generators, remove the hex nuts and mounting screw for the protective end cap. See Fig. 15. Remove end cap.

   NOTE—
   The new compact generator terminal B+ (battery positive) is marked B1+ at the generator terminal. See Fig. 15.

2. Remove voltage regulator mounting bolts and voltage regulator assembly with carbon brushes. See Fig. 16.

3. Measure length of carbon brushes and compare to specification provided above. See Fig. 17.

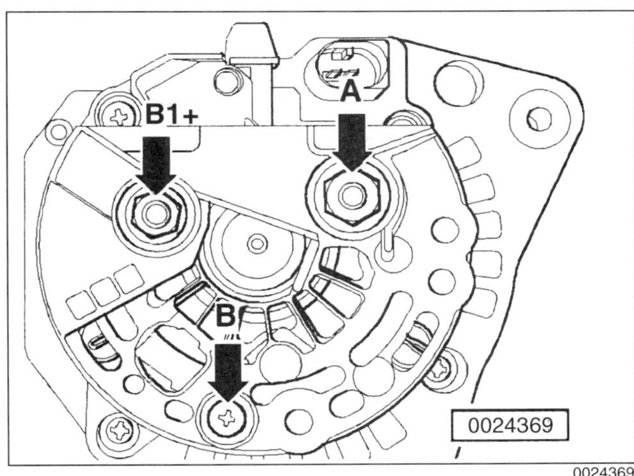

0024369

Fig. 15. Remove nuts (**arrows A** and **B1+**) and mounting screw (**arrow B**) to remove protective end cap of new compact generator.

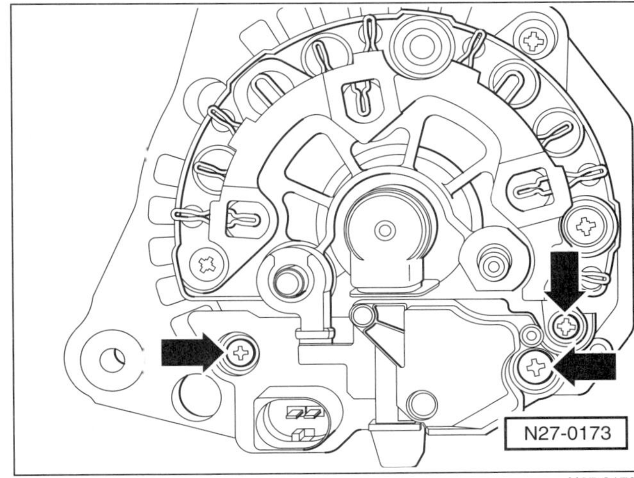

N27-0173

Fig. 16. Mounting bolts (**arrows**) for voltage regulator assembly.

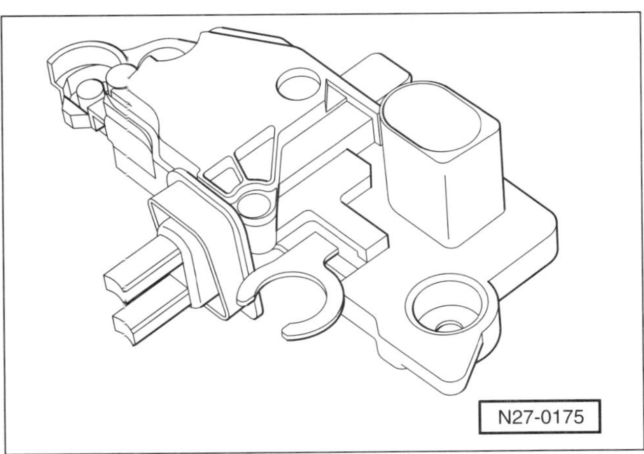

N27-0175

Fig. 17. Voltage regulator with carbon brushes on 2000 and later m.y.

2001 m.y.

For model year 2001, a modified compact generator is used. The terminal designations are shown in Fig. 18. The new generators have no removable rear cap to service the voltage regulator. If the voltage regulator is faulty the entire generator will need to be replaced.

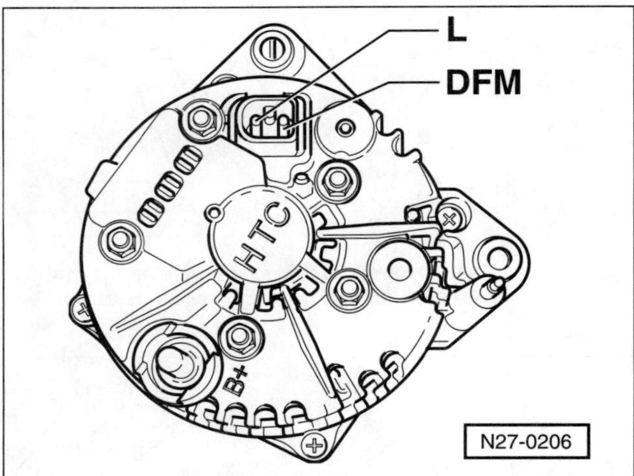

N27-0206

Fig. 18. Rear view of m.y. 2001 compact generator.

STARTER SERVICE

The starter is located below the engine on the left-hand (driver's) side, bolted to the forward part of the transmission. The starter and solenoid are removed together as an assembly. The solenoid can be separated from the starter motor once the starter has been removed. Although the starter is generally replaced as an exchange unit, the solenoid and other parts are available from an authorized Volkswagen dealer.

All vehicles have a lock-out relay for the starter which is controlled by the alarm system. For location of relays, see **97 Wiring Diagrams, Fuses and Relays**.

In addition, vehicles equipped with manual transmissions have a starter lock-out function requiring the clutch pedal to be depressed before the starter can be activated. This system consists of a pedal switch and a relay on the fuse-relay panel. See Fig. 19.

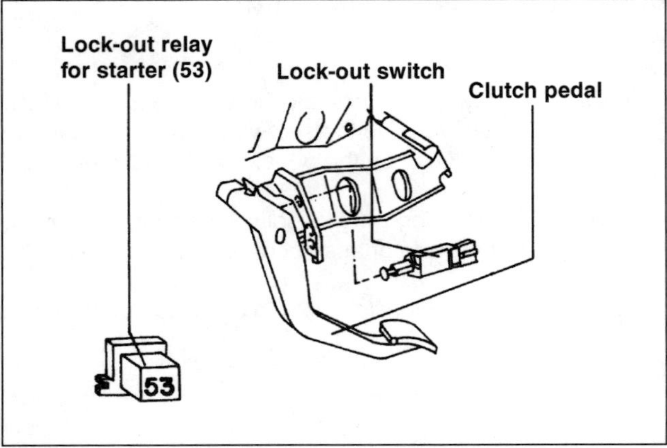

0024256

Fig. 19. Starter lock-out switch and relay for vehicles with manual transmission.

Vehicles equipped with automatic transmissions have a park/neutral position relay that prevents the vehicles from being started if the gear selector is not in the P (Park) or N (Neutral) position.

Before troubleshooting the starter, make sure the battery is fully charged and the battery cables and ground connections are free of corrosion and in good condition. Troubleshooting information for the starting system appears in **Table c**.

NOTE —
Starter cranking speed is affected by engine oil viscosity, especially in cold weather. Make sure the correct oil is in the engine. See **0 Maintenance**.

Specification

- Starter rating
  - 1.8L and 2.0L engines. . . . . 1.1 kW (1.48 hp)
  - 1.9L and 2.8L engines. . . . . 2.0 kW (2.68 hp)

Table c. Starter System Troubleshooting

Symptom	Probable cause	Corrective action
1. Starter does not operate when ignition switch is turned to START	a. Ignition switch or wire leading from ignition switch to solenoid faulty (less than 8 volts to solenoid)	a. Test for voltage at terminal 50 of solenoid with ignition at START. If not at least 8 volts, test for voltage at terminal 50 of ignition switch with switch at START. Replace ignition switch or eliminate open circuit between ignition switch and solenoid.
	b. Automatic transmission Park/Neutral position (PNP) relay faulty	b. Test relay. See **97 Wiring Diagrams, Fuses and Relays** and **37 Automatic Transmission.**
	c. Starter lock-out switch or relay faulty (manual transmission only)	c. Test switch and relay. See **97 Wiring Diagrams, Fuses and Relays.**
2. Starter turns slowly or fails to turn engine	a. Dirty, loose, or corroded starter connections	a. Clean, and tighten connections. If necessary check voltage drop between the battery and the starter as described in **9 Electrical System—General.**
	b. Dirty, loose, or corroded ground strap between engine and body	b. Remove and clean or replace strap
	c. Starter worn or faulty	c. Repair or replace starter
3. Starter operates, but does not turn engine	a. Flywheel or driveplate teeth missing or damaged	a. Replace flywheel or driveplate. See **1 ENGINE.**
	b. Starter drive or armature shaft faulty	b. Repair or replace starter
	c. Solenoid mechanism faulty	c. Replace starter solenoid

Starter, removing and installing

1. Disconnect battery ground (GND) strap from battery negative (-) terminal. See the **Cautions** at the beginning of this repair group regarding battery disconnection.

   NOTE —
   Be sure to have the anti-theft radio code on hand before disconnecting the battery.

2. Remove battery and battery tray as described earlier.
3. Disconnect starter harness connector and connection at terminal 50 and terminal 30 (battery positive (+) cable). See Fig. 20.

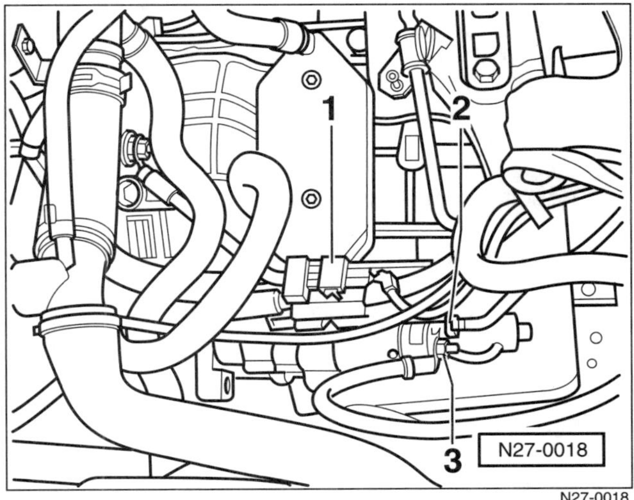

Fig. 20. Disconnect starter harness connector (**1**) and connections at terminal 50 (**2**) and terminal 30 (**3**).

4. Remove upper mounting bolt for starter.
5. Remove lower sound absorber panel(s) (belly pan).
6. Remove brackets and retainers for power steering lines and place connected lines to side.
7. Remove lower starter mounting bolt and starter. See Fig. 21.

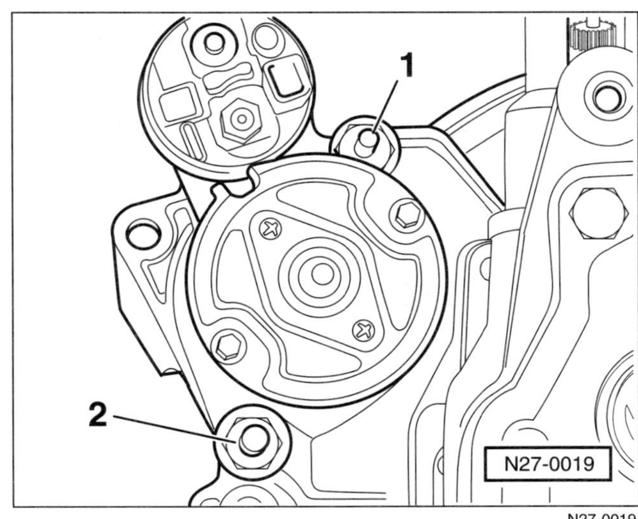

Fig. 21. Starter mounting bolts; upper (**1**) and lower (**2**).

Tightening torque
- Starter to engine block . . . . 65 Nm (48 ft-lb)

Starter terminal designation

- Switched battery positive (+) from ignition/starter switch . . . . terminal 50
- Battery positive (+), hot at all times . . . . . . terminal 30

8. Installation is the reverse of removal. Be sure to install a new starter bushing as described below.

Tightening torque

- Battery positive (+) cable to starter . . .13 Nm (10 ft lb)

Starter bushing, removing and installing

1. Remove starter as describe above.

2. Use Volkswagen special tool VW 228b, or similar to extract the starter bushing. See Fig. 22.

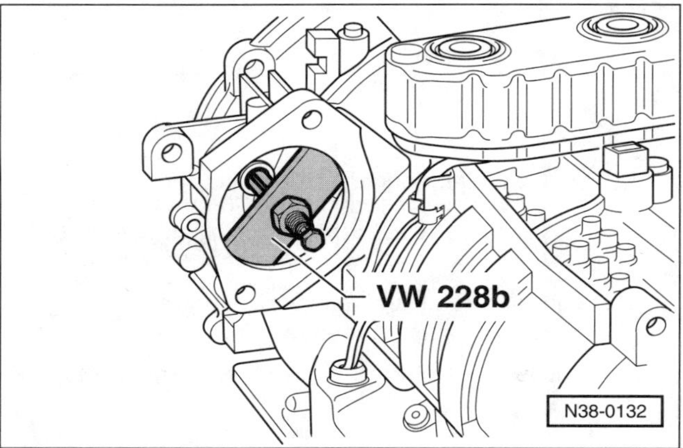

N38-0132

Fig. 22. Starter bushing being removed with special tool VW 228b. Automatic transmission shown, manual is similar.

3. Use Volkswagen special tool VW 222a or similar to install a new starter bushing. See Fig. 23.

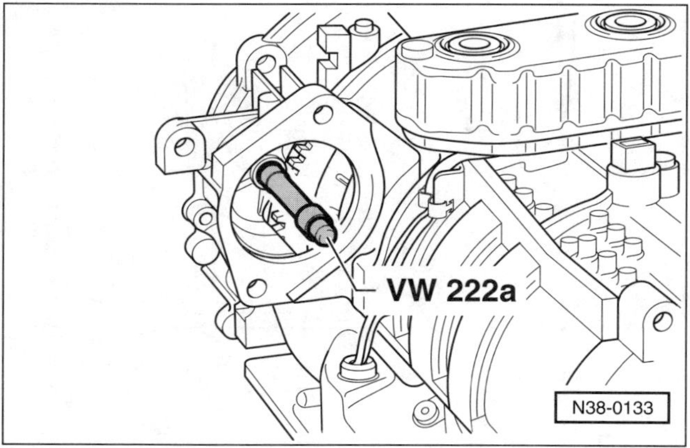

N38-0133

Fig. 23. Starter bushing being installed with special tool VW 222a. Automatic transmission shown, manual is similar.

QUALITY REVIEW

CRUISE CONTROL

All cruise control system functions are controlled by the engine control module (ECM). The processing of electronic engine controls and cruise control functions are integrated in the ECM. Other than the cruise control switches on the steering column, the clutch and brake pedal switches and related wiring and fuses, there are no separate cruise control components to be serviced.

As the electronic throttle control operations (with the exception of the 2.0L AEG engine) are monitored by OnBoard Diagnostic (OBD), Diagnostic Trouble Codes (DTCs) pertaining to engine electronics that are stored in the DTC memory may be relevant to cruise control function. Always check DTC memory using a scan tool first before troubleshooting the cruise control system. See **ST Scan Tool Codes** at the back of this manual.

If the ECM has been replaced on all but the AEG 2.0L engine the cruise control system may need to be activated using a scan tool such as the VAG 1551, 1552, 5051 or equivalent. **Table D** shows the various activation and deactivation codes for the cruise control system and the ECM.

Table d. Cruise control and ECM activation codes

Engine (code) and model year	Activation code	Deactivation code
1.8L (AWD) and 2.8L (AFP) - m.y. 1999	00003	00004
1.9L (ALH) - m.y.1999➤	11463	16167
1.8L (AWD/AWW) - m.y. 2000➤	11463	16167
2.0L (AVH/AZG) - m.y. 2000➤	11463	16167
2.8L (AFP) - m.y. 2000➤	11463	16167

QUALITY REVIEW

When you have finished working under the hood and around other areas of the vehicle, it is advisable to take a moment to quality check or review your work. This helps to insure that the operation or repair has been completed properly with all affected systems functioning within normal parameters. These may include the following:

- Ensure battery is securely mounted, cables connections are tight, and battery cover is in place.

If the battery has been disconnected:

- Re-code radio and set clock.
- Check the operation of power windows and reset as necessary, see **57 Doors**.
- Reset basic setting for automatic transmission (as applicable) using VAG 1551/1552 or a suitable scan tool, or see **37 Automatic Transmission**.
- Reset basic settings for engine and OBD II readiness codes as required using VAG 1551/1552 or a suitable scan tool. See **23 Fuel Injection–Diesel (1.9L engine)** or **24 Fuel Injection–Motronic** for the appropriate engine.

28a Ignition System–Gasoline

GENERAL

The ignition functions of the 1.8L, 2.0L and 2.8L gasoline engines are controlled by the Motronic engine management system. The Engine Control Module (ECM) computes ignition timing based on inputs from various sensors. Crankshaft speed from the crankshaft position sensor (G28) and engine load from the mass air flow sensor (G70) are the two main inputs used to calculate the basic ignition timing point. The other sensors, including the two knock sensors, are used by the ECM to modify and correct the ignition timing point to changing operating conditions.

> ***WARNING —***
> *Disconnecting the negative (–) battery cable may erase fault codes and basic settings in the engine management and automatic transmission control modules. Some driveability problems may be noticed until the system re-adapts to operating conditions. OBD II readiness codes, which may be required for emissions testing, may also be erased. Convenience electronics (alarm system, interior light control, power locks, mirrors, and windows) will need to be re-set using a VAG 1551/1552 or equivalent scan tool.*

Fuel Systems–Gasoline

- 1.8L (AWD, AWW) . . . . . Motronic ME 7.5
- 2.0L (AEG) . . . . . Motronic 5.9.2
- 2.0L (AVH, AZG) . . . . . Motronic ME 7.5
- 2.8L (AFP) . . . . . Motronic ME 7.1

NOTE —
The Motronic fuel systems are all OBD II compliant. It is recommended that fault diagnosis and troubleshooting be carried out using Volkswagen scan tools VAG 1551, 1552, 5051, or an equivalent aftermarket scan tool. See **ST Scan Tool Codes** *at the back of this manual for a list of diagnostic trouble codes (DTCs) and scan tool suppliers.*

Service precautions

Ignition system service and repair work must be carried out carefully. The ignition system contains sensitive electronic components. To guard against system damage, and for personal and general safety, the following warnings and cautions apply to any ignition system troubleshooting, maintenance or repair work.

> ***WARNING —***
> - *Ignition systems operate in a dangerous voltage range that could prove to be fatal if exposed terminals or live parts are contacted. Use extreme caution when working on a vehicle with the ignition on or the engine running.*
> - *Connect and disconnect ignition system wires, terminal connectors and test equipment leads only while the ignition is off unless specifically instructed otherwise. Do not touch or disconnect any of the high voltage wires from the coil pack or spark plugs while the engine is running or being cranked by the starter.*

Disabling ignition system

If the engine must be turned at starter speed without starting, the ignition system should be disabled to prevent the discharge of dangerously high voltage. This should be done any time repairs or maintenance are performed on the engine with the ignition key on or if the starter needs to be operated without running the engine. The ignition coils are mounted low on the front of the cylinder block behind the secondary air injection pump.

1. Disconnect harness connector from ignition coil Power Output Stage.
   - On 1.8L engine, disconnect 4-pin harness connector from each ignition coil output stage. See Fig. 1.
   - On 2.0L (AEG) engine, disconnect 4-pin harness connector at ignition coil output stage. See Fig. 2.
   - On 2.0L (AVH, AZG) engine, disconnect 6-pin harness connector at ignition coil output stage. See Fig. 3.
   - On 2.8L engine, disconnect the 5-pin ignition coil harness connector. See Fig. 4.

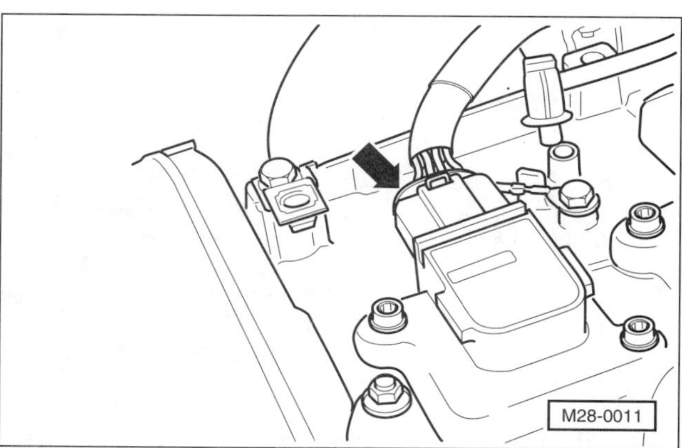

M28-0011

Fig. 1. Disconnect the four ignition coil connectors for each cylinder (**arrow**) on 1.8L engine to disable ignition system. (Cyl. 1 shown)

0024275

Fig. 2. Disconnect ignition coil connector (**arrow**) on 2.0L (AEG) engine to disable ignition system. Secondary air pump has been removed for clarity.

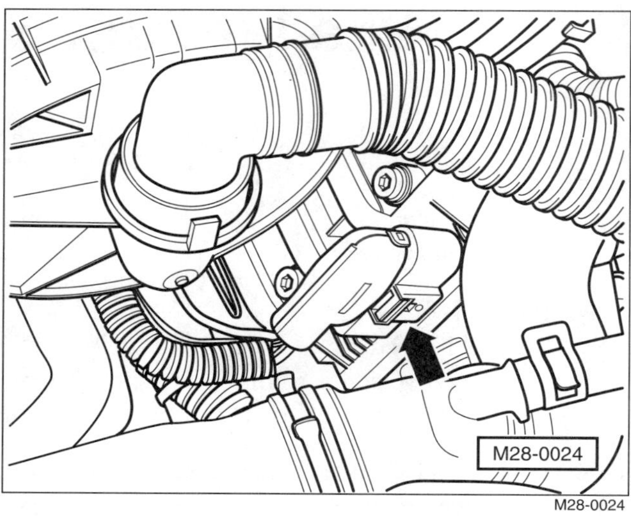

M28-0024

Fig. 3. Disconnect ignition coil output stage harness connector (**arrow**) on 2.0L (AVH/AZG) engine to disable ignition system.

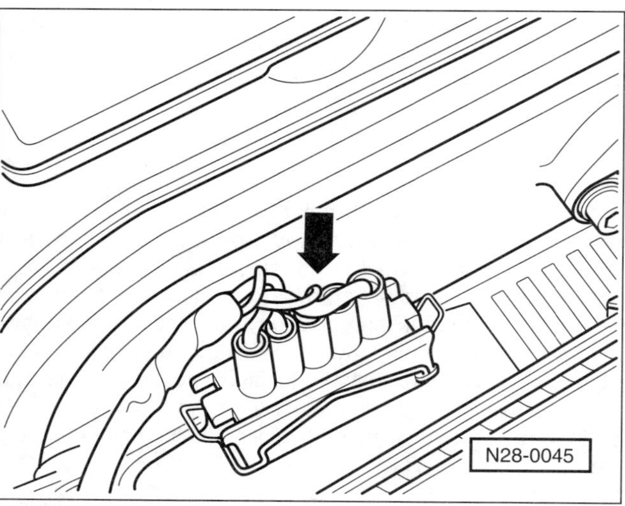

N28-0045

Fig. 4. Disconnect ignition coil connector (**arrow**) on 2.8L engine to disable ignition system.

2. Remove fuse 32 (for fuel injectors). See Fig. 5.

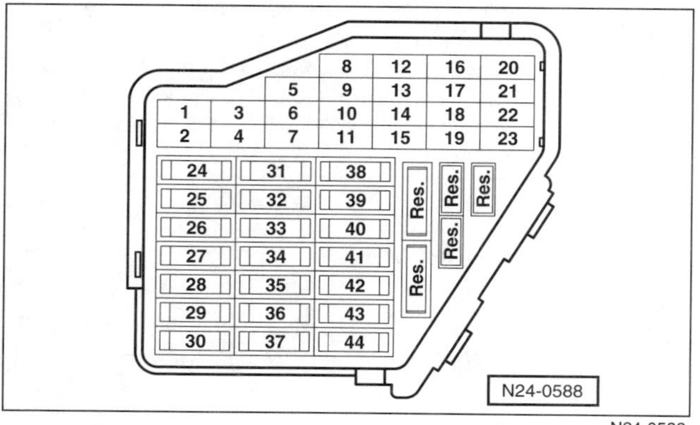

N24-0588

Fig. 5. Fuse 32 protects fuel injector circuit for all engine versions.

IGNITION SYSTEM TROUBLESHOOTING

Poor driveability may have a variety of causes. The fault may lie with the ignition system, the fuel system, parts of the emission control system, or a combination of the three. Because of the interrelated functions of these systems, it is often difficult to know where to begin looking for problems. For this reason, when troubleshooting always consider these systems in unison, as one major system.

A complete failure of the ignition system to produce spark at the spark plugs is self-evident. For other problems such as rough idle, misfiring, or poor starting the cause may not be so clear. The engine management system has a built in diagnostic circuit that monitors the ignition system components and detects and stores system faults. Before troubleshooting the ignition system, always check for diagnostic trouble codes (DTCs) using a suitable scan tool such as VAG 1551/1552 or equivalent

> ***NOTE —***
> *Continued operation of the engine with a misfire will result in serious damage to the catalytic converter.*

Quick-check of ignition system

The first step in troubleshooting a no-start condition is to determine whether the problem is caused by the ignition system or some other system, such as a fuel delivery problem. This is done by checking that the spark plugs are firing. If no spark is present, a more detailed testing of the ignition system is necessary.

To make the check, turn the ignition off and remove a spark plug connector from a spark plug. Connect the plug connector to a known good spark plug. Position the plug so that the outer electrode is grounded on the engine. For accurate test results, the battery should be fully charged.

> ***CAUTION —***
> *Never let the spark plug gap (between electrode and ground) exceed 5 mm (0.20 in.) when checking for a spark, as the power output stage may be damaged. Always ground the plug on the engine when checking for spark.*

While a helper actuates the starter, look and listen for a spark at the plug. A bright blue spark indicates a healthy ignition system. If there is no spark, visually ensure that the engine speed sensor plug is connected properly and that the speed sensor is secured into the mount in the cylinder block. If the above inspection reveals no obvious defects, then test the ignition coil output stage and the ignition coil as described later.

Specification
- Ignition firing order, (4-cylinder engines) 1-3-4-2
- Ignition firing order, (6-cylinder engine) . . . 1-5-3-6-2-4

> ***WARNING —***
> - *Do not hold the spark plug or its connector during the test, even if using insulated pliers.*
> - *If ignition system failure is not the problem, the engine may start during this test. Be prepared to switch the ignition off immediately. Running the engine with a spark plug wire disconnected may damage the catalytic converter.*

Spark plug wires/connectors, checking

On the 2.0L and 2.8L engines spark plug wires suppress radio frequency (RF) interference through the use of resistors built in to the ends.

The turbocharged 1.8L engines use individual ignition coil power output stages at each cylinder that eliminate the need for spark plug wires, however the resistance of the spark plug connector can be measured.

1. On 2.0L and 2.8L engines disable ignition system as described earlier by disconnecting harness connector from ignition coil pack. On 1.8L remove individual ignition coil/plug connector assemblies.

2. Disconnect spark plug wire from spark plug using appropriate tool, as applicable. For 1.8L engine, carefully twist off spark plug from end of ignition coil.

3. Disconnect spark plug wire from ignition coil.

4. Measure resistance of spark plug wires with connectors (2.0L or 2.8L engines) or just the connector itself (1.8L engine).

Specification
- Resistance of spark plug wire with connectors
  - 2.0L engine . . . . 4000 to 8000 ohms
  - 2.8L engine . . . . 4000 to 6000 ohms
- Resistance of spark plug connector
  - 1.8L engine . . . . 2000 ohms

IGNITION SYSTEM (1.8L ENGINE)

The ignition system of the 1.8L engine requires little or no periodic maintenance due to the distributor-less nature of its design. Most of the components are monitored by the engine management system and a failure will cause a fault (DTC) to be stored in the engine control module. Engine misfiring can even result in a DTC being stored due to the potential for damage to the catalytic converter. For 1.8L engine ignition system components, see Fig. 6.

Ignition system components (1.8L engine)

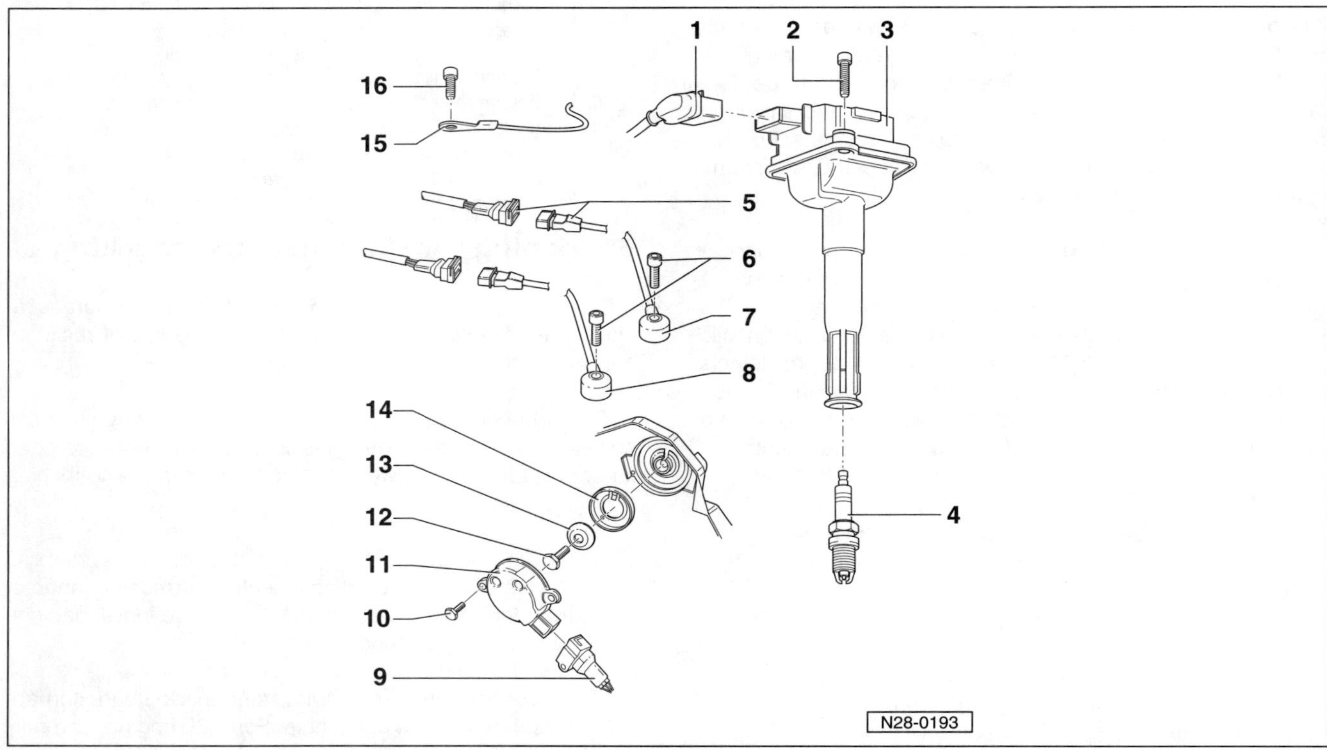

Fig. 6. Primary and secondary ignition system components of the 1.8L engine. AWD shown, AWW is similar.

1. **4-pin harness connector**
   - Separate connectors for each coil
2. **Bolt**
   - Tighten to 10 Nm (7 ft lb)
3. **Ignition coil pack (N70, N127, N291, N292)**
   - Separate coil for each cylinder
   - With power output stages
4. **Spark plug**
   - Tighten to 30 Nm (22 ft-lb)
   - Remove and install with 5/8 (16x mm) spark plug socket
5. **Harness connector**
   - AWD engine: 3-pin
   - AWW engine: 2-pin
   - Black for knock sensor 1
   - Brown for knock sensor 2
6. **Bolts**
   - Tighten to 20 Nm (14 ft lb)
7. **Knock sensor 1 (G61)**
   - Sensor and connector terminals are gold-plated
   - Mounting locations, **see** (A)
8. **Knock sensor 2 (G66)**
   - Sensor and connector terminals are gold-plated
   - Mounting locations, **see** (B)
9. **3-pin harness connector**
   - Check for voltage between terminals 1 and 3 with ignition on; specification: minimum 4.5 volts
10. **Bolt**
    - Tighten to 10 Nm (7 ft lb)
11. **Camshaft position sensor 2 (G163)**
    - Shutter wheel (rotor) mounted on camshaft
    - Mounted on front of cylinder head near intake camshaft, **see** (B)
12. **Bolt**
    - Tighten to 25 Nm (18 ft lb)
13. **Washer**
    - Conical shape
14. **Shutter wheel**
    - For camshaft position sensor
    - Note installation position
15. **Ground wire**
    - Remove and install only with ignition switched off
16. **Bolt**
    - Tighten to 20 Nm (15 ft lb)
    - Tightening torque influences function of knock sensor

A Knock sensors, mounting locations (1.8L engine)

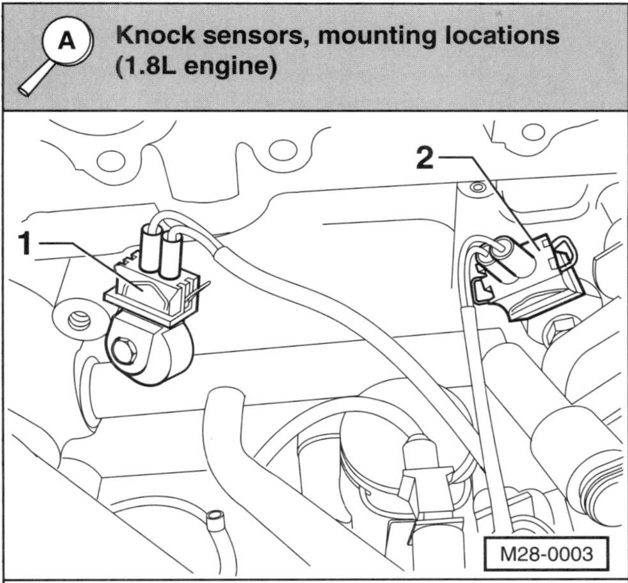

M28-0003

- **Knock sensor 1 (G61) monitors cylinders 1 and 2. and is mounted to the toothed belt end of cylinder block on the intake side.**
- **Knock sensor 2 (G66) monitors cylinders 3 and 4 and is mounted to the transmission end of cylinder block on the intake side.**
- **Correct torque is critical for proper operation: Tighten to 20 Nm (15 ft-lb).**
- **Knock sensors begin functioning at engine speeds over 2000 rpm and 40% loads.**

B Camshaft position sensor (1.8L engine)

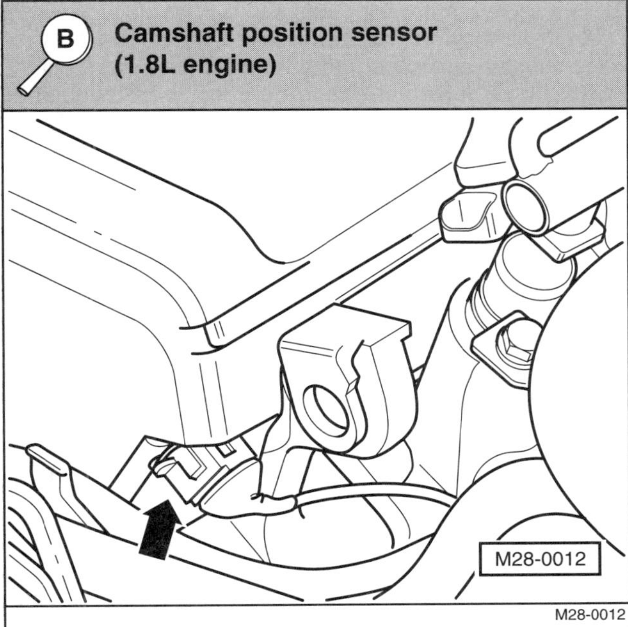

M28-0012

- **Camshaft position sensor is mounted to the front of the cylinder head on the intake side behind the upper toothed belt guard (arrow).**
- **Shutter wheel/rotor is mounted on the intake end of the camshaft.**

Spark plugs, removing and installing (1.8L engine)

Spark plugs are generally replaced during scheduled maintenance services. Due to engine design, and the shape of the cylinder head, spark plug replacement can easily be accomplished after removal of the ignition coils.

1. Switch ignition off.
2. Remove upper sound absorber panel.
3. Disconnect 4-pin harness connector from cylinder #1 ignition coil power output stage.
4. Remove cylinder #1 ignition coil. See Fig. 7.

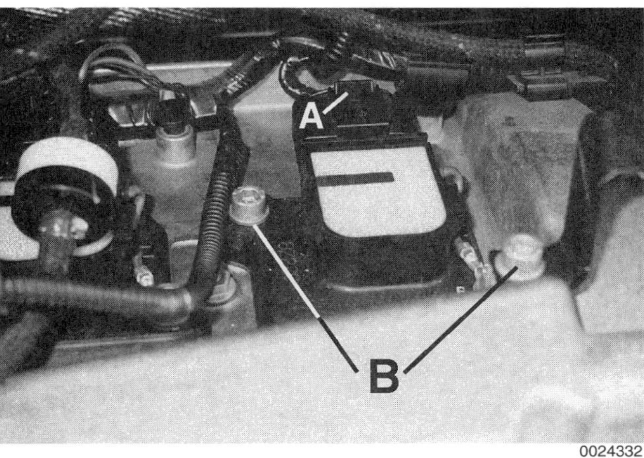

0024332

Fig. 7. Disconnect harness connector (**A**) and remove bolts (**B**) to remove ignition coil. AWD engine shown, AWW is similar.

5. Remove the spark plug with a 5/8 in. (16x mm) spark plug socket and an extension.
6. Check gap on new spark plug and install.
7. Install ignition coil and harness connector.

Specifications
- Spark Plugs (1.8L engine)
  - Original equipment number. 101-000-063-AA
  - Manufacturers number . . . . NGK PFR 6 Q
- Gap. . . . . .0.80 mm max.(0.031 in)
- Tightening torque . . . . 30 Nm (22 ft-lb)

8. Repeat for each remaining cylinder.
9. Install upper engine cover.

Ignition coils and power output stage, testing (1.8L engine)

Individual ignition coils each with a power output stage are mounted above each spark plug. The power output stage takes the low power signal from the ECM and boosts it to a level usable by the ignition coils. The power output stage cannot be directly tested, but the signal from the ECM along with power and ground can be easily tested.

1. Disable ignition system by disconnecting 4-pin harness connector from ignition coil as shown earlier. See Fig. 1.

2. Connect an accurate digital voltmeter to disconnected connector at terminals 1 and 4. See Fig. 8.

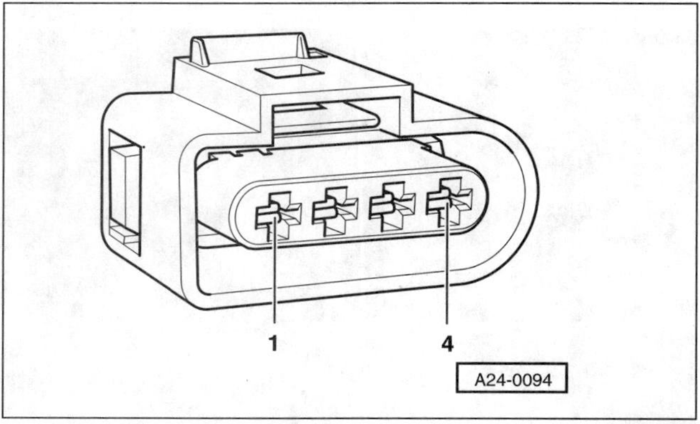

A24-0094

Fig. 8. Disconnected 4-pin harness connector to ignition coil. Connect voltmeter between terminals 1 and 4.

3. Switch on ignition and read voltage.

4. Repeat for terminals 1 and 2.

5. If voltage is present, proceed to next step. If no voltage is present, check for breaks or open circuits in the wiring, see **97 Wiring Diagrams, Fuses and Relays**.

Specification

- Voltage supply
  power output stage. . . . . 11.5 Volts minimum

---

6. Switch off ignition.

7. Remove fuse 32 (for fuel injectors) as shown earlier. See Fig. 5.

8. Connect an LED test light (such as VAG 1527B) to the disconnected connector at terminals 2 and 3.

CAUTION —

- *Use a high-quality digital automotive multimeter and an LED test light to make the tests. An analog (swing-needle) meter and conventional test light should not be used as they can permanently damage electronic components.*

- *Always connect and disconnect the ECM connector and meter probes with the ignition off to avoid damage to electronic components.*

9. Operate starter and check for a signal from the ECM. LED test light must flicker.
   - If LED test light flickers, signal from ECM is good.
   - If test light does not flicker, check for break in wiring, see **97 Wiring Diagrams, Fuses and Relays.** If no faults are found, check ECM for DTCs with a suitable scan tool.

10. Repeat procedure for each ignition coil.

NOTE —

- *Ignition coils and power output stages are a combined unit.*

- *Ignition coil primary and secondary resistance cannot be measured.*

If no faults are found with the supply voltage, impulse signal or wiring, then the faulty ignition coils should be replaced.

IGNITION SYSTEM (2.0L ENGINE)

The ignition system of the 2.0L engine require little or no periodic maintenance due to the distributor-less nature of the system. Most of the components are monitored by their respective engine management system and a failure will cause a fault (DTC) to be stored in the engine control module. Engine misfiring can even result in a DTC being stored due to the potential for damage to the catalytic converter. The various components of the 2.0L engine (code AEG) ignition system are shown in Fig. 9. For the 2.0L with engine code AVH or AZG see Fig. 13.

Ignition system components (AEG engine)

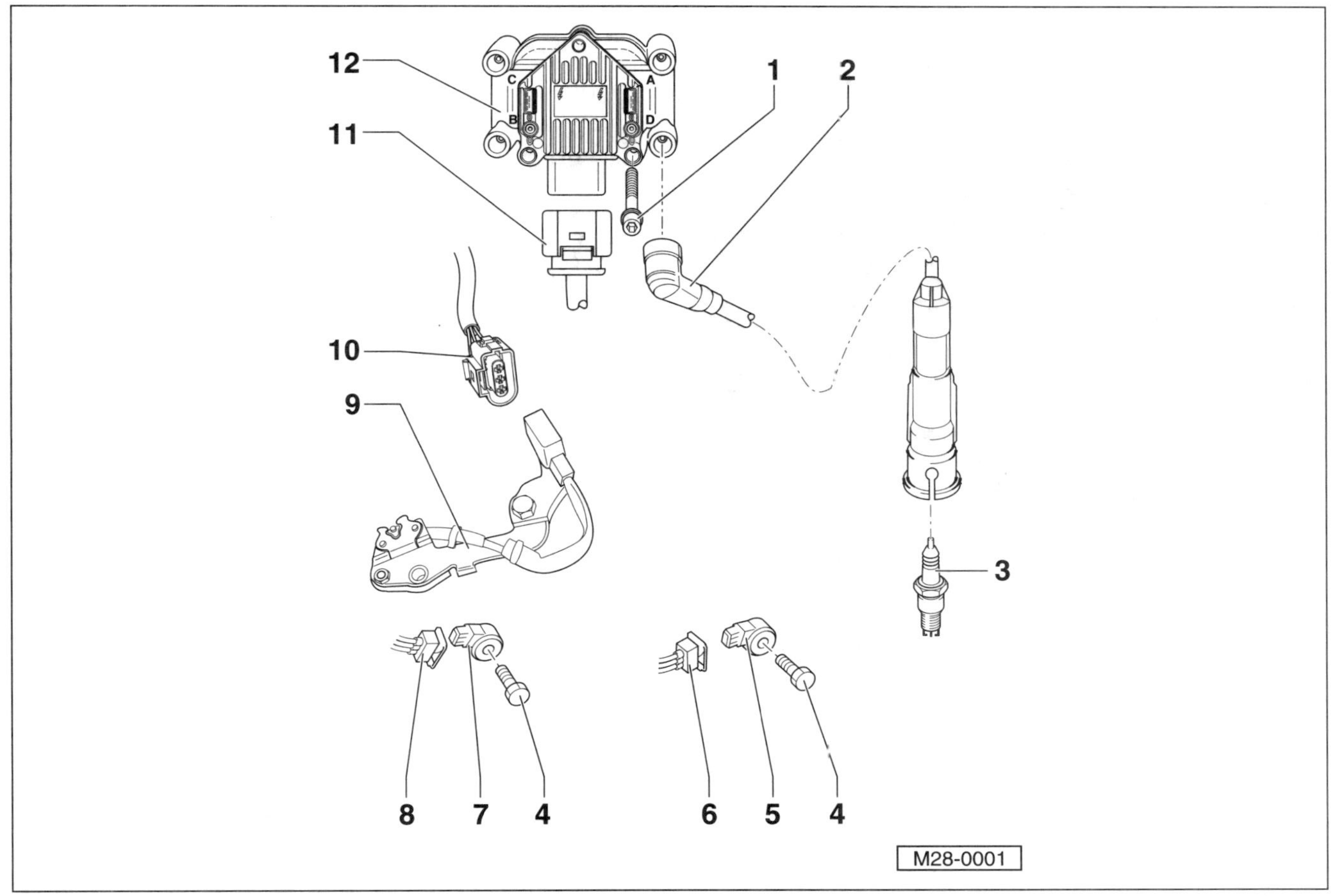

M28-0001

Fig. 9. Primary and secondary ignition system components of the 2.0L (AEG) engine.

1. **Bolt**
   - Tighten to 10 Nm (7 ft-lb)
2. **Ignition wire**
   - RF suppressor
   - Resistance: 4-8kΩ
   - Remove with special tool T10029
3. **Spark plug**
   - Tighten to 30 Nm (22 ft-lb)
   - Remove and install with 5/8 (16x mm) spark plug socket
4. **Bolt**
   - Tighten to 20 Nm (15 ft-lb)
   - Tightening torque influences knock sensor function
5. **Knock sensor 2 (G66)**
   - Sensor and connector terminals are gold-plated
   - Resistance: ∞Ω
6. **2-pin harness connector**
   - Brown with gold-plated terminals
7. **Knock sensor 1 (G61)**
   - Sensor and connector terminals are gold plated
   - Resistance: ∞Ω
8. **2-pin harness connector**
   - Black with gold-plated terminals
9. **Camshaft position sensor (G40)**
   - Mounted on cylinder head behind camshaft sprocket, **see** (A)
   - Shutter wheel (rotor) mounted on camshaft sprocket
10. **3-pin harness connector**
    - Check for voltage between terminals 1 and 3 with ignition on; specification: minimum 4.5 volts
    - For camshaft position sensor (G40)
11. **4-pin harness connector**
    - Black
12. **Ignition coil pack (N152)**
    - With integral power output stage
    - Marked for ignition cables:
      A = Cylinder 1
      B = Cylinder 3
      C = Cylinder 2
      D = Cylinder4

A Camshaft position sensor (AEG engine)

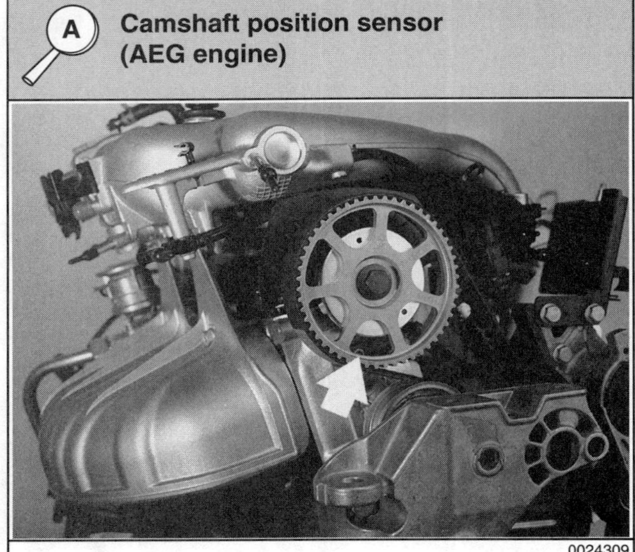

- **Camshaft position sensor is mounted to the front of the cylinder head behind the camshaft drive sprocket (arrow).**
- **Shutter wheel/rotor is permanently mounted on the camshaft drive sprocket.**

Ignition coils and power output stage, testing (AEG engine)

Double-ended ignition coils are mounted in a common housing together with a power output stage. AEG engines use 2 double-ended coils. The power output stage takes the low power signal from the ECM and boosts it to a level usable by the ignition coils. The signal to fire a spark plug results in both spark plugs on that particular coil firing at the same time. One spark is "wasted" by the un-used cylinder because it occurs at a time when it is not needed. The other simultaneous spark is used to fire the mixture in the normal manner. The un-used spark causes no additional wear on the spark plug because it occurs at a time when there is minimal heat and pressure on the spark plug. The power output stage cannot be directly tested, but the signal from the ECM along with power and ground can be easily tested. The ignition coil can also be checked as follows.

1. Disconnect 4-pin harness connector from ignition coil power output stage as shown earlier. See Fig. 2.

2. Connect a voltmeter to disconnected connector at terminals 2 and 4. See Fig. 10.

3. Switch on ignition and read voltage. If voltage is present, proceed to next step. If no voltage is present, check for breaks, high resistance or open circuits in the wiring, **see 97 Wiring Diagrams, Fuses and Relays.**

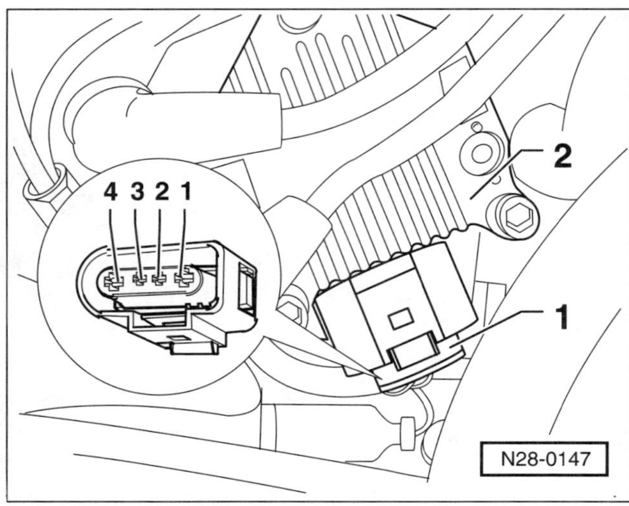

N28-0147

Fig. 10. Disconnect 4-pin harness connector (**1**) to power output stage (**2**). Connect voltmeter between pins 2 and 4.

Specification
- Voltage supply power output stage . . . . 11.5 Volts minimum

4. Switch off ignition.

5. Remove fuse 32 (for fuel injectors) as shown earlier. See Fig. 5.

6. Connect an LED test light (such as VAG 1527B) to disconnected harness connector at terminals 2 and 4.

> ***CAUTION—***
> - *Use a high-quality digital automotive multimeter and an LED test light to make the tests. An analog (swing-needle) meter and conventional test light should not be used as they can permanently damage electronic components.*
> - *Always connect and disconnect the ECM connector and meter probes with the ignition off to avoid damage to electronic components.*

7. Operate starter and check for a signal from the ECM. LED test light must flicker.

8. Repeat steps 6 and 7 with the LED test light in terminals 3 and 4.
   - If LED test light flickers, signal from ECM is good.
   - If test light does not flicker, check for break in wiring, **see 97 Wiring Diagrams, Fuses and Relays.** If no faults are found, check ECM for DTCs with a suitable scan tool.

The secondary (high voltage) side of the ignition coil can also be checked with an ohmmeter.

1. Label and disconnect spark plug wires from coil terminals.

2. Connect an accurate ohmmeter between terminals 3 and 2 and take reading. Repeat for terminals 1 and 4. See Fig. 11.

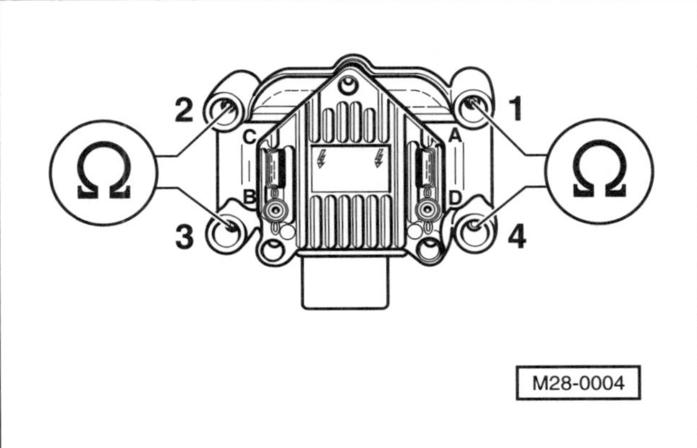

M28-0004

Fig. 11. Connect an ohmmeter to ignition coil terminals as shown. Resistance should be within specification. Open circuits and short circuits to ground are not acceptable.

3. Compare to specification.

Specification

- Ignition coil secondary resistance at 20°C (68°F) . . . . .4000 to 6000 ohms

---

4. Reconnect all terminals disconnected for testing and replace all parts removed. Install new components as needed.

> ***NOTE —***
> - *Ignition coils and power output stages are a combined unit.*
> - *Ignition coil primary resistance cannot be measured.*

If no faults are found with the supply voltage, impulse signal, wiring, and resistance at coil, then the ignition coil pack should be replaced.

Spark plugs, removing and installing (2.0L engine)

Spark plugs are generally replaced during scheduled maintenance services. On 2.0L engines, due to the design of the combustion chambers and the shape of the cylinder head, spark plug replacement can easily be accomplished without removal of the intake manifold. See Fig. 12.

0024276

Fig. 12. Spark plug wires shown with upper section of intake manifold removed for clarity. Note that spark plugs for cylinders **1** and **2** are angled to the left and that spark plugs for cylinders **3** and **4** are angled to the right.

1. Remove the upper engine cover.

2. Remove the spark plug wire from cylinder no. 1 with a suitable tool such as Volkswagen special tool 3277 or T10029. Do not pull on the wire.

> ***NOTE —***
> *It may be necessary to unplug the injector wire and gently turn the injector in the mounts for access.*

3. Remove the spark plug with a 5/8 in. (16x mm) spark plug socket and an extension. Inspect condition of spark plug electrode, it should be brown to grayish-tan color with slight electrode wear.

4. Check gap on new spark plug and install, re-install injector wire and plug wire.

Specifications

- Spark Plugs (AEG engine)
  - Original equipment number. 101-000-033-AA
  - Manufacturer's number . . . . NGK BKUR 6 ET-10
- Spark Plugs (AVH/AZG engine)
  - Original equipment number. 101-000-062-AB
  - Manufacturer's number . . . . PZFR 5 D-11
- Gap. . . . . .0.90 to 1.10 mm (.035 to .043 in)
- Tightening torque . . . . 30 Nm (22 ft-lb)

---

5. Repeat for each remaining cylinder.

6. Install upper engine cover.

The ignition system components for the 2.0L engine with engine code AVH or AZG are shown in Fig. 13.

Ignition system components (AVH/AZG engine)

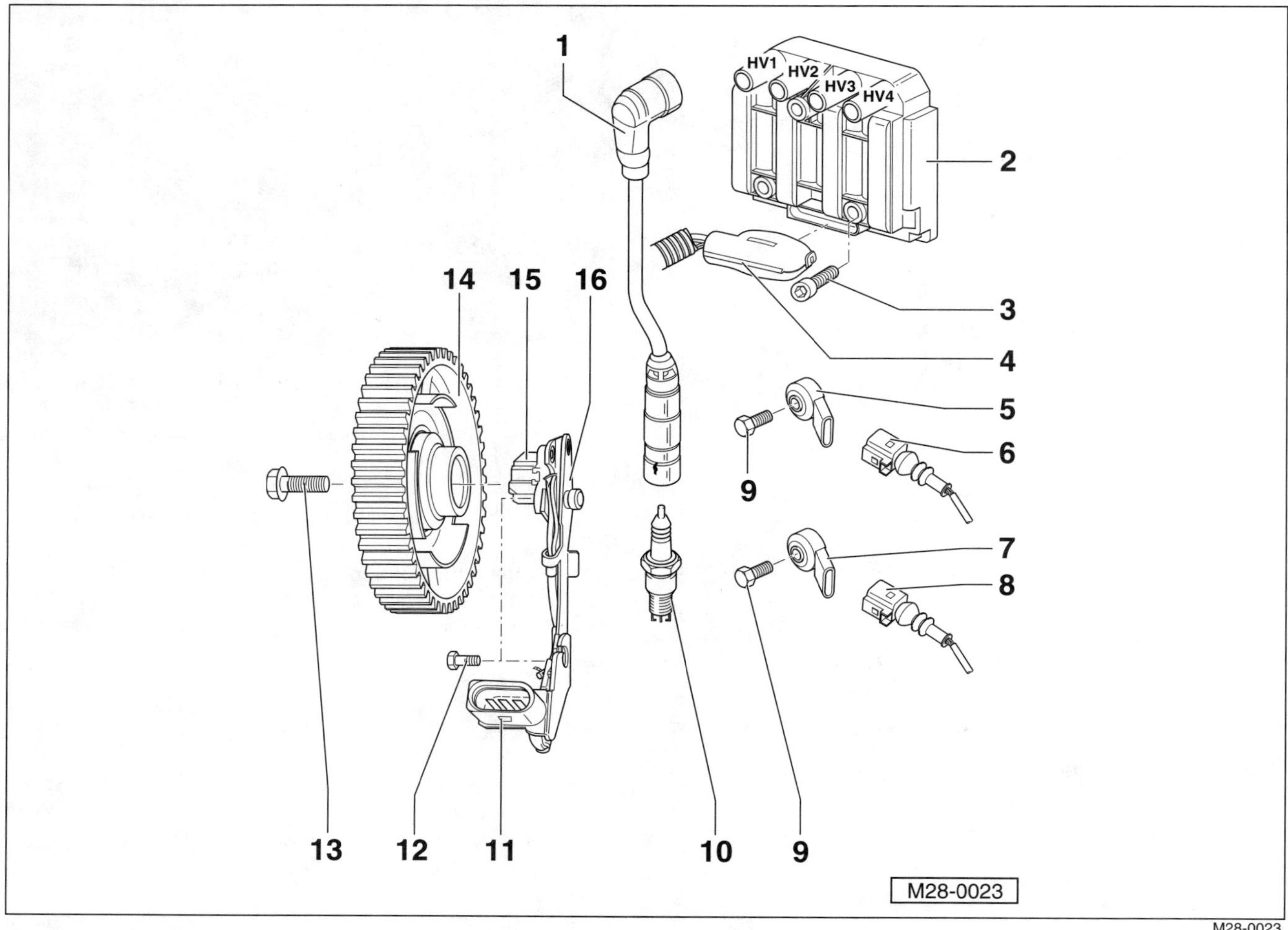

M28-0023

Fig. 13. Ignition system components for the 2.0L (AVH/AZG) engine.

1. **Ignition wire**
   - With suppression and spark plug connector
   - Resistance: 4-8kΩ
   - Remove with special tool T10029
2. **Ignition coil s (N70, N127, N291, N292)**
   - With integral power output stage
   - Marked for ignition cables:
     HV1 = Cylinder 1
     HV2 = Cylinder 2
     HV3 = Cylinder 3
     HV4 = Cylinder 4
   - Checking supply voltage and activation, **see** Ⓐ
3. **Bolt**
   - Tighten to 10 Nm (7 ft-lb)
4. **6-pin harness connector**
5. **Knock sensor 1 (G61)**
   - Sensor and connector terminals are gold plated
   - Resistance: ∞Ω
6. **2-pin harness connector**
   - For knock sensor 1
   - Gold plated terminals
   - Mark before disconnecting
7. **Knock sensor 2 (G66)**
   - Sensor and connector terminals are gold-plated
   - Resistance: ∞Ω
8. **2-pin harness connector**
   - For knock sensor 2
   - Gold plated terminals
   - Mark before disconnecting
9. **Bolt**
   - Tighten to 20 Nm (15 ft-lb)
   - Tightening torque influences knock sensor function
10. **Spark plug**
    - Tighten to 30 Nm (22 ft-lb)
    - Remove and install with 5/8 (16x mm) spark plug socket and extension

(continued on next page)

11. 3-pin harness connector
- With gold-plated terminals

12. Bolt
- Tighten to 10 Nm (7 ft-lb)

13. Bolt
- Tighten to 100 Nm (74 ft-lb)
- Use counter-hold tool 3415 to loosen and tighten

14. Camshaft sprocket
- With shutter wheel (rotor) for camshaft position sensor

15. Camshaft position sensor (G40)

16. Bracket

A Ignition coils, checking supply voltage and activation (AVH/AZG 2.0L engine)

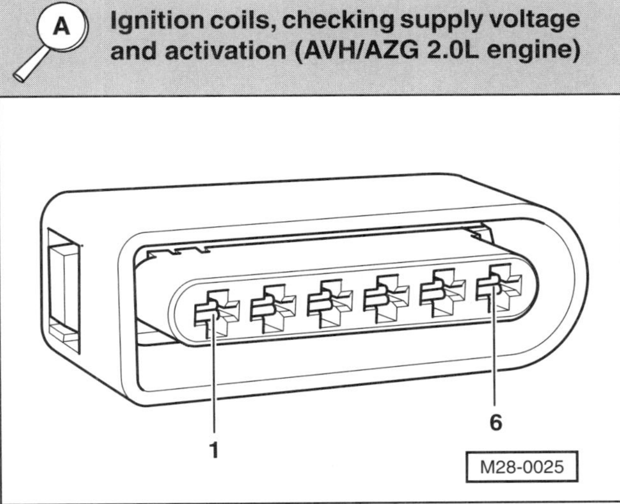

M28-0025

- **With ignition off, disconnect the 6-pin harness connector (shown above) from ignition coils.**
- **Turn ignition on and read voltage using a digital voltmeter at terminals 1 and 6 of the connector.**
  Specification: min. 11.5 volts
- **To check activation, first remove fuse 32 to stop voltage supply to fuel injectors (prevent engine from running).**
- **During activation test do not touch the connecting parts of the ignition coils or test cables.**
- **Use an LED test light (VAG 1527 B or equivalent) and test across the following terminals while a second technician operates the starter. The LED should flicker.**
  terminals 1 & 2 (ignition output 1)
  terminals 1 & 3 (ignition output 2)
  terminals 1 & 4 (ignition output 3)
  terminals 1 & 5 (ignition output 4)
- **If test light does not flicker, check wiring for open circuits, short to ground or positive, using wiring diagrams.**
- **Each wire should have a maximum resistance of 1.5Ω.**
- **If voltage is present at terminals 1 and 6 and all wiring is OK, replace ignition coils with output stage.**
- **Switch off ignition before reconnecting harness connector.**

IGNITION SYSTEM (2.8L ENGINE)

The ignition system of the AFP (2.8L) engine requires little or no periodic maintenance due to the distributor-less nature of the system. Most of the components are monitored by their respective engine management system and a failure will cause a fault (DTC) to be stored in the engine control module. Engine misfiring can even result in a DTC being stored due to the potential for damage to the catalytic converter. The various components of the 2.8L ignition system are shown in Fig. 14.

Ignition system components (2.8L engine)

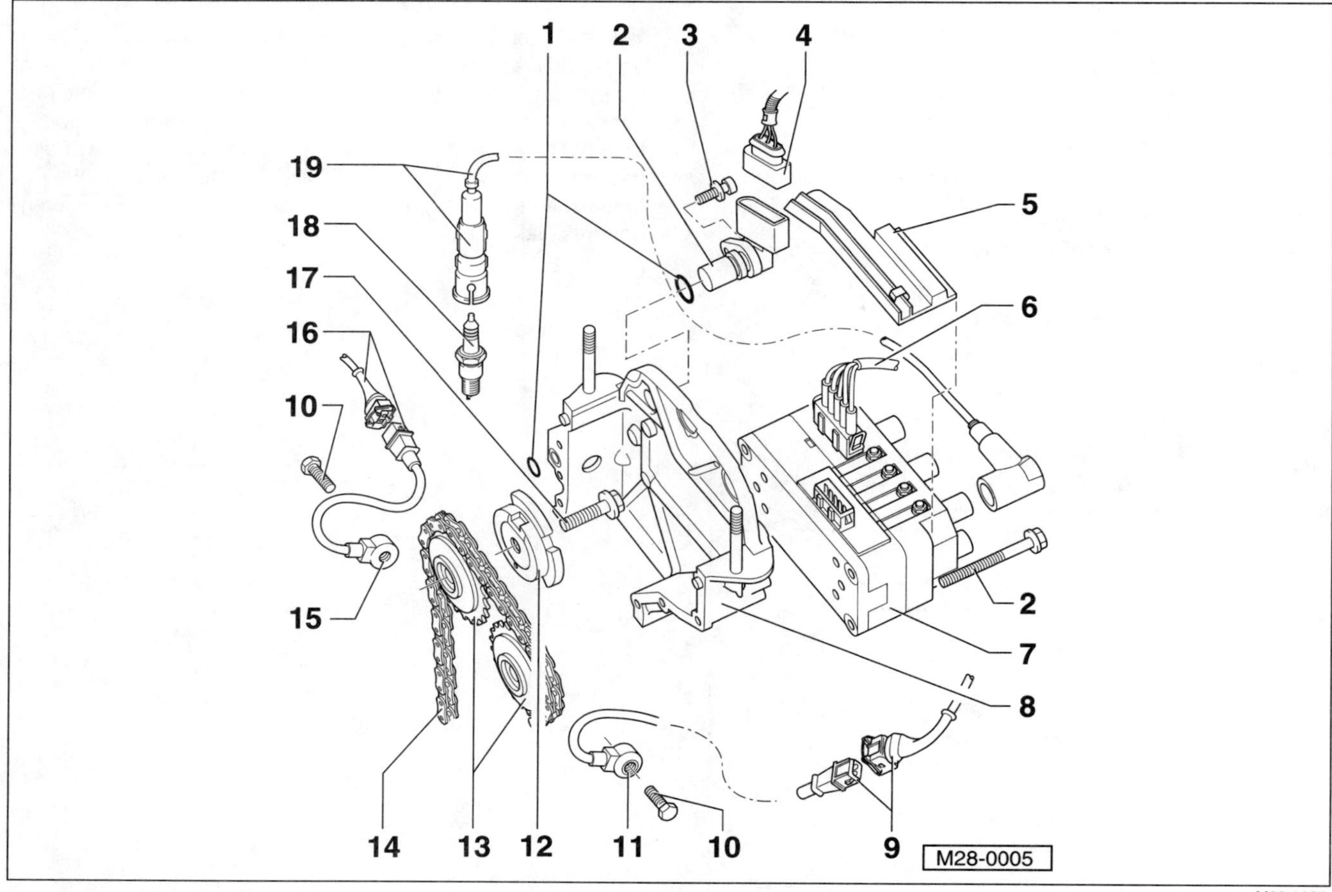

M28-0005

Fig. 14. Primary and secondary ignition system components of the 2.8L engine.

1. **O-ring seals**
   - Always replace
2. **Camshaft position sensor (G40)**
   - Mounted on camshaft sprocket cover at exhaust side camshaft
   - Shutter wheel (rotor) mounted on exhaust side camshaft
   - Sensor and connector terminals are gold-plated
3. **Bolt**
   - Tighten to 10 Nm (7 ft-lb)
4. **3-pin harness connector**
   - For camshaft position sensor (G40)
   - Sensor and connector terminals are gold-plated
   - Check for voltage between terminals 1 and 3 with ignition on; specification: minimum 4.5 volts
5. **Cable guide**
   - For ignition coil
6. **5-pin harness connector**
   - Black
7. **Ignition coil pack (N152)**
   - With power output stages
   - Marked for ignition cables
   - Use caution to avoid incorrect installation
8. **Cover, camshaft sprocket**
9. **3-pin harness connector**
   - Brown
   - Terminals gold plated
   - Checking resistance between terminals, **see** Ⓐ
10. **Bolts**
    - Tighten to 20 Nm (15 ft-lb)
    - Tightening torque influences knock sensor function
11. **Knock sensor 2 (G66)**
    - Location: intake side of cylinder block
    - Sensor and connector terminals are gold-plated
12. **Shutter wheel**
    - For camshaft position sensor
    - Note installation position
    - Contact area between camshaft sprocket and shutter wheel must be clean and dry at installation

(continued on next page)

(continued from previous page)

13. Camshaft chain sprockets

14. Camshaft drive chain, upper, double row

15. Knock sensor 1 (G61)
- Location: exhaust side of cylinder block
- Sensor and connector terminals are gold-plated

16. 3-pin harness connector
- White
- Terminals gold plated

17. Camshaft chain sprocket bolt
- Tighten to 100 Nm (74 ft-lb)
- Note 24 mm hex on camshaft to counter-hold
- Do not use plastic alignment tool 3268 to counter-hold
- Lightly oil bolt head contact surface before installing

18. Spark plug
- Tighten to 25 Nm (18 ft lb)
- Remove and install with 5/8 (16x mm) spark plug socket

19. Spark plug wire
- With RF suppressor and spark plug connector
- Resistance: 4-6kΩ
- Individual lengths for each cylinder
- Remove with special tool T10029
- Do not pull on wire
- Attached to coil pack with water resistant sealant

A Knock sensor harness connector, checking resistance

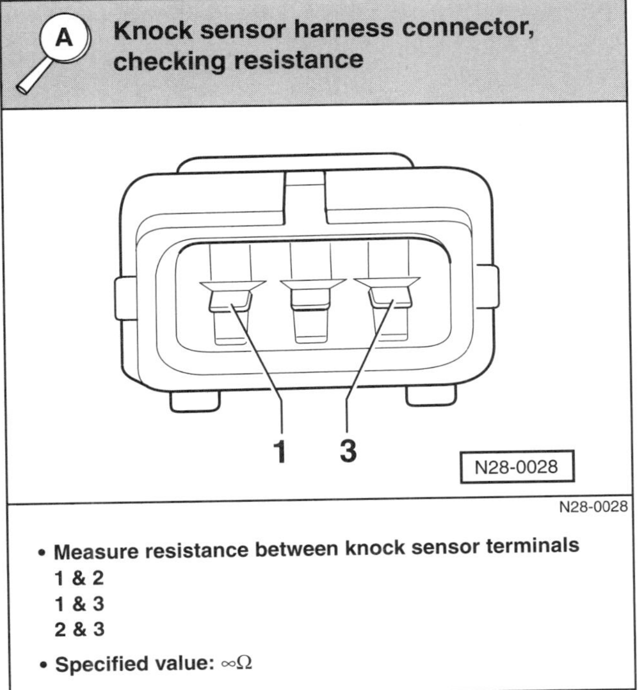

N28-0028

- **Measure resistance between knock sensor terminals**
  1 & 2
  1 & 3
  2 & 3
- **Specified value: ∞Ω**

Spark plugs, removing and installing (2.8L engine)

Spark plugs are generally replaced during scheduled maintenance services. On 2.8L engines, Volkswagen special tool T10029 must be used to remove the wires due to the design of the spark plug connector. See Fig. 15.

0024362

Fig. 15. Remove spark plug connectors with special tool T10029 as shown to avoid damage to spark plug connector. Do not pull on wires.

1. Remove the spark plug wire from cylinder no. 1 with a suitable tool such as Volkswagen special tool T10029. Do not pull on the wire.

2. Remove the spark plug with a 5/8 in. (16x mm) spark plug socket and an extension. Inspect condition of spark plug electrode, it should be brown to grayish-tan color with slight electrode wear.

3. Check gap on new spark plug and re-install plug wire.

Specifications
- Spark Plugs (2.8L engine)
  Original equipment number....... 101-000-035-AH
  Manufacturer's number.........NGK BKR 5 EKUP
- Gap.................... 0.70 mm max. (0.027 in)
- Tightening torque................ 25 Nm (18 ft-lb)

4. Repeat for each remaining cylinder.

Ignition coils and power output stage, testing (2.8L engine)

Double-ended ignition coils are mounted in a common housing together with a power output stage. 2.8L engines use 3 double-ended coils. The power output stage takes the low power signal from the ECM and boosts it to a level usable by the ignition coils. The signal to fire a spark plug results in both spark plugs on that particular coil firing at the same time. One spark is "wasted" by the un-used cylinder because it occurs at a time when it is not needed. The other simultaneous spark is used to fire the mixture in the normal manner. The un-used spark causes no additional wear on the spark plug because it occurs at a time when there is minimal heat and pressure on the spark plug. The power output stage cannot be directly tested, but the signal from the ECM along with power and ground can be easily tested as follows.

1. Disable ignition system by disconnecting 5-pin harness connector from ignition coil power output stage as shown earlier. See Fig. 4.

2. Connect a digital voltmeter to across connector terminals 1 and 5. See Fig. 16.

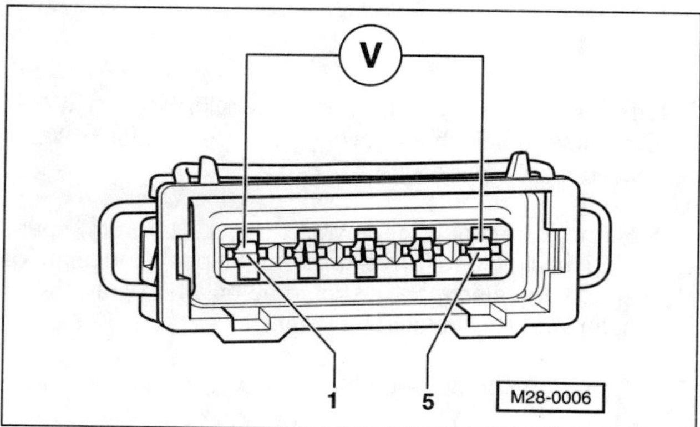

M28-0006

Fig. 16. Measure voltage across terminals 1 and 5 of coil pack harness connector with ignition on.

3. Switch on ignition and read voltage. If voltage is present, proceed to next step. If no voltage is present, check for breaks, high resistance or open circuits in the wiring, **see 97 Wiring Diagrams, Fuses and Relays.**

Specification

- Voltage supply power output stage. . . . . 11.5 Volts minimum

---

4. Switch off ignition.

5. Remove fuse 32 (for fuel injectors) as shown earlier. See Fig. 5.

6. Connect an LED test light (such as VAG 1527B) to the disconnected harness connector at terminals 2 and 5.

> ***CAUTION —***
> - *Use a high-quality digital automotive multimeter and an LED test light to make the tests. An analog (swing-needle) meter and conventional test light should not be used as they can damage components.*
> - *Always connect and disconnect the ECM connector and meter probes with the ignition off to avoid damage to components.*

7. Operate starter and check for a signal from the ECM. LED test light must flicker.

8. Repeat steps 6 and 7 with the LED test light in terminals 3 and 5, and 4 and 5.
   - If LED test light flickers the signal from ECM is good.
   - If test light does not flicker, check for break in wiring, **see 97 Wiring Diagrams, Fuses and Relays.** If no faults are found, check ECM for DTCs with a suitable scan tool. See **ST Scan Tool Codes** at back of book.

The secondary (high voltage) side of the ignition coil can also be checked with an ohmmeter.

1. Label and disconnect spark plug wires from coil pack.

2. Connect an accurate ohmmeter between terminals 1 and 6 and take reading. Repeat for terminals 3 and 4 and for terminals 2 and 5. See Fig. 17.

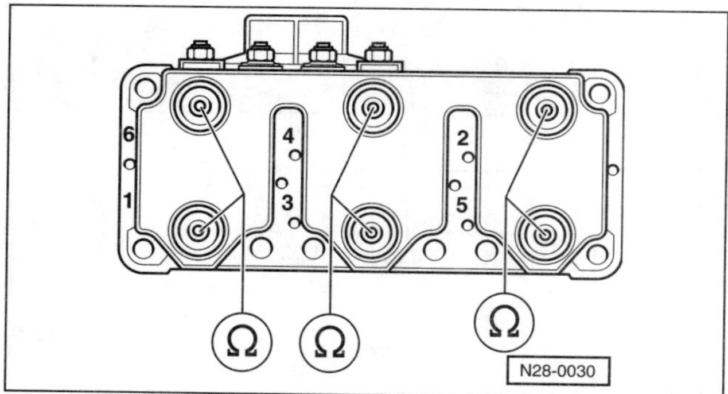

N28-0030

Fig. 17. Connect an ohmmeter to ignition coil terminals as shown. Resistance should be within specification. Open circuits and short circuits to ground are not acceptable.

3. Compare to specification.

Specification

- Ignition coil secondary resistance at 20°C (68°F) . . . . 3600 to 4400 Ω

If no faults are found with the supply voltage, impulse signal, wiring, and resistance at coil, then the ignition coil pack should be replaced.

28b Ignition System–Diesel

GENERAL

The ignition system of a diesel engine is based on heat generated by the compression of air in the cylinder. Fuel is injected into this hot air at a precise time to obtain ignition and the exact time is varied by the injection pump to obtain ignition advance. Diesel engines are therefore said to be compression-ignition engines. As a result of this design, diesel engines do not require spark plugs and their associated components. A cold diesel engine can be difficult to start, however, because the compression heat generated is quickly dissipated into the surrounding structure leaving the combustion chamber too cold to support combustion. Extra heat is required to overcome this cold starting limitation. The Volkswagen 1.9L diesel engine uses glow plugs to provide the additional heat required during a cold start.

> ***CAUTION —***
> *Disconnecting the negative (–) battery cable may erase fault codes and basic settings in the engine management and automatic transmission control modules. Some driveability problems may be noticed until the system re-adapts to operating conditions. OBD II readiness codes, which may be required for emissions testing, may also be erased. Convenience electronics (alarm system, interior light control, power locks, mirrors, and windows) may need to be re-set using a VAG 1551/1552 or equivalent scan tool.*

NOTE —
The TDI engine management system found on the 1.9L engines has a built in diagnostic circuit that detects and stores a limited number of system faults related to the glow plug system. These faults are known as Diagnostic Trouble Codes (DTCs). It is recommended that fault diagnosis and troubleshooting be carried out using the special Volkswagen scan tool VAG 1551/1552 or equivalent.

Service precautions

Ignition system service and repair work must be carried out carefully. The ignition system contains sensitive electronic components. To guard against system damage, and for general safety, the following warnings apply to any ignition system troubleshooting, maintenance or repair work.

> ***WARNING —***
> *Glow plug systems operate at high current levels. For this reason, always insure that electrical connections that have been disturbed during testing are properly secured when done.*

> ***CAUTION —***
> *Disconnecting engine management components with the key in the "on" position during some procedures will cause diagnostic trouble codes to be stored in the engine control module. Erasing these DTCs and resetting the readiness code will require Volkswagen scan tool VAG 1551/1552 or equivalent.*

DIESEL GLOW PLUG SYSTEM

The TDI diesel engine uses four glow plugs. Because of the TDI combustion chamber design, the glow plugs are installed in a vertical manner and are fitted with push-on electrical connectors similar to spark plug connectors. The glow plugs assist combustion during cold starts by providing additional heat for ignition. Due to the efficiency of the TDI engine design, the additional heat that the glow plugs provide is not needed until temperatures drop to approximately 48°F (9°C). This function is known as preglow. In addition to preglowing, the glow plugs will continue to operate after the engine is started. This is known as afterglowing and is used to reduce engine noise, improve idle quality and reduce hydrocarbon emissions. The afterglow function is enabled after every start, both hot and cold until the specified time has expired or the engine speed exceeds 2,500 rpm.

The glow plug system is controlled by the Engine Control Module (ECM) and the Engine Coolant Temperature (ECT) sensor. The period of preglow depends on the temperature of the engine coolant as determined by the ECT. A dash mounted indicator light signals the driver that preglowing is operating. See Fig. 1. Preglowing is not linked to operation of the driver's door as in some earlier Volkswagen diesel systems.

> ***WARNING —***
> *Disconnecting engine management components for this procedure will cause diagnostic trouble codes to be stored in the engine control module. Erasing these DTCs and resetting the readiness code will require Volkswagen scan tool VAG 1551/1552 or equivalent.*

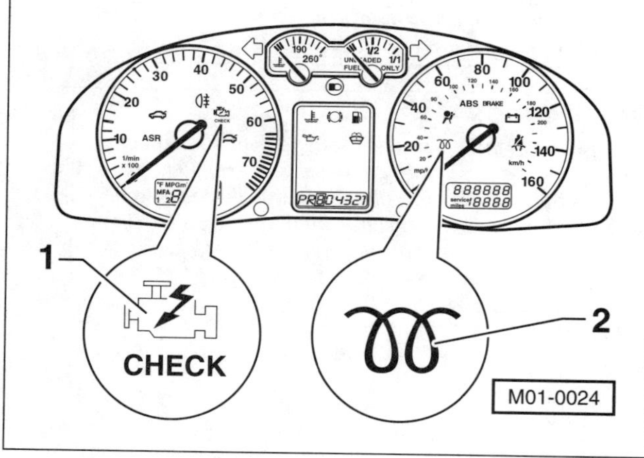

M01-0024

Fig. 1. Glow plug warning light (**2**) and Malfunction indicator light (**1**) on instrument cluster.

NOTE —
- *For more information on troubleshooting diesel cold starting problems, see* **23 Fuel Injection—Diesel (1.9L engine)**.
- *See* **97 Wiring Diagrams, Fuses and Relays** *for a complete wiring diagram of the glow plug electrical circuits.*

Testing and replacing glow plugs

Basic checks of the glow plug system are similar to earlier diesel systems.

1. Remove upper engine cover.
2. Disconnect the harness connector from the Engine Coolant Temperature (ECT) sensor. See Fig. 2.

   NOTE —
   Disconnecting the ECT harness connector simulates a cold engine when the ignition key is switched on.

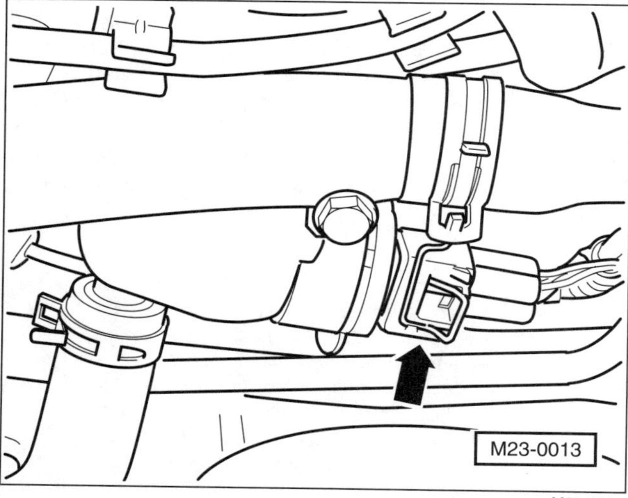

M23-0013

Fig. 2. Engine coolant temperature sensor (**arrow**) in the radiator hose. Disconnecting the harness connector simulates a cold engine and operates the glow plugs for the maximum length of time.

3. Disconnect the bus connector from the glow plugs by gently pulling it off. See Fig. 3.
4. Connect an accurate voltmeter between the bus connector for cylinder #1 and ground.
5. Turn on the key and observe battery voltage. Voltage should be present for approximately 20 seconds.
6. Repeat for remaining cylinders.
7. If no voltage is present, check glow plug fuses, see **97 Wiring Diagrams, Fuses and Relays.**

Fig. 3. Glow plug bus connector (**1**) shown attached to each glow plug (**arrows**).

> ***NOTE —***
> *Glow plug fuses are located in the fuse holder on the battery cover.*

8. If voltage is present, switch off ignition.

9. Connect a suitable test light to battery positive and touch the other end to the disconnected terminal on the glow plug. See Fig. 4. The low resistance of the glow plug will cause the test light to light up if the glow plug is good.

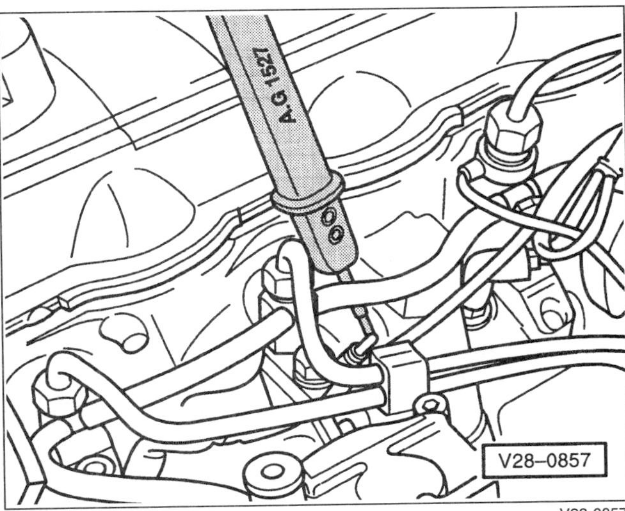

Fig. 4. A test light with one terminal connected to the battery and the other terminal touching glow plug #2. The test light will light if the glow plug is good.

10. Replace defective glow plugs using a 10mm deep socket and suitable extension or use Volkswagen special tool 3220. Torque replacement glow plugs to specification.

Tightening torque
- TDI glow plug in cylinder head . . . . . . 15 Nm (11 ft-lb)

> ***NOTE —***
> *Advanced testing of the glow plug system requires the use of Volkswagen scan tool VAG 1551 or 1552 or equivalent.*

COOLANT GLOW PLUGS/AUXILIARY HEATER

Because of its outstanding efficiency, the 1.9L TDI engine develops very little waste heat. In certain circumstances, there may not be sufficient heat with manual transmission vehicles to warm the vehicle interior. An auxiliary heater consisting of three coolant glow plugs is installed to provide additional coolant heat when needed. See Fig. 5. The coolant glow plugs are operated by two coolant glow plug relays which are controlled by the engine control module. The coolant glow plug relays are located under the hood.

The coolant glow plugs can operate in one of three modes depending on the amount of heat required. Coolant glow plug #1 can operate separately, or #2 and #3 together, or all three at the same time.

Testing and replacing coolant glow plugs

Complete testing of the coolant glow plug system requires the use of Volkswagen scan tool VAG 1551/1552 or equivalent. The coolant glow plugs can, however, be checked in the same manner as the glow plugs used for starting.

1. Visually inspect the fuse for the coolant glow plugs in the fuse holder on battery cover. See **97 Wiring Diagrams, Fuses and Relays**. Replace as required.

2. Pull the electrical connectors off of the coolant glow plugs. See Fig. 5.

3. Connect a suitable test light to battery positive and touch the other end to the end of the coolant glow plug. The light will glow due to the low resistance of the glow plug if it is good. Faulty coolant glow plugs will not light the test light.

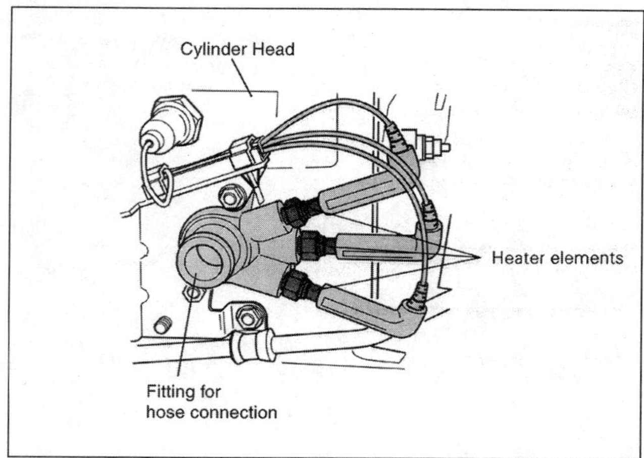

Fig. 5. Coolant glow plugs (**heater elements**) in the flange on the end of the cylinder head with the electrical connectors in place. Early version shown, ALH engine is similar.

4. If defective glow plugs are found, unscrew and replace as necessary. Coolant will leak out of the system when unscrewing glow plugs.

> ***WARNING —***
>
> - *Hot coolant can scald and result in serious personal injury. Do not work on the cooling system until it has fully cooled.*
> - *At normal operating temperature the cooling system is pressurized. Allow the system to cool as long as possible before opening—a minimum of an hour—then release the cap very slowly to allow safe release of pressure.*
> - *Releasing the cooling system pressure lowers the coolant's boiling point, and the coolant may boil suddenly. Use heavy gloves and wear eye and face protection to guard against scalding.*
> - *Use extreme care when working at or near the cooling fan when the engine is hot. The fan can come on at any time–even if the ignition key is off.*
> - *Use extreme care when draining and disposing of engine coolant. Coolant is poisonous and lethal. Children and pets are attracted to coolant because of its sweet smell and taste. See a doctor or veterinarian immediately if any amount of coolant is ingested.*

5. Re-attach electrical connectors and replace lost coolant.

QUALITY REVIEW

When you have finished working under the hood and around other areas of the vehicle, it is advisable to take a moment to quality check or review your work. This helps to insure that the operation or repair has been completed properly with all affected systems functioning within normal parameters. These may include the following:

- Make sure that there are no fuel or coolant leaks.
- Make sure that the coolant is at the proper concentration and level.
- Ensure that all cable ties and hose clamps that were removed as part of the repair are replaced.
- Be sure to wipe up any diesel fuel spills using soap and water as necessary, especially on any rubber or painted surfaces.
- Make sure that all components involved in the repair are positioned correctly and function properly.
- Make sure that the radiator fans cycles properly.
- Make sure all tools and shop cloths are removed.
- Clean grease and fingerprints from painted surfaces, steering wheel and shifter.
- Road test vehicle as required to confirm proper cooling system operation.

30 Clutch

GENERAL

Servicing of the clutch assembly requires that the transmission be removed from the engine. Special tools and equipment are required to remove the transmission and service the clutch. See **34 Manual Transmission** for transmission removal procedures. Read the procedures through to fully understand the scope and nature of the job.

> ***WARNING —***
> - *The cars covered by this manual use an airbag system that automatically deploys the airbags in the event of a frontal or side impact. The airbags are inflated by an explosive device. Handled improperly or without adequate safeguards, the system can be very dangerous. Special precautions must be observed prior to any work at or near the steering wheel or steering column, including the pedal assembly. See* **69 Seatbelts, Airbags**.
> - *To guard against personal injury or airbag system failure, only trained Volkswagen service technicians should test, disassemble or service the airbag system.*

> ***CAUTION —***
> *Disconnecting the negative (–) battery cable may erase fault codes and basic settings in the engine management and automatic transmission control modules. Some driveability problems may be noticed until the system re-adapts to operating conditions. OBD II readiness codes, which may be required for emissions testing, may also be erased. Convenience electronics (alarm system, interior light control, power locks, mirrors, and windows) may need to be re-set using a VAG 1551/1552 or equivalent scan tool.*

CLUTCH ACTUATING MECHANISM

Fig. 1 shows components of the pedal assembly. Be sure to lubricate all bearings and friction surfaces with poly-resin grease (VW Part No. G 052 142 A2). Always replace self-locking nuts and circlips during repairs.

> ***CAUTION —***
> *Before working on the pedal cluster, obtain anti-theft radio code and then disconnect battery ground (–) strap.*

Pedal Cluster, assembly

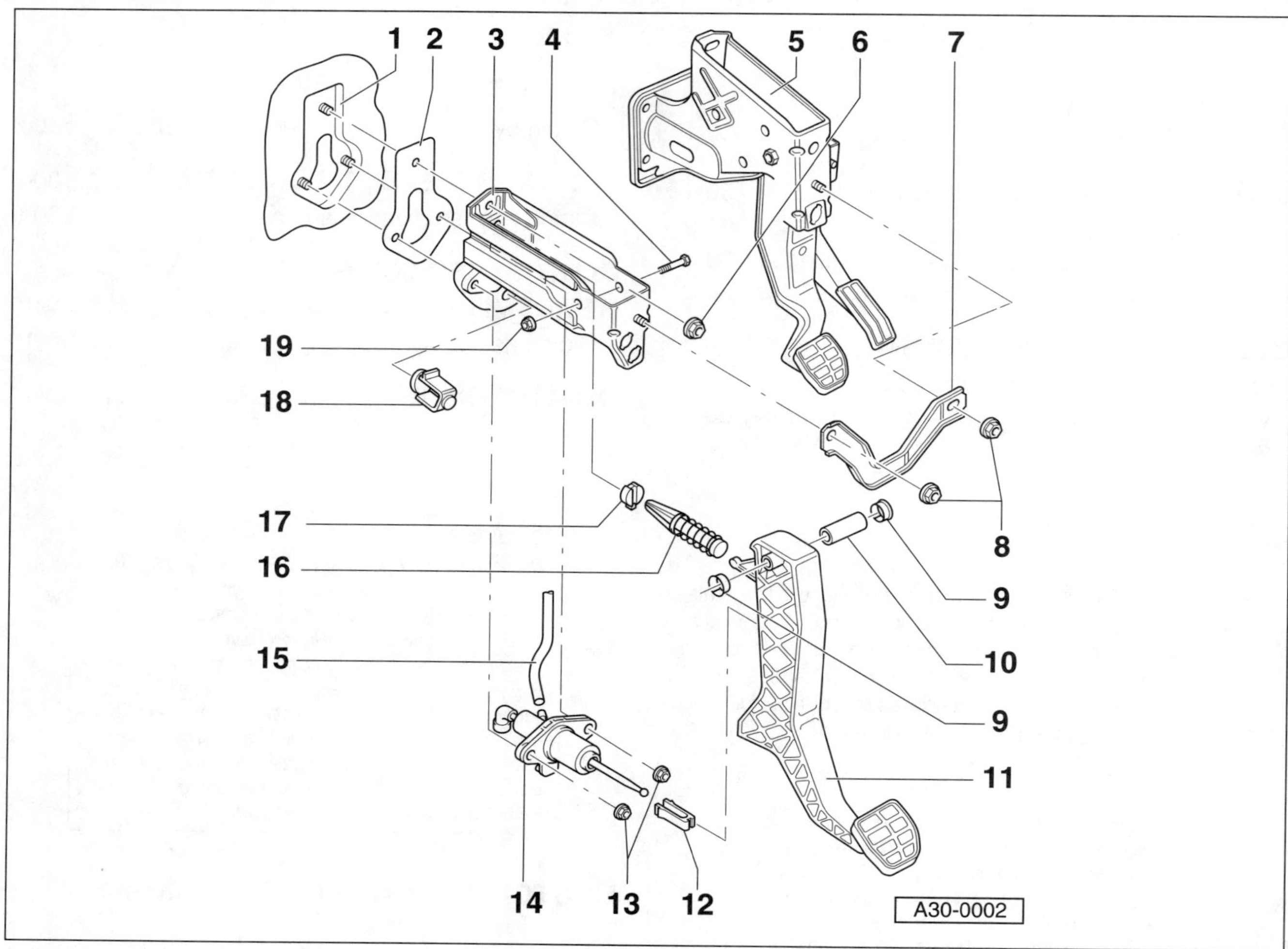

A30-0002

Fig. 1. Clutch actuating mechanism and related parts.

1. **Bulkhead**
2. **Seal**
   - Always replace
3. **Clutch pedal mounting bracket**
4. **Pivot bolt**
5. **Accelerator and brake pedal mounting bracket**
6. **Self-locking nut**
   - Tighten to 25 Nm (18 ft-lb)
   - Always replace
7. **Connecting plate**
8. **Self-locking nut**
   - Tighten to 25 Nm (18 ft-lb)
   - Always replace
9. **Bushing**
10. **Fulcrum pin**
11. **Clutch pedal**
12. **Retainer**
13. **Self-locking nut**
    - Tighten to 25 Nm (18 ft-lb)
    - Always replace
14. **Clutch master cylinder**
15. **Supply hose**
    - from brake fluid reservoir
16. **Over-center spring**
17. **Over-center spring mount**
    - See Clutch master cylinder, removing and installing
18. **Clutch pedal stop**
19. **Self-locking nut**
    - Tighten to 25 Nm (18 ft-lb)
    - Always replace

Over-center spring, removing and installing

1. Remove drivers side lower trim to access pedal assembly.

2. Compress clutch pedal over-center spring by pushing clutch pedal forward, then install retaining clamp. See Fig. 2.

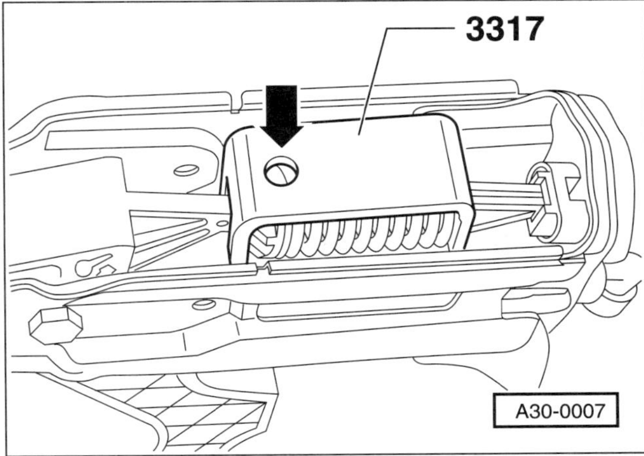

A30-0007

Fig. 2. Volkswagen special tool 3317 (retaining clamp) installed to compress clutch pedal over-center spring. Hole (**arrow**) should be positioned toward clutch pedal.

3. Move clutch pedal to rest position and remove over-center spring with retaining clamp still installed.

4. To install over-center spring, push clutch pedal forward and insert over-center spring (with retaining clamp) into rear mount. Operate clutch pedal until spring seats on mounting lug of clutch pedal. See Fig. 3.

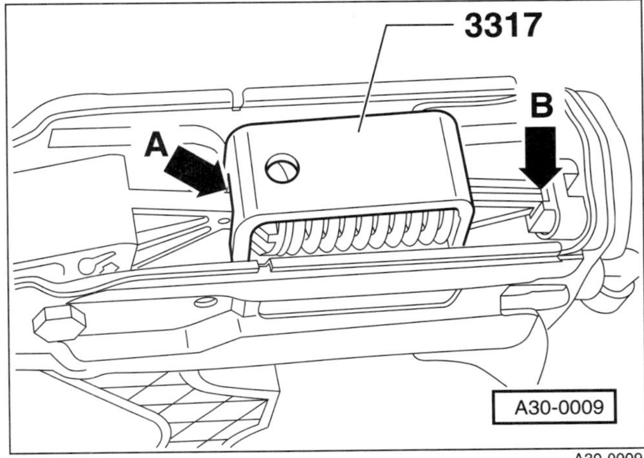

A30-0009

Fig. 3. Install over-center spring with retaining clamp into rear mount (**B**), then operate clutch pedal to seat mounting lug (**A**).

5. Remove retaining clamp while moving clutch pedal to rest position.

Clutch pedal, removing and installing

1. Remove clutch pedal over-center spring.

2. Separate clutch pedal from clutch master cylinder, see **Clutch master cylinder, removing and installing**.

3. Push master cylinder operating rod toward engine compartment onto stop.

4. Remove clutch pedal mounting bolt. See items 4 and 19 in Fig. 1, given earlier.

5. Install clutch pedal and mounting bolt.

6. Install clutch over-center spring as described earlier.

7. Ensure that retainer is correctly installed on master cylinder operating rod. Press clutch pedal down to engage retainer. See Fig. 4.

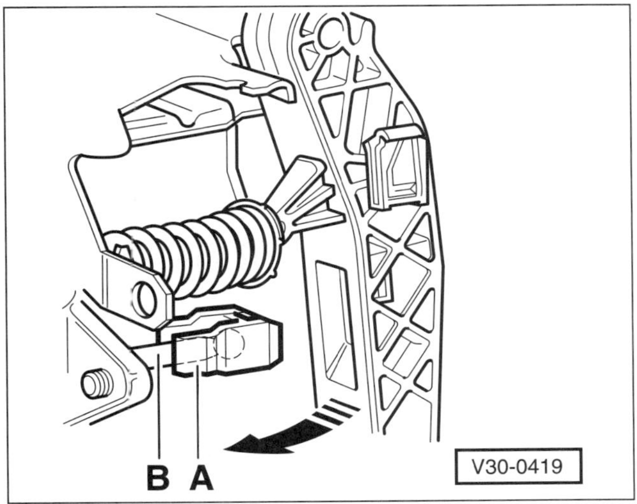

V30-0419

Fig. 4. Retainer (**A**) must be installed on the master cylinder operating rod (**B**). Press clutch in direction of **arrow** to engage retainer.

8. Remove over-center spring retaining clamp.

9. Bleed clutch system if hydraulic fluid level is below MIN marking on brake fluid reservoir. See **Clutch hydraulic system, bleeding**.

10. Fill brake fluid reservoir up to MAX marking.

Specification

- Hydraulic (brake) fluid. .DOT 4

11. Be sure to quality check your work, see **Quality Review** at the end of this repair group.

CLUTCH HYDRAULIC SYSTEM

Clutch hydraulic system, assembly

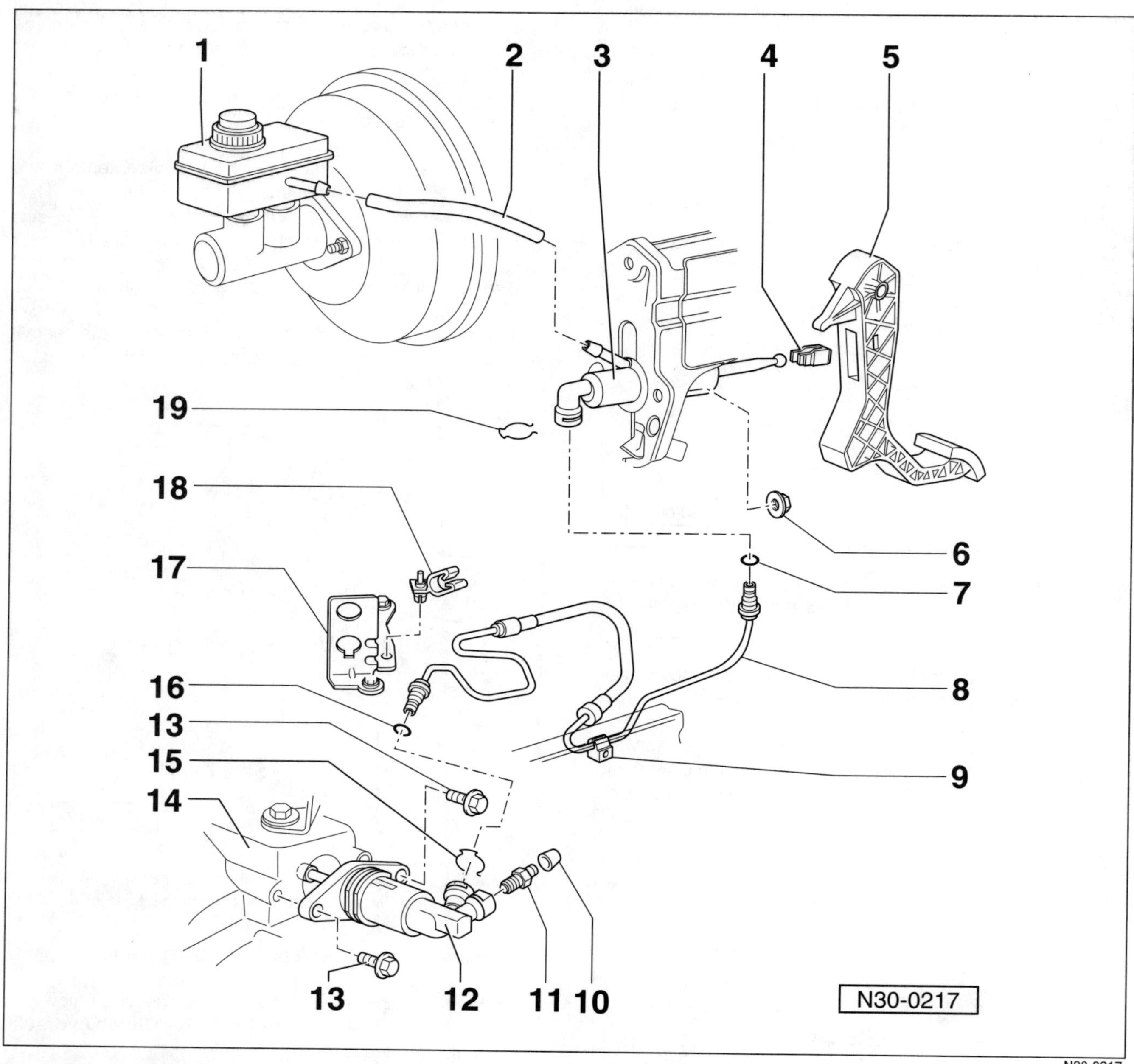

N30-0217

Fig. 5. Clutch hydraulic system and related components.

1. **Hydraulic (brake) fluid reservoir**
2. **Supply hose**
3. **Master cylinder**
4. **Retainer**
   - Replace only with master cylinder removed
   - Removing **see** (A), installing **see** (B)
5. **Clutch pedal**
6. **Self-locking nut**
   - Tighten to 25 Nm (18 ft-lb)
   - Always replace
7. **O-ring**
   - Coat with hydraulic fluid
   - Pull into line/hose connection
8. **Hydraulic line/hose assembly**

(continued from previous page)

9. **Bracket**
   - Attached to body
10. **Dust cap**
11. **Bleeder valve**
12. **Slave cylinder**
   - Remove the following components before removing slave cylinder (see **34 Manual Transmission**):
     - gear selector cable from selector lever
     - relay lever and actuating arm for gate selector cable
   - After installing adjust gear selector mechanism
13. **Bolt**
   - Tighten to 25 Nm (18 ft-lb)
   - With collar
14. **Transmission**
15. **Clip**
16. **O-ring**
   - Coat with hydraulic fluid
   - Pull onto/hose connection
17. **Cable support bracket**
18. **Hose bracket**
   - Secure to cable support bracket
19. **Clip**

A Clutch master cylinder retainer, removing

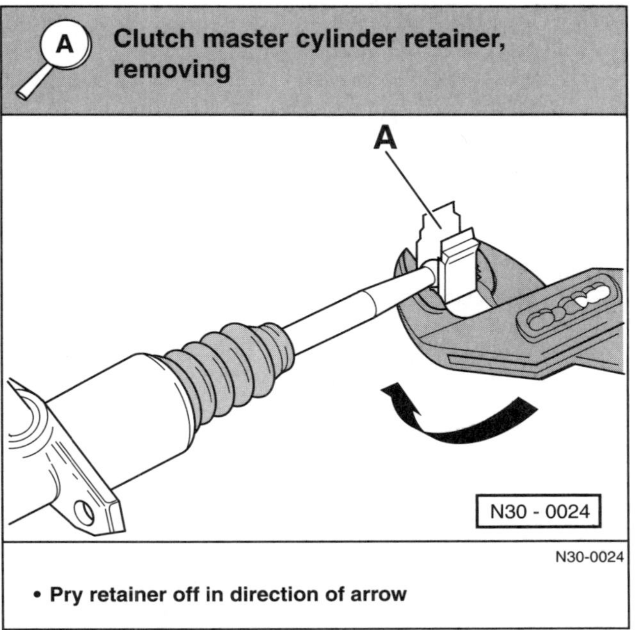

N30-0024

- **Pry retainer off in direction of arrow**

B Master cylinder operating rod retainer, installing

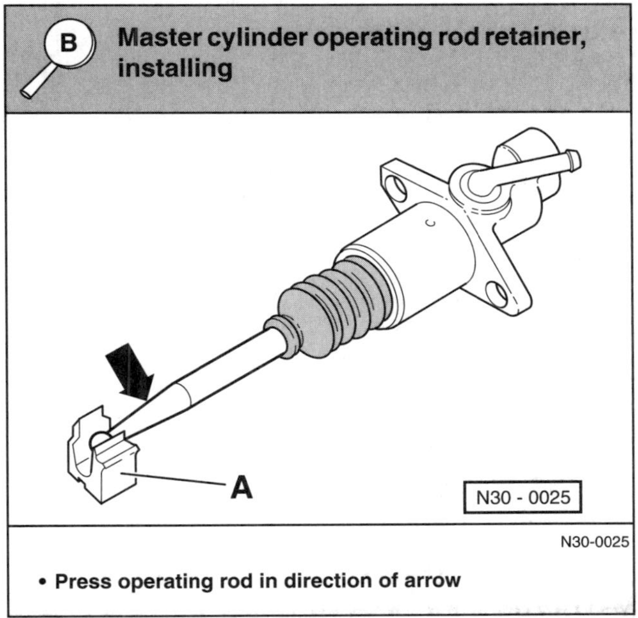

N30-0025

- **Press operating rod in direction of arrow**

Clutch master cylinder, removing and installing

1. Disconnect battery ground (GND) strap from battery negative (–) terminal. See the **Cautions** at the beginning of this repair group regarding battery disconnection.

   NOTE —
   Be sure to have the anti-theft radio code on hand before disconnecting the battery.

2. Remove intake air hose and harness connector from Mass Air Flow (MAF) sensor.

3. Remove mounting bolts for air cleaner and lift out air cleaner assembly. See Fig. 6.

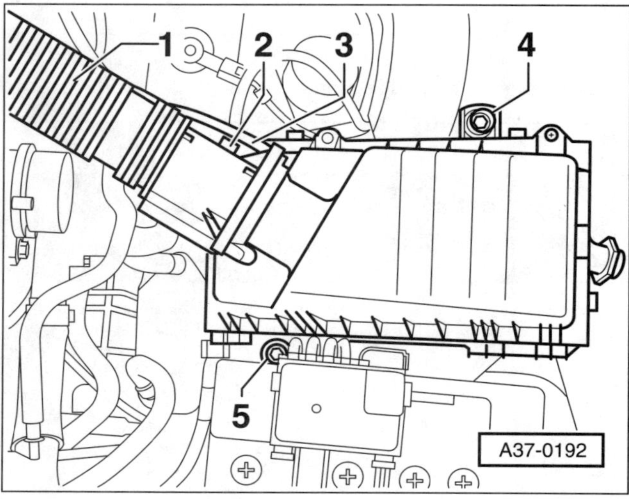

A37-0192

Fig. 6. Remove intake air hose (**1**), harness connector (**2**), small hose (**3**), and air cleaner mounting bolts (**4, 5**).

4. Remove hydraulic fluid reservoir supply hose and seal end to prevent dirt or moisture from entering.

5. Pry out clip for brake line and hose assembly at master cylinder. See Fig. 7.

6. Disconnect hydraulic brake line/hose assembly from rear of master cylinder and seal end to prevent dirt or moisture from entering.

7. Remove drivers side lower trim to access pedal assembly.

8. Remove connecting plate for clutch and brake pedal assemblies, then remove self-locking nuts for clutch pedal mounting bracket. See Fig. 8.

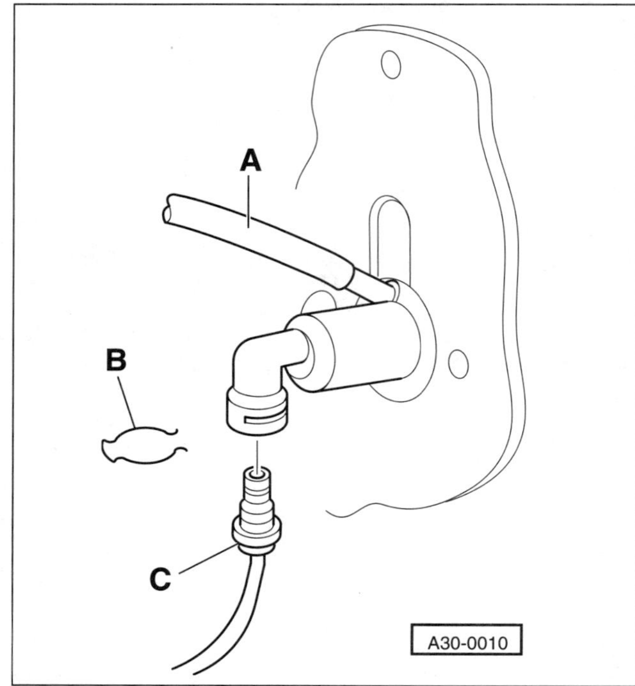

A30-0010

Fig. 7. Remove supply hose (**A**), pry out clip (**B**) and remove brake line/hose assembly (**C**).

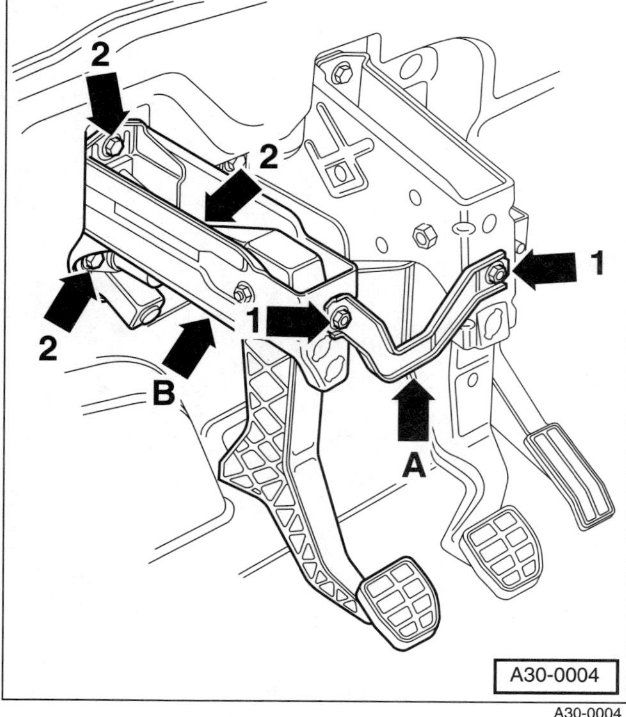

A30-0004

Fig. 8. Remove nuts (**1**) for connecting plate (**A**) and nuts (**2**) for mounting bracket (**B**). Lower two nuts (**2**) also secure clutch master cylinder to bulkhead.

9. Separate master cylinder operating rod from clutch pedal as follows:
   - Insert Volkswagen special tool 3309 (release tool) in clutch peal cutout with inscription "top/oben" pointing away from clutch pedal.
   - Position Volkswagen special tool 10-208A (valve shim pliers) or similar, in recess on sides of clamp and press clamp together. See Fig. 9.

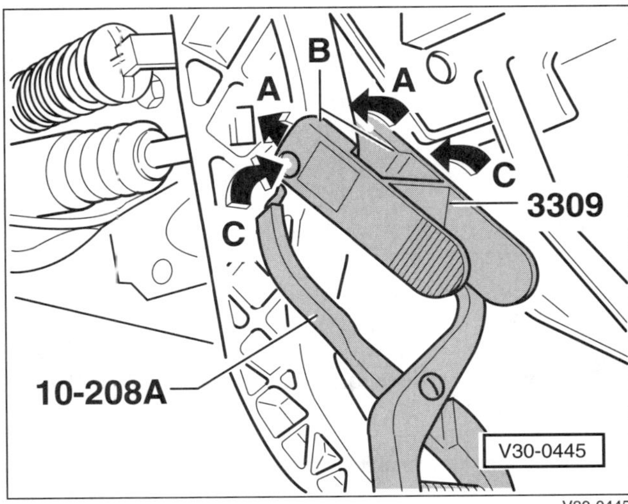

V30-0445

Fig. 9. Volkswagen special tool 3309 positioned in clutch pedal cutout (**A**) with "top/oben" (**B**) pointing away from pedal. Use special pliers 10-208A to press clamp together (**C**).

10. Turn clutch pedal stop counterclockwise and remove. See Fig. 10.

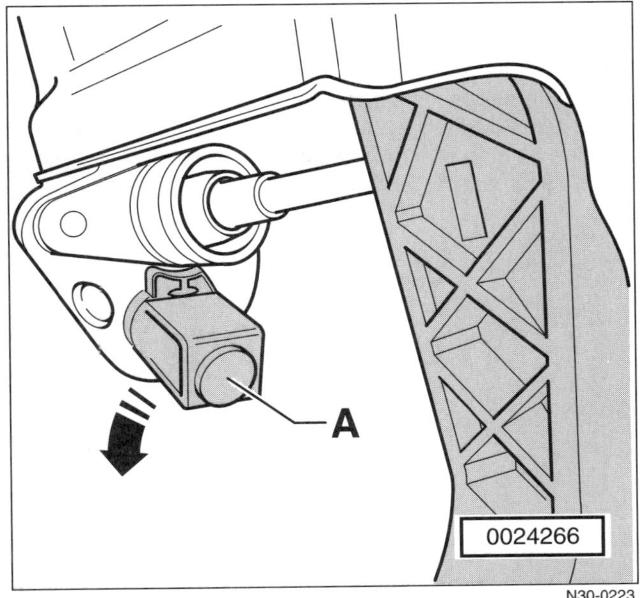

N30-0223

Fig. 10. Turn clutch pedal stop (**A**) in direction of **arrow** and remove.

11. Push master cylinder down onto stop and swing downward out of mounting bracket.

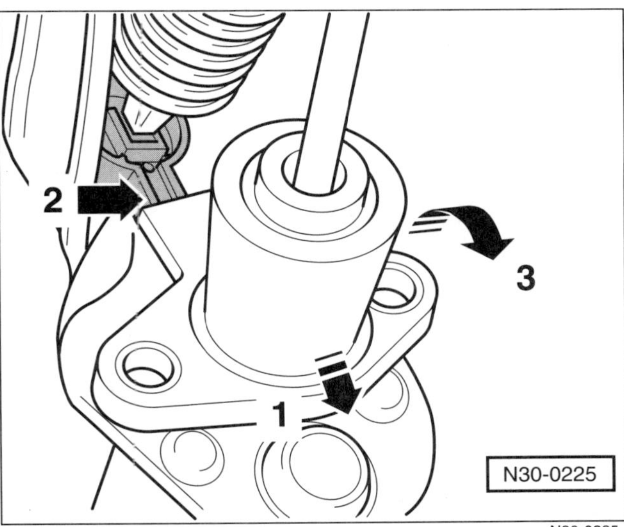

N30-0225

Fig. 11. Remove master cylinder by pushing down (**1**) and swinging downward (**3**).

NOTE —

*The master cylinder must not be blocked in the upper area by the over-center spring mount (**arrow 2** above).*

12. Installation is reverse of removal, noting the following:
   - When installing master cylinder be sure to position clutch pedal retainer properly as shown earlier. See Fig. 4.
   - Position master cylinder behind slave cylinder and install mounting nuts.
   - Install clutch pedal stop with arm pointing towards master cylinder. See Fig. 12.
   - Bleed clutch system after installing master cylinder, see **Clutch hydraulic system, bleeding**.
   - Be sure to quality check your work, see **Quality Review** at the end of this repair group.

Tightening torque

- Clutch master cylinder mounting nuts (always replace) . . . . 25 Nm (18 ft-lb)

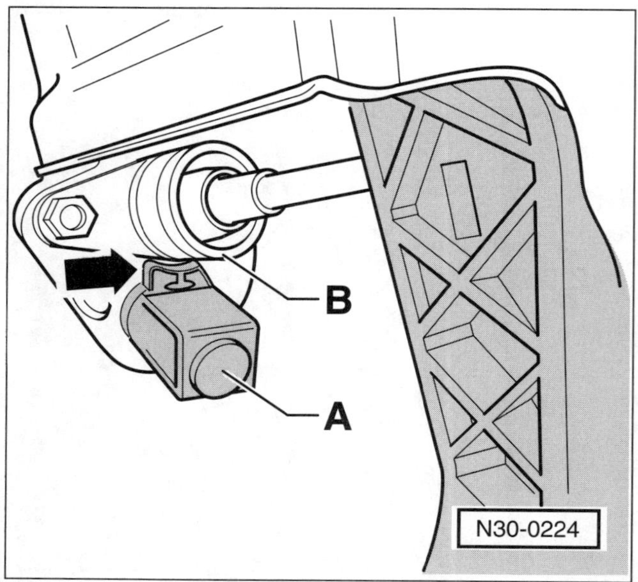

N30-0224

Fig. 12. Clutch pedal stop (**A**) installed with arm (**arrow**) positioned against slave cylinder (**B**).

Clutch hydraulic system, bleeding

Bleed clutch hydraulic system using VAG 1869 or US 1116 brake filling and bleeding unit or equivalent power bleeding equipment.

1. To bleed system, connect approximately 670 mm (26 in.) of bleeder hose to pressure hose fitting on collector bottle of power bleeder.

2. Connect bleeder hose to slave cylinder and open bleeder valve to bleed system. See Fig. 13.

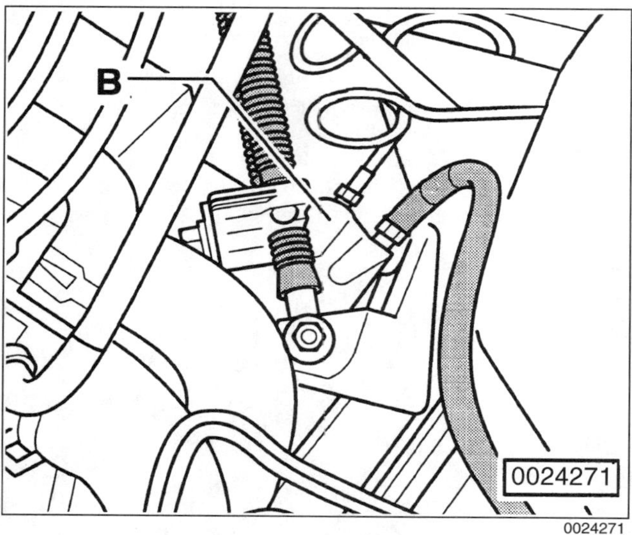

0024271

Fig. 13. Connect bleeder hose to slave cylinder (**B**) and open bleeder valve.

3. Depress clutch pedal several times after completing bleeding process.

4. Top off hydraulic fluid in reservoir.

Specification

- Hydraulic (brake) fluid. . . . . .DOT 4

CLUTCH RELEASE MECHANISM

Fig. 14 shows the clutch release mechanism components. The clutch slave cylinder can be replaced with the transmission installed in the car. Replacement of the other clutch release components require that the transmission be removed from the car. See **34 Manual Transmission** for transmission removal and replacement procedures.

Clutch release mechanism, assembly

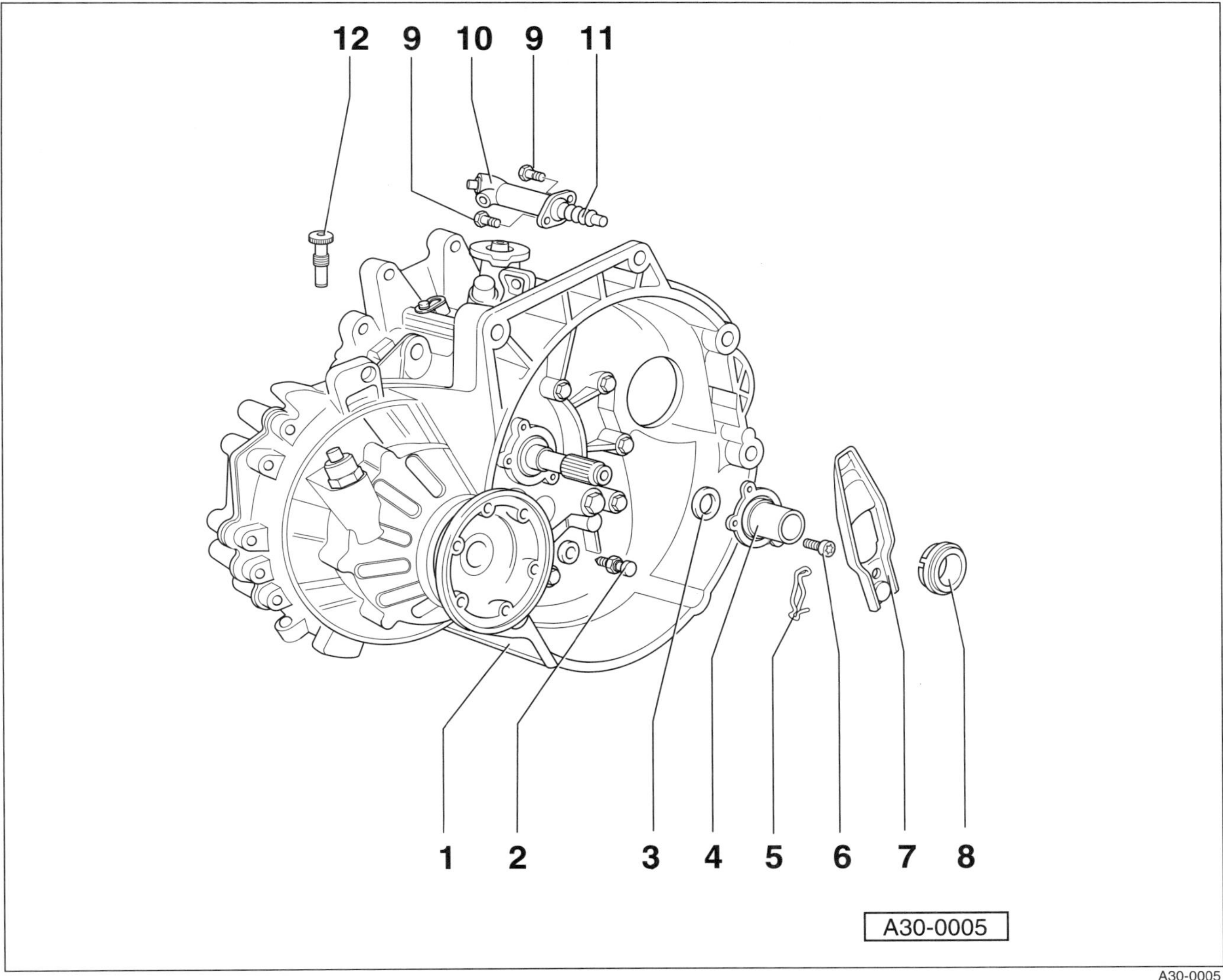

Fig. 14. Clutch release mechanism.

1. **Transmission**
2. **Ball stud**
   - Tighten to 25 Nm (18 ft lb)
   - Lubricate with MoS_2
3. **Input shaft oil seal**
4. **Guide sleeve**
   - With vulcanized O-ring
   - If damaged, replace guide sleeve and O-ring
   - Lubricate guide sleeve in area of release bearing with MoS_2 grease
5. **Retaining spring**
   - Secure to clutch release lever
6. **Bolt**
   - Tighten to 20 Nm (15 ft-lb)
7. **Clutch release lever**
8. **Release bearing**
   - Do not wash bearing out, only wipe
   - Replace noisy bearings
   - Lubricate surfaces which contact release lever with MoS_2 grease
9. **Bolt**
   - Tighten to 20 Nm (15 ft-lb)
10. **Slave cylinder**
11. **Plunger**
    - Grease end of plunger with MoS_2 grease
12. **Assembly bolt**
    - Secures clutch release lever when installing trans.
    - Remove after transmission has been installed
    - An M8 x 35 bolt can be used in place of assembly bolt

CLUTCH, SERVICING (TRANSMISSION REMOVED)

Clutch assembly

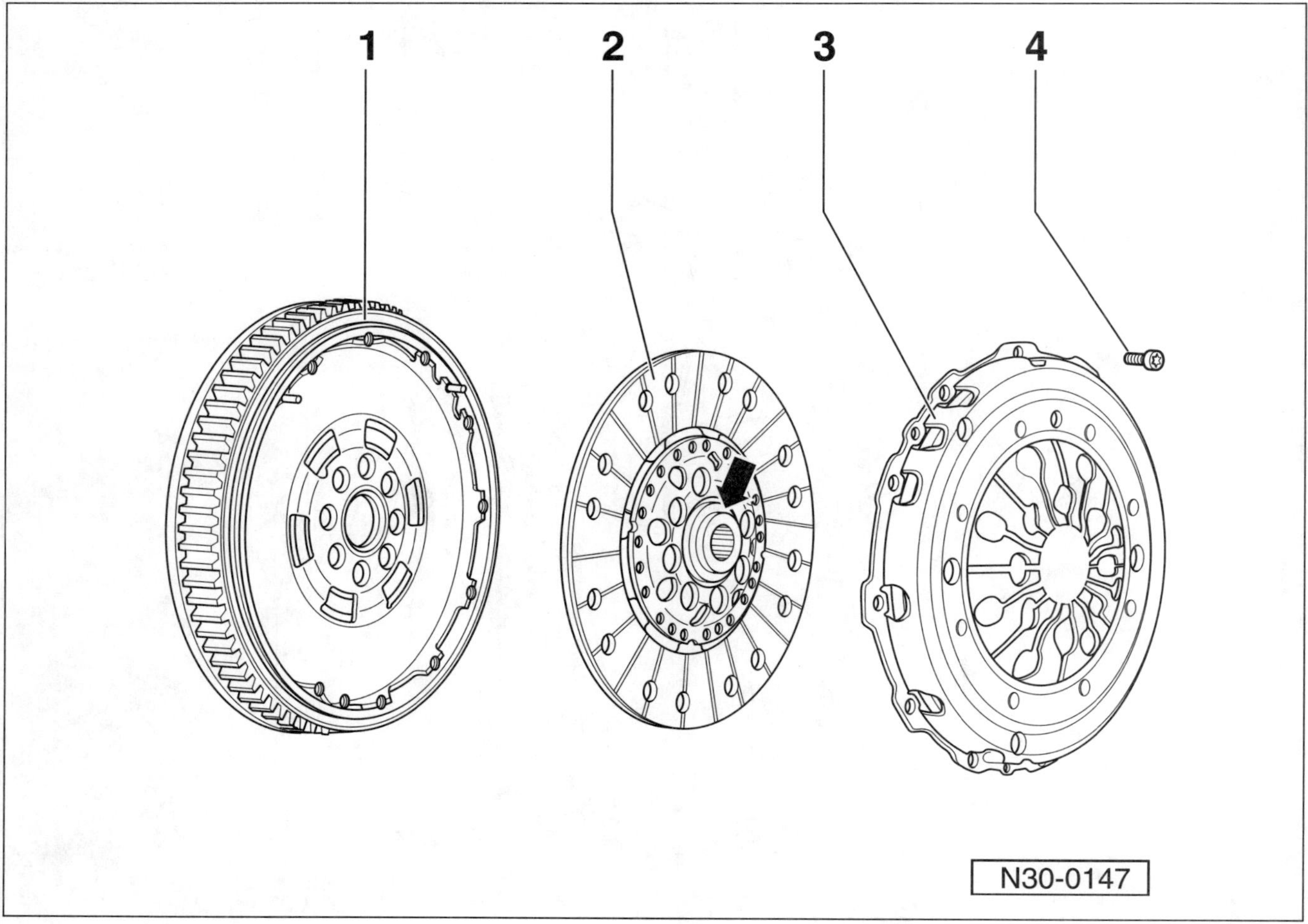

N30-0147

Fig. 15. Clutch assembly.

1. **Flywheel**
   - Make sure centering pins fit tightly
   - Contact surfaces for clutch disc must be free of grooves, oil and grease
   - Removing/installing, see **13 Crankshaft/Cylinder Block**
2. **Clutch disc**
   - Installation position with two-piece flywheel: shorter hub end (**arrow**) points toward pressure plate
   - Installation position with one-piece flywheel: spring cage faces pressure plate
   - Clean and lightly grease splines
   - After light greasing, move clutch plate back and forth on input shaft until hub moves freely on shaft
   - Centering, **see** (A)
3. **Pressure plate**
   - Removing and installing, **see** (A)
   - Clean contact surface only
   - Check ends of diaphragm spring, **see** (B)
4. **Bolt**
   - Select correct flywheel bolt for two- or one-piece flywheel
   - Loosen and tighten gradually and diagonally
   - Two-piece flywheel:
     Tighten to 13 Nm (10 ft-lb)
   - One-piece flywheel:
     Tighten to 20 Nm (15 ft-lb)

NOTE —

- *Replace clutch plates and pressure plates that have damaged or loose rivets.*
- *Select the correct clutch plate and pressure plate according to engine code.*

A) **Clutch disc, centering**
Pressure plate, removing/installing

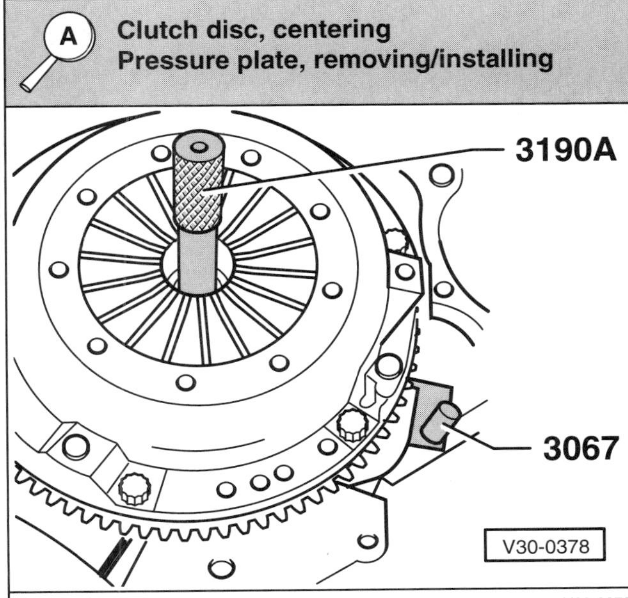

V30-0378

- **VW special tool 3190A being used to center clutch disc**
- **Loosen and tighten bolts gradually and diagonally**
- **When removing, reverse position of flywheel locking tool (VW 3067 shown)**
- **Pressure plate contact surface and clutch disc must make full contact with flywheel.**

B) **Diaphragm spring, checking ends**

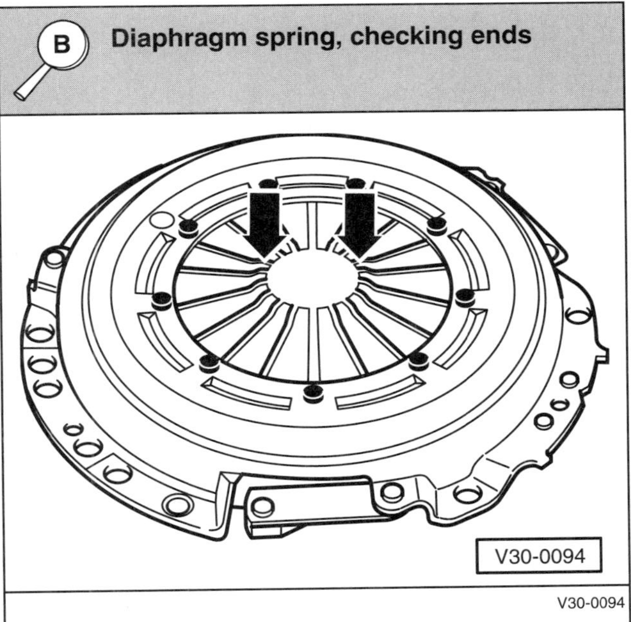

V30-0094

- **Check pressure plate diaphragm spring for wear (arrows)**
- **Maximum wear: up to half of original diaphragm spring thickness**

QUALITY REVIEW

When you have finished working under the hood and around other areas of the vehicle, it is advisable to take a moment to quality check or review your work. This helps to insure that the operation or repair has been completed properly with all affected systems functioning within normal parameters. These may include the following:

- Make sure that all components involved in the repair are positioned correctly and function properly.
- Make sure all tools and shop cloths are removed.
- Be sure to top off hydraulic (brake) fluid.
- Be careful not to spill hydraulic fluid as it can damage painted surfaces. Wipe up any spills immediately.
- Check for smooth operation of clutch pedal.
- Before road testing vehicle, confirm that clutch operates properly.
- Road test the vehicle to check operation of clutch and transmission.

34 Manual Transmission

TABLES

GENERAL

This repair group covers repair information for the cable-operated gear shift mechanism and the removal and installation of the 02J manual transmission. This repair group does not cover transaxle or transmission teardown and disassembly.

The close ratio 02J transmission uses a hydraulic clutch release mechanism and a cable operated shift mechanism.

NOTE —

- *For information on the hydraulic and mechanical components of the clutch, see* **30 Clutch**.
- *For information on drive axles, including drive flange oil seals, see* **39 Differential and Final Drive**.
- *To check manual transmission oil, see* **0 Maintenance**.

CAUTION —

- *Before working on the transmission or gear selector lever mechanism disconnect the negative (–) battery cable.*
- *Disconnecting the negative (–) battery cable may erase fault codes and basic settings in the engine management and automatic transmission control modules. Some driveability problems may be noticed until the system re-adapts to operating conditions. OBD II readiness codes, which may be required for emissions testing, may also be erased. Convenience electronics (alarm system, interior light control, power locks, mirrors, and windows) may need to be re-set using a VAG 1551/1552 or equivalent scan tool.*
- *Be sure to have the anti-theft radio code on hand before disconnecting the battery.*

Transmission code location

The transmission code and production number can be found stamped on the transmission case near the shift linkage. See illustration below. The transmission code letters can also be found on the vehicle data plate.

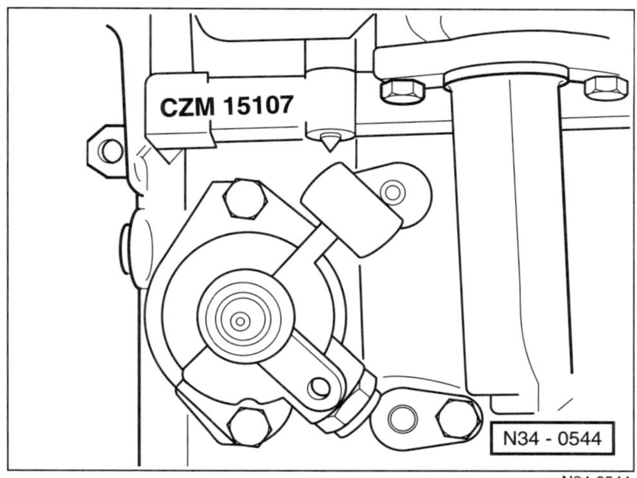

N34-0544

Transmission code letters and date of manufacture. Example above is a code **CZM**, manufactured on the **15**th day of the **10**th month in 199**7.**

Table a lists the engine applications, gear ratios, and other data for the various manual transmissions.

Table a. O2J manual transmission specifications

Code letters	EBQ, EMT, EGX, FBW	DQY, EBJ, EGR	DZQ, EBP, EGT, EKG, EKH, EMS, EZK, FBV	DZC, EHC, EGF, EWW, FBY, FCF
Engine application, horsepower	1.8L, 150hp	1.9L, 90hp	2.0L, 115hp	2.8L, 176hp
Ratio: Z_2:Z_1				
Final drive	63:16 = 3.938	61:18 = 3.389	72:17 = 4.235	61:18: 3.389
1st gear	33:10 = 3.300	34:9 = 3.788	34:9 = 3.778	29:8 = 3.625
2nd gear	35:18 = 1.944	36:17 = 2.118	36:17 = 2.118	29:14 = 2.071
3rd gear	34:26 = 1.308	34:25 = 1.360	34:25 = 1.360	28:19 = 1.474
4th gear	35:34 = 1.029	34:35 = 0.971	35:34 = 1.029	27:26 = 1.038
5th gear	36:43 = 0.837	34:45 = 0.756	36:43 = 0.837	27:32 = 0.844
Reverse gear	18:9 x 36:20 = 3.600	18:9 x 36:20 = 3.600	18:9 x 36:20 = 3.600	15:8 x 36:20 = 3.389
Lubricant				
Capacity	2.0 liters (2.1 qt.)			
Specification	G50 synthetic oil, SAE 75W/90			
Clutch control	hydraulic			
Clutch disc diameter	219 mm	219 mm	215 mm	228 mm
Ratio, overall in top gear	3.296	2.562	3.545	2.860

GEAR SELECTOR MECHANISM

The cable shift linkage has been re-designed for the “A4” Golf and Jetta models. Fig. 1. shows the shift knob. The shift lever with housing and selector cables are shown in Fig. 2. and Fig. 3. Access to the gear selector mechanism may be difficult without partially removing the exhaust system, see **26 Exhaust System and Emission Controls**.

Shift lever knob assembly

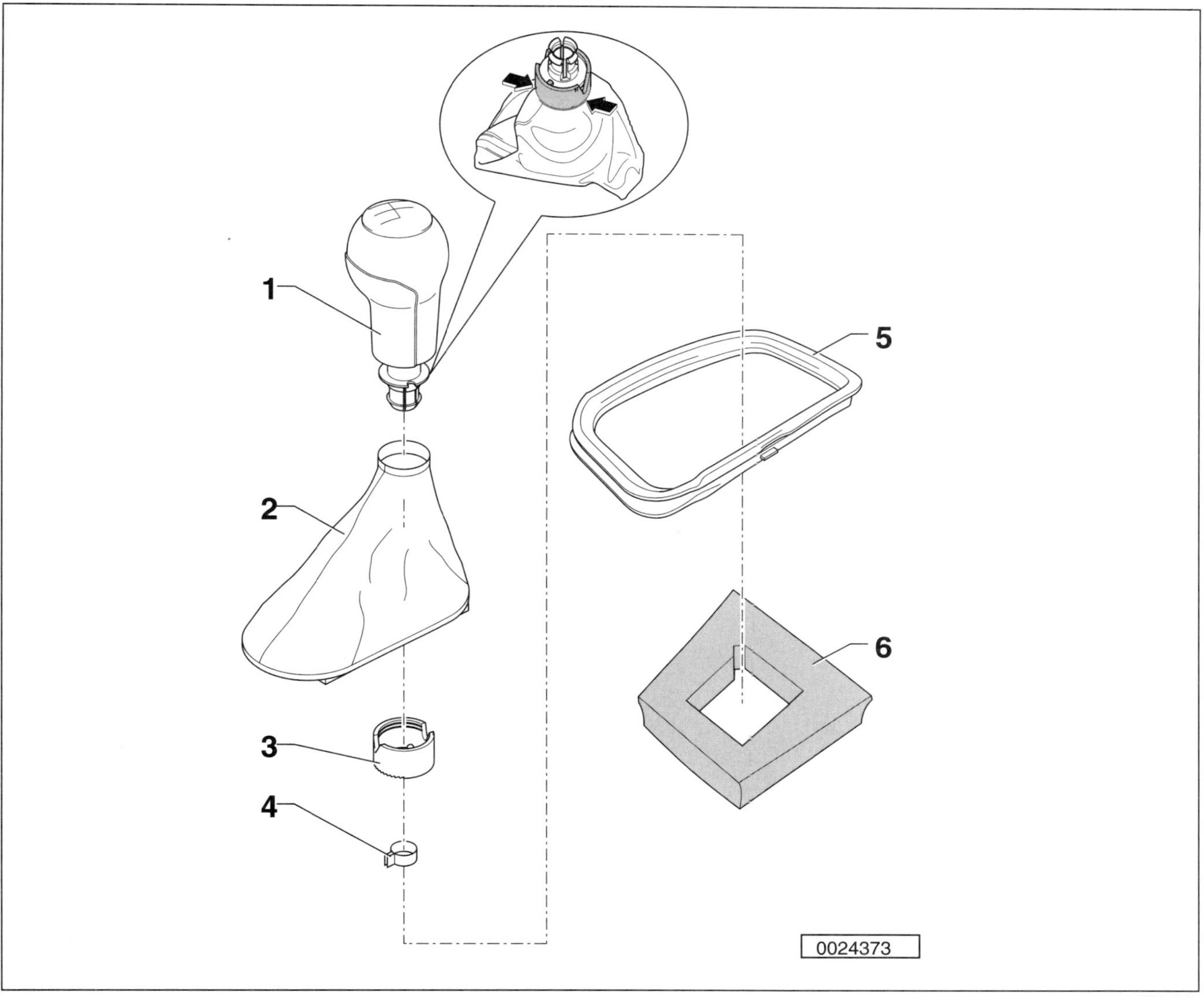

Fig. 1. Shift knob and shift .

1. **Shift lever knob**
   - Screw on and off together with boot
2. **Boot**
   - Remove and install together with shift lever knob
   - Removing:
     Pry boot up (see Fig. 7.) and turn boot inside out.
     Cut clamp (item 4) to remove gear lever knob from gear lever.
     Carefully pry retaining sleeve legs with small screwdriver in direction of **arrows** (see inset) while simultaneously pulling gear lever knob out.
   - Installing
     Insert gear lever knob in boot.
     Push sleeve onto gear lever knob and engage.
     Install knob and boot together on gear lever.
3. **Retaining sleeve**
4. **Clamp**
   - Cut clip to remove gear lever knob from gear lever
   - Use hose clamp pliers (VAG 1275 or equivalent) to install
5. **Frame**
6. **Noise insulation**

Shift lever and housing

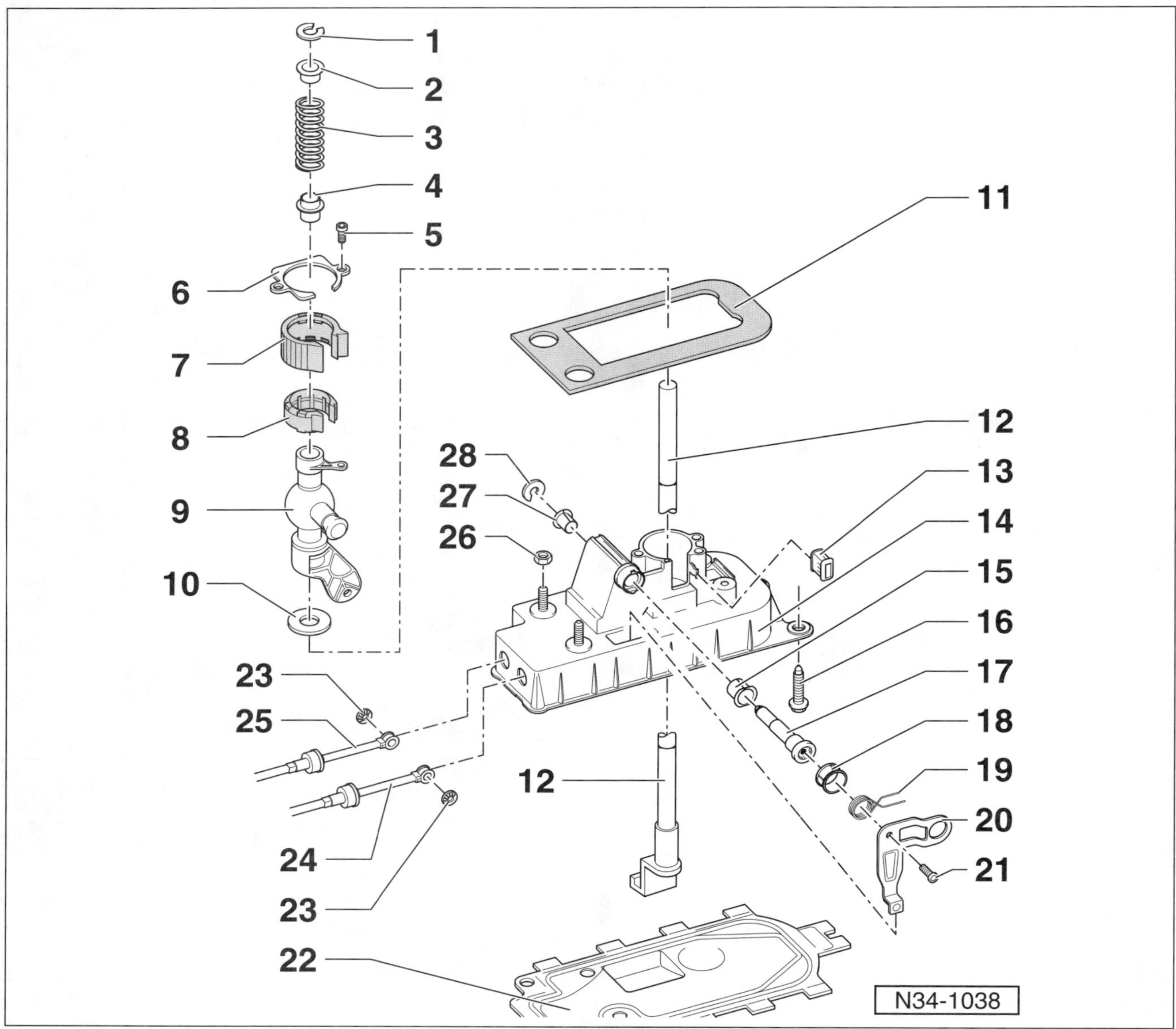

N34-1038

Fig. 2. Shift lever, housing and related components.

NOTE —
Lubricate all mountings and sliding surfaces with Polyuric grease (VW part no. G 052 142 A2, or equivalent).

1. **Circlip**
   - Removing and installing, **see** (A)
2. **Bushing**
3. **Spring**
4. **Bushing**
5. **Torx bolt**
   - Tighten to 5 Nm (44 in-lb)
6. **Cover**
7. **Insulation**
8. **bearing housing**
9. **Shift lever guide**
10. **Insulating washer**
11. **Gasket**
    - Between shift lever housing and floor
    - Self-adhesive, bonded to shift lever housing
12. **Shift lever**

13. **Damper**
14. **Bushing**
15. **Shift lever housing**
16. **Bolt**
    - Tighten to 25 Nm (18 ft-lb)
17. **Pivot pin**
18. **Guide bushing**
19. **Spring**
    - Installing, **see** (B)
20. **Gate selector bracket**
21. **Torx bolt**
    - Tighten to 5 Nm (44 in-lb)
22. **Floor plate**
    - Bend up clips to remove
    - Always replace
23. **Lock washer**
24. **Gate selector cable**
25. **Gear change cable**
    - Press onto shift lever guide
26. **Nut**
    - Tighten to 25 Nm (18 ft-lb)
27. **Bushing**
28. **Lock washer**

(A) Circlip, removing and installing

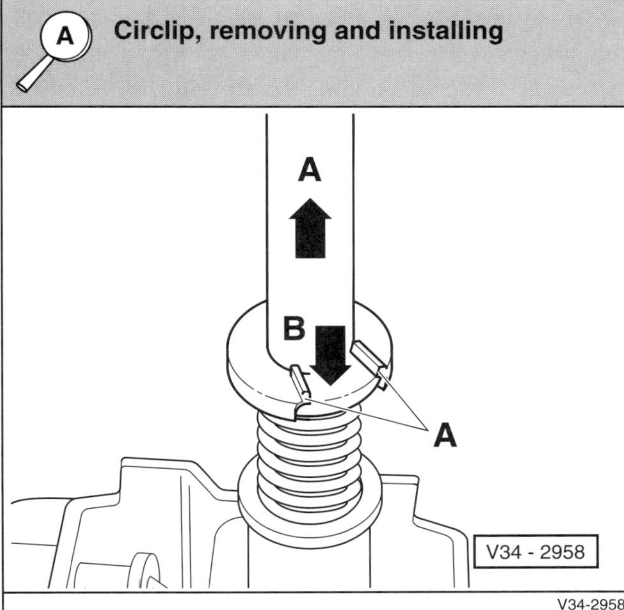

V34-2958

- **Pull shift lever up (direction of arrow A) while pushing down on spacer bushing (arrow B) to release spring tension.**
- **Remove circlip (A).**

NOTE —
Do not tilt spacer bushing when pushing down. Carefully release pressure at groove in gear lever for clip.

(B) Gate selector bracket spring, installing

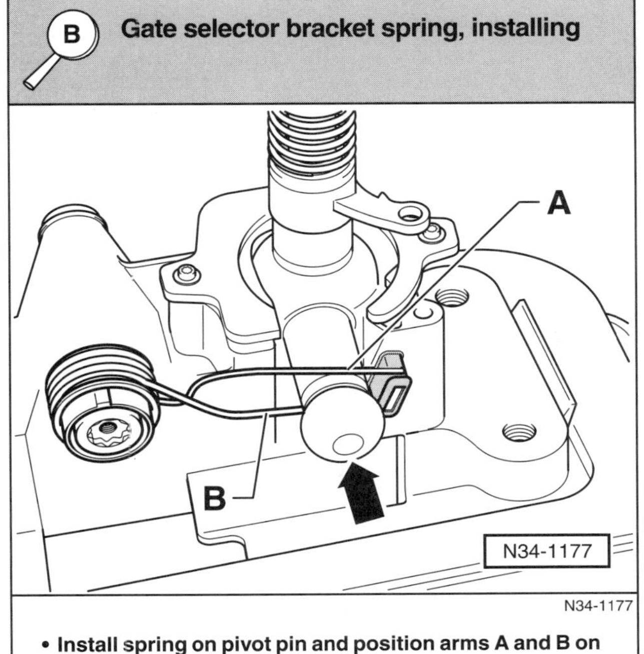

N34-1177

- **Install spring on pivot pin and position arms A and B on shift lever guide (arrow) as shown.**

Gear selector cables, assembly

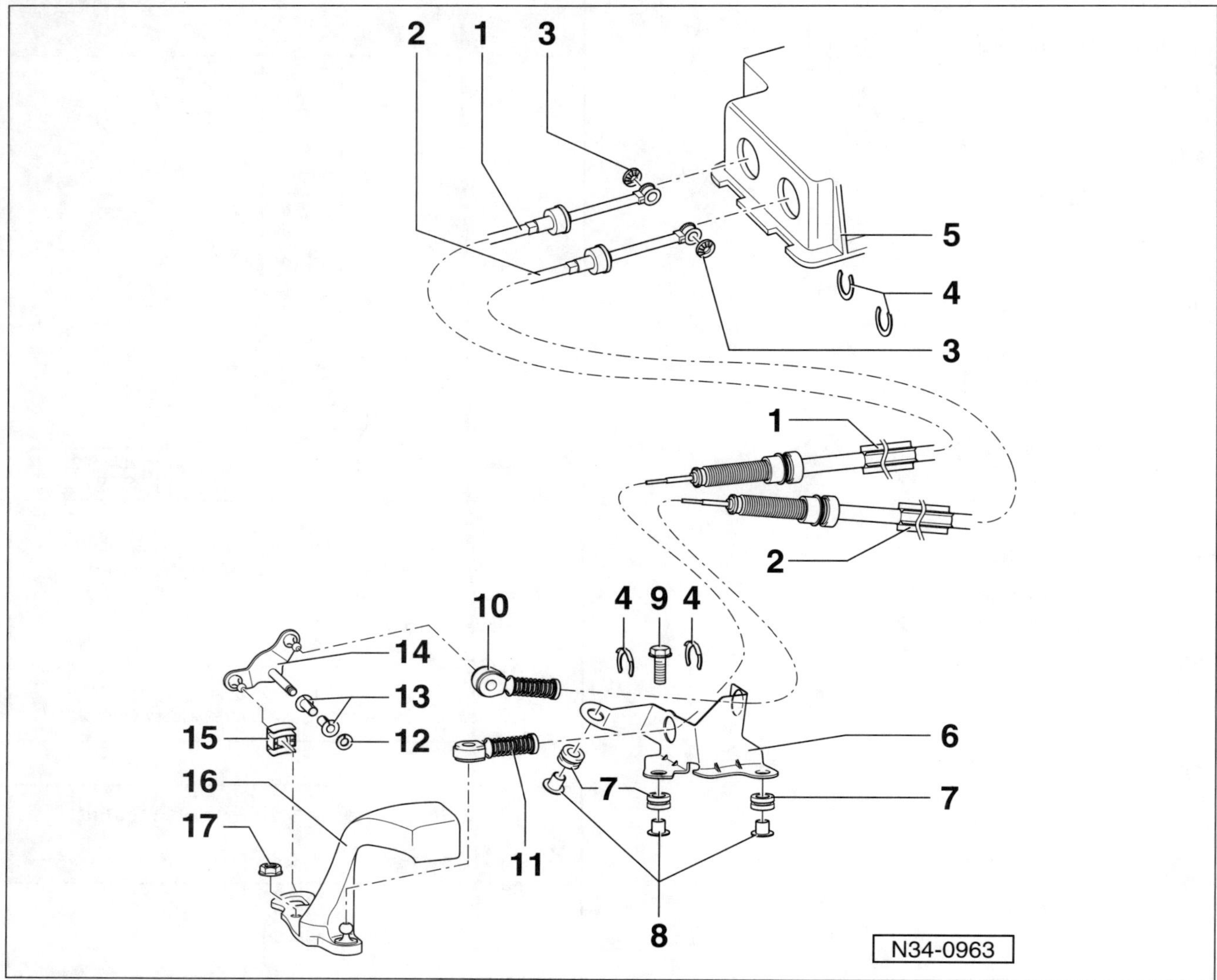

N34-0963

Fig. 3. Gear selector cables and related parts.

1. **Gear change cable**
   - Press onto shift lever guide
   - Installation position, **see** Ⓐ
2. **Gate selector cable**
   - To gate selector bracket
   - Installation position, **see** Ⓐ
3. **Circlip**
4. **Circlip**
   - When removing do not damage cables
5. **Shift lever housing**
6. **Support bracket**
7. **Grommet**
   - Between support bracket and transmission
8. **Spacer**
9. **Bolt**
   - Tighten to 25 Nm (18 ft-lb)
   - For support bracket
10. **Cable engagement piece**
    - For gate selector cable to relay lever
11. **Cable engagement piece**
    - For gear change cable to gear selector
12. **Circlip**
13. **Bushing**
14. **Relay lever**
    - Installation position **see** Ⓑ

(continued from previous page)

15. Insert

16. Gear shift lever

- With dampening weight
- Install so that gap in spline partition aligns with selector shaft
- Adjust selector mechanism after installing
- Installation position **see** (B)

17. Self-locking nut

- Tighten to 25 Nm (18 ft lb)

NOTE —

During reassembly, lubricate all mounting and contact surfaces with polycarbomide grease (VW part no. G 052 142 A2). As the final step, adjust the gear selector mechanism, see **Gear selector mechanism, adjusting**.

(A) Gear selector mechanism, installation position

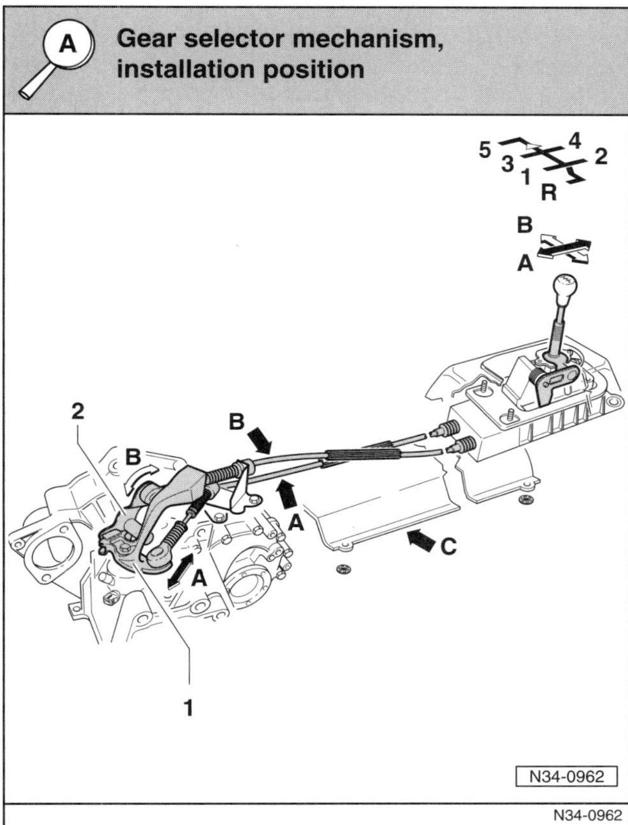

N34-0962

- **Gear change cable (A) controls forward/back travel.**
- **Gate selector cable (B) controls side-to-side travel.**
- **Heat shield (C) protects cables from exhaust.**
- **Gear selector lever is (1) and relay lever is (2).**

(B) Gear selector lever and relay lever, installation position

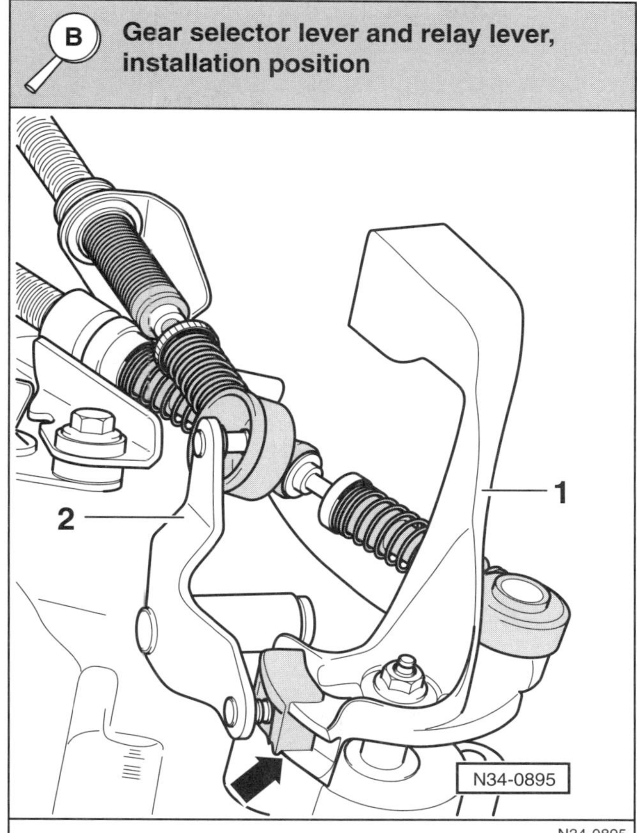

N34-0895

1. **Gear selector lever with dampening weight**
2. **Relay lever**
   - Locates in guide rail of gear shift lever (**arrow**)
   - Lubricate with MoS_2 grease

Gear selector mechanism, adjusting

NOTE —
Special VW tools are required to accurately adjust the shift mechanism. Read the procedure through to determine what tools will be necessary.

1. Place transmission in neutral.
2. Remove intake hose and harness connector from Mass Air Flow (MAF) sensor. Remove air cleaner mounting bolts and pull out air cleaner. See Fig. 4.

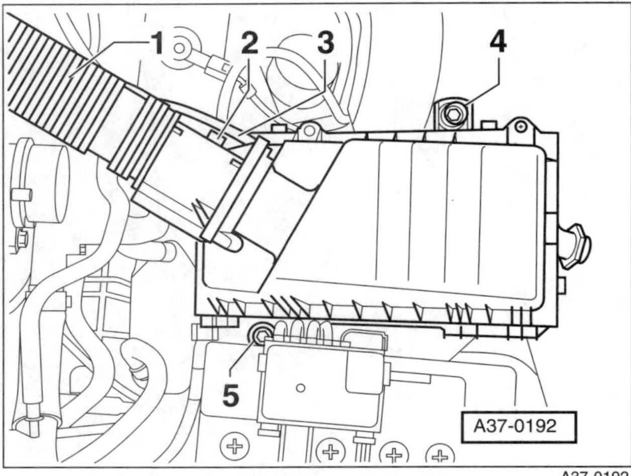

A37-0192

Fig. 4. Remove intake air hose (**1**), harness connector (**2**), and air cleaner mounting bolts (**3**, **4**).

3. Working at transmission, pull locking mechanism at gear selector lever and gate selector lever toward the front until reaching stop. Engage levers by twisting to left. See Fig. 5.

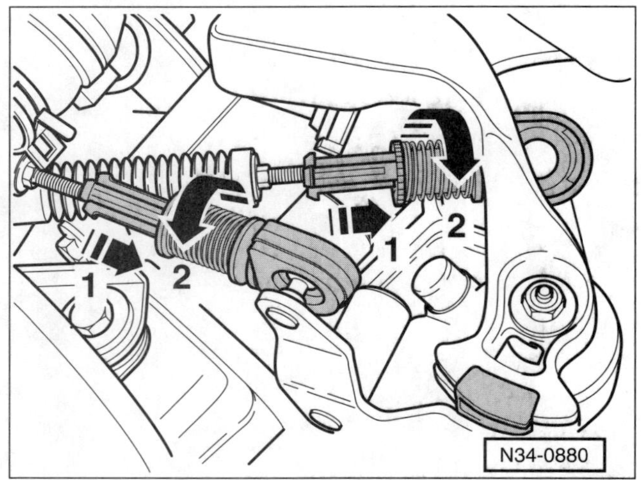

N34-0880

Fig. 5. Pull gear and gate selector levers forward to stop (**arrows 1**) and engage by twisting to the left (**arrows 2**).

4. Secure selector shaft by pressing down on shaft and turning locking lever clockwise. See Fig. 6.

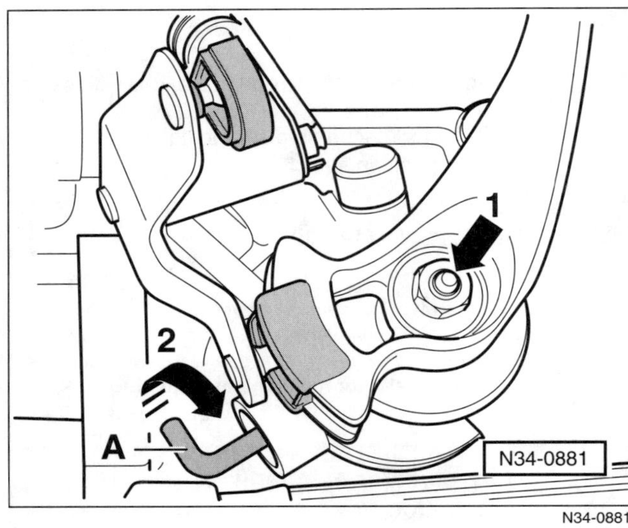

N34-0881

Fig. 6. Secure selector shaft by pressing down on shaft (**arrow 1**) and turning lever (**A**) in direction of **arrow 2**.

5. Carefully pry boot off center console. See Fig. 7.

A34-0026

Fig. 7. Pry gear shift boot off at **arrows**.

6. If installed, pull rubber cover toward shift lever knob.

7. Working in shift lever housing, secure selector shaft with T10027 inserting pin (VW special tool T10027 or equivalent) through two holes. See Fig. 8.

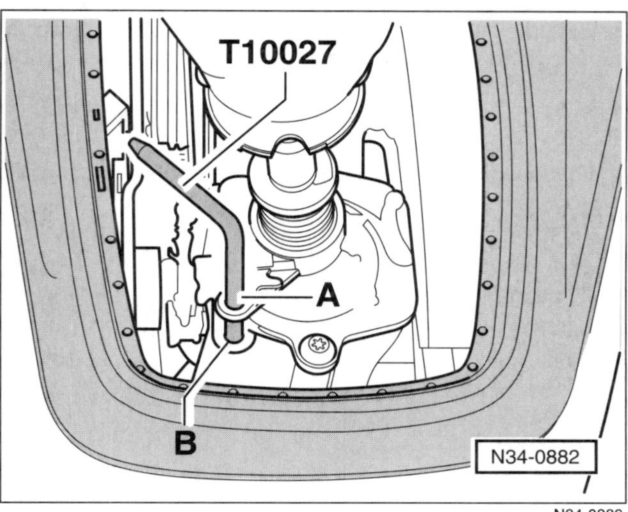

Fig. 8. Install insertion pin (VW special tool no T10027) through hole (**A**) and into hole (**B**).

8. Turn locking mechanism on gear and gate selector cable toward the right until reaching stop. Spring will push locking mechanism into starting position. See Fig. 9.

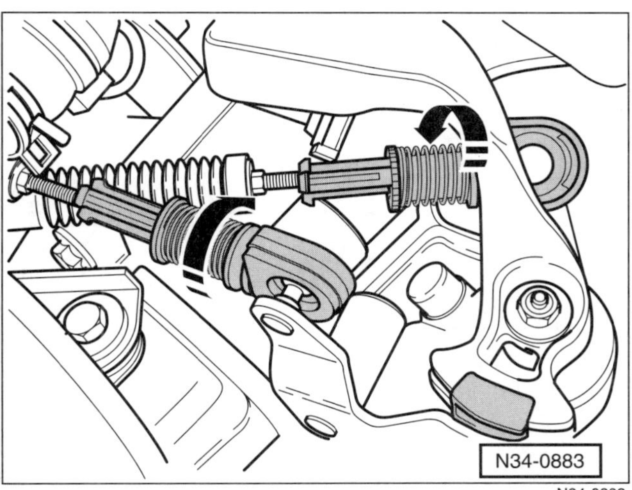

Fig. 9. Turn ends of gear and gate selector cables to right (**arrows**) until reaching stop.

9. Turn locking lever back to original position. See Fig. 10.

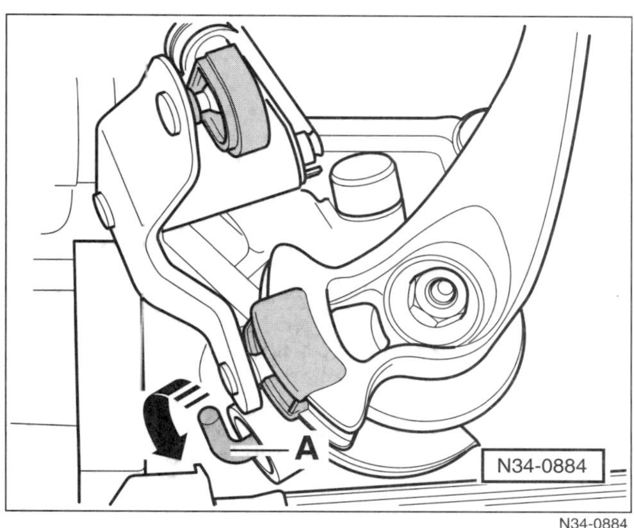

Fig. 10. Turn lever (**A**) back to original position (direction of **arrow**).

10. Check whether selector shaft moves properly. See Fig. 11.

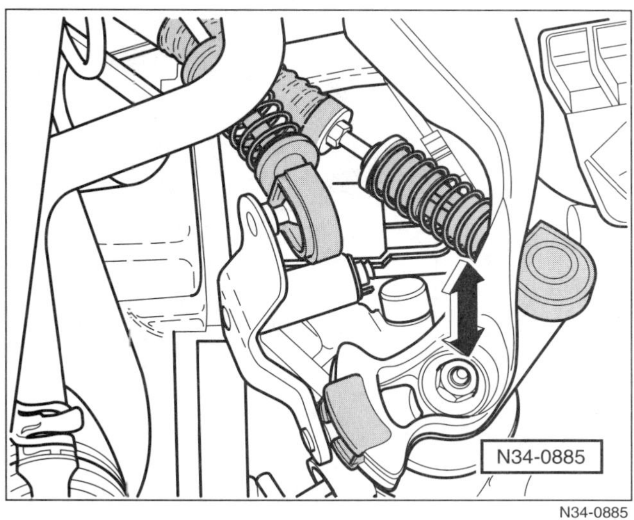

Fig. 11. Check selector shaft for proper movement (direction of **arrow**).

11. Remove insertion pin from inside shift lever housing. See Fig. 8.

12. Install shift lever boot and rubber cover as applicable.

13. Be sure to quality check your work, see **Quality Review** at the end of this repair group.

Gear selector mechanism, functional check

1. With transmission in neutral, make sure shift lever is in 3rd/4th gear gate.
2. Depress clutch pedal.
3. Select each gear several times, checking all gears. Pay particular attention to operation of reverse gear.

NOTE —
Should any gear fail to engage smoothly after being selected repeatedly, the selector shaft play (lift) should be checked as described below.

4. Have a helper select 1st gear and then press shift lever to left stop, then release. At same time, observe selector shaft on transmission. The selector shaft must move approximately 1 mm (0.04 in.). See Fig. 12.

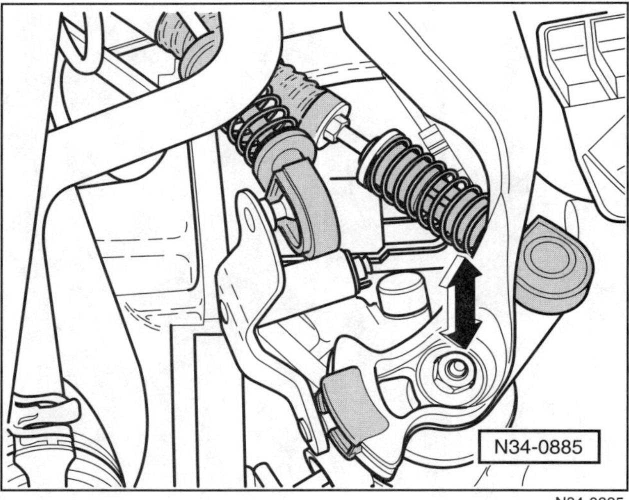

N34-0885

Fig. 12. When moving shift lever to 1st gear stop, transmission selector lever should move in direction of arrow approximately 1.0 mm (0.04 in.).

5. If any faults are found, see **Gear selector mechanism, adjusting**.

TRANSMISSION, REMOVING AND INSTALLING

This procedure describes the removal and installation of the manual transmission. Special engine lifting and jacking equipment is needed to support and reposition the engine as the transmission is removed from below.

Volkswagen recommended special tools

- VW 457/1 support rails
- 10-222A transmission support kit
- 10-222A/8 adapter
- 3282 transmission support
- 3282/8 adjustment plate
- 3300A engine support
- 3336 transmission lifting beam
- VAG 1331 torque wrench
- VAG 1332 torque wrench
- VAG 1383A engine/transmission jack
- VAS 5024 mounting pliers

Special tools, modifying

One of the Volkswagen recommended special tools will need to be modified as follows.

To secure support rail VW 457/1 to the subframe a new hole is required. See Fig. 13.

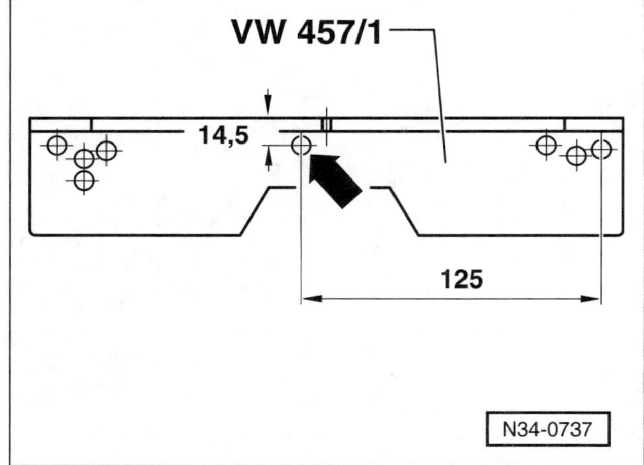

N34-0737

Fig. 13. Drill an 8.5 mm (0.335 in.) diameter hole (**arrow**) in VW 457/1 support rail. Dimensions are provided in mm.

Transmission, removing

1. Remove engine cover.

2. Disconnect battery ground (GND) strap from battery negative (–) terminal. See the **Cautions** at the beginning of this repair group regarding battery disconnection.

   NOTE —

   Be sure to have the anti-theft radio code on hand before disconnecting the battery.

3. Remove intake hose and harness connector from Mass Air Flow (MAF) sensor.

4. Remove air cleaner mounting bolts and pull out air cleaner. See Fig. 14.

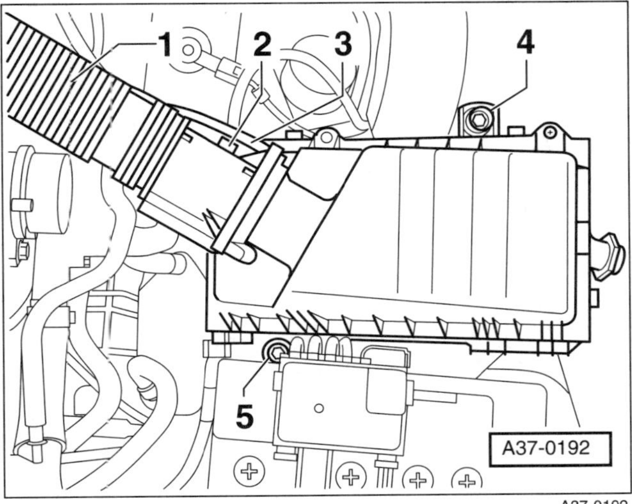

A37-0192

Fig. 14. Remove intake air hose (**1**), harness connector (**2**), and air cleaner mounting bolts (**3**, **4**).

5. Disconnect harness connector from vehicle speed sensor and back-up light switch. See Fig. 15.

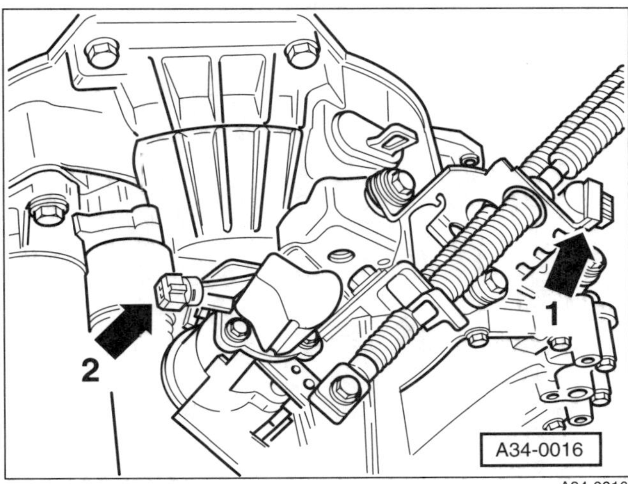

A34-0016

Fig. 15. Vehicle speed sensor (**1**) and backup light switch (**2**) harness connectors to be disconnected from transmission.

6. Remove gear and gate selector cables at transmission by prying off from ball connection with 13mm wrench. See Fig. 16.

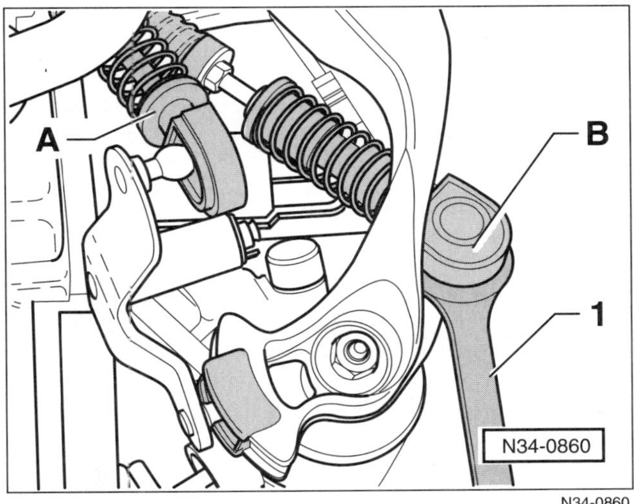

N34-0860

Fig. 16. Remove gear change cable (**B**) and gate selector cable (**A**) by prying off from ball connection with 13mm wrench (**1**).

7. Remove cable retaining bracket from transmission. See Fig. 17.

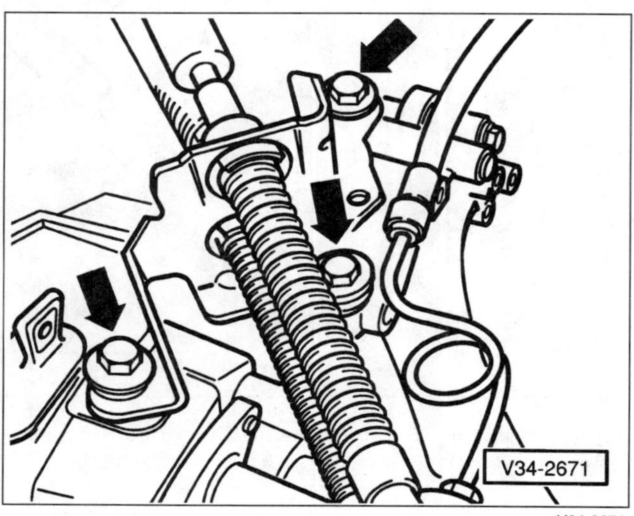

V34-2671

Fig. 17. Cable retaining bracket mounting bolts (**arrows**).

> ***NOTE —***
> *If necessary unclip hydraulic hose at cable support bracket before removing bracket.*

8. Remove slave cylinder and secure to side with wire. Do not disconnect hydraulic lines. See Fig. 18.

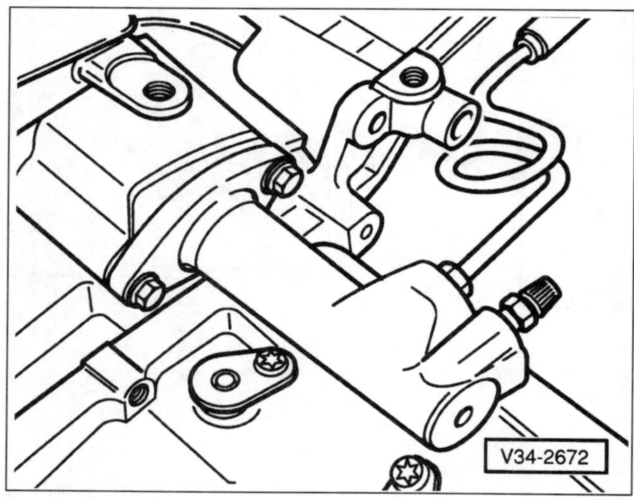

V34-2672

Fig. 18. Clutch slave cylinder on transmission.

> ***CAUTION —***
> *Do not depress clutch pedal with slave cylinder removed.*

9. Remove cable retainer and upper mounting bolt on starter. See Fig. 19.

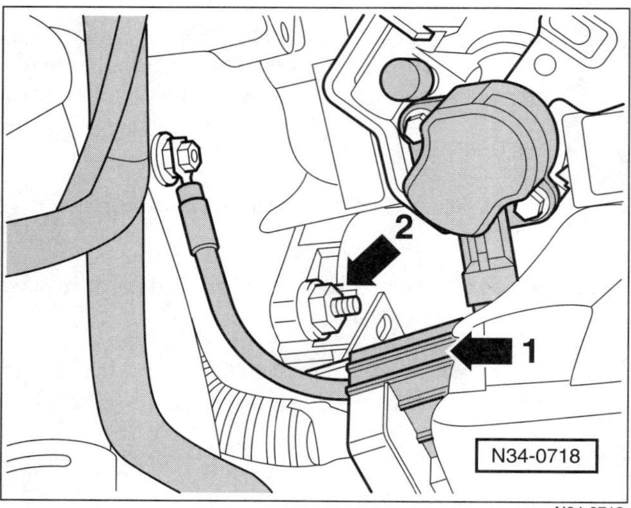

N34-0718

Fig. 19. Remove cable retainer (**arrow 1**) and upper mounting bolt (**arrow 2**) on starter.

10. Remove ground strap at engine-to-transmission upper securing bolt.

11. Remove upper engine-to-transmission mounting bolts.

12. On vehicles with 1.9L TDI (ALH engine), remove intake air duct between intake air cooler and turbocharger, see **21 Turbocharger and Intercooler**.

13. Attach engine lifting equipment (VW sling 10-222A with appropriate adapters and legs as shown below). Adjust the lifting sling until the weight of the engine is fully supported. For 4-cylinder vehicles see Fig. 20. For 6-cylinder vehicles see Fig. 21.

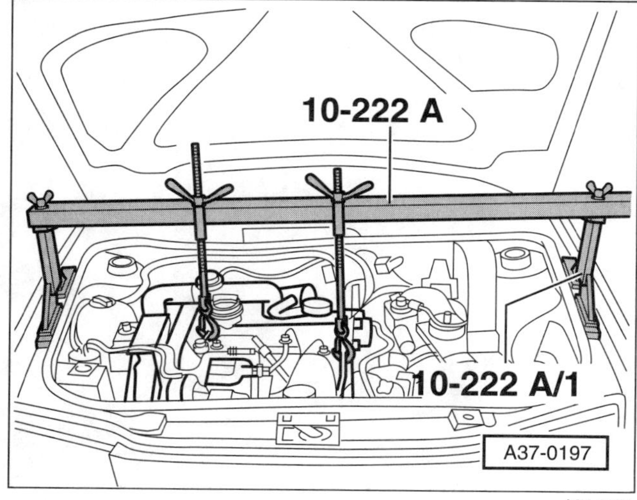

A37-0197

Fig. 20. Engine lifting equipment used to support weight of 4-cylinder engine. Numbers shown are for VW special tools.

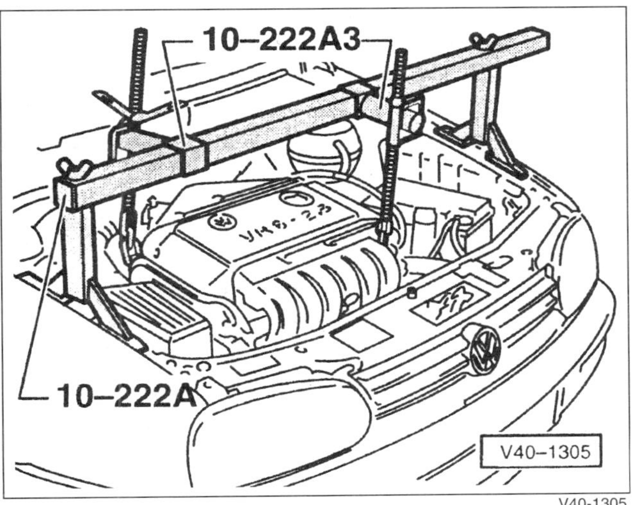

V40-1305

Fig. 21. Engine lifting equipment used to support weight of 6-cylinder engine. Numbers shown are for VW special tools.

> ***CAUTION —***
> - *Before installing the engine lifting hooks, disconnect all hoses and wiring in the vicinity of the engine lifting eyes, to prevent damage.*
> - *Do not position engine sling legs on the fender mounting bolts.*

14. Raise car and support with jack stands or lift. See **0 Maintenance** for proper lifting procedure.

> ***WARNING —***
> *Observe all warnings and cautions associated with lifting vehicle in* **0 Maintenance**.

15. Remove lower sound absorber panels (belly pans). See Fig. 22.

NOTE —
Sound insulator fasteners may best be removed and installed with needle nose pliers.

16. Remove power steering line from starter and transmission mounts.

NOTE —
Use care not to damage the power steering line.

17. Remove starter, see **27 Engine Electrical**.

18. Remove right inner drive axle boot protective cover from engine, if installed. See Fig. 23.

19. Turn wheels all the way to the left.

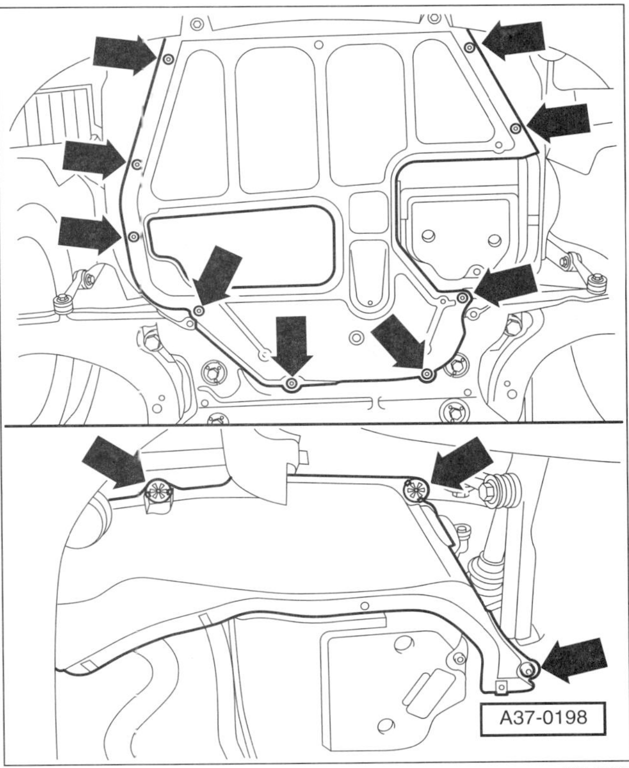

A37-0198

Fig. 22. Remove lower sound insulator panels by unscrewing fasteners (**arrows**). AEG engine shown, others similar.

0024260

Fig. 23. Remove bolts (**arrows**) for drive axle boot protective cover.

20. Disconnect drive axles from drive flanges and tie up as high as possible.

NOTE —
When tying up axle shafts use care not to damage the paint on the body panels or the axle boots.

21. Remove flywheel small cover plate behind right axle flange, if installed. See Fig. 24.

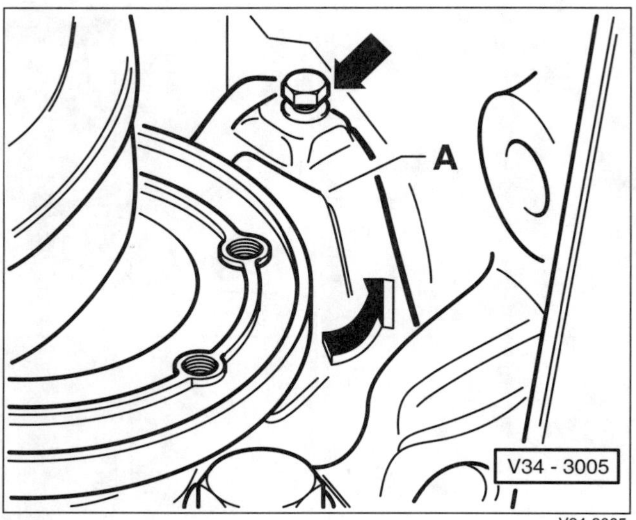

Fig. 24. Remove flywheel small cover plate (**A**) behind right axle flange (**arrows**), if installed.

22. If installed, remove lower flywheel cover plate.

23. Separate exhaust system at front exhaust pipe and remove from subframe as necessary, see **26 Exhaust System/Emission Controls**.

24. Remove bolts for pendulum mount. See Fig. 25.

Fig. 25. Remove pendulum mounting bolts (**A** and **B**).

25. Remove transmission support from transmission and bolts from left assembly mount. See Fig. 26.

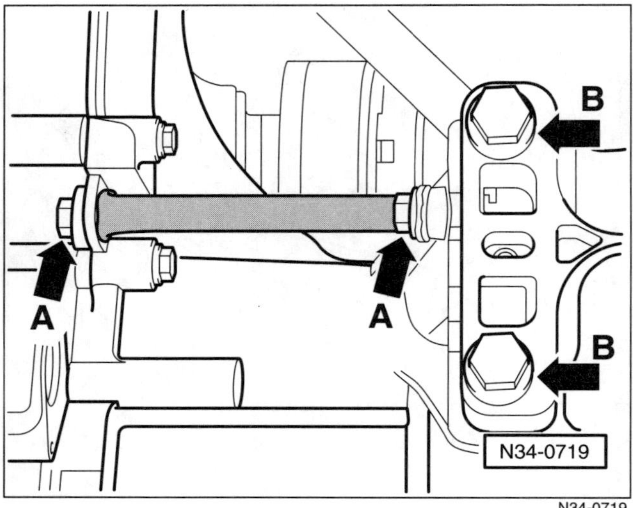

Fig. 26. Remove transmission support (**arrows A**) and left assembly mount bolts (**arrows B**).

26. Incline engine/transmission assembly by lowering it via left-side spindle of support bar.

27. Remove bolts for transmission mount. See Fig. 27.

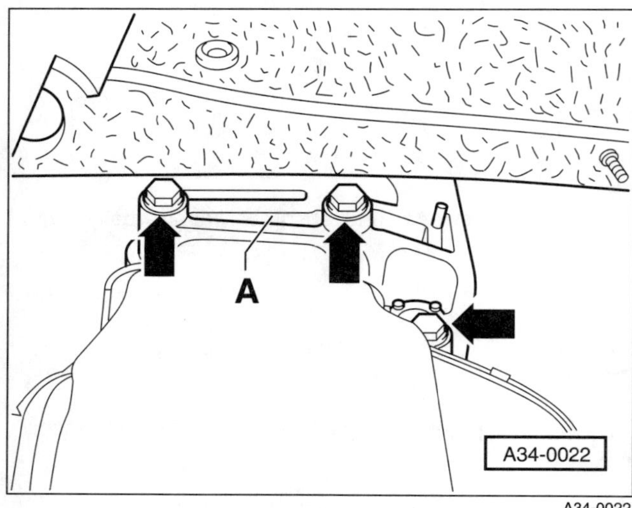

Fig. 27. Remove bolts (**arrows**) for transmission mount (**A**).

28. Obtain two M8x25 bolts and spacers totalling 6mm (1/4 in.) thickness to use with both bolts.

29. Bolt support rail (VW 457/1 or equivalent) to the pendulum support securing holes on subframe. See Fig. 28.

NOTE —
- *Volkswagen special tool 457/1 must be modified as described earlier under* **Special tools, modifying**.
- *Spacers totaling a thickness of 6 mm must be inserted between the subframe and the support rail VW 457/1.*

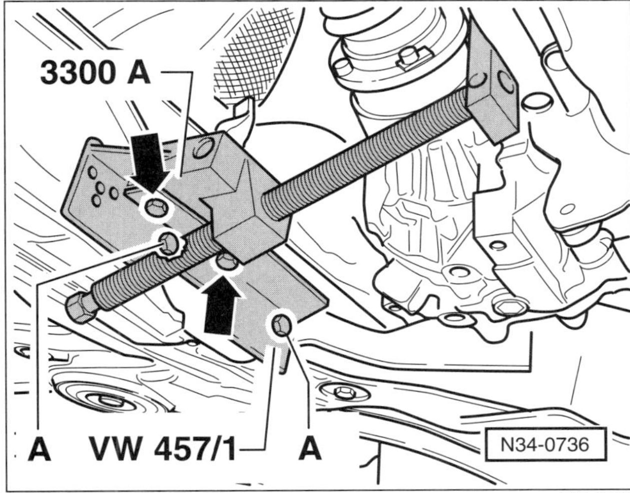

N34-0736

Fig. 28. Use two M8 x 25 bolts (**A**) to attach support rail to the pendulum mount securing holes on subframe. Install support 3300A to support rail (**arrows**). Numbers shown are for VW special tools.

30. Install support (VW 3300A) to support rail (VW 457/1) and secure. Refer to Fig. 28.

31. Press engine/transmission assembly forward carefully.

NOTE —
Do not damage power steering line when moving engine/transmission assembly.

32. Assemble transmission jack with support 3282, adjustment plate 3282/8 (same as for 02A transmission) and support elements. See Fig. 29.
    - Place adjustment plate 3282/8 on transmission support 3282. (Adjustment plate only fits in one position).
    - Position transmission support arms according to holes in adjustment plate.

NOTE —
Arrow on adjustment plate 3282/8 should point toward front of vehicle.

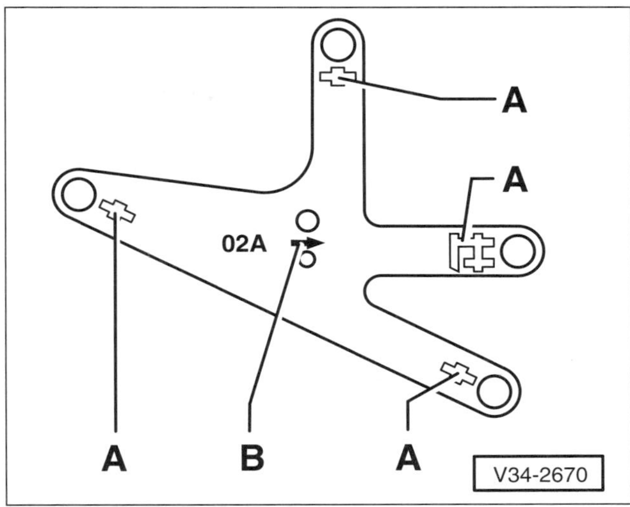

V34-2670

Fig. 29. Adjustment plate 3282/8 to be used with Volkswagen transmission jack 3282. Position transmission support arms at **A**. Arrow (**B**) should point toward front of vehicle.

33. Place transmission jack under vehicle. See Fig. 30.

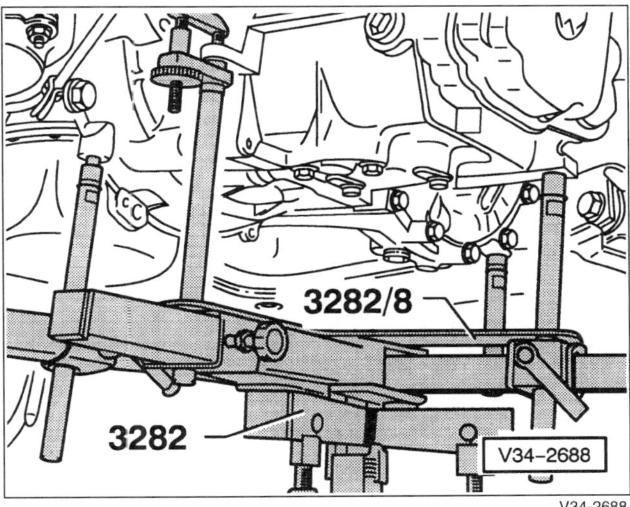

V34-2688

Fig. 30. Transmission jack correctly placed under transmission. Numbers shown are for VW transmission jack and adapters.

34. Align adjustment plate parallel to transmission and lock safety supports on transmission jack.

35. Remove lower engine/transmission securing bolts.

> ***WARNING —***
> *Before unbolting lower engine-to-transmission mounting bolts be sure to support the weight of the vehicle at all four corners with jack stands designed for that purpose. Removal of the transmission can upset the weight balance of the vehicle and cause it to fall off the lift.*

36. Press transmission off alignment dowel sleeves and carefully swing toward subframe. See Fig. 31.

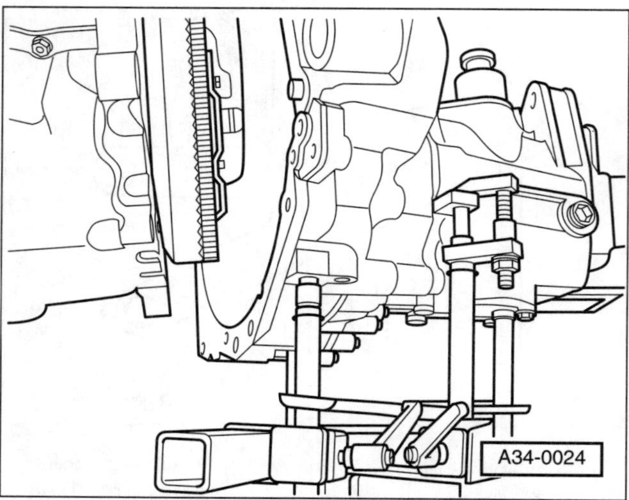

A34-0024

Fig. 31. Press transmission off dowel sleeves and carefully swing toward sub-frame.

37. Lower transmission carefully while guiding right flange shaft past flywheel. Guide left flange shaft past subframe. See Fig. 32.

NOTE—

- *When lowering the transmission change its position using the transmission support 3282 spindles.*
- *Do not damage the power steering line when lowering the transmission.*

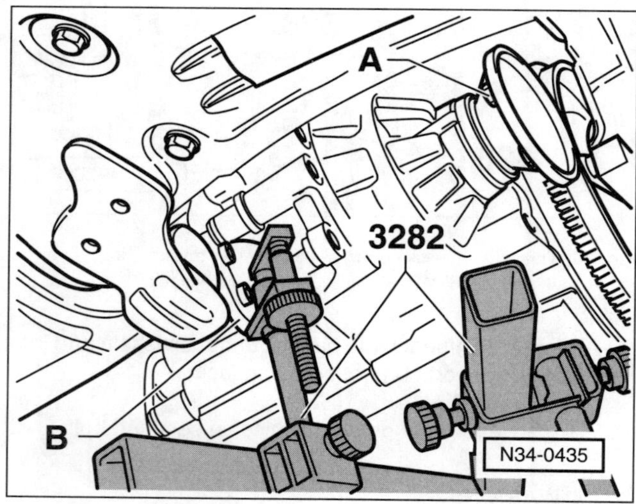

N43-0435

Fig. 32. Lower transmission carefully while guiding right flange shaft (**A**) past flywheel. Guide left flange shaft (**B**) past subframe.

Transmission, installing

Install the transmission in the reverse order of removal. Check that all engine-to-transmission dowel pins are installed in the engine block. Replace any that are missing. Clean the hub splines of the transmission input shaft and apply a light coat of MoS2 grease before installing. If replacing the transmission assembly, transfer the vehicle speed sensor, the back-up light switch, and the transmission relay lever to the new transmission.

On 4-cylinder engines, check that intermediate plate is installed correctly. See Fig. 33.

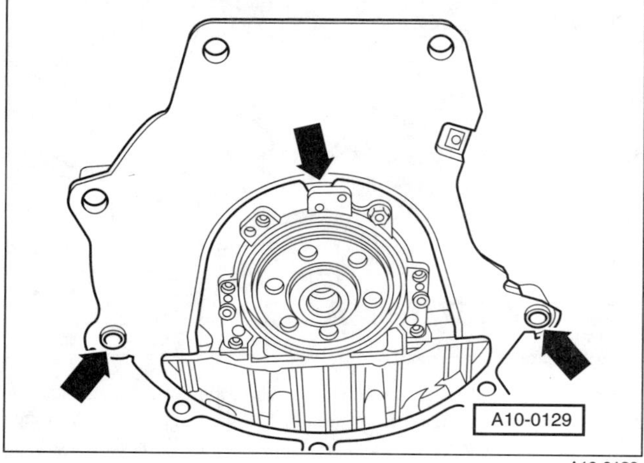

A10-0129

Fig. 33. On 4-cylinder engines, install intermediate plate on sealing flange and slide onto dowel sleeves (**arrows**).

Before installing transmission to engine, press the clutch release lever toward transmission case and secure lever in position using a M8 x 35 bolt. See Fig. 34. Remove bolt after transmission has been installed. The hole will be sealed by the third cable support bracket securing bolt or plugged.

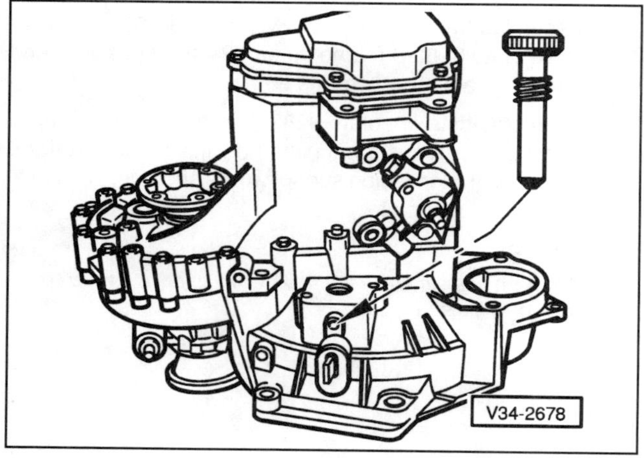

V34-2678

Fig. 34. Press clutch release lever into operating position and secure by inserting M8 x 35 bolt through bellhousing. Remove bolt once transmission is installed.

Transmission-to-engine bolt specifications and tightening torques for 4-cylinder engines are listed in **Table b**. See Fig. 35.

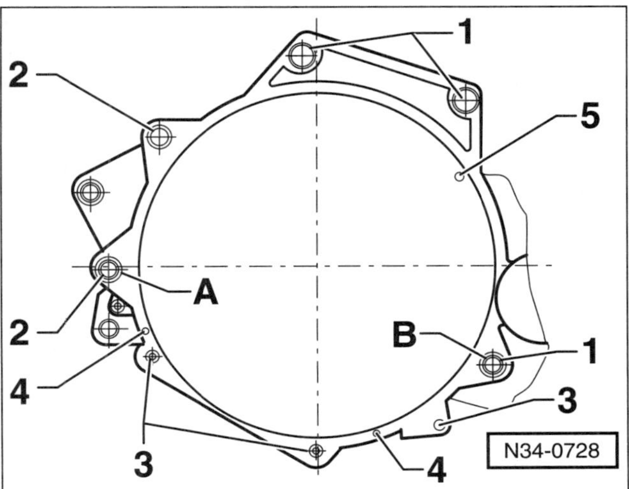

N34-0728

Fig. 35. Engine-to-transmission mounting bolt locations for 4-cylinder engines to be used in conjunction with **Table b**. Alignment dowel sleeves shown at **A** and **B**.

Table b. 4-cylinder transmission to engine fasteners

Fastener	Size	Qty.	Tightening torque
1	M12 X 55	3	80 Nm (59 ft-lb)
2*	M12 X 150	2	80 Nm (59 ft-lb)
3**	M10 X 50	3	40 Nm (30 ft-lb)
4***	M7 X 12	2	10 Nm (7 ft-lb)
5****	M7 X 12	1	10 Nm (7 ft-lb)

* Also starter to transmission
** Only on engines with an aluminum oil pan
*** Large cover plate for flywheel, only on engines with sheet steel oil pan (painted black)
**** Small cover plate for flywheel

Transmission-to-engine bolt specifications and tightening torques for 6-cylinder engines are listed in **Table c**. See Fig. 36.

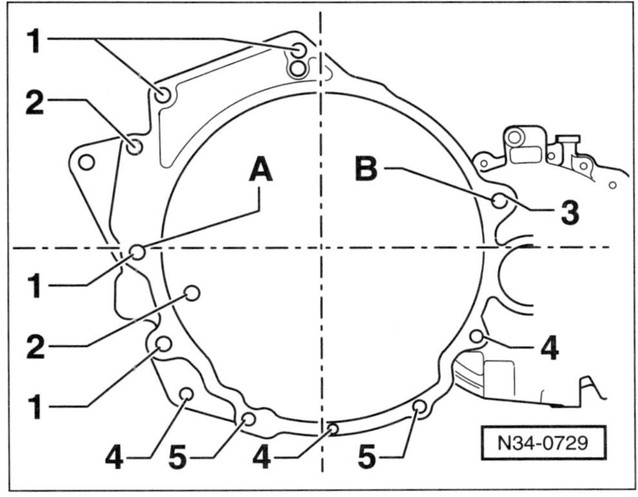

N34-0729

Fig. 36. Engine-to-transmission mounting bolt locations for 6-cylinder engines to be used in conjunction with **Table b**. Alignment dowel sleeves shown at **A** and **B**.

Table c. 6-cylinder transmission to engine fasteners

Fastener	Size	Qty.	Tightening torque
1	M12 X 55	4	80 Nm (59 ft-lb)
2*	M12 X 55	2	80 Nm (59 ft-lb)
3	M12 X 65	1	80 Nm (59 ft-lb)
4**	M10 X 60	3	40 Nm (30 ft-lb)
5***	M7 X 12	2	10 Nm (7 ft-lb)

* Also starter to transmission
** Only on engines with an aluminum oil pan, on some engines M10 x 50 bolts are installed, tighten them to 25 Nm (18 ft-lb)
*** Large cover plate for flywheel, only on engines with sheet steel oil pan (painted black)

Remaining transmission installation tightening torques are given below with corresponding Fig. # as necessary for clarification.

Tightening torques

Always replace all stretch bolts
(stretch bolts have plus ¼ turn (90°) specification)

- Transmission mount to transmission (See Fig. 27.) . . . . 50 Nm (37 ft-lb) plus ¼ turn (90°)
- Transmission to body
  - (**arrow A**, See Fig. 26.) . . . . 25 Nm (18 ft-lb)
  - (**arrow B**, See Fig. 26.) . . . . 60 Nm (44 ft-lb) plus ¼ turn (90°)
- Pendulum mount to body (**arrow A**, See Fig. 25.) . . . . 20 Nm (15 ft-lb) plus ¼ turn (90°)
- Pendulum mount bracket (**arrow B**, See Fig. 25.) . . . . 40 Nm (30 ft-lb) plus ¼ turn (90°)
- Axle shaft to axle flange. . . . . 40 Nm (30 ft-lb)
- Balance weight to transmission selector lever . . . . 25 Nm (18 ft-lb)
- Clutch slave cylinder mounting bolts . 25 Nm (18 ft-lb)
- CV joint to drive flange on transmission
  - M8. . . . . 40 Nm (30 ft-lb)
  - M10. . . . . 80 Nm (59 ft-lb)
- Drive axle boot protective cover to engine block. . . . . 35 Nm (26 ft-lb)
- Engine-to-transmission bolts, M10. . . 60 Nm (44 ft-lb)
- Engine-to-transmission bolts, M12. . . 80 Nm (59 ft-lb)
- Selector cable support bracket to transmission. . . . . 25 Nm (18 ft-lb)
- Selector cable bolt to transmission lever . . . . 25 Nm (18 ft-lb)
- Starter to transmission. . . . . 80 Nm (59 ft-lb)

Quality Review

When you have finished working under the hood and around other areas of the vehicle, it is advisable to take a moment to quality check or review your work. This helps to insure that the operation or repair has been completed properly with all affected systems functioning within normal parameters. These may include the following:

- Make sure that there are no air, vacuum or exhaust leaks.
- Make sure that all components involved in the repair are positioned correctly and function properly.
- Make sure all tools and shop cloths are removed.
- Install the engine/transmission mounts so that they are free of tension. See **10 Engine–Removing and Installing** for specific engine/transaxle installation procedures.
- Check the transmission oil level. See **0 Maintenance**.
- Adjust gear selector mechanism, see **Gear selector mechanism, adjusting**.
- Check the operation of the clutch hydraulics. See **30 Clutch**.
- Top off transmission with appropriate gear oil, see **0 Maintenance**.
- Road test vehicle and check for proper gear selection and transmission operation.

37 Automatic Transmission

TABLES

GENERAL

Cars covered by this manual with automatic transmissions are equipped with the 01M 4-speed automatic transmission. The 01M automatic transmission is controlled electro-hydraulically and features adaptive programming and On-Board Diagnostic (OBD) capabilities.

NOTE —
- *For information on drive axles, including drive flange oil seals, see* **39 Differential and Final Drive**.
- *ATF draining and filling procedures, including ATF screen (filter) replacement, is covered in* **0 Maintenance**.

CAUTION —
- *Before working on the transmission or gear selector mechanism, disconnect the negative (–) battery cable.*
- *Disconnecting the negative (–) battery cable may erase fault codes and basic settings in the engine management and automatic transmission control modules. Some driveability problems may be noticed until the system re-adapts to operating conditions. OBD II readiness codes, which may be required for emissions testing, may also be erased. Convenience electronics (alarm system, interior light control, power locks, mirrors, and windows) will need to be re-set using a VAG 1551/1552 or equivalent scan tool.*

Transmission code location

The transmission code and production number can be found stamped on the transmission case near the Automatic Transmission Fluid (ATF) cooler. See illustration below. The transmission code letters can also be found on the vehicle data plate.

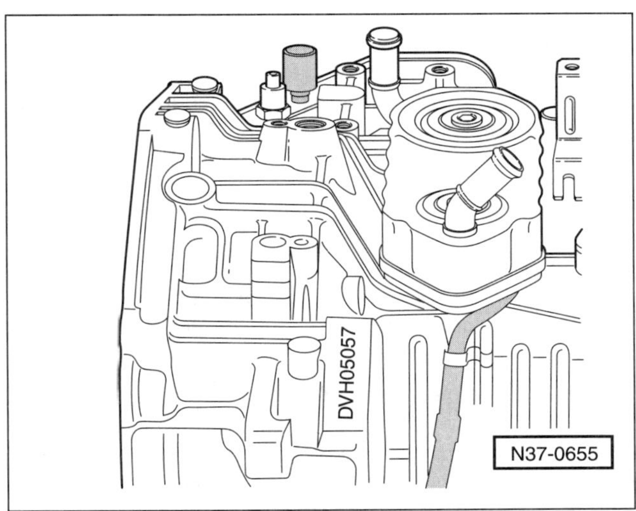

N37-0655

Transmission code letters and date of manufacture. Example above is a code **DVH**, manufactured on the 5th (**05**) day of the 5th (**05**) month in 199**7**.

Table a lists the engine applications, gear ratios, and other data for the various automatic transmissions.

Table a. 01M automatic transmission specifications

Code letters		ELU, EPL, FDC	ECN, ELT, EPB, FDB	ECV, ELY, EPG, FDF	ECM, ENZ, EPJ, FCZ
Engine application		1.8L, 150hp	1.9L, 90hp	2.0L, 115hp	2.8L, 174hp
Ratio:	Final drive	4.533	3.700	4.875	4.267
	Intermediate drive	0.978	0.978	1.033	0.978
	1st gear	2.714	2.714	2.714	2.714
	2nd gear	1.441	1.441	1.551	1.441
	3rd gear	1.000	1.000	1.000	1.000
	4th gear	0.742	0.742	0.679	0.742
	Reverse	2.884	2.884	2.111	2.884
Torque converter code		QCDC	QCDC	QADC, QBDC	QCDR, QDDT
Valve body code		QFB, QEB,			
Trans. Lubricant	Initial filling	5.3 Liters (5.6 qt.)			
	Oil change	approx. 3.0 Liters (3.2 qt.)			
	Specification	VW ATF			
Final drive lubricant	Initial filling	0.75 Liters (0.8 qt.)			
	Oil change	Filled for life, no change			
	Specification	Synthetic oil, SAE 75/90W			
Drive shaft		tripodic			

BASIC SETTINGS

The automatic Transmission Control Module (TCM) and the Engine Control Module (ECM) share data concerning engine and transmission operation. One piece of data that the TCM may not always "know" is the full throttle position. This is known as a basic setting. The basic setting influences automatic transmission shifting and is set at the time that the vehicle is new. The basic setting will be lost if the battery is disconnected or runs down, or if the TCM is disconnected. It will change if the TCM or the throttle control module is replaced. In these circumstances, the basic settings must be restored to insure proper automatic transmission operation.

Basic settings, restoring

Basic settings can be restored using a suitable scan tool and following the manufacturer's instructions or by using the procedure outlined below. In either case, the kickdown switch on the accelerator cable must function properly.

1. Switch on the ignition but do not start the engine.

2. Push the accelerator pedal all the way to the floor and hold it there for a minimum of 5 seconds.

NOTE —
Be sure that floor mats do not prevent the accelerator pedal from being completely depressed.

3. Release the accelerator pedal and switch off the ignition.

Basic requirements

1. Check that the ATF level is correct. Check that fluid is clean and of correct type. See **0 Maintenance**.

CAUTION —
The 01M transmission uses a special VW-only ATF. If the fluid was changed, check to make sure that the correct fluid was installed. VW ATF is yellowish in color.

2. Make a visual check of the components shown in Fig. 1. Check the wiring and harness connectors for loose, damaged or corroded wiring. Check that all related grounds are firmly connected and in good condition. Consult the wiring diagrams shown in **97 Wiring Diagrams, Fuses and Relays**.

3. Check the shift mechanism for proper function. See **Shift Mechanism**.

4. Review the list given below.
   - Engine control module (ECM) replaced
   - New, reconditioned, or used engine installed
   - New or altered/adjusted throttle housing
   - New or altered/adjusted throttle position sensor
   - Transmission control module (TCM) replaced

If any of the above conditions are met, the TCM must be reset to its "basic settings" using the VAG 1551/1552 scan tool or the procedure described above. If the TCM basic settings are not re-established, driveability problems may be encountered.

5. If no faults are found up to this point, the next logical step is to have an authorized VW dealer check for faults using the special VW scan tool, VAG 1551 or 1552. If the transmission problem is electrical/electronic in nature, specific DTCs will most likely be stored in memory.

NOTE —
- *Volkswagen identifies electrical components by a letter/number code in the electrical schematics. These component codes are given in the numbered list below as an aid in using the wiring diagrams. See* **97 Wiring Diagrams, Fuses, and Relays**.
- *If engine or transmission control modules are replaced, the system must be returned to basic setting.*

Automatic transmission electronic/electrical components

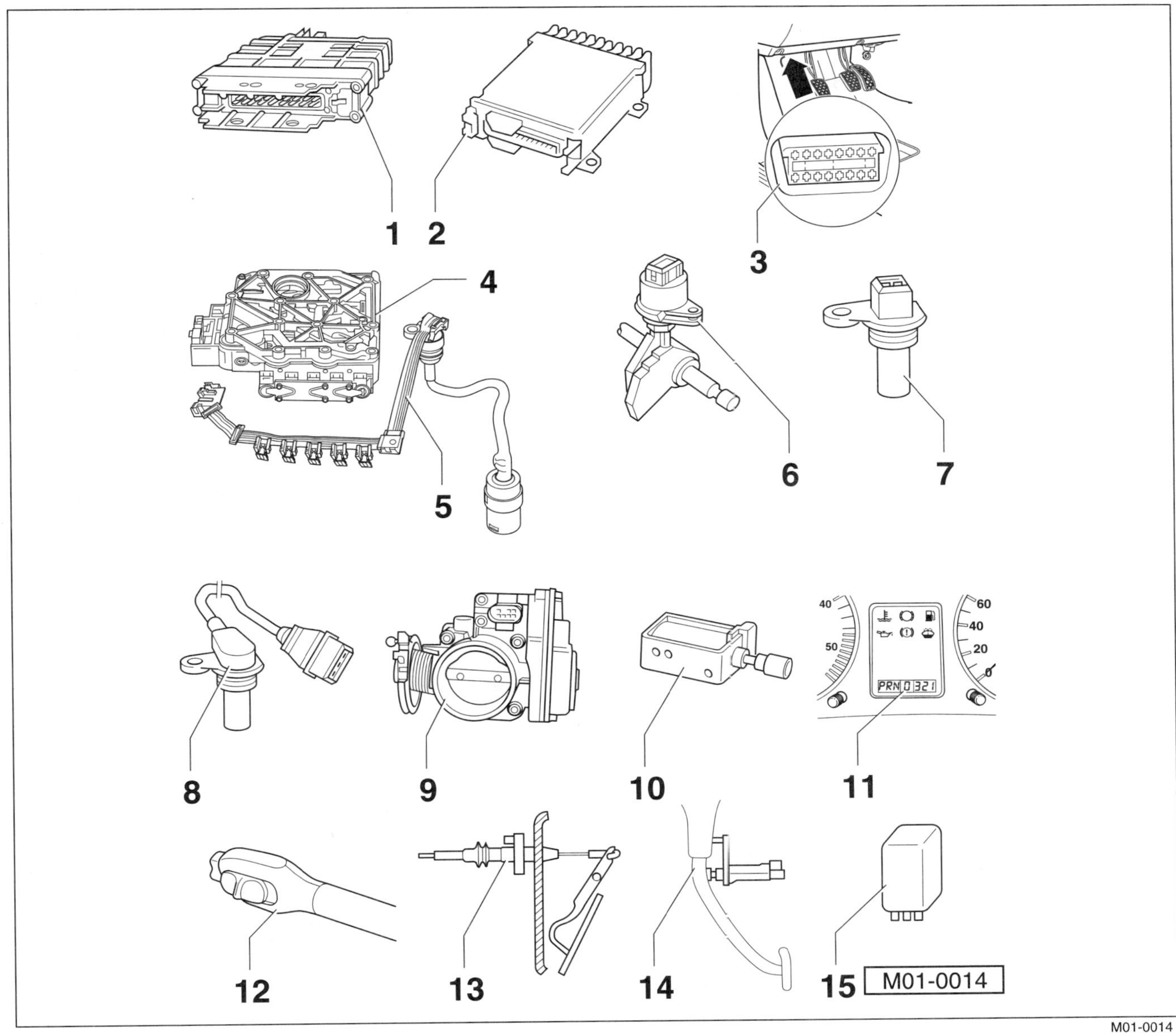

Fig. 1. Electrical/electronic components for automatic transmission.

1. **Transmission control module (J217)**
   - Located in center/right plenum
   - Factory coded, no user changes possible
   - Removing, **see** (A)
2. **Engine control module**
   - Located in center plenum
   - Removing and installing, see **23 Fuel Injection–Diesel (ALH engine)** or **24 Fuel Injection–Motronic** (for appropriate engine)
3. **Data Link Connector (DLC)**
   - Located under dashboard on driver's side
4. **Valve body**
   - Located above oil pan
   - Solenoid valves (N88, N89, N90, N91, N92, N93, N94) are attached to the valve body
   - Valves are checked by On-Board Diagnostics (OBD)
5. **Conductor strip with integrated transmission fluid temperature sensor (G93)**
   - Located in oil pan, on valve body
   - Checked by OBD
   - Can be replaced without removing valve body or transmission

(continued on following page)

(continued from previous page)

6. **Multi-function transmission range switch (F125)**
   - Removing and installing, **see** (B)
   - Checked by OBD
7. **Transmission vehicle speed sensor (G38)**
   - Located on top of transmission
   - Removing and installing, **see** (C)
   - Checked by OBD
8. **Vehicle speed sensor (G68)**
   - Location, removing and installing **see** (E)
   - Checked by OBD
9. **Throttle position sensor (G69)**
   - Checked by OBD
   - Gasoline engines: located on throttle valve housing, part of throttle valve control module (J338)
   - Diesel engines: throttle valve signal is generated in the throttle position sensor (G79) located near accelerator pedal
   - Function, **see** (D)
10. **Shift lock solenoid (N110)**
    - Location, see **Shift mechanism, assembly**
    - Checked by OBD
11. **Transmission range selector lever display (Y5)**
    - Located in instrument cluster
12. **Cruise control switch (E45)**
13. **Kick down switch (F8)**
    - Engines with accelerator cable (gasoline): kickdown switch is integrated into cable and located on bulkhead in engine compartment
    - Engines without accelerator cable (diesel): kickdown signal is generated in the throttle position sensor (G79) located near accelerator pedal
14. **Brake light switch (F)**
    - Located on pedal cluster
15. **Park/Neutral Position (PNP) relay (J226)**
    - Located on additional relay panel under instrument panel, left side
    - Marked with number "175"

(A) Transmission control module (TCM), removing

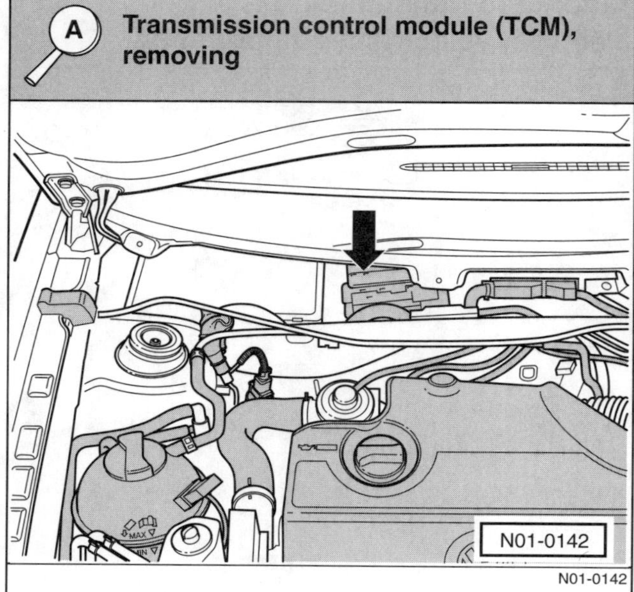

N01-0142

- **Switch off ignition.**
- **Remove wiper arms, rubber plenum seal, and inner plenum cover.**
- **Release multi-pin connector lock and slide connector off toward center of vehicle.**
- **Remove TCM mounting screws that are below connector.**

(B) Multi-function transmission range switch, removing and installing

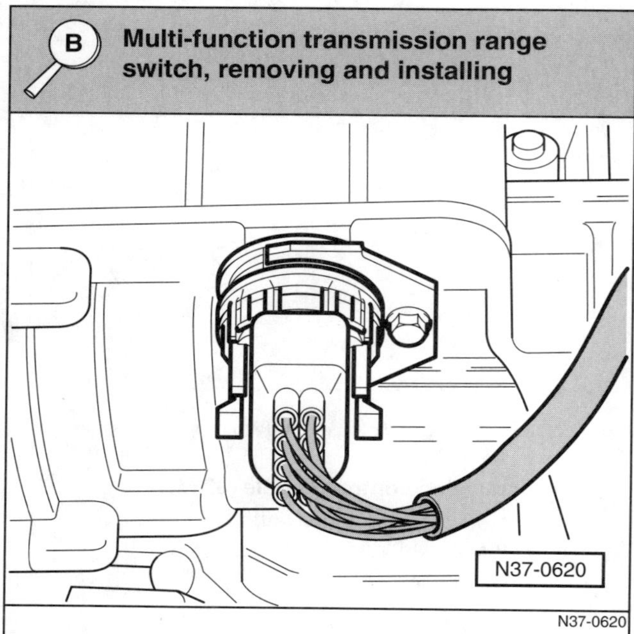

N37-0620

- **Switch off ignition, remove harness connector, bolt, and retaining bracket.**
- **When installing, replace seal.**
- **Tighten retaining clamp bolt to 10 Nm (7 ft-lb).**

C Transmission vehicle speed sensor, removing and installing

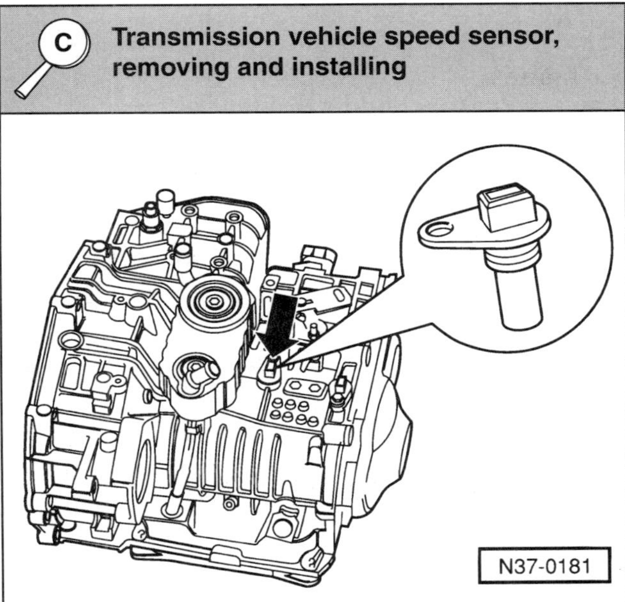

N37-0181

- Switch off ignition, remove harness connector and retaining bolt.
- When installing, replace seal.
- Tighten retaining clamp bolt to 10 Nm (7 ft-lb).

D Throttle position (TP) sensor, function

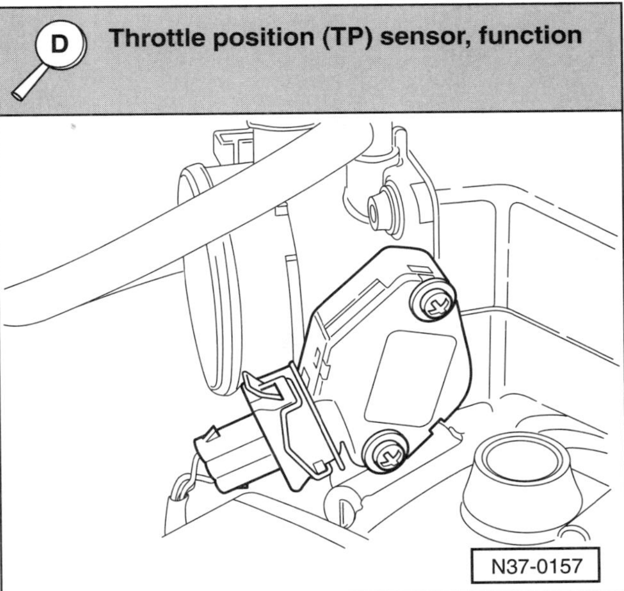

N37-0157

- Sends signal to engine control module which sends signal to the transmission control module.
- On vehicles with CAN-bus system, the TCM receives the TP signal from the CAN-bus.
- On vehicles without CAN-bus, the signal is made available via a wire from the engine control module.
- The on-board diagnostics of the transmission only checks the signal, not the TP sensor. On vehicles without CAN-bus the wire for the signal is also checked.

E Vehicle speed sensor, removing and installing

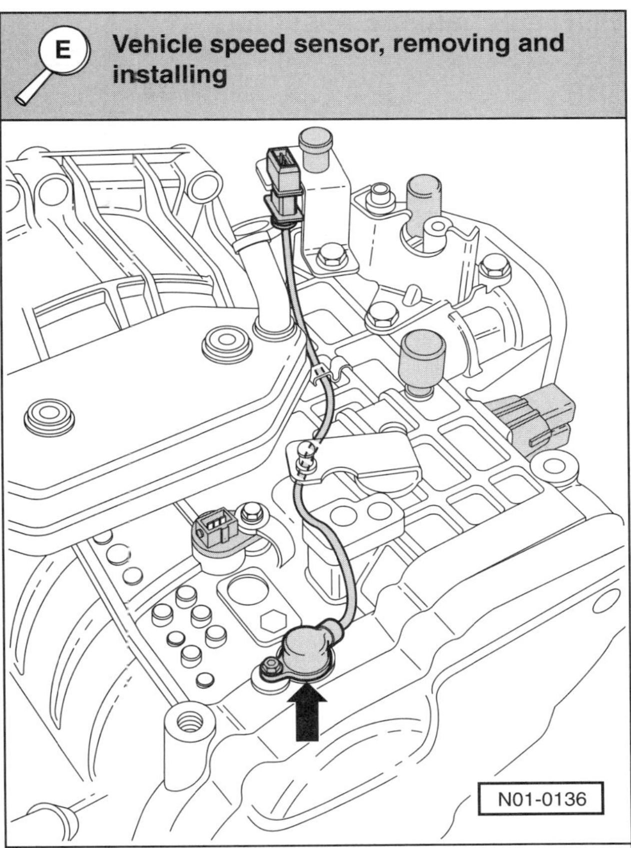

N01-0136

- When transmission is installed the sensor is covered by left transmission mount.
- Transmission must be unbolted from mounts and lowered approximately 2.5 in. to access sensor, see Transmission, Removing and Installing, given later.
- Disconnect harness connector from sensor and remove sensor retaining bolt.
- When installing, replace seal.
- Tighten retaining bolt to 10 Nm (7 ft-lb).

SHIFT MECHANISM

The selector lever handle and shift mechanism components are shown in Fig. 2.

Shift mechanism, assembly

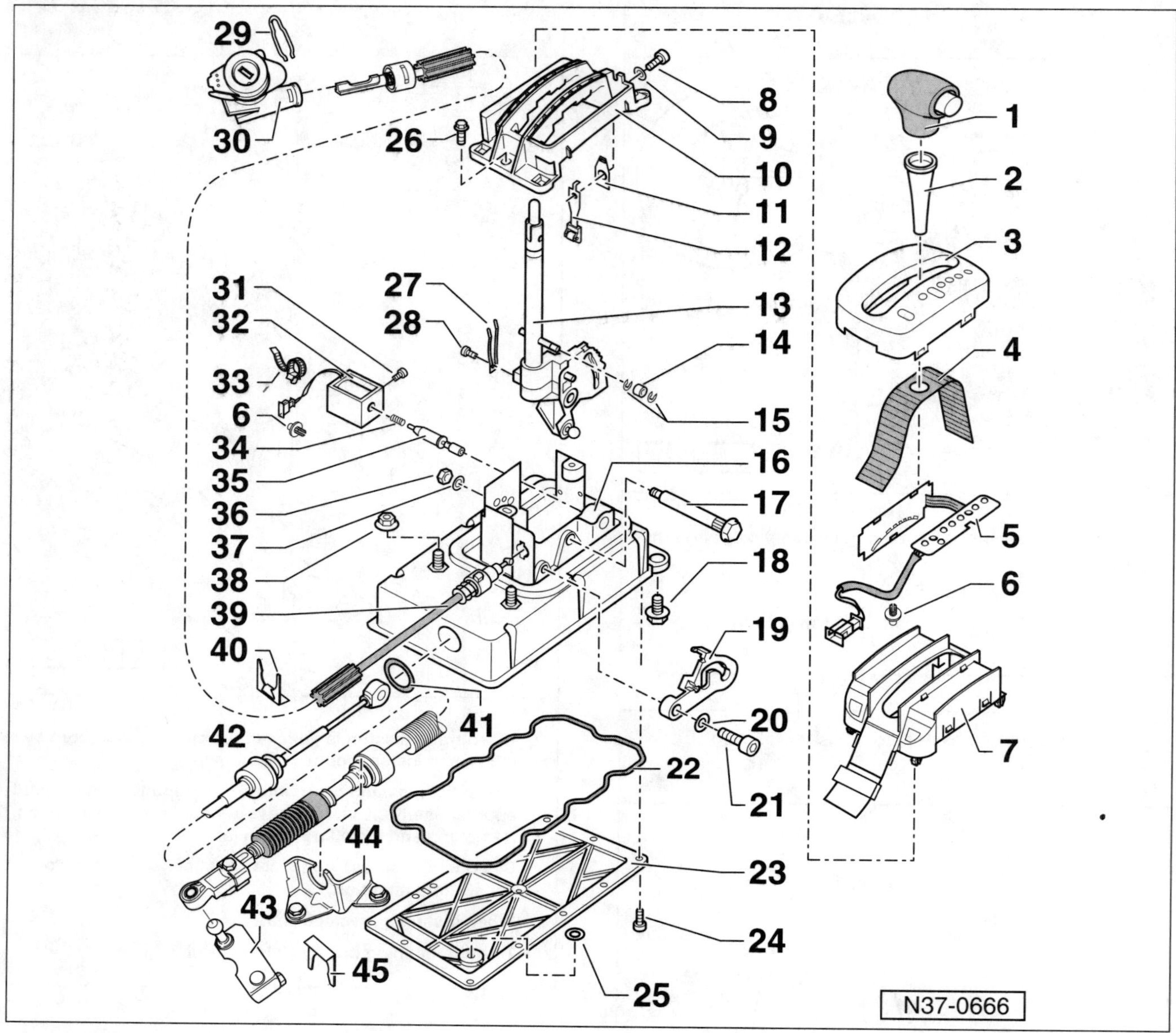

N37-0666

Fig. 2. Shift mechanism for automatic transmission.

NOTE —

Lubricate mounting points and contact surfaces with grease (VW part no. G 052 142 A2).

1. **Selector lever handle**
   - Removing: push sleeve (item 2) down and while depressing knob, remove handle upward
   - Installing: while depressing knob, install handle until lock engages. Push sleeve up to lock.
2. **Sleeve**
   - Locks selector lever handle
   - Prevents selector lever handle from being pulled off
3. **Cover**
   - With selector indicator
   - Snapped into bracket (item 7)
4. **Cover strip**
   - Insert in bracket (item 7)
5. **Selector lever position display**
   - Printed circuit for selector lever position illuminated display is held in position by clips
6. **Retainer**
   - To position connector in bracket (item 7)

(continued from previous page)

7. **Bracket**
   - Carefully pry off at corners
   - Push into cover strip (item 4)
   - Installation position: ribs must face down
   - Carefully position printed circuits and wiring (item 5)
   - When installing be careful not to damage contact springs (item 27) for selector lever position display

8. **Bolt**
   - Tighten to 7 Nm (62 in-lb)
   - Attaches locating spring (item 12) and plate (item 11) to bracket (item 7)

9. **Washer**

10. **Locking segment**
    - Place on centering elements of selector lever housing

11. **Plate**

12. **Locating spring with roller**
    - Engages in detent in selector lever

13. **Selector lever**
    - With pull rod, spring, detent, contact spring for selector lever position and locking cable release

14. **Roller**
    - For releasing locking cable

15. **Circlip**

16. **Selector lever housing**
    - Does not need not be removed to replace most individual parts, with the exception of selector lever and shift lock solenoid

17. **Splined fulcrum pin**
    - Apply grease to shank
    - Do not turn when installing selector lever

18. **Bolt**
    - Tighten to 25 Nm (18 ft-lb)

19. **Locking lever**
    - For locking cable
    - For locking selector lever in "**P**"

20. **Washer**

21. **Bolt**

22. **Gasket**
    - Always replace

23. **Cover**
    - For selector lever housing

24. **Bolt (qty. 14)**

25. **O-ring**
    - Always replace

26. **Bolt (qty. 2)**
    - Tighten to 8 Nm (71 in-lb)

27. **Contact spring**
    - For selector lever position display

28. **Bolt**
    - Tighten to 4 Nm (35 in-lb)
    - Place selector lever in "**P**" to loosen and tighten

29. **Clip**

30. **Steering lock**

31. **Bolt (qty. 2)**
    - Attaches solenoid to selector lever housing

32. **Shift lock solenoid (N110)**
    - Checked via OBD
    - Remove/install only with selector lever in position "**1**"
    - Look out for spring and locking pin when removing
    - Install together with locking pin and spring while moving selector lever slightly back and forth

33. **Cable tie**
    - Attaches wiring/solenoid to selector lever housing
    - Always replace

34. **Spring**

35. **Locking pin**

36. **Nut**
    - Tighten to 13 Nm (10 ft-lb)
    - Always replace

37. **Washer**

38. **Nut (qty. 2)**
    - Tighten to 25 Nm (18 ft-lb)
    - Always replace

39. **Shift-lock cable**
    - Do not kink
    - See **Automatic Shift Lock**, given later

40. **Clip**
    - Always replace
    - Mounts selector lever cable to selector lever housing
    - Install angled end toward inside of selector housing

41. **Gasket**
    - Always replace

42. **Selector lever cable**
    - Do not bend or kink
    - If outer cable sleeve is damaged, replace selector lever cable.
    - Lightly grease ball socket and cable ends before installing

43. **Lever**
    - For selector shaft

44. **Support bracket**
    - For mounting selector lever cable on transmission

45. **Clip**
    - Always replace

Selector lever cable, checking and adjusting

1. Switch ignition off and set parking brake.
2. Open hood and locate selector lever cable and selector shaft lever on transmission.
3. Remove selector cable retaining clip from support bracket at transmission. See Fig. 3.

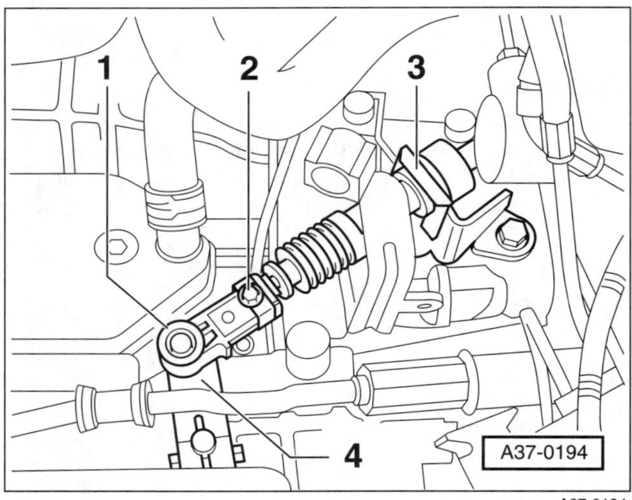

A37-0194

Fig. 3. Selector lever cable (**1**), adjustment bolt (**2**), retaining clip (**3**), selector shaft lever (**4**) on 01M automatic transmission.

4. Use a screwdriver to pry selector lever cable off selector shaft lever and move cable aside so that the end is free to move.
5. Move selector lever from "**P**" to "**1**" and check that shift mechanism and selector lever cable move freely. If necessary replace selector lever cable or service shift mechanism.
6. Check protective bellows at front of selector cable for damage. If protective bellow is damaged, replace selector cable.
7. To adjust cable, install retaining clip and selector lever cable on selector shaft lever. Move selector lever to "**P**".
8. Loosen adjustment bolt. See Fig. 3.
9. Place selector shaft lever into position "**P**" on transmission then tighten adjustment bolt. Shift through all gear positions and check for smooth operation.

NOTE —
*With selector lever in "**P**" position, the transmission locking lever must engage, locking both front wheels.*

Tightening torque
- Selector lever adjustment bolt . . . . 8 Nm (71 in-lb)

AUTOMATIC SHIFT LOCK

Automatic shift-lock is used on cars with automatic transmission. Turning the ignition key on and off operates a bowden cable to lock and unlock the selector lever. See Fig. 4.

When the key is turned to the off position (shift lever in **P**), the cable pushes the stop lever into the shift lever. This locks the lever button and also allows the ignition key to be withdrawn from the lock cylinder. The key can only be removed from the ignition with the lever in the "**P**" position. With the key out of the ignition, the selector lever cannot be shifted out of "**P**" position.

When the key is in the **ON** position, the cable pulls the stop lever away from the shift lever, allowing the shift lever to be moved out of park.

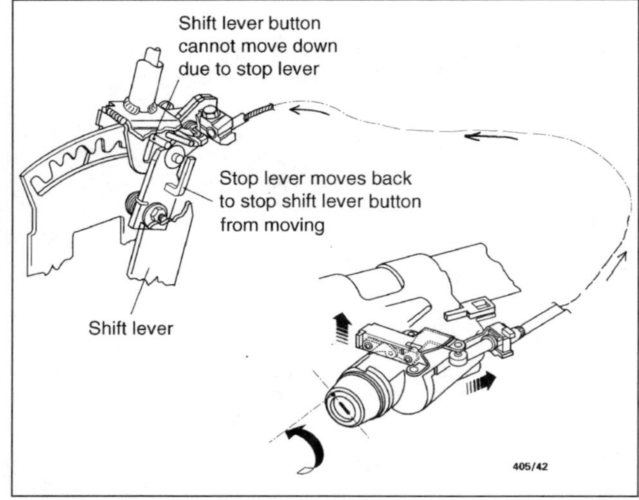

405/42

Fig. 4. Automatic shift lock shown in the "key-off" position.

Shift-lock cable, removing and installing

The shift-lock cable is routed through the dashboard and under the center console. Be sure to route the cable correctly when installing. See Fig. 5.

1. Disconnect battery ground (GND) strap from battery negative (–) terminal. See the **Cautions** at the beginning of this repair group regarding battery disconnection.

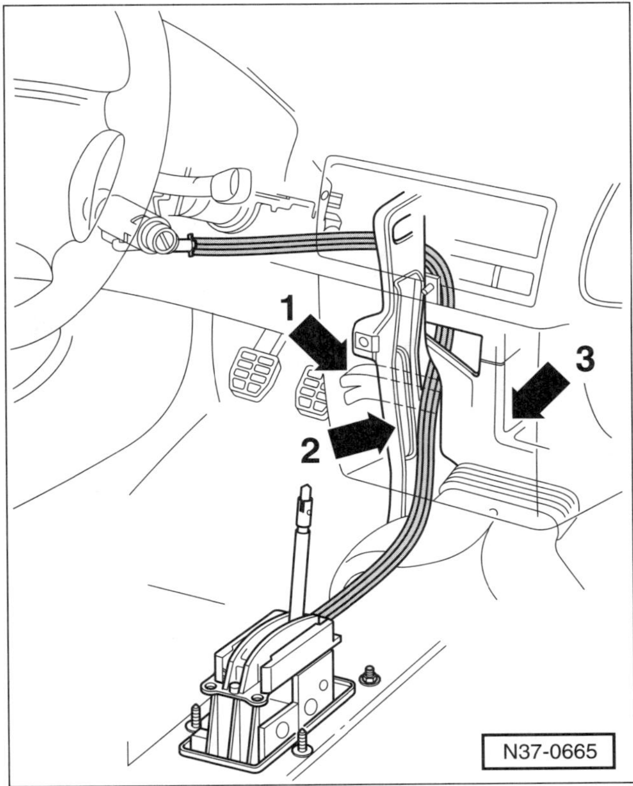

N37-0665

Fig. 5. Installation position of shift-lock cable showing footwell vents (**1**), instrument panel support (**2**), and heater unit (**3**).

NOTE —
Be sure to have the anti-theft radio code on hand before disconnecting the battery.

2. Remove steering wheel, handle for steering height and reach adjustment and cover for ignition/starter lock, see **48 Steering**.

3. Turn ignition **ON** and move selector lever to "**P**".

4. Remove shift-lock cable clip and pull cable out of ignition/steering lock assembly. See Fig. 6.

5. Push down sleeve on selector lever handle.

6. While depressing knob, remove selector lever handle by pulling upward.

7. Remove center console and extension, see **70 Trim–Interior**.

8. Disconnect shift-lock cable from locking lever at selector mechanism.

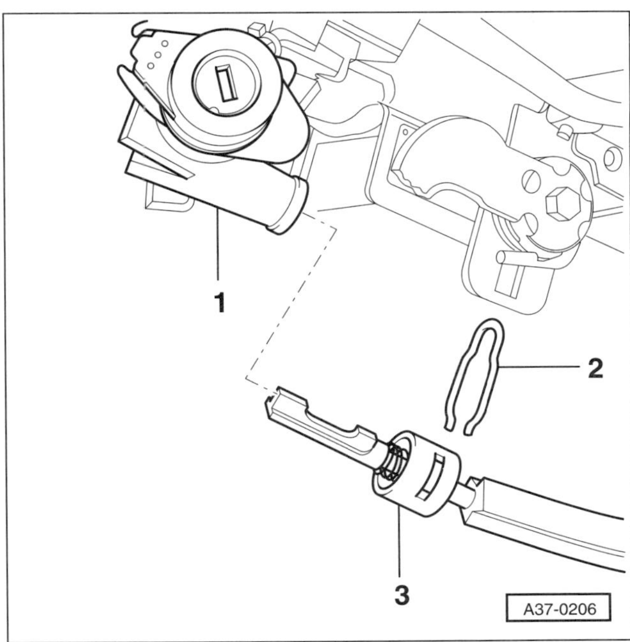

A37-0206

Fig. 6. Remove clip (**2**) for shift-lock cable (**3**) and pull out of steering lock (**1**).

9. Press tabs of shift lock cable retaining clip together and pull locking cable out of selector mechanism. See arrows in Fig. 7.

10. To install, move selector lever to "**P**".

CAUTION —
- *Be sure to route cable correctly when installing.*
- *Do not kink cable.*
- *Be sure to adjust cable after installation.*

11. Press shift-lock cable into support bracket on selector lever housing until tabs on retaining clip spread. See arrows in Fig. 7.

12. Attach locking cable in locking lever.

13. Turn ignition **ON**.

14. Push locking cable into ignition/steering lock assembly.

15. Install clip onto cable.

NOTE —
Be sure that clip is properly located.

Shift-lock cable, adjusting

> ***CAUTION —***
> *Follow the adjustment procedure exactly as outlined.*

1. Remove ignition key.
2. Remove center console and extension, see **70 Trim–Interior**.
3. Working at center console, slide cable sleeve forward and release clip by pushing up. See Fig. 7.

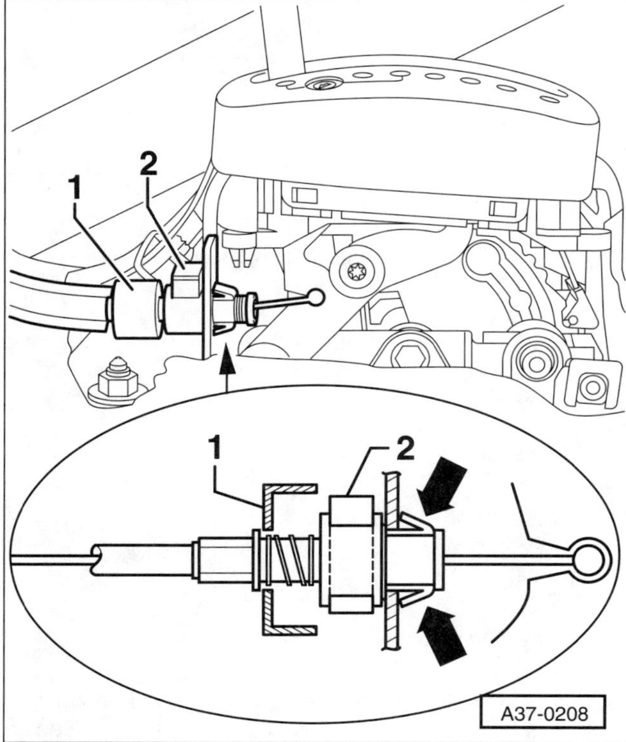

A37-0208

Fig. 7. Slide sleeve (**1**) forward and release clip (**2**) by pushing up. **Arrows** are for removal and installation of shift-lock cable clip.

4. Remove harness connector at rear of selector lever housing. Remove selector lever sleeve and selector lever housing. Carefully pry up at four corners of shift lever bracket and remove. See Fig. 8.

> ***NOTE —***
> *Be careful not to damage contact spring for shift lever position indicator.*

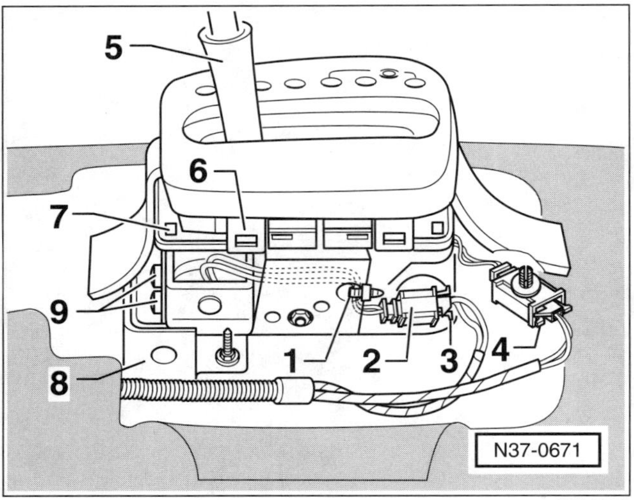

N37-0671

Fig. 8. Remove connector (**4**), pull sleeve (**5**) up, release housing at retaining tabs (**6**), and pry off bracket at corners (**7**).

5. Slide 0.8 mm feeler gauge between locking lever and selector lever roller.
6. Pull outer sleeve of shift-lock cable slightly forward in direction of travel and push red clip down until it engages. See Fig. 9.

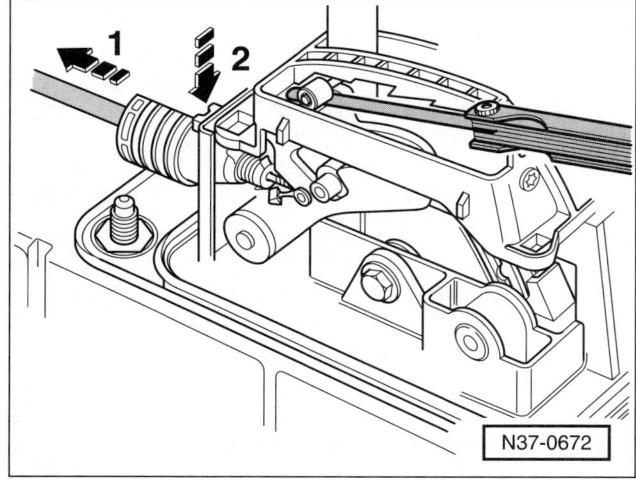

N37-0672

Fig. 9. Slide 0.8 mm feeler gauge between locking lever and selector lever roller. Pull shift-lock cable outer sleeve forward slightly (**1**) and push clip down (**2**) until it engages.

7. Push sliding sleeve over clip.
8. Check for proper ignition key removal.
9. Replace center console and extension.

TRANSMISSION, REMOVING AND INSTALLING

This procedure describes the removal and installation of the automatic transmission. Special engine lifting and jacking equipment is needed to support and reposition the engine as the transmission is removed from below.

Volkswagen recommended special tools
- VW 457/1 support rails
- 10-222A transmission support kit
- 3094 hose clamps
- 3282 transmission support
- 3282/2 adjustment plate
- 3300A engine support
- 3336 transmission lifting beam
- VAG 1331 torque wrench
- VAG 1332 torque wrench
- VAG 1383A engine/transmission jack
- V/175 socket

Special tools, modifying

One of the Volkswagen recommended special tools will need to be modified as follows. To secure support rail VW 457/1 to the subframe a new hole is required. See Fig. 10.

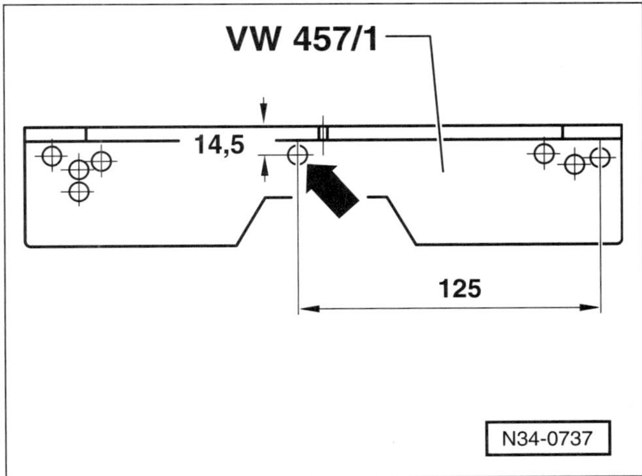

Fig. 10. Drill an 8.5 mm (0.335 in.) diameter hole (**arrow**) in VW 457/1 support rail. Dimensions are provided in mm.

Transmission, removing

1. Remove engine cover.

2. Disconnect battery ground (GND) strap from battery negative (–) terminal. See the **Cautions** at the beginning of this repair group regarding battery disconnection.

   NOTE —
   Be sure to have the anti-theft radio code on hand before disconnecting the battery.

3. Disconnect battery positive (+) cable and remove battery and battery tray. See **27 Engine Electrical**.

4. Remove intake hose and harness connector from Mass Air Flow (MAF) sensor.

5. Remove vacuum hose to air cleaner near MAF sensor.

6. Remove air cleaner mounting bolts and pull out air cleaner housing. See Fig. 11.

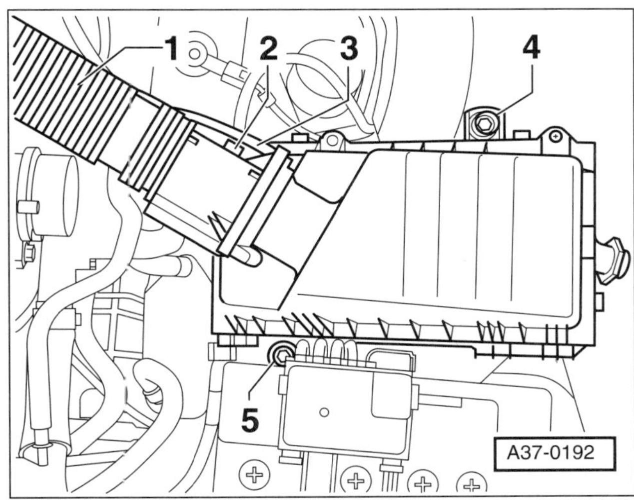

Fig. 11. Remove intake air hose (**1**), harness connector (**2**), and air cleaner mounting bolts (**3**, **4**).

7. Disconnect harness connector for solenoid valves, vehicle speed sensor, multi-function transmission range sensor, and transmission vehicle speed sensor. See Fig. 12.

8. Remove wiring harness from retainer on transmission and move aside.

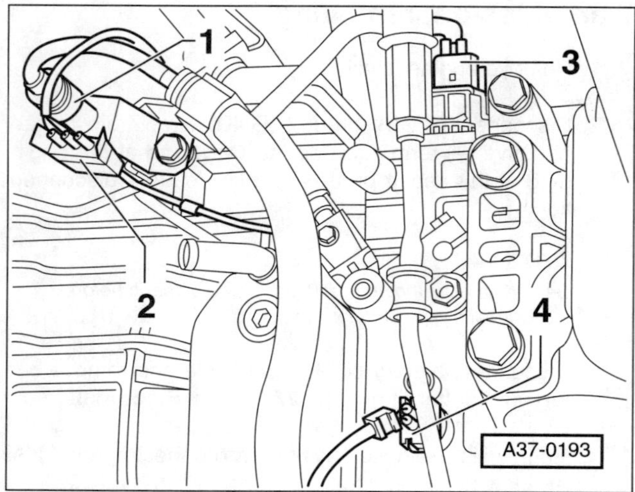

A37-0193

Fig. 12. Harness connectors for solenoid valves (**1**), vehicle speed sensor (**2**), multi-function transmission range switch (**3**), and transmission vehicle speed sensor (**4**) to be disconnected from transmission.

9. Remove bracket for power steering hose with retainer for wiring harness from transmission.

10. Move selector lever to "**P**". Using a screwdriver, pry selector lever cable off selector shaft lever.

11. Remove clip at selector lever cable support bracket and remove selector lever cable. See Fig. 13.

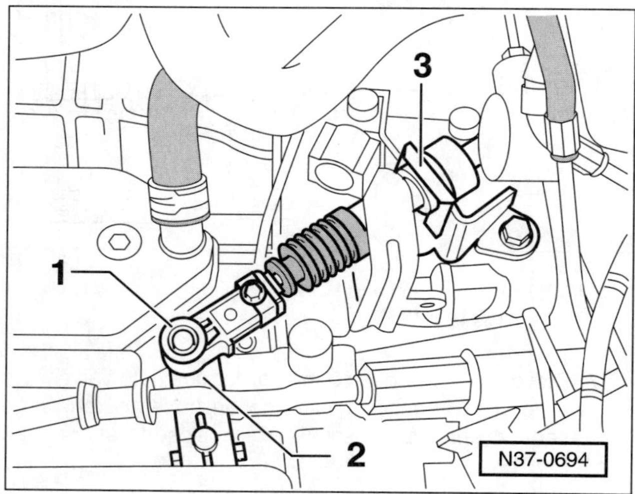

N37-0694

Fig. 13. Pry selector lever cable (**1**) off lever/selector shaft lever (**2**). Remove clip (**3**) and selector lever cable.

NOTE —

Do not kink selector lever cable.

12. For all vehicles, disconnect ground cable from upper engine/transmission bolt, electrical connections at starter motor and harness connector on top of starter motor. See Fig. 14.

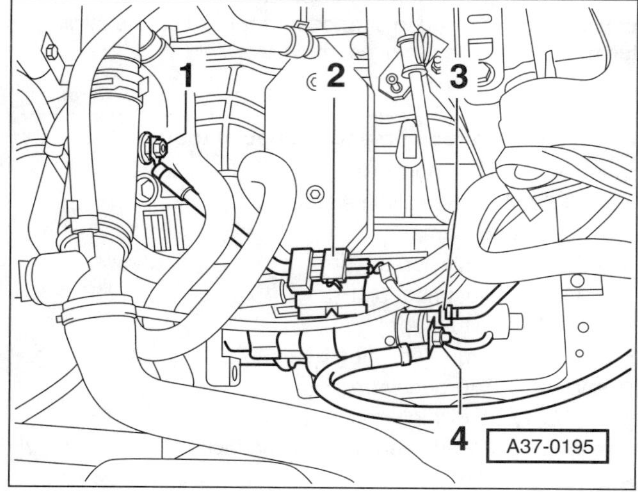

A37-0195

Fig. 14. Disconnect ground cable (**1**) from upper engine/transmission bolt, electrical connections at starter motor (**3** and **4**), and harness connector on top of starter motor (**2**).

13. Pull harness connector out of retainer on top of starter motor and remove retainer.

14. Remove upper starter mounting bolt.

15. Clamp-off ATF cooler hoses and detach at ATF cooler. Seal ATF cooler with clean plugs. See Fig. 15.

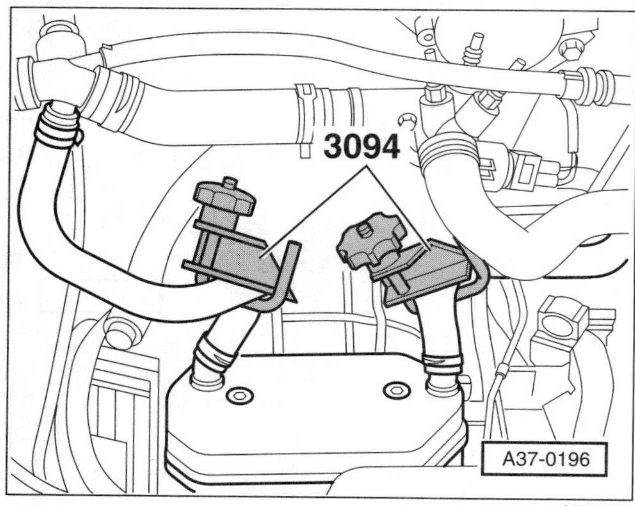

A37-0196

Fig. 15. Volkswagen special tool 3094 being used to clamp off ATF hoses.

16. Remove upper engine/transmission bolts.

17. Attach engine lifting equipment (VW sling 10-222A with appropriate adapters and legs as shown below). Adjust the lifting sling until the weight of the engine is fully supported. For 4-cylinder vehicles see Fig. 16. For 6-cylinder vehicles Fig. 17.

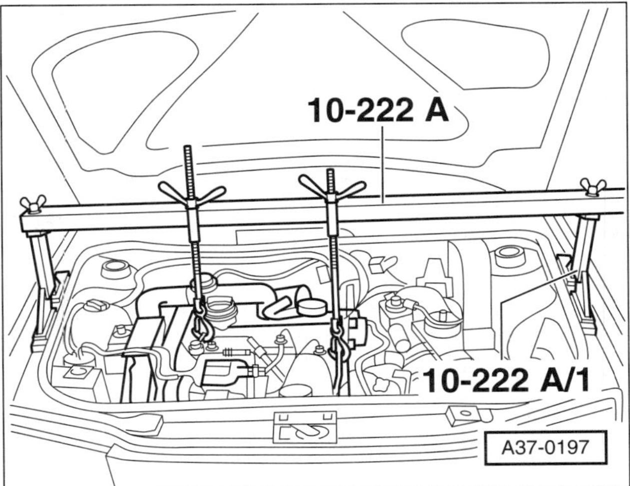

A37-0197

Fig. 16. Engine lifting equipment used to support weight of 4-cylinder engine. Numbers shown are for VW special tools.

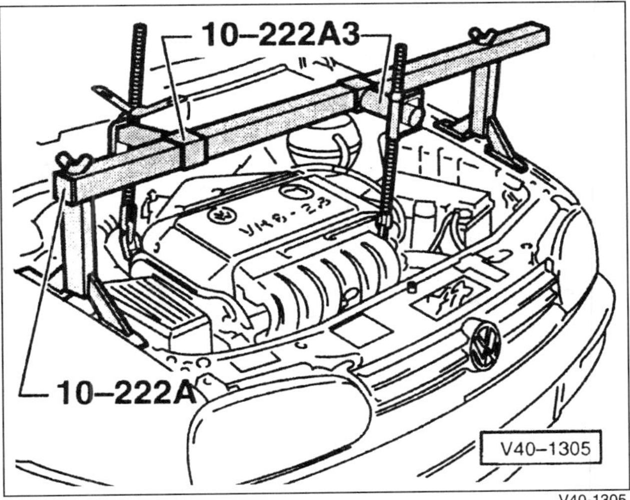

V40-1305

Fig. 17. Engine lifting equipment used to support weight of 6-cylinder engine. Numbers shown are for VW special tools.

> ***CAUTION —***
> - *Before installing the engine lifting hooks, disconnect all hoses and wiring in the vicinity of the engine lifting eyes, to prevent damage.*
> - *Do not position engine sling legs on the fender mounting bolts.*

18. Loosen left front wheel bolts.

19. Raise car and support with jack stands or lift. See **0 Maintenance** for proper lifting procedure.

> ***WARNING —***
> *Observe all warnings and cautions associated with lifting vehicle in* **0 Maintenance**.

20. Remove left front wheel.

21. Remove lower sound absorber panels (belly pans). See Fig. 18.

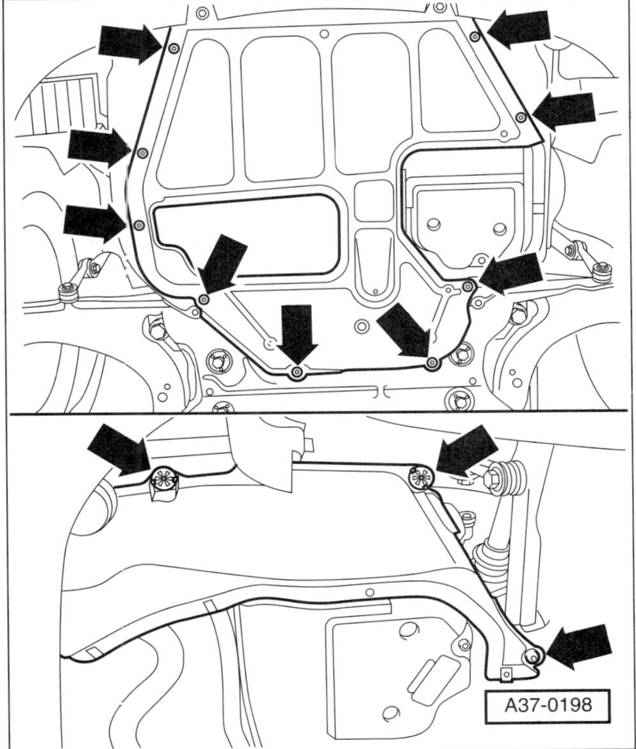

A37-0198

Fig. 18. Remove screws (**arrows**) for belly pan.

> ***NOTE —***
> *Sound insulator fasteners may best be removed and installed with needle nose pliers.*

22. On vehicles with 1.9L TDI engine, remove intake air duct between intake air cooler and turbocharger, see **21 Turbocharger and Intercooler**.

23. Remove ATF pan protective cover. See Fig. 19.

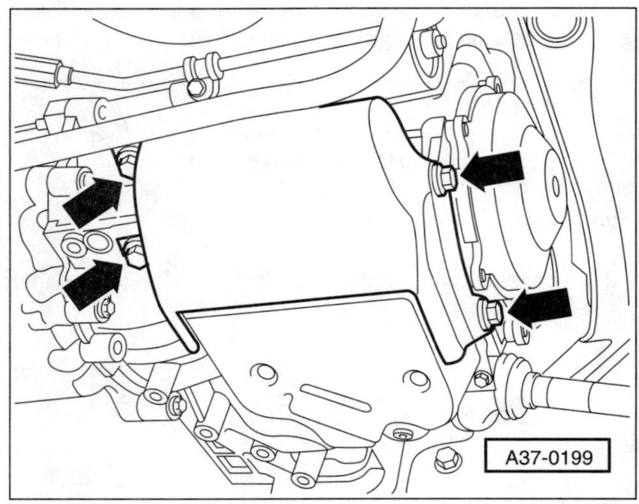

A37-0199

Fig. 19. Unbolt ATF pan protective cover (**arrows**).

24. Remove bracket for power steering line near starter lower mounting bolt. Remove starter lower mounting bolt and starter. See Fig. 20.

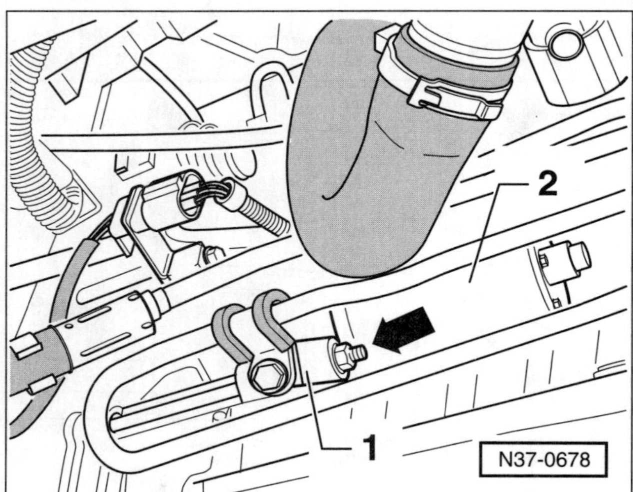

N37-0678

Fig. 20. Remove bracket (**1**) for power steering line and lower starter bolt (**arrow**). Remove starter (**2**).

NOTE—

Use care not to damage the power steering line.

25. Remove right inner drive axle boot protective cover from engine, if installed. See Fig. 21.

26. Disconnect drive shafts from transmission flanges and tie up as high as possible.

NOTE—

When tying up axle shafts use care not to damage the paint on the body panels or the axle boots.

0024260

Fig. 21. Remove bolts (**arrows**) for drive axle boot protective cover.

27. Remove bolts for pendulum mount. See Fig. 22.

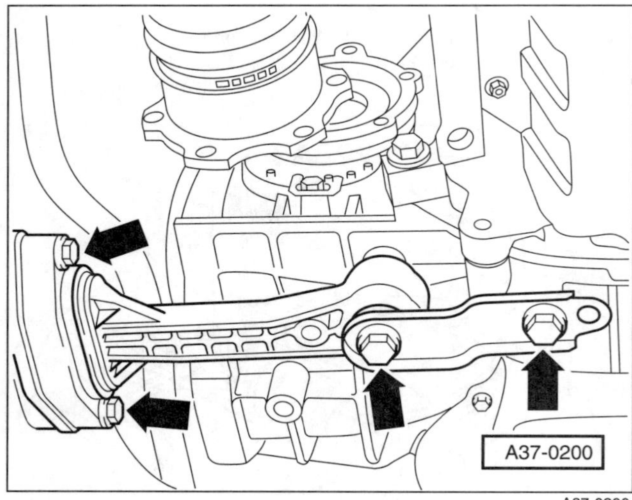

A37-0200

Fig. 22. Remove pendulum mounting bolts (**arrows**).

28. Remove caps for torque converter nuts.

29. Remove torque converter nuts (qty. 3) with special socket (V/175 or equivalent). See Fig. 23.

NOTE—

Turn crankshaft 120° to access each nut.

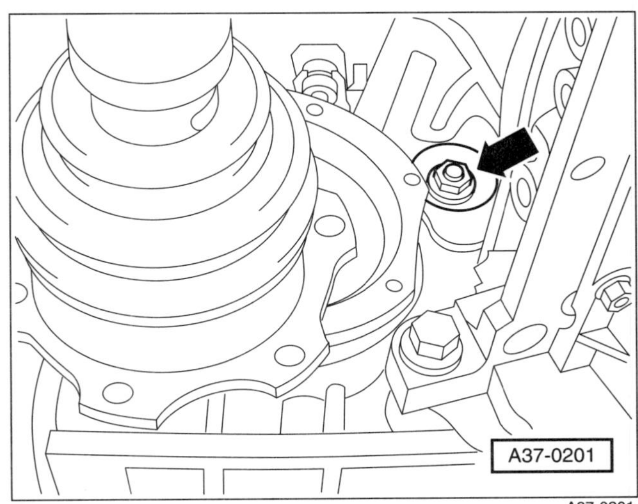

Fig. 23. Remove torque converter nuts (**arrow**).

30. Turn steering fully to left.

31. Mark installation position of ball joint bolts on left control arm.

32. Remove left control arm bolts. See Fig. 24.

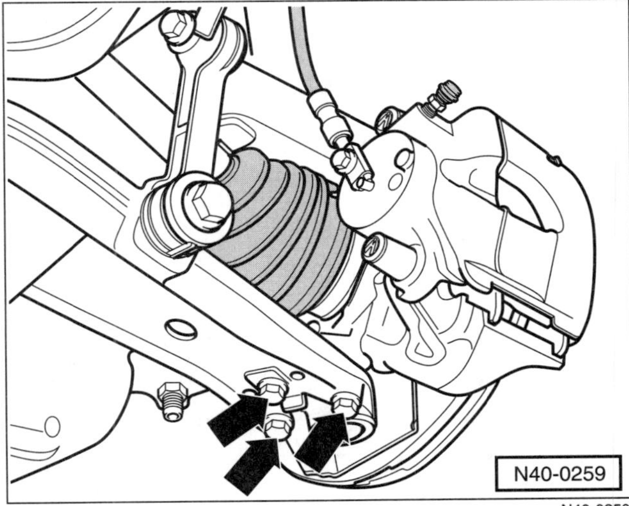

Fig. 24. Remove control arm bolts (**arrows**).

33. Unbolt left stabilizer coupling rod from control arm and turn coupling rod upward. Swing wheel bearing housing outward and guide left drive shaft out between subframe and transmission. Lift drive shaft and secure to suspension strut with wire. See Fig. 25.

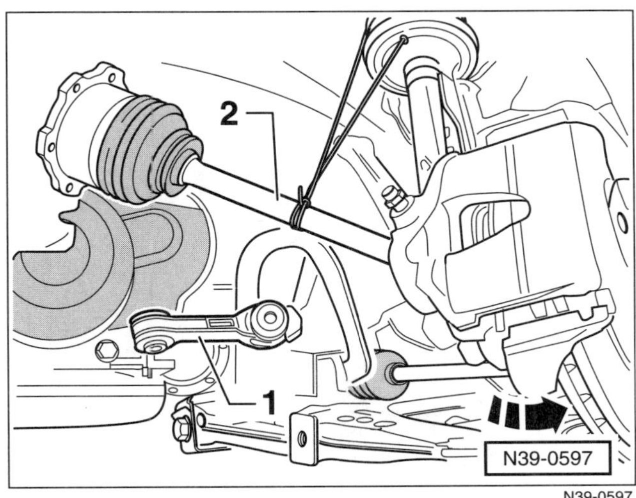

Fig. 25. Remove stabilizer coupling rod (**1**), swing wheel bearing housing outward (**arrow**), and move left drive shaft (**2**) away from transmission.

34. Disconnect exhaust at down pipe. Remove front exhaust support if necessary, see **26 Exhaust System/Emission Controls**.

35. Remove mounting bolts for left engine/transmission mount. See Fig. 26.

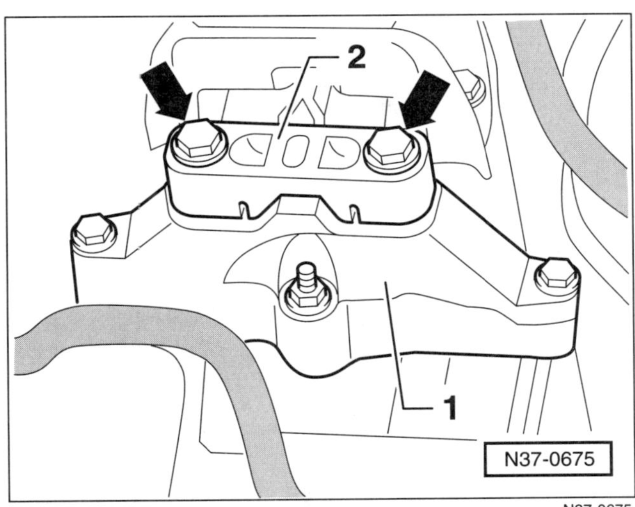

Fig. 26. Remove bolts (**arrows**) of left engine/transmission mount (**2**) from left support (**1**).

36. Carefully tilt engine/transmission assembly by lowering left-side spindle of support bar (VW 10-222A, or equivalent) by approximately 60 mm (2.3 in.).

37. Remove left support from transmission. See Fig. 27.

N37-0676

Fig. 27. Remove bolts and nut (**arrows**) for left support (**1**).

38. Bolt support rail (VW 457/1 or equivalent) to the pendulum support securing holes on subframe. See Fig. 28.

NOTE —

- *Volkswagen special tool 457/1 must be modified as described earlier under* **Special tools, modifying**.
- *Spacers totaling a thickness of 6 mm must be inserted between the subframe and the support rail VW 457/1.*

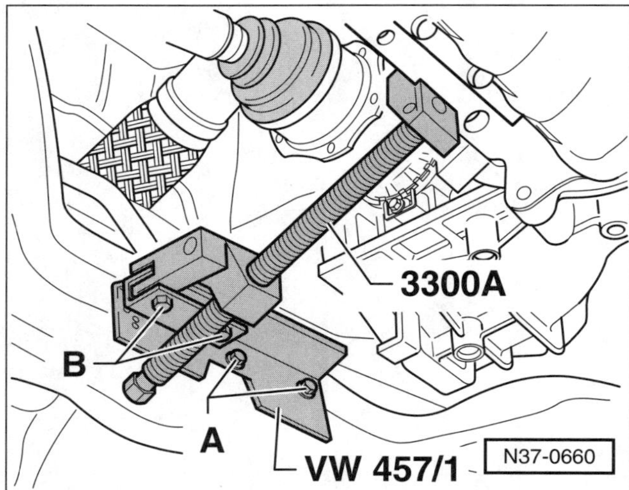

N37-0660

Fig. 28. Use two M8 x 25 bolts (**A**) to attach support rail to the pendulum mount securing holes on subframe. Install support 3300A to support rail and tighten with bolts (**B**). Numbers shown are for VW special tools.

39. Install support (VW 3300A) to support rail (VW 457/1) and secure. Refer to Fig. 28.

40. Press engine/transmission assembly forward carefully.

NOTE —

Do not damage power steering line when moving engine/transmission assembly.

41. Assemble transmission jack with support 3282, adjustment plate 3282/2 and support elements. See Fig. 29.

- Place adjustment plate 3282/2 on transmission support 3282. (Adjustment plate only fits in one position).
- Position transmission support arms according to holes in adjustment plate.

NOTE —

Arrow on adjustment plate 3282/2 should point toward front of vehicle.

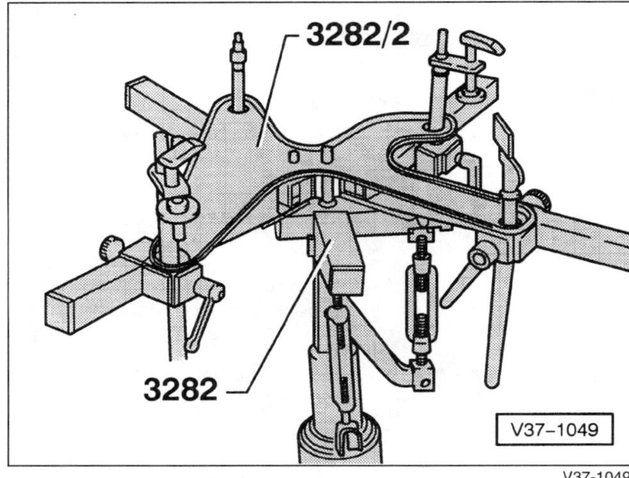

V37-1049

Fig. 29. Volkswagen transmission jack 3282 with adjustment plate 3282/2.

42. Place transmission jack under transmission. See Fig. 30.

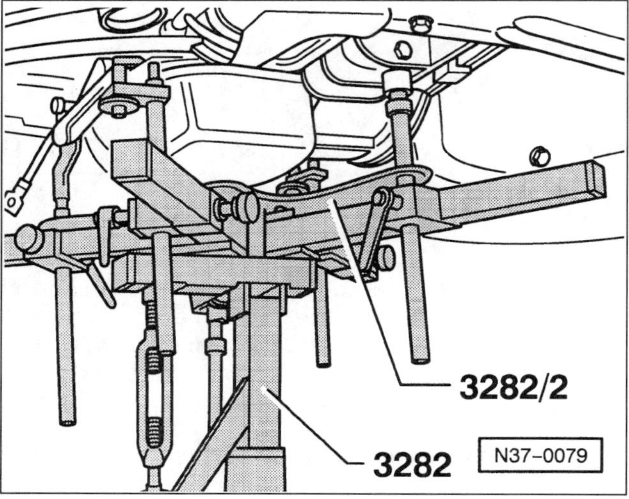

N37-0079

Fig. 30. Transmission jack correctly placed under transmission. Numbers shown are for VW transmission jack and adapters.

43. Align adjustment plate parallel to transmission and lock safety supports on transmission jack.

44. Place safety support pin on oil pan and secure it to transmission housing. See Fig. 31.

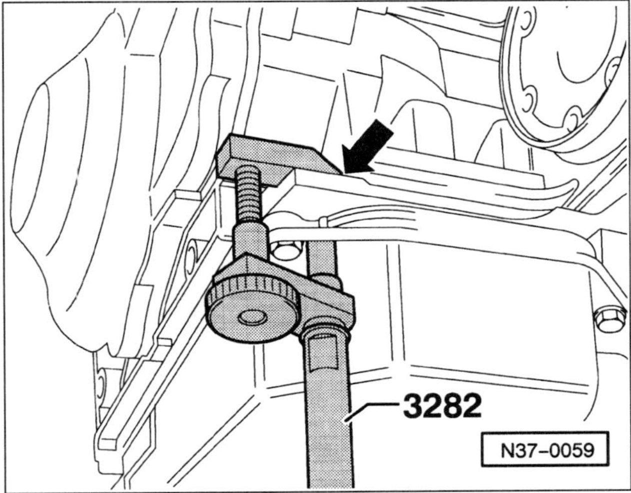

N37-0059

Fig. 31. Safety support pin placed on oil pan and secured to transmission housing (**arrow**).

45. Turn right transmission output flange to the right until flat section is vertical. See Fig. 32.

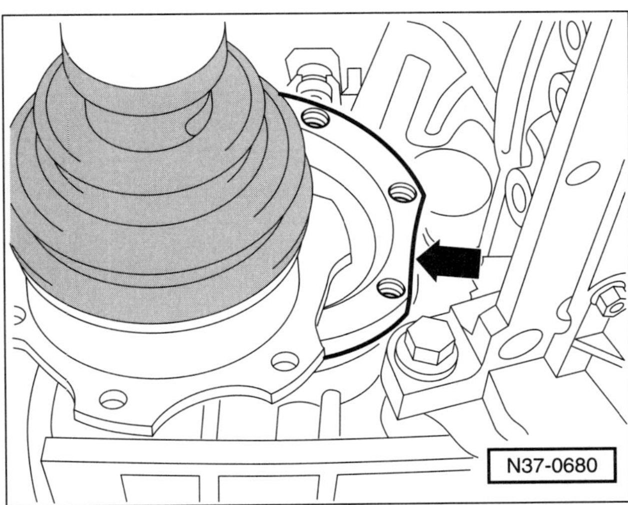

N37-0680

Fig. 32. Turn transmission flange to the right until flat section (**arrow**) is vertical.

46. Remove lower engine/transmission securing bolts.

47. Separate transmission from engine while pushing torque converter away from drive plate.

48. Lower transmission slightly.

> ***WARNING —***
> *Before unbolting lower engine-to-transmission mounting bolts be sure to support the weight of the vehicle at all four corners with jack stands designed for that purpose. Removal of the transmission can upset the weight balance of the vehicle and cause it to fall off the lift.*

> ***CAUTION —***
> *On automatic transmissions, the torque converter should come off with the transmission. Secure the torque converter to the transmission to prevent damage.*

NOTE —
While lowering transmission, guide power steering pressure line past transmission.

49. Tilt transmission using transmission jack spindle and while lowering ensure cover (wheel housing side) is guided closely past wheel housing.

50. Swivel transmission and carefully lower.

NOTE —
- *While lowering transmission, guide right axle joint at engine past support 3300 A.*
- *Be careful not to let multi-function switch contact engine/transmission mount.*

Transmission, installing

NOTE —
If torque converter has been removed, the torque converter seal will need to be replaced as described later.

The transmission is installed in the reverse order of removal, noting the following:

1. When installing torque converter, be sure that both drive pins engage in the ATF pump inner wheel recesses.

2. Before installing transmission, be sure that the dowel sleeves are correctly located.

3. When installing transmission, check torque converter contact pattern on drive plate.

4. Replace selector cable locking circlip.

5. Adjust selector lever cable, see **Selector lever cable, checking and adjusting**.

6. Check and top up ATF level.

7. Connect VAG 1551/1552, or equivalent, and check diagnostic trouble code memory.

8. Have the front wheels professionally aligned once installation is complete.

Use the following tightening torques when installing the automatic transmission.

Tightening torques

- Drive shaft to transmission drive flange . . . . 40 Nm (30 ft-lb)
- Torque converter to drive plate. . . . . . 60 Nm (44 ft-lb)
- Transmission to engine
  (M10) . . . . 60 Nm (44 ft-lb)
  (M12) . . . . 80 Nm (59 ft-lb)
- Transmission to oil pan (M10) . . . . . . 25 Nm (18 ft-lb)
- Ball joint to control arm . . . . 35 Nm (26 ft-lb)
- Coupling rod to control arm . . . . 45 Nm (33 ft-lb)
- Left mount to transmission. . . . . 25 Nm (18 ft-lb)
- Wheel bolts to wheel hub. . . . . 120 Nm (89 ft-lb)
- Protective cover for drive axle boot to engine block. . . . . 35 Nm (26 ft-lb)

Remaining transmission installation tightening torques are given below with corresponding Fig. # as necessary for clarification.

Tightening torques

Always replace all bolts

- Transmission to body
  (bolts **A**, See Fig. 33.). . . . . 60 Nm (44 ft-lb) plus ¼ turn (90°)
  (bolts **B**, See Fig. 33.). . . . . 40 Nm (30 ft-lb) plus ¼ turn (90°)
- Pendulum mount to body
  (bolts **A**, See Fig. 34.) . . . . 20 Nm (15 ft-lb) plus ¼ turn (90°)
- Pendulum mount bracket
  (bolts **B**, See Fig. 34.) . . . . 40 Nm (30 ft-lb) plus ¼ turn (90°)

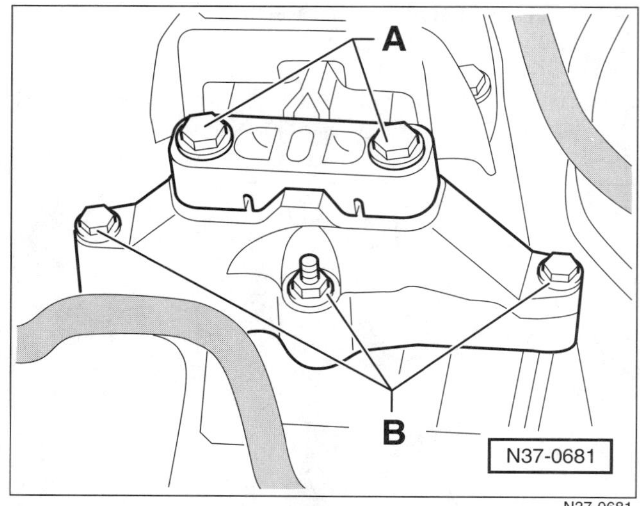

N37-0681

Fig. 33. Transmission to body mount.

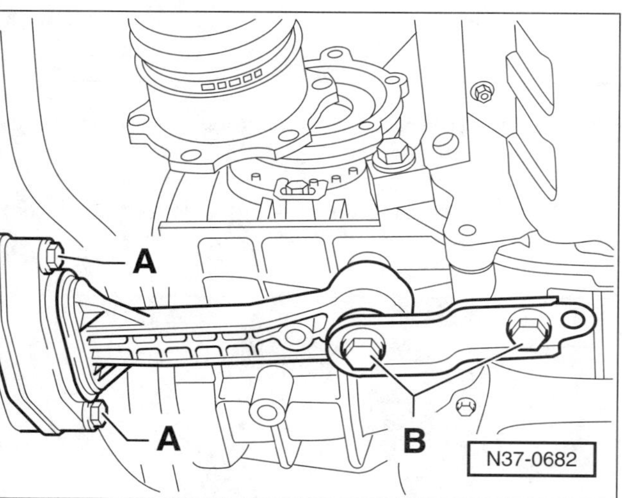

N37-0682

Fig. 34. Rear transmission pendulum mount.

TORQUE CONVERTER

When replacing the torque converter, always note the torque converter code number. The code number can be found in one of two places. See Fig. 35. and Fig. 36. The replacement torque converter must have the same code number, as it is matched to the transmission/engine application.

> ***CAUTION —***
> *When installing the torque converter, make sure that both drive pins engage in the recesses in the ATF pump inner wheel.*

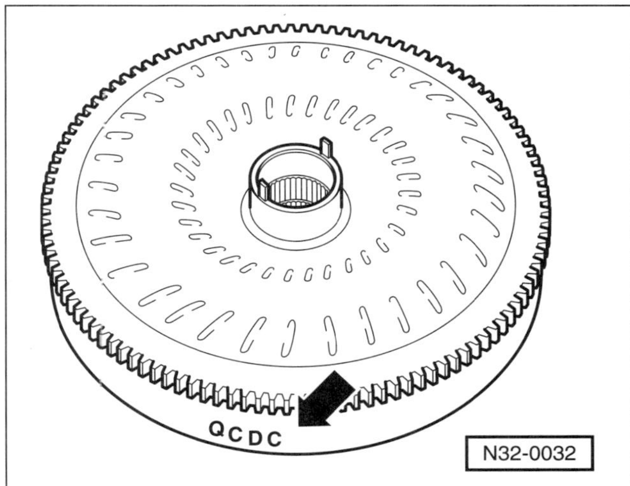

N32-0032

Fig. 35. Torque converter code letter location (**arrow**).

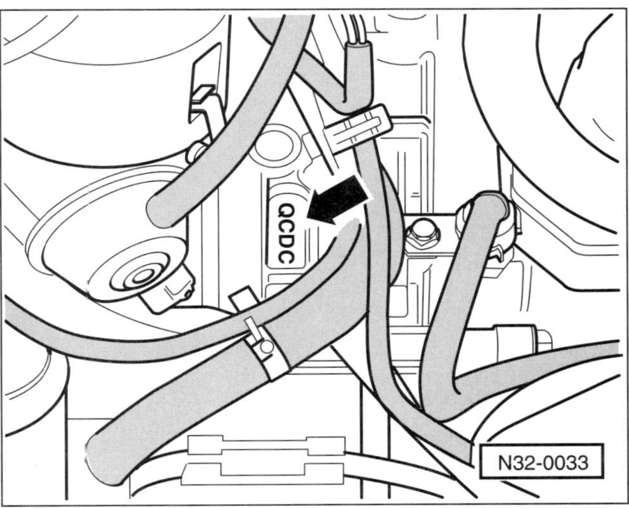

N32-0033

Fig. 36. Torque converter code letters visible through access hole with transmission installed (**arrow**).

If the torque converter has become contaminated by particles resulting from wear or abrasion, or in the course of a major overhaul of the transmission, always flush the torque converter with clean ATF. The torque converter can be flushed with commercially-available extraction equipment, such as EZ1 fluid evacuator, or Volkswagen special tools VAG 1358A and VAG 1358 A/1 probe.

Torque converter oil seal, replacing (transmission removed)

1. Remove the torque converter seal using a seal extractor. See Fig. 37.

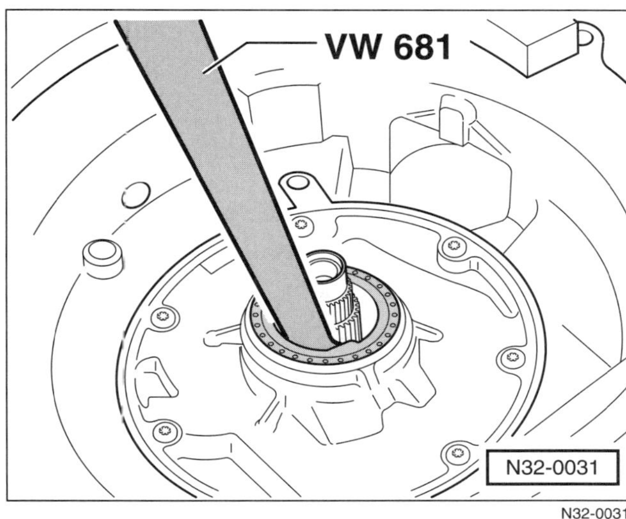

N32-0031

Fig. 37. Torque converter seal being removed from bell housing. Volkswagen special tool VW 681 shown.

2. Using a seal driver, drive seal in until flush. See Fig. 38.

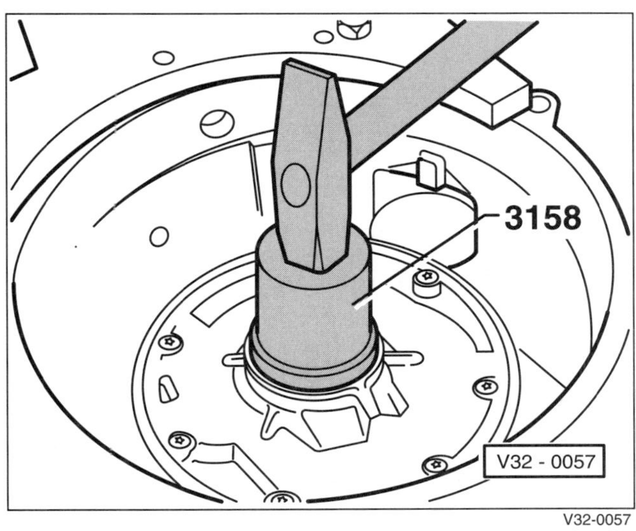

V32-0057

Fig. 38. Installing torque converter seal with seal driver. Volkswagen special tool 3158 shown.

ATF COOLER

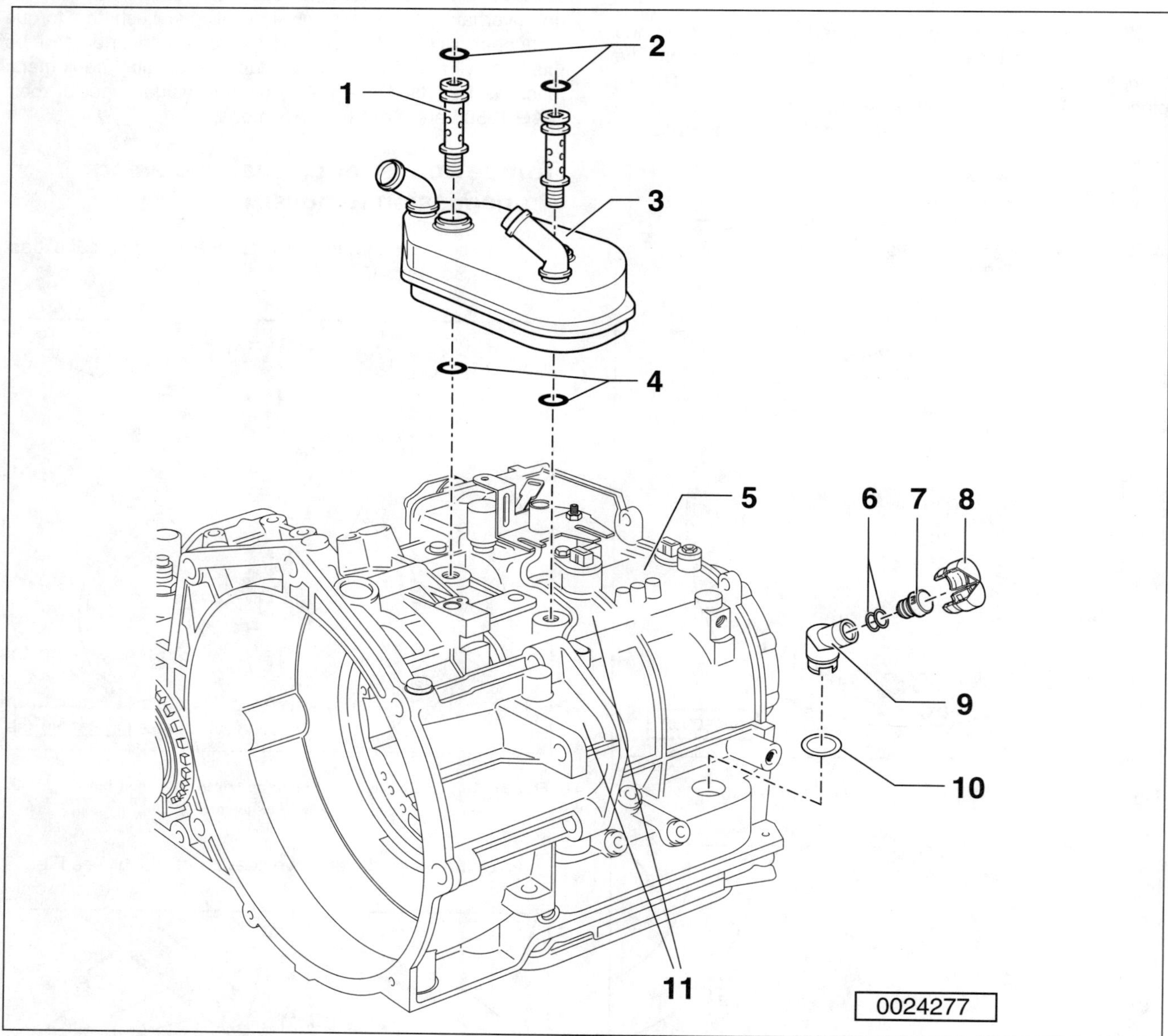

0024277

Fig. 39. ATF cooler for automatic transmission.

1. **Banjo bolt**
   - Tighten to 35 Nm (26 ft-lb)
2. **O-ring**
   - Always replace
3. **ATF cooler**
4. **O-ring**
   - Always replace
5. **Transmission housing**
6. **Seal**
   - Always replace
7. **Plug**
8. **Cap**
   - To secure ATF level plug after checking ATF level
   - Always replace
9. **ATF filler tube**
10. **O-ring**
    - Always replace
11. **Location of transmission code and production number**

39 Differential and Final Drive

GENERAL

This repair group covers replacement of the drive flange oil seals in the final drive unit. Disassembly of the final drive unit is not covered in this section. The final drive for the automatic transmission is filled with gear oil and this repair group details checking that fluid. On cars with manual transmission, the final drive unit shares the same gear oil as the transmission. For information on checking, draining and filling the manual transmission and final drive oil, see **0 Maintenance**.

MANUAL TRANSMISSION

The layout of the 02J manual transmission and final drive is shown in Fig. 1.

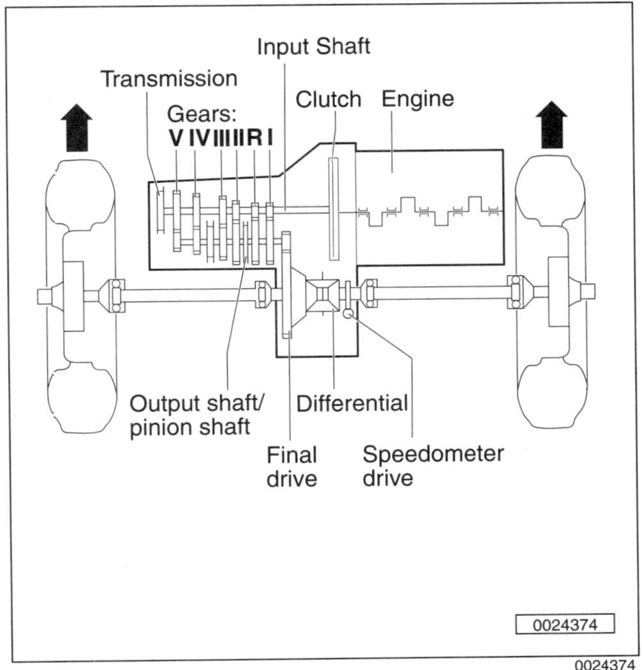

Fig. 1. O2J manual transmission layout. **Arrow** points in direction of travel.

Drive flange oil seal, replacing

NOTE —

- *A slide hammer with a puller hook may be needed to remove the drive flange oil seals. Alternatively, a seal removal tool may be used.*
- *An installation drift (VW special tool 3106, or equivalent) is also necessary for installing the drive flange oil seal as shown later in Fig. 7.*

1. If replacing the left-side drive flange seal, remove the left side drive axle as described in **40 Front Suspension and Drive Axles**.
2. If replacing the right-side drive flange seal, turn the steering wheel completely to right (full-lock). Remove the right inner drive axle boot protective cover, if installed. See Fig. 2. Disconnect drive axle from transmission drive flange.

Fig. 2. Remove bolts (**arrows**) for drive axle boot protective cover.

3. Push drive axle upward as far as possible and suspend with stiff wire or heavy-duty tie wrap.

> **CAUTION —**
> *Avoid damaging protective surface on the drive axle.*

4. Place drip tray underneath drive flange.

5. Install two bolts into CV joint mounting holes of drive flange and counter-hold with screwdriver. Remove counter-sunk allen-head bolt from center of drive flange. See Fig. 3.

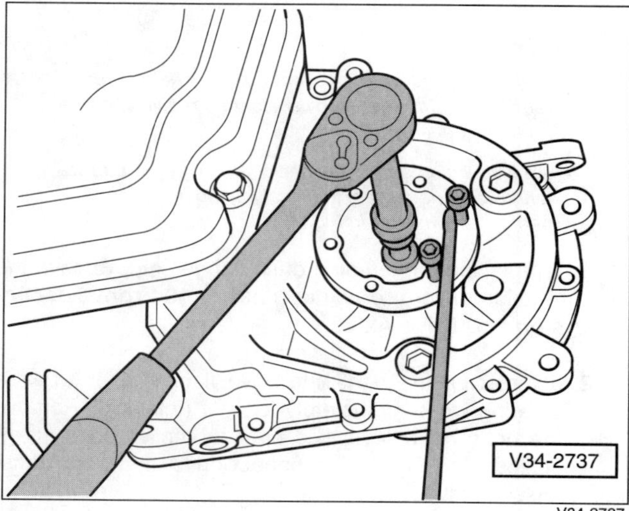

V34-2737

Fig. 3. Remove drive flange mounting bolt while counter-holding drive flange using screwdriver and bolts in CV joint mounting holes.

6. Remove drive flange shaft with spring.

7. Using sliding hammer and appropriate hook or seal removal tool, pull out drive flange oil seal. See Fig. 4.

> **CAUTION —**
> - *Do not damage sleeve when removing oil seal.*
> - *If sleeve is damaged, replace as shown in Fig. 5.*

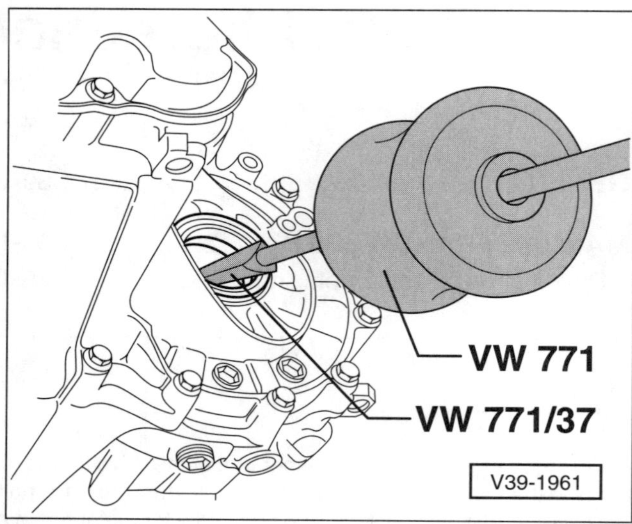

V39-1961

Fig. 4. Removing drive flange oil seal with slide hammer and hook (Volkswagen special tool numbers shown).

8. If drive flange sleeve is damaged, pry out the old sleeve with a screwdriver and install new sleeve with thrust pad and threaded rod with bolt. See Fig. 5.

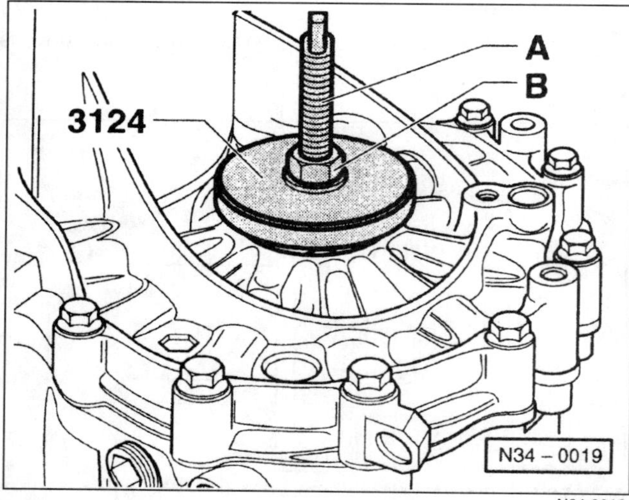

N34-0019

Fig. 5. If necessary, install new drive flange sleeve with thrust pad (VW special tool 3124), threaded rod (**A**) from assembly tool (VW special tool 3066 or equivalent) and M12 nut with washer. Turn nut (**B**) until sleeve contacts stop.

9. Fill space between lips of new oil seal with multi-purpose (MoS2) grease. Oil seal dimensions are indicated in Fig. 6.

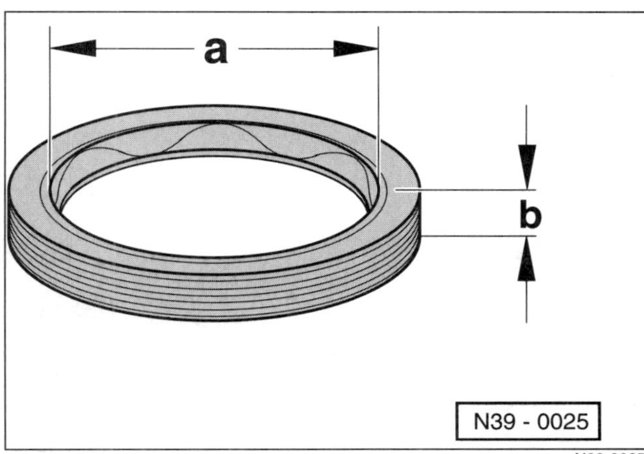

N39-0025

Fig. 6. Drive flange oil seal for 02J manual transmission.

Drive flange oil seal dimensions
- Inner diameter (**a**) .... 48.0 mm (1.890 in.)
- Height (**b**).................... 7.0 mm (0.276 in.)
- Outer diameter (not indicated) . . . 62.0 mm (2.441 in.)

10. Using seal driver, drive seal in against shoulder. See Fig. 7.

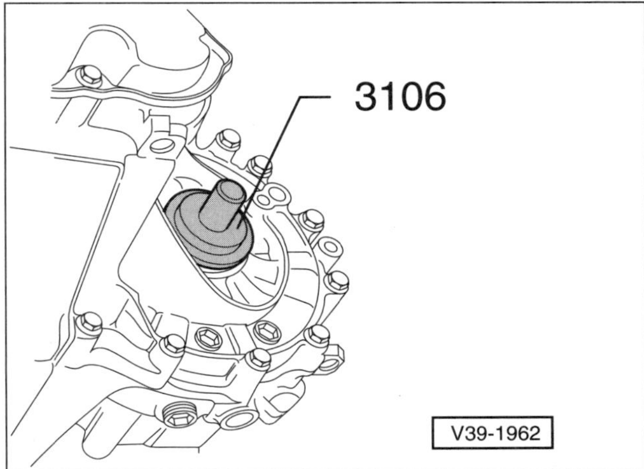

V39-1962

Fig. 7. Drive flange oil seal being installed with seal driver (Volkswagen special tool 3106).

11. Remainder of installation is the reverse of removal. Be sure to top up gear oil, see **0 Maintenance**. Tightening torques are given below.

Tightening torques
- Drive flange to transmission (counter-sunk allen head bolt) ...... 25 Nm (18 ft-lb)
- Drive axle to flange .... 40 Nm (30 ft-lb)
- Drive axle boot protective cover to engine block.................. 35 Nm (26 ft-lb)

AUTOMATIC TRANSMISSION

A cut-away view of the final drive in the 01M automatic transmission is shown in Fig. 8.

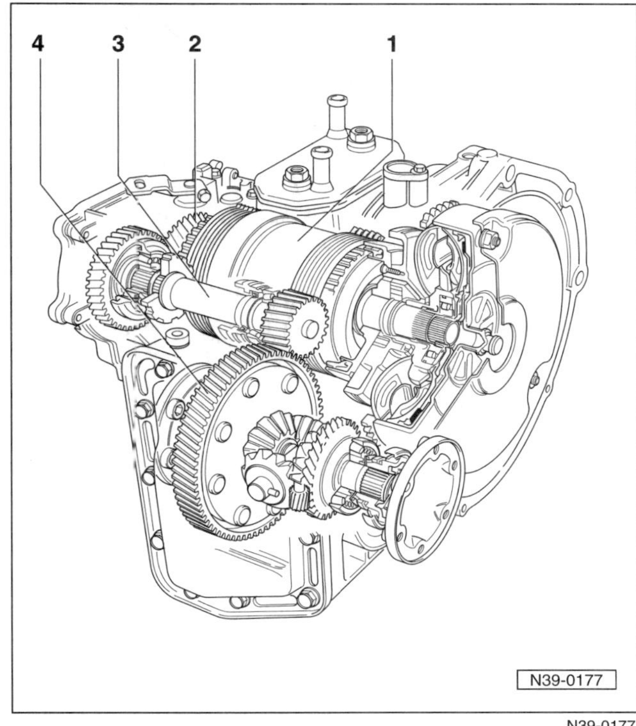

N39-0177

Fig. 8. Cut-away view of final drive unit in 01M automatic transmission. Planetary gear shown at (**1**), input gear (**2**), drive pinion (**3**), and differential at (**4**).

Final drive oil level, checking

On cars with automatic transmission, the final drive oil level should be checked regularly as specified in **0 Maintenance**. It is checked by removing the speedometer drive gear from the transmission housing and using the drive gear as a dipstick. The car should be on a level surface when making the check.

NOTE —

Volkswagen does not specify a final drive lubricant replacement interval. If the fluid needs to be drained, it can be drawn off using a fluid extraction/pumping system.

1. Remove harness connector from speedometer drive gear. Unscrew drive gear from transmission housing.

NOTE —

The speedometer drive gear is mounted through the top left-hand side of transmission, above the final drive end cover.

2. Clean speedometer drive gear using a clean cloth. Then install and remove drive gear to check the oil level. See Fig. 9.

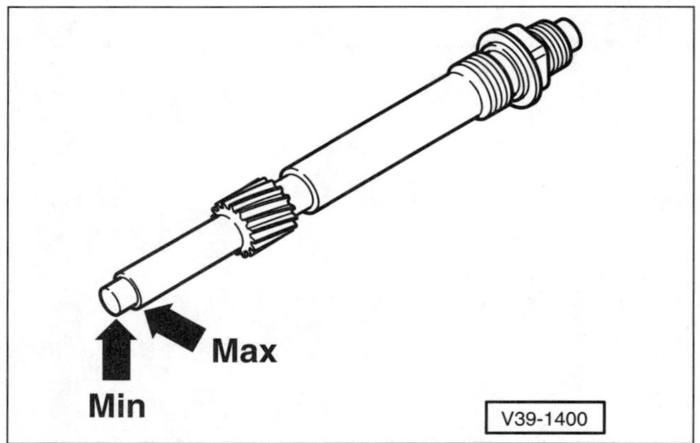

V39-1400

Fig. 9. Speedometer drive gear used to check final drive oil level. Level should be between **Min** and **Max** marks.

3. Add lubricant as necessary. Reinstall speedometer drive gear.

NOTE —
The difference between the "Min" and "Max" marks on the speedometer drive gear is approx. 0.1 liter (3.4 fl. oz.).

Final drive lubricant (automatic transmission)
- Specification. . . . . SAE 75W/90 synthetic gear oil
- Capacity . . . . 0.75 liters (0.79 qt.)

Drive flange oil seal, replacing

1. Remove noise insulation trays (belly pans) from underneath engine.

2. If replacing right-hand oil seal, lift vehicle and support with appropriate jack stands as necessary. Then proceed as follows:
   - Remove pendulum support from subframe.
   - Remove drive axle boot protective cover as shown earlier in Fig. 2.
   - Unbolt drive axle from drive flange. Move drive axle to one side and hold axle in place using stiff wire.

3. If replacing left-hand oil seal, loosen left front wheel bolts with vehicle on the ground. Lift vehicle, support with appropriate jack stands as necessary and remove wheel. Then proceed as follows:
   - Disconnect drive axle from drive flange.
   - Remove pendulum support from sub-frame. See Fig. 10.

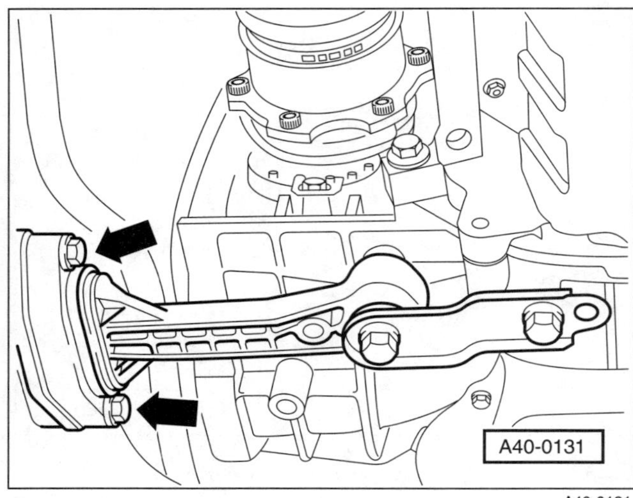

A40-0131

Fig. 10. Remove bolts (**arrows**) to remove pendulum support from subframe.

- Mark position of ball joint on left control arm and remove ball joint mounting bolts. See Fig. 11.

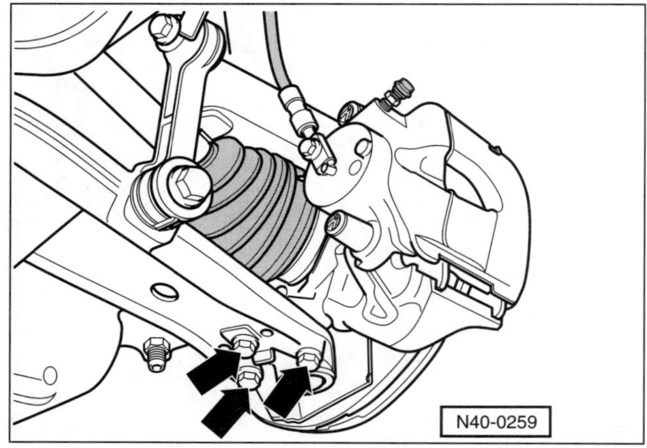

N40-0259

Fig. 11. Mark installation position of ball joint and remove bolts (**arrows**).

- Unbolt left side stabilizer bar connecting link from control arm and turn upward. Swing wheel bearing housing outward. Guide drive axle out between subframe and transmission while helper pushes engine/transmission assembly forward slightly. Secure drive axle to suspension strut with wire. See Fig. 12.

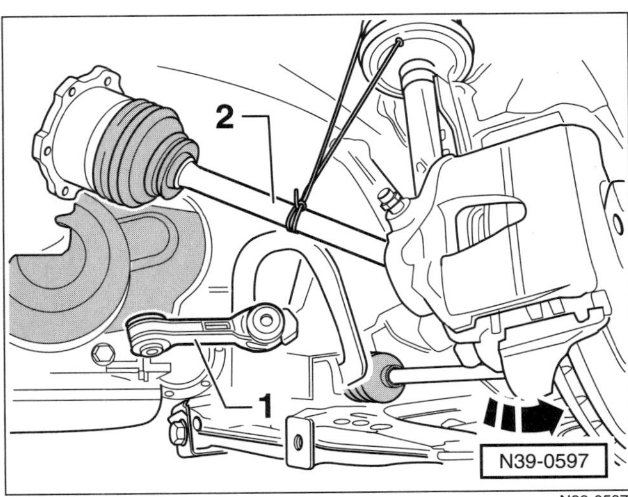

N39-0597

Fig. 12. Unbolt left side stabilizer bar connecting link (**1**) from control arm and turn upward. Swing wheel bearing housing outward (**arrow**). Notice drive axle (**2**) secured to suspension strut with wire.

Continued for left- and right-side oil seals

4. Pry off cover in center of drive flange by piercing center of cover with screwdriver.

5. Mount puller to drive flange with two 8x35mm bolts. Install a center spindle with nut through puller that will thread into output shaft (M10 thread). Turn spindle to press drive flange in slightly and remove drive flange retaining circlip. See Fig. 13.

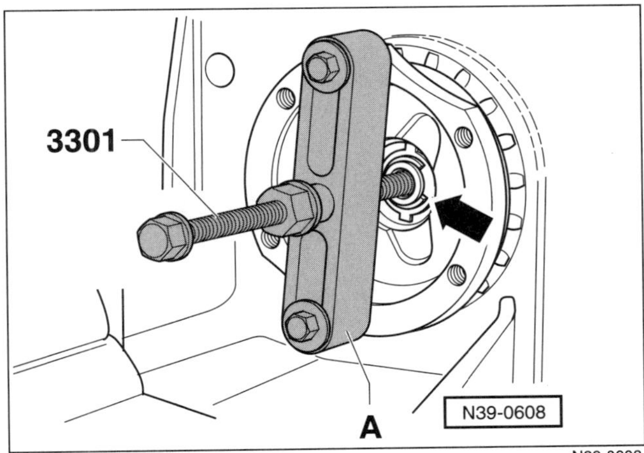

N39-0608

Fig. 13. Puller (**A**) (Kukko 18-0 shown with spindle and nut from VW special tool 3301) bolted to flange with 8x35mm bolts. Turn center spindle to press drive flange in slightly in order to remove circlip (**arrow**).

> ***NOTE —***
> *Volkswagen special tool 3109 can also be used to press flange in to remove circlip.*

6. Unthread center spindle from output shaft and remove from puller. Remove dished washer, noting orientation.

7. Install regular spindle into puller and place drip tray underneath flange. Turn spindle against output shaft to pull drive flange off. See Fig. 14.

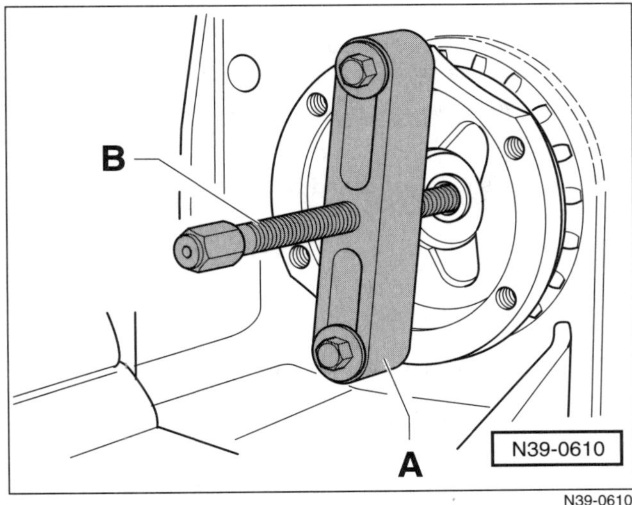

N39-0610

Fig. 14. Kukko two-arm puller (**A**) and standard center spindle (**B**) being used to pull out drive flange.

> ***NOTE —***
> *Drive flange can also be removed with special tool VW 391.*

8. Remove drive flange oil seal with seal removal tool (VW 681 or equivalent).

9. Carefully drive new seal into position against stop using seal installation tool. See Fig. 15.

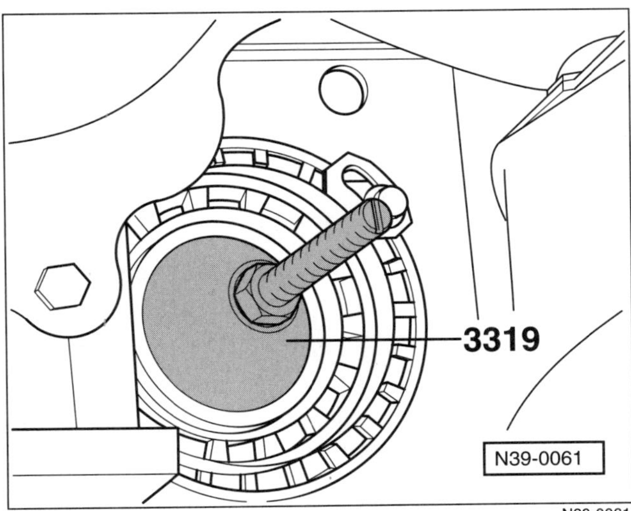

N39-0061

Fig. 15. VW special tool no. 3319 being used to install new oil seal. Center spindle is M10 threaded rod approx. 80 mm (3 in.) long.

10. Fill space between new oil seal and dust lip with multi-purpose grease.

11. Install drive flange using puller (Kukko 18-0, or equivalent) and center spindle that threads into output shaft. See Fig. 13., given earlier.

   NOTE —

   - *Place dished washer onto center spindle of puller with concave side facing in toward the differential.*
   - *Drive flange can also be installed with special tool VW 3109.*

12. Install dished washer and circlip onto output shaft.

   NOTE —

   Install dished washer so that the concave faces in, toward the differential.

13. Seal drive flange using a new sealing cover.

14. Remaining installation is the reverse of removal. Tightening torques are given below.

Tightening torques

- Drive axle to drive flange . . . . 40 Nm (30 ft-lb)
- Ball joint to control arm . . . . 35 Nm (25 ft-lb)
- Connecting link to control arm . . . . . . 45 Nm (33 ft-lb)
- Pendulum support to sub-frame. . . . . 20 Nm (15 ft-lb) + 1/4 turn (90°)
- Wheel bolts to hub . . . . 120 Nm (89 ft-lb)

15. Check final drive oil level as described earlier.

40 Front Suspension and Drive Axles

TABLES

GENERAL

Special tools, equipment and procedures are required for most front suspension repair and component replacement. In addition, front wheel alignment is almost always disturbed when suspension components are removed or replaced.

This section covers repairs to the front suspension and related components. For rear suspension servicing and repair information, see **42 Rear Suspension**. For wheel alignment specifications, see **44 Wheels, Tires, Wheel Alignment**.

Also covered are the drive axle assemblies with Constant Velocity (CV) joints as installed in vehicles with manual transmissions, as well as drive axles with triple rotor joints installed in vehicles with automatic transmissions.

> ***WARNING —***
> - *Do not re-use any fasteners that are worn or deformed in normal use. Most fasteners are designed to be used only once and become unreliable and may fail when used a second time. This includes, but is not limited to, nuts, bolts, washers, circlips cotter pins, self-locking nuts and bolts. For replacements, always use new parts.*
> - *Do not reinstall bolts and nuts coated with undercoating wax, as correct tightening torque cannot be ensured. Always clean the threads of removed bolts and nuts that are to be re-used with a suitable solvent before installation. Ensure that new parts are clean.*

> ***WARNING —***
> - *Do not use standard nuts and bolts in place of green colored parts. The green color denotes a special anti-corrosion process known as "dacromet" or "delta-tone". Torque specifications are given based on use of these parts only.*
> - *Always replaced rusted or corroded bolts, nuts and washers even if not specifically indicated.*
> - *DO NOT attempt to straighten or weld suspension struts, wheel bearing housings, control arms or any other wheel locating or load bearing components of the front suspension.*

> ***CAUTION —***
> *If a vehicle has to be moved (rolled) after removing the drive axle, install an outer constant velocity joint into the wheel bearing/housing and tighten the nut to 50 Nm (37 ft-lb). Otherwise the wheel bearing will be damaged.*

SUBFRAME AND CONTROL ARMS

The control arms and the subframe are mounted in replaceable rubber bushings that are subject to wear. The subframe supports the steering gear and the lower engine/transmission pendulum mount. Always understand and observe the warnings and cautions listed above before working on the suspension components. Fig. 1 shows the subframe, stabilizer bar and control arm assembly.

Subframe/stabilizer bar/control arm assembly

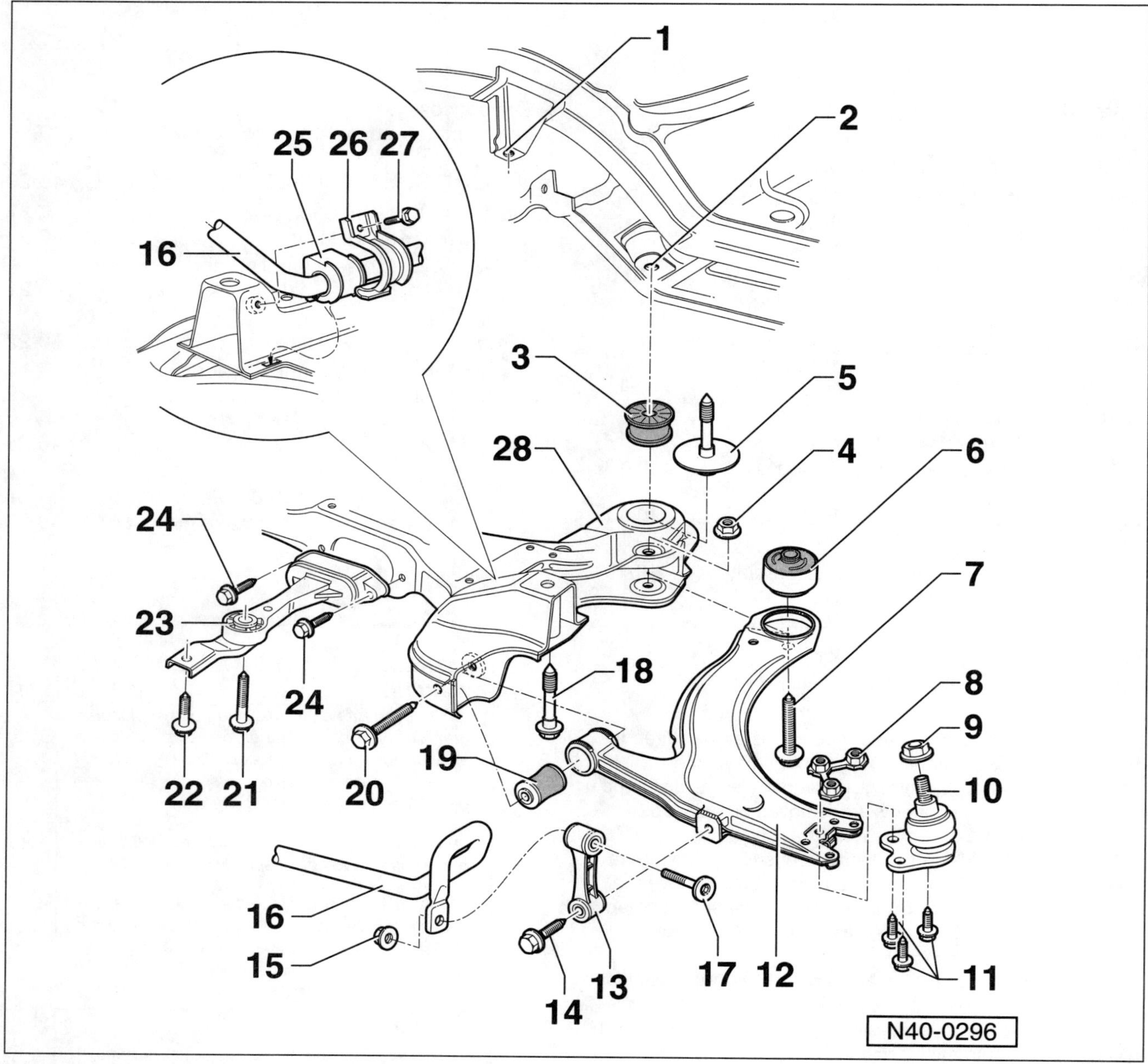

N40-0296

Fig. 1. Subframe with left control arm and related components.

1. **Subframe retaining bracket (on body)**
2. **Welded nut (in body)**
3. **Rear bonded rubber bushing for subframe**
4. **Nut, self-locking**
   - Always replace
5. **Bolt**
   - Always replace
   - Tighten to 100 Nm (74 ft-lb) + ¼-turn (90°)
6. **Rear bonded rubber bushing for control arm**
   - Installed position, **see** (A)
   - Pressing out/in, **see** (B)
7. **Bolt**
   - Always replace
   - Tighten to 70 Nm (52 ft-lb) + ¼-turn (90°)
8. **Nut plate**
9. **Nut, self-locking**
   - Always replace
   - Tighten to 45 Nm (33 ft-lb)

(continued from previous page)

10. Ball joint
- Checking, **see** Ⓒ

11. Bolts
- Always replace
- Tighten to 20 Nm (15 ft-lb) + ¼-turn (90°)

12. Control arm

13. Stabilizer connecting link

14. Bolt
- Tighten to 45 Nm (33 ft-lb)

15. Nut, self-locking
- Always replace
- Tighten to 30 Nm (22 ft-lb)

16. Stabilizer bar
- Subframe must be lowered to remove and install

17. Bolt

18. Bolt
- Always replace
- Tighten to 100 Nm (74 ft-lb) + ¼-turn (90°)

19. Front bonded rubber bushing for control arm
- Pressing out, **see** Ⓓ
- Pressing in, **see** Ⓔ

20. Bolt
- Always replace
- Tighten to 70 Nm (52 ft-lb) + ¼-turn (90°)

21. Bolt
- Always replace
- Tighten to 50 Nm (37 ft-lb) + ¼-turn (90°)

22. Bolt
- Always replace
- Tighten to 50 Nm (37 ft-lb) + ¼-turn (90°)

23. Pendulum support

24. Bolts
- Always replace
- Tighten to 25 Nm (18 ft-lb) + 1/4-turn (90°)

25. Stabilizer bar bushing

26. Stabilizer bar mounting bracket

27. Bolt
- Tighten to 25 Nm (18 ft-lb)

28. Subframe
- If damaged, do not repair threads in sub-frame for front control arm bolt

Ⓐ Rear bushing for control arm, installed position

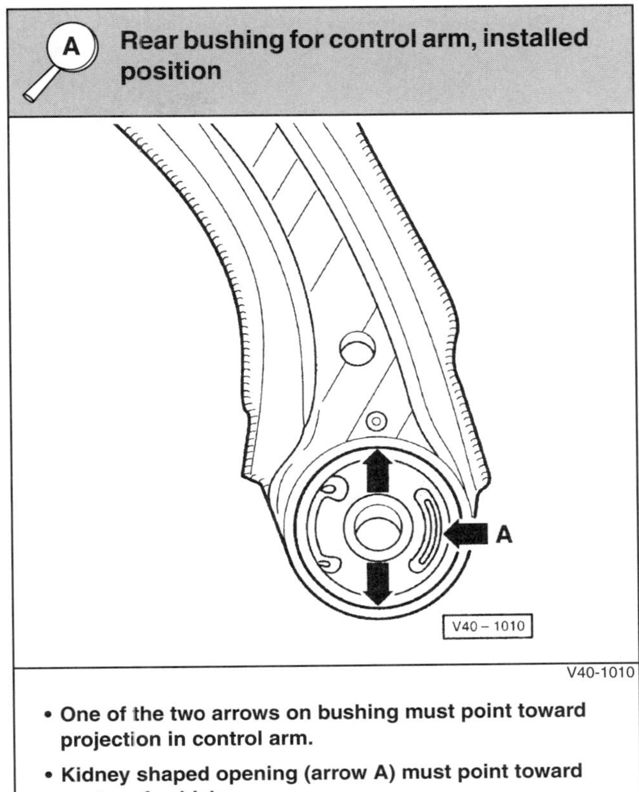

V40-1010

- **One of the two arrows on bushing must point toward projection in control arm.**
- **Kidney shaped opening (arrow A) must point toward center of vehicle.**

Ⓑ Rear bushing for control arm, pressing out/in

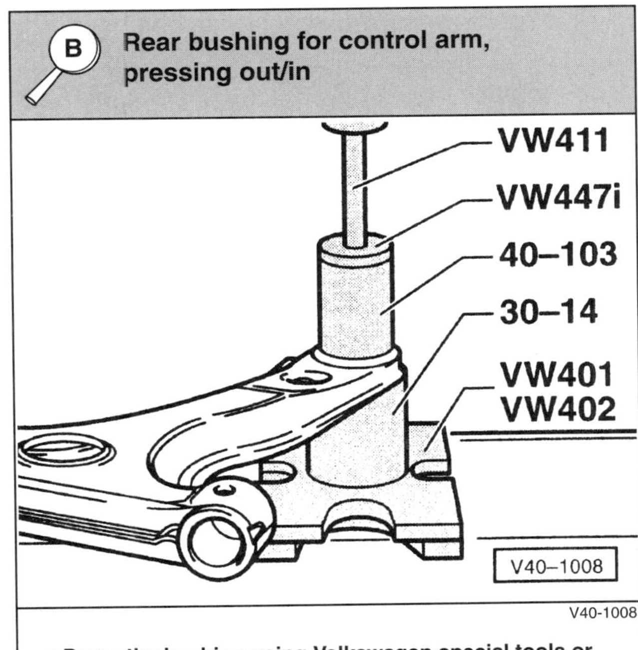

V40-1008

- **Press the bushing using Volkswagen special tools or equivalent, as shown.**
- **Set-up is the same for removal and installation.**

C Ball joint, checking axial and radial play

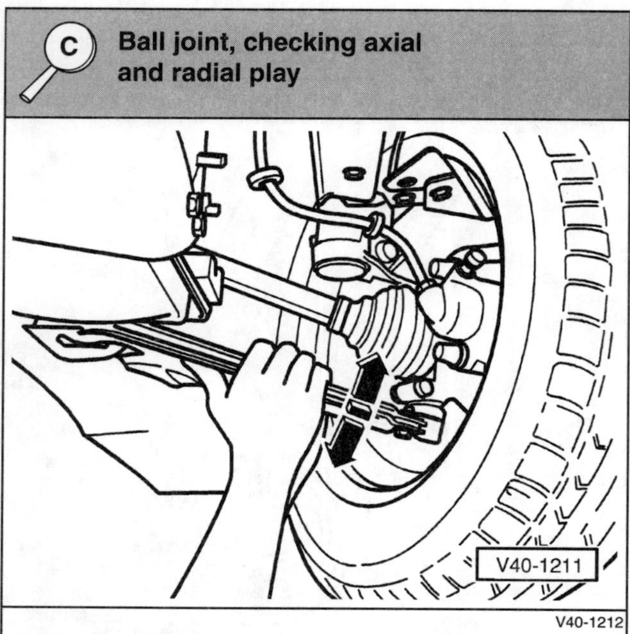

V40-1212

- Forcibly pull ball joint down and press up again (arrows) to check axial play.
- Forcibly push lower part of wheel in and out to check radial play.
- There must not be any perceptible play as a result of either check. Do not confuse with upper suspension strut mount or wheel bearing play.
- Replace ball joint if dust boot is damaged.

D Pressing out front bonded rubber bushing for control arm

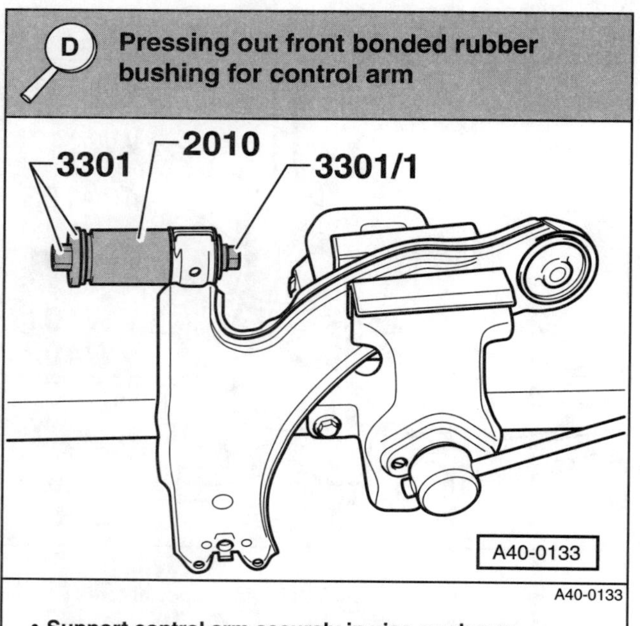

A40-0133

- Support control arm securely in vise as shown.

E Pressing in front bonded rubber bushing for control arm

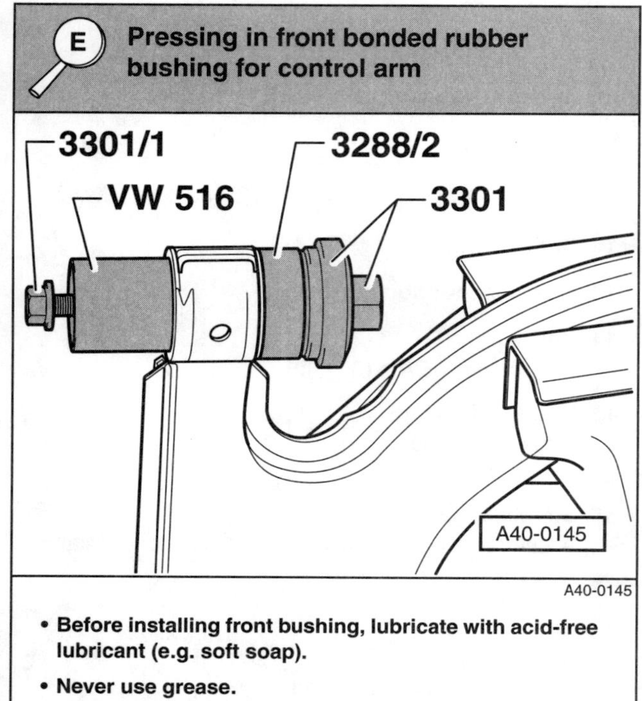

A40-0145

- Before installing front bushing, lubricate with acid-free lubricant (e.g. soft soap).
- Never use grease.

Ball joint, removing and installing

Replacement of the ball joint affects front wheel alignment. Be sure to have the front wheels aligned as the final step in the job.

1. With vehicle on the ground, loosen 12-point axle nut.
2. Lift vehicle and support with appropriate jackstands to relieve load on front axles.
3. Remove lower sound insulation panels (belly pans).
4. Mark the installed position of the ball joint in relation to the control arm. Then remove ball joint bolts. See Fig. 2.

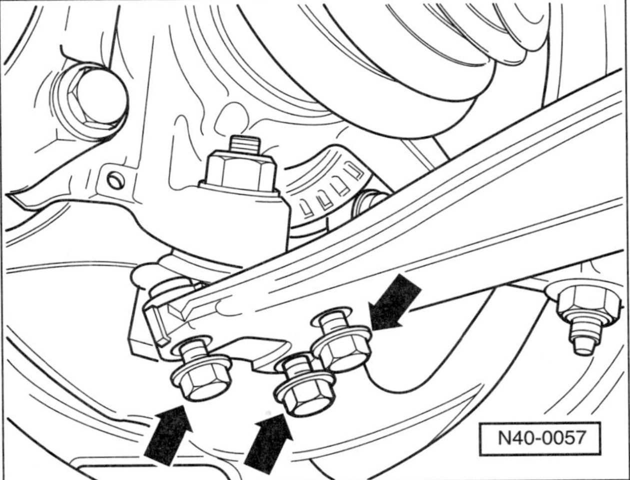

N40-0057

Fig. 2. Ball joint mounting bolts (arrows). Mark installed position of ball joint to control arm before loosening bolts.

5. Press axle shaft out with Volkswagen special tool 3283, or equivalent. See Fig. 3.

> ***CAUTION —***
> - *When pressing drive axle out make sure that sufficient clearance is available.*
> - *Do not allow drive axle to hand by inner CV joint or triple rotor joint to avoid damaging bearing surfaces. Tie drive axle to stabilizer bar or other suspension component if it is to remain attached to drive flange.*
> - *Do not flex inner CV or triple-roller joint more than 25° from its original angle.*

6. Pull wheel bearing housing with ball joint out from control arm.

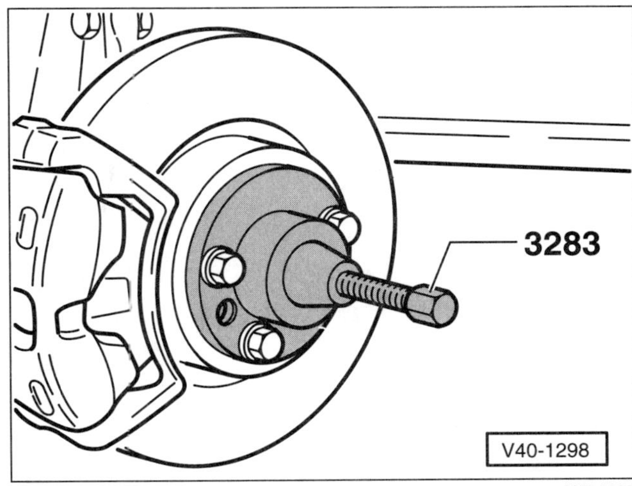

V40-1298

Fig. 3. Press axle shaft out of wheel hub with VW special tool 3283 or equivalent.

7. Swing wheel bearing housing/rotor assembly and suspension strut outwards and support in position using a block of wood, or equivalent. See Fig. 4.

> ***NOTE —***
> *Wedge block of wood between strut and body to prevent damage to undercoating.*

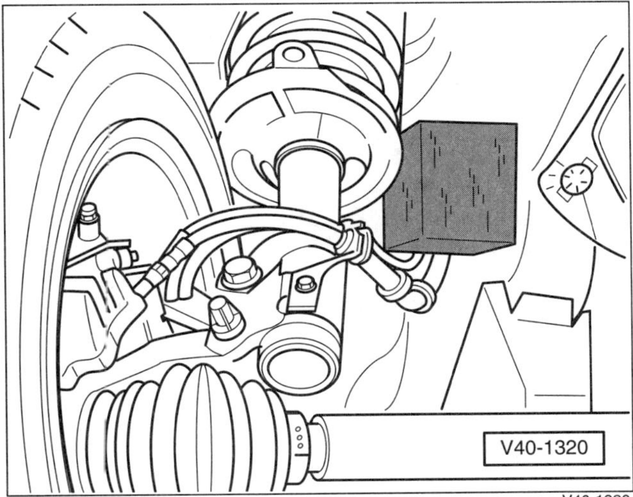

V40-1320

Fig. 4. Swing wheel bearing housing/rotor assembly with strut away from vehicle and support with wood block as shown.

8. Install ball joint puller and remove ball joint. See Fig. 5.

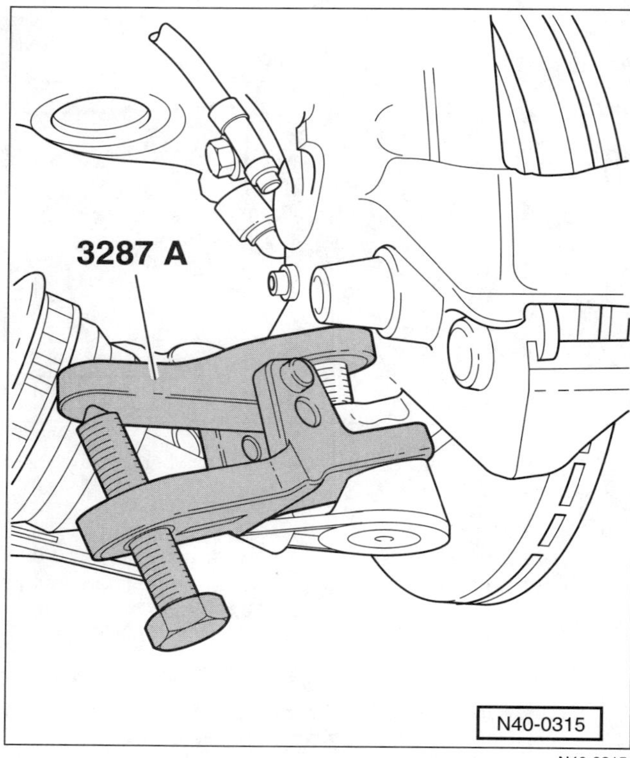

Fig. 5. Install ball joint puller (VW special tool 3287 A shown) to remove ball joint.

> ***NOTE —***
> *To remove ball joint, pre-tension slightly with ball joint puller and lightly tap out ball joint with a hammer. Ball joint should slide out of housing.*

> ***WARNING —***
> - *Place engine/transmission jack underneath ball joint to prevent if from falling out unexpectedly.*
> - *Leave ball joint nut threaded on few turns to protect ball joint threads.*

9. On cars with base suspension, remove the ball joint clamping nut and bolt. Remove the ball joint from the wheel bearing housing.

10. On cars with plus suspension, loosen the nut on top of the ball joint, but do not fully remove it. Press the ball joint loose. Remove the press and the ball joint. See Fig. 6.

> ***CAUTION —***
> *Use care when pressing the ball joint out of the wheel bearing housing. Once the ball joint breaks loose, the press will want to fall to the ground.*

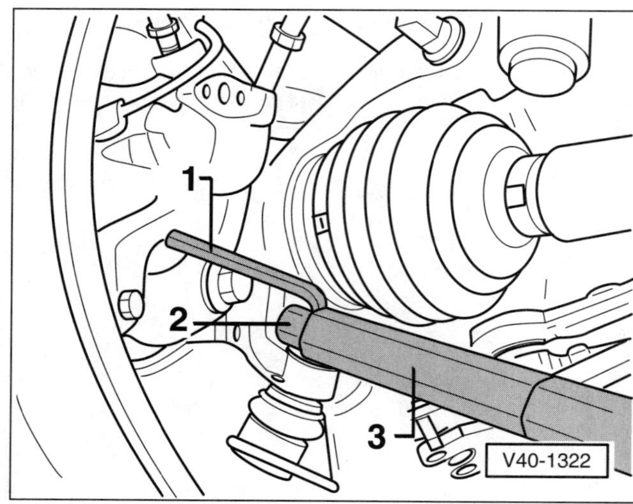

Fig. 6. Install ball joint using Torx wrench T40 (1), torque wrench (3) with 18mm box wrench insert (2).

11. Remaining installation is the reverse of removal noting the following:
    - Make sure the matching marks made earlier for the ball joint on the control arm are exactly aligned before tightening bolts.
    - Use a new 12-point nut for bolting the drive axle to the wheel hub. See tightening procedures given later under **Front wheel bearing housing assembly**.
    - Check and adjust front wheel alignment.

Tightening torques
- Ball joint to control arm (always replace. . . . . .20 Nm (15 ft-lb) + 90°
- Ball joint to wheel bearing housing. . . 45 Nm (33 ft-lb)
- 12-point nut for drive axle to wheel hub. . . . . .50 Nm (37 ft-lb) + 30°

WHEEL BEARINGS

Removal and/or replacement of the front wheel bearings requires special tools and equipment. Note that the wheel bearing is destroyed any time it is removed. Always understand and observe the warnings and cautions listed at the beginning of this section. Fig. 7. shows the front wheel bearing housing with related suspension components.

Front wheel bearing housing assembly

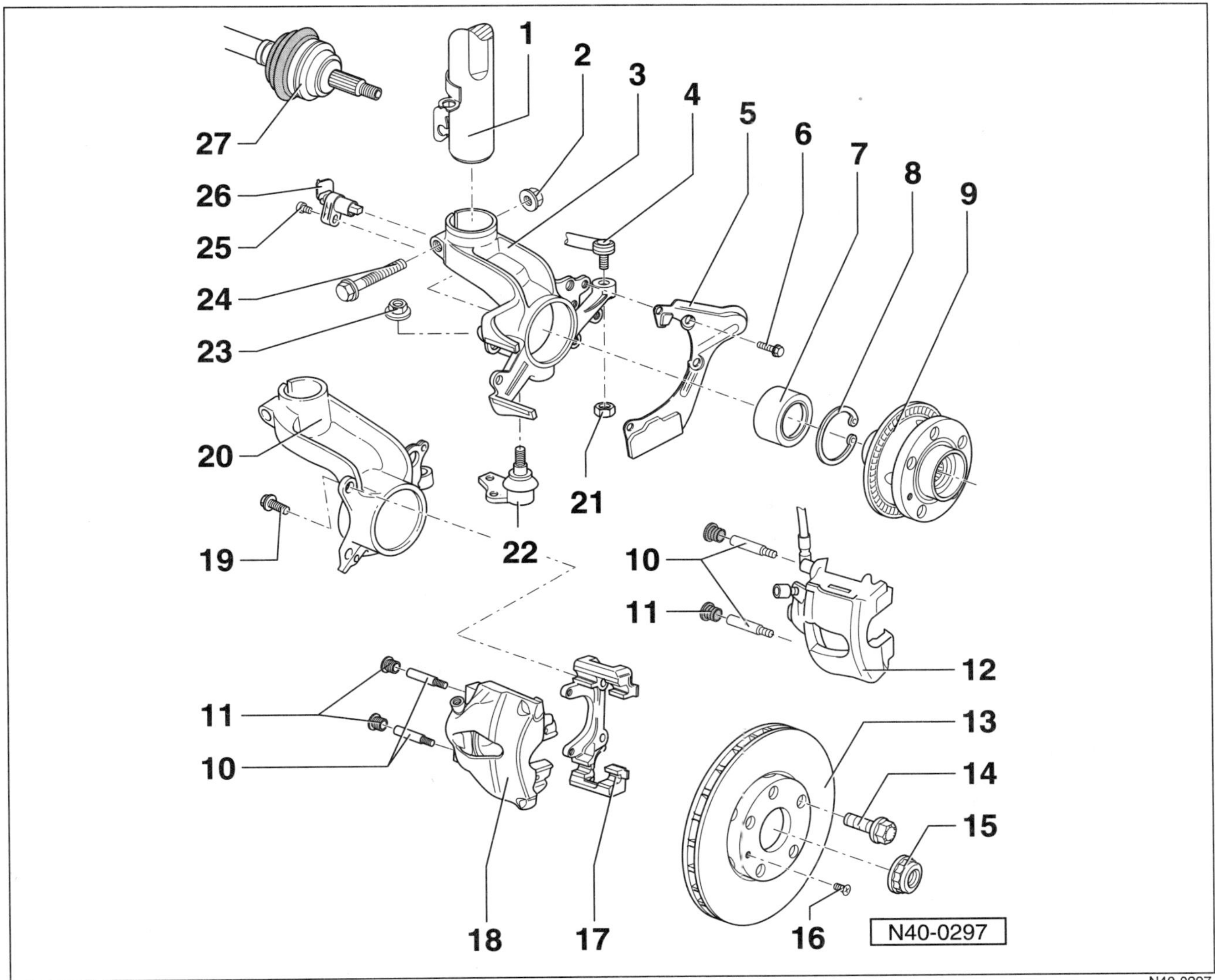

Fig. 7. Front wheel bearing with related components on the left side.

1. **Suspension strut**
2. **Nut, self-locking**
   - Always replace
   - Tighten to 60 Nm (44 ft-lb) + ¼-turn (90°)
   - Never less than 90°
   - Turning angle tolerance 90°–120°
3. **Wheel bearing housing**
   - Installed on cars with ALH (1.9 L) and AEG (2.0 L)
4. **Tie rod end**
5. **Splash plate**
6. **Bolt**
   - Tighten to 10 Nm (7 ft-lb)
7. **Wheel bearing**
   - Always replace (bearing is destroyed when removed)
   - Pressing out, **see** Ⓐ
   - Pressing in, **see** Ⓑ
8. **Circlip**
   - Make sure clip is correctly seated
9. **Wheel hub with ABS wheel speed sensor rotor**
   - Rotor welded to wheel hub
   - Pressing out of wheel bearing housing, **see** Ⓒ
   - Pressing hub into wheel bearing, **see** Ⓓ
   - Pulling out bearing race, **see** Ⓔ
10. **Guide pins**
    - Tighten to 28 Nm (21 ft-lb)

(continued on following page)

(continued from previous page)

11. Protective caps

12. Brake caliper
- Installed on cars with ALH (1.9 L) and AEG (2.0 L)
- Do not loosen the brake hose when working on the front suspension
- Do not allow the caliper to hang by the brake hose. The unsupported weight can stretch and damage the hose. Suspend the brake caliper using a piece of wire or similar.

13. Ventilated brake disc (rotor)

14. Wheel (lug) bolts
- Tighten to 120 Nm (87 ft-lb)

15. Axle nut, self-locking
- Always replace
- Any paint residue and/or corrosion on threads of outer joint must be removed before nut is installed
- Recommended tightening procedure, **see** (F)
- Alternate tightening procedure, **see** (G)

16. Screw
- Tighten to 4 Nm (35 in-lb)

17. Brake carrier
- Installed on cars with AFP (2.8 L) and AWD (1.8 L)

18. Brake caliper
- Installed on cars with AFP (2.8 L) and AWD (1.8 L)
- Do not loosen the brake hose when working on the front suspension
- Do not allow the caliper to hang by brake hose. The unsupported weight can stretch and damage hose. Suspend brake caliper using a piece of wire or similar.

19. Bolt, self-locking
- Tighten to 125 Nm (92 ft-lb)
- Clean ribs on under side of bolt head

20. Wheel bearing housing
- Installed on cars with AFP (2.8 L) and AWD (1.8 L)

21. Nut, self-locking
- Always replace
- Tighten to 45 Nm (33 ft-lb)

22. Ball joint

23. Nut, self-locking
- Always replace
- Tighten to 45 Nm (33 ft-lb)

24. Bolt
- Always replace

25. Bolt
- Tighten to 8 Nm (71 in-lb)

26. ABS wheel speed sensor

27. Drive axle
- Pressing drive axle out/in from wheel hub, **see** (H)

(A) Wheel bearing, pressing out

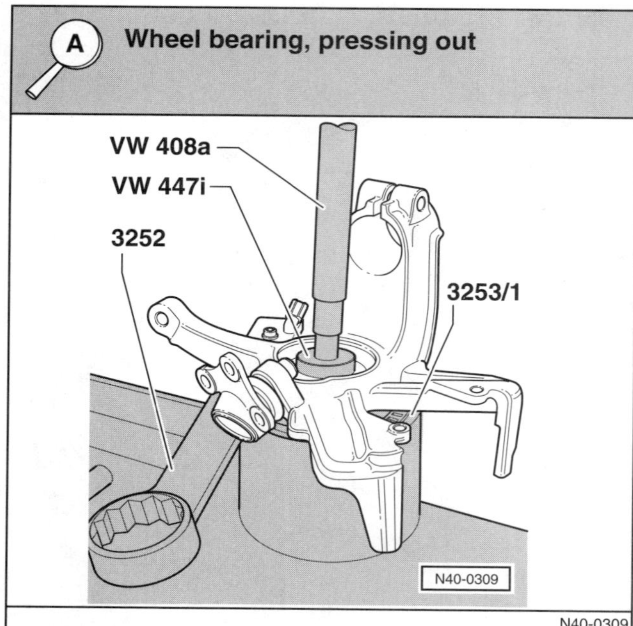

N40-0309

- **Press the bushing using Volkswagen special tools or equivalent, as shown.**

(B) Wheel bearing, pressing in

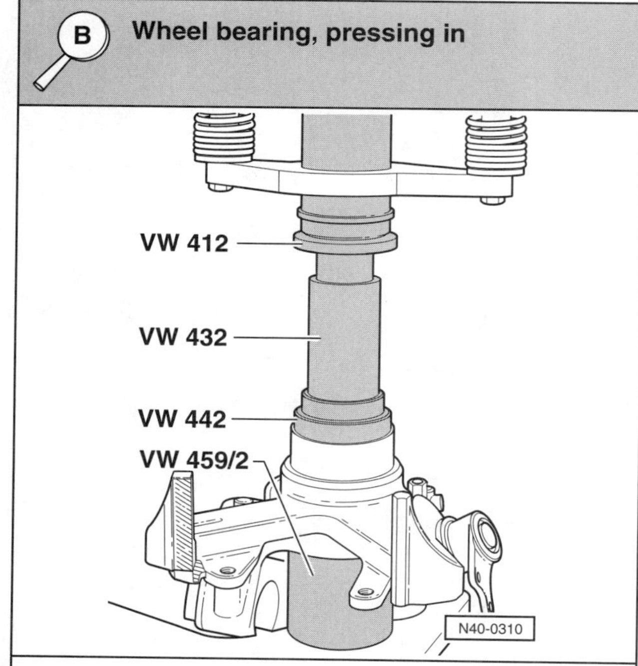

N40-0310

- **Lubricate bearing with grease (VW part no. N 052 723 00) before installation. Grease comes with VW repair kit.**
- **Install circlip in housing with open end at the bottom of the wheel bearing housing.**
- **Be sure that circlip is properly seated.**
- **Press the bushing using Volkswagen special tools or equivalent, as shown.**

C Wheel hub, pressing out of housing

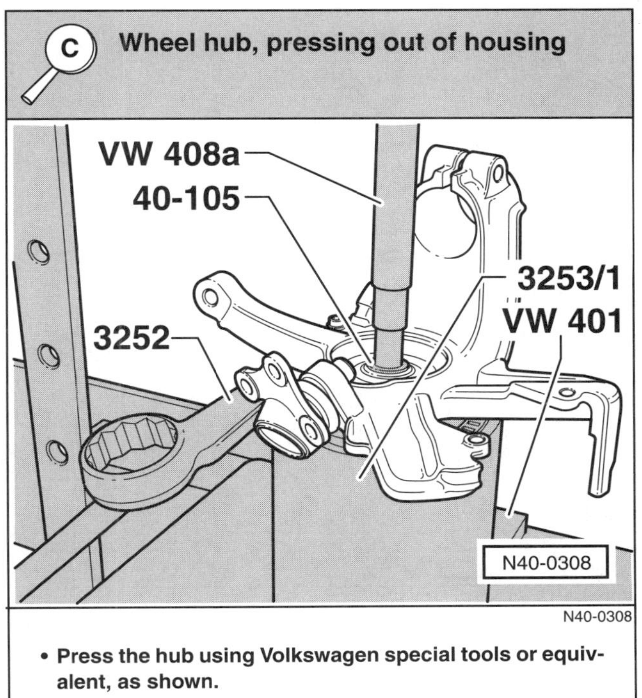

N40-0308

- Press the hub using Volkswagen special tools or equivalent, as shown.

D Wheel hub, pressing into wheel bearing housing

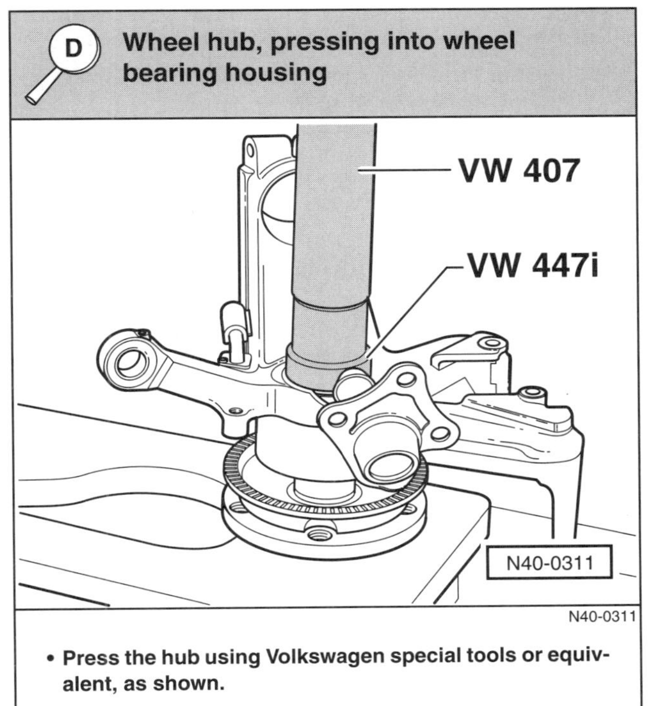

N40-0311

- Press the hub using Volkswagen special tools or equivalent, as shown.

E Bearing race, pulling out of wheel hub

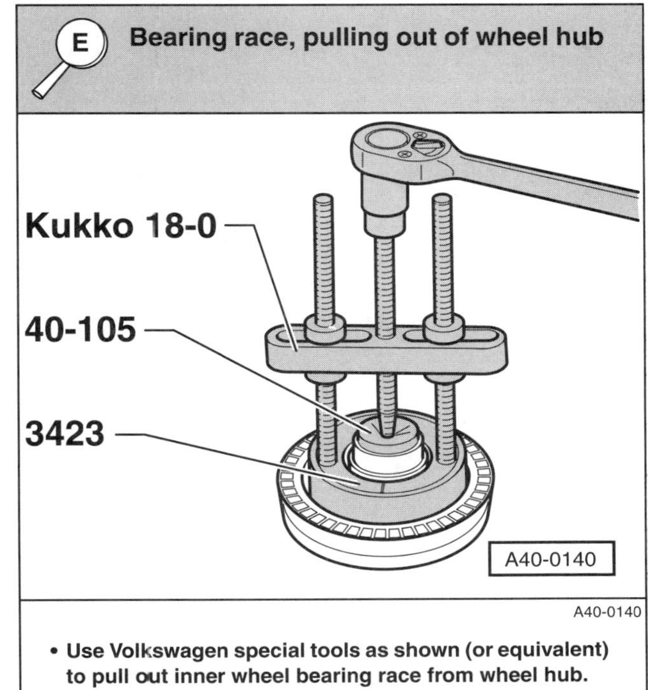

A40-0140

- Use Volkswagen special tools as shown (or equivalent) to pull out inner wheel bearing race from wheel hub.

F Axle nut, final tightening - recommended procedure

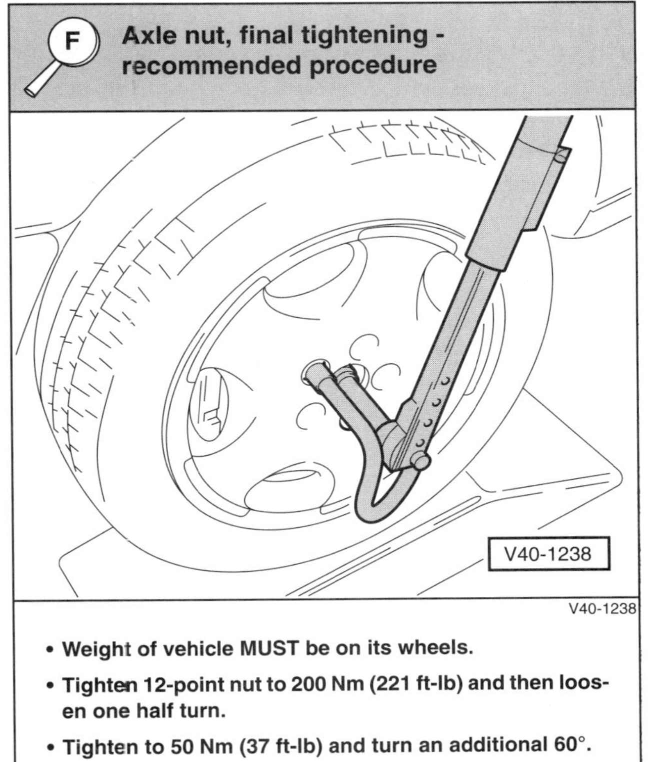

V40-1238

- Weight of vehicle MUST be on its wheels.
- Tighten 12-point nut to 200 Nm (221 ft-lb) and then loosen one half turn.
- Tighten to 50 Nm (37 ft-lb) and turn an additional 60°.

G Axle nut, final tightening - alternate procedure

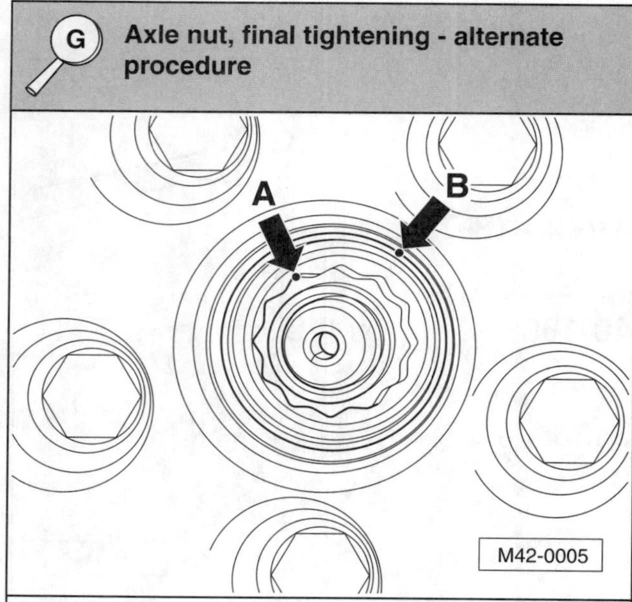

M42-0005

- **Weight of vehicle MUST be on its wheels.**
- **Tighten 12-point nut to 200 Nm (148 ft-lb) and then loosen one half-turn.**
- **Make a mark on nut point with line (arrow A).**
- **Make a second mark on the wheel hub (arrow B) two nut points away from the first. (The distance between each nut point on a 12-point nut is 30°)**
- **Tighten the axle nut until both marks line up.**

H Drive axle/constant velocity joint, pressing out

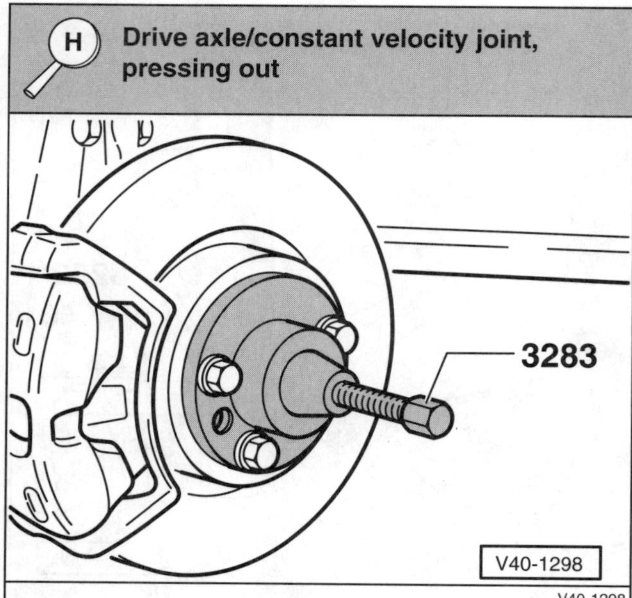

V40-1298

- **Press end of axle out using Volkswagen special tools or equivalent, as shown.**
- **Be sure there is sufficient clearance before pressing.**
- **Do not allow drive axle to hang from inner CV joint or triple rotor joint to avoid damaging bearing. Tie up axle to stabilizer bar or another suspension component.**
- **Do not flex the inner CV joint or triple rotor joint more than 25° from its original angle.**

> ***WARNING —***
> *Loosen and tighten axle nuts only when weight of vehicle is on the wheels. The leverage required for this operation is sufficient to topple the vehicle to the ground if supported on a lift or jack stands.*

SUSPENSION STRUTS

Removal and/or replacement of the front suspension struts requires special tools and equipment. Note that the strut is a sealed unit integral with the shock absorber. Always understand and observe the warnings and cautions listed at the beginning of this section. Fig. 8. shows the front strut with related components.

Front suspension strut assembly

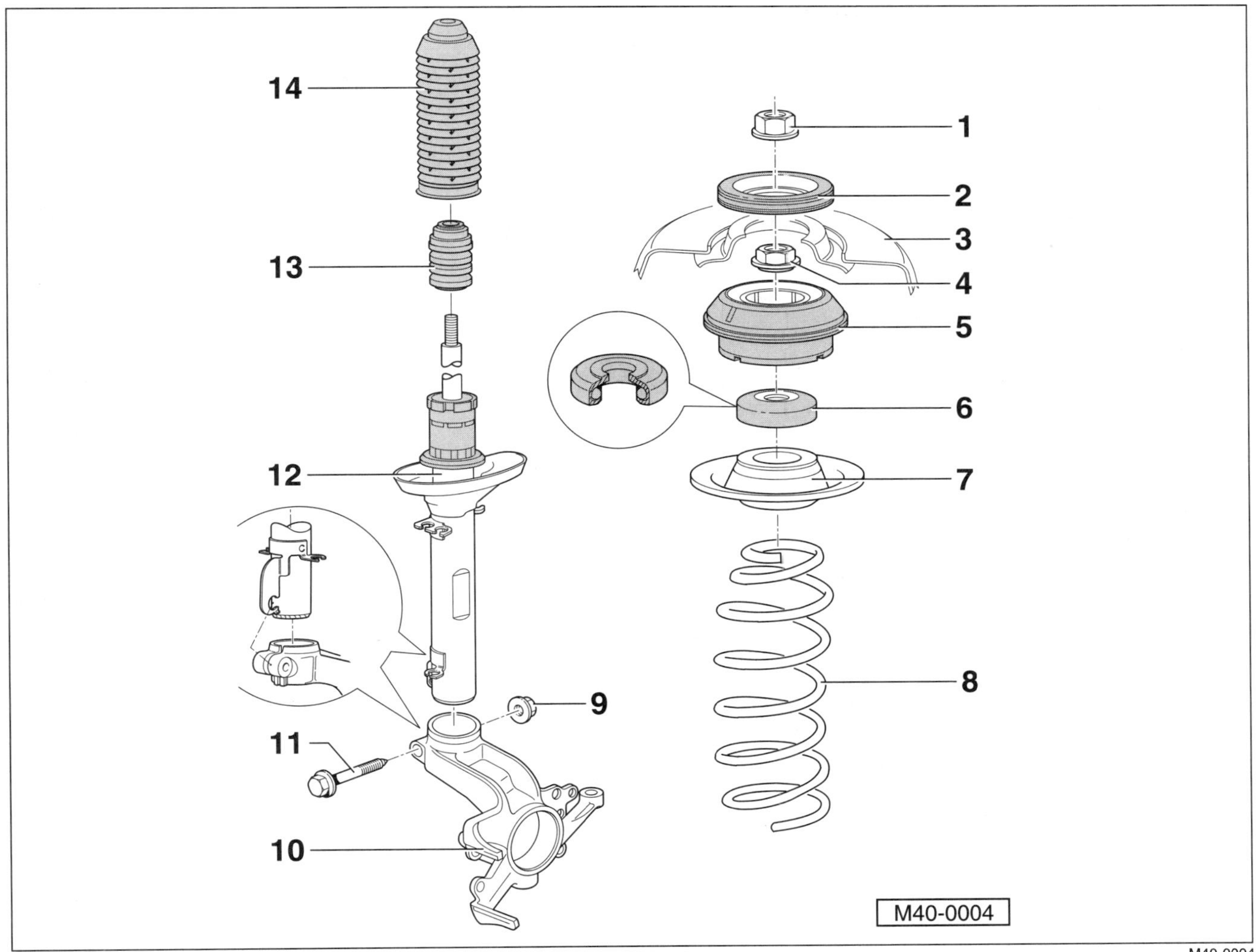

M40-0004

Fig. 8. Suspension strut with coil spring and related components.

1. **Outer nut, self-locking**
   - Always replace
   - Tighten to 60 Nm (44 ft-lb)
2. **Stop plate**
3. **Suspension strut turret**
   - Welded to inner wheel housing
4. **Inner nut**
   - Tighten to 60 Nm (44 ft-lb)
5. **Suspension strut mount, upper**
6. **Axial ball bearing**
7. **Spring plate**
   - Only on vehicles with heavy duty suspension (1GB)
   - Suspension part no., if relevant, can be found on vehicle data label in luggage compartment or owner's manual
8. **Coil spring**
   - Note color-code marking for identification
   - Outer surface of spring must not be damaged
9. **Nut, self-locking**
   - Always replace
   - Tighten to 60 Nm (44 ft-lb) + ¼-turn (90°)
   - Never less than 90°
   - Turning angle tolerance 90°–120°
10. **Wheel bearing housing**
11. **Bolt**
    - Always replace
12. **Shock absorber**
    - Can be replaced individually
    - Slight traces of oil do not necessitate replacement
13. **Buffer stop**
14. **Protective sleeve**

Front suspension struts, removing and installing

> **WARNING —**
> - Suspension strut springs are compressed and under pressure when installed on struts.
> - DO NOT attempt to disassemble or repair suspension without proper tools and experience. Serious injury will result from using improper tools or procedures.
> - Suspension strut is removed and installed as an assembly. DO NOT disassemble or attempt repair while assembly is still installed in vehicle.
> - Front wheel alignment may be altered during suspension strut repairs. Wheel alignment should be checked and adjusted any time repairs are made to the suspension strut area.

1. Raise vehicle and properly support.

> **WARNING —**
> - Be sure to use jack stands designed for the purpose.
> - Jack stands should be on a level hard surface.
> - If a vehicle lift/hoist is used, be sure vehicle is lifted according to manufacturer's instructions.

2. Remove lower sound absorber panels and front wheels.
3. Remove both guide pins from brake caliper. See Fig. 9.

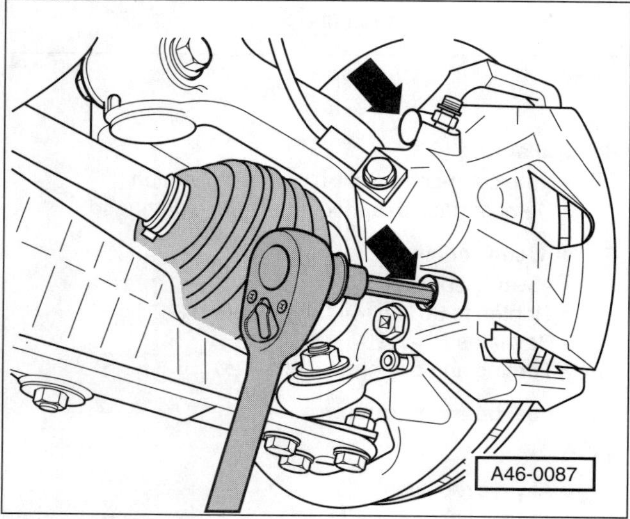

A46-0087

Fig. 9. Remove guide pins (arrows) from brake caliper and support caliper with a wire hanger.

4. Remove brake caliper and suspend using wire.

> ***NOTE —***
> - *Suspend the brake caliper using a piece of wire or heavy duty tie wrap.*
> - *Do not allow the caliper to hang by the brake hose. The unsupported weight can stretch and damage the hose.*

5. Unbolt stabilizer bar connecting link from control arm.
6. Remove ABS wheel speed sensor wire from its bracket on the strut and disconnect harness connector at sensor with a gentle pull.
7. Remove right side drive axle inner boot protective cover from engine block. Disconnect right side drive axle from transmission drive flange. Tie up drive axle to prevent damage.

> ***NOTE —***
> *It is necessary to disconnect right side drive axle so suspension can achieve full droop.*

8. Remove bolt and nut from wheel bearing housing at suspension strut connection. See Fig. 10.

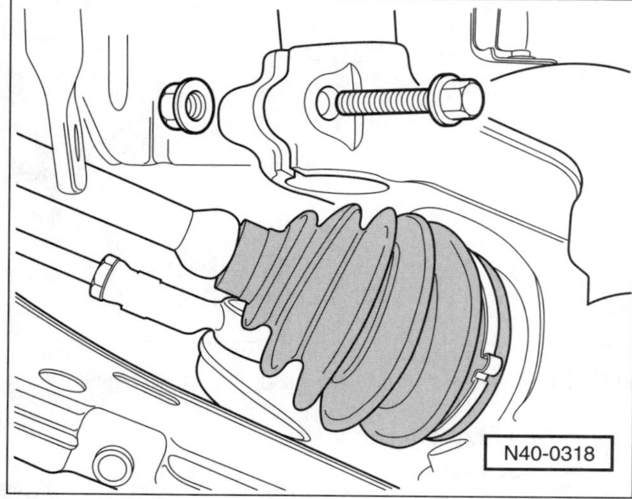

N40-0318

Fig. 10. Bolt and nut securing wheel bearing housing and suspension strut.

9. Insert Volkswagen special spreader tool 3424 into gap in wheel bearing housing and turn ¼-turn in either direction to spread apart. See Fig. 11.

> ***NOTE —***
> *A socket-drive screwdriver bit may be used with care to pry the strut clamp apart if special tool 3424 is not available.*

10. Push brake disc in direction of suspension strut by hand to prevent shock absorber tube from canting in wheel bearing housing opening.

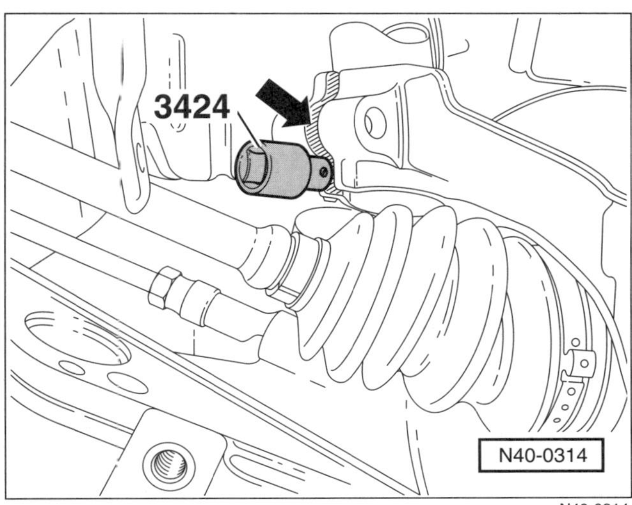

N40-0314

Fig. 11. Volkswagen special tool 3424 (arrow) shown inserted into gap in wheel bearing housing. Turn with a ½-inch ratchet.

11. Pull wheel bearing housing down and clear of shock absorber.

12. Remove wiper arms and cowl panel, see **92 Wipers and Washers.**

13. Remove outer nut and stop plate for upper shock absorber mount using Volkswagen special tools or equivalent. See Fig. 12.

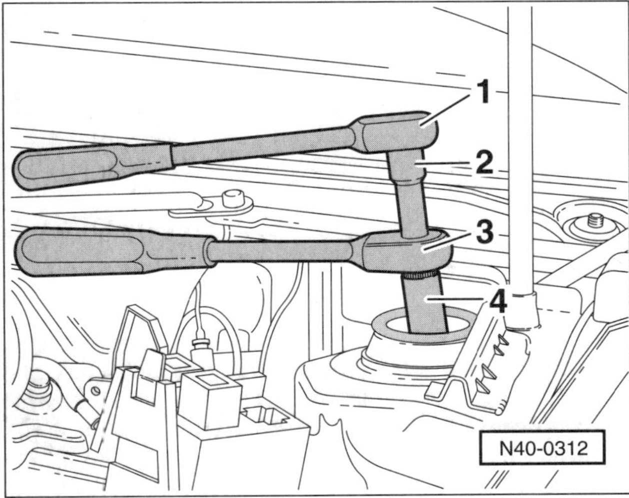

N40-0312

Fig. 12. Set-up for removing suspension strut from vehicle using tools from Volkswagen special tool kit T10001; (1) ½-inch ratchet, (2) T10001/8, (3) T10001/11, (4) T10001/5.

NOTE—
A special offset box wrench or a socket with part of the side ground away can be used to turn the outer strut nut while holding the inner nut with a hex wrench, as an alternative to the VW special tools.

14. Carefully remove suspension strut from below.

15. Before installing strut assembly, remove any dirt from mating areas.

NOTE—
If necessary, use a lubricant that will evaporate quickly such as WD-40 to clean components. Do not use grease.

16. Install top mounting bolt of strut using special tools, or equivalent, as shown earlier in Fig. 12.

17. Raise the control arm with a threaded support stand or floor jack until bolt hole in wheel bearing housing aligns with pinch bolt locating tab on the bottom of the strut.

18. Install a new self-locking lower strut mounting bolt.

19. Remaining installation is the reverse of removal.

Tightening torque
- Outer nut on top of strut (always replace) . . . . 60 Nm (44 ft-lb)
- Lower strut mounting bolt (always replace) . . . . . . 60 Nm (44 ft-lb) +¼ turn (90°)
- Drive axle to drive flange . . . . .see **Drive Axles**
- Drive axle boot protective cover to engine block . . . . 35 Nm (26 ft-lb)
- Brake caliper guide pins . . . . 28 Nm (21 ft-lb)

Coil spring, removing and installing

1. Using VAG1752 spring compressor, or equivalent, compress coil spring until upper spring seat is free. See Fig. 13.

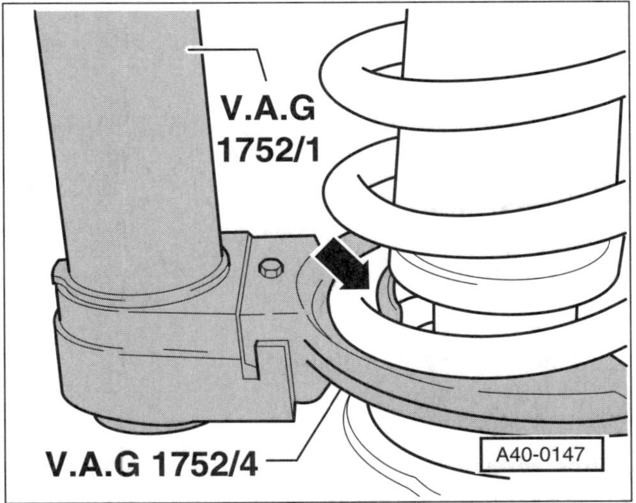

A40-0147

Fig. 13. Insure that coil spring is seated securely (arrow) into Volkswagen spring compressor VAG 1752/4.

2. With coil spring properly compressed, remove inner nut. See Fig. 14.

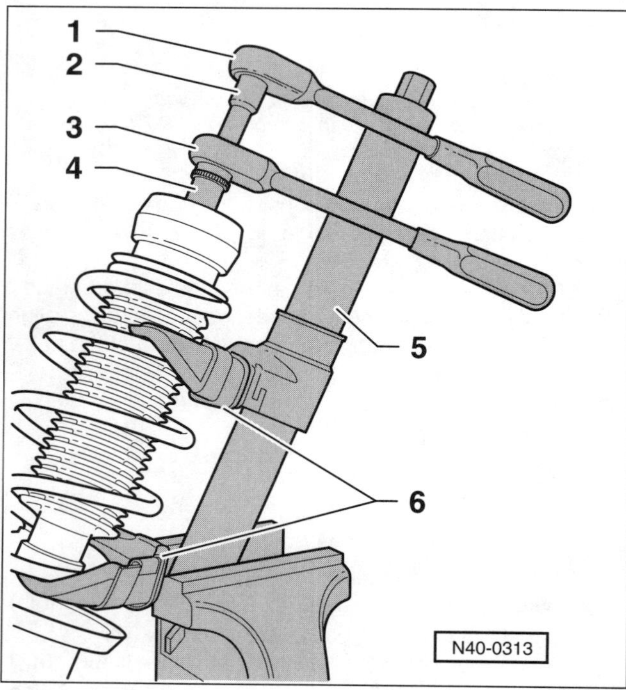

N40-0313

Fig. 14. Set-up for removing coil spring from suspension strut using Volkswagen special tools; (1) ½-inch ratchet, (2) T10001/8, (3) T10001/11, (4) T10001/5, (5) VAG 1752, (6) VAG 1752/4. Volkswagen special tool 3186 is also suitable.

> ***WARNING —***
> *Do not remove inner nut from top of strut assembly without a spring compressor.*

3. Remove components of suspension strut keeping parts in order as they are removed.

4. When re-installing coil spring, fit end of coil against stop in lower spring seat on strut. Fig. 15.

5. If coil springs are to be replaced, note identifying paint marks on coils for proper matching. See Fig. 16.

6. Installation is the reverse of disassembly.

Tightening torque

- Inner suspension strut nut . . . . 60 Nm (44 ft-lb)
- Outer suspension strut nut (always replace) . . . . 60 Nm (44 ft-lb)

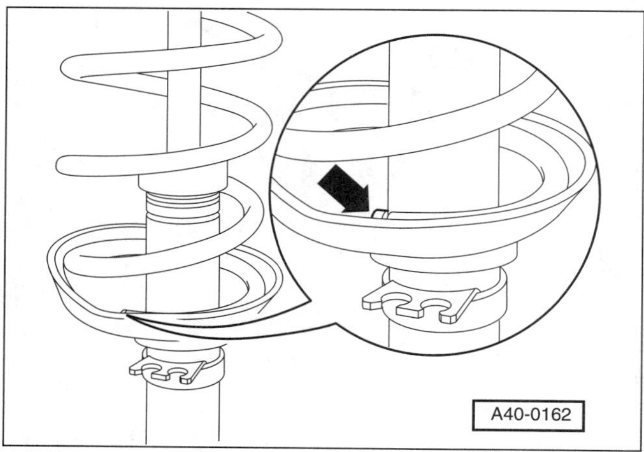

A40-0162

Fig. 15. Install end of coil spring against stop (arrow) in lower spring seat on strut.

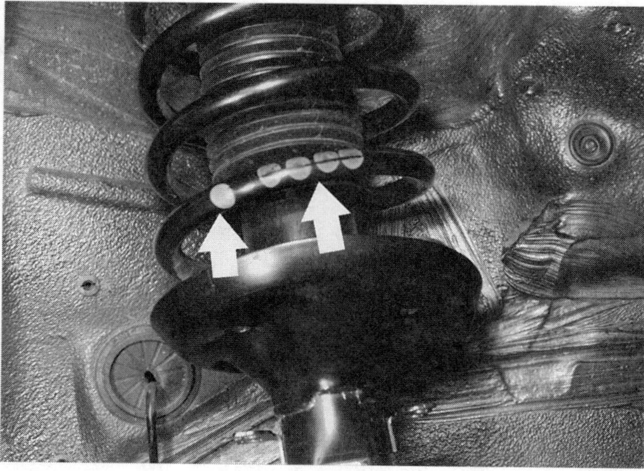

0024281

Fig. 16. Colored paint marks (arrows) are used to identify coil springs with different spring rates.

DRIVE AXLES

Removal and/or replacement of the front axle with constant velocity or triple rotor joints requires special tools and equipment. In some cases, constant velocity and triple rotor joints are supplied only with axles. Lubricate all axle joints with special high temperature molybdenum-disulfide "moly" grease. Always understand and observe the warnings and cautions listed at the beginning of this section.

Specification

- Molybdenum-disulfide constant velocity and triple rotor joint lubricant
  VW part # G 000 603 . . . . 90 G (3.2 oz.)
  VW part # G 000 633 . . . . 120 G (4.2 oz.)

Assembly views are shown in Fig. 17. for CV joint axles and Fig. 18. for triple rotor joint axles.

Drive axles with constant velocity joints, assembly

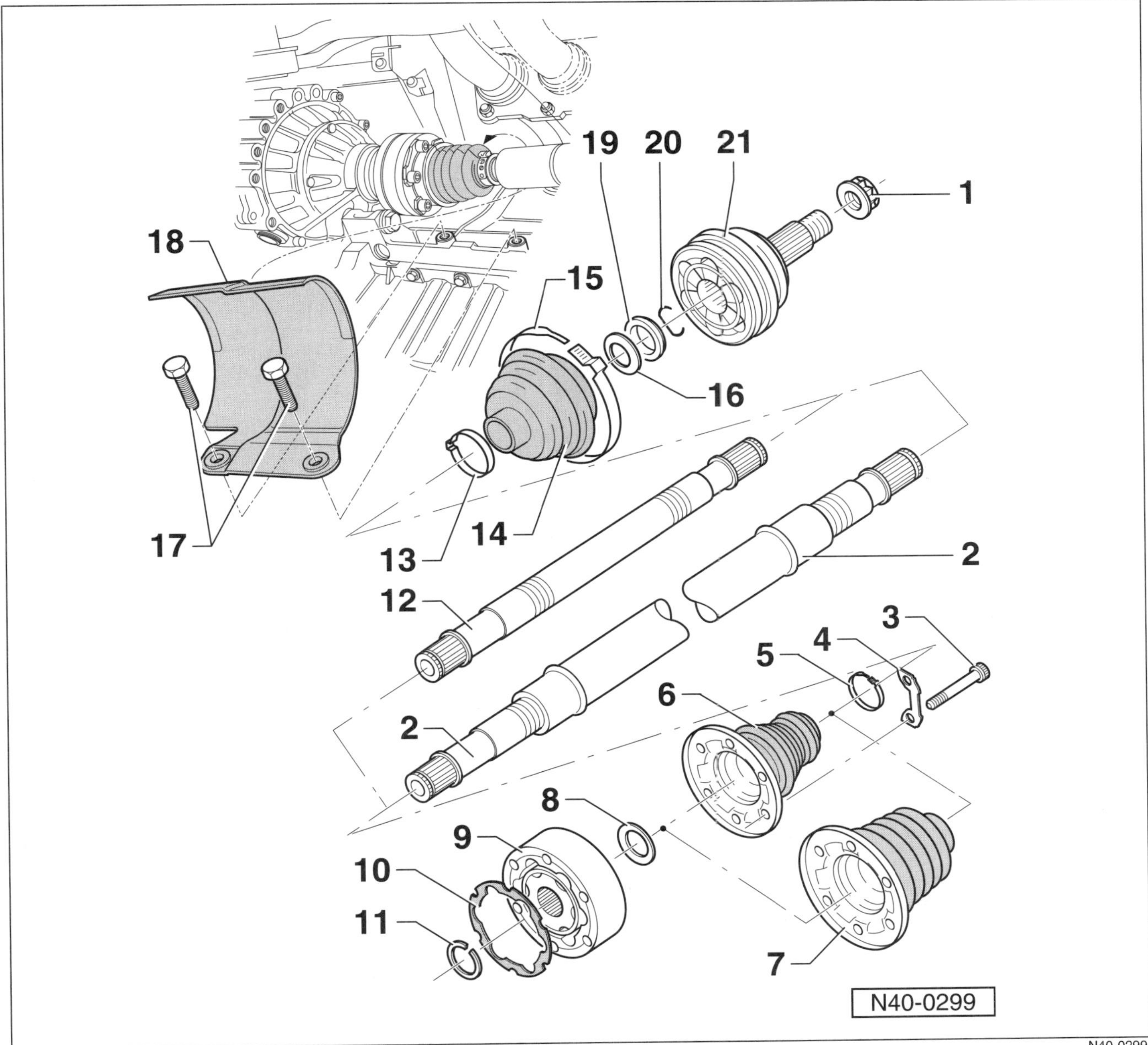

Fig. 17. Constant velocity (CV) joints with axles and related components on manual transmission equipped vehicles.

1. **Axle nut, self-locking**
   - Always replace
   - Any paint residue and/or corrosion on threads of outer joint must be removed before nut is installed
   - For tightening procedure see **Front wheel bearing housing assembly** given earlier
2. **Axle shaft, right side (tube shaft)**
3. **Bolt**
   - Tighten to 40 Nm (30 ft-lb)
4. **Lock plate**
5. **Clamp**
   - Always replace
6. **CV joint boot, inner**
   - Material: Hytrel (Polyelastomer)
   - No vent hole
   - Check for tears and chafing
   - Drive off CV joint using drift

(continued on following page)

(continued from previous page)

7. **CV joint boot, inner**
   - Material: Rubber
   - With vent hole
   - Check for tears and chafing
   - Drive off CV joint using drift
   - Installation position for left drive axle, **see** (A)
   - Installation position for right drive axle, **see** (B)
8. **Spring washer**
   - Installation position, **see** (C)
9. **Inner CV joint**
   - Only replace complete unit
   - Support ball hub and press off of axle
   - Install with chamfer on inner diameter of hub facing stop on axle shaft
   - Press up to stop
   - Install new circlip
10. **Gasket**
    - Always replace
    - Adhesive surface on CV joint must be free of oil and grease
    - Remove protective foil and stick gasket onto CV joint.
11. **Circlip**
12. **Axle shaft, left side (solid shaft)**
13. **Clamp**
    - Always replace
14. **CV joint boot, outer**
    - Check for tears and chafing
    - Material: Hytrel (Polyelastomer)
15. **Clamp**
    - Always replace
16. **Spring washer**
    - Installation position, **see** (D)
17. **Bolts**
    - Tighten to 35 Nm (26 ft-lb)
18. **Protective cover**
19. **Thrust washer**
    - Installation position, **see** (D)
20. **Circlip**
    - Always replace
    - Install in shaft groove
21. **Outer CV joint**
    - Only replace complete unit
    - Drive off axle with plastic/brass/aluminum hammer
    - Drive onto shaft up to stop using plastic/brass/aluminum hammer

(A) Left (solid) axle CV joint boot, installed position

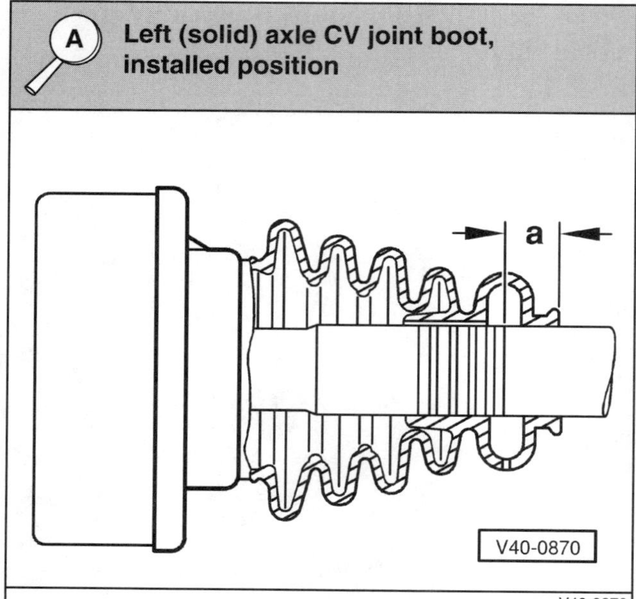

V40-0870

- **Note edge location of boot before disassembly with paint or tape mark. Do not mark by scratching axle.**
- **Install to dimension (a); 17 mm (0.669 in)**

(B) Right (hollow) axle CV joint boot, installed position

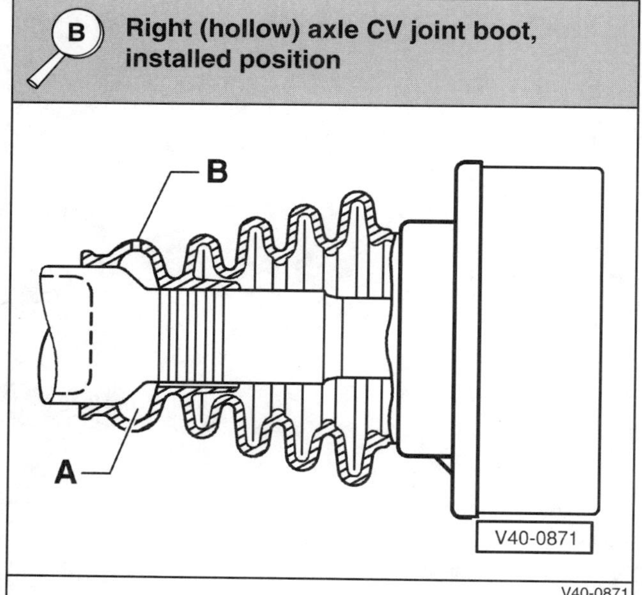

V40-0871

- **Position boot to allow for vent chamber (A).**
- **Vent hole (B) must open into vent chamber (A).**

C **Spring washer on inner CV joints, installed position**

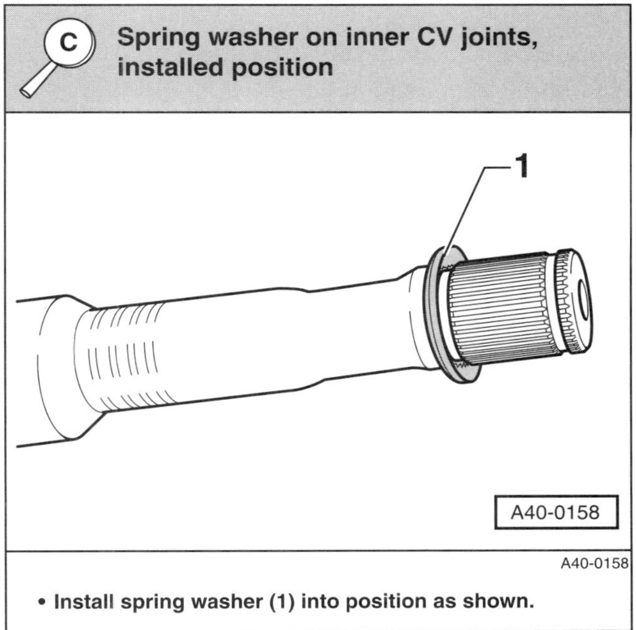

A40-0158

- Install spring washer (1) into position as shown.

D **Spring washer and thrust washer on outer CV joints, installed position**

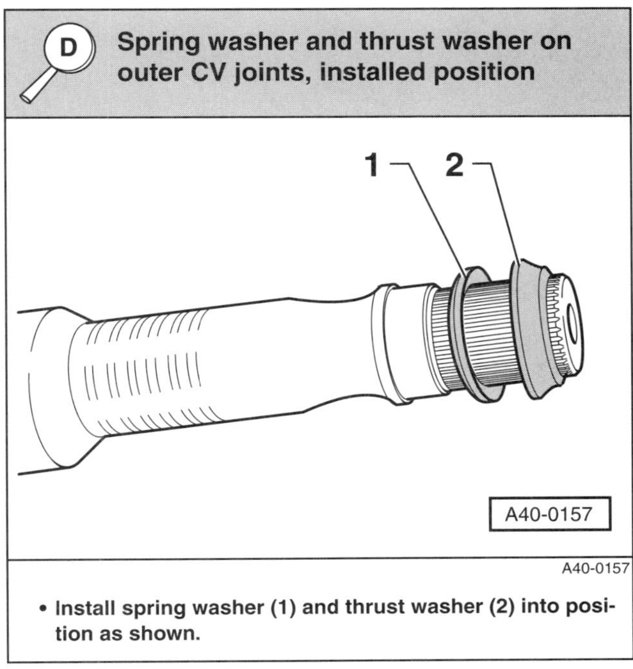

A40-0157

- Install spring washer (1) and thrust washer (2) into position as shown.

Drive axles with triple rotor joint, assembly

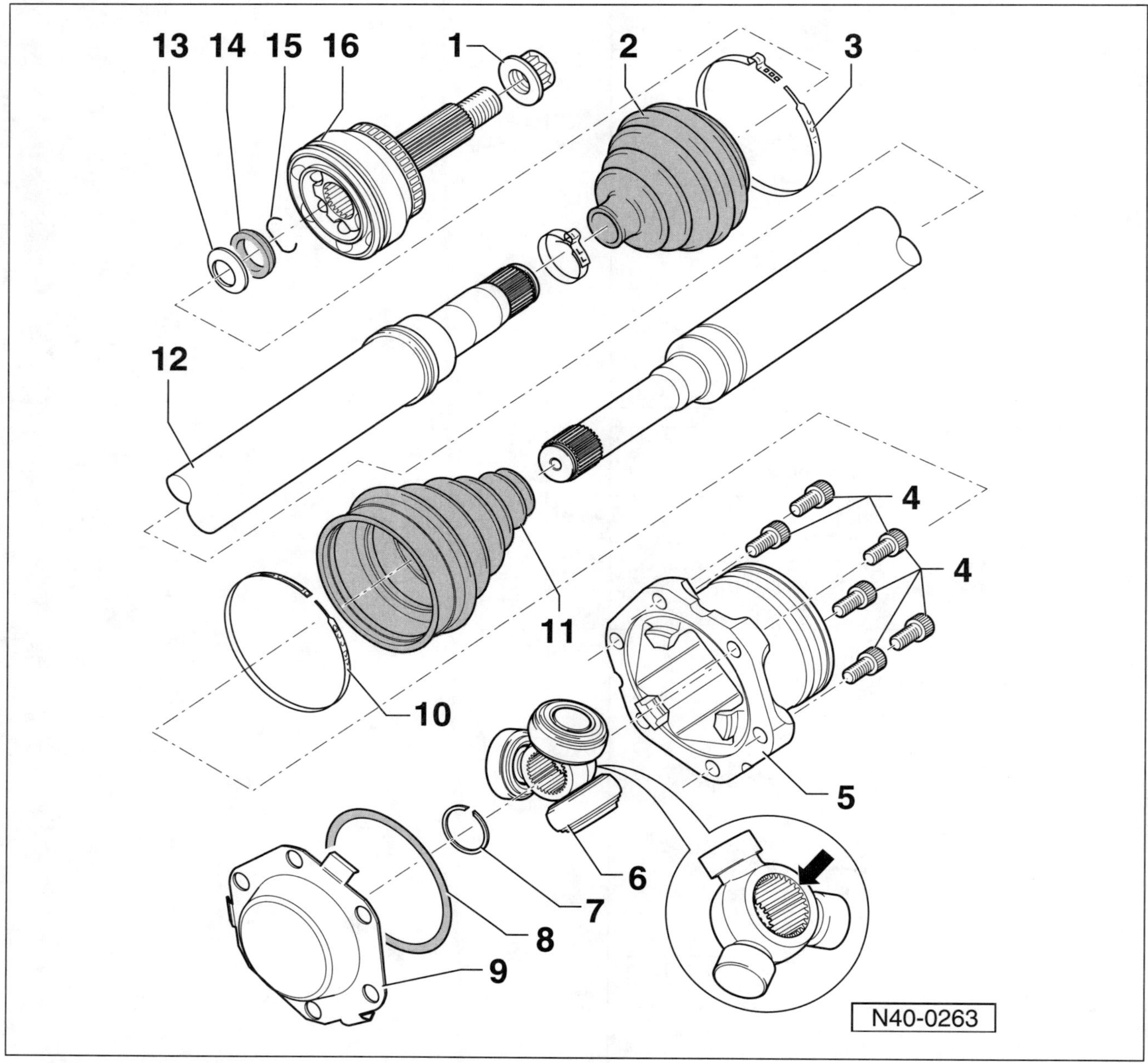

N40-0263

Fig. 18. Triple rotor joints with axle and related components on vehicles equipped with automatic transmission.

1. **Axle nut, self-locking**
   - Always replace
   - Any paint residue and/or corrosion on threads of outer joint must be removed before nut is installed
   - For tightening procedure see **Front wheel bearing housing assembly** given earlier
2. **CV joint boot, outer**
   - Check for tears and chafing
3. **Clamp**
   - Always replace
4. **Multi-point socket head bolt**
   - (M8) tighten to 40 Nm (30 ft-lb)
   - (M10) tighten to 80 Nm (59 ft-lb)
5. **Triple rotor joint housing**
   - Also called "tripot" and "tripod" joints
   - Only replace complete unit
   - Use caution on re-assembly to prevent axle from inadvertently falling apart, **see** Ⓐ

(continued from previous page)

6. **Triple rotor star (hub)**
   - Chamfer faces opposite end of drive axle
7. **Circlip**
   - Always replace
   - Install in shaft groove
8. **O-ring**
   - Always replace
9. **Cover**
   - Always replace
10. **Clamp**
    - For triple-rotor joint
    - Only installed to left side on production vehicles
11. **Triple rotor joint boot**
12. **Drive axle**
13. **Spring washer**
    - Installation position, larger diameter faces thrust washer
14. **Thrust washer**
15. **Circlip**
    - Always replace
    - Install in shaft groove
16. **Outer constant velocity (CV) joint**
    - Only replace complete unit
    - Drive off of axle with plastic/brass/aluminum hammer
    - Drive onto shaft up to stop using plastic/brass/aluminum hammer

A Triple rotor joint, installation precautions

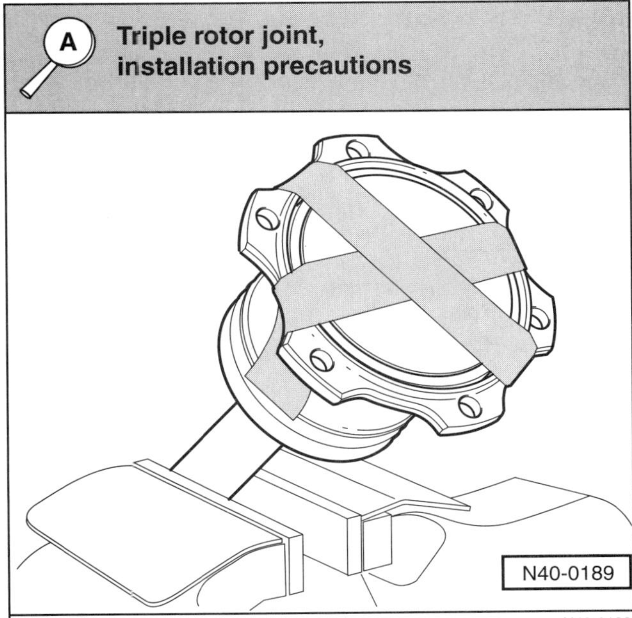

N40-0189

- **Secure triple rotor joint with adhesive tape as shown to prevent housing from accidently sliding down axle shaft.**
- **Remove tape just prior to bolting securely to drive flange.**

CV JOINTS, SERVICING

The components of each CV joint are precisely matched during manufacture and they cannot be serviced individually. The joint can be disassembled to replace the grease or to check the balls and ball tracks for wear and damage. See **table a** for CV joint dimensions and grease quantity.

> ***CAUTION —***
> - *CV joints must be removed from the axle shaft prior to disassembly.*
> - *DO NOT re-use drive axle circlips or CV boot clamps.*
> - *DO NOT interchange parts between CV joints.*

Table a. CV joint dimensions and grease quantity

Outer joint diameter	Total grease	Proportions	
		Joint	Boot
mm/in.	g/oz	g/oz	g/oz
81 (3.2)	80 (2.8)	40 (1.4)	40 (1.4)
90 (3.5)	120 (4.2)	80 (2.8)	40 (1.4)
Inner joint			
94 (3.7)	90 (3.2)	40 (1.4)	50 (1.8)
100 (3.9)	120 (4.2)	50 (1.8)	70 (2.5)

Outer CV joint and boot, removing and installing

1. Remove drive axle from car. See **Drive Axles**.
2. Mark position of CV boot on drive axle.
3. Remove drive axle boot clamps. Disconnect boot from CV joint and cut boot from drive axle.
4. Carefully drive CV joint off drive axle with firm blow from soft mallet. See Fig. 19.
5. Remove thrust washer and dished washer.
6. Clean drive axle. Install new circlip on drive axle.

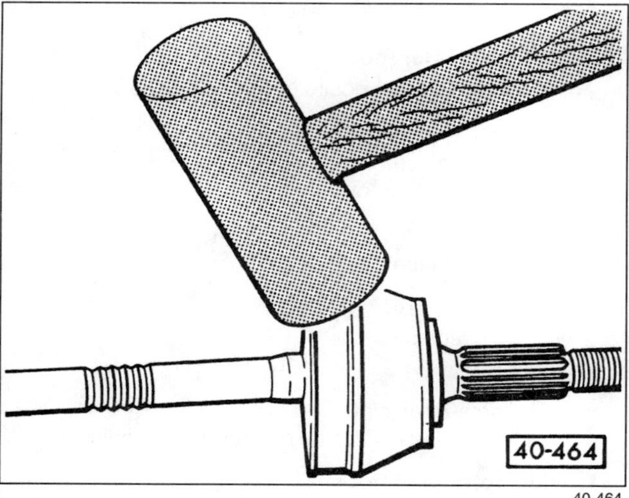

40-464

Fig. 19. CV joint being driven off axle with soft mallet.

7. Slide inner (small) CV boot clamp onto drive axle.
8. Slide new CV boot onto drive axle. Position CV boot on axle, aligning marks made earlier.
9. Pack CV boot with CV joint grease, see **table a**.
10. Install dished washer and thrust washer onto axle. Dished washer outer diameter faces thrust washer.
11. Pack CV joint with grease, see **table a**.
12. Using a soft mallet drive the CV joint onto the axle until the circlip is seated (springs into groove).
13. Install grease packed boot to CV joint. Boot should fit into groove in CV joint.
14. Install outer clamp and crimp.

    NOTE —
    Special pliers should be used to crimp CV boot clamps. Use Snap-On YA 3080 pliers, or equivalent.

15. Lift the boot slightly off the joint to ventilate and equalize pressure. Then slide inner clamp onto boot and crimp.

Outer CV joint, disassembling and assembling

1. Remove CV joint as described above.
2. Mark position of ball hub in relation to ball cage and housing with electric scriber.
3. Swivel ball hub and ball cage so that balls are exposed. See Fig. 20.

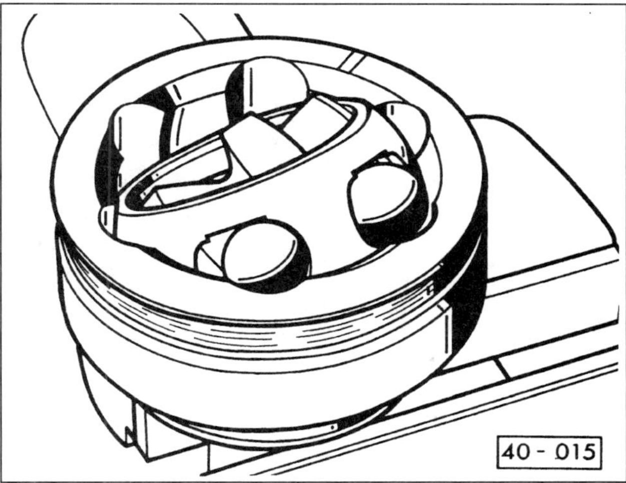

40-015

Fig. 20. Ball track swivelled for ball removal.

4. Remove each ball in turn, swiveling the ball hub and cage as necessary.
5. Turn cage until rectangular openings on either side of ball cage align with joint housing and lift out ball cage together with hub. See Fig. 21.

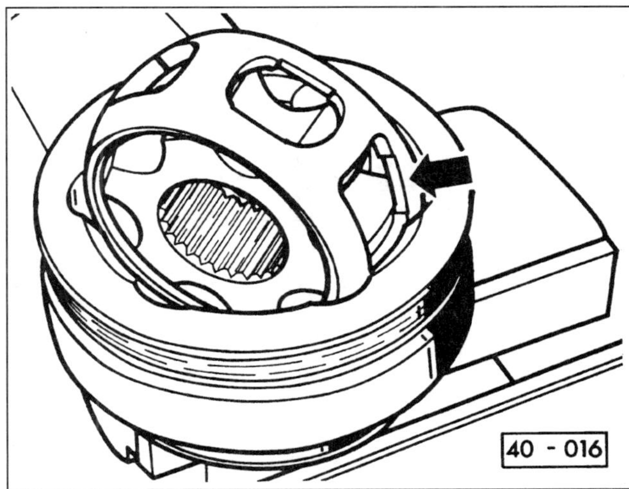

40-016

Fig. 21. Rectangular openings (arrow) aligned with housing.

6. Remove ball hub from ball cage by swinging segment of hub into rectangular opening of cage and tilting hub out of cage. See Fig. 22.

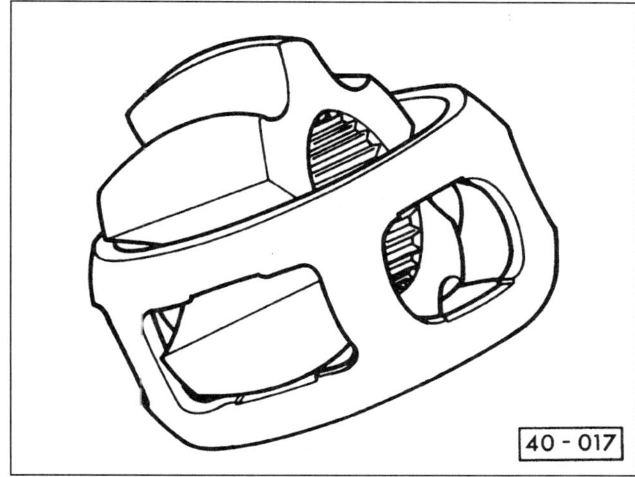

40-017

Fig. 22. Hub being aligned with rectangular opening in cage.

7. Check housing, hub, cage, and balls for pitting and signs of seizure.

NOTE —

- *The six balls of each joint belong to one tolerance group.*
- *Check stub axle, hub, cage and balls for small indentations (pitting) and signs of seizure.*
- *Excessive backlash in the joint will be noticed as a knock when changing from acceleration to overrun or vice versa. Replace the joint if necessary.*
- *Do not replace the joint because of a polished appearance or because ball tracks are visible.*

8. Insert ball hub into ball cage at rectangular opening as shown above in Fig. 22.
9. Pack CV joint housing with grease, see **table a** given earlier.
10. Install cage together with hub into joint housing while aligning rectangular openings in ball cage. Make sure marks made earlier align when installing the cage into the housing.
11. Press in balls separately from alternate sides. Ensure original position of hub in relation to cage.
12. Install CV joint to drive axle as described previously.

Inner CV joint and boot, removing and installing

1. Remove drive axle from car. See **Drive Axles**.
2. Mark the position of the inner CV boot on the drive axle.
3. Wipe away the grease from the end of the drive axle. Remove the circlip holding the inner CV joint to the end of the drive axle.
4. Using a drift, tap off the CV joint boot protective cap The cap is pressed onto the CV joint.
5. While supporting the ball hub, press the drive axle out of the CV joint. Remove the dished washer from the axle. See Fig. 23.

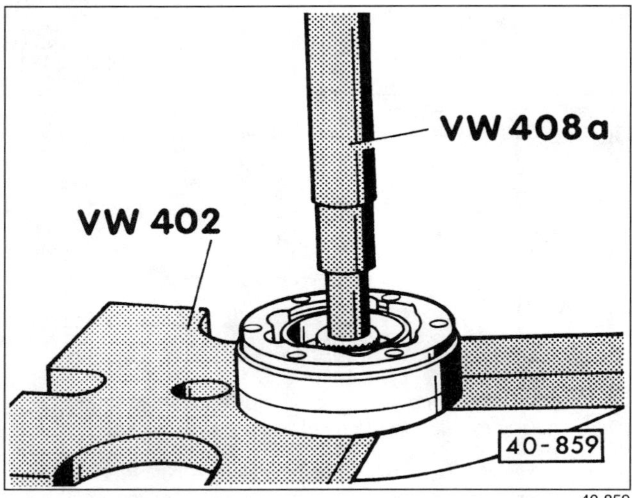

40-859

Fig. 23. Axle shaft being pressed out of inner CV joint. Numbers indicate VW special tools.

6. Remove the CV boot clamp and slide the boot off.
7. Clean drive axle.
8. Slide inner (small) CV boot clamp onto axle.
9. Slide CV boot onto drive axle.
10. Pack boot with grease, see **table a** given earlier.
11. Install dished washer so that dished washer outer diameter faces CV joint.
12. Pack CV joint with grease, see **table a** given earlier.
13. Press CV joint onto axle and install circlip. See Fig. 24.

NOTE —
Chamfer on inner ball hub (splined diameter) must face the contact shoulder on the drive axle.

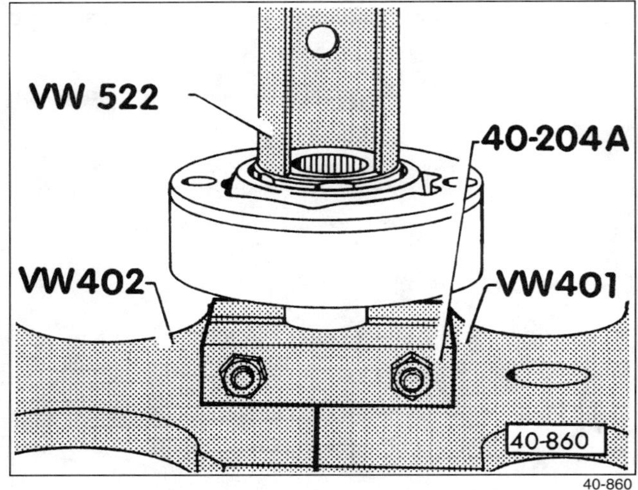

40-860

Fig. 24. Inner CV joint being pressed onto drive axle. Numbers indicate Volkswagen special tools.

14. Slide axle flange bolts through protective cap and into openings in CV joint. Press protective cap onto CV joint.
15. Slide inner clamp onto boot and crimp.

NOTE —
Special pliers should be used to crimp CV boot clamps. Use Snap-On YA 3080 pliers, or equivalent.

Inner CV joint, disassembling and assembling

1. Remove CV joint from drive axle as described previously.
2. Mark position of ball hub in relation to ball cage and housing with electric scriber.
3. Swivel ball hub and ball cage 90°. Pull ball hub together with cage and balls from housing. See Fig. 25.

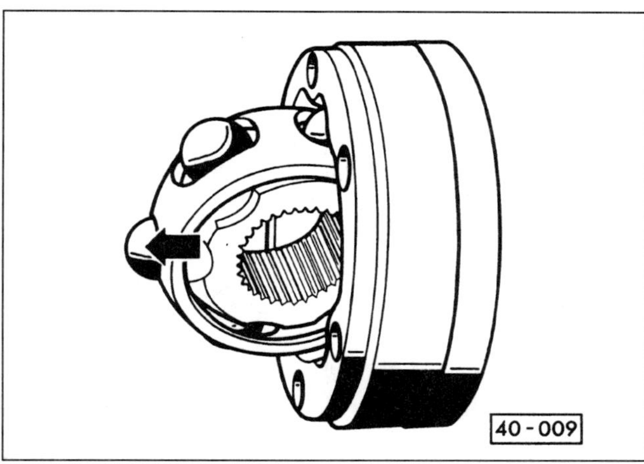

40-009

Fig. 25. Ball hub and cage being removed from housing. Pull in direction of arrow.

4. Press balls out of cage. Tilt ball hub so that ball tracks are aligned with edge of ball cage and remove hub from cage. See Fig. 26.

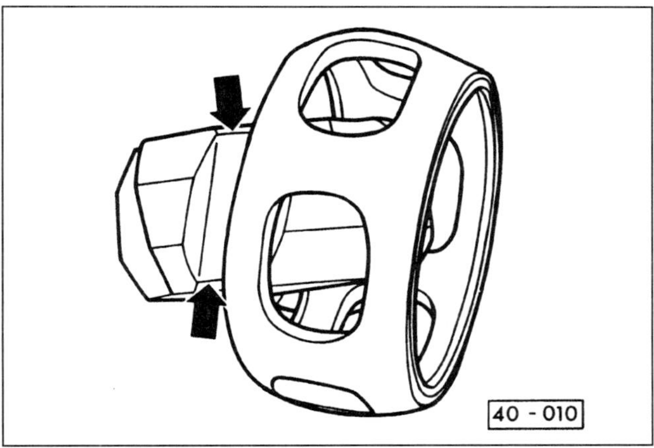

40-010

Fig. 26. Align ball tracks (**arrows**) on hub with ball cage edge when installing hub into cage.

5. Check housing, hub, cage, and balls for pitting and signs of seizure.

NOTE —

- *The six balls of each joint belong to one tolerance group.*
- *Check stub axle, hub, cage and balls for small indentations (pitting) and signs of seizure.*
- *Excessive backlash in the joint will be noticed as a knock when changing from acceleration to overrun or vice versa. Replace the joint if necessary.*
- *Do not replace the joint because of a polished appearance or because ball tracks are visible.*

6. Insert ball hub over both chamfers into ball cage.

7. Align ball hub to cage using marks made earlier. Press balls into cage. See Fig. 27.

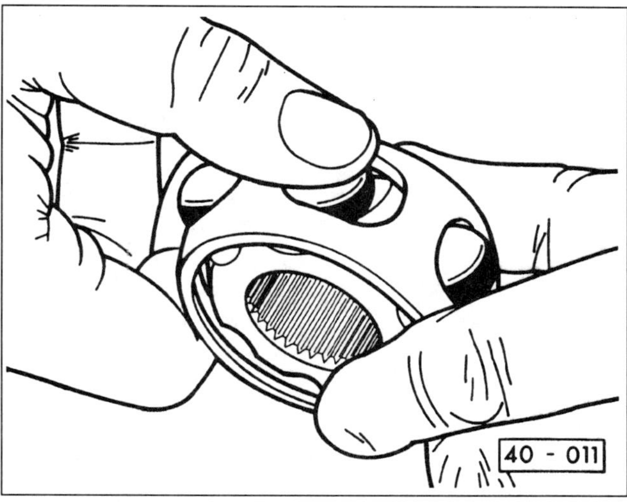

40-011

Fig. 27. Balls being pressed into cage.

8. Insert hub with cage and balls into joint at right angles, ensuring the following (See Fig. 28.):
   - Wide ball groove in outer ring (**a**) and narrow groove in hub (**b**) are together on one side when hub is pivoted into housing.
   - Matching marks on hub, cage, and housing are aligned.
   - Chamfer on inside diameter of ball hub faces larger diameter of joint.

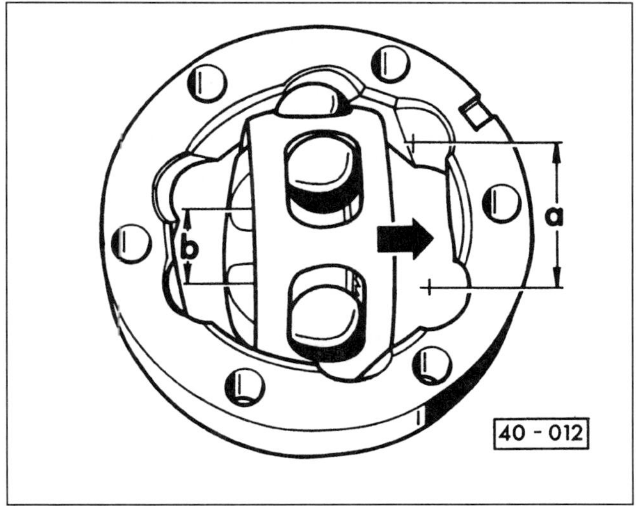

40-012

Fig. 28. Hub assembly correctly in housing with wide ball groove in housing (a) and a narrow groove in hub (b) together on one side.

9. Swivel ball hub with cage and balls into housing. Pivoting hub and cage until balls align. See Fig. 29.

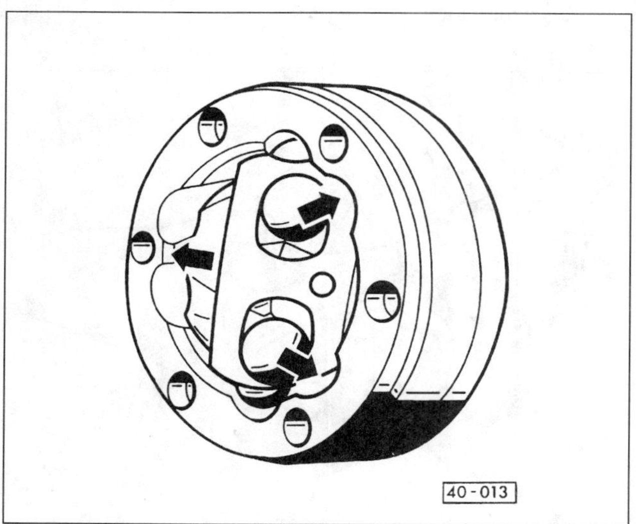

40-013

Fig. 29. Ball hub correctly installed into housing. Pivot hub out of cage (arrows) until balls are spaced to fit grooves.

10. Press cage firmly by hand until hub swings fully into position. See Fig. 30.

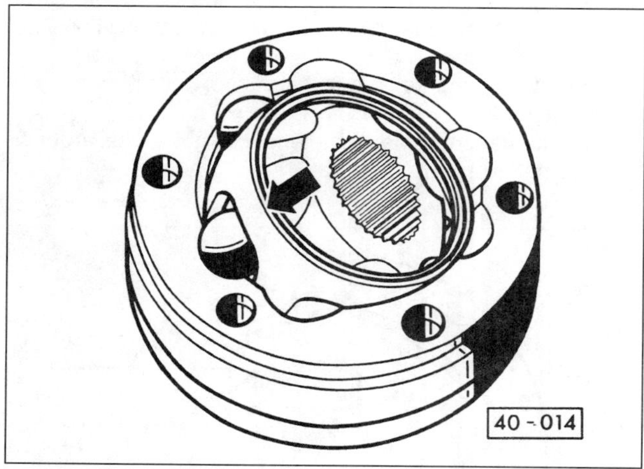

40-014

Fig. 30. Press cage firmly at arrow until hub swings fully into position.

> ***NOTE —***
> *The joint is correctly assembled when the ball hub can be moved in and out over the full range of axial movement by hand.*

11. Pack CV joint with grease, see **table a** given earlier. Pack grease from both sides of CV joint and pack CV boot with remaining grease.

12. Install CV joint to axle using a new circlip.

QUALITY REVIEW

QUALITY REVIEW

When you have finished working under the hood and around other areas of the vehicle, it is advisable to take a moment to quality check or review your work. This helps to insure that the operation or repair has been completed properly with all affected systems functioning within normal parameters. These may include the following:

- Ensure that all cable ties and clamps that were removed as part of the repair are replaced.
- Ensure that all fasteners and hardware were replaced and torqued as specified.
- Make sure that all other components involved in the repair are positioned correctly, properly torqued and function properly.
- Make sure that all tools, shop cloths, fender covers and protective tapes are removed before closing the hood.
- Clean grease and fingerprints from painted surfaces, steering wheel and shifter.

42 Rear Suspension

GENERAL

Special tools, equipment and procedures are required for most front suspension repair and component replacement. In addition, wheel alignment is almost always disturbed when suspension components are removed or replaced.

This section covers repairs to the rear suspension and related components. For front suspension servicing and repair information, see **40 Front Suspension**. For wheel alignment specifications, see **44 Wheels, Tires, Wheel Alignment**.

> ***WARNING —***
> - *Do not re-use any fasteners that are worn or deformed in normal use. Most fasteners are designed to be used only once and become unreliable and may fail when used a second time. This includes, but is not limited to, nuts, bolts, washers, circlips, cotter pins, self-locking nuts and bolts. For replacements, always use new parts.*
> - *Do not reinstall bolts and nuts coated with undercoating wax, as correct tightening torque cannot be ensured. Always clean the threads of removed bolts and nuts that are to be re-used with a suitable solvent before installation. Ensure that new parts are clean.*

> ***WARNING —***
> - *Do not use standard nuts and bolts in place of green colored parts. The green color denotes a special anti-corrosion process known as "dacromet" or "delta-tone". Torque specifications are given based on use of these parts only.*
> - *Always replaced rusted or corroded bolts, nuts and washers even if not specifically indicated.*
> - *DO NOT attempt to straighten or weld suspension struts, wheel bearing housings, control arms or any other wheel locating or load bearing components of the front suspension.*

REAR SUSPENSION

The beam-type rear axle is a one-piece welded assembly consisting of an axle beam, trailing arms, stabilizer bar, and coil spring seat. Rear wheel stub axles are bolted to the trailing arms. Coil springs are mounted low on the beam with the upper spring seats attached to the rear body structure. Gas-pressure telescopic rear shock absorbers are bolted to the outside of the wheel wells and are easily removed independent of the springs. Rear wheel bearings are sealed into the hub assembly and are not serviceable. Fig. 1 shows the rear suspension with related components.

42

Rear suspension overview

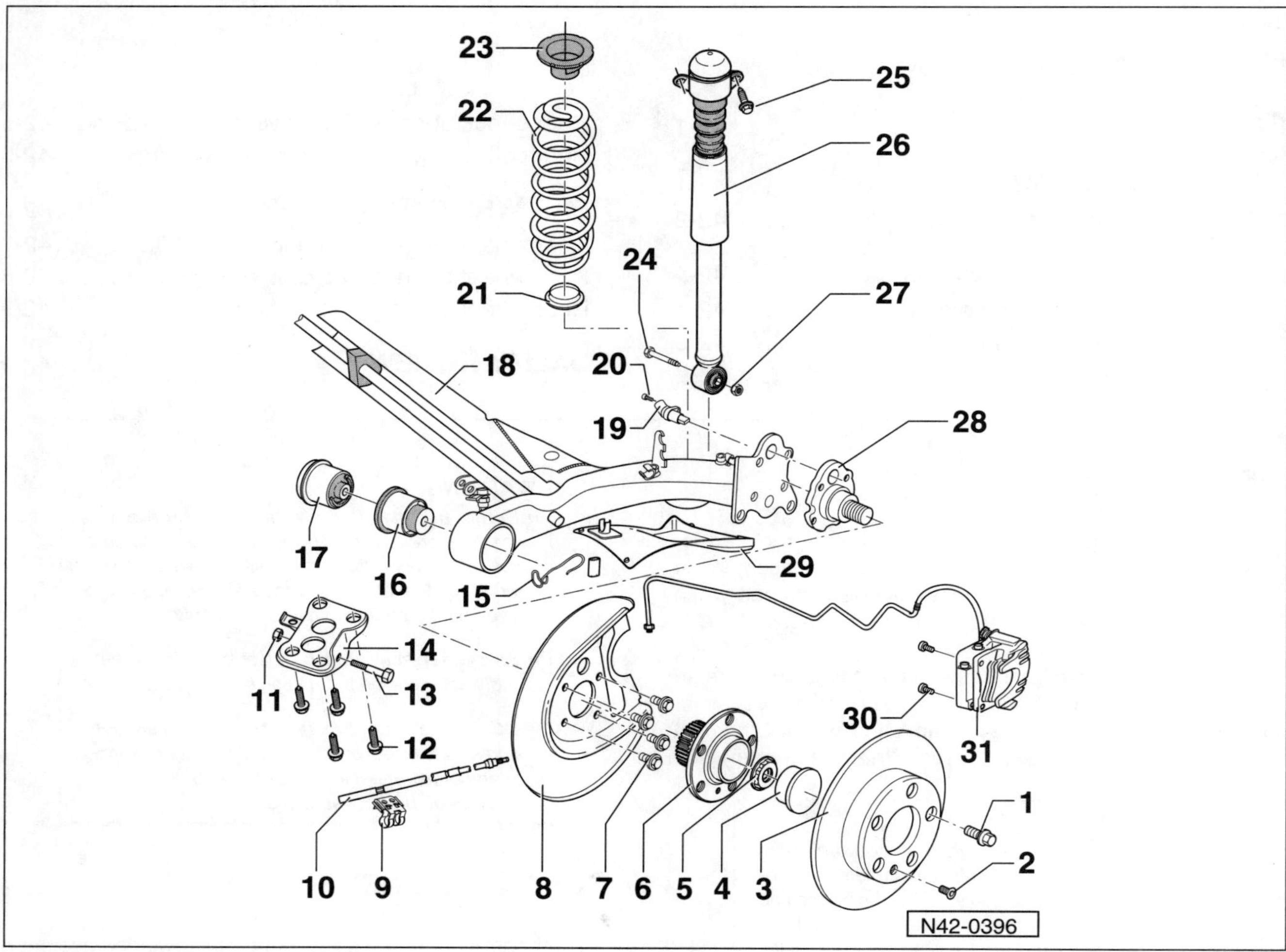

N42-0396

Fig. 1. Rear axle beam with left side suspension and brake components.

1. **Wheel lug bolts**
   - Tighten to 120 Nm (89 ft-lb)
2. **Screw**
   - Tighten to 4 Nm (35 in-lb)
3. **Brake disc (rotor)**
4. **Dust cap**
   - Always replace
   - Proper function and long service life can only be ensured by the perfect seal of a new dust cap
5. **Nut, self-locking**
   - Always replace
   - Tighten to 175 Nm (129 ft-lb)
6. **Wheel bearing/hub unit with ABS wheel speed sensor rotor**
   - Wheel bearing, wheel hub and wheel speed sensor rotor are installed together in housing
   - Wheel bearing/hub unit is maintenance and adjustment free
7. **Bolt**
   - Always replace
   - Tighten to 60 Nm (44 ft-lb)
8. **Splash shield**
9. **Parking brake cable bracket**
10. **Parking brake cable**
11. **Nut, self-locking**
    - Always replace
    - Tighten to 80 Nm (59 ft-lb)
12. **Bolt**
    - Always replace
    - Tighten to 75 Nm (55 ft-lb)
    - If threads in welded nut in longitudinal member (rear body structure) are damaged, repair using Heli-Coil
    - Do not repair more than one welded nut on each side with Heli-Coils

(continued from previous page)

13. Bolt
- Always replace
- Tighten to 80 Nm (59 ft-lb)

14. Rear axle mounting bracket
- Check, and if necessary adjust rear axle total toe after installation
- If possible do not loosen when removing rear axle

15. Parking brake cable bracket

16. Bonded rubber bushing
- Installed position, **see** Ⓐ

17. Hydraulic bonded rubber bushing
- Not installed on all vehicles
- Removing and installing, **see** Ⓑ

18. Axle beam
- Stub axle contact surfaces and threaded holes must be free of paint and dirt

19. ABS wheel speed sensor

20. Bolt
- Tighten to 8 Nm (71 in-lb)

21. Spacer bushing
- Material: zinc
- Check for damage

22. Coil spring
- Note color-code marking for identification

23. Spring seat, upper
- End of coil spring must lie against spring seat stop, see **Rear coil spring, removing and installing**

24. Lower shock bolt
- Always replace
- Tighten to 60 Nm (44 ft-lb)

25. Upper shock bolt
- Always replace
- Tighten to 75 Nm (55 ft-lb)

26. Shock absorber
- Gas pressure
- Can be replaced individually

27. Nut
- Always replace
- Axle beam must be centered when tightening nut to insure proper shock bushing preload
- Load car rear with weight of one person when tightening

28. Stub axle
- Do not attempt to straighten stub axle
- Do not attempt to re-cut threads

29. Stone protection plate

30. Bolts
- Always replace
- Tighten to 65 Nm (48 ft-lb)

31. Rear brake caliper

A Bonded rubber axle beam bushing, installed position

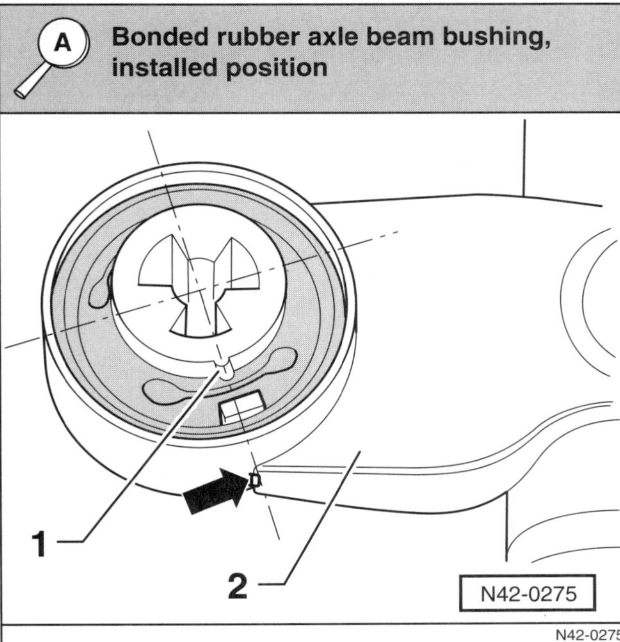

N42-0275

- **Identification mark (1) on face of bonded rubber bushing must align with edge of trailing arm (arrow) on axle beam (2).**

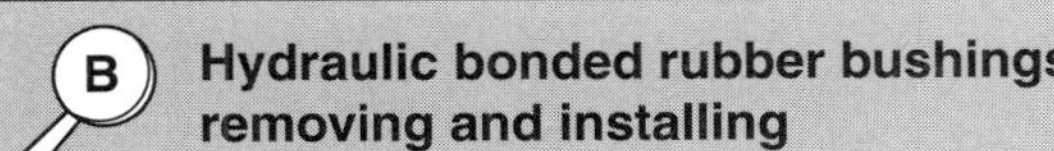

B Hydraulic bonded rubber bushings, removing and installing

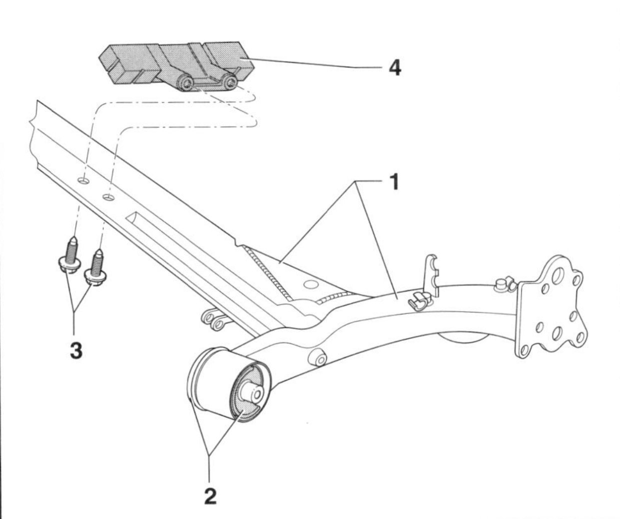

N42-0406

- **If bushing (2) is damaged, the entire rear axle beam (1) must be replaced.**
- **Vibration damper (4) is only on axles equipped with hydraulic bonded rubber bushings (axles with solid rubber bushings do not have damper).**
- **Rear axle beam with hydraulic bushings installed is supplied as a replacement part by Volkswagen.**

REAR SHOCK ABSORBERS

Rear shock absorber assembly

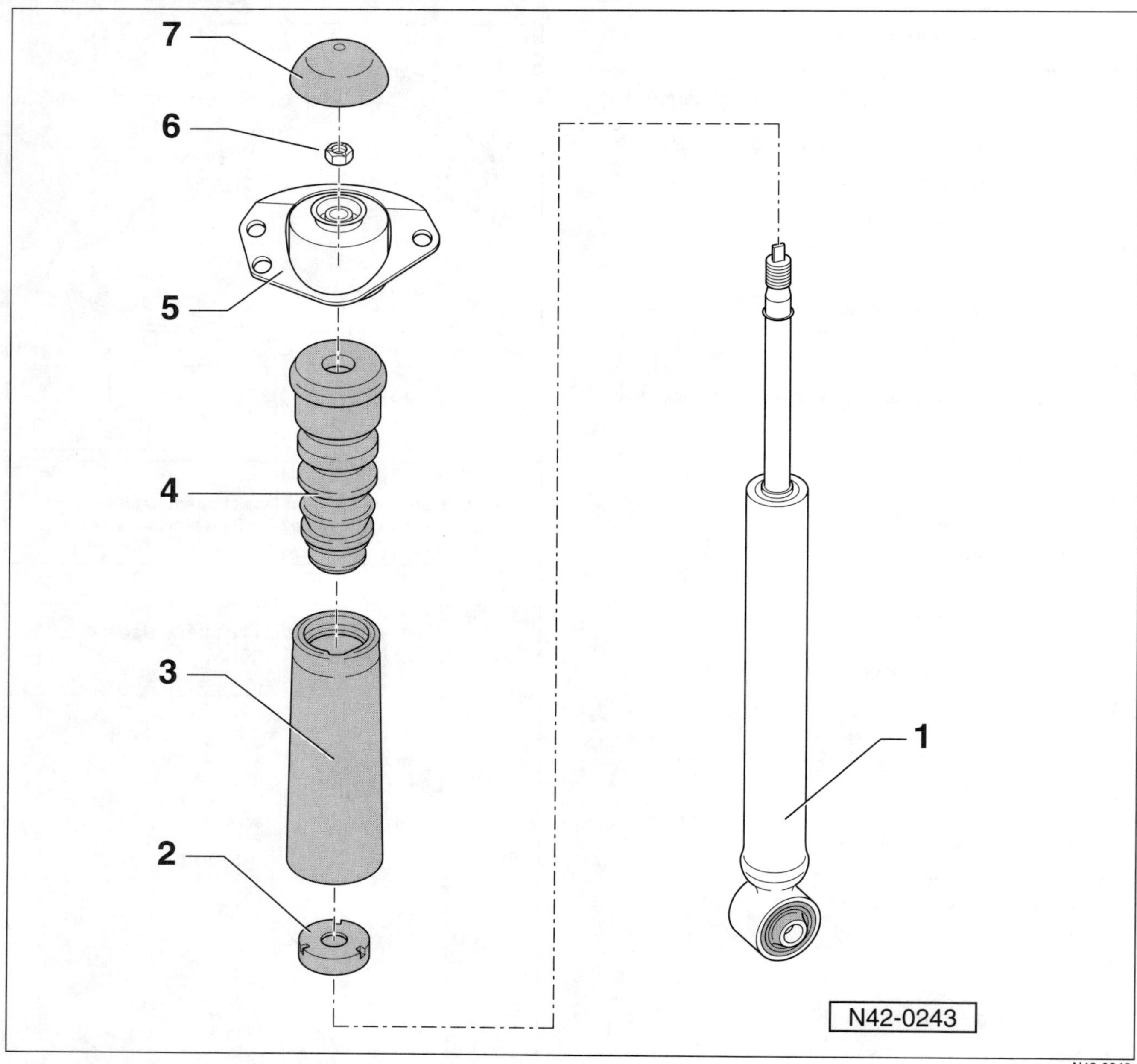

Fig. 2. Rear shock absorber and related components with upper mount.

1. **Gas-filled shock absorber**
   - Can be replaced individually
   - Slight traces of oil do not necessitate replacement
2. **Protective cap**
3. **Protective tube**
4. **Bump stop**
5. **Upper shock absorber mount**
6. **Nut, self-locking**
   - Always replace
   - Tighten to 25 Nm (18 ft-lb)
7. **Protective sleeve**

Rear shock absorber, checking

1. Remove shock absorber as described below.
2. Compress shock absorber by hand. Piston rod must move over its complete length smoothly and with even force.
3. If gas pressure is sufficient, piston rod will return to its fully extended position.
4. If piston rod does not return to its fully extended position and there is no loss of oil, then shock absorber is still OK.

Rear shock absorber, removing and installing

1. Raise vehicle slightly with a lift or floor jack, but leave weight of vehicle on the wheels.

NOTE —

Rear suspension must not be allowed to extend fully. Spring will fall out when shock absorber is unbolted if some vehicle weight is not supported by the rear wheel.

2. Remove upper shock mounting bolts. See Fig. 3.

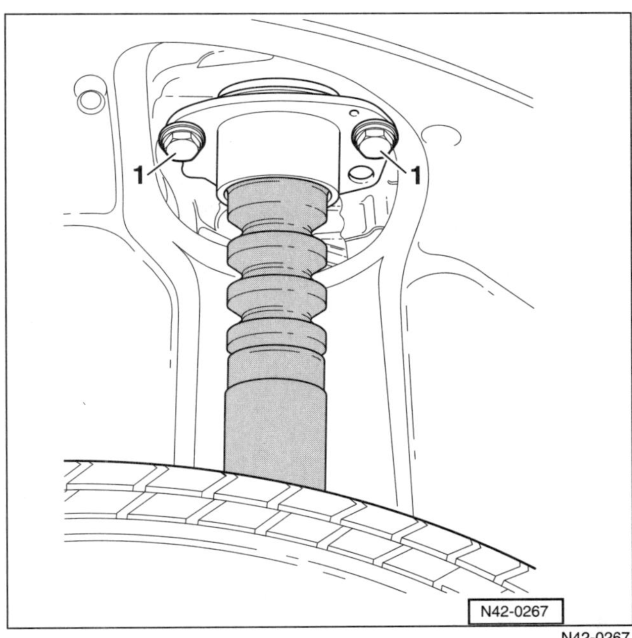

N42-0267

Fig. 3. Remove bolts (**1**) with the vehicle still resting on its wheels.

3. Raise vehicle slightly to relieve coil spring pressure.
4. Remove lower shock absorber bolt on rear axle. See Fig. 4.
5. Remove shock absorber.

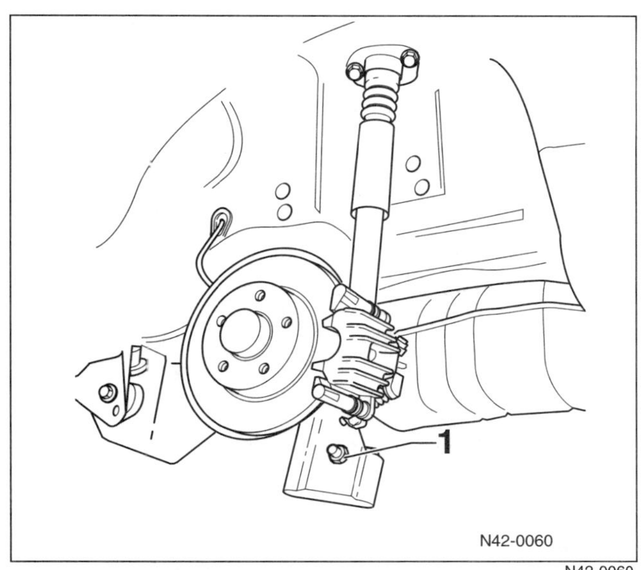

N42-0060

Fig. 4. Remove lower shock bolt (**1**) holding shock to axle beam. Wheel and coil spring shown removed for clarity, but can remain installed.

6. Remove upper shock mount. See Fig. 5.

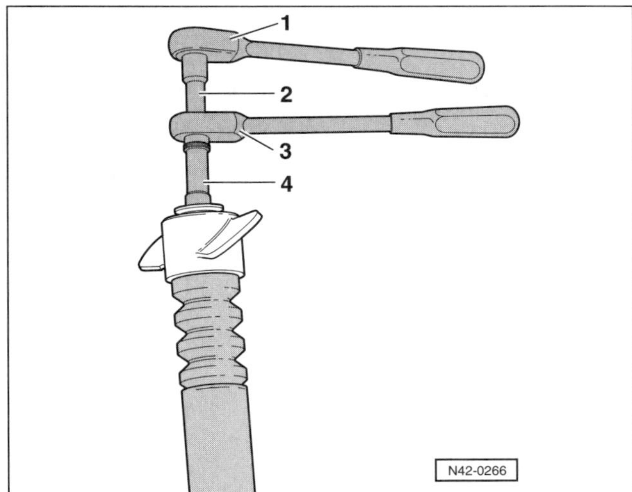

N42-0266

Fig. 5. Set-up for removing nut holding upper shock mount using Volkswagen special tools; (**1**) ½-inch ratchet, (**2**) T10001/9, (**3**) T10001/11, (**4**) T10001/1. Volkswagen special tool 3079 is also suitable.

7. Installation is the reverse of removal.

Tightening torque

- Upper shock bolt (M10) always replace . . . . 75 Nm (55 ft-lb)
- Lower shock bolt and nut (M10) always replace . . . . 60 Nm (44 ft-lb)

Rear coil spring, removing and installing

1. Disconnect harness connector for ABS wheel speed sensor (as applicable).

2. Unclip wheel speed sensor wiring from retainer. See Fig. 6.

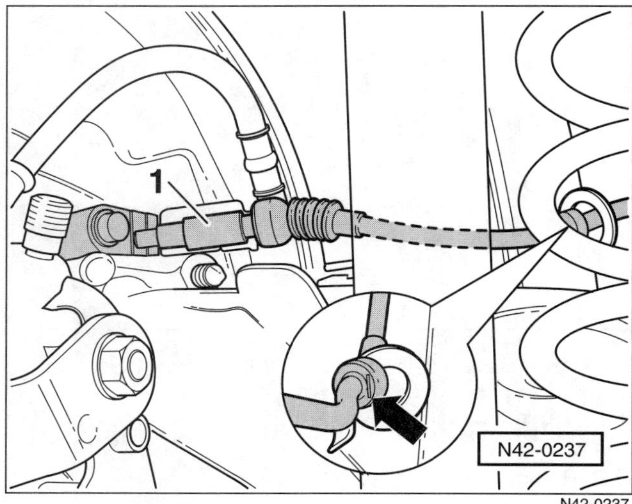

Fig. 6. Unplug ABS wheel speed sensor (**1**) as required and unclip sensor wiring from retainer (**arrow**).

3. Raise vehicle slightly with a lift or floor jack, but leave vehicle resting on its wheels.

4. Remove upper shock mounting bolts as shown earlier. See Fig. 3.

5. Raise vehicle further to relieve coil spring pressure.

6. Remove coil spring.

7. Installation is the reverse of removal, noting the following:
   - Make sure spacer bushing (zinc) is not damaged, replace if necessary.
   - Position end of coil spring against stop in upper spring seat. See Fig. 7.

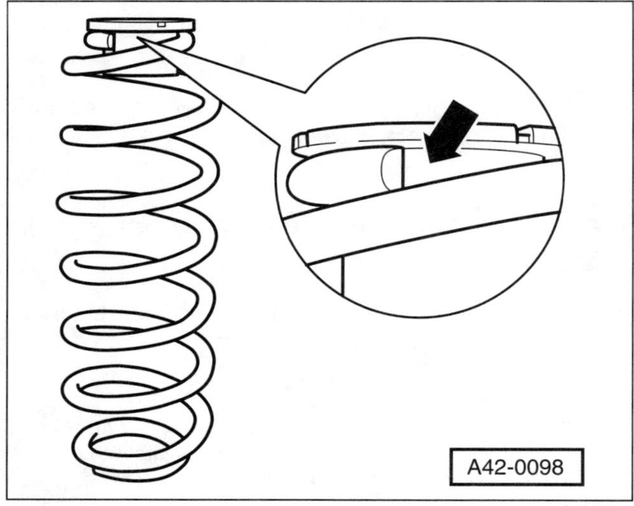

Fig. 7. Install end of spring against stop (**arrow**) in upper spring seat.

- Install spring together with spring seat.
- Press rear axle upward using transmission jack.

> ***WARNING —***
> *If vehicle is supported on a vehicle lift or hoist, ensure that transmission jack does not push up on the suspension sufficient to topple the vehicle off.*

- Using new bolts, bolt shock absorber to body.

Tightening torque
- Upper shock bolt (M10)
  always replace . . . . 75 Nm (55 ft-lb)

REAR WHEEL BEARINGS

Inner and outer rear wheel bearings along with the hub and ABS speed sensor rotor are combined into a single integrated assembly. This assembly must be replaced as a complete unit as there are no individually serviceable components. See Fig. 8.

Rear wheel bearing/hub unit, assembly

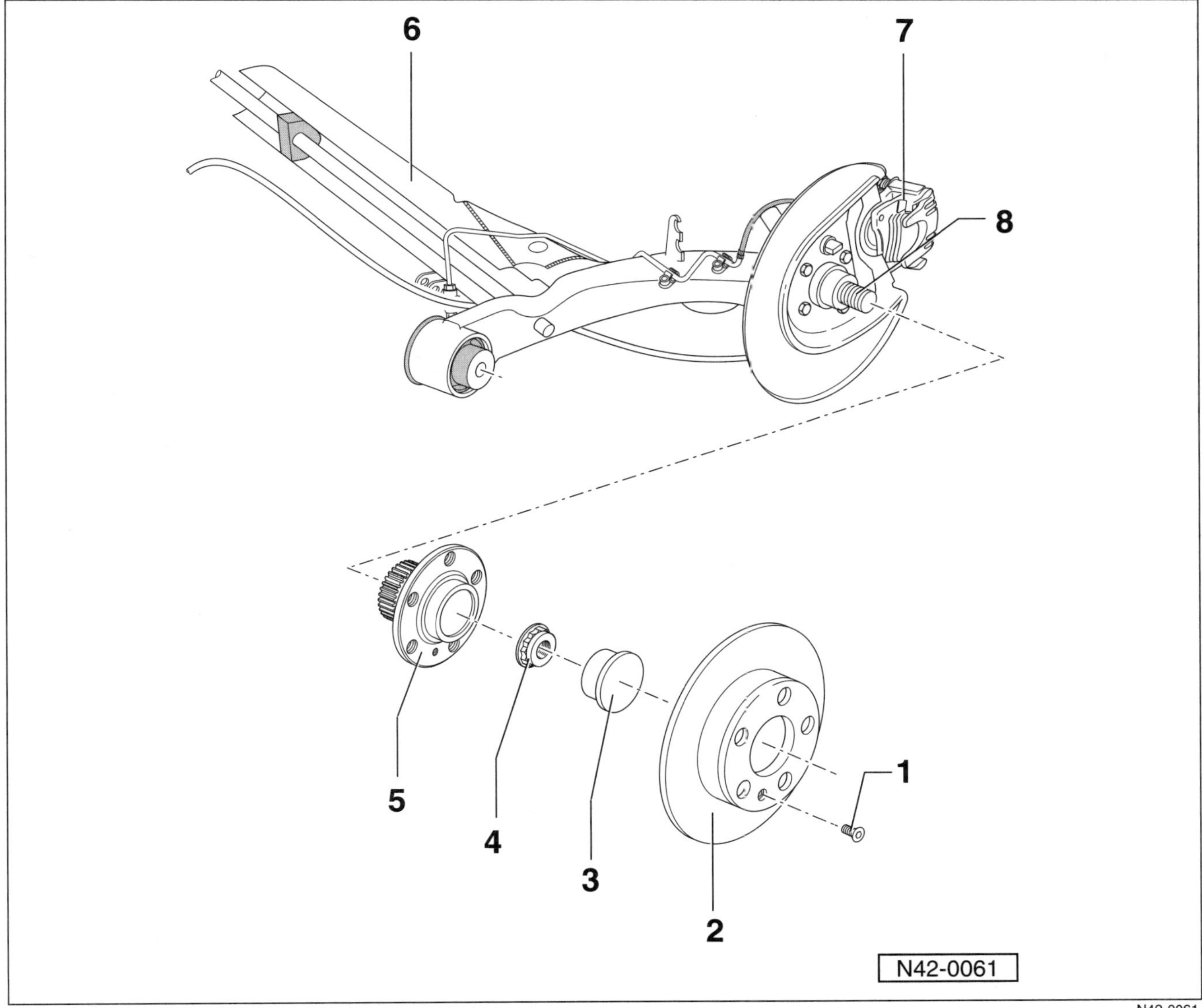

N42-0061

Fig. 8. Left rear wheel bearing/hub unit assembly and related components. Right side is similar.

1. **Screw**
2. **Brake disc (rotor)**
3. **Dust cap**
   - Always replace
   - Proper function and long service life can only be ensured by the perfect seal of a new dust cap
4. **Nut, self-locking, 12-point**
   - Always replace
   - Tighten to 175 Nm (129 ft-lb)
5. **Wheel bearing/hub unit with ABS wheel speed sensor rotor**
   - Wheel bearing, wheel hub and wheel speed sensor rotor are installed together in housing
   - Wheel bearing/hub unit is maintenance and adjustment free
6. **Axle beam assembly**
7. **Rear brake caliper**
8. **Stub axle**
   - Do not attempt to straighten stub axle
   - Do not attempt to re-cut threads

Rear wheel bearing/hub unit, removing

1. Remove wheel assembly.

2. Remove rear hub dust cap from seat on rotor. See Fig. 9.

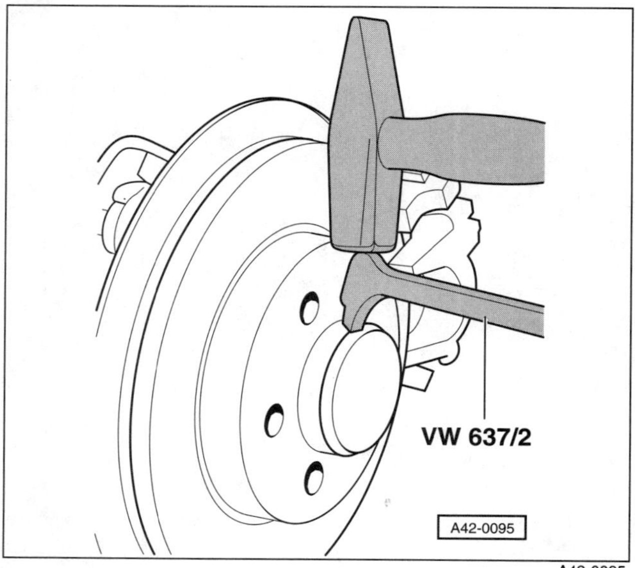

A42-0095

Fig. 9. Tap on dust cap with suitable tools to loosen, then remove using cap puller.

3. Remove brake caliper. See Fig. 10.

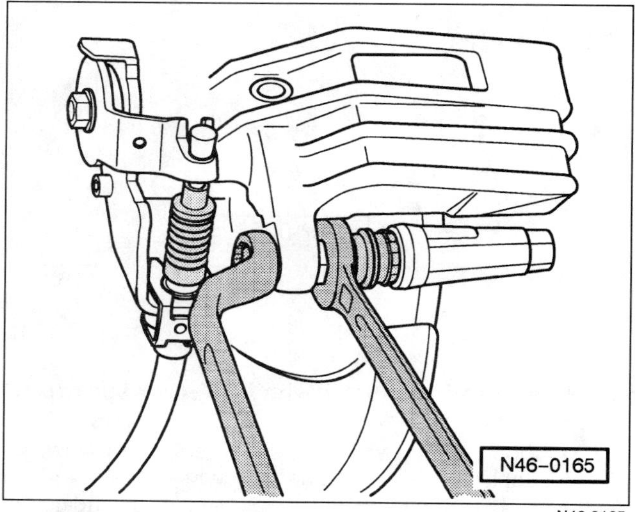

N46-0165

Fig. 10. Counterhold guide pins and remove mounting bolts from brake caliper.

> ***CAUTION —***
> *Do not allow the caliper to hang by the brake hose. The unsupported weight can stretch and damage the hose.*

4. Remove locating screw from brake disc (rotor) and remove brake disc.

5. Remove 12-point nut at center of hub assembly.

6. Using a suitable puller, remove bearing/hub unit. See Fig. 11.

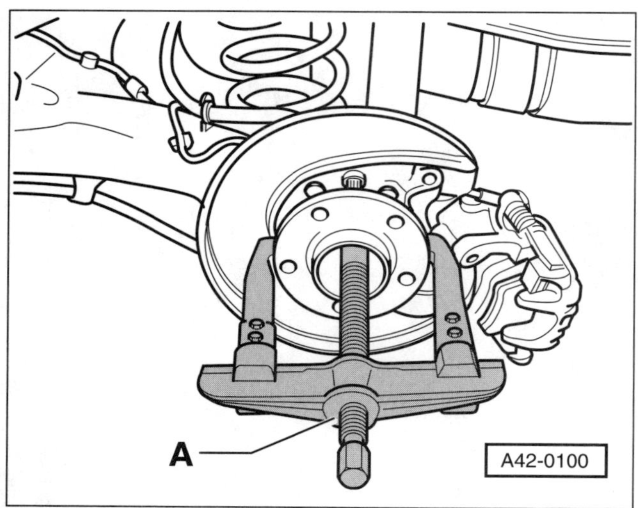

A42-0100

Fig. 11. Kukko 20/2 puller (**A**) shown pulling off bearing/hub unit.

7. Pulling the bearing/hub unit may leave the inner wheel bearing on the stub axle. Using a suitable puller, carefully remove the inner bearing. See Fig. 12.

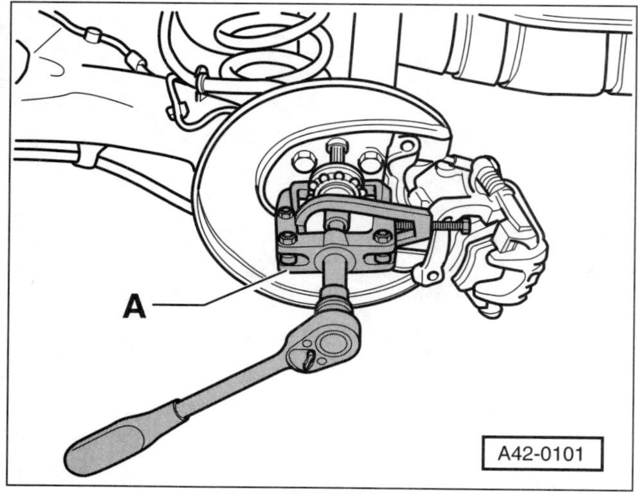

A42-0101

Fig. 12. Kukko 204-2 puller (**A**) shown pulling off inner wheel bearing. Use only a puller with leg clamps to prevent the jaws from spreading and damaging the bearing.

8. Remove stub axle.

Rear wheel bearing/hub unit, installing

1. Install stub axle to axle beam with new bolts.

Tightening torque

- Stub axle bolts to axle beam (M10) always replace . . . . 60 Nm (44 ft-lb)

---

2. Place inner wheel bearing into hub (if applicable) and install wheel bearing/hub unit as far as possible onto stub axle.

3. Attach Volkswagen assembly tool 3420 and pull wheel bearing/hub unit all the way onto stub axle. See Fig. 13.

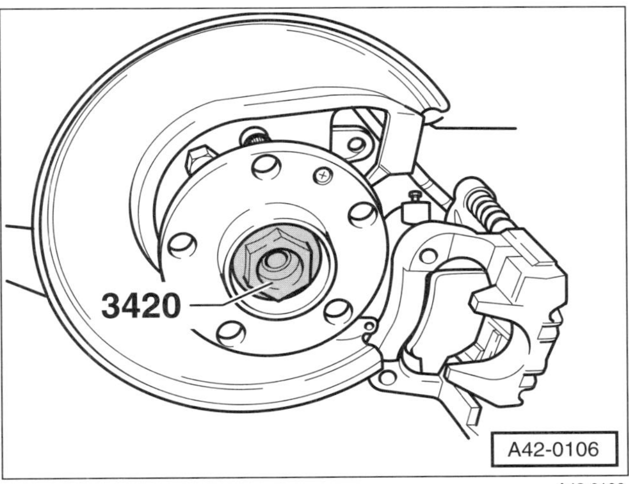

A42-0106

Fig. 13. Volkswagen special tool 3420 shown installed to pull wheel bearing/hub unit onto stub axle.

4. Remove Volkswagen assembly tool 3420 and install a new self-locking 12-point nut.

Tightening torque

- Stub axle nut, self-locking, shouldered (M20) always replace . . . . 175 Nm (129 ft-lb)
- Screw, brake rotor (M6) . . . . 4 Nm (35 in-lb)
- Bolt, brake caliper . . . . 65 Nm (48 ft-lb)
- Wheel bolt to wheel hub. . . . . 120 Nm (87 ft-lb)

---

5. Install brake disc (rotor) and caliper.

6. Install new dust cap. See Fig. 14.

> ***NOTE —***
> *Use care when installing new dust cap as dented and damaged dust caps allow moisture contamination that shortens bearing life.*

7. Install and torque wheel assembly.

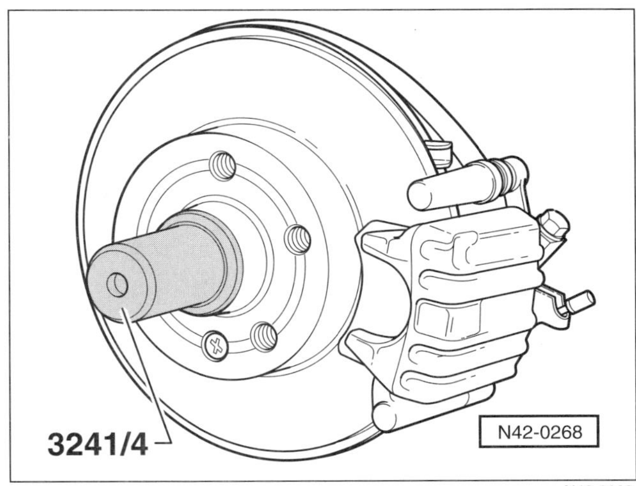

N42-0268

Fig. 14. Volkswagen special tool 3241/4 shown in place to drive new dust cap onto hub.

QUALITY REVIEW

When you have finished working under the vehicle and around other areas, it is advisable to take a moment to quality check or review your work. This helps to insure that the operation or repair has been completed properly with all affected systems functioning within normal parameters. These may include the following:

- Ensure that all cable ties and clamps that were removed as part of the repair are replaced.
- Ensure that all fasteners and hardware were replaced and torqued as specified.
- Make sure that all other components involved in the repair are positioned correctly, properly torqued and function properly.
- Make sure that all tools, shop cloths, fender covers and protective tapes are removed before closing the hood.
- Clean grease and fingerprints from painted surfaces, steering wheel and shifter.

44 Wheels–Tires, Wheel Alignment

TABLES

GENERAL

This repair group covers basic tire, wheel, and wheel alignment information. Also covered here is wheel alignment specifications to be used in conjunction with professional alignment tools and measuring equipment.

Wheels and tires

Wheels and tires approved by the manufacturer have been matched to the vehicle and contribute largely to road handling and driving characteristics. To retain the handling characteristics, it is recommended that the tires be replaced only with tires having the same specifications with regard to size, design, load carrying capacity, speed rating, tread pattern, tread depth, etc. This information can be found on the tire's sidewall. See Fig. 1. Various tire and wheel applications can be found in **Table a**.

Volkswagen recommends that the tires be rotated front to back, with the tires remaining on the same side of the vehicle. Only when tires show unusual wear should they be rotated diagonally. See **0 Maintenance** for maintenance schedules regarding tire rotation.

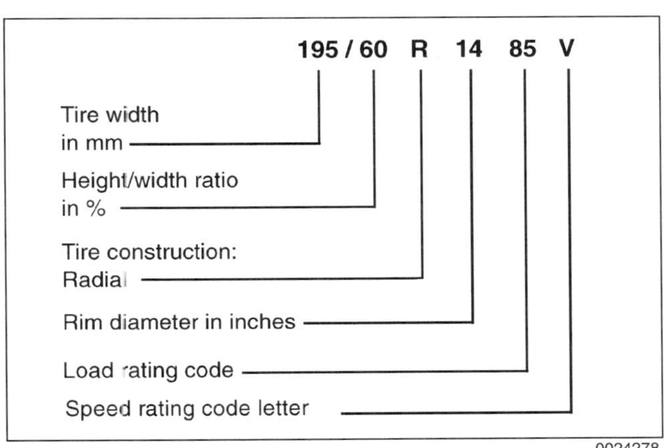

Fig. 1. Tire sidewalls are marked with important tire specifications.

Tightening torque

- Wheel bolt to hub (diagonally and evenly) . . . . 120 Nm (87 ft-lb)

Table a. Wheel and Tire applications

Wheel	Tire size	Wheel	Offset (mm)	Track width (mm)	Snow chains permissible
Standard	195/65 R 15 91 H	6 J x 15	38	1516 front 1494 rear	Yes
Optional	205/55 R 16 91 H	6½ J x 16	42	1508 front 1486 rear	No
Temporary spare	T 125/70 R 18 99 M	3½ J x 18 6½ J x 15	38	n/a	No

WHEEL ALIGNMENT

Tire pressures, tire wear, and wheel alignment will all influence how the car feels and responds on the road. For stability and control, all four wheels and tires must be in good condition, balanced, and be properly aligned. Precise wheel alignment can only be accomplished when the tires, the suspension, and the steering are in good condition. Reputable wheel alignment technicians will always inspect the front and rear suspension and the steering for worn parts before an alignment, and will recommend that any necessary repairs be made before proceeding. The important front wheel alignment angles are camber, caster, and toe. In the rear, the important angles are camber, toe and thrust line. Although rear alignment angles are not generally adjustable, they should be checked because of the effect that they have on rear tire wear and straight-line stability of the vehicle.

Camber is the angle that the wheels tilt from vertical when viewed from front or rear. See Fig. 2. Wheels which tilt out at the top have positive (+) camber. Wheels that tilt in at the top have negative (–) camber. On the Volkswagens covered by this manual, camber is non-adjustable and corrections must be made by moving the front subframe slightly.

Camber influences cornering, directional stability, and tire wear. Different camber on the two front wheels may cause the car to pull to one side. Incorrectly adjusted camber will cause uneven tire wear.

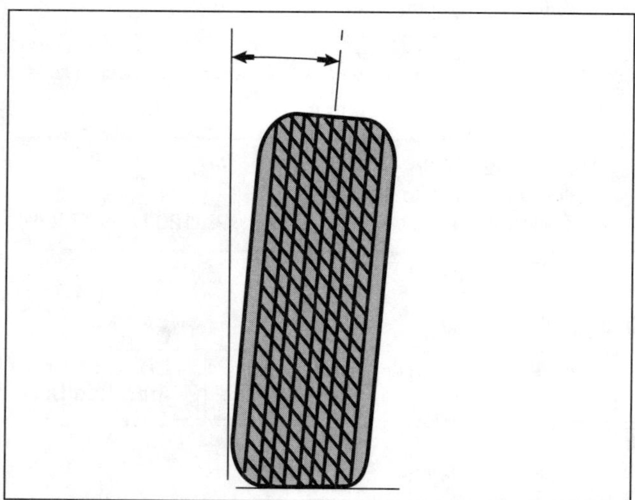

Fig. 2. Camber is the wheel/tire deviation from vertical as viewed from front or rear.

Caster is the angle at which the steering axis deviates from vertical. See Fig. 3. Most cars are designed with positive caster, which improves directional stability and tends to make the steering more self-centering. Caster angle should be checked as part of wheel alignment, but it is not adjustable on cars covered by this manual.

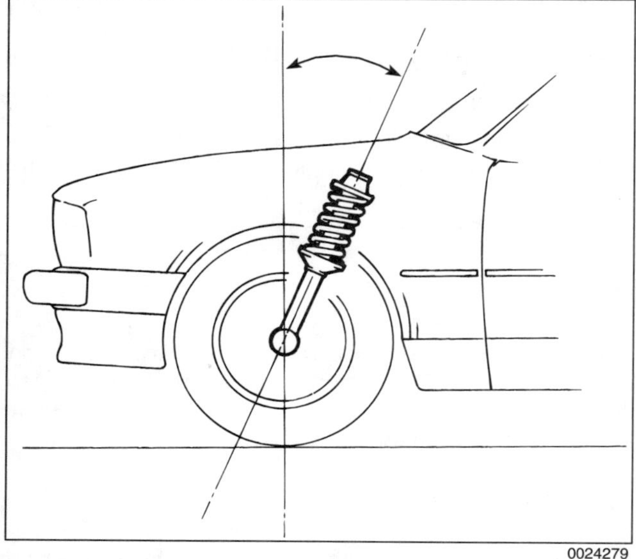

Fig. 3. Caster is the angle of steering axis inclination from vertical.

Toe is a measurement of the amount that two wheels on the same axle point toward each other (toe-in) or away from each other (toe-out). Toe affects directional stability and tire wear. Toe also affects response to steering input. Too much toe will cause tires to "scrub" and to wear unevenly and quickly. Too little toe may cause the car to be less stable and wander at highway speeds. See Fig. 4.

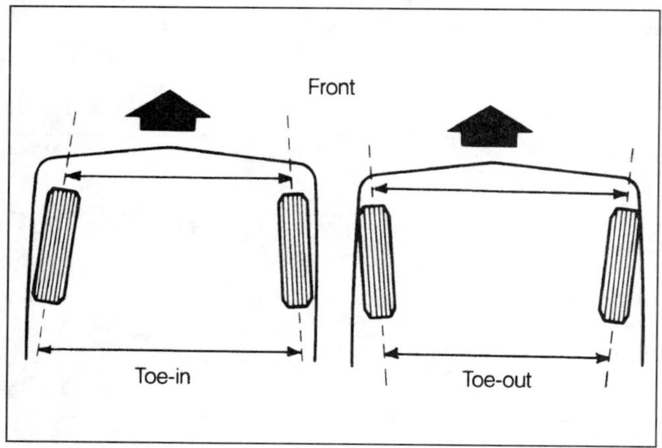

Fig. 4. Front wheel toe.

Wheel alignment, checking

Accurate wheel alignment will best be obtained by having your Volkswagen dealer or a certified alignment shop perform the procedure. Following are a list of required conditions and alignment specifications.

> ***CAUTION—***
> - *It is recommended that both the front and rear axles are measured (thrust angle) when carrying out alignment measurements.*
> - *If the installation position of the rear axle (which affects the direction of travel of the vehicle) is not taken into account the steering wheel may not be centered.*

Before evaluating alignment, be sure that steering wheel and steering column are aligned. See Fig. 5.

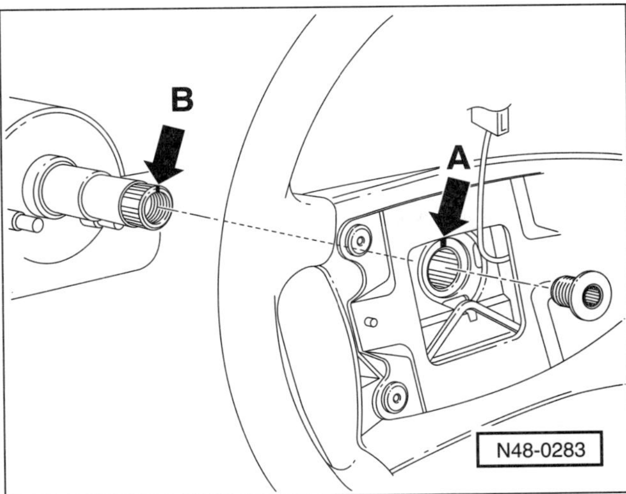

Fig. 5. Mark on steering wheel (**A**) and steering column (**B**) should always line up.

NOTE—
Steering columns supplied as a replacement parts do not have a center punch mark.

> ***WARNING—***
> - *Do not remove air bag without reviewing cautions and warnings in* **69 Seatbelts, Airbags**.
> - *To remove steering wheel and airbag, see* **48 Steering**.

Tightening torque
- Steering wheel bolt to steering column . . . . 50 Nm (37 ft-lb)

Wheel alignment should be checked whenever vehicle is not tracking properly, if there is tire wear on one side, or if there has been damage from an accident. An alignment should also be performed when the following suspension components have been replaced:

- Front lower control arm
- Front wheel bearing housing
- Front tie rod or tie rod end
- Steering gear
- Sub-frame
- Front shock absorber
- Rear axle assembly
- Rear sub-assemblies
- Rear lower or upper control arm
- Rear trailing arm

It is not necessary to do an alignment when the rear shocks or coil springs are replaced.

Alignment requirements

- Vehicle at curb weight
- Fuel tank full
- Spare wheel and vehicle tools are stored at correct locations
- Fluid reservoir for windshield/headlight washer system full
- Equal tread depth for both tires on each axle, with difference between two not more than 2 mm (0.079 in.)
- Tires inflated to correct pressure
- Test equipment must be properly adjusted and attached to vehicle. Observe all instructions, cautions and warnings of the test equipment manual.
- Vehicle accurately positioned, suspension bounced and rocked several times
- Suspension, steering and steering linkage in proper condition; without excessive play or damage
- Do not check alignment before vehicle has been driven 600 to 1200 miles (1000 to 2000 km) so as to allow coil springs to settle

NOTE—
The vehicle alignment should not be checked before the vehicle has completed 1000-2000 km (600-1200 miles) so that the coil springs can have a chance to settle.

Wheel alignment specifications

Table b. Wheel Alignment Data—Front Suspension

Suspension (version)	**Base suspension (1 GC, 1GJ)**	**Sport suspension (1GD, G76)**
Total toe [1] (wheels not pressed)	0° ± 10'	
Camber [1] (in straight-ahead position)	–30' ± 30'	–33' ± 30'
Maximum permissible difference between left and right	max. 30'	
Toe angle difference at 20° lock from left to right	+1° 30' ± 20'	+1° 31' ± 20'
Caster (not adjustable)	+7° 40' ± 30'	+7° 50' ± 30'
Maximum permissible difference between left and right	30'	30'

[1]Camber adjustments are not possible. Corrections are possible by moving the subframe slightly. Adjustment approx. 10′ to 15′.

Table c. Wheel Alignment Data—Rear Suspension

Suspension (version)	**Base suspension (1JA, 1JD)**	**Sport suspension (1JC, UA9)**
Camber	–1°27' ± 20'	
Maximum permissible difference between left and right	30'	
Total toe (with specified camber)	+20' ± 10'	+25' ± 10'
Maximum permissible deviation from direction of travel (thrust angle)	20'	

Suspension type

Various suspension versions are available and the data label in spare wheel recess or in the glovebox owner's manual identifies the suspension type. See Fig. 6.

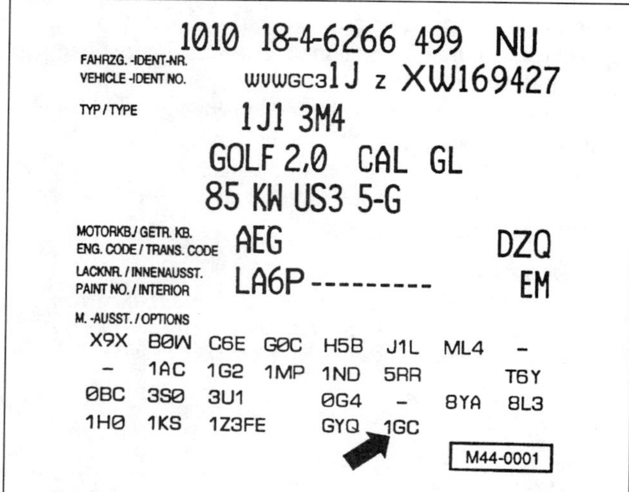

M44-0001

Fig. 6. Example of vehicle data label and suspension type (**arrow**).

Front suspension types
- Base suspension 1GC
- Suspension for engine above 175 hp. 1GJ
- Sport suspension 1GD, G76

Thrust angle, calculating

Thrust angle (deviation from direction of travel) can be calculated using one of the two following examples. The result is the deviation of the actual running direction from the longitudinal center line of the vehicle.

If alignment readings for rear toe are both positive or both negative (+/+ or -/-), subtract smaller figure from larger figure to determine total toe angle, then divide by 2.

Example:
- Left rear wheel track. . . . .+ 15'
- Right rear wheel track. . . . .+ 5'

15' - 5' = 10'

10' ÷ 2 = 5'

- Thrust angle (deviation from direction of travel): 5′

If alignment readings for rear toe are different signs, one positive and one negative (+/-), add two figures to determine total toe angle, then divide by 2.

Example:
- Left rear wheel track. . . . .+ 15'
- Right rear wheel track. . . . . - 5'

15' + 5' = 20'

10' ÷ 2 = 10'

- Thrust angle (deviation from direction of travel): 10′

45 Anti-lock Brakes (ABS)

GENERAL

This repair group covers the ITT (Teves) Mark 20 IE and Mark 60 IE anti-lock brake systems (ABS), ABS with electronic differential lock (EDL), and ABS/EDL with automatic slip regulation (ASR) found on the vehicles covered by this manual. These systems include specially matched control module software that regulates rear axle brake pressure which eliminates the need for an axle-mounted mechanical brake pressure regulator. Brake pedal pressure is boosted pneumatically by a vacuum brake booster in these dual-diagonal systems.

The EDL system operates automatically and in conjunction with the ABS. At speeds up to 25 mph, if a difference of approx. 100rpm is detected between the drive wheels (i.e. one drive wheel is on a slippery surface), that wheel will be braked in a controlled manner and more of the engine's power will be directed to the other wheel via the differential to achieve greater traction.

NOTE —

- *The ABS system features built-in diagnostic circuitry that detects and stores Diagnostic Trouble Code (DTC) information. When the system detects a fault, a DTC is generated and stored in the ABS control module's permanent memory. These fault codes can be accessed through the data link connector using Volkswagen scan tool VAG 1551/1552*
- *If an ABS malfunction is stored, the ABS warning light comes on. ABS and EDL functions may be switched off depending on the nature of the fault. However, normal vacuum and hydraulic brake function is retained.*

WARNING —

- *ABS is a vehicle safety system; appropriate knowledge and special equipment are necessary to properly work on the system.*
- *The ABS system must be bled after repairs requiring opening of the brake hydraulic system. See* **47 Brakes-Hydraulic System.**
- *If you drive an ABS-equipped vehicle after a fault has been detected by the On-Board Diagnostics, keep in mind that the function of the brake system may be limited and there is a risk of accident. The brake pressure at the rear wheels is no longer controlled by the Electronic Brake Distribution (EBD) function. This can result in excessive braking at the rear, and the vehicle may skid unexpectedly under braking.*

Special precautions for ABS or ABS/EDL equipped vehicles

The ABS control module processes precise, low-level electronic signals and can be very sensitive to changes in the power supply and the environment. The following precautions apply to vehicles with ABS.

WARNING —

- *When driving or riding in an airbag-equipped vehicle, NEVER hold the scan tool or other test equipment in your hands or lap while in motion. Objects between you and the airbag increase the risk of injury in an accident.*
- *During a test drive in an air-bag equipped vehicle, test equipment must always be fastened to and operated from the rear seat by a helper.*
- *Brake fluid is poisonous!*

CAUTION—

- *When working on the electrical sections of the ABS, only disconnect harness connectors with the ignition switched off.*
- *If the ABS warning light illuminates, there is a fault in the system. Determine the cause of the malfunction using the On-Board Diagnostic (OBD) program. Check the fault memory with a suitable scan tool such as Volkswagen scan tool VAG 1551/1552 or equivalent before proceeding.*
- *Certain faults will only be detected and stored as DTCs at speeds greater than 20 kph (13 mph).*
- *The ABS and brake system warning lights are not capable of monitoring all brake system functions; visual inspections are still required for the system.*
- *Brake fluid must not contact any painted surfaces; it will remove paint.*
- *Brake fluid absorbs moisture from the surrounding air and must be replaced every two years. Use only new brake fluid that complies with Federal Motor Vehicle Safety Standards 116, DOT 4.*
- *Do not use silicone-based brake fluids (DOT 5). This fluid is incompatible with the brake system and even the smallest trace can cause severe corrosion.*
- *Absolute cleanliness is required when working on the ABS system. Do not use any products that contain mineral oil such as oil, grease, etc.*
- *Thoroughly clean all connections and the area immediately around them before loosening. Do not use aggressive cleaning agents such as brake cleaner, gasoline or thinners.*
- *Place removed parts on a clean surface and cover them. Only use clean plastic covering or paper. Do not use rags that may contain lint.*
- *Carefully seal or cover opened components if repairs cannot be completed immediately.*
- *After separating the control module from the hydraulic unit, use the transportation protection for the valve dome.*
- *Only install replacement parts from original packaging. Only remove the parts from the package immediately before installation.*
- *Do not work with compressed air nearby whenever the hydraulic system is open. Do not move the vehicle with the hydraulic system open.*
- *Be very careful not to let any brake fluid enter any wiring harness connectors.*
- *Do not re-use fasteners that are worn or deformed from normal use.*

ABS COMPONENTS

The ITT (Teves) Mark 20 IE and Mark 60 IE Anti-Lock brake systems (ABS) and ABS/EDL system use electronic, electrical, hydraulic and mechanical components. For an overview of the major electronic and electrical components, see Fig. 1. For an overview of the major hydraulic and mechanical components, see Fig. 2.

NOTE—

Volkswagen identifies electrical components by a letter and/or a number in the electrical schematics. See **97 Wiring Diagrams, Fuses and Relays**. *These electrical identifiers are listed in parenthesis as an aid to electrical troubleshooting.*

Electrical/electronic ABS components

The following numbered list applies to Fig. 1.

1. **ABS and ABS/ASR hydraulic unit (N55)**
   - Consists of following components:
     Hydraulic pump (V64)
     Valve block with inlet/outlet valves
   - Do not separate above components from each other
   - If exchanging, use plugs from new unit to seal openings

   Two different models:
   - Mark 60 IE is mounted vertically and has a 47-pin control unit bolted to hydraulic unit
   - Mark 20 IE is mounted horizontally and has a 25-pin control unit bolted to hydraulic unit
     Distinguishing ABS, ABS/EDL and ABS/EDL/ASR units, **see** (A)
2. **ABS control module (J104)**
   - Mounted to hydraulic unit
   - Hydraulic unit and control module form one unit that can only be separated when removed from vehicle
   - New control modules (replacement parts) are not coded and must be coded after installation
   - Disconnect harness connector only with ignition switched off
   - Check for Diagnostic Trouble Codes (DTCs) with scan tool before disconnecting harness connector
3. **Brake light switch (F)**
   - Open circuit in rest position
   - Removing and adjusting, see **96 Lights, Accessories–Interior**
   - Checking resistance, **see** (B)
4. **ABS warning light (K47)**
   - Operation, **see** (C)
5. **Brake system warming light (K118)**
   - Operation, **see** (C)
6. **ESP control lamp (K155)**
   - Only for vehicles with anti-slip regulation (ASR)
   - Warning light comes on and goes out when vehicle is started as a system self test
   - Light is on continuously when ASR not engaged (manually turned off or malfunction)
   - Light flashes when ASR is in operation while driving

Electrical/electronic ABS components

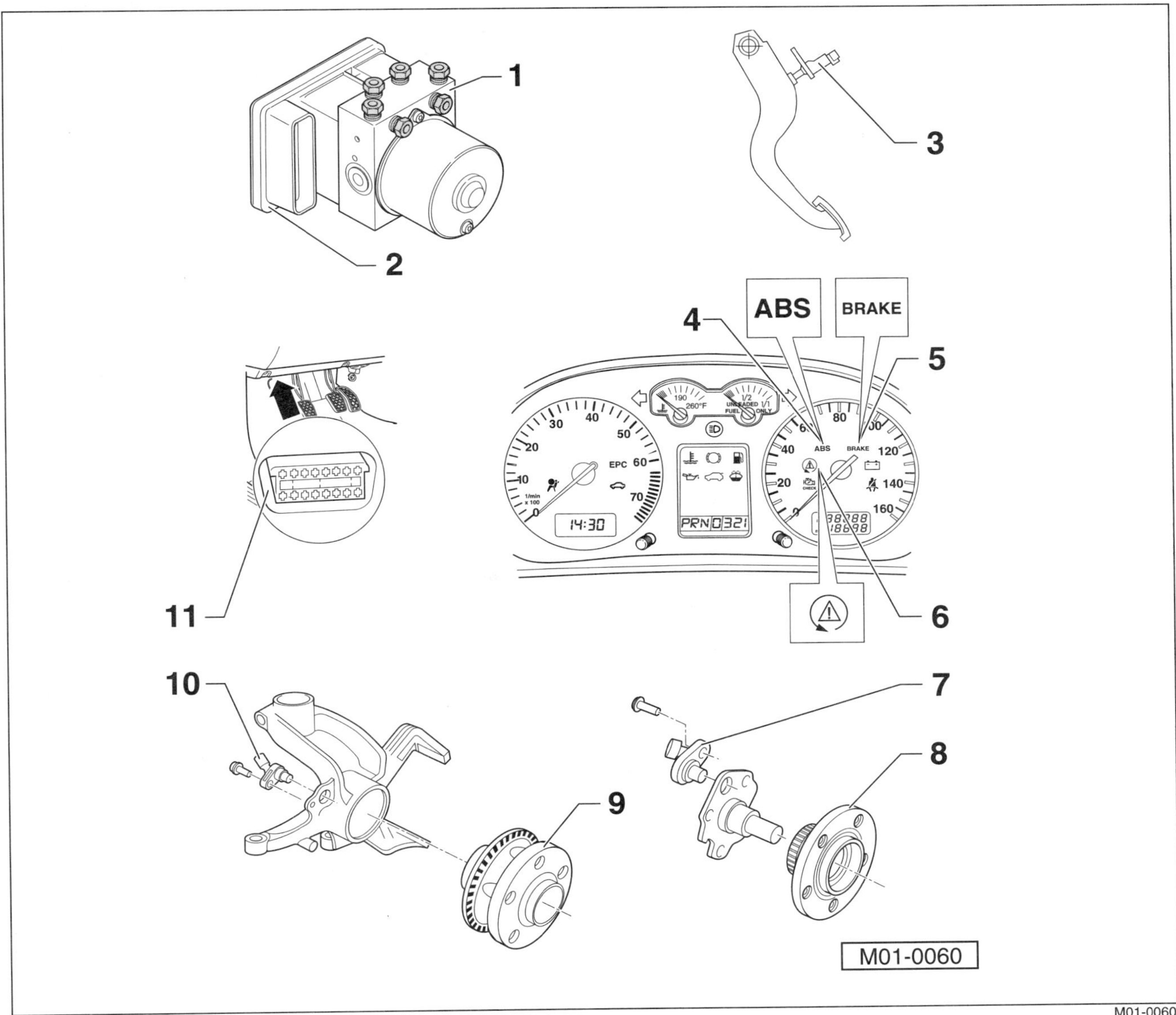

M01-0060

Fig. 1. Major electrical/electronic components of the ABS and ABS/EDL system.

7. **ABS wheel speed sensor, rear right/left (G44/G46)**
   - Clean inner surface in wheel bearing housing before installing and lubricate with grease (VW part no. G 000 650 or equivalent)
   - Check to be sure wiring is not twisted in wheel well before connecting
   - Tighten mounting bolt to 10 Nm (89 in-lb)
8. **Rear wheel hub with ABS wheel speed sensor rotor**
   - Rotor and speed sensors for left and right rear sides are identical
   - Rotor welded to wheel hub
9. **Front wheel hub with ABS wheel speed sensor rotor**
   - Rotor and speed sensors for left and right rear sides are identical
   - Rotor welded to wheel hub
10. **ABS wheel speed sensor, front right/left (G45/G47)**
    - Clean inner surface in wheel bearing housing before installing and lubricate with grease (VW part no. G 000 650 or equivalent)
    - Check to be sure wiring is not twisted in wheel well before connecting
    - Tighten mounting bolt to 10 Nm (89 in-lb)
11. **Data Link Connector (DLC)**
    - Located in left lower area of dash panel

A ABS, ABS/EDL, ABS/EDL/ASR hydraulic unit, distinguishing features

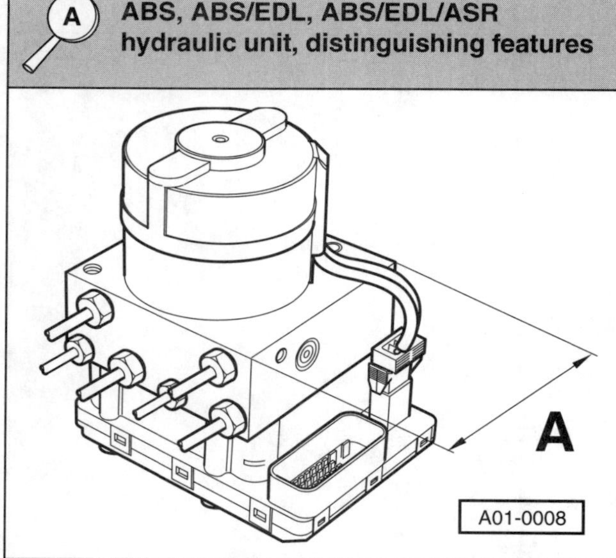

A01-0008

ITT Mark 20 IE hydraulic unit

- **Dimension (A) on ABS-only unit is 100mm (3.9 in)**
- **Dimension (A) on ABS/EDL unit is 130mm (5.1 in)**
- **Dimension (A) on ABS/EDL/ASR unit is 130mm (5.1 in)**

B Brake light switch, checking resistance

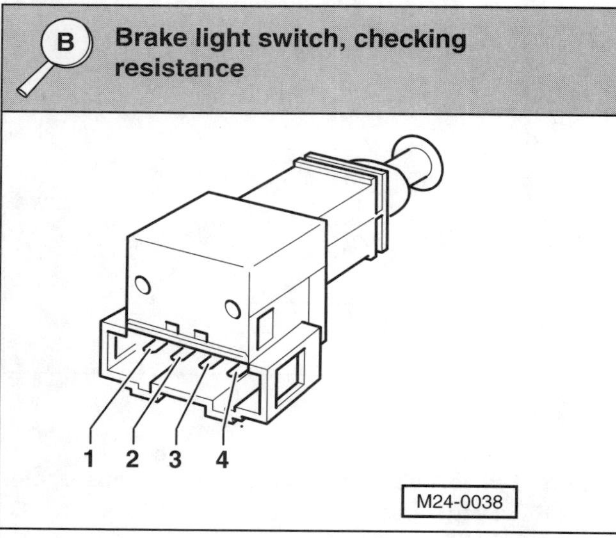

- **Measure resistance between terminals 1 & 4**
  Specification:
  Brake pedal depressed: max. 1.5Ω
  Brake pedal not depressed: ∞Ω
- **Measure resistance between terminals 2 & 3**
  Specification:
  Brake pedal depressed: ∞Ω
  Brake pedal not depressed: max. 1.5Ω

C Brake system warning lights

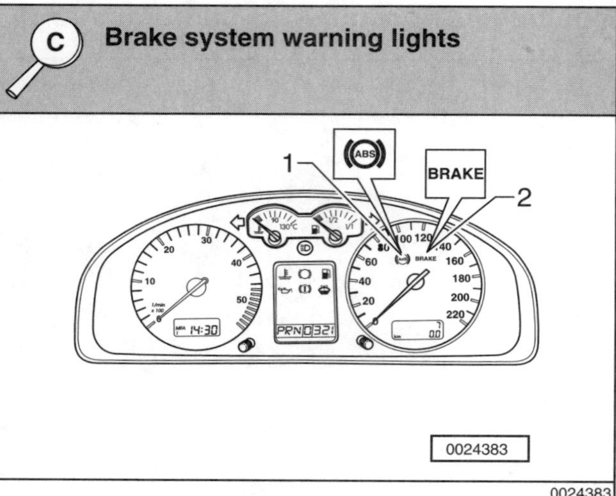

0024383

NOTE —

On vehicles with ABS/EDL where the EDL is not functioning, it could be the result of incorrectly adjusted brake light switch.

ABS warning light (1):

- **Lights momentarily and goes out if key is switched on and ABS system is functioning within normal parameters (as a self test).**
- **Lights if supply voltage drops below 10.0 volts.**
- **Lights if ABS system has a malfunction (ABS system is automatically switched off if light is on).**
- **Light goes out (after restart) when vehicle speed exceeds 20 km/h (13 mph) to indicate wheel speed sensor malfunction.**
- **Lights if EDL system is not functioning.**
- **May light if instrument cluster or wiring malfunction is present.**

Brake warning light (2):

- **Lights momentarily and goes out if key is switched on and parking brake is not applied (as a self test).**
- **Lights if key is switched on and parking brake is applied.**
- **Lights if parking brake switch is inoperative, incorrectly adjusted or if there is a malfunction if the wiring.**
- **Lights if key is switched on and parking brake is not applied if brake fluid level is low (may flicker).**

WARNING —

- *If ABS warning light (1) and brake warning light (2) light up together, it is possible rear wheels will lock-up early under hard braking. This could cause loss of vehicle control and may be due to the electronic brake pressure distribution not functioning. Have your vehicle serviced immediately by an authorized Volkswagen dealer or a qualified independent repair shop.*
- *If the brake warning light (2) does not light up when the engine is cranking or the parking brake is applied, there may be a malfunction in the electrical system. Do not drive vehicle without diagnosing the problem.*

Hydraulic/mechanical ABS components

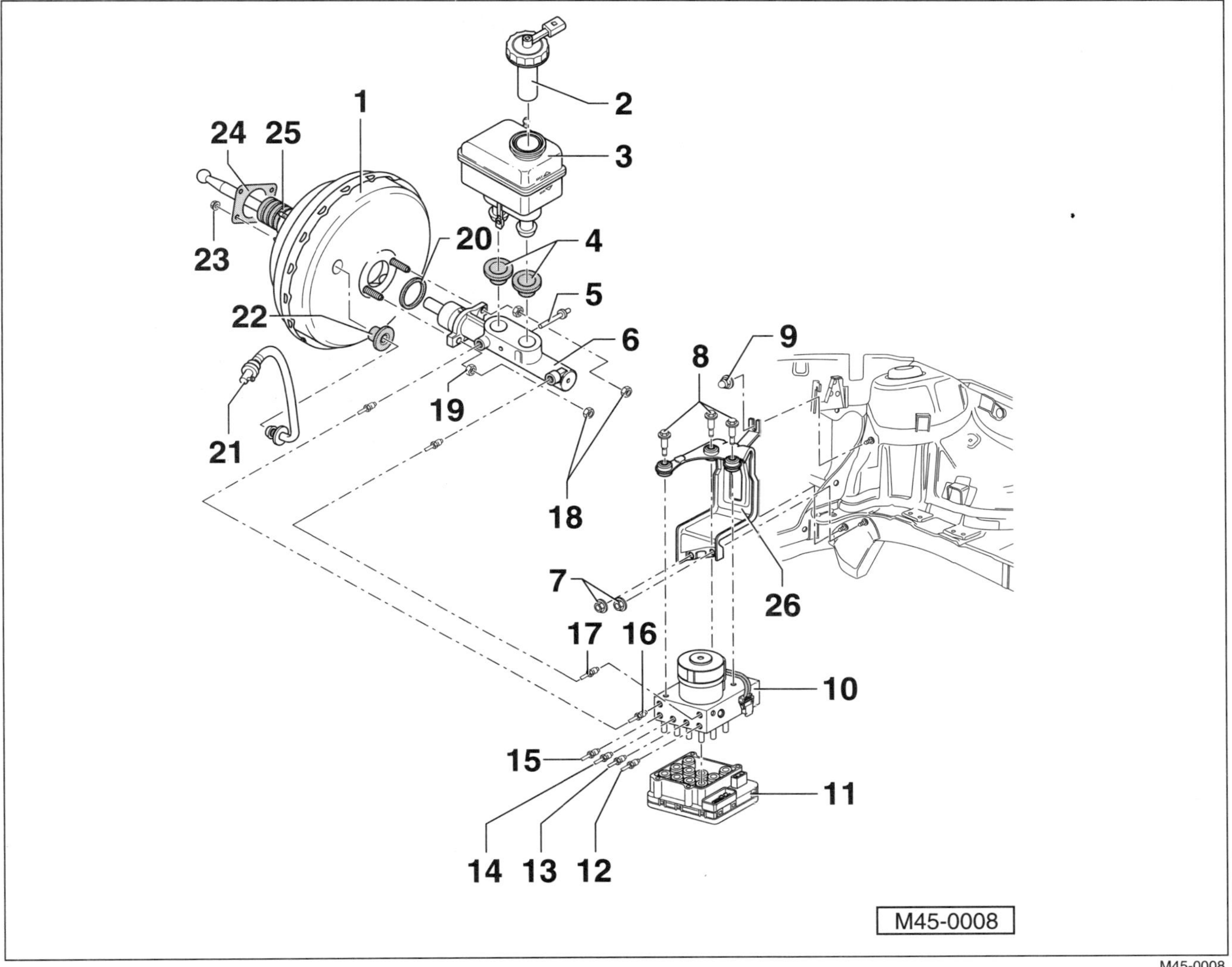

M45-0008

Fig. 2. Major hydraulic/mechanical components of the ABS system.

1. **Brake booster**
   - On gasoline engines vacuum is taken from intake manifold
   - Diesel engines have a vacuum pump to create required vacuum
   - Complete master cylinders and brake boosters can be replaced separately
   - Functional check:
     With engine off, depress brake pedal several times to exhaust vacuum in the unit.
     Depress brake pedal and start engine. If booster is functioning properly, brake pedal should give noticeably underfoot.
     If pedal does not give, replace brake booster.

2. **Cap**
   - With fluid level sensor

3. **Brake fluid reservoir**
   - Also supplies brake fluid to hydraulic clutch for manual transmission

4. **Sealing plug**
   - Moisten with brake fluid and press into reservoir

5. **Retainer pin**
   - Insert through brake master cylinder

6. **Tandem brake master cylinder**
   - Cannot be repaired
   - If faulty, replace as complete unit

7. **Nut, self-locking**
   - Always replace
   - Tighten to 20 Nm (15 ft-lb)

8. **Bolt**
   - Tighten to 9 Nm (80 in-lb)

9. **Nut**
   - Tighten to 9 Nm (80 in-lb)

(continued on following page)

Hydraulic/mechanical ABS components (continued)

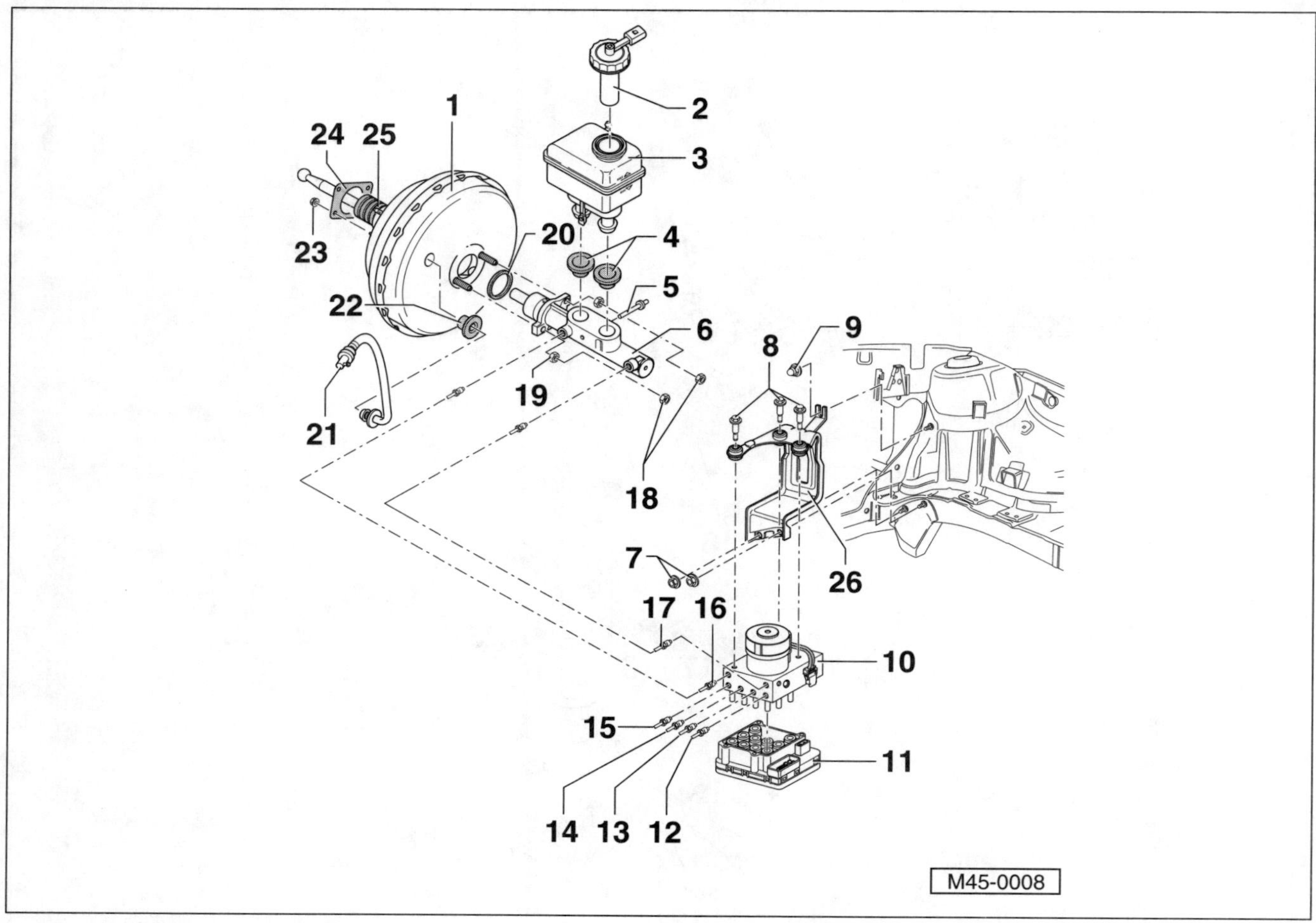

(continued from previous page)

10. ABS/EDL hydraulic unit

11. ABS control module

- Hydraulic unit must be removed as an assembly before removing control module

12. Brake line connection

- Hydraulic unit to left front brake caliper

13. Brake line connection

- Hydraulic unit to right rear cylinder/caliper

14. Brake line connection

- Hydraulic unit to left rear cylinder/caliper

15. Brake line connection

- Hydraulic unit to right front brake caliper

16. Brake line

- Brake master cylinder/primary piston circuit to hydraulic unit

17. Brake line

- Master brake cylinder/secondary piston circuit to hydraulic unit

18. Nut, self-locking

- Always replace
- Tighten to 20 Nm (15 ft-lb)

19. Nut, self-locking

- Always replace
- Tighten to 20 Nm (15 ft-lb)

20. Seal

- Always replace

21. Vacuum hose

- Insert into brake booster

22. Sealing plug

23. Nut, self-locking

- Always replace
- Tighten to 20 Nm (15 ft-lb)

24. Seal

- For brake booster

25. Boot

- Ensure proper seating

26. Bracket

Hydraulic unit, removing and installing

1. Disconnect battery ground (GND) strap from battery negative (–) terminal.

NOTE —
Be sure to have the anti-theft radio code on hand before disconnecting the battery.

2. Disconnect mass air flow sensor harness connector at air filter tube.
3. Remove air filter housing.
4. On 1.9L diesel engines, remove relay panel above brake booster.
5. Remove as much brake fluid as possible from fluid reservoir using a brake bleeder bottle.
6. Depress brake pedal several times and hold in position using VAG 1869/2 brake pedal actuator, or equivalent.
7. Connect brake bleeder bottle hose to bleed screw of left front brake caliper and open bleed screw.
8. Once fluid stops running out of bleed screw, close screw.
9. Release ABS control module harness connector and secure cable out of way. See Fig. 3.

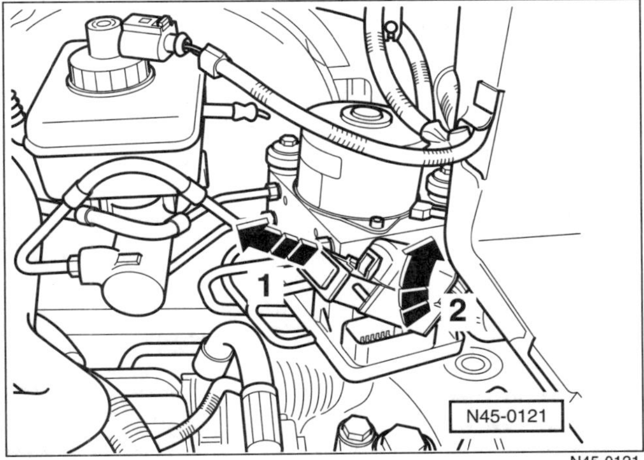

N45-0121

Fig. 3. Release ABS control module harness connector (**arrow 1**) and remove by tilting up (**arrow 2**).

10. Place plastic covering under control module and hydraulic unit. Do not use rags.

CAUTION —
Do not let brake fluid enter electrical connectors.

11. Disconnect brake lines from hydraulic unit and suspend with wire. See Fig. 4.

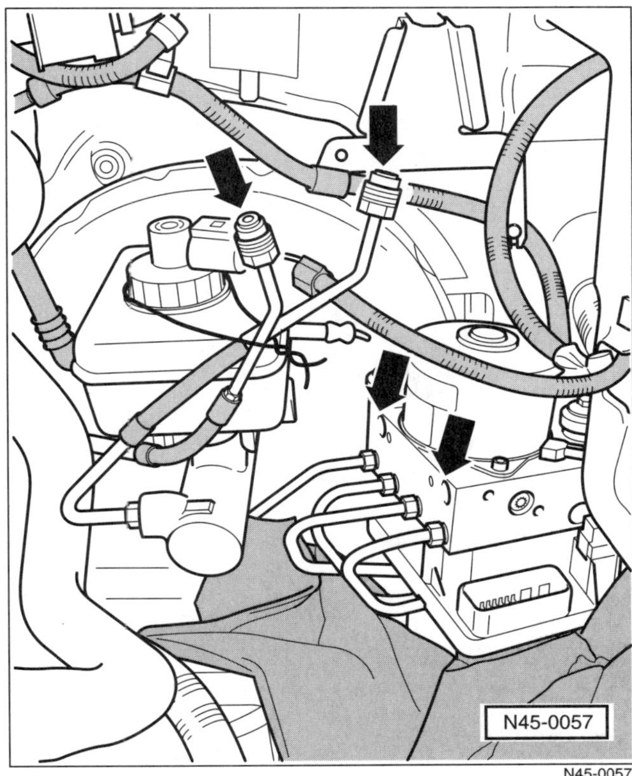

N45-0057

Fig. 4. Disconnect brake lines (**arrows**) and suspend with wire.

12. Disconnect remaining brake lines from hydraulic unit.
13. Seal brake lines and threaded holes using plugs from repair kit, Volkswagen Part # 1H0 698 311A.
14. Remove bolts from bracket for hydraulic unit. See Fig. 5.

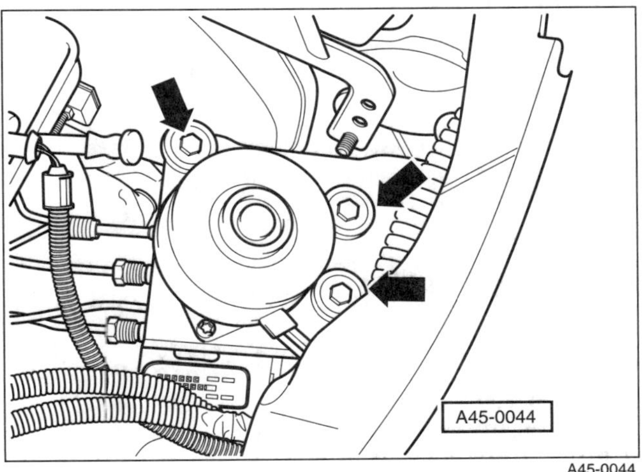

A45-0044

Fig. 5. Remove bolts (**arrows**) from bracket for hydraulic unit.

15. Remove hydraulic unit with control module attached.

16. To remove control module from hydraulic unit, first disconnect harness connector for hydraulic pump motor from control module.

17. Remove bolts from bottom of control module. Pull control module and hydraulic unit straight apart to separate. See Fig. 6.

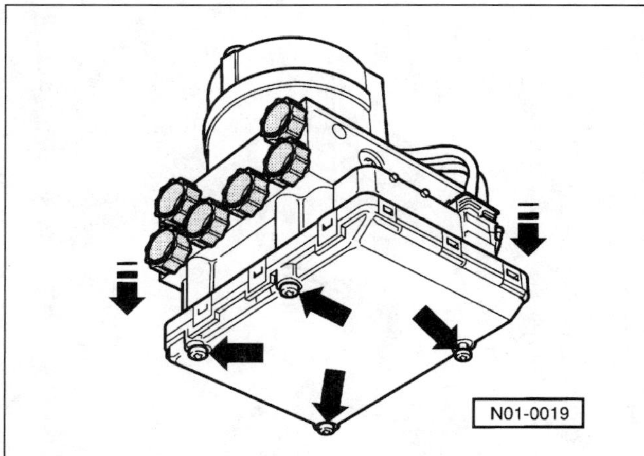

N01-0019

Fig. 6. Remove control module mounting bolts (**solid arrows**). Pull control module straight down to separate (**dashed arrows**).

> ***CAUTION —***
> - *When removing or assembling the control module and hydraulic unit, be sure that the hydraulic unit valve dome is not tilted against the control module solenoid valves.*
> - *Cover control module coils with plastic cover. Do not use rags.*
> - *After separating the control module and hydraulic unit, use transportation protection for the valve dome.*
> - *Only remove sealing plugs on the new hydraulic unit just before installing the corresponding brake line.*
> - *If the sealing plugs are removed too early, brake fluid can escape. The unit may no longer be sufficiently filled or adequately bled.*

18. Use new bolts to attach control module to hydraulic unit. Tighten to specification listed below.

19. Re-connect harness connector for hydraulic pump motor.

20. Install ABS hydraulic unit onto mounting bracket.

21. Hand tighten brake lines to hydraulic unit first. After tightening brake lines, then tighten hydraulic unit lines.

22. Remaining installation is the reverse of removal.

23. Fill brake fluid reservoir and bleed brake system as described in **47 Brakes–Hydraulic System**.

24. Be sure to quality check your work, see **Quality Review** at the end of this repair group.

Tightening torques
- Control module to hydraulic unit always replace (M4) . . . . 4 Nm (35 in-lb)
- Hydraulic unit bolt to bracket (M6) . . . . 8 Nm (71 in-lb)
- Master cylinder nut to booster (M8) . . 20 Nm (15 ft-lb)
- Brake lines to ABS unit (M10/M12) . . 15 Nm (11 ft-lb)
- Mounting bracket to body (M8). . . . . . 20 Nm (15 ft-lb)

ABS CONTROL MODULE

The ABS control module is attached to the bottom of the ABS hydraulic unit located in the engine compartment. Control unit replacement is only possible if the hydraulic unit has been removed.

Vehicles equipped with ABS link the ABS control module to the engine control module and the automatic transmission control module (where applicable). Linking the systems allows certain types of vehicle data to be shared for functional and diagnostic purposes. Linking systems to share data is generally known as multiplexing. Volkswagen uses a 2-wire system called a CAN-bus. See Fig. 7.

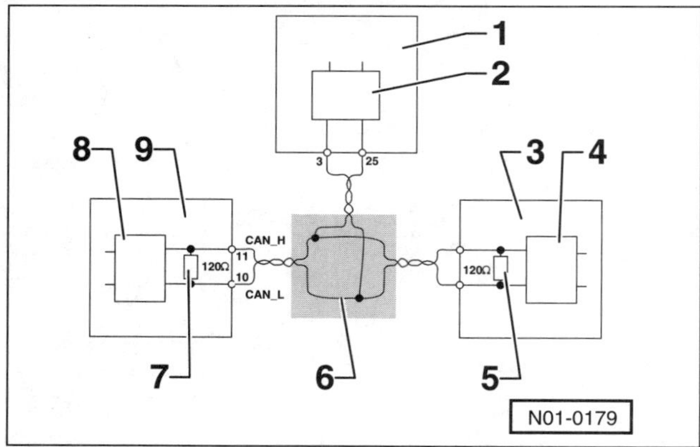

N01-0179

Fig. 7. Schematic view of linked control modules if all systems were installed in a given vehicle. Numbers identify various components.

1. **Automatic transmission control module (TCM)**
2. **Communications circuitry**
3. **Engine control module (ECM)**
4. **Communications circuitry**
5. **Terminating impedance**
6. **CAN-bus multiplexing**
7. **Terminating impedance**
8. **Communications circuitry**
9. **Anti -lock brakes control module (ABS)**

Most service and repair to the ABS system requires the use of a scan tool such as the Volkswagen VAG 1551/1552 or equivalent. Access is via the Data Link Connector (DLC) under the dashboard. This includes coding of replacement control modules. Replacement control modules are shipped uncoded and will not function properly when installed in an uncoded condition. Because of the specialized nature of these repairs, servicing should be referred to an authorized Volkswagen dealer or qualified independent repair shop. ABS control module coding numbers are shown in **Table a** for the Teves Mark 20 IE system and **Table b** for the Teves Mark 60 IE system.

Table a. ABS control module coding (Mark 20 system)

Engine (Code)	System	Control Module Code
2.0L (AEG)	ABS	03504
2.0L (AEG)	ABS/EDL	13504
1.9L (ALH)	ABS	03504
1.9L (ALH)	ABS/EDL	13504
1.9L (ALH)	ABS/EDL/ASR	13204
2.8L (AFP)	ABS	03504
2.8L (AFP)	ABS/EDL	13504
2.8L (AFP)	ABS/EDL/ASR	13204

Table b. ABS control module coding (Mark 60 system)

System	Control Module Code
ABS	04097
ABS/ASR	18945

NOTE —
The Teves (ITT) Mark 60 IE brake system was introduced as a running model change on the Jetta in 2001 from vehicle # 9M-1-094 323. The system was also introduced on the Golf and GTI models but no specific vehicle numbers were available at the time of publication. See Fig. 1. for more information in determining system type.

WHEEL SPEED SENSORS

Each wheel has a separate speed sensor to supply data to the ABS control module. Each sensor is also monitored by the control module and malfunctions will cause a DTC to be stored. The system checks the sensors for proper resistance when the ignition is first switched on and again for proper signal when the vehicle is in motion.

Front wheel speed sensor, replacing

1. Raise car and support with jack stands or lift. See **0 Maintenance** for proper lifting procedure.

> ***WARNING —***
> *Observe all warnings and cautions associated with lifting vehicle in* **0 Maintenance**.

2. Disconnect harness connector from wheel speed sensor.

3. Remove bolt from wheel bearing housing. See Fig. 8.

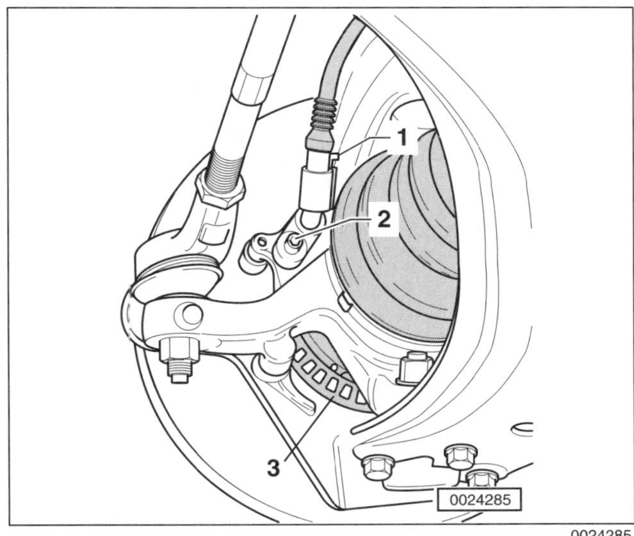

0024285

Fig. 8. Front ABS wheel speed sensor harness connector (**1**), securing bolt (**2**) and sensor rotor (**3**).

4. Remove sensor from bearing housing.

Specification
- ABS wheel speed sensor resistance, front and rear . . . . 1000-1300 ohms

5. Before installing sensor into bearing housing, clean mounting hole and lubricate with grease (VW part no. G 000 650 or equivalent).

6. Install sensor and bolt, reconnect harness connector.

Tightening torque
- Wheel speed sensor mounting bolt, front and rear, M6 . . . . 8 Nm (71 in-lb)

7. Turn wheels fully to left and then to right. Check sensor wiring for interference and clearance.

Front ABS rotor, checking

1. Raise car and support with jack stands or lift. See **0 Maintenance** for proper lifting procedure.

> ***WARNING —***
> *Observe all warnings and cautions associated with lifting vehicle in* **0 Maintenance**.

2. Rotate brake disc and check whether wheel speed sensor is damaged or dirty. Check rotor runout. See Fig. 9.

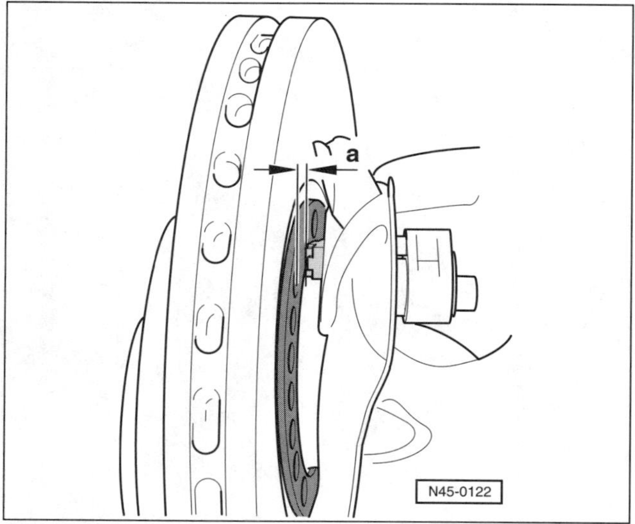

N45-0122

Fig. 9. Turn wheel hub and measure distance (**a**) between rotor and speed sensor at various places around the rotor.

ABS rotor runout

- Distance between ABS rotor and speed sensor . . . . 0.3 mm (0.0118 in.)

---

3. If rotor is damaged or runout is excessive, remove wheel hub with rotor and replace. See **40 Front Suspension and Drive Axles**.

Rear wheel speed sensor, replacing

1. Raise car and support with jack stands or lift. See **0 Maintenance** for proper lifting procedure.

> ***WARNING —***
> *Observe all warnings and cautions associated with lifting vehicle in* **0 Maintenance**.

2. Disconnect harness connector from wheel speed sensor.

3. Remove ABS wheel sensor mounting bolt from stub axle. See Fig. 10.

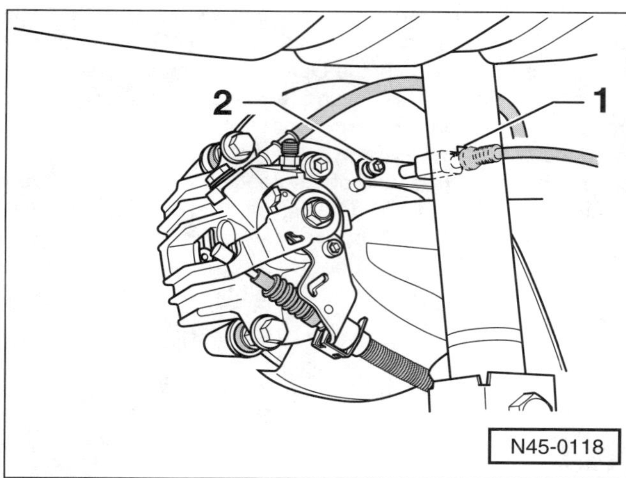

N45-0118

Fig. 10. Rear ABS wheel speed sensor harness connector (**1**) and securing bolt (**2**).

4. Pull ABS wheel speed sensor out of stub axle.

5. Before installing sensor into bearing housing, clean mounting hole and lubricate with grease (VW part no. G 000 650 or equivalent).

6. Install sensor and bolt, reconnect harness connector.

7. Check sensor wiring for interference and clearance around suspension components.

QUALITY REVIEW

When you have finished working under the hood and around other areas of the vehicle, it is advisable to take a moment to quality check or review your work. This helps to insure that the operation or repair has been completed properly with all affected systems functioning within normal parameters. These may include the following:

- During the final road test make at least one controlled brake test where the brake pedal is felt to pulsate (ABS operation).
- Ensure that all cable ties and clamps that were removed as part of the repair are replaced.
- Ensure that all fasteners and hardware were replaced and torqued as specified.
- Check and adjust brake fluid level.
- Make sure that all other components involved in the repair are positioned correctly, properly torqued and function properly.
- Make sure that all tools, shop cloths, fender covers and protective tapes are removed before closing the hood.
- Clean grease and fingerprints from painted surfaces, steering wheel and shifter.

46 Brakes–Mechanical Components

GENERAL

This repair groups covers service and repair to the brake friction components; brake pads and rotors. Also included here is parking brake service.

Cars covered by this manual are equipped with disc brakes on all four wheels. Some cars with four-wheel disc brakes are also equipped with anti-lock brakes (ABS).

NOTE —

- *For brake caliper and rear brake wheel cylinder repair information, see* **47 Brakes–Hydraulic System**.
- *For information on the ABS hydraulic unit and ABS service, see* **45 Anti-Lock Brakes (ABS)**.
- *Brake fluid should be flushed from the system every two years. See* **47 Brakes–Hydraulic System**.

WARNING —

- *A properly functioning brake system is essential to safe driving. If the red brake/parking warning light or ABS warning light illuminates while driving, it is imperative that the system be given a thorough check, even if braking action still seems satisfactory. The brakes should be inspected regularly.*
- *Brake fluid is poisonous. Wear safety glasses when working with brake fluid, and wear rubber gloves to prevent brake fluid from entering the bloodstream through cuts or scratches. Do not siphon brake fluid by mouth.*
- *New brake pads and shoes require some break-in. Allow for slightly longer stopping distances for the first 100 to 150 miles of city driving, and avoid hard stops.*

CAUTION —

- *All brake work must be done with cleanliness, careful attention to specifications, and proper working procedures. If you lack the skills, the tools, or a clean workplace for servicing the brake system, we suggest you leave these repairs to an authorized VW dealer or other qualified shop.*
- *After replacing brake components, depress the brake pedal firmly several times to seat the brakes in their normal operating position.The pedal should be firm and at its normal height, if not, further work is required before driving vehicle.*
- *Brake fluid is very damaging to paint. Immediately wipe up any brake fluid that spills on the vehicle.*

FRONT BRAKES

Two types of front discs are used on the cars covered by this manual. Repair procedures vary depending on caliper/rotor application. See the appropriate (FS III or FN 3) assembly view.

Caliper application	
• 1.8L (1.8L engine)	FN 3
• 1.9L (1.9L engine)	FS III
• 2.0L (2.0L engine)	FS III
• 2.8L (2.8L engine)	FN 3

Rotors should be inspected for cracks, scoring, glazing and warpage. Rotors must be replaced (in pairs) if either disc is worn below the minimum thickness specification or if any of the above listed defects are found.

NOTE —
The minimum brake rotor thickness specification is stamped into the rotor's hub and also listed in the appropriate illustration.

Front brake assembly (FS III caliper)

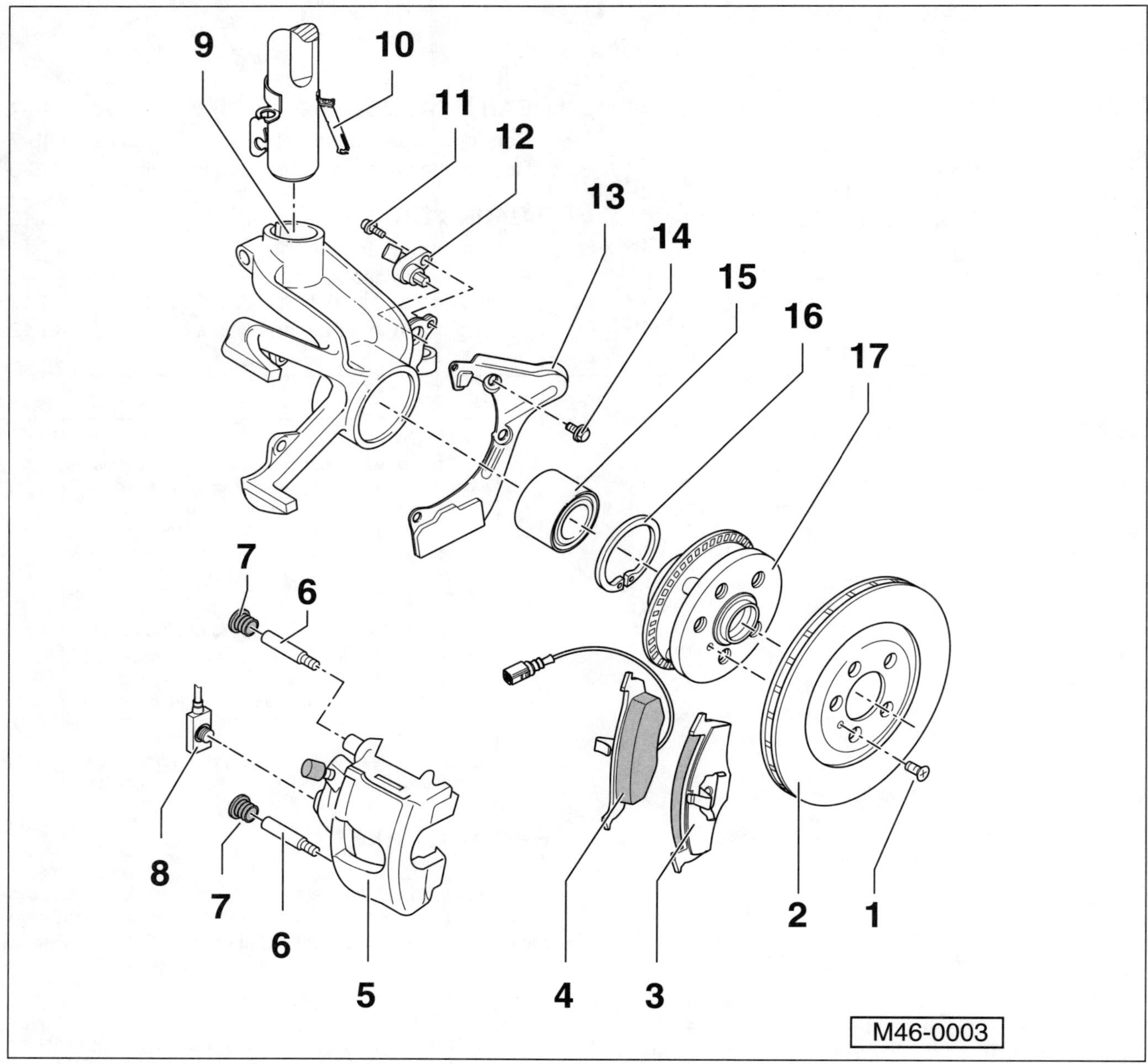

M46-0003

Fig. 1. Front brake assembly with FS III brake caliper.

1. **Screw**
   - Tighten to 4 Nm (35 in-lb)
2. **Brake disc**
   - Diameter: 280 mm (11.02 in.)
   - Thickness: 22 mm (0.866 in.)
   - Wear limit: 20 mm (0.748 in.)
   - When worn always replace on both sides
   - Remove brake caliper before removing disc
   - Never remove brake discs from hub by using force. If necessary use penetrating fluid, otherwise brake discs can be damaged.
3. **Outer brake pad**
   - Thickness 14 mm (0.551 in.)
   - Checking thickness, see **0 Maintenance**
   - Always replace all pads on one axle at same time
   - Wear limit: 7 mm (0.276 in.) including backing plate
4. **Inner brake pad with brake wear indicator**
   - Thickness 14 mm (0.551 in.)
   - Checking thickness, see **0 Maintenance**
   - Always replace all pads on one axle at same time
   - Wear limit: 7 mm (0.276 in.) including backing plate

(continued from previous page)

5. **Brake caliper**
   - Do not loosen hydraulic line when replacing pads
6. **Guide pin**
   - Tighten to 28 Nm (21 ft-lb)
7. **Protective cap**
8. **Brake hose with union and banjo bolt**
   - Tighten to 35 Nm (26 ft-lb)
9. **Wheel bearing housing**
10. **Pad wear sensor connector bracket**
    - It is not necessary to remove harness connector from bracket when replacing brake pad wear indicator
11. **Socket-head bolt**
    - Tighten to 8 Nm (71 in-lb)
12. **ABS wheel speed sensor**
    - Before inserting sensor, clean hole inner surface and coat with grease (VW part no. G 000 650)
13. **Splash shield**
14. **Bolt**
    - Tighten to 10 Nm (7 ft-lb)
15. **Wheel bearing**
    - Replace each time after removing
    - Pressing out and in, see **40 Front Suspension and Drive Axles**
16. **Circlip**
17. **Wheel hub with rotor**
    - Removing and installing, see **40 Front Suspension and Drive Axles**

Front brake pads, removing and installing (FS III caliper)

1. Raise car and support with jack stands or lift. See **0 Maintenance** for proper lifting procedure.

> ***WARNING —***
> *Observe all warnings and cautions associated with lifting vehicle in* **0 Maintenance***.*

2. Remove front wheels.

3. Remove guide pin protective caps.

4. Remove both guide pins from brake caliper.

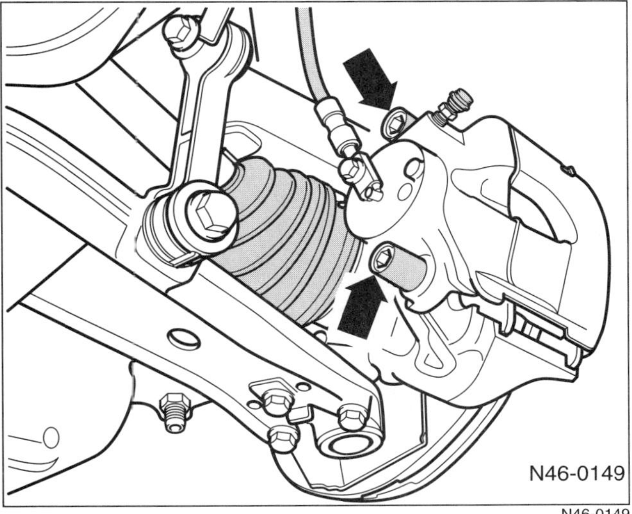

N46-0149

Fig. 2. Remove caliper guide pins (**arrows**)

5. Remove brake caliper housing and hang up with wire.

> ***CAUTION —***
> - *Do not allow caliper to hang by the brake hose. The unsupported weight can stretch and damage the hose.*
> - *Do not disconnect the brake hose from the caliper when removing brake pads.*

6. Remove brake pads from brake caliper housing.

7. Before installing new pads extract some of the brake fluid from the brake fluid reservoir.

> ***WARNING —***
> *Brake fluid is poisonous. Never siphon by mouth.*

> ***CAUTION —***
> *A full brake fluid reservoir may allow brake fluid to flow out and cause damage when pistons are pushed back.*

8. Press piston into caliper housing. See Fig. 3.

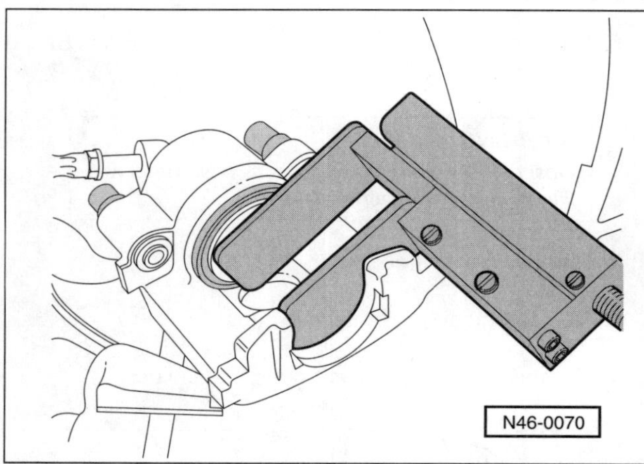

N46-0070

Fig. 3. Caliper piston being pressed into caliper using VW special tool.

9. Install brake pads with retaining spring in brake caliper housing.

10. Install brake caliper onto wheel bearing housing.
    - Position lower brake caliper housing on first.
    - The brake caliper housing tab must be behind the wheel bearing housing guide. See Fig. 4.

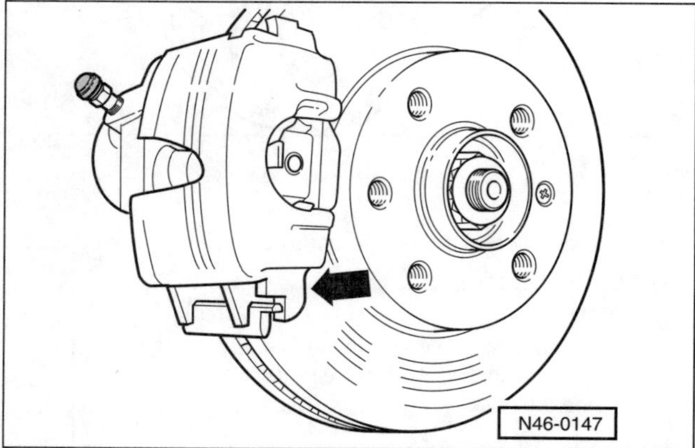

N46-0147

Fig. 4. Brake caliper housing tab (**arrow**) must be behind the wheel bearing housing guide.

11. Mount brake caliper housing to brake carrier with both guide pins and install guide pin protective caps.

12. Install wheels and lower vehicle.

Tightening torques
- Brake caliper to bearing housing . . . . 28 Nm (21 ft-lb)
- Wheel bolt to hub . . . . 120 Nm (89 ft-lb)

---

13. Depress brake pedal firmly several times to seat brake pads to brake disc. Check brake fluid level.

Front brake assembly (FN 3 caliper)

The followiong numbered list applies to Fig. 5.

1. **Screw**
   - Tighten to 4 Nm (35 in-lb)
2. **Brake disc**
   - Diameter: 288 mm (11.34 in.)
   - Thickness: 25 mm (0.984 in.)
   - Wear limit: 22 mm (0.866 in.)
   - When worn always replace brake disc pairs on both sides
3. **Outer brake pad**
   - Thickness: 14 mm (0.551 in.)
   - Checking thickness, see **0 Maintenance**
   - Always replace all pads on one axle at same time
   - Wear limit: 7 mm (0.276 in.) including backing plate
4. **Inner brake pad**
   - Thickness: 14 mm (0.551 in.)
   - Checking thickness, see **0 Maintenance**
   - Always replace all pads on one axle at same time
   - Wear limit: 7 mm (0.276 in.) including backing plate
5. **Retaining spring**
   - Insert in both brake caliper housings
6. **Brake carrier**
   - Supplied as replacement part
   - If protective caps are damaged, use repair kit
   - Use grease packet supplied to lubricate guide pins
7. **Brake caliper housing**
   - Do not disconnect brake hose when changing brake pads
8. **Guide pins**
   - Tighten to 28 Nm (21 ft-lb)
9. **Protective cap**
10. **Brake hose with union and banjo bolt**
    - Tighten to 35 Nm (26 ft-lb)
11. **Ribbed bolt**
    - Tighten to 125 Nm (92 ft-lb)
12. **Wheel bearing housing**
13. **Pad wear sensor connector bracket**
    - It is not necessary to remove harness connector from bracket when replacing brake pad wear indicator
14. **Socket-head bolt**
    - Tighten to 8 Nm (70 in-lb)
15. **ABS wheel speed sensor**
    - Before inserting sensor, clean hole inner surface and coat with grease (VW part no. G 000 650)
16. **Splash shield**

(continued on following page)

Front brake assembly (FN 3 caliper)

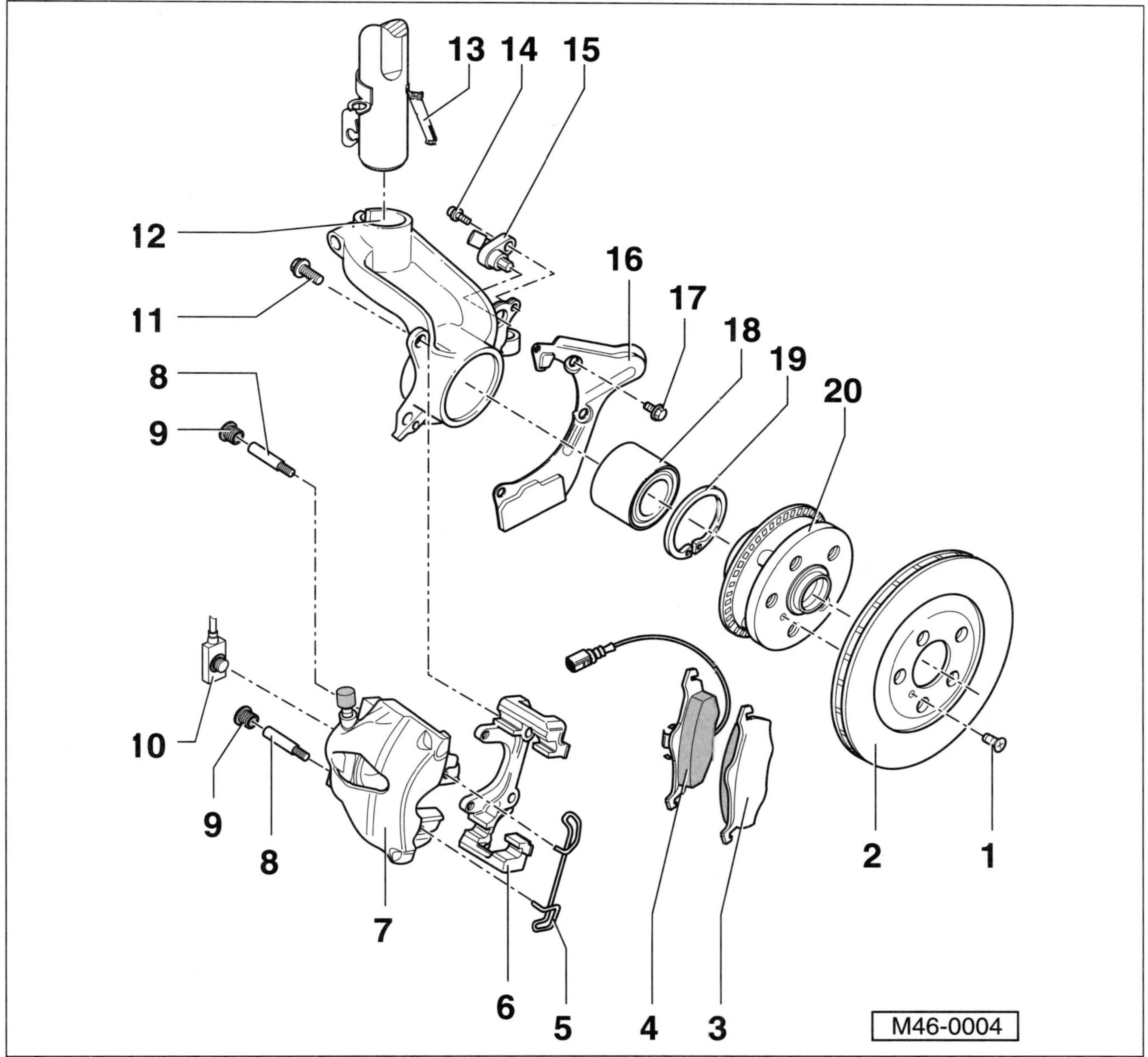

Fig. 5. Front brake assembly with FN 3 brake caliper.

17. Bolt
- Tighten to 10 Nm (7 ft-lb)

18. Wheel bearing
- Replace each time after removing
- Removing and installing, see **40 Front Suspension and Drive Axles**

19. Circlip

20. Wheel hub with rotor
- Removing and installing, see **40 Front Suspension and Drive Axles**

Front brake pads, removing and installing (FN 3 caliper)

1. Raise car and support with jack stands or lift. See **0 Maintenance** for proper lifting procedure.

> ***WARNING —***
> *Observe all warnings and cautions associated with lifting vehicle in* **0 Maintenance**.

2. Remove front wheels.
3. Remove guide pin protective caps.
4. Using a screwdriver, pry brake pad retaining spring out of brake caliper housing and remove.

> ***WARNING —***
> *Wear appropriate eye protection when removing retaining spring.*

5. Remove both guide pins from brake caliper. See Fig. 6.

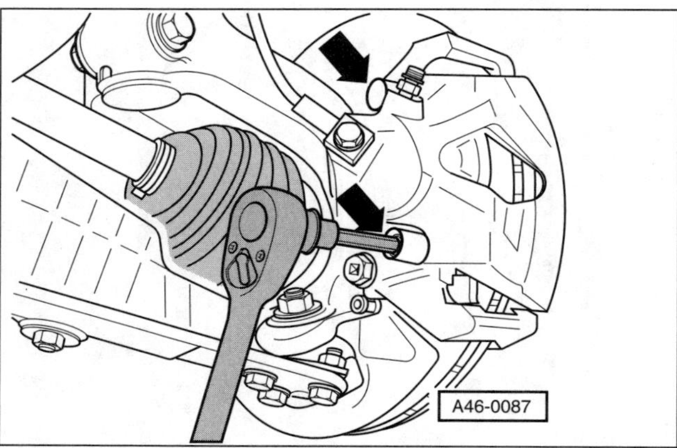

A46-0087

Fig. 6. Remove caliper guide pins (**arrows**).

6. Remove brake caliper housing and hang up with wire.

> ***CAUTION —***
> - *Do not allow caliper to hang by the brake hose. The unsupported weight can stretch and damage the hose.*
> - *Do not disconnect the brake hose from the caliper when removing brake pads.*

7. Remove brake pads.
8. Clean brake caliper housing, especially bonding surface for brake pad. Surfaces must be free of adhesive or grease residue.
9. Before installing new pads extract some of the brake fluid from the brake fluid reservoir.

> ***WARNING —***
> *Brake fluid is poisonous. Never siphon brake fluid by mouth.*

> ***CAUTION —***
> *A full brake fluid reservoir may allow brake fluid to flow out and cause damage when pistons are pushed back.*

10. Be sure to install correct brake pads into left and right caliper. See Fig. 7.

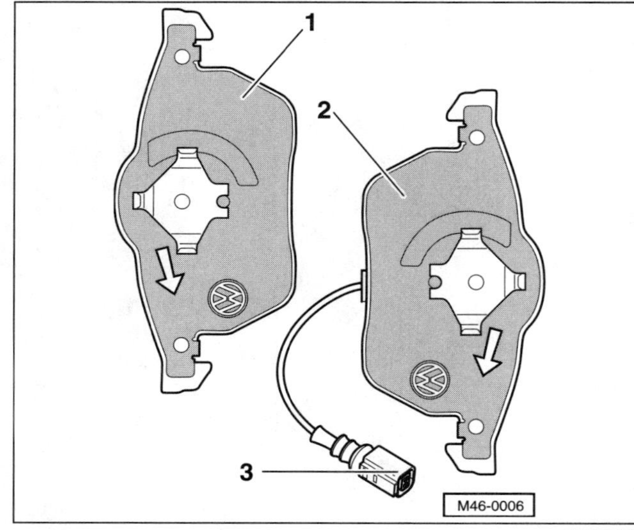

N46-0006

Fig. 7. Right-hand piston side brake pad (**1**) and left-hand piston side brake pad (**2**). **Arrow** on brake pad backing plate must point downward when installed in caliper.

11. Press piston into caliper housing and install brake pads.
12. Install outer brake pad in brake caliper.
13. Pull protective foil off outer brake pad backing plate.
14. Install brake caliper housing with both guide pins to brake carrier.
15. Install guide pin protective caps.
16. Insert retaining spring into brake caliper housing.
17. Install wheels and lower vehicle.

Tightening torques
- Brake caliper to bearing housing . . . . 28 Nm (21 ft-lb)
- Wheel bolt to hub . . . . 120 Nm (89 ft-lb)

---

18. Depress brake pedal firmly several times to seat brake pads to brake disc. Check brake fluid level and add as necessary.

REAR BRAKES

Rear disc brake assembly

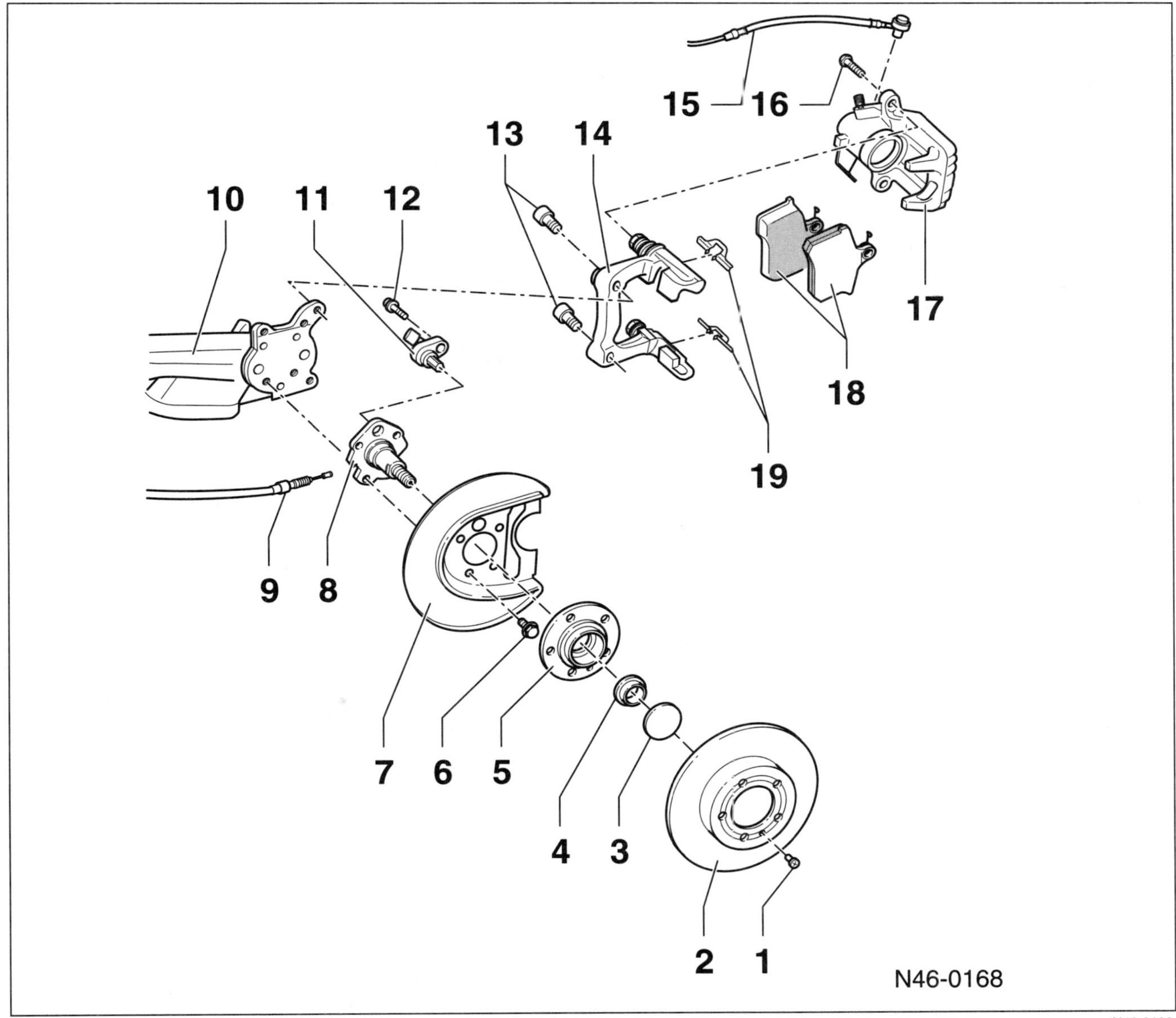

N46-0168

Fig. 8. Rear disc brake assembly.

1. **Screw**
   - Tighten to 4 Nm (35 in-lb)
2. **Brake disc**
   - Diameter: 232 mm (9.13 in.)
   - Thickness: 9 mm (0.354 in.)
   - Wear limit: 7 mm (0.275 in.)
   - When worn, always replace on both sides.
3. **Cap**
   - Removing and installing, see **42 Rear Suspension**
4. **Self-locking nut**
   - Tighten to 175 Nm (129 ft-lb)
   - Always replace after removing
5. **Wheel hub with wheel bearing and ABS rotor**
   - Always replace after removing
   - Only replace as complete unit
   - Removing and installing, see **42 Rear Suspension**
6. **Bolt**
   - Tighten to 60 Nm (44 ft-lb)
   - With dished spring washer

(continued on following page)

(continued from previous page)

7. **Splash shield**
8. **Stub axle**
9. **Parking brake cable**
10. **Axle beam**
11. **ABS wheel speed sensor**
    - Before inserting sensor, clean installation hole inner surface and coat with grease (VW part no. G 000 650)
12. **Socket-head bolt**
    - Tighten to 8 Nm (71 in-lb)
13. **Socket-head bolt**
    - Tighten to 65 Nm (48 ft-lb)
14. **Brake carrier with guide pins and protective cap**
    - Supplied as replacement part assembled with sufficient grease on guide pins
    - If protective caps or guide pins are damaged use repair kit
    - Use grease packet supplied to lubricate guide pins.
15. **Brake hose with union and banjo bolt**
    - With seals
    - Tighten to 35 Nm (26 ft-lb)
    - Do not disconnect brake hose when changing brake pads
16. **Self-locking bolt**
    - Tighten to 35 Nm (26 ft-lb)
    - Always replace
17. **Brake caliper**
    - Adjust parking brake cable after maintenance or replacement.
    - Do not pull parking brake before adjusting it
18. **Brake pads**
    - Thickness: 12 mm (0.472 in.)
    - Checking thickness, see **0 Maintenance**
    - Always replace all pads on one axle at same time
19. **Pad retaining springs**
    - Always replace springs when changing pads

Rear brake pads, removing and installing

NOTE —
If re-using brake pads, mark pad position before removing. Reinstall brake pads in their original position to prevent uneven braking.

1. Raise car and support with jack stands or lift. See **0 Maintenance** for proper lifting procedure.

WARNING —
Observe all warnings and cautions associated with lifting vehicle in **0 Maintenance***.*

1. Remove rear wheels.
2. Remove retaining clip for parking brake cable. Press brake lever downward and unhook parking brake cable. See Fig. 9.

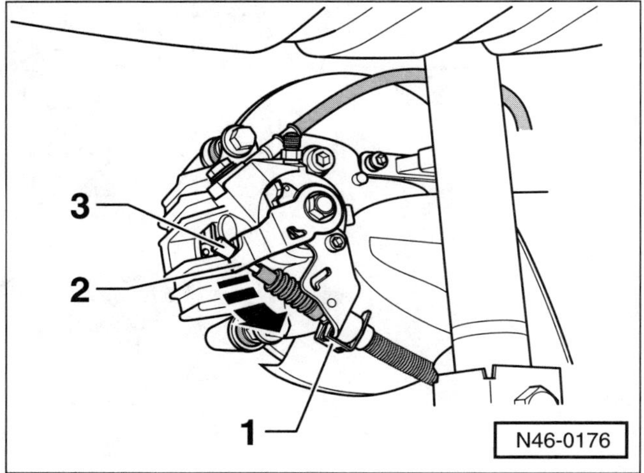

N46-0176

Fig. 9. Remove clip (**1**), press brake lever (**2**) in direction of **arrow** and unhook parking brake cable (**3**).

3. Remove bolts from brake caliper housing while counterholding guide pins. Remove brake caliper and hang up with wire. See Fig. 10.

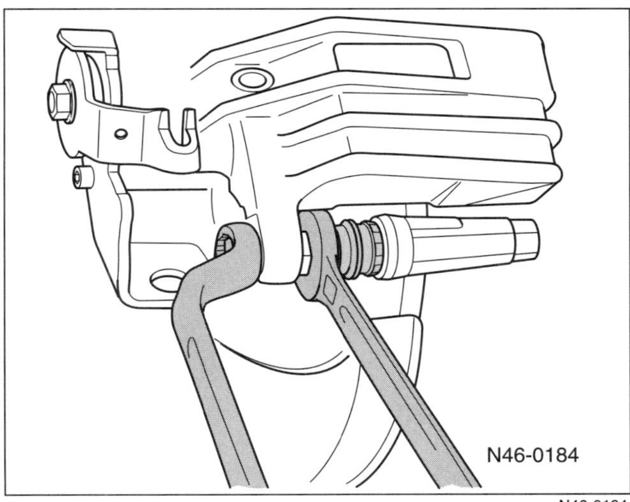

N46-0184

Fig. 10. Caliper mounting bolt being removed. Use wrench to counter-hold guide pin when removing mounting bolt.

> ***CAUTION —***
> - *Do not allow caliper to hang by the brake hose. The unsupported weight can stretch and damage the hose.*
> - *Do not disconnect the brake hose from the caliper when removing brake pads.*

4. Remove brake pads and pad retaining springs. See Fig. 11.

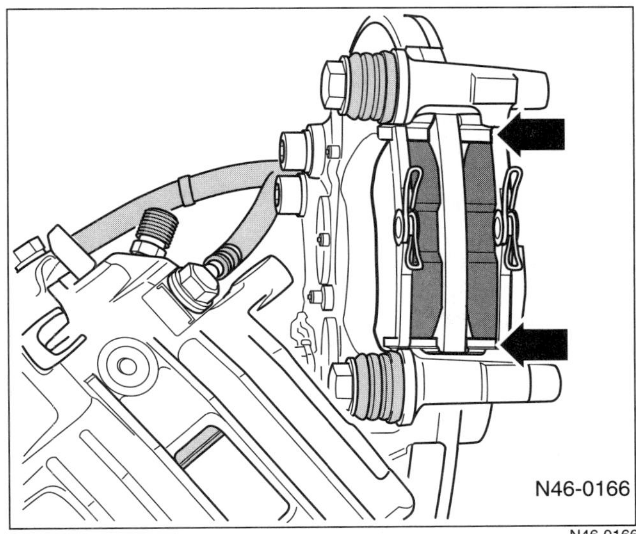

N46-0166

Fig. 11. Remove pads and retaining springs (**arrows**).

5. Clean brake caliper housing, especially bonding surface for brake pad. Bonding surfaces must be free of adhesive and grease residues.

6. Before installing new pads extract some of the brake fluid from the brake fluid reservoir.

> ***WARNING —***
> *Brake fluid is poisonous. Never siphon brake fluid by mouth.*

> ***CAUTION —***
> - *A full brake fluid reservoir may allow brake fluid to flow out and cause damage when pistons are pushed back.*
> - *Use a bleeder bottle or plastic bottle which is used only for brake fluid.*

7. Reset caliper's automatic adjustment mechanism by turning piston clockwise while pushing in. See Fig. 12.

> ***CAUTION —***
> - *If the piston is not reset correctly, or if the brake pedal is operated with the caliper removed, the automatic adjustment mechanism will be destroyed.*
> - *Always remove some brake fluid from the reservoir before resetting and pushing the caliper piston in. When the piston is pushed in, fluid is forced up into the reservoir.*

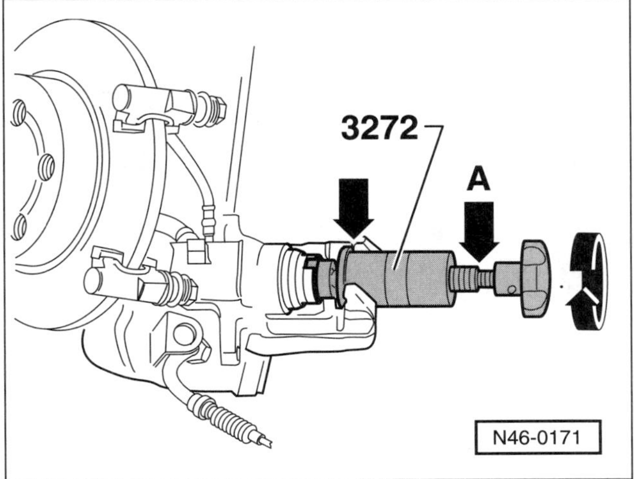

N46-0171

Fig. 12. Automatic adjustment mechanism being reset using Volkswagen special tool 3272. Turn piston clockwise (**rotational arrow**) while pushing piston in. An open-ended wrench can be used on flats (**A**) if necessary.

8. Pull protective foil off outer brake pad backing plate.

9. Insert brake pads and brake pad retaining springs into brake carrier.

10. Install brake caliper housing with new self-locking bolts.

> ***WARNING —***
> *Always replace the self-locking caliper mounting bolts with the ones in the repair kit.*

Tightening torque
- Brake caliper to brake carrier. . . . . . . 35 Nm (26 ft-lb)

11. Connect parking brake cable to lever on caliper and install retaining clip.

12. Adjust parking brake if necessary, see **Parking brake, adjusting** given later.

> ***NOTE —***
> *Operate the foot brake first after adjusting the parking brake.*

13. Install rear wheels and lower vehicle.

14. Depress brake pedal firmly several times to seat brake pads to brake disc. Check brake fluid level and add as necessary.

PARKING BRAKE

The cable-operated parking brake mechanically actuates the rear caliper pistons independent of the hydraulic brake system. Because of the automatic rear wheel brake adjustment there is normally no need to adjust the parking brake. The parking brake must be adjusted only if the parking brake cables, brake calipers or brake discs are replaced.

Parking brake, adjusting

1. Remove center console extension, see **68 Body Interior Equipment**.

2. Raise car and support with jack stands or lift. See **0 Maintenance** for proper lifting procedure.

> ***WARNING —***
> *Observe all warnings and cautions associated with lifting vehicle in* **0 Maintenance**.

3. Release parking brake.

4. Firmly depress brake pedal once.

5. Pull parking brake lever to fourth notch.

6. Tighten parking brake cable adjusting nut until both rear wheels are difficult to turn by hand. See Fig. 13.

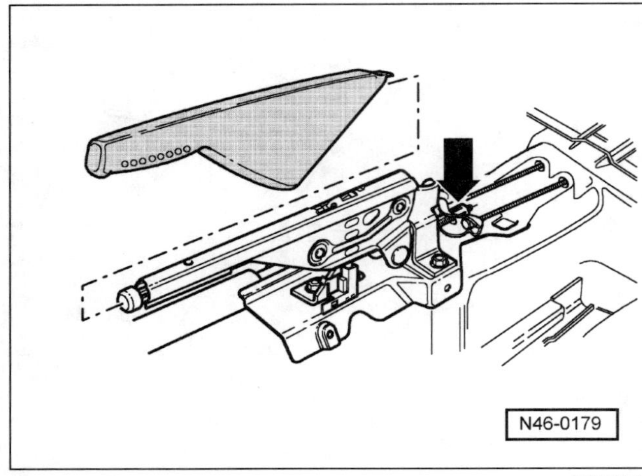

N46-0179

Fig. 13. Tighten adjustment nuts (**arrow**) until both rear wheel are difficult to turn by hand.

7. Release parking brake and check that both wheels turn freely. If necessary turn adjusting nut back slightly.

8. Install center console extension.

9. Lower vehicle.

Parking brake cables, removing and installing

1. Remove center console extension, see **68 Body Interior Equipment**.

2. Release parking brake.

3. Loosen parking brake adjustment nut (shown in Fig. 13) until parking brake cable can be unhooked from compensator.

4. Raise car and support with jack stands or lift. See **0 Maintenance** for proper lifting procedure.

> ***WARNING —***
> *Observe all warnings and cautions associated with lifting vehicle in* **0 Maintenance**.

5. Remove retaining clip for parking brake cable. Press brake lever downward and unhook parking brake cable as shown earlier in Fig. 9.

6. Unclip parking brake cable from retainers. See Fig. 14.

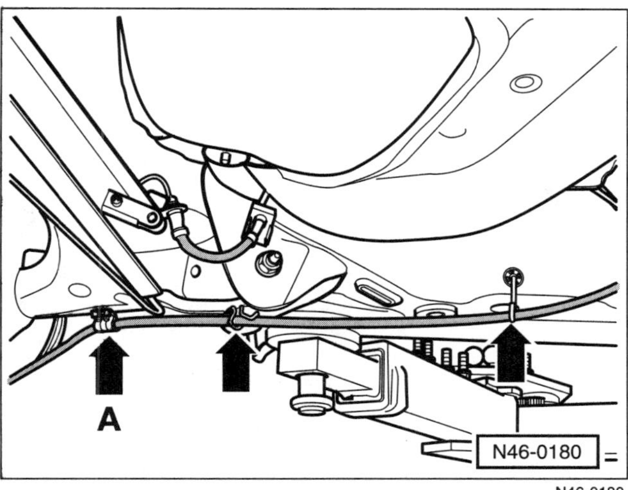

N46-0180

Fig. 14. Parking brake cable retainer on rear axle (**arrow A**) and additional retainers (**arrows**)

7. Pull parking brake cable out of guide tube. See Fig. 15.

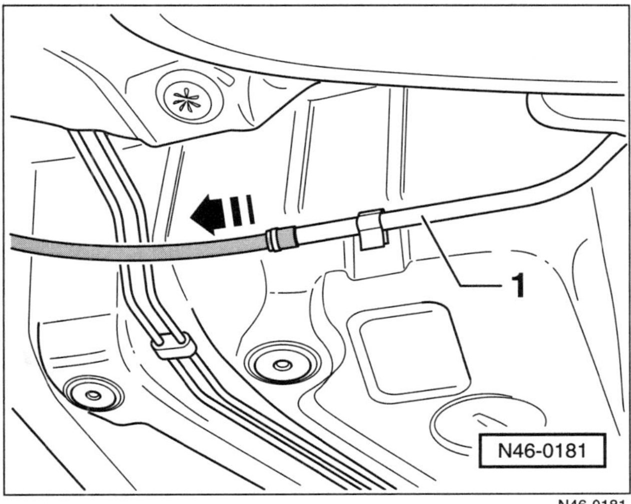

N46-0181

Fig. 15. Pull parking brake cable out of guide tube (**1**) in direction of **arrow**.

8. Begin installation by sliding parking brake cable into guide tube.

9. Connect parking brake cable to lever on caliper and install retaining clip. See Fig. 16.

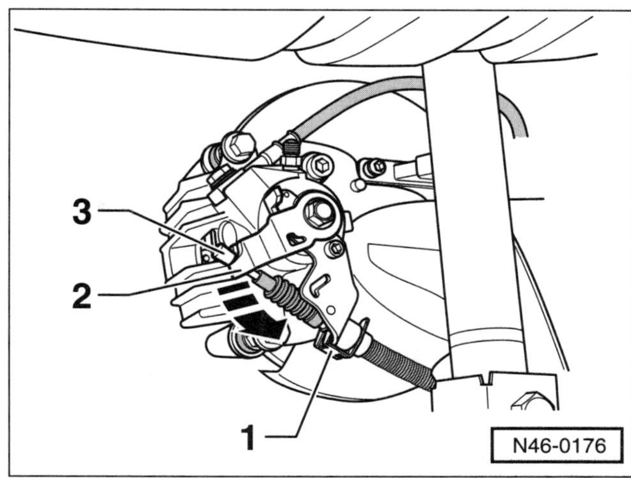

N46-0176

Fig. 16. Press brake lever (**2**) in direction of **arrow** and attach parking brake cable (**3**) and retaining clip (**1**).

10. Clip parking brake cable into retainer on rear axle.

> ***NOTE —***
> *Parking brake cable clamp ring must lie in middle of clip.*

11. Hook parking brake cable into remaining retainers.

12. Hook parking brake cable into compensator at parking brake lever.

13. Install parking brake cable adjustment nut.

14. Adjust parking brake, see **Parking brake, adjusting** given earlier.

15. Lower vehicle.

16. Install center console extension.

Parking brake lever assembly

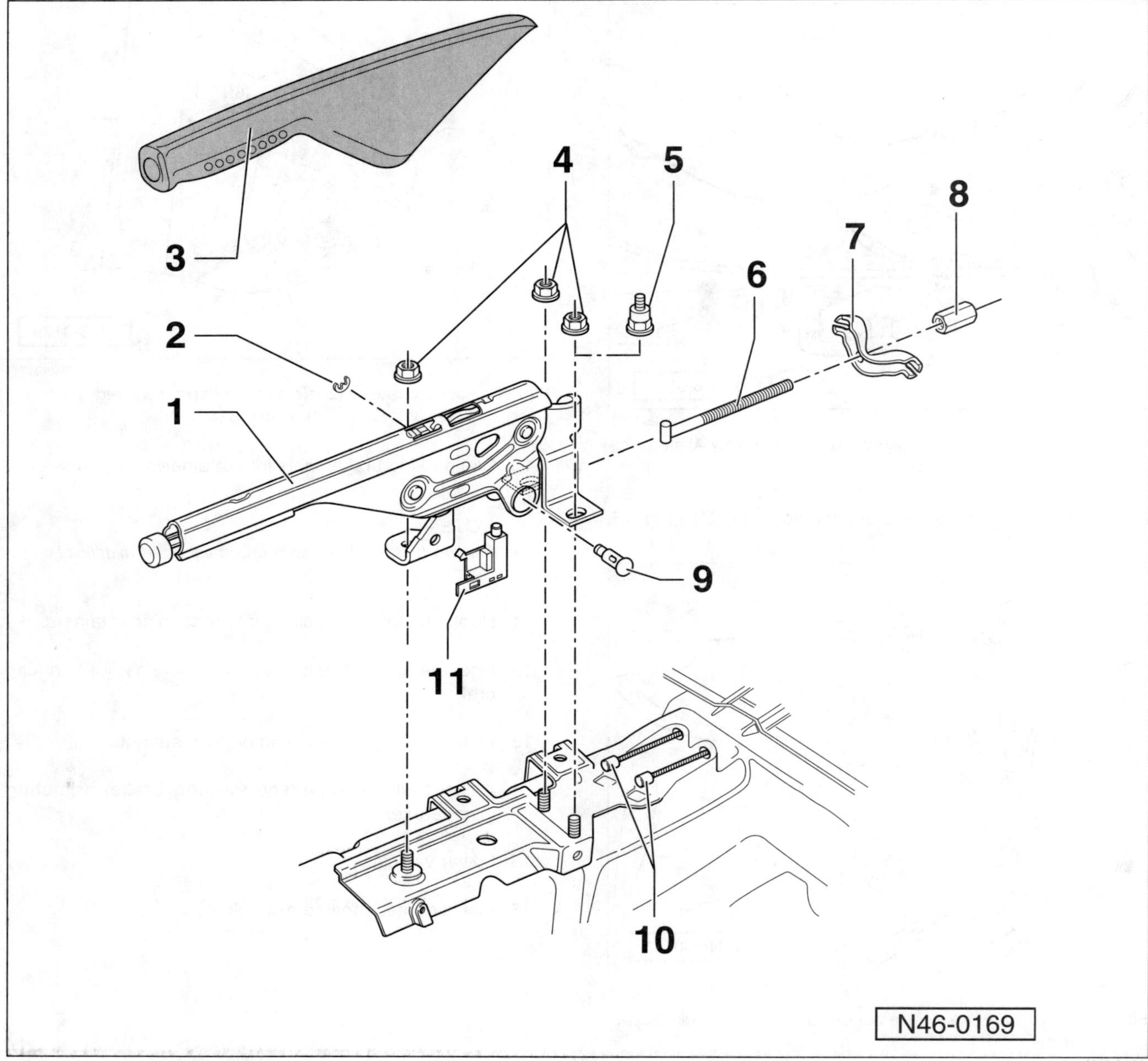

N46-0169

Fig. 17. Parking brake lever and related components.

1. **Parking brake lever**
   - Before removing remove center console
2. **Circlip**
3. **Parking brake lever trim**
   - Pull off toward front
4. **Nuts**
   - Tighten to 25 Nm (18 ft-lb)
5. **Adapter**
   - For vehicles with center armrest
6. **Pull rod**
7. **Compensator**
8. **Adjusting nut**
9. **Fulcrum pin**
   - Holds pull rod (item 6) in parking brake
10. **Parking brake cables**
11. **Parking brake warning light switch**

47 Brakes–Hydraulic System

GENERAL

This repair group covers service and repair to the hydraulic and vacuum-assist brake system components. Also included here is brake bleeding. Cars covered by this manual are equipped with front and rear disc brakes. Some cars are also equipped with anti-lock brakes (ABS).

> ***CAUTION —***
> - *This repair group does not cover the anti-lock braking system hydraulic unit (with integral master cylinder). For information on the ABS system see* **45 Anti-Lock Brakes (ABS)**.

Brake service precautions

The following warnings and cautions should be read before servicing the brake hydraulic system:

> ***WARNING —***
> - *A properly functioning brake system is essential to safe driving. If the red brake/parking warning light or the ABS warning light illuminates while driving, it is imperative that the system be given a thorough check, even if braking action still seems satisfactory. The brakes should be inspected regularly.*
> - *Brake fluid absorbs moisture from the air and must be replaced every two years. Use only new, approved brake fluid that complies with MVSS 116 DOT 4. Do not use silicone-based brake fluid (DOT 5). Even the smallest traces can cause severe corrosion in the brake system.*
> - *Brake fluid is poisonous. Wear safety glasses and rubber gloves when working with brake fluid. Prevent brake fluid from entering the bloodstream through cuts or scratches. Do not siphon brake fluid by mouth.*

> ***CAUTION —***
> - *Always disconnect battery negative (–) cable when working at or near pedal cluster.*
> - *Disconnecting the negative (–) battery cable may erase fault codes and basic settings in the engine management and automatic transmission control modules. Some driveability problems may be noticed until the system re-adapts to operating conditions. OBD II readiness codes, which may be required for emissions testing, may also be erased. Convenience electronics (alarm system, interior light control, power locks, mirrors, and windows) may need to be re-set using a VAG 1551/1552 or equivalent scan tool.*
> - *Before disconnecting the battery be sure to obtain the anti-theft radio code.*
> - *After replacing brake components, depress the brake pedal firmly several times to seat the brakes in their normal operating position. The pedal should be firm and at its normal height, if not, further work is required before driving vehicle.*
> - *Brake fluid is very damaging to paint.*

FRONT BRAKE CALIPER

Two types of front calipers are used on the cars covered by this manual. Repair procedures vary depending on caliper application. See the appropriate (FS III or FN 3) assembly view.

Front caliper application

- 2.0L, 1.9L . . . . . FS III
- 2.8L, 1.8L . . . . . FN 3

Front brake caliper (FS III) assembly

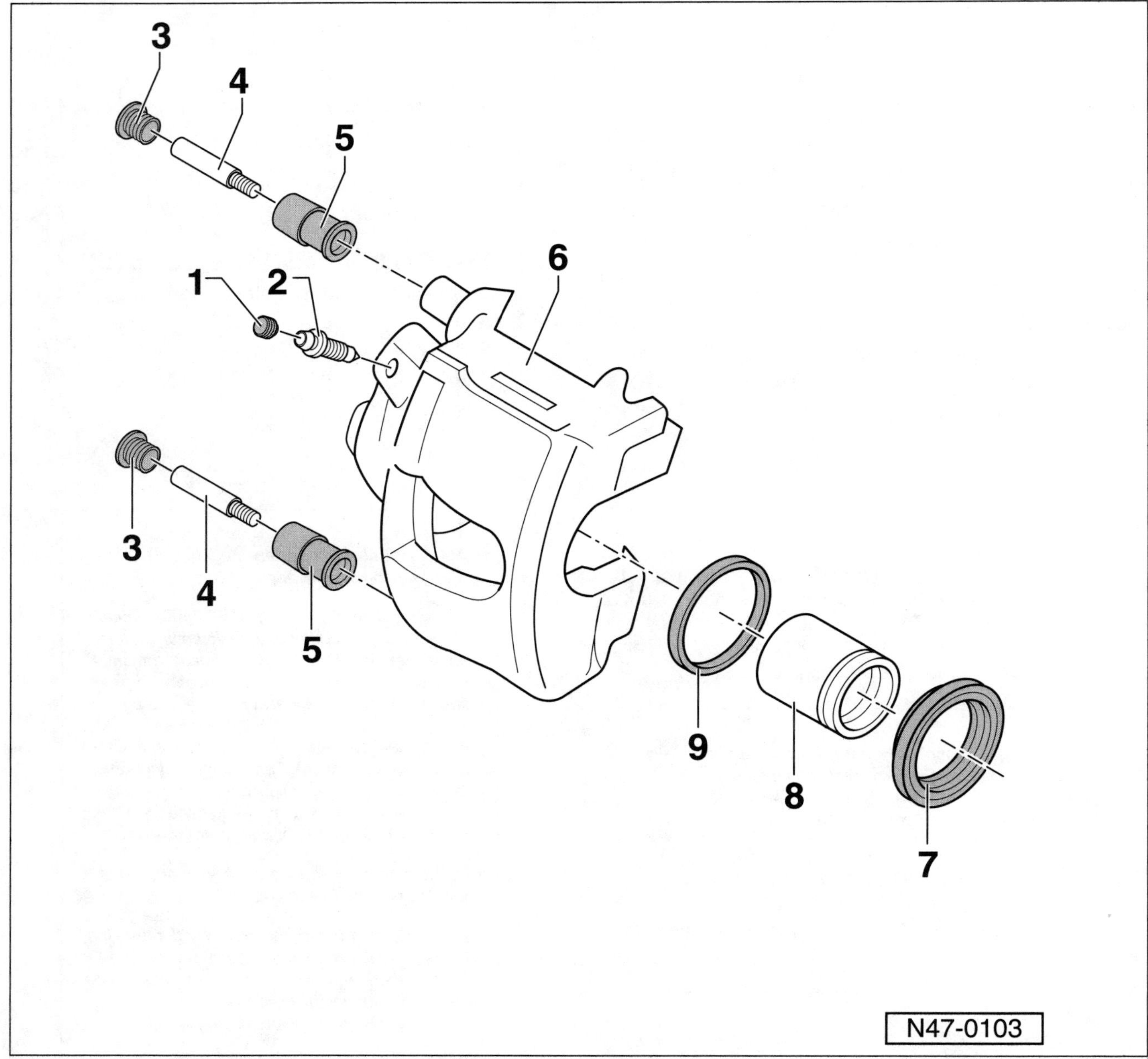

Fig. 1. FS III front brake caliper, piston and piston seals.

NOTE —
- *Install all parts in repair kit.*
- *New brake calipers are filled with brake fluid and are pre-bled.*
- *When assembling, apply a thin coat of grease (VW part no. G052 150 A2) to brake cylinders, pistons and seals.*

1. **Dust boot**
   - Do not damage when inserting piston
2. **Piston**
3. **Brake caliper housing**
4. **Piston seal**

Front brake caliper (FN 3) assembly

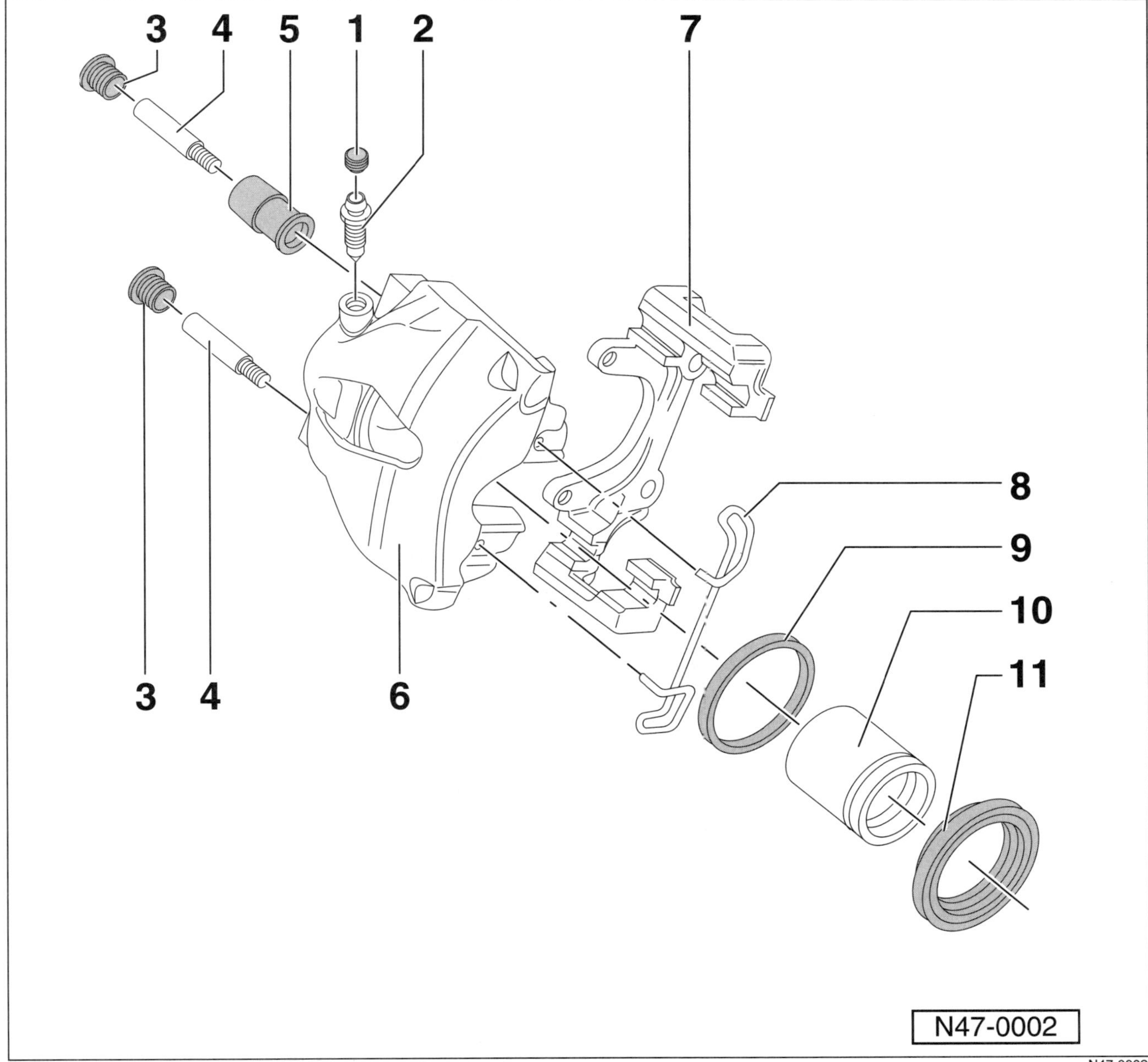

Fig. 2. FN 3 front brake caliper, piston and piston seals.

NOTE —

- *Install all parts in repair kit.*
- *New brake calipers are filled with brake fluid and are pre-bled.*
- *When assembling, apply a thin coat of grease (VW part no. G052 150 A2) to brake cylinders, pistons and seals.*

1. **Dust cap**
2. **Bleeder valve**
   - Apply thin coat of brake fluid to threads when installing
3. **Cap**
   - Insert in mounting bushing
4. **Guide pin**
   - Tighten to 28 Nm (21 ft-lb)

(continued on following page)

(continued from previous page)

5. **Mounting bushing**
   - Insert into brake caliper housing
6. **Brake caliper housing**
7. **Brake carrier**
8. **Retaining spring**
   - Insert with both ends in holes in brake caliper housing
9. **Piston seal**
10. **Piston**
    - Apply thin coat of brake fluid to piston before inserting
    - Piston diameter: 54 mm (2.125 in.)
11. **Dust boot**
    - Do not damage when inserting piston

Front caliper piston, removing and installing

1. Remove brake caliper and pads as described in **46 Brakes–Mechanical Components**.

2. Force piston out of brake caliper housing using compressed air. See Fig. 3.

V47-0406

Fig. 3. Use compressed air at **arrow** to force piston out of caliper.

> ***CAUTION —***
> - *Place a piece of wood in the recess to prevent damaging the piston.*
> - *Use only enough air pressure to force piston out.*

> ***WARNING —***
> *Always wear safety goggles when working with compressed air.*

3. Carefully remove piston seal using a plastic wedge. See Fig. 4.

> ***CAUTION —***
> *When removing, use care to ensure that the cylinder bore is not damaged.*

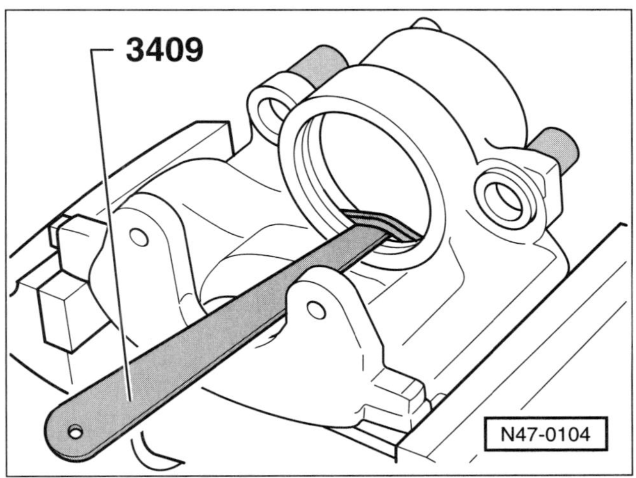

N47-0104

Fig. 4. Volkswagen special tool 3409 (wedge) being used to remove piston seal.

4. Clean caliper and piston with fresh brake fluid.

5. Install new piston seal in caliper.

6. Lubricate piston and cylinder bore lightly using grease (VW part no. G052 150 A2).

7. Install dust boot with outer sealing lip on piston. See Fig. 5.

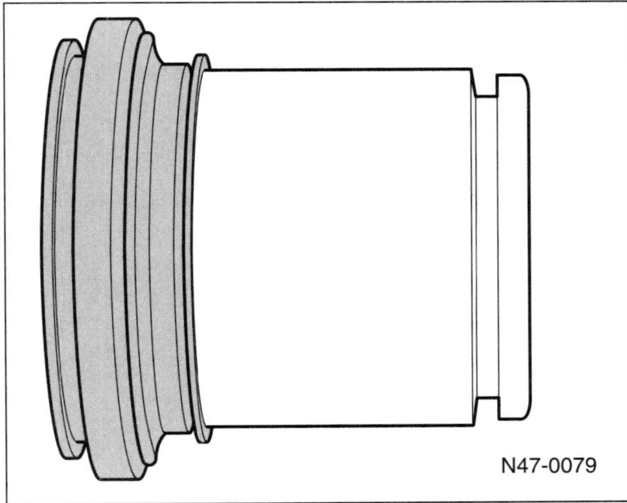

N47-0079

Fig. 5. Installation position of dust boot on piston.

8. Hold piston in front of caliper and insert inner sealing lip into grove in cylinder using a plastic wedge. See Fig. 6.

9. Press piston into brake caliper housing using piston re-setting tool. See Fig. 7.

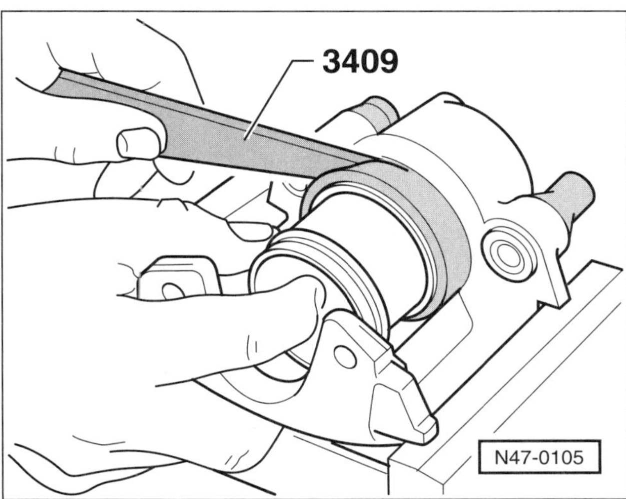

N47-0105

Fig. 6. Use wedge (VW 3409) to insert sealing lip into cylinder while installing piston.

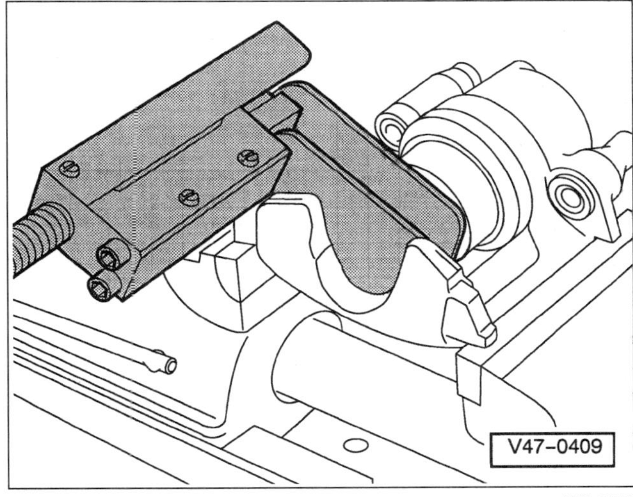

V47-0409

Fig. 7. Piston being pressed into brake caliper housing. Be sure that sealing lip of dust boot slips into the piston groove.

NOTE —

The outer sealing lip of the dust boot must slip into the piston groove.

10. Be sure to quality check your work.

Rear brake caliper assembly

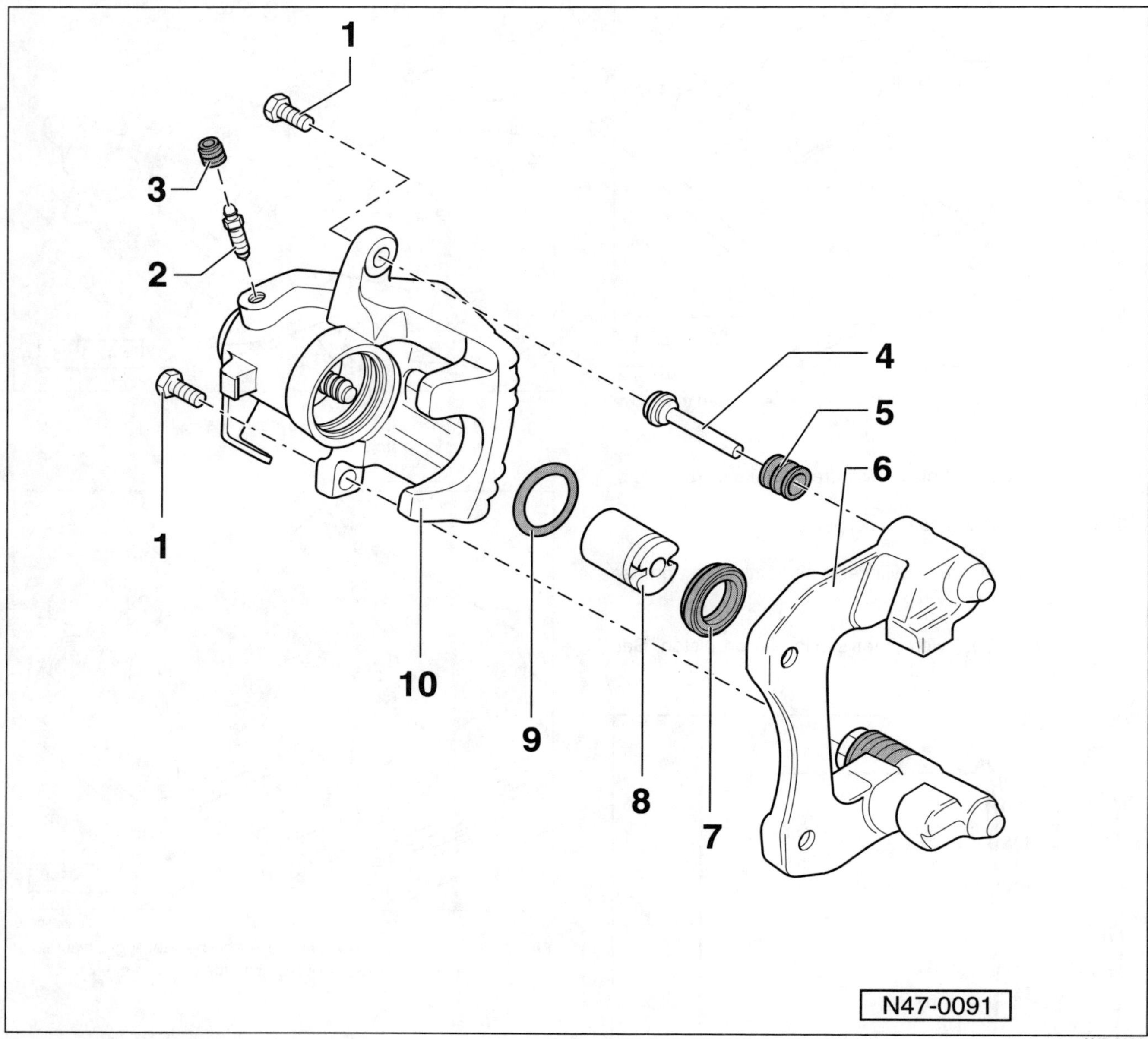

N47-0091

Fig. 8. Rear brake caliper.

NOTE —
- *Install all parts in repair kit.*
- *New brake calipers are filled with brake fluid and are pre-bled.*
- *When assembling, apply a thin coat of grease (VW part no. G052 150 A2) to brake cylinders, pistons and seals.*
- *When repairing, be sure to pre-bleed brake calipers (without brake pads) before installing, see* **Rear caliper piston, removing and installing**.

1. **Self-locking bolt**
   - Tighten to 35 Nm (26 ft-lb)
   - Always replace
   - When loosening and tightening, counter-hold on guide pin
2. **Bleeder screw**
   - Apply thin coat of grease (VW part no. G052 150 A2) to threads before installing
3. **Dust cap**

(continued form previous page)

4. **Guide pins**
   - Apply thin coat of grease (VW part no. G052 150 A2) before installing protective cap
5. **Protective cap**
   - Pull onto brake carrier and guide pin
6. **Brake carrier with guide pin and protective cap**
   - Replacement part is assembled with sufficient grease on guide pins.
   - If protective caps or guide pins are damaged, install repair kit. Use grease packet supplied to lubricate guide pins.
7. **Dust boot**
   - Pull outer sealing lip onto piston
8. **Piston with automatic adjustment**
   - Apply thin coat of grease (VW part no. G052 150 A2) before installing
9. **Piston seal**
10. **Brake caliper housing**
    - With parking brake cable lever
    - If fluid is leaking at parking brake cable lever, replace brake caliper housing
    - After repairing, pre-bleed caliper housing, see **Rear caliper piston, removing and installing**

Rear caliper piston, removing and installing

1. Remove piston from brake caliper housing by turning knurled wheel on piston resetting and removal tool counter-clockwise. See Fig. 9.

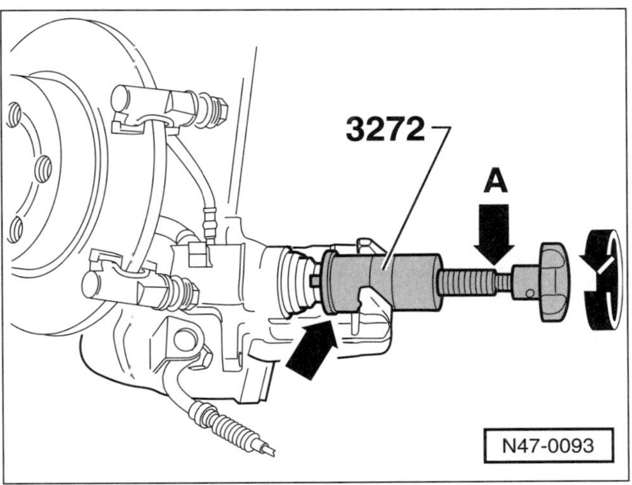

N47-0093

Fig. 9. Volkswagen special tool 3272 being used to remove rear caliper piston. Install tool with collar (**arrow**) positioned before the piston. If piston is difficult to move, use 13 mm wrench on flat spots (**arrow A**) of tool.

2. Remove seal using plastic wedge. See Fig. 10.

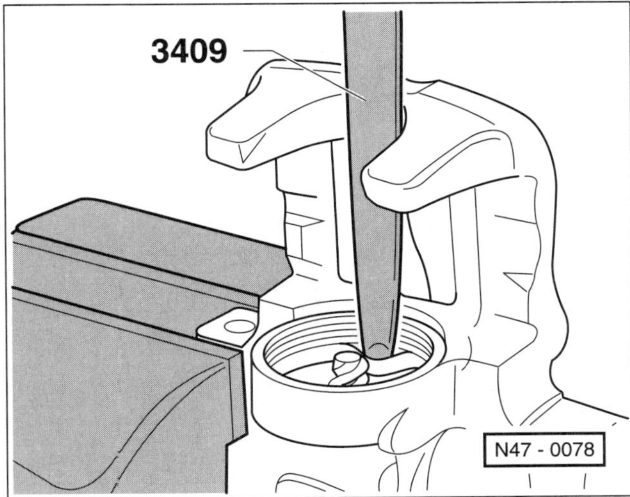

N47-0078

Fig. 10. Volkswagen special tool 3409 (wedge) being used to remove piston seal.

> ***CAUTION —***
> *When removing, use care to ensure that the cylinder bore is not damaged.*

3. Clean caliper and piston with fresh brake fluid.

4. Install new piston seal in caliper.

5. Lubricate piston and cylinder bore lightly using grease (VW part no. G052 150 A2).

6. Install dust boot with outer sealing lip on piston. See Fig. 11.

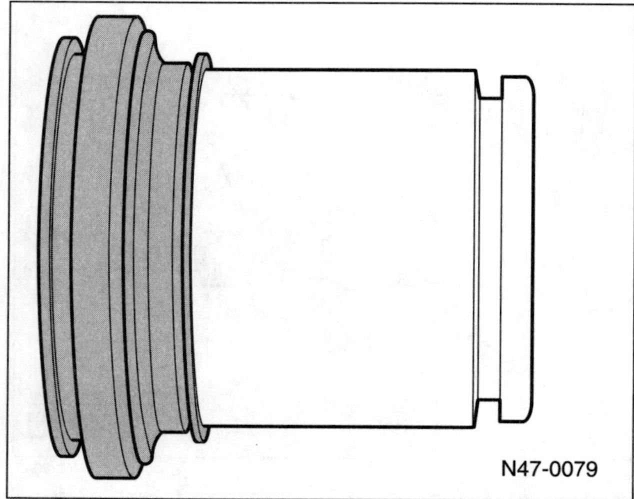

N47-0079

Fig. 11. Installation position of dust boot on piston.

7. Hold piston in front of caliper and insert inner sealing lip into grove in cylinder using a plastic wedge. See Fig. 12.

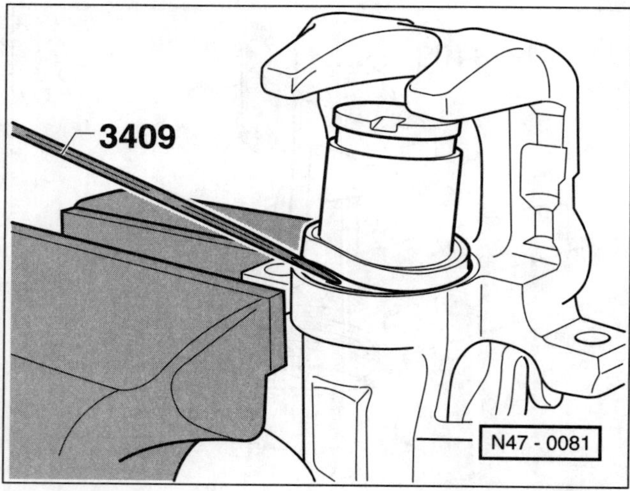

N47-0081

Fig. 12. Use wedge (VW 3409) to insert sealing lip into cylinder while installing piston.

8. Reset caliper's automatic adjustment mechanism by turning the piston clockwise while pushing piston in. See Fig. 13.

9. Pre-bleed caliper by opening bleeder screw and fill a standard bleeder bottle with brake fluid until bubble-free fluid flows from brake hose connection.

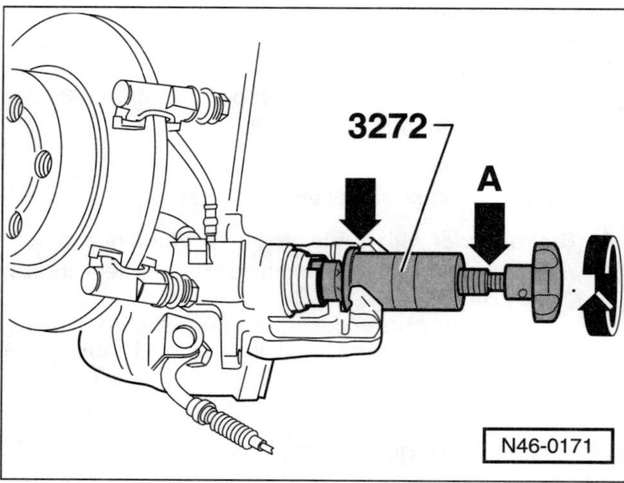

N46-0171

Fig. 13. Automatic adjustment mechanism being reset using Volkswagen special tool 3272. Turn piston clockwise (**rotational arrow**) while pushing piston in.

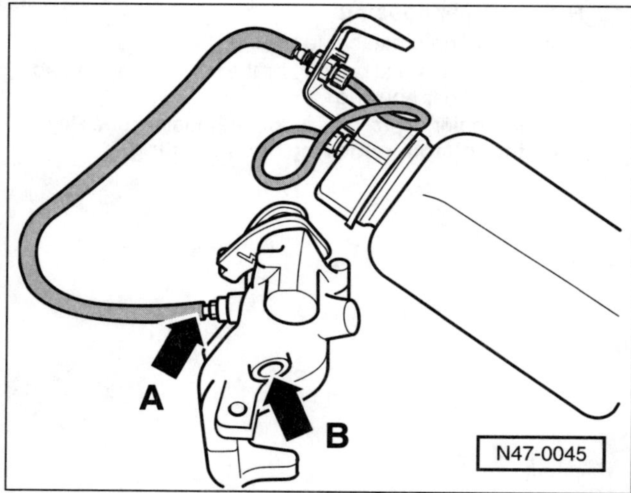

N47-0045

Fig. 14. Pre-bleed caliper by opening bleeder screw (**arrow A**) and fill bleeder bottle with brake fluid until bubble-free fluid flows from brake hose connection (**arrow B**).

CAUTION—

- *If the piston is not reset correctly, or if the brake pedal is operated with the caliper removed, the automatic adjustment mechanism will be destroyed.*
- *Always remove some brake fluid from the reservoir before resetting and pushing the caliper piston in. When the piston is pushed in, fluid is forced up into the reservoir.*

10. Close bleeder screw.

11. Be sure to quality check your work.

Brake pressure regulator assembly

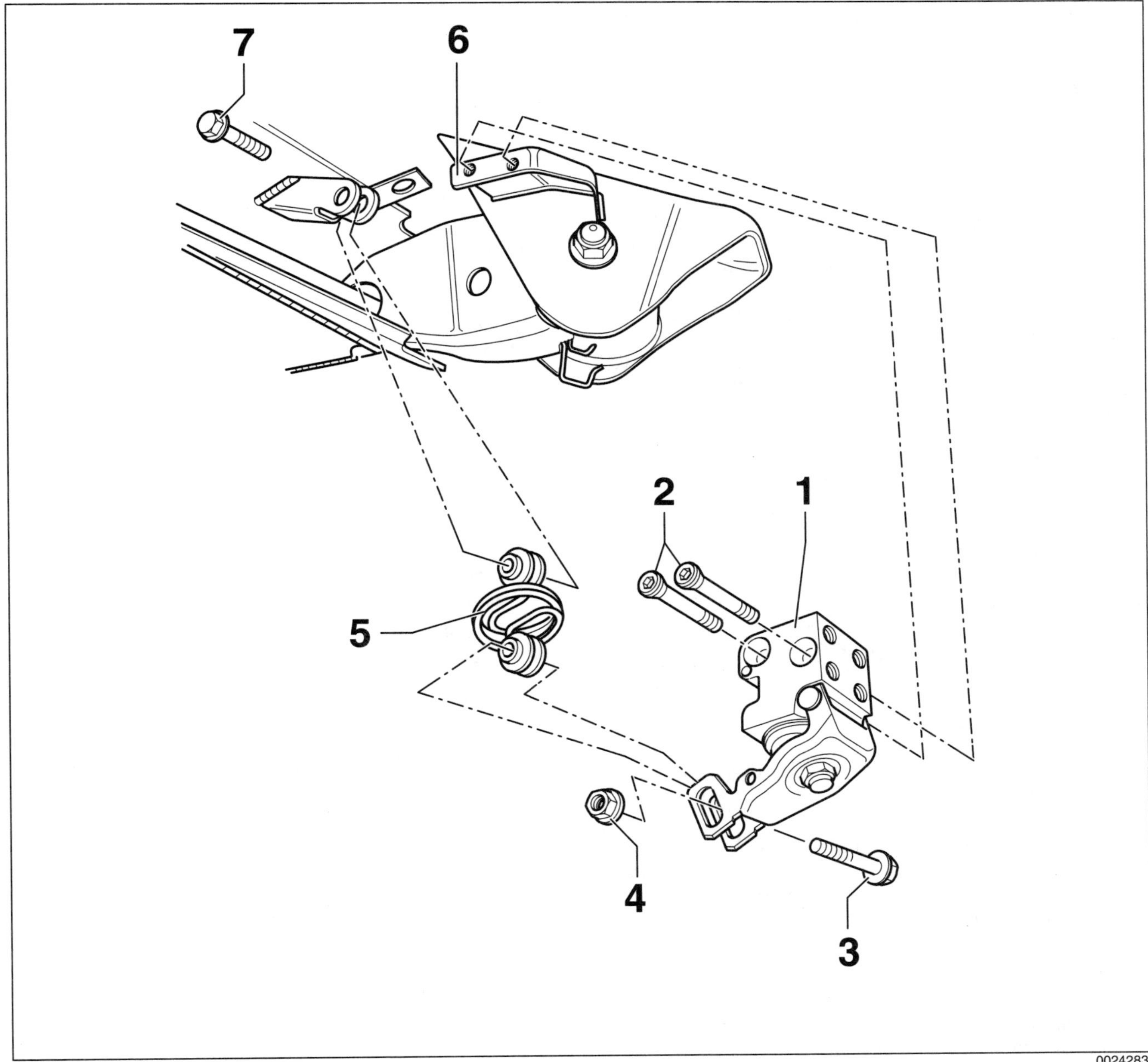

Fig. 15. Brake pressure regulator installed on the rear axle of non-ABS equipped cars.

1. **Brake pressure regulator**
2. **Socket-head bolt**
   - Tighten to 21 Nm (15 ft-lb)
3. **Bolt**
   - Tighten to 21Nm (15 ft-lb)
4. **Nut**
   - Tighten to 21 Nm (15 ft-lb)
5. **Spring**
6. **Mounting bracket**
7. **Bolt**
   - Tighten to 16 Nm (12 ft-lb)

Brake pressure regulator, checking

Cars without ABS have a brake pressure regulator mounted on a bracket attached to the rear axle. This load-sensing regulator is controlled from the rear axle by a spring. When the axle changes position, due to a heavy load or during hard braking, the pressure regulator varies the pressure to the rear brakes.

> ***NOTE —***
> *The brake pressure regulator should be checked and if necessary adjusted following repairs to the rear suspension, or when there is excessive rear brake wear.*

With the car resting on all four wheels and the fuel tank full, observe the pressure regulator while a helper depresses and quickly releases the brake pedal. The regulator should move slightly when the brake is quickly released. If not, the regulator is faulty and should be replaced.

> ***NOTE —***
> *For this check to be accurate, the car should be emptied of all cargo and occupants, except driver.*

Testing and adjusting the pressure-regulating function requires measuring brake system pressure at each wheel caliper using two pressure gauges. Because of the need for this specialized equipment, we recommend having this test performed by an authorized Volkswagen dealer.

BRAKE BLEEDING

The procedure given here applies to all vehicles covered in this manual with and without ABS.

The brake system can be bled using a pressure bleeder or manually using a helper. Pressure bleeding, if the equipment is available, is the fastest. Manual bleeding requires a helper, but is easy and requires no special tools.

> ***CAUTION —***
> - *Brake fluid absorbs moisture from the air and must be replaced every two years, see* **0 Maintenance**.
> - *Use only new, approved brake fluid that complies with MVSS 116 DOT 4. Do not use silicone-based brake fluid (DOT 5). Even the smallest traces can cause severe corrosion in the brake system.*
> - *Brake fluid is poisonous. Wear safety glasses and rubber gloves when working with brake fluid. Prevent brake fluid from entering the bloodstream through cuts or scratches. Do not siphon brake fluid by mouth.*
> - *Brake fluid is very damaging to paint. Immediately wipe up any brake fluid that spills on the vehicle.*
> - *The brake fluid level in the reservoir must not fall below the MIN mark during bleeding.*

> ***NOTE —***
> - *On non-ABS cars, the brake pressure regulator lever must be pressed toward the rear during rear brake bleeding.*
> - *Depress the brake pedal several times during the bleeding operation.*

Bleeding, with pressure bleeder

Pressure bleeding using Volkswagen special tool US1116 or equivalent is the preferred method of removing air from all brake systems because it does a more thorough purge.

1. Connect pressure bleeder with regulated compressed air supply to fluid reservoir according to manufacturer's instructions.

> ***CAUTION —***
> *Do not exceed filling pressure of 1 bar (14.5 psi) when filling brake fluid using pressure bleeder US 1116. The brake system will not be completely bled if excessive pressure is used.*

2. Connect hose from bleeder bottle to caliper/wheel cylinder bleeder screw and bleed brakes in following sequence:
   - Right rear caliper
   - Left rear caliper
   - Right front caliper
   - Left front caliper
3. Brake fluid should be allowed to flow from the bleeder valve/screw until it runs clear.

Bleeding, manually

1. Connect hose from bleeder bottle to brake bleeder screw at the right rear caliper or wheel cylinder.

> ***CAUTION —***
> *The brake fluid level in the reservoir must not fall below the MIN mark during bleeding.*

2. Have a helper pump the brake pedal several times and then hold pedal down.
3. Open bleeder screw at the caliper or wheel cylinder and collect fluid.
4. Close bleeder screw and then release brake pedal. Repeat operation until brake fluid runs clear and flows without air bubbles.
5. Repeat the above procedure at the remaining wheels, using the following sequence:
   - Left rear caliper
   - Right front caliper
   - Left front caliper

MASTER CYLINDER/BRAKE BOOSTER

Master cylinder/brake booster assembly

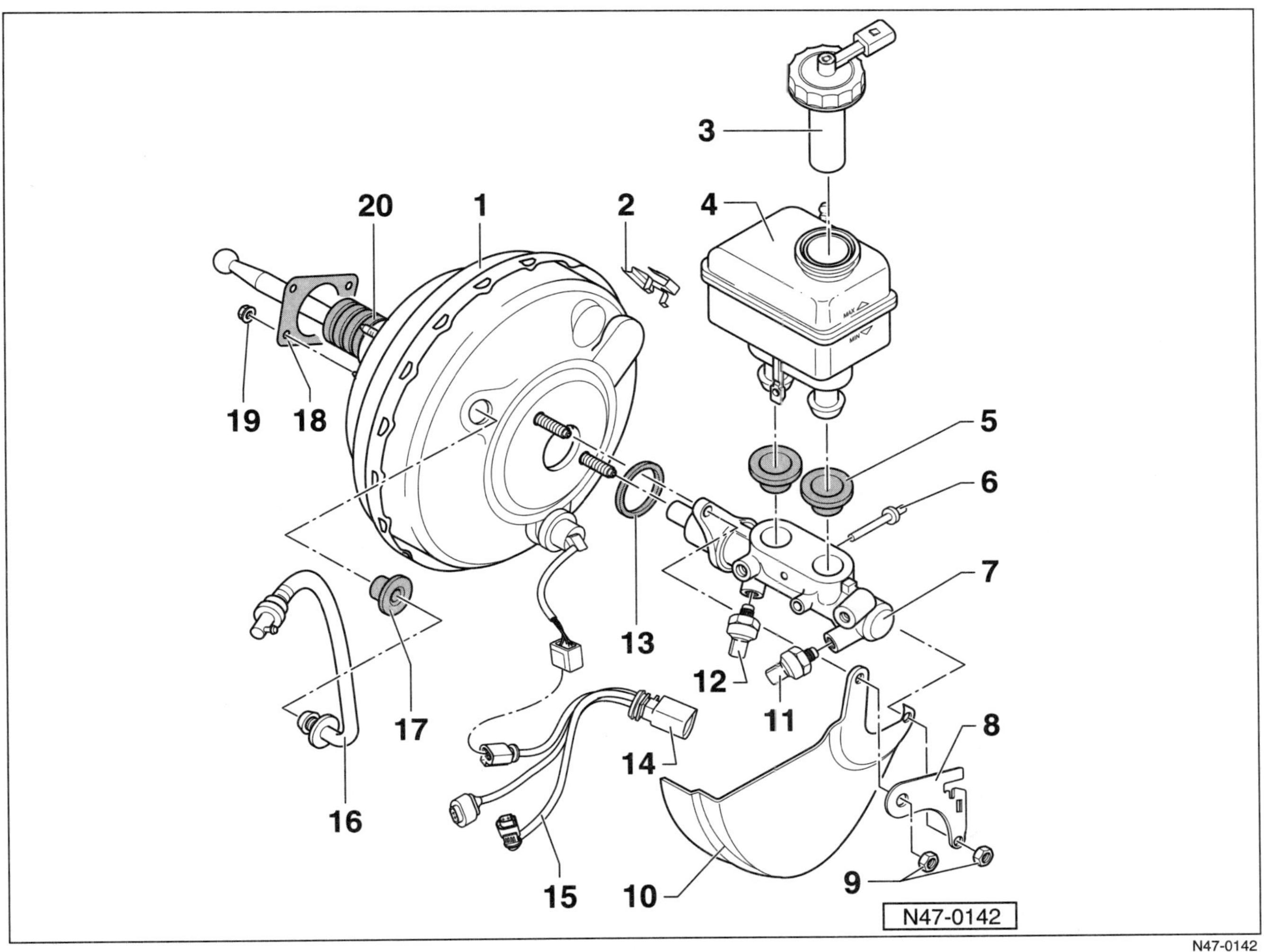

N47-0142

Fig. 16. Brake master cylinder with brake booster for vehicles with ABS/EDS/ASR/ESP.

1. **Brake Booster**
   - Can be replaced separately from master cylinder
   - Gasoline engine: vacuum supplied by intake manifold
   - Diesel (1.9L engine): pump supplies vacuum, **see** Ⓐ
   - Functional check:
     With engine off, depress brake pedal firmly several times (to exhaust vacuum in unit).
     Depress brake pedal with average foot pressure, hold and start engine. If brake booster is working properly, pedal will give slightly under foot.
   - If booster is not functioning replace complete brake booster
   - Checking vacuum check valve (1.9L engine), **see** Ⓑ
2. **Bracket**
   - Mounted on edge of brake booster
   - Used to hold wiring connector (item 14)
3. **Cover**
4. **Brake fluid reservoir**
5. **Sealing plug**
   - Moisten with brake fluid and press into reservoir
6. **Retainer pin**
   - Install through brake master cylinder
7. **Brake master cylinder**
   - Cannot be repaired. If faulty, replace as complete unit
8. **Holding plate**
   - Used to retain wiring harness (item 15)
9. **Self-locking nut**
   - Tighten to 20 Nm (15 ft-lb)
   - Always replace

(continued on following page)

(continued from previous page)

10. Heat shield
- May not be installed in some vehicles

11. Sender 1 for brake booster (G201)

12. Sensor 2 for brake booster (G214)

13. Sealing ring
- Always replace

14. Connecting housing

15. Wiring harness

16. Vacuum hose
- Insert into brake booster

17. Sealing plug

18. Gasket
- For brake booster

19. Self-locking nut
- Tighten to 20 Nm (15 ft-lb)
- Always replace

20. Boot
- Must be seated correctly or may cause air noise

A Vacuum pump for brake booster (1.9L engine), removing and installing

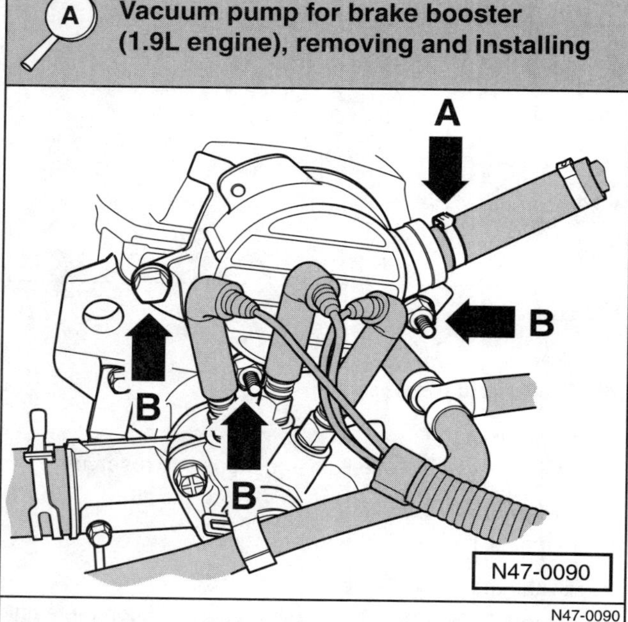

N47-0090

- **Remove retainer for wiring harness from vacuum pump.**
- **Loosen vacuum hose clamp (arrow A) and remove hose from pump.**
- **Remove bolts (arrow B) on flange and remove pump.**
- **When installing vacuum pump be sure that follower engages correctly with camshaft.**
- **Install bolts (arrows B) on cylinder head flange and secure vacuum hose with clamp (arrow A).**

NOTE —
Volkswagen identifies electrical components by a letter and/or a number in the electrical schematics. See **97 Wiring Diagrams, Fuses and Relays***. These electrical identifiers are listed in parenthesis as an aid to electrical troubleshooting.*

B Vacuum check valve, checking (1.9L engine)

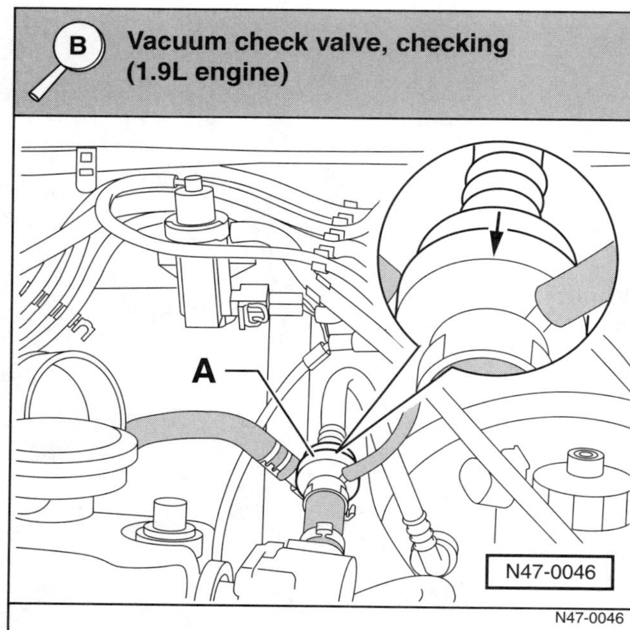

N47-0046

- **Air must pass through in direction of arrow.**
- **Check valve (A) must stay closed (no air passes through) if supplied from opposite direction.**

Brake master cylinder, removing and installing

1. Disconnect battery ground (GND) strap from battery negative (–) terminal. See the **Cautions** at the beginning of this repair group regarding battery disconnection.

NOTE —
Be sure to have the anti-theft radio code on hand before disconnecting the battery.

2. Disconnect mass air flow (MAF) sensor harness connector and remove air filter mounting bolts and air filter.

3. On vehicles with diesel engine, remove relay panel above brake booster.

4. Spread sufficient lint-free cloths in area of plenum chamber and on engine and transmission to catch any escaping brake fluid.

WARNING —
- *Brake fluid is poisonous.*
- *To draw off brake fluid from the reservoir, use a bleeder bottle which is used only for brake fluid. Never siphon brake fluid by mouth.*

5. Using bleeder bottle, draw off as much brake fluid as possible from brake fluid reservoir.

6. Clamp clutch master cylinder supply hose with special tool (VW 3094 or equivalent).

7. Remove clutch master cylinder supply hose from brake fluid reservoir.

8. Disconnect brake fluid level sensor wiring connector.

9. On vehicles with automatic transmission, disconnect wiring connectors from master cylinder pressure sensors. See Fig. 17.

10. Disconnect brake lines on brake master cylinder and seal with plugs from repair kit, (VW part no. 1H0 698 311 A).

NOTE —
Volkswagen part numbers are given for reference only. Always consult with your Volkswagen Parts Department or aftermarket parts specialist for the latest parts information.

11. Remove nuts securing brake master cylinder to brake booster.

12. Remove heat shield if installed.

13. Carefully remove brake master cylinder from brake booster.

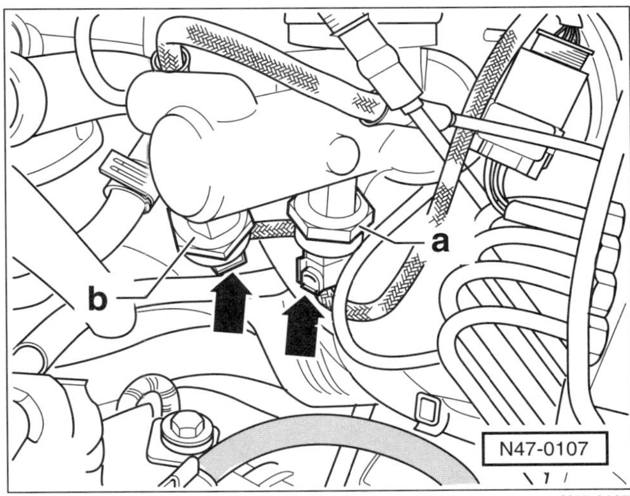

N47-0107

Fig. 17. Disconnect wiring from pressure sensors (a and b) on cars with automatic transmission.

14. Install master cylinder in reverse order of removal, noting the following:
    - When connecting brake master cylinder and brake booster be sure that the push rod is correctly located in the master cylinder.
    - After installing, bleed brakes as described earlier. Bleed clutch, see **30 Clutch**.

15. Be sure to quality check your work.

Brake booster, removing and installing

1. Disconnect battery ground (GND) strap from battery negative (–) terminal. See the **Cautions** at the beginning of this repair group regarding battery disconnection.

NOTE —
Be sure to have the anti-theft radio code on hand before disconnecting the battery.

Vehicles with manual transmission

2. Clamp clutch master cylinder supply hose with special tool (VW 3094 or equivalent).

3. Remove clutch master cylinder supply hose from brake fluid reservoir.

Vehicles with automatic transmission

4. Disconnect harness connector as shown in Fig. 18.

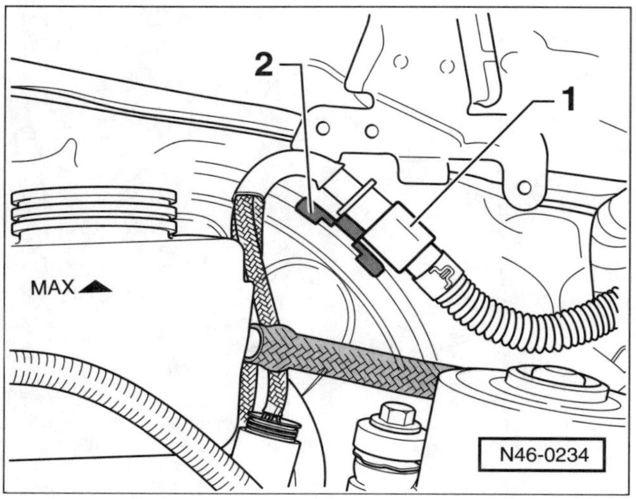

N46-0234

Fig. 18. On vehicles with automatic transmission, remove harness connector (**1**) from retainer (**2**) and separate connector.

All vehicles

5. Remove ABS control module and hydraulic unit, see **45 Anti-lock Brakes (ABS)**.

6. Disconnect vacuum hose from brake booster.

Vehicles with Diesel TDI engine

7. Remove wiring harness retainer from vacuum pump.

All vehicles

8. Remove trim below instrument panel. See Fig. 19.

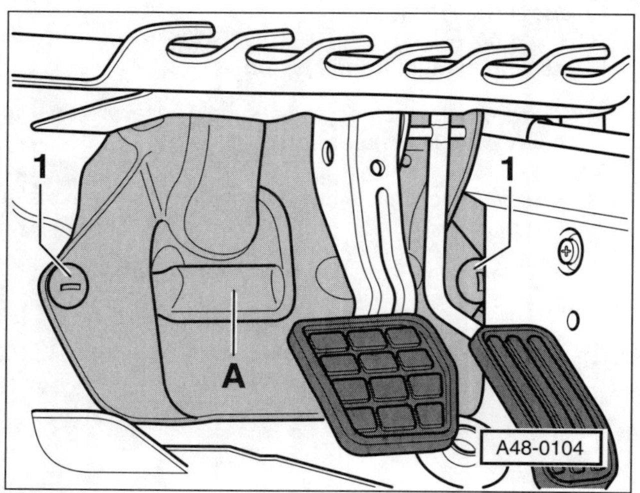

A48-0104

Fig. 19. Remove screws (**1**) and cover (**A**) on vehicles with TDI engine.

Vehicles with manual transmission

9. Remove connecting plate between clutch and brake pedals. See Fig. 20.

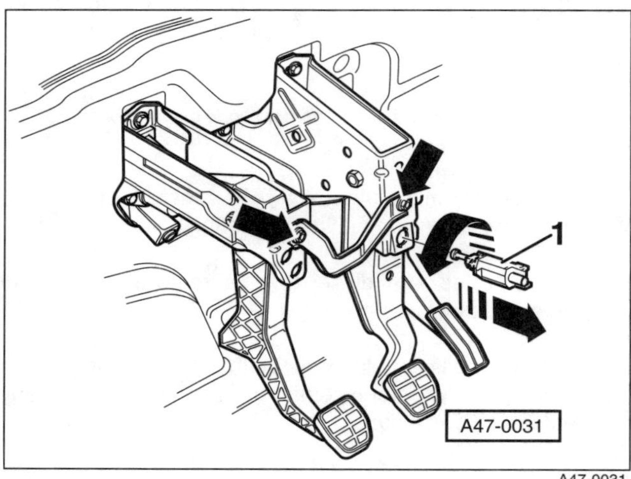

A47-0031

Fig. 20. On vehicles with manual transmission remove connecting plate between clutch and brake pedals. Remove brake light switch (**1**) by rotating and pulling out.

All vehicles

10. Remove brake light switch and separate brake pedal from brake booster.

11. Remove brake booster mounting nuts. See Fig. 21.

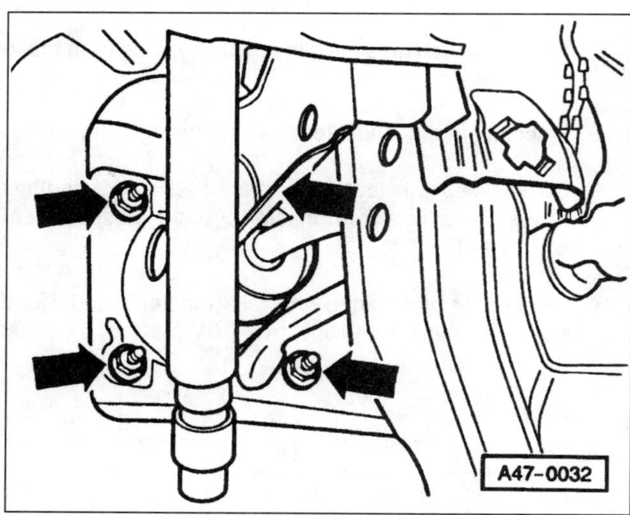

A47-0032

Fig. 21. Remove brake booster mounting nuts (**arrows**).

12. Guide brake booster with brake master cylinder out forward to remove.

13. Install brake master cylinder with brake booster in reverse order of removal noting the following:

- Adjust brake light switch see **96 Lights, Accessories–Interior**.

48 Steering

GENERAL

Power assisted rack and pinion steering is available on all vehicles covered by this manual. A vane type pump driven by the ribbed V-belt provides hydraulic pressure to the steering gear. Service of the steering gear, including repair of housing seal leaks is by replacement only. The power steering gear is available only as a complete assembly.

Special tools, equipment and procedures are required for most steering repair and component replacement. In addition, front wheel alignment is almost always disturbed when steering tie rods or steering gear are removed or replaced.

WARNING —

- *Do not re-use any fasteners that are worn or deformed in normal use. Most fasteners are designed to be used only once and become unreliable and may fail when used a second time. This includes, but is not limited to, nuts, bolts, washers, circlips, cotter pins, self-locking nuts and bolts. For replacements, always use new parts.*
- *Do not reinstall bolts and nuts coated with undercoating wax as correct tightening torque cannot be ensured. Always clean the threads of removed bolts and nuts that are to be re-used with a suitable solvent before installation. Ensure that new parts are clean.*

WARNING —

- *Do not use standard nuts and bolts in place of green colored parts. The green color denotes a special anti-corrosion process known as "dacromet" or "delta-tone". Torque specifications are given based on use of these parts only.*
- *Always replaced rusted or corroded bolts, nuts and washers even if not specifically indicated.*
- *DO NOT attempt to straighten or weld suspension struts, wheel bearing housings, control arms or any other wheel locating or load bearing components of the front suspension.*

CAUTION —

Disconnecting the negative (–) battery cable may erase fault codes and basic settings in the engine management and automatic transmission control modules. Some driveability problems may be noticed until the system re-adapts to operating conditions. OBD II readiness codes, which may be required for emissions testing, may also be erased. Convenience electronics (alarm system, interior light control, power locks, mirrors, and windows) may need to be re-set using a VAG 1551/1552 or equivalent scan tool.

Special precautions for airbag equipped vehicles

Airbag systems can enhance passenger safety in the event of a collision. To accomplish this task, they rely on sensitive electronic circuits and fast-acting deployment devices. Special service precautions must be followed to prevent possible serious bodily injury to the repair technician and others involved in the handling and storage of airbag components and to insure proper operation in the event of a collision.

> ***WARNING —***
>
> - *Before working on any airbag, steering wheel or steering column component, always **disconnect the battery first.***
> - *No waiting time is required after disconnecting the battery.*
> - *Airbags are inflated by an explosive device. Handled improperly or without adequate safeguards and training, the system can be very dangerous. Special precautions must be observed prior to any work at or near the steering wheel and steering column, including the pedal assembly.*
> - *The airbag is a vehicle safety system. To guard against personal injury or airbag system failure, only trained Volkswagen service technicians should test, disassemble or service the airbag system.*
> - *Airbag units that have been dropped onto a hard surface must not be installed. Always replace any airbag system component that has been mechanically or physically damaged (example: dented or cracked).*
> - *Make sure that no one is in the passenger compartment when connecting the battery Ground (GND) strap to the battery negative (–) terminal.*
> - *A technician must be electrostatically discharged before picking up or touching any airbag unit. This is accomplished by touching a suitable metal ground such as a water or heating pipe or metal frame. If in the vehicle, this is accomplished by touching a suitable chassis ground such as a door latch or striker.*
> - *Install new airbag unit as soon as the unit is removed from the packaging. Reinstall in packaging if work will not be completed immediately.*
> - *Do not leave any undeployed airbag unit unattended. If work is interrupted, store airbag unit in a secure location where it cannot be disturbed.*
> - *Undeployed airbag units that have been replaced must only be stored and shipped in packaging designed specifically for the purpose such as that found with the replacement unit.*
> - *Undeployed airbag units that have been replaced must be properly identified as such.*

> ***WARNING —***
>
> - *The storage and transportation of airbag units must be in accordance with all applicable federal, state and local rules and regulations.*
> - *Airbag units that have been removed during the course of repairs must be stored with the padded side facing up and in a secure location where it cannot be disturbed.*
> - *Observe all cautions, warnings and notes before starting repairs involving airbag systems.*

STEERING WHEEL WITH AIRBAG

All vehicles covered by this manual are equipped with multiple airbags. The driver's airbag unit is installed in the center area of the steering wheel. Because removal of the steering wheel is often required for repairs to the steering column, the driver's airbag unit will be covered in this section. For further details on the airbag unit, see **69 Seatbelts, Airbags.** Fig. 1. and Fig. 2. show the four and three spoke steering wheel assemblies.

Four spoke steering wheel

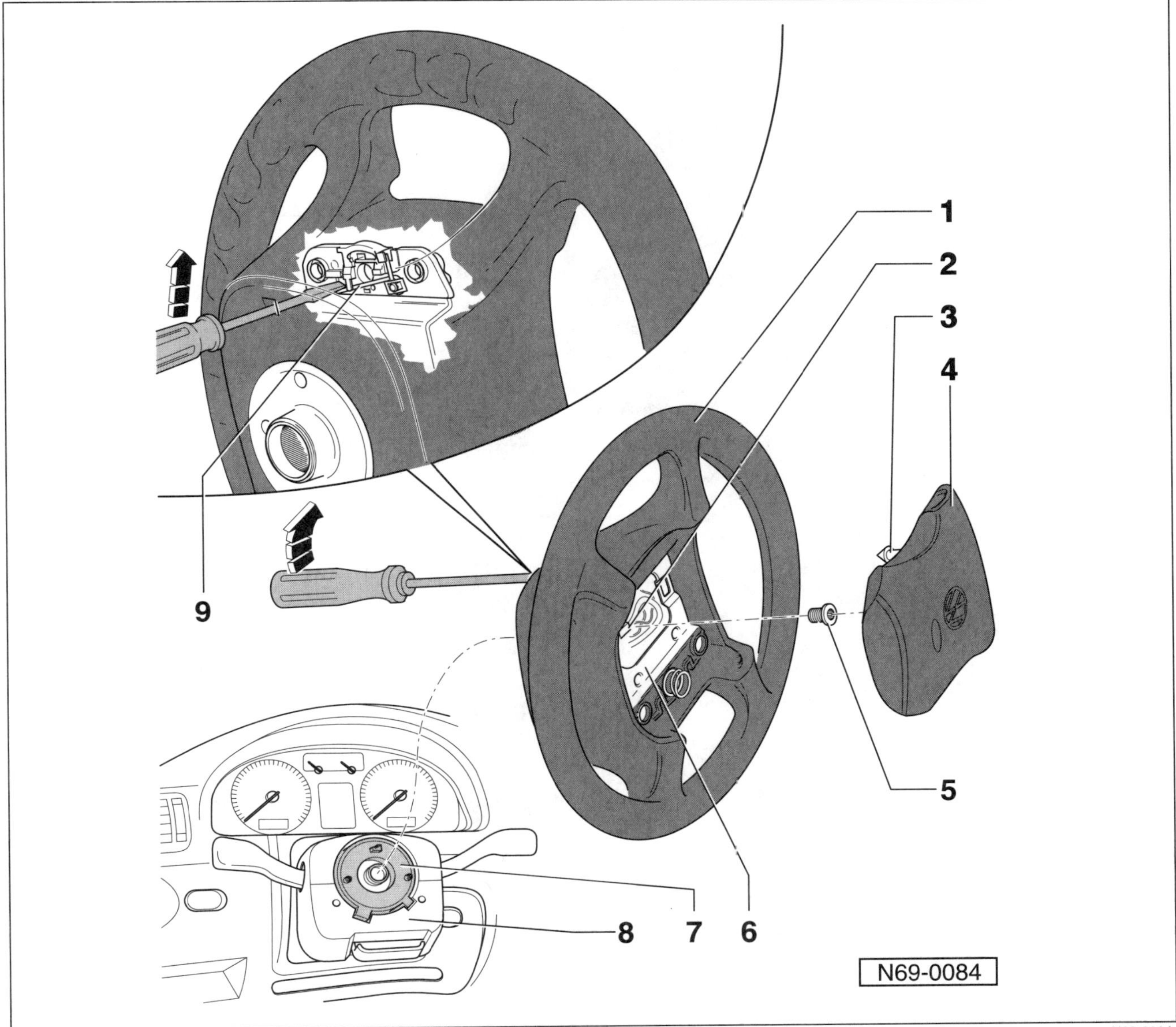

Fig. 1. Four spoke steering wheel with airbag and related components.

1. **Steering wheel**
2. **Harness connector for airbag**
3. **Locking lugs**
   - Release from rear of steering wheel
4. **Airbag unit**
5. **Bolt, multi-point socket-head**
   - Tighten to 50 Nm (37 ft-lb) with locking compound
   - Can be reused up to 5 times
   - Mark with center punch after each installation
6. **Securing plate**
7. **Spiral spring with slip ring**
8. **Steering column trim**
9. **Spring clip**

Three spoke steering wheel

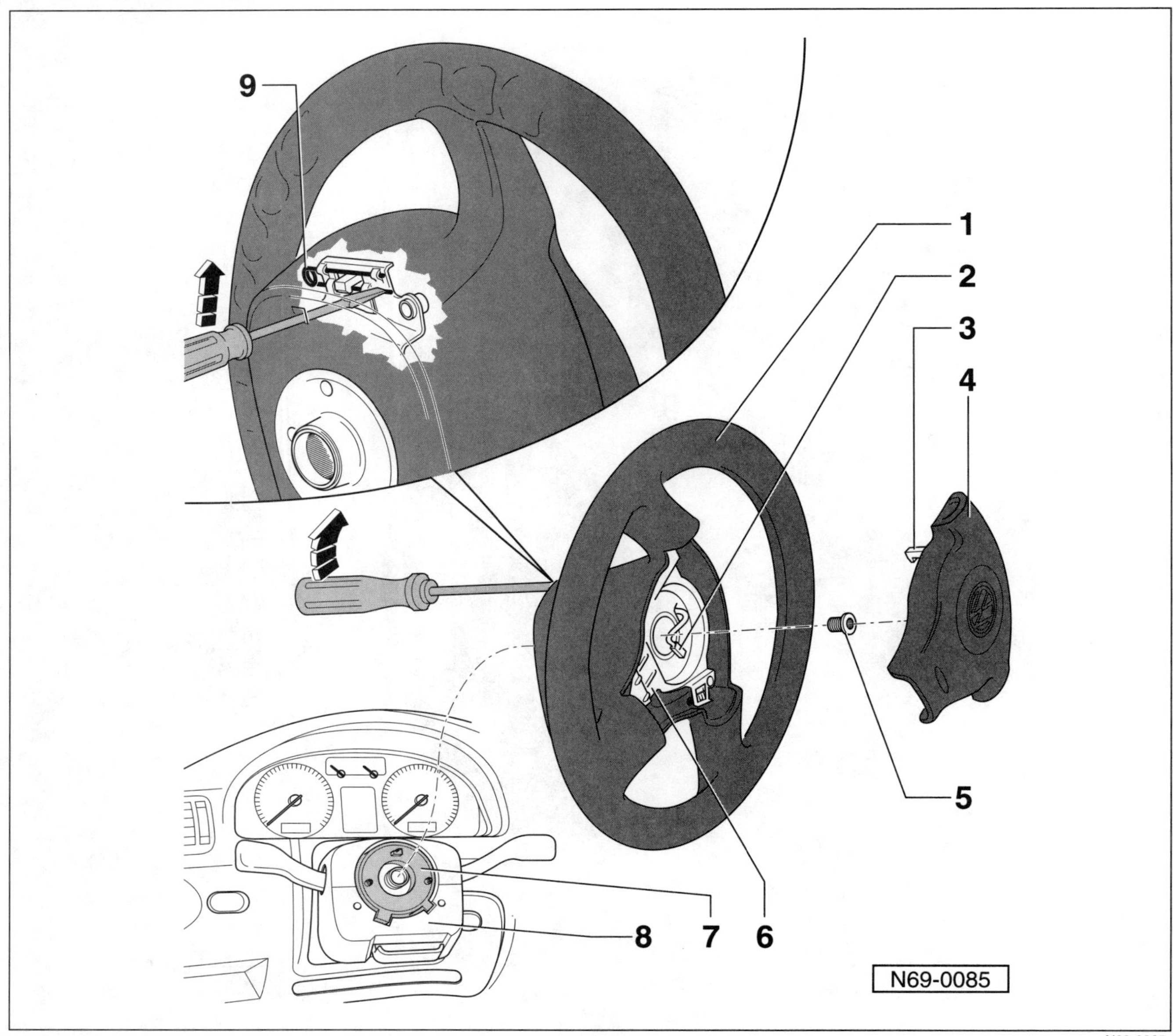

N69-0085

Fig. 2. Three spoke steering wheel with airbag and related components.

1. **Steering wheel**
2. **Harness connector for airbag**
3. **Locking lugs**
   • Release from rear of steering wheel
4. **Airbag unit**
5. **Bolt, multi-point socket-head**
   • Tighten to 50 Nm (37 ft-lb) with locking compound
   • Can be reused up to 5 times
   • Mark with center punch after each installation
6. **Securing plate**
7. **Spiral spring with slip ring**
8. **Steering column trim**
9. **Spring clip**

Airbag unit in steering wheel, removing

Removal of the steering wheel airbag unit is accomplished by inserting a tool into openings in the dashboard side of the steering wheel.

1. Disconnect battery ground (GND) strap from battery negative (–) terminal. See the **Cautions** at the beginning of this repair group regarding battery disconnection.

   NOTE —
   Be sure to have the anti-theft radio code on hand before disconnecting the battery.

2. Release steering column adjustment lever.
3. Turn steering wheel until a spoke is vertical. Extend steering wheel fully and move to uppermost position.
4. Lock steering column adjustment lever.
5. Using a screwdriver approximately 175 mm (7 in.) long, insert approximately 45 mm (1¾ in.) from reverse side into hole on dashboard side of steering wheel hub.
6. Press screwdriver in direction of arrow to press back spring clip (Fig. 1 or 2, item 9) and release locking lug (Fig. 1 or 2, item 3) of airbag unit.
7. Turn steering wheel back ½ turn (180°) and release second locking lug on opposite side.
8. Turn steering wheel to center position (wheels straight ahead).
9. Disconnect harness connector from airbag unit.
10. Place removed airbag unit in a secure location with padding side facing up.

Airbag unit in steering wheel, installing

NOTE —
Only use airbags and steering wheels designed to operate together and of same manufacture.

1. Install instrument cluster, if applicable.
2. Reconnect harness connector for airbag unit.
3. Position airbag unit on steering wheel and snap into place.

   NOTE —
   Airbag unit locking lugs must be heard and felt to snap into place.

4. Switch ignition on.

   WARNING —
   - *Make sure the passenger compartment is not occupied before connecting the battery Ground (GND) strap.*
   - *Observe all cautions, warnings and notes when completing repairs involving airbag systems.*

5. Connect battery ground (GND) strap to battery negative (–) terminal.

Steering wheel, inner assembly

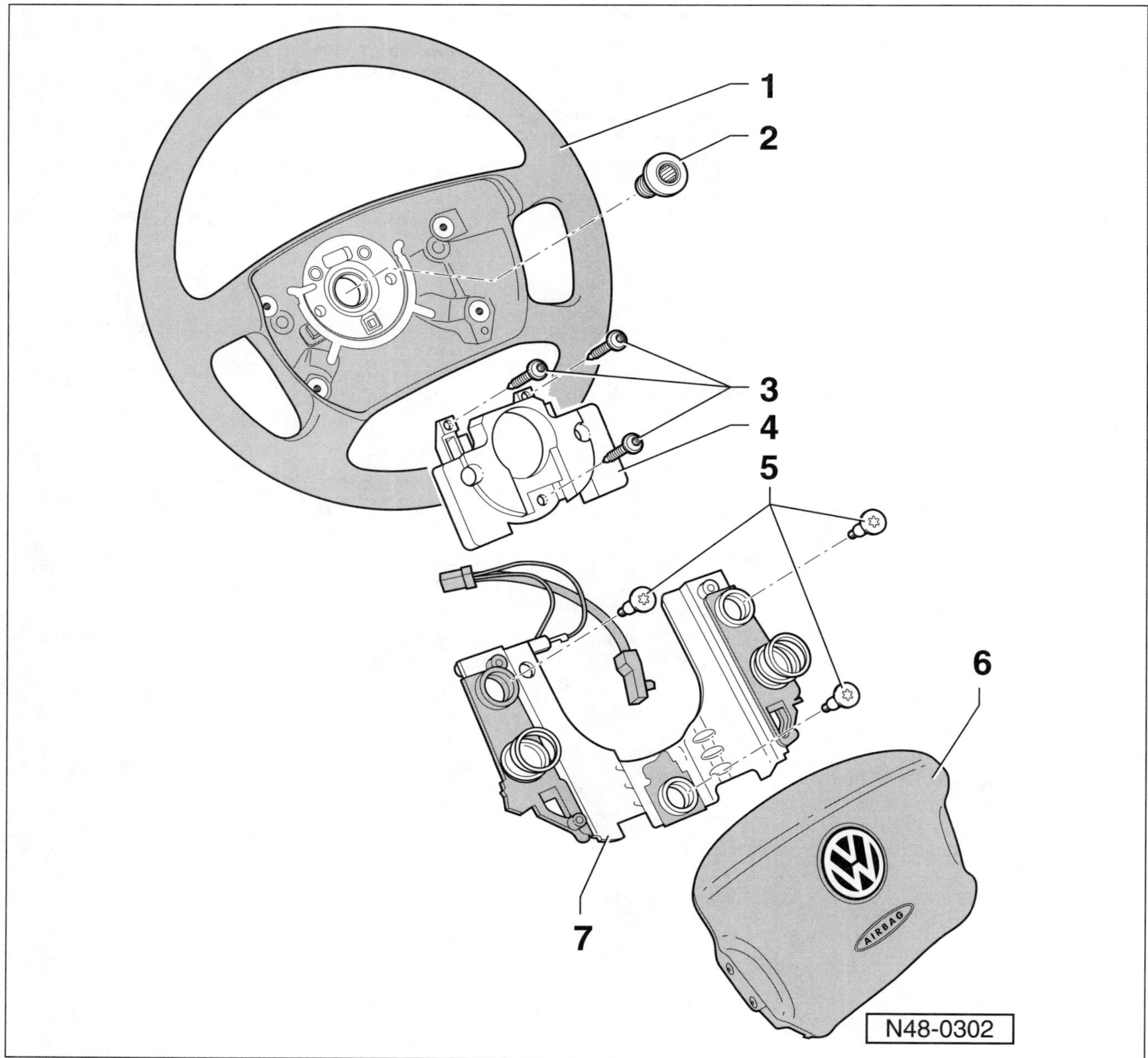

N48-0302

Fig. 3. Four spoke steering wheel and related inner components. Three spoke steering wheels are similar.

1. **Steering wheel**
   - Installed position, **see** Ⓐ
2. **Bolt, multi-point socket-head**
   - Tighten to 50 Nm (37 ft-lb) with locking compound
   - Can be reused up to 5 times
   - Mark with center punch after each installation
3. **Bolts, Torx®**
4. **Vibration damper**
   - Installed on vehicles equipped with ALH engine and automatic transmission
5. **Bolts, Torx®**
   - Tighten to 5 Nm (44 in-lb)
6. **Airbag unit**
7. **Securing plate**

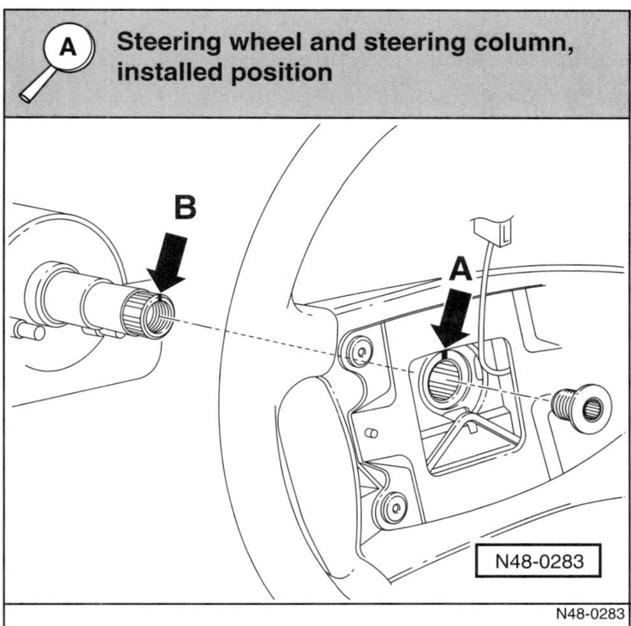

N48-0283

- **Center punch mark on steering wheel (A) must align with center punch mark on steering column (B).**
- **Replacement steering columns do not have center punch marks.**

STEERING COLUMN

The vehicles covered by this manual are equipped with a steering column that is height adjustable and telescopic. Defective steering columns must be replaced as a complete assembly as no internal repair parts are available from Volkswagen. Two different steering columns have been used from vehicle # 1JXB 095035. When replacing a steering column, always use one from the same manufacturer as the original. The two different steering columns are identified in Fig. 4.

The steering column, cross member and related components are shown in Fig. 5. and Fig. 7.

Steering column, versions

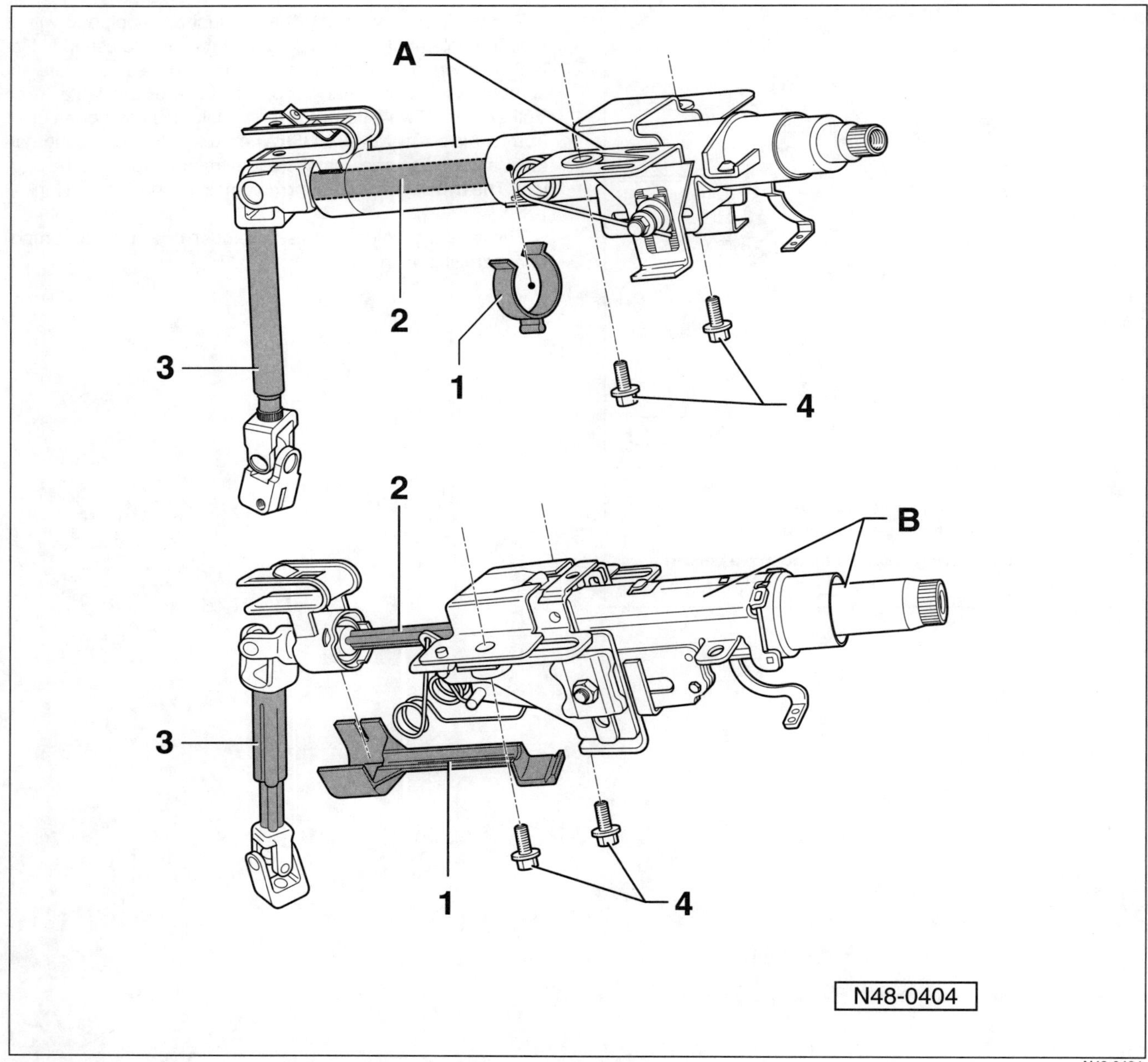

N48-0404

Fig. 4. Steering columns manufactured by Nacam (**A**) and Krupp Presta (**B**).

1. **Transportation device**
   - Remove first after steering column is installed
2. **Steering column**
   - Column is not visible on Nacam version
3. **Steering column universal joint shaft**
4. **Hex bolts**
   - Tighten to 25 Nm (18 ft-lb)
   - Install with locking fluid

Steering column (Nacam), assembly

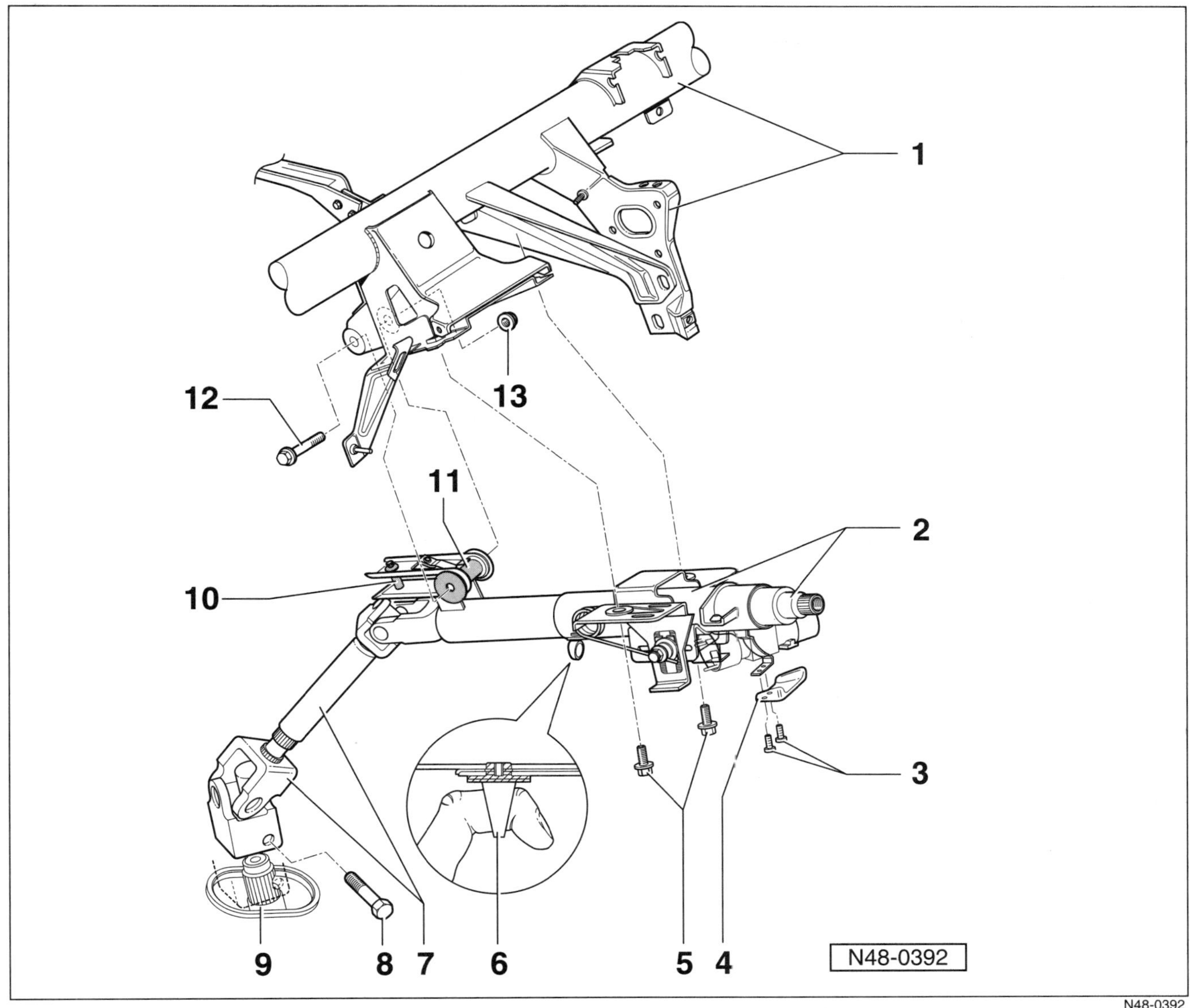

N48-0392

Fig. 5. Nacam steering column and attachment points to body crossmember.

1. **Crossmember for steering column**
2. **Steering column**
   - Secure steering column before removal, **see** Ⓐ
   - Check for damage, **see** Ⓑ
3. **Bolts**
4. **Handle**
   - Lock/unlock column adjustment
5. **Bolts**
   - Tighten to 25 Nm (18 ft-lb)
6. **Transportation securing device**
   - Remove after column has been installed into vehicle
7. **Steering column universal joint shaft**
8. **Bolt**
   - Tighten to 20 Nm (15 ft-lb) + 1/4-turn (90°)
9. **Steering gear pinion shaft**
10. **Shear bolt**
11. **Pin**
12. **Bolt**
13. **Nut**
    - Tighten to 10 Nm (7 ft-lb)

Steering column (Krupp Presta), assembly

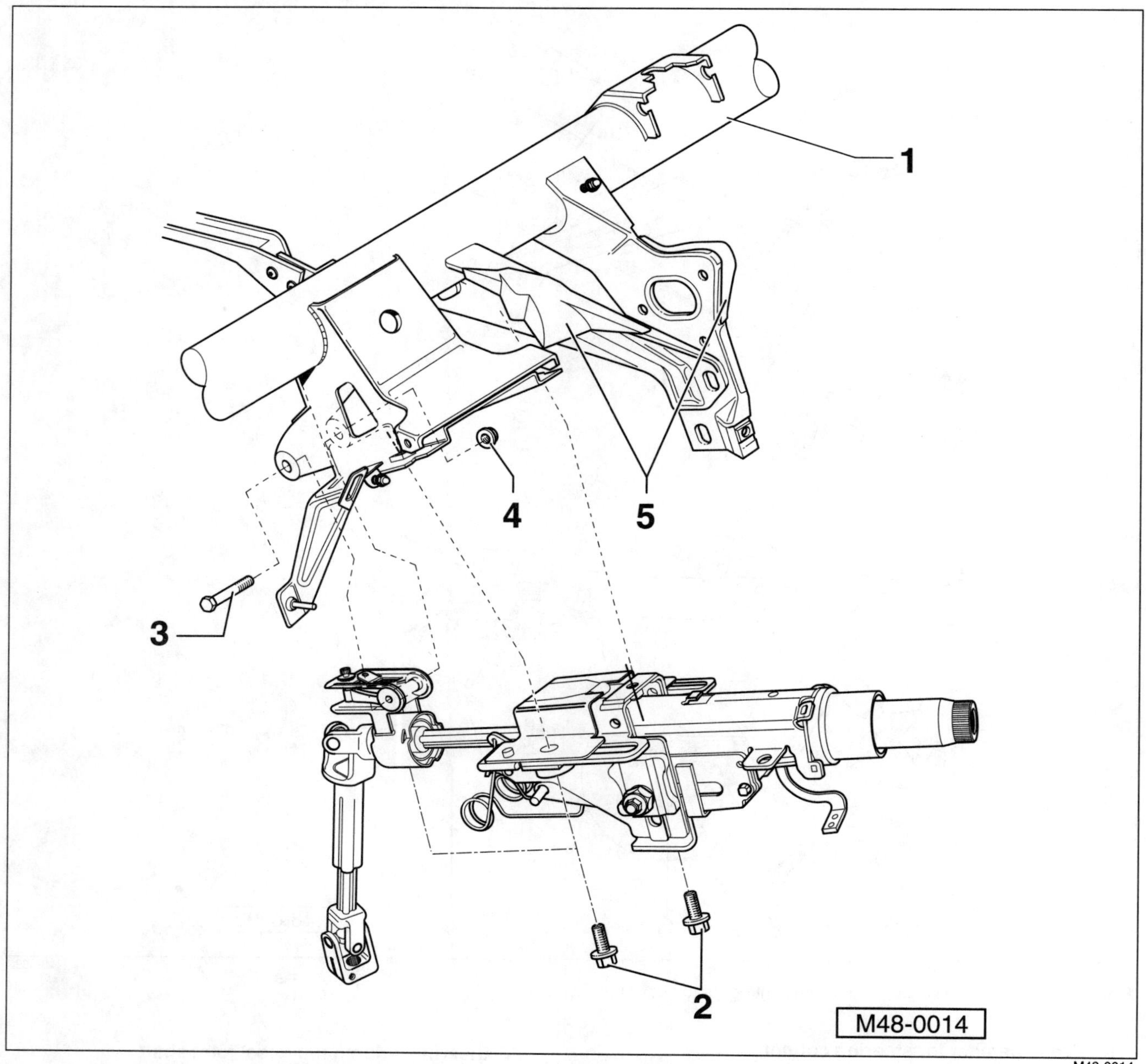

Fig. 6. Krupp Presta steering column and attachment points to body crossmember.

1. **Crossmember for steering column**
   - Secure steering column before removal, **see** Ⓐ
   - Check for damage, **see** Ⓑ
2. **Bolts**
   - Tighten to 25 Nm (18 ft-lb)
3. **Hex bolt**
4. **Hex nut**
   - Tighten to 10 Nm (7 ft-lb)
5. **Plastic cover**

A Steering column, securing before removing

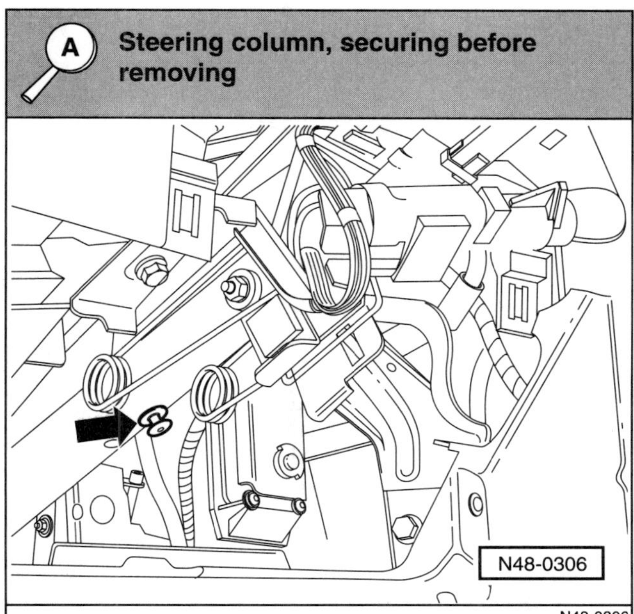

N48-0306

- Assembly aid is required to prevent upper and lower sections of steering column from pulling apart during removal.
- Splined sections can separate and cause rattling noises unless installed in original positions.
- Push or pull steering column slightly to align holes and insert suitable clip or pin into hole (arrow).

B Steering column, inspecting for damage

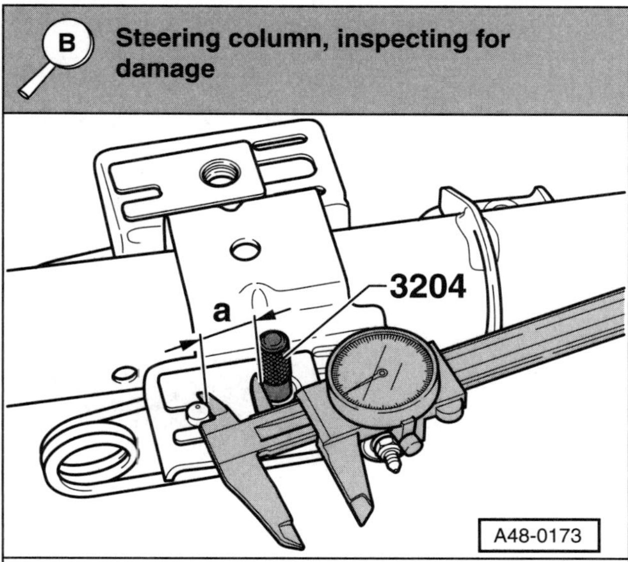

A48-0173

- Visually inspect for damage.
- Disconnect steering column universal joint shaft and check for smooth operation (without binding) of steering shaft.
- Check that steering column can be adjusted for full range of height and telescopic adjustment.
- Check gap (a) with alignment pin inserted in hole. Maximum distance from edge to edge is 23 mm (0.906 in).

Steering column crossmember, assembly

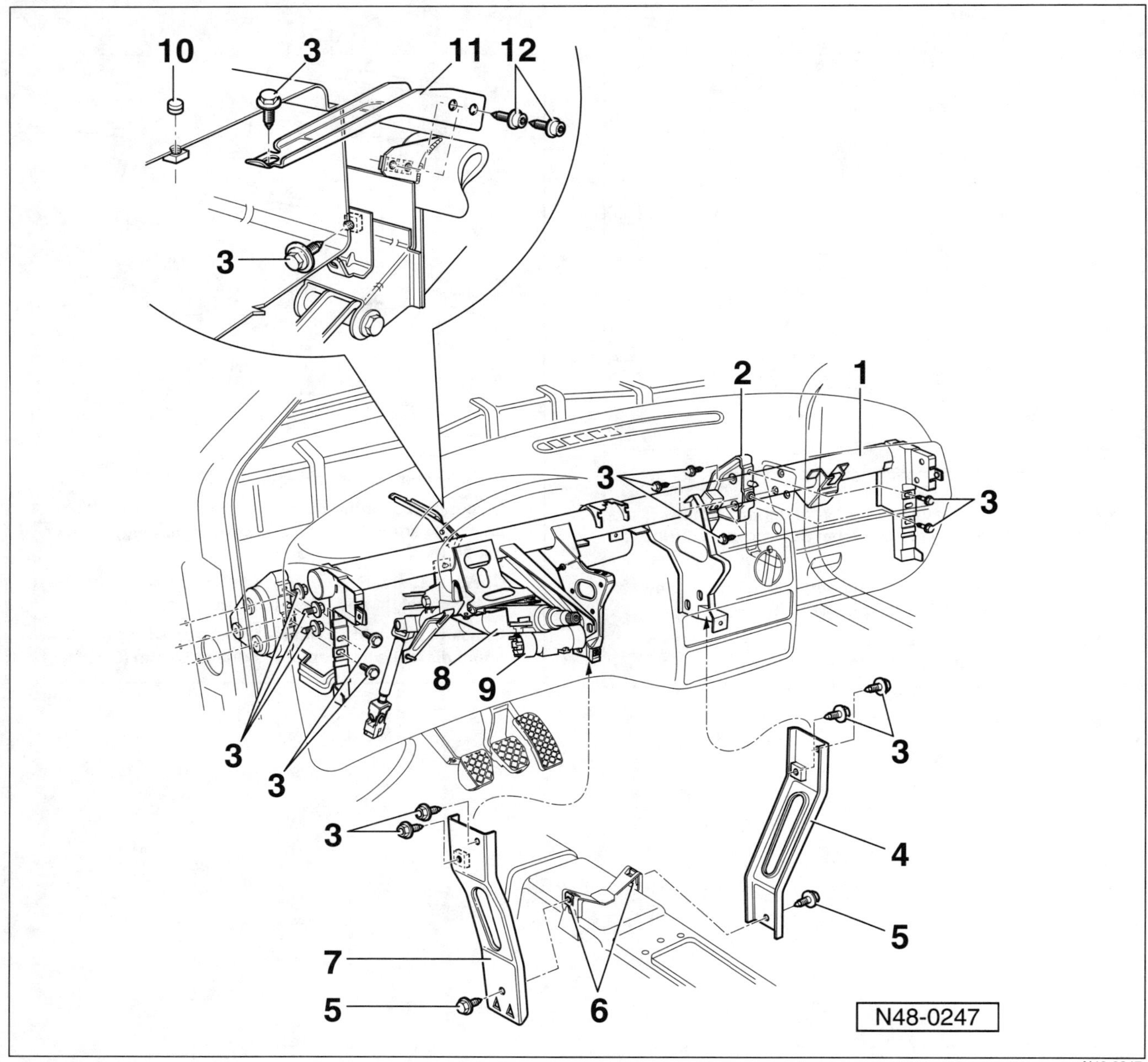

N48-0247

Fig. 7. Steering column crossmember and related components.

1. **Steering column crossmember**
2. **Adjustment brackets**
3. **Hex bolts**
   - Tighten to 25 Nm (18 ft-lb)
4. **Support, right**
5. **Bolts**
6. **Speed nuts**
7. **Support, left**
8. **Steering column assembly**
9. **Steering lock housing**
10. **Sealing plug**
11. **Support for bulkhead**
12. **Bolts**
    - Tighten to 10 Nm (89 in-lb)

Steering column switches and lock housing, removing and installing

> ***WARNING —***
> *Observe all cautions, warnings and notes before starting repairs involving airbag systems.*

1. Turn the wheels to the straight ahead position.
2. Disconnect battery ground (GND) strap from battery negative (–) terminal. See the **Cautions** at the beginning of this repair group regarding battery disconnection.

   NOTE —
   Be sure to have the anti-theft radio code on hand before disconnecting the battery.

3. Remove airbag unit in steering wheel as described earlier.
4. Remove steering wheel as described earlier.
5. Remove adjustment handle and lower and upper trim. See Fig. 8.

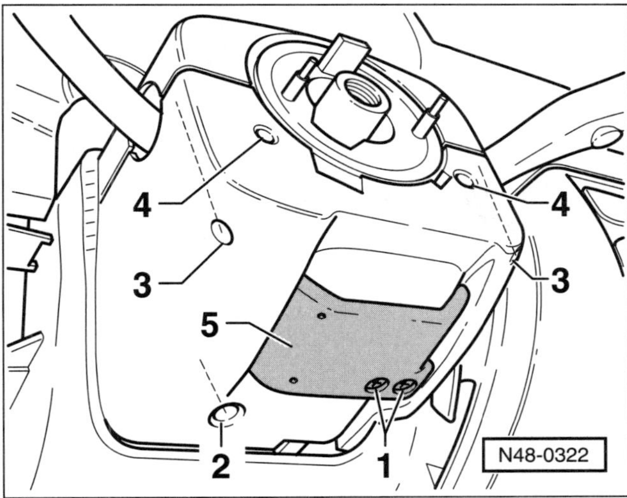

N48-0322

Fig. 8. Steering column as seen from below. Remove handle screws (**1**), handle (**5**), and securing screws (**2**), (**3**), (**4**).

6. Remove upper steering column switch trim. See Fig. 9.

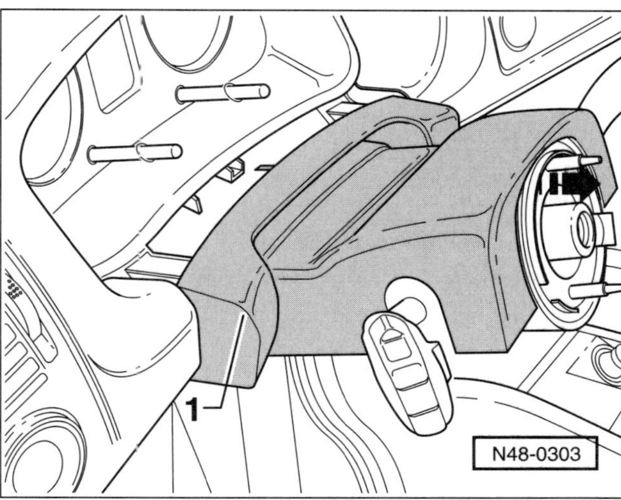

N48-0303

Fig. 9. Remove upper steering column switch trim (**1**).

7. Unplug harness connector and release locking lugs on spiral spring/slip ring and pull off. See Fig. 10.

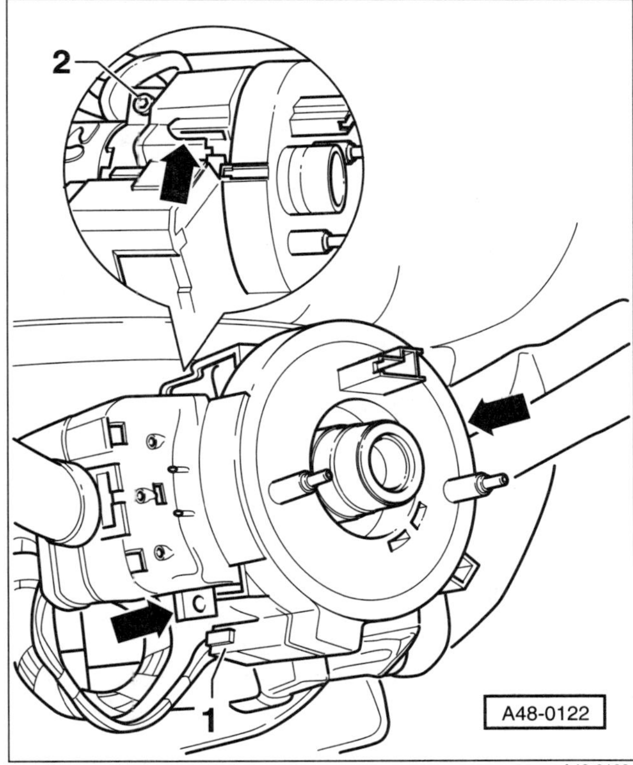

A48-0122

Fig. 10. Remove spiral spring/slip ring by releasing lugs (**arrows**) and unplugging harness connector (**1**).

8. Remove securing bolt for steering column switch, unplug switch assembly and slide off steering column. See Fig. 11.

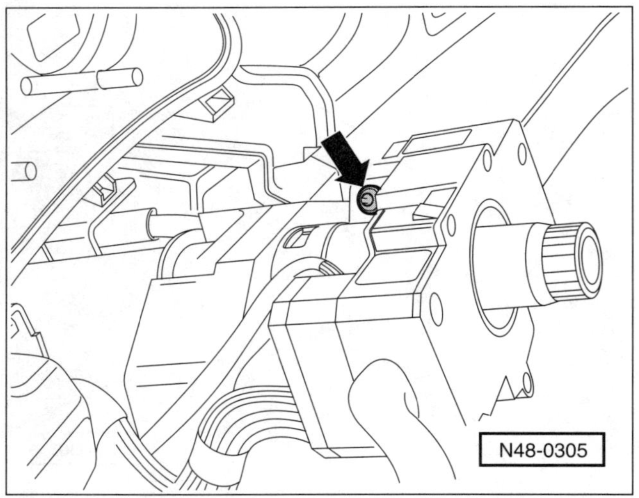

N48-0305

Fig. 11. Remove steering column switch securing bolt (**arrow**) and slide switch assembly off column.

9. Remove plastic cover over shear bolts. See Fig. 12.

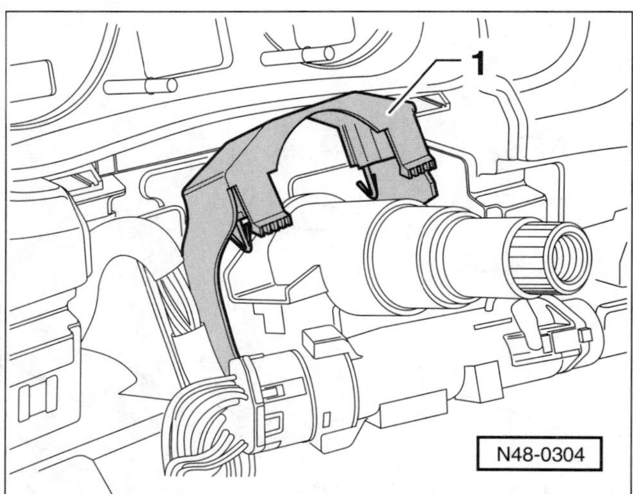

N48-0304

Fig. 12. Unclip plastic cover (**1**) over shear bolts and pull up to remove.

10. On vehicles with automatic transmission, unhook shift lock cable by placing shift lever in park, and turning ignition key to the on position. Press wire retaining clip upward or downward (depending on installed position) while pulling out on locking cable. See Fig. 13.

11. Cut off shear head bolts using a suitable sharp chisel. See Fig. 14.

12. Unplug harness connector on ignition switch and slide lock housing off of column.

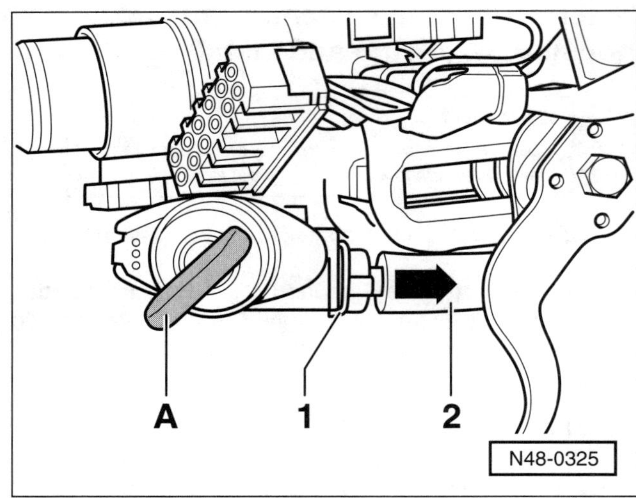

N48-0325

Fig. 13. On cars with automatic transmission, turn key (**A**) to ignition on position. Pull wire clip (**1**) up or down to release ignition lock cable and pull lock cable (**2**) out (direction of **arrow**).

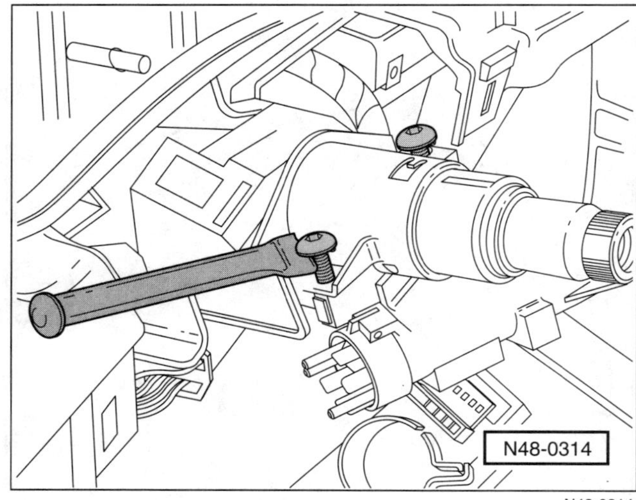

N48-0314

Fig. 14. Chisel off both shear bolts to remove them.

13. Begin installation by installing lock housing onto steering column with new shear bolts. Bolts are correctly torqued when hex head on bolt shears off.

14. Install plastic cover over shear bolts.

15. On vehicles with automatic transmission, connect shift lock cable by placing shift lever in park, and turning ignition key to the on position. Slide locking cable onto steering lock housing until wire clip engages. See Fig. 15.

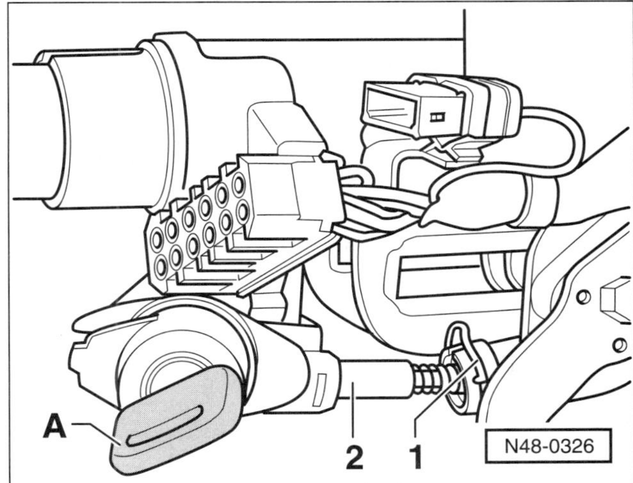

N48-0326

Fig. 15. Side view of ignition lock showing key (**A**). Slide shift lock cable (**2**) onto housing until wire clip (**1**) engages.

16. Install steering column switch assembly.

17. Install spiral spring/slip ring.

18. Temporarily install steering wheel and adjust distance between spiral spring/slip ring and steering wheel. Adjustment is made by sliding switch assembly on steering column and locking in place with securing screw. See Fig. 16.

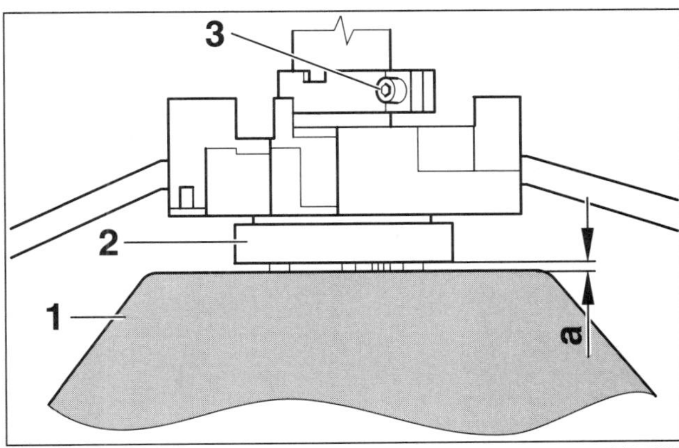

A48-0128

Fig. 16. Temporarily install steering wheel (**1**) and adjust gap (**a**) by sliding spiral spring/slip ring (**2**) and switch assembly. Tighten securing screw (**3**) when proper gap is obtained.

Specification

- Clearance between steering wheel and spiral spring/slipring . . . . approx. 2½ mm (0.1 in)

19. Remove steering wheel and install steering column trim.

20. Remainder of installation is the reverse of removal.

Tightening torque

- Steering wheel bolt. . . . . 50 Nm (37 ft-lb)

> ***WARNING —***
> *Observe all cautions, warnings and notes when completing repairs involving airbag systems.*

Ignition lock cylinder and switch, removing and installing

> ***WARNING —***
> *Observe all cautions, warnings and notes before starting repairs involving airbag systems.*

1. Disconnect battery ground strap.

2. Remove airbag unit and steering wheel as described earlier.

3. Remove upper and lower steering column trim as described earlier.

4. Insert ignition key into lock cylinder and turn to ignition **ON** position. See Fig. 17.

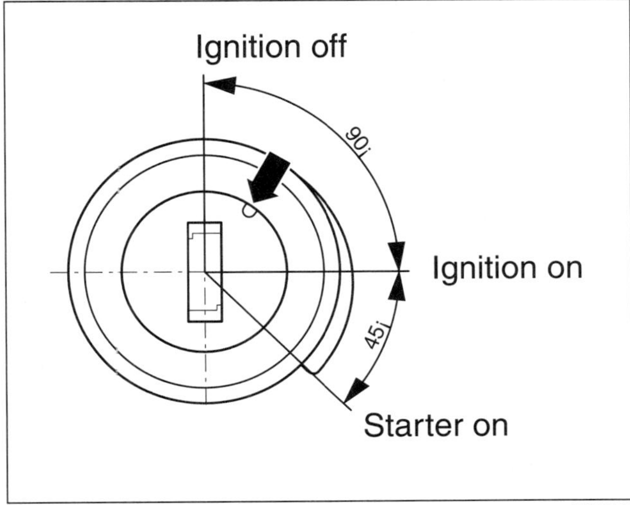

0024290

Fig. 17. Insert wire tool into opening (**arrow**) to remove lock cylinder.

5. Insert a wire tool approximately 1.2 mm (0.047 in) in diameter into the opening in the face of the lock cylinder. See Fig. 17.

NOTE —
A large paper clip or a 3/64 inch drill bit are suitable for inserting into lock cylinder opening.

6. Release lock cylinder by gently pulling on key while pushing in on wire tool. See Fig. 18.

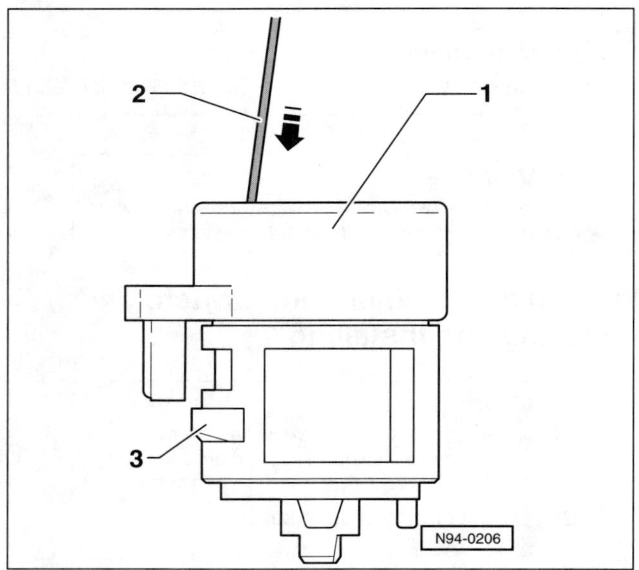

N94-0206

Fig. 18. Remove ignition lock cylinder by pushing in (**arrow**) on wire tool (**2**) while pulling gently on key. Wire tool (**2**) will release locking tab (**3**) and allow lock cylinder to slide out.

7. Disconnect harness connector from ignition switch.

8. Remove sealant (paint) from ignition switch securing screws. See Fig. 19.

9. Loosen ignition switch securing screws and pull ignition switch out from steering lock housing.

NOTE —
- *When installing ignition/starter lock switch ensure that it is in the same position as the lock cylinder, e.g. "ignition on".*
- *Be sure to use locking compound on ignition switch securing screws when installing.*

10. Install ignition lock cylinder by inserting key into lock cylinder and turning key into the same position used on removal.

11. Insert wire tool into opening and slide assembly fully into ignition lock housing until seated.

12. Remove wire tool and check for smooth operation of ignition lock and cylinder.

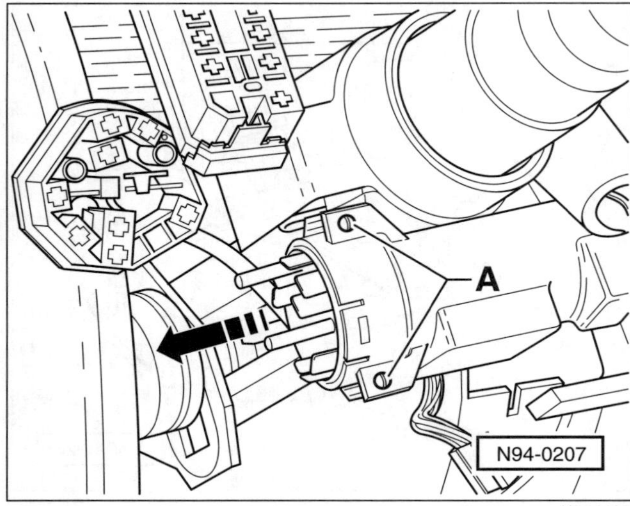

N94-0207

Fig. 19. Remove screws (**A**) and remove switch in direction of **arrow**.

13. Installation is reverse of removal for remaining components.

> ***WARNING —***
> *Observe all cautions, warnings and notes when completing repairs involving airbag systems.*

POWER STEERING GEAR

The power rack and pinion steering gear is not serviceable, malfunctioning units must be replaced. An exploded view of the power steering gear is shown in Fig. 20.

Specifications
- Special steering rack grease . . . . . . .AOF 063 000 04
- Power steering hydraulic oil . . . . G 002 000
- Power steering hydraulic oil quantity. . . . . 0.7 - 0.9 L (23.6 - 30.4 oz.)

Tightening torque
- Power steering gear to subframe (M8) always replace . . . . . . .20 Nm (15 ft-lb) + ¼ turn (90°)
- Subframe to body (M14) always replace . . . . . .100 Nm (74 ft-lb) + ¼ turn (90°)
- Universal joint to steering gear pinion always replace (M8) . . . . 30 Nm (22 ft-lb)
- Return line banjo bolt (M16). . . . . 45 Nm (33 ft-lb)
- Pressure hose banjo bolt (M14) . . . . . 40 Nm (30 ft-lb)
- Pendulum support to transmission (M8) always replace . . . . . . .40 Nm (30 ft-lb) + ¼ turn (90°)
- Tie rod end to wheel bearing housing (M12) always replace . . . . 45 Nm (33 ft-lb)

Power steering gear, assembly

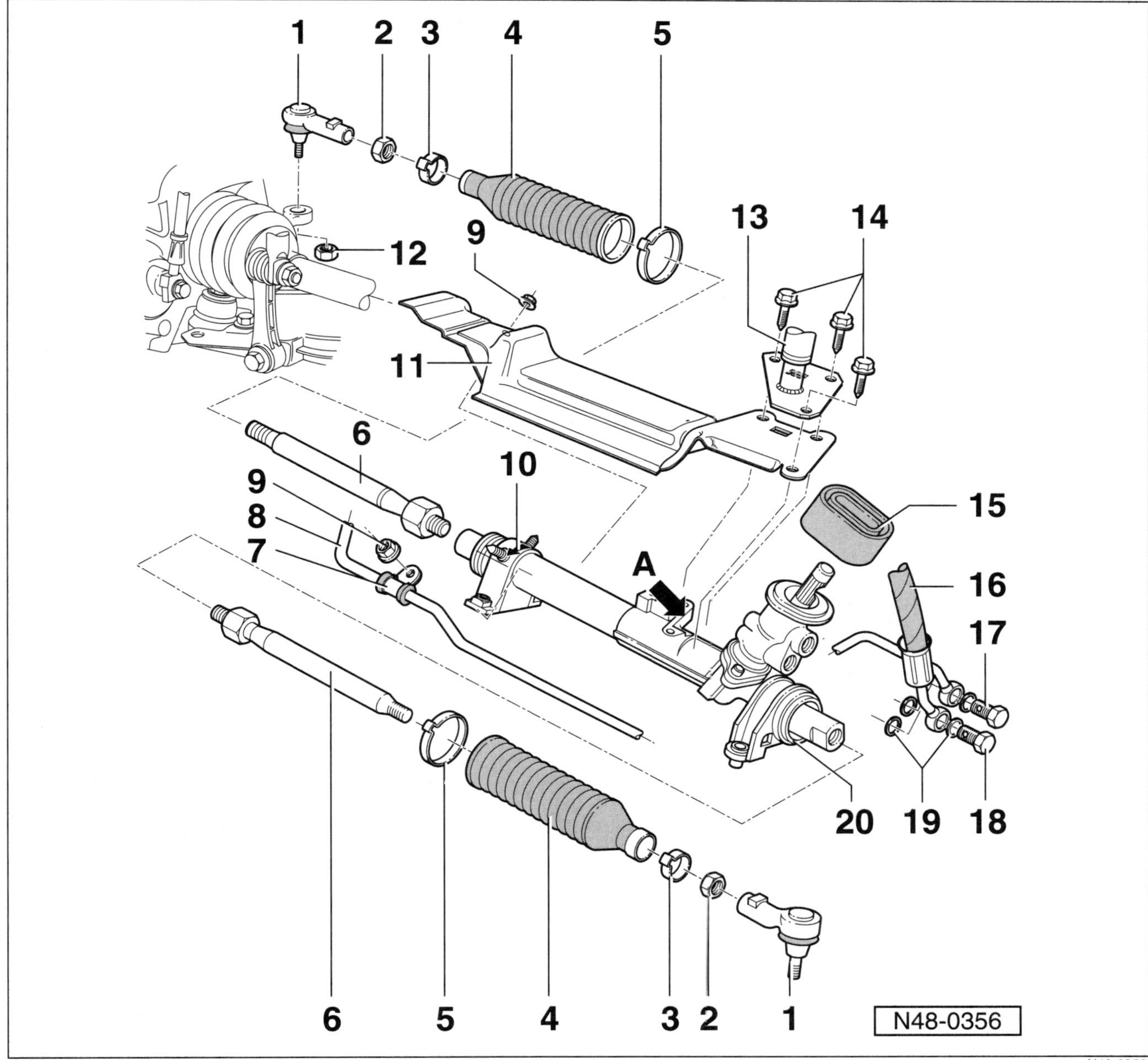

N48-0356

Fig. 20. Power steering gear with related steering components.

1. **Tie rod end**
   - Removing, **see** Ⓐ
2. **Nut**
   - Tighten to 50 Nm (37 ft lb)
3. **Clamp**
   - Always replace
   - Use special clamp pliers (VAG 1275 or equivalent) to install
4. **Boot**
   - Must not be twisted while adjusting toe
   - Remove steering gear to replace
5. **Clamp**
   - Always replace
   - Use special clamp pliers (VAG 1275 or equivalent) to install
6. **Tie rod**
   - Tighten to 75 Nm (55 ft-lb)
   - Replacement parts are supplied preset
   - Check vehicle alignment if replaced
7. **Clamp with rubber sleeve**

(continued on following page)

(continued from previous page)

8. **Hydraulic return line**
   - Installing, **see** (B)
9. **Nut**
   - Tighten to 22 Nm (16 ft-lb)
10. **Mounting bracket with rubber bushing**
    - Arrow on bracket points forward
    - Replace if threads in welded nut are damaged
11. **Heat shield**
12. **Nut, self-locking**
    - Tighten to 45 Nm (33 ft-lb)
13. **Selector mechanism bearing bracket**
    - Center on support (**arrow A**) with heat shield (item 11)
14. **Bolts**
    - Tighten to 24 Nm (18 ft-lb)
15. **Gasket**
16. **Hydraulic pressure hose**
17. **Banjo bolt**
    - Tighten to 45 Nm (33 ft-lb)
18. **Banjo bolt**
    - Tighten to 40 Nm (30 ft-lb)
19. **Seals**
    - Always replace
20. **Power steering gear**
    - Center before installing, **see** (C)
    - Adjusting, **see** (D)

(A) Tie rod, removing

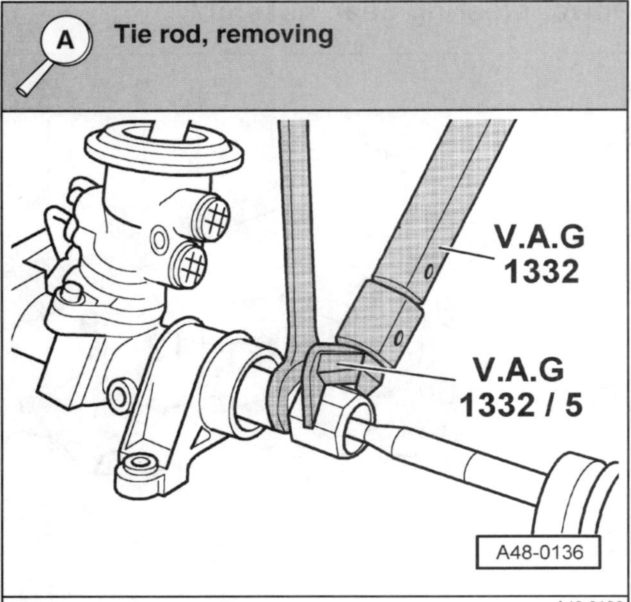

A48-0136

- **Steering gear must be removed before removing tie rods.**
- **Seal power steering line connections on steering gear.**
- **Clean area around steering gear boot.**
- **Open boot clamps and push boot back.**
- **Clamp steering gear in vice and remove tie rod using appropriate tools as shown above.**

(B) Power steering return line, installing

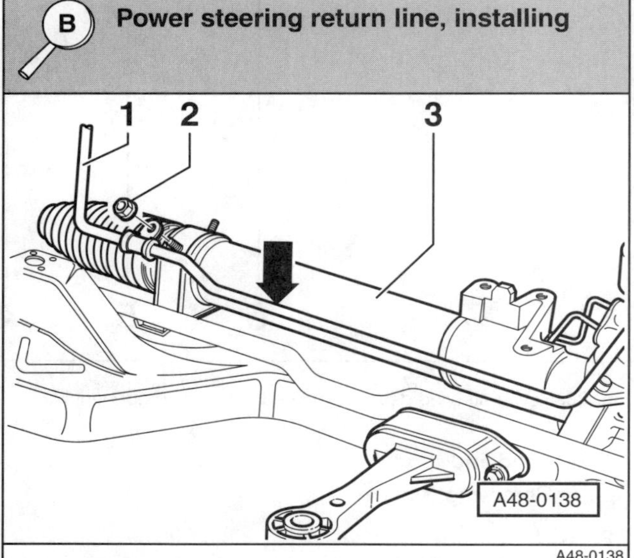

A48-0138

- **When installing power steering return line, a gap (arrow) of approx. 10 mm (0.39 in) must exist between return line (1) and steering gear (3).**
- **Tighten nut (2) to 22 Nm (16 ft-lb).**

C Power steering rack, determining center position

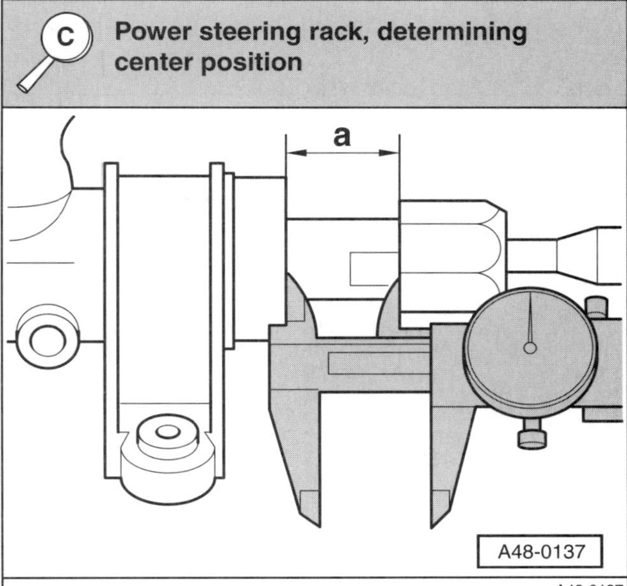

A48-0137

- Center position must be identified before installation.
- Slide rack until dimension (a) is obtained.
- Dimension (a) = 30.5 mm (1.20 in).

D Power steering gear, adjusting

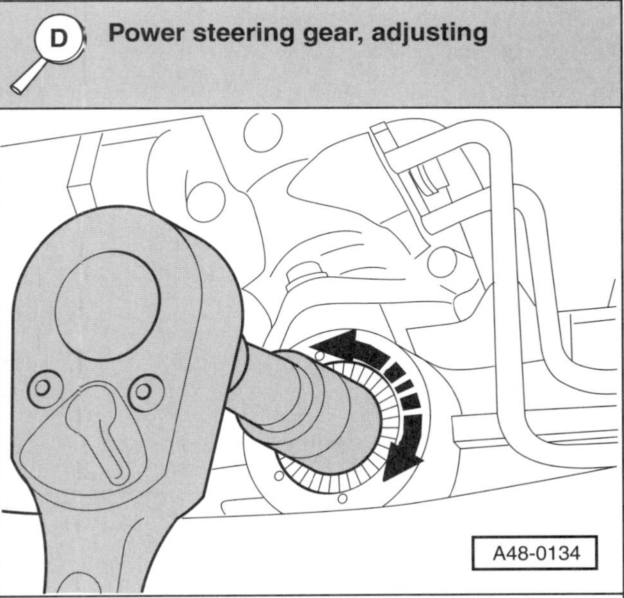

A48-0134

- Use of a helper is necessary to adjust steering gear.
- Raise vehicle and position front wheels straight ahead.
- Turning steering wheel back and forth (approx. 30° from center) will produce a knocking noise if play is excessive.
- Carefully turn adjustment screw in until knocking noise can no longer be heard from inside vehicle.
- Road test vehicle to ensure steering returns to center without sticking.
- Secure lock nut for adjustment screw with a punch mark.

POWER STEERING HYDRAULIC HOSES

Power steering lines, overview

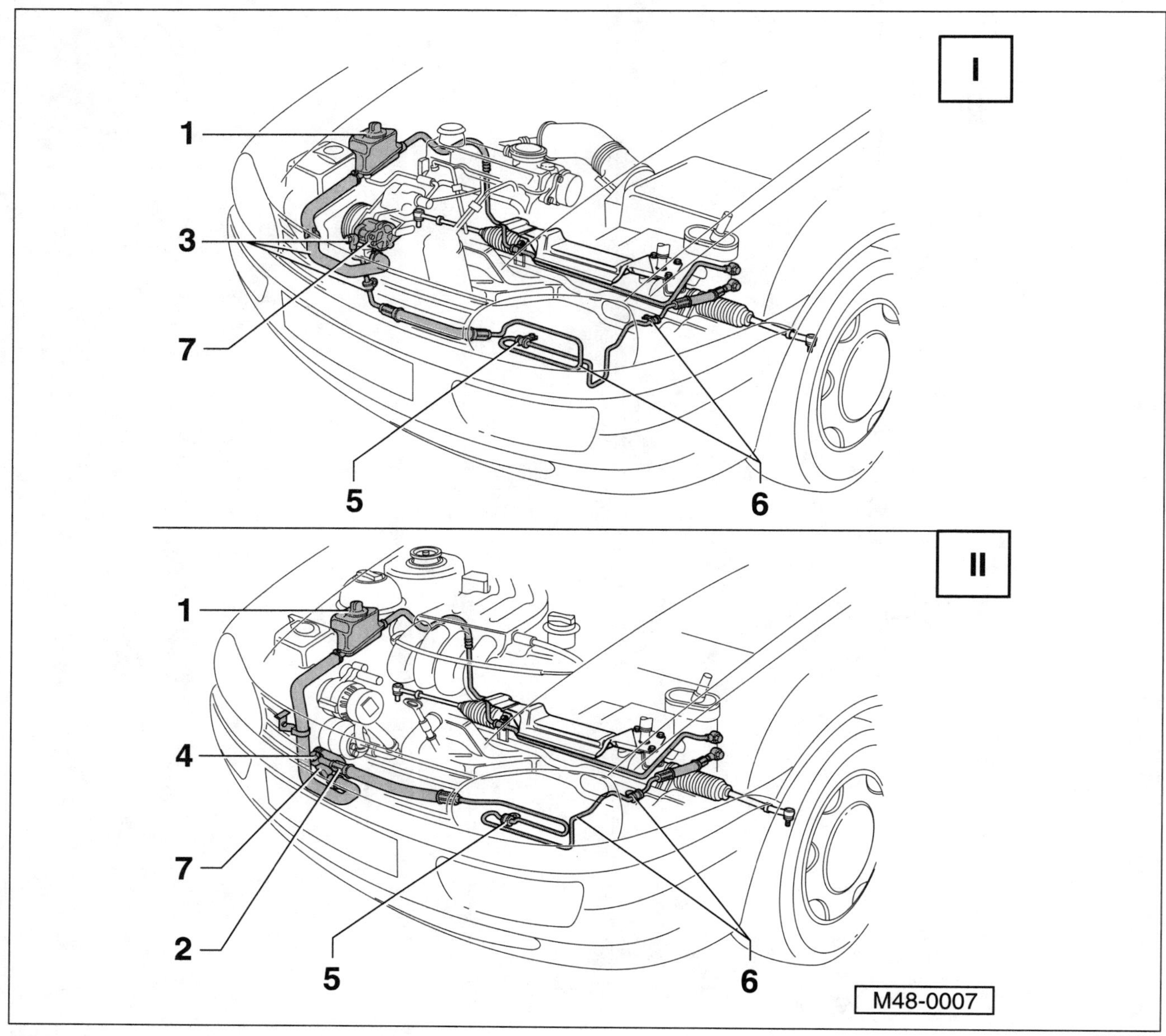

M48-0007

Fig. 21. Overview of power steering hydraulic components for vehicles with power steering pump in upper area of engine compartment (**I** at top) and vehicles with power steering pump in lower area of engine compartment (**II** at bottom).

1. **Fluid reservoir**
2. **Pressure hose/line**
   - Vehicles with TDI engine and A/C
3. **Pressure hose/line**
   - Vehicles with TDI engine and no A/C
4. **Pressure hose/line**
   - Vehicles with TDI engine and A/C
5. **Pressure hose/line**
   - On 5-speed manual transmission 02J
6. **Pressure hose/line**
   - On automatic transmission
7. **Pressure hose/line**
   - Fill before installing

Power steering fluid reservoir, assembly

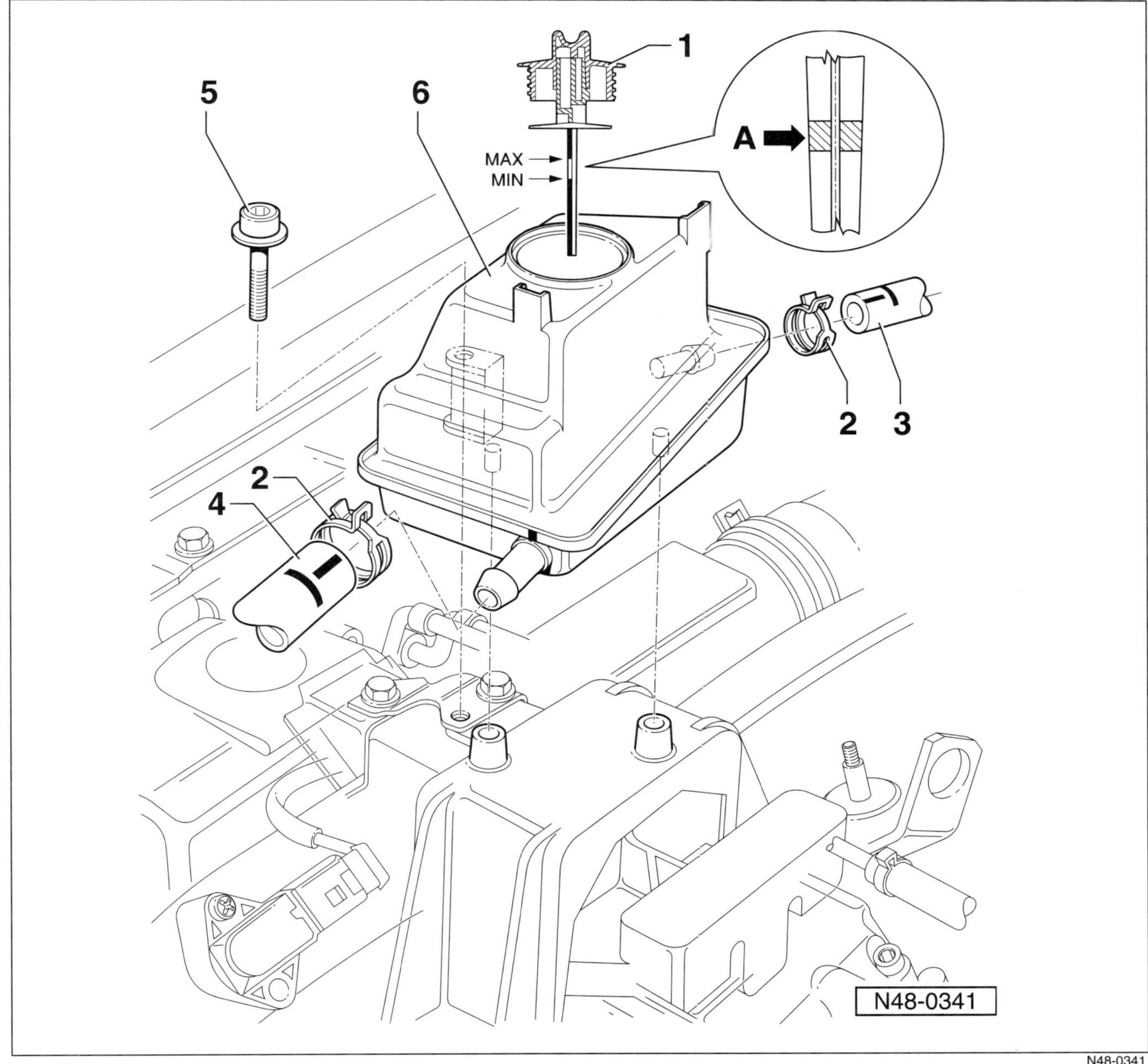

N48-0341

Fig. 22. Power steering fluid reservoir shown with related components.

1. **Cap with dip stick**
   - Twist to open using suitable tool as required
   - Screw cap on fully to check oil level
   - Oil level with engine warm, approx. 50°C (122°F): between **MIN** and **MAX** marks (**arrow A**)
   - Oil level with engine cold: not over **MIN** marking
2. **Spring clamp**
3. **Suction hose**
4. **Return hose**
5. **Bolt**
   - Tighten to 10 Nm (7 ft-lb)
6. **Reservoir**

Power steering hoses (gasoline engines with A/C)

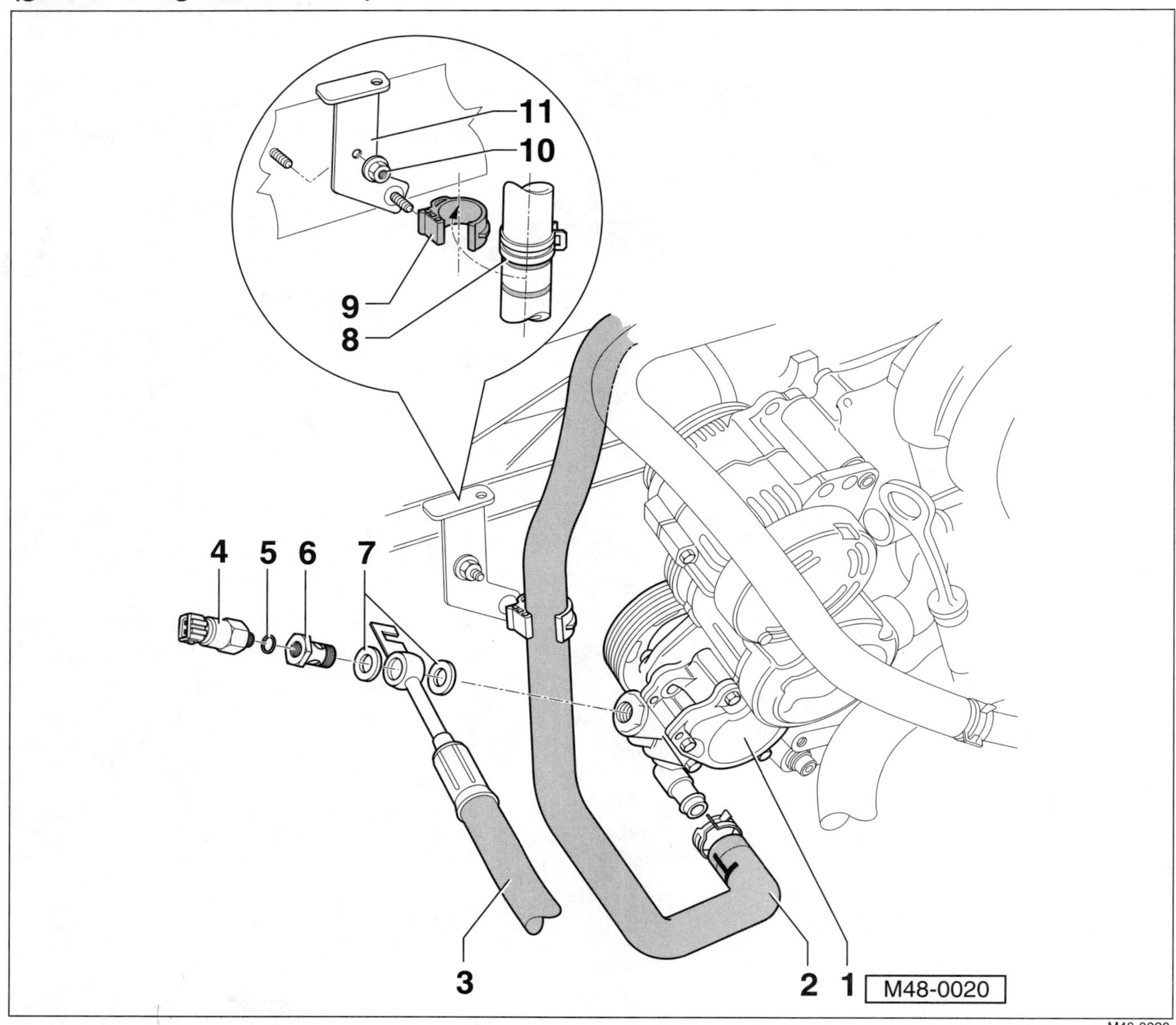

Fig. 23. Power steering hose detail on gasoline engines equipped with A/C.

1. **Power steering pump**
   - Fill with oil before installing
2. **Suction hose**
3. **Pressure hose**
4. **Pressure switch**
   - Only on 1.8L engine
   - Switches at 40 bar (580 psi)
   - Tighten to 15 Nm (11 ft-lb)
5. **Seal**
   - Only on 1.8L engine
   - Always replace
6. **Banjo bolt**
   - Without pressure switch (item 4) on 2.0L and 2.8L
   - Tighten to 30 Nm (22 ft-lb)
7. **Seals**
   - Always replace
8. **Suction hose**
   - White or yellow ring must seat within retainer (item 9)
9. **Retainer**
10. **Bolt**
11. **Mounting bracket**

Power steering hoses (diesel engine with A/C)

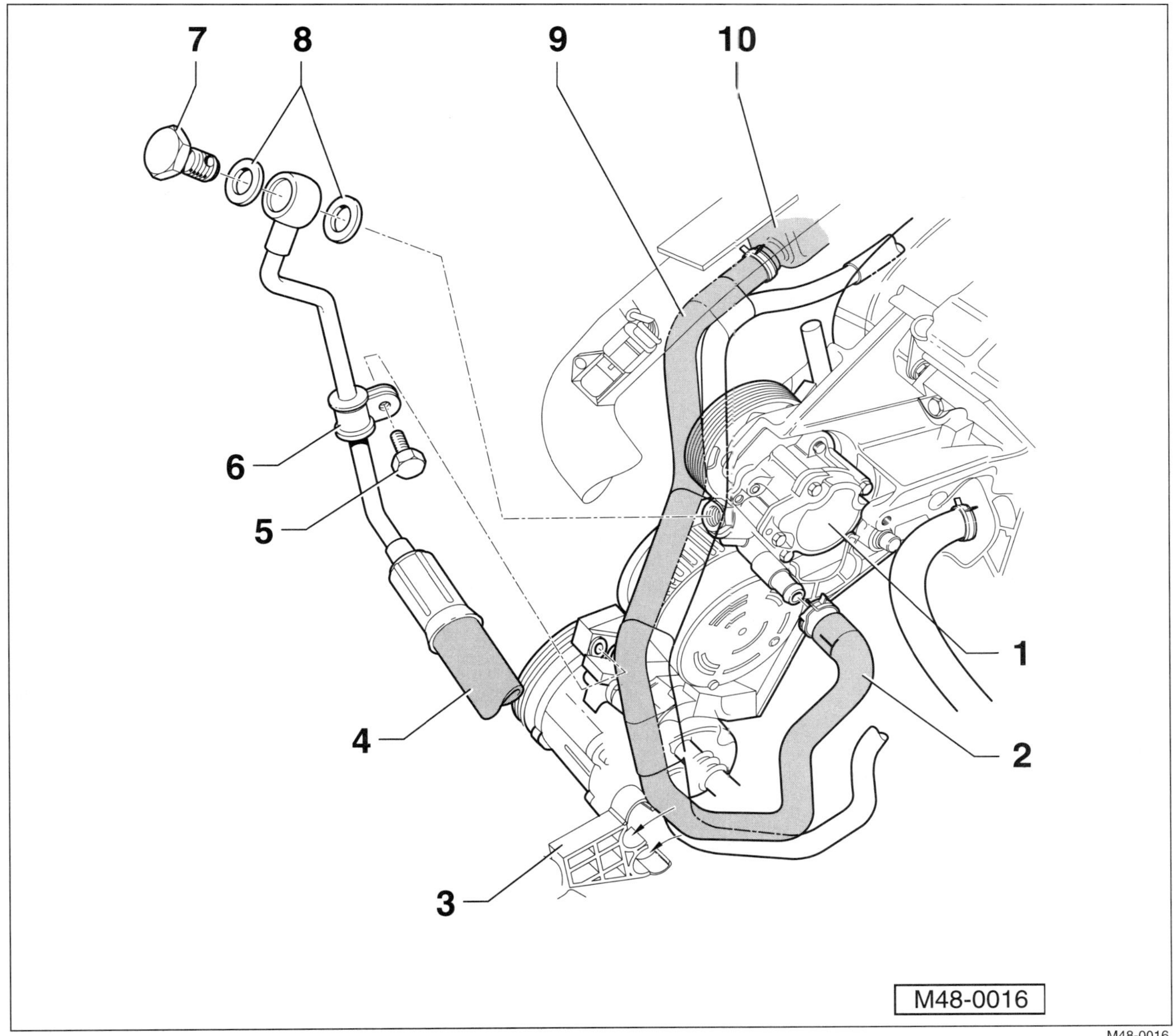

M48-0016

Fig. 24. Power steering hose detail on 1.9L diesel engines equipped with A/C.

1. **Power steering pump**
   - Fill with oil before installing
2. **Suction hose**
3. **Mounting bracket**
4. **Pressure hose**
5. **Bolt**
   - Tighten to 10 Nm (7 ft-lb)
6. **Clamp**
7. **Banjo bolt**
   - Tighten to 30 Nm (22 ft-lb)
8. **Seals**
   - Always replace
9. **Suction hose**
10. **Fluid reservoir**

Pressure hose, mounting to manual transmission

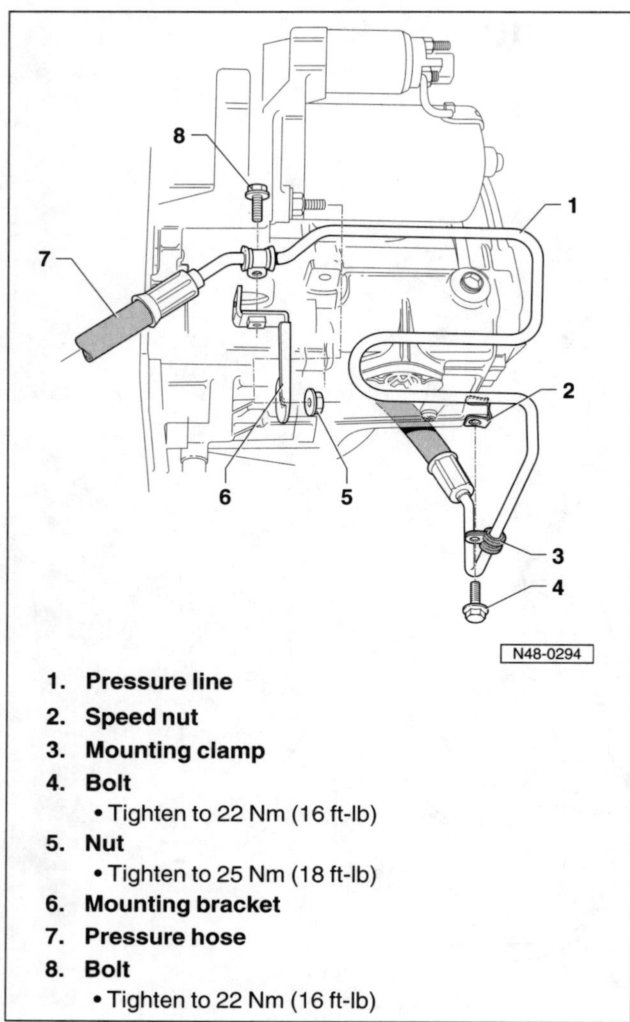

N48-0294

Fig. 25. Power steering pressure hose assembly mounting detail on vehicles equipped with manual transmissions.

Pressure hose, mounting to automatic transmission

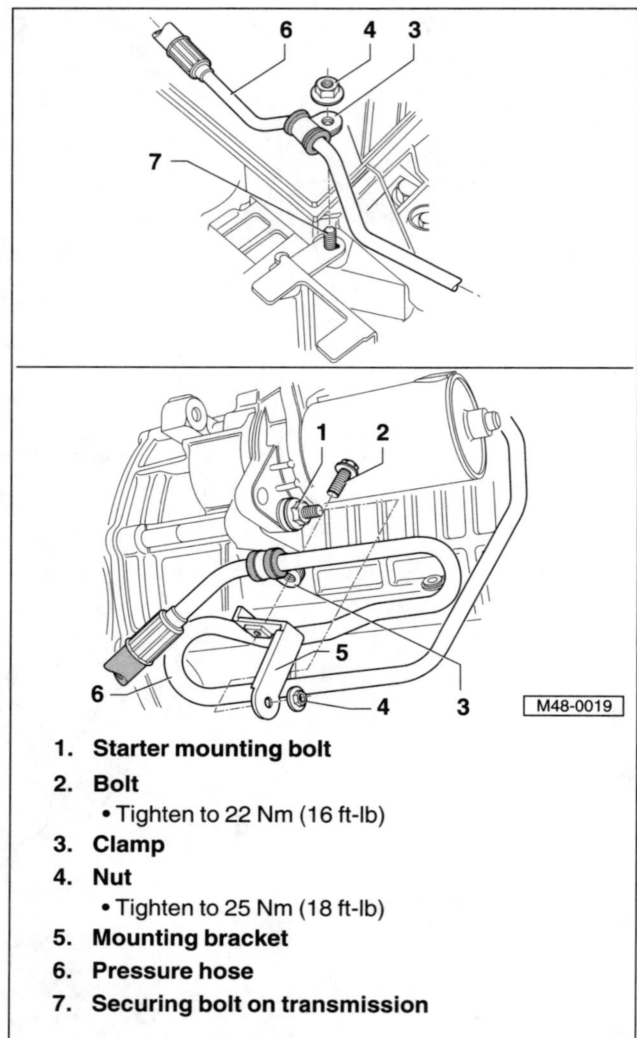

M48-0019

Fig. 26. Power steering pressure hose assembly mounting detail on vehicles equipped with automatic transmissions.

POWER STEERING PUMP

Different power steering pump positions and belt routings are used on the vehicles covered by this manual depending on engine type and equipment level. For vehicles with power steering pump mounted lower on the bracket see Fig. 27. For vehicles with power steering pump mounted higher on the bracket see Fig. 28.

Specification

- Power steering pump pressures at idle
  Gasoline engines . . . . 85-95 bar (1233-1378 psi)
  Diesel engines . . . . 96-105 bar (1392-1523 psi)

Power steering pump assembly, (pump in lower mounting bracket)

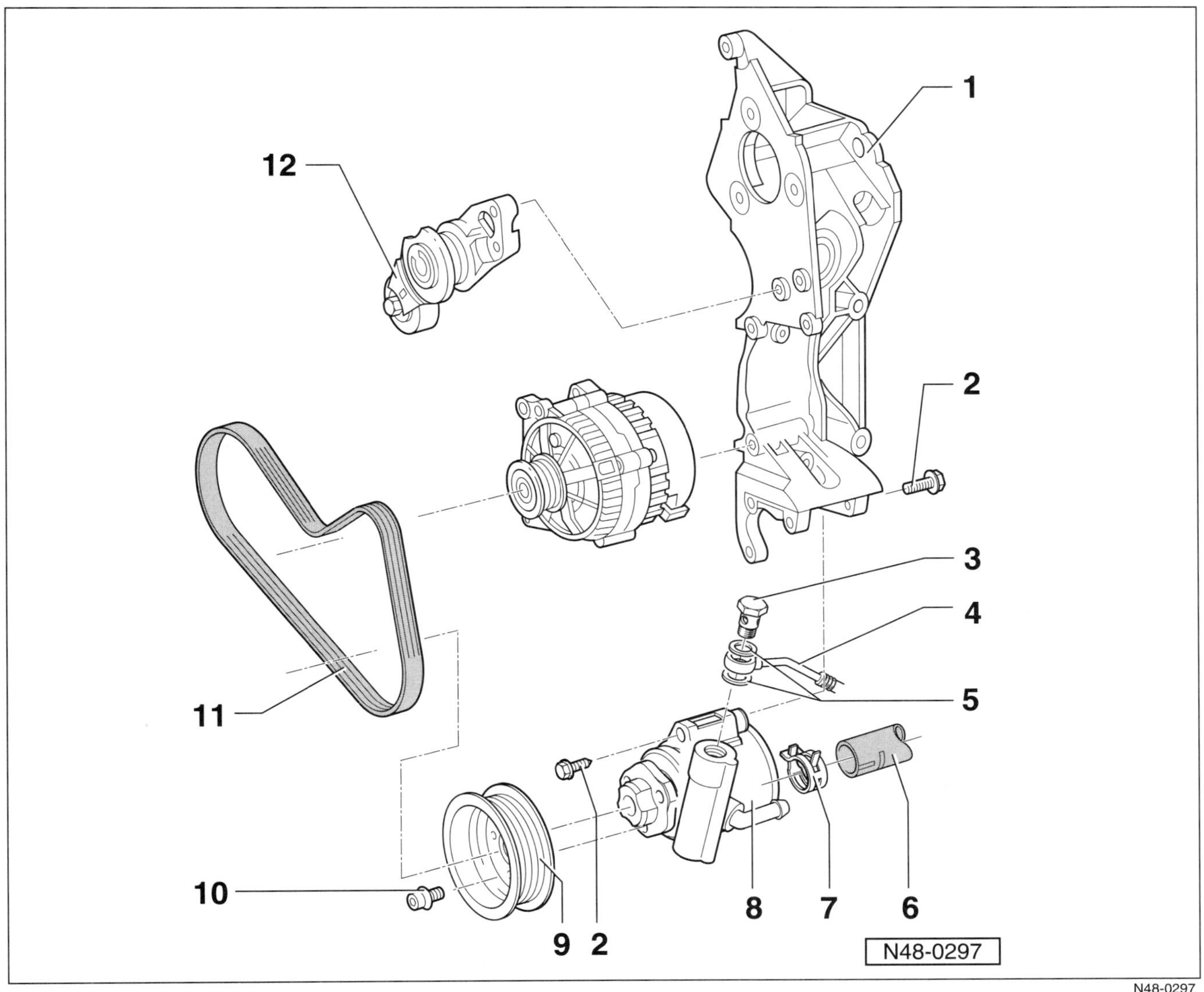

N48-0297

Fig. 27. Power steering pump and components mounted to lower section of bracket.

1. **Bracket (diesel shown, gasoline similar)**
2. **Bolts**
   - Tighten to 25 Nm (18 ft-lb)
3. **Banjo bolt**
   - Tighten to 30 Nm (22 ft-lb)
4. **Pressure hose assembly**
5. **Seals**
   - Always replace
6. **Suction hose**
7. **Spring clamp**
8. **Power steering pump**
   - Fill with oil before installing
9. **Belt pulley**
10. **Bolt**
    - Tighten to 25 Nm (18 ft-lb)
11. **Ribbed V-belt**
    - Using a crayon or marker, mark the direction of travel before removing the ribbed belt
    - Reinstalling a used belt in the opposite direction could damage the belt
    - Make sure belt is correctly seated in the pulleys when installing
12. **Ribbed V-belt tensioner**

Power steering pump assembly, (pump in upper mounting bracket)

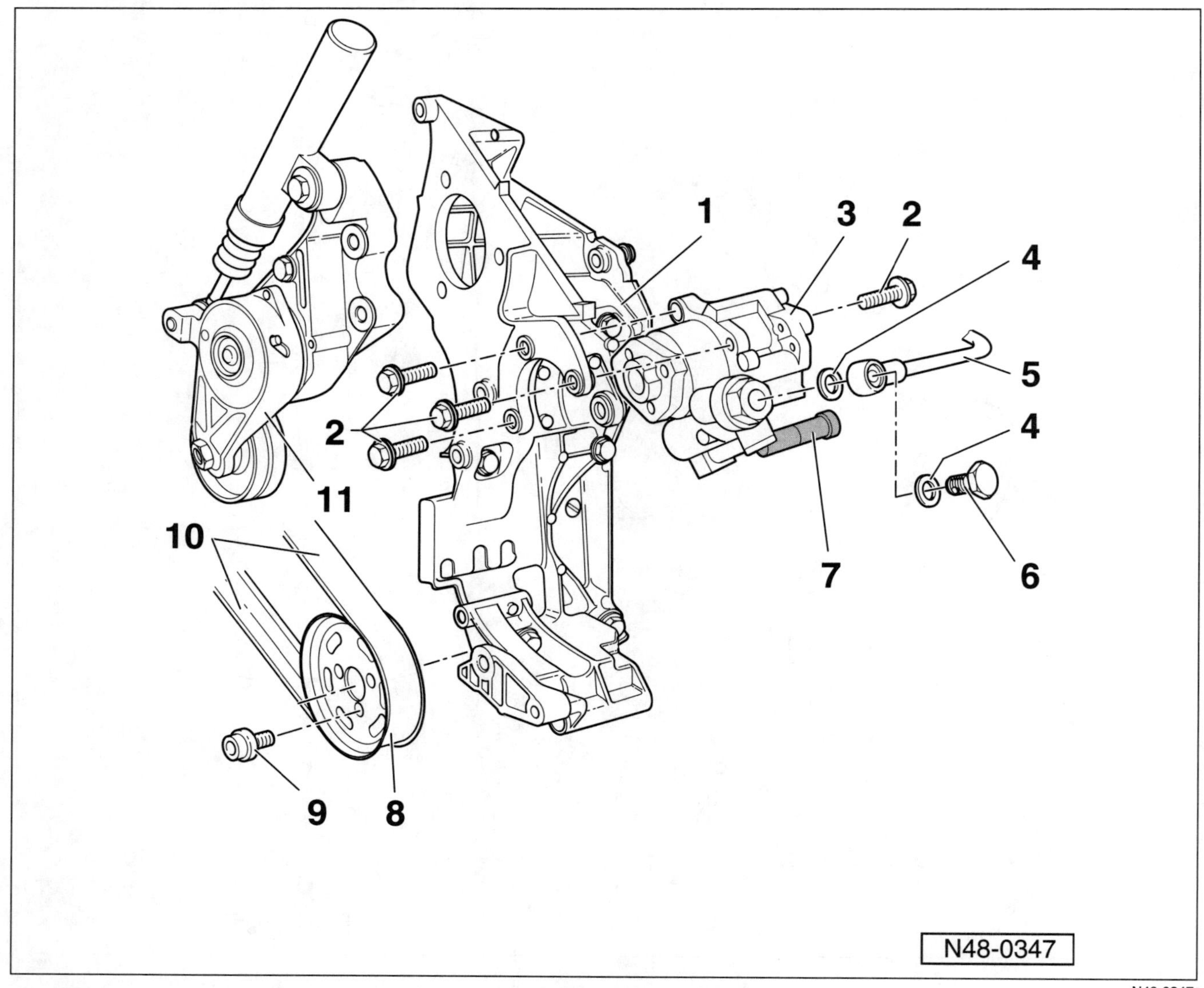

N48-0347

Fig. 28. Power steering components mounted to upper section of bracket.

1. **Bracket**
2. **Bolts**
   - Tighten to 25 Nm (18 ft-lb)
3. **Power steering pump**
   - Fill with oil before installing
4. **Seals**
   - Always replace
5. **Banjo Bolt**
   - Tighten to 30 Nm (22 ft-lb)
6. **Pressure hose assembly**
7. **Bolt**
   - Tighten to 22 Nm (16 ft-lb)
8. **Belt pulley**
9. **Socket-head bolt**
   - Tighten to 25 Nm (18 ft-lb)
10. **Ribbed V-belt**
    - Using a crayon or marker, mark the direction of travel before removing the ribbed belt
    - Reinstalling a used belt in the opposite direction could damage the belt
    - Make sure belt is correctly seated in the pulleys when installing
11. **Ribbed V-belt tensioner**

50 Body–Front

GENERAL

This repair group covers the front body section, front fender and radiator support removal and installation. The radiator support can be removed from the car as one unit to facilitate repairs, such as engine removal.

> ***WARNING —***
> *Disconnecting the negative (–) battery cable may erase fault codes and basic settings in the engine management and automatic transmission control modules. Some driveability problems may be noticed until the system re-adapts to operating conditions. OBD II readiness codes, which may be required for emissions testing, may also be erased. Convenience electronics (alarm system, interior light control, power locks, mirrors, and windows) may need to be re-set using a VAG 1551/1552 or equivalent scan tool.*

NOTE —
Volkswagen refers to the radiator support as a lock carrier.

FRONT BODY COMPONENTS

The front fenders are both part of the front clip which must be removed as a complete assembly. See Fig. 1.

Front fender assembly

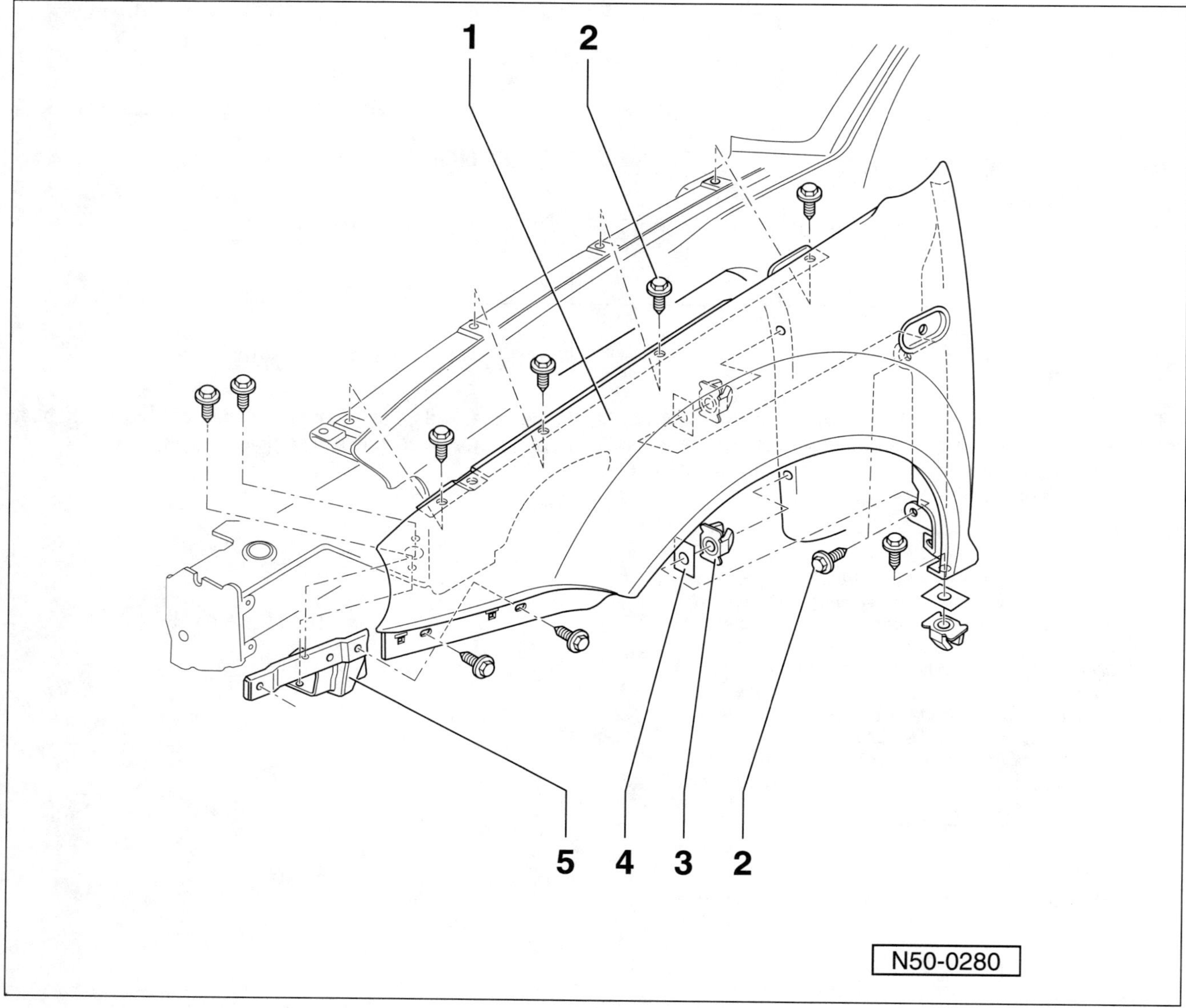

N50-0280

Fig. 1. Front body assembly with fenders must be removed as a complete unit.

1. **Fender**
   - Dimensions, **see** Ⓐ or Ⓑ
   - Removing:
     Remove bumper cover, see **63 Bumpers**
     Remove wheel housing liner, see **66 Body–Exterior Equipment**
     Heat fender in area of A-pillar with hot air blower to help with removal
   - Before installing screws on fender, fit a zinc intermediate piece (VW part no. AKL 381 035 50) to each bolt position contact area

NOTE —
Volkswagen part numbers are given for reference only. Always consult with your Volkswagen Parts Department or aftermarket parts specialist for the latest parts information.

2. **Bolt**
   - Qty. 9
   - Tighten to 6 Nm (53 in-lb)
3. **Spring nut**
4. **Seal**
5. **Bracket**
   - Bolted to front of longitudinal member

(A) Fender dimensions, Golf/GTI

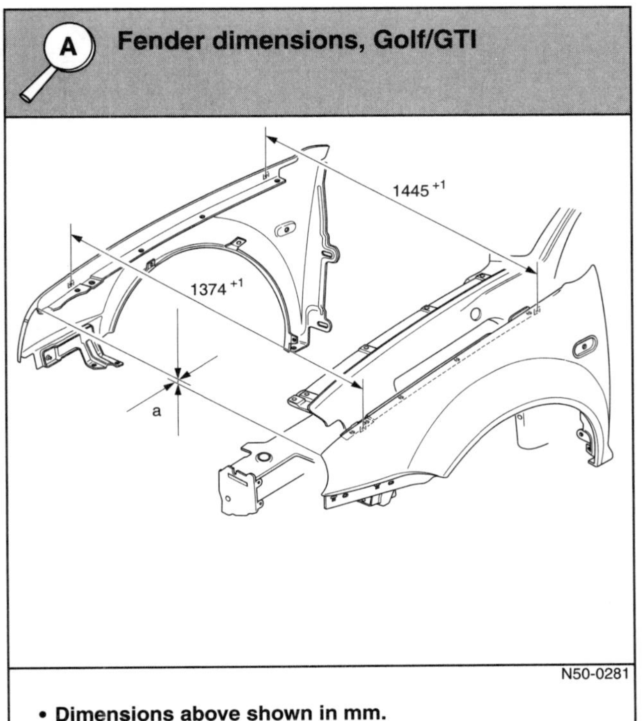

N50-0281

- Dimensions above shown in mm.
- Offset between fender horizontal and vertical points
  a = 0 - 2 mm (0.0787 in.)

(B) Fender dimensions, Jetta

1445 +1

1409 +1

a

M50-0005

M50-00005

- Dimensions above shown in mm.
- Offset between fender horizontal and vertical points
  a = 0 - 2 mm (0.0787 in.)

Lock carrier, removing and installing

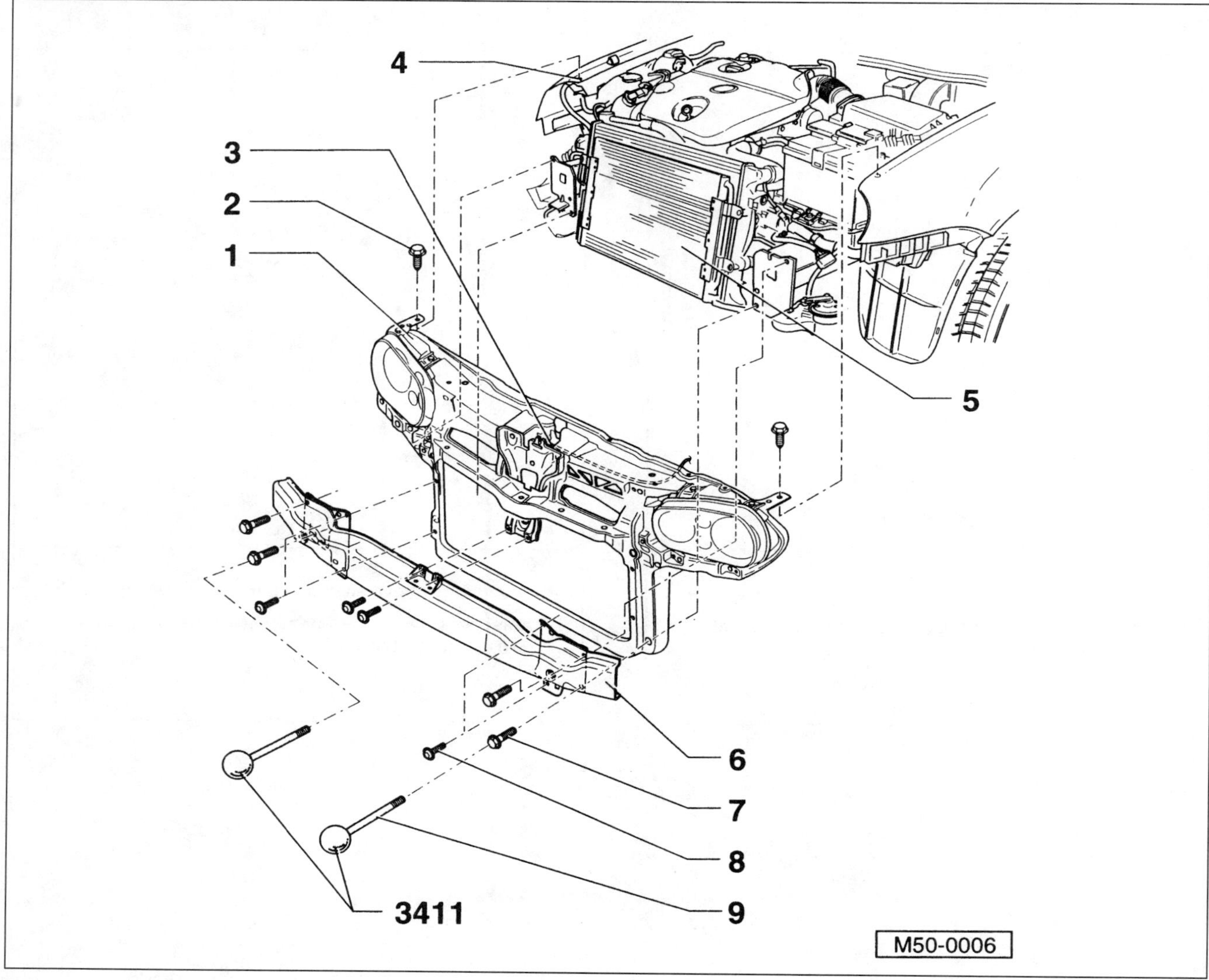

M50-0006

Fig. 2. Front lock carrier (radiator support) and related components.

1. **Lock carrier with attachments**
   - Removing:
     Disconnect bowden cable (item 3) and harness connectors on lock
     Disconnect harness connector from headlights
     Remove front bumper and bumper carrier, see **63 Bumpers**
     Disconnect headlight washer system at T-connection
     Unbolt radiator and condenser from lock carrier and secure in engine compartment
   - Align lock carrier to floor pan members when installing
2. **Bolt**
   - Qty. 2
   - Tighten to 8 Nm (71 in-lb)
3. **Bowden cable**
4. **Hole in side panel**
5. **Radiator and condenser**
   - Do not hang condenser by lines/hoses
   - Do not kink condenser lines/hoses
6. **Bumper beam**
7. **Bolt**
   - Qty. 4
   - Tighten to 8 Nm (71 ft-lb)
8. **Bolt**
   - Qty. 4
   - Tighten to 9 Nm (80 in-lb)
9. **Guide rods 3411**
   - VW special tool for holding lock carrier in service position

Lock carrier, service position

The lock carrier can be moved forward to allow easier access for various service procedures.

1. Remove front bumper cover, see **63 Bumpers**.
2. Disconnect bowden cable on hood lock.
3. Remove one lock carrier mounting bolt from each floor pan member and install VW special tool 3411 (guide rods), or equivalent. See Fig. 2.
4. Remove remaining lock carrier mounting bolts and pull lock carrier forward.

FRONT NOISE INSULATION

Gasoline and diesel equipped vehicles have different lower sound absorption panels (belly pans) as shown in Fig. 3. and Fig. 4.

Noise insulation (gasoline engines)

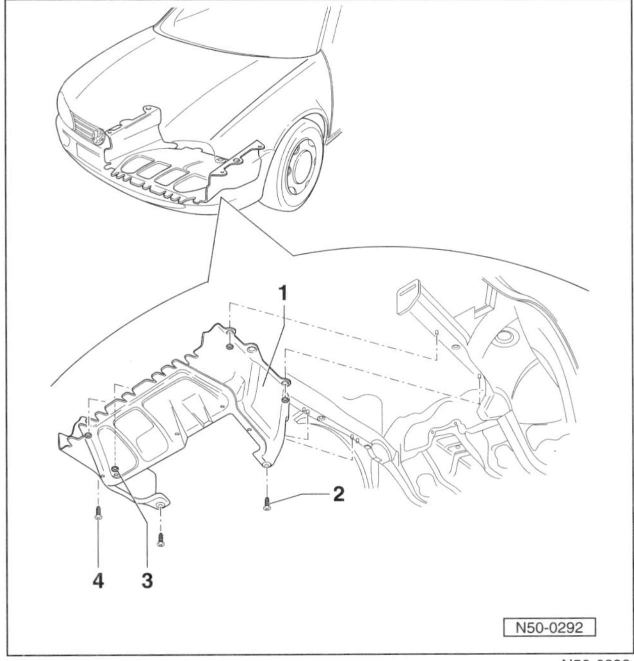

N50-0292

Fig. 3. Noise insulation assembly (**1**) bolted to lock carrier in gasoline equipped vehicles. Mounting hardware also shown (**2**, **3**, and **4**).

Noise insulation (diesel engines)

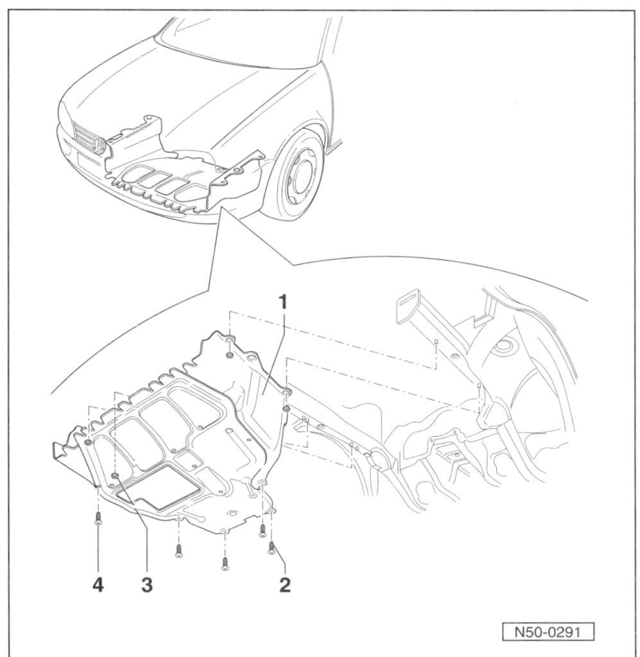

N50-0291

Fig. 4. Noise insulation assembly (**1**) bolted to lock carrier in diesel equipped vehicles. Mounting hardware also shown (**2**, **3**, and **4**).

55 Hood and Lids

GENERAL

The front hood and rear hatch are easily removed with the aid of a helper. Where applicable, the support strut(s) should first be disconnected. See Fig. 1. Be sure to mark the lid location in reference to the hinges for proper alignment during installation.

> ***NOTE —***
> *If strut is to be re-used do not remove retaining clip completely.*

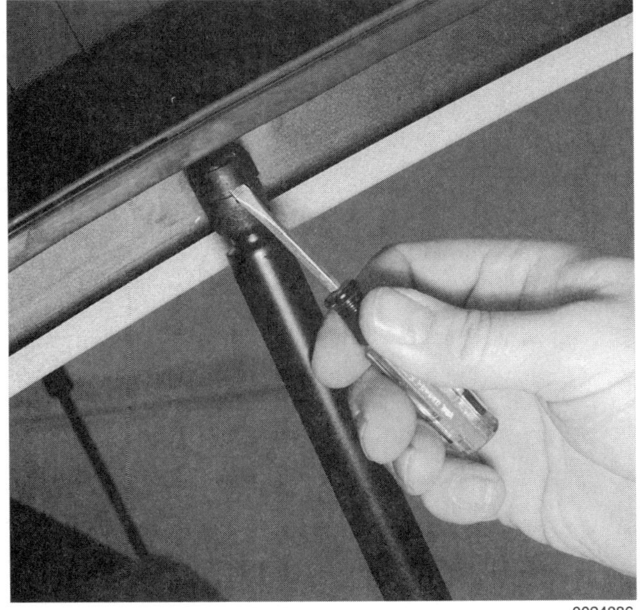

0024286

Fig. 1. After prying up strut retaining clip with screwdriver, as shown, remove strut from ball stud. Do not remove clip completely.

FRONT HOOD

Hood assembly

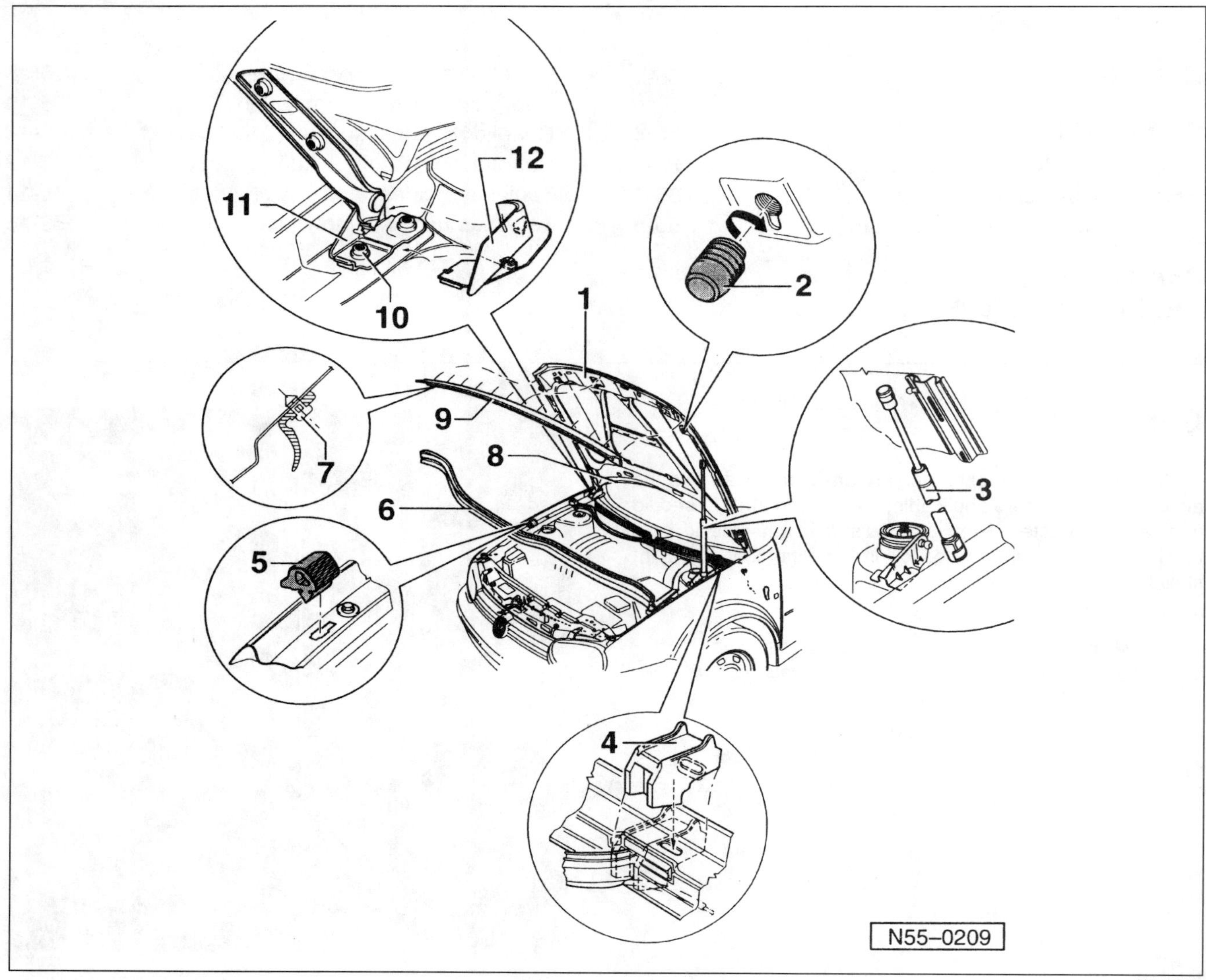

N55-0209

Fig. 2. Front hood assembly.

1. **Hood**
   - Removing:
     Remove windshield washer hoses and jets
     Take out bolts (item 9) and remove hood
2. **Rubber stop**
   - Adjust hood height to fenders using rubber stops
3. **Gas-filled strut**
4. **Cushion**
5. **Rubber stop**
6. **Plenum seal**
   - Pushed onto flange
7. **Clip**
8. **Spray jet/hose**
   - Removing, see **92 Wipers and Washers**
9. **Guide piece**
10. **Bolt**
    - Tighten to 23 Nm (17 ft-lb)
11. **Hinge**
    - Hood can be aligned between fenders by moving hinges within the slotted holes
    - After installation or adjusting, treat hinges and bolts with corrosion protection
12. **Hinge cover**
    - Clipped on, pull off at right angles

Hood release cable assembly

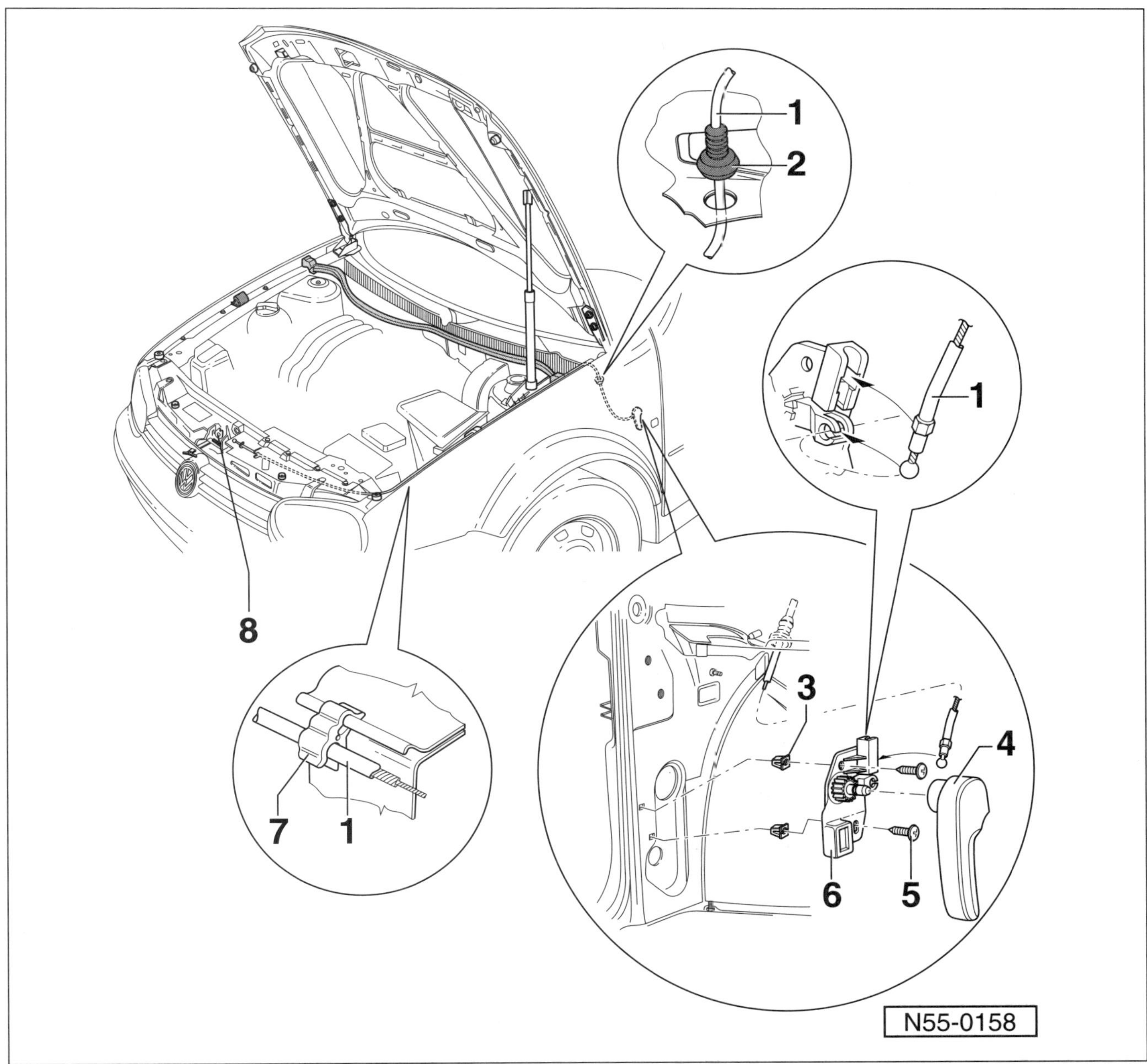

N55-0158

Fig. 3. Hood release cable and related hardware.

1. **Hood release (bowden) cable**
   - Removing:
     Remove release lever (item 4)
     Remove cable from clip at lock (item 8) and engine compartment (item 7)
     Remove lower A-pillar trim, see **70 Trim–Interior**
     Tie string (approx. 39 in.) to cable at hood release and pull cable out at release lever end
   - Use the same string to pull new cable into place
2. **Grommet**
3. **Spreader nut**
4. **Release lever**
   - Removing and installing, **see** Ⓐ
5. **Self-tapping screw**
6. **Lever bracket**
   - Cable attached
7. **Cable clip**
8. **Hood lock**

Release lever, removing and installing

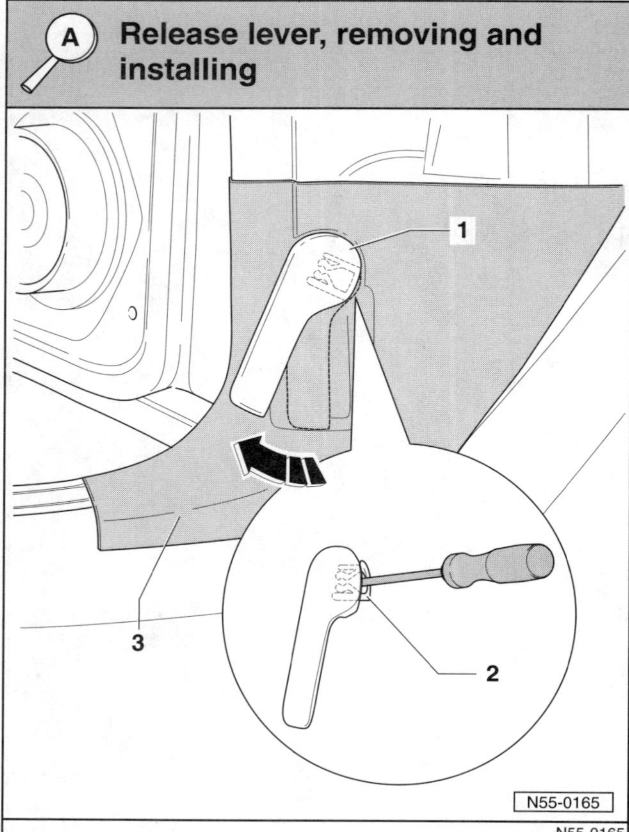

N55-0165

- Pull back release lever (1) approx. 2 cm (0.8 in.)
- Insert small screwdriver into gap between release lever and clip (2)
- Let go of release lever and pry clip off (clip falls behind trim)
- Unclip trim (3) from bracket at center and from sill panel
- To install, clip trim (3) into sill first
- Push clip (2) completely into release lever and press release lever onto bracket
- Check operation of release lever

Hood lock assembly

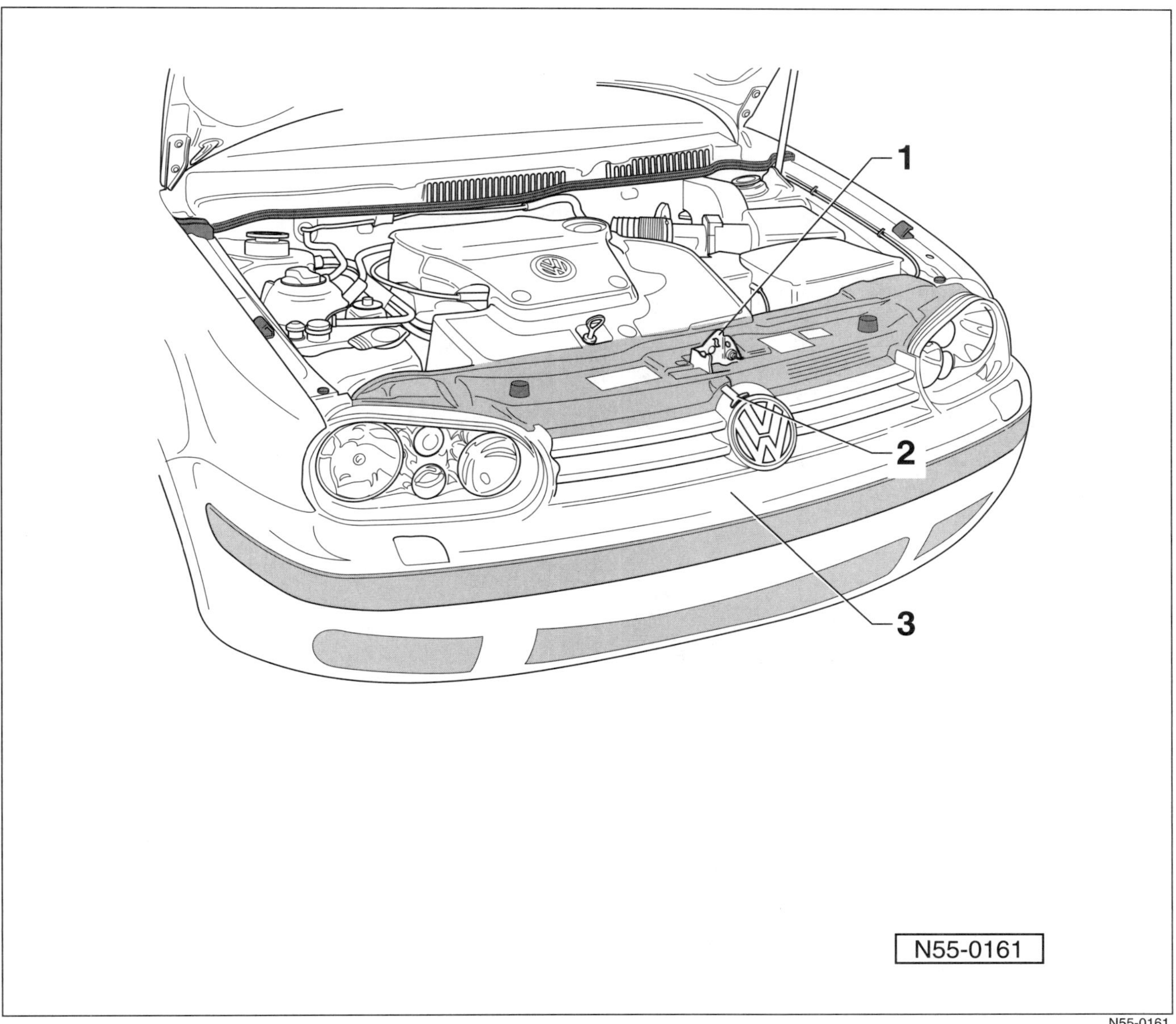

N55-0161

Fig. 4. Hood lock assembly.

1. **Hood lock**
   - Adjust with slotted mounting holes
   - Removing:
     Remove radiator grille and bumper
     Remove lock support, **see** Ⓐ
     Remove hood lock, **see** Ⓑ

2. **Release lever**

3. **Bumper**

A Hood lock support, removing

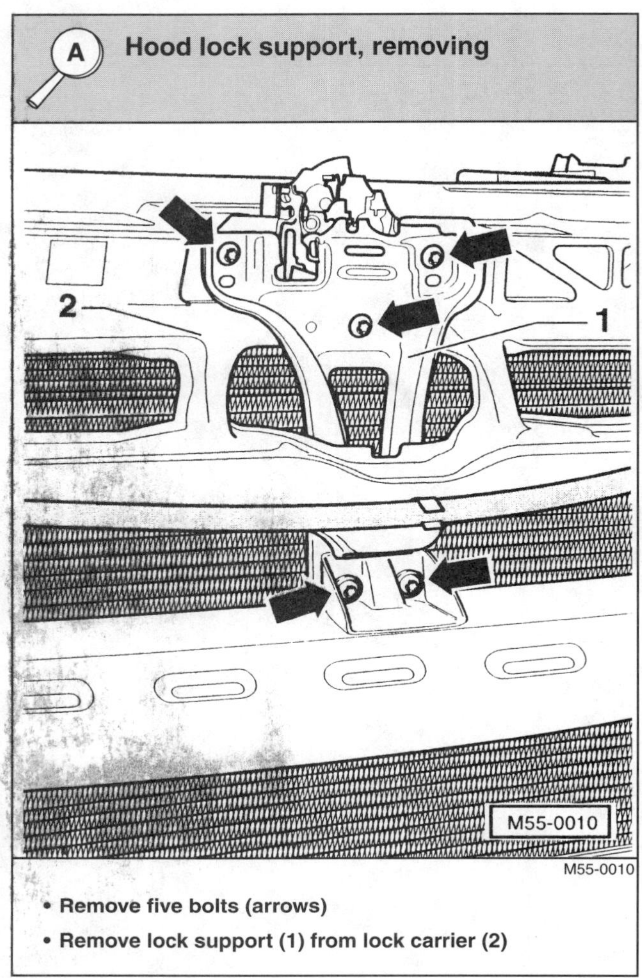

M55-0010

- Remove five bolts (arrows)
- Remove lock support (1) from lock carrier (2)

B Hood lock, removing

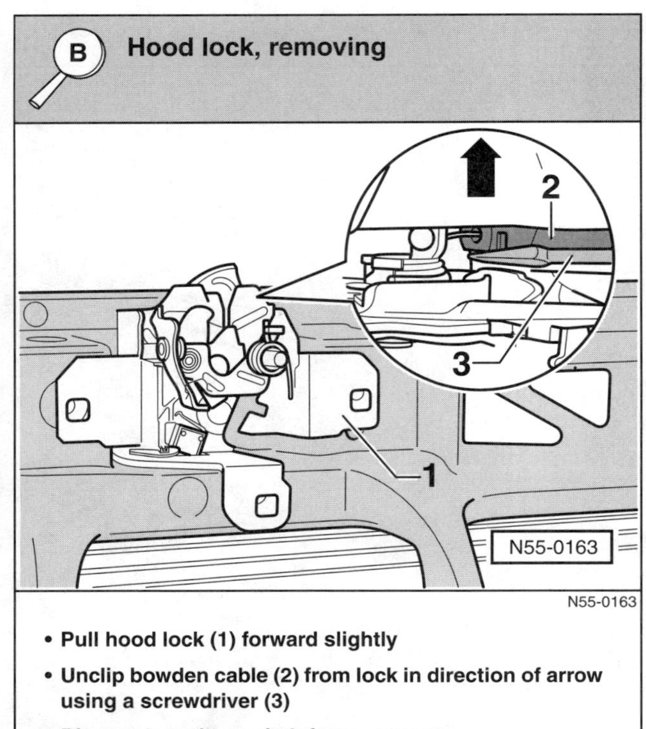

N55-0163

- Pull hood lock (1) forward slightly
- Unclip bowden cable (2) from lock in direction of arrow using a screwdriver (3)
- Disconnect microswitch from connector.

REAR LIDS

Rear hatch/lid, adjusting

The rear hatch or rear lid (trunk) is properly adjusted when the shut lines are even all around and the hatch/lid does not project to far in or out. All contours must align when the rear hatch/lid is closed.

> ***NOTE —***
> - *The vehicle must be standing on its wheels when adjusting the rear lid.*
> - *The following illustrations are for Golf/GTI vehicles, Jettas are very similar.*

1. Turn adjustment buffer trough 90° with an open end wrench (24 mm) and remove from hole in lid. See Fig. 5.

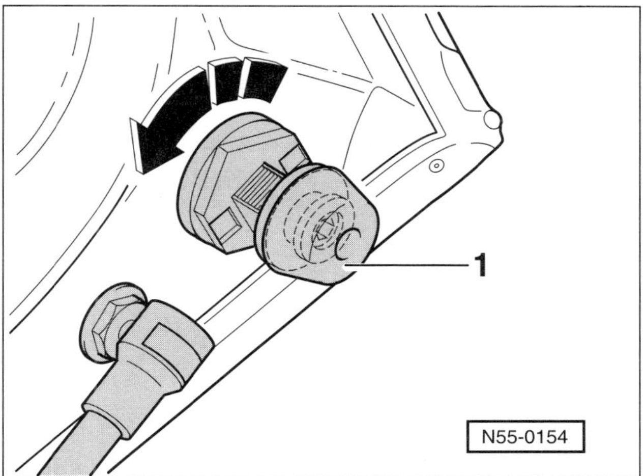

N55-0154

Fig. 5. Use 24 mm open end wrench to rotate buffer 90° (**arrow**) and remove from lid. Remove rubber stop (**1**) from screw.

2. Remove rubber stop from buffer adjustment screw and unscrew locking screw using 3mm hex key until notched slide can be pulled out.

3. Pull notched slide out of housing and set buffer stop height to 12.5 mm (0.49 in). See Fig. 6.

4. Install rubber stop and buffer assembly into rear lid and turn adjustment buffer trough 90° in the opposite direction necessary for removal.

5. For Golf/GTI only, unscrew cap from blind rivet on left and right sides of hatch opening. See Fig. 7.

6. Close rear lid using light pressure at center and holding handle (as applicable for Golf/GTI).

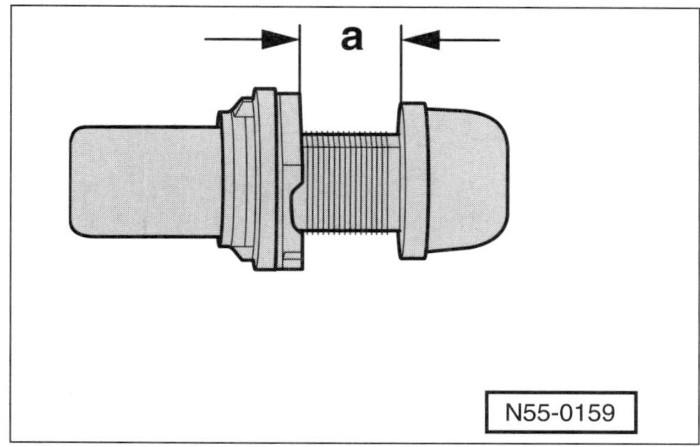

N55-0159

Fig. 6. Pull notched slide out of housing and set dimension **a** to 12.5 mm (0.49 in).

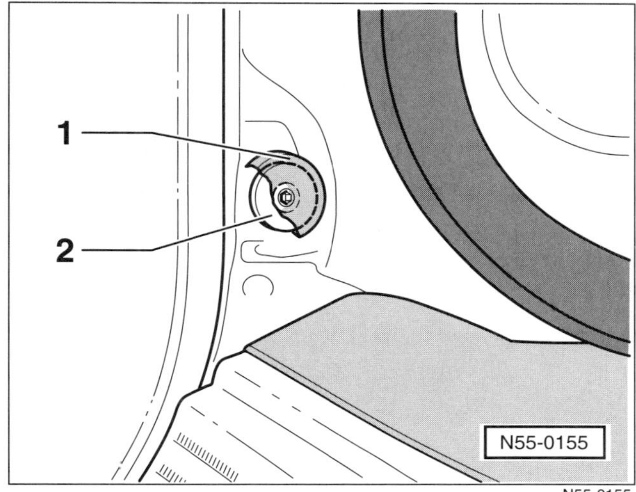

N55-0155

Fig. 7. For Golf/GTI, unscrew cap (**1**) from blind rivet (**2**) on left and right sides of hatch opening.

7. For Golf/GTI check for a gap of 5mm between rear lid and side panel using Volkswagen special tool 3371 adjustment gauge or equivalent.

8. Open rear lid and replace caps on blind rivet (as applicable for Golf/GTI).

9. Tighten locking screw on adjustment buffers.

Tightening torque
- Rear lid adjustment buffer locking screw . . . . 1.5 Nm (13 in-lb)

---

10. Check that rear hatch closes without too much force and doesn't have any up or down movement when in locked position. When unlocking, the lid will pop up slightly due to pre-tension on hinge.

Rear hatch assembly (Golf)

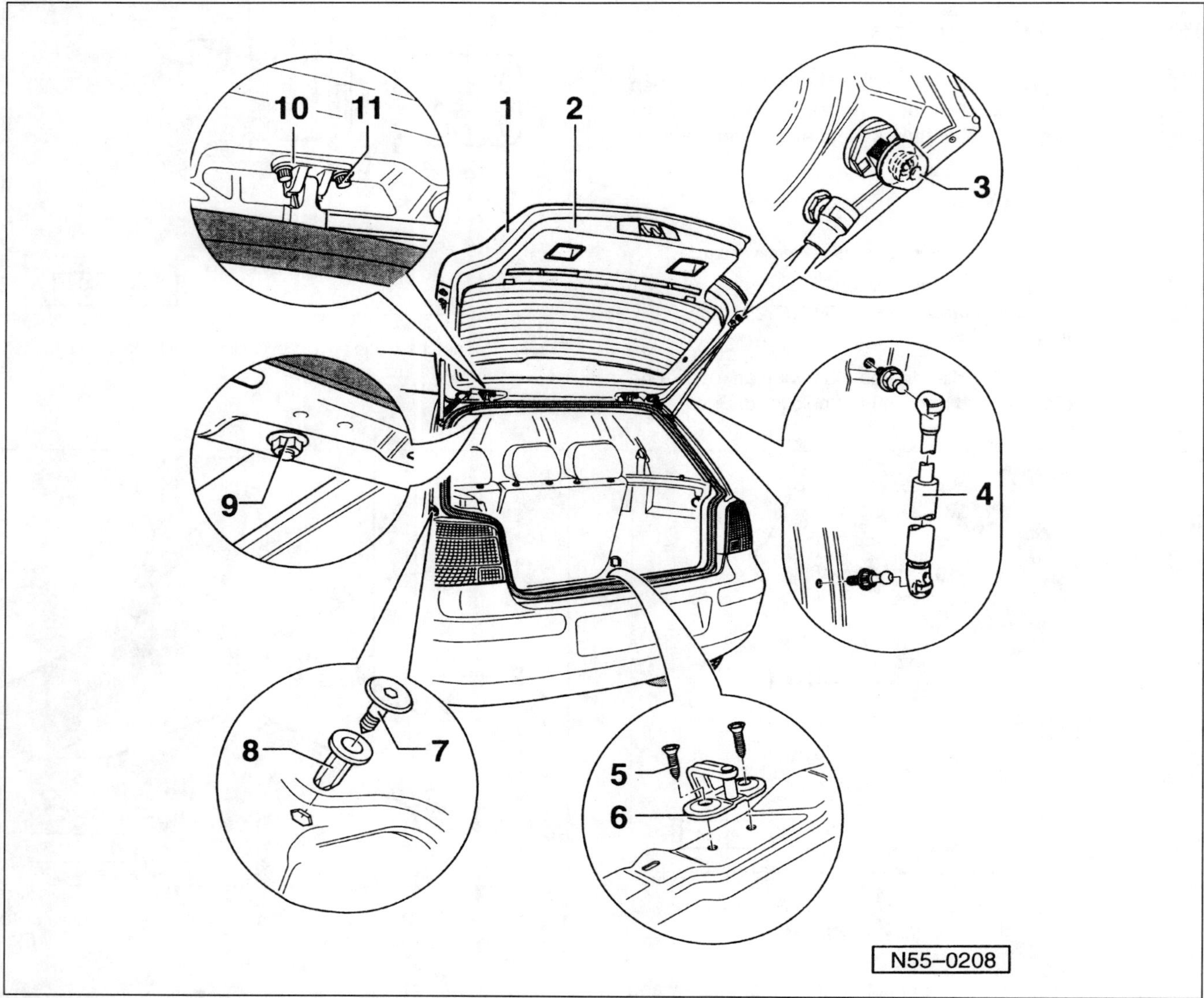

N55-0208

Fig. 8. Rear hatch and related hardware.

1. **Rear hatch**
2. **Trim**
   - Removing and installing, see **70 trim–Interior**
3. **Rubber stop**
4. **Gas-filled strut**
   - Removing and installing, **see** Ⓐ
5. **Screw**
   - Tighten to 22 Nm (16 ft-lb)
6. **Lock plate**
   - Adjusting - within oversized holes
7. **Cap**
8. **Blind nut**
9. **Hex nut**
10. **Hinge**
11. **Bolt**
    - Tighten to 22 Nm (16 ft-lb)

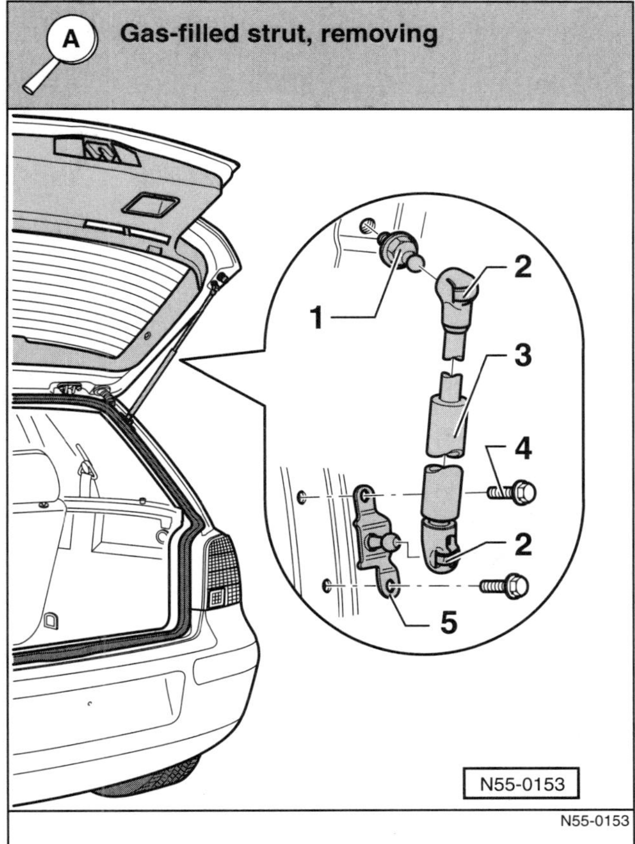

N55-0153

- **Lift retaining clip (2) with a screwdriver and pull gas strut off ball head stud (1).**
- **Do not remove retaining clip completely if gas strut is to be re-used.**

Rear hatch lock assembly (Golf)

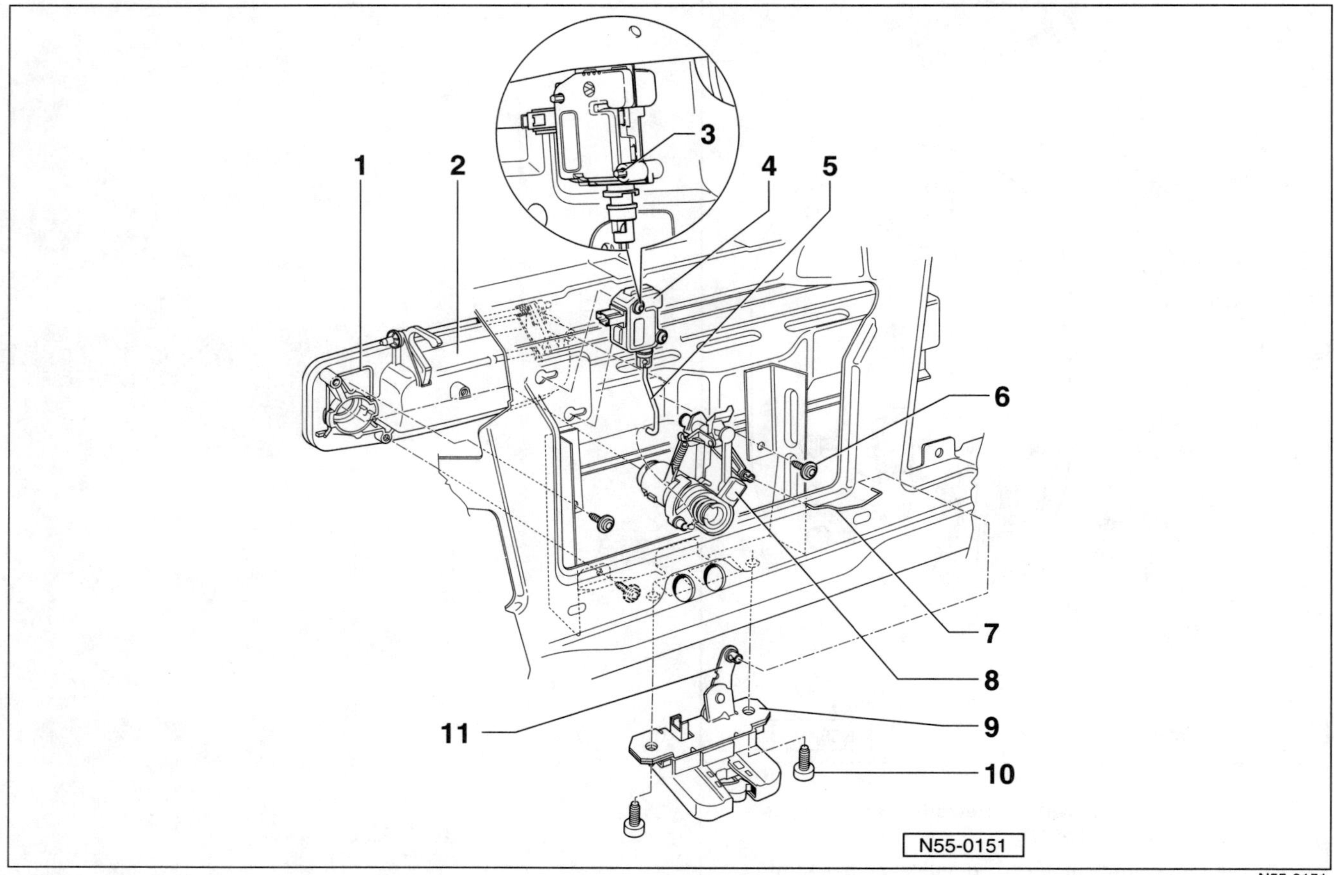

N55-0151

Fig. 9. Rear hatch lock and related components.

1. **Securing clip**
2. **Handle**
   - Removing:
     Unclip rear hatch trim (handle is secured with one cross-head screw)
     Unclip pull rod (item 5)
     Pry out securing clip (item 1) and take lock cylinder out of handle
     Disconnect harness connector for rear interior light and, if applicable, unclip central locking operating rod
     Remove torx bolts (item 6) and remove handle from rear hatch
3. **Actuator securing bolt**
   - Release and tighten with VW special tool T 10010 socket
4. **Central locking actuator**
   - Unscrew actuator with VW special tool T10010 socket
5. **Pull rod**
6. **Torx screw**
7. **Operating rod**
   - Press relay lever (item 11) against stop and insert operating rod without tension
8. **Lock cylinder housing**
   - Removing:
     Unclip rear hatch trim (handle is secured with one cross-head screw)
     Unclip pull rod (item 5)
     Pry out securing clip (item 1) and take lock cylinder out of handle
   - Installing:
     Engage securing clip
     Install lock cylinder housing to handle trim and engage (a clicking must be heard)
9. **Lock**
   - Removing:
     Remove rear hatch trim, see **70 Trim–Interior**
     Disconnect harness connector
     Unclip operating rod (item 7), unscrew bolt (item 10) and remove lock from rear hatch
   - When installing, locate striker catch in detent
10. **Countersunk bolt**
    - Tighten to 20 Nm (15 ft-lb)
11. **Relay lever**

Rear lid (trunk) assembly (Jetta)

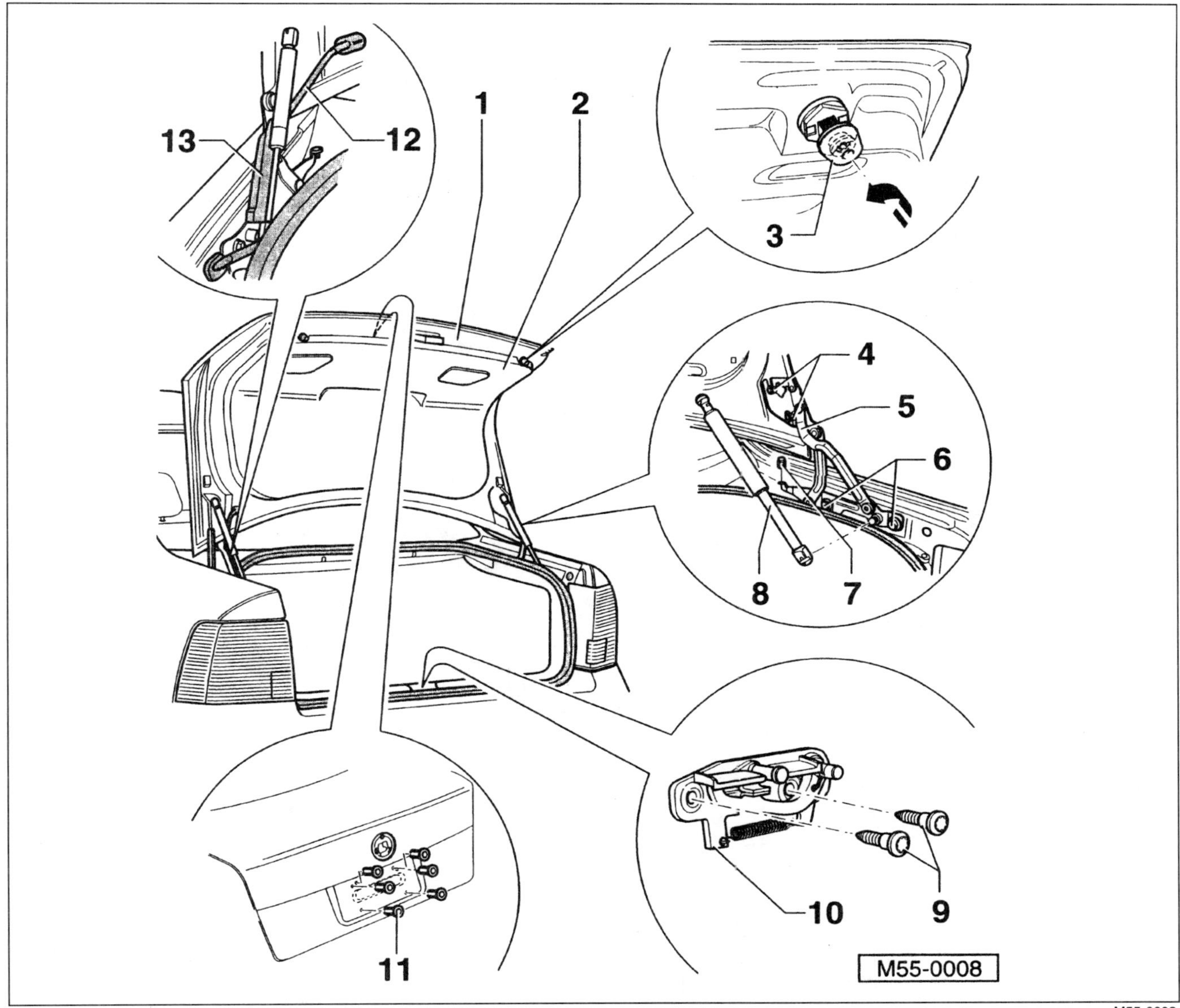

M55-0008

Fig. 10. Rear lid and related hardware on Jetta models.

1. **Rear lid**
2. **Trim**
   - Removing and installing, see **70 Trim–Interior**
3. **Adjustment stop**
4. **Hex nut**
   - Tighten to 22 Nm (16 ft-lb)
5. **Hinge**
6. **Bolt**
   - Tighten to 22 Nm (16 ft-lb)
7. **Rubber stop**
8. **Gas-filled strut**
   - Removing and installing, same as Golf as described earlier
9. **Bolt**
   - Tighten to 22 Nm (16 ft-lb)
10. **Lock plate**
    - Adjusting, move within oversize holes
11. **Rivet nut**
    - Install with rivet nut installation tool VAG 1765 B or equivalent
12. **Wiring**
13. **Hinge cover**

Rear lid lock assembly (Jetta)

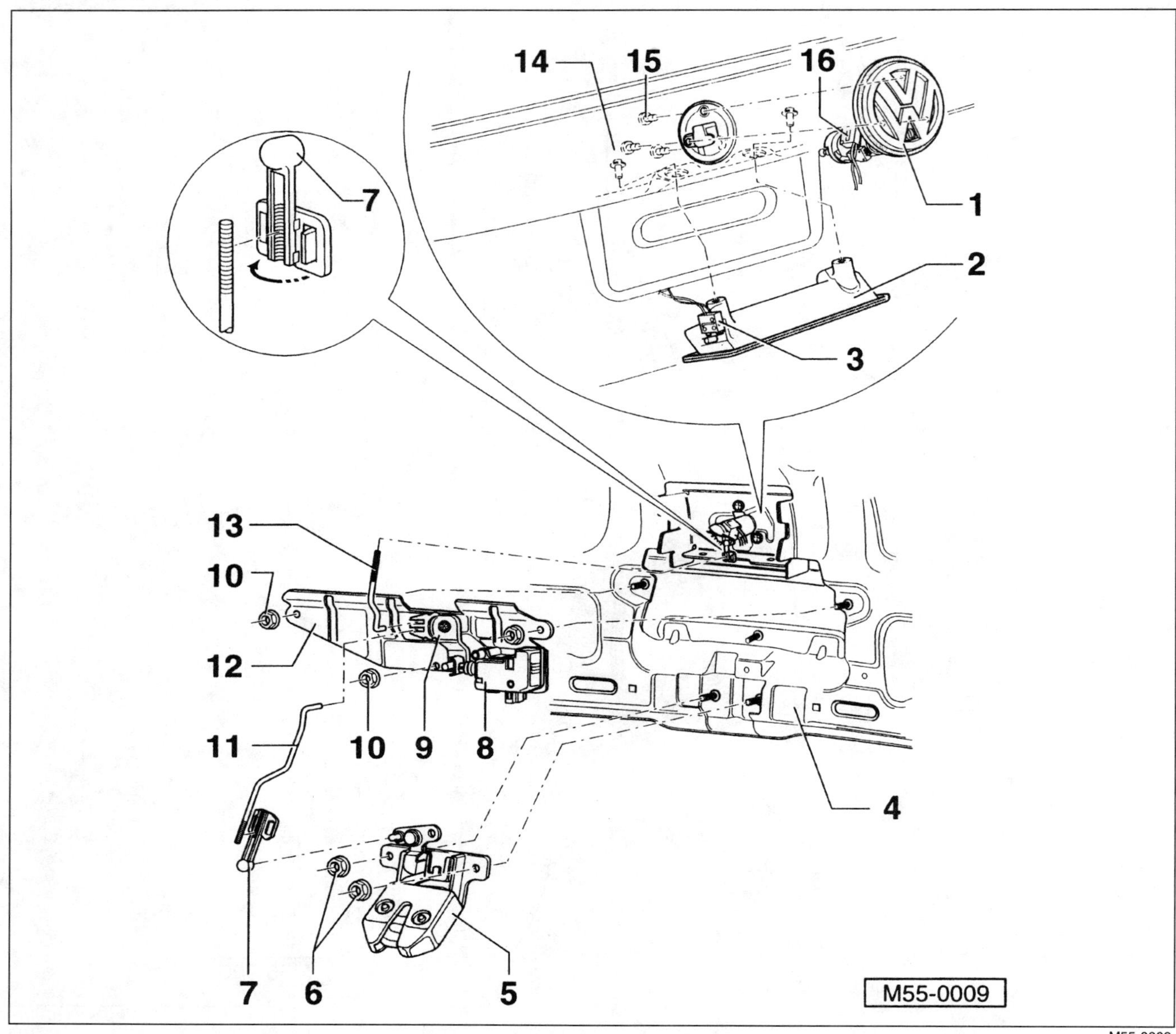

M55-0009

Fig. 11. Rear lid lock and related hardware on Jetta models.

1. **Lock cylinder housing**
   - Removing:
     Remove lock trim, see **70 Trim–Interior**
     Remove bolts (item 15)
     Disconnect wiring for switch (item 16)
     Remove lock cylinder housing
2. **Handle**
   - Removing:
     Remove lock trim, see **70 Trim–Interior**
     Remove bolt (item 14)
     Disconnect wiring for switch (item 3)
     Remove handle from lock
3. **Rear lid release switch**
4. **Rear lid**
5. **Lock**
   - Removing:
     Remove lock trim, see **70 Trim–Interior**
     Disconnect wiring from lock
     Unclip actuator rod (item 11)
     Remove hex nuts (item 6) and remove lock
6. **Hex nut**
   - Tighten to 7 Nm (62 in-lb)
7. **Linkage lever**

(continued on following page)

(continued from previous page)

8. **Rear lid release motor**
   - Removing:
     Remove lock trim, see **70 Trim–Interior**
     Disconnect wiring from motor
     Unclip actuator rod (item 11) from lock
     Unclip actuator rod (item 13) from lock cylinder
     Remove hex nuts (item 10) and bracket (item 12)
     Remove rear lid release motor from bracket

9. **Linkage lever**

10. **Hex nut**
    - Tighten to 7 Nm (62 in-lb)

11. **Actuator rod**
    - Press linkage lever (item 9) against stop on motor (item 8) and hook in actuator rod without tension

12. **Support bracket**

13. **Actuator rod**
    - Press linkage lever (item 9) against stop on motor (item 8) and hook in actuator rod without tension

14. **Bolt**
    - Tighten to 7 Nm (62 in-lb)

15. **Bolt**
    - Tighten to 7 Nm (62 in-lb)

16. **Rear lid release switch**

Tank flap unit assembly (Golf)

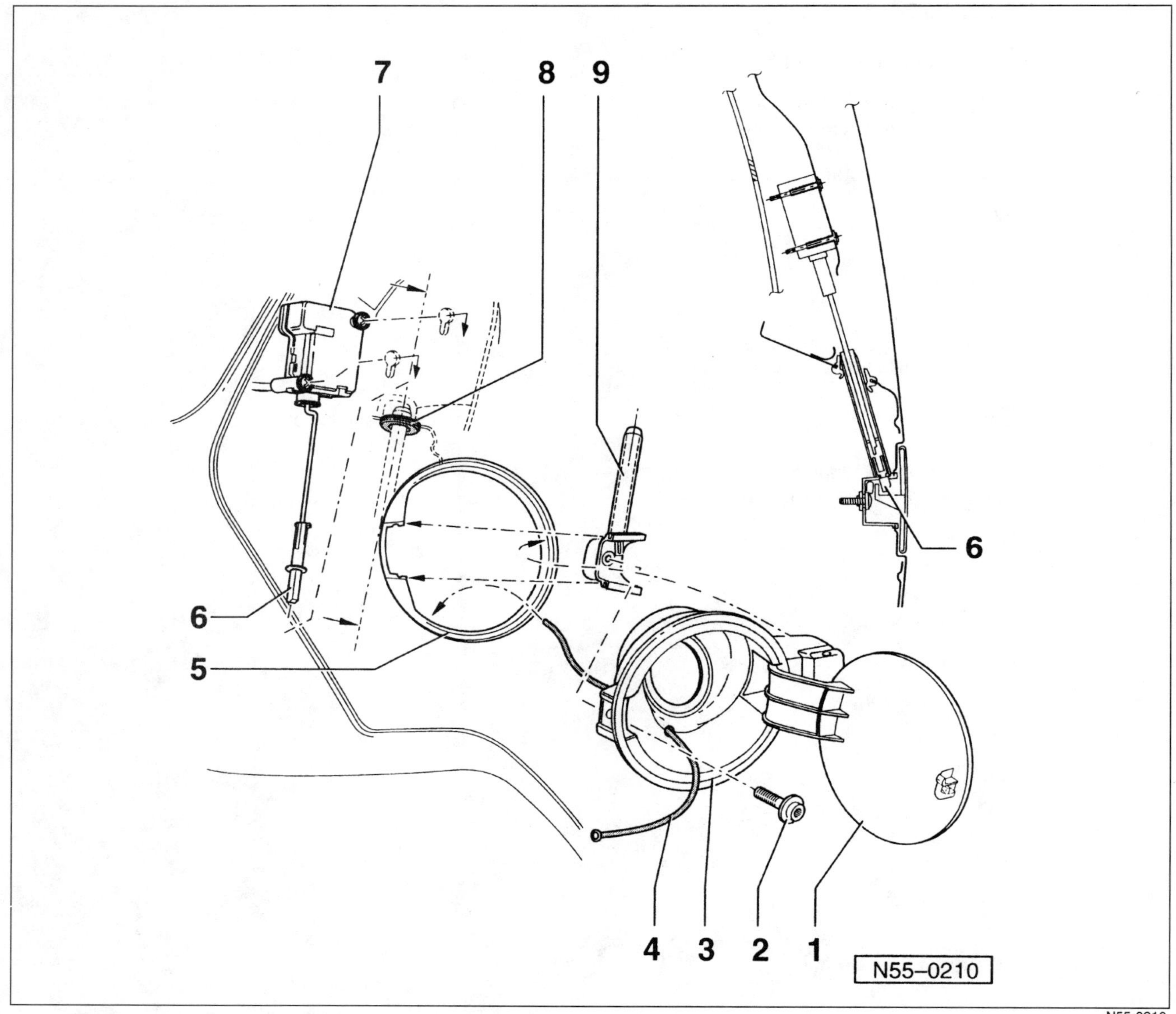

N55-0210

Fig. 12. Fuel filler flap and related components on Golf/GTI models.

1. **Tank flap unit**
   - Removing:
     Unscrew tank filler cap
     Press back lock rod by operating remote release
     Remove bolt (item 2)
     Pull rubber part off fuel tank filler and swing flap unit out of quarter panel
   - Installing:
     Assembly piece (item 9) and actuator unit (item 7) should already be installed
     Install tank flap unit (rubber part rolled up) with hinge side first
     Secure tank flap unit and assembly piece
2. **Bolt**
3. **Tank flap cup**
   - Can only be removed as part of tank flap unit
   - Press out securing pin in tank flap unit to remove
4. **Drain tube**
5. **Side piece**
6. **Release rod**
7. **Actuator unit for tank flap**
8. **Seal**
9. **Assembly piece**
   - Assists in removal and installation

Tank flap unit assembly (Jetta)

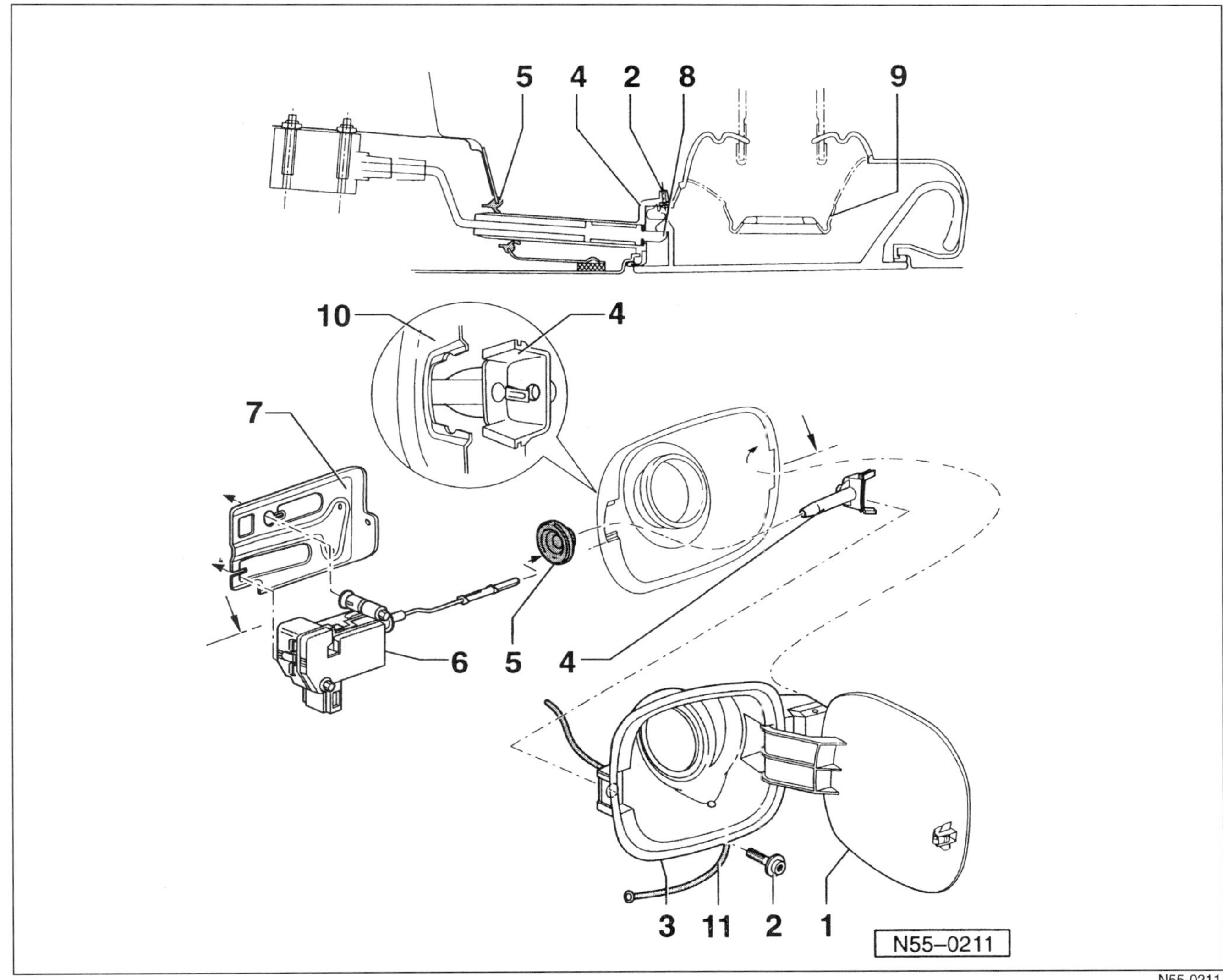

N55-0211

Fig. 13. Fuel filler flap and related components on Jetta models.

1. **Tank flap unit**
   - Removing:
     Unscrew tank filler cap
     Press back lock rod by operating remote release
     Remove cross-head screw (item 1)
     Pull rubber part off fuel tank filler and swing flap unit out of quarter panel
   - Installing:
     Assembly piece (item 4) and actuator unit (item 6) should already be installed
     Install tank flap unit (rubber part rolled up) with hinge side first
     Secure tank flap unit and assembly piece
2. **Bolt**
3. **Tank flap cup**
   - Can only be removed as part of tank flap unit
   - Press out securing pin in tank flap unit to remove
4. **Assembly piece**
   - Pushed into quarter panel
5. **Seal**
6. **Actuator unit for tank flap**
7. **Quarter panel**
8. **Release rod**
9. **Rubber part**
   - Rolled up on assembly
10. **Side piece**
11. **Drain tube**

57 Front Doors

GENERAL

This repair group covers removal and installation of the front door assemblies, the front door glass and window regulators, and service to the door lock assemblies including the central locking system. Special tools and equipment are required for some operations. For removal of door panels see **70 Trim–Interior**.

> ***WARNING —***
> *Disconnecting the negative (–) battery cable may erase fault codes and basic settings in the engine management and automatic transmission control modules. Some driveability problems may be noticed until the system re-adapts to operating conditions. OBD II readiness codes, which may be required for emissions testing, may also be erased. Convenience electronics (alarm system, interior light control, power locks, mirrors, and windows) may need to be re-set using a VAG 1551/1552 or equivalent scan tool.*

Power windows

Models equipped with power windows feature the ability to raise and lower both front windows by using the key in the front door lock. By holding the key in the locked position for more than 1 second, either window that was in the down position will be raised to the closed position in addition to locking the vehicle. This feature is known as convenience close.

As a ventilation aid in hot weather, both front windows can be lowered. By holding the key in the unlock position for more than 2 seconds, both front windows will be lowered at the same time in addition to unlocking the vehicle.

Power windows also feature pinch protection and one-touch up and one-touch down operation. The power windows will remain functional for approximately 10 minutes after the ignition is shut off provided that a door is not opened. The one-touch up feature is deactivated when the ignition is switched off.

Central locking

All models are available with central locking that is activated by insertion of the key into an outside door, by activation of a locking switch from within, or by the keyless remote.

When opening a locked vehicle from the outside with the key, there are two options. If the key is turned once, only that particular door will unlock. If the key is quickly turned twice, both doors will be unlocked. This safety feature is known as selective unlocking.

DOORS

The doors are designed with a split hinge that can be slid apart. After disconnecting the appropriate electrical connectors and the door check, the complete door can easily be removed from the vehicle as required. For an overview of the door hinges, latches and related components, see Fig. 1. Most of the internal components of the doors including the window regulators and window glass are assembled into a modular assembly known as an assembly carrier. For an overview of the window glass and related components see Fig. 19.

57

Door assembly

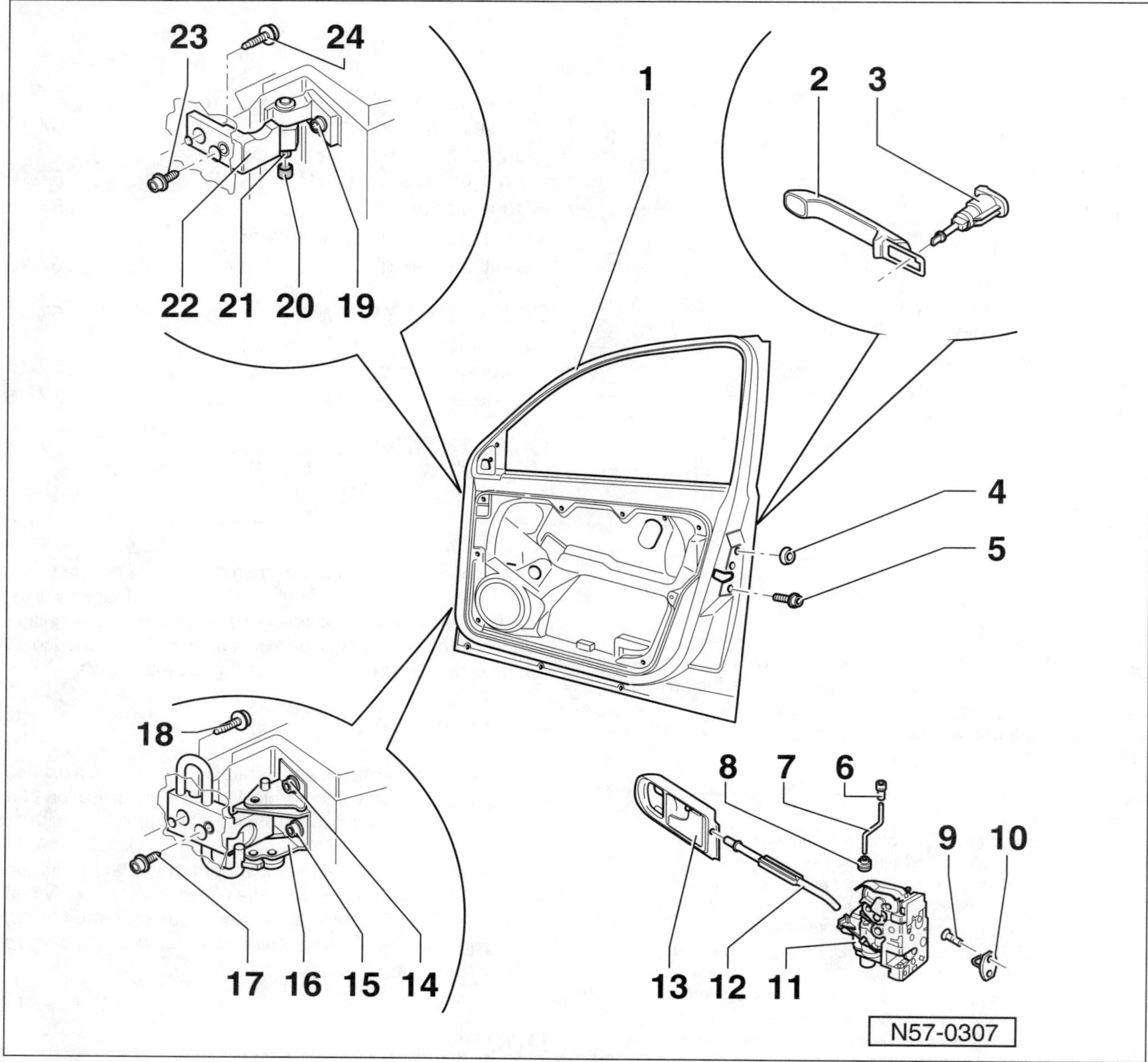

N57-0307

Fig. 1. Door hinges, latches and related components shown for the right side. Left side is similar.

NOTE —
- *The instrument panel must be removed to remove and adjust the upper door hinges.*
- *Always replace the hinge bolts if loosened.*

1. **Door**
2. **Door handle with base**
3. **Lock cylinder housing**
4. **Cover cap**
5. **Bolt**
    - Tighten to 18 Nm (13 ft-lb)
    - Install with locking compound
6. **Locking button**
7. **Locking rod**
8. **Rubber boot**
9. **Bolt**
    - Tighten to 20 Nm (15 ft-lb)

(continued from previous page)

10. Striker plate

11. Door lock assembly

12. Bowden cable

13. Interior release handle

14. Multi-point socket head bolt
- M8 x 28
- Tighten to 20 Nm (15 ft-lb) + ¼ turn (90°)
- Always replace bolt after loosening

15. Multi-point socket head bolt
- M8 x 28
- Tighten to 20 Nm (15 ft-lb) + ¼ turn (90°)
- Always replace bolt after loosening

16. Door hinge with arrester
- Hinge is divided

17. Multi-point socket head bolt
- M8 x 28
- Install from inside vehicle
- Remove A-pillar lower trim, see **70 Trim–Interior**
- Tighten to 20 Nm (15 ft-lb) + ¼ turn (90°)
- Always replace bolt after loosening

18. Multi-point socket head bolt
- M8 x 28
- Tighten to 20 Nm (15 ft-lb) + ¼ turn (90°)
- Always replace bolt after loosening

19. Multi-point socket head bolt
- M8 x 28
- Tighten to 20 Nm (15 ft-lb) + ¼ turn (90°)
- Always replace bolt after loosening

20. Cover cap

21. Bolt
- Tighten to 13 Nm (10 ft-lb)

22. Door hinge
- Hinge is divided

23. Multi-point socket head bolt
- M8 x 22
- Install from inside vehicle
- To loosen or tighten bolt, remove and install instrument panel, see **70 Trim–Interior**
- Tighten to 20 Nm (15 ft-lb) + ¼ turn (90°)
- Always replace bolt after loosening

24. Multi-point socket head bolt
- M8 x 28
- Tighten to 20 Nm (15 ft-lb) + ¼ turn (90°)
- Always replace bolt after loosening

Door, removing and installing

The following steps refer to Fig. 2.

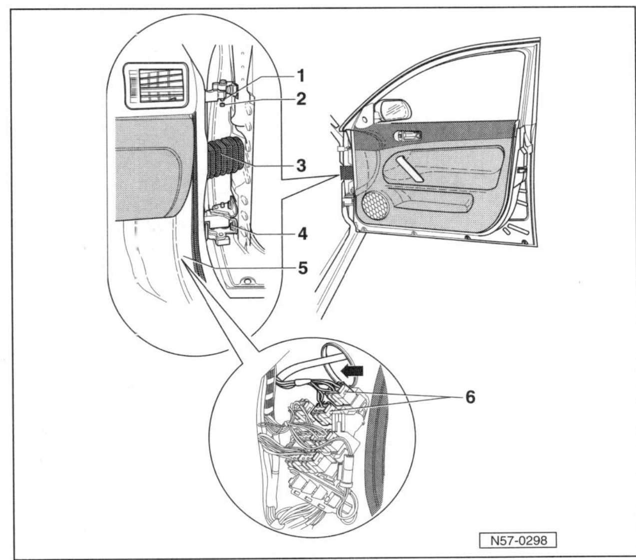

N57-0298

Fig. 2. Varicus components involved in door removal.

1. Remove lower A-pillar lower trim (item **5** above), see **70 Trim–Interior**.
2. Disconnect harness connectors (item **6** above).
3. Remove wiring harness boot (item **3** above) at A-pillar and carefully work wiring harness connectors through opening (**arrow** above).

> ***CAUTION —***
> *Do not close door with harness connectors between door and A-pillar. They will be crushed.*

4. Pry off cover cap (item **2** above) and remove bolt (item **1** above) from upper hinge pin.
5. Remove lower bolt (item **4** above) from hinge using VW special tool 3320 door adjusting wrench and 3320/2 box spanner. Always replace this bolt upon installation.
6. Carefully lift door upward and out of hinge brackets.
7. Installation is the reverse of removal. The hinges must be loosened to adjust the door. The instrument panel must be removed to loosen door hinge on upper A-pillar. Use VW special tool 3320 door adjusting wrench and 3320/2 box spanner to adjust the door.

Tightening torques
- Upper hinge bolt . . . . 13 Nm (10 ft-lb)
- Lower hinge bolt (always replace) . . . . . . 20 Nm (15 ft-lb) + ¼ turn (90°)

Door handle and lock assembly

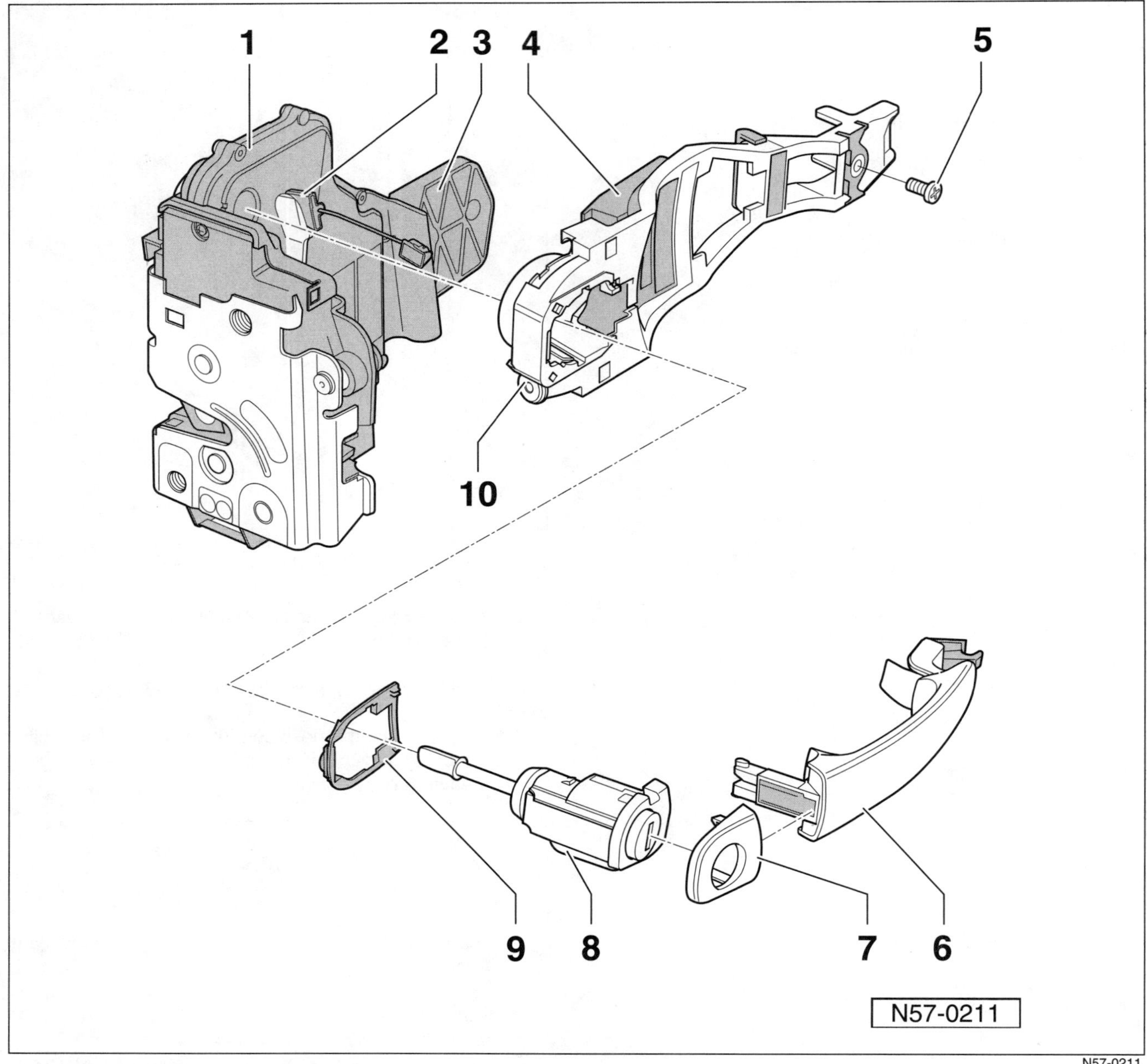

N57-0211

Fig. 3. Right side door lock, outside door handle and related components. Left side is similar.

1. **Door lock**
   - The door lock can only be removed with the carrier assembly
2. **Cable**
   - Outside door handle release
3. **Retaining bracket**
   - Bolted and riveted to carrier assembly and door lock
4. **Handle bracket**
   - Removing:
     Door handle, lock cylinder housing and assembly carrier are removed first
     Remove screw (item 5) and slide bracket slightly to rear and remove from door
5. **Screw**
   - Tighten to 8.5 Nm (76 in-lb)

(continued from previous page)

6. **Door handle with base**
7. **Lock cylinder cover (trim)**
8. **Lock cylinder housing**
   - Only supplied with lock cylinder and keys.
9. **Gasket**
10. **Multi-point socket head bolt**
    - Requires special socket insert tool T10011 or equivalent, **see** (A)
    - Loosening this screw releases the lock cylinder housing, allowing it to be pulled out of handle bracket.
    - Bolt must not be threaded in without lock cylinder housing installed or locking ring may fall into door.

> ***CAUTION —***
> *Loosen multi-point socket head bolt only. If bolt is removed, door lock must be removed to realign.*

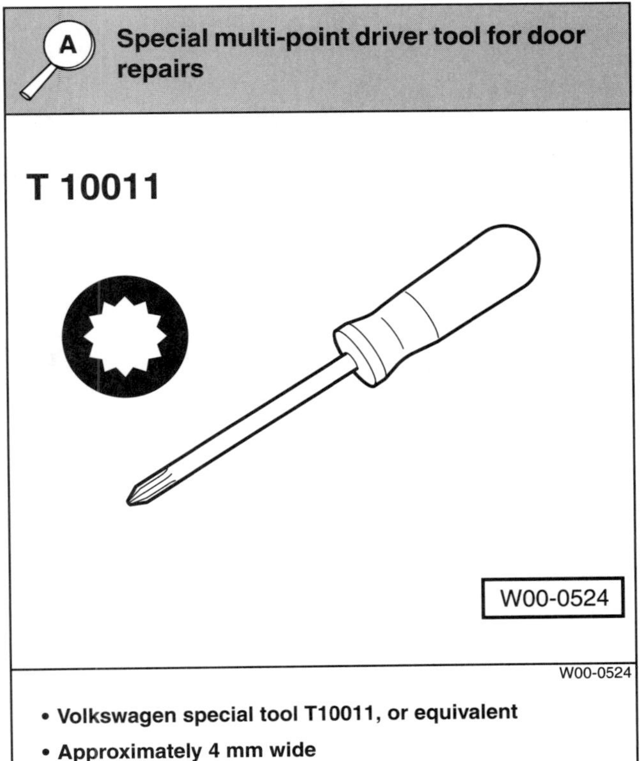

A
Special multi-point driver tool for door repairs
T 10011
W00-0524
W00-0524
• Volkswagen special tool T10011, or equivalent
• Approximately 4 mm wide

Lock cylinder housing, removing

1. Carefully pry out cover cap on edge of door. See Fig. 4.

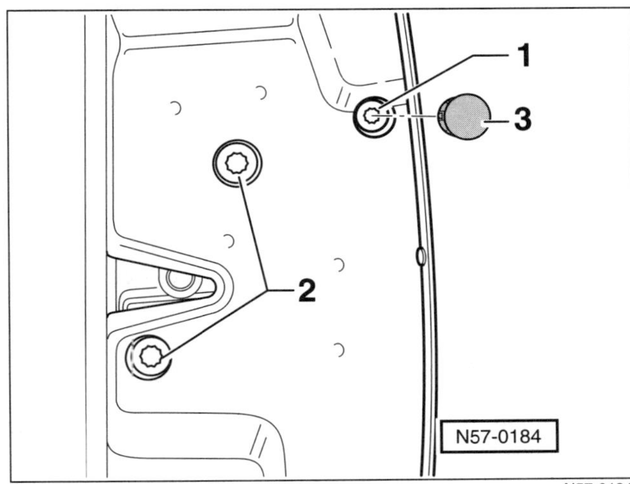

Fig. 4. Carefully pry out cover cap (**3**) to access multi-point socket head bolt (**1**). Do not loosen bolts (**2**) for door lock unit.

2. Pull door handle open and hold.
3. Loosen multi-point socket bolt to the stop with Volkswagen special tool T10011, or equivalent, to release lock cylinder housing. Lock cylinder housing is released before screw comes out. See Fig. 5.

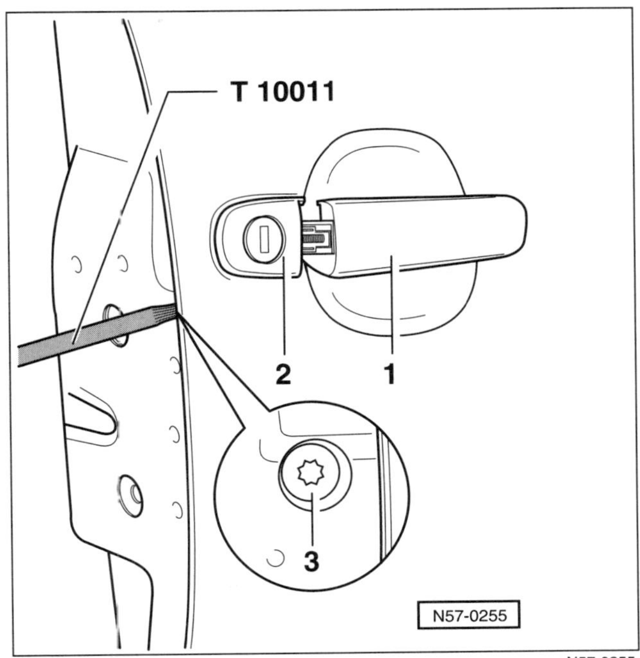

Fig. 5. Hold door handle (**1**) open and use special tool T10011 to loosen multi-point socket head bolt (**3**). Do not remove bolt but only loosen until lock cylinder housing (**2**) is released.

> **CAUTION —**
> *Loosen multi-point socket head bolt only. If screw is removed, the door lock must be removed to re-install.*

NOTE —
The door handle will remain open on its own if the multi-point socket head bolt is loosened properly.

4. Pull lock cylinder housing straight out.

NOTE —
Inserting the key into lock cylinder aids in removing the lock cylinder housing.

Lock cylinder housing, installing

1. Ensure that door handle has remained opened from the removal procedure.
2. Carefully install lock cylinder housing into opening in door.
3. Tighten multi-point socket bolt. As screw is tightened, an audible noise should be heard indicating correct seating of lock cylinder housing and tensioning of door handle spring.
4. Operate key and door handle to ensure correct operation.
5. Reinstall sealing plug.

Door handle, removing

1. Remove lock cylinder housing as described earlier.
2. Remove cable clip from door handle lock release with a pick or a small screwdriver. See Fig. 6.

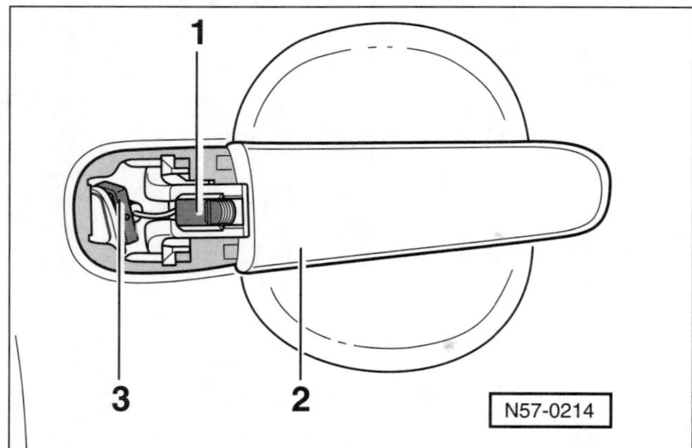

N57-0214

Fig. 6. Outside door handle (**2**) shown with lock cylinder housing removed. Pry out cable clip (**1**) with a pick or screwdriver. When installing door handle, do not pull lock operating lever (**3**).

3. Swing rear of door handle out of door, pivoting from front of handle.

NOTE —
By pivoting door handle out, door handle spring is tensioned and locked. After door handle is installed, spring tension is released.

Door handle, installing

NOTE —
Replacement door handles are supplied finished in primer only and must be painted prior to installation.

1. Place Volkswagen special tool T 10034 through door handle opening and hook it under lock spring. See Fig. 7.

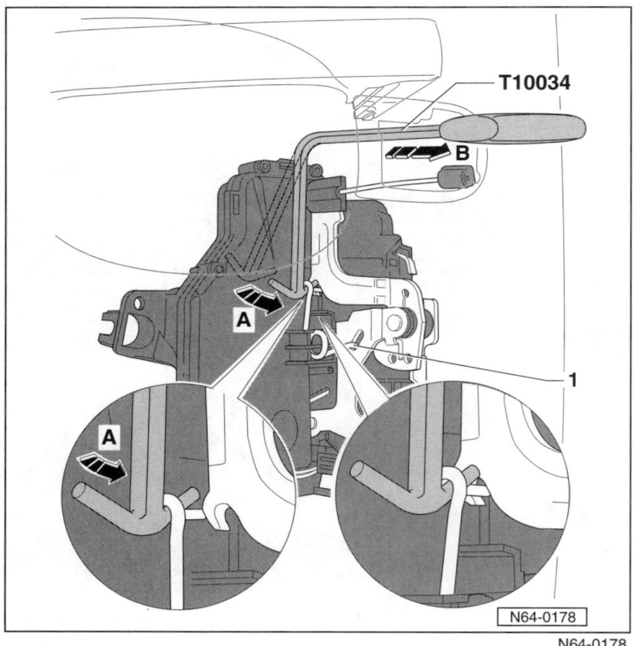

N64-0178

Fig. 7. Hook VW special tool T 10034 under (**arrow A**) lock spring (**1**) and into door lock mechanism by pulling tool (**arrow B**).

2. Position lock spring up into door lock mechanism by pulling special tool outward. See Fig. 7.
3. Slip front of door handle into door opening and swing rear of door handle into position against door.
4. Snap cable clip into slot in door handle taking care not to pull cable tight.

NOTE —
When installing cable clip, do not pull lock operating lever while pushing on door handle.

5. Install lock cylinder housing and check door handle function. Door will not open if bowden cable is not correctly installed and adjusted.

Door lock, removing

The window regulator, door glass, door speaker and door lock are secured to the door assembly carrier. The door lock can only be removed after the assembly carrier is removed.

> ***NOTE —***
> *The assembly carrier can only be removed when the door window clamping brackets of the window regulator are unscrewed. This is accomplished by lowering the door window to the height of the holes in assembly carrier and loosening the clamping brackets.*

1. Remove door trim panel. **See 70 Trim–Interior.**
2. Remove lock cylinder housing as given earlier.
3. Remove cable clip from door handle. See Fig. 8.

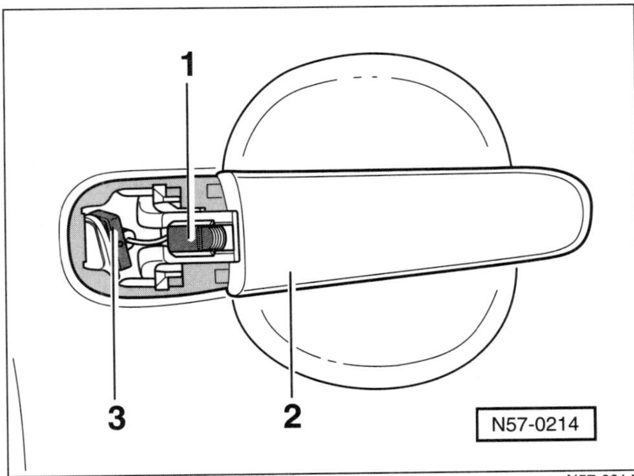

Fig. 8. Pry out cable clip (**1**) with a pick or screwdriver.

4. Pry out sealing plugs in door assembly carrier to gain access to window glass securing bolts. See Fig. 9.
5. Lower window until window glass securing bolts are accessible.

> ***NOTE —***
> *If the power window motor is not working it can be removed to allow the window to be slid down.*

6. Loosen window glass securing bolts and carefully press glass securing clamps apart.

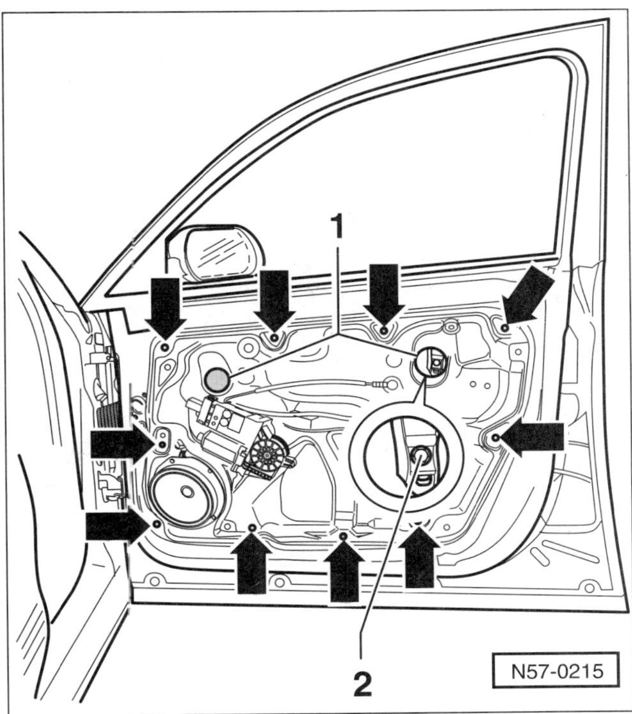

Fig. 9. Passenger side door shown with trim panel removed. Remove rubber sealing plugs (**1**) to access window glass securing bolts (**2**). Assembly carrier mounting bolts shown at **arrows**.

7. Push window glass upward in the track. Secure the window glass in up position with strips of suitable adhesive tape stuck to inside glass, looped over door frame and stuck to the outside glass.
8. Remove hood release lever on left side, as required. **See 55 Hoods and Lids.**
9. Remove lower A-pillar trim. **See 70 Body–Interior Trim.**
10. Disconnect multi-pin harness connectors and position wires out of way for removal of assembly carrier. See Fig. 10.

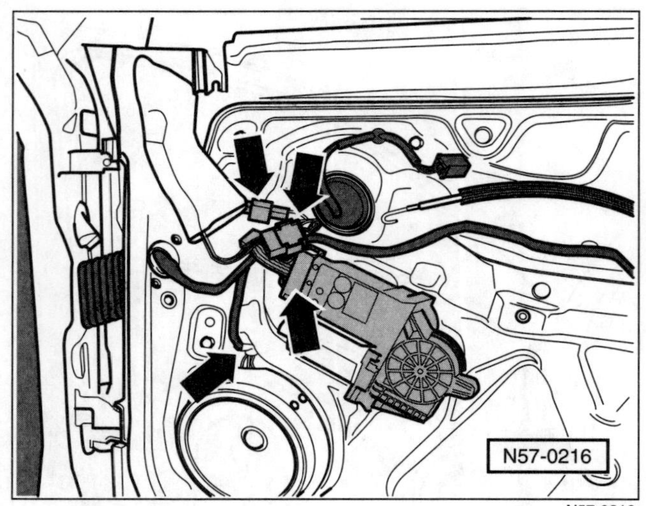

Fig. 10. Disconnect harness connectors (**arrows**) and move wiring out of way for assembly carrier removal.

11. Remove door lock mounting bolts. See Fig. 11.

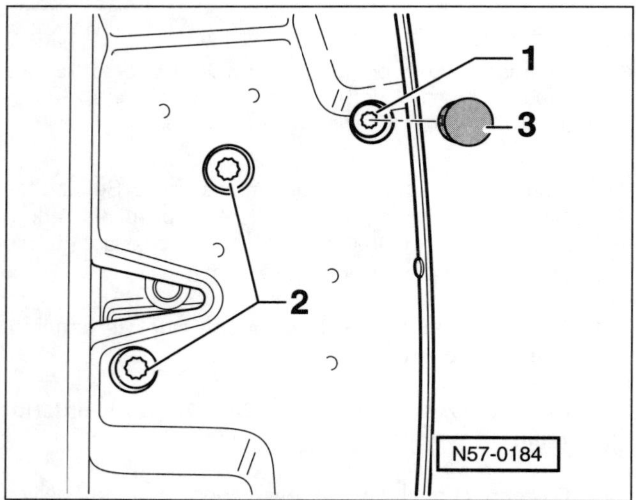

Fig. 11. Remove door lock mounting bolts (**2**) on edge of door.

12. Remove assembly carrier mounting bolts (**arrows** in Fig. 9.)

13. Pull top of door assembly carrier from door, lift and pull out of door toward hinges.

14. Turn assembly carrier and pull off connection to door lock.

15. Drive out door lock securing clips with a drift. See Fig. 12.

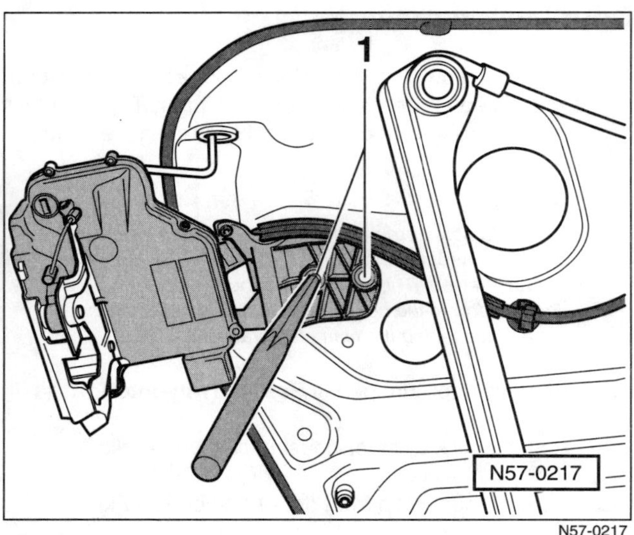

Fig. 12. Drive out clips (**1**) securing door lock to assembly carrier.

16. Disconnect inside release cable from clip on assembly carrier and carefully pry door lock off assembly carrier using a screwdriver. See Fig. 13.

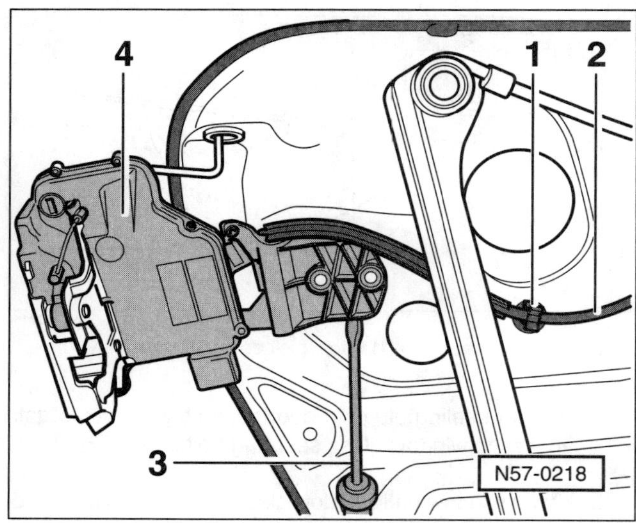

Fig. 13. Disconnect inside release cable (**2**) from clip (**1**) and pry retaining bracket for door lock (**4**) off carrier with a screwdriver (**3**).

NOTE —

The door lock retaining bracket is a separate part. It is not part of the items supplied with the door lock. It is secured to the door lock with a bolt and a pop rivet.

17. Disconnect door lock rod and inside release cable to remove door lock from assembly carrier. See Fig. 14.

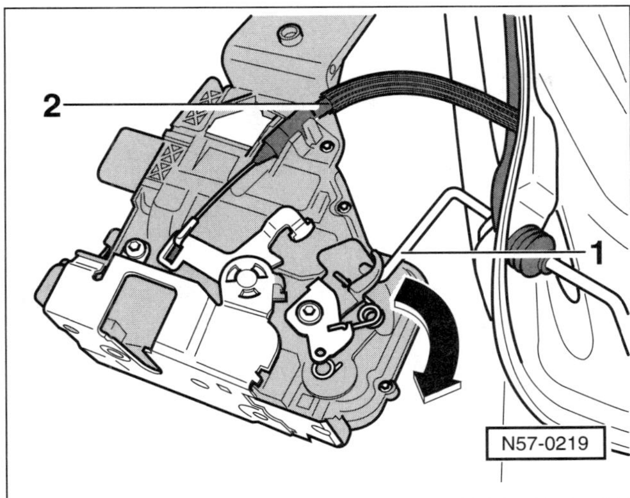

N57-0219

Fig. 14. Disconnect door lock rod (**1**) by turning door lock in direction of arrow. Unsnap inside release cable (**2**) and remove from eyelet in lever.

Door lock, installing

1. Prepare door lock assembly. See Fig. 15.

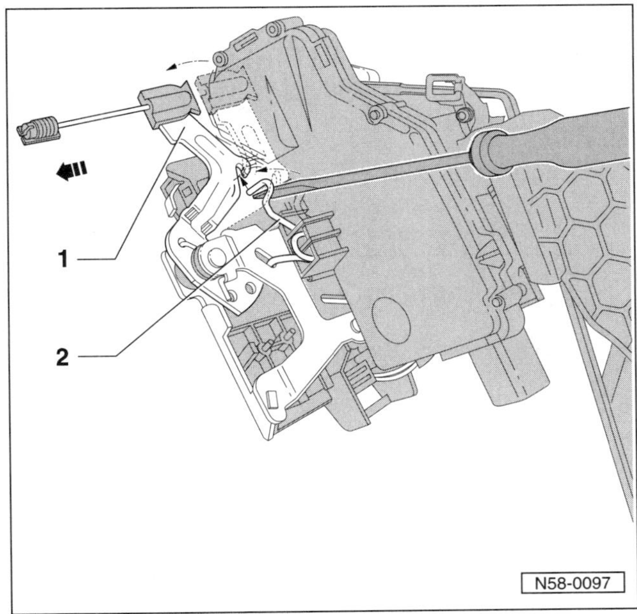

N58-0097

Fig. 15. Pull lock operating lever (**1**) in direction of **arrow**. Hook spring (**2**) into slot on operating lever, **small arrows**.

> ***NOTE —***
> *Connecting the operating lever locks the mechanism and prevents incorrect attachment of the outside handle cable later.*

2. Attach door lock rod and inside release cable.
3. Attach door lock to door assembly carrier.
4. Insert assembly carrier in door.
5. Loosely install all door carrier assembly bolts and then tighten bolts in sequence. See Fig. 16.

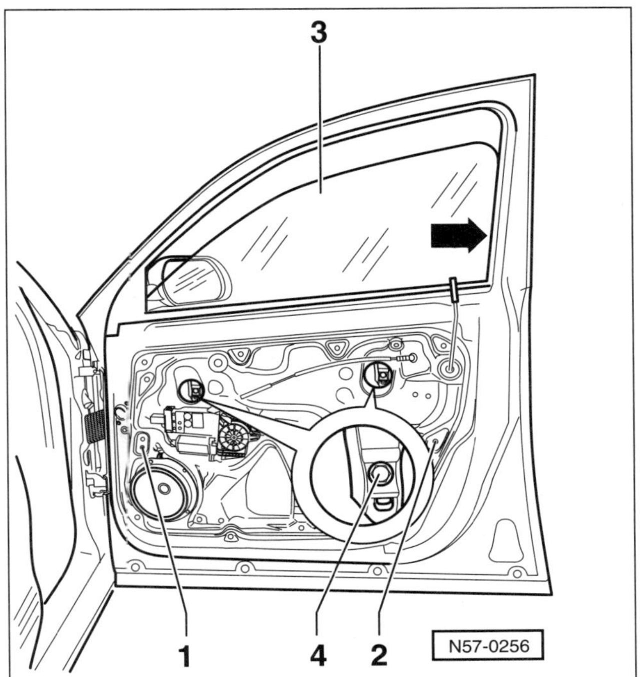

N57-0256

Fig. 16. Install assembly carrier mounting bolts and tighten bolts **1** and **2** first. Position door window (**3**) into window guide (**arrow**) and tighten window glass securing clamps (**4**).

Tightening torque
- Assembly carrier to door . . . . 8 Nm (71 ft-lb)
- Window glass securing clamp bolts . . 10 Nm (89 in-lb)

6. Remove adhesive tape securing window glass and carefully guide glass down into securing clamps.
7. Adjust window glass in securing clamps and tighten.
8. Remainder of installation is the reverse of disassembly.
9. Check operation of window before final installation of door trim panel.

Lock button, right front and left rear, removing and installing

> ***CAUTION —***
> *Failure to follow this procedure may result in loosening of the locking rods in the doors requiring complete disassembly to repair.*

1. Remove lock button by turning ½ turn (180°) counter-clockwise.
2. Pull lock button upward and off. See Fig. 17.

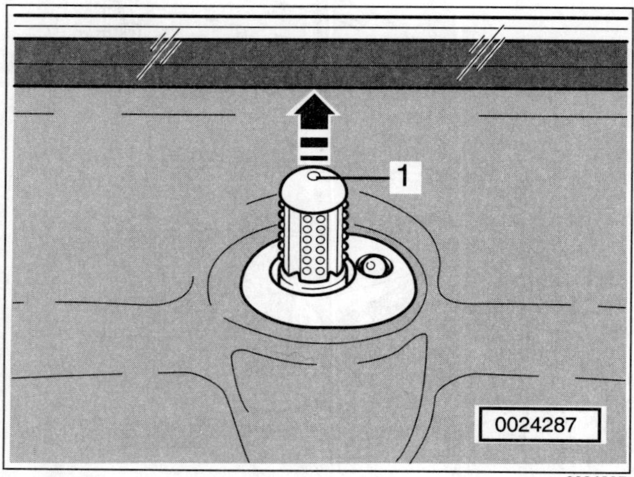

0024287

Fig. 17. Lock button shown with index (**1**) mark turned to the inside. Pull up to remove.

3. Install lock button on lock rod with index mark (small dot on top) toward vehicle interior. See Fig. 18.
4. Push lock button onto lock rod until fluted section is flush with door trim.
5. Turn lock button ½ turn (180°) counter-clockwise.

> ***NOTE —***
> *Lock button in the locked position can be flush with the door trim panel to approximately 2 mm (0.078 in.) above door trim panel.*

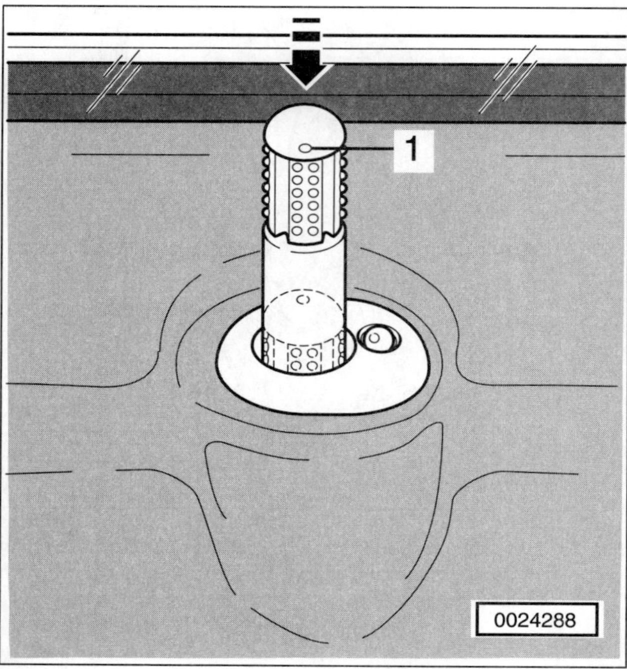

0024288

Fig. 18. Lock button shown with index mark (**1**) turned to the inside. Push button down and turn (180°).

Lock button, left front and right rear, removing and installing

> ***CAUTION —***
> *Failure to follow this procedure may result in loosening of the locking rods in the doors requiring complete disassembly to repair.*

1. Remove lock button by turning ½ turn (180°) clockwise.
2. Pull lock button upward and off. See Fig. 17.
3. Install lock button on lock rod with index mark (small dot on top) toward vehicle interior. See Fig. 18.
4. Push lock button onto lock rod until fluted section is flush with door trim.
5. Turn lock button ½ turn (180°) clockwise.

> ***NOTE —***
> *Lock button in the locked position can be flush with the door trim panel to approximately 2 mm (0.078 in.) above door trim panel.*

Door window assembly

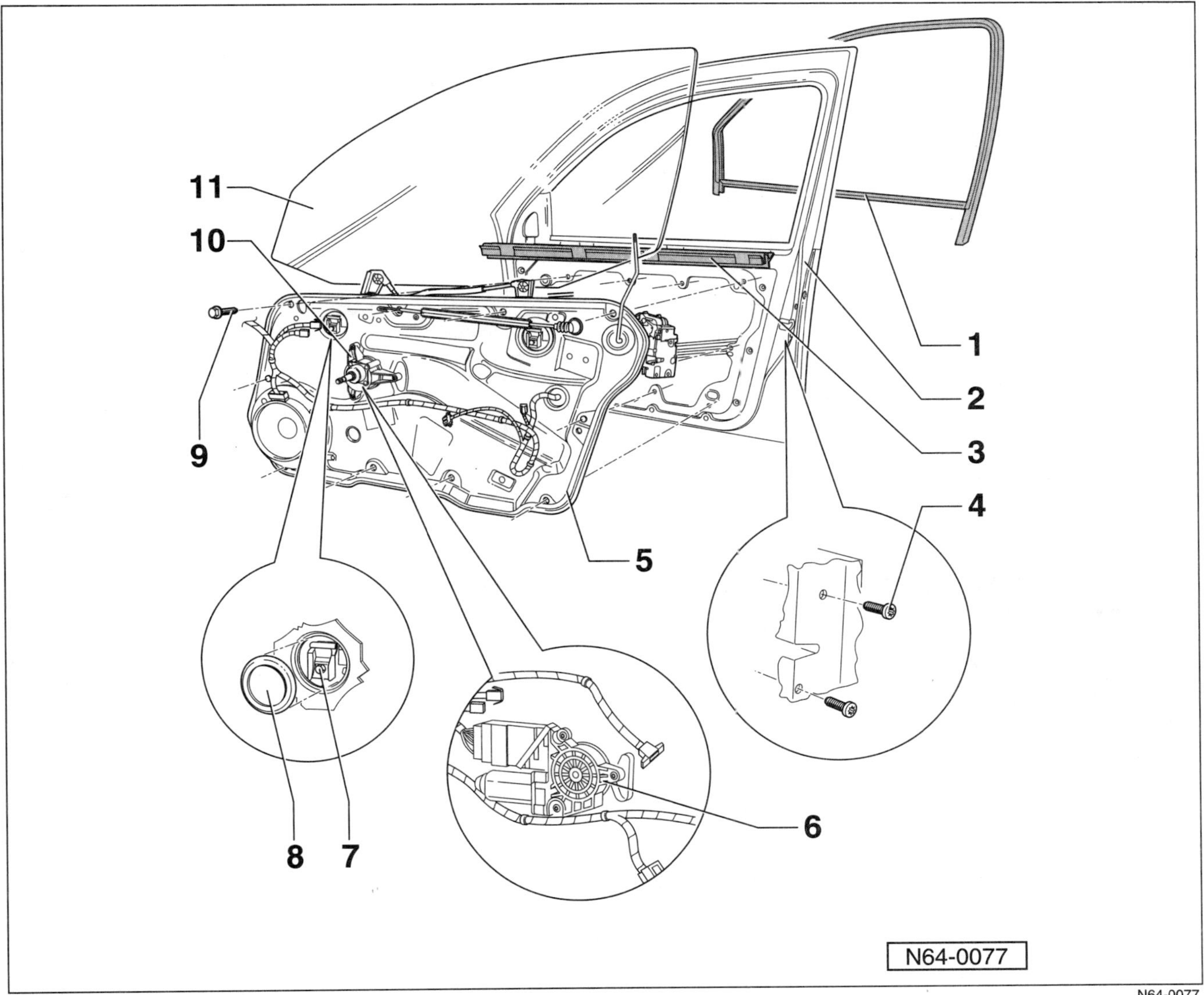

N64-0077

Fig. 19. Door window glass and related components shown for the right side. Left side is similar

1. **Window channel**
   - Pushed into door frame opening
2. **Door**
3. **Window slot seal, inner**
   - Pushed onto door frame
4. **Bolt**
   - Tighten to 20 Nm (15 ft-lb)
   - Install with locking compound
5. **Door assembly carrier**
   - Window regulator is part of assembly carrier
6. **Motor for window regulator**
   - Attached to carrier assembly from the front
7. **Bolt**
   - Tighten to 10 Nm (7 ft-lb)
8. **Cover cap**
9. **Bolt**
   - Tighten to 8 Nm (71 in-lb)
10. **Crank drive for manual window regulator**
    - Attached to carrier assembly from the front
11. **Door window**

Door window glass, removing

NOTE —

Window glass must be operable in order to remove door assembly carrier. Any malfunction that prevents the windows (manual or power) from being lowered must be corrected before proceeding.

1. Remove door trim panel. **See 70 Trim–Interior.**

2. Pry out sealing plugs in door assembly carrier to gain access to window glass securing bolts. See Fig. 20.

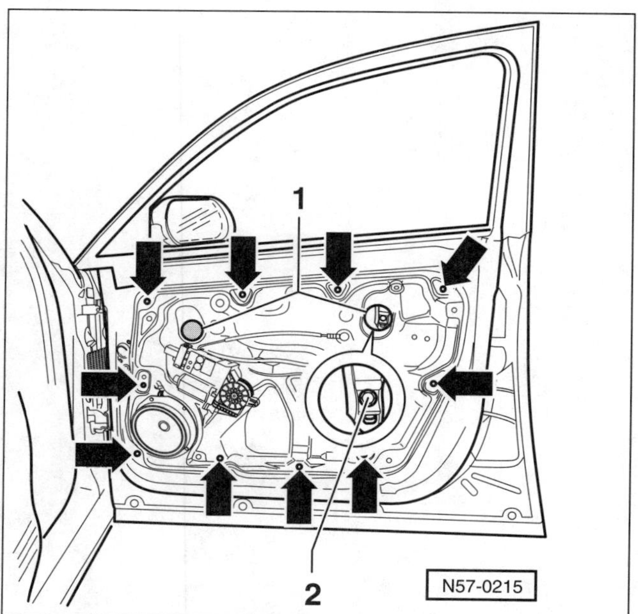

N57-0215

Fig. 20. Passenger side door shown with trim panel removed. Remove rubber sealing plugs (**1**) to access window glass securing bolts (**2**).

3. Lower window until window glass securing bolts are accessible.

NOTE —

If the power window motor is not working it can be removed to allow the window to be slid down.

4. Loosen window glass securing bolts and carefully press glass securing clamps apart.

NOTE —

If glass is being replaced due to breakage, remove door assembly carrier as given earlier and remove all broken shards of glass to prevent rattling noises in door.

5. Carefully lower the window regulator.

6. Lift the window glass up and pivot forward. See Fig. 21.

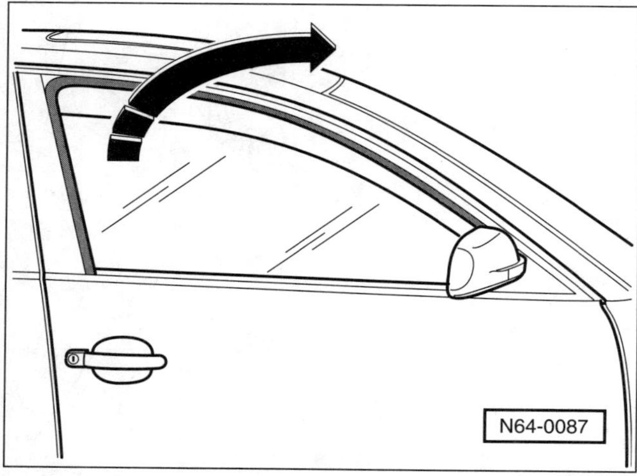

N64-0087

Fig. 21. Remove door window glass by lifting up while tilting forward (**arrow**).

7. Place removed window glass in a secure location.

Door window glass, installing

1. Slide forward part of window glass into opening and pivot glass downward, reversing the removal procedure.

2. Raise window regulator until window glass securing bolts are visible in access holes on door assembly carrier.

3. Guide glass down into securing clamps and adjust window glass in securing clamps and tighten. See Fig. 22.

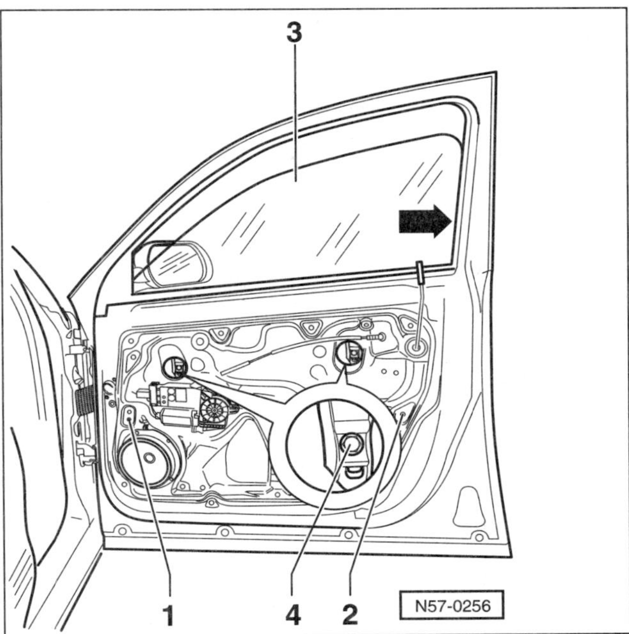

N57-0256

Fig. 22. Gently press window (**3**) in direction of **arrow** and tighten securing clamp bolts (**4**). Items **1** and **2** in illustration are not applicable

4. Remainder of installation is the reverse of disassembly.

5. Check operation of window before final installation of door trim panel.

Tightening torque
- Window glass securing bolts . . . . 10 Nm (89 in-lb)

COMFORT SYSTEM

The vehicles covered by this manual are available with central locking, anti-theft alarm system, keyless remote system and power mirrors. This combination of inter-connected systems is known as the Comfort System. See Fig. 23.

NOTE —
- *The comfort system features built-in diagnostic circuitry that detects and stores Diagnostic Trouble Code (DTC) information. When the system detects a fault, a DTC is generated and stored in the comfort system central control module memory. This may result in failure of the system to operate properly. Proper diagnosis of fault codes can be accessed through the data link connector using Volkswagen scan tool VAG 1551/1552 or equivalent.*
- *Additional diagnostic information is available in a data-stream format to aid in troubleshooting. This valuable information can only be accessed by scan tools such as the Volkswagen VAG 1551/1552 or equivalent. Evaluation and interpretation of this information fall outside the scope of this service manual.*
- *Volkswagen identifies electrical components by a letter and/or a number in the electrical schematics. See* **97 Wiring Diagrams, Fuses and Relays**. *These electrical identifiers are listed in parenthesis as an aid to electrical troubleshooting.*

Comfort system and central locking, component overview

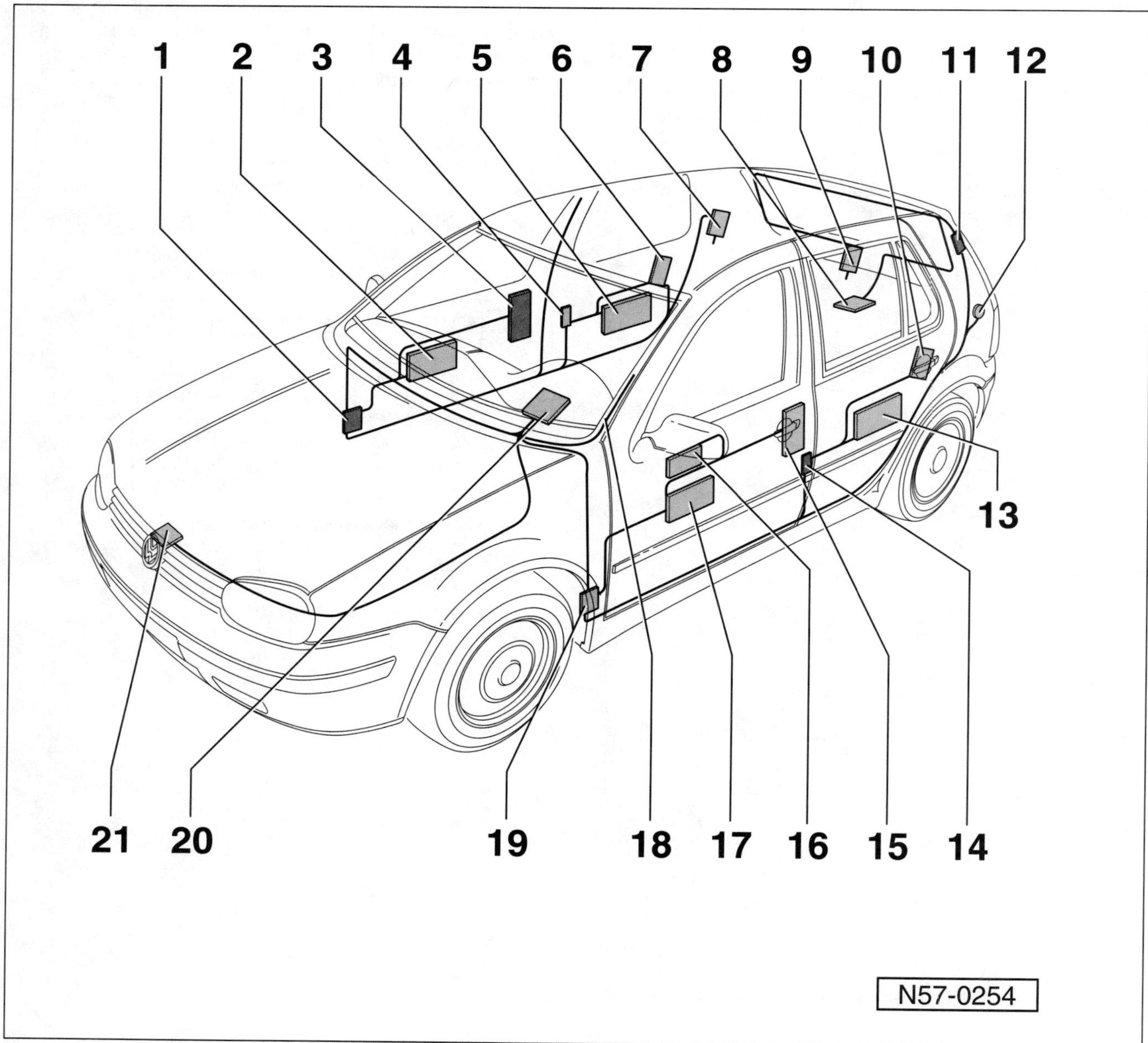

N57-0254

Fig. 23. Overview of major components of central locking, power windows, anti-theft alarm and keyless remote system.

1. **Connector station**
   - Location: right side lower A-pillar, **see** Ⓐ
2. **Door control module, front right**
   - For comfort system only
   - Integrated into window motor
3. **Lock unit, front right**
   - Secured to assembly carrier
   - Electric central locking is integrated into door lock module
4. **Connector station**
   - Location: lower B-pillar

(continued from previous page)

5. **Door control module, right rear**
   - For comfort system only
   - Integrated into window motor
6. **Door lock, right rear**
   - Secured to assembly carrier
   - Electric central locking is integrated into door lock module
7. **Motor, fuel tank filler flap (V155)**
   - Location: under C-pillar trim
8. **Rear lid lock**
   - Bolted to rear lid
   - Remove with special socket T 10010
9. **Rear lid actuator**
   - Bolted to rear lid
   - Remove with special socket T 10010
10. **Door lock, left rear**
    - Secured to assembly carrier
    - Electric central locking is integrated into door lock module
11. **Connector station**
    - Location: rear roof area, covered by roof trim
12. **Anti-theft alarm horn**
    - Location: in area of C-pillar, covered by trim
13. **Door control module, left rear**
    - For comfort system only
    - Integrated into window motor
14. **Connector station**
    - Location: lower B-pillar
15. **Door lock, left front**
    - Secured to assembly carrier
    - Electric central locking is integrated into door lock module
16. **Controls**
    - Installed in door trim
17. **Door control module, left front**
    - For comfort system only
    - Integrated into window motor
18. **Antenna for radio frequency remote control**
    - Under left A-pillar trim
19. **Connector station**
    - Location: lower A-pillar, covered by trim in footwell
20. **Central control module**
    - Bolted to bracket on steering column under instrument panel
21. **Hood lock**
    - Contact switch for anti-theft alarm
    - Location: in lock carrier

A Connector station in A-pillar

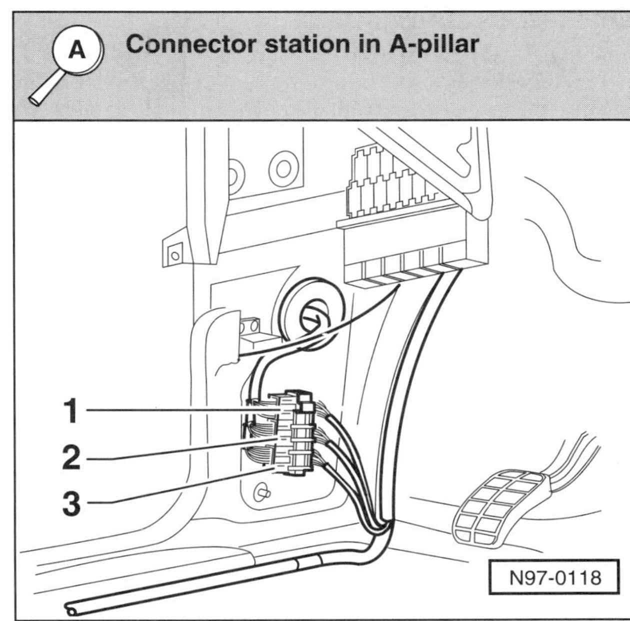

N97-0118

- **Connector station is located in the front footwell behind trim panel. Driver side shown, passenger side is a mirror image of above.**

Terminal identification:

1 - Central locking

2 - Electric windows, red

3 - electric mirror adjustment, blue

Keyless remote control

A battery-powered keyless remote transmitter is included with all vehicles equipped with the keyless remote system. Up to 4 keyless remotes can be purchased and programmed into the system. See Fig. 24.

The four functions of the keyless remote transmitter are:

- Lock the vehicle and arm the alarm.
- Unlock the vehicle and disarm the alarm.
- Disarm the alarm and open the trunk or hatch. The system will rearm when the trunk or hatch is closed if the alarm system had previously been armed.
- Red panic button to trigger the alarm at any time.

The selective unlock feature of the central locking and the convenience close feature of the power windows do not function with the keyless remote system.

As a security feature, if the vehicle has been unlocked using the keyless remote transmitter and a door is not opened within approximately 30 seconds, the system will re-lock all of the doors and re-arm the alarm system.

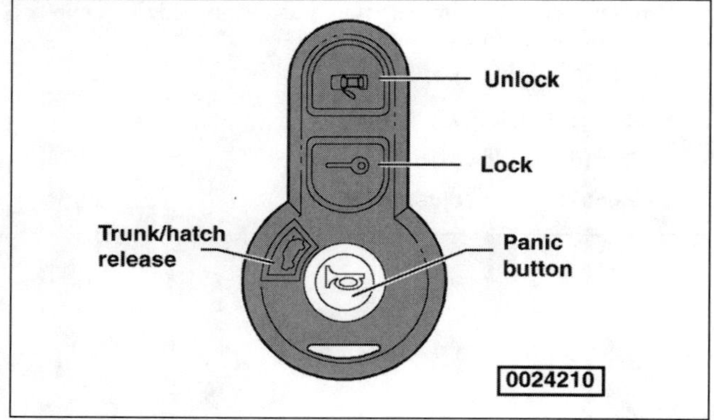

0024210

Fig. 24. Four function keyless remote transmitter.

QUALITY REVIEW

When you have finished working on the vehicle, it is advisable to take a moment to quality check or review your work. This helps to insure that the operation or repair has been completed properly with all affected systems functioning within normal parameters. These may include the following:

- Ensure that all cable ties and clamps that were removed as part of the repair are replaced.
- Ensure that all fasteners and hardware were replaced and torqued as specified.
- Make sure that all other components involved in the repair are positioned correctly and function properly.
- Make sure that all tools, shop cloths, fender covers and protective tapes are removed before closing the hood.
- Clean grease and fingerprints from painted surfaces, steering wheel and shifter.
- Unlock anti-theft radio and reset the clock.

58 Rear Doors

GENERAL

This repair group covers removal and installation of the rear door assemblies, the rear door glass and window regulators, and service to the rear door lock assemblies. Special tools and equipment are required for some operations. For removal of door trim panels see **70 Trim–Interior**.

> ***WARNING —***
> *Disconnecting the negative (–) battery cable may erase fault codes and basic settings in the engine management and automatic transmission control modules. Some driveability problems may be noticed until the system re-adapts to operating conditions. OBD II readiness codes, which may be required for emissions testing, may also be erased. Convenience electronics (alarm system, interior light control, power locks, mirrors, and windows) may need to be re-set using a VAG 1551/1552 or equivalent scan tool.*

DOORS

The doors are designed with a split hinge that can be slid apart. After disconnecting the appropriate electrical connectors and the door check, the complete door can easily be removed from the vehicle as required. For an overview of the rear door hinges, latches and related components, see Fig. 1. Most of the internal components of the doors including the window regulators and window glass are assembled into a modular assembly known as a door assembly carrier.

Rear door assembly

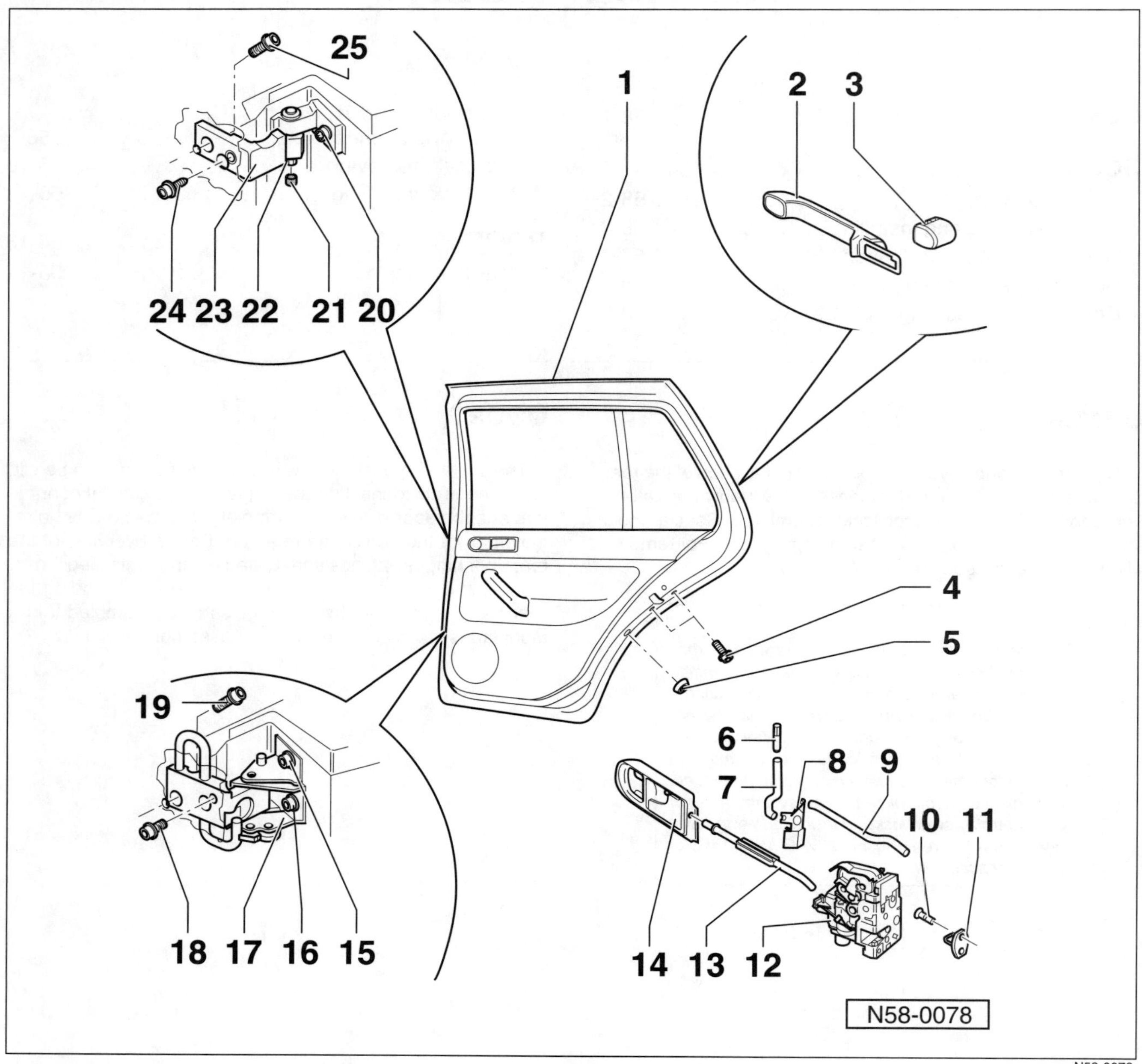

N58-0078

Fig. 1. Door hinges, latches and related components shown for the right side. Left side is similar.

> ***NOTE —***
> *Always replace the hinge bolts if loosened.*

1. **Door**
2. **Door handle with base**
3. **Lock cylinder housing**
4. **Bolt**
   - Tighten to 18 Nm (13 ft-lb)
   - Install with locking compound
5. **Cover cap**
6. **Locking button**
7. **Locking rod**
8. **Bell crank**
9. **Locking rod**
10. **Bolt**
    - Tighten to 20 Nm (15 ft-lb)

(continued from previous page)

11. Striker plate

12. Door lock assembly

13. Bowden cable

14. Interior release handle

15. Multi-point socket head bolt
- M8 x 28
- Tighten to 20 Nm (15 ft-lb) + ¼ turn (90°)
- Always replace bolt after loosening

16. Multi-point socket head bolt
- M8 x 28
- Only remove this bolt from hinge to remove door
- Tighten to 20 Nm (15 ft-lb) + ¼ turn (90°)
- Always replace bolt after loosening

17. Door hinge with check
- Hinge is divided

18. Multi-point socket head bolt
- M8 x 28
- Install from inside vehicle
- Remove B-pillar lower trim, see **70 Trim–Interior**
- Tighten to 20 Nm (15 ft-lb) + ¼ turn (90°)
- Always replace bolt after loosening

19. Multi-point socket head bolt
- M8 x 28
- Tighten to 20 Nm (15 ft-lb) + ¼ turn (90°)
- Always replace bolt after loosening

20. Multi-point socket head bolt
- M8 x 28
- Tighten to 20 Nm (15 ft-lb) + ¼ turn (90°)
- Always replace bolt after loosening

21. Cover cap

22. Bolt
- Tighten to 13 Nm (10 ft-lb)

23. Door hinge
- Hinge is divided

24. Multi-point socket head bolt
- M8 x 22
- Install from inside vehicle
- To loosen or tighten bolt, remove B-pillar lower trim, see **70 Trim–Interior**
- Tighten to 20 Nm (15 ft-lb) + ¼ turn (90°)
- Always replace bolt after loosening

25. Multi-point socket head bolt
- M8 x 28
- Tighten to 20 Nm (15 ft-lb) + ¼ turn (90°)
- Always replace bolt after loosening

Door, removing and installing

The following steps refer to Fig. 2.

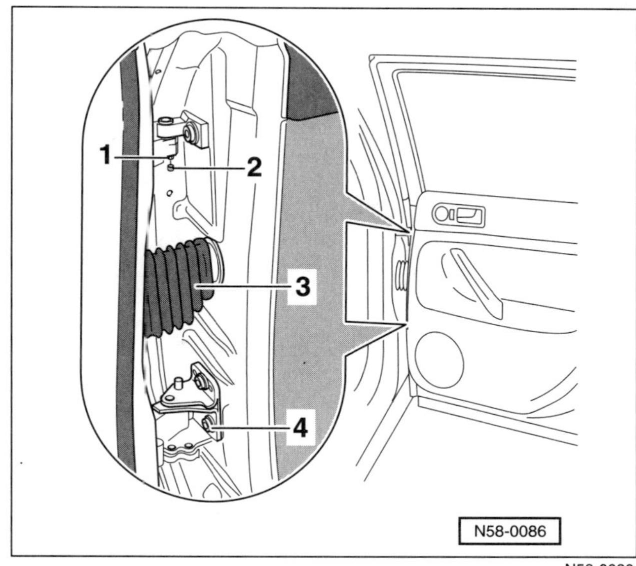

N58-0086

Fig. 2. Various components involved in rear door removal.

1. Remove lower B-pillar upper and lower trim, see **70 Trim–Interior**.

2. Disconnect harness connectors under rubber boot (item **3** above) on B-pillar.

> ***CAUTION —***
> *Do not close door with harness connectors between door and B-pillar. They will be crushed.*

3. Pry off cover cap (item **2** above) and remove bolt (item **1** above) from upper hinge.

4. Remove lower bolt (item **4** above) from hinge. Always replace this bolt upon installation.

5. Carefully lift door upward and out of hinge brackets.

6. Installation is the reverse of removal. The hinges must be loosened to adjust the door. Use VW special tool 3320 door adjusting wrench and 3320/2 box spanner to adjust the door.

Tightening torques
- Upper hinge bolt . . . . 13 Nm (10 ft-lb)
- Lower hinge bolt (always replace) . . . . . . 20 Nm (15 ft-lb) + ¼ turn (90°)

Door handle and lock assembly

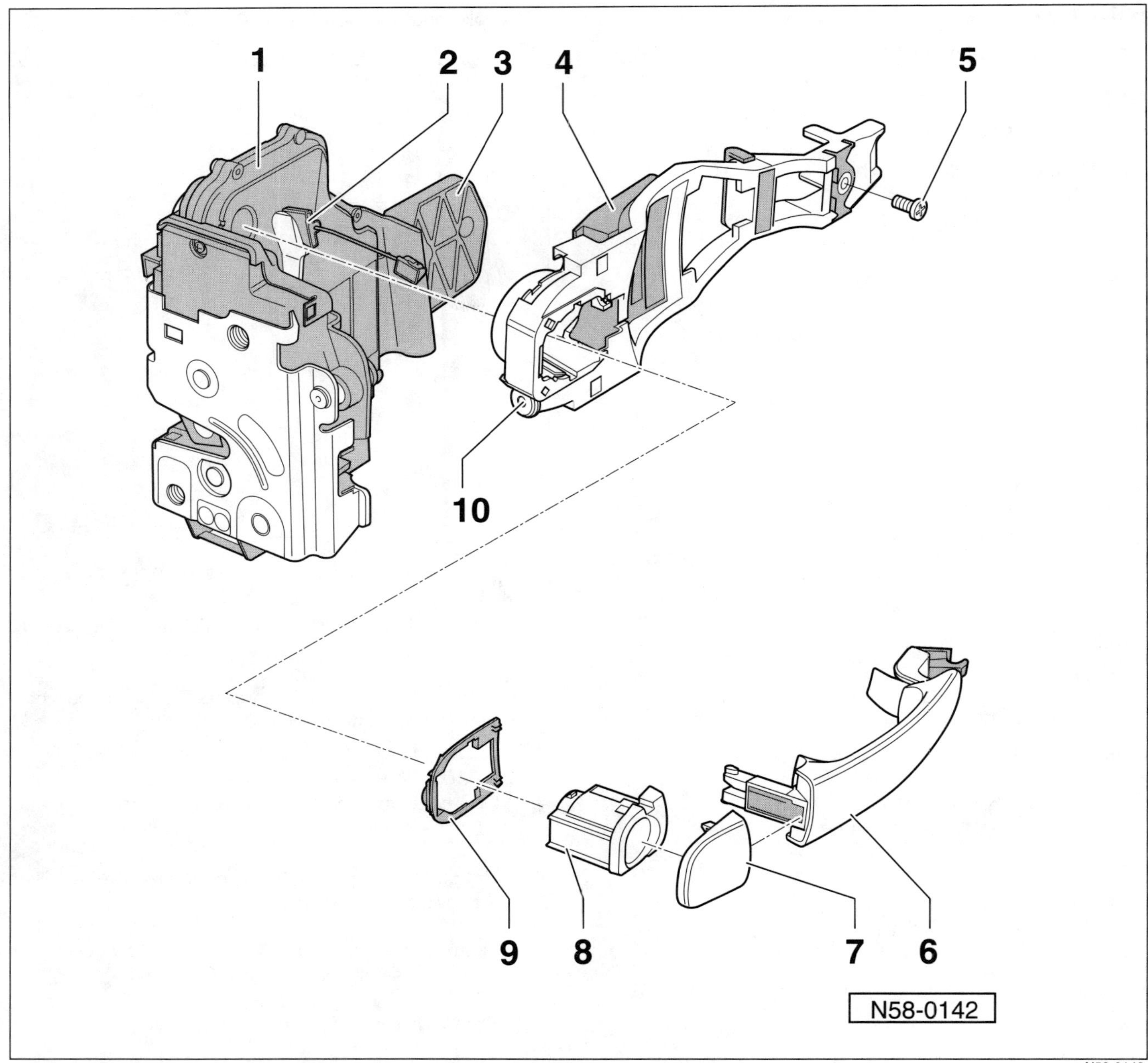

Fig. 3. Right side door lock, outside door handle and related components. Left side is similar.

1. **Door lock**
   - The door lock can only be removed with the carrier assembly
2. **Cable**
   - Outside door handle release
3. **Retaining bracket**
   - Bolted and riveted to carrier assembly and door lock
   - Not supplied with replacement door lock
4. **Handle bracket**
   - Removing:
     Door handle, lock cylinder housing and assembly carrier are removed first
     Remove screw (item 5) and slide bracket slightly to rear and remove from door
5. **Screw**

(continued from previous page)

6. **Door handle with base**
7. **Lock cylinder cover (trim)**
8. **Lock cylinder housing**
9. **Gasket**
10. **Multi-point socket head bolt**
    - Requires special socket insert tool T10011 or equivalent, **see** Ⓐ
    - Loosening this screw releases the lock cylinder housing, allowing it to be pulled out of handle bracket.
    - Bolt must not be threaded in without lock cylinder housing installed or locking ring may fall into door.

> ***CAUTION —***
> *Loosen multi-point socket head bolt only. If bolt is removed, door lock must be removed to realign.*

Ⓐ Special multi-point driver tool for door repairs

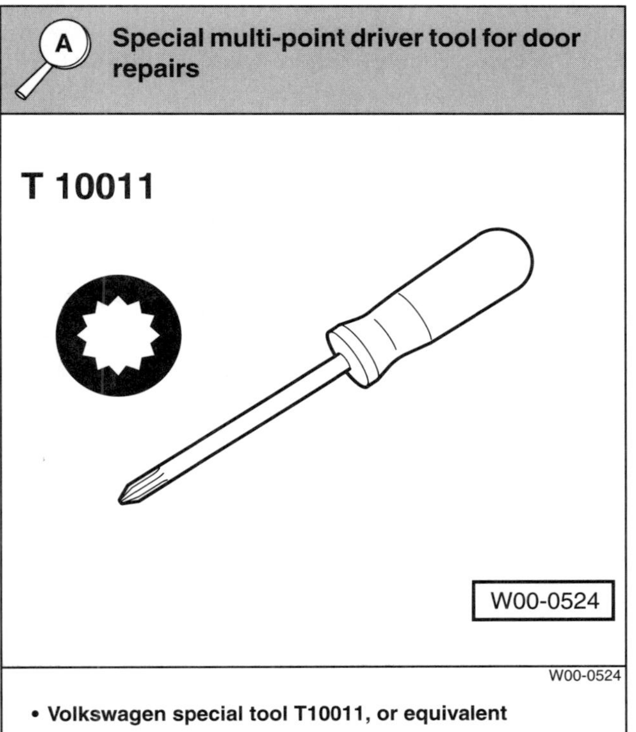

W00-0524

- **Volkswagen special tool T10011, or equivalent**
- **Approximately 4 mm wide**

Door handle, removing

1. Pull door seal away from door edge in area of door handle.

2. Pull door handle to open position and hold. Unscrew door handle mounting bolt to stop with VW special tool socket insert T 10011, or equivalent. This releases the lock cylinder housing.

> ***CAUTION —***
> *Loosen multi-point socket head bolt only. If bolt is removed, door lock must be removed to realign.*

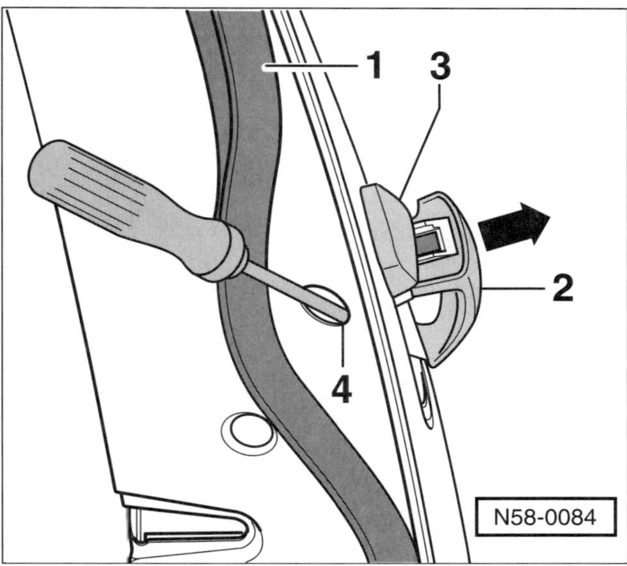

N58-0084

Fig. 4. Peel back door seal (**1**) and pull door handle (**2**) in direction of **arrow**. Unscrew mounting bolt (**4**) and until lock cylinder (**3**) is released.

3. Pull out lock cylinder housing at right angles to door.

4. Remove cable clip from door handle lock release with a pick or a small screwdriver. See Fig. 5.

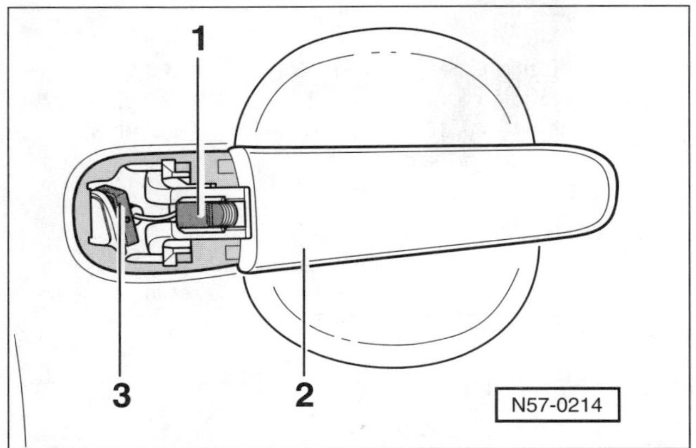

N57-0214

Fig. 5. Outside door handle (**2**) shown with lock cylinder housing removed. Pry out cable clip (**1**) with a pick or screwdriver. When installing door handle, do not pull lock operating lever (**3**).

5. Swing rear of door handle out of door, pivoting from front of handle.

> ***NOTE —***
> *By pivoting door handle out, door handle spring is tensioned and locked. After door handle is installed, spring tension is released.*

Door handle, installing

> ***NOTE —***
> *Replacement door handles are supplied finished in primer only and must be painted prior to installation.*

1. Place Volkswagen special tool T 10034 through door handle opening and hook it under lock spring. See Fig. 6.
2. Position lock spring up into door lock mechanism by pulling special tool outward. See Fig. 6.

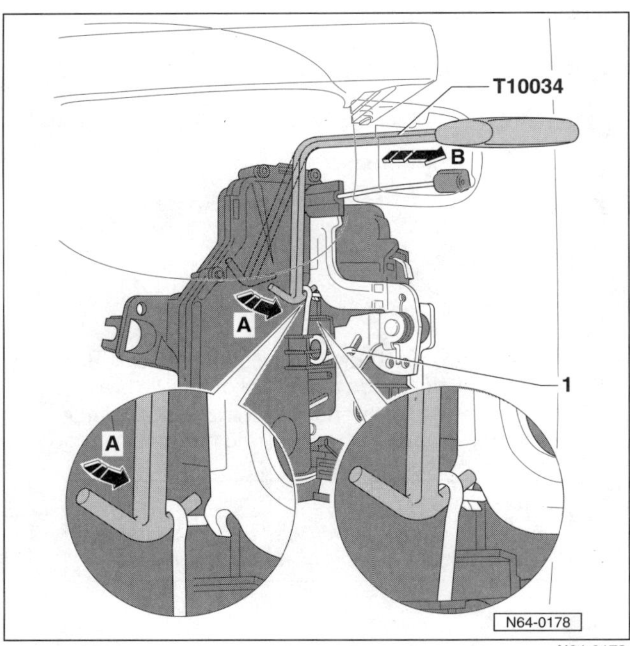

N64-0178

Fig. 6. Hook VW special tool T 10034 under (**arrow A**) lock spring (**1**) and into door lock mechanism by pulling tool (**arrow B**).

3. Slip front of door handle into door opening and swing rear of door handle into position against door.
4. Snap cable clip into slot in door handle taking care not to pull cable tight.

> ***NOTE —***
> *When installing cable clip, do not pull lock operating lever while pushing on door handle.*

5. Install lock cylinder housing and check door handle function. Door will not open if bowden cable is not correctly installed and adjusted.

Rear door windows, removing and installing

1. Remove door trim panel. **See 70 Trim–Interior.**

2. Pry out sealing plug in door assembly carrier to gain access to window glass securing bolts. See Fig. 7.

3. Lower window until window glass spreader pin and spreader plug are accessible through cut-out in window regulator.

NOTE —
If the power window motor is not working it can be removed to allow the window to be slid down.

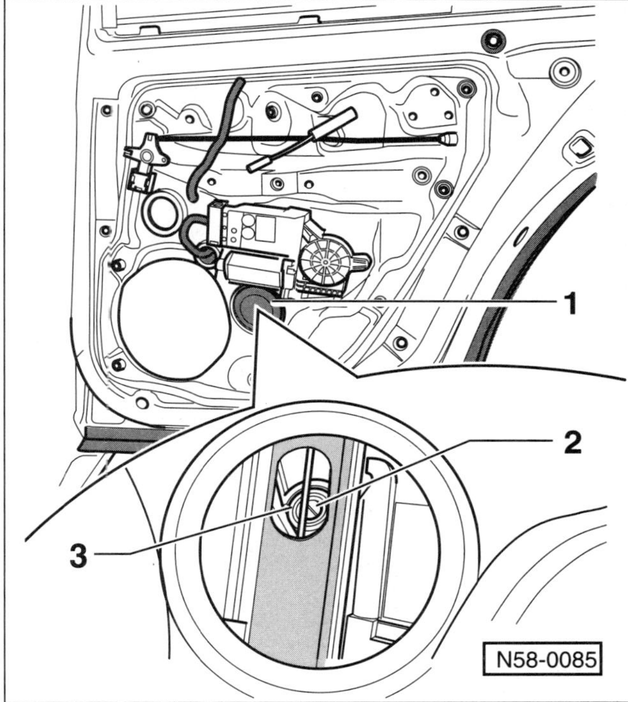

N58-0085

Fig. 7. Passenger side door shown with trim panel removed. Remove rubber sealing plug (**1**) to access window glass spreader pin (**2**) and spreader plug (**3**).

4. Thread a 5 mm bolt (approx. 70 mm long) into the window spreader pin and pull pin out from spreader plug.

5. Thread an 8 mm bolt (approx. 80 mm long) into spreader plug.

NOTE —
Use only light pressure when threading bolt into spreader plug or the plug may fall into the door.

6. Pull spreader plug out from window guide and window while pressing regulator bowden cable out of way with a screwdriver.

7. Pull window seal away from quarter window frame.

8. Pry out cover cap and remove quarter window mounting bolt. See Fig. 8.

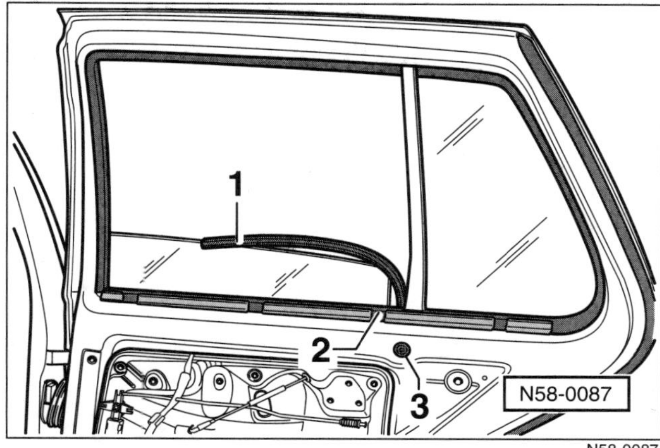

N58-0087

Fig. 8. Pull seal (**1**) away from quarter window frame down to door window shaft seal (**2**). Pry out cover (**3**) and remove bolt underneath.

9. Use screwdriver to lift locking tab at bottom of quarter window frame. Pull out filler piece below locking tab. See Fig. 9.

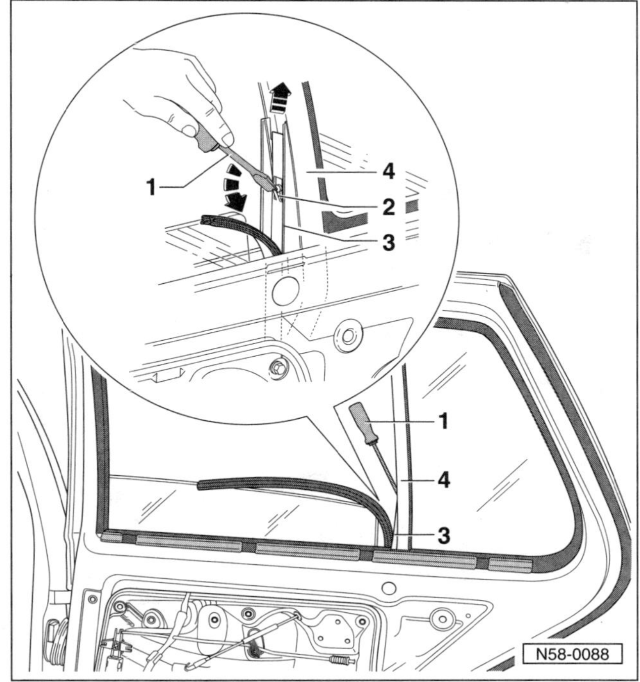

N58-0088

Fig. 9. Lift locking tab (**2**) and pull out filler piece (**3**) from quarter window frame (**4**).

10. Grip door window shaft inner seal with pliers and twist inward and down slightly to pull seal out of door flange. See Fig. 10.

NOTE—
Use of a plastic wedge will help window shaft seal pull away and prevent damage to door from pliers.

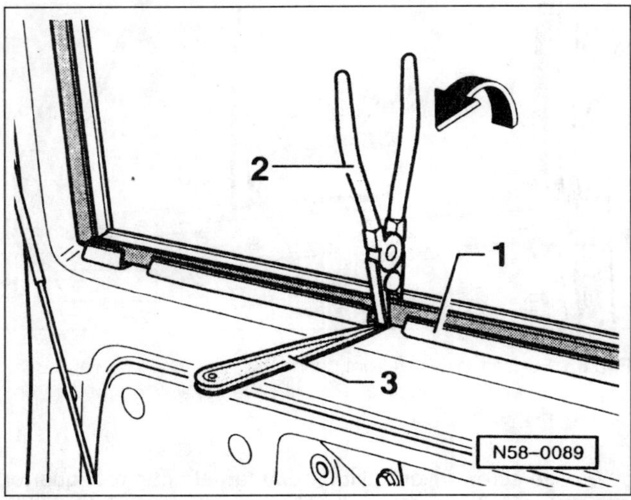

Fig. 10. Grip window shaft inner seal (**1**) with pliers (**2**). Rotate pliers in direction of **arrow** while lifting seal out of door flange. Use of a plastic wedge (**3**) is advised.

11. Slide door window upward and pull inward out of door. See Fig. 11.

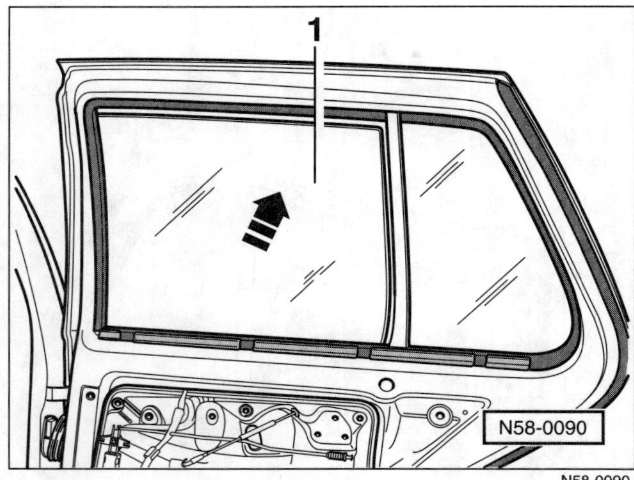

Fig. 11. Slide door window up and pull inward from door frame.

12. Place door window glass in a safe place.

13. To continue with quarter widow removal, pull window guide off in area of upper quarter window frame. See Fig. 12.

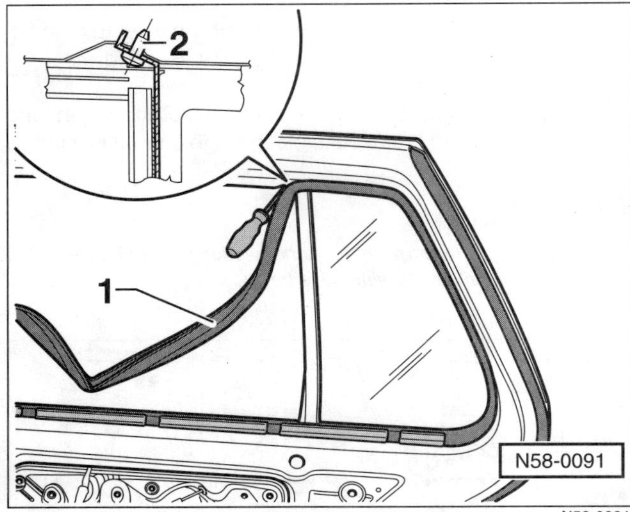

Fig. 12. Pull window frame guide (**1**) down near quarter window frame. Remove screw (**2**) at top of frame, if installed.

NOTE—
The screw at the top of the quarter window frame is gradually being discontinued by the factory. The quarter window frame without a screw is just clipped into the top of door.

14. Remove quarter window frame lower mounting bolt from edge of door. See Fig. 13.

15. Remove quarter window frame as shown in Fig. 13.

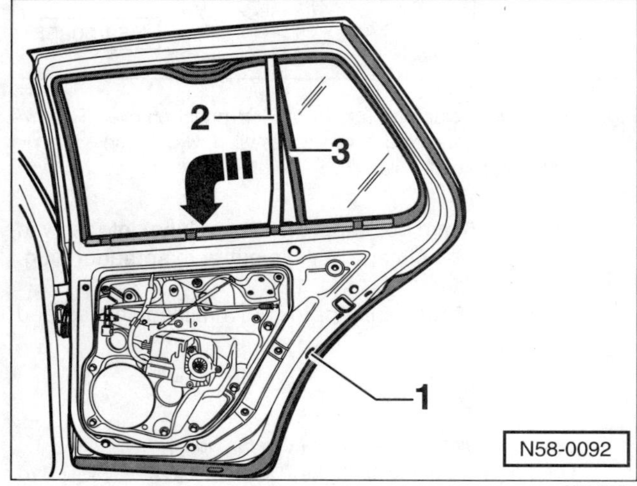

Fig. 13. Remove bolt (**1**) and pivot quarter window frame (**2**) off from quarter window seal (**3**). Pull quarter window frame down from upper window guide.

NOTE —

If the rear door window and quarter window frame are being removed in order to remove the door lock assembly, proceed to **Door lock, removing** *at this point. To continue with removal of rear quarter window proceed with the steps below.*

16. Pull window guide off door flange. Turn lower area of window guide 90° toward exterior and pull window shaft seal upward off door. See Fig. 14.

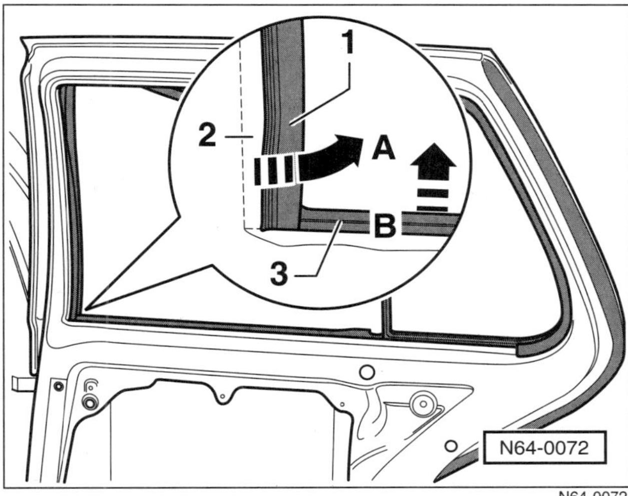

Fig. 14. Pull off window guide (**1**) from door flange (**2**) by rotating 90° (**arrow A**). Remove window shaft seal upward (**arrow B**).

17. Remove quarter window from door by rotating out of door frame. See Fig. 15.

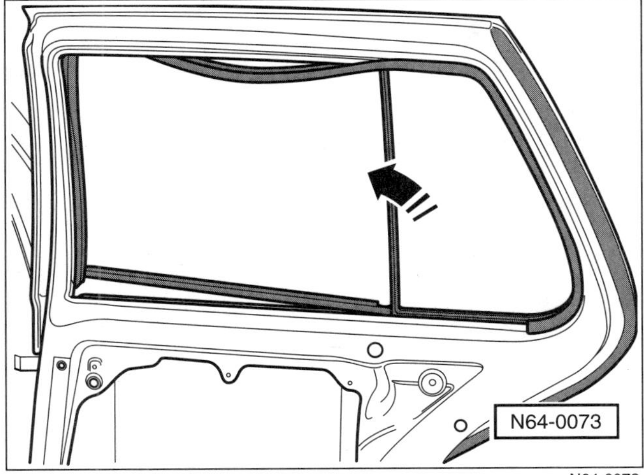

Fig. 15. Remove rear quarter window in direction of **arrow**.

18. To install quarter window, insert into door frame.

NOTE —

Dishwashing soap can be used as a lubricant to help install the quarter window.

19. Install window guide into window shaft by rotating 90° from exterior. Press bottom of window shaft seal downward onto door flange and press into door frame. See Fig. 16.

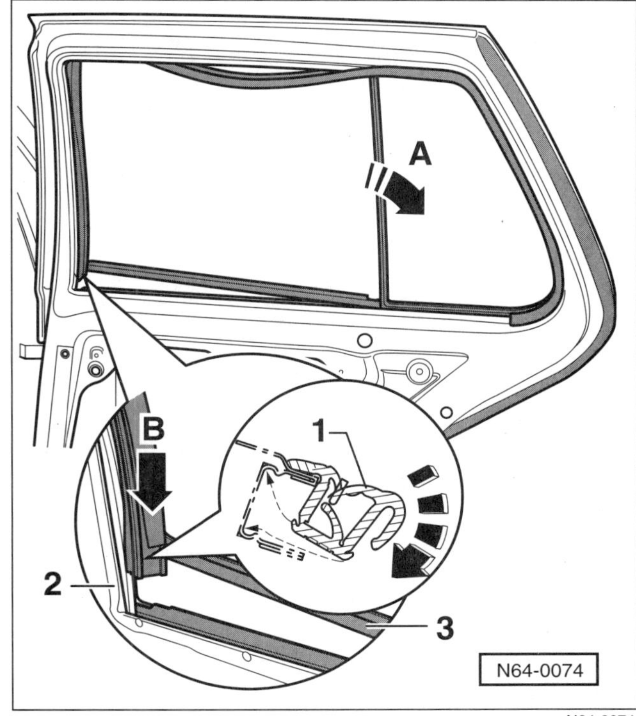

Fig. 16. Insert quarter window (arrow A). Install window guide (**1**) into window shaft by rotating down 90° (**arrow**) from exterior. Press bottom of window shaft seal downward (**arrow B**) onto door flange (**2**) and press into door frame.

20. Install quarter window frame and door window guide in reverse order of removal.

21. Install door window into door and insert spreader plug and spreader pin into window. See Fig. 17.
    - Position spreader plug projection on each side of window.
    - Guide window into door.
    - Insert window into lift rail guides slot.
    - Lightly tap top of window so that window is positioned properly in lift rail.

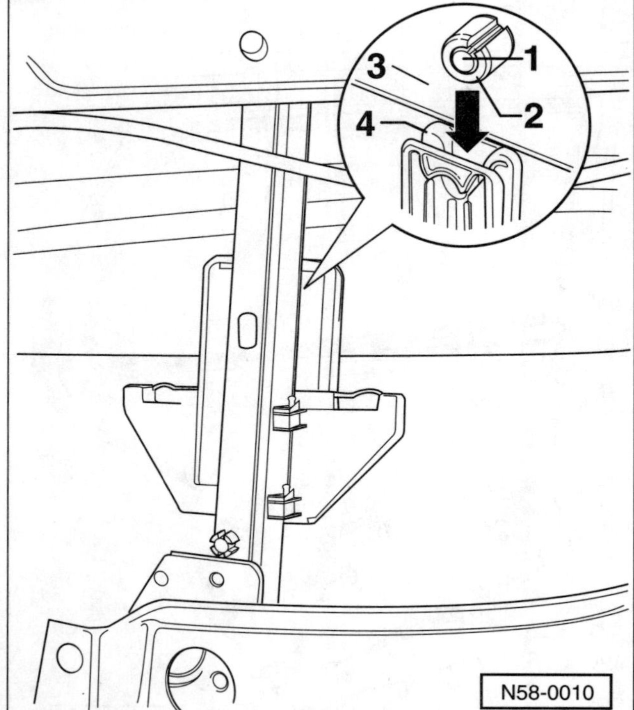

N58-0010

Fig. 17. Insert spreader plug (**2**) and spreader pin (**1**) into window. Guide window into door and insert into lift rail guide slot (**4**). Lightly tap top of window to seat in lift rail (**arrow**).

22. Guide electrical wiring through boot in door and secure retaining clips in door panel.

23. Loosely install all door carrier assembly bolts and then tighten two bolts shown in Fig. 18. Tighten remaining bolts to specification.

Tightening torque
- Assembly carrier to door .... 8 Nm (71 in-lb)

24. Check for proper operation of door window before installing interior door panel.

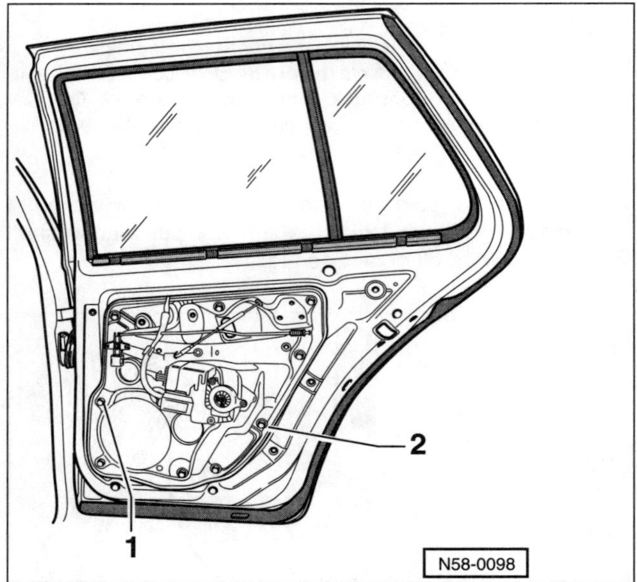

N58-0098

Fig. 18. Install assembly carrier and tighten bolts (**1** and **2**) first.

Door lock, removing

The window regulator, door glass, door speaker and door lock are secured to the door assembly carrier. The door lock can only be removed after the door assembly carrier is removed. Additionally, the rear door window and the rear quarter window frame must also be removed for sufficient clearance in door to remove lock unit.

1. Remove door trim panel. **See 70 Trim–Interior.**

2. Remove lock cylinder housing as described earlier, see **Door handle, removing**.

3. Remove door window, window guide on quarter window frame and quarter window frame as described above.

NOTE—
It is not necessary to remove the rear quarter window.

4. Pull rubber boot off from B-pillar in door jamb and disconnect harness connectors under boot. See Fig. 19.

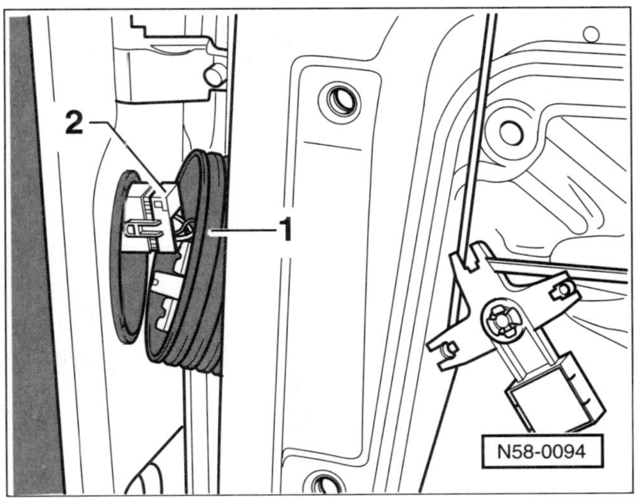

N58-0094

Fig. 19. Pull off rubber boot (**1**) at B-pillar and disconnect harness connector (**2**).

5. Remove assembly carrier mounting bolts and mounting bolts for lock assembly. See Fig. 20.

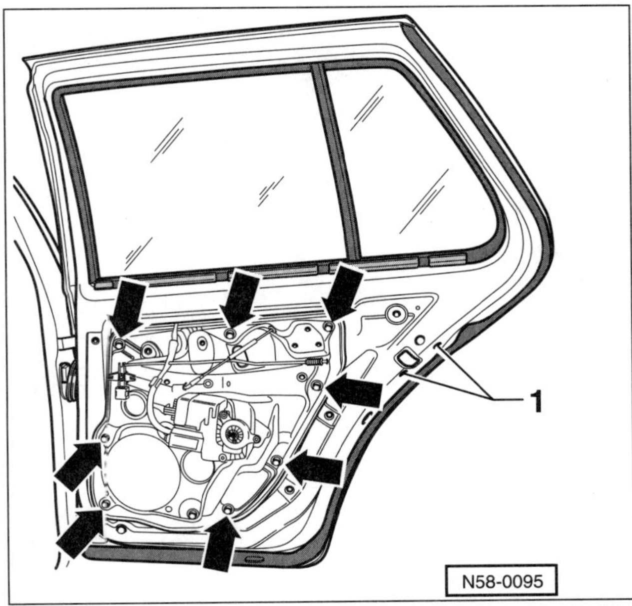

N58-0095

Fig. 20. Remove assembly carrier mounting bolts (**arrows**) and mounting bolts (**1**) for lock assembly.

6. Pull top of assembly carrier off from door, lift and pull out of door toward hinges.

7. Turn assembly carrier and release wiring clips from reinforcing plate in door. Pull wiring out of boot and remove assembly carrier with door lock assembly attached.

8. Drive out door lock securing clips with a drift. See Fig. 21.

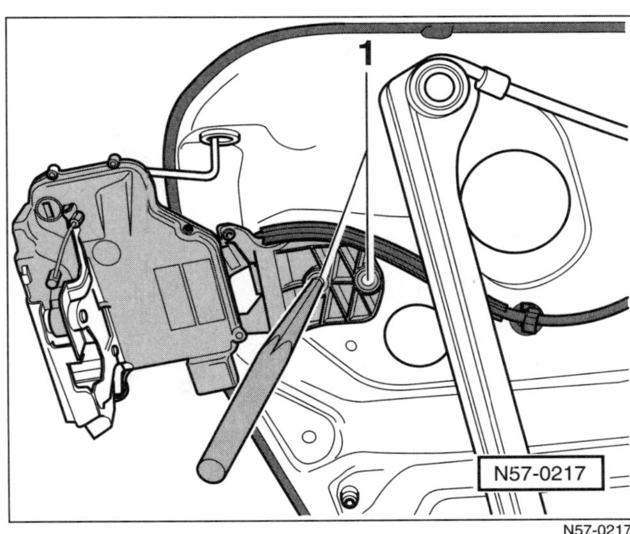

N57-0217

Fig. 21. Drive out clips (**1**) securing door lock to assembly carrier. Front door shown, rear door is similar.

9. Disconnect inside release cable from clip on assembly carrier and carefully pry door lock off assembly carrier using a screwdriver. See Fig. 22.

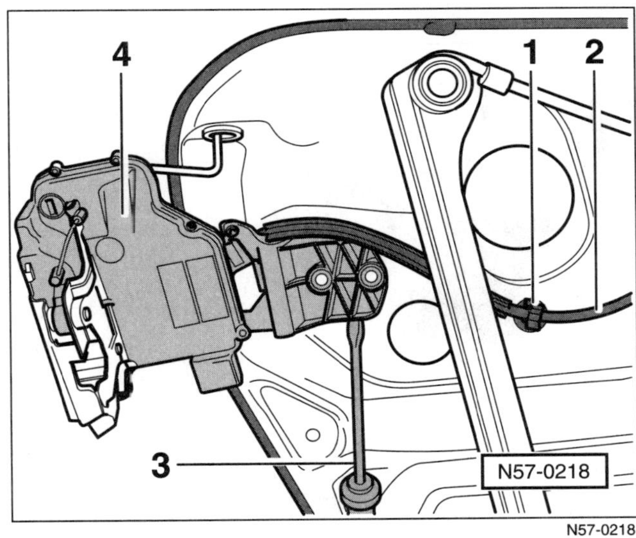

N57-0218

Fig. 22. Disconnect inside release cable (**2**) from clip (**1**) and pry retaining bracket for door lock (**4**) off carrier with a screwdriver (**3**). Front door shown, rear door is similar.

NOTE —

The door lock retaining bracket is a separate part. It is not part of the items supplied with a replacement door lock. It is secured to the door lock with a bolt and a pop rivet.

10. Disconnect door lock rod and inside release cable. See Fig. 23.

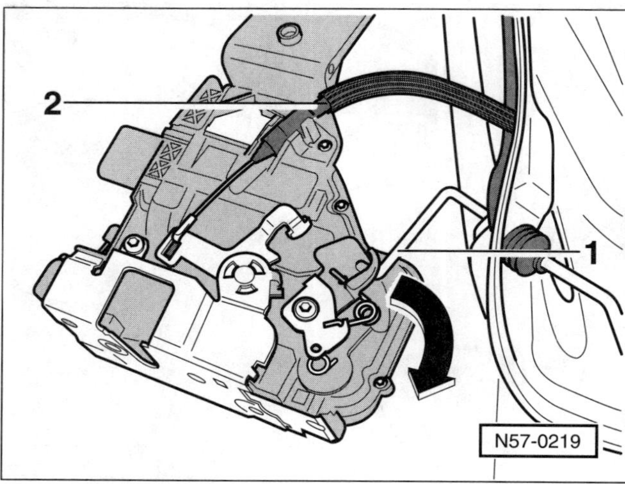

N57-0219

Fig. 23. Disconnect door lock rod (**1**) by turning door lock in direction of arrow. Unsnap inside release cable (**2**) and remove from eyelet in lever. Front door shown, rear door is similar.

Door lock, installing

1. Prepare door lock assembly. See Fig. 24.

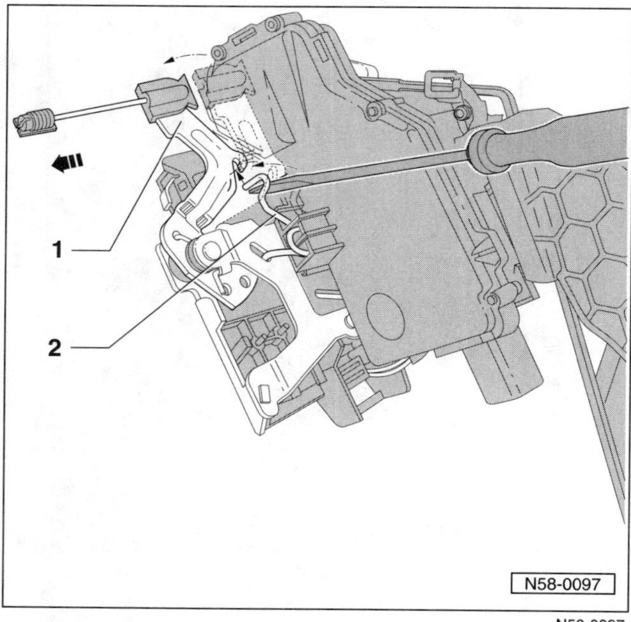

N58-0097

Fig. 24. Pull lock operating lever (**1**) in direction of **arrow**. Hook spring (**2**) into slot on operating lever, **small arrows**.

NOTE —

Connecting the operating lever locks the mechanism and prevents incorrect attachment of the outside handle cable later.

2. Attach door lock rod and inside release cable.
3. Attach door lock to door assembly carrier.
4. Insert assembly carrier in door.
5. Loosely install all door carrier assembly bolts and then tighten two bolts shown in Fig. 25. Tighten remaining bolts to specification.

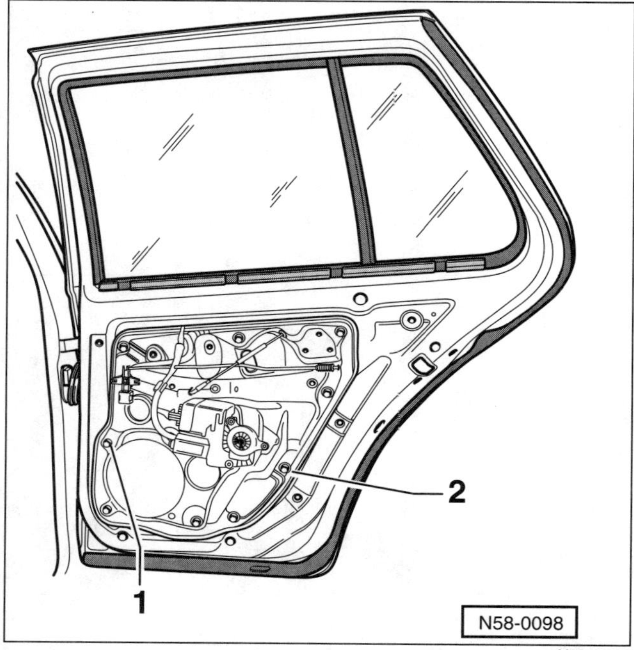

N58-0098

Fig. 25. Install assembly carrier and tighten bolts (**1** and **2**) first.

Tightening torque

- Assembly carrier to door . . . . 8 Nm (71 ft-lb)

6. Guide electrical wiring through boot into door. Secure all wiring retaining clips and install rubber boot between door and B-pillar.
7. Install quarter window frame and door window guide in reverse order of removal, see **Rear windows, removing and installing**.

8. Install door window into door and insert spreader plug and spreader pin into window. See Fig. 26.
   - Position spreader plug projection on each side of window.
   - Guide window into door.
   - Insert window into lift rail guides slot.
   - Lightly tap top of window so that window is positioned properly in lift rail.

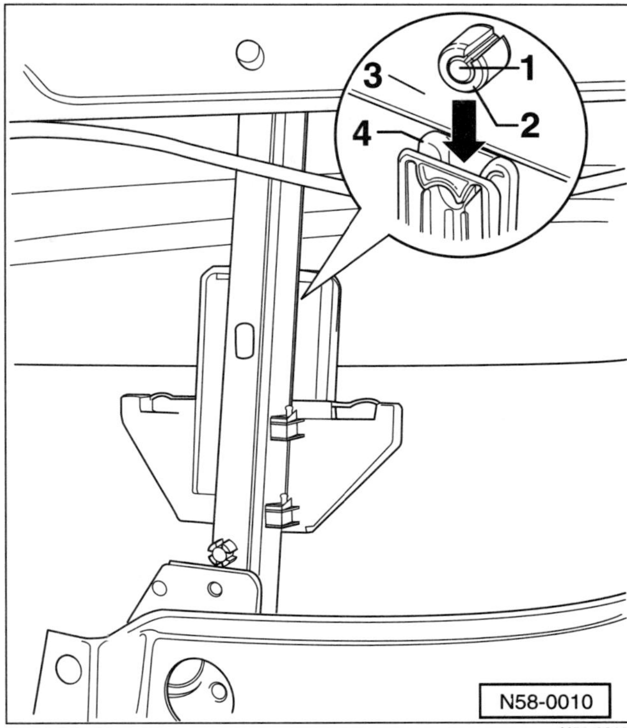

N58-0010

Fig. 26. Insert spreader plug (**2**) and spreader pin (**1**) into window. Guide window into door and insert into lift rail guide slot (**4**). Lightly tap top of window to seat in lift rail (**arrow**).

9. Remainder of installation is the reverse of disassembly.

10. Check operation of window before final installation of door trim panel.

DOOR SEALS

The inner and outer rear door seals are shown in Fig. 27. Various interior trim pieces must be removed to replace the door seals, see **70 Trim–Interior**.

Rear door seals

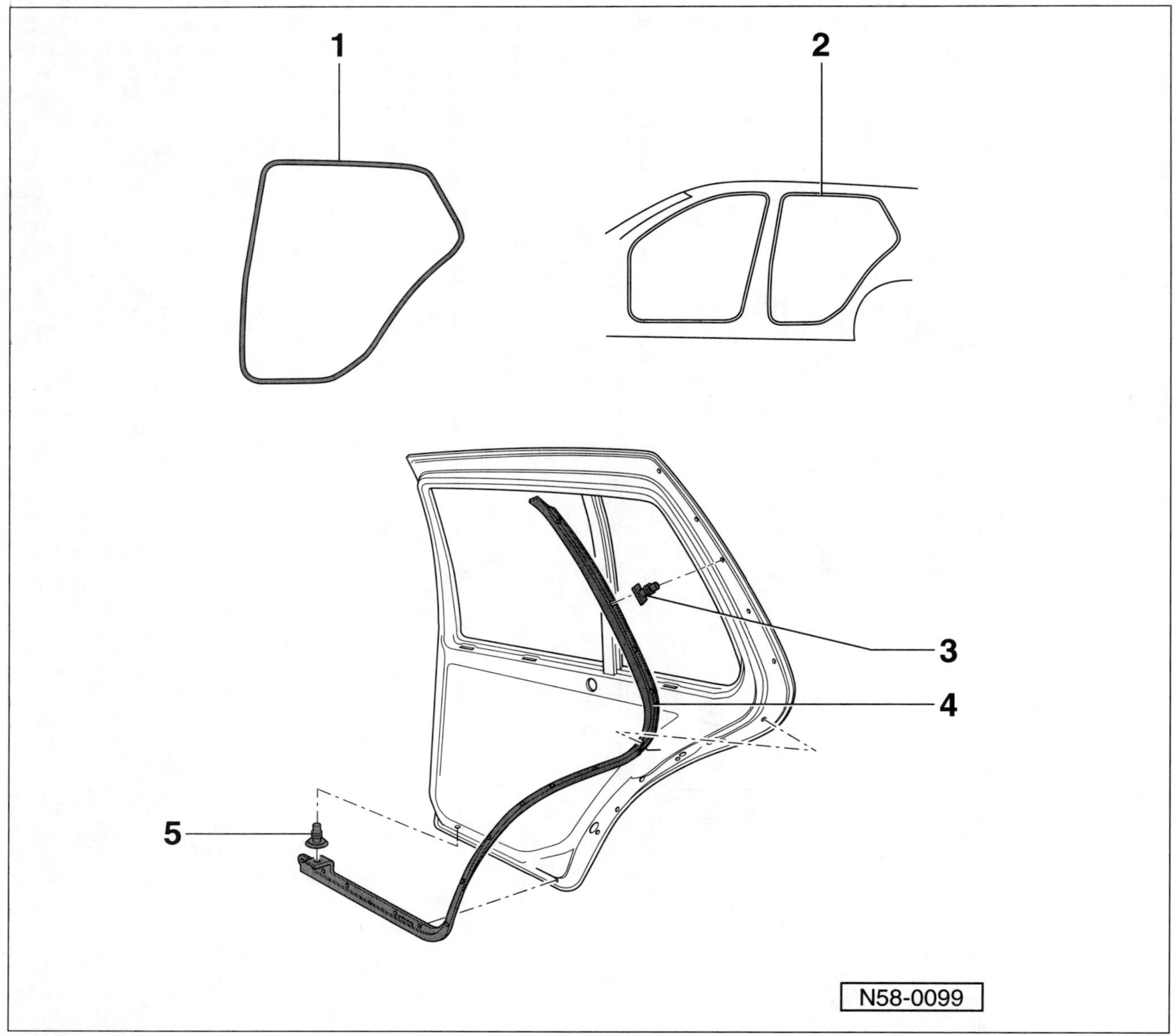

Fig. 27. Inner and outer rear door seals.

1. **Inner door seal**
   - Start at upper radius of door cut-out when installing
2. **Inner door seal for 4-door models**
3. **Clip**
   - Inserted in door seal
4. **Outer door seal**
5. **Clip**
   - Inserted in door seal

60 Sunroof

GENERAL

The power sunroof is a two-way design that tilts open or slides back into the roof. The sunroof is a glass panel with an interior sliding shade (headliner). An electronic control unit is combined with the sunroof motor and regulates the motor operation.

Function

The sunroof is opened and closed by switching the ignition on and turning the rotary switch. In addition, the sunroof may be tilted or closed by pushing or pulling the switch. After switching off the ignition the sunroof can be opened or closed until either the driver's or front passenger's door is opened. Marks on the rotary switch are for preset opening positions of the glass panel. Any other intermediate opening position can be selected by turning the switch clockwise. To tilt or close the sunroof, push or pull the switch until desired position is reached. The sunroof switch is shown in Fig. 1.

Additionally, there is an emergency lock function in the sunroof switch. If there are lock problems, the sunroof can be locked by pressing the pre-selector actuator, which must be in the "sunroof closed" position. During emergency lock function the closing force limiter of the sunroof is switched off.

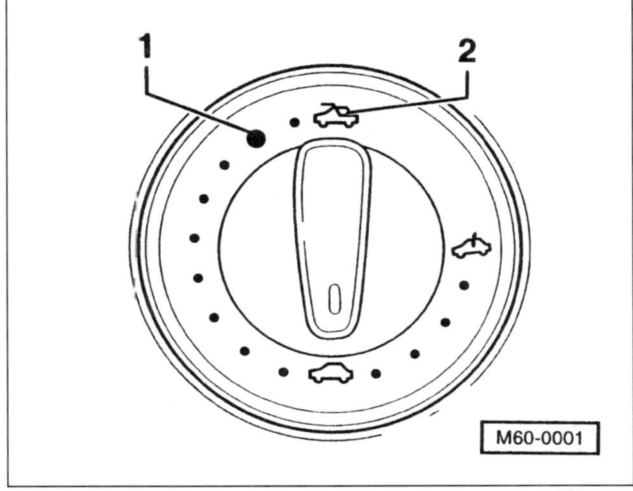

M60-0001

Fig. 1. Comfort position (**1**) prevents wind noises that are more noticeable than in the fully open position (**2**).

The drive for the sunroof is also protected by a running time limit to prevent overheating. This protection mechanism responds after an uninterrupted actuation of approx. 2 minutes. After a cool down phase the mechanism is then operational again.

Distinguishing features

There are two different sunroofs which have been installed in the vehicles covered by this manual. They are supplied by Webasto and Rockwell. While there are no functional or operational differences between the sunroofs it is important to know which type is installed before doing any maintenance, repair, or ordering replacement parts. When replacing a complete sunroof it can be either type. To determine which type of sunroof is installed, tilt open the rear of the sunroof with operating switch and observe the water channel. The distinguishing features are shown in Fig. 2. and Fig. 3.

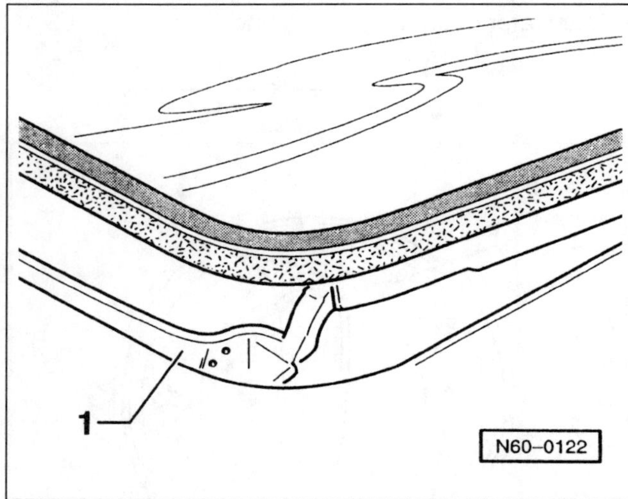

N60-0122

Fig. 2. Webasto sunroofs have a water channel (**1**) that is connected with a glass cover at rear edge.

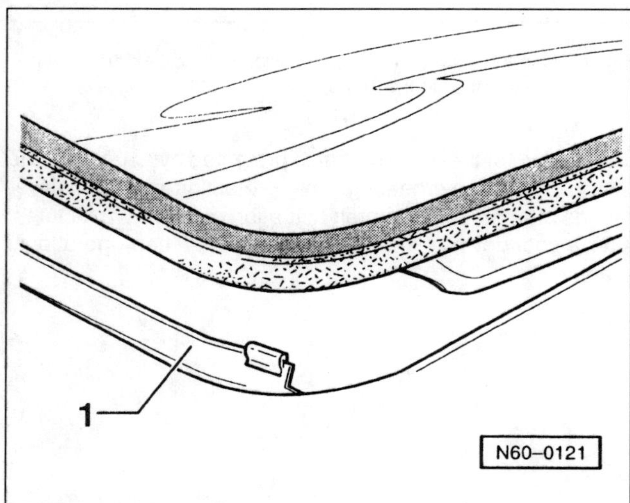

N60-0121

Fig. 3. Rockwell sunroofs do not have a glass cover to connect the water channel (**1**).

SUNROOF, SERVICING

Glass panel, removing and installing

1. Slide sliding headliner to rear position.

2. Tilt sunroof open.

3. Remove lower trim from side of sunroof.
   - For Webasto sunroofs, unclip lower trim at rear and slide trim forward to remove. See Fig. 4.
   - For Rockwell sunroofs, unclip lower trim at front and pull inward to center of vehicle and unhook at rear. See Fig. 5.

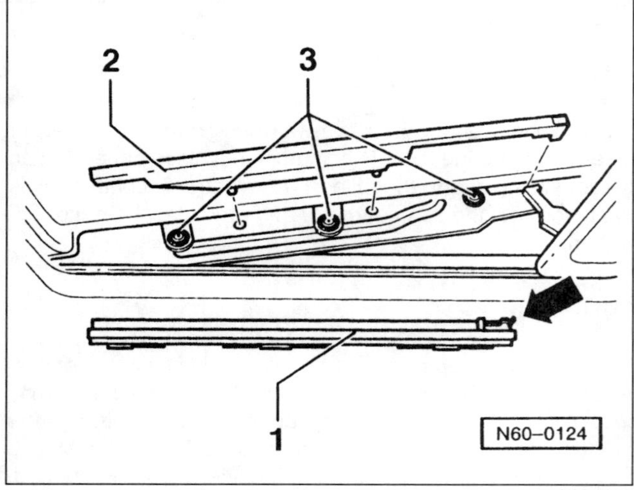

N60-0124

Fig. 4. Webasto sunroof lower trim (**1**), upper trim (**2**) and glass panel mounting screws (**3**).

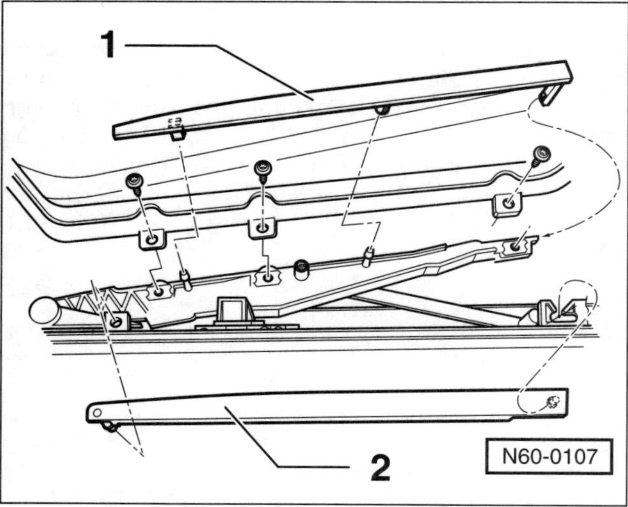

N60-0107

Fig. 5. Rockwell sunroof upper trim (**1**), lower trim (**2**) and glass panel mounting screws.

4. Unclip front and center of upper trim and unhook at rear.

   NOTE —
   For Webasto sunroofs refer to Fig. 4. For Rockwell sunroofs refer to Fig. 5.

5. Remove glass panel mounting screws (Torx insert T 25) and remove glass panel upward.

   NOTE —
   For Rockwell sunroofs, the sunroof must not be moved to the "Open" position when removed. The water channel will not be compressed by the glass panel and can jam inside the roof.

6. Before installing glass panel, ensure that the sunroof switch is in the "0 position" (sunroof closed).

7. Align guide rail pin with marking tab(s).
   - For Webasto sunroofs see Fig. 6.
   - For Rockwell sunroofs see Fig. 7.

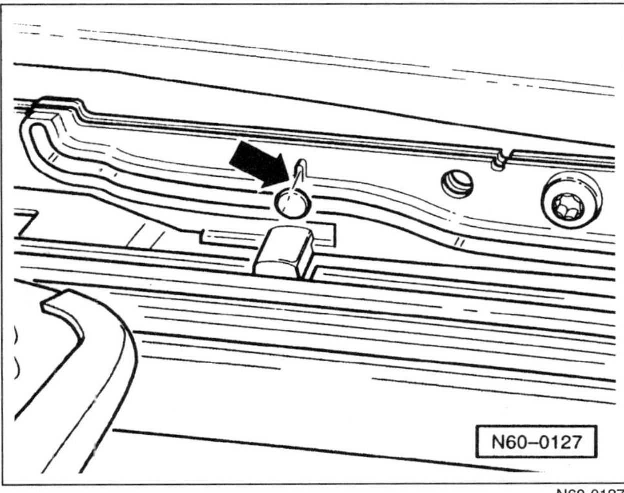

N60-0127

Fig. 6. For Webasto sunroof, align guide rail pin with marking tab (**arrow**).

   NOTE —
   On Rockwell sunroofs, the slotted guide rail must be located in the guide rails (cannot be moved by hand). If not, adjust parallel movement as shown later, see **Rockwell sunroof assembly**.

8. Position glass panel from above and install mounting screws on each side.

Tightening torque
- Glass panel to slotted guide rail. . . . .4.5 Nm (40 in-lb)

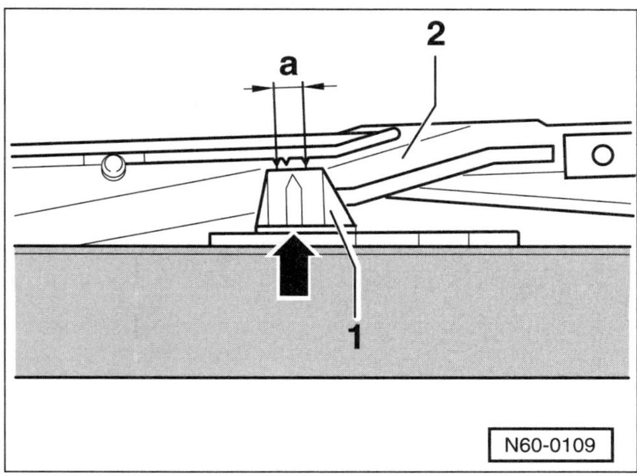

N60-0109

Fig. 7. For Rockwell sunroof, align mark (**arrow**) on rear guide (**1**) within marks (**dimension a**) on the slotted guide rail (**2**).

Glass panel, adjusting height

1. Tilt sunroof open and slide headliner to rear.

2. Remove upper and lower trim pieces and loosen glass panel mounting screws as described above, see **Glass panel, removing and installing**. Do not remove glass panel.

3. Run glass panel into closed position, then open and close again. (The correct order is important for adjustment).

4. Carry out front and rear height adjustment as shown in Fig. 8. and Fig. 9.

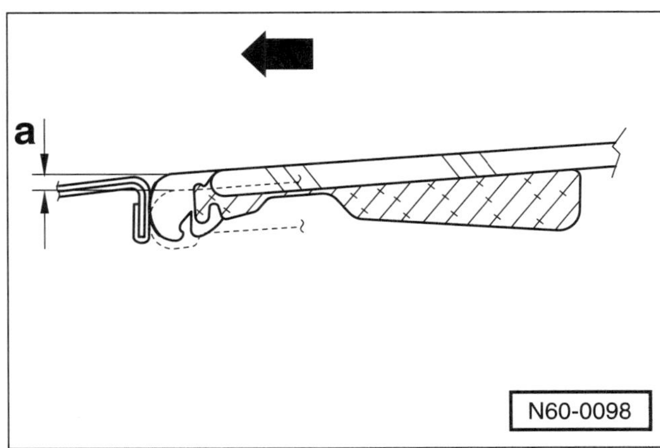

N60-0098

Fig. 8. Front of sunroof panel should be 1mm (dimension **a**) lower than body (roof). **Arrow** indicates direction of travel.

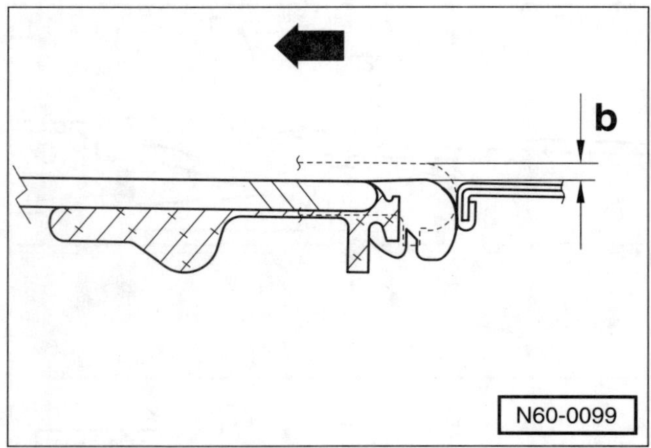

N60-0099

Fig. 9. Rear of sunroof panel should be 1mm (dimension **b**) higher than body (roof). **Arrow** indicates direction of travel.

5. Tighten glass panel mounting screws and replace trim pieces.

NOTE —
Always tighten left and right-hand glass panel screws symmetrically.

Tightening torque
- Glass panel to slotted guide rail. . . . .4.5 Nm (40 in-lb)

Sliding headliner, removing

1. Remove sunroof gals panel as described earlier.

2. Slide headliner to rear.

3. Remove front mounting bolts on left and right-hand sides of headliner. Pull slide out forward over stop. See Fig. 10.

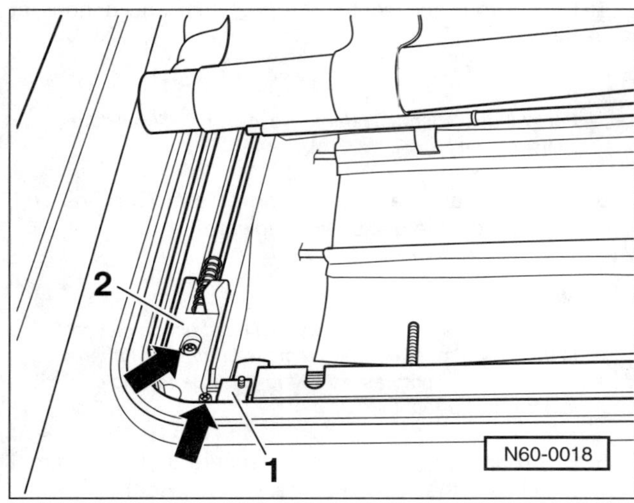

A60-0018

Fig. 10. Remove front mounting bolts (**arrow**) on left and right-hand sides of headliner. Pull slide out forward over stop (**1**).

4. Remove rear mounting bolts on left and right-hand sides of headliner. Pull out slide to rear and remove sliding headliner. See Fig. 11.

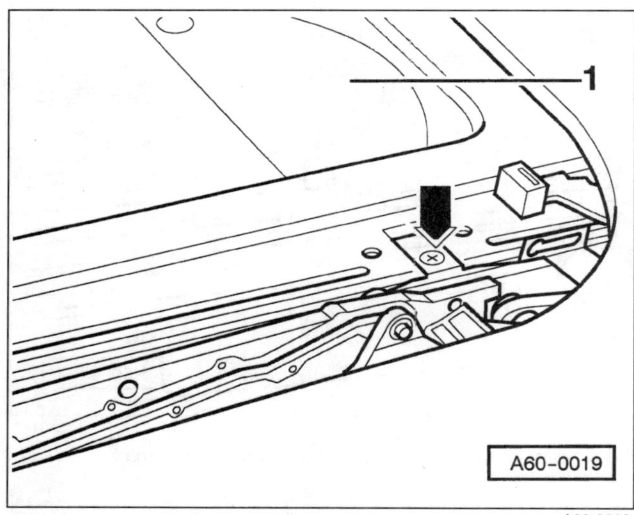

A60-0019

Fig. 11. Remove rear mounting bolts (**arrow**) on left and right-hand sides of headliner. Pull out slide to rear and remove sliding headliner (**1**).

Drive motor for sunroof, adjusting ("0" position)

It is necessary to adjust the "0" position if the drive motor was removed when not in "0" position or if the sunroof was locked by emergency actuation or opened in that mode.

1. If not already done, pry out trim panel for drive motor and remove drive motor mounting bolts and pull drive motor down. Leave electrical harness connector attached to drive motor. See Fig. 12.

N60-0104

Fig. 12. Remove sunroof drive motor mounting screws (**arrows**).

2. Select "tilt roof" by turning sunroof rotary switch. Select "closed roof" by turning sunroof rotary switch. Select "opened roof" with sunroof rotary switch. Select "closed roof" again with sunroof rotary switch.

3. "0" position can checked by looking through the small window in the motor. If the two notches align, the motor is at the "0" position. See Fig. 13.

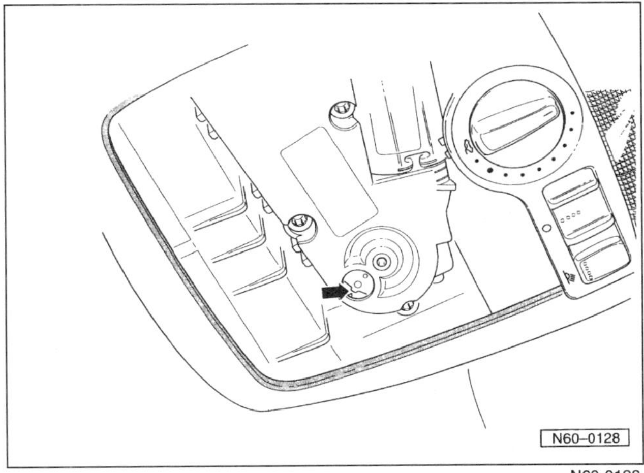

N60-0128

Fig. 13. Drive motor is in "0" position when notches align (**arrow**).

4. Install drive motor in "0" position. Be sure that sunroof is closed before installing motor.

Sunroof switch, removing

1. Unclip domelight lens at front and remove. See Fig. 14.

N60-0083

Fig. 14. Unclip domelight lens (**1**) at front and remove in direction of **arrows**.

2. Remove switch mounting screws and pull out sunroof switch. See Fig. 15.

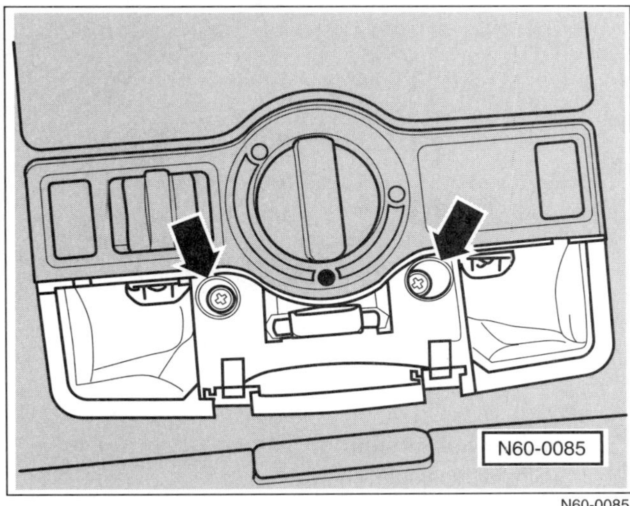

N60-0085

Fig. 15. Remove sunroof switch mounting screws (**arrows**).

3. Disconnect harness connector and remove switch.

Webasto sunroof assembly

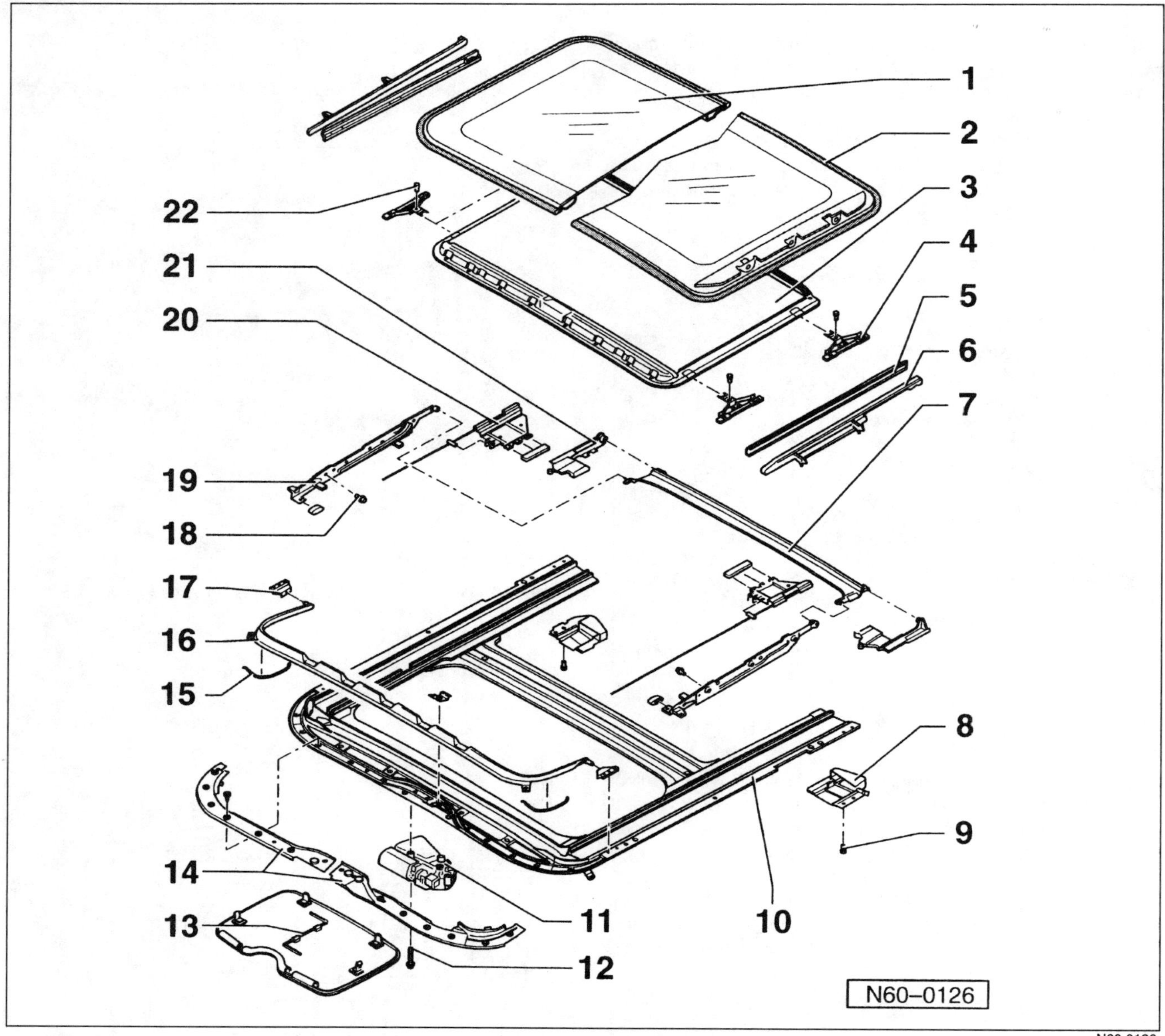

N60-0126

Fig. 16. Webasto sunroof and related components.

1. **Glass panel for sunroof**
   - Single pane safety glass
   - Parallel movement, checking and adjusting, **see** (A)
2. **Panel seal**
   - Replacing, **see** (B)
3. **Sliding headliner**
4. **Slide**
5. **Lower trim**
6. **Upper trim**
7. **Water channel**
   - Removed together with slotted guide rail
8. **End piece**
   - Use butyl adhesive sealing cord (VW part no. AKL 450 005 05) to seal
9. **Bolt**
10. **Carrier unit**
    - U-frame with guide channels
    - If required, guide channels are to be greased with special grease, G 000 450 02 only

(continued from previous page)

11. Drive motor

12. Bolt

13. Cover
- With Allen key for emergency opening

14. Channel cover

15. Wind deflector spring

16. Wind deflector
- Removing, **see** (C)

17. Wind deflector mount

18. Glass panel mounting screw
- Torx T25
- Tighten to 4.5 Nm (40 in-lb)

19. Slotted guide rail

20. Guide with cable

21. Slotted water channel

22. Countersunk screws
- Micro encapsulated
- Always replace
- Tighten to 3.5 Nm (31 in-lb)

(A) Sunroof parallel movement, checking and adjusting

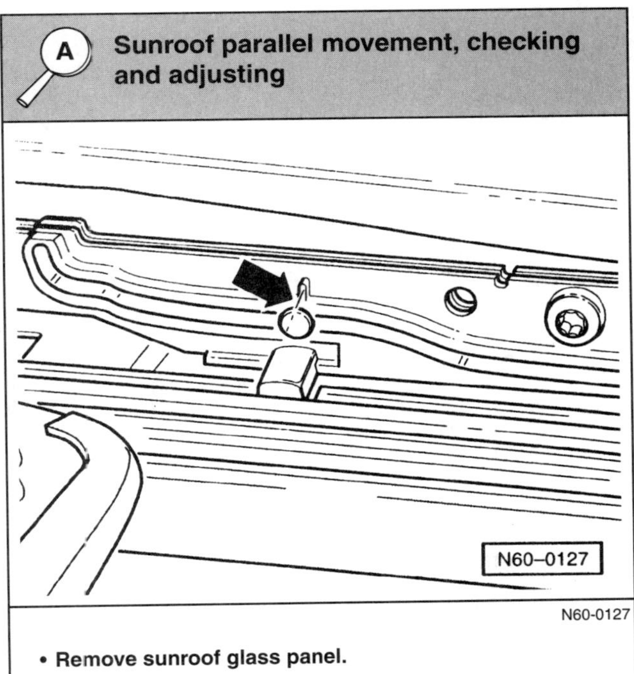

N60-0127

- **Remove sunroof glass panel.**
- **Guide rail pin must align with marking tab (arrow).**
- **To adjust, remove sunroof drive motor and check for "0" position.**

(B) Panel seal, replacing

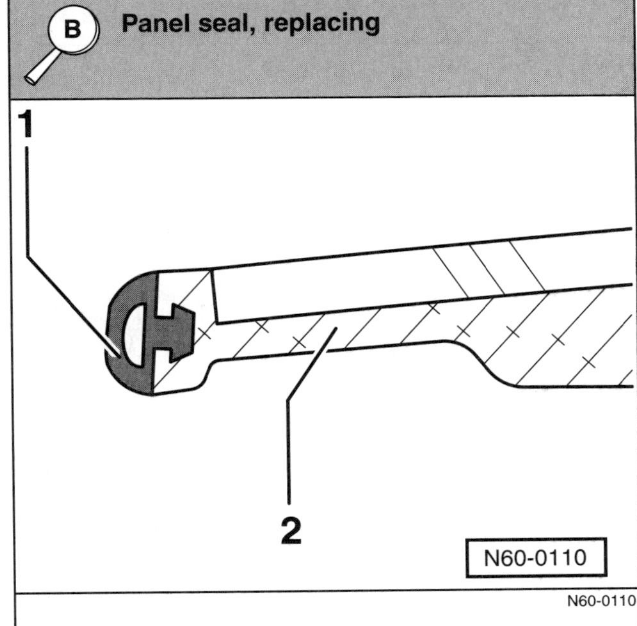

N60-0110

- **Pull seal (1) off glass panel.**
- **Center new seal in glass panel (2) and press in.**

(C) Wind deflector, removing

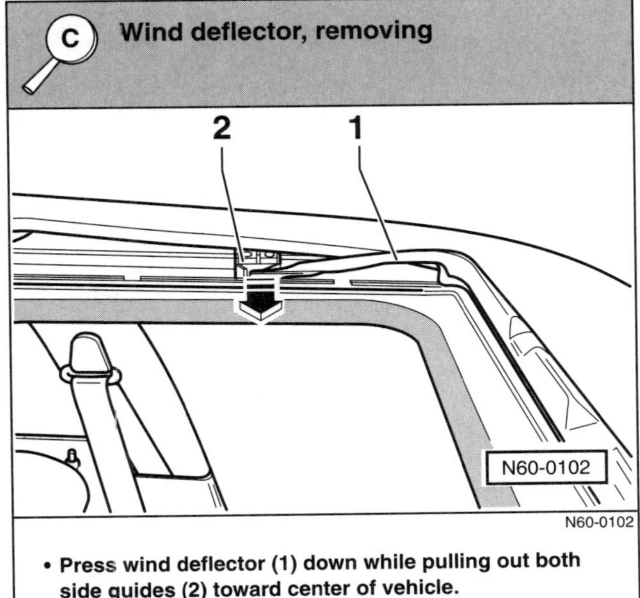

N60-0102

- **Press wind deflector (1) down while pulling out both side guides (2) toward center of vehicle.**
- **Remove wind deflector.**

Rockwell sunroof assembly

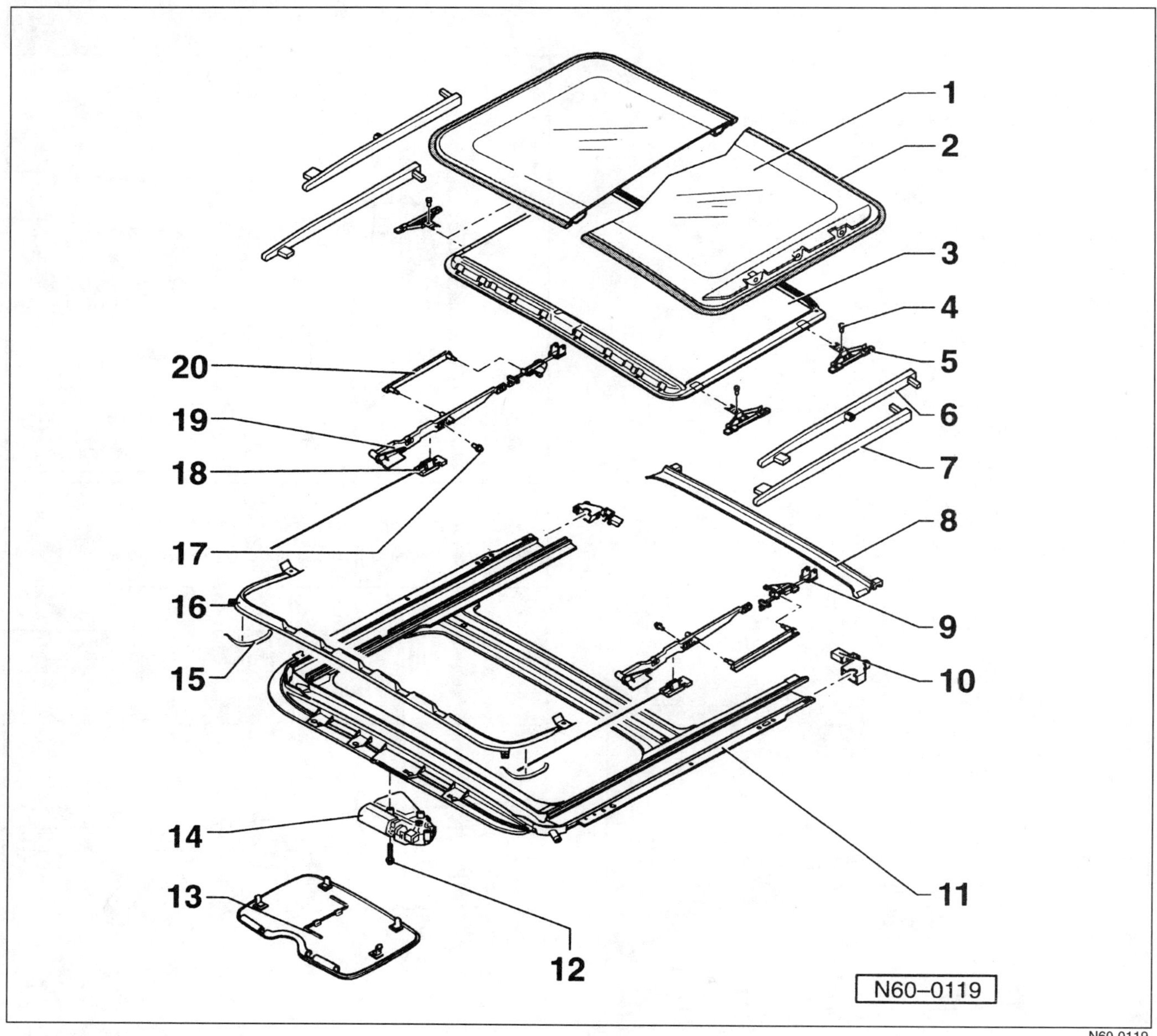

N60-0119

Fig. 17. Rockwell sunroof and related components.

1. **Glass panel for sunroof**
   - Single pane safety glass
   - Parallel movement, checking and adjusting, **see** (A)
2. **Panel seal**
   - Adjusting/replacing, **see** (B)
3. **Sliding headliner**
4. **Countersunk screws**
   - Micro encapsulated
   - Always replace
   - Tighten to 3.5 Nm (31 in-lb)
5. **Slide**
6. **Upper trim**
7. **Lower trim**
8. **Water channel**
   - Removed together with slotted guide rail
9. **Guide locking hook**
10. **End piece**
    - Use butyl adhesive sealing cord (VW part no. AKL 450 005 05) to seal

(continued from previous page)

11. Carrier unit
- U-frame with guide channels
- If required, guide channels are to be greased with special grease, G 000 450 02 only

12. Bolt

13. Cover
- With Allen key for emergency opening

14. Drive motor

15. Wind deflector spring

16. Wind deflector
- Removing, **see** (C)

17. Glass panel mounting screw
- Torx T25
- Tighten to 4.5 Nm (40 in-lb)

18. Rear guide
- Removed with slotted guide rail

19. Slotted guide rail

20. Spacer
- Removed with slotted guide rail

(A) Sunroof parallel movement, checking and adjusting

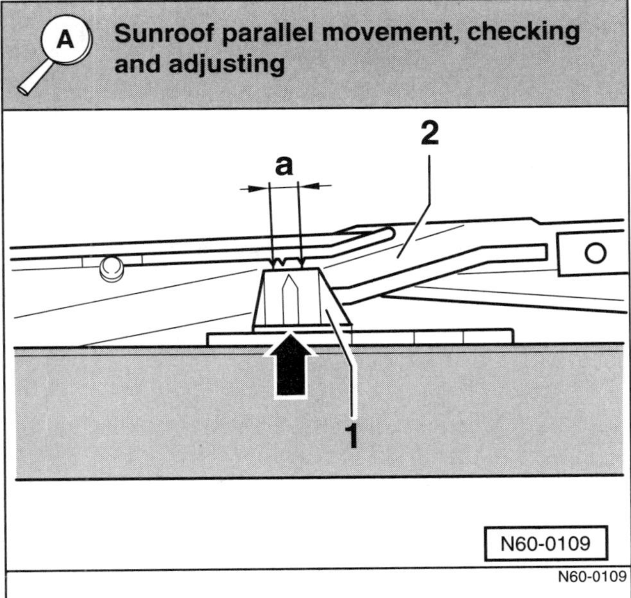

N60-0109

- **Remove sunroof glass panel.**
- **The mark (arrow) on the rear guide upper section (1) must lie within the marks (dimension a) on the guide rail. Check both sides.**
- **The slotted guide rail (2) must be located in the guide (cannot be moved by hand).**
- **To adjust, remove drive motor and slide guide upper part (1) from front to rear, centering between marks.**
- **Install drive motor in "0" position and check adjustment.**

(B) Panel seal, adjusting and replacing

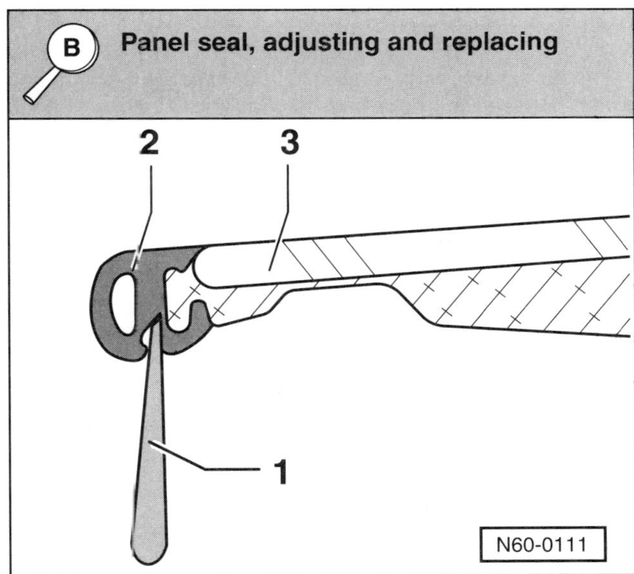

N60-0111

- **Glass panel (3) must be removed to adjust panel seal.**
- **Check for uniform spacing between panel seal (2) and body using a 0.3 mm thick strip of paper (i.e. business card).**
- **Use a wedge (1) to push panel seal apart if spacing is too thin, or to push seal closer if spacing is too large.**
- **To replace seal, pull off from glass panel and install new seal from bottom to top, starting at rear center.**

(C) Wind deflector, removing

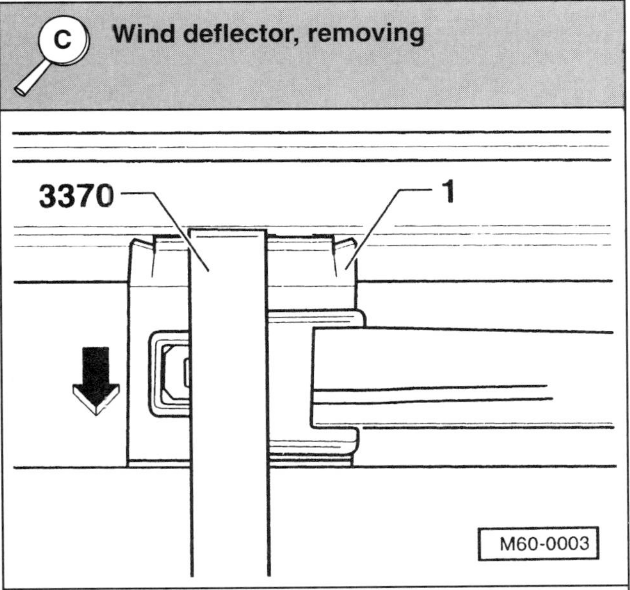

M60-0003

- **Open sunroof completely and place assembly tool 3370 between roof and wind deflector and remove deflector on right and left sides by pulling tool.**
- **Pry wind deflector mount (1) out of carrier unit on left and right sides carefully with a screwdriver.**

Front water drain hoses, cleaning

The front water drain hoses are routed in the A-pillars and empty between the door and the A-pillar. Cleaning is done from the sunroof panel opening. A flexible cable that is approx. 230 cm (90 in.) long is necessary for cleaning the drain hose. The drain hose and grommet are shown in Fig. 18.

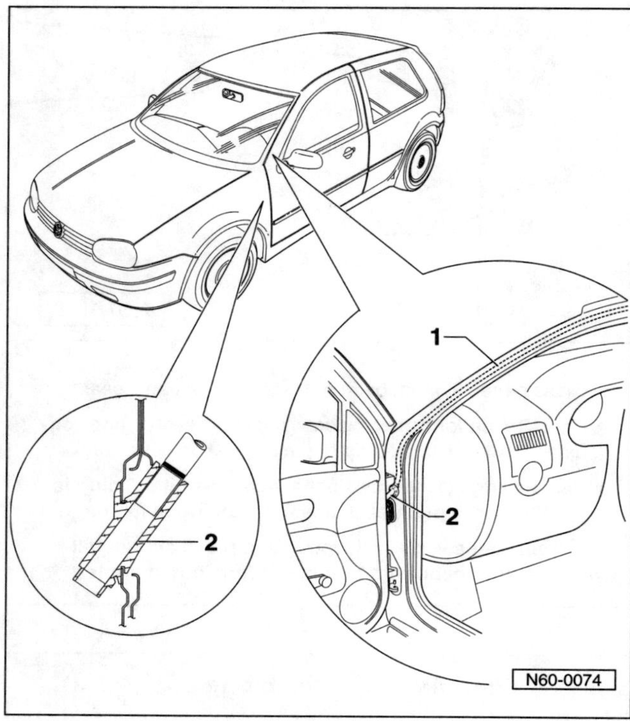

N60-0074

Fig. 18. Front water drain hose (**1**) and hose grommet (**2**).

Rear water drain hoses, cleaning

The rear water drain hoses are routed in the C-pillars and empty behind the bumper under the tail light cluster. Cleaning is done from the lower end of the hose. The rear bumper must be removed to clean the rear drain hoses, see **63 Bumpers**. A flexible cable that is approx. 230 cm (90 in.) long is necessary for cleaning the drain hose. The drain hose and grommet are shown in Fig. 19.

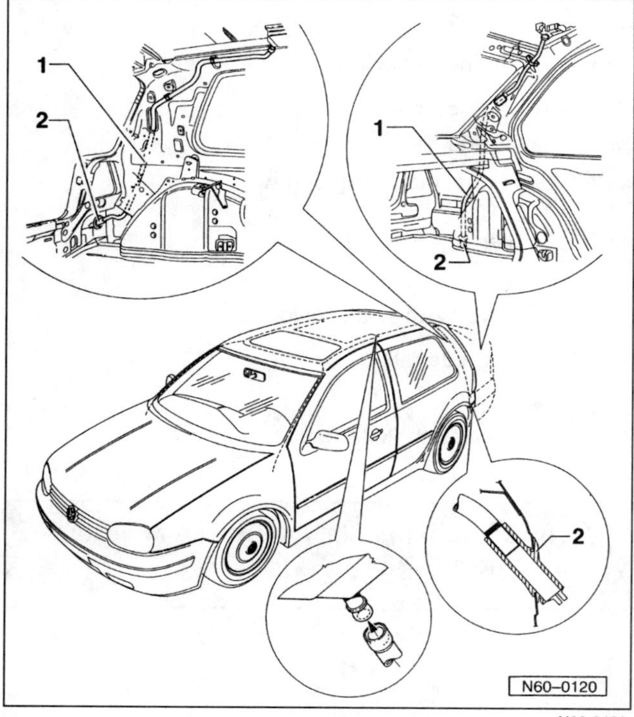

N60-0120

Fig. 19. Rear water drain hose (**1**) and hose grommet (**2**).

63 Bumpers

GENERAL

The bumpers consist of a cross-member that is bolted directly to the body structure. The bumper cover must first be removed to access the bumper beam. It is also necessary to remove the front bumper cover and front bumper beam to move the radiator support (lock carrier) to the service position, see **50 Body–Front**.

BUMPERS, SERVICING

Hood release lever, removing

Before removing the front bumper cover the hood release lever must first be removed.

1. Open hood and swing retaining clip for hood release lever upward. See Fig. 1.

2. Pull release lever with a screwdriver and remove front hood lock.

3. Pull release lever and guide out of radiator support (lock carrier).

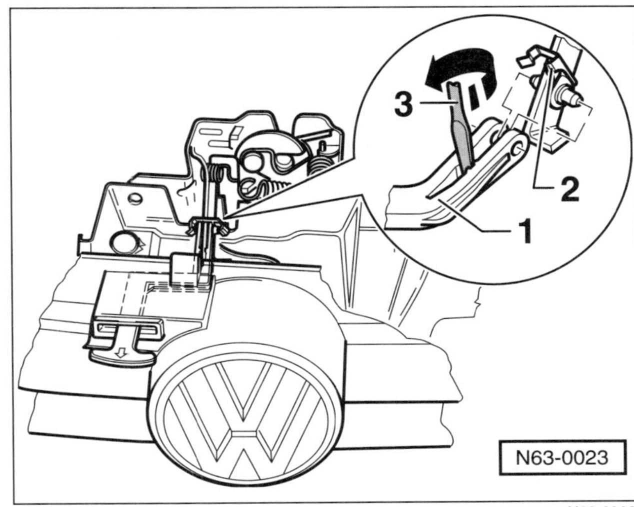

N63-0023

Fig. 1. Swing clip (**2**) upward, pull release lever (**1**) with screwdriver (**3**) in direction of **arrow**. Remove release lever and guide.

To continue with removal of front bumper cover refer to Fig. 2. The rear bumper cover is shown in Fig. 4.

63

Front bumper assembly

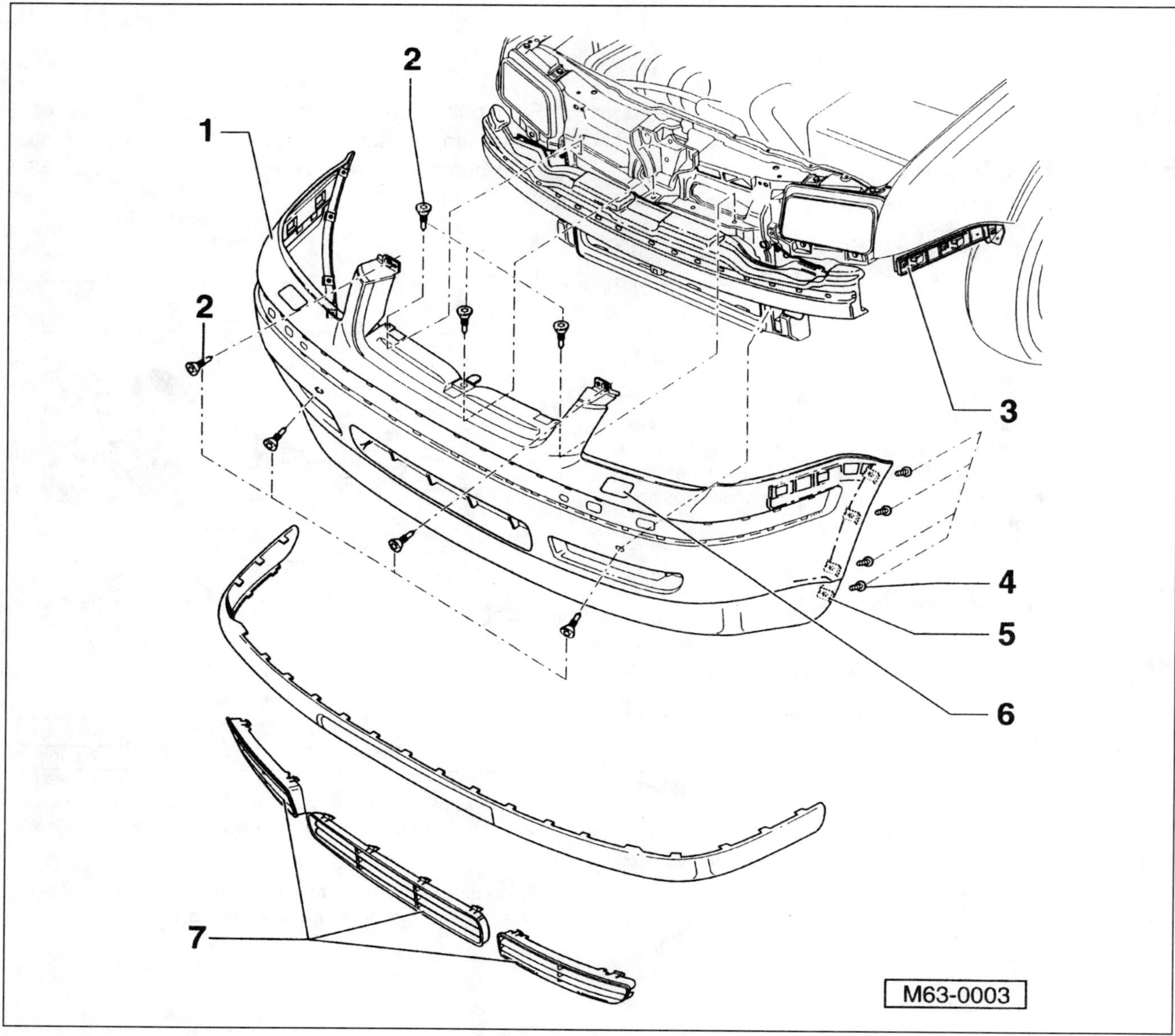

M63-0003

Fig. 2. Front bumper assembly.

1. **Bumper cover**
   - Removing:
     Separate release lever from hood lock, see Fig. 1.
     Remove radiator grille, see **66 Body–Exterior**
     Unclip and remove headlight washer covers (item 6)
     Remove mounting bolts from wheel housing (item 4)
     Unclip outer air guides (item 7)
     Remove mounting screws (item 2)
     Remove guides (item 3) from right and left sides
     Disconnect wiring from temperature sensor
2. **Bolt**
   - Qty. 7
   - Tighten to 6.5 Nm (57 in-lb)
3. **Guide**
   - To remove/install bumper, pull out or push in parallel to guides at left and right
4. **Screw**
   - Qty. 4 per side
5. **Speed nut**
6. **Cover for headlight washer**
7. **Air guide grille**
   - Clipped into bumper cover

Front bumper beam assembly

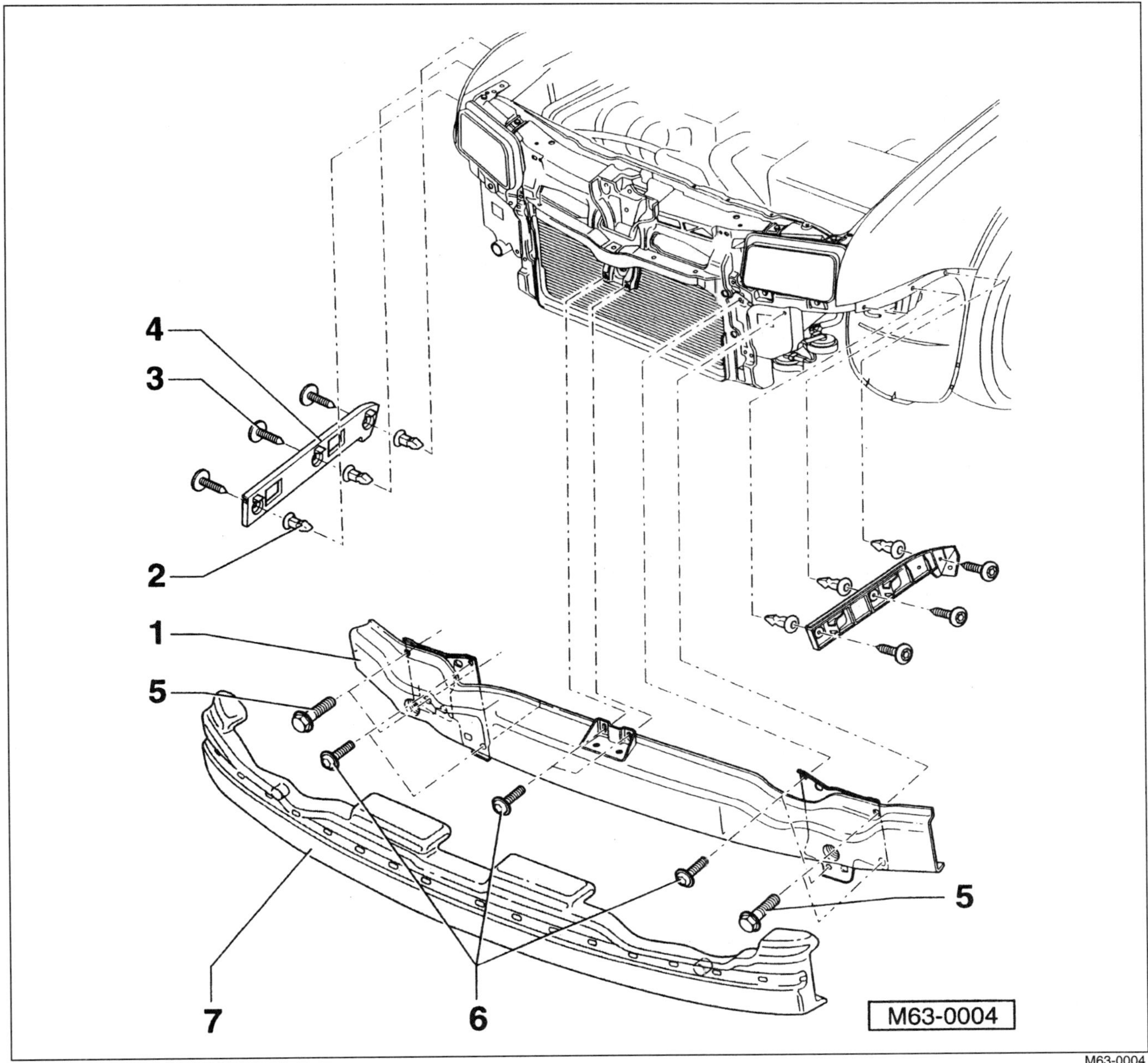

M63-0004

Fig. 3. Front bumper beam and related components.

1. **Bumper beam**
2. **Spreader nut**
   - Qty. 3
3. **Screw**
   - Qty. 3
4. **Guide**
   - To remove/install bumper, pull out or push in parallel to guides at left and right
5. **Bolt**
   - Qty. 4
   - Tighten to 20 Nm (15 ft-lb)
6. **Bolt**
   - Qty. 6
   - Tighten to 8 Nm (71 in-lb)
7. **Impact damper**
   - Connected to bumper beam

Rear bumper assembly

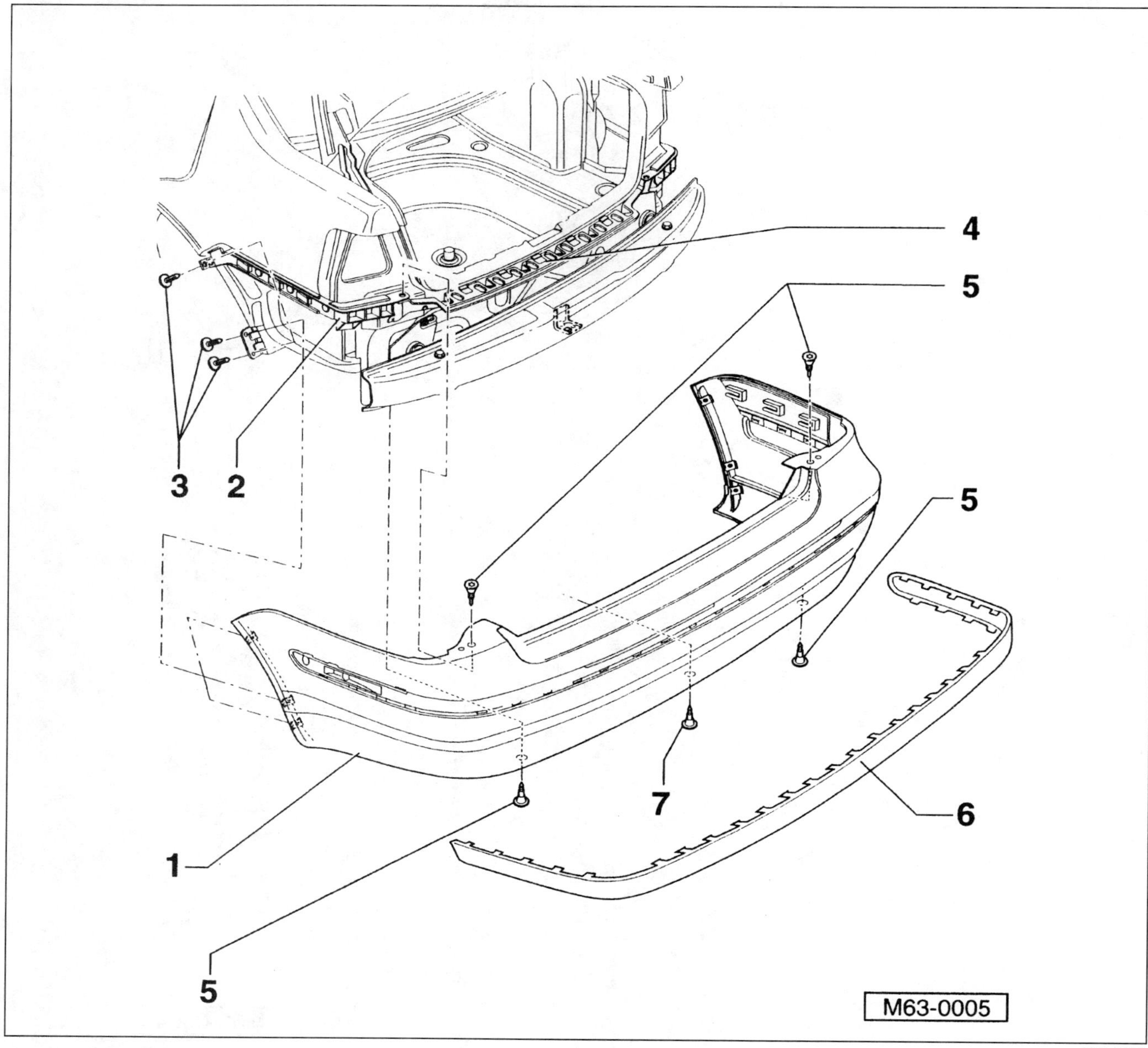

Fig. 4. Rear bumper assembly.

1. **Bumper cover**
   - Removing:
     Remove mounting bolts from wheel housing (item 3)
     Remove tail light assemblies, see **94 Lights, Accessories–Exterior**
     On Golf/GTI, disconnect harness connector for license plate light under left tail light
     Remove mounting bolts (item 5)
2. **Guide**
   - To remove/install bumper, pull out or push in parallel to guides at left and right
3. **Bolt**
   - Qty. 4
4. **Mounting strip**
5. **Bolt**
   - Qty. 4
   - Tighten to 15 Nm (11 ft-lb)
6. **Impact strip**
7. **Bolt**
   - Tighten to 15 Nm (11 ft-lb)
   - Only for Jetta bumper

Rear bumper beam assembly

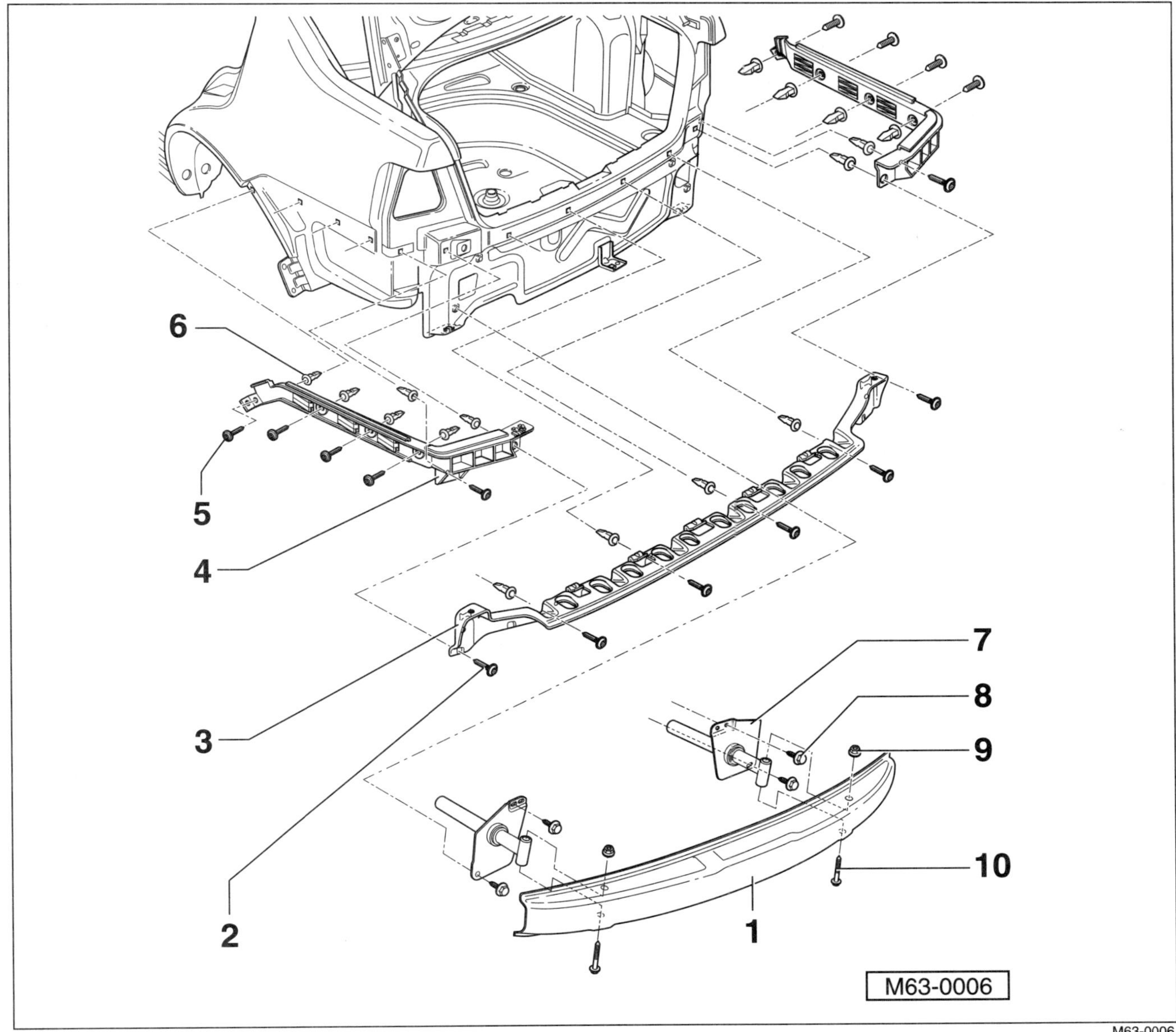

M63-0006

Fig. 5. Fear bumper beam and related components.

1. **Bumper beam**
2. **Screw**
   - Qty. 6
3. **Mounting strip**
4. **Guide**
   - To remove/install bumper, pull out or push in parallel to guides at left and right
5. **Screw**
   - Qty. 4
   - Tighten to 20 Nm (15 ft-lb)
6. **Spreader nut**
   - Qty. 6
7. **Impact absorber**
8. **Bolt**
   - Qty. 4
   - Tighten to 20 Nm (15 ft-lb)
9. **Nut**
10. **Bolt**

66 Body–Exterior Equipment

GENERAL

This repair group covers various exterior equipment including side-view mirrors, wheel housing liners, roof moldings and front grille trim.

SIDE-VIEW MIRROR

Mirror housing, removing and installing

1. Fold mirror housing forward to ease removal.

2. Position mirror glass totally vertical to avoid catching mirror housing on glass when removing.

3. Use screwdriver to release housing retaining clip on bottom of actuator bracket. See Fig. 1.

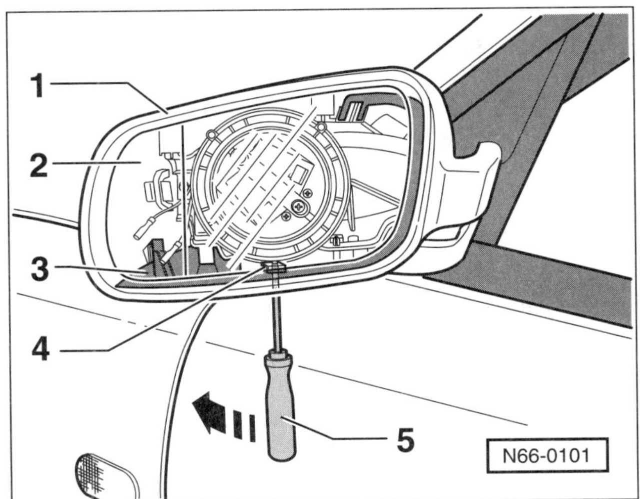

Fig. 1. Position mirror glass (**2**) vertical. Press screwdriver (**5**) in direction of **arrow** to release housing retaining clip (**4**).

4. Pull mirror housing upward off mirror carrier. See Fig. 2.

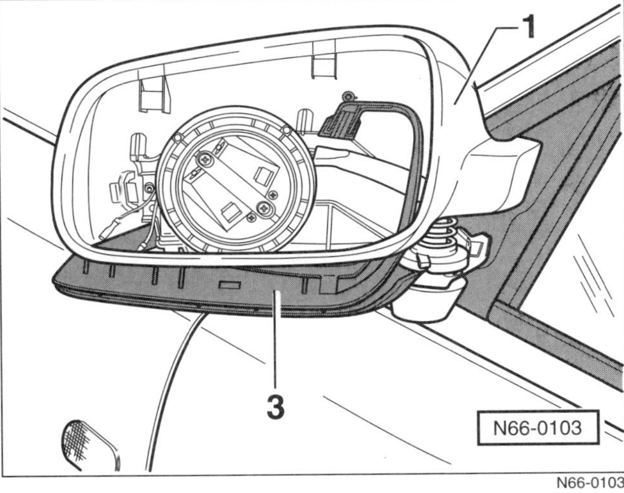

Fig. 2. Pull mirror housing (**1**) upward off mirror carrier (**3**).

Most of the vehicles covered by this manual come equipped with power mirror adjustment. Power mirrors are adjusted with a joy stick that is installed in the driver's door panel. This joystick will adjust either the driver or passenger side mirror. An exploded view of the side-view mirror with power adjustment is provided in Fig. 3.

Vehicles with manually adjusted mirrors have a joy stick on each front door panel that operates cables to adjust each side-view mirror. An exploded view of the manual side-view mirror assembly is shown in Fig. 4.

Side-view mirror assembly (power mirrors)

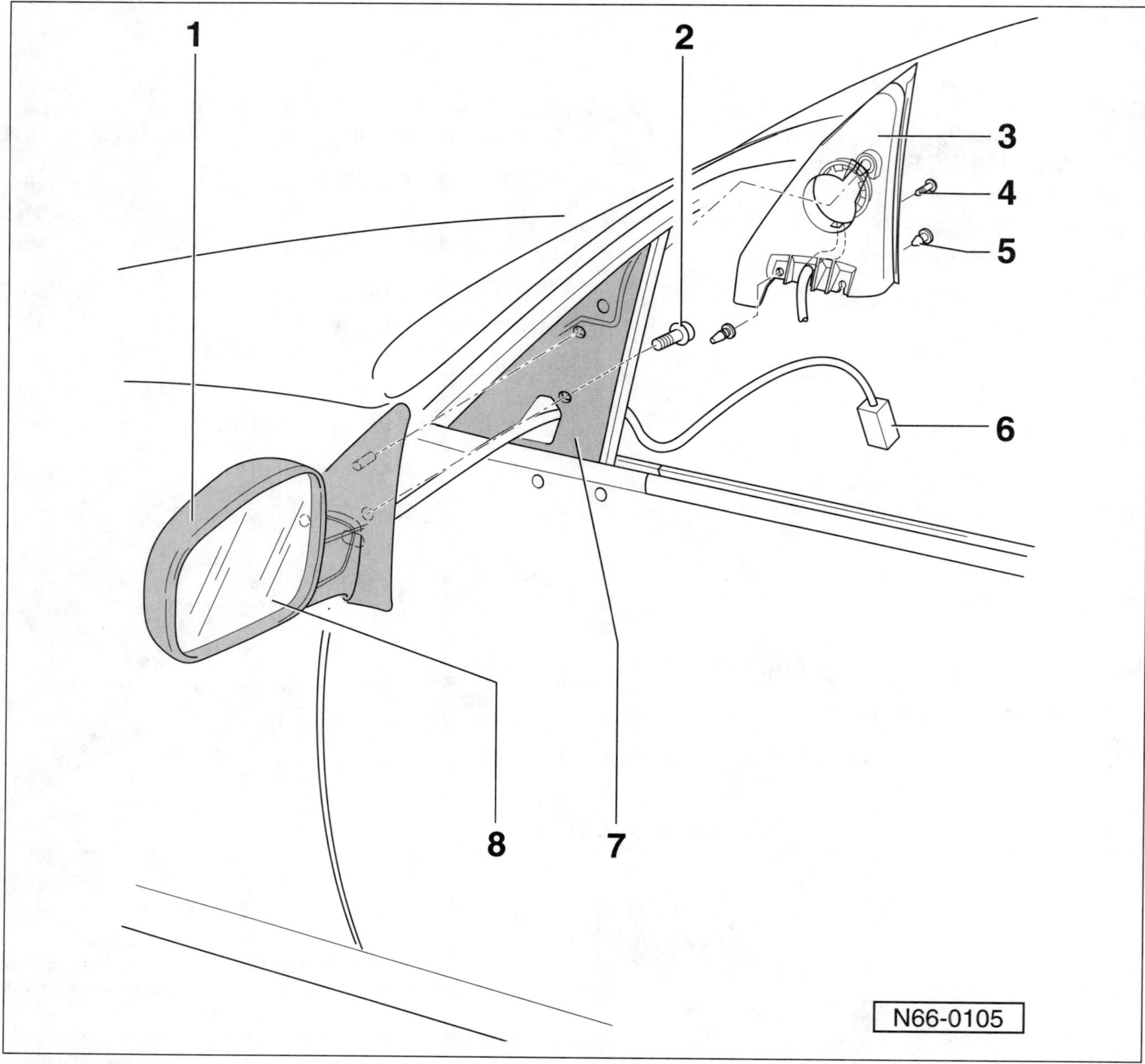

N66-0105

Fig. 3. Side-view mirror assembly for power mirrors.

1. **Mirror housing**
2. **Bolt**
   - Tighten to 10 Nm (7 ft-lb)
3. **Cover**
4. **Bolt**
5. **Clip**
6. **Harness connector**
7. **Insulation**
8. **Mirror glass**
   - Removing:
     Protect inside bottom of mirror from damage with tape
     Pivot top of mirror into housing
     Pry off mirror from tab in housing using VW special tool 80-200 (pry lever) through bottom edge of glass
   - Installing:
     Position mirror glass guide studs into mounts and press center of mirror to install

Side-view mirror assembly (manual mirrors)

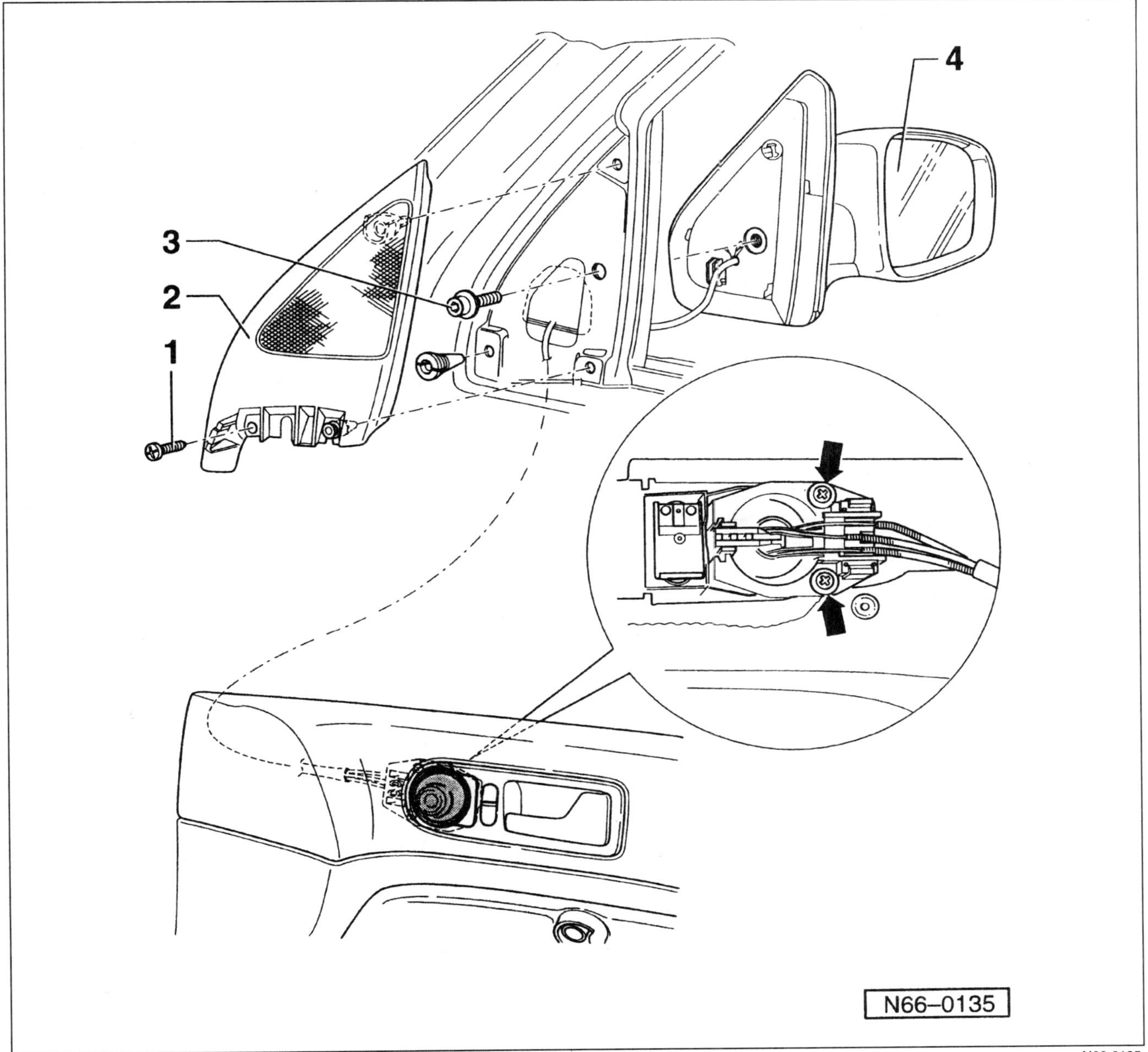

N66-0135

Fig. 4. Side-view mirror assembly (manual mirrors).

1. **Screw**
   - Remove front door trim to access screw, see **70 Trim–Interior**
2. **Trim piece**
   - With stereo speaker, as applicable
3. **Mounting bolt**
4. **Mirror assembly**
   - Removing:
     Remove mirror adjuster mounting bolts (**arrows**)
     Remove screw (item 1)
     Disconnect harness connector for stereo speaker
     Remove trim piece (item 2)
     Remove sound deadener from mirror base
     Remove bolt (item 3) and separate mirror assembly from door

WHEEL HOUSING LINERS

Front wheel housing liner

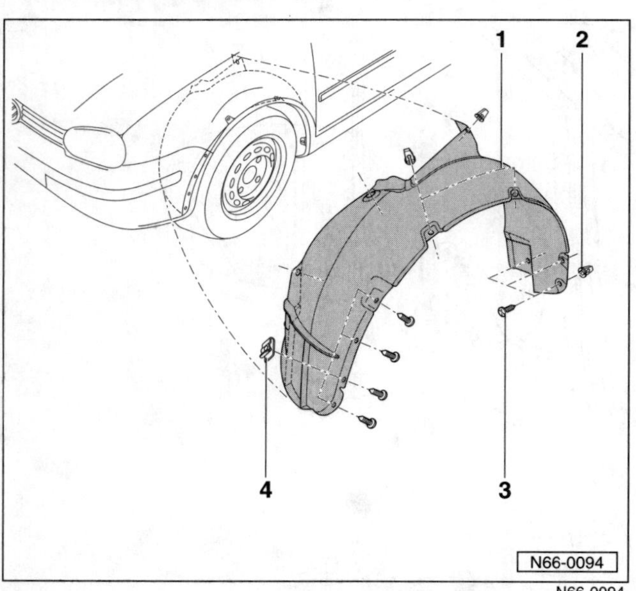

N66-0094

Fig. 5. Front wheel housing liner and related hardware.

The numbered list below applies to Fig. 5.

1. **Wheel housing liner**
   - Removal:
     Remove wheel
     (when installing tighten lug bolts to 120 Nm (89 ft-lb)
     Remove screws (item 3)–(qty. 12) and wheel housing liner
2. **Spreader nut**
3. **Screw**
4. **Speed nut**
   - On bumper cover

   NOTE —

   Wheel housing liners may differ slightly depending on equipment, with regard to position and number of mounting elements.

Rear wheel housing liner

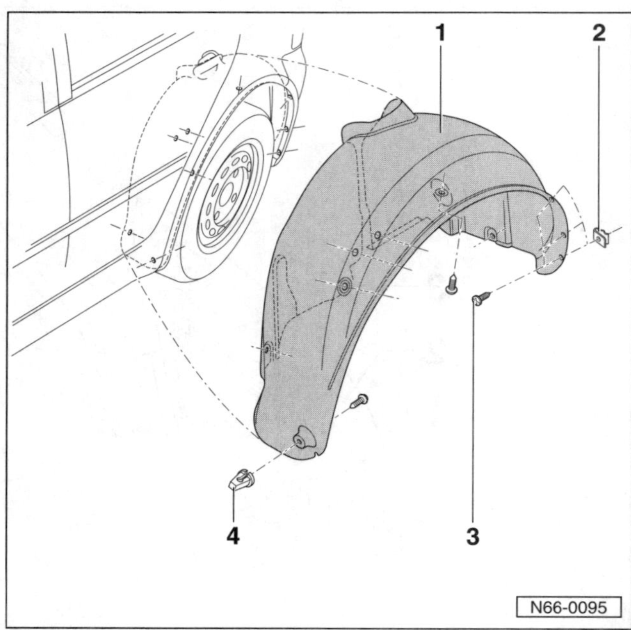

N66-0095

Fig. 6. Rear wheel housing liner and related hardware.

The numbered list below applies to Fig. 6.

1. **Wheel housing liner**
   - Removal:
     Remove wheel
     (when installing tighten lug bolts to 120 Nm (89 ft-lb)
     Remove screws (item 3)–(qty. 7) and wheel housing liner
2. **Speed nut**
   - On bumper cover
3. **Screw**
4. **Spreader nut**

   NOTE —

   Wheel housing liners may differ slightly depending on equipment, with regard to position and number of mounting elements.

EXTERIOR MOLDINGS

Roof moldings, overview

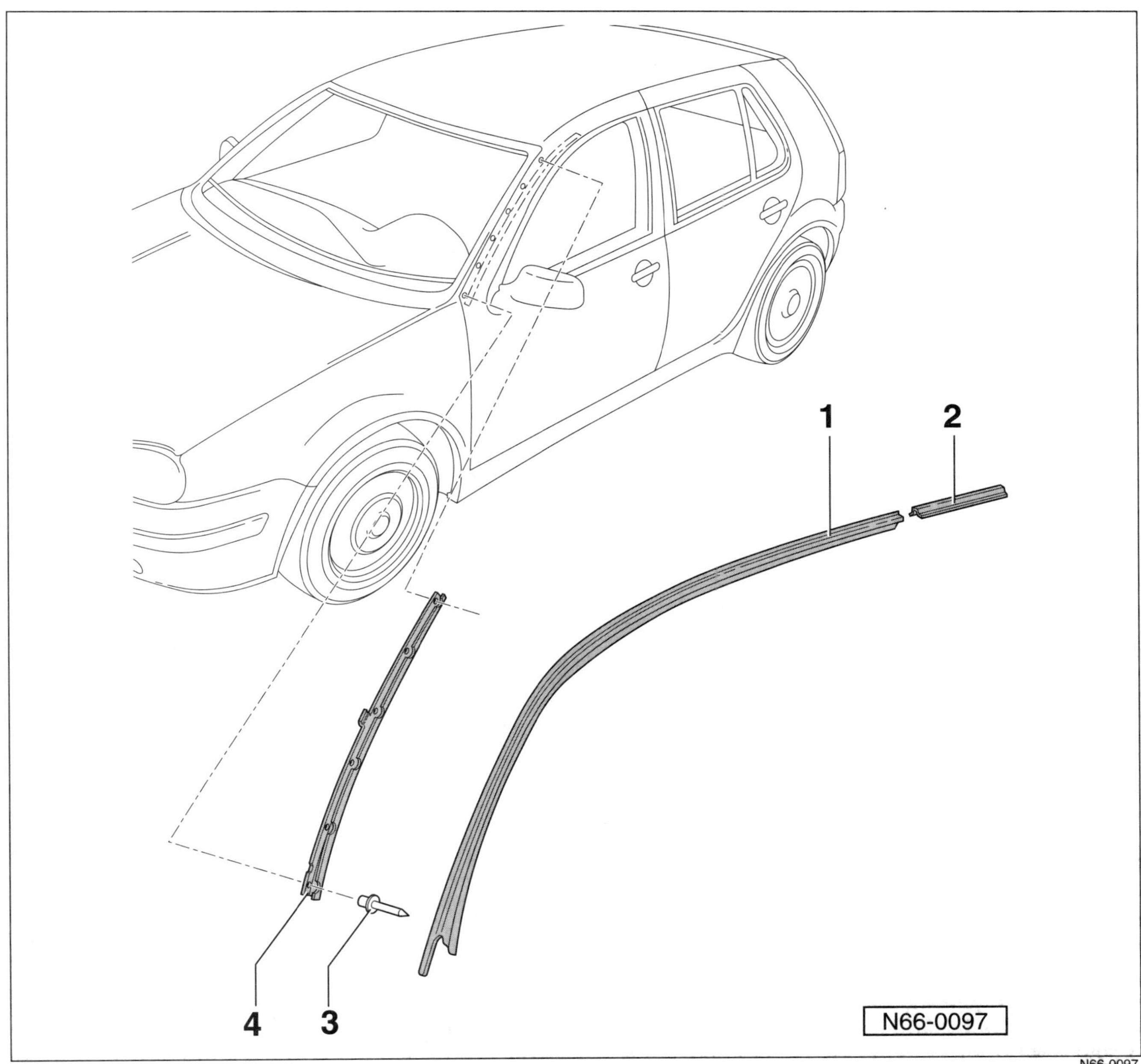

N66-0097

Fig. 7. Details of various roof moldings on Golf/Jetta.

1. **Roof molding**
   - With cover strip (item 2).
   - Do not bend roof molding
   - To remove, start at windshield, carefully pry off with soft plastic wedge
   - To install, align molding on B-pillar (2-door) or C-pillar (4-door) and assemble moving forward

2. **Cover strip**
   - Installing:
     Insert cover strip into pocket of roof molding onto stop, then press into roof channel
     A lubricant may be used to ease assembly

3. **Pop rivet**

4. **Angled strip**

Side moldings, overview

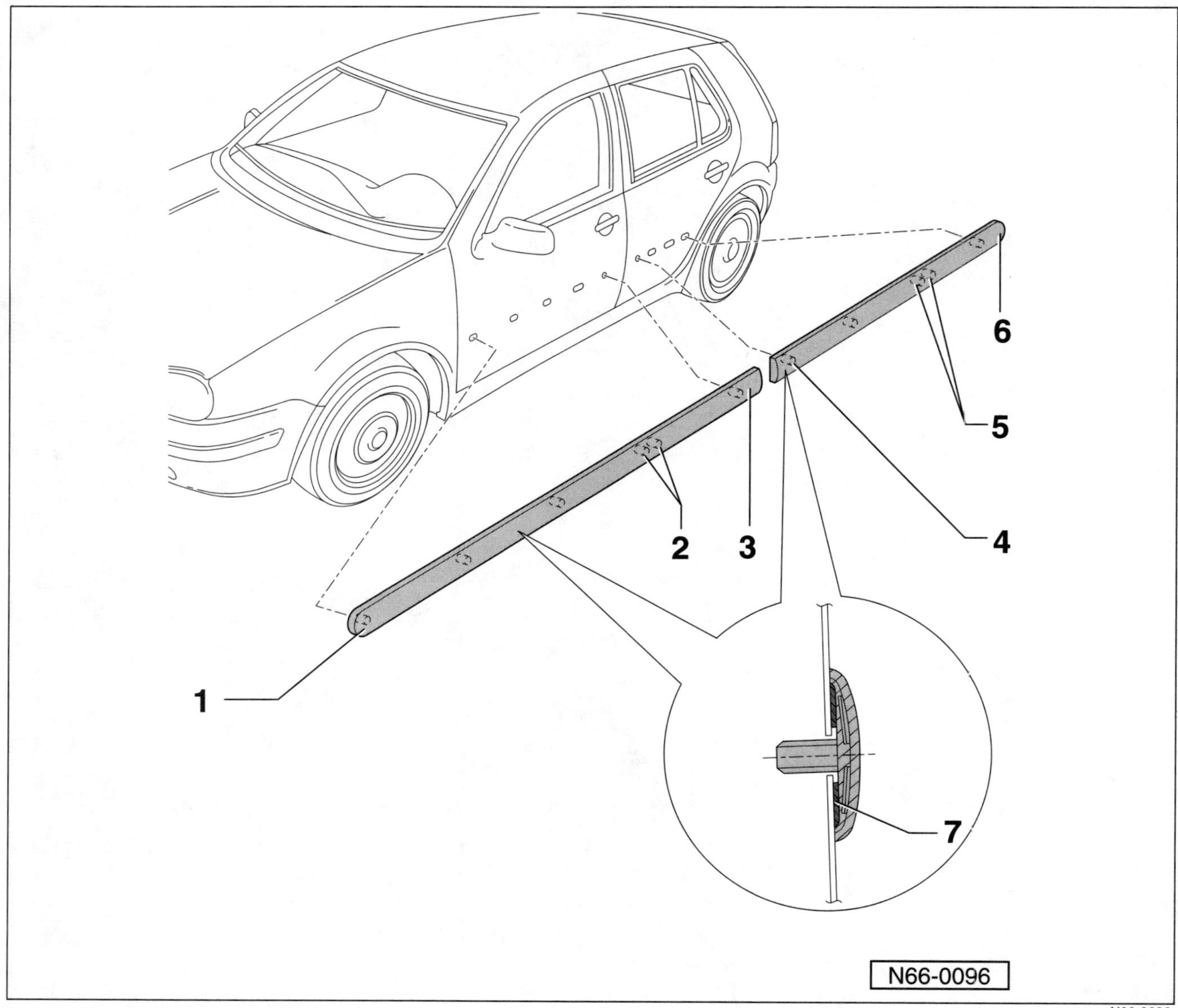

N66-0096

Fig. 8. Protective side moldings on Golf/Jetta.

1. **Front door protective side molding**
   - Left and right-hand protective side moldings have different hole patterns
   - Self-adhesive backing
   - Warm up molding and backing with hot air blower before installing
   - Working temperature when attaching moldings should be at least 20°C (68 °F)
   - Clean exterior panels with solvent, treat with silicone remover and rub dry
   - Use locating tabs (item 3 and 4) to position molding
2. **Pins**
   - Prevents twisting of molding
3. **Locating tab**
4. **Locating tab**
5. **Pins**
   - Prevents twisting of molding
6. **Rear door protective side molding**
   - Left and right-hand protective side moldings have different hole patterns
   - Self-adhesive backing
   - Use locating tabs (item 3 and 4) to position molding
7. **Protective foil**

FRONT GRILLE

Front grille assembly

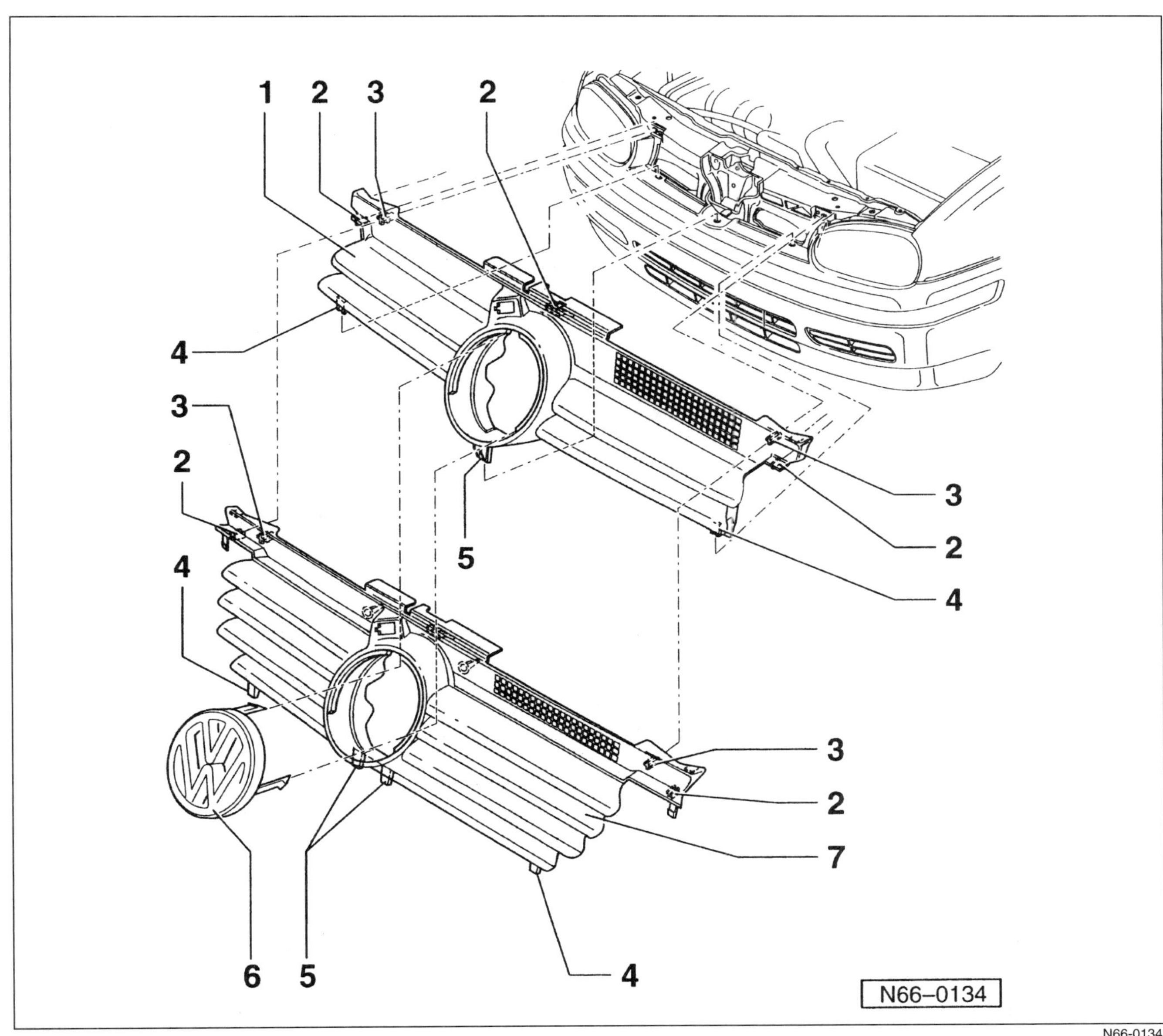

N66-0134

Fig. 9. Front grille assembly for Golf or Jetta.

1. **Golf grille**
2. **Attachment clip**
3. **Pin**
4. **Locking tab**
5. **Locating tab**
6. **VW emblem**
   - Clipped onto grille
7. **Jetta grille**

To remove grille, separate hood release lever from hood lock as shown in **63 Bumpers**. Unlock attachment clips (item 2) with a screwdriver. Pull pins (item 3) out of upper radiator support and remove grille from top.

To install, align radiator grille with center locator (item 5). Insert lower tabs (item 4) in bumper cover and clip in upper area. Install pins (item 3).

69 Seatbelts, Airbags

TABLE

GENERAL

This repair group covers emergency tensioning (pyrotechnic) seat belt assemblies and airbag system components. This repair group does not cover airbag system or pyrotechnic seat belt fault diagnosis or repair. Service and repair to these systems requires special test equipment, knowledge and training and should only be carried out by an authorized Volkswagen Dealer. Before starting repairs involving these systems, always read and observe all warnings, cautions and notes.

> ***WARNING —***
> *Disconnecting the negative (–) battery cable may erase fault codes and basic settings in the engine management and automatic transmission control modules. Some driveability problems may be noticed until the system re-adapts to operating conditions. OBD II readiness codes, which may be required for emissions testing, may also be erased. Convenience electronics (alarm system, interior light control, power locks, mirrors, and windows) may need to be re-set using a VAG 1551/1552 or equivalent scan tool.*

SEATBELTS

The vehicles covered by this manual use an inertia reel-type lap/shoulder belt combination to restrain the front seat passengers. In addition, these belts are self-tensioning through the use of an electric or pyrotechnic device. Deployment of the tensioner is by means of either a mechanical trigger or in conjunction with the airbag system (electric). Rear seat passengers are protected by an inertia reel-type lap/shoulder belt combination. A warning light in the instrument cluster illuminates when the ignition is first switched on as a reminder to buckle up. See Fig. 1.

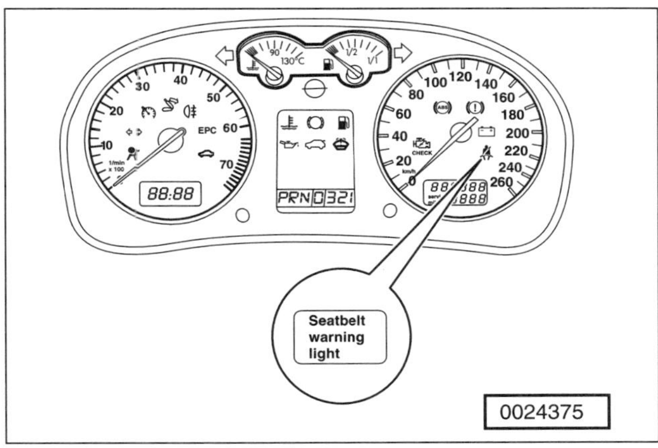

0024375

Fig. 1. Seat belt warning light will be illuminated when ignition is switched on. It will stay illuminated for approximately 6 seconds and then go out if the seatbelt is not buckled. It should not come on at any other time.

Special precautions for pyrotechnic seatbelt equipped vehicles

Emergency tensioning front seat belt systems can enhance passenger safety in the event of a collision provided that the seat belts are used. Special service precautions must be followed to prevent possible serious bodily injury to the repair technician and others involved in the handling and storage of pyrotechnic seatbelt components and to insure proper operation in the event of a collision.

> ***WARNING —***
>
> - *Before working on pyrotechnic seatbelt components linked to airbag systems, **disconnect the battery first.***
> - *Pyrotechnic seat belts are activated by an explosive device. Handled improperly or without adequate safeguards and training, the system can be very dangerous. Special precautions must be observed when working on or near the seatbelts.*
> - *Seat belts are vehicle safety systems. To guard against personal injury or system failure, only trained Volkswagen service Technicians should test, disassemble or service the pyrotechnic seat belt systems.*
> - *Install new seatbelt unit as soon as the unit is removed from the packaging. Reinstall in packaging if work will not be completed immediately.*
> - *Do not leave any pyrotechnic seatbelt unit unattended. If work is interrupted, store seatbelt unit in a secure location where it cannot be disturbed.*
> - *The storage and transportation of airbag units must be in accordance with all applicable Federal, State and Local rules and regulations.*
> - *Observe all cautions, warnings and notes before starting repairs involving airbag systems.*
> - *Belt tensioners that have been deployed can be disposed of as normal scrap.*
> - *Do not use tools with a hammer-type action to disassemble the belt tensioner.*
> - *The pyrotechnic seatbelt propellant has no expiration date, and it has an unlimited, maintenance-free life.*
> - *The belt tensioner unit must not be exposed to grease, cleaning solutions or similar substances.*
> - *Belt tensioner units must not be exposed to temperatures above 100°C (212°F), even for short periods.*
> - *Belt tensioner components may not be opened or repaired; always use new parts.*
> - *Belt tensioner units which have been dropped on the must not be installed into a vehicle.*
> - *Belt tensioner units that show evidence of mechanical or physical damaged (dents, cracks) must be replaced.*
> - *Pyrotechnic seatbelt units which have not been deployed should be marked and returned to the manufacturer for disposal using original seatbelt shipping container.*

Seatbelts, inspecting

Any time that a New Beetle is involved in an accident, all of the seatbelts should be checked for damage and proper operation.

> ***WARNING —***
> *After every accident the seat belt system must be inspected systematically. If damage is found when inspecting the check points, the customer must be advised regarding the necessity of replacing the seatbelts.*

Webbing (belt material), checking

- Pull belt completely out.
- Inspect webbing for dirt and soiling; wash as needed using a mild soap solution.
- Inspect for damage according to Fig. 2. Fig. 3. or Fig. 4.

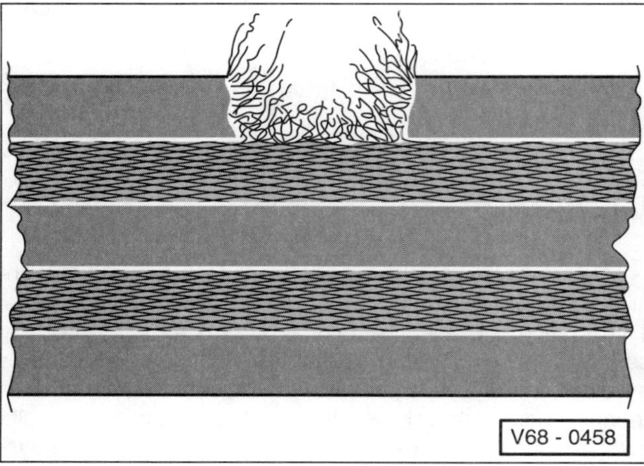

V68-0458

Fig. 2. Seatbelt webbing showing example of cuts, chafing and tears. If vehicle was in an accident replace complete seatbelt assembly with buckle. If vehicle was not in an accident and damage is from other sources, it is ok to replace only the belt.

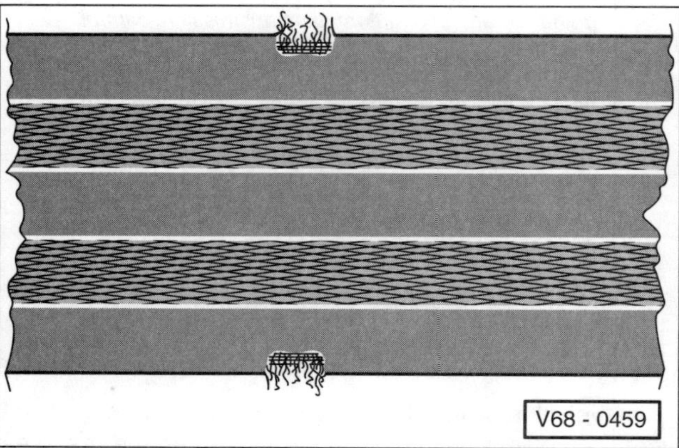

V68-0459

Fig. 3. Seatbelt webbing showing example of torn edges. If vehicle was in an accident replace complete seatbelt assembly with buckle. If vehicle was not in an accident and damage is from other sources, it is permissible to replace only the belt.

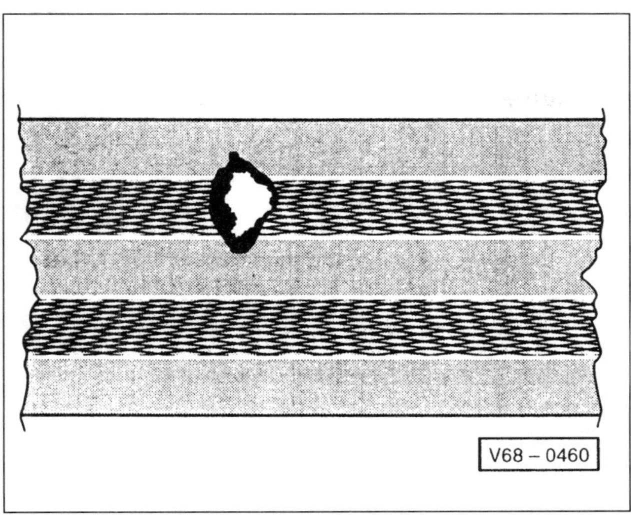

V68-0460

Fig. 4. Seatbelt webbing showing example of burns from cigarettes etc. It is permissible to replace only the belt in this case.

Inertia reel, checking

- Pull belt out of reel with a firm and sudden jerk. Seatbelt should lock immediately.
- Road test from 20 km/h (13 mph) by applying brakes suddenly to simulate an emergency stop. Seatbelt should lock immediately.
- If belt does not lock, check mounting position and correct as necessary.
- If belt does not lock and mounting is in order, replace complete seatbelt assembly.

> ***WARNING —***
> *For safety reasons, the road test should be done on a traffic-free stretch of road or parking lot to ensure safety to the vehicle and driver as well as other vehicles and pedestrians.*

Belt buckle latch, checking

- Inspect belt latch and buckle for cracks and breaks.
- If there is any indication of cracking or breakage, replace complete seatbelt assembly
- Inspect belt latch and buckle for proper operation by inserting latch into buckle a minimum of 5 times. Latch should engage buckle firmly and securely with an audible clicking sound and should not pull apart.
- If latch and buckle do not engage smoothly or firmly, or come apart when pulled, replace complete seatbelt assembly.

Belt buckle release, checking

- Engage latch and buckle with no tension on the belt (slack) and push release button a minimum of 5 times. Latch must spring out of belt buckle on its own.
- If latch fails to spring out of belt buckle, replace complete seatbelt assembly.

Belt guides and latch tongue, checking

- Inspect plastic guides for deformation, scoring and fractures due to accident. Do not confuse smooth wear marks which are normal due to frequent use.
- If deformation, scoring or fractures are present, replace complete seatbelt assembly.

Seatbelt mounting components and anchorage points, checking

- Check latch and bracket for deformation and/or stretching.
- Check function of height adjuster.
- Check anchorage points on B-pillar, seat and floor for distortion, damage and proper torque.
- If distortion or damage is present, repair or replace components as required. Torque fasteners to specification.

Automatic retractor mechanism, checking

- Check retractor mechanism for smooth operation when seatbelt is pulled out and smooth operation when belt is reeled in.
- Ensure that seatbelts equipped with child seat feature operate properly when seatbelt is pulled completely out.
- Ensure that seatbelt is not twisted.
- If retractor mechanism does not operate properly, replace seat belt retractor.
- If front pyrotechnic seatbelts do not retract, they have been deployed and are no longer usable. They must be replaced.

Front seatbelt assembly

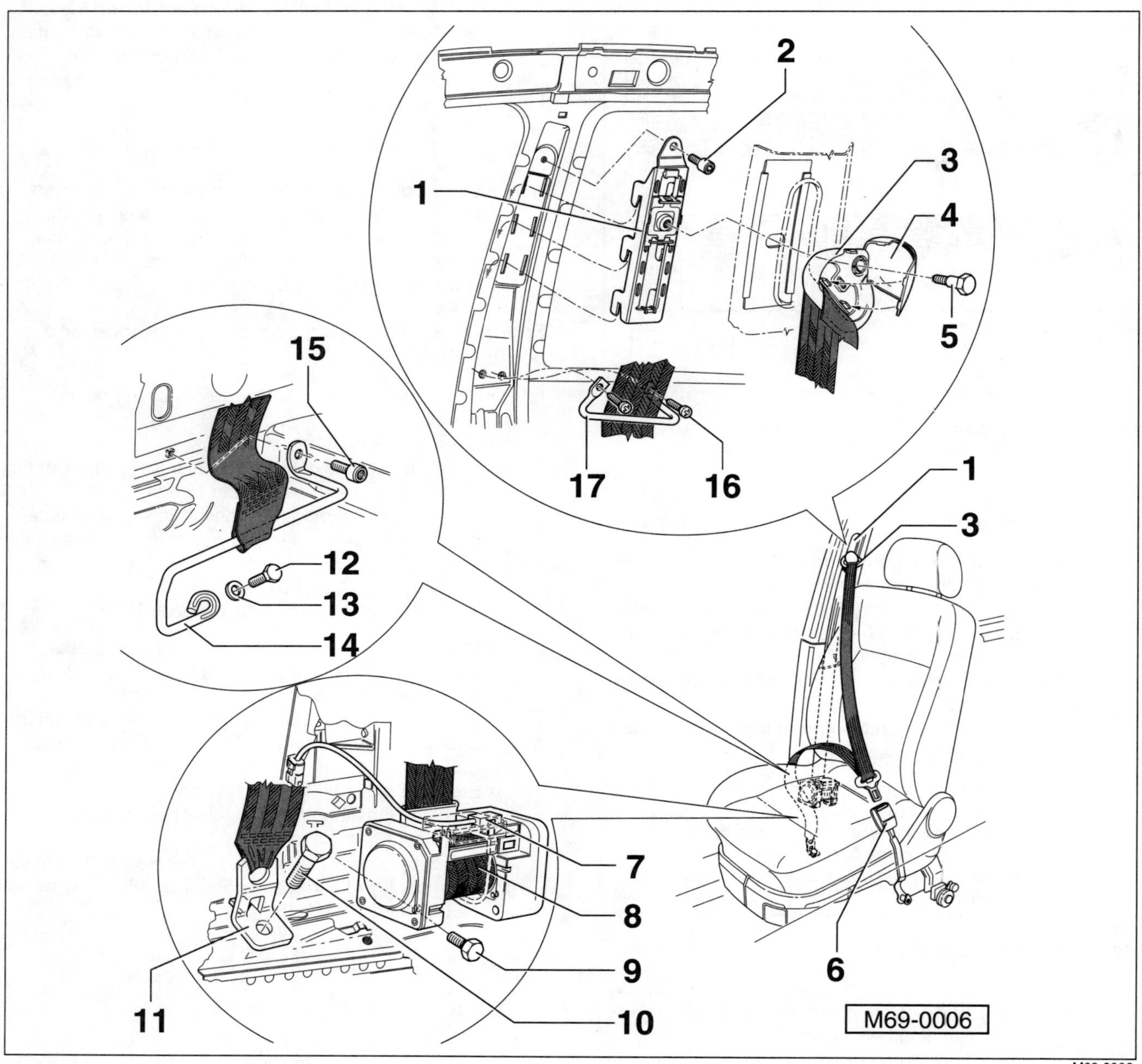

Fig. 5. Front seatbelt tensioner shown with related components.

> ***WARNING —***
> *Observe all cautions, warnings and notes before starting repairs involving airbag systems.*

> ***CAUTION —***
> *Before starting any body disassembly, straightening or other body repair work, the belt tensioning units must be removed.*

1. **Belt height adjuster**
   - To remove height adjustment mechanism, first remove trim on top of B-pillar
2. **Screw**
   - Tighten to 23 Nm (17 ft-lb)
3. **Belt relay/guide**
4. **Belt relay/guide cover**

(continued from previous page)

5. **Bolt**
   - Tighten to 40 Nm (30 ft-lb)

6. **Front belt buckle (latch)**

7. **Connector**
   - For electrically deployed belt tensioner only

8. **Seat belt with belt tensioner**
   - Two different seatbelt tensioners are installed depending on vehicle production date
   - Mechanically activated with pyrotechnic tensioner for vehicles without side airbags
   - Electrically deployed via airbag system for vehicles with side airbags
   - After an accident in which one or both belt tensioners have been deployed (triggered), both seat belts must be replaced (the belts will no longer retract)
   - Retaining tabs determine position of belt reel in mount
   - To remove, first remove lower B-panel trim and sill panel trim, see **70 Trim–Interior**
   - The disposal of old components that have not been deployed (triggered) is done by the manufacturer

9. **Bolt**
   - Tighten to 40 Nm (30 ft-lb)
   - Loosen bolt to prevent belt tensioner from deploying during repairs (mechanical tensioner only)
   - Tighten bolt to return tensioner to operational condition after repairs (mechanical tensioner only)

10. **Bolt**
    - Only on 4-door models
    - Tighten to 40 Nm (30 ft-lb)

11. **Lower belt mount**
    - Tighten to 1.5 Nm (13 in-lb)

12. **Bolt**
    - Only on 2-door models
    - Tighten to 40 Nm (30 ft-lb)

13. **Washer**
    - Only on 2-door models

14. **Guide bracket**
    - Only on 2-door models

15. **Bolt**
    - Only on 2-door models
    - Tighten to 23 Nm (17 ft-lb)

16. **Screw**

17. **Belt guide**
    - Secured with two screws

Rear seat belt assembly

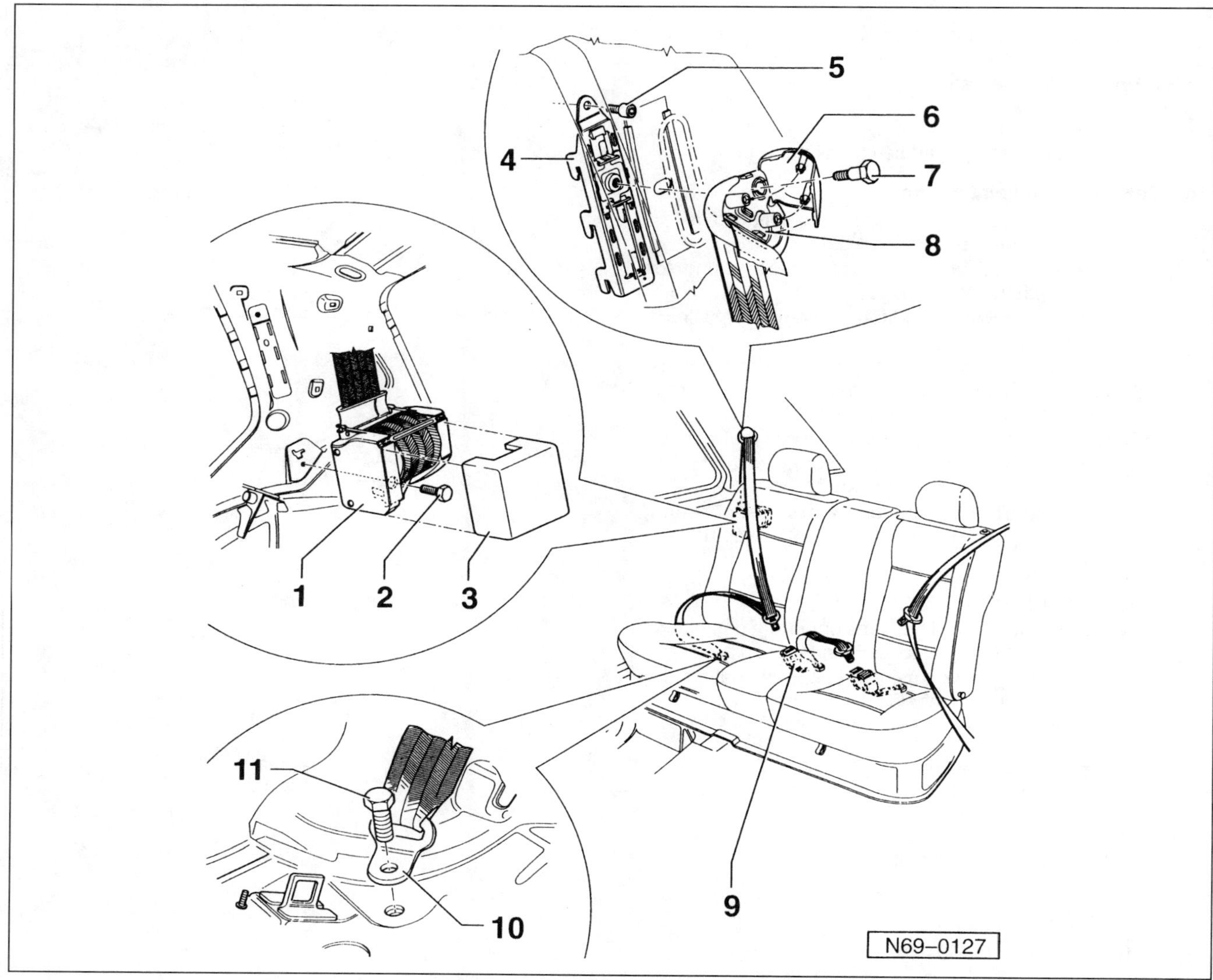

Fig. 6. Rear seatbelt assemblies shown with related components.

N69-0127

1. **Belt inertia reel**
   - Retaining tabs determine position of belt reel in mount
   - Removing:
     Pull up rear seat bottom and fold forward
     Release rear seat back rest and fold forward
     Remove support for luggage compartment cover, see **70 Trim –Interior**
     Unclip luggage compartment trim in area of belt inertia reel
     Remove belt inertia reel (item 1), belt relay (item 8), and lower anchorage (item 10)
2. **Bolt**
   - Tighten to 40 Nm (30 ft-lb)
3. **Sound deadener**
   - On belt inertia reel
4. **Belt height adjuster**
   - Remove C-pillar trim to access, see **70 Trim–Interior**
5. **Socket head screw**
   - Tighten to 23 Nm (17 ft-lb)
6. **Cover cap for belt guide**
7. **Bolt**
   - Tighten to 40 Nm (30 ft-lb)
8. **Belt guide**
9. **Belt latch**
10. **Lower anchorage**
11. **Bolt**
    - Tighten to 40 Nm (30 ft-lb)

Center rear seat belt assembly

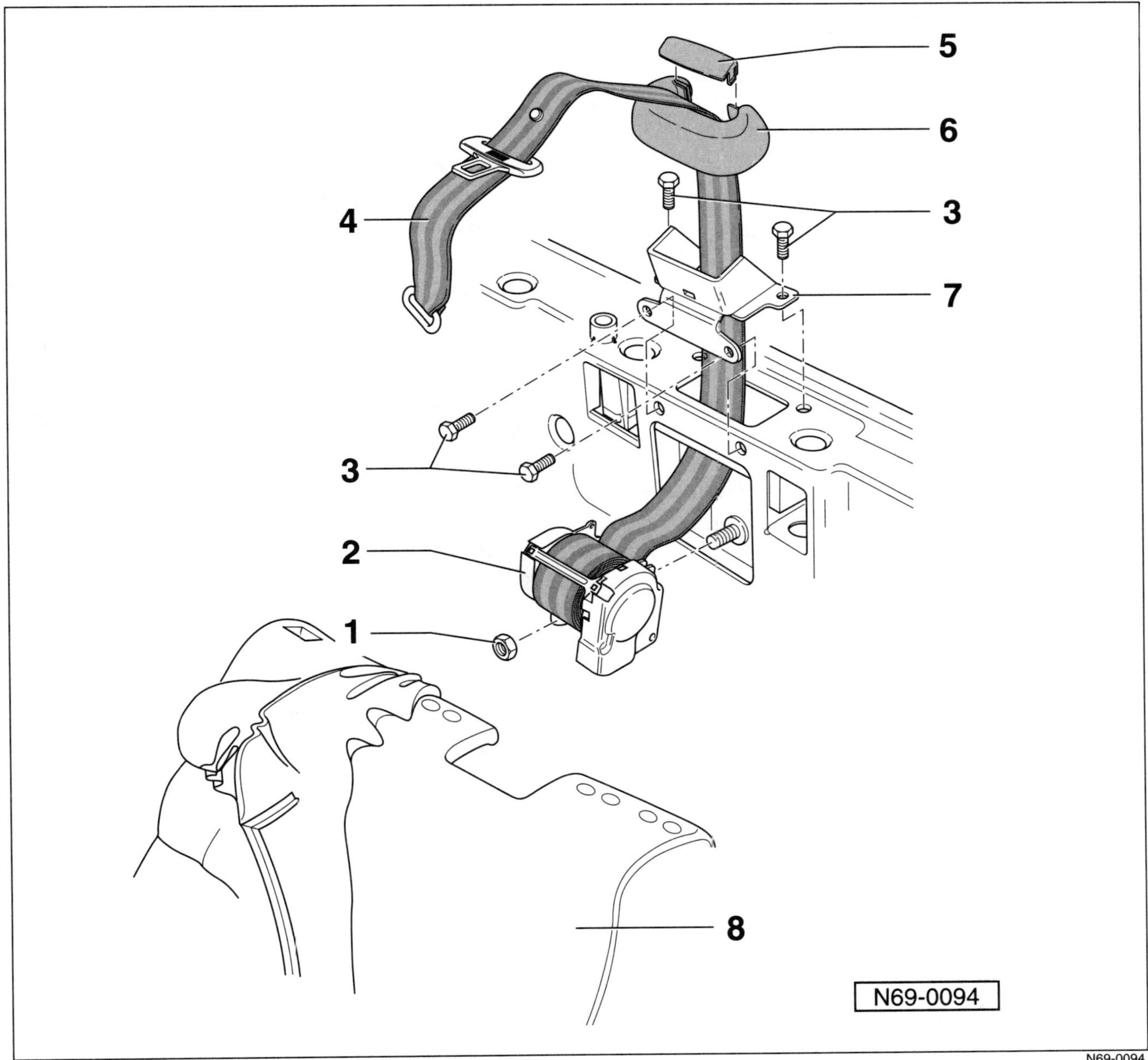

Fig. 7. Center seatbelt in rear seat of Golf/Jetta.

1. **Nut**
   - Tighten to 40 Nm (30 ft-lb)
2. **Belt inertia reel**
   - Removing, **see** (B)
3. **Mounting bolts**
   - Qty. 4
   - Tighten to 23 Nm (17 ft-lb)
4. **Seatbelt**
5. **Cover**
   - Remove first when removing seatbelt
   - Removing, **see** (A)
6. **Belt guide**
7. **Belt mount**
8. **Rear seat backrest**

A Rear center seatbelt guide, removing

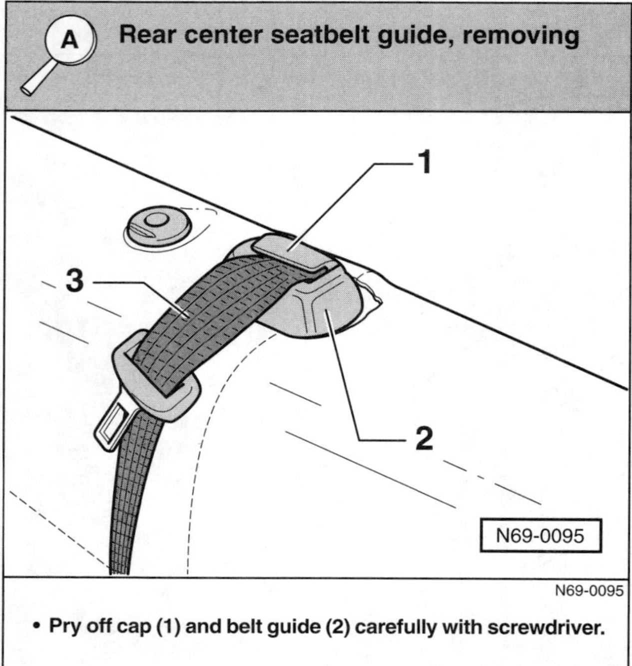

N69-0095

- Pry off cap (1) and belt guide (2) carefully with screwdriver.

B Rear center belt reel, removing

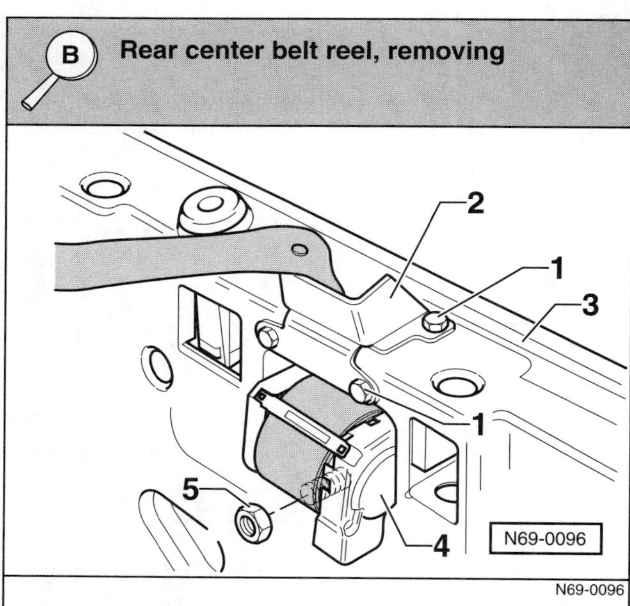

N69-0096

- Remove cap and belt guide as shown above.
- Unhook seatbelt from lower mount.
- Remove head restraint guides, see 72 Seats.
- Release seat back rest cover and padding, see 72 Seats.
- Remove belt reel mounting bolts (1) and remove seat belt mount (2) from backrest frame (3).
- Remove hex nut (5) and unhook inertia reel (4) from backrest frame.
- Guide seat belt with belt tongue downward from backrest frame.

Child restraint LATCH guidance fixture, installing

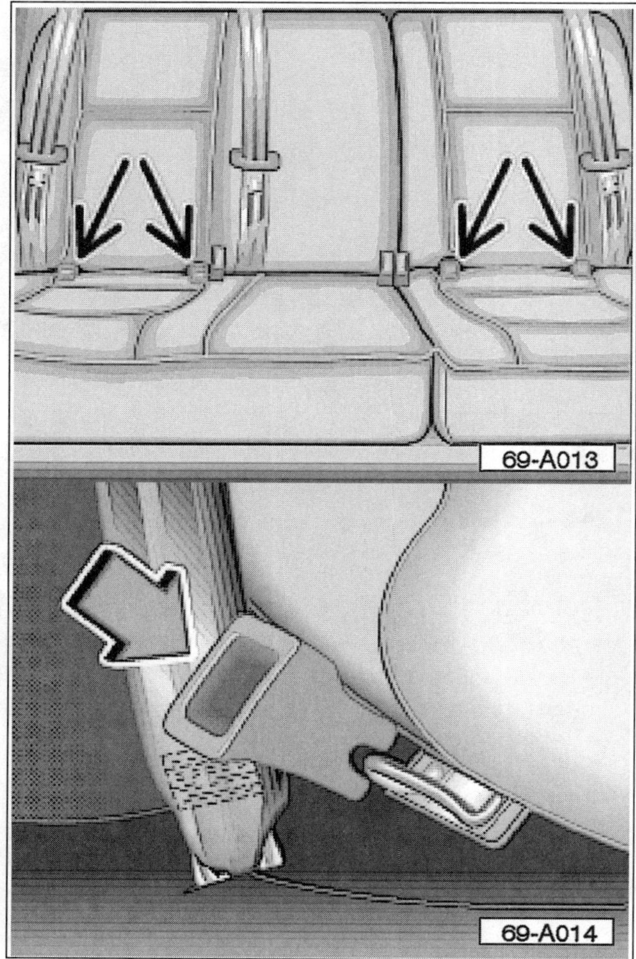

69-A013, 69-A014

Fig. 8. Locate four anchorage bars between rear seat back and cushion (**arrows**, top illustration). Install LATCH guidance fixture (**arrow**, bottom illustration) by snapping over anchorage bars. Part number on LATCH guidance fixture must face down when installed.

AIRBAGS

Diagnostics, component testing and repair of the airbag system should only be carried out by properly trained Volkswagen technicians using specialized test equipment.

When the ignition key is turned on, the airbag warning light will illuminate for approximately 5 seconds. See Fig. 9. The illuminated light indicates the self-test of the air bag electronic control module, and all of the related electronic components. If all monitored systems are operating normally, the light will go out. If the warning light does not go out after approximately 5 seconds, or if it comes on at any time while driving, the system has detected a fault and will not operate. In this case, the vehicle should be inspected by an authorized Volkswagen Dealer.

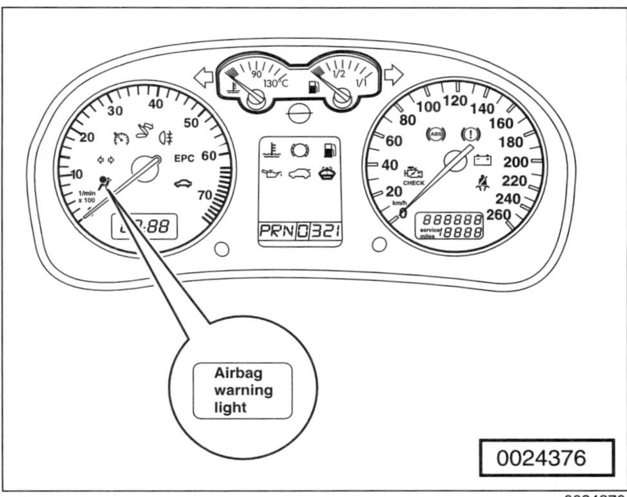

0024376

Fig. 9. Airbag warning light in instrument cluster.

If the vehicle has been involved in an accident where the airbag was deployed, Volkswagen specifies that the following components must be replaced:

- All airbag units that have been deployed
- Passenger side airbag support
- Airbag control module and sensors
- Airbag spiral spring/slip ring
- Deployed front seatbelt tensioners

In addition, the following must also be replaced if necessary:

- All damaged components including, but not limited to, seat frames, seat covers and rear seatbelts

In the event of an accident where the airbags have not been deployed, observe the airbag system warning light. If the airbag system warning light does not indicate a fault, it is not necessary to replace any airbag components.

Airbag equipped vehicles have a fuel crash shut-off. This is intended to reduce the risk of vehicle fire following a crash by switching off the fuel pump via the fuel pump relay.

Special precautions for airbag equipped vehicles

Special service precautions must be followed to prevent possible serious bodily injury to the repair technician and others involved in the handling and storage of airbag components and to insure proper operation in the event of a collision. For an overview of the airbag system. See Fig. 10.

WARNING —

- *Before working on any airbag, steering wheel or steering column component, always **disconnect the battery first.***
- *No waiting time is required after disconnecting the battery. Airbag systems can be worked on immediately.*
- *Airbags are inflated by an explosive device. Handled improperly or without adequate safeguards and training, the system can be very dangerous. Special precautions must be observed prior to any work at or near the steering wheel and steering column including the pedal assembly.*
- *The airbag is a vehicle safety system. To guard against personal injury or airbag system failure, only factory trained Volkswagen service technicians should test, disassemble or service the airbag system.*
- *Airbag units that have been dropped onto a hard surface must not be installed. Always replace any airbag system component that has been mechanically or physically damaged (example: dented or cracked).*
- *Make sure that no one is in the passenger compartment when connecting the battery Ground (GND) strap.*
- *A technician must be electrostatically discharged before picking up or touching any airbag unit. This is accomplished by touching a suitable metal ground such as a water or heating pipe or metal frame. If in the vehicle, this is accomplished by touching a suitable chassis ground such as a door latch or striker.*
- *Install new airbag unit as soon as the unit is removed from the packaging. Reinstall in packaging if work will not be completed immediately.*
- *Do not leave any undeployed airbag unit unattended. If work is interrupted, store airbag unit in a secure location where it cannot be disturbed.*
- *Undeployed airbag units that have been replaced must only be stored and shipped in packaging designed specifically for the purpose, such as packaging found with the replacement unit.*
- *Undeployed airbag units that have been replaced must be properly identified as such.*
- *The storage and transportation of airbag units must be in accordance with all applicable Federal, State and Local rules and regulations.*
- *Airbag units that have been removed during the course of repairs must be stored with the padded side facing up and in a secure location where it cannot be disturbed.*
- *Observe all cautions, warnings and notes before starting repairs involving airbag systems.*

Airbag system, overview

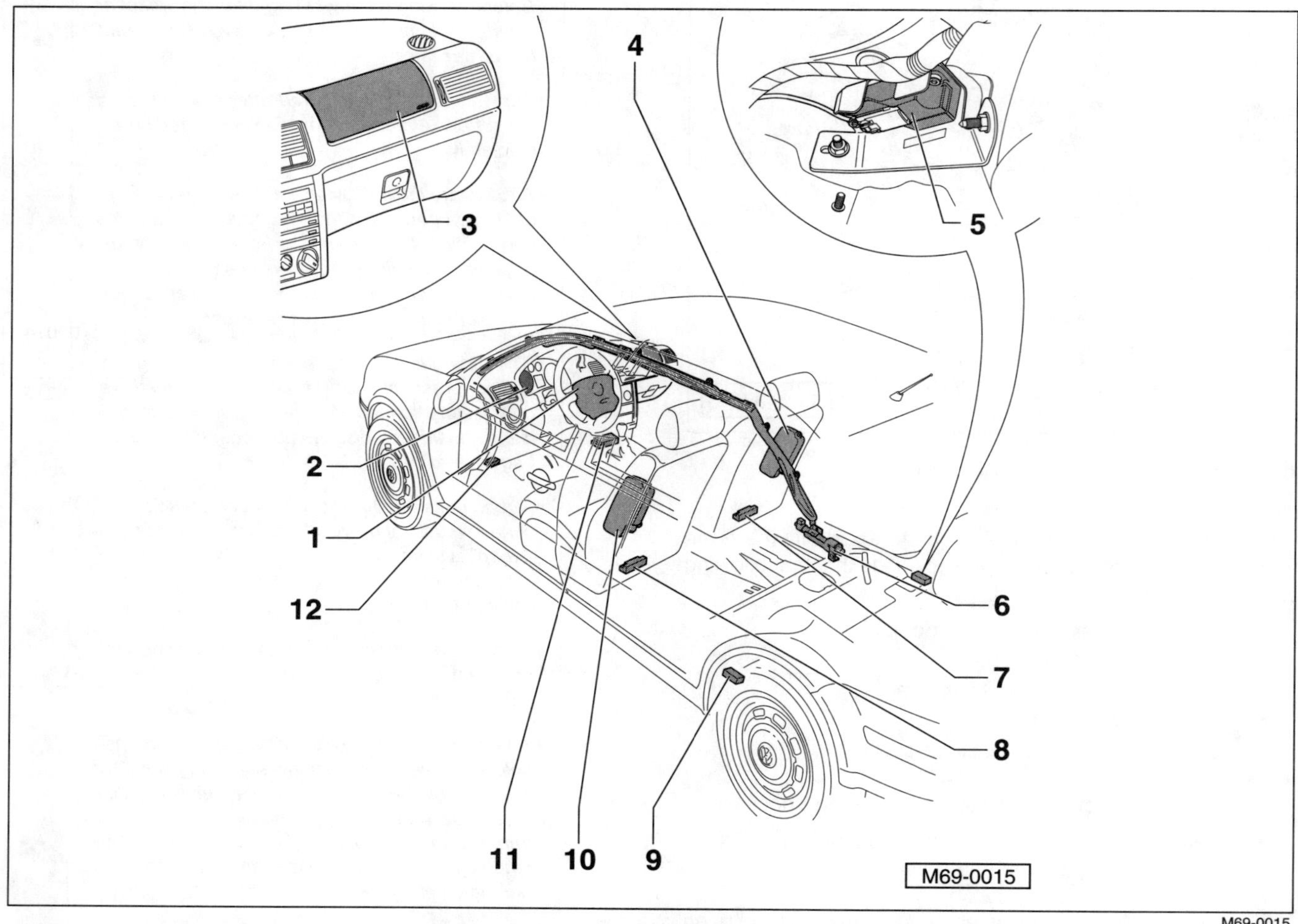

M69-0015

Fig. 10. Airbag system shown with related components including seatbelt tensioners where applicable.

1. **Airbag unit, driver's side**
   - With airbag igniter (N95)
2. **Airbag malfunction indicator lamp (K75)**
   - Location: in instrument cluster
3. **Airbag unit, front passenger**
   - With airbag igniter (N131)
4. **Side airbag unit, front passenger**
   - With airbag igniter (N200)
   - Location: in right front seat backrest frame
5. **Impact sensor, rear passenger side**
   - Location: bolted to body under rear wheelhouse trim
6. **Side curtain protection**
   - Driver side Jetta model shown
   - Located in driver and passenger side roof pillars
7. **Impact sensor, side airbag, front passenger (G180)**
   - Location: bolted to right front floor crossmember under passenger seat
8. **Impact sensor, side airbag, driver (G179)**
   - Location: bolted to left front floor crossmember under driver seat
9. **Impact sensor, rear driver side**
   - Location: bolted to body under rear wheelhouse trim
10. **Side airbag unit, driver side**
    - With airbag igniter (N199)
    - Location: in left front seat backrest frame
11. **Airbag control module (J234)**
    - Location: on tunnel under center console
12. **Data link connector**
    - Location: left lower side of instrument panel
    - If replacing any airbag unit or airbag control module, consult your authorized Volkswagen Dealer's Parts Department for the proper registration procedure

Airbag control module

The airbag control module is mounted to the floor on the tunnel near the base of the bulkhead. See Fig. 11. To access the control module, remove the footwell trim, see **70 Trim–Interior**. Be sure to disconnect battery ground (GND) strap from battery negative (–) terminal before removing control module. See the **Cautions** at the beginning of this repair group regarding battery disconnection.

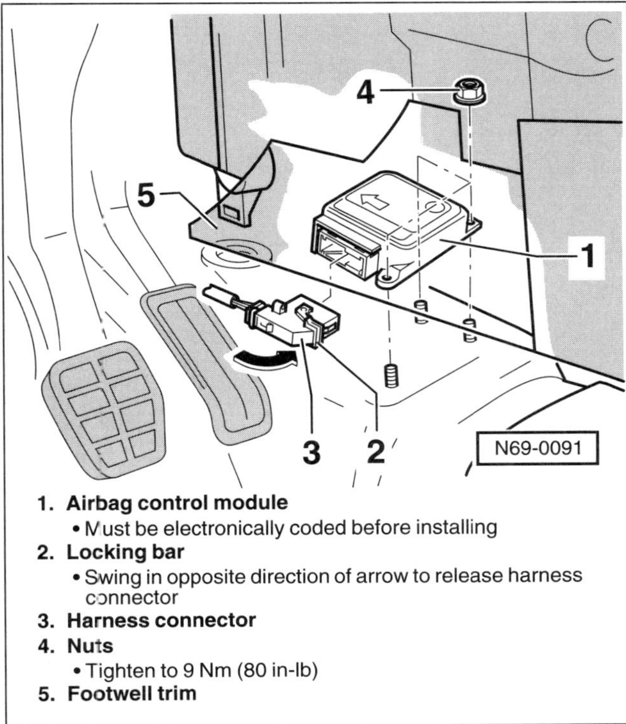

1. **Airbag control module**
   - Must be electronically coded before installing
2. **Locking bar**
   - Swing in opposite direction of arrow to release harness connector
3. **Harness connector**
4. **Nuts**
   - Tighten to 9 Nm (80 in-lb)
5. **Footwell trim**

N69-0091

Fig. 11. Airbag control module mounting position on tunnel.

> ***WARNING —***
>
> - *Observe all cautions, warnings and notes before starting repairs involving airbag systems.*
> - *Disconnect battery Ground (GND) strap before disconnecting or removing the airbag control module.*

Most service and repair to the airbag system requires the use of a scan tool such as the Volkswagen VAG 1551/1552 or equivalent. Access for diagnosis, including coding of replacement control modules is via the Data Link Connector (DLC) which is below the driver's side of the dashboard. Replacement airbag control modules are shipped uncoded and will not function when installed. Because of the specialized nature of these repairs, servicing should be referred to an authorized Volkswagen Dealer or qualified independent repair shop. Proper airbag control module coding is derived from the airbag control module part number as reported by the scan tool. For a listing of possible airbag control module codings, refer to **Table a**. Always verify vehicle equipment when installing and coding a new airbag control module.

Table a. Airbag control module coding

Vehicle equipment	Part No.	Index	Code No.
Only driver's airbag	1J0 909 603	AP	16720
Only driver's airbag	6Q0 909 601	OB	12354
Driver's/passenger airbag	1J0 909 603	AN	16718
Driver's/passenger airbag	6Q0 909 601	OC	12355
Driver's/passenger airbag	6Q0 909 601	12	12594
Driver's/passenger airbag USA	6Q0 909 601	OD	12356
Driver's/passenger airbag USA	1J0 909 603	J	00074
Driver's/passenger's airbag with kneebar USA (Mexico production)	6Q0 909 601	OM	12365
Driver's/passenger airbag USA (Brazil production)	1J0 909 601	13	12595
Driver's and side airbags	1JO 909 608	AS	16723
Driver's/passenger's and side airbags	1JO 909 608	AR	16722
Driver's/and side airbags + electric belt tensioner	1J0 909 609	B	00066

> ***NOTE —***
>
> *Volkswagen part numbers are given for reference only! Always consult with your Volkswagen Parts Department or aftermarket parts specialist for the latest parts information.*

Airbag unit in 4-spoke steering wheel, distinguishing features

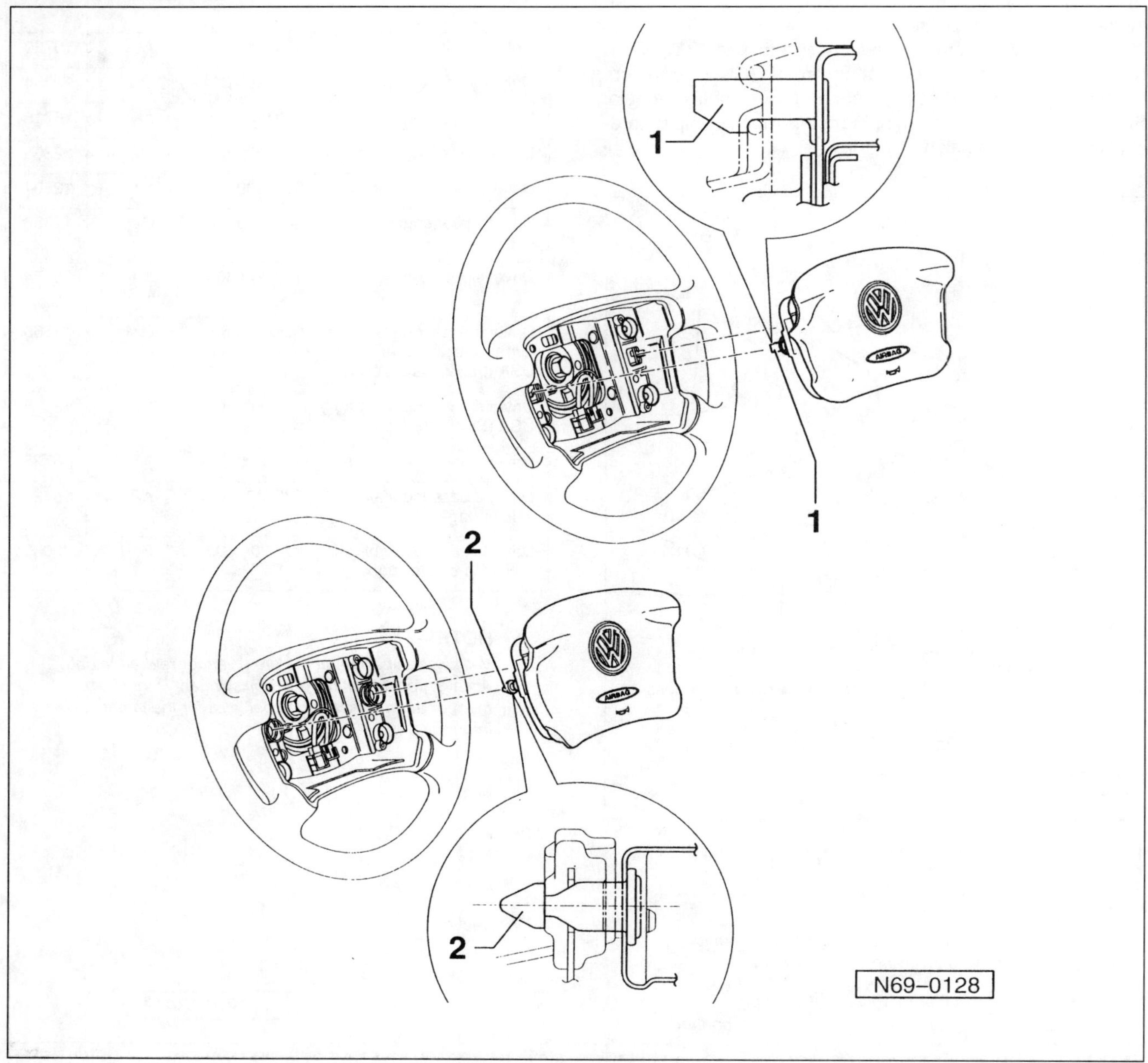

N69-0128

Fig. 12. Steering wheel shown with Petri and TRW airbags.

1. **Petri airbag, mounting stud**
   - Rectangular, see inset
2. **TRW airbag, mounting stud**
   - Stepped, see inset

> ***WARNING —***
> *Use only 4-spoke steering wheels, airbags and replacement parts supplied by the same manufacturer due to the different mounting studs of the various airbags.*

4-spoke steering wheel and airbag

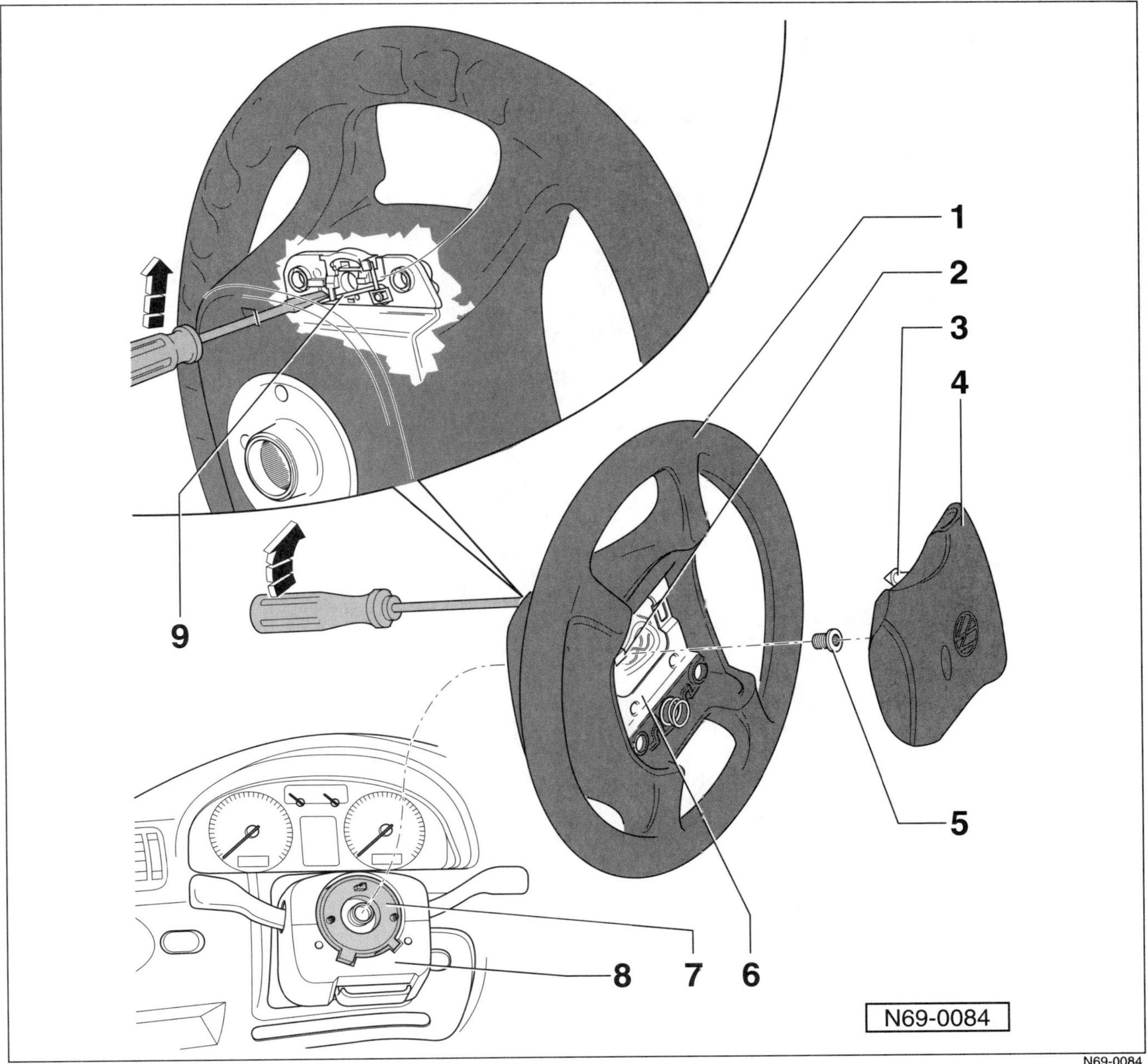

Fig. 13. 4-spoke steering wheel and airbag.

1. **Steering wheel**
2. **Connector**
3. **Locking lug**
   - Release from rear of steering wheel
4. **Airbag unit**
   - Because of differing engaging mechanisms, only steering wheel and airbags units from the same supplier can be installed, see Fig. 12.
5. **Bolt, multi-point socket-head**
   - Tighten to 50 Nm (37 ft-lb) with locking compound
   - Can be reused up to 5 times
   - Mark with center punch after each installation
6. **Securing plate**
7. **Spiral spring with slip ring**
8. **Steering column trim**
9. **Spring clip**

3-spoke steering wheel and airbag

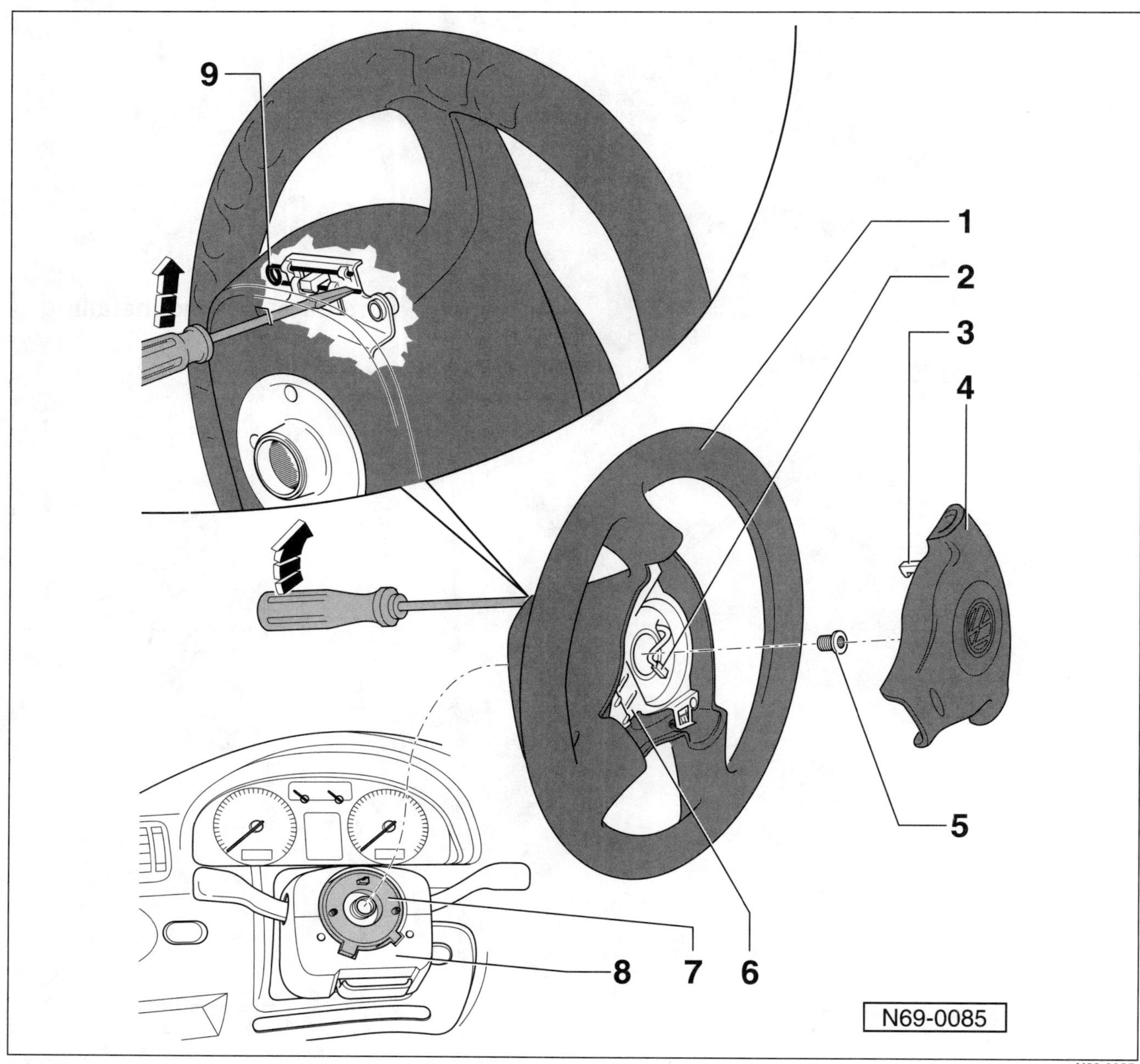

Fig. 14. 3-spoke steering wheel and airbag.

1. **Steering wheel**
2. **Connector**
3. **Locking lug**
   - Release from rear of steering wheel
4. **Airbag unit**
5. **Bolt, multi-point socket-head**
   - Tighten to 50 Nm (37 ft-lb) with locking compound
   - Can be reused up to 5 times
   - Mark with center punch after each installation
6. **Securing plate**
7. **Spiral spring with slip ring**
8. **Steering column trim**
9. **Spring clip**

Airbag unit in steering wheel, removing and installing

Removal of the steering wheel airbag unit is accomplished by inserting a tool into openings in the dashboard side of the steering wheel.

> ***WARNING —***
> *Observe all cautions, warnings and notes before starting repairs involving airbag systems.*

1. Disconnect battery ground (GND) strap from battery negative (–) terminal. See the **Cautions** at the beginning of this repair group regarding battery disconnection.

2. Release steering column adjustment lever.

3. Turn steering wheel until a spoke is vertical. Extend steering column out fully toward driver.

4. Secure steering column adjustment lever.

5. Using a screwdriver approximately 175 mm (7 in.) long, insert approximately 45 mm (1¾ in.) from reverse side into hole on dashboard side of steering wheel hub. See Fig. 13. or Fig. 14.

   NOTE —
   If a screwdriver with a very short handle is used, it is possible to eliminate step 2 and leave the instrument cluster in place.

6. Press screwdriver upward to press back spring clip and release locking lug of airbag unit. See Fig. 13. or Fig. 14.

7. Turn steering wheel back ½ turn (180°) and release second locking lug on opposite side.

8. Turn steering wheel to center position (wheels straight ahead).

9. Disconnect harness connector from airbag unit.

10. Place the removed airbag unit in a secure location with the padding side facing up.

11. Begin installation by connecting harness connector for airbag unit.

12. Position airbag unit on steering wheel and snap into place.

    NOTE —
    Airbag unit locking lugs must be heard and felt to snap into place.

13. Switch ignition on.

14. Connect battery ground strap.

> ***CAUTION —***
> *Make sure the passenger compartment is not occupied before connecting the battery Ground (GND) strap.*

> ***WARNING —***
> *Observe all cautions, warnings and notes when completing repairs involving airbag systems.*

Airbag slip ring, removing and installing

> ***WARNING —***
> *Observe all cautions, warnings and notes before starting repairs involving airbag systems.*

1. Turn the wheels to the straight ahead position.

2. Disconnect battery ground (GND) strap from battery negative (–) terminal. See the **Cautions** at the beginning of this repair group regarding battery disconnection.

3. Remove airbag unit in steering wheel as described earlier.

4. Remove steering wheel.

5. Remove steering column upper trim. See Fig. 15.

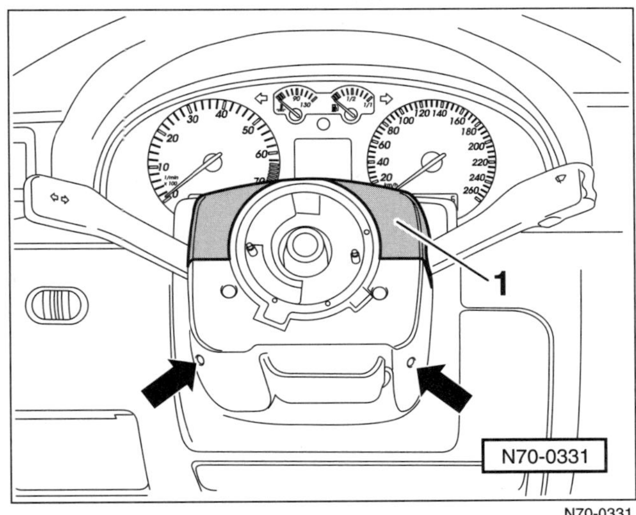

N70-0331

Fig. 15. Remove screws (**arrows**) for upper steering column trim.

6. Remove steering column lower trim. See Fig. 16.

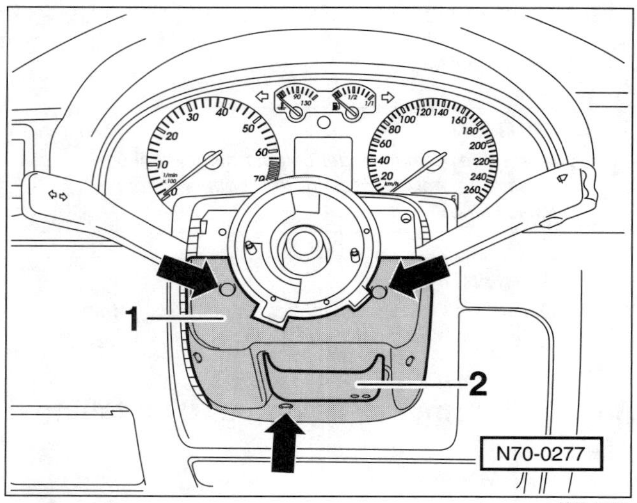

N70-0277

Fig. 16. Remove screws (**arrows**), release steering height adjustment lever (**2**), and pull off steering column lower trim (**1**).

7. Unplug harness connector and release locking lugs on slip ring and pull off. See Fig. 17.

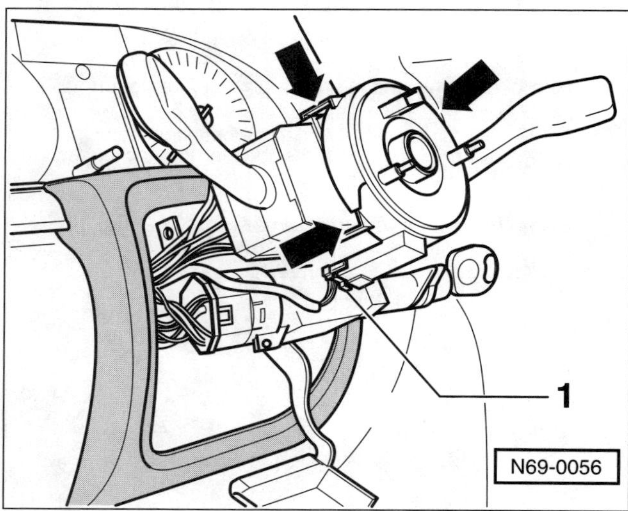

N68-0058

Fig. 17. Remove spiral spring/slip ring by releasing lugs (**arrows**) and unplugging harness connector (**1**).

NOTE —

Steering wheel must be in center position (wheels pointed straight ahead) when harness connector and slip ring are removed and installed.

8. Installation is the reverse of removal.

WARNING —

Observe all cautions, warnings and notes when completing repairs involving airbag systems.

Side airbag units

Both driver's and passenger's front seats are equipped with airbags mounted in the seat backrest frames. These airbags are designed to deploy under certain side impact conditions and are triggered by separate sensors mounted to the front floor crossmembers under the front seats. Before removing the front seats, a special safety harness must be installed to prevent accidental deployment of the airbag units. See Fig. 18.

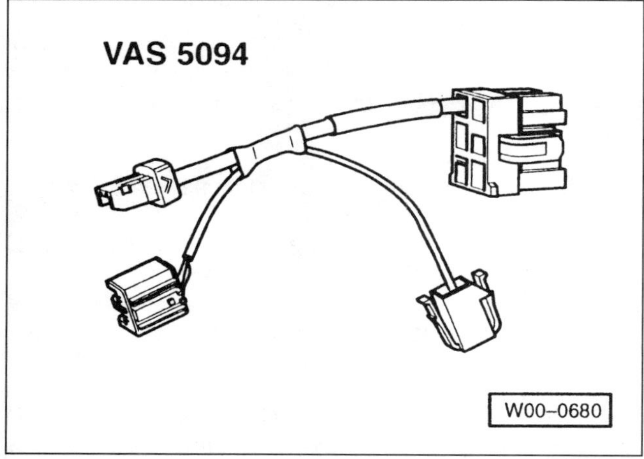

W00-0680

Fig. 18. Special tool VAS 5094 must be installed on seats before removal or repairs.

WARNING —

- *Observe all cautions, warnings and notes before starting and when completing repairs involving airbag system.*
- *Volkswagen of America specifically warns against the installation of aftermarket upholstery on any vehicle equipped with side airbags. The factory-installed upholstery is designed to separate in specific places at specific rates, and in specific directions. Installation of non-factory upholstery including, but not limited to, "beads" and "sheepskins", may cause seat mounted airbags to deploy when they are not supposed to; fail to deploy when they should; or to deploy in some manner other than designed. This is a safety hazard and could result in serious injury or death to occupants of the vehicle.*

An assembly view of the side airbag unit is shown in Fig. 19.

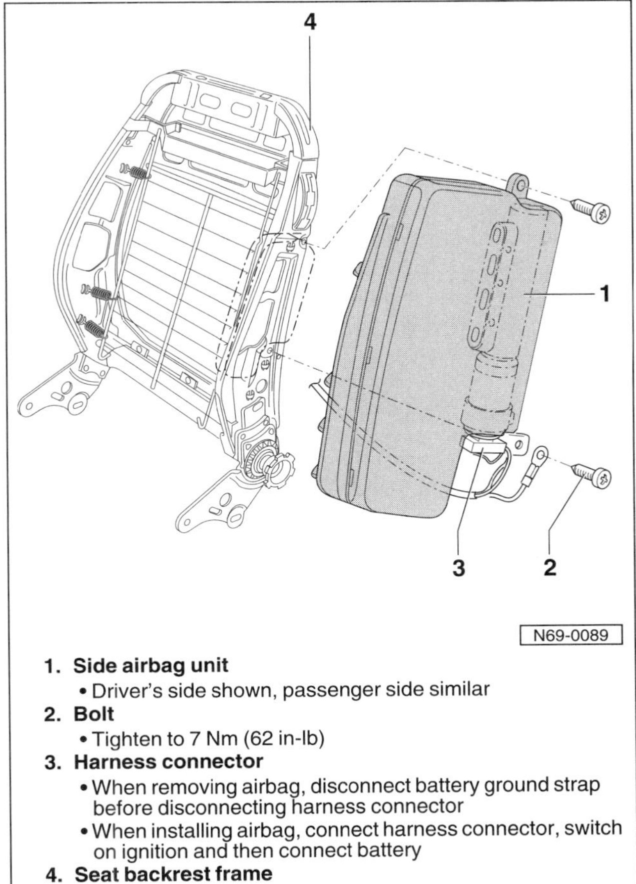

1. **Side airbag unit**
   - Driver's side shown, passenger side similar
2. **Bolt**
   - Tighten to 7 Nm (62 in-lb)
3. **Harness connector**
   - When removing airbag, disconnect battery ground strap before disconnecting harness connector
   - When installing airbag, connect harness connector, switch on ignition and then connect battery
4. **Seat backrest frame**

N69-0089

Fig. 19. Side airbag unit as installed in driver's seat backrest. Passenger side is similar.

Impact sensor, side airbag, overview

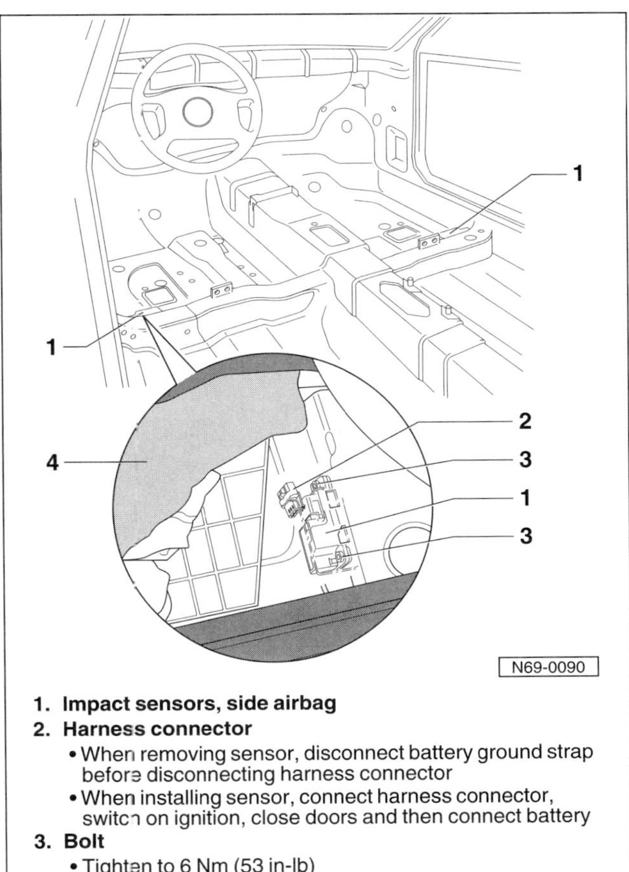

1. **Impact sensors, side airbag**
2. **Harness connector**
   - When removing sensor, disconnect battery ground strap before disconnecting harness connector
   - When installing sensor, connect harness connector, switch on ignition, close doors and then connect battery
3. **Bolt**
   - Tighten to 6 Nm (53 in-lb)
4. **Carpeting and sound absorber padding**

N69-0090

Fig. 20. Impact sensors for side airbags shown in position on the floor crossmember under the seats.

Airbag unit, front passenger, assembly

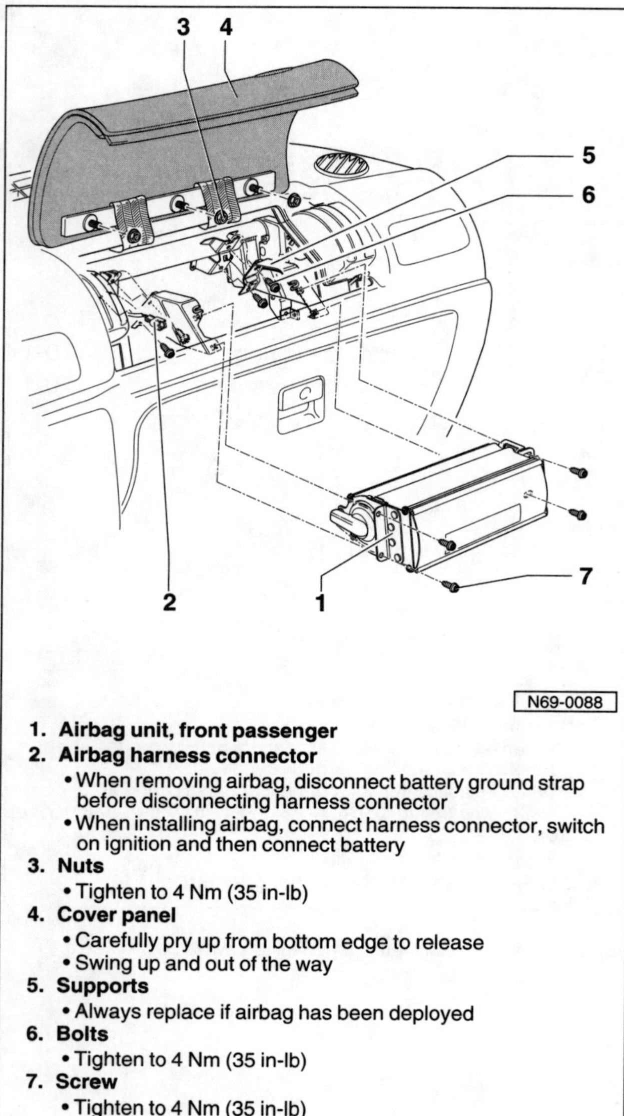

1. **Airbag unit, front passenger**
2. **Airbag harness connector**
   - When removing airbag, disconnect battery ground strap before disconnecting harness connector
   - When installing airbag, connect harness connector, switch on ignition and then connect battery
3. **Nuts**
   - Tighten to 4 Nm (35 in-lb)
4. **Cover panel**
   - Carefully pry up from bottom edge to release
   - Swing up and out of the way
5. **Supports**
   - Always replace if airbag has been deployed
6. **Bolts**
   - Tighten to 4 Nm (35 in-lb)
7. **Screw**
   - Tighten to 4 Nm (35 in-lb)

N69-0088

Fig. 21. Airbag and related components for front seat passenger.

70 Trim–Interior

GENERAL

This repair group covers interior equipment and trim panels, including center console and instrument panel removal. For interior lights and accessories see **96 Lights, Accessories–Interior**.

CENTER CONSOLE

Assembly views of the center console and center console extension are provided in Fig. 1. and Fig. 2. Removal and installation instructions are provided as well.

CAUTION —

- *Disconnect battery ground (GND) strap from battery negative (–) terminal before working on any components of the electrical system.*
- *Be sure to have radio anti-theft code on hand before disconnecting battery.*
- *Disconnecting the negative (–) battery cable may erase fault codes and basic settings in the engine management and automatic transmission control modules. Some driveability problems may be noticed until the system re-adapts to operating conditions. OBD II readiness codes, which may be required for emissions testing, may also be erased.*

Center console assembly

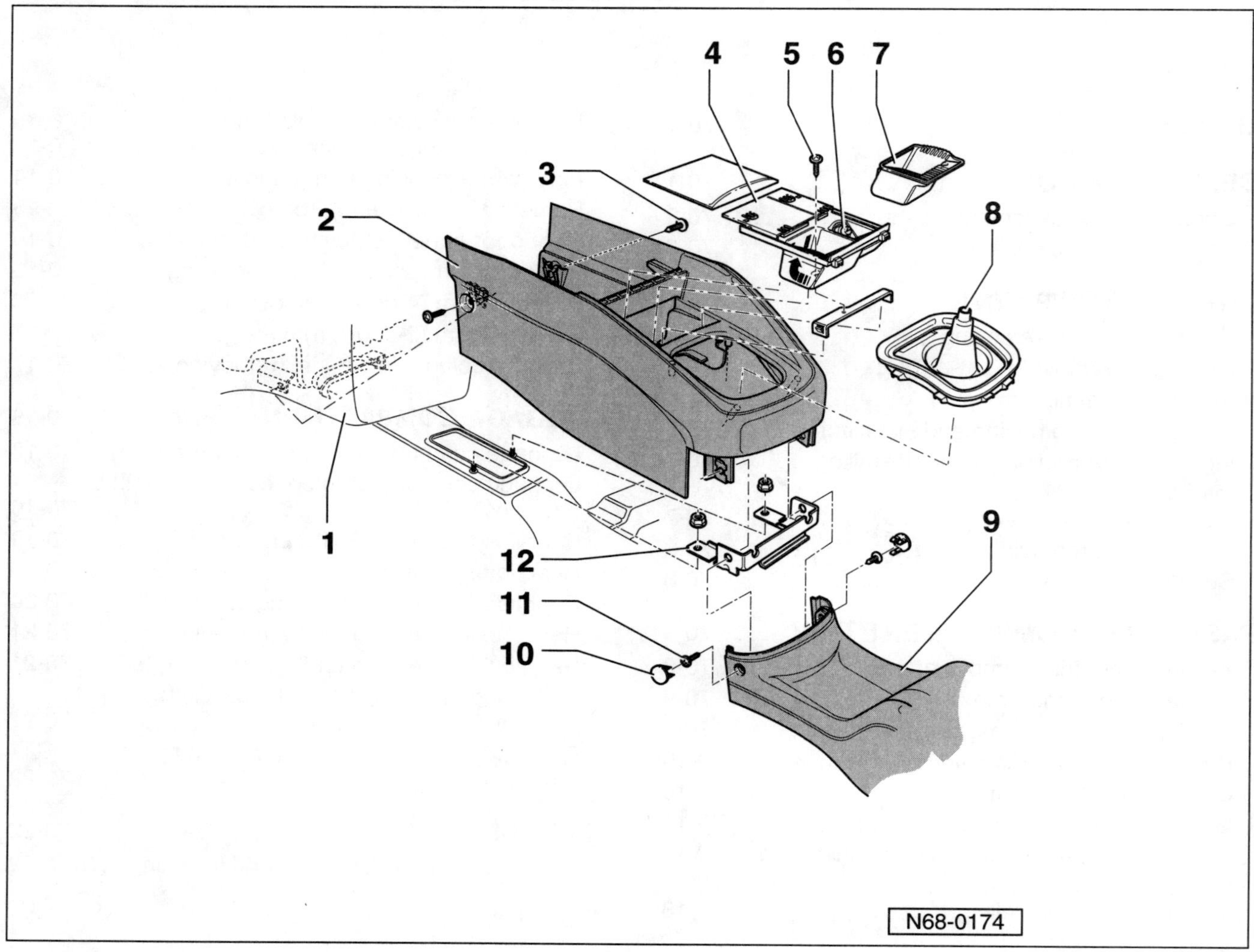

N68-0174

Fig. 1. Center console components. Manual transmission version shown, automatic is similar.

1. **Instrument panel**
2. **Center console**
   - It is not necessary to remove shifter trim plate on vehicles with automatic transmission before removing center console. Automatic shift lever knob will need to be removed, see **37 Automatic Transmission**
   - Removing:
     Unclip cover caps (item **10**) and remove screws (item **11**)
     Unclip shifter boot (item **8**) and pull up
     Pull out ashtray insert (item **7**) and remove screw (item **5**)
     Slide ashtray forward, close lid and pull out (**arrow**) until it is possible to disconnect cigarette lighter connector (item **6**)
     Remove screws (item **3**) and pull center console upward over shift lever to remove
3. **Screws**
   - Qty. 2
4. **Ashtray**
5. **Screw**
6. **Cigarette lighter**
7. **Ashtray insert**
8. **Shifter boot**
9. **Center console extension**
10. **Screw cover**
    - Qty. 2
11. **Screw**
    - Qty. 2
12. **Mounting bracket**

Center console extension

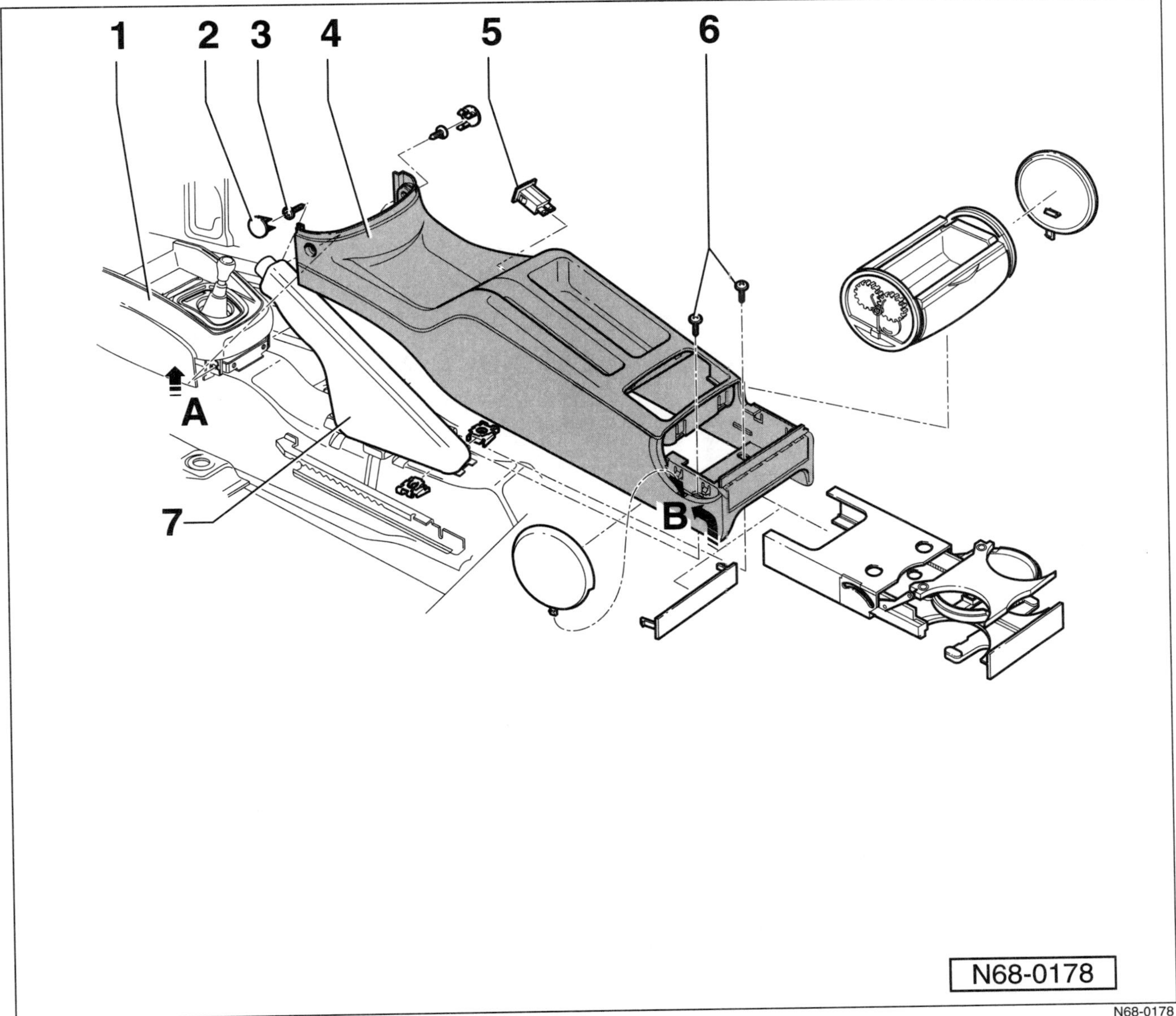

Fig. 2. Center console extension behind emergency brake handle.

1. **Center console**
2. **Cover caps**
3. **Screws**
   - Qty. 2
4. **Center console extension**
   - It is not necessary to remove shifter trim plate on vehicles with automatic transmission before removing center console.
   - Removing:
     If equipped, remove center armrest, **see** Ⓐ
     Remove rear ashtray, **see** Ⓑ
   - Center console extension, removing (continued):
     Remove rear cupholder, **see** Ⓒ
     Pry off cover caps (item **2**)
     Remove screws (item **3**) and pull up parking brake
     Release extension from center console
     Pull up front of extension (**arrow A**), guide rear over center armrest support and pull connector off fuel fill flap switch (item **5**)
     Pull center console extension off forward over parking brake lever (item **7**)
5. **Fuel flap switch**
6. **Screws**
7. **Parking brake lever**

A Front center armrest, removing

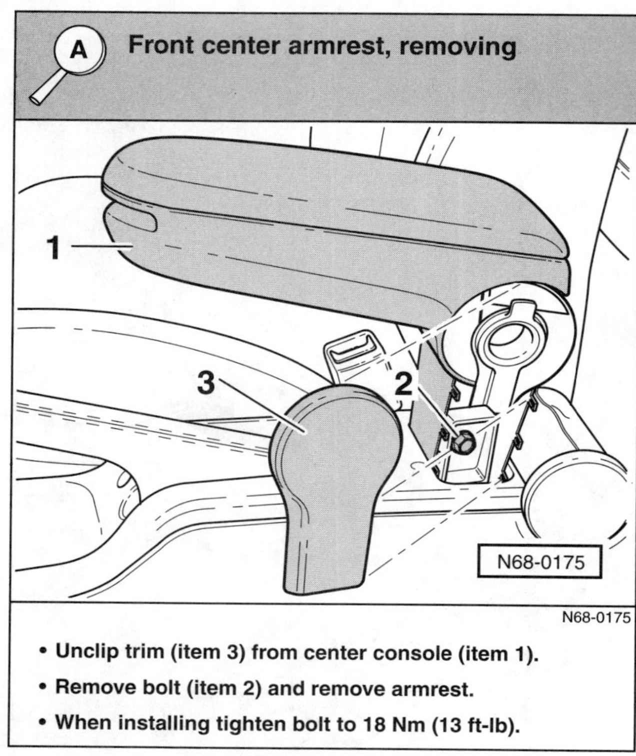

N68-0175

- Unclip trim (item 3) from center console (item 1).
- Remove bolt (item 2) and remove armrest.
- When installing tighten bolt to 18 Nm (13 ft-lb).

B Rear ashtray, removing

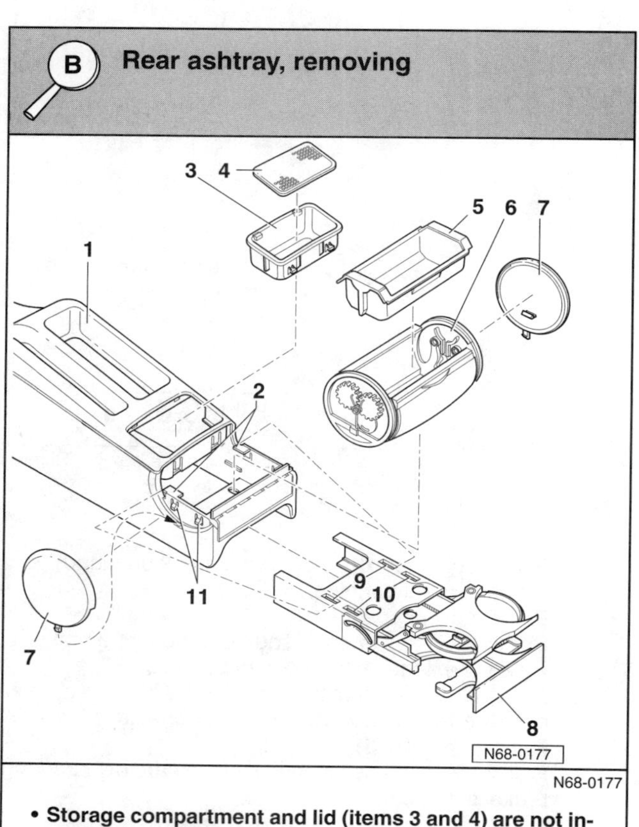

N68-0177

- Storage compartment and lid (items 3 and 4) are not installed on vehicles with center armrest.
- Remove cover caps (item 7).
- Release ashtray at and right locking lugs (item 11).

C Rear cupholder, removing and installing

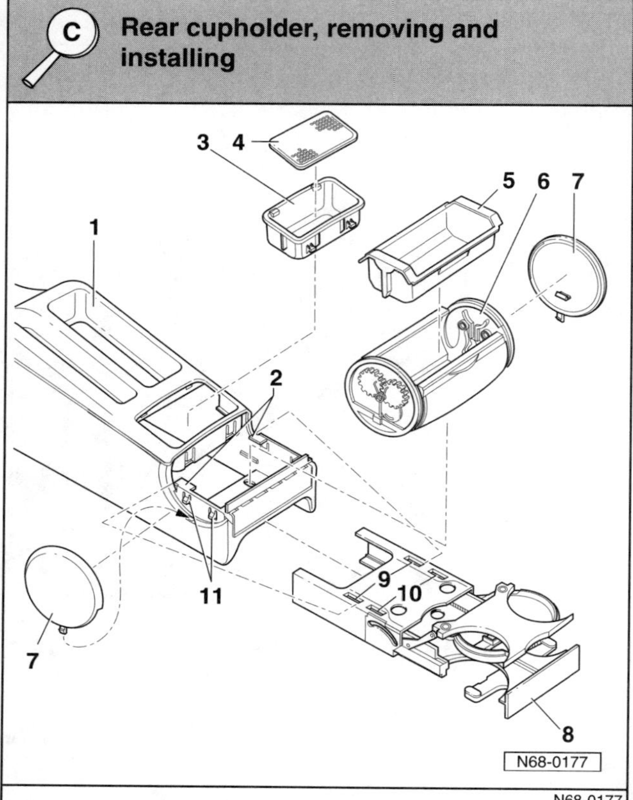

N68-0177

- Remove rear ashtray.
- Press down retaining hooks (item 9) and pull cupholder out from center console (item 1).
- To install, guide cupholder into center console until retaining hooks (item 10) meet retaining lugs (item 2).
- Bend up retaining hooks (item 9) slightly.
- Install ashtray (item 6).

INTERIOR EQUIPMENT

Front cup holder, removing

1. Fold up trim panel for front cup holder.

2. Press retaining clips at sides of cup holder assembly with flat tip screwdriver and unclip. See Fig. 3.

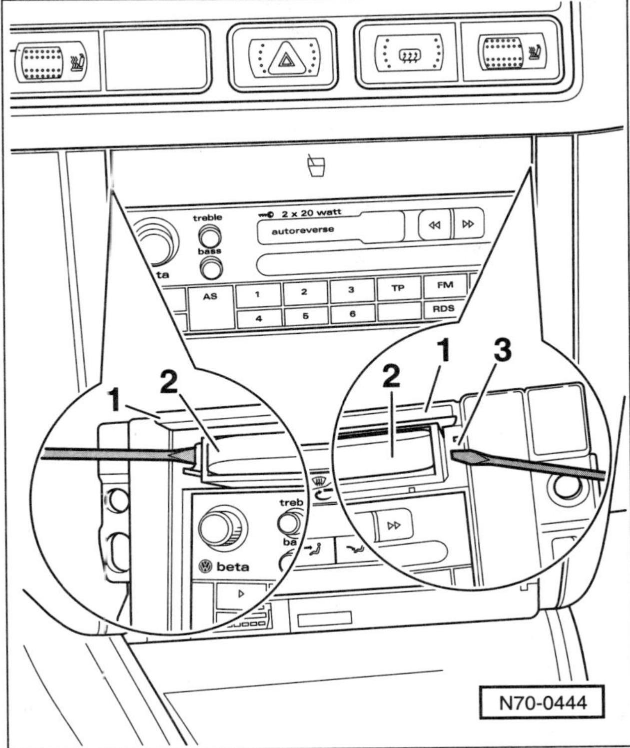

N70-0444

Fig. 3. Fold up cupholder trim (**1**), press retaining clips (**2** and **3**) and pull out cup holder assembly.

3. Pull out cup holder.

Glove box, removing

1. Carefully pry off right side instrument panel cover at mounting clips. See Fig. 4.

2. Remove center console as described earlier.

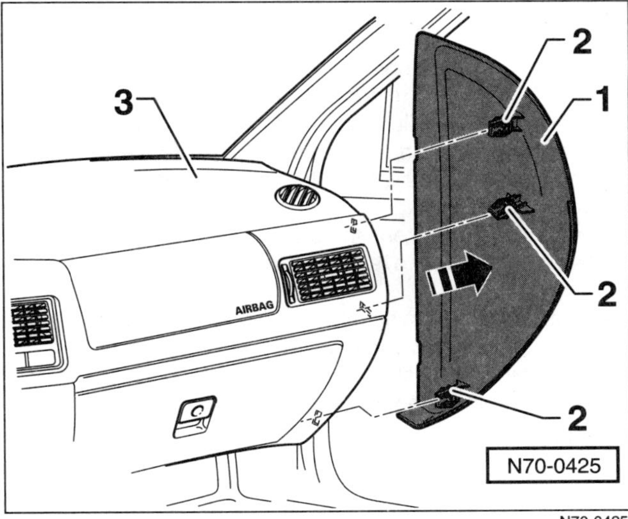

N70-0425

Fig. 4. Pry out right side instrument panel cover (**1**) at clips (**2**).

3. Remove the glovebox retaining screws and the glove box. See Fig. 5.

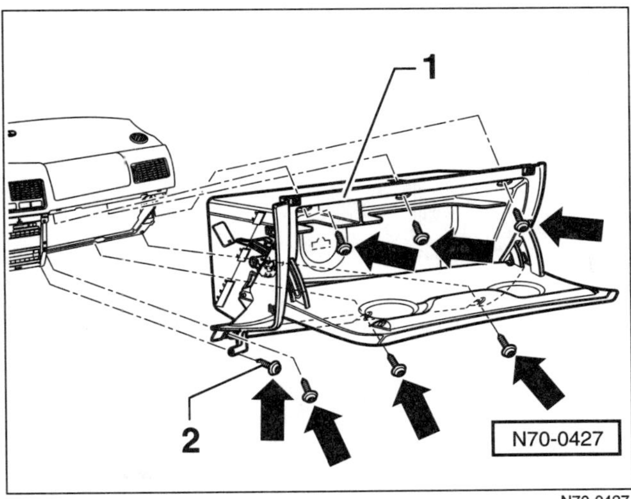

N70-0427

Fig. 5. Remove retaining screws (**arrows**) and glove box (**1**). Screw (**2**) is located underneath center console.

> ***NOTE —***
> *Glovebox mounting screw (item 2 above) secures the glovebox to carrier and is located behind center console.*

4. Disconnect harness connector for glove box light.

Automatic dimming interior mirror

The automatic interior mirror darkens when the driver is "blinded" from behind. It consists of a mirror element and two photo sensors. The electronic circuitry recognizes light incidence for the front and rear through the photo sensors. If the light incidence is greater from the rear than from the front the circuitry applies voltage to the conductive coating. An increase in voltage darkens the electrolyte and less of the light incidence is reflected to the driver's eye.

The automatic dimming function can be checked by switching on the ignition, covering the front photo sensor (item **3** below) and shining a flashlight at the rear photo sensor (item **2** below). The mirror should darken if reverse gear is not engaged. See Fig. 6.

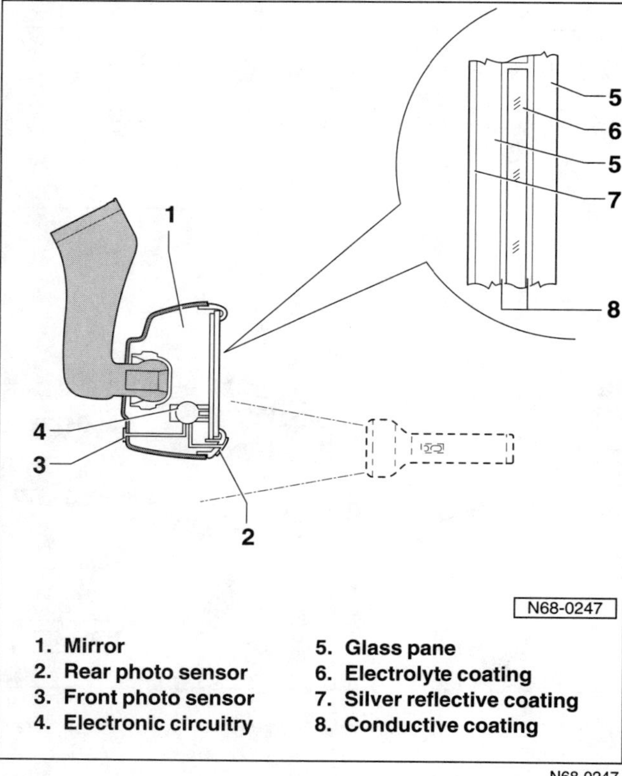

N68-0247

Fig. 6. Automatic dimming interior mirror with component list.

NOTE —

When selecting reverse gear the dimming function of the mirror is switched off enabling the mirror to be effectively used to back up the vehicle (i.e. from a dark garage).

Interior mirror, removing and installing

1. Press mirror downward at an angle off retaining plate (spring clip in mirror base). See Fig. 7.

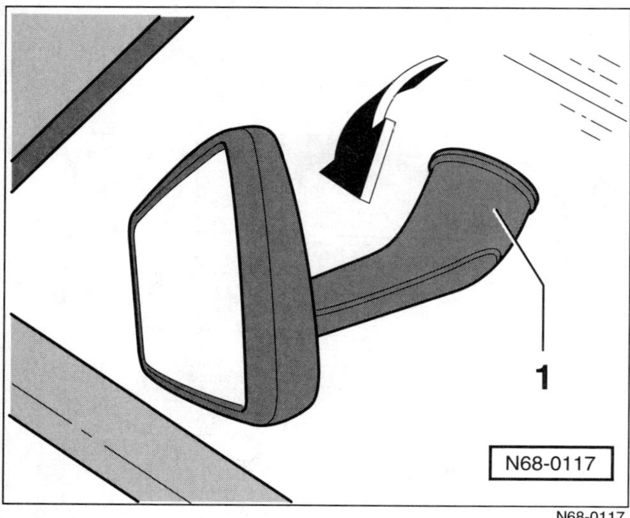

N68-0117

Fig. 7. Rotate mirror (**1**) downward (**arrow**) and counter-clockwise to release it from retaining plate.

NOTE —

- *In cold weather, warm the windshield first by running the defroster on high for a few minutes.*
- *To aid in removal, rotate mirror counter-clockwise as you pull it down.*

2. To install, position mirror 90° from installed position and turn clockwise on mount until locking spring clicks into place.

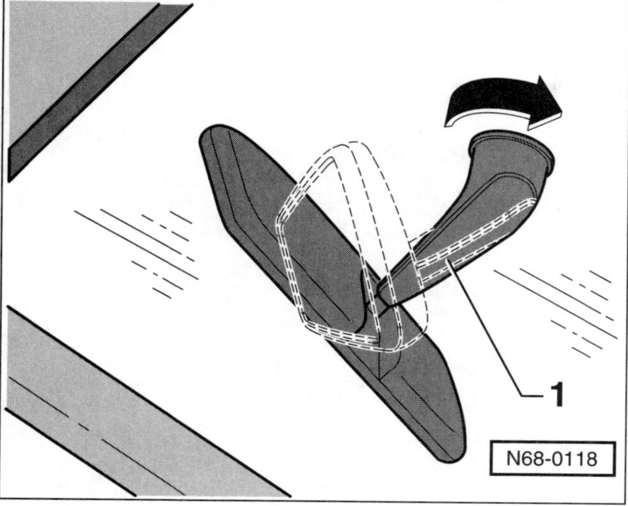

N68-0118

Fig. 8. Place mirror (**1**) on mount and rotate clockwise (**arrow**) until locking spring clicks into place.

Interior mirror retaining plate, installing

If the mirror retaining plate separates from the windshield it must be re-attached using Volkswagen glass-metal adhesive kit (part no. D 000 703 A1) or equivalent.

1. Remove retaining plate from mirror base.
2. Remove PUR adhesive from retaining plate with wire brush.
3. Grind off three spacer protrusions on bonding surface using sandpaper (360/400 grit) on flat surface.

NOTE —
Keep sanded surface clean and free of grease.

4. Scrape PUR adhesive material and primer from windshield down to ceramic layer using glass scraper. See Fig. 9.

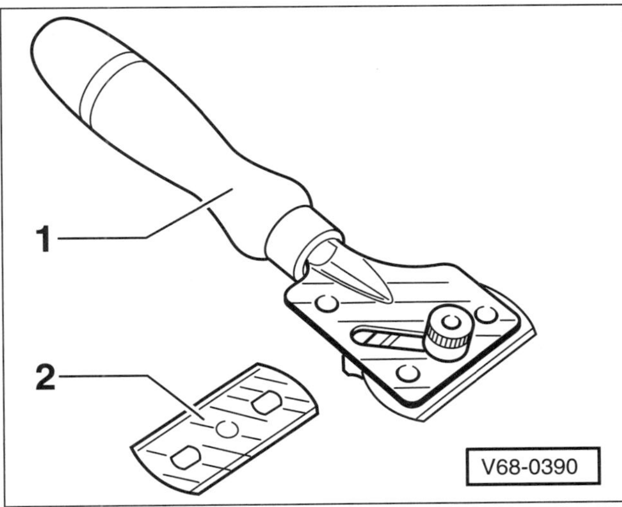

V68-0390

Fig. 9. Commercial glass scraper (**1**) with blade (**2**).

CAUTION —
Do not damage ceramic coating. Scratches will remain permanently visible.

5. Clean bonding area with adhesive remover (VW part no. D 002 000 10) or cleaning solution (VW part no. D 009 401 04). Allow cleaner to dry at least 10 minutes.

NOTE —
Volkswagen part numbers are given for reference only. Always consult with your Volkswagen Parts Department or aftermarket parts specialist for the latest parts information.

6. Cut nylon mesh fabric to exactly the size of mirror retaining plate.
7. Apply adhesive evenly and smoothly to retaining plate.

WARNING —
Wear hand protection (rubber gloves) when working with adhesive.

8. Apply nylon mesh fabric to adhesive on retaining plate.
9. Apply adhesive to exposed surface of nylon mesh.
10. Within 30 seconds of applying adhesive to nylon mesh, press retaining plate firmly (do not use force) against windshield. Hold in place for 15 seconds.
11. Remove excess adhesive with a cloth.
12. Wait at least 15 minutes before installing mirror onto retaining plate.

Interior mirror with rain sensor, removing and installing

1. Pry left and right side trim covers on neck of mirror apart.
2. Pull out wiring harness connector and disconnect.
3. Pull mirror base down off windshield. See Fig. 10.

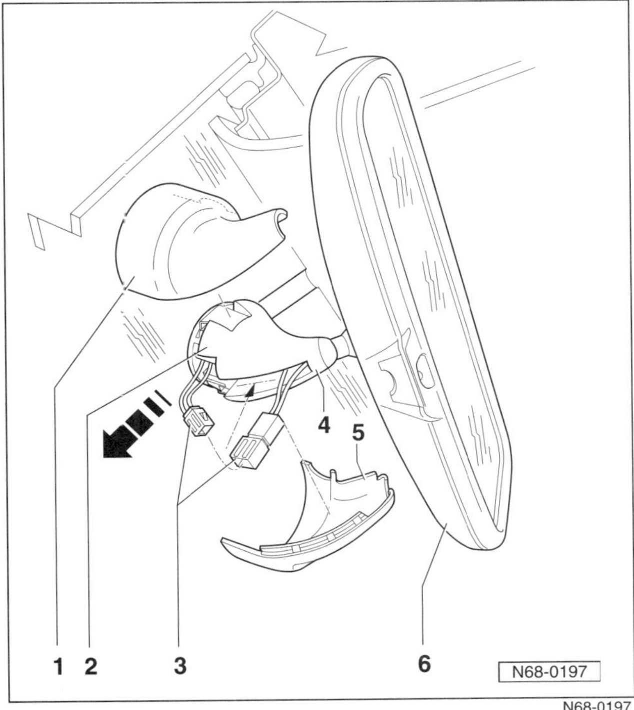

N68-0197

Fig. 10. Pry apart trim (**1** and **5**), disconnect harness connector (**3**) and pull mirror base (**4**) and mirror (**6**) off windshield (**arrow**).

4. Install in reverse order of removal.

Roof handle, removing

1. Fold handle down.

2. Pry cover up with screwdriver. Remove mounting screws and handle. See Fig. 11.

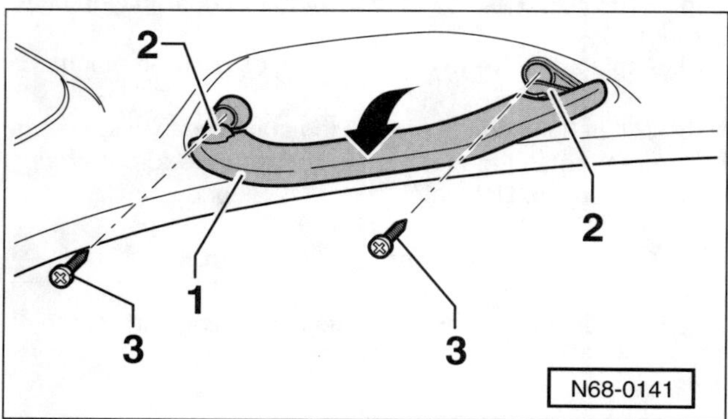

N68-0141

Fig. 11. Fold roof handle (**1**) down, pry open caps (**2**) and remove screws (**3**).

Sun visors, removing

1. Release sun visor from inner mount (item 2, Fig. 12.).

2. Pry off outer mount cover cap and remove screw.

3. Swing sun visor outer mount (item 4, Fig. 12.) down from roof and separate harness connector (item 3, Fig. 12.)

4. Pry off inner mount cover cap and remove screw and mount.

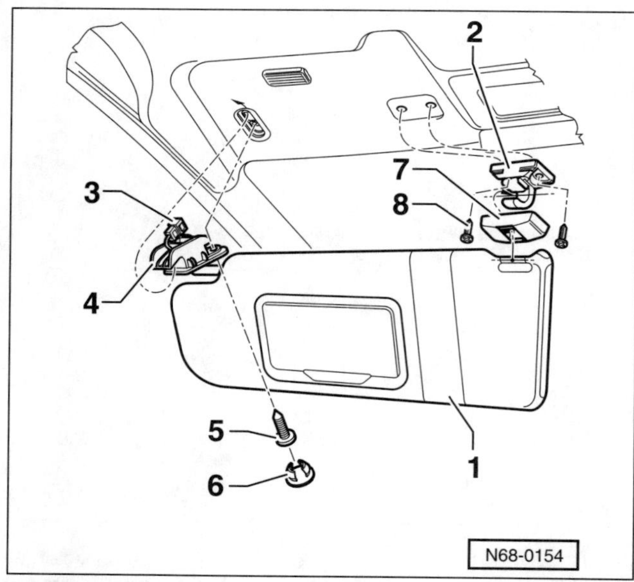

N68-0154

Fig. 12. Sun visor and related mounting hardware.

NOTE—
The center sun visor (above interior mirror) can be removed by folding it down and removing the self-tapping mounting screws from roof frame.

PASSENGER COMPARTMENT TRIM

Details of the passenger compartment interior trim panels are shown in Fig. 13. through Fig. 34. Unless otherwise noted, installation is the reverse of removal.

NOTE—
It is advisable to use a special non-marring trim removal tool (plastic bone) to pry various trim panels out without damaging paint or other adjacent panels.

A-pillar upper trim, removing

1. Pull door inner seal off A-pillar.

2. Starting at top, unclip trim from A-pillar. Lift up to remove. See Fig. 13.

3. Before installing trim, check clips on A-pillar and replace as necessary.

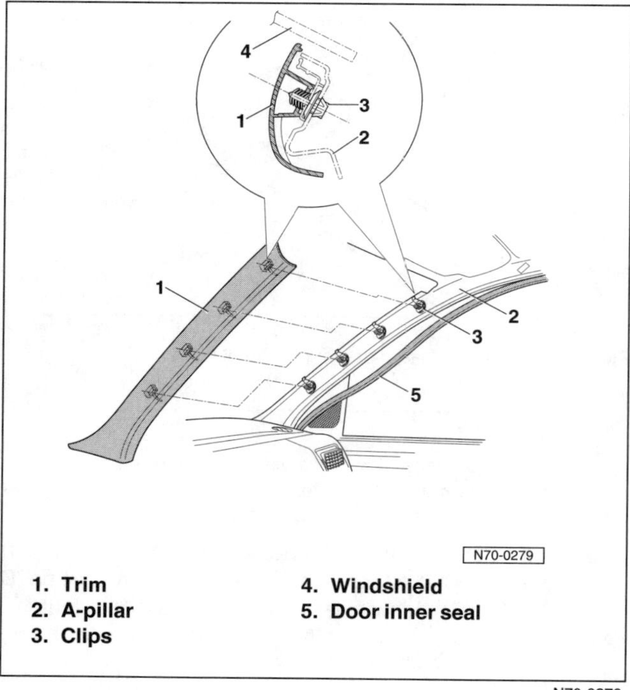

N70-0279

Fig. 13. A-pillar upper trim on left side.

4. After installing trim, make sure door seal is seated correctly.

A-pillar lower trim, removing

1. Remove hood release lever (as applicable for driver's side). See **55 Hoods and Lids**.

2. Unclip top part of A-pillar lower trim and release bottom from sill panel trim. See Fig. 14.

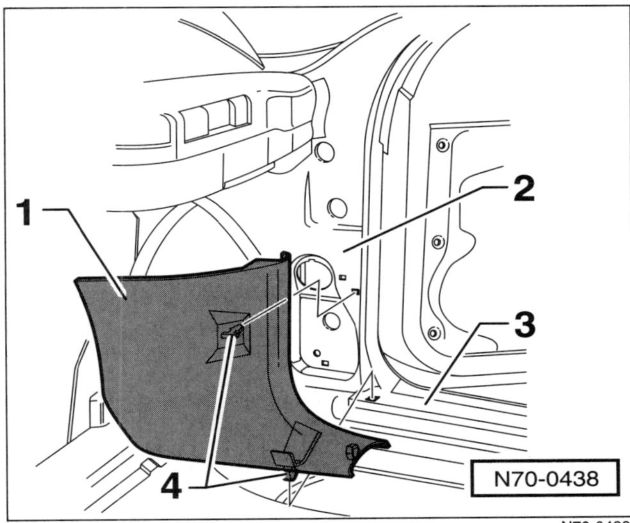

N70-0438

Fig. 14. Unclip top of trim (**1**) first, then unclip from sill (**3**). Trim is secured to body with two panel clips (**4**).

> ***NOTE —***
> *It may be necessary to remove side panel of dashboard (See Fig. 4.) and glovebox (See Fig. 5.) to access top part of A-pillar lower trim.*

B-pillar upper trim, removing

1. Pull inner door seal off B-pillar.

2. Pry off seatbelt relay cover, remove retaining bolt and seatbelt relay.

3. Release lower B-pillar trim at top.

4. Pry B-pillar trim off at sides and then in center. See Fig. 15.

5. Before installing upper B-pillar trim check condition of retaining clips and replace as necessary.

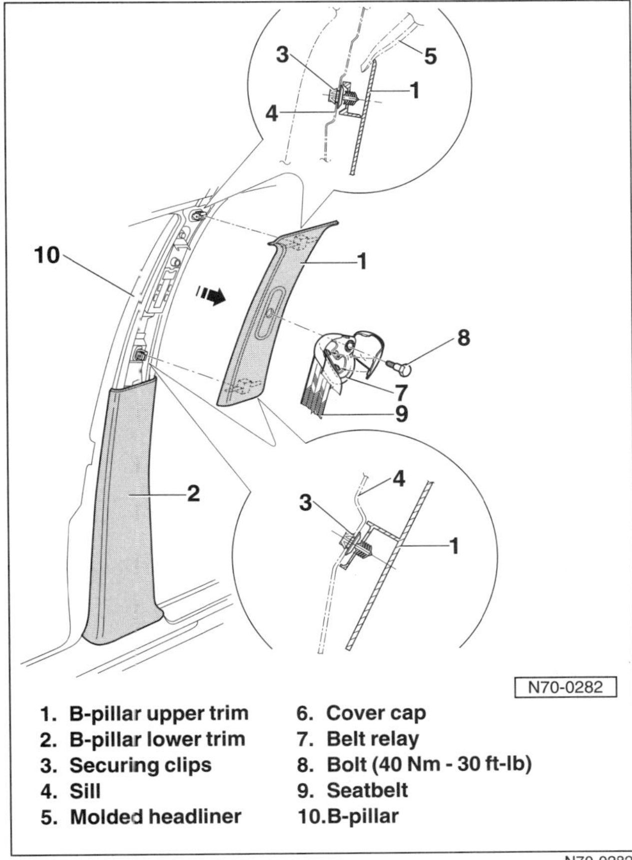

N70-0282

Fig. 15. Upper B-pillar trim and mounting hardware.

B-pillar lower trim, removing

1. Pry B-pillar trim off at sides and then in center.

2. Pull B-pillar trim upwards to release locking hooks from sill panel trim. See Fig. 16.

3. Before installing lower B-pillar trim check condition of retaining clips and replace as necessary.

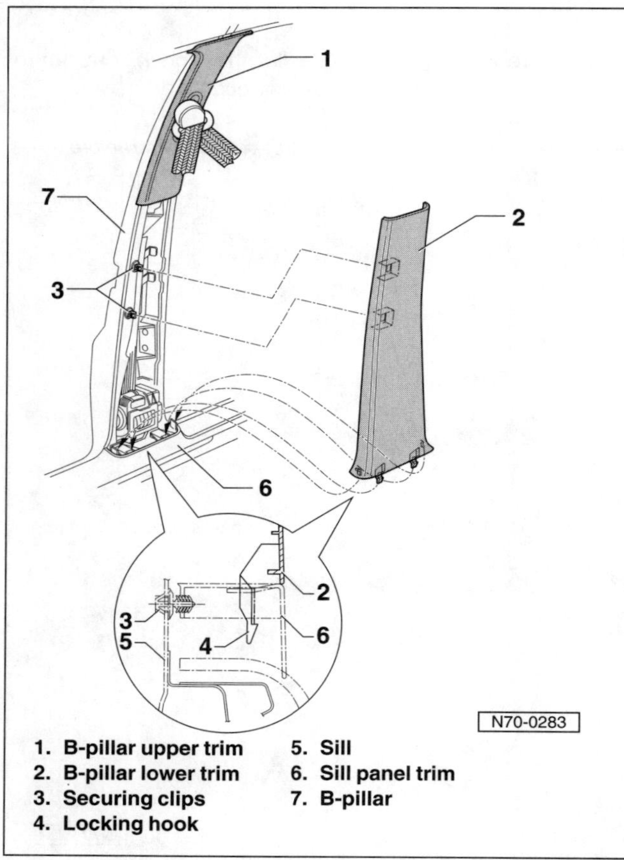

Fig. 16. Lower B-pillar trim and mounting hardware.

C-pillar trim (Golf), removing

1. Remove seatbelt relay by prying off trim cover and removing mounting bolt.

2. Remove luggage compartment cover support as described later.

3. Unclip plugs (item 8 in Fig. 17.) from C-pillar.

4. Remove lower trim (item 7 in Fig. 17.) from over C-pillar.

5. Remove speed nuts (item 3 in Fig. 17.) from studs.

NOTE —

Speed nuts are located near wheel housing flange and are covered by C-pillar trim. See Fig. 17.

6. Unclip trim from C-pillar.

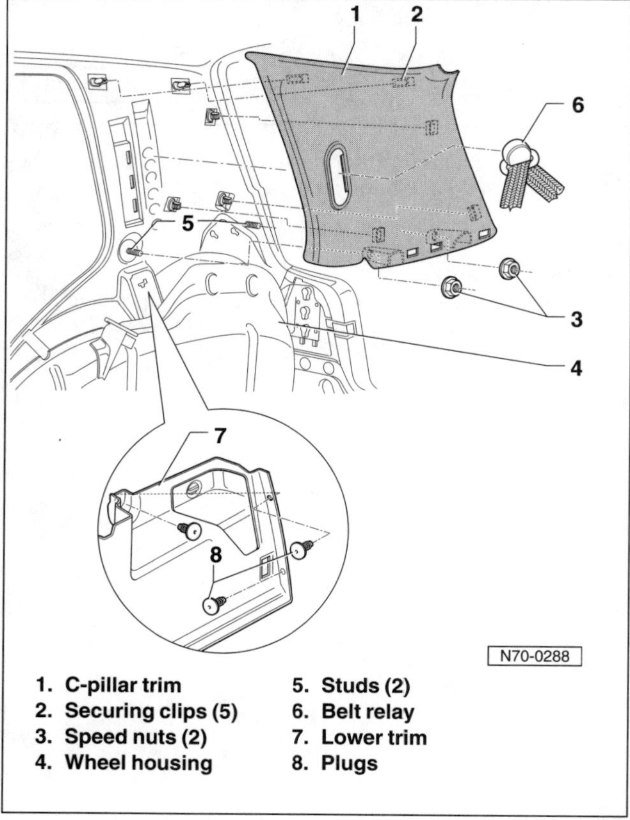

Fig. 17. Golf C-pillar trim and mounting hardware.

C-pillar trim (Jetta), removing

1. Remove seatbelt relay by prying off trim cover and removing mounting bolt. Remove washer and spacer from behind belt relay.

2. Remove parcel shelf trim as described later.

3. Unclip trim from C-pillar. See Fig. 18.

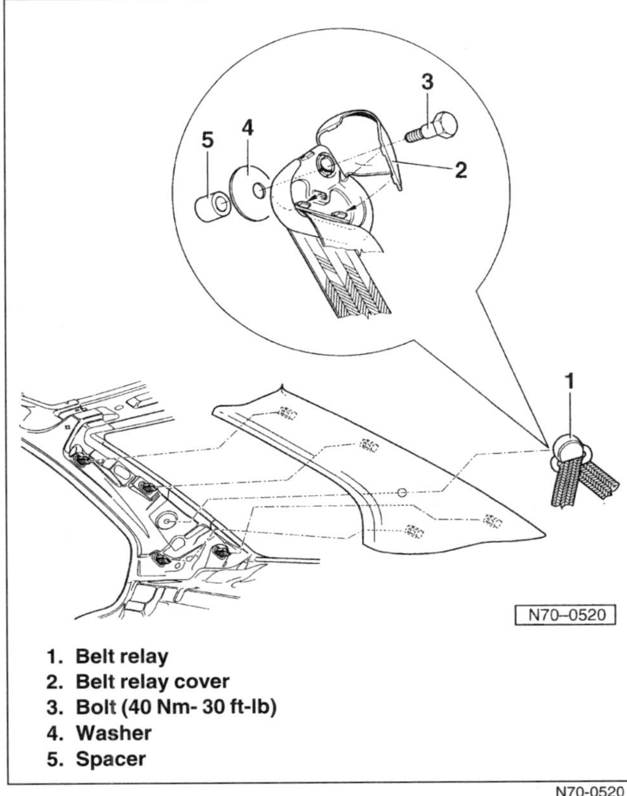

Fig. 18. Jetta C-pillar trim and mounting hardware.

Driver's door panel, removing and installing

NOTE —

Removing and installing driver's door panel for vehicles with manual windows is the same as the removing and installing passenger side door panel as described later.

1. Disconnect battery ground (GND) strap from battery negative (–) terminal. See the **Cautions** at the beginning of this repair group regarding battery disconnection.

NOTE —

Be sure to have the anti-theft radio code on hand before disconnecting the battery.

2. Use a screwdriver with a thin blade to carefully pry inner trim piece out of electric window control panel. See Fig. 19.

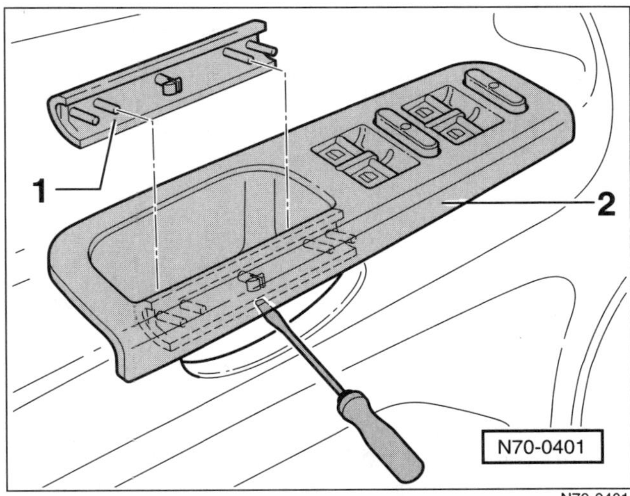

Fig. 19. Insert screwdriver into lower separating joint between inner trim piece (**1**) and window control panel (**2**). Carefully pry off toward door.

3. Unclip window control panel from door panel and lift upwards.

NOTE —

Do not grasp in grip depression (where inner trim was) when pulling off grip recess as a strut secured to door trim is underneath.

4. Press locking lug under front of window control panel and remove from door panel. See Fig. 20.

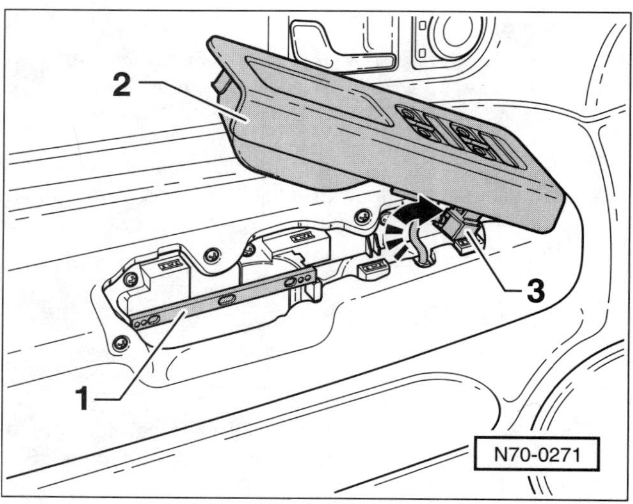

N70-0271

Fig. 20. Unclip window control panel (**2**) at rear, lift upward and release locking lug (**3**) by pressing in direction of **arrow**.

5. Remove door panel mounting screws and unclip panel from door using Volkswagen special tool 3392 or equivalent. Lift door panel upwards and out of window slot. See Fig. 21.

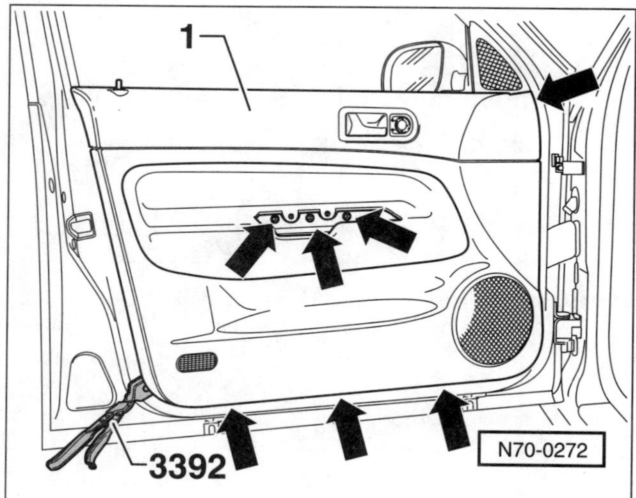

N70-0272

Fig. 21. Remove screws (**arrows**) and pry door panel (**1**) away from door with VW special tool 3392, or equivalent.

6. Unclip cable guide from door latch with screwdriver, pull cable out from retainer and unhook cable hook. See Fig. 22.

7. Disconnect harness connectors from door panel switches.

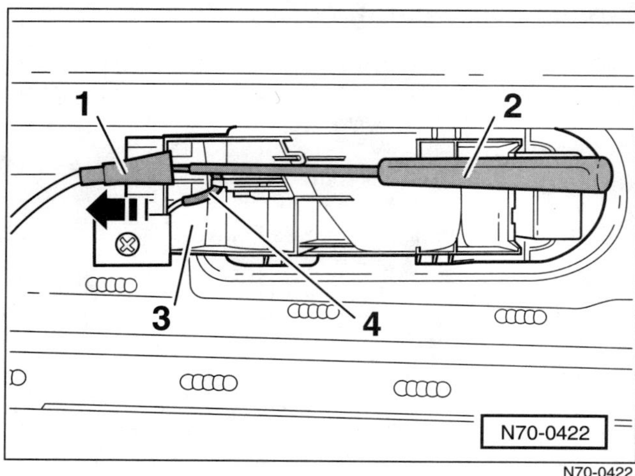

N70-0422

Fig. 22. Unclip cable guide (**1**) with screwdriver (**2**), pull out from retainer (**3**) in direction of **arrow** and unhook cable hook (**4**).

8. Install door panel in reverse order of removal, noting the following:
   - Pull window slot seal off door panel and insert into window slot before installing panel. See Fig. 23.
   - Check door trim clips before installing door panel and replace if necessary.
   - After connecting battery, check vehicle equipment (radio, clock, electric windows).
   - If ECM is subjected to low voltage with ignition on, DTC memory and readiness code must be checked using VAG scan tool 1551/5051, or equivalent.

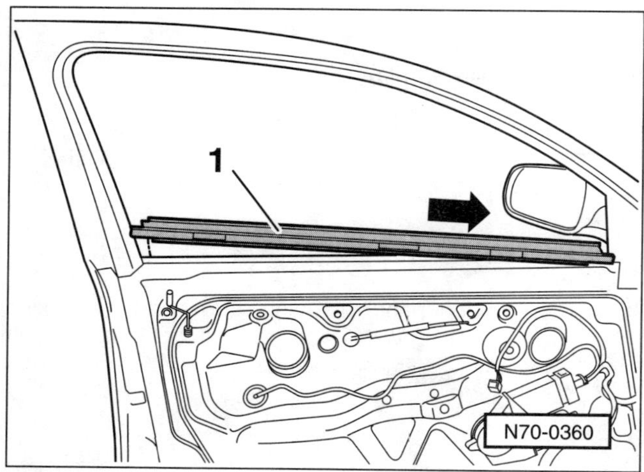

N70-0360

Fig. 23. Remove window slot seal (**1**) from door panel and insert (in direction of **arrow**) into window slot before installing door panel.

Passenger door panel, removing and installing

NOTE —
Removing and installing driver's door panel for vehicles with manual windows is the same as the removing and installing passenger side door panel as described below.

1. Disconnect battery ground (GND) strap from battery negative (–) terminal. See the **Cautions** at the beginning of this repair group regarding battery disconnection.

NOTE —
Be sure to have the anti-theft radio code on hand before disconnecting the battery.

2. Pry out door grab handle trim with screwdriver. See Fig. 24.

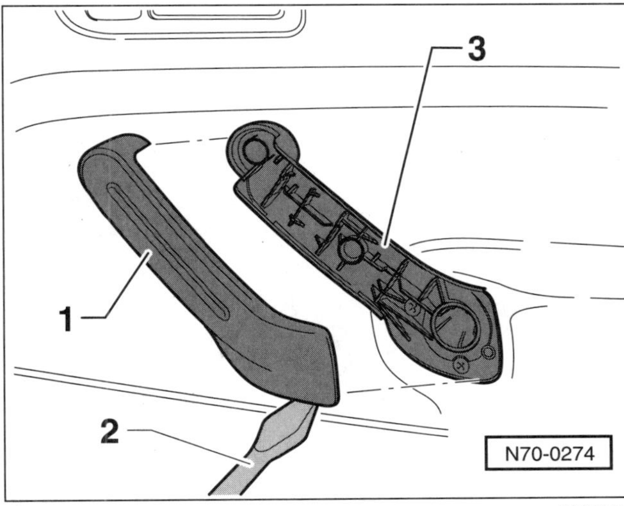

N70-0274

Fig. 24. Pry off door handle trim (**1**) with screwdriver (**2**).

3. Remove door panel mounting screws and unclip panel from door using Volkswagen special tool 3392 or equivalent. Lift door panel upwards and out of window slot. See Fig. 25.

4. Unclip cable guide from door latch with screwdriver, pull cable out from retainer and unhook cable hook. See Fig. 22. given earlier.

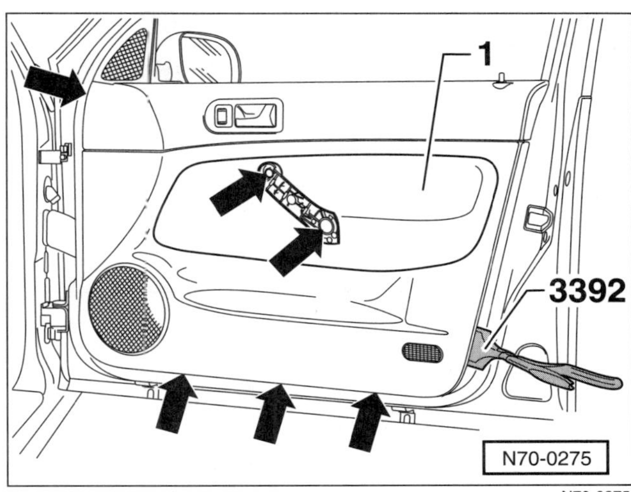

N70-0275

Fig. 25. Remove screws (**arrows**) and pry door panel (**1**) away from door with VW special tool 3392, or equivalent.

5. Disconnect harness connectors from door panel switches.

6. Installation is the reverse of removal, noting the following:
   - Pull window slot seal off door panel and insert into window slot before installing panel. See Fig. 23. given earlier.
   - Check door trim clips before installing door panel and replace if necessary.
   - After connecting battery, check vehicle equipment (radio, clock, electric windows).

NOTE —
If ECM is subjected to low voltage with ignition on, DTC memory and readiness code must be checked using VAG scan tool 1551/5051, or equivalent.

Front door window triangular trim (with speaker), removing

1. Remove door panel as described above.

2. Separate speaker harness connector in door.

3. Remove mounting screw at bottom of triangular trim. See Fig. 26.

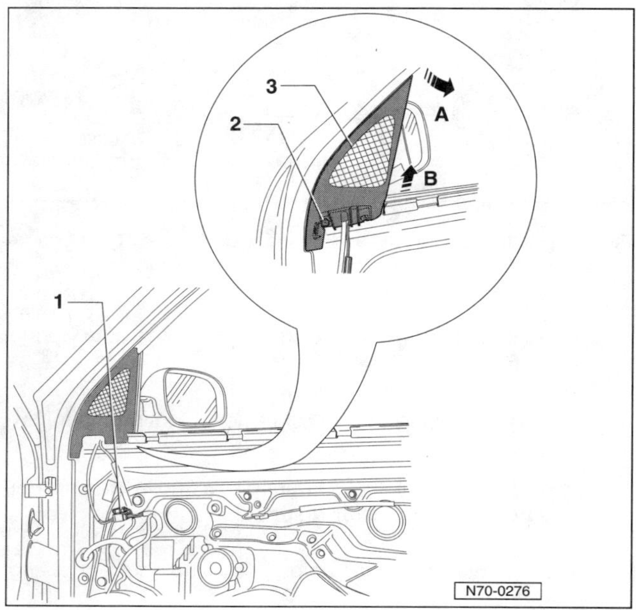

N70-0276

Fig. 26. Remove mounting screw (**1**) and pull off trim in direction of **arrow A** and **B**.

4. Pull speaker off at top and separate from door.

Inner wheel housing trim, removing

1. Remove parcel shelf trim (Jetta only).

2. Fold seat cushion and backrest forward.

3. Unscrew press button at bottom of inner wheel housing trim.

4. For Jetta only, remove plug at top of wheel housing trim using Volkswagen 3392 removal pliers or equivalent. See Fig. 27.

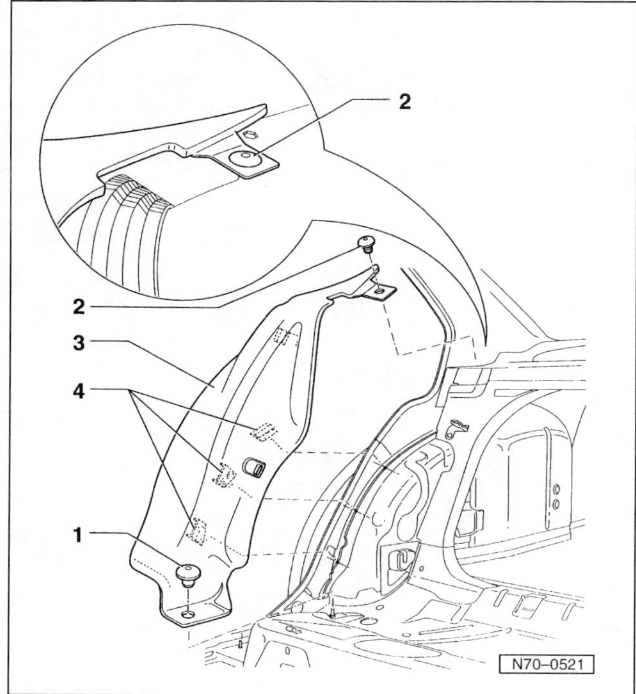

N70-0521

Fig. 27. Inner wheel housing trim for Jetta. Golf is similar with the exception of upper plug (**2**). Press button is shown at **1**.

5. Unclip trim panel from retaining clips and remove.

Parcel shelf trim (Jetta), removing

1. Fold rear seat backrest forward.
2. Separate harness connector for center mounted brake light. See Fig. 28.
3. Unclip and remove parcel shelf.

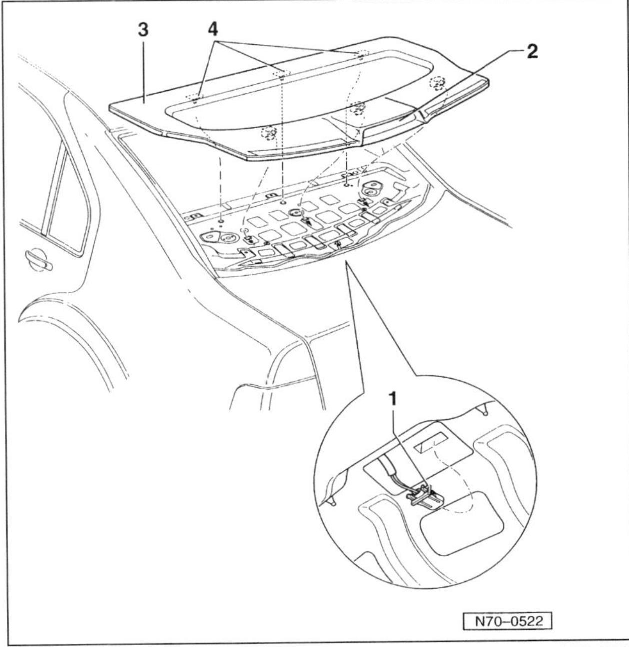

N70-0522

Fig. 28. Jetta parcel shelf trim (**3**), retaining clips (**4**), and center brake light (**2**) harness connector (**1**).

4. Check trim clips before installing and replace if necessary.

Rear door panel, removing and installing

1. Disconnect battery ground (GND) strap from battery negative (–) terminal. See **Cautions** at the beginning of this repair group regarding battery disconnection.

NOTE —
Be sure to have the anti-theft radio code on hand before disconnecting the battery.

2. Pry out door grab handle trim with screwdriver as shown earlier in Fig. 24.
3. Remove door panel mounting screws and unclip panel at sides with Volkswagen 3392 assembly pliers, or equivalent. See Fig. 29.
4. Lift door trim upward off window slot.

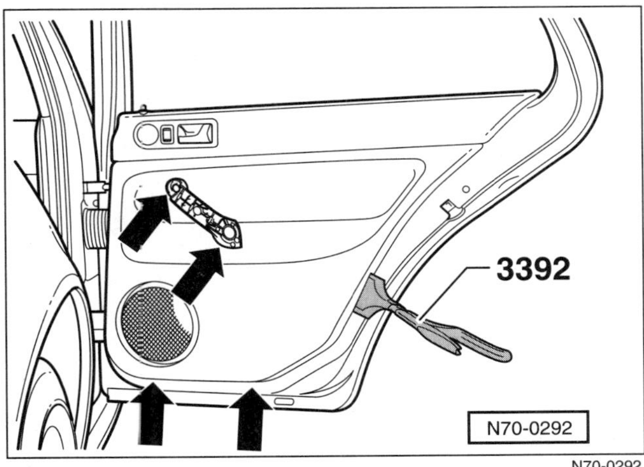

N70-0292

Fig. 29. Remove door panel mounting screws (**arrows**) and pry off panel at sides.

5. Unclip cable guide from door latch with screwdriver, pull cable out from retainer and unhook cable hook. See Fig. 22. given earlier.
6. Disconnect harness connectors from door panel switches.
7. Installation is reverse of removal, noting the following:
   - Pull window slot seal off door panel and insert into window slot before installing panel. See Fig. 30.
   - Check door trim clips before installing door panel and replace if necessary.
   - After connecting battery, check vehicle equipment (radio, clock, electric windows).

NOTE —
If ECM is subjected to low voltage with ignition on, DTC memory and readiness code must be checked using VAG scan tool 1551/5051, or equivalent.

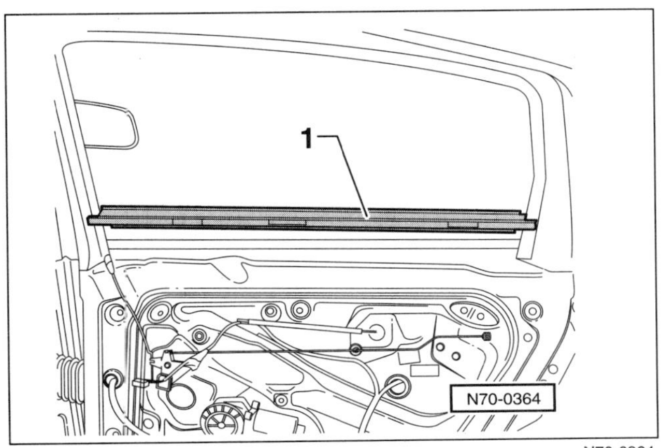

N70-0364

Fig. 30. Insert window slot seal (**1**) into window slot before installing door panel.

Rear side trim (2-door Golf), removing

1. Remove rear seat and backrest, see **72 Seats**.
2. Unclip side panel trim from B-pillar and speaker bracket. See Fig. 31.

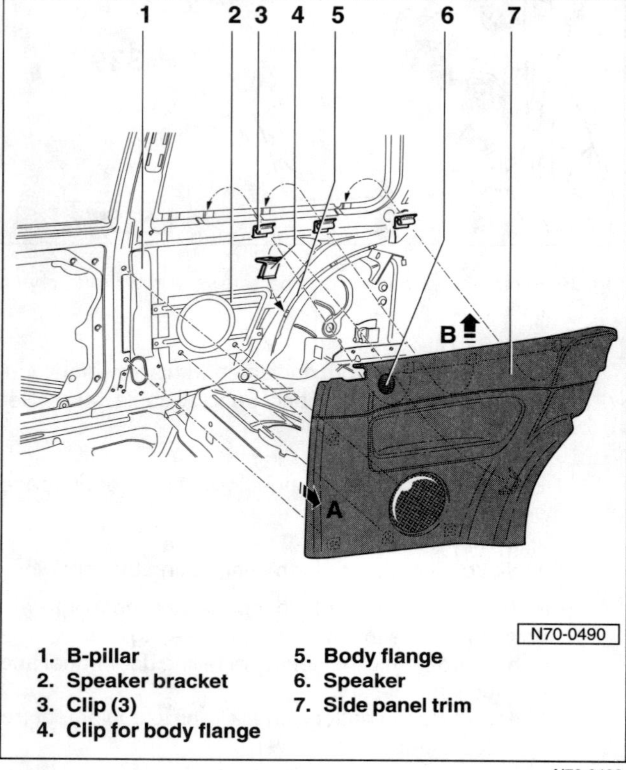

N70-0490

Fig. 31. 2-door Golf rear side panel trim and various components. Pull panel away at **arrow A** and lift up (**arrow B**).

3. Pull up side panel slightly and separate harness connector for speaker (if applicable).
4. Installation is reverse of removal, noting the following:
   - Check door trim clips before installing door panel and replace if necessary.
   - Clip for body flange (item 4 in Fig. 31.) secures the side panel trim to the wheel housing body flange.

Sill panel trim (4-door), removing

1. Fold rear seat bottom and backrest forward.
2. Remove A-pillar, B-pillar, and inner wheel housing trim as described earlier.
3. Unclip sill panel on left and right sides of B-pillar by pulling upward. Remove sill panel by pulling toward center of car. See Fig. 32.

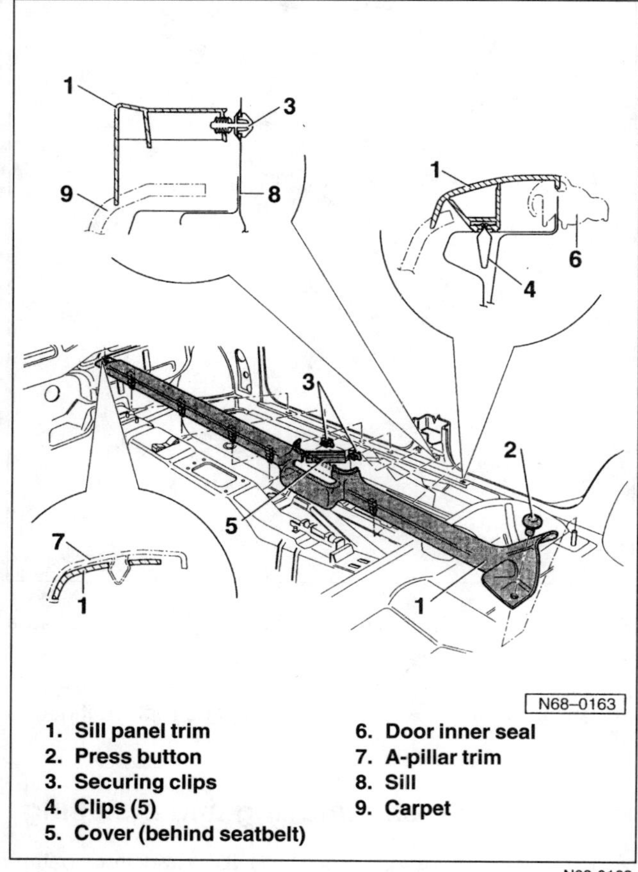

N68-0163

Fig. 32. Sill panel trim for four door vehicles and various components.

Sill panel trim (2-door), removing

1. Remove rear seat cushion and backrest, see **72 Seats**.
2. Remove rear side trim as described earlier.
3. Remove press button at rear of sill panel trim. See Fig. 33.

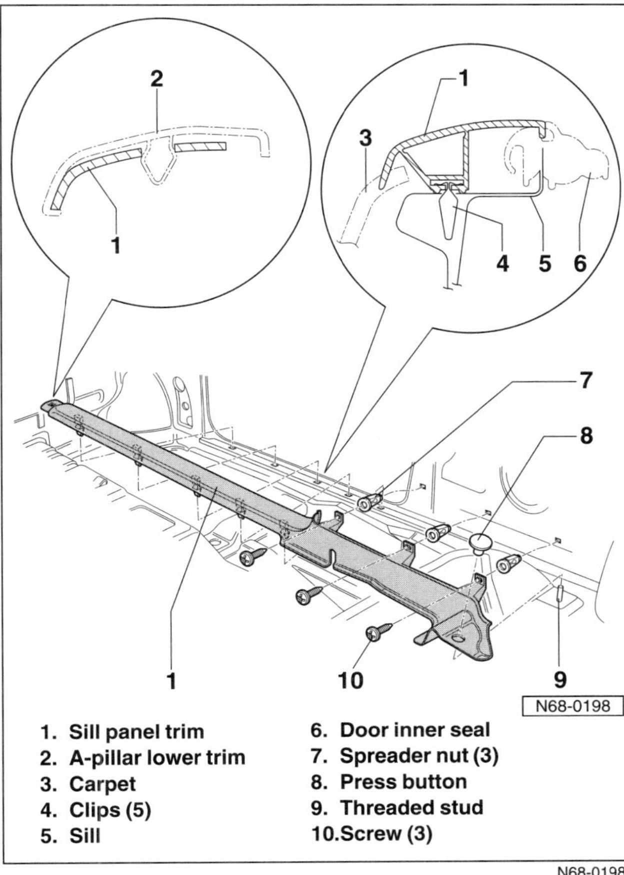

N68-0198

Fig. 33. Sill panel trim for two door vehicles and various components.

4. Remove sill panel mounting screws.
5. Starting at the front, unclip sill panel from lower A-pillar and remove.

Steering column lower trim, removing

1. Remove lower mounting screws for trim panel directly underneath steering column and unclip top of trim. See Fig. 34.
2. Remove mounting screws for trim panel to the right of steering column and unclip panel from top.

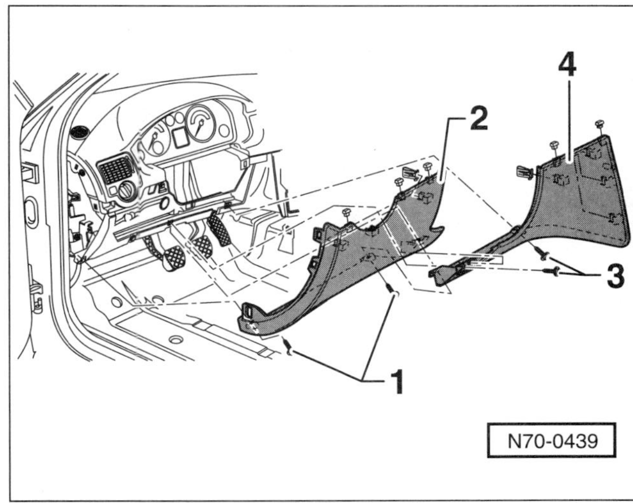

N70-0439

Fig. 34. Remove screws (**1**) and trim panel (**2**) to access screws (**3**) and remove trim panel (**4**).

LUGGAGE COMPARTMENT TRIM

Luggage compartment cover support (Golf)

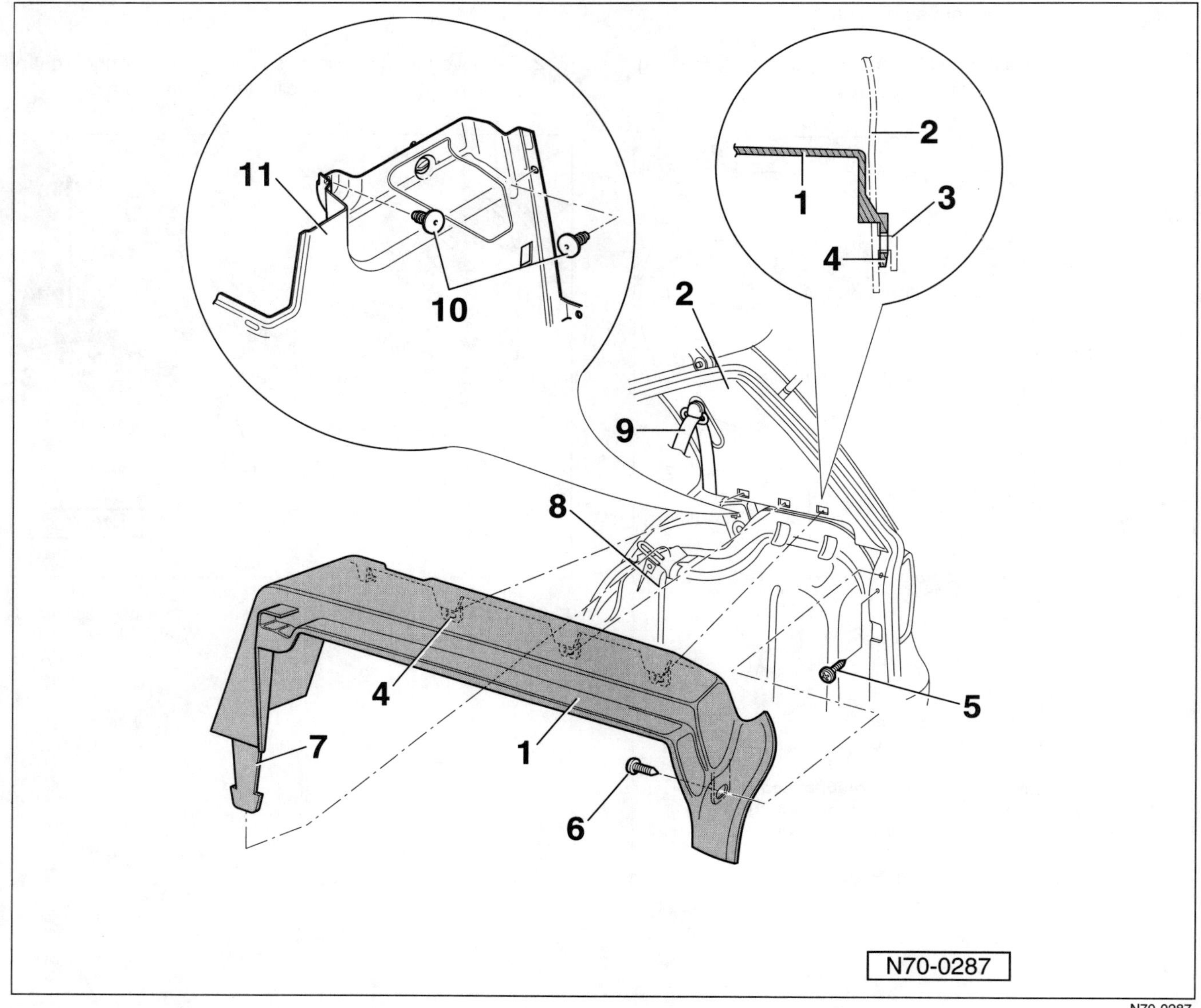

N70-0287

Fig. 35. Luggage compartment cover support for Golf/GTI.

1. **Support**
   - Removing:
     Remove screw (item 5)
     Unclip lock carrier trim from C-pillar and pull out clips (item 10)
     Remove screw (item 6)
     Unclip support (item 1) upwards, starting at rear
     Pull support (item 1) out of wheel housing (item 8), including locking pin (item 7)
2. **C-pillar trim**
3. **Locking lug on C-pillar trim**
4. **Locking hook on support**
5. **Screw**
6. **Screw**
7. **Locking pin**
8. **Wheel housing**
9. **Seat belt**
10. **Clips**
11. **Luggage compartment trim**

Luggage compartment floor covering (Golf), removing

1. Fold rear seat cushion and backrest forward.

2. Pull luggage compartment floor covering out toward rear from under rear seat backrest. See Fig. 36.

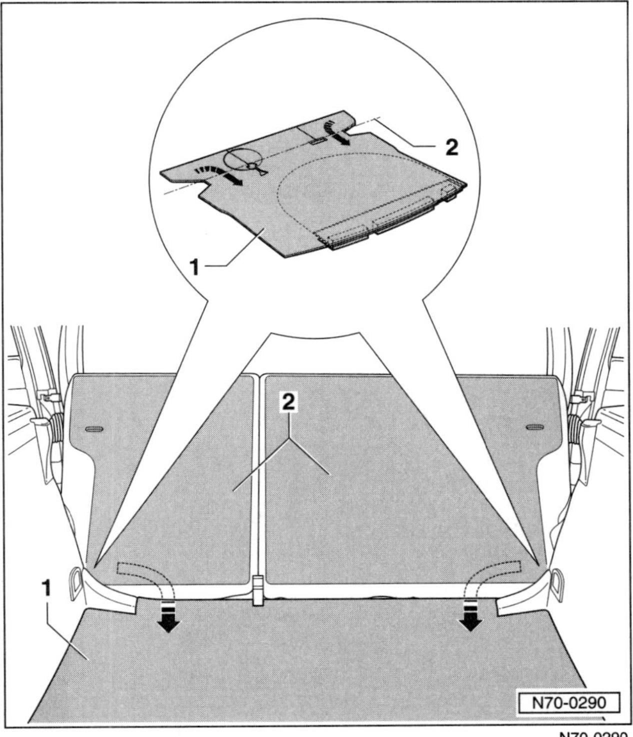

N70-0290

Fig. 36. Pull floor covering for Golf luggage compartment (**1**) in direction of **arrows** with rear seat backrest (**2**) folded forward.

Rear lid lower trim (Golf), removing

1. Remove two mounting screws from bottom of rear lid lower trim.

2. Unclip trim from rear lid and from upper trim at sides. See Fig. 37.

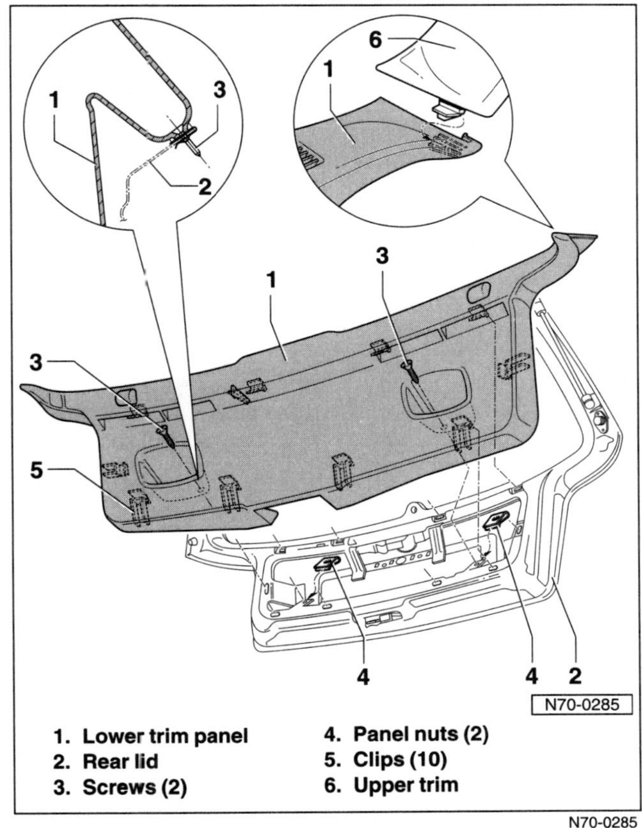

N70-0285

Fig. 37. Golf lower rear lid trim and related components.

Rear lid upper trim (Golf), removing

1. Remove rear lid lower trim as described above.
2. Pull spreader pin out from rear shelf retainer on left and right hand sides. See Fig. 38.
3. Unclip trim from along sides and then at top.

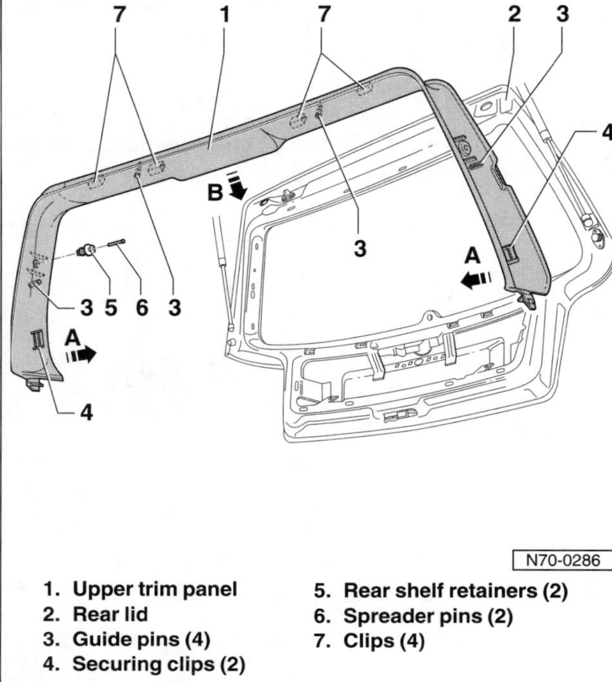

N70-0286

Fig. 38. Golf upper rear lid trim and list of components. After removing spreader pins (**6**) and retainers (**5**), pull out trim at sides (**arrow A**) and at top (**arrow B**).

Rear lid trim (Jetta), removing and installing

1. Open rear lid and remove emergency warning triangles from rear lid trim, if applicable, by opening locking device that holds triangles in place. See Fig. 39.
2. Remove retaining screws and slide locking device upward to remove. See Fig. 40.
3. Remove retaining screws for rear lid trim and release trim in area of handle molding and remove. See Fig. 41.
4. Installation is the reverse of removal. Check condition of spreader nuts in rear lid and replace as necessary.

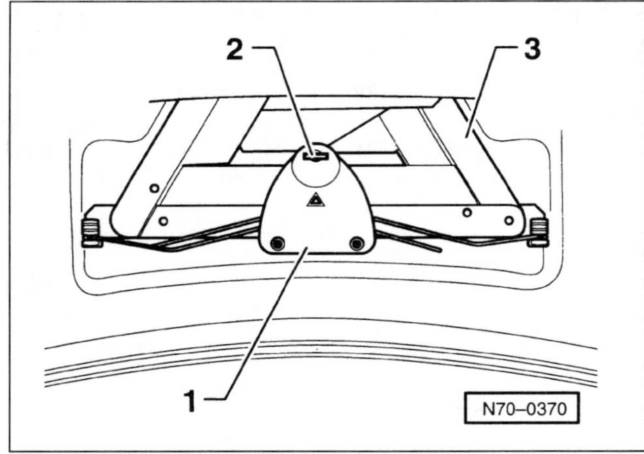

N70-0370

Fig. 39. Open locking device (**2**), fold open retainer (**1**) and remove emergency triangles (**3**), if equipped.

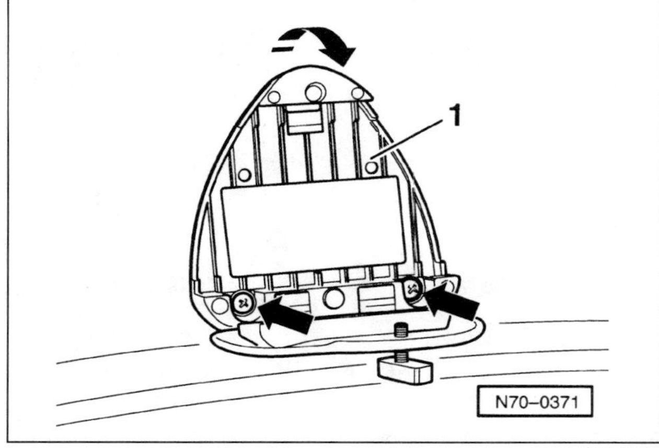

N70-0371

Fig. 40. Remove retaining screws (**bottom arrows**) and locking device (**1**) by sliding upward and out (**top arrow**).

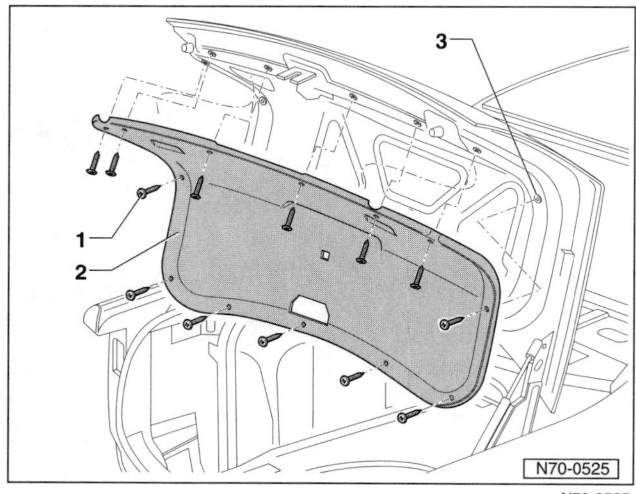

N70-0525

Fig. 41. Remove screws (**1**) and release rear lid trim (**2**) at molded handle and remove from rear lid.

Rear lock carrier trim (Golf), removing

1. Open rear hatch and release rear lock carrier trim from cross panel at top first and then at bottom. See Fig. 42.

2. Pull lock carrier trim upward off cross panel.

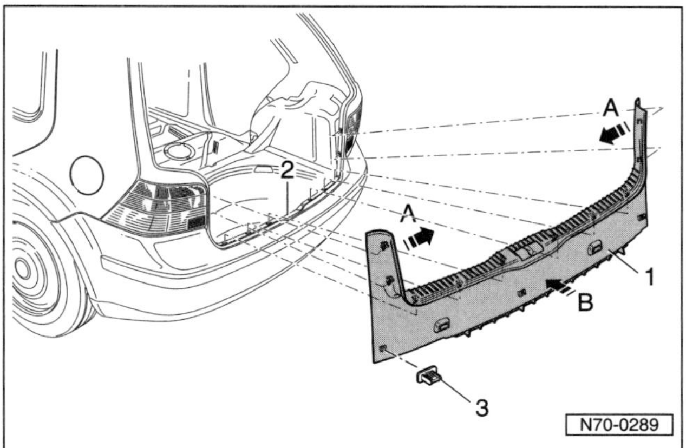

N70-0289

Fig. 42. Release rear lock carrier trim (**1**) from cross panel (**2**) at top first (**arrows A**) and then at bottom (**arrow B**).

Rear lock carrier trim (Jetta), removing

1. Open trunk and release rear lock carrier trim from lock carrier at top first and then at bottom. See Fig. 43.

2. Pull lock carrier trim upward off lock carrier.

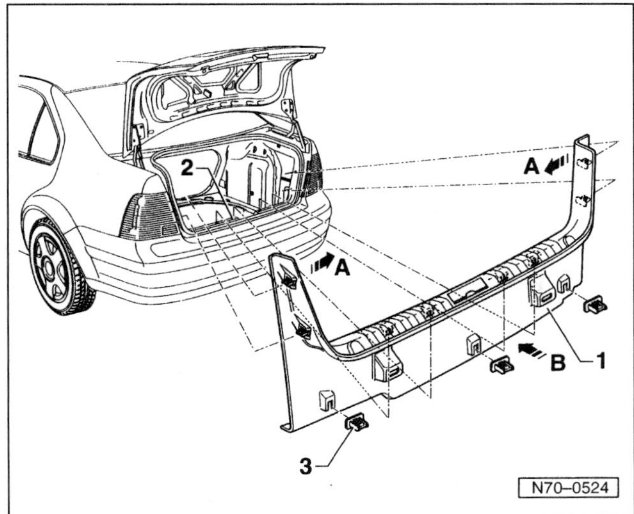

N70-0524

Fig. 43. Release rear lock carrier trim (**1**) from cross panel (**2**) at top first (**arrows A**) and then at bottom (**arrow B**).

Right luggage compartment trim (Golf), removing

1. Remove right rear seat backrest, see **72 Seats**.

2. Remove inner wheel housing trim as described earlier.

3. Remove rear lock carrier trim as described above.

4. Remove tie down hook mounting screws and tie down hooks.

5. Pull out three trim panel retaining plugs. See Fig. 44.

6. Remove trim panel and disconnect harness connector for 12 V accessory socket.

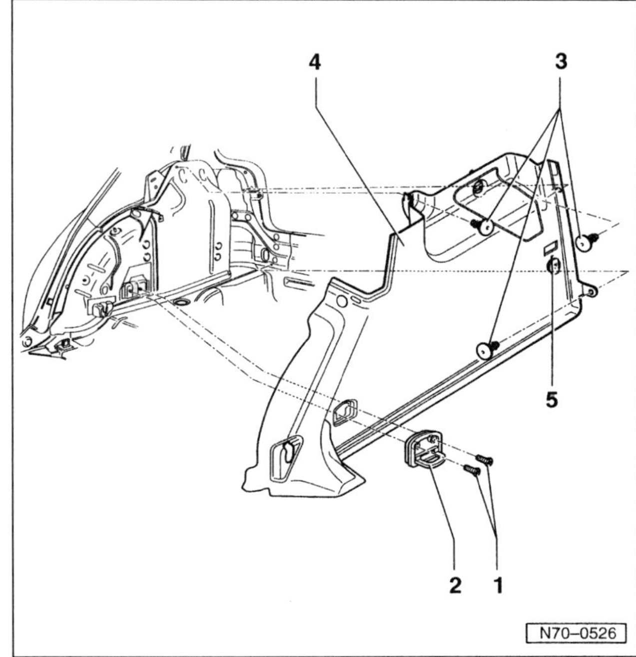

N70-0526

Fig. 44. Remove mounting screws (**1**), tie down hook (**2**), pull out three plugs (**3**), remove panel and disconnect harness connector for 12 V accessory socket (**5**).

Right luggage compartment trim (Jetta), removing

1. Remove rear seat backrest, see **72 Seats**.
2. Remove inner wheel housing trim as described earlier.
3. Remove rear lock carrier trim as described above.
4. Remove tie down hook mounting screws and tie down hooks.
5. Pull out three trim panel retaining plugs. See Fig. 45.
6. Remove trim panel and disconnect harness connector for 12 V accessory socket.

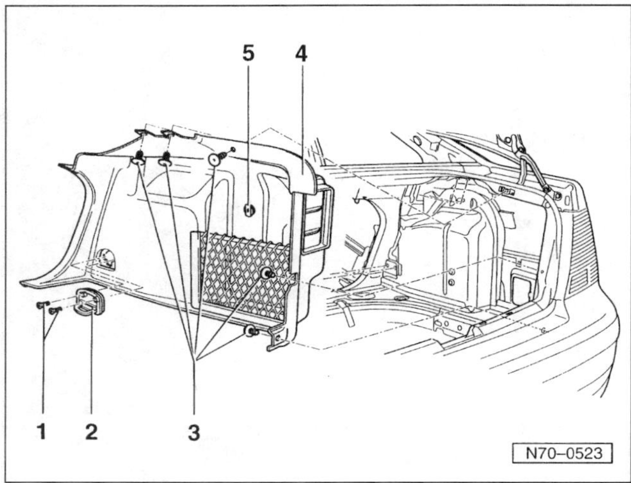

N70-0523

Fig. 45. Remove mounting screws (**1**), tie down hook (**2**), pull out three plugs (**3**), remove panel and disconnect harness connector for 12 V accessory socket (**5**).

INSTRUMENT PANEL

Instrument panel, removing and installing

WARNING —

- *Disconnect the battery Ground strap (GND) from negative (–) battery terminal before working on the electrical system.*
- *Disconnecting the negative (–) battery cable may erase fault codes and basic settings in the engine management and automatic transmission control modules. Some driveability problems may be noticed until the system re-adapts to operating conditions. OBD II readiness codes, which may be required for emissions testing, may also be erased. Convenience electronics (alarm system, interior light control, power locks, mirrors, and windows) may need to be re-set using a VAG 1551/5051 or equivalent scan tool.*

NOTE —

- *Be sure to have the anti-theft radio code on hand before disconnecting the battery.*
- *Removal of the instrument panel requires removing the radio. Volkswagen special tool 3316 is necessary for removing the factory radio.*

1. Remove steering wheel and driver's airbag unit as described in **48 Steering** and **69 Seatbelts, Airbags**.
2. Remove center console as described earlier.
3. Remove screws holding upper steering column switch trim in place and remove trim. See Fig. 46.

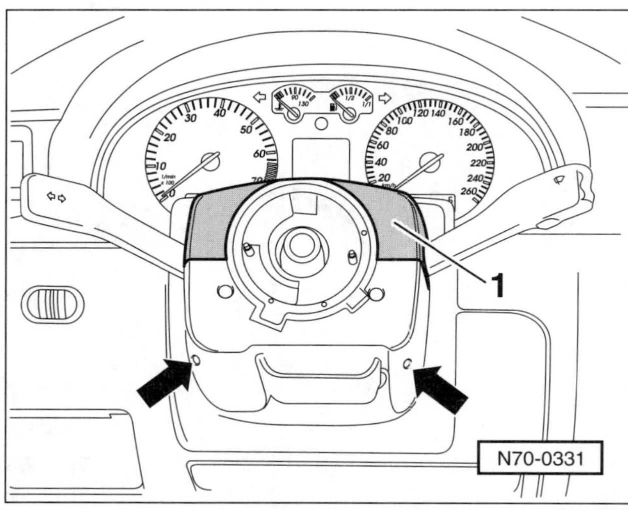

N70-0331

Fig. 46. Remove screws (**arrows**) and upper steering column switch trim (**1**).

4. Remove screws from lower steering column switch trim and steering wheel height adjustment lever. See Fig. 47.

5. Remove steering column height adjustment handle and release (pull down) height adjustment lever. Remove lower steering column switch trim.

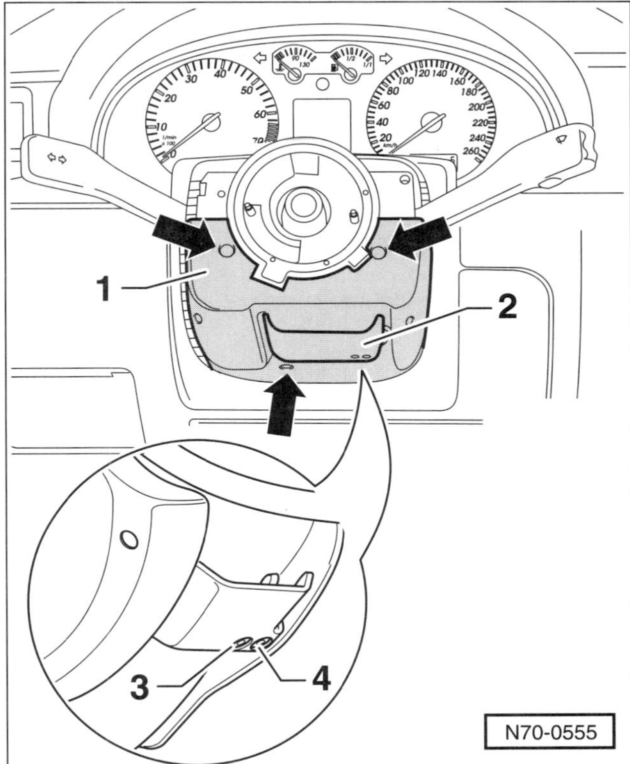

N70-0555

Fig. 47. Remove screws (**arrows**) and height adjustment handle mounting screws (**3** and **4**) and handle (**2**). Remove lower steering column switch trim (**1**).

6. Remove bolt behind steering column switch assembly.

7. Disconnect harness connectors from steering column switch assembly.

8. Remove steering column switch assembly. See Fig. 48.

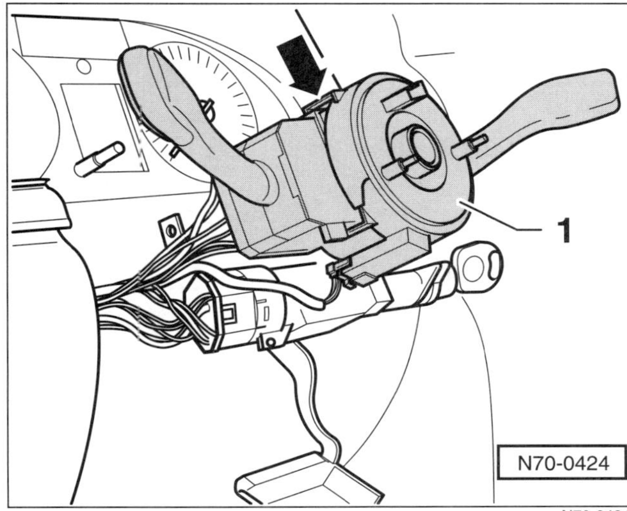

N70-0424

Fig. 48. Remove bolt (**arrows**) and disconnect harness connectors and remove switch assembly (**1**).

9. Unclip and remove left and right-side instrument panel trim pieces with a screwdriver. See Fig. 49.

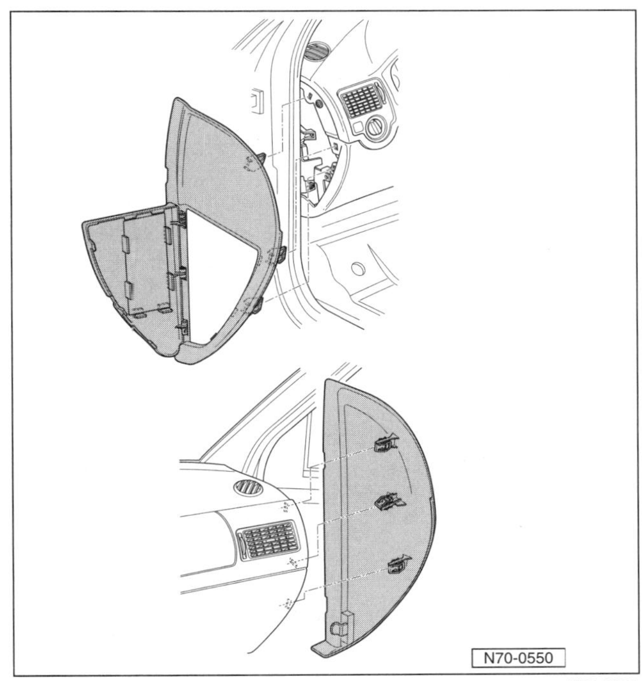

N70-0550

Fig. 49. Use a screwdriver to unclip and remove dashboard end panels.

10. Remove mounting screws above and below fuse panel. See Fig. 50.

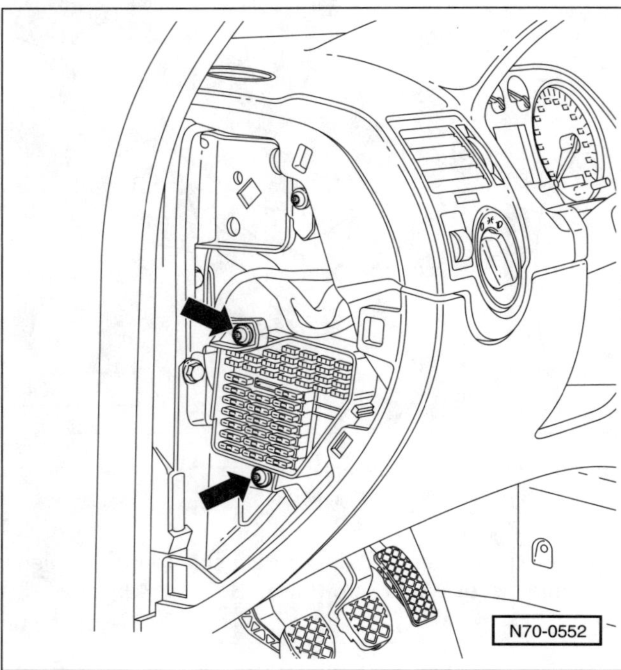

N70-0552

Fig. 50. Remove two screws (**arrows**).

11. Remove steering column lower trim as shown earlier in Fig. 34.

12. Remove mounting screws and reinforcement plate from below steering column. See Fig. 51.

N68-0443

Fig. 51. Remove mounting screws (**arrows**) and reinforcement plate (**1**) from below steering column.

13. Remove glovebox as described earlier, see **Glove box, removing**.

14. Slide Volkswagen radio release special tools 3316 into slots until they engage. See Fig. 52.

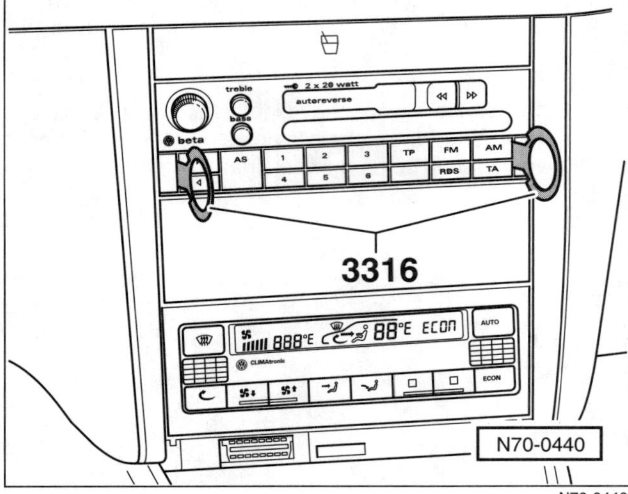

N70-0440

Fig. 52. Volkswagen special tools being used to remove radio.

15. Pull radio out of instrument panel using grip rings of release tools and disconnect harness connectors on back of radio.

NOTE —

- *Do not push the radio release tool 3316 to the side or tilt it.*
- *Press the locating tabs on the side of the radio inward to remove the release tools.*
- *Do not install radio with release tools in place.*

16. For vehicles without radio, remove radio block-off trim.

17. Remove trim panel for climate control unit.

NOTE —

VW special trim removal tool 3370 can be used to remove trim, or equivalent tool with hooked end. See Fig. 53.

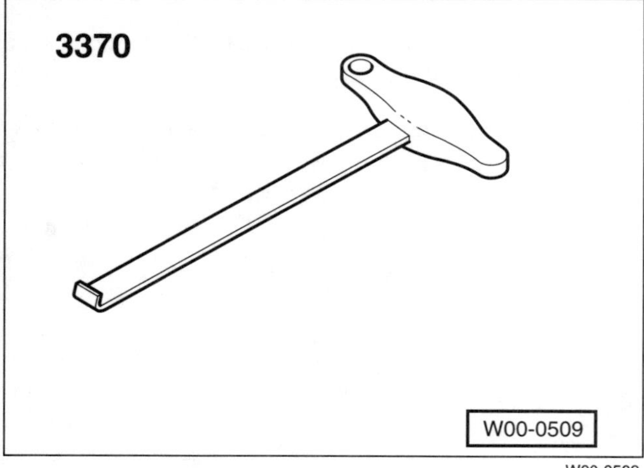

W00-0509

Fig. 53. VW special trim removal tool 3319.

18. Remove mounting screws and climate control unit. See Fig. 54.

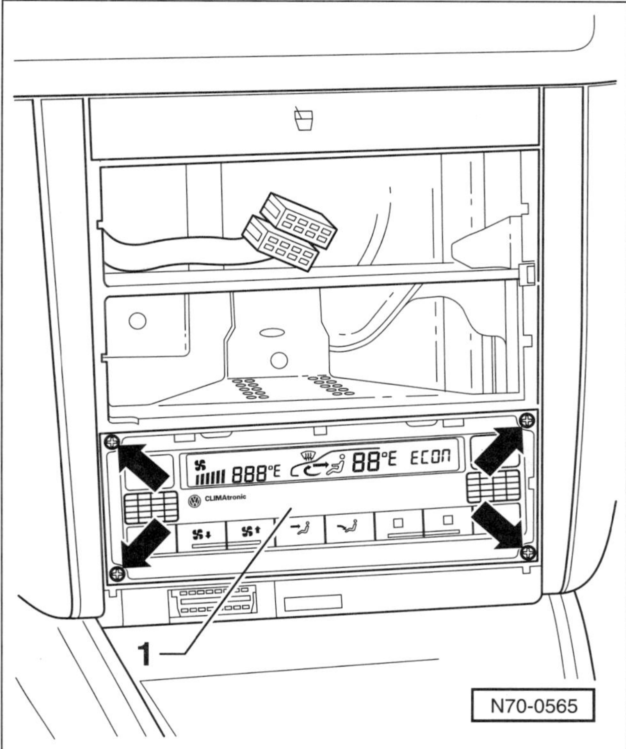

N70-0565

Fig. 54. Remove mounting screws (**arrows**) for Climatronic control unit (**1**). Non-climatronic unit is similar.

NOTE —
For non-climatronic control unit, remove mounting screws and press control unit with attached cables into instrument panel.

19. Remove mounting screws and radio/climate control unit carrier from center of dash. See Fig. 55.

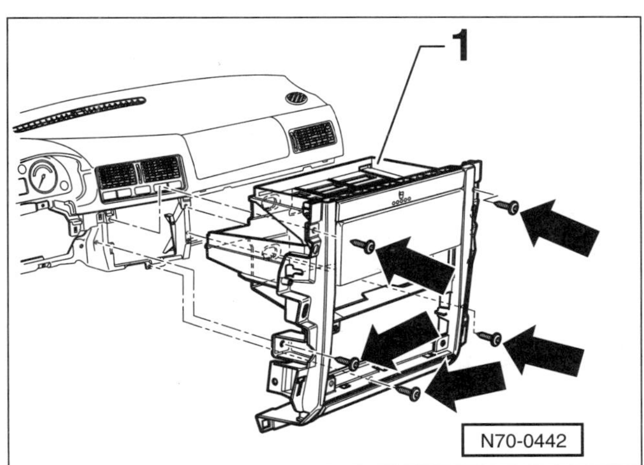

N70-0442

Fig. 55. Remove screws (**arrows**) and carrier unit (**1**).

20. Remove mounting screws and footwell trim panel. See Fig. 56.

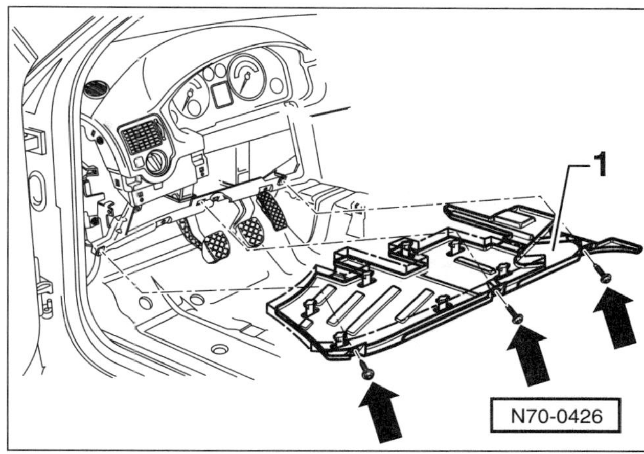

N70-0426

Fig. 56. Remove mounting screws (**arrows**) and footwell trim panel (**1**).

NOTE —
Footwell trim panel can also be secured with clips rather than screws.

21. Remove mounting screws in bottom of instrument cluster. Lower cluster slightly and pull out from instrument panel. Disconnect harness connectors on back of cluster and remove. See Fig. 57.

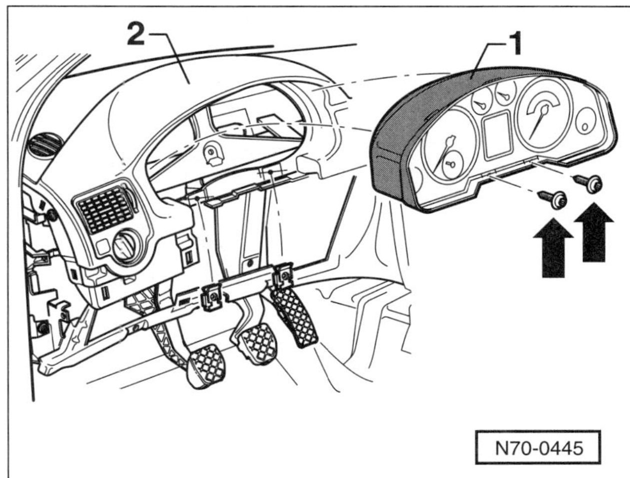

N70-0445

Fig. 57. Remove screws (**arrows**), lower cluster slightly (**1**) and pull out from instrument panel (**2**).

22. Unclip temperature sensor (Climatronic) from top of instrument panel and separate harness connector. See Fig. 58.

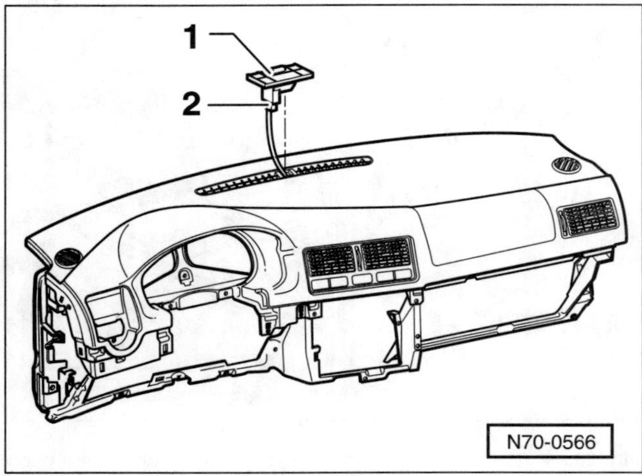

N70-0566

Fig. 58. For vehicles with Climatronic, unclip temperature sensor (**1**), and separate harness connector (**2**).

23. Remove instrument panel mounting screws. See Fig. 59.

24. Remove instrument panel from crossmember.

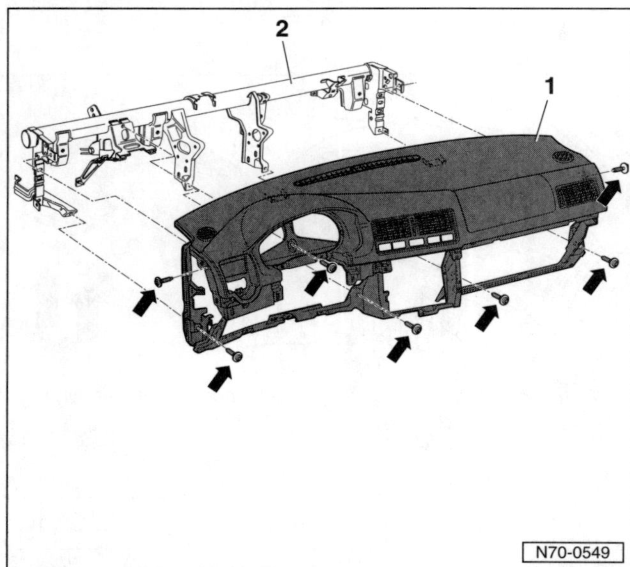

N70-0549

Fig. 59. Remove screws (**arrows**) and pull instrument panel away from cross-member (**2**).

25. Install instrument panel in reverse order of removal, noting the following:
    - Always replace steering wheel mounting bolt when installing steering wheel.
    - After connecting battery check operation of vehicle equipment (radio, clock, power windows).
    - After connecting battery, readiness code for the ECM will need to be re-set using VAG 1551/5051 scan tool or equivalent.
    - If airbag malfunction indicator lamp (MIL) signals a malfunction after installing instrument panel, the Diagnostic Trouble Code (DTC) memory must be erased and checked again with VAG 1551/5051 scan tool or equivalent.

QUALITY REVIEW

When you have finished working under the hood and around other areas of the vehicle, it is advisable to take a moment to quality check or review your work. This helps to insure that the operation or repair has been completed properly with all affected systems functioning within normal parameters. These may include the following:

- Ensure that all cable ties and clamps that were removed as part of the repair are replaced.
- Ensure that all fasteners and hardware were replaced and torqued as specified.
- Make sure that all other components involved in the repair are positioned correctly, properly torqued and function properly.
- Make sure that all tools, shop cloths, fender covers and protective tapes are removed.
- Clean grease and fingerprints from painted surfaces, steering wheel, upholstery and shifter.
- Make sure that seatbelt and airbag warning lights function correctly.
- Unlock anti-theft radio and reset the clock.

72 Seats

FRONT SEATS

Both driver and passenger front seats are equipped with airbags mounted in the seat backrest frames. These airbags are designed to deploy under certain side impact conditions and are triggered by separate sensors mounted to the front floor crossmembers under the front seats. Before removing the front seats, a safety device (VAS 5094) must be installed to prevent accidental deployment of the airbag units.

> ***WARNING —***
> - *Observe all cautions, warnings and notes before starting repairs involving airbag systems, see* **69 Seatbelts, Airbags**.
> - *Volkswagen of America specifically warns against the installation of aftermarket upholstery on any vehicle equipped with side airbags. The factory-installed upholstery is designed to separate in specific places at specific rates, and in specific directions. Installation of non-factory upholstery including, but not limited to, "beads" and "sheepskins", may cause seat mounted airbags to deploy when they are not supposed to; fail to deploy when they should; or to deploy in some manner other than designed. This is a safety hazard and could result in serious injury or death to occupants of the vehicle.*

Front seat, removing and installing

1. Disconnect the battery ground (–) strap before working on the electrical system.

> ***CAUTION —***
> *Disconnecting the negative (–) battery cable may erase fault codes and basic settings in the engine management and automatic transmission control modules. Some driveability problems may be noticed until the system re-adapts to operating conditions. OBD II readiness codes, which may be required for emissions testing, may also be erased. Convenience electronics (alarm system, interior light control, power locks, mirrors, and windows) may need to be re-set using a VAG 1551/5051 or equivalent scan tool.*

NOTE —
- *The removal and installation procedures may have to be modified slightly depending on equipment variations.*
- *Obtain the radio code before disconnecting the battery.*

2. Slide seat forward.

3. Remove screw cover (**1**) and screw (**2**). See Fig. 1.

NOTE —
The items in parenthesis for steps 3 through 8 refer to Fig. 1.

4. Unclip cover strip (**3**) from inner seat rail (**arrow A**) and remove toward rear (**arrow B**).

5. Remove screw cover (**4**) and screw (**5**).

6. Unclip cover strip (**6**) from outer seat rail (**arrow C**) and remove by sliding forward (**arrow D**).

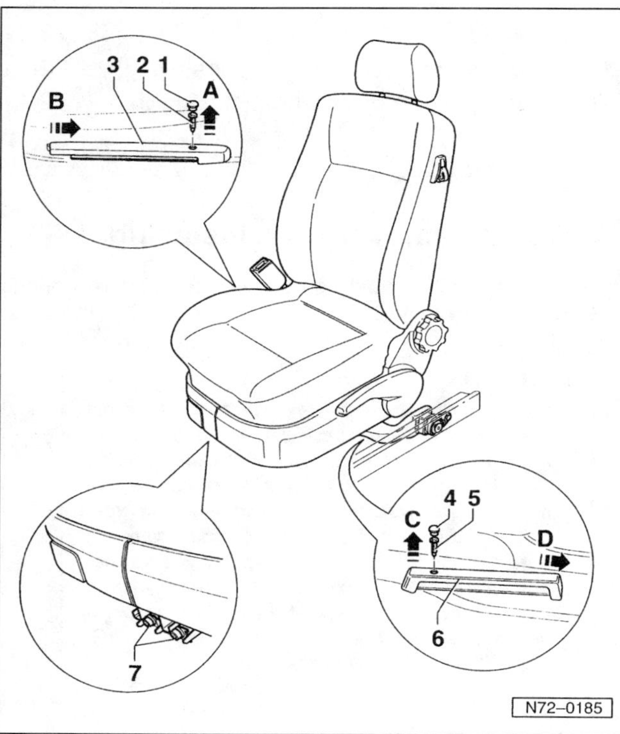

N72-0185

Fig. 1. Front seat with removal and installation details.

7. Slide seat to rear.

8. Remove retaining bolts (**7**). See Fig. 1.

Tightening torque
- Front seat retaining bolts . . . . 23 Nm (17 ft-lb)

9. Separate side airbag wiring harness connector (**1**) at seat connector station (**2**). See Fig. 2.

NOTE —
The items in parenthesis for steps 9 through 11 refer to Fig. 2.

WARNING —
Before disconnecting the side airbag connector for the seat, a technician must discharge him/herself electrostatically by briefly touching door striker or vehicle body.

10. Separate connector (**3**) for seat heating (as applicable) and seat adjustment connector (as applicable).

11. Insert connector (**4**) of Volkswagen special tool VAS 5094 airbag adapter into connector housing (**5**).

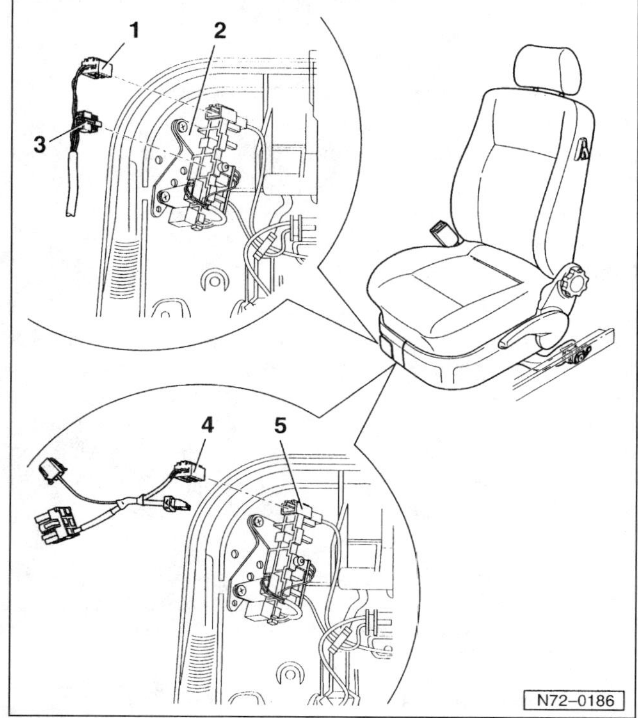

N72-0186

Fig. 2. Airbag adapter VAS 5094 (**4**) must be installed when removing seats to prevent accidental discharge of the side airbag.

WARNING —
Failure to install VAS 5094 could result in deployment of the side airbag.

12. Slide seat out of guide rails.

13. Install in reverse order of removal, noting the following:
    - After all components are installed, switch ignition on.
    - Connect battery ground strap.

WARNING —
Make sure the passenger compartment is not occupied before connecting the battery ground strap.

- After connecting the battery ground (–), ensure proper operation of vehicle equipment (radio, clock, power windows).

Front seat assembly

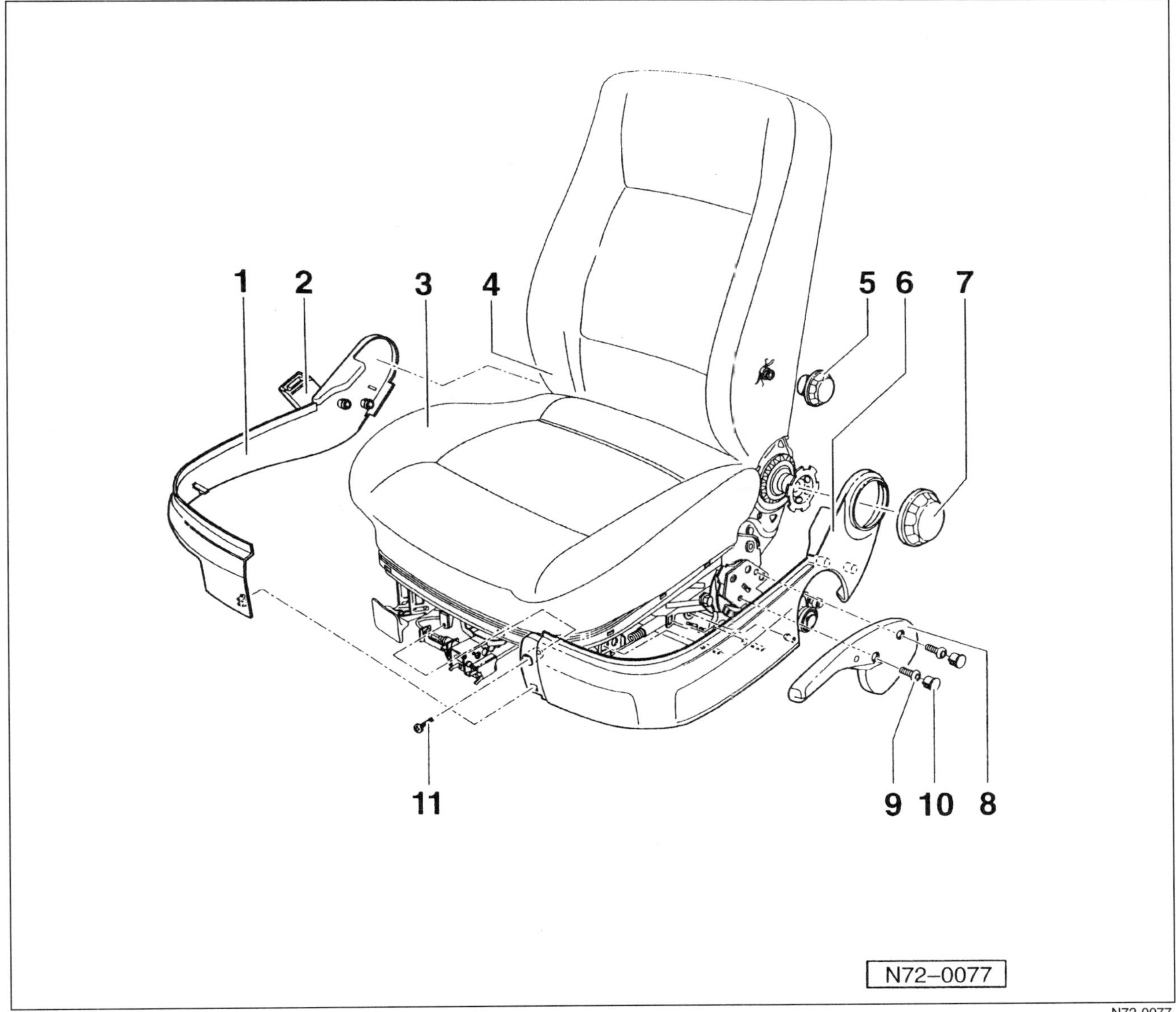

N72-0077

Fig. 3. Front seat for vehicles with four doors, two door models similar.

1. **Seat trim, right**
2. **Belt lock**
3. **Seat bottom**
4. **Backrest**
   - Removal:
     Remove seat belt lock (item 2)
     Remove seat from vehicle
     Pull off adjusting knob (item 7)
     Remove adjusting lever (item 8)
     Pull off trim (item 1)
     Remove screw and left-side trim (item 11and 6)
     For remainder of removal procedure see Ⓐ
5. **Adjusting knob (lumbar support)**
6. **Seat trim, left**
7. **Adjusting knob (backrest)**
8. **Adjusting lever (seat height)**
9. **Screws**
10. **Cap**
    - Qty. 2
11. **Screw**
    - Qty. 2

A Front backrest, removing and installing (continued)

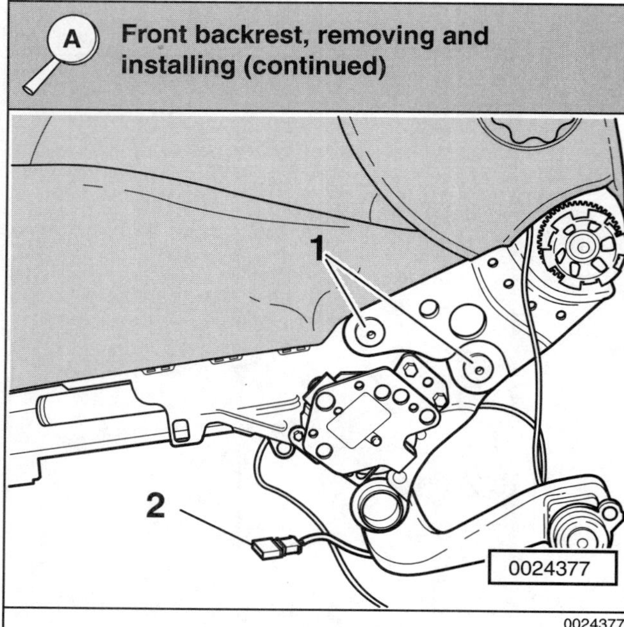

0024377

- Unclip wiring guides under seat.
- Disconnect wiring connector (2) for backrest heating, if equipped.
- Remove bolts (1) from both sides of seat and take off backrest.
- When installing, bolts (4) must be secured with thread locking compound and tightened to 24 Nm (18 ft-lb).

Head restraint guides, removing

1. Remove head restraint from backrest by pulling the restraint up until it stops. Then, press the release button on the side of head restraint while pulling the head restraint up and out. See Fig. 4.

BUS-056C

Fig. 4. Press button (**arrow**) while pulling headrest up and out from seat backrest.

2. Press in locking lugs on head restraint guides and pull out guides from backrest. See Fig. 5.

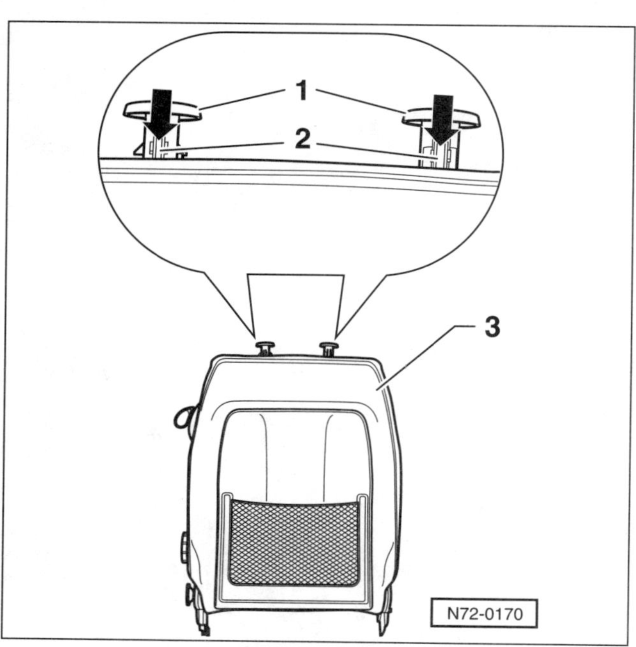

N72-0157

Fig. 5. Press in locking lugs (**2**) and pull out head restraint guides (**1**) from backrest (**3**).

Locking backrest assembly (Golf 2-door)

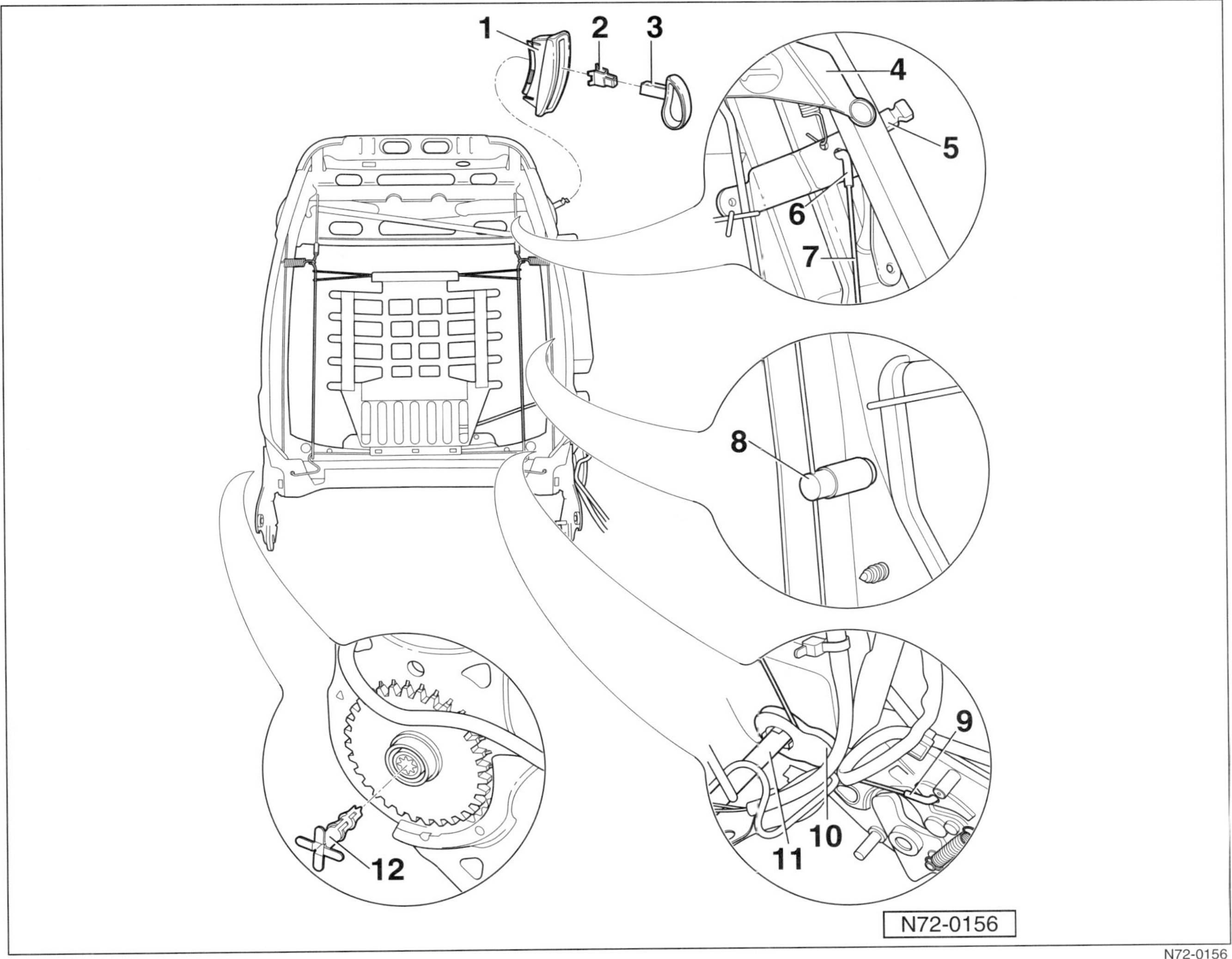

N72-0156

Fig. 6. Front seat backrest for 2-door Golf/GTI with details of release mechanism.

1. **Cover**
2. **Clip**
3. **Grip**
4. **Backrest frame**
5. **Locking lever**
6. **Cable upper hook**
7. **Cable**
   - Removing:
     Remove seat and backrest as described earlier
     Pry off grip (item 3) and unclip cover (item 1)
     Remove cover and padding, as described later
     Break off the four small tabs of the locking sleeve (item 12) and drive sleeve into transfer rod (item 11) using punch
   - Removing cable (continued)
     Press locking lever (item 5) down and pull out cable hook (item 6)
     Unclip cable center guide (item 8) from backrest frame (item 4)
     Pull transfer rod (item 11) out from backrest frame enough to allow lower cable guide (item 10) to be unhcoked
     Unhook cable hook (item 9) and pull cable (item 7) out from backrest frame
8. **Cable center guide**
9. **Cable lower hook**
10. **Cable lower guide**
11. **Transfer rod**
12. **Locking sleeve**
    - Always replace when replacing cable (item 7)

Seat height adjuster assembly

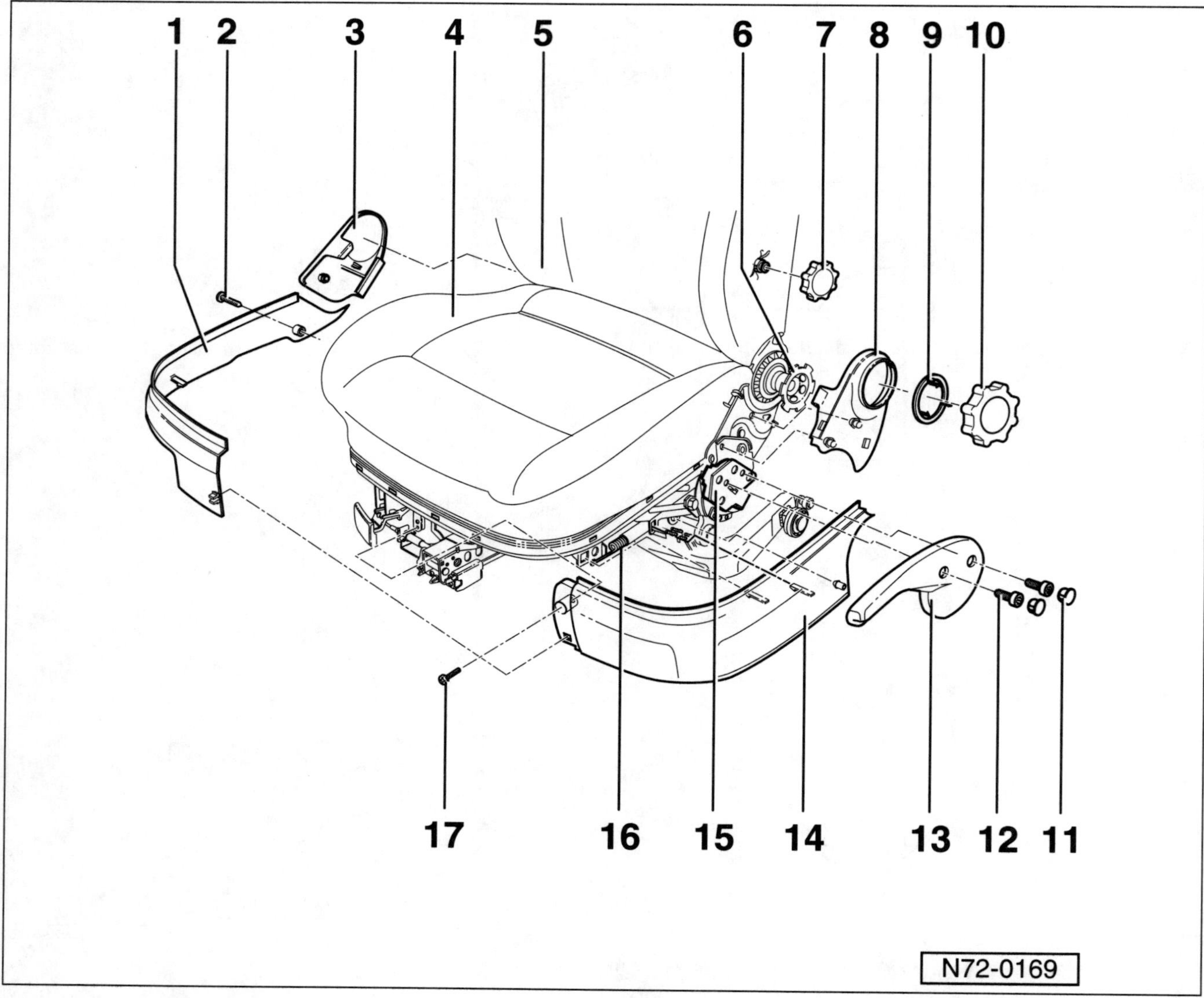

N72-0169

Fig. 7. Seat height adjuster and related components of driver seat. Passenger seat is a mirror image of above.

1. **Seat trim, inner front**
2. **Screw**
3. **Seat trim, inner rear**
4. **Seat bottom**
5. **Backrest**
6. **Transfer rod**
   - For backrest adjustment
7. **Adjusting knob**
8. **Seat trim, outer rear**
9. **Spacer**
10. **Adjusting knob**
    - For backrest angle
11. **Cover cap (2)**
12. **Screw (2)**
13. **Adjusting lever**
    - For seat height
14. **Seat trim, outer front**
15. **Seat height adjusting element**
16. **Spring (2)**
17. **Screw**

Seat height adjuster, removing and installing

1. Remove front seat as described earlier.
2. Remove mounting screws and inner front trim piece (item 2 in Fig. 7.)
3. Unclip cover caps, remove screws and adjusting lever (items 11, 12, 13 in Fig. 7.)
4. Remove front mounting screw and front outer trim piece (items 17 and 14 in Fig. 7.)
5. Unhook spring at bottom front corners of seat. Remove mounting bolts and pull seat adjuster out of mounting frame. See Fig. 8.

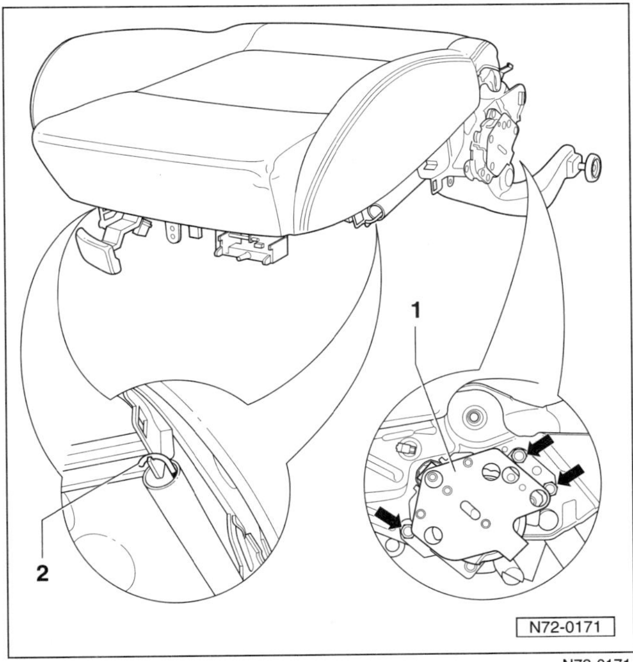

N72-0171

Fig. 8. Unhook springs (**2**) carefully, remove bolts (**arrows**) and pull seat height adjuster (**1**) out from seat frame.

6. Installation is the reverse of removal.

Tightening torque
- Seat adjuster to seat frame . . . . 10 Nm (7 ft-lb)

Front seat backrest cover and padding, removing and installing

NOTE —
The front seat backrest cover must be removed to access the lumbar support mechanism and the cable and mechanism for the locking backrest on 2-door Golf/GTI models.

1. Remove head restraint, seat and backrest as described earlier.
2. Unclip bottom of trim on rear of backrest and unhook upwards.
3. Use a screwdriver to separate beading strip of backrest cover from front of seat cover. See Fig. 9.

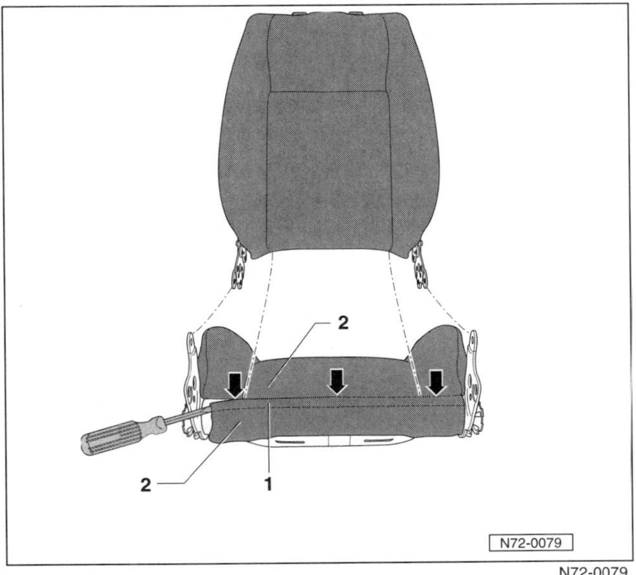

N72-0079

Fig. 9. Separate cover (**2**) beading strip (**1**) using screwdriver (**arrows**).

4. Unhook tensioning wire for seat cover. See Fig. 10.

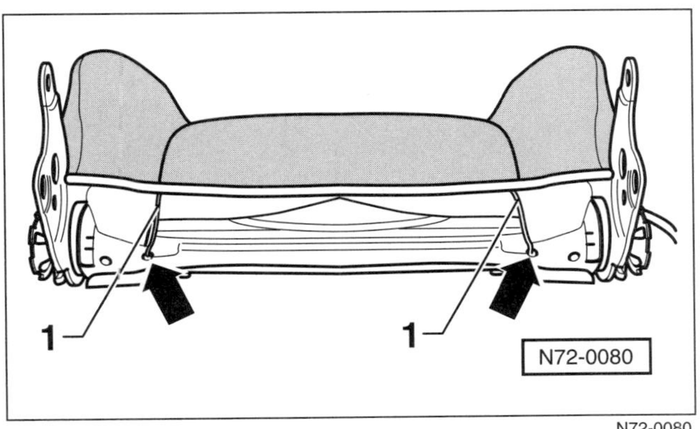

N72-0080

Fig. 10. Unhook tensioning wire (**1**) for seat cover at **arrows**.

5. Pry off adjustment knob on side of seat.

6. Pull cover up and release from tensioning frame. Pull cover up over padding and head restraint guides. See Fig. 11.

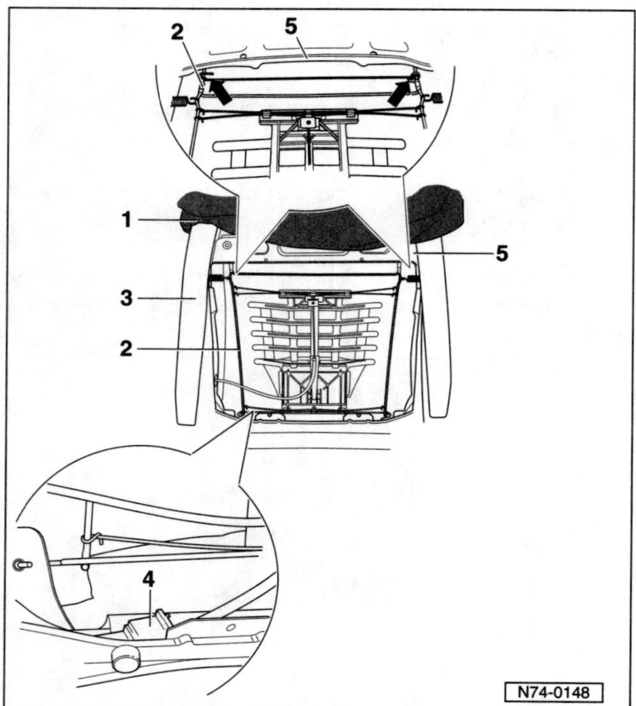

N74-0148

Fig. 11. Pull up cover (**1**), release from tensioning frame (**2**), pull up over padding (**3**) and head restraint guides. Separate backrest heater harness connector (**4**) and pull padding off backrest (**5**).

NOTE —

Seat padding is connected to lumbar frame with Velcro®.

7. Separate harness connector for backrest heater, if applicable.

8. Pull padding off backrest.

9. Installation is the reverse of removal.

Electrically Adjustable Front Seats

Some vehicles are equipped with electrically adjustable front seats that have the ability to adjust the seat in 8 different directions. Hence they are also referred to as 8-way adjustable seats.

8-way seat adjusting unit, removing

1. Remove seat and belt lock as described earlier.

2. Remove screw cover and screw at the lower front of seat.

3. Unclip seat trim on right-hand side.

4. Remove mounting screws for left-side trim. See Fig. 12.

5. Separate harness connector for 8-way adjustable switch and unclip left-side trim.

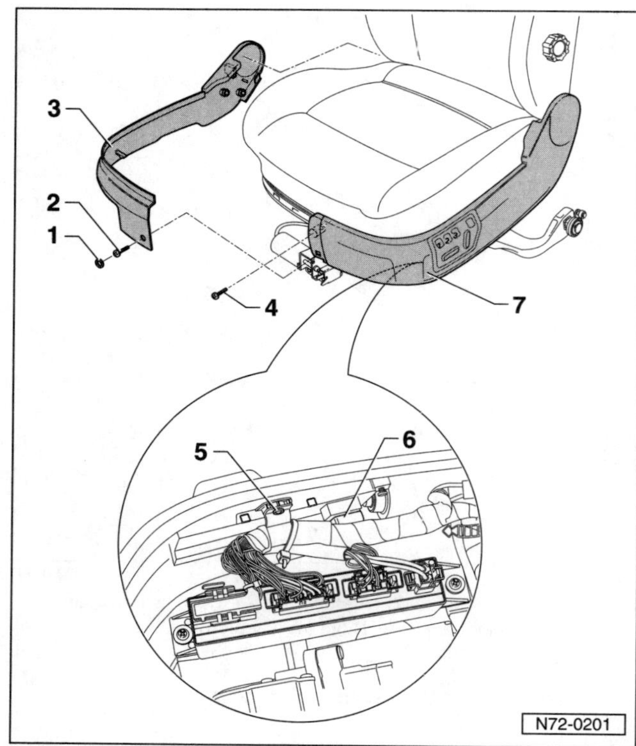

N72-0201

Fig. 12. Remove cover (**1**), screw (**2**), right-side trim (**3**), screws (**4** and **5**), separate connector (**6**) and remove left-side trim (**7**).

6. Remove two screws on either side of 8-way adjusting unit and remove unit. See Fig. 13.

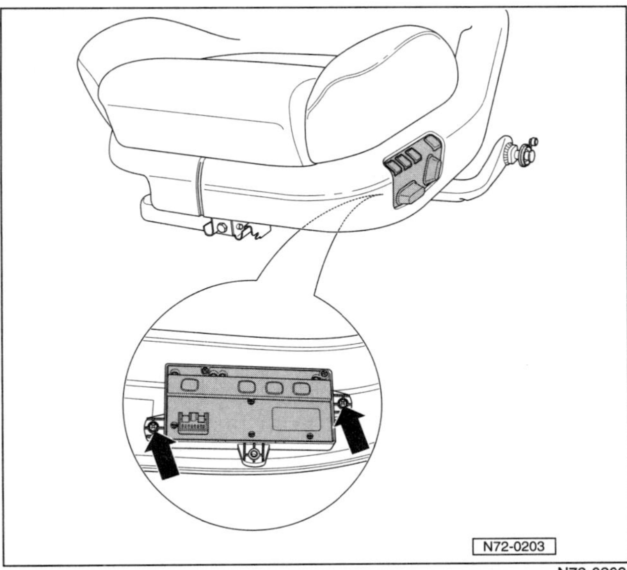

N72-0203

Fig. 13. Remove screws (**arrows**) and 8-way adjusting unit.

8-way adjustable seat control unit, removing

1. Remove seat as described earlier.

2. Separate the four harness connectors from the 8-way adjustable control unit. See Fig. 14.

3. Remove control unit mounting screws and control unit.

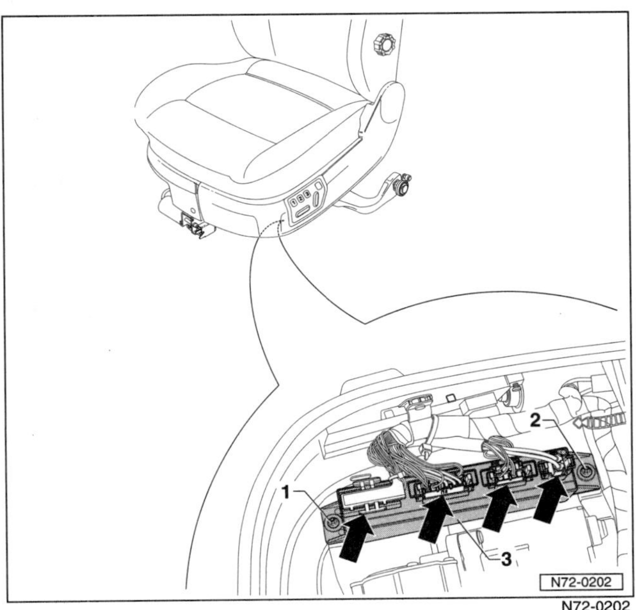

N72-0202

Fig. 14. Separate harness connectors (**arrows**) remove screws (**1** and **2**) and remove control unit (**3**).

8-way seat fore/aft adjustment, removing

1. Remove seat as described earlier.

2. Separate fore/aft harness connector with screwdriver. See Fig. 15.

3. Remove eight mounting screws (four on each side) and pull seat fore/aft adjustment mechanism out. See Fig. 15.

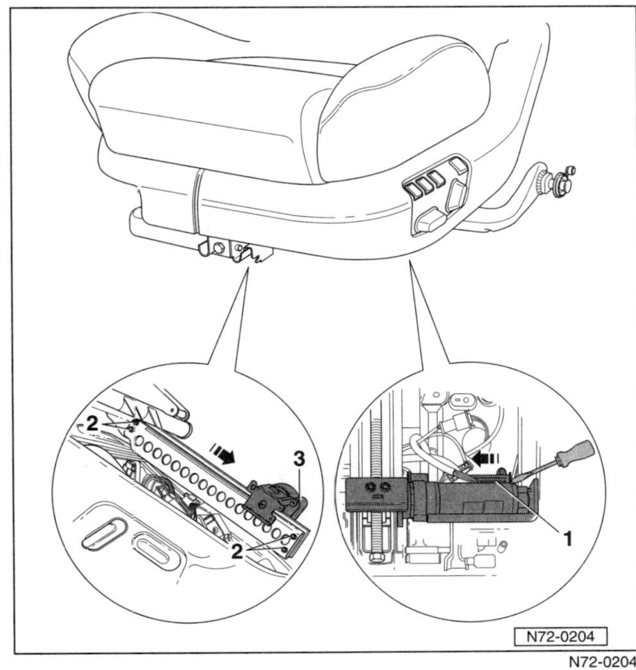

N72-0204

Fig. 15. Separate connector (**1**) by prying with screwdriver in direction of **arrow**. Remove mounting screws (**2**) and fore/aft mechanism in direction of **arrow**.

8-way seat rear height adjustment drive, removing

1. Remove seat and trim as described earlier.
2. Separate rear height adjustment harness connector with screwdriver. See Fig. 16.
3. Remove three mounting screws and rear height adjustment drive unit. See Fig. 16.

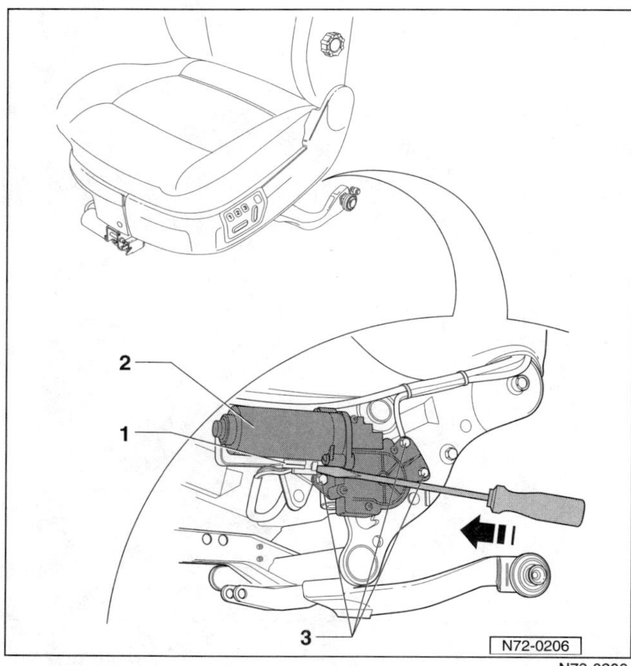

N72-0206

Fig. 16. Separate connector (**1**) by prying with screwdriver in direction of **arrow**. Remove mounting screws (**3**) and rear adjustment drive motor (**2**).

8-way seat backrest adjustment drive, removing

1. Remove seat and trim as described earlier.
2. Release backrest cover at bottom and roll up, see Fig. 9. and Fig. 10. given earlier.
3. Separate backrest adjustment harness connector with screwdriver. See Fig. 17.
4. Pry off securing washer and drive shaft into backrest frame approx. 15 cm (6 in.) with hammer and drift. Remove drive unit mounting nut and drive unit. See Fig. 17.

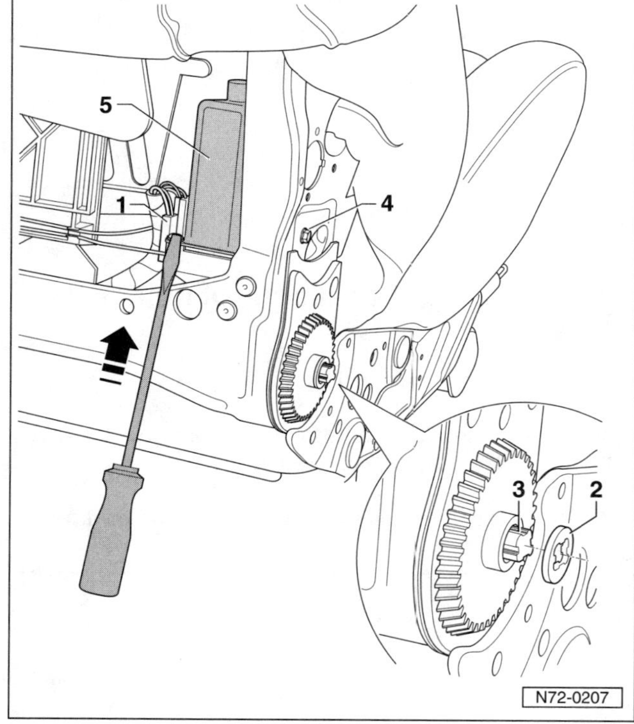

N72-0207

Fig. 17. Separate connector (**1**) by prying with screwdriver in direction of **arrow**. Pry off securing washer (**2**) and drive shaft (**3**) into backrest frame approx. 15 cm (6 in.) with hammer and drift. Remove nut (**4**) and drive (**5**).

REAR SEATS

Rear seat bottom, removing and installing

1. Lift seat cushion and pull forward.
2. Unhook seat retaining rods from retainers. See Fig. 18.

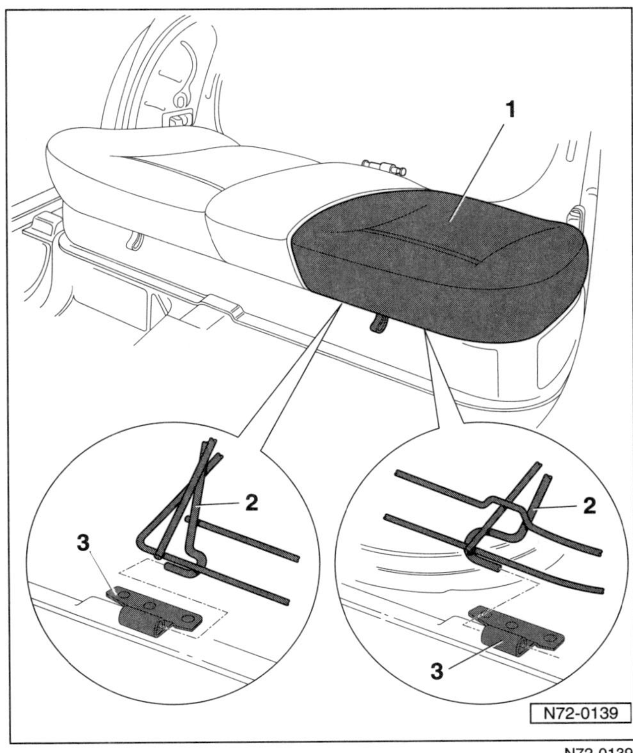

N72-0139

Fig. 18. Unhook rods (**2**) from retainers (**3**) to remove rear seat cushion. Left-side cushion shown, right-side is identical.

3. To install, hook rods into retainers, fold seat cushion back and push down at front.

Rear seat backrest, removing and installing

1. Fold backrest forward.
2. Using a screwdriver, press back backrest retaining hooks on right and left sides and pull backrest up out of mount. See Fig. 19.

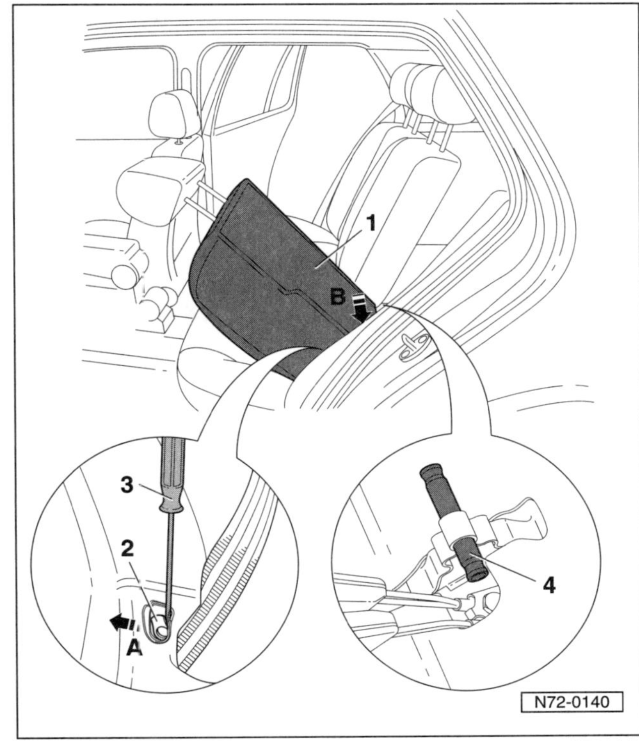

N72-0140

Fig. 19. Use a screwdriver (**3**) to press retaining hooks (**2**) in direction of **arrow A**. Lift backrest (**1**) up slightly and pull off from center mount (**4**) at **arrow B**.

3. Installation is reverse of removal.

80 Heating and Ventilation

GENERAL

This section primarily applies to heating and vetillation components of the HVAC system. For those vehicles with A/C, the refrigerant must first be discharged using specialized equipment before working on most of the heating and ventilation components, see **87 Air Conditioning**.

This section also covers removal and installation of the heating and ventillation controls for vehicles equipped with manual A/C. For vehicles equipped with electronic A/C (Climatronic), see **87 Air Conditioning**.

> ***WARNING —***
> *The cooling system is pressurized when the engine is warm. Wear gloves and other protection and carefully release system pressure if necessary, before performing repairs.*

> ***CAUTION —***
> *Disconnecting the negative (–) battery cable may erase fault codes and basic settings in the engine management and automatic transmission control modules. Some driveability problems may be noticed until the system re-adapts to operating conditions. OBD II readiness codes, which may be required for emissions testing, may also be erased. Convenience electronics (alarm system, interior light control, power locks, mirrors, and windows) may need to be re-set using a VAG 1551/5051 or equivalent scan tool.*

HEATING AND VENTILATION CONTROLS

Passenger compartment air is vented to the outside through openings in the parcel shelf (Jetta) below the rear window. In order for the ventilation system to work properly, these openings must not be blocked.

For an overview of the major heating and ventilation system components, see Fig. 1.

Passenger compartment components, overview

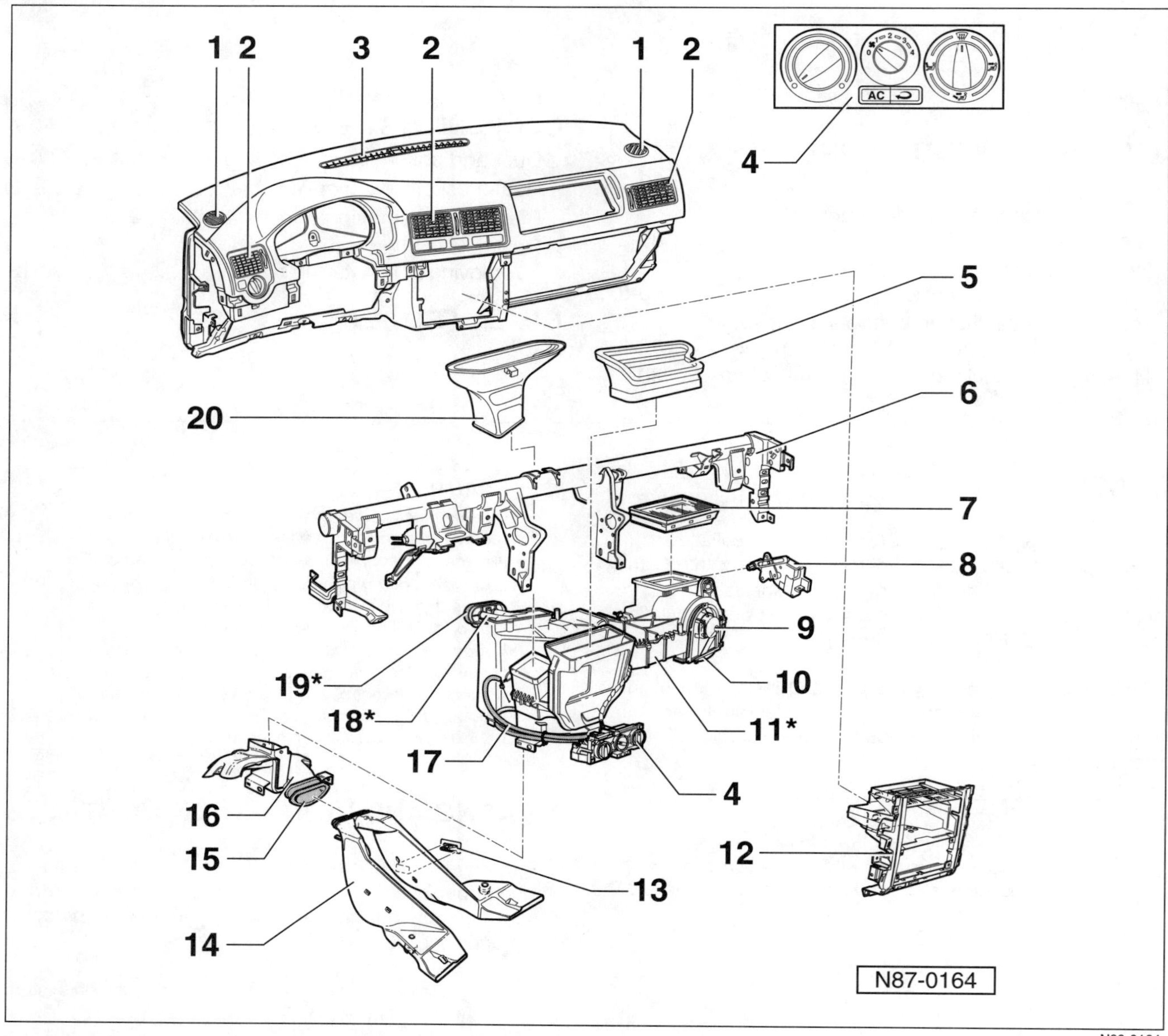

N80-0164

Fig. 1. Major components related to the heating and ventilation system located in the passenger compartment.

1. **Side window air outlet**
   - Removing, **see** Ⓐ
2. **Dashboard air outlets**
   - Removing, **see** Ⓑ
3. **Defroster air outlet**
4. **Heating and ventilation controls**
   - With A/C switch, as applicable
   - With fresh air blower fan switch (E9)
   - With fresh air and recirculation switch (E184)
5. **Intermediate duct**
6. **Instrument panel cross member, see** Ⓒ
7. **Dust and pollen filter**
   - Covers outside air inlet to passenger compartment
   - Filters all incoming air
8. **Servo motor for recirculation door (V154)**
9. **Blower fan (V2)**
10. **Blower fan series resistance pack (N24)**
    - With thermal fuse

(continued from previous page)

11. Heating and ventilation unit

- Removing:
  Remove instrument panel, see 70 Trim–Interior
  Loosen instrument panel cross member, **see** Ⓒ
  Carefully pinch off both coolant hoses to heater core and disconnect hoses
  Seal off heater core to prevent coolant from running out
  Remove heating and ventilation unit

> ***WARNING —***
> *The cooling system is pressurized when the engine is warm. Wear gloves and other protection and carefully release system pressure, if necessary, before performing repairs.*

12. Center trim

13. Footwell air outlet

14. Rear footwell air outlet

15. Gasket

16. Connecting duct

- With driver's side footwell air outlet
- Removing, **see** Ⓓ

17. Cables

- Color code yellow - air distribution control knob to central flap
- Color code green - air distribution control knob to footwell/defrost flap
- Color code beige - temperature control knob to temperature flap

18. Heater core

- Always replace coolant after removal/replacement

19. Heater core/bulkhead seal

20. Defroster duct

- Instrument panel must be removed and support beam loosened to replace duct
- Note installed position, **see** Ⓔ

Ⓐ Side window fixed air vents, removing and installing

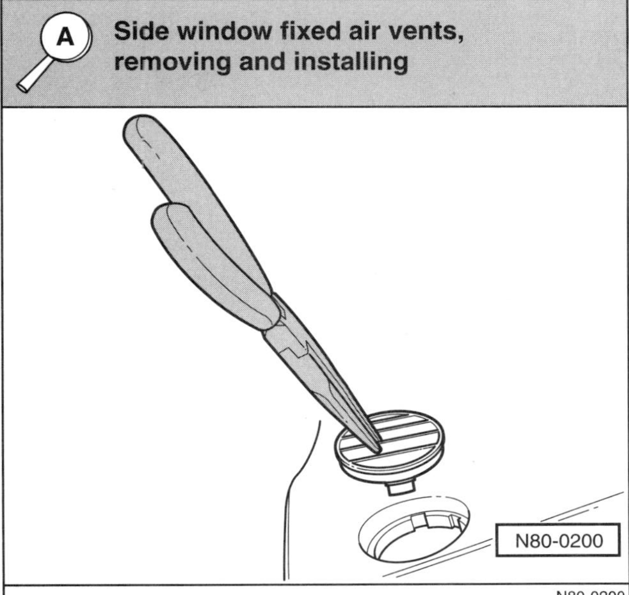

N80-0200

- **Protect vanes of vent before removing.**
- **Apply cloth tape to the pliers or vanes or use needle nose pliers with plastic or rubber protective jaws.**
- **Carefully remove air outlet by pulling out with needle nose pliers.**

Ⓑ Air outlets, removing

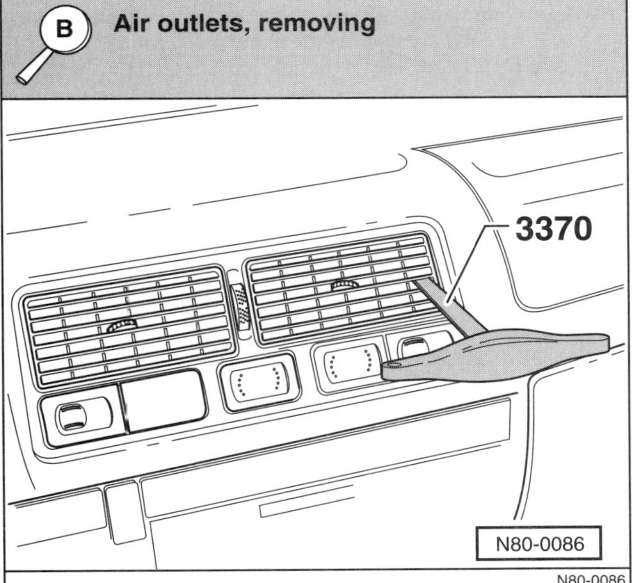

N80-0086

- **Attach Volkswagen special tool 3370, or equivalent, at center of right or left side of air outlet pull out.**
- **An illustration of special tool 3370 is shown in 70 Trim–Interior in the Instrument Panel section.**

C Instrument panel crossmember, loosening and tightening

N80-0256

- Remove securing bolts (arrows).
  Tightening torque: 25 Nm (18 ft-lb)
- To access or remove heating and ventilation unit, lift cross member in direction of arrow A and support unit.
- To prevent damage to the steering column, work should be done with aid of another technician.
- If removed component(s) are not to be reinstalled immediately, re-secure the cross member to the bulkhead.
- Any wiring harnesses released from their retainers must be secured again at the same point, using the same method of securing.

D Connecting duct, removing

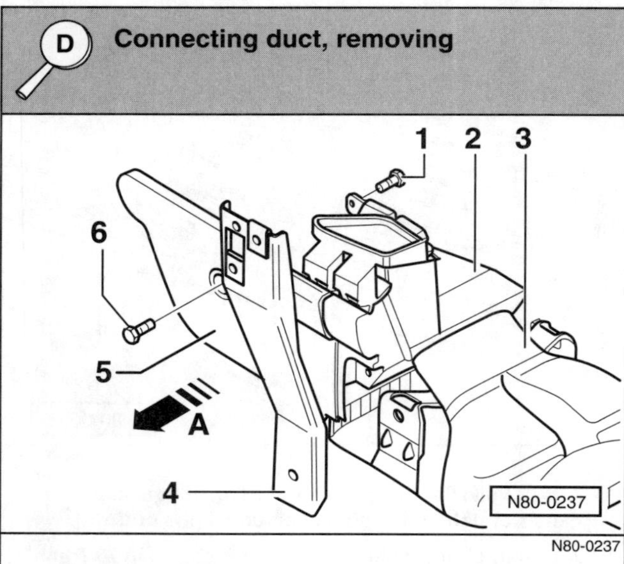

N80-0237

- Remove glove box and steering column lower trim, see 70 Trim–Interior.
- Remove bracket (4), bolt (6), and cover (5).
- Remove bolt (1) and connecting duct (2) in direction of arrow. Leave rear footwell duct (3) in place.

E Defroster duct, installation position

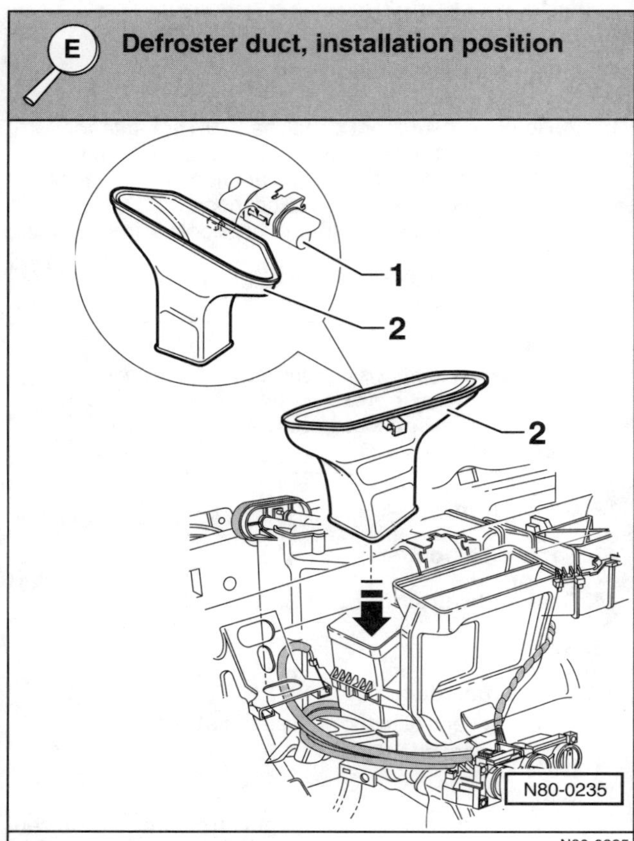

N80-0235

- Attach defroster duct (2) to heater unit.
- At the same time position defroster duct in instrument panel cross-member (1).

Heating and ventilation controls (manual A/C system)

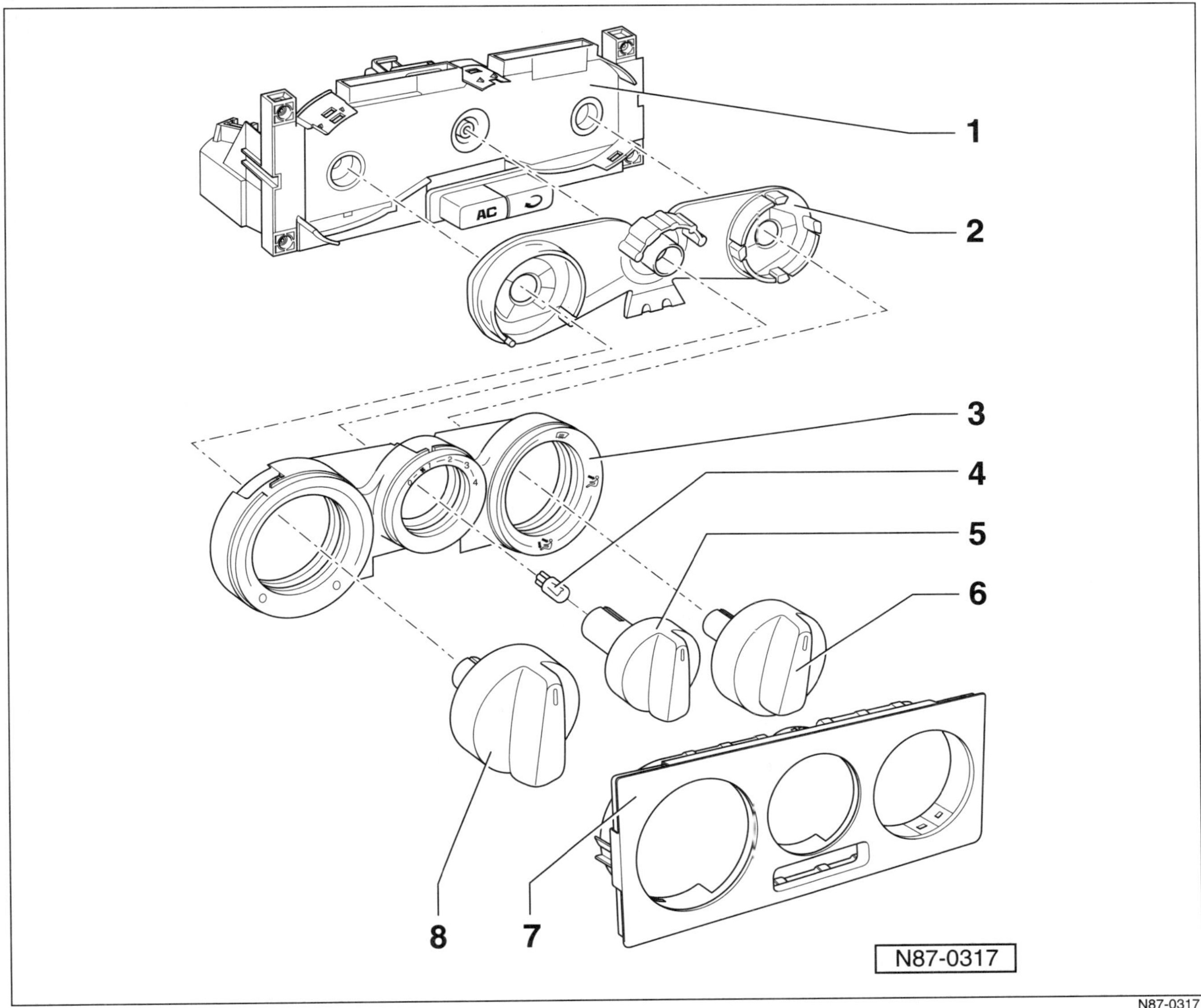

Fig. 2. Heating and ventilation controls for vehicles without the digital Climatronic system.

1. **Heating and A/C control unit**
   - With fresh air blower switch and recirculation switch
2. **Illumination filter**
3. **Trim panel**
4. **Fresh air control lever light**
   - 12V, 1.2W
   - Unclip trim panel (item 7) and rotary control (item 5) to remove
5. **Rotary control**
   - For blower speed
   - Use pliers with plastic or rubber protection on jaws to pull off
6. **Rotary control**
   - For air distribution
   - Use pliers with plastic or rubber protection on jaws to pull off
7. **Trim panel**
8. **Rotary control**
   - For interior temperature control
   - Use pliers with plastic or rubber protection on jaws to pull off

Heating and ventilation controls, removing and installing (manual A/C system)

1. Remove glove box, lower steering column trim and center console, see **70 Trim–Interior**.

2. Pull off HVAC control trim panel with VW special tool 3370, or equivalent. See Fig. 3.

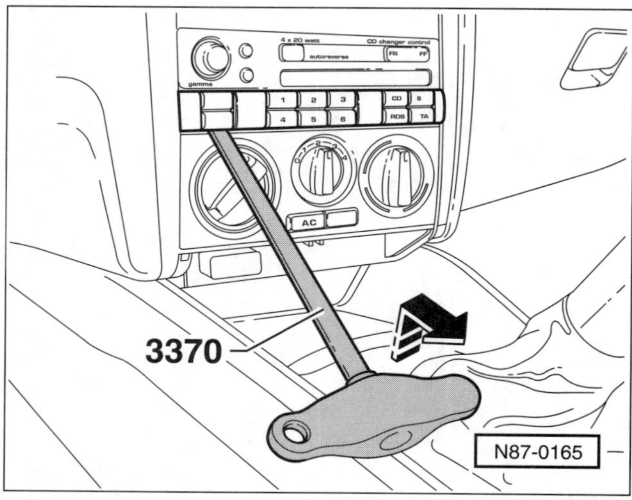

N87-0165

Fig. 3. Remove heating control trim panel with VW special tool 3370, or equivalent.

> ***NOTE —***
> *An illustration of VW special tool 3370 can be found in 70 Trim–Interior in the Instrument Panel section.*

3. Remove HVAC control unit mounting screws. See Fig. 4.

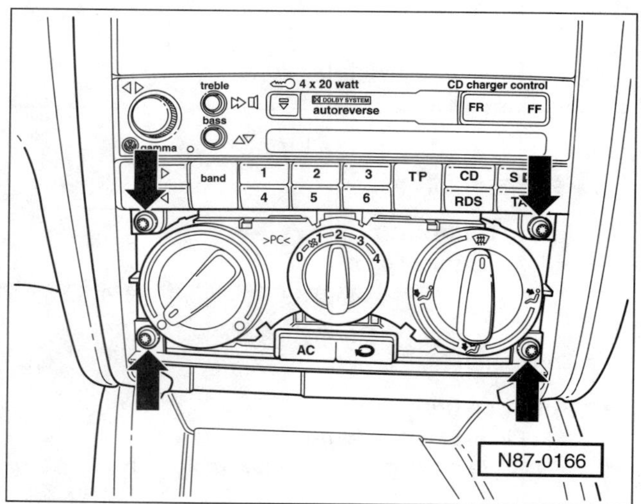

N87-0166

Fig. 4. Remove mounting screws (**arrows**).

4. Unclip cables and detach from control unit.

5. Disconnect harness connector and remove control unit.

6. Before installing controls, check operation of cables by moving each cable back and forth. Replace cables with damage or stiff/binding operation.

7. Attach color coded cable to correct control arm. See Fig. 5.

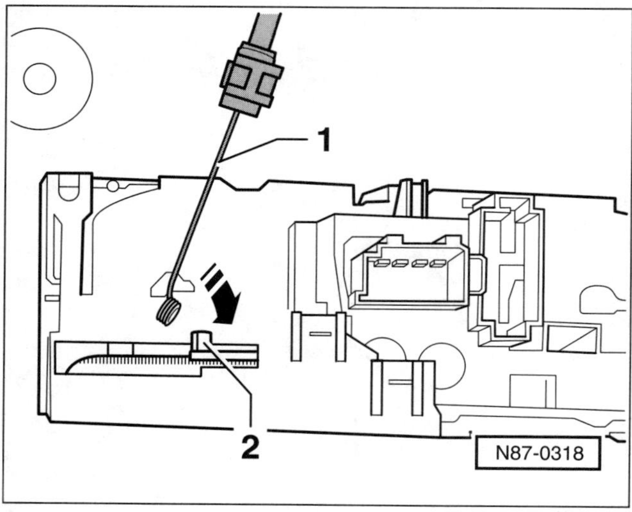

N87-0318

Fig. 5. Attach cable (**1**) to control lever (**2**).

8. Snap each cable into appropriate retainer. See Fig. 6.

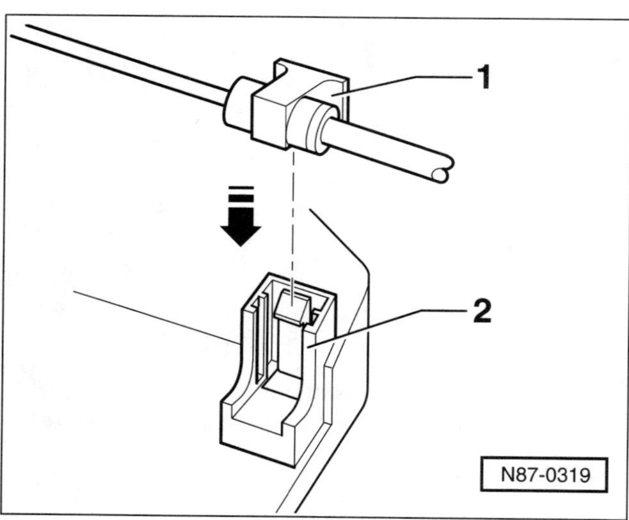

N87-0319

Fig. 6. Press cable (**1**) fully into retainer (**2**) until it engages.

9. Install harness connector.

10. Fit controls into instrument panel opening and install mounting screws.

11. Adjust cables as needed. See Fig. 7.

Heating and ventilation controls, adjusting

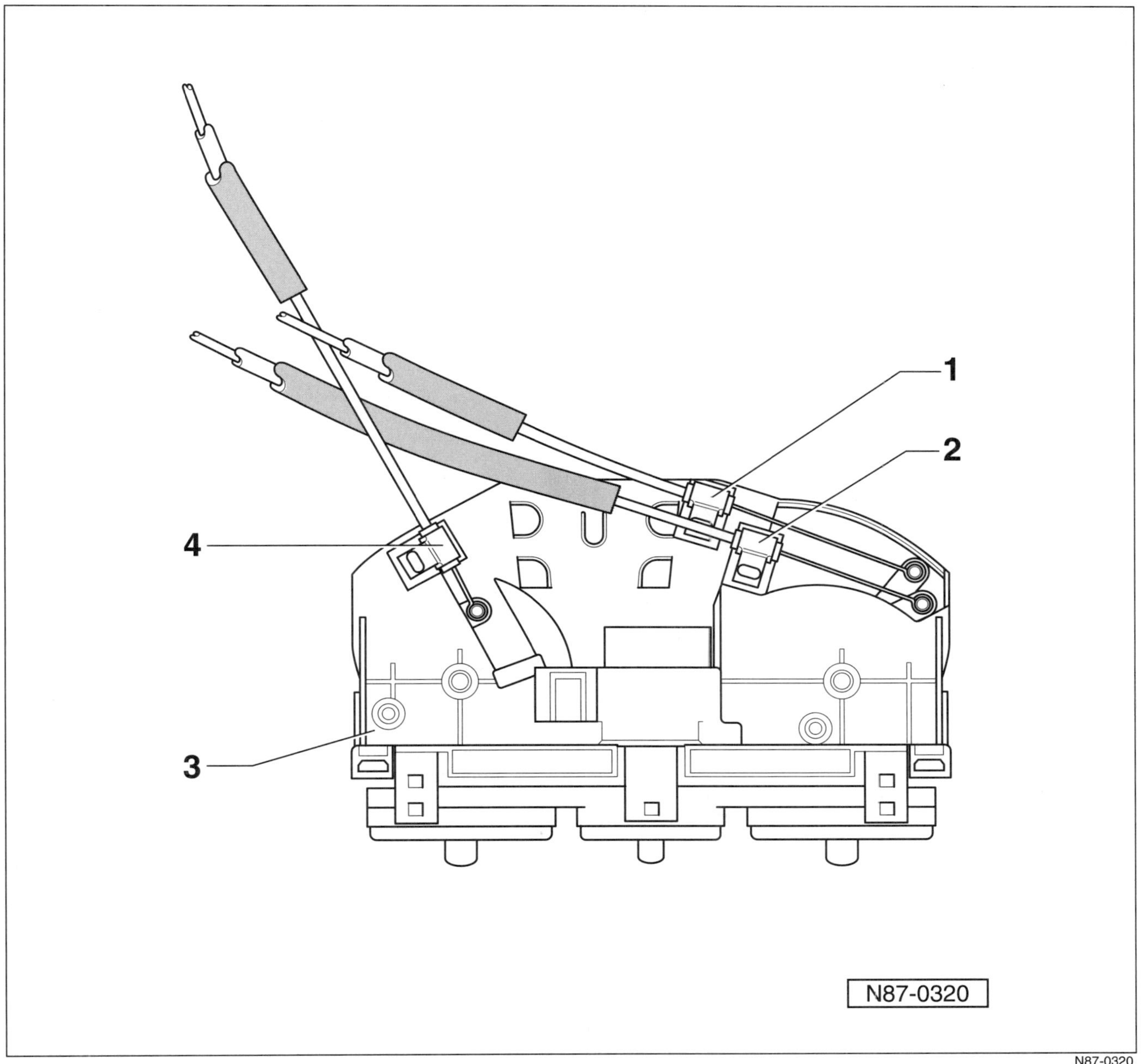

N87-0320

Fig. 7. Heating and ventilation control shown with assembled control cables.

1. **Central flap cable**
    - From air distribution rotary control to central flap
    - Cable sleeve color code: Yellow
    - Adjusting, **see** Ⓐ
2. **Footwell/defrost flap cable**
    - From air distribution rotary control to footwell/defrost flap
    - Cable sleeve color code: Green
    - Adjusting, **see** Ⓑ
3. **Heating and ventilation controls**
    - First attach cables to removed controls then to appropriate levers
    - All air flaps must be heard to move onto end stops when operating controls
4. **Temperature flap cable**
    - From temperature rotary control to temperature flap
    - Cable sleeve color code: Beige
    - Adjusting, **see** Ⓒ

A Central flap cable, installing and adjusting

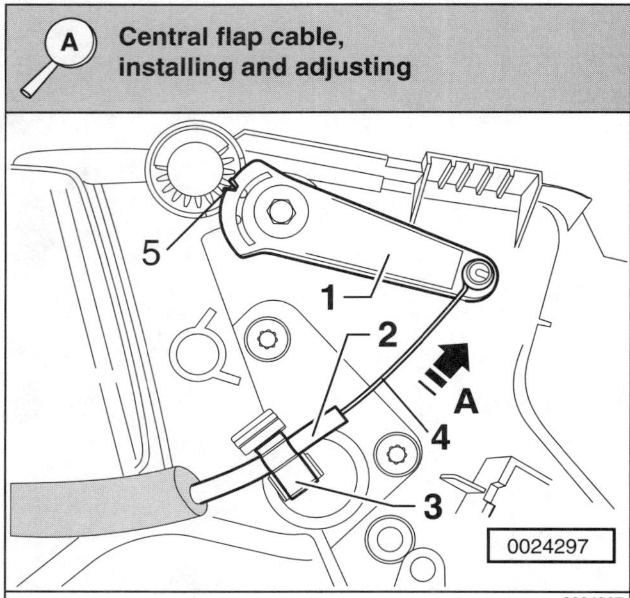

0024297

- Cable sleeve color code: yellow.
- Install/adjust with controls installed, connecting duct removed and flap lever correctly indexed (5).
- Turn air distribution rotary control knob fully counter-clockwise against stop.
- Attach center wire of cable (4) to the central flap lever (1).
- Press central flap lever against stop (arrow A) and attach outer cable (2) with clip (3).
- Turn air distribution rotary control knob fully to left and right against stops.
- When turning the rotary control knob both end stops must be reached.

B Footwell/defrost flap cable, installing and adjusting

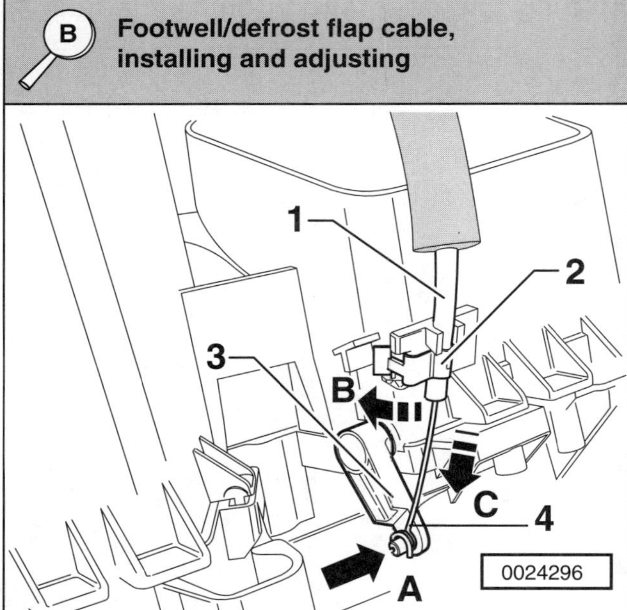

0024296

- Cable sleeve color code: green
- Install/adjust with controls installed.
- Turn air distribution rotary control knob fully counter-clockwise against stop.
- Attach center wire of cable (4) to the footwell/defrost flap lever (3) at arrow (A).
- Press footwell/defrost flap lever against stop (arrow C) and secure outer cable (1) with clip (2) (arrow B).
- Turn air distribution rotary control knob fully to left and right against stops.
- When turning the rotary control knob both end stops must be reached.

Temperature flap cable, installing and adjusting

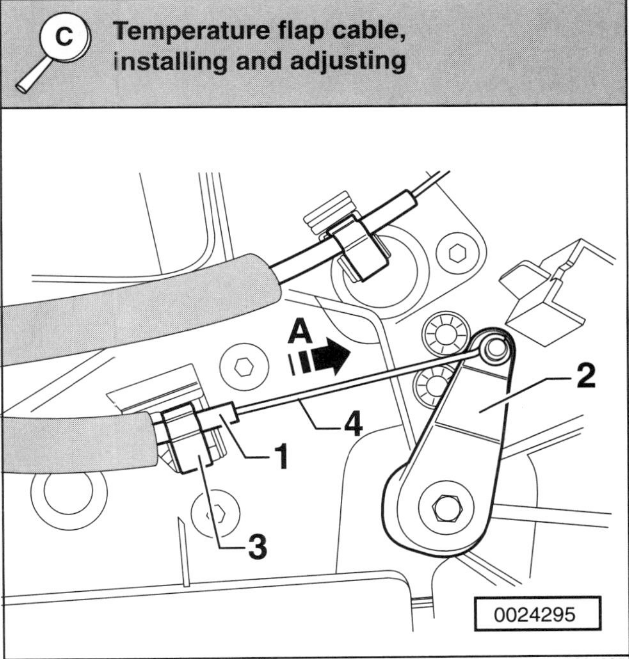

0024295

- Cable sleeve color code: beige.
- Install/adjust with controls installed and connecting duct removed.
- Turn temperature rotary control knob fully counter-clockwise against stop.
- Attach center wire of cable (4) to the temperature flap lever (2).
- Push temperature flap lever (2) against stop (arrow A) and secure outer cable (1) with clip (3).
- Turn temperature rotary control knob fully to left and right against stops.
- When turning the rotary control knob both end stops must be reached.

HEATING AND VENTILATION COMPONENTS

Dust and pollen filter, removing and installing

The dust and pollen filter is located in the far right side of the plenum (the area between the engine compartment and the passenger compartment). It is covered by trim panels removed from behind the engine compartment of the vehicle. See Fig. 8.

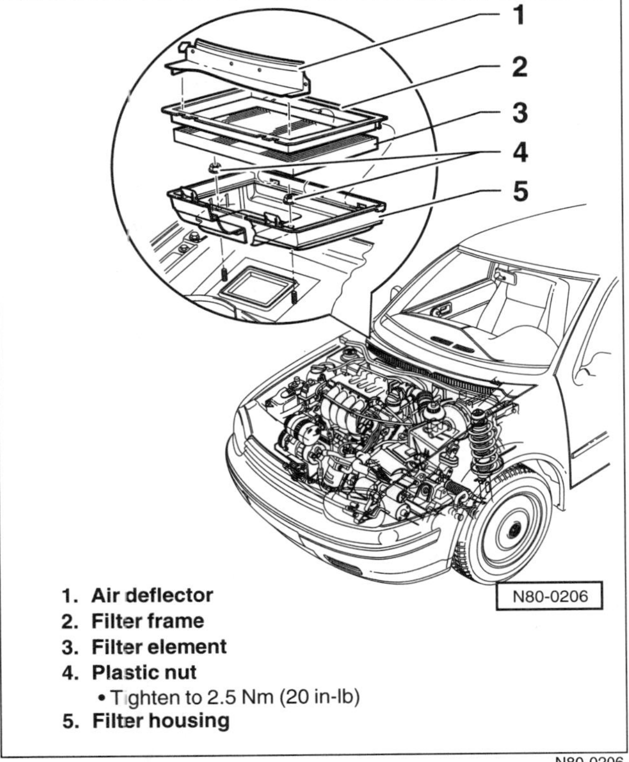

1. **Air deflector**
2. **Filter frame**
3. **Filter element**
4. **Plastic nut**
   - Tighten to 2.5 Nm (20 in-lb)
5. **Filter housing**

N80-0206

Fig. 8. Exploded view of dust and pollen filter assembly.

1. Open hood and remove rubber gasket between engine compartment and plenum. Unclip and remove plastic plenum cover.
2. Depress tabs at front edge of dust and pollen filter frame (item 2 in Fig. 8.)
3. Lift and pull filter element with frame out toward front.
4. When installing, position filter element into frame. Insert frame with locating pins correctly oriented into filter housing and clip into place.
5. Install remaining components in the reverse of removal.

Heater assembly, overview

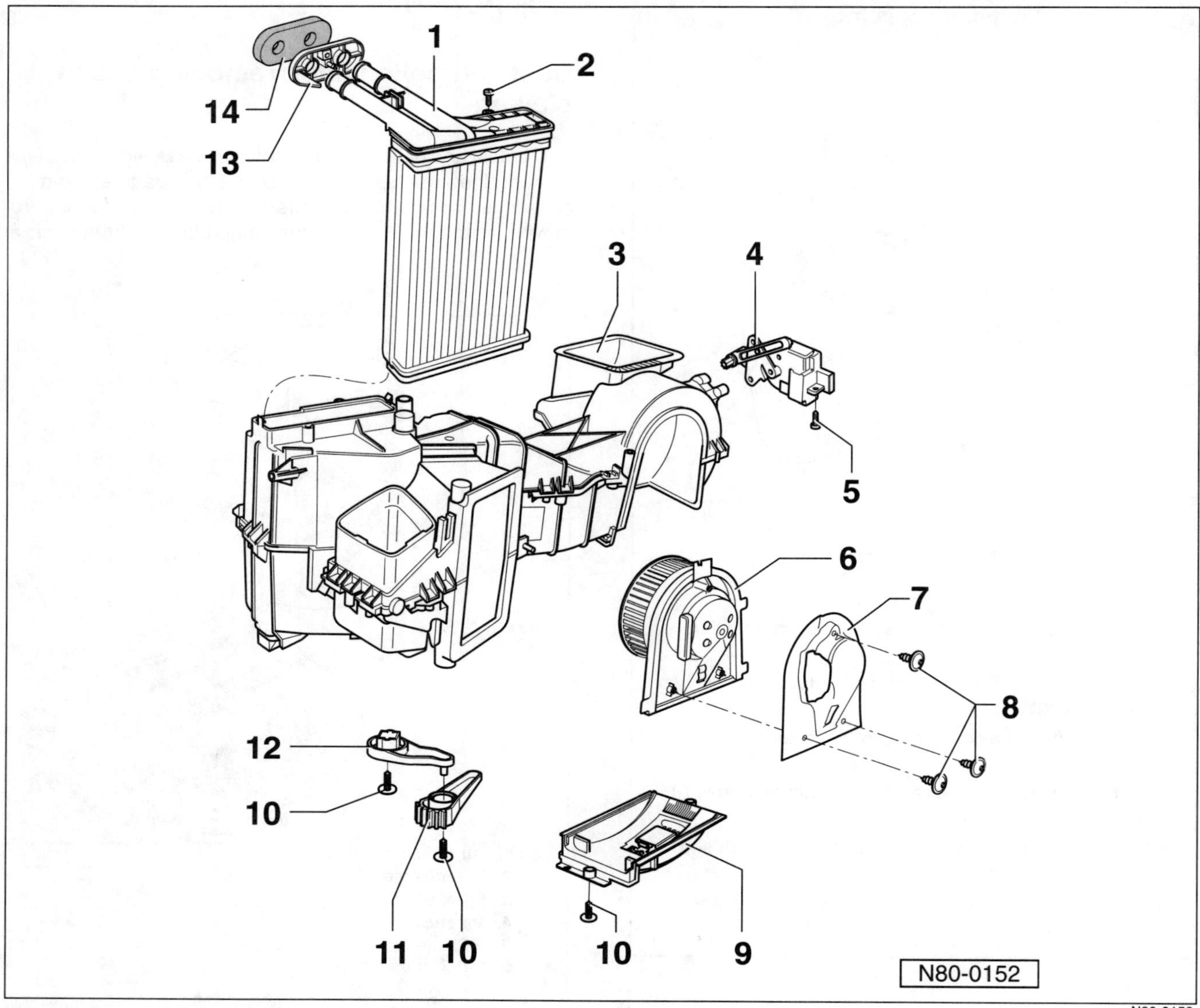

N80-0152

Fig. 9. Heater core shown with housing and related components for vehicles without A/C.

1. **Heater core**
   - Drain coolant before removal
   - Always use new coolant after replacement
   - Secured to housing with retainer clips
2. **Screw, self-tapping**
   - Use if retainer clips break
3. **Air distribution housing**
   - With air distribution flaps
4. **Servo motor for recirculation flap (V154)**
5. **Screw, self-tapping**
6. **Blower fan (V2)**
7. **Cover**
8. **Screw, self-tapping**
9. **Series resistor pack (N24)**
10. **Screw, self-tapping**
11. **Central flap lever**
    - Installed position, **see** Ⓐ
12. **Temperature flap lever**
13. **Base plate**
14. **Heater core bulkhead seal**
    - Installed position, **see** Ⓑ

A Central flap lever, installing and adjusting

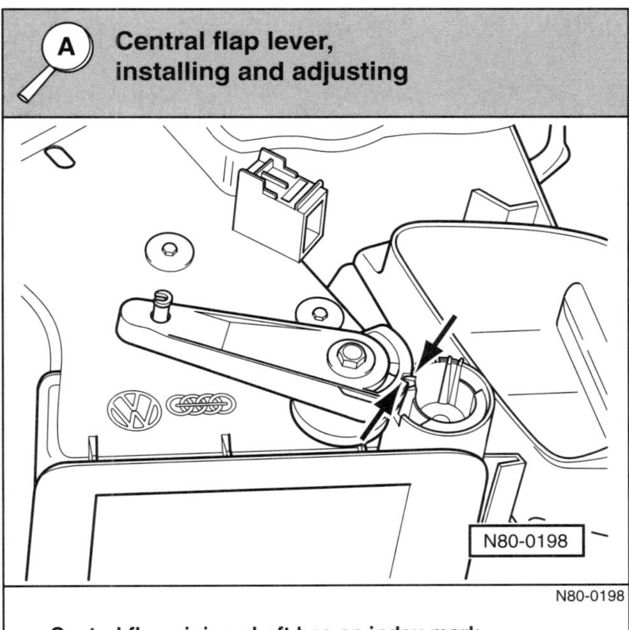

N80-0198

- Central flap pinion shaft has an index mark.
- Install the lever so that index notches on lever and pinion shaft are aligned (arrows).

B Heater core bulkhead seal, installed position

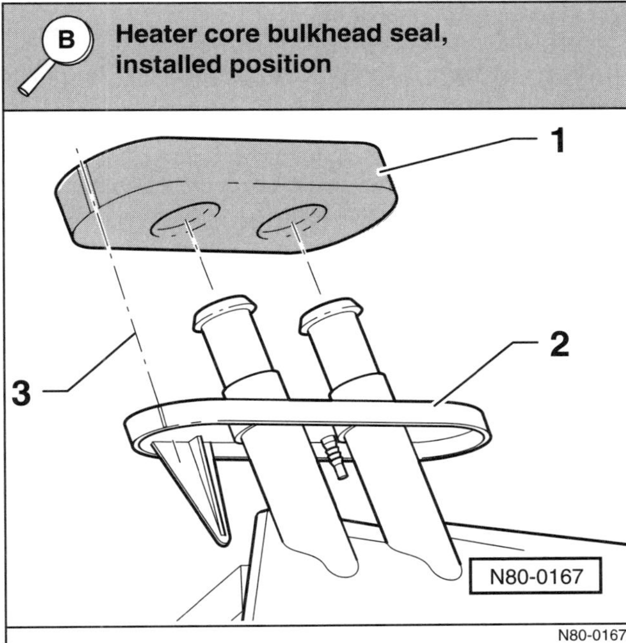

N80-0167

- Seal between heater core and bulkhead has a positioning mark on the side.
- Install seal (1) so that the notches on the seal and notches on the base plate (2) are aligned (3).

Blower fan, removing and installing

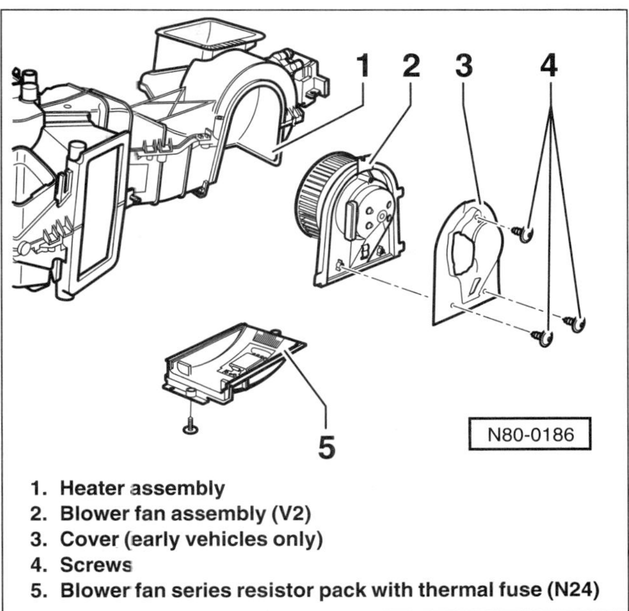

1. **Heater assembly**
2. **Blower fan assembly (V2)**
3. **Cover (early vehicles only)**
4. **Screws**
5. **Blower fan series resistor pack with thermal fuse (N24)**

N80-0186

Fig. 10. Blower fan with related mounting components.

1. Remove glove box, see **70 Trim–Interior**
2. Remove screws (4) and cover (3) where applicable.

   NOTE —
   The numbers in parenthesis in the procedure steps refer to Fig. 10.

3. Remove lower cover containing series resistor pack (5) and disconnect harness connector.
4. Disconnect harness connector from blower fan (2).
5. Pull blower fan out and downward.
6. Installation is the reverse of removal.

Recirculation flap servo, removing and installing

1. Remove glove box, see **70 Trim–Interior**.
2. Disconnect harness connector from flap servo.
3. Remove securing screw and swing motor downwards. See Fig. 11.

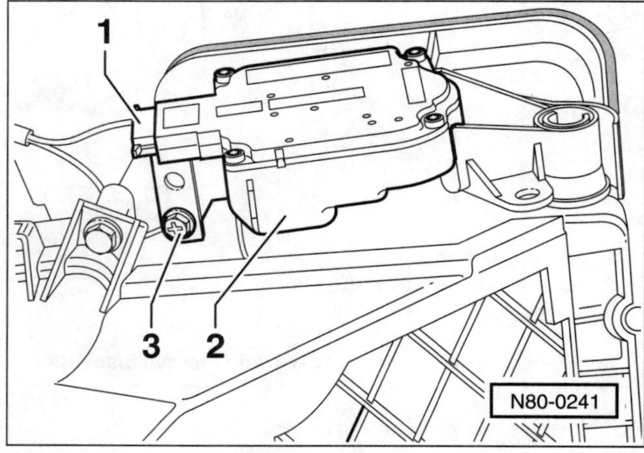

Fig. 11. Recirculation flap servo (**2**) shown in installed position. Unplug harness connector (**1**) and remove securing screw (**3**).

4. Disconnect motor from recirculation flap lever.
5. Before installing a new servo, attach harness connector to the new servo and switch on ignition.

NOTE —
Replacement servos are supplied with operating levers in the "recirculation" position.

6. Operate switch for recirculation flap and observe lever position.
7. When center position of travel is reached, quickly unplug the harness connector and switch off ignition.
8. Install servo onto recirculation flap shaft.

NOTE —
If it is difficult to align and fit the servo to the recirculation flap shaft, remove the blower fan and position the flap and shaft as required.

9. When servo has been installed onto recirculation flap shaft, move motor into mounting position and install securing screw. See Fig. 12.
10. Install harness connector.

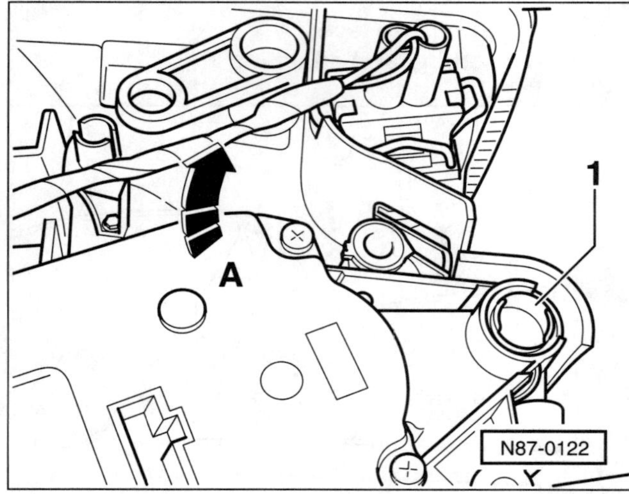

Fig. 12. When servo is installed onto recirculation flap shaft (**1**), move servo in direction of arrow (**A**) to installed position and secure with mounting screw.

11. Install glove box and remainder of removed components.

QUALITY REVIEW

When you have finished working under the hood and around other areas of the vehicle, it is advisable to take a moment to quality check or review your work. This helps to insure that the operation or repair has been completed properly with all affected systems functioning within normal parameters. These may include the following:

- Ensure that all cable ties and clamps that were removed as part of the repair are replaced.
- Ensure that all fasteners and hardware were replaced and torqued as specified.
- Make sure that all other components involved in the repair are positioned correctly, properly torqued and function properly.
- Make sure that all tools, shop cloths, fender covers and protective tapes are removed before closing the hood.
- Clean grease and fingerprints from painted surfaces, steering wheel, upholstery and shifter.
- Make sure that warm/hot air is delivered by the appropriate air vents when the heater is switched on.
- Unlock anti-theft radio and reset the clock.

87 Air Conditioning

TABLES

GENERAL

This section covers the Air Conditioning (A/C) refrigerant system and related components. Service and adjustment to the ventilation control cables is covered in **80 Heating and Ventilation.**

> ***CAUTION —***
> *Disconnecting the negative (–) battery cable may erase fault codes and basic settings in the engine management and automatic transmission control modules. Some driveability problems may be noticed until the system re-adapts to operating conditions. OBD II readiness codes, which may be required for emissions testing, may also be erased. Convenience electronics (alarm system, interior light control, power locks, mirrors, and windows) may need to be re-set using a VAG 1551/5051 or equivalent scan tool.*

The refrigerant system of the vehicles covered by this manual are designed to work only with a refrigerant known as R-134a. In this section, the refrigerant will always be referred to as R-134a, however, this chemical is marketed and sold under several trade designations such as: Tetrafluoroethane, $CH_2F\ CF_3$, H-KW 134a, SUVA® 134a, and ARCTON® 134a.

Other refrigerants may be available in the marketplace, however, Volkswagen specifically recommends that no other refrigerant be used. Serious damage will usually result and performance will be reduced.

Special precautions for A/C systems

The air conditioning system is filled with refrigerant R-134a under pressure. The unique characteristics of this chemical necessitate special servicing and handling procedures which may be governed by Federal, State, Provincial and Local regulations.

WARNING —

- *Work in a well ventilated area. Refrigerant gases are heavier than air, displace oxygen and may cause suffocation in areas of poor air circulation, for example under the vehicle.*

- *Pressurized R134a refrigerant in the presence of oxygen may form a combustible mixture. Never introduce compressed air into any R-134a container (full or empty), capped off A/C component, or piece of service equipment.*

- *As of January 1, 1992 any person who services a motor vehicle air conditioner in the USA MUST, by law, be properly trained and certified and use approved refrigerant recycling equipment. Technicians must complete an EPA approved recycling course to be certified.*

- *State, Provincial and Local governments may have additional requirements regarding air conditioning servicing. Always comply with all applicable laws and regulations.*

- *The A/C system is filled with refrigerant gas which is under pressure.*

- *Avoid breathing refrigerant vapors. Exposure may irritate eyes, nose and throat.*

- *Always be careful that refrigerant does not come in contact with your skin. Always wear hand and eye protection (gloves and goggles) when working around the A/C system. If refrigerant has come in contact with your skin or eyes:*
  - *Do not rub skin or eyes.*
  - *Immediately flush with cool water for 15 minutes.*
  - *Rush to a doctor or hospital.*
  - *Do not attempt to treat yourself.*

- *Keep refrigerant containers stored below 50°C (122°F) and use care to avoid dropping.*

- *DO NOT warm refrigerant containers with an open flame. If refrigerant needs to be warmed, place bottom of tank in warm water.*

- *Do not expose any component of the A/C system to high temperatures above 80°C (176°F) or open flames. Excessive heat will cause system pressure increases which could burst the system.*

- *Switch on exhaust/ventilation systems when working on the refrigerant system.*

- *Keep refrigerant away from open flames. Poisonous gas will be produced if it burns. Do not smoke when refrigerant gases are present for the same reason.*

- *Electric welding near refrigerant hoses causes R-134a to decompose from ultraviolet light. Discharge system before electric welding.*

CAUTION —

- *Always use an Underwriter's Laboratory (UL) approved refrigerant recovery/recycling/recharging unit such as Kent-Moore ACR4, or equivalent, whenever servicing an R-134a A/C system.*

- *Do not steam clean condensers or evaporators. Use only cold water or compressed air on the outside of the component.*

- *Refrigerant oils used for the R-134a system and R-12 (FREON®) systems are NOT compatible. Use only the specified synthetic oil (Polyalkylene Glycol/PAG) for the R-134a refrigerant system. DO NOT use R-12 system oil in an R-134a system or R-134a system oil in an R-12 system. If the refrigerant oils are mixed, system contamination will occur and compressor failure may result.*

- *R-134a refrigerant system oil (PAG oil) absorbs moisture very rapidly. Moisture combines with the refrigerant to form acids which will damage the system. Use only the specified oil from a sealed container and ALWAYS reseal oil container immediately after use. DO NOT use oil if it has become contaminated with moisture.*

- *Only use R-134a in Volkswagen A/C systems. Never use substitute or "drop-in" replacement refrigerants. Vehicle safety will be compromised and severe damage to vehicle and servicing equipment will result.*

- *Immediately plug open connections on A/C components to prevent dirt and especially moisture contamination. Likewise, DO NOT remove new components from packaging until ready to install. Immediately tighten component connections after installation.*

- *Always use separate refrigerant recovery/recycling/recharging servicing equipment for R-12 and R-134a systems. DO NOT use one piece of equipment for both R-12 and R-134a systems. The residual traces of refrigerant will contaminate and damage the equipment. Servicing equipment includes recovery/recycling/recharging unit, charging station, vacuum pump, manifold gauges, etc. Use only equipment designed to meet Society of Automotive Engineers (SAE) standards.*

- *Always replace O-rings, DO NOT reuse. Use only the correct size and type of O-rings specified for use with R-134a refrigerant. Lubricate O-ring with refrigerant oil before installing.*

- *Always replace damaged and/or leaking A/C system components. Do not attempt repair by soldering or welding.*

- *Always reinstall caps over A/C service valves.*

- *Work area must be extremely clean when working on A/C system components.*

A/C refrigerant circuit

Fig. 1 shows the basic schematic layout of the air conditioning system found in the vehicles covered by this manual. The variable displacement compressor compresses the R-134a refrigerant and moves it from the discharge port in a gaseous state to the condenser. The condenser is mounted in the front of the vehicle where air from the radiator fans or the motion of the vehicle passes through it. The motion of the air removes the heat from the refrigerant and a change of state from gas to liquid occurs. The liquid refrigerant flows to the receiver-drier where it is temporarily stored and a desiccant removes any moisture. The refrigerant then moves past a sight glass (early vehicles only) and a high pressure service port to the expansion valve unit. The expansion valve has a small internal orifice which sprays the liquid refrigerant into the evaporator. The resulting change of state from liquid to gas and the associated pressure drop causes the evaporator to become cold. Air from inside the passenger compartment is passed over the evaporator by a fan where it gives up its heat and becomes cold. It is then distributed through the vent system. The gaseous refrigerant passes back through a port on the expansion valve, past a low pressure service port and damper and finally back to the suction side of the compressor to be compressed again. See Fig. 1.

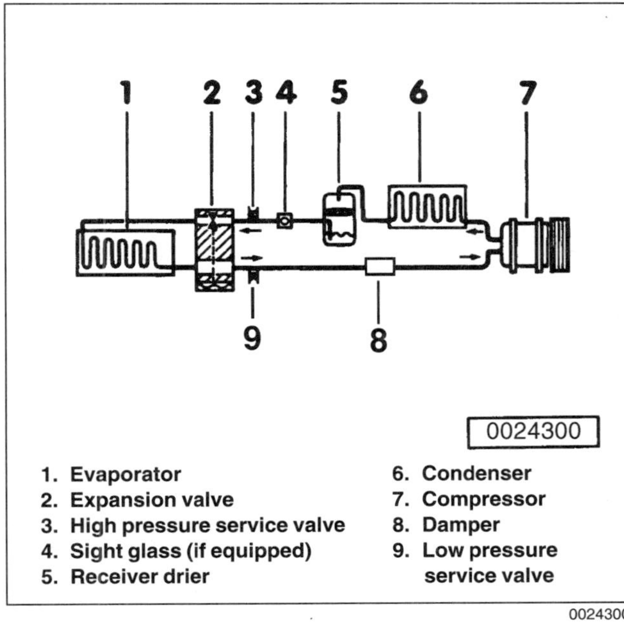

Fig. 1. Air conditioning refrigerant system schematic. Arrows indicate direction of refrigerant flow.

Several other components are used to control and protect the system in addition to those mentioned above. The compressor runs when needed by means of an electro-magnetic clutch which is in turn controlled by several relays. A pressure switch in the refrigerant line also controls operation of the compressor clutch and the radiator cooling fans. A pressure relief valve is mounted to the compressor cylinder head plate. Switches for operation are mounted within easy reach of the driver and fuses and relays are mounted under the instrument panel.

A/C REFRIGERANT SYSTEM

The air conditioning system is comprised of components that can be grouped into several areas. This heading covers those components that are used to handle and contain the R-134a refrigerant. See Fig. 2.

> ***WARNING —***
> *Observe all cautions, warnings and notes before starting repairs involving air conditioning system.*

NOTE —
Volkswagen identifies electrical components by a letter and/or a number in the electrical schematics. See **97 Wiring Diagrams, Fuses and Relays***. These electrical identifiers are listed in parenthesis as an aid to electrical troubleshooting.*

A/C refrigerant system, component overview

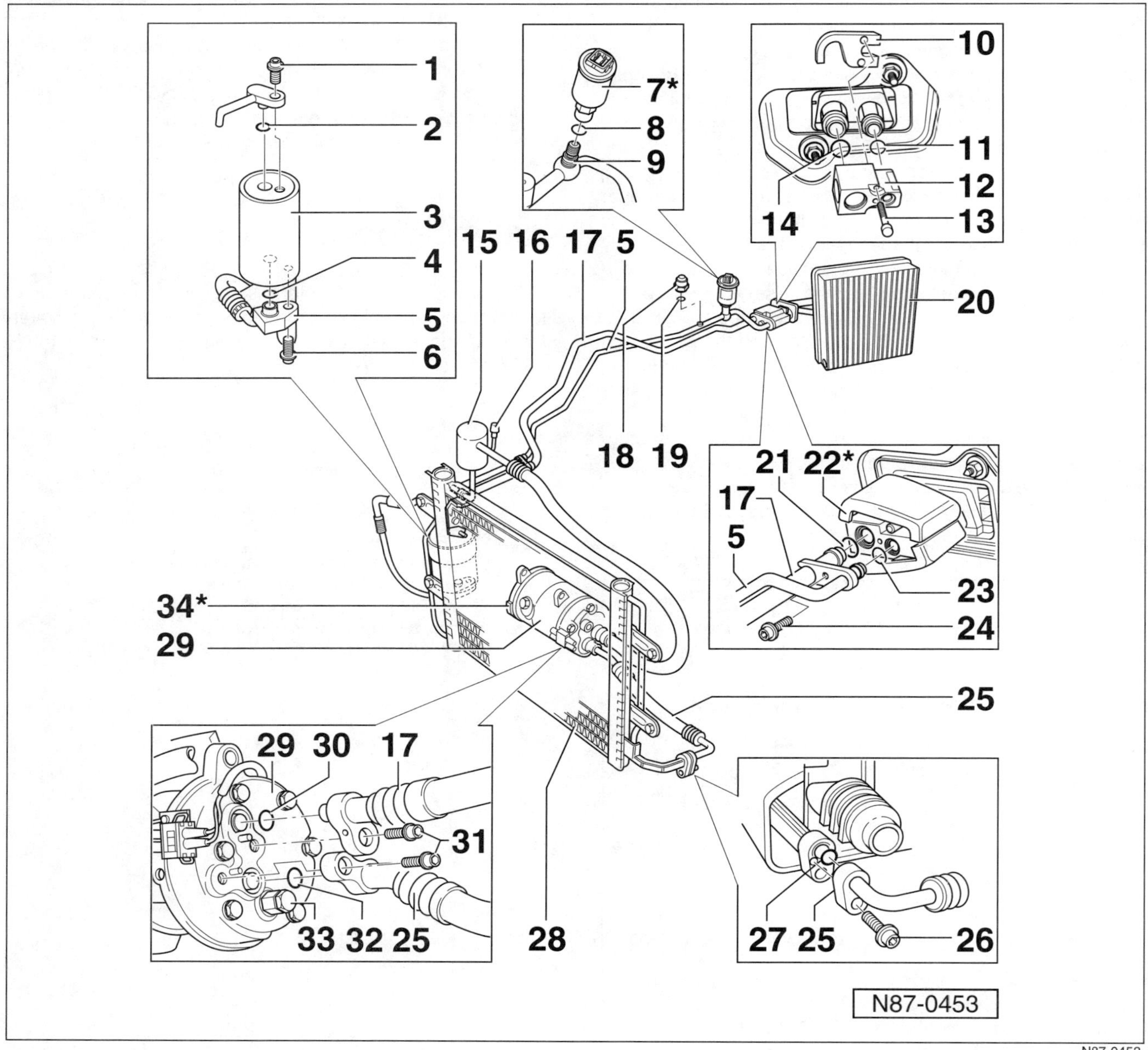

N87-0453

Fig. 2. A/C system components. Discharge A/C system with appropriate recovery/recycling unit before removing all components, except those indicated with an asterisk (*).

1. **Bolt**
   - Tighten to 15 Nm (11 ft-lb)
2. **O-ring, see** Ⓐ
   - Always replace
   - 10.8 mm x 1.8 mm
3. **Receiver drier, see** Ⓑ
   - Always replace
   - Location: attached to right side of condenser
4. **O-ring**
   - Always replace
   - 10.8 mm x 1.8 mm
5. **Liquid refrigerant line**
   - Location: between receiver drier outlet and expansion valve inlet
6. **Bolt**
   - Tighten to 15 Nm (11 ft-lb)

(continued from previous page)

7. **A/C pressure switch (F129), or high pressure sensor (G65)***
   - Location: liquid refrigerant line near expansion valve
   - Pressure switch (F129) and pressure sensor (G65) can be removed without discharging the A/C system
   - Checking pressure switch (F129), **see** (C)
   - Pressure sensor (G65) is monitored by the ECM
   - G65 supplies refrigerant system pressure signal to coolant fan control module (J239) and ECM
8. **O-ring**
   - Always replace
   - 10.8 mm x 1.8 mm
9. **Schrader valve**
10. **Threaded plate**
11. **O-ring**
    - Always replace
    - 10.8 mm x 1.8 mm
12. **Expansion valve**
    - Location: near bulkhead on right side of engine compartment
    - Hole for refrigerant lines at bulkhead must be sealed against splash water
13. **Bolt**
    - Tighten to 8 Nm (71 in-lb)
14. **O-ring**
    - Always replace
    - 14.0 mm x 1.8 mm
15. **Damper**
16. **Low pressure service valve**
    - Only use Kent Moore ACR4 or equivalent
    - Assembly, **see** (D)
17. **Refrigerant hose**
    - From expansion valve to compressor
    - With damper
18. **High pressure service valve port**
    - Only use Kent Moore ACR4 or equivalent
    - Assembly, **see** (E)
19. **O-ring**
    - Always replace
    - 10.8 mm x 1.8 mm
20. **Evaporator**
    - Location: in heater/evaporator housing
21. **O-ring**
    - Always replace
    - 16.7 mm x 1.8 mm
22. **Insulation***
    - Wrapped around expansion valve
23. **O-ring**
    - Always replace
    - 7.6 mm x 1.8 mm
24. **Bolt**
    - Tighten to 8 Nm (71 in-lb)
25. **High pressure refrigerant line**
    - From compressor to condenser
26. **Bolt**
    - Tighten to 15 Nm (11 ft lb)
27. **O-ring**
    - Always replace
    - 10.8 mm x 1.8 mm
28. **Condenser**
    - Location: ahead of radiator
29. **Compressor**
    - Location: attached to mounting bracket on engine
    - Replacement compressors are filled with the total system refrigerant oil quantity
30. **O-ring**
    - Always replace
    - 14.3 mm x 2.4 mm
31. **Bolt**
    - Tighten to 20 Nm (15 ft-lb)
32. **O-ring**
    - Always replace
    - 10.8 mm x 1.8 mm
33. **Pressure relief valve**
    - Location: on compressor cylinder head plate
    - Checking, **see** (F)
34. **A/C compressor clutch (N25)***
    - Location: attached to front of A/C compressor
    - Type: Sanden

A O-rings

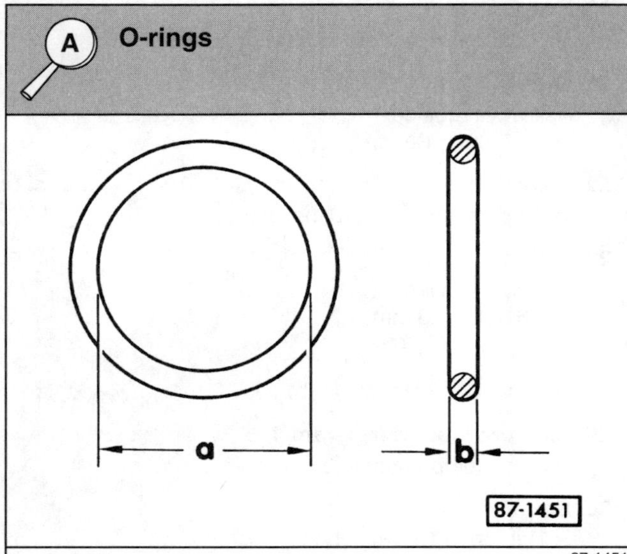

87-1451

- Note inner diameter (a) and thickness (b).
- Lubricate with PAG oil before installing.
- Always replace during repairs, never reuse.
- Only use O-rings that are compatible with R-134a.
- May be color coded green, red, violet or black.

B Receiver drier

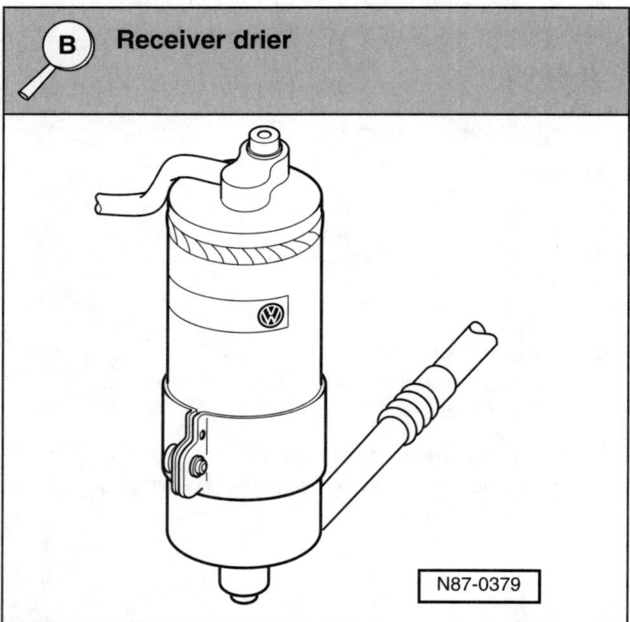

N87-0379

- Reservoir for liquid refrigerant.
- Contains desiccant to absorb moisture from refrigerant.
- Must have green identification markings to indicate compatibility with R-134a.
- Never use R-12 FREON parts.
- To ensure optimum system operation, always replace every time refrigerant system is opened.

C A/C pressure switch

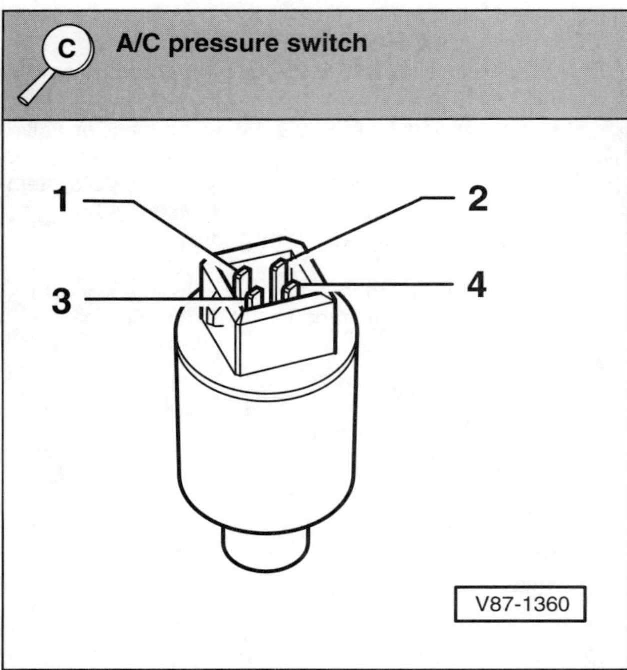

V87-1360

- Can be replaced without discharging refrigerant due to schraeder valve in threaded fitting.
- Switches A/C clutch off when refrigerant pressure exceeds 32 bar (464 psi) and resets when pressure drops to 24 bar (348 psi).
- Switches A/C clutch off when refrigerant pressure falls below 1.2 bar (17.4 psi).
- Switches radiator coolant fan to second speed when pressure reaches 16 bar (232 psi).
- Terminals 1 and 2 switch A/C clutch.
- Terminals 3 and 4 switch radiator coolant fan.
- Checking: with the engine running and switch installed, briefly bridge terminal 1 and 2 of connector. If the A/C clutch engages, the refrigerant circuit is empty.

D Low pressure service valve assembly

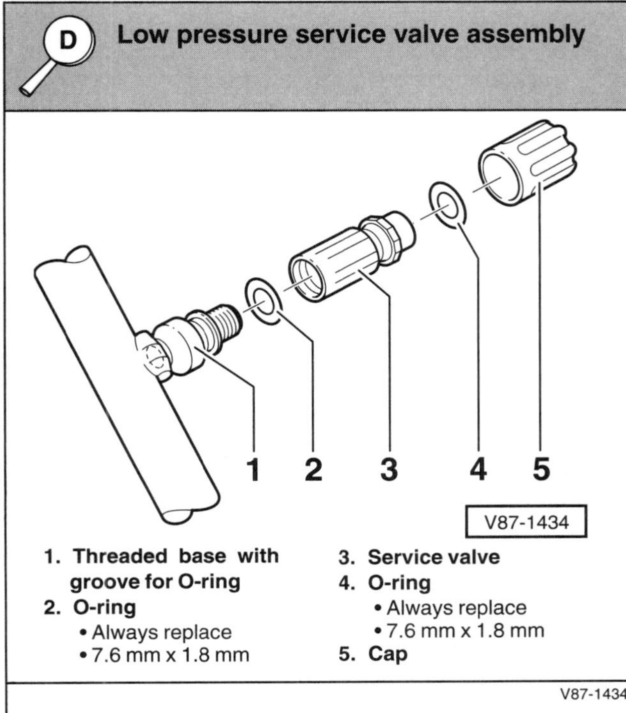

1. Threaded base with groove for O-ring
2. O-ring
   - Always replace
   - 7.6 mm x 1.8 mm
3. Service valve
4. O-ring
   - Always replace
   - 7.6 mm x 1.8 mm
5. Cap

V87-1434

- Discharge refrigerant system before replacing valve.
- Protect all components against dirt and moisture contamination with suitable plastic caps.

E High pressure service valve assembly

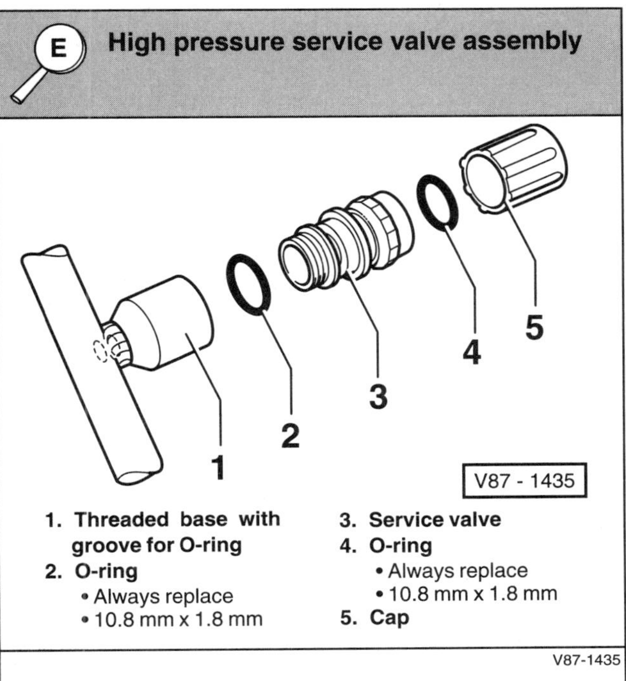

1. Threaded base with groove for O-ring
2. O-ring
   - Always replace
   - 10.8 mm x 1.8 mm
3. Service valve
4. O-ring
   - Always replace
   - 10.8 mm x 1.8 mm
5. Cap

V87-1435

- Discharge refrigerant system before replacing valve.
- Protect all components against dirt and moisture contamination with suitable plastic caps.

F Pressure relief valve

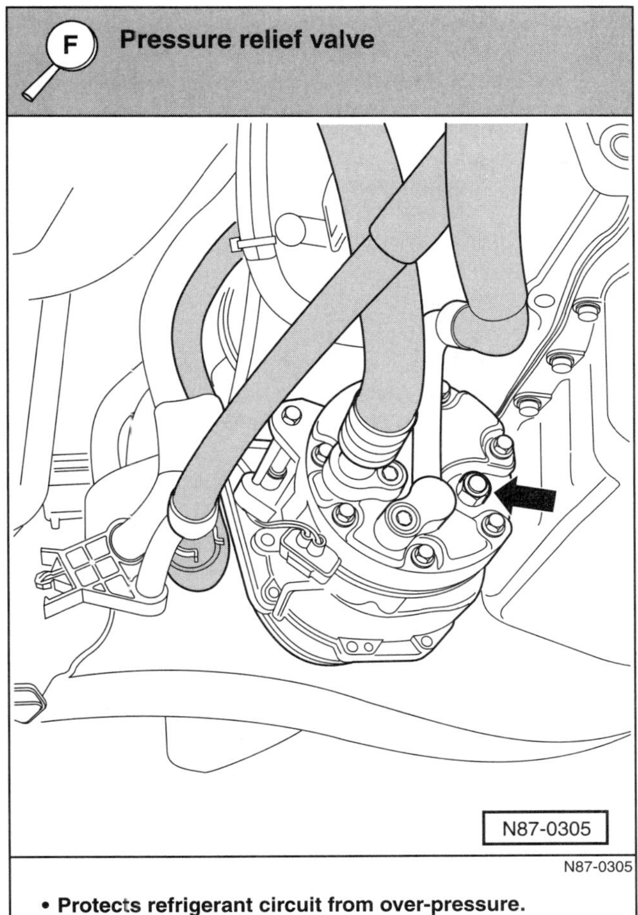

N87-0305

- Protects refrigerant circuit from over-pressure.
- Opens to vent pressures over 40 bar (580 psi) and then closes to prevent total refrigerant loss.
- Adhesive plate (arrow) is pushed out if valve has opened.

A/C refrigerant R-134a

Refrigerant R-134a has the following characteristics:

- Colorless and is invisible as a gas.
- R-134a when viewed through the sight glass may appear milky due to the mixture of refrigerant and lubricating oil (PAG oil).
- Escaped R-134a gases are heavier than air and will gather first in low places, such as under the car.
- R-134a refrigerant gas displaces oxygen and may cause suffocation in low areas or areas of poor air circulation.
- Refrigerant R-134a will deteriorate some plastics. Therefore, when making system repairs, use only genuine VW replacement parts or parts which are specified for use with R-134a refrigerant.
- R-134a in an enclosed container will have a specific temperature/pressure relationship.
- Refrigerant R-134a is not poisonous in any state (liquid or gas) and is safe when used properly.
- Refrigerant R-134a, in its pure state, is chemically stable and will not attack iron, copper, brass or aluminum. However, the mixture of R-134a and PAG oil may deteriorate certain metals (copper). Therefore, when making system repairs, use only genuine VW replacement parts or parts which are specified for use with R-134a refrigerant.
- Liquid R-134a refrigerant will absorb only very minute quantities of moisture. However, R-134a vapor can absorb large amounts of moisture.
- R-134a refrigerant is not flammable.
- DO NOT exceed maximum rated capacity of refrigerant stored in containers.
- Use halogen leak detector Hitec HI400A-TEL or equivalent to check for R-134a system leaks. This tool can also be used to detect leaks in R-12 systems. Many currently available R-12 leak detectors cannot detect R-134a refrigerant leaks. See Fig. 3.

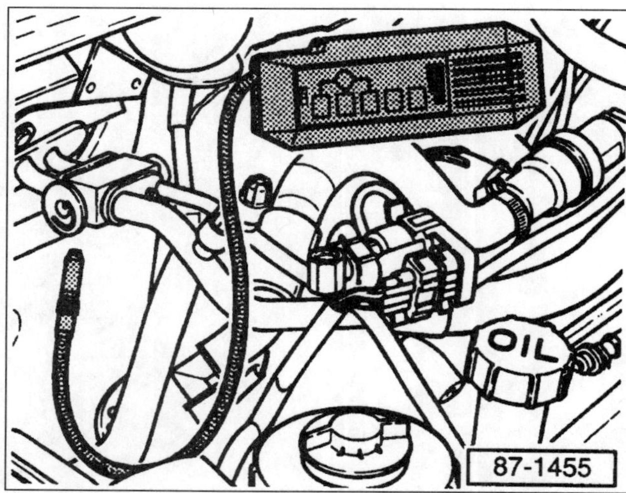

87-1455

Fig. 3. Leak detector such as the Hitec HI400A-TEL (shown) or equivalent, being used to check for refrigerant leaks. Always follow the leak detector manufacturer's instructions.

NOTE —
- *Refrigerant gas dissipates very quickly. To make the job easier, avoid drafty or windy areas when checking for leaks.*
- *If the refrigerant system is discharged (empty), it is permissible to temporarily recharge the system with approx. 100 g (3.5 oz) of refrigerant in order to check for leaks. When the source of the leak is found, this refrigerant must be recovered from the system before repairs are started.*

Refrigerant oil, PAG

A special Polyalkylene Glycol (PAG) synthetic oil is used in R-134a systems. This oil is NOT compatible with mineral based oils used in older R-12 systems. Refer to **Special precautions for A/C systems**. For specifications and quantity, see **Table a**.

Table a. A/C system capacities

Fluid & Specification	Quantity
Refrigerant, R-134a	700 g + 50 g (24.7 + 1.8 oz.)
Oil, PAG, SP-10 (G 052 154 A2)	135 cc ± 15 cc (4.6 oz. ± .5 oz.)

NOTE —
- *Replacement compressors from Volkswagen are supplied with 135 cc of refrigerant oil.*
- *Volkswagen part numbers are given for reference only. Always consult with your Volkswagen Parts Department or aftermarket parts specialist for the latest parts information.*
- *A label on the lock carrier in the engine compartment indicates the refrigerant type and capacity and should be consulted before starting any servicing or repairs.*

Refrigerant lines and hoses

Lines and hoses are fastened together with threaded couplings and fittings. They are retained to the bodywork or components with specially isolated hose clamps. During servicing, all couplings, fittings and related fasteners must be torqued to specification.

A/C refrigerant system, replacing components

Replacement A/C compressors, evaporators and condensers supplied by the authorized Volkswagen dealer parts departments are filled with Nitrogen. If gas (Nitrogen) does not escape when component is first opened, the component may be faulty (leaking), do not install. Additionally, replacement A/C compressors are filled with the total refrigerant oil quantity needed for the entire refrigerant system.

Always replace the receiver drier whenever the refrigerant system has been left open. Install immediately after opening to prevent moisture contamination of drier desiccant. Moreover, keep refrigerant system and other replacement components sealed for as long as possible to minimize the chance of dirt and moisture contamination. Even the slightest amount of trapped moisture can freeze within the system causing blockage and erratic performance. Always plug any open refrigerant line connections to prevent dirt and moisture contamination during the repair especially if the repair will not be completed immediately.

If the system has been discharged due to a damaged or leaking component (refrigerant hose/line, compressor, evaporator, condenser, etc.), flush the refrigerant system first with compressed air, then with nitrogen (available locally) and collect the oil that runs out. This will remove the refrigerant oil which may be saturated with moisture.

> ***CAUTION —***
> *DO NOT flush R-134a refrigerant system with any other type of refrigerant such as R-12 or R-11. Other refrigerants are not compatible with refrigerant R-134a/PAG oil and will cause total system contamination!*

If the compressor is not replaced after flushing the system, fill the compressor with the correct type and quantity of refrigerant oil for the total system as specified in **Table a**. If a new Sanden compressor is used, do not add any additional oil as the total amount of oil required is already in the compressor. Refrigerant oil is distributed in most major parts of the refrigerant system. For approximate capacities, see **Table b**.

Table b. Refrigerant oil distribution

Component	Approximate amount of oil in component - % of total
Compressor	67.5 cc (2.3 oz) - 50%
Condenser	13.5 cc (0.46 oz) - 10%
Suction line	13.5 cc (0.46 oz) - 10%
Discharge line	--
Evaporator	27 cc (0.92 oz) - 20%
Receiver-drier	13.5 cc (0.46 oz) - 10%

> ***WARNING —***
> *Dispose of contaminated refrigerant oil following laws governing hazardous waste disposal. Do not combine any refrigerant oil with any other old oils such as engine oil or transmission fluid unless approved by the appropriate governing body.*

Condenser assembly, overview

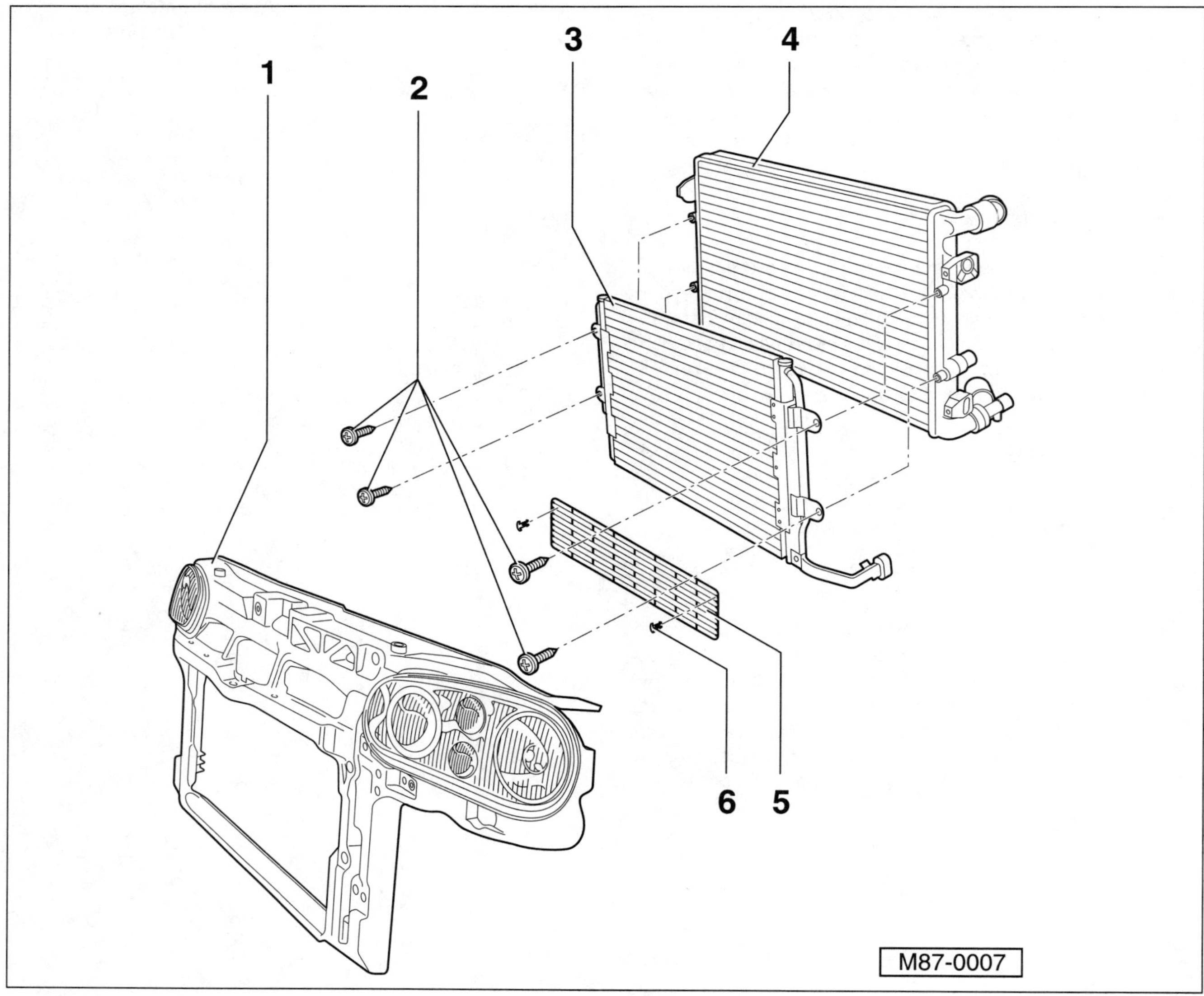

M87-0007

Fig. 4. A/C condenser shown with related mounting components.

> ***WARNING —***
> *Observe all cautions, warnings and notes before starting repairs involving air conditioning systems.*

1. **Lock carrier**
   - Bring into service position for condenser removal
2. **Screws**
   - Tighten to 8 Nm (71 in-lb)
3. **Condenser**
   - Discharge and recover refrigerant before removal
   - Disconnect refrigerant lines at condenser
4. **Radiator**
   - Drain coolant before removal
   - Always use new coolant after replacement
   - Seal open refrigerant lines immediately
   - Inspect for bent and obstructed fins and physical damage before installing
   - Always replace O-rings for refrigerant lines
5. **Grille**
   - Where applicable
6. **Clips**
   - Where applicable

Evaporator/heater assembly, overview

The A/C evaporator and the heater core are encased in a multi-piece housing inside the vehicle. See Fig. 5. Access is from the interior and requires A/C refrigerant discharge and removal of the instrument panel and instrument panel cross-member. See **70 Trim–Interior**.

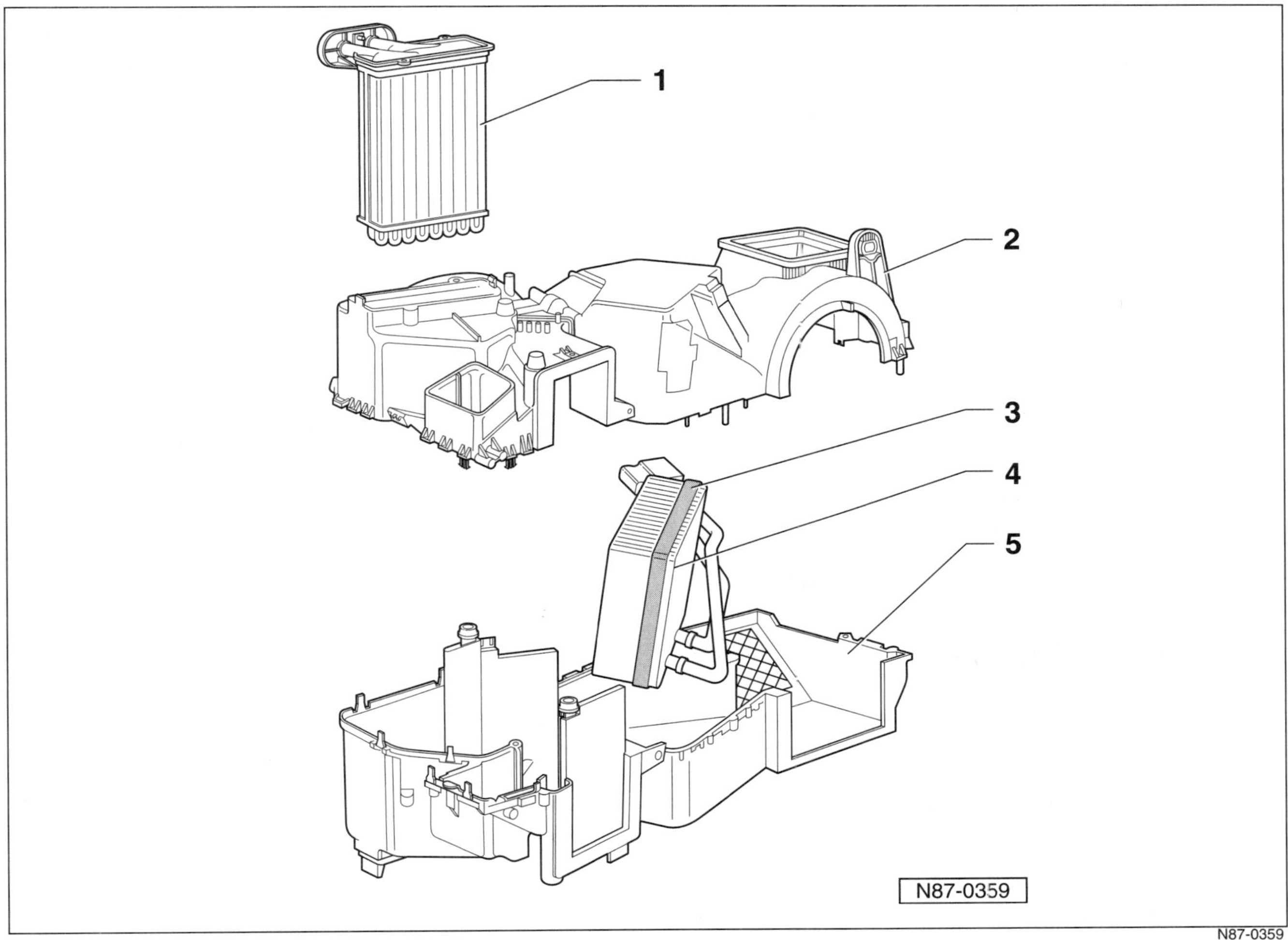

N87-0359

Fig. 5. A/C evaporator shown with heater core and housing.

> ***WARNING —***
> *Observe all cautions, warnings and notes before starting repairs involving air conditioning systems.*

NOTE —
Availability of individual air conditioning components may be limited. Complete assemblies may be required.

1. **Heater core**
   - Drain coolant before removal
   - Always use new coolant after replacement

2. **Housing, upper section**
   - With fresh/recirculating air flap

3. **Evaporator seal**
   - Install seal to top and sides only, not to bottom
   - Secure with glue
   - Condensate MUST be free to drain out from the bottom of the housing under the evaporator.

4. **Evaporator**
   - Discharge and recover refrigerant before removal
   - Disconnect refrigerant lines at expansion valve
   - Seal open refrigerant lines immediately
   - Inspect for bent and obstructed fins and physical damage before installing
   - Always replace O-rings for refrigerant lines

5. **Housing, lower section**

A/C system odor, checking

An unpleasant smell or "musty" odor can be emitted from any automotive air conditioning system under certain conditions. Many times this "musty" odor is caused by residual condensate in and around the A/C evaporator mixing with airborne pollutants. This environment is suitable for the formation and growth of bacteria and/or fungi which can cause undesirable odors. Condensation is normally formed as part of the air conditioning process and must be allowed to flow out of the system.

To minimize the growth of bacteria and/or fungi, there are several steps that can be performed:

- Water drain(s) in the bottom of the plenum chamber(s) under the hood must be open and free of any debris.
- The bulkhead between the engine compartment and the passenger compartment must be sealed along with any cable grommets passing through the bulkhead.
- The evaporator water (condensate) drain must open freely. This valve is located behind the bulkhead insulation.

If the above steps fail to correct an odor problem, professional preparation and treatment using a commercially available product such as Airsept Air Conditioning Treatment™ should be performed. Special tools, equipment and training are required to properly apply Airsept™ Products. These procedures are outside the scope of this repair manual.

A/C REFRIGERANT SYSTEM SERVICING

In accordance with SAE and industry standards, Volkswagen air conditioners are equipped with service fittings that accept standard R-134a charging equipment. Connecting gauges to the refrigerant system and measuring the various pressures during operation is a valuable and accurate way to troubleshoot. The pressures and associated temperatures in the A/C system will vary depending on engine speed (rpm), coolant fan speed, engine coolant temperature, A/C clutch engagement, outside temperature, humidity, etc. and can give an accurate indication of system performance.

> ***WARNING —***
> *Observe all cautions, warnings and notes before starting repairs involving air conditioning systems.*

A/C refrigerant system, testing with pressure gauges

Due to the constant temperature/pressure relationship of refrigerant R-134a, approximate high side and low side system temperature can be determined based on system pressures, see **Table c**.

Table c. R-134a temperature/pressure relationship

Temperature in °C (°F)	Pressure in bar (psi)
-30 (-22)	0.0 (0.0)
-20 (-4)	0.3 (4.4)
-10 (14)	1.0 (14.5)
0 (32)	1.9 (27.5)
10 (50)	3.1 (45.0)
20 (68)	4.7 (68.2)
30 (86)	6.7 (97.2)
40 (104)	9.1 (132.0)
50 (122)	12.2 (177.0)
60 (140)	15.8 (229.0)
70 (158)	20.2 (293.0)

Commercially available manifold gauge sets are specifically calibrated for R-134a and should be connected to the system according to the manufacturers instructions. All commercially available refrigerant recovery, recycling and recharging equipment also have gauges that are appropriate for R-134a and are suitable for system testing.

Pressure and temperature measurements should be made using the following conditions:

- Engine running at 1,500 rpm with A/C switched on.
- Blower fan control set to highest speed.
- A/C temperature control set to maximum cooling and recirculation switched on.
- All passenger compartment air outlets open fully.

For pressure and temperature specifications of the various components, see **Table d**.

Table d. Pressure and temperature specifications[a]

Component	Refrigerant state	Approximate pressure	Approximate temperature
Evaporator, inlet to outlet	Vapor to gas	1.2 bar (17.4 psi)[b]	-7°C (19°F)[c]
Low pressure service valve port	Gas		-1°C (30°F)
Compressor, low pressure (suction) side	Gas		
Compressor, high pressure (discharge) side	Gas	14 bar (203 psi)	65°C (149°F)
Condenser	Gas to vapor to liquid		55°C (131°F) at outlet
Receiver drier	Liquid		55°C (131°F)
Sight glass (where equipped)	Liquid		
High pressure service valve port	Liquid		
Expansion valve	Liquid to vapor	Inlet: 14 bar (203 psi) Outlet: 1.2 bar (17.4 psi)	Inlet: 55°C (131°F) Outlet: -7°C (19°F)

a. Pressure and temperature specifications are based on: 1) Engine speed at 1,500 rpm, 2) Blower fan set to high speed, 3) A/C controls set to maximum cooling.

b. Pressure maintained in the refrigerant system by the variable displacement compressor despite variables in temperature, load and engine speeds (RPM).

c. Temperature maintained in the refrigerant system by the variable displacement compressor despite variable in temperature, load and engine speeds (RPM).

A/C system, troubleshooting

If the A/C system does not cool sufficiently there are a number of different checks that can be done to determine which component might be at fault.

> ***NOTE —***
> - *Ensure that the electrical system is OK and the air flow distribution system (controls and cables) are OK.*
> - *Manual A/C system controls and cables are covered in* **80 Heating and Ventilation**. *Electronic A/C system (Climatronic) controls and flap motors are covered later in this section.*

If A/C does not cool at all, cooling is insufficient at all driving speeds or there is no cooling after a period of driving, check the following:

- A/C system must be fully charged, if necessary discharge system, evacuate and recharge.
- Condenser and radiator must be clean and free of obstructions (spray clean if necessary).
- Air distribution can be adjusted correctly (all air distribution flaps reach end positions) using control knobs or Climatronic control unit.
- Wiring is OK as per 97 **Wiring Diagrams, Fuses and Relays**.
- Outside (ambient) air temperature is between 20-30° (68-86°F)
- Drive belts for A/C compressor and generator in good condition and properly tensioned, see **0 Maintenance**.

If all of the above conditions are met proceed to test the A/C system as follows.

1. Start engine and set temperature control to maximum "cold" (manual A/C) or "LO" (Climatronic).

2. For manual A/C, press "A/C" button and select second blower speed. For Climatronic, select minimum blower speed (manual override) by pressing "decrease blower speed" button and observing blower speed display in control head.

3. Adjust air distribution to instrument panel outlets and insert thermometer into center outlet and raise engine speed to approx. 1500 RPM.

> ***NOTE —***
> *Outside (ambient) air temperature should be between 20-25°C (68-77°F) for A/C temperature drop test. For higher ambient temperatures and/or higher humidity, air temperature from center instrument panel vent can be slightly higher than specified below.*

A/C air temperature

- Maximum temperature at center outlet after 1 minute . . . . 10°C (50°F)

4. If specified A/C air temperature is not obtained after running A/C for 1 minute, shut off A/C and engine. Connect refrigerant recovery/recyling/recharging unit (Kent-Moore ACR[4] or equivalent) to high and low pressure service valves of A/C system.

5. Disconnect harness connector from coolant fan and start engine.

6. Set temperature control to maximum "hot" (manual A/C) or "HI" (Climatronic).

7. Press "A/C" button and select highest blower speed (manual A/C only).

8. Adjust air distribution to footwell outlets and raise engine speed to approx. 1500 RPM.

9. Read A/C system high pressure.

Normal system high pressure
- Within 30 seconds . . . . 232 psi (16 bar)

10. If specificified pressure is not obtained, set temperature control to maximum "cold" (manual A/C) or "LO" (Climatronic).

11. Press "A/C" button and select first blower speed (manual A/C) or select minimum blower speed with the manual override by pressing "decrease blower speed" (Climatronic).

12. Adjust air distribution to instrument panel outlets and raise engine speed to approx. 1500 RPM.

13. Read A/C system low pressure.

Normal system low pressure
- Within 30 seconds . . . . 22-36 psi (1.5-2.5 bar)

14. If specified pressure is not obtained, compare the results of the various tests (temperature drop, high pressure and low pressure) to **Table e** for possible causes and corrective measures.

A/C refrigerant system, discharging and charging

Before starting repairs involving opening of the refrigerant system, the refrigerant must first be removed. It is not permissible to vent the refrigerant into the atmosphere for environmental, legal and economic reasons. In addition, due to the lack of a sight glass in most vehicles, a measured amount of refrigerant must be installed to insure that the system is fully charged. Equipment suitable for this purpose is available from several manufacturers. All refrigerant servicing equipment attaches to the high and low pressure service valve ports, but exact connection details and operation may differ slightly between individual equipment manufacturers. Always follow the equipment manufacturer's instructions regarding connections to the vehicle. See Fig. 6.

After discharging and recovering the refrigerant, proceed with repairs as required. Do not leave the refrigerant system open. Seal openings to keep dirt and especially moisture from entering. When repairs have been completed, the system must be evacuated for a minimum of 30 minutes. This will "pull the system down" by creating a vacuum. It will remove all traces of the old refrigerant ensuring an accurate recharge. More importantly, however, it will remove any moisture that may have entered the system.

When the system has been repaired and properly evacuated, add refrigerant oil if required and recharge according to the equipment manufacturers instructions. Consult **Table a.** A/C system capacities, given earlier.

Table e. Temperature drop and pressure tests

Temperature drop result	High pressure result	Low pressure result	Possible causes	Corrective measures
Normal	Normal	Normal	None	---
Too high	Normal	Normal	Temperature flap postion incorrect	Adjust temperature flap cable, see **80 Heating and Ventilation**
Too high	Too low	Normal	Compressor	Replace compressor
Normal	Too low	Normal	Compressor	Replace compressor
Normal	Normal	Too high or too low	Expansion valve or compressor	Clean/replace expansion valve or replace compressor
Too high	Normal	Too high or too low		
Normal	Too high or too low	Too high or too low		

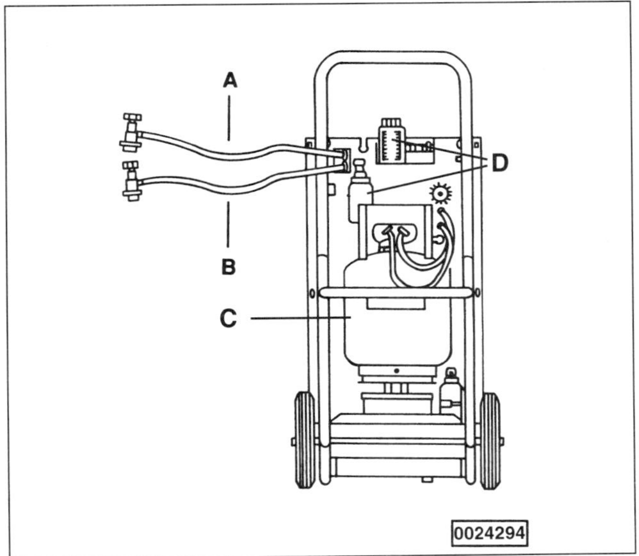

0024294

Fig. 6. Rear view of R-134a equipment supplied by Kent-Moore. High pressure hose (**A**) is color coded red and low pressure hose (**B**) is color coded blue. Equipment also has a built-in tank for R-134a (**C**) and provisions for adding PAG oil (**D**).

After the system has been recharged, switch on the ignition, but do not start the engine. Switch on the A/C and manually rotate the A/C compressor approximately 10 turns before starting the engine to insure adequate compressor lubrication. Start the engine with the A/C switched OFF. After idle speed has stabilized, switch A/C ON and let the engine idle with the compressor running for a minimum of two minutes before raising engine speed. This will allow the refrigerant oil to properly circulate to all parts of the system.

A/C refrigerant system, flushing

Certain circumstances may require complete removal of the refrigerant and refrigerant oil. This process is known as flushing and is accomplished with nitrogen and compressed air. Compressed nitrogen with regulators and adapters are available locally. Flushing is usually needed under the following conditions:

- Refrigerant oil is dark and viscous (thick) or shows metallic particles.
- Too much refrigerant oil is known to be in the system following compressor replacement.
- Do not know how much refrigerant oil is in the system.
- Moisture, dirt or other impurities have entered the refrigerant system, (i.e. following an accident).
- Unable to pull a constant vacuum during evacuation of a leak-free system due to excessive moisture in system.
- Refrigerant system has been open longer than the time required for normal repairs, (i.e. following an accident).
- Based on temperature and pressure measurements, system is diagnosed with moisture contamination.
- Compressor is replaced due to noises or internal damage.

If flushing the system, observe the following points:

- When using compressed nitrogen always use a pressure regulator and the proper adaptor hoses and fittings.
- During flushing, use existing exhaust/ventilation systems to draw off the gas mixture escaping from A/C system.
- Use compressed air and nitrogen (available locally) to remove moisture, impurities and old refrigerant oil from A/C refrigerant system.
- First blow out old refrigerant oil and dirt with compressed air, then dry components with nitrogen.
- DO NOT blow compressed air and nitrogen through the compressor or expansion valve. Only blow compressed air and nitrogen through disconnected, free flowing components (i.e. disconnected hose, condenser, evaporator, etc.)
- DO NOT blow compressed air and nitrogen into a capped off A/C component. Pressurized R-134a refrigerant in the presence of oxygen may form a combustible mixture.
- Always flush components in opposite direction of refrigerant flow.
- Flush evaporator through the low pressure line with the high pressure line removed.
- If any component has dark thick deposits that cannot be removed with compressed air, replace component.
- Thin light gray deposits in refrigerant lines and hoses are normal and do not impair the function of the system.
- Always replace receiver drier and restrictor after flushing.
- Dispose of contaminated refrigerant (PAG) oil following laws governing hazardous waste disposal. Do not combine PAG oil with any other old oils such as engine oil or transmission fluid.

WARNING —

- *DO NOT flush R-134a refrigerant system with any other type of refrigerant such as R-12 or R-11. Other refrigerants are not compatible with refrigerant R-134a/PAG oil and will cause total system contamination!*
- *DO NOT blow compressed air and nitrogen through the compressor or expansion valve. Only blow compressed air and nitrogen through disconnected, free flowing components (i.e. disconnected hose, condenser, evaporator, etc.).*
- *DO NOT blow compressed air and nitrogen into a capped off A/C component. Pressurized R-134a refrigerant in the presence of oxygen may form a combustible mixture.*

A/C, HEATING AND VENTILATION CONTROLS

An exploded view of the heating and ventilation components in the passenger compartment for vehicles equipped with the electronic (Climatronic) air conditioning system is shown in Fig. 7.

A/C passenger compartment components, overview (Climatronic)

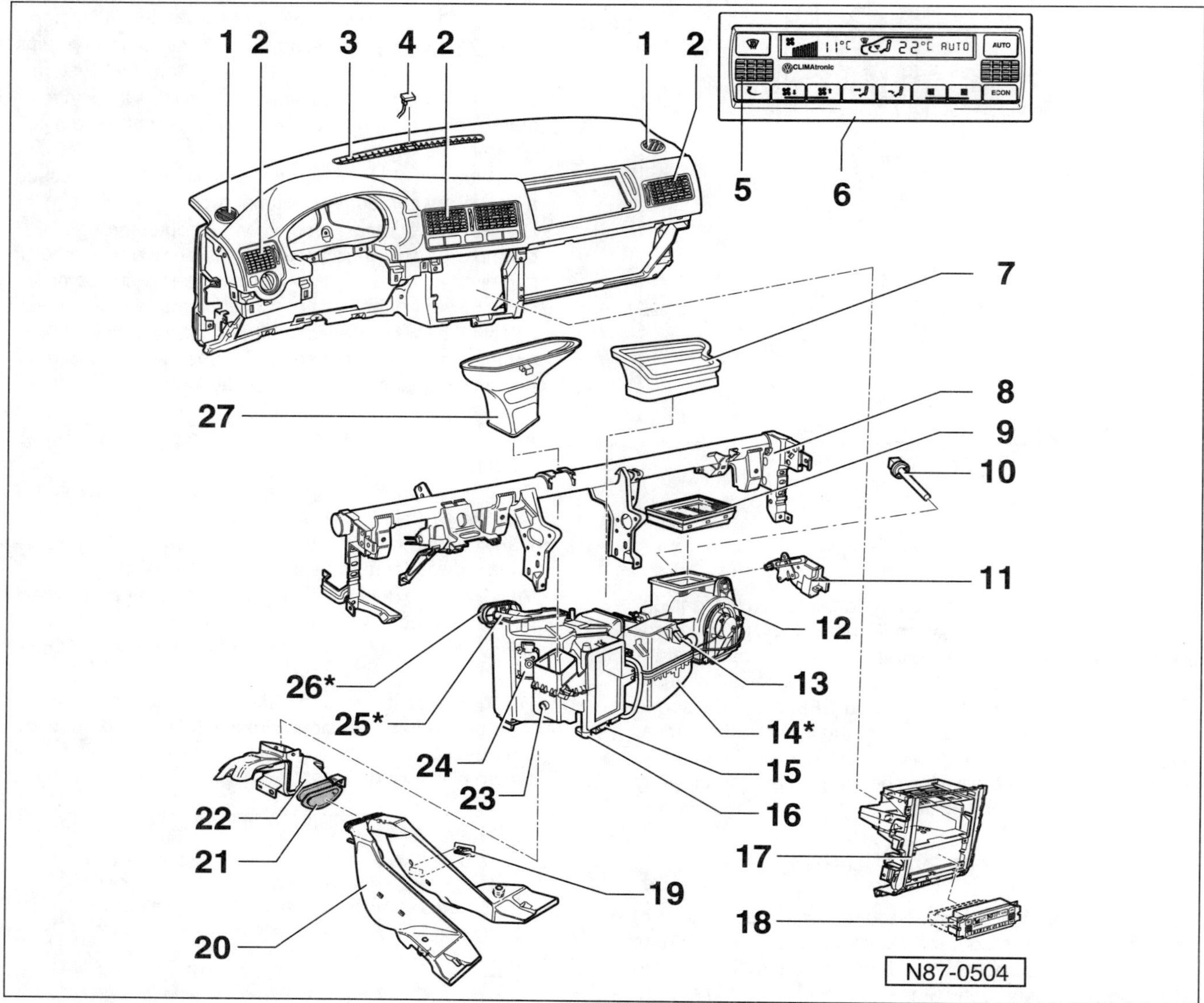

N87-0504

Fig. 7. Major components related to the Climatronic A/C system located in the passenger compartment. Components identified with an asterisk (*) cannot be removed until refrigerant system is discharged.

NOTE —

- *For an assembly view of passenger compartment components for vehicles without Climatronic, see* **80 Heating and Ventilation**.
- *Volkswagen identifies electrical components by a letter and/or a number in the electrical schematics. See* **97 Wiring Diagrams, Fuses and Relays**. *These electrical identifiers are listed in parenthesis as an aid to electrical troubleshooting.*

1. **Side window air outlet**
   - Removing, see **80 Heating and Ventilation**

2. **Dashboard air outlets**
   - Removing, see **80 Heating and Ventilation**

3. **Defroster air outlet**
   - Must remove instrument panel to remove, see **70 Trim –Interior**

4. **Sunlight photo sensor (G107)**
   - Controls temperature flap and fresh air blower speed depending on light intensity
   - Climatronic control module will assume a fixed value in the event of sensor failure
   - Removing, **see** Ⓐ

(continued from previous page)

5. **Instrument panel temperature sensor (G56) with interior temperature sensor fan (V42)**
   - Climatronic control unit, A/C control head and instrument panel temp. sensor with fan are integrated into a single unit which cannot be serviced separately
   - Controls temperature flap and fresh air blower
   - Climatronic control module will assume a fixed value of 24°C (75°F) in the event of sensor failure

6. **A/C control head unit**
   - Climatronic control unit, A/C control head and instrument panel temp. sensor with fan are integrated into a single unit which cannot be serviced separately
   - Replacing and adjusting:
     Code Climatronic control module, function 07 and then initiate basic setting, function 04 using VAG scan tool 1551/5051 or equivalent

7. **Intermediate duct**

8. **Instrument panel cross member**
   - Loosening and tightening, see **80 Heating and Ventilation**

9. **Dust and pollen filter**
   - With activated charcoal filter
   - Removing and installing, see **80 Heating and Ventilation**

10. **Fresh air intake duct temperature sensor (G89)**
    - Controls temperature flap and fresh air blower
    - If sensor malfunctions, outside temperature sensor value is used instead
    - Replacing:
      Remove glove box, see **70 Trim–Interior**
      Reach behind heating and A/C unit and turn sensor 90° and pull out
    - Lubricate seal with oil when installing

11. **Air flow flap motor (V71)**
    - Also operates fresh and recirculating air flap
    - Replacing and adjusting:
      Initiate basic setting, function 04 using VAG scan tool 1551/5051 or equivalent

12. **Fresh air blower fan (V2)**

13. **Fresh air blower control module (J126)**
    - Controls fresh air blower speed depending on voltage signal
    - Replacing, **see** (B)

14. **Heating and A/C unit***
    - Refrigerant must be discharged before removing
    - With heater core and evaporator

15. **Central air flap motor (V70)**
    - Replacing and adjusting:
      Initiate basic setting, function 04 using VAG scan tool 1551/5051 or equivalent

16. **Temperature regulator flap motor**
    - Replacing and adjusting:
      Initiate basic setting, function 04 using VAG scan tool 1551/5051 or equivalent

17. **Center trim**

18. **Climatronic control module**
    - Climatronic control unit, A/C control head and instrument panel temp. sensor with fan are integrated into a single unit which cannot be serviced separately
    - After replacing:
      Always code Climatronic control module, function 07 and then initiate basic setting, function 04 using VAG scan tool 1551/5051 or equivalent

19. **Footwell air outlet**
    - Passenger side only

20. **Rear footwell air duct**

21. **Gasket**

22. **Connecting duct**
    - With driver's side footwell air outlet
    - Removing, see **80 Heating and Ventilation**

23. **Footwell air outlet temperature sensor (G192)**
    - Controls air distribution defrost/footwell and fresh air blower speed depending on air outlet temperature measurement
    - In the event of sensor failure, operation will continue assuming a default value of 80°C (176°F)
    - Removing and installing, **see** (C)

24. **Footwell/defroster flap motor (V85)**
    - Replacing and adjusting:
      Initiate basic setting, function 04 using VAG scan tool 1551/5051 or equivalent

25. **Heater core***
    - Refrigerant must be discharged before removing

26. **Heater core/bulkhead seal ***
    - Refrigerant must be discharged before removing
    - Note installed position

27. **Defroster duct**
    - Replacing:
      Remove instrument panel, see **70 Trim–Interior**
      Loosen instrument panel cross member, see **80 Heating and Ventilation**

A Sunlight photo sensor, removing

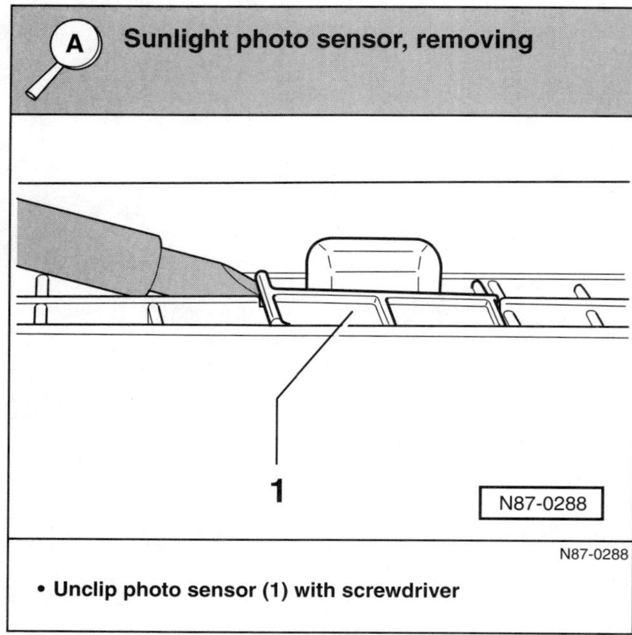

N87-0288

- **Unclip photo sensor (1) with screwdriver**

B Control module for fresh air blower, removing

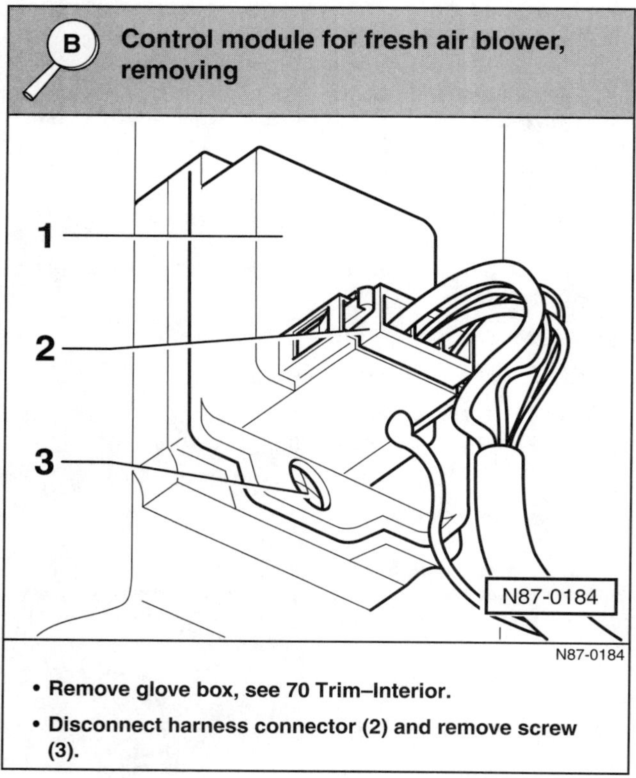

N87-0184

- **Remove glove box, see 70 Trim–Interior.**
- **Disconnect harness connector (2) and remove screw (3).**

C Footwell air outlet temperature sensor, removing and installing

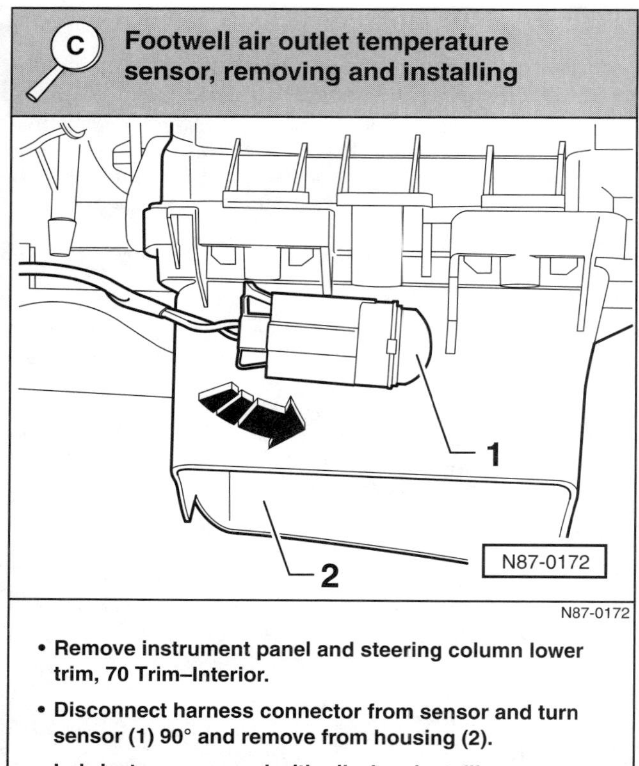

N87-0172

- **Remove instrument panel and steering column lower trim, 70 Trim–Interior.**
- **Disconnect harness connector from sensor and turn sensor (1) 90° and remove from housing (2).**
- **Lubricate sensor seal with oil when installing.**

Fresh air blower, removing

1. Remove glove box, see **70 Trim–Interior.**
2. Remove plastic foam cover below A/C unit. See Fig. 8.
3. Remove mounting bolts and blower fan lower cover. See Fig. 8.

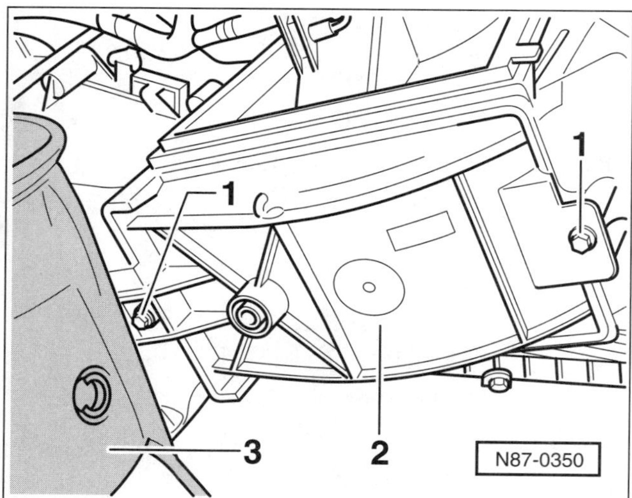

N87-0350

Fig. 8. Remove plastic foam cover (**3**), bolts (**1**) and blower fan lower cover (**2**).

4. Disconnect harness connector for blower fan and pull fan downward to remove. See Fig. 9.

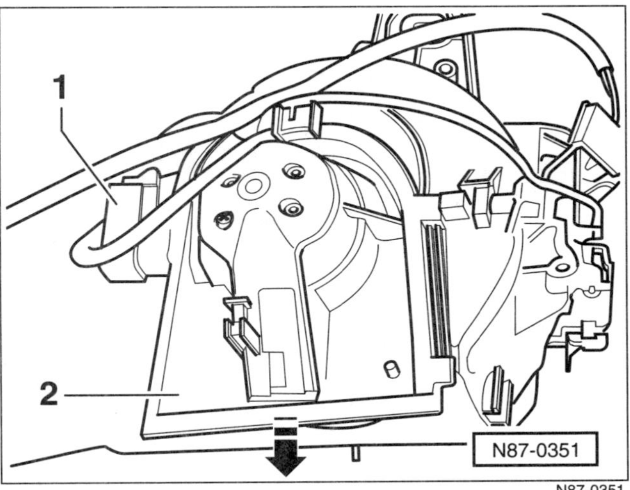

N87-0351

Fig. 9. Disconnect harness connector (**1**) and remove blower motor (**2**) in a downward direction (**arrow**).

A/C, heating and ventilation control head, removing and installing (Climatronic)

> ***WARNING —***
> *Observe all cautions, warnings and notes before starting repairs involving air conditioning systems.*

NOTE —
To remove heating and ventilation controls in vehicles without Climatronic, see **80 Heating and Ventilation**.

1. Remove trim around control head with plastic trim removal tool or screwdriver with protected tip. See Fig. 10.

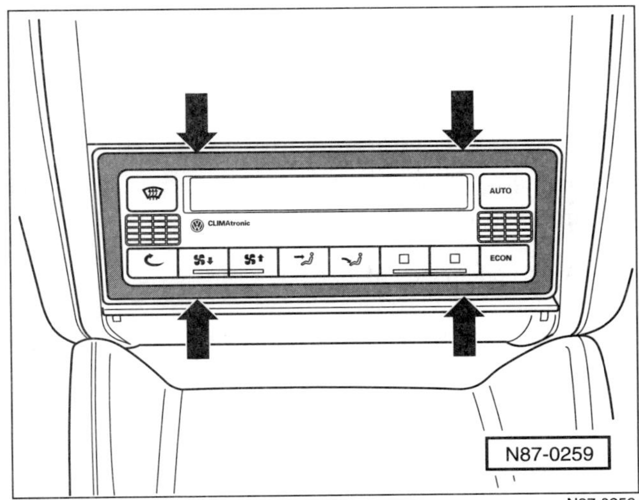

N87-0259

Fig. 10. Carefully pry out trim panel at **arrows**.

2. Remove control head mounting screws. See Fig. 11.

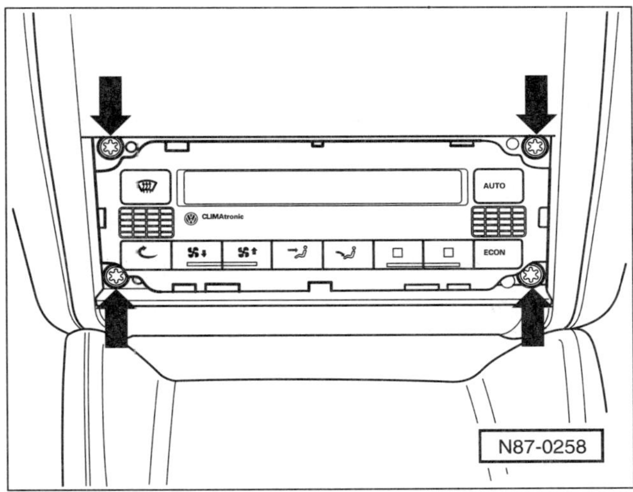

N87-0258

Fig. 11. Check control cable operation with controls removed. Move cables in and out (**arrows**) several times.

3. Pull out A/C control head and disconnect electrical harness connectors. Remove control head.

4. Installation is the reverse of removal.

NOTE —
The control module will need to be coded using VAG scan tool 1551/5051, or equivalent, with function 07 and the basic setting initiated with function 04.

AIR FLAP MOTORS (CLIMATRONIC)

The Climatronic A/C control head is programmed to set the various air flow flaps within the heater/evaporator housing to specific positions in response to passenger requirements and sensor inputs. The flap servo motors move the flaps.

Position sensors provide feedback to the control unit so it knows where the various flaps are positioned. The control unit reads varying voltage signals from potentiometers which are attached to the flaps. As the potentiometer sweeps past a fixed resistor, the voltage drop across the resistor changes. The control unit matches the incoming voltage signals to values held in memory. When the voltage matches the programmed value the control head switches off the current to the flap motor.

The values held in memory come from full sweep movements of the potentiometers that were retained during basic settings (function 04) using the VAG 1551/5051 scan tool, or equivalent.

NOTE —
- *Before replacing any components of the Climatronic A/C system, the system should be diagnosed using a VAG 1551/5051 scan tool, or equivalent.*
- *After replacing any of the flap motors, it will be necessary to initiate basic setting (function 04) using a VAG 1551/5051 scan tool, or equivalent.*
- *For vehicles without Climatronic, the cable operated flaps are covered in* **80 Heating and Ventilation**.
- *Volkswagen identifies electrical components by a letter and/or a number in the electrical schematics. See* **97 Wiring Diagrams, Fuses and Relays**. *These electrical identifiers are listed in parenthesis as an aid to electrical troubleshooting.*

Air flow flap motor (V71), removing and installing

1. Disconnect battery ground (GND) strap from battery negative (–) terminal. See the **Cautions** at the beginning of this repair group regarding battery disconnection.

NOTE —
Be sure to have the anti-theft radio code on hand before disconnecting the battery.

2. Remove the glove box, see **70 Trim–Interior.**
3. Use a screwdriver to carefully unclip the air flow flap rod from lever. See Fig. 12.

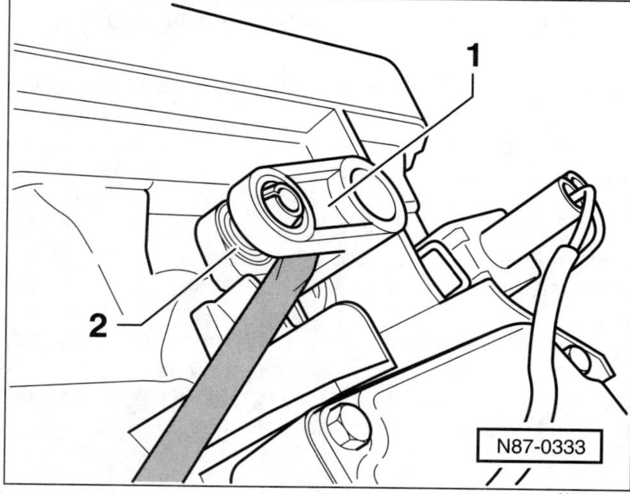

N87-0333

Fig. 12. Unclip air flow flap rod (**1**) from lever (**2**).

4. Disconnect harness connector for flap motor and remove mounting bolt.
5. Lower flap motor while pulling off from fresh air/recirculating air flap shaft. See Fig. 13.

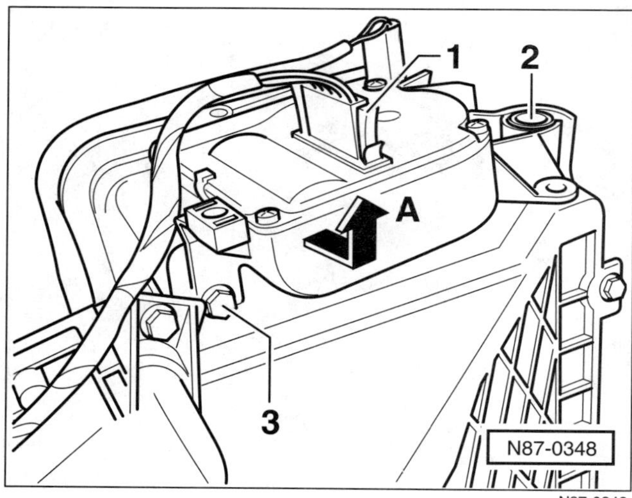

N87-0348

Fig. 13. Disconnect harness connector (**1**), remove bolt (**3**) and pull motor off fresh air/recirculating flap shaft (**2**) in direction of **arrow A**.

6. To install motor, connect harness connector to flap motor and switch on ignition.
7. Operate button for fresh air/recirculating air.

NOTE —
Replacement flap motors from Volkswagen are supplied in the "recirculating air" position.

8. When the center position has been reached by the flap, disconnect electrical harness connector from flap motor.
9. Insert flap motor onto fresh air/recirculating air flap shaft. See Fig. 14.

NOTE —
If the flap motor cannot be attached to the fresh air/recirculating air flap shaft, remove the fresh air blower and attach flap by hand.

10. Turn flap motor in a clockwise direction and install mounting bolts. See Fig. 14.
11. Attach operating rod for air flow flap.
12. Install harness connector and initiate basic setting (function 04) with VAG 1551/5051 scan tool, or equivalent.

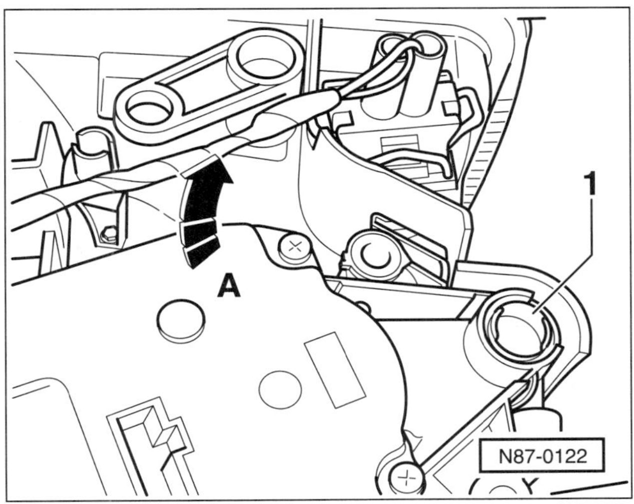

N87-0122

Fig. 14. Insert flap motor onto fresh air/recirculating air flap shaft (**1**), rotate motor in direction of **arrow A** and install mounting bolts.

Temperature flap motor (V68), removing and installing

1. Remove glove box, lower steering column trim and center console, see **70 Trim–Interior**.
2. Remove connecting duct to rear footwell air duct, see **80 Heating and Ventilation**.
3. Disconnect harness connector from flap motor and use a screwdriver to carefully unclip operating rod from flap lever. See Fig. 15.
4. Remove mounting screws and flap motor.

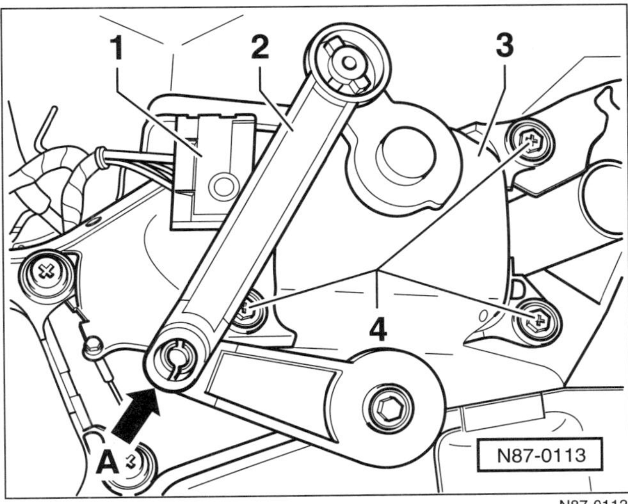

N87-0113

Fig. 15. Disconnect harness connector (**1**), unclip operating rod (**2**) from flap lever (**arrow A**), remove screws (**4**) and flap motor (**3**).

5. Install in reverse order of removal.
6. Initiate basic setting (function 04) with VAG 1551/5051 scan tool, or equivalent.

Central flap motor (V70), removing and installing

1. Remove glove box, lower steering column trim and center console, see **70 Trim–Interior**.
2. Remove connecting duct to rear footwell air duct, see **80 Heating and Ventilation**.
3. Disconnect harness connector from flap motor and use a screwdriver to carefully unclip operating rod from flap lever.
4. Remove mounting bolts for motor.
5. Turn operating rod to remove from flap motor and remove flap motor. See Fig. 16.

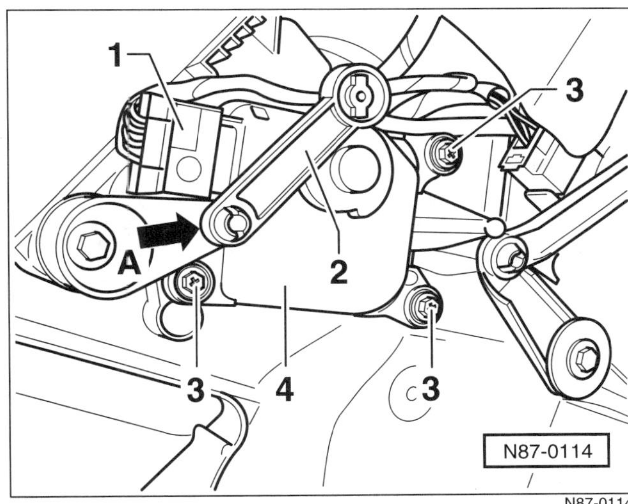

N87-0114

Fig. 16. Disconnect harness connector (**1**) and unclip operating rod (**2**) from flap lever (**arrow A**). Remove screws (**3**), turn operating rod to release from motor and remove flap motor (**4**).

6. Install in reverse order of removal.
7. Initiate basic setting (function 04) with VAG 1551/5051 scan tool, or equivalent.

Footwell/defrost flap motor (V85), removing and installing

1. Remove lower steering column trim, **70 Trim–Interior**.
2. Disconnect harness connector from flap motor.
3. Remove mounting screws for flap motor.
4. Turn flap motor to disengage from operating rod. See Fig. 17.

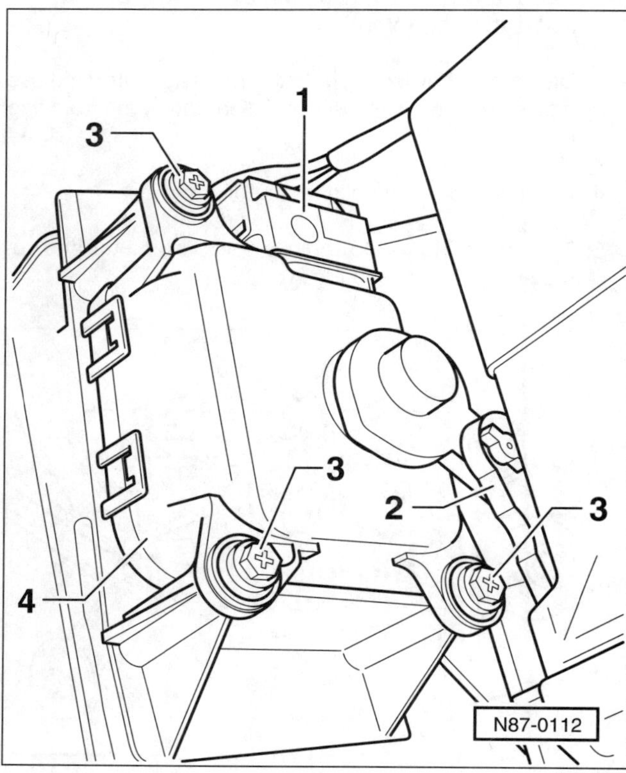

N87-0112

Fig. 17. Disconnect harness connector (**1**), remove screws (**3**), rotate motor to release from operating rod (**2**) and remove flap motor (**4**).

5. Remove flap motor from housing.
6. Install in reverse order of removal.
7. Initiate basic setting (function 04) with VAG 1551/5051 scan tool, or equivalent.

A/C COMPONENTS, UNDERHOOD

> ***WARNING —***
> *Observe all cautions, warnings and notes before starting repairs involving air conditioning systems.*

NOTE —
Components identified with an asterisk (*) can only be removed after discharging the refrigerant.

The following numbered list applies to Fig. 18.

1. **Damper***
   - In refrigerant hose (item 2).
2. **Refrigerant hose***
   - From expansion valve to compressor
3. **Refrigerant pipe***
   - From receiver dryer to expansion valve
4. **Service valve (evacuating/charging)***
   - Use Kent Moore ACR4 recovery unit, or equivalent
5. **A/C pressure switch (F129) or high pressure sensor (G65)***
   - Can be removed without discharging refrigerant
   - Tighten to 8 Nm (71 in-lb)
   - Always replace O-ring
   - Checking pressure switch (F129), see **A/C refrigerant system, component overview** given earlier
   - G65 supplies refrigerant system pressure signal to coolant fan control module (J239) and ECM
6. **Expansion valve***
7. **Dust and pollen filter**
   - With activated charcoal filter
   - Removing and installing, see **80 Heating and Ventilation**
8. **Ambient air temperature switch (F38) or outside temperature sensor (G17)**
   - F38 on manual A/C system only:
     Switches off A/C clutch (N25) at low ambient air temperatures to prevent damage
     Switches clutch off at -1°C (30°F)
     Switches back on at 7°C (45°F)
   - G17 (not shown) on Climatronic only:
     Located behind driver side headlight
     In the event of a malfunction, fresh air intake duct sensor (G89) takes over. If both sensors are malfunctioning, operation continues assuming a value of 10°C (50°F). Air recirculation is not possible and A/C control head will indicate "--"
9. **A/C thermal cut-out switch (F163)**
   - Switches off A/C clutch (N25) at excessively high coolant temperature
   - Switches clutch off at 119°C (246°F)
   - Switches clutch back on at 112°C (234°F)

A/C components, underhood overview

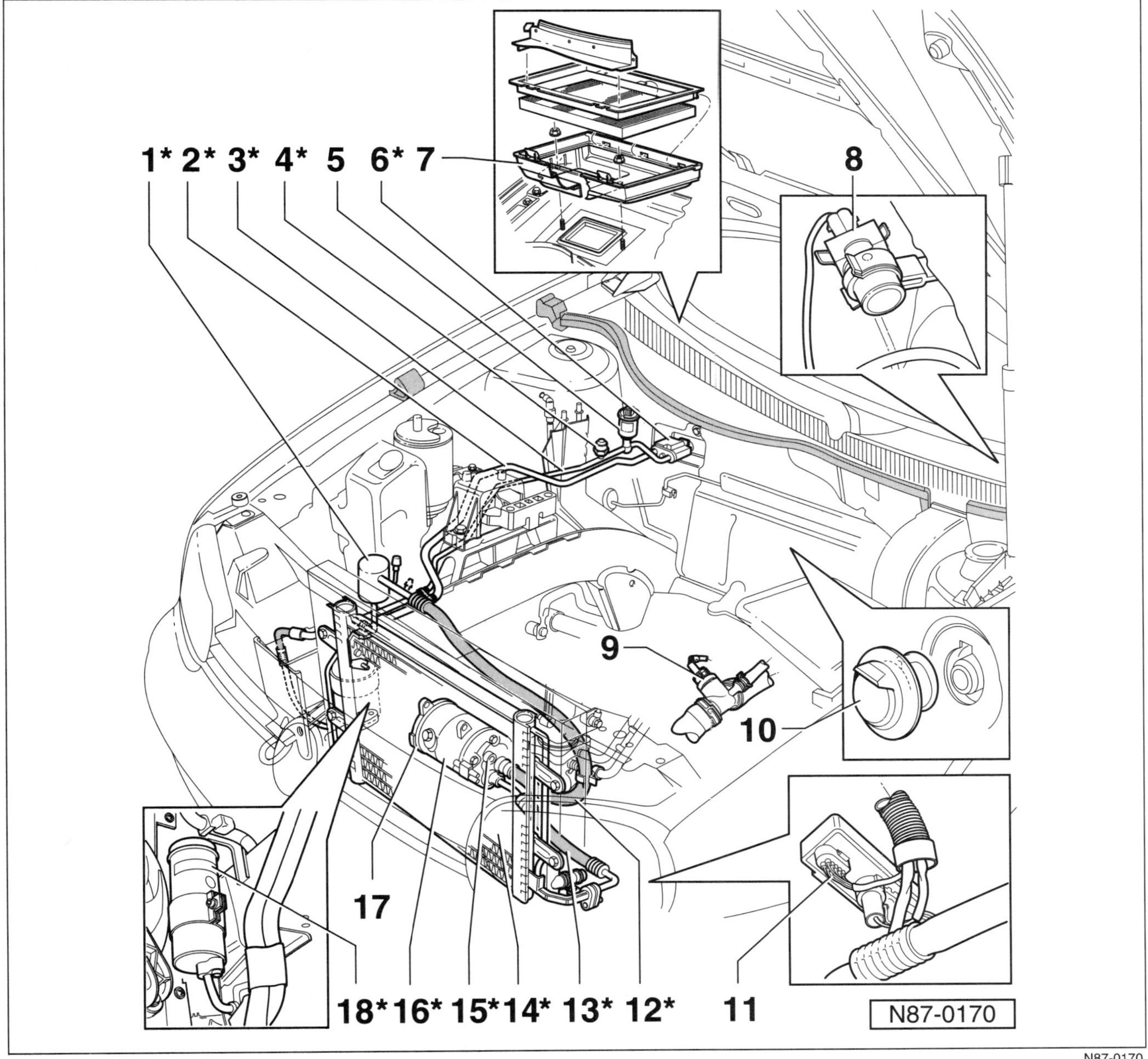

N87-0170

Fig. 18. A/C components in the engine compartment. Manual A/C shown, Climatronic differences are noted in component list.

10. Evaporator water drain valve
- Location: Under insulation flap on bulkhead
- Checking, **see** Ⓐ

11. Coolant fan control module (J293)
- Location: lower left side of engine compartment near radiator
- Controls all A/C clutch functions and A/C related radiator fan functions

12. Refrigerant hose*

13. Refrigerant hose*

14. Condenser*

15. Pressure relief valve*

16. Compressor*

17. A/C compressor clutch (N25)

18. Receiver drier*

(A) Evaporator water drain valve, checking

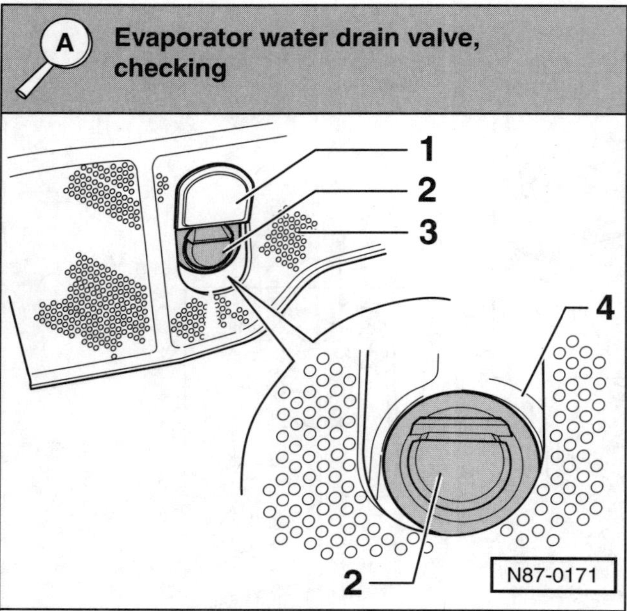

N87-0171

- Fold cover (1) in bulkhead insulation mat (3) upwards.
- Remove drain valve (2) from opening in bulkhead (4).
- The water drain valve flap and body must not be stuck together.
- Insulation mat must not be deformed or damaged in the area of water drain valve.
- The opening in the drain valve body must point downwards with the flap hinge at the top.
- When the insulation cover (1) is closed it must be flush with the insulation matting (3). If the insulation cover (1) is pushed in too far, the water drain valve flap can become jammed.

A/C compressor mounting bracket assembly (2.0L engine)

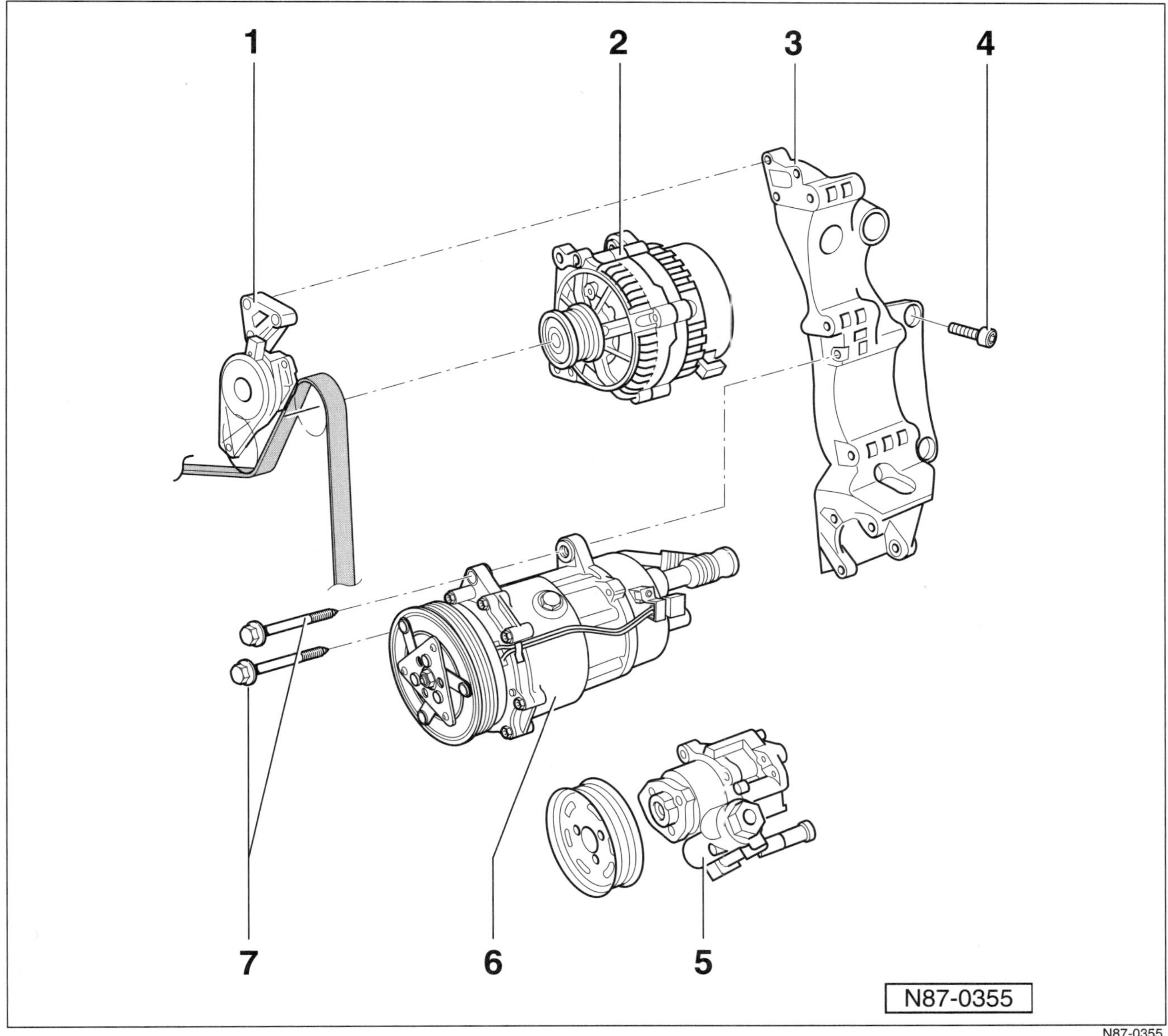

Fig. 19. Mounting bracket and related components for A/C equipped 2.0L engine.

1. **Tensioning roller, ribbed V-belt**
2. **Generator (GEN) and pulley**
3. **Bracket**
   - Compressor bracket and related components can be removed and installed without having to open the refrigerant circuit
   - Mounting for generator, A/C compressor and power steering pump
   - Remove compressor from bracket, swing away and secure in engine compartment with wire
4. **Bolts**
   - Tighten to 50 Nm (37 ft-lb)
5. **Power steering pump**
6. **A/C compressor**
7. **Bolts**
   - Tighten to 45 Nm (33 ft-lb)

A/C compressor mounting bracket assembly (1.9L engine)

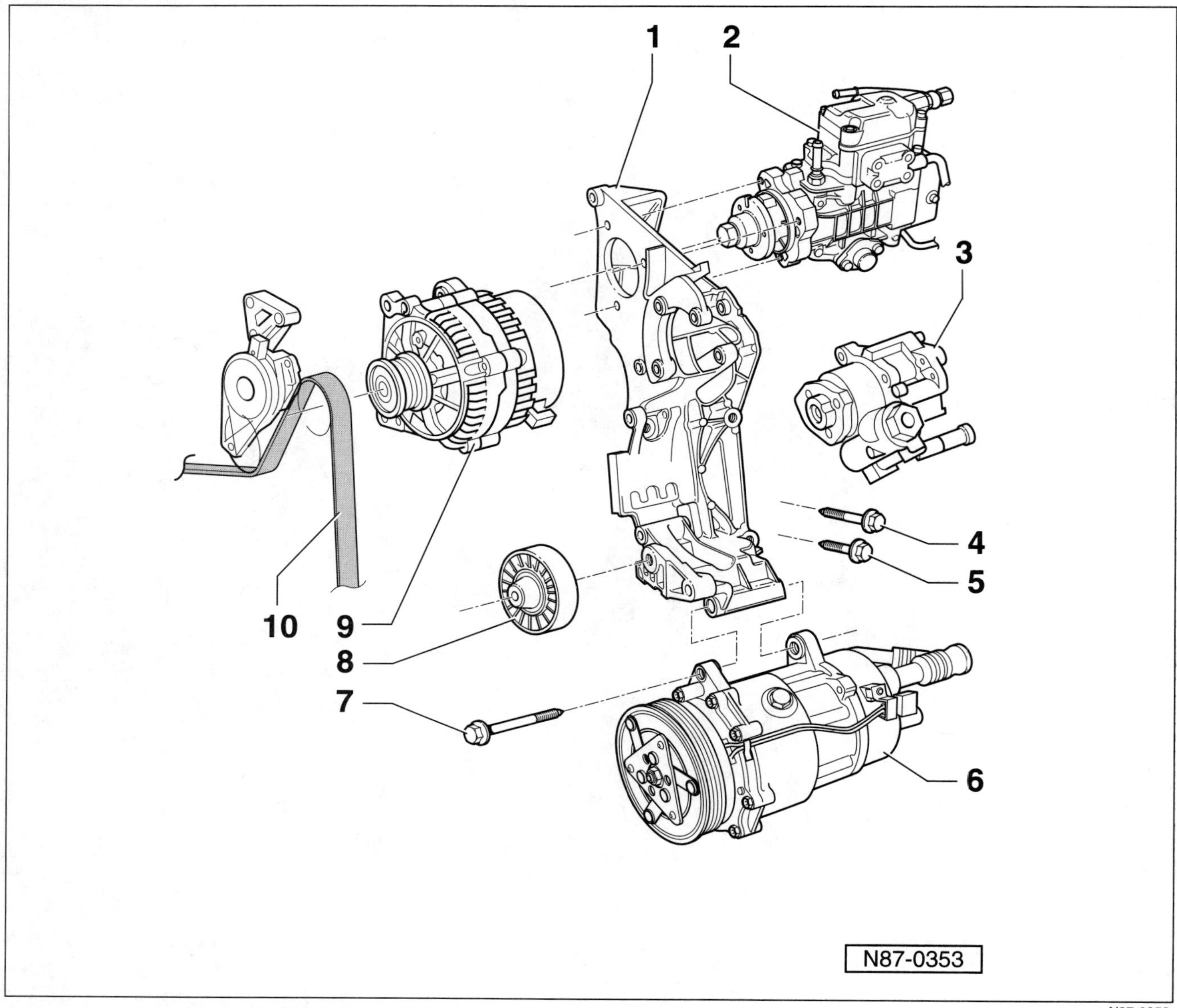

N87-0353

Fig. 20. Mounting bracket and related components for A/C equipped 1.9L engines.

1. **Bracket**
   - The compressor bracket and related components can be removed and installed without having to open the refrigerant circuit.
   - Mounting for generator, compressor, power steering pump, diesel injection pump.
   - Remove compressor from bracket, swing away and secure in engine compartment with wire.
2. **Diesel injection pump**
3. **Power steering pump**
4. **Bolts**
   - Tighten to 45 Nm (33 ft-lb)
5. **Bolts**
   - Tighten to 45 Nm (33 ft-lb)
6. **Compressor**
7. **Bolt**
   - Tighten to 45 Nm (33 ft-lb)
8. **Idler pulley, see** Ⓐ
9. **Generator (GEN) and pulley**
10. **Ribbed V-belt**
    - Routing, **see** Ⓑ

A Idler pulley, assembly

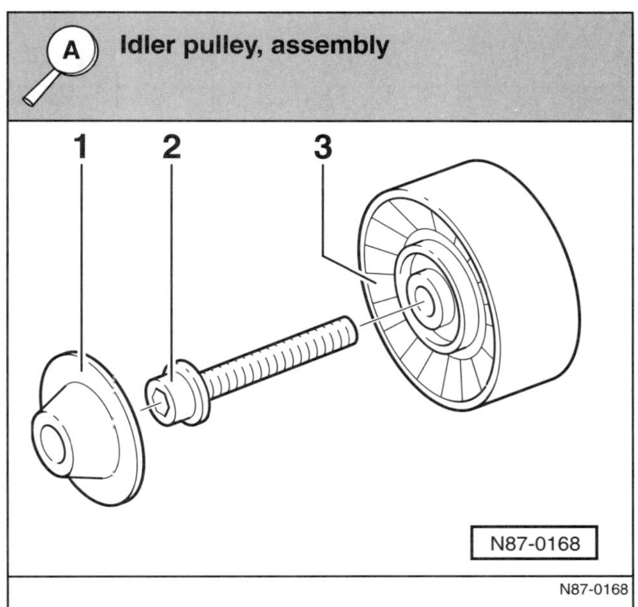

N87-0168

1. Protective cap
2. Bolt, tighten to 25 Nm (18 ft-lb)
3. Idler roller with bearings

B Ribbed V-belt, routing

N87-0167

N87-0167

- Always mark the running direction before removing and install in the same direction.
- When installing the belt ensure it is correctly seated in the pulley.

A/C compressor mounting bracket assembly (2.8L engine)

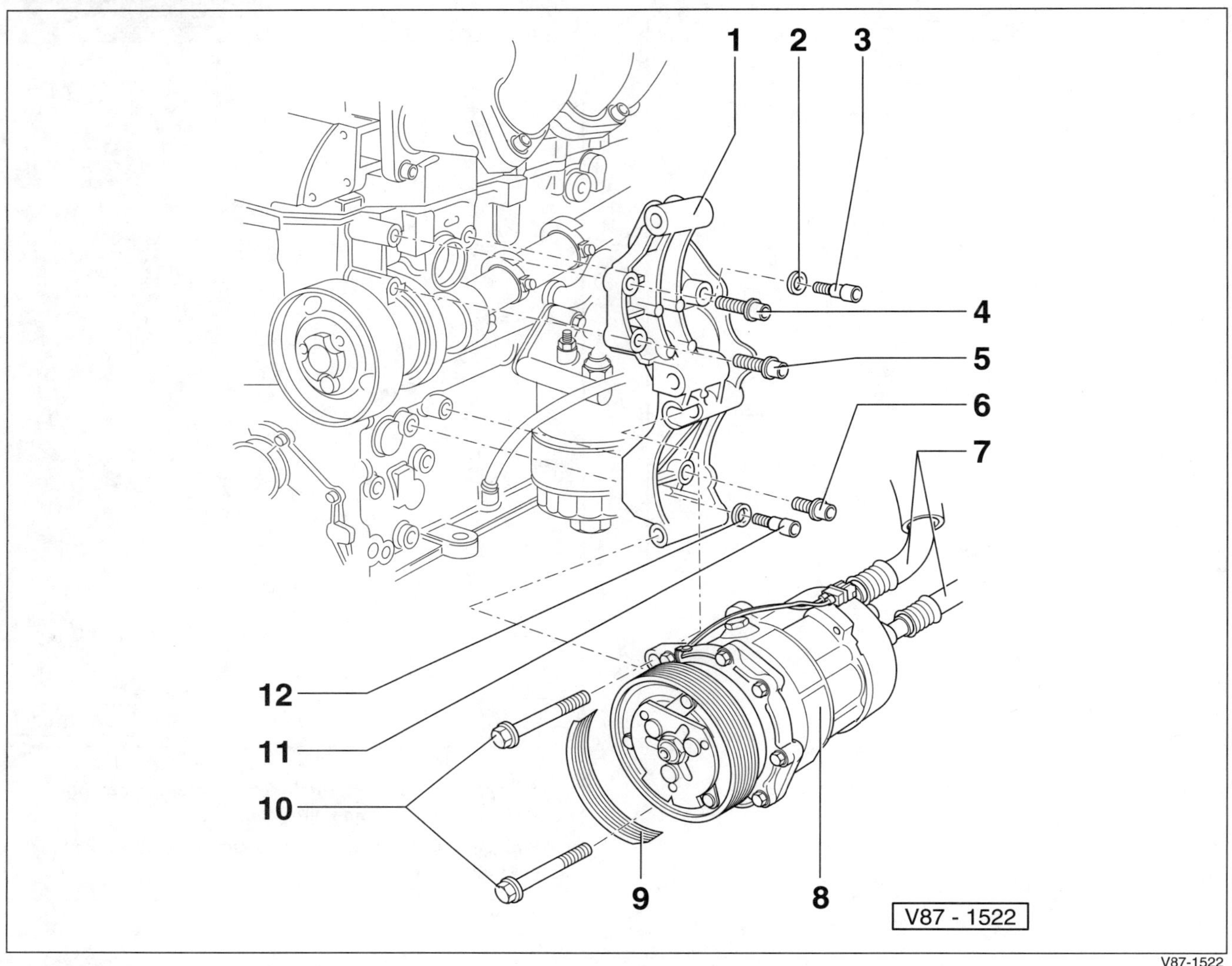

V87-1522

Fig. 21. Mounting bracket and related components for A/C equipped 2.8L engines.

1. **Bracket**
   - The compressor bracket and related components can be removed and installed without having to open the refrigerant circuit.
   - Remove compressor from bracket, swing away and secure in engine compartment with wire.
   - When installing, first install bolts (items 3 and 11)
2. **Washer**
3. **Bolt (M8 x 30)**
   - Tighten to 25 Nm (18 ft-lb)
4. **Allen head bolt (M8 x 30)**
   - Tighten to 25 Nm (18 ft-lb)
5. **Allen head bolt (M8 x 30)**
   - Tighten to 25 Nm (18 ft-lb)
6. **Allen head bolt (M8 x 30)**
   - Tighten to 25 Nm (18 ft-lb)
7. **Refrigerant hoses**
8. **Compressor with A/C clutch**
9. **Ribbed belt**
10. **Bolt (M10 x 112)**
    - Tighten to 45 Nm (33 ft-lb)
11. **Bolt (M8 x 20)**
    - Tighten to 25 Nm (18 ft-lb)
12. **Washer**

A/C compressor overview

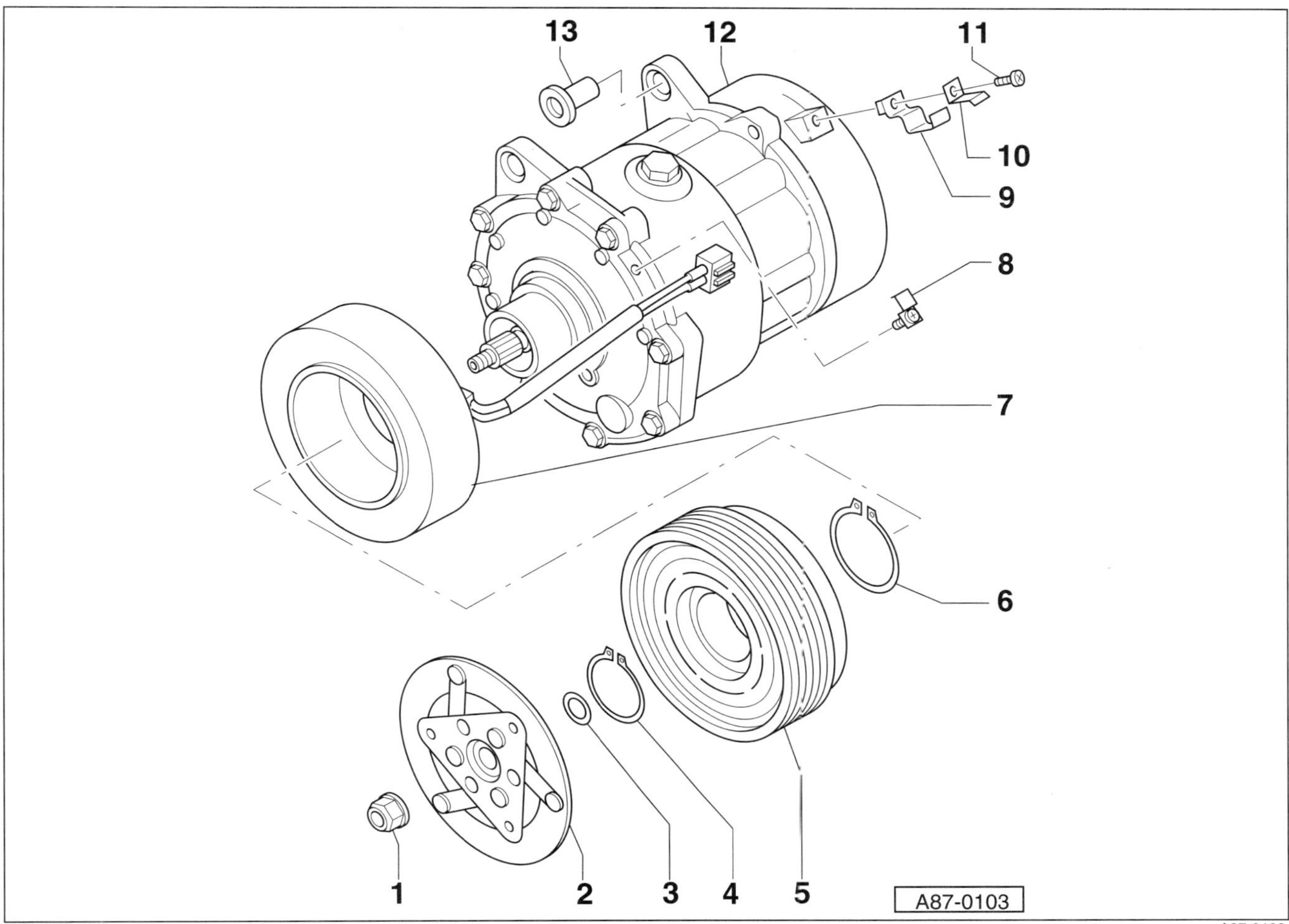

A87-0103

Fig. 22. Sanden compressor and A/C clutch.

1. **Nut, self locking**
   - Always replace
   - Tighten to 15 Nm (11 ft-lb)
   - Use two pin spanner wrench (with 4mm pins) to counterhold clutch plate while loosening nut
2. **Clutch plate**
   - Removing, **see** Ⓐ
3. **Shims**
   - Used to adjust gap between clutch plate and pulley, **see** Ⓒ
4. **Circlip**
   - Always replace
   - Note installation position: flat side faces compressor
   - Ensure correct seating in groove
5. **Clutch pulley**
   - Refrigerant circuit does not need to be discharged to service A/C clutch.
6. **Circlip**
   - Always replace
   - Note installation position: flat side faces compressor
   - Ensure correct seating in groove
7. **Clutch coil**
   - Thermo-fuse integrated into clutch coil protects the A/C clutch in the event of overheating due to a binding compressor. The clutch coil circuit is interrupted.
   - Note installation position, **see** Ⓑ
8. **Retainer**
   - With screw
9. **Retainer**
10. **Retainer**
11. **Screw**
12. **Compressor**
13. **Threaded bushing**

A A/C clutch plate, removing

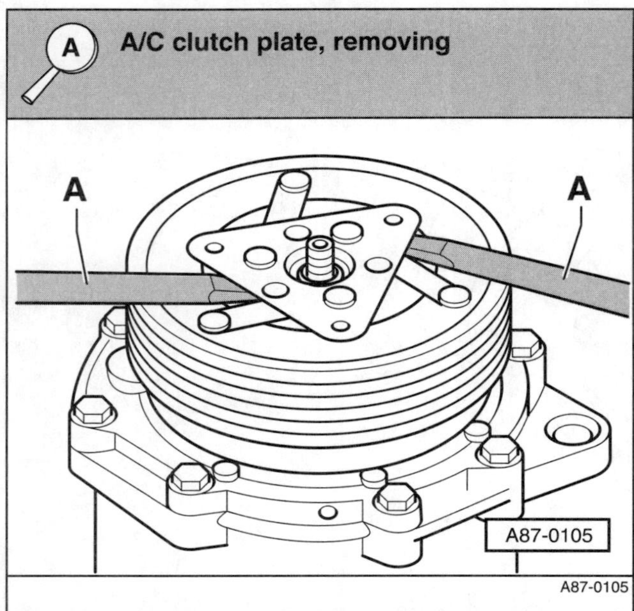

A87-0105

- Loosen self-locking nut that holds clutch plate while counter-holding clutch plate with two-pin spanner wrench.
- Carefully pry off clutch plate using two large screwdrivers (A) as shown.

B A/C clutch coil, installed position

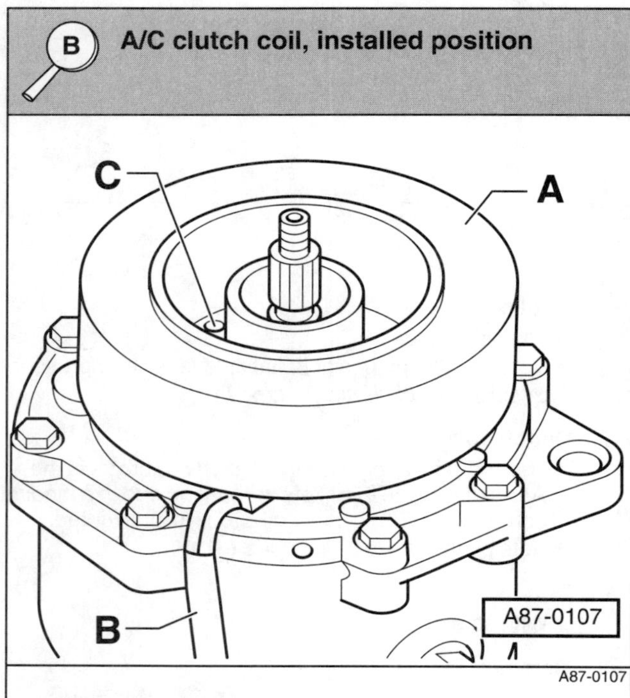

A87-0107

- Install coil (A) onto compressor.
- Locate locking tab on coil and position into recess (C) in face of compressor.
- Ensure proper routing of coil wiring harness (B).

C A/C clutch plate gap, checking

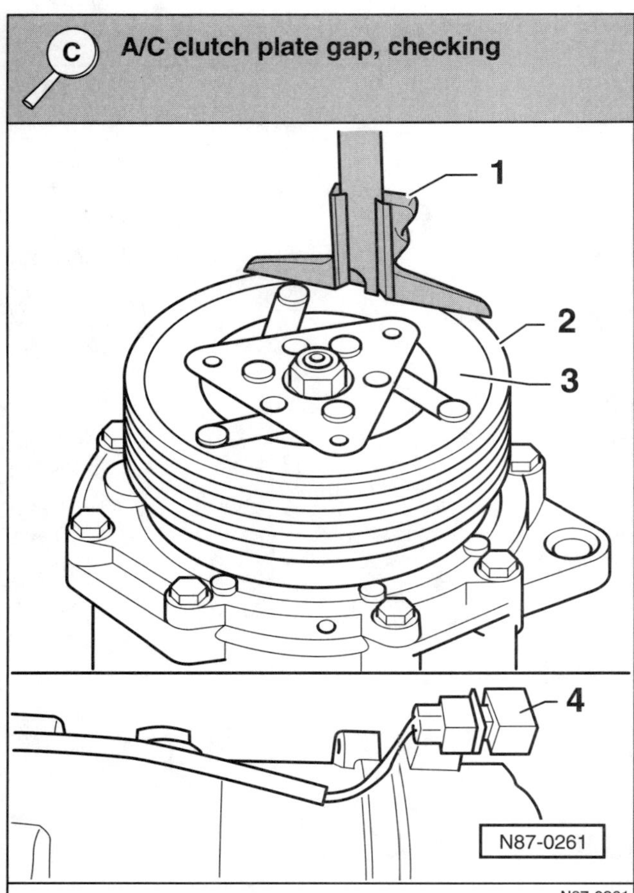

N87-0261

- Gap between clutch plate and clutch pulley when clutch is not energized: 0.4 - 0.8 mm (0.015 - 0.032 in).
- Using depth gauge (1), measure gap between top of clutch plate (3) and clutch pulley (2) at three equally spaced locations. Measurements must not deviate from each other.
- If gap between clutch plate and clutch pulley is not within specification, remove clutch plate and add or remove shims as needed.
- When installing, ensure that wiring harness and harness connector (4) are secured under securing clips.

9 Electrical System

GENERAL

This group covers a brief description of the principal parts of the electrical system. Also covered here is general electrical system troubleshooting.

Voltage and polarity

Volkswagen electrical systems are 12-volt direct current (DC) negative-ground systems. A voltage regulator controls the output of the alternator to approximately 13.5 volts. All circuits are grounded by direct or indirect connection to the negative (–) terminal of the battery. A number of ground connections throughout the car connect the wiring harness to chassis ground. These circuits are completed by the battery cable or ground strap between the body and the battery negative (–) terminal.

Electrical system safety precautions

Please read the following warnings and cautions before doing any work on your electrical system.

> ***WARNING —***
> - *Ignition systems operate in a dangerous voltage range that could prove to be fatal if exposed terminals or live parts are contacted. Use extreme caution when working on a vehicle with the ignition on or the engine running.*
> - *On cars equipped with Airbags, special precautions apply to any electrical system testing or repair. The airbag unit is an explosive device and must be handled with extreme care. Before starting any work on an airbag equipped car, refer to the warnings and cautions in* **69 Seatbelts, Airbags**.
> - *Before operating the starter without starting the engine (as when making a compression test), disable ignition system as described in* **28a Ignition System**.

> ***CAUTION —***
> - *Always switch the ignition off and disconnect the negative (–) battery cable before removing any electrical components.*
> - *Before disconnecting battery be sure to obtain radio anti-theft code.*
> - *Connect and disconnect ignition system wires, multiple connectors, and ignition test equipment leads only while the ignition is switched off.*
> - *Do not disconnect battery while the engine is running. Never reverse the battery terminal connections. Even a momentary wrong connection can damage the alternator or electrical components. If the polarity markings on the battery are not visible, confirm the polarity of battery using a voltmeter.*
> - *Always remove the battery cables before quick-charging the battery. Never use a quick-charger as a booster for starting the car. Do not exceed 16.5 volts at the battery.*
> - *Many solid-state modules operate on very low current and can be permanently damaged if exposed to static discharge. Always handle the modules using proper static prevention equipment and techniques.*
> - *Always switch a test meter to the appropriate function and range before making test connections.*
> - *Disconnect the battery before doing any electric welding on the car.*
> - *Do not wash the engine while it is running, or anytime the ignition is switched on.*
> - *Do not try to start the engine of a car which has been heated above 176°F (80°C), (for example, in a paint drying booth) until allowing it to cool to normal temperature.*

Electrical test equipment

Many of the electrical tests described in this manual call for measuring voltage, current or resistance using a digital multimeter (DMM). DMMs are preferred for precise measurements and for electronics work because they are generally more accurate than analog meters. The DMM is also safe for most solid state components whereas an analog meter can damage some components.

An LED test light is a safe, inexpensive tool that can be used to perform many simple electrical tests that would otherwise require a multimeter. The LED indicates when voltage is present between any two test-points in a circuit.

> ***CAUTION —***
> - *Choose test equipment carefully. Use a meter with at least 10 megohm input impedance, or an LED test light. An analog meter (swing-needle) or a test light with a normal incandescent bulb may draw enough current to damage sensitive electronic components.*
> - *An analog meter must not be used to measure resistance on solid state components such as control units or time delay relays.*
> - *Always disconnect the battery before making resistance (ohm) measurements on the circuit.*

Wiring diagrams, fuses and relays

Nearly all parts of the wiring harness connect to components of the electrical system with keyed, push-on connectors that lock into place. Notable exceptions are the heavy battery cables and the alternator wiring.

With the exception of the charging system, all electrical power is routed from the ignition switch or the battery through the fuse panel, located in the passenger compartment behind the driver side left knee bar. Fuses prevent excessive current from damaging components and wiring. Fuses are color coded to indicate their different current capacities. Most relays are electro-mechanical switches that operate on low current to switch a high-current circuit on and off.

The wiring diagrams shown in **97 Wiring Diagrams, Fuses and Relays** are organized according to model year and engine type, with complete diagrams for each year.

ELECTRICAL TROUBLESHOOTING

Four things are required for current to flow in any electrical circuit: a voltage source, wires or connections to transport the voltage, a consumer or device that uses the electricity, and a connection to ground or a return to the voltage source. Most problems can be found using only a digital multimeter (volt/ohm/amp meter) to check for voltage supply, for breaks in the wiring (infinite resistance/no continuity), or for a path to ground that completes the circuit.

Electric current is logical in its flow, always moving from the voltage source toward ground. Keeping this in mind, electrical faults can be located through a process of elimination. When troubleshooting a complex circuit, separate the circuit into smaller parts. Be sure to analyze the problem. Use the wiring diagrams to determine the most likely cause of the problem. Get an understanding of how the circuit works by following the circuit from ground back to the power source.

> ***CAUTION —***
> *When making test connections at connectors and components, use care to avoid spreading or damaging the connectors or terminals. Some electrical tests may require jumper wires to bypass components. When connecting jumper wires, use blade connectors at the wire ends that match the size of the terminal being tested. The small internal contacts are easily spread apart, and this can cause intermittent or faulty connections that can lead to more problems.*

Voltage and ground, checking

Checking for the presence of voltage or ground is usually the first step in troubleshooting a problem circuit. For example, if a parking light does not work, a check for voltage at the bulb socket will quickly determine if the circuit is functioning properly or if the bulb itself is faulty. If voltage and ground are found at the socket, then the bulb is most likely faulty.

Another valuable troubleshooting technique is a voltage drop test. This is a good test to perform if current is flowing through the circuit but the circuit is not operating correctly. Sluggish wipers or dim headlights are examples of this. A voltage drop test will help to pinpoint a corroded ground strap or a faulty switch. Normally, there should be less than 1 volt drop across most wires or closed switches. A voltage drop across a connector or short cable should not exceed 0.5 volts.

A voltage drop is caused by higher than normal resistance in a circuit. This additional resistance actually decreases or stops the flow of current. Some common sources of voltage drops are faulty wires or switches, dirty or corroded connections or contacts, and loose or corroded ground wires and ground connections.

A voltage drop can be checked only when current is flowing through the circuit, such as by operating the starter motor or turning on the headlights. Making a voltage drop test requires measuring the voltage in the circuit and comparing it to what the voltage should be. Since these measurements are usually small, a digital voltmeter should be used to ensure accurate readings. If a voltage drop is suspected, turn the circuit on and measure the voltage at the circuit's load.

NOTE —

- *A voltage drop test is generally more accurate than a simple resistance check because the resistances involved are often too small to measure with most ohmmeters. For example, a resistance as small as 0.02 ohms would result in a 3 Volt drop in a typical 150 amp starter circuit (150 amps x 0.02 ohms = 3 volts).*
- *Keep in mind that voltage with the key on and voltage with the engine running are not the same. With the ignition on and the engine off (battery voltage), voltage should be approximately 12.6 volts. With the engine running (charging voltage), voltage should be approximately 14.0 volts. Measure voltage at the battery with the ignition on and then with the engine running to get exact measurements.*

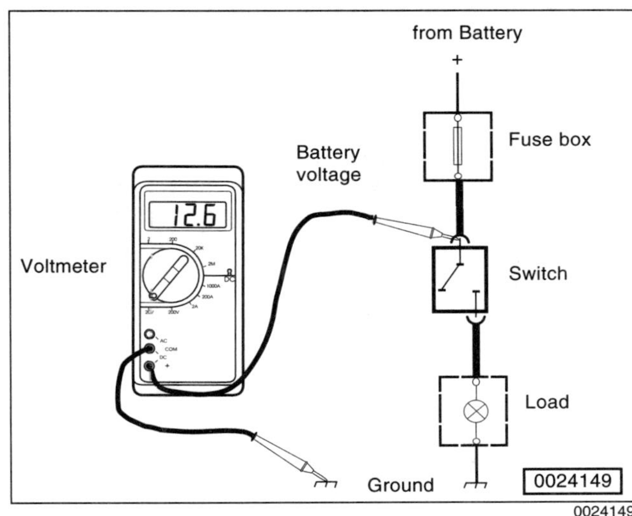

0024149

Fig. 1. Voltmeter being used to check for voltage.

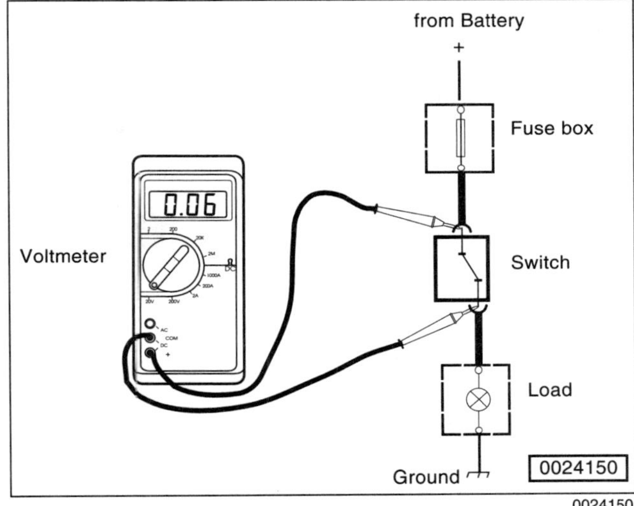

0024150

Fig. 2. Voltmeter being used to check for voltage drop across switch.

Voltage, measuring

1. Set voltage meter to 20V DC scale and connect negative lead to a reliable ground point on car.
2. Connect voltmeter positive lead to the point in the circuit you wish to measure. See Fig. 1.
3. If a reading is obtained, there is voltage at that point in the circuit. The voltage reading should not deviate more than 1 volt from voltage at battery. If the voltage is less than this, there is probably a fault in the circuit, such as a corroded connector or a loose ground wire.

Voltage drop, testing

1. Connect digital voltmeter positive lead to positive (+) connector of component to be tested.
2. Connect voltmeter negative lead to the negative (–) connector of component being tested. See Fig. 2.
3. With power on and circuit working, meter shows the voltage drop (difference between the two points). This value should not exceed 1 volt.

NOTE —

The maximum voltage drop in an automotive circuit, as recommended by the Society of Automotive Engineers (SAE), is as follows: 0 Volts for small wire connections; 0.1 Volts for high current connections; 0.2 Volts for high current cables; and 0.3 Volts for switch or solenoid contacts. On longer wires or cables, the drop may be slightly higher. In any case, a voltage drop of more than 1.0 Volt usually indicates a problem.

Continuity, checking

The continuity test can be used to check the basic integrity of a circuit or switch. Because most automotive circuits are designed to have little or no resistance, a circuit or part of a circuit can be easily checked for faults using an ohmmeter. An open circuit or a circuit with high resistance will not allow current to flow. A circuit with little or no resistance allows current to flow easily.

> ***CAUTION —***
> *Do not use an analog (swing-needle) ohmmeter to check circuit resistance or continuity on any electronic (solid-state) components. The internal power source used in most analog meters can damage solid state components. Use only a high quality digital ohmmeter having high input impedance when checking electronic components.*

When checking continuity, the ignition should be off. On circuits that are powered at all times, the battery should be disconnected. Using the appropriate wiring diagram, a circuit can be easily tested for faulty connections, wires, switches, relays, and engine sensors by checking for continuity. Fig. 3 shows a continuity test being made on a brake light switch.

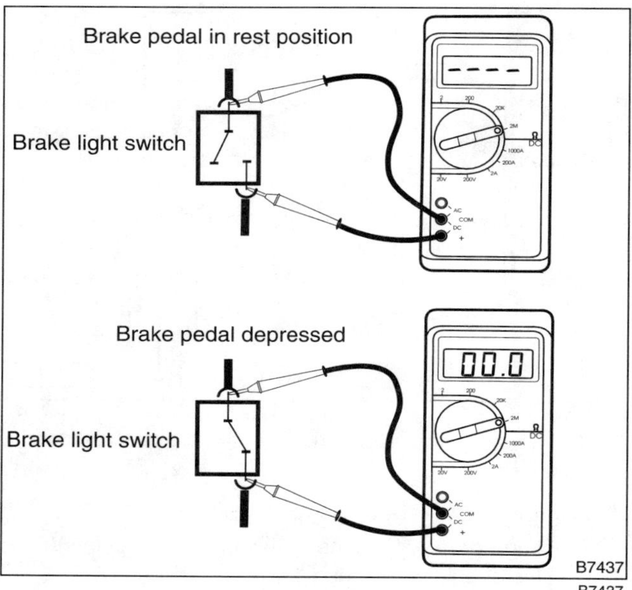

B7437

Fig. 3. Brake light switch being tested for continuity (battery disconnected). With brake pedal in rest position (switch open) there is no continuity (infinite ohms). With the pedal depressed (switch closed) there is continuity (zero ohms).

Short circuits, checking

A short circuit is exactly what the name implies. The circuit takes a shorter path than it was designed to take. The most common short that causes problems is a short to ground where the insulation on a positive (+) wire wears away and the metal wire is exposed. When the wire rubs against a metal part of the car or other ground source, the circuit is shorted to ground. If the exposed wire is live (positive battery voltage), the direct current flow to ground will blow a fuse or damage an unfused circuit.

> ***CAUTION —***
> - *On circuits protected with large fuses (25 amp and greater), the wires or circuit components may be damaged before the fuse blows. Always check for damage before replacing fuses of this rating.*
> - *When replacing blown fuses, use only fuses having the correct rating. Always confirm the correct fuse rating printed on the fuse panel cover.*

Short circuit test with voltmeter

1. Remove blown fuse from circuit.
2. Disconnect harness connector from circuit load or consumer.
3. Using a voltmeter, connect test leads across fuse terminals. See Fig. 4. Make sure power is present in circuit. If necessary, turn key on.

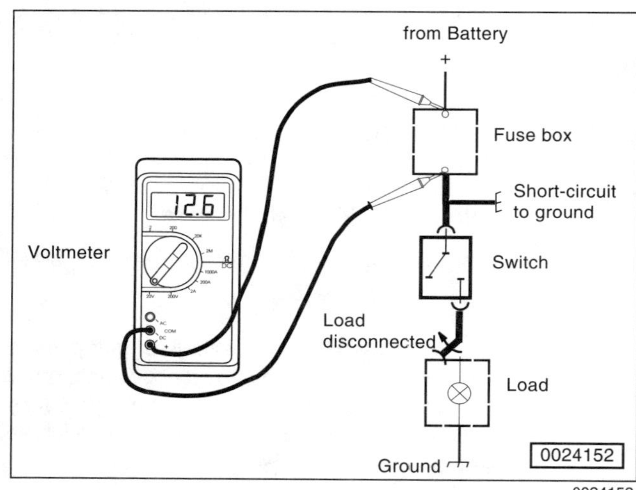

0024152

Fig. 4. Voltmeter being used to find short circuit.

4. If voltage is indicated at voltmeter, there is a short to ground somewhere in the circuit.
5. If voltage is not indicated, work from wire harness nearest to fuse panel and move or wiggle wires while observing meter. Continue to move down harness until meter displays a reading. This is the location of the short to ground.
6. Inspect wire harness at this point for any faults. If no faults are visible, carefully slice open harness cover or wire insulation for further inspection. Repair any faults found.

90 Instruments

GENERAL

The instrument cluster contains an electronic speedometer and tachometer with an LCD digital odometer/trip odometer and clock display. Vehicles with automatic transmission also have a gear selector display. Some vehicles also have an optional multi-function indicator (MFI) incorporated into the clock display window which will indicate outside temperature, momentary fuel consumption, average fuel consumption, distance driven, average driving speed and time driven.

The speedometer receives an electronic signal from a Hall sender on the transmission. Mileage is permanently held in memory and will be retained if power to the instrument cluster is interrupted.

Individual components for the instrument cluster are not available from Volkswagen and therefore disassembly of the cluster is not recommended. The illumination for the instrument cluster is provided by several blue light emitting diodes (LEDs) that are not serviceable. Remanufactured instrument cluster assemblies are available through the Volkswagen parts department.

> ***NOTE —***
> *Some versions of the instrument cluster may use a miniature light bulb to provide illumination for certain displays. These bulbs are replaceable separately.*

> ***CAUTION —***
> *Disconnecting the negative (–) battery cable may erase fault codes and basic settings in the engine management and automatic transmission control modules. Some driveability problems may be noticed until the system re-adapts to operating conditions. OBD II readiness codes, which may be required for emissions testing, may also be erased. Convenience electronics (alarm system, interior light control, power locks, mirrors, and windows) may need to be re-set using a VAG 1551/1552 or equivalent scan tool.*

INSTRUMENT CLUSTER

If the instrument cluster is to be replaced it will be necessary to use a VAG 1551/1552 or 5051 scan tool, or equivalent. The scan tool is used to code the instrument cluster and diagnostic interface for the data bus as well as adapting the odometer display, service interval data, vehicle immobilizer (if equipped) and reactivate the radio anti-theft system (if equipped). If you do not have a proper scan tool and/or experience then it is recommended that the vehicle be taken to an authorized Volkswagen dealer or properly equipped independent repair shop for instrument cluster replacement.

Malfunction recognition and display

The instrument cluster has On-Board Diagnostic (OBD) capability, which is an aid to troubleshooting.

If the instrument cluster control module detects a malfunction with the odometer or speedometer that is non-repairable, then "dEF" will appear in the trip recorder display. Replacement of the instrument cluster will be necessary.

If the instrument cluster control module detects a malfunction and nothing is displayed on the trip recorder display, carry out the following work before removing the instrument cluster:

1. Check DTC memory with VAG1551/1552 or equivalent scan tool .
2. Read service interval display values and odometer reading with VAG1551/1552 or equivalent scan tool and note the values.

If the malfunction indicates that the instrument cluster requires replacement, the recorded values can be entered in the new instrument cluster.

Instrument cluster, removing and installing

> ***WARNING —***
> - *Special safety precautions apply to vehicles equipped with airbags.*
> - *Refer to airbag **CAUTIONS** and **WARNINGS** in* **69 Seatbelts, Airbags**.

> ***CAUTION —***
> - *Disconnect battery ground (GND) strap from battery negative (–) terminal.*
> - *Be sure to have the anti-theft radio code on hand before disconnecting the battery.*
> - *Disconnecting the negative (–) battery cable may erase fault codes and basic settings in the engine management and automatic transmission control modules. Some driveability problems may be noticed until the system re-adapts to operating conditions. OBD II readiness codes, which may be required for emissions testing, may also be erased. Convenience electronics (alarm system, interior light control, power locks, mirrors, and windows) may need to be re-set using a VAG 1551/1552 or equivalent scan tool.*
> - *See* **Malfunction recognition and display** *given earlier before removing instrument cluster.*

NOTE —
- *If replacing the instrument cluster, be sure to note the mileage indicated in the old cluster before removal.*
- *For ease of illustration the steering wheel is not shown in the following illustrations. It is not necessary to remove the steering wheel to remove the instrument cluster.*

1. Release steering wheel position lock, pull steering wheel out completely and lock again in lowest position.
2. Pull trim piece above steering column out from instrument panel. See Fig. 1.
3. Remove instrument cluster mounting screws. See Fig. 2.
4. Tilt instrument cluster slightly toward passenger compartment.
5. Disconnect harness connectors at rear of instrument cluster.
6. Remove instrument cluster.
7. Installation is reverse of removal. After completing installation check function of instrument cluster.

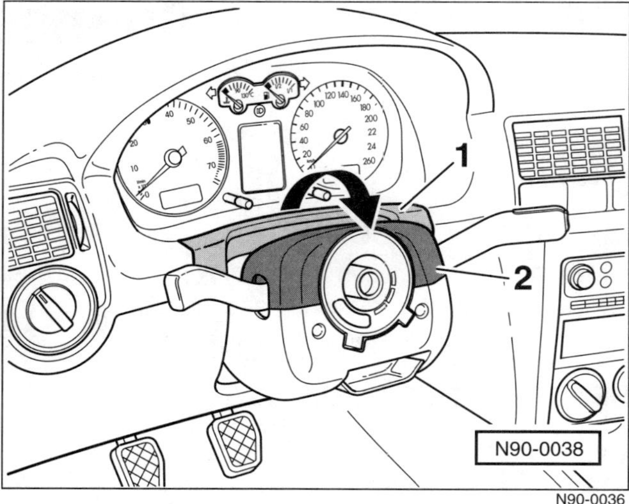

Fig. 1. Pull trim piece (**1**) out from instrument cluster and place on steering column switch upper cover (**2**).

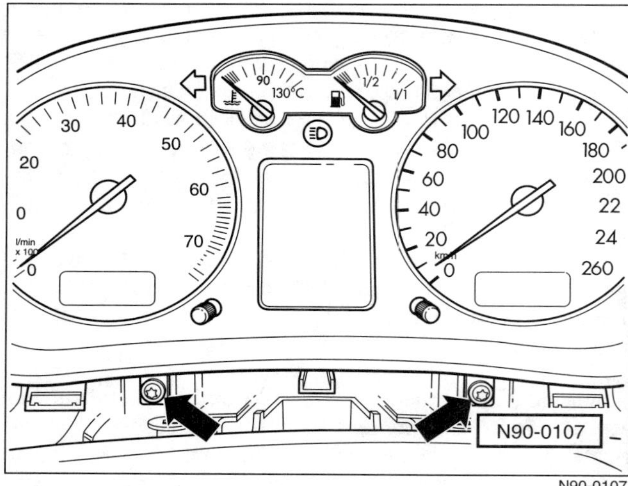

Fig. 2. Remove instrument cluster mounting screws (**arrows**).

NOTE —
- *Due to the large number of instrument cluster variations it always advisable to order a replacement cluster using the part number on the back of the cluster.*
- *Replacement clusters can have the odometer mileage adjusted to match the mileage of the original cluster. Because of the specialized nature of these repairs, servicing should be referred to an authorized Volkswagen dealer or qualified independent repair shop.*
- *If the instrument cluster has been replaced because it was faulty, and a functional check does not display a malfunction the instrument cluster will need to be coded with VAG 1551/1552 scan tool or equivalent, see* **Table a**.

Table a. Instrument cluster coding values

Digit position					Equipment variation
1	2	3	4	5	
0	1				Brake pad wear indicator
0	2				Seat belt warning
0	4				Windshield washer fluid warning
1	6				Navigation system
		1			Europe (EU)[1]
		2			USA market (US)
		3			Canada market (CDN)
		4			Great Britain (GB)[1]
		5			Japan (JP)[1]
		6			Saudi Arabia (SA)[1]
		7			Australia (AUS)[1]
			0		Vehicles with fixed service intervals without oil level thermal sensor (G266), PR-Nr.: QG0[1] (from 05.00 production)
			1		Vehicles with flexible service intervals (WIV) with oil level thermal sensor (G266), PR-Nr.: QG1[1] (from 05.00 production)
			2		Vehicles with fixed service intervals with oil level thermal sensor (G266), PR-Nr.: QG2[1] (from 05.00 production)
			3		Vehicles without service interval display (USA/Canada, from 05.00 production)
			4		4-cylinder (05.99 to 04.00 production)
			5		5-cylinder (05.99 to 04.00 production)[1]
			6		6-cylinder (05.99 to 04.00 production)
					Code number for number of impulses from vehicle speed sensor to read 1 mile:
				1	4345 (1.4L with manual transmission)[1]
				2	3528 (all other engine/trans. combinations)
				3	4134 (1.6L, 1.9L SDI with manual trans.)[1]
				4	3648 (1.9 L TDI with 02M manual transmission) (all engines with 5-speed automatic transmission, 6-speed manual, or all wheel drive)[1]

1) Not currently applicable to North American market vehicles

NOTE —
If more than one code for optional equipment is to be entered in digit postion 1 and 2, then code numbers must be added together. i.e. Brake pad wear indicator and washer fluid warning would be 01 + 04 = 05.

Multi-pin connector terminal assignment

NOTE —
- *The instrument cluster must not be disassembled.*
- *For troubleshooting specific systems and circuits see* **Wiring Diagrams, Fuses and Relays**.

The back of the instrument cluster has a blue and a green 32-pin connector, see Fig. 3. **Table b** and **Table c** identify the various terminals for these connectors.

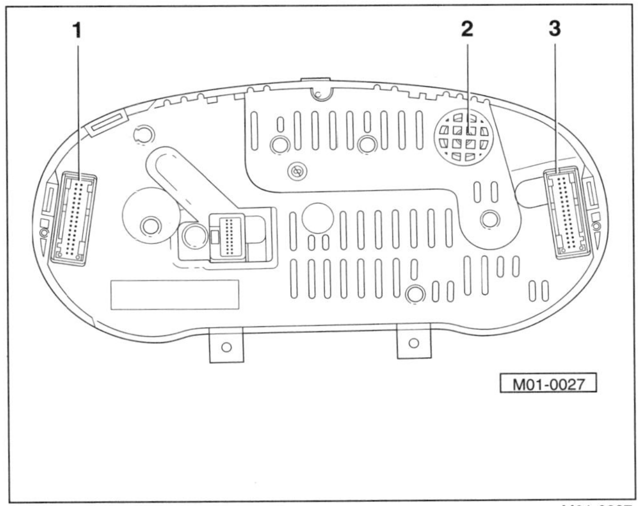

M01-0027

Fig. 3. Green (**1**) and blue (**3**) 32-pin connectors on back of instrument cluster. Warning buzzer is shown at **2**.

Table b. Instrument cluster 32-pin connector (green) terminal identification

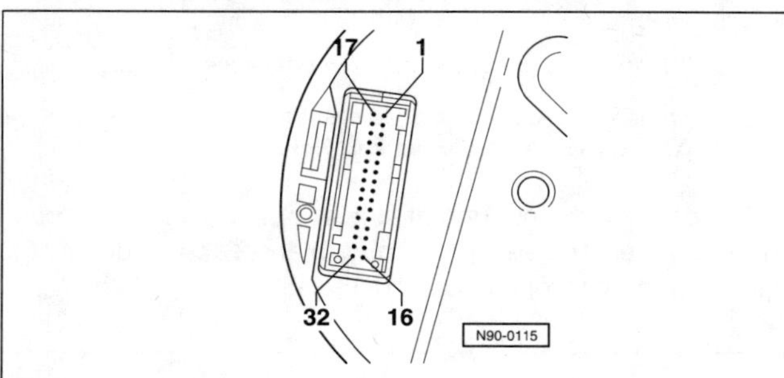

Terminal	Circuit
1	Open
2	Reading coil for immobilizer 1 (where applicable)
3	Warning lamp for side lights
4	Data bus (CAN), screening for input signals
5	W-wire
6	Low level washer fluid
7	Brake pad wear
8	External buzzer Open from 05.99 production
9	External gong Open from 05.99 production
10	Fuel reserve warning Open from 05.99 production
11	Signal for vehicle stationary
12	Air conditioning system cut-off
13	Parking brake indicator light (K14)
14	Warning light for traction control/vehicle stability
15	Malfunction light for electric accelerator mechanism, Open from 05.99 production

Table b. Instrument cluster 32-pin connector (green) terminal identification

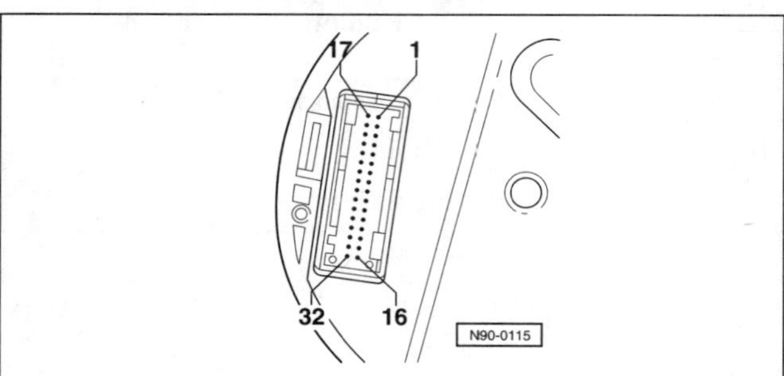

Terminal	Circuit
16	Immobilizer relay output Open from 05.99 production
17	Reading coil for immobilizer 2 (where applicable)
18	Oil temperature and oil level warning signals
19	Data bus (CAN), high input signal
20	Data bus (CAN), low input signal
21	Oil temp. warning signal (cars w/out oil level warning), Open from 05.99 production
22	Open Input signal from hood switch from 05.99 prod.
23	MFI call up button - top (display switches down)
24	MFI call up button - bottom (display switches up)
25	MFI memory switch - reset
26	Ambient temperature sensor
27	Data bus (CAN), high output signal
28	Data bus (CAN), low output signal
29	Data bus (CAN) screening for output signals, Open from 05.99 production
30	Output signal 2 from electronic speedometer, Open from 05.99 production
31	Selector lever display, Open from 05.99 production
32	Fuel consumption signal, Open from 05.99 production

Table c. Instrument cluster 32-pin connector (blue) terminal identification

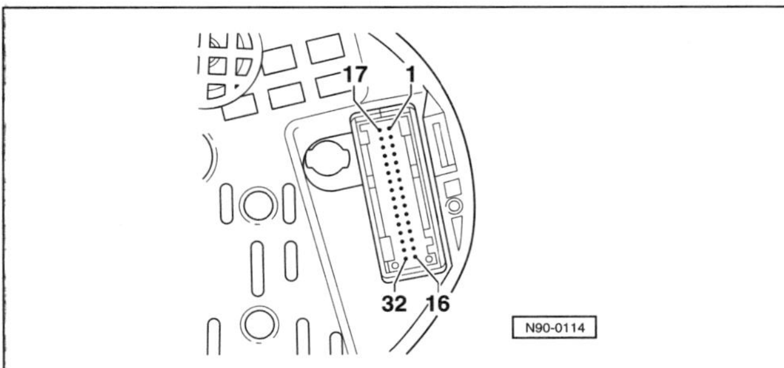

Table c. Instrument cluster 32-pin connector (blue) terminal identification

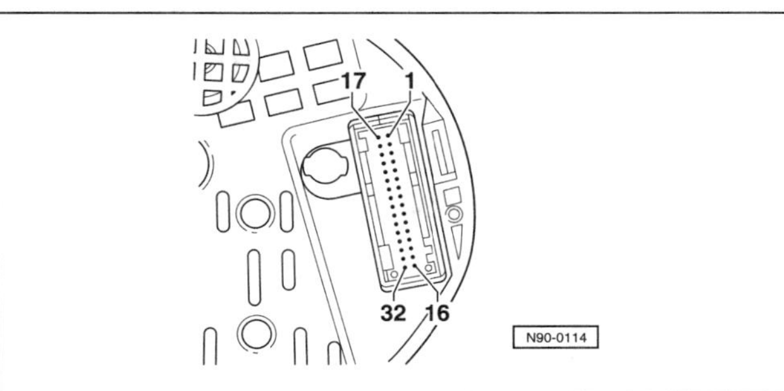

Terminal	Circuit
1	Terminal 15, positive
2	Right turn signal indicator light (K94)
3	Output signal 1 from electronic speedometer
4	Warning lamp for trailer towing
5	Fuel gauge (G1)
6	Airbag
7	Terminal 31, sender Ground (GND)
8	Engine coolant temperature gauge (G3)
9	Terminal 31, Ground (GND)
10	Oil pressure switch (F1)
11	RPM signal Open from 05.99 production
12	Generator warning light (K2), terminal 61
13	Glow plug indicator light (K29) (Diesel only) Control light for rear seat backrest lock from 05.99 production (only certain countries)
14	Rear fog light indicator light (K13)
15	Open
16	Warning light for rear lid open (only certain countries)
17	Headlight high beam indicator light (K1), terminal 56a
18	Left turn signal indicator light (K65)
19	ABS warning light (K47)
20	Instrument cluster illumination, terminal 58b
21	Signal for open driver's door
22	Engine Coolant Level (ECL) sensor (G32)
23	Terminal 30, (B+)
24	Terminal 31, Ground (GND)
25	On-Board Diagnostic (K-wire)
26	Parking light right, signal for “lights on” warning buzzer
27	Parking light left, signal for “lights on” warning buzzer
28	Speedometer Vehicle Speed Sensor (VSS) (G22)
29	Warning light for brake system
30	S-contact
31	Seat belt warning system
32	Emission warning lamp (only certain countries) Open from 05.99 production

SERVICE INTERVAL DISPLAY

The service interval display (if equipped) is visible in the display window at the bottom of the speedometer. Based on information obtained from a time recorder and two distance recorders this system will let the driver know if regular service is required. The flashing display will show distance travelled and **service OIL** or **service INSP** in the display window.

Service interval display
- **service OIL** . . change engine oil, see **0 Maintenance**
- **service INSP** . . . . inspection service every 12 months or every 30,000 km (20,000 miles), see **0 Maintenance**

After service has been carried out, each service affected must be called-up individually and reset. This can be done using the VAG scan tool 1551/1552 or by using the procedure below.

Service interval display, resetting

1. Switch off ignition.

2. Press and hold button at bottom left of speedometer. See Fig. 4.

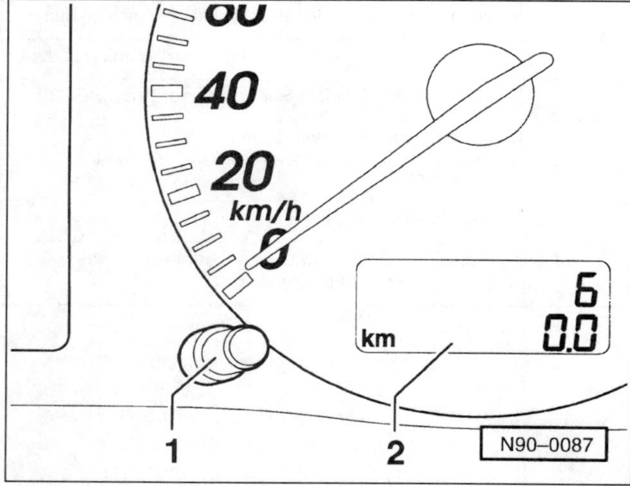

N90-0087

Fig. 4. Switch off ignition, press and hold button (**1**), switch ignition on and release button. Service interval display is shown at **2**.

3. Switch ignition on and release button.

4. The text "**service OIL**" will appear in the display window. On 2000 m.y. cars, the message "SERVICE NOW" will appear in the instrument clusters with center display.
   - To reset oil service display continue with next step.
   - To change display to "**service INSP**" press the button shown in Fig. 4. again.

5. To reset either function (**service OIL or service INSP**) turn adjusting knob at lower right side of tachometer to the right. See Fig. 5.

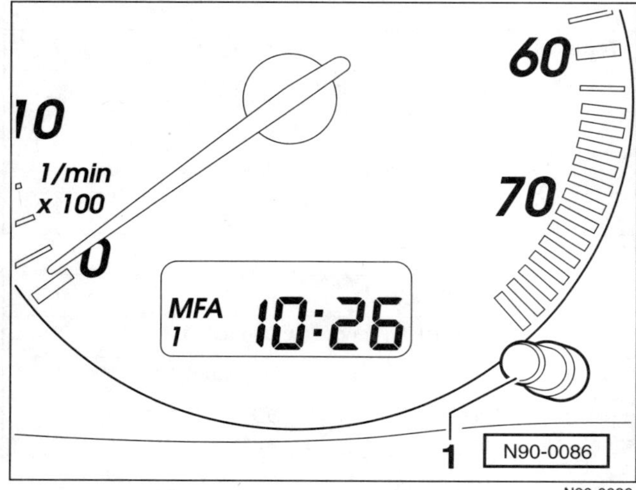

N90-0086

Fig. 5. Turn adjusting knob (**1**) next to tachometer to the right.

6. The service display shown in the display window is now reset and "service _ _ _" will appear in display window.

7. Switch off ignition. Service display is now reset until next scheduled service interval is reached.

91 Radio

TABLES

GENERAL

This section covers the Volkswagen factory installed stereo radio sound systems. For specific circuit tracing, it is necessary to see **97 Wiring Diagrams, Fuses and Relays**.

> ***CAUTION —***
> *Disconnecting the negative (–) battery cable may erase fault codes and basic settings in the engine management and automatic transmission control modules. Some driveability problems may be noticed until the system re-adapts to operating conditions. OBD II readiness codes, which may be required for emissions testing, may also be erased. Convenience electronics (alarm system, interior light control, power locks, mirrors, and windows) may need to be re-set using a VAG 1551/1552 or equivalent scan tool.*

> ***WARNING —***
> - *Be sure to have the anti-theft radio code on hand before disconnecting the battery.*
> - *Before working on any part of the electrical system, always disconnect the battery ground strap first.*

Radio reception

Radio stations send out electromagnetic signals from transmitting towers. When these signals move past an automobile, a small electrical impulse is induced in the antenna and sent to the radio for detection and amplification. The radio takes these small electrical impulses and converts them to a level sufficient to operate a speaker.

AM (amplitude modulation) radio signals travel in two ways; ground waves and sky waves. Ground waves travel through

> ***CAUTION —***
> - *The radio is wired to the vehicle alarm system. If the alarm system is armed, removing the radio will activate the alarm even if the proper tools are used. Do not attempt to remove the radio without disarming the alarm.*
> - *The factory installed connectors are designed for genuine Volkswagen radios. If installing a different radio, remember that the radio may not fit properly into the space provided, the electrical connections may not be compatible and different terminals may be needed.*
> - *Keep in mind that factory installed radios are electronically linked to the ignition, alarm and data link circuits.*

the air and follow the curve of the earth. Sky waves spread up into the sky until they reach the ionosphere where they are reflected back to earth. Depending on the power of the transmitting station, this reflection or “skip”, enables AM radio waves to travel great distances. FM (frequency modulation) radio waves are not reflected by the atmosphere and travel in what is known as “line of sight”. Therefore, FM broadcasts do not travel as far as AM broadcasts.

Radio reception will be affected by the height of the transmitting antenna, station power and conditions between radio stations and the vehicle radio. Radio signals are also affected by the weather, mountains, buildings, tunnels and other barriers. Best reception is when the vehicle antenna can “see” the station's transmitting antenna. That is, however, rarely the case. Normally, the signal picked up by the vehicle antenna has been reflected by many solid objects. This makes the transmission path longer or shorter and delays or weakens the signal.

Several impediments can prevent optimum radio reception in any vehicle and can include:

Fading

- Signal fading is typical on AM when driving through an underpass or near large buildings or objects. FM does not tend to fade as much as AM. In the same location where AM fades, FM may come in strong and clear because the shorter radio waves are reflected by metal objects such as buildings and bridges.

Flutter-fence effect

- In weak FM reception areas you may hear short pops of hissing background noise with otherwise good reception of the radio program. This "flutter" noise is like the sound burst that occurs when passing poles or posts close to the side of the road. This flutter effect may cause the stereo indicator to flicker because the signal has fallen below the minimum level to operate the stereo decoder. In even more remote areas such as in the desert or in hilly or mountain areas, it may not be possible to receive some AM or FM radio stations at all.

Multi-Path Cancellation

- Flutter and distortion is also caused by a mixing of several signals coming from different directions as a result of reflection from various objects. Mixing or cancellation effects often happen in cities even when close to the radio station transmitting towers and when transmitting towers are in close proximity to each other.

Interference

- Ignition or accessory interference, flutter, distortion and background noise can be caused by the ignition system or electrical accessories in the vehicle. In addition to internal sources, noise can also be caused by outside sources such as electrical power lines, other radio wave transmitters and other vehicles.

Interference suppression

The majority of the electrical consumers in the vehicle have radio suppression built in. All vehicles also include additional suppression measures in the following areas and components:

- Coolant fans (V7)
- Windshield wiper motor (V)
- Rear window wiper motor (V12), as applicable

NOTE —

Volkswagen identifies electrical components by a letter and/or a number in the electrical schematics. See **97 Wiring Diagrams, Fuses and Relays**. *These electrical identifiers are listed in parenthesis as an aid to electrical troubleshooting.*

RADIO SYSTEM

Radio system, description

The radio system consists of a radio head unit and cassette tape player with bass loudspeakers (woofers) in the front doors and rear side panels. Domed treble loudspeakers (tweeters) are installed in each front door exterior mirror triangular cover as well as the in the rear trim/door panels. The system also includes an amplified roof mounted antenna.

A 6-Disc CD changer is available as optional equipment, and (if equipped) is located in left side of the luggage compartment behind the rear seat. All vehicles are pre-wired from the factory for this unit only. In addition, some vehicles may be equipped with an in-dash single CD-player.

Some vehicles are equipped with an optional Premium/Monsoon radio system. The radio head unit is very similar to the standard Sound System unit and all service procedures in this section apply to all factory installed components of either type of system. The differences of the Premium/Monsoon head unit are shown in Fig. 1.

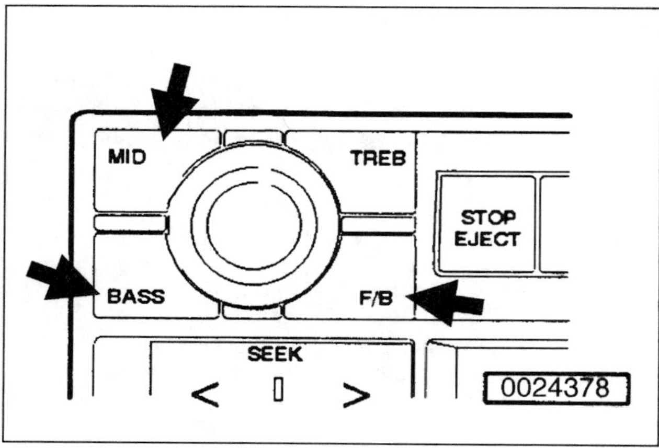

0024378

Fig. 1. Factory installed Premium/Monsoon radio head unit has different control buttons (**arrows**) as shown above.

Volkswagen radios are capable of communicating with scan tool VAG 1551/1552 through the Data Link Connector (DLC). Radios can store Diagnostic Trouble Codes, (DTCs), and must be coded via the scan tool in order to function properly. The correct code varies depending on the type of vehicle, the type of antenna and the CD changer, if applicable.

NOTE —

- *Radio malfunctions and equipment changes requiring the use of scan tool VAG 1551/1552 should be handled by an authorized Volkswagen dealer or other qualified repair facility.*
- *Only factory approved accessory radios and radio equipment (available from Volkswagen of America, Inc.) should be installed. This ensures proper installation and minimizes risk of damaging vehicle electrical system and On-Board Diagnostic functions.*

Radio head unit, removing and installing

> ***CAUTION —***
> *Observe all cautions and warnings in* **9 Electrical System** *before starting repairs involving the electrical system.*

1. Slide Volkswagen radio release tools 3316 into radio release slots until they engage the release mechanism. See Fig. 2.

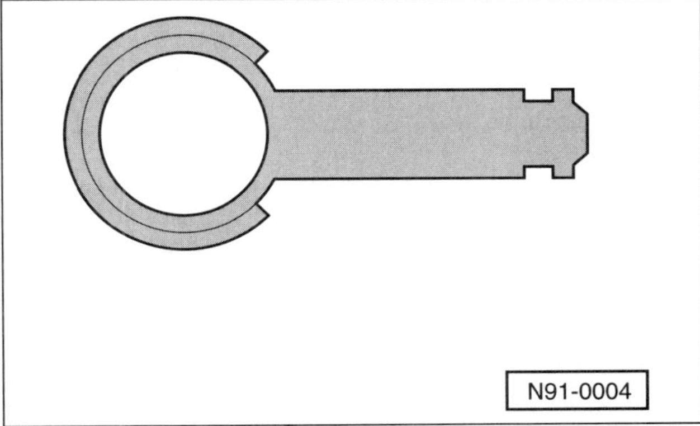

N91-0004

Fig. 2. The radio release tool 3316 consists of two identical parts used to remove the factory radio unit.

2. Pull radio out of instrument panel using grip rings of release tools. See Fig. 3.

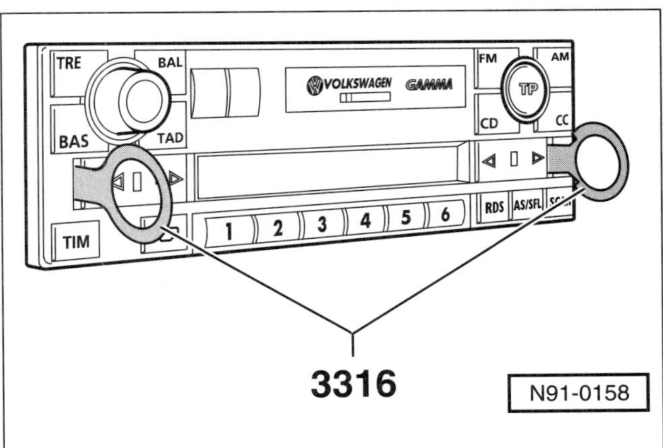

N91-0158

Fig. 3. Radio release tools shown in proper position to remove radio.

> ***NOTE —***
> - *The radio release tool 3316 must not be pushed to the side or tilted. Pull straight out.*
> - *Remove release tools before reinstalling radio head unit.*
> - *To remove the release tools from the radio the locating lugs on the side of the radio must be pressed inward.*

3. Remove antenna connector and harness connectors on back of radio head unit.

4. To install radio head unit, remove release tools.

5. Connect harness and antenna connectors to radio head unit.

6. Carefully slide radio head unit straight into instrument panel until it engages properly in assembly frame.

7. If new (or exchange) radio head unit has been installed, be sure to leave new radio code card in vehicle.

Speakers, removing and installing

1. To remove domed treble speaker in front door, remove door trim panel first, see **70 Trim–Interior**.

2. Disconnect harness connector for speaker and remove mounting screw.

3. Carefully slide triangular mirror cover upwards and remove speaker. See Fig. 4.

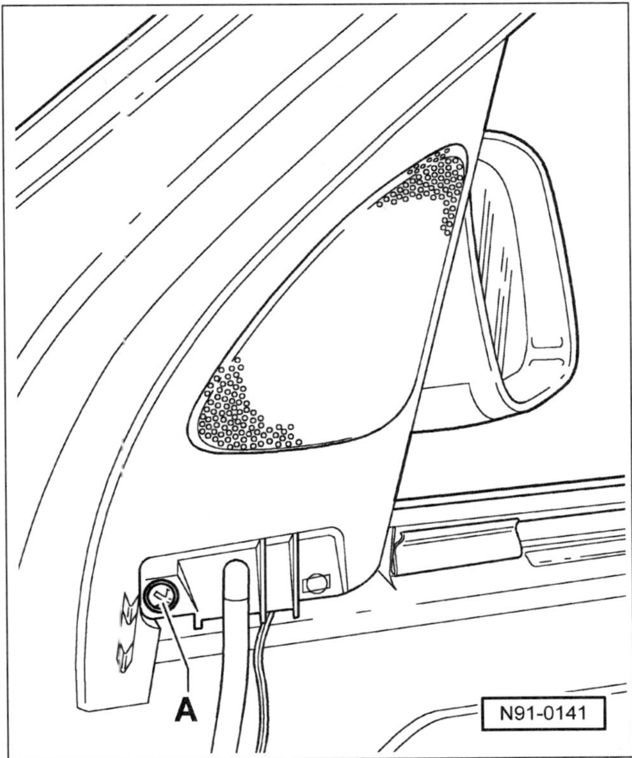

N91-0141

Fig. 4. Remove mounting screw (**A**) and slide trim piece upward

4. Install domed treble front door speaker in reverse order of removal.

5. The rear treble (tweeter) speakers are integrated into the rear trim panel, or rear door panel on 4-door models. The panel must be removed first to remove the rear tweeter, see **70 Trim–Interior**.

6. The rear bass speakers (woofers) are also attached to the rear trim/door panel which must first be removed, see **70 Trim–Interior**.

7. Disconnect harness connector from rear door speaker.

8. Carefully drill out rivets that hold speaker to trim panel. See Fig. 5.

NOTE —

- *To prevent corrosion, make sure that all metal particles from drilling are removed from inside the door.*
- *If the paint on door frame is damaged during drilling, touch-up immediately.*

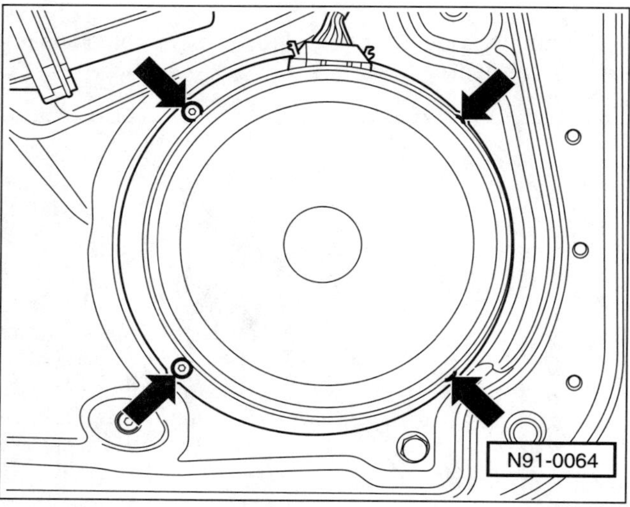

N91-0064

Fig. 5. Drill out rivets (**arrows**) to remove rear bass speaker.

9. Install rubber gasket between speaker and trim panel. Use new rivets of proper length and diameter to install speaker.

Radio anti-theft system, description

All factory installed and supplied radios are equipped with an electronic anti-theft system. The anti-theft system is activated and electronically de-activates (locks) the radio as soon as any of the following occur:

- Voltage supply (terminal 30) drops below a predetermined minimum voltage value.
- The radio unit is disconnected from voltage supply (terminal 30) such as when removing radio head unit or if the fuse blows.
- Vehicle battery has been disconnected.

A radio which is locked by the electronic anti-theft system has the word "SAFE" in the display window when the radio is switched on. After 3 seconds, the word "SAFE" will be replaced by the number "1000" indicating readiness to unlock.

In addition to electronic anti-theft locking, the radio is linked to the alarm system. The alarm horn will sound if the alarm has been set and the radio is removed.

Radio anti-theft system, unlocking

If the radio has been electronically locked as described above, it can be unlocked using the following procedure. The radio will only work if the correct code number for the anti-theft system is entered. The anti-theft code can be found along with the radio number on the radio card provided with the vehicle.

NOTE —

For security reasons, the radio card should not be left in the vehicle. Ask the customer for the code before starting repairs. Never leave the radio card in the car.

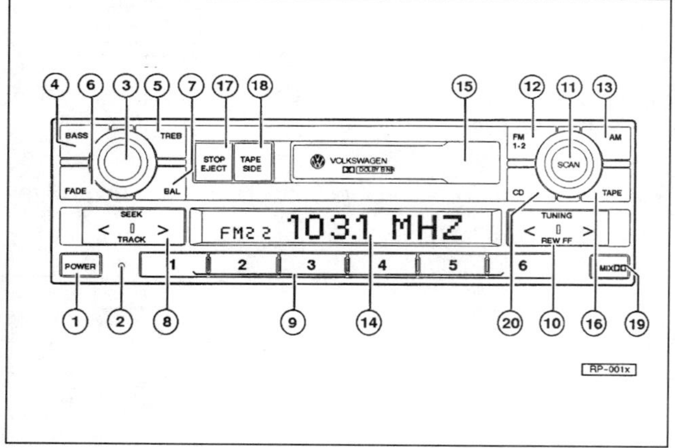

RP-001x

Fig. 6. Standard sound System radio head unit showing controls. Several circled numbers are referenced in text. Premium/Monsoon system is similar.

To unlock the radio anti-theft feature, perform the following steps:

1. Obtain correct anti-theft code number from radio card.

2. Switch radio on (**1**).

NOTE —

Numbers in parenthesis in procedure steps refer to Fig. 6.

3. "SAFE" will appear in the display window (**14**). After 3 seconds, the number "1000" will appear in the display window.

4. Use station preset buttons 1 to 4 (**9**) to enter 4 digit code number.
   - Press preset button 1 to enter first digit in code number, preset button 2 for second digit and so on.
   - To enter code number, press applicable button repeatedly until desired number appears on display.
   - The value range for each of the 4 digits is between 0 and 9.
   - If a button is pressed beyond desired number, sequence will start over at 0 after 9 is pressed.
5. When entire code is entered, press right side of "Seek" button (**8**) for about 2 seconds, until audible signal is heard.
   - If wrong code was accidentally entered, display window will show "SAFE"; flashing at first and then remaining on.
   - Coding procedure may be repeated a second time (the number of coding attempts will be shown on display window). If wrong code is entered again, radio will be disabled for an hour. If this happens, leave radio ON and key in ignition for one hour. After the hour has elapsed, you will have two more attempts to unlock system. Unsuccessful attempts will cause the cycle to be repeated.
   - The cycle is: 2 attempts, 1 hour locked.

Radio anti-theft system, first activation

On new radios the anti-theft coding is not active. The electronic anti-theft system only becomes active after entering the correct code number factory assigned to that particular unit. If the radio is disconnected from the voltage supply before the anti-theft system is activated, it will not electronically lock. Radio head units that have not had the anti-theft system activation done initially will not have the blinking LED (**2**) when the key is removed. Note the following points:

- Each radio is assigned a unique code.
- If the radio has been replaced, the new code must be used.
- The customer must be informed that the code number has changed.

Perform steps in the exact order given below. Numbers in parenthesis refer to Fig. 4.

1. Obtain correct anti-theft code number from radio card.
2. Switch radio on (**1**).
3. "SAFE" will appear in the display window (**14**). After 3 seconds, the number "1000" will appear in display window.
4. Use station preset buttons 1 to 4 (**9**) to enter 4 digit code number.
   - Press preset button 1 to enter first digit in the code number, preset button 2 for second digit and so on.
   - To enter code number, press applicable button repeatedly until desired number appears on display.
   - Value range for each of the 4 digits is between 0 and 9.
   - If a button is pressed beyond the desired number, sequence will start over at 0 after 9 is pressed.
5. When entire code is entered, press right side of "Seek" button (**8**) for about 2 seconds, until audible signal is heard.
   - If a wrong code was accidentally entered, display window will show "SAFE"; flashing at first and then remaining on.
   - Coding procedure may be repeated a second time (the number of coding attempts will be shown on the display window). If wrong code is entered again, radio will be disabled for an hour. If this happens, leave radio ON and key in the ignition for one hour. After the hour has elapsed, you will have two more attempts to unlock system. Unsuccessful attempts will cause cycle to be repeated.
   - The cycle is: 2 attempts, 1 hour locked.

Radio head unit, coding

The radio is controlled by a microprocessor which has extensive On-Board Diagnostic (OBD) capability. To take full advantage of the OBD capabilities, the head unit must be coded to match the equipment level of the vehicle. Failure to code the radio head upon the addition of a CD changer will prevent it from being included in the On-Board Diagnostics, however, it will operate properly. Conversely, failure to change the code after removing a CD changer will cause erroneous DTCs to be stored in the radio head unit memory. Access to the radio head unit is via the Data Link Connector (DLC). Because of the specialized nature of these repairs, coding should be referred to an authorized Volkswagen Dealer or qualified independent repair shop. See **Table a**.

Table a. Radio head unit codes

System	Radio head unit code
Car model (xx below)	01- Golf 02- Jetta
Without CD changer	xx401
With CD changer	xx403
i.e. Jetta with CD changer code = 02403	

Table b lists the terminal assignments for the multi-pin connector on the back of the radio.

Table b. Radio head unit terminal assignments

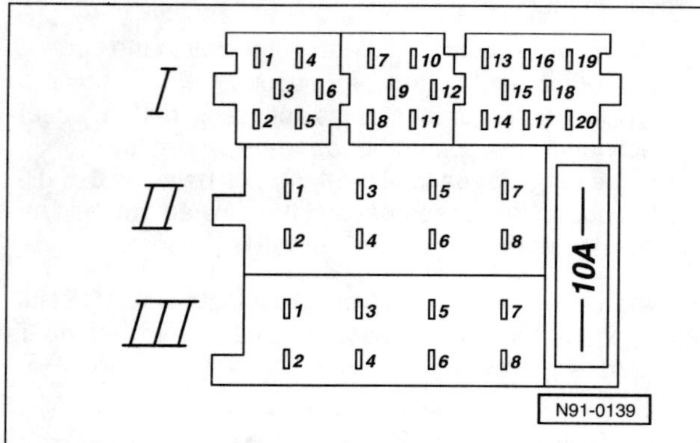

Terminal	Circuit
	Harness connector I, T20, part 1, yellow
1	Line out, L/R
2	Line out, R/R
3	Ground (GND)
4	Line out, L/F
5	Line out, R/F
6	Switched positive (B+ out) for sound amplifier
	Harness connector I, T20, part 2, green
7	Telephone input signal, TEL+
8	Second display, CLOCK
9	Second display, DATA
10	Second display, ENA
11	Remote control, REM
12	Telephone input signal, TEL-
	Harness connector I, T20, part 3, blue
13	CD changer - DATA IN
14	CD changer - DATA OUT
15	CD changer - CLOCK
16	CD changer - Positive (B+ in), terminal 30
17	CD changer - Control signal, turn-on
18	CD changer - Ground (GND) and shield
19	CD changer - Line out, left (CD/L)
20	CD changer - Line out, right (CD/R)

Table b. Radio head unit terminal assignments

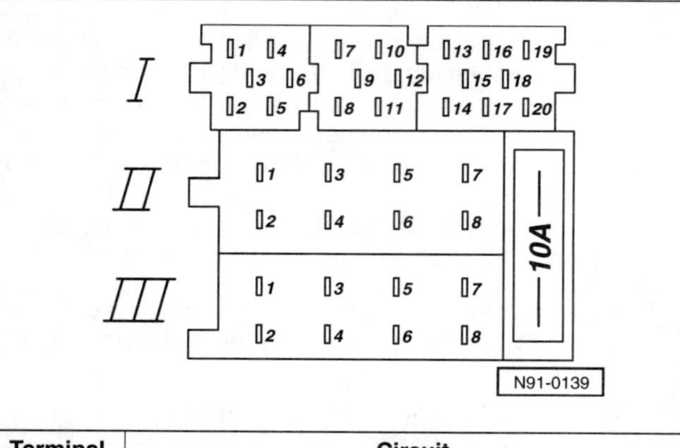

Terminal	Circuit
	Harness connector II, T8a, brown
1	R/R speaker +
2	R/R speaker -
3	R/F speaker +
4	R/F speaker -
5	L/F speaker +
6	L/F speaker -
7	L/R speaker +
8	L/R speaker -
	Harness connector III, T8, black
1	Gala (volume adaptation)
2	Telephone mute circuit
3	Data Link Connector (DLC), K wire
4	Ignition switch (SU contact)
5	Anti-theft system control signal, SAFE (terminal 30)
6	Illumination (terminal 58b)
7	Battery positive (B+) (terminal 30)
8	Battery ground, (GND) (terminal 31)

Amplified antenna, roof mounted

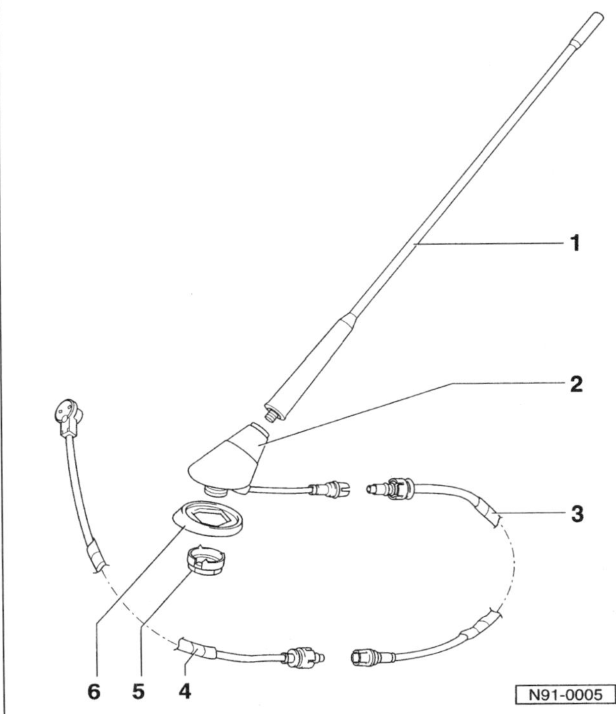

1. **Antenna mast**
2. **Antenna base**
   - With amplifier
   - Lower molded headliner at rear to access base
3. **Antenna cable**
   - From roof antenna to front of center console
   - Current to operate the amplifier is supplied from the radio head unit through the center coaxial conductor. No separate 12 volt power lead is used.
4. **Antenna cable**
   - From front of center console to radio head unit
5. **Nut with serrated washer**
   - Special M14 nut with attached serrated grounding washer
   - Serrated washer is attached to nut with plastic ring
   - Apply contact grease to inside of roof in area of the serrated washer to insure good electrical grounding
   - Tighten to: 7 Nm (62 in lb)
6. **Gasket**
   - Ensure correct positioning to provide water tight seal.

N91-0005

Fig. 7. Roof mounted amplified antenna shown with related components. Roof mounting provides optimal reception. Antenna shown for vehicles without optional telephone or navigational system (currently unavailable options).

> ***CAUTION—***
> *Observe all cautions and warnings in* **9 Electrical System** *before starting repairs involving the electrical system.*

CD PLAYER/CHANGER

With the increased popularity of compact discs (CDs), the addition of a dash mounted player or a trunk mounted changer is a common option. As a result of this popularity, all Volkswagens are factory wired for an optional 6 disc CD changer. Only genuine Volkswagen supplied changers are compatible with the radio head unit and the additional wiring. Installed location is in the left rear area of the luggage compartment just behind the rear seat.

CD player, removing and installing

> ***NOTE—***
> *Some vehicles are equipped with a single disc CD player in the dashboard. For vehicles with a multiple disc CD changer, see* **CD changer, removing and installing**, *given later.*

1. Remove radio head unit as described above.
2. Slide Volkswagen radio release tools 3316 into radio release slots until they engage the release mechanism.
3. Pull CD player out of the dashboard panel using the grip rings of the release tools. See Fig. 8.

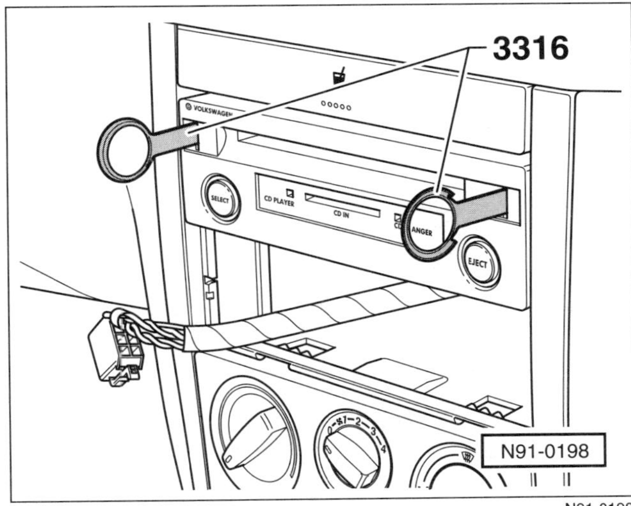

N91-0198

Fig. 8. Radio release tools shown in proper position to release single disc CD player.

4. Disconnect harness connectors from back of CD player and radio. Remove CD player.
5. To install CD player, remove release tools, connect harness connector and slide player into slot until it clicks into place.

CD player terminal assignment

The multi-pin connections on the back of the CD player are listed in **Table c**.

> ***NOTE —***
> *The multi-pin connector "A" shown below is identical to the multi-pin connection I, part 3, blue on "Premium IV and "Premium V" radios.*

Table c. CD changer terminal assignment

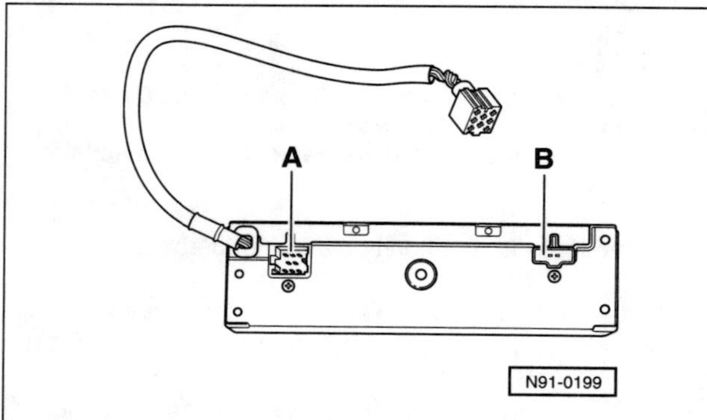

Terminal	Circuit
	Multi-pin connector "A"
13	CD changer - DATA IN
14	CD changer - DATA OUT
15	CD changer - CLOCK IN
16	CD changer - Positive (B+ in), terminal 30
17	CD changer - Control signal, turn-on
18	CD changer - Ground (GND) and shield
19	CD changer - Line out, left (CD/L)
20	CD changer - Line out, right (CD/R)
	Multi-pin connector "B"
1	CD changer ground (terminal 31)
2	Illumination for CD changer (terminal 58d)

CD changer, removing and installing

The factory supplied CD changer is located in the left side of the luggage compartment, behind a protective flap.

> ***NOTE —***
> - *Always confirm CD changer and radio compatibility with your Volkswagen parts department or aftermarket parts specialist.*
> - *The CD changer is installed horizontally in Golf/GTI models and vertically in Jetta models.*

> ***CAUTION —***
> *Observe all cautions and warnings in* **9 Electrical System** *before starting repairs involving the electrical system.*

1. Remove protective flap at left side of luggage compartment by turning retaining knobs counterclockwise. See Fig. 9.

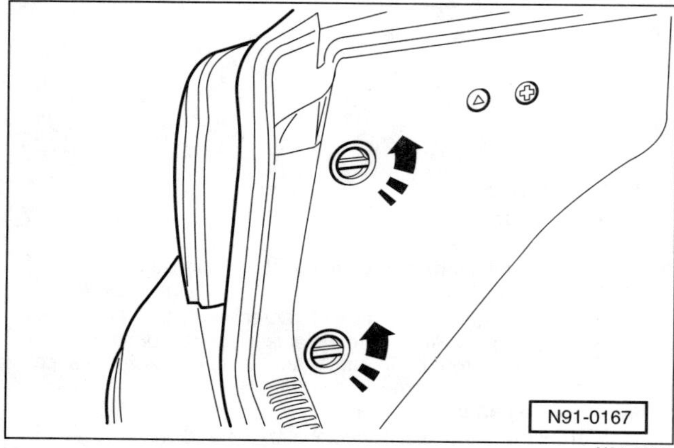

N91-0167

Fig. 9. Turn retaining knobs in direction of **arrows** and open flap.

2. Disconnect harness connector below CD changer and unclip from retaining bracket. See Fig. 10.

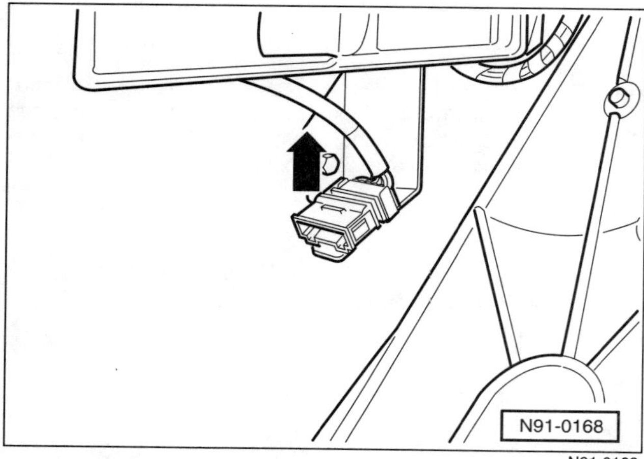

N91-0168

Fig. 10. Disconnect harness connector and unclip from retaining bracket in direction of **arrow**.

3. Remove securing bolts for CD changer and remove changer from mounting bracket. See Fig. 11.

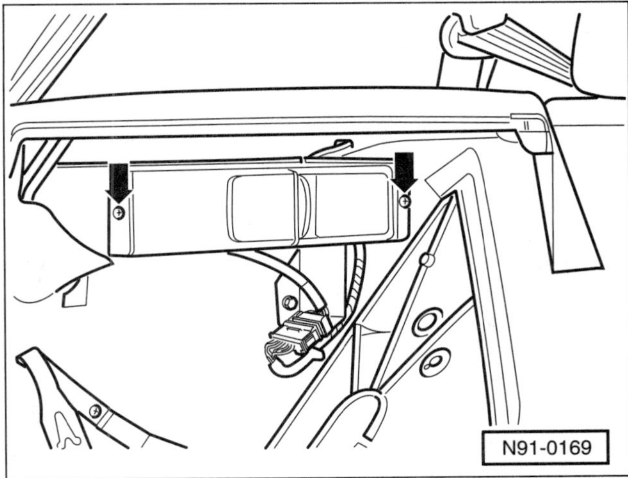

N91-0169

Fig. 11. Remove CD changer mounting bolts (**arrows**) and changer.

4. To remove CD changer mounting bracket, remove securing bolts and bracket. See Fig. 12.

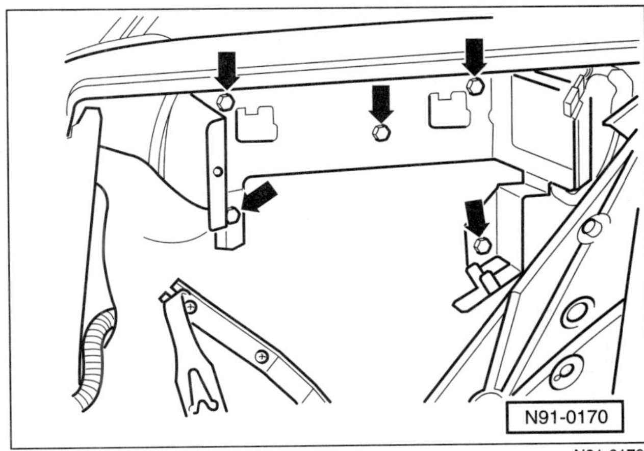

N91-0170

Fig. 12. Remove CD changer bracket mounting bolts (**arrows**).

Tightening torque
- CD changer bracket to body . . . . 5 Nm (44 in-lb)

---

5. Install components in reverse order of removal.

6. If installing new (first time) CD changer, code radio head unit for addition of CD changer with VAG 1551/1552 scan tool or equivalent.

MULTI-FUNCTION STEERING WHEEL

The multi-function steering wheel available as an option from May 2000 allows the various functions of the radio and cruise control system to be selected from the steering wheel. The system includes an operating unit in the steering wheel with two sets of buttons on the left and right sides of the wheel and a control module. Additionally on cars with diesel engines there is a balance weight installed in the multi-function steering wheel to prevent transmission of vibrations from the engine. For an overview of the components in this system see Fig. 13.

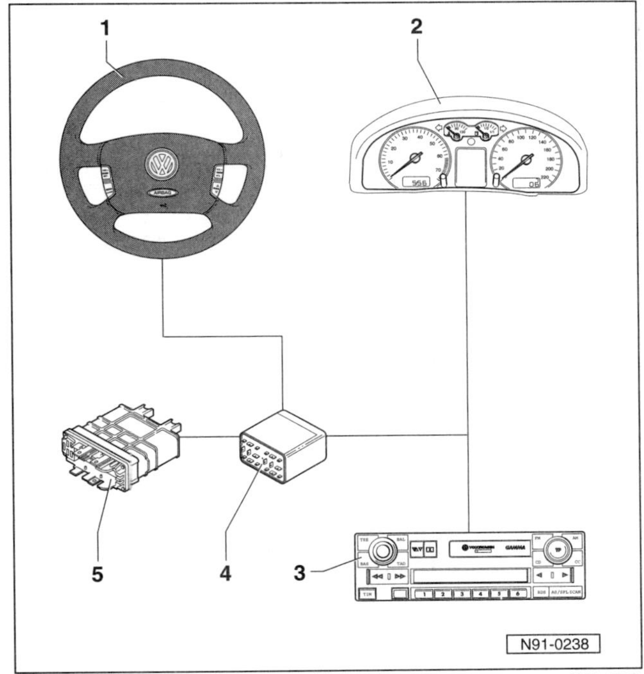

N91-0238

Fig. 13. Multi-function steering wheel and list of components.

1. **Multi-function steering wheel**
   - With integrated operating unit (E221)
2. **Instrument cluster**
   - Control module with display unit in instrument cluster (J285)
3. **Radio or radio/navigation system**
4. **Multi-function steering wheel control module (J453)**
   - Installed on relay carrier, see **97 Wiring Diagrams, Fuses and Relays**
   - Connector assignment, see **table d**
5. **Engine control module**

Table d. Multi-function steering wheel control module terminal assignment

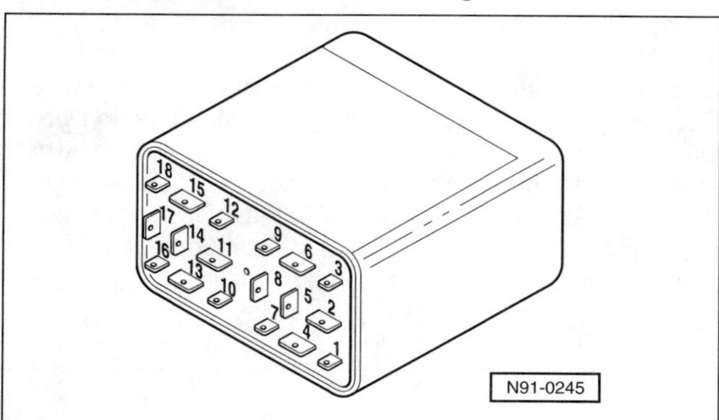

Terminal	Circuit
1	Comfort CAN low
2	Vacant
3	Comfort CAN high
4	Vacant
5	Radio, serial data
6	K-wire, diagnosis
7	CCS - resume, accelerating
8	CAN ground
9	Vacant
10	Ground (-) (terminal 31)
11	Double tone horn relay
12	Battery (+) with ignition on (terminal 15)
13	Battery (+) (terminal 30)
14	Vacant
15	Terminal 58d
16	CCS+ (SET/delay)
17	Heating inlet "ON"
18	CAN bus to operating unit in steering wheel

Multi-function steering wheel operating unit, removing and installing

1. Disconnect battery ground (GND) strap from battery negative (–) terminal. See the **Cautions** at the beginning of this repair group regarding battery disconnection.

2. Remove airbag from steering wheel, see **69 Seatbelts, Airbags**.

3. Remove mounting bolts for multi-function operating unit. See Fig. 14.

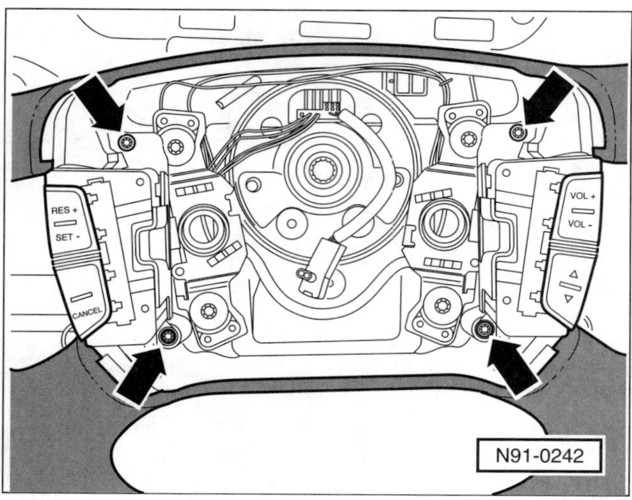

N91-0242

Fig. 14. Remove mounting bolts (**arrows**) for multi-function operating unit in steering wheel.

4. Disconnect harness connectors on operating unit and remove unit. See Fig. 15.

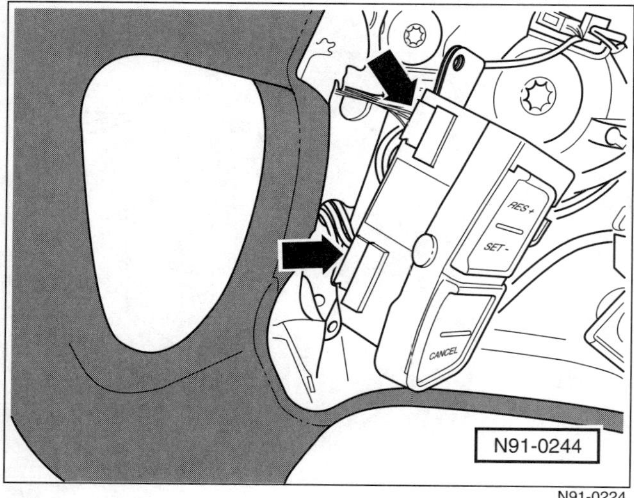

N91-0224

Fig. 15. Disconnect harness connectors (**arrows**) on operating unit and remove unit.

5. Install in reverse order of removal.

92 Wipers and Washers

GENERAL

The front windshield wipers are operated by the wiper switch on the steering column. There is a small lever on the top of the wiper switch which adjusts the interval when the wipers are in delay mode. Pulling the wiper switch back toward the passenger compartment operates the washer and the wipers automatically.

Some vehicles are equipped with heated washer nozzles which do not have a separate switch and are automatically activated (with ignition switched on) depending on outside temperature.

WIPERS AND WASHERS

CAUTION —
- *Worn or dirty wiper blades will reduce visibility, making driving hazardous. Clean blades regularly to remove road film and car wash wax build-up. Use an alcohol based cleaning solution and a lint free cloth to wipe along the rubber blade.*
- *Clean all inside and outside glass regularly. Use an alcohol based cleaning solution and wipe dry with a lint free cloth.*
- *Do not use the wiper/washer in freezing weather without first warming the windshield with the defroster. Otherwise the washer solution may freeze on the windshield and obscure your vision.*
- *To prevent scratching the glass avoid running the wiper blades over a dry windshield. A scratched windshield will reduce visibility and increase glare.*

Rubber wiper inserts, replacing

1. Free end of wiper insert from retaining hooks by squeezing metal strip in insert with pliers.
2. Slide rubber insert from retaining hooks.
3. Slide rubber insert into lower retaining hooks of wiper blade.

NOTE —
If necessary, transfer metal strips from old insert to new insert. Notches in metal strips must face rubber and engage rubber lugs in groove.

4. Squeeze metal strips at open end of rubber insert using pliers and install insert into hooks so that hook engages rubber retaining slot on insert. See Fig. 1.

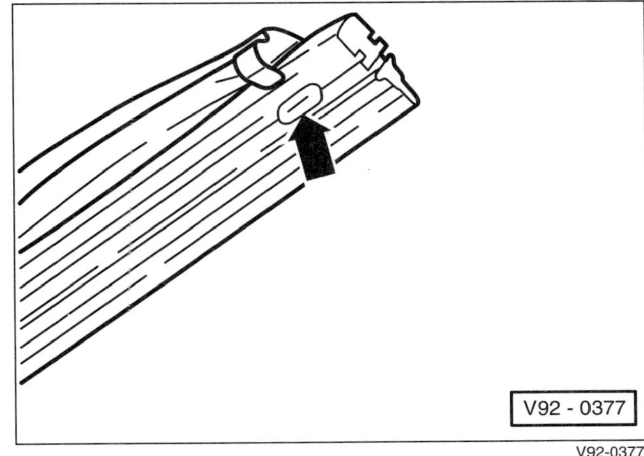

V92-0377

Fig. 1. Install rubber insert so that hook engages rubber retaining slot (**arrow**).

Wiper arm, front, removing and installing

1. Be sure wipers are set at park position.

2. Pry off protective cap and loosen wiper arm mounting nut, but do not remove completely. See Fig. 2.

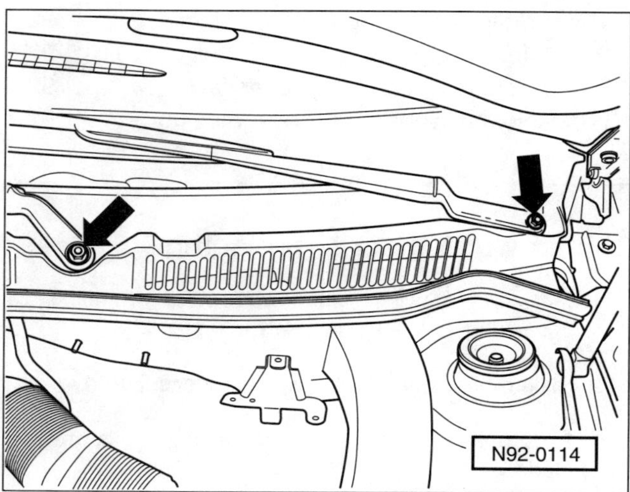

N92-0114

Fig. 2. Loosen wiper arm mounting nuts (**arrows**) but do not remove yet.

3. Move wiper arm slightly to release from tapered mounting shaft.

4. Remove mounting nut and take off wiper arm.

5. When installing wiper arm, be sure to carefully align end of arm onto tapered shaft before tightening mounting bolt.

6. Install driver's side wiper arm as shown in Fig. 3.

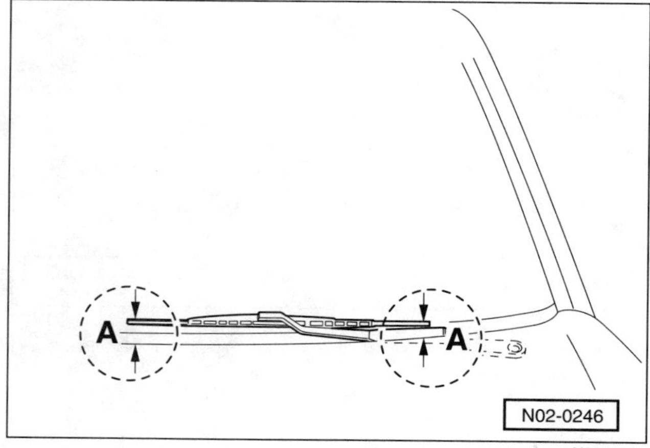

N02-0246

Fig. 3. Driver's side wiper arm position; dimension **A** = 25 ± 5mm measured at ends of wiper blades.

7. Install passenger side wiper arm as shown in Fig. 4.

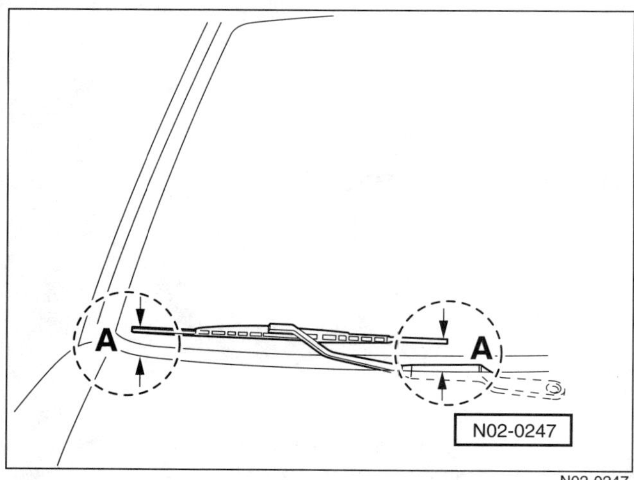

N02-0247

Fig. 4. Passenger side wiper arm position; dimension **A** = 25 ± 5mm measured at ends of wiper blades.

Tightening torque

• Wiper arm to shaft . . . . 20 Nm (15 ft-lb)

Wiper motor, removing and installing

1. Make sure the wiper arms are in park position. Only then can wiper arm end position be correctly set when reinstalling.

2. Disconnect battery ground (GND) strap from battery negative (–) terminal.

NOTE —
Be sure to have the anti-theft radio code on hand before disconnecting the battery.

CAUTION —
Disconnecting the negative (–) battery cable may erase fault codes and basic settings in the engine management and automatic transmission control modules. Some driveability problems may be noticed until the system re-adapts to operating conditions. OBD II readiness codes, which may be required for emissions testing, may also be erased. Convenience electronics (alarm system, interior light control, power locks, mirrors, and windows) may need to be re-set using a VAG 1551/1552 or equivalent scan tool.

3. Remove wiper arms as described above.

4. Pull up plenum panel rubber gasket and remove.

5. Remove dust and pollen filter cover.

6. Unclip trim on inner fender at both sides. See Fig. 5.

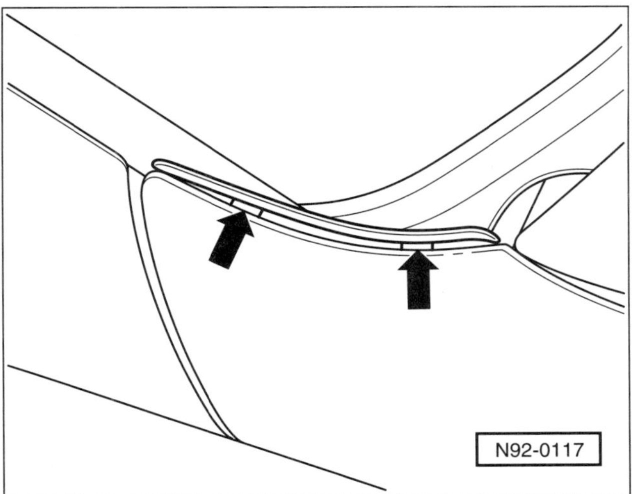

N92-0117

Fig. 5. Unclip inner fender trim at **arrows**.

7. Carefully pry cowl panel upward and off.

NOTE —
The cowl panel is attached to a window guide underneath the windshield.

8. Disconnect wiper motor harness connector and remove wiper motor assembly mounting nuts and washers. See Fig. 6.

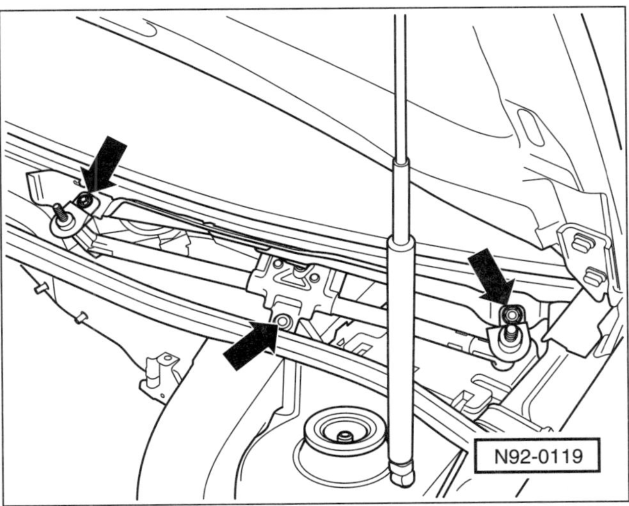

N92-0119

Fig. 6. Remove wiper motor assembly nuts and washers (**arrows**).

9. Remove complete wiper motor assembly from cowl.

10. Pry connecting rods off wiper motor crank using large screwdriver.

11. Remove M8 hex nut for crank arm from wiper motor drive shaft.

12. Unbolt wiper motor-to-frame mounting bolts. See Fig. 7.

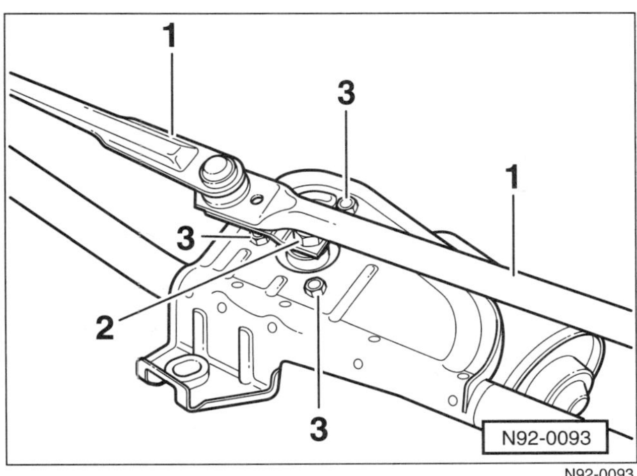

N92-0093

Fig. 7. Pry off connecting rods (**1**), remove nut for crank arm (**2**) and motor-to-frame mounting bolts (**3**).

13. Remove wiper motor from wiper frame.

14. Begin installation by connecting harness connector to wiper motor and operating wiper switch briefly to ensure that motor is in park position.

15. Disconnect harness connector again and install wiper motor-to-frame mounting bolts.

Tightening torque
- Wiper motor to frame . . . . 8 Nm (71 in-lb)

16. Install crank and align so that connecting rods are in line. See Fig. 8.

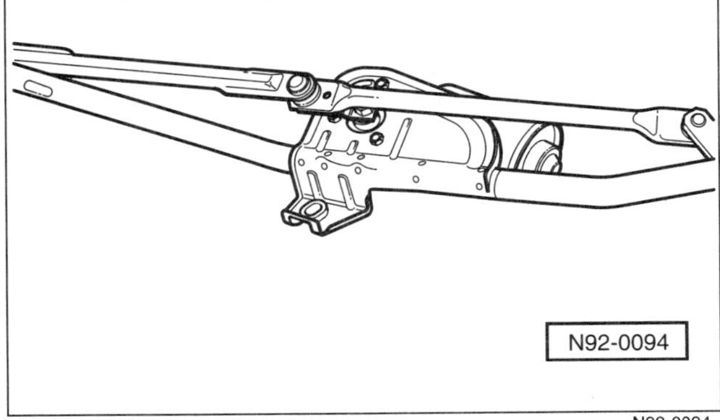

N92-0094

Fig. 8. Install wiper motor crank so that wiper arms line up as shown.

17. Tighten crank arm nut and press rods back onto crank.

Tightening torque

- Wiper motor crank arm nut . . . . 20 Nm (15 ft-lb)

18. Install wiper motor assembly into cowl and connect harness connector for motor.

19. Install wiper arms as described previously.

20. Install ends of cowl panel under rubber strip at bottom of A-pillar. See Fig. 9.

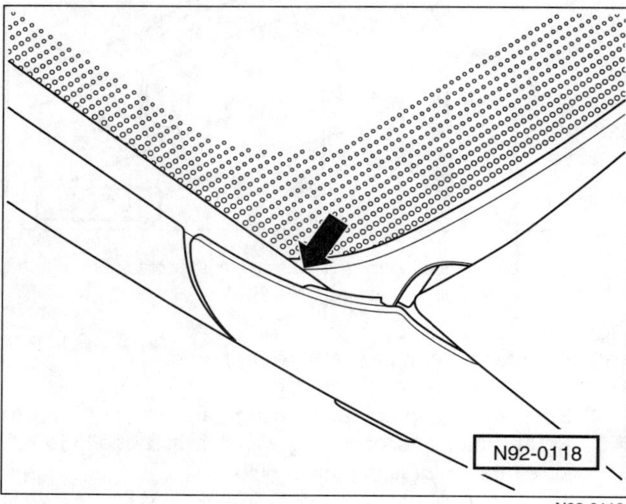

N92-0118

Fig. 9. Install ends of cowl panel under rubber strip (**arrow**) at bottom of A-pillar.

21. Install rubber gasket for cowl and check operation of wipers.

Rear wiper assembly

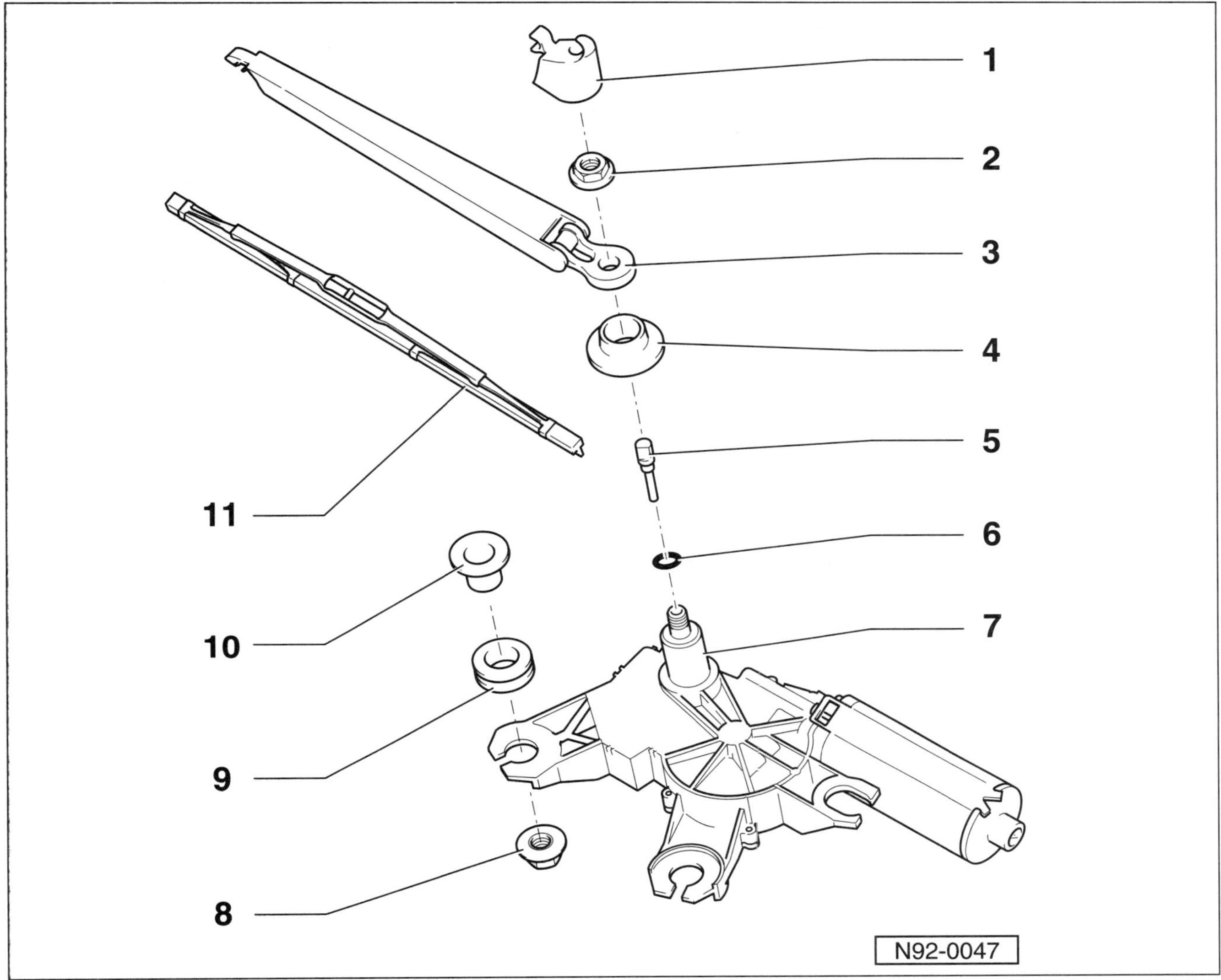

N92-0047

Fig. 10. Rear windshield wiper arm and motor for Golf and GTI models.

1. **Cover cap**
2. **Nut (13mm)**
   - Tighten to 15 Nm (11 ft-lb)
3. **Wiper arm**
   - Adjust gap between wiper rubber and lower edge of window to 25 mm
4. **Seal**
5. **Washer jet**
   - Use VW special tool 3125 A window washer adjusting tool, or equivalent to adjust spray pattern
   - Do not use a needle or similar object to adjust jet as the passages in the spray jets will be damaged
   - To replace spray jet, fold wiper arm mounting nut cap open and pull out jet with needle nose pliers
6. **Seal**
7. **Wiper motor**
   - Removing:
     Remove rear wiper arm, rear trim panel, harness connector, washer fluid line and three mounting nuts (item 8) for motor
8. **Mounting nuts**
9. **Rubber grommet**
   - Ensure grommet seats properly in rear hatch when installing wiper motor assembly
10. **Spacer**
11. **Wiper blade**

Windshield washer system overview

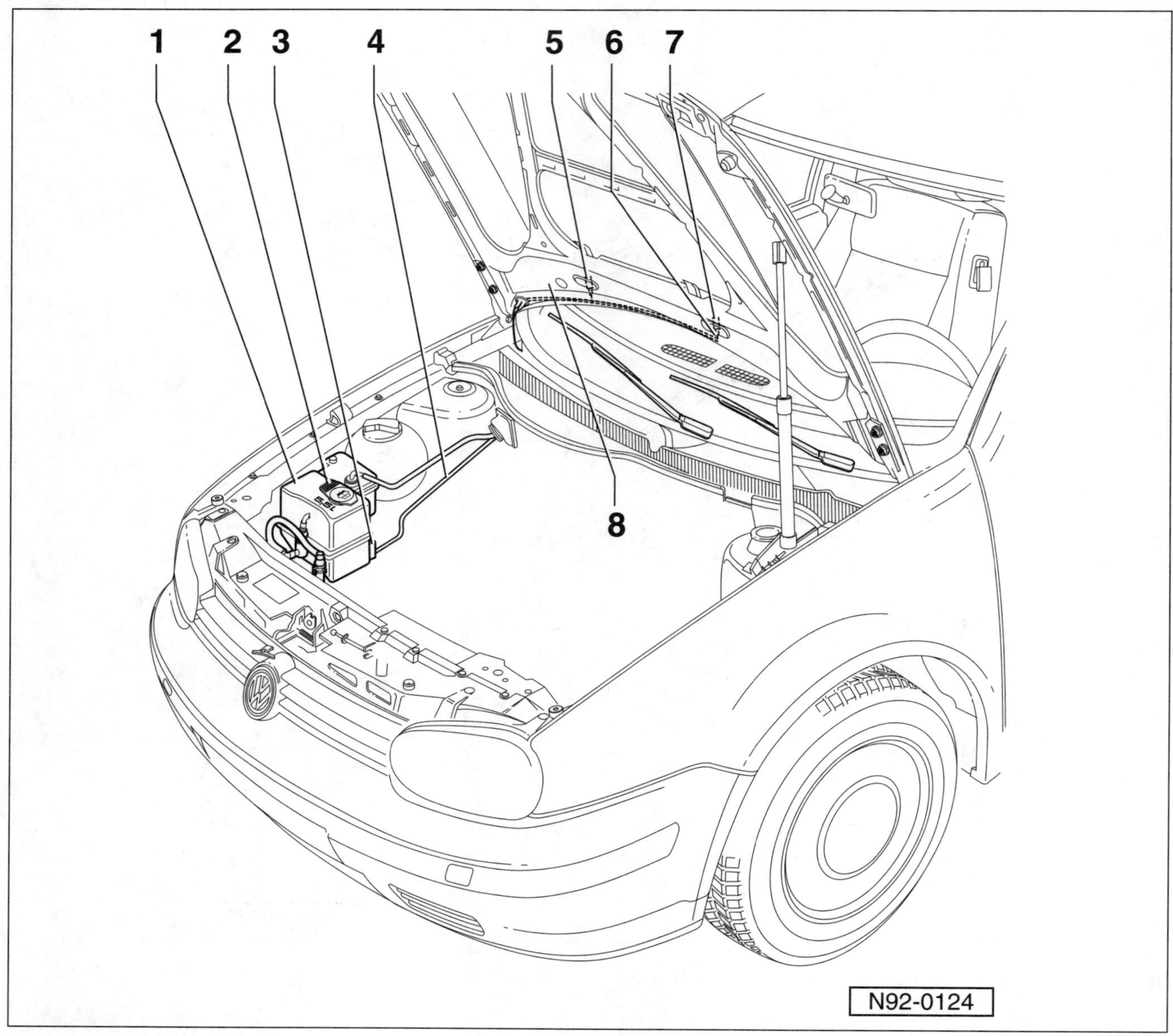

N92-0124

Fig. 11. Windshield washer system and related components.

1. **Windshield washer system reservoir**
   - Capacity 5.5 liters
   - For windshield and headlights, as applicable
2. **Container cap**
3. **Windshield washer system pump**
4. **Hose**
5. **Spray jet**
   - Removing, **see** Ⓐ
   - Adjusting, **see** Ⓑ
6. **Spray jet**
   - Removing, **see** Ⓐ
   - Adjusting, **see** Ⓑ
7. **Cover**
8. **Junction**
   - Behind cover cap

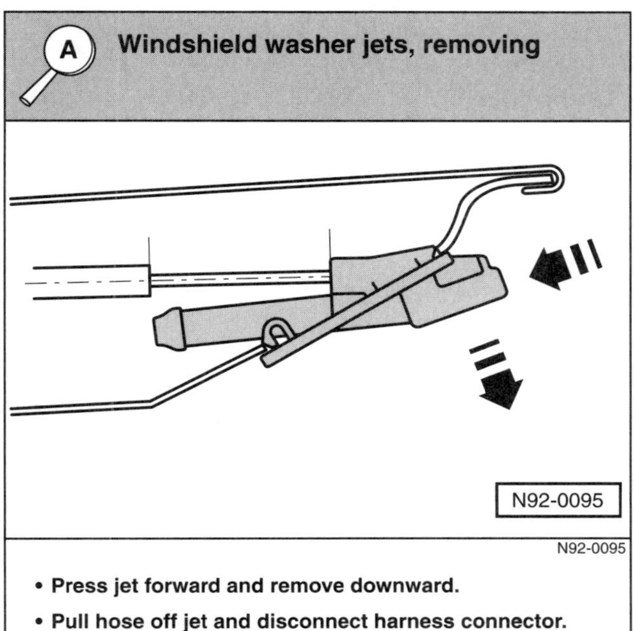

- **Press jet forward and remove downward.**
- **Pull hose off jet and disconnect harness connector.**

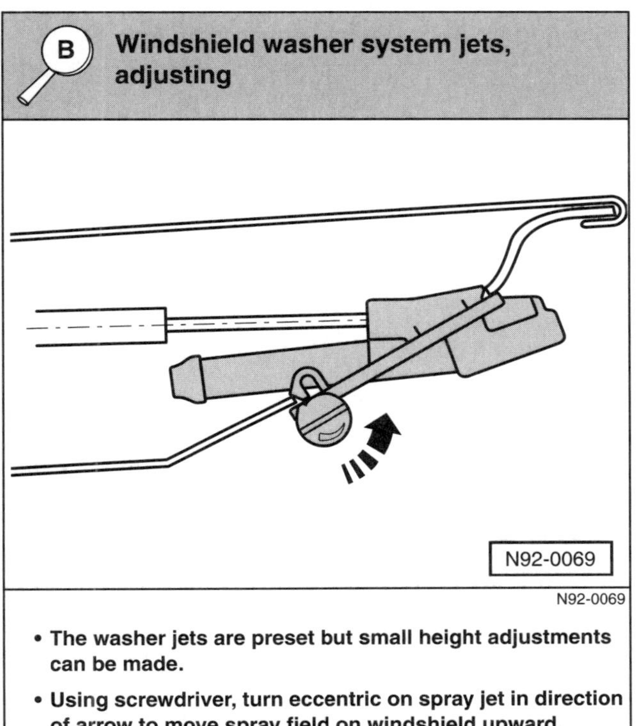

B
Windshield washer system jets, adjusting
N92-0069
N92-0069

- **The washer jets are preset but small height adjustments can be made.**
- **Using screwdriver, turn eccentric on spray jet in direction of arrow to move spray field on windshield upward.**
- **The spray jets must not be cleaned opposite to direction of spray, e.g. blown through from front.**

Windshield washer reservoir, removing

1. Remove mounting bolts for coolant expansion tank and position tank out of way with coolant hoses still connected. See Fig. 12.

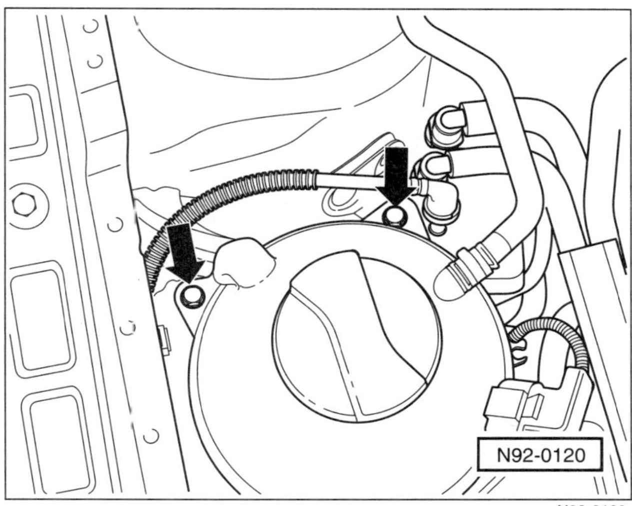

Fig. 12. Remove bolts (**arrows**) and place coolant expansion tank to side with hoses still connected.

2. Remove mounting bolts for activated charcoal filter housing and place to side with hoses still attached. See Fig. 13.

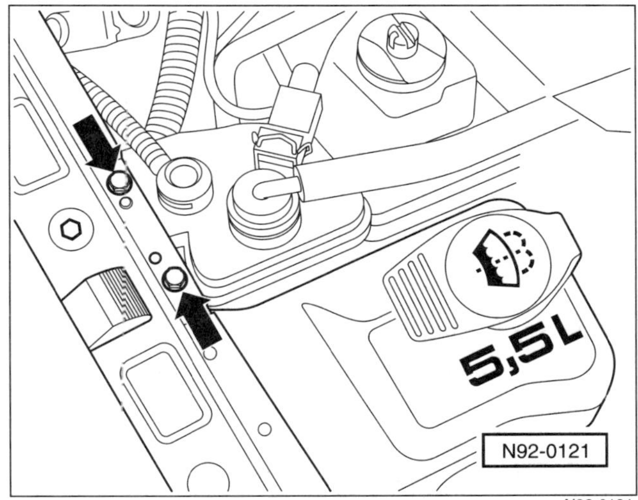

Fig. 13. Remove bolts (**arrows**) for activated charcoal filter housing and place to side with hoses still connected.

3. Remove lower plastic mounting nut from bottom of washer fluid tank. See Fig. 14.

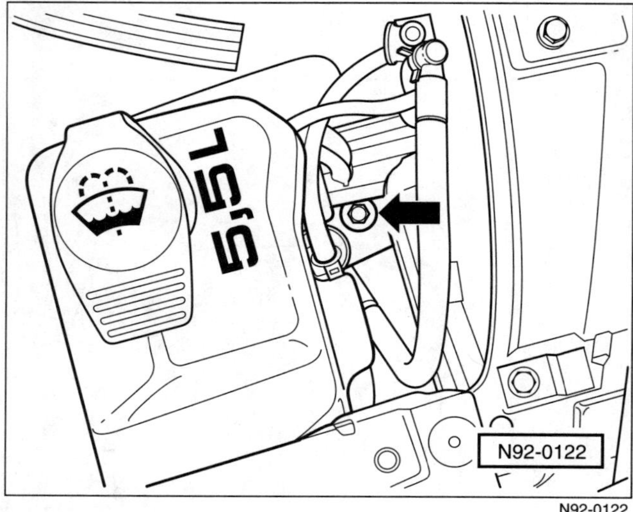

N92-0122

Fig. 14. Remove plastic nut (**arrow**) from bottom of washer fluid tank.

4. Remove upper plastic mounting nut from top of washer fluid reservoir. See Fig. 15.

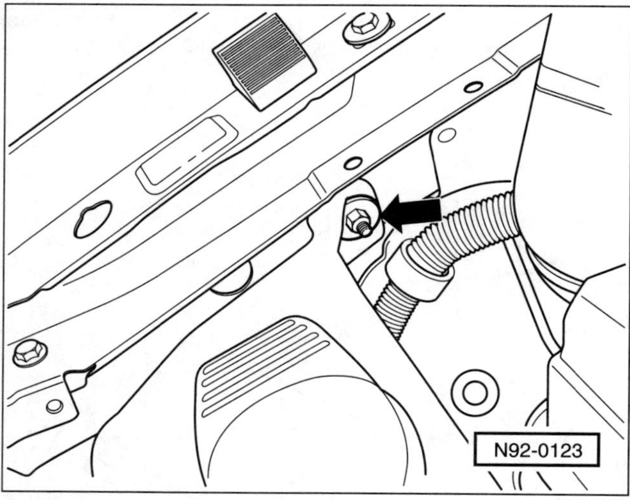

N92-0123

Fig. 15. Remove plastic nut (**arrow**) from top of washer fluid tank.

5. Pull hose and electrical connections off windshield washer pump and remove reservoir.

94 Lights, Accessories–Exterior

GENERAL

The Jetta and Golf/GTI headlights are styled differently but function the same. The headlight housings enclose the high and low beam lights as well as turn signal and parking lights. The headlights are projector beam lamps for improved lighting and the assemblies are covered with a plastic chip resistant lens.

Fog lights are standard on all GLX models and the GLS version of the GTI. These are also housed in the headlight assembly. Models without fog lights have the fog light openings blocked off. The components of the Golf/GTI headlight assembly are shown in Fig. 1.

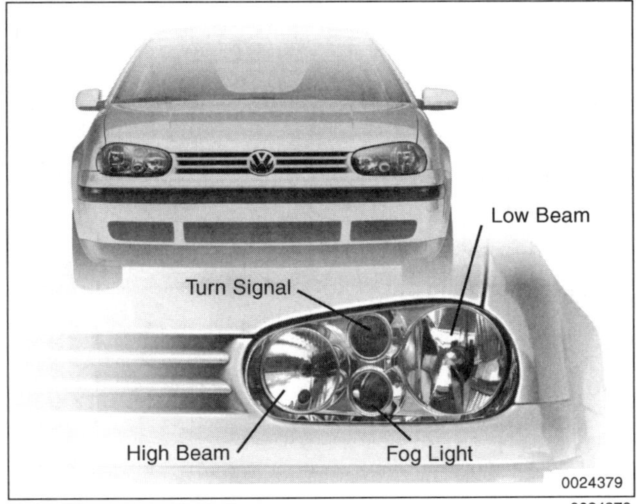

0024379

Fig. 1. Headlight components for Golf/GTI. Jettas have the high and low beams incorporated into one dual filament bulb.

This repair group covers removal, installation and replacing of the exterior lights and bulbs.

> ***CAUTION —***
> - *Before working on the electrical system disconnect battery ground (GND) strap from battery negative (–) terminal.*
> - *Be sure to have the anti-theft radio code on hand before disconnecting the battery.*
> - *Disconnecting the negative (–) battery cable may erase fault codes and basic settings in the engine management and automatic transmission control modules. Some driveability problems may be noticed until the system re-adapts to operating conditions. OBD II readiness codes, which may be required for emissions testing, may also be erased. Convenience electronics (alarm system, interior light control, power locks, mirrors, and windows) may need to be re-set using a VAG 1551/1552 or equivalent scan tool.*

GOLF/GTI EXTERIOR LIGHTS

The headlight assembly for Golf and GTI models is shown in Fig. 2.

> ***NOTE —***
> *After working on any component of the headlight system that could affect the headlight level setting be sure to adjust the headlights as described later.*

94

Headlight assembly (Golf/GTI)

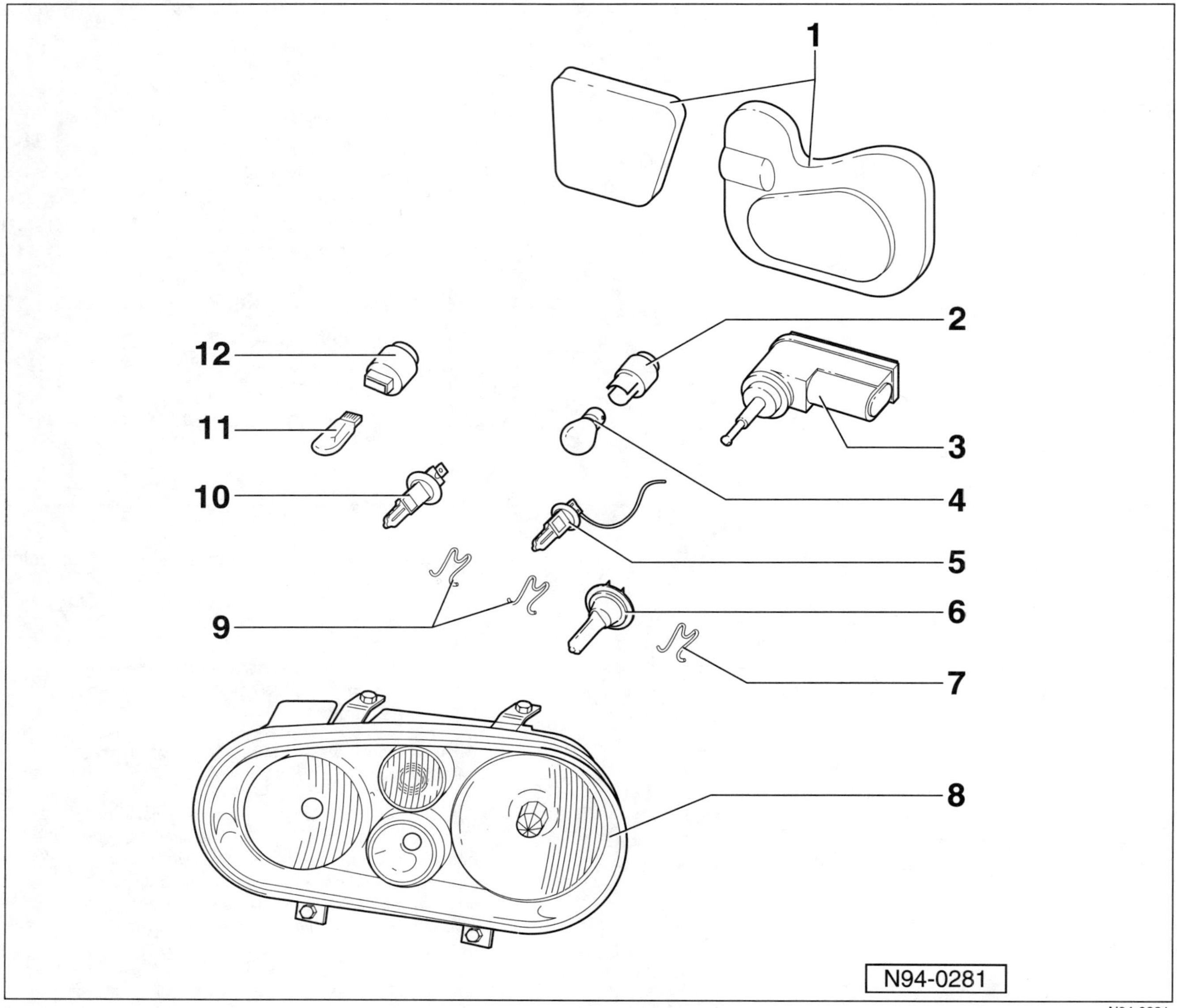

N94-0281

Fig. 2. Headlight assembly for Golf and GTI.

1. **Sealing caps**
2. **Turn signal bulb holder**
3. **Headlight beam range control positioning motor**
   - Adjusts headlight beam based on vehicle load
   - Not currently available on U.S. models
4. **Turn signal bulb**
   - 12V, 21W
5. **Fog light bulb**
   - As applicable
   - H3 12V, 55W
6. **Low beam bulb**
   - H7 12V, 55W
7. **Spring clip**
8. **Headlight housing**
9. **Spring clip**
10. **High beam bulb**
    - H7 12V, 55W
11. **Parking light bulb**
    - 12V, 5W
12. **Parking light bulb holder**

Headlight aim, adjusting

Adjusting the headlights is best accomplished with a commercial headlight adjusting unit. The vertical and horizontal adjustment wheels are shown in Fig. 3.

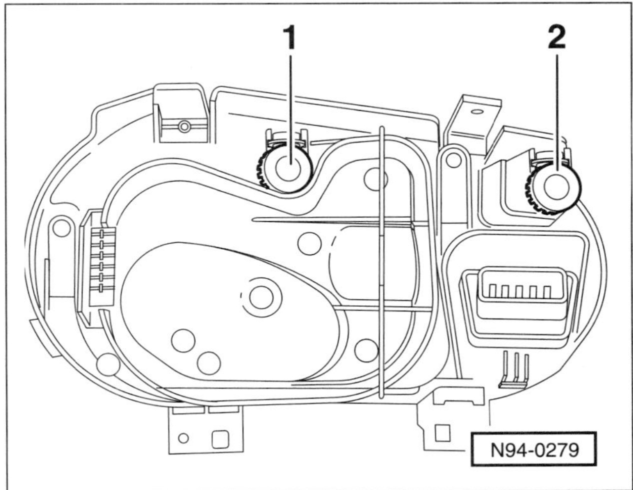

N94-0279

Fig. 3. Horizontal adjustment (**1**) and vertical adjustment (**2**) on driver's side headlight. Passenger side is oriented the same way.

> ***NOTE —***
> *Headlight adjustments are done using a screwdriver on the vertical and horizontal adjustment screws that turn the adjustment wheels on the back of headlight. See Fig. 4.*

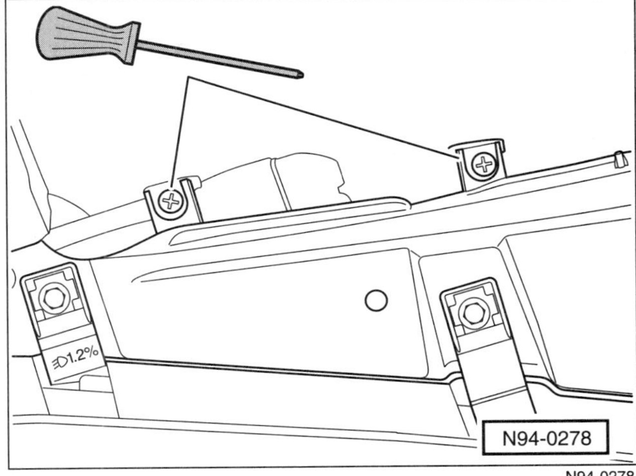

N94-0278

Fig. 4. Adjustment screws for horizontal and vertical settings of headlight.

Headlights, removing and installing

1. Remove bumper cover, see **63 Bumpers**.
2. Remove headlight mounting screws. See Fig. 5.

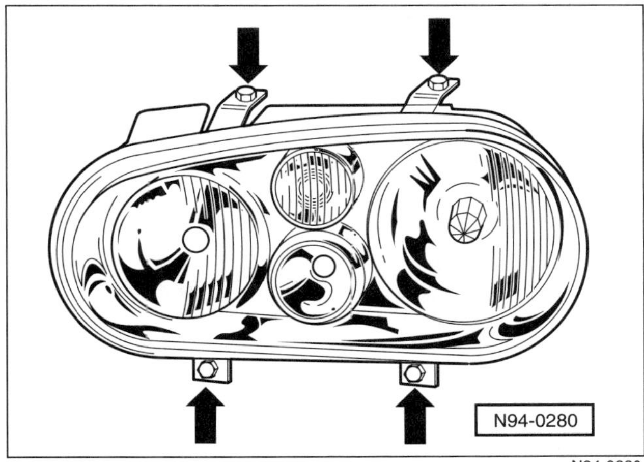

N94-0280

Fig. 5. Remove headlight mounting screws (**arrows**).

3. Pull headlight slightly forward and disconnect harness connector from back. Remove headlight.
4. Install headlight in reverse order of removal.

Headlight bulbs, replacing

> ***NOTE —***
> - *Do not touch bulb glass with bare skin when replacing bulb. Fingers leave traces of grease on glass which can cause bulb to cloud over or burn out prematurely.*
> - *On vehicles with headlight washer system, move hoses to one side if necessary.*

1. If replacing low beam, turn signal, or fog light bulb, release spring clip on back of headlight and remove larger sealing cover for those bulbs. See Fig. 6.

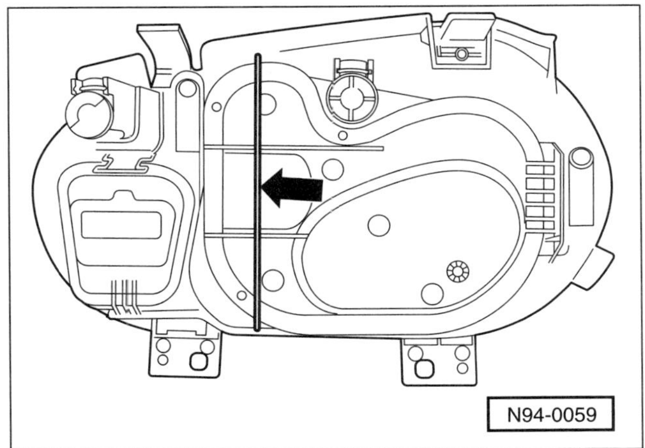

N94-0059

Fig. 6. Release spring clip (**arrow**) and remove sealing cover for turn signal, fog light and high beam bulb.

2. To replace low beam bulb, pull harness connector off back of bulb and push retaining clip over retaining lugs and release clip. Pull bulb out of reflector. See Fig. 7.

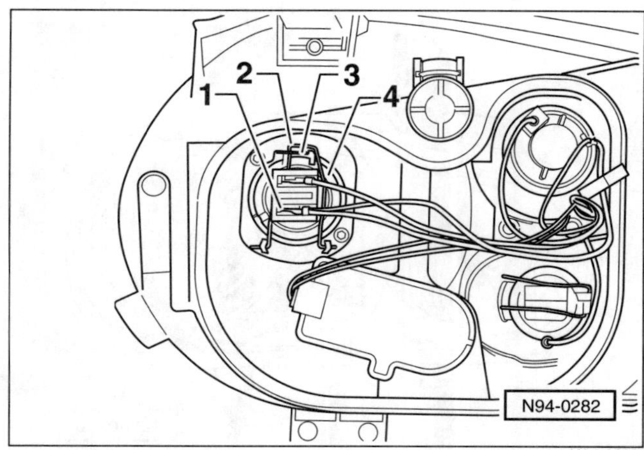

N94-0282

Fig. 7. Pull off low beam bulb harness connector (**1**) and push retaining clip (**2**) over lugs (**3**) to release clip and remove bulb (**4**).

3. To replace turn signal bulb, turn bulb holder to left and pull out of housing. Remove bulb from holder. See Fig. 8.

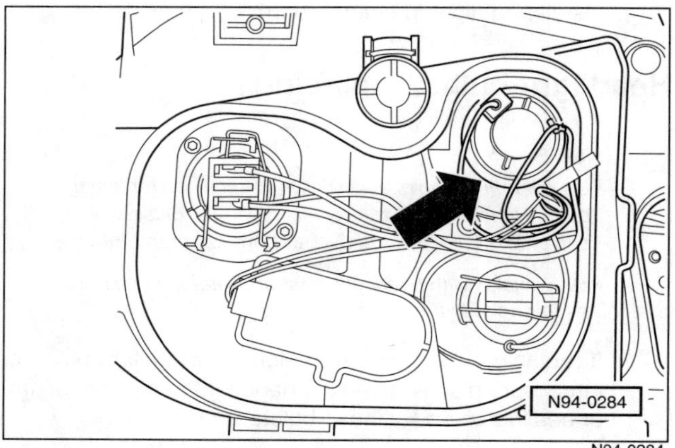

N94-0284

Fig. 8. Rotate turn signal bulb holder (**arrow**) to left and pull out.

4. To replace fog light bulb, pull harness connector off bulb and push retaining clip over retaining lugs and release clip. Pull bulb out of reflector. See Fig. 9.

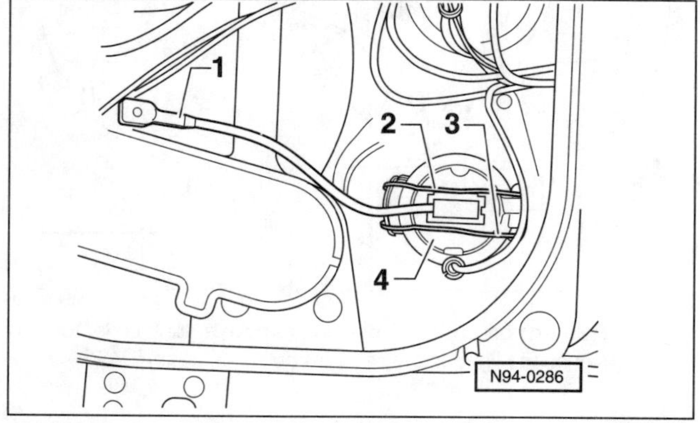

N94-0286

Fig. 9. Pull off fog light bulb harness connector (**1**) and push retaining clip (**2**) over lugs (**3**) to release clip and remove bulb (**4**).

5. If replacing high beam bulb only, release spring clip on back of headlight and remove sealing cover for high beam bulb. See Fig. 10.

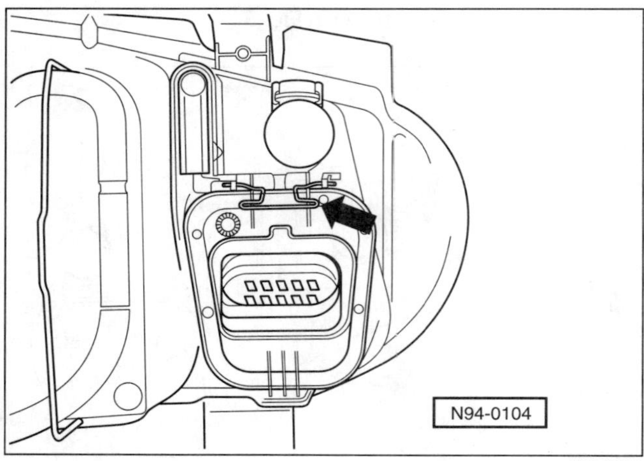

N94-0104

Fig. 10. Release spring clip (**arrow**) and take off sealing cover for high beam bulb.

6. Pull harness connector off bulb and push retaining clip over retaining lugs and release clip. Pull bulb out of reflector. See Fig. 11.

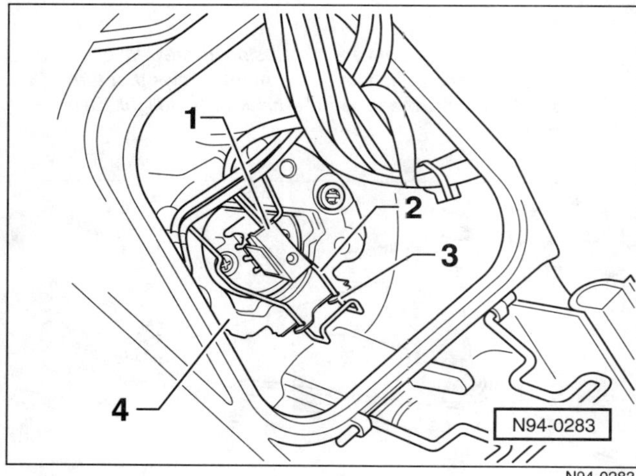

N94-0283

Fig. 11. Pull off harness connector (**1**) and push retaining clip (**2**) over lugs (**3**) to release clip and remove bulb (**4**).

7. When installing new bulbs be sure lugs on the bulb plate align with the cut-outs in the reflector, or for turn signal bulb ensure bulb holder engages in housing.

8. Secure bulb retaining clip (as applicable), push harness connector back onto bulb and replace sealing cap and spring clip.

9. Check headlight aim and operation of all bulbs.

Taillight assembly (Golf/GTI)

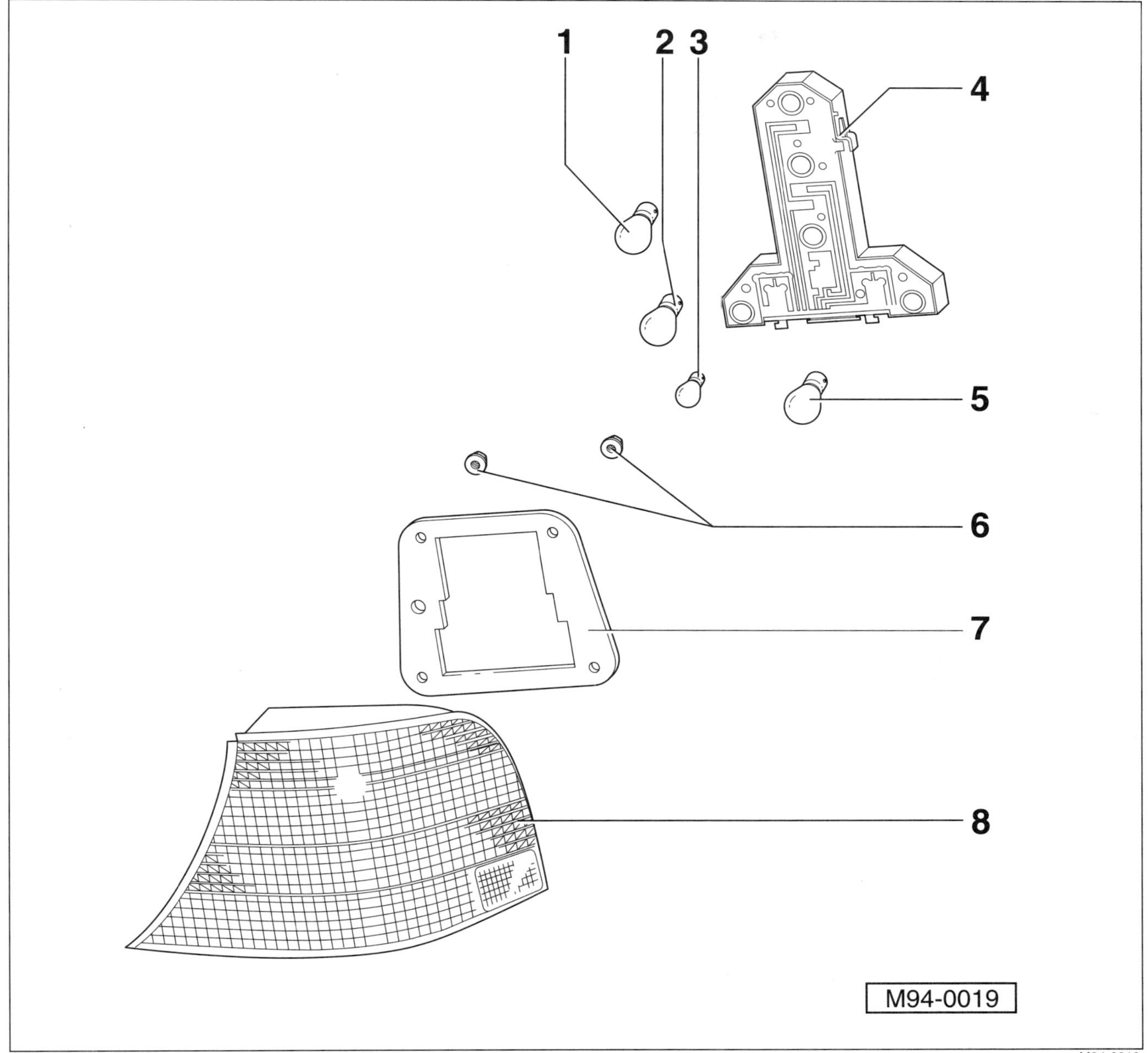

Fig. 12. Taillight assembly for Golf/GTI vehicles.

1. **Brake light bulb**
   - 12V, 21W
2. **Turn signal bulb**
   - 12V, 21W
3. **Taillight bulb**
   - 12V, 10W
4. **Bulb holder**
   - Removing and installing, **see** Ⓐ
5. **Reverse light bulb**
   - 12V, 21W
6. **Hex nuts**
7. **Gasket**
8. **Taillight housing**
   - Removing and installing, **see** Ⓑ

A Taillight bulb holder, removing and installing

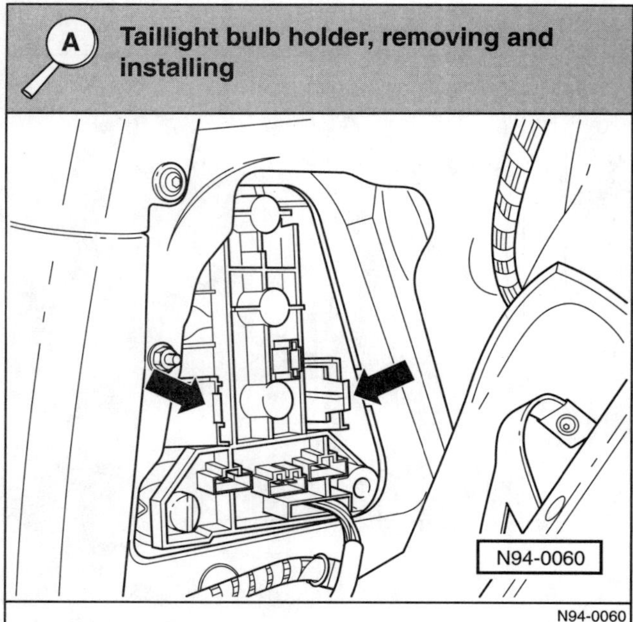

N94-0060

- **Pull off harness connector.**
- **Release retainer clips (arrows) and pull bulb holder out.**
- **Install in reverse order of removal.**

B Taillight housing, removing and installing

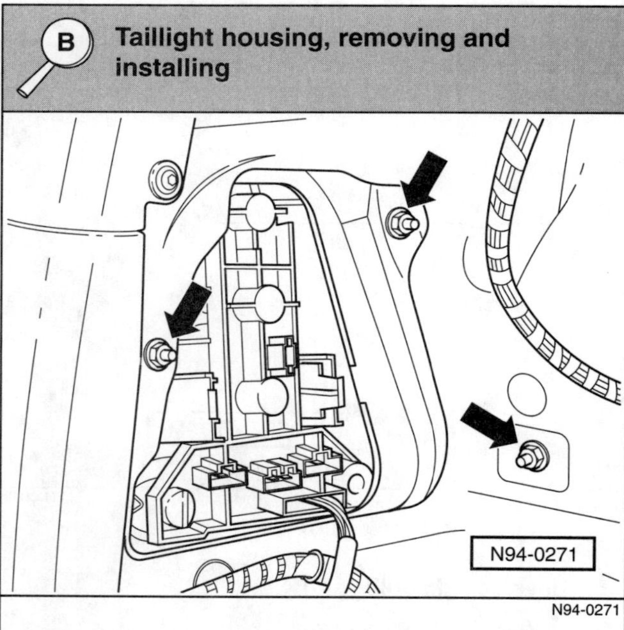

N94-0271

- **Remove rear luggage compartment trim for appropriate side, see 70 Trim–Interior.**
- **Remove bulb holder as shown above.**
- **Remove securing nuts (arrows) and pull off tail light assembly.**
- **When installing, tighten securing nuts to 3 Nm (27 in-lb).**

High-mount brake light, removing and installing

1. Remove upper and lower rear lid trim, see **70 Trim–Interior**.

2. Remove securing screws for high-mount brake light and pull off harness connector. See Fig. 13.

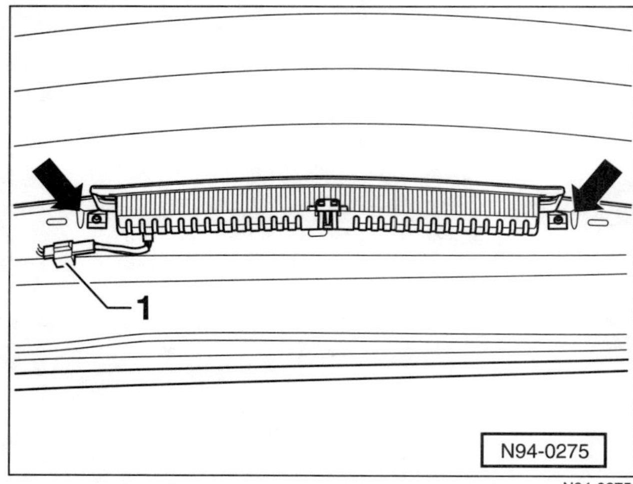

N94-0275

Fig. 13. Remove mounting screws (**arrows**) and harness connector (**1**) for high-mount brake light.

3. Unclip retaining clips from short sides of bulb housing.

4. Unclip retaining clips from long sides of bulb housing and remove housing. See Fig. 14.

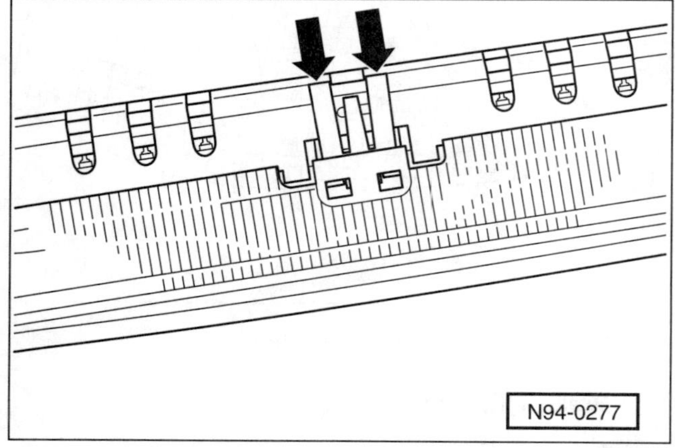

N94-0277

Fig. 14. Unclip retaining clips (**arrows**) from long sides of bulb housing.

NOTE —

The bulb holder is a circuit board with 32 soldered LED's which are covered by a plastic strip. Changing an individual LED is not recommended and Volkswagen only provides the complete bulb holder as a replacement part.

5. Install housing in reverse order of removal.

JETTA EXTERIOR LIGHTS

Headlight assembly (Jetta)

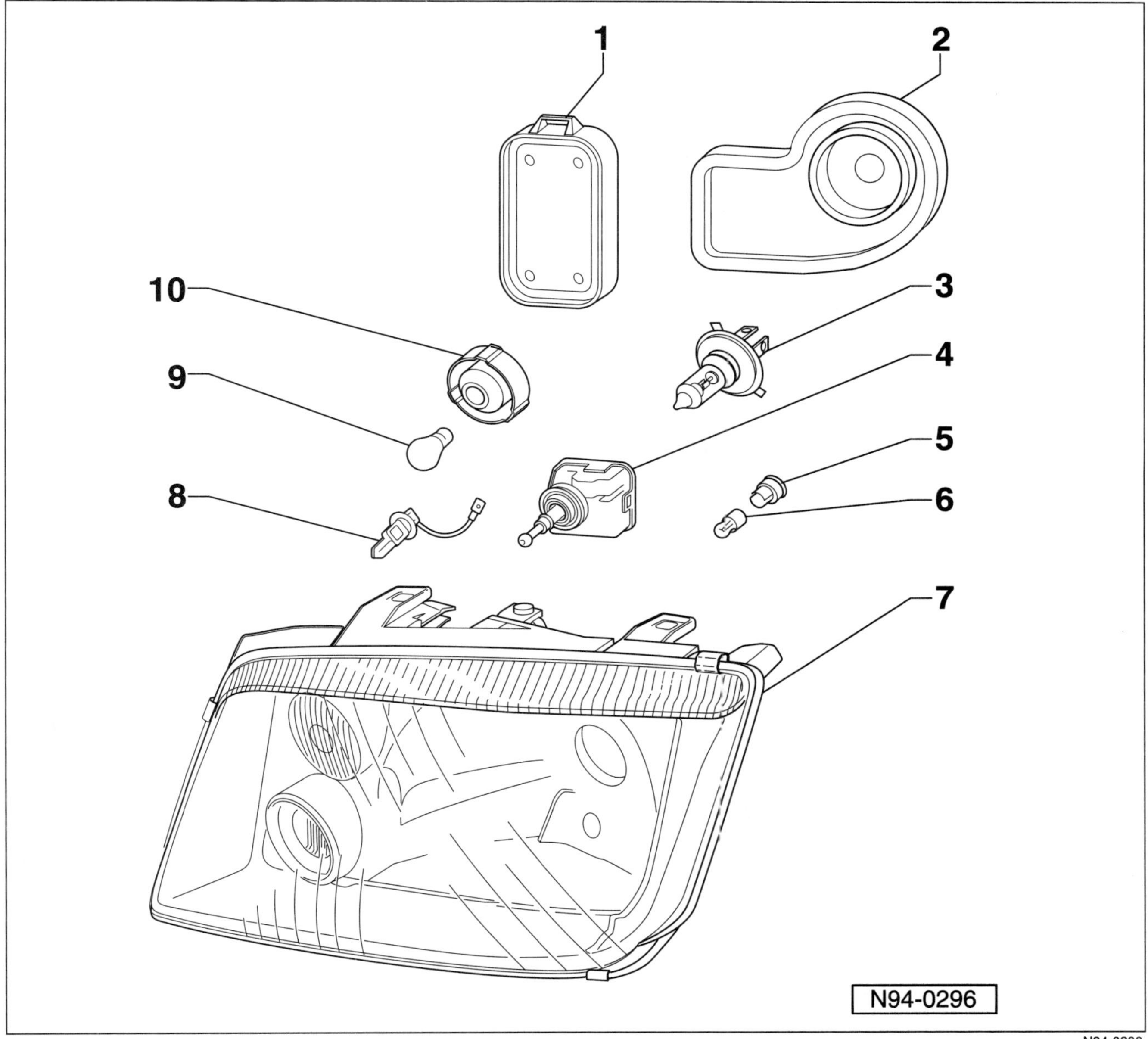

Fig. 15. Headlight assembly for Jetta.

1. **Sealing cap**
2. **Sealing cap**
3. **Dual filament bulb for high and low beam lights**
   - H4, 12V, 60/55W
4. **Headlight beam range control positioning motor**
   - Adjusts headlight beam based on vehicle load
   - Not currently available on U.S. models
5. **Side light bulb holder**
   - Not applicable for US/CDN models
6. **Side light bulb**
   - Not applicable for US/CDN models
   - 12V, 5W
7. **Headlight housing**
8. **Fog light bulb**
   - H3, 12V, 55W
9. **Turn signal/parking light bulb**
   - 12V, 21W/5W
10. **Turn signal/parking light bulb holder**

Headlight aim, adjusting

Adjusting the headlights is best accomplished with a commercial headlight adjusting unit. The vertical and horizontal adjustment screws are shown in Fig. 16.

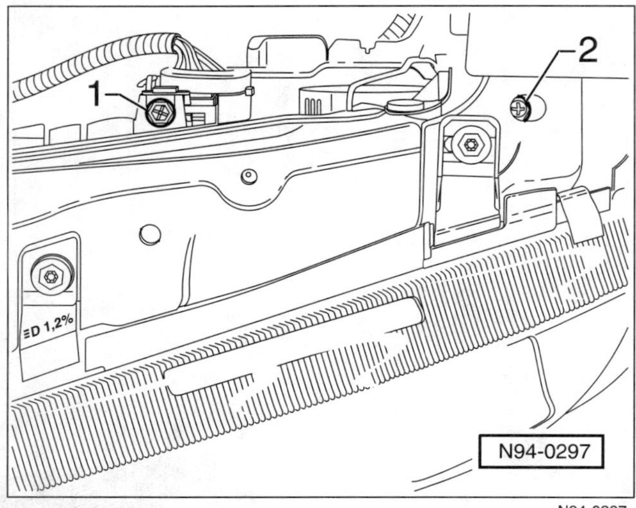

N94-0297

Fig. 16. Horizontal adjustment (**1**) and vertical adjustment (**2**) on driver's side headlight. Passenger side is oriented the same way.

> ***NOTE —***
> *Headlight adjustments are done using a screwdriver on the vertical and horizontal adjustment screws that turn the adjustment wheels on the back of headlight. See Fig. 17.*

Headlights, removing and installing

1. Remove bumper cover, see **63 Bumpers**.
2. Remove mounting screws for headlight upper cover in engine compartment and remove cover. See Fig. 17.
3. Remove upper mounting screws for headlight housing.
4. Disconnect harness connector from back of headlight.

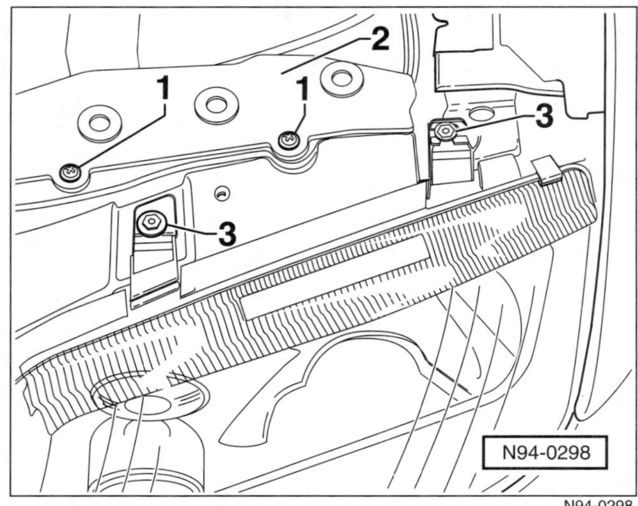

N94-0298

Fig. 17. Remove upper cover mounting screws (**1**), upper cover (**2**) and headlight housing upper mounting screws (**3**).

5. Remove headlight housing lower mounting screws. See Fig. 18.

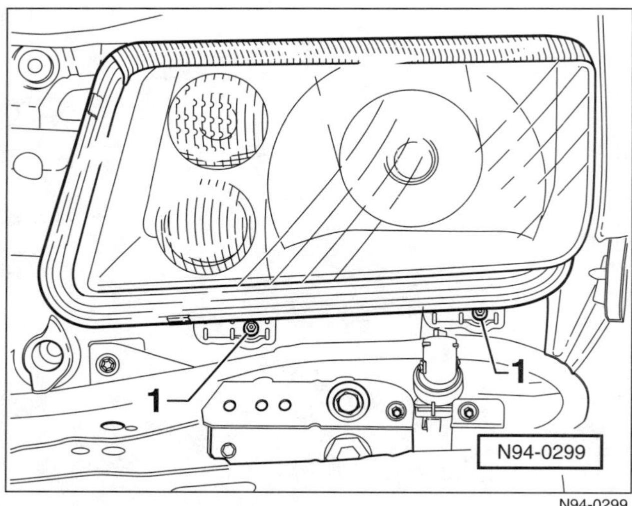

N94-0299

Fig. 18. Remove lower mounting screws (**1**) for headlight.

6. Remove headlight housing by pulling out forward.
7. Installation is the reverse of removal.
8. Check headlight aim as necessary.

Headlight bulbs, replacing

NOTE —

- *Do not touch bulb glass with bare skin when replacing bulb. Fingers leave traces of grease on the glass which can cause the bulb to cloud over or burn out prematurely.*
- *On vehicles with headlight washer system, move hoses to one side if necessary.*

1. If replacing high/low beam bulb or side light bulb, release spring clip on back of headlight and remove larger sealing cover for those bulbs. See Fig. 19.

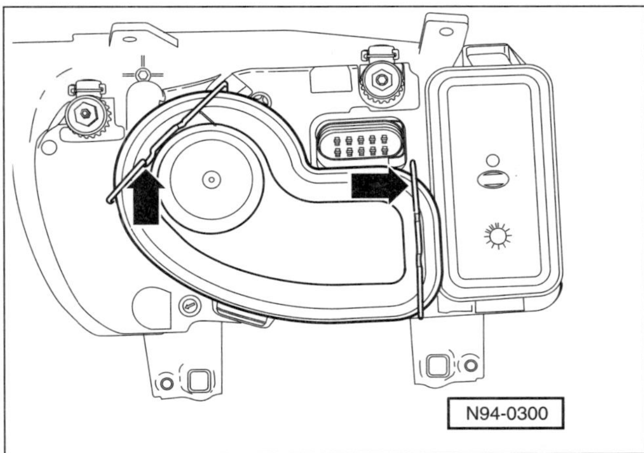

N94-0300

Fig. 19. Release spring clip (**arrow**) and remove sealing cover for high/low beam bulb and side light bulb.

2. To replace high/low beam bulb, pull harness connector off back of bulb and push retaining clip over retaining lugs and release clip. Pull bulb out of reflector. See Fig. 20.

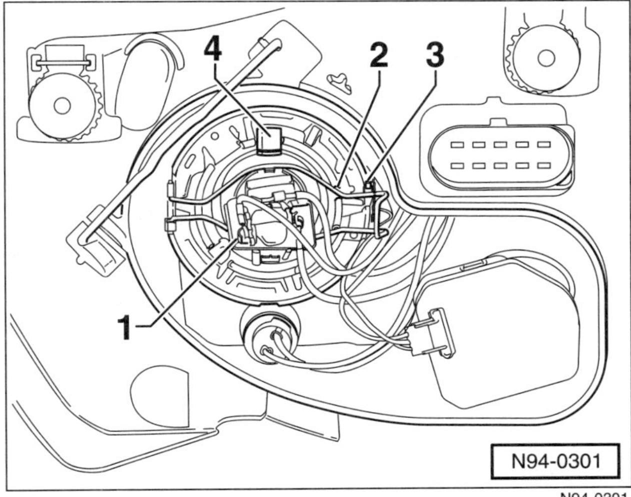

N94-0301

Fig. 20. Pull off high/low beam bulb harness connector (**1**) and push retaining clip (**2**) over lugs (**3**) to release clip and remove bulb (**4**).

3. To replace side light bulb, pull bulb holder out of housing and remove bulb from holder. See Fig. 21.

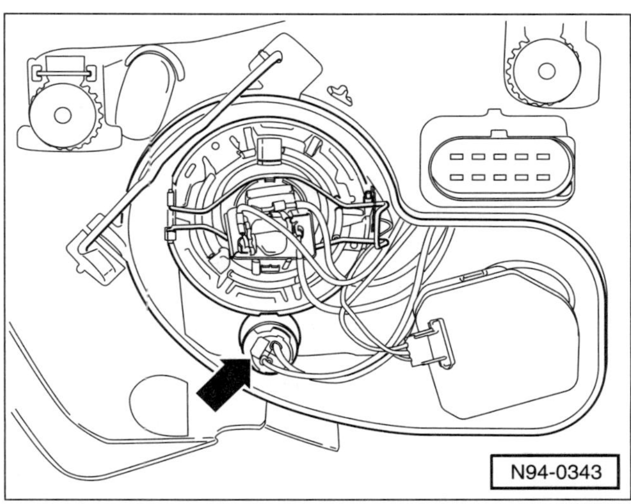

N94-0343

Fig. 21. Pull turn signal bulb holder (**arrow**) out from housing.

4. To replace front turn signal or fog light bulb, release spring clip on back of headlight and remove smaller sealing cover for turn signal and fog light bulbs. See Fig. 22.

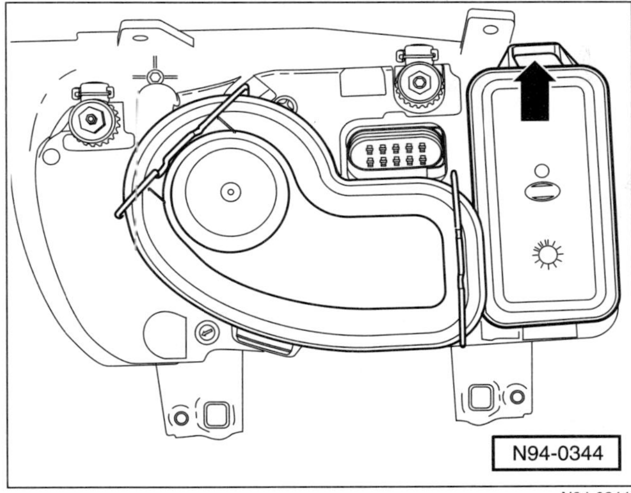

N94-0344

Fig. 22. Release spring clip (**arrow**) and take off smaller sealing cover for turn signal and fog light bulbs.

5. To replace turn signal bulb, turn bulb holder to left and pull out of housing. Remove bulb from holder. See Fig. 23.

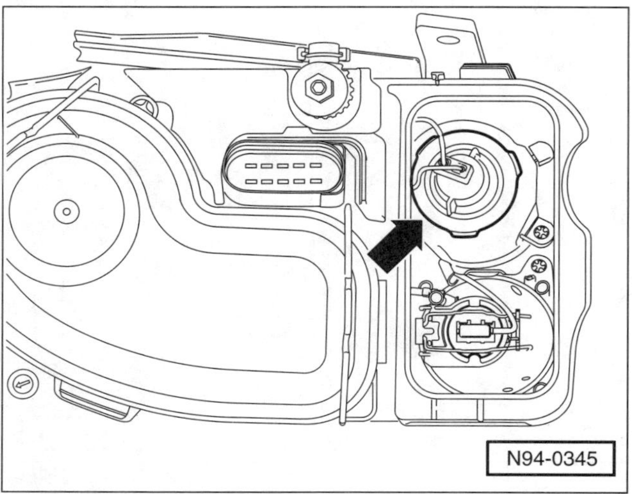

N94-0345

Fig. 23. Rotate turn signal bulb holder (**arrow**) to left and pull out.

6. To replace fog light bulb, pull harness connector off bulb and push retaining clip over retaining lugs and release clip. Pull bulb out of reflector. See Fig. 24.

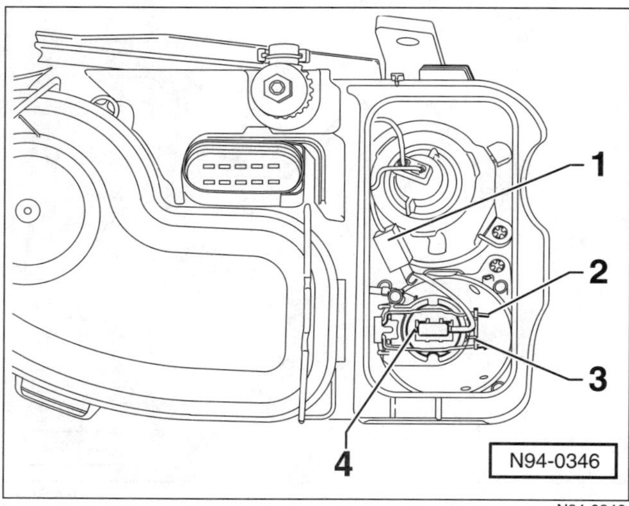

N94-0346

Fig. 24. Pull off fog light bulb harness connector (**1**) and push retaining clip (**2**) over lugs (**3**) to release clip and remove bulb (**4**).

7. When installing new bulbs be sure lugs on the bulb plate align with the cut-outs in the reflector, or for turn signal bulb ensure bulb holder engages in housing.

8. Secure bulb retaining clip (as applicable), push harness connector back onto bulb and replace sealing cap and spring clip.

9. Check headlight aim and operation of all bulbs.

High-mount brake light, removing and installing

1. Remove harness connector from back of high-mount brake light.

1. Remove rear parcel shelf with high-mount brake light, see **70 Trim–Interior**.

2. Unclip high-mount brake light from rear parcel shelf. See Fig. 25.

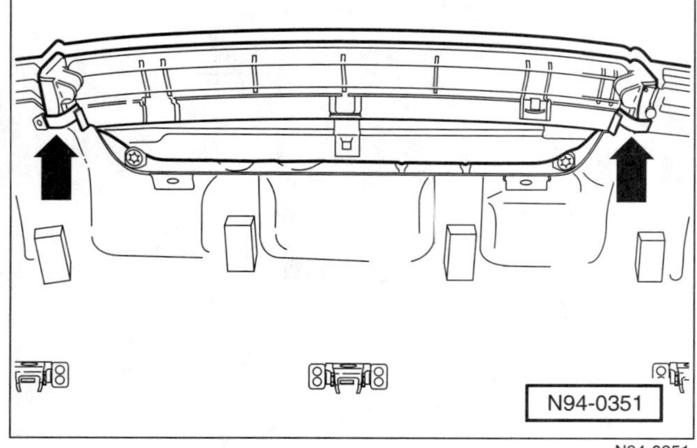

N94-0351

Fig. 25. Unclip high-mount brake light from rear parcel shelf at **arrows**.

3. Unclip bulb holder from high-mount brake light housing. See Fig. 26.

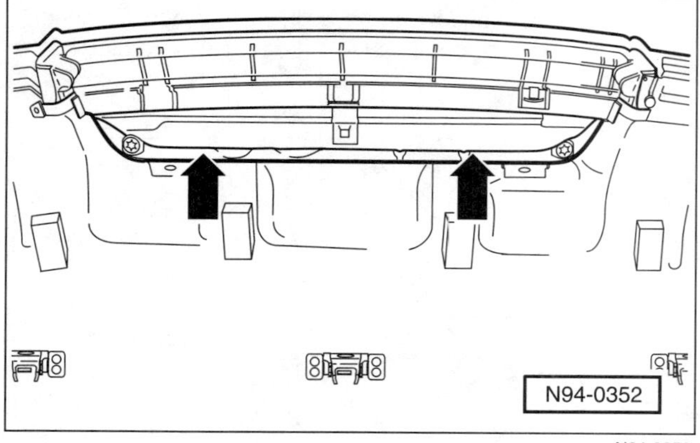

N94-0352

Fig. 26. Unclip bulb holder at **arrows** from high-mount brake light housing.

NOTE —

The bulb holder is a circuit board with 18 soldered LED's which are covered by a plastic strip. Changing an individual LED is not recommended and Volkswagen only provides the complete bulb holder as a replacement part.

4. Install housing in reverse order of removal.

Taillight assembly (Jetta)

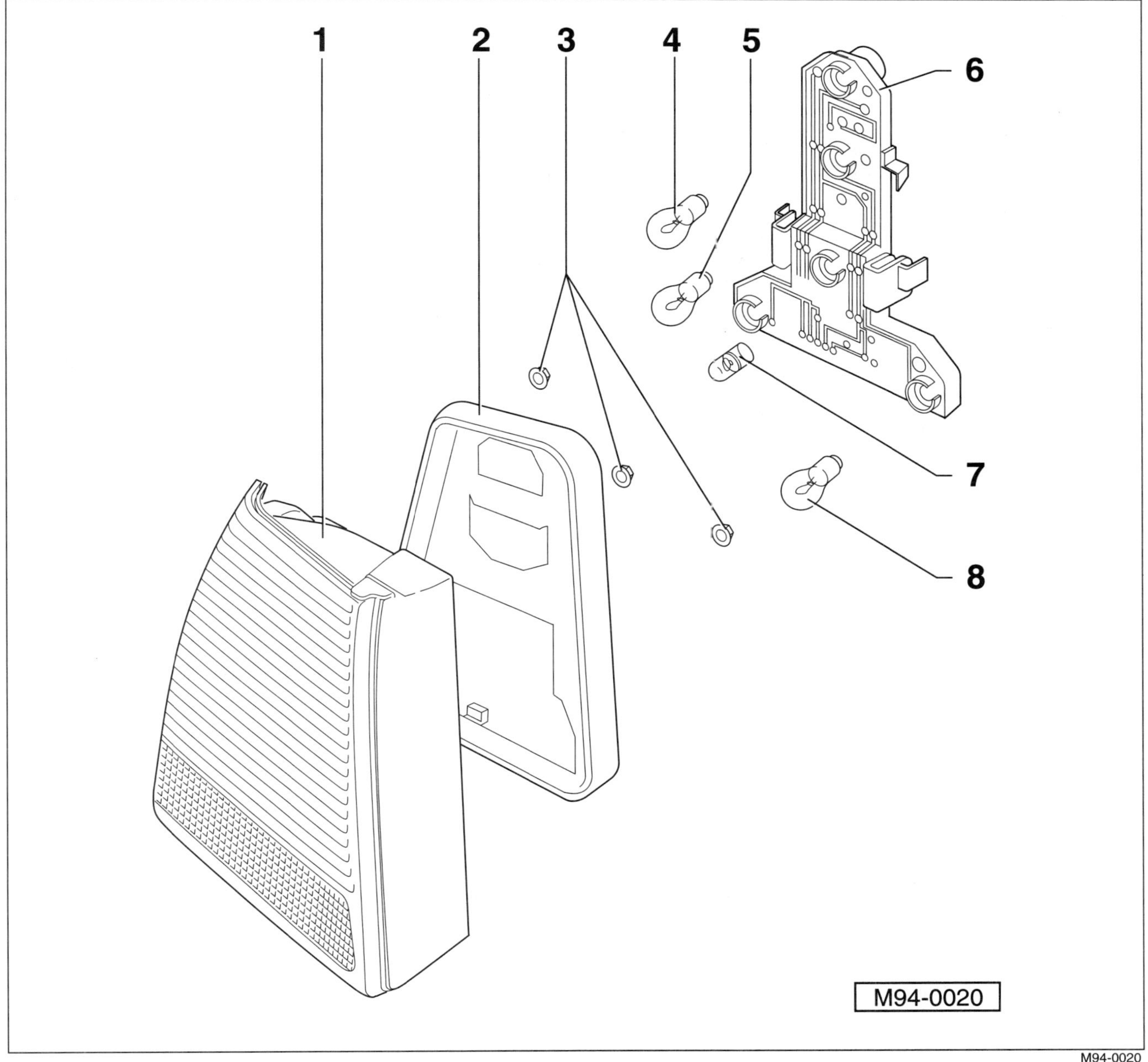

M94-0020

Fig. 27. Taillight assembly for Jetta vehicles. Sedan shown, wagon similar.

1. **Taillight housing**
   - Removing and installing, **see** Ⓐ
2. **Gasket**
3. **Hex nuts (3)**
4. **Brake light bulb**
   - 12V, 21W
5. **Turn signal bulb**
   - 12V, 21W
6. **Bulb holder**
   - Removing and installing, **see** Ⓑ
7. **Tail light bulb**
   - 12V, 5W
8. **Reverse light bulb**
   - 12V, 21W

A Taillight housing, removing and installing

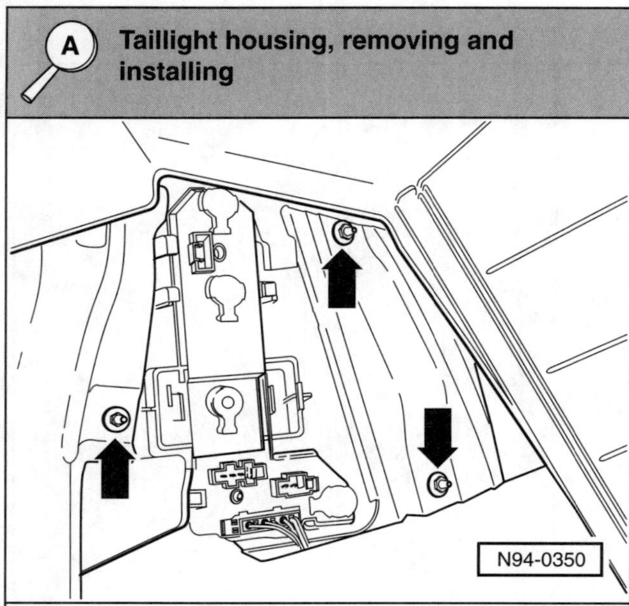

N94-0350

- **Remove rear luggage compartment trim for appropriate side, see 70 Trim–Interior.**
- **Remove bulb holder as shown below.**
- **Remove securing nuts (arrows) and pull off tail light assembly.**
- **When installing, tighten securing nuts to 3 Nm (27 in-lb).**

B Taillight bulb holder, removing and installing

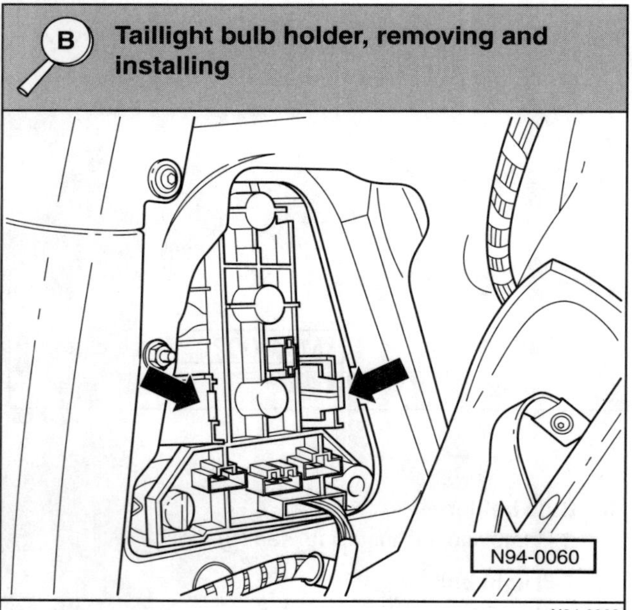

N94-0060

- **Pull off harness connector.**
- **Release retainer clips (arrows) and pull bulb holder out.**
- **Install in reverse order of removal.**

GOLF/GTI/JETTA EXTERIOR LIGHTS

This section contains procedures for components that are common to all the vehicles covered by this manual.

Headlight upper securing lugs, servicing

NOTE —

If the headlight upper securing tabs have broken off it is possible to replace the tabs with a repair kit from Volkswagen.

1. Remove headlight as previously described.
2. Sand down broken headlight tab flat.
3. Position replacement tab onto headlight securing tab socket and secure with mounting screw. See Fig. 28.

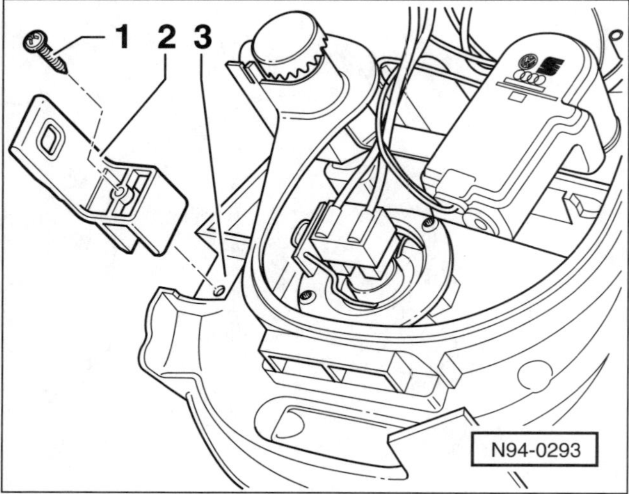

N94-0293

Fig. 28. Position replacement tab (**2**) into securing tab socket (**3**) and secure with screw (**1**).

4. Install headlight and check aim, adjust as necessary.

Side mounted turn signals, removing and installing

NOTE —
Use extreme caution when removing side-mounted turn signal since it can only be removed in one direction and it is difficult to recognize on which side of the turn signal the spring clip or mounting pin sits.

1. Using a plastic pry tool, carefully press turn signal toward spring clip side and remove. See Fig. 29.

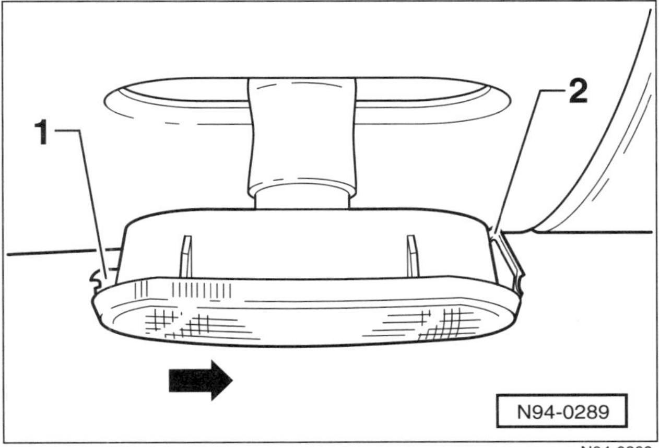

N94-0289

Fig. 29. Carefully press turn signal at mounting side (**1**) in direction of **arrow** against force of spring clip (**2**).

NOTE —
Protect paint surface using adhesive tape if necessary.

2. Pull rubber holder and push-fit bulb from bulb housing.
3. Remove bulb by pulling from holder and replace if necessary.
4. To install, place rubber holder and push-fit bulb onto bulb housing.
5. Carefully install turn signal into body panel and check for proper operation of turn signal.

License plate light, removing and installing

1. Remove mounting screws for license plate light. See Fig. 30.

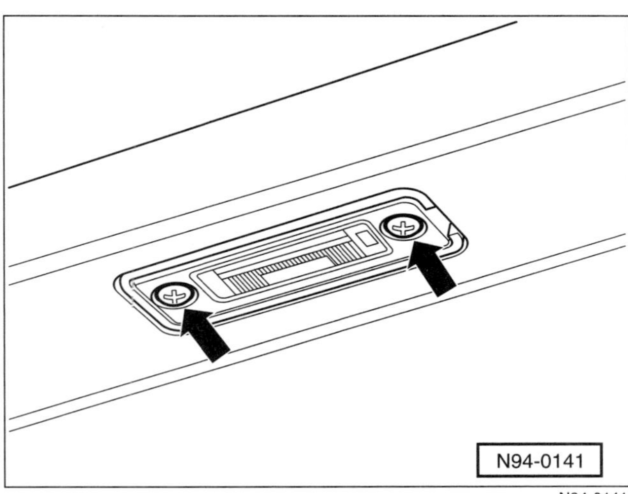

N94-0141

Fig. 30. Remove mounting screws (**arrows**) for license plate light.

2. Remove license plate light lens with bulb and disconnect harness connector.
3. Remove bulb (12V/5W) and replace as necessary.

CAUTION —
Do not touch the glass portion of the bulb with bare hands. The moisture and/or grease from fingers that evaporates on the bulb during operation, can cause the glass to cloud over.

4. When installing license plate light, be sure that the small silver covered strip is oriented toward the rear bumper. See Fig. 31.

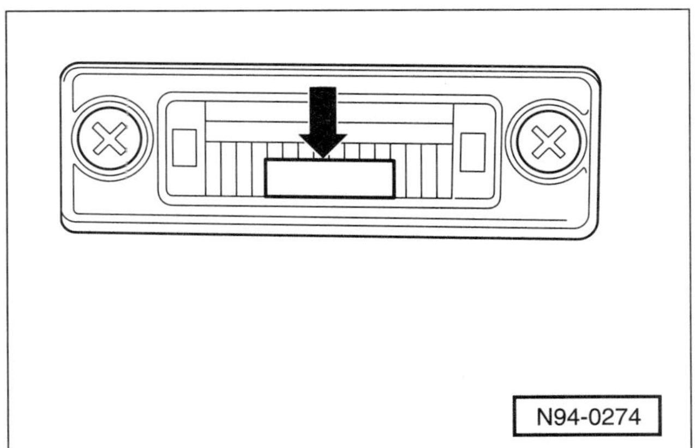

N94-0274

Fig. 31. The small silver covered strip (**arrow**) on the license plate light should be oriented toward the rear bumper.

96 Lights, Accessories–Interior

GENERAL

This section covers electrical light switches and accessories located in the passenger compartment. Items such as radio, heating and A/C that require detailed coverage have their own repair groups. See **97 Wiring Diagrams, Fuses and Relays** for additional information.

> ***CAUTION —***
> - *Before working on electrical system disconnect negative (–) battery cable.*
> - *Before disconnecting battery be sure to obtain radio anti-theft code.*

INTERIOR LIGHTS AND SWITCHES

> ***NOTE —***
> - *The luggage compartment light switch is integrated into the trunk lock and cannot be replaced separately. If the luggage compartment light switch is faulty the complete trunk lock must be replaced, see* **70 Trim–Interior**.
> - *The door contact switch is integrated into the door lock and cannot be replaced individually. The complete door lock must be replaced if the door contact switch is faulty, see* **70 Trim–Interior**.
> - *For steering column switches, see* **48 Steering**.

Headlight switch, removing and installing

1. Turn rotary knob of light switch to "0" position.
2. Press rotary knob inward and turn slightly to right.
3. Hold rotary knob in this position, pull on rotary knob and remove light switch from instrument panel. See Fig. 1.

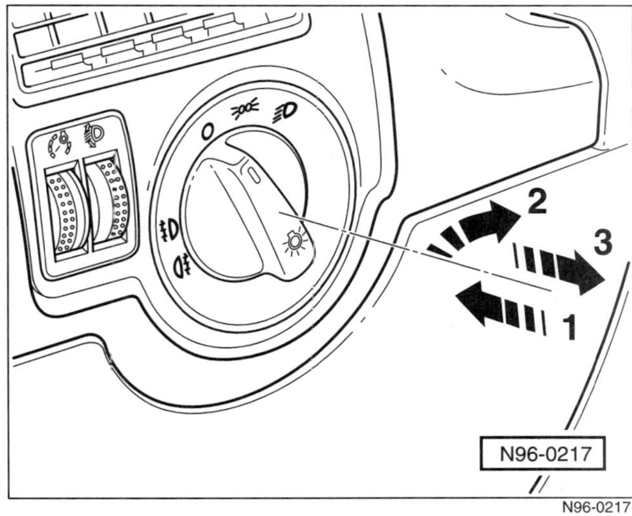

Fig. 1. Turn light switch to "0" position, press knob inward (**arrow 1**), turn slightly to right (**arrow 2**), pull on knob to remove (**arrow 3**).

4. Disconnect harness connector.

5. To install, first connect harness connector.

6. Hold light switch and press rotary knob inward and turn slightly to right. Hold rotary knob in this position and slide light switch into instrument panel. See Fig. 2.

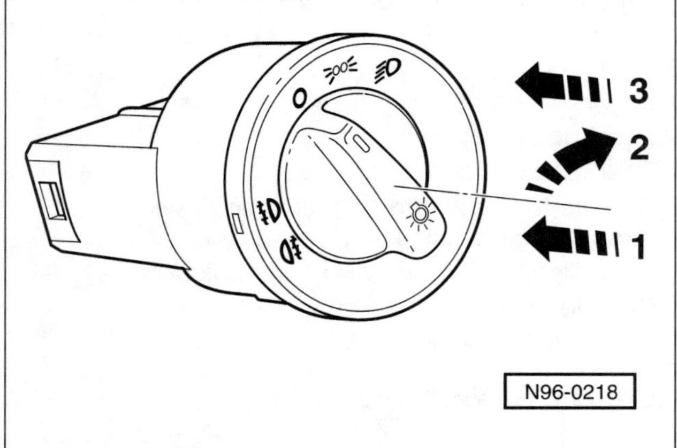

N96-0218

Fig. 2. To install light switch, press knob inward (**arrow 1**), turn slightly to right (**arrow 2**) and slide into instrument panel (**arrow 3**).

7. Turn rotary knob to "0" position, release and engage switch.

Instrument panel light dimmer switch, removing and installing

1. Place screwdriver behind switch housing and carefully pry switch carefully out of locking device. See Fig. 3.

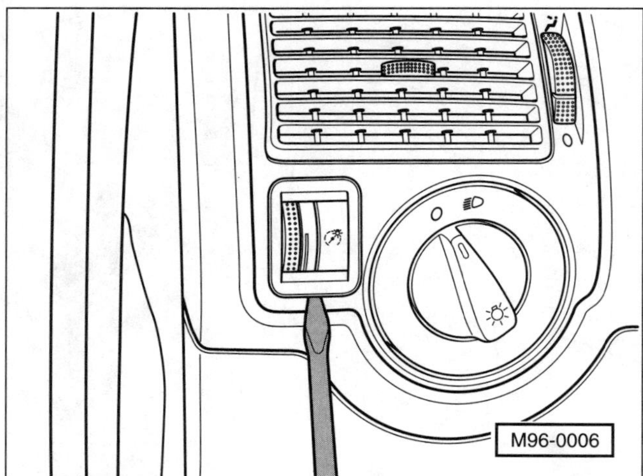

M96-0005

Fig. 3. Dimmer switch being removed from instrument panel.

> ***NOTE —***
> *Use adhesive tape around switch on dashboard and/or on screwdriver to prevent marring of trim.*

2. Disconnect harness connector.

3. To install, first connect harness connector.

4. Insert switch into locking device and engage.

Mirror adjustment switch, removing and installing

1. Remove interior door trim, see **70 Trim–Interior**.

2. Disconnect harness connector from switch.

3. Pry mounting frame outward on long side of switch and remove switches from mounting frame. See Fig. 4.

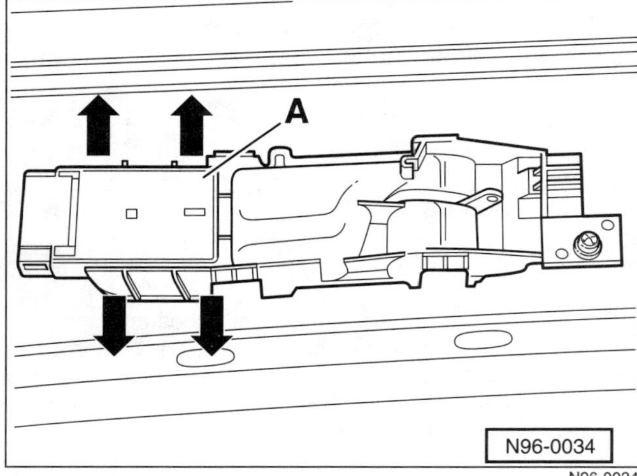

N96-0034

Fig. 4. Pry mounting frame outward (**arrows**) to remove mirror adjustment switch (**A**).

4. To install, insert switch in mounting frame and engage.

5. Connect harness connector.

6. Install interior door trim.

Interior lock and window lifter switches–driver's position, removing and installing

> ***NOTE —***
> *The interior lock and electric window switches in the driver's door panel cannot be removed individually. The complete window control unit must be removed as described below.*

1. Remove window control unit with door pull handle from the driver's door panel as shown in **70 Trim–Interior, Driver's door panel, removing and installing**.

2. Disconnect harness connector from back of window control unit.

3. Remove mounting screws for window control unit and pull out control unit. See Fig. 5.

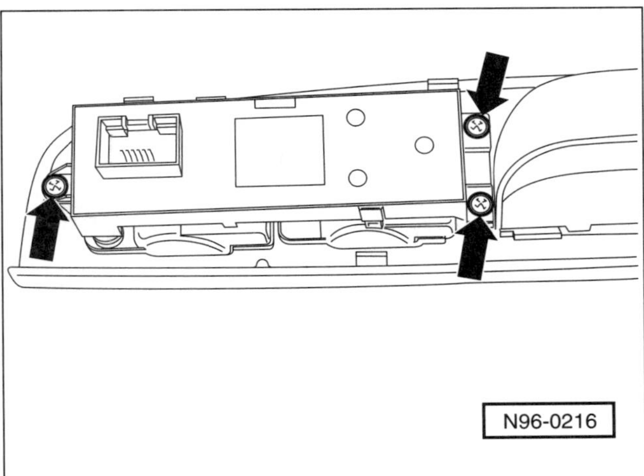

N96-0216

Fig. 5. Remove mounting screws (**arrows**) for window control unit.

4. Install in reverse order of removal.

Interior lock and window lifter switch–passenger positions, removing and installing

NOTE —
Removing and installing the front and rear passenger electric window switches (on four door vehicles) is the same.

1. Remove interior door trim, see **70 Trim–Interior**.
2. Disconnect harness connector from switch.
3. Release switch housing by pressing sideways out from locking device in mounting frame and remove. See Fig. 6.

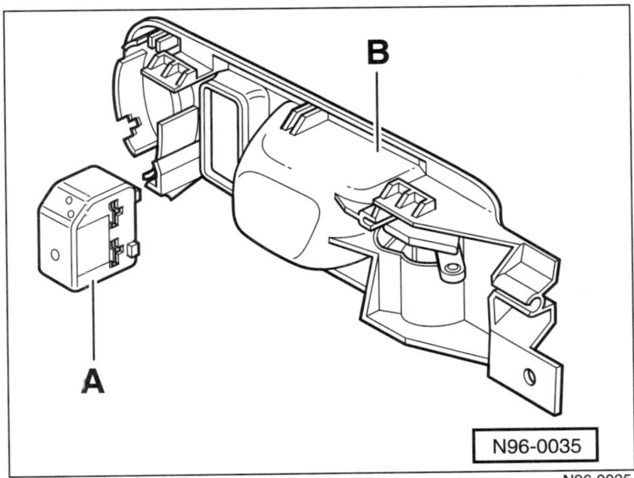

N96-0035

Fig. 6. Release interior lock switch housing (**A**) by pressing sideways out from mounting frame (**B**) locking device.

4. To install, first connect harness connector.
5. Insert switch in recess of mounting frame and engage.
6. Install door trim.

Instrument panel switches–center, removing and installing

NOTE —
- *Removing and installing is the same procedure for all switches. Only the hazard warning light switch is described here.*
- *The switch must be pulled out from the instrument panel in order to disconnect harness connector.*
- *A wooden or plastic wedge should be used to prevent damage to plastic trim and adjacent switches.*
- *It may be necessary to remove a switch on the left of the relevant switch in order to pull out the wiring sufficiently.*
- *Depending on vehicle options, there may be covers in place of some switches. The covers can be removed in the same manner as the switches.*

1. Protect instrument panel and adjacent switches with adhesive tape if necessary.
2. To remove switch for heated seats carefully pry out switch using flat plastic wedge or screwdriver. See Fig. 7.

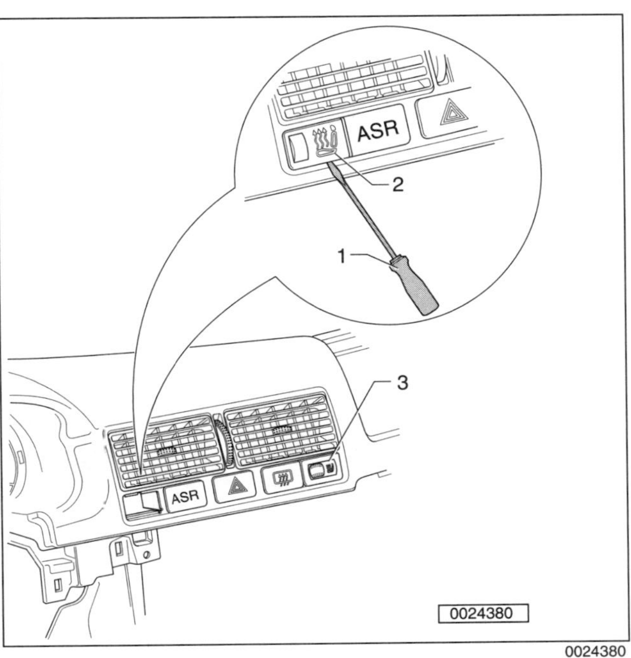

0024380

Fig. 7. Remove heated seat switch using screwdriver (**1**) or plastic wedge. Switch for driver's seat is at position **2** and for passenger at position **3**.

NOTE—
Heated seat control module is part of heated seat switch.

3. Disengage and disconnect harness connector from back of switch. Remove switch.

4. To remove switch for rear window defrost, emergency flasher or ASR (Anti-Slip Regulation) it is necessary to use Volkswagen special tool T10034 to pull switch out.

NOTE—
- *Do not use a screwdriver to remove rear window defrost, emergency flasher, or ASR switches due to the stronger springs in their release mechanisms.*
- *Before removing the ASR or rear window defrost switch, remove the seat heater switch or switch hole cover next to each switch as described above.*

5. Reach behind the ASR switch and use the tip of special tool T10034 to release spring loaded retaining button and pull switch out from dash. See Fig. 8.

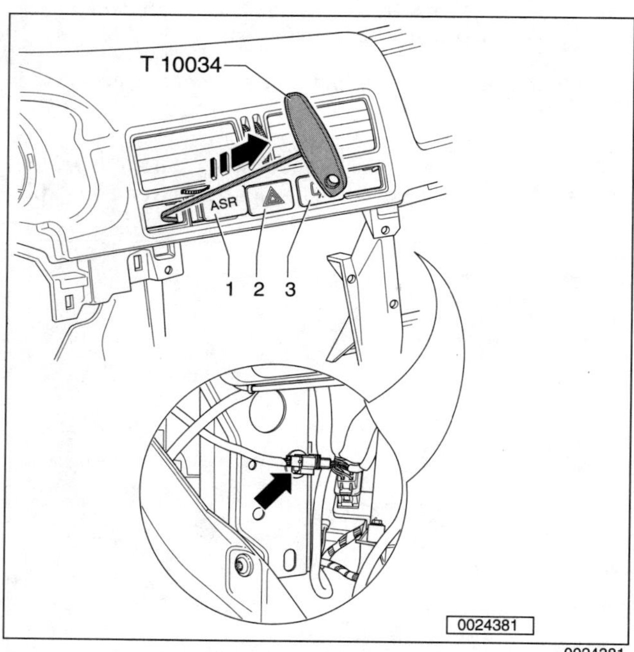

0024381

Fig. 8. Remove ASR (**1**), emergency flasher (**2**), or rear window defrost (**3**) switches with VW special tool T10034.

6. Disengage and remove harness connector. Remove switch.

7. Repeat for emergency flasher and rear window defrost switches as necessary.

8. To install, first connect harness connector and lock down retaining mechanism.

9. Insert switch into dash and engage properly.

Interior light and sunroof switch, removing and installing

NOTE—
Ignore references to sunroof switch in procedure below for vehicles not equipped with a sunroof.

1. Carefully pry out interior light lens and remove.

2. Remove mounting screws for interior light/sunroof switch assembly.

3. Use a screwdriver at retaining clips to release assembly from headliner. See Fig. 9.

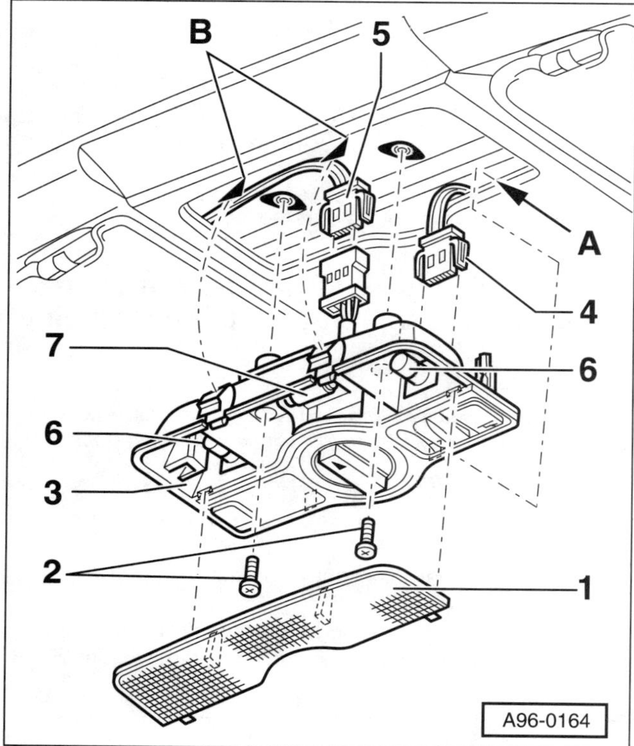

N96-0222

Fig. 9. Interior light/sunroof switch assembly. Remove screws (**2**) and pry out assembly at retaining clips (**B**). When installing, position retaining hooks into headliner (**A**) at rear first.

4. Disconnect harness connectors from light and sunroof switch.

NOTE—
To replace sunroof switch, the entire interior light/sunroof switch assembly must be replaced.

5. To install, connect harness connectors and position retaining hooks at rear of assembly into headliner. Push up front part of assembly until retaining clips engage.

6. Remaining installation is the reverse of removal. See **60 Sunroof** for sunroof motor replacement and sunroof components.

Various other interior lights shown below can all be removed by carefully prying out with a screwdriver as shown in the following illustrations:

Door warning light

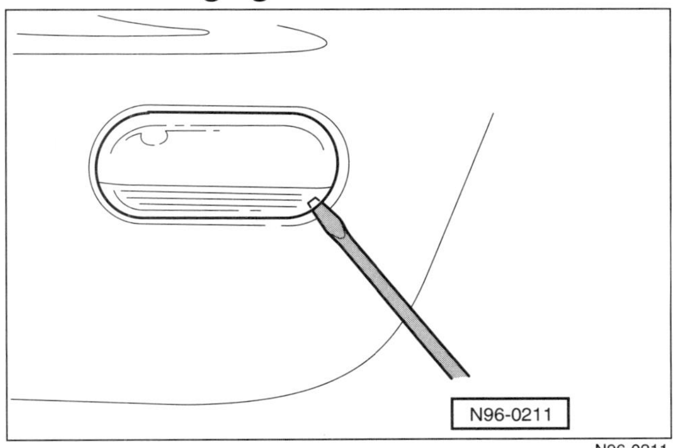

N96-0211

Fig. 10. Insert screwdriver behind lens and pry out.

Glove compartment light

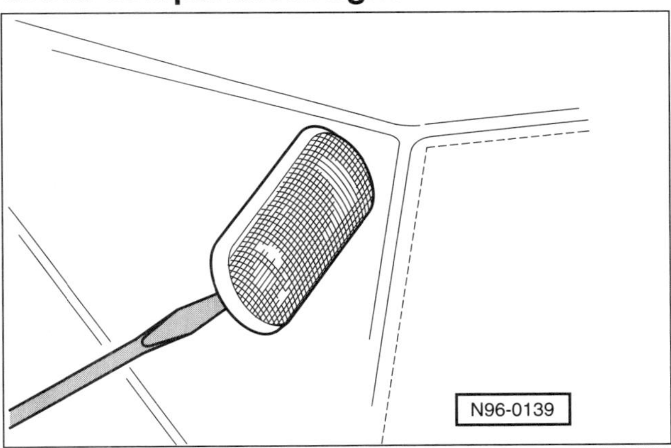

N96-0139

Fig. 11. Pry out glovebox light as shown. Check for proper operation after installing light to ensure light goes out when door is closed.

Luggage compartment light

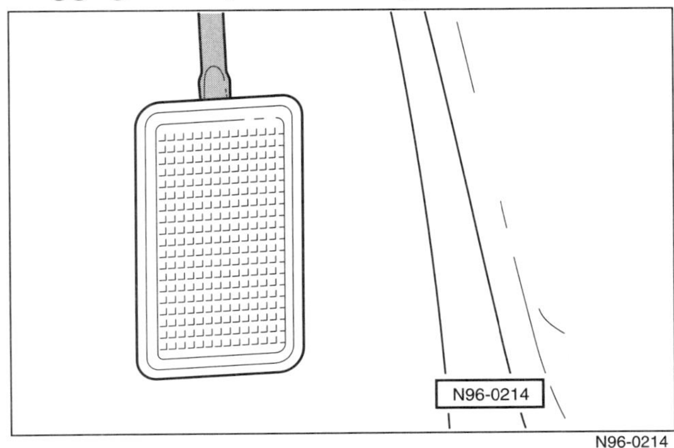

N96-0214

Fig. 12. Pry out lens from top with screwdriver.

Rear reading light

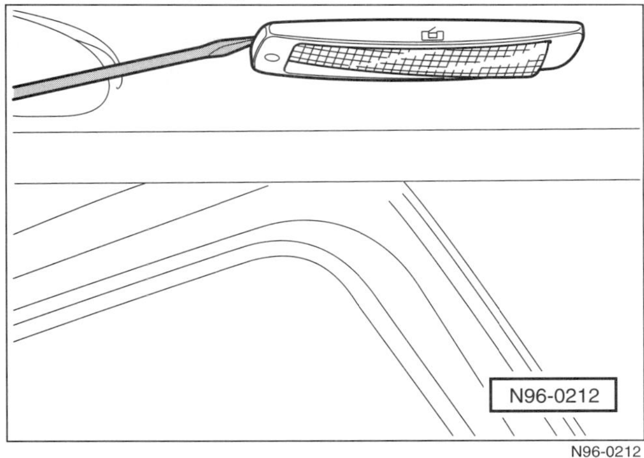

N96-0212

Fig. 13. Insert screwdriver into lens recess and pry out reading light.

Remote fuel tank door/rear lid unlock switch, removing and installing

NOTE —

The switches for remote fuel tank door and remote rear trunk lid are shown in Fig. 14.

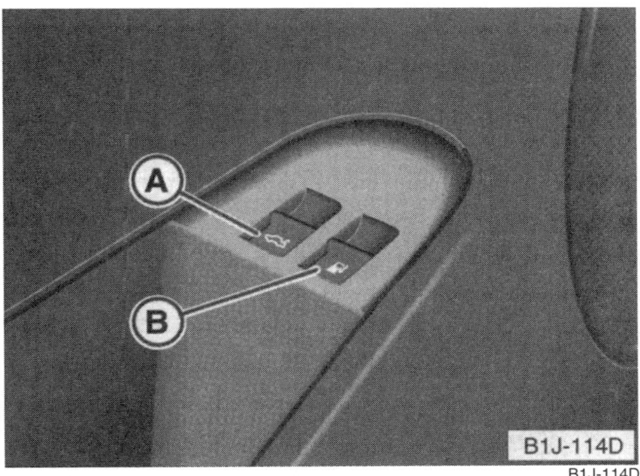

B1J-114D

Fig. 14. Remote fuel tank door (**B**) and rear lid unlock (**A**) switches in driver's side door panel.

1. Remove interior door trim, see **70 Trim–Interior**.
2. Disconnect harness connector from back of switches.
3. Release switch housing by pressing locking tabs and remove from door trim.
4. To install, insert switch into door trim and engage.
5. Connect harness connector.
6. Install door trim.

Brake light switch, removing and adjusting

The brake light switch is located above brake pedal in pedal bracket.

> ***CAUTION —***
> *Shut off engine and apply parking brake before removing brake light switch.*

NOTE —
- *It is necessary to first remove brake light switch to adjust it.*
- *Once removed, the brake light switch plunger should extend fully out. If not, switch is defective.*

1. Remove brake light switch by rotating it 90° clockwise.
2. Press brake pedal down as far as possible by hand.
3. Guide brake light switch through pedal bracket opening until plunger contacts brake pedal.
4. Lock in position by turning 90° counter-clockwise.
5. Release brake pedal and check function of brake lights. For electrical check of switch, see **45 Anti-Lock Brakes**.

Rear lid handle release button, removing and installing (Jetta)

1. Remove trim for rear lock housing, see **70 Trim–Interior**.
2. Unclip rear lock harness connectors from retaining clips and separate connectors. See Fig. 15.

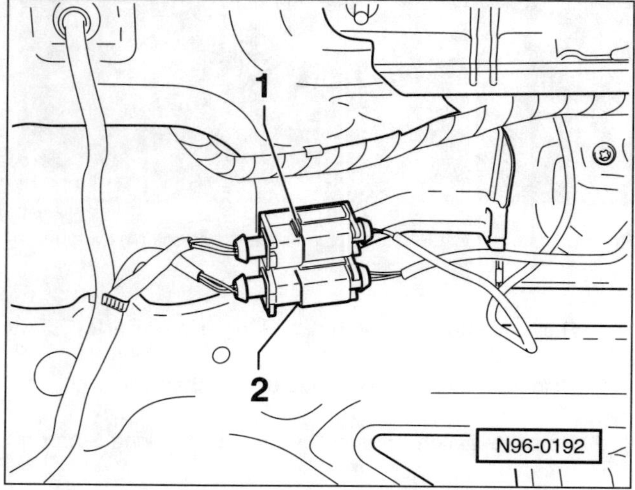

N96-0192

Fig. 15. Unclip rear lock harness connectors (**1** and **2**).

3. Unclip operating rod from lock cylinder.
4. Remove lock cylinder mounting screws. Remove lock cylinder in upward direction. See Fig. 16.

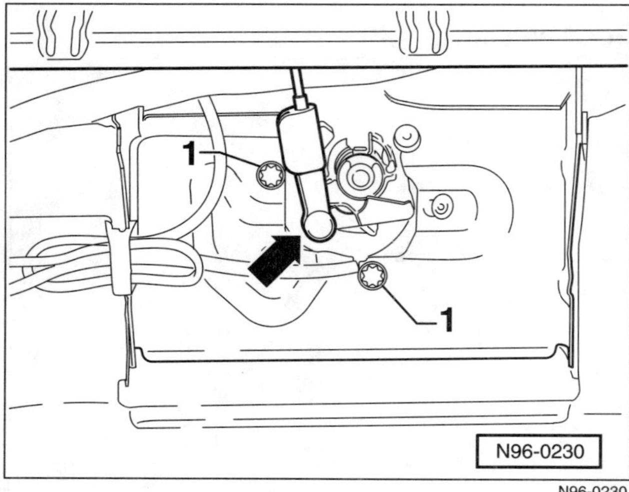

N96-0230

Fig. 16. Unclip operating rod (**arrow**) and lock cylinder mounting screws (**1**).

5. Remove mounting screws for rear lid handle release button and remove handle. See Fig. 17.

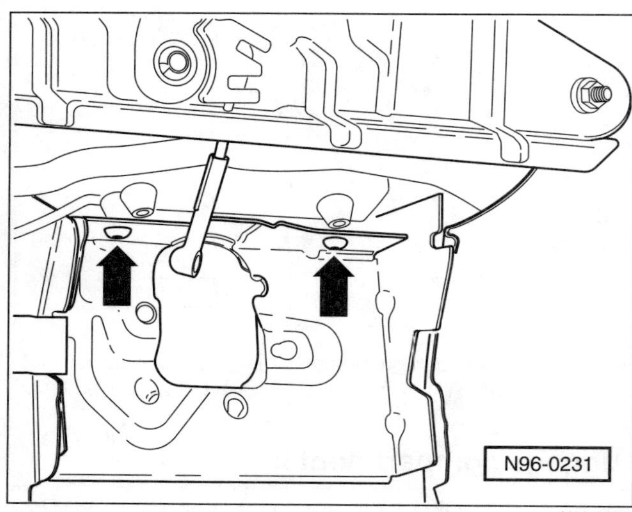

N96-0231

Fig. 17. Remove mounting screws (**arrows**) for rear lid handle release button.

6. Installation is the reverse of removal.

QUALITY REVIEW

When you have finished working under the hood and around other areas of the vehicle, it is advisable to take a moment to quality check or review your work. This helps to insure that the operation or repair has been completed properly with all affected systems functioning within normal parameters.

97 Wiring Diagrams, Fuses and Relays

TABLES

GENERAL

This section contains wiring diagrams for 1999 and later m.y. (model year) vehicles covered by this manual.

> ***WARNING —***
> *Special airbag precautions apply to any electrical system testing or repair. The airbag unit is an explosive device and must be handled with extreme care. Before starting any work on the vehicle, refer to the warnings and cautions in* **69 Seatbelts, Airbags***.*

NOTE —
Standardized terms for automotive components are used throughout this manual, including alternator which should always be referred to as a generator.

> ***CAUTION —***
> - *Before working on the electrical system always switch the ignition off and disconnect battery ground strap from battery negative (–) terminal.*
> - *Be sure to have the anti-theft radio code on hand before disconnecting the battery.*
> - *Disconnecting the negative (–) battery cable may erase fault codes and basic settings in the engine management and automatic transmission control modules. Some driveability problems may be noticed until the system re-adapts to operating conditions. OBD II readiness codes, which may be required for emissions testing, may also be erased.*

FUSES AND RELAYS

Fuse panels

The central electric panel (fuse panel) is located behind an access panel on left edge of the instrument panel. It contains both standard size fuses and mini-fuses. The use of mini-fuses allows protection of individual circuits.

There is also a main fuse box located on top of the battery in the engine compartment. It contains special fuses for high current applications and prevents the main wiring harness in the event of a short circuit. See Fig. 1. To access these fuses, squeeze tabs of plastic fuse cover and pull upward.

> ***NOTE —***
> *Volkswagen identifies electrical components by a letter and/or a number in the electrical schematics. These electrical identifiers are listed in parenthesis as an aid to electrical troubleshooting.*

Main fuse box on top of battery

- Standard fuse applications
  - Coolant fan, single speed (S180) 30A
  - ABS (S179) 30A
  - ABS-hydraulic pump (S178) 30A
- Metal fuse applications
  - Generator (S177)
    - 90 Amp 110A
    - 120 Amp 150A
  - Interior relay panel (S176) 110A
  - Coolant fan and control module (S164) 40A
  - Fuel pump relay or glow plug relay (S163) 50A
  - Secondary air injection relay or coolant pre-heating relays (S162) 50A

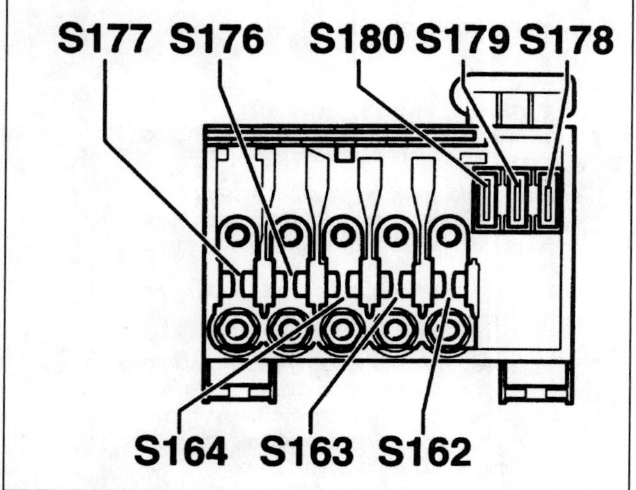

Fig. 1. Main fuse box on top of battery with fuse identification.

> ***WARNING —***
> *Metal fuses in the main fuse box should be changed by an authorized Volkswagen service professional.*

> ***NOTE —***
> - *Fuse application and amperage may vary depending on equipment level.*
> - *All fuses are identified in the wiring diagrams with the prefix of S, i.e. fuse #4 is S4.*
> - *"RES" in the central electric panel refers to reserve, or places for spare fuses.*

Fuse colors and amperage

- Green 30A
- White 25A
- Yellow 20A
- Blue 15A
- Red 10A
- Brown 7.5A
- Beige 5A
- Violet 3A

The fuses in the central electric panel are identified in **Table a**.

Table a. Fuse identification

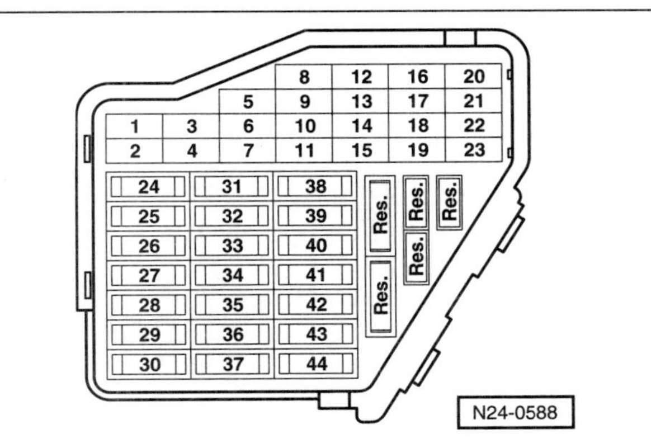

Table a. Fuse identification

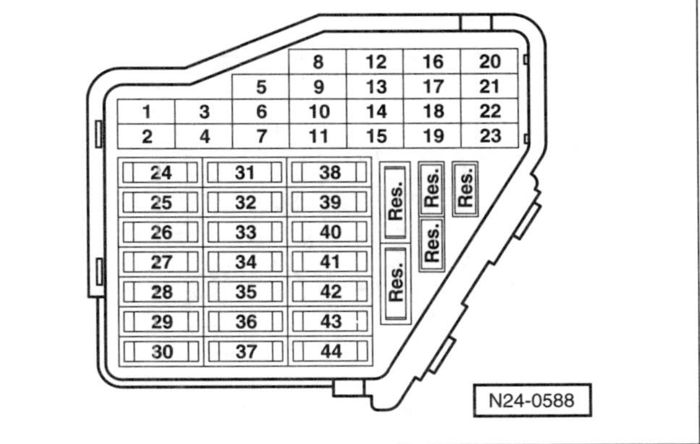
8 12 16 20
5 9 13 17 21
1 3 6 10 14 18 22
2 4 7 11 15 19 23
24 31 38
25 32 39
26 33 40
27 34 41
28 35 42
29 36 43
30 37 44
Res.
Res.
Res.
Res.
Res.
N24-0588

Position	Description	Amperage
1	Heated washer nozzles, glove compartment light	10
2	Turn signal system	10
3	Fog light relay	5
4	License plate light	5
5	Comfort system, cruise control, Climatronic, A/C, heated seat control modules, day/night dimming mirror, control module and control unit for multi-function steering wheel	7.5
6	Central locking system	5
7	Back-up lights, speedometer vehicle speed sensor	10
8	open	-
9	Anti-lock brakes (ABS)	5
10	ECM, gasoline engine ECM, diesel engine (m.y. 2000 >)	10 5
11	Instrument cluster, shift lock solenoid	5
12	B+ (battery positive voltage) for Data Link Connector (DLC)	7.5
13	Brake lights	10
14	Interior lights, central locking system	10
15	Instrument cluster, automatic transmission control module (TCM)	5
16	A/C clutch, after-run coolant pump	10
17	open	-
18	High beam right	10
19	High beam left	10
20	Low beam right	15
21	Low beam left	15
22	Parking and side marker lights, right	5
23	Parking and side marker lights, left	5
24	Front wiper motor, washer pump	20
25	Fresh air blower, Climatronic, A/C	25
26	Rear window defogger	25
27	Rear wiper motor	15
28	Fuel pump, gasoline	15
29	Engine control module (ECM), gasoline Engine control module (ECM), diesel	15 10
30	Sunroof control module	20
31	Automatic transmission control module	20
32	Fuel Injectors (gasoline) ECM (diesel)	10 15
33	Headlight washer system	20
34	Engine control elements	10
35	12V power outlet (in luggage comp.)	30
36	Fog lights	15
37	Radio terminal 86S, instrument cluster	10
38	Central locking system (with power windows) luggage compartment light, remote fuel tank door, rear lid unlock	15
39	Emergency flashers	15
40	Dual tone horn	20
41	Cigarette lighter	15
42	Radio system	25
43	Engine control elements	10
44	Heated seats	15

NOTE —

Fuses number 23 through 44 are identified in wiring diagrams with an additional prefix of 2 (i.e. fuse #40 is S240).

Relay positions

The relay panel is located under the left side of the instrument panel. There are three fuses on the lower relay panel which are identified in **Table b**. The relays are also identified in **Table b**.

Table b. Relay panel identification

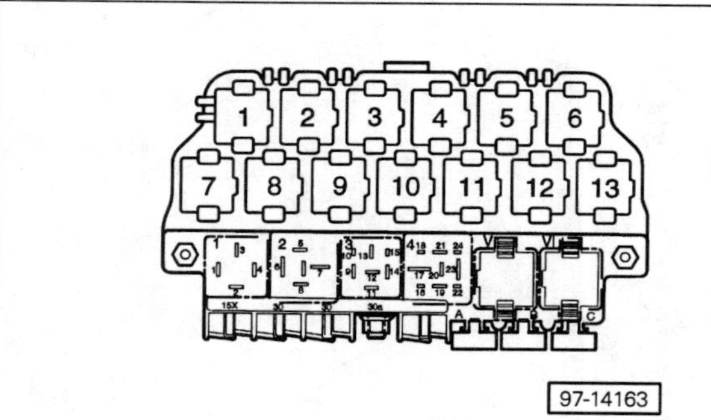

Position	Description	Number on relay
	Lower relay panel	
1	Dual horn relay	53
2	Load reduction relay	18/100
3	open	-
4	Fuel pump relay	409
V, VI	Wiper/Washer intermittent relay vehicles without headlight washer system vehicles with headlight washer system Vehicles with rain sensor	 377 389 192
	Fuses on lower relay panel	
A	Power (Memory) seat circuit breaker	-
B	open	-
C	Power windows, central locking, heated power mirrors	-
	Relays on upper (auxiliary) relay panel	
1	open	-
2	Rear lid remote unlock motor relay	79
3	Anti-theft starter lock relay (clutch pedal switch)	185, 53
4	Fog light relay	53
5	multi-function steering wheel relay (as applicable)	-
6	multi-function steering wheel relay (as applicable)	-
7	Daytime running lights (from April 1999)	173
8	Daytime running lights (through March 1999)	173
9	open	-
10	Glow plug relay	180
11	Park/Neutral position relay	175
12	Power supply (terminal 30b, B+) relay	109
13	open	-

There are also additional fuses above the relay panel which are identified in **Table c**.

Table c. Fuses above relay panel

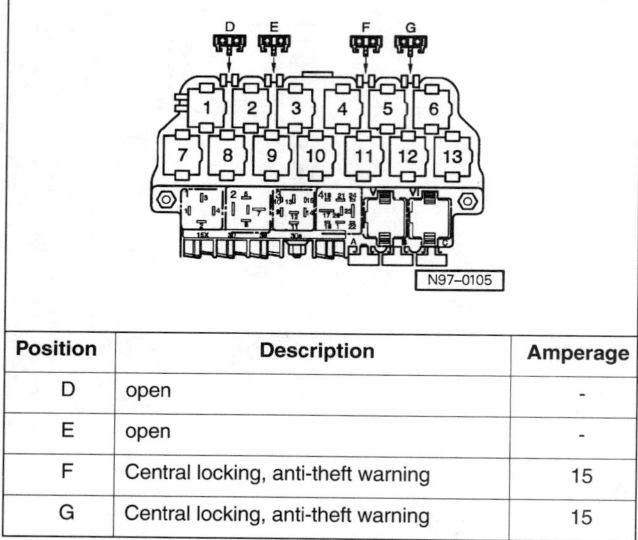

Position	Description	Amperage
D	open	-
E	open	-
F	Central locking, anti-theft warning	15
G	Central locking, anti-theft warning	15

Fuse panel, removing and installing

1. Disconnect battery ground (GND) strap from battery negative (–) terminal. See the **Cautions** at the beginning of this repair group regarding battery disconnection.
2. Pry off fuse panel cover from left side of dashboard.
3. Remove steering column lower trim, see **70 Trim–Interior**.
4. Remove fuse panel mounting screws. Press retaining clips on top and bottom of fuse panel and push panel inward to remove. See Fig. 2.

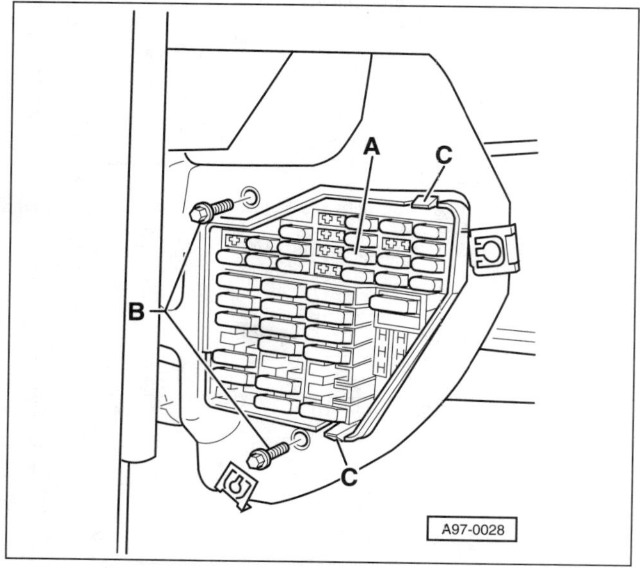

A97-0028

Fig. 2. Remove mounting screws (**B**), press retaining clips (**C**) and push fuse panel (**A**) inward to remove.

Relay panel, removing and installing

1. Disconnect battery ground (GND) strap from battery negative (–) terminal. See the **Cautions** at the beginning of this repair group regarding battery disconnection.

2. Remove steering column lower trim, see **70 Trim–Interior**.

3. Remove mounting nuts on either side of relay panel and disconnect screw-on wire connections at bottom of panel. Pull down panel to remove. See Fig. 3.

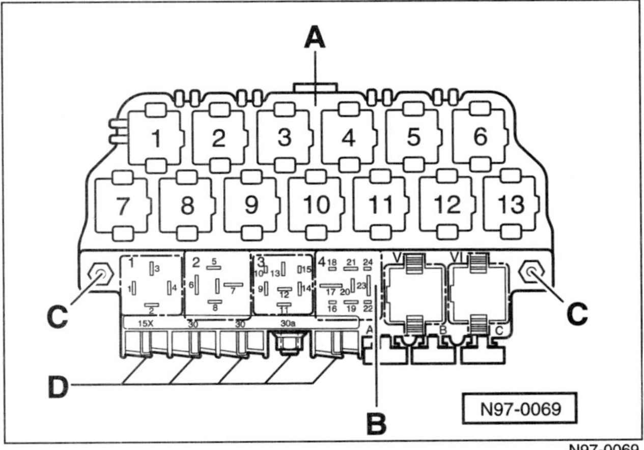

N97-0069

Fig. 3. Remove mounting nuts (**C**) and loosen screw-on connections (**D**) to remove central electric (**B**) and relay panel (**A**).

CONNECTOR STATIONS

Various connector stations are located throughout the vehicles covered by this manual. Some of those connector stations are shown below.

Lower A-pillar

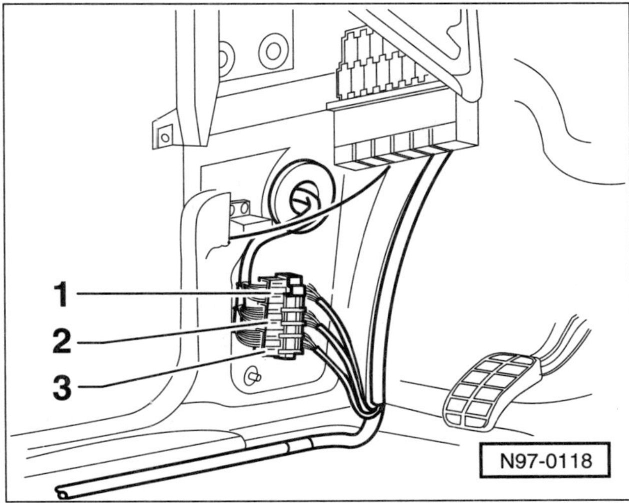

N97-0118

Fig. 4. Connector station in driver's side lower A-pillar. Passenger side is a mirror image of above. Brown connector (**1**) is for central locking system, blue connector (**2**) is for power mirrors, black connector (**3**) is for loudspeaker and power windows.

C-pillar (Golf/GTI)

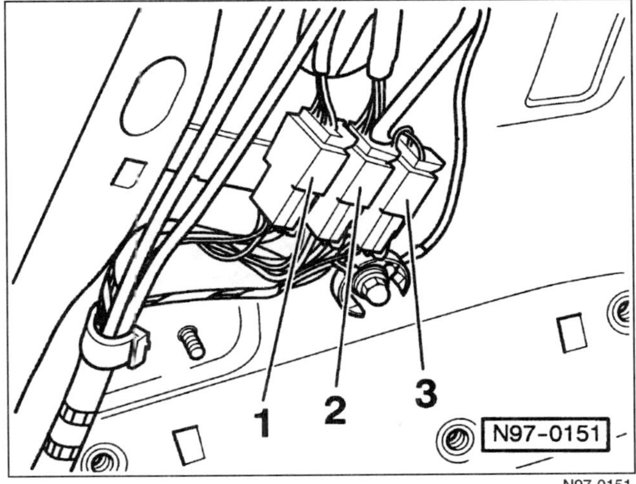

N97-0151

Fig. 5. Connector station on C-pillar of Golf/GTI. Black connector (**1**) is for heated rear window, luggage compartment light, high mount brake light, and rear window defrost. Pink connector (**2**) is for rear wiper motor. Brown connector (**3**) is for central locking and rear lid unlock motor.

C-pillar (Jetta)

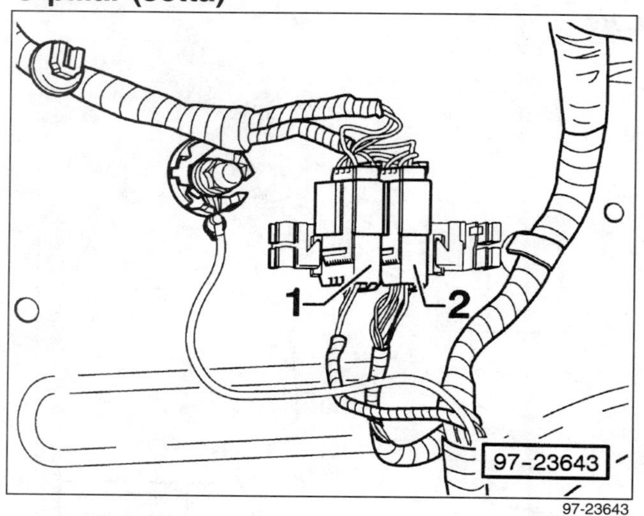

97-23643

Fig. 6. Connector station on C-pillar of Jettas. Black connector (**1**) is for license plate light and luggage compartment light. Brown connector (**2**) is for central locking and rear lid unlock motor.

GROUND LOCATIONS

Various ground locations are identified in the figures shown below. Be sure to inspect these for clean tight connections when troubleshooting electrical problems.

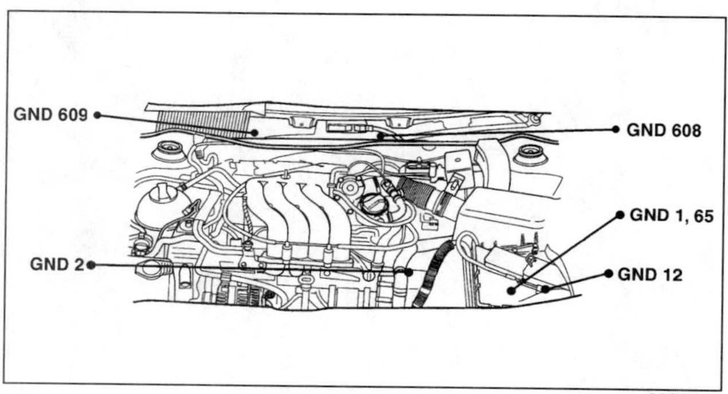

0024382

Fig. 7. Ground locations in the engine compartment. **GND 1**, **12**, and **65** are located below battery tray. **GND 2** is on transmission, near engine block. **GND 608** is in the left side of the plenum in front of the ECM. **GND 609** is in the right side of the plenum in front of the dust and pollen filter housing.

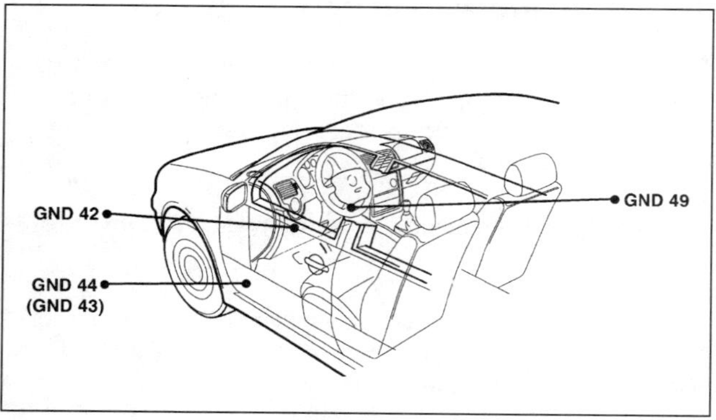

0024383

Fig. 8. Ground locations inside vehicle. **GND 42** is above driver's footwell, to left of pedal cluster. **GND 44** is at the bottom of left-side A-pillar. **GND 43** is at the bottom of right-side A-pillar. **GND 49** is on the steering column, left side, above lock cylinder housing.

0024384

Fig. 9. Ground locations in rear of vehicle. **GND 50** is in luggage compartment, left side, below C-pillar.

0024385

Fig. 10. Ground locations in front of vehicle. **GND 77** and **78** are on the lower left and right B-pillars, above seat belt reel.

COMPONENT LOCATIONS

Table d. Component locations

Component (code)	Application	Location and additional information
ABS control module (J104)	all with ABS	to left of vacuum brake booster, on bottom of hydraulic unit
ABS wheel speed sensors: right rear (G44), left rear (G46) right front (G45), left front (G47)	all with ABS	 at appropriate rear stub axle in appropriate front wheel bearing housing
A/C cut-out thermal switch (F163)	all with A/C	in "T" in coolant line, between radiator and engine cylinder head
After-run coolant pump (V51)	2.8L	on cylinder head, left rear
Airbag control module (J234)	all	on center tunnel, front, beneath heater housing
Airbag igniter, driver side (N95)	all	mounted on steering wheel
Airbag igniter, passenger side (N131)	all	instrument panel, above glovebox
Airbag spiral spring (F138)	all	on steering column, with wiring for horn contact
Alarm horn (H8)	central locking	in plenum, left side
Ambient temperature switch (F38)	all with A/C	in plenum, left side
Back-up light switch (F4)	all manual	top of transmission, on front selector mechanism housing
Brake fluid level warning switch (F34)	all	in brake fluid reservoir cap
Brake light switch (F)	all	above brake pedal, integral with (F47)
Brake vacuum vent valve switch (F47)	all	above brake pedal, integral with (F), for cruise control
Camshaft position sensor (G40)	4-cylinder 6-cylinder	on cylinder head, right side, behind camshaft sprocket on cylinder head, left side, behind ignition coil
Change-over valve for intake manifold flap (N239)	1.9L	back of intake manifold
Closed throttle position switch (F60)	2.0L (AEG) 1.9L	on throttle body on bulkhead, above accelerator pedal, part of throttle position sensor
Clutch pedal position switch (F194)	all manual	above clutch pedal
Clutch vacuum vent valve switch (F36)	all manual	above clutch pedal
Cold start injector (N108)	1.9L	on bottom of diesel injection pump
Comfort system central control module (J393)	comfort system	above pedal cluster, to left of steering column
Connectors, 2-pin for engine glow plugs (T2a) for needle lift sensor (T2b) (T2c)	1.9L	 in engine compartment, left side, behind air cleaner housing in front of engine block, to left of diesel injection pump in engine compartment, left side, behind air cleaner housing
Connector, 3-pin for RPM sensor (T3)	2.0L 1.9L 2.8L	in front of engine cylinder block, above oil filter flange in front of engine block, to left of diesel injection pump in front of engine, left side, below secondary air injection pump
Connector, 4-pin for 02S (T4c)	gasoline	on bottom right side floor panel, inside protective housing
Connector, 4-pin for A/C clutch & generator (T4)	all	above starter
Connector, 4-pin for HO2S (T4b)	gasoline	on bottom right side floor panel, inside protective housing
Connector, 6-pin brown (T6)	all	in connector station in plenum, left side beneath windshield wiper linkage
Connector, 10-pin (T10a)	all	in engine compartment, left side, to rear of air cleaner housing, in guide
Connectors, 10-pin: orange (T10) green (T10d) black (T10e) grey (T10g) blue (T10h)	all	in connector station in plenum, left side beneath windshield wiper linkage
Connectors, 10-pin for door components black (T10i) black (T10k) black (T10l) black (T10m) brown (T10n) brown (T10p) blue (T10c) blue (T10r)	all with power windows and locks	 bottom of driver side A-pillar bottom of passenger side A-pillar driver side B-pillar passenger side B-pillar bottom of driver side A-pillar bottom of passenger side A-pillar bottom of driver side A-pillar bottom of passenger side A-pillar

Table d. Component locations

Component (code)	Application	Location and additional information
Connector, 12-pin for CD changer	all	luggage compartment left side
Connector, 12-pin for solenoid valves and ATF temperature sensor	all automatics	on top of final drive housing
Coolant fan control module (J293)	all	engine compartment. lower left below front support
Coolant fan control thermal switch (F18)	all	back of radiator, bottom left
Coolant preheating relay, low heat output (J359)	1.9L	engine compartment, left rear under protective cover
Coolant preheating relay, high heat output (J360)	1.9L	engine compartment, left rear under protective cover
Crash sensor for side airbag driver side (G179) passenger side (G180)	all with side airbags	 under driver's seat and carpet under front passenger's seat and carpet
Door control module driver side (J386) passenger side (J387) left rear (J388) right rear (J389)	all with power windows	in door, on component carrier, integral with window motor
EGR vacuum regulator solenoid valve (N18)	1.9L	engine compartment, rear, left side, to right of wastegate bypass valve
Engine control module (J220)	all	in plenum, center
Engine coolant level sensor (G32)	all	in coolant reservoir (expansion tank)
Engine coolant temperature sensor (G2)	all	in coolant flange on cylinder head, left side, integral with (G62)
Engine coolant temperature sensor (G62)	all	in coolant flange on cylinder head, left side, integral with (G2)
Engine speed (RPM) sensor (G28)	all	on front of engine block, lower left, near transmission flange
Evaporative emission canister purge regulator valve (N80)	gasoline	in engine compartment, right side, next to coolant reservoir
Fresh air blower (V2)	all	in front of glove box
Fresh air blower series resistance with fuse (N24)	all	in front of glove box, beneath fresh air blower
Fresh/recirculating air door servo motor (V154)	all	in front of glove box, to right of fresh air blower housing
Fuel cut-off valve (N109)	1.9L	on top of diesel injection pump, left side
Fuel gauge sender (G)	all	in fuel tank, beneath rear seat, part of fuel pump module (gasoline only)
Fuel pump (G6)	gasoline	in fuel tank, beneath rear seat, part of fuel pump module
Fuel tank lid unlock (V155)	all	luggage compartment, right side, behind wheel housing
Fuel temperature sensor (G81)	1.9L	on front of diesel injection pump, integral with modulating piston displacement sensor and quantity adjuster
Generator (C)	all	front of engine, right side
Hood alarm switch (F120)	central locking	on hood latch mechanism
Ignition coil (N152)	4-cyl. gasoline 6-cyl. gasoline	on front of engine block, left side on cylinder head, left side
Intake air temperature sensor (G72)	2.0L 1.9L, 1.8L	in intake air duct, to right of air cleaner housing in intake air duct between charge air cooler and intake manifold
Intake manifold change-over valve (N156)	6-cylinder	in front of engine, left side, above oil filter housing
Kick down switch for automatic transmission (F8)	1.9L 2.0L	on bulkhead above accelerator pedal, component of throttle position sensor in engine compartment, to right of vacuum brake booster
Knock sensor 1 (G61)	4-cyl. gasoline 6-cyl. gasoline	on front of engine cylinder block, right side on engine cylinder block, right rear, below exhaust manifold
Knock sensor 2 (G66)	4-cyl. gasoline 6-cyl. gasoline	on front of engine cylinder block, behind ignition coil on engine cylinder block, left front, above engine oil cooler
Leak detection pump (V144)	gasoline	inside right-rear wheelhousing, toward rear, near fuel-filler neck
Lock unit for central locking driver side (F220), passenger side (F221) left rear (F222), right rear (F223)	central locking	component of door lock assembly, includes motor and switches
Manifold absolute pressure sensor (G71)	1.8L and 1.9L	in intake air duct between charge air cooler and intake manifold
Mass air flow sensor (G70)	all	in intake air duct, to right of air cleaner housing

Table d. Component locations

Component (code)	Application	Location and additional information
Modulating piston displacement sensor (G149)	1.9L	on front of diesel injection pump, integral with fuel temperature sensor and quantity adjuster
Multi-function transmission range switch (F125)	all automatics	rear of transmission housing, top
Needle lift sensor (G80)	1.9L	front of cylinder head, part of cylinder no. 3 fuel injector
Oil pressure switch (F1)	4-cylinder 6-cylinder	front of engine on oil filter flange on top of oil filter housing
Oxygen sensor ahead of catalytic converter, heated (G39)	gasoline	in exhaust system, ahead of catalytic converter
Oxygen sensor behind catalytic converter (G130)	gasoline	in exhaust system, at back of catalytic converter
Parking brake warning switch (F9)	all	central tunnel, below parking brake lever
Positive crankcase ventilation heating element (N79)	gasoline diesel	in hose between cylinder head cover and intake air duct, near throttle body in PCV hose between cylinder head cover and intake air duct
Quantity adjuster (N146)	1.9L	on front of diesel injection pump, integral with fuel temperature sensor and displacement sensor
Rear lid unlock motor (V139)	Jetta	rear lid, attached to rear lock cylinder carrier
Seat belt tensioner igniter driver side (N153) passenger side (N154)	all	bottom of B-pillar
Secondary air injection solenoid valve (N112)	4-cyl. gasoline 6-cyl. gasoline	in engine compartment, left side, above brake fluid reservoir in front of engine, left side, above oil cooler housing
Secondary air injection motor (V101)	gasoline	in engine compartment, left side
Secondary air injection pump relay (J299)	gasoline	engine compartment, left side, behind air cleaner housing, under protective cover
Shift lock solenoid (N110)	all automatics	on central tunnel, with gear selector mechanism
Side airbag igniter, driver side (N199)	side airbags	on left side of driver seat backrest, beneath seat cover
Side airbag igniter, passenger side (N200)	side airbags	on right side of passenger seat backrest, beneath seat cover
Speedometer vehicle speed sensor (G22)	all	top of final drive housing
Throttle position actuator (V60)	gasoline	mounted on throttle body, part of throttle valve control module
Throttle position sensor (G69)	2.0L (AEG)	mounted on throttle body, component of throttle valve control module
Throttle position sensor (G79)	all with electronic throttle	on bulkhead, above accelerator pedal, integral with kick-down switch and closed throttle position switch
Throttle position sensor (G88)	gasoline	mounted on throttle body, component of throttle valve control module
Throttle valve control module (J338)	gasoline	mounted on throttle body, contains CTP switch, TP sensors and TP actuator
Transmission control module (J217)	all automatics	in plenum, right side
Transmission vehicle speed sensor (G38)	all automatics	top of transmission housing, to left of transmission cooler
Trunk lock alarm/central locking switch	central locking	on trunk lock cylinder, in rear lid
Vehicle speed sensor (G68)	all automatics	top of transmission housing, below transmission mount
Voltage regulator (C1)	all	on back of generator, later model regulators cannot be replaced separately
Wastegate bypass regulator valve (N75)	1.9L	engine compartment, rear, left side, to left of EGR solenoid valve
Window regulator motor driver side front (V147) passenger side front (V148) driver side rear (V26), passenger side rear (V27)	all with power windows	in door on component carrier, integral with door control module
Windshield and rear window (Golf only) washer pump (V59)	all	on windshield washer fluid reservoir
Windshield washer fluid level sensor (G33)	all	in windshield washer fluid reservoir

USING WIRING DIAGRAMS

The wiring diagrams are oriented on the pages in a 2-up horizontal format in order to facilitate easier tracking of the various circuits which frequently run across several pages.

This electrical wiring diagram section has been organized based on the way the electrical wiring diagrams were originally distributed. Each wiring diagram page appears in its original and complete form, including original page numbers or technical bulletin numbers. In addition, every page contains a unique Repair Manual page number to facilitate indexing and easy access to individual circuits.

The electrical wiring diagram section has several comprehensive indexes designated by model year and identified by black page tabs. These indexes list the various components and electrical systems on a particular vehicle model, or systems that are common to all models. The actual wiring diagrams themselves follow the indexes.

The diagram below shows important wiring diagram information.

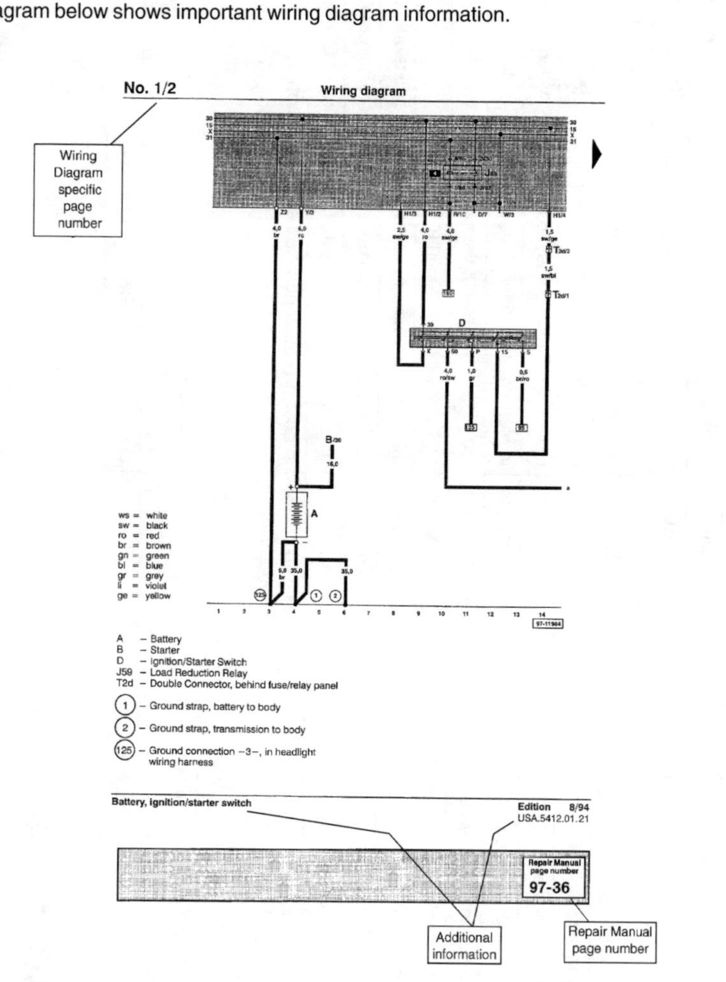

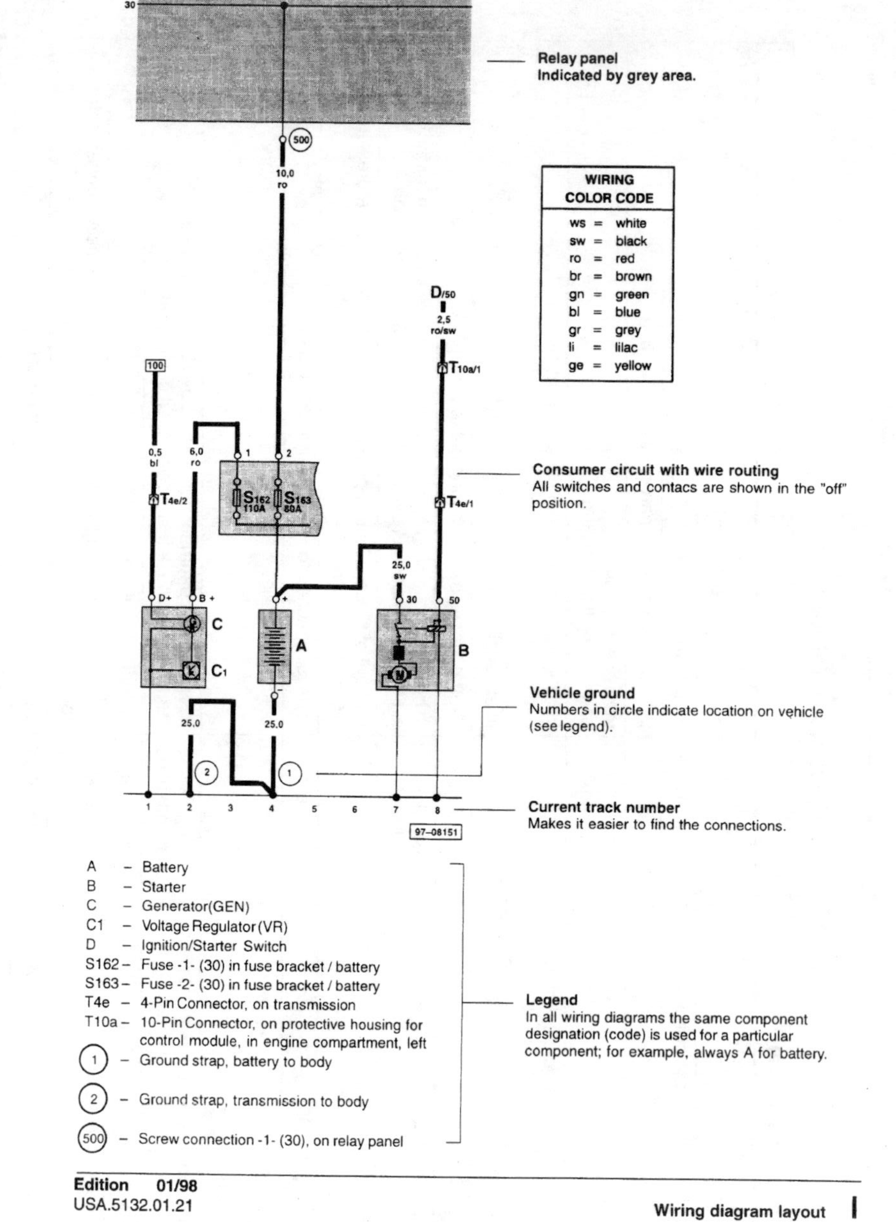

Relay panel
Indicated by grey area.
WIRING COLOR CODE
ws = white
sw = black
ro = red
br = brown
gn = green
bl = blue
gr = grey
li = lilac
ge = yellow
Consumer circuit with wire routing
All switches and contacs are shown in the "off" position.
Vehicle ground
Numbers in circle indicate location on vehicle (see legend).
Current track number
Makes it easier to find the connections.
Legend
In all wiring diagrams the same component designation (code) is used for a particular component; for example, always A for battery.
A – Battery
B – Starter
C – Generator(GEN)
C1 – Voltage Regulator (VR)
D – Ignition/Starter Switch
S162 – Fuse -1- (30) in fuse bracket / battery
S163 – Fuse -2- (30) in fuse bracket / battery
T4e – 4-Pin Connector, on transmission
T10a – 10-Pin Connector, on protective housing for control module, in engine compartment, left
1 – Ground strap, battery to body
2 – Ground strap, transmission to body
500 – Screw connection -1- (30), on relay panel

Edition 01/98
USA.5132.01.21

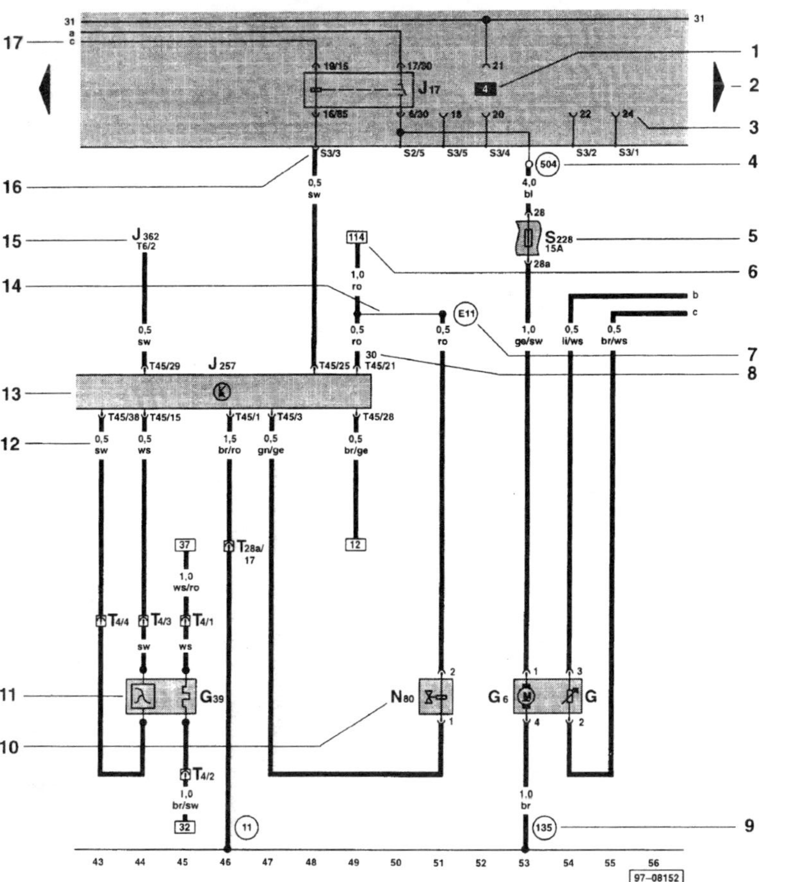

Edition 01/98
USA.5132.01.21

How to read wiring diagrams

1 – **Relay location number**
Indicates location on relay panel.

2 – **Arrow**
Indicates wiring circuit is continued on the previous and/or next page.

3 – **Connection designation – relay control module on relay panel**
Shows the individual terminals in a multi-point connector.
For example: contact 24 on terminal **4** on relay panel.

4 – **Diagram of threaded pin on relay panel**
White circle shows a detachable connection.

5 – **Fuse designation**
For example: S228 = Fuse number 228, 15 amps, in relay panel

6 – **Reference of wire continuation (current track number)**
Number in frame indicates current track where wire is continued.

7 – **Wire connection designation in wiring harness**
Location of wire connections are indicated in the legend.

8 – **Terminal designation**
Designation which appears on actual component and/or terminal number of a multi-point connector

9 – **Ground connection designation in wire harness**
Locations of ground connections are indicated in legend.

10 – **Component designation**
Use legend at bottom of page to identify the component code.

11 – **Component symbols (see Symbols used in wiring diagrams)**

12 – **Wire cross-section size (in mm^2) and wire colours**
Abbreviations are explaining in colour chart beside the wiring diagram.

13 – **Component symbol with open drawing side**
Indicated component is continued on another wiring diagram. The number of corresponding wiring diagram can taken from list of contents.

14 – **Internal connections (thin lines)**
These connections are **not** wires. Internal connections are current carrying and are listed to allow tracing of current flow inside components and wiring harness.

15 – **Reference of continuation of wire to component**
For example: Control module for anti-theft immobilizer J362 on 6-Pin Connector, terminal 2

16 – **Relay panel connectors**
Shows wiring of multi-point or single connectors on relay panel
For example: S3/3 – Multi-point connector S3, terminal 3

17 – **Reference of internal connection continuation**
Letters indicate where connection continues on the previous and/or next page.

Wiring diagram terminal (circuit) identification

Several wiring circuits in the vehicle's electrical system are identified with a number or letter designation. These circuits are identified the same in all wiring diagrams and are most commonly shown near the top of each page in the fuse/relay panel portion of the wiring diagram. The circuit designations may also be used to identify switch connector terminals (switch circuits). Following are the most common numbered/lettered circuits:

Terminal (circuit) 1-	Ignition coil/ignition distributor low voltage (typically used as an Engine Speed (RPM) signal for the tachometer)
Terminal (circuit) 15-	Switched Battery Positive Voltage (B+) from ignition/starter switch
Terminal (circuit) 30-	Battery Positive Voltage (B+), hot at all times
Terminal (circuit) 31-	Ground (GND)
Terminal (circuit) 50-	Starter control; switched B+ from ignition/starter switch
Terminal (circuit) 56-	Switched headlight B+ from light switch
Terminal (circuit) 58-	Switched parking light, taillight, illumination B+ from light switch
Terminal (circuit) S (SU)-	Key in ignition circuit; switched B+ from ignition/starter switch
Terminal (circuit) X-	Load reduction circuit; switched B+ from load reduction relay

Edition 01/98
USA.5132.01.21

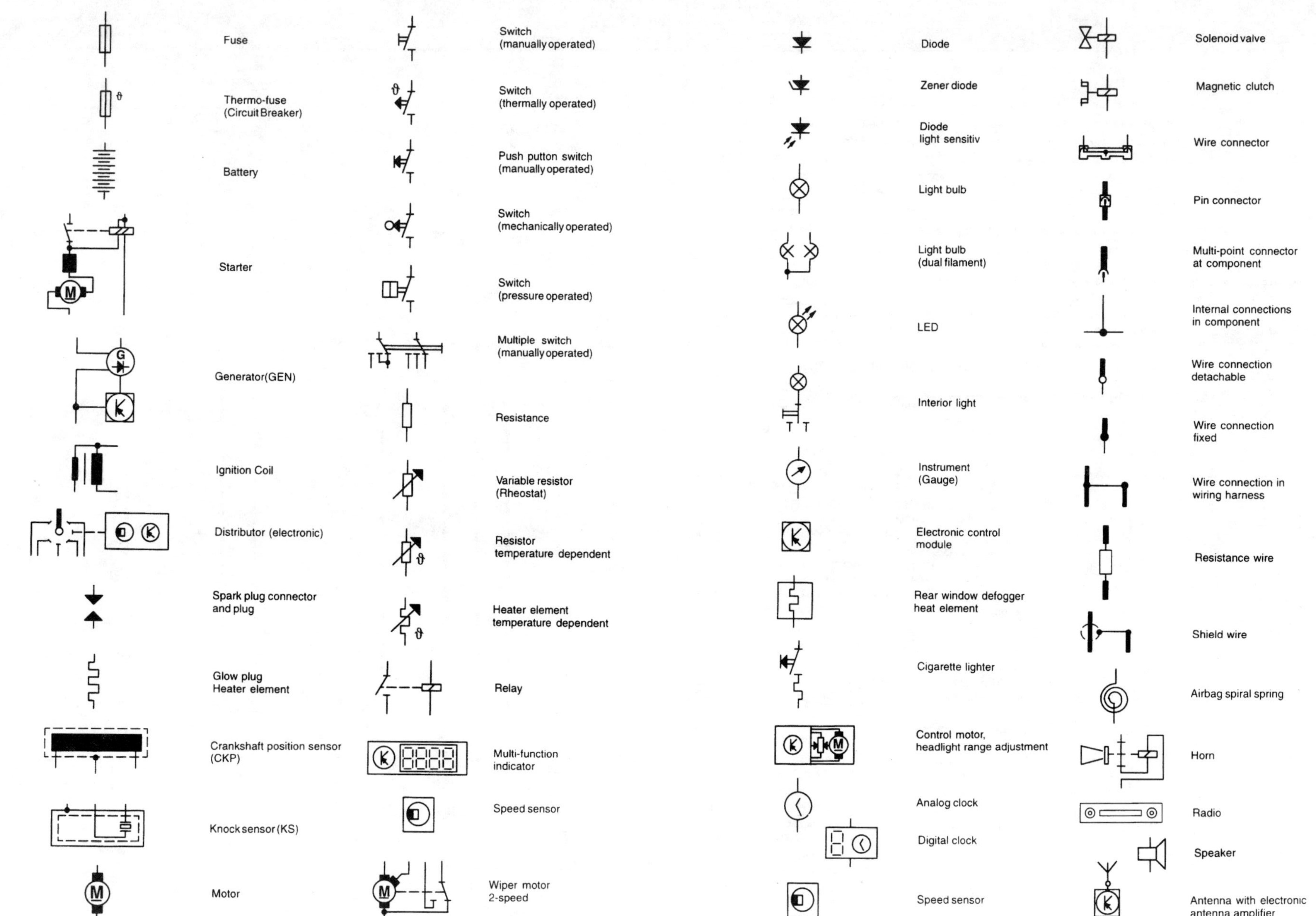

Fuse
Thermo-fuse (Circuit Breaker)
Battery
Starter
Generator(GEN)
Ignition Coil
Distributor (electronic)
Spark plug connector and plug
Glow plug Heater element
Crankshaft position sensor (CKP)
Knock sensor (KS)
Motor
Switch (manually operated)
Switch (thermally operated)
Push putton switch (manually operated)
Switch (mechanically operated)
Switch (pressure operated)
Multiple switch (manually operated)
Resistance
Variable resistor (Rheostat)
Resistor temperature dependent
Heater element temperature dependent
Relay
Multi-function indicator
Speed sensor
Wiper motor 2-speed
Diode
Zener diode
Diode light sensitiv
Light bulb
Light bulb (dual filament)
LED
Interior light
Instrument (Gauge)
Electronic control module
Rear window defogger heat element
Cigarette lighter
Control motor, headlight range adjustment
Analog clock
Digital clock
Speed sensor
Solenoid valve
Magnetic clutch
Wire connector
Pin connector
Multi-point connector at component
Internal connections in component
Wire connection detachable
Wire connection fixed
Wire connection in wiring harness
Resistance wire
Shield wire
Airbag spiral spring
Horn
Radio
Speaker
Antenna with electronic antenna amplifier

Symbols used in wiring diagrams

Standard equipment, from Sept. 1998

2.0L engine (code AEG), from Sept.1998

Electrical Wiring Diagram Index

1.9L engine (code ALH) w/manual transmission from Sept. 1998

	Wiring Diagram page number	Repair Manual page number
● **1.9L - Engine – Turbo Diesel Fuel Injection (DFI)/66KW, code ALH, (with manual transmission), from September 1998**	4/1	97-90
– Battery, ignition/starter switch	1/2	97-47
– Instrument cluster, starting interlock relay, clutch pedal position (CPP) switch, generator (GEN) warning light	1/3	97-48
– Generator (GEN)	4/2	97-91
– Glow plug relay, starter, glow plugs (engine)	4/3	97-92
– Diesel direct fuel injection (DFI) engine control module (ECM), power supply (terminal 30, B+) relay	4/4	97-93
– Diesel direct fuel injection (DFI) engine control module (ECM), closed throttle position (CTP) switch, intake air temperature (IAT) sensor, manifold absolute pressure (MAP) sensor	4/5	97-94
– Diesel direct fuel injection (DFI) engine control module (ECM), engine speed (RPM) sensor, engine coolant temperature (ECT) sensor, needle lift sensor	4/6	97-95
– Diesel direct fuel injection (DFI) engine control module (ECM), quantity adjuster, mass air flow (MAF) sensor, fuel temperature sensor, modulating piston displacement sensor	4/7	97-96
– Diesel direct fuel injection (DFI) engine control module (ECM), cold start injector, fuel cut-off valve, wastegate bypass regulator valve, EGR vacuum regulator solenoid valve	4/8	97-97
– Diesel direct fuel injection (DFI) engine control module (ECM), cruise control switch, brake vacuum vent valve switch, brake light switch, clutch vacuum vent valve switch	4/9	97-98
– Diesel direct fuel injection (DFI) engine control module (ECM)	4/10	97-99
– Diesel direct fuel Injection (DFI) engine control module (ECM), fuel level sensor, glow plugs (coolant), engine coolant level (ECL) sensor	4/11	97-100
– Instrument cluster, oil pressure switch, speedometer vehicle speed sensor, engine coolant level/temperature (ECL/ECT) warning light, glow plug indicator light	4/12	97-101
– Instrument cluster, multi-function indicator (MFI), engine coolant temperature (ECT) gauge, fuel gauge, speedometer, malfunction indicator lamp (MIL), outside air temperature sensor	4/13	97-102

1.9L engine (code ALH) w/auto. transmission from Sept. 1998

	Wiring Diagram page number	Repair Manual page number
● **1.9L - Engine – Turbo Diesel Fuel Injection (DFI)/66KW, code ALH, (with automatic transmission), from September 1998**	5/1	97-104
– Generator (GEN)	5/2	97-105
– Glow plug relay, starter, glow plugs (engine)	5/3	97-106
– Diesel direct fuel injection (DFI) engine control module (ECM), power supply (terminal 30, B+) relay	5/4	97-107
– Diesel direct fuel injection (DFI) engine control module (ECM), closed throttle position (CTP) switch, intake air temperature (IAT) sensor, manifold absolute pressure (MAP) sensor	5/5	97-108
- Diesel direct fuel injection (DFI) engine control module (ECM), engine speed (RPM) sensor, engine coolant temperature (ECT) sensor, needle lift sensor	5/6	97-109
- Diesel direct fuel injection (DFI) engine control module (ECM), quantity adjuster, mass air flow (MAF) sensor, fuel temperature sensor, modulating piston displacement sensor	5/7	97-110
- Diesel direct fuel injection (DFI) engine control module (ECM), cold start injector, fuel cut-off valve, wastegate bypass regulator valve, EGR vacuum regulator solenoid valve	5/8	97-111
- Diesel direct fuel injection (DFI) engine control module (ECM), cruise control switch, brake vacuum vent valve switch, brake light switch	5/9	97-112
- Diesel direct fuel injection (DFI) engine control module (ECM)	5/10	97-113
- Diesel direct fuel Injection (DFI) engine control module (ECM), fuel level sensor, engine coolant level (ECL) sensor, positive crankcase ventilation (PCV) heating element	5/11	97-114
- Instrument cluster, oil pressure switch, speedometer vehicle speed sensor, engine coolant level/temperature (ECL/ECT) warning light, glow plug indicator light	5/12	97-115
- Instrument cluster, multi-function indicator (MFI), engine coolant temperature (ECT) gauge, fuel gauge, speedometer, malfunction indicator lamp (MIL), outside air temperature sensor	5/13	97-116

2.8L engine (code AFP), from Dec. 1998

1999 m.y. additional electrical wiring diagrams

Electrical Wiring Diagram Index

Standard equipment, from May 1999

	Wiring Diagram page number	Repair Manual page number
● **Golf/Jetta - Standard Equipment, from May 1999**	29/1	97-252
- Battery, ignition/starter switch	29/2	97-253
- Instrument cluster, clutch pedal position (CPP) switch, starting interlock relay	29/3	97-254
- Instrument cluster, tachometer, speedometer, odometer display antitheft immobilizer, warning light for anti-theft imobilizer sensor	29/4	97-255
- Instrument cluster, generator (GEN) warning light, digital clock, low fuel level warning light	29/5	97-256
- Instrument cluster, left front brake pad wear sensor, brake pad wear indicator light, headlight high beam indicator light	29/6	97-257
- Instrument cluster, parking brake warning light switch, brake fluid level warning switch, low windshield washer fluid level indication, left and right turn signal indicator lights	29/7	97-258
- Turn signal switch, headlight dimmer/flasher switch, left front turn signal light, light for side marker front left, left headlight	29/8	97-259
- Emergency flasher switch, turn signal relay, right front turn signal light, light for side marker front right, right headlight	29/9	97-260
- Back-up light switch, left rear turn signal light, left back-up light, left brake/tail light, high-mount brake light (Golf only)	29/10	97-261
- Brake light switch, right rear turn signal light, right back-up light, right brake/tail light, high-mount brake light (Jetta only)	29/11	97-262
- Data Link Connector (DLC) radio connection, cigarette lighter	29/12	97-263
- Light switch, rear fog light switch, instrument panel vent illumination	29/13	97-264
- License plate light	29/14	97-265
- Dual tone horn, fuel tank door remote	29/15	97-266
- Instrument panel light dimmer switch, glove compartment light, rear window defogger switch, heated rear window	29/16	97-267
- Fresh air blower switch, fresh air/recirculating flap switch, fresh air blower	29/17	97-268
- Motor for rear windshield wiper, windshield and rear window washer pump	29/18	97-269
- Windshield wiper/washer switch, windshield wiper intermittent regulator, windshield wiper motor, wiper/washer intermittent relay	29/19	97-270

2.0L engine (code AEG), from May 1999

	Wiring Diagram page number	Repair Manual page number
● **2.0L - Engine - Motronic Multiport Fuel Injection (MFI)/85 kW, code AEG, from May 1999**	30/1	97-272
- Battery, ignition/starter switch	29/2	97-253
- Instrument cluster, clutch pedal position (CPP) switch, starting interlock relay	29/3	97-254
- Generator (GEN), starter	30/2	97-273
- Motronic engine control module (ECM), ignition system	30/3	97-274
- Motronic engine control module (ECM), camshaft position (CMP) sensor, engine coolant temperature (ECT) sensor, knock sensor (KS) 1	30/4	97-275
- Motronic engine control module (ECM), throttle valve control module, knock sensor (KS) 2, engine speed (RPM) sensor	30/5	97-276
- Motronic engine control module (ECM), injectors	30/6	97-277
- Motronic engine control module (ECM), leak detection pump (LDP), positive crankcase ventilation (PCV) heating element,	30/7	97-278
- Motronic engine control module (ECM), secondary air injection (AIR) pump motor, secondary air injection (AIR) solenoid valve	30/8	97-279
- Motronic engine control module (ECM), mass air flow (MAF) sensor, heated oxygen sensor (HO2S), evaporative emission (EVAP) canister purge regulator valve	30/9	97-280
- Fuel pump (FP), fuel level sensor, engine coolant level (ECL) sensor	30/10	97-281
- Instrument cluster, oil pressure switch, speedometer vehicle speed sensor, generator (GEN) warning light, engine coolant level/temperature (ECL/ECT) warning light	30/11	97-282
- Instrument cluster, multi-function indicator (MFI), engine coolant temperature (ECT) gauge, fuel gauge, malfunction indicator lamp (MIL), outside air temperature sensor	30/12	97-283

1.9L engine (code ALH) w/manual transmission from May 1999

1.9L engine (code ALH) w/auto. transmission from May 1999

Electrical Wiring Diagram Index

2.8L engine (code AFP), from May 1999

1.8L engine (code AWD), from Nov. 1999

2000 m.y. additional electrical wiring diagrams

THIS PAGE INTENTIONALLY LEFT

BLANK

Electrical Wiring Diagram Index

Golf/Jetta sedan standard equipment from May 2000

Golf/Jetta wagon standard equipment from January 2001

1.8L engine (code AWW) from June 2000

1.8L engine (code AWP) from June 2001

Electrical Wiring Diagram Index

1.9L engine (code ALH) w/manual transmission from May 1999

1.9L engine (code ALH) w/auto. transmission from May 1999

2.0L engine (code AEG), from May 1999

2.0L engine (code AVH/AZG), from August 2000

2.8L engine (code AFP), from May 1999

THIS PAGE INTENTIONALLY LEFT

BLANK

2001 m.y. additional electrical wiring diagrams

	Wiring Diagram page number	Repair Manual page number
• **Airbag systems,** from May 1999	34/1	97-326
• **Airbag systems,** from October 2000	50/1	97-468
• **Air conditioning (manual control, not Climatronic),** from May 1999		
1.9L - Engine - Turbo Diesel Fuel Injection (DFI)/66 kW, code ALH	38/1	97-348
1.8L - Engine - Motronic Multiport Fuel Injection (MFI)/110 kW, code AWW	38/1	97-348
2.0L - Engine - Motronic Multiport Fuel Injection (MFI)/85 kW, code AEG, AVH, AZG	38/1	97-348
2.8L - Engine - Motronic Multiport Fuel Injection (MFI)/130 kW, code AFP	38/1	97-348
• **Anti-lock brake system (ABS), Anti-lock brake system (ABS) with electronic differential lock (EDL) and anti-slip control (ASC),** from September 1998	9/1	97-134
• **Anti-lock brake system (ABS), Anti-lock brake system (ABS) with electronic differential lock (EDL) and anti-slip control (ASC),** from August 2000	48/1	97-446
• **Anti-theft warning system (Jetta Wagon),** from January 2001		
see Comfort System (without power windows)	53/1	97-514
see Comfort System (with power windows)	54/1	97-528
• **Anti-theft warning system (Golf/Jetta Sedan),** from May 1999		
see Comfort System (without power windows)	42/1	97-384
see Comfort System (with power windows)	43/1	97-398
• **Anti-theft immobilizer (Jetta Wagon),** from January 2001	51/4	97-477
• **Anti-theft immobilizer (Golf/Jetta Sedan),** from May 2000	52/4	97-497
• **Automatic transmission,** from May 1999		
1.9L - Engine - Turbo Diesel Fuel Injection (DFI)/66 kW, code ALH	36/1	97-338
1.8L - Engine - Motronic Multiport Fuel Injection (MFI)/110 kW, code AWW	35/1	97-330
2.0L - Engine - Motronic Multiport Fuel Injection (MFI)/85 kW, code AEG, AVH, AZG	35/1	97-330
2.8L - Engine - Motronic Multiport Fuel Injection (MFI)/130 kW, code AFP	35/1	97-330
• **CD changer wiring preparation (Radio system),** from September 1998	28/1	97-248
• **Central locking system with remote control (Jetta Wagon),** from January 2001		
see Comfort System (without power windows)	53/1	97-514
see Comfort System (with power windows)	54/1	97-528
• **Central locking system with remote control (Golf/Jetta Sedan),** from May 1999		
see Comfort System (without power windows)	42/1	97-384
see Comfort System (with power windows)	43/1	97-398
• **Climatronic (automatic climate control),** from May 1999		
2.8L - Engine - Motronic Multiport Fuel Injection (MFI)/130 kW, code AFP	39/1	97-354
• **Comfort System (without power windows), Jetta Wagon,** from January 2001	53/1	97-514
• **Comfort System (without power windows), Golf/Jetta Sedan,** from May 1999	42/1	97-384
• **Comfort System (with power windows), Jetta Wagon,** from January 2001	54/1	97-528
• **Comfort System (with power windows), Golf/Jetta Sedan,** from May 1999	43/1	97-398
• **Coolant Fan, single speed,** from September 1998	11/1	97-144
• **Coolant Fan, two speeds,** from September 1998	12/1	97-146
• **Coolant Fan (with after-run coolant pump),** from May 1999		
2.8L - Engine - Motronic Multiport Fuel Injection (MFI)/130 kW, code AFP	37/1	97-344
• **Cruise control**		
1.8L - Engine - Motronic Multiport Fuel Injection (MFI)/110 kW, code AWW	47/13	97-440
1.9L - Engine - Turbo Diesel Fuel Injection (DFI)/66 kW, code ALH, manual transmission	32/10	97-307
1.9L - Engine - Turbo Diesel Fuel Injection (DFI)/66 kW, code ALH, automatic transmission	33/10	97-321
2.0L - Engine - Motronic Multiport Fuel Injection (MFI)/85 kW, code AEG	44/1	97-416
2.0L - Engine - Motronic Multiport Fuel Injection (MFI)/85 kW, code AVH, AZG	49/12	97-463
2.8L - Engine - Motronic Multiport Fuel Injection (MFI)/130 kW, code AFP	31/9	97-292
• **Daytime running lights,** from May 2000	61/1	97-620
• **Fog lights,** from May 2000	60/1	97-614
• **Fuel tank lid unlock system (Jetta Wagon),** from January 2001		
see Comfort System (without power windows)	53/1	97-514
see Comfort System (with power windows)	54/1	97-528
• **Fuel tank lid unlock system (Golf/Jetta Sedan),** from May 1999		
see Comfort System (without power windows)	42/1	97-384
see Comfort System (with power windows)	43/1	97-398
• **Headlight washer,** from May 2000	59/1	97-610
• **Heated seats,** from September 1998	19/1	97-182
• **Heated leather seats,** from September 1998	20/1	97-186
• **Heated outside mirrors (Jetta Wagon),** from January 2001		
see Comfort System (without power windows)	53/1	97-514
see Comfort System (with power windows)	54/1	97-528
• **Heated outside mirrors (Golf/Jetta Sedan),** from May 1999		
see Comfort System (without power windows)	42/1	97-384
see Comfort System (with power windows)	43/1	97-398
• **Heated power mirrors (Jetta Wagon),** from January 2001, see Comfort System (with power windows)	54/1	97-528
• **Heated power mirrors (Golf/Jetta Sedan),** from May 1999, see Comfort System (with power windows)	43/1	97-398

2001 m.y. additional electrical wiring diagrams (continued)

	Wiring Diagram page number	Repair Manual page number
• **Interior lights (Jetta Wagon),** from January 2001		
see Comfort System (without power windows)	53/1	97-514
see Comfort System (with power windows)	54/1	97-528
• **Interior lights (Golf/Jetta Sedan),** from May 1999		
see Comfort System (without power windows)	42/1	97-384
see Comfort System (with power windows)	43/1	97-398
• **Interior rear view mirror (self-dimming),** from September 1998	24/1	97-202
• **Luggage compartment light (Jetta Wagon),** from January 2001		
see Comfort System (without power windows)	53/1	97-514
see Comfort System (with power windows)	54/1	97-528
• **Luggage compartment light (Golf/Jetta Sedan),** from May 1999		
see Comfort System (without power windows)	42/1	97-384
see Comfort System (with power windows)	43/1	97-398
• **Multi-function steering wheel for cruise control and radio,** from May 2000	46/1	97-424
• **Power seats and mirror adjustment with Memory,** from September 1998	26/1	97-220
• **Power sunroof (Jetta Wagon),** from January 2001		
see Comfort System (without power windows)	53/1	97-514
see Comfort System (with power windows)	54/1	97-528
• **Power sunroof (Golf/Jetta Sedan),** from May 1999		
see Comfort System (without power windows)	42/1	97-384
see Comfort System (with power windows)	43/1	97-398
• **Power outlet (12V),** from September 1998	22/1	97-192
• **Power windows (Jetta Wagon),** from January 2001, see Comfort System (with power windows)	54/1	97-528
• **Power windows (Golf/Jetta Sedan),** from May 1999, see Comfort System (with power windows)	43/1	97-398
• **Radio system (with CD changer wiring preparation),** from September 1998	28/1	97-248
• **Radio system "Monsoon" (with CD changer wiring preparation),** from May 1999	40/1	97-362
• **Rain-sensor,** from September 1998	24/1	97-202
• **Rear lid unlock system (Jetta Wagon),** from January 2001		
see Comfort System (without power windows)	53/1	97-514
see Comfort System (with power windows)	54/1	97-528
• **Rear lid unlock system (Golf/Jetta Sedan),** from May 1999		
see Comfort System (without power windows)	42/1	97-384
see Comfort System (with power windows)	43/1	97-398
• **Seat belt control,** from May 1999	34/1	97-326
• **Seat belt control,** from October 2000	50/1	97-468
• **Seat belt tensioner,** from September 1998	34/1	97-326
• **Seat belt tensioner,** from October 2000	50/1	97-468
• **Warning light for rear lid unlocked (Jetta Wagon),** from January 2001		
see Comfort System (without power windows)	53/1	97-514
see Comfort System (with power windows)	54/1	97-528
• **Warning light for rear lid unlocked (Golf/Jetta Sedan),** from May 1999		
see Comfort System (without power windows)	42/1	97-384
see Comfort System (with power windows)	43/1	97-398
• **Washer nozzle heaters,** from September 1998	21/1	97-190

2002 m.y. additional electrical wiring diagrams

	Wiring Diagram page number	Repair Manual page number
● **Airbag systems,** from October 2000	50/1	97-468
● **Air conditioning (manual control, not Climatronic),** from May 1999		
1.9L - Engine - Turbo Diesel Fuel Injection (DFI)/66 kW, code ALH	38/1	97-348
1.8L - Engine - Motronic Multiport Fuel Injection (MFI)/110 kW, code AWW	38/1	97-348
1.8L - Engine - Motronic Multiport Fuel Injection (MFI)/132 kW, code AWP	38/1	97-348
2.0L - Engine - Motronic Multiport Fuel Injection (MFI)/85 kW, code AEG, AVH, AZG	38/1	97-348
2.8L - Engine - Motronic Multiport Fuel Injection (MFI)/130 kW, code AFP	38/1	97-348
● **Anti-lock brake system (ABS), Anti-lock brake system (ABS) with electronic differential lock (EDL) and anti-slip control (ASC),** from August 2000	48/1	97-446
● **Anti-theft warning system (Jetta Wagon),** from May 2001		
see Comfort System (without power windows)	55/1	97-546
see Comfort System (with power windows)	56/1	97-560
● **Anti-theft warning system (Golf/Jetta Sedan),** from May 2001		
see Comfort System (without power windows)	57/1	97-578
see Comfort System (with power windows)	58/1	97-592
● **Anti-theft immobilizer (Jetta Wagon),** from January 2001	51/4	97-477
● **Anti-theft immobilizer (Golf/Jetta Sedan),** from May 2000	52/4	97-497
● **Automatic transmission, 4 speed automatic,** from May 1999		
1.9L - Engine - Turbo Diesel Fuel Injection (DFI)/66 kW, code ALH	36/1	97-338
1.8L - Engine - Motronic Multiport Fuel Injection (MFI)/110 kW, code AWW	35/1	97-330
2.0L - Engine - Motronic Multiport Fuel Injection (MFI)/85 kW, code AEG, AVH, AZG	35/1	97-330
2.8L - Engine - Motronic Multiport Fuel Injection (MFI)/130 kW, code AFP	35/1	97-330
● **Automatic transmission, 5 speed automatic with Tiptronic,** from June 2001		
1.8L - Engine - Motronic Multiport Fuel Injection (MFI)/132 kW, code AWP	35/1	97-330
● **CD changer wiring preparation (Radio system),** from September 1998	28/1	97-248
● **Central locking system with remote control (Jetta Wagon),** from May 2001		
see Comfort System (without power windows)	55/1	97-546
see Comfort System (with power windows)	56/1	97-560
● **Central locking system with remote control (Golf/Jetta Sedan),** from May 1999		
see Comfort System (without power windows)	57/1	97-578
see Comfort System (with power windows)	58/1	97-592
● **Climatronic (automatic climate control),** from May 1999		
2.8L - Engine - Motronic Multiport Fuel Injection (MFI)/130 kW, code AFP	39/1	97-354
● **Comfort System (without power windows), Jetta Wagon,** from May 2001	55/1	97-546
● **Comfort System (without power windows), Golf/Jetta Sedan,** from May 1999	57/1	97-578
● **Comfort System (with power windows), Jetta Wagon,** from May 2001	56/1	97-560
● **Comfort System (with power windows), Golf/Jetta Sedan,** from May 2001	58/1	97-592
● **Coolant Fan, single speed,** from September 1998	11/1	97-144
● **Coolant Fan, two speeds,** from September 1998	12/1	97-146
● **Coolant Fan (with after-run coolant pump),** from May 1999		
2.8L - Engine - Motronic Multiport Fuel Injection (MFI)/130 kW, code AFP	37/1	97-344
● **Cruise control**		
1.8L - Engine - Motronic Multiport Fuel Injection (MFI)/110 kW, code AWW	47/13	97-440
1.8L - Engine - Motronic Multiport Fuel Injection (MFI)/132 kW, code AWP	62/13	97-640
1.9L - Engine - Turbo Diesel Fuel Injection (DFI)/66 kW, code ALH, manual transmission	32/10	97-307
1.9L - Engine - Turbo Diesel Fuel Injection (DFI)/66 kW, code ALH, automatic transmission	33/10	97-321
2.0L - Engine - Motronic Multiport Fuel Injection (MFI)/85 kW, code AEG	44/1	97-416
2.0L - Engine - Motronic Multiport Fuel Injection (MFI)/85 kW, code AVH, AZG	49/12	97-463
2.8L - Engine - Motronic Multiport Fuel Injection (MFI)/130 kW, code AFP	31/9	97-292
● **Daytime running lights,** from May 2000	61/1	97-620
● **Fog lights,** from May 2000	60/1	97-614
● **Fuel tank lid unlock system (Jetta Wagon),** from May 2001		
see Comfort System (without power windows)	55/1	97-546
see Comfort System (with power windows)	56/1	97-560
● **Fuel tank lid unlock system (Golf/Jetta Sedan),** from May 2001		
see Comfort System (without power windows)	57/1	97-578
see Comfort System (with power windows)	58/1	97-592
● **Headlight washer,** from May 2000	59/1	97-610
● **Heated seats,** from September 1998	19/1	97-182
● **Heated leather seats,** from September 1998	20/1	97-186
● **Heated outside mirrors (Jetta Wagon),** from May 2001		
see Comfort System (without power windows)	55/1	97-546
see Comfort System (with power windows)	56/1	97-560
● **Heated outside mirrors (Golf/Jetta Sedan),** from May 2001		
see Comfort System (without power windows)	57/1	97-578
see Comfort System (with power windows)	58/1	97-592
● **Heated power mirrors (Jetta Wagon),** from May 2001, see Comfort System (with power windows)	56/1	97-560
● **Heated power mirrors (Golf/Jetta Sedan),** from May 2001, see Comfort System (with power windows)	58/1	97-592

2002 m.y. additional electrical wiring diagrams (continued)

	Wiring Diagram page number	Repair Manual page number
● **Interior lights (Jetta Wagon),** from May 2001		
see Comfort System (without power windows)	55/1	97-546
see Comfort System (with power windows)	56/1	97-560
● **Interior lights (Golf/Jetta Sedan),** from May 2001		
see Comfort System (without power windows)	57/1	97-578
see Comfort System (with power windows)	58/1	97-592
● **Interior rear view mirror (self-dimming),** from September 1998	24/1	97-202
● **Luggage compartment light (Jetta Wagon),** from May 2001		
see Comfort System (without power windows)	55/1	97-546
see Comfort System (with power windows)	56/1	97-560
● **Luggage compartment light (Golf/Jetta Sedan),** from May 2001		
see Comfort System (without power windows)	57/1	97-578
see Comfort System (with power windows)	58/1	97-592
● **Multi-function steering wheel for cruise control and radio,** from May 2000	46/1	97-424
● **Power seats and mirror adjustment with Memory,** from September 1998	26/1	97-220
● **Power sunroof (Jetta Wagon),** from May 2001		
see Comfort System (without power windows)	55/1	97-546
see Comfort System (with power windows)	56/1	97-560
● **Power sunroof (Golf/Jetta Sedan),** from May 2001		
see Comfort System (without power windows)	57/1	97-578
see Comfort System (with power windows)	58/1	97-592
● **Power outlet (12V),** from September 1998	22/1	97-192
● **Power windows (Jetta Wagon),** from May 2001, see Comfort System (with power windows)	56/1	97-560
● **Power windows (Golf/Jetta Sedan),** from May 2001, see Comfort System (with power windows)	58/1	97-592
● **Radio system (with CD changer wiring preparation),** from September 1998	28/1	97-248
● **Radio system "Monsoon" (with CD changer wiring preparation),** from May 1999	40/1	97-362
● **Rain-sensor,** from September 1998	24/1	97-202
● **Rear lid unlock system (Jetta Wagon),** from May 2001		
see Comfort System (without power windows)	55/1	97-546
see Comfort System (with power windows)	56/1	97-560
● **Rear lid unlock system (Golf/Jetta Sedan),** from May 2001		
see Comfort System (without power windows)	57/1	97-578
see Comfort System (with power windows)	58/1	97-592
● **Seat belt control,** from October 2000	50/1	97-468
● **Seat belt tensioner,** from October 2000	50/1	97-468
● **Warning light for rear lid unlocked/door ajar indicator lamp (Jetta Wagon),** from May 2001		
see Comfort System (without power windows)	55/1	97-546
see Comfort System (with power windows)	56/1	97-560
● **Warning light for rear lid unlocked/door ajar indicator lamp (Golf/Jetta Sedan),** from May 2001		
see Comfort System (without power windows)	57/1	97-578
see Comfort System (with power windows)	58/1	97-592
● **Washer nozzle heaters,** from September 1998	21/1	97-190

THIS PAGE INTENTIONALLY LEFT

BLANK

THIS PAGE INTENTIONALLY LEFT

BLANK

Golf /Jetta - Standard Equipment,

from September 1998

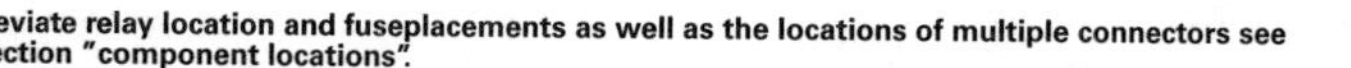

Deviate relay location and fuseplacements as well as the locations of multiple connectors see section "component locations".

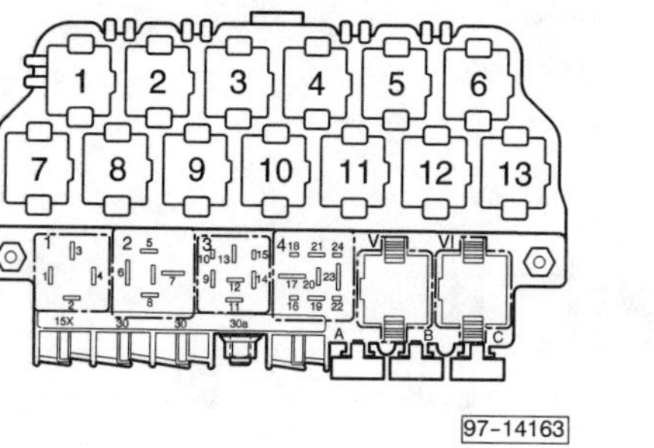

Relay location on the thirteenfold auxiliary relay panel, above relay panel:

- **3** Starting Interlock Relay (185)

Relay panel:

- **1** Dual Horn Relay (53)
- **2** Load Reduction Relay (18)/(100)
- **V**
- **VI** Wiper/Washer Intermittent Relay (377)

Note: Number in parentheses indicates production control number stamped on relay housing.

Fuse colors

30 A - green
25 A - white
20 A - yellow
15 A - blue
10 A - red
7,5 A - brown
5 A - beige
3 A - violet

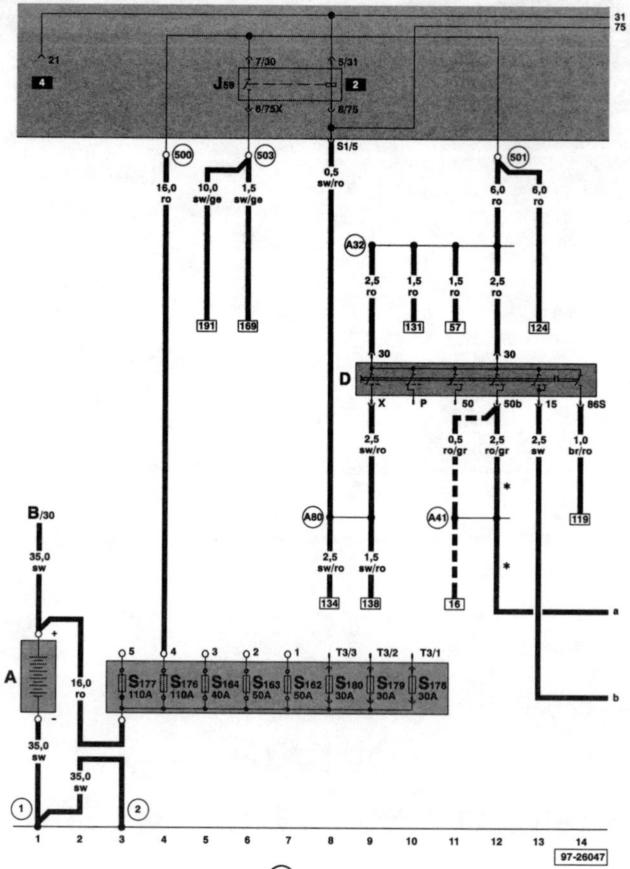

ws = white
sw = black
ro = red
br = brown
gn = green
bl = blue
gr = grey
li = lilac
ge = yellow

97-26047

A - Battery
B - Starter
D - Ignition/Starter Switch
J59 - Load Reduction Relay
S162 - Fuse -1- (30) in fuse bracket/battery
S163 - Fuse -2- (30) in fuse bracket/battery
S164 - Fuse -3- (30) in fuse bracket/battery
S176 - Fuse -4- (30) in fuse bracket/battery
S177 - Fuse -5- (30) in fuse bracket/battery
S178 - Fuse -6- (30) in fuse bracket/battery
S179 - Fuse -7- (30) in fuse bracket/battery
S180 - Fuse -8- (30) in fuse bracket/battery
T3 - 3-Pin Connector

(1) - Ground strap, battery to body

(2) - Ground strap, transmission to body
(500) - Threaded connection -1- (30) on the relay plate
(501) - Threaded connection -2- (30) on the relay plate
(503) - Threaded connection -2- (75x) on the relay plate
(A32) - Plus connection (30), in instrument panel wiring harness
(A41) - Plus connection (50), in instrument panel wiring harness (gasoline engine only)
(A80) - Connector -1- (X) in instrument panel wiring harness
* - Manual transmission only
--- Automatic transmission only

Battery, ignition/starter switch

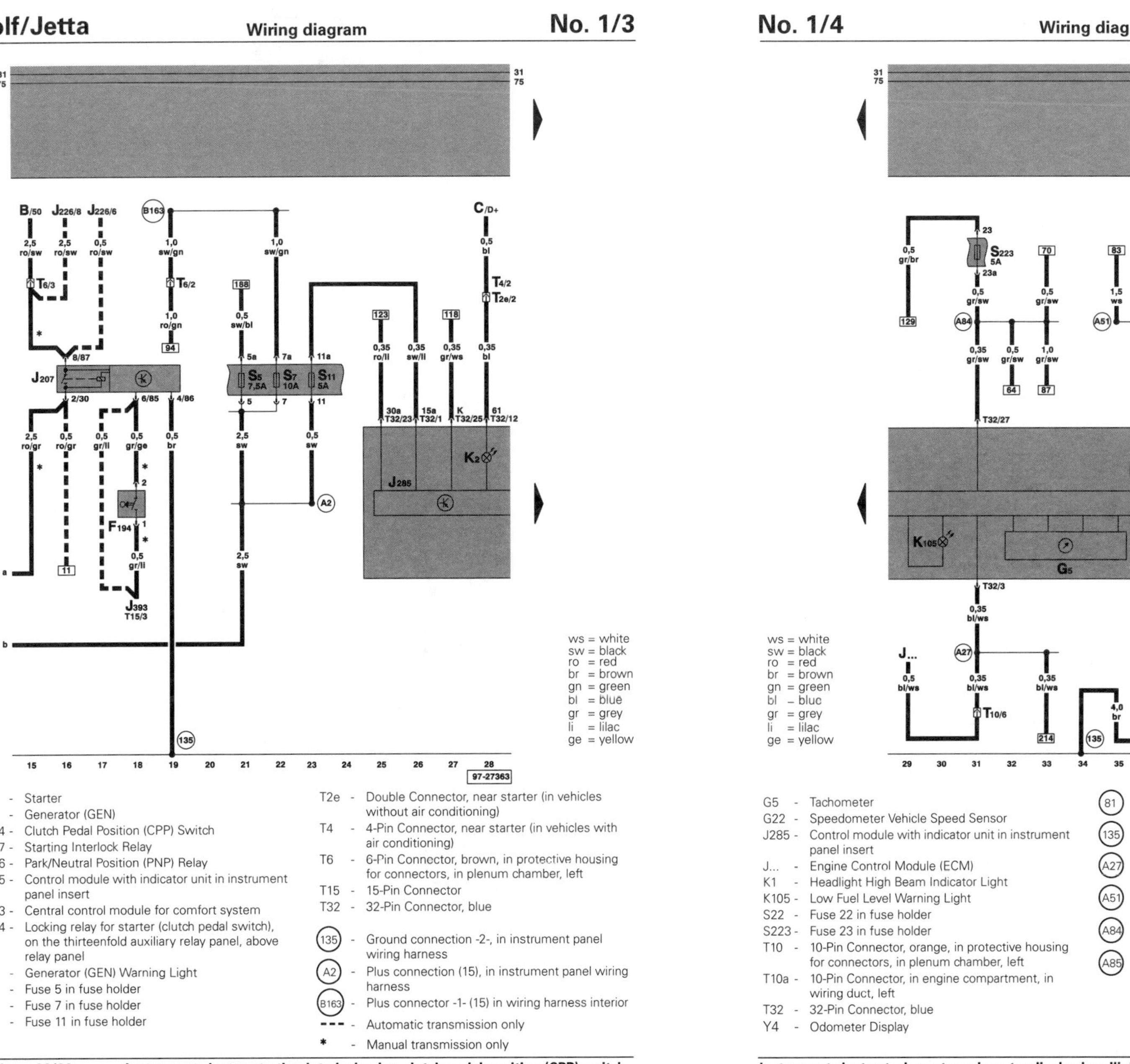

ws = white
sw = black
ro = red
br = brown
gn = green
bl = blue
gr = grey
li = lilac
ge = yellow

B - Starter
C - Generator (GEN)
F194 - Clutch Pedal Position (CPP) Switch
J207 - Starting Interlock Relay
J226 - Park/Neutral Position (PNP) Relay
J285 - Control module with indicator unit in instrument panel insert
J393 - Central control module for comfort system
J434 - Locking relay for starter (clutch pedal switch), on the thirteenfold auxiliary relay panel, above relay panel
K2 - Generator (GEN) Warning Light
S5 - Fuse 5 in fuse holder
S7 - Fuse 7 in fuse holder
S11 - Fuse 11 in fuse holder
T2e - Double Connector, near starter (in vehicles without air conditioning)
T4 - 4-Pin Connector, near starter (in vehicles with air conditioning)
T6 - 6-Pin Connector, brown, in protective housing for connectors, in plenum chamber, left
T15 - 15-Pin Connector
T32 - 32-Pin Connector, blue

(135) - Ground connection -2-, in instrument panel wiring harness
(A2) - Plus connection (15), in instrument panel wiring harness
(B163) - Plus connector -1- (15) in wiring harness interior
- - - - Automatic transmission only
* - Manual transmission only

Edition 06/00
USA.5102.06.21

Instrument cluster, starting interlock relay, clutch pedal position (CPP) switch, generator (GEN) warning light

ws = white
sw = black
ro = red
br = brown
gn = green
bl = blue
gr = grey
li = lilac
ge = yellow

G5 - Tachometer
G22 - Speedometer Vehicle Speed Sensor
J285 - Control module with indicator unit in instrument panel insert
J... - Engine Control Module (ECM)
K1 - Headlight High Beam Indicator Light
K105 - Low Fuel Level Warning Light
S22 - Fuse 22 in fuse holder
S223 - Fuse 23 in fuse holder
T10 - 10-Pin Connector, orange, in protective housing for connectors, in plenum chamber, left
T10a - 10-Pin Connector, in engine compartment, in wiring duct, left
T32 - 32-Pin Connector, blue
Y4 - Odometer Display

(81) - Ground connection -1-, in instrument panel wiring harness
(135) - Ground connection -2-, in instrument panel wiring harness
(A27) - Wire connection (vehicle speed signal), in instrument panel wiring harness
(A51) - Wire connection (56), in instrument panel wiring harness
(A84) - Connector (58L) in instrument panel wiring harness
(A85) - Connector (58R) in instrument panel wiring harness

Instrument cluster, tachometer, odometer display headlight high beam indicator light, low fuel level warning light

Edition 06/00
USA.5102.06.21

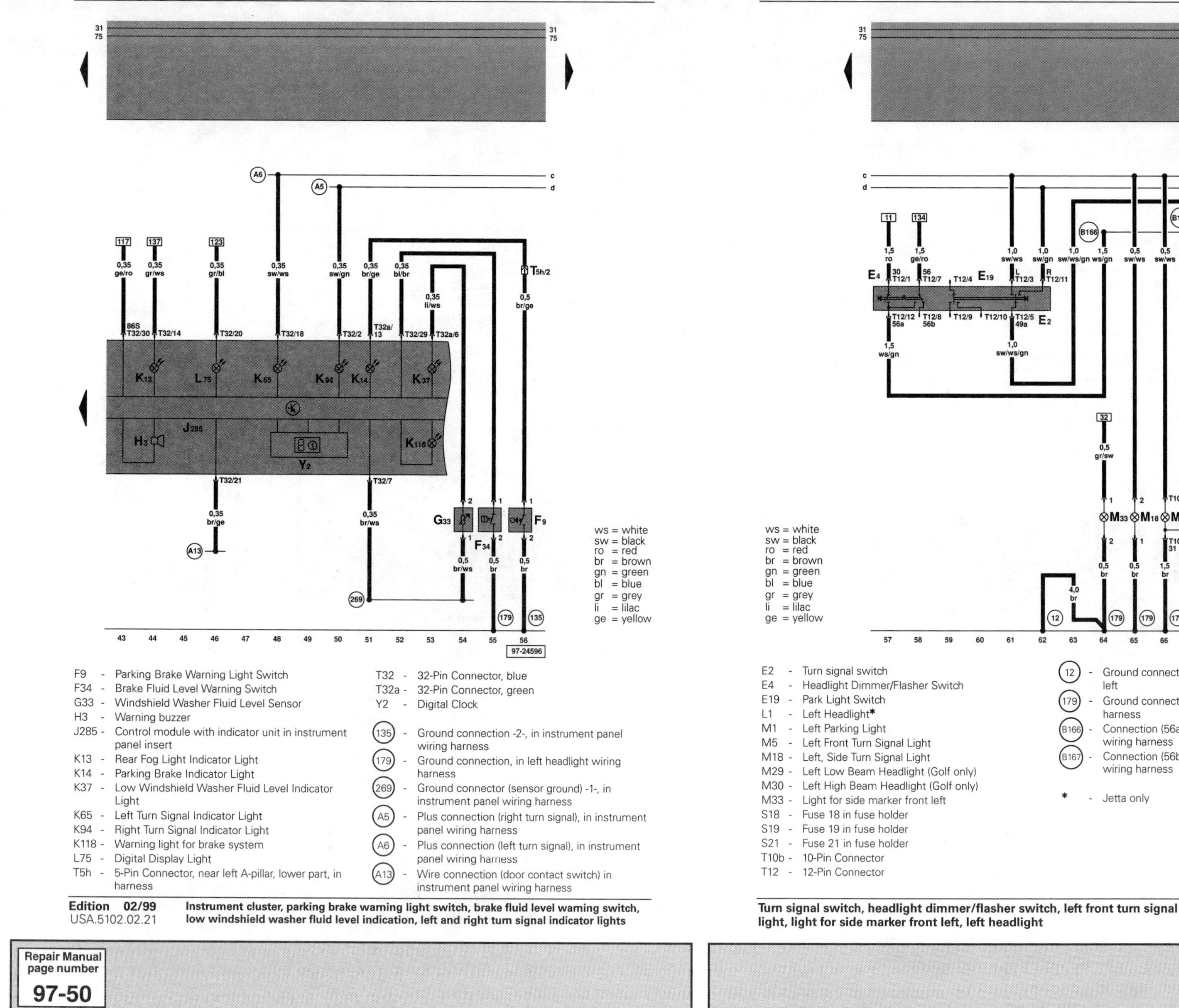

ws = white
sw = black
ro = red
br = brown
gn = green
bl = blue
gr = grey
li = lilac
ge = yellow

F9 - Parking Brake Warning Light Switch
F34 - Brake Fluid Level Warning Switch
G33 - Windshield Washer Fluid Level Sensor
H3 - Warning buzzer
J285 - Control module with indicator unit in instrument panel insert
K13 - Rear Fog Light Indicator Light
K14 - Parking Brake Indicator Light
K37 - Low Windshield Washer Fluid Level Indicator Light
K65 - Left Turn Signal Indicator Light
K94 - Right Turn Signal Indicator Light
K118 - Warning light for brake system
L75 - Digital Display Light
T5h - 5-Pin Connector, near left A-pillar, lower part, in harness
T32 - 32-Pin Connector, blue
T32a - 32-Pin Connector, green
Y2 - Digital Clock

(135) - Ground connection -2-, in instrument panel wiring harness
(179) - Ground connection, in left headlight wiring harness
(269) - Ground connector (sensor ground) -1-, in instrument panel wiring harness
(A5) - Plus connection (right turn signal), in instrument panel wiring harness
(A6) - Plus connection (left turn signal), in instrument panel wiring harness
(A13) - Wire connection (door contact switch) in instrument panel wiring harness

Instrument cluster, parking brake warning light switch, brake fluid level warning switch, low windshield washer fluid level indication, left and right turn signal indicator lights

ws = white
sw = black
ro = red
br = brown
gn = green
bl = blue
gr = grey
li = lilac
ge = yellow

E2 - Turn signal switch
E4 - Headlight Dimmer/Flasher Switch
E19 - Park Light Switch
L1 - Left Headlight*
M1 - Left Parking Light
M5 - Left Front Turn Signal Light
M18 - Left, Side Turn Signal Light
M29 - Left Low Beam Headlight (Golf only)
M30 - Left High Beam Headlight (Golf only)
M33 - Light for side marker front left
S18 - Fuse 18 in fuse holder
S19 - Fuse 19 in fuse holder
S21 - Fuse 21 in fuse holder
T10b - 10-Pin Connector
T12 - 12-Pin Connector

(12) - Ground connection, in engine compartment, left
(179) - Ground connection, in left headlight wiring harness
(B166) - Connection (56a) in passenger compartment wiring harness
(B167) - Connection (56b) in passenger compartment wiring harness

* - Jetta only

Turn signal switch, headlight dimmer/flasher switch, left front turn signal light, light for side marker front left, left headlight

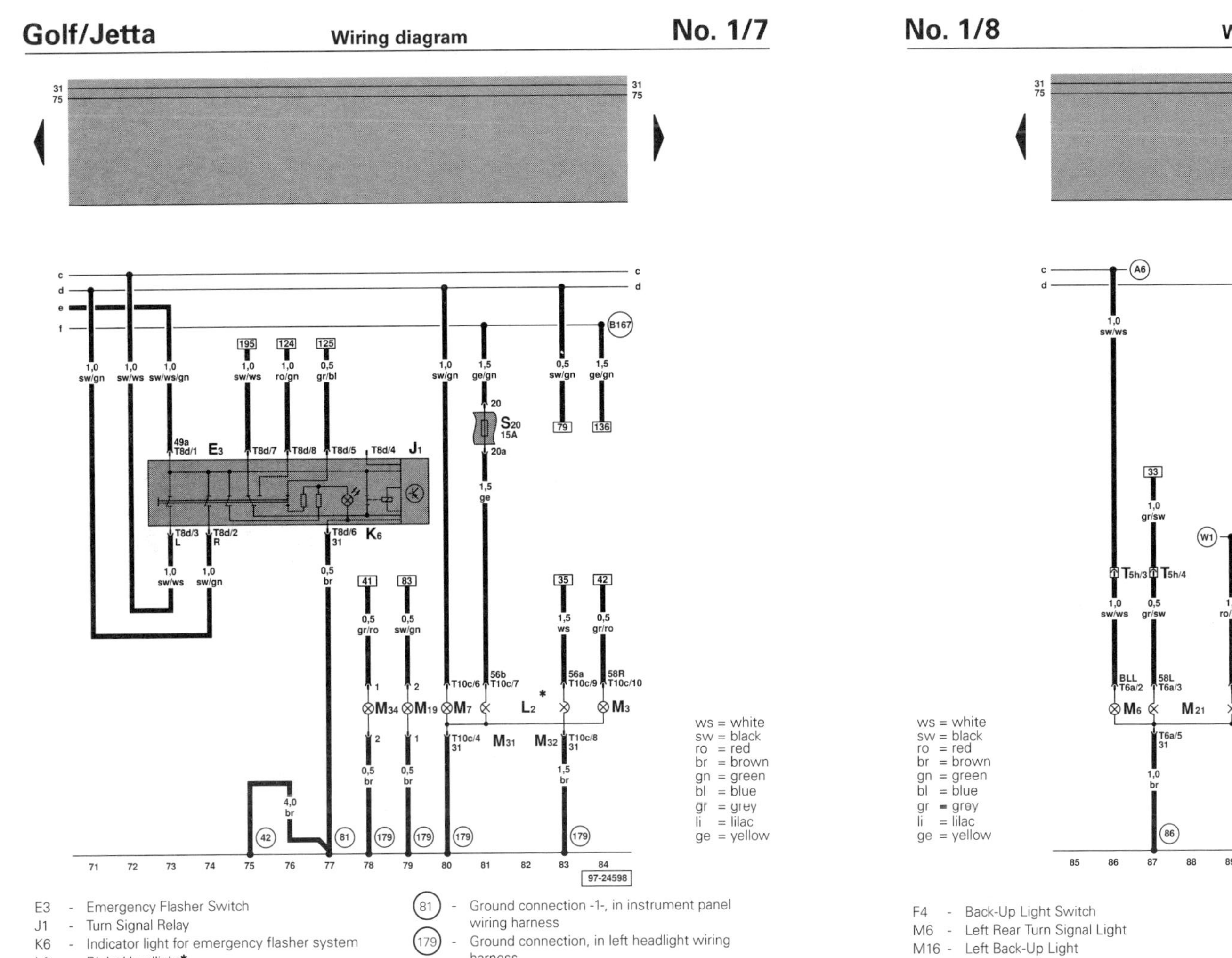

ws = white
sw = black
ro = red
br = brown
gn = green
bl = blue
gr = grey
li = lilac
ge = yellow

E3 - Emergency Flasher Switch
J1 - Turn Signal Relay
K6 - Indicator light for emergency flasher system
L2 - Right Headlight*
M3 - Right Parking Light
M7 - Right Front Turn Signal Light
M19 - Right, Side Turn Signal Light
M31 - Right Low Beam Headlight (Golf only)
M32 - Right High Beam Headlight (Golf only)
M34 - Light for side marker front right
S20 - Fuse 20 in fuse holder
T8d - 8-Pin Connector
T10c - 10-Pin Connector

(42) - Ground connection, beside steering column

(81) - Ground connection -1-, in instrument panel wiring harness
(179) - Ground connection, in left headlight wiring harness
(B167) - Connection (56b), in passenger compartment wiring harness

* - Jetta only

Emergency flasher switch, turn signal relay, right front turn signal light, light for side marker front right, right headlight

ws = white
sw = black
ro = red
br = brown
gn = green
bl = blue
gr = grey
li = lilac
ge = yellow

F4 - Back-Up Light Switch
M6 - Left Rear Turn Signal Light
M16 - Left Back-Up Light
M21 - Left Brake/Tail Light
M25 - High-mount Brake Light (32 light emitting diodes)
T5 - 5-Pin Connector, black, connector station C-pillar, left
T5a - 5-Pin Connector, pink, connector station C-pillar, left (Golf only)
T5h - 5-Pin Connector, near left A-pillar, lower part, in harness
T6a - 6-Pin Connector
T10 - 10-Pin Connector, orange, in protective housing for connectors, in plenum chamber, left

(86) - Ground connection -1-, in rear wiring harness
(98) - Ground connection, in rear lid wiring harness
(A6) - Plus connection (left turn signal), in instrument panel wiring harness
(B182) - Connection (RF), in passenger compartment wiring harness
(W1) - Plus connection (54), in rear wiring harness
(W28) - Plus connector -2- (54), in wiring harness taillight assembly

-•-•- Golf only

Back-up light switch, left rear turn signal light, left back-up light, left brake/tail light, high-mount brake light (Golf only)

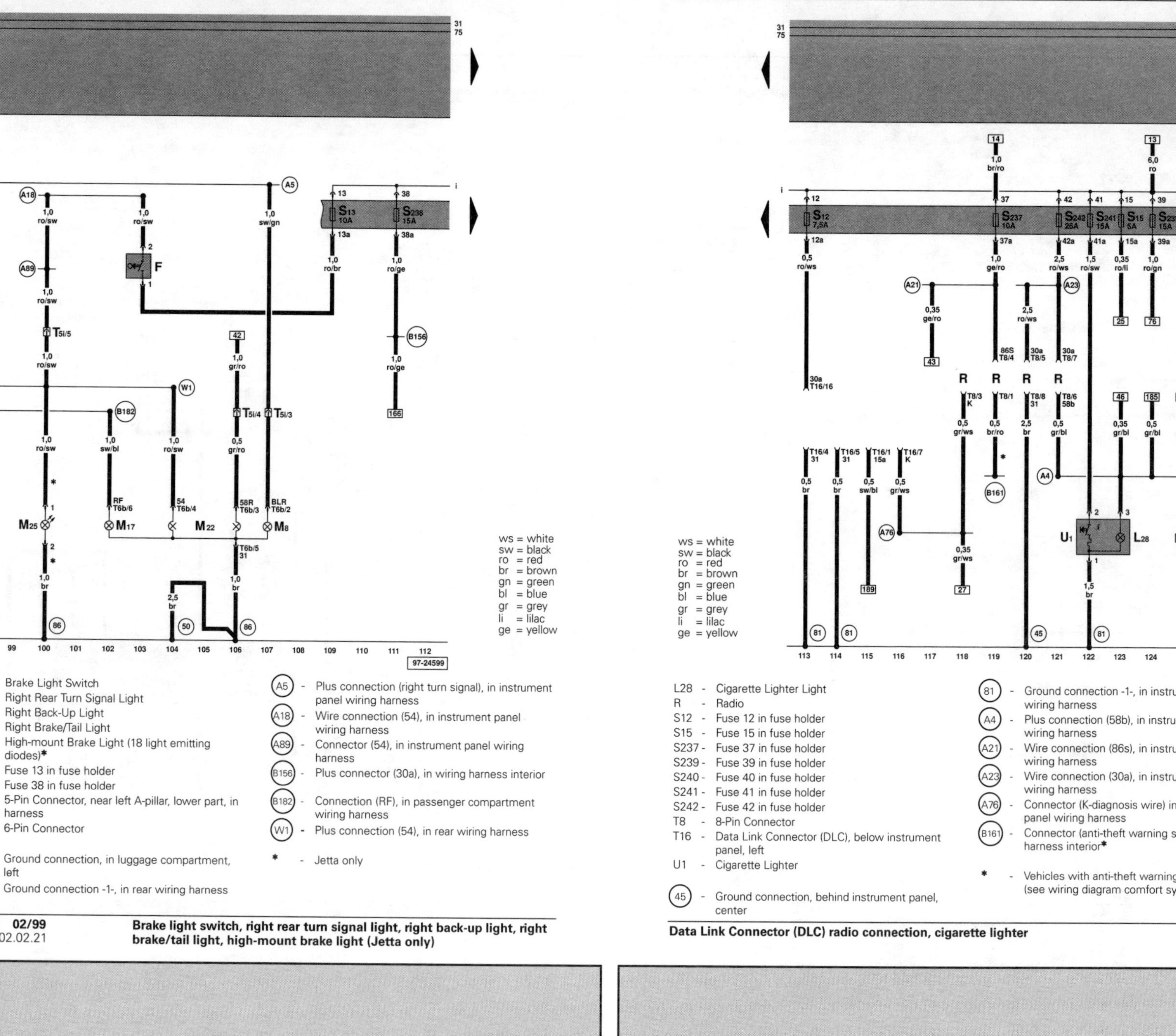

ws = white
sw = black
ro = red
br = brown
gn = green
bl = blue
gr = grey
li = lilac
ge = yellow

F - Brake Light Switch
M8 - Right Rear Turn Signal Light
M17 - Right Back-Up Light
M22 - Right Brake/Tail Light
M25 - High-mount Brake Light (18 light emitting diodes)*
S13 - Fuse 13 in fuse holder
S238 - Fuse 38 in fuse holder
T5i - 5-Pin Connector, near left A-pillar, lower part, in harness
T6b - 6-Pin Connector

(50) - Ground connection, in luggage compartment, left
(86) - Ground connection -1-, in rear wiring harness

(A5) - Plus connection (right turn signal), in instrument panel wiring harness
(A18) - Wire connection (54), in instrument panel wiring harness
(A89) - Connector (54), in instrument panel wiring harness
(B156) - Plus connector (30a), in wiring harness interior
(B182) - Connection (RF), in passenger compartment wiring harness
(W1) - Plus connection (54), in rear wiring harness

* - Jetta only

Edition 02/99
USA.5102.02.21

Brake light switch, right rear turn signal light, right back-up light, right brake/tail light, high-mount brake light (Jetta only)

ws = white
sw = black
ro = red
br = brown
gn = green
bl = blue
gr = grey
li = lilac
ge = yellow

L28 - Cigarette Lighter Light
R - Radio
S12 - Fuse 12 in fuse holder
S15 - Fuse 15 in fuse holder
S237 - Fuse 37 in fuse holder
S239 - Fuse 39 in fuse holder
S240 - Fuse 40 in fuse holder
S241 - Fuse 41 in fuse holder
S242 - Fuse 42 in fuse holder
T8 - 8-Pin Connector
T16 - Data Link Connector (DLC), below instrument panel, left
U1 - Cigarette Lighter

(45) - Ground connection, behind instrument panel, center

(81) - Ground connection -1-, in instrument panel wiring harness
(A4) - Plus connection (58b), in instrument panel wiring harness
(A21) - Wire connection (86s), in instrument panel wiring harness
(A23) - Wire connection (30a), in instrument panel wiring harness
(A76) - Connector (K-diagnosis wire) in instrument panel wiring harness
(B161) - Connector (anti-theft warning system), in wiring harness interior*

* - Vehicles with anti-theft warning system only (see wiring diagram comfort system)

Data Link Connector (DLC) radio connection, cigarette lighter

Edition 02/99
USA.5102.02.21

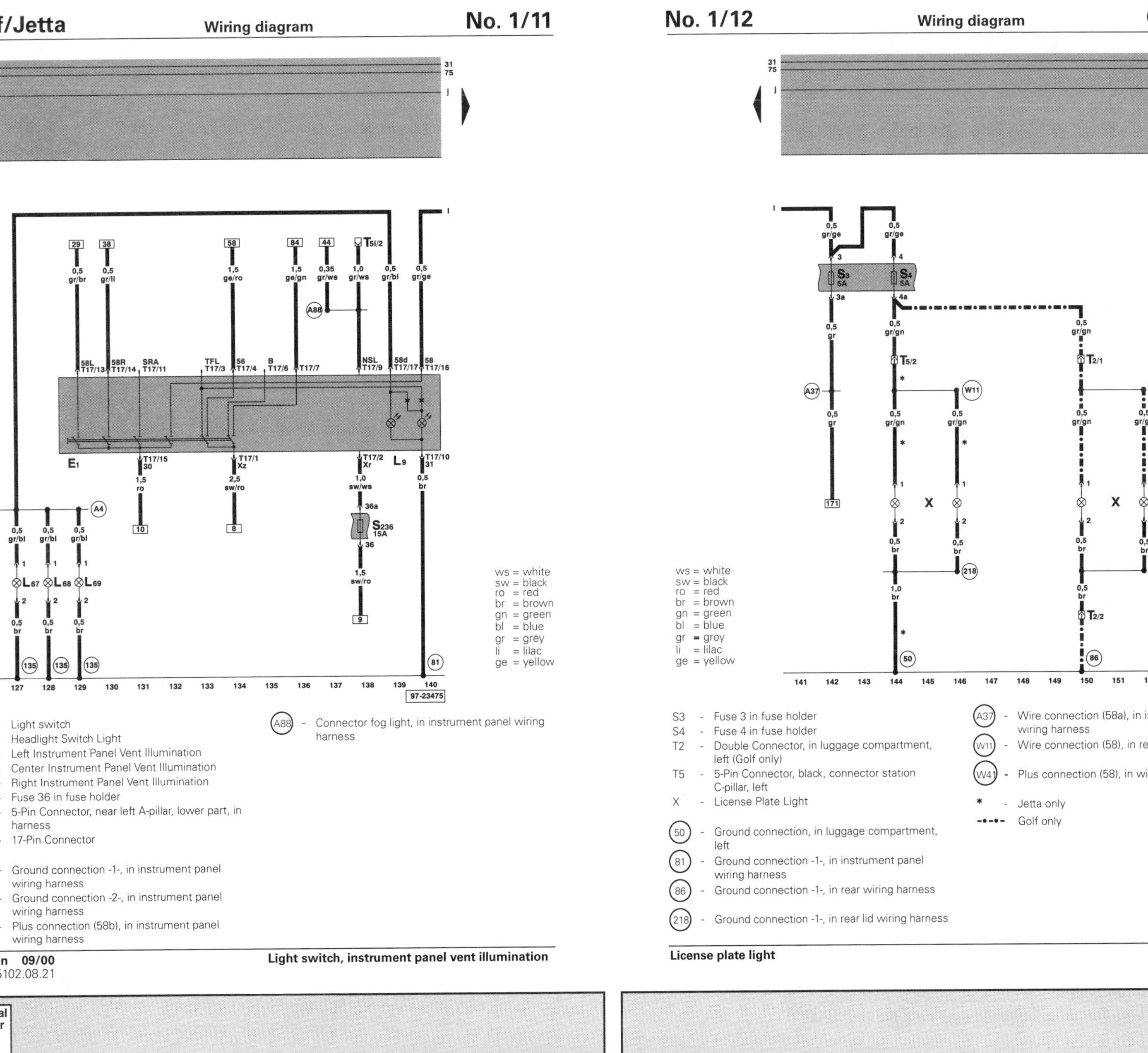

ws = white
sw = black
ro = red
br = brown
gn = green
bl = blue
gr = grey
li = lilac
ge = yellow

- E1 - Light switch
- L9 - Headlight Switch Light
- L67 - Left Instrument Panel Vent Illumination
- L68 - Center Instrument Panel Vent Illumination
- L69 - Right Instrument Panel Vent Illumination
- S236 - Fuse 36 in fuse holder
- T5i - 5-Pin Connector, near left A-pillar, lower part, in harness
- T17 - 17-Pin Connector
- (81) - Ground connection -1-, in instrument panel wiring harness
- (135) - Ground connection -2-, in instrument panel wiring harness
- (A4) - Plus connection (58b), in instrument panel wiring harness
- (A88) - Connector fog light, in instrument panel wiring harness

Light switch, instrument panel vent illumination

ws = white
sw = black
ro = red
br = brown
gn = green
bl = blue
gr = groy
li = lilac
ge = yellow

- S3 - Fuse 3 in fuse holder
- S4 - Fuse 4 in fuse holder
- T2 - Double Connector, in luggage compartment, left (Golf only)
- T5 - 5-Pin Connector, black, connector station C-pillar, left
- X - License Plate Light
- (50) - Ground connection, in luggage compartment, left
- (81) - Ground connection -1-, in instrument panel wiring harness
- (86) - Ground connection -1-, in rear wiring harness
- (218) - Ground connection -1-, in rear lid wiring harness
- (A37) - Wire connection (58a), in instrument panel wiring harness
- (W11) - Wire connection (58), in rear lid wiring harness
- (W41) - Plus connection (58), in wiring harness
- * - Jetta only
- -•-•- Golf only

License plate light

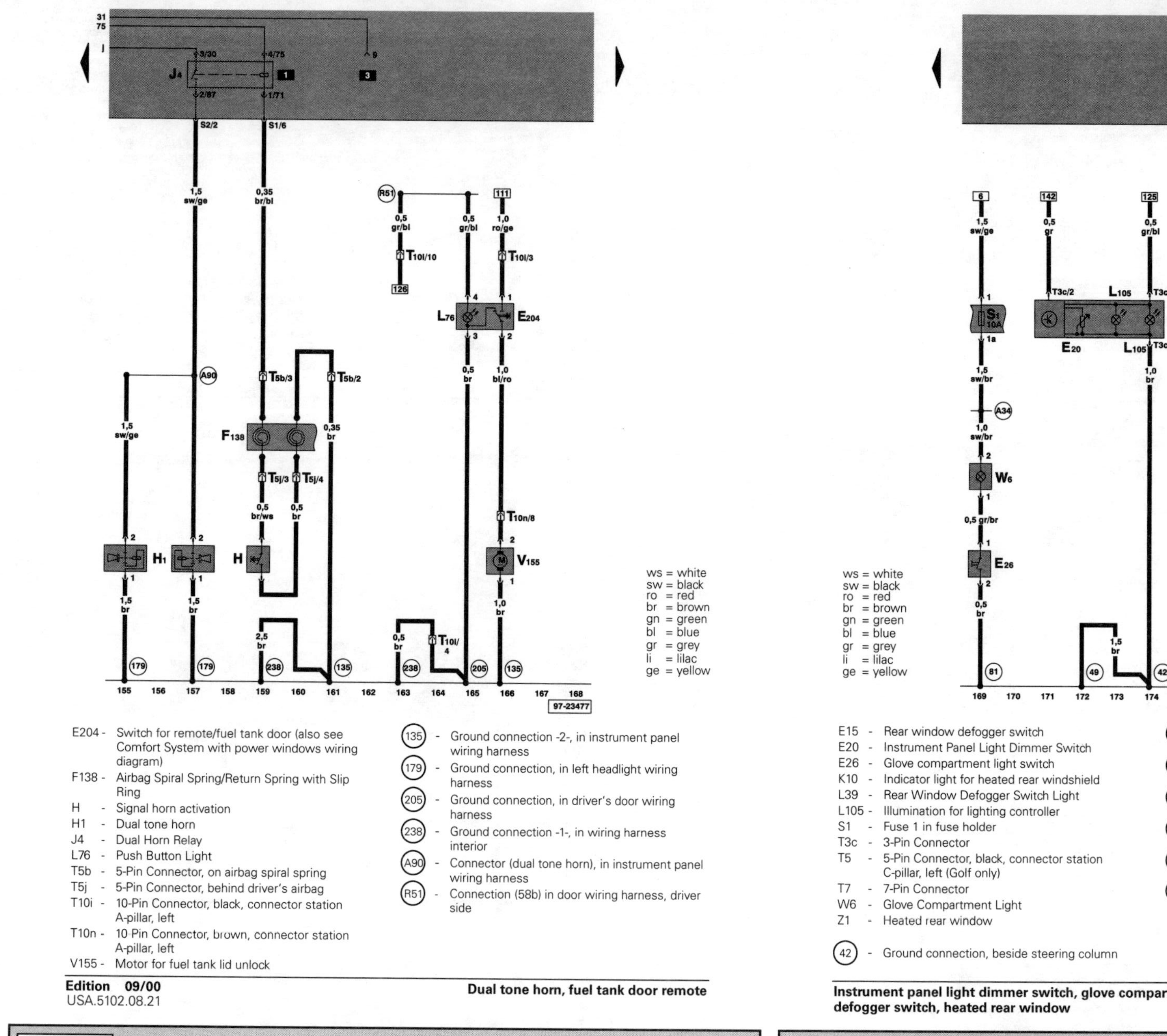

ws = white
sw = black
ro = red
br = brown
gn = green
bl = blue
gr = grey
li = lilac
ge = yellow

- E204 - Switch for remote/fuel tank door (also see Comfort System with power windows wiring diagram)
- F138 - Airbag Spiral Spring/Return Spring with Slip Ring
- H - Signal horn activation
- H1 - Dual tone horn
- J4 - Dual Horn Relay
- L76 - Push Button Light
- T5b - 5-Pin Connector, on airbag spiral spring
- T5j - 5-Pin Connector, behind driver's airbag
- T10i - 10-Pin Connector, black, connector station A-pillar, left
- T10n - 10 Pin Connector, brown, connector station A-pillar, left
- V155 - Motor for fuel tank lid unlock

- (135) - Ground connection -2-, in instrument panel wiring harness
- (179) - Ground connection, in left headlight wiring harness
- (205) - Ground connection, in driver's door wiring harness
- (238) - Ground connection -1-, in wiring harness interior
- (A90) - Connector (dual tone horn), in instrument panel wiring harness
- (R51) - Connection (58b) in door wiring harness, driver side

Edition 09/00
USA.5102.08.21

Dual tone horn, fuel tank door remote

ws = white
sw = black
ro = red
br = brown
gn = green
bl = blue
gr = grey
li = lilac
ge = yellow

- E15 - Rear window defogger switch
- E20 - Instrument Panel Light Dimmer Switch
- E26 - Glove compartment light switch
- K10 - Indicator light for heated rear windshield
- L39 - Rear Window Defogger Switch Light
- L105 - Illumination for lighting controller
- S1 - Fuse 1 in fuse holder
- T3c - 3-Pin Connector
- T5 - 5-Pin Connector, black, connector station C-pillar, left (Golf only)
- T7 - 7-Pin Connector
- W6 - Glove Compartment Light
- Z1 - Heated rear window

- (42) - Ground connection, beside steering column
- (49) - Ground connection, on steering column
- (50) - Ground connection, in luggage compartment, left
- (81) - Ground connection -1-, in instrument panel wiring harness
- (86) - Ground connection -1-, in rear wiring harness
- (219) - Ground connection -2-, in rear lid wiring harness
- (A34) - Wire connection (75x), in instrument panel wiring harness

- * - Jetta only
- -•-•- - Golf only

Instrument panel light dimmer switch, glove compartment light, rear window defogger switch, heated rear window

Edition 09/00
USA.5102.08.21

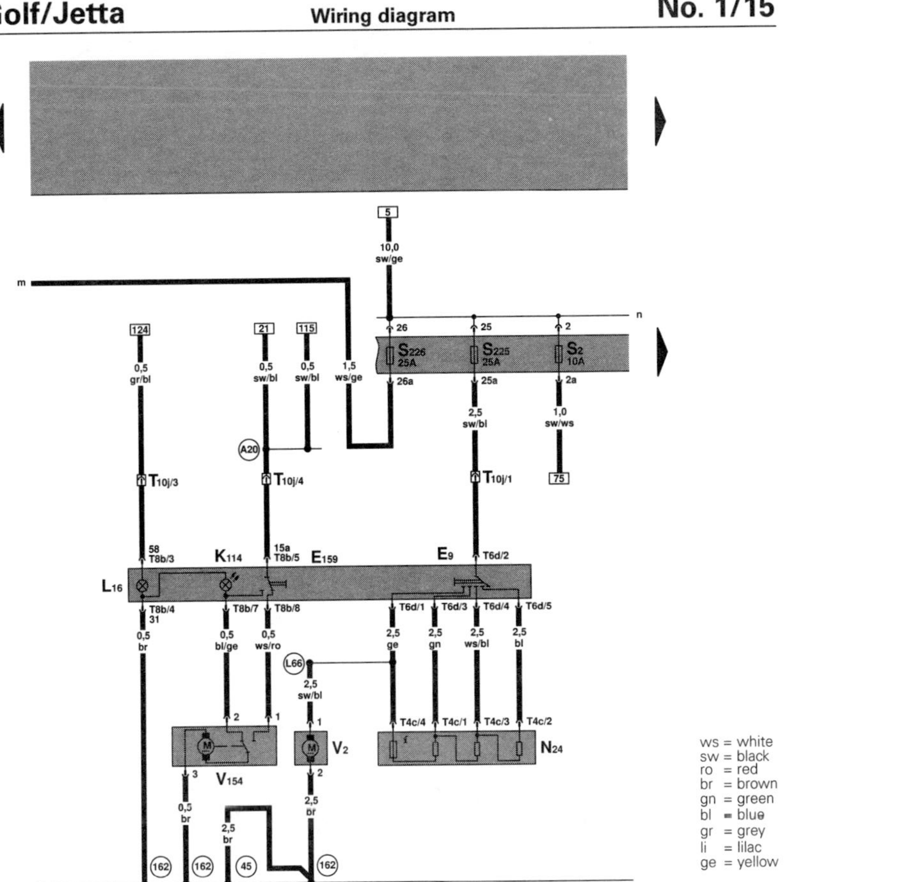

ws = white
sw = black
ro = red
br = brown
gn = green
bl = blue
gr = grey
li = lilac
ge = yellow

E9 - Fresh Air Blower Switch
E159 - Fresh Air/Recirculating Flap Switch
K114 - Fresh Air and Recirculating Air Mode Indicator Light
L16 - Fresh Air Control Lever Light
N24 - Fresh Air Blower Series Resistance With Fuse
S2 - Fuse 2 in fuse holder
S225 - Fuse 25 in fuse holder
S226 - Fuse 26 in fuse holder
T4c - 4-Pin Connector
T6d - 6-Pin Connector
T8b - 8-Pin Connector
T10j - 10-Pin Connector, behind instrument panel, center
V2 - Fresh Air Blower
V154 - Servo motor for fresh-/recirculating air door

(45) - Ground connection, behind instrument panel, center
(162) - Ground connection, in blower motor wiring harness
(A20) - Wire connection (15a), in instrument panel wiring harness
(L66) - Connector, in wiring harness heater blower

Fresh air blower switch, fresh air/recirculating flap switch, fresh air blower

ws = white
sw = black
ro = red
br = brown
gn = green
bl = blue
gr = grey
li = lilac
ge = yellow

S224 - Fuse 24 in fuse holder
S227 - Fuse 27 in fuse holder
T5a - 5-Pin Connector, pink, connector station C-pillar, left (Golf only)
T5h - 5-Pin Connector, near left A-pillar, lower part, in harness
T5i - 5-Pin Connector, near left A-pillar, lower part, in harness
V12 - Motor for rear windshield wiper
V59 - Windshield and Rear Window Washer Pump

(98) - Ground connection, in rear lid wiring harness

(A96) - Connector (53a), in instrument panel wiring harness

(A97) - Connector (53), in instrument panel wiring harness
(A102) - Connector (windshield wiper), in instrument panel wiring harness

-•-•- Golf only

Motor for rear windshield wiper, windshield and rear window washer pump

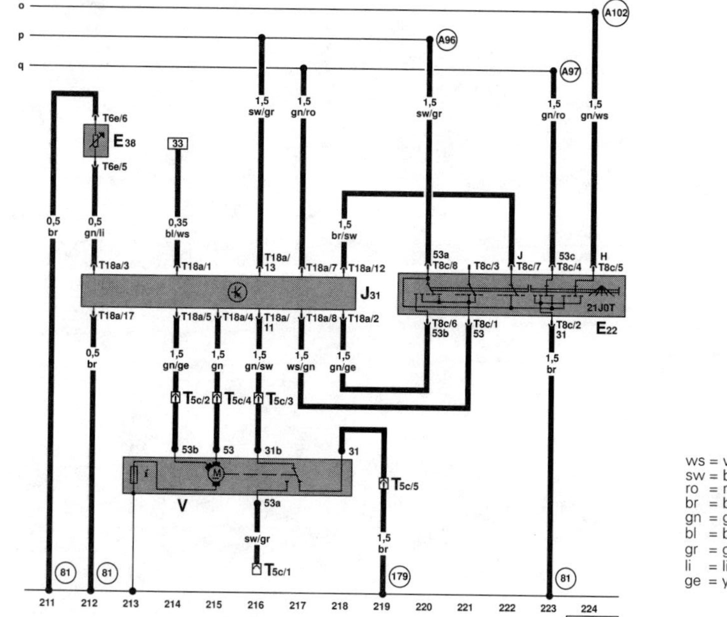

ws = white
sw = black
ro = red
br = brown
gn = green
bl = blue
gr = grey
li = lilac
ge = yellow

E22 - Windshield Wiper/Washer Switch
E38 - Windshield Wiper Intermittent Regulator
J31 - Wiper/Washer Intermittent Relay, on relais panel
T5c - 5-Pin Connector, on windshield wiper motor
T6e - 6-Pin Connector
T8c - 8-Pin Connector
T18a - 18-Pin Connector
V - Windshield Wiper Motor

(81) - Ground connection -1-, in instrument panel wiring harness
(179) - Ground connection, in left headlight wiring harness
(A96) - Connector (53a), in instrument panel wiring harness
(A97) - Connector (53), in instrument panel wiring harness
(A102) - Connector (windshield wiper), in instrument panel wiring harness

Edition 12/98
USA.5102.01.21

Windshield wiper/washer switch, windshield wiper intermittent regulator, windshield wiper motor, wiper/washer intermittent relay

THIS PAGE INTENTIONALLY LEFT BLANK

2.0L - Engine - Motronic Multiport Fuel Injection (MFI)/85 kW, code AEG,

from September 1998

Deviate relay location and fuseplacements as well as the locations of multiple connectors see section "component locations".

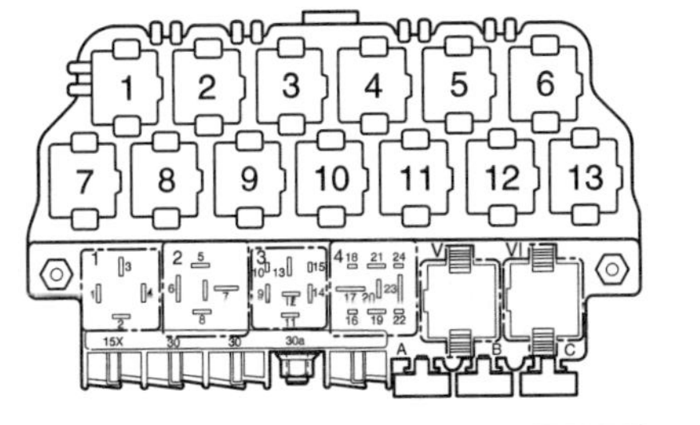

Relay location on the thirteenfold auxiliary relay panel, above relay panel:

Relay panel:

2 Load Reduction Relay (100)

4 Fuel Pump (FP) Relay (409)

Note: Number in parentheses indicates production control number stamped on relay housing.

Fuse colors

30 A - green
25 A - white
20 A - yellow
15 A - blue
10 A - red
7,5 A - brown
5 A - beige
3 A - violet

ws = white
sw = black
ro = red
br = brown
gn = green
bl = blue
gr = grey
li = lilac
ge = yellow

97-26049

A - Battery
B - Starter
C - Generator (GEN)
C1 - Voltage Regulator (VR)
D - Ignition/Starter Switch
J59 - Load Reduction Relay
J207 - Starting Interlock Relay
J226 - Park/Neutral Position (PNP) Relay
S162 - Fuse -1- (30) in fuse bracket/battery
S163 - Fuse -2- (30) in fuse bracket/battery
S176 - Fuse -4- (30) in fuse bracket/battery
S177 - Fuse -5- (30) in fuse bracket/battery
T2e - Double Connector, near starter (vehicles without air conditioning)
T4 - 4-Pin Connector, near starter (vehicles with air conditioning only)

T6 - 6-Pin Connector, brown, in protective housing for connectors, in plenum chamber, left

(81) - Ground connection -1-, in instrument panel wiring harness
(500) - Threaded connection -1- (30) on the relay plate
(501) - Threaded connection -2- (30) on the relay plate
(502) - Threaded connection -1- (30a) on the relay plate
(A41) - Plus connection (50), in instrument panel wiring harness

* - Manual transmission only
--- Automatic transmission only

Generator (GEN), starter

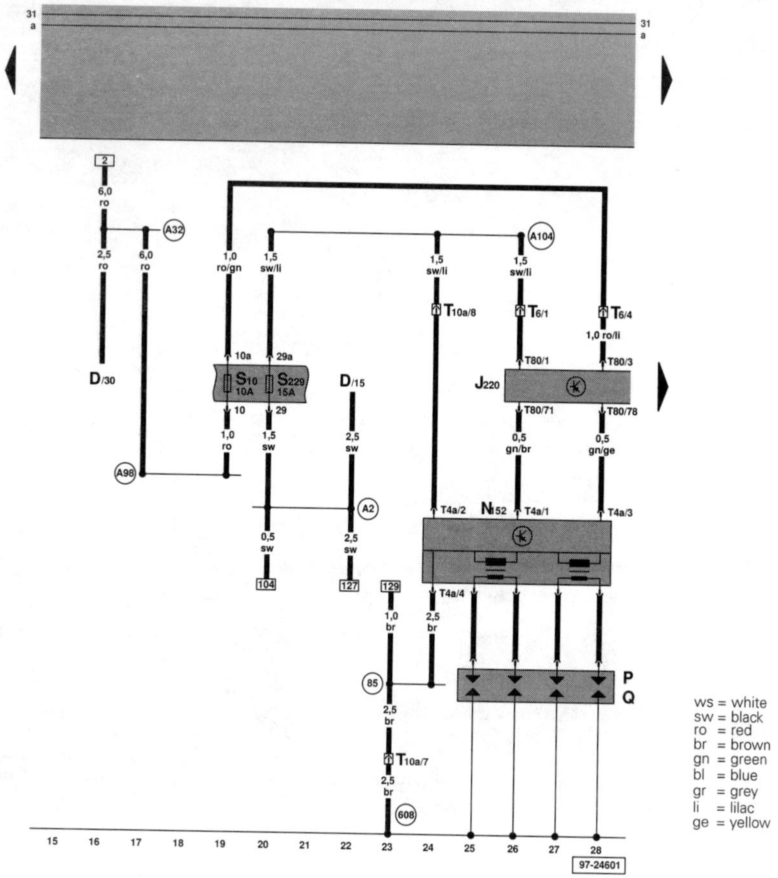

ws = white
sw = black
ro = red
br = brown
gn = green
bl = blue
gr = grey
li = lilac
ge = yellow

D - Ignition/Starter Switch
J220 - Motronic Engine Control Module (ECM), in plenum chamber, center
N152 - Ignition Coil
P - Spark Plug Connectors
Q - Spark Plugs
S10 - Fuse 10 in fuse holder
S229 - Fuse 29 in fuse holder
T4a - 4-Pin Connector
T6 - 6-Pin Connector, brown, in protective housing for connectors, in plenum chamber, left
T10a - 10-Pin Connector, in engine compartment, in wiring duct, left
T80 - Connector, 80 point

(608) - Ground connection (in center plenum chamber)
(85) - Ground connection -1-, in engine compartment wiring harness
(A2) - Plus connection (15), in instrument panel wiring harness
(A32) - Plus connection (30), in instrument panel wiring harness
(A98) - Plus connector -4- (30), in instrument panel wiring harness
(A104) - Plus connector -2- (15), in instrument panel wiring harness

Motronic engine control module (ECM), ignition system

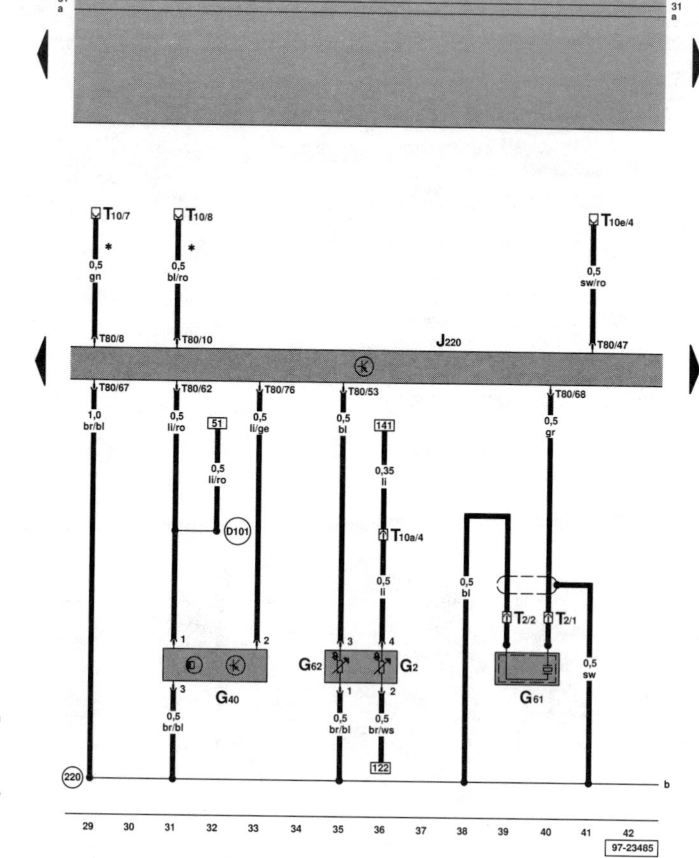

ws = white
sw = black
ro = red
br = brown
gn = green
bl = blue
gr = grey
li = lilac
ge = yellow

G2 - Engine Coolant Temperature (ECT) Sensor
G40 - Camshaft Position (CMP) Sensor
G61 - Knock Sensor (KS) 1
G62 - Engine Coolant Temperature (ECT) Sensor
J220 - Motronic Engine Control Module (ECM), in plenum chamber, center
T2 - Double Connector, in engine compartment, rear
T10 - 10-Pin Connector, orange, in protective housing for connectors, in plenum chamber, left
T10a - 10-Pin Connector, in engine compartment, in wiring duct, left
T10e - 10-Pin Connector, black, in protective housing for connectors, in plenum chamber, left
T80 - Connector, 80 point

(220) - Ground connection (sensor ground), in engine compartment wiring harness
(D101) - Wire connection -1-, in engine compartment wiring harness
* - A/C connection

Motronic engine control module (ECM), camshaft position (CMP) sensor, engine coolant temperature (ECT) sensor, knock sensor (KS) 1

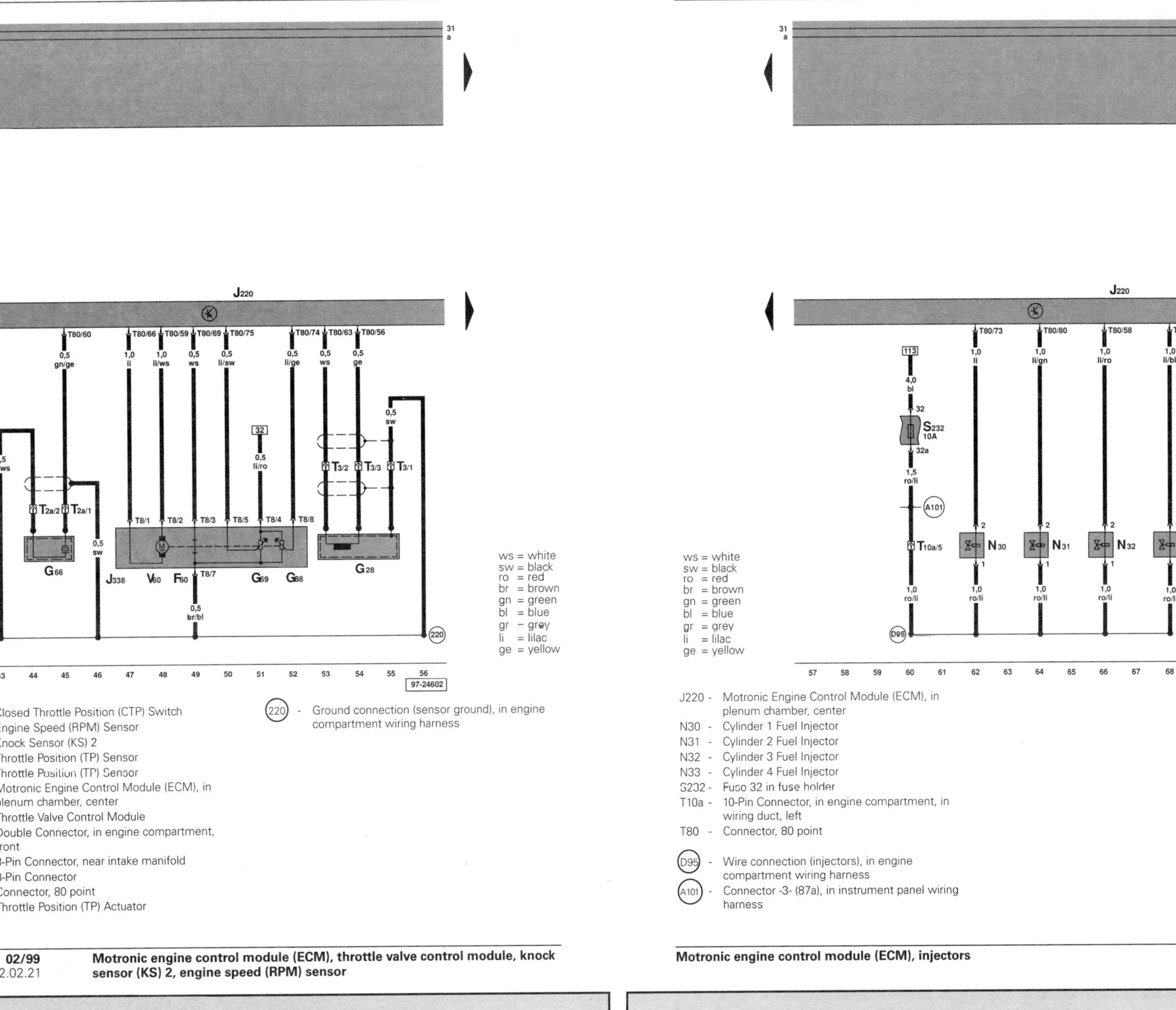

ws = white
sw = black
ro = red
br = brown
gn = green
bl = blue
gr = grey
li = lilac
ge = yellow

F60 - Closed Throttle Position (CTP) Switch
G28 - Engine Speed (RPM) Sensor
G66 - Knock Sensor (KS) 2
G69 - Throttle Position (TP) Sensor
G88 - Throttle Position (TP) Sensor
J220 - Motronic Engine Control Module (ECM), in plenum chamber, center
J338 - Throttle Valve Control Module
T2a - Double Connector, in engine compartment, front
T3 - 3-Pin Connector, near intake manifold
T8 - 8-Pin Connector
T80 - Connector, 80 point
V60 - Throttle Position (TP) Actuator

(220) - Ground connection (sensor ground), in engine compartment wiring harness

Edition 02/99
USA.5102.02.21

Motronic engine control module (ECM), throttle valve control module, knock sensor (KS) 2, engine speed (RPM) sensor

ws = white
sw = black
ro = red
br = brown
gn = green
bl = blue
gr = grey
li = lilac
ge = yellow

J220 - Motronic Engine Control Module (ECM), in plenum chamber, center
N30 - Cylinder 1 Fuel Injector
N31 - Cylinder 2 Fuel Injector
N32 - Cylinder 3 Fuel Injector
N33 - Cylinder 4 Fuel Injector
S232 - Fuse 32 in fuse holder
T10a - 10-Pin Connector, in engine compartment, in wiring duct, left
T80 - Connector, 80 point

(D95) - Wire connection (injectors), in engine compartment wiring harness
(A101) - Connector -3- (87a), in instrument panel wiring harness

Motronic engine control module (ECM), injectors

Edition 02/99
USA.5102.02.21

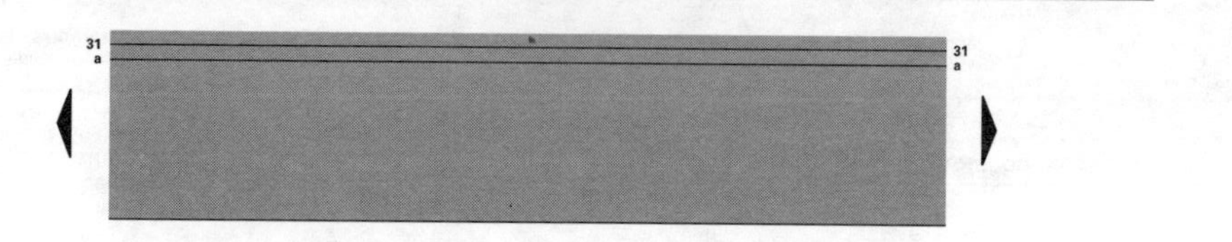

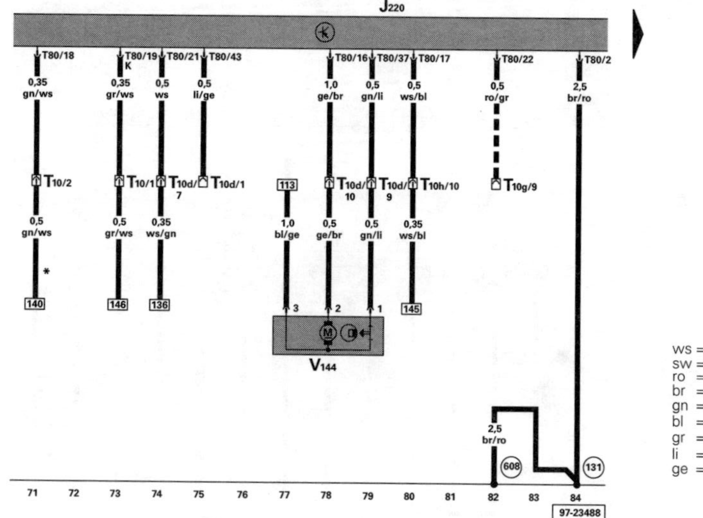

ws = white
sw = black
ro = red
br = brown
gn = green
bl = blue
gr = grey
li = lilac
ge = yellow

- J220 - Motronic Engine Control Module (ECM), in plenum chamber, center
- T10 - 10-Pin Connector, orange, in protective housing for connectors, in plenum chamber, left
- T10d - 10-Pin Connector, green, in protective housing for connectors, in plenum chamber, left
- T10h - 10-Pin Connector, blue, in protective housing for connectors, in plenum chamber, left
- T10g - 10-Pin Connector, grey, in protective housing for connectors, in plenum chamber, left
- T80 - Connector, 80 point
- V144 - Leak detection pump (LDP)
- (608) - Ground Connection (in center plenum chamber)
- (131) - Ground connection -2-, in engine compartment wiring harness
- * - Vehicles with Multi-Function Indicator (MFI) only
- --- Automatic transmission only

Motronic engine control module (ECM), leak detection pump (LDP)

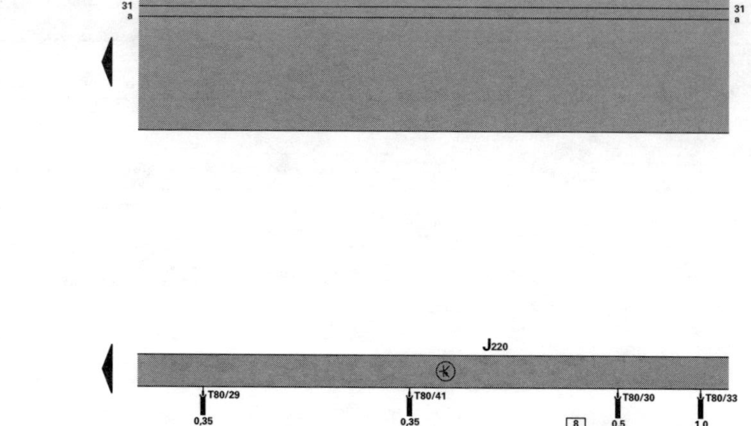

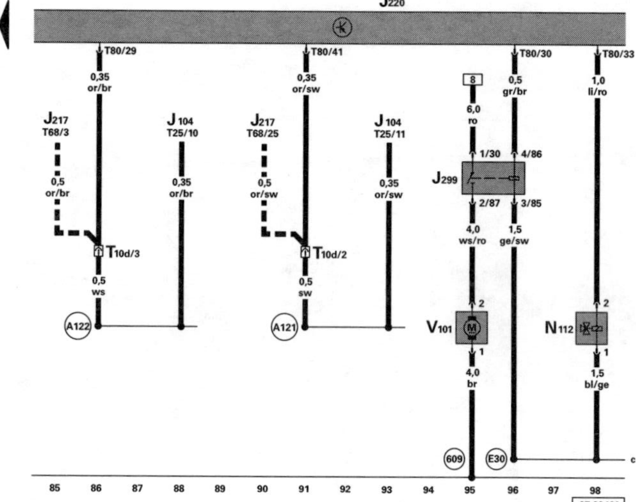

ws = white
sw = black
ro = red
br = brown
gn = green
bl = blue
gr = grey
li = lilac
ge = yellow
or = orange

- J104 - ABS Control Module (w/EDL), in engine compartment, left
- J217 - Transmission Control Module (TCM), in plenum chamber, center
- J220 - Motronic Engine Control Module (ECM), in plenum chamber, center
- J299 - Secondary Air Injection (AIR) Pump Relay, in protective housing, in engine compartment, left, production control number (100)
- N112 - Secondary Air Injection (AIR) Solenoid Valve
- T10d - 10-Pin Connector, green, in protective housing for connectors, in plenum chamber, left
- T25 - 25-Pin Connector, on ABS Control Module (w/EDL)
- T68 - 68-Pin Connector, on Transmission Control Module (TCM)
- T80 - Connector, 80 point
- V101 - Secondary Air Injection (AIR) Pump Motor
- (609) - Ground Connection (in right plenum chamber)
- (A121) - Connection (high bus), in instrument panel wiring harness
- (A122) - Connection (low bus), in instrument panel wiring harness
- (E30) - Connector (87a), in wiring harness engine
- --- Automatic transmission only

Motronic engine control module (ECM), secondary air injection (AIR) pump motor, secondary air injection (AIR) solenoid valve

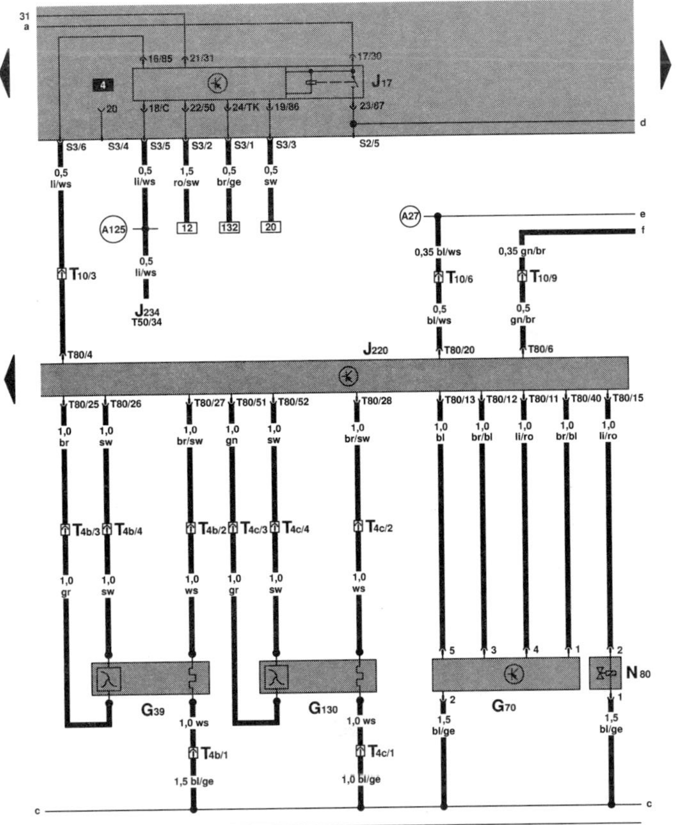

ws = white
sw = black
ro = red
br = brown
gn = green
bl = blue
gr = grey
li = lilac
ge = yellow

G39 - Heated Oxygen Sensor (HO2S)
G70 - Mass Air Flow (MAF) Sensor
G130 - Oxygen Sensor (O2S) behind Three Way Catalytic Converter (TWC)
J17 - Fuel Pump (FP) Relay
J220 - Motronic Engine Control Module (ECM), in plenum chamber, center
J234 - Airbag Control Module
N80 - Evaporative Emission (EVAP) Canister Purge Regulator Valve
T4b - 4-Pin Connector, in protective housing for connectors under right floor
T4c - 4-Pin Connector, in protective housing for connectors under right floor
T10 - 10-Pin Connector, orange, in protective housing for connectors, in plenum chamber, left
T50 - 50-Pin Connector
T80 - Connector, 80 point
(A125) - Connection (crash signal) in instrument panel wiring harness
(A27) - Wire Connection (vehicle speed signal), in instrument panel wiring harness

Motronic engine control module (ECM), mass air flow (MAF) sensor, heated oxygen sensor (HO2S), evaporative emission (EVAP) canister purge regulator valve

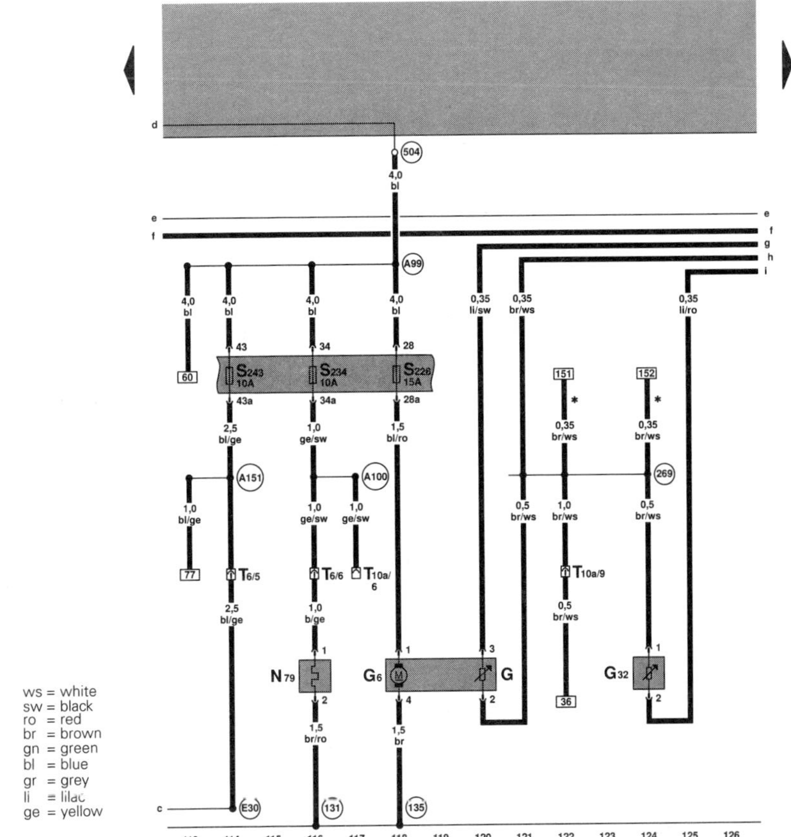

ws = white
sw = black
ro = red
br = brown
gn = green
bl = blue
gr = grey
li = lilac
ge = yellow

G - Fuel Level Sensor
G6 - Fuel Pump (FP)
G32 - Engine Coolant Level (ECL) Sensor
N79 - Positive Crankcase Ventilation (PCV) Heating Element
S228 - Fuse 28 in fuse holder
S234 - Fuse 34 in fuse holder
S243 - Fuse 43 in fuse holder
T6 - 6-Pin Connector, brown, in protective housing for connectors, in plenum chamber, left
T10a - 10-Pin Connector, in engine compartment, in wiring duct, left
(131) - Ground connection -2-, in engine compartment wiring harness
(135) - Ground connection -2-, in instrument panel wiring harness
(269) - Ground connection (sensor ground) -1-, in instrument panel wiring harness
(504) - Threaded connection -1- (87) on the relay plate
(E30) - Connector (87a), in wiring harness engine
(A99) - Connector -1- (87), in instrument panel wiring harness
(A100) - Connector -2- (87), in instrument panel wiring harness
(A151) - Connector -4- (87), in instrument panel wiring harness
* - Vehicles with Multi-Function Indicator (MFI) only

Fuel pump (FP), fuel level sensor, positive crankcase ventilation (PCV) heating element, engine coolant level (ECL) sensor

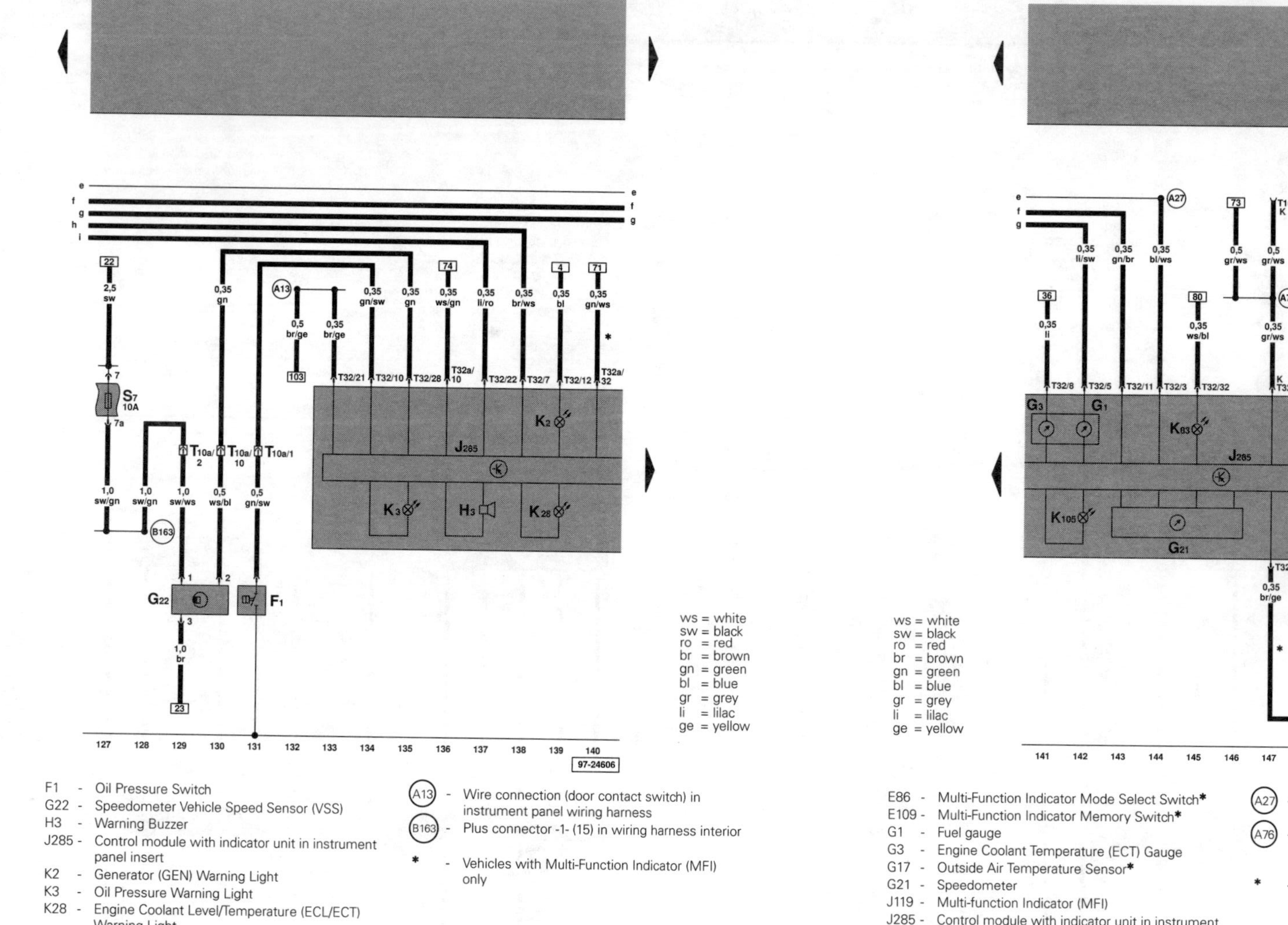

ws = white
sw = black
ro = red
br = brown
gn = green
bl = blue
gr = grey
li = lilac
ge = yellow

F1 - Oil Pressure Switch
G22 - Speedometer Vehicle Speed Sensor (VSS)
H3 - Warning Buzzer
J285 - Control module with indicator unit in instrument panel insert
K2 - Generator (GEN) Warning Light
K3 - Oil Pressure Warning Light
K28 - Engine Coolant Level/Temperature (ECL/ECT) Warning Light
S7 - Fuse 7 in fuse holder
T10a - 10-Pin Connector, in engine compartment, in wiring duct, left
T32 - 32-Pin Connector, blue
T32a - 32-Pin Connector, green

(A13) - Wire connection (door contact switch) in instrument panel wiring harness
(B163) - Plus connector -1- (15) in wiring harness interior
* - Vehicles with Multi-Function Indicator (MFI) only

Instrument cluster, oil pressure switch, speedometer vehicle speed sensor, generator (GEN) warning light, engine coolant level/temperature (ECL/ECT) warning light

ws = white
sw = black
ro = red
br = brown
gn = green
bl = blue
gr = grey
li = lilac
ge = yellow

E86 - Multi-Function Indicator Mode Select Switch*
E109 - Multi-Function Indicator Memory Switch*
G1 - Fuel gauge
G3 - Engine Coolant Temperature (ECT) Gauge
G17 - Outside Air Temperature Sensor*
G21 - Speedometer
J119 - Multi-function Indicator (MFI)
J285 - Control module with indicator unit in instrument panel insert
K83 - Malfunction Indicator Lamp (MIL)
K105 - Low Fuel Level Warning Light
T6e - 6-Pin Connector
T16 - Data Link Connector (DLC), below instrument panel, left
T32 - 32-Pin Connector, blue
T32a - 32-Pin Connector, green

(A27) - Wire Connection (vehicle speed signal), in instrument panel wiring harness
(A76) - Connector (K-diagnosis wire), in instrument panel wiring harness
* - Vehicles with Multi-Function Indicator (MFI) only

Instrument cluster, multi-function indicator (MFI), engine coolant temperature (ECT) gauge, fuel gauge, malfunction indicator lamp (MIL), outside air temperature sensor

2.8L - Engine - Motronic Multiport Fuel Injection (MFI)/130 kW, code AFP,

from December 1998

Deviate relay location and fuseplacements as well as the locations of multiple connectors see section "component locations".

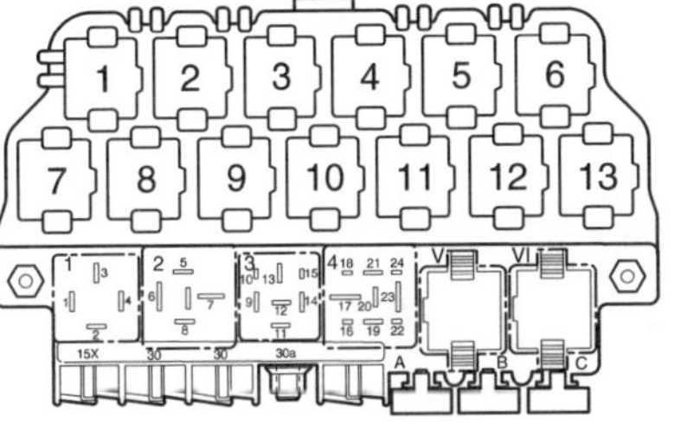

97-14163

Relay location on the thirteenfold auxiliary relay panel, above relay panel:

Relay panel:

- **2** Load Reduction Relay (100)
- **4** Fuel Pump (FP) Relay (409)

Note: Number in parentheses indicates production control number stamped on relay housing.

Fuse colors

30 A - green
25 A - white
20 A - yellow
15 A - blue
10 A - red
7.5 A - brown
5 A - beige
3 A - violet

ws = white
sw = black
ro = red
br = brown
gn = green
bl = blue
gr = grey
li = lilac
ge = yellow

97-26051

A - Battery
B - Starter
C - Generator (GEN)
C1 - Voltage Regulator (VR)
D - Ignition/Starter Switch
J59 - Load Reduction Relay
J207 - Starting Interlock Relay
J226 - Park/Neutral Position (PNP) Relay
S162 - Fuse -1- (30) in fuse bracket/battery
S163 - Fuse -2- (30) in fuse bracket/battery
S176 - Fuse -4- (30) in fuse bracket/battery
S177 - Fuse -5- (30) in fuse bracket/battery
T2e - Double Connector, near starter (vehicles without air conditioning)
T4 - 4-Pin Connector, near starter (vehicles with air conditioning only)
T6 - 6-Pin Connector, brown, in protective housing for connectors, in plenum chamber, left

(81) - Ground connection -1-, in instrument panel wiring harness
(500) - Threaded connection -1- (30) on the relay plate
(502) - Threaded connection -1- (30a) on the relay plate
(A41) - Plus connection (50), in instrument panel wiring harness

* - Manual transmission only
--- Automatic transmission only

Generator (GEN), starter

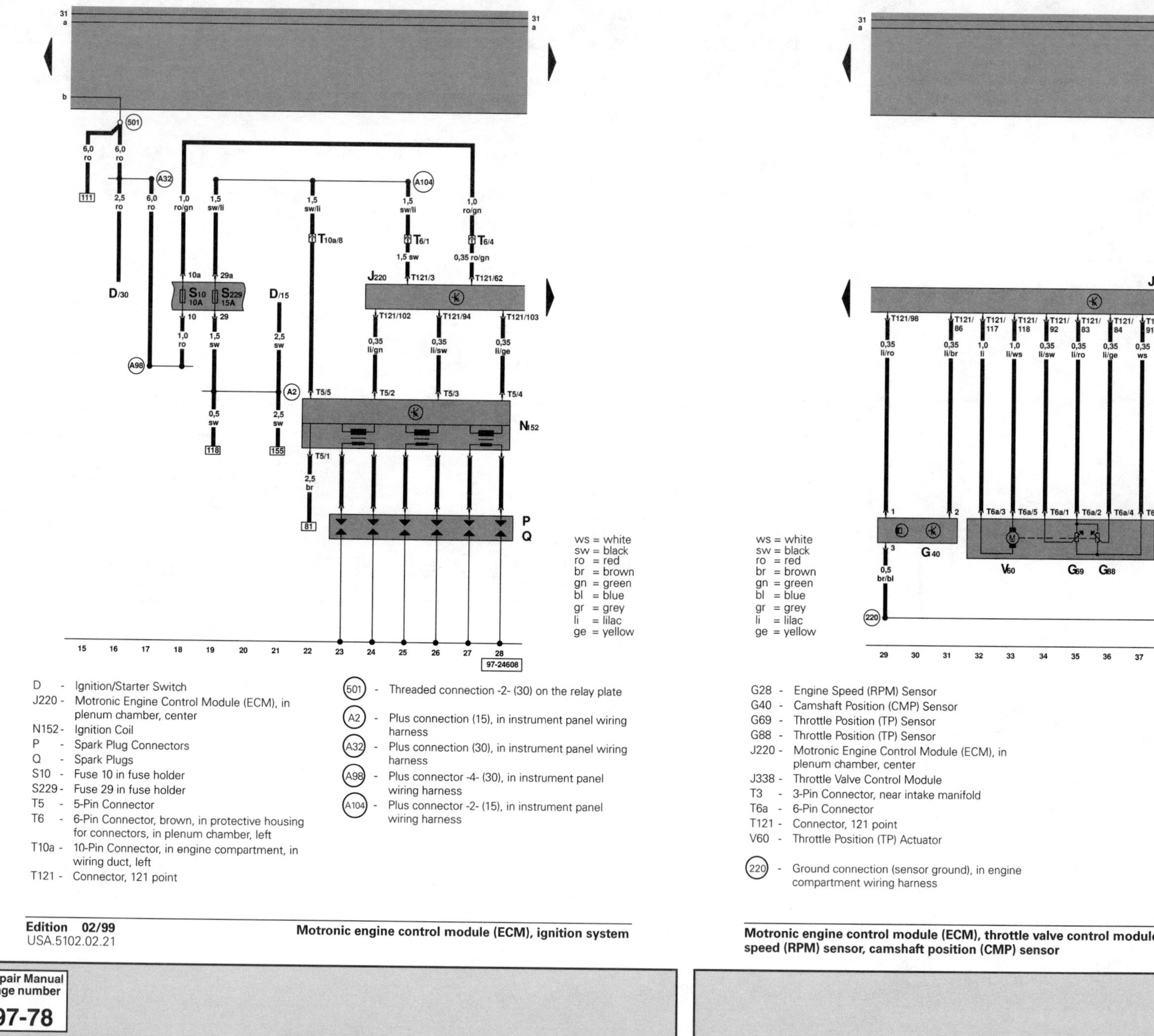

ws = white
sw = black
ro = red
br = brown
gn = green
bl = blue
gr = grey
li = lilac
ge = yellow

D - Ignition/Starter Switch
J220 - Motronic Engine Control Module (ECM), in plenum chamber, center
N152 - Ignition Coil
P - Spark Plug Connectors
Q - Spark Plugs
S10 - Fuse 10 in fuse holder
S229 - Fuse 29 in fuse holder
T5 - 5-Pin Connector
T6 - 6-Pin Connector, brown, in protective housing for connectors, in plenum chamber, left
T10a - 10-Pin Connector, in engine compartment, in wiring duct, left
T121 - Connector, 121 point

(501) - Threaded connection -2- (30) on the relay plate
(A2) - Plus connection (15), in instrument panel wiring harness
(A32) - Plus connection (30), in instrument panel wiring harness
(A98) - Plus connector -4- (30), in instrument panel wiring harness
(A104) - Plus connector -2- (15), in instrument panel wiring harness

Motronic engine control module (ECM), ignition system

ws = white
sw = black
ro = red
br = brown
gn = green
bl = blue
gr = grey
li = lilac
ge = yellow

G28 - Engine Speed (RPM) Sensor
G40 - Camshaft Position (CMP) Sensor
G69 - Throttle Position (TP) Sensor
G88 - Throttle Position (TP) Sensor
J220 - Motronic Engine Control Module (ECM), in plenum chamber, center
J338 - Throttle Valve Control Module
T3 - 3-Pin Connector, near intake manifold
T6a - 6-Pin Connector
T121 - Connector, 121 point
V60 - Throttle Position (TP) Actuator

(220) - Ground connection (sensor ground), in engine compartment wiring harness

Motronic engine control module (ECM), throttle valve control module, engine speed (RPM) sensor, camshaft position (CMP) sensor

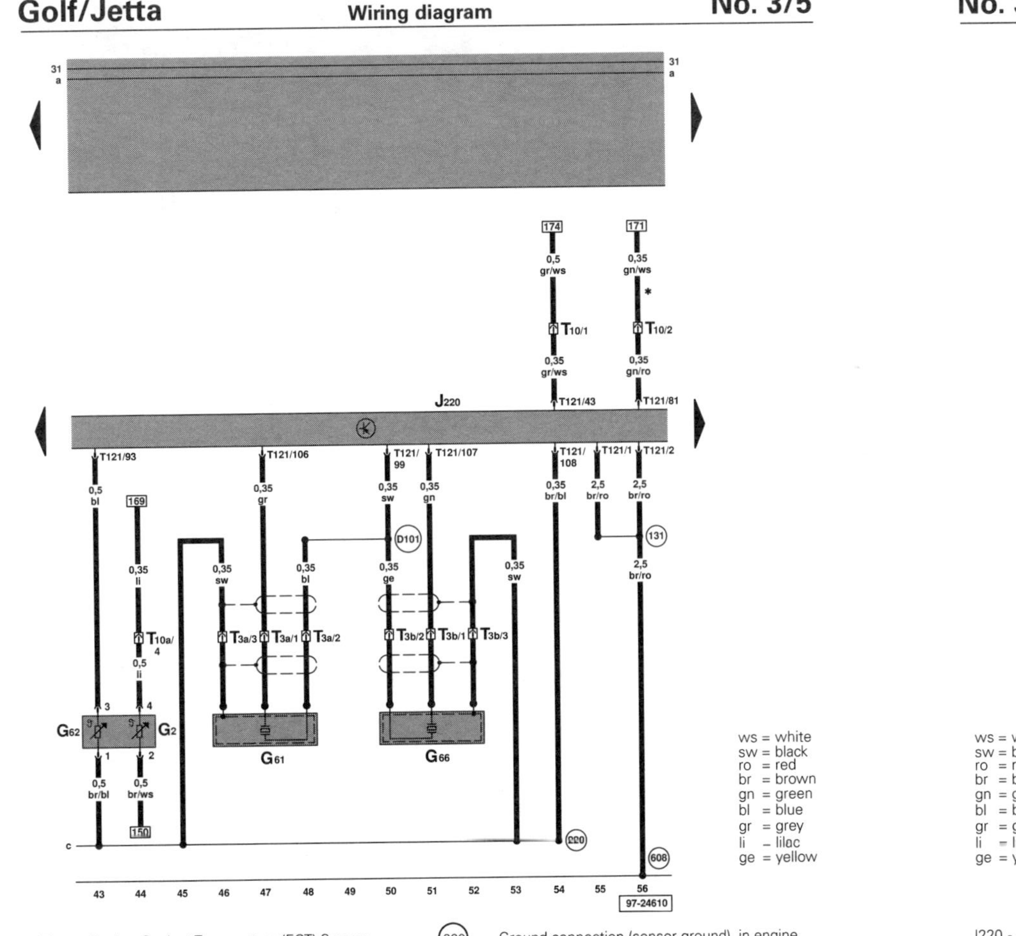

ws = white
sw = black
ro = red
br = brown
gn = green
bl = blue
gr = grey
li = lilac
ge = yellow

G2 - Engine Coolant Temperature (ECT) Sensor
G61 - Knock Sensor (KS) 1
G62 - Engine Coolant Temperature (ECT) Sensor
G66 - Knock Sensor (KS) 2
J220 - Motronic Engine Control Module (ECM), in plenum chamber, center
T3a - 3-Pin Connector, in engine compartment, rear
T3b - 3-Pin Connector, in engine compartment, front
T10 - 10-Pin Connector, orange, in protective housing for connectors, in plenum chamber, left
T10a - 10-Pin Connector, in engine compartment, in wiring duct, left
T121 - Connector, 121 point

(608) - Ground connection (in center plenum chamber)

(220) - Ground connection (sensor ground), in engine compartment wiring harness
(131) - Ground connection -2-, in engine compartment wiring harness
(D101) - Wire connection -1-, in engine compartment wiring harness

* - Vehicles with Multi-Function Indicator (MFI) only

Edition 02/99 USA.5102.02.21

Motronic engine control module (ECM), knock sensor (KS) 1, knock sensor (KS) 2, engine coolant temperature (ECT) sensor

ws = white
sw = black
ro = red
br = brown
gn = green
bl = blue
gr = grey
li = lilac
ge = yellow

J220 - Motronic Engine Control Module (ECM), in plenum chamber, center
N30 - Cylinder 1 Fuel Injector
N31 - Cylinder 2 Fuel Injector
N32 - Cylinder 3 Fuel Injector
N33 - Cylinder 4 Fuel Injector
N83 - Cylinder 5 Fuel Injector
N84 - Cylinder 6 Fuel Injector
S232 - Fuse 32 in fuse holder
T10a - 10-Pin Connector, in engine compartment, in wiring duct, left
T121 - Connector, 121 point

(A101) - Connector -3- (87a), in instrument panel wiring harness

(D95) - Wire connection (injectors), in engine compartment wiring harness

Motronic engine control module (ECM), injectors

Edition 02/99 USA.5102.02.21

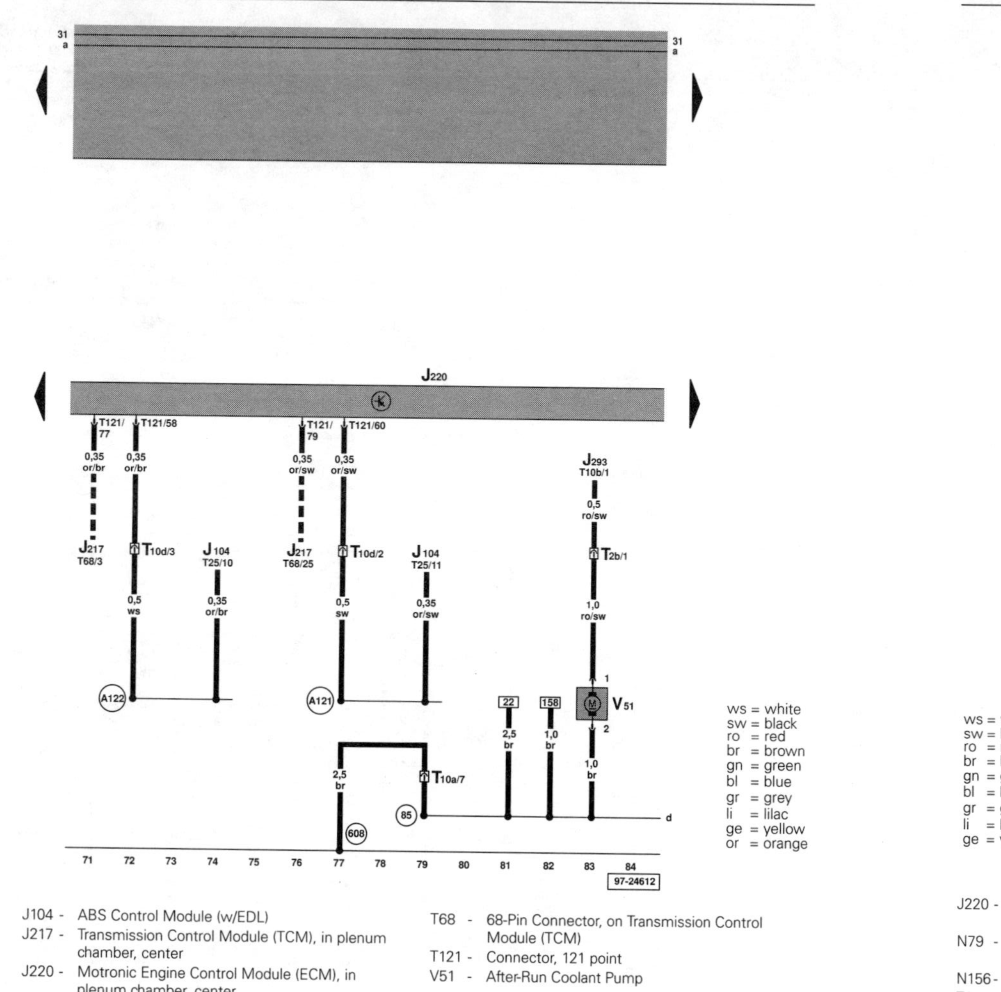

ws = white
sw = black
ro = red
br = brown
gn = green
bl = blue
gr = grey
li = lilac
ge = yellow
or = orange

J104 - ABS Control Module (w/EDL)
J217 - Transmission Control Module (TCM), in plenum chamber, center
J220 - Motronic Engine Control Module (ECM), in plenum chamber, center
J293 - Coolant FC (Fan Control) Control Module
T2b - Double Connector, in engine compartment, in wiring duct, left
T10a - 10-Pin Connector, in engine compartment, in wiring duct, left
T10b - 10-Pin Connector, on Coolant FC (Fan Control) Control Module
T10d - 10-Pin Connector, green, in protective housing for connectors, in plenum chamber, left
T25 - 25-Pin Connector, on ABS Control Module (w/EDL)
T68 - 68-Pin Connector, on Transmission Control Module (TCM)
T121 - Connector, 121 point
V51 - After-Run Coolant Pump

(608) - Ground connection (in center plenum chamber)
(85) - Ground connection -1-, in engine compartment wiring harness
(A121) - Connection (high bus), in instrument panel wiring harness
(A122) - Connection (low bus), in instrument panel wiring harness

--- Automatic transmission only

Motronic engine control module (ECM), after-run coolant pump

ws = white
sw = black
ro = red
br = brown
gn = green
bl = blue
gr = grey
li = lilac
ge = yellow

J220 - Motronic Engine Control Module (ECM), in plenum chamber, center
N79 - Positive Crankcase Ventilation (PCV) Heating Element
N156 - Intake Manifold Change-Over Valve
T6 - 6-Pin Connector, brown, in protective housing for connectors, in plenum chamber, left
T10 - 10-Pin Connector, orange, in protective housing for connectors, in plenum chamber, left
T10a - 10-Pin Connector, in engine compartment, in wiring duct, left
T10d - 10-Pin Connector, green, in protective housing for connectors, in plenum chamber, left
T10h - 10-Pin Connector, blue, in protective housing for connectors, in plenum chamber, left
T121 - Connector, 121 point
V144 - Leak detection pump (LDP)

(85) - Ground connection -1-, in engine compartment wiring harness
(A100) - Connector -2- (87), in instrument panel wiring harness
(D102) - Wire connection -2-, in engine compartment wiring harness

* - A/C connection

--- Automatic transmission only

Motronic engine control module (ECM), leak detection pump (LDP), intake manifold change-over valve, positive crankcase ventilation (PCV) heating element

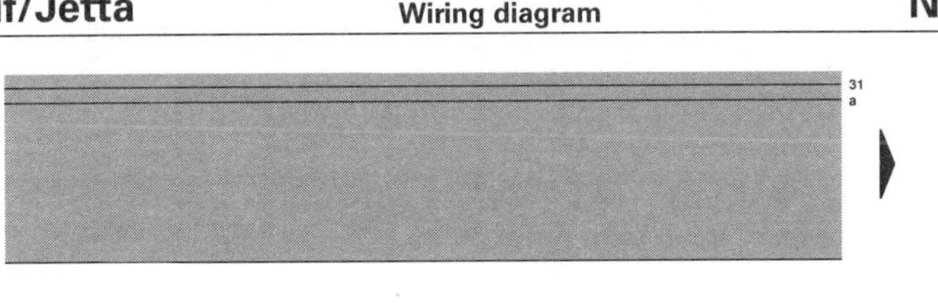

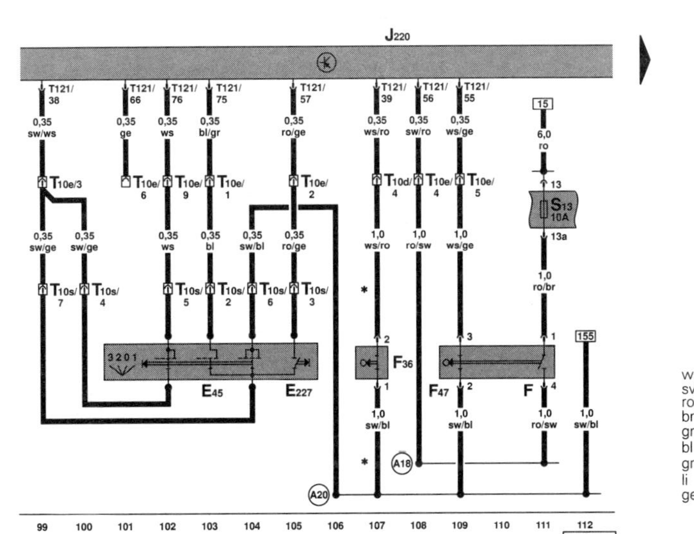

ws = white
sw = black
ro = red
br = brown
gn = green
bl = blue
gr = grey
li = lilac
ge = yellow

E45 - Cruise Control Switch
E227 - Cruise Control Push Button (SET)
F - Brake Light Switch
F36 - Clutch Vacuum Vent Valve Switch
F47 - Brake Vacuum Vent Valve Switch for cruise control
J220 - Motronic Engine Control Module (ECM), in plenum chamber, center
S13 - Fuse 13 in fuse holder
T10d - 10-Pin Connector, green, in protective housing for connectors, in plenum chamber, left
T10e - 10-Pin Connector, black, in protective housing for connectors, in plenum chamber, left
T10s - 10-Pin Connector, near steering column
T121 - Connector, 121 point

(A18) - Wire connection (54), in instrument panel

(A20) - Wire connection (15a), in instrument panel wiring harness

* - Manual transmission only

Motronic engine control module (ECM), cruise control switch, brake light switch, clutch vacuum vent valve switch, brake vacuum vent valve switch

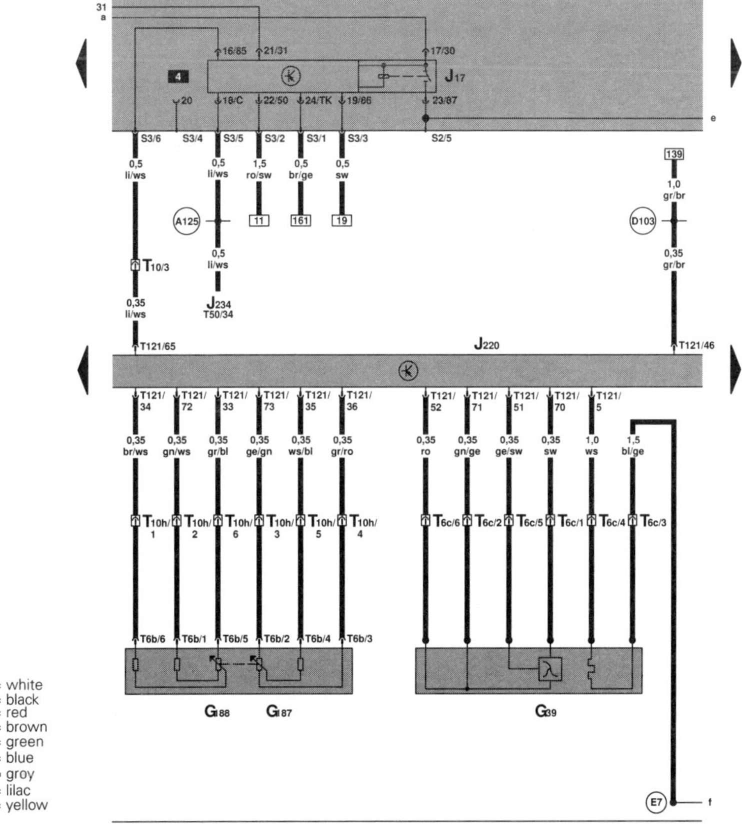

ws = white
sw = black
ro = red
br = brown
gn = green
bl = blue
gr = groy
li = lilac
ge = yellow

G39 - Heated Oxygen Sensor (HO2S)
G187 - Angle sensor -1- for throttle drive (power accelerator actuation)
G188 - Angle sensor -2- for throttle drive (power accelerator actuation)
J17 - Fuel Pump (FP) Relay
J220 - Motronic Engine Control Module (ECM), in plenum chamber, center
J234 - Airbag Control Module
T6b - 6-Pin Connector
T6c - 6-Pin Connector, in protective housing for connectors, in engine compartment, rear
T10 - 10-Pin Connector, orange, in protective housing for connectors, in plenum chamber, left
T10h - 10-Pin Connector, blue, in protective housing for connectors, in plenum chamber, left
T50 - 50-Pin Connector
T121 - Connector, 121 point

(A125) - Connection (crash signal) in instrument panel wiring harness

(D103) - Wire connection -3-, in engine compartment wiring harness

(E7) - Plus connection (87a), in Motronic Multiport Fuel Injection (MFI) wiring harness

Motronic engine control module (ECM), angle sensors for throttle drive (power accelerator actuation), heated oxygen sensor (HO2S)

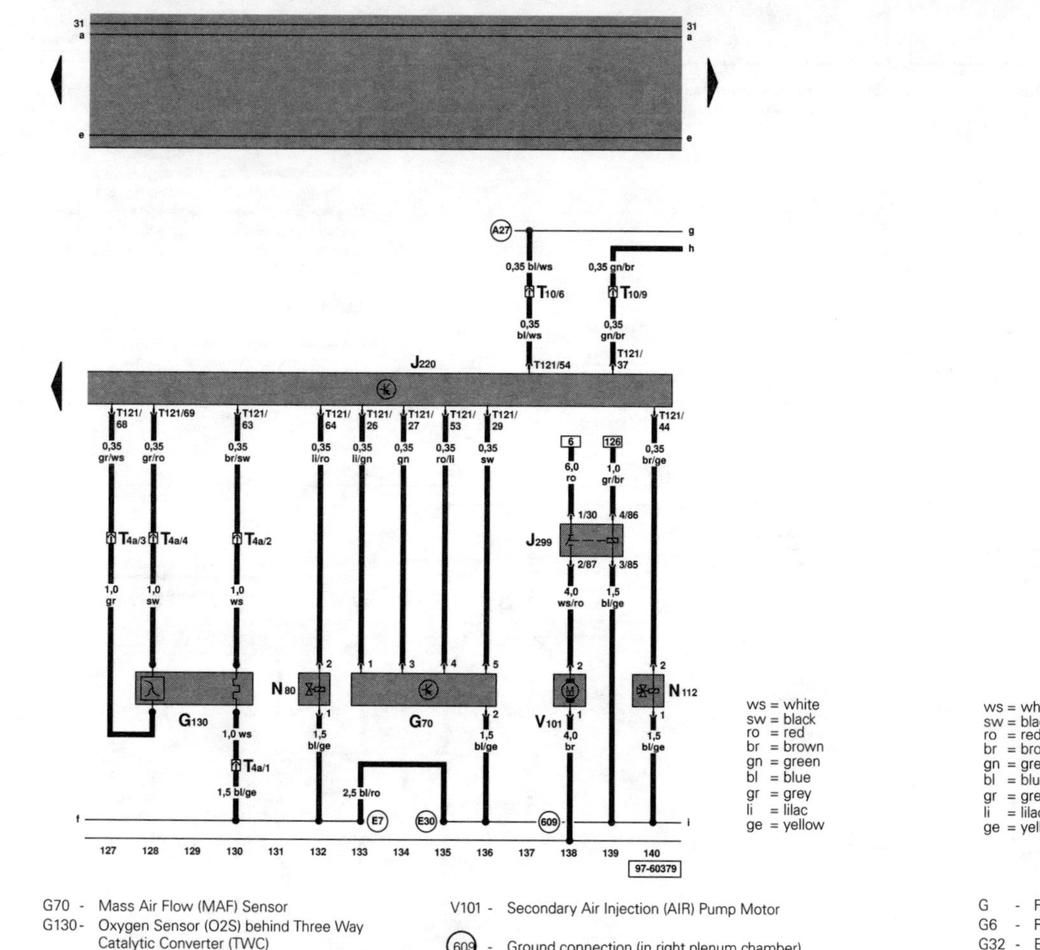

ws = white
sw = black
ro = red
br = brown
gn = green
bl = blue
gr = grey
li = lilac
ge = yellow

G70 - Mass Air Flow (MAF) Sensor
G130 - Oxygen Sensor (O2S) behind Three Way Catalytic Converter (TWC)
J220 - Motronic Engine Control Module (ECM), in plenum chamber, center
J299 - Secondary Air Injection (AIR) Pump Relay, in protective housing, in engine compartment, left, production control number (100)
N80 - Evaporative Emission (EVAP) Canister Purge Regulator Valve
N112 - Secondary Air Injection (AIR) Solenoid Valve
T4a - 4-Pin Connector, in protective housing for connectors, in engine compartment, rear
T10 - 10-Pin Connector, orange, in protective housing for connectors, in plenum chamber, left
T121 - Connector, 121 point

V101 - Secondary Air Injection (AIR) Pump Motor
(609) - Ground connection (in right plenum chamber)
(A27) - Wire Connection (vehicle speed signal), in instrument panel wiring harness
(E7) - Plus connection (87a), in Motronic Multiport Fuel Injection (MFI) wiring harness
(E30) - Connector (87a), in wiring harness engine

Edition 02/99
USA.5102.02.21

Motronic engine control module (ECM), secondary air injection (AIR) pump system, oxygen sensor (O2S) behind three way catalytic converter (TWC)

ws = white
sw = black
ro = red
br = brown
gn = green
bl = blue
gr = grey
li = lilac
ge = yellow

G - Fuel Level Sensor
G6 - Fuel Pump (FP)
G32 - Engine Coolant Level (ECL) Sensor
S228 - Fuse 28 in fuse holder
S234 - Fuse 34 in fuse holder
S243 - Fuse 43 in fuse holder
T6 - 6-Pin Connector, brown, in protective housing for connectors, in plenum chamber, left
T10a - 10-Pin Connector, in engine compartment, in wiring duct, left
(135) - Ground connection -2-, in instrument panel wiring harnes

(269) - Ground connection (sensor ground) -1-, in instrument panel wiring harness
(504) - Threaded connection -1- (87) on the relay plate
(E30) - Connector (87a), in wiring harness engine
(A99) - Connector -1- (87), in instrument panel wiring harness
(A151) - Connector -4- (87), in instrument panel wiring harness
* - Vehicles with Multi-Function Indicator (MFI) only

Fuel pump (FP), fuel level sensor, engine coolant level (ECL) sensor

Edition 02/99
USA.5102.02.21

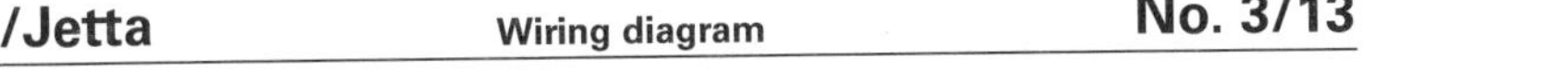

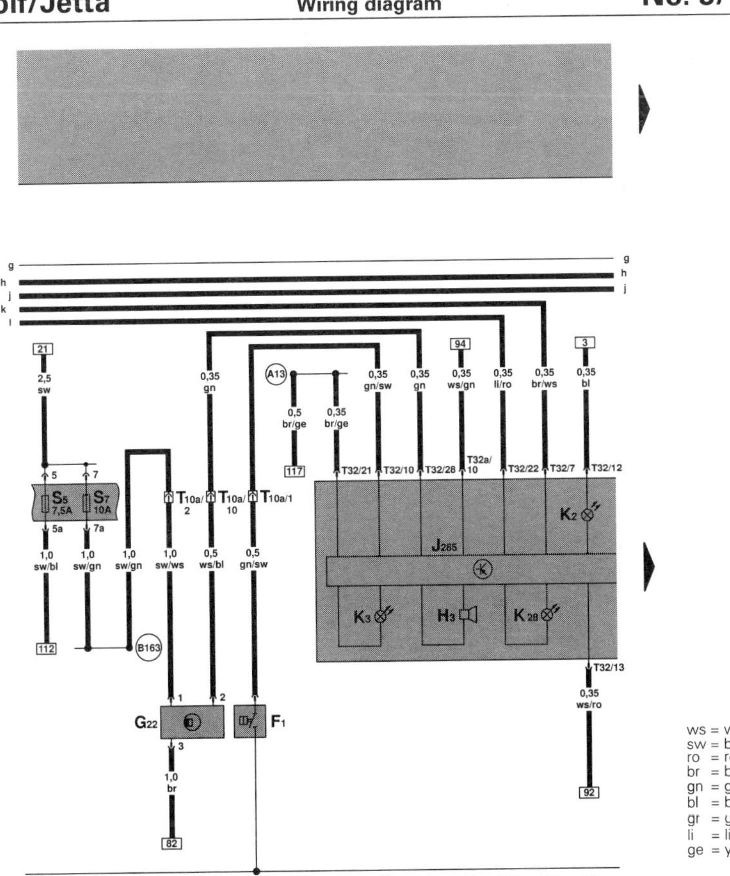

ws = white
sw = black
ro = red
br = brown
gn = green
bl = blue
gr = grey
li = lilac
ge = yellow

F1 - Oil Pressure Switch
G22 - Speedometer Vehicle Speed Sensor (VSS)
H3 - Warning Buzzer
J285 - Control module with indicator unit in instrument panel insert
K2 - Generator (GEN) Warning Light
K3 - Oil Pressure Warning Light
K28 - Engine Coolant Level/Temperature (ECL/ECT) Warning Light
S5 - Fuse 5 in fuse holder
S7 - Fuse 7 in fuse holder
T10a - 10-Pin Connector, in engine compartment, in wiring duct, left
T32 - 32-Pin Connector, blue
T32a - 32-Pin Connector, green

(A13) - Wire connection (door contact switch) in instrument panel wiring harness
(B163) - Plus connector -1- (15) in wiring harness interior

Instrument cluster, oil pressure switch, speedometer vehicle speed sensor, generator (GEN) warning light, engine coolant level/temperature ECL/ECT) warning light

ws = white
sw = black
ro = red
br = brown
gn = green
bl = blue
gr = grey
li = lilac
ge = yellow

169 170 171 172 173 174 175 176 177 178 179 180 181 182
97-24618

E86 - Multi-Function Indicator Mode Select Switch*
E109 - Multi-Function Indicator Memory Switch*
G1 - Fuel gauge
G3 - Engine Coolant Temperature (ECT) Gauge
G17 - Outside Air Temperature Sensor*
G21 - Speedometer
J119 - Multi-function Indicator (MFI)
J285 - Control module with indicator unit in instrument panel insert
K83 - Malfunction Indicator Lamp (MIL)
K105 - Low Fuel Level Warning Light
T6e - 6-Pin Connector
T16 - Data Link Connector (DLC), below instrument panel, left
T32 - 32-Pin Connector, blue
T32a - 32-Pin Connector, green

(A27) - Wire Connection (vehicle speed signal), in instrument panel wiring harness
(A76) - Connector (K-diagnosis wire), in instrument panel wiring harness

* - Vehicles with Multi-Function Indicator (MFI) only

Instrument cluster, multi-function indicator (MFI), engine coolant temperature (ECT) gauge, fuel gauge, malfunction indicator lamp (MIL), outside air temperature sensor

1.9L - Engine - Turbo Diesel Fuel Injection (DFI)/66KW, code ALH, (with manual transmission),

from September 1998

Deviate relay location and fuseplacements as well as the locations of multiple connectors see section "component locations".

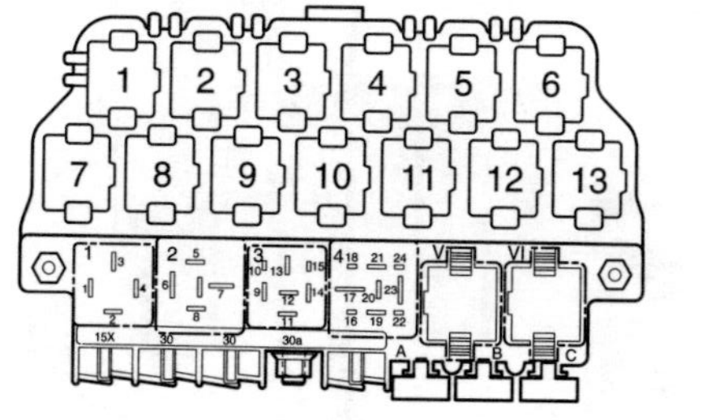

Relay location on the thirteenfold auxiliary relay panel, above relay panel:

- **10** Glow Plug Relay (180)
- **12** Power Supply (Terminal 30, B+) Relay (109)

Relay panel:

- **2** Load Reduction Relay (18)

Note: Number in parentheses indicates production control number stamped on relay housing.

Fuse colors

30 A - green
25 A - white
20 A - yellow
15 A - blue
10 A - red
7,5 A - brown
5 A - beige
3 A - violet

ws = white
sw = black
ro = red
br = brown
gn = green
bl = blue
gr = grey
li = lilac
ge = yellow

97-23494

A - Battery
C - Generator (GEN)
C1 - Voltage Regulator (VR)
D - Ignition/Starter Switch
J59 - Load Reduction Relay
S162 - Fuse -1- (30) in fuse bracket/battery
S163 - Fuse -2- (30) in fuse bracket/battery
S176 - Fuse -4- (30) in fuse bracket/battery
S177 - Fuse -5- (30) in fuse bracket/battery
T2e - Double Connector, near starter (vehicles without air conditioning)
T4 - 4-Pin Connector, near starter (vehicles with air conditioning only)

(81) - Ground connection -1-, in instrument panel wiring harness

(500) - Threaded connection -1- (30) on the relay plate

(501) - Threaded connection -2- (30) on the relay plate

(A32) - Plus connection (30), in instrument panel wiring harness

(A98) - Plus connector -4- (30), in instrument panel wiring harness

Generator (GEN)

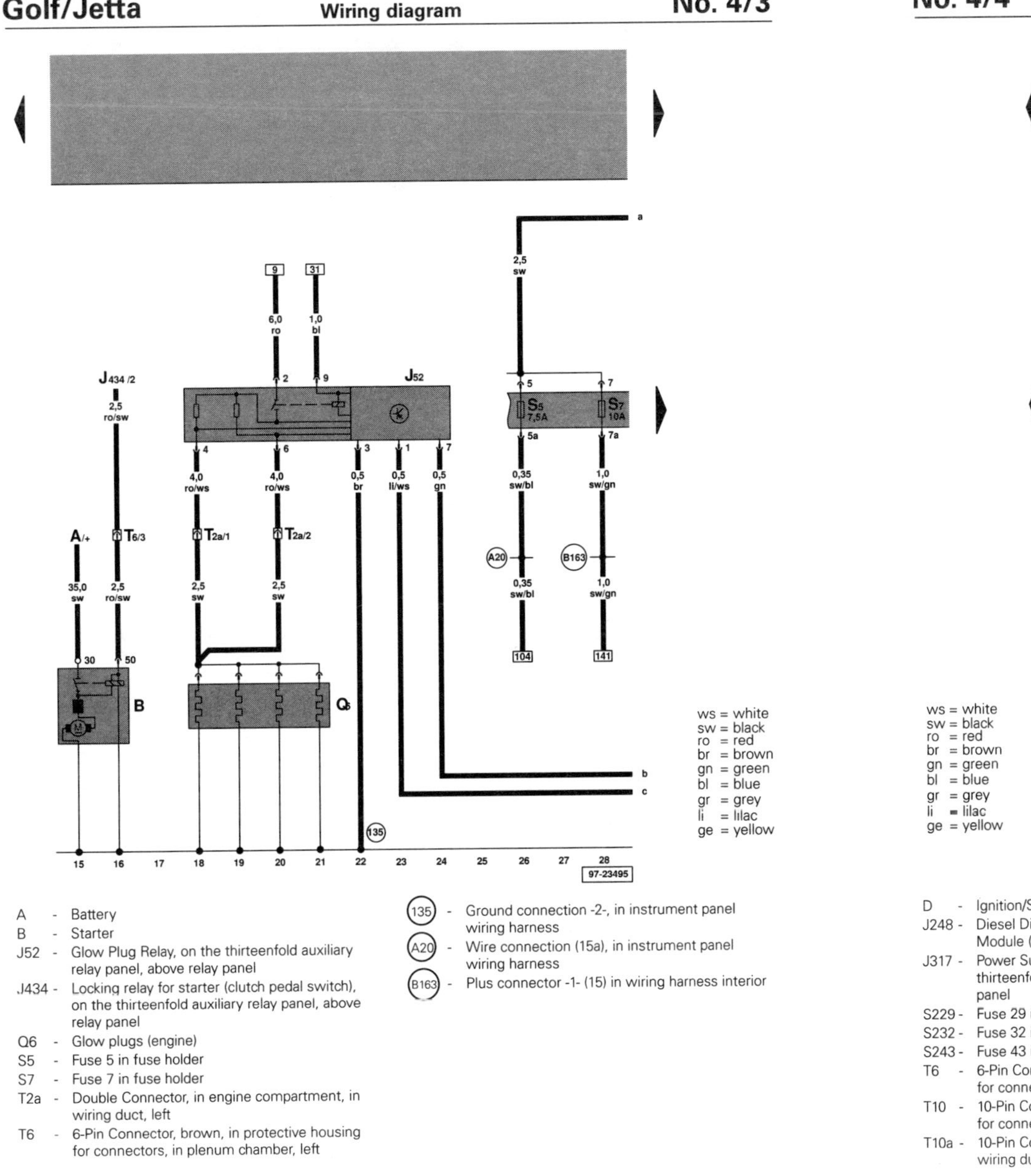

ws = white
sw = black
ro = red
br = brown
gn = green
bl = blue
gr = grey
li = lilac
ge = yellow

A - Battery
B - Starter
J52 - Glow Plug Relay, on the thirteenfold auxiliary relay panel, above relay panel
J434 - Locking relay for starter (clutch pedal switch), on the thirteenfold auxiliary relay panel, above relay panel
Q6 - Glow plugs (engine)
S5 - Fuse 5 in fuse holder
S7 - Fuse 7 in fuse holder
T2a - Double Connector, in engine compartment, in wiring duct, left
T6 - 6-Pin Connector, brown, in protective housing for connectors, in plenum chamber, left

(135) - Ground connection -2-, in instrument panel wiring harness
(A20) - Wire connection (15a), in instrument panel wiring harness
(B163) - Plus connector -1- (15) in wiring harness interior

ws = white
sw = black
ro = red
br = brown
gn = green
bl = blue
gr = grey
li = lilac
ge = yellow

D - Ignition/Starter Switch
J248 - Diesel Direct Fuel Injection (DFI) Engine Control Module (ECM), in plenum chamber, center
J317 - Power Supply (Terminal 30, B+) Relay, on the thirteenfold auxiliary relay panel, above relay panel
S229 - Fuse 29 in fuse holder
S232 - Fuse 32 in fuse holder
S243 - Fuse 43 in fuse holder
T6 - 6-Pin Connector, brown, in protective housing for connectors, in plenum chamber, left
T10 - 10-Pin Connector, orange, in protective housing for connectors, in plenum chamber, left
T10a - 10-Pin Connector, in engine compartment, in wiring duct, left
T10e - 10-Pin Connector, black, in protective housing for connectors, in plenum chamber, left
T10h - 10-Pin Connector, blue, in protective housing for connectors, in plenum chamber, left
T80 - Connector, 80 point

(A2) - Plus connection (15), in instrument panel wiring harness
(A71) - Connector (86), in instrument panel wiring harness
(A104) - Plus connector -2- (15), in instrument panel wiring harness
(B168) - Connection (86) in passenger compartment wiring harness

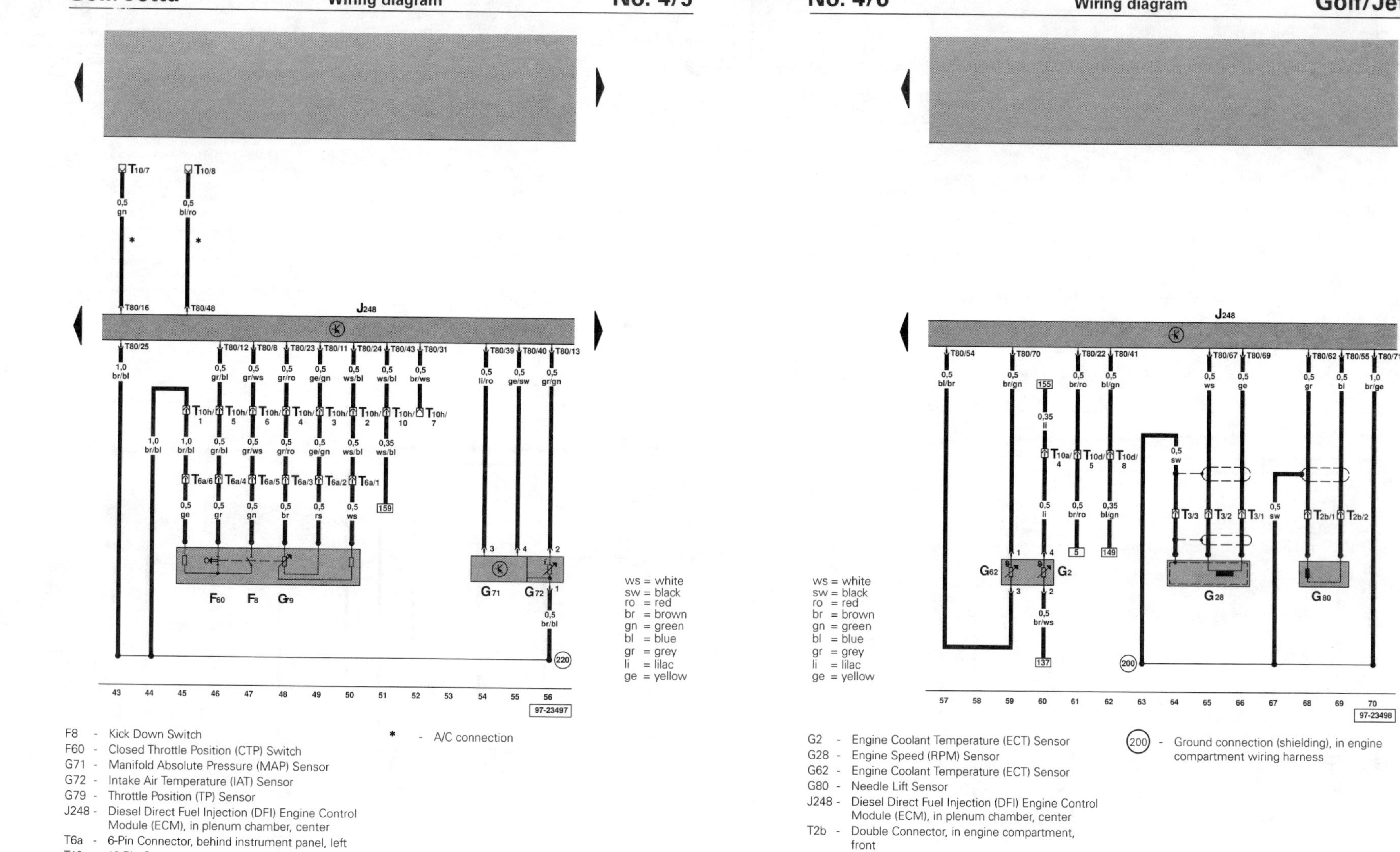

ws = white
sw = black
ro = red
br = brown
gn = green
bl = blue
gr = grey
li = lilac
ge = yellow

F8 - Kick Down Switch
F60 - Closed Throttle Position (CTP) Switch
G71 - Manifold Absolute Pressure (MAP) Sensor
G72 - Intake Air Temperature (IAT) Sensor
G79 - Throttle Position (TP) Sensor
J248 - Diesel Direct Fuel Injection (DFI) Engine Control Module (ECM), in plenum chamber, center
T6a - 6-Pin Connector, behind instrument panel, left
T10 - 10-Pin Connector, orange, in protective housing for connectors, in plenum chamber, left
T10h - 10-Pin Connector, blue, in protective housing for connectors, in plenum chamber, left
T80 - Connector, 80 point

(220) - Ground connection (sensor ground), in engine compartment wiring harness

* - A/C connection

Diesel direct fuel injection (DFI) engine control module (ECM), closed throttle position (CTP) switch, intake air temperature (IAT) sensor, manifold absolute pressure (MAP) sensor

ws = white
sw = black
ro = red
br = brown
gn = green
bl = blue
gr = grey
li = lilac
ge = yellow

G2 - Engine Coolant Temperature (ECT) Sensor
G28 - Engine Speed (RPM) Sensor
G62 - Engine Coolant Temperature (ECT) Sensor
G80 - Needle Lift Sensor
J248 - Diesel Direct Fuel Injection (DFI) Engine Control Module (ECM), in plenum chamber, center
T2b - Double Connector, in engine compartment, front
T3 - 3-Pin Connector, in engine compartment, front
T10a - 10-Pin Connector, in engine compartment, in wiring duct, left
T10d - 10-Pin Connector, green, in protective housing for connectors, in plenum chamber, left
T80 - Connector, 80 point

(200) - Ground connection (shielding), in engine compartment wiring harness

Diesel direct fuel injection (DFI) engine control module (ECM), engine speed (RPM) sensor, engine coolant temperature (ECT) sensor, needle lift sensor

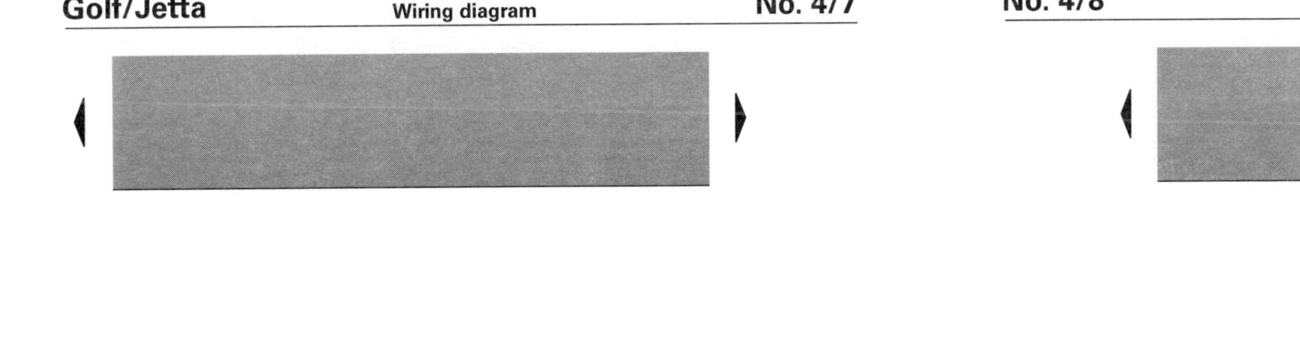

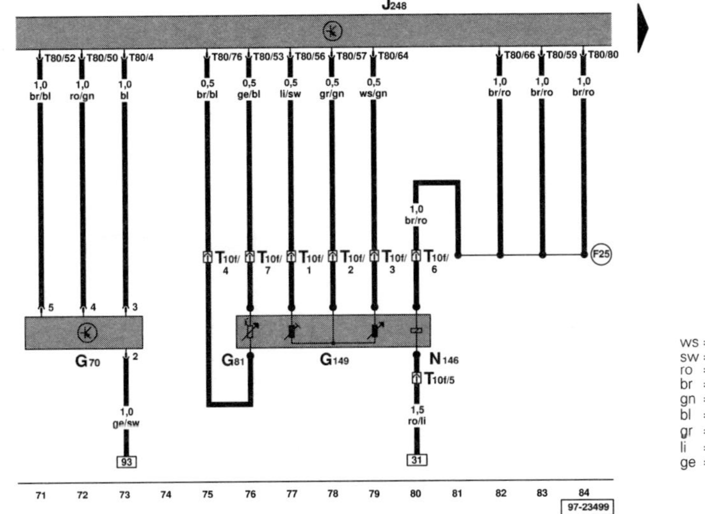

ws = white
sw = black
ro = red
br = brown
gn = green
bl = blue
gr = grey
li = lilac
ge = yellow

- G70 - Mass Air Flow (MAF) Sensor
- G81 - Fuel Temperature Sensor
- G149 - Modulating Piston Displacement Sensor
- J248 - Diesel Direct Fuel Injection (DFI) Engine Control Module (ECM), in plenum chamber, center
- N146 - Quantity Adjuster
- T10f - 10-Pin Connector, in engine compartment, front
- T80 - Connector, 80 point
- (F25) - Wire connection -1-, in Diesel Direct Fuel Injection (DFI) system wiring harness

Edition 12/98
USA.5102.01.21

Diesel direct fuel injection (DFI) engine control module (ECM), quantity adjuster, mass air flow (MAF) sensor, fuel temperature sensor, modulating piston displacement sensor

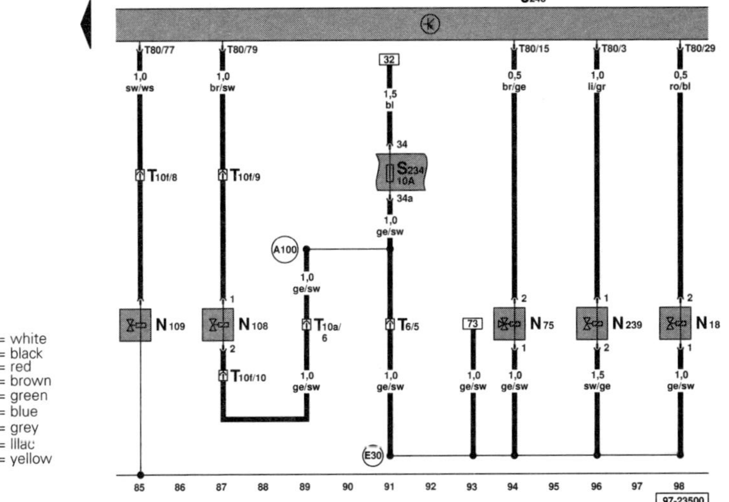

ws = white
sw = black
ro = red
br = brown
gn = green
bl = blue
gr = grey
li = lilac
ge = yellow

- J248 - Diesel Direct Fuel Injection (DFI) Engine Control Module (ECM), in plenum chamber, center
- N18 - EGR Vacuum Regulator Solenoid Valve
- N75 - Wastegate Bypass Regulator Valve
- N108 - Cold Start Injector
- N109 - Fuel Cut-off Valve
- N239 - Change-over valve for intake manifold flap
- S234 - Fuse 34 in fuse holder
- T6 - 6-Pin Connector, brown, in protective housing for connectors, in plenum chamber, left
- T10a - 10-Pin Connector, in engine compartment, in wiring duct, left
- T10f - 10-Pin Connector, in engine compartment, front
- T80 - Connector, 80 point
- (A100) - Connector -2- (87), in instrument panel wiring harness
- (E30) - Connector (87a), in wiring harness engine

Diesel direct fuel injection (DFI) engine control module (ECM), cold start injector, fuel cut-off valve, wastegate bypass regulator valve, EGR vacuum regulator solenoid valve

Edition 12/98
USA.5102.01.21

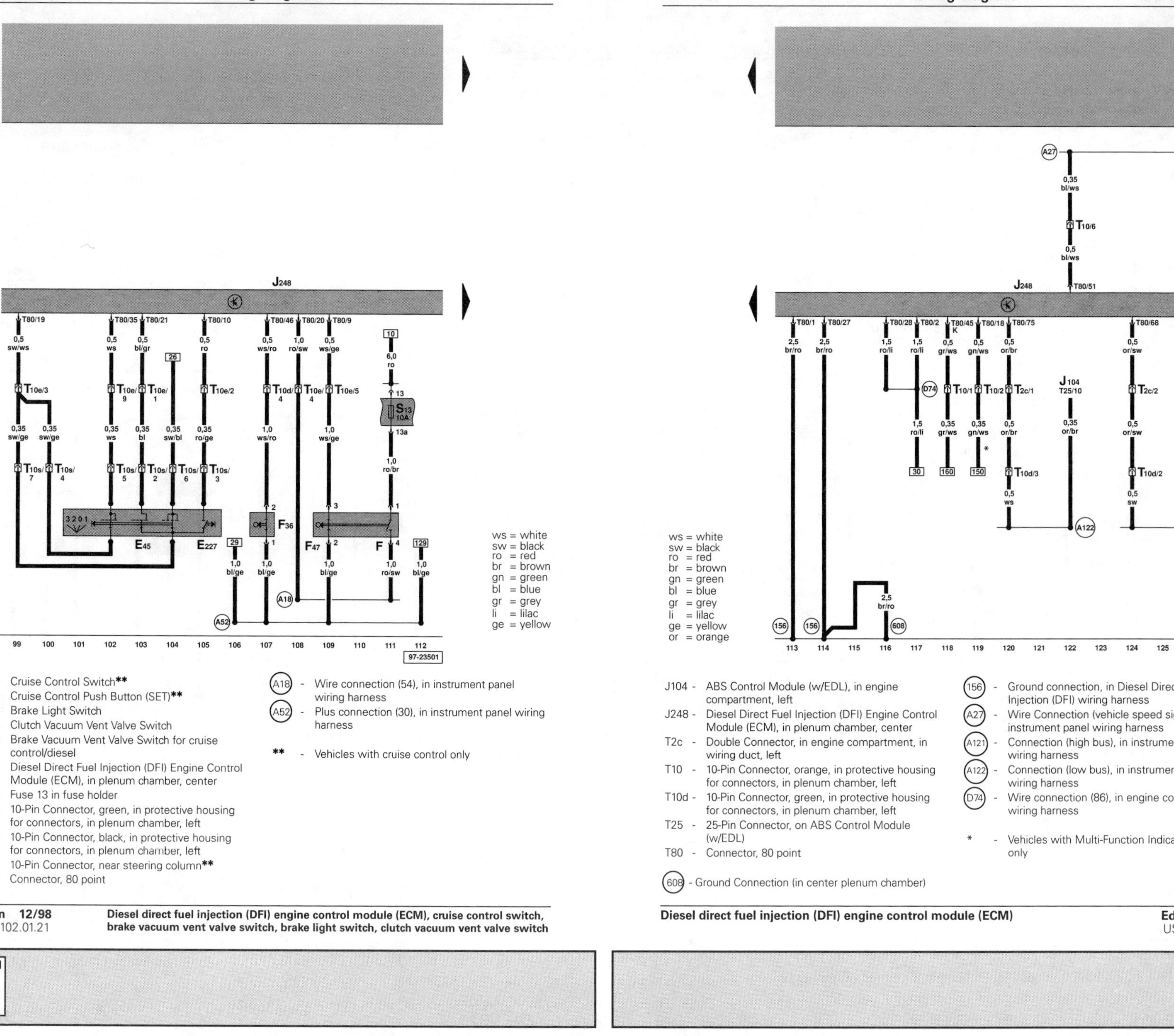

ws = white
sw = black
ro = red
br = brown
gn = green
bl = blue
gr = grey
li = lilac
ge = yellow

- E45 - Cruise Control Switch**
- E227 - Cruise Control Push Button (SET)**
- F - Brake Light Switch
- F36 - Clutch Vacuum Vent Valve Switch
- F47 - Brake Vacuum Vent Valve Switch for cruise control/diesel
- J248 - Diesel Direct Fuel Injection (DFI) Engine Control Module (ECM), in plenum chamber, center
- S13 - Fuse 13 in fuse holder
- T10d - 10-Pin Connector, green, in protective housing for connectors, in plenum chamber, left
- T10e - 10-Pin Connector, black, in protective housing for connectors, in plenum chamber, left
- T10s - 10-Pin Connector, near steering column**
- T80 - Connector, 80 point

- (A18) - Wire connection (54), in instrument panel wiring harness
- (A52) - Plus connection (30), in instrument panel wiring harness
- ** - Vehicles with cruise control only

Diesel direct fuel injection (DFI) engine control module (ECM), cruise control switch, brake vacuum vent valve switch, brake light switch, clutch vacuum vent valve switch

ws = white
sw = black
ro = red
br = brown
gn = green
bl = blue
gr = grey
li = lilac
ge = yellow
or = orange

- J104 - ABS Control Module (w/EDL), in engine compartment, left
- J248 - Diesel Direct Fuel Injection (DFI) Engine Control Module (ECM), in plenum chamber, center
- T2c - Double Connector, in engine compartment, in wiring duct, left
- T10 - 10-Pin Connector, orange, in protective housing for connectors, in plenum chamber, left
- T10d - 10-Pin Connector, green, in protective housing for connectors, in plenum chamber, left
- T25 - 25-Pin Connector, on ABS Control Module (w/EDL)
- T80 - Connector, 80 point
- (608) - Ground Connection (in center plenum chamber)

- (156) - Ground connection, in Diesel Direct Fuel Injection (DFI) wiring harness
- (A27) - Wire Connection (vehicle speed signal), in instrument panel wiring harness
- (A121) - Connection (high bus), in instrument panel wiring harness
- (A122) - Connection (low bus), in instrument panel wiring harness
- (D74) - Wire connection (86), in engine compartment wiring harness
- * - Vehicles with Multi-Function Indicator (MFI) only

Diesel direct fuel injection (DFI) engine control module (ECM)

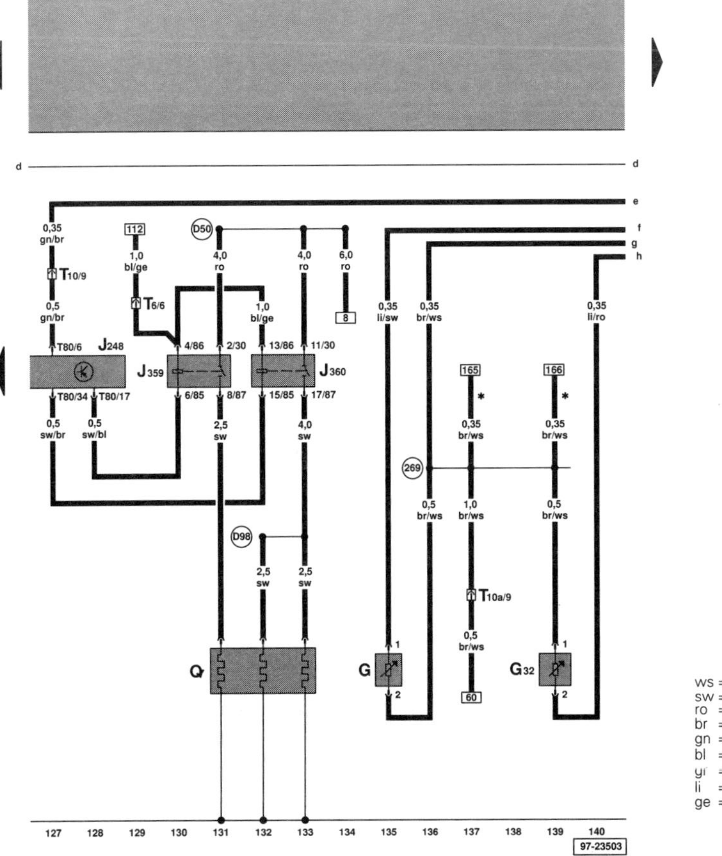

G - Fuel Level Sensor

G32 - Engine Coolant Level (ECL) Sensor

J248 - Diesel Direct Fuel Injection (DFI) Engine Control Module (ECM), in plenum chamber, center

J359 - Relay for preheating coolant, low heat output, in protective housing, in engine compartment, left, production control number (53)

J360 - Relay for preheating coolant, high heat output, in protective housing, in engine compartment, left, production control number (53)

Q7 - Glow plugs (coolant)

T6 - 6-Pin Connector, brown, in protective housing for connectors, in plenum chamber, left

T10 - 10-Pin Connector, orange, in protective housing for connectors, in plenum chamber, left

T10a - 10-Pin Connector, in engine compartment, in wiring duct, left

T80 - Connector, 80 point

(269) - Ground connection (sensor ground) -1-, in instrument panel wiring harness

(D50) - Plus connection (30), in engine compartment wiring harness

(D98) - Wire connection (glow plugs), in engine compartment wiring harness

* - Vehicles with Multi-Function Indicator (MFI) only

Diesel direct fuel Injection (DFI) engine control module (ECM), fuel level sensor, glow plugs (coolant), engine coolant level (ECL) sensor

ws = white
sw = black
ro = red
br = brown
gn = green
bl = blue
gr = groy
li = lilac
ge = yellow

F1 - Oil Pressure Switch

G22 - Speedometer Vehicle Speed Sensor (VSS)

H3 - Warning Buzzer

J285 - Control module with indicator unit in instrument panel insert

K2 - Generator (GEN) Warning Light

K3 - Oil Pressure Warning Light

K28 - Engine Coolant Level/Temperature (ECL/ECT) Warning Light

K29 - Glow Plug Indicator Light

T10a - 10-Pin Connector, in engine compartment, in wiring duct, left

T32 - 32-Pin Connector, blue

T32a - 32-Pin Connector, green

(608) - Ground Connection (in center plenum chamber)

* - Vehicles with Multi-Function Indicator (MFI) only

Instrument cluster, oil pressure switch, speedometer vehicle speed sensor, engine coolant level/temperature (ECL/ECT) warning light, glow plug indicator light

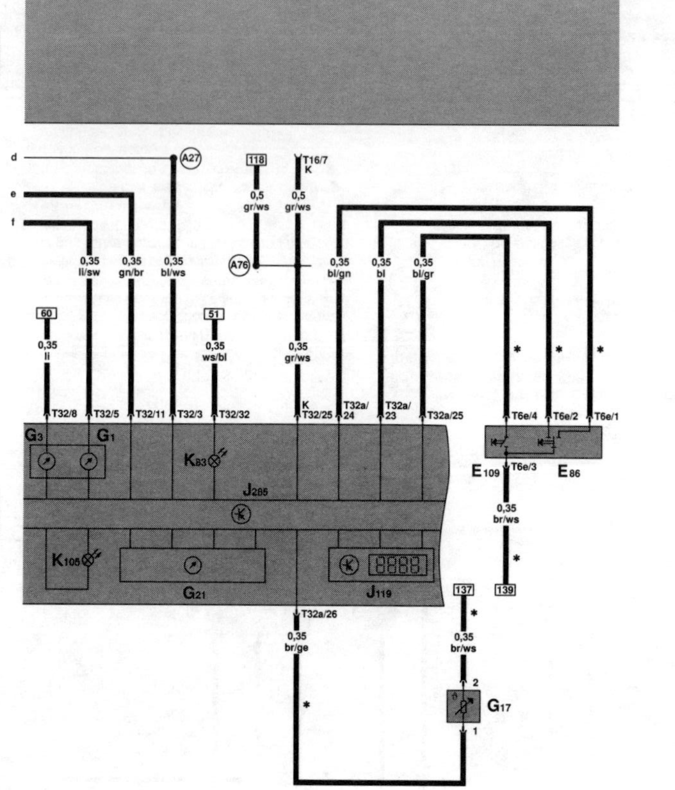

ws = white
sw = black
ro = red
br = brown
gn = green
bl = blue
gr = grey
li = lilac
ge = yellow

E86 - Multi-Function Indicator Mode Select Switch
E109 - Multi-Function Indicator Memory Switch
G1 - Fuel gauge
G3 - Engine Coolant Temperature (ECT) Gauge
G17 - Outside Air Temperature Sensor
G21 - Speedometer
J119 - Multi-function Indicator (MFI)
J285 - Control module with indicator unit in instrument panel insert
K83 - Malfunction Indicator Lamp (MIL)
K105 - Low Fuel Level Warning Light
T6e - 6-Pin Connector
T16 - Data Link Connector (DLC), below instrument panel, center
T32 - 32-Pin Connector, blue
T32a - 32-Pin Connector, green

(A27) - Wire Connection (vehicle speed signal), in instrument panel wiring harness
(A76) - Connector (K-diagnosis wire), in instrument panel wiring harness

* - Vehicles with Multi-Function Indicator (MFI) only

Edition 12/98 USA.5102.01.21 **Instrument cluster, multi-function indicator (MFI), engine coolant temperature (ECT) gauge, fuel gauge, speedometer, malfunction indicator lamp (MIL), outside air temperature sensor**

THIS PAGE INTENTIONALLY LEFT

BLANK

1.9L - Engine - Turbo Diesel Fuel Injection (DFI)/66KW, code ALH, (with automatic transmission),

from September 1998

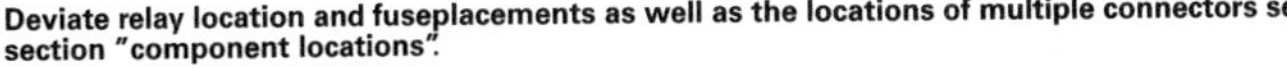

Deviate relay location and fuseplacements as well as the locations of multiple connectors see section "component locations".

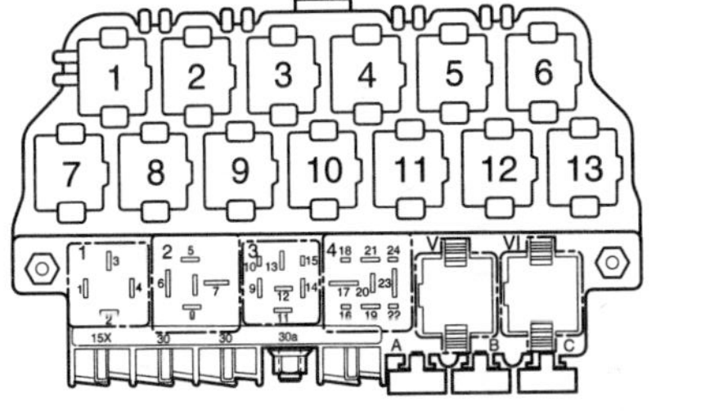

97-14163

Relay location on the thirteenfold auxiliary relay panel, above relay panel:

- **10** Glow Plug Relay (180)
- **12** Power Supply (Terminal 30, B+) Relay (109)

Relay panel:

- **2** Load Reduction Relay (18)

Note: Number in parentheses indicates production control number stamped on relay housing.

Fuse colors

30 A - green
25 A - white
20 A - yellow
15 A - blue
10 A - red
7,5 A - brown
5 A - beige
3 A - violet

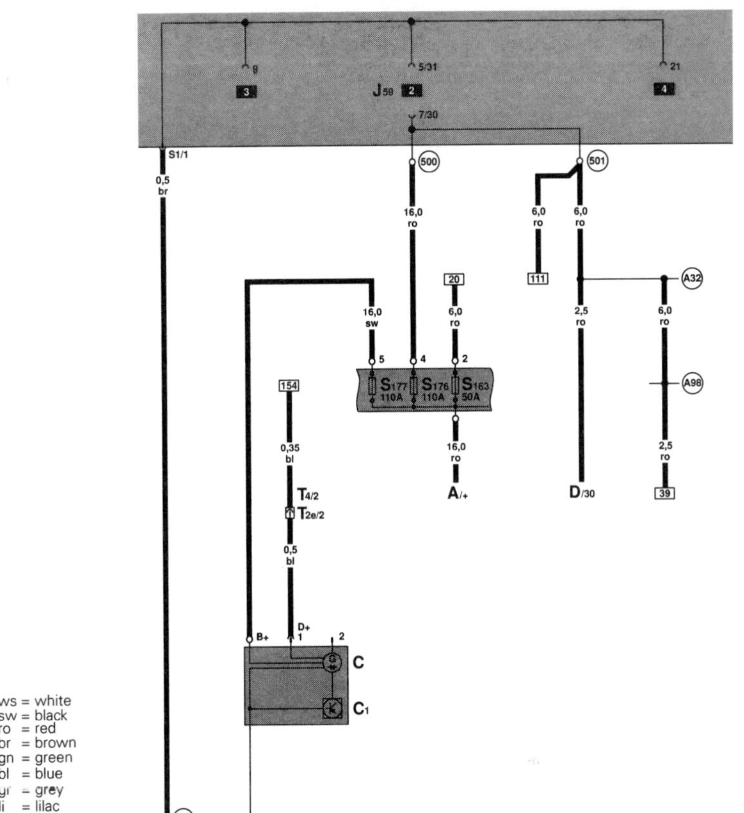

ws = white
sw = black
ro = red
br = brown
gn = green
bl = blue
gr = grey
li = lilac
ge = yellow

A - Battery
C - Generator (GEN)
C1 - Voltage Regulator (VR)
D - Ignition/Starter Switch
J59 - Load Reduction Relay
S162 - Fuse -1- (30) in fuse bracket/battery
S163 - Fuse -2- (30) in fuse bracket/battery
S176 - Fuse -4- (30) in fuse bracket/battery
S177 - Fuse -5- (30) in fuse bracket/battery
T2e - Double Connector, near starter (vehicles without air conditioning)
T4 - 4-Pin Connector, near starter (vehicles with air conditioning only)

(81) - Ground connection -1-, in instrument panel wiring harness

(500) - Threaded connection -1- (30) on the relay plate

(501) - Threaded connection -2- (30) on the relay plate

(A32) - Plus connection (30), in instrument panel wiring harness

(A98) - Plus connector -4- (30), in instrument panel wiring harness

Generator (GEN)

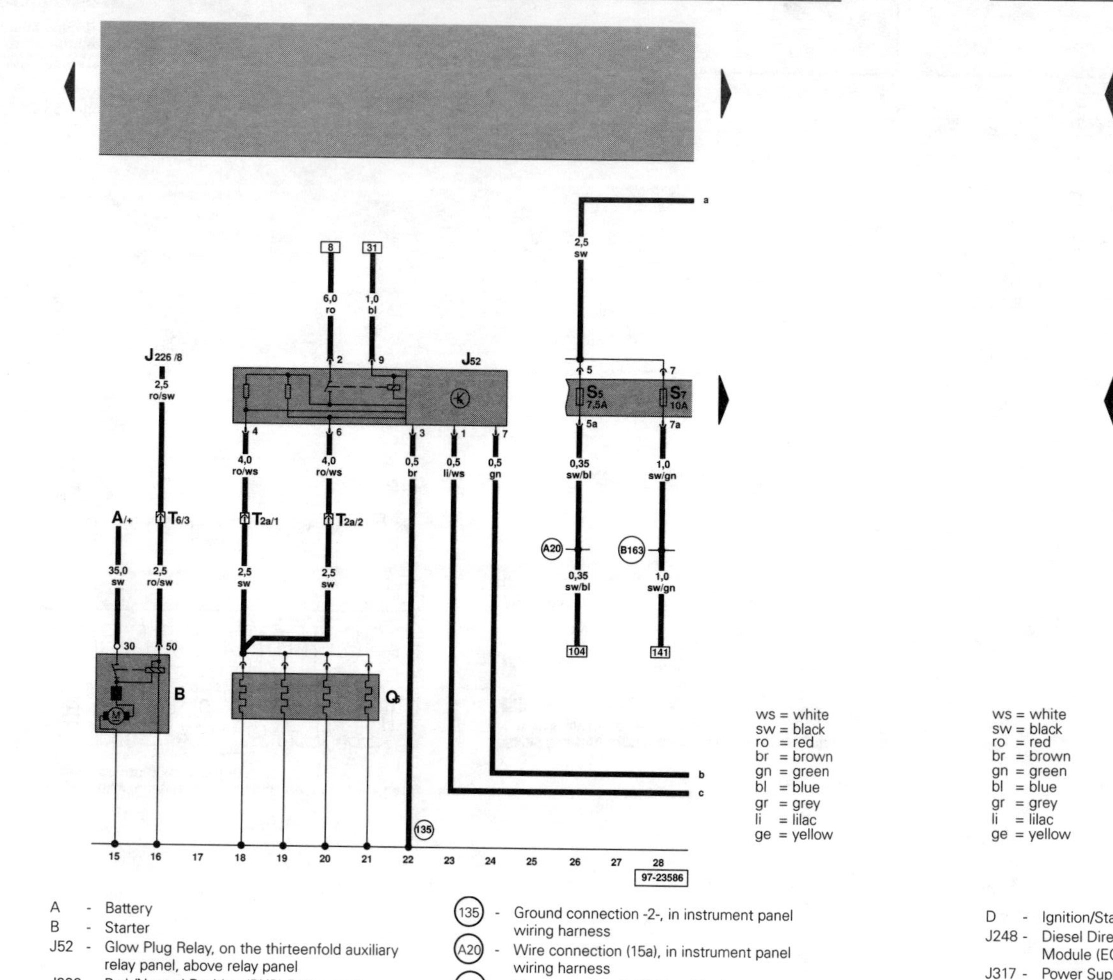

ws = white
sw = black
ro = red
br = brown
gn = green
bl = blue
gr = grey
li = lilac
ge = yellow

A - Battery
B - Starter
J52 - Glow Plug Relay, on the thirteenfold auxiliary relay panel, above relay panel
J226 - Park/Neutral Position (PNP) Relay, on the thirteenfold auxiliary relay panel, above relay panel
Q6 - Glow plugs (engine)
S5 - Fuse 5 in fuse holder
S7 - Fuse 7 in fuse holder
T2a - Double Connector, in engine compartment, in wiring duct, left
T6 - 6-Pin Connector, brown, in protective housing for connectors, in plenum chamber, left

(135) - Ground connection -2-, in instrument panel wiring harness
(A20) - Wire connection (15a), in instrument panel wiring harness
(B163) - Plus connector -1- (15) in wiring harness interior

Glow plug relay, starter, glow plugs (engine)

ws = white
sw = black
ro = red
br = brown
gn = green
bl = blue
gr = grey
li = lilac
ge = yellow

D - Ignition/Starter Switch
J248 - Diesel Direct Fuel Injection (DFI) Engine Control Module (ECM), in plenum chamber, center
J317 - Power Supply (Terminal 30, B+) Relay, on the thirteenfold auxiliary relay panel, above relay panel
S229 - Fuse 29 in fuse holder
S232 - Fuse 32 in fuse holder
S243 - Fuse 43 in fuse holder
T6 - 6-Pin Connector, brown, in protective housing for connectors, in plenum chamber, left
T10 - 10-Pin Connector, orange, in protective housing for connectors, in plenum chamber, left
T10a - 10-Pin Connector, in engine compartment, in wiring duct, left
T10e - 10-Pin Connector, black, in protective housing for connectors, in plenum chamber, left
T10h - 10-Pin Connector, blue, in protective housing for connectors, in plenum chamber, left
T80 - Connector, 80 point

(A2) - Plus connection (15), in instrument panel wiring harness
(A71) - Connector (86), in instrument panel wiring harness
(A104) - Plus connector -2- (15), in instrument panel wiring harness
(B168) - Connection (86) in passenger compartment wiring harness

Diesel direct fuel injection (DFI) engine control module (ECM), power supply (terminal 30, B+) relay

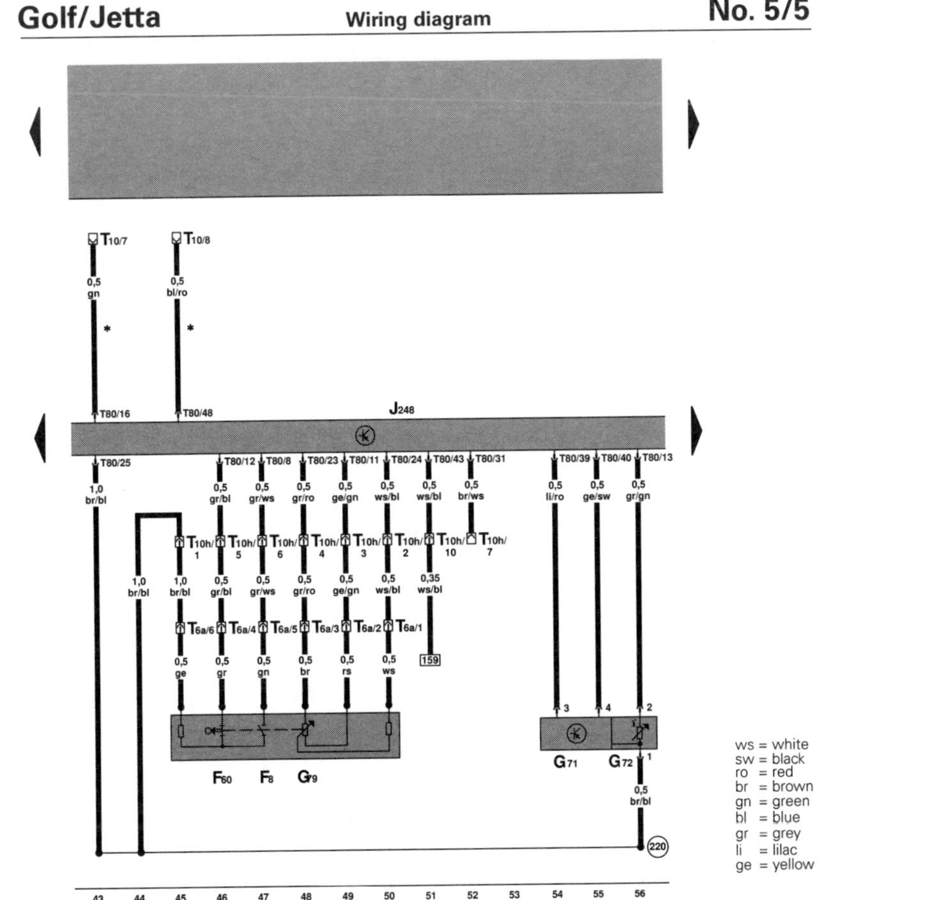

ws = white
sw = black
ro = red
br = brown
gn = green
bl = blue
gr = grey
li = lilac
ge = yellow

F8 - Kick Down Switch
F60 - Closed Throttle Position (CTP) Switch
G71 - Manifold Absolute Pressure (MAP) Sensor
G72 - Intake Air Temperature (IAT) Sensor
G79 - Throttle Position (TP) Sensor
J248 - Diesel Direct Fuel Injection (DFI) Engine Control Module (ECM), in plenum chamber, center
T6a - 6-Pin Connector, behind instrument panel, left
T10 - 10-Pin Connector, orange, in protective housing for connectors, in plenum chamber, left
T10h - 10-Pin Connector, blue, in protective housing for connectors, in plenum chamber, left
T80 - Connector, 80 point

(220) - Ground connection (sensor ground), in engine compartment wiring harness

* - A/C connection

Diesel direct fuel injection (DFI) engine control module (ECM), closed throttle position (CTP) switch, intake air temperature (IAT) sensor, manifold absolute pressure (MAP) sensor

ws = white
sw = black
ro = red
br = brown
gn = green
bl = blue
gr = grey
li = lilac
ge = yellow

57 58 59 60 61 62 63 64 65 66 67 68 69 70
97-23588

G2 - Engine Coolant Temperature (ECT) Sensor
G28 - Engine Speed (RPM) Sensor
G62 - Engine Coolant Temperature (ECT) Sensor
G80 - Needle Lift Sensor
J248 - Diesel Direct Fuel Injection (DFI) Engine Control Module (ECM), in plenum chamber, center
T2b - Double Connector, in engine compartment, front
T3 - 3-Pin Connector, in engine compartment, front
T10a - 10-Pin Connector, in engine compartment, in wiring duct, left
T10d - 10-Pin Connector, green, in protective housing for connectors, in plenum chamber, left
T80 - Connector, 80 point

(156) - Ground connection, in Diesel Direct Fuel Injection (DFI) wiring harness
(200) - Ground connection (shielding), in engine compartment wiring harness

Diesel direct fuel injection (DFI) engine control module (ECM), engine speed (RPM) sensor, engine coolant temperature (ECT) sensor, needle lift sensor

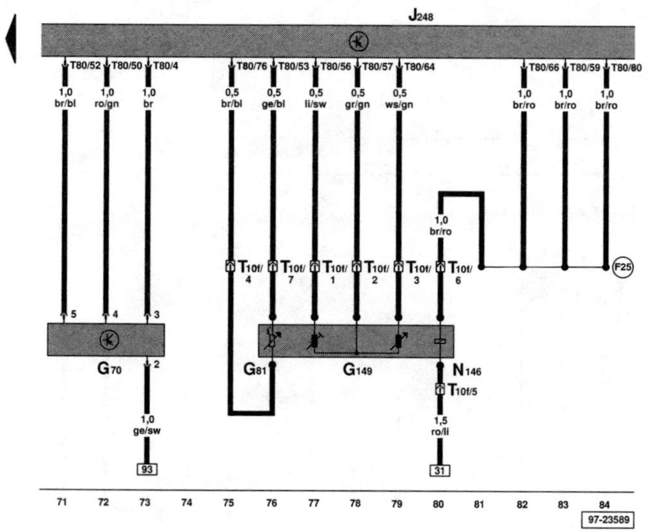

J248

T80/52 T80/50 T80/4 T80/76 T80/53 T80/56 T80/57 T80/64 T80/66 T80/59 T80/80

1,0 br/bl 1,0 ro/gn 1,0 br 0,5 br/bl 0,5 ge/bl 0,5 li/sw 0,5 gr/gn 0,5 ws/gn 1,0 br/ro 1,0 br/ro 1,0 br/ro

1,0 br/ro

T10f/4 T10f/7 T10f/1 T10f/2 T10f/3 T10f/6 F25

G70 G81 G149 N146 T10f/5

1,0 ge/sw 93 1,5 ro/li 31

71 72 73 74 75 76 77 78 79 80 81 82 83 84

97-23589

ws = white
sw = black
ro = red
br = brown
gn = green
bl = blue
gr = grey
li = lilac
ge = yellow

G70 - Mass Air Flow (MAF) Sensor
G81 - Fuel Temperature Sensor
G149 - Modulating Piston Displacement Sensor
J248 - Diesel Direct Fuel Injection (DFI) Engine Control Module (ECM), in plenum chamber, center
N146 - Quantity Adjuster
T10f - 10-Pin Connector, in engine compartment, front
T80 - Connector, 80 point

(F25) - Wire connection -1-, in Diesel Direct Fuel Injection (DFI) system wiring harness

Diesel direct fuel injection (DFI) engine control module (ECM), quantity adjuster, mass air flow (MAF) sensor, fuel temperature sensor, modulating piston displacement sensor

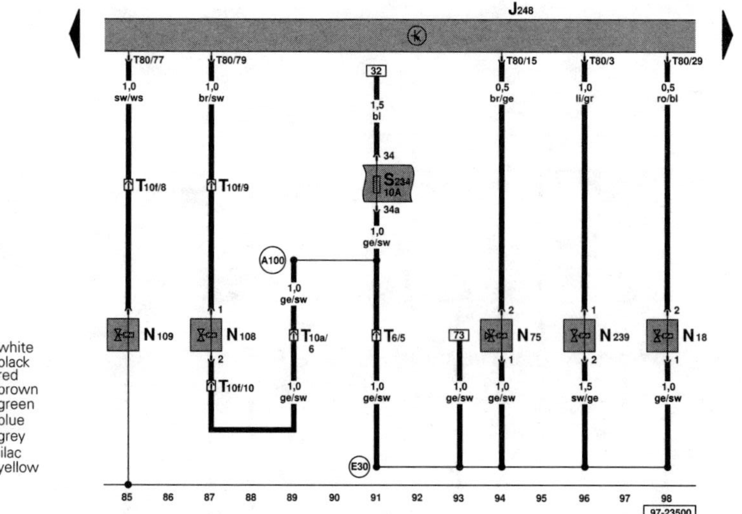

ws = white
sw = black
ro = red
br = brown
gn = green
bl = blue
gr = grey
li = lilac
ge = yellow

J248 - Diesel Direct Fuel Injection (DFI) Engine Control Module (ECM), in plenum chamber, center
N18 - EGR Vacuum Regulator Solenoid Valve
N75 - Wastegate Bypass Regulator Valve
N108 - Cold Start Injector
N109 - Fuel Cut-off Valve
N239 - Change-over valve for intake manifold flap
S234 - Fuse 34 in fuse holder
T6 - 6-Pin Connector, brown, in protective housing for connectors, in plenum chamber, left
T10a - 10-Pin Connector, in engine compartment, in wiring duct, left
T10f - 10-Pin Connector, in engine compartment, front
T80 - Connector, 80 point

(A100) - Connector -2- (87), in instrument panel wiring harness
(E30) - Connector (87a), in wiring harness engine

Diesel direct fuel injection (DFI) engine control module (ECM), cold start injector, fuel cut-off valve, wastegate bypass regulator valve, EGR vacuum regulator solenoid valve

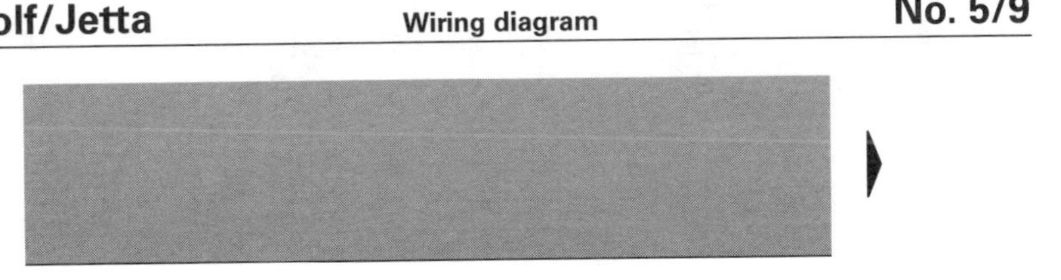

ws = white
sw = black
ro = red
br = brown
gn = green
bl = blue
gr = grey
li = lilac
ge = yellow

E45 - Cruise Control Switch**
E227 - Cruise Control Push Button (SET)**
F - Brake Light Switch
F47 - Brake Vacuum Vent Valve Switch for cruise control/diesel
J248 - Diesel Direct Fuel Injection (DFI) Engine Control Module (ECM), in plenum chamber, center
S13 - Fuse 13 in fuse holder
T10e - 10-Pin Connector, black, in protective housing for connectors, in plenum chamber, left
T10s - 10-Pin Connector, near steering column**
T80 - Connector, 80 point

A18 - Wire connection (54), in instrument panel wiring harness

A52 - Plus connection (30), in instrument panel wiring harness

** - Vehicles with cruise control only

Diesel direct fuel injection (DFI) engine control module (ECM), cruise control switch, brake vacuum vent valve switch, brake light switch

ws = white
sw = black
ro = red
br = brown
gn = green
bl = blue
gr = grey
li = lilac
ge = yellow
or = orange

J104 - ABS Control Module (w/EDL), in engine compartment, left
J248 - Diesel Direct Fuel Injection (DFI) Engine Control Module (ECM), in plenum chamber, center
J217 - Transmission Control Module (TCM), in plenum chamber, center
T2c - Double Connector, in engine compartment, in wiring duct, left
T10 - 10-Pin Connector, orange, in protective housing for connectors, in plenum chamber, left
T10d - 10-Pin Connector, green, in protective housing for connectors, in plenum chamber, left
T25 - 25-Pin Connector, on ABS Control Module (w/EDL)
T68 - 68-Pin Connector
T80 - Connector, 80 point

A121 - Connection (high bus), in instrument panel wiring harness
A122 - Connection (low bus), in instrument panel wiring harness
D74 - Wire connection (86), in engine compartment wiring harness

* - Vehicles with Multi-Function Indicator (MFI) only

Diesel direct fuel injection (DFI) engine control module (ECM)

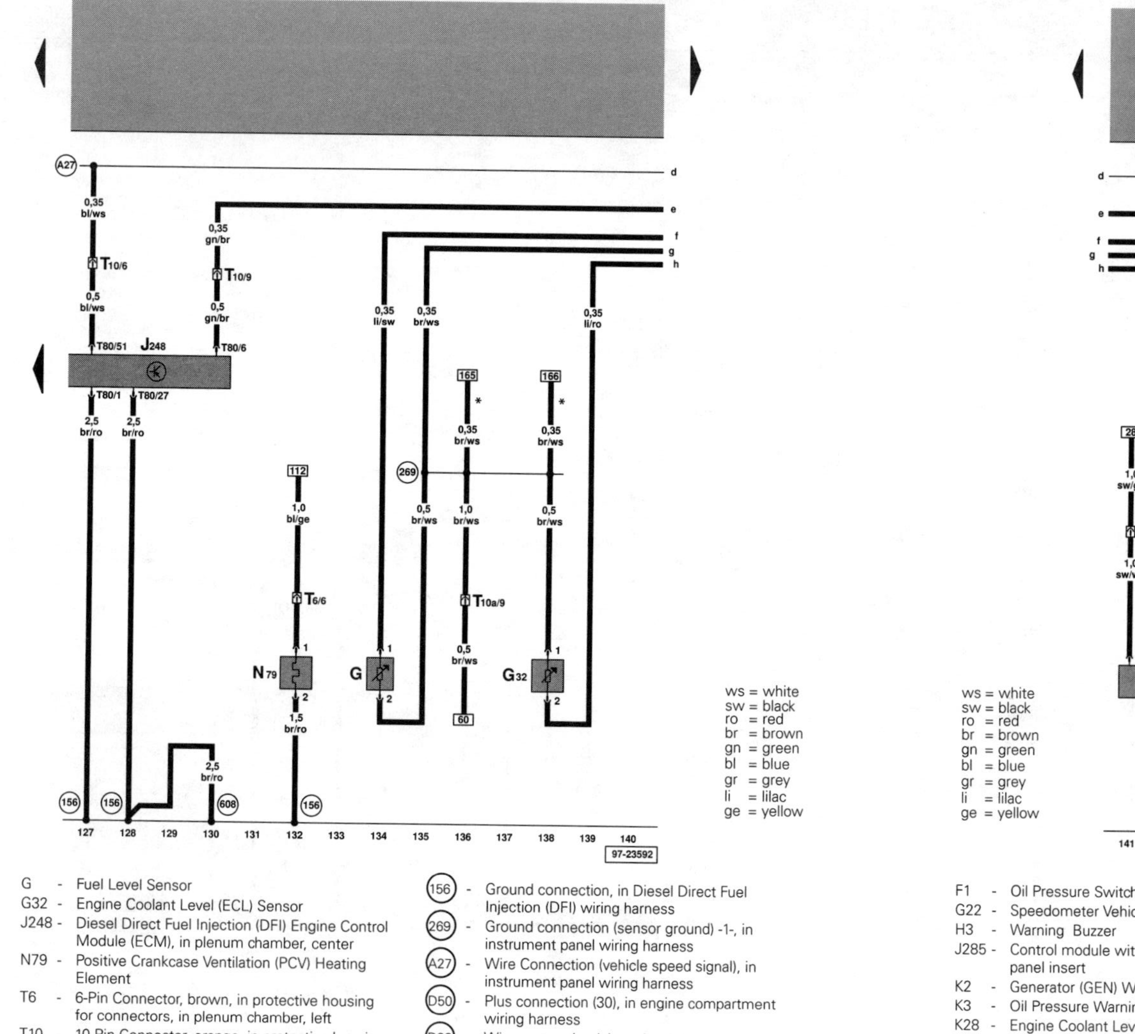

G - Fuel Level Sensor
G32 - Engine Coolant Level (ECL) Sensor
J248 - Diesel Direct Fuel Injection (DFI) Engine Control Module (ECM), in plenum chamber, center
N79 - Positive Crankcase Ventilation (PCV) Heating Element
T6 - 6-Pin Connector, brown, in protective housing for connectors, in plenum chamber, left
T10 - 10-Pin Connector, orange, in protective housing for connectors, in plenum chamber, left
T10a - 10-Pin Connector, in engine compartment, in wiring duct, left
T80 - Connector, 80 point

(608) - Ground Connection (in center plenum chamber)

(156) - Ground connection, in Diesel Direct Fuel Injection (DFI) wiring harness
(269) - Ground connection (sensor ground) -1-, in instrument panel wiring harness
(A27) - Wire Connection (vehicle speed signal), in instrument panel wiring harness
(D50) - Plus connection (30), in engine compartment wiring harness
(D98) - Wire connection (glow plugs), in engine compartment wiring harness

* - Vehicles with Multi-Function Indicator (MFI) only

Diesel direct fuel Injection (DFI) engine control module (ECM), fuel level sensor, engine coolant level (ECL) sensor, positive crankcase ventilation (PCV) heating element

ws = white
sw = black
ro = red
br = brown
gn = green
bl = blue
gr = grey
li = lilac
ge = yellow

141 142 143 144 145 146 147 148 149 150 151 152 153 154
97-23593

F1 - Oil Pressure Switch
G22 - Speedometer Vehicle Speed Sensor (VSS)
H3 - Warning Buzzer
J285 - Control module with indicator unit in instrument panel insert
K2 - Generator (GEN) Warning Light
K3 - Oil Pressure Warning Light
K28 - Engine Coolant Level/Temperature (ECL/ECT) Warning Light
K29 - Glow Plug Indicator Light
T10a - 10-Pin Connector, in engine compartment, in wiring duct, left
T32 - 32-Pin Connector, blue
T32a - 32-Pin Connector, green

(608) - Ground Connection (in center plenum chamber)

* - Vehicles with Multi-Function Indicator (MFI) only

Instrument cluster, oil pressure switch, speedometer vehicle speed sensor, engine coolant level/temperature (ECL/ECT) warning light, glow plug indicator light

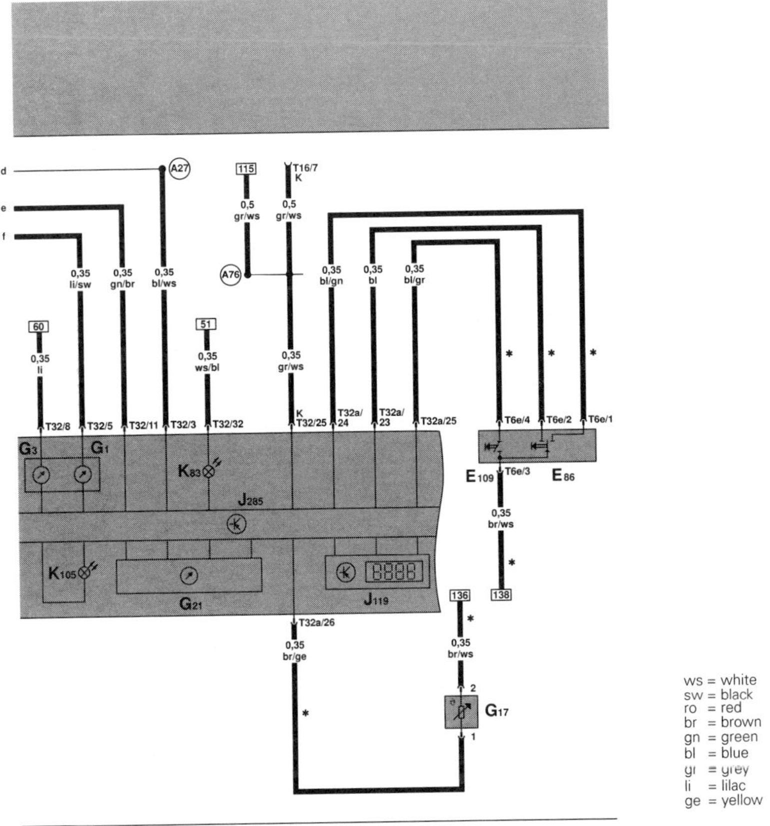

ws = white
sw = black
ro = red
br = brown
gn = green
bl = blue
gr = grey
li = lilac
ge = yellow

E86 - Multi-Function Indicator Mode Select Switch
E109 - Multi-Function Indicator Memory Switch
G1 - Fuel gauge
G3 - Engine Coolant Temperature (ECT) Gauge
G17 - Outside Air Temperature Sensor
G21 - Speedometer
J119 - Multi-function Indicator (MFI)
J285 - Control module with indicator unit in instrument panel insert
K83 - Malfunction Indicator Lamp (MIL)
K105 - Low Fuel Level Warning Light
T6e - 6-Pin Connector
T16 - Data Link Connector (DLC), below instrument panel, center
T32 - 32-Pin Connector, blue
T32a - 32-Pin Connector, green

(A27) - Wire Connection (vehicle speed signal), in instrument panel wiring harness
(A76) - Connector (K-diagnosis wire), in instrument panel wiring harness

* - Vehicles with Multi-Function Indicator (MFI) only

Edition 12/98
USA.5102.01.21

Instrument cluster, multi-function indicator (MFI), engine coolant temperature (ECT) gauge, fuel gauge, speedometer, malfunction indicator lamp (MIL), outside air temperature sensor

THIS PAGE INTENTIONALLY LEFT

BLANK

Automatic transmission, 4 speed automatic,

from September 1998

- **2.0L - Engine - Motronic Multiport Fuel Injection (MFI)/85 kW, code AEG**
- **2.8L - Engine - Motronic Multiport Fuel Injection (MFI)/130 kW, code AFP**

Deviate relay location and fuseplacements as well as the locations of multiple connectors see section "component locations".

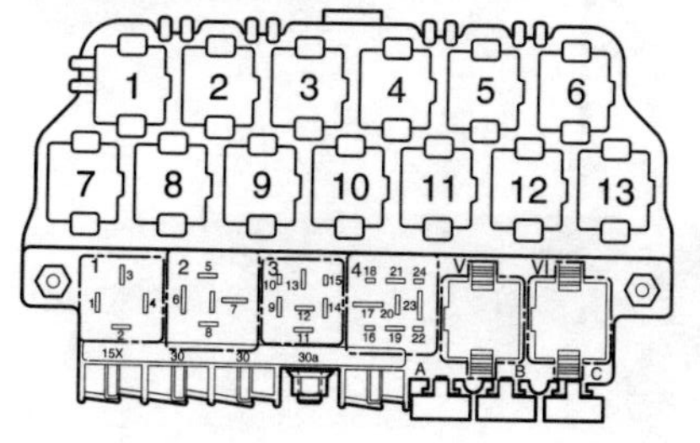

97–14163

Relay location on the thirteenfold auxiliary relay panel, above relay panel:

11 Park/Neutral Position (PNP) Relay (175)

Relay panel:

Note: Number in parentheses indicates production control number stamped on relay housing.

Fuse colors

30 A - green
25 A - white
20 A - yellow
15 A - blue
10 A - red
7,5 A - brown
5 A - beige
3 A - violet

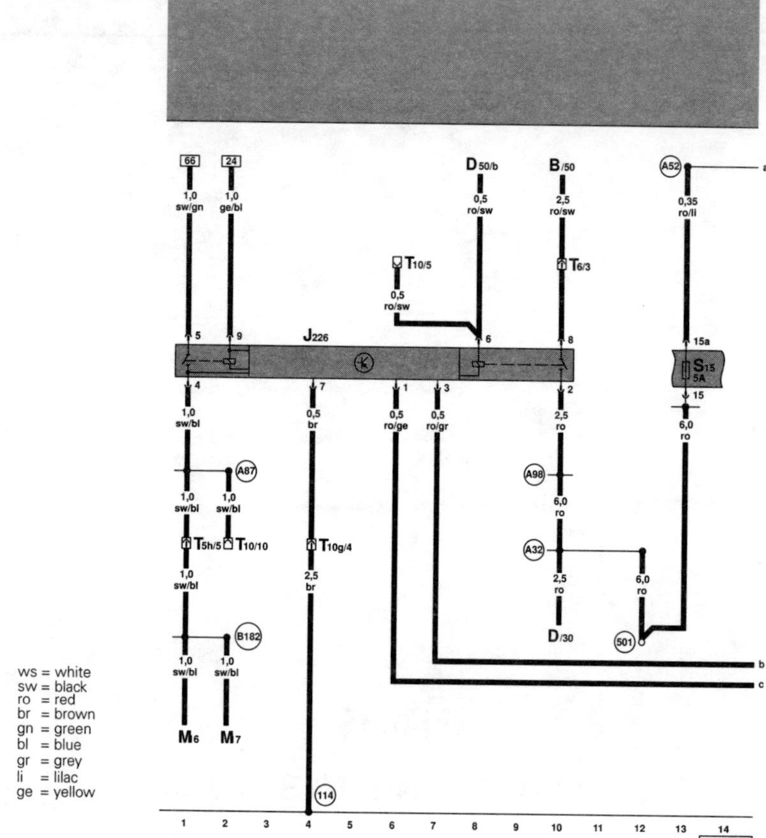

ws = white
sw = black
ro = red
br = brown
gn = green
bl = blue
gr = grey
li = lilac
ge = yellow

B - Starter
D - Ignition/Starter Switch
J226 - Park/Neutral Position (PNP) Relay, on the thirteenfold auxiliary relay panel, above relay panel
M16 - Left Back-Up Light
M17 - Right Back-Up Light
S15 - Fuse 15 in fuse holder
T5h - 5-Pin Connector, near left A-pillar, lower part, in harness
T6 - 6-Pin Connector, brown, in protective housing for connectors, in plenum chamber, left
T10 - 10-Pin Connector, orange, in protective housing for connectors, in plenum chamber, left
T10g - 10-Pin Connector, grey, in protective housing for connectors, in plenum chamber, left

(114) - Ground connection, in automatic transmission wiring harness
(501) - Threaded connection -2- (30) on the relay plate
(A32) - Plus connection (30), in instrument panel wiring harness
(A52) - Plus connection (30a), in instrument panel wiring harness
(A87) - Connector (RF), in instrument panel wiring harness
(A98) - Plus connector -4- (30), in instrument panel wiring harness
(B182) - Connection (RF), in passenger compartment wiring harness

Park/neutral position (PNP) relay

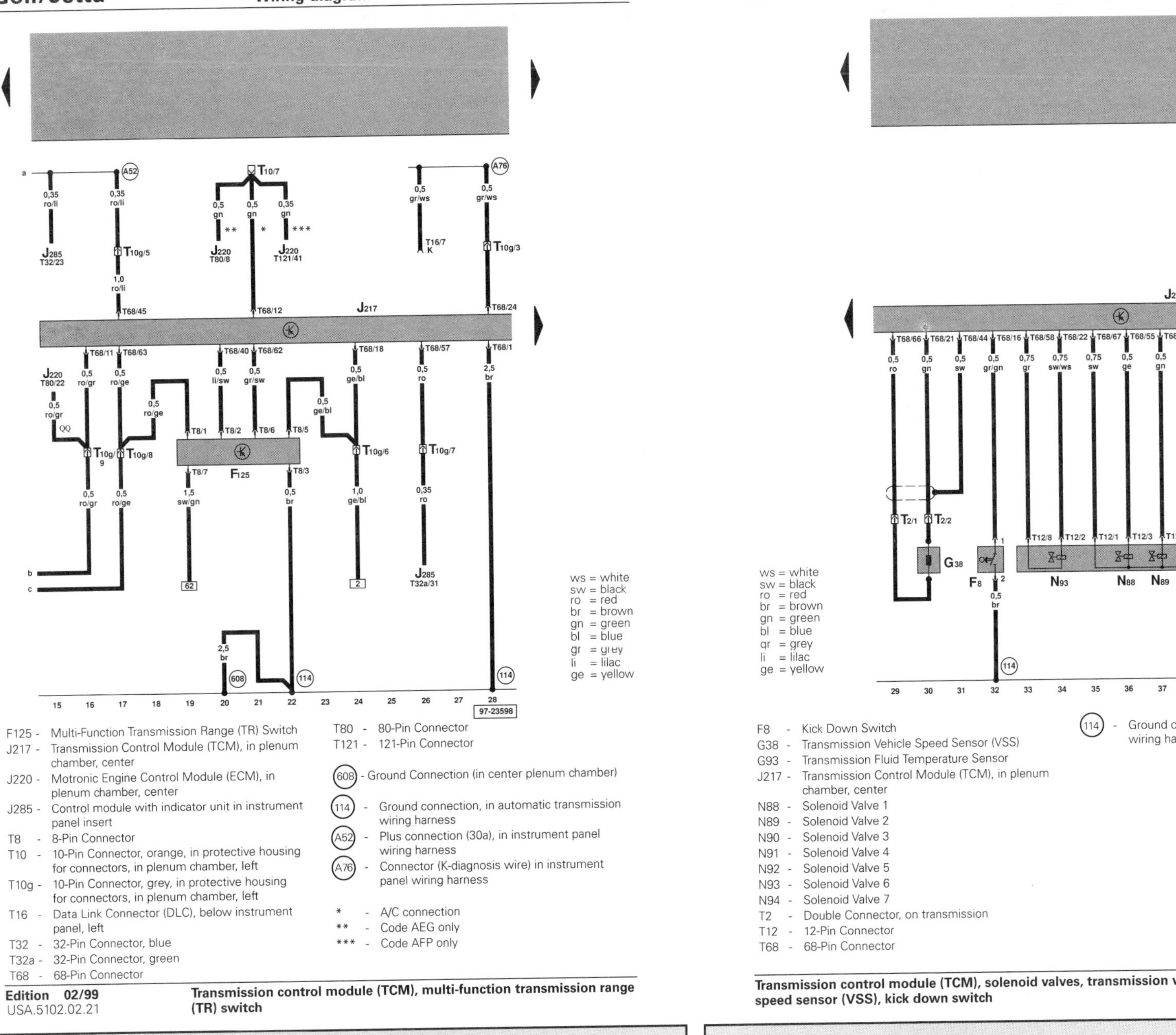

ws = white
sw = black
ro = red
br = brown
gn = green
bl = blue
gr = grey
li = lilac
ge = yellow

F125 - Multi-Function Transmission Range (TR) Switch
J217 - Transmission Control Module (TCM), in plenum chamber, center
J220 - Motronic Engine Control Module (ECM), in plenum chamber, center
J285 - Control module with indicator unit in instrument panel insert
T8 - 8-Pin Connector
T10 - 10-Pin Connector, orange, in protective housing for connectors, in plenum chamber, left
T10g - 10-Pin Connector, grey, in protective housing for connectors, in plenum chamber, left
T16 - Data Link Connector (DLC), below instrument panel, left
T32 - 32-Pin Connector, blue
T32a - 32-Pin Connector, green
T68 - 68-Pin Connector
T80 - 80-Pin Connector
T121 - 121-Pin Connector

(608) - Ground Connection (in center plenum chamber)
(114) - Ground connection, in automatic transmission wiring harness
(A52) - Plus connection (30a), in instrument panel wiring harness
(A76) - Connector (K-diagnosis wire) in instrument panel wiring harness

* - A/C connection
** - Code AEG only
*** - Code AFP only

Edition 02/99
USA.5102.02.21

Transmission control module (TCM), multi-function transmission range (TR) switch

ws = white
sw = black
ro = red
br = brown
gn = green
bl = blue
gr = grey
li = lilac
ge = yellow

F8 - Kick Down Switch
G38 - Transmission Vehicle Speed Sensor (VSS)
G93 - Transmission Fluid Temperature Sensor
J217 - Transmission Control Module (TCM), in plenum chamber, center
N88 - Solenoid Valve 1
N89 - Solenoid Valve 2
N90 - Solenoid Valve 3
N91 - Solenoid Valve 4
N92 - Solenoid Valve 5
N93 - Solenoid Valve 6
N94 - Solenoid Valve 7
T2 - Double Connector, on transmission
T12 - 12-Pin Connector
T68 - 68-Pin Connector

(114) - Ground connection, in automatic transmission wiring harness

Transmission control module (TCM), solenoid valves, transmission vehicle speed sensor (VSS), kick down switch

Edition 12/98
USA.5102.01.21

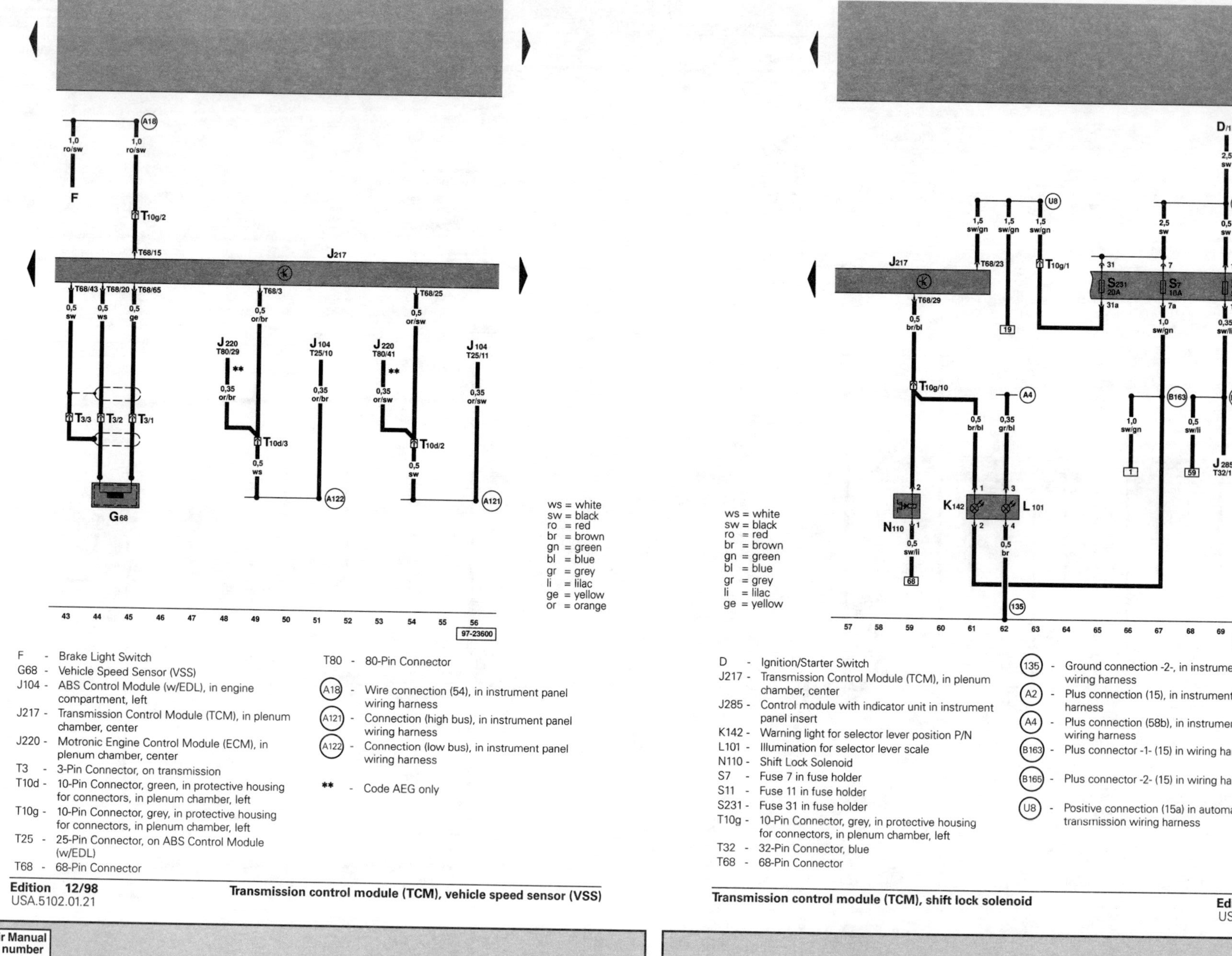

ws = white
sw = black
ro = red
br = brown
gn = green
bl = blue
gr = grey
li = lilac
ge = yellow
or = orange

F - Brake Light Switch
G68 - Vehicle Speed Sensor (VSS)
J104 - ABS Control Module (w/EDL), in engine compartment, left
J217 - Transmission Control Module (TCM), in plenum chamber, center
J220 - Motronic Engine Control Module (ECM), in plenum chamber, center
T3 - 3-Pin Connector, on transmission
T10d - 10-Pin Connector, green, in protective housing for connectors, in plenum chamber, left
T10g - 10-Pin Connector, grey, in protective housing for connectors, in plenum chamber, left
T25 - 25-Pin Connector, on ABS Control Module (w/EDL)
T68 - 68-Pin Connector
T80 - 80-Pin Connector
(A18) - Wire connection (54), in instrument panel wiring harness
(A121) - Connection (high bus), in instrument panel wiring harness
(A122) - Connection (low bus), in instrument panel wiring harness
** - Code AEG only

Edition 12/98
USA.5102.01.21

Transmission control module (TCM), vehicle speed sensor (VSS)

ws = white
sw = black
ro = red
br = brown
gn = green
bl = blue
gr = grey
li = lilac
ge = yellow

D - Ignition/Starter Switch
J217 - Transmission Control Module (TCM), in plenum chamber, center
J285 - Control module with indicator unit in instrument panel insert
K142 - Warning light for selector lever position P/N
L101 - Illumination for selector lever scale
N110 - Shift Lock Solenoid
S7 - Fuse 7 in fuse holder
S11 - Fuse 11 in fuse holder
S231 - Fuse 31 in fuse holder
T10g - 10-Pin Connector, grey, in protective housing for connectors, in plenum chamber, left
T32 - 32-Pin Connector, blue
T68 - 68-Pin Connector
(135) - Ground connection -2-, in instrument panel wiring harness
(A2) - Plus connection (15), in instrument panel wiring harness
(A4) - Plus connection (58b), in instrument panel wiring harness
(B163) - Plus connector -1- (15) in wiring harness interior
(B165) - Plus connector -2- (15) in wiring harness interior
(U8) - Positive connection (15a) in automatic transmission wiring harness

Transmission control module (TCM), shift lock solenoid

Edition 12/98
USA.5102.01.21

Automatic transmission, 4 speed automatic,

from September 1998

- **1.9L - Engine - Turbo Diesel Fuel Injection (DFI)/66 kW, code ALH**

Deviate relay location and fuseplacements as well as the locations of multiple connectors see section "component locations".

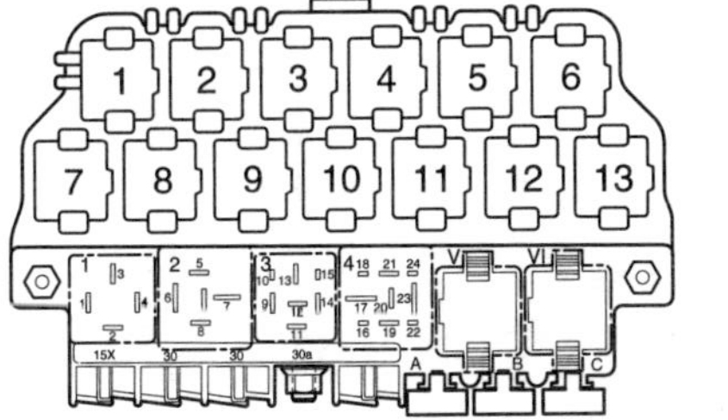

Relay location on the thirteenfold auxiliary relay panel, above relay panel:

11 Park/Neutral Position (PNP) Relay (175)

Relay panel:

Note: Number in parentheses indicates production control number stamped on relay housing.

Fuse colors

30 A - green
25 A - white
20 A - yellow
15 A - blue
10 A - red
7,5 A - brown
5 A - beige
3 A - violet

97-26089

ws = white
sw = black
ro = red
br = brown
gn = green
bl = blue
gr = grey
li = lilac
ge = yellow

B - Starter
D - Ignition/Starter Switch
J226 - Park/Neutral Position (PNP) Relay, on the thirteenfold auxiliary relay panel, above relay panel
M16 - Left Back-Up Light
M17 - Right Back-Up Light
S15 - Fuse 15 in fuse holder
T5h - 5-Pin Connector, near left A-pillar, lower part, in harness
T6 - 6-Pin Connector, brown, in protective housing for connectors, in plenum chamber, left
T10 - 10-Pin Connector, orange, in protective housing for connectors, in plenum chamber, left
T10g - 10-Pin Connector, grey, in protective housing for connectors, in plenum chamber, left

(114) - Ground connection, in automatic transmission wiring harness
(501) - Threaded connection -2- (30) on the relay plate
(A32) - Plus connection (30), in instrument panel wiring harness
(A52) - Plus connection (30a), in instrument panel wiring harness
(A87) - Connector (RF), in instrument panel wiring harness
(A98) - Plus connector -4- (30), in instrument panel wiring harness
(B182) - Connection (RF), in passenger compartment wiring harness

Park/neutral position (PNP) relay

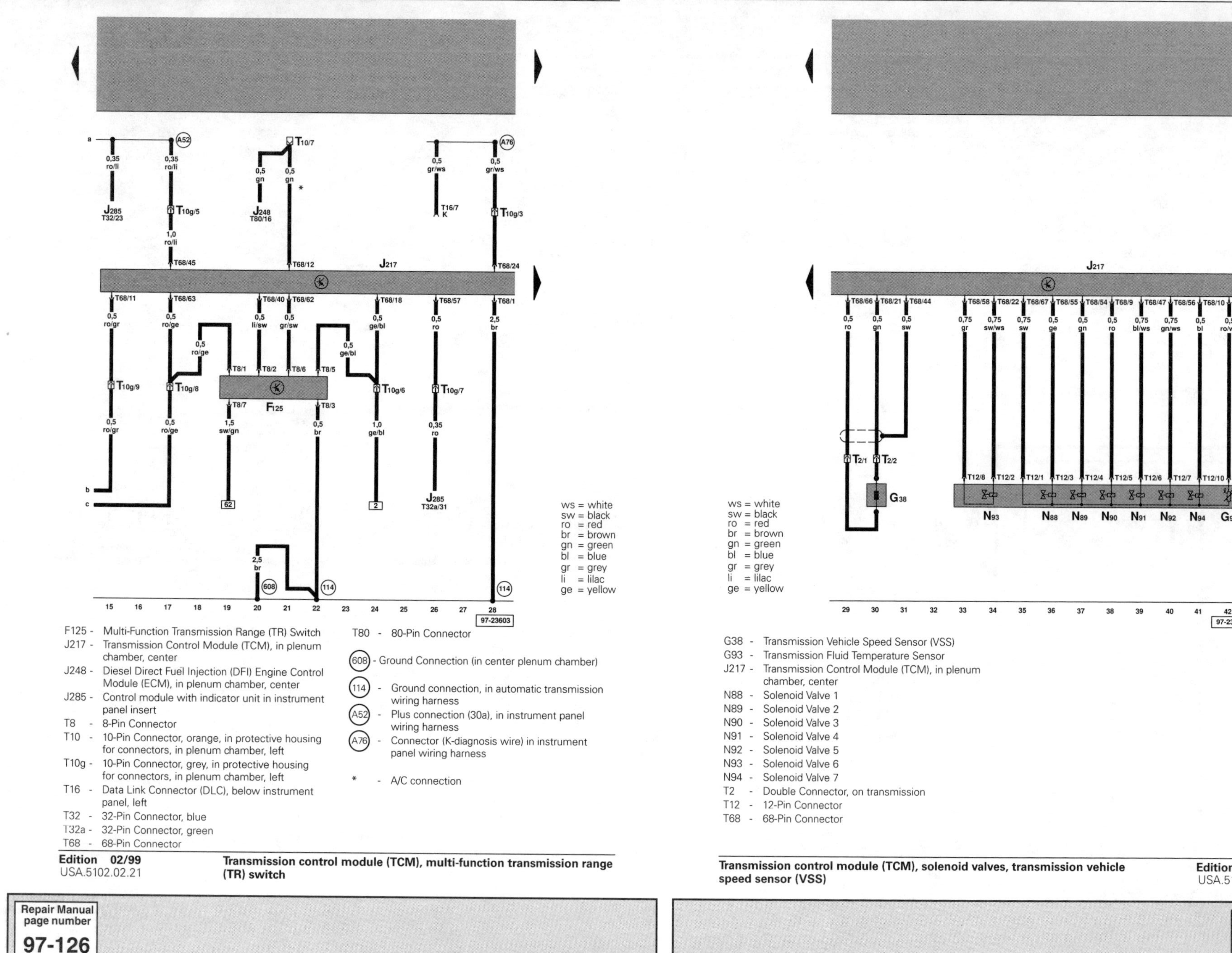

ws = white
sw = black
ro = red
br = brown
gn = green
bl = blue
gr = grey
li = lilac
ge = yellow

F125 - Multi-Function Transmission Range (TR) Switch
J217 - Transmission Control Module (TCM), in plenum chamber, center
J248 - Diesel Direct Fuel Injection (DFI) Engine Control Module (ECM), in plenum chamber, center
J285 - Control module with indicator unit in instrument panel insert
T8 - 8-Pin Connector
T10 - 10-Pin Connector, orange, in protective housing for connectors, in plenum chamber, left
T10g - 10-Pin Connector, grey, in protective housing for connectors, in plenum chamber, left
T16 - Data Link Connector (DLC), below instrument panel, left
T32 - 32-Pin Connector, blue
T32a - 32-Pin Connector, green
T68 - 68-Pin Connector
T80 - 80-Pin Connector

(608) - Ground Connection (in center plenum chamber)

(114) - Ground connection, in automatic transmission wiring harness

(A52) - Plus connection (30a), in instrument panel wiring harness

(A76) - Connector (K-diagnosis wire) in instrument panel wiring harness

* - A/C connection

Transmission control module (TCM), multi-function transmission range (TR) switch

ws = white
sw = black
ro = red
br = brown
gn = green
bl = blue
gr = grey
li = lilac
ge = yellow

G38 - Transmission Vehicle Speed Sensor (VSS)
G93 - Transmission Fluid Temperature Sensor
J217 - Transmission Control Module (TCM), in plenum chamber, center
N88 - Solenoid Valve 1
N89 - Solenoid Valve 2
N90 - Solenoid Valve 3
N91 - Solenoid Valve 4
N92 - Solenoid Valve 5
N93 - Solenoid Valve 6
N94 - Solenoid Valve 7
T2 - Double Connector, on transmission
T12 - 12-Pin Connector
T68 - 68-Pin Connector

Transmission control module (TCM), solenoid valves, transmission vehicle speed sensor (VSS)

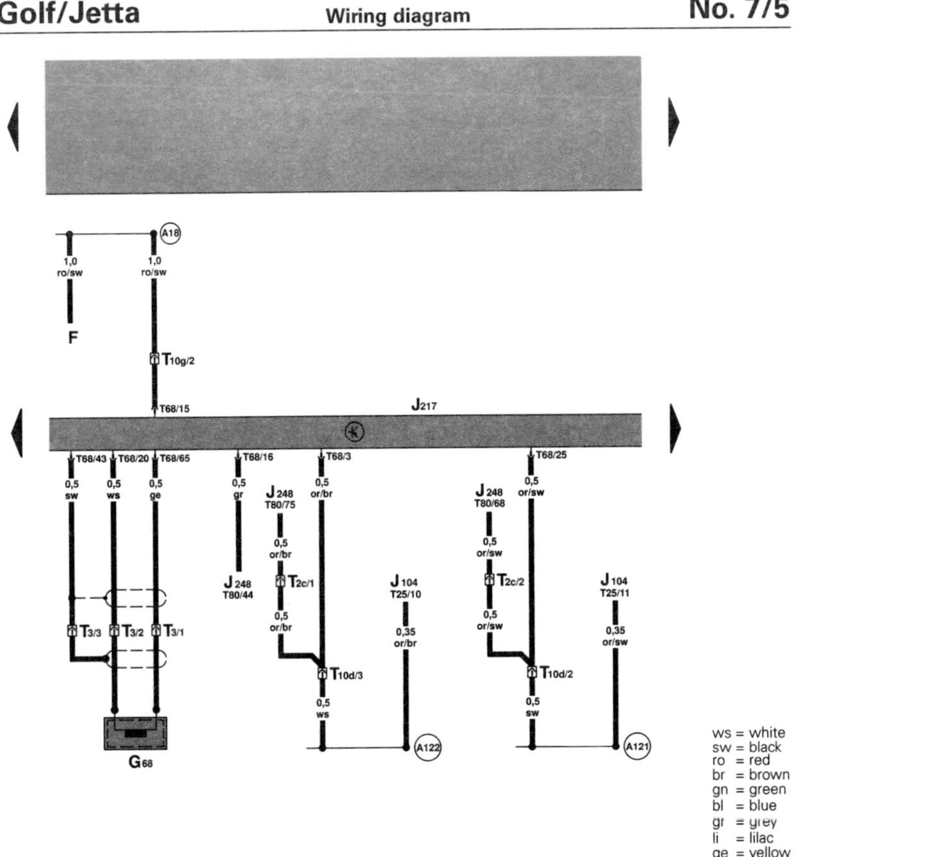

ws = white
sw = black
ro = red
br = brown
gn = green
bl = blue
gr = grey
li = lilac
ge = yellow
or = orange

F - Brake Light Switch
G68 - Vehicle Speed Sensor (VSS)
J104 - ABS Control Module (w/EDL), in engine compartment, left
J217 - Transmission Control Module (TCM), in plenum chamber, center
J248 - Diesel Direct Fuel Injection (DFI) Engine Control Module (ECM), in plenum chamber, center
T2c - Double Connector, in engine compartment, in wiring duct, left
T3 - 3-Pin Connector, on transmission
T10d - 10-Pin Connector, green, in protective housing for connectors, in plenum chamber, left
T10g - 10-Pin Connector, grey, in protective housing for connectors, in plenum chamber, left
T25 - 25-Pin Connector, on ABS Control Module (w/EDL)
T68 - 68-Pin Connector
T80 - 80-Pin Connector

(A18) - Wire connection (54), in instrument panel wiring harness
(A121) - Connection (high bus), in instrument panel wiring harness
(A122) - Connection (low bus), in instrument panel wiring harness

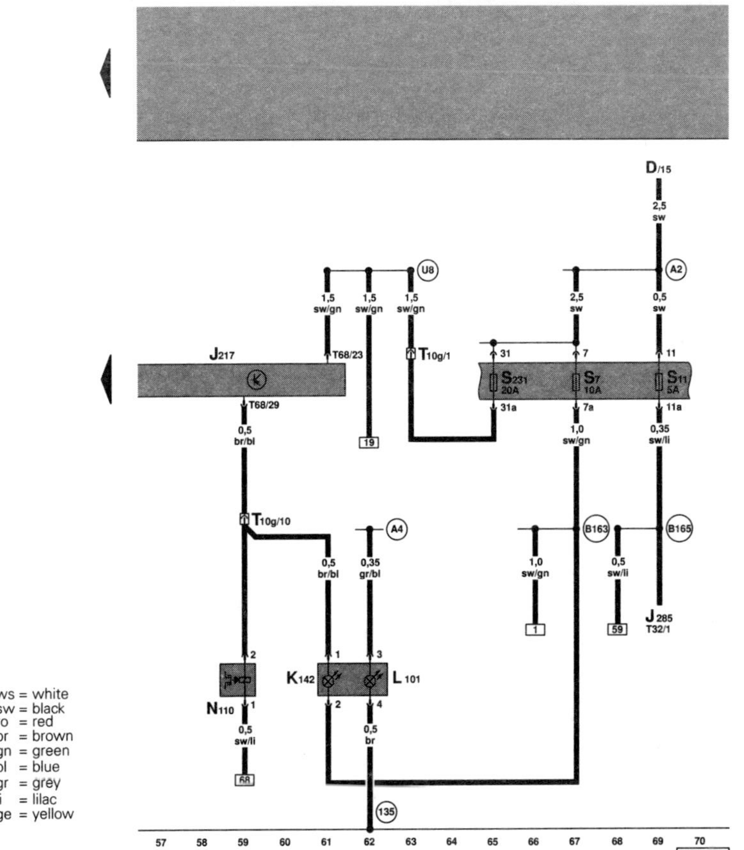

ws = white
sw = black
ro = red
br = brown
gn = green
bl = blue
gr = grey
li = lilac
ge = yellow

D - Ignition/Starter Switch
J217 - Transmission Control Module (TCM), in plenum chamber, center
J285 - Control module with indicator unit in instrument panel insert
K142 - Warning light for selector lever position P/N
L101 - Illumination for selector lever scale
N110 - Shift Lock Solenoid
S7 - Fuse 7 in fuse holder
S11 - Fuse 11 in fuse holder
S231 - Fuse 31 in fuse holder
T10g - 10-Pin Connector, grey, in protective housing for connectors, in plenum chamber, left
T32 - 32-Pin Connector, blue
T68 - 68-Pin Connector

(135) - Ground connection -2-, in instrument panel wiring harness
(A2) - Plus connection (15), in instrument panel wiring harness
(A4) - Plus connection (58b), in instrument panel wiring harness
(B163) - Plus connector -1- (15) in wiring harness interior
(B165) - Plus connector -2- (15) in wiring harness interior
(U8) - Positive connection (15a) in automatic transmission wiring harness

Cruise control,

from September 1998

- **2.0L - Engine - Motronic Multiport Fuel Injection (MFI)/85 kW, code AEG**

Deviate relay location and fuseplacements as well as the locations of multiple connectors see section "component locations".

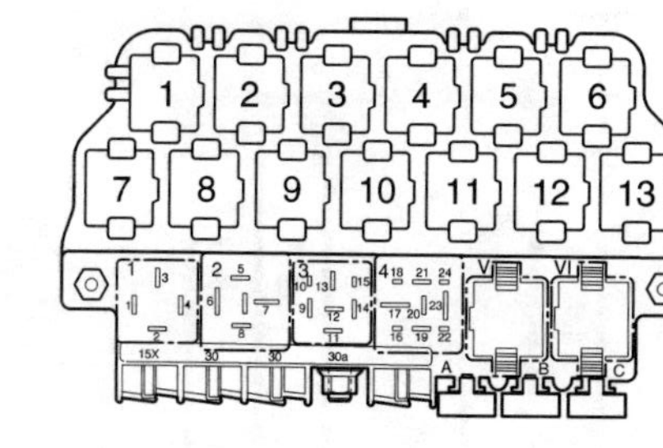

97-14163

Relay location on the thirteenfold auxiliary relay panel, above relay panel:

Relay panel:

2 Load Reduction Relay (100)

Note: Number in parentheses indicates production control number stamped on relay housing.

Fuse colors

30 A - green
25 A - white
20 A - yellow
15 A - blue
10 A - red
7,5 A - brown
5 A - beige
3 A - violet

ws = white
sw = black
ro = red
br = brown
gn = green
bl = blue
gr = grey
li = lilac
ge = yellow

97-27400

D - Ignition/Starter Switch
F - Brake Light Switch
F36 - Clutch Vacuum Vent Valve Switch
F47 - Brake Vacuum Vent Valve Switch for cruise control
J59 - Load Reduction Relay
J220 - Motronic Engine Control Module (ECM), in plenum chamber, center
S5 - Fuse 5 in fuse holder
S13 - Fuse 13 in fuse holder
S176 - Fuse -4- (30) in fuse bracket/battery
T10d - 10-Pin Connector, green, in protective housing for connectors, in plenum chamber, left
T10e - 10-Pin Connector, black, in protective housing for connectors, in plenum chamber, left
T80 - 80-Pin Connector

(500) - Threaded connection -1- (30) on the relay plate
(501) - Threaded connection -2- (30) on the relay plate
(A2) - Plus connection (15), in instrument panel wiring harness
(A18) - Wire connection (54), in instrument panel wiring harness
(A20) - Wire connection (15a), in instrument panel wiring harness
* - Manual transmission only
--- Automatic transmission only

Motronic engine control module (ECM), brake light switch, clutch vacuum vent valve switch, brake vacuum vent valve switch for cruise control

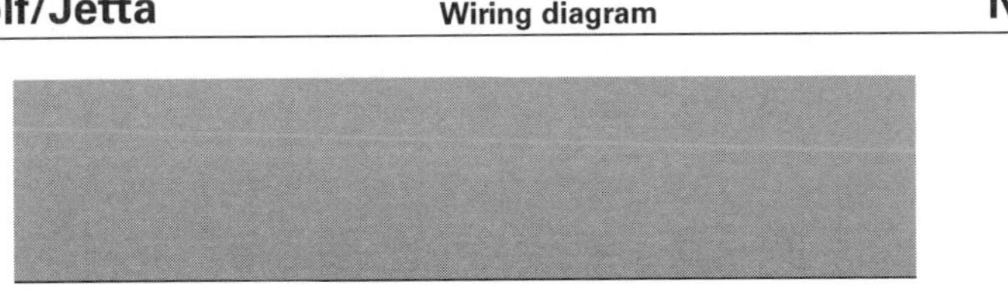

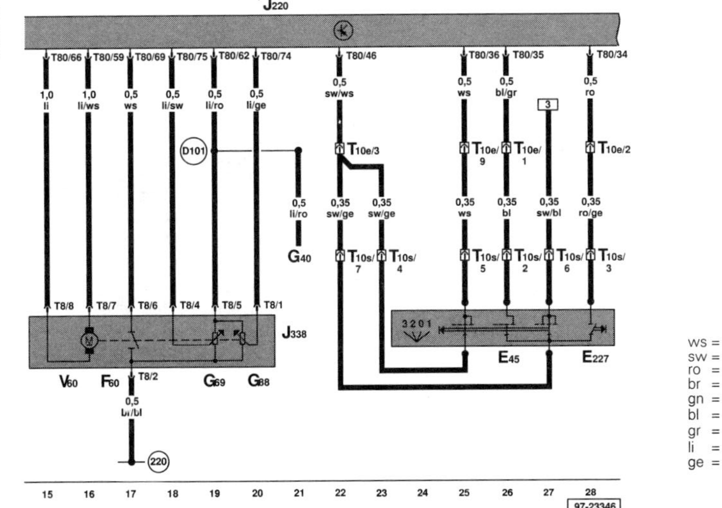

ws = white
sw = black
ro = red
br = brown
gn = green
bl = blue
gr = grey
li = lilac
ge = yellow

- E45 - Cruise Control Switch
- E227 - Cruise Control Push Button (SET)
- F60 - Closed Throttle Position (CTP) Switch
- G40 - Camshaft Position (CMP) Sensor
- G69 - Throttle Position (TP) Sensor
- G88 - Throttle Position (TP) Sensor
- J220 - Motronic Engine Control Module (ECM), in plenum chamber, center
- J338 - Throttle Valve Control Module
- T8 - 8-Pin Connector
- T10e - 10-Pin Connector, black, in protective housing for connectors, in plenum chamber, left
- T10s - 10-Pin Connector, near steering column
- T80 - 80-Pin Connector
- V60 - Throttle Position (TP) Actuator

- (220) - Ground connection (sensor ground), in engine compartment wiring harness
- (D101) - Wire connection -1-, in engine compartment wiring harness

Motronic engine control module (ECM), cruise control switch, throttle valve control module

THIS PAGE INTENTIONALLY LEFT BLANK

Anti-lock brake system (ABS), Anti-lock brake system (ABS) with electronic differential lock (EDL) and anti-slip control (ASC),

from September 1998

Deviate relay location and fuseplacements as well as the locations of multiple connectors see section "component locations".

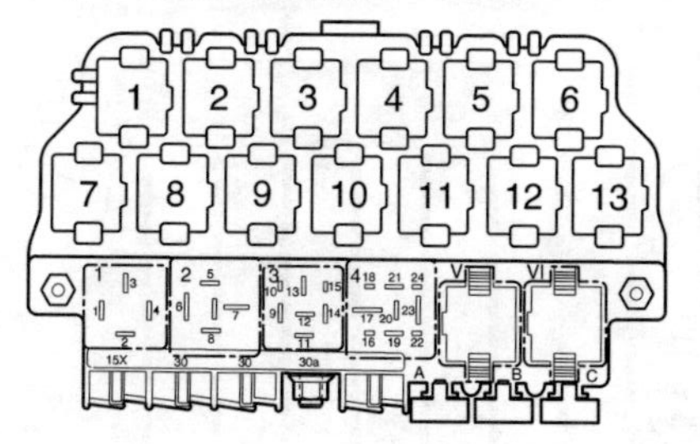

Fuse colors

30 A - green
25 A - white
20 A - yellow
15 A - blue
10 A - red
7,5 A - brown
5 A - beige
3 A - violet

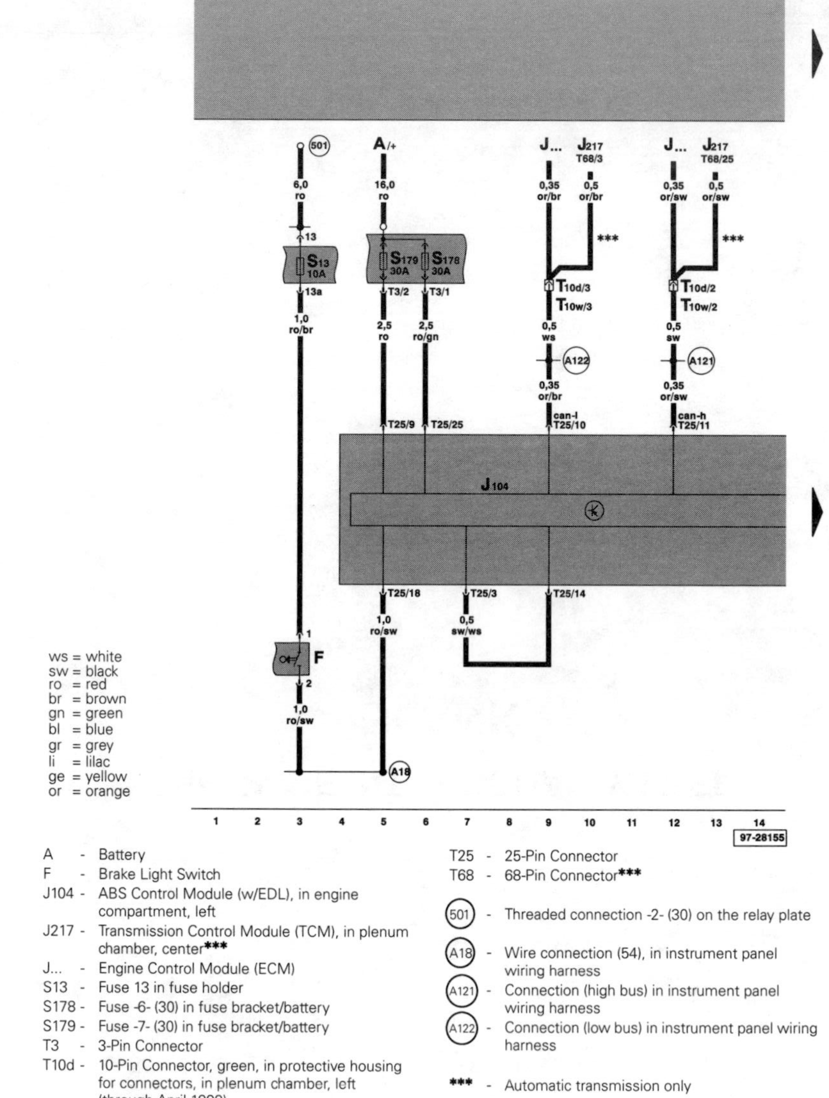

ws = white
sw = black
ro = red
br = brown
gn = green
bl = blue
gr = grey
li = lilac
ge = yellow
or = orange

A - Battery
F - Brake Light Switch
J104 - ABS Control Module (w/EDL), in engine compartment, left
J217 - Transmission Control Module (TCM), in plenum chamber, center***
J... - Engine Control Module (ECM)
S13 - Fuse 13 in fuse holder
S178 - Fuse -6- (30) in fuse bracket/battery
S179 - Fuse -7- (30) in fuse bracket/battery
T3 - 3-Pin Connector
T10d - 10-Pin Connector, green, in protective housing for connectors, in plenum chamber, left (through April 1999)
T10w - 10-Pin Connector, white, in protective housing for connectors, in plenum chamber, left (beginning May 1999)
T25 - 25-Pin Connector
T68 - 68-Pin Connector***

(501) - Threaded connection -2- (30) on the relay plate
(A18) - Wire connection (54), in instrument panel wiring harness
(A121) - Connection (high bus) in instrument panel wiring harness
(A122) - Connection (low bus) in instrument panel wiring harness

*** - Automatic transmission only

ABS control module (w/EDL), brake light switch

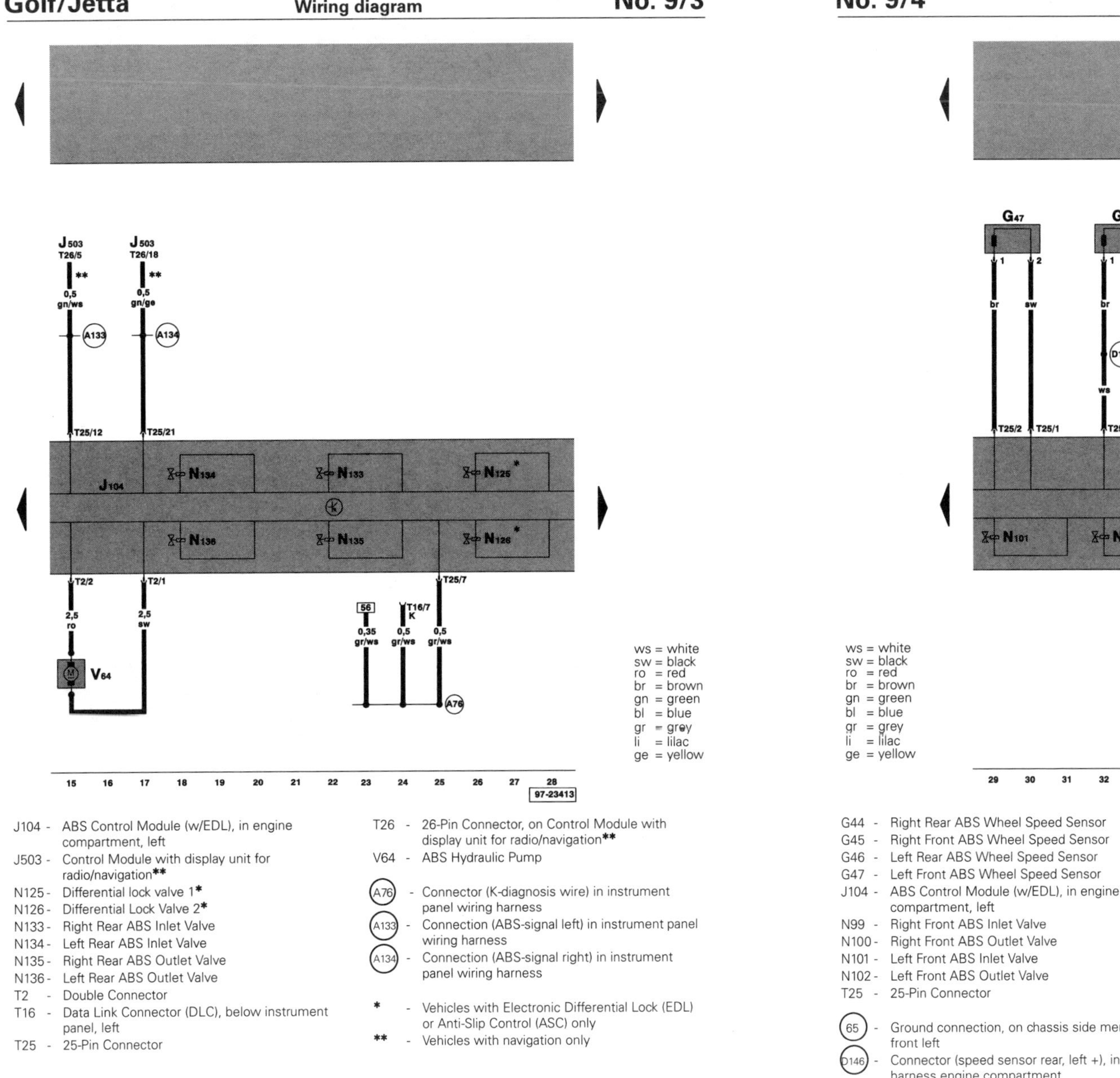

ws = white
sw = black
ro = red
br = brown
gn = green
bl = blue
gr = grey
li = lilac
ge = yellow

J104 - ABS Control Module (w/EDL), in engine compartment, left
J503 - Control Module with display unit for radio/navigation**
N125 - Differential lock valve 1*
N126 - Differential Lock Valve 2*
N133 - Right Rear ABS Inlet Valve
N134 - Left Rear ABS Inlet Valve
N135 - Right Rear ABS Outlet Valve
N136 - Left Rear ABS Outlet Valve
T2 - Double Connector
T16 - Data Link Connector (DLC), below instrument panel, left
T25 - 25-Pin Connector
T26 - 26-Pin Connector, on Control Module with display unit for radio/navigation**
V64 - ABS Hydraulic Pump
A76 - Connector (K-diagnosis wire) in instrument panel wiring harness
A133 - Connection (ABS-signal left) in instrument panel wiring harness
A134 - Connection (ABS-signal right) in instrument panel wiring harness
* - Vehicles with Electronic Differential Lock (EDL) or Anti-Slip Control (ASC) only
** - Vehicles with navigation only

ABS control module (w/EDL), ABS hydraulic pump

ws = white
sw = black
ro = red
br = brown
gn = green
bl = blue
gr = grey
li = lilac
ge = yellow

G44 - Right Rear ABS Wheel Speed Sensor
G45 - Right Front ABS Wheel Speed Sensor
G46 - Left Rear ABS Wheel Speed Sensor
G47 - Left Front ABS Wheel Speed Sensor
J104 - ABS Control Module (w/EDL), in engine compartment, left
N99 - Right Front ABS Inlet Valve
N100 - Right Front ABS Outlet Valve
N101 - Left Front ABS Inlet Valve
N102 - Left Front ABS Outlet Valve
T25 - 25-Pin Connector
65 - Ground connection, on chassis side member, front left
D146 - Connector (speed sensor rear, left +), in wiring harness engine compartment
D147 - Connector (speed sensor rear, left -), in wiring harness engine compartment
D148 - Connector (speed sensor rear, right +), in wiring harness engine compartment
D149 - Connector (speed sensor rear, right -), in wiring harness engine compartment

ABS control module (w/EDL), front and rear speed sensor

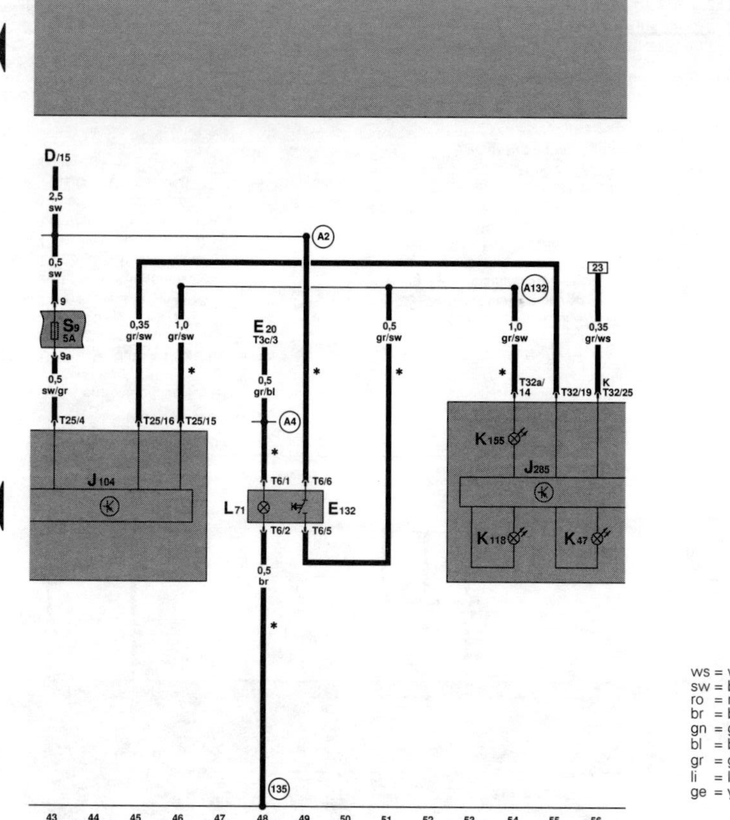

ws = white
sw = black
ro = red
br = brown
gn = green
bl = blue
gr = grey
li = lilac
ge = yellow

- D - Ignition/Starter Switch
- E20 - Instrument Panel Light Dimmer Switch
- E132 - Anti-Slip Control Switch*
- J104 - ABS Control Module (w/EDL), in engine compartment, left
- J285 - Control module with indicator unit in instrument panel insert
- K47 - ABS Warning Light
- K118 - Warning light for brake system
- K155 - Warning light for Anti-Slip Control (ASC)*
- L71 - Anti-Slip Control Switch Illumination*
- S9 - Fuse 9 in fuse holder
- T3c - 3-Pin Connector
- T6 - 6-Pin Connector*
- T25 - 25-Pin Connector
- T32 - 32-Pin Connector, blue
- T32a - 32-Pin Connector, green
- (135) - Ground connection -2-, in instrument panel wiring harness
- (A2) - Plus connection (15), in instrument panel wiring harness
- (A4) - Plus connection (58b), in instrument panel wiring harness
- (A132) - Connection (ASC), in instrument panel wiring harness
- * - Vehicles with Anti-Slip Control (ASC) only

Edition 12/98
USA.5102.01.21

ABS control module (w/EDL), anti-slip control switch, ABS warning light, warning light for brake system, warning light for ASC

THIS PAGE INTENTIONALLY LEFT
BLANK

Airbag systems,

from September 1998

- **Driver- and front passsenger airbag**
- **Side airbag**
- **Seat belt tensioner**
- **Seat belt control**

Deviate relay location and fuseplacements as well as the locations of multiple connectors see section "component locations".

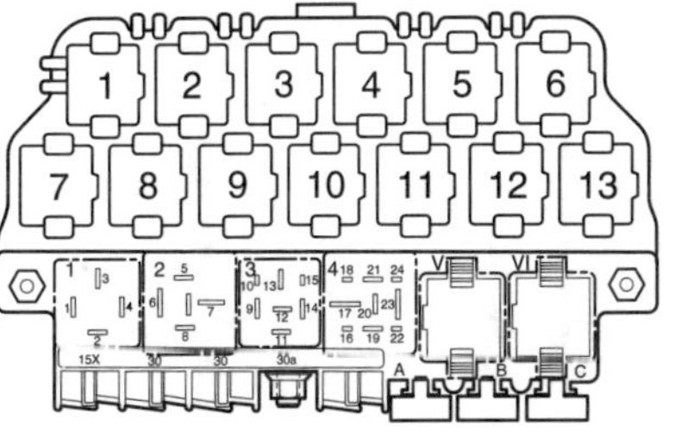

Relay location on the thirteenfold auxiliary relay panel, above relay panel:

Relay panel:

1 Dual Horn Relay (53)

Note: Number in parentheses indicates production control number stamped on relay housing.

Fuse colors

30 A - green
25 A - white
20 A - yellow
15 A - blue
10 A - red
7,5 A - brown
5 A - beige
3 A - violet

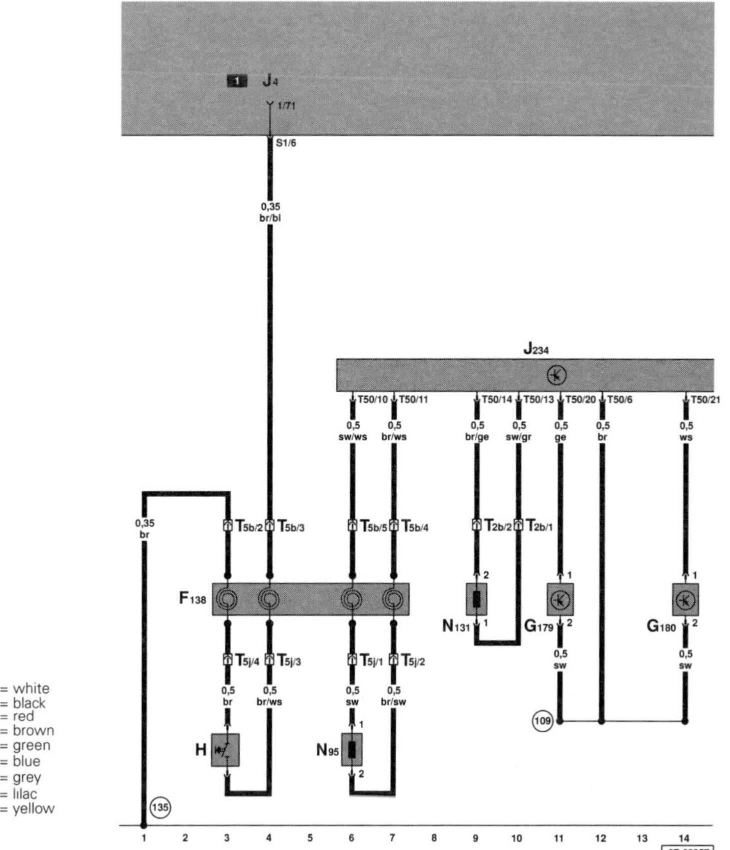

ws = white
sw = black
ro = red
br = brown
gn = green
bl = blue
gr = grey
li = lilac
ge = yellow

F138 - Airbag Spiral Spring/Return Spring With Slip Ring
G179 - Crash sensor for side airbag, driver's side
G180 - Crash sensor for side airbag, passenger side
H - Signal horn activation
J4 - Dual Horn Relay
J234 - Airbag Control Module, behind console, lower part
N95 - Driver's Side Airbag Igniter
N131 - Passenger's Side Airbag Igniter 1
T2b - 2-Pin Connector, on passenger's side airbag igniter 1
T5b - 5-Pin Connector, beside steering column
T5j - 5-Pin Connector, behind driver's airbag
T50 - 50-Pin Connector

(109) - Ground connection, in airbag wiring harness
(135) - Ground connection -2-, in instrument panel wiring harness

Airbag control module, airbag spiral spring/return spring with slip ring, crash sensor for side airbag, airbag igniter

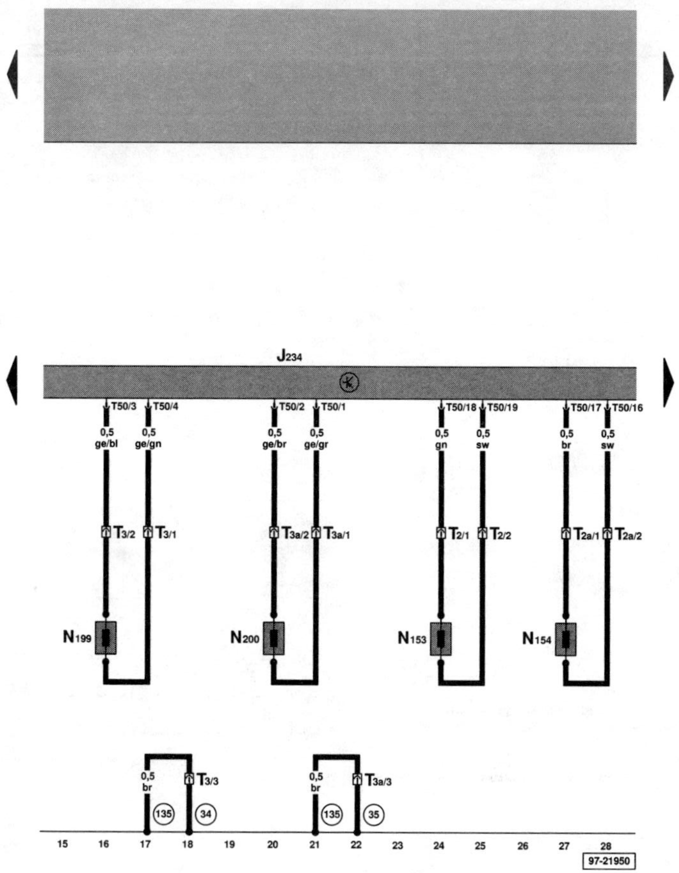

ws = white
sw = black
ro = red
br = brown
gn = green
bl = blue
gr = grey
li = lilac
ge = yellow

J234 - Airbag Control Module, behind console, lower part
N153 - Left Seat Belt Tensioner Igniter
N154 - Right Seat Belt Tensioner Igniter
N199 - Igniter for side airbag, driver's side
N200 - Igniter for side airbag, passenger side
T2 - Double Connector, below driver's seat
T2a - Double Connector, below driver's seat
T3 - 3-Pin Connector, below driver's seat
T3a - 3-Pin Connector, below passenger's seat
T50 - 50-Pin Connector

(34) - Ground connection, below driver's seat

(35) - Ground connection, below passenger's seat

(135) - Ground connection -2-, in instrument panel wiring harness

Airbag control module, seat belt tensioner igniter, igniter for side airbag

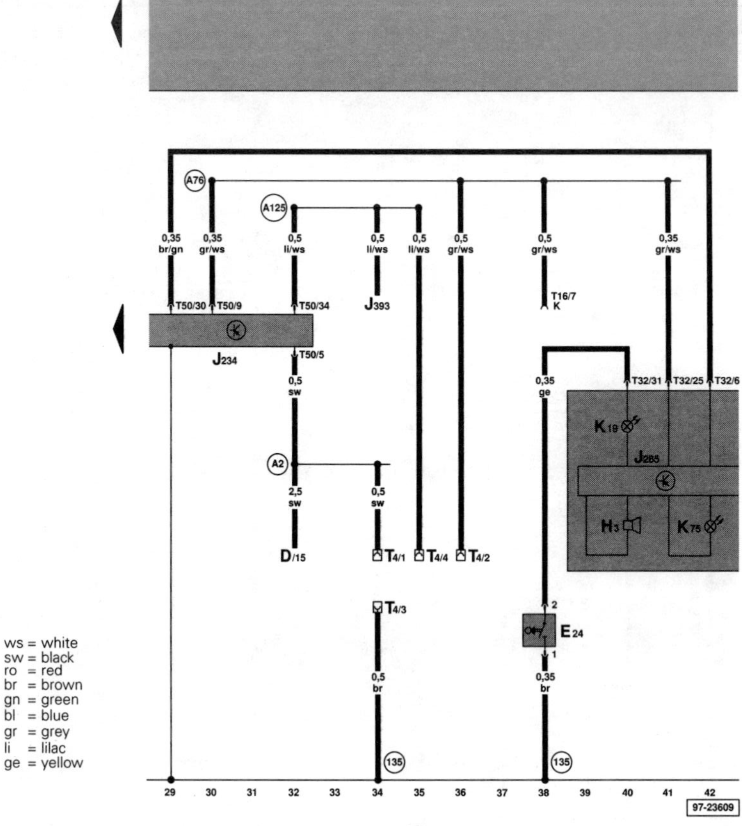

ws = white
sw = black
ro = red
br = brown
gn = green
bl = blue
gr = grey
li = lilac
ge = yellow

D - Ignition/Starter Switch
E24 - Left Seat Belt Switch
H3 - Warning Buzzer
J234 - Airbag Control Module, behind console, lower part
J285 - Control module with indicator unit in instrument panel insert
J393 - Central control module for comfort system, behind instrument panel, left
K19 - Seat Belt Warning Light
K75 - Airbag Malfunction Indicator Lamp (MIL)
T4 - 4-Pin Connector, behind instrument panel, right
T16 - Data Link Connector (DLC), below instrument panel, left
T32 - 32-Pin Connector, blue
T50 - 50-Pin Connector

(135) - Ground connection -2-, in instrument panel wiring harness
(A2) - Plus connection (15), in instrument panel wiring harness
(A76) - Connector (K-diagnosis wire) in instrument panel wiring harness
(A125) - Connection (crash signal) in instrument panel wiring harness

Airbag control module, left seat belt switch, seat belt warning light, airbag malfunction indicator lamp (MIL)

Coolant Fan (single speed),

from September 1998

Deviate relay location and fuseplacements as well as the locations of multiple connectors see section "component locations".

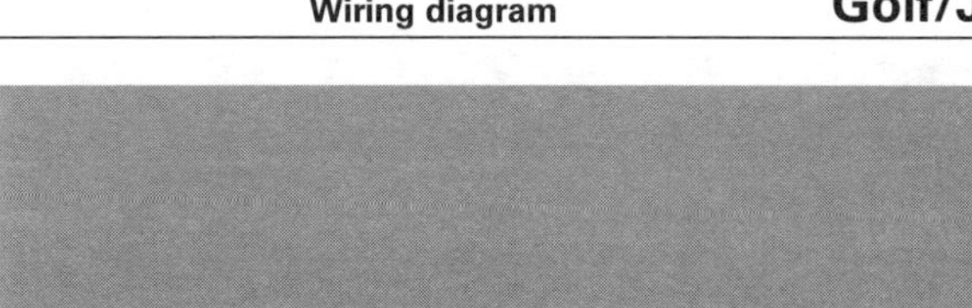

Fuse colors

30 A - green
25 A - white
20 A - yellow
15 A - blue
10 A - red
7,5 A - brown
5 A - beige
3 A - violet

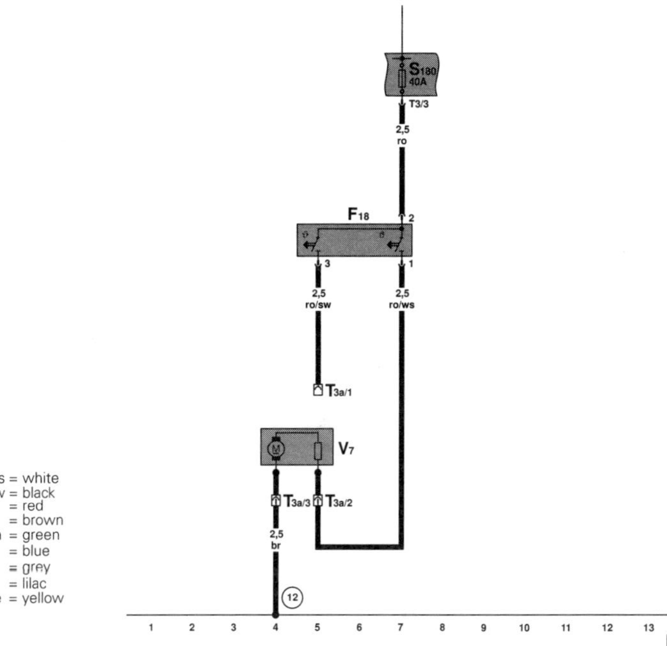

ws = white
sw = black
ro = red
br = brown
gn = green
bl = blue
gr = grey
li = lilac
ge = yellow

A - Battery
F18 - Coolant Fan Control (FC) Thermal Switch
S180 - Fuse -8- (30) in fuse bracket/battery
T3 - 3-Pin Connector
T3a - 3-Pin Connector, in engine compartment, left front
V7 - Coolant Fan

(12) - Ground connection, in engine compartment, left

Coolant fan, coolant fan control (FC) thermal switch

Coolant Fan (two speeds),

from September 1998

Deviate relay location and fuseplacements as well as the locations of multiple connectors see section "component locations".

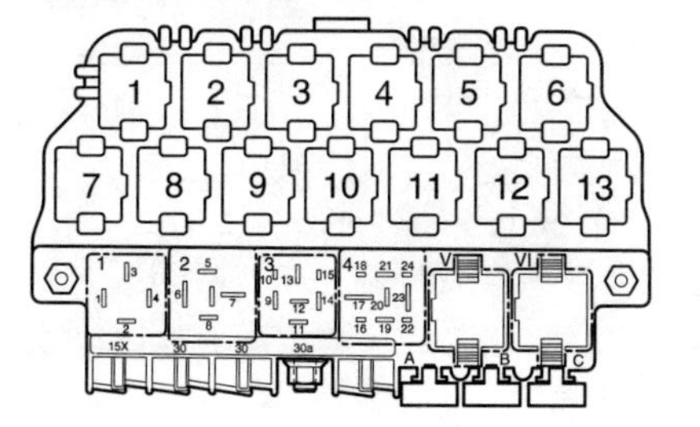

Fuse colors

30 A - green
25 A - white
20 A - yellow
15 A - blue
10 A - red
7,5 A - brown
5 A - beige
3 A - violet

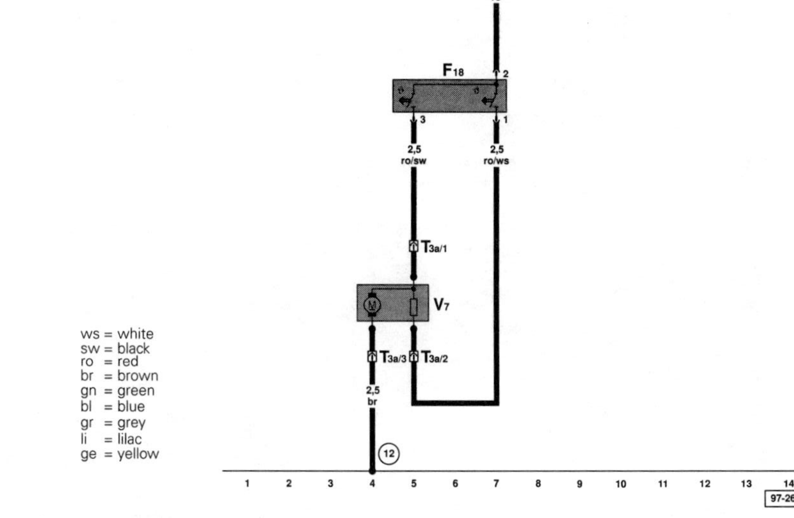

ws = white
sw = black
ro = red
br = brown
gn = green
bl = blue
gr = grey
li = lilac
ge = yellow

A - Battery
F18 - Coolant Fan Control (FC) Thermal Switch
S180 - Fuse -8- (30) in fuse bracket/battery
T3 - 3-Pin Connector
T3a - 3-Pin Connector, in engine compartment, left front
V7 - Coolant Fan

(12) - Ground connection, in engine compartment, left

Coolant fan, coolant fan control (FC) thermal switch

Coolant Fans,

from December 1998

- **2.8L - Engine - Motronic Multiport Fuel Injection (MFI)/130 kW, code AFP**

Deviate relay location and fuseplacements as well as the locations of multiple connectors see section "component locations".

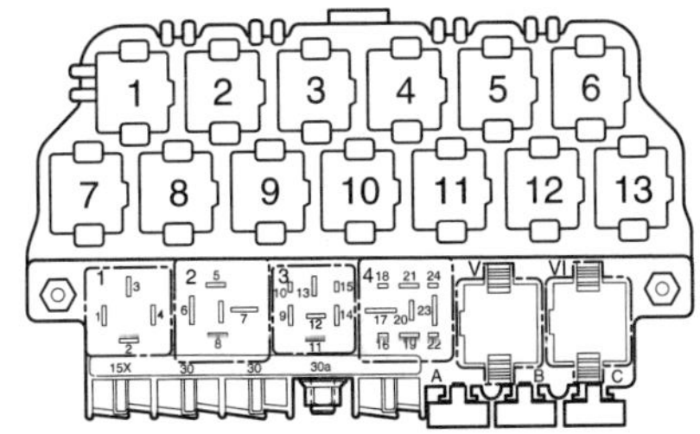

Fuse colors

30 A - green
25 A - white
20 A - yellow
15 A - blue
10 A - red
7,5 A - brown
5 A - beige
3 A - violet

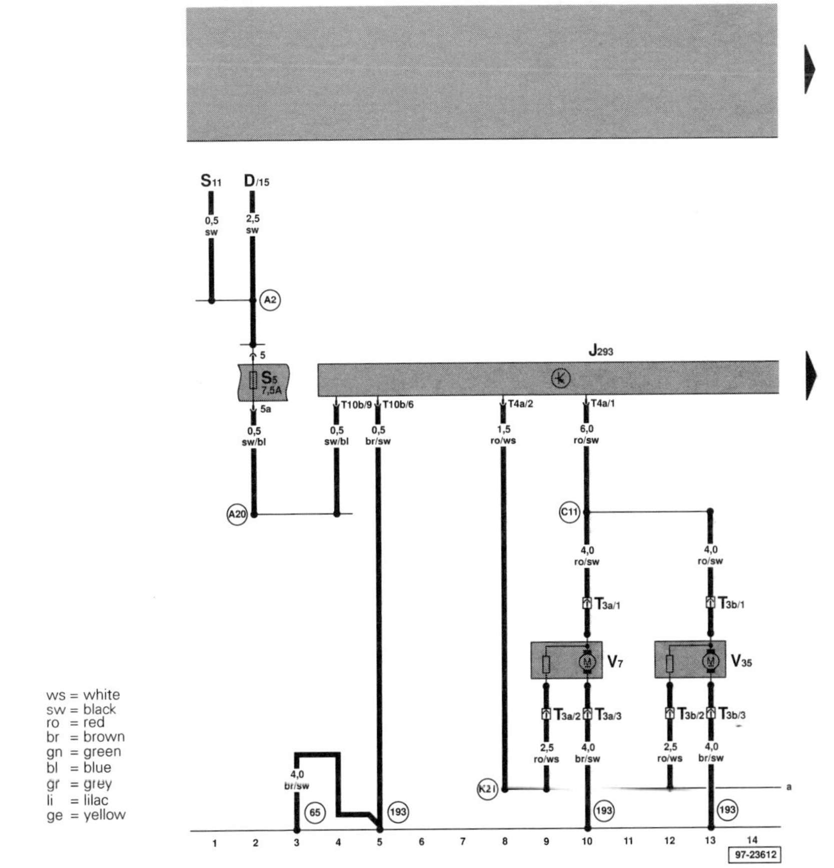

ws = white
sw = black
ro = red
br = brown
gn = green
bl = blue
gr = grey
li = lilac
ge = yellow

D - Ignition/Starter Switch
J293 - Coolant Fan Control (FC) Control Module, in engine compartment, left
S5 - Fuse 5 in fuse holder
S11 - Fuse 11 in fuse holder
T3a - 3-Pin Connector, in engine compartment, left
T3b - 3-Pin Connector, in engine compartment, left
T4a - 4-Pin Connector
T10b - 10-Pin Connector
V7 - Left Coolant Fan
V35 - Right Coolant Fan

(65) - Ground connection, on chassis side member, front left
(193) - Ground connection -1-, in coolant fan wiring harness

(A2) - Plus connection (15), in instrument panel wiring harness
(A20) - Wire connection (15a), in instrument panel wiring harness
(C11) - Wire connection, in coolant fan wiring harness
(K21) - Wire connection -1-, in coolant fan wiring harness

Coolant fan control (FC) control module, coolant fan

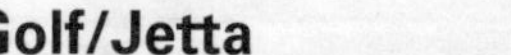

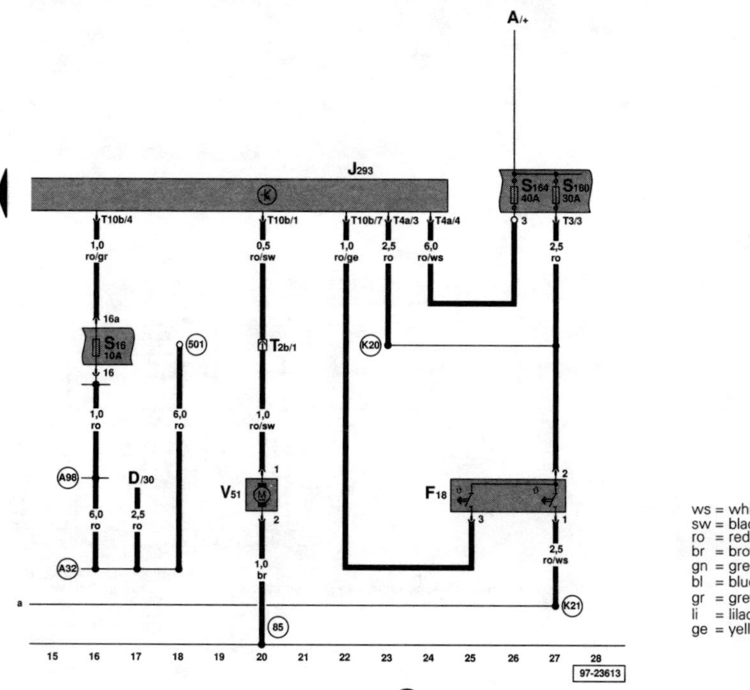

ws = white
sw = black
ro = red
br = brown
gn = green
bl = blue
gr = grey
li = lilac
ge = yellow

A - Battery
D - Ignition/Starter Switch
F18 - Coolant Fan Control (FC) Thermal Switch
J293 - Coolant Fan Control (FC) Control Module, in engine compartment, left
S16 - Fuse 16 in fuse holder
S164 - Fuse -3- (30) in fuse bracket/battery
S180 - Fuse -8- (30) in fuse bracket/battery
T2b - Double Connector, in engine compartment, in wiring duct, left
T3 - 3-Pin Connector
T4a - 4-Pin Connector
T10b - 10-Pin Connector
V51 - After-Run Coolant Pump

(85) - Ground connection -1-, in engine compartment wiring harness
(501) - Threaded connection -2- (30) on the relay plate
(A32) - Plus connection (30), in instrument panel wiring harness
(A98) - Plus connector -4- (30), in instrument panel wiring harness
(K20) - Plus connection -1- (30), in coolant fan wiring harness
(K21) - Wire connection -1-, in coolant fan wiring harness

Edition 12/98 USA.5102.01.21 **Coolant fan control (FC) control module, coolant fan control (FC) thermal switch, after-run coolant pump**

THIS PAGE INTENTIONALLY LEFT BLANK

Air conditioning (manual control),

from September 1998

- **1.9L - Engine - Turbo Diesel Fuel Injection (DFI)/66 kW, code ALH**
- **2.0L - Engine - Motronic Multiport Fuel Injection (MFI)/85 kW, code AEG**

Deviate relay location and fuseplacements as well as the locations of multiple connectors see section "component locations".

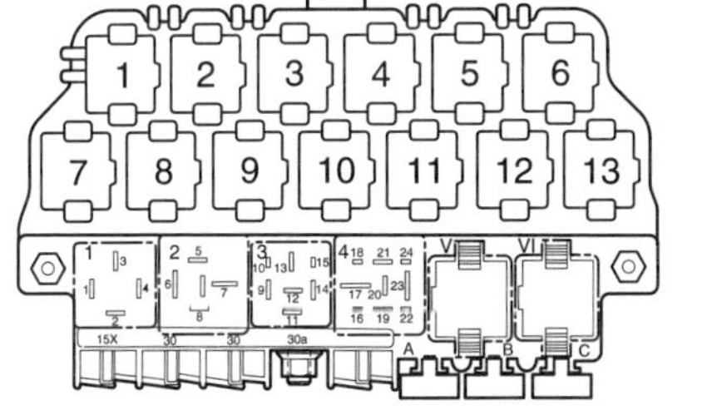

Fuse colors

30 A - green
25 A - white
20 A - yellow
15 A - blue
10 A - red
7,5 A - brown
5 A - beige
3 A - violet

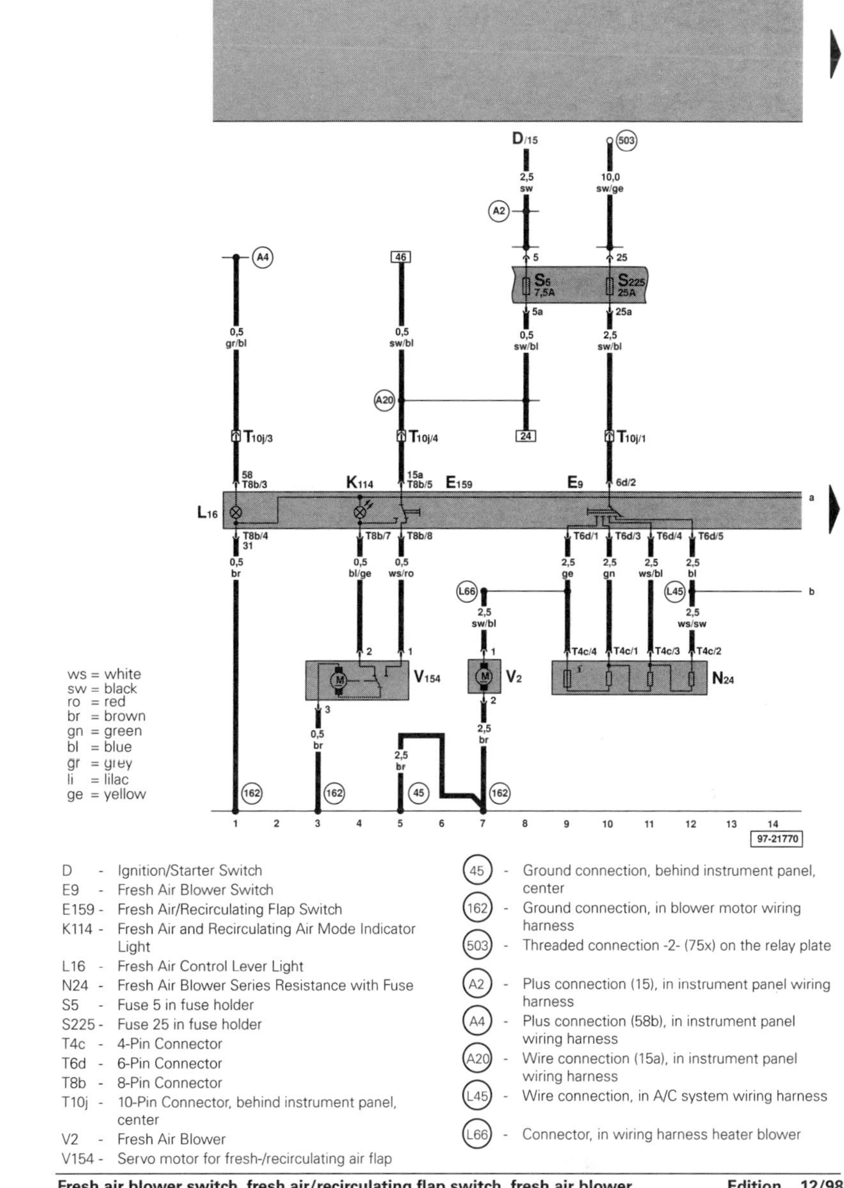

ws = white
sw = black
ro = red
br = brown
gn = green
bl = blue
gr = grey
li = lilac
ge = yellow

D - Ignition/Starter Switch
E9 - Fresh Air Blower Switch
E159 - Fresh Air/Recirculating Flap Switch
K114 - Fresh Air and Recirculating Air Mode Indicator Light
L16 - Fresh Air Control Lever Light
N24 - Fresh Air Blower Series Resistance with Fuse
S5 - Fuse 5 in fuse holder
S225 - Fuse 25 in fuse holder
T4c - 4-Pin Connector
T6d - 6-Pin Connector
T8b - 8-Pin Connector
T10j - 10-Pin Connector, behind instrument panel, center
V2 - Fresh Air Blower
V154 - Servo motor for fresh-/recirculating air flap

(45) - Ground connection, behind instrument panel, center
(162) - Ground connection, in blower motor wiring harness
(503) - Threaded connection -2- (75x) on the relay plate
(A2) - Plus connection (15), in instrument panel wiring harness
(A4) - Plus connection (58b), in instrument panel wiring harness
(A20) - Wire connection (15a), in instrument panel wiring harness
(L45) - Wire connection, in A/C system wiring harness
(L66) - Connector, in wiring harness heater blower

Fresh air blower switch, fresh air/recirculating flap switch, fresh air blower, servo motor for fresh-/recirculating air flap

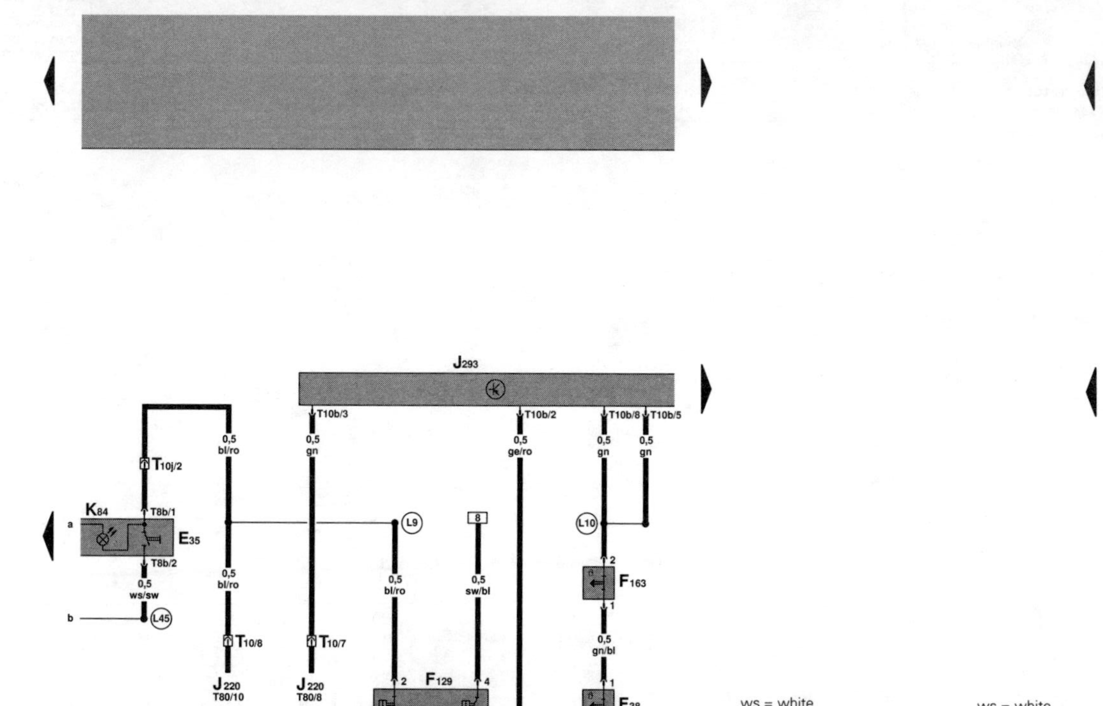

ws = white
sw = black
ro = red
br = brown
gn = green
bl = blue
gr = grey
li = lilac
ge = yellow

E35 - A/C Switch
F38 - Ambient Temperature Switch
F129 - A/C Pressure Switch
F163 - A/C Cut-Out Thermal Switch
J220 - Motronic Engine Control Module (ECM), in plenum chamber, center
J248 - Diesel Direct Fuel Injection (DFI) Engine Control Module (ECM), in plenum chamber, center
J293 - Coolant Fan Control (FC) Control Module, in engine compartment, left
K84 - A/C Indicator Light
T8b - 8-Pin Connector
T10 - 10-Pin Connector, orange, in protective housing for connectors, in plenum chamber, left
T10b - 10-Pin Connector
T10j - 10-Pin Connector, behind instrument panel, center
T80 - Connector, 80 point
(L9) - Wire connection -1-, in A/C wiring harness
(L10) - Wire connection -2-, in A/C wiring harness
(L45) - Wire connection, in A/C system wiring harness

Coolant fan control (FC) control module, A/C switch, ambient temperature switch, A/C pressure switch, A/C cut-out thermal switch

J293
T10b/6 T4a/2 T4a/1 T10b/10
0,5 br/sw
1,5 ro/ws
6,0 ro/sw
1,0 gn/sw
C11
T4/3
4,0 ro/sw
T3a/1
T3b/1
N25
V7
V35
1,0 br/sw
T3a/2 T3a/3 T3b/2 T3b/3 T4/4
2,5 ro/ws
4,0 br/sw
K21
193
65
29 30 31 32 33 34 35 36 37 38 39 40 41 42
97-23615

ws = white
sw = black
ro = red
br = brown
gn = green
bl = blue
gr = grey
li = lilac
ge = yellow

J293 - Coolant Fan Control (FC) Control Module, in engine compartment, left
N25 - A/C Clutch
T3a - 3-Pin Connector, in engine compartment, left
T3b - 3-Pin Connector, in engine compartment, left
T4 - 4-Pin Connector, near starter
T4a - 4-Pin Connector
T10b - 10-Pin Connector
V7 - Left Coolant Fan
V35 - Right Coolant Fan
(65) - Ground connection, on chassis side member, front left
(193) - Ground connection -1-, in coolant fan wiring harness
(C11) - Wire connection, in coolant fan wiring harness
(K21) - Wire connection -1-, in coolant fan wiring harness

Coolant fan control (FC) control module, A/C clutch, coolant fan

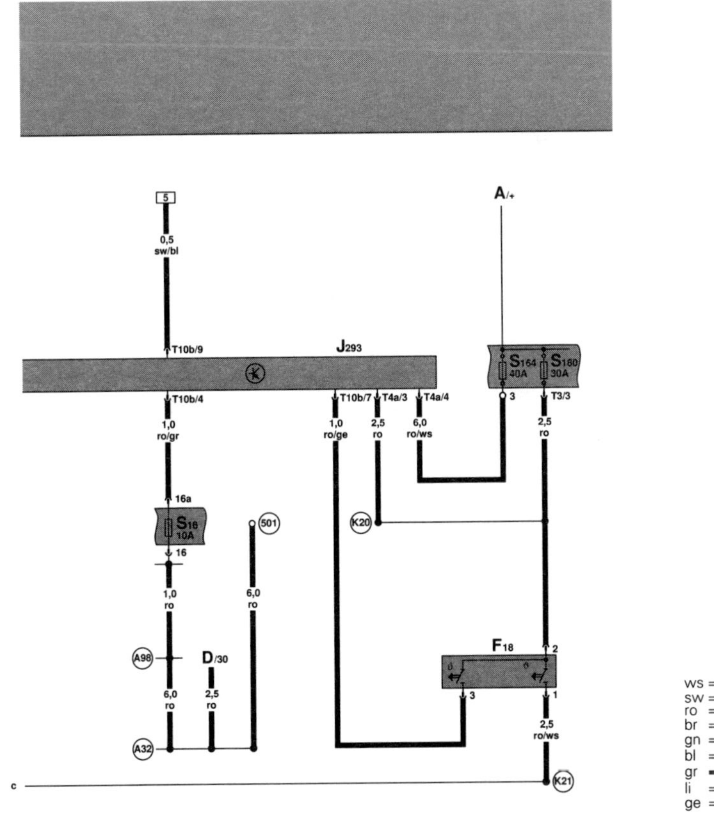

ws = white
sw = black
ro = red
br = brown
gn = green
bl = blue
gr = grey
li = lilac
ge = yellow

A - Battery
D - Ignition/Starter Switch
F18 - Coolant Fan Control (FC) Thermal Switch
J293 - Coolant Fan Control (FC) Control Module, in engine compartment, left
S16 - Fuse 16 in fuse holder
S164 - Fuse -3- (30) in fuse bracket/battery
S180 - Fuse -8- (30) in fuse bracket/battery
T3 - 3-Pin Connector
T4a - 4-Pin Connector
T10b - 10-Pin Connector

(501) - Threaded connection -2- (30) on the relay plate

(A32) - Plus connection (30), in instrument panel wiring harness

(A98) - Plus connector -4- (30), in instrument panel wiring harness

(K20) - Plus connection -1- (30), in coolant fan wiring harness

(K21) - Wire connection -1-, in coolant fan wiring harness

THIS PAGE INTENTIONALLY LEFT BLANK

Air conditioning (manual control),

from December 1998

- **2.8L - Engine - Motronic Multiport Fuel Injection (MFI)/130 kW, code AFP**

Deviate relay location and fuseplacements as well as the locations of multiple connectors see section "component locations".

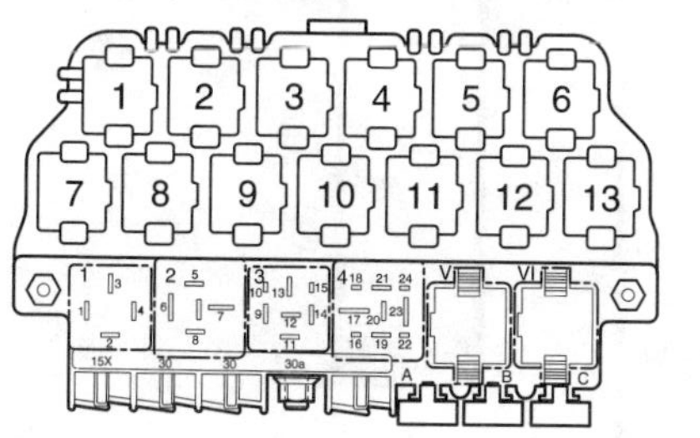

Fuse colors

30 A - green
25 A - white
20 A - yellow
15 A - blue
10 A - red
7,5 A - brown
5 A - beige
3 A - violet

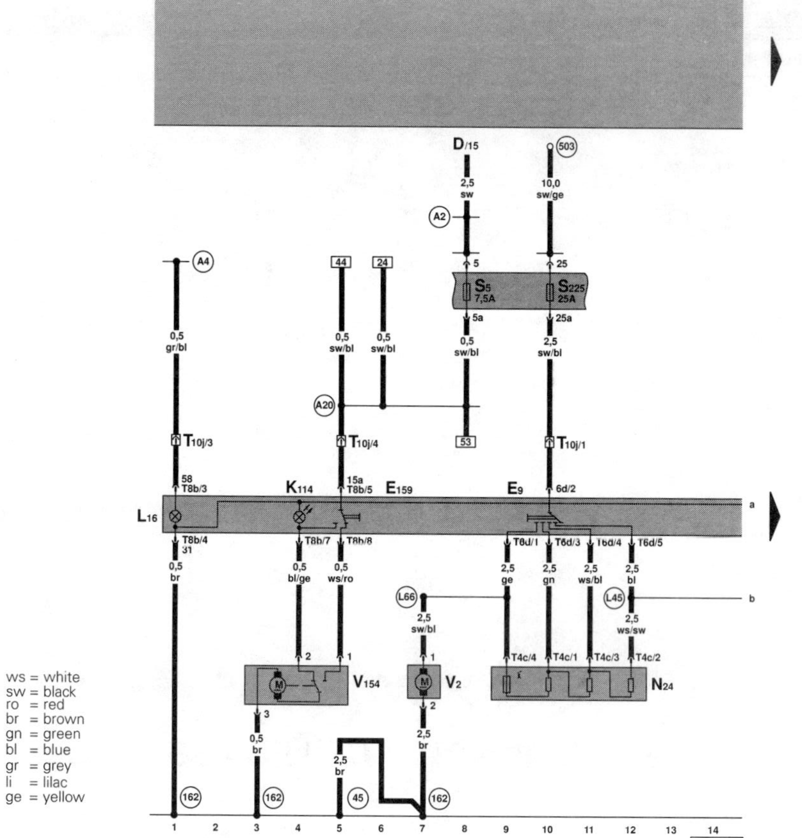

ws = white
sw = black
ro = red
br = brown
gn = green
bl = blue
gr = grey
li = lilac
ge = yellow

D - Ignition/Starter Switch
E9 - Fresh Air Blower Switch
E159 - Fresh Air/Recirculating Flap Switch
K114 - Fresh Air and Recirculating Air Mode Indicator Light
L16 - Fresh Air Control Lever Light
N24 - Fresh Air Blower Series Resistance with Fuse
S5 - Fuse 5 in fuse holder
S225 - Fuse 25 in fuse holder
T4c - 4-Pin Connector
T6d - 6-Pin Connector
T8b - 8-Pin Connector
T10j - 10-Pin Connector, behind instrument panel, center
V2 - Fresh Air Blower
V154 - Servo motor for fresh-/recirculating air flap

(45) - Ground connection, behind instrument panel, center
(162) - Ground connection, in blower motor wiring harness
(503) - Threaded connection -2- (75x) on the relay plate
(A2) - Plus connection (15), in instrument panel wiring harness
(A4) - Plus connection (58b), in instrument panel wiring harness
(A20) - Wire connection (15a), in instrument panel wiring harness
(L45) - Wire connection, in A/C system wiring harness
(L66) - Connector, in wiring harness heater blower

Fresh air blower switch, fresh air/recirculating flap switch, fresh air blower, servo motor for fresh-/recirculating air flap

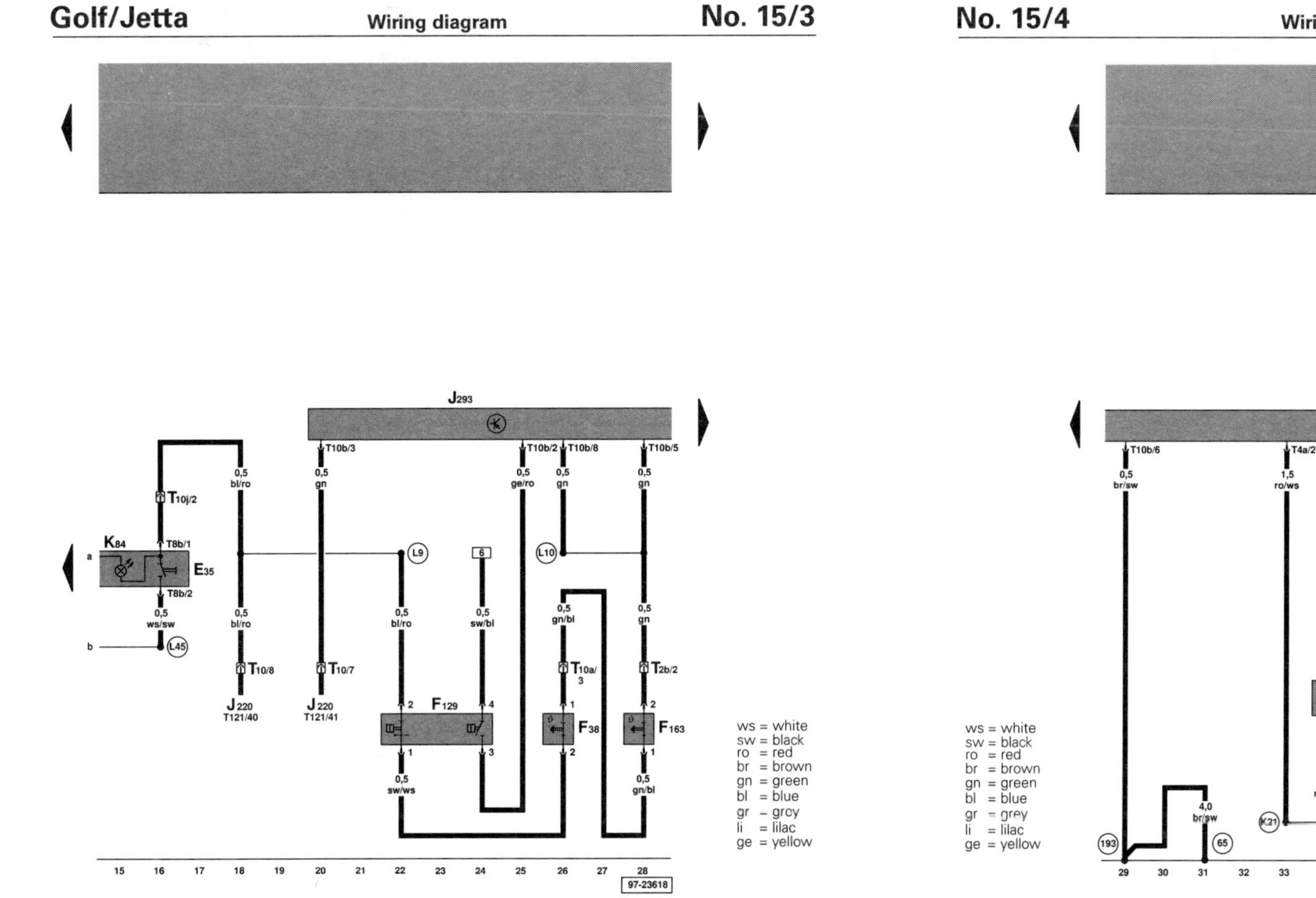

ws = white
sw = black
ro = red
br = brown
gn = green
bl = blue
gr = grey
li = lilac
ge = yellow

E35 - A/C Switch
F38 - Ambient Temperature Switch
F129 - A/C Pressure Switch
F163 - A/C Cut-Out Thermal Switch
J220 - Motronic Engine Control Module (ECM), in plenum chamber, center
J293 - Coolant Fan Control (FC) Control Module, in engine compartment, left
K84 - A/C Indicator Light
T2b - Double Connector, in engine compartment, in wiring duct, left
T8b - 8-Pin Connector
T10 - 10-Pin Connector, orange, in protective housing for connectors, in plenum chamber, left
T10a - 10-Pin Connector, in engine compartment, in wiring duct, left
T10b - 10-Pin Connector
T10j - 10-Pin Connector, behind instrument panel, center
T121 - Connector, 121 point

(L9) - Wire connection -1-, in A/C wiring harness

(L10) - Wire connection -2-, in A/C wiring harness

(L45) - Wire connection, in A/C system wiring harness

Coolant fan control (FC) control module, A/C switch, ambient temperature switch, A/C cut-out thermal switch, A/C pressure switch

ws = white
sw = black
ro = red
br = brown
gn = green
bl = blue
gr = grey
li = lilac
ge = yellow

J293 - Coolant Fan Control (FC) Control Module, in engine compartment, left
N25 - A/C Clutch
T3a - 3-Pin Connector, in engine compartment, left
T3b - 3-Pin Connector, in engine compartment, left
T4 - 4-Pin Connector, near starter
T4a - 4-Pin Connector
T10b - 10-Pin Connector
V7 - Left Coolant Fan
V35 - Right Coolant Fan

(65) - Ground connection, on chassis side member, front left

(193) - Ground connection -1-, in coolant fan wiring harness

(C11) - Wire connection, in coolant fan wiring harness

(K21) - Wire connection -1-, in coolant fan wiring harness

Coolant fan control (FC) control module, A/C clutch, coolant fan

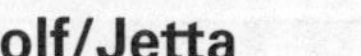

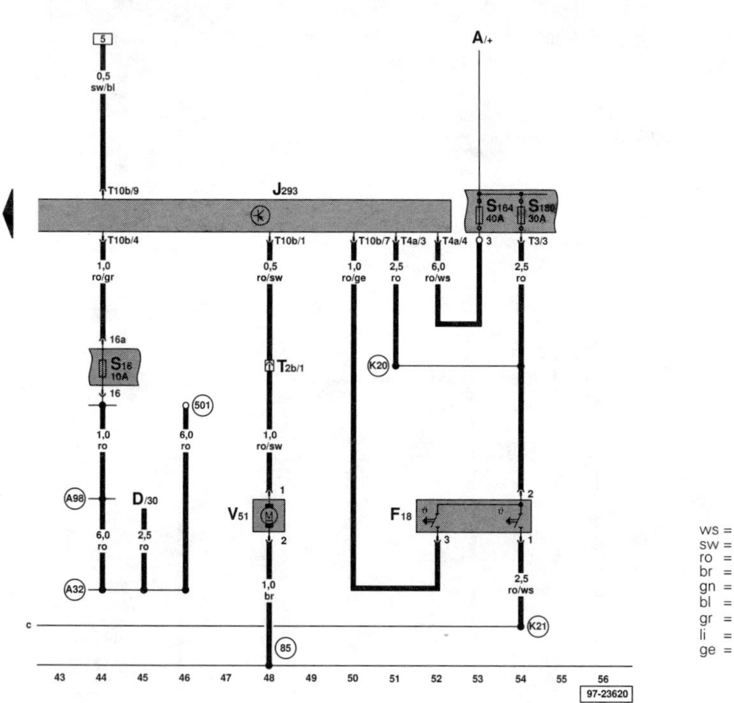

ws = white
sw = black
ro = red
br = brown
gn = green
bl = blue
gr = grey
li = lilac
ge = yellow

- A - Battery
- D - Ignition/Starter Switch
- F18 - Coolant Fan Control (FC) Thermal Switch
- J293 - Coolant Fan Control (FC) Control Module, in engine compartment, left
- S16 - Fuse 16 in fuse holder
- S164 - Fuse -3- (30) in fuse bracket/battery
- S180 - Fuse -8- (30) in fuse bracket/battery
- T2b - Double Connector, in engine compartment, in wiring duct, left
- T3 - 3-Pin Connector
- T4a - 4-Pin Connector
- T10b - 10-Pin Connector
- V51 - After-Run Coolant Pump

- (85) - Ground connection -1-, in engine compartment wiring harness
- (501) - Threaded connection -2- (30) on the relay plate
- (A32) - Plus connection (30), in instrument panel wiring harness
- (A98) - Plus connector -4- (30), in instrument panel wiring harness
- (K20) - Plus connection -1- (30), in coolant fan wiring harness
- (K21) - Wire connection -1-, in coolant fan wiring harness

Edition 12/98 USA.5102.01.21 **Coolant fan control (FC) control module, coolant fan control (FC) thermal switch, after-run coolant pump**

THIS PAGE INTENTIONALLY LEFT

BLANK

Daytime running lights,

from September 1998

Deviate relay location and fuseplacements as well as the locations of multiple connectors see section "component locations".

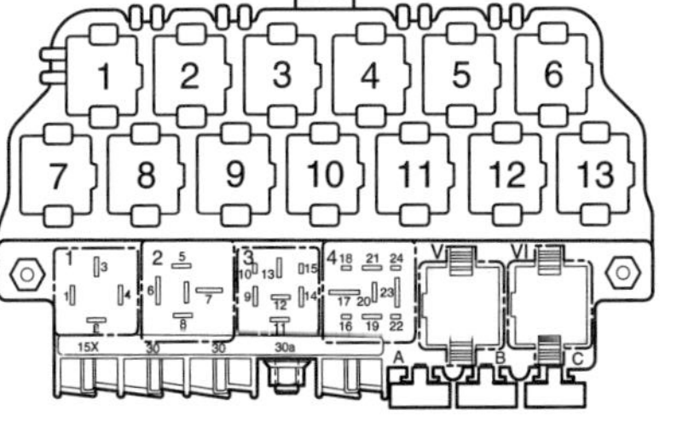

Relay location on the thirteenfold auxiliary relay panel, above relay panel:

- **7** Daytime Running Lights Change-over Relay (173), from April 1999
- **8** Daytime Running Lights Change-over Relay (173), trough March 1999

Relay panel:

Note: Number in parentheses indicates production control number stamped on relay housing.

Fuse colors

30 A - green
25 A - white
20 A - yellow
15 A - blue
10 A - red
7,5 A - brown
5 A - beige
3 A - violet

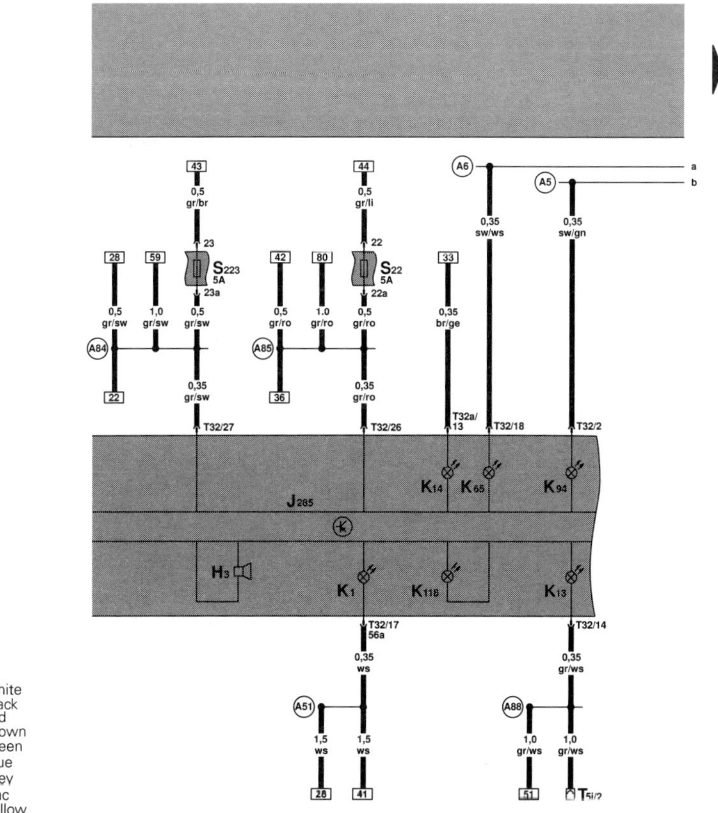

ws = white
sw = black
ro = red
br = brown
gn = green
bl = blue
gr = grey
li = lilac
ge = yellow

H3 - Warning buzzer
J285 - Control module with indicator unit in instrument panel insert
K1 - Headlight High Beam Indicator Light
K13 - Rear Fog Light Indicator Light
K14 - Parking Brake Indicator Light
K65 - Left Turn Signal Indicator Light
K94 - Right Turn Signal Indicator Light
K118 - Warning light for brake system
S22 - Fuse 22 in fuse holder
S223 - Fuse 23 in fuse holder
T5i - 5-Pin Connector, near left A-pillar, lower part, in harness
T32 - 32-Pin Connector, blue
T32a - 32-Pin Connector, green

(A5) - Plus connection (right turn signal), in instrument panel wiring harness
(A6) - Plus connection (left turn signal), in instrument panel wiring harness
(A51) - Wire connection (56), in instrument panel wiring harness
(A84) - Connector (58L) in instrument panel wiring harness
(A85) - Connector (58R) in instrument panel wiring harness
(A88) - Connector fog light, in instrument panel wiring harness

Instrument cluster, left and right turn signal indicator lights, parking brake indicator light, warning light for brake system, headlight high beam indicator light

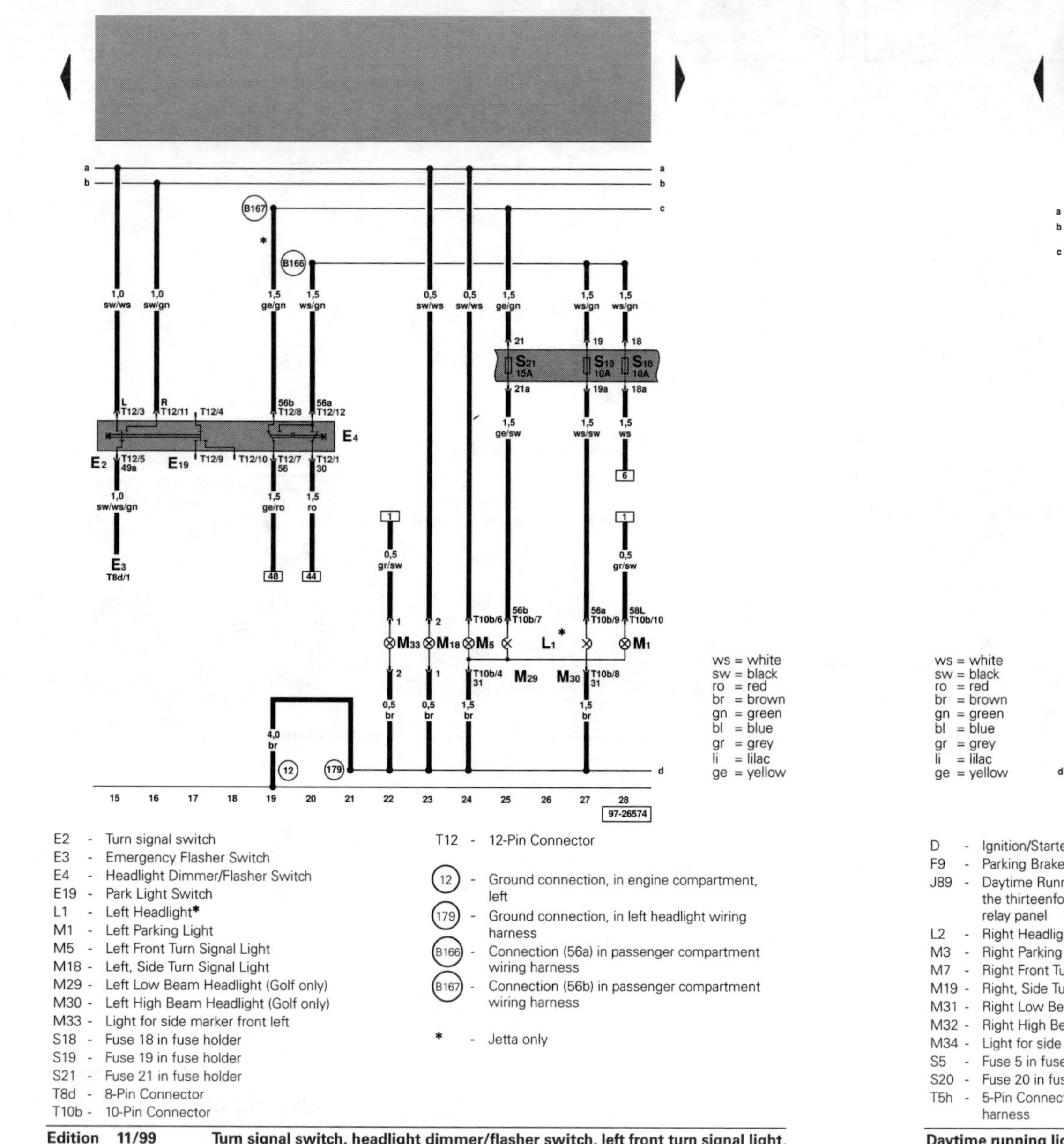

ws = white
sw = black
ro = red
br = brown
gn = green
bl = blue
gr = grey
li = lilac
ge = yellow

E2 - Turn signal switch
E3 - Emergency Flasher Switch
E4 - Headlight Dimmer/Flasher Switch
E19 - Park Light Switch
L1 - Left Headlight*
M1 - Left Parking Light
M5 - Left Front Turn Signal Light
M18 - Left, Side Turn Signal Light
M29 - Left Low Beam Headlight (Golf only)
M30 - Left High Beam Headlight (Golf only)
M33 - Light for side marker front left
S18 - Fuse 18 in fuse holder
S19 - Fuse 19 in fuse holder
S21 - Fuse 21 in fuse holder
T8d - 8-Pin Connector
T10b - 10-Pin Connector
T12 - 12-Pin Connector

(12) - Ground connection, in engine compartment, left
(179) - Ground connection, in left headlight wiring harness
(B166) - Connection (56a) in passenger compartment wiring harness
(B167) - Connection (56b) in passenger compartment wiring harness

* - Jetta only

Turn signal switch, headlight dimmer/flasher switch, left front turn signal light, light for side marker front left, left headlight

ws = white
sw = black
ro = red
br = brown
gn = green
bl = blue
gr = grey
li = lilac
ge = yellow

D - Ignition/Starter Switch
F9 - Parking Brake Warning Light Switch
J89 - Daytime Running Lights Change-over Relay, on the thirteenfold auxiliary relay panel, above relay panel
L2 - Right Headlight*
M3 - Right Parking Light
M7 - Right Front Turn Signal Light
M19 - Right, Side Turn Signal Light
M31 - Right Low Beam Headlight (Golf only)
M32 - Right High Beam Headlight (Golf only)
M34 - Light for side marker front right
S5 - Fuse 5 in fuse holder
S20 - Fuse 20 in fuse holder
T5h - 5-Pin Connector, near left A-pillar, lower part, in harness
T10c - 10-Pin Connector

(135) - Ground connection -2-, in instrument panel wiring harness
(179) - Ground connection, in left headlight wiring harness
(A2) - Plus connection (15), in instrument panel wiring harness
(A20) - Wire connection (15a), in instrument panel wiring harness

* - Jetta only

Daytime running lights change-over relay, parking brake warning light switch, right front turn signal light, light for side marker front right, right headlight

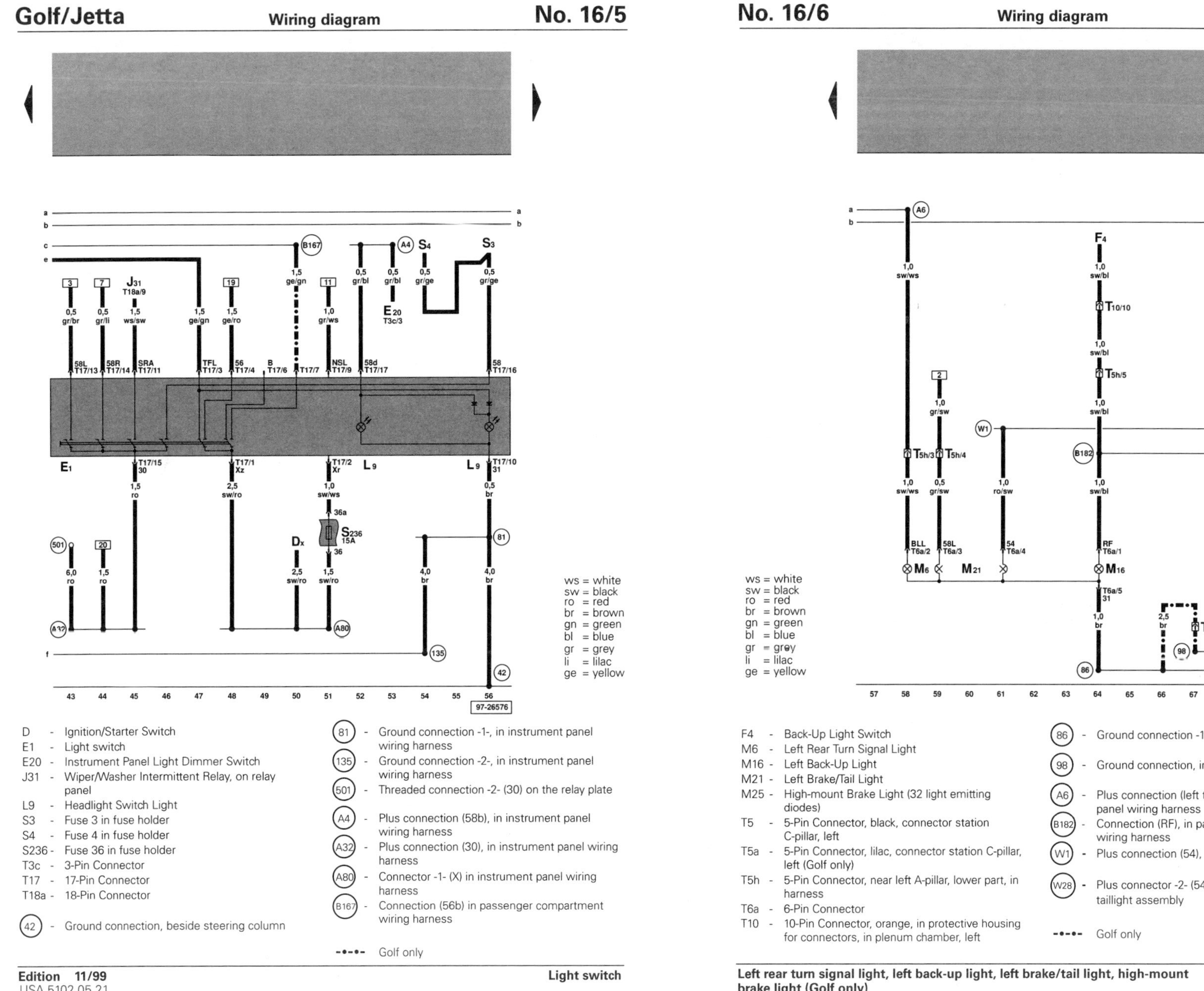

ws = white
sw = black
ro = red
br = brown
gn = green
bl = blue
gr = grey
li = lilac
ge = yellow

- D - Ignition/Starter Switch
- E1 - Light switch
- E20 - Instrument Panel Light Dimmer Switch
- J31 - Wiper/Washer Intermittent Relay, on relay panel
- L9 - Headlight Switch Light
- S3 - Fuse 3 in fuse holder
- S4 - Fuse 4 in fuse holder
- S236 - Fuse 36 in fuse holder
- T3c - 3-Pin Connector
- T17 - 17-Pin Connector
- T18a - 18-Pin Connector
- (42) - Ground connection, beside steering column
- (81) - Ground connection -1-, in instrument panel wiring harness
- (135) - Ground connection -2-, in instrument panel wiring harness
- (501) - Threaded connection -2- (30) on the relay plate
- (A4) - Plus connection (58b), in instrument panel wiring harness
- (A32) - Plus connection (30), in instrument panel wiring harness
- (A80) - Connector -1- (X) in instrument panel wiring harness
- (B167) - Connection (56b) in passenger compartment wiring harness
- -•-•- Golf only

Light switch

ws = white
sw = black
ro = red
br = brown
gn = green
bl = blue
gr = grey
li = lilac
ge = yellow

- F4 - Back-Up Light Switch
- M6 - Left Rear Turn Signal Light
- M16 - Left Back-Up Light
- M21 - Left Brake/Tail Light
- M25 - High-mount Brake Light (32 light emitting diodes)
- T5 - 5-Pin Connector, black, connector station C-pillar, left
- T5a - 5-Pin Connector, lilac, connector station C-pillar, left (Golf only)
- T5h - 5-Pin Connector, near left A-pillar, lower part, in harness
- T6a - 6-Pin Connector
- T10 - 10-Pin Connector, orange, in protective housing for connectors, in plenum chamber, left
- (86) - Ground connection -1-, in rear wiring harness
- (98) - Ground connection, in rear lid wiring harness
- (A6) - Plus connection (left turn signal), in instrument panel wiring harness
- (B182) - Connection (RF), in passenger compartment wiring harness
- (W1) - Plus connection (54), in rear wiring harness
- (W28) - Plus connector -2- (54), in wiring harness taillight assembly
- -•-•- Golf only

Left rear turn signal light, left back-up light, left brake/tail light, high-mount brake light (Golf only)

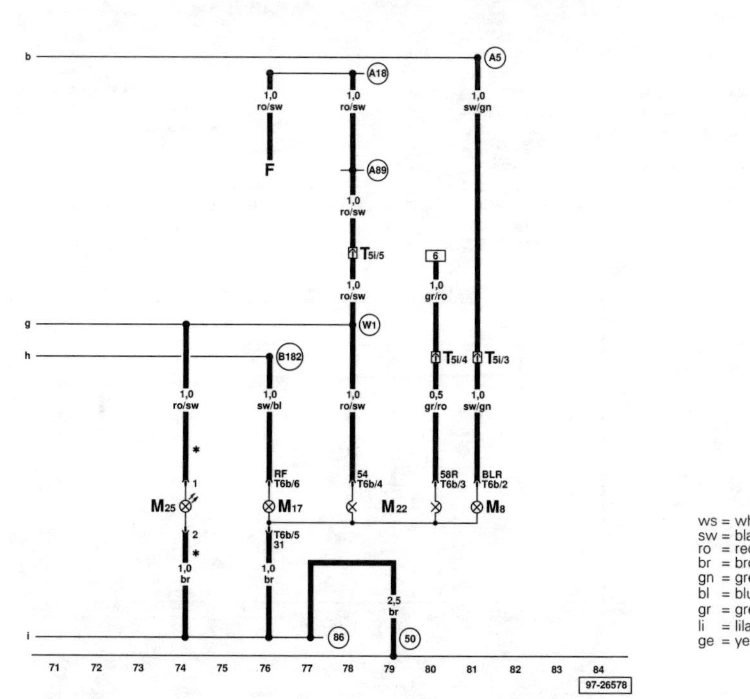

ws = white
sw = black
ro = red
br = brown
gn = green
bl = blue
gr = grey
li = lilac
ge = yellow

F - Brake Light Switch
M8 - Right Rear Turn Signal Light
M17 - Right Back-Up Light
M22 - Right Brake/Tail Light
M25 - High-mount Brake Light (18 light emitting diodes)*
T5i - 5-Pin Connector, near left A-pillar, lower part, in harness
T6b - 6-Pin Connector

(50) - Ground connection, in luggage compartment, left
(86) - Ground connection -1-, in rear wiring harness

(A5) - Plus connection (right turn signal), in instrument panel wiring harness

(A18) - Wire connection (54), in instrument panel wiring harness
(A89) - Connector (54), in instrument panel wiring harness
(B182) - Connection (RF), in passenger compartment wiring harness
(W1) - Plus connection (54), in rear wiring harness
* - Jetta only

Edition 11/99 USA.5102.05.21 **Right rear turn signal light, right back-up light, right brake/tail light, high-mount brake light (Jetta only)**

THIS PAGE INTENTIONALLY LEFT
BLANK

Fog lights,

from September 1998

Deviate relay location and fuseplacements as well as the locations of multiple connectors see section "component locations".

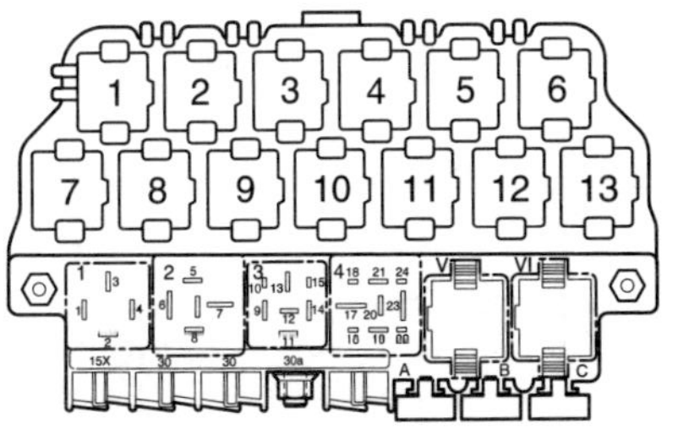

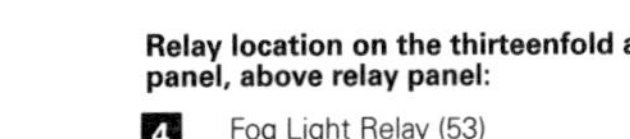

Relay location on the thirteenfold auxiliary relay panel, above relay panel:

4 Fog Light Relay (53)

Relay panel:

Note: Number in parentheses indicates production control number stamped on relay housing.

Fuse colors

30 A - green
25 A - white
20 A - yellow
15 A - blue
10 A - red
7,5 A - brown
5 A - beige
3 A - violet

Edition 11/99
USA.5102.05.21

ws = white
sw = black
ro = red
br = brown
gn = green
bl = blue
gr = grey
li = lilac
ge = yellow

J285 - Control module with indicator unit in instrument panel insert
K1 - Headlight High Beam Indicator Light
K13 - Rear Fog Light Indicator Light
K65 - Left Turn Signal Indicator Light
K94 - Right Turn Signal Indicator Light
L1 - Left Headlight*
L22 - Left Front Fog Light
M1 - Left Parking Light
M5 - Left Front Turn Signal Light
M18 - Left, Side Turn Signal Light
M29 - Left Low Beam Headlight (Golf only)
M30 - Left High Beam Headlight (Golf only)
M33 - Light for side marker front left
S19 - Fuse 19 in fuse holder
S21 - Fuse 21 in fuse holder

T10b - 10-Pin Connector
T32 - 32-Pin Connector, blue

(179) - Ground connection, in left headlight wiring harness
(A5) - Plus connection (right turn signal), in instrument panel wiring harness
(A6) - Plus connection (left turn signal), in instrument panel wiring harness
(A84) - Connector (58L), in instrument panel wiring harness
(B166) - Connection (56a), in passenger compartment wiring harness
(B167) - Connection (56b), in passenger compartment wiring harness
* - Jetta only

97-26579

Instrument cluster, headlight high beam indicator light, turn signal indicator lights, left headlight light, light for side marker front left, left front fog light

Edition 11/99
USA.5102.05.21

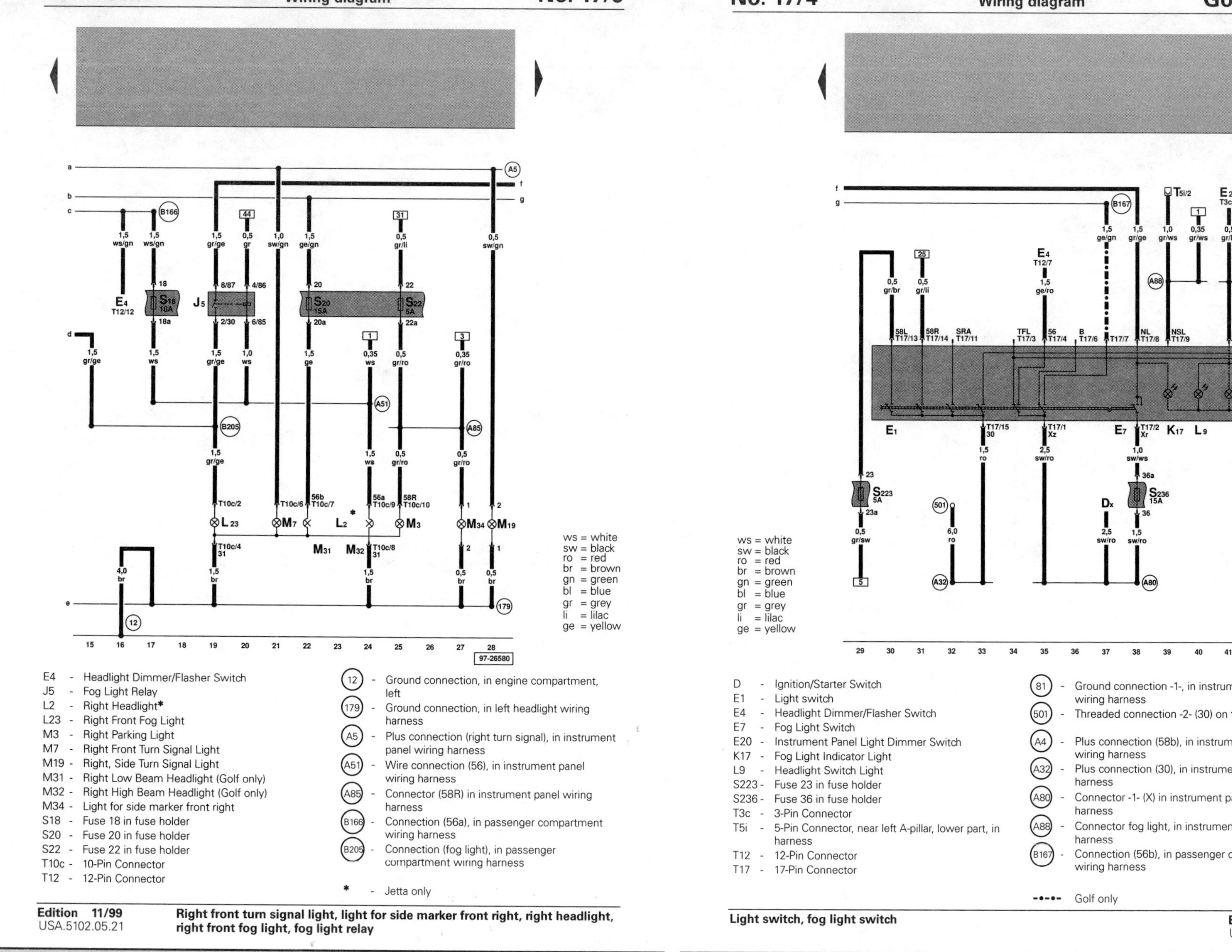

ws = white
sw = black
ro = red
br = brown
gn = green
bl = blue
gr = grey
li = lilac
ge = yellow

E4 - Headlight Dimmer/Flasher Switch
J5 - Fog Light Relay
L2 - Right Headlight*
L23 - Right Front Fog Light
M3 - Right Parking Light
M7 - Right Front Turn Signal Light
M19 - Right, Side Turn Signal Light
M31 - Right Low Beam Headlight (Golf only)
M32 - Right High Beam Headlight (Golf only)
M34 - Light for side marker front right
S18 - Fuse 18 in fuse holder
S20 - Fuse 20 in fuse holder
S22 - Fuse 22 in fuse holder
T10c - 10-Pin Connector
T12 - 12-Pin Connector

(12) - Ground connection, in engine compartment, left
(179) - Ground connection, in left headlight wiring harness
(A5) - Plus connection (right turn signal), in instrument panel wiring harness
(A51) - Wire connection (56), in instrument panel wiring harness
(A85) - Connector (58R) in instrument panel wiring harness
(B166) - Connection (56a), in passenger compartment wiring harness
(B205) - Connection (fog light), in passenger compartment wiring harness

* - Jetta only

Right front turn signal light, light for side marker front right, right headlight, right front fog light, fog light relay

ws = white
sw = black
ro = red
br = brown
gn = green
bl = blue
gr = grey
li = lilac
ge = yellow

D - Ignition/Starter Switch
E1 - Light switch
E4 - Headlight Dimmer/Flasher Switch
E7 - Fog Light Switch
E20 - Instrument Panel Light Dimmer Switch
K17 - Fog Light Indicator Light
L9 - Headlight Switch Light
S223 - Fuse 23 in fuse holder
S236 - Fuse 36 in fuse holder
T3c - 3-Pin Connector
T5i - 5-Pin Connector, near left A-pillar, lower part, in harness
T12 - 12-Pin Connector
T17 - 17-Pin Connector

(81) - Ground connection -1-, in instrument panel wiring harness
(501) - Threaded connection -2- (30) on the relay plate
(A4) - Plus connection (58b), in instrument panel wiring harness
(A32) - Plus connection (30), in instrument panel wiring harness
(A80) - Connector -1- (X) in instrument panel wiring harness
(A88) - Connector fog light, in instrument panel wiring harness
(B167) - Connection (56b), in passenger compartment wiring harness

-•-•- Golf only

Light switch, fog light switch

ws = white
sw = black
ro = red
br = brown
gn = green
bl = blue
gr = grey
li = lilac
ge = yellow

S3 - Fuse 3 in fuse holder
S4 - Fuse 4 in fuse holder
T2 - Double Connector, in luggage compartment, left (Golf only)
T5 - 5-Pin Connector, black, connector station C-pillar, left
X - License Plate Light

(50) - Ground connection, in luggage compartment, left
(86) - Ground connection -1-, in rear wiring harness
(218) - Ground connection -1-, in rear lid wiring harness
(A37) - Wire connection (58a), in instrument panel wiring harness

(W11) - Wire connection (58), in rear lid wiring harness
(W41) - Plus connection (58), in wiring harness
* - Jetta only
-•-•- Golf only

THIS PAGE INTENTIONALLY LEFT BLANK

Headlight washer,

from September 1998

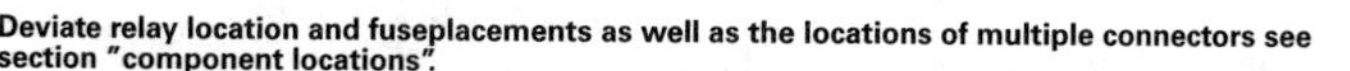

Deviate relay location and fuseplacements as well as the locations of multiple connectors see section "component locations".

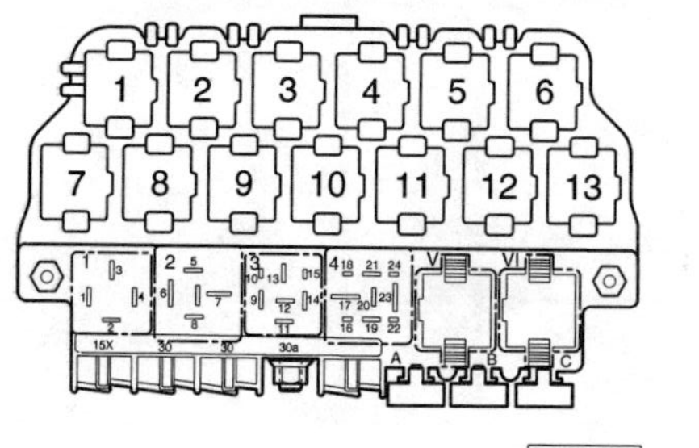

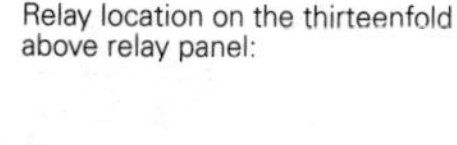

Relay location on the thirteenfold auxiliary relay panel, above relay panel:

Relay panel:

V **VI** Wiper/Washer Intermittent Relay (389)

Note: Number in parentheses indicates production control number stamped on relay housing.

Fuse colors

- 30 A - green
- 25 A - white
- 20 A - yellow
- 15 A - blue
- 10 A - red
- 7,5 A - brown
- 5 A - beige
- 3 A - violet

Edition 03/01
USA.5102.10.21

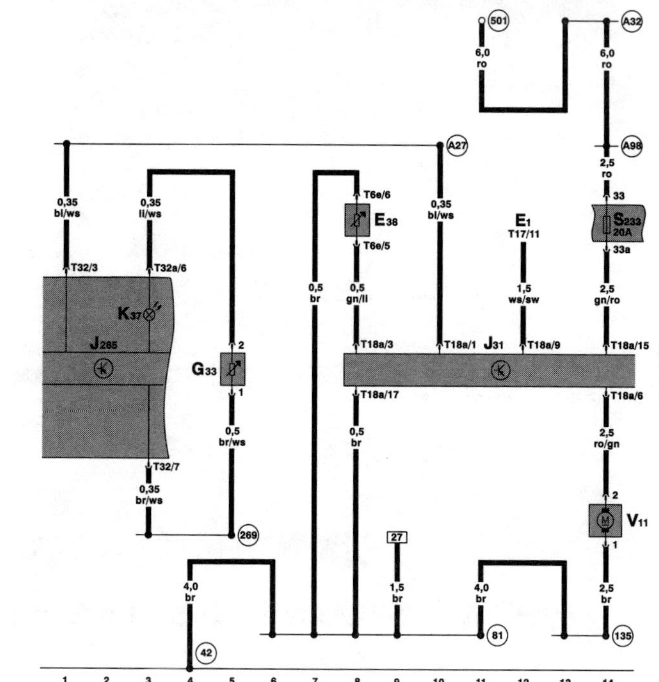

ws = white
sw = black
ro = red
br = brown
gn = green
bl = blue
gr = grey
li = lilac
ge = yellow
or = orange

E1 - Light switch
E38 - Windshield Wiper Intermittent Regulator
G33 - Windshield Washer Fluid Level Sensor
J31 - Wiper/Washer Intermittent Relay, on relais panel
J285 - Control module with indicator unit in instrument panel insert
K37 - Low Windshield Washer Fluid Level Indicator Light
S233 - Fuse 33 in fuse holder
T6e - 6-Pin Connector
T17 - 17-Pin Connector
T18a - 18-Pin Connector
T32 - 32-Pin Connector, blue
T32a - 32-Pin Connector, green
V11 - Headlight Washer Pump

(42) - Ground connection, beside steering column
(81) - Ground connection -1-, in instrument panel wiring harness
(135) - Ground connection -2-, in instrument panel wiring harness
(269) - Ground connector (sensor ground) -1-, in instrument panel wiring harness
(501) - Threaded connection -2- (30) on the relay plate
(A27) - Wire connection (vehicle speed signal), in instrument panel wiring harness
(A32) - Plus connection (30), in instrument panel wiring harness
(A98) - Plus connector -4- (30), in instrument panel wiring harness

Wiper/washer intermittent relay, windshield wiper intermittent regulator, windshield washer fluid level sensor, headlight washer pump, instrument cluster

Edition 03/01
USA.5102.10.21

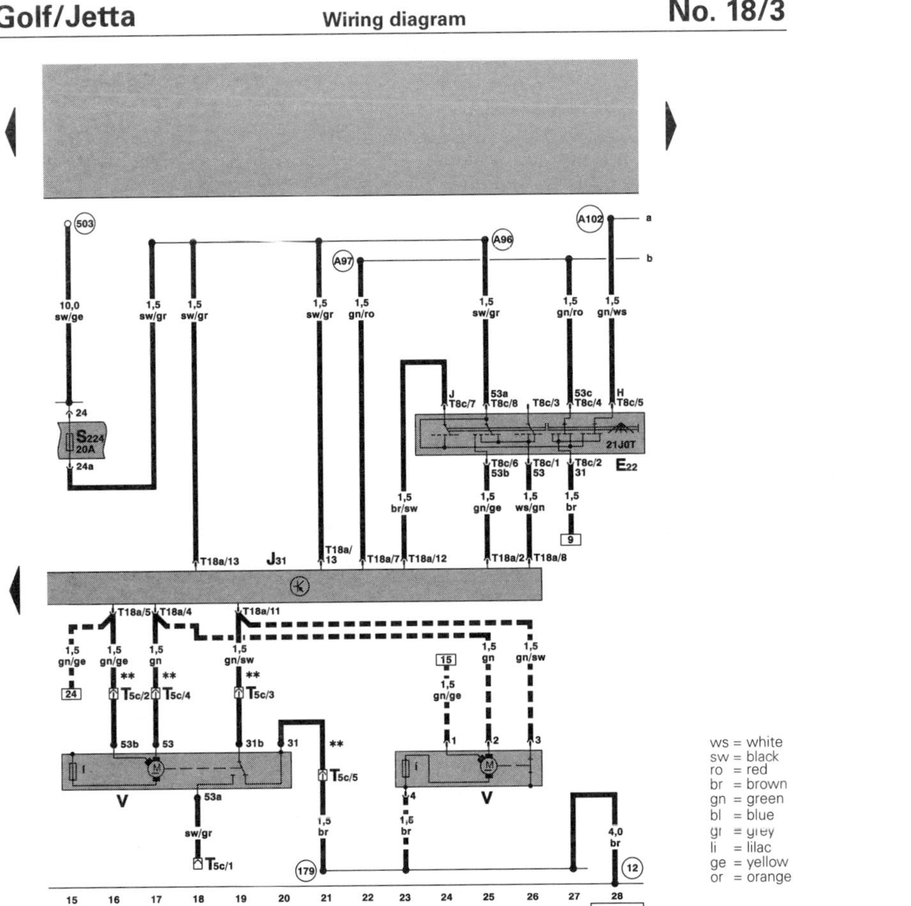

ws = white
sw = black
ro = red
br = brown
gn = green
bl = blue
gr = grey
li = lilac
ge = yellow
or = orange

E22 - Windshield Wiper/Washer Switch
J31 - Wiper/Washer Intermittent Relay, on relais panel
S224 - Fuse 24 in fuse holder
T5c - 5-Pin Connector, on windshield wiper motor
T8c - 8-Pin Connector
T18a - 18-Pin Connector
V - Windshield Wiper Motor

(12) - Ground connection, in engine compartment, left
(179) - Ground connection, in left headlight wiring harness
(503) - Threaded connection -2- (75x) on the relay plate

(A96) - Connector (53a), in instrument panel wiring harness
(A97) - Connector (53), in instrument panel wiring harness
(A102) - Connector (windshield wiper), in instrument panel wiring harness

** - Through August 2000
- - - Beginning September 2000

Wiper/washer intermittent relay, windshield wiper/washer switch, windshield wiper motor

T5a - 5-Pin Connector, pink, connector station C-pillar, left (Golf only)
T5h - 5-Pin Connector, near left A-pillar, lower part, in harness
T5i - 5-Pin Connector, near left A-pillar, lower part, in harness
V12 - Motor for rear windshield wiper
V59 - Windshield and Rear Window Washer Pump

(50) - Ground connection, in luggage compartment, left
(86) - Ground connection -1-, in rear wiring harness
(98) - Ground connection, in rear lid wiring harness

(A97) - Connector (53), in instrument panel wiring harness
(A102) - Connector (windshield wiper), in instrument panel wiring harness

-•-•- Golf only

Motor for rear windshield wiper, windshield and rear window washer pump

Heated seats,

from September 1998

Deviate relay location and fuseplacements as well as the locations of multiple connectors see section "component locations".

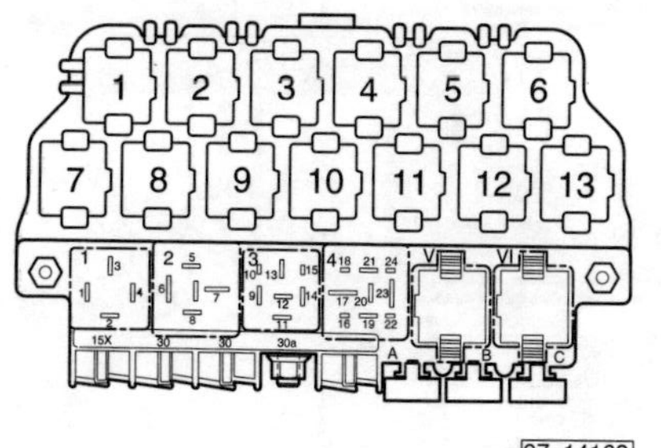

Fuse colors

30 A - green
25 A - white
20 A - yellow
15 A - blue
10 A - red
7,5 A - brown
5 A - beige
3 A - violet

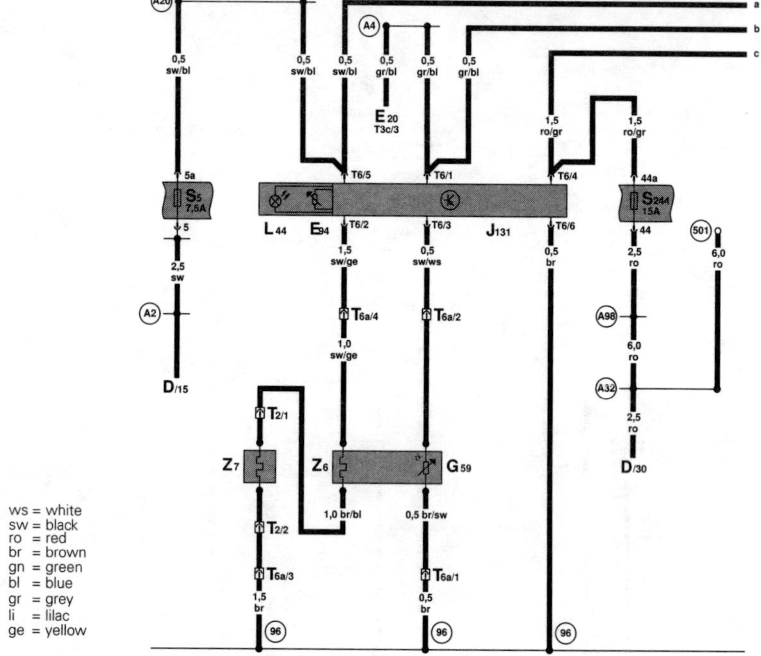

ws = white
sw = black
ro = red
br = brown
gn = green
bl = blue
gr = grey
li = lilac
ge = yellow

- D - Ignition/Starter Switch
- E20 - Instrument Panel Light Dimmer Switch
- E94 - Adjuster for heated driver's seat
- G59 - Driver's Heated Seat Temperature Sensor
- J131 - Driver's Heated Seat Control Module
- L44 - Heated Seat Switch Illumination Light
- S5 - Fuse 5 in fuse holder
- S244 - Fuse 44 in fuse holder
- T2 - Double Connector, below driver's seat
- T3c - 3-Pin Connector
- T6 - 6-Pin Connector
- T6a - 6-Pin Connector, green, below driver's seat
- Z6 - Driver's Seat Heating Element
- Z7 - Driver's Backrest Heating Element

- (96) - Ground connection -1-, in heated seats wiring harness
- (501) - Threaded connection -2- (30) on the relay plate
- (A2) - Plus connection (15), in instrument panel wiring harness
- (A4) - Plus connection (58b), in instrument panel wiring harness
- (A20) - Wire connection (15a), in instrument panel wiring harness
- (A32) - Plus connection (30), in instrument panel wiring harness
- (A98) - Plus connector -4- (30), in instrument panel wiring harness

Driver's heated seat control module, driver's heated seat temperature sensor, driver's seat heating element, driver's backrest heating element

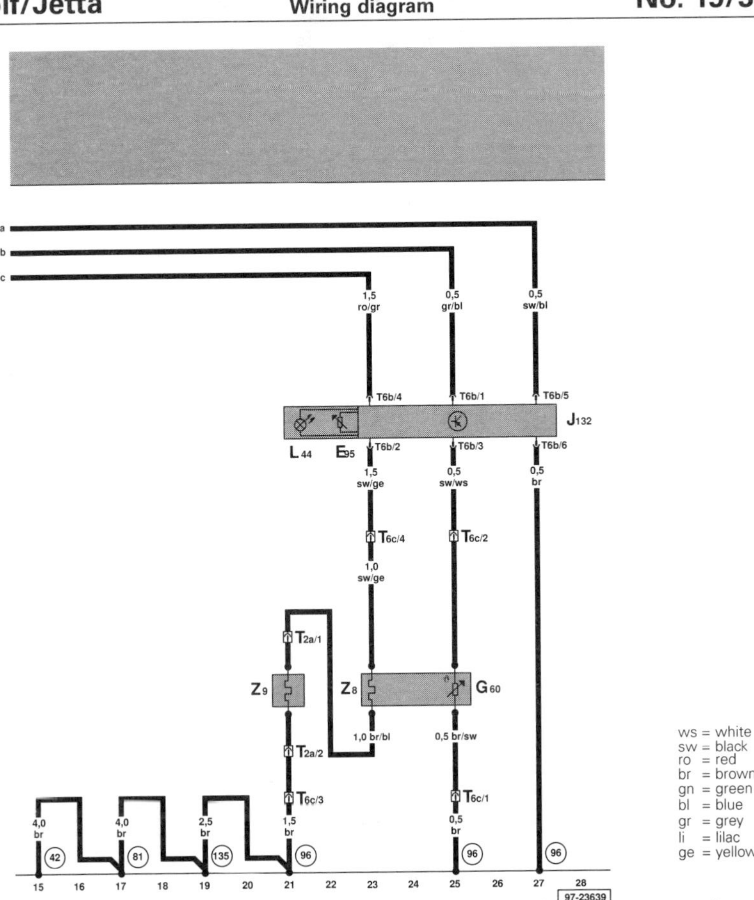

ws = white
sw = black
ro = red
br = brown
gn = green
bl = blue
gr = grey
li = lilac
ge = yellow

E95 - Adjuster for heated passenger seat
G60 - Passenger's Heated Seat Temperature Sensor
J132 - Passenger's Heated Seat Control Module
L44 - Heated Seat Switch Illumination Light
T2a - Double Connector, below passenger's seat
T6b - 6-Pin Connector
T6c - 6-Pin Connector, green, below passenger's seat
Z8 - Passenger's Seat Heating Element
Z9 - Passenger's Backrest Heating Element

(42) - Ground connection, beside steering column

(81) - Ground connection -1-, in instrument panel wiring harness

(96) - Ground connection -1-, in heated seats wiring harness

(135) - Ground connection -2-, in instrument panel wiring harness

Passenger's heated seat control module, passenger's heated seat temperature sensor, passenger's seat heating element, passenger's backrest heating element

THIS PAGE INTENTIONALLY LEFT
BLANK

Heated leather seats,

from September 1998

Deviate relay location and fuseplacements as well as the locations of multiple connectors see section "component locations".

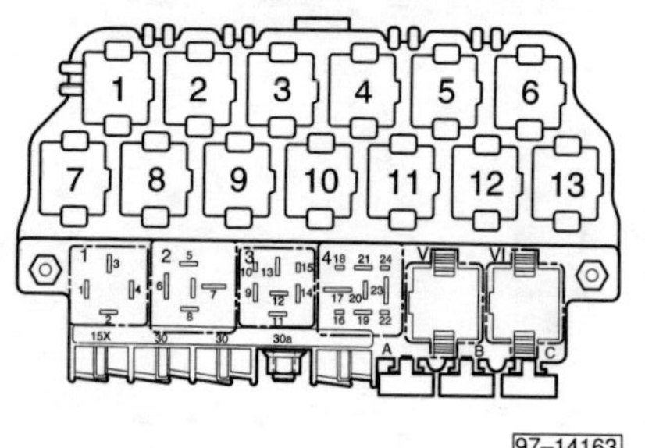

Fuse colors

30 A - green
25 A - white
20 A - yellow
15 A - blue
10 A - red
7,5 A - brown
5 A - beige
3 A - violet

ws = white
sw = black
ro = red
br = brown
gn = green
bl = blue
gr = grey
li = lilac
ge = yellow

97-23640

T2 - Double Connector, below driver's seat
T2b - Double Connector, below driver's seat
T6a - 6-Pin Connector, green, below driver's seat
Z7 - Driver's Seat Backrest Heater
Z31 - Driver's Seat Side Bolster Heater
Z40 - Driver's Seat Side Bolster Heater 2

(96) - Ground connection -1-, in heated seats wiring harness
(135) - Ground connection -2-, in instrument panel wiring harness
(136) - Ground connection -2-, in heated seats wiring harness
(O4) - Plus connection (30a), in heated seats wiring harness

Driver's seat backrest and side bolster heaters

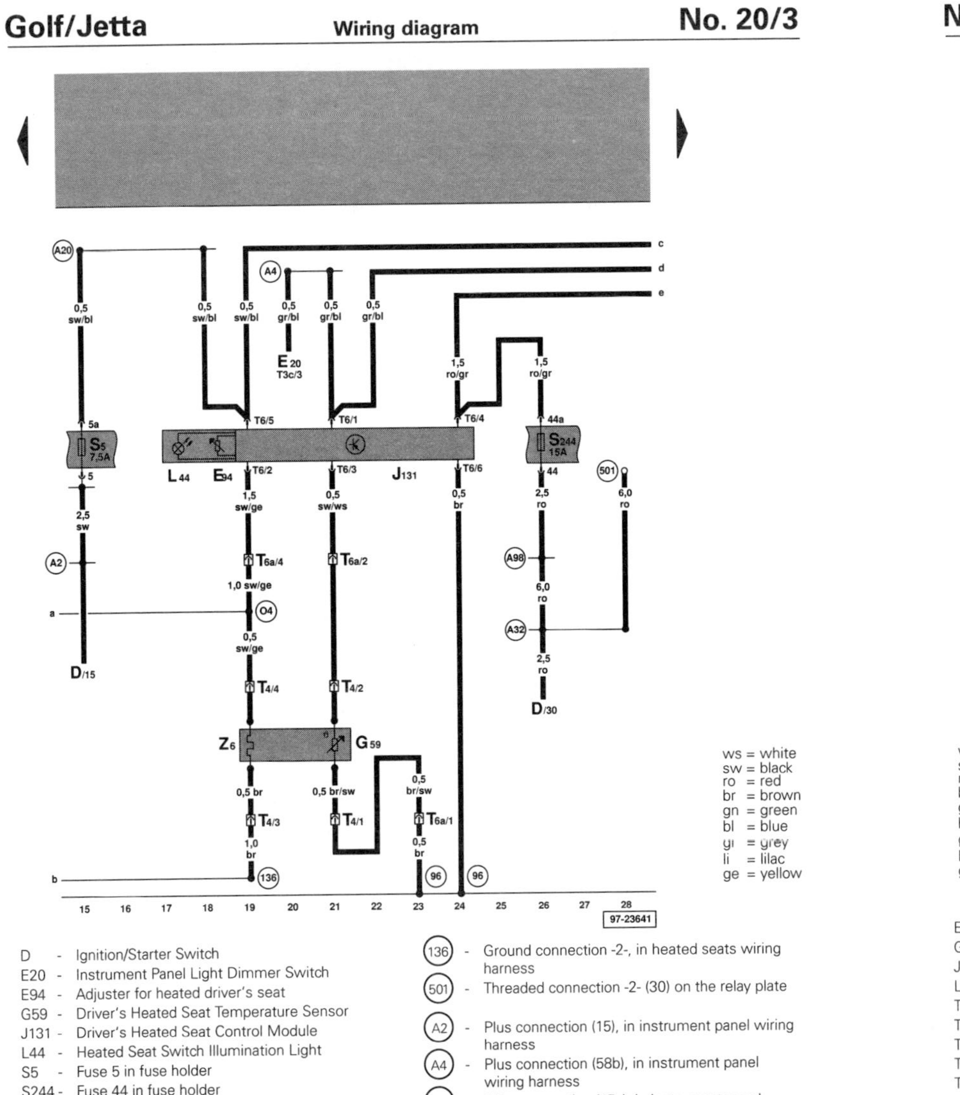

ws = white
sw = black
ro = red
br = brown
gn = green
bl = blue
gr = grey
li = lilac
ge = yellow

D - Ignition/Starter Switch
E20 - Instrument Panel Light Dimmer Switch
E94 - Adjuster for heated driver's seat
G59 - Driver's Heated Seat Temperature Sensor
J131 - Driver's Heated Seat Control Module
L44 - Heated Seat Switch Illumination Light
S5 - Fuse 5 in fuse holder
S244 - Fuse 44 in fuse holder
T3c - 3-Pin Connector
T4 - 4-Pin Connector, below driver's seat
T6 - 6-Pin Connector
T6a - 6-Pin Connector, green, below driver's seat
Z6 - Driver's Seat Heater

(96) - Ground connection -1-, in heated seats wiring harness

(136) - Ground connection -2-, in heated seats wiring harness
(501) - Threaded connection -2- (30) on the relay plate
(A2) - Plus connection (15), in instrument panel wiring harness
(A4) - Plus connection (58b), in instrument panel wiring harness
(A20) - Wire connection (15a), in instrument panel wiring harness
(A32) - Plus connection (30), in instrument panel wiring harness
(A98) - Plus connector -4- (30), in instrument panel wiring harness
(O4) - Plus connection (30a), in heated seats wiring harness

Edition 12/98
USA.5102.01.21

Driver's heated seat control module, driver's heated seat temperature sensor, driver's seat heater

ws = white
sw = black
ro = red
br = brown
gn = green
bl = blue
gr = grey
li = lilac
ge = yellow

E95 - Adjuster for heated passenger seat
G60 - Passenger's Heated Seat Temperature Sensor
J132 - Passenger's Heated Seat Control Module
L44 - Heated Seat Switch Illumination Light
T2a - Double Connector, below passenger's seat
T2c - Double Connector, below passenger's seat
T4a - 4-Pin Connector, below passenger's seat
T6b - 6-Pin Connector
T6c - 6-Pin Connector, green, below passenger's seat
Z8 - Passenger's Seat Heater
Z9 - Passenger's Seat Backrest Heater
Z33 - Passenger's Seat Side Bolster Heater
Z41 - Passengers Seat Side Bolster Heater 2

(96) - Ground connection -1-, in heated seats wiring harness

(145) - Ground connection -3-, in heated seats wiring harness
(O10) - Plus connector -2- (30a), in wiring harness heated seat

Passenger's heated seat control module, passenger's heated seat temperature sensor, passenger's seat heater, backrest and side bolster heaters

Edition 12/98
USA.5102.01.21

Washer nozzle heaters,

from September 1998

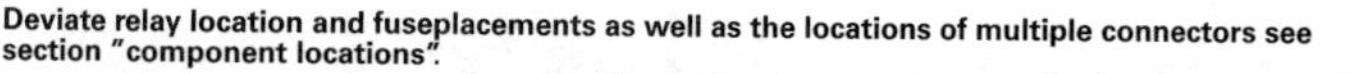

Deviate relay location and fuseplacements as well as the locations of multiple connectors see section "component locations".

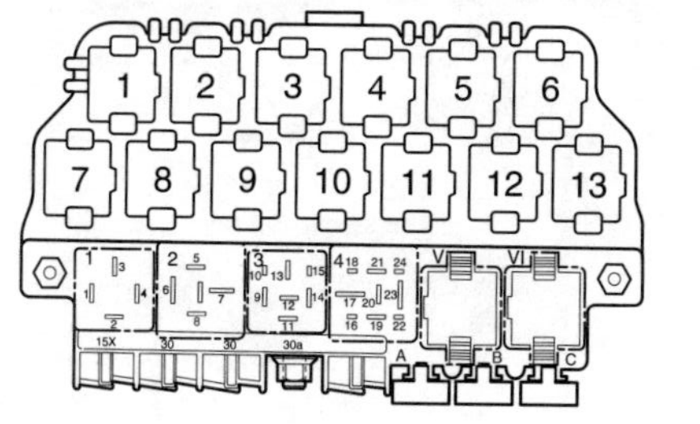

Relay location on the thirteenfold auxiliary relay panel, above relay panel:

Relay panel:

2 Load Reduction Relay (18)

Note: Number in parentheses indicates production control number stamped on relay housing.

Fuse colors

30 A - green
25 A - white
20 A - yellow
15 A - blue
10 A - red
7,5 A - brown
5 A - beige
3 A - violet

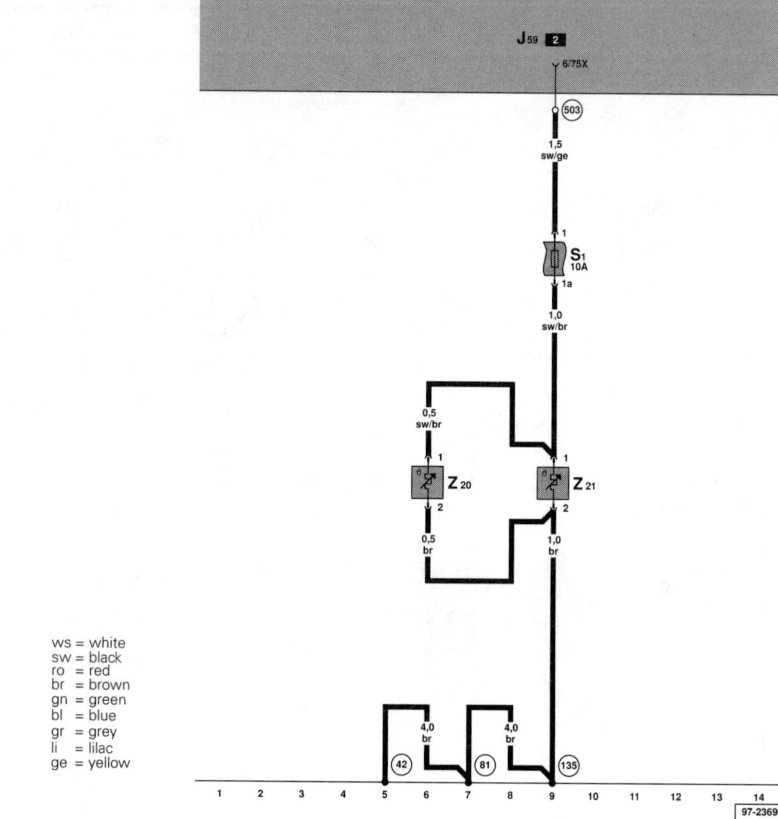

ws = white
sw = black
ro = red
br = brown
gn = green
bl = blue
gr = grey
li = lilac
ge = yellow

J59 - Load Reduction Relay
S1 - Fuse 1 in fuse holder
Z20 - Left Washer Nozzle Heater
Z21 - Right Washer Nozzle Heater

(42) - Ground connection, beside steering column

(81) - Ground connection -1-, in instrument panel wiring harness

(135) - Ground connection -2-, in instrument panel wiring harness

(501) - Threaded connection -2- (30) on the relay plate

Power outlet (12V),

from September 1998

Deviate relay location and fuseplacements as well as the locations of multiple connectors see section "component locations".

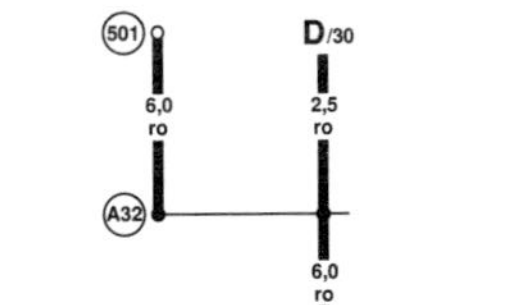

Fuse colors

30 A - green
25 A - white
20 A - yellow
15 A - blue
10 A - red
7,5 A - brown
5 A - beige
3 A - violet

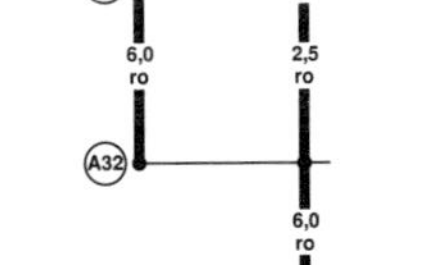

ws = white
sw = black
ro = red
br = brown
gn = green
bl = blue
gr = grey
li = lilac
ge = yellow

D - Ignition/Starter Switch
S235 - Fuse 35 in fuse holder
T3 - 3-Pin Connector
U5 - 12 V-Socket, in luggage compartment, right

(50) - Ground connection, in luggage compartment, left
(86) - Ground connection -1-, in rear wiring harness
(501) - Threaded connection -2- (30) on the relay plate
(A32) - Plus connection (30), in instrument panel wiring harness
(A98) - Plus connector -4- (30), in instrument panel wiring harness

12 V-Socket

Climatronic (automatic climate control),

from December 1998

- **2.8L - Engine - Motronic Multiport Fuel Injection (MFI)/130 kW, code AFP**

Deviate relay location and fuseplacements as well as the locations of multiple connectors see section "component locations".

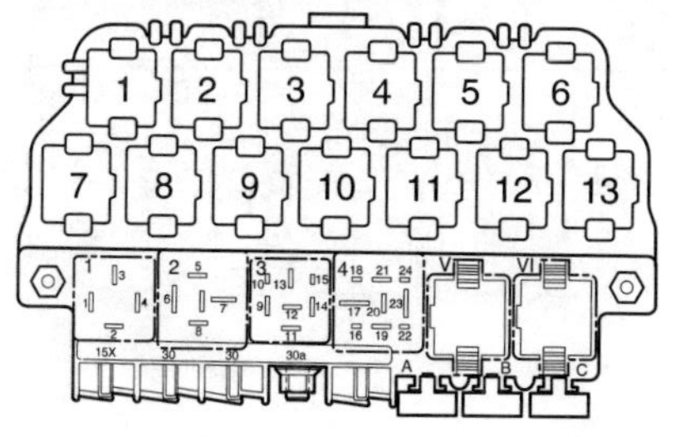

Fuse colors

30 A - green
25 A - white
20 A - yellow
15 A - blue
10 A - red
7,5 A - brown
5 A - beige
3 A - violet

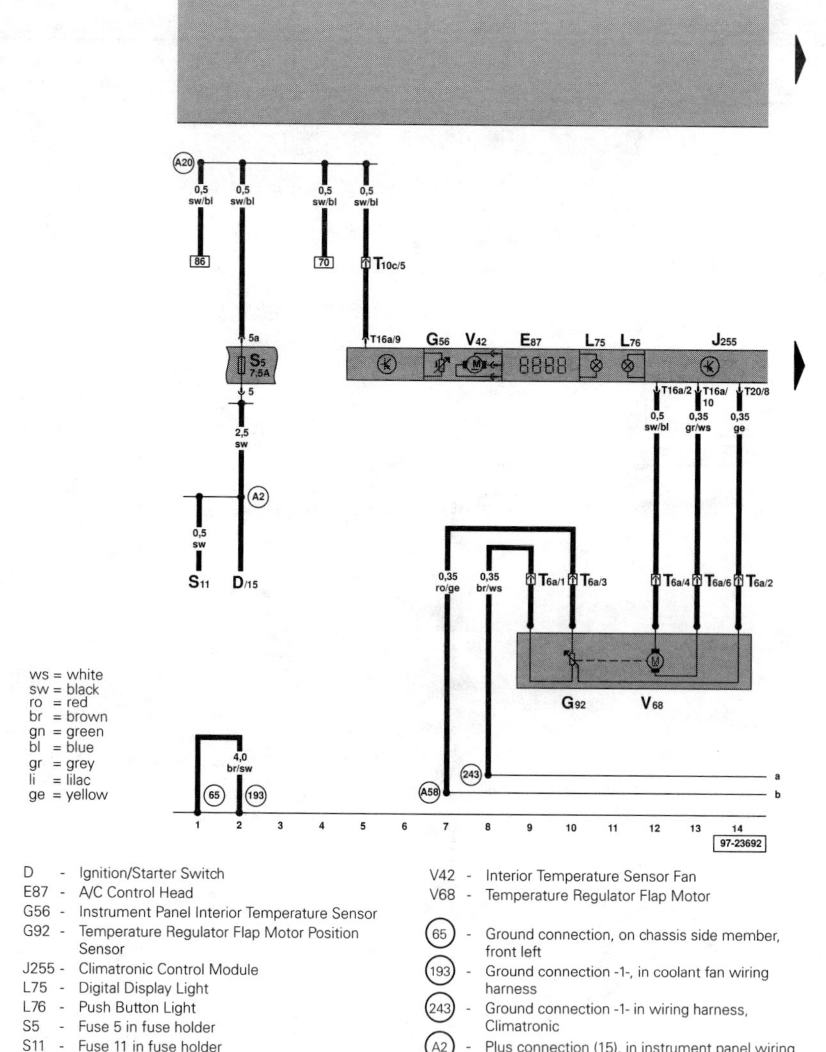

ws = white
sw = black
ro = red
br = brown
gn = green
bl = blue
gr = grey
li = lilac
ge = yellow

D - Ignition/Starter Switch
E87 - A/C Control Head
G56 - Instrument Panel Interior Temperature Sensor
G92 - Temperature Regulator Flap Motor Position Sensor
J255 - Climatronic Control Module
L75 - Digital Display Light
L76 - Push Button Light
S5 - Fuse 5 in fuse holder
S11 - Fuse 11 in fuse holder
T6a - 6-Pin Connector, behind instrument panel, center
T10c - 10-Pin Connector, behind instrument panel, center
T16a - 16-Pin Connector
T20 - 20-Pin Connector
V42 - Interior Temperature Sensor Fan
V68 - Temperature Regulator Flap Motor

(65) - Ground connection, on chassis side member, front left
(193) - Ground connection -1-, in coolant fan wiring harness
(243) - Ground connection -1- in wiring harness, Climatronic
(A2) - Plus connection (15), in instrument panel wiring harness
(A20) - Wire connection (15a), in instrument panel wiring harness
(A58) - Wire connection (5 V), in instrument cluster wiring harness

Climatronic control module, temperature regulator flap motor position sensor

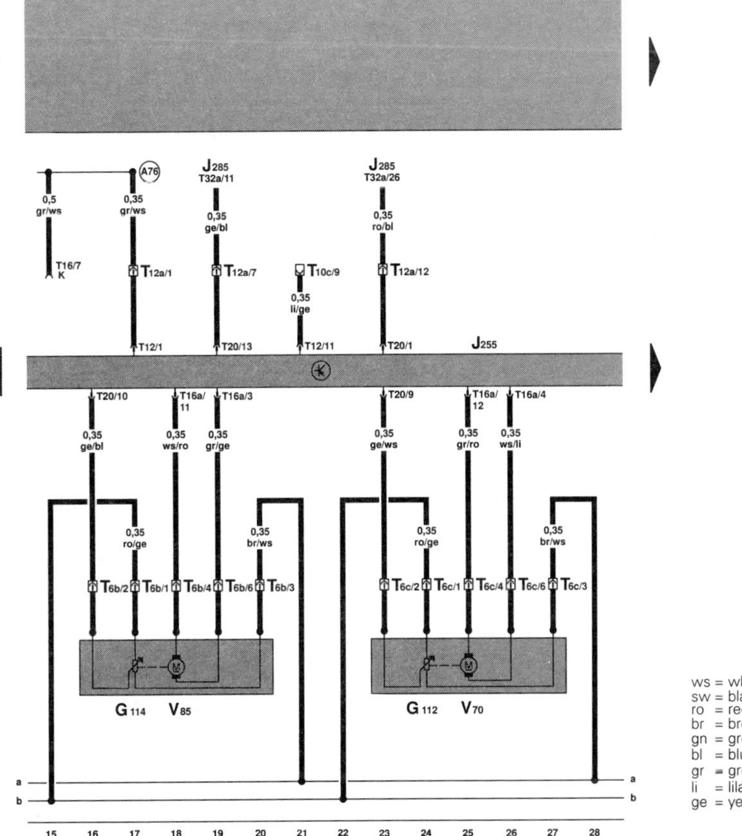

ws = white
sw = black
ro = red
br = brown
gn = green
bl = blue
gr = groy
li = lilac
ge = yellow

G112 - Central Flap Motor Position Sensor
G114 - Footwell/Defrost Flap Motor Position Sensor
J255 - Climatronic Control Module
J285 - Control module with indicator unit in instrument panel insert
T6b - 6-Pin Connector, behind instrument panel, center
T6c - 6-Pin Connector, behind instrument panel, center
T10c - 10-Pin Connector, behind instrument panel, center
T12 - 12-Pin Connector
T12a - 12-Pin Connector, behind instrument panel, center
T16 - Data Link Connector (DLC), below instrument panel, left
T16a - 16-Pin Connector
T20 - 20-Pin Connector
T32a - 32-Pin Connector, green
V70 - Central Air Flap Motor
V85 - Footwell/Defroster Flap Motor
(A76) - Connector (K-diagnosis wire) in instrument panel wiring harness

Climatronic control module, central flap motor position sensor, central air flap motor, footwell/defrost flap motor position sensor, footwell/defrost flap motor

ws = white
sw = black
ro = red
br = brown
gn = green
bl = blue
gr = grey
li = lilac
ge = yellow

G89 - Fresh Air Intake Duct Temperature Sensor, below instrument panel, right
G113 - Back Pressure Flap Motor Position Sensor
G192 - Sender for outlet temperature, floor outlet
J220 - Motronic Engine Control Module (ECM), in plenum chamber, center
J255 - Climatronic Control Module
J285 - Control module with indicator unit in instrument panel insert
T5 - 5-Pin Connector, behind instrument panel, center
T10 - 10-Pin Connector, orange, in protective housing for connectors, in plenum chamber, left
T10c - 10-Pin Connector, behind instrument panel, center
T12 - 12-Pin Connector
T16a - 16-Pin Connector
T16b - 16-Pin Connector
T20 - 20-Pin Connector
T32 - 32-Pin Connector, blue
T121 - Connector, 121 point, on Motronic Engine Control Module (ECM)
V71 - Air Flow Flap Motor
(A45) - Wire connection (RPM-signal), in instrument panel wiring harness
(A58) - Wire connection (5 V), in instrument cluster wiring harness

Climatronic control module, fresh air intake duct temperature sensor, sender for outlet temperature, air flow flap motor, back pressure flap motor position sensor

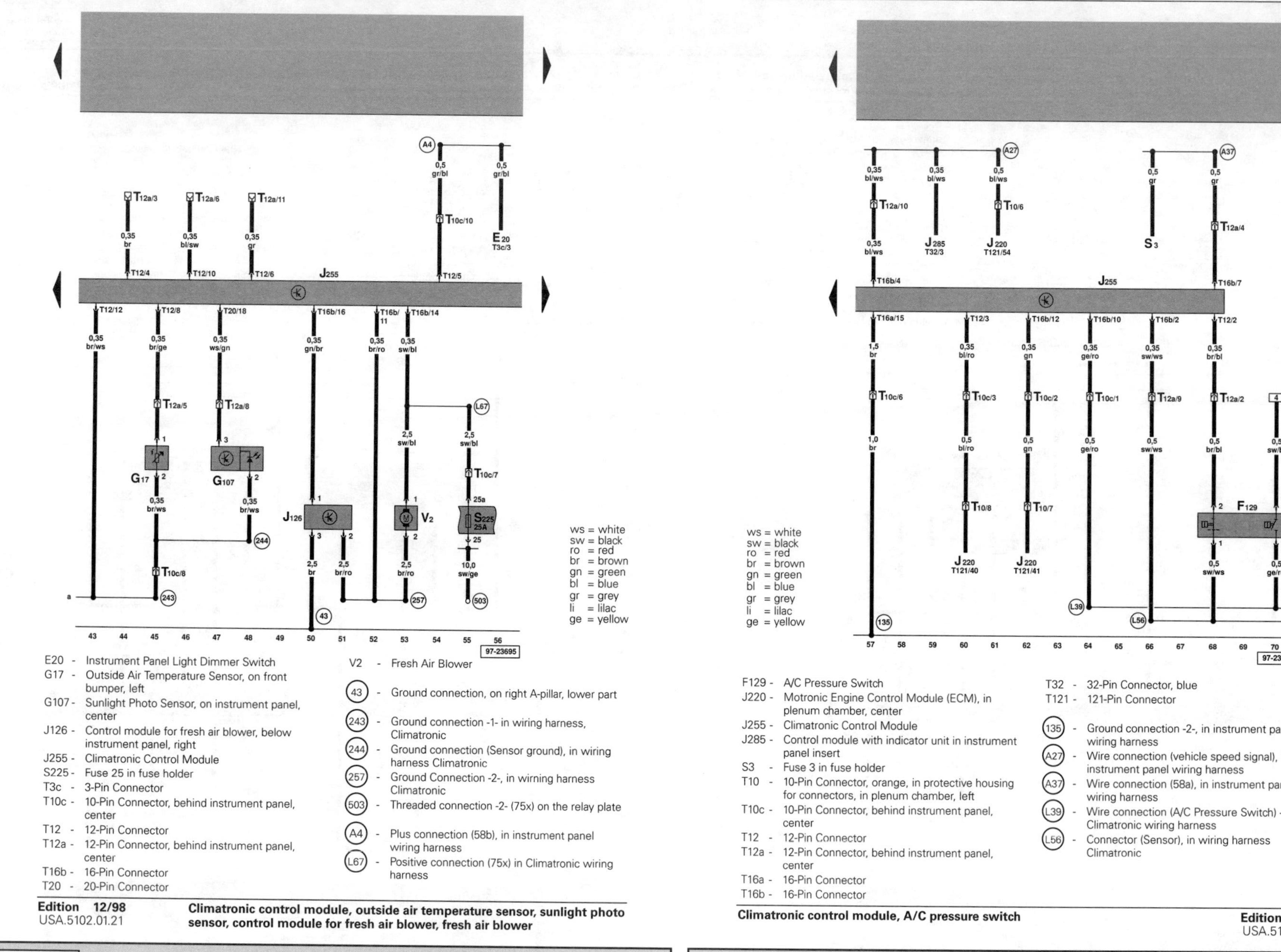

ws = white
sw = black
ro = red
br = brown
gn = green
bl = blue
gr = grey
li = lilac
ge = yellow

E20 - Instrument Panel Light Dimmer Switch
G17 - Outside Air Temperature Sensor, on front bumper, left
G107 - Sunlight Photo Sensor, on instrument panel, center
J126 - Control module for fresh air blower, below instrument panel, right
J255 - Climatronic Control Module
S225 - Fuse 25 in fuse holder
T3c - 3-Pin Connector
T10c - 10-Pin Connector, behind instrument panel, center
T12 - 12-Pin Connector
T12a - 12-Pin Connector, behind instrument panel, center
T16b - 16-Pin Connector
T20 - 20-Pin Connector

V2 - Fresh Air Blower

(43) - Ground connection, on right A-pillar, lower part
(243) - Ground connection -1- in wiring harness, Climatronic
(244) - Ground connection (Sensor ground), in wiring harness Climatronic
(257) - Ground Connection -2-, in wirning harness Climatronic
(503) - Threaded connection -2- (75x) on the relay plate
(A4) - Plus connection (58b), in instrument panel wiring harness
(L67) - Positive connection (75x) in Climatronic wiring harness

Climatronic control module, outside air temperature sensor, sunlight photo sensor, control module for fresh air blower, fresh air blower

ws = white
sw = black
ro = red
br = brown
gn = green
bl = blue
gr = grey
li = lilac
ge = yellow

F129 - A/C Pressure Switch
J220 - Motronic Engine Control Module (ECM), in plenum chamber, center
J255 - Climatronic Control Module
J285 - Control module with indicator unit in instrument panel insert
S3 - Fuse 3 in fuse holder
T10 - 10-Pin Connector, orange, in protective housing for connectors, in plenum chamber, left
T10c - 10-Pin Connector, behind instrument panel, center
T12 - 12-Pin Connector
T12a - 12-Pin Connector, behind instrument panel, center
T16a - 16-Pin Connector
T16b - 16-Pin Connector

T32 - 32-Pin Connector, blue
T121 - 121-Pin Connector

(135) - Ground connection -2-, in instrument panel wiring harness
(A27) - Wire connection (vehicle speed signal), in instrument panel wiring harness
(A37) - Wire connection (58a), in instrument panel wiring harness
(L39) - Wire connection (A/C Pressure Switch) -1-, in Climatronic wiring harness
(L56) - Connector (Sensor), in wiring harness Climatronic

Climatronic control module, A/C pressure switch

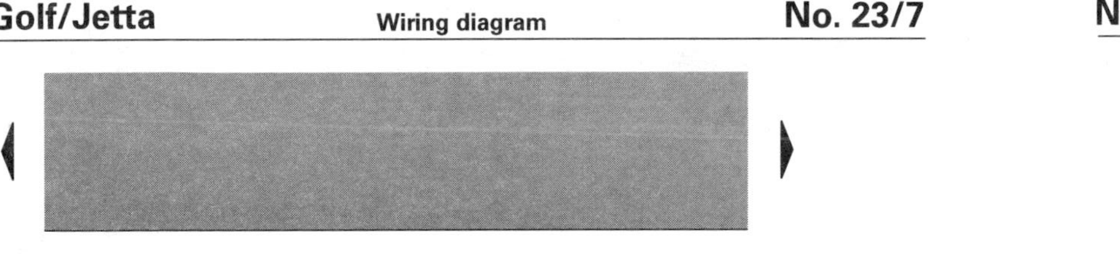

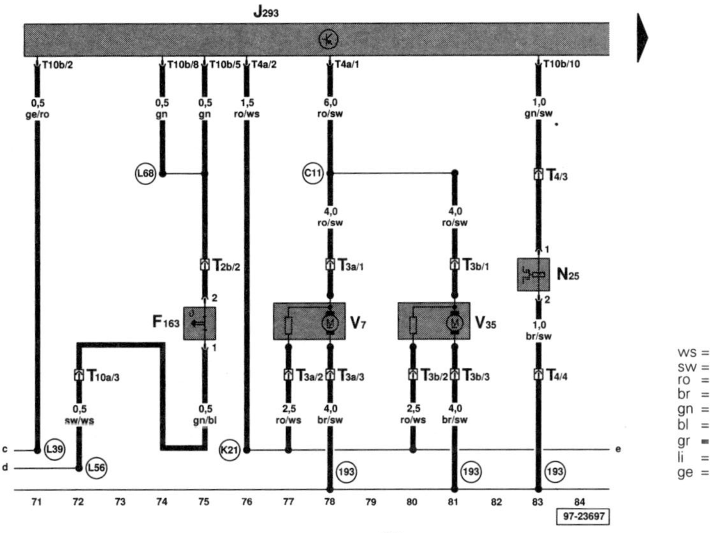

ws = white
sw = black
ro = red
br = brown
gn = green
bl = blue
gr = grey
li = lilac
ge = yellow

F163 - A/C Cut-Out Thermal Switch
J293 - Coolant Fan Control (FC) Control Module, in engine compartment, left
N25 - A/C Clutch
T2b - Double Connector, in engine compartment, in wiring duct, left
T3a - 3-Pin Connector, in engine compartment, left
T3b - 3-Pin Connector, in engine compartment, left
T4 - 4-Pin Connector, near starter
T4a - 4-Pin Connector
T10a - 10-Pin Connector, in engine compartment, in wiring duct, left
T10b - 10-Pin Connector
V7 - Left Coolant Fan
V35 - Right Coolant Fan

(193) - Ground connection -1-, in coolant fan wiring harness
(C11) - Wire connection, in coolant fan wiring harness
(K21) - Wire connection -1-, in coolant fan wiring harness
(L39) - Wire connection (A/C Pressure Switch) -1-, in Climatronic wiring harness
(L56) - Connector (Sensor), in wiring harness Climatronic
(L68) - Connection 2 (sensor) in Climatronic wiring harness

Coolant fan control (FC) control module, A/C cut-out thermal switch, A/C clutch, coolant fan

ws = white
sw = black
ro = red
br = brown
gn = green
bl = blue
gr = grey
li = lilac
ge = yellow

A - Battery
D - Ignition/Starter Switch
F18 - Coolant Fan Control (FC) Thermal Switch
J293 - Coolant Fan Control (FC) Control Module, in engine compartment, left
S16 - Fuse 16 in fuse holder
S164 - Fuse -3- (30) in fuse bracket/battery
S180 - Fuse -8- (30) in fuse bracket/battery
T2b - Double Connector, in engine compartment, in wiring duct, left
T3 - 3-Pin Connector
T4a - 4-Pin Connector
T10b - 10-Pin Connector
V51 - After-Run Coolant Pump

(85) - Ground connection -1-, in engine compartment wiring harness
(193) - Ground connection -1-, in coolant fan wiring harness
(501) - Threaded connection -2- (30) on the relay plate
(A32) - Plus connection (30), in instrument panel wiring harness
(A98) - Plus connector -4- (30), in instrument panel wiring harness
(K20) - Plus connection -1- (30), in coolant fan wiring harness
(K21) - Wire connection -1-, in coolant fan wiring harness

Coolant fan control (FC) control module, coolant fan control (FC) thermal switch, after-run coolant pump

Interior rear view mirror (self-dimming), rain-sensor,

from September 1998

Deviate relay location and fuseplacements as well as the locations of multiple connectors see section "component locations".

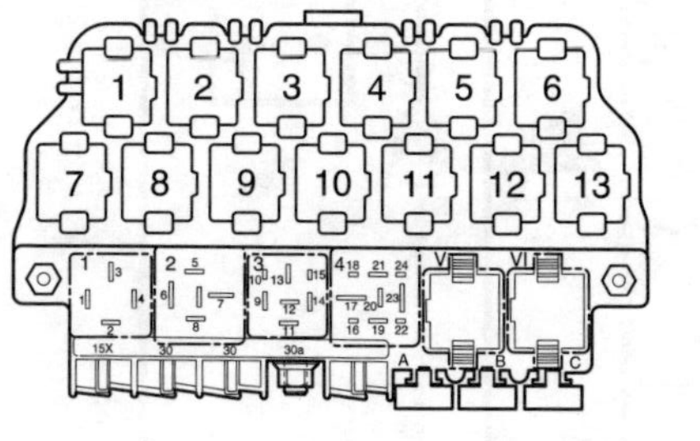

Relay location on the thirteenfold auxiliary relay panel, above relay panel:

Relay panel:

V

VI Wiper/Washer Intermittent Relay (192)

Note: Number in parentheses indicates production control number stamped on relay housing.

Fuse colors

30 A - green
25 A - white
20 A - yellow
15 A - blue
10 A - red
7,5 A - brown
5 A - beige
3 A - violet

Edition 12/98
USA.5102.01.21

ws = white
sw = black
ro = red
br = brown
gn = green
bl = blue
gr = grey
li = lilac
ge = yellow

D - Ignition/Starter Switch
E38 - Windshield Wiper Intermittent Regulator
F4 - Back-Up Light Switch
G213 - Rain-Sensor
J31 - Wiper/Washer Intermittent Relay, on relais panel
S5 - Fuse 5 in fuse holder
T4 - 4-Pin Connector, near front interior light
T6 - 6-Pin Connector, near front interior light
T6a - 6-Pin Connector, near front interior light
T6e - 6-Pin Connector
T10 - 10-Pin Connector, orange, in protective housing for connectors, in plenum chamber, left
T18a - 18-Pin Connector
Y7 - Automatic day/night interior mirror

(81) - Ground connection -1-, in instrument panel wiring harness
(135) - Ground connection -2-, in instrument panel wiring harness
(303) - Ground connection -rain-sensor/mirror-, in wiring harness interior
(A2) - Plus connection (15), in instrument panel wiring harness
(A20) - Wire connection (15a), in instrument panel wiring harness
(A87) - Connector (reverse lamp), in instrument panel wiring harness

Wiper/washer intermittent relay, windshield wiper intermittent regulator, rain-sensor, automatic day/night interior mirror

Edition 12/98
USA.5102.01.21

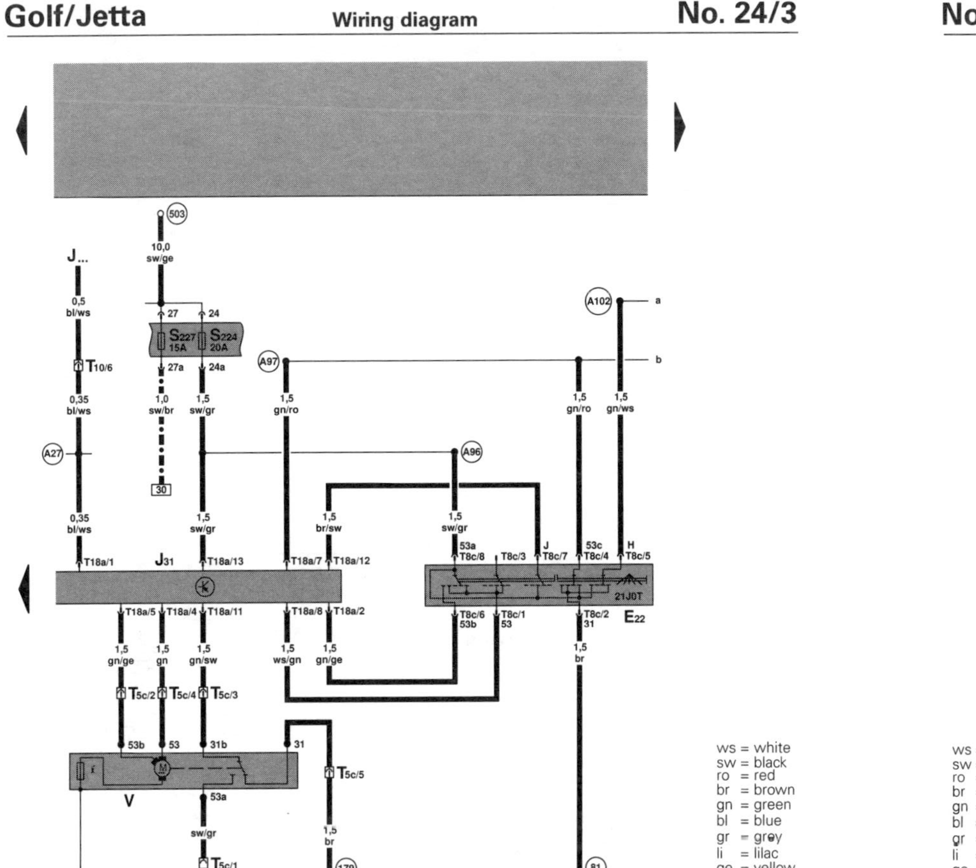

ws = white
sw = black
ro = red
br = brown
gn = green
bl = blue
gr = grey
li = lilac
ge = yellow

E22 - Windshield Wiper/Washer Switch
J31 - Wiper/Washer Intermittent Relay, on relais panel
J... - Engine Control Module (ECM)
S224 - Fuse 24 in fuse holder
S227 - Fuse 27 in fuse holder
T5c - 5-Pin Connector, on windshield wiper motor
T8c - 8-Pin Connector
T10 - 10-Pin Connector, orange, in protective housing for connectors, in plenum chamber, left
T18a - 18-Pin Connector
V - Windshield Wiper Motor

(81) - Ground connection -1-, in instrument panel wiring harness

(179) - Ground connection, in left headlight wiring harness
(503) - Threaded connection -2- (75x) on the relay plate
(A27) - Wire Connection (vehicle speed signal), in instrument panel wiring harness
(A96) - Connector (53a), in instrument panel wiring harness
(A97) - Connector (53), in instrument panel wiring harness
(A102) - Connector (windshield wiper), in instrument panel wiring harness

-•-•- Golf only

Wiper/washer intermittent relay, windshield wiper/washer switch, windshield wiper motor

ws = white
sw = black
ro = red
br = brown
gn = green
bl = blue
gr = grey
li = lilac
ge = yellow

T5a - 5-Pin Connector, pink, connector station C-pillar, left (Golf only)
T5h - 5-Pin Connector, near left A-pillar, lower part, in harness
T5i - 5-Pin Connector, near left A-pillar, lower part, in harness
V12 - Motor for rear windshield wiper
V59 - Windshield and Rear Window Washer Pump

(86) - Ground connection -1-, in rear wiring harness

(98) - Ground connection, in rear lid wiring harness

(A97) - Connector (53), in instrument panel wiring harness

(A102) - Connector (windshield wiper), in instrument panel wiring harness

-•-•- Golf only

Motor for rear windshield wiper, windshield and rear window washer pump

Comfort system (vehicles without power windows),

from September 1998

- **Anti-theft warning system**
- **Central locking system with remote control**
- **Fuel tank lid unlock system**
- **Heated outside mirrors**
- **Interior lights**
- **Luggage compartment light**
- **Power sunroof**
- **Rear lid unlock system**

Deviate relay location and fuseplacements as well as the locations of multiple connectors see section "component locations".

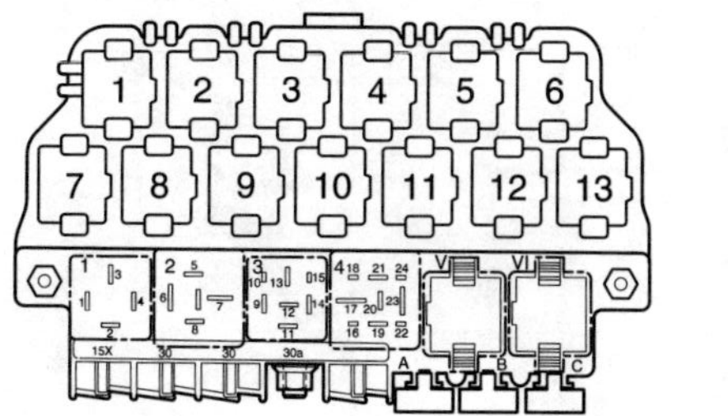

Relay location on the thirteenfold auxiliary relay panel, above relay panel:

2 Relay for motor remote unlock rear lid (79)

Relay panel:

Note: Number in parentheses indicates production control number stamped on relay housing.

Fuse colors

30 A - green
25 A - white
20 A - yellow
15 A - blue
10 A - red
7,5 A - brown
5 A - beige
3 A - violet

ws = white
sw = black
ro = red
br = brown
gn = green
bl = blue
gr = grey
li = lilac
ge = yellow

97-26583

E20 - Instrument Panel Light Dimmer Switch
E204 - Switch for remote/fuel tank door
J398 - Relay for motor remote unlock rear lid, on the thirteenfold auxiliary relay panel, above relay panel (through January 1999)*
L76 - Push Button Light
T3c - 3-Pin Connector
T5d - 5-Pin Connector, brown, connector station C-pillar, left
T10i - 10-Pin Connector, black, connector station A-pillar, left
T10k - 10-Pin Connector, black, connector station A-pillar, right
T10n - 10-Pin Connector, brown, connector station A-pillar, left
V139 - Motor to unlock rear lid*
V155 - Motor for fuel tank lid unlock

(42) - Ground connection, beside steering column
(81) - Ground connection -1-, in instrument panel wiring harness
(135) - Ground connection -2-, in instrument panel wiring harness
(238) - Ground connection -1-, in wiring harness interior
(A4) - Plus connection (58b), in instrument panel wiring harness
(R51) - Connection (58b) in door wiring harness, driver side
-•-- - Through January 1999
* - Jetta only
- - - Beginning February 1999

Switch for remote/fuel tank door, motor for fuel tank lid unlock, relay for motor remote unlock rear lid, motor to unlock rear lid

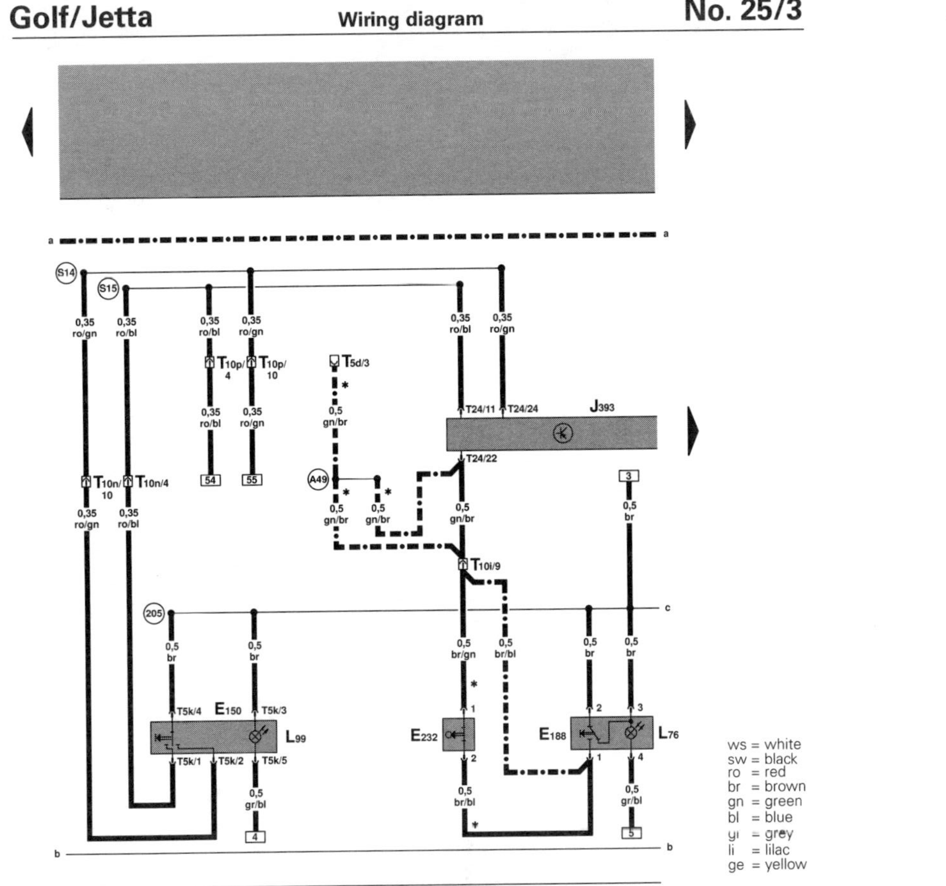

ws = white
sw = black
ro = red
br = brown
gn = green
bl = blue
gr = grey
li = lilac
ge = yellow

15 16 17 18 19 20 21 22 23 24 25 26 27 28

E150 - Switch for interior lock, driver side
E188 - Switch for remote unlock, rear lid, driver side
E232 - Key switch for switching off remote unlock rear lid
J393 - Central control module for comfort system, behind instrument panel, left
L76 - Push Button Light
L99 - Lighting for switch interior lock
T5d - 5-Pin Connector, brown, connector station C-pillar, left
T5k - 5-Pin Connector
T10i - 10-Pin Connector, black, connector station A-pillar, left
T10n - 10-Pin Connector, brown, connector station A-pillar, left
T10p - 10-Pin Connector, brown, connector station A-pillar, right
T24 - 24-Pin Connector
(205) - Ground connection, in driver's door wiring harness
(A49) - Wire connection -1-, in instrument panel wiring harness
(S14) - Wire connection (open), in central locking system wiring harness
(S15) - Wire connection (closed), in central locking system wiring harness

-•-- - Through January 1999
* - Jetta only
-•-•- Golf only

Central control module for comfort system, switch for interior lock (driver side), switch for remote unlock rear lid

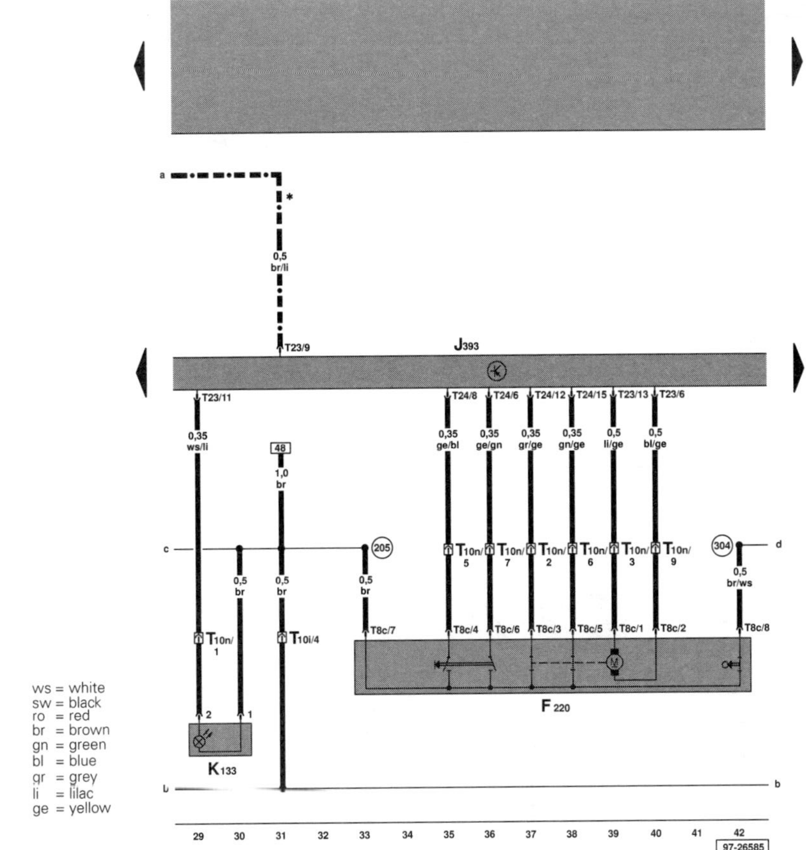

ws = white
sw = black
ro = red
br = brown
gn = green
bl = blue
gr = grey
li = lilac
ge = yellow

29 30 31 32 33 34 35 36 37 38 39 40 41 42

F220 - Lock unit for central locking, driver side
J393 - Central control module for comfort system, behind instrument panel, left
K133 - Warning light for central locking -SAFE-
T8c - 8-Pin Connector
T10i - 10-Pin Connector, black, connector station A-pillar, left
T10n - 10-Pin Connector, brown, connector station A-pillar, left
T23 - 23-Pin Connector
T24 - 24-Pin Connector
(205) - Ground connection, in driver's door wiring harness
(304) - Ground connector -3-, in wiring harness door cable - driver side

* - Jetta only
-•-- - Through January 1999

Central control module for comfort system, lock unit for central locking, warning light for central locking -SAFE-

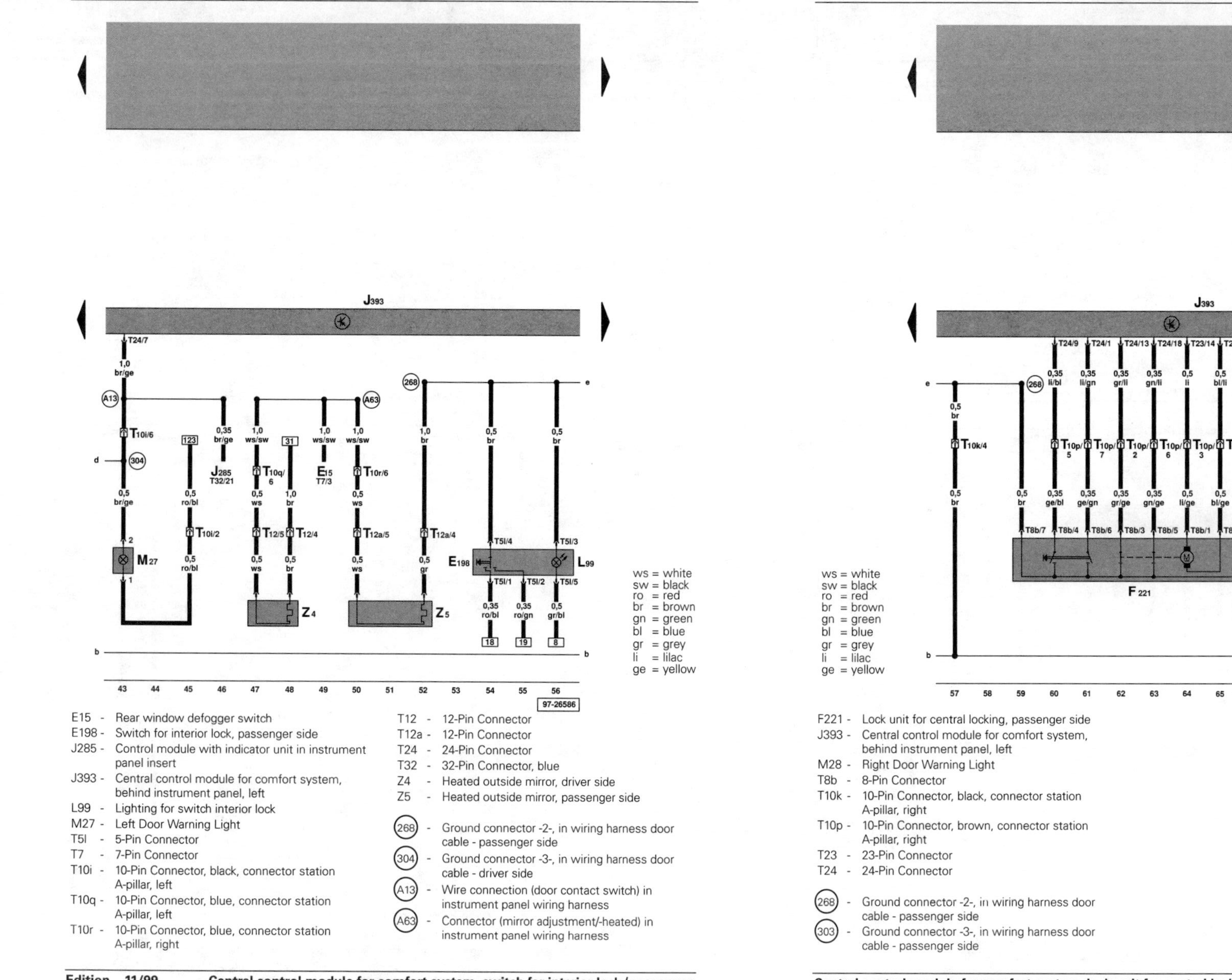

ws = white
sw = black
ro = red
br = brown
gn = green
bl = blue
gr = grey
li = lilac
ge = yellow

- E15 - Rear window defogger switch
- E198 - Switch for interior lock, passenger side
- J285 - Control module with indicator unit in instrument panel insert
- J393 - Central control module for comfort system, behind instrument panel, left
- L99 - Lighting for switch interior lock
- M27 - Left Door Warning Light
- T5l - 5-Pin Connector
- T7 - 7-Pin Connector
- T10i - 10-Pin Connector, black, connector station A-pillar, left
- T10q - 10-Pin Connector, blue, connector station A-pillar, left
- T10r - 10-Pin Connector, blue, connector station A-pillar, right
- T12 - 12-Pin Connector
- T12a - 12-Pin Connector
- T24 - 24-Pin Connector
- T32 - 32-Pin Connector, blue
- Z4 - Heated outside mirror, driver side
- Z5 - Heated outside mirror, passenger side
- (268) - Ground connector -2-, in wiring harness door cable - passenger side
- (304) - Ground connector -3-, in wiring harness door cable - driver side
- (A13) - Wire connection (door contact switch) in instrument panel wiring harness
- (A63) - Connector (mirror adjustment/-heated) in instrument panel wiring harness

Central control module for comfort system, switch for interior lock (passenger side), left door warning light, heated outside mirrors

ws = white
sw = black
ro = red
br = brown
gn = green
bl = blue
gr = grey
li = lilac
ge = yellow

- F221 - Lock unit for central locking, passenger side
- J393 - Central control module for comfort system, behind instrument panel, left
- M28 - Right Door Warning Light
- T8b - 8-Pin Connector
- T10k - 10-Pin Connector, black, connector station A-pillar, right
- T10p - 10-Pin Connector, brown, connector station A-pillar, right
- T23 - 23-Pin Connector
- T24 - 24-Pin Connector
- (268) - Ground connector -2-, in wiring harness door cable - passenger side
- (303) - Ground connector -3-, in wiring harness door cable - passenger side

Central control module for comfort system, lock unit for central locking (passenger side), right door warning light

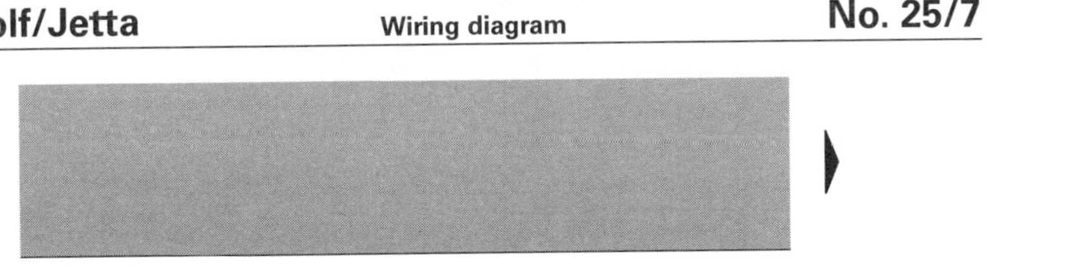

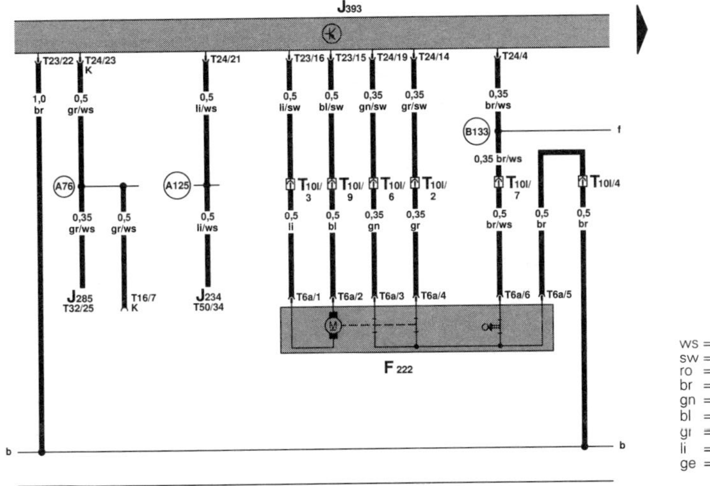

ws = white
sw = black
ro = red
br = brown
gn = green
bl = blue
gr = grey
li = lilac
ge = yellow

F222 - Lock unit for central locking, rear, left
J234 - Airbag Control Module, behind console, lower part
J285 - Control module with indicator unit in instrument panel insert
J393 - Central control module for comfort system, behind instrument panel, left
T6a - 6-Pin Connector
T10l - 10-Pin Connector, black, connector station B-pillar, left
T16 - Data Link Connector (DLC), below instrument panel, left
T23 - 23-Pin Connector
T24 - 24-Pin Connector
T32 - 32-Pin Connector, blue
T50 - 50-Pin Connector

(A76) - Connector (K-diagnosis wire) in instrument panel wiring harness
(A125) - Connection (crash signal) in instrument panel wiring harness
(B133) - Connector (central locking open), in wiring harness interior

Central control module for comfort system, lock unit for central locking (rear left)

ws = white
sw = black
ro = red
br = brown
gn = green
bl = blue
gr = grey
li = lilac
ge = yellow

F124 - Trunk Lock Alarm/Central Locking Switch
F223 - Lock unit for central locking, rear, right
J393 - Central control module for comfort system, behind instrument panel, left
T2 - Double Connector, in rear lid
T5d - 5-Pin Connector, brown, connector station C-pillar, left
T6b - 6-Pin Connector
T10m - 10-Pin Connector, black, connector station B-pillar, right
T23 - 23-Pin Connector
T24 - 24-Pin Connector
V53 - Decklid Central Locking System Motor (Golf only)

(218) - Ground connection -1-, in rear lid wiring harness
(219) - Ground connection -2-, in rear lid wiring harness
(B133) - Connector (central locking open), in wiring harness interior

* - Jetta only
--- - Beginning February 1999
-•-•- - Golf only

Central control module for comfort system, lock unit for central locking (rear right), trunk lock alarm/central locking switch, decklid central locking system motor

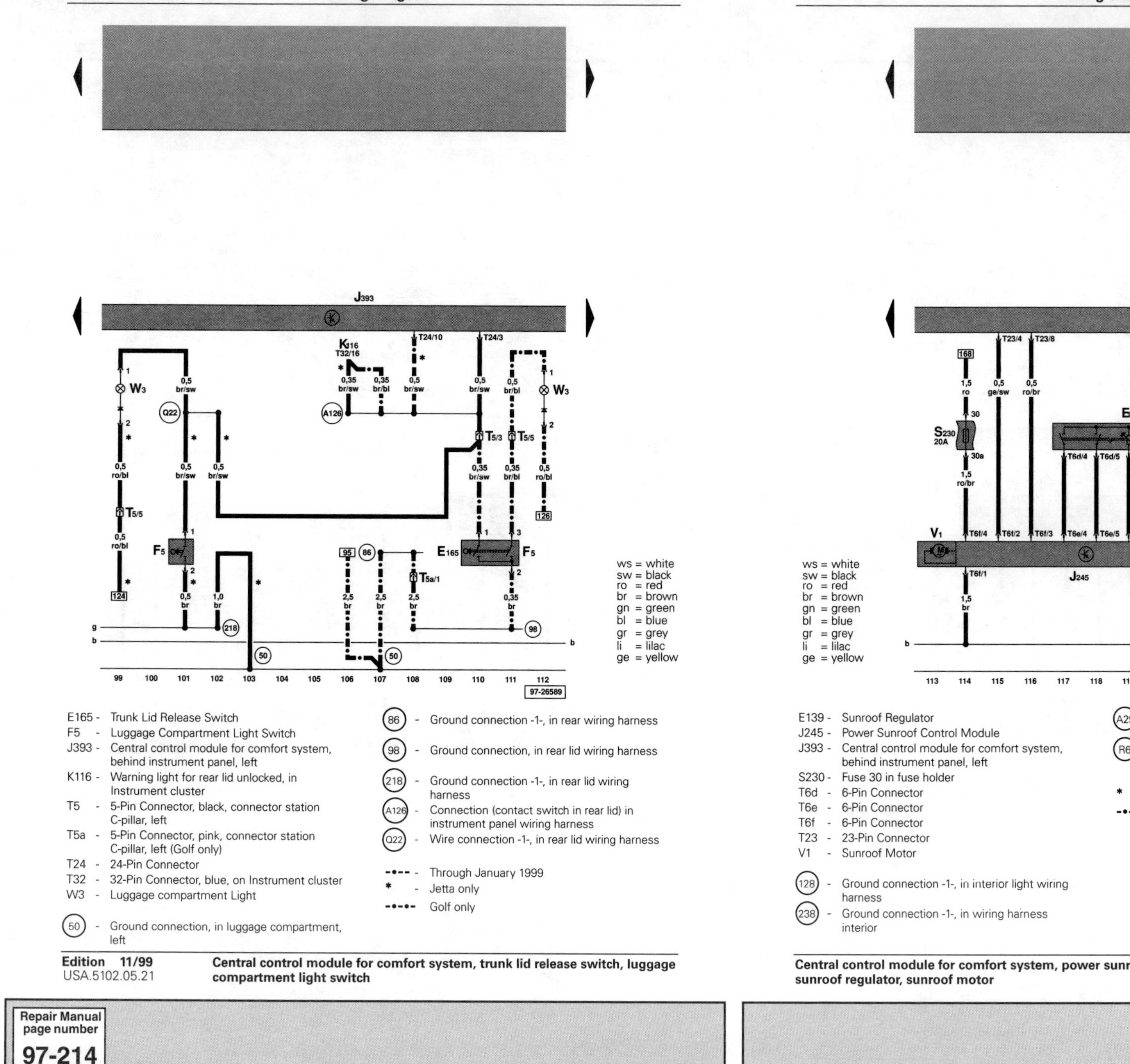

ws = white
sw = black
ro = red
br = brown
gn = green
bl = blue
gr = grey
li = lilac
ge = yellow

E165 - Trunk Lid Release Switch
F5 - Luggage Compartment Light Switch
J393 - Central control module for comfort system, behind instrument panel, left
K116 - Warning light for rear lid unlocked, in Instrument cluster
T5 - 5-Pin Connector, black, connector station C-pillar, left
T5a - 5-Pin Connector, pink, connector station C-pillar, left (Golf only)
T24 - 24-Pin Connector
T32 - 32-Pin Connector, blue, on Instrument cluster
W3 - Luggage compartment Light

(50) - Ground connection, in luggage compartment, left

(86) - Ground connection -1-, in rear wiring harness

(98) - Ground connection, in rear lid wiring harness

(218) - Ground connection -1-, in rear lid wiring harness

(A126) - Connection (contact switch in rear lid) in instrument panel wiring harness

(Q22) - Wire connection -1-, in rear lid wiring harness

-•-- - Through January 1999
* - Jetta only
--•-•-- - Golf only

Edition 11/99
USA.5102.05.21

Central control module for comfort system, trunk lid release switch, luggage compartment light switch

ws = white
sw = black
ro = red
br = brown
gn = green
bl = blue
gr = grey
li = lilac
ge = yellow

E139 - Sunroof Regulator
J245 - Power Sunroof Control Module
J393 - Central control module for comfort system, behind instrument panel, left
S230 - Fuse 30 in fuse holder
T6d - 6-Pin Connector
T6e - 6-Pin Connector
T6f - 6-Pin Connector
T23 - 23-Pin Connector
V1 - Sunroof Motor

(128) - Ground connection -1-, in interior light wiring harness

(238) - Ground connection -1-, in wiring harness interior

(A29) - Wire connection (interior light), in instrument panel wiring harness

(R6) - Plus connection -1-, in interior light wiring harness

* - Jetta only
--•-•-- - Golf only

Central control module for comfort system, power sunroof control module, sunroof regulator, sunroof motor

Edition 11/99
USA.5102.05.21

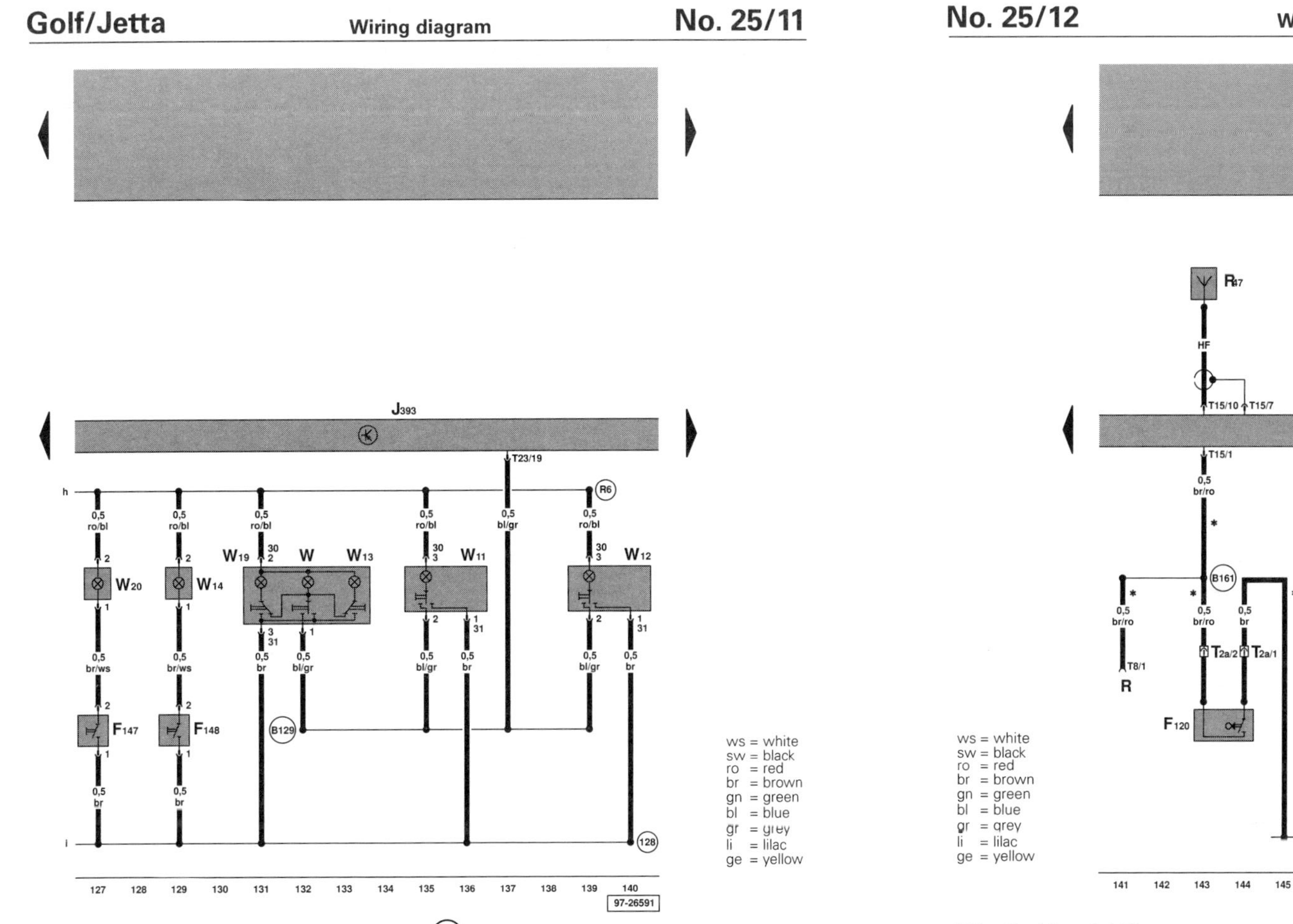

ws = white
sw = black
ro = red
br = brown
gn = green
bl = blue
gr = grey
li = lilac
ge = yellow

- F147 - Left Make-Up Mirror Light Switch
- F148 - Right Make-Up Mirror Light Switch
- J393 - Central control module for comfort system, behind instrument panel, left
- W - Front Interior Light
- W11 - Left Rear Reading Light
- W12 - Right Rear Reading Light
- W13 - Right Front Map/Reading Light
- W14 - Right Make-up Mirror Light
- W19 - Left Front Reading Light
- W20 - Left Make-up Mirror Light
- T23 - 23-Pin Connector
- (128) - Ground connection -1-, in interior light wiring harness
- (B129) - Connector (interior light 3/L) in wiring harness interior
- (R6) - Plus connection -1-, in interior light wiring harness

Edition 11/99 **Central control module for comfort system, Interior lights, make-up mirror lights**
USA.5102.05.21

ws = white
sw = black
ro = red
br = brown
gn = green
bl = blue
gr = grey
li = lilac
ge = yellow

- F120 - Hood Alarm Switch*
- F194 - Clutch Pedal Position (CPP) Switch**
- H8 - Alarm Horn*
- J207 - Starting Interlock Relay
- J285 - Control module with indicator unit in instrument panel insert
- J393 - Central control module for comfort system, behind instrument panel, left
- R - Radio
- R47 - Antenna wire for central locking and antitheft warning system
- T2a - Double Connector, near headlight, right
- T8 - 8-Pin Connector, on radio
- T15 - 15-Pin Connector
- T23 - 23-Pin Connector
- T32 - 32-Pin Connector, blue, on Instrument cluster
- (12) - Ground connection, in engine compartment, left
- (179) - Ground connection, in left headlight wiring harness
- (A5) - Plus connection (right turn signal), in instrument panel wiring harness
- (A6) - Plus connection (left turn signal), in instrument panel wiring harness
- (A13) - Wire connection (door contact switch) in instrument panel wiring harness
- (B161) - Connector (anti-theft warning system), in wiring harness interior
- * - Vehicles with anti-theft warning system only
- ** - Manual transmission only
- --- - Automatic transmission only

Central control module for comfort system, antitheft warning system, antenna wire for central locking and antitheft warning system **Edition 11/99**
USA.5102.05.21

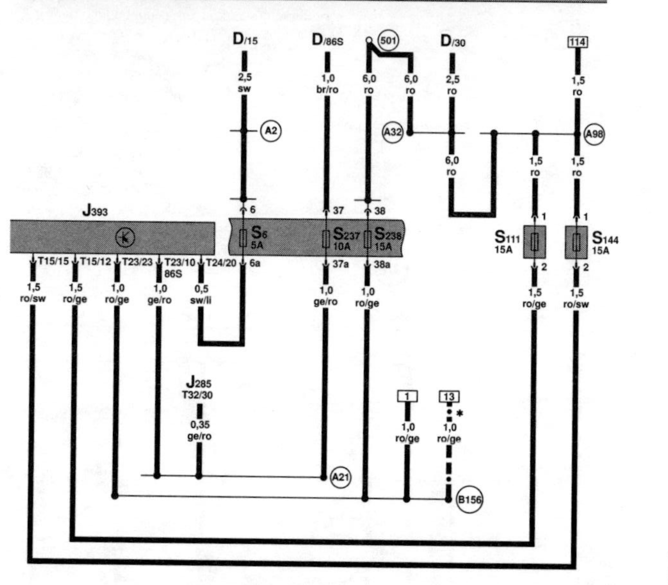

ws = white
sw = black
ro = red
br = brown
gn = green
bl = blue
gr = grey
li = lilac
ge = yellow

- D - Ignition/Starter Switch
- J285 - Control module with indicator unit in instrument panel insert
- J393 - Central control module for comfort system, behind instrument panel, left
- S6 - Fuse 6 in fuse holder
- S111 - Alarm System and Anti-Theft Fuse, above the thirteenfold auxiliary relay panel
- S144 - Fuse for central locking/anti-theft warning system, above the thirteenfold auxiliary relay panel
- S237 - Fuse 37 in fuse holder
- S238 - Fuse 38 in fuse holder
- T15 - 15-Pin Connector
- T23 - 23-Pin Connector
- T24 - 24-Pin Connector
- T32 - 32-Pin Connector, blue
- (501) - Threaded connection -2- (30) on the relay plate
- (A2) - Plus connection (15), in instrument panel wiring harness
- (A21) - Wire connection (86s), in instrument panel wiring harness
- (A32) - Plus connection (30), in instrument panel wiring harness
- (A98) - Plus connector -4- (30), in instrument panel wiring harness
- (B156) - Plus connector (30a), in wiring harness interior
- * - Jetta only
- -•-- - Through January 1999

Edition 11/99
USA.5102.05.21

Central control module for comfort system

THIS PAGE INTENTIONALLY LEFT
BLANK

Power seats and mirror adjustment with memory,

from September 1998

Deviate relay location and fuseplacements as well as the locations of multiple connectors see section "component locations".

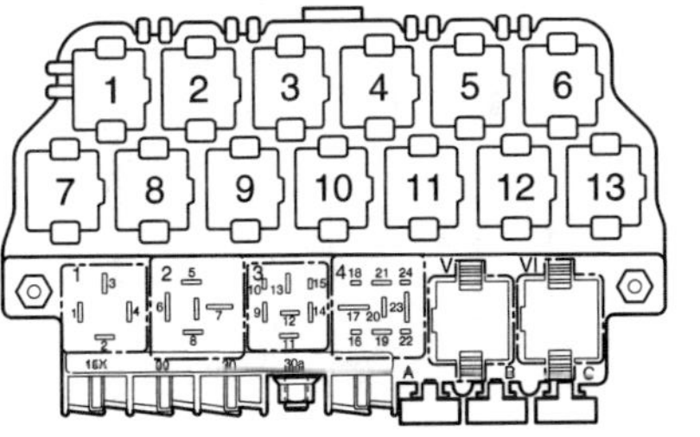

Relay location on the thirteenfold auxiliary relay panel, above relay panel:

Relay panel:

2 Load Reduction Relay (18)/ (100)

Note: Number in parentheses indicates production control number stamped on relay housing.

Fuse colors

30 A - green
25 A - white
20 A - yellow
15 A - blue
10 A - red
7,5 A - brown
5 A - beige
3 A - violet

J136

T28/11 0,35 ge/sw T16c/6 E218
T28/10 0,35 ge/ro T16c/5 E219
T28/9 0,35 ge/bl T16c/4 E220
T28/13 0,35 gn/sw T16c/10 E212
T28/12 0,35 ws/sw T16c/9 E213
T28/14 0,35 ws/ro T16c/7 E208
T28/24 0,35 gn/ro T16c/8 E209
T28/25 0,35 ws/bl T16c/11 E210
T28/28 0,35 gn/bl T16c/12 E211
T28/26 0,35 gn T16c/14
T28/27 0,35 ws/gn T16c/13 E96
T28/20 0,35 br/bl T16c/2
T28/15 0,35 ro/br T16c/3
T28/23 0,35 ro T16c/1 E190

1 2 3 4 5 6 7 8 9 10 11 12 13 14

97-23210

ws = white
sw = black
ro = red
br = brown
gn = green
bl = blue
gr = grey
li - lilac
ge = yellow

E96 - Driver's Backrest Adjustment Switch
E190 - Emergency Shut-Off Switch for Memory
E208 - Button for front height adjustment, upwards, driver seat
E209 - Button for front height adjustment, downwards, driver seat
E210 - Button for rear height adjustment, upwards, driver seat
E211 - Button for rear height adjustment, downwards, driver seat
E212 - Button for length adjustment, forward, driver seat
E213 - Button for length adjustment, backward, driver seat
E218 - Button for driver 1, memory seat
E219 - Button for driver 2, memory seat
E220 - Button for driver 3, memory seat
J136 - Memory Seat Control Module, below driver's seat
T16c - 16-Pin Connector
T28 - 28-Pin Connector

Memory seat control module, button for front -and rear height adjustment, button for length adjustment, driver's backrest adjustment switch, emergency shut-off switch for memory

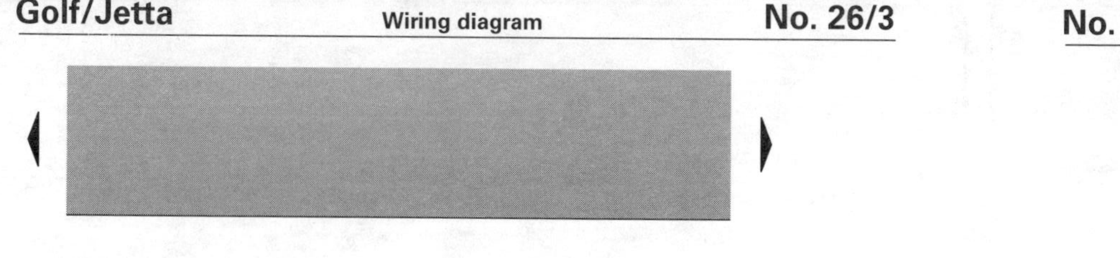

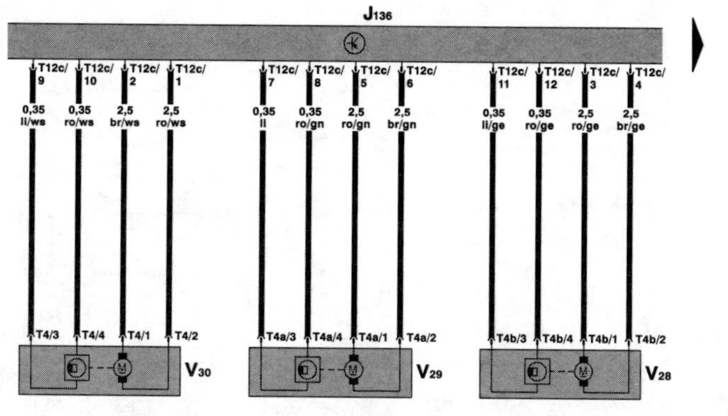

ws = white
sw = black
ro = red
br = brown
gn = green
bl = blue
gr = grey
li = lilac
ge = yellow

15 16 17 18 19 20 21 22 23 24 25 26 27 28

97-28649

J136 - Memory Seat Control Module, below driver's seat
T4 - 4-Pin Connector
T4a - 4-Pin Connector
T4b - 4-Pin Connector
T12c - 12-Pin Connector
V28 - Driver's seat fore/aft adjusting motor
V29 - Motor for front height adjustment, driver seat
V30 - Motor for rear height adjustment, driver seat

Memory seat control module, driver's seat fore/aft adjusting motor, motor for front height adjustment (driver seat), motor for rear height adjustment (driver seat)

ws = white
sw = black
ro = red
br = brown
gn = green
bl = blue
gr = grey
li = lilac
ge = yellow

29 30 31 32 33 34 35 36 37 38 39 40 41 42

97-28650

F4 - Back-Up Light Switch
J136 - Memory Seat Control Module
J226 - Park/Neutral Position (PNP) Relay
T4c - 4-Pin Connector
T6g - 6-Pin Connector, red, below driver's seat
T8d - 8-Pin Connector
T10 - 10-Pin Connector, orange, in protective housing for connectors, in plenum chamber, left
T10u - 10-Pin Connector, brown, below driver's seat
T28 - 28-Pin Connector
V45 - Motor for seatback adjustment, driver seat

A34 - Wire connection (75x), in instrument panel wiring harness
A87 - Connector (RF), in instrument panel wiring harness

W39 - Connection -1- (mirror memory), in floor wiring harness
W45 - Connection -2- (mirror memory), in floor wiring harness

* - Manual transmission only
--- Automatic transmission only

Memory seat control module, motor for seatback adjustment (driver seat)

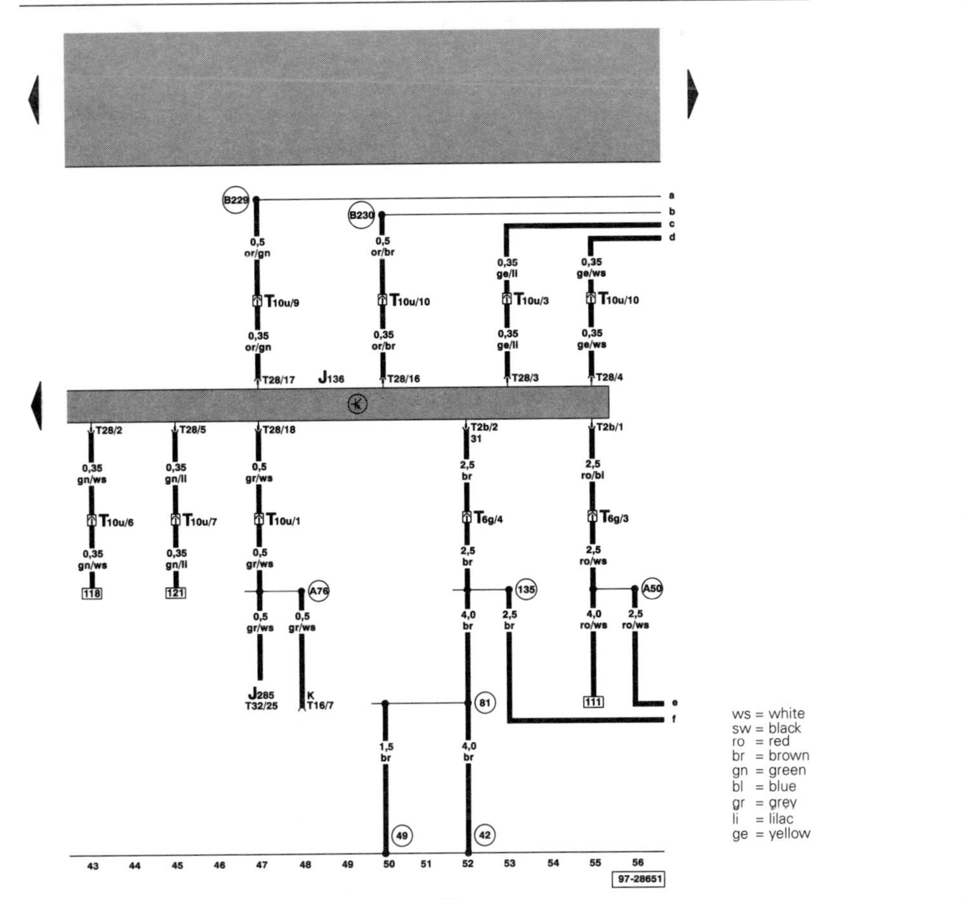

ws = white
sw = black
ro = red
br = brown
gn = green
bl = blue
gr = grey
li = lilac
ge = yellow

J136 - Memory Seat Control Module, below driver's seat
J285 - Control module with indicator unit in instrument panel insert
T2b - Double Connector
T6g - 6-Pin Connector, red, below driver's seat
T10u - 10-Pin Connector, brown, below driver's seat
T16 - 16-Pin Connector, On Board Diagnostic (OBD), below instrument panel, left
T28 - 28-Pin Connector
T32 - 32-Pin Connector, blue

(42) - Ground connection, beside steering column

(49) - Ground connection on steering column

(81) - Ground connection -1-, in instrument panel wiring harness

(135) - Ground connection -2-, in instrument panel wiring harness

(A50) - Plus connection (30a), in instrument panel wiring harness

(A76) - Connector (K-diagnosis wire) in instrument panel wiring harness

(B229) - Connection (high bus), in instrument panel wiring harness

(B230) - Connection (low bus), in instrument panel wiring harness

Edition 12/00
USA.5102.09.21

Memory seat control module

ws = white
sw = black
ro = red
br = brown
gn = green
bl = blue
gr = grey
li = lilac
ge = yellow

57 58 59 60 61 62 63 64 65 66 67 68 69 70
97-28652

E64 - Passenger's Seat Fore/Aft Adjusting Switch
E65 - Passenger's Seat Front Height Adjusting Switch
E66 - Passenger's Seat Rear Height Adjusting Switch
E98 - Passenger Backrest Adjustment Switch
T2c - Double Connector
T4d - 4-Pin Connector
T4e - 4-Pin Connector
T4f - 4-Pin Connector
T4g - 4-Pin Connector
T6h - 6-Pin Connector, red, below passenger's seat
T8f - 8-Pin Connector
V31 - Passenger's Seat Fore/Aft Adjusting Motor
V32 - Passenger's Seat Front Height Adjusting Motor
V33 - Passenger's Seat Rear Height Adjusting Motor
V46 - Passenger's Backrest Adjusting Motor

Passenger's seat fore/aft adjustment, passenger's seat front height adjustment, passenger's seat rear height adjustment, passenger backrest adjustment

Edition 12/00
USA.5102.09.21

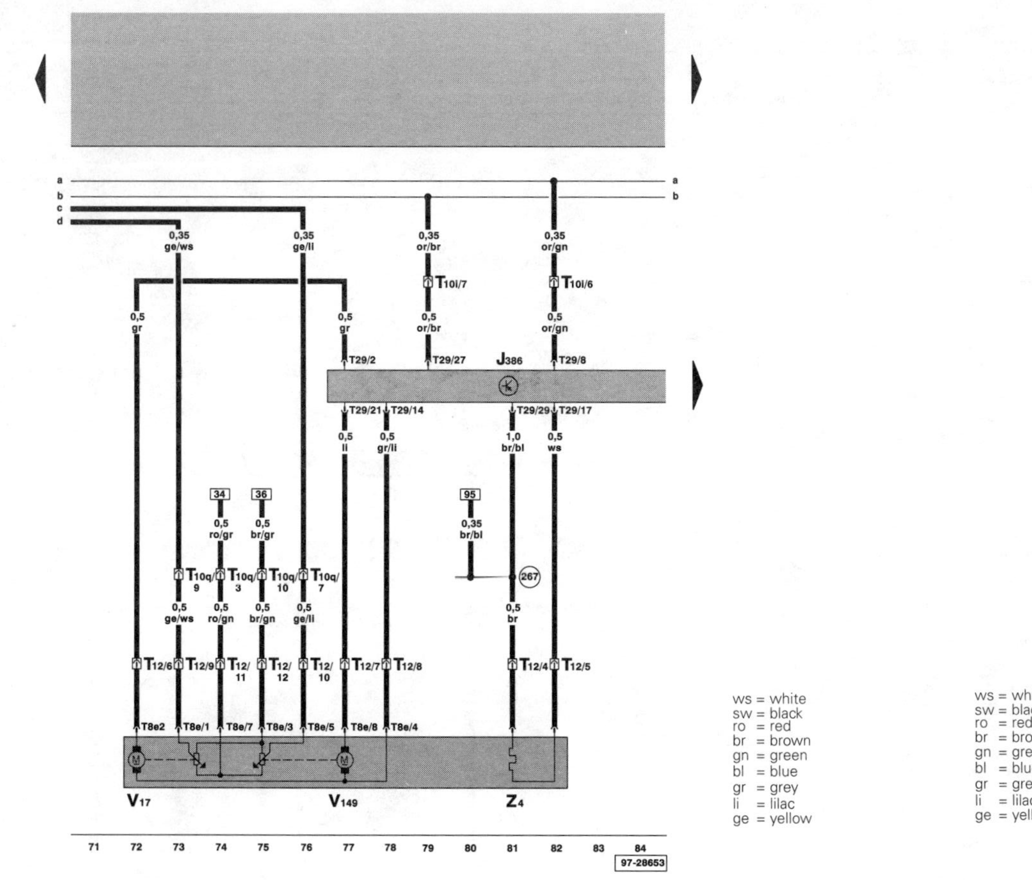

ws = white
sw = black
ro = red
br = brown
gn = green
bl = blue
gr = grey
li = lilac
ge = yellow

J386 - Door control module, driver side
T8e - 8-Pin Connector
T10i - 10-Pin Connector, black, connector station A-pillar, left
T10q - 10-Pin Connector, blue, connector station A-pillar, left
T12 - 12-Pin Connector
T29 - 29-Pin Connector
V17 - Driver's Side Mirror Adjustment Motor
V149 - Motor for mirror adjustment, driver side
Z4 - Heated outside mirror, driver side

(267) - Ground connector -2-, in wiring harness door cable - driver side

Door control module (driver side), power mirror (driver side), heated outside mirror (driver side)

ws = white
sw = black
ro = red
br = brown
gn = green
bl = blue
gr = grey
li = lilac
ge = yellow

E20 - Instrument Panel Light Dimmer Switch
E43 - Mirror Adjustment Switch
E48 - Mirror Selector Switch
E231 - Switch for outside mirror heating
E263 - Mirror fold-away Switch*
J386 - Door control module, driver side
J393 - Central control module for comfort system, behind instrument panel, left
L78 - Mirror Adjusting Switch Light
T3c - 3-Pin Connector
T10i - 10-Pin Connector, black, connector station A-pillar, left
T10q - 10-Pin Connector, blue, connector station A-pillar, left
T10t - 10-Pin Connector
T23 - 23-Pin Connector
T29 - 29-Pin Connector

(A4) - Plus connection (58b), in instrument panel wiring harness
(A20) - Wire connection (15a), in instrument panel wiring harness
(R51) - Connection (58b), in driver's door wiring harness

* - Only on vehicles with mirror fold-away function
--- Only on vehicles with separate switch for outside mirror heating

Door control module (driver side), mirror selector switch, mirror adjustment switch, switch for outside mirror heating

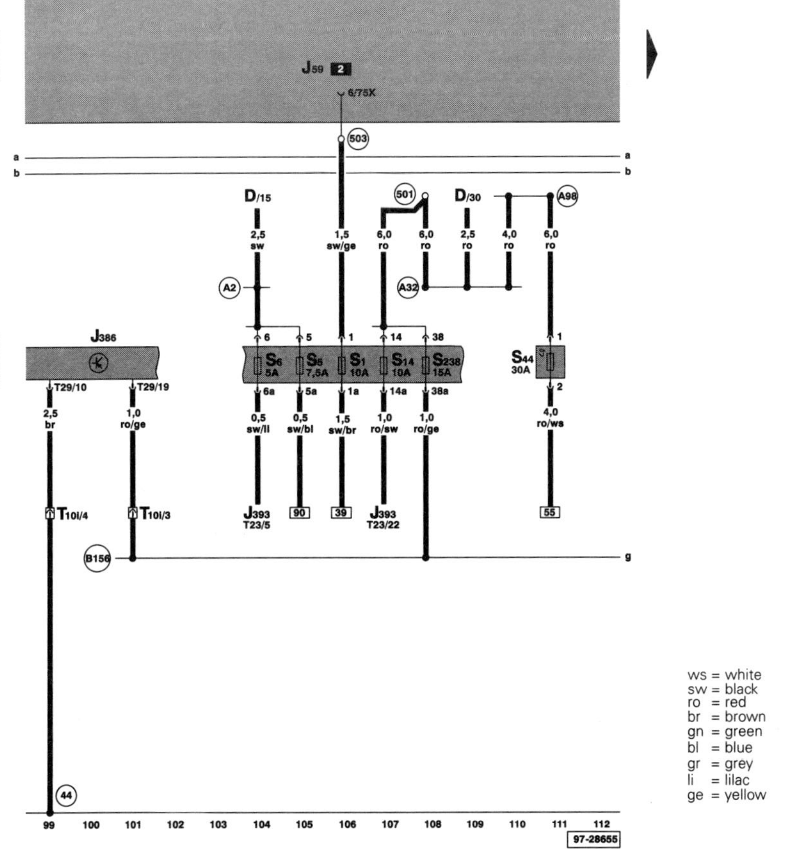

ws = white
sw = black
ro = red
br = brown
gn = green
bl = blue
gr = grey
li = lilac
ge = yellow

- D - Ignition/Starter Switch
- J59 - Load Reduction Relay
- J386 - Door control module, driver side
- J393 - Central control module for comfort system, behind instrument panel, left
- S1 - Fuse 1 in fuse holder
- S5 - Fuse 5 in fuse holder
- S6 - Fuse 6 in fuse holder
- S14 - Fuse 14 in fuse holder
- S44 - Power (Memory) Seat Circuit Breaker, on relay panel
- S238 - Fuse 38 in fuse holder
- T10i - 10-Pin Connector, black, connector station A-pillar, left
- T23 - 23-Pin Connector
- T29 - 29-Pin Connector

- (44) - Ground connection, on left A-pillar, lower part
- (501) - Threaded connection -2- (30) on the relay plate
- (503) - Threaded connection -2- (75x) on the relay plate
- (A2) - Plus connection (15), in instrument panel wiring harness
- (A32) - Plus connection (30), in instrument panel wiring harness
- (A98) - Plus connector -4- (30), in instrument panel wiring harness
- (B156) - Plus connector (30a), in wiring harness interior

THIS PAGE INTENTIONALLY LEFT
BLANK

Comfort System (vehicles with power windows),

from September 1998

- **Anti-theft warning system**
- **Central locking system with remote control**
- **Fuel tank lid unlock system**
- **Heated power mirrors**
- **Interior lights**
- **Luggage compartment light**
- **Power sunroof**
- **Power windows**
- **Rear lid unlock system**

Deviate relay location and fuseplacements as well as the locations of multiple connectors see section "component locations".

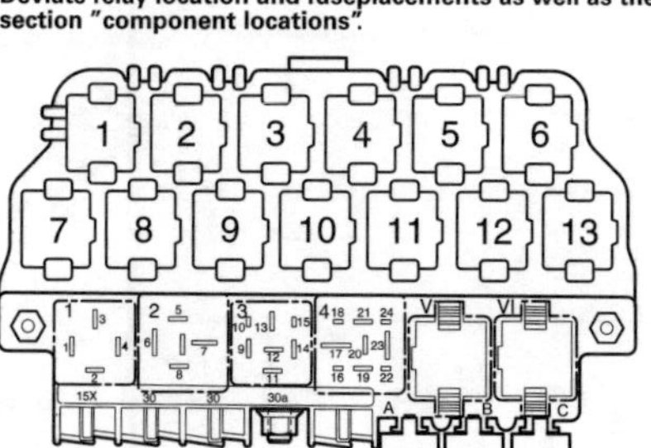

Relay location on the thirteenfold auxiliary relay panel, above relay panel:

2 Relay for motor remote unlock rear lid (79)

Relay panel:

Note: Number in parentheses indicates production control number stamped on relay housing.

Fuse colors

30 A - green
25 A - white
20 A - yellow
15 A - blue
10 A - red
7,5 A - brown
5 A - beige
3 A - violet

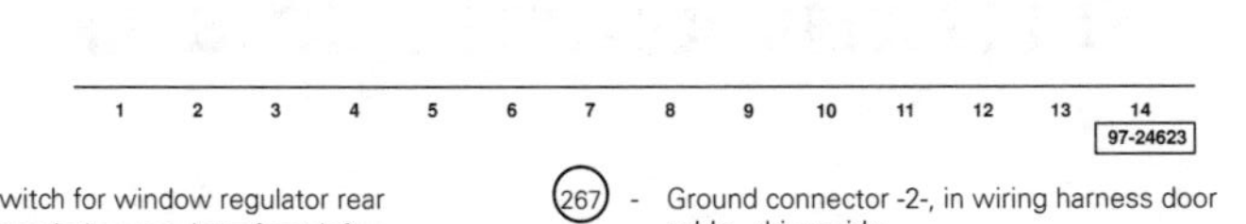

ws = white
sw = black
ro = red
br = brown
gn = green
bl = blue
gr = grey
li = lilac
ge = yellow

E39 - Safety switch for window regulator rear
E40 - Switch for window regulator front left
E53 - Switch for window regulator rear left, driver
E55 - Switch for window regulator rear right, driver
E81 - Switch for window regulator front right, driver
E150 - Switch for interior lock, driver side
J386 - Door control module, driver side
L76 - Push Button Light
S37 - Fuse for window regulator (circuit breaker), on thirteen position auxiliary relay panel
T10i - 10-Pin Connector, black, connector station A-pillar, left
T16a - 16-Pin Connector
T29 - 29-Pin Connector
V147 - Motor for window regulator, driver side

(267) - Ground connector -2-, in wiring harness door cable - driver side
(B110) - Connection (30), window regulator) in wiring harness interior

Door control module (driver side), switch for window regulator, safety switch for window regulator rear, switch for interior lock (driver side)

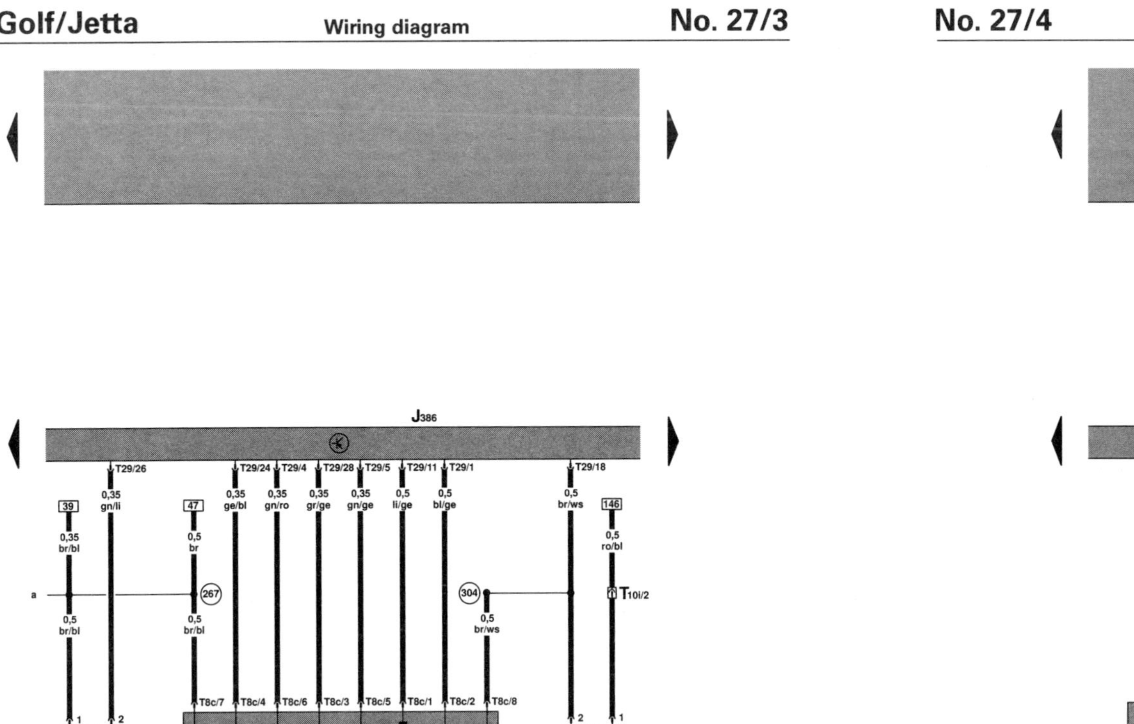

ws = white
sw = black
ro = red
br = brown
gn = green
bl = blue
gr = grey
li = lilac
ge = yellow

F220 - Lock unit for central locking, driver side
J386 - Door control module, driver side
K133 - Warning light for central locking -SAFE-
M27 - Left Door Warning Light
T8c - 8-Pin Connector
T10i - 10-Pin Connector, black, connector station A-pillar, left
T29 - 29-Pin Connector

(267) - Ground connector -2-, in wiring harness door cable - driver side
(304) - Ground connector -3-, in wiring harness door cable - driver side

Edition 11/99
USA.5102.05.21

Door control module (driver side), lock unit for central locking (driver side), warning light for central locking -SAFE-, left door warning light

ws = white
sw = black
ro = red
br = brown
gn = green
bl = blue
gr = grey
li = lilac
ge = yellow

E43 - Mirror Adjustment Switch
E48 - Mirror Selector Switch
E231 - Switch for outside mirror heating
E263 - Mirror fold-away Switch*
J386 - Door control module, driver side
L78 - Mirror Adjusting Switch Light
T10i - 10-Pin Connector, black, connector station A-pillar, left
T10q - 10-Pin Connector, blue, connector station A-pillar, left
T10t - 10-Pin Connector
T29 - 29-Pin Connector

(44) - Ground connection, on left A-pillar, lower part

(205) - Ground connection, in driver's door wiring harness
(A20) - Wire connection (15a), in instrument panel wiring harness

* - If equipped
--- - Vehicles with seperate heated outside mirrors only

Door control module (driver side), mirror adjustment switch, mirror selector switch, switch for outside mirror heating

Edition 11/99
USA.5102.05.21

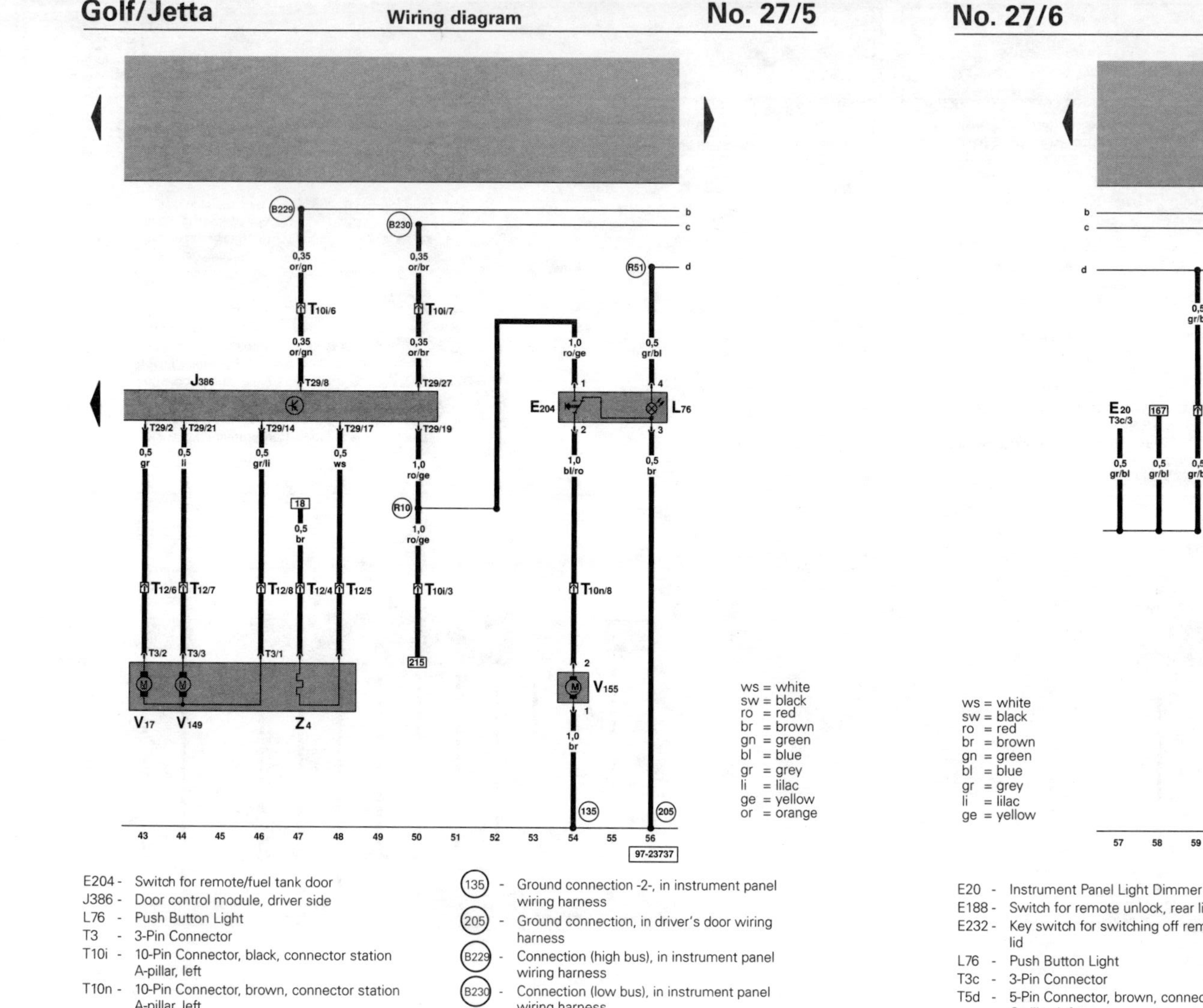

ws = white
sw = black
ro = red
br = brown
gn = green
bl = blue
gr = grey
li = lilac
ge = yellow
or = orange

E204 - Switch for remote/fuel tank door
J386 - Door control module, driver side
L76 - Push Button Light
T3 - 3-Pin Connector
T10i - 10-Pin Connector, black, connector station A-pillar, left
T10n - 10-Pin Connector, brown, connector station A-pillar, left
T12 - 12-Pin Connector
T29 - 29-Pin Connector
V17 - Driver's Side Mirror Adjustment Motor
V149 - Motor for mirror adjustment, driver side
V155 - Motor for fuel tank lid unlock
Z4 - Heated outside mirror, driver side

(135) - Ground connection -2-, in instrument panel wiring harness
(205) - Ground connection, in driver's door wiring harness
(B229) - Connection (high bus), in instrument panel wiring harness
(B230) - Connection (low bus), in instrument panel wiring harness
(R10) - Plus connection -1- (30a), in driver's door wiring harness
(R51) - Connection (58b), in driver's door wiring harness

Door control module (driver side), switch for remote/fuel tank door, motor for fuel tank lid unlock, power mirror (driver side), heated outside mirror (driver side)

E20
L76
E188
E232
A4
A49
R51
97-23738

ws = white
sw = black
ro = red
br = brown
gn = green
bl = blue
gr = grey
li = lilac
ge = yellow

E20 - Instrument Panel Light Dimmer Switch
E188 - Switch for remote unlock, rear lid, driver side
E232 - Key switch for switching off remote unlock rear lid
L76 - Push Button Light
T3c - 3-Pin Connector
T5d - 5-Pin Connector, brown, connector station C-pillar, left
T10i - 10-Pin Connector, black, connector station A-pillar, left

(205) - Ground connection, in driver's door wiring harness
(A4) - Plus connection (58b), in instrument panel wiring harness

(A49) - Wire connection -1-, in instrument panel wiring harness
(R51) - Connection (58b), in driver's door wiring harness

* - Jetta only
-•-•- Golf only

Switch for remote unlock rear lid (driver side), key switch for switching off remote unlock rear lid

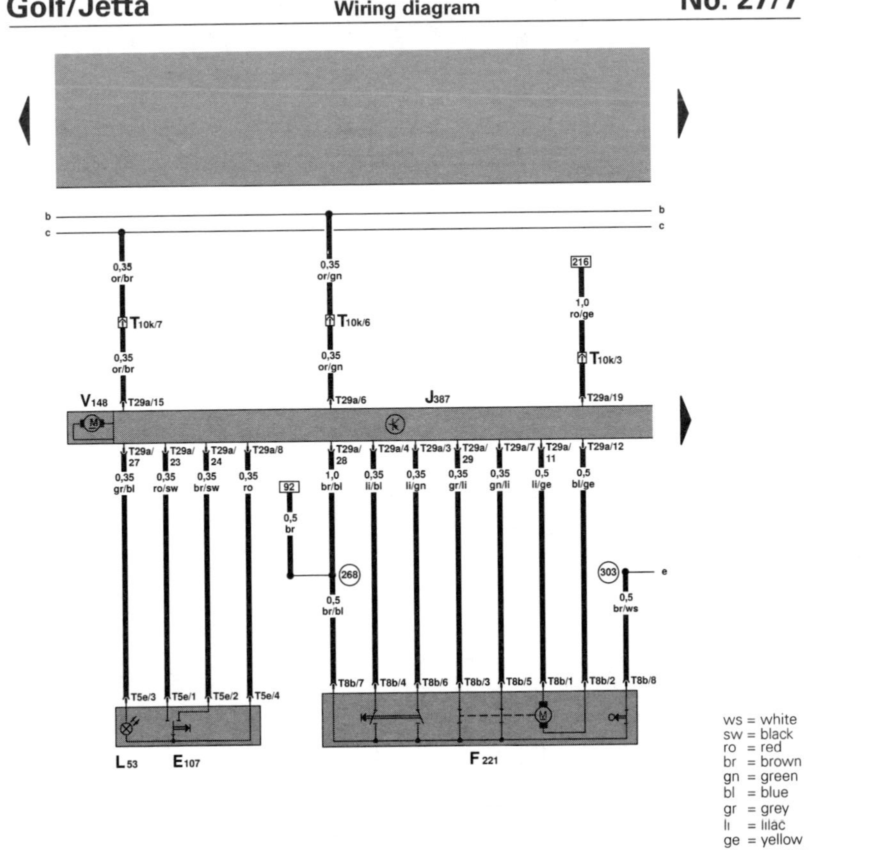

E107 - Switch for window regulator, in passenger door
F221 - Lock unit for central locking, passenger side
J387 - Door control module, passenger side
L53 - Power Window Switch Light
T5e - 5-Pin Connector
T8b - 8-Pin Connector
T10k - 10-Pin Connector, black, connector station A-pillar, right
T29a - 29-Pin Connector
V148 - Motor for window regulator, passenger side

(268) - Ground connector -2-, in wiring harness door cable - passenger side
(303) - Ground connector -3-, in wiring harness door cable - passenger side

Door control module (passenger side), switch for window regulator (passenger door), lock unit for central locking (passenger side)

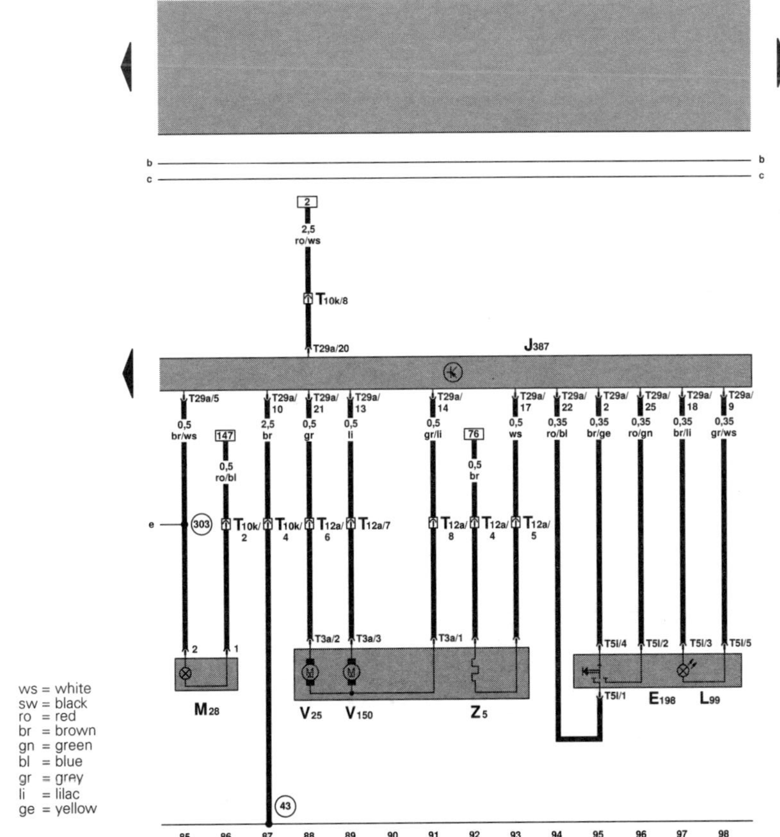

E198 - Switch for interior lock, passenger side
J387 - Door control module, passenger side
L99 - Lighting for switch interior lock
M28 - Right Door Warning Light
T3a - 3-Pin Connector
T5l - 5-Pin Connector
T10k - 10-Pin Connector, black, connector station A-pillar, right
T12a - 12-Pin Connector
T29a - 29-Pin Connector
V25 - Passenger's Side Mirror Adjustment Motor
V150 - Motor for mirror adjustment, passenger side
Z5 - Heated outside mirror, passenger side

(43) - Ground connection, on right A-pillar, lower part

(303) - Ground connector -3-, in wiring harness door cable - passenger side

Door control module (passenger side), switch for interior lock (passenger side), right door warning light, power mirror (passenger side), heated outside mirror

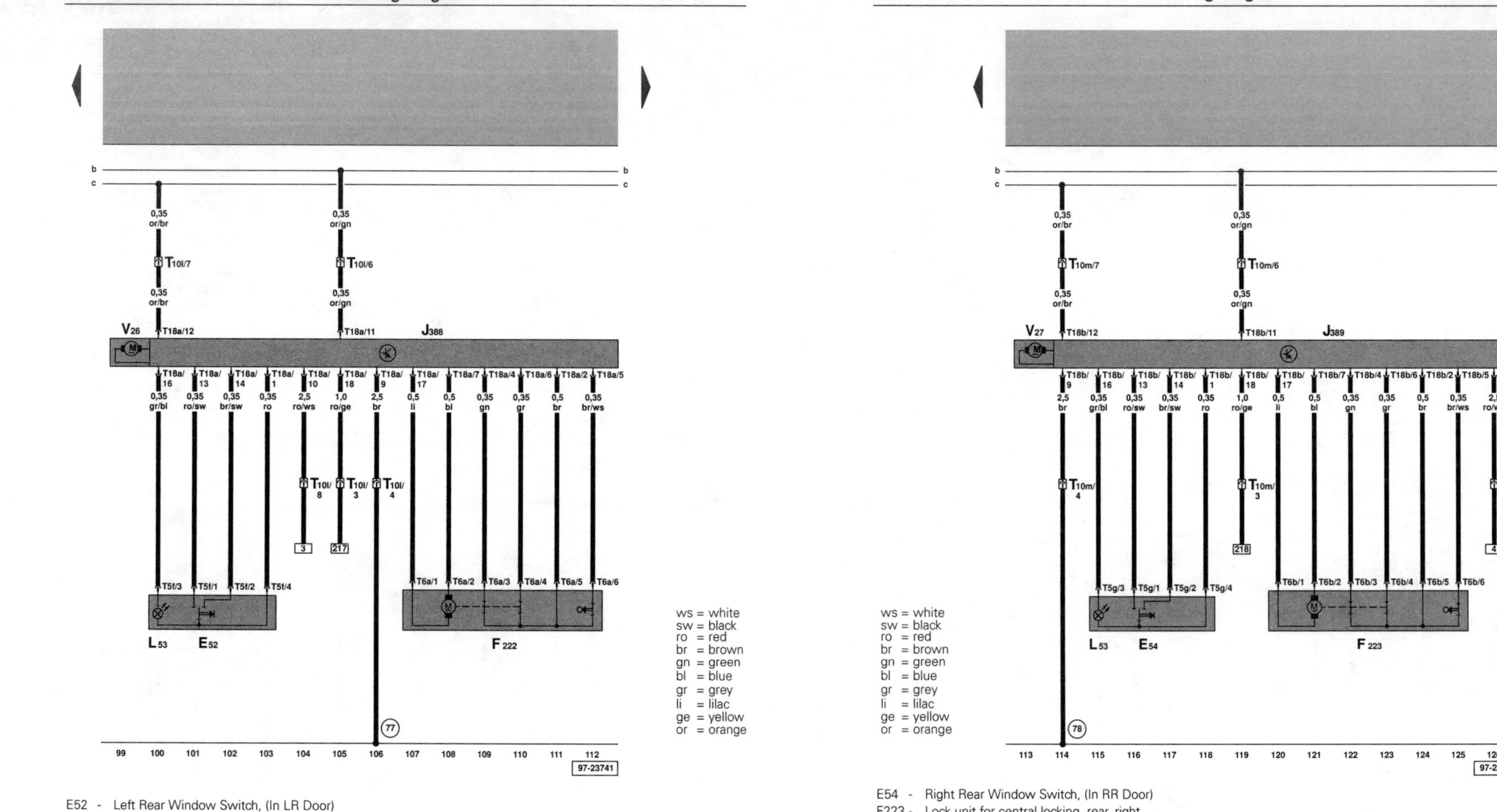

ws = white
sw = black
ro = red
br = brown
gn = green
bl = blue
gr = grey
li = lilac
ge = yellow
or = orange

- E52 - Left Rear Window Switch, (In LR Door)
- F222 - Lock unit for central locking, rear, left
- J388 - Door control module, rear, left
- L53 - Power Window Switch Light
- T5f - 5-Pin Connector
- T6a - 6-Pin Connector
- T10l - 10-Pin Connector, black, connector station B-pillar, left
- T18a - 18-Pin Connector
- V26 - Motor for window regulator, rear, left
- (77) - Ground connection, on left B-pillar, lower part

ws = white
sw = black
ro = red
br = brown
gn = green
bl = blue
gr = grey
li = lilac
ge = yellow
or = orange

- E54 - Right Rear Window Switch, (In RR Door)
- F223 - Lock unit for central locking, rear, right
- J389 - Door control module, rear, right
- L53 - Power Window Switch Light
- T5g - 5-Pin Connector
- T6b - 6-Pin Connector
- T10m - 10-Pin Connector, black, connector station B-pillar, right
- T18b - 18-Pin Connector
- V27 - Motor for window regulator, rear, right
- (78) - Ground connection, on right B-pillar, lower part

Door control module (rear left), left rear window switch (In LR Door), lock unit for central locking (rear left), motor for window regulator (rear left)

Door control module (rear right), right rear window switch (In RR Door), lock unit for central locking (rear right), motor for window regulator (rear right)

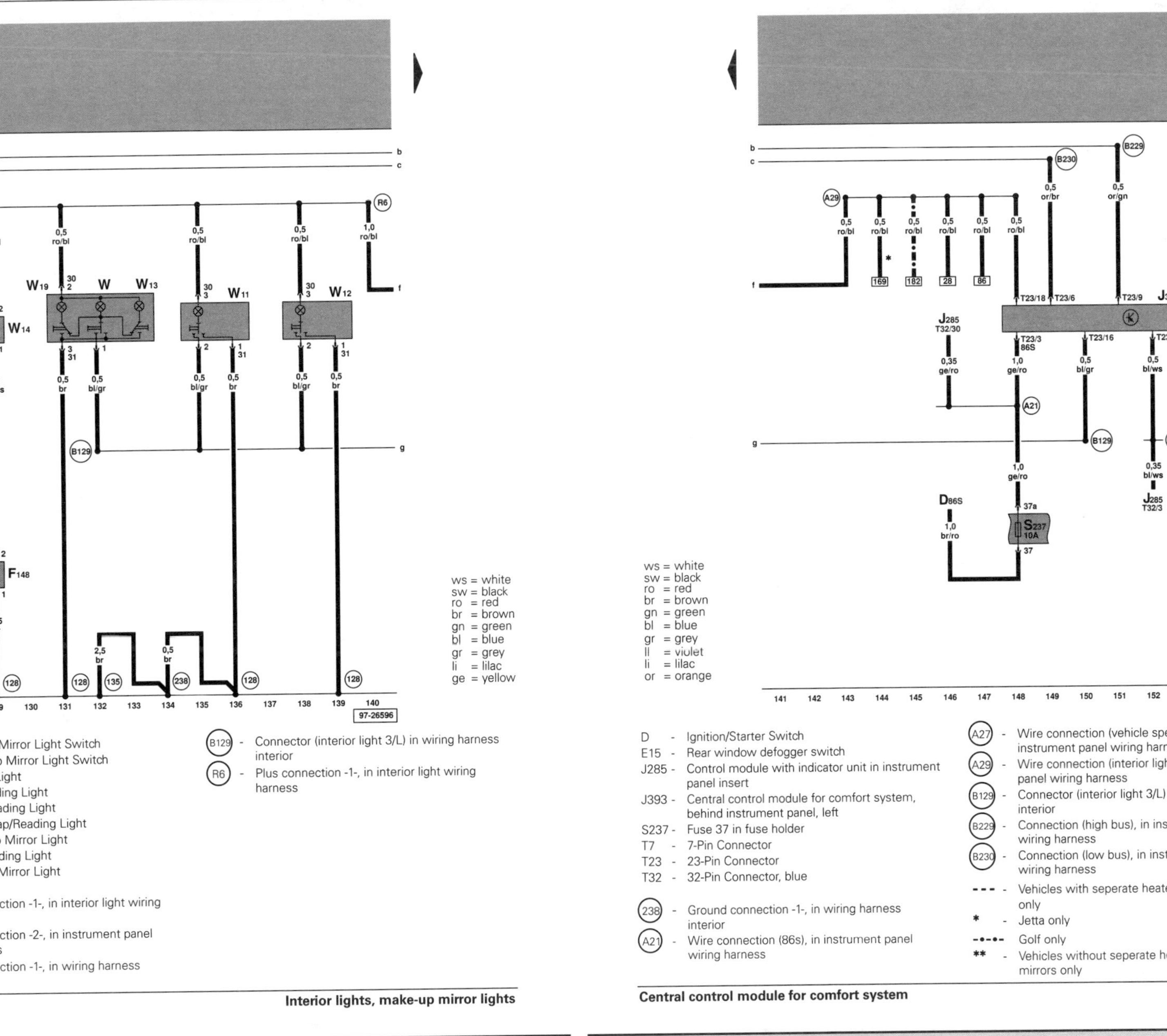

F147 - Left Make-Up Mirror Light Switch
F148 - Right Make-Up Mirror Light Switch
W - Front Interior Light
W11 - Left Rear Reading Light
W12 - Right Rear Reading Light
W13 - Right Front Map/Reading Light
W14 - Right Make-up Mirror Light
W19 - Left Front Reading Light
W20 - Left Make-up Mirror Light

(128) - Ground connection -1-, in interior light wiring harness
(135) - Ground connection -2-, in instrument panel wiring harness
(238) - Ground connection -1-, in wiring harness interior
(B129) - Connector (interior light 3/L) in wiring harness interior
(R6) - Plus connection -1-, in interior light wiring harness

ws = white
sw = black
ro = red
br = brown
gn = green
bl = blue
gr = grey
li = lilac
ge = yellow

Interior lights, make-up mirror lights

ws = white
sw = black
ro = red
br = brown
gn = green
bl = blue
gr = grey
ll = violet
li = lilac
or = orange

D - Ignition/Starter Switch
E15 - Rear window defogger switch
J285 - Control module with indicator unit in instrument panel insert
J393 - Central control module for comfort system, behind instrument panel, left
S237 - Fuse 37 in fuse holder
T7 - 7-Pin Connector
T23 - 23-Pin Connector
T32 - 32-Pin Connector, blue

(238) - Ground connection -1-, in wiring harness interior
(A21) - Wire connection (86s), in instrument panel wiring harness
(A27) - Wire connection (vehicle speed signal), in instrument panel wiring harness
(A29) - Wire connection (interior light), in instrument panel wiring harness
(B129) - Connector (interior light 3/L) in wiring harness interior
(B229) - Connection (high bus), in instrument panel wiring harness
(B230) - Connection (low bus), in instrument panel wiring harness

--- - Vehicles with seperate heated outside mirrors only
* - Jetta only
-•-•- - Golf only
** - Vehicles without seperate heated outside mirrors only

Central control module for comfort system

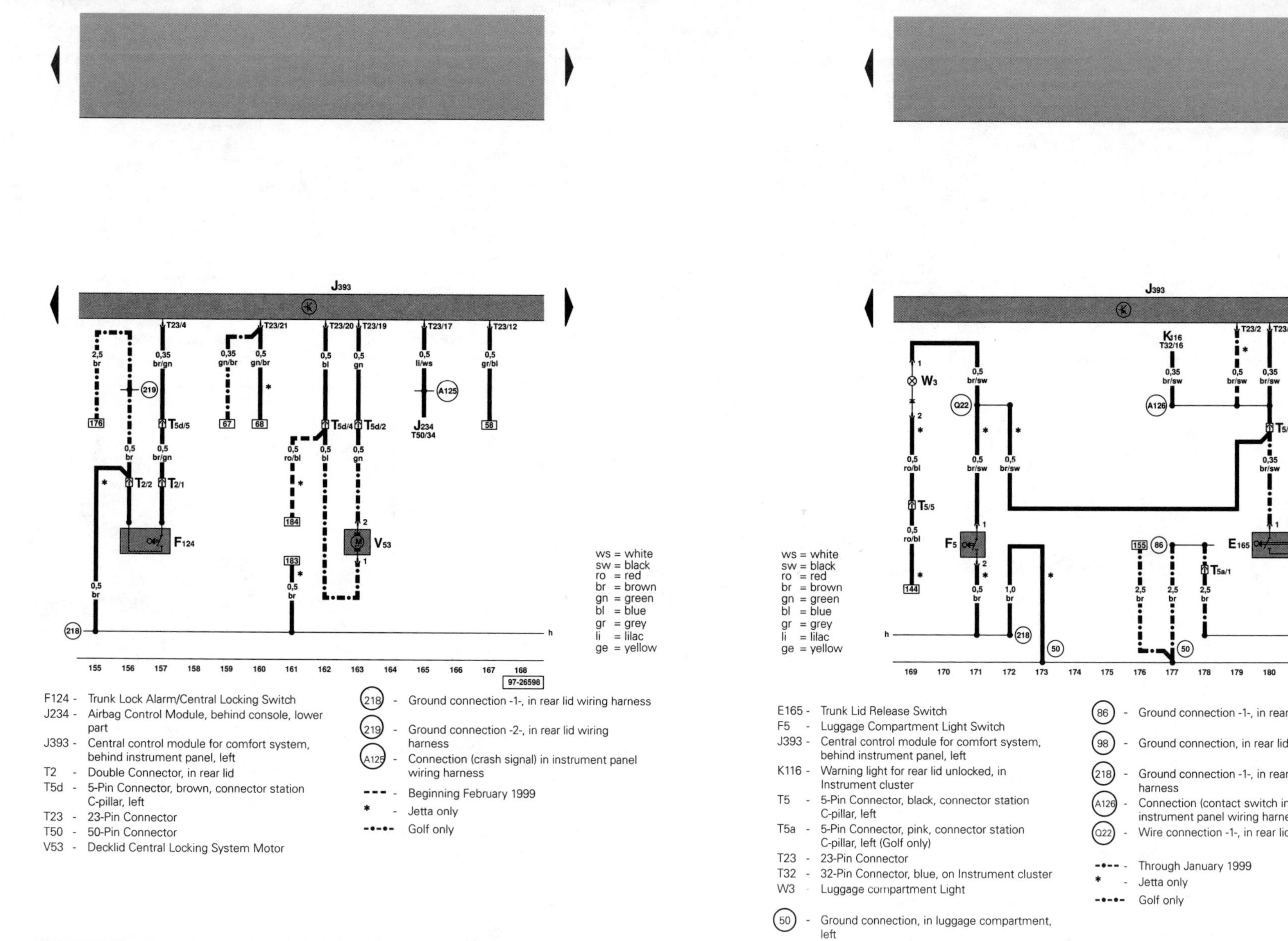

ws = white
sw = black
ro = red
br = brown
gn = green
bl = blue
gr = grey
li = lilac
ge = yellow

F124 - Trunk Lock Alarm/Central Locking Switch
J234 - Airbag Control Module, behind console, lower part
J393 - Central control module for comfort system, behind instrument panel, left
T2 - Double Connector, in rear lid
T5d - 5-Pin Connector, brown, connector station C-pillar, left
T23 - 23-Pin Connector
T50 - 50-Pin Connector
V53 - Decklid Central Locking System Motor

(218) - Ground connection -1-, in rear lid wiring harness
(219) - Ground connection -2-, in rear lid wiring harness
(A125) - Connection (crash signal) in instrument panel wiring harness

--- - Beginning February 1999
* - Jetta only
-•-•- - Golf only

Central control module for comfort system, trunk lock alarm/central locking switch, decklid central locking system motor

ws = white
sw = black
ro = red
br = brown
gn = green
bl = blue
gr = grey
li = lilac
ge = yellow

E165 - Trunk Lid Release Switch
F5 - Luggage Compartment Light Switch
J393 - Central control module for comfort system, behind instrument panel, left
K116 - Warning light for rear lid unlocked, in Instrument cluster
T5 - 5-Pin Connector, black, connector station C-pillar, left
T5a - 5-Pin Connector, pink, connector station C-pillar, left (Golf only)
T23 - 23-Pin Connector
T32 - 32-Pin Connector, blue, on Instrument cluster
W3 - Luggage compartment Light

(50) - Ground connection, in luggage compartment, left

(86) - Ground connection -1-, in rear wiring harness
(98) - Ground connection, in rear lid wiring harness
(218) - Ground connection -1-, in rear lid wiring harness
(A126) - Connection (contact switch in rear lid) in instrument panel wiring harness
(Q22) - Wire connection -1-, in rear lid wiring harness

-•-- - Through January 1999
* - Jetta only
-•-•- - Golf only

Central control module for comfort system, trunk lid release switch, luggage compartment light

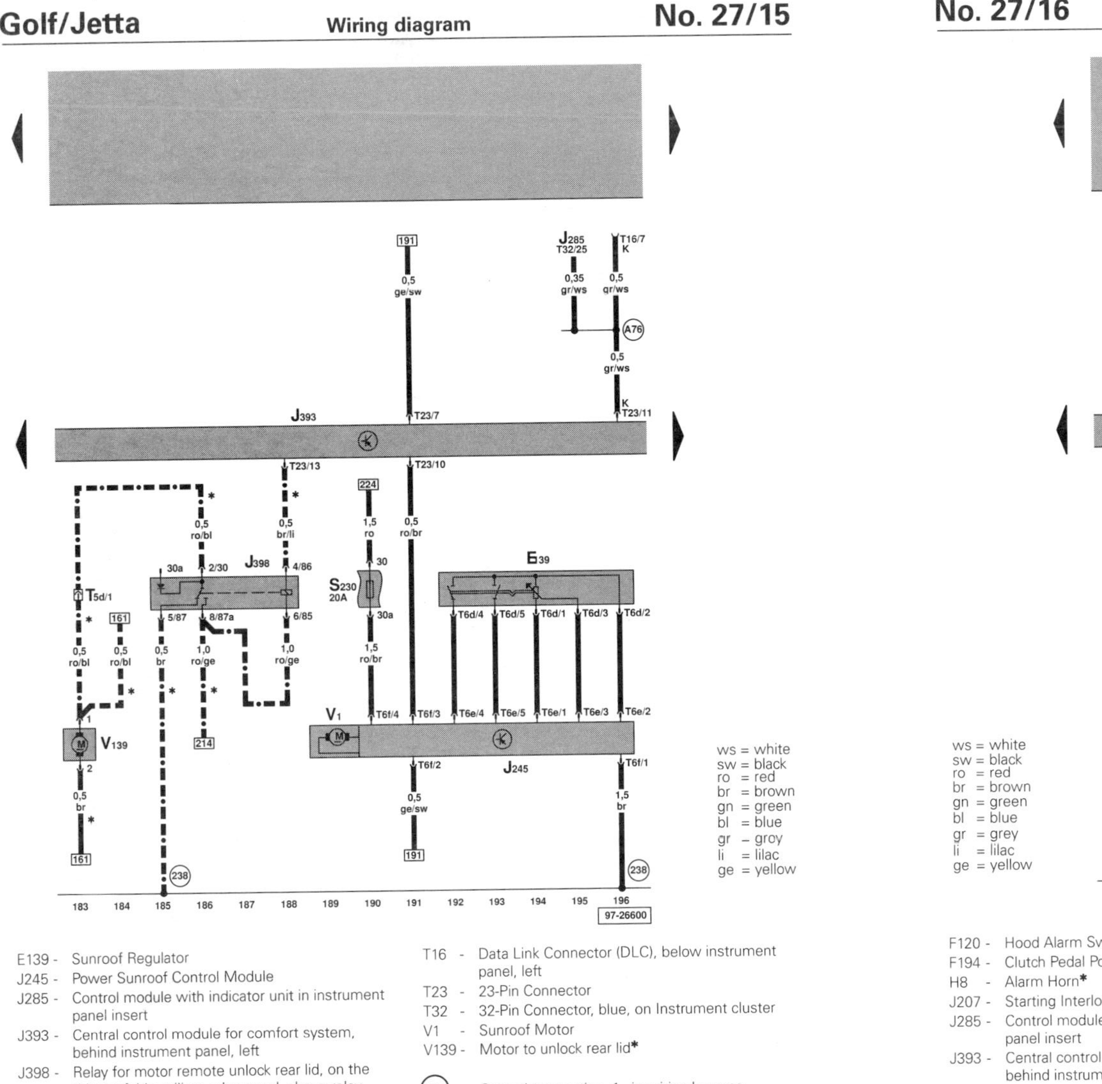

ws = white
sw = black
ro = red
br = brown
gn = green
bl = blue
gr = groy
li = lilac
ge = yellow

E139 - Sunroof Regulator
J245 - Power Sunroof Control Module
J285 - Control module with indicator unit in instrument panel insert
J393 - Central control module for comfort system, behind instrument panel, left
J398 - Relay for motor remote unlock rear lid, on the thirteenfold auxiliary relay panel, above relay panel*
S230 - Fuse 30 in fuse holder
T5d - 5-Pin Connector, brown, connector station C-pillar, left
T6d - 6-Pin Connector
T6e - 6-Pin Connector
T6f - 6-Pin Connector
T16 - Data Link Connector (DLC), below instrument panel, left
T23 - 23-Pin Connector
T32 - 32-Pin Connector, blue, on Instrument cluster
V1 - Sunroof Motor
V139 - Motor to unlock rear lid*

(238) - Ground connection -1-, in wiring harness interior
(A76) - Connector (K-diagnosis wire) in instrument panel wiring harness

-•-- - Through January 1999
* - Jetta only
- - - Beginning February 1999

Central control module for comfort system, power sunroof control module, sunroof regulator, sunroof motor, relay for motor remote unlock rear lid, motor to unlock rear lid

ws = white
sw = black
ro = red
br = brown
gn = green
bl = blue
gr = grey
li = lilac
ge = yellow

F120 - Hood Alarm Switch*
F194 - Clutch Pedal Position (CPP) Switch**
H8 - Alarm Horn*
J207 - Starting Interlock Relay
J285 - Control module with indicator unit in instrument panel insert
J393 - Central control module for comfort system, behind instrument panel, left
R - Radio
R47 - Antenna wire for central locking and antitheft warning system
T2a - Double Connector, near headlight, right
T8 - 8-Pin Connector, on radio
T15 - 15-Pin Connector
T23 - 23-Pin Connector
T32 - 32-Pin Connector, blue, on Instrument cluster

(12) - Ground connection, in engine compartment, left
(179) - Ground connection, in left headlight wiring harness
(A5) - Plus connection (right turn signal), in instrument panel wiring harness
(A6) - Plus connection (left turn signal), in instrument panel wiring harness
(A13) - Wire connection (door contact switch) in instrument panel wiring harness
(B161) - Connector (anti-theft warning system), in wiring harness interior
* - Vehicles with anti-theft warning system only
** - Manual transmission only
- - - - Automatic transmission only

Central control module for comfort system, antitheft warning system, antenna wire for central locking and antitheft warning system

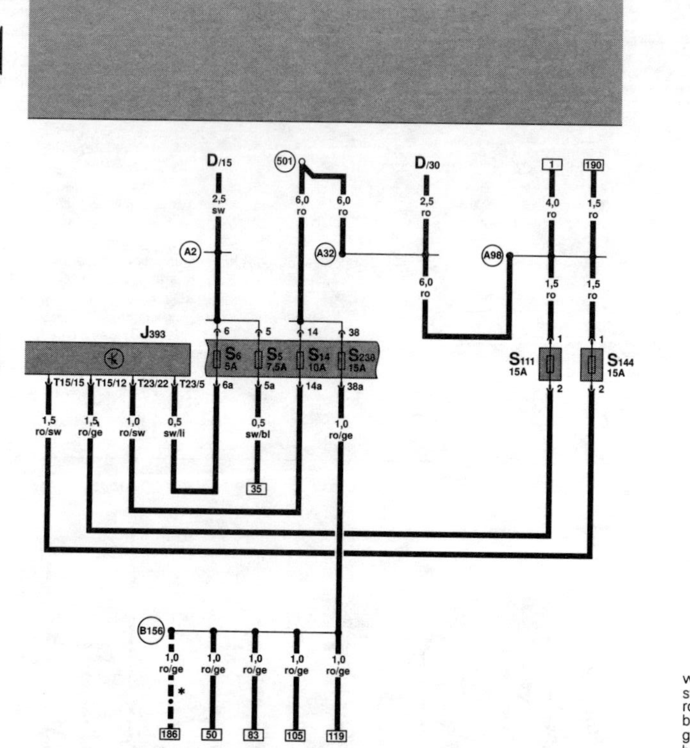

ws = white
sw = black
ro = red
br = brown
gn = green
bl = blue
gr = grey
li = lilac
ge = yellow

D - Ignition/Starter Switch
J393 - Central control module for comfort system, behind instrument panel, left
S5 - Fuse 5 in fuse holder
S6 - Fuse 6 in fuse holder
S14 - Fuse 14 in fuse holder
S111 - Alarm System and Anti-Theft Fuse, above the thirteenfold auxiliary relay panel
S144 - Fuse for central locking/anti-theft warning system, above the thirteenfold auxiliary relay panel
S238 - Fuse 38 in fuse holder
T15 - 15-Pin Connector
T23 - 23-Pin Connector

(501) - Threaded connection -2- (30) on the relay plate
(A2) - Plus connection (15), in instrument panel wiring harness
(A32) - Plus connection (30), in instrument panel wiring harness
(A98) - Plus connector -4- (30), in instrument panel wiring harness
(B156) - Plus connector (30a), in wiring harness interior

* - Jetta only
-•-- - Through January 1999

THIS PAGE INTENTIONALLY LEFT BLANK

Radio system (with CD changer wiring preparation)

from September 1998

Deviate relay location and fuseplacements as well as the locations of multiple connectors see section "component locations".

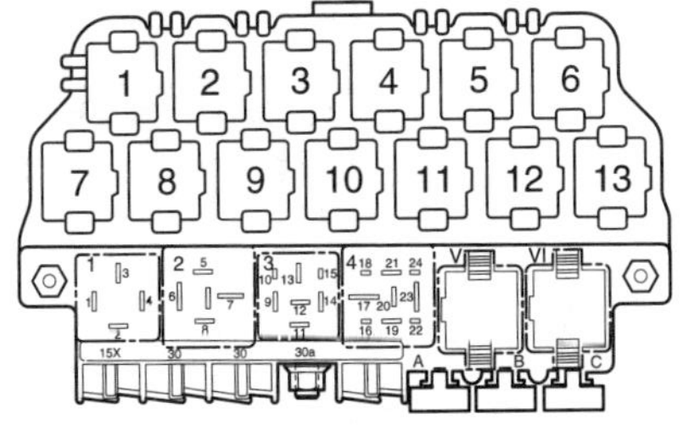

Fuse colors

30 A - green
25 A - white
20 A - yellow
15 A - blue
10 A - red
7,5 A - brown
5 A - beige
3 A - violet

ws = white
sw = black
ro = red
br = brown
gn = green
bl = blue
gr = grey
li = lilac
ge = yellow

97-24528

R - Radio
R11 - Antenna
R20 - Treble speaker, left front
R21 - Bass speaker, left front
R24 - Antenna Amplifier
R41 - CD Changer Unit
T1 - Single Connector
T8a - 8-Pin Connector
T10i - 10-Pin Connector, black, connector station A-pillar, left
T12 - 12-Pin Connector
T20 - 20-Pin Connector, on Radio

(45) - Ground connection, behind instrument panel, center

(255) - Ground connection, -1-, in wiring harness radio

(V14) - Wire connection (shielding), in CD-changer wiring harness

Radio, wiring harness from radio to CD changer unit, loud speaker (left front)

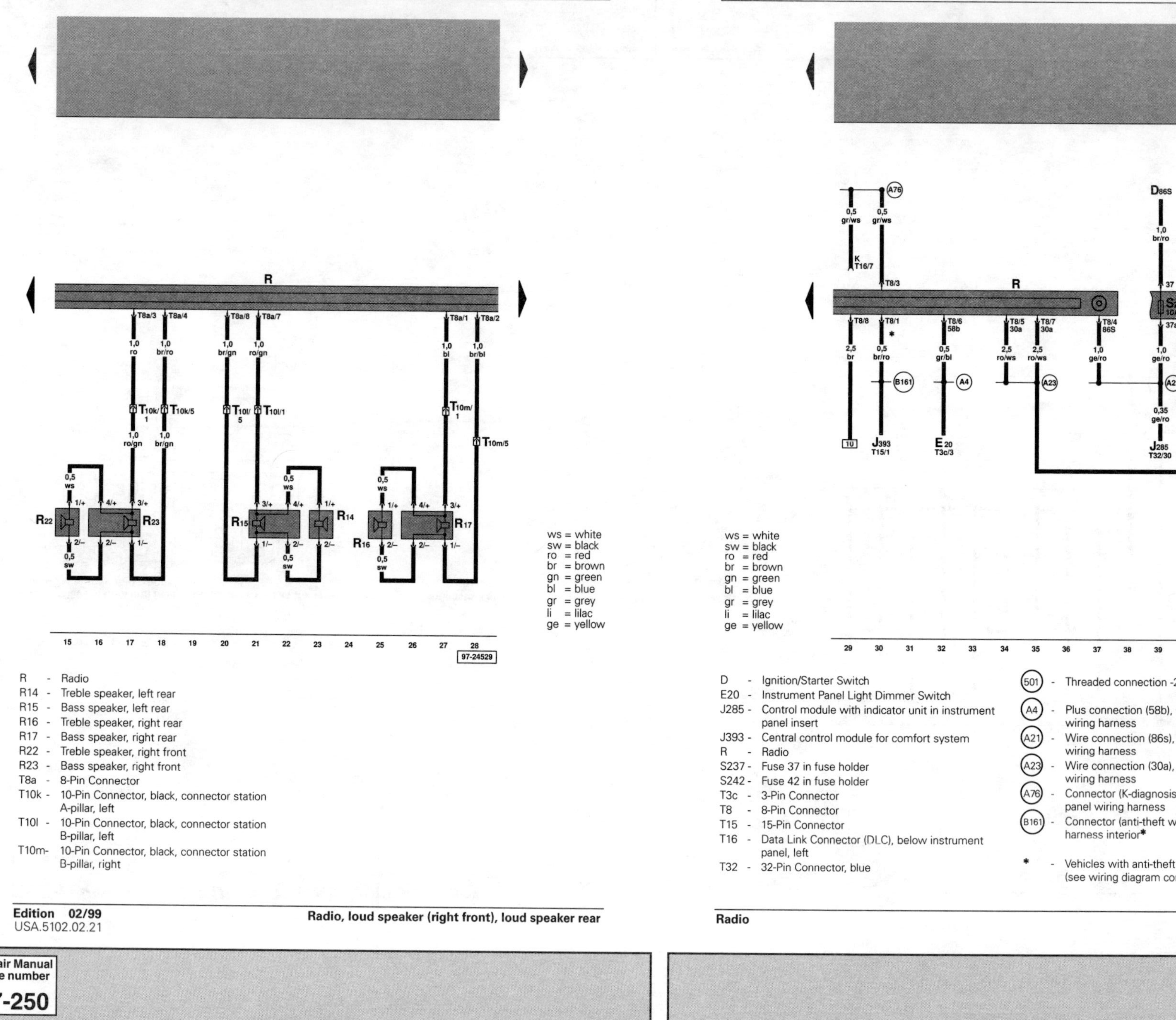

ws = white
sw = black
ro = red
br = brown
gn = green
bl = blue
gr = grey
li = lilac
ge = yellow

R - Radio
R14 - Treble speaker, left rear
R15 - Bass speaker, left rear
R16 - Treble speaker, right rear
R17 - Bass speaker, right rear
R22 - Treble speaker, right front
R23 - Bass speaker, right front
T8a - 8-Pin Connector
T10k - 10-Pin Connector, black, connector station A-pillar, left
T10l - 10-Pin Connector, black, connector station B-pillar, left
T10m- 10-Pin Connector, black, connector station B-pillar, right

ws = white
sw = black
ro = red
br = brown
gn = green
bl = blue
gr = grey
li = lilac
ge = yellow

D - Ignition/Starter Switch
E20 - Instrument Panel Light Dimmer Switch
J285 - Control module with indicator unit in instrument panel insert
J393 - Central control module for comfort system
R - Radio
S237 - Fuse 37 in fuse holder
S242 - Fuse 42 in fuse holder
T3c - 3-Pin Connector
T8 - 8-Pin Connector
T15 - 15-Pin Connector
T16 - Data Link Connector (DLC), below instrument panel, left
T32 - 32-Pin Connector, blue

(501) - Threaded connection -2- (30) on the relay plate
(A4) - Plus connection (58b), in instrument panel wiring harness
(A21) - Wire connection (86s), in instrument panel wiring harness
(A23) - Wire connection (30a), in instrument panel wiring harness
(A76) - Connector (K-diagnosis wire) in instrument panel wiring harness
(B161) - Connector (anti-theft warning system), in wiring harness interior*

* - Vehicles with anti-theft warning system only (see wiring diagram comfort system)

Golf /Jetta - Standard Equipment,

from May 1999

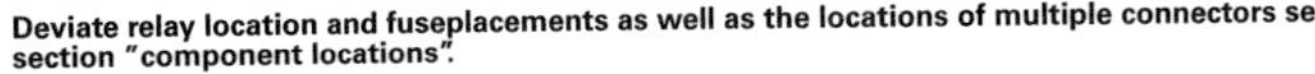

Deviate relay location and fuseplacements as well as the locations of multiple connectors see section "component locations".

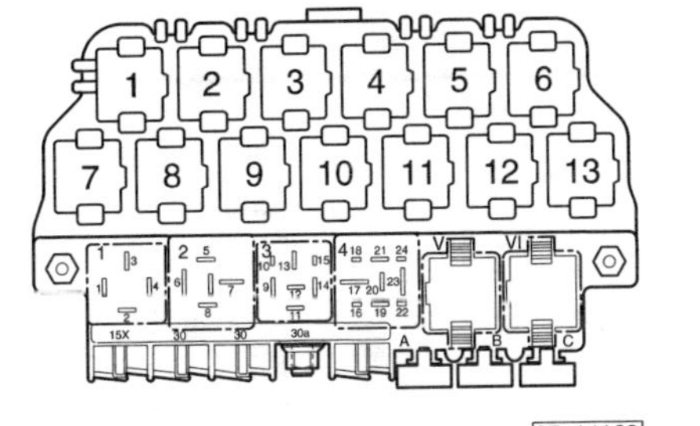

Relay location on the thirteenfold auxiliary relay panel, above relay panel:

3 Starting Interlock Relay (53)

Relay panel:

1 Dual Horn Relay (53)

2 Load Reduction Relay (18)/(100)

V Wiper/Washer Intermittent Relay (377)

VI

Note: Number in parentheses indicates production control number stamped on relay housing.

Fuse colors

30 A - green
25 A - white
20 A - yellow
15 A - blue
10 A - red
7,5 A - brown
5 A - beige
3 A - violet

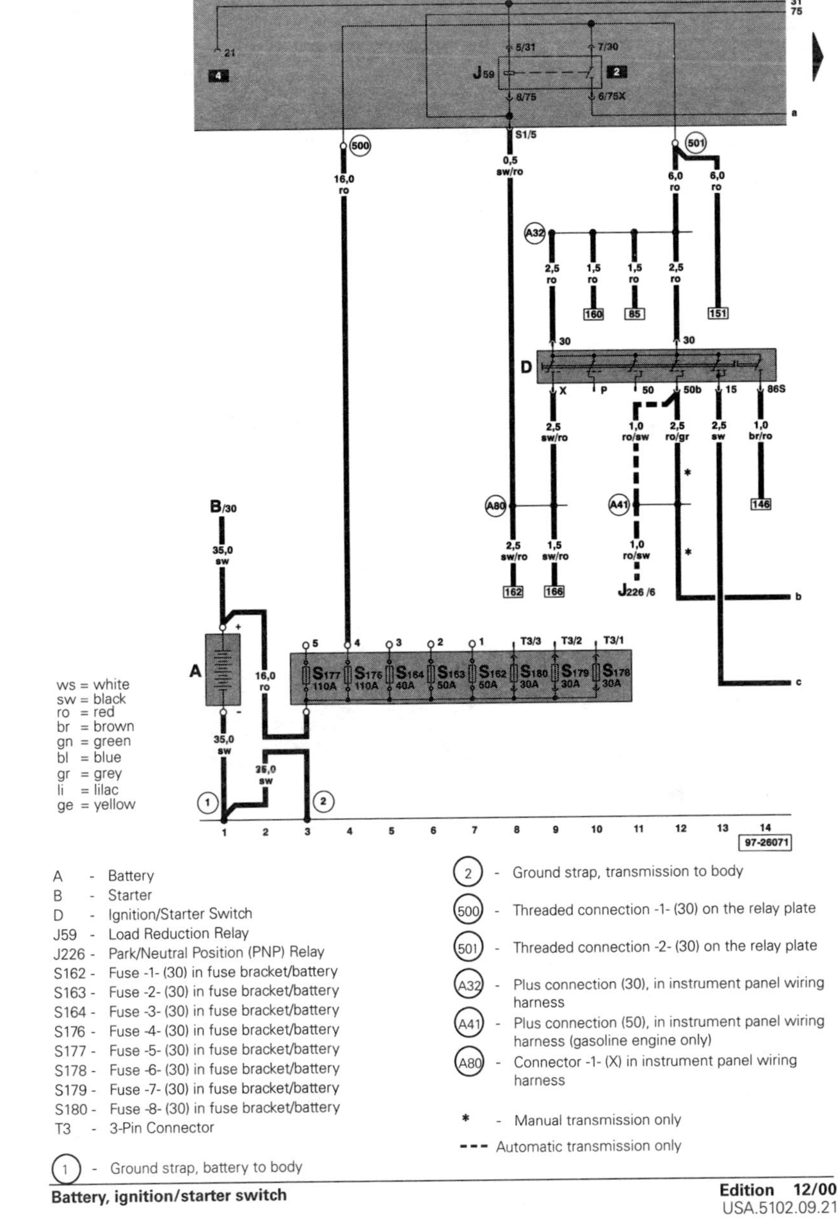

ws = white
sw = black
ro = red
br = brown
gn = green
bl = blue
gr = grey
li = lilac
ge = yellow

A - Battery
B - Starter
D - Ignition/Starter Switch
J59 - Load Reduction Relay
J226 - Park/Neutral Position (PNP) Relay
S162 - Fuse -1- (30) in fuse bracket/battery
S163 - Fuse -2- (30) in fuse bracket/battery
S164 - Fuse -3- (30) in fuse bracket/battery
S176 - Fuse -4- (30) in fuse bracket/battery
S177 - Fuse -5- (30) in fuse bracket/battery
S178 - Fuse -6- (30) in fuse bracket/battery
S179 - Fuse -7- (30) in fuse bracket/battery
S180 - Fuse -8- (30) in fuse bracket/battery
T3 - 3-Pin Connector

(1) - Ground strap, battery to body

(2) - Ground strap, transmission to body

(500) - Threaded connection -1- (30) on the relay plate

(501) - Threaded connection -2- (30) on the relay plate

(A32) - Plus connection (30), in instrument panel wiring harness

(A41) - Plus connection (50), in instrument panel wiring harness (gasoline engine only)

(A80) - Connector -1- (X) in instrument panel wiring harness

* - Manual transmission only

--- Automatic transmission only

Battery, ignition/starter switch

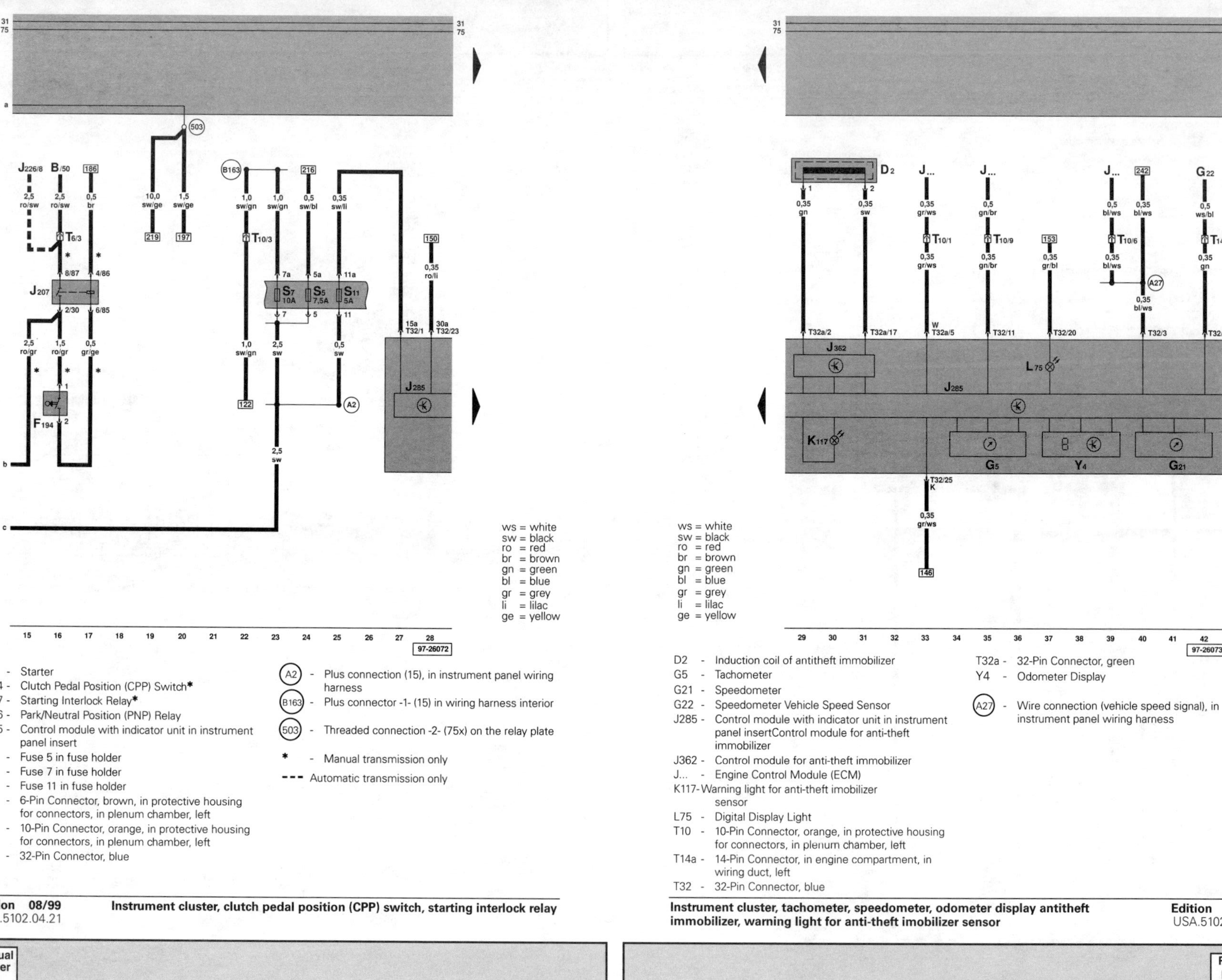

ws = white
sw = black
ro = red
br = brown
gn = green
bl = blue
gr = grey
li = lilac
ge = yellow

B - Starter
F194 - Clutch Pedal Position (CPP) Switch*
J207 - Starting Interlock Relay*
J226 - Park/Neutral Position (PNP) Relay
J285 - Control module with indicator unit in instrument panel insert
S5 - Fuse 5 in fuse holder
S7 - Fuse 7 in fuse holder
S11 - Fuse 11 in fuse holder
T6 - 6-Pin Connector, brown, in protective housing for connectors, in plenum chamber, left
T10 - 10-Pin Connector, orange, in protective housing for connectors, in plenum chamber, left
T32 - 32-Pin Connector, blue

(A2) - Plus connection (15), in instrument panel wiring harness
(B163) - Plus connector -1- (15) in wiring harness interior
(503) - Threaded connection -2- (75x) on the relay plate
* - Manual transmission only
--- Automatic transmission only

Instrument cluster, clutch pedal position (CPP) switch, starting interlock relay

ws = white
sw = black
ro = red
br = brown
gn = green
bl = blue
gr = grey
li = lilac
ge = yellow

D2 - Induction coil of antitheft immobilizer
G5 - Tachometer
G21 - Speedometer
G22 - Speedometer Vehicle Speed Sensor
J285 - Control module with indicator unit in instrument panel insertControl module for anti-theft immobilizer
J362 - Control module for anti-theft immobilizer
J... - Engine Control Module (ECM)
K117- Warning light for anti-theft immobilizer sensor
L75 - Digital Display Light
T10 - 10-Pin Connector, orange, in protective housing for connectors, in plenum chamber, left
T14a - 14-Pin Connector, in engine compartment, in wiring duct, left
T32 - 32-Pin Connector, blue
T32a - 32-Pin Connector, green
Y4 - Odometer Display

(A27) - Wire connection (vehicle speed signal), in instrument panel wiring harness

Instrument cluster, tachometer, speedometer, odometer display antitheft immobilizer, warning light for anti-theft imobilizer sensor

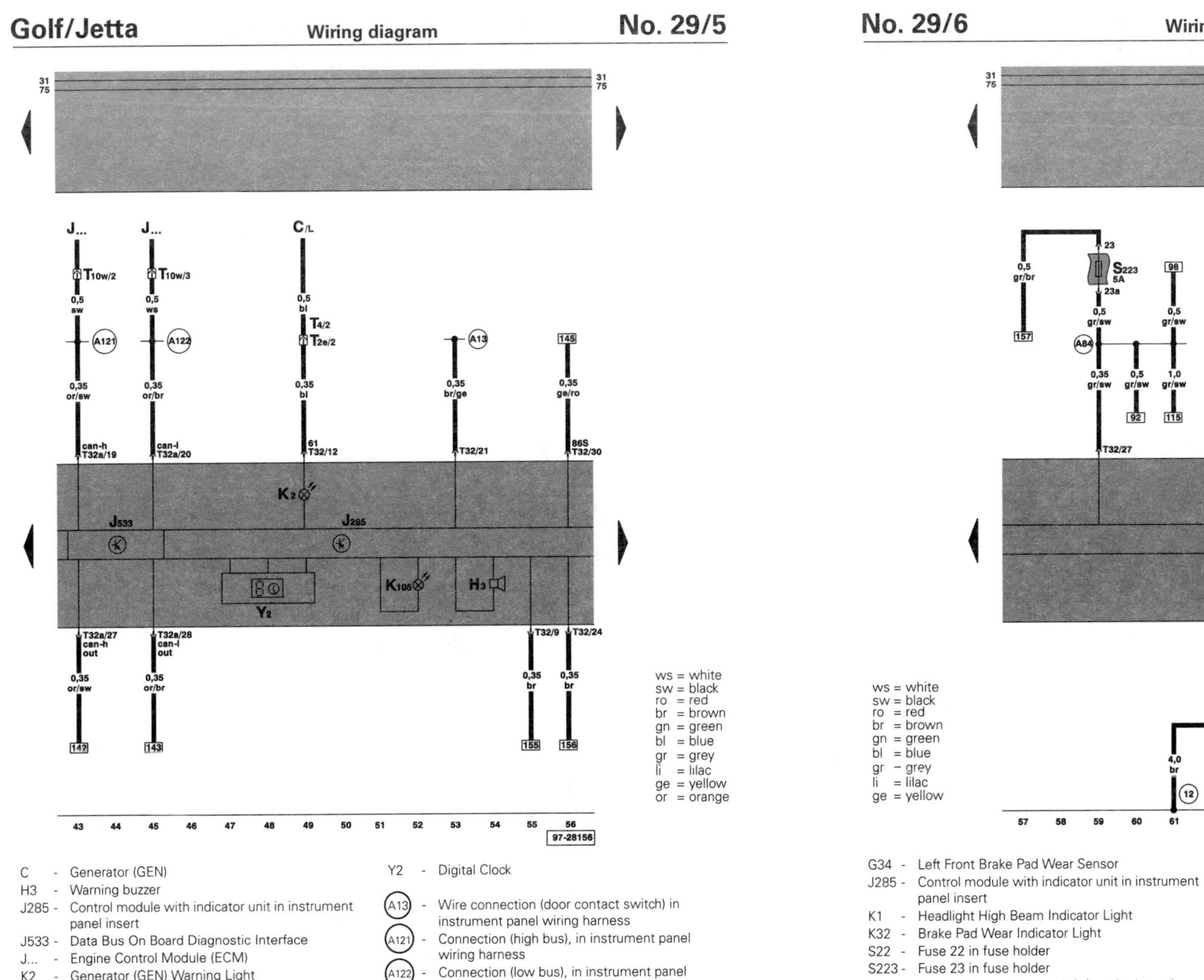

ws = white
sw = black
ro = red
br = brown
gn = green
bl = blue
gr = grey
li = lilac
ge = yellow
or = orange

C - Generator (GEN)
H3 - Warning buzzer
J285 - Control module with indicator unit in instrument panel insert
J533 - Data Bus On Board Diagnostic Interface
J... - Engine Control Module (ECM)
K2 - Generator (GEN) Warning Light
K105 - Low Fuel Level Warning Light
T2e - Double Connector, near starter (in vehicles without air conditioning)
T4 - 4-Pin Connector, near starter (in vehicles with air conditioning)
T10w - 10-Pin Connector, white, in protective housing for connectors, in plenum chamber, left
T32 - 32-Pin Connector, blue
T32a - 32-Pin Connector, green

Y2 - Digital Clock

(A13) - Wire connection (door contact switch) in instrument panel wiring harness
(A121) - Connection (high bus), in instrument panel wiring harness
(A122) - Connection (low bus), in instrument panel wiring harness

Instrument cluster, generator (GEN) warning light, digital clock, low fuel level warning light

ws = white
sw = black
ro = red
br = brown
gn = green
bl = blue
gr = grey
li = lilac
ge = yellow

G34 - Left Front Brake Pad Wear Sensor
J285 - Control module with indicator unit in instrument panel insert
K1 - Headlight High Beam Indicator Light
K32 - Brake Pad Wear Indicator Light
S22 - Fuse 22 in fuse holder
S223 - Fuse 23 in fuse holder
T2c - Double Connector, near left front brake pad wear sensor
T32 - 32-Pin Connector, blue
T32a - 32-Pin Connector, green

(12) - Ground connection, in engine compartment, left
(179) - Ground connection, in left headlight wiring harness

(A51) - Wire connection (56), in instrument panel wiring harness
(A84) - Connector (58L) in instrument panel wiring harness
(A85) - Connector (58R) in instrument panel wiring harness

Instrument cluster, left front brake pad wear sensor, brake pad wear indicator light, headlight high beam indicator light

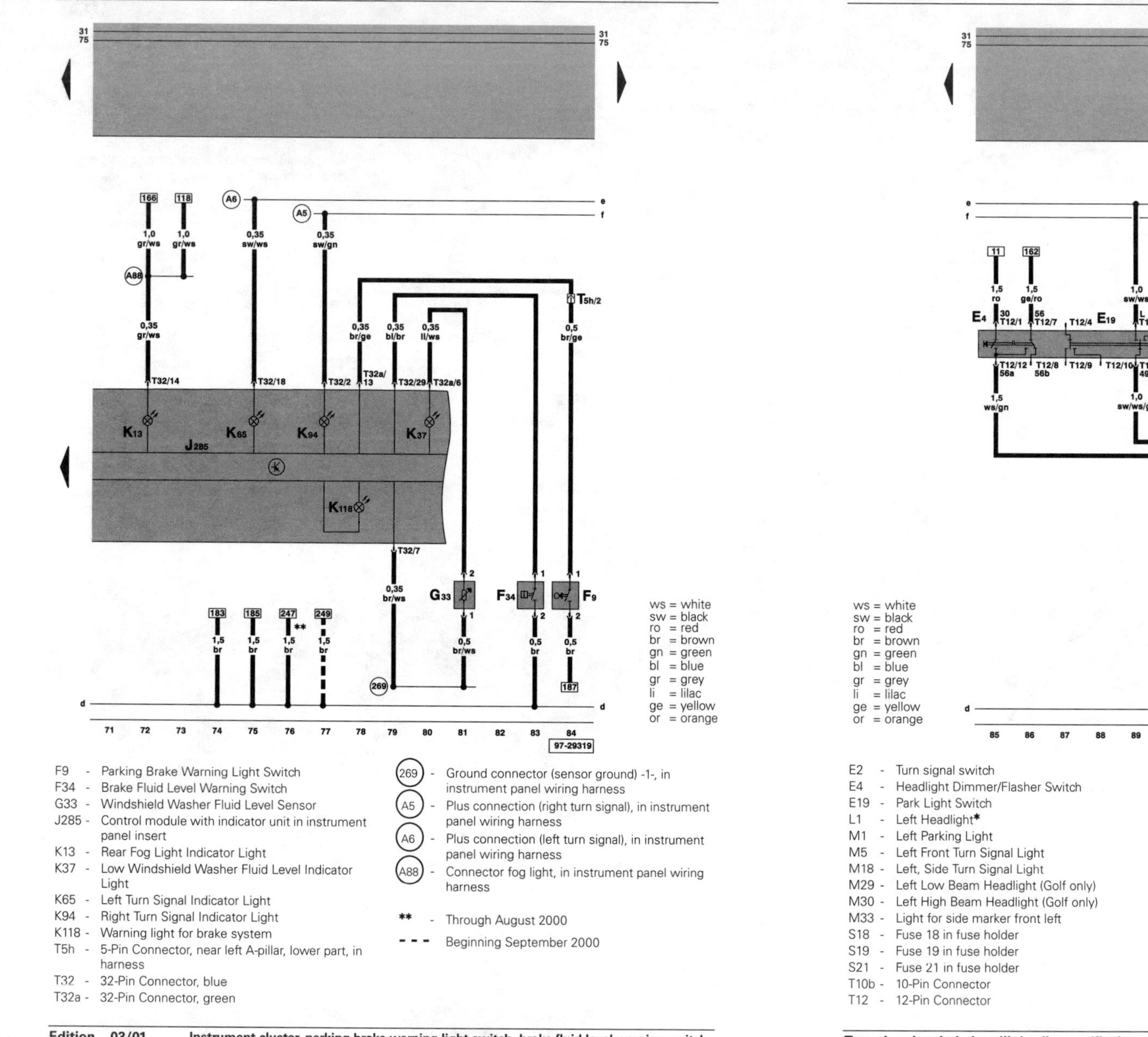

ws = white
sw = black
ro = red
br = brown
gn = green
bl = blue
gr = grey
li = lilac
ge = yellow
or = orange

F9 - Parking Brake Warning Light Switch
F34 - Brake Fluid Level Warning Switch
G33 - Windshield Washer Fluid Level Sensor
J285 - Control module with indicator unit in instrument panel insert
K13 - Rear Fog Light Indicator Light
K37 - Low Windshield Washer Fluid Level Indicator Light
K65 - Left Turn Signal Indicator Light
K94 - Right Turn Signal Indicator Light
K118 - Warning light for brake system
T5h - 5-Pin Connector, near left A-pillar, lower part, in harness
T32 - 32-Pin Connector, blue
T32a - 32-Pin Connector, green

(269) - Ground connector (sensor ground) -1-, in instrument panel wiring harness
(A5) - Plus connection (right turn signal), in instrument panel wiring harness
(A6) - Plus connection (left turn signal), in instrument panel wiring harness
(A88) - Connector fog light, in instrument panel wiring harness

** - Through August 2000
- - - Beginning September 2000

Edition 03/01
USA.5102.10.21

Instrument cluster, parking brake warning light switch, brake fluid level warning switch, low windshield washer fluid level indication, left and right turn signal indicator lights

ws = white
sw = black
ro = red
br = brown
gn = green
bl = blue
gr = grey
li = lilac
ge = yellow
or = orange

E2 - Turn signal switch
E4 - Headlight Dimmer/Flasher Switch
E19 - Park Light Switch
L1 - Left Headlight*
M1 - Left Parking Light
M5 - Left Front Turn Signal Light
M18 - Left, Side Turn Signal Light
M29 - Left Low Beam Headlight (Golf only)
M30 - Left High Beam Headlight (Golf only)
M33 - Light for side marker front left
S18 - Fuse 18 in fuse holder
S19 - Fuse 19 in fuse holder
S21 - Fuse 21 in fuse holder
T10b - 10-Pin Connector
T12 - 12-Pin Connector

(B166) - Connection (56a) in passenger compartment wiring harness
(B167) - Connection (56b) in passenger compartment wiring harness

* - Jetta only

Turn signal switch, headlight dimmer/flasher switch, left front turn signal light, light for side marker front left, left headlight

Edition 03/00
USA.5102.10.21

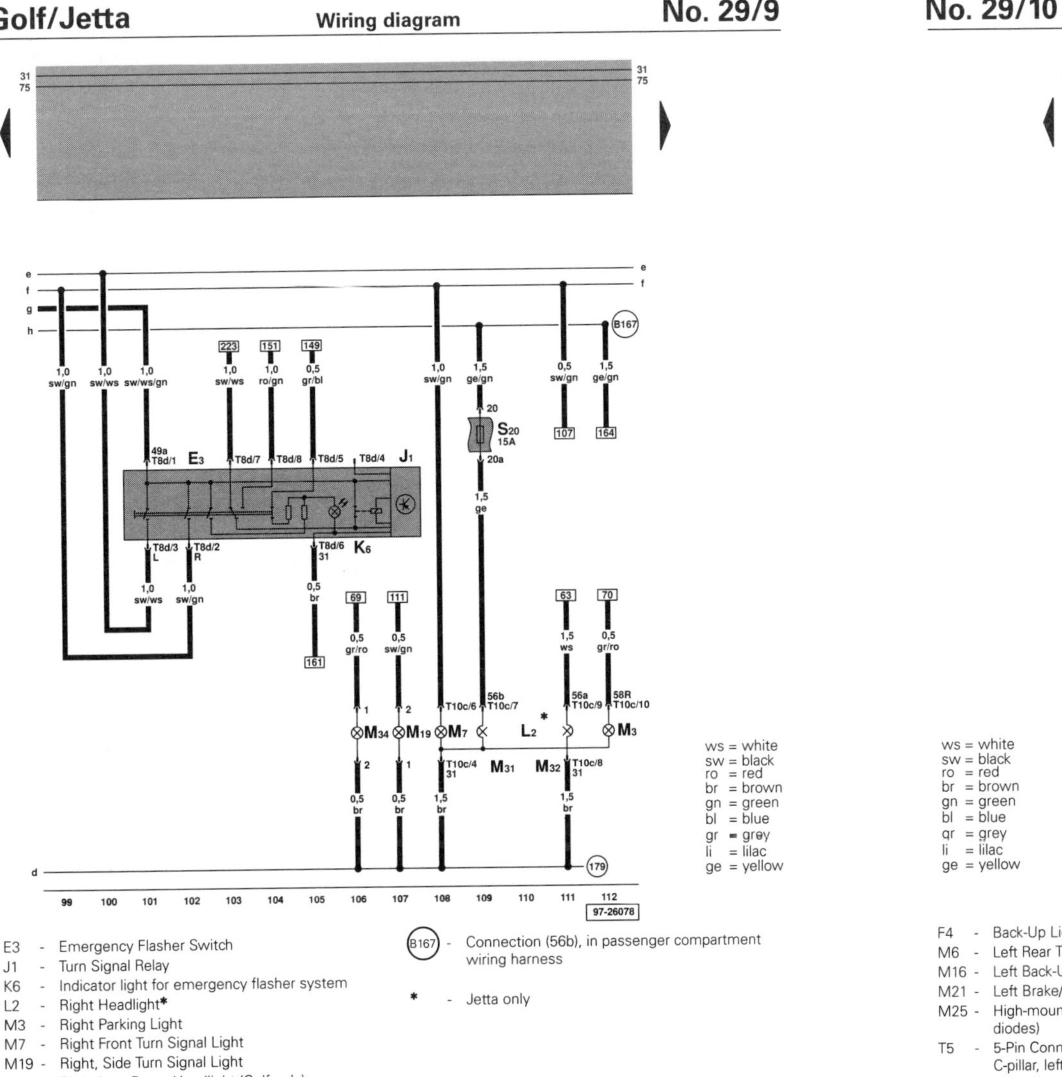

ws = white
sw = black
ro = red
br = brown
gn = green
bl = blue
gr = grey
li = lilac
ge = yellow

E3 - Emergency Flasher Switch
J1 - Turn Signal Relay
K6 - Indicator light for emergency flasher system
L2 - Right Headlight*
M3 - Right Parking Light
M7 - Right Front Turn Signal Light
M19 - Right, Side Turn Signal Light
M31 - Right Low Beam Headlight (Golf only)
M32 - Right High Beam Headlight (Golf only)
M34 - Light for side marker front right
S20 - Fuse 20 in fuse holder
T8d - 8-Pin Connector
T10c - 10-Pin Connector

(179) - Ground connection, in left headlight wiring harness

(B167) - Connection (56b), in passenger compartment wiring harness

* - Jetta only

Emergency flasher switch, turn signal relay, right front turn signal light, light for side marker front right, right headlight

ws = white
sw = black
ro = red
br = brown
gn = green
bl = blue
gr = grey
li = lilac
ge = yellow

F4 - Back-Up Light Switch
M6 - Left Rear Turn Signal Light
M16 - Left Back-Up Light
M21 - Left Brake/Tail Light
M25 - High-mount Brake Light (32 light emitting diodes)
T5 - 5-Pin Connector, black, connector station C-pillar, left
T5a - 5-Pin Connector, pink, connector station C-pillar, left (Golf only)
T5h - 5-Pin Connector, near left A-pillar, lower part, in harness
T5i - 5-Pin Connector, near left A-pillar, lower part, in harness
T6a - 6-Pin Connector
T10 - 10-Pin Connector, orange, in protective housing for connectors, in plenum chamber, left

(86) - Ground connection -1-, in rear wiring harness

(98) - Ground connection, in rear lid wiring harness

(A6) - Plus connection (left turn signal), in instrument panel wiring harness

(B182) - Connection (RF), in passenger compartment wiring harness

(W1) - Plus connection (54), in rear wiring harness

(W28) - Plus connector -2- (54), in wiring harness taillight assembly

-•-•- Golf only

Back-up light switch, left rear turn signal light, left back-up light, left brake/tail light, high-mount brake light (Golf only)

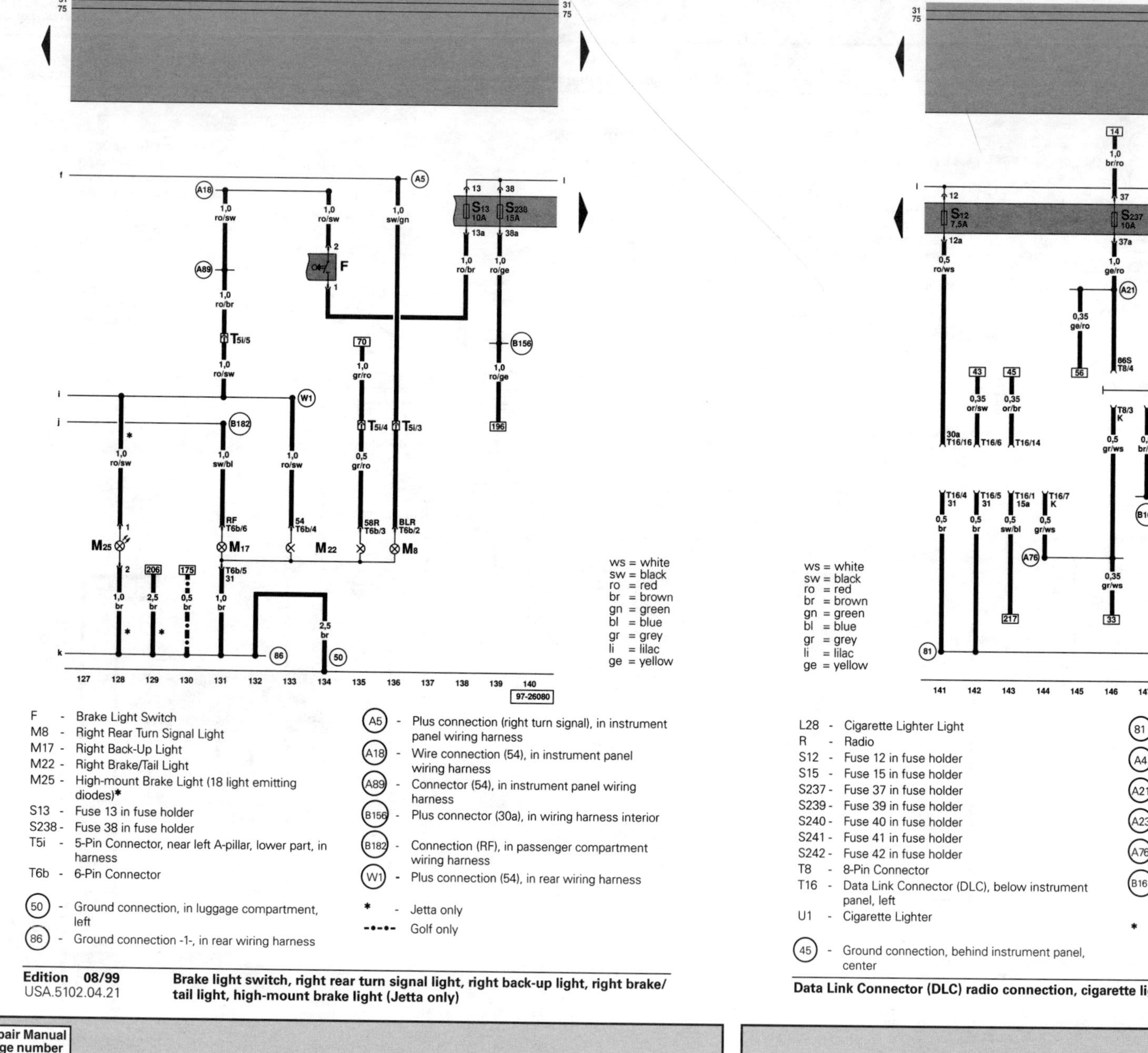

ws = white
sw = black
ro = red
br = brown
gn = green
bl = blue
gr = grey
li = lilac
ge = yellow

F - Brake Light Switch
M8 - Right Rear Turn Signal Light
M17 - Right Back-Up Light
M22 - Right Brake/Tail Light
M25 - High-mount Brake Light (18 light emitting diodes)*
S13 - Fuse 13 in fuse holder
S238 - Fuse 38 in fuse holder
T5i - 5-Pin Connector, near left A-pillar, lower part, in harness
T6b - 6-Pin Connector

(50) - Ground connection, in luggage compartment, left
(86) - Ground connection -1-, in rear wiring harness

(A5) - Plus connection (right turn signal), in instrument panel wiring harness
(A18) - Wire connection (54), in instrument panel wiring harness
(A89) - Connector (54), in instrument panel wiring harness
(B156) - Plus connector (30a), in wiring harness interior
(B182) - Connection (RF), in passenger compartment wiring harness
(W1) - Plus connection (54), in rear wiring harness

* - Jetta only
-•-•- Golf only

Edition 08/99
USA.5102.04.21

Brake light switch, right rear turn signal light, right back-up light, right brake/tail light, high-mount brake light (Jetta only)

ws = white
sw = black
ro = red
br = brown
gn = green
bl = blue
gr = grey
li = lilac
ge = yellow

L28 - Cigarette Lighter Light
R - Radio
S12 - Fuse 12 in fuse holder
S15 - Fuse 15 in fuse holder
S237 - Fuse 37 in fuse holder
S239 - Fuse 39 in fuse holder
S240 - Fuse 40 in fuse holder
S241 - Fuse 41 in fuse holder
S242 - Fuse 42 in fuse holder
T8 - 8-Pin Connector
T16 - Data Link Connector (DLC), below instrument panel, left
U1 - Cigarette Lighter

(45) - Ground connection, behind instrument panel, center

(81) - Ground connection -1-, in instrument panel wiring harness
(A4) - Plus connection (58b), in instrument panel wiring harness
(A21) - Wire connection (86s), in instrument panel wiring harness
(A23) - Wire connection (30a), in instrument panel wiring harness
(A76) - Connector (K-diagnosis wire) in instrument panel wiring harness
(B161) - Connector (anti-theft warning system), in wiring harness interior*

* - Vehicles with anti-theft warning system only (see wiring diagram comfort system/ central locking)

Data Link Connector (DLC) radio connection, cigarette lighter

Edition 08/99
USA.5102.04.21

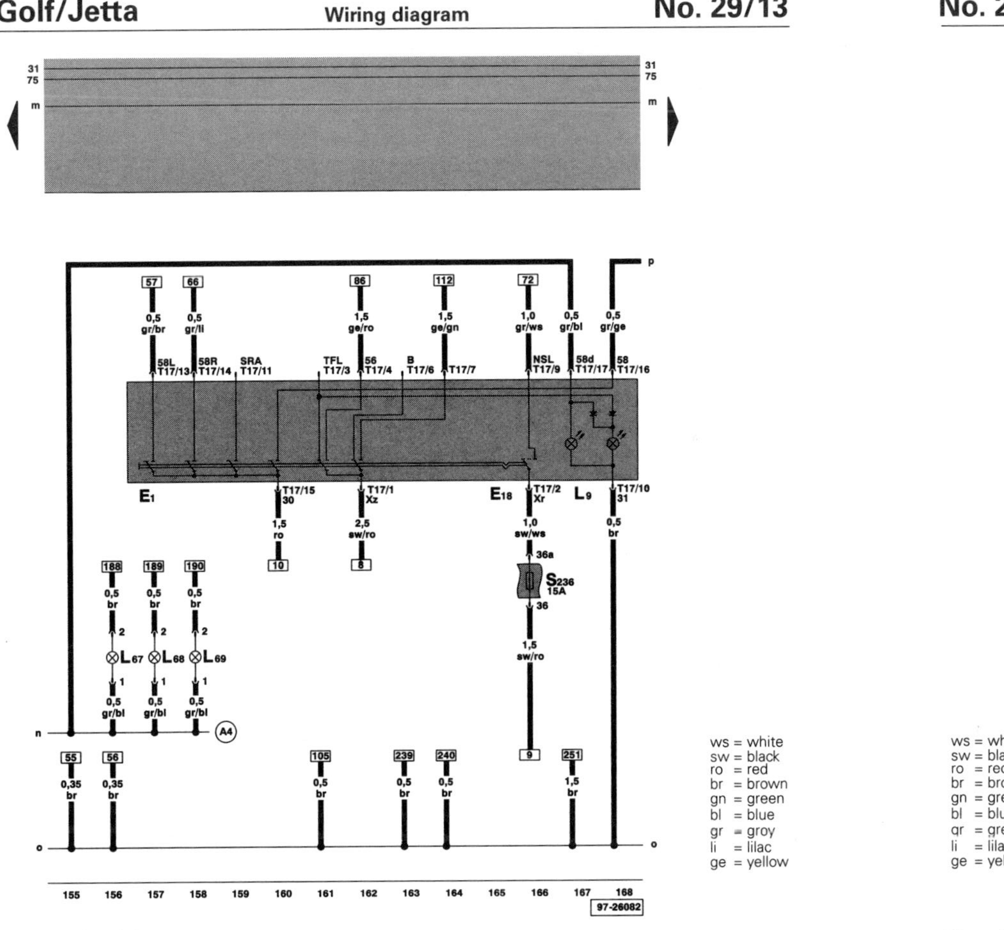

ws = white
sw = black
ro = red
br = brown
gn = green
bl = blue
gr = groy
li = lilac
ge = yellow

E1 - Light switch
E18 - Rear Fog Light Switch
L9 - Headlight Switch Light
L67 - Left Instrument Panel Vent Illumination
L68 - Center Instrument Panel Vent Illumination
L69 - Right Instrument Panel Vent Illumination
S236 - Fuse 36 in fuse holder
T17 - 17-Pin Connector

(A4) - Plus connection (58b), in instrument panel wiring harness

Light switch, rear fog light switch, instrument panel vent illumination

ws = white
sw = black
ro = red
br = brown
gn = green
bl = blue
gr = grey
li = lilac
ge = yellow

S3 - Fuse 3 in fuse holder
S4 - Fuse 4 in fuse holder
T2 - Double Connector, in luggage compartment, left (Golf only)
T5 - 5-Pin Connector, black, connector station C-pillar, left
X - License Plate Light

(49) - Ground connection, on steering column

(50) - Ground connection, in luggage compartment, left

(218) - Ground connection -1-, in rear lid wiring harness

(A37) - Wire connection (58a), in instrument panel wiring harness

(W11) - Wire connection (58), in rear lid wiring harness

(W41) - Plus connection (58), in wiring harness

* - Jetta only

-•-•- Golf only

License plate light

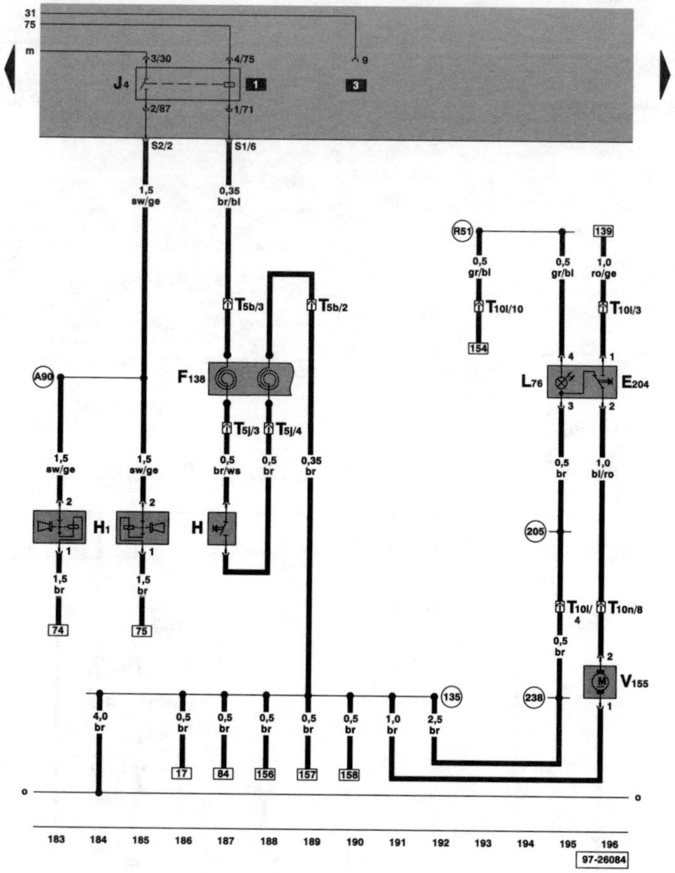

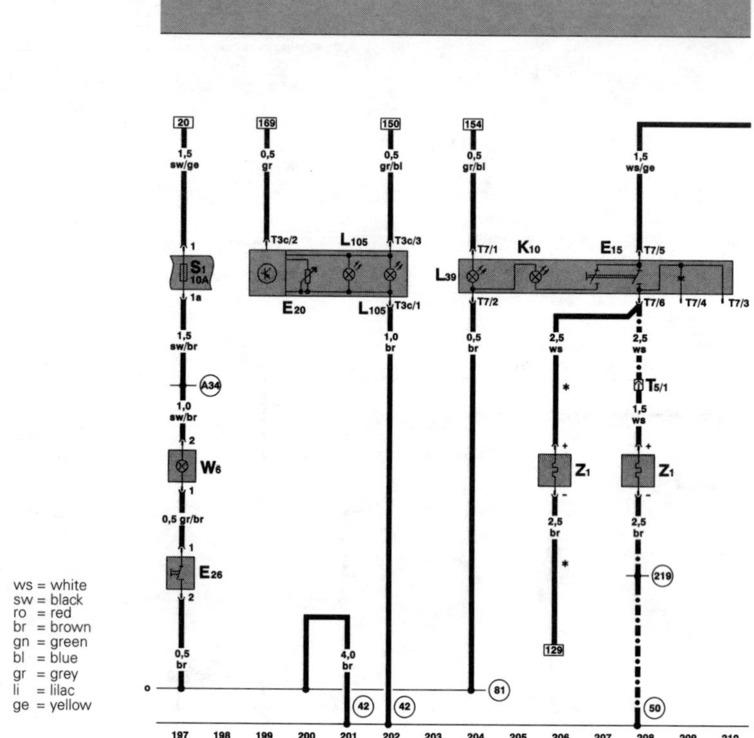

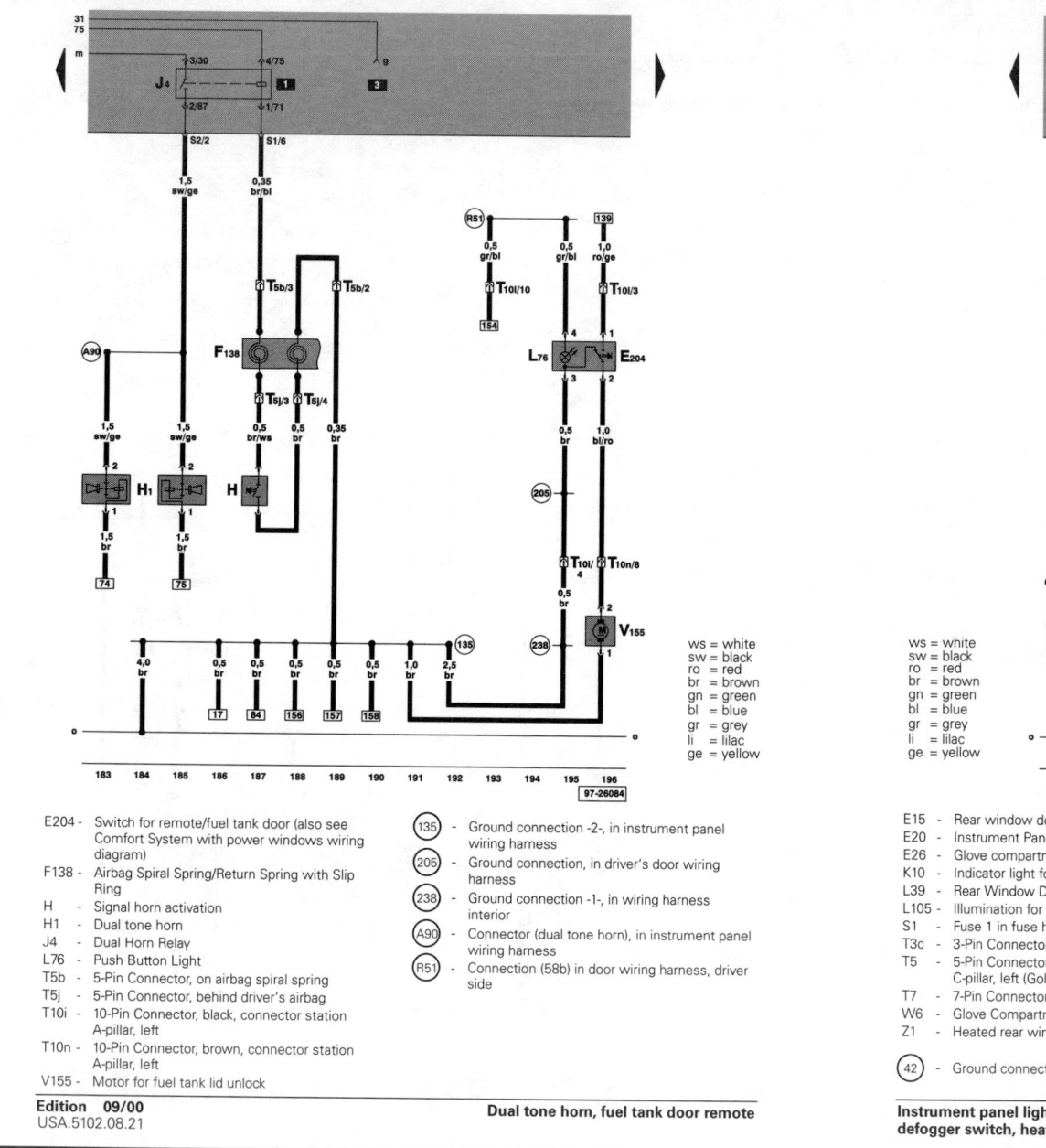

ws = white
sw = black
ro = red
br = brown
gn = green
bl = blue
gr = grey
li = lilac
ge = yellow

E204 - Switch for remote/fuel tank door (also see Comfort System with power windows wiring diagram)
F138 - Airbag Spiral Spring/Return Spring with Slip Ring
H - Signal horn activation
H1 - Dual tone horn
J4 - Dual Horn Relay
L76 - Push Button Light
T5b - 5-Pin Connector, on airbag spiral spring
T5j - 5-Pin Connector, behind driver's airbag
T10i - 10-Pin Connector, black, connector station A-pillar, left
T10n - 10-Pin Connector, brown, connector station A-pillar, left
V155 - Motor for fuel tank lid unlock

(135) - Ground connection -2-, in instrument panel wiring harness
(205) - Ground connection, in driver's door wiring harness
(238) - Ground connection -1-, in wiring harness interior
(A90) - Connector (dual tone horn), in instrument panel wiring harness
(R51) - Connection (58b) in door wiring harness, driver side

Dual tone horn, fuel tank door remote

ws = white
sw = black
ro = red
br = brown
gn = green
bl = blue
gr = grey
li = lilac
ge = yellow

197 198 199 200 201 202 203 204 205 206 207 208 209 210
97-28159

E15 - Rear window defogger switch
E20 - Instrument Panel Light Dimmer Switch
E26 - Glove compartment light switch
K10 - Indicator light for heated rear windshield
L39 - Rear Window Defogger Switch Light
L105 - Illumination for lighting controller
S1 - Fuse 1 in fuse holder
T3c - 3-Pin Connector
T5 - 5-Pin Connector, black, connector station C-pillar, left (Golf only)
T7 - 7-Pin Connector
W6 - Glove Compartment Light
Z1 - Heated rear window

(42) - Ground connection, beside steering column

(50) - Ground connection, in luggage compartment, left
(81) - Ground connection -1-, in instrument panel wiring harness
(219) - Ground connection -2-, in rear lid wiring harness
(A34) - Wire connection (75x), in instrument panel wiring harness

* - Jetta only
-•-•- Golf only

Instrument panel light dimmer switch, glove compartment light, rear window defogger switch, heated rear window

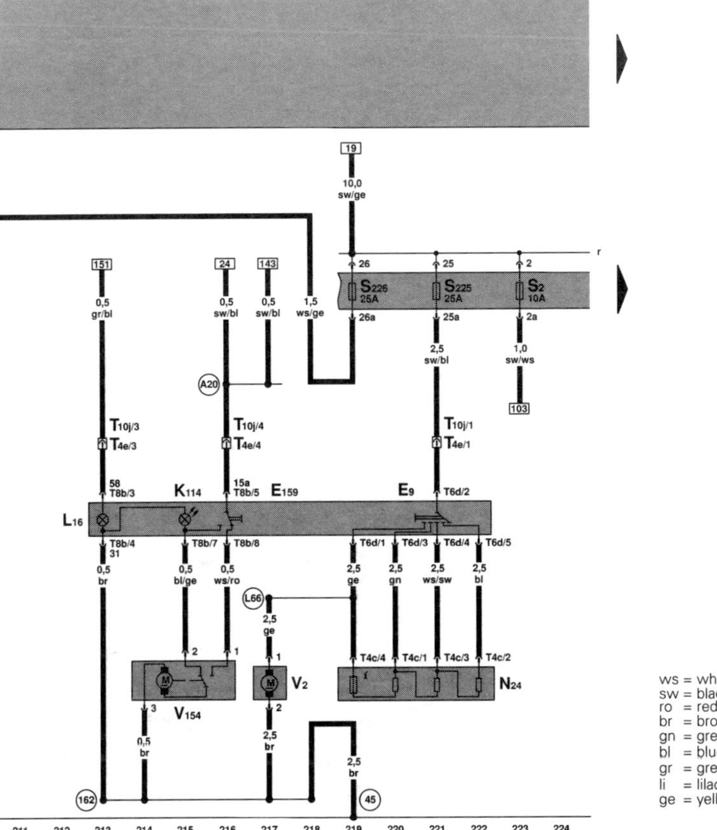

ws = white
sw = black
ro = red
br = brown
gn = green
bl = blue
gr = grey
li = lilac
ge = yellow

E9 - Fresh Air Blower Switch
E159 - Fresh Air/Recirculating Flap Switch
K114 - Fresh Air and Recirculating Air Mode Indicator Light
L16 - Fresh Air Control Lever Light
N24 - Fresh Air Blower Series Resistance With Fuse
S2 - Fuse 2 in fuse holder
S225 - Fuse 25 in fuse holder
S226 - Fuse 26 in fuse holder
T4c - 4-Pin Connector
T4e - 4-Pin Connector (in vehicles without air conditioning)
T6d - 6-Pin Connector
T8b - 8-Pin Connector
T10j - 10-Pin Connector, behind instrument panel, center (in vehicles with air conditioning)

V2 - Fresh Air Blower
V154 - Servo motor for fresh-/recirculating air door

(45) - Ground connection, behind instrument panel, center
(162) - Ground connection, in blower motor wiring harness
(A20) - Wire connection (15a), in instrument panel wiring harness
(L66) - Connector, in wiring harness heater blower

Fresh air blower switch, fresh air/recirculating flap switch, fresh air blower

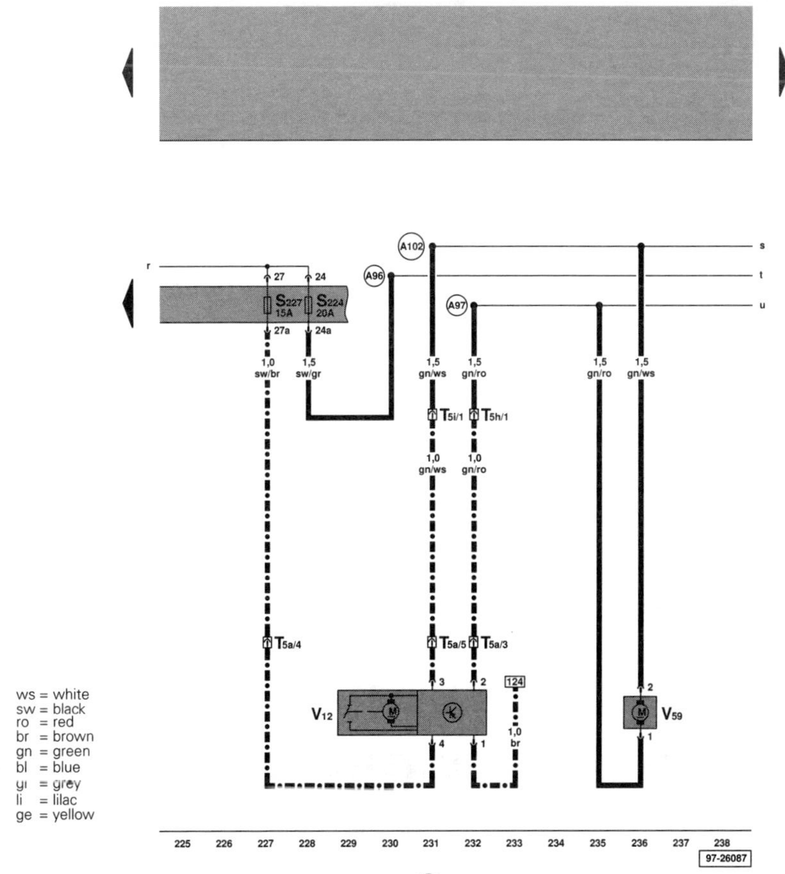

ws = white
sw = black
ro = red
br = brown
gn = green
bl = blue
gr = grey
li = lilac
ge = yellow

S224 - Fuse 24 in fuse holder
S227 - Fuse 27 in fuse holder
T5a - 5-Pin Connector, pink, connector station C-pillar, left (Golf only)
T5h - 5-Pin Connector, near left A-pillar, lower part, in harness
T5i - 5-Pin Connector, near left A-pillar, lower part, in harness
V12 - Motor for rear windshield wiper
V59 - Windshield and Rear Window Washer Pump

(A96) - Connector (53a), in instrument panel wiring harness
(A97) - Connector (53), in instrument panel wiring harness

(A102) - Connector (windshield wiper), in instrument panel wiring harness

-•-•- Golf only

Motor for rear windshield wiper, windshield and rear window washer pump

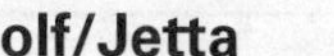

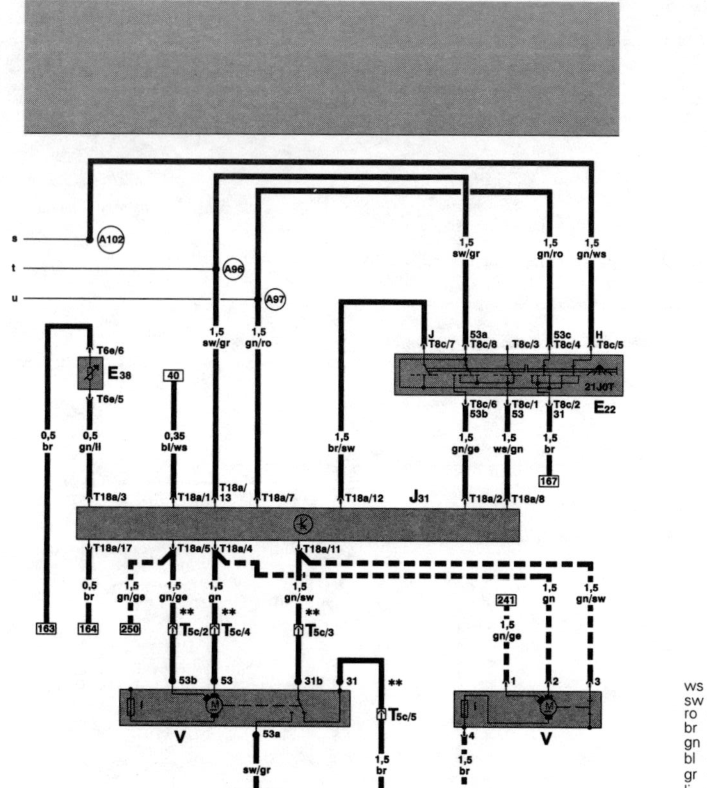

ws = white
sw = black
ro = red
br = brown
gn = green
bl = blue
gr = grey
li = lilac
ge = yellow
or = orange

E22 - Windshield Wiper/Washer Switch
E38 - Windshield Wiper Intermittent Regulator
J31 - Wiper/Washer Intermittent Relay, on relais panel
T5c - 5-Pin Connector, on windshield wiper motor
T6e - 6-Pin Connector
T8c - 8-Pin Connector
T18a - 18-Pin Connector
V - Windshield Wiper Motor

A96 - Connector (53a), in instrument panel wiring harness
A97 - Connector (53), in instrument panel wiring harness
A102 - Connector (windshield wiper), in instrument panel wiring harness

** - Through August 2000
- - - Beginning September 2000

Windshield wiper/washer switch, windshield wiper intermittent regulator, windshield wiper motor, wiper/washer intermittent relay

THIS PAGE INTENTIONALLY LEFT
BLANK

2.0L - Engine - Motronic Multiport Fuel Injection (MFI)/85 kW, code AEG,

from May 1999

Deviate relay location and fuseplacements as well as the locations of multiple connectors see section "component locations".

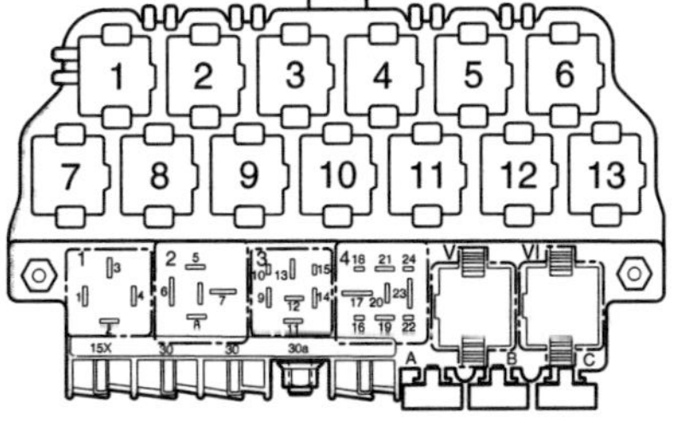

Relay location on the thirteenfold auxiliary relay panel, above relay panel:

Relay panel:

- **2** Load Reduction Relay (100)
- **4** Fuel Pump (FP) Relay (409)

Note: Number in parentheses indicates production control number stamped on relay housing.

Fuse colors

30 A - green
25 A - white
20 A - yellow
15 A - blue
10 A - red
7,5 A - brown
5 A - beige
3 A - violet

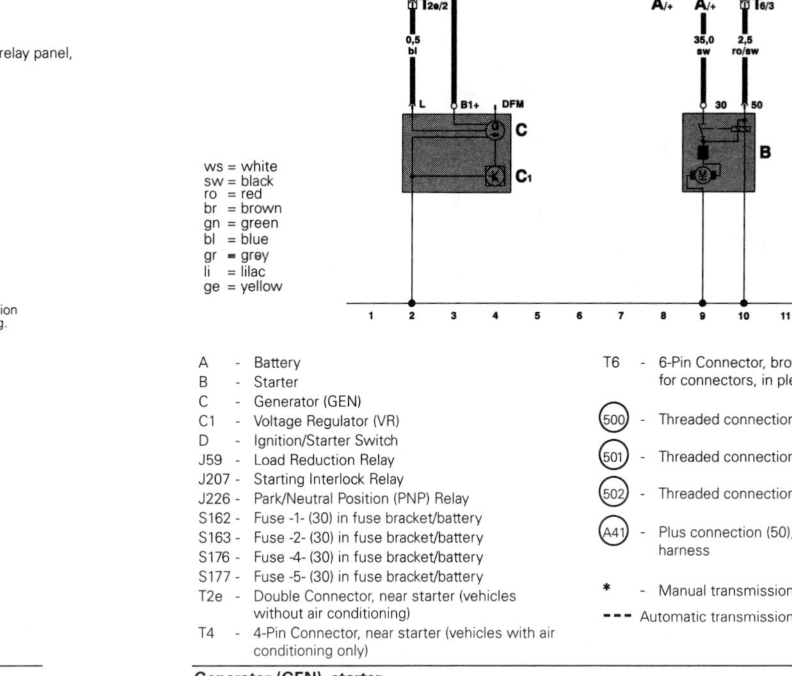

ws = white
sw = black
ro = red
br = brown
gn = green
bl = blue
gr = grey
li = lilac
ge = yellow

A - Battery
B - Starter
C - Generator (GEN)
C1 - Voltage Regulator (VR)
D - Ignition/Starter Switch
J59 - Load Reduction Relay
J207 - Starting Interlock Relay
J226 - Park/Neutral Position (PNP) Relay
S162 - Fuse -1- (30) in fuse bracket/battery
S163 - Fuse -2- (30) in fuse bracket/battery
S176 - Fuse -4- (30) in fuse bracket/battery
S177 - Fuse -5- (30) in fuse bracket/battery
T2e - Double Connector, near starter (vehicles without air conditioning)
T4 - 4-Pin Connector, near starter (vehicles with air conditioning only)
T6 - 6-Pin Connector, brown, in protective housing for connectors, in plenum chamber, left
(500) - Threaded connection -1- (30) on the relay plate
(501) - Threaded connection -2- (30) on the relay plate
(502) - Threaded connection -1- (30a) on the relay plate
(A41) - Plus connection (50), in instrument panel wiring harness
* - Manual transmission only
--- Automatic transmission only

Generator (GEN), starter

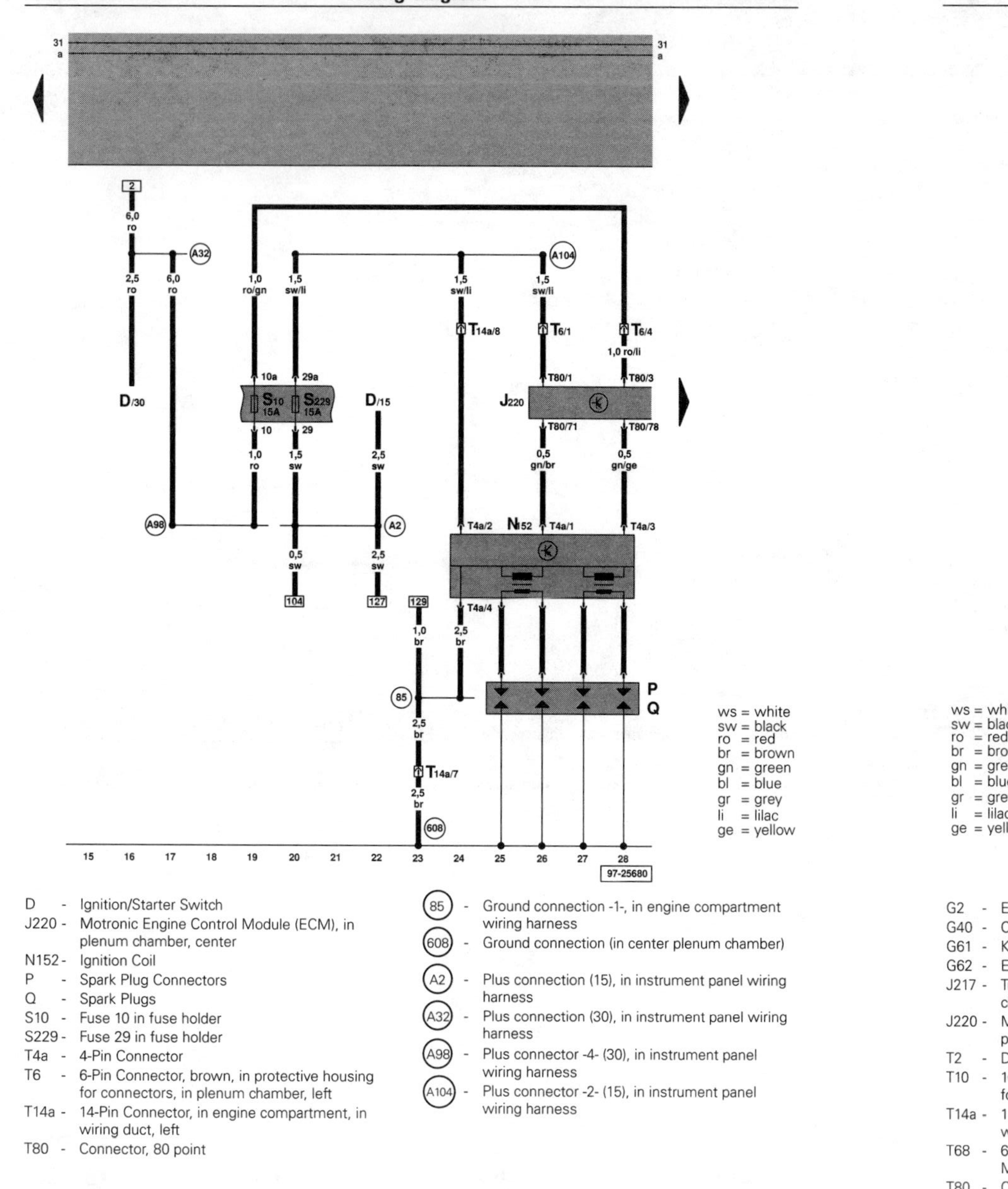

ws = white
sw = black
ro = red
br = brown
gn = green
bl = blue
gr = grey
li = lilac
ge = yellow

97-25680

D - Ignition/Starter Switch
J220 - Motronic Engine Control Module (ECM), in plenum chamber, center
N152 - Ignition Coil
P - Spark Plug Connectors
Q - Spark Plugs
S10 - Fuse 10 in fuse holder
S229 - Fuse 29 in fuse holder
T4a - 4-Pin Connector
T6 - 6-Pin Connector, brown, in protective housing for connectors, in plenum chamber, left
T14a - 14-Pin Connector, in engine compartment, in wiring duct, left
T80 - Connector, 80 point

(85) - Ground connection -1-, in engine compartment wiring harness
(608) - Ground connection (in center plenum chamber)
(A2) - Plus connection (15), in instrument panel wiring harness
(A32) - Plus connection (30), in instrument panel wiring harness
(A98) - Plus connector -4- (30), in instrument panel wiring harness
(A104) - Plus connector -2- (15), in instrument panel wiring harness

ws = white
sw = black
ro = red
br = brown
gn = green
bl = blue
gr = grey
li = lilac
ge = yellow

97-25681

G2 - Engine Coolant Temperature (ECT) Sensor
G40 - Camshaft Position (CMP) Sensor
G61 - Knock Sensor (KS) 1
G62 - Engine Coolant Temperature (ECT) Sensor
J217 - Transmission Control Module (TCM), in plenum chamber, center
J220 - Motronic Engine Control Module (ECM), in plenum chamber, center
T2 - Double Connector, in engine compartment, rear
T10 - 10-Pin Connector, orange, in protective housing for connectors, in plenum chamber, left
T14a - 14-Pin Connector, in engine compartment, in wiring duct, left
T68 - 68-Pin Connector, on Transmission Control Module (TCM)
T80 - Connector, 80 point

(220) - Ground connection (sensor ground), in engine compartment wiring harness
(D101) - Wire connection -1-, in engine compartment wiring harness

** - A/C connection
--- Automatic transmission only

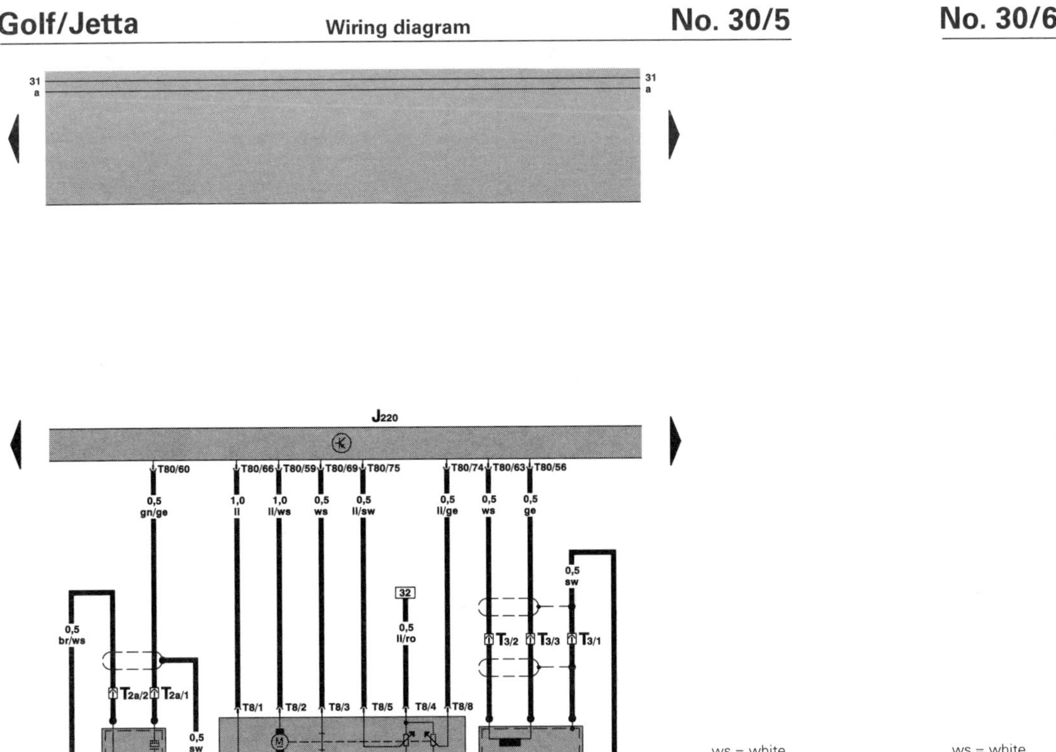

ws = white
sw = black
ro = red
br = brown
gn = green
bl = blue
gr = grey
li = lilac
ge = yellow
or = orange

F60 - Closed Throttle Position (CTP) Switch
G28 - Engine Speed (RPM) Sensor
G66 - Knock Sensor (KS) 2
G69 - Throttle Position (TP) Sensor
G88 - Throttle Position (TP) Sensor
J220 - Motronic Engine Control Module (ECM), in plenum chamber, center
J338 - Throttle Valve Control Module***
T2a - Double Connector, in engine compartment, front
T3 - 3-Pin Connector, near intake manifold
T8 - 8-Pin Connector***
T80 - Connector, 80 point
V60 - Throttle Position (TP) Actuator

(220) - Ground connection (sensor ground), in engine compartment wiring harness

*** - Vehicles with cruise control see also wiring diagram Cruise Control No. 44/1

Motronic engine control module (ECM), throttle valve control module, knock sensor (KS) 2, engine speed (RPM) sensor

ws = white
sw = black
ro = red
br = brown
gn = green
bl = blue
gr = grey
li = lilac
ge = yellow
or = orange

J220 - Motronic Engine Control Module (ECM), in plenum chamber, center
N30 - Cylinder 1 Fuel Injector
N31 - Cylinder 2 Fuel Injector
N32 - Cylinder 3 Fuel Injector
N33 - Cylinder 4 Fuel Injector
S232 - Fuse 32 in fuse holder
T14a - 14-Pin Connector, in engine compartment, in wiring duct, left
T80 - Connector, 80 point

(D95) - Wire connection (injectors), in engine compartment wiring harness
(A101) - Connector -3- (87a), in instrument panel wiring harness

Motronic engine control module (ECM), injectors

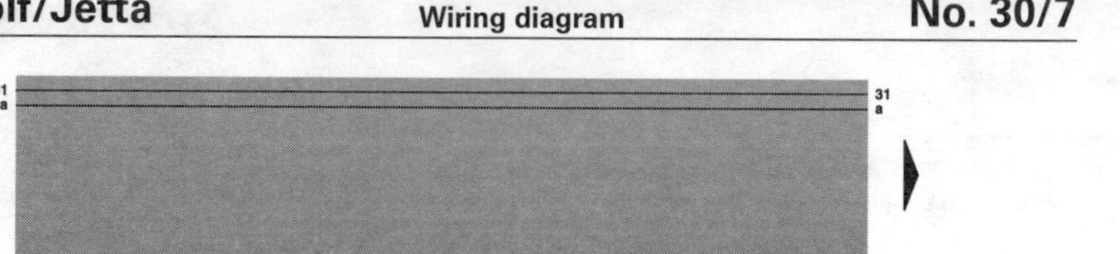

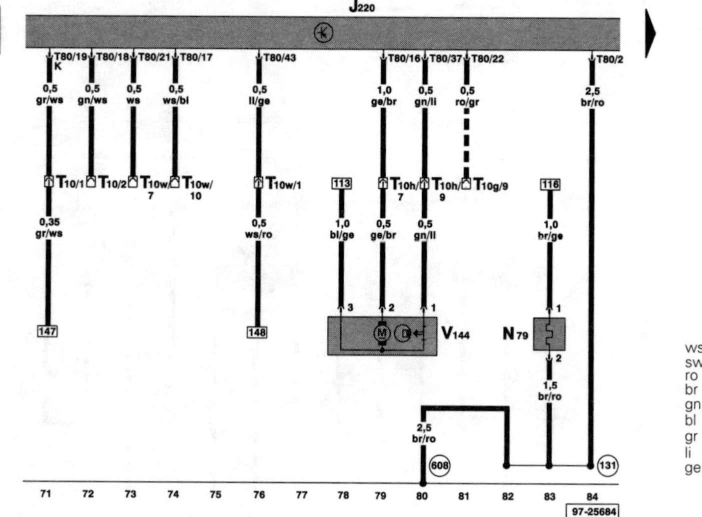

ws = white
sw = black
ro = red
br = brown
gn = green
bl = blue
gr = grey
li = lilac
ge = yellow

J220 - Motronic Engine Control Module (ECM), in plenum chamber, center
N79 - Positive Crankcase Ventilation (PCV) Heating Element
T10 - 10-Pin Connector, orange, in protective housing for connectors, in plenum chamber, left
T10g - 10-Pin Connector, grey, in protective housing for connectors, in plenum chamber, left
T10h - 10-Pin Connector, blue, in protective housing for connectors, in plenum chamber, left
T10w - 10-Pin Connector, white, in protective housing for connectors, in plenum chamber, left
T80 - Connector, 80 point
V144 - Leak detection pump (LDP)

(131) - Ground connection -2-, in engine compartment wiring harness
(608) - Ground Connection (in center plenum chamber)

--- Automatic transmission only

Motronic engine control module (ECM), leak detection pump (LDP), positive crankcase ventilation (PCV) heating element

ws = white
sw = black
ro = red
br = brown
gn = green
bl = blue
gr = grey
li = lilac
ge = yellow
or = orange

J104 - ABS Control Module (w/EDL), in engine compartment, left
J217 - Transmission Control Module (TCM), in plenum chamber, center
J220 - Motronic Engine Control Module (ECM), in plenum chamber, center
J299 - Secondary Air Injection (AIR) Pump Relay, in protective housing, in engine compartment, left, production control number (100)
N112 - Secondary Air Injection (AIR) Solenoid Valve
T10w - 10-Pin Connector, white, in protective housing for connectors, in plenum chamber, left
T25 - 25-Pin Connector, on ABS Control Module (through July 2000)
T47a - 47-Pin Connector, on ABS Control Module (beginning August 2000)
T68 - 68-Pin Connector, on Transmission Control Module (TCM)
T80 - Connector, 80 point
V101 - Secondary Air Injection (AIR) Pump Motor

(609) - Ground Connection (in right plenum chamber)
(A121) - Connection (high bus), in instrument panel wiring harness
(A122) - Connection (low bus), in instrument panel wiring harness
(E30) - Connector (87a), in wiring harness engine

--- Automatic transmission only

Motronic engine control module (ECM), secondary air injection (AIR) pump motor, secondary air injection (AIR) solenoid valve

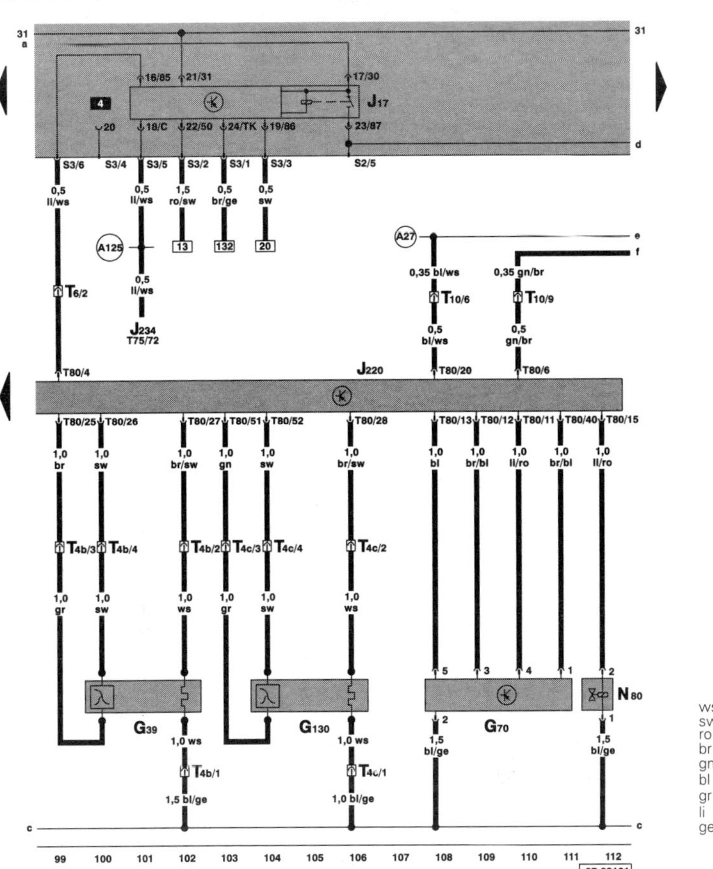

ws = white
sw = black
ro = red
br = brown
gn = green
bl = blue
gr = grey
li = lilac
ge = yellow

G39 - Heated Oxygen Sensor (HO2S)
G70 - Mass Air Flow (MAF) Sensor
G130 - Oxygen Sensor (O2S) behind Three Way Catalytic Converter (TWC)
J17 - Fuel Pump (FP) Relay
J220 - Motronic Engine Control Module (ECM), in plenum chamber, center
J234 - Airbag Control Module
N80 - Evaporative Emission (EVAP) Canister Purge Regulator Valve
T4b - 4-Pin Connector, in protective housing for connectors under right floor
T4c - 4-Pin Connector, in protective housing for connectors under right floor
T6 - 6-Pin Connector, brown, in protective housing for connectors, in plenum chamber, left
T10 - 10-Pin Connector, orange, in protective housing for connectors, in plenum chamber, left
T75 - 75-Pin Connector
T80 - Connector, 80 point

(A27) - Wire Connection (vehicle speed signal), in instrument panel wiring harness
(A125) - Connection (crash signal) in instrument panel wiring harness

Motronic engine control module (ECM), mass air flow (MAF) sensor, heated oxygen sensor (HO2S), evaporative emission (EVAP) canister purge regulator valve

ws = white
sw = black
ro = red
br = brown
gn = green
bl = blue
gr = grey
li = lilac
ge = yellow

G - Fuel Level Sensor
G6 - Fuel Pump (FP)
G32 - Engine Coolant Level (ECL) Sensor
S228 - Fuse 28 in fuse holder
S234 - Fuse 34 in fuse holder
S243 - Fuse 43 in fuse holder
T6 - 6-Pin Connector, brown, in protective housing for connectors, in plenum chamber, left
T14a - 14-Pin Connector, in engine compartment, in wiring duct, left

(42) - Ground connection, beside steering column
(81) - Ground connection -1-, in instrument panel wiring harness
(135) - Ground connection -2-, in instrument panel wiring harness
(269) - Ground connection (sensor ground) -1-, in instrument panel wiring harness
(504) - Threaded connection -1- (87) on the relay plate
(A99) - Connector -1- (87), in instrument panel wiring harness
(A100) - Connector -2- (87), in instrument panel wiring harness
(A151) - Connector -4- (87), in instrument panel wiring harness
(E30) - Connector (87a), in wiring harness engine

* - Vehicles with Multi-Function Indicator (MFI) only

Fuel pump (FP), fuel level sensor, engine coolant level (ECL) sensor

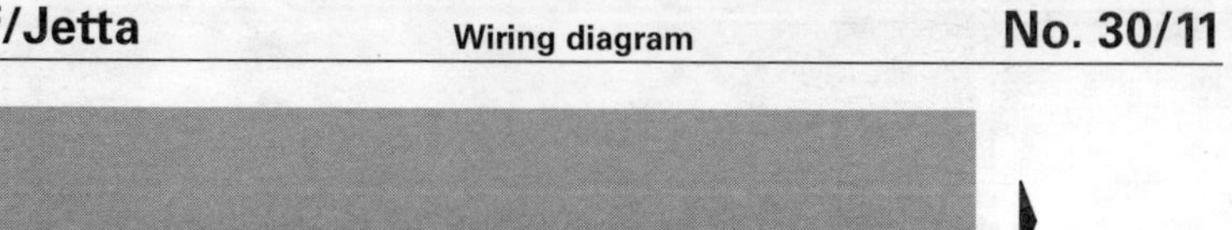

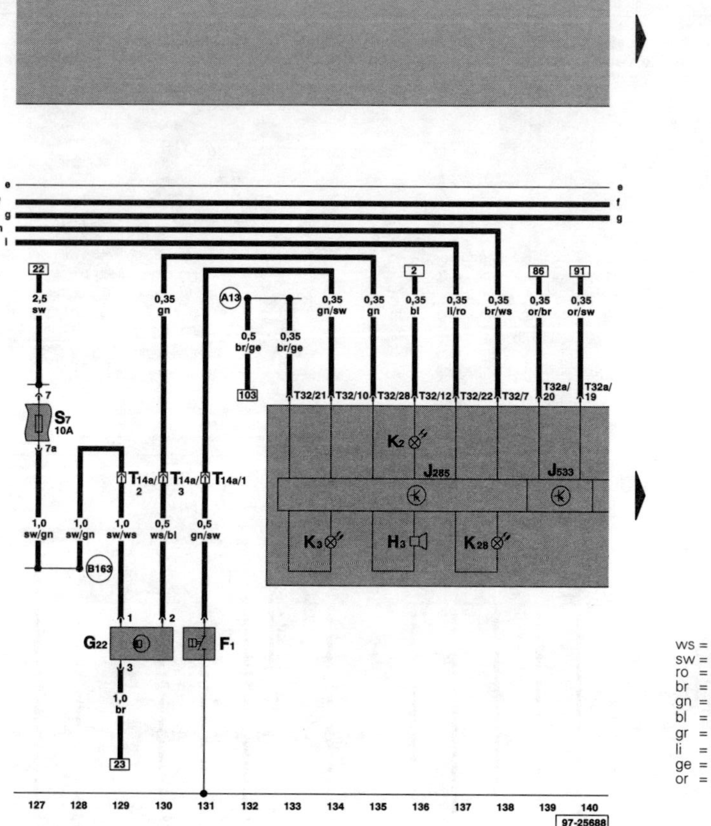

ws = white
sw = black
ro = red
br = brown
gn = green
bl = blue
gr = grey
li = lilac
ge = yellow
or = orange

- F1 - Oil Pressure Switch
- G22 - Speedometer Vehicle Speed Sensor (VSS)
- H3 - Warning Buzzer
- J285 - Control module with indicator unit in instrument panel insert
- J533 - Data Bus On Board Diagnostic Interface
- K2 - Generator (GEN) Warning Light
- K3 - Oil Pressure Warning Light
- K28 - Engine Coolant Level/Temperature (ECL/ECT) Warning Light
- S7 - Fuse 7 in fuse holder
- T14a - 14-Pin Connector, in engine compartment, in wiring duct, left
- T32 - 32-Pin Connector, blue

- (A13) - Wire connection (door contact switch) in instrument panel wiring harness
- (B163) - Plus connector -1- (15) in wiring harness interior

Edition 09/00
USA.5102.08.21

Instrument cluster, oil pressure switch, speedometer vehicle speed sensor, generator (GEN) warning light, engine coolant level/temperature (ECL/ECT) warning light

ws = white
sw = black
ro = red
br = brown
gn = green
bl = blue
gr = grey
li = lilac
ge = yellow

- E86 - Multi-Function Indicator Mode Select Switch*
- E109 - Multi-Function Indicator Memory Switch*
- G1 - Fuel gauge
- G3 - Engine Coolant Temperature (ECT) Gauge
- G5 - Tachometer
- G17 - Outside Air Temperature Sensor*
- G21 - Speedometer
- J119 - Multi-function Indicator (MFI)
- J285 - Control module with indicator unit in instrument panel insert
- K83 - Malfunction Indicator Lamp (MIL)
- K105 - Low Fuel Level Warning Light
- T6e - 6-Pin Connector
- T16 - Data Link Connector (DLC), below instrument panel, left
- T32 - 32-Pin Connector, blue
- T32a - 32-Pin Connector, green

- (A27) - Wire Connection (vehicle speed signal), in instrument panel wiring harness
- (A76) - Connector (K-diagnosis wire), in instrument panel wiring harness

- * - Vehicles with Multi-Function Indicator (MFI) only

Instrument cluster, multi-function indicator (MFI), engine coolant temperature (ECT) gauge, fuel gauge, malfunction indicator lamp (MIL), outside air temperature sensor

Edition 09/00
USA.5102.08.21

2.8L - Engine - Motronic Multiport Fuel Injection (MFI)/130 kW, code AFP,

from May 1999

Deviate relay location and fuseplacements as well as the locations of multiple connectors see section "component locations".

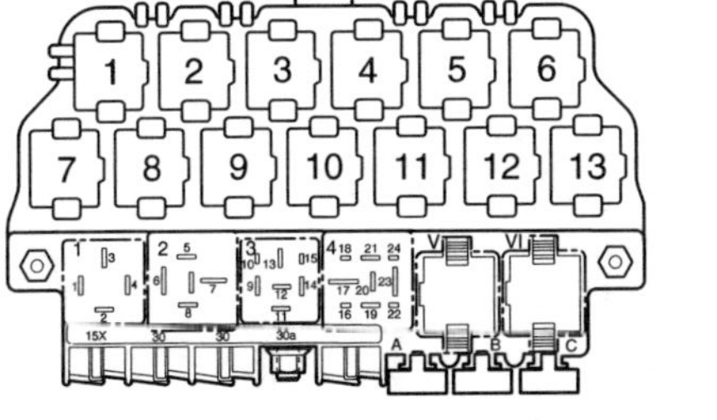

Relay location on the thirteenfold auxiliary relay panel, above relay panel:

Relay panel:

2 Load Reduction Relay (100)

4 Fuel Pump (FP) Relay (409)

Note: Number in parentheses indicates production control number stamped on relay housing.

Fuse colors

30 A - green
25 A - white
20 A - yellow
15 A - blue
10 A - red
7,5 A - brown
5 A - beige
3 A - violet

ws = white
sw = black
ro = red
br = brown
gn = green
bl = blue
gr = grey
li = lilac
ge = yellow

A - Battery
B - Starter
C - Generator (GEN)
C1 - Voltage Regulator (VR)
D - Ignition/Starter Switch
J59 - Load Reduction Relay
J207 - Starting Interlock Relay
J226 - Park/Neutral Position (PNP) Relay
S162 - Fuse -1- (30) in fuse bracket/battery
S163 - Fuse -2- (30) in fuse bracket/battery
S176 - Fuse -4- (30) in fuse bracket/battery
S177 - Fuse -5- (30) in fuse bracket/battery
T2e - Double Connector, near starter (vehicles without air conditioning)
T4 - 4-Pin Connector, near starter (vehicles with air conditioning only)

T6 - 6-Pin Connector, brown, in protective housing for connectors, in plenum chamber, left

(500) - Threaded connection -1- (30) on the relay plate

(502) - Threaded connection -1- (30a) on the relay plate

(A41) - Plus connection (50), in instrument panel wiring harness

* - Manual transmission only

--- Automatic transmission only

Generator (GEN), starter

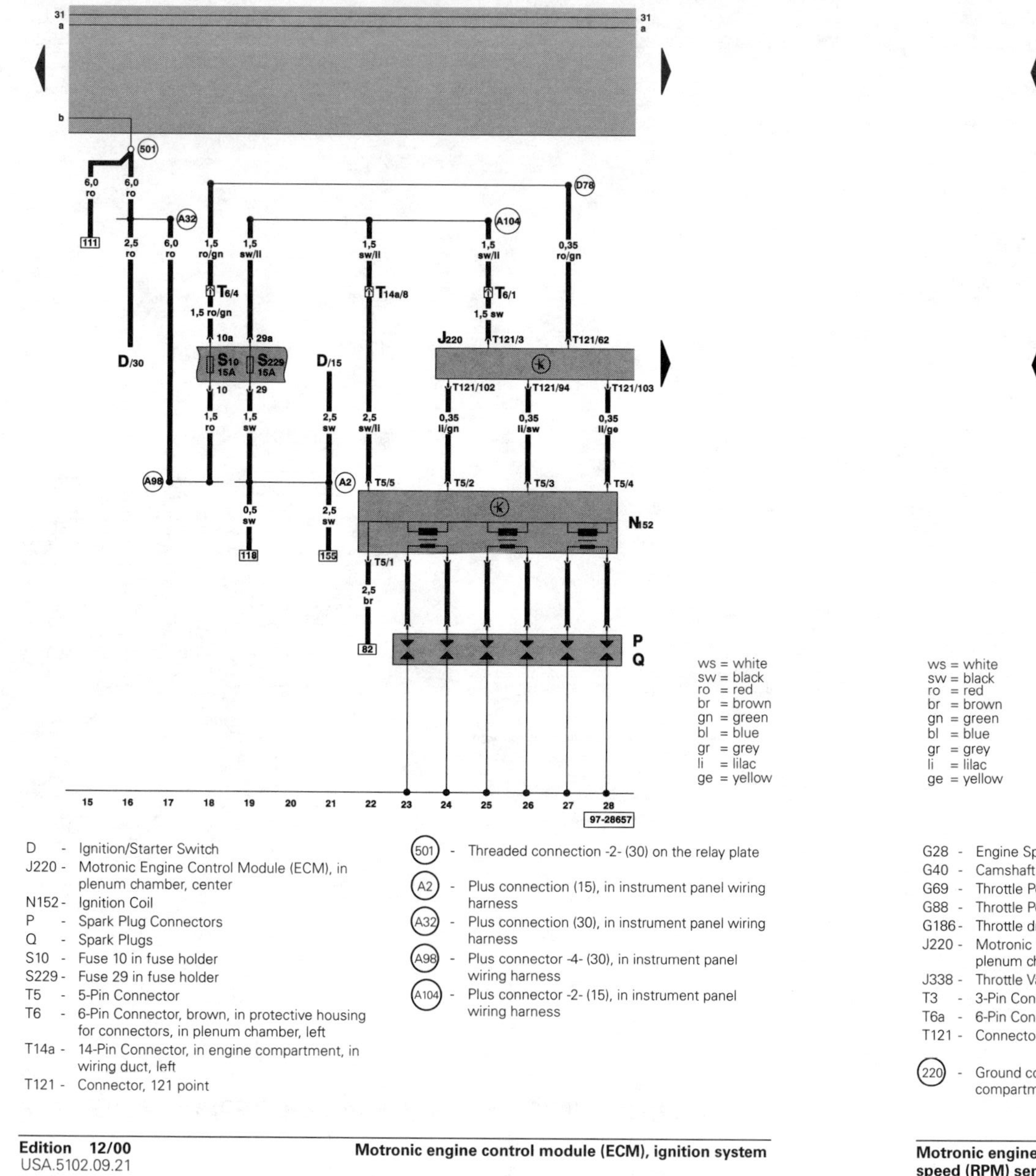

ws = white
sw = black
ro = red
br = brown
gn = green
bl = blue
gr = grey
li = lilac
ge = yellow

- D - Ignition/Starter Switch
- J220 - Motronic Engine Control Module (ECM), in plenum chamber, center
- N152 - Ignition Coil
- P - Spark Plug Connectors
- Q - Spark Plugs
- S10 - Fuse 10 in fuse holder
- S229 - Fuse 29 in fuse holder
- T5 - 5-Pin Connector
- T6 - 6-Pin Connector, brown, in protective housing for connectors, in plenum chamber, left
- T14a - 14-Pin Connector, in engine compartment, in wiring duct, left
- T121 - Connector, 121 point

- (501) - Threaded connection -2- (30) on the relay plate
- (A2) - Plus connection (15), in instrument panel wiring harness
- (A32) - Plus connection (30), in instrument panel wiring harness
- (A98) - Plus connector -4- (30), in instrument panel wiring harness
- (A104) - Plus connector -2- (15), in instrument panel wiring harness

Motronic engine control module (ECM), ignition system

ws = white
sw = black
ro = red
br = brown
gn = green
bl = blue
gr = grey
li = lilac
ge = yellow

- G28 - Engine Speed (RPM) Sensor
- G40 - Camshaft Position (CMP) Sensor
- G69 - Throttle Position (TP) Sensor
- G88 - Throttle Position (TP) Sensor
- G186 - Throttle drive (power accelerator actuation)
- J220 - Motronic Engine Control Module (ECM), in plenum chamber, center
- J338 - Throttle Valve Control Module
- T3 - 3-Pin Connector, near intake manifold
- T6a - 6-Pin Connector
- T121 - Connector, 121 point

- (220) - Ground connection (sensor ground), in engine compartment wiring harness

Motronic engine control module (ECM), throttle valve control module, engine speed (RPM) sensor, camshaft position (CMP) sensor

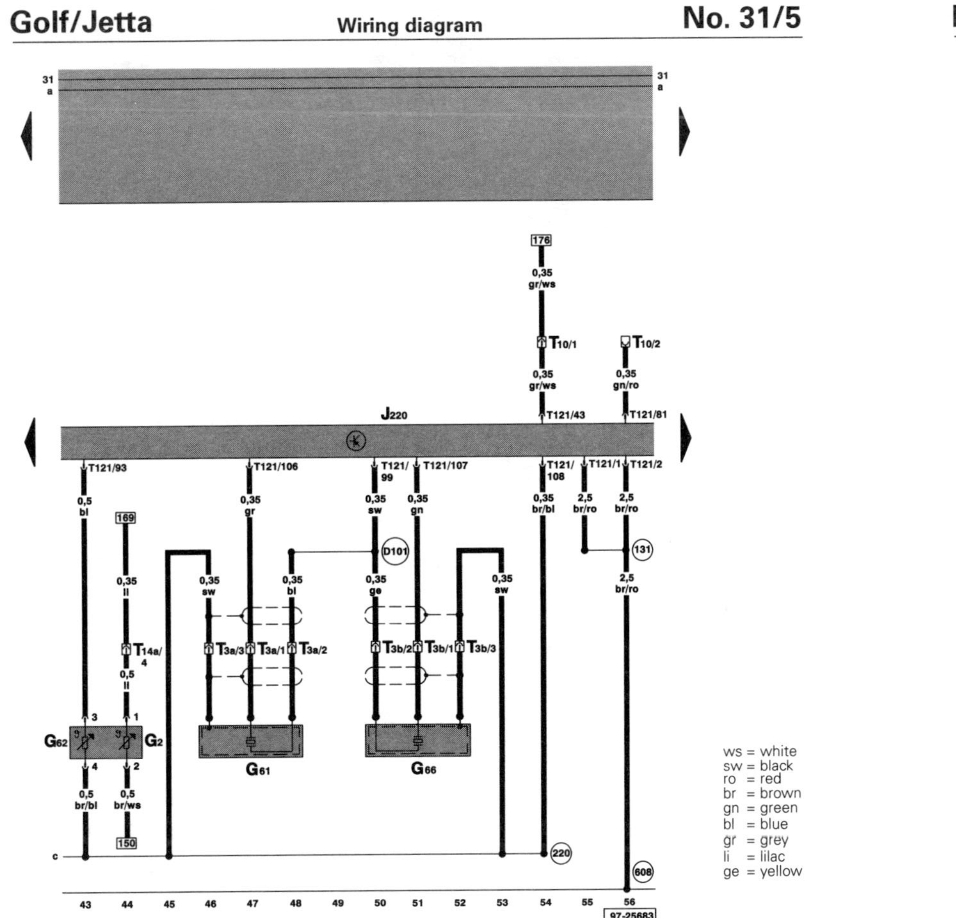

ws = white
sw = black
ro = red
br = brown
gn = green
bl = blue
gr = grey
li = lilac
ge = yellow

G2 - Engine Coolant Temperature (ECT) Sensor
G61 - Knock Sensor (KS) 1
G62 - Engine Coolant Temperature (ECT) Sensor
G66 - Knock Sensor (KS) 2
J220 - Motronic Engine Control Module (ECM), in plenum chamber, center
T3a - 3-Pin Connector, in engine compartment, rear
T3b - 3-Pin Connector, in engine compartment, front
T10 - 10-Pin Connector, orange, in protective housing for connectors, in plenum chamber, left
T14a - 14-Pin Connector, in engine compartment, in wiring duct, left
T121 - Connector, 121 point

(131) - Ground connection -2-, in engine compartment wiring harness

(220) - Ground connection (sensor ground), in engine compartment wiring harness
(608) - Ground connection (in center plenum chamber)
(D101) - Wire connection -1-, in engine compartment wiring harness

Edition 06/00 USA.5102.06.21 **Motronic engine control module (ECM), knock sensor (KS) 1, knock sensor (KS) 2, engine coolant temperature (ECT) sensor**

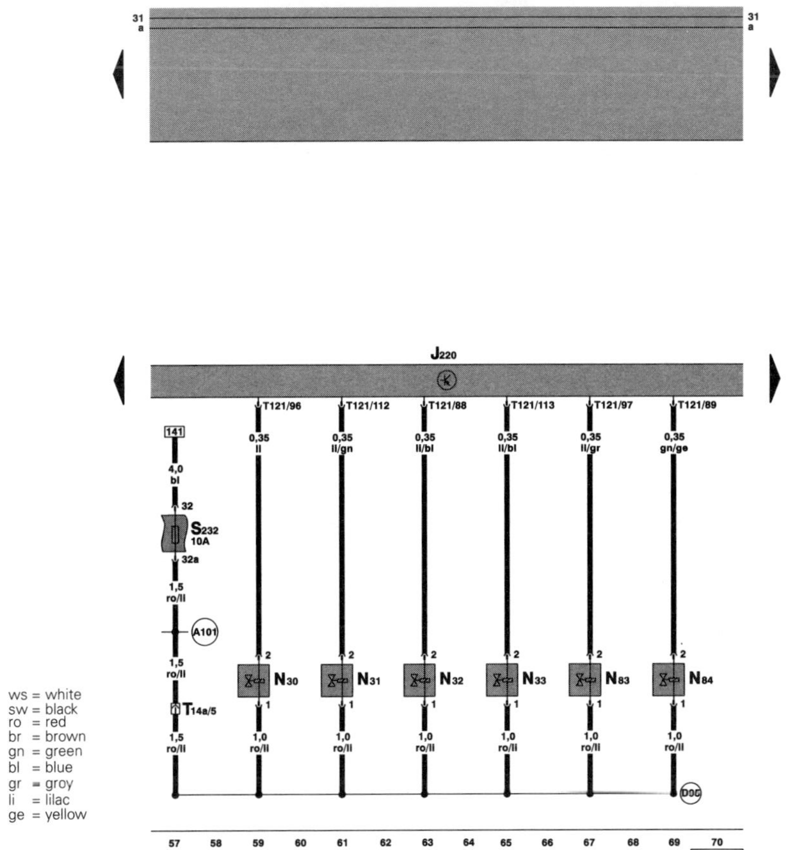

ws = white
sw = black
ro = red
br = brown
gn = green
bl = blue
gr = grey
li = lilac
ge = yellow

J220 - Motronic Engine Control Module (ECM), in plenum chamber, center
N30 - Cylinder 1 Fuel Injector
N31 - Cylinder 2 Fuel Injector
N32 - Cylinder 3 Fuel Injector
N33 - Cylinder 4 Fuel Injector
N83 - Cylinder 5 Fuel Injector
N84 - Cylinder 6 Fuel Injector
S232 - Fuse 32 in fuse holder
T14a - 14-Pin Connector, in engine compartment, in wiring duct, left
T121 - Connector, 121 point

(A101) - Connector -3- (87a), in instrument panel wiring harness

(D95) - Wire connection (injectors), in engine compartment wiring harness

Motronic engine control module (ECM), injectors **Edition 06/00** USA.5102.06.21

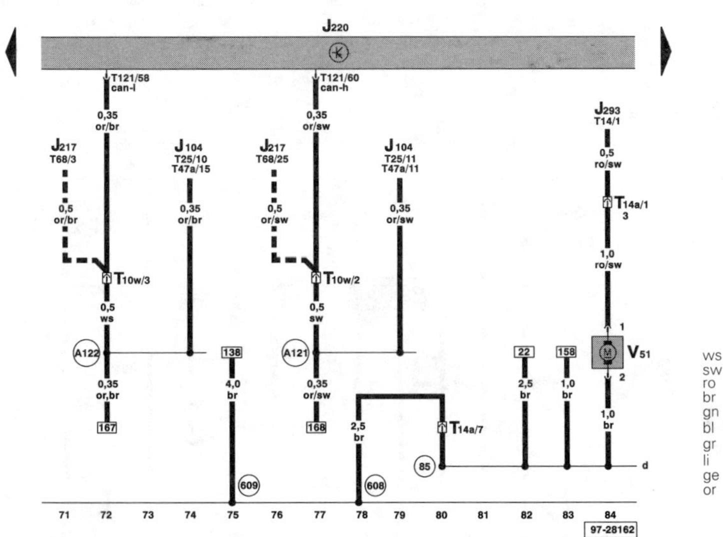

ws = white
sw = black
ro = red
br = brown
gn = green
bl = blue
gr = grey
li = lilac
ge = yellow
or = orange

J104 - ABS Control Module (w/EDL)
J217 - Transmission Control Module (TCM), in plenum chamber, center
J220 - Motronic Engine Control Module (ECM), in plenum chamber, center
J293 - Coolant FC (Fan Control) Control Module
T10w - 10-Pin Connector, white, in protective housing for connectors, in plenum chamber, left
T14 - 14-Pin Connector, on Coolant FC (Fan Control) Control Module
T14a - 14-Pin Connector, in engine compartment, in wiring duct, left
T25 - 25-Pin Connector, on ABS Control Module (through July 2000)
T47a - 47-Pin Connector, on ABS Control Module (beginning August 2000)
T68 - 68-Pin Connector, on Transmission Control Module (TCM)
T121 - Connector, 121 point
V51 - After-Run Coolant Pump
(85) - Ground connection -1-, in engine compartment wiring harness
(608) - Ground connection (in center plenum chamber)
(609) - Ground connection (in right plenum chamber)
(A121) - Connection (high bus), in instrument panel wiring harness
(A122) - Connection (low bus), in instrument panel wiring harness
--- Automatic transmission only

Edition 09/00
USA.5102.08.21

Motronic engine control module (ECM), after-run coolant pump

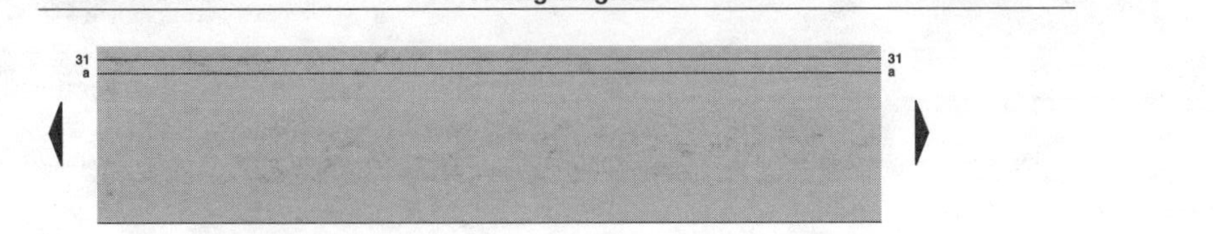

ws = white
sw = black
ro = red
br = brown
gn = green
bl = blue
gr = grey
li = lilac
ge = yellow

J217 - Transmission Control Module (TCM), in plenum chamber, center
J220 - Motronic Engine Control Module (ECM), in plenum chamber, center
N79 - Positive Crankcase Ventilation (PCV) Heating Element
N156 - Intake Manifold Change-Over Valve
N314 - Brake Booster Vacuum Valve
T6 - 6-Pin Connector, brown, in protective housing for connectors, in plenum chamber, left
T10 - 10-Pin Connector, orange, in protective housing for connectors, in plenum chamber, left
T10h - 10-Pin Connector, blue, in protective housing for connectors, in plenum chamber, left
T10w - 10-Pin Connector, white, in protective housing for connectors, in plenum chamber, left
T14a - 14-Pin Connector, in engine compartment, in wiring duct, left
T68 - 68-Pin Connector, on Transmission Control Module (TCM)
T121 - Connector, 121 point
V144 - Leak detection pump (LDP)
(85) - Ground connection -1-, in engine compartment wiring harness
(A100) - Connector -2- (87), in instrument panel wiring harness
(D102) - Wire connection -2-, in engine compartment wiring harness
** - A/C connection
*** - Coolant Fan Control Control Module connection
--- Automatic transmission only

Motronic engine control module (ECM), leak detection pump (LDP), intake manifold change-over valve, (PCV) heating element, brake booster vacuum valve

Edition 09/00
USA.5102.08.21

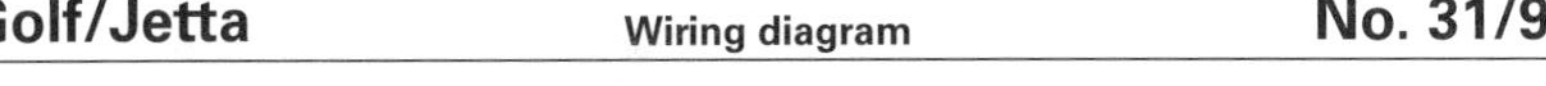

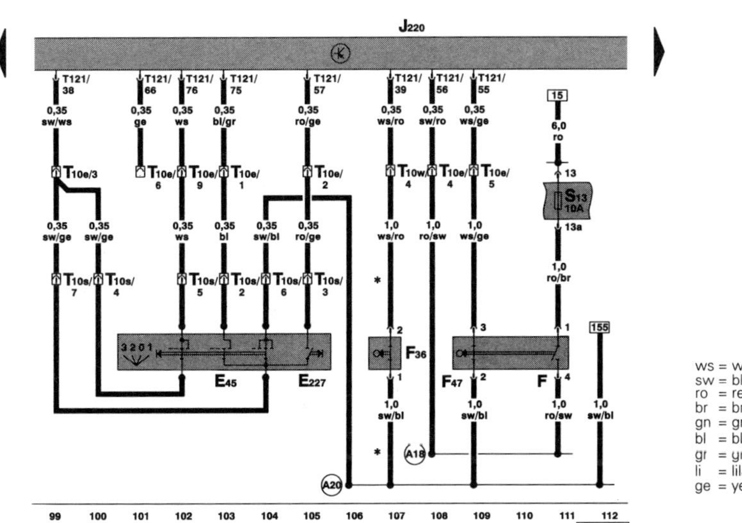

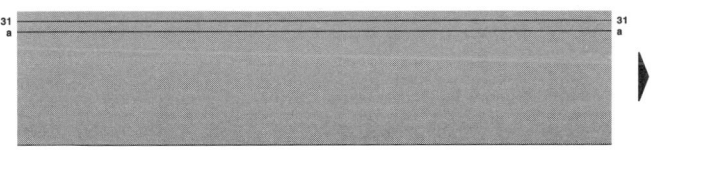

ws = white
sw = black
ro = red
br = brown
gn = green
bl = blue
gr = grey
li = lilac
ge = yellow

E45 - Cruise Control Switch
E227 - Cruise Control Push Button (SET)
F - Brake Light Switch
F36 - Clutch Vacuum Vent Valve Switch
F47 - Brake Vacuum Vent Valve Switch for cruise control
J220 - Motronic Engine Control Module (ECM), in plenum chamber, center
S13 - Fuse 13 in fuse holder
T10e - 10-Pin Connector, black, in protective housing for connectors, in plenum chamber, left
T10s - 10-Pin Connector, near steering column
T10w - 10-Pin Connector, white, in protective housing for connectors, in plenum chamber, left
T121 - Connector, 121 point

A18 - Wire connection (54), in instrument panel
A20 - Wire connection (15a), in instrument panel wiring harness
* - Manual transmission only

Motronic engine control module (ECM), cruise control switch, brake light switch, clutch vacuum vent valve switch, brake vacuum vent valve switch

ws = white
sw = black
ro = red
br = brown
gn = green
bl = blue
gr = grey
li = lilac
ge = yellow
or = orange

G39 - Heated Oxygen Sensor (HO2S)
G187 - Angle sensor -1- for throttle drive (power accelerator actuation)
G188 - Angle sensor -2- for throttle drive (power accelerator actuation)
J17 - Fuel Pump (FP) Relay
J220 - Motronic Engine Control Module (ECM), in plenum chamber, center
J234 - Airbag Control Module
T6 - 6-Pin Connector, brown, in protective housing for connectors, in plenum chamber, left
T6b - 6-Pin Connector
T6c - 6-Pin Connector, in protective housing for connectors under right floor
T10h - 10-Pin Connector, blue, in protective housing for connectors, in plenum chamber, left
T75 - 75-Pin Connector
T121 - Connector, 121 point

A125 - Connection (crash signal) in instrument panel wiring harness
E7 - Plus connection (87a), in Motronic Multiport Fuel Injection (MFI) wiring harness

Motronic engine control module (ECM), angle sensors for throttle drive (power accelerator actuation), heated oxygen sensor (HO2S)

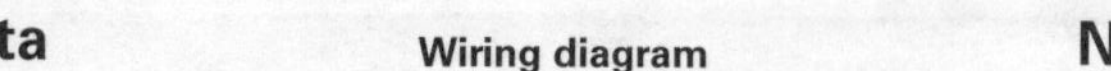

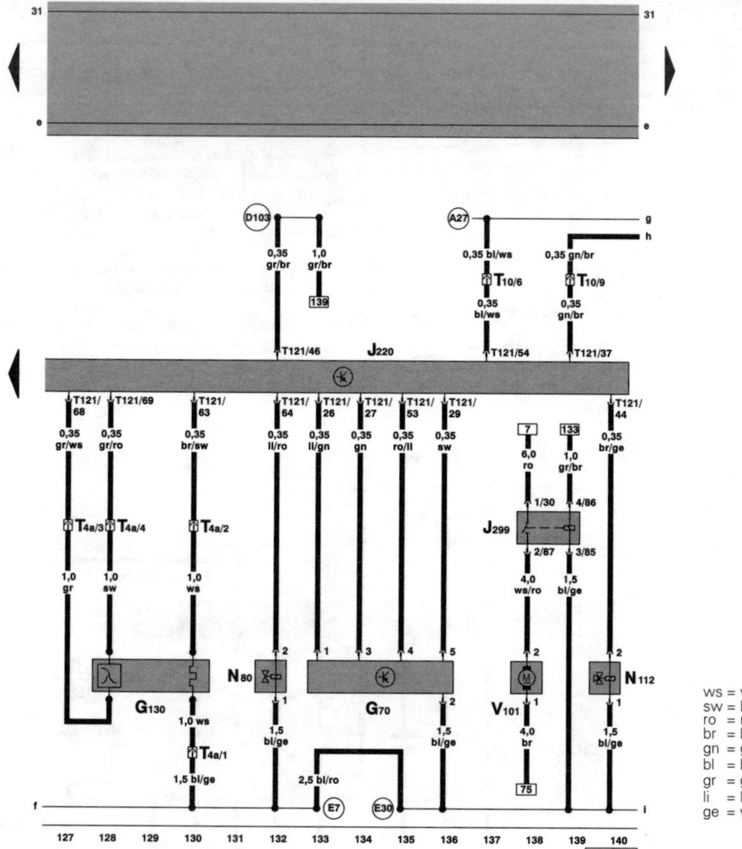

ws = white
sw = black
ro = red
br = brown
gn = green
bl = blue
gr = grey
li = lilac
ge = yellow

G70 - Mass Air Flow (MAF) Sensor
G130 - Oxygen Sensor (O2S) behind Three Way Catalytic Converter (TWC)
J220 - Motronic Engine Control Module (ECM), in plenum chamber, center
J299 - Secondary Air Injection (AIR) Pump Relay, in protective housing, in engine compartment, left, production control number (100)
N80 - Evaporative Emission (EVAP) Canister Purge Regulator Valve
N112 - Secondary Air Injection (AIR) Solenoid Valve
T4a - 4-Pin Connector, in protective housing for connectors under right
T10 - 10-Pin Connector, orange, in protective housing for connectors, in plenum chamber, left
T121 - Connector, 121 point
V101 - Secondary Air Injection (AIR) Pump Motor
(A27) - Wire Connection (vehicle speed signal), in instrument panel wiring harness
(D103) - Wire connection -3-, in engine compartment wiring harness
(E7) - Plus connection (87a), in Motronic Multiport Fuel Injection (MFI) wiring harness
(E30) - Connector (87a), in wiring harness engine

Motronic engine control module (ECM), secondary air injection (AIR) pump system, oxygen sensor (O2S) behind three way catalytic converter (TWC)

ws = white
sw = black
ro = red
br = brown
gn = green
bl = blue
gr = grey
li = lilac
ge = yellow

G - Fuel Level Sensor
G6 - Fuel Pump (FP)
G32 - Engine Coolant Level (ECL) Sensor
S228 - Fuse 28 in fuse holder
S234 - Fuse 34 in fuse holder
S243 - Fuse 43 in fuse holder
T6 - 6-Pin Connector, brown, in protective housing for connectors, in plenum chamber, left
T14a - 14-Pin Connector, in engine compartment, in wiring duct, left
(42) - Ground connection, beside steering column
(81) - Ground connection -1-, in instrument panel wiring harness
(135) - Ground connection -2-, in instrument panel wiring harnes
(269) - Ground connection (sensor ground) -1-, in instrument panel wiring harness
(504) - Threaded connection -1- (87) on the relay plate
(E30) - Connector (87a), in wiring harness engine
(A99) - Connector -1- (87), in instrument panel wiring harness
(A151) - Connector -4- (87), in instrument panel wiring harness
* - Vehicles with Multi-Function Indicator (MFI) only

Fuel pump (FP), fuel level sensor, engine coolant level (ECL) sensor

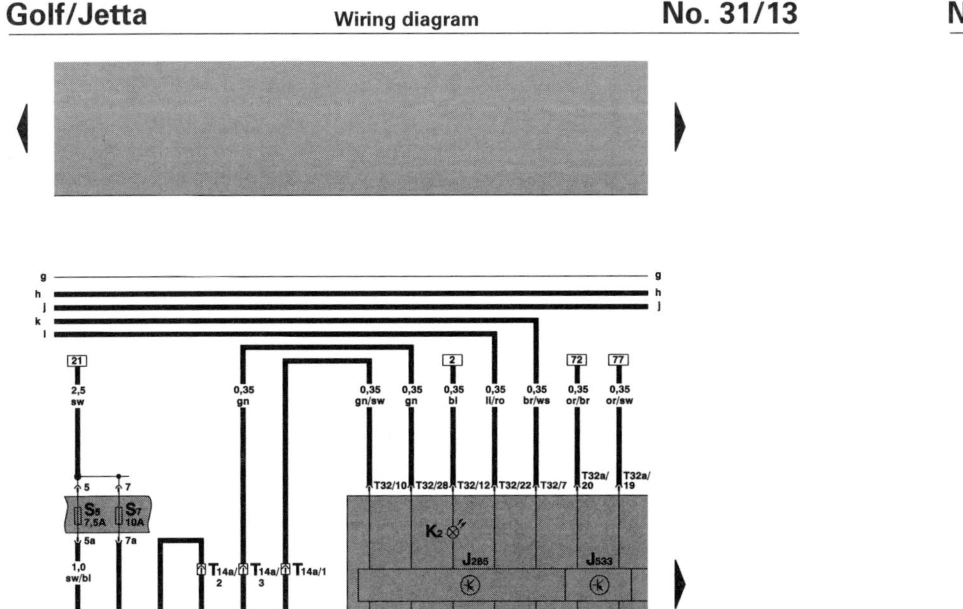

ws = white
sw = black
ro = red
br = brown
gn = green
bl = blue
gr = grey
li = lilac
ge = yellow
or = orange

F1 - Oil Pressure Switch
G22 - Speedometer Vehicle Speed Sensor (VSS)
H3 - Warning Buzzer
J285 - Control module with indicator unit in instrument panel insert
J533 - Data Bus On Board Diagnostic Interface
K2 - Generator (GEN) Warning Light
K3 - Oil Pressure Warning Light
K28 - Engine Coolant Level/Temperature (ECL/ECT) Warning Light
S5 - Fuse 5 in fuse holder
S7 - Fuse 7 in fuse holder
T14a - 14-Pin Connector, in engine compartment, in wiring duct, left
T32 - 32-Pin Connector, blue
T32a - 32-Pin Connector, green

(A13) - Wire connection (door contact switch) in instrument panel wiring harness
(B163) - Plus connector -1- (15) in wiring harness interior

Edition 06/00 USA.5102.06.21

Instrument cluster, oil pressure switch, speedometer vehicle speed sensor, generator (GEN) warning light, engine coolant level/temperature (ECL/ECT) warning light

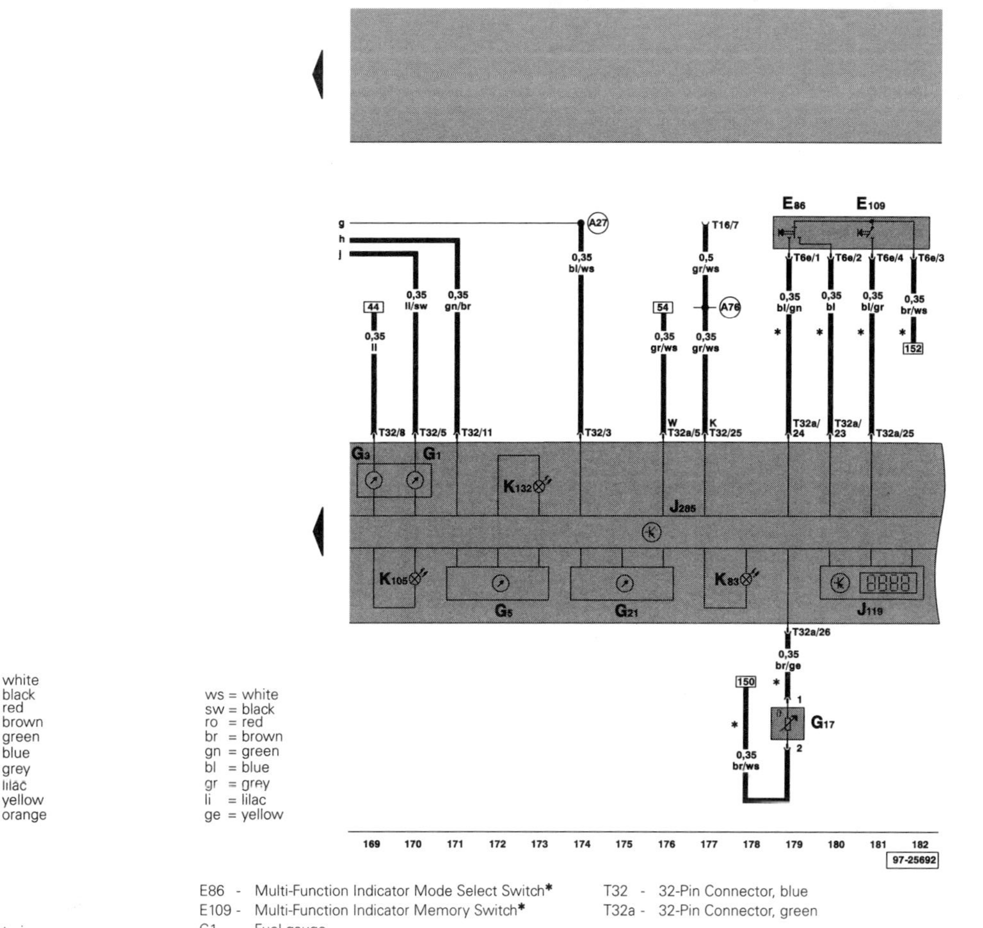

ws = white
sw = black
ro = red
br = brown
gn = green
bl = blue
gr = grey
li = lilac
ge = yellow

E86 - Multi-Function Indicator Mode Select Switch*
E109 - Multi-Function Indicator Memory Switch*
G1 - Fuel gauge
G3 - Engine Coolant Temperature (ECT) Gauge
G5 - Tachometer
G17 - Outside Air Temperature Sensor*
G21 - Speedometer
J119 - Multi-function Indicator (MFI)
J285 - Control module with indicator unit in instrument panel insert
K83 - Malfunction Indicator Lamp (MIL)
K105 - Low Fuel Level Warning Light
K132 - Electronic Power Control (EPC) Warning Lamp
T6e - 6-Pin Connector
T16 - Data Link Connector (DLC), below instrument panel, left
T32 - 32-Pin Connector, blue
T32a - 32-Pin Connector, green

(A27) - Wire Connection (vehicle speed signal), in instrument panel wiring harness
(A76) - Connector (K-diagnosis wire), in instrument panel wiring harness

* - Vehicles with Multi-Function Indicator (MFI) only

Instrument cluster, multi-function indicator (MFI), engine coolant temperature (ECT) gauge, fuel gauge, malfunction indicator lamp (MIL), electronic power control (EPC) warning lamp

Edition 06/00 USA.5102.06.21

1.9L - Engine - Turbo Diesel Fuel Injection (DFI)/66KW, code ALH, (with manual transmission),

from May 1999

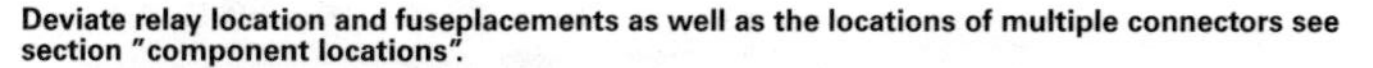

Deviate relay location and fuseplacements as well as the locations of multiple connectors see section "component locations".

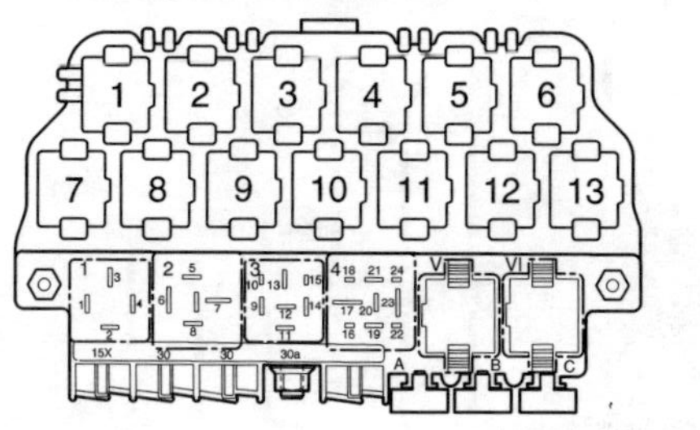

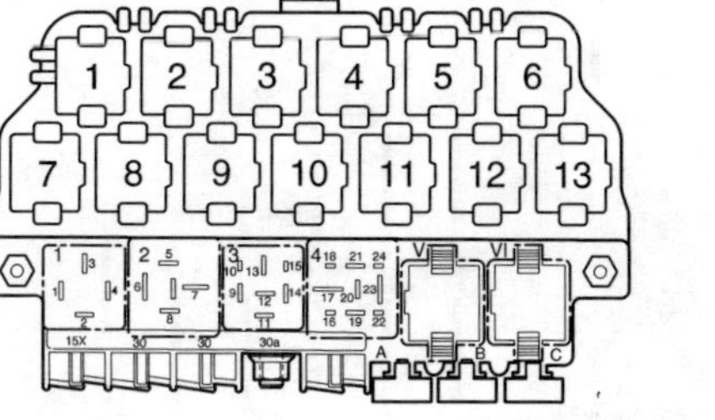

Relay location on the thirteenfold auxiliary relay panel, above relay panel:

- **10** Glow Plug Relay (180)
- **12** Power Supply (Terminal 30, B+) Relay (109)

Relay panel:

- **2** Load Reduction Relay (100)

Note: Number in parentheses indicates production control number stamped on relay housing.

Fuse colors

30 A - green
25 A - white
20 A - yellow
15 A - blue
10 A - red
7,5 A - brown
5 A - beige
3 A - violet

ws = white
sw = black
ro = red
br = brown
gn = green
bl = blue
gr = grey
li = lilac
ge = yellow

A - Battery
B - Starter
C - Generator (GEN)
C1 - Voltage Regulator (VR)
D - Ignition/Starter Switch
J207 - Starting Interlock Relay
S162 - Fuse -1- (30) in fuse bracket/battery
S163 - Fuse -2- (30) in fuse bracket/battery
S176 - Fuse -4- (30) in fuse bracket/battery
S177 - Fuse -5- (30) in fuse bracket/battery
T2e - Double Connector, near starter (vehicles without air conditioning)
T4 - 4-Pin Connector, near starter (vehicles with air conditioning only)
T6 - 6-Pin Connector, brown, in protective housing for connectors, in plenum chamber, left

(42) - Ground connection, beside steering column
(81) - Ground connection -1-, in instrument panel wiring harness
(135) - Ground connection -2-, in instrument panel wiring harness
(500) - Threaded connection -1- (30) on the relay plate

Generator (GEN), starter

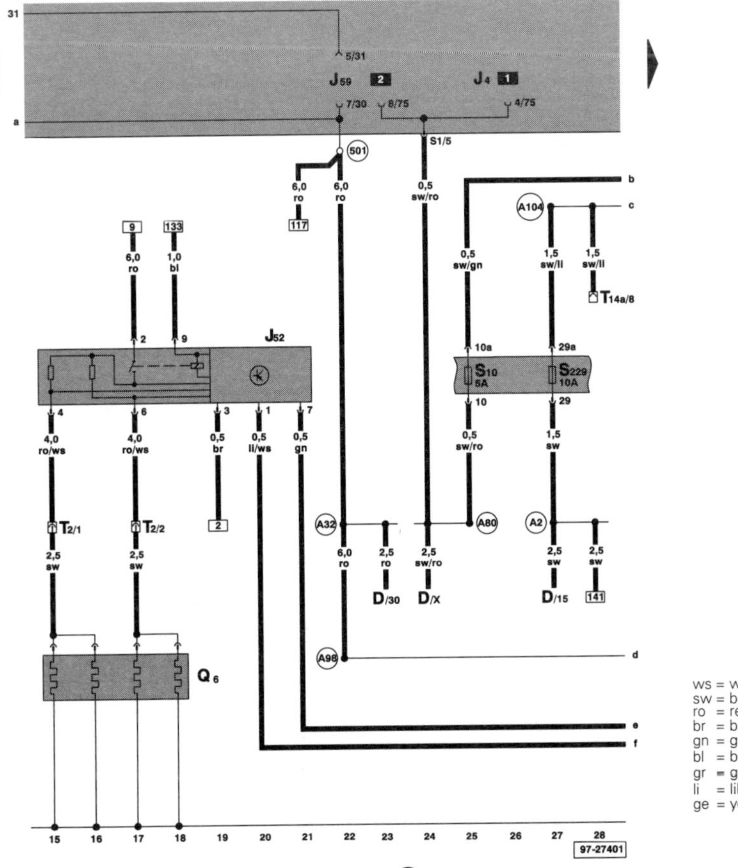

ws = white
sw = black
ro = red
br = brown
gn = green
bl = blue
gr = grey
li = lilac
ge = yellow

- D - Ignition/Starter Switch
- J4 - Dual Horn Relay
- J52 - Glow Plug Relay, on the thirteenfold auxiliary relay panel, above relay panel
- J59 - Load Reduction Relay
- Q6 - Glow plugs (engine)
- S10 - Fuse 10 in fuse holder
- S229 - Fuse 29 in fuse holder
- T2 - Double Connector, in engine compartment, in wiring duct, left
- T14a - 14-Pin Connector, in engine compartment, in wiring duct, left
- (501) - Threaded connection -2- (30) on the relay plate
- (A2) - Plus connection (15), in instrument panel wiring harness
- (A32) - Plus connection (30), in instrument panel wiring harness
- (A80) - Connector -1- (X) in instrument panel wiring harness
- (A98) - Plus connector -4- (30), in instrument panel wiring harness
- (A104) - Plus connector -2- (15), in instrument panel wiring harness

Glow plug relay, glow plugs (engine)

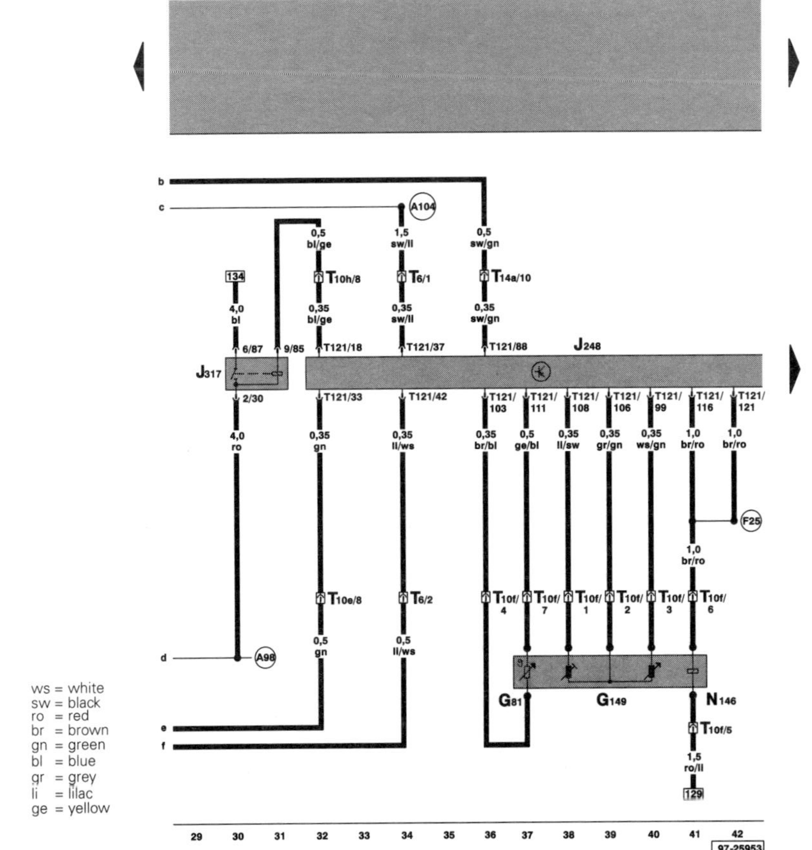

ws = white
sw = black
ro = red
br = brown
gn = green
bl = blue
gr = grey
li = lilac
ge = yellow

- G81 - Fuel Temperature Sensor
- G149 - Modulating Piston Displacement Sensor
- J248 - Diesel Direct Fuel Injection (DFI) Engine Control Module (ECM), in plenum chamber, center
- J317 - Power Supply (Terminal 30, B+) Relay, on the thirteenfold auxiliary relay panel, above relay panel
- N146 - Quantity Adjuster
- T6 - 6-Pin Connector, brown, in protective housing for connectors, in plenum chamber, left
- T10e - 10-Pin Connector, black, in protective housing for connectors, in plenum chamber, left
- T10f - 10-Pin Connector, in engine compartment, front
- T10h - 10-Pin Connector, blue, in protective housing for connectors, in plenum chamber, left
- T14a - 14-Pin Connector, in engine compartment, in wiring duct, left
- T121 - Connector, 121 point
- (A104) - Plus connector -2- (15), in instrument panel wiring harness
- (A98) - Plus connector -4- (30), in instrument panel wiring harness
- (F25) - Wire connection -1-, in Diesel Direct Fuel Injection (DFI) system wiring harness

Diesel direct fuel injection (DFI) engine control module (ECM), power supply (terminal 30, B+) relay, fuel temperature sensor, quantity adjuster, modulating piston displacement sensor

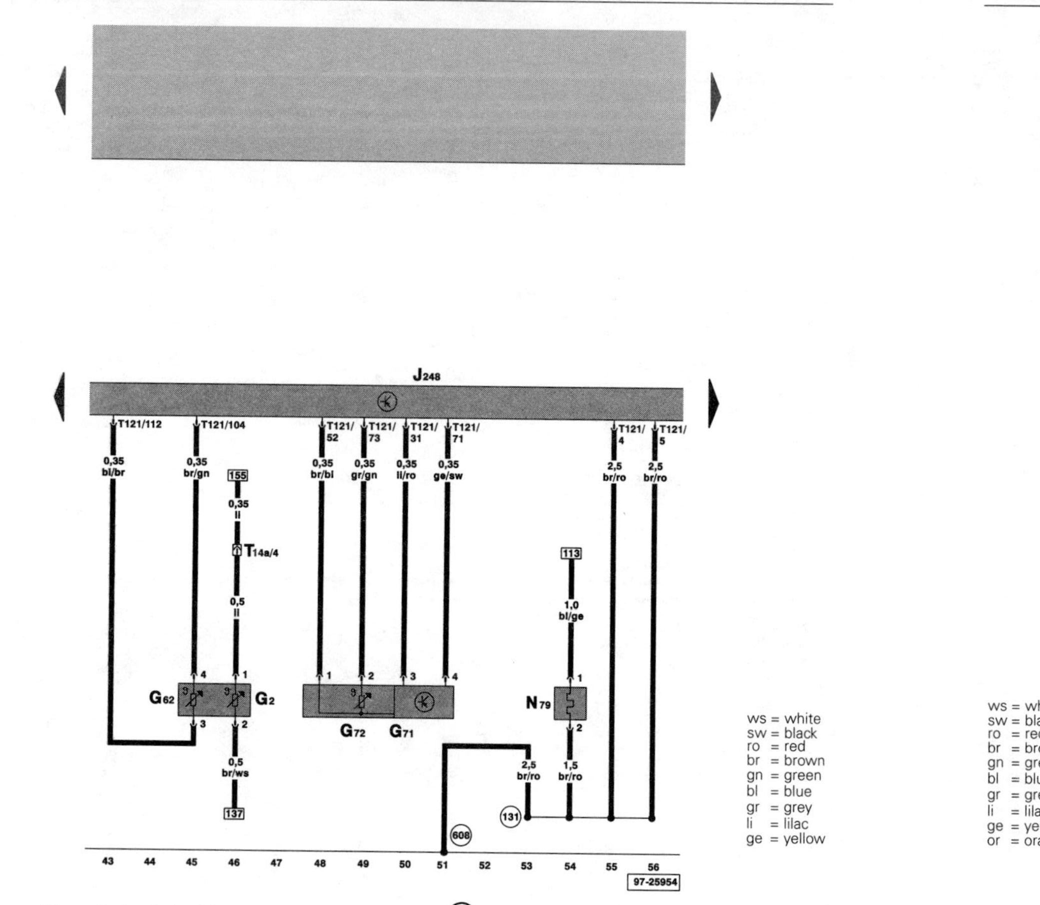

ws = white
sw = black
ro = red
br = brown
gn = green
bl = blue
gr = grey
li = lilac
ge = yellow

G2 - Engine Coolant Temperature (ECT) SensorPositive Crankcase Ventilation (PCV) Heating Element
G62 - Engine Coolant Temperature (ECT) Sensor
G71 - Manifold Absolute Pressure (MAP) Sensor
G72 - Intake Air Temperature (IAT) Sensor
J248 - Diesel Direct Fuel Injection (DFI) Engine Control Module (ECM), in plenum chamber, center
N79 - Positive Crankcase Ventilation (PCV) Heating Element
T14a - 14-Pin Connector, in engine compartment, in wiring duct, left
T121 - Connector, 121 point

(131) - Ground connection -2-, in engine compartment wiring harness

(608) - Ground Connection (in center plenum chamber)

Diesel direct fuel injection (DFI) engine control module (ECM), engine coolant temperature (ECT) sensor, intake air temperature (IAT) sensor, manifold absolute pressure (MAP) sensor

ws = white
sw = black
ro = red
br = brown
gn = green
bl = blue
gr = grey
li = lilac
ge = yellow
or = orange

J104 - ABS Control Module (w/EDL), in engine compartment, left
J248 - Diesel Direct Fuel Injection (DFI) Engine Control Module (ECM), in plenum chamber, center
T6 - 6-Pin Connector, brown, in protective housing for connectors, in plenum chamber, left
T10 - 10-Pin Connector, orange, in protective housing for connectors, in plenum chamber, left
T10w - 10-Pin Connector, white, in protective housing for connectors, in plenum chamber, left
T25 - 25-Pin Connector, on ABS Control Module (through July 2000)
T47a - 47-Pin Connector, on ABS Control Module (beginning August 2000)
T121 - Connector, 121 point

(A121) - Connection (high bus), in instrument panel wiring harness
(A122) - Connection (low bus), in instrument panel wiring harness
(D74) - Wire connection (86), in engine compartment wiring harness

* - Coolant Fan Control (FC) Control Module connection
** - A/C connection

Diesel direct fuel injection (DFI) engine control module (ECM)

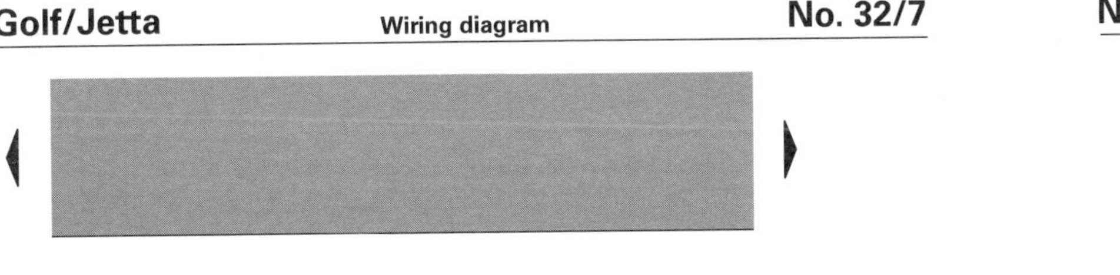

ws = white
sw = black
ro = red
br = brown
gn = green
bl = blue
gr = grey
li = lilac
ge = yellow

F8 - Kick Down Switch
F60 - Closed Throttle Position (CTP) Switch
G28 - Engine Speed (RPM) Sensor
G79 - Throttle Position (TP) Sensor
G80 - Needle Lift Sensor
J248 - Diesel Direct Fuel Injection (DFI) Engine Control Module (ECM), in plenum chamber, center
T2a - Double Connector, in engine compartment, front
T3 - 3-Pin Connector, in engine compartment, front
T6a - 6-Pin Connector
T10h - 10-Pin Connector, blue, in protective housing for connectors, in plenum chamber, left
T121 - Connector, 121 point

(200) - Ground connection (shielding), in engine compartment wiring harness

Diesel direct fuel injection (DFI) engine control module (ECM), kick down switch, (CTP) switch, engine speed (RPM) sensor, throttle position (TP) sensor, needle lift sensor

ws = white
sw = black
ro = red
br = brown
gn = green
bl = blue
gr = grey
li = lilac
ge = yellow

G70 - Mass Air Flow (MAF) Sensor
J248 - Diesel Direct Fuel Injection (DFI) Engine Control Module (ECM), in plenum chamber, center
N18 - EGR Vacuum Regulator Solenoid Valve
N75 - Wastegate Bypass Regulator Valve
N239 - Change-over valve for intake manifold flap
T5 - 5-Pin Connector
T10 - 10-Pin Connector, orange, in protective housing for connectors, in plenum chamber, left
T10w - 10-Pin Connector, white, in protective housing for connectors, in plenum chamber, left
T121 - Connector, 121 point

(E29) - Connector, in wiring harness engine

(DFI) engine control module (ECM), mass air flow sensor, change-over valve for intake manifold flap, wastegate bypass regulator valve, EGR vacuum regulator solenoid valve

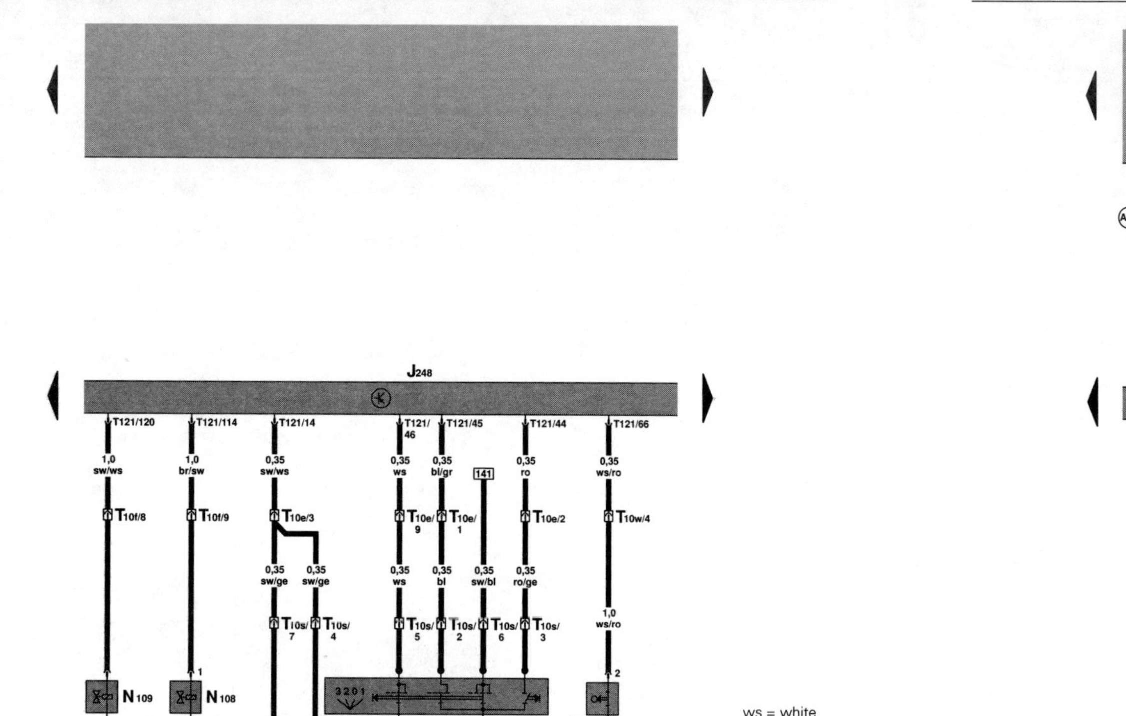

ws = white
sw = black
ro = red
br = brown
gn = green
bl = blue
gr = grey
li = lilac
ge = yellow

- E45 - Cruise Control Switch**
- E227 - Cruise Control Push Button (SET)**
- F36 - Clutch Vacuum Vent Valve Switch
- J248 - Diesel Direct Fuel Injection (DFI) Engine Control Module (ECM), in plenum chamber, center
- N108 - Cold Start Injector
- N109 - Fuel Cut-off Valve
- T10e - 10-Pin Connector, black, in protective housing for connectors, in plenum chamber, left
- T10f - 10-Pin Connector, in engine compartment, front
- T10s - 10-Pin Connector, near steering column**
- T10w - 10-Pin Connector, white, in protective housing for connectors, in plenum chamber, left
- T121 - Connector, 121 point
- (A155) - Connector -2- (86), in instrument panel wiring harness
- ** - Vehicles with cruise control only

Diesel direct fuel injection (DFI) engine control module (ECM), cruise control switch, clutch vacuum vent valve switch, cold start injector, fuel cut-off valve

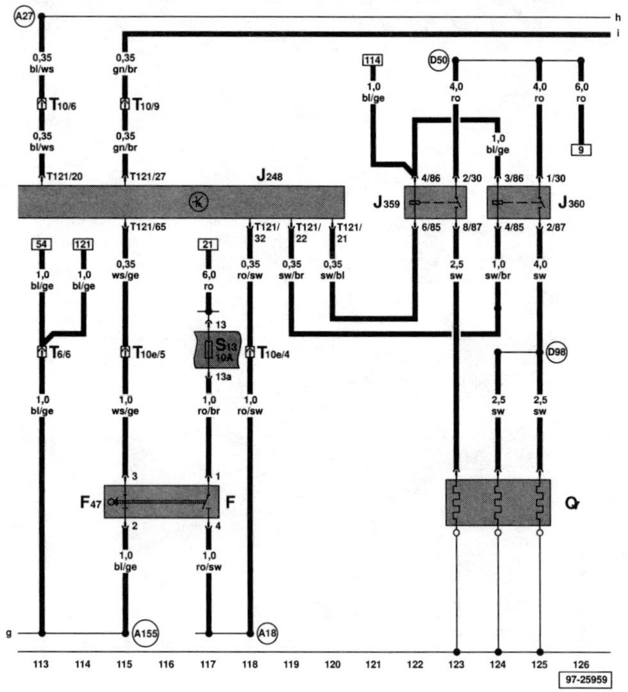

ws = white
sw = black
ro = red
br = brown
gn = green
bl = blue
gr = grey
li = lilac
ge = yellow

- F - Brake Light Switch
- F47 - Brake Vacuum Vent Valve Switch for cruise control/diesel
- J248 - Diesel Direct Fuel Injection (DFI) Engine Control Module (ECM), in plenum chamber, center
- J359 - Relay for preheating coolant, low heat output, in protective housing, in engine compartment, left, production control number (53)
- J360 - Relay for preheating coolant, high heat output, in protective housing, in engine compartment, left, production control number (53)
- Q7 - Glow plugs (coolant)
- S13 - Fuse 13 in fuse holder
- T6 - 6-Pin Connector, brown, in protective housing for connectors, in plenum chamber, left
- T10 - 10-Pin Connector, orange, in protective housing for connectors, in plenum chamber, left
- T10e - 10-Pin Connector, black, in protective housing for connectors, in plenum chamber, left
- T121 - Connector, 121 point
- (A18) - Wire connection (54), in instrument panel wiring harness
- (A27) - Wire Connection (vehicle speed signal), in instrument panel wiring harness
- (A155) - Connector -2- (86), in instrument panel wiring harness
- (D50) - Plus connection (30), in engine compartment wiring harness
- (D98) - Wire connection (glow plugs), in engine compartment wiring harness

Diesel direct fuel injection (DFI) engine control module (ECM), brake light switch, brake vacuum vent valve switch for cruise control/diesel, glow plugs (coolant)

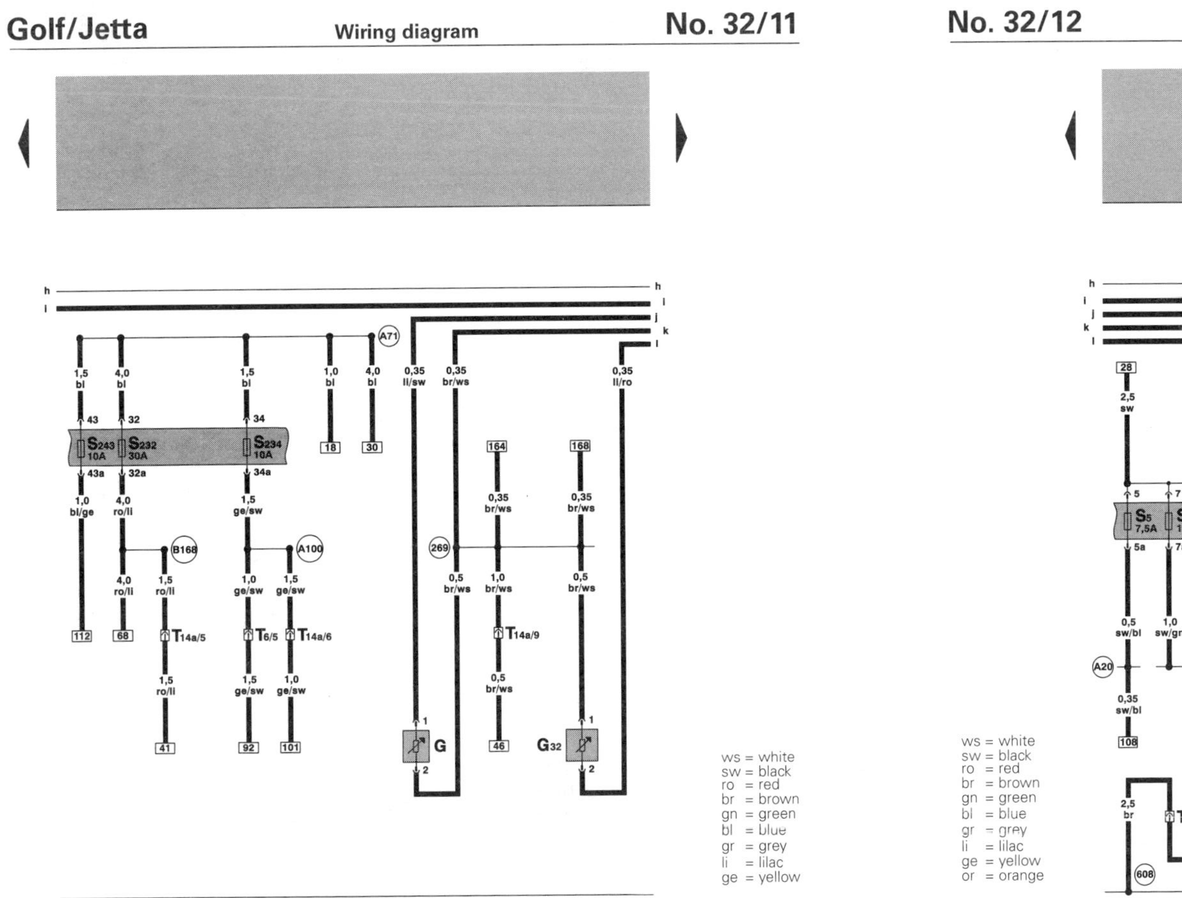

ws = white
sw = black
ro = red
br = brown
gn = green
bl = blue
gr = grey
li = lilac
ge = yellow

G - Fuel Level Sensor
G32 - Engine Coolant Level (ECL) Sensor
S232 - Fuse 32 in fuse holder
S234 - Fuse 34 in fuse holder
S243 - Fuse 43 in fuse holder
T6 - 6-Pin Connector, brown, in protective housing for connectors, in plenum chamber, left
T14a - 14-Pin Connector, in engine compartment, in wiring duct, left

(269) - Ground connection (sensor ground) -1-, in instrument panel wiring harness
(A71) - Connector (86), in instrument panel wiring harness
(A100) - Connector -2- (87), in instrument panel wiring harness

(B168) - Connection (86) in passenger compartment wiring harness

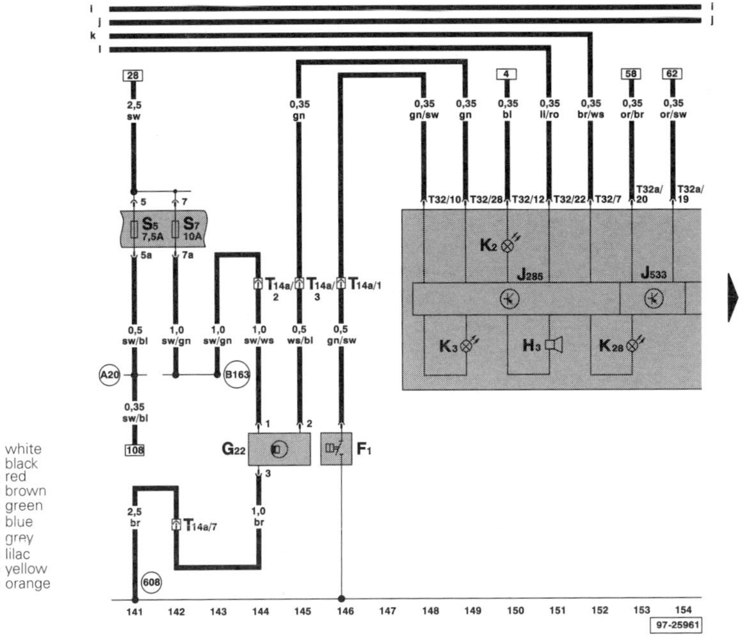

ws = white
sw = black
ro = red
br = brown
gn = green
bl = blue
gr = grey
li = lilac
ge = yellow
or = orange

F1 - Oil Pressure Switch
G22 - Speedometer Vehicle Speed Sensor (VSS)
H3 - Warning Buzzer
J285 - Control module with indicator unit in instrument panel insert
J533 - Data Bus On Board Diagnostic Interface
K2 - Generator (GEN) Warning Light
K3 - Oil Pressure Warning Light
K28 - Engine Coolant Level/Temperature (ECL/ECT) Warning Light
S5 - Fuse 5 in fuse holder
S7 - Fuse 7 in fuse holder
T14a - 14-Pin Connector, in engine compartment, in wiring duct, left
T32 - 32-Pin Connector, blue
T32a - 32-Pin Connector, green

(608) - Ground Connection (in center plenum chamber)
(A20) - Wire connection (15a), in instrument panel wiring harness
(B163) - Plus connector -1- (15) in wiring harness interior

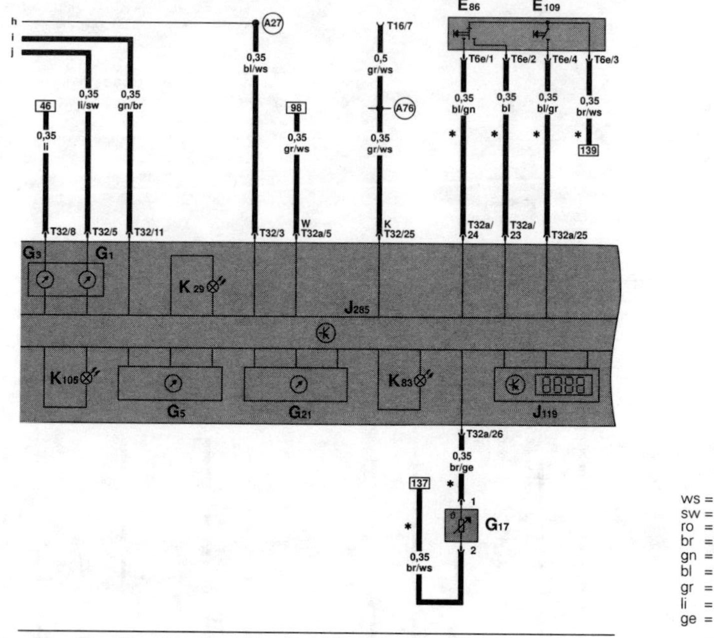

ws = white
sw = black
ro = red
br = brown
gn = green
bl = blue
gr = grey
li = lilac
ge = yellow

E86 - Multi-Function Indicator Mode Select Switch*
E109 - Multi-Function Indicator Memory Switch*
G1 - Fuel gauge
G3 - Engine Coolant Temperature (ECT) Gauge
G5 - Tachometer
G17 - Outside Air Temperature Sensor*
G21 - Speedometer
J119 - Multi-function Indicator (MFI)
J285 - Control module with indicator unit in instrument panel insert
K29 - Glow Plug Indicator Light
K83 - Malfunction Indicator Lamp (MIL)
K105 - Low Fuel Level Warning Light
T6e - 6-Pin Connector
T16 - Data Link Connector (DLC), below instrument panel, left

T32 - 32-Pin Connector, blue
T32a - 32-Pin Connector, green

(A27) - Wire Connection (vehicle speed signal), in instrument panel wiring harness
(A76) - Connector (K-diagnosis wire), in instrument panel wiring harness

* - Vehicles with Multi-Function Indicator (MFI) only

Instrument cluster, engine coolant temperature (ECT) gauge, fuel gauge, tachometer, speedometer, glow plug indicator light

THIS PAGE INTENTIONALLY LEFT

BLANK

1.9L - Engine - Turbo Diesel Fuel Injection (DFI)/66KW, code ALH, (with automatic transmission),

from May 1999

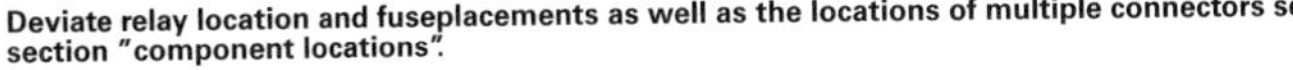

Deviate relay location and fuseplacements as well as the locations of multiple connectors see section "component locations".

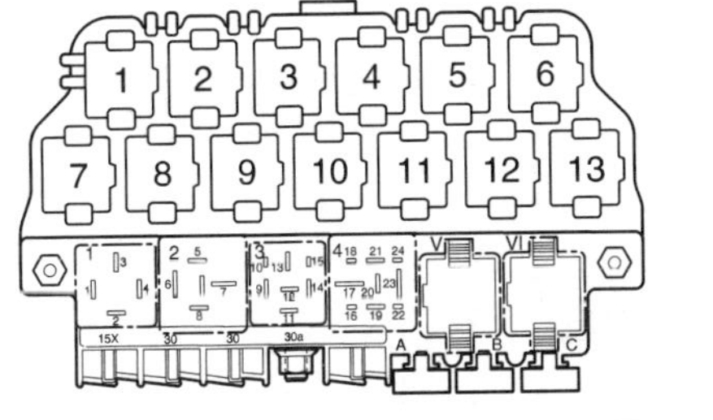

97-14163

Relay location on the thirteenfold auxiliary relay panel, above relay panel:

- **10** Glow Plug Relay (180)
- **12** Power Supply (Terminal 30, B+) Relay (109)

Relay panel:

- **2** Load Reduction Relay (100)

Note: Number in parentheses indicates production control number stamped on relay housing.

Fuse colors

- 30 A - green
- 25 A - white
- 20 A - yellow
- 15 A - blue
- 10 A - red
- 7,5 A - brown
- 5 A - beige
- 3 A - violet

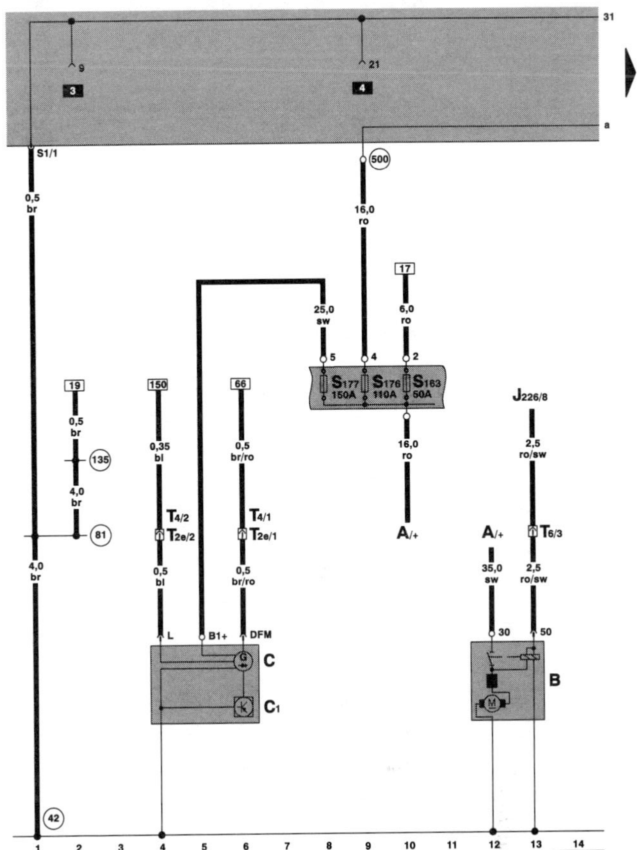

- ws = white
- sw = black
- ro = red
- br = brown
- gn = green
- bl = blue
- gr = grey
- li = lilac
- ge = yellow

97-26024

- A - Battery
- B - Starter
- C - Generator (GEN)
- C1 - Voltage Regulator (VR)
- J226 - Park/Neutral Position (PNP) Relay, on the thirteenfold auxiliary relay panel, above relay panel
- S163 - Fuse -2- (30) in fuse bracket/battery
- S176 - Fuse -4- (30) in fuse bracket/battery
- S177 - Fuse -5- (30) in fuse bracket/battery
- T2e - Double Connector, near starter (vehicles without air conditioning)
- T4 - 4-Pin Connector, near starter (vehicles with air conditioning only)
- T6 - 6-Pin Connector, brown, in protective housing for connectors, in plenum chamber, left

- (42) - Ground connection, beside steering column
- (81) - Ground connection -1-, in instrument panel wiring harness
- (135) - Ground connection -2-, in instrument panel wiring harness
- (500) - Threaded connection -1- (30) on the relay plate

Generator (GEN), starter

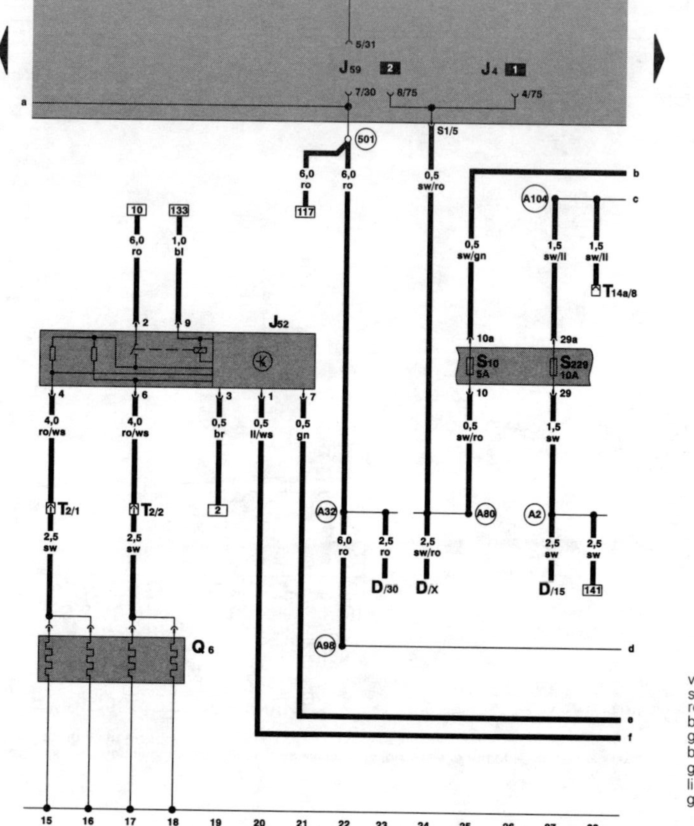

ws = white
sw = black
ro = red
br = brown
gn = green
bl = blue
gr = grey
li = lilac
ge = yellow

- D - Ignition/Starter Switch
- J4 - Dual Horn Relay
- J52 - Glow Plug Relay, on the thirteenfold auxiliary relay panel, above relay panel
- J59 - Load Reduction Relay
- Q6 - Glow plugs (engine)
- S10 - Fuse 10 in fuse holder
- S229 - Fuse 29 in fuse holder
- T2 - Double Connector, in engine compartment, in wiring duct, left
- T14a - 14-Pin Connector, in engine compartment, in wiring duct, left
- (501) - Threaded connection -2- (30) on the relay plate
- (A2) - Plus connection (15), in instrument panel wiring harness
- (A32) - Plus connection (30), in instrument panel wiring harness
- (A80) - Connector -1- (X) in instrument panel wiring harness
- (A98) - Plus connector -4- (30), in instrument panel wiring harness
- (A104) - Plus connector -2- (15), in instrument panel wiring harness

Glow plug relay, glow plugs (engine)

ws = white
sw = black
ro = red
br = brown
gn = green
bl = blue
gr = grey
li = lilac
ge = yellow

- G81 - Fuel Temperature Sensor
- G149 - Modulating Piston Displacement Sensor
- J248 - Diesel Direct Fuel Injection (DFI) Engine Control Module (ECM), in plenum chamber, center
- J317 - Power Supply (Terminal 30, B+) Relay, on the thirteenfold auxiliary relay panel, above relay panel
- N146 - Quantity Adjuster
- T6 - 6-Pin Connector, brown, in protective housing for connectors, in plenum chamber, left
- T10e - 10-Pin Connector, black, in protective housing for connectors, in plenum chamber, left
- T10f - 10-Pin Connector, in engine compartment, front
- T10h - 10-Pin Connector, blue, in protective housing for connectors, in plenum chamber, left
- T14a - 14-Pin Connector, in engine compartment, in wiring duct, left
- T121 - Connector, 121 point
- (A104) - Plus connector -2- (15), in instrument panel wiring harness
- (A98) - Plus connector -4- (30), in instrument panel wiring harness
- (F25) - Wire connection -1-, in Diesel Direct Fuel Injection (DFI) system wiring harness

Diesel direct fuel injection (DFI) engine control module (ECM), power supply (terminal 30, B+) relay, fuel temperature sensor, quantity adjuster, modulating piston displacement sensor

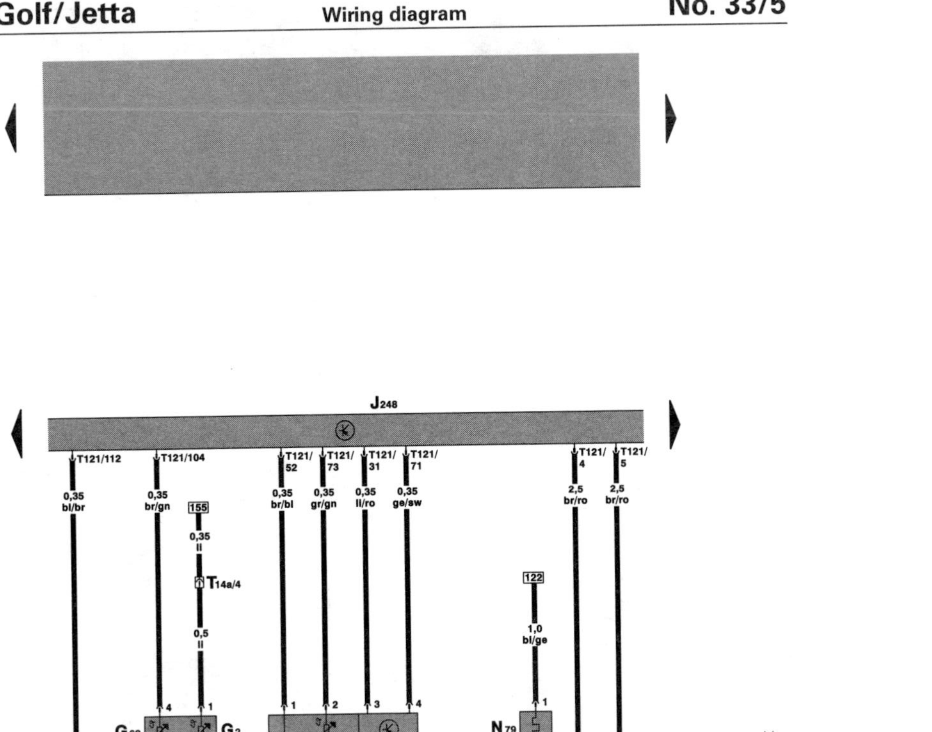

ws = white
sw = black
ro = red
br = brown
gn = green
bl = blue
gr = grey
li = lilac
ge = yellow

G2 - Engine Coolant Temperature (ECT) SensorPositive Crankcase Ventilation (PCV) Heating Element
G62 - Engine Coolant Temperature (ECT) Sensor
G71 - Manifold Absolute Pressure (MAP) Sensor
G72 - Intake Air Temperature (IAT) Sensor
J248 - Diesel Direct Fuel Injection (DFI) Engine Control Module (ECM), in plenum chamber, center
N79 - Positive Crankcase Ventilation (PCV) Heating Element
T14a - 14-Pin Connector, in engine compartment, in wiring duct, left
T121 - Connector, 121 point

(131) - Ground connection -2-, in engine compartment wiring harness

(608) - Ground Connection (in center plenum chamber)

Diesel direct fuel injection (DFI) engine control module (ECM), engine coolant temperature (ECT) sensor, intake air temperature (IAT) sensor, manifold absolute pressure (MAP) sensor

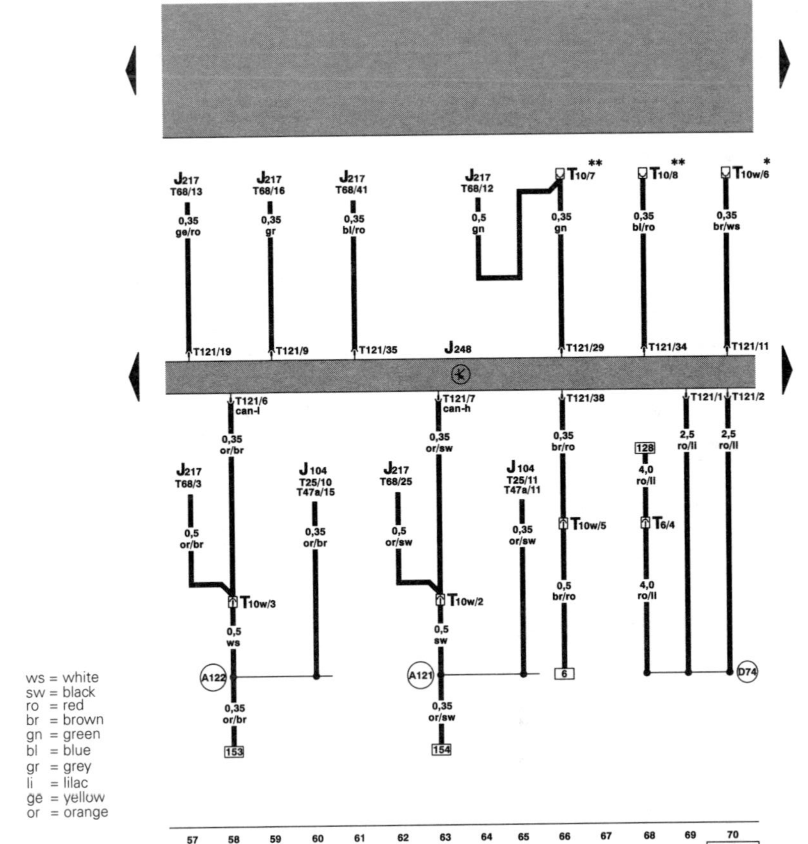

ws = white
sw = black
ro = red
br = brown
gn = green
bl = blue
gr = grey
li = lilac
ge = yellow
or = orange

J104 - ABS Control Module (w/EDL), in engine compartment, left
J217 - Transmission Control Module (TCM), in plenum chamber, center
J248 - Diesel Direct Fuel Injection (DFI) Engine Control Module (ECM), in plenum chamber, center
T6 - 6-Pin Connector, brown, in protective housing for connectors, in plenum chamber, left
T10 - 10-Pin Connector, orange, in protective housing for connectors, in plenum chamber, left
T10w- 10-Pin Connector, white, in protective housing for connectors, in plenum chamber, left
T25 - 25-Pin Connector, on ABS Control Module (through July 2000)
T47a - 47-Pin Connector, on ABS Control Module (beginning August 2000)
T68 - 68-Pin Connector
T121 - Connector, 121 point

(A121) - Connection (high bus), in instrument panel wiring harness
(A122) - Connection (low bus), in instrument panel wiring harness
(D74) - Wire connection (86), in engine compartment wiring harness

* - Coolant Fan Control (FC) Control Module connection
** - A/C connection

Diesel direct fuel injection (DFI) engine control module (ECM)

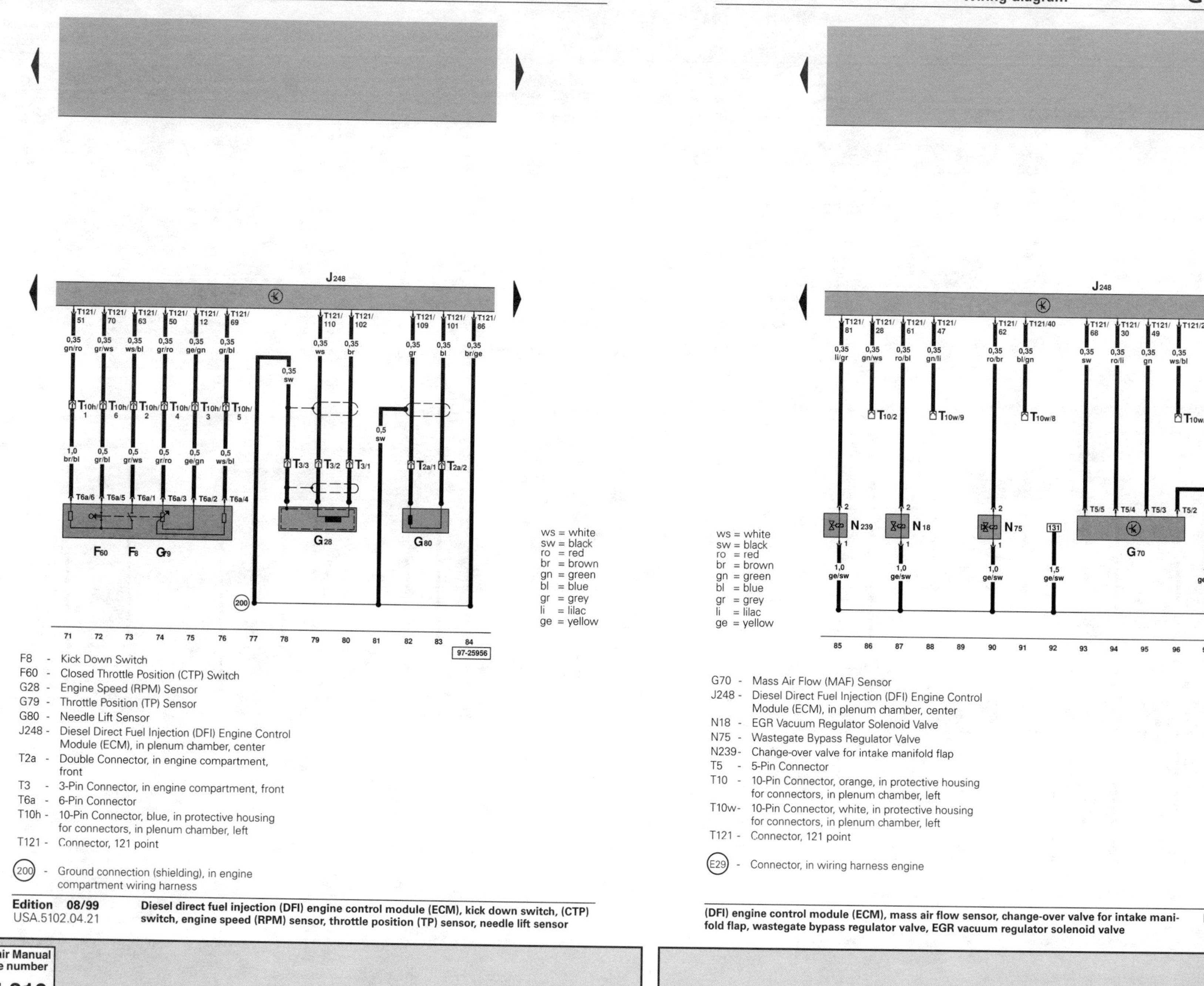

ws = white
sw = black
ro = red
br = brown
gn = green
bl = blue
gr = grey
li = lilac
ge = yellow

- F8 - Kick Down Switch
- F60 - Closed Throttle Position (CTP) Switch
- G28 - Engine Speed (RPM) Sensor
- G79 - Throttle Position (TP) Sensor
- G80 - Needle Lift Sensor
- J248 - Diesel Direct Fuel Injection (DFI) Engine Control Module (ECM), in plenum chamber, center
- T2a - Double Connector, in engine compartment, front
- T3 - 3-Pin Connector, in engine compartment, front
- T6a - 6-Pin Connector
- T10h - 10-Pin Connector, blue, in protective housing for connectors, in plenum chamber, left
- T121 - Connector, 121 point
- (200) - Ground connection (shielding), in engine compartment wiring harness

Diesel direct fuel injection (DFI) engine control module (ECM), kick down switch, (CTP) switch, engine speed (RPM) sensor, throttle position (TP) sensor, needle lift sensor

ws = white
sw = black
ro = red
br = brown
gn = green
bl = blue
gr = grey
li = lilac
ge = yellow

- G70 - Mass Air Flow (MAF) Sensor
- J248 - Diesel Direct Fuel Injection (DFI) Engine Control Module (ECM), in plenum chamber, center
- N18 - EGR Vacuum Regulator Solenoid Valve
- N75 - Wastegate Bypass Regulator Valve
- N239 - Change-over valve for intake manifold flap
- T5 - 5-Pin Connector
- T10 - 10-Pin Connector, orange, in protective housing for connectors, in plenum chamber, left
- T10w - 10-Pin Connector, white, in protective housing for connectors, in plenum chamber, left
- T121 - Connector, 121 point
- (E29) - Connector, in wiring harness engine

(DFI) engine control module (ECM), mass air flow sensor, change-over valve for intake manifold flap, wastegate bypass regulator valve, EGR vacuum regulator solenoid valve

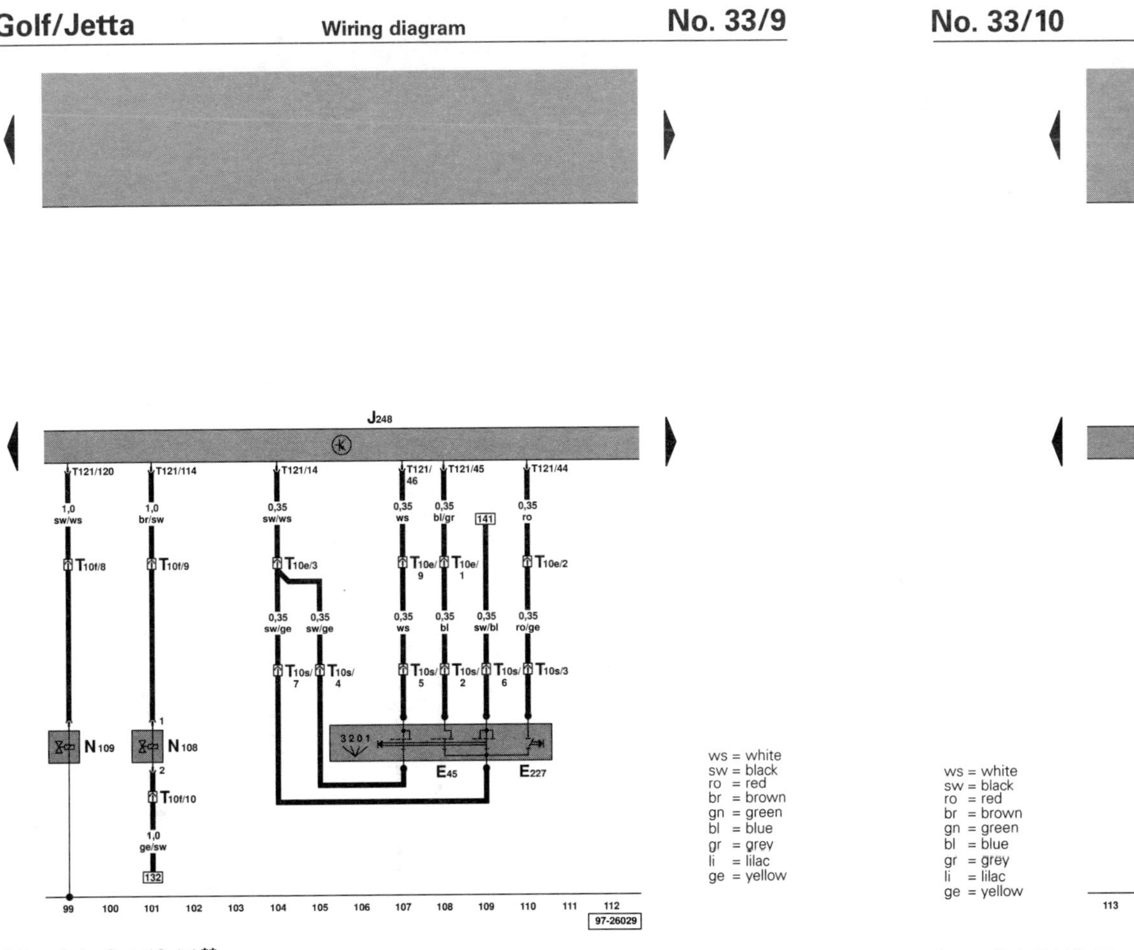

ws = white
sw = black
ro = red
br = brown
gn = green
bl = blue
gr = grey
li = lilac
ge = yellow

- E45 - Cruise Control Switch**
- E227 - Cruise Control Push Button (SET)**
- J248 - Diesel Direct Fuel Injection (DFI) Engine Control Module (ECM), in plenum chamber, center
- N108 - Cold Start Injector
- N109 - Fuel Cut-off Valve
- T10e - 10-Pin Connector, black, in protective housing for connectors, in plenum chamber, left
- T10f - 10-Pin Connector, in engine compartment, front
- T10s - 10-Pin Connector, near steering column**
- T121 - Connector, 121 point

** - Vehicles with cruise control only

Diesel direct fuel injection (DFI) engine control module (ECM), cruise control switch, fuel cut-off valve

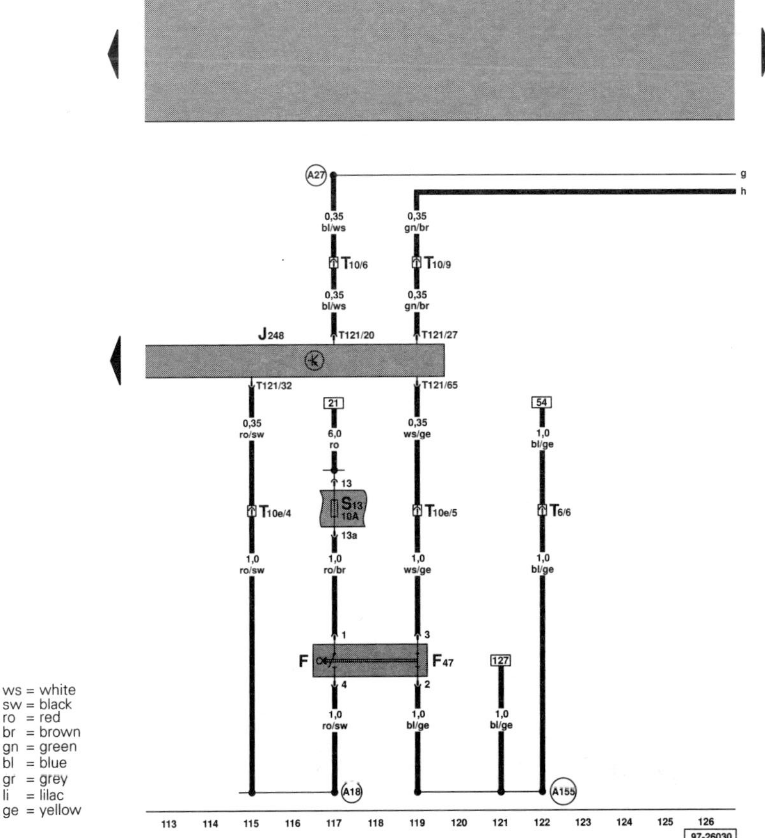

ws = white
sw = black
ro = red
br = brown
gn = green
bl = blue
gr = grey
li = lilac
ge = yellow

- F - Brake Light Switch
- F47 - Brake Vacuum Vent Valve Switch for cruise control/diesel
- J248 - Diesel Direct Fuel Injection (DFI) Engine Control Module (ECM), in plenum chamber, center
- S13 - Fuse 13 in fuse holder
- T6 - 6-Pin Connector, brown, in protective housing for connectors, in plenum chamber, left
- T10 - 10-Pin Connector, orange, in protective housing for connectors, in plenum chamber, left
- T10e - 10-Pin Connector, black, in protective housing for connectors, in plenum chamber, left
- T121 - Connector, 121 point
- (A18) - Wire connection (54), in instrument panel wiring harness
- (A27) - Wire Connection (vehicle speed signal), in instrument panel wiring harness
- (A155) - Connector -2- (86), in instrument panel wiring harness

Diesel direct fuel injection (DFI) engine control module (ECM), brake light switch, brake vacuum vent valve switch for cruise control/diesel

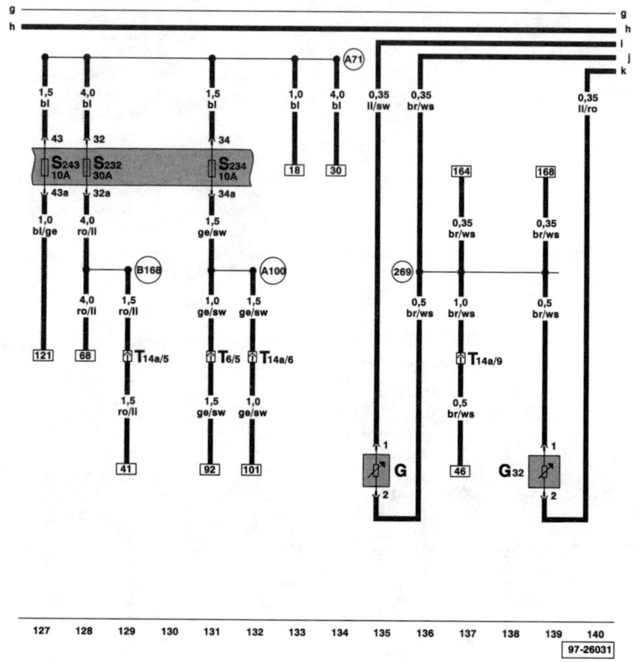

ws = white
sw = black
ro = red
br = brown
gn = green
bl = blue
gr = grey
li = lilac
ge = yellow

- G - Fuel Level Sensor
- G32 - Engine Coolant Level (ECL) Sensor
- S232 - Fuse 32 in fuse holder
- S234 - Fuse 34 in fuse holder
- S243 - Fuse 43 in fuse holder
- T6 - 6-Pin Connector, brown, in protective housing for connectors, in plenum chamber, left
- T14a - 14-Pin Connector, in engine compartment, in wiring duct, left
- (269) - Ground connection (sensor ground) -1-, in instrument panel wiring harness
- (A71) - Connector (86), in instrument panel wiring harness
- (A100) - Connector -2- (87), in instrument panel wiring harness
- (B168) - Connection (86) in passenger compartment wiring harness

Fuel level sensor, engine coolant level (ECL) sensor

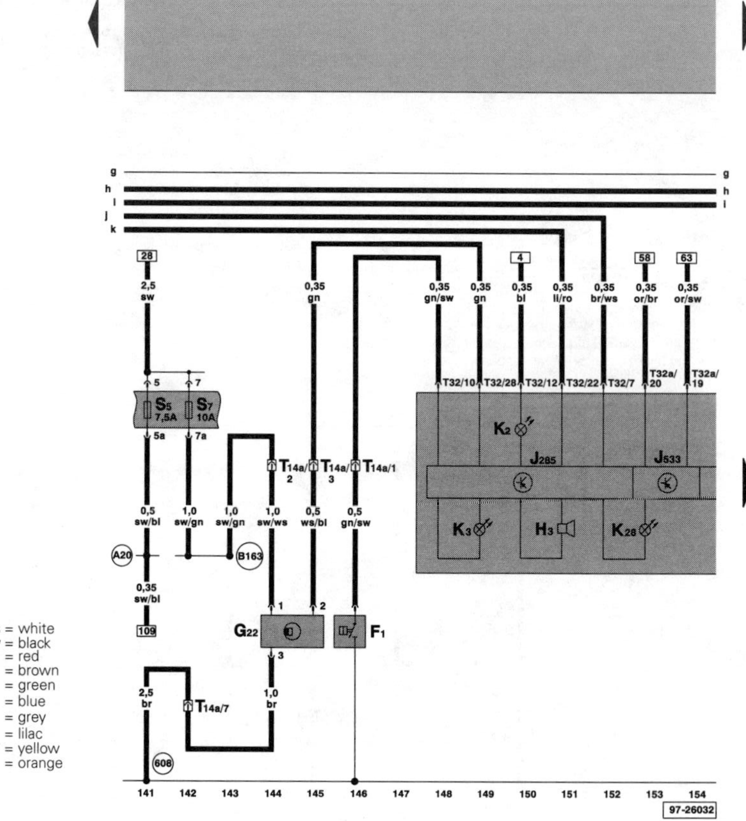

ws = white
sw = black
ro = red
br = brown
gn = green
bl = blue
gr = grey
li = lilac
ge = yellow
or = orange

- F1 - Oil Pressure Switch
- G22 - Speedometer Vehicle Speed Sensor (VSS)
- H3 - Warning Buzzer
- J285 - Control module with indicator unit in instrument panel insert
- J533 - Data Bus On Board Diagnostic Interface
- K2 - Generator (GEN) Warning Light
- K3 - Oil Pressure Warning Light
- K28 - Engine Coolant Level/Temperature (ECL/ECT) Warning Light
- S5 - Fuse 5 in fuse holder
- S7 - Fuse 7 in fuse holder
- T14a - 14-Pin Connector, in engine compartment, in wiring duct, left
- T32 - 32-Pin Connector, blue
- T32a - 32-Pin Connector, green
- (608) - Ground Connection (in center plenum chamber)
- (A20) - Wire connection (15a), in instrument panel wiring harness
- (B163) - Plus connector -1- (15) in wiring harness interior

Instrument cluster, oil pressure switch, speedometer vehicle speed sensor, generator (GEN) warning light, engine coolant level/temperature (ECL/ECT) warning light

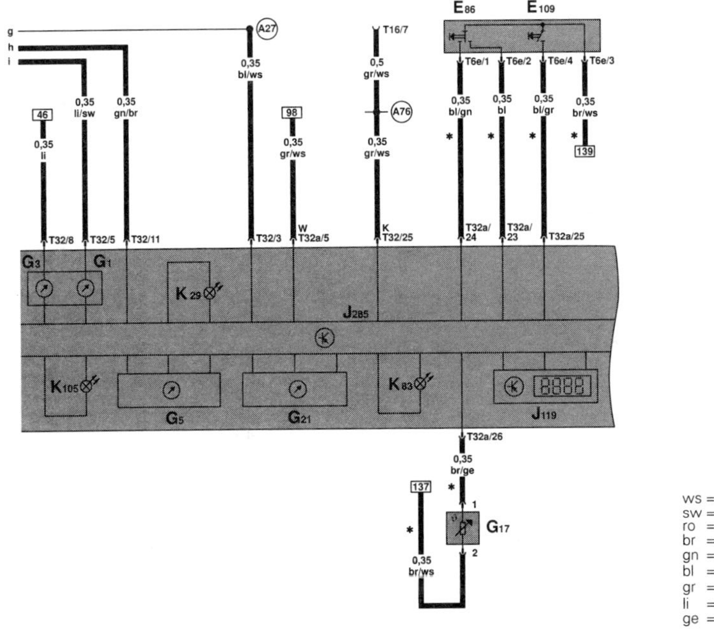

ws = white
sw = black
ro = red
br = brown
gn = green
bl = blue
gr = grey
li = lilac
ge = yellow

E86 - Multi-Function Indicator Mode Select Switch*
E109 - Multi-Function Indicator Memory Switch*
G1 - Fuel gauge
G3 - Engine Coolant Temperature (ECT) Gauge
G5 - Tachometer
G17 - Outside Air Temperature Sensor*
G21 - Speedometer
J119 - Multi-function Indicator (MFI)
J285 - Control module with indicator unit in instrument panel insert
K29 - Glow Plug Indicator Light
K83 - Malfunction Indicator Lamp (MIL)
K105 - Low Fuel Level Warning Light
T6e - 6-Pin Connector
T16 - Data Link Connector (DLC), below instrument panel, left

T32 - 32-Pin Connector, blue
T32a - 32-Pin Connector, green

(A27) - Wire Connection (vehicle speed signal), in instrument panel wiring harness
(A76) - Connector (K-diagnosis wire), in instrument panel wiring harness

* - Vehicles with Multi-Function Indicator (MFI) only

Edition 08/99
USA.5102.04.21

Instrument cluster, engine coolant temperature (ECT) gauge, fuel gauge, tachometer, speedometer, glow plug indicator light

THIS PAGE INTENTIONALLY LEFT

BLANK

Airbag systems,

from May 1999

- **Driver- and front passsenger airbag**
- **Head airbag**
- **Side airbag**
- **Seat belt tensioner**
- **Seat belt control**

Deviate relay location and fuseplacements as well as the locations of multiple connectors see section "component locations".

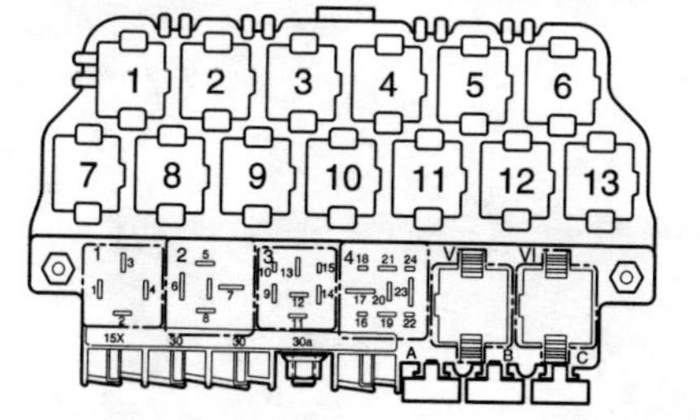

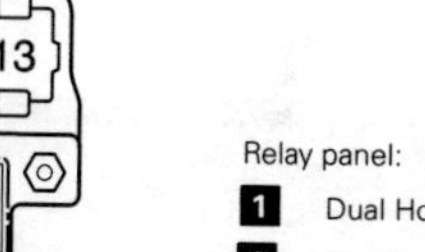

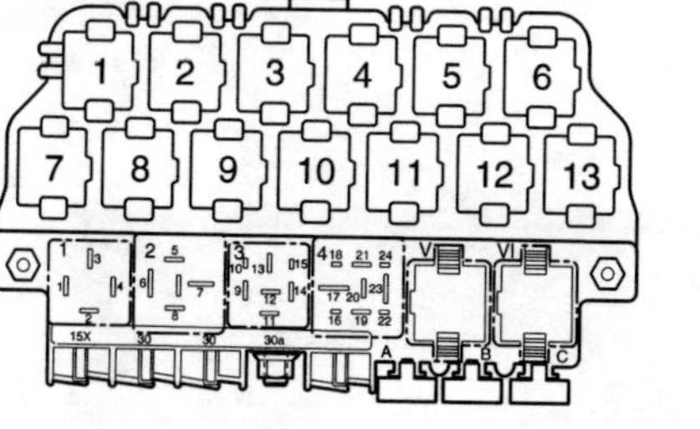

Relay location on the thirteenfold auxiliary relay panel, above relay panel:

Relay panel:

- **1** Dual Horn Relay (53)
- **4** Fuel Pump (FP) Relay (409)

Note: Number in parentheses indicates production control number stamped on relay housing.

Fuse colors

30 A - green
25 A - white
20 A - yellow
15 A - blue
10 A - red
7,5 A - brown
5 A - beige
3 A - violet

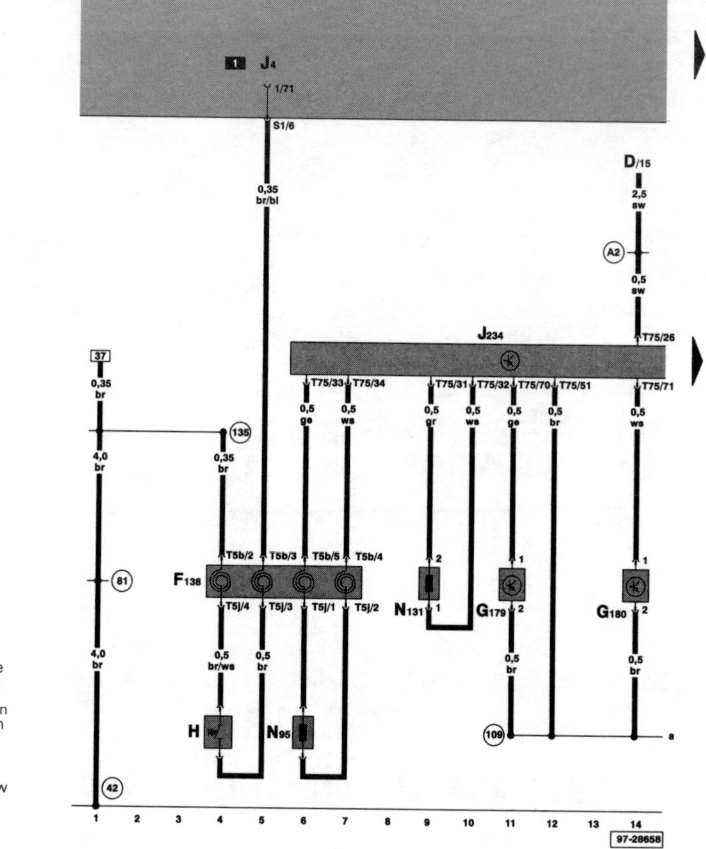

ws = white
sw = black
ro = red
br = brown
gn = green
bl = blue
gr = grey
li = lilac
ge = yellow

D - Ignition/Starter Switch
F138 - Airbag Spiral Spring/Return Spring With Slip Ring
G179 - Crash sensor for side airbag, driver's side
G180 - Crash sensor for side airbag, passenger side
H - Signal horn activation
J4 - Dual Horn Relay
J234 - Airbag Control Module, behind console, lower part
N95 - Driver's Side Airbag Igniter
N131 - Passenger's Side Airbag Igniter 1
T5b - 5-Pin Connector
T5j - 5-Pin Connector
T75 - 75-Pin Connector

(42) - Ground connection, beside steering column
(81) - Ground connection -1-, in instrument panel wiring harness
(109) - Ground connection, in airbag wiring harness
(135) - Ground connection -2-, in instrument panel wiring harness
(A2) - Plus connection (15), in instrument panel wiring harness

Airbag control module, airbag spiral spring/return spring with slip ring, crash sensor for side airbag, airbag igniter, signal horn activation

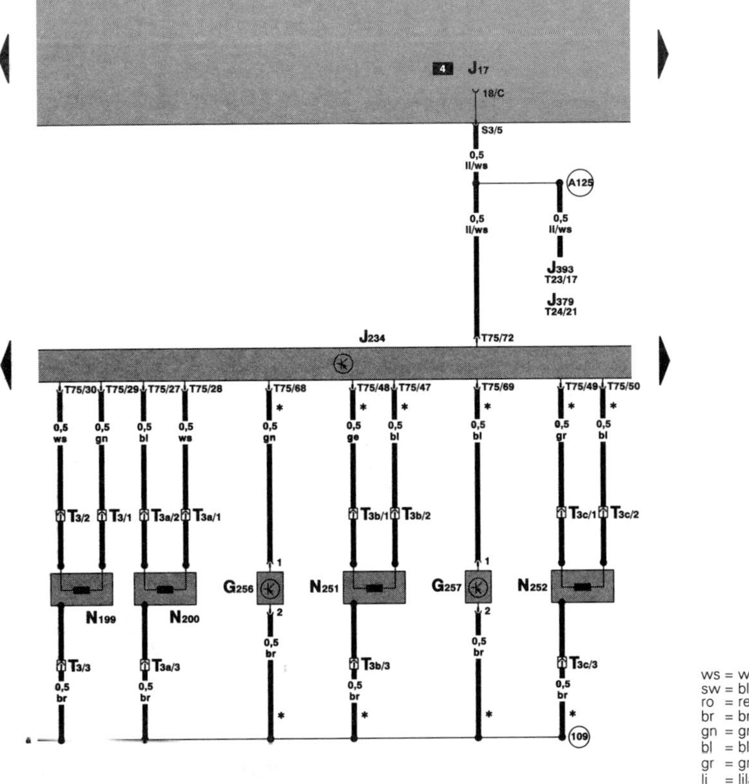

ws = white
sw = black
ro = red
br = brown
gn = green
bl = blue
gr = grey
li = lilac
ge = yellow

15 16 17 18 19 20 21 22 23 24 25 26 27 28

97-27572

G256 - Left Rear Side Airbag Crash Sensor*
G257 - Right Rear Side Airbag Crash Sensor*
J17 - Fuel Pump (FP) Relay (gasoline engine only)
J234 - Airbag Control Module, behind console, lower part
J379 - Control module for central locking and anti-theft-system
J393 - Central control module for comfort system
N199 - Igniter for side airbag, driver's side
N200 - Igniter for side airbag, passenger side
N251 - Igniter for head airbag, driver side*
N252 - Detonator for head airbag, passenger side*
T3 - 3-Pin Connector, below driver's seat
T3a - 3-Pin Connector, below passenger's seat
T3b - 3-Pin Connector, behind C-pillar trim, left
T3c - 3-Pin Connector, behind C-pillar trim, right
T23 - 23-Pin Connector
T24 - 24-Pin Connector
T75 - 75-Pin Connector

(109) - Ground connection, in airbag wiring harness

(A125) - Connection (crash signal) in instrument panel wiring harness

* - Vehicles with head airbag only (beginning May 2000)

Edition 07/00 USA.5102.07.21 **Airbag control module, igniter for side airbag, left and right rear side airbag crash sensors, igniter for head airbag (driver side), detonator for head airbag (passenger side)**

ws = white
sw = black
ro = red
br = brown
gn = green
bl = blue
gr = grey
li = lilac
ge = yellow
or = orange

29 30 31 32 33 34 35 36 37 38 39 40 41 42

97-27573

E24 - Left Seat Belt Switch
H3 - Warning Buzzer
J234 - Airbag Control Module, behind console, lower part
J285 - Control module with indicator unit in instrument panel insert
J533 - Data Bus On Board Diagnostic Interface
K19 - Seat Belt Warning Light
K75 - Airbag Malfunction Indicator Lamp (MIL)
N153 - Left Seat Belt Tensioner Igniter
N154 - Right Seat Belt Tensioner Igniter
T2 - Double Connector, below driver's seat
T2a - Double Connector, below passenger's seat
T16 - Data Link Connector (DLC), below instrument panel, left
T32 - 32-Pin Connector, blue
T32a - 32-Pin Connector, green
T75 - 75-Pin Connector

(A76) - Connector (K-diagnosis wire) in instrument panel wiring harness

(A121) - Connection (high bus), in instrument panel wiring harness

(A122) - Connection (low bus), in instrument panel wiring harness

Airbag control module, left seat belt switch, seat belt tensioner igniter, seat belt warning light, airbag malfunction indicator lamp (MIL) **Edition 07/00** USA.5102.07.21

Automatic transmission, 4 speed automatic,

from May 1999

- **1.8L - Engine - Motronic Multiport Fuel Injection (MFI)/110 kW, code AWD, AWW**
- **2.0L - Engine - Motronic Multiport Fuel Injection (MFI)/85 kW, code AEG, AVH, AZG**
- **2.8L - Engine - Motronic Multiport Fuel Injection (MFI)/130 kW, code AFP**

Deviate relay location and fuseplacements as well as the locations of multiple connectors see section "component locations".

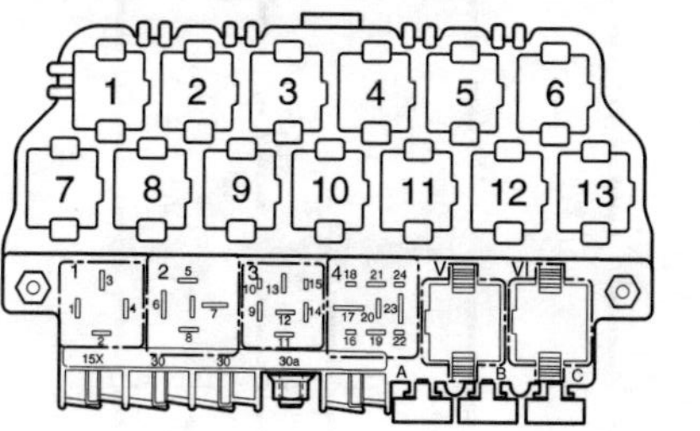

97-14163

Relay location on the thirteenfold auxiliary relay panel, above relay panel:

11 Park/Neutral Position (PNP) Relay (175)

Relay panel:

4 Fuel Pump (FP) Relay (409)

Note: Number in parentheses indicates production control number stamped on relay housing.

Fuse colors

30 A - green
25 A - white
20 A - yellow
15 A - blue
10 A - red
7,5 A - brown
5 A - beige
3 A - violet

ws = white
sw = black
ro = red
br = brown
gn = green
bl = blue
gr = grey
li = lilac
ge = yellow

97-28165

- B - Starter
- D - Ignition/Starter Switch
- J17 - Fuel Pump (FP) Relay
- J226 - Park/Neutral Position (PNP) Relay, on the thirteenfold auxiliary relay panel, above relay panel
- M16 - Left Back-Up Light
- M17 - Right Back-Up Light
- S15 - Fuse 15 in fuse holder
- T5h - 5-Pin Connector, near left A-pillar, lower part, in harness
- T6 - 6-Pin Connector, brown, in protective housing for connectors, in plenum chamber, left
- T10 - 10-Pin Connector, orange, in protective housing for connectors, in plenum chamber, left
- T10g - 10-Pin Connector, grey, in protective housing for connectors, in plenum chamber, left
- (114) - Ground connection, in automatic transmission wiring harness
- (501) - Threaded connection -2- (30) on the relay plate
- (A32) - Plus connection (30), in instrument panel wiring harness
- (A41) - Plus connection (50), in instrument panel wiring harness
- (A87) - Connector (RF), in instrument panel wiring harness
- (A98) - Plus connector -4- (30), in instrument panel wiring harness
- (B182) - Connection (RF), in passenger compartment wiring harness

Park/neutral position (PNP) relay

ws = white
sw = black
ro = red
br = brown
gn = green
bl = blue
gr = grey
li = lilac
ge = yellow

F125 - Multi-Function Transmission Range (TR) Switch
J217 - Transmission Control Module (TCM), in plenum chamber, center
J220 - Motronic Engine Control Module (ECM), in plenum chamber, center
J285 - Control module with indicator unit in instrument panel insert
T8 - 8-Pin Connector
T10 - 10-Pin Connector, orange, in protective housing for connectors, in plenum chamber, left
T10g - 10-Pin Connector, grey, in protective housing for connectors, in plenum chamber, left
T16 - Data Link Connector (DLC), below instrument panel, left
T32 - 32-Pin Connector, blue
T68 - 68-Pin Connector
T80 - 80-Pin Connector
T121 - 121-Pin Connector

(A52) - Plus connection (30a), in instrument panel wiring harness
(A76) - Connector (K-diagnosis wire) in instrument panel wiring harness

* - 2.0L-Engine - code AEG only
** - A/C connection
*** - 1.8L-Engine - code AWD, AWW only
2.0L-Engine - code AVH, AZG only
2.8L-Engine - code AFP only

Transmission control module (TCM), multi-function transmission range (TR) switch

ws = white
sw = black
ro = red
br = brown
gn = green
bl = blue
gr = grey
li = lilac
ge = yellow

F8 - Kick Down Switch*
G38 - Transmission Vehicle Speed Sensor (VSS)
G93 - Transmission Fluid Temperature Sensor
J217 - Transmission Control Module (TCM), in plenum chamber, center
N88 - Solenoid Valve 1
N89 - Solenoid Valve 2
N90 - Solenoid Valve 3
N91 - Solenoid Valve 4
N92 - Solenoid Valve 5
N93 - Solenoid Valve 6
N94 - Solenoid Valve 7
T2 - Double Connector, on transmission
T12 - 12-Pin Connector
T68 - 68-Pin Connector

(114) - Ground connection, in automatic transmission wiring harness
(608) - Ground Connection (in center plenum chamber)

* - 2.0L-Engine - code AEG only

Transmission control module (TCM), solenoid valves, transmission vehicle speed sensor (VSS), transmission fluid temperature sensor, kick down switch

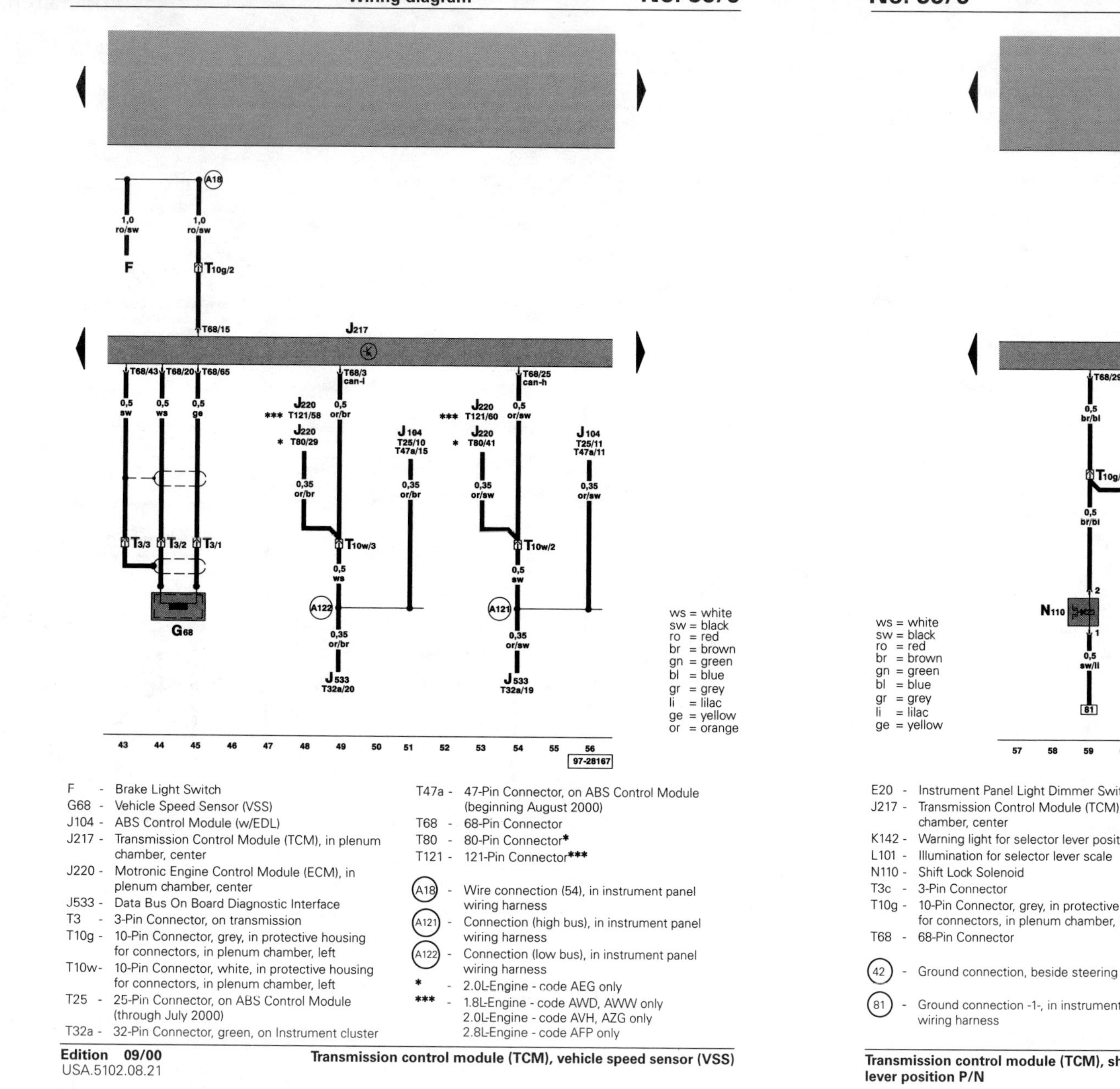

ws = white
sw = black
ro = red
br = brown
gn = green
bl = blue
gr = grey
li = lilac
ge = yellow
or = orange

F - Brake Light Switch
G68 - Vehicle Speed Sensor (VSS)
J104 - ABS Control Module (w/EDL)
J217 - Transmission Control Module (TCM), in plenum chamber, center
J220 - Motronic Engine Control Module (ECM), in plenum chamber, center
J533 - Data Bus On Board Diagnostic Interface
T3 - 3-Pin Connector, on transmission
T10g - 10-Pin Connector, grey, in protective housing for connectors, in plenum chamber, left
T10w - 10-Pin Connector, white, in protective housing for connectors, in plenum chamber, left
T25 - 25-Pin Connector, on ABS Control Module (through July 2000)
T32a - 32-Pin Connector, green, on Instrument cluster
T47a - 47-Pin Connector, on ABS Control Module (beginning August 2000)
T68 - 68-Pin Connector
T80 - 80-Pin Connector*
T121 - 121-Pin Connector***

(A18) - Wire connection (54), in instrument panel wiring harness
(A121) - Connection (high bus), in instrument panel wiring harness
(A122) - Connection (low bus), in instrument panel wiring harness
* - 2.0L-Engine - code AEG only
*** - 1.8L-Engine - code AWD, AWW only
2.0L-Engine - code AVH, AZG only
2.8L-Engine - code AFP only

Transmission control module (TCM), vehicle speed sensor (VSS)

ws = white
sw = black
ro = red
br = brown
gn = green
bl = blue
gr = grey
li = lilac
ge = yellow

E20 - Instrument Panel Light Dimmer Switch
J217 - Transmission Control Module (TCM), in plenum chamber, center
K142 - Warning light for selector lever position P/N
L101 - Illumination for selector lever scale
N110 - Shift Lock Solenoid
T3c - 3-Pin Connector
T10g - 10-Pin Connector, grey, in protective housing for connectors, in plenum chamber, left
T68 - 68-Pin Connector

(42) - Ground connection, beside steering column

(81) - Ground connection -1-, in instrument panel wiring harness

(135) - Ground connection -2-, in instrument panel wiring harness
(A4) - Plus connection (58b), in instrument panel wiring harness

Transmission control module (TCM), shift lock solenoid, warning light for selector lever position P/N

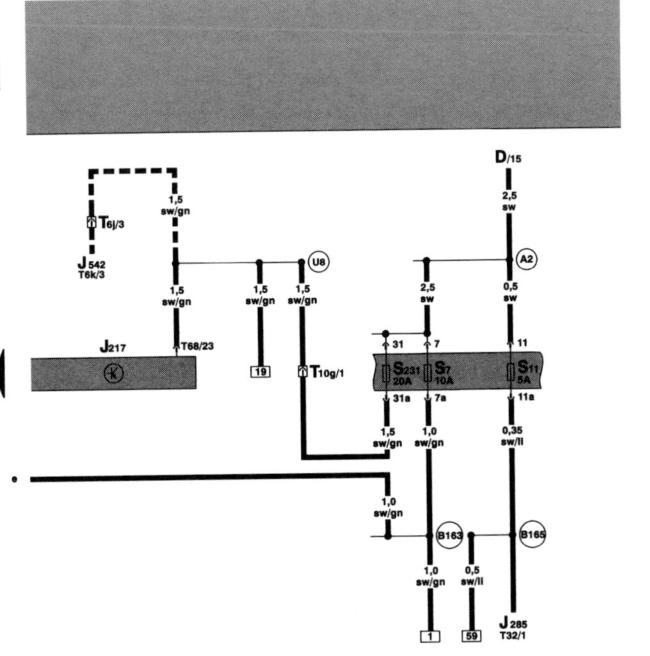

ws = white
sw = black
ro = red
br = brown
gn = green
bl = blue
gr = grey
li = lilac
ge = yellow

D - Ignition/Starter Switch
J217 - Transmission Control Module (TCM), in plenum chamber, center
J285 - Control module with indicator unit in instrument panel insert
J542 - Brake Booster Control Module
S7 - Fuse 7 in fuse holder
S11 - Fuse 11 in fuse holder
S231 - Fuse 31 in fuse holder
T6j - 6-Pin Connector, in engine compartment left
T6k - 6-Pin Connector
T10g - 10-Pin Connector, grey, in protective housing for connectors, in plenum chamber, left
T32 - 32-Pin Connector, blue
T68 - 68-Pin Connector

(A2) - Plus connection (15), in instrument panel wiring harness
(B163) - Plus connector -1- (15) in wiring harness interior
(B165) - Plus connector -2- (15) in wiring harness interior
(U8) - Plus connection (15a) in automatic transmission wiring harness

--- 1.8L-Engine - code AWW only

THIS PAGE INTENTIONALLY LEFT BLANK

Automatic transmission, 4 speed automatic,

from May 1999

- **1.9L - Engine - Turbo Diesel Fuel Injection (DFI)/66 kW, code ALH**

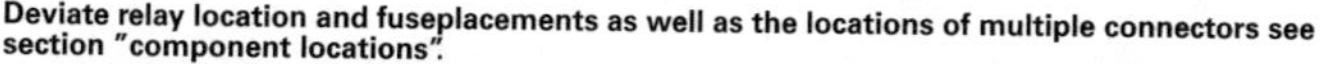

Deviate relay location and fuseplacements as well as the locations of multiple connectors see section "component locations".

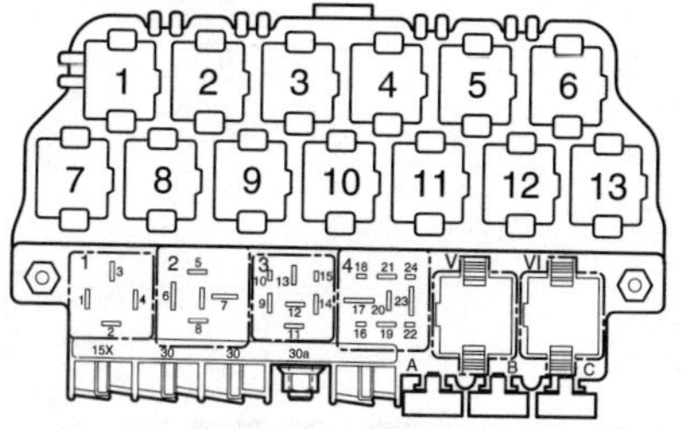

Relay location on the thirteenfold auxiliary relay panel, above relay panel:

11 Park/Neutral Position (PNP) Relay (175)

Relay panel:

Note: Number in parentheses indicates production control number stamped on relay housing.

Fuse colors

30 A - green
25 A - white
20 A - yellow
15 A - blue
10 A - red
7,5 A - brown
5 A - beige
3 A - violet

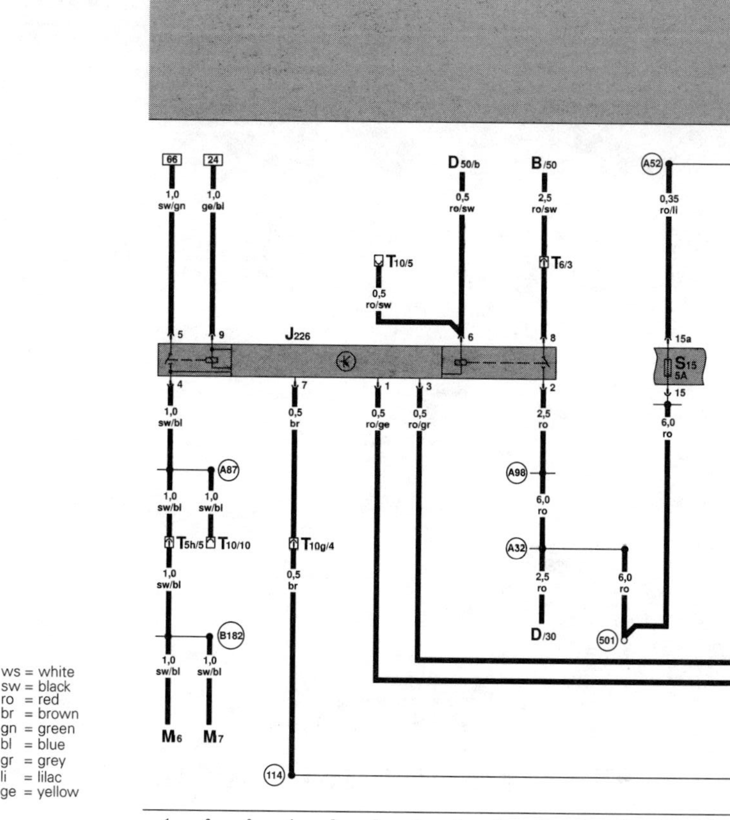

ws = white
sw = black
ro = red
br = brown
gn = green
bl = blue
gr = grey
li = lilac
ge = yellow

B - Starter
D - Ignition/Starter Switch
J226 - Park/Neutral Position (PNP) Relay, on the thirteenfold auxiliary relay panel, above relay panel
M16 - Left Back-Up Light
M17 - Right Back-Up Light
S15 - Fuse 15 in fuse holder
T5h - 5-Pin Connector, near left A-pillar, lower part, in harness
T6 - 6-Pin Connector, brown, in protective housing for connectors, in plenum chamber, left
T10 - 10-Pin Connector, orange, in protective housing for connectors, in plenum chamber, left
T10g - 10-Pin Connector, grey, in protective housing for connectors, in plenum chamber, left

(114) - Ground connection, in automatic transmission wiring harness
(501) - Threaded connection -2- (30) on the relay plate
(A32) - Plus connection (30), in instrument panel wiring harness
(A52) - Plus connection (30a), in instrument panel wiring harness
(A87) - Connector (RF), in instrument panel wiring harness
(A98) - Plus connector -4- (30), in instrument panel wiring harness
(B182) - Connection (RF), in passenger compartment wiring harness

Park/neutral position (PNP) relay

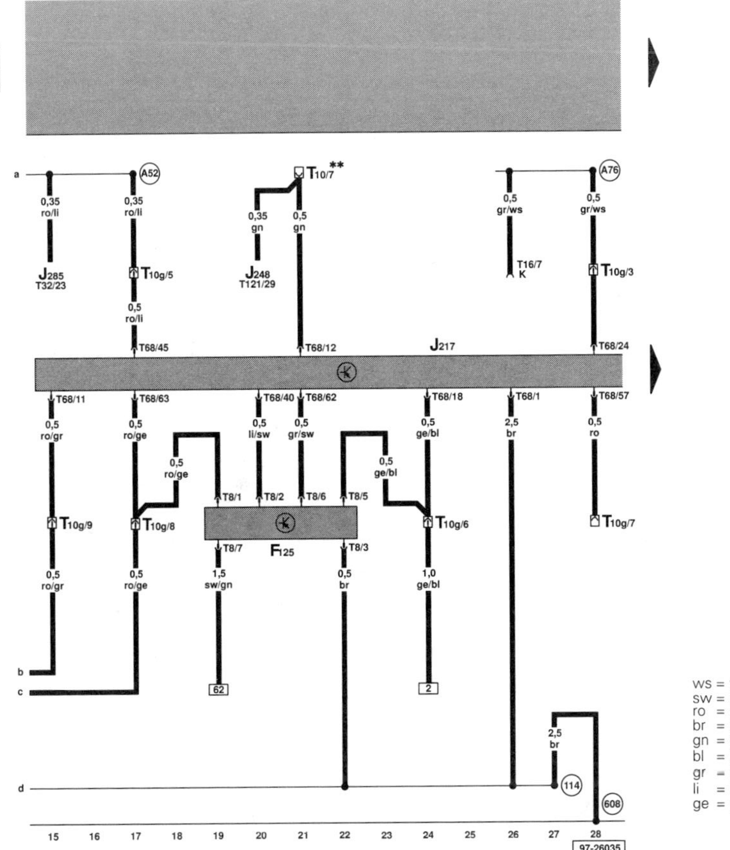

F125 - Multi-Function Transmission Range (TR) Switch
J217 - Transmission Control Module (TCM), in plenum chamber, center
J248 - Diesel Direct Fuel Injection (DFI) Engine Control Module (ECM), in plenum chamber, center
J285 - Control module with indicator unit in instrument panel insert
T8 - 8-Pin Connector
T10 - 10-Pin Connector, orange, in protective housing for connectors, in plenum chamber, left
T10g - 10-Pin Connector, grey, in protective housing for connectors, in plenum chamber, left
T16 - Data Link Connector (DLC), below instrument panel, left
T32 - 32-Pin Connector, blue
T68 - 68-Pin Connector
T121 - 121-Pin Connector
(608) - Ground Connection (in center plenum chamber)
(114) - Ground connection, in automatic transmission wiring harness
(A52) - Plus connection (30a), in instrument panel wiring harness
(A76) - Connector (K-diagnosis wire) in instrument panel wiring harness
** - A/C connection

Transmission control module (TCM), multi-function transmission range (TR) switch

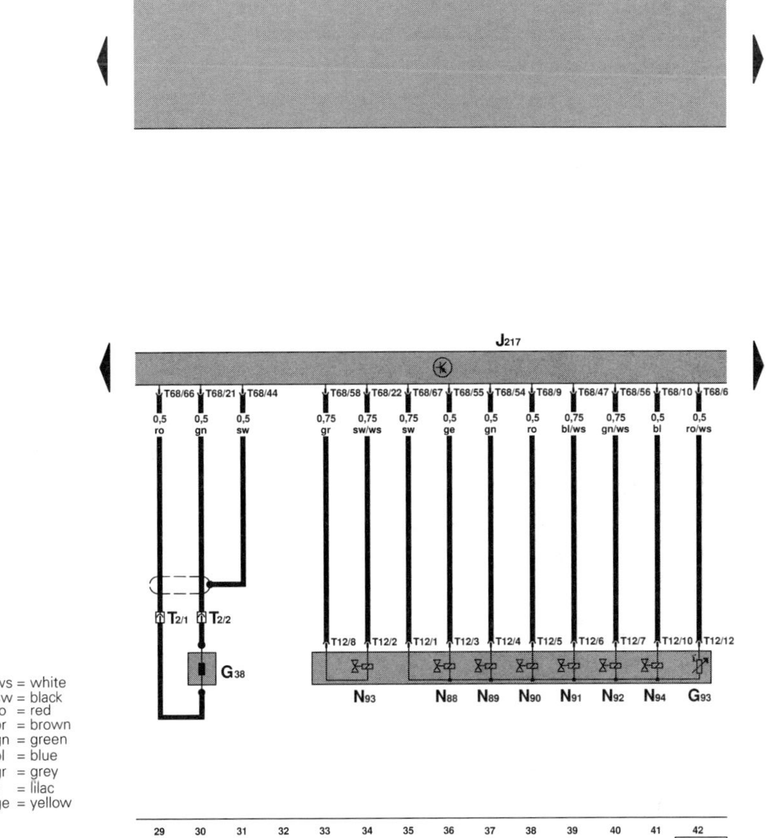

G38 - Transmission Vehicle Speed Sensor (VSS)
G93 - Transmission Fluid Temperature Sensor
J217 - Transmission Control Module (TCM), in plenum chamber, center
N88 - Solenoid Valve 1
N89 - Solenoid Valve 2
N90 - Solenoid Valve 3
N91 - Solenoid Valve 4
N92 - Solenoid Valve 5
N93 - Solenoid Valve 6
N94 - Solenoid Valve 7
T2 - Double Connector, on transmission
T12 - 12-Pin Connector
T68 - 68-Pin Connector

Transmission control module (TCM), solenoid valves, transmission vehicle speed sensor (VSS), transmission fluid temperature sensor

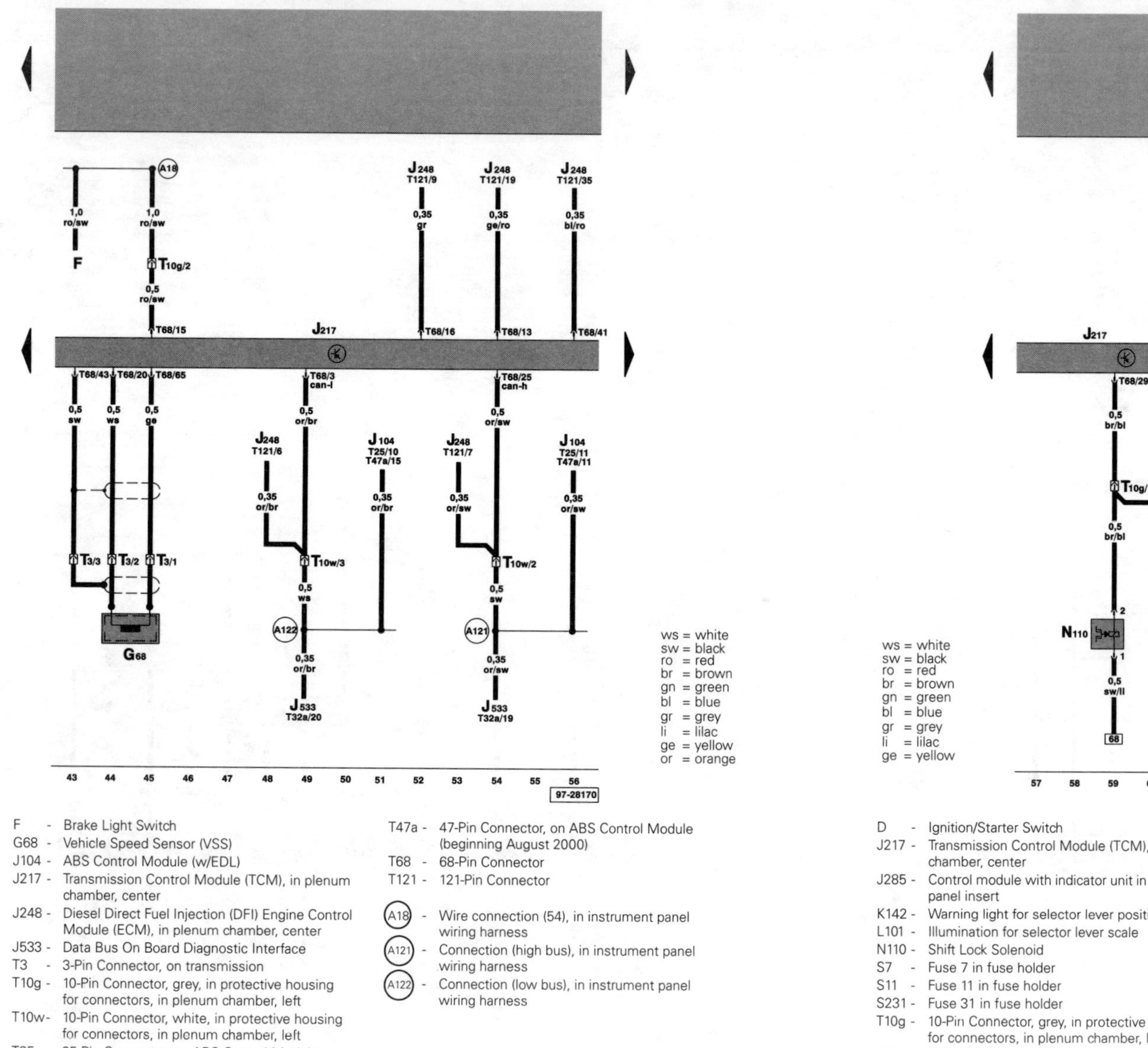

ws = white
sw = black
ro = red
br = brown
gn = green
bl = blue
gr = grey
li = lilac
ge = yellow
or = orange

F - Brake Light Switch
G68 - Vehicle Speed Sensor (VSS)
J104 - ABS Control Module (w/EDL)
J217 - Transmission Control Module (TCM), in plenum chamber, center
J248 - Diesel Direct Fuel Injection (DFI) Engine Control Module (ECM), in plenum chamber, center
J533 - Data Bus On Board Diagnostic Interface
T3 - 3-Pin Connector, on transmission
T10g - 10-Pin Connector, grey, in protective housing for connectors, in plenum chamber, left
T10w - 10-Pin Connector, white, in protective housing for connectors, in plenum chamber, left
T25 - 25-Pin Connector, on ABS Control Module (through July 2000)
T32a - 32-Pin Connector, green, on Instrument cluster
T47a - 47-Pin Connector, on ABS Control Module (beginning August 2000)
T68 - 68-Pin Connector
T121 - 121-Pin Connector
(A18) - Wire connection (54), in instrument panel wiring harness
(A121) - Connection (high bus), in instrument panel wiring harness
(A122) - Connection (low bus), in instrument panel wiring harness

Edition 09/00
USA.5102.08.21

Transmission control module (TCM), vehicle speed sensor (VSS)

ws = white
sw = black
ro = red
br = brown
gn = green
bl = blue
gr = grey
li = lilac
ge = yellow

D - Ignition/Starter Switch
J217 - Transmission Control Module (TCM), in plenum chamber, center
J285 - Control module with indicator unit in instrument panel insert
K142 - Warning light for selector lever position P/N
L101 - Illumination for selector lever scale
N110 - Shift Lock Solenoid
S7 - Fuse 7 in fuse holder
S11 - Fuse 11 in fuse holder
S231 - Fuse 31 in fuse holder
T10g - 10-Pin Connector, grey, in protective housing for connectors, in plenum chamber, left
T32 - 32-Pin Connector, blue
T68 - 68-Pin Connector
(42) - Ground connection, beside steering column
(81) - Ground connection -1-, in instrument panel wiring harness
(135) - Ground connection -2-, in instrument panel wiring harness
(A2) - Plus connection (15), in instrument panel wiring harness
(A4) - Plus connection (58b), in instrument panel wiring harness
(B163) - Plus connector -1- (15) in wiring harness interior
(B165) - Plus connector -2- (15) in wiring harness interior
(U8) - Plus connection (15a) in automatic transmission wiring harness

Transmission control module (TCM), shift lock solenoid, warning light for selector lever position P/N

Edition 09/00
USA.5102.08.21

Coolant Fans,

from May 1999

- **2.8L - Engine - Motronic Multiport Fuel Injection (MFI)/130 kW, code AFP**

Deviate relay location and fuseplacements as well as the locations of multiple connectors see section "component locations".

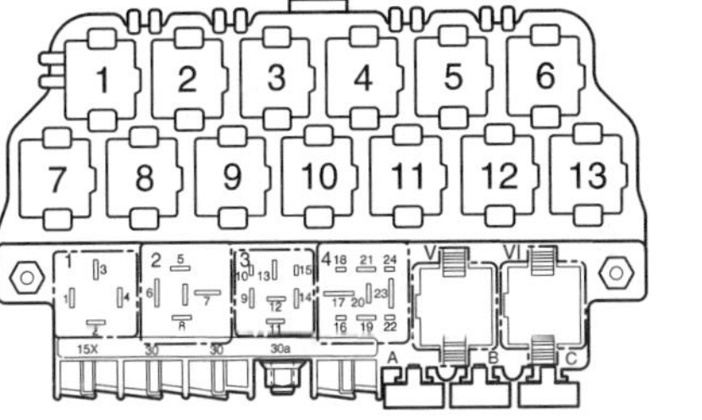

97-14163

Relay location on the thirteenfold auxiliary relay panel, above relay panel:

Relay panel:

2 Load Reduction Relay (100)

Note: Number in parentheses indicates production control number stamped on relay housing.

Fuse colors

30 A - green
25 A - white
20 A - yellow
15 A - blue
10 A - red
7,5 A - brown
5 A - beige
3 A - violet

ws = white
sw = black
ro = red
br = brown
gn = green
bl = blue
gr = grey
li = lilac
ge = yellow

97-28670

- A - Battery
- D - Ignition/Starter Switch
- F18 - Coolant Fan Control (FC) Thermal Switch
- J293 - Coolant Fan Control (FC) Control Module, in engine compartment, left
- J59 - Load Reduction Relay
- S5 - Fuse 5 in fuse holder
- S16 - Fuse 16 in fuse holder
- S164 - Fuse -3- (30) in fuse bracket/battery
- S178 - Fuse -4- (30) in fuse bracket/battery
- S180 - Fuse -8- (30) in fuse bracket/battery
- T4a - 4-Pin Connector
- T14 - 14-Pin Connector
- (500) - Threaded connection -1- (30) on the relay plate
- (501) - Threaded connection -2- (30) on the relay plate
- (A2) - Plus connection (15), in instrument panel wiring harness
- (A20) - Wire connection (15a), in instrument panel wiring harness
- (A32) - Plus connection (30), in instrument panel wiring harness
- (A98) - Plus connector -4- (30), in instrument panel wiring harness
- (K20) - Plus connection -1- (30), in coolant fan wiring harness
- (K21) - Wire connection -1-, in coolant fan wiring harness

Coolant fan control (FC) control module, coolant fan control (FC) thermal switch

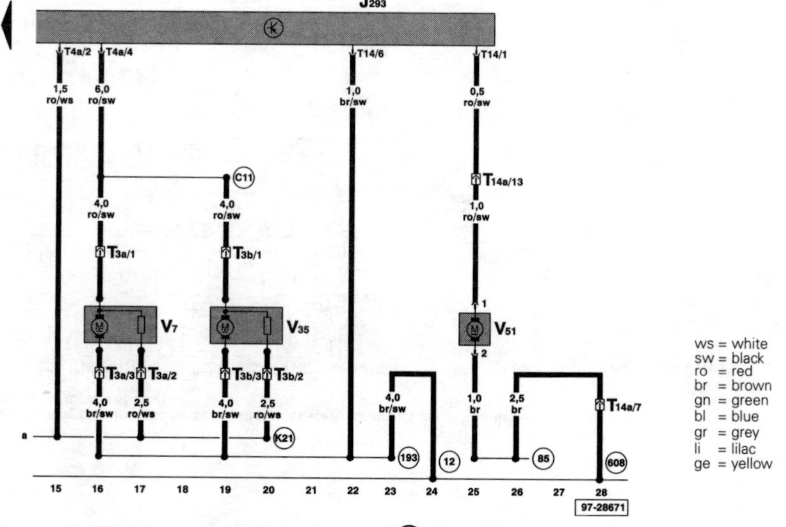

ws = white
sw = black
ro = red
br = brown
gn = green
bl = blue
gr = grey
li = lilac
ge = yellow

J293 - Coolant Fan Control (FC) Control Module, in engine compartment, left
T3a - 3-Pin Connector, in engine compartment, left
T3b - 3-Pin Connector, in engine compartment, left
T4a - 4-Pin Connector
T14 - 14-Pin Connector
T14a - 14-Pin Connector, in engine compartment, in wiring duct, left
V7 - Left Coolant Fan
V35 - Right Coolant Fan
V51 - After-Run Coolant Pump

(12) - Ground connection, in engine compartment, left
(85) - Ground connection -1-, in engine compartment wiring harness
(193) - Ground connection -1-, in coolant fan wiring harness
(608) - Ground Connection (in center plenum chamber)
(C11) - Wire connection, in coolant fan wiring harness
(K21) - Wire connection -1-, in coolant fan wiring harness

Edition 12/00
USA.5102.09.21

Coolant fan control (FC) control module, after-run coolant pump, coolant fan

THIS PAGE INTENTIONALLY LEFT BLANK

Air conditioning (manual control)

from May 1999

Deviate relay location and fuseplacements as well as the locations of multiple connectors see section "component locations".

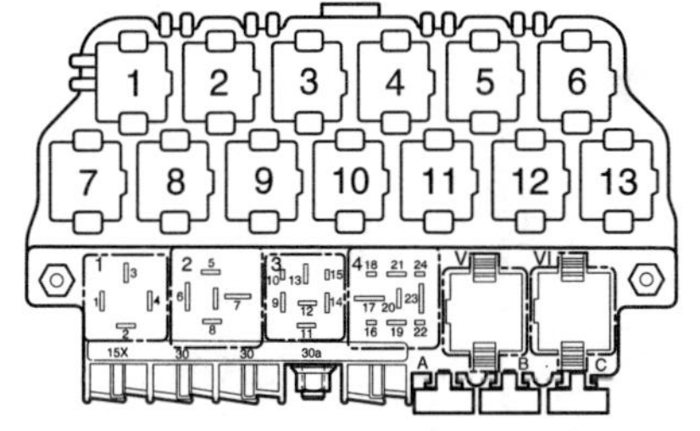

Fuse colors

30 A - green
25 A - white
20 A - yellow
15 A - blue
10 A - red
7,5 A - brown
5 A - beige
3 A - violet

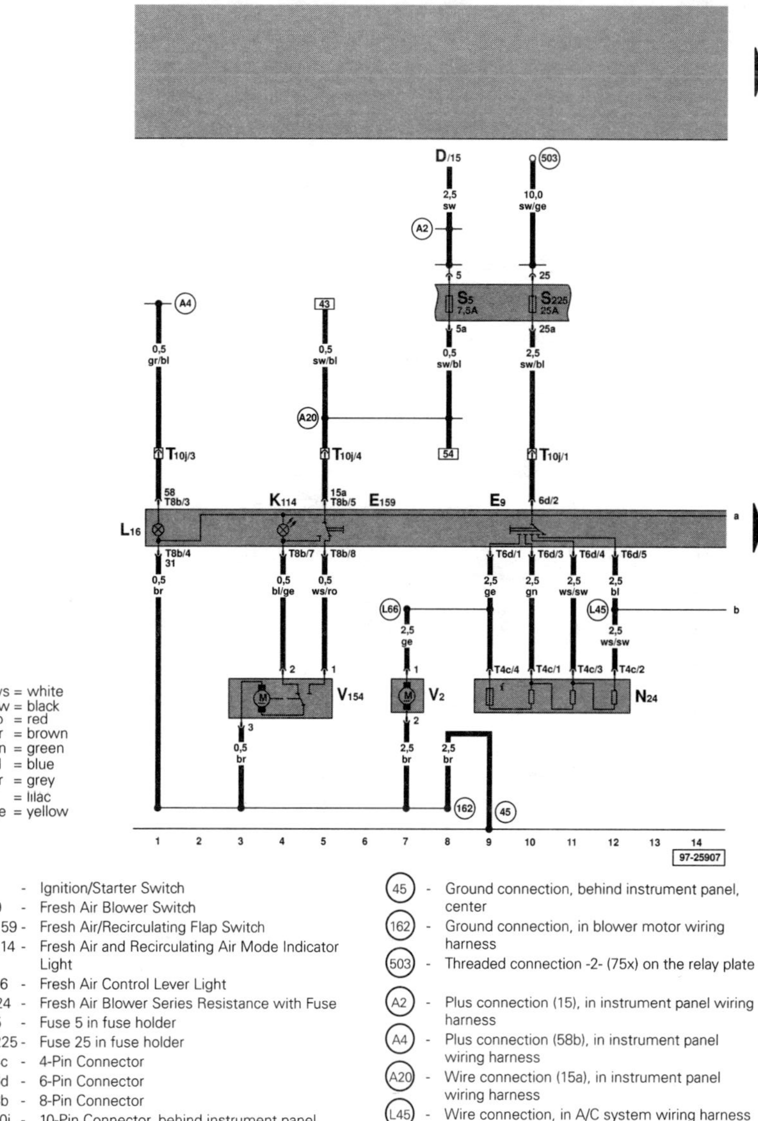

ws = white
sw = black
ro = red
br = brown
gn = green
bl = blue
gr = grey
li = lilac
ge = yellow

D - Ignition/Starter Switch
E9 - Fresh Air Blower Switch
E159 - Fresh Air/Recirculating Flap Switch
K114 - Fresh Air and Recirculating Air Mode Indicator Light
L16 - Fresh Air Control Lever Light
N24 - Fresh Air Blower Series Resistance with Fuse
S5 - Fuse 5 in fuse holder
S225 - Fuse 25 in fuse holder
T4c - 4-Pin Connector
T6d - 6-Pin Connector
T8b - 8-Pin Connector
T10j - 10-Pin Connector, behind instrument panel, center
V2 - Fresh Air Blower
V154 - Servo motor for fresh-/recirculating air flap

(45) - Ground connection, behind instrument panel, center
(162) - Ground connection, in blower motor wiring harness
(503) - Threaded connection -2- (75x) on the relay plate

(A2) - Plus connection (15), in instrument panel wiring harness
(A4) - Plus connection (58b), in instrument panel wiring harness
(A20) - Wire connection (15a), in instrument panel wiring harness
(L45) - Wire connection, in A/C system wiring harness
(L66) - Connector, in wiring harness heater blower

Fresh air blower switch, fresh air/recirculating flap switch, fresh air blower, servo motor for fresh-/recirculating air flap

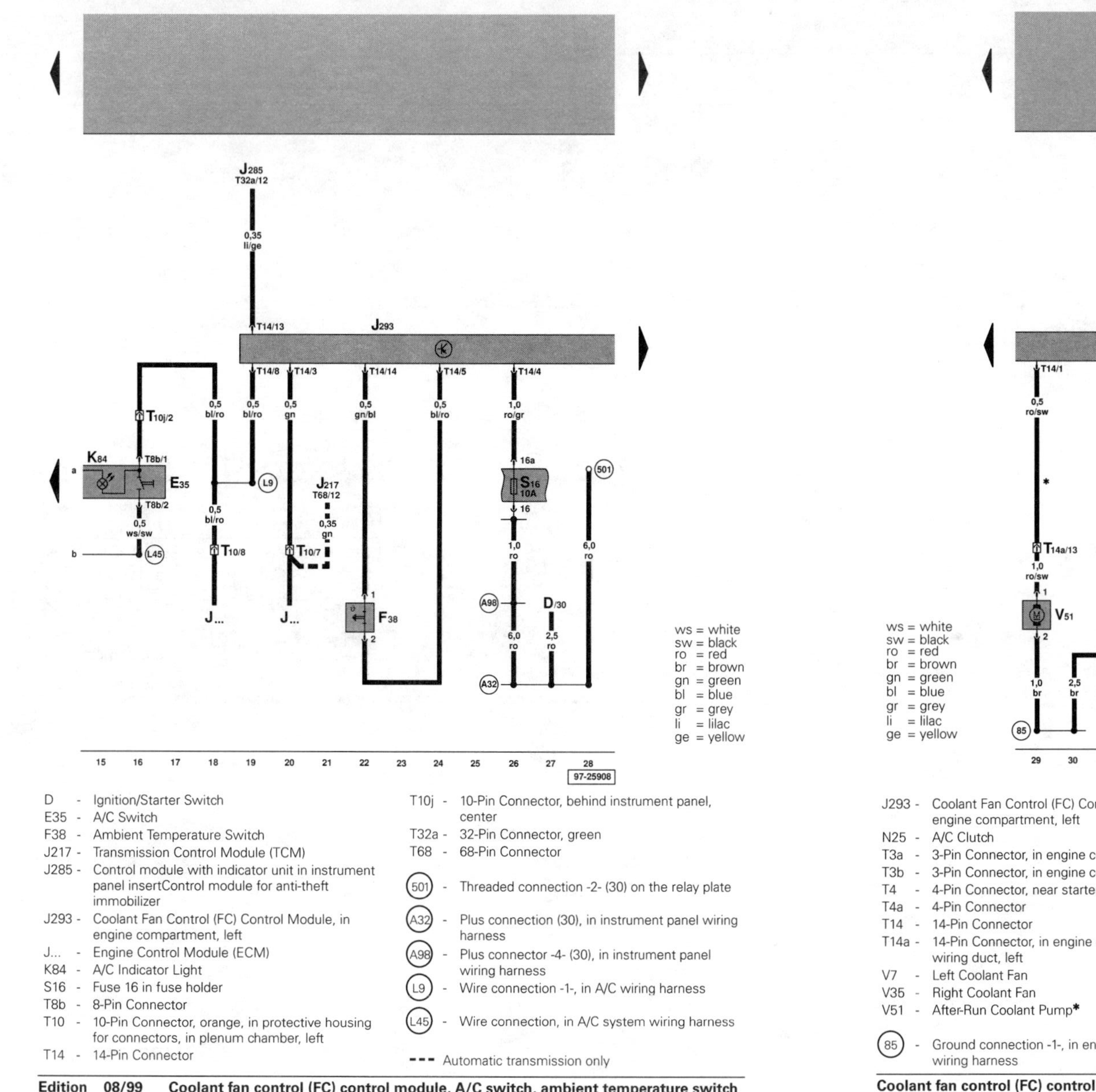

D - Ignition/Starter Switch
E35 - A/C Switch
F38 - Ambient Temperature Switch
J217 - Transmission Control Module (TCM)
J285 - Control module with indicator unit in instrument panel insertControl module for anti-theft immobilizer
J293 - Coolant Fan Control (FC) Control Module, in engine compartment, left
J... - Engine Control Module (ECM)
K84 - A/C Indicator Light
S16 - Fuse 16 in fuse holder
T8b - 8-Pin Connector
T10 - 10-Pin Connector, orange, in protective housing for connectors, in plenum chamber, left
T14 - 14-Pin Connector
T10j - 10-Pin Connector, behind instrument panel, center
T32a - 32-Pin Connector, green
T68 - 68-Pin Connector

(501) - Threaded connection -2- (30) on the relay plate

(A32) - Plus connection (30), in instrument panel wiring harness

(A98) - Plus connector -4- (30), in instrument panel wiring harness

(L9) - Wire connection -1-, in A/C wiring harness

(L45) - Wire connection, in A/C system wiring harness

--- Automatic transmission only

Edition 08/99 USA.5102.04.21 **Coolant fan control (FC) control module, A/C switch, ambient temperature switch**

J293 - Coolant Fan Control (FC) Control Module, in engine compartment, left
N25 - A/C Clutch
T3a - 3-Pin Connector, in engine compartment, left
T3b - 3-Pin Connector, in engine compartment, left
T4 - 4-Pin Connector, near starter
T4a - 4-Pin Connector
T14 - 14-Pin Connector
T14a - 14-Pin Connector, in engine compartment, in wiring duct, left
V7 - Left Coolant Fan
V35 - Right Coolant Fan
V51 - After-Run Coolant Pump*

(85) - Ground connection -1-, in engine compartment wiring harness

(193) - Ground connection -1-, in coolant fan wiring harness

(608) - Ground connection (in center plenum chamber)

(C11) - Wire connection, in coolant fan wiring harness

(K21) - Wire connection -1-, in coolant fan wiring harness

* - 2.8L-Engine - code AFP only

Coolant fan control (FC) control module, A/C clutch, coolant fan, after-run coolant pump **Edition 08/99** USA.5102.04.21

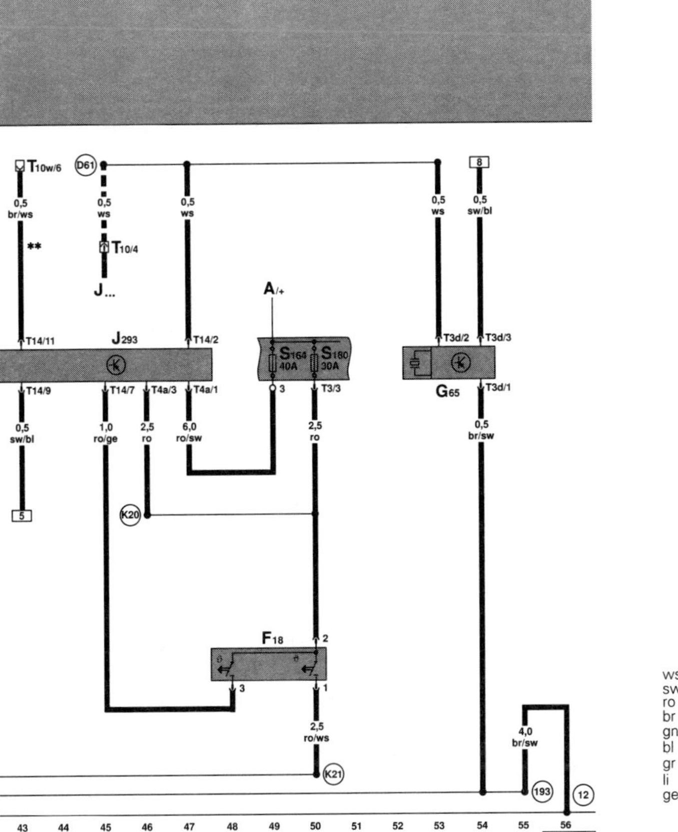

ws = white
sw = black
ro = red
br = brown
gn = green
bl = blue
gr = grey
li = lilac
ge = yellow

A - Battery
F18 - Coolant Fan Control (FC) Thermal Switch
G65 - High Pressure Sensor
J293 - Coolant Fan Control (FC) Control Module, in engine compartment, left
J... - Engine Control Module (ECM)
S164 - Fuse -3- (30) in fuse bracket/battery
S180 - Fuse -8- (30) in fuse bracket/battery
T3 - 3-Pin Connector
T3d - 3-Pin Connector
T4a - 4-Pin Connector
T10 - 10-Pin Connector, orange, in protective housing for connectors, in plenum chamber, left
T10w - 10-Pin Connector, white, in protective housing for connectors, in plenum chamber, left
T14 - 14-Pin Connector

(12) - Ground connection, in engine compartment, left
(193) - Ground connection -1-, in coolant fan wiring harness
(K20) - Plus connection -1- (30), in coolant fan wiring harness
(K21) - Wire connection -1-, in coolant fan wiring harness
(D61) - wire connection (A/C), in engine compartment wiring harness

** - 1.9L-Engine - code ALH only
--- - 1.8L-Engine - code AWD only
2.8L-Engine - code AFP only

Coolant fan control (FC) control module, coolant fan control (FC) thermal switch, high pressure sensor

THIS PAGE INTENTIONALLY LEFT
BLANK

Climatronic (automatic climate control),

from May 1999

- **2.8L - Engine - Motronic Multiport Fuel Injection (MFI)/130 kW, code AFP**

Deviate relay location and fuseplacements as well as the locations of multiple connectors see section "component locations".

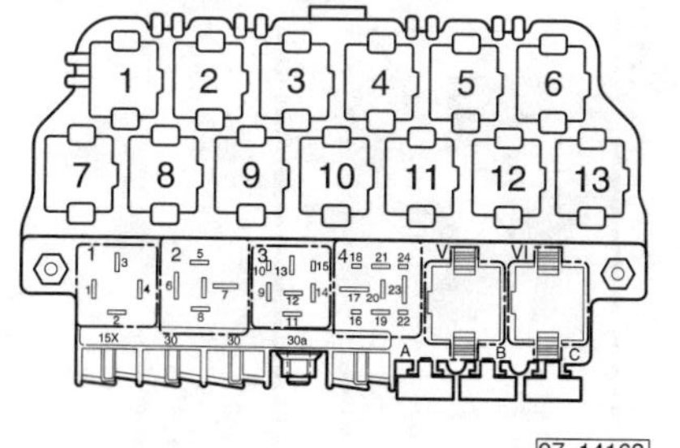

Fuse colors

30 A - green
25 A - white
20 A - yellow
15 A - blue
10 A - red
7,5 A - brown
5 A - beige
3 A - violet

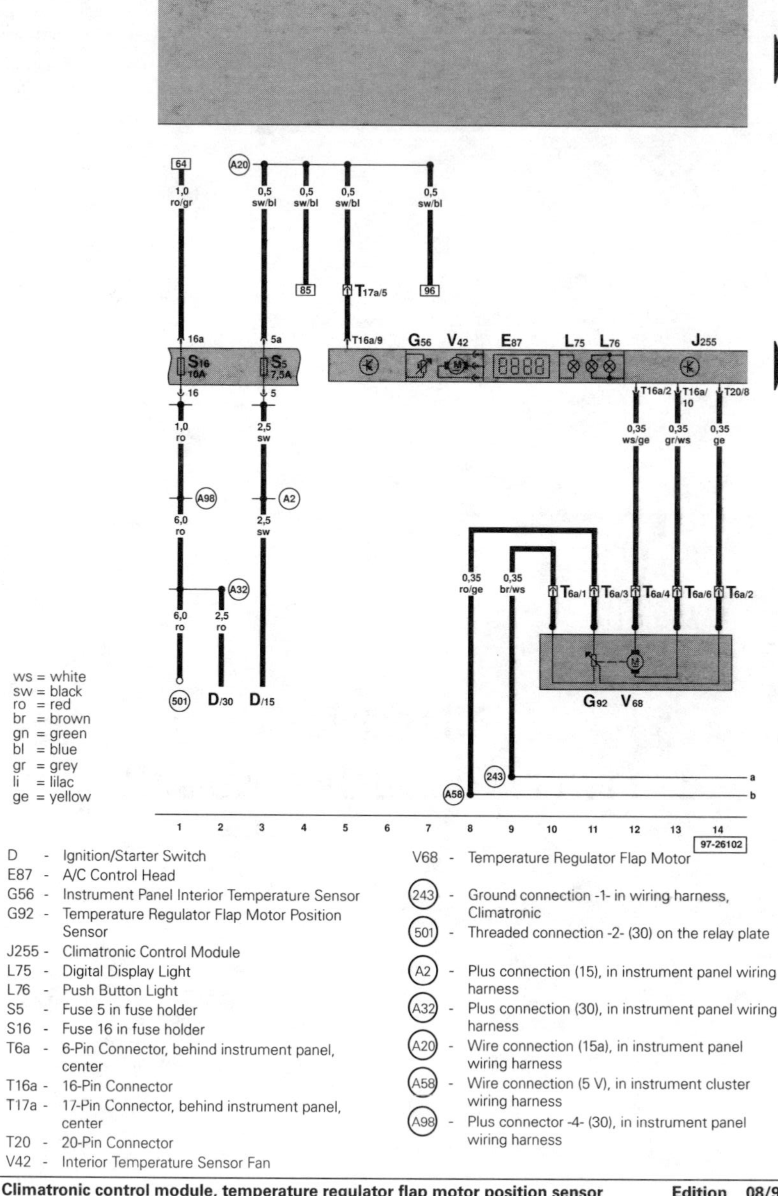

ws = white
sw = black
ro = red
br = brown
gn = green
bl = blue
gr = grey
li = lilac
ge = yellow

D - Ignition/Starter Switch
E87 - A/C Control Head
G56 - Instrument Panel Interior Temperature Sensor
G92 - Temperature Regulator Flap Motor Position Sensor
J255 - Climatronic Control Module
L75 - Digital Display Light
L76 - Push Button Light
S5 - Fuse 5 in fuse holder
S16 - Fuse 16 in fuse holder
T6a - 6-Pin Connector, behind instrument panel, center
T16a - 16-Pin Connector
T17a - 17-Pin Connector, behind instrument panel, center
T20 - 20-Pin Connector
V42 - Interior Temperature Sensor Fan
V68 - Temperature Regulator Flap Motor

(243) - Ground connection -1- in wiring harness, Climatronic
(501) - Threaded connection -2- (30) on the relay plate
(A2) - Plus connection (15), in instrument panel wiring harness
(A32) - Plus connection (30), in instrument panel wiring harness
(A20) - Wire connection (15a), in instrument panel wiring harness
(A58) - Wire connection (5 V), in instrument cluster wiring harness
(A98) - Plus connector -4- (30), in instrument panel wiring harness

Climatronic control module, temperature regulator flap motor position sensor

ws = white
sw = black
ro = red
br = brown
gn = green
bl = blue
gr = grey
li = lilac
ge = yellow

G112 - Central Flap Motor Position Sensor
G114 - Footwell/Defrost Flap Motor Position Sensor
J255 - Climatronic Control Module
J285 - Control module with indicator unit in instrument panel insert
T6b - 6-Pin Connector, behind instrument panel, center
T6c - 6-Pin Connector, behind instrument panel, center
T12 - 12-Pin Connector
T12a - 12-Pin Connector, behind instrument panel, center
T16 - Data Link Connector (DLC), below instrument panel, left
T16a - 16-Pin Connector
T20 - 20-Pin Connector
T32a - 32-Pin Connector, green
V70 - Central Air Flap Motor
V85 - Footwell/Defroster Flap Motor

(A76) - Connector (K-diagnosis wire) in instrument panel wiring harness

97-25920

Edition 08/99
USA.5102.04.21

Climatronic control module, central flap motor position sensor, central air flap motor, footwell/defrost flap motor position sensor, footwell/defrost flap motor

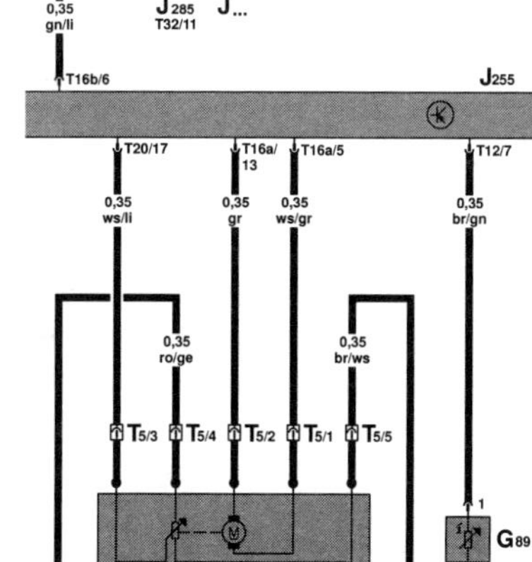

ws = white
sw = black
ro = red
br = brown
gn = green
bl = blue
gr = groy
li = lilac
ge = yellow

G89 - Fresh Air Intake Duct Temperature Sensor, below instrument panel, right
G113 - Back Pressure Flap Motor Position Sensor
G192 - Sender for outlet temperature, floor outlet
J255 - Climatronic Control Module
J285 - Control module with indicator unit in instrument panel insert
J... - Engine Control Module (ECM)
T5 - 5-Pin Connector, behind instrument panel, center
T10 - 10-Pin Connector, orange, in protective housing for connectors, in plenum chamber, left
T17a - 17-Pin Connector, behind instrument panel, center
T12 - 12-Pin Connector
T16a - 16-Pin Connector
T16b - 16-Pin Connector
T20 - 20-Pin Connector
T32 - 32-Pin Connector, blue
V71 - Air Flow Flap Motor

(A45) - Wire connection (RPM-signal), in instrument panel wiring harness
(A58) - Wire connection (5 V), in instrument cluster wiring harness

97-25921

Climatronic control module, fresh air intake duct temperature sensor, sender for outlet temperature, air flow flap motor, back pressure flap motor position sensor

Edition 08/98
USA.5102.04.21

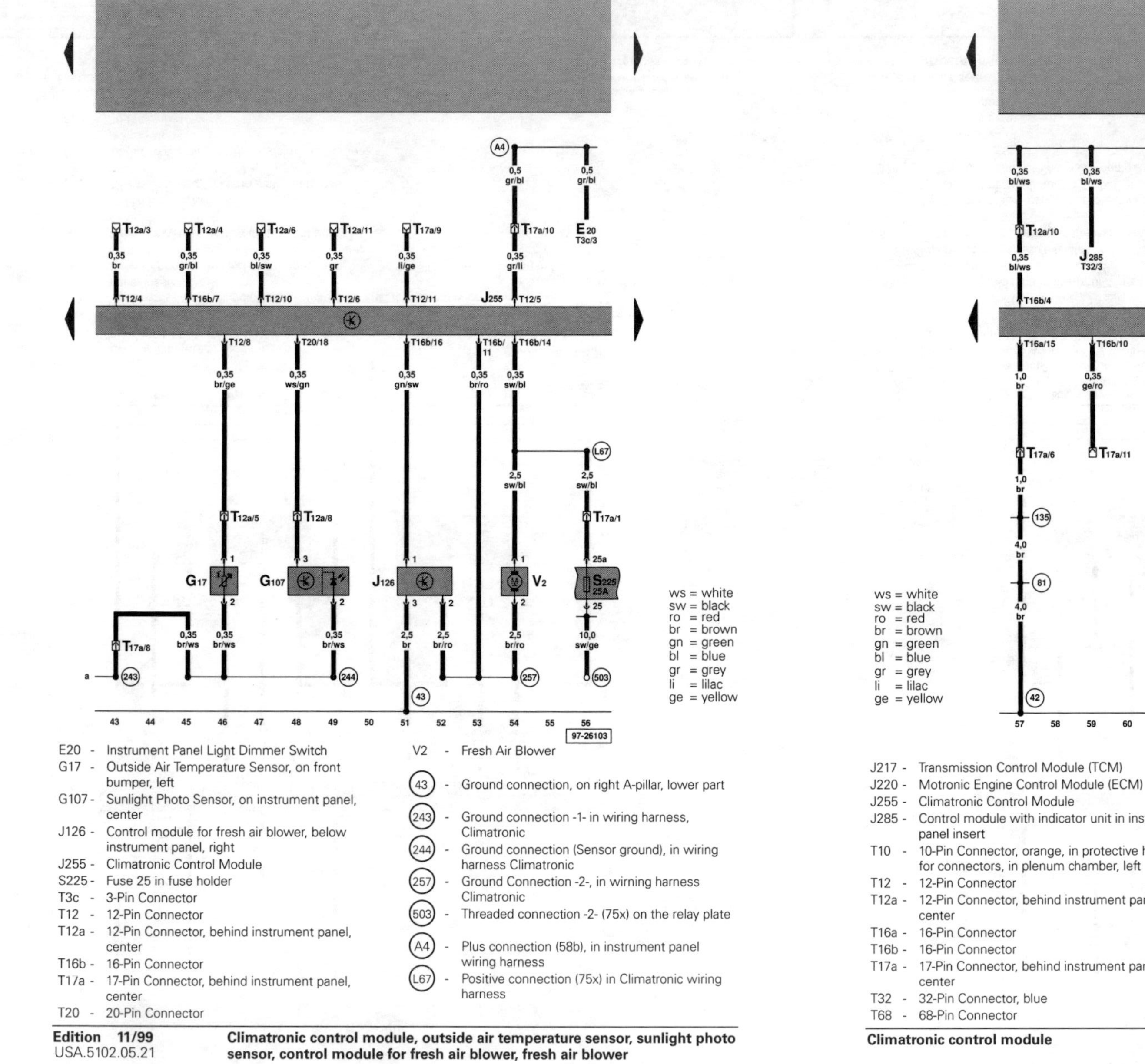

ws = white
sw = black
ro = red
br = brown
gn = green
bl = blue
gr = grey
li = lilac
ge = yellow

E20 - Instrument Panel Light Dimmer Switch
G17 - Outside Air Temperature Sensor, on front bumper, left
G107 - Sunlight Photo Sensor, on instrument panel, center
J126 - Control module for fresh air blower, below instrument panel, right
J255 - Climatronic Control Module
S225 - Fuse 25 in fuse holder
T3c - 3-Pin Connector
T12 - 12-Pin Connector
T12a - 12-Pin Connector, behind instrument panel, center
T16b - 16-Pin Connector
T17a - 17-Pin Connector, behind instrument panel, center
T20 - 20-Pin Connector
V2 - Fresh Air Blower
(43) - Ground connection, on right A-pillar, lower part
(243) - Ground connection -1- in wiring harness, Climatronic
(244) - Ground connection (Sensor ground), in wiring harness Climatronic
(257) - Ground Connection -2-, in wirning harness Climatronic
(503) - Threaded connection -2- (75x) on the relay plate
(A4) - Plus connection (58b), in instrument panel wiring harness
(L67) - Positive connection (75x) in Climatronic wiring harness

Edition 11/99
USA.5102.05.21

Climatronic control module, outside air temperature sensor, sunlight photo sensor, control module for fresh air blower, fresh air blower

ws = white
sw = black
ro = red
br = brown
gn = green
bl = blue
gr = grey
li = lilac
ge = yellow

J217 - Transmission Control Module (TCM)
J220 - Motronic Engine Control Module (ECM)
J255 - Climatronic Control Module
J285 - Control module with indicator unit in instrument panel insert
T10 - 10-Pin Connector, orange, in protective housing for connectors, in plenum chamber, left
T12 - 12-Pin Connector
T12a - 12-Pin Connector, behind instrument panel, center
T16a - 16-Pin Connector
T16b - 16-Pin Connector
T17a - 17-Pin Connector, behind instrument panel, center
T32 - 32-Pin Connector, blue
T68 - 68-Pin Connector
T121 - Connector, 121 point
(42) - Ground connection, beside steering column
(81) - Ground connection -1-, in instrument panel wiring harness
(135) - Ground connection -2-, in instrument panel wiring harness
(A27) - Wire connection (vehicle speed signal), in instrument panel wiring harness
(A68) - Connector (30, A/C), in instrument panel wiring harness
- - - - Automatic transmission only

Climatronic control module

Edition 11/99
USA.5102.05.21

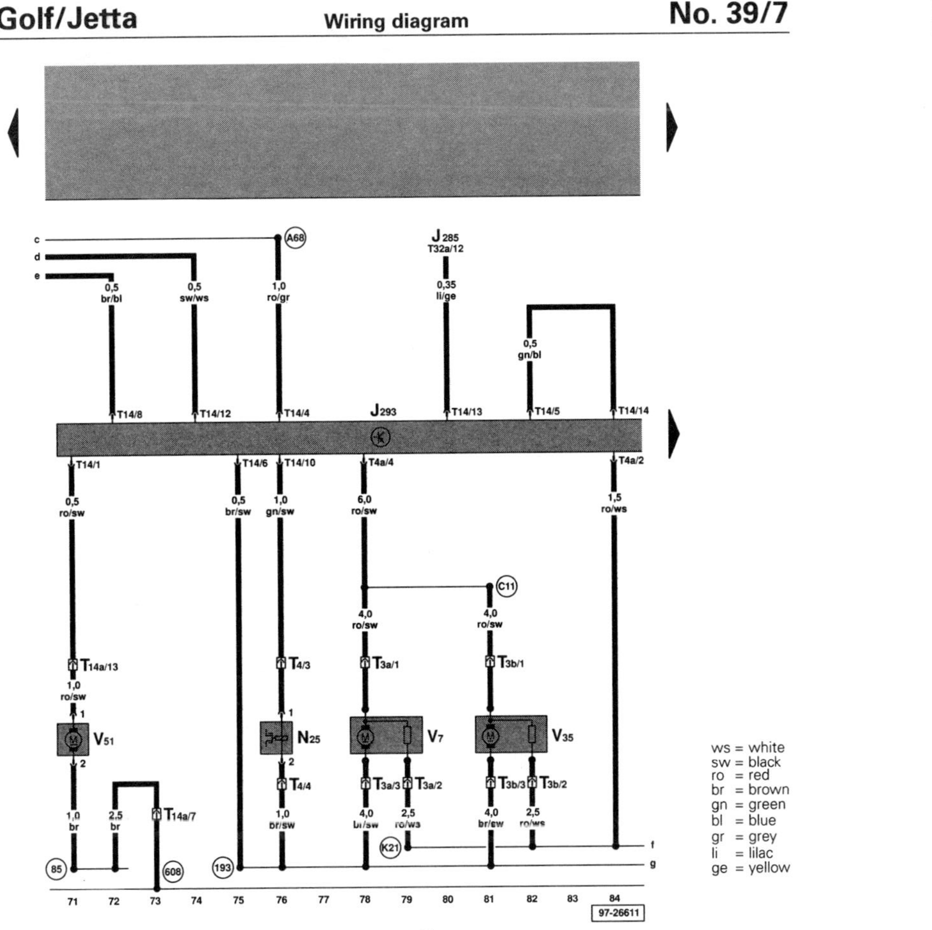

ws = white
sw = black
ro = red
br = brown
gn = green
bl = blue
gr = grey
li = lilac
ge = yellow

J285 - Control module with indicator unit in instrument panel insert
J293 - Coolant Fan Control (FC) Control Module, in engine compartment, left
N25 - A/C Clutch
T3a - 3-Pin Connector, in engine compartment, left
T3b - 3-Pin Connector, in engine compartment, left
T4 - 4-Pin Connector, near starter
T4a - 4-Pin Connector
T14 - 14-Pin Connector
T14a - 14-Pin Connector, in engine compartment, in wiring duct, left
T32a - 32-Pin Connector, green
V7 - Left Coolant Fan
V35 - Right Coolant Fan
V51 - After-Run Coolant Pump

(85) - Ground connection -1-, in engine compartment wiring harness
(193) - Ground connection -1-, in coolant fan wiring harness
(608) - Ground connection (in center plenum chamber)
(A68) - Connector (30, A/C), in instrument panel wiring harness
(C11) - Wire connection, in coolant fan wiring harness
(K21) - Wire connection -1-, in coolant fan wiring harness

ws = white
sw = black
ro = red
br = brown
gn = green
bl = blue
gr = grey
li = lilac
ge = yellow

A - Battery
F18 - Coolant Fan Control (FC) Thermal Switch
G65 - High Pressure Sensor
J220 - Motronic Engine Control Module (ECM)
J293 - Coolant Fan Control (FC) Control Module, in engine compartment, left
S164 - Fuse -3- (30) in fuse bracket/battery
S180 - Fuse -8- (30) in fuse bracket/battery
T3 - 3-Pin Connector
T3d - 3-Pin Connector
T4a - 4-Pin Connector
T10 - 10-Pin Connector, orange, in protective housing for connectors, in plenum chamber, left
T10w - 10-Pin Connector, white, in protective housing for connectors, in plenum chamber, left
T14 - 14-Pin Connector
T121 - Connector, 121 point

(12) - Ground connection, in engine compartment, left
(193) - Ground connection -1-, in coolant fan wiring harness
(K20) - Plus connection -1- (30), in coolant fan wiring harness
(K21) - Wire connection -1-, in coolant fan wiring harness
(D61) - wire connection (A/C), in engine compartment wiring harness

Radio system "Monsoon" (with CD changer wiring preparation)

from May 1999

Deviate relay location and fuseplacements as well as the locations of multiple connectors see section "component locations".

97–14163

Fuse colors

- 30 A - green
- 25 A - white
- 20 A - yellow
- 15 A - blue
- 10 A - red
- 7,5 A - brown
- 5 A - beige
- 3 A - violet

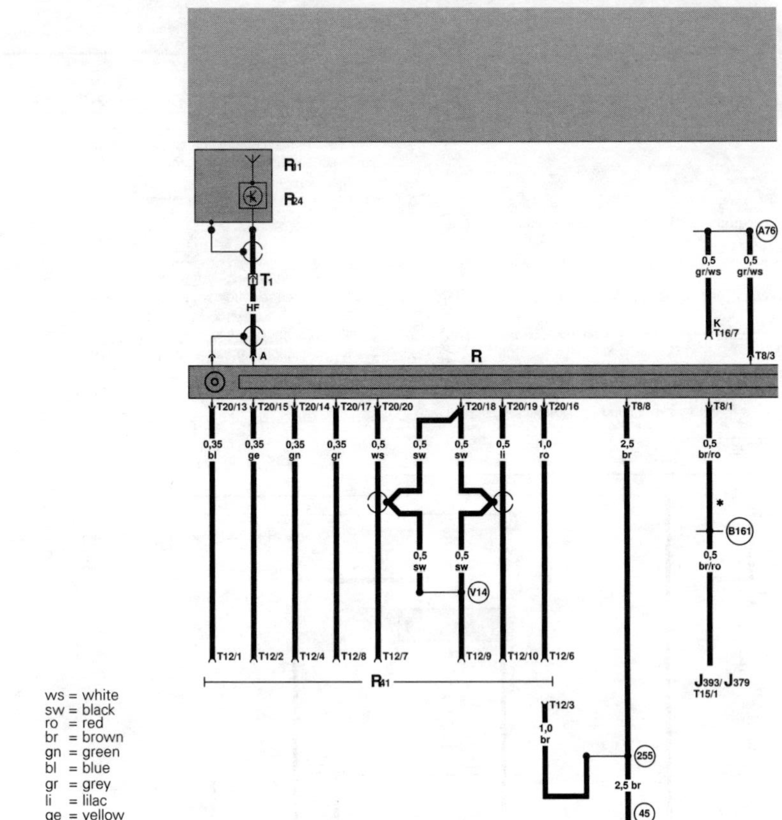

ws = white
sw = black
ro = red
br = brown
gn = green
bl = blue
gr = grey
li = lilac
ge = yellow

- J379 - Control module for central locking and anti-theft-system
- J393 - Central control module for comfort system
- R - Radio
- R11 - Antenna
- R24 - Antenna Amplifier
- R41 - CD Changer Unit
- T1 - Single Connector
- T8 - 8-Pin Connector
- T8a - 8-Pin Connector
- T12 - 12-Pin Connector
- T15 - 15-Pin Connector
- T16 - Data Link Connector (DLC), below instrument panel, left
- T20 - 20-Pin Connector, on Radio

- (45) - Ground connection, behind instrument panel, center
- (255) - Ground connection, -1-, in wiring harness radio
- (A76) - Connector (K-diagnosis wire) in instrument panel wiring harness
- (B161) - Connector (anti-theft warning system), in wiring harness interior*
- (V14) - Wire connection (shielding), in CD-changer wiring harness
- * - Vehicles with anti-theft warning system only (see wiring diagram comfort system/ central locking)

Radio, wiring harness from radio to CD changer unit

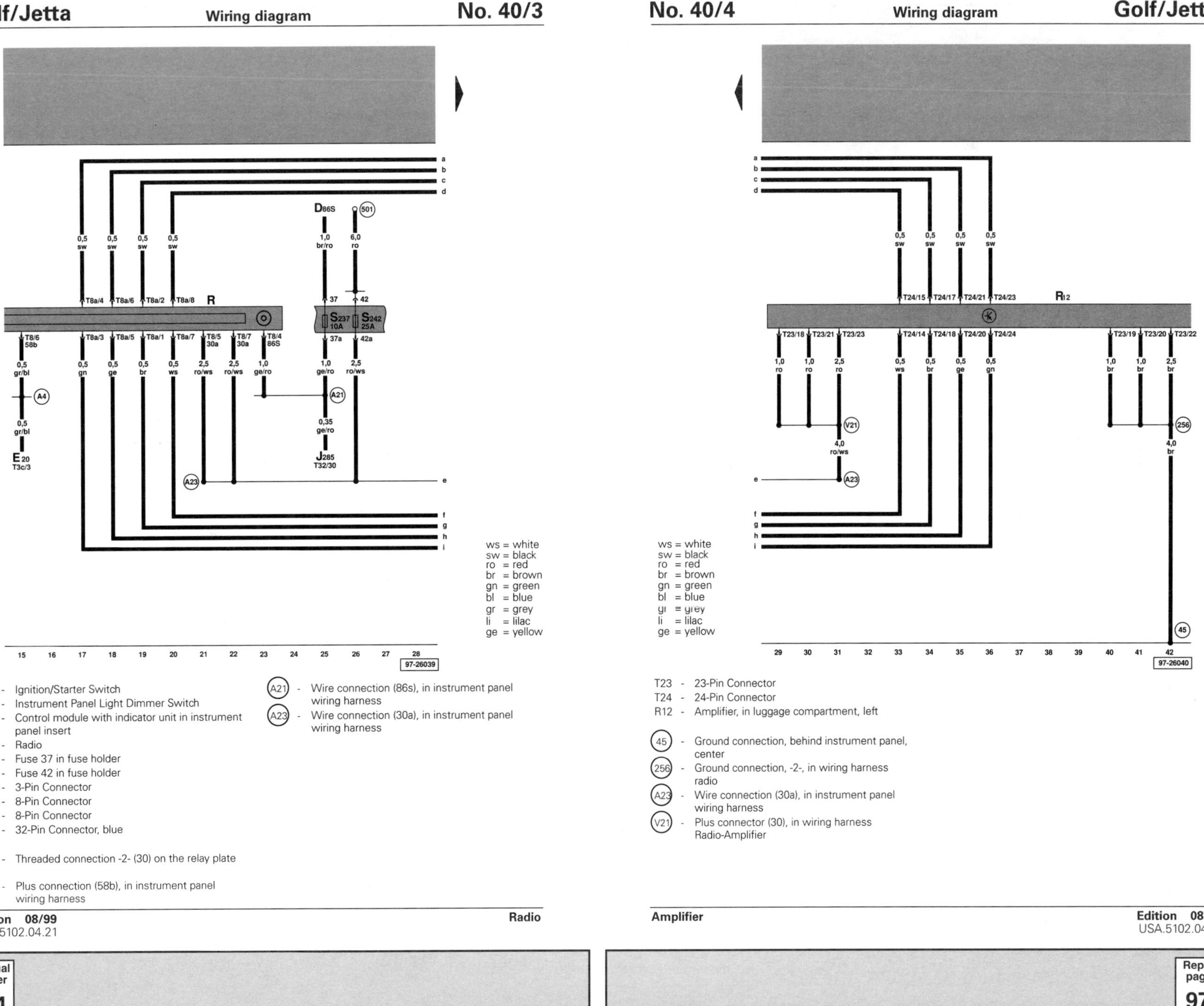

ws = white
sw = black
ro = red
br = brown
gn = green
bl = blue
gr = grey
li = lilac
ge = yellow

D - Ignition/Starter Switch
E20 - Instrument Panel Light Dimmer Switch
J285 - Control module with indicator unit in instrument panel insert
R - Radio
S237 - Fuse 37 in fuse holder
S242 - Fuse 42 in fuse holder
T3c - 3-Pin Connector
T8 - 8-Pin Connector
T8a - 8-Pin Connector
T32 - 32-Pin Connector, blue

(501) - Threaded connection -2- (30) on the relay plate

(A4) - Plus connection (58b), in instrument panel wiring harness

(A21) - Wire connection (86s), in instrument panel wiring harness

(A23) - Wire connection (30a), in instrument panel wiring harness

ws = white
sw = black
ro = red
br = brown
gn = green
bl = blue
gr = grey
li = lilac
ge = yellow

T23 - 23-Pin Connector
T24 - 24-Pin Connector
R12 - Amplifier, in luggage compartment, left

(45) - Ground connection, behind instrument panel, center

(256) - Ground connection, -2-, in wiring harness radio

(A23) - Wire connection (30a), in instrument panel wiring harness

(V21) - Plus connector (30), in wiring harness Radio-Amplifier

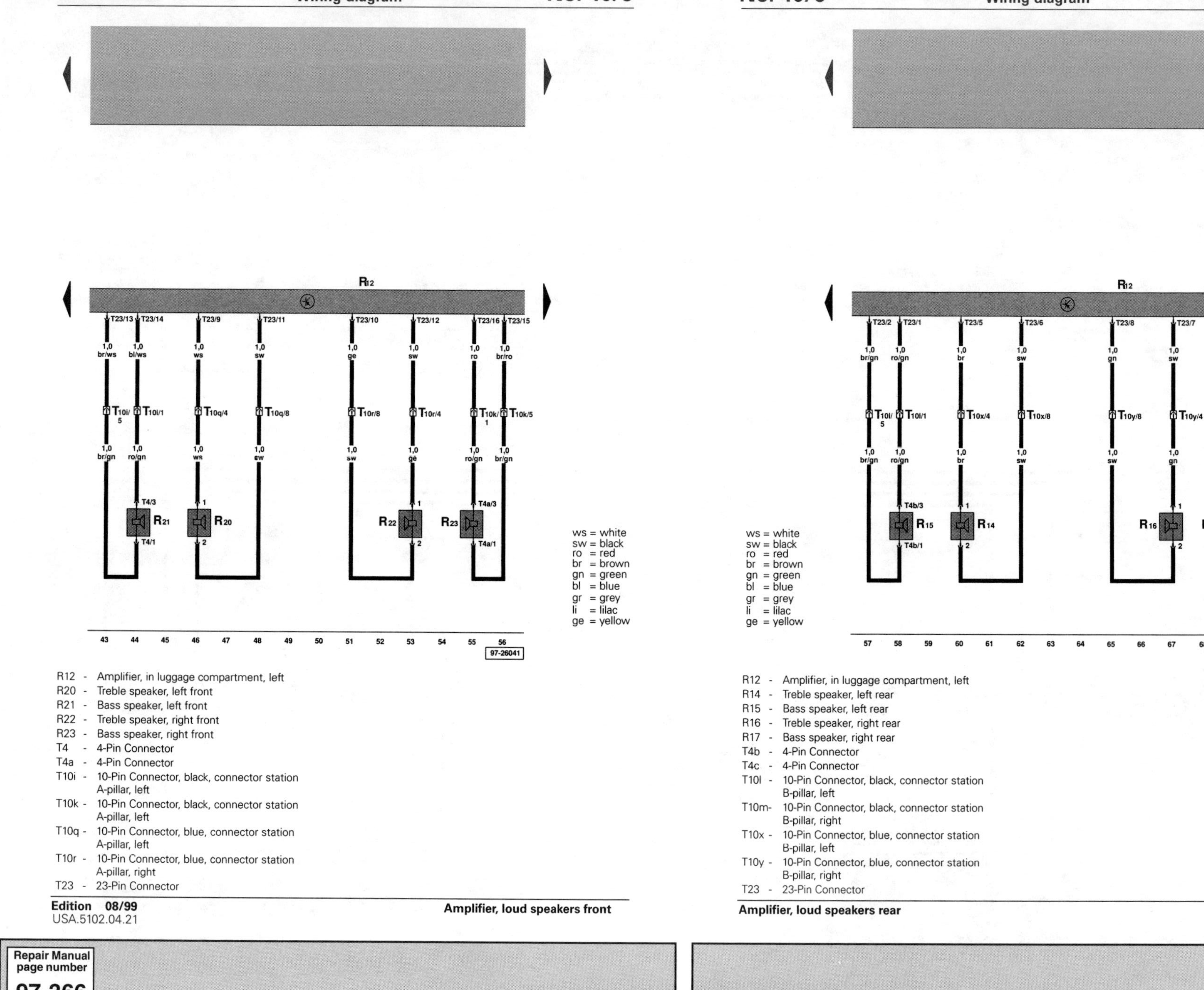

ws = white
sw = black
ro = red
br = brown
gn = green
bl = blue
gr = grey
li = lilac
ge = yellow

R12 - Amplifier, in luggage compartment, left
R20 - Treble speaker, left front
R21 - Bass speaker, left front
R22 - Treble speaker, right front
R23 - Bass speaker, right front
T4 - 4-Pin Connector
T4a - 4-Pin Connector
T10i - 10-Pin Connector, black, connector station A-pillar, left
T10k - 10-Pin Connector, black, connector station A-pillar, left
T10q - 10-Pin Connector, blue, connector station A-pillar, left
T10r - 10-Pin Connector, blue, connector station A-pillar, right
T23 - 23-Pin Connector

Amplifier, loud speakers front

ws = white
sw = black
ro = red
br = brown
gn = green
bl = blue
gr = grey
li = lilac
ge = yellow

R12 - Amplifier, in luggage compartment, left
R14 - Treble speaker, left rear
R15 - Bass speaker, left rear
R16 - Treble speaker, right rear
R17 - Bass speaker, right rear
T4b - 4-Pin Connector
T4c - 4-Pin Connector
T10l - 10-Pin Connector, black, connector station B-pillar, left
T10m- 10-Pin Connector, black, connector station B-pillar, right
T10x - 10-Pin Connector, blue, connector station B-pillar, left
T10y - 10-Pin Connector, blue, connector station B-pillar, right
T23 - 23-Pin Connector

Amplifier, loud speakers rear

1.8L - Engine - Motronic Multiport Fuel Injection (MFI)/110 kW, code AWD,

from November 1999

Deviate relay location and fuseplacements as well as the locations of multiple connectors see section "component locations".

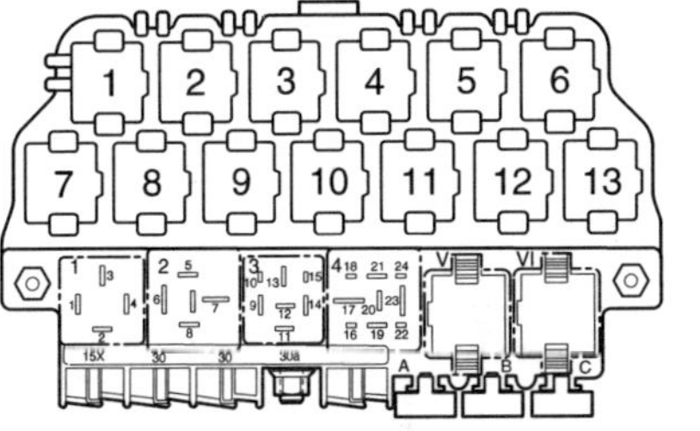
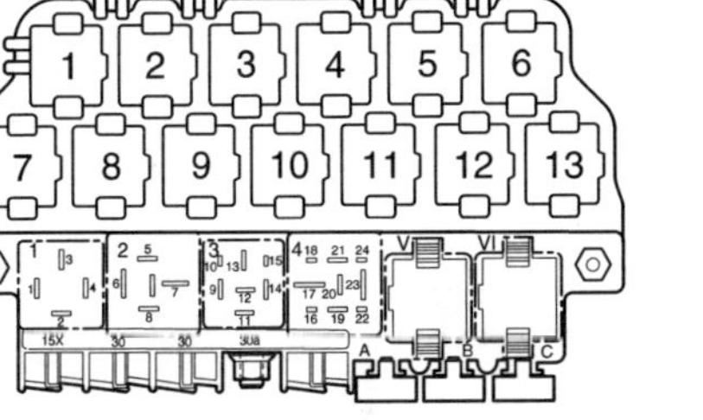

Relay location on the thirteenfold auxiliary relay panel, above relay panel:

Relay panel:

- **2** Load Reduction Relay (100)
- **4** Fuel Pump (FP) Relay (409)

Note: Number in parentheses indicates production control number stamped on relay housing.

Fuse colors

30 A - green
25 A - white
20 A - yellow
15 A - blue
10 A - red
7,5 A - brown
5 A - beige
3 A - violet

ws = white
sw = black
ro = red
br = brown
gn = green
bl = blue
gr = grey
li = lilac
ge = yellow

A - Battery
B - Starter
C - Generator (GEN)
C1 - Voltage Regulator (VR)
D - Ignition/Starter Switch
J59 - Load Reduction Relay
J207 - Starting Interlock Relay
J226 - Park/Neutral Position (PNP) Relay
S162 - Fuse -1- (30) in fuse bracket/battery
S163 - Fuse -2- (30) in fuse bracket/battery
S176 - Fuse -4- (30) in fuse bracket/battery
S177 - Fuse -5- (30) in fuse bracket/battery
T2e - Double Connector, near starter (vehicles without air conditioning)
T4 - 4-Pin Connector, near starter (vehicles with air conditioning only)
T6 - 6-Pin Connector, brown, in protective housing for connectors, in plenum chamber, left
(500) - Threaded connection -1- (30) on the relay plate
(502) - Threaded connection -1- (30a) on the relay plate
(A41) - Plus connection (50), in instrument panel wiring harness
* - Manual transmission only
--- Automatic transmission only

97-28659

Generator (GEN), starter

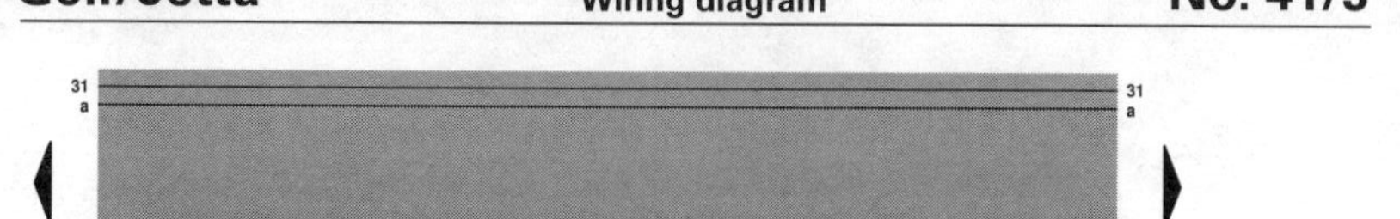

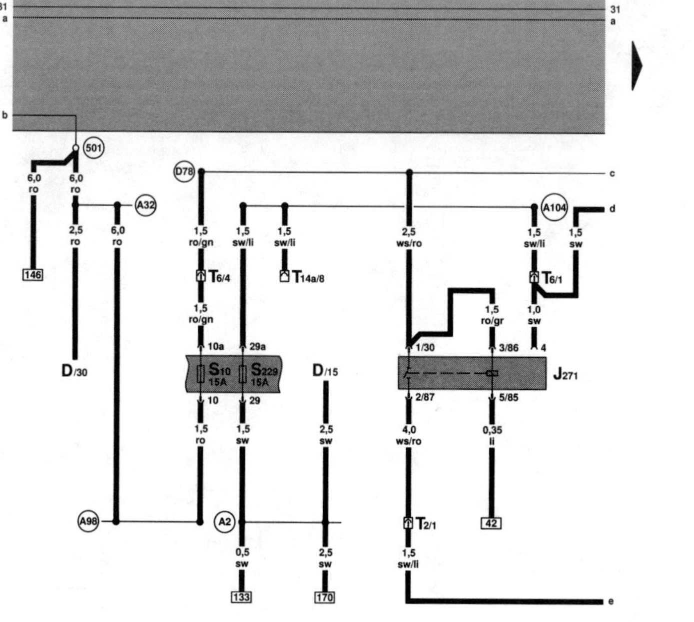

ws = white
sw = black
ro = red
br = brown
gn = green
bl = blue
gr = grey
li = lilac
ge = yellow

97-26184

D - Ignition/Starter Switch

J271 - Motronic engine control module (ECM) power supply relay, in protective housing, in engine compartment, left, production control number (428)

S10 - Fuse 10 in fuse holder

S229 - Fuse 29 in fuse holder

T2 - 2-Pin Connector, in engine compartment, left

T6 - 6-Pin Connector, brown, in protective housing for connectors, in plenum chamber, left

T14a - 14-Pin Connector, in engine compartment, in wiring duct, left

(501) - Threaded connection -2- (30) on the relay plate

(A2) - Plus connection (15), in instrument panel wiring harness

(A32) - Plus connection (30), in instrument panel wiring harness

(A98) - Plus connector -4- (30), in instrument panel wiring harness

(A104) - Plus connector -2- (15), in instrument panel wiring harness

(D78) - Plus connector -1- (30a), in engine compartment wiring harness

ws = white
sw = black
ro = red
br = brown
gn = green
bl = blue
gr = grey
li = lilac
ge = yellow

97-26185

J220 - Motronic Engine Control Module (ECM), in plenum chamber, center

N70 - Ignition Coil 1 with Power Output Stage

N127 - Ignition Coil 2 with Power Output Stage

N291 - Ignition Coil 3 with Power Output Stage

N292 - Ignition Coil 4 with Power Output Stage

P - Spark Plug Connectors

Q - Spark Plugs

T4a - 4-Pin Connector

T4b - 4-Pin Connector

T4c - 4-Pin Connector

T4d - 4-Pin Connector

T121 - Connector, 121 point

(15) - Ground connection, on cylinder head

(85) - Ground connection -1-, in engine compartment wiring harness

(281) - Ground connector -1-, in wiring harness engine pre-wiring

(D52) - Plus connector (15a), in engine compartment wiring harness

(D78) - Plus connector -1- (30a), in engine compartment wiring harness

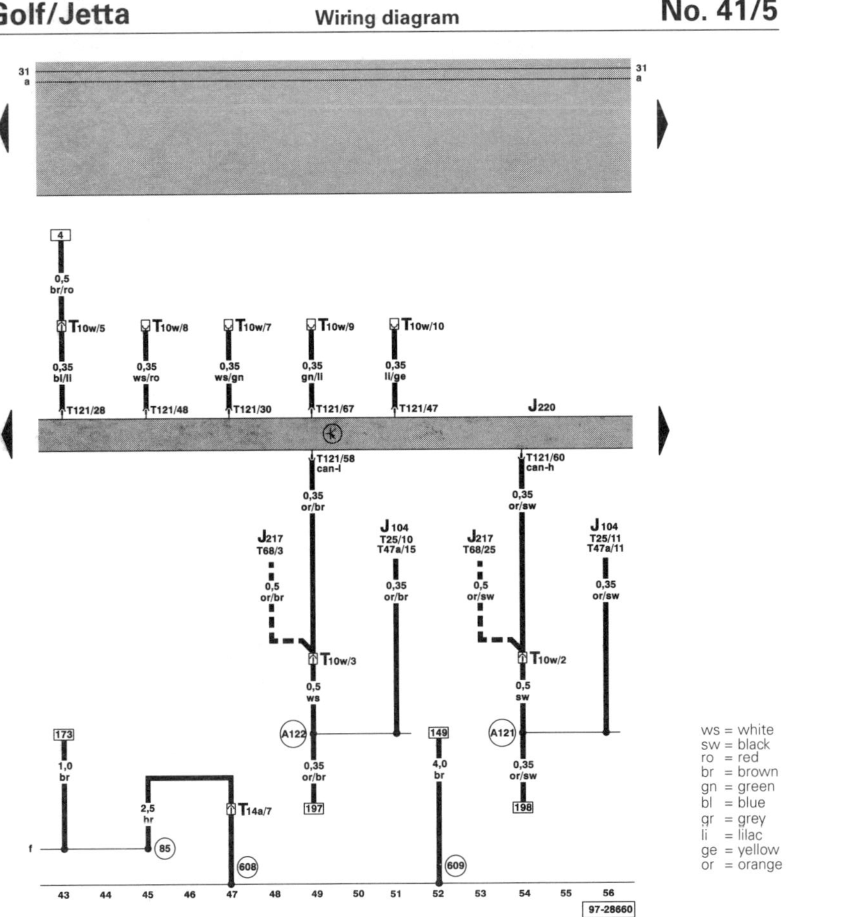

ws = white
sw = black
ro = red
br = brown
gn = green
bl = blue
gr = grey
li = lilac
ge = yellow
or = orange

J104 - ABS Control Module (w/EDL), in engine compartment, left
J217 - Transmission Control Module (TCM), in plenum chamber, center
J220 - Motronic Engine Control Module (ECM), in plenum chamber, center
T10w - 10-Pin Connector, white, in protective housing for connectors, in plenum chamber, left
T14a - 14-Pin Connector, in engine compartment, in wiring duct, left
T25 - 25-Pin Connector, on ABS Control Module (through July 2000)
T47a - 47-Pin Connector, on ABS Control Module (beginning August 2000)
T68 - 68-Pin Connector, on Transmission Control Module (TCM)
T121 - Connector, 121 point

(85) - Ground connection -1-, in engine compartment wiring harness
(608) - Ground Connection (in center plenum chamber)
(609) - Ground Connection (in right plenum chamber)
(A121) - Connection (high bus), in instrument panel wiring harness
(A122) - Connection (low bus), in instrument panel wiring harness

--- Automatic transmission only

ws = white
sw = black
ro = red
br = brown
gn = green
bl = blue
gr = grey
li = lilac
ge = yellow

G2 - Engine Coolant Temperature (ECT) Sensor
G31 - Charge Air Pressure Sensor
G62 - Engine Coolant Temperature (ECT) Sensor
G163 - Camshaft Position (CMP) Sensor 2
J220 - Motronic Engine Control Module (ECM), in plenum chamber, center
N75 - Wastegate Bypass Regulator Valve
N249 - Recirculating valve for turbocharger
T4g - 4-Pin Connector
T10 - 10-Pin Connector, orange, in protective housing for connectors, in plenum chamber, left
T14a - 14-Pin Connector, in engine compartment, in wiring duct, left
T121 - Connector, 121 point

(220) - Ground connection (sensor ground), in engine compartment wiring harness
(D101) - Wire connection -1-, in engine compartment wiring harness
(D102) - Wire connection -2-, in engine compartment wiring harness

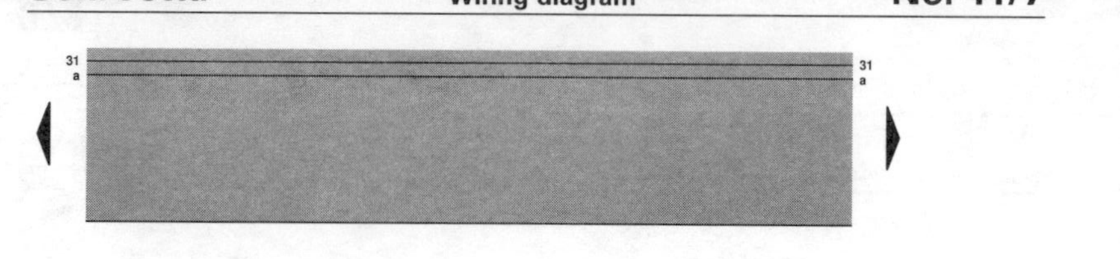

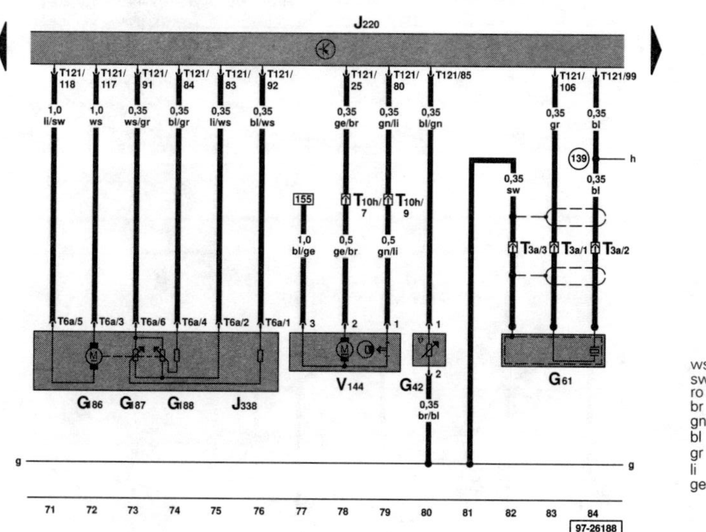

ws = white
sw = black
ro = red
br = brown
gn = green
bl = blue
gr = grey
li = lilac
ge = yellow

G42 - Intake Air Temperature (IAT) Sensor
G61 - Knock Sensor (KS) 1
G186 - Throttle drive (power accelerator actuation)
G187 - Angle sensor -1- for throttle drive (power accelerator actuation)
G188 - Angle sensor -2- for throttle drive (power accelerator actuation)
J220 - Motronic Engine Control Module (ECM), in plenum chamber, center
J338 - Throttle Valve Control Module
T3a - 3-Pin Connector, in engine compartment, front
T6a - 6-Pin Connector
T10h - 10-Pin Connector, blue, in protective housing for connectors, in plenum chamber, left
T121 - Connector, 121 point

V144 - Leak detection pump (LDP)

(139) - Ground connection (sensor Ground), in Motronic Multiport Fuel Injection (MFI) wiring harness

Motronic engine control module (ECM), angle sensor for throttle drive (power accelerator actuation), intake air temperature (IAT) sensor, knock sensor (KS) 1, leak detection pump (LDP)

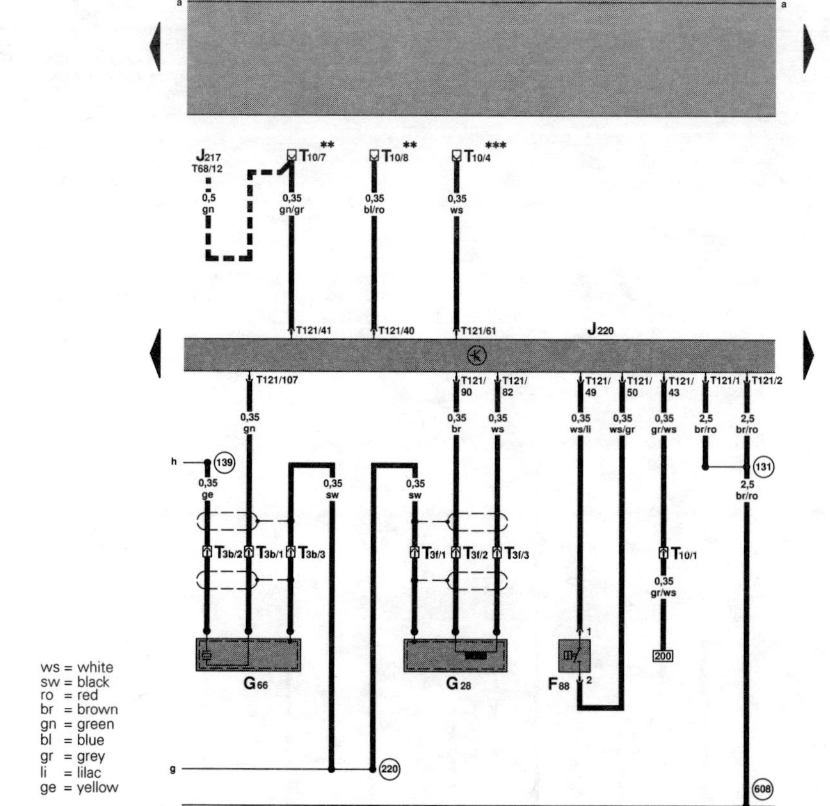

ws = white
sw = black
ro = red
br = brown
gn = green
bl = blue
gr = grey
li = lilac
ge = yellow

F88 - Pressure switch/power steering
G28 - Engine Speed (RPM) Sensor
G66 - Knock Sensor (KS) 2
J217 - Transmission Control Module (TCM), in plenum chamber, center
J220 - Motronic Engine Control Module (ECM), in plenum chamber, center
T3b - 3-Pin Connector, in engine compartment, front
T3f - 3-Pin Connector, in engine compartment, front
T10 - 10-Pin Connector, orange, in protective housing for connectors, in plenum chamber, left
T68 - Connector, 68 point
T121 - Connector, 121 point

(131) - Ground connection -2-, in engine compartment wiring harness

(139) - Ground connection (sensor Ground), in Motronic Multiport Fuel Injection (MFI) wiring harness
(220) - Ground connection (sensor ground), in engine compartment wiring harness
(608) - Ground Connection (in center plenum chamber)

** - A/C connection
*** - Coolant Fan Control Module connection
- - - - Automatic transmission only

Motronic engine control module (ECM), pressure switch/power steering, engine speed (RPM) sensor, knock sensor (KS) 2

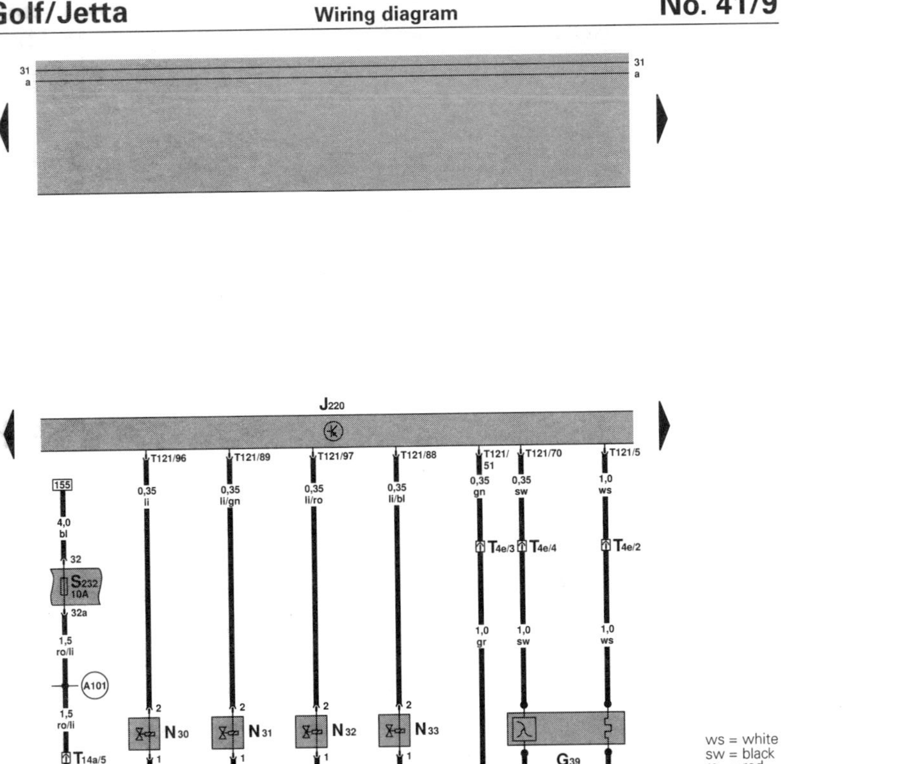

ws = white
sw = black
ro = red
br = brown
gn = green
bl = blue
gr = grey
li = lilac
ge = yellow

G39 - Heated Oxygen Sensor (HO2S)
J220 - Motronic Engine Control Module (ECM), in plenum chamber, center
N30 - Cylinder 1 Fuel Injector
N31 - Cylinder 2 Fuel Injector
N32 - Cylinder 3 Fuel Injector
N33 - Cylinder 4 Fuel Injector
S232 - Fuse 32 in fuse holder
T4e - 4-Pin Connector, in protective housing for connectors under right floor
T14a - 14-Pin Connector, in engine compartment, in wiring duct, left
T121 - Connector, 121 point

(A101) - Connector -3- (87a), in instrument panel wiring harness

(D95) - Wire connection (injectors), in engine compartment wiring harness
(E30) - Connector (87a), in wiring harness engine

Edition 11/99 USA.5102.05.21 **Motronic engine control module (ECM), heated oxygen sensor (HO2S), injectors**

ws = white
sw = black
ro = red
br = brown
gn = green
bl = blue
gr = grey
li = lilac
ge = yellow

G79 - Throttle Position (TP) Sensor
G130 - Oxygen Sensor (O2S) behind Three Way Catalytic Converter (TWC)
G185 - Sender -2- for accelerator pedal position
J220 - Motronic Engine Control Module (ECM), in plenum chamber, center
N80 - Evaporative Emission (EVAP) Canister Purge Regulator Valve
T4f - 4-Pin Connector, in protective housing for connectors under right floor
T6b - 6-Pin Connector
T10h - 10-Pin Connector, blue, in protective housing for connectors, in plenum chamber, left
T121 - Connector, 121 point

Motronic engine control module (ECM), throttle position (TP) sensor, oxygen sensor (O2S) behind three way catalytic converter (TWC), evaporative emission (EVAP) canister purge

Edition 11/99 USA.5102.05.21

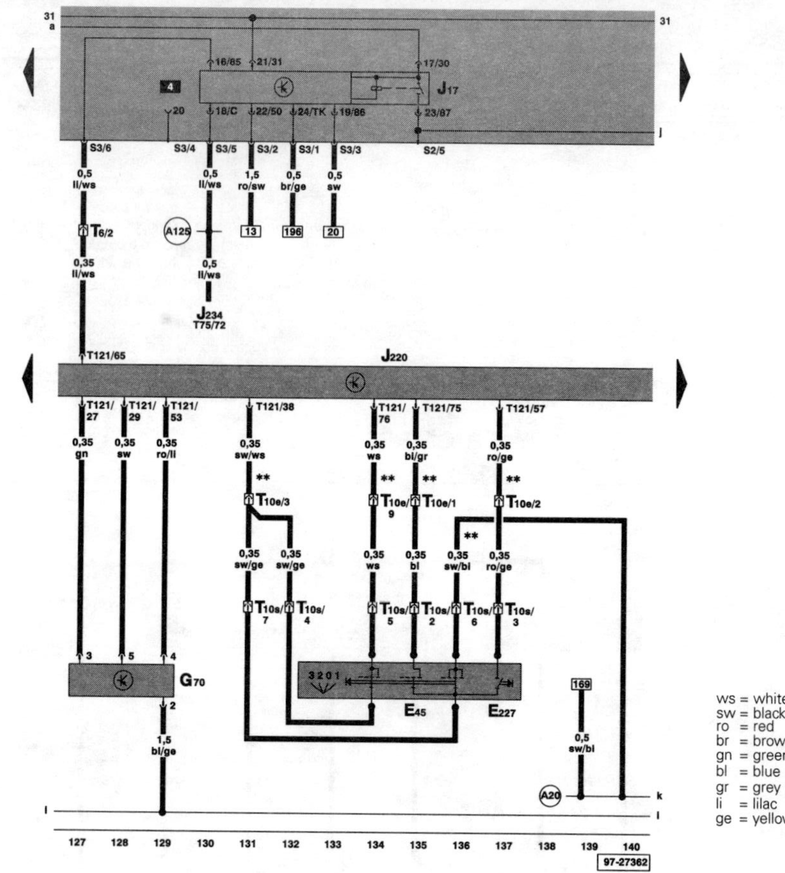

ws = white
sw = black
ro = red
br = brown
gn = green
bl = blue
gr = grey
li = lilac
ge = yellow

E45 - Cruise Control Switch**
E227 - Cruise Control Push Button (SET)**
G70 - Mass Air Flow (MAF) Sensor
J17 - Fuel Pump (FP) Relay
J220 - Motronic Engine Control Module (ECM), in plenum chamber, center
J234 - Airbag Control Module
T6 - 6-Pin Connector, brown, in protective housing for connectors, in plenum chamber, left
T10e - 10-Pin Connector, black, in protective housing for connectors, in plenum chamber, left
T10s - 10-Pin Connector, near steering column
T75 - 75-Pin Connector
T121 - Connector, 121 point

(A20) - Wire connection (15a), in instrument panel wiring harness
(A125) - Connection (crash signal) in instrument panel wiring harness

** - Vehicles with cruise control only

Edition 06/00 USA.5102.06.21 **Motronic engine control module (ECM), fuel pump (FP) relay, cruise control switch, mass air flow (MAF) sensor**

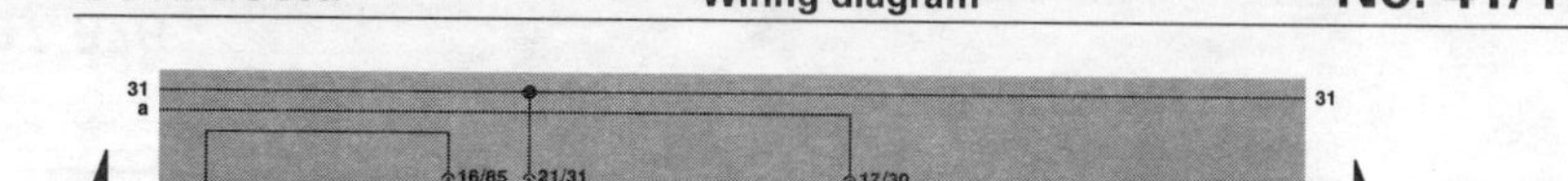

ws = white
sw = black
ro = red
br = brown
gn = green
bl = blue
gr = grey
li = lilac
ge = yellow

F - Brake Light Switch
F36 - Clutch Vacuum Vent Valve Switch
F47 - Brake Vacuum Vent Valve Switch for cruise control
J220 - Motronic Engine Control Module (ECM), in plenum chamber, center
J299 - Secondary Air Injection (AIR) Pump Relay, in protective housing, in engine compartment, left, production control number (100)
N112 - Secondary Air Injection (AIR) Solenoid Valve
S13 - Fuse 13 in fuse holder
T10 - 10-Pin Connector, orange, in protective housing for connectors, in plenum chamber, left
T10e - 10-Pin Connector, black, in protective housing for connectors, in plenum chamber, left
T10w - 10-Pin Connector, white, in protective housing for connectors, in plenum chamber, left
T121 - Connector, 121 point
V101 - Secondary Air Injection (AIR) Pump Motor

(A18) - Wire connection (54), in instrument panel
(A20) - Wire connection (15a), in instrument panel wiring harness
(A27) - Wire Connection (vehicle speed signal), in instrument panel wiring harness

* - Manual transmission only

Motronic engine control module (ECM), secondary air injection (AIR) pump system, brake light switch, clutch vacuum vent valve switch, brake vacuum vent valve switch **Edition 06/00** USA.5102.06.21

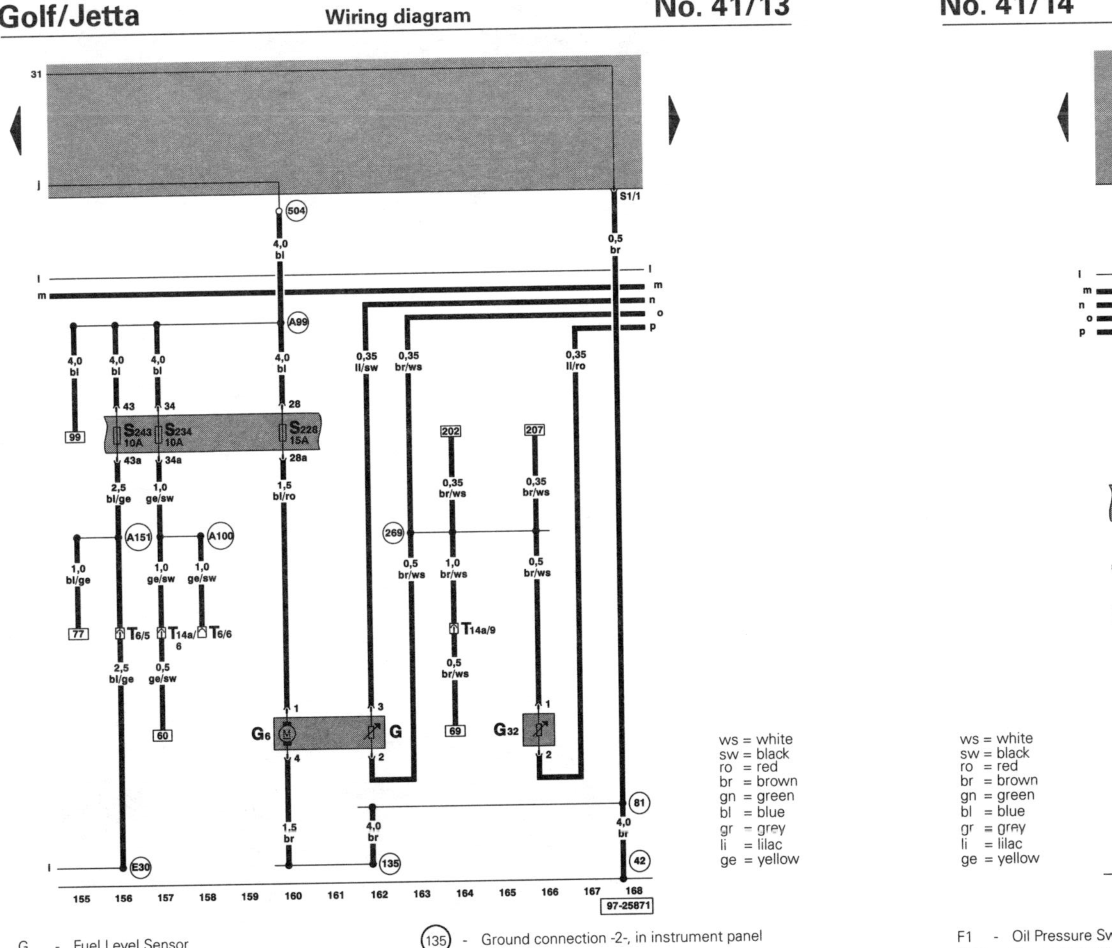

ws = white
sw = black
ro = red
br = brown
gn = green
bl = blue
gr = grey
li = lilac
ge = yellow

G - Fuel Level Sensor
G6 - Fuel Pump (FP)
G32 - Engine Coolant Level (ECL) Sensor
S228 - Fuse 28 in fuse holder
S234 - Fuse 34 in fuse holder
S243 - Fuse 43 in fuse holder
T6 - 6-Pin Connector, brown, in protective housing for connectors, in plenum chamber, left
T14a - 14-Pin Connector, in engine compartment, in wiring duct, left

(42) - Ground connection, beside steering column

(81) - Ground connection -1-, in instrument panel wiring harness

(135) - Ground connection -2-, in instrument panel wiring harnes

(269) - Ground connection (sensor ground) -1-, in instrument panel wiring harness

(504) - Threaded connection -1- (87) on the relay plate

(A99) - Connector -1- (87), in instrument panel wiring harness

(A100) - Connector -2- (87), in instrument panel wiring harness

(A151) - Connector -4- (87), in instrument panel wiring harness

(E30) - Connector (87a), in wiring harness engine

Fuel pump (FP), fuel level sensor, engine coolant level (ECL) sensor

ws = white
sw = black
ro = red
br = brown
gn = green
bl = blue
gr = grey
li = lilac
ge = yellow

F1 - Oil Pressure Switch
G22 - Speedometer Vehicle Speed Sensor (VSS)
J285 - Control module with indicator unit in instrument panel insert
K3 - Oil Pressure Warning Light
K38 - Engine Oil Level Indicator Light
S5 - Fuse 5 in fuse holder
S7 - Fuse 7 in fuse holder
T14a - 14-Pin Connector, in engine compartment, in wiring duct, left
T32 - 32-Pin Connector, blue

(B163) - Plus connector -1- (15) in wiring harness interior

Instrument cluster, oil pressure switch, speedometer vehicle speed sensor (VSS), oil pressure warning light

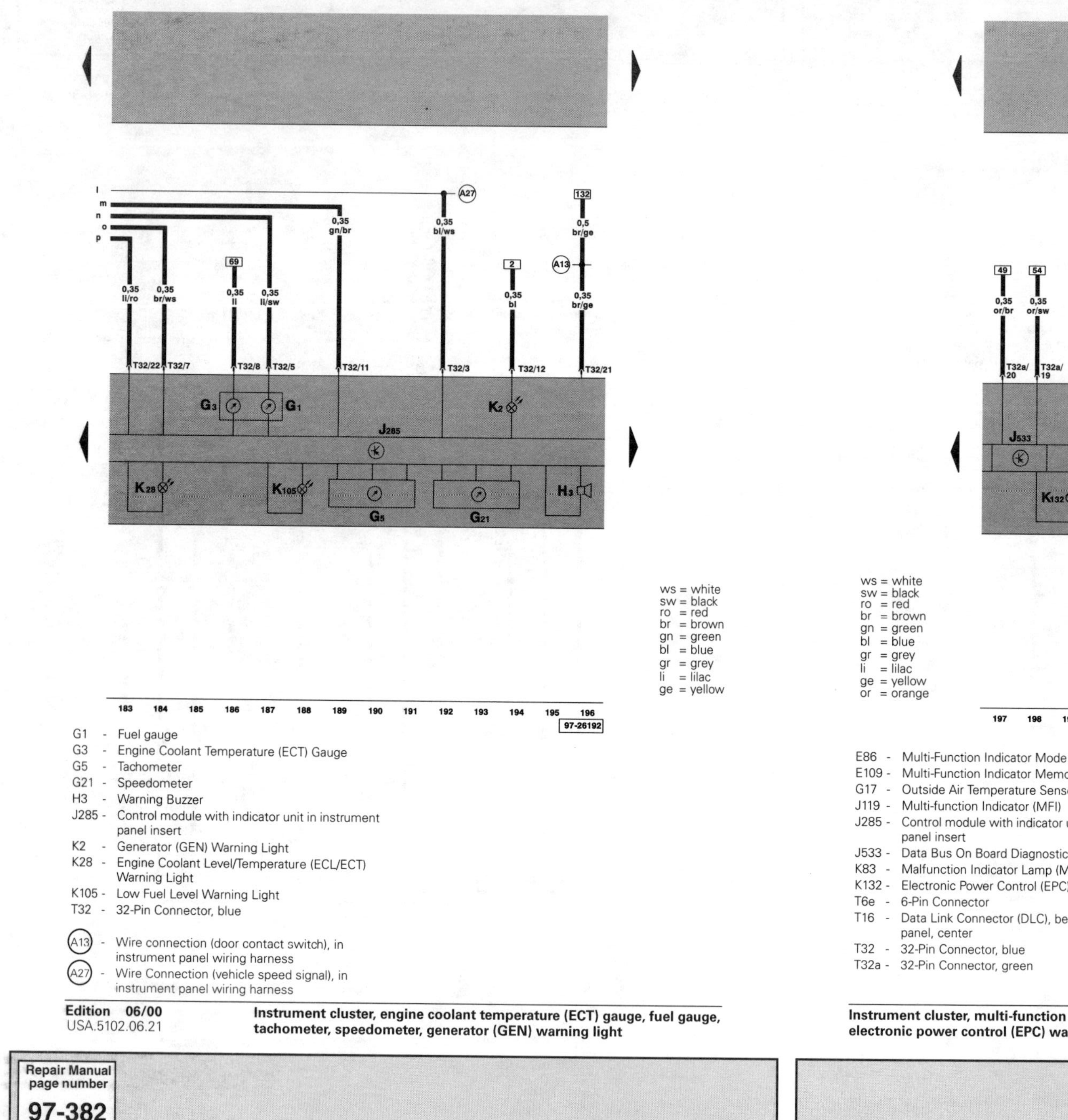

ws = white
sw = black
ro = red
br = brown
gn = green
bl = blue
gr = grey
li = lilac
ge = yellow

G1 - Fuel gauge
G3 - Engine Coolant Temperature (ECT) Gauge
G5 - Tachometer
G21 - Speedometer
H3 - Warning Buzzer
J285 - Control module with indicator unit in instrument panel insert
K2 - Generator (GEN) Warning Light
K28 - Engine Coolant Level/Temperature (ECL/ECT) Warning Light
K105 - Low Fuel Level Warning Light
T32 - 32-Pin Connector, blue

(A13) - Wire connection (door contact switch), in instrument panel wiring harness
(A27) - Wire Connection (vehicle speed signal), in instrument panel wiring harness

Instrument cluster, engine coolant temperature (ECT) gauge, fuel gauge, tachometer, speedometer, generator (GEN) warning light

ws = white
sw = black
ro = red
br = brown
gn = green
bl = blue
gr = grey
li = lilac
ge = yellow
or = orange

E86 - Multi-Function Indicator Mode Select Switch
E109 - Multi-Function Indicator Memory Switch
G17 - Outside Air Temperature Sensor
J119 - Multi-function Indicator (MFI)
J285 - Control module with indicator unit in instrument panel insert
J533 - Data Bus On Board Diagnostic Interface
K83 - Malfunction Indicator Lamp (MIL)
K132 - Electronic Power Control (EPC) Warning Lamp
T6e - 6-Pin Connector
T16 - Data Link Connector (DLC), below instrument panel, center
T32 - 32-Pin Connector, blue
T32a - 32-Pin Connector, green

(A76) - Connector (K-diagnosis wire), in instrument panel wiring harness

Instrument cluster, multi-function indicator (MFI), outside air temperature sensor, electronic power control (EPC) warning lamp

Comfort system (vehicles without power windows),

from May 1999

- Anti-theft warning system
- Central locking system with remote control
- Fuel tank lid unlock system
- Heated outside mirrors
- Interior lights
- Luggage compartment light
- Power sunroof
- Rear lid unlock system

Deviate relay location and fuseplacements as well as the locations of multiple connectors see section "component locations".

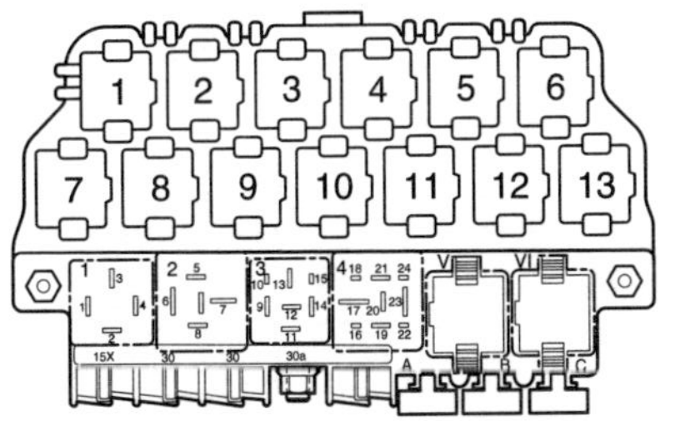

Fuse colors

30 A - green
25 A - white
20 A - yellow
15 A - blue
10 A - red
7,5 A - brown
5 A - beige
3 A - violet

ws = white
sw = black
ro = red
br = brown
gn = green
bl = blue
gr = grey
li = lilac
ge = yellow

97-26438

E20 - Instrument Panel Light Dimmer Switch
E204 - Switch for remote/fuel tank door
L76 - Push Button Light
T3c - 3-Pin Connector
T10i - 10-Pin Connector, black, connector station A-pillar, left
T10k - 10-Pin Connector, black, connector station A-pillar, right
T10n - 10-Pin Connector, brown, connector station A-pillar, left
V155 - Motor for fuel tank lid unlock

(42) - Ground connection, beside steering column

(81) - Ground connection -1-, in instrument panel wiring harness

(135) - Ground connection -2-, in instrument panel wiring harness
(238) - Ground connection -1-, in wiring harness interior
(A4) - Plus connection (58b), in instrument panel wiring harness
(R51) - Connection (58b) in door wiring harness, driver side

Switch for remote/fuel tank door, motor for fuel tank lid unlock

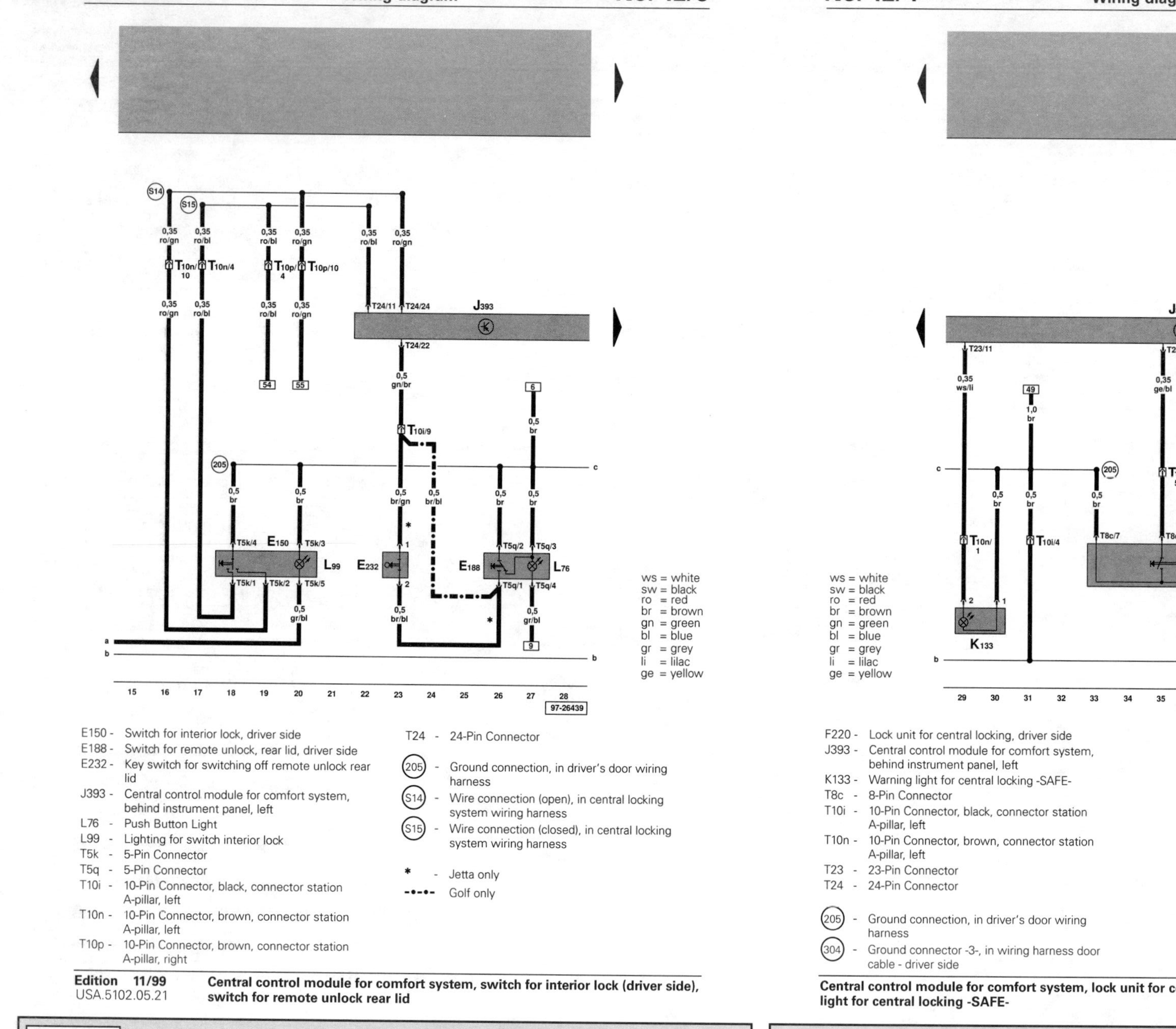

ws = white
sw = black
ro = red
br = brown
gn = green
bl = blue
gr = grey
li = lilac
ge = yellow

E150 - Switch for interior lock, driver side
E188 - Switch for remote unlock, rear lid, driver side
E232 - Key switch for switching off remote unlock rear lid
J393 - Central control module for comfort system, behind instrument panel, left
L76 - Push Button Light
L99 - Lighting for switch interior lock
T5k - 5-Pin Connector
T5q - 5-Pin Connector
T10i - 10-Pin Connector, black, connector station A-pillar, left
T10n - 10-Pin Connector, brown, connector station A-pillar, left
T10p - 10-Pin Connector, brown, connector station A-pillar, right
T24 - 24-Pin Connector

(205) - Ground connection, in driver's door wiring harness
(S14) - Wire connection (open), in central locking system wiring harness
(S15) - Wire connection (closed), in central locking system wiring harness

* - Jetta only
-•-•- Golf only

Edition 11/99
USA.5102.05.21

Central control module for comfort system, switch for interior lock (driver side), switch for remote unlock rear lid

ws = white
sw = black
ro = red
br = brown
gn = green
bl = blue
gr = grey
li = lilac
ge = yellow

F220 - Lock unit for central locking, driver side
J393 - Central control module for comfort system, behind instrument panel, left
K133 - Warning light for central locking -SAFE-
T8c - 8-Pin Connector
T10i - 10-Pin Connector, black, connector station A-pillar, left
T10n - 10-Pin Connector, brown, connector station A-pillar, left
T23 - 23-Pin Connector
T24 - 24-Pin Connector

(205) - Ground connection, in driver's door wiring harness
(304) - Ground connector -3-, in wiring harness door cable - driver side

Central control module for comfort system, lock unit for central locking, warning light for central locking -SAFE-

Edition 11/99
USA.5102.05.21

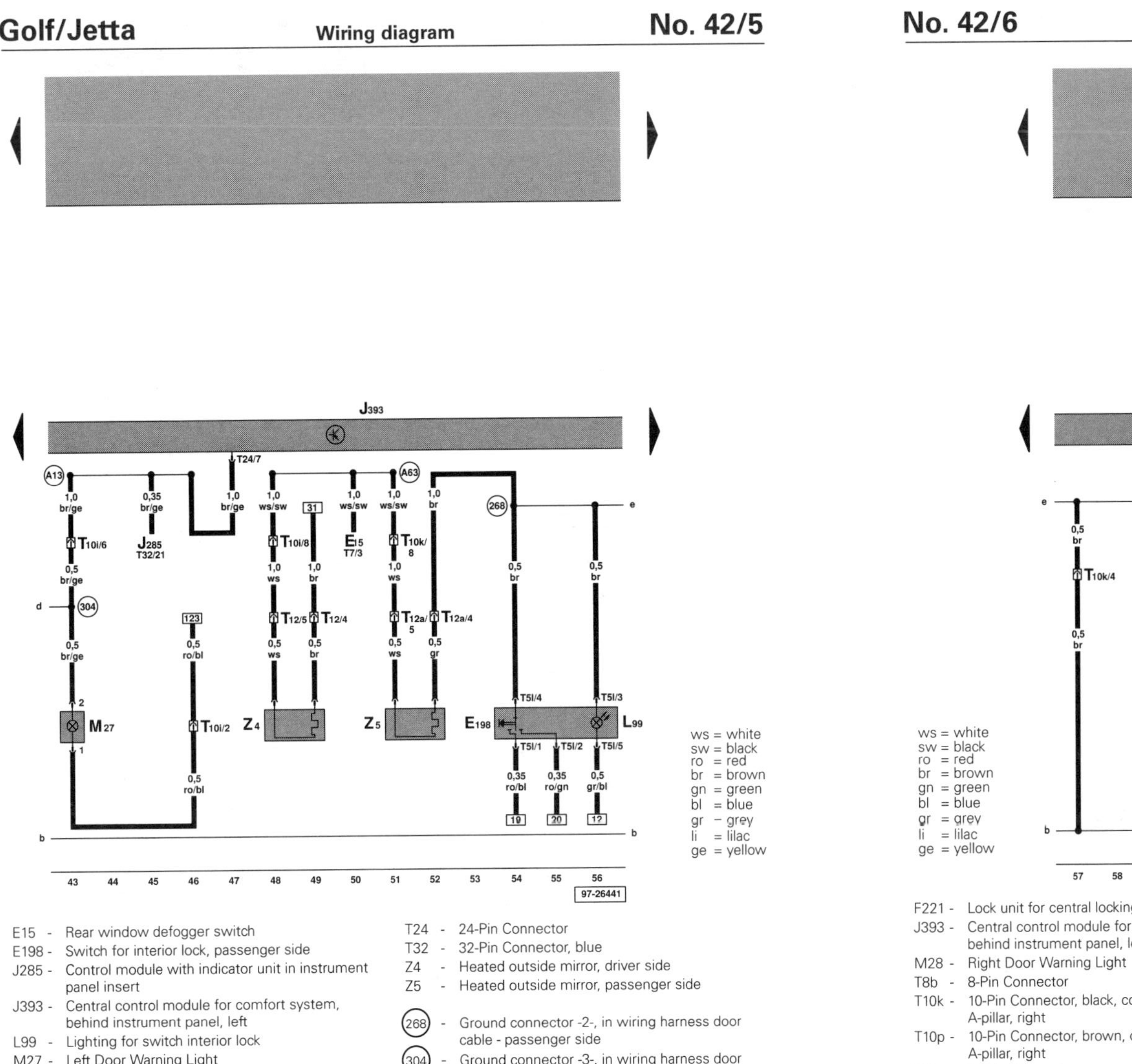

ws = white
sw = black
ro = red
br = brown
gn = green
bl = blue
gr = grey
li = lilac
ge = yellow

E15 - Rear window defogger switch
E198 - Switch for interior lock, passenger side
J285 - Control module with indicator unit in instrument panel insert
J393 - Central control module for comfort system, behind instrument panel, left
L99 - Lighting for switch interior lock
M27 - Left Door Warning Light
T5l - 5-Pin Connector
T7 - 7-Pin Connector
T10i - 10-Pin Connector, black, connector station A-pillar, left
T10k - 10-Pin Connector, black, connector station A-pillar, right
T12 - 12-Pin Connector
T12a - 12-Pin Connector
T24 - 24-Pin Connector
T32 - 32-Pin Connector, blue
Z4 - Heated outside mirror, driver side
Z5 - Heated outside mirror, passenger side
(268) - Ground connector -2-, in wiring harness door cable - passenger side
(304) - Ground connector -3-, in wiring harness door cable - driver side
(A13) - Wire connection (door contact switch) in instrument panel wiring harness
(A63) - Connector (mirror adjustment/-heated) in instrument panel wiring harness

Central control module for comfort system, switch for interior lock (passenger side), left door warning light, heated outside mirrors

ws = white
sw = black
ro = red
br = brown
gn = green
bl = blue
gr = grey
li = lilac
ge = yellow

F221 - Lock unit for central locking, passenger side
J393 - Central control module for comfort system, behind instrument panel, left
M28 - Right Door Warning Light
T8b - 8-Pin Connector
T10k - 10-Pin Connector, black, connector station A-pillar, right
T10p - 10-Pin Connector, brown, connector station A-pillar, right
T23 - 23-Pin Connector
T24 - 24-Pin Connector
(268) - Ground connector -2-, in wiring harness door cable - passenger side
(303) - Ground connector -3-, in wiring harness door cable - passenger side

Central control module for comfort system, lock unit for central locking (passenger side), right door warning light

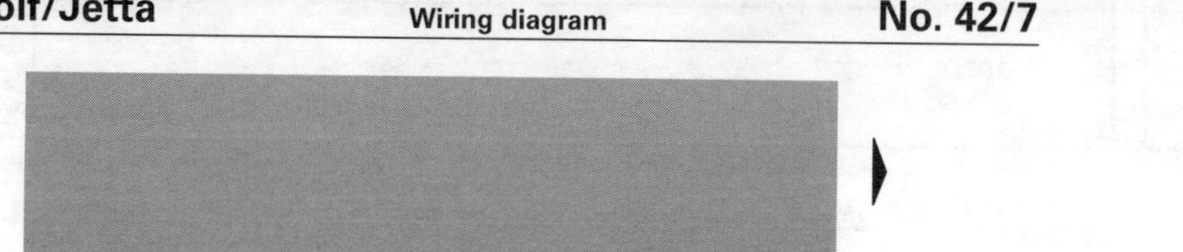

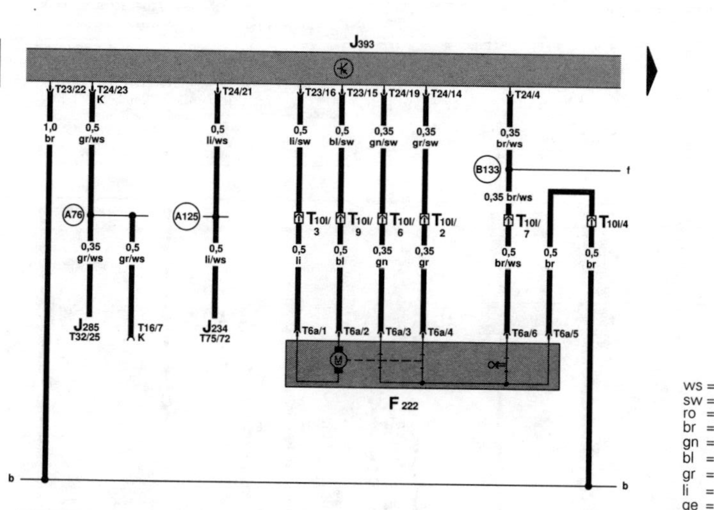

ws = white
sw = black
ro = red
br = brown
gn = green
bl = blue
gr = grey
li = lilac
ge = yellow

F222 - Lock unit for central locking, rear, left
J234 - Airbag Control Module, behind console, lower part
J285 - Control module with indicator unit in instrument panel insert
J393 - Central control module for comfort system, behind instrument panel, left
T6a - 6-Pin Connector
T10l - 10-Pin Connector, black, connector station B-pillar, left
T16 - Data Link Connector (DLC), below instrument panel, left
T23 - 23-Pin Connector
T24 - 24-Pin Connector
T32 - 32-Pin Connector, blue
T75 - 75-Pin Connector

(A76) - Connector (K-diagnosis wire) in instrument panel wiring harness
(A125) - Connection (crash signal) in instrument panel wiring harness
(B133) - Connector (central locking open), in wiring harness interior

Edition 11/99 USA.5102.05.21 **Central control module for comfort system, lock unit for central locking (rear left)**

ws = white
sw = black
ro = red
br = brown
gn = green
bl = blue
gr = grey
li = lilac
ge = yellow

85 86 87 88 89 90 91 92 93 94 95 96 97 98
97-26444

F124 - Trunk Lock Alarm/Central Locking Switch
F223 - Lock unit for central locking, rear, right
J393 - Central control module for comfort system, behind instrument panel, left
T2 - Double Connector, in rear lid
T5d - 5-Pin Connector, brown, connector station C-pillar, left
T6b - 6-Pin Connector
T10m - 10-Pin Connector, black, connector station B-pillar, right
T23 - 23-Pin Connector
T24 - 24-Pin Connector
V53 - Decklid Central Locking System Motor (Golf only)
V139 - Motor to unlock rear lid*

(218) - Ground connection -1-, in rear lid wiring harness
(219) - Ground connection -2-, in rear lid wiring harness
(B133) - Connector (central locking open), in wiring harness interior

* - Jetta only
-•-•- Golf only

Central control module for comfort system, lock unit for central locking (rear right), trunk lock alarm/central locking switch, decklid central locking system motor **Edition 11/99** USA.5102.05.21

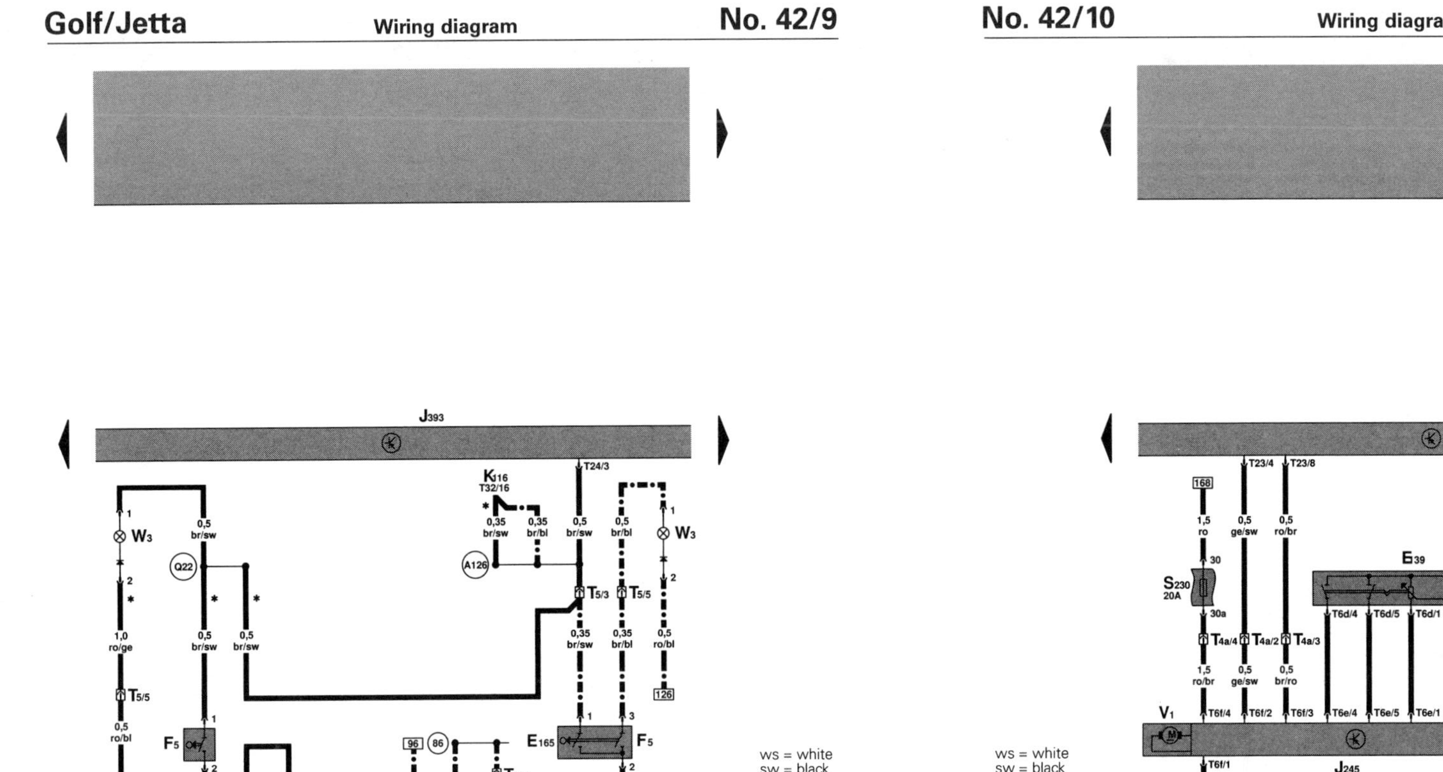

ws = white
sw = black
ro = red
br = brown
gn = green
bl = blue
gr = grey
li = lilac
ge = yellow

E165 - Trunk Lid Release Switch
F5 - Luggage Compartment Light Switch
J393 - Central control module for comfort system, behind instrument panel, left
K116 - Warning light for rear lid unlocked, in Instrument cluster
T5 - 5-Pin Connector, black, connector station C-pillar, left
T5a - 5-Pin Connector, pink, connector station C-pillar, left (Golf only)
T24 - 24-Pin Connector
T32 - 32-Pin Connector, blue, on Instrument cluster
W3 - Luggage compartment Light

(50) - Ground connection, in luggage compartment, left

(86) - Ground connection -1-, in rear wiring harness

(98) - Ground connection, in rear lid wiring harness

(218) - Ground connection -1-, in rear lid wiring harness

(A126) - Connection (contact switch in rear lid) in instrument panel wiring harness

(Q22) - Wire connection -1-, in rear lid wiring harness

* - Jetta only

-•-•- Golf only

Central control module for comfort system, trunk lid release switch, luggage compartment light switch

ws = white
sw = black
ro = red
br = brown
gn = green
bl = blue
gr = grey
li = lilac
ge = yellow

E139 - Sunroof Regulator
J245 - Power Sunroof Control Module
J393 - Central control module for comfort system, behind instrument panel, left
S230 - Fuse 30 in fuse holder
T4a - 4-Pin Connector, behind instrument panel, left
T6d - 6-Pin Connector
T6e - 6-Pin Connector
T6f - 6-Pin Connector
T8e - 8-Pin Connector, behind instrument panel, left
T23 - 23-Pin Connector
V1 - Sunroof Motor

(128) - Ground connection -1-, in interior light wiring harness

(238) - Ground connection -1-, in wiring harness interior

(A29) - Wire connection (interior light), in instrument panel wiring harness

(R6) - Plus connection -1-, in interior light wiring harness

* - Jetta only

-•-•- Golf only

Central control module for comfort system, power sunroof control module, sunroof regulator, sunroof motor

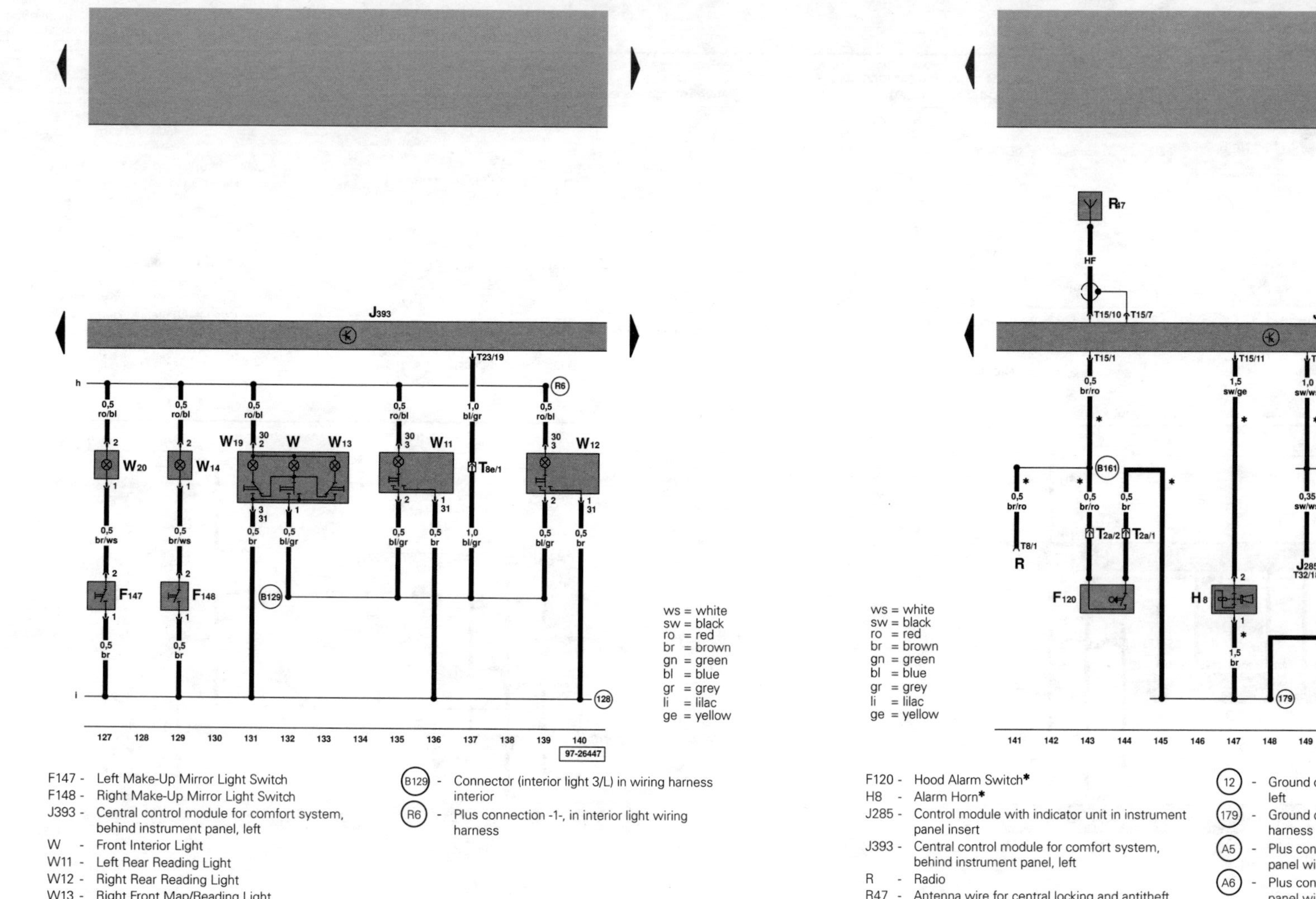

ws = white
sw = black
ro = red
br = brown
gn = green
bl = blue
gr = grey
li = lilac
ge = yellow

- F147 - Left Make-Up Mirror Light Switch
- F148 - Right Make-Up Mirror Light Switch
- J393 - Central control module for comfort system, behind instrument panel, left
- W - Front Interior Light
- W11 - Left Rear Reading Light
- W12 - Right Rear Reading Light
- W13 - Right Front Map/Reading Light
- W14 - Right Make-up Mirror Light
- W19 - Left Front Reading Light
- W20 - Left Make-up Mirror Light
- T8e - 8-Pin Connector, behind instrument panel, left
- T23 - 23-Pin Connector
- (128) - Ground connection -1-, in interior light wiring harness
- (B129) - Connector (interior light 3/L) in wiring harness interior
- (R6) - Plus connection -1-, in interior light wiring harness

Central control module for comfort system, Interior lights, make-up mirror lights

ws = white
sw = black
ro = red
br = brown
gn = green
bl = blue
gr = grey
li = lilac
ge = yellow

- F120 - Hood Alarm Switch*
- H8 - Alarm Horn*
- J285 - Control module with indicator unit in instrument panel insert
- J393 - Central control module for comfort system, behind instrument panel, left
- R - Radio
- R47 - Antenna wire for central locking and antitheft warning system
- T2a - Double Connector, near headlight, right
- T8 - 8-Pin Connector, on radio
- T15 - 15-Pin Connector
- T23 - 23-Pin Connector
- T32 - 32-Pin Connector, blue, on Instrument cluster
- (12) - Ground connection, in engine compartment, left
- (179) - Ground connection, in left headlight wiring harness
- (A5) - Plus connection (right turn signal), in instrument panel wiring harness
- (A6) - Plus connection (left turn signal), in instrument panel wiring harness
- (A27) - Wire connection (vehicle speed signal), in instrument panel wiring harness
- (B161) - Connector (anti-theft warning system), in wiring harness interior
- * - Vehicles with anti-theft warning system only

Central control module for comfort system, antitheft warning system, antenna wire for central locking and antitheft warning system

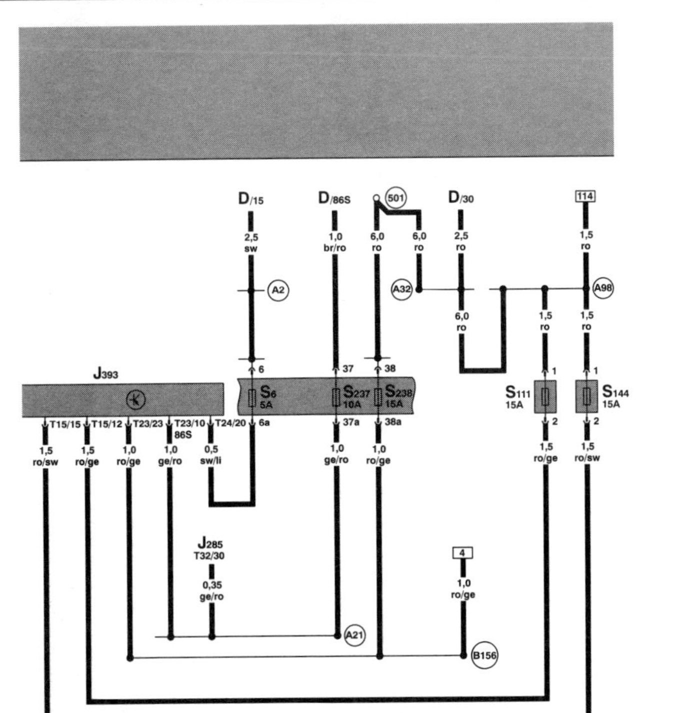

ws = white
sw = black
ro = red
br = brown
gn = green
bl = blue
gr = grey
li = lilac
ge = yellow

D - Ignition/Starter Switch
J285 - Control module with indicator unit in instrument panel insert
J393 - Central control module for comfort system, behind instrument panel, left
S6 - Fuse 6 in fuse holder
S111 - Alarm System and Anti-Theft Fuse, above the thirteenfold auxiliary relay panel
S144 - Fuse for central locking/anti-theft warning system, above the thirteenfold auxiliary relay panel
S237 - Fuse 37 in fuse holder
S238 - Fuse 38 in fuse holder
T15 - 15-Pin Connector
T23 - 23-Pin Connector
T24 - 24-Pin Connector
T32 - 32-Pin Connector, blue
(501) - Threaded connection -2- (30) on the relay plate
(A2) - Plus connection (15), in instrument panel wiring harness
(A21) - Wire connection (86s), in instrument panel wiring harness
(A32) - Plus connection (30), in instrument panel wiring harness
(A98) - Plus connector -4- (30), in instrument panel wiring harness
(B156) - Plus connector (30a), in wiring harness interior

THIS PAGE INTENTIONALLY LEFT
BLANK

Comfort System (vehicles with power windows),

from May 1999

- Anti-theft warning system
- Central locking system with remote control
- Fuel tank lid unlock system
- Heated power mirrors
- Interior lights
- Luggage compartment light
- Power sunroof
- Power windows
- Rear lid unlock system

Deviate relay location and fuseplacements as well as the locations of multiple connectors see section "component locations".

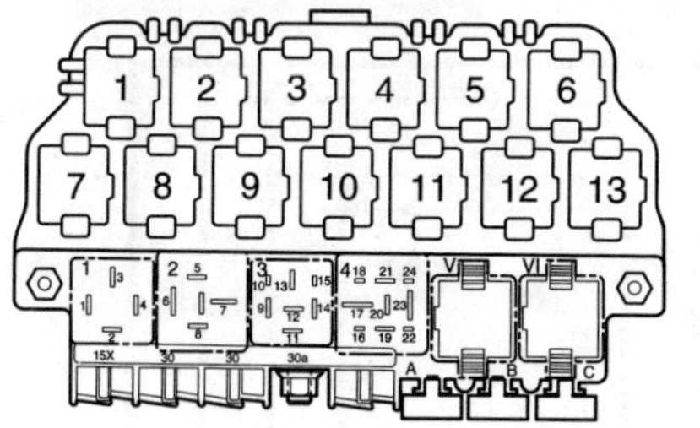

Fuse colors

30 A - green
25 A - white
20 A - yellow
15 A - blue
10 A - red
7,5 A - brown
5 A - beige
3 A - violet

ws = white
sw = black
ro = red
br = brown
gn = green
bl = blue
gr = grey
li = lilac
ge = yellow

97-26450

E39 - Safety switch for window regulator rear
E40 - Switch for window regulator front left
E53 - Switch for window regulator rear left, driver
E55 - Switch for window regulator rear right, driver
E81 - Switch for window regulator front right, driver
E150 - Switch for interior lock, driver side
J386 - Door control module, driver side
L76 - Push Button Light
S37 - Fuse for window regulator (circuit breaker), on thirteen position auxiliary relay panel
T10i - 10-Pin Connector, black, connector station A-pillar, left
T16a - 16-Pin Connector
T29 - 29-Pin Connector
V147 - Motor for window regulator, driver side

(267) - Ground connector -2-, in wiring harness door cable - driver side
(B110) - Connection (30), window regulator) in wiring harness interior

Door control module (driver side), switch for window regulator, safety switch for window regulator rear, switch for interior lock (driver side)

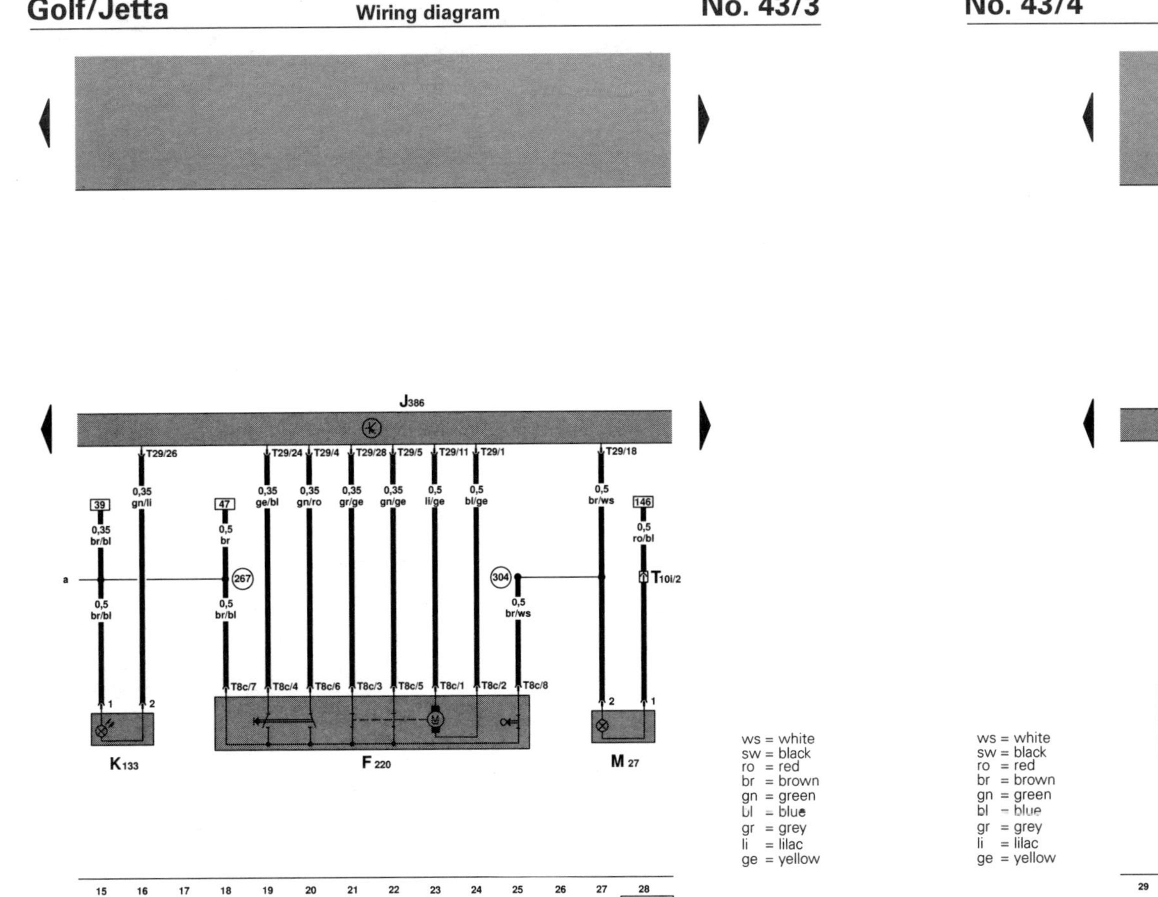

ws = white
sw = black
ro = red
br = brown
gn = green
bl = blue
gr = grey
li = lilac
ge = yellow

F220 - Lock unit for central locking, driver side
J386 - Door control module, driver side
K133 - Warning light for central locking -SAFE-
M27 - Left Door Warning Light
T8c - 8-Pin Connector
T10i - 10-Pin Connector, black, connector station A-pillar, left
T29 - 29-Pin Connector

(267) - Ground connector -2-, in wiring harness door cable - driver side
(304) - Ground connector -3-, in wiring harness door cable - driver side

Door control module (driver side), lock unit for central locking (driver side), warning light for central locking -SAFE-, left door warning light

ws = white
sw = black
ro = red
br = brown
gn = green
bl = blue
gr = grey
li = lilac
ge = yellow

E43 - Mirror Adjustment Switch
E48 - Mirror Selector Switch
E231 - Switch for outside mirror heating
E263 - Mirror fold-away Switch*
J386 - Door control module, driver side
L78 - Mirror Adjusting Switch Light
T10q - 10-Pin Connector, blue, connector station A-pillar, left
T10t - 10-Pin Connector
T29 - 29-Pin Connector

(A20) - Wire connection (15a), in instrument panel wiring harness

* - If equipped
- - - - Vehicles with seperate heated outside mirrors only

Door control module (driver side), mirror adjustment switch, mirror selector switch, switch for outside mirror heating

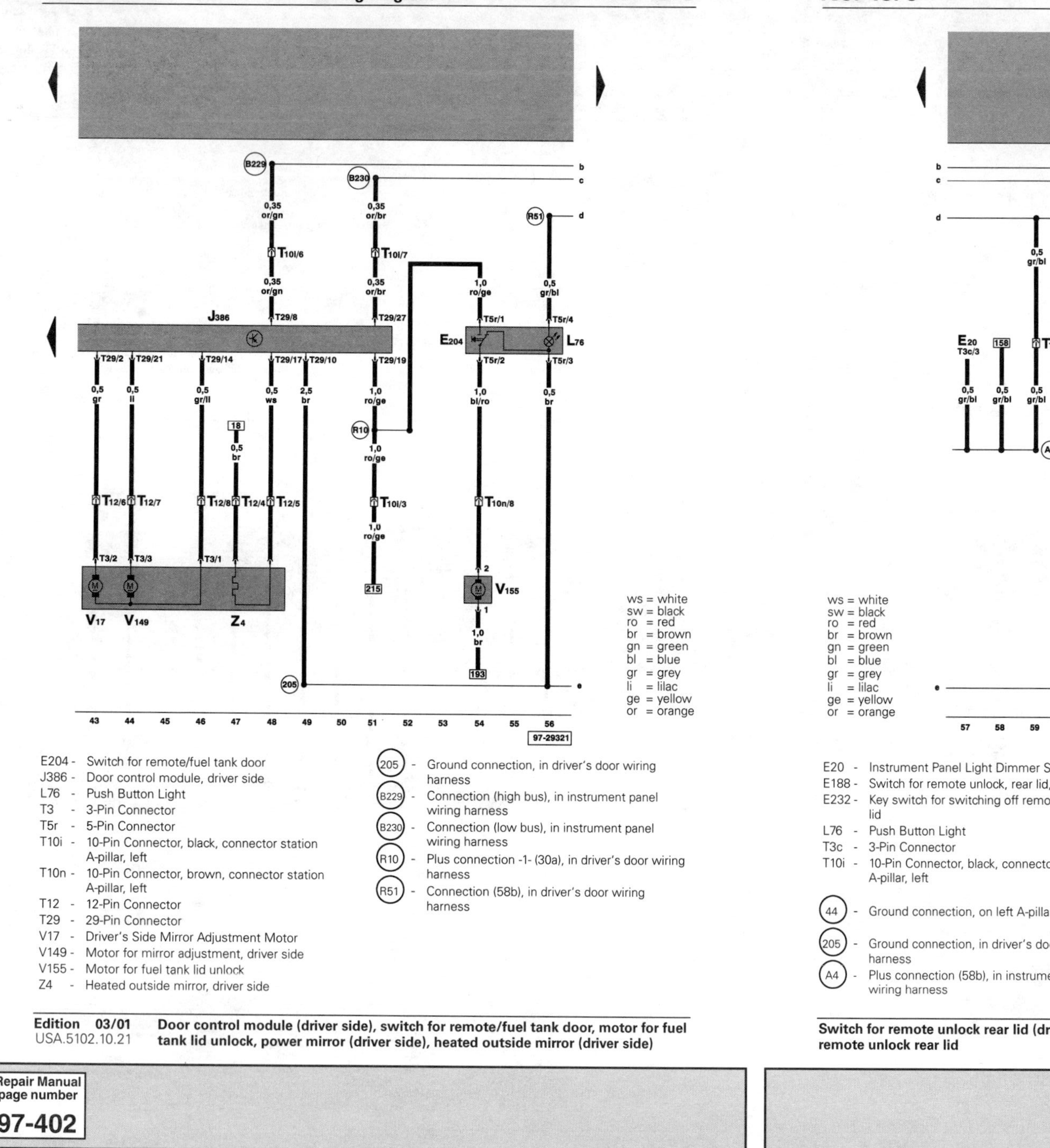

ws = white
sw = black
ro = red
br = brown
gn = green
bl = blue
gr = grey
li = lilac
ge = yellow
or = orange

- E204 - Switch for remote/fuel tank door
- J386 - Door control module, driver side
- L76 - Push Button Light
- T3 - 3-Pin Connector
- T5r - 5-Pin Connector
- T10i - 10-Pin Connector, black, connector station A-pillar, left
- T10n - 10-Pin Connector, brown, connector station A-pillar, left
- T12 - 12-Pin Connector
- T29 - 29-Pin Connector
- V17 - Driver's Side Mirror Adjustment Motor
- V149 - Motor for mirror adjustment, driver side
- V155 - Motor for fuel tank lid unlock
- Z4 - Heated outside mirror, driver side

- (205) - Ground connection, in driver's door wiring harness
- (B229) - Connection (high bus), in instrument panel wiring harness
- (B230) - Connection (low bus), in instrument panel wiring harness
- (R10) - Plus connection -1- (30a), in driver's door wiring harness
- (R51) - Connection (58b), in driver's door wiring harness

Door control module (driver side), switch for remote/fuel tank door, motor for fuel tank lid unlock, power mirror (driver side), heated outside mirror (driver side)

ws = white
sw = black
ro = red
br = brown
gn = green
bl = blue
gr = grey
li = lilac
ge = yellow
or = orange

- E20 - Instrument Panel Light Dimmer Switch
- E188 - Switch for remote unlock, rear lid, driver side
- E232 - Key switch for switching off remote unlock rear lid
- L76 - Push Button Light
- T3c - 3-Pin Connector
- T10i - 10-Pin Connector, black, connector station A-pillar, left

- (44) - Ground connection, on left A-pillar, lower part
- (205) - Ground connection, in driver's door wiring harness
- (A4) - Plus connection (58b), in instrument panel wiring harness
- (R51) - Connection (58b), in driver's door wiring harness
- * - Jetta only

Switch for remote unlock rear lid (driver side), key switch for switching off remote unlock rear lid

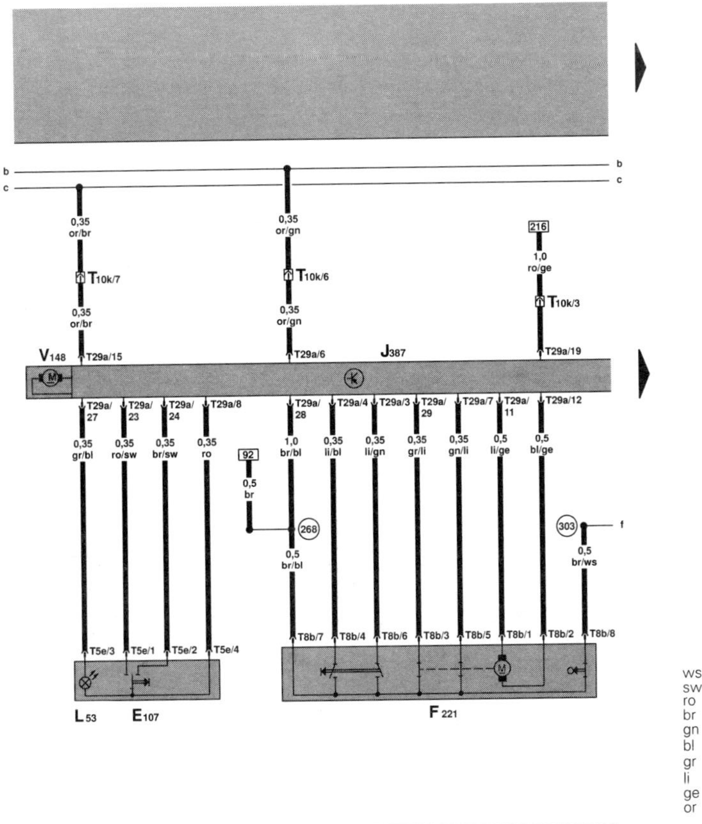

ws = white
sw = black
ro = red
br = brown
gn = green
bl = blue
gr = grey
li = lilac
ge = yellow
or = orange

E107 - Switch for window regulator, in passenger door
F221 - Lock unit for central locking, passenger side
J387 - Door control module, passenger side
L53 - Power Window Switch Light
T5e - 5-Pin Connector
T8b - 8-Pin Connector
T10k - 10-Pin Connector, black, connector station A-pillar, right
T29a - 29-Pin Connector
V148 - Motor for window regulator, passenger side

(268) - Ground connector -2-, in wiring harness door cable - passenger side
(303) - Ground connector -3-, in wiring harness door cable - passenger side

Door control module (passenger side), switch for window regulator (passenger door), lock unit for central locking (passenger side)

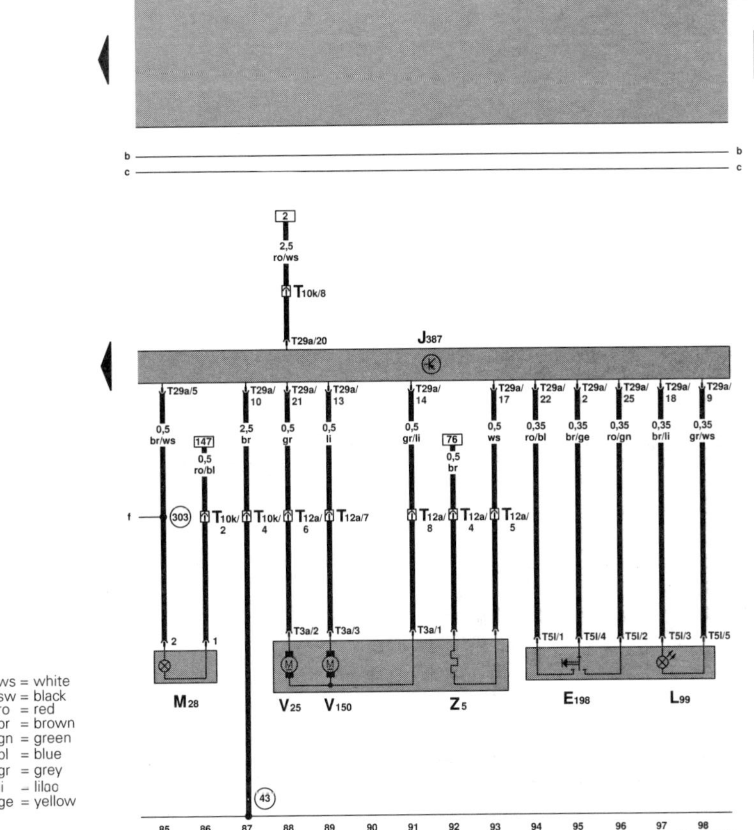

ws = white
sw = black
ro = red
br = brown
gn = green
bl = blue
gr = grey
li = lilac
ge = yellow

E198 - Switch for interior lock, passenger side
J387 - Door control module, passenger side
L99 - Lighting for switch interior lock
M28 - Right Door Warning Light
T3a - 3-Pin Connector
T5l - 5-Pin Connector
T10k - 10-Pin Connector, black, connector station A-pillar, right
T12a - 12-Pin Connector
T29a - 29-Pin Connector
V25 - Passenger's Side Mirror Adjustment Motor
V150 - Motor for mirror adjustment, passenger side
Z5 - Heated outside mirror, passenger side

(43) - Ground connection, on right A-pillar, lower part

(303) - Ground connector -3-, in wiring harness door cable - passenger side

Door control module (passenger side), switch for interior lock (passenger side), right door warning light, power mirror (passenger side), heated outside mirror

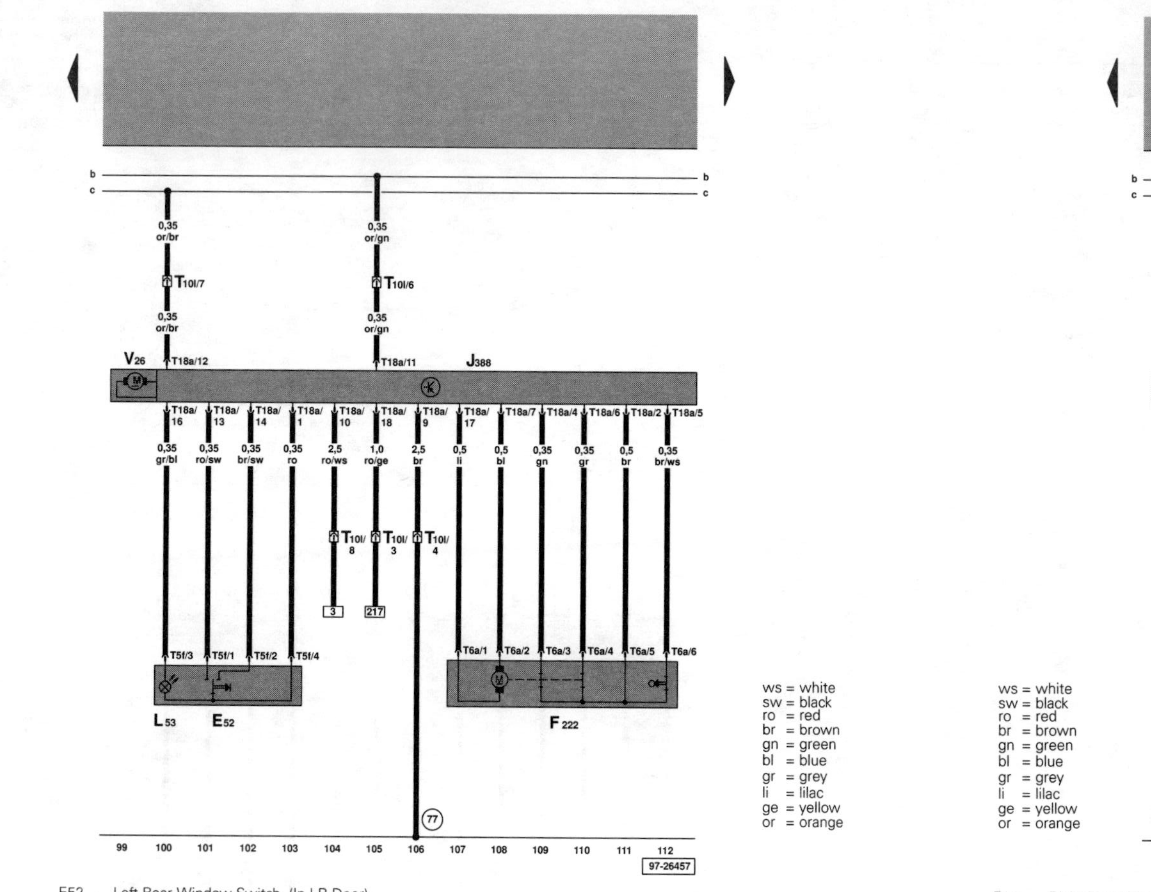

ws = white
sw = black
ro = red
br = brown
gn = green
bl = blue
gr = grey
li = lilac
ge = yellow
or = orange

E52 - Left Rear Window Switch, (In LR Door)
F222 - Lock unit for central locking, rear, left
J388 - Door control module, rear, left
L53 - Power Window Switch Light
T5f - 5-Pin Connector
T6a - 6-Pin Connector
T10l - 10-Pin Connector, black, connector station B-pillar, left
T18a - 18-Pin Connector
V26 - Motor for window regulator, rear, left

(77) - Ground connection, on left B-pillar, lower part

Door control module (rear left), left rear window switch (In LR Door), lock unit for central locking (rear left), motor for window regulator (rear left)

ws = white
sw = black
ro = red
br = brown
gn = green
bl = blue
gr = grey
li = lilac
ge = yellow
or = orange

E54 - Right Rear Window Switch, (In RR Door)
F223 - Lock unit for central locking, rear, right
J389 - Door control module, rear, right
L53 - Power Window Switch Light
T5g - 5-Pin Connector
T6b - 6-Pin Connector
T10m- 10-Pin Connector, black, connector station B-pillar, right
T18b - 18-Pin Connector
V27 - Motor for window regulator, rear, right

(78) - Ground connection, on right B-pillar, lower part

Door control module (rear right), right rear window switch (In RR Door), lock unit for central locking (rear right), motor for window regulator (rear right)

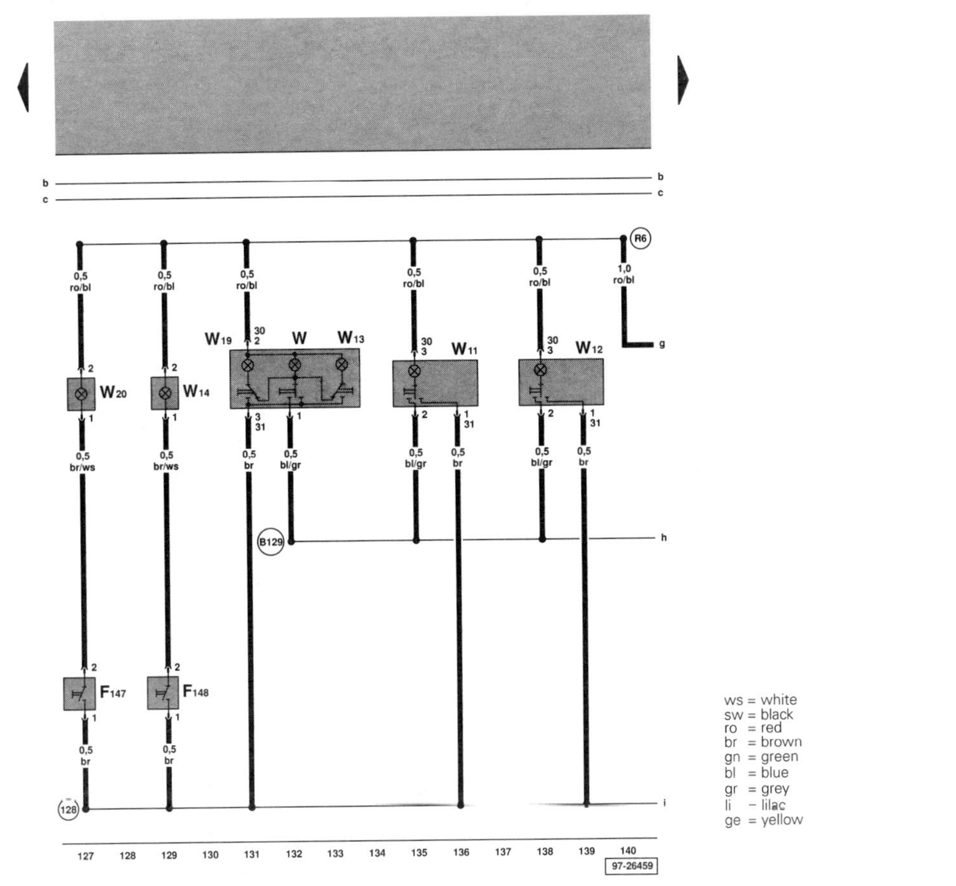

F147 - Left Make-Up Mirror Light Switch
F148 - Right Make-Up Mirror Light Switch
W - Front Interior Light
W11 - Left Rear Reading Light
W12 - Right Rear Reading Light
W13 - Right Front Map/Reading Light
W14 - Right Make-up Mirror Light
W19 - Left Front Reading Light
W20 - Left Make-up Mirror Light

(128) - Ground connection -1-, in interior light wiring harness
(B129) - Connector (interior light 3/L) in wiring harness interior
(R6) - Plus connection -1-, in interior light wiring harness

Edition 11/99
USA.5102.05.21

Interior lights, make-up mirror lights

ws = white
sw = black
ro = red
br = brown
gn = green
bl = blue
gr = grey
li = violet
li = lilac
or = orange

D - Ignition/Starter Switch
J285 - Control module with indicator unit in instrument panel insert
J393 - Central control module for comfort system, behind instrument panel, left
S237 - Fuse 37 in fuse holder
T8e - 8-Pin Connector, behind instrument panel, left
T23 - 23-Pin Connector
T32 - 32-Pin Connector, blue

(128) - Ground connection -1-, in interior light wiring harness
(238) - Ground connection -1-, in wiring harness interior
(A21) - Wire connection (86s), in instrument panel wiring harness

(A27) - Wire connection (vehicle speed signal), in instrument panel wiring harness
(A29) - Wire connection (interior light), in instrument panel wiring harness
(B129) - Connector (interior light 3/L) in wiring harness interior
(B229) - Connection (high bus), in instrument panel wiring harness
(B230) - Connection (low bus), in instrument panel wiring harness

* - Jetta only
--•--•-- - Golf only

Central control module for comfort system

Edition 11/99
USA.5102.05.21

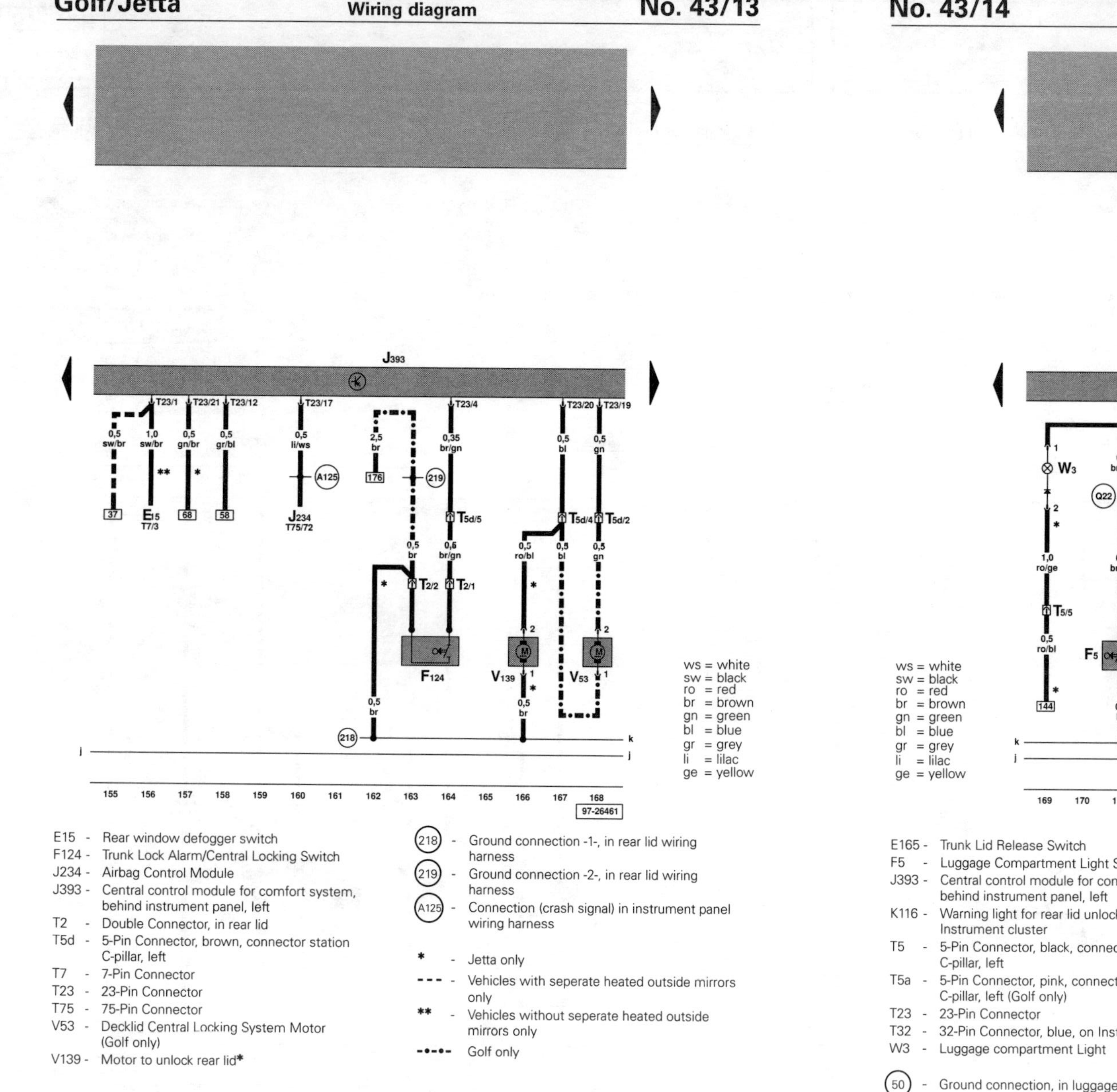

ws = white
sw = black
ro = red
br = brown
gn = green
bl = blue
gr = grey
li = lilac
ge = yellow

E15 - Rear window defogger switch
F124 - Trunk Lock Alarm/Central Locking Switch
J234 - Airbag Control Module
J393 - Central control module for comfort system, behind instrument panel, left
T2 - Double Connector, in rear lid
T5d - 5-Pin Connector, brown, connector station C-pillar, left
T7 - 7-Pin Connector
T23 - 23-Pin Connector
T75 - 75-Pin Connector
V53 - Decklid Central Locking System Motor (Golf only)
V139 - Motor to unlock rear lid*

(218) - Ground connection -1-, in rear lid wiring harness
(219) - Ground connection -2-, in rear lid wiring harness
(A125) - Connection (crash signal) in instrument panel wiring harness

* - Jetta only
--- - Vehicles with seperate heated outside mirrors only
** - Vehicles without seperate heated outside mirrors only
-•-•- Golf only

Central control module for comfort system, trunk lock alarm/central locking switch, decklid central locking system motor, motor to unlock rear lid

ws = white
sw = black
ro = red
br = brown
gn = green
bl = blue
gr = grey
li = lilac
ge = yellow

E165 - Trunk Lid Release Switch
F5 - Luggage Compartment Light Switch
J393 - Central control module for comfort system, behind instrument panel, left
K116 - Warning light for rear lid unlocked, in Instrument cluster
T5 - 5-Pin Connector, black, connector station C-pillar, left
T5a - 5-Pin Connector, pink, connector station C-pillar, left (Golf only)
T23 - 23-Pin Connector
T32 - 32-Pin Connector, blue, on Instrument cluster
W3 - Luggage compartment Light

(50) - Ground connection, in luggage compartment, left

(86) - Ground connection -1-, in rear wiring harness
(98) - Ground connection, in rear lid wiring harness
(218) - Ground connection -1-, in rear lid wiring harness
(A126) - Connection (contact switch in rear lid) in instrument panel wiring harness
(Q22) - Wire connection -1-, in rear lid wiring harness

* - Jetta only
-•-•- Golf only

Central control module for comfort system, trunk lid release switch, luggage compartment light

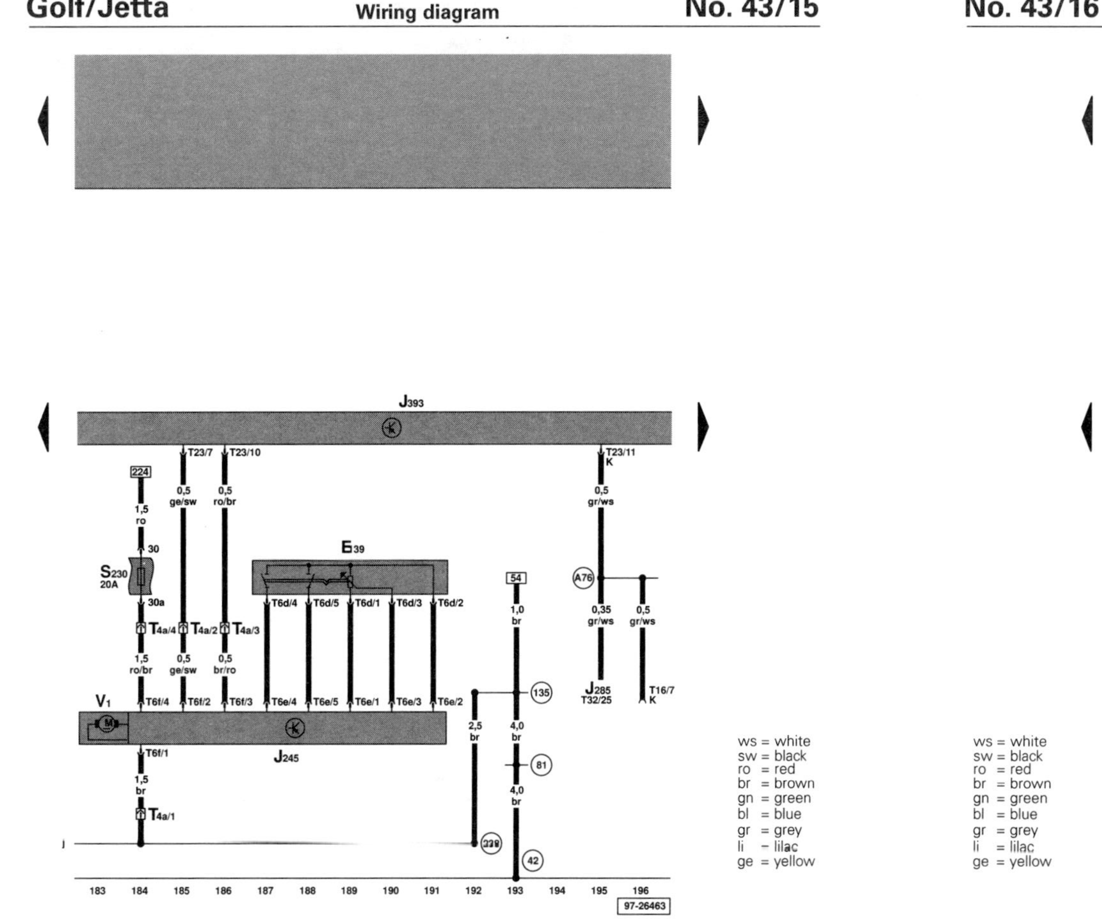

ws = white
sw = black
ro = red
br = brown
gn = green
bl = blue
gr = grey
li = lilac
ge = yellow

E139 - Sunroof Regulator
J245 - Power Sunroof Control Module
J285 - Control module with indicator unit in instrument panel insert
J393 - Central control module for comfort system, behind instrument panel, left
S230 - Fuse 30 in fuse holder
T4a - 4-Pin Connector, behind instrument panel, left
T6d - 6-Pin Connector
T6e - 6-Pin Connector
T6f - 6-Pin Connector
T16 - Data Link Connector (DLC), below instrument panel, left
T23 - 23-Pin Connector
T32 - 32-Pin Connector, blue, on Instrument cluster
V1 - Sunroof Motor

(42) - Ground connection, beside steering column
(81) - Ground connection -1-, in instrument panel wiring harness
(135) - Ground connection -2-, in instrument panel wiring harness
(238) - Ground connection -1-, in wiring harness interior
(A76) - Connector (K-diagnosis wire) in instrument panel wiring harness

Central control module for comfort system, power sunroof control module, sunroof regulator, sunroof motor

ws = white
sw = black
ro = red
br = brown
gn = green
bl = blue
gr = grey
li = lilac
ge = yellow

F120 - Hood Alarm Switch*
H8 - Alarm Horn*
J285 - Control module with indicator unit in instrument panel insert
J393 - Central control module for comfort system, behind instrument panel, left
R - Radio
R47 - Antenna wire for central locking and antitheft warning system
T2a - Double Connector, near headlight, right
T8 - 8-Pin Connector, on radio
T15 - 15-Pin Connector
T23 - 23-Pin Connector
T32 - 32-Pin Connector, blue, on Instrument cluster

(12) - Ground connection, in engine compartment, left
(179) - Ground connection, in left headlight wiring harness
(A5) - Plus connection (right turn signal), in instrument panel wiring harness
(A6) - Plus connection (left turn signal), in instrument panel wiring harness
(A13) - Wire connection (door contact switch) in instrument panel wiring harness
(B161) - Connector (anti-theft warning system), in wiring harness interior
* - Vehicles with anti-theft warning system only

Central control module for comfort system, antitheft warning system, antenna wire for central locking and antitheft warning system

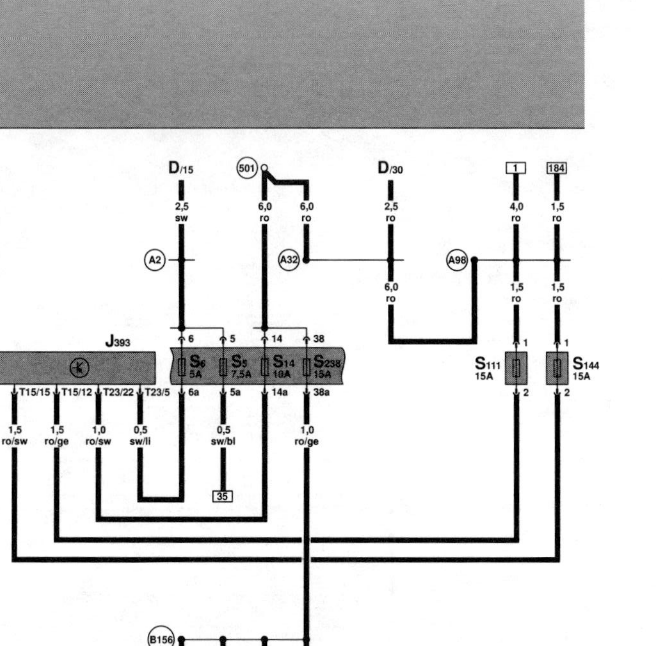

ws = white
sw = black
ro = red
br = brown
gn = green
bl = blue
gr = grey
li = lilac
ge = yellow

D - Ignition/Starter Switch
J393 - Central control module for comfort system, behind instrument panel, left
S5 - Fuse 5 in fuse holder
S6 - Fuse 6 in fuse holder
S14 - Fuse 14 in fuse holder
S111 - Alarm System and Anti-Theft Fuse, above the thirteenfold auxiliary relay panel*
S144 - Fuse for central locking/anti-theft warning system, above the thirteenfold auxiliary relay panel*
S238 - Fuse 38 in fuse holder
T15 - 15-Pin Connector
T23 - 23-Pin Connector

(501) - Threaded connection -2- (30) on the relay plate
(A2) - Plus connection (15), in instrument panel wiring harness
(A32) - Plus connection (30), in instrument panel wiring harness
(A98) - Plus connector -4- (30), in instrument panel wiring harness
(B156) - Plus connector (30a), in wiring harness interior
* - Vehicles with anti-theft warning system only

THIS PAGE INTENTIONALLY LEFT
BLANK

Cruise control,

from May 1999

- **2.0L - Engine - Motronic Multiport Fuel Injection (MFI)/85 kW, code AEG**

Deviate relay location and fuseplacements as well as the locations of multiple connectors see section "component locations".

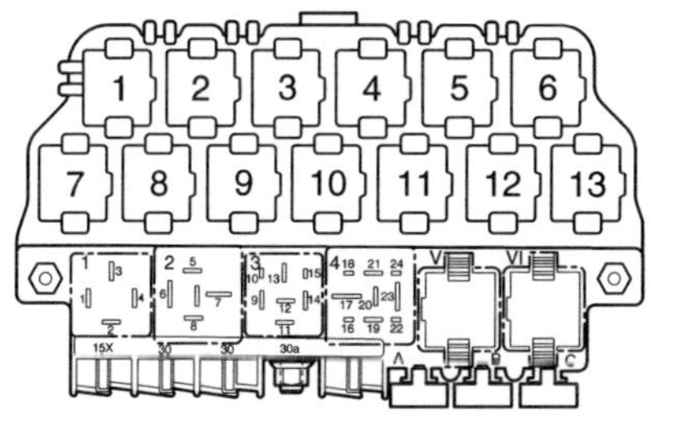
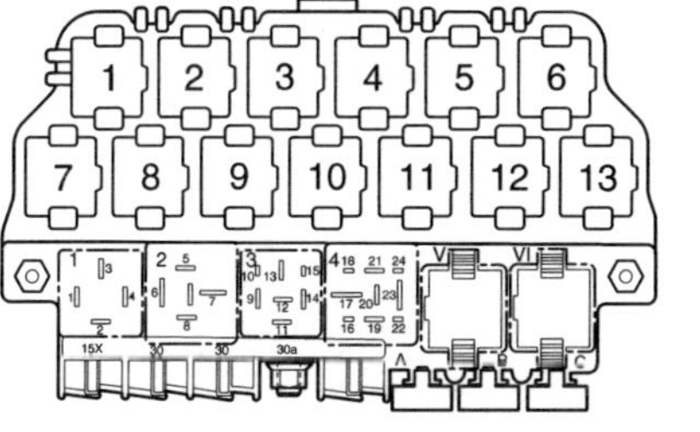

97-14163

Relay location on the thirteenfold auxiliary relay panel, above relay panel:

Relay panel:

2 Load Reduction Relay (100)

Note: Number in parentheses indicates production control number stamped on relay housing.

Fuse colors

30 A - green
25 A - white
20 A - yellow
15 A - blue
10 A - red
7,5 A - brown
5 A - beige
3 A - violet

97-27403

ws = white
sw = black
ro = red
br = brown
gn = green
bl = blue
gr = grey
ll = lilac
ge = yellow

D - Ignition/Starter Switch
F - Brake Light Switch
F36 - Clutch Vacuum Vent Valve Switch
F47 - Brake Vacuum Vent Valve Switch for cruise control
J59 - Load Reduction Relay
J220 - Motronic Engine Control Module (ECM), in plenum chamber, center
S5 - Fuse 5 in fuse holder
S13 - Fuse 13 in fuse holder
S176 - Fuse -4- (30) in fuse bracket/battery
T10e - 10-Pin Connector, black, in protective housing for connectors, in plenum chamber, left
T10w - 10-Pin Connector, white, in protective housing for connectors, in plenum chamber, left
T80 - 80-Pin Connector

(500) - Threaded connection -1- (30) on the relay plate
(501) - Threaded connection -2- (30) on the relay plate
(A2) - Plus connection (15), in instrument panel wiring harness
(A18) - Wire connection (54), in instrument panel wiring harness
(A20) - Wire connection (15a), in instrument panel wiring harness

* - Manual transmission only
--- Automatic transmission only

Motronic engine control module (ECM), brake light switch, clutch vacuum vent valve switch, brake vacuum vent valve switch for cruise control

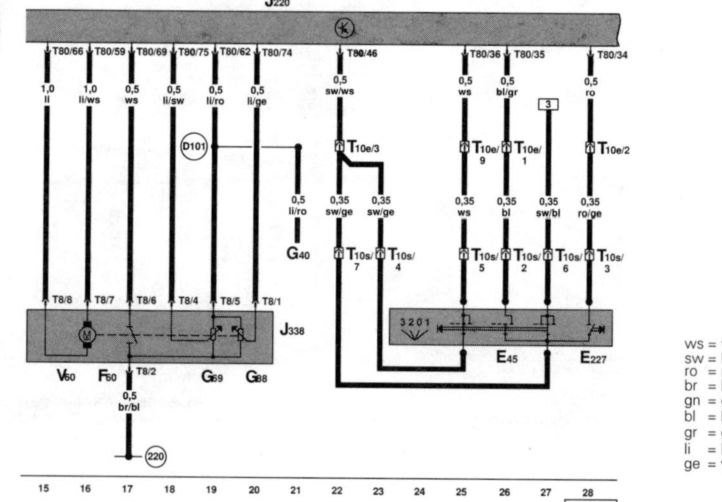

ws = white
sw = black
ro = red
br = brown
gn = green
bl = blue
gr = grey
li = lilac
ge = yellow

E45 - Cruise Control Switch
E227 - Cruise Control Push Button (SET)
F60 - Closed Throttle Position (CTP) Switch
G40 - Camshaft Position (CMP) Sensor
G69 - Throttle Position (TP) Sensor
G88 - Throttle Position (TP) Sensor
J220 - Motronic Engine Control Module (ECM), in plenum chamber, center
J338 - Throttle Valve Control Module
T8 - 8-Pin Connector
T10e - 10-Pin Connector, black, in protective housing for connectors, in plenum chamber, left
T10s - 10-Pin Connector, near steering column
T80 - 80-Pin Connector
V60 - Throttle Position (TP) Actuator

(220) - Ground connection (sensor ground), in engine compartment wiring harness
(D101) - Wire connection -1-, in engine compartment wiring harness

Motronic engine control module (ECM), cruise control switch, throttle valve control module

THIS PAGE INTENTIONALLY LEFT
BLANK

Airbag systems for vehicles with overlay wiring harness repair

from September 1998

applies to vehicles through model year 1999 only.

- ☆ **Driver- and front passsenger airbag**
- ☆ **Side airbag**
- ☆ **Seat belt tensioner**
- ☆ **Seat belt control**

Deviate relay location and fuseplacements as well as the locations of multiple connectors see section • component locations•.

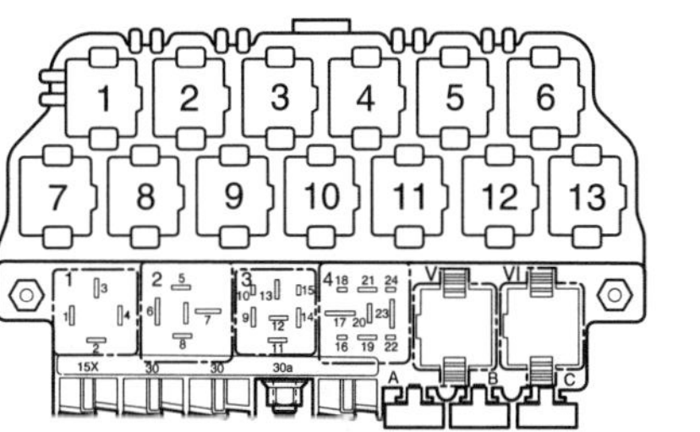

Relay location on the thirteenfold auxiliary relay panel, above relay panel:

Relay panel:

1 Dual Horn Relay (53)

Note: Number in parentheses indicates production control number stamped on relay housing.

Fuse colors

30 A - green
25 A - white
20 A - yellow
15 A - blue
10 A - red
7,5 A - brown
5 A - beige
3 A - violet

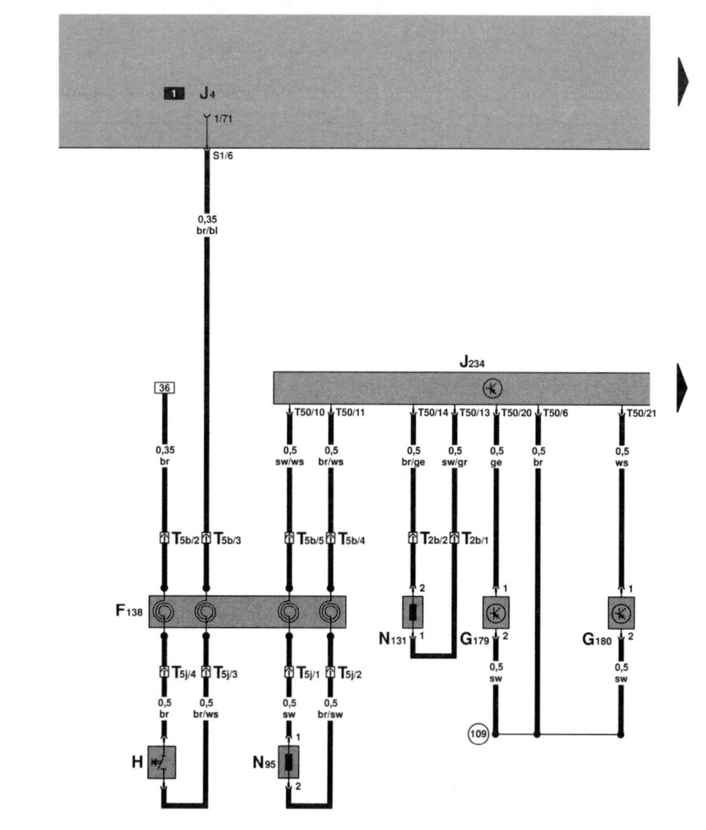

ws = white
sw = black
ro = red
br = brown
gn = green
bl = blue
gr = grey
li = lilac
ge = yellow

F138 - Airbag spiral spring/return spring with slip ring
G179 - Crash sensor for side airbag, driver•s side
G180 - Crash sensor for side airbag, passenger side
H - Signal horn activation
J4 - Dual Horn Relay
J234 - Airbag Control Module, behind console, lower part
N95 - Driver•s Side Airbag Igniter
N131 - Passenger•s Side Airbag Igniter 1
T2b - 2-Pin Connector, on passenger•s side airbag igniter 1
T5b - 5-Pin Connector, beside steering column
T5j - 5-Pin Connector, behind driver•s airbag
T50 - 50-Pin Connector

(109) - Ground connection, in airbag wiring harness

Airbag control module, airbag spiral spring/return spring with slip ring, crash sensor for side airbag, airbag igniter

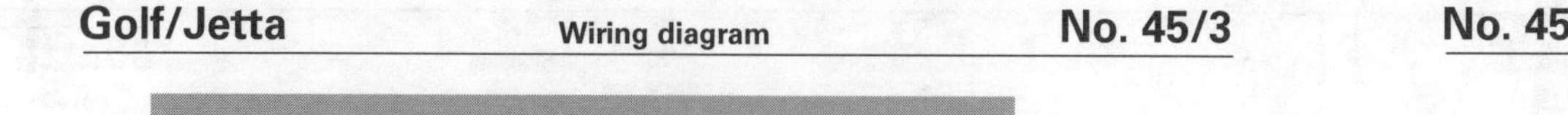

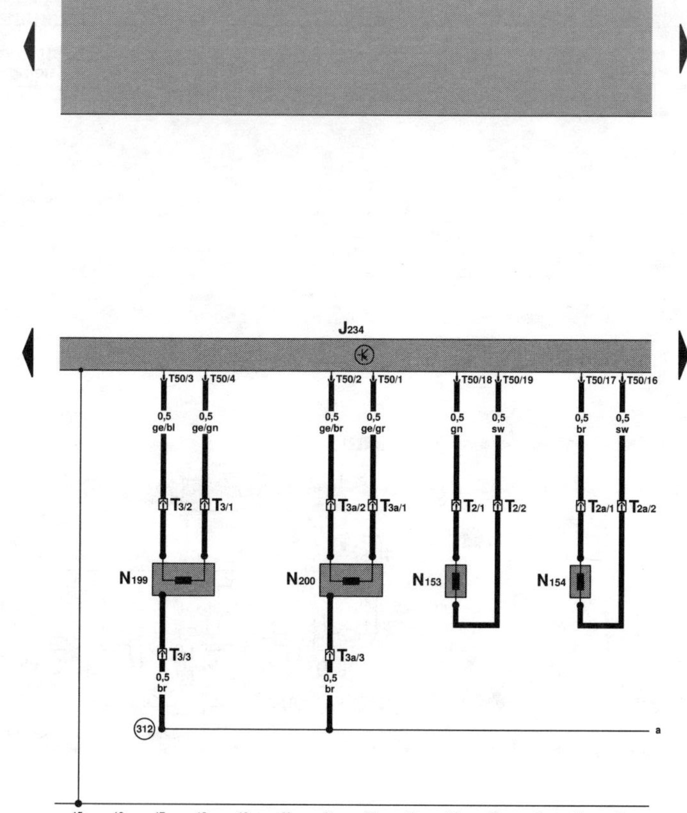

ws = white
sw = black
ro = red
br = brown
gn = green
bl = blue
gr = grey
li = lilac
ge = yellow

J234 - Airbag Control Module, behind console, lower part
N153 - Left Seat Belt Tensioner Igniter
N154 - Right Seat Belt Tensioner Igniter
N199 - Igniter for side airbag, driver's side
N200 - Igniter for side airbag, passenger side
T2 - Double Connector, below driver's seat
T2a - Double Connector, below driver's seat
T3 - 3-Pin Connector, below driver's seat
T3a - 3-Pin Connector, below passenger's seat
T50 - 50-Pin Connector

(312) - Ground connection, in airbag wiring harness

Airbag control module, seat belt tensioner igniter, igniter for side airbag

J234 A76 T50/30 T50/5 T50/34 T50/9 K T16/7 K T32/31 T32/25 T32/6
0,35 br/gn 0,5 gr/ws 0,5 gr/ws 0,35 gr/ws 0,35 br/gn
0,5 br 0,5 sw 0,35 li/ws 0,35 gr/ws 0,35 ge
T4/3 T4/1 T4/4 T4/2
K19 J285 H3 K75 E24
A2 A125 3
2,5 sw 0,5 li/ws 0,35 br 0,35 br 4,0 br 4,0 br
D/15 J393 81 135 42 312 a
29 30 31 32 33 34 35 36 37 38 39 40 41 42
97-26661

ws = white
sw = black
ro = red
br = brown
gn = green
bl = blue
gr = grey
li = lilac
ge = yellow

D - Ignition/Starter Switch
E24 - Left Seat Belt Switch
H3 - Warning Buzzer
J234 - Airbag Control Module, behind console, lower part
J285 - Control module with indicator unit in instrument panel insert
J393 - Central control module for comfort system
K19 - Seat Belt Warning Light
K75 - Airbag Malfunction Indicator Lamp (MIL)
T4 - 4-Pin Connector, behind instrument panel right (connection for repair wiring harness)
T16 - Data Link Connector (DLC), below instrument panel, left
T32 - 32-Pin Connector, blue
T50 - 50-Pin Connector

(42) - Ground connection, beside steering column
(81) - Ground connection -1-, in instrument panel wiring harness
(135) - Ground connection -2-, in instrument panel wiring harness
(312) - Ground connection, in airbag wiring harness
(A2) - Plus connection (15), in instrument panel wiring harness
(A76) - Connector (K-diagnosis wire) in instrument panel wiring harness
(A125) - Connection (crash signal) in instrument panel wiring harness

Airbag control module, left seat belt switch, seat belt warning light, airbag malfunction indicator lamp (MIL), connection for repair wiring harness

Multi-function steering wheel for cruise control and radio

from May 2000

Deviate relay location and fuseplacements as well as the locations of multiple connectors see section "component locations".

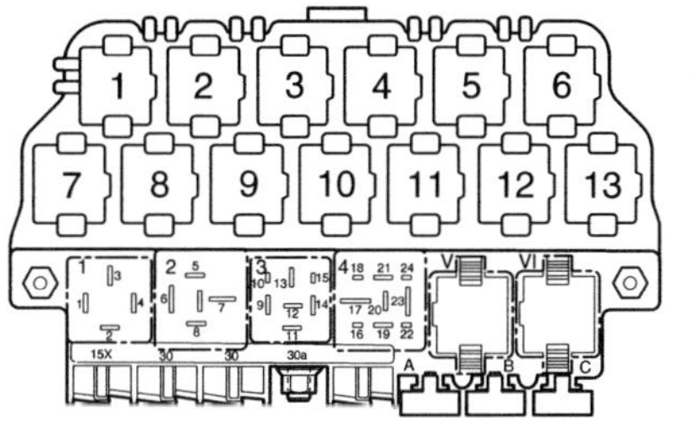
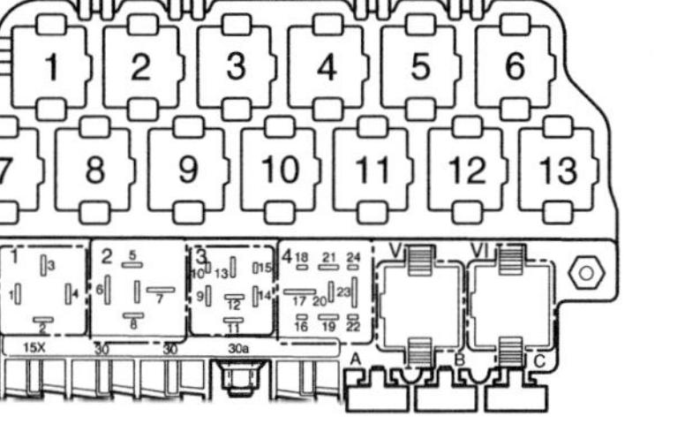

Relay location on the thirteenfold auxiliary relay panel, above relay panel:

Relay panel:

- **2** Load Reduction Relay (100)
- **4** Fuel Pump (FP) Relay (409)

Note: Number in parentheses indicates production control number stamped on relay housing.

Fuse colors

30 A - green
25 A - white
20 A - yellow
15 A - blue
10 A - red
7,5 A - brown
5 A - beige
3 A - violet

ws = white
sw = black
ro = red
br = brown
gn = green
bl = blue
gr = grey
li = lilac
ge = yellow

E221 - Control unit in steering wheel
F138 - Airbag Spiral Spring/Return Spring with Slip Ring
H - Signal horn activation
J234 - Airbag Control Module
L45 - Operating Unit Light
N95 - Driver's Side Airbag Igniter
T5b - 5-Pin Connector, on airbag spiral spring
T5j - 5-Pin Connector, behind driver's airbag
T75 - 75-Pin Connector

(42) - Ground connection, beside steering column

(81) - Ground connection -1-, in instrument panel wiring harness

(135) - Ground connection -2-, in instrument panel wiring harness

(A20) - Wire connection (15a), in instrument panel wiring harness

Control unit in steering wheel, signal horn activation, airbag spiral spring/return spring with slip ring, driver's side airbag igniter

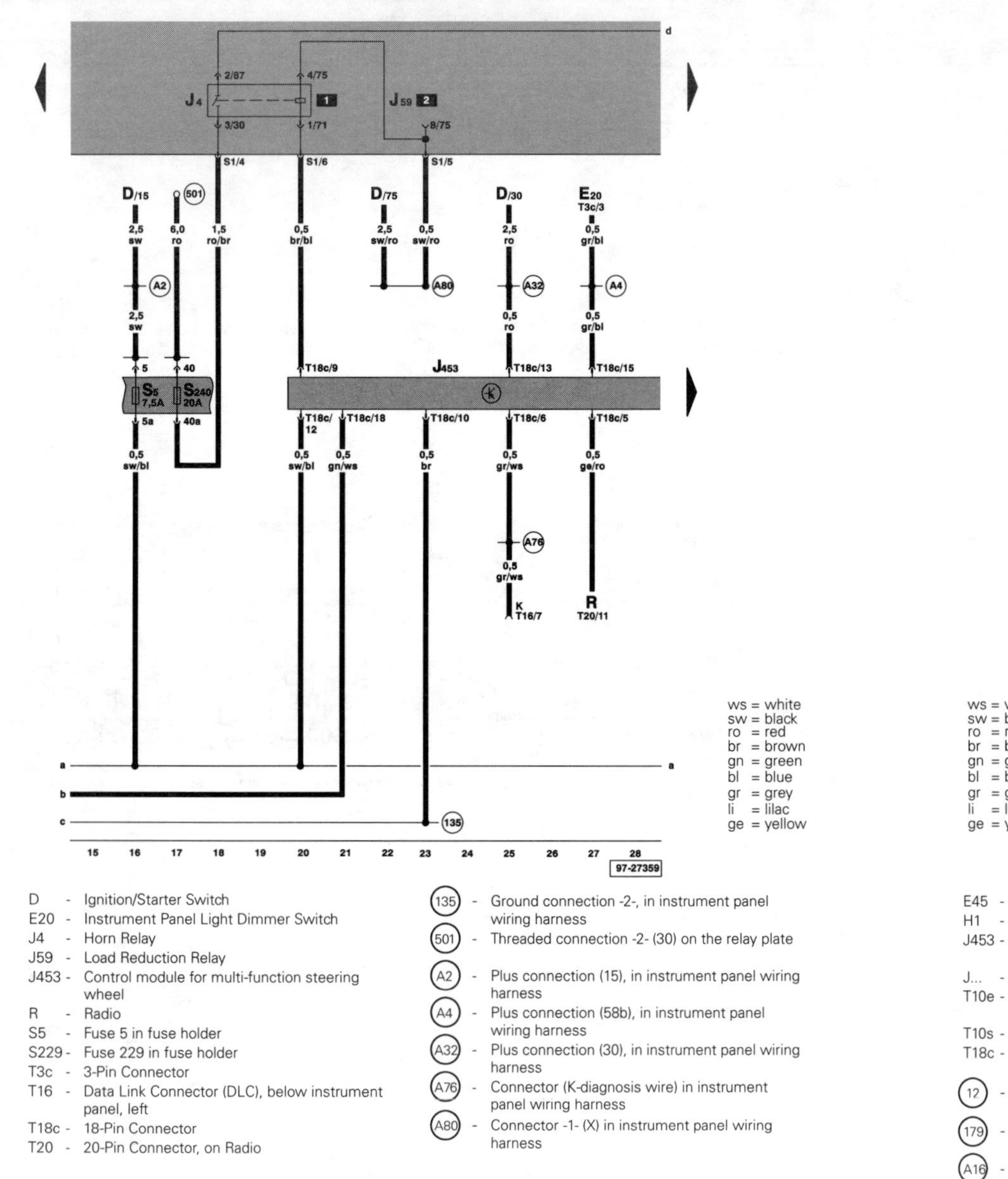

ws = white
sw = black
ro = red
br = brown
gn = green
bl = blue
gr = grey
li = lilac
ge = yellow

- D - Ignition/Starter Switch
- E20 - Instrument Panel Light Dimmer Switch
- J4 - Horn Relay
- J59 - Load Reduction Relay
- J453 - Control module for multi-function steering wheel
- R - Radio
- S5 - Fuse 5 in fuse holder
- S229 - Fuse 229 in fuse holder
- T3c - 3-Pin Connector
- T16 - Data Link Connector (DLC), below instrument panel, left
- T18c - 18-Pin Connector
- T20 - 20-Pin Connector, on Radio

- (135) - Ground connection -2-, in instrument panel wiring harness
- (501) - Threaded connection -2- (30) on the relay plate
- (A2) - Plus connection (15), in instrument panel wiring harness
- (A4) - Plus connection (58b), in instrument panel wiring harness
- (A32) - Plus connection (30), in instrument panel wiring harness
- (A76) - Connector (K-diagnosis wire) in instrument panel wiring harness
- (A80) - Connector -1- (X) in instrument panel wiring harness

Control module for multi-function steering wheel, horn relay

ws = white
sw = black
ro = red
br = brown
gn = green
bl = blue
gr = grey
li = lilac
ge = yellow

- E45 - Cruise Control Switch
- H1 - Dual tone horn
- J453 - Control module for multi-function steering wheel
- J... - Engine Control Module (ECM)
- T10e - 10-Pin Connector, black, in protective housing for connectors, in plenum chamber, left*
- T10s - 10-Pin Connector, near steering column
- T18c - 18-Pin Connector

- (12) - Ground connection, in engine compartment, left
- (179) - Ground connection, in left headlight wiring harness
- (A16) - Wire connection (cruise control), in instrument panel wiring harness
- (A20) - Wire connection (15a), in instrument panel wiring harness
- (A90) - Connector (two-tone horn), in instrument panel wiring harness
- * - See also wiring diagram cruise control/ motor

Control module for multi-function steering wheel, dual tone horn, cruise control switch

1.8L - Engine - Motronic Multiport Fuel Injection (MFI)/110 kW, code AWW,

from June 2000

Deviate relay location and fuseplacements as well as the locations of multiple connectors see section "component locations".

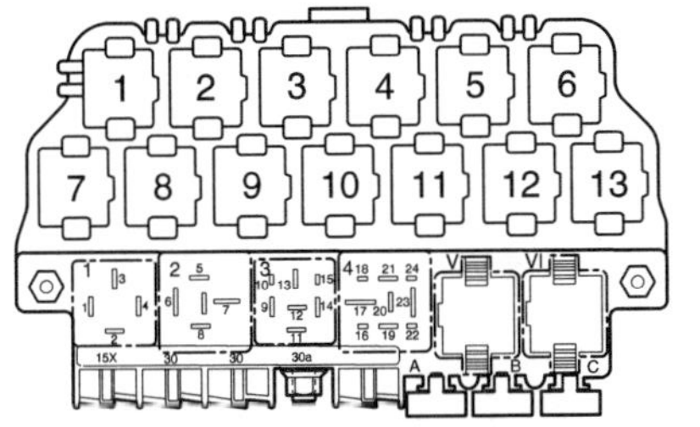

Relay location on the thirteenfold auxiliary relay panel, above relay panel:

Relay panel:

2 Load Reduction Relay (100)

4 Fuel Pump (FP) Relay (409)

Note: Number in parentheses indicates production control number stamped on relay housing.

Fuse colors

30 A - green
25 A - white
20 A - yellow
15 A - blue
10 A - red
7,5 A - brown
5 A - beige
3 A - violet

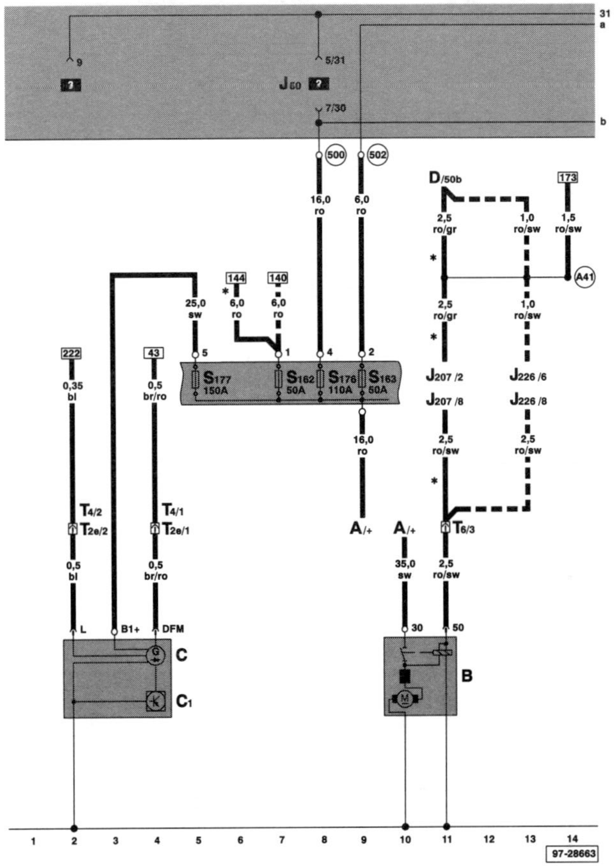

ws = white
sw = black
ro = red
br = brown
gn = green
bl = blue
gr = grey
li = lilac
ge = yellow

97-28663

A - Battery
B - Starter
C - Generator (GEN)
C1 - Voltage Regulator (VR)
D - Ignition/Starter Switch
J59 - Load Reduction Relay
J207 - Starting Interlock Relay
J226 - Park/Neutral Position (PNP) Relay
S162 - Fuse -1- (30) in fuse bracket/battery
S163 - Fuse -2- (30) in fuse bracket/battery
S176 - Fuse -4- (30) in fuse bracket/battery
S177 - Fuse -5- (30) in fuse bracket/battery
T2e - Double Connector, near starter (vehicles without air conditioning)
T4 - 4-Pin Connector, near starter (vehicles with air conditioning only)
T6 - 6-Pin Connector, brown, in protective housing for connectors, in plenum chamber, left

(500) - Threaded connection -1- (30) on the relay plate

(502) - Threaded connection -1- (30a) on the relay plate

(A41) - Plus connection (50), in instrument panel wiring harness

* - Manual transmission only

--- Automatic transmission only

Generator (GEN), starter

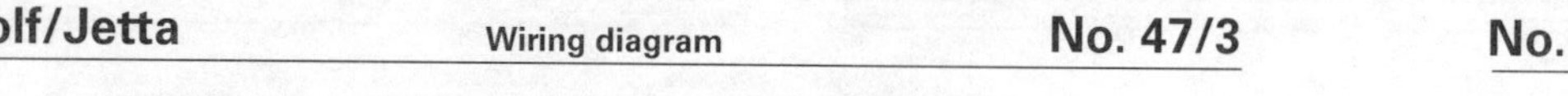

ws = white
sw = black
ro = red
br = brown
gn = green
bl = blue
gr = grey
li = lilac
ge = yellow

15 16 17 18 19 20 21 22 23 24 25 26 27 28

97-27549

D - Ignition/Starter Switch
J271 - Motronic engine control module (ECM) power supply relay, in protective housing, in engine compartment, left, production control number (428)
S10 - Fuse 10 in fuse holder
S229 - Fuse 29 in fuse holder
S231 - Fuse 31 in fuse holder
T2 - 2-Pin Connector, in engine compartment, left
T6 - 6-Pin Connector, brown, in protective housing for connectors, in plenum chamber, left
T14a - 14-Pin Connector, in engine compartment, in wiring duct, left

(501) - Threaded connection -2- (30) on the relay plate

(A2) - Plus connection (15), in instrument panel wiring harness
(A32) - Plus connection (30), in instrument panel wiring harness
(A98) - Plus connector -4- (30), in instrument panel wiring harness
(A104) - Plus connector -2- (15), in instrument panel wiring harness
(D78) - Plus connector -1- (30a), in engine compartment wiring harness

--- Automatic transmission only

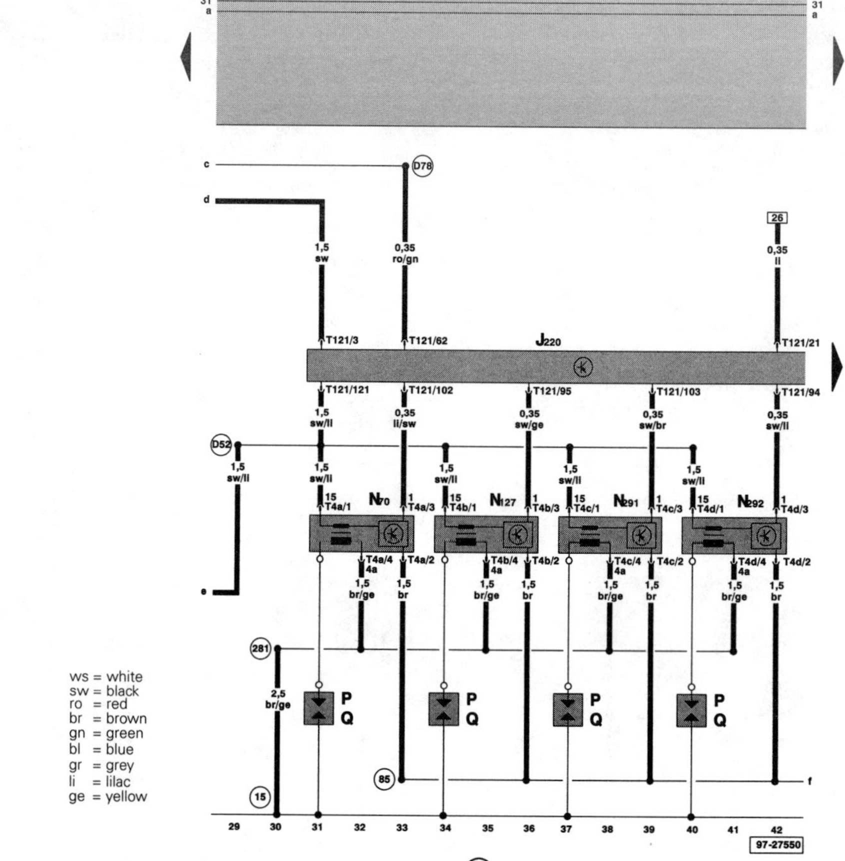

ws = white
sw = black
ro = red
br = brown
gn = green
bl = blue
gr = grey
li = lilac
ge = yellow

29 30 31 32 33 34 35 36 37 38 39 40 41 42

97-27550

J220 - Motronic Engine Control Module (ECM), in plenum chamber, center
N70 - Ignition Coil 1 with Power Output Stage
N127 - Ignition Coil 2 with Power Output Stage
N291 - Ignition Coil 3 with Power Output Stage
N292 - Ignition Coil 4 with Power Output Stage
P - Spark Plug Connectors
Q - Spark Plugs
T4a - 4-Pin Connector
T4b - 4-Pin Connector
T4c - 4-Pin Connector
T4d - 4-Pin Connector
T121 - Connector, 121 point

(15) - Ground connection, on cylinder head

(85) - Ground connection -1-, in engine compartment wiring harness
(281) - Ground connector -1-, in wiring harness engine pre-wiring
(D52) - Plus connector (15a), in engine compartment wiring harness
(D78) - Plus connector -1- (30a), in engine compartment wiring harness

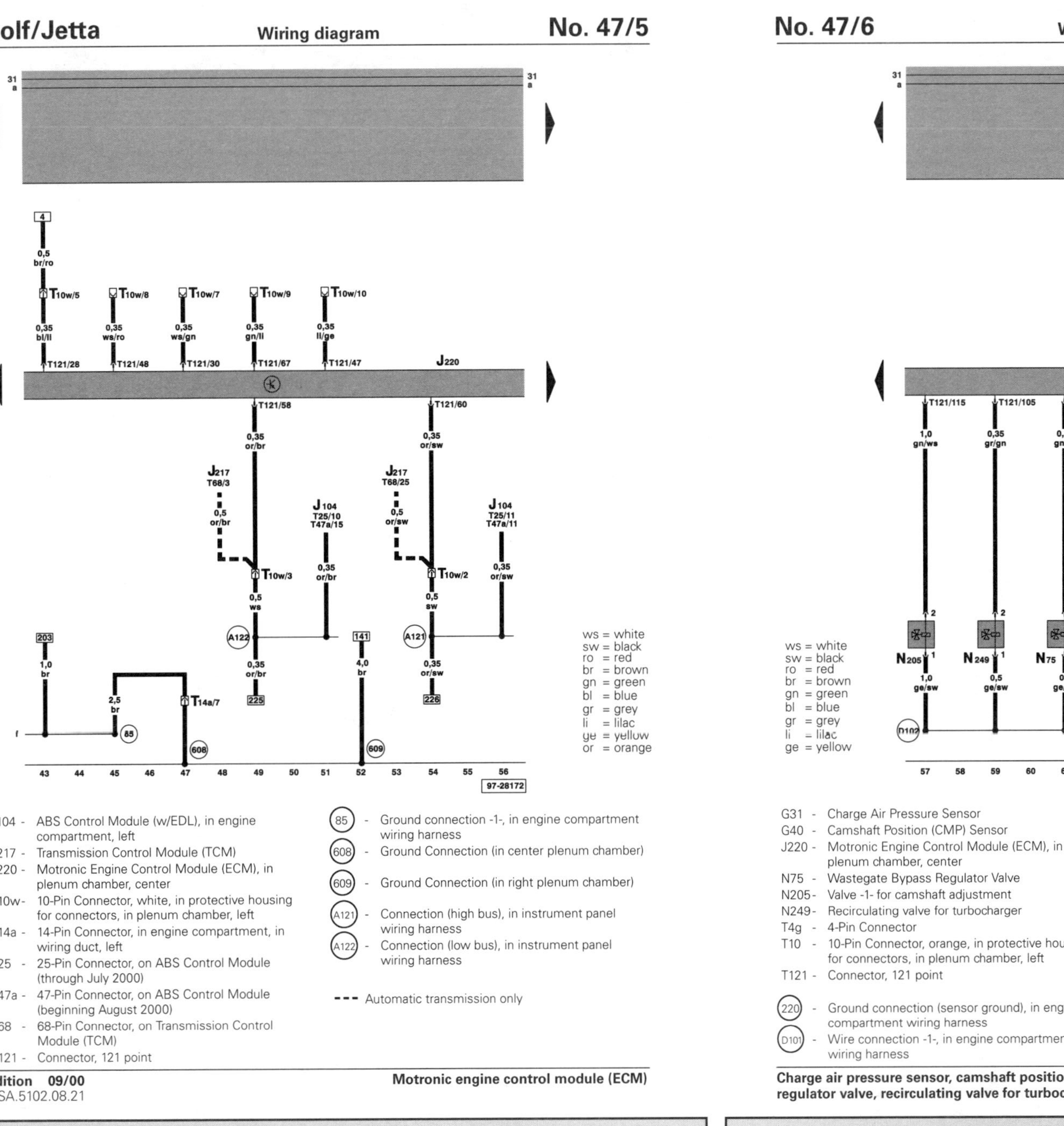

ws = white
sw = black
ro = red
br = brown
gn = green
bl = blue
gr = grey
li = lilac
ge = yellow
or = orange

J104 - ABS Control Module (w/EDL), in engine compartment, left
J217 - Transmission Control Module (TCM)
J220 - Motronic Engine Control Module (ECM), in plenum chamber, center
T10w- 10-Pin Connector, white, in protective housing for connectors, in plenum chamber, left
T14a - 14-Pin Connector, in engine compartment, in wiring duct, left
T25 - 25-Pin Connector, on ABS Control Module (through July 2000)
T47a - 47-Pin Connector, on ABS Control Module (beginning August 2000)
T68 - 68-Pin Connector, on Transmission Control Module (TCM)
T121 - Connector, 121 point

(85) - Ground connection -1-, in engine compartment wiring harness
(608) - Ground Connection (in center plenum chamber)
(609) - Ground Connection (in right plenum chamber)
(A121) - Connection (high bus), in instrument panel wiring harness
(A122) - Connection (low bus), in instrument panel wiring harness

--- Automatic transmission only

Motronic engine control module (ECM)

ws = white
sw = black
ro = red
br = brown
gn = green
bl = blue
gr = grey
li = lilac
ge = yellow

G31 - Charge Air Pressure Sensor
G40 - Camshaft Position (CMP) Sensor
J220 - Motronic Engine Control Module (ECM), in plenum chamber, center
N75 - Wastegate Bypass Regulator Valve
N205 - Valve -1- for camshaft adjustment
N249 - Recirculating valve for turbocharger
T4g - 4-Pin Connector
T10 - 10-Pin Connector, orange, in protective housing for connectors, in plenum chamber, left
T121 - Connector, 121 point

(220) - Ground connection (sensor ground), in engine compartment wiring harness
(D101) - Wire connection -1-, in engine compartment wiring harness
(D102) - Wire connection -2-, in engine compartment wiring harness

Charge air pressure sensor, camshaft position (CMP) sensor, wastegate bypass regulator valve, recirculating valve for turbocharger, valve for camshaft adjustment

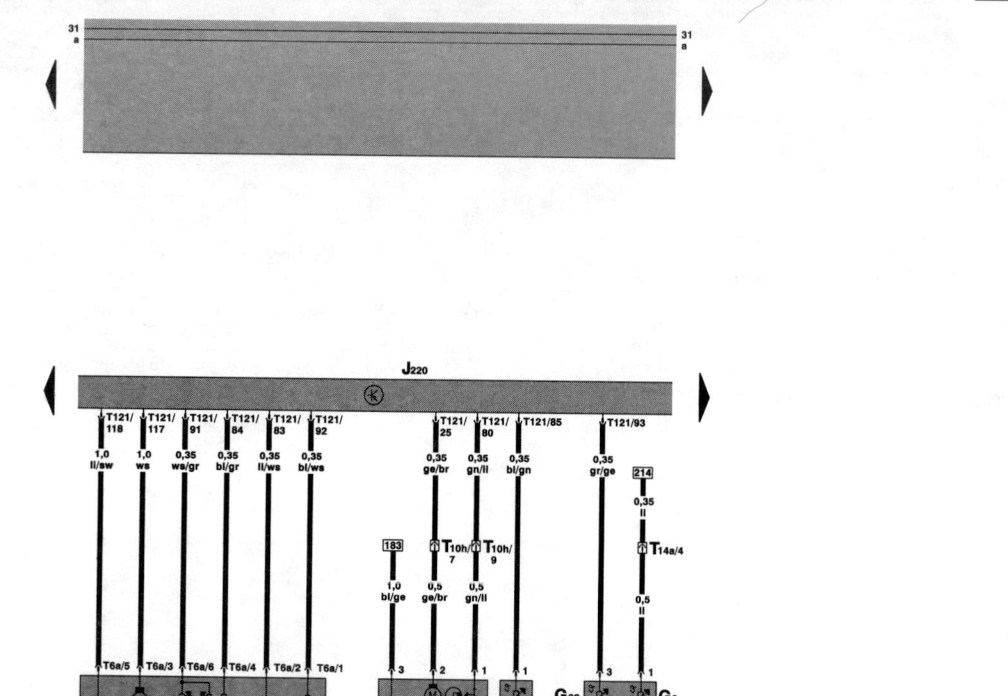

ws = white
sw = black
ro = red
br = brown
gn = green
bl = blue
gr = grey
li = lilac
ge = yellow

G2 - Engine Coolant Temperature (ECT) Sensor
G42 - Intake Air Temperature (IAT) Sensor
G62 - Engine Coolant Temperature (ECT) Sensor
G186 - Throttle drive (power accelerator actuation)
G187 - Angle sensor -1- for throttle drive (power accelerator actuation)
G188 - Angle sensor -2- for throttle drive (power accelerator actuation)
J220 - Motronic Engine Control Module (ECM), in plenum chamber, center
J338 - Throttle Valve Control Module
T6a - 6-Pin Connector
T10h - 10-Pin Connector, blue, in protective housing for connectors, in plenum chamber, left
T14a - 14-Pin Connector, in engine compartment, in wiring duct, left
T121 - Connector, 121 point
V144 - Leak detection pump (LDP)

Edition 07/00
USA.5102.07.21

Motronic engine control module (ECM), angle sensor for throttle drive (power accelerator actuation), intake air temperature (IAT) sensor, (ECT) sensor, leak detection pump (LDP)

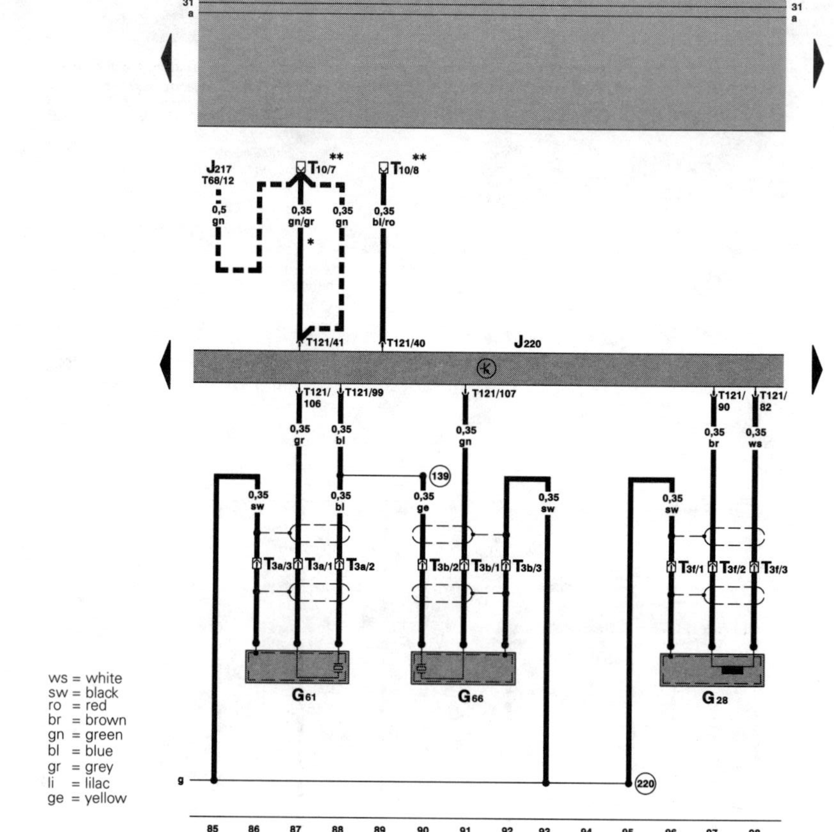

ws = white
sw = black
ro = red
br = brown
gn = green
bl = blue
gr = grey
li = lilac
ge = yellow

G28 - Engine Speed (RPM) Sensor
G61 - Knock Sensor (KS) 1
G66 - Knock Sensor (KS) 2
J217 - Transmission Control Module (TCM)
J220 - Motronic Engine Control Module (ECM), in plenum chamber, center
T3a - 3-Pin Connector, in engine compartment, front
T3b - 3-Pin Connector, in engine compartment, front
T3f - 3-Pin Connector, in engine compartment, front
T10 - 10-Pin Connector, orange, in protective housing for connectors, in plenum chamber, left
T68 - Connector, 68 point
T121 - Connector, 121 point

(139) - Ground connection (sensor Ground), in Motronic Multiport Fuel Injection (MFI) wiring harness
(220) - Ground connection (sensor ground), in engine compartment wiring harness

* - Manual transmission only
** - A/C connection
--- Automatic transmission only

Motronic engine control module (ECM), engine speed (RPM) sensor, knock sensor (KS) 1, knock sensor (KS) 2

Edition 07/00
USA.5102.07.21

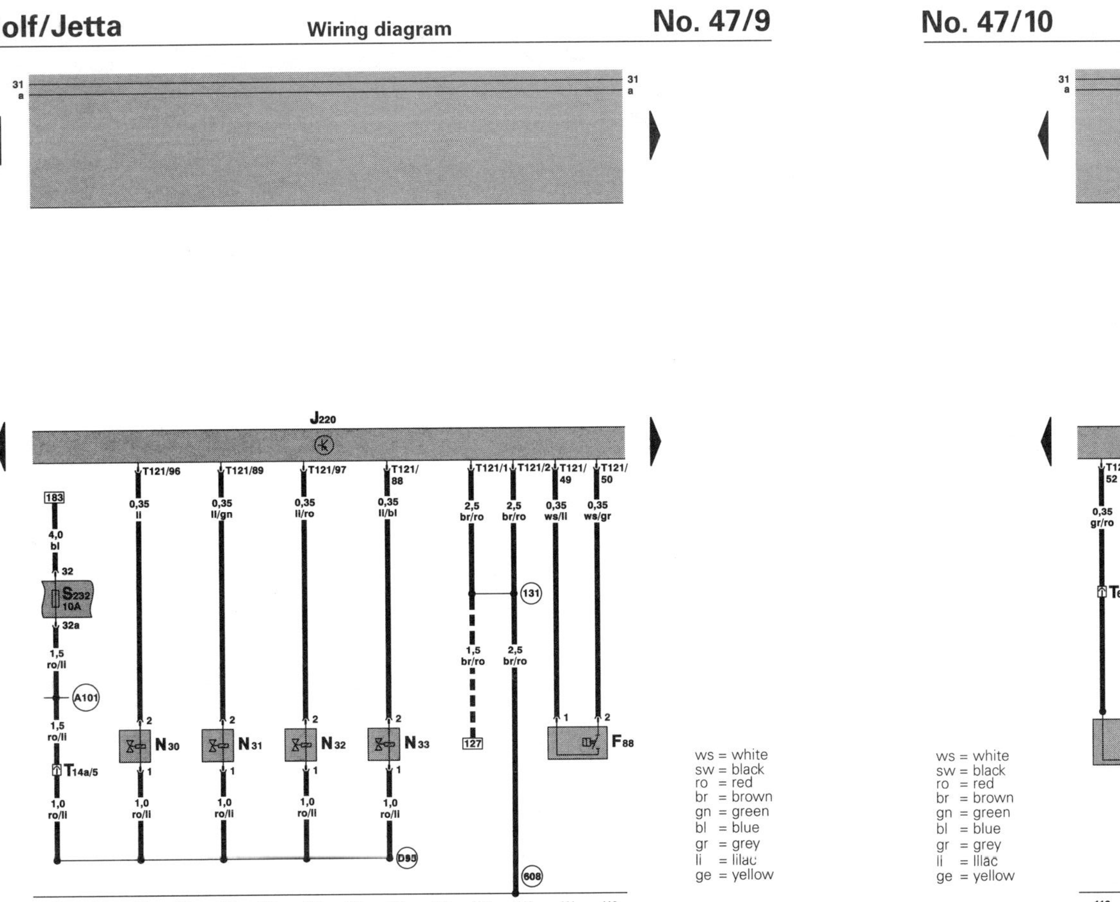

ws = white
sw = black
ro = red
br = brown
gn = green
bl = blue
gr = grey
li = lilac
ge = yellow

F88 - Pressure switch/power steering
J220 - Motronic Engine Control Module (ECM), in plenum chamber, center
N30 - Cylinder 1 Fuel Injector
N31 - Cylinder 2 Fuel Injector
N32 - Cylinder 3 Fuel Injector
N33 - Cylinder 4 Fuel Injector
S232 - Fuse 32 in fuse holder
T14a - 14-Pin Connector, in engine compartment, in wiring duct, left
T121 - Connector, 121 point

(131) - Ground connection -2-, in engine compartment wiring harness
(608) - Ground Connection (in center plenum chamber)

(A101) - Connector -3- (87a), in instrument panel wiring harness
(D95) - Wire connection (injectors), in engine compartment wiring harness

--- Automatic transmission only

Edition 07/00 USA.5102.07.21 **Motronic engine control module (ECM), pressure switch/power steering, injectors**

ws = white
sw = black
ro = red
br = brown
gn = green
bl = blue
gr = grey
li = lilac
ge = yellow

G39 - Heated Oxygen Sensor (HO2S)
G130 - Oxygen Sensor (O2S) behind Three Way Catalytic Converter (TWC)
J220 - Motronic Engine Control Module (ECM), in plenum chamber, center
N80 - Evaporative Emission (EVAP) Canister Purge Regulator Valve
T4f - 4-Pin Connector, in protective housing for connectors under right floor
T6c - 6-Pin Connector, in protective housing for connectors under right floor
T121 - Connector, 121 point

(E30) - Connector (87a), in wiring harness engine

Heated oxygen sensor (HO2S), oxygen sensor (O2S) behind three way catalytic converter (TWC), evaporative emission (EVAP) canister purge regulator valve

Edition 07/00 USA.5102.07.21

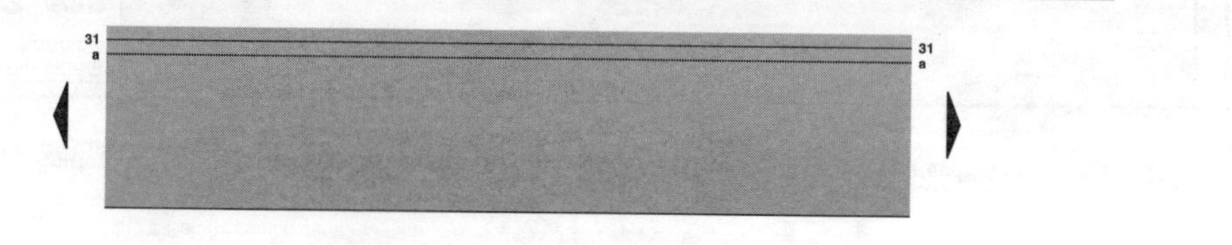

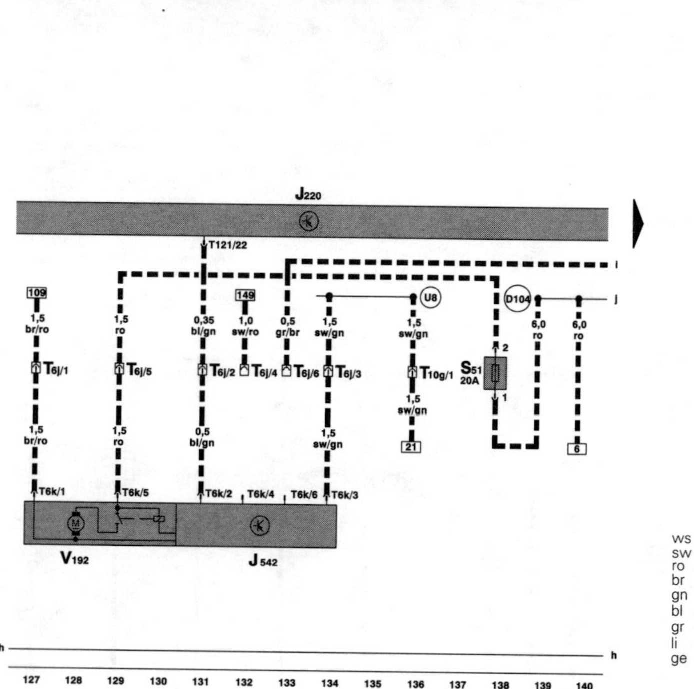

ws = white
sw = black
ro = red
br = brown
gn = green
bl = blue
gr = grey
li = lilac
ge = yellow

J220 - Motronic Engine Control Module (ECM), in plenum chamber, center
J542 - Brake Booster Control Module
S51 - Fuse, in protective housing, in engine compartment, left
T6j - 6-Pin Connector, in engine compartment left
T6k - 6-Pin Connector
T10g - 10-Pin Connector, grey, in protective housing for connectors, in plenum chamber, left
T121 - Connector, 121 point
V192 - Brake System Vacuum Pump

D104 - Plus connection -2- (30a), in engine compartment wiring harness
U8 - Plus Connection (15a) in automatic transmission wiring harness

--- Automatic transmission only

Edition 12/00
USA.5102.09.21

Motronic engine control module (ECM), brake booster control module, brake system vacuum pump

ws = white
sw = black
ro = red
br = brown
gn = green
bl = blue
gr = grey
li = lilac
ge = yellow

F - Brake Light Switch
F47 - Brake Vacuum Vent Valve Switch for cruise control
J220 - Motronic Engine Control Module (ECM), in plenum chamber, center
J299 - Secondary Air Injection (AIR) Pump Relay, in protective housing, in engine compartment, left, production control number (100)
N112 - Secondary Air Injection (AIR) Solenoid Valve
S13 - Fuse 13 in fuse holder
S130 - Fuse for secondary air pump, in protective housing, in engine compartment, left
T2f - Double Connector, in engine compartment left
T10e - 10-Pin Connector, black, in protective housing for connectors, in plenum chamber, left
T121 - Connector, 121 point

V101 - Secondary Air Injection (AIR) Pump Motor
A18 - Wire connection (54), in instrument panel
A20 - Wire connection (15a), in instrument panel wiring harness
D103 - Wire connection -3-, in engine compartment wiring harness
D104 - Plus connection -2- (30a), in engine compartment wiring harness

* - Manual transmission only
--- Automatic transmission only

Motronic engine control module (ECM), secondary air injection (AIR) pump system, brake light switch, brake vacuum vent valve switch for cruise control

Edition 12/00
USA.5102.09.21

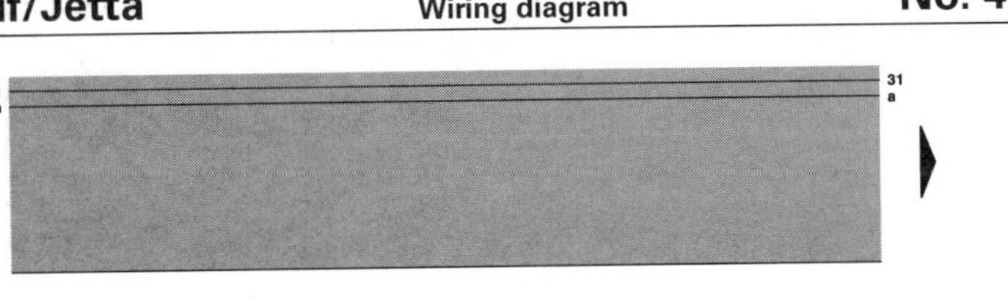

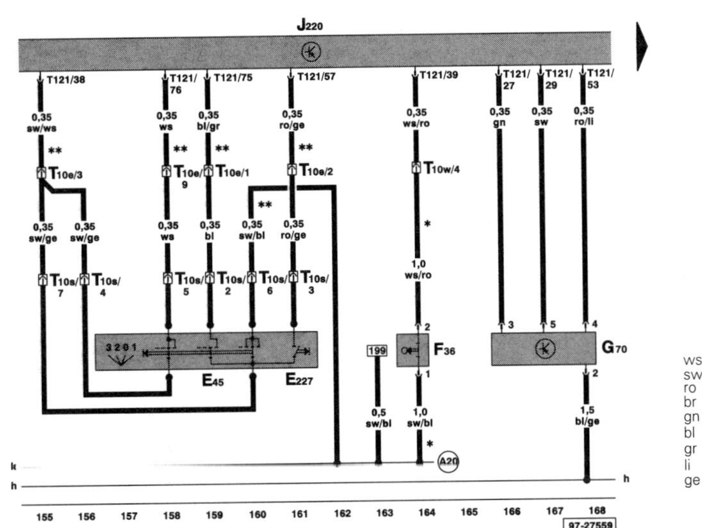

ws = white
sw = black
ro = red
br = brown
gn = green
bl = blue
gr = grey
li = lilac
ge = yellow

E45 - Cruise Control Switch**
E227 - Cruise Control Push Button (SET)**
F36 - Clutch Vacuum Vent Valve Switch
G70 - Mass Air Flow (MAF) Sensor
J220 - Motronic Engine Control Module (ECM), in plenum chamber, center
T10e - 10-Pin Connector, black, in protective housing for connectors, in plenum chamber, left
T10s - 10-Pin Connector, near steering column
T10w - 10-Pin Connector, white, in protective housing for connectors, in plenum chamber, left
T121 - Connector, 121 point

(A20) - Wire connection (15a), in instrument panel wiring harness

* - Manual transmission only
** - Vehicles with cruise control only

Edition 07/00
USA.5102.07.21

Motronic engine control module (ECM), cruise control switch, mass air flow (MAF) sensor, clutch vacuum vent valve switch

ws = white
sw = black
ro = red
br = brown
gn = green
bl = blue
gr = grey
li = lilac
ge = yellow

G79 - Throttle Position (TP) Sensor
G185 - Sender -2- for accelerator pedal position
J17 - Fuel Pump (FP) Relay
J220 - Motronic Engine Control Module (ECM), in plenum chamber, center
J234 - Airbag Control Module
T6 - 6-Pin Connector, brown, in protective housing for connectors, in plenum chamber, left
T6b - 6-Pin Connector
T10 - 10-Pin Connector, orange, in protective housing for connectors, in plenum chamber, left
T10h - 10-Pin Connector, blue, in protective housing for connectors, in plenum chamber, left
T75 - 75-Pin Connector
T121 - Connector, 121 point

(A27) - Wire Connection (vehicle speed signal), in instrument panel wiring harness
(A125) - Connection (crash signal) in instrument panel wiring harness

Motronic engine control module (ECM), throttle position (TP) sensor, fuel pump (FP) relay

Edition 07/00
USA.5102.07.21

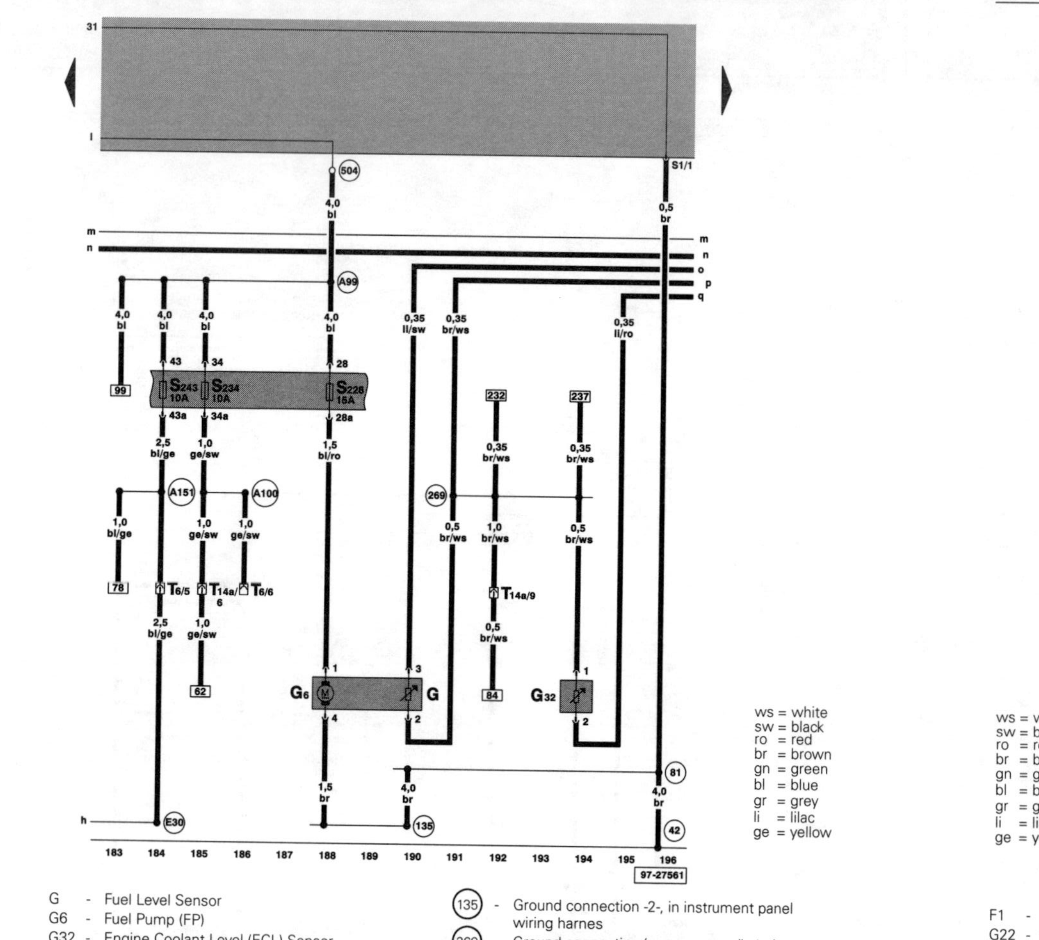

ws = white
sw = black
ro = red
br = brown
gn = green
bl = blue
gr = grey
li = lilac
ge = yellow

G - Fuel Level Sensor
G6 - Fuel Pump (FP)
G32 - Engine Coolant Level (ECL) Sensor
S228 - Fuse 28 in fuse holder
S234 - Fuse 34 in fuse holder
S243 - Fuse 43 in fuse holder
T6 - 6-Pin Connector, brown, in protective housing for connectors, in plenum chamber, left
T14a - 14-Pin Connector, in engine compartment, in wiring duct, left

(42) - Ground connection, beside steering column

(81) - Ground connection -1-, in instrument panel wiring harness

(135) - Ground connection -2-, in instrument panel wiring harnes

(269) - Ground connection (sensor ground) -1-, in instrument panel wiring harness

(504) - Threaded connection -1- (87) on the relay plate

(A99) - Connector -1- (87), in instrument panel wiring harness

(A100) - Connector -2- (87), in instrument panel wiring harness

(A151) - Connector -4- (87), in instrument panel wiring harness

(E30) - Connector (87a), in wiring harness engine

Fuel pump (FP), fuel level sensor, engine coolant level (ECL) sensor

ws = white
sw = black
ro = red
br = brown
gn = green
bl = blue
gr = grey
li = lilac
ge = yellow

F1 - Oil Pressure Switch
G22 - Speedometer Vehicle Speed Sensor (VSS)
J285 - Control module with indicator unit in instrument panel insert
K3 - Oil Pressure Warning Light
K38 - Engine Oil Level Indicator Light
S5 - Fuse 5 in fuse holder
S7 - Fuse 7 in fuse holder
T14a - 14-Pin Connector, in engine compartment, in wiring duct, left
T32 - 32-Pin Connector, blue

(B163) - Plus connector -1- (15) in wiring harness interior

Instrument cluster, oil pressure switch, speedometer vehicle speed sensor (VSS), oil pressure warning light

ws = white
sw = black
ro = red
br = brown
gn = green
bl = blue
gr = grey
li = lilac
ge = yellow

211 212 213 214 215 216 217 218 219 220 221 222 223 224 97-27563

G1 - Fuel gauge
G3 - Engine Coolant Temperature (ECT) Gauge
G5 - Tachometer
G21 - Speedometer
H3 - Warning Buzzer
J285 - Control module with indicator unit in instrument panel insert
K2 - Generator (GEN) Warning Light
K28 - Engine Coolant Level/Temperature (ECL/ECT) Warning Light
K105 - Low Fuel Level Warning Light
T32 - 32-Pin Connector, blue

(A13) - Wire connection (door contact switch), in instrument panel wiring harness
(A27) - Wire Connection (vehicle speed signal), in instrument panel wiring harness

Instrument cluster, engine coolant temperature (ECL/ECT) gauge, fuel gauge, tachometer, speedometer, generator (GEN) warning light, low fuel level warning light

ws = white
sw = black
ro = red
br = brown
gn = green
bl = blue
gr = grey
li = lilac
ge = yellow
or = orange

225 226 227 228 229 230 231 232 233 234 235 236 237 238 97-27564

E86 - Multi-Function Indicator Mode Select Switch
E109 - Multi-Function Indicator Memory Switch
G17 - Outside Air Temperature Sensor
J119 - Multi-function Indicator (MFI)
J285 - Control module with indicator unit in instrument panel insert
J533 - Data Bus On Board Diagnostic Interface
K31 - Cruise Control Indicator Light
K83 - Malfunction Indicator Lamp (MIL)
K132 - Electronic Power Control (EPC) Warning Lamp
T6e - 6-Pin Connector
T16 - Data Link Connector (DLC), below instrument panel, left
T32 - 32-Pin Connector, blue
T32a - 32-Pin Connector, green

(A76) - Connector (K-diagnosis wire), in instrument panel wiring harness

Instrument cluster, multi-function indicator (MFI), outside air temperature sensor, electronic power control (EPC) warning lamp, cruise control indicator light, malfunction indicator lamp

Anti-lock brake system (ABS), Anti-lock brake system (ABS) with electronic differential lock (EDL) and anti-slip control (ASC),

from August 2000

Deviate relay location and fuseplacements as well as the locations of multiple connectors see section "component locations".

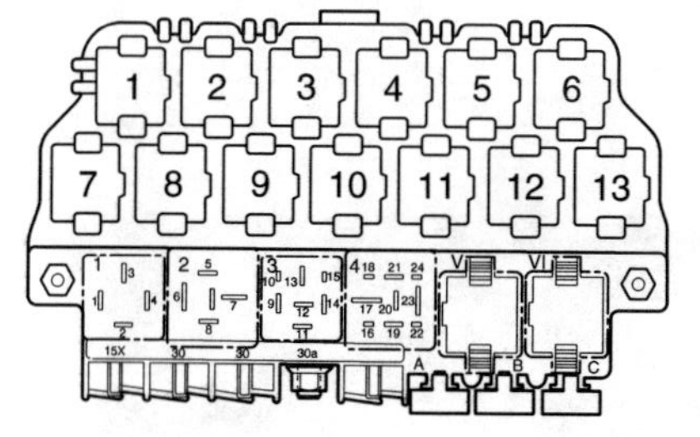

Fuse colors

30 A - green
25 A - white
20 A - yellow
15 A - blue
10 A - red
7,5 A - brown
5 A - beige
3 A - violet

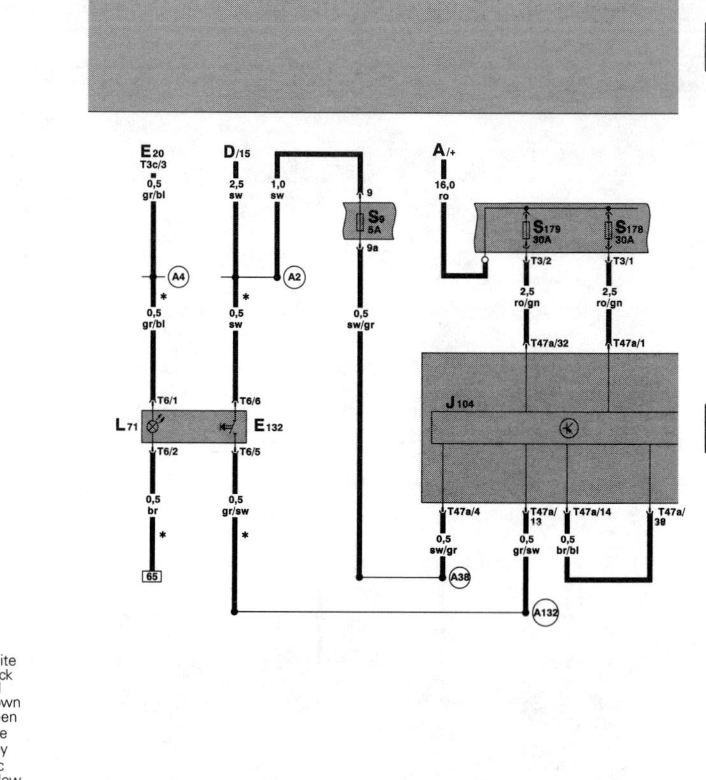

ws = white
sw = black
ro = red
br = brown
gn = green
bl = blue
gr = grey
li = lilac
ge = yellow
or = orange

A - Battery
D - Ignition/Starter Switch
E20 - Instrument Panel Light Dimmer Switch
E132 - ESP/Anti-Slip Control Switch*
J104 - ABS Control Module (w/EDL), in engine compartment, left
L71 - Anti-Slip Control Switch Illumination*
S9 - Fuse 9 in fuse holder
S178 - Fuse -6- (30) in fuse bracket/battery
S179 - Fuse -7- (30) in fuse bracket/battery
T3 - 3-Pin Connector
T3c - 3-Pin Connector
T6 - 6-Pin Connector*
T47a - 47-Pin Connector

A2 - Plus connection (15), in instrument panel wiring harness
A4 - Plus connection (58b), in instrument panel wiring harness
A38 - Plus connection -2- (15a), in instrument panel wiring harness
A132 - Connection (ASC), in instrument panel wiring harness

* - Vehicles with ESP/Anti-Slip Control (ASC) only

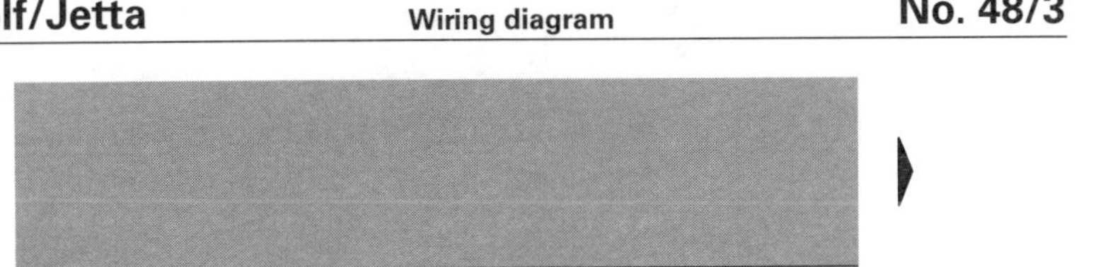

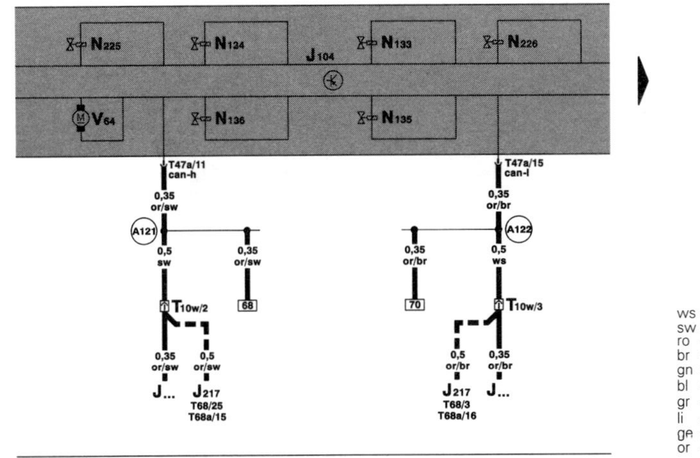

ws = white
sw = black
ro = red
br = brown
gn = green
bl = blue
gr = grey
li = lilac
ge = yellow
or = orange

J104 - ABS Control Module (w/EDL), in engine compartment, left
J217 - Transmission Control Module (TCM), in plenum chamber, center
J... - Engine Control Module (ECM)
N133 - Right Rear ABS Inlet Valve
N134 - Left Rear ABS Inlet Valve
N135 - Right Rear ABS Outlet Valve
N136 - Left Rear ABS Outlet Valve
N225 - Pilot valve -1- traction control
N226 - Pilot valve -2- traction control
T10w - 10-Pin Connector, white, in protective housing for connectors, in plenum chamber, left
T47a - 47-Pin Connector
T68 - 68-Pin Connector, on transmission control module (TCM) (4 speed automatic)
T68a - 68-Pin Connector, on Transmission Control Module (TCM) (5 speed automatic with Tiptronic)
V64 - ABS Hydraulic Pump

(A121) - Connection (high bus), in instrument panel wiring harness
(A122) - Connection (low bus), in instrument panel wiring harness

- - - Automatic transmission only

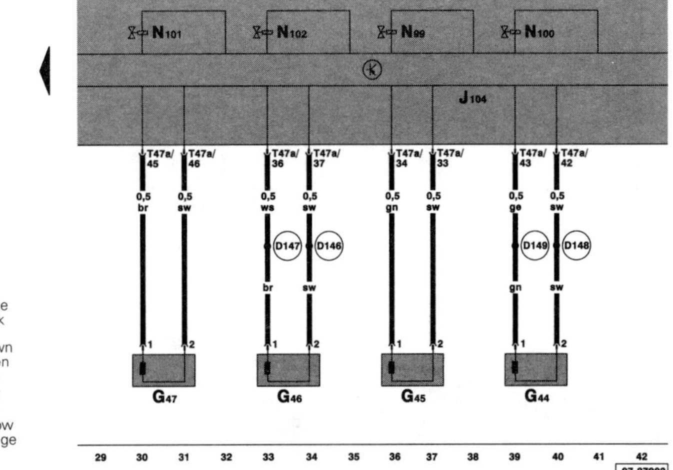

ws = white
sw = black
ro = red
br = brown
gn = green
bl = blue
gr = grey
li = lilac
ge = yellow
or = orange

G44 - Right Rear ABS Wheel Speed Sensor
G45 - Right Front ABS Wheel Speed Sensor
G46 - Left Rear ABS Wheel Speed Sensor
G47 - Left Front ABS Wheel Speed Sensor
J104 - ABS Control Module (w/EDL), in engine compartment, left
N99 - Right Front ABS Inlet Valve
N100 - Right Front ABS Outlet Valve
N101 - Left Front ABS Inlet Valve
N102 - Left Front ABS Outlet Valve
T47a - 47-Pin Connector

(D146) - Connector (speed sensor rear, left +), in wiring harness engine compartment
(D147) - Connector (speed sensor rear, left -), in wiring harness engine compartment
(D148) - Connector (speed sensor rear, right +), in wiring harness engine compartment
(D149) - Connector (speed sensor rear, right -), in wiring harness engine compartment

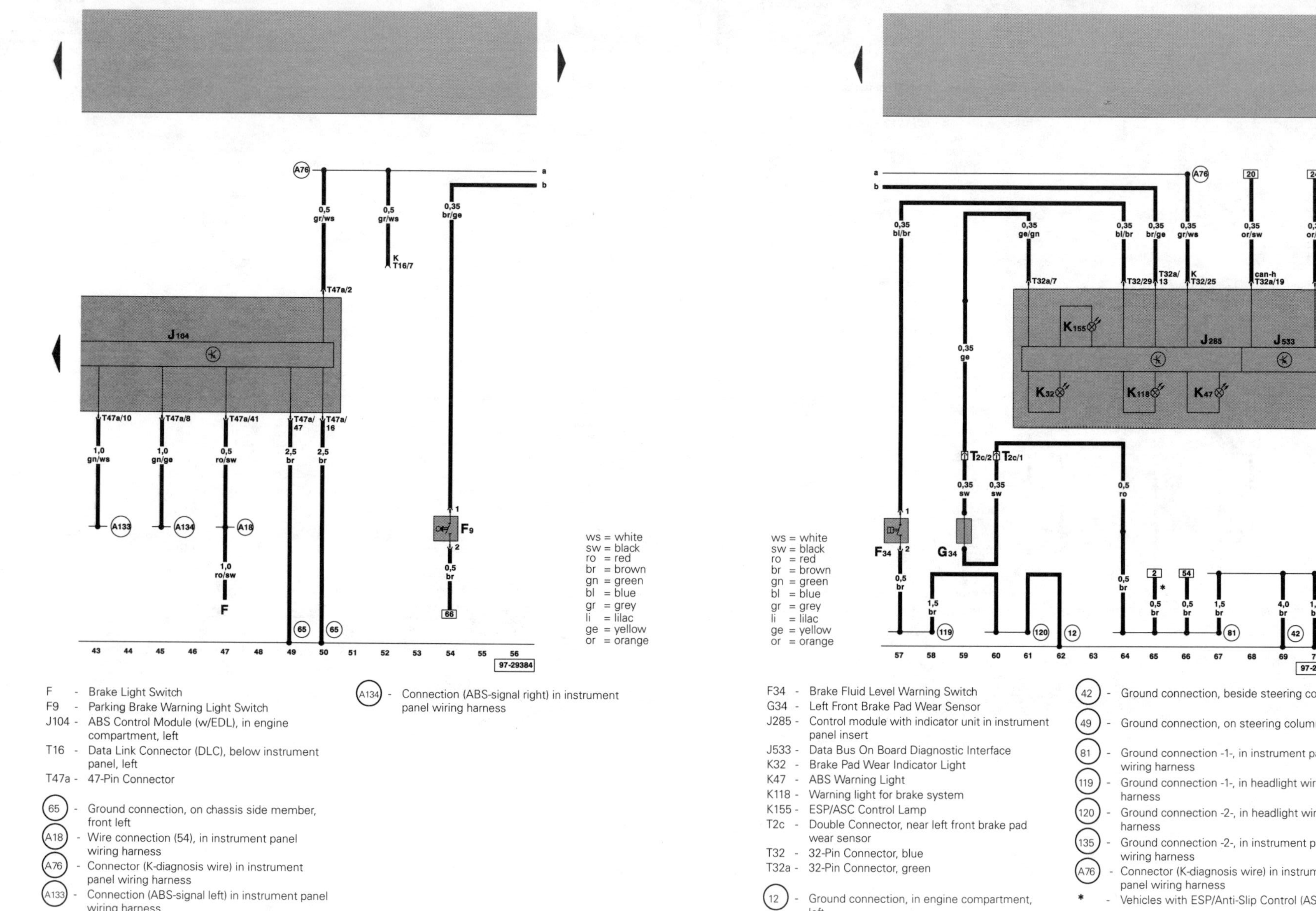

ws = white
sw = black
ro = red
br = brown
gn = green
bl = blue
gr = grey
li = lilac
ge = yellow
or = orange

F - Brake Light Switch
F9 - Parking Brake Warning Light Switch
J104 - ABS Control Module (w/EDL), in engine compartment, left
T16 - Data Link Connector (DLC), below instrument panel, left
T47a - 47-Pin Connector

(65) - Ground connection, on chassis side member, front left
(A18) - Wire connection (54), in instrument panel wiring harness
(A76) - Connector (K-diagnosis wire) in instrument panel wiring harness
(A133) - Connection (ABS-signal left) in instrument panel wiring harness
(A134) - Connection (ABS-signal right) in instrument panel wiring harness

Edition 03/01
USA.5102.10.21

ABS control module (w/EDL), parking brake warning light switch

ws = white
sw = black
ro = red
br = brown
gn = green
bl = blue
gr = grey
li = lilac
ge = yellow
or = orange

F34 - Brake Fluid Level Warning Switch
G34 - Left Front Brake Pad Wear Sensor
J285 - Control module with indicator unit in instrument panel insert
J533 - Data Bus On Board Diagnostic Interface
K32 - Brake Pad Wear Indicator Light
K47 - ABS Warning Light
K118 - Warning light for brake system
K155 - ESP/ASC Control Lamp
T2c - Double Connector, near left front brake pad wear sensor
T32 - 32-Pin Connector, blue
T32a - 32-Pin Connector, green

(12) - Ground connection, in engine compartment, left
(42) - Ground connection, beside steering column
(49) - Ground connection, on steering column
(81) - Ground connection -1-, in instrument panel wiring harness
(119) - Ground connection -1-, in headlight wiring harness
(120) - Ground connection -2-, in headlight wiring harness
(135) - Ground connection -2-, in instrument panel wiring harness
(A76) - Connector (K-diagnosis wire) in instrument panel wiring harness
* - Vehicles with ESP/Anti-Slip Control (ASC) only

Instrument cluster, left front brake pad wear sensor, brake pad wear indicator light, ESP/ASC control lamp, ABS warning light, warning light for brake system

Edition 03/01
USA.5102.10.21

2.0L - Engine - Motronic Multiport Fuel Injection (MFI)/85 kW, code AVH,

from August 2000

2.0L - Engine - Motronic Multiport Fuel Injection (MFI)/85 kW, code AZG,

from October 2000

Deviate relay location and fuseplacements as well as the locations of multiple connectors see section "component locations".

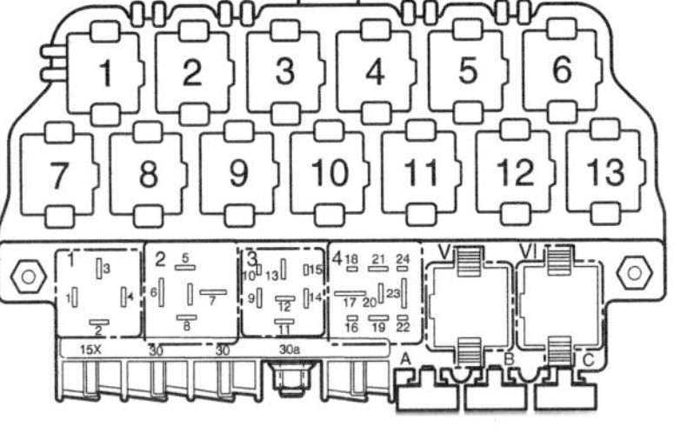

Relay location on the thirteenfold auxiliary relay panel, above relay panel:

Relay panel:

- **2** Load Reduction Relay (100)
- **4** Fuel Pump (FP) Relay (409)

Note: Number in parentheses indicates production control number stamped on relay housing.

Fuse colors

30 A - green
25 A - white
20 A - yellow
15 A - blue
10 A - red
7,5 A - brown
5 A - beige
3 A - violet

ws = white
sw = black
ro = red
br = brown
gn = green
bl = blue
gr = grey
li = lilac
ge – yellow

97-27906

A - Battery
B - Starter
C - Generator (GEN)
C1 - Voltage Regulator (VR)
D - Ignition/Starter Switch
J59 - Load Reduction Relay
J207 - Starting Interlock Relay
J226 - Park/Neutral Position (PNP) Relay
S162 - Fuse -1- (30) in fuse bracket/battery
S163 - Fuse -2- (30) in fuse bracket/battery
S176 - Fuse -4- (30) in fuse bracket/battery
S177 - Fuse -5- (30) in fuse bracket/battery
T2e - Double Connector, near starter (vehicles without air conditioning)
T4 - 4-Pin Connector, near starter (vehicles with air conditioning only)
T6 - 6-Pin Connector, brown, in protective housing for connectors, in plenum chamber, left
(500) - Threaded connection -1- (30) on the relay plate
(502) - Threaded connection -1- (30a) on the relay plate
(A41) - Plus connection (50), in instrument panel wiring harness
* - Manual transmission only
--- Automatic transmission only

Generator (GEN), starter

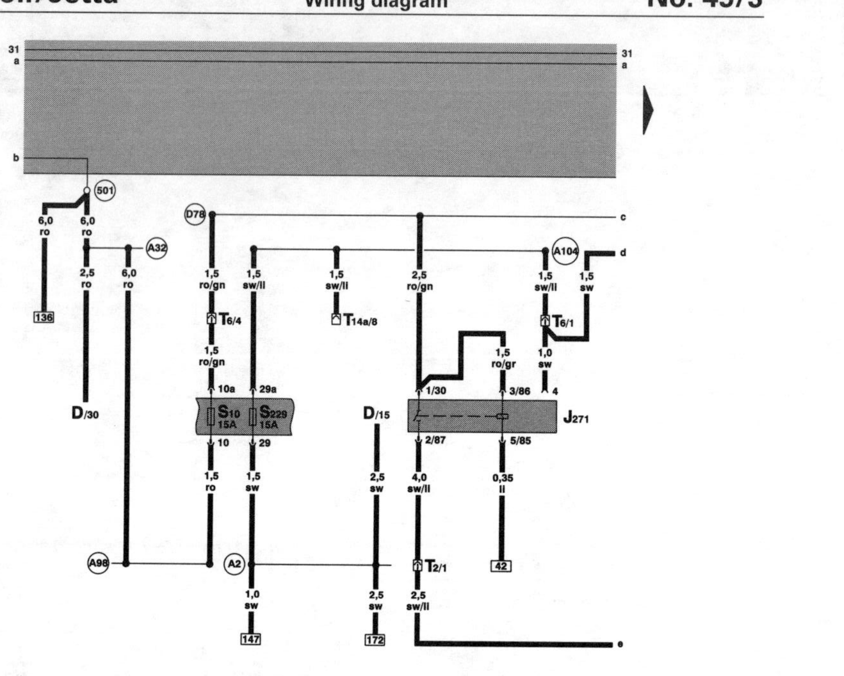

ws = white
sw = black
ro = red
br = brown
gn = green
bl = blue
gr = grey
li = lilac
ge = yellow

D - Ignition/Starter Switch
J271 - Motronic engine control module (ECM) power supply relay, in protective housing, in engine compartment, left, production control number (428)
S10 - Fuse 10 in fuse holder
S229 - Fuse 29 in fuse holder
T2 - 2-Pin Connector, in engine compartment, left
T6 - 6-Pin Connector, brown, in protective housing for connectors, in plenum chamber, left
T14a - 14-Pin Connector, in engine compartment, in wiring duct, left

(501) - Threaded connection -2- (30) on the relay plate

(A2) - Plus connection (15), in instrument panel wiring harness
(A32) - Plus connection (30), in instrument panel wiring harness
(A98) - Plus connector -4- (30), in instrument panel wiring harness
(A104) - Plus connector -2- (15), in instrument panel wiring harness
(D78) - Plus connector -1- (30a), in engine compartment wiring harness

ws = white
sw = black
ro = red
br = brown
gn = green
bl = blue
gr = grey
li = lilac
ge = yellow

J220 - Motronic Engine Control Module (ECM), in plenum chamber, center
N70 - Ignition Coil 1 with Power Output Stage
N127 - Ignition Coil 2 with Power Output Stage
N291 - Ignition Coil 3 with Power Output Stage
N292 - Ignition Coil 4 with Power Output Stage
P - Spark Plug Connectors
Q - Spark Plugs
T6d - 6-Pin Connector
T121 - Connector, 121 point

(85) - Ground connection -1-, in engine compartment wiring harness
(D52) - Plus connector (15a), in engine compartment wiring harness

(D78) - Plus connector -1- (30a), in engine compartment wiring harness

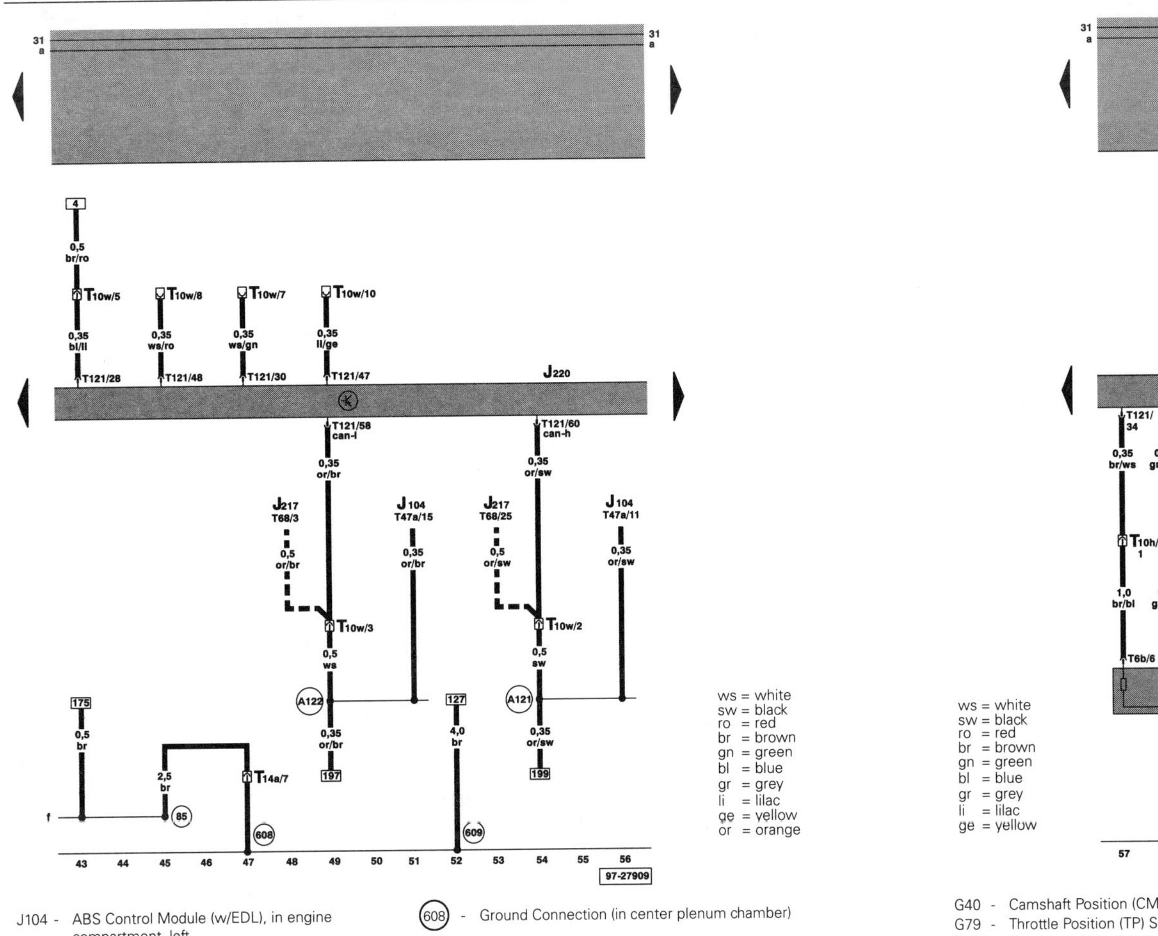

ws = white
sw = black
ro = red
br = brown
gn = green
bl = blue
gr = grey
li = lilac
ge = yellow
or = orange

J104 - ABS Control Module (w/EDL), in engine compartment, left
J217 - Transmission Control Module (TCM)
J220 - Motronic Engine Control Module (ECM), in plenum chamber, center
T10w - 10-Pin Connector, white, in protective housing for connectors, in plenum chamber, left
T14a - 14-Pin Connector, in engine compartment, in wiring duct, left
T47a - 47-Pin Connector, on ABS Control Module
T68 - 68-Pin Connector, on Transmission Control Module (TCM)
T121 - Connector, 121 point

(85) - Ground connection -1-, in engine compartment wiring harness

(608) - Ground Connection (in center plenum chamber)
(609) - Ground Connection (in right plenum chamber)
(A121) - Connection (high bus), in instrument panel wiring harness
(A122) - Connection (low bus), in instrument panel wiring harness

- - - Automatic transmission only

Motronic engine control module (ECM)

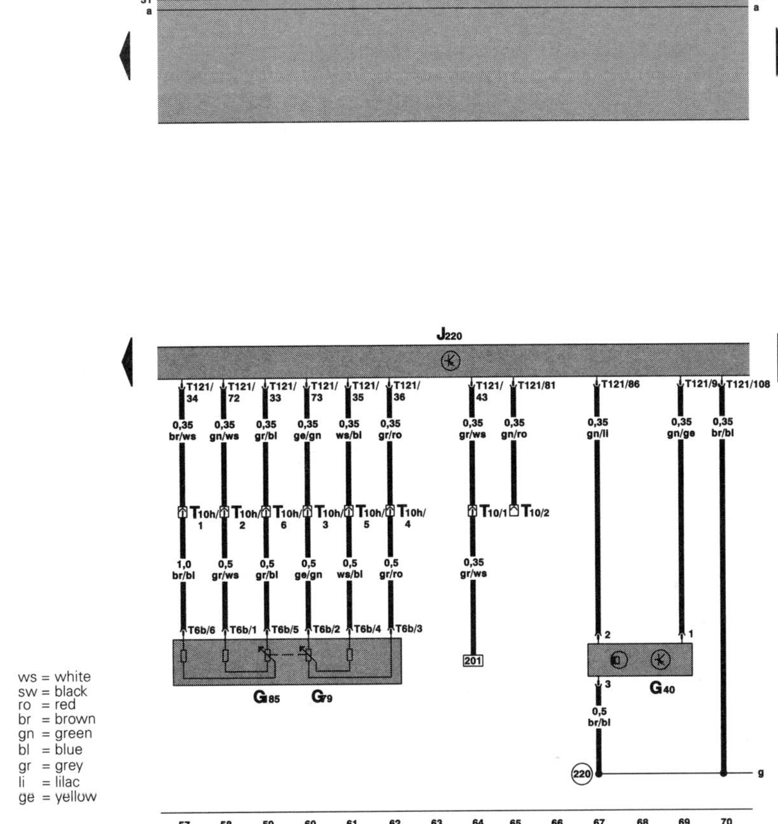

ws = white
sw = black
ro = red
br = brown
gn = green
bl = blue
gr = grey
li = lilac
ge = yellow

G40 - Camshaft Position (CMP) Sensor
G79 - Throttle Position (TP) Sensor
G185 - Sender -2- for accelerator pedal position
J220 - Motronic Engine Control Module (ECM), in plenum chamber, center
T6b - 6-Pin Connector
T10 - 10-Pin Connector, orange, in protective housing for connectors, in plenum chamber, left
T10h - 10-Pin Connector, blue, in protective housing for connectors, in plenum chamber, left
T121 - Connector, 121 point

(220) - Ground connection (sensor ground), in engine compartment wiring harness

Motronic engine control module (ECM), throttle position (TP) sensor, camshaft position (CMP) sensor

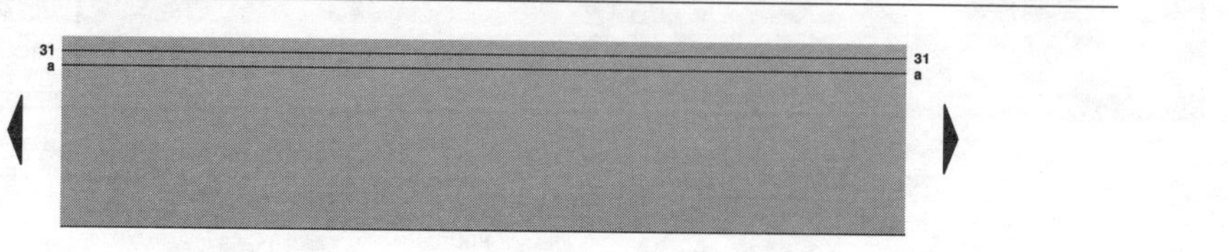

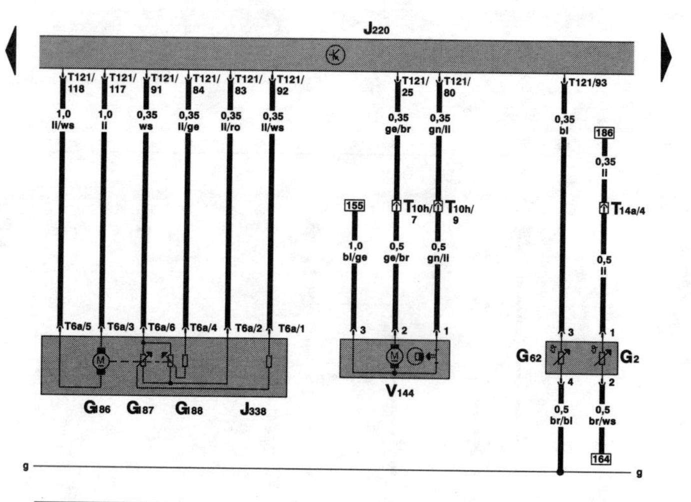

ws = white
sw = black
ro = red
br = brown
gn = green
bl = blue
gr = grey
li = lilac
ge = yellow

G2 - Engine Coolant Temperature (ECT) Sensor
G62 - Engine Coolant Temperature (ECT) Sensor
G186 - Throttle drive (power accelerator actuation)
G187 - Angle sensor -1- for throttle drive (power accelerator actuation)
G188 - Angle sensor -2- for throttle drive (power accelerator actuation)
J220 - Motronic Engine Control Module (ECM), in plenum chamber, center
J338 - Throttle Valve Control Module
T6a - 6-Pin Connector
T10h - 10-Pin Connector, blue, in protective housing for connectors, in plenum chamber, left
T14a - 14-Pin Connector, in engine compartment, in wiring duct, left
T121 - Connector, 121 point

V144 - Leak detection pump (LDP)

Motronic engine control module (ECM), angle sensor for throttle drive (power accelerator actuation), (ECT) sensor, leak detection pump (LDP)

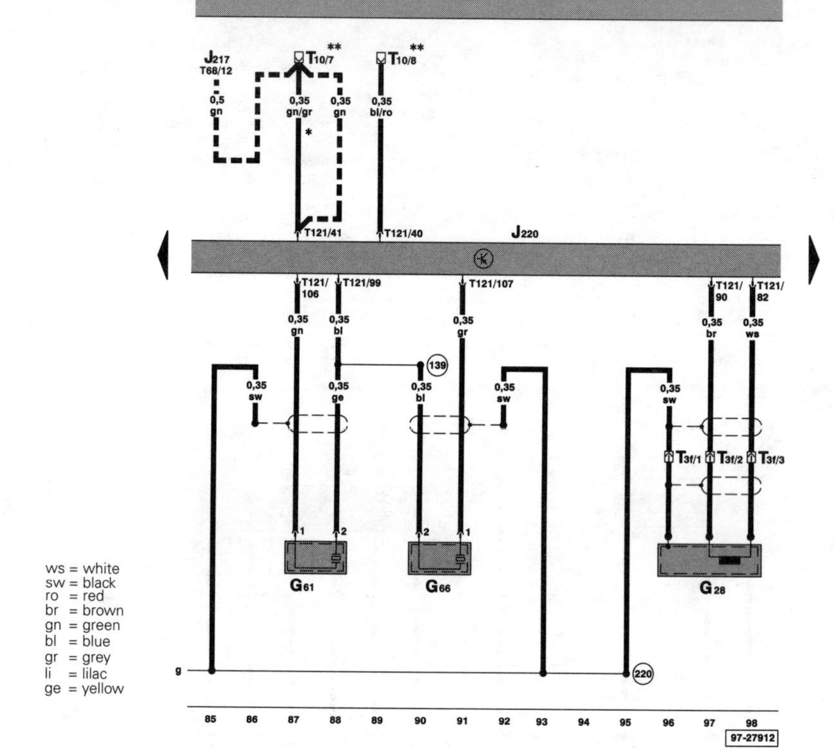

ws = white
sw = black
ro = red
br = brown
gn = green
bl = blue
gr = grey
li = lilac
ge = yellow

G28 - Engine Speed (RPM) Sensor
G61 - Knock Sensor (KS) 1
G66 - Knock Sensor (KS) 2
J217 - Transmission Control Module (TCM)
J220 - Motronic Engine Control Module (ECM), in plenum chamber, center
T3f - 3-Pin Connector, in engine compartment, front
T10 - 10-Pin Connector, orange, in protective housing for connectors, in plenum chamber, left
T68 - Connector, 68 point
T121 - Connector, 121 point

(139) - Ground connection (sensor Ground), in Motronic Multiport Fuel Injection (MFI) wiring harness

(220) - Ground connection (sensor ground), in engine compartment wiring harness

* - Manual transmission only
** - A/C connection
--- Automatic transmission only

Motronic engine control module (ECM), engine speed (RPM) sensor, knock sensor (KS) 1, knock sensor (KS) 2

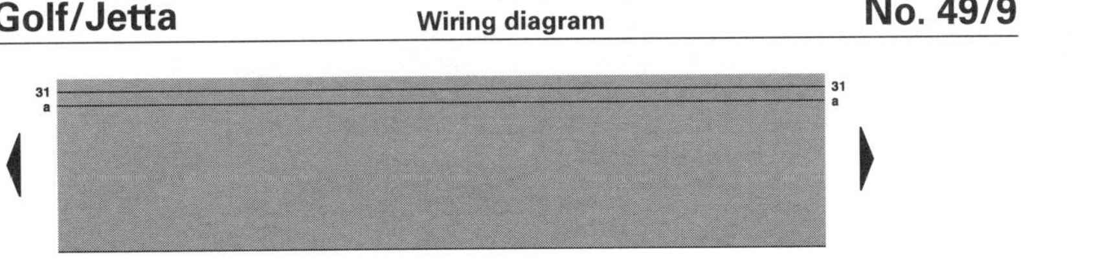

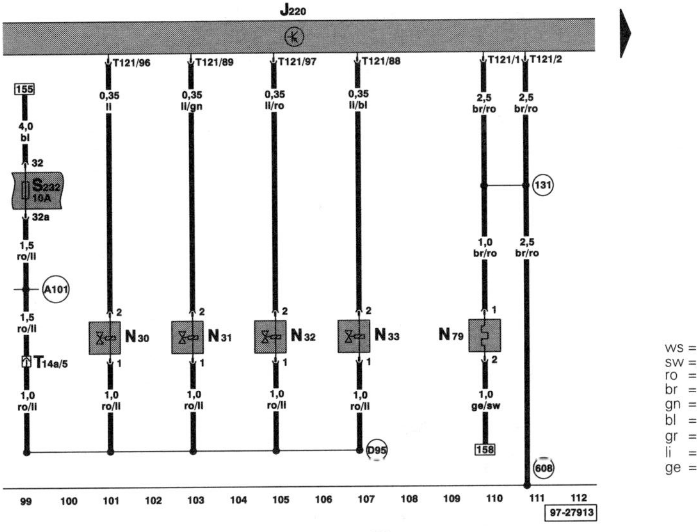

ws = white
sw = black
ro = red
br = brown
gn = green
bl = blue
gr = grey
li = lilac
ge = yellow

- J220 - Motronic Engine Control Module (ECM), in plenum chamber, center
- N30 - Cylinder 1 Fuel Injector
- N31 - Cylinder 2 Fuel Injector
- N32 - Cylinder 3 Fuel Injector
- N33 - Cylinder 4 Fuel Injector
- N79 - Positive Crankcase Ventilation (PCV) Heating Element
- S232 - Fuse 32 in fuse holder
- T14a - 14-Pin Connector, in engine compartment, in wiring duct, left
- T121 - Connector, 121 point
- (131) - Ground connection -2-, in engine compartment wiring harness
- (608) - Ground connection (in center plenum chamber)
- (A101) - Connector -3- (87a), in instrument panel wiring harness
- (D95) - Wire connection (injectors), in engine compartment wiring harness

Edition 09/00 USA.5102.08.21 **Motronic engine control module (ECM), injectors, positive crankcase ventilation (PCV) heating element**

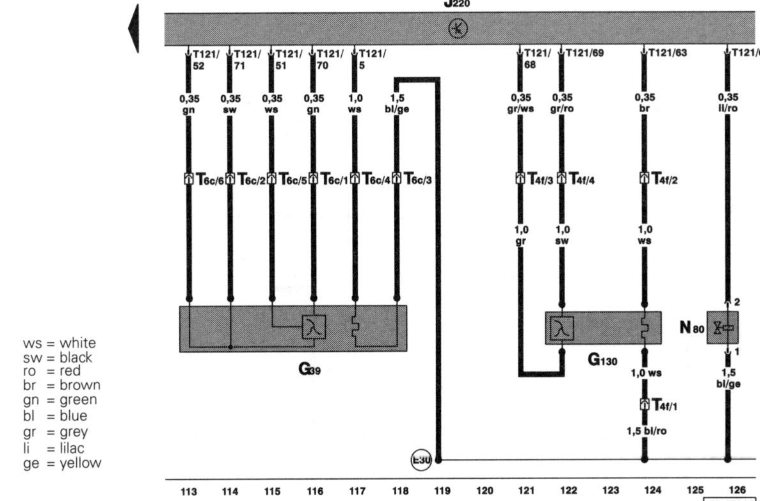

ws = white
sw = black
ro = red
br = brown
gn = green
bl = blue
gr = grey
li = lilac
ge = yellow

- G39 - Heated Oxygen Sensor (HO2S)
- G130 - Oxygen Sensor (O2S) behind Three Way Catalytic Converter (TWC)
- J220 - Motronic Engine Control Module (ECM), in plenum chamber, center
- N80 - Evaporative Emission (EVAP) Canister Purge Regulator Valve
- T4f - 4-Pin Connector, in protective housing for connectors under right floor
- T6c - 6-Pin Connector, in protective housing for connectors under right floor
- T121 - Connector, 121 point
- (E30) - Connector (87a), in wiring harness engine

Heated oxygen sensor (HO2S), oxygen sensor (O2S) behind three way catalytic converter (TWC), evaporative emission (EVAP) canister purge regulator valve **Edition 09/00** USA.5102.08.21

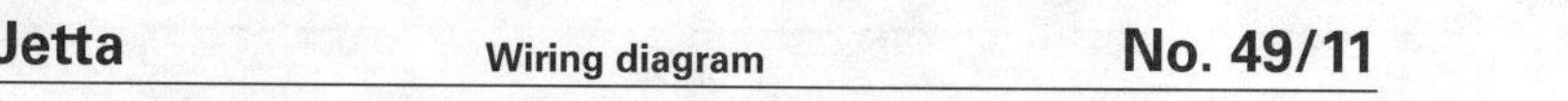

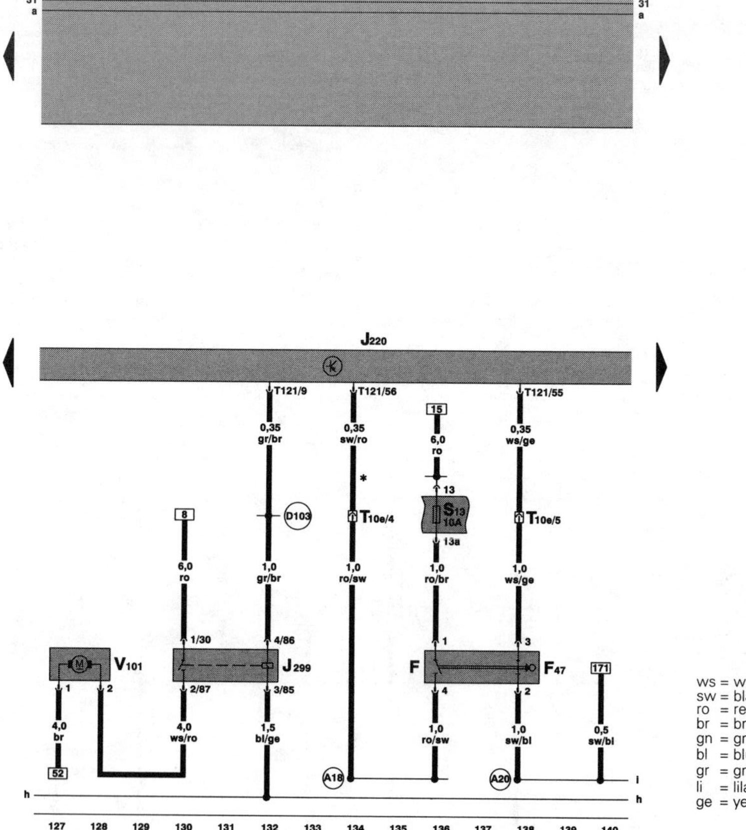

ws = white
sw = black
ro = red
br = brown
gn = green
bl = blue
gr = grey
li = lilac
ge = yellow

F - Brake Light Switch
F47 - Brake Vacuum Vent Valve Switch for cruise control
J220 - Motronic Engine Control Module (ECM), in plenum chamber, center
J299 - Secondary Air Injection (AIR) Pump Relay, in protective housing, in engine compartment, left, production control number (100)
S13 - Fuse 13 in fuse holder
T10e - 10-Pin Connector, black, in protective housing for connectors, in plenum chamber, left
T121 - Connector, 121 point
V101 - Secondary Air Injection (AIR) Pump Motor

(A18) - Wire connection (54), in instrument panel

(A20) - Wire connection (15a), in instrument panel wiring harness
(D103) - Wire connection -3-, in engine compartment wiring harness

* - Manual transmission only

Motronic engine control module (ECM), secondary air injection (AIR) pump motor, secondary air injection (AIR) pump relay

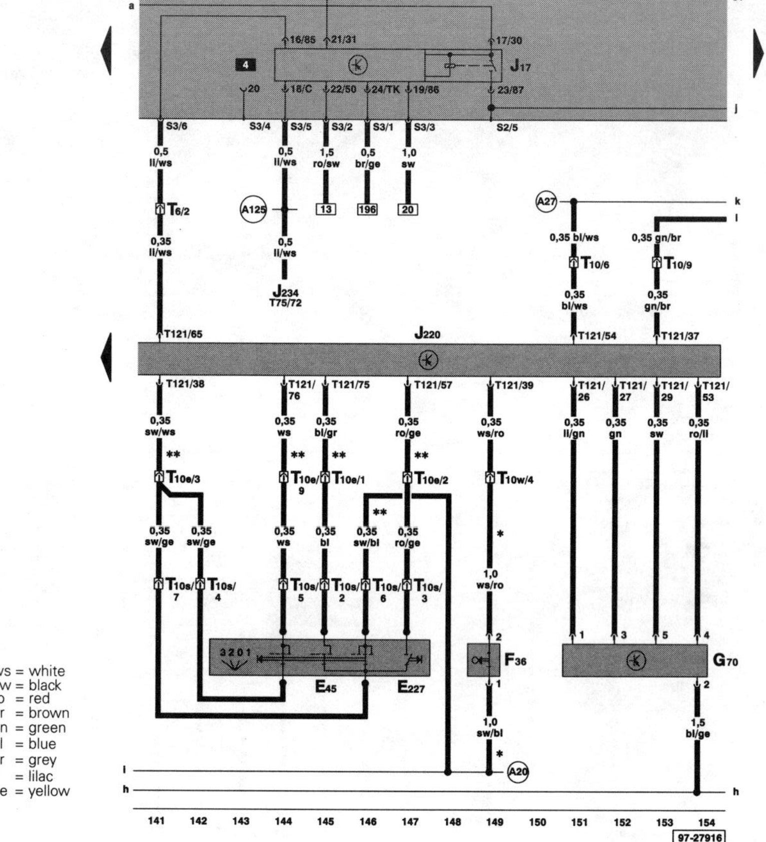

ws = white
sw = black
ro = red
br = brown
gn = green
bl = blue
gr = grey
li = lilac
ge = yellow

E45 - Cruise Control Switch**
E227 - Cruise Control Push Button (SET)**
F36 - Clutch Vacuum Vent Valve Switch**
G70 - Mass Air Flow (MAF) Sensor
J17 - Fuel Pump (FP) Relay
J220 - Motronic Engine Control Module (ECM), in plenum chamber, center
J234 - Airbag Control Module
T6 - 6-Pin Connector, brown, in protective housing for connectors, in plenum chamber, left
T10 - 10-Pin Connector, orange, in protective housing for connectors, in plenum chamber, left
T10e - 10-Pin Connector, black, in protective housing for connectors, in plenum chamber, left
T10s - 10-Pin Connector, near steering column
T10w - 10-Pin Connector, white, in protective housing for connectors, in plenum chamber, left
T75 - 75-Pin Connector
T121 - Connector, 121 point

(A20) - Wire connection (15a), in instrument panel wiring harness
(A27) - Wire Connection (vehicle speed signal), in instrument panel wiring harness
(A125) - Connection (crash signal) in instrument panel wiring harness

* - Manual transmission only
** - Vehicles with cruise control only

Motronic engine control module (ECM), cruise control switch, mass air flow (MAF) sensor, clutch vacuum vent valve switch, fuel pump (FP) relay

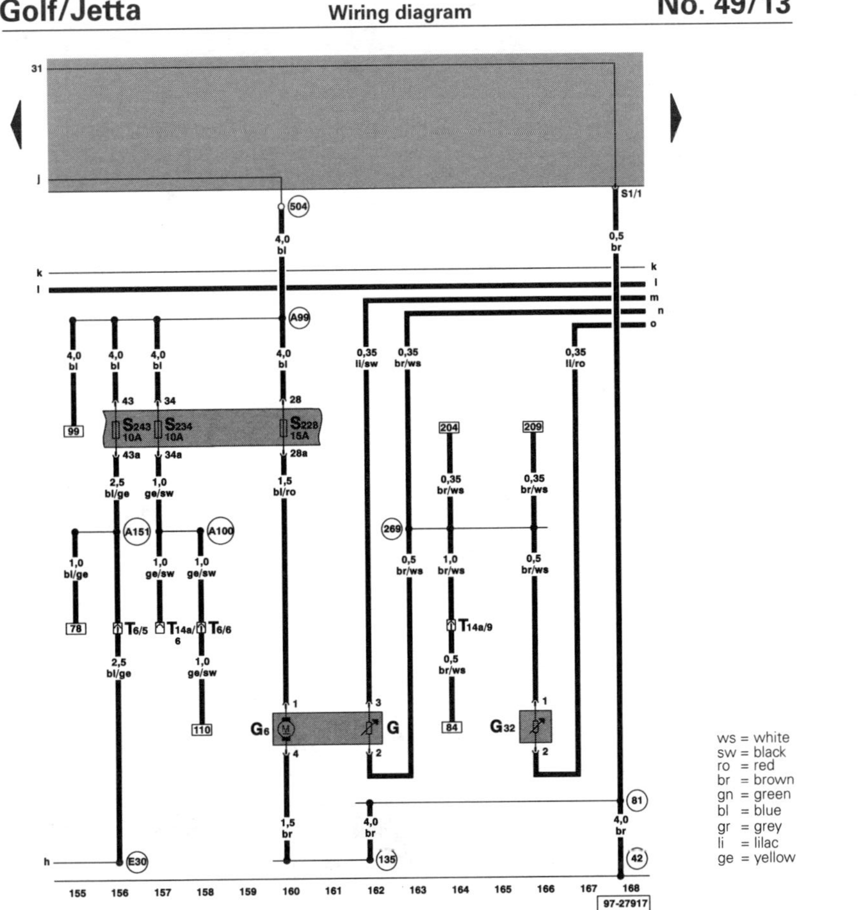

ws = white
sw = black
ro = red
br = brown
gn = green
bl = blue
gr = grey
li = lilac
ge = yellow

G - Fuel Level Sensor
G6 - Fuel Pump (FP)
G32 - Engine Coolant Level (ECL) Sensor
S228 - Fuse 28 in fuse holder
S234 - Fuse 34 in fuse holder
S243 - Fuse 43 in fuse holder
T6 - 6-Pin Connector, brown, in protective housing for connectors, in plenum chamber, left
T14a - 14-Pin Connector, in engine compartment, in wiring duct, left

(42) - Ground connection, beside steering column

(81) - Ground connection -1-, in instrument panel wiring harness

(135) - Ground connection -2-, in instrument panel wiring harnes

(269) - Ground connection (sensor ground) -1-, in instrument panel wiring harness

(504) - Threaded connection -1- (87) on the relay plate

(A99) - Connector -1- (87), in instrument panel wiring harness

(A100) - Connector -2- (87), in instrument panel wiring harness

(A151) - Connector -4- (87), in instrument panel wiring harness

(E30) - Connector (87a), in wiring harness engine

Fuel pump (FP), fuel level sensor, engine coolant level (ECL) sensor

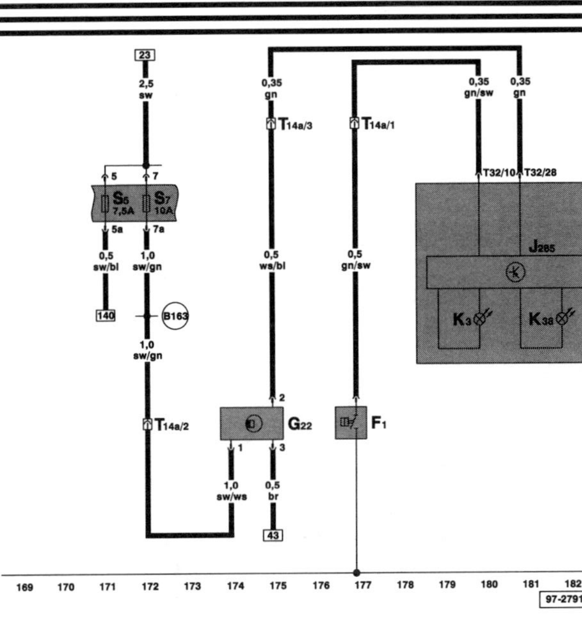

ws = white
sw = black
ro = red
br = brown
gn = green
bl = blue
gr = grey
li = lilac
ge = yellow

F1 - Oil Pressure Switch
G22 - Speedometer Vehicle Speed Sensor (VSS)
J285 - Control module with indicator unit in instrument panel insert
K3 - Oil Pressure Warning Light
K38 - Engine Oil Level Indicator Light
S5 - Fuse 5 in fuse holder
S7 - Fuse 7 in fuse holder
T14a - 14-Pin Connector, in engine compartment, in wiring duct, left
T32 - 32-Pin Connector, blue

(B163) - Plus connector -1- (15) in wiring harness interior

Instrument cluster, oil pressure switch, speedometer vehicle speed sensor (VSS), oil pressure warning light

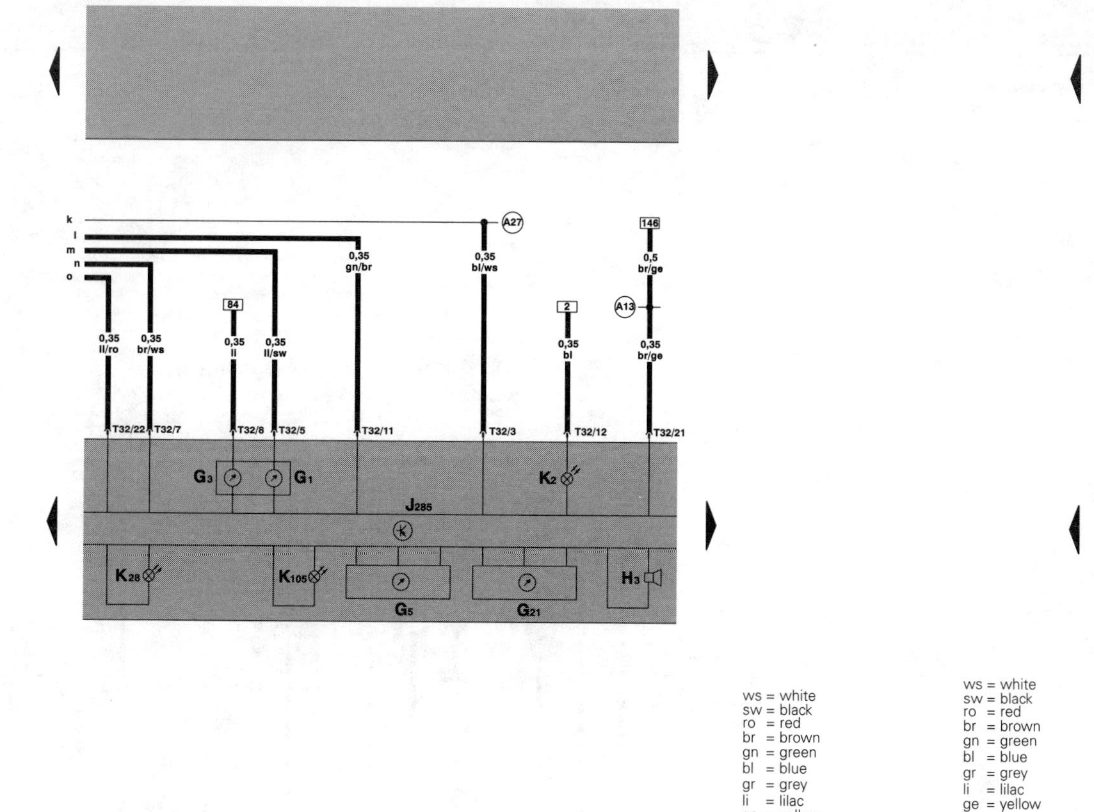

ws = white
sw = black
ro = red
br = brown
gn = green
bl = blue
gr = grey
li = lilac
ge = yellow

G1 - Fuel gauge
G3 - Engine Coolant Temperature (ECT) Gauge
G5 - Tachometer
G21 - Speedometer
H3 - Warning Buzzer
J285 - Control module with indicator unit in instrument panel insert
K2 - Generator (GEN) Warning Light
K28 - Engine Coolant Level/Temperature (ECL/ECT) Warning Light
K105 - Low Fuel Level Warning Light
T32 - 32-Pin Connector, blue

(A13) - Wire connection (door contact switch), in instrument panel wiring harness
(A27) - Wire Connection (vehicle speed signal), in instrument panel wiring harness

Edition 09/00
USA.5102.08.21

Instrument cluster, engine coolant temperature (ECL/ECT) gauge, fuel gauge, tachometer, speedometer, generator (GEN) warning light, low fuel level warning light

ws = white
sw = black
ro = red
br = brown
gn = green
bl = blue
gr = grey
li = lilac
ge = yellow
or = orange

197 198 199 200 201 202 203 204 205 206 207 208 209 210
97-27920

E86 - Multi-Function Indicator Mode Select Switch
E109 - Multi-Function Indicator Memory Switch
G17 - Outside Air Temperature Sensor
J119 - Multi-function Indicator (MFI)
J285 - Control module with indicator unit in instrument panel insert
J533 - Data Bus On Board Diagnostic Interface
K31 - Cruise Control Indicator Light
K83 - Malfunction Indicator Lamp (MIL)
K132 - Electronic Power Control (EPC) Warning Lamp
T6e - 6-Pin Connector
T16 - Data Link Connector (DLC), below instrument panel, left
T32 - 32-Pin Connector, blue
T32a - 32-Pin Connector, green

(A76) - Connector (K-diagnosis wire), in instrument panel wiring harness

* - Vehicles with Multi-Function Indicator (MFI) only

Instrument cluster, multi-function indicator (MFI), outside air temperature sensor, electronic power control (EPC) warning lamp, cruise control indicator light, malfunction indicator lamp

Edition 09/00
USA.5102.08.21

Airbag systems,

from October 2000

- Driver- and front passsenger airbag
- Head airbag
- Side airbag
- Seat belt tensioner
- Seat belt control

Deviate relay location and fuseplacements as well as the locations of multiple connectors see section "component locations".

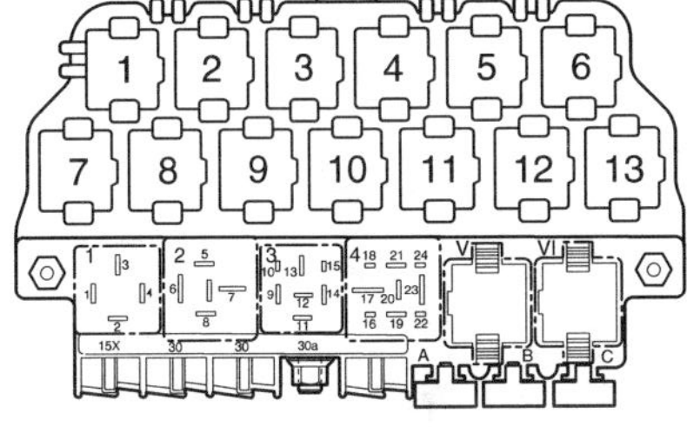

97-14163

Relay location on the thirteenfold auxiliary relay panel, above relay panel:

Relay panel:

1 Dual Horn Relay (53)

4 Fuel Pump (FP) Relay (409)

Note: Number in parentheses indicates production control number stamped on relay housing.

Fuse colors

30 A - green
25 A - white
20 A - yellow
15 A - blue
10 A - red
7,5 A - brown
5 A - beige
3 A - violet

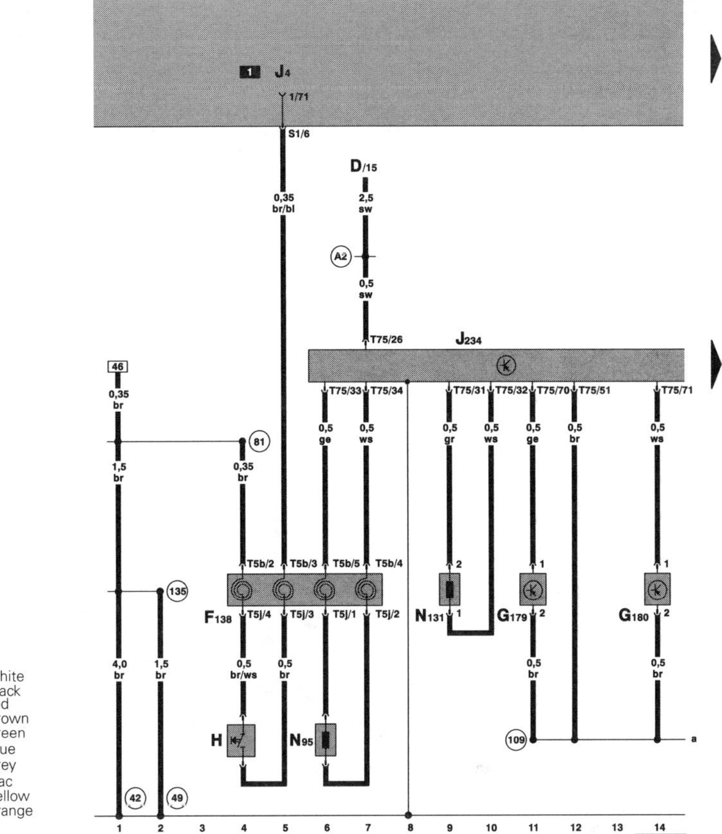

ws = white
sw = black
ro = red
br = brown
gn = green
bl = blue
gr = grey
li = lilac
ge = yellow
or = orange

D - Ignition/Starter Switch
F138 - Airbag Spiral Spring/Return Spring With Slip Ring
G179 - Crash sensor for side airbag, driver's side
G180 - Crash sensor for side airbag, passenger side
H - Signal horn activation
J4 - Dual Horn Relay
J234 - Airbag Control Module, behind console, lower part
N95 - Driver's Side Airbag Igniter
N131 - Passenger's Side Airbag Igniter 1
T5b - 5-Pin Connector
T5j - 5-Pin Connector
T75 - 75-Pin Connector

(42) - Ground connection, beside steering column
(49) - Ground connection, on steering column
(81) - Ground connection -1-, in instrument panel wiring harness
(109) - Ground connection, in airbag wiring harness
(135) - Ground connection -2-, in instrument panel wiring harness
(A2) - Plus connection (15), in instrument panel wiring harness

Airbag control module, airbag spiral spring/return spring with slip ring, crash sensor for side airbag, airbag igniter, signal horn activation

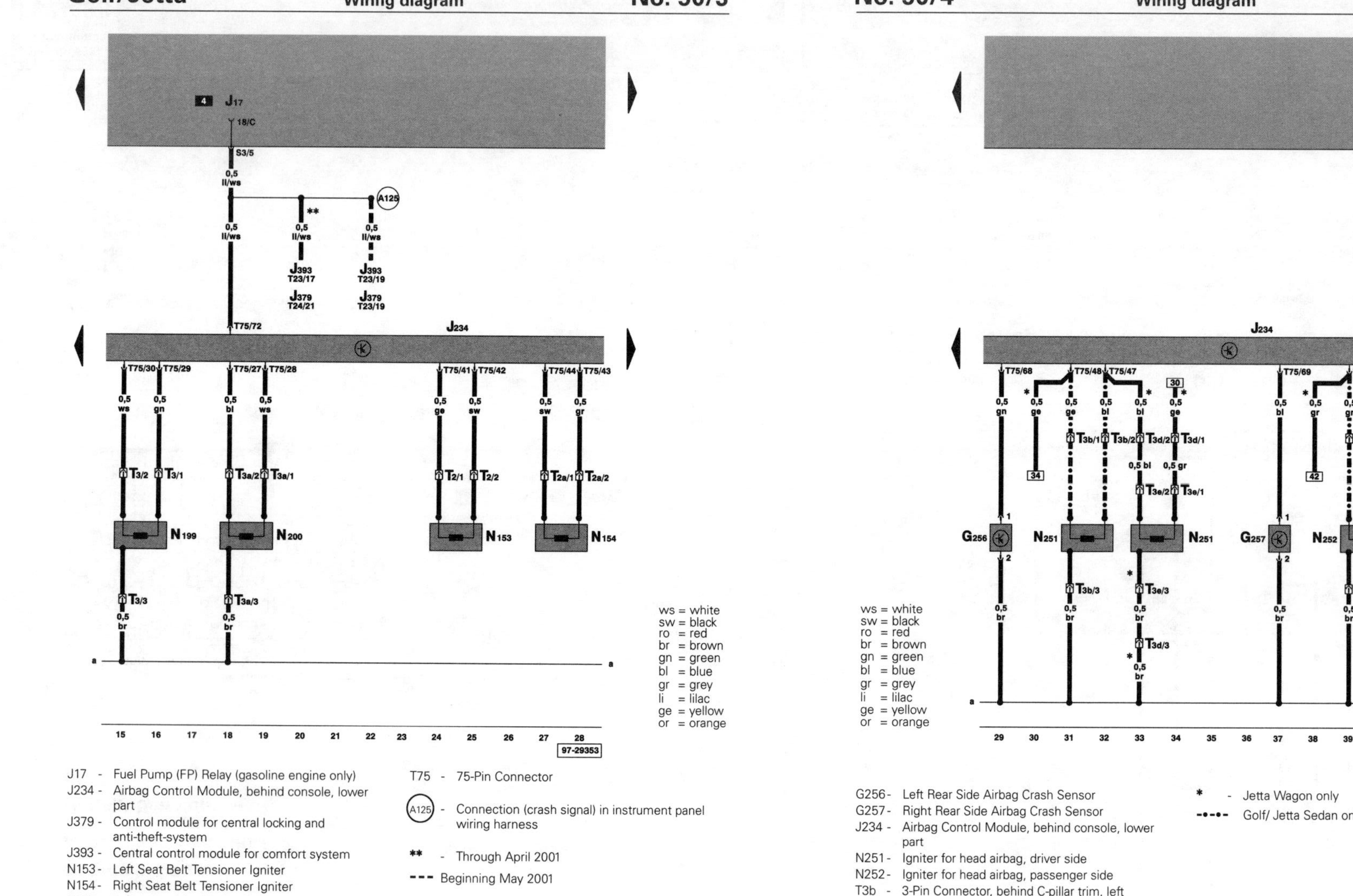

ws = white
sw = black
ro = red
br = brown
gn = green
bl = blue
gr = grey
li = lilac
ge = yellow
or = orange

J17 - Fuel Pump (FP) Relay (gasoline engine only)
J234 - Airbag Control Module, behind console, lower part
J379 - Control module for central locking and anti-theft-system
J393 - Central control module for comfort system
N153 - Left Seat Belt Tensioner Igniter
N154 - Right Seat Belt Tensioner Igniter
N199 - Igniter for side airbag, driver's side
N200 - Igniter for side airbag, passenger side
T2 - Double Connector, below driver's seat
T2a - Double Connector, below passenger's seat
T3 - 3-Pin Connector, below driver's seat
T3a - 3-Pin Connector, below passenger's seat
T23 - 23-Pin Connector
T24 - 24-Pin Connector
T75 - 75-Pin Connector
(A125) - Connection (crash signal) in instrument panel wiring harness
** - Through April 2001
--- Beginning May 2001

Airbag control module, seat belt tensioner igniter, igniter for side airbags

ws = white
sw = black
ro = red
br = brown
gn = green
bl = blue
gr = grey
li = lilac
ge = yellow
or = orange

G256 - Left Rear Side Airbag Crash Sensor
G257 - Right Rear Side Airbag Crash Sensor
J234 - Airbag Control Module, behind console, lower part
N251 - Igniter for head airbag, driver side
N252 - Igniter for head airbag, passenger side
T3b - 3-Pin Connector, behind C-pillar trim, left
T3c - 3-Pin Connector, behind C-pillar trim, right
T3d - 3-Pin Connector, near connector station D-pillar, left
T3e - 3-Pin Connector, behind D-pillar trim, left
T3f - 3-Pin Connector, near connector station D-pillar, right
T3g - 3-Pin Connector, behind D-pillar trim, right
T75 - 75-Pin Connector
* - Jetta Wagon only
-•-•- Golf/ Jetta Sedan only

Airbag control module, left and right rear side airbag crash sensors, igniter for head airbag (driver side), igniter for head airbag (passenger side)

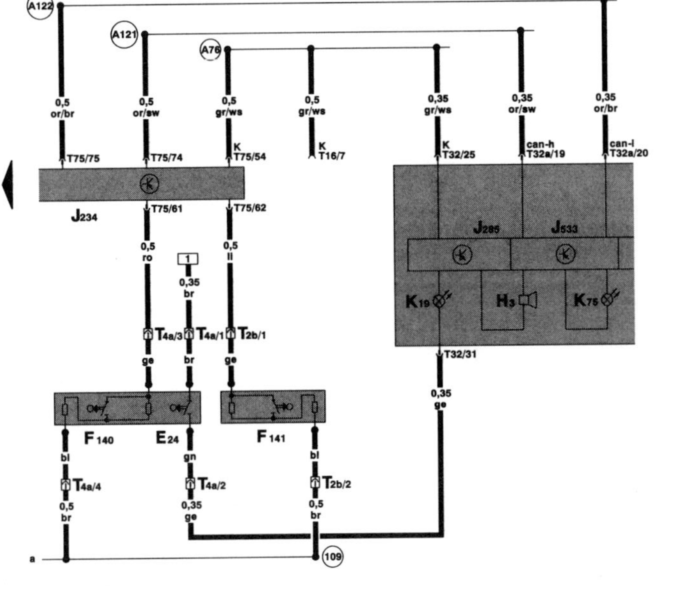

ws = white
sw = black
ro = red
br = brown
gn = green
bl = blue
gr = grey
li = lilac
ge = yellow
or = orange

E24 - Left Seat Belt Switch
F140 - Left Front Seat Belt Microswitch*
F141 - Right Front Seat Belt Microswitch*
H3 - Warning Buzzer
J234 - Airbag Control Module, behind console, lower part
J285 - Control module with indicator unit in instrument panel insert
J533 - Data Bus On Board Diagnostic Interface
K19 - Seat Belt Warning Light
K75 - Airbag Malfunction Indicator Lamp (MIL)
T2b - Double Connector, below passenger's seat
T4a - 4-Pin Connector, below driver's seat
T16 - Data Link Connector (DLC), below instrument panel, left
T32 - 32-Pin Connector, blue
T32a - 32-Pin Connector, green
T75 - 75-Pin Connector

(109) - Ground connection, in airbag wiring harness
(A76) - Connector (K-diagnosis wire) in instrument panel wiring harness
(A121) - Connection (high bus), in instrument panel wiring harness
(A122) - Connection (low bus), in instrument panel wiring harness

* - Scan Tool display text for these component codes may be different than indicated

Edition 03/01
USA.5102.10.21

Airbag control module, seat belt warning light, airbag malfunction indicator lamp (MIL), left seat belt switch, left and right front seat belt microswitches

THIS PAGE INTENTIONALLY LEFT BLANK

Jetta Wagon - Standard Equipment,

from January 2001

Deviate relay location and fuseplacements as well as the locations of multiple connectors see section "component locations".

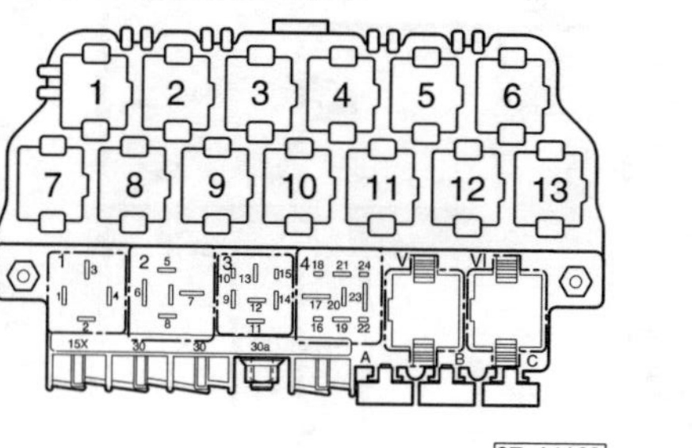

97-14163

Relay location on the thirteenfold auxiliary relay panel, above relay panel:

- **3** Starting Interlock Relay (53)

Relay panel:

- **1** Dual Horn Relay (53)
- **2** Load Reduction Relay (100)
- **V** Wiper/Washer Intermittent Relay (377)
- **VI**

Note: Number in parentheses indicates production control number stamped on relay housing.

Fuse colors

- 30 A - green
- 25 A - white
- 20 A - yellow
- 15 A - blue
- 10 A - red
- 7,5 A - brown
- 5 A - beige
- 3 A - violet

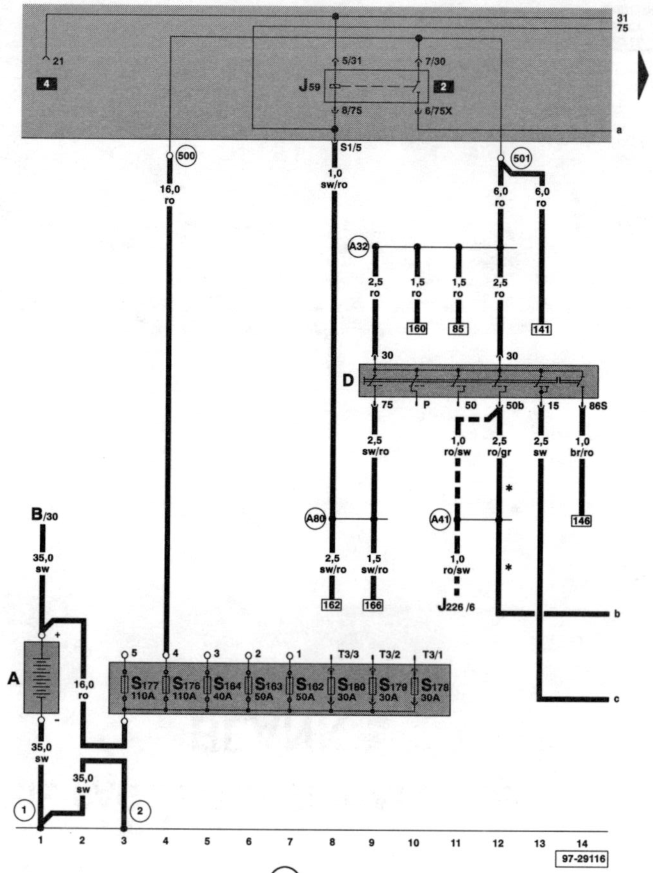

97-29116

- ws = white
- sw = black
- ro = red
- br = brown
- gn = green
- bl = blue
- gr = grey
- li = lilac
- ge = yellow
- or = orange

- A - Battery
- B - Starter
- D - Ignition/Starter Switch
- J59 - Load Reduction Relay
- J226 - Park/Neutral Position (PNP) Relay
- S162 - Fuse -1- (30) in fuse bracket/battery
- S163 - Fuse -2- (30) in fuse bracket/battery
- S164 - Fuse -3- (30) in fuse bracket/battery
- S176 - Fuse -4- (30) in fuse bracket/battery
- S177 - Fuse -5- (30) in fuse bracket/battery
- S178 - Fuse -6- (30) in fuse bracket/battery
- S179 - Fuse -7- (30) in fuse bracket/battery
- S180 - Fuse -8- (30) in fuse bracket/battery
- T3 - 3-Pin Connector
- (1) - Ground strap, battery to body
- (2) - Ground strap, transmission to body
- (500) - Threaded connection -1- (30) on the relay plate
- (501) - Threaded connection -2- (30) on the relay plate
- (A32) - Plus connection (30), in instrument panel wiring harness
- (A41) - Plus connection (50), in instrument panel wiring harness (gasoline engine only)
- (A80) - Connector -1- (X) in instrument panel wiring harness
- * - Manual transmission only
- --- Automatic transmission only

Battery, ignition/starter switch

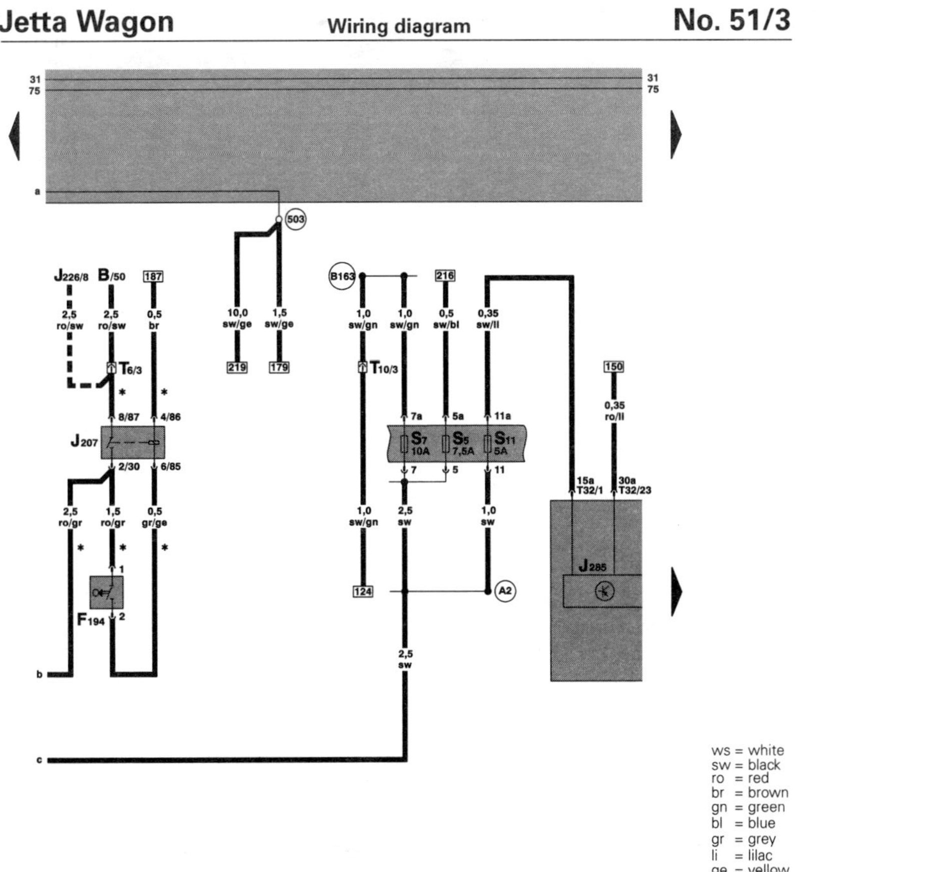

ws = white
sw = black
ro = red
br = brown
gn = green
bl = blue
gr = grey
li = lilac
ge = yellow
or = orange

B - Starter
F194 - Clutch Pedal Position (CPP) Switch*
J207 - Starting Interlock Relay*
J226 - Park/Neutral Position (PNP) Relay
J285 - Control module with indicator unit in instrument panel insert
S5 - Fuse 5 in fuse holder
S7 - Fuse 7 in fuse holder
S11 - Fuse 11 in fuse holder
T6 - 6-Pin Connector, brown, in protective housing for connectors, in plenum chamber, left
T10 - 10-Pin Connector, orange, in protective housing for connectors, in plenum chamber, left
T32 - 32-Pin Connector, blue

(503) - Threaded connection -2- (75x) on the relay plate
(A2) - Plus connection (15), in instrument panel wiring harness
(B163) - Plus connector -1- (15) in wiring harness interior
* - Manual transmission only
--- Automatic transmission only

Instrument cluster, clutch pedal position (CPP) switch, starting interlock relay

31
75
D2
J...
J...
J...
242
G22
T10/1
T10/9
153
T10/6
T14a/3
A27
T32a/2
T32a/17
T32a/5
T32/11
T32/20
T32/3
T32/28
J362
J285
L75
K117
G5
Y4
G21
T32/25
146
29 30 31 32 33 34 35 36 37 38 39 40 41 42
97-29118

ws = white
sw = black
ro = red
br = brown
gn = green
bl = blue
gr = grey
li = lilac
ge = yellow
or = orange

D2 - Induction coil of anti-theft immobilizer
G5 - Tachometer
G21 - Speedometer
G22 - Speedometer Vehicle Speed Sensor
J285 - Control module with indicator unit in instrument panel insert
J362 - Control module for anti-theft immobilizer
J... - Engine Control Module (ECM)
K117 - Warning light for anti-theft immobilizer sensor
L75 - Digital Display Light
T10 - 10-Pin Connector, orange, in protective housing for connectors, in plenum chamber, left
T14a - 14-Pin Connector, in engine compartment, in wiring duct, left
T32 - 32-Pin Connector, blue

T32a - 32-Pin Connector, green
Y4 - Odometer Display

(A27) - Wire connection (vehicle speed signal), in instrument panel wiring harness

Instrument cluster, tachometer, speedometer, odometer display, anti-theft immobilizer, warning light for anti-theft immobilizer sensor

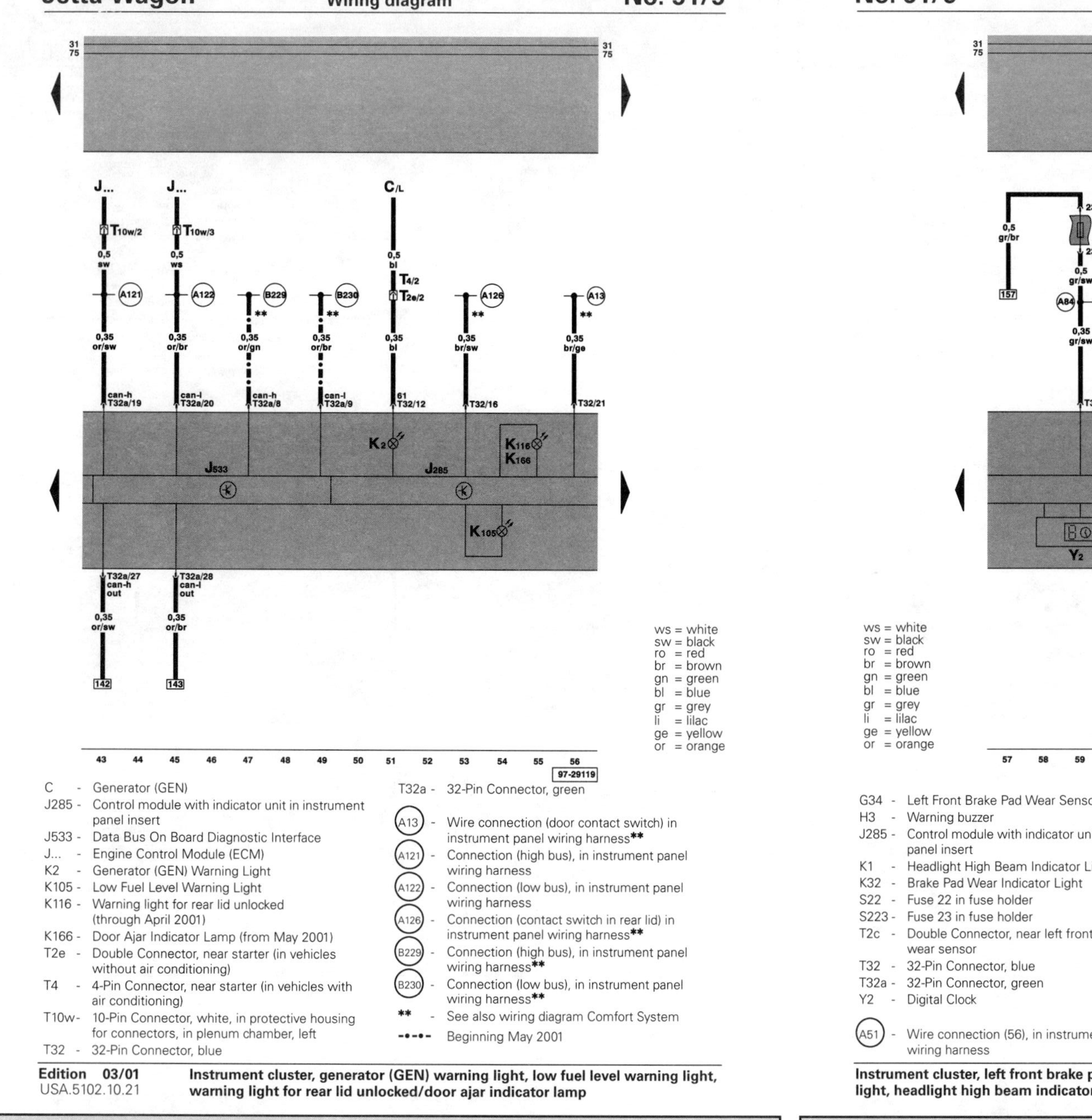

ws = white
sw = black
ro = red
br = brown
gn = green
bl = blue
gr = grey
li = lilac
ge = yellow
or = orange

- C - Generator (GEN)
- J285 - Control module with indicator unit in instrument panel insert
- J533 - Data Bus On Board Diagnostic Interface
- J... - Engine Control Module (ECM)
- K2 - Generator (GEN) Warning Light
- K105 - Low Fuel Level Warning Light
- K116 - Warning light for rear lid unlocked (through April 2001)
- K166 - Door Ajar Indicator Lamp (from May 2001)
- T2e - Double Connector, near starter (in vehicles without air conditioning)
- T4 - 4-Pin Connector, near starter (in vehicles with air conditioning)
- T10w - 10-Pin Connector, white, in protective housing for connectors, in plenum chamber, left
- T32 - 32-Pin Connector, blue
- T32a - 32-Pin Connector, green
- (A13) - Wire connection (door contact switch) in instrument panel wiring harness**
- (A121) - Connection (high bus), in instrument panel wiring harness
- (A122) - Connection (low bus), in instrument panel wiring harness
- (A126) - Connection (contact switch in rear lid) in instrument panel wiring harness**
- (B229) - Connection (high bus), in instrument panel wiring harness**
- (B230) - Connection (low bus), in instrument panel wiring harness**
- ** - See also wiring diagram Comfort System
- --•-•- - Beginning May 2001

Instrument cluster, generator (GEN) warning light, low fuel level warning light, warning light for rear lid unlocked/door ajar indicator lamp

ws = white
sw = black
ro = red
br = brown
gn = green
bl = blue
gr = grey
li = lilac
ge = yellow
or = orange

- G34 - Left Front Brake Pad Wear Sensor
- H3 - Warning buzzer
- J285 - Control module with indicator unit in instrument panel insert
- K1 - Headlight High Beam Indicator Light
- K32 - Brake Pad Wear Indicator Light
- S22 - Fuse 22 in fuse holder
- S223 - Fuse 23 in fuse holder
- T2c - Double Connector, near left front brake pad wear sensor
- T32 - 32-Pin Connector, blue
- T32a - 32-Pin Connector, green
- Y2 - Digital Clock
- (A51) - Wire connection (56), in instrument panel wiring harness
- (A84) - Connector (58L) in instrument panel wiring harness
- (A85) - Connector (58R) in instrument panel wiring harness

Instrument cluster, left front brake pad wear sensor, brake pad wear indicator light, headlight high beam indicator light, digital clock

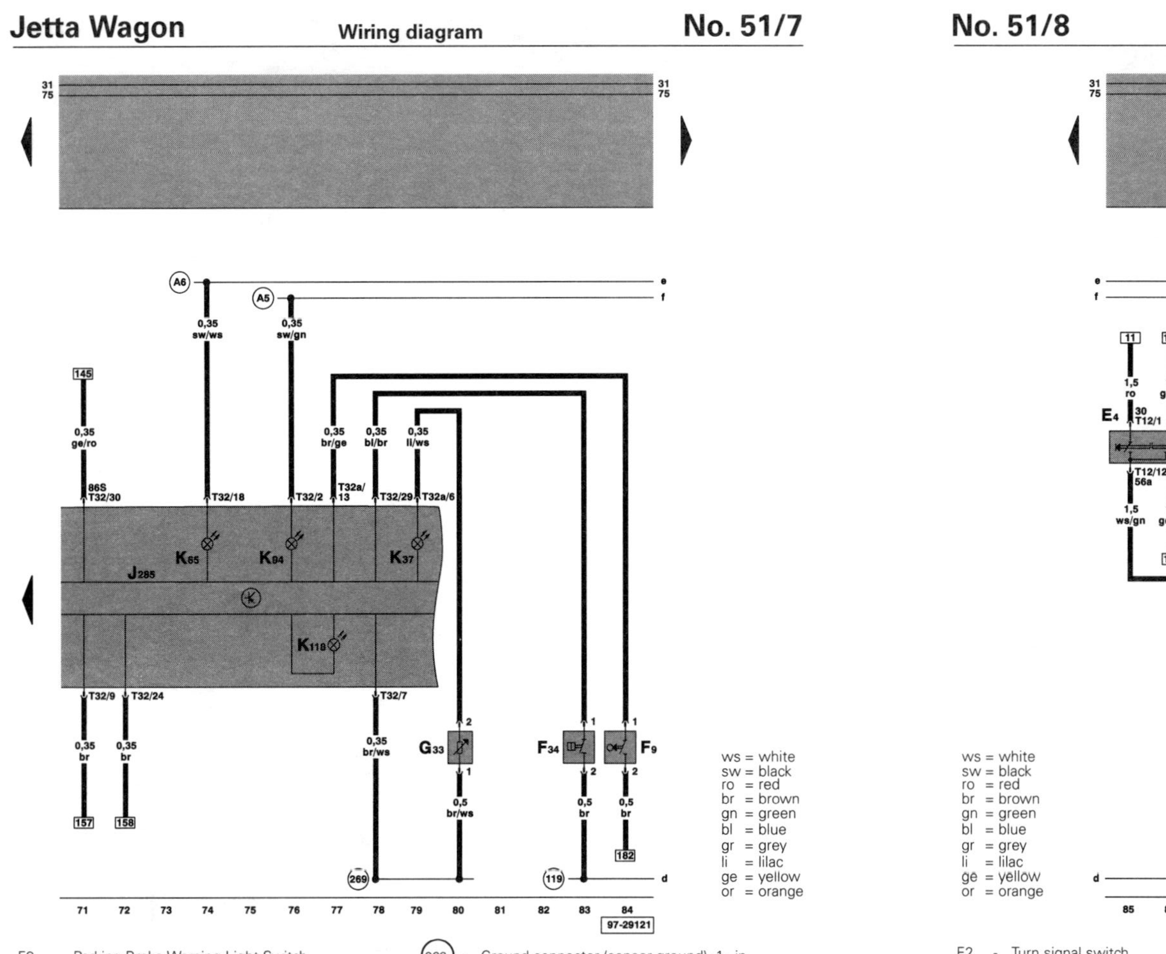

ws = white
sw = black
ro = red
br = brown
gn = green
bl = blue
gr = grey
li = lilac
ge = yellow
or = orange

F9 - Parking Brake Warning Light Switch
F34 - Brake Fluid Level Warning Switch
G33 - Windshield Washer Fluid Level Sensor
J285 - Control module with indicator unit in instrument panel insert
K37 - Low Windshield Washer Fluid Level Indicator Light
K65 - Left Turn Signal Indicator Light
K94 - Right Turn Signal Indicator Light
K118 - Warning light for brake system
T32 - 32-Pin Connector, blue
T32a - 32-Pin Connector, green

(119) - Ground connection -1-, in headlight wiring harness

(269) - Ground connector (sensor ground) -1-, in instrument panel wiring harness

(A5) - Plus connection (right turn signal), in instrument panel wiring harness

(A6) - Plus connection (left turn signal), in instrument panel wiring harness

Instrument cluster, parking brake warning light switch, brake fluid level warning switch, low windshield washer fluid level indication, left and right turn signal indicator lights

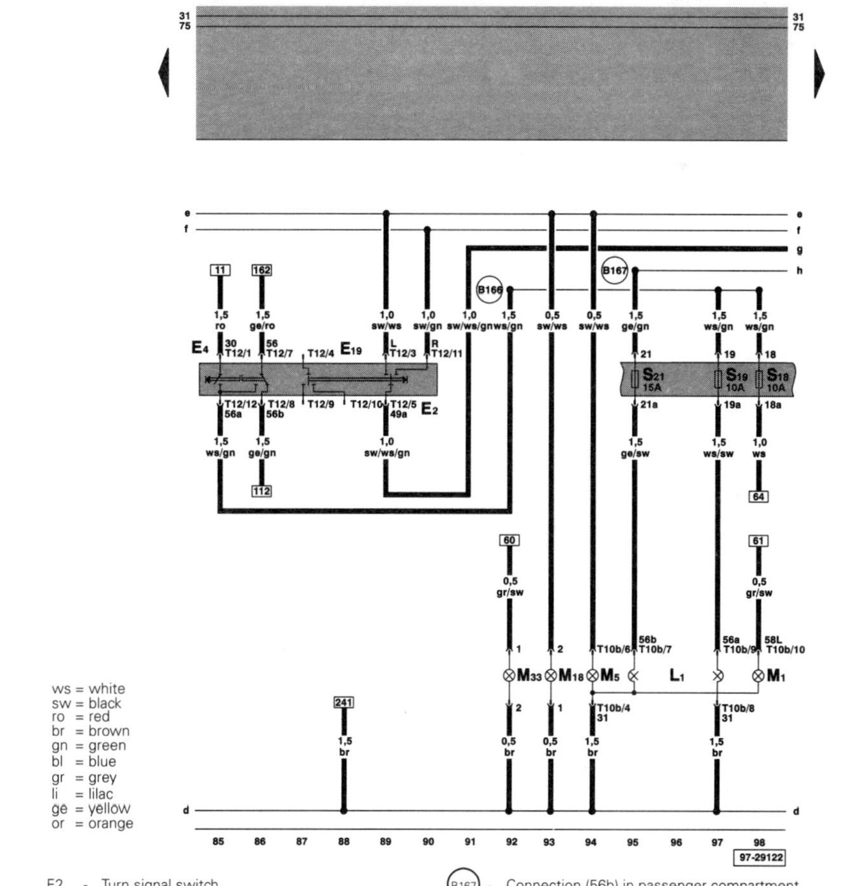

ws = white
sw = black
ro = red
br = brown
gn = green
bl = blue
gr = grey
li = lilac
ge = yellow
or = orange

E2 - Turn signal switch
E4 - Headlight Dimmer/Flasher Switch
E19 - Park Light Switch
L1 - Left Headlight
M1 - Left Parking Light
M5 - Left Front Turn Signal Light
M18 - Left, Side Turn Signal Light
M33 - Light for side marker front left
S18 - Fuse 18 in fuse holder
S19 - Fuse 19 in fuse holder
S21 - Fuse 21 in fuse holder
T10b - 10-Pin Connector
T12 - 12-Pin Connector

(B166) - Connection (56a) in passenger compartment wiring harness

(B167) - Connection (56b) in passenger compartment wiring harness

Turn signal switch, headlight dimmer/flasher switch, left front turn signal light, light for side marker front left, left headlight

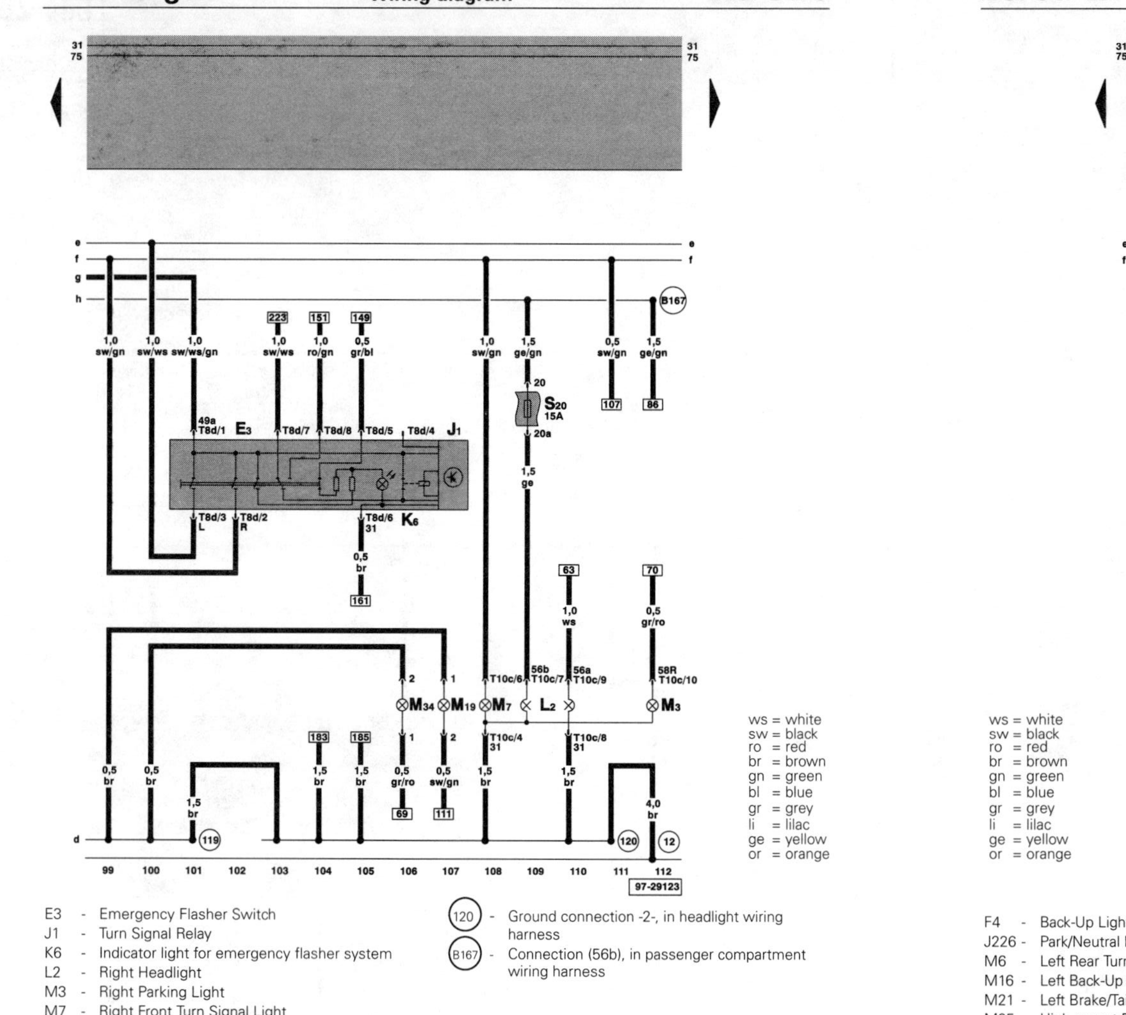

ws = white
sw = black
ro = red
br = brown
gn = green
bl = blue
gr = grey
li = lilac
ge = yellow
or = orange

- E3 - Emergency Flasher Switch
- J1 - Turn Signal Relay
- K6 - Indicator light for emergency flasher system
- L2 - Right Headlight
- M3 - Right Parking Light
- M7 - Right Front Turn Signal Light
- M19 - Right, Side Turn Signal Light
- M34 - Light for side marker front right
- S20 - Fuse 20 in fuse holder
- T8d - 8-Pin Connector
- T10c - 10-Pin Connector
- (12) - Ground connection, in engine compartment, left
- (119) - Ground connection -1-, in headlight wiring harness
- (120) - Ground connection -2-, in headlight wiring harness
- (B167) - Connection (56b), in passenger compartment wiring harness

Edition 03/01
USA.5102.10.21

Emergency flasher switch, turn signal relay, right front turn signal light, light for side marker front right, right headlight

ws = white
sw = black
ro = red
br = brown
gn = green
bl = blue
gr = grey
li = lilac
ge = yellow
or = orange

- F4 - Back-Up Light Switch
- J226 - Park/Neutral Position (PNP) Relay
- M6 - Left Rear Turn Signal Light
- M16 - Left Back-Up Light
- M21 - Left Brake/Tail Light
- M25 - High-mount Brake Light (18 light emitting diodes)
- T5 - 5-Pin Connector, black, connector station D-pillar, left
- T5h - 5-Pin Connector, near left A-pillar, lower part, in harness
- T6a - 6-Pin Connector
- T10 - 10-Pin Connector, orange, in protective housing for connectors, in plenum chamber, left
- (50) - Ground connection, in luggage compartment, left
- (86) - Ground connection -1-, in rear wiring harness
- (218) - Ground connection -1-, in rear lid wiring harness
- (A6) - Plus connection (left turn signal), in instrument panel wiring harness
- (A87) - Connector (reverse lamp), in instrument panel wiring harness
- (B182) - Connection (RF), in passenger compartment wiring harness
- (W1) - Plus connection (54), in rear wiring harness
- * - Manual transmission only
- --- Automatic transmission only

Back-up light switch, left rear turn signal light, left back-up light, left brake/tail light, high-mount brake light

Edition 03/01
USA.5102.10.21

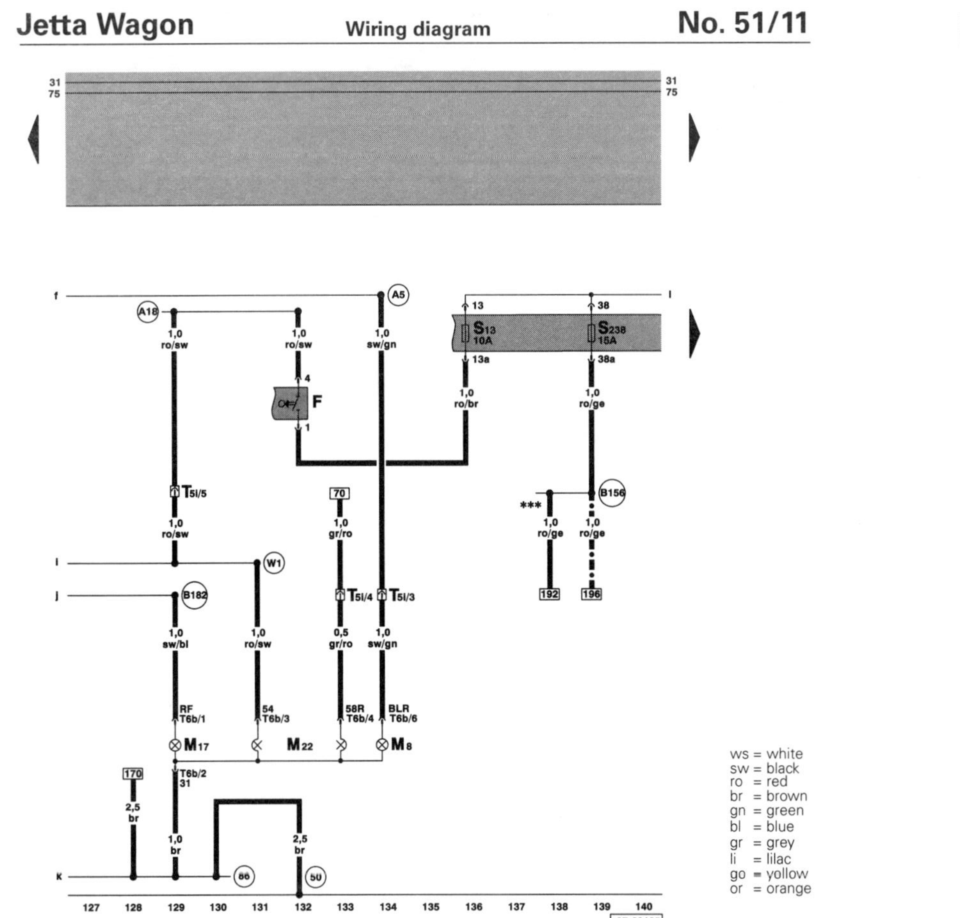

ws = white
sw = black
ro = red
br = brown
gn = green
bl = blue
gr = grey
li = lilac
go = yellow
or = orange

F - Brake Light Switch
M8 - Right Rear Turn Signal Light
M17 - Right Back-Up Light
M22 - Right Brake/Tail Light
S13 - Fuse 13 in fuse holder
S238 - Fuse 38 in fuse holder
T5i - 5-Pin Connector, near left A-pillar, lower part, in harness
T6b - 6-Pin Connector

(50) - Ground connection, in luggage compartment, left

(86) - Ground connection -1-, in rear wiring harness

(A5) - Plus connection (right turn signal), in instrument panel wiring harness

(A18) - Wire connection (54), in instrument panel wiring harness

(B156) - Plus connector (30a), in wiring harness interior

(B182) - Connection (RF), in passenger compartment wiring harness

(W1) - Plus connection (54), in rear wiring harness

*** - Through April 2001

-•-•- - Beginning May 2001

Edition 03/01
USA.5102.10.21

Brake light switch, right rear turn signal light, right back-up light, right brake/tail light

ws = white
sw = black
ro = red
br = brown
gn = green
bl = blue
gr = grey
li = lilac
ge = yellow
or = orange

L28 - Cigarette Lighter Light
R - Radio
S12 - Fuse 12 in fuse holder
S15 - Fuse 15 in fuse holder
S237 - Fuse 37 in fuse holder
S239 - Fuse 39 in fuse holder
S240 - Fuse 40 in fuse holder
S241 - Fuse 41 in fuse holder
S242 - Fuse 42 in fuse holder
T8 - 8-Pin Connector
T16 - Data Link Connector (DLC), below instrument panel, left
U1 - Cigarette Lighter

(45) - Ground connection, behind instrument panel, center

(81) - Ground connection -1-, in instrument panel wiring harness

(A4) - Plus connection (58b), in instrument panel wiring harness

(A21) - Wire connection (86s), in instrument panel wiring harness

(A23) - Wire connection (30a), in instrument panel wiring harness

(A76) - Connector (K-diagnosis wire) in instrument panel wiring harness

(B161) - Connector (anti-theft warning system), in wiring harness interior*

* - Vehicles with anti-theft warning system only (see wiring diagram comfort system/ central locking)

Data Link Connector (DLC), radio connection, cigarette lighter

Edition 03/01
USA.5102.10.21

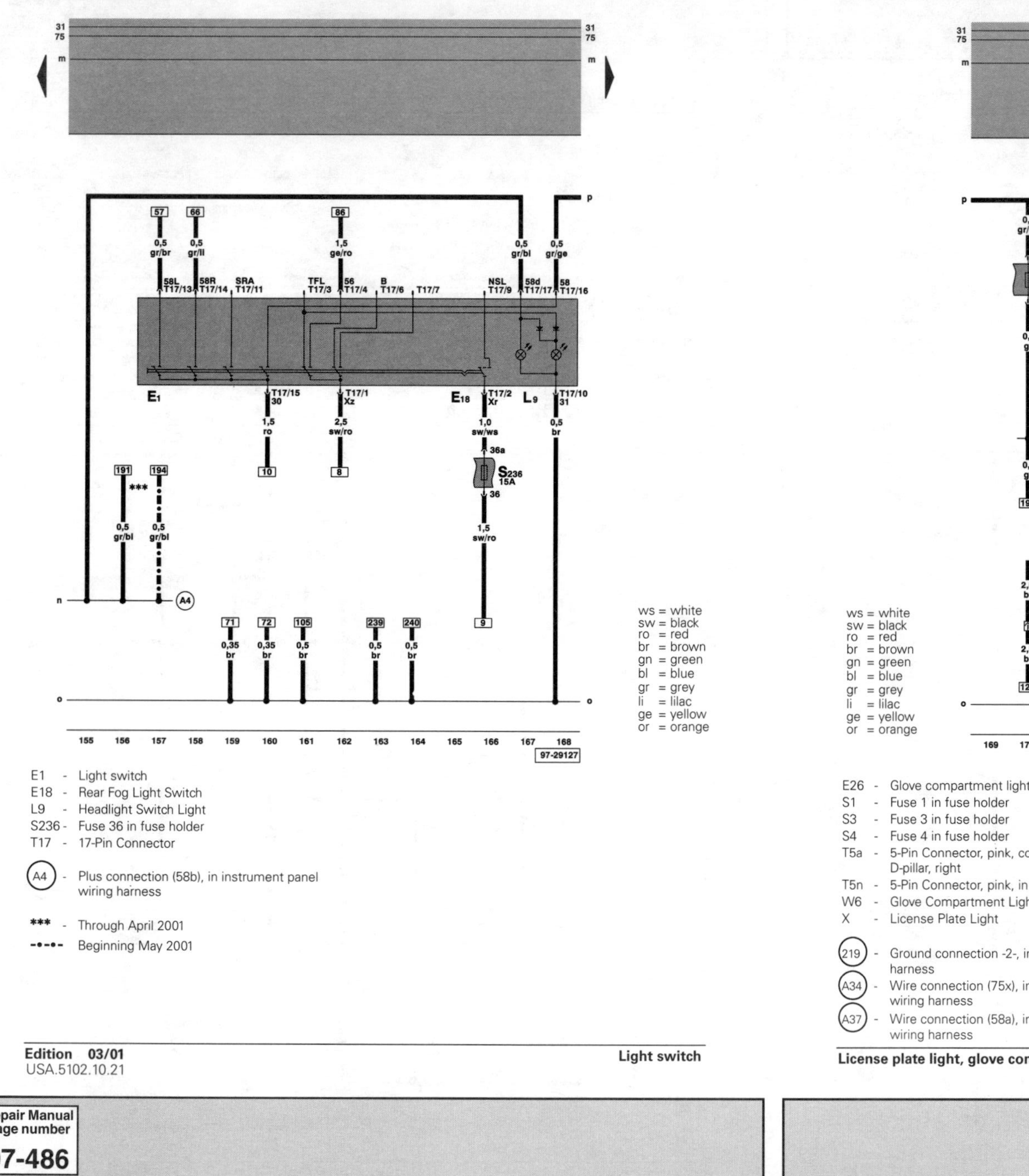

ws = white
sw = black
ro = red
br = brown
gn = green
bl = blue
gr = grey
li = lilac
ge = yellow
or = orange

E1 - Light switch
E18 - Rear Fog Light Switch
L9 - Headlight Switch Light
S236 - Fuse 36 in fuse holder
T17 - 17-Pin Connector

(A4) - Plus connection (58b), in instrument panel wiring harness

*** - Through April 2001

-•-•- - Beginning May 2001

ws = white
sw = black
ro = red
br = brown
gn = green
bl = blue
gr = grey
li = lilac
ge = yellow
or = orange

E26 - Glove compartment light switch
S1 - Fuse 1 in fuse holder
S3 - Fuse 3 in fuse holder
S4 - Fuse 4 in fuse holder
T5a - 5-Pin Connector, pink, connector station D-pillar, right
T5n - 5-Pin Connector, pink, in rear lid
W6 - Glove Compartment Light
X - License Plate Light

(219) - Ground connection -2-, in rear lid wiring harness
(A34) - Wire connection (75x), in instrument panel wiring harness
(A37) - Wire connection (58a), in instrument panel wiring harness

(W11) - Wire connection (58), in rear lid wiring harness

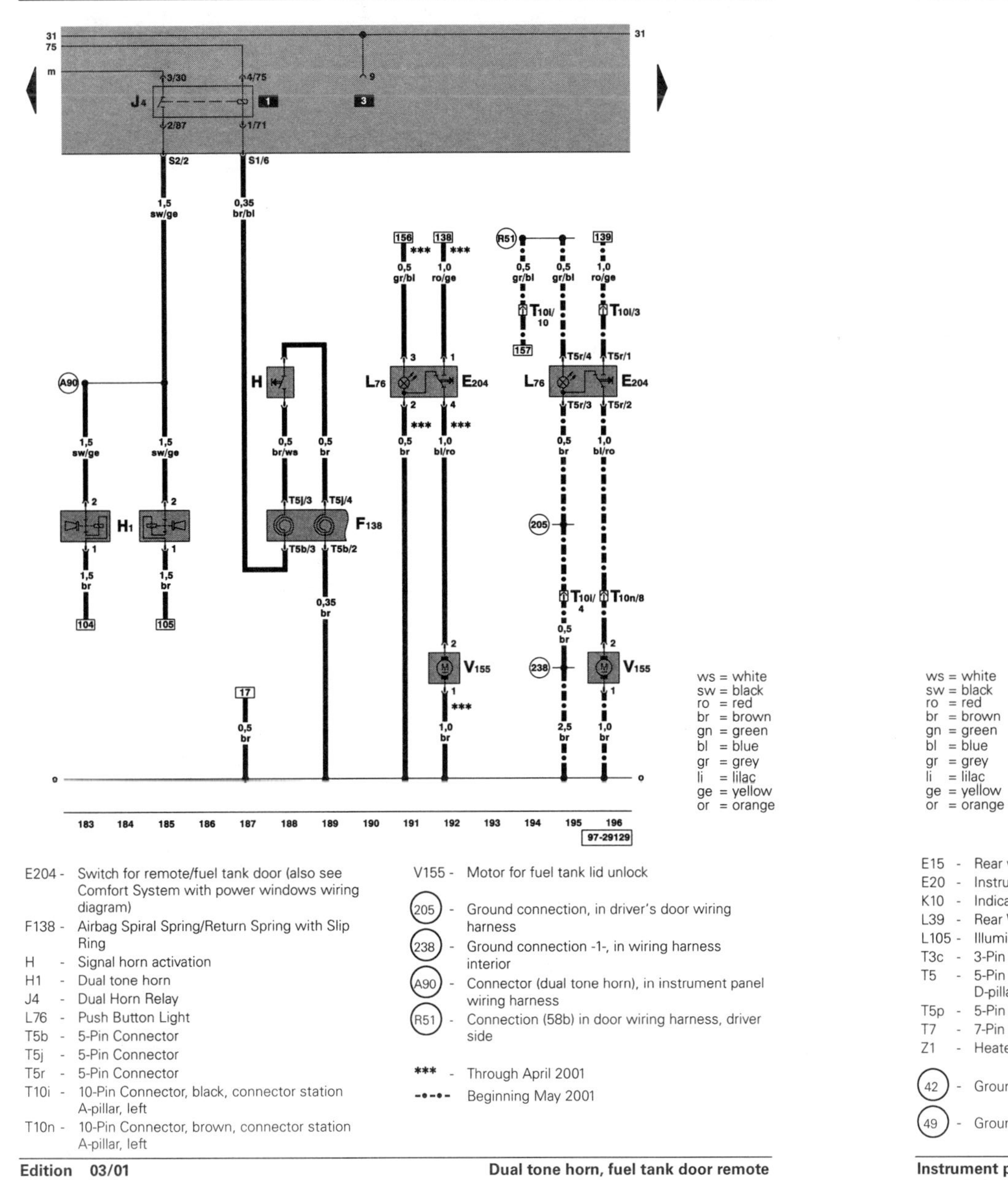

ws = white
sw = black
ro = red
br = brown
gn = green
bl = blue
gr = grey
li = lilac
ge = yellow
or = orange

E204 - Switch for remote/fuel tank door (also see Comfort System with power windows wiring diagram)
F138 - Airbag Spiral Spring/Return Spring with Slip Ring
H - Signal horn activation
H1 - Dual tone horn
J4 - Dual Horn Relay
L76 - Push Button Light
T5b - 5-Pin Connector
T5j - 5-Pin Connector
T5r - 5-Pin Connector
T10i - 10-Pin Connector, black, connector station A-pillar, left
T10n - 10-Pin Connector, brown, connector station A-pillar, left

V155 - Motor for fuel tank lid unlock

(205) - Ground connection, in driver's door wiring harness

(238) - Ground connection -1-, in wiring harness interior

(A90) - Connector (dual tone horn), in instrument panel wiring harness

(R51) - Connection (58b) in door wiring harness, driver side

*** - Through April 2001

-•-•- - Beginning May 2001

Dual tone horn, fuel tank door remote

ws = white
sw = black
ro = red
br = brown
gn = green
bl = blue
gr = grey
li = lilac
ge = yellow
or = orange

E15 - Rear window defogger switch
E20 - Instrument Panel Light Dimmer Switch
K10 - Indicator light for heated rear windshield
L39 - Rear Window Defogger Switch Light
L105 - Illumination for lighting controller
T3c - 3-Pin Connector
T5 - 5-Pin Connector, black, connector station D-pillar, left
T5p - 5-Pin Connector, black, in rear lid
T7 - 7-Pin Connector
Z1 - Heated rear window

(42) - Ground connection, beside steering column

(49) - Ground connection, on steering column

(81) - Ground connection -1-, in instrument panel wiring harness

(135) - Ground connection -2-, in instrument panel wiring harness

Instrument panel light dimmer switch, rear window defogger switch, heated rear window

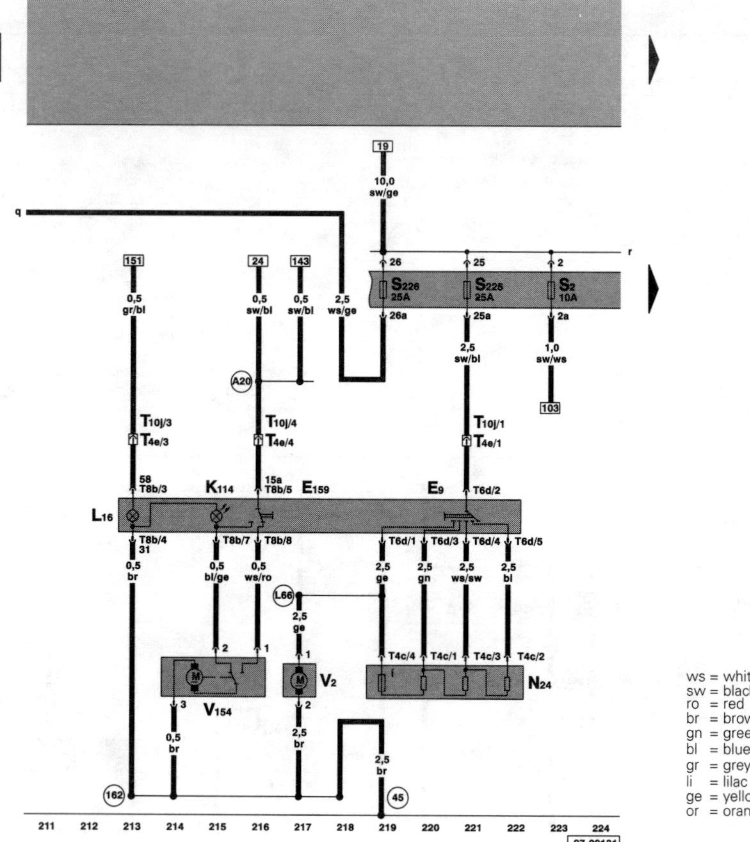

ws = white
sw = black
ro = red
br = brown
gn = green
bl = blue
gr = grey
li = lilac
ge = yellow
or = orange

E9 - Fresh Air Blower Switch
E159 - Fresh Air/Recirculating Flap Switch
K114 - Fresh Air and Recirculating Air Mode Indicator Light
L16 - Fresh Air Control Lever Light
N24 - Fresh Air Blower Series Resistance With Fuse
S2 - Fuse 2 in fuse holder
S225 - Fuse 25 in fuse holder
S226 - Fuse 26 in fuse holder
T4c - 4-Pin Connector
T4e - 4-Pin Connector, behind instrument panel, center (in vehicles without air conditioning)
T6d - 6-Pin Connector
T8b - 8-Pin Connector
T10j - 10-Pin Connector, behind instrument panel, center (in vehicles with air conditioning)

V2 - Fresh Air Blower
V154 - Servo motor for fresh-/recirculating air door

(45) - Ground connection, behind instrument panel, center
(162) - Ground connection, in blower motor wiring harness
(A20) - Wire connection (15a), in instrument panel wiring harness
(L66) - Connector, in wiring harness heater blower

Fresh air blower switch, fresh air/recirculating flap switch, fresh air blower

ws = white
sw = black
ro = red
br = brown
gn = green
bl = blue
gr = grey
li = lilac
ge = yellow
or = orange

S224 - Fuse 24 in fuse holder
S227 - Fuse 27 in fuse holder
T5a - 5-Pin Connector, black, connector station D-pillar, right
T5n - 5-Pin Connector, pink, in rear lid
T5h - 5-Pin Connector, near left A-pillar, lower part, in harness
T5i - 5-Pin Connector, near left A-pillar, lower part, in harness
V12 - Motor for rear windshield wiper
V59 - Windshield and Rear Window Washer Pump

(A96) - Connector (53a), in instrument panel wiring harness
(A97) - Connector (53), in instrument panel wiring harness

(A102) - Connector (windshield wiper), in instrument panel wiring harness

Motor for rear windshield wiper, windshield and rear window washer pump

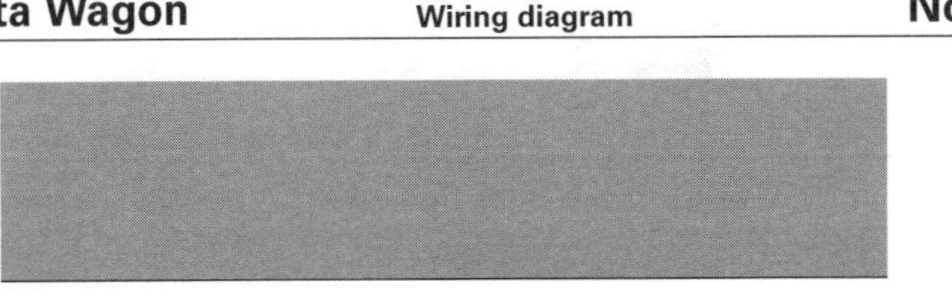

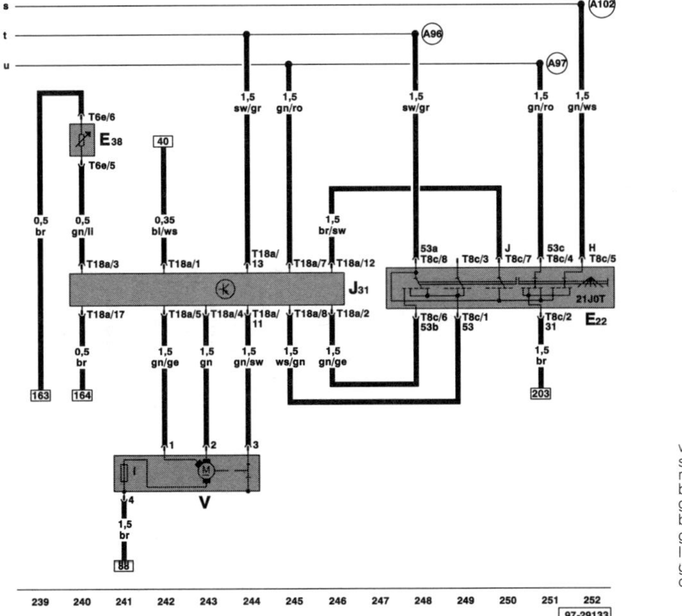

ws = white
sw = black
ro = red
br = brown
gn = green
bl = blue
gr = grey
li = lilac
ge = yellow
or = orange

- E22 - Windshield Wiper/Washer Switch
- E38 - Windshield Wiper Intermittent Regulator
- J31 - Wiper/Washer Intermittent Relay, on relais panel
- T6e - 6-Pin Connector
- T8c - 8-Pin Connector
- T18a - 18-Pin Connector
- V - Windshield Wiper Motor

- (A96) - Connector (53a), in instrument panel wiring harness
- (A97) - Connector (53), in instrument panel wiring harness
- (A102) - Connector (windshield wiper), in instrument panel wiring harness

Windshield wiper/washer switch, windshield wiper intermittent regulator, windshield wiper motor, wiper/washer intermittent relay

THIS PAGE INTENTIONALLY LEFT

BLANK

Golf /Jetta - Standard Equipment,

from May 2000

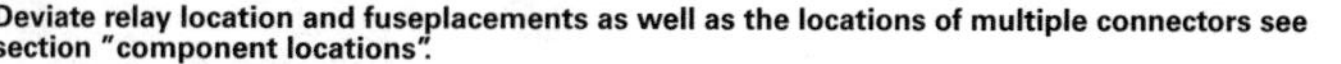

Deviate relay location and fuseplacements as well as the locations of multiple connectors see section "component locations".

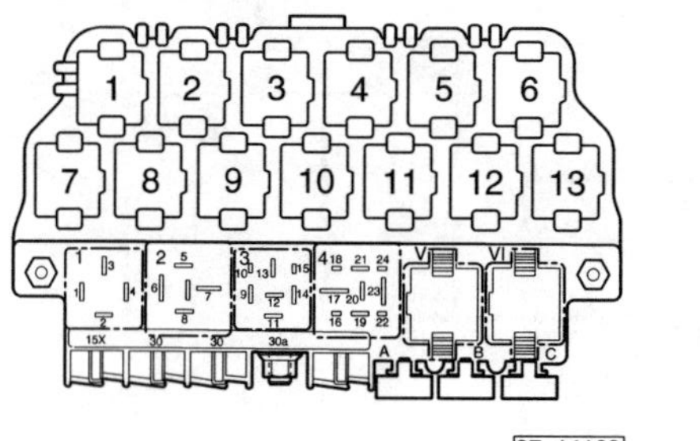

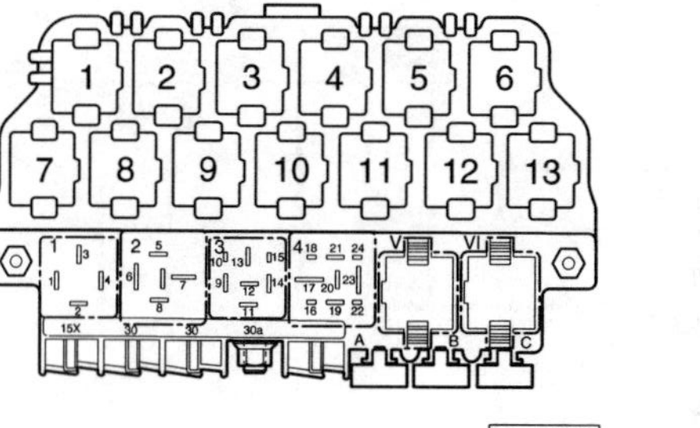

Relay location on the thirteenfold auxiliary relay panel, above relay panel:

3 Starting Interlock Relay (53)

Relay panel:

1 Dual Horn Relay (53)

2 Load Reduction Relay (100)

V **VI** Wiper/Washer Intermittent Relay (377)

Note: Number in parentheses indicates production control number stamped on relay housing.

Fuse colors

30 A - green
25 A - white
20 A - yellow
15 A - blue
10 A - red
7,5 A - brown
5 A - beige
3 A - violet

ws = white
sw = black
ro = red
br = brown
gn = green
bl = blue
gr = grey
li = lilac
ge = yellow
or = orange

A - Battery
B - Starter
D - Ignition/Starter Switch
J59 - Load Reduction Relay
J226 - Park/Neutral Position (PNP) Relay
S162 - Fuse -1- (30) in fuse bracket/battery
S163 - Fuse -2- (30) in fuse bracket/battery
S164 - Fuse -3- (30) in fuse bracket/battery
S176 - Fuse -4- (30) in fuse bracket/battery
S177 - Fuse -5- (30) in fuse bracket/battery
S178 - Fuse -6- (30) in fuse bracket/battery
S179 - Fuse -7- (30) in fuse bracket/battery
S180 - Fuse -8- (30) in fuse bracket/battery
T3 - 3-Pin Connector

(1) - Ground strap, battery to body
(2) - Ground strap, transmission to body
(500) - Threaded connection -1- (30) on the relay plate
(501) - Threaded connection -2- (30) on the relay plate
(A32) - Plus connection (30), in instrument panel wiring harness
(A41) - Plus connection (50), in instrument panel wiring harness (gasoline engine only)
(A80) - Connector -1- (X) in instrument panel wiring harness

* - Manual transmission only
--- Automatic transmission only

Battery, ignition/starter switch

97-29199

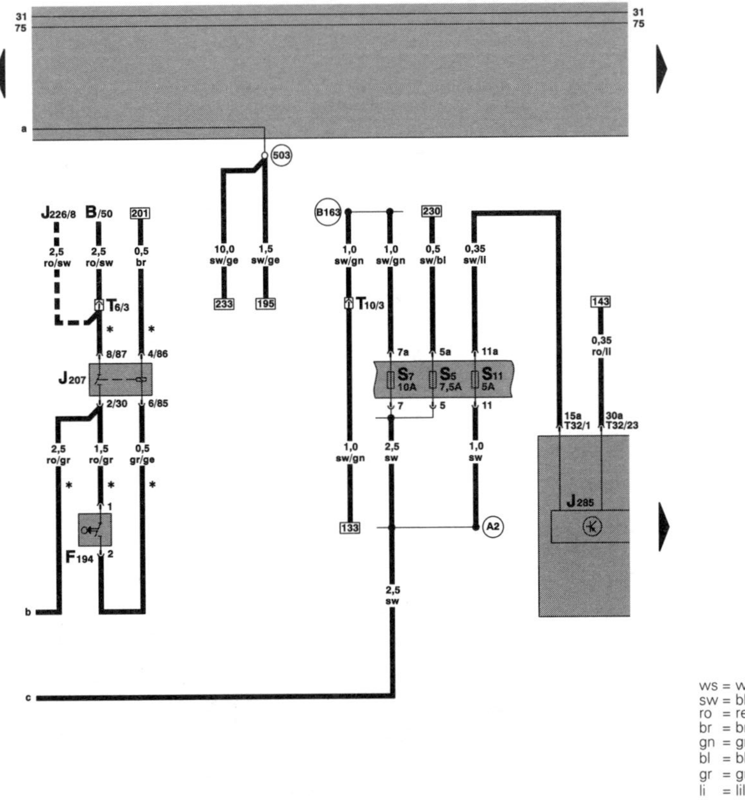

ws = white
sw = black
ro = red
br = brown
gn = green
bl = blue
gr = grey
li = lilac
ge = yellow
or = orange

B - Starter
F194 - Clutch Pedal Position (CPP) Switch*
J207 - Starting Interlock Relay*
J226 - Park/Neutral Position (PNP) Relay
J285 - Control module with indicator unit in instrument panel insert
S5 - Fuse 5 in fuse holder
S7 - Fuse 7 in fuse holder
S11 - Fuse 11 in fuse holder
T6 - 6-Pin Connector, brown, in protective housing for connectors, in plenum chamber, left
T10 - 10-Pin Connector, orange, in protective housing for connectors, in plenum chamber, left
T32 - 32-Pin Connector, blue

(503) - Threaded connection -2- (75x) on the relay plate
(A2) - Plus connection (15), in instrument panel wiring harness
(B163) - Plus connector -1- (15) in wiring harness interior
* - Manual transmission only
--- Automatic transmission only

Instrument cluster, clutch pedal position (CPP) switch, starting interlock relay

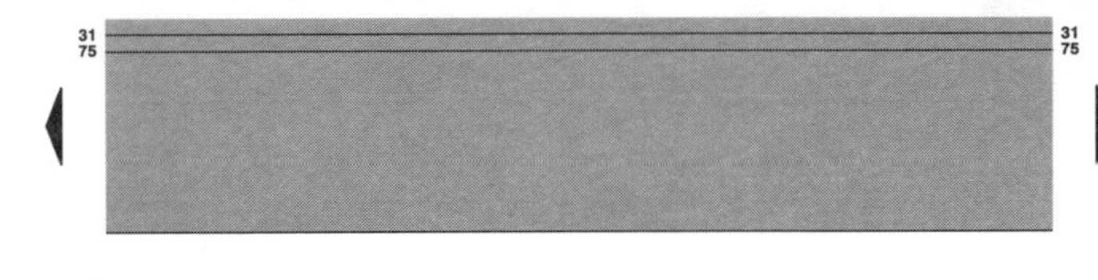

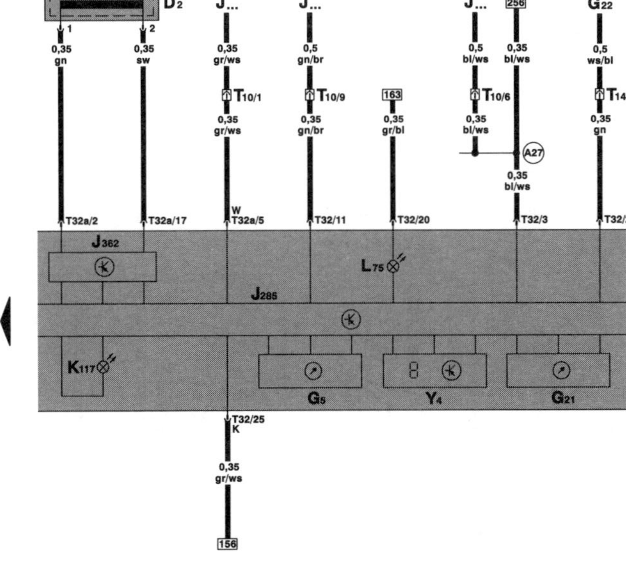

ws = white
sw = black
ro = red
br = brown
gn = green
bl = blue
gr = grey
li = lilac
ge = yellow
or = orange

D2 - Induction coil of anti-theft immobilizer
G5 - Tachometer
G21 - Speedometer
G22 - Speedometer Vehicle Speed Sensor
J285 - Control module with indicator unit in instrument panel insert
J362 - Control module for anti-theft immobilizer
J... - Engine Control Module (ECM)
K117 - Warning light for anti-theft immobilizer sensor
L75 - Digital Display Light
T10 - 10-Pin Connector, orange, in protective housing for connectors, in plenum chamber, left
T14a - 14-Pin Connector, in engine compartment, in wiring duct, left
T32 - 32-Pin Connector, blue
T32a - 32-Pin Connector, green

Y4 - Odometer Display
(A27) - Wire connection (vehicle speed signal), in instrument panel wiring harness

Instrument cluster, tachometer, speedometer, odometer display, anti-theft immobilizer, warning light for anti-theft immobilizer sensor

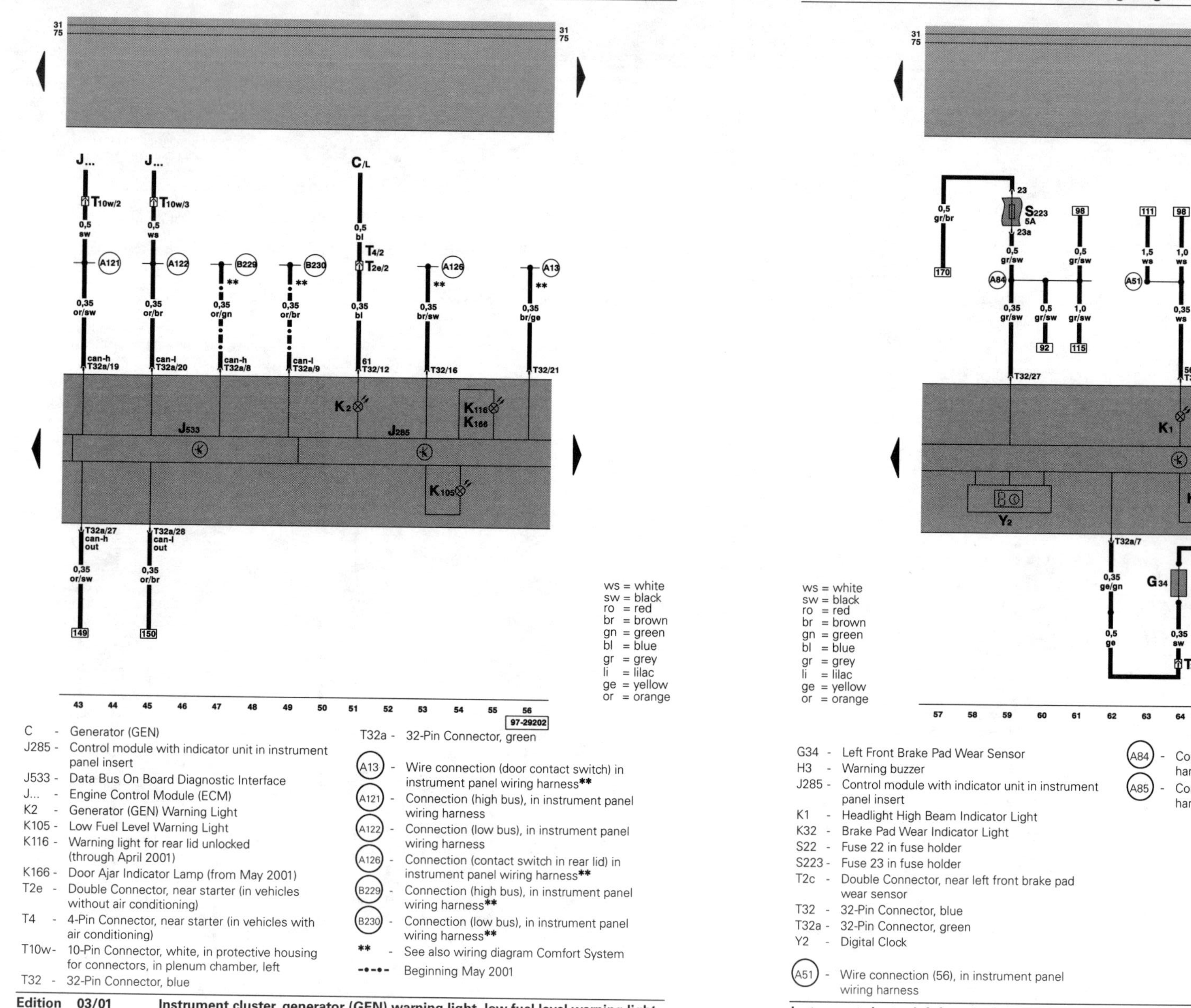

ws = white
sw = black
ro = red
br = brown
gn = green
bl = blue
gr = grey
li = lilac
ge = yellow
or = orange

43 44 45 46 47 48 49 50 51 52 53 54 55 56

97-29202

- C - Generator (GEN)
- J285 - Control module with indicator unit in instrument panel insert
- J533 - Data Bus On Board Diagnostic Interface
- J... - Engine Control Module (ECM)
- K2 - Generator (GEN) Warning Light
- K105 - Low Fuel Level Warning Light
- K116 - Warning light for rear lid unlocked (through April 2001)
- K166 - Door Ajar Indicator Lamp (from May 2001)
- T2e - Double Connector, near starter (in vehicles without air conditioning)
- T4 - 4-Pin Connector, near starter (in vehicles with air conditioning)
- T10w - 10-Pin Connector, white, in protective housing for connectors, in plenum chamber, left
- T32 - 32-Pin Connector, blue
- T32a - 32-Pin Connector, green
- (A13) - Wire connection (door contact switch) in instrument panel wiring harness**
- (A121) - Connection (high bus), in instrument panel wiring harness
- (A122) - Connection (low bus), in instrument panel wiring harness
- (A126) - Connection (contact switch in rear lid) in instrument panel wiring harness**
- (B229) - Connection (high bus), in instrument panel wiring harness**
- (B230) - Connection (low bus), in instrument panel wiring harness**
- ** - See also wiring diagram Comfort System
- -•-•- - Beginning May 2001

Edition 03/01
USA.5102.10.21

Instrument cluster, generator (GEN) warning light, low fuel level warning light, warning light for rear lid unlocked/door ajar indicator lamp

ws = white
sw = black
ro = red
br = brown
gn = green
bl = blue
gr = grey
li = lilac
ge = yellow
or = orange

57 58 59 60 61 62 63 64 65 66 67 68 69 70

97-29203

- G34 - Left Front Brake Pad Wear Sensor
- H3 - Warning buzzer
- J285 - Control module with indicator unit in instrument panel insert
- K1 - Headlight High Beam Indicator Light
- K32 - Brake Pad Wear Indicator Light
- S22 - Fuse 22 in fuse holder
- S223 - Fuse 23 in fuse holder
- T2c - Double Connector, near left front brake pad wear sensor
- T32 - 32-Pin Connector, blue
- T32a - 32-Pin Connector, green
- Y2 - Digital Clock
- (A51) - Wire connection (56), in instrument panel wiring harness
- (A84) - Connector (58L) in instrument panel wiring harness
- (A85) - Connector (58R) in instrument panel wiring harness

Instrument cluster, left front brake pad wear sensor, brake pad wear indicator light, headlight high beam indicator light, digital clock

Edition 03/01
USA.5102.10.21

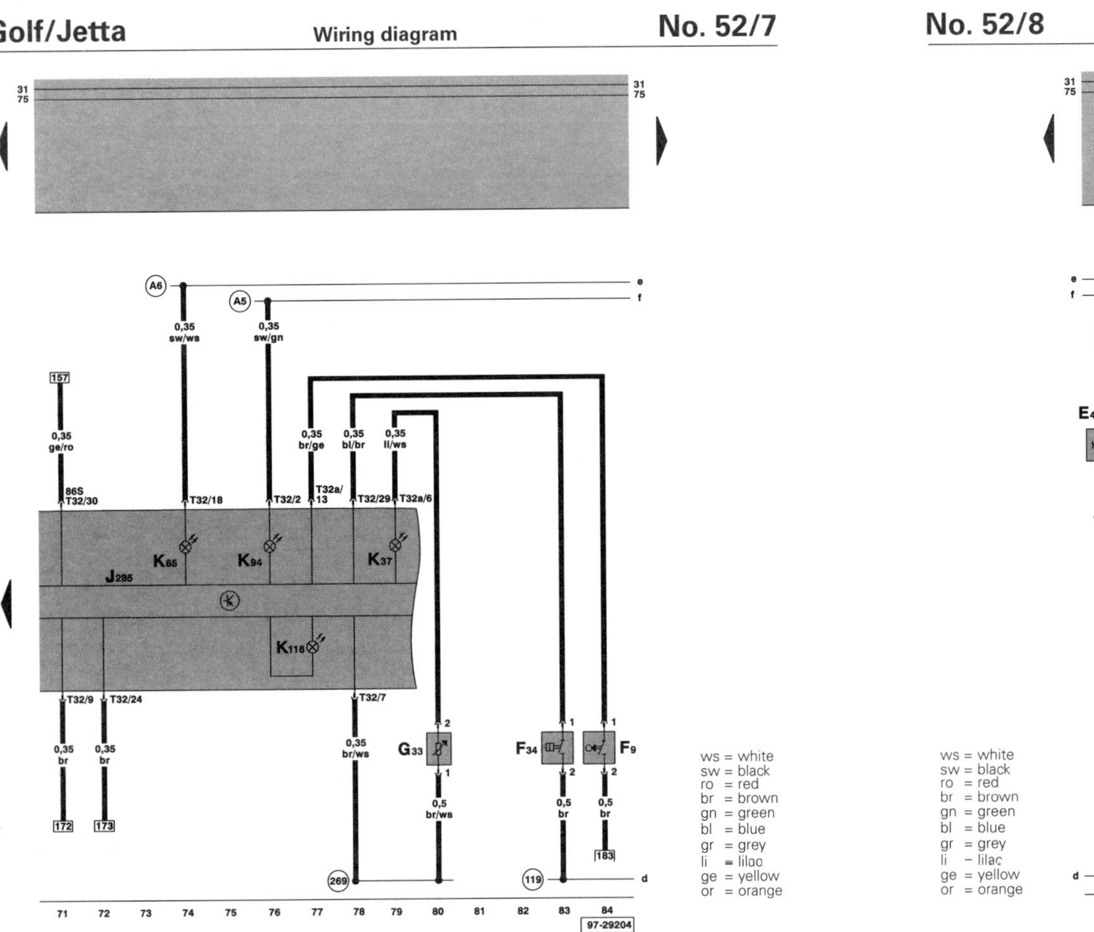

ws = white
sw = black
ro = red
br = brown
gn = green
bl = blue
gr = grey
li = lilac
ge = yellow
or = orange

F9 - Parking Brake Warning Light Switch
F34 - Brake Fluid Level Warning Switch
G33 - Windshield Washer Fluid Level Sensor
J285 - Control module with indicator unit in instrument panel insert
K37 - Low Windshield Washer Fluid Level Indicator Light
K65 - Left Turn Signal Indicator Light
K94 - Right Turn Signal Indicator Light
K118 - Warning light for brake system
T32 - 32-Pin Connector, blue
T32a - 32-Pin Connector, green

(119) - Ground connection -1-, in headlight wiring harness

(269) - Ground connector (sensor ground) -1-, in instrument panel wiring harness
(A5) - Plus connection (right turn signal), in instrument panel wiring harness
(A6) - Plus connection (left turn signal), in instrument panel wiring harness

Instrument cluster, parking brake warning light switch, brake fluid level warning switch, low windshield washer fluid level indication, left and right turn signal indicator lights

ws = white
sw = black
ro = red
br = brown
gn = green
bl = blue
gr = grey
li = lilac
ge = yellow
or = orange

E2 - Turn signal switch
E4 - Headlight Dimmer/Flasher Switch
E19 - Park Light Switch
L1 - Left Headlight*
M1 - Left Parking Light
M5 - Left Front Turn Signal Light
M18 - Left, Side Turn Signal Light
M29 - Left Low Beam Headlight (Golf only)
M30 - Left High Beam Headlight (Golf only)
M33 - Light for side marker front left
S18 - Fuse 18 in fuse holder
S19 - Fuse 19 in fuse holder
S21 - Fuse 21 in fuse holder
T10b - 10-Pin Connector
T12 - 12-Pin Connector

(B166) - Connection (56a) in passenger compartment wiring harness
(B167) - Connection (56b) in passenger compartment wiring harness

* - Jetta only

Turn signal switch, headlight dimmer/flasher switch, left front turn signal light, light for side marker front left, left headlight

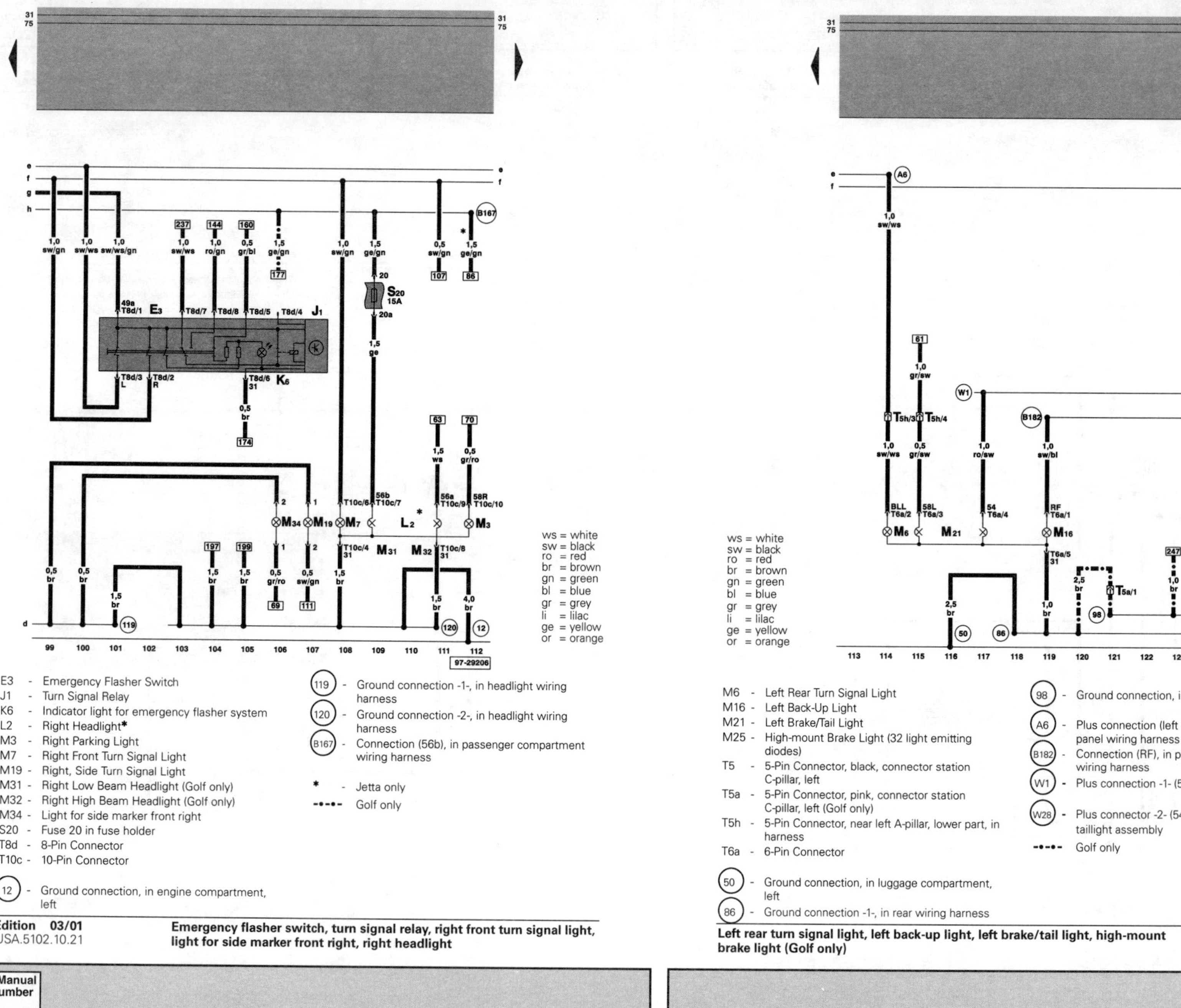

ws = white
sw = black
ro = red
br = brown
gn = green
bl = blue
gr = grey
li = lilac
ge = yellow
or = orange

E3 - Emergency Flasher Switch
J1 - Turn Signal Relay
K6 - Indicator light for emergency flasher system
L2 - Right Headlight*
M3 - Right Parking Light
M7 - Right Front Turn Signal Light
M19 - Right, Side Turn Signal Light
M31 - Right Low Beam Headlight (Golf only)
M32 - Right High Beam Headlight (Golf only)
M34 - Light for side marker front right
S20 - Fuse 20 in fuse holder
T8d - 8-Pin Connector
T10c - 10-Pin Connector

(12) - Ground connection, in engine compartment, left

(119) - Ground connection -1-, in headlight wiring harness
(120) - Ground connection -2-, in headlight wiring harness
(B167) - Connection (56b), in passenger compartment wiring harness

* - Jetta only
-•-•- Golf only

Edition 03/01
USA.5102.10.21

Emergency flasher switch, turn signal relay, right front turn signal light, light for side marker front right, right headlight

ws = white
sw = black
ro = red
br = brown
gn = green
bl = blue
gr = grey
li = lilac
ge = yellow
or = orange

M6 - Left Rear Turn Signal Light
M16 - Left Back-Up Light
M21 - Left Brake/Tail Light
M25 - High-mount Brake Light (32 light emitting diodes)
T5 - 5-Pin Connector, black, connector station C-pillar, left
T5a - 5-Pin Connector, pink, connector station C-pillar, left (Golf only)
T5h - 5-Pin Connector, near left A-pillar, lower part, in harness
T6a - 6-Pin Connector

(50) - Ground connection, in luggage compartment, left
(86) - Ground connection -1-, in rear wiring harness

(98) - Ground connection, in rear lid wiring harness
(A6) - Plus connection (left turn signal), in instrument panel wiring harness
(B182) - Connection (RF), in passenger compartment wiring harness
(W1) - Plus connection -1- (54), in rear wiring harness
(W28) - Plus connector -2- (54), in wiring harness taillight assembly
-•-•- Golf only

Left rear turn signal light, left back-up light, left brake/tail light, high-mount brake light (Golf only)

Edition 03/01
USA.5102.10.21

F - Brake Light Switch
F4 - Back-Up Light Switch
J226 - Park/Neutral Position (PNP) Relay
M8 - Right Rear Turn Signal Light
M17 - Right Back-Up Light
M22 - Right Brake/Tail Light
M25 - High-mount Brake Light (18 light emitting diodes)*
T5h - 5-Pin Connector, near left A-pillar, lower part, in harness
T5i - 5-Pin Connector, near left A-pillar, lower part, in harness
T6b - 6-Pin Connector
T10 - 10-Pin Connector, orange, in protective housing for connectors, in plenum chamber, left

(86) - Ground connection -1-, in rear wiring harness
(A5) - Plus connection (right turn signal), in instrument panel wiring harness
(A18) - Wire connection (54), in instrument panel wiring harness
(A87) - Connector (reverse lamp), in instrument panel wiring harness
(B182) - Connection (RF), in passenger compartment wiring harness
(W1) - Plus connection -1- (54), in rear wiring harness

* - Jetta only
** - Manual transmission only
--- Automatic transmission only

ws = white
sw = black
ro = red
br = brown
gn = green
bl = blue
gr = grey
li = lilac
ge = yellow
or = orange

97-29208

Back-up light switch, brake light switch, right rear turn signal light, right back-up light, right brake/tail light

ws = white
sw = black
ro = red
br = brown
gn = green
bl = blue
gr = grey
li = lilac
ge = yellow
or = orange

97-29209

S12 - Fuse 12 in fuse holder
S13 - Fuse 13 in fuse holder
S15 - Fuse 15 in fuse holder
S238 - Fuse 38 in fuse holder
S239 - Fuse 39 in fuse holder
T16 - Data Link Connector (DLC), below instrument panel, left

(81) - Ground connection -1-, in instrument panel wiring harness
(A76) - Connector (K-diagnosis wire) in instrument panel wiring harness
(B156) - Plus connector (30a), in wiring harness interior

Data Link Connector (DLC)

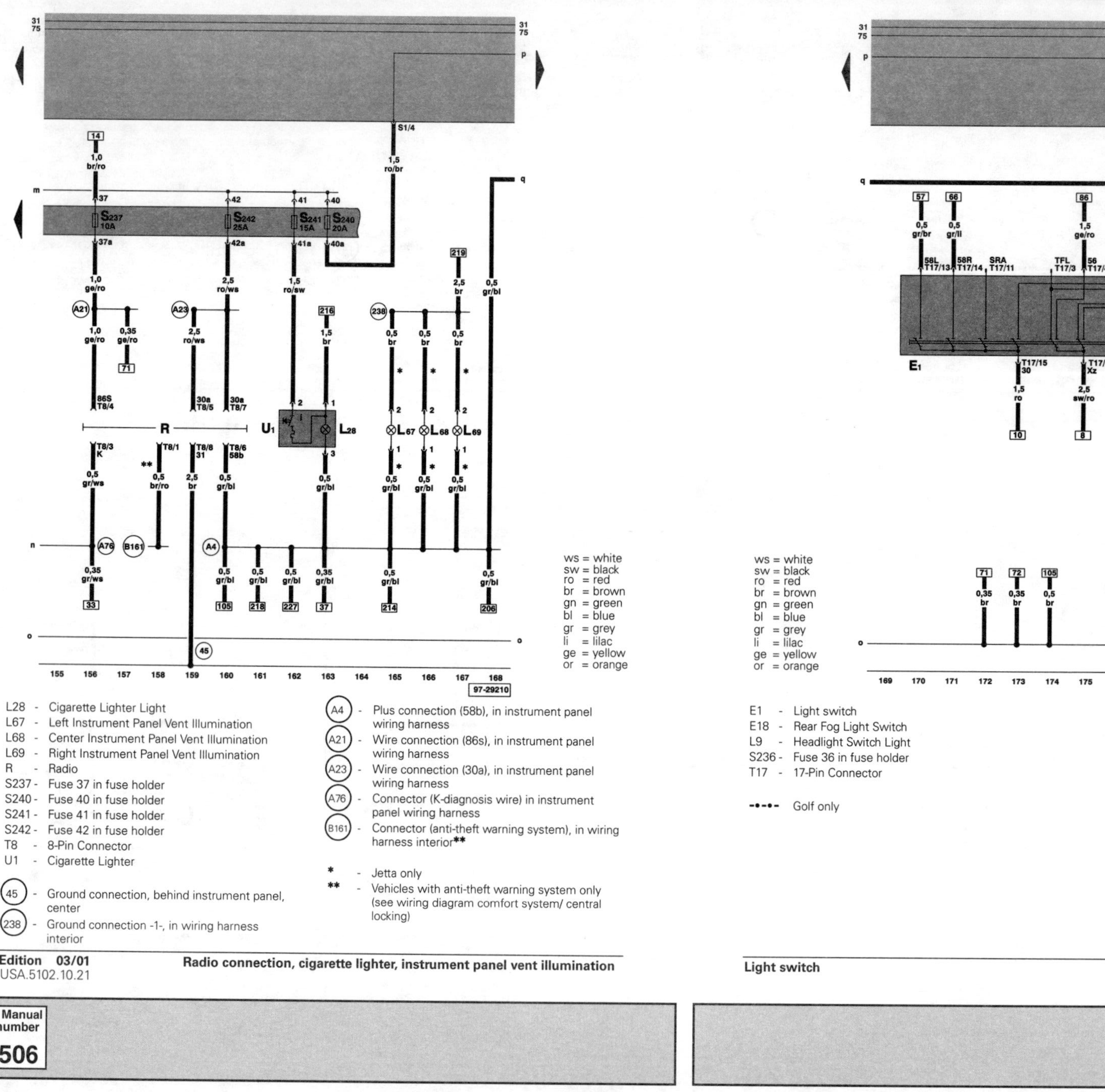

ws = white
sw = black
ro = red
br = brown
gn = green
bl = blue
gr = grey
li = lilac
ge = yellow
or = orange

L28 - Cigarette Lighter Light
L67 - Left Instrument Panel Vent Illumination
L68 - Center Instrument Panel Vent Illumination
L69 - Right Instrument Panel Vent Illumination
R - Radio
S237 - Fuse 37 in fuse holder
S240 - Fuse 40 in fuse holder
S241 - Fuse 41 in fuse holder
S242 - Fuse 42 in fuse holder
T8 - 8-Pin Connector
U1 - Cigarette Lighter

(45) - Ground connection, behind instrument panel, center
(238) - Ground connection -1-, in wiring harness interior

(A4) - Plus connection (58b), in instrument panel wiring harness
(A21) - Wire connection (86s), in instrument panel wiring harness
(A23) - Wire connection (30a), in instrument panel wiring harness
(A76) - Connector (K-diagnosis wire) in instrument panel wiring harness
(B161) - Connector (anti-theft warning system), in wiring harness interior**

* - Jetta only
** - Vehicles with anti-theft warning system only (see wiring diagram comfort system/ central locking)

Radio connection, cigarette lighter, instrument panel vent illumination

ws = white
sw = black
ro = red
br = brown
gn = green
bl = blue
gr = grey
li = lilac
ge = yellow
or = orange

E1 - Light switch
E18 - Rear Fog Light Switch
L9 - Headlight Switch Light
S236 - Fuse 36 in fuse holder
T17 - 17-Pin Connector

-•-•- Golf only

Light switch

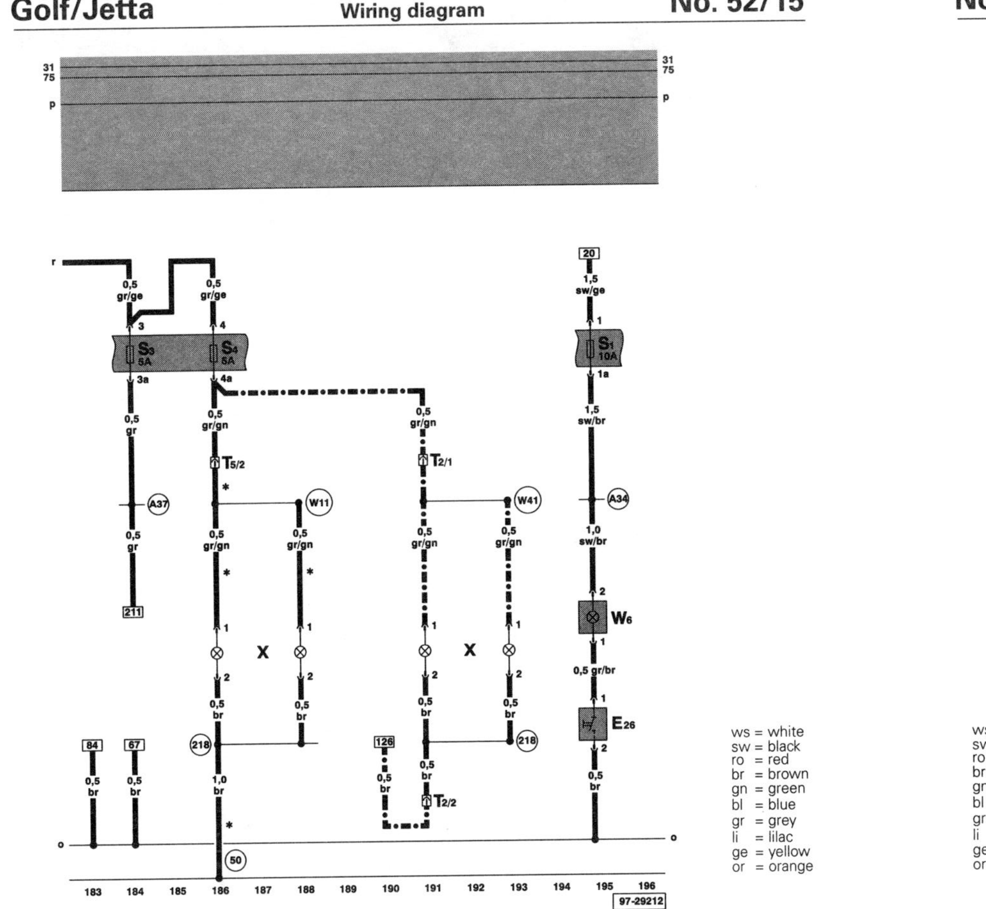

ws = white
sw = black
ro = red
br = brown
gn = green
bl = blue
gr = grey
li = lilac
ge = yellow
or = orange

E26 - Glove compartment light switch
S1 - Fuse 1 in fuse holder
S3 - Fuse 3 in fuse holder
S4 - Fuse 4 in fuse holder
T2 - Double Connector, in luggage compartment, left (Golf only)
T5 - 5-Pin Connector, black, connector station C-pillar, left
W6 - Glove Compartment Light
X - License Plate Light

(50) - Ground connection, in luggage compartment, left
(218) - Ground connection -1-, in rear lid wiring harness

(A34) - Wire connection (75x), in instrument panel wiring harness
(A37) - Wire connection (58a), in instrument panel wiring harness
(W11) - Wire connection (58), in rear lid wiring harness
(W41) - Plus connection (58), in wiring harness

* - Jetta only
--•-•- - Golf only

License plate light, glove compartment light

ws = white
sw = black
ro = red
br = brown
gn = green
bl = blue
gr = grey
li = lilac
ge = yellow
or = orange

E204 - Switch for remote/fuel tank door (also see Comfort System with power windows wiring diagram)
F138 - Airbag Spiral Spring/Return Spring with Slip Ring
H - Signal horn activation
H1 - Dual tone horn
J4 - Dual Horn Relay
L76 - Push Button Light
T5b - 5-Pin Connector
T5j - 5-Pin Connector
T5r - 5-Pin Connector
T10i - 10-Pin Connector, black, connector station A-pillar, left
T10n - 10-Pin Connector, brown, connector station A-pillar, left

V155 - Motor for fuel tank lid unlock

(205) - Ground connection, in driver's door wiring harness
(238) - Ground connection -1-, in wiring harness interior
(A90) - Connector (dual tone horn), in instrument panel wiring harness
(R51) - Connection (58b) in door wiring harness, driver side

Dual tone horn, fuel tank door remote

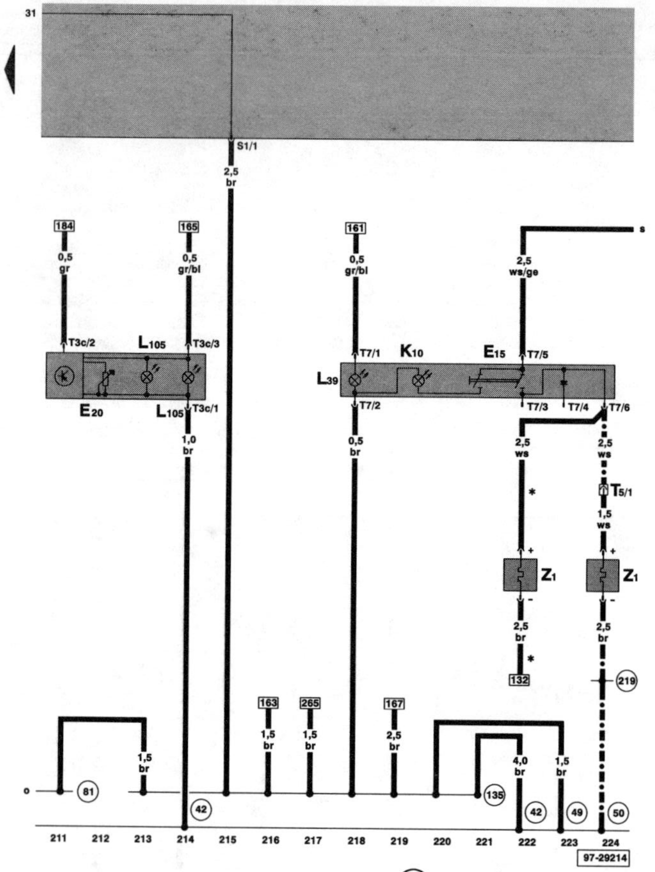

ws = white
sw = black
ro = red
br = brown
gn = green
bl = blue
gr = grey
li = lilac
ge = yellow
or = orange

E15 - Rear window defogger switch
E20 - Instrument Panel Light Dimmer Switch
K10 - Indicator light for heated rear windshield
L39 - Rear Window Defogger Switch Light
L105 - Illumination for lighting controller
T3c - 3-Pin Connector
T5 - 5-Pin Connector, black, connector station C-pillar, left
T7 - 7-Pin Connector
Z1 - Heated rear window

(42) - Ground connection, beside steering column
(49) - Ground connection, on steering column
(50) - Ground connection, in luggage compartment, left
(81) - Ground connection -1-, in instrument panel wiring harness
(135) - Ground connection -2-, in instrument panel wiring harness
(219) - Ground connection -2-, in rear lid wiring harness

* - Jetta only
--•--•-- - Golf only

Edition 03/01
USA.5102.10.21

Instrument panel light dimmer switch, rear window defogger switch, heated rear window

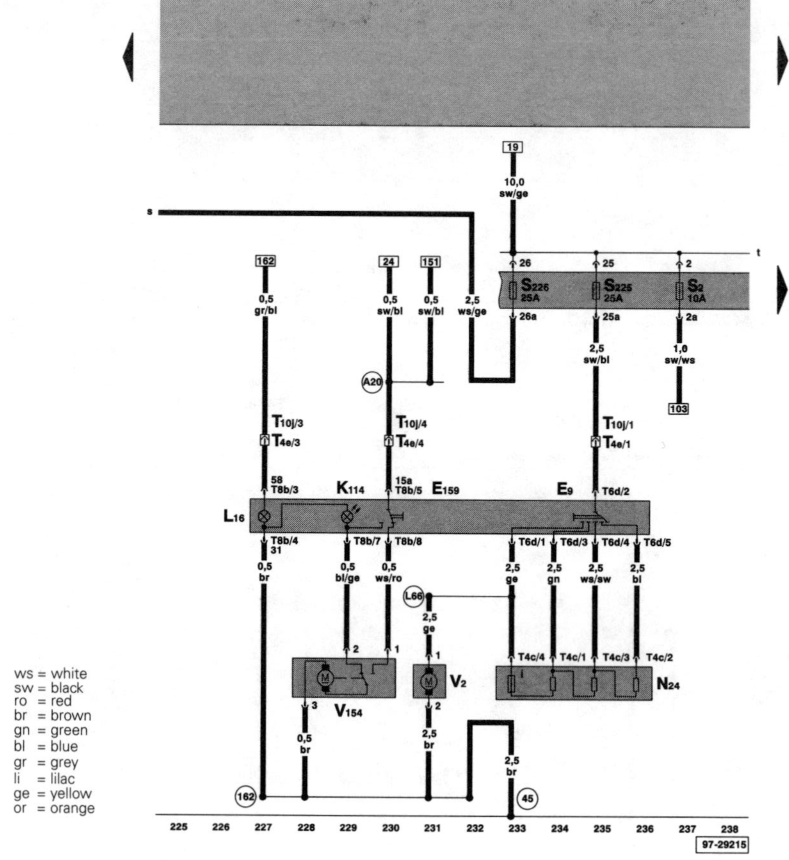

ws = white
sw = black
ro = red
br = brown
gn = green
bl = blue
gr = grey
li = lilac
ge = yellow
or = orange

E9 - Fresh Air Blower Switch
E159 - Fresh Air/Recirculating Flap Switch
K114 - Fresh Air and Recirculating Air Mode Indicator Light
L16 - Fresh Air Control Lever Light
N24 - Fresh Air Blower Series Resistance With Fuse
S2 - Fuse 2 in fuse holder
S225 - Fuse 25 in fuse holder
S226 - Fuse 26 in fuse holder
T4c - 4-Pin Connector
T4e - 4-Pin Connector, behind instrument panel, center (in vehicles without air conditioning)
T6d - 6-Pin Connector
T8b - 8-Pin Connector
T10j - 10-Pin Connector, behind instrument panel, center (in vehicles with air conditioning)
V2 - Fresh Air Blower
V154 - Servo motor for fresh-/recirculating air door

(45) - Ground connection, behind instrument panel, center
(162) - Ground connection, in blower motor wiring harness
(A20) - Wire connection (15a), in instrument panel wiring harness
(L66) - Connector, in wiring harness heater blower

Fresh air blower switch, fresh air/recirculating flap switch, fresh air blower

Edition 03/01
USA.5102.10.21

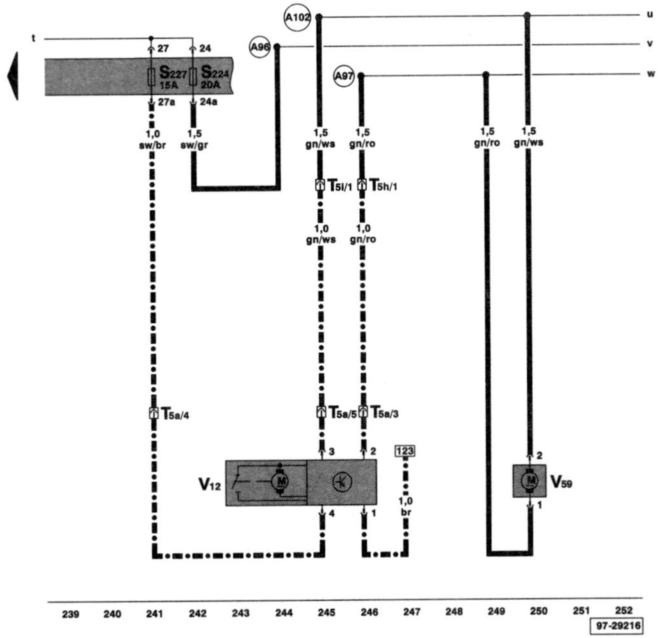

ws = white
sw = black
ro = red
br = brown
gn = green
bl = blue
gr = grey
li = lilac
ge = yellow
or = orange

S224 - Fuse 24 in fuse holder
S227 - Fuse 27 in fuse holder
T5a - 5-Pin Connector, pink, connector station C-pillar, left
T5h - 5-Pin Connector, near left A-pillar, lower part, in harness
T5i - 5-Pin Connector, near left A-pillar, lower part, in harness
V12 - Motor for rear windshield wiper
V59 - Windshield and Rear Window Washer Pump

(A96) - Connector (53a), in instrument panel wiring harness
(A97) - Connector (53), in instrument panel wiring harness
(A102) - Connector (windshield wiper), in instrument panel wiring harness

-•-•- Golf only

Motor for rear windshield wiper, windshield and rear window washer pump

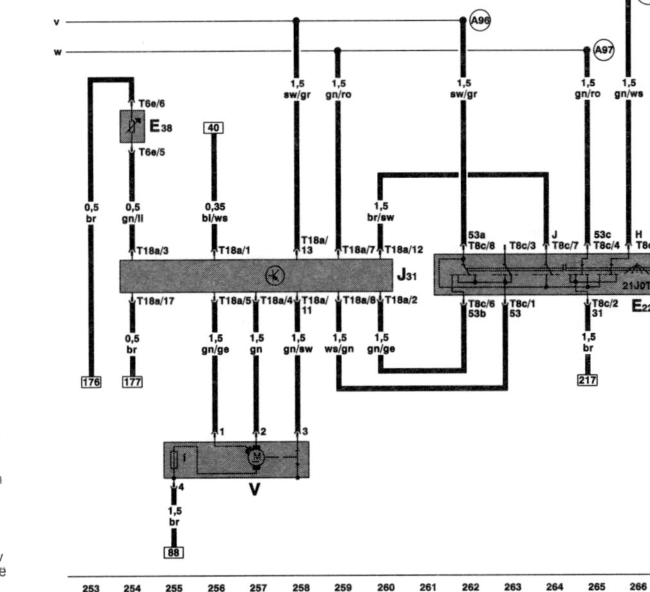

ws = white
sw = black
ro = red
br = brown
gn = green
bl = blue
gr = grey
li = lilac
ge = yellow
or = orange

E22 - Windshield Wiper/Washer Switch
E38 - Windshield Wiper Intermittent Regulator
J31 - Wiper/Washer Intermittent Relay, on relais panel
T6e - 6-Pin Connector
T8c - 8-Pin Connector
T18a - 18-Pin Connector
V - Windshield Wiper Motor

(A96) - Connector (53a), in instrument panel wiring harness
(A97) - Connector (53), in instrument panel wiring harness
(A102) - Connector (windshield wiper), in instrument panel wiring harness

Windshield wiper/washer switch, windshield wiper intermittent regulator, windshield wiper motor, wiper/washer intermittent relay

Comfort system (vehicles without power windows),

from January 2001

- **Anti-theft warning system**
- **Central locking system with remote control**
- **Fuel tank lid unlock system**
- **Heated outside mirrors**
- **Interior lights**
- **Luggage compartment light**
- **Power sunroof**
- **Rear lid unlock system**

Deviate relay location and fuseplacements as well as the locations of multiple connectors see section "component locations".

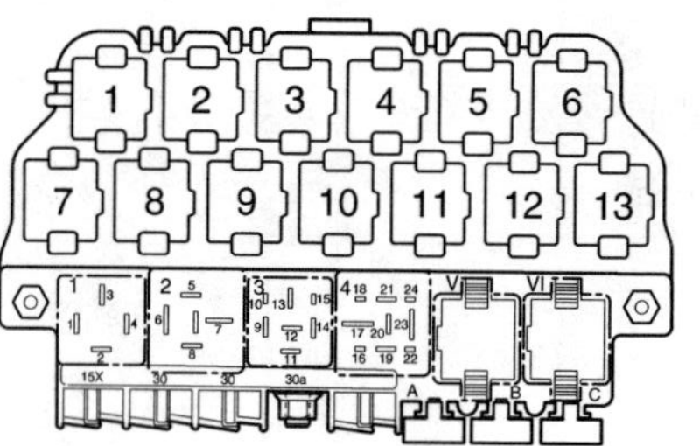

97-14163

Relay location on the thirteenfold auxiliary relay panel, above relay panel:

2 Relay for motor remote unlock rear lid (79)

Relay panel:

Note: Number in parentheses indicates production control number stamped on relay housing.

Fuse colors

30 A - green
25 A - white
20 A - yellow
15 A - blue
10 A - red
7,5 A - brown
5 A - beige
3 A - violet

ws = white
sw = black
ro = red
br = brown
gn = green
bl = blue
gr = grey
li = lilac
ge = yellow
or = orange

97-29218

- E20 - Instrument Panel Light Dimmer Switch
- E204 - Switch for remote/fuel tank door
- L76 - Push Button Light
- T3c - 3-Pin Connector
- T10i - 10-Pin Connector, black, connector station A-pillar, left
- T10k - 10-Pin Connector, black, connector station A-pillar, right
- V155 - Motor for fuel tank lid unlock
- (42) - Ground connection, beside steering column
- (49) - Ground connection, on steering column
- (81) - Ground connection -1-, in instrument panel wiring harness
- (135) - Ground connection -2-, in instrument panel wiring harness
- (238) - Ground connection -1-, in wiring harness interior
- (A4) - Plus connection (58b), in instrument panel wiring harness

Switch for remote/fuel tank door, motor for fuel tank lid unlock

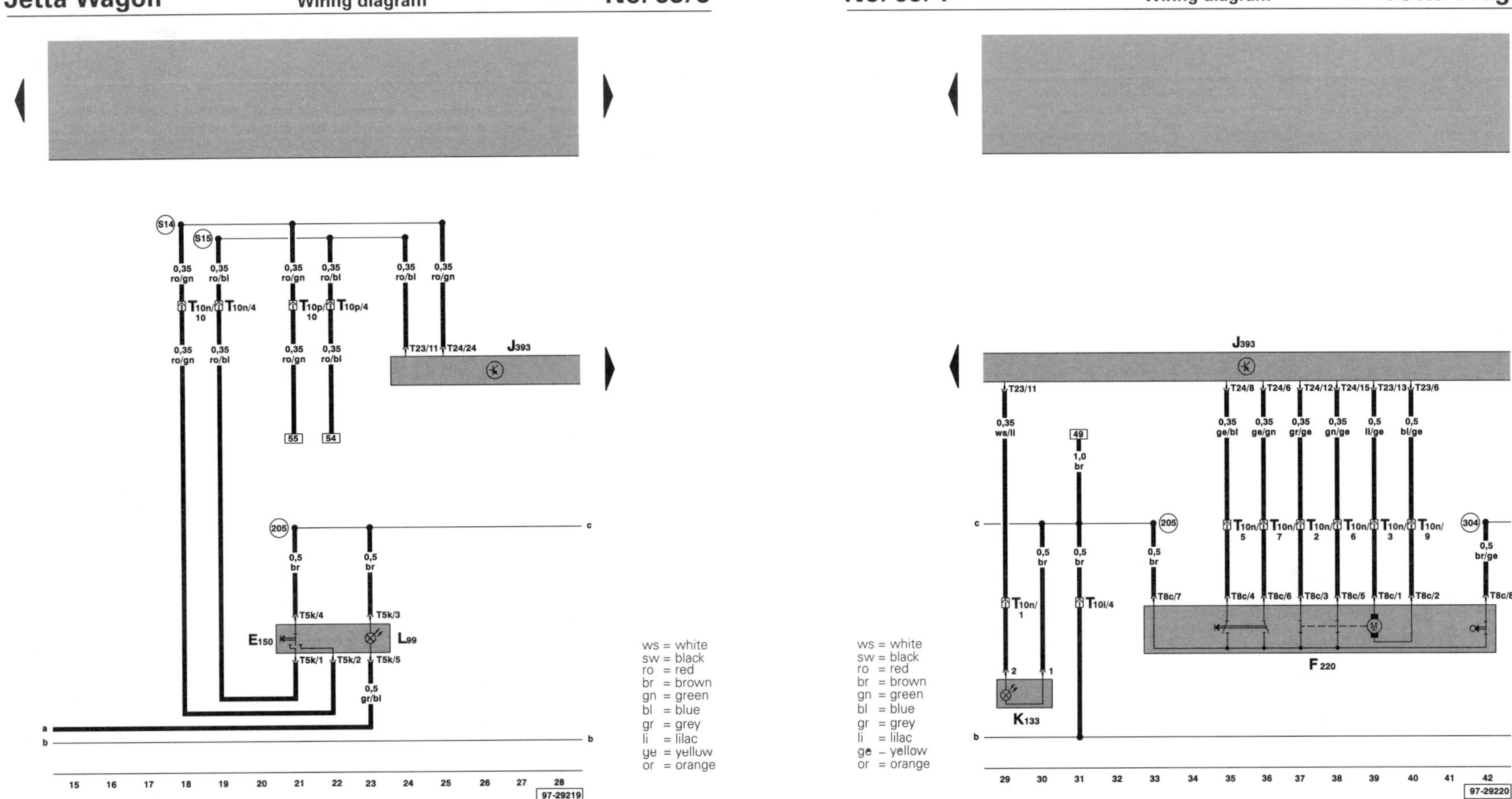

ws = white
sw = black
ro = red
br = brown
gn = green
bl = blue
gr = grey
li = lilac
ge = yellow
or = orange

E150 - Switch for interior lock, driver side
J393 - Central control module for comfort system, behind instrument panel, left
L99 - Lighting for switch interior lock
T5k - 5-Pin Connector
T10n - 10-Pin Connector, brown, connector station A-pillar, left
T10p - 10-Pin Connector, brown, connector station A-pillar, right
T23 - 23-Pin Connector
T24 - 24-Pin Connector

(205) - Ground connection, in driver's door wiring harness
(S14) - Wire connection (open), in central locking system wiring harness
(S15) - Wire connection (closed), in central locking system wiring harness

Edition 03/01
USA.5102.10.21

Central control module for comfort system, switch for interior lock (driver side)

F220 - Lock unit for central locking, driver side
J393 - Central control module for comfort system, behind instrument panel, left
K133 - Warning light for central locking -SAFE-
T8c - 8-Pin Connector
T10i - 10-Pin Connector, black, connector station A-pillar, left
T10n - 10-Pin Connector, brown, connector station A-pillar, left
T23 - 23-Pin Connector
T24 - 24-Pin Connector

(205) - Ground connection, in driver's door wiring harness
(304) - Ground connector -3-, in wiring harness door cable - driver side

Central control module for comfort system, lock unit for central locking (driver side), warning light for central locking -SAFE-

Edition 03/01
USA.5102.10.21

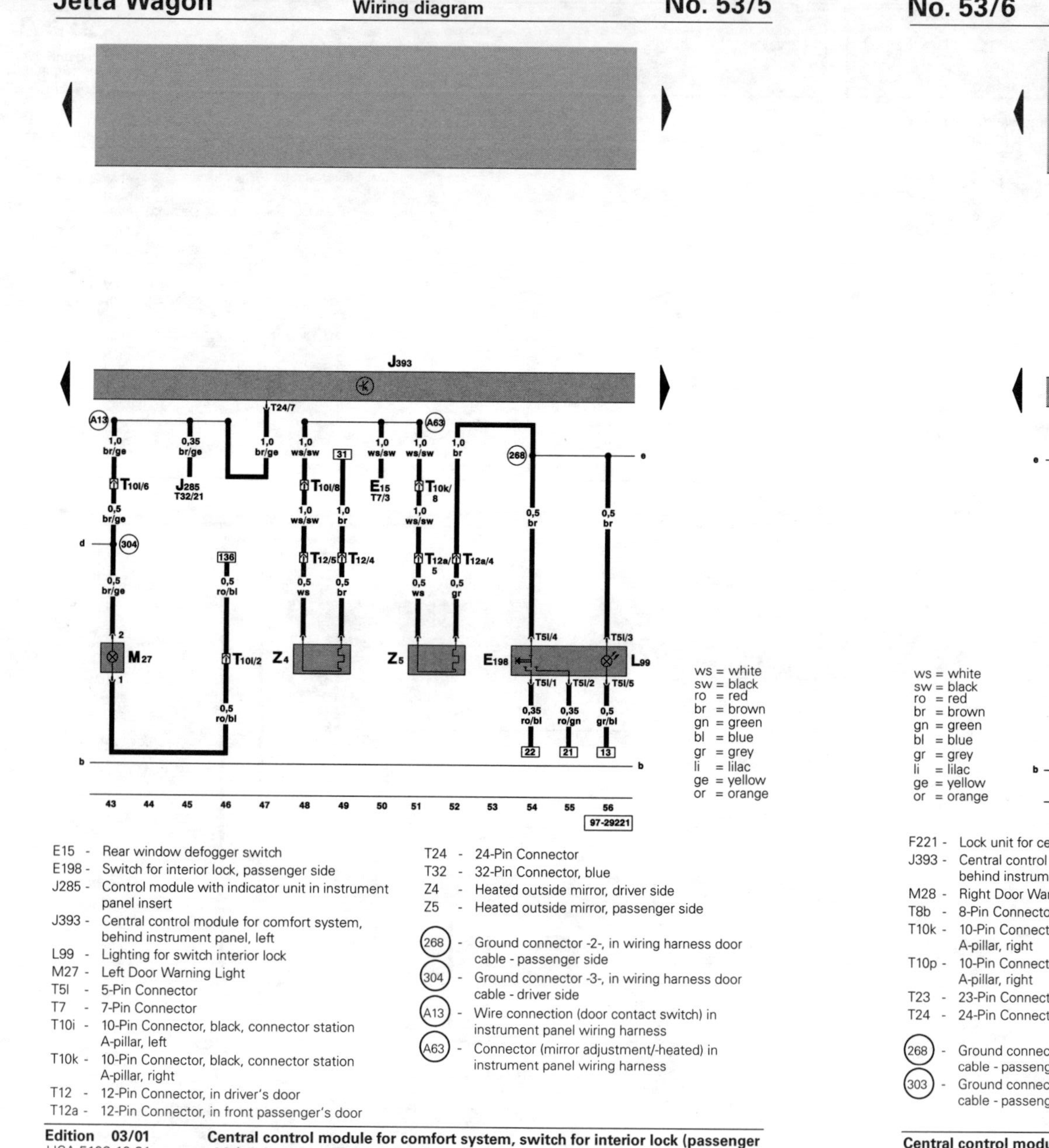

E15 - Rear window defogger switch
E198 - Switch for interior lock, passenger side
J285 - Control module with indicator unit in instrument panel insert
J393 - Central control module for comfort system, behind instrument panel, left
L99 - Lighting for switch interior lock
M27 - Left Door Warning Light
T5l - 5-Pin Connector
T7 - 7-Pin Connector
T10i - 10-Pin Connector, black, connector station A-pillar, left
T10k - 10-Pin Connector, black, connector station A-pillar, right
T12 - 12-Pin Connector, in driver's door
T12a - 12-Pin Connector, in front passenger's door
T24 - 24-Pin Connector
T32 - 32-Pin Connector, blue
Z4 - Heated outside mirror, driver side
Z5 - Heated outside mirror, passenger side

(268) - Ground connector -2-, in wiring harness door cable - passenger side
(304) - Ground connector -3-, in wiring harness door cable - driver side
(A13) - Wire connection (door contact switch) in instrument panel wiring harness
(A63) - Connector (mirror adjustment/-heated) in instrument panel wiring harness

Central control module for comfort system, switch for interior lock (passenger side), left door warning light, heated outside mirrors

J393

ws = white
sw = black
ro = red
br = brown
gn = green
bl = blue
gr = grey
li = lilac
ge = yellow
or = orange

F221 - Lock unit for central locking, passenger side
J393 - Central control module for comfort system, behind instrument panel, left
M28 - Right Door Warning Light
T8b - 8-Pin Connector
T10k - 10-Pin Connector, black, connector station A-pillar, right
T10p - 10-Pin Connector, brown, connector station A-pillar, right
T23 - 23-Pin Connector
T24 - 24-Pin Connector

(268) - Ground connector -2-, in wiring harness door cable - passenger side
(303) - Ground connector -3-, in wiring harness door cable - passenger side

Central control module for comfort system, lock unit for central locking (passenger side), right door warning light

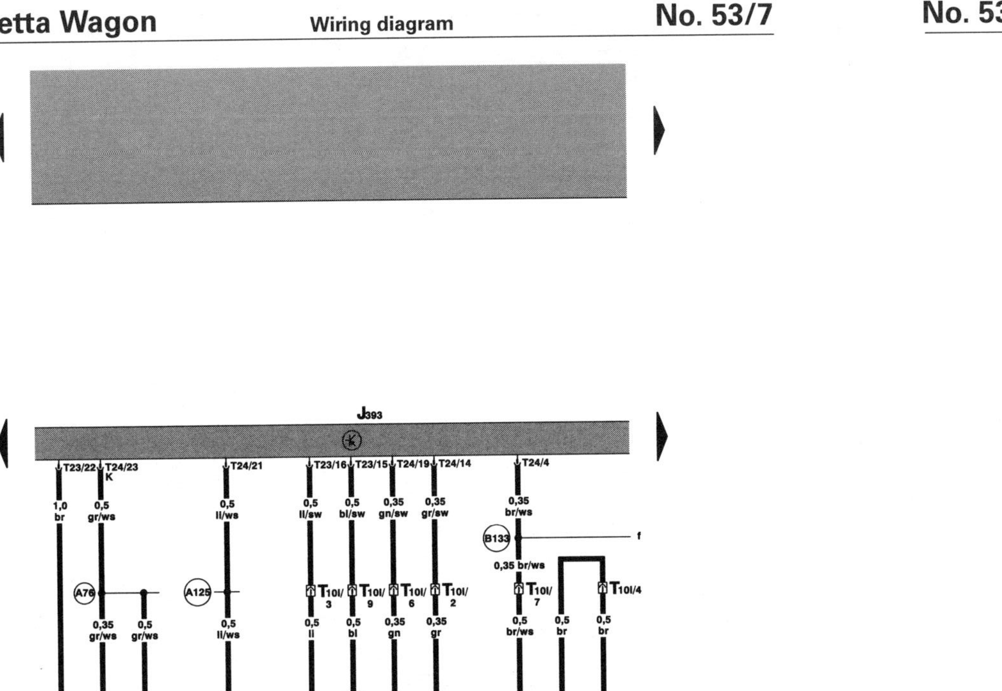

ws = white
sw = black
ro = red
br = brown
gn = green
bl = blue
gr = grey
li = lilac
ge = yellow
or = orange

F222 - Lock unit for central locking, rear, left
J234 - Airbag Control Module, behind console, lower part
J285 - Control module with indicator unit in instrument panel insert
J393 - Central control module for comfort system, behind instrument panel, left
T6a - 6-Pin Connector
T10l - 10-Pin Connector, black, connector station B-pillar, left
T16 - Data Link Connector (DLC), below instrument panel, left
T23 - 23-Pin Connector
T24 - 24-Pin Connector
T32 - 32-Pin Connector, blue
T75 - 75-Pin Connector

(A76) - Connector (K-diagnosis wire) in instrument panel wiring harness
(A125) - Connection (crash signal) in instrument panel wiring harness
(B133) - Connector (central locking open), in wiring harness interior

Central control module for comfort system, lock unit for central locking (rear left)

ws = white
sw = black
ro = red
br = brown
gn = green
bl = blue
gr = grey
li = lilac
ge = yellow
or = orange

F223 - Lock unit for central locking, rear, right
J393 - Central control module for comfort system, behind instrument panel, left
J398 - Relay for motor remote unlock rear lid, on the thirteenfold auxiliary relay panel, above relay panel
T6b - 6-Pin Connector
T10m - 10-Pin Connector, black, connector station B-pillar, right
T23 - 23-Pin Connector
T24 - 24-Pin Connector

(B133) - Connector (central locking open), in wiring harness interior

Central control module for comfort system, lock unit for central locking (rear right), relay for motor remote unlock rear lid

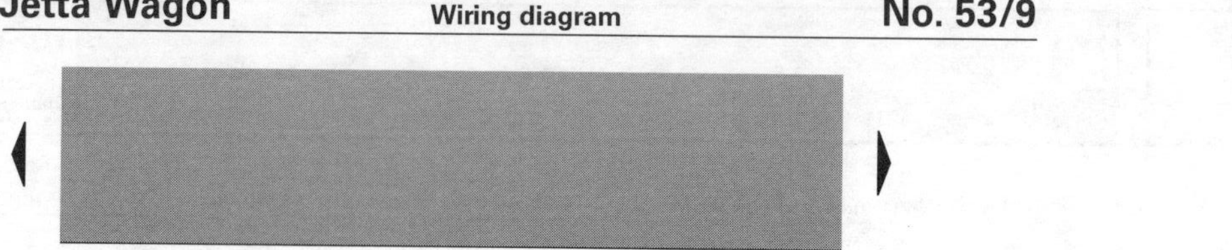

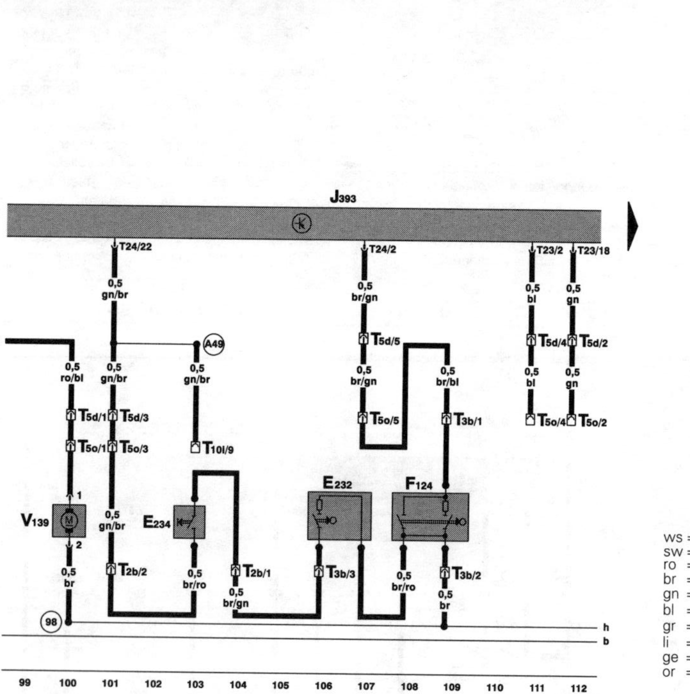

E232 - Rear Lid Remote Lock Key Switch
E234 - Switch for unlocking, rear lid handle
F124 - Trunk Lock Alarm/Central Locking Switch
J393 - Central control module for comfort system, behind instrument panel, left
T2b - Double Connector, in rear lid
T3b - 3-Pin Connector, in rear lid
T5d - 5-Pin Connector, brown, connector station D-pillar, right
T5o - 5-Pin Connector, brown, in rear lid
T10i - 10-Pin Connector, black, connector station A-pillar, left
T23 - 23-Pin Connector
T24 - 24-Pin Connector
V139 - Motor to unlock rear lid

(98) - Ground connection, in rear lid wiring harness
(A49) - Wire connection -1-, in instrument panel wiring harness

Central control module for comfort system, rear lid remote lock key switch, switch for unlocking (rear lid handle), trunk lock alarm/central locking switch, motor to unlock rear lid

ws = white
sw = black
ro = red
br = brown
gn = green
bl = blue
gr = grey
li = lilac
ge = yellow
or = orange

E165 - Trunk Lid Release Switch
F5 - Luggage Compartment Light Switch
J393 - Central control module for comfort system, behind instrument panel, left
K116 - Warning light for rear lid unlocked, in Instrument cluster
T5 - 5-Pin Connector, black, connector station D-pillar, left
T5p - 5-Pin Connector, black, in rear lid
T24 - 24-Pin Connector
T32 - 32-Pin Connector, blue, on Instrument cluster
W3 - Luggage compartment Light
W18 - Left Luggage Compartment Light

(50) - Ground connection, in luggage compartment, left

(98) - Ground connection, in rear lid wiring harness
(218) - Ground connection -1-, in rear lid wiring harness
(A126) - Connection (contact switch in rear lid) in instrument panel wiring harness
(Q22) - Wire connection -1-, in rear lid wiring harness
(Q44) - Wire connection -2-, in tailgate wiring harness

Central control module for comfort system, trunk lid release switch, luggage compartment light switch, luggage compartment light

ws	= white
sw	= black
ro	= red
br	= brown
gn	= green
bl	= blue
gr	= grey
li	= lilac
ge	= yellow
or	= orange

E139 - Sunroof Regulator
J245 - Power Sunroof Control Module
J393 - Central control module for comfort system, behind instrument panel, left
S230 - Fuse 30 in fuse holder
T4a - 4-Pin Connector, behind instrument panel, left
T6d - 6-Pin Connector
T6e - 6-Pin Connector
T6f - 6-Pin Connector
T8e - 8-Pin Connector, behind instrument panel, left
T23 - 23-Pin Connector
V1 - Sunroof Motor

(128) - Ground connection -1-, in interior light wiring harness

(238) - Ground connection -1-, in wiring harness interior
(A29) - Wire connection (interior light), in instrument panel wiring harness
(R6) - Plus connection -1-, in interior light wiring harness

Central control module for comfort system, power sunroof control module, sunroof regulator, sunroof motor

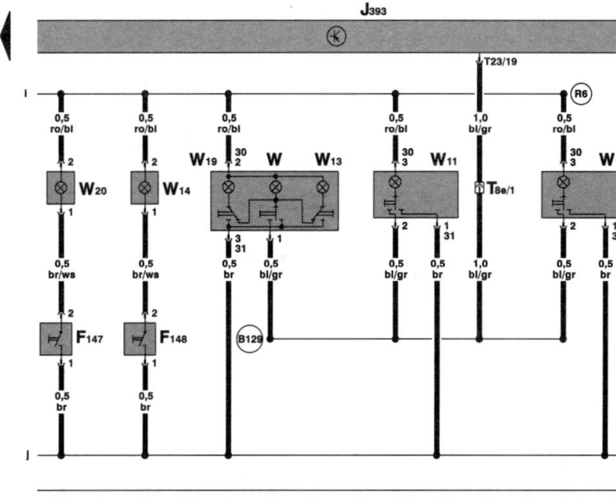

ws	= white
sw	= black
ro	= red
br	= brown
gn	= green
bl	= blue
gr	= grey
li	= lilac
ge	= yellow
or	= orange

F147 - Left Make-Up Mirror Light Switch
F148 - Right Make-Up Mirror Light Switch
J393 - Central control module for comfort system, behind instrument panel, left
T8e - 8-Pin Connector, behind instrument panel, left
T23 - 23-Pin Connector
W - Front Interior Light
W11 - Left Rear Reading Light
W12 - Right Rear Reading Light
W13 - Right Front Map/Reading Light
W14 - Right Make-up Mirror Light
W19 - Left Front Reading Light
W20 - Left Make-up Mirror Light

(128) - Ground connection -1-, in interior light wiring harness

(B129) - Connector (interior light 3/L) in wiring harness interior
(R6) - Plus connection -1-, in interior light wiring harness

Central control module for comfort system, interior lights, make-up mirror lights

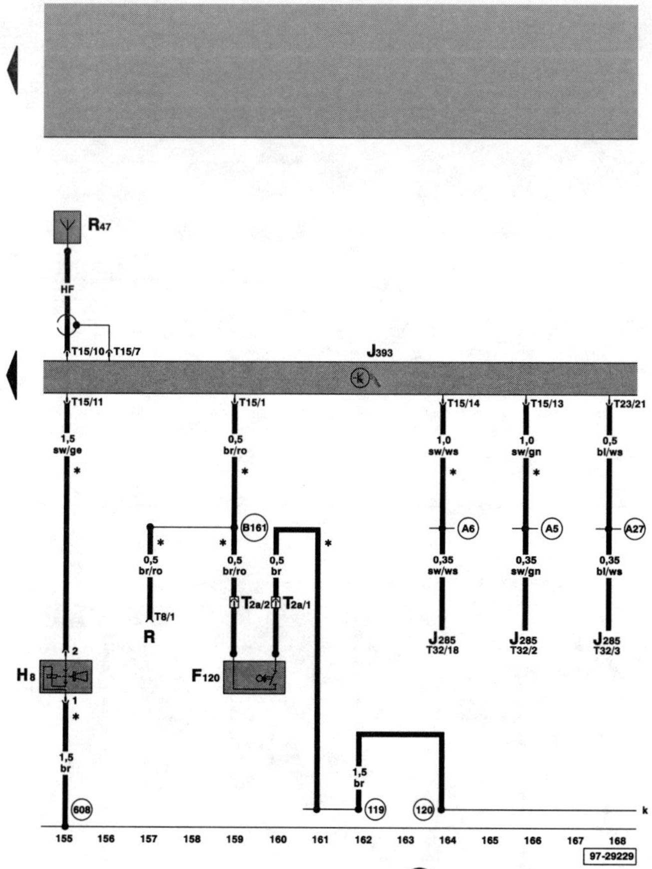

ws = white
sw = black
ro = red
br = brown
gn = green
bl = blue
gr = grey
li = lilac
ge = yellow
or = orange

F120 - Hood Alarm Switch*
H8 - Alarm Horn*
J285 - Control module with indicator unit in instrument panel insert
J393 - Central control module for comfort system, behind instrument panel, left
R - Radio
R47 - Antenna wire for central locking and antitheft warning system
T2a - Double Connector, near headlight, right
T8 - 8-Pin Connector, on radio
T15 - 15-Pin Connector
T23 - 23-Pin Connector
T32 - 32-Pin Connector, blue, on instrument cluster

(119) - Ground connection -1-, in headlight wiring harness
(120) - Ground connection -2-, in headlight wiring harness
(608) - Ground connection (in center plenum chamber)
(A5) - Plus connection (right turn signal), in instrument panel wiring harness
(A6) - Plus connection (left turn signal), in instrument panel wiring harness
(A27) - Wire connection (vehicle speed signal), in instrument panel wiring harness
(B161) - Connector (anti-theft warning system), in wiring harness interior

* - Vehicles with anti-theft warning system only

Central control module for comfort system, antitheft warning system, antenna wire for central locking and antitheft warning system

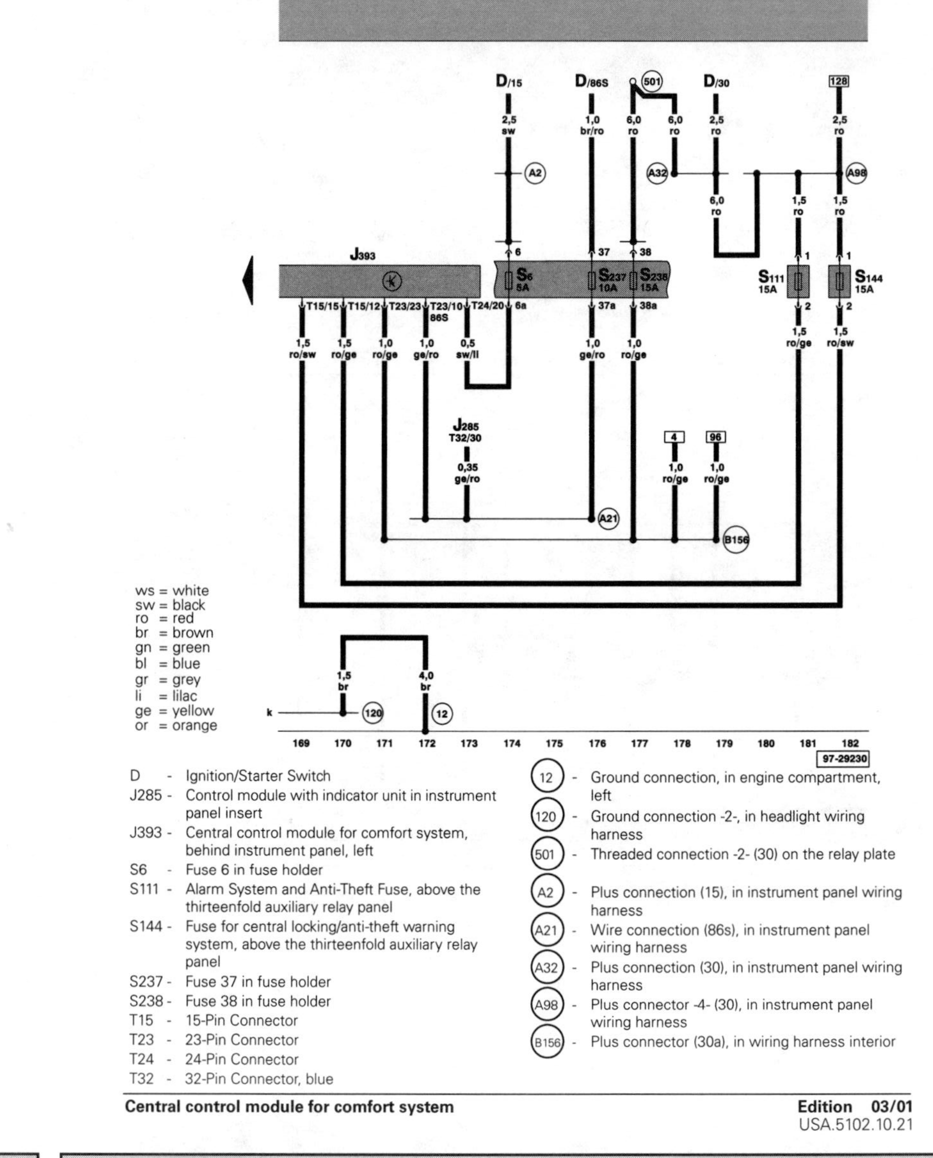

ws = white
sw = black
ro = red
br = brown
gn = green
bl = blue
gr = grey
li = lilac
ge = yellow
or = orange

D - Ignition/Starter Switch
J285 - Control module with indicator unit in instrument panel insert
J393 - Central control module for comfort system, behind instrument panel, left
S6 - Fuse 6 in fuse holder
S111 - Alarm System and Anti-Theft Fuse, above the thirteenfold auxiliary relay panel
S144 - Fuse for central locking/anti-theft warning system, above the thirteenfold auxiliary relay panel
S237 - Fuse 37 in fuse holder
S238 - Fuse 38 in fuse holder
T15 - 15-Pin Connector
T23 - 23-Pin Connector
T24 - 24-Pin Connector
T32 - 32-Pin Connector, blue

(12) - Ground connection, in engine compartment, left
(120) - Ground connection -2-, in headlight wiring harness
(501) - Threaded connection -2- (30) on the relay plate
(A2) - Plus connection (15), in instrument panel wiring harness
(A21) - Wire connection (86s), in instrument panel wiring harness
(A32) - Plus connection (30), in instrument panel wiring harness
(A98) - Plus connector -4- (30), in instrument panel wiring harness
(B156) - Plus connector (30a), in wiring harness interior

Central control module for comfort system

Comfort System (vehicles with power windows),

from January 2001

- Anti-theft warning system
- Central locking system with remote control
- Fuel tank lid unlock system
- Heated power mirrors
- Interior lights
- Luggage compartment light
- Power sunroof
- Power windows
- Rear lid unlock system

Deviate relay location and fuseplacements as well as the locations of multiple connectors see section "component locations".

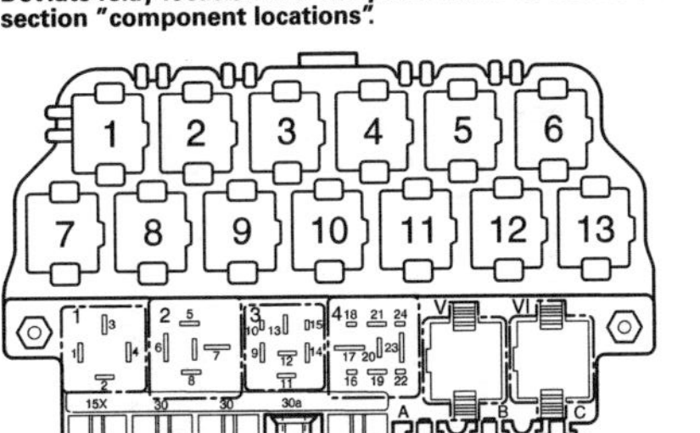

Relay location on the thirteenfold auxiliary relay panel, above relay panel:

2 Relay for motor remote unlock rear lid (79)

Relay panel:

Note: Number in parentheses indicates production control number stamped on relay housing.

Fuse colors

30 A - green
25 A - white
20 A - yellow
15 A - blue
10 A - red
7,5 A - brown
5 A - beige
3 A - violet

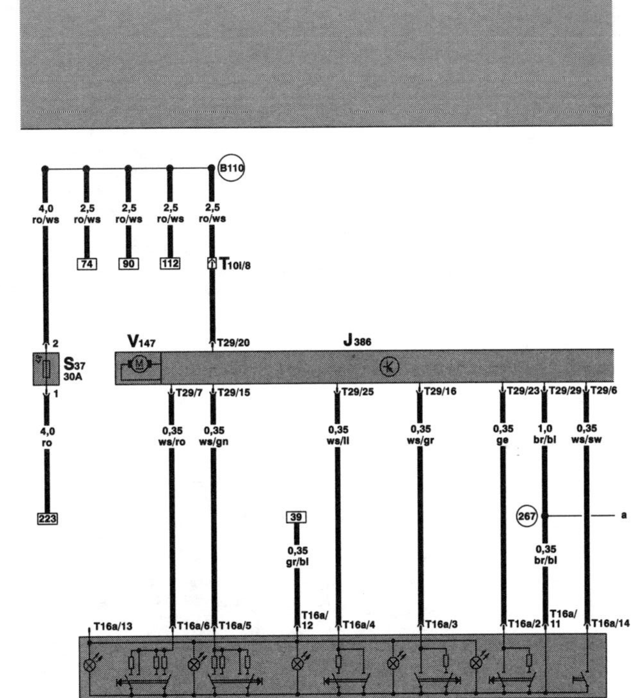

ws = white
sw = black
ro = red
br = brown
gn = green
bl = blue
gr = grey
li = lilac
ge = yellow
or = orange

E39 - Safety switch for window regulator rear
E40 - Switch for window regulator front left
E53 - Switch for window regulator rear left, driver
E55 - Switch for window regulator rear right, driver
E81 - Switch for window regulator front right, driver
E150 - Switch for interior lock, driver side
J386 - Door control module, driver side
L76 - Push Button Light
S37 - Fuse for window regulator (circuit breaker), on thirteen position auxiliary relay panel
T10i - 10-Pin Connector, black, connector station A-pillar, left
T16a - 16-Pin Connector
T29 - 29-Pin Connector
V147 - Motor for window regulator, driver side

(267) - Ground connector -2-, in wiring harness door cable - driver side
(B110) - Connection (30, window regulator) in wiring harness interior

Door control module (driver side), switch for window regulator, safety switch for window regulator rear, switch for interior lock (driver side)

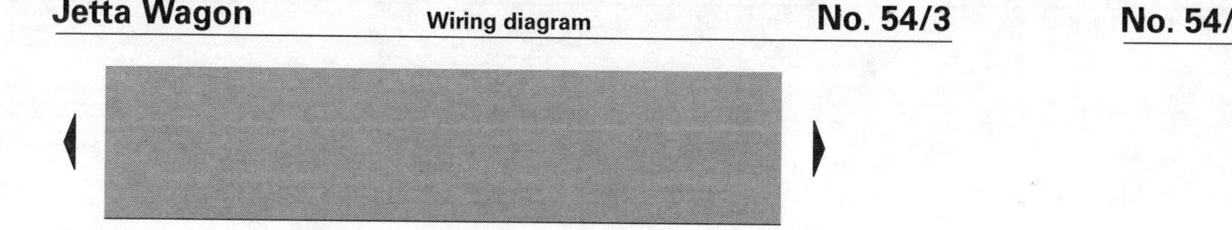

Wire colors	
ws	white
sw	black
ro	red
br	brown
gn	green
bl	blue
gr	grey
li	lilac
ge	yellow
or	orange

F220 - Lock unit for central locking, driver side
J386 - Door control module, driver side
K133 - Warning light for central locking -SAFE-
M27 - Left Door Warning Light
T8c - 8-Pin Connector
T10i - 10-Pin Connector, black, connector station A-pillar, left
T29 - 29-Pin Connector

(267) - Ground connector -2-, in wiring harness door cable - driver side
(304) - Ground connector -3-, in wiring harness door cable - driver side

Edition 03/01
USA.5102.10.21

Door control module (driver side), lock unit for central locking (driver side), warning light for central locking -SAFE-, left door warning light

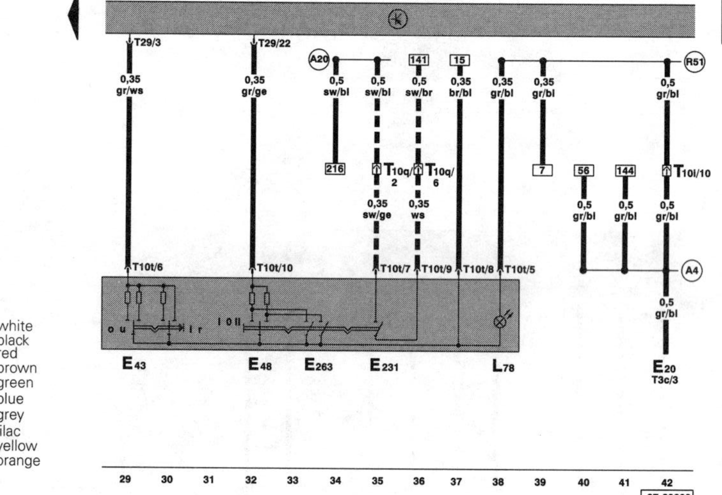

Wire colors	
ws	white
sw	black
ro	red
br	brown
gn	green
bl	blue
gr	grey
li	lilac
ge	yellow
or	orange

E20 - Instrument Panel Light Dimmer Switch
E43 - Mirror Adjustment Switch
E48 - Mirror Selector Switch
E231 - Switch for outside mirror heating
E263 - Mirror fold-away Switch*
J386 - Door control module, driver side
L78 - Mirror Adjusting Switch Light
T3c - 3-Pin Connector
T10i - 10-Pin Connector, black, connector station A-pillar, left
T10q - 10-Pin Connector, blue, connector station A-pillar, left
T10t - 10-Pin Connector
T29 - 29-Pin Connector

(A4) - Plus connection (58b), in instrument panel wiring harness
(A20) - Wire connection (15a), in instrument panel wiring harness
(R51) - Connection (58b), in driver's door wiring harness

* - Mirror fold-away function for some export countrys only

--- Vehicles with seperate heated outside mirrors only

Door control module (driver side), mirror adjustment switch, mirror selector switch, switch for outside mirror heating

Edition 03/01
USA.5102.10.21

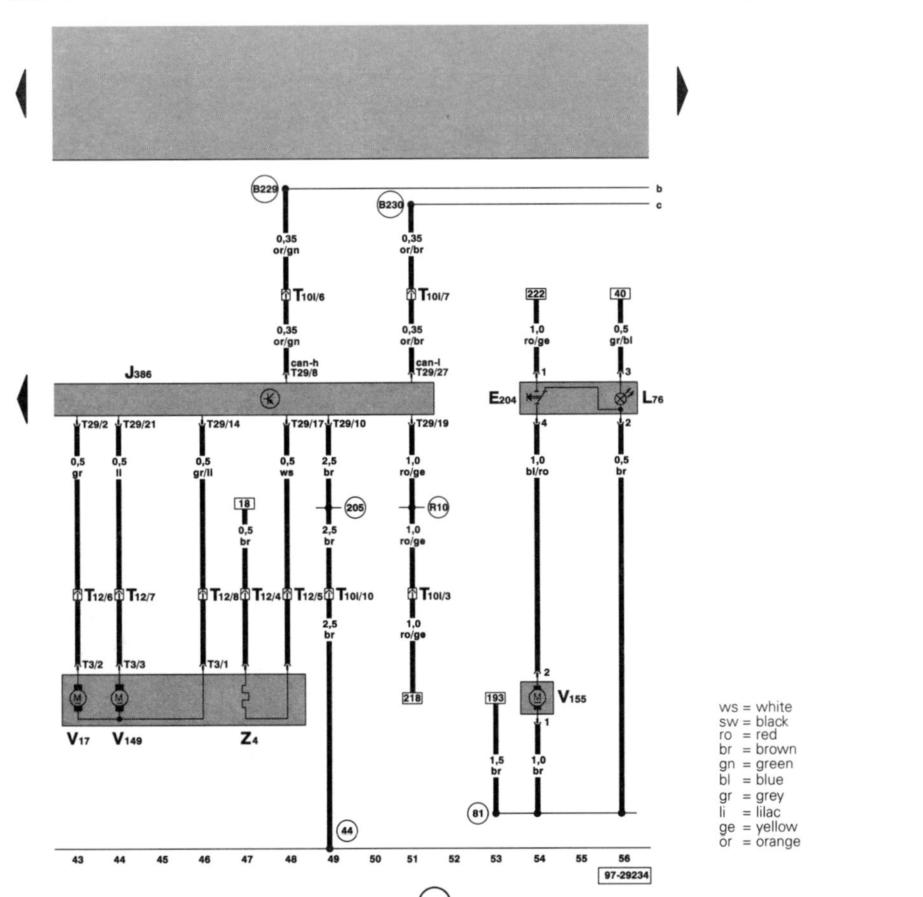

ws = white
sw = black
ro = red
br = brown
gn = green
bl = blue
gr = grey
li = lilac
ge = yellow
or = orange

E204 - Switch for remote/fuel tank door
J386 - Door control module, driver side
L76 - Push Button Light
T3 - 3-Pin Connector
T10i - 10-Pin Connector, black, connector station A-pillar, left
T12 - 12-Pin Connector
T29 - 29-Pin Connector
V17 - Driver's Side Mirror Adjustment Motor
V149 - Motor for mirror adjustment, driver side
V155 - Motor for fuel tank lid unlock
Z4 - Heated outside mirror, driver side

(44) - Ground connection, on left A-pillar, lower part

(81) - Ground connection -1-, in instrument panel wiring harness
(205) - Ground connection, in driver's door wiring harness
(B229) - Connection (high bus), in instrument panel wiring harness
(B230) - Connection (low bus), in instrument panel wiring harness
(R10) - Plus connection -1- (30a), in driver's door wiring harness

Door control module (driver side), power mirror (driver side), heated outside mirror (driver side), Switch for remote/fuel tank door, motor for fuel tank lid unlock

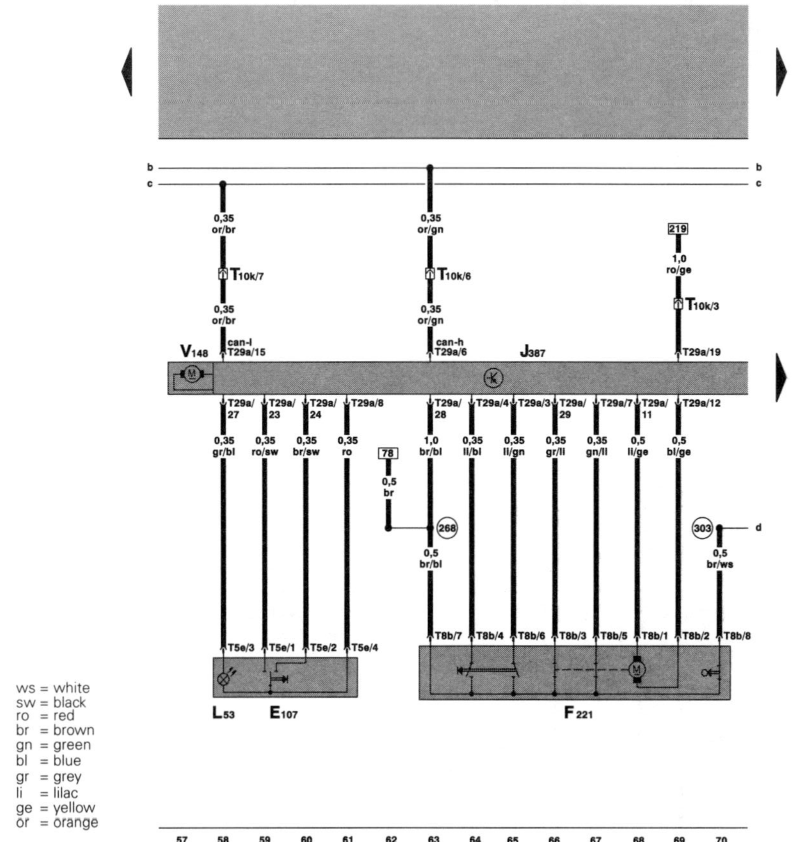

ws = white
sw = black
ro = red
br = brown
gn = green
bl = blue
gr = grey
li = lilac
ge = yellow
or = orange

E107 - Switch for window regulator, in passenger door
F221 - Lock unit for central locking, passenger side
J387 - Door control module, passenger side
L53 - Power Window Switch Light
T5e - 5-Pin Connector
T8b - 8-Pin Connector
T10k - 10-Pin Connector, black, connector station A-pillar, right
T29a - 29-Pin Connector
V148 - Motor for window regulator, passenger side

(268) - Ground connector -2-, in wiring harness door cable - passenger side
(303) - Ground connector -3-, in wiring harness door cable - passenger side

Door control module (passenger side), switch for window regulator (passenger door), lock unit for central locking (passenger side)

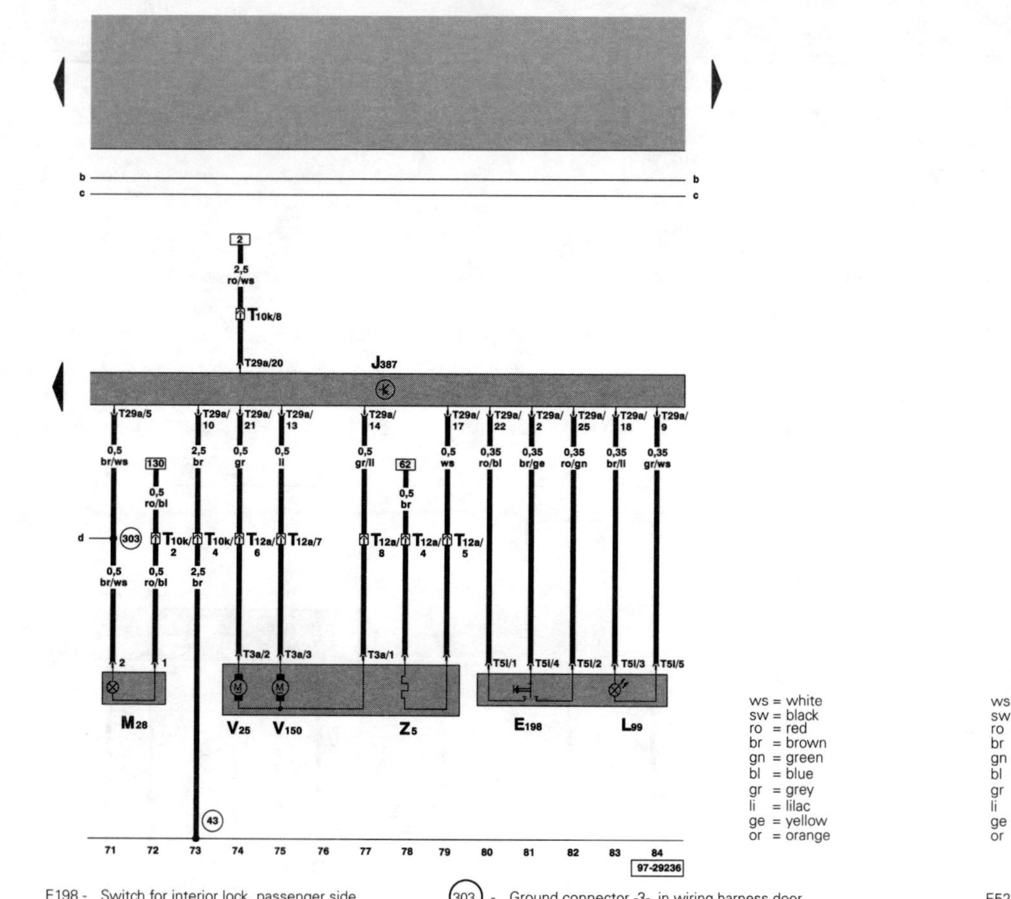

ws = white
sw = black
ro = red
br = brown
gn = green
bl = blue
gr = grey
li = lilac
ge = yellow
or = orange

E198 - Switch for interior lock, passenger side
J387 - Door control module, passenger side
L99 - Lighting for switch interior lock
M28 - Right Door Warning Light
T3a - 3-Pin Connector
T5l - 5-Pin Connector
T10k - 10-Pin Connector, black, connector station A-pillar, right
T12a - 12-Pin Connector
T29a - 29-Pin Connector
V25 - Passenger's Side Mirror Adjustment Motor
V150 - Motor for mirror adjustment, passenger side
Z5 - Heated outside mirror, passenger side

(43) - Ground connection, on right A-pillar, lower part

(303) - Ground connector -3-, in wiring harness door cable - passenger side

Door control module (passenger side), switch for interior lock (passenger side), right door warning light, power mirror (passenger side), heated outside mirror

ws = white
sw = black
ro = red
br = brown
gn = green
bl = blue
gr = grey
li = lilac
ge = yellow
or = orange

E52 - Left Rear Window Switch, (In LR Door)
F222 - Lock unit for central locking, rear, left
J388 - Door control module, rear, left
L53 - Power Window Switch Light
T5f - 5-Pin Connector
T6a - 6-Pin Connector
T10l - 10-Pin Connector, black, connector station B-pillar, left
T18a - 18-Pin Connector
V26 - Motor for window regulator, rear, left

(77) - Ground connection, on left B-pillar, lower part

Door control module (rear left), left rear window switch (In LR Door), lock unit for central locking (rear left), motor for window regulator (rear left)

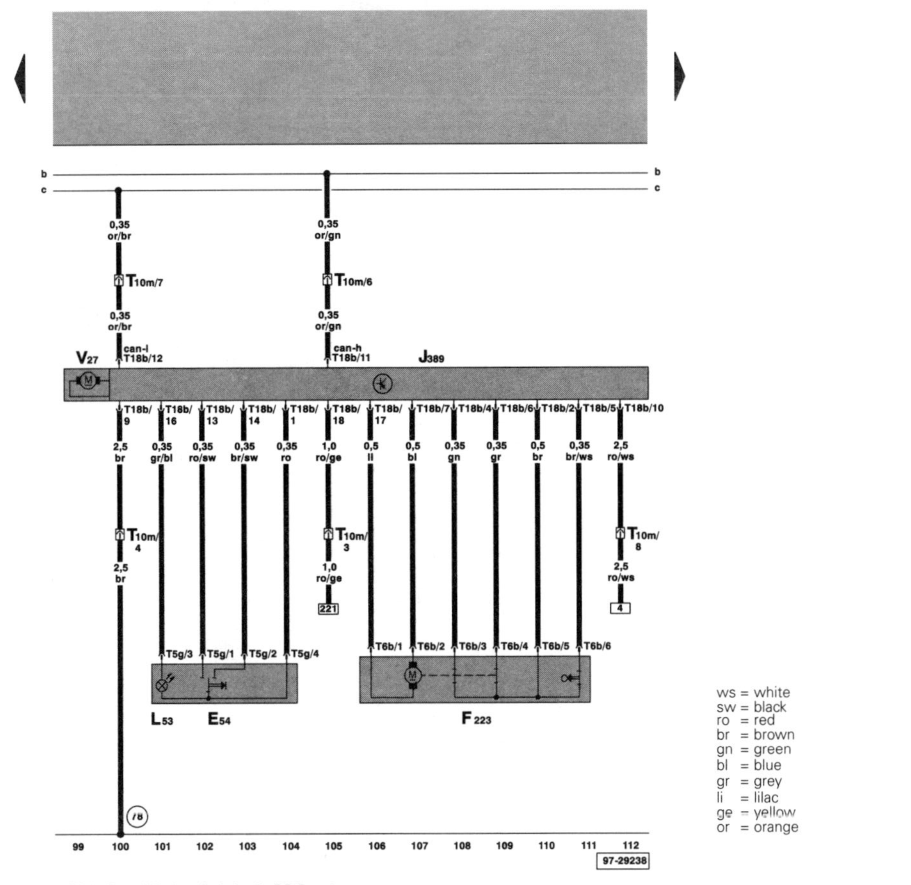

ws = white
sw = black
ro = red
br = brown
gn = green
bl = blue
gr = grey
li = lilac
ge = yellow
or = orange

E54 - Right Rear Window Switch, (In RR Door)
F223 - Lock unit for central locking, rear, right
J389 - Door control module, rear, right
L53 - Power Window Switch Light
T5g - 5-Pin Connector
T6b - 6-Pin Connector
T10m - 10-Pin Connector, black, connector station B-pillar, right
T18b - 18-Pin Connector
V27 - Motor for window regulator, rear, right

(78) - Ground connection, on right B-pillar, lower part

Door control module (rear right), right rear window switch (In RR Door), lock unit for central locking (rear right), motor for window regulator (rear right)

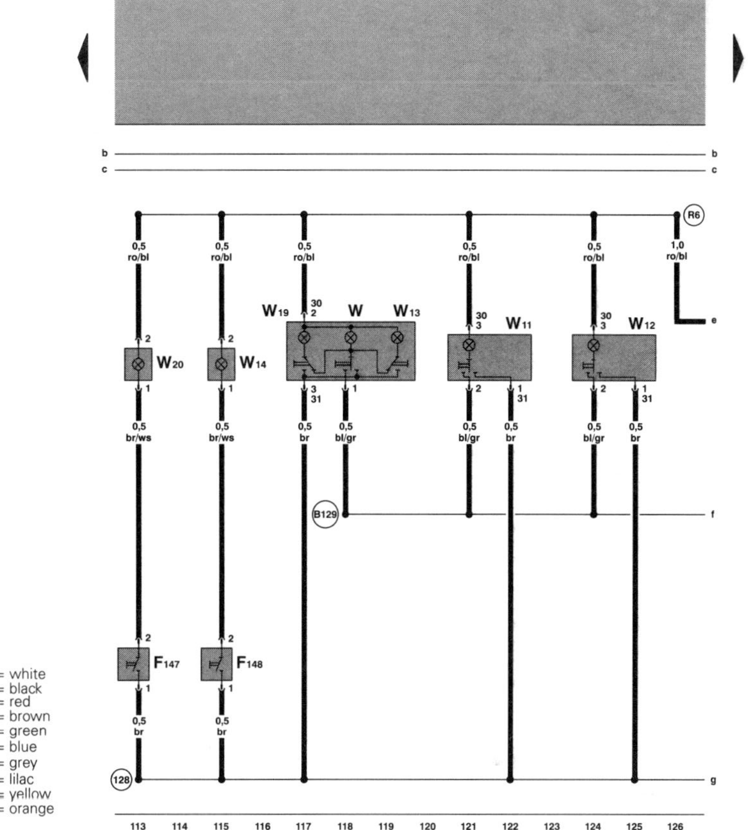

ws = white
sw = black
ro = red
br = brown
gn = green
bl = blue
gr = grey
li = lilac
ge = yellow
or = orange

F147 - Left Make-Up Mirror Light Switch
F148 - Right Make-Up Mirror Light Switch
W - Front Interior Light
W11 - Left Rear Reading Light
W12 - Right Rear Reading Light
W13 - Right Front Map/Reading Light
W14 - Right Make-up Mirror Light
W19 - Left Front Reading Light
W20 - Left Make-up Mirror Light

(128) - Ground connection -1-, in interior light wiring harness
(B129) - Connector (interior light 3/L) in wiring harness interior
(R6) - Plus connection -1-, in interior light wiring harness

Interior lights, make-up mirror lights

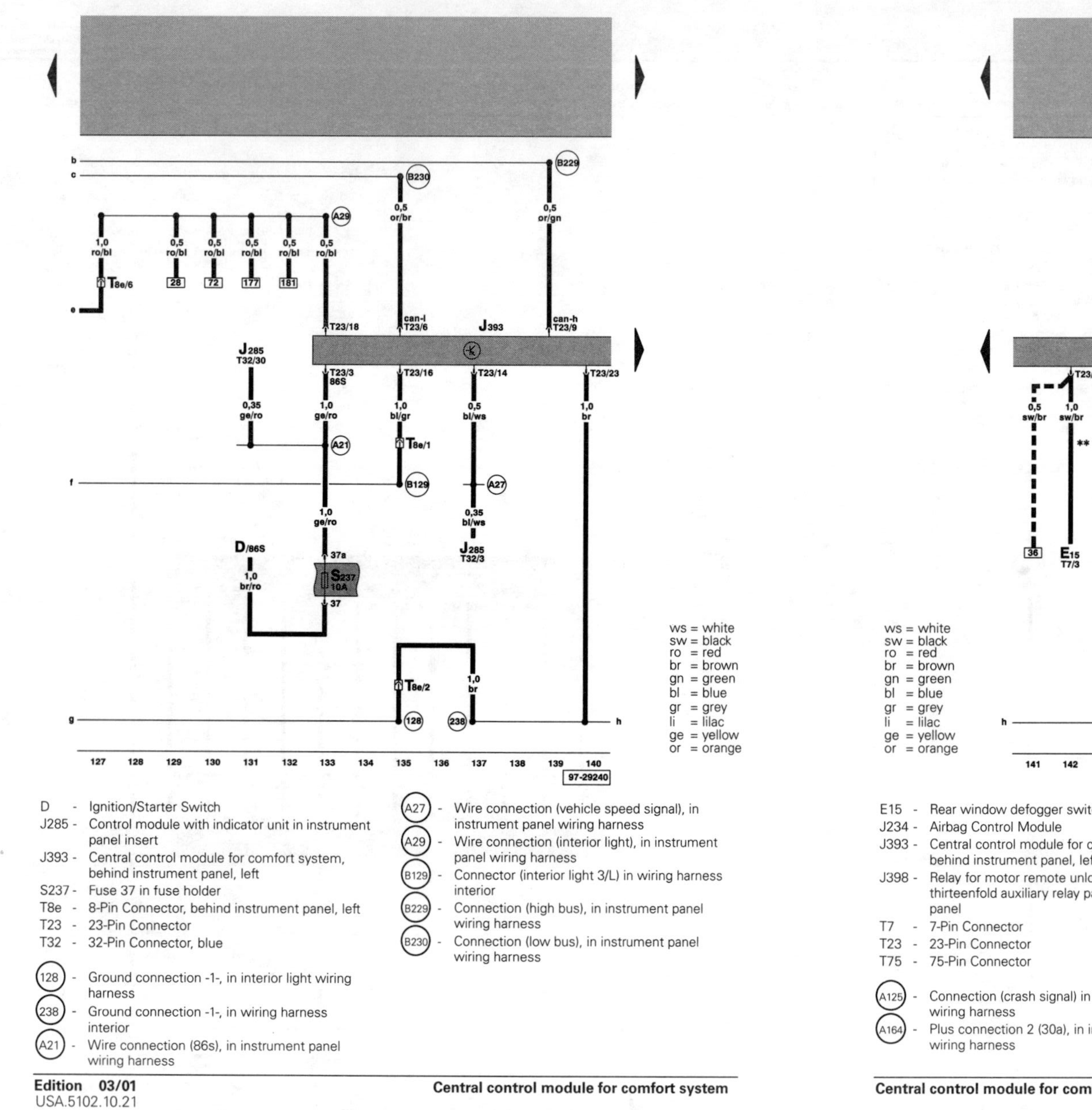

ws = white
sw = black
ro = red
br = brown
gn = green
bl = blue
gr = grey
li = lilac
ge = yellow
or = orange

D - Ignition/Starter Switch
J285 - Control module with indicator unit in instrument panel insert
J393 - Central control module for comfort system, behind instrument panel, left
S237 - Fuse 37 in fuse holder
T8e - 8-Pin Connector, behind instrument panel, left
T23 - 23-Pin Connector
T32 - 32-Pin Connector, blue

(128) - Ground connection -1-, in interior light wiring harness
(238) - Ground connection -1-, in wiring harness interior
(A21) - Wire connection (86s), in instrument panel wiring harness
(A27) - Wire connection (vehicle speed signal), in instrument panel wiring harness
(A29) - Wire connection (interior light), in instrument panel wiring harness
(B129) - Connector (interior light 3/L) in wiring harness interior
(B229) - Connection (high bus), in instrument panel wiring harness
(B230) - Connection (low bus), in instrument panel wiring harness

ws = white
sw = black
ro = red
br = brown
gn = green
bl = blue
gr = grey
li = lilac
ge = yellow
or = orange

E15 - Rear window defogger switch
J234 - Airbag Control Module
J393 - Central control module for comfort system, behind instrument panel, left
J398 - Relay for motor remote unlock rear lid, on the thirteenfold auxiliary relay panel, above relay panel
T7 - 7-Pin Connector
T23 - 23-Pin Connector
T75 - 75-Pin Connector

(A125) - Connection (crash signal) in instrument panel wiring harness
(A164) - Plus connection 2 (30a), in instrument panel wiring harness

--- Vehicles with seperate heated outside mirrors only
** - Vehicles without seperate heated outside mirrors only

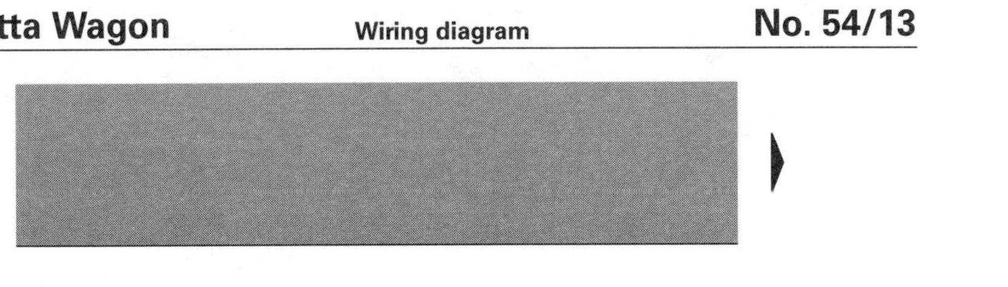

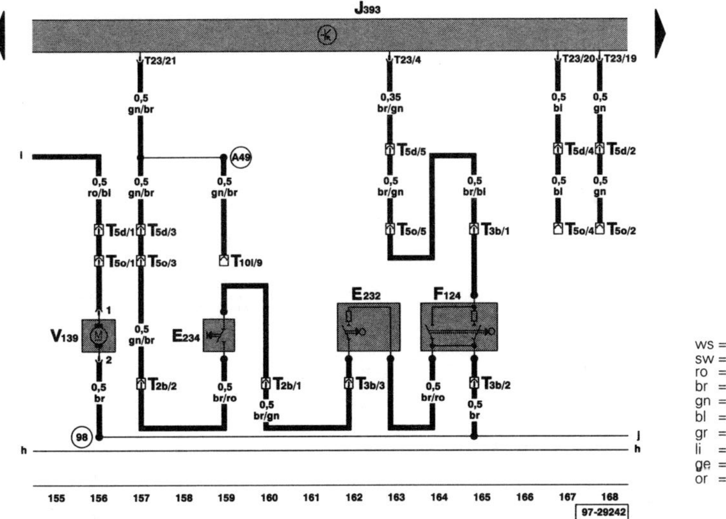

ws = white
sw = black
ro = red
br = brown
gn = green
bl = blue
gr = grey
li = lilac
ge = yellow
or = orange

E232 - Rear Lid Remote Lock Key Switch
E234 - Switch for unlocking, rear lid handle
F124 - Trunk Lock Alarm/Central Locking Switch
J393 - Central control module for comfort system, behind instrument panel, left
T2b - Double Connector, in rear lid
T3b - 3-Pin Connector, in rear lid
T5d - 5-Pin Connector, brown, connector station D-pillar, right
T5o - 5-Pin Connector, brown, in rear lid
T10i - 10-Pin Connector, black, connector station A-pillar, left
T23 - 23-Pin Connector
V139 - Motor to unlock rear lid

(98) - Ground connection, in rear lid wiring harness

(A49) - Wire connection -1-, in instrument panel wiring harness

Central control module for comfort system, rear lid remote lock key switch, switch for unlocking (rear lid handle), trunk lock alarm/central locking switch, motor to unlock rear lid

ws = white
sw = black
ro = red
br = brown
gn = green
bl = blue
gr = grey
li = lilac
ge = yellow
or = orange

169 170 171 172 173 174 175 176 177 178 179 180 181 182
97-29243

E165 - Trunk Lid Release Switch
F5 - Luggage Compartment Light Switch
J393 - Central control module for comfort system, behind instrument panel, left
K116 - Warning light for rear lid unlocked, in Instrument cluster
T5 - 5-Pin Connector, black, connector station D-pillar, left
T5p - 5-Pin Connector, black, in rear lid
T23 - 23-Pin Connector
T32 - 32-Pin Connector, blue, on Instrument cluster
W3 - Luggage compartment Light
W18 - Left Luggage Compartment Light

(50) - Ground connection, in luggage compartment, left

(98) - Ground connection, in rear lid wiring harness

(218) - Ground connection -1-, in rear lid wiring harness

(A126) - Connection (contact switch in rear lid) in instrument panel wiring harness

(Q22) - Wire connection -1-, in rear lid wiring harness

(Q44) - Wire connection -2-, in tailgate wiring harness

Central control module for comfort system, trunk lid release switch, luggage compartment light switch, luggage compartment light

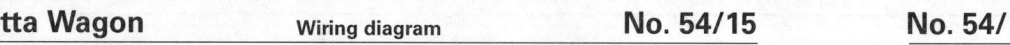

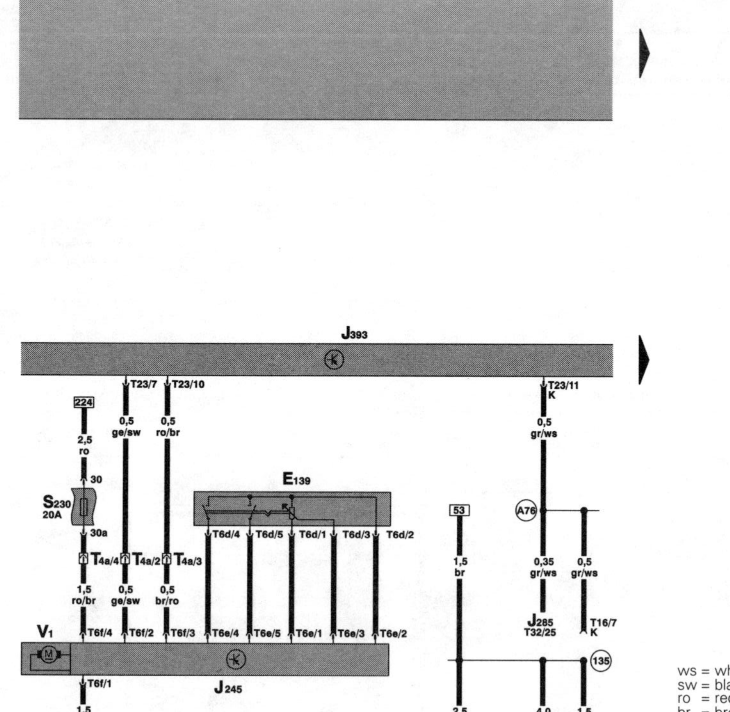

ws = white
sw = black
ro = red
br = brown
gn = green
bl = blue
gr = grey
li = lilac
ge = yellow
or = orange

- E139 - Sunroof Regulator
- J245 - Power Sunroof Control Module
- J285 - Control module with indicator unit in instrument panel insert
- J393 - Central control module for comfort system, behind instrument panel, left
- S230 - Fuse 30 in fuse holder
- T4a - 4-Pin Connector, behind instrument panel, left
- T6d - 6-Pin Connector
- T6e - 6-Pin Connector
- T6f - 6-Pin Connector
- T16 - Data Link Connector (DLC), below instrument panel, left
- T23 - 23-Pin Connector
- T32 - 32-Pin Connector, blue, on Instrument cluster
- V1 - Sunroof Motor

- (42) - Ground connection, beside steering column
- (49) - Ground connection, on steering column
- (135) - Ground connection -2-, in instrument panel wiring harness
- (238) - Ground connection -1-, in wiring harness interior
- (A76) - Connector (K-diagnosis wire) in instrument panel wiring harness

Edition 03/01
USA.5102.10.21

Central control module for comfort system, power sunroof control module, sunroof regulator, sunroof motor

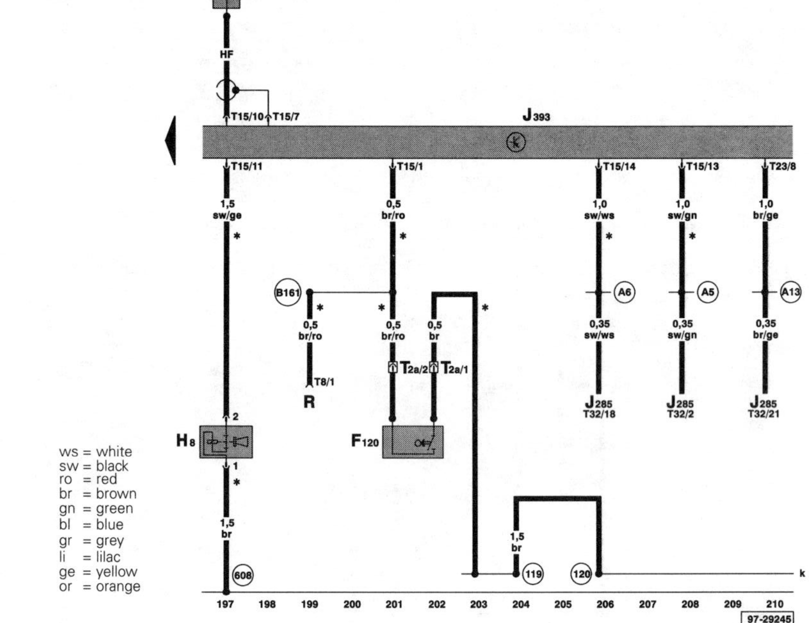

ws = white
sw = black
ro = red
br = brown
gn = green
bl = blue
gr = grey
li = lilac
ge = yellow
or = orange

- F120 - Hood Alarm Switch*
- H8 - Alarm Horn*
- J285 - Control module with indicator unit in instrument panel insert
- J393 - Central control module for comfort system, behind instrument panel, left
- R - Radio
- R47 - Antenna wire for central locking and antitheft warning system
- T2a - Double Connector, near headlight, right
- T8 - 8-Pin Connector, on radio
- T15 - 15-Pin Connector*
- T23 - 23-Pin Connector
- T32 - 32-Pin Connector, blue, on instrument cluster

- (119) - Ground connection -1-, in headlight wiring harness
- (120) - Ground connection -2-, in headlight wiring harness
- (608) - Ground connection (in center plenum chamber)
- (A5) - Plus connection (right turn signal), in instrument panel wiring harness
- (A6) - Plus connection (left turn signal), in instrument panel wiring harness
- (A13) - Wire connection (door contact switch) in instrument panel wiring harness
- (B161) - Connector (anti-theft warning system), in wiring harness interior

* - Vehicles with anti-theft warning system only

Central control module for comfort system, antitheft warning system, antenna wire for central locking and antitheft warning system

Edition 03/01
USA.5102.10.21

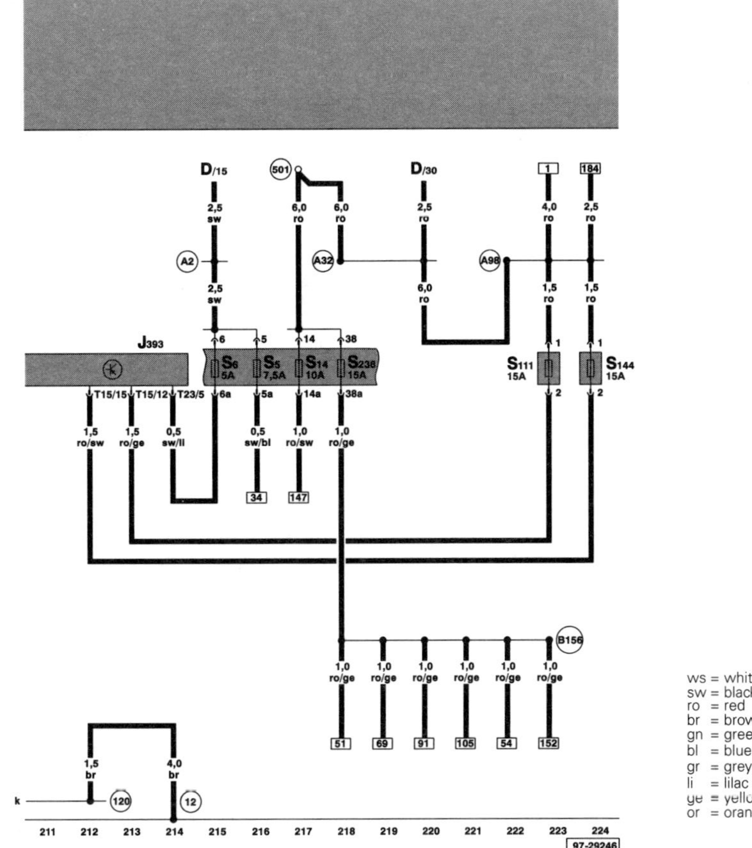

ws = white
sw = black
ro = red
br = brown
gn = green
bl = blue
gr = grey
li = lilac
ge = yellow
or = orange

- D - Ignition/Starter Switch
- J393 - Central control module for comfort system, behind instrument panel, left
- S5 - Fuse 5 in fuse holder
- S6 - Fuse 6 in fuse holder
- S14 - Fuse 14 in fuse holder
- S111 - Alarm System and Anti-Theft Fuse, above the thirteenfold auxiliary relay panel*
- S144 - Fuse for central locking/anti-theft warning system, above the thirteenfold auxiliary relay panel*
- S238 - Fuse 38 in fuse holder
- T15 - 15-Pin Connector*
- T23 - 23-Pin Connector

- (12) - Ground connection, in engine compartment, left
- (120) - Ground connection -2-, in headlight wiring harness
- (501) - Threaded connection -2- (30) on the relay plate
- (A2) - Plus connection (15), in instrument panel wiring harness
- (A32) - Plus connection (30), in instrument panel wiring harness
- (A98) - Plus connector -4- (30), in instrument panel wiring harness
- (B156) - Plus connector (30a), in wiring harness interior

* - Vehicles with anti-theft warning system only

THIS PAGE INTENTIONALLY LEFT BLANK

Comfort system (vehicles without power windows),

from May 2001

- Anti-theft warning system
- Central locking system with remote control
- Fuel tank lid unlock system
- Heated outside mirrors
- Interior lights
- Luggage compartment light
- Power sunroof
- Rear lid unlock system

Deviate relay location and fuseplacements as well as the locations of multiple connectors see section "component locations".

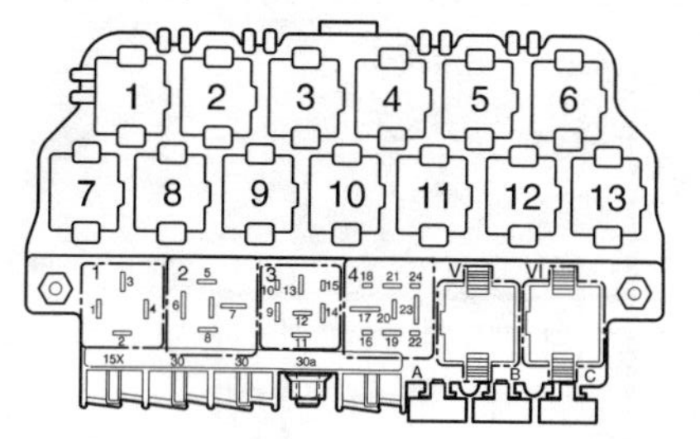

Fuse colors

30 A - green
25 A - white
20 A - yellow
15 A - blue
10 A - red
7,5 A - brown
5 A - beige
3 A - violet

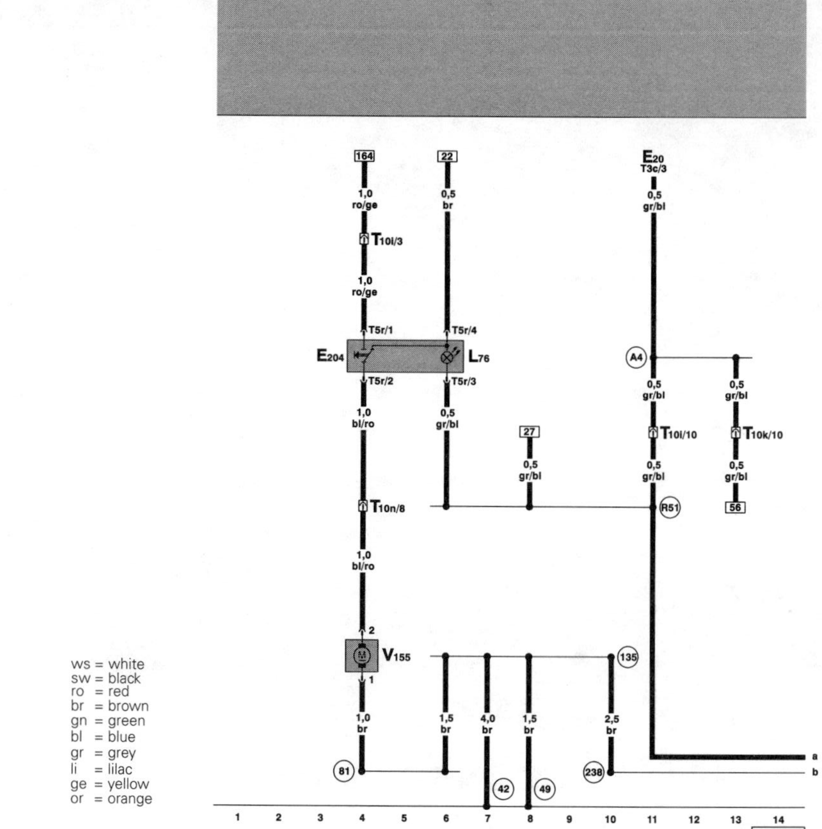

ws = white
sw = black
ro = red
br = brown
gn = green
bl = blue
gr = grey
li = lilac
ge = yellow
or = orange

E20 - Instrument Panel Light Dimmer Switch
E204 - Switch for remote/fuel tank door
L76 - Push Button Light
T3c - 3-Pin Connector
T5r - 5-Pin Connector
T10i - 10-Pin Connector, black, connector station A-pillar, left
T10k - 10-Pin Connector, black, connector station A-pillar, right
T10n - 10-Pin Connector, brown, connector station A-pillar, left
V155 - Motor for fuel tank lid unlock

(42) - Ground connection, beside steering column

(49) - Ground connection, on steering column

(81) - Ground connection -1-, in instrument panel wiring harness

(135) - Ground connection -2-, in instrument panel wiring harness

(238) - Ground connection -1-, in wiring harness interior

(A4) - Plus connection (58b), in instrument panel wiring harness

(R51) - Connection (58b) in door wiring harness, driver side

Switch for remote/fuel tank door, motor for fuel tank lid unlock

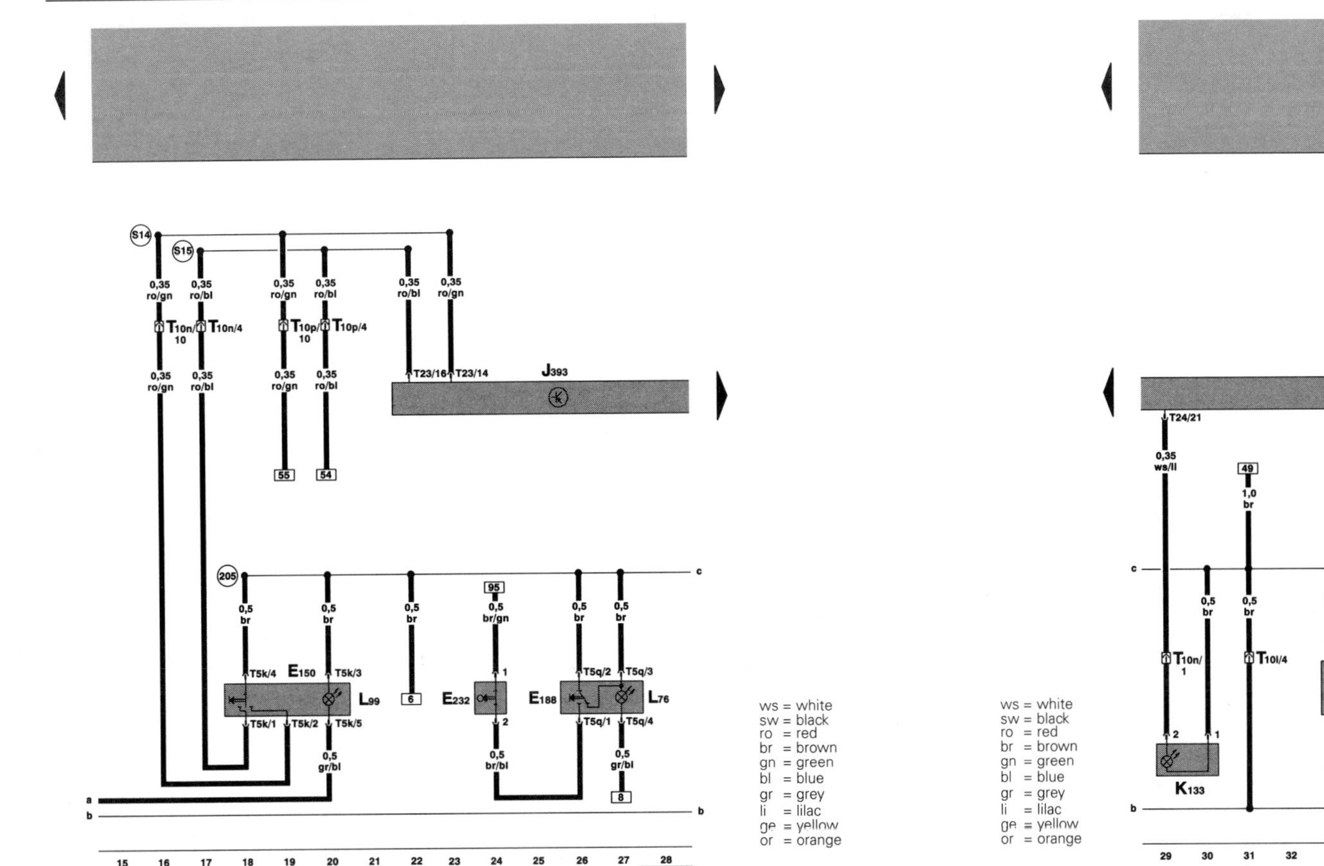

ws = white
sw = black
ro = red
br = brown
gn = green
bl = blue
gr = grey
li = lilac
ge = yellow
or = orange

E150 - Switch for interior lock, driver side
E188 - Switch for remote unlock, rear lid, driver side
E232 - Key switch for switching off remote unlock rear lid
J393 - Central control module for comfort system, behind instrument panel, left
L76 - Push Button Light
L99 - Lighting for switch interior lock
T5k - 5-Pin Connector
T5q - 5-Pin Connector
T10n - 10-Pin Connector, brown, connector station A-pillar, left
T10p - 10-Pin Connector, brown, connector station A-pillar, right
T23 - 23-Pin Connector

(205) - Ground connection, in driver's door wiring harness
(S14) - Wire connection (open), in central locking system wiring harness
(S15) - Wire connection (closed), in central locking system wiring harness

Central control module for comfort system, switch for interior lock (driver side), switch for remote unlock rear lid

ws = white
sw = black
ro = red
br = brown
gn = green
bl = blue
gr = grey
li = lilac
ge = yellow
or = orange

F220 - Lock unit for central locking, driver side
J393 - Central control module for comfort system, behind instrument panel, left
K133 - Warning light for central locking -SAFE-
T8c - 8-Pin Connector
T10i - 10-Pin Connector, black, connector station A-pillar, left
T10n - 10-Pin Connector, brown, connector station A-pillar, left
T24 - 24-Pin Connector

(205) - Ground connection, in driver's door wiring harness
(304) - Ground connector -3-, in wiring harness door cable - driver side

Central control module for comfort system, lock unit for central locking, warning light for central locking -SAFE-

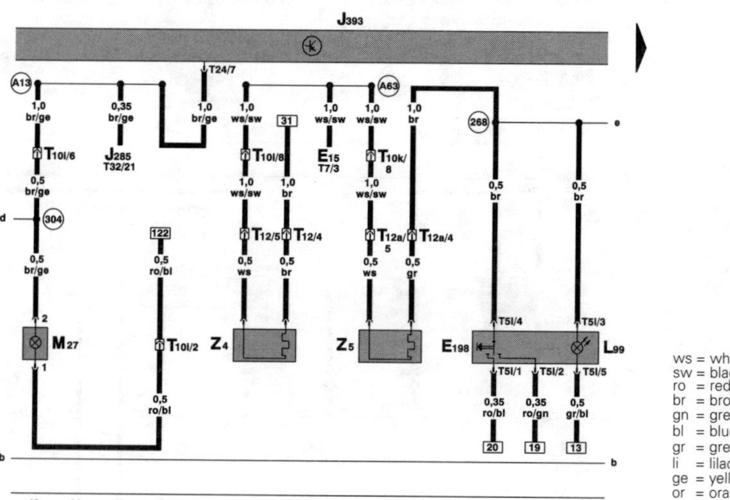

ws = white
sw = black
ro = red
br = brown
gn = green
bl = blue
gr = grey
li = lilac
ge = yellow
or = orange

E15 - Rear window defogger switch
E198 - Switch for interior lock, passenger side
J285 - Control module with indicator unit in instrument panel insert
J393 - Central control module for comfort system, behind instrument panel, left
L99 - Lighting for switch interior lock
M27 - Left Door Warning Light
T5l - 5-Pin Connector
T7 - 7-Pin Connector
T10i - 10-Pin Connector, black, connector station A-pillar, left
T10k - 10-Pin Connector, black, connector station A-pillar, right
T12 - 12-Pin Connector, in driver's door
T12a - 12-Pin Connector, in front passenger's door
T24 - 24-Pin Connector
T32 - 32-Pin Connector, blue
Z4 - Heated outside mirror, driver side
Z5 - Heated outside mirror, passenger side
(268) - Ground connector -2-, in wiring harness door cable - passenger side
(304) - Ground connector -3-, in wiring harness door cable - driver side
(A13) - Wire connection (door contact switch) in instrument panel wiring harness
(A63) - Connector (mirror adjustment/-heated) in instrument panel wiring harness

Central control module for comfort system, switch for interior lock (passenger side), left door warning light, heated outside mirrors

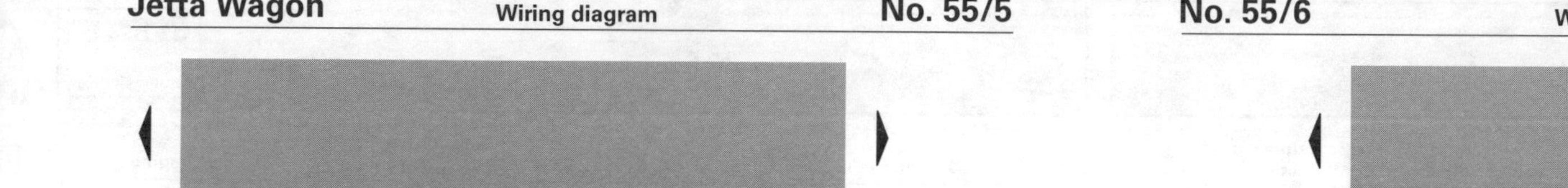

ws = white
sw = black
ro = red
br = brown
gn = green
bl = blue
gr = grey
li = lilac
ge = yellow
or = orange

F221 - Lock unit for central locking, passenger side
J393 - Central control module for comfort system, behind instrument panel, left
M28 - Right Door Warning Light
T8b - 8-Pin Connector
T10k - 10-Pin Connector, black, connector station A-pillar, right
T10p - 10-Pin Connector, brown, connector station A-pillar, right
T24 - 24-Pin Connector
(268) - Ground connector -2-, in wiring harness door cable - passenger side
(303) - Ground connector -3-, in wiring harness door cable - passenger side

Central control module for comfort system, lock unit for central locking (passenger side), right door warning light

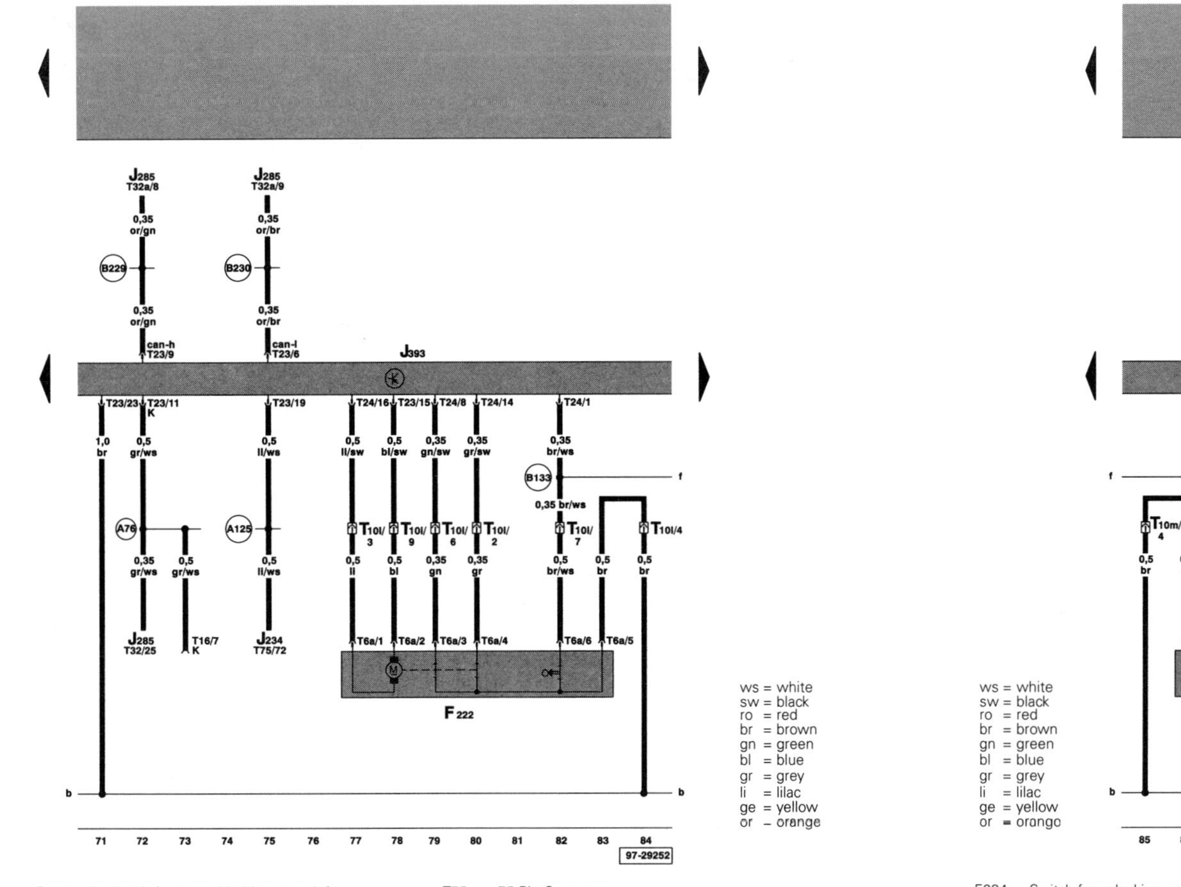

ws = white
sw = black
ro = red
br = brown
gn = green
bl = blue
gr = grey
li = lilac
ge = yellow
or = orange

- F222 - Lock unit for central locking, rear, left
- J234 - Airbag Control Module, behind console, lower part
- J285 - Control module with indicator unit in instrument panel insert
- J393 - Central control module for comfort system, behind instrument panel, left
- T6a - 6-Pin Connector
- T10l - 10-Pin Connector, black, connector station B-pillar, left
- T16 - Data Link Connector (DLC), below instrument panel, left
- T23 - 23-Pin Connector
- T24 - 24-Pin Connector
- T32 - 32-Pin Connector, blue
- T32a - 32-Pin Connector, green
- T75 - 75-Pin Connector
- (A76) - Connector (K-diagnosis wire) in instrument panel wiring harness
- (A125) - Connection (crash signal) in instrument panel wiring harness
- (B133) - Connector (central locking open), in wiring harness interior
- (B229) - Connection (high bus), in instrument panel wiring harness
- (B230) - Connection (low bus), in instrument panel wiring harness

Central control module for comfort system, lock unit for central locking (rear left)

ws = white
sw = black
ro = red
br = brown
gn = green
bl = blue
gr = grey
li = lilac
ge = yellow
or = orange

- E234 - Switch for unlocking, rear lid handle
- F223 - Lock unit for central locking, rear, right
- J393 - Central control module for comfort system, behind instrument panel, left
- T5d - 5-Pin Connector, brown, connector station D-pillar, right
- T5o - 5-Pin Connector, brown, in rear lid
- T5p - 5-Pin Connector, black, in rear lid
- T6b - 6-Pin Connector
- T10i - 10-Pin Connector, black, connector station A-pillar, left
- T10m - 10-Pin Connector, black, connector station B-pillar, right
- T23 - 23-Pin Connector
- T24 - 24-Pin Connector
- V139 - Motor to unlock rear lid
- (50) - Ground connection, in luggage compartment, left
- (98) - Ground connection, in rear lid wiring harness
- (218) - Ground connection -1-, in rear lid wiring harness
- (A49) - Wire connection -1-, in instrument panel wiring harness
- (B133) - Connector (central locking open), in wiring harness interior
- (W16) - Connector (contact switch) in lock cylinder for rear hatch central locking), in wiring harness, rear

Central control module for comfort system, lock unit for central locking (rear right), switch for unlocking (rear lid handle), motor to unlock rear lid

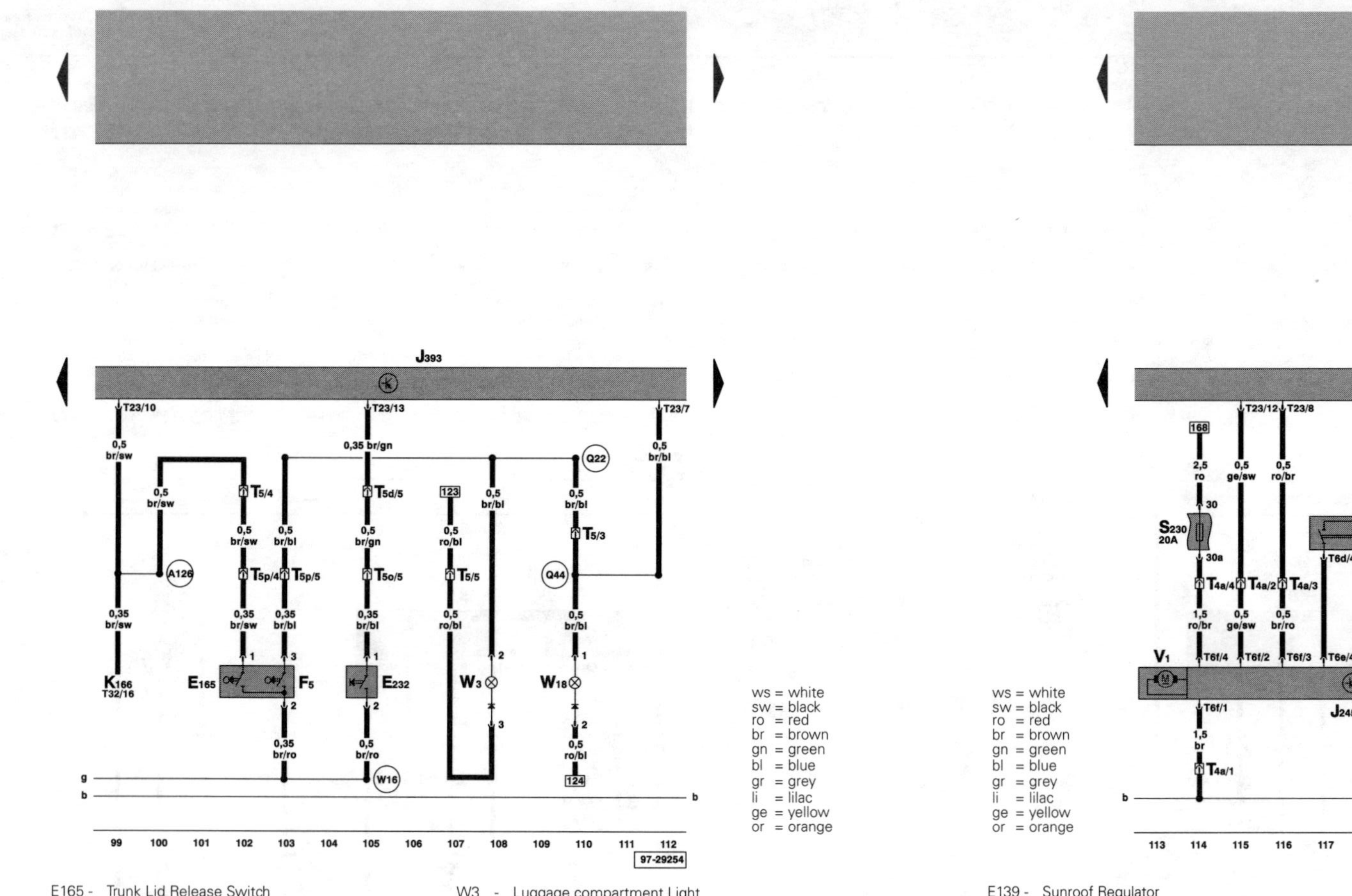

ws = white
sw = black
ro = red
br = brown
gn = green
bl = blue
gr = grey
li = lilac
ge = yellow
or = orange

E165 - Trunk Lid Release Switch
E232 - Rear Lid Remote Lock Key Switch
F5 - Luggage Compartment Light Switch
J393 - Central control module for comfort system, behind instrument panel, left
K166 - Door Ajar Indicator Lamp, in instrument cluster
T5 - 5-Pin Connector, black, connector station D-pillar, left
T5d - 5-Pin Connector, brown, connector station D-pillar, right
T5o - 5-Pin Connector, brown, in rear lid
T5p - 5-Pin Connector, black, in rear lid
T23 - 23-Pin Connector
T24 - 24-Pin Connector
T32 - 32-Pin Connector, blue, on Instrument cluster

W3 - Luggage compartment Light
W18 - Left Luggage Compartment Light

(A126) - Connection (contact switch in rear lid) in instrument panel wiring harness
(Q22) - Wire connection -1-, in rear lid wiring harness
(Q44) - Wire connection -2-, in tailgate wiring harness
(W16) - Connector (contact switch) in lock cylinder for rear hatch central locking), in wiring harness, rear

Central control module for comfort system, trunk lid release switch, luggage compartment light switch, luggage compartment light, rear lid remote lock key switch

ws = white
sw = black
ro = red
br = brown
gn = green
bl = blue
gr = grey
li = lilac
ge = yellow
or = orange

E139 - Sunroof Regulator
J245 - Power Sunroof Control Module
J393 - Central control module for comfort system, behind instrument panel, left
S230 - Fuse 30 in fuse holder
T4a - 4-Pin Connector, behind instrument panel, left
T6d - 6-Pin Connector
T6e - 6-Pin Connector
T6f - 6-Pin Connector
T8e - 8-Pin Connector, behind instrument panel, left
T23 - 23-Pin Connector
V1 - Sunroof Motor

(128) - Ground connection -1-, in interior light wiring harness

(238) - Ground connection -1-, in wiring harness interior
(A29) - Wire connection (interior light), in instrument panel wiring harness
(R6) - Plus connection -1-, in interior light wiring harness

Central control module for comfort system, power sunroof control module, sunroof regulator, sunroof motor

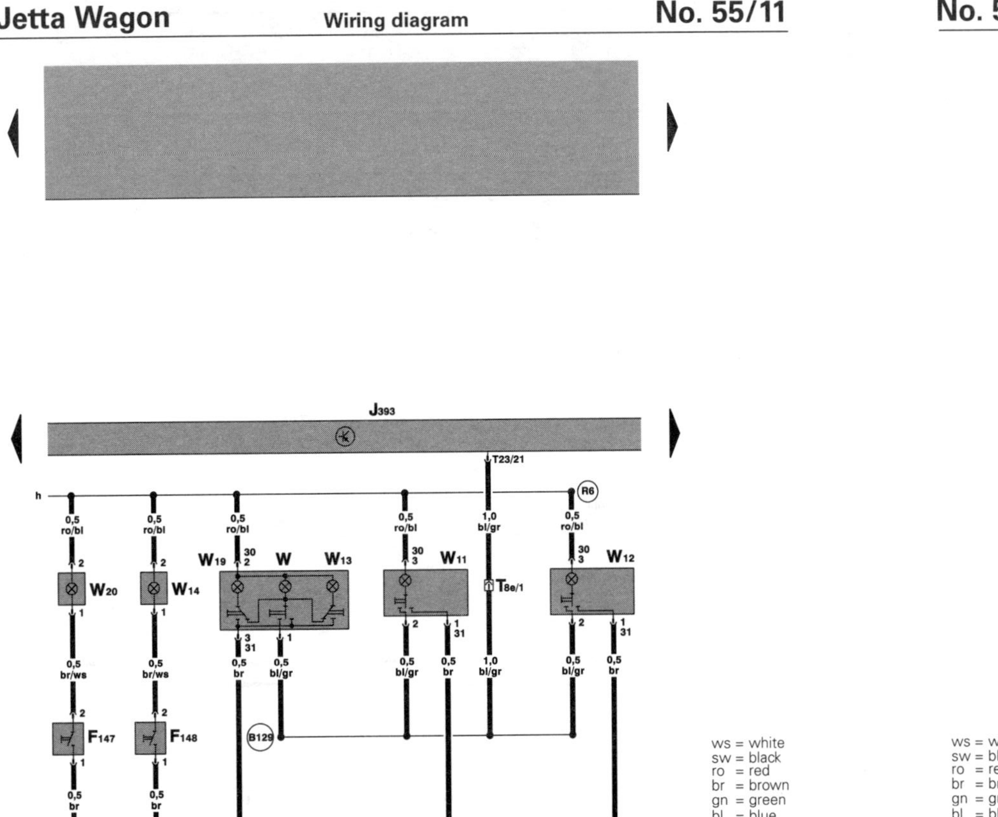

ws = white
sw = black
ro = red
br = brown
gn = green
bl = blue
gr = grey
li = lilac
ge = yellow
or = orange

F147 - Left Make-Up Mirror Light Switch
F148 - Right Make-Up Mirror Light Switch
J393 - Central control module for comfort system, behind instrument panel, left
W - Front Interior Light
W11 - Left Rear Reading Light
W12 - Right Rear Reading Light
W13 - Right Front Map/Reading Light
W14 - Right Make-up Mirror Light
W19 - Left Front Reading Light
W20 - Left Make-up Mirror Light
T8e - 8-Pin Connector, behind instrument panel, left
T23 - 23-Pin Connector

(128) - Ground connection -1-, in interior light wiring harness

(B129) - Connector (interior light 3/L) in wiring harness interior
(R6) - Plus connection -1-, in interior light wiring harness

Edition 03/01
USA.5102.10.21

Central control module for comfort system, interior lights, make-up mirror lights

R47
HF
T15/10 T15/7
J393
T15/11 T15/5 T15/15 T15/14 T23/15
1,5 sw/ge
0,5 br/ro
1,0 sw/ws
1,0 sw/gn
0,5 bl/ws
B161 A6 A5 A27
0,5 br/ro
0,5 br
0,35 sw/ws
0,35 sw/gn
0,35 bl/ws
T8/1
R
T2a/2 T2a/1
J285 T32/18
J285 T32/2
J285 T32/3
H8
F120
1,5 br
608 119 120
141 142 143 144 145 146 147 148 149 150 151 152 153 154
97-29257

ws = white
sw = black
ro = red
br = brown
gn = green
bl = blue
gr = grey
li = lilac
ge = yellow
or = orange

F120 - Hood Alarm Switch*
H8 - Alarm Horn*
J285 - Control module with indicator unit in instrument panel insert
J393 - Central control module for comfort system, behind instrument panel, left
R - Radio
R47 - Antenna wire for central locking and antitheft warning system
T2a - Double Connector, near headlight, right
T8 - 8-Pin Connector, on radio
T15 - 15-Pin Connector
T23 - 23-Pin Connector
T32 - 32-Pin Connector, blue, on instrument cluster

(119) - Ground connection -1-, in headlight wiring harness
(120) - Ground connection -2-, in headlight wiring harness
(608) - Ground connection (in center plenum chamber)
(A5) - Plus connection (right turn signal), in instrument panel wiring harness
(A6) - Plus connection (left turn signal), in instrument panel wiring harness
(A27) - Wire connection (vehicle speed signal), in instrument panel wiring harness
(B161) - Connector (anti-theft warning system), in wiring harness interior

* - Vehicles with anti-theft warning system only

Central control module for comfort system, antitheft warning system, antenna wire for central locking and antitheft warning system

Edition 03/01
USA.5102.10.21

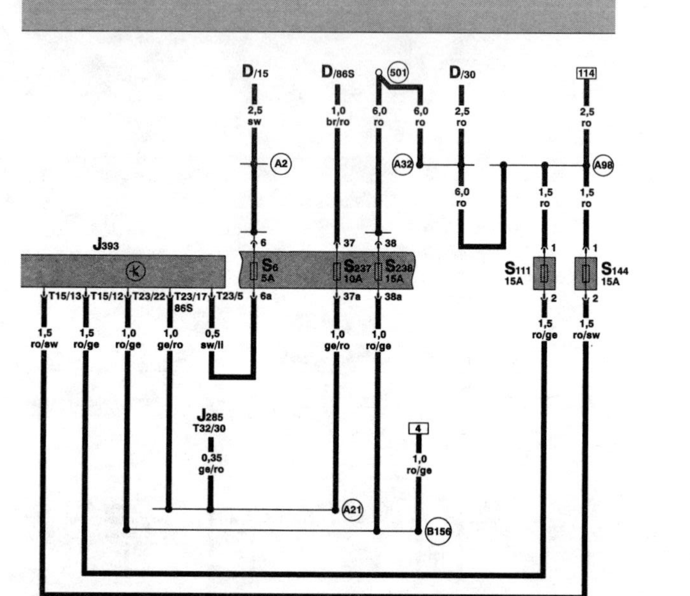

D - Ignition/Starter Switch
J285 - Control module with indicator unit in instrument panel insert
J393 - Central control module for comfort system, behind instrument panel, left
S6 - Fuse 6 in fuse holder
S111 - Alarm System and Anti-Theft Fuse, above the thirteenfold auxiliary relay panel
S144 - Fuse for central locking/anti-theft warning system, above the thirteenfold auxiliary relay panel
S237 - Fuse 37 in fuse holder
S238 - Fuse 38 in fuse holder
T15 - 15-Pin Connector
T23 - 23-Pin Connector
T32 - 32-Pin Connector, blue

(12) - Ground connection, in engine compartment, left
(120) - Ground connection -2-, in headlight wiring harness
(501) - Threaded connection -2- (30) on the relay plate
(A2) - Plus connection (15), in instrument panel wiring harness
(A21) - Wire connection (86s), in instrument panel wiring harness
(A32) - Plus connection (30), in instrument panel wiring harness
(A98) - Plus connector -4- (30), in instrument panel wiring harness
(B156) - Plus connector (30a), in wiring harness interior

Edition 03/01
USA.5102.10.21

Central control module for comfort system

THIS PAGE INTENTIONALLY LEFT

BLANK

Comfort System (vehicles with power windows),

from May 2001

- Anti-theft warning system
- Central locking system with remote control
- Fuel tank lid unlock system
- Heated power mirrors
- Interior lights
- Luggage compartment light
- Power sunroof
- Power windows
- Rear lid unlock system

Deviate relay location and fuseplacements as well as the locations of multiple connectors see section "component locations".

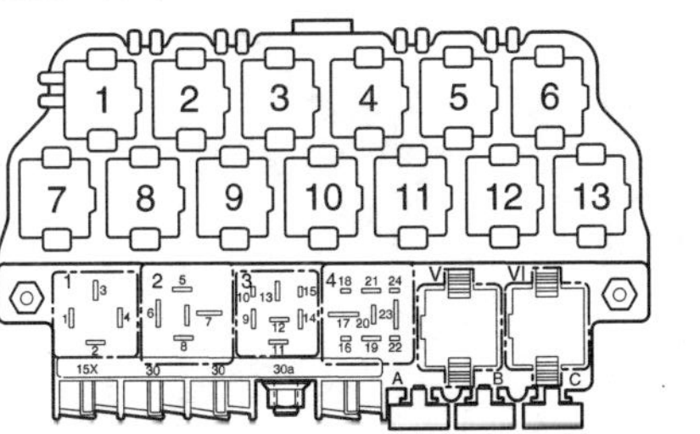

Fuse colors

30 A - green
25 A - white
20 A - yellow
15 A - blue
10 A - red
7,5 A - brown
5 A - beige
3 A - violet

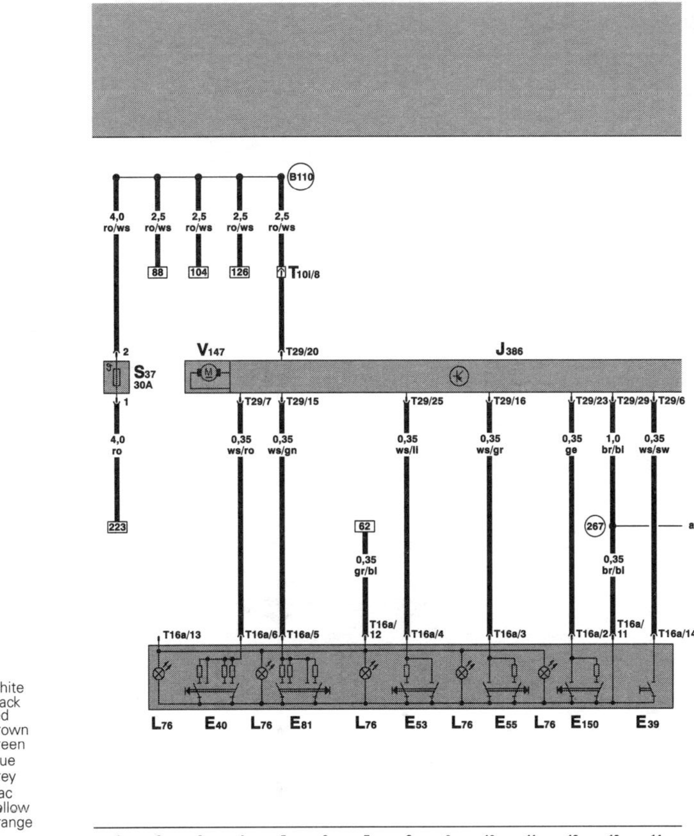

ws = white
sw = black
ro = red
br = brown
gn = green
bl = blue
gr = grey
li = lilac
ge = yellow
or = orange

E39 - Safety switch for window regulator rear
E40 - Switch for window regulator front left
E53 - Switch for window regulator rear left, driver
E55 - Switch for window regulator rear right, driver
E81 - Switch for window regulator front right, driver
E150 - Switch for interior lock, driver side
J386 - Door control module, driver side
L76 - Push Button Light
S37 - Fuse for window regulator (circuit breaker), on thirteen position auxiliary relay panel
T10i - 10-Pin Connector, black, connector station A-pillar, left
T16a - 16-Pin Connector
T29 - 29-Pin Connector
V147 - Motor for window regulator, driver side

(267) - Ground connector -2-, in wiring harness door cable - driver side
(B110) - Connection (30, window regulator) in wiring harness interior

Door control module (driver side), switch for window regulator, safety switch for window regulator rear, switch for interior lock (driver side)

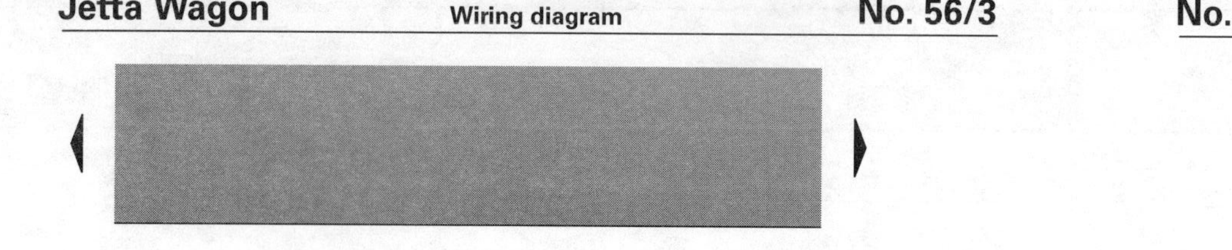

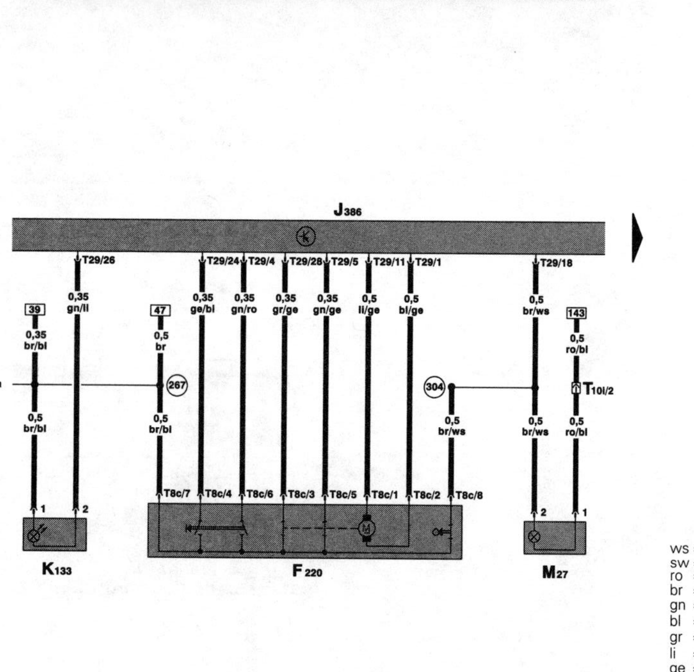

ws = white
sw = black
ro = red
br = brown
gn = green
bl = blue
gr = grey
li = lilac
ge = yellow
or = orange

15 16 17 18 19 20 21 22 23 24 25 26 27 28

97-29260

F220 - Lock unit for central locking, driver side
J386 - Door control module, driver side
K133 - Warning light for central locking -SAFE-
M27 - Left Door Warning Light
T8c - 8-Pin Connector
T10i - 10-Pin Connector, black, connector station A-pillar, left
T29 - 29-Pin Connector

267 - Ground connector -2-, in wiring harness door cable - driver side
304 - Ground connector -3-, in wiring harness door cable - driver side

Door control module (driver side), lock unit for central locking (driver side), warning light for central locking -SAFE-, left door warning light

J386

T29/3 T29/22 A20 155 216 T10q/2 T10q/6 15 61

T10t/6 T10t/10 T10t/7 T10t/9 T10t/8 T10t/5

E43 E48 E263 E231 L78

ws = white
sw = black
ro = red
br = brown
gn = green
bl = blue
gr = grey
li = lilac
ge = yellow
or = orange

29 30 31 32 33 34 35 36 37 38 39 40 41 42

97-29261

E43 - Mirror Adjustment Switch
E48 - Mirror Selector Switch
E231 - Switch for outside mirror heating
E263 - Mirror fold-away Switch*
J386 - Door control module, driver side
L78 - Mirror Adjusting Switch Light
T10q - 10-Pin Connector, blue, connector station A-pillar, left
T10t - 10-Pin Connector
T29 - 29-Pin Connector

(A20) - Wire connection (15a), in instrument panel wiring harness

* - Mirror fold-away function for some export countrys only

--- Vehicles with seperate heated outside mirrors only

Door control module (driver side), mirror adjustment switch, mirror selector switch, switch for outside mirror heating

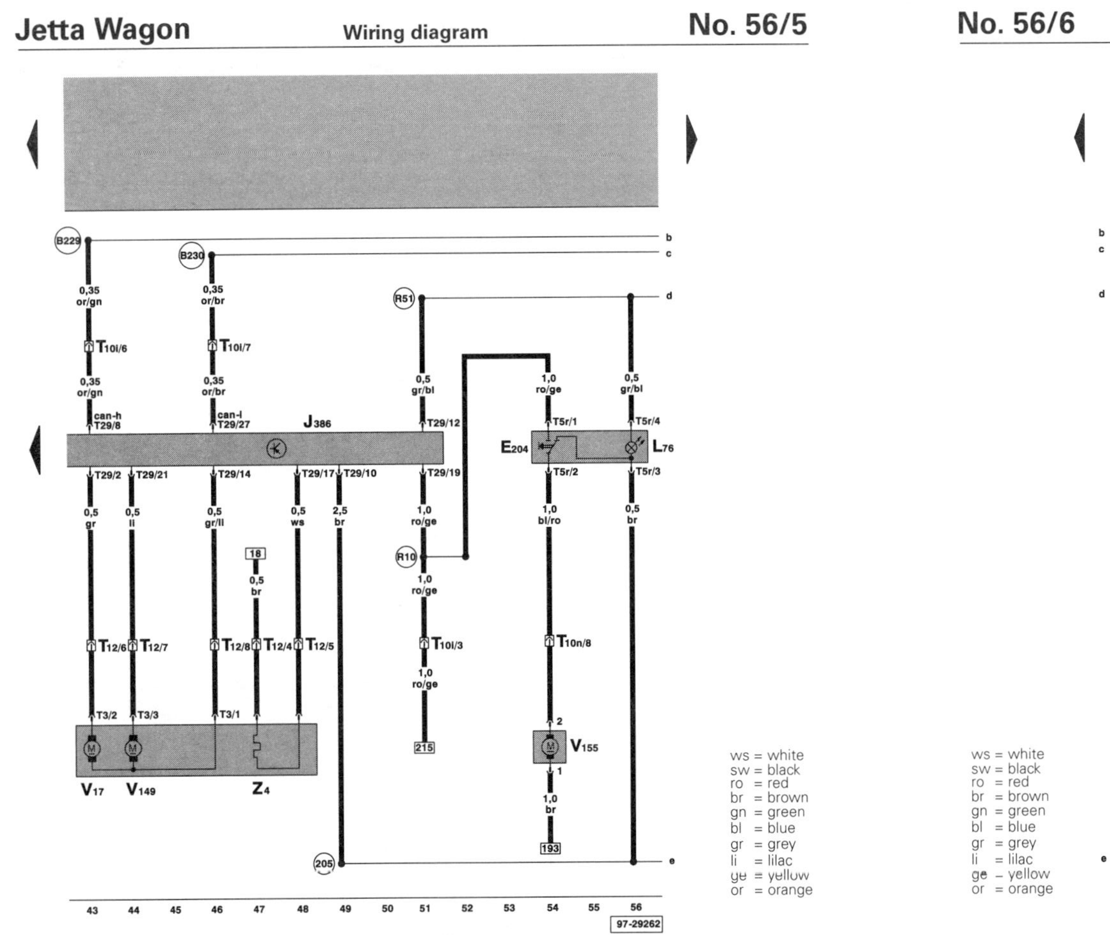

ws = white
sw = black
ro = red
br = brown
gn = green
bl = blue
gr = grey
li = lilac
ge = yellow
or = orange

E204 - Switch for remote/fuel tank door
J386 - Door control module, driver side
L76 - Push Button Light
T3 - 3-Pin Connector
T5r - 5-Pin Connector
T10i - 10-Pin Connector, black, connector station A-pillar, left
T10n - 10-Pin Connector, brown, connector station A-pillar, left
T12 - 12-Pin Connector
T29 - 29-Pin Connector
V17 - Driver's Side Mirror Adjustment Motor
V149 - Motor for mirror adjustment, driver side
V155 - Motor for fuel tank lid unlock
Z4 - Heated outside mirror, driver side

(205) - Ground connection, in driver's door wiring harness
(B229) - Connection (high bus), in instrument panel wiring harness
(B230) - Connection (low bus), in instrument panel wiring harness
(R10) - Plus connection -1- (30a), in driver's door wiring harness
(R51) - Connection (58b), in driver's door wiring harness

Edition 03/01
USA.5102.10.21

Door control module (driver side), switch for remote/fuel tank door, motor for fuel tank lid unlock, power mirror (driver side), heated outside mirror (driver side)

97-29263

ws = white
sw = black
ro = red
br = brown
gn = green
bl = blue
gr = grey
li = lilac
ge = yellow
or = orange

E20 - Instrument Panel Light Dimmer Switch
E188 - Switch for remote unlock, rear lid, driver side
E232 - Key switch for switching off remote unlock rear lid
L76 - Push Button Light
T3c - 3-Pin Connector
T5q - 5-Pin Connector
T10i - 10-Pin Connector, black, connector station A-pillar, left

(44) - Ground connection, on left A-pillar, lower part
(205) - Ground connection, in driver's door wiring harness
(A4) - Plus connection (58b), in instrument panel wiring harness
(R51) - Connection (58b), in driver's door wiring harness

Switch for remote unlock rear lid (driver side), key switch for switching off remote unlock rear lid

Edition 03/01
USA.5102.10.21

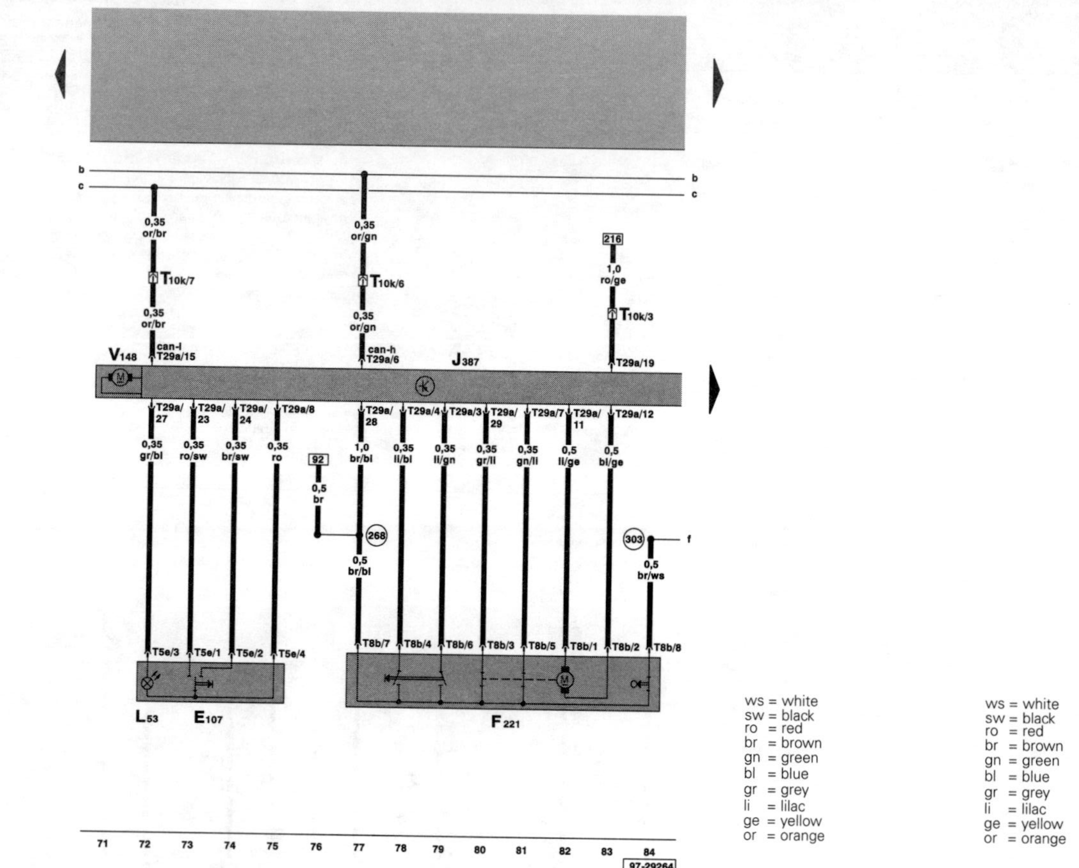

ws = white
sw = black
ro = red
br = brown
gn = green
bl = blue
gr = grey
li = lilac
ge = yellow
or = orange

E107 - Switch for window regulator, in passenger door
F221 - Lock unit for central locking, passenger side
J387 - Door control module, passenger side
L53 - Power Window Switch Light
T5e - 5-Pin Connector
T8b - 8-Pin Connector
T10k - 10-Pin Connector, black, connector station A-pillar, right
T29a - 29-Pin Connector
V148 - Motor for window regulator, passenger side

(268) - Ground connector -2-, in wiring harness door cable - passenger side
(303) - Ground connector -3-, in wiring harness door cable - passenger side

Edition 03/01
USA.5102.10.21

Door control module (passenger side), switch for window regulator (passenger door), lock unit for central locking (passenger side)

ws = white
sw = black
ro = red
br = brown
gn = green
bl = blue
gr = grey
li = lilac
ge = yellow
or = orange

E198 - Switch for interior lock, passenger side
J387 - Door control module, passenger side
L99 - Lighting for switch interior lock
M28 - Right Door Warning Light
T3a - 3-Pin Connector
T5l - 5-Pin Connector
T10k - 10-Pin Connector, black, connector station A-pillar, right
T12a - 12-Pin Connector
T29a - 29-Pin Connector
V25 - Passenger's Side Mirror Adjustment Motor
V150 - Motor for mirror adjustment, passenger side
Z5 - Heated outside mirror, passenger side

(43) - Ground connection, on right A-pillar, lower part

(303) - Ground connector -3-, in wiring harness door cable - passenger side

Door control module (passenger side), switch for interior lock (passenger side), right door warning light, power mirror (passenger side), heated outside mirror

Edition 03/01
USA.5102.10.21

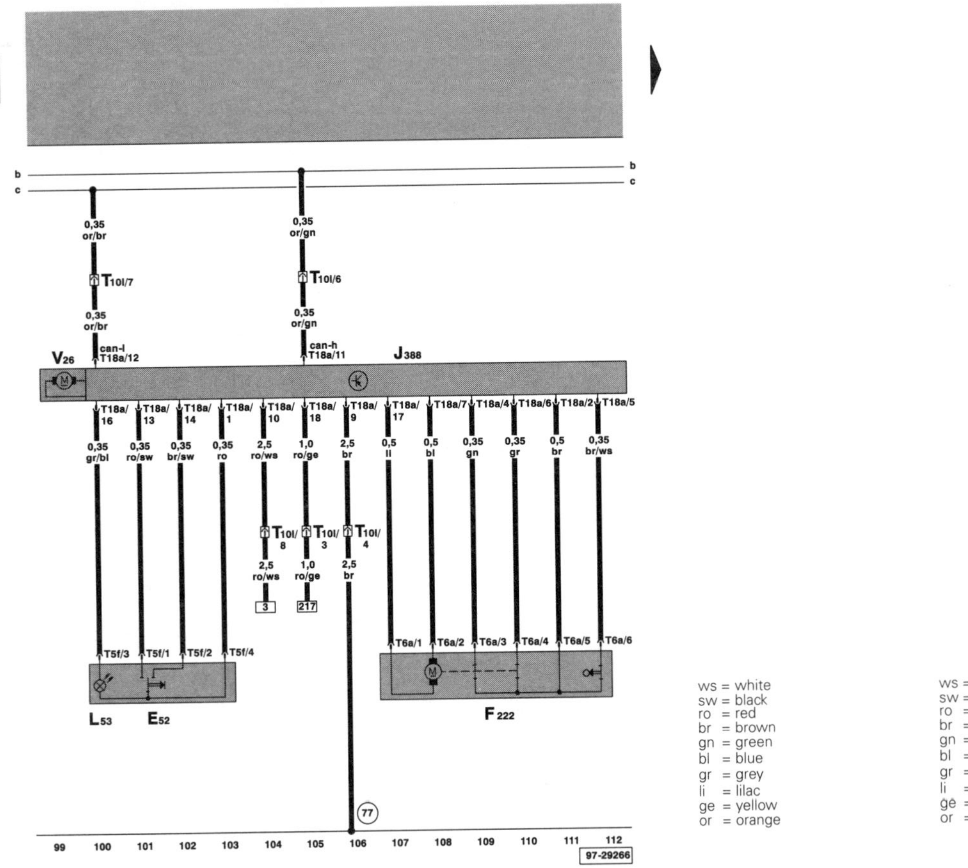

ws = white
sw = black
ro = red
br = brown
gn = green
bl = blue
gr = grey
li = lilac
ge = yellow
or = orange

E52 - Left Rear Window Switch, (In LR Door)
F222 - Lock unit for central locking, rear, left
J388 - Door control module, rear, left
L53 - Power Window Switch Light
T5f - 5-Pin Connector
T6a - 6-Pin Connector
T10l - 10-Pin Connector, black, connector station B-pillar, left
T18a - 18-Pin Connector
V26 - Motor for window regulator, rear, left

(77) - Ground connection, on left B-pillar, lower part

Door control module (rear left), left rear window switch (In LR Door), lock unit for central locking (rear left), motor for window regulator (rear left)

ws = white
sw = black
ro = red
br = brown
gn = green
bl = blue
gr = grey
li = lilac
ge = yellow
or = orange

E54 - Right Rear Window Switch, (In RR Door)
F223 - Lock unit for central locking, rear, right
J389 - Door control module, rear, right
L53 - Power Window Switch Light
T5g - 5-Pin Connector
T6b - 6-Pin Connector
T10m- 10-Pin Connector, black, connector station B-pillar, right
T18b - 18-Pin Connector
V27 - Motor for window regulator, rear, right

(78) - Ground connection, on right B-pillar, lower part

Door control module (rear right), right rear window switch (In RR Door), lock unit for central locking (rear right), motor for window regulator (rear right)

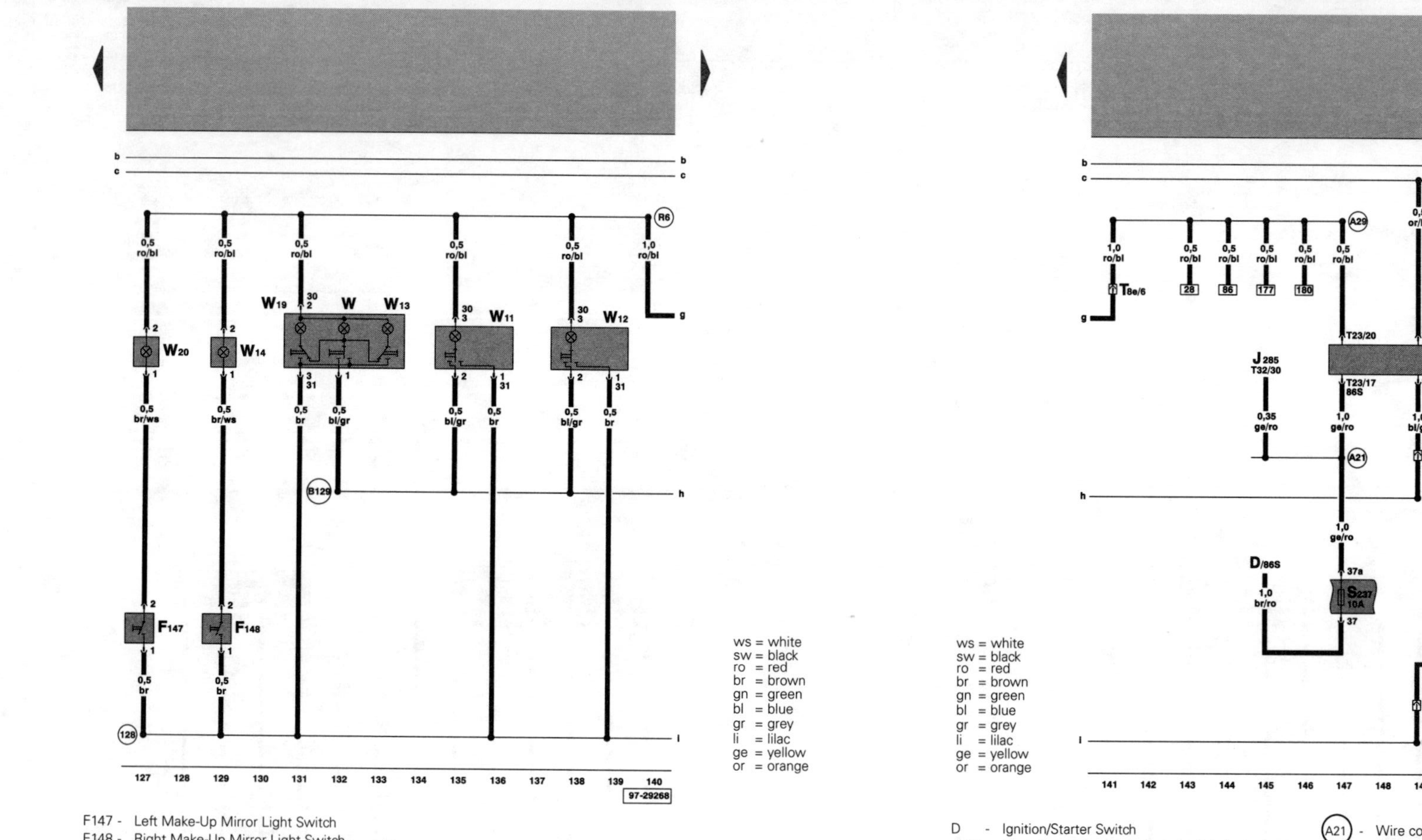

ws = white
sw = black
ro = red
br = brown
gn = green
bl = blue
gr = grey
li = lilac
ge = yellow
or = orange

F147 - Left Make-Up Mirror Light Switch
F148 - Right Make-Up Mirror Light Switch
W - Front Interior Light
W11 - Left Rear Reading Light
W12 - Right Rear Reading Light
W13 - Right Front Map/Reading Light
W14 - Right Make-up Mirror Light
W19 - Left Front Reading Light
W20 - Left Make-up Mirror Light

(128) - Ground connection -1-, in interior light wiring harness
(B129) - Connector (interior light 3/L) in wiring harness interior
(R6) - Plus connection -1-, in interior light wiring harness

Interior lights, make-up mirror lights

ws = white
sw = black
ro = red
br = brown
gn = green
bl = blue
gr = grey
li = lilac
ge = yellow
or = orange

D - Ignition/Starter Switch
J285 - Control module with indicator unit in instrument panel insert
J393 - Central control module for comfort system, behind instrument panel, left
S237 - Fuse 37 in fuse holder
T8e - 8-Pin Connector, behind instrument panel, left
T23 - 23-Pin Connector
T32 - 32-Pin Connector, blue
T32a - 32-Pin Connector, green

(128) - Ground connection -1-, in interior light wiring harness
(238) - Ground connection -1-, in wiring harness interior

(A21) - Wire connection (86s), in instrument panel wiring harness
(A27) - Wire connection (vehicle speed signal), in instrument panel wiring harness
(A29) - Wire connection (interior light), in instrument panel wiring harness
(B129) - Connector (interior light 3/L) in wiring harness interior
(B229) - Connection (high bus), in instrument panel wiring harness
(B230) - Connection (low bus), in instrument panel wiring harness

Central control module for comfort system

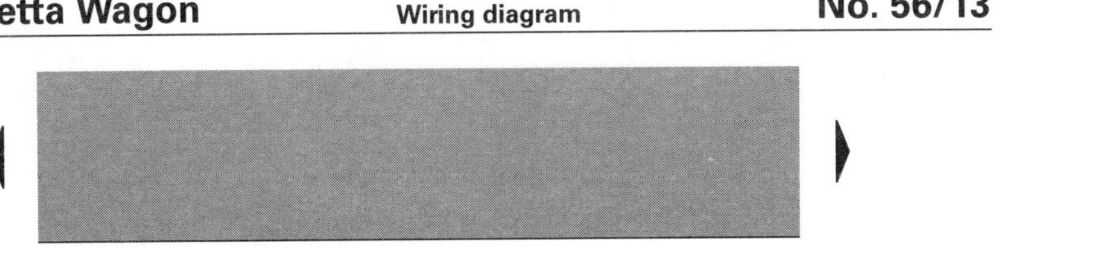

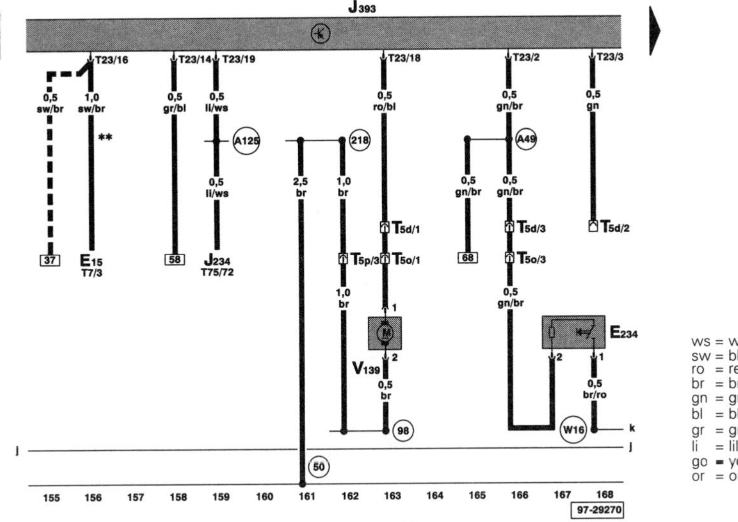

ws = white
sw = black
ro = red
br = brown
gn = green
bl = blue
gr = grey
li = lilac
go = yellow
or = orange

E15 - Rear window defogger switch
E234 - Switch for unlocking, rear lid handle
J234 - Airbag Control Module
J393 - Central control module for comfort system, behind instrument panel, left
T5d - 5-Pin Connector, brown, connector station D-pillar, right
T5o - 5-Pin Connector, brown, in rear lid
T5p - 5-Pin Connector, black, in rear lid
T7 - 7-Pin Connector
T23 - 23-Pin Connector
T75 - 75-Pin Connector
V139 - Motor to unlock rear lid

(50) - Ground connection, in luggage compartment, left

(98) - Ground connection, in rear lid wiring harness

(218) - Ground connection -1-, in rear lid wiring harness

(A49) - Wire connection -1-, in instrument panel wiring harness

(A125) - Connection (crash signal) in instrument panel wiring harness

(W16) - Connector (contact switch) in lock cylinder for rear hatch central locking), in wiring harness, rear

--- Vehicles with seperate heated outside mirrors only

** - Vehicles without seperate heated outside mirrors only

Central control module for comfort system, switch for unlocking (rear lid handle), motor to unlock rear lid

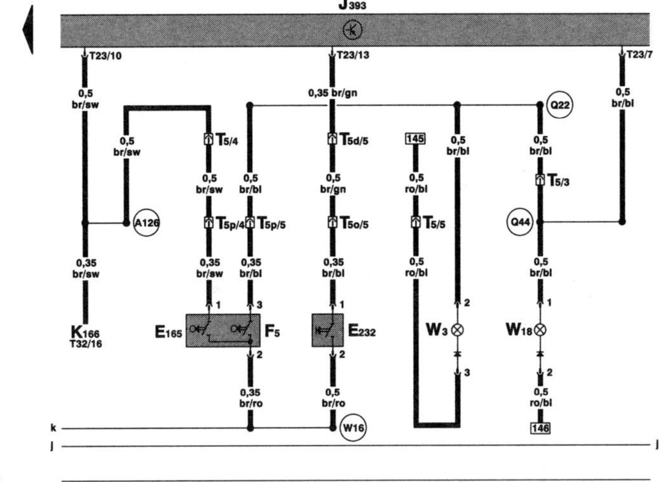

ws = white
sw = black
ro = red
br = brown
gn = green
bl = blue
gr = grey
li = lilac
ge - yellow
or = orange

E165 - Trunk Lid Release Switch
E232 - Rear Lid Remote Lock Key Switch
F5 - Luggage Compartment Light Switch
J393 - Central control module for comfort system, behind instrument panel, left
K166 - Door Ajar Indicator Lamp, in instrument cluster
T5 - 5-Pin Connector, black, connector station D-pillar, left
T5d - 5-Pin Connector, brown, connector station D-pillar, right
T5o - 5-Pin Connector, brown, in rear lid
T5p - 5-Pin Connector, black, in rear lid
T23 - 23-Pin Connector
T24 - 24-Pin Connector
T32 - 32-Pin Connector, blue, on Instrument cluster

W3 - Luggage compartment Light
W18 - Left Luggage Compartment Light

(A126) - Connection (contact switch in rear lid) in instrument panel wiring harness

(Q22) - Wire connection -1-, in rear lid wiring harness

(Q44) - Wire connection -2-, in tailgate wiring harness

(W16) - Connector (contact switch) in lock cylinder for rear hatch central locking), in wiring harness, rear

Central control module for comfort system, trunk lid release switch, luggage compartment light

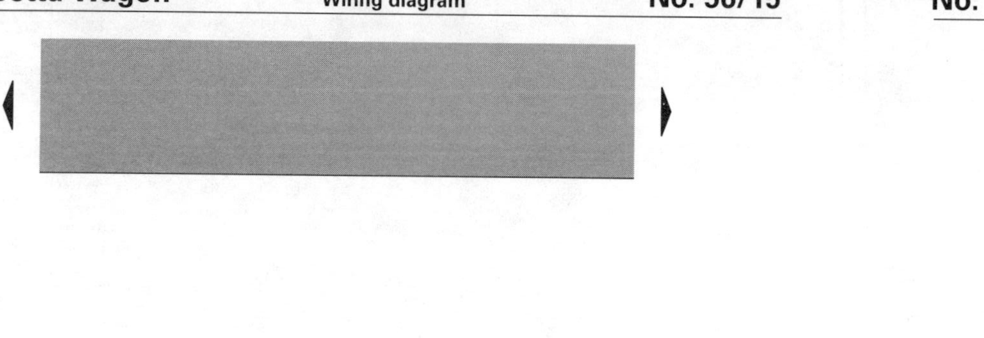

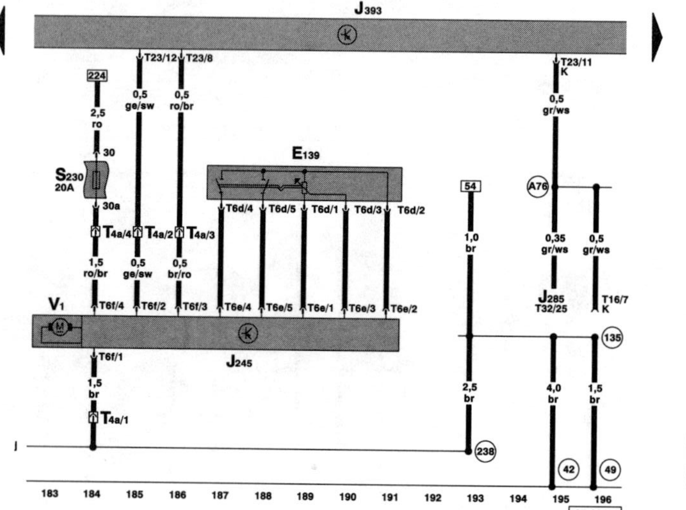

ws = white
sw = black
ro = red
br = brown
gn = green
bl = blue
gr = grey
li = lilac
ge = yellow
or = orange

E139 - Sunroof Regulator
J245 - Power Sunroof Control Module
J285 - Control module with indicator unit in instrument panel insert
J393 - Central control module for comfort system, behind instrument panel, left
S230 - Fuse 30 in fuse holder
T4a - 4-Pin Connector, behind instrument panel, left
T6d - 6-Pin Connector
T6e - 6-Pin Connector
T6f - 6-Pin Connector
T16 - Data Link Connector (DLC), below instrument panel, left
T23 - 23-Pin Connector
T32 - 32-Pin Connector, blue, on Instrument cluster
V1 - Sunroof Motor

(42) - Ground connection, beside steering column
(49) - Ground connection, on steering column
(81) - Ground connection -1-, in instrument panel wiring harness
(135) - Ground connection -2-, in instrument panel wiring harness
(238) - Ground connection -1-, in wiring harness interior
(A76) - Connector (K-diagnosis wire) in instrument panel wiring harness

Central control module for comfort system, power sunroof control module, sunroof regulator, sunroof motor

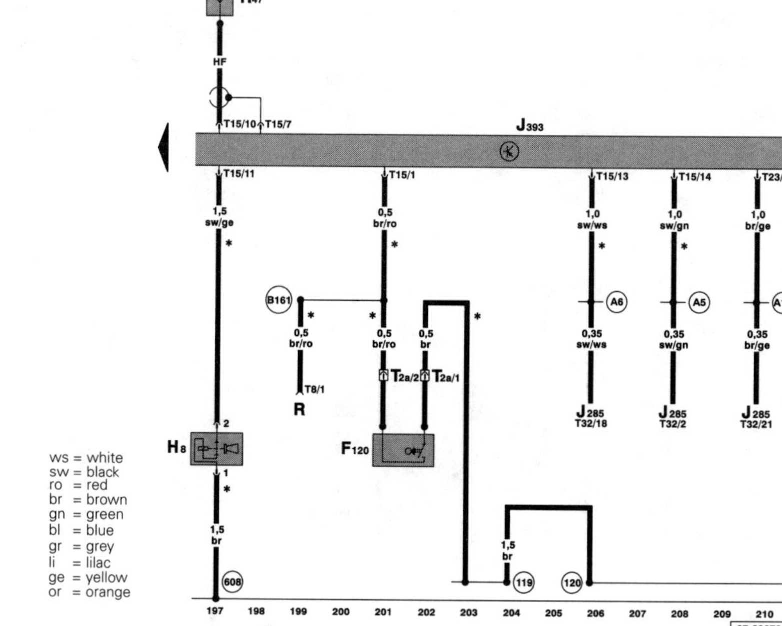

ws = white
sw = black
ro = red
br = brown
gn = green
bl = blue
gr = grey
li = lilac
ge = yellow
or = orange

F120 - Hood Alarm Switch*
H8 - Alarm Horn*
J285 - Control module with indicator unit in instrument panel insert
J393 - Central control module for comfort system, behind instrument panel, left
R - Radio
R47 - Antenna wire for central locking and antitheft warning system
T2a - Double Connector, near headlight, right
T8 - 8-Pin Connector, on radio
T15 - 15-Pin Connector*
T23 - 23-Pin Connector
T32 - 32-Pin Connector, blue, on instrument cluster

(119) - Ground connection -1-, in headlight wiring harness
(120) - Ground connection -2-, in headlight wiring harness
(608) - Ground connection (in center plenum chamber)
(A5) - Plus connection (right turn signal), in instrument panel wiring harness
(A6) - Plus connection (left turn signal), in instrument panel wiring harness
(A13) - Wire connection (door contact switch) in instrument panel wiring harness
(B161) - Connector (anti-theft warning system), in wiring harness interior

* - Vehicles with anti-theft warning system only

Central control module for comfort system, antitheft warning system, antenna wire for central locking and antitheft warning system

ws = white
sw = black
ro = red
br = brown
gn = green
bl = blue
gr = grey
li = lilac
ge = yellow
or = orange

D - Ignition/Starter Switch
J393 - Central control module for comfort system, behind instrument panel, left
S5 - Fuse 5 in fuse holder
S6 - Fuse 6 in fuse holder
S14 - Fuse 14 in fuse holder
S111 - Alarm System and Anti-Theft Fuse, above the thirteenfold auxiliary relay panel*
S144 - Fuse for central locking/anti-theft warning system, above the thirteenfold auxiliary relay panel*
S238 - Fuse 38 in fuse holder
T15 - 15-Pin Connector*
T23 - 23-Pin Connector

(12) - Ground connection, in engine compartment, left
(120) - Ground connection -2-, in headlight wiring harness
(501) - Threaded connection -2- (30) on the relay plate
(A2) - Plus connection (15), in instrument panel wiring harness
(A32) - Plus connection (30), in instrument panel wiring harness
(A98) - Plus connector -4- (30), in instrument panel wiring harness
(B156) - Plus connector (30a), in wiring harness interior

* - Vehicles with anti-theft warning system only

THIS PAGE INTENTIONALLY LEFT
BLANK

Comfort system (vehicles without power windows),

from May 2001

- Anti-theft warning system
- Central locking system with remote control
- Fuel tank lid unlock system
- Heated outside mirrors
- Interior lights
- Luggage compartment light
- Power sunroof
- Rear lid unlock system

Deviate relay location and fuseplacements as well as the locations of multiple connectors see section "component locations".

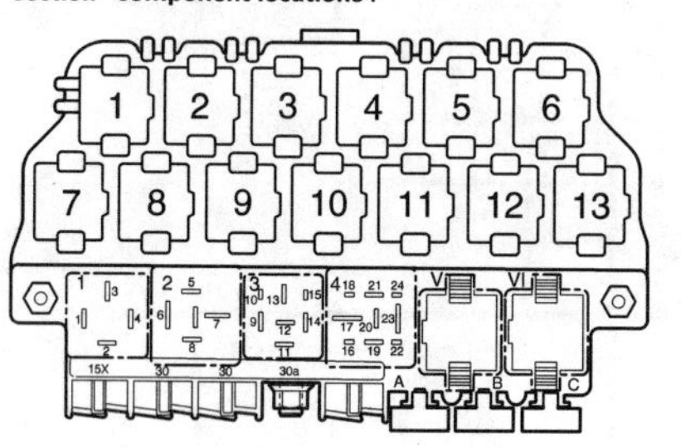

Fuse colors

30 A - green
25 A - white
20 A - yellow
15 A - blue
10 A - red
7,5 A - brown
5 A - beige
3 A - violet

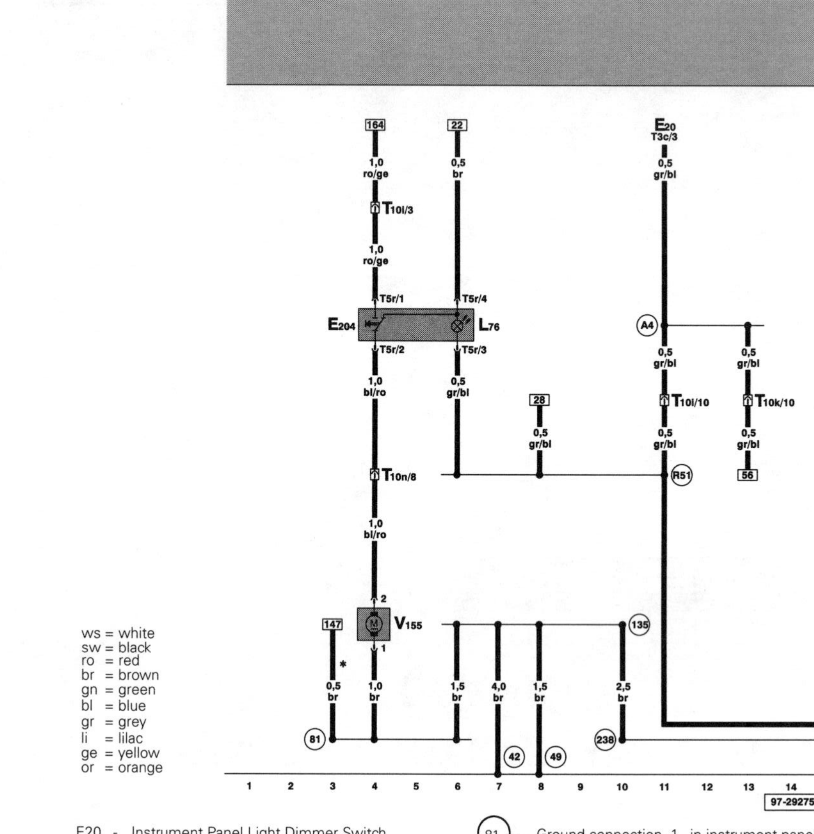

E20 - Instrument Panel Light Dimmer Switch
E204 - Switch for remote/fuel tank door
L76 - Push Button Light
T3c - 3-Pin Connector
T5r - 5-Pin Connector
T10i - 10-Pin Connector, black, connector station A-pillar, left
T10k - 10-Pin Connector, black, connector station A-pillar, right
T10n - 10-Pin Connector, brown, connector station A-pillar, left
V155 - Motor for fuel tank lid unlock

(42) - Ground connection, beside steering column

(49) - Ground connection, on steering column

(81) - Ground connection -1-, in instrument panel wiring harness

(135) - Ground connection -2-, in instrument panel wiring harness

(238) - Ground connection -1-, in wiring harness interior

(A4) - Plus connection (58b), in instrument panel wiring harness

(R51) - Connection (58b) in door wiring harness, driver side

* - Vehicles with anti-theft warning system only

Switch for remote/fuel tank door, motor for fuel tank lid unlock

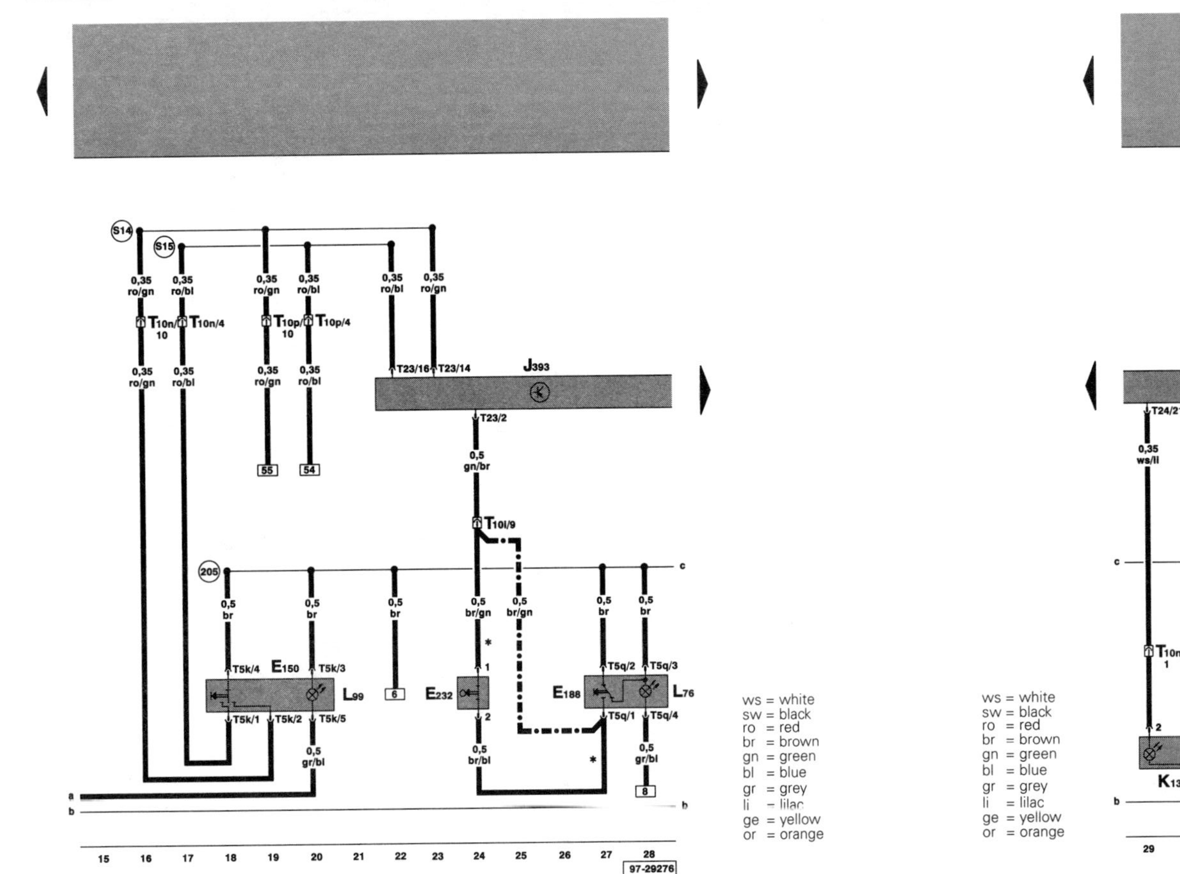

ws = white
sw = black
ro = red
br = brown
gn = green
bl = blue
gr = grey
li = lilac
ge = yellow
or = orange

E150 - Switch for interior lock, driver side
E188 - Switch for remote unlock, rear lid, driver side
E232 - Key switch for switching off remote unlock rear lid
J393 - Central control module for comfort system, behind instrument panel, left
L76 - Push Button Light
L99 - Lighting for switch interior lock
T5k - 5-Pin Connector
T5q - 5-Pin Connector
T10i - 10-Pin Connector, black, connector station A-pillar, left
T10n - 10-Pin Connector, brown, connector station A-pillar, left
T10p - 10-Pin Connector, brown, connector station A-pillar, right
T23 - 23-Pin Connector
(205) - Ground connection, in driver's door wiring harness
(S14) - Wire connection (open), in central locking system wiring harness
(S15) - Wire connection (closed), in central locking system wiring harness
* - Jetta only
-•-•- Golf only

Central control module for comfort system, switch for interior lock (driver side), switch for remote unlock rear lid

ws = white
sw = black
ro = red
br = brown
gn = green
bl = blue
gr = grey
li = lilac
ge = yellow
or = orange

F220 - Lock unit for central locking, driver side
J393 - Central control module for comfort system, behind instrument panel, left
K133 - Warning light for central locking -SAFE-
T8c - 8-Pin Connector
T10i - 10-Pin Connector, black, connector station A-pillar, left
T10n - 10-Pin Connector, brown, connector station A-pillar, left
T24 - 24-Pin Connector
(205) - Ground connection, in driver's door wiring harness
(304) - Ground connector -3-, in wiring harness door cable - driver side

Central control module for comfort system, lock unit for central locking, warning light for central locking -SAFE-

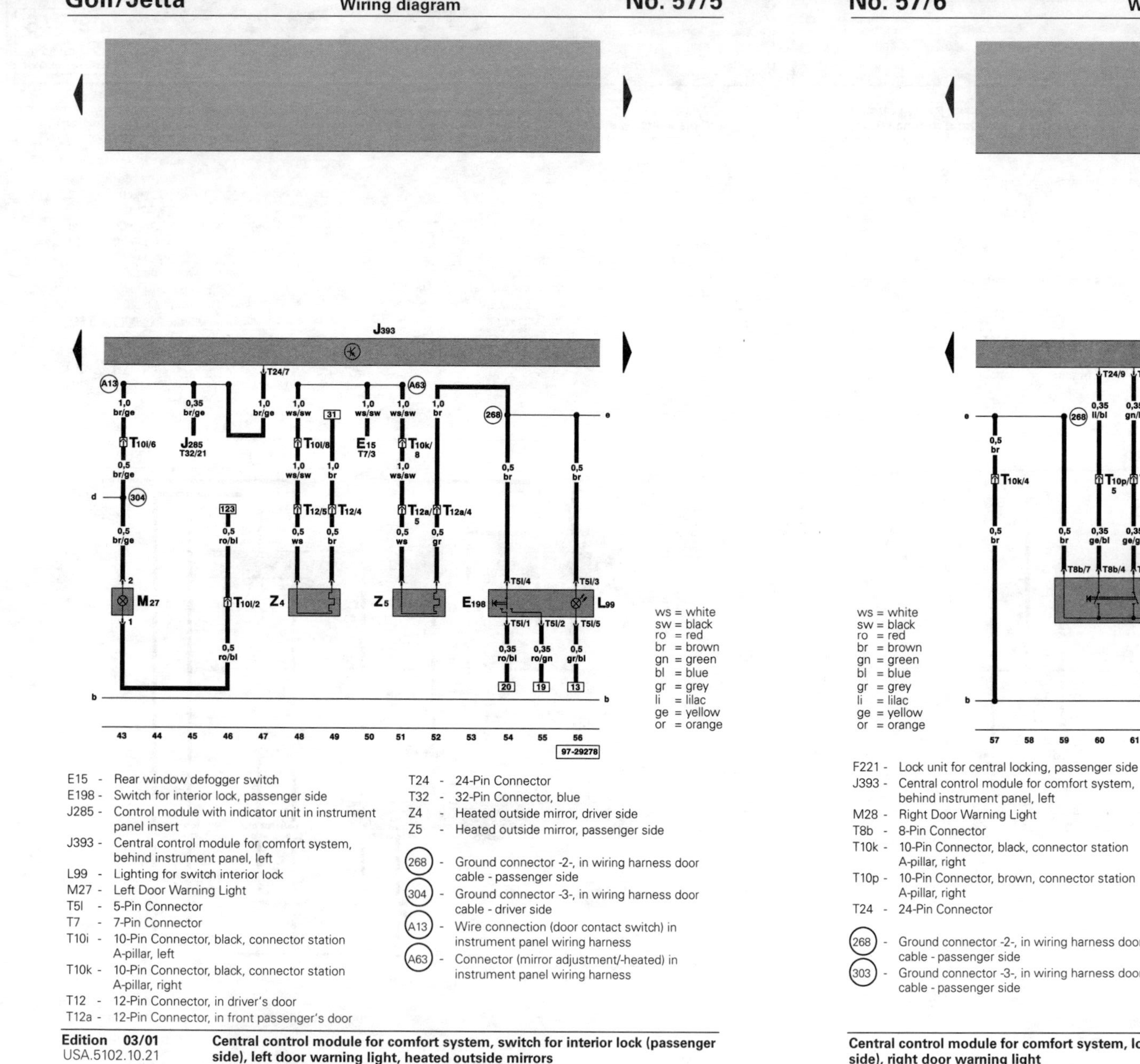

ws = white
sw = black
ro = red
br = brown
gn = green
bl = blue
gr = grey
li = lilac
ge = yellow
or = orange

E15 - Rear window defogger switch
E198 - Switch for interior lock, passenger side
J285 - Control module with indicator unit in instrument panel insert
J393 - Central control module for comfort system, behind instrument panel, left
L99 - Lighting for switch interior lock
M27 - Left Door Warning Light
T5l - 5-Pin Connector
T7 - 7-Pin Connector
T10i - 10-Pin Connector, black, connector station A-pillar, left
T10k - 10-Pin Connector, black, connector station A-pillar, right
T12 - 12-Pin Connector, in driver's door
T12a - 12-Pin Connector, in front passenger's door
T24 - 24-Pin Connector
T32 - 32-Pin Connector, blue
Z4 - Heated outside mirror, driver side
Z5 - Heated outside mirror, passenger side

(268) - Ground connector -2-, in wiring harness door cable - passenger side
(304) - Ground connector -3-, in wiring harness door cable - driver side
(A13) - Wire connection (door contact switch) in instrument panel wiring harness
(A63) - Connector (mirror adjustment/-heated) in instrument panel wiring harness

Central control module for comfort system, switch for interior lock (passenger side), left door warning light, heated outside mirrors

ws = white
sw = black
ro = red
br = brown
gn = green
bl = blue
gr = grey
li = lilac
ge = yellow
or = orange

F221 - Lock unit for central locking, passenger side
J393 - Central control module for comfort system, behind instrument panel, left
M28 - Right Door Warning Light
T8b - 8-Pin Connector
T10k - 10-Pin Connector, black, connector station A-pillar, right
T10p - 10-Pin Connector, brown, connector station A-pillar, right
T24 - 24-Pin Connector

(268) - Ground connector -2-, in wiring harness door cable - passenger side
(303) - Ground connector -3-, in wiring harness door cable - passenger side

Central control module for comfort system, lock unit for central locking (passenger side), right door warning light

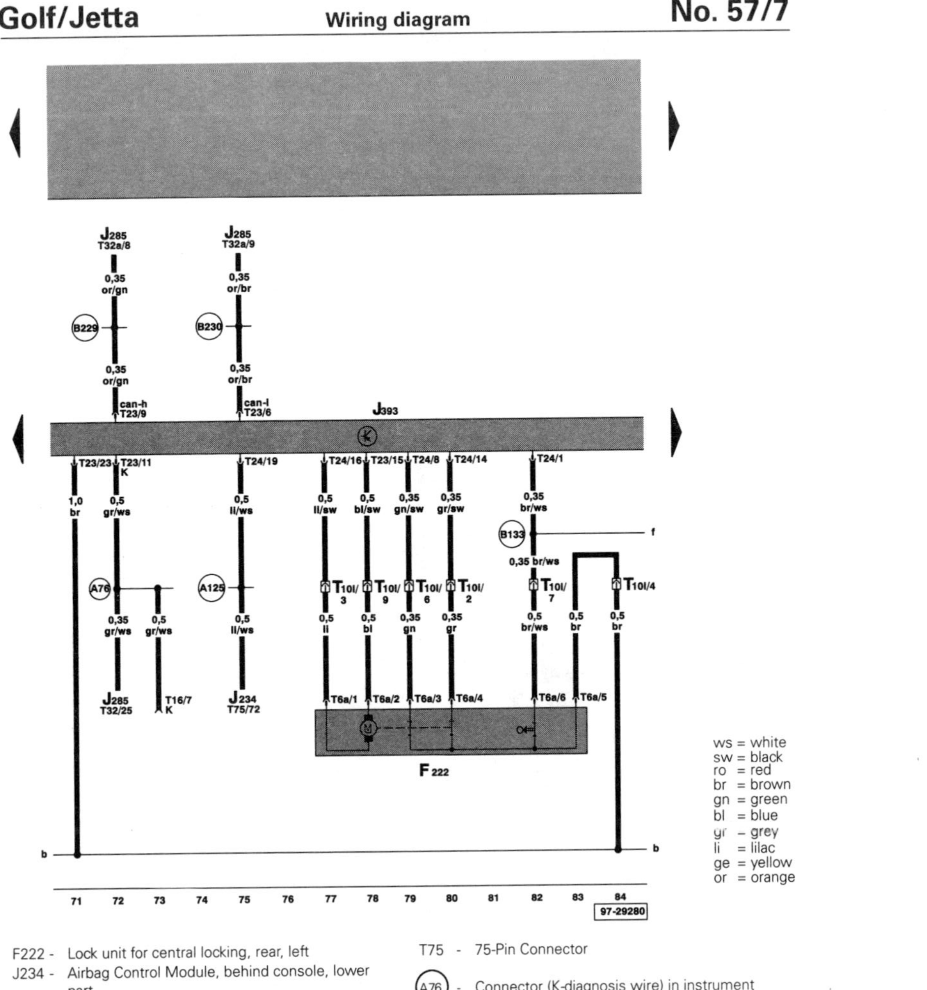

ws = white
sw = black
ro = red
br = brown
gn = green
bl = blue
gr = grey
li = lilac
ge = yellow
or = orange

F222 - Lock unit for central locking, rear, left
J234 - Airbag Control Module, behind console, lower part
J285 - Control module with indicator unit in instrument panel insert
J393 - Central control module for comfort system, behind instrument panel, left
T6a - 6-Pin Connector
T10l - 10-Pin Connector, black, connector station B-pillar, left
T16 - Data Link Connector (DLC), below instrument panel, left
T23 - 23-Pin Connector
T24 - 24-Pin Connector
T32 - 32-Pin Connector, blue
T32a - 32-Pin Connector, green
T75 - 75-Pin Connector

(A76) - Connector (K-diagnosis wire) in instrument panel wiring harness
(A125) - Connection (crash signal) in instrument panel wiring harness
(B133) - Connector (central locking open), in wiring harness interior
(B229) - Connection (high bus), in instrument panel wiring harness
(B230) - Connection (low bus), in instrument panel wiring harness

Edition 03/01 USA.5102.10.21 **Central control module for comfort system, lock unit for central locking (rear left)**

ws = white
sw = black
ro = red
br = brown
gn = green
bl = blue
gr = grey
li = lilac
ge = yellow
or = orange

F124 - Trunk Lock Alarm/Central Locking Switch
F223 - Lock unit for central locking, rear, right
J393 - Central control module for comfort system, behind instrument panel, left
T2 - Double Connector, in rear lid
T5d - 5-Pin Connector, brown, connector station C-pillar, left
T6b - 6-Pin Connector
T10m- 10-Pin Connector, black, connector station B-pillar, right
T23 - 23-Pin Connector
T24 - 24-Pin Connector
V53 - Decklid Central Locking System Motor (Golf only)
V139 - Motor to unlock rear lid*

(218) - Ground connection -1-, in rear lid wiring harness
(219) - Ground connection -2-, in rear lid wiring harness
(B133) - Connector (central locking open), in wiring harness interior

* - Jetta only
-•-•- Golf only

Central control module for comfort system, lock unit for central locking (rear right), trunk lock alarm/central locking switch, decklid central locking system motor **Edition 03/01** USA.5102.10.21

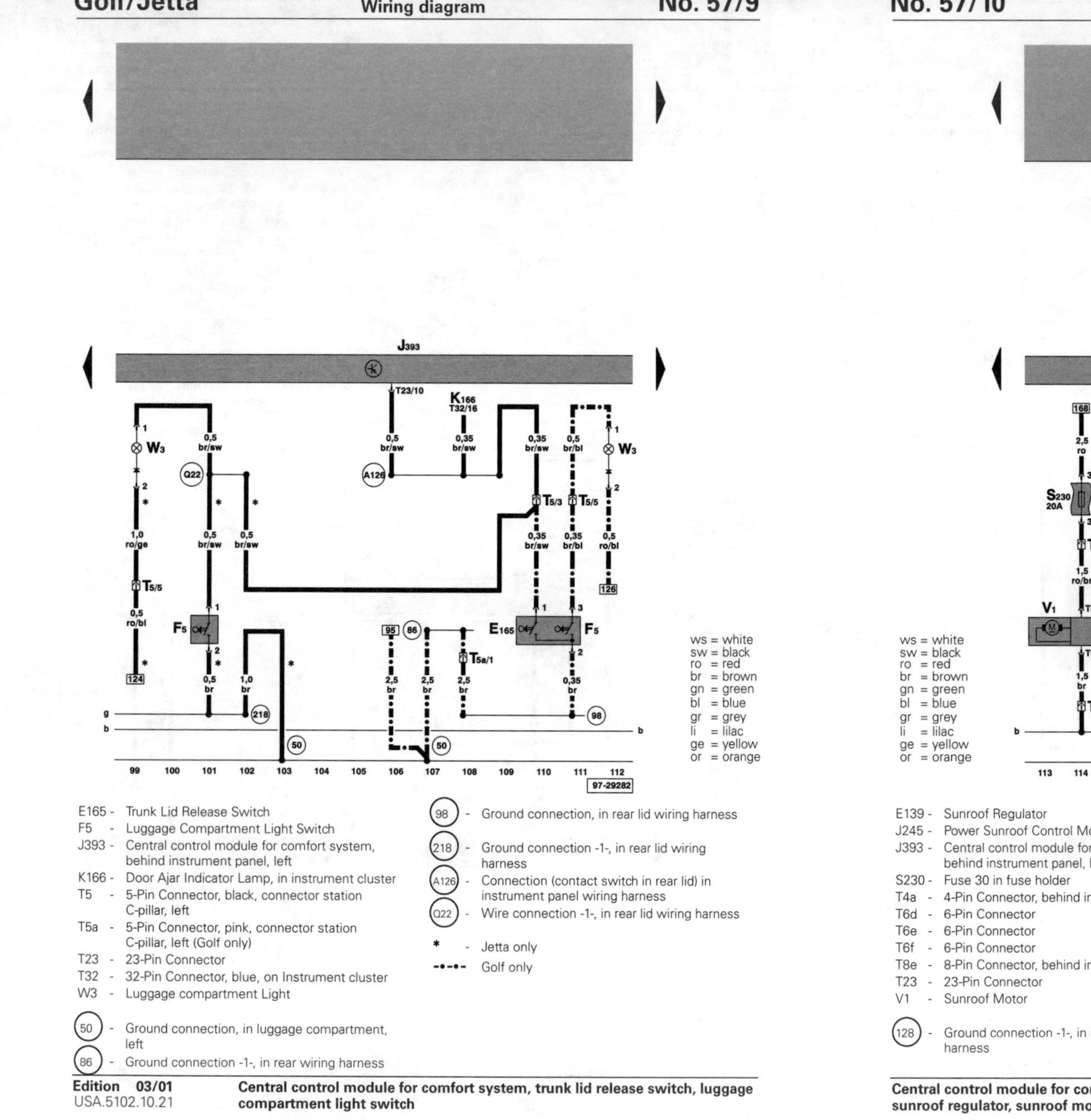

ws = white
sw = black
ro = red
br = brown
gn = green
bl = blue
gr = grey
li = lilac
ge = yellow
or = orange

E165 - Trunk Lid Release Switch
F5 - Luggage Compartment Light Switch
J393 - Central control module for comfort system, behind instrument panel, left
K166 - Door Ajar Indicator Lamp, in instrument cluster
T5 - 5-Pin Connector, black, connector station C-pillar, left
T5a - 5-Pin Connector, pink, connector station C-pillar, left (Golf only)
T23 - 23-Pin Connector
T32 - 32-Pin Connector, blue, on Instrument cluster
W3 - Luggage compartment Light

(50) - Ground connection, in luggage compartment, left
(86) - Ground connection -1-, in rear wiring harness
(98) - Ground connection, in rear lid wiring harness
(218) - Ground connection -1-, in rear lid wiring harness
(A126) - Connection (contact switch in rear lid) in instrument panel wiring harness
(Q22) - Wire connection -1-, in rear lid wiring harness

* - Jetta only
--•--•-- - Golf only

Central control module for comfort system, trunk lid release switch, luggage compartment light switch

ws = white
sw = black
ro = red
br = brown
gn = green
bl = blue
gr = grey
li = lilac
ge = yellow
or = orange

E139 - Sunroof Regulator
J245 - Power Sunroof Control Module
J393 - Central control module for comfort system, behind instrument panel, left
S230 - Fuse 30 in fuse holder
T4a - 4-Pin Connector, behind instrument panel, left
T6d - 6-Pin Connector
T6e - 6-Pin Connector
T6f - 6-Pin Connector
T8e - 8-Pin Connector, behind instrument panel, left
T23 - 23-Pin Connector
V1 - Sunroof Motor

(128) - Ground connection -1-, in interior light wiring harness
(238) - Ground connection -1-, in wiring harness interior
(A29) - Wire connection (interior light), in instrument panel wiring harness
(R6) - Plus connection -1-, in interior light wiring harness

* - Jetta only
--•--•-- - Golf only

Central control module for comfort system, power sunroof control module, sunroof regulator, sunroof motor

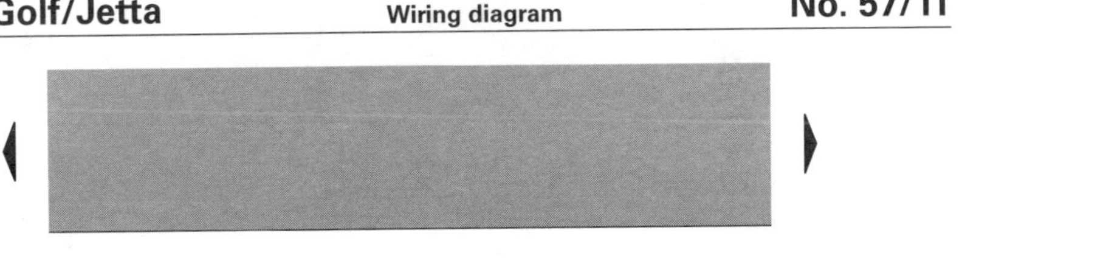

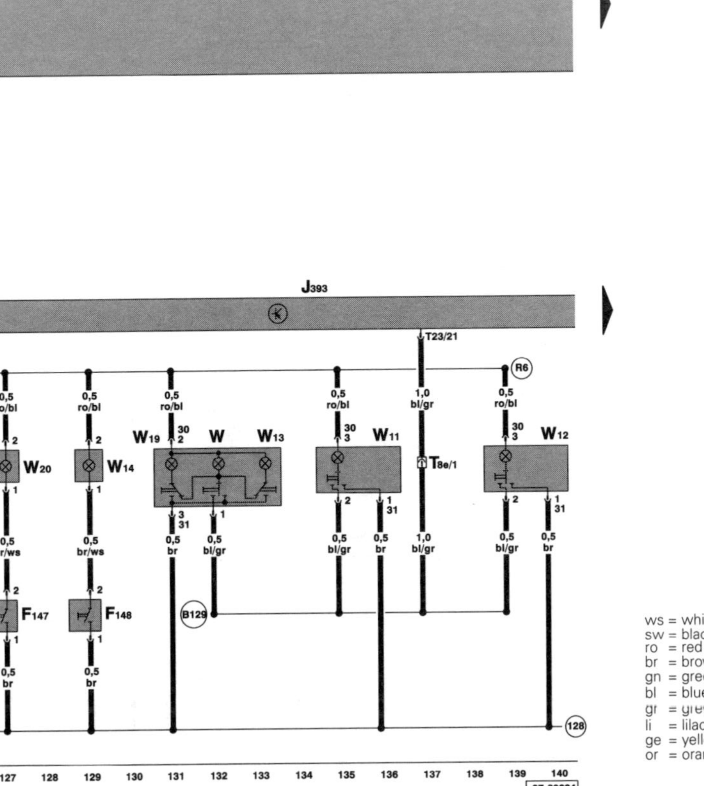

ws = white
sw = black
ro = red
br = brown
gn = green
bl = blue
gr = grey
li = lilac
ge = yellow
or = orange

F147 - Left Make-Up Mirror Light Switch
F148 - Right Make-Up Mirror Light Switch
J393 - Central control module for comfort system, behind instrument panel, left
W - Front Interior Light
W11 - Left Rear Reading Light
W12 - Right Rear Reading Light
W13 - Right Front Map/Reading Light
W14 - Right Make-up Mirror Light
W19 - Left Front Reading Light
W20 - Left Make-up Mirror Light
T8e - 8-Pin Connector, behind instrument panel, left
T23 - 23-Pin Connector

(128) - Ground connection -1-, in interior light wiring harness

(B129) - Connector (interior light 3/L) in wiring harness interior
(R6) - Plus connection -1-, in interior light wiring harness

Edition 03/01 USA.5102.10.21 **Central control module for comfort system, interior lights, make-up mirror lights**

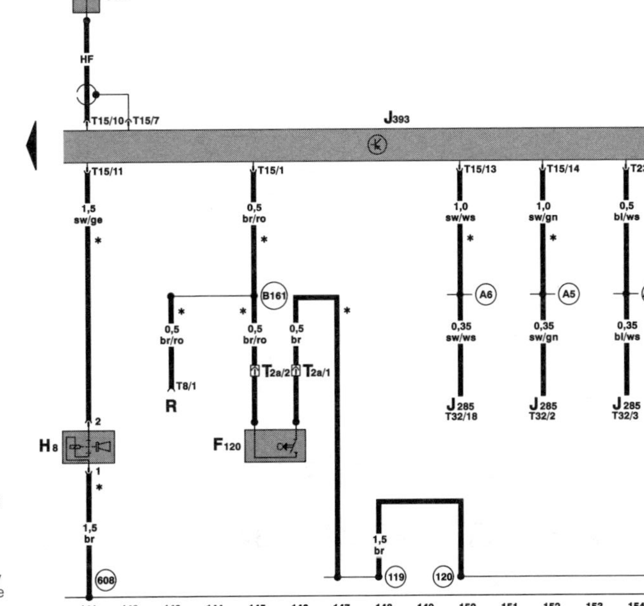

ws = white
sw = black
ro = red
br = brown
gn = green
bl = blue
gr = grey
li = lilac
ge = yellow
or = orange

F120 - Hood Alarm Switch*
H8 - Alarm Horn*
J285 - Control module with indicator unit in instrument panel insert
J393 - Central control module for comfort system, behind instrument panel, left
R - Radio
R47 - Antenna wire for central locking and antitheft warning system
T2a - Double Connector, near headlight, right
T8 - 8-Pin Connector, on radio
T15 - 15-Pin Connector
T23 - 23-Pin Connector
T32 - 32-Pin Connector, blue, on instrument cluster

(119) - Ground connection -1-, in headlight wiring harness
(120) - Ground connection -2-, in headlight wiring harness
(608) - Ground connection (in center plenum chamber)
(A5) - Plus connection (right turn signal), in instrument panel wiring harness
(A6) - Plus connection (left turn signal), in instrument panel wiring harness
(A27) - Wire connection (vehicle speed signal), in instrument panel wiring harness
(B161) - Connector (anti-theft warning system), in wiring harness interior

* - Vehicles with anti-theft warning system only

Central control module for comfort system, antitheft warning system, antenna wire for central locking and antitheft warning system **Edition 03/01** USA.5102.10.21

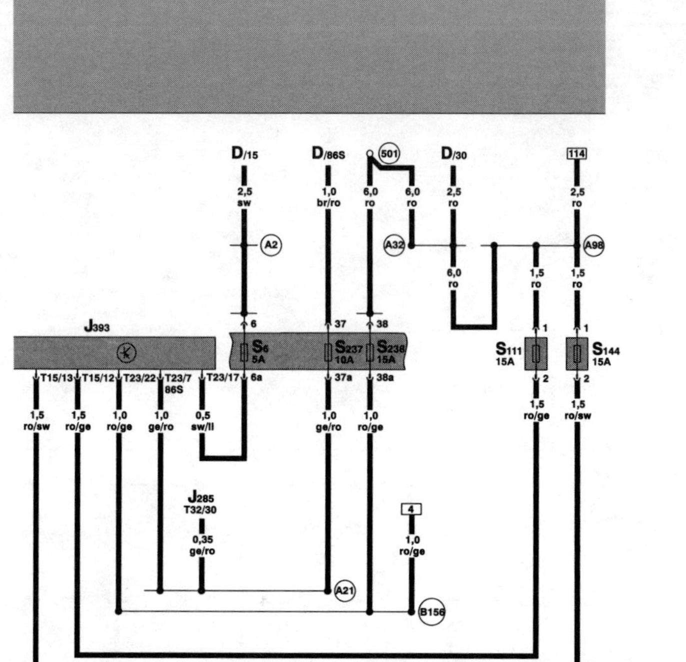

D - Ignition/Starter Switch
J285 - Control module with indicator unit in instrument panel insert
J393 - Central control module for comfort system, behind instrument panel, left
S6 - Fuse 6 in fuse holder
S111 - Alarm System and Anti-Theft Fuse, above the thirteenfold auxiliary relay panel
S144 - Fuse for central locking/anti-theft warning system, above the thirteenfold auxiliary relay panel
S237 - Fuse 37 in fuse holder
S238 - Fuse 38 in fuse holder
T15 - 15-Pin Connector
T23 - 23-Pin Connector
T32 - 32-Pin Connector, blue

(12) - Ground connection, in engine compartment, left
(120) - Ground connection -2-, in headlight wiring harness
(501) - Threaded connection -2- (30) on the relay plate
(A2) - Plus connection (15), in instrument panel wiring harness
(A21) - Wire connection (86s), in instrument panel wiring harness
(A32) - Plus connection (30), in instrument panel wiring harness
(A98) - Plus connector -4- (30), in instrument panel wiring harness
(B156) - Plus connector (30a), in wiring harness interior

Central control module for comfort system

Edition 03/01
USA.5102.10.21

THIS PAGE INTENTIONALLY LEFT BLANK

Comfort System (vehicles with power windows),

from May 2001

- Anti-theft warning system
- Central locking system with remote control
- Fuel tank lid unlock system
- Heated power mirrors
- Interior lights
- Luggage compartment light
- Power sunroof
- Power windows
- Rear lid unlock system

Deviate relay location and fuseplacements as well as the locations of multiple connectors see section "component locations".

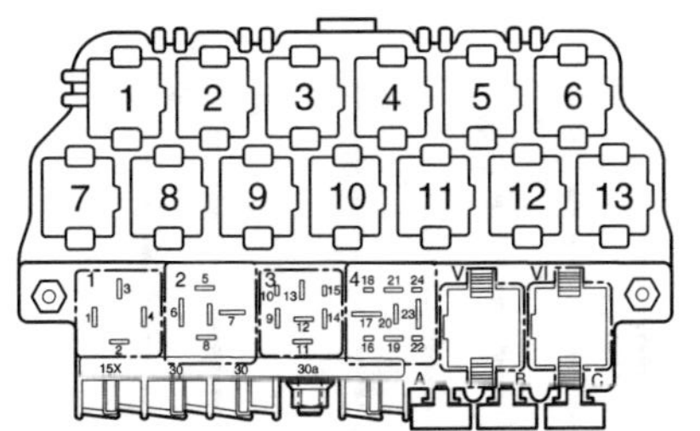

Fuse colors

30 A - green
25 A - white
20 A - yellow
15 A - blue
10 A - red
7,5 A - brown
5 A - beige
3 A - violet

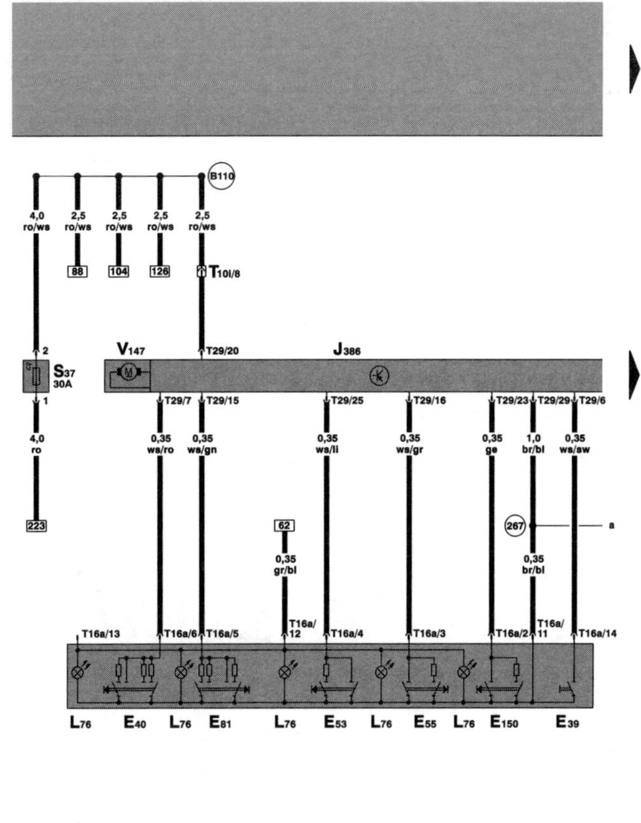

ws = white
sw = black
ro = red
br = brown
gn = green
bl = blue
gr = grey
li = lilac
ge = yellow
or = orange

1 2 3 4 5 6 7 8 9 10 11 12 13 14

97-29287

E39 - Safety switch for window regulator rear
E40 - Switch for window regulator front left
E53 - Switch for window regulator rear left, driver
E55 - Switch for window regulator rear right, driver
E81 - Switch for window regulator front right, driver
E150 - Switch for interior lock, driver side
J386 - Door control module, driver side
L76 - Push Button Light
S37 - Fuse for window regulator (circuit breaker), on thirteen position auxiliary relay panel
T10i - 10-Pin Connector, black, connector station A-pillar, left
T16a - 16-Pin Connector
T29 - 29-Pin Connector
V147 - Motor for window regulator, driver side

(267) - Ground connector -2-, in wiring harness door cable - driver side
(B110) - Connection (30), window regulator) in wiring harness interior

Door control module (driver side), switch for window regulator, safety switch for window regulator rear, switch for interior lock (driver side)

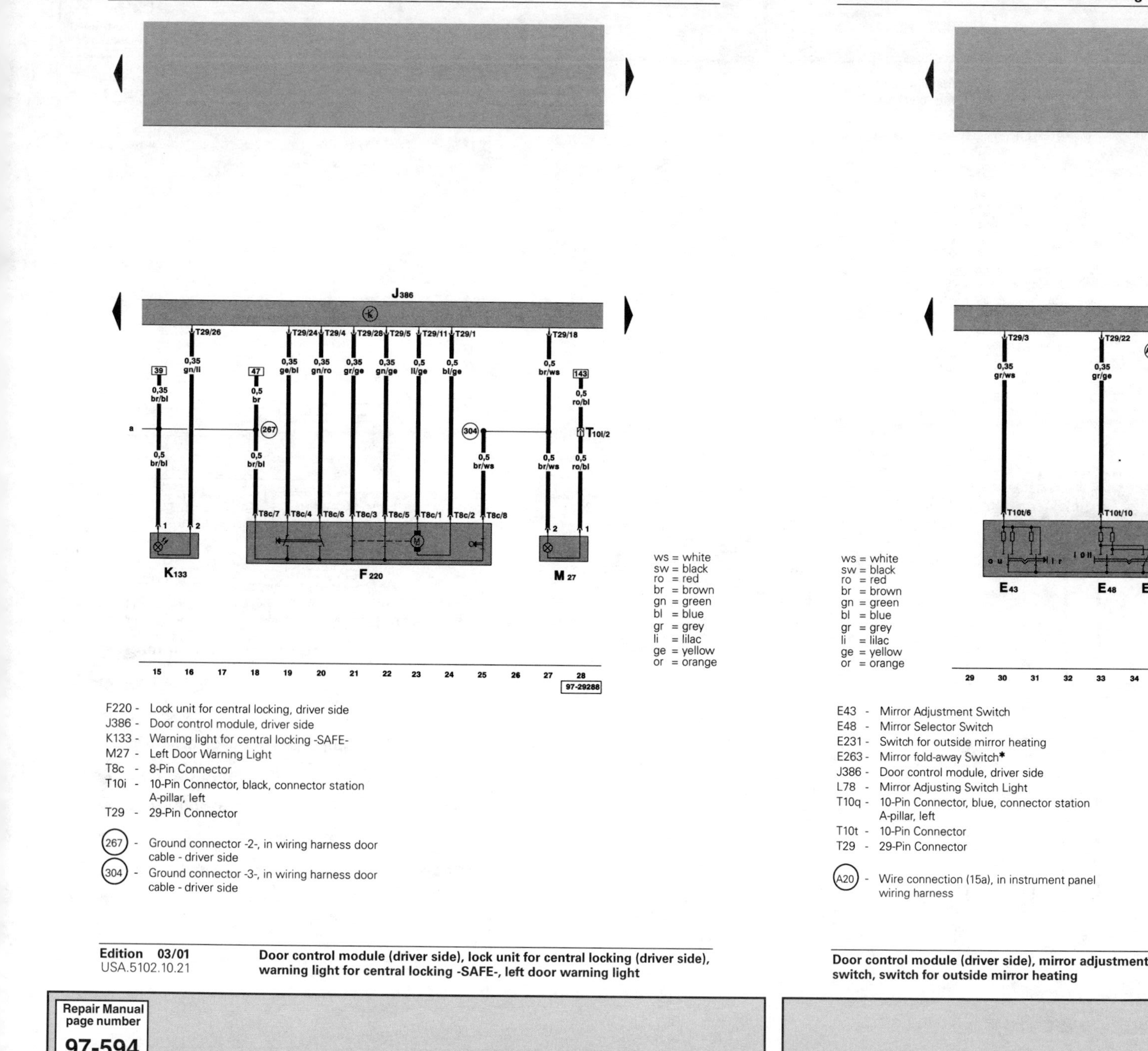

ws = white
sw = black
ro = red
br = brown
gn = green
bl = blue
gr = grey
li = lilac
ge = yellow
or = orange

F220 - Lock unit for central locking, driver side
J386 - Door control module, driver side
K133 - Warning light for central locking -SAFE-
M27 - Left Door Warning Light
T8c - 8-Pin Connector
T10i - 10-Pin Connector, black, connector station A-pillar, left
T29 - 29-Pin Connector

(267) - Ground connector -2-, in wiring harness door cable - driver side
(304) - Ground connector -3-, in wiring harness door cable - driver side

Door control module (driver side), lock unit for central locking (driver side), warning light for central locking -SAFE-, left door warning light

ws = white
sw = black
ro = red
br = brown
gn = green
bl = blue
gr = grey
li = lilac
ge = yellow
or = orange

E43 - Mirror Adjustment Switch
E48 - Mirror Selector Switch
E231 - Switch for outside mirror heating
E263 - Mirror fold-away Switch*
J386 - Door control module, driver side
L78 - Mirror Adjusting Switch Light
T10q - 10-Pin Connector, blue, connector station A-pillar, left
T10t - 10-Pin Connector
T29 - 29-Pin Connector

(A20) - Wire connection (15a), in instrument panel wiring harness

* - Mirror fold-away function for some export countrys only

--- Vehicles with seperate heated outside mirrors only

Door control module (driver side), mirror adjustment switch, mirror selector switch, switch for outside mirror heating

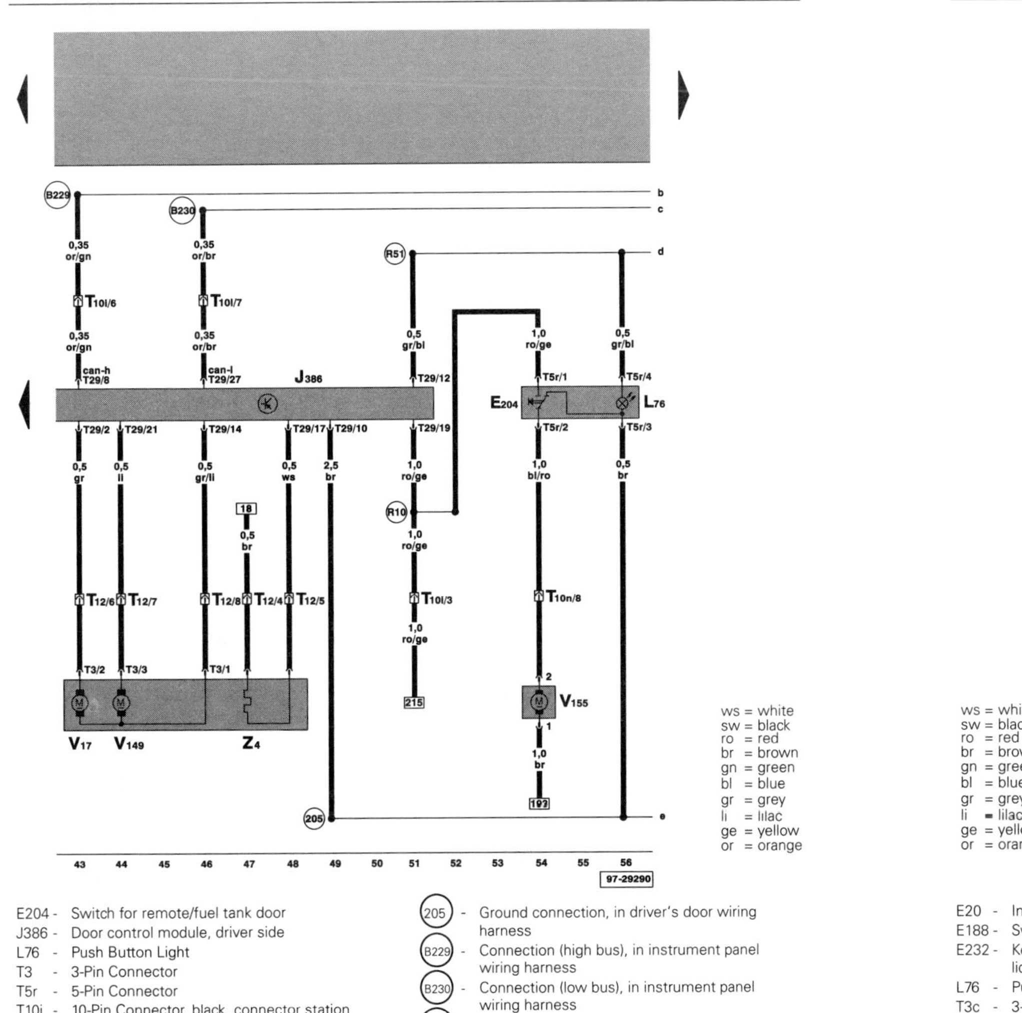

ws = white
sw = black
ro = red
br = brown
gn = green
bl = blue
gr = grey
li = lilac
ge = yellow
or = orange

E204 - Switch for remote/fuel tank door
J386 - Door control module, driver side
L76 - Push Button Light
T3 - 3-Pin Connector
T5r - 5-Pin Connector
T10i - 10-Pin Connector, black, connector station A-pillar, left
T10n - 10-Pin Connector, brown, connector station A-pillar, left
T12 - 12-Pin Connector
T29 - 29-Pin Connector
V17 - Driver's Side Mirror Adjustment Motor
V149 - Motor for mirror adjustment, driver side
V155 - Motor for fuel tank lid unlock
Z4 - Heated outside mirror, driver side

(205) - Ground connection, in driver's door wiring harness
(B229) - Connection (high bus), in instrument panel wiring harness
(B230) - Connection (low bus), in instrument panel wiring harness
(R10) - Plus connection -1- (30a), in driver's door wiring harness
(R51) - Connection (58b), in driver's door wiring harness

Door control module (driver side), switch for remote/fuel tank door, motor for fuel tank lid unlock, power mirror (driver side), heated outside mirror (driver side)

ws = white
sw = black
ro = red
br = brown
gn = green
bl = blue
gr = grey
li = lilac
ge = yellow
or = orange

E20 - Instrument Panel Light Dimmer Switch
E188 - Switch for remote unlock, rear lid, driver side
E232 - Key switch for switching off remote unlock rear lid
L76 - Push Button Light
T3c - 3-Pin Connector
T5q - 5-Pin Connector
T10i - 10-Pin Connector, black, connector station A-pillar, left

(44) - Ground connection, on left A-pillar, lower part
(205) - Ground connection, in driver's door wiring harness
(A4) - Plus connection (58b), in instrument panel wiring harness
(R51) - Connection (58b), in driver's door wiring harness

Switch for remote unlock rear lid (driver side), key switch for switching off remote unlock rear lid

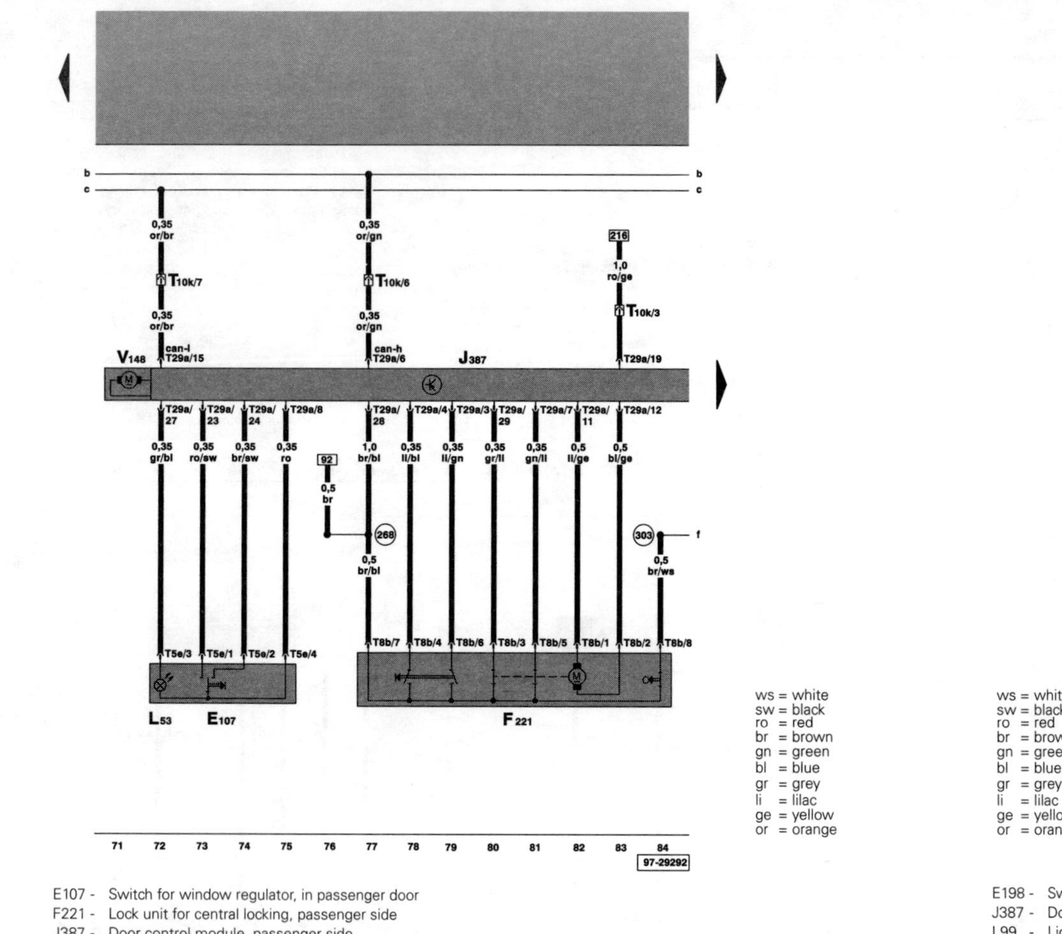

ws = white
sw = black
ro = red
br = brown
gn = green
bl = blue
gr = grey
li = lilac
ge = yellow
or = orange

E107 - Switch for window regulator, in passenger door
F221 - Lock unit for central locking, passenger side
J387 - Door control module, passenger side
L53 - Power Window Switch Light
T5e - 5-Pin Connector
T8b - 8-Pin Connector
T10k - 10-Pin Connector, black, connector station A-pillar, right
T29a - 29-Pin Connector
V148 - Motor for window regulator, passenger side

(268) - Ground connector -2-, in wiring harness door cable - passenger side
(303) - Ground connector -3-, in wiring harness door cable - passenger side

Door control module (passenger side), switch for window regulator (passenger door), lock unit for central locking (passenger side)

ws = white
sw = black
ro = red
br = brown
gn = green
bl = blue
gr = grey
li = lilac
ge = yellow
or = orange

E198 - Switch for interior lock, passenger side
J387 - Door control module, passenger side
L99 - Lighting for switch interior lock
M28 - Right Door Warning Light
T3a - 3-Pin Connector
T5l - 5-Pin Connector
T10k - 10-Pin Connector, black, connector station A-pillar, right
T12a - 12-Pin Connector
T29a - 29-Pin Connector
V25 - Passenger's Side Mirror Adjustment Motor
V150 - Motor for mirror adjustment, passenger side
Z5 - Heated outside mirror, passenger side

(43) - Ground connection, on right A-pillar, lower part

(303) - Ground connector -3-, in wiring harness door cable - passenger side

Door control module (passenger side), switch for interior lock (passenger side), right door warning light, power mirror (passenger side), heated outside mirror

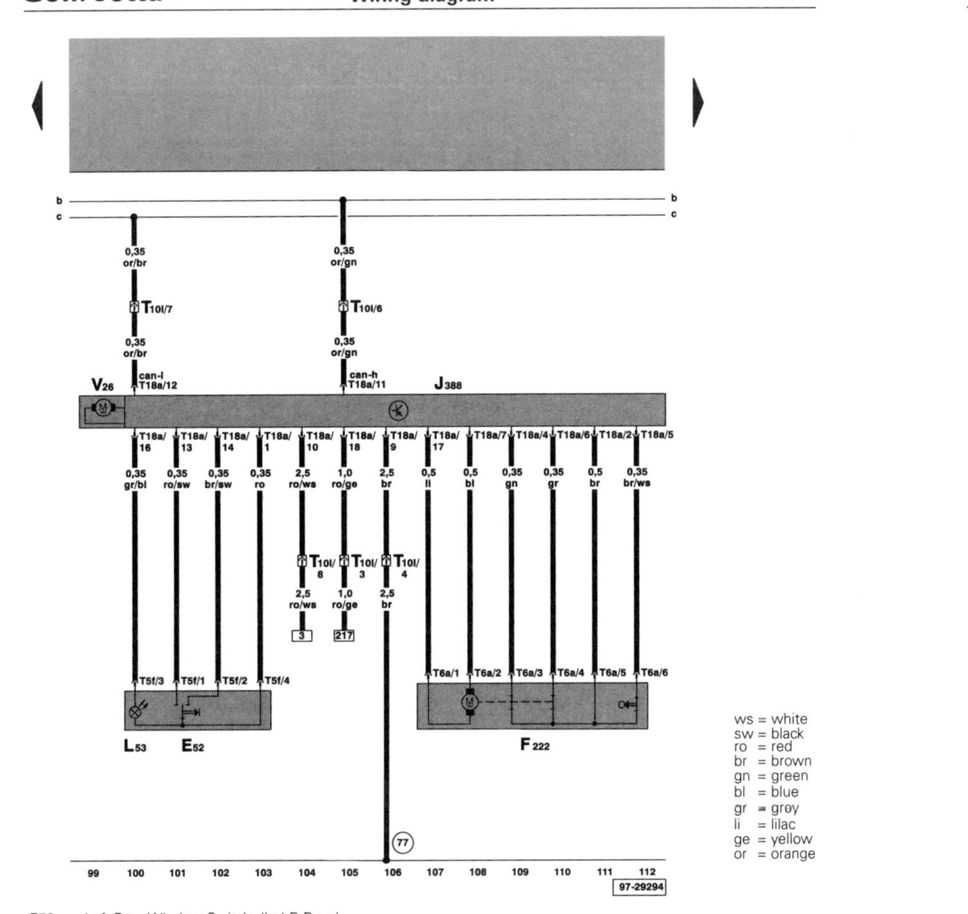

ws = white
sw = black
ro = red
br = brown
gn = green
bl = blue
gr = grey
li = lilac
ge = yellow
or = orange

E52 - Left Rear Window Switch, (In LR Door)
F222 - Lock unit for central locking, rear, left
J388 - Door control module, rear, left
L53 - Power Window Switch Light
T5f - 5-Pin Connector
T6a - 6-Pin Connector
T10l - 10-Pin Connector, black, connector station B-pillar, left
T18a - 18-Pin Connector
V26 - Motor for window regulator, rear, left

(77) - Ground connection, on left B-pillar, lower part

ws = white
sw = black
ro = red
br = brown
gn = green
bl = blue
gr = grey
li = lilac
ge = yellow
or = orange

E54 - Right Rear Window Switch, (In RR Door)
F223 - Lock unit for central locking, rear, right
J389 - Door control module, rear, right
L53 - Power Window Switch Light
T5g - 5-Pin Connector
T6b - 6-Pin Connector
T10m - 10-Pin Connector, black, connector station B-pillar, right
T18b - 18-Pin Connector
V27 - Motor for window regulator, rear, right

(78) - Ground connection, on right B-pillar, lower part

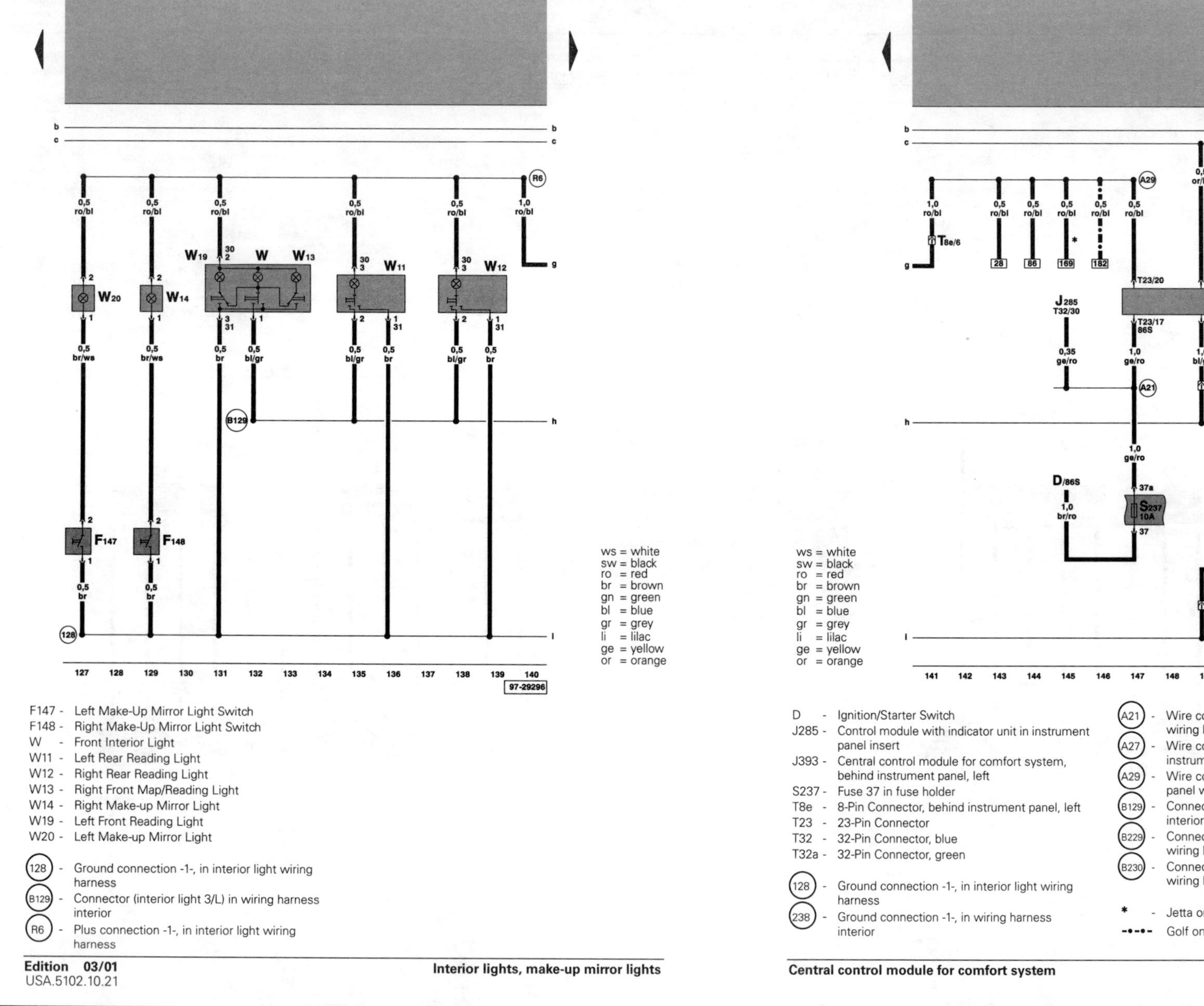

ws = white
sw = black
ro = red
br = brown
gn = green
bl = blue
gr = grey
li = lilac
ge = yellow
or = orange

F147 - Left Make-Up Mirror Light Switch
F148 - Right Make-Up Mirror Light Switch
W - Front Interior Light
W11 - Left Rear Reading Light
W12 - Right Rear Reading Light
W13 - Right Front Map/Reading Light
W14 - Right Make-up Mirror Light
W19 - Left Front Reading Light
W20 - Left Make-up Mirror Light

(128) - Ground connection -1-, in interior light wiring harness
(B129) - Connector (interior light 3/L) in wiring harness interior
(R6) - Plus connection -1-, in interior light wiring harness

Interior lights, make-up mirror lights

ws = white
sw = black
ro = red
br = brown
gn = green
bl = blue
gr = grey
li = lilac
ge = yellow
or = orange

D - Ignition/Starter Switch
J285 - Control module with indicator unit in instrument panel insert
J393 - Central control module for comfort system, behind instrument panel, left
S237 - Fuse 37 in fuse holder
T8e - 8-Pin Connector, behind instrument panel, left
T23 - 23-Pin Connector
T32 - 32-Pin Connector, blue
T32a - 32-Pin Connector, green

(128) - Ground connection -1-, in interior light wiring harness
(238) - Ground connection -1-, in wiring harness interior

(A21) - Wire connection (86s), in instrument panel wiring harness
(A27) - Wire connection (vehicle speed signal), in instrument panel wiring harness
(A29) - Wire connection (interior light), in instrument panel wiring harness
(B129) - Connector (interior light 3/L) in wiring harness interior
(B229) - Connection (high bus), in instrument panel wiring harness
(B230) - Connection (low bus), in instrument panel wiring harness

* - Jetta only
-•-•- - Golf only

Central control module for comfort system

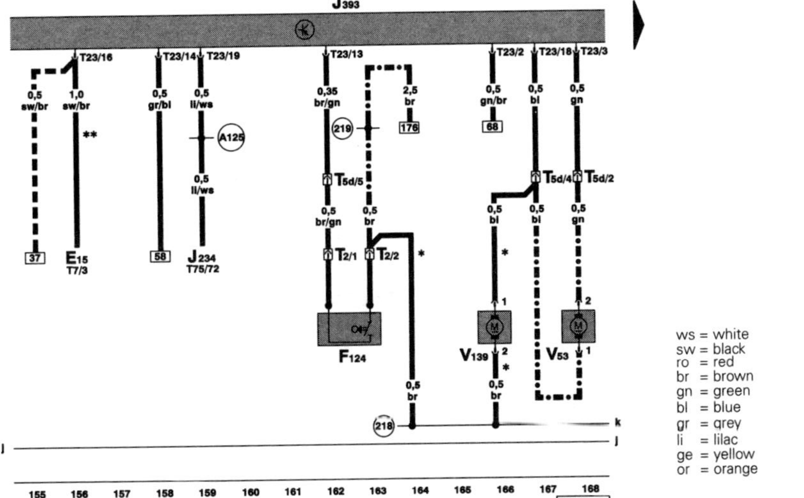

ws = white
sw = black
ro = red
br = brown
gn = green
bl = blue
gr = grey
li = lilac
ge = yellow
or = orange

E15 - Rear window defogger switch
F124 - Trunk Lock Alarm/Central Locking Switch
J234 - Airbag Control Module, behind console, lower part
J393 - Central control module for comfort system, behind instrument panel, left
T2 - Double Connector, in rear lid
T5d - 5-Pin Connector, brown, connector station C-pillar, left
T7 - 7-Pin Connector
T23 - 23-Pin Connector
T75 - 75-Pin Connector
V53 - Decklid Central Locking System Motor (Golf only)
V139 - Motor to unlock rear lid*

(218) - Ground connection -1-, in rear lid wiring harness
(219) - Ground connection -2-, in rear lid wiring harness
(A125) - Connection (crash signal) in instrument panel wiring harness

* - Jetta only
--- Vehicles with seperate heated outside mirrors only
** - Vehicles without seperate heated outside mirrors only
-•-•- Golf only

Central control module for comfort system, switch for unlocking (rear lid handle), motor to unlock rear lid

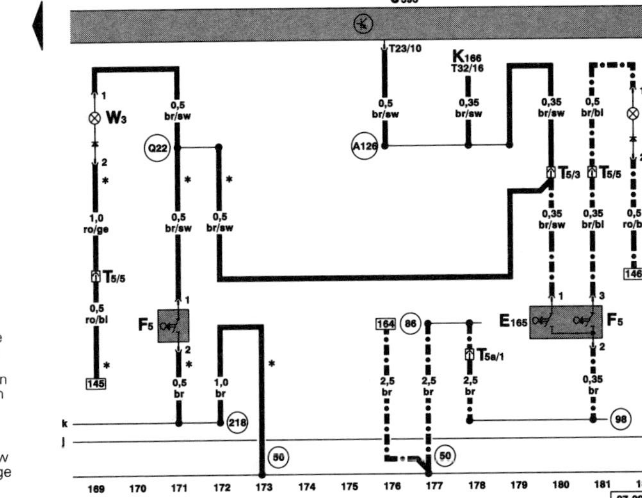

ws = white
sw = black
ro = red
br = brown
gn = green
bl = blue
gr = grey
li = lilac
ge = yellow
or = orange

E165 - Trunk Lid Release Switch
F5 - Luggage Compartment Light Switch
J393 - Central control module for comfort system, behind instrument panel, left
K166 - Door Ajar Indicator Lamp, in instrument cluster
T5 - 5-Pin Connector, black, connector station C-pillar, left
T5a - 5-Pin Connector, pink, connector station C-pillar, left (Golf only)
T23 - 23-Pin Connector
T32 - 32-Pin Connector, blue, on Instrument cluster
W3 - Luggage compartment Light

(50) - Ground connection, in luggage compartment, left
(86) - Ground connection -1-, in rear wiring harness
(98) - Ground connection, in rear lid wiring harness
(218) - Ground connection -1-, in rear lid wiring harness
(A126) - Connection (contact switch in rear lid) in instrument panel wiring harness
(Q22) - Wire connection -1-, in rear lid wiring harness

* - Jetta only
-•-•- Golf only

Central control module for comfort system, trunk lid release switch, luggage compartment light switch

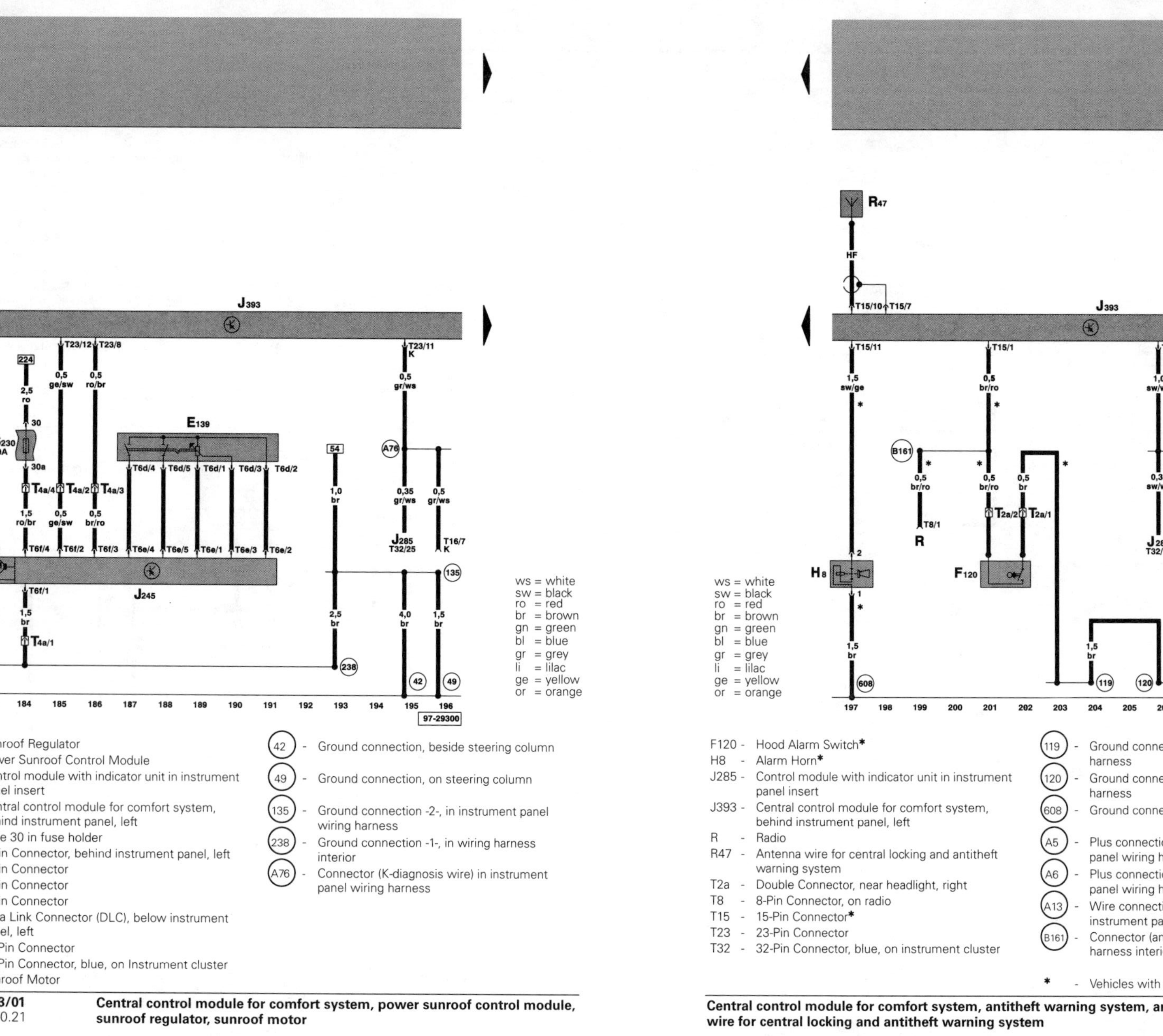

ws = white
sw = black
ro = red
br = brown
gn = green
bl = blue
gr = grey
li = lilac
ge = yellow
or = orange

E139 - Sunroof Regulator
J245 - Power Sunroof Control Module
J285 - Control module with indicator unit in instrument panel insert
J393 - Central control module for comfort system, behind instrument panel, left
S230 - Fuse 30 in fuse holder
T4a - 4-Pin Connector, behind instrument panel, left
T6d - 6-Pin Connector
T6e - 6-Pin Connector
T6f - 6-Pin Connector
T16 - Data Link Connector (DLC), below instrument panel, left
T23 - 23-Pin Connector
T32 - 32-Pin Connector, blue, on Instrument cluster
V1 - Sunroof Motor

(42) - Ground connection, beside steering column
(49) - Ground connection, on steering column
(135) - Ground connection -2-, in instrument panel wiring harness
(238) - Ground connection -1-, in wiring harness interior
(A76) - Connector (K-diagnosis wire) in instrument panel wiring harness

Edition 03/01
USA.5102.10.21

Central control module for comfort system, power sunroof control module, sunroof regulator, sunroof motor

ws = white
sw = black
ro = red
br = brown
gn = green
bl = blue
gr = grey
li = lilac
ge = yellow
or = orange

F120 - Hood Alarm Switch*
H8 - Alarm Horn*
J285 - Control module with indicator unit in instrument panel insert
J393 - Central control module for comfort system, behind instrument panel, left
R - Radio
R47 - Antenna wire for central locking and antitheft warning system
T2a - Double Connector, near headlight, right
T8 - 8-Pin Connector, on radio
T15 - 15-Pin Connector*
T23 - 23-Pin Connector
T32 - 32-Pin Connector, blue, on instrument cluster

(119) - Ground connection -1-, in headlight wiring harness
(120) - Ground connection -2-, in headlight wiring harness
(608) - Ground connection (in center plenum chamber)
(A5) - Plus connection (right turn signal), in instrument panel wiring harness
(A6) - Plus connection (left turn signal), in instrument panel wiring harness
(A13) - Wire connection (door contact switch) in instrument panel wiring harness
(B161) - Connector (anti-theft warning system), in wiring harness interior

* - Vehicles with anti-theft warning system only

Central control module for comfort system, antitheft warning system, antenna wire for central locking and antitheft warning system

Edition 03/01
USA.5102.10.21

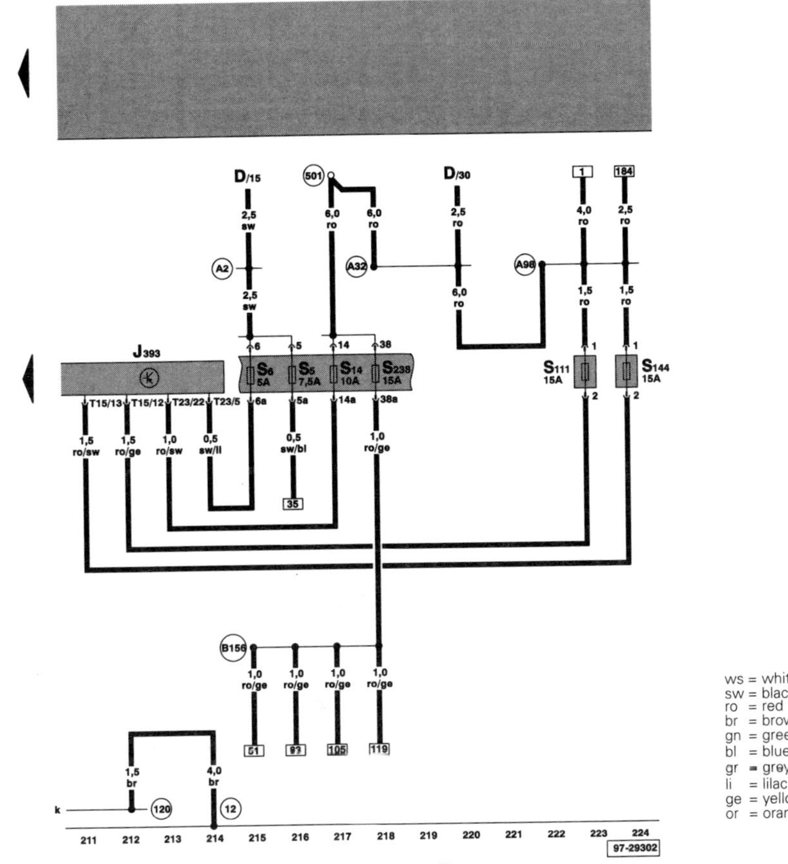

ws = white
sw = black
ro = red
br = brown
gn = green
bl = blue
gr = grey
li = lilac
ge = yellow
or = orange

D - Ignition/Starter Switch
J393 - Central control module for comfort system, behind instrument panel, left
S5 - Fuse 5 in fuse holder
S6 - Fuse 6 in fuse holder
S14 - Fuse 14 in fuse holder
S111 - Alarm System and Anti-Theft Fuse, above the thirteenfold auxiliary relay panel*
S144 - Fuse for central locking/anti-theft warning system, above the thirteenfold auxiliary relay panel*
S238 - Fuse 38 in fuse holder
T15 - 15-Pin Connector*
T23 - 23-Pin Connector

(12) - Ground connection, in engine compartment, left
(120) - Ground connection -2-, in headlight wiring harness
(501) - Threaded connection -2- (30) on the relay plate
(A2) - Plus connection (15), in instrument panel wiring harness
(A32) - Plus connection (30), in instrument panel wiring harness
(A98) - Plus connector -4- (30), in instrument panel wiring harness
(B156) - Plus connector (30a), in wiring harness interior

* - Vehicles with anti-theft warning system only

Headlight washer,

from May 2000

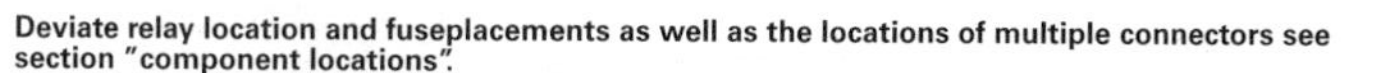

Deviate relay location and fuseplacements as well as the locations of multiple connectors see section "component locations".

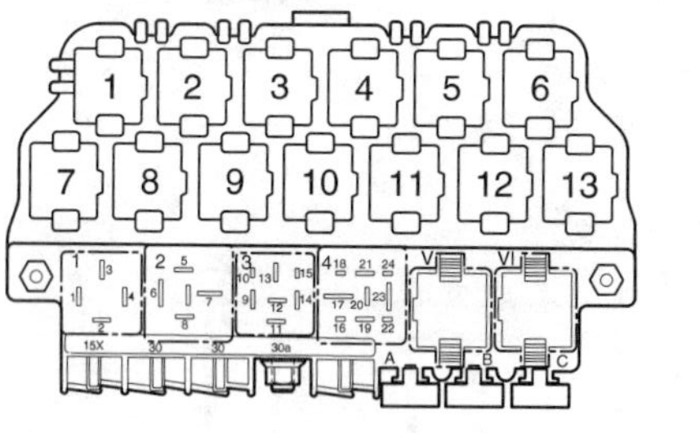

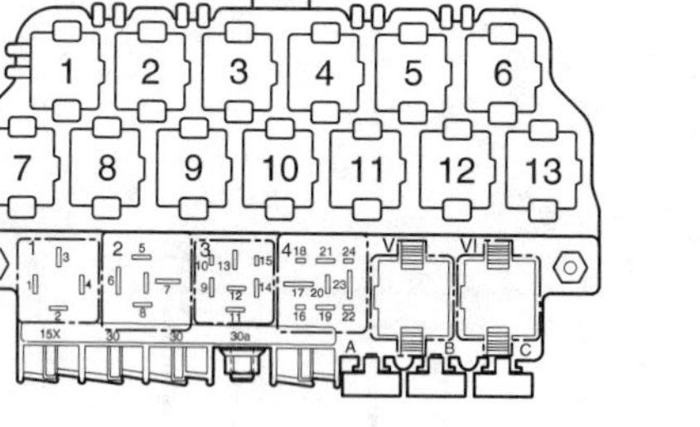

Relay location on the thirteenfold auxiliary relay panel, above relay panel:

Relay panel:

V
VI Wiper/Washer Intermittent Relay (389)

Note: Number in parentheses indicates production control number stamped on relay housing.

Fuse colors

30 A - green
25 A - white
20 A - yellow
15 A - blue
10 A - red
7,5 A - brown
5 A - beige
3 A - violet

Edition 03/01
USA.5102.10.21

ws = white
sw = black
ro = red
br = brown
gn = green
bl = blue
gr = grey
li = lilac
ge = yellow
or = orange

E1 - Light switch
E38 - Windshield Wiper Intermittent Regulator
G33 - Windshield Washer Fluid Level Sensor
J31 - Wiper/Washer Intermittent Relay, on relais panel
J285 - Control module with indicator unit in instrument panel insert
K37 - Low Windshield Washer Fluid Level Indicator Light
S233 - Fuse 33 in fuse holder
T6e - 6-Pin Connector
T17 - 17-Pin Connector
T18a - 18-Pin Connector
T32 - 32-Pin Connector, blue
T32a - 32-Pin Connector, green
V11 - Headlight Washer Pump

(81) - Ground connection -1-, in instrument panel wiring harness
(135) - Ground connection -2-, in instrument panel wiring harness
(269) - Ground connector (sensor ground) -1-, in instrument panel wiring harness
(501) - Threaded connection -2- (30) on the relay plate
(A27) - Wire connection (vehicle speed signal), in instrument panel wiring harness
(A32) - Plus connection (30), in instrument panel wiring harness
(A98) - Plus connector -4- (30), in instrument panel wiring harness

Wiper/washer intermittent relay, windshield wiper intermittent regulator, windshield washer fluid level sensor, headlight washer pump, instrument cluster

Edition 03/01
USA.5102.10.21

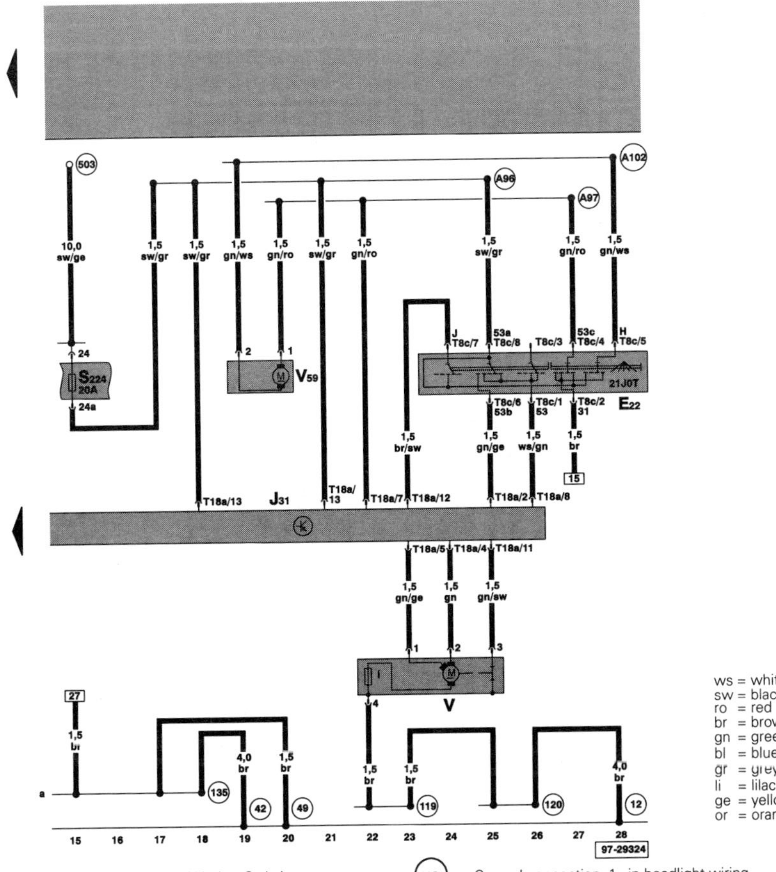

ws = white
sw = black
ro = red
br = brown
gn = green
bl = blue
gr = grey
li = lilac
ge = yellow
or = orange

E22 - Windshield Wiper/Washer Switch
J31 - Wiper/Washer Intermittent Relay, on relais panel
S224 - Fuse 24 in fuse holder
T8c - 8-Pin Connector
T18a - 18-Pin Connector
V - Windshield Wiper Motor
V59 - Windshield and Rear Window Washer Pump

(12) - Ground connection, in engine compartment, left
(42) - Ground connection, beside steering column
(49) - Ground connection, on steering column

(119) - Ground connection -1-, in headlight wiring harness
(120) - Ground connection -2-, in headlight wiring harness
(135) - Ground connection -2-, in instrument panel wiring harness
(503) - Threaded connection -2- (75x) on the relay plate

(A96) - Connector (53a), in instrument panel wiring harness
(A97) - Connector (53), in instrument panel wiring harness
(A102) - Connector (windshield wiper), in instrument panel wiring harness

Fog lights,

from May 2000

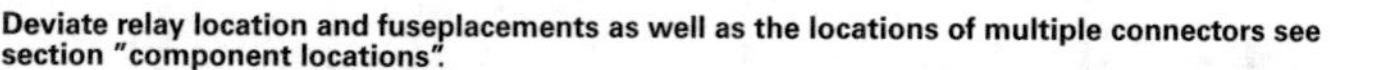
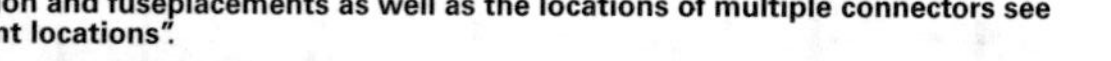

Deviate relay location and fuseplacements as well as the locations of multiple connectors see section "component locations".

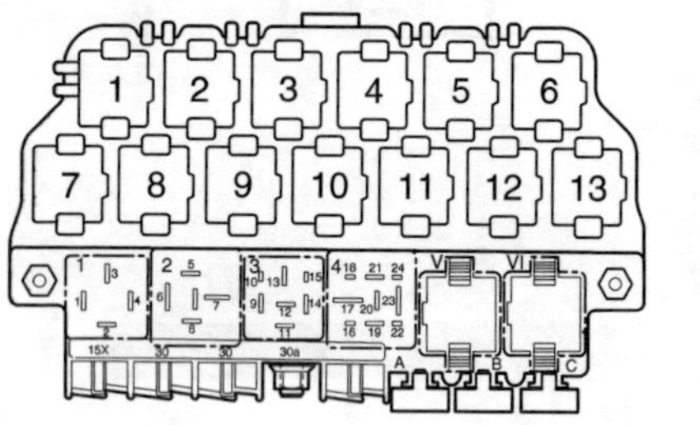
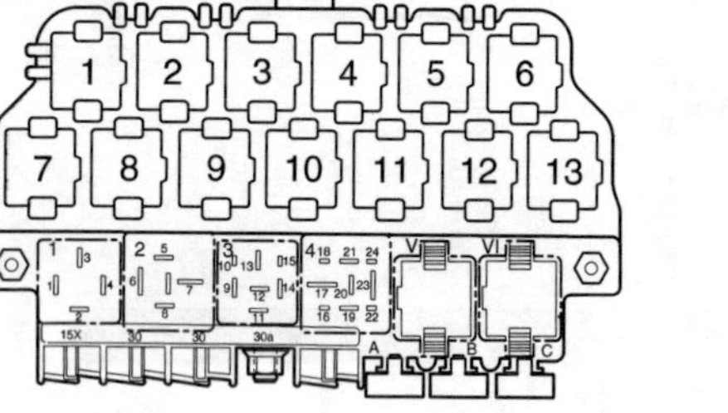

Relay location on the thirteenfold auxiliary relay panel, above relay panel:

4 Fog Light Relay (53)

Relay panel:

Note: Number in parentheses indicates production control number stamped on relay housing.

Fuse colors

30 A - green
25 A - white
20 A - yellow
15 A - blue
10 A - red
7,5 A - brown
5 A - beige
3 A - violet

ws = white
sw = black
ro = red
br = brown
gn = green
bl = blue
gr = grey
li = lilac
ge = yellow
or = orange

97-29325

E4 - Headlight Dimmer/Flasher Switch
J5 - Fog Light Relay
L1 - Left Headlight*
L22 - Left Front Fog Light
M1 - Left Parking Light
M5 - Left Front Turn Signal Light
M18 - Left, Side Turn Signal Light
M29 - Left Low Beam Headlight (Golf only)
M30 - Left High Beam Headlight (Golf only)
M33 - Light for side marker front left
S18 - Fuse 18 in fuse holder
S19 - Fuse 19 in fuse holder
S21 - Fuse 21 in fuse holder
T10b - 10-Pin Connector
T12 - 12-Pin Connector

(119) - Ground connection -1-, in headlight wiring harness
(A6) - Plus connection (left turn signal), in instrument panel wiring harness
(A51) - Wire connection (56), in instrument panel wiring harness
(B166) - Connection (56a), in passenger compartment wiring harness
(B167) - Connection (56b), in passenger compartment wiring harness
(B205) - Connection (fog light), in passenger compartment wiring harness

* - Jetta only

Left headlight light, light for side marker front left, fog light relay, left front fog light, left parking light

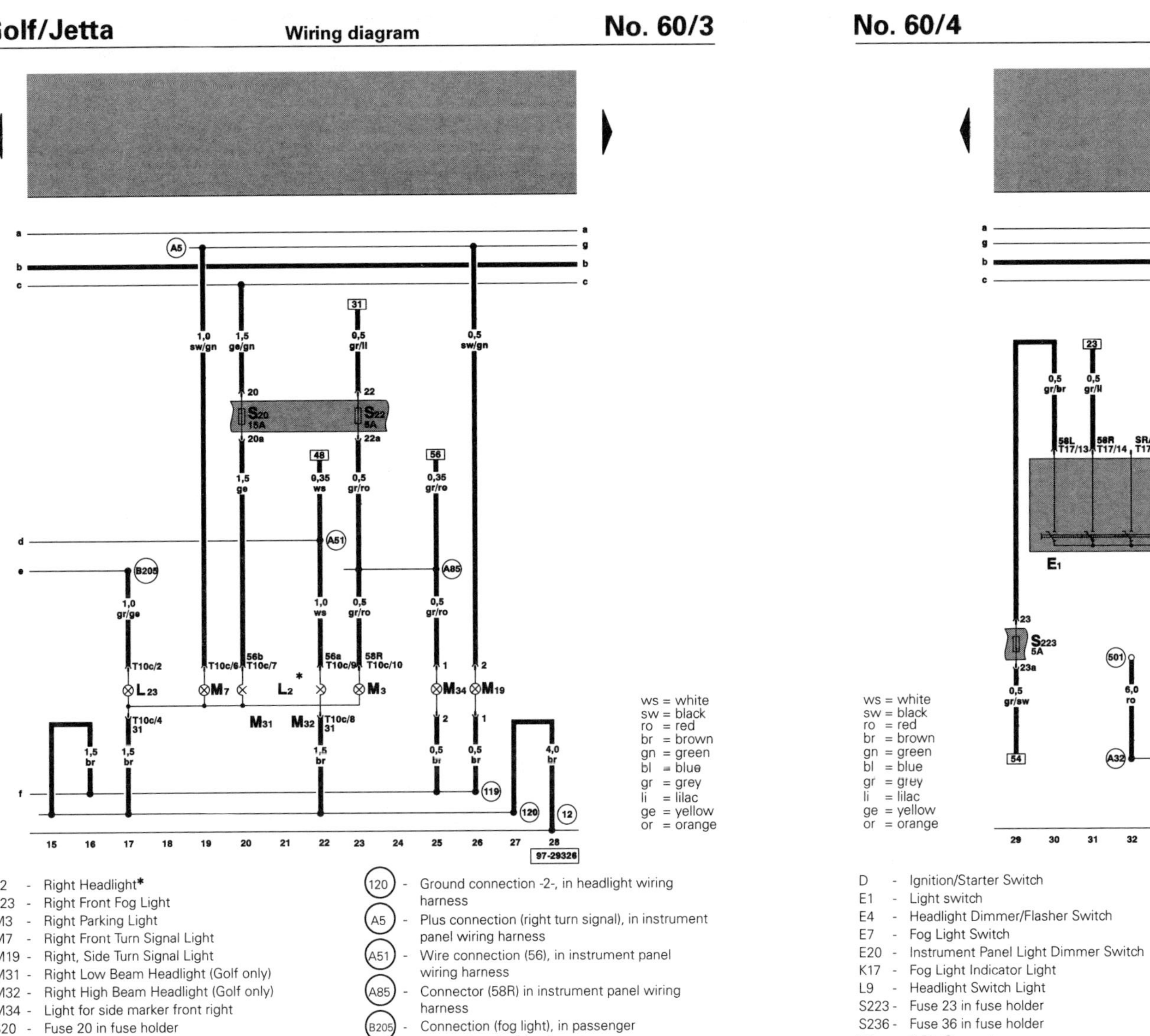

ws = white
sw = black
ro = red
br = brown
gn = green
bl = blue
gr = grey
li = lilac
ge = yellow
or = orange

- L2 - Right Headlight*
- L23 - Right Front Fog Light
- M3 - Right Parking Light
- M7 - Right Front Turn Signal Light
- M19 - Right, Side Turn Signal Light
- M31 - Right Low Beam Headlight (Golf only)
- M32 - Right High Beam Headlight (Golf only)
- M34 - Light for side marker front right
- S20 - Fuse 20 in fuse holder
- S22 - Fuse 22 in fuse holder
- T10c - 10-Pin Connector

- (12) - Ground connection, in engine compartment, left
- (119) - Ground connection -1-, in headlight wiring harness
- (120) - Ground connection -2-, in headlight wiring harness
- (A5) - Plus connection (right turn signal), in instrument panel wiring harness
- (A51) - Wire connection (56), in instrument panel wiring harness
- (A85) - Connector (58R) in instrument panel wiring harness
- (B205) - Connection (fog light), in passenger compartment wiring harness

- * - Jetta only

Right front turn signal light, light for side marker front right, right headlight, right front fog light, right parking light

ws = white
sw = black
ro = red
br = brown
gn = green
bl = blue
gr = grey
li = lilac
ge = yellow
or = orange

- D - Ignition/Starter Switch
- E1 - Light switch
- E4 - Headlight Dimmer/Flasher Switch
- E7 - Fog Light Switch
- E20 - Instrument Panel Light Dimmer Switch
- K17 - Fog Light Indicator Light
- L9 - Headlight Switch Light
- S223 - Fuse 23 in fuse holder
- S236 - Fuse 36 in fuse holder
- T3c - 3-Pin Connector
- T12 - 12-Pin Connector
- T17 - 17-Pin Connector

- (81) - Ground connection -1-, in instrument panel wiring harness
- (501) - Threaded connection -2- (30) on the relay plate
- (A4) - Plus connection (58b), in instrument panel wiring harness
- (A32) - Plus connection (30), in instrument panel wiring harness
- (A80) - Connector -1- (X) in instrument panel wiring harness
- (B167) - Connection (56b), in passenger compartment wiring harness

- -•-•- Golf only

Light switch, fog light switch

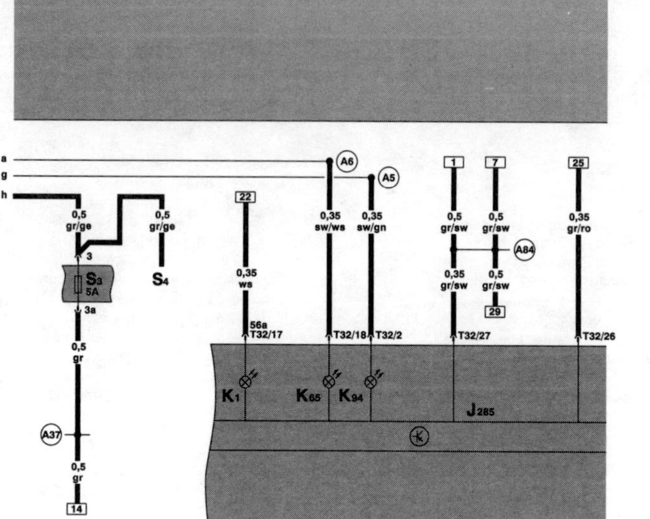

ws = white
sw = black
ro = red
br = brown
gn = green
bl = blue
gr = grey
li = lilac
ge = yellow
or = orange

J285 - Control module with indicator unit in instrument panel insert
K1 - Headlight High Beam Indicator Light
K65 - Left Turn Signal Indicator Light
K94 - Right Turn Signal Indicator Light
S3 - Fuse 3 in fuse holder
S4 - Fuse 4 in fuse holder
T32 - 32-Pin Connector, blue

(42) - Ground connection, beside steering column

(49) - Ground connection, on steering column

(81) - Ground connection -1-, in instrument panel wiring harness

(135) - Ground connection -2-, in instrument panel wiring harness

(A5) - Plus connection (right turn signal), in instrument panel wiring harness

(A6) - Plus connection (left turn signal), in instrument panel wiring harness

(A37) - Wire connection (58a), in instrument panel wiring harness

(A84) - Connector (58L), in instrument panel wiring harness

Edition 03/01 **Instrument cluster, headlight high beam indicator light, turn signal indicator lights**
USA.5102.10.21

THIS PAGE INTENTIONALLY LEFT

BLANK

Daytime running lights,

from May 2000

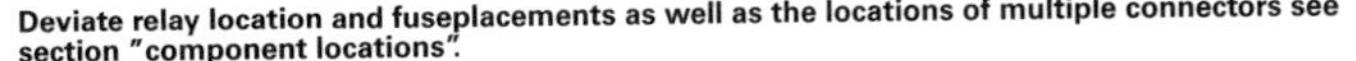

Deviate relay location and fuseplacements as well as the locations of multiple connectors see section "component locations".

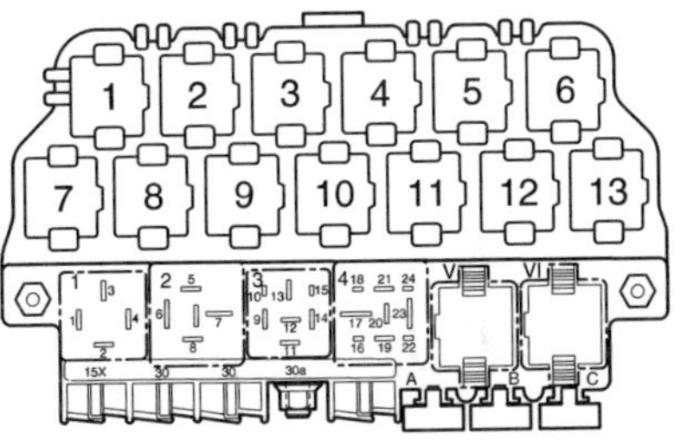

Relay location on the thirteenfold auxiliary relay panel, above relay panel:

7 Daytime Running Lights Change-over Relay (173)

Relay panel:

Note: Number in parentheses indicates production control number stamped on relay housing.

Fuse colors

30 A - green
25 A - white
20 A - yellow
15 A - blue
10 A - red
7,5 A - brown
5 A - beige
3 A - violet

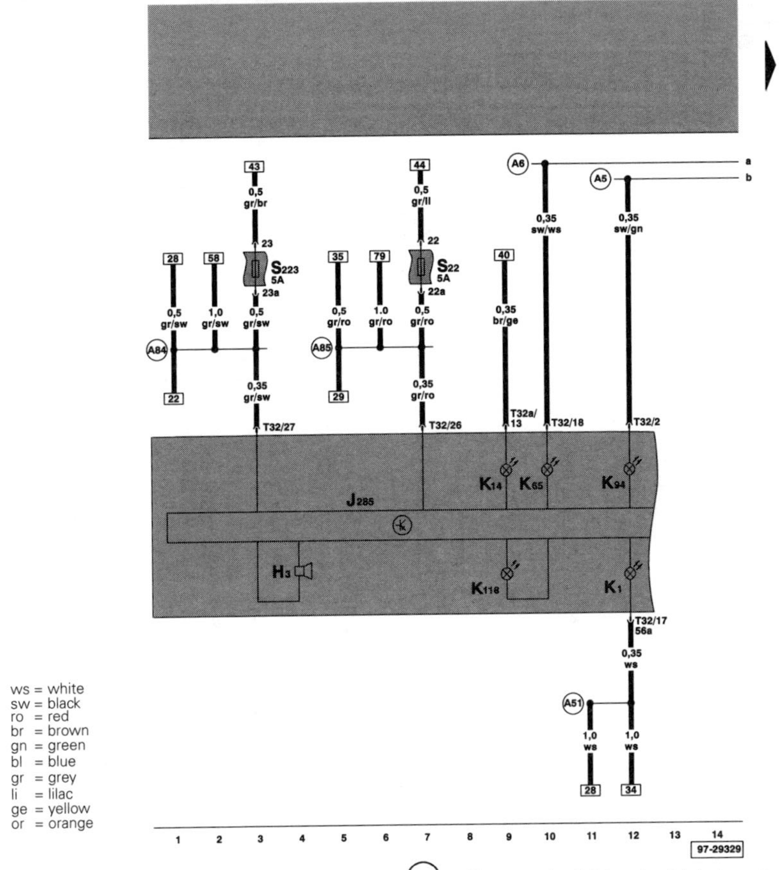

ws = white
sw = black
ro = red
br = brown
gn = green
bl = blue
gr = grey
li = lilac
ge = yellow
or = orange

H3 - Warning buzzer
J285 - Control module with indicator unit in instrument panel insert
K1 - Headlight High Beam Indicator Light
K14 - Parking Brake Indicator Light
K65 - Left Turn Signal Indicator Light
K94 - Right Turn Signal Indicator Light
K118 - Warning light for brake system
S22 - Fuse 22 in fuse holder
S223 - Fuse 23 in fuse holder
T32 - 32-Pin Connector, blue
T32a - 32-Pin Connector, green

(A5) - Plus connection (right turn signal), in instrument panel wiring harness

(A6) - Plus connection (left turn signal), in instrument panel wiring harness
(A51) - Wire connection (56), in instrument panel wiring harness
(A84) - Connector (58L) in instrument panel wiring harness
(A85) - Connector (58R) in instrument panel wiring harness

Instrument cluster, left and right turn signal indicator lights, parking brake indicator light, warning light for brake system, headlight high beam indicator light

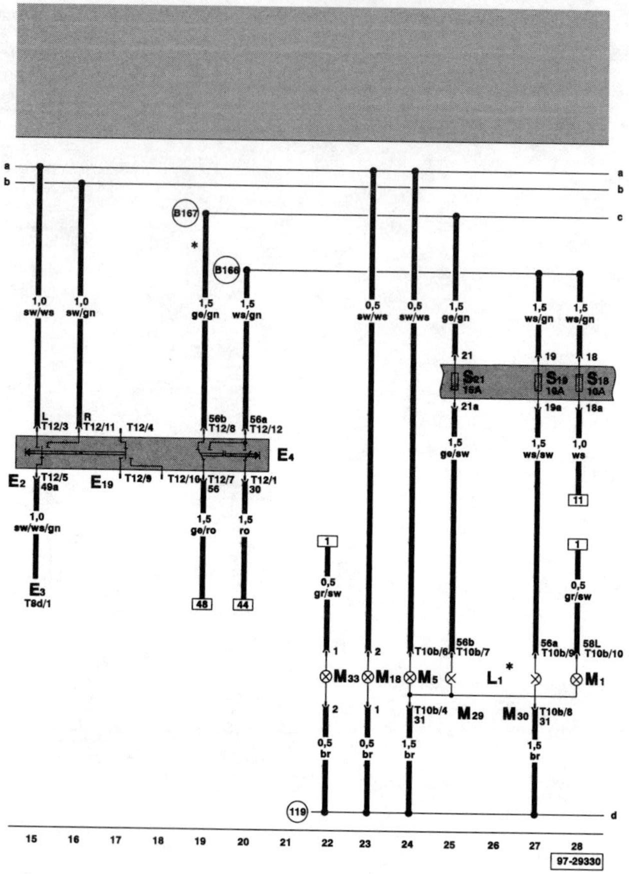

ws = white
sw = black
ro = red
br = brown
gn = green
bl = blue
gr = grey
li = lilac
ge = yellow
or = orange

- E2 - Turn signal switch
- E3 - Emergency Flasher Switch
- E4 - Headlight Dimmer/Flasher Switch
- E19 - Park Light Switch
- L1 - Left Headlight*
- M1 - Left Parking Light
- M5 - Left Front Turn Signal Light
- M18 - Left, Side Turn Signal Light
- M29 - Left Low Beam Headlight (Golf only)
- M30 - Left High Beam Headlight (Golf only)
- M33 - Light for side marker front left
- S18 - Fuse 18 in fuse holder
- S19 - Fuse 19 in fuse holder
- S21 - Fuse 21 in fuse holder
- T8d - 8-Pin Connector
- T10b - 10-Pin Connector
- T12 - 12-Pin Connector
- (119) - Ground connection -1-, in headlight wiring harness
- (B166) - Connection (56a) in passenger compartment wiring harness
- (B167) - Connection (56b) in passenger compartment wiring harness
- * - Jetta only

Turn signal switch, headlight dimmer/flasher switch, left front turn signal light, light for side marker front left, left headlight

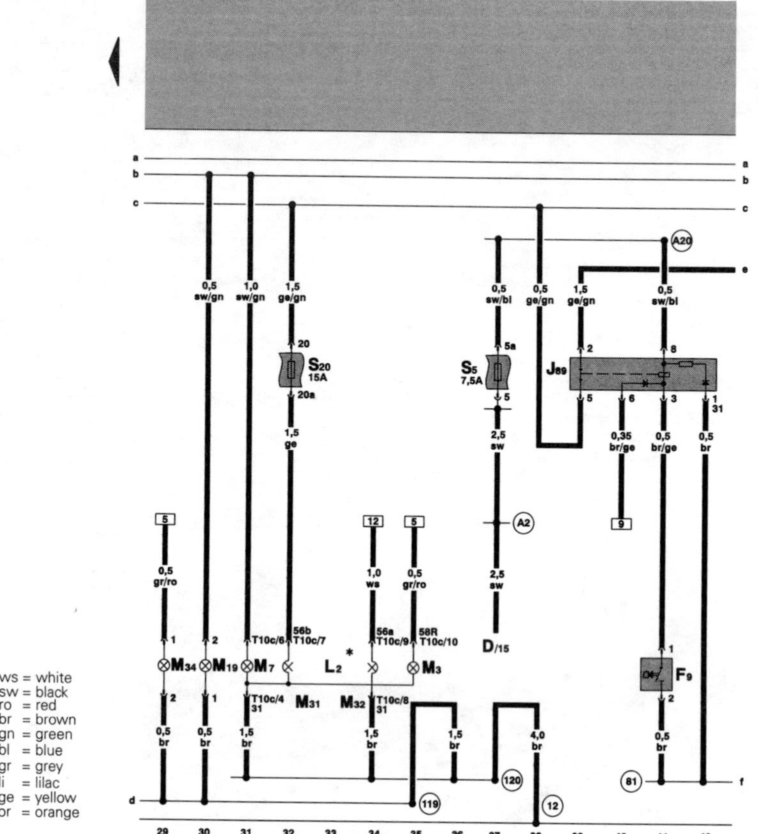

ws = white
sw = black
ro = red
br = brown
gn = green
bl = blue
gr = grey
li = lilac
ge = yellow
or = orange

- D - Ignition/Starter Switch
- F9 - Parking Brake Warning Light Switch
- J89 - Daytime Running Lights Change-over Relay, on the thirteenfold auxiliary relay panel, above relay panel
- L2 - Right Headlight*
- M3 - Right Parking Light
- M7 - Right Front Turn Signal Light
- M19 - Right, Side Turn Signal Light
- M31 - Right Low Beam Headlight (Golf only)
- M32 - Right High Beam Headlight (Golf only)
- M34 - Light for side marker front right
- S5 - Fuse 5 in fuse holder
- S20 - Fuse 20 in fuse holder
- T10c - 10-Pin Connector
- (12) - Ground connection, in engine compartment, left
- (81) - Ground connection -1-, in instrument panel wiring harness
- (119) - Ground connection -1-, in headlight wiring harness
- (120) - Ground connection -2-, in headlight wiring harness
- (A2) - Plus connection (15), in instrument panel wiring harness
- (A20) - Wire connection (15a), in instrument panel wiring harness
- * - Jetta only

Daytime running lights change-over relay, parking brake warning light switch, right front turn signal light, light for side marker front right, right headlight

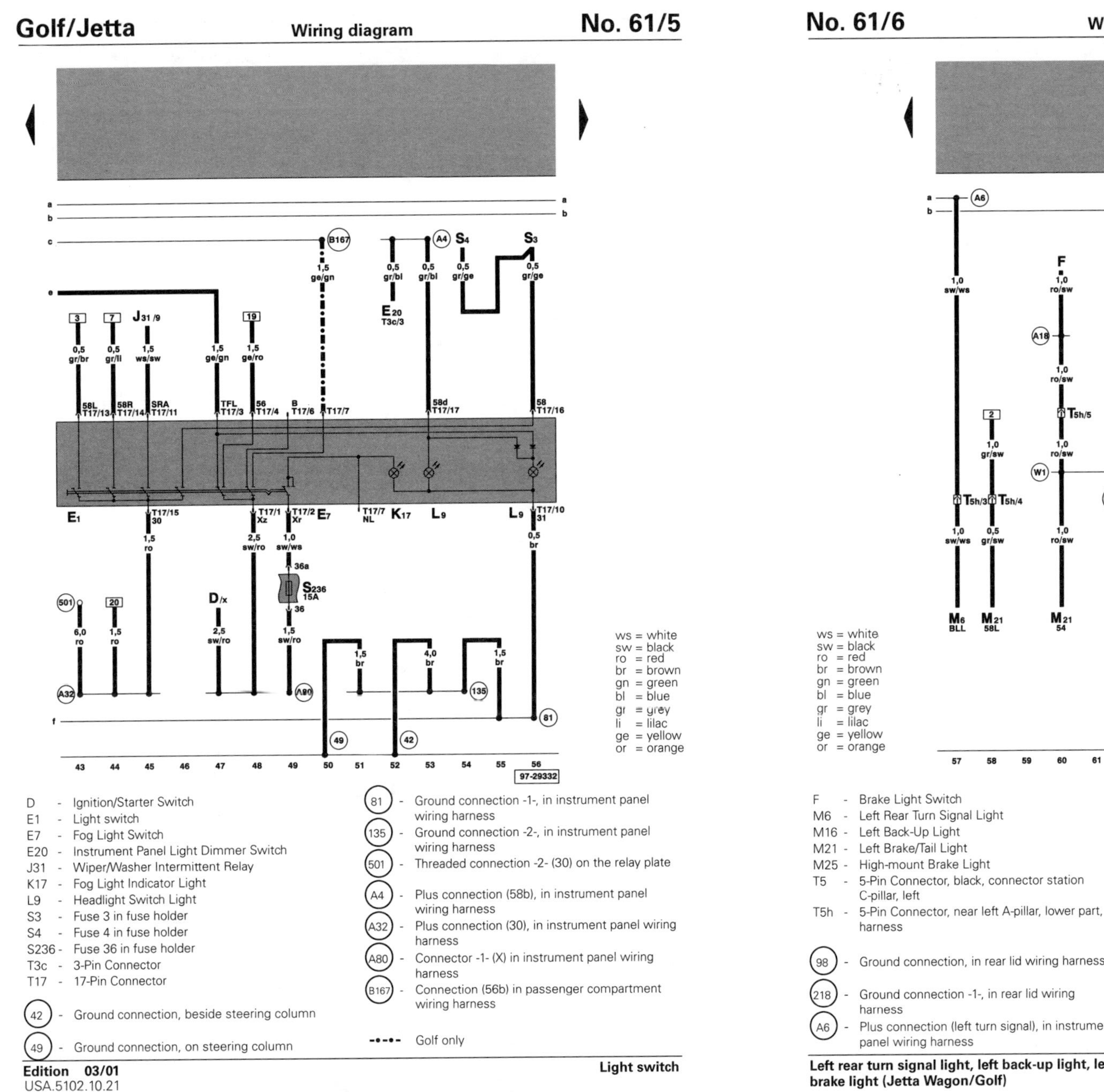

ws = white
sw = black
ro = red
br = brown
gn = green
bl = blue
gr = grey
li = lilac
ge = yellow
or = orange

- D - Ignition/Starter Switch
- E1 - Light switch
- E7 - Fog Light Switch
- E20 - Instrument Panel Light Dimmer Switch
- J31 - Wiper/Washer Intermittent Relay
- K17 - Fog Light Indicator Light
- L9 - Headlight Switch Light
- S3 - Fuse 3 in fuse holder
- S4 - Fuse 4 in fuse holder
- S236 - Fuse 36 in fuse holder
- T3c - 3-Pin Connector
- T17 - 17-Pin Connector
- (42) - Ground connection, beside steering column
- (49) - Ground connection, on steering column
- (81) - Ground connection -1-, in instrument panel wiring harness
- (135) - Ground connection -2-, in instrument panel wiring harness
- (501) - Threaded connection -2- (30) on the relay plate
- (A4) - Plus connection (58b), in instrument panel wiring harness
- (A32) - Plus connection (30), in instrument panel wiring harness
- (A80) - Connector -1- (X) in instrument panel wiring harness
- (B167) - Connection (56b) in passenger compartment wiring harness
- -•-•- Golf only

Light switch

ws = white
sw = black
ro = red
br = brown
gn = green
bl = blue
gr = grey
li = lilac
ge = yellow
or = orange

- F - Brake Light Switch
- M6 - Left Rear Turn Signal Light
- M16 - Left Back-Up Light
- M21 - Left Brake/Tail Light
- M25 - High-mount Brake Light
- T5 - 5-Pin Connector, black, connector station C-pillar, left
- T5h - 5-Pin Connector, near left A-pillar, lower part, in harness
- (98) - Ground connection, in rear lid wiring harness
- (218) - Ground connection -1-, in rear lid wiring harness
- (A6) - Plus connection (left turn signal), in instrument panel wiring harness
- (A18) - Wire connection (54), in instrument panel wiring harness
- (B182) - Connection (RF), in passenger compartment wiring harness
- (W1) - Plus connection (54), in rear wiring harness
- (W28) - Plus connector -2- (54), in wiring harness taillight assembly
- -•-•- Golf only
- --- Jetta Wagon only

Left rear turn signal light, left back-up light, left brake/tail light, high-mount brake light (Jetta Wagon/Golf)

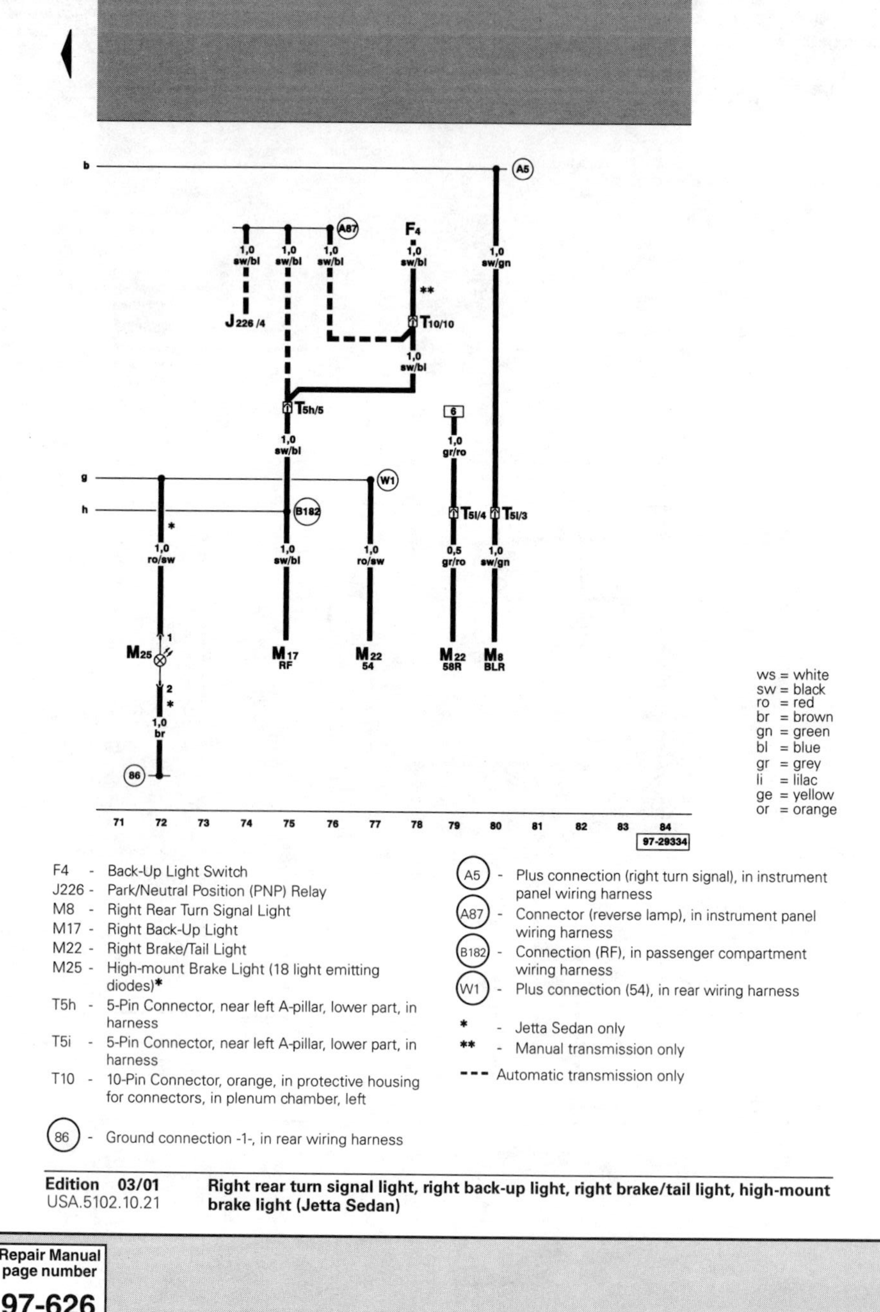

ws = white
sw = black
ro = red
br = brown
gn = green
bl = blue
gr = grey
li = lilac
ge = yellow
or = orange

F4 - Back-Up Light Switch
J226 - Park/Neutral Position (PNP) Relay
M8 - Right Rear Turn Signal Light
M17 - Right Back-Up Light
M22 - Right Brake/Tail Light
M25 - High-mount Brake Light (18 light emitting diodes)*
T5h - 5-Pin Connector, near left A-pillar, lower part, in harness
T5i - 5-Pin Connector, near left A-pillar, lower part, in harness
T10 - 10-Pin Connector, orange, in protective housing for connectors, in plenum chamber, left

(86) - Ground connection -1-, in rear wiring harness

(A5) - Plus connection (right turn signal), in instrument panel wiring harness
(A87) - Connector (reverse lamp), in instrument panel wiring harness
(B182) - Connection (RF), in passenger compartment wiring harness
(W1) - Plus connection (54), in rear wiring harness

* - Jetta Sedan only
** - Manual transmission only
--- Automatic transmission only

Edition 03/01
USA.5102.10.21

Right rear turn signal light, right back-up light, right brake/tail light, high-mount brake light (Jetta Sedan)

1.8L - Engine - Motronic Multiport Fuel Injection (MFI)/132 kW, code AWP,

from May 2001

Deviate relay location and fuseplacements as well as the locations of multiple connectors see section "component locations".

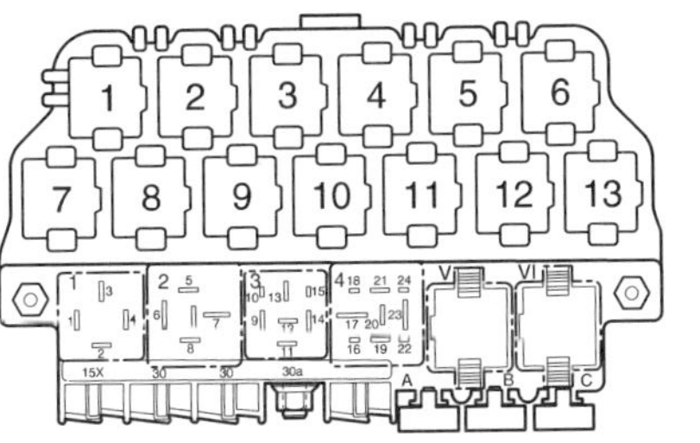

Relay location on the thirteenfold auxiliary relay panel, above relay panel:

Relay panel:

- **2** Load Reduction Relay (100)
- **4** Fuel Pump (FP) Relay (400)

Note: Number in parentheses indicates production control number stamped on relay housing.

Fuse colors

30 A - green
25 A - white
20 A - yellow
15 A - blue
10 A - red
7,5 A - brown
5 A - beige
3 A - violet

ws = white
sw = black
ro = red
br = brown
gn = green
bl = blue
gr = grey
ll = lilac
ge = yellow
or = orange

A - Battery
B - Starter
C - Generator (GEN)
C1 - Voltage Regulator (VR)
D - Ignition/Starter Switch
J59 - Load Reduction Relay
J207 - Starting Interlock Relay
J226 - Park/Neutral Position (PNP) Relay
S162 - Fuse -1- (30) in fuse bracket/battery
S163 - Fuse -2- (30) in fuse bracket/battery
S176 - Fuse -4- (30) in fuse bracket/battery
S177 - Fuse -5- (30) in fuse bracket/battery
T2e - Double Connector, near starter (vehicles without air conditioning)
T4 - 4-Pin Connector, near starter (vehicles with air conditioning only)
T6 - 6-Pin Connector, brown, in protective housing for connectors, in plenum chamber, left
(500) - Threaded connection -1- (30) on the relay plate
(502) - Threaded connection -1- (30a) on the relay plate
(A41) - Plus connection (50), in instrument panel wiring harness
* - Manual transmission only
--- Automatic transmission only

Generator (GEN), starter

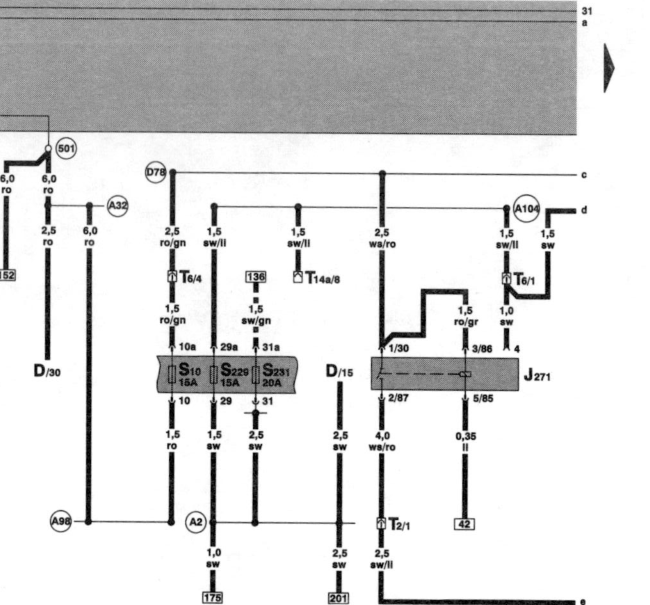

ws = white
sw = black
ro = red
br = brown
gn = green
bl = blue
gr = grey
li = lilac
ge = yellow
or = orange

15 16 17 18 19 20 21 22 23 24 25 26 27 28

97-29336

- D - Ignition/Starter Switch
- J271 - Motronic engine control module (ECM) power supply relay, in protective housing, in engine compartment, left, production control number (428)
- S10 - Fuse 10 in fuse holder
- S229 - Fuse 29 in fuse holder
- S231 - Fuse 31 in fuse holder
- T2 - 2-Pin Connector, in engine compartment, left
- T6 - 6-Pin Connector, brown, in protective housing for connectors, in plenum chamber, left
- T14a - 14-Pin Connector, in engine compartment, in wiring duct, left
- (501) - Threaded connection -2- (30) on the relay plate
- (A2) - Plus connection (15), in instrument panel wiring harness
- (A32) - Plus connection (30), in instrument panel wiring harness
- (A98) - Plus connector -4- (30), in instrument panel wiring harness
- (A104) - Plus connector -2- (15), in instrument panel wiring harness
- (D78) - Plus connector -1- (30a), in engine compartment wiring harness

--- Automatic transmission only

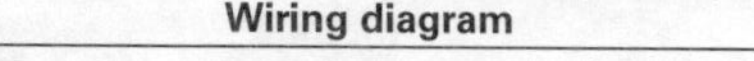

ws = white
sw = black
ro = red
br = brown
gn = green
bl = blue
gr = grey
li = lilac
ge = yellow
or = orange

29 30 31 32 33 34 35 36 37 38 39 40 41 42

97-29337

- J220 - Motronic Engine Control Module (ECM), in plenum chamber, center
- N70 - Ignition Coil 1 with Power Output Stage
- N127 - Ignition Coil 2 with Power Output Stage
- N291 - Ignition Coil 3 with Power Output Stage
- N292 - Ignition Coil 4 with Power Output Stage
- P - Spark Plug Connectors
- Q - Spark Plugs
- T4a - 4-Pin Connector
- T4b - 4-Pin Connector
- T4c - 4-Pin Connector
- T4d - 4-Pin Connector
- T121 - Connector, 121 point
- (15) - Ground connection, on cylinder head
- (85) - Ground connection -1-, in engine compartment wiring harness
- (281) - Ground connector -1-, in wiring harness engine pre-wiring
- (D52) - Plus connector (15a), in engine compartment wiring harness
- (D78) - Plus connector -1- (30a), in engine compartment wiring harness

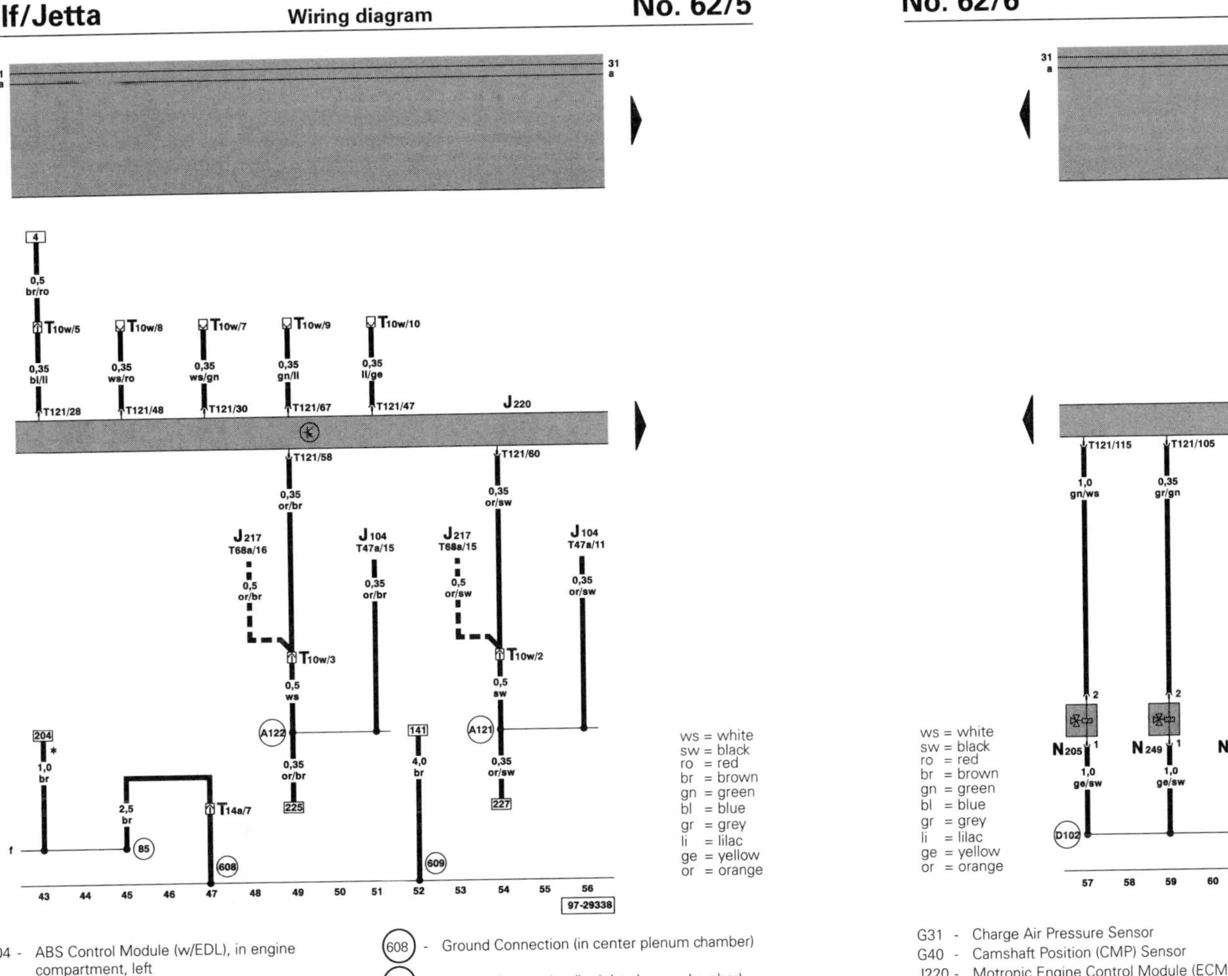

ws = white
sw = black
ro = red
br = brown
gn = green
bl = blue
gr = grey
li = lilac
ge = yellow
or = orange

J104 - ABS Control Module (w/EDL), in engine compartment, left
J217 - Transmission Control Module (TCM)
J220 - Motronic Engine Control Module (ECM), in plenum chamber, center
T10w- 10-Pin Connector, white, in protective housing for connectors, in plenum chamber, left
T14a - 14-Pin Connector, in engine compartment, in wiring duct, left
T47a - 47-Pin Connector, on ABS Control Module
T68a - 68-Pin Connector, on Transmission Control Module (TCM)
T121 - Connector, 121 point

(85) - Ground connection -1-, in engine compartment wiring harness

(608) - Ground Connection (in center plenum chamber)
(609) - Ground Connection (in right plenum chamber)
(A121) - Connection (high bus), in instrument panel wiring harness
(A122) - Connection (low bus), in instrument panel wiring harness

* - Manual transmission only
--- Automatic transmission only

Motronic engine control module (ECM)

ws = white
sw = black
ro = red
br = brown
gn = green
bl = blue
gr = grey
li = lilac
ge = yellow
or = orange

G31 - Charge Air Pressure Sensor
G40 - Camshaft Position (CMP) Sensor
J220 - Motronic Engine Control Module (ECM), in plenum chamber, center
N75 - Wastegate Bypass Regulator Valve
N205- Valve -1- for camshaft adjustment
N249- Recirculating valve for turbocharger
T4g - 4-Pin Connector
T10 - 10-Pin Connector, orange, in protective housing for connectors, in plenum chamber, left
T121 - Connector, 121 point

(220) - Ground connection (sensor ground), in engine compartment wiring harness
(D101) - Wire connection -1-, in engine compartment wiring harness
(D102) - Wire connection -2-, in engine compartment wiring harness

Charge air pressure sensor, camshaft position (CMP) sensor, wastegate bypass regulator valve, recirculating valve for turbocharger, valve for camshaft adjustment

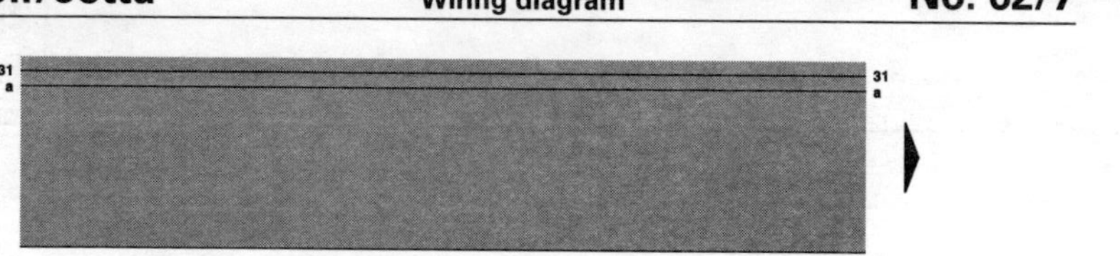

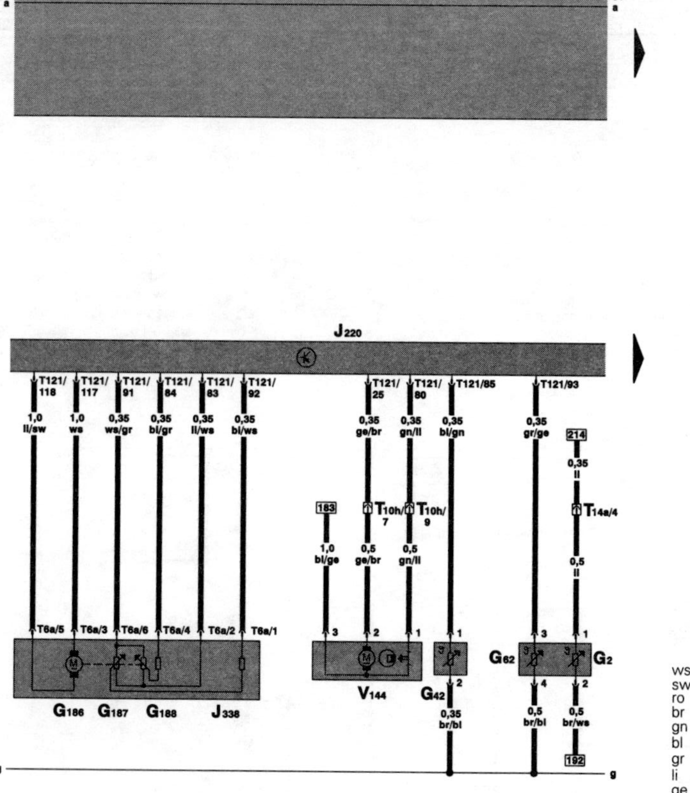

ws = white
sw = black
ro = red
br = brown
gn = green
bl = blue
gr = grey
li = lilac
ge = yellow
or = orange

G2 - Engine Coolant Temperature (ECT) Sensor
G42 - Intake Air Temperature (IAT) Sensor
G62 - Engine Coolant Temperature (ECT) Sensor
G186 - Throttle drive (power accelerator actuation)
G187 - Angle sensor -1- for throttle drive (power accelerator actuation)
G188 - Angle sensor -2- for throttle drive (power accelerator actuation)
J220 - Motronic Engine Control Module (ECM), in plenum chamber, center
J338 - Throttle Valve Control Module
T6a - 6-Pin Connector
T10h - 10-Pin Connector, blue, in protective housing for connectors, in plenum chamber, left
T14a - 14-Pin Connector, in engine compartment, in wiring duct, left
T121 - Connector, 121 point
V144 - Leak detection pump (LDP)

Edition 03/01
USA.5102.10.21

Motronic engine control module (ECM), angle sensor for throttle drive (power accelerator actuation), intake air temperature (IAT) sensor, (ECT) sensor, leak detection pump (LDP)

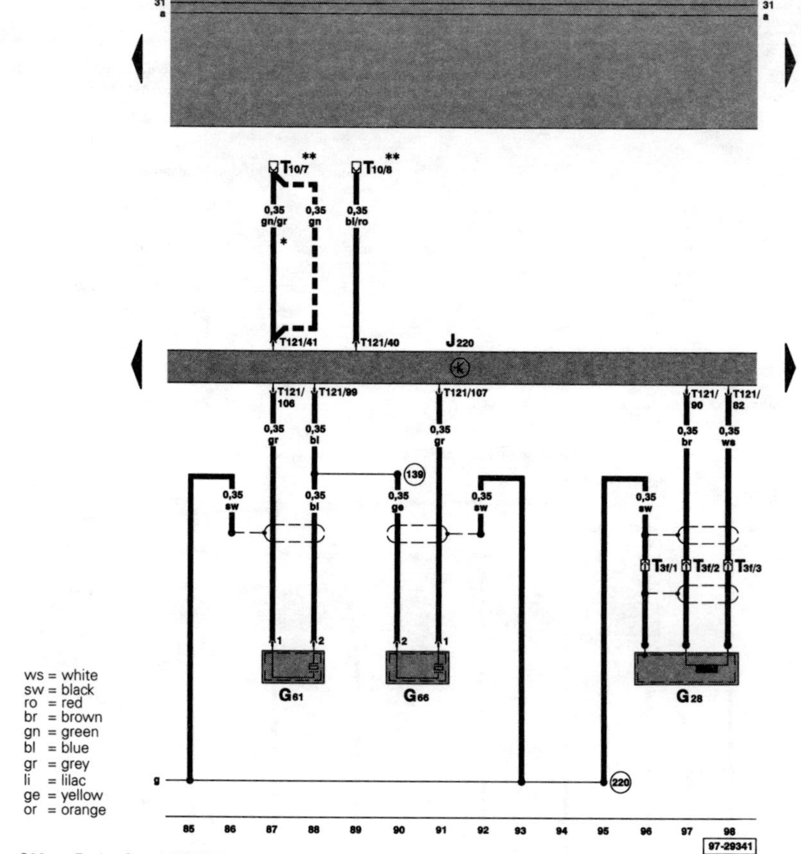

ws = white
sw = black
ro = red
br = brown
gn = green
bl = blue
gr = grey
li = lilac
ge = yellow
or = orange

G28 - Engine Speed (RPM) Sensor
G61 - Knock Sensor (KS) 1
G66 - Knock Sensor (KS) 2
J220 - Motronic Engine Control Module (ECM), in plenum chamber, center
T3f - 3-Pin Connector, in engine compartment, front
T10 - 10-Pin Connector, orange, in protective housing for connectors, in plenum chamber, left
T121 - Connector, 121 point
(139) - Ground connection (sensor Ground), in Motronic Multiport Fuel Injection (MFI) wiring harness
(220) - Ground connection (sensor ground), in engine compartment wiring harness

* - Manual transmission only
** - A/C connection
--- Automatic transmission only

Motronic engine control module (ECM), engine speed (RPM) sensor, knock sensor (KS) 1, knock sensor (KS) 2

Edition 03/01
USA.5102.10.21

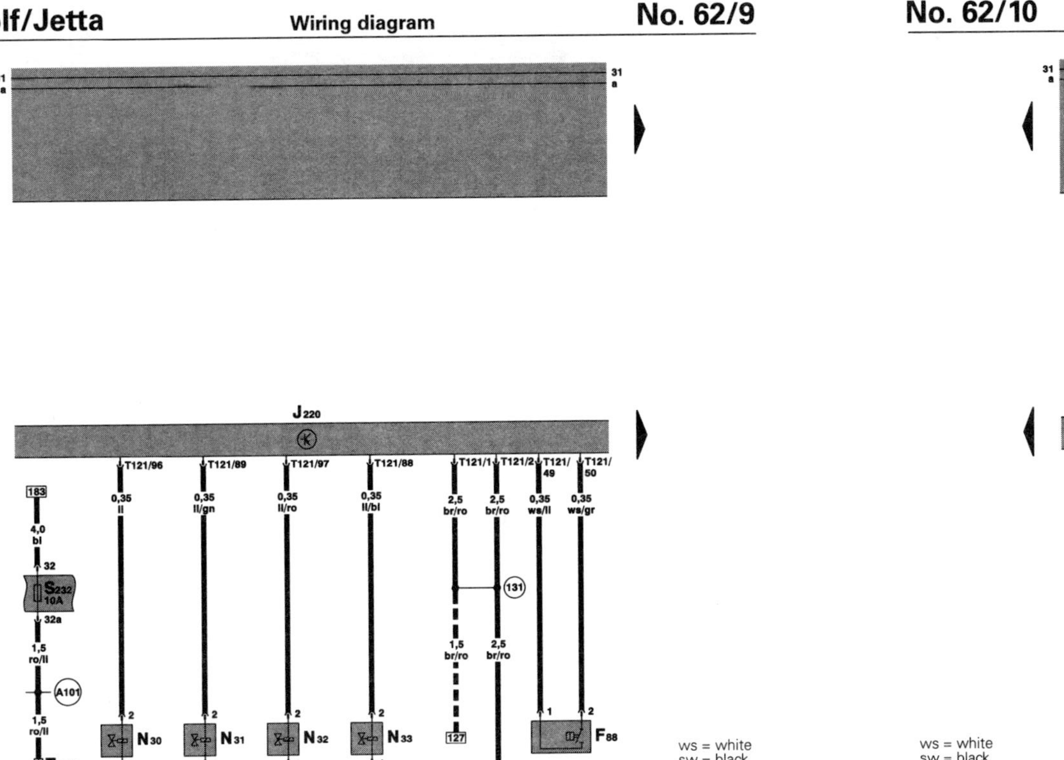

ws = white
sw = black
ro = red
br = brown
gn = green
bl = blue
gr = grey
li = lilac
ge = yellow
or = orange

F88 - Pressure switch/power steering
J220 - Motronic Engine Control Module (ECM), in plenum chamber, center
N30 - Cylinder 1 Fuel Injector
N31 - Cylinder 2 Fuel Injector
N32 - Cylinder 3 Fuel Injector
N33 - Cylinder 4 Fuel Injector
S232 - Fuse 32 in fuse holder
T14a - 14-Pin Connector, in engine compartment, in wiring duct, left
T121 - Connector, 121 point

(131) - Ground connection -2-, in engine compartment wiring harness
(608) - Ground Connection (in center plenum chamber)

(A101) - Connector -3- (87a), in instrument panel wiring harness
(D95) - Wire connection (injectors), in engine compartment wiring harness

--- Automatic transmission only

Motronic engine control module (ECM), pressure switch/power steering, injectors

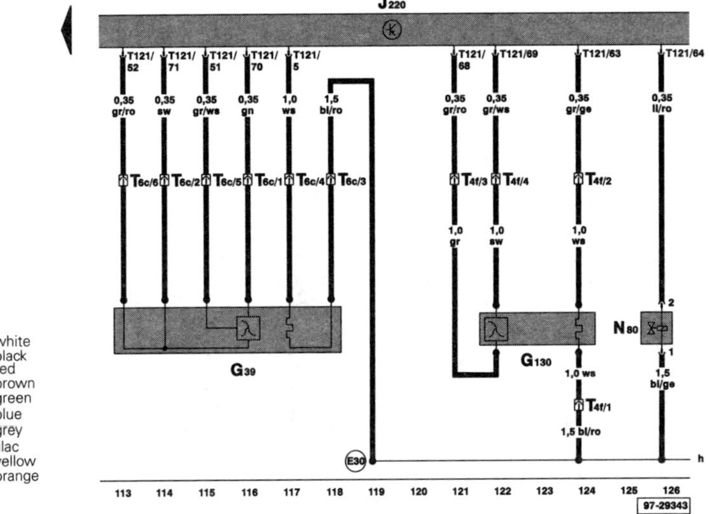

ws = white
sw = black
ro = red
br = brown
gn = green
bl = blue
gr = grey
li = lilac
ge = yellow
or = orange

G39 - Heated Oxygen Sensor (HO2S)
G130 - Oxygen Sensor (O2S) behind Three Way Catalytic Converter (TWC)
J220 - Motronic Engine Control Module (ECM), in plenum chamber, center
N80 - Evaporative Emission (EVAP) Canister Purge Regulator Valve
T4f - 4-Pin Connector, in protective housing for connectors under right floor
T6c - 6-Pin Connector, in protective housing for connectors under right floor
T121 - Connector, 121 point

(E30) - Connector (87a), in wiring harness engine

Motronic engine control module (ECM), heated oxygen sensor (HO2S), oxygen sensor (O2S) behind three way catalytic converter (TWC), (EVAP) canister purge regulator valve

ws = white
sw = black
ro = red
br = brown
gn = green
bl = blue
gr = grey
li = lilac
ge = yellow
or = orange

- J220 - Motronic Engine Control Module (ECM), in plenum chamber, center
- J542 - Brake Booster Control Module
- S51 - Fuse, in protective housing, in engine compartment, left
- T6j - 6-Pin Connector, in engine compartment left
- T6k - 6-Pin Connector
- T10g - 10-Pin Connector, grey, in protective housing for connectors, in plenum chamber, left
- T121 - Connector, 121 point
- V192 - Brake System Vacuum Pump
- (D104) - Plus connection -2- (30a), in engine compartment wiring harness
- (U8) - Plus Connection (15a) in automatic transmission wiring harness

--- Automatic transmission only

Edition 03/01
USA.5102.10.21

Motronic engine control module (ECM), brake booster control module, brake system vacuum pump

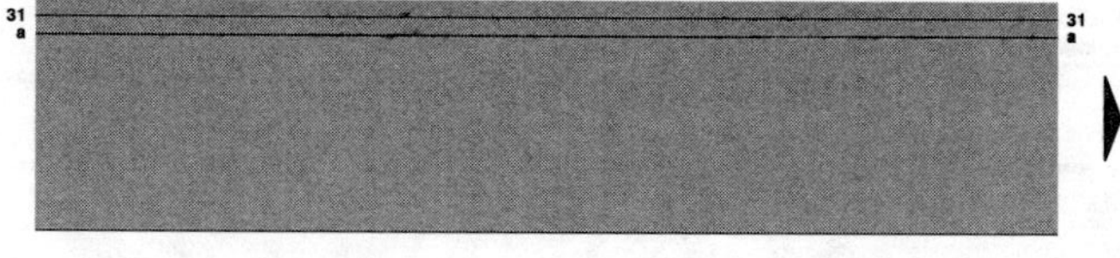

ws = white
sw = black
ro = red
br = brown
gn = green
bl = blue
gr = grey
li = lilac
ge = yellow
or = orange

- F - Brake Light Switch
- F47 - Brake Vacuum Vent Valve Switch for cruise control
- J220 - Motronic Engine Control Module (ECM), in plenum chamber, center
- J299 - Secondary Air Injection (AIR) Pump Relay, in protective housing, in engine compartment, left, production control number (100)
- N112 - Secondary Air Injection (AIR) Solenoid Valve
- S13 - Fuse 13 in fuse holder
- S130 - Fuse for secondary air pump, in protective housing, in engine compartment, left
- T2f - Double Connector, in engine compartment left
- T10e - 10-Pin Connector, black, in protective housing for connectors, in plenum chamber, left
- T121 - Connector, 121 point
- V101 - Secondary Air Injection (AIR) Pump Motor
- (A18) - Wire connection (54), in instrument panel
- (A20) - Wire connection (15a), in instrument panel wiring harness
- (D103) - Wire connection -3-, in engine compartment wiring harness
- (D104) - Plus connection -2- (30a), in engine compartment wiring harness

* - Manual transmission only

--- Automatic transmission only

Motronic engine control module (ECM), secondary air injection (AIR) pump system, brake light switch, brake vacuum vent valve switch for cruise control

Edition 03/01
USA.5102.10.21

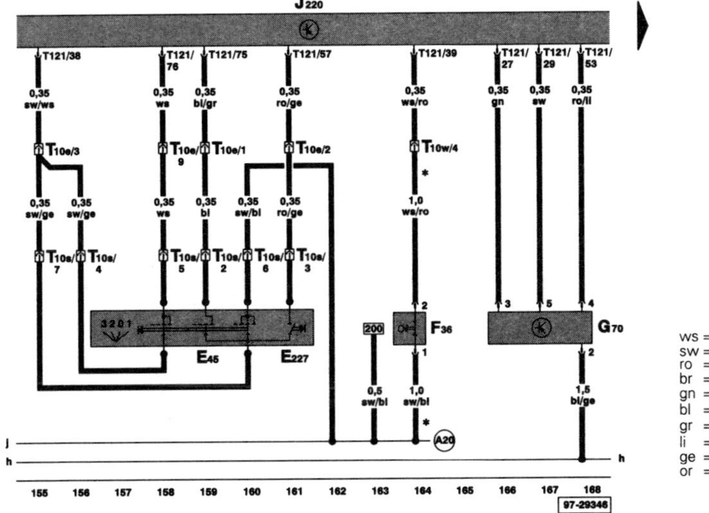

ws = white
sw = black
ro = red
br = brown
gn = green
bl = blue
gr = grey
li = lilac
ge = yellow
or = orange

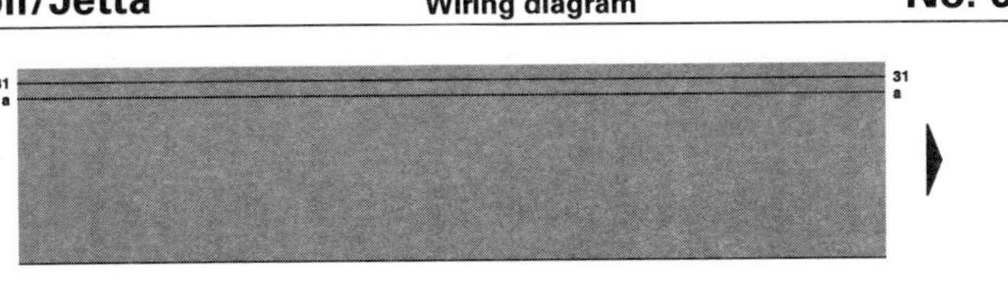

- E45 - Cruise Control Switch
- E227 - Cruise Control Push Button (SET)
- F36 - Clutch Vacuum Vent Valve Switch
- G70 - Mass Air Flow (MAF) Sensor
- J220 - Motronic Engine Control Module (ECM), in plenum chamber, center
- T10e - 10-Pin Connector, black, in protective housing for connectors, in plenum chamber, left
- T10s - 10-Pin Connector, near steering column
- T10w - 10-Pin Connector, white, in protective housing for connectors, in plenum chamber, left
- T121 - Connector, 121 point
- (A20) - Wire connection (15a), in instrument panel wiring harness

* - Manual transmission only

Motronic engine control module (ECM), cruise control switch, mass air flow (MAF) sensor, clutch vacuum vent valve switch

ws = white
sw = black
ro = red
br = brown
gn = green
bl = blue
gr = grey
li = lilac
ge = yellow
or = orange

- G79 - Throttle Position (TP) Sensor
- G185 - Sender -2- for accelerator pedal position
- J17 - Fuel Pump (FP) Relay
- J217 - Transmission Control Module (TCM)
- J220 - Motronic Engine Control Module (ECM), in plenum chamber, center
- J234 - Airbag Control Module
- T6 - 6-Pin Connector, brown, in protective housing for connectors, in plenum chamber, left
- T6b - 6-Pin Connector
- T10 - 10-Pin Connector, orange, in protective housing for connectors, in plenum chamber, left
- T10h - 10-Pin Connector, blue, in protective housing for connectors, in plenum chamber, left
- T68a - 68-Pin Connector, on Transmission Control Module (TCM)
- T75 - 75-Pin Connector
- T121 - Connector, 121 point
- (A27) - Wire Connection (vehicle speed signal), in instrument panel wiring harness
- (A125) - Connection (crash signal) in instrument panel wiring harness

* - Manual transmission only

--- Automatic transmission only

Motronic engine control module (ECM), throttle position (TP) sensor, fuel pump (FP) relay

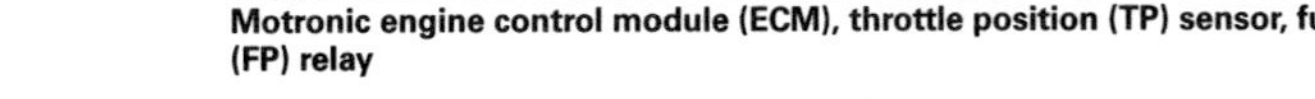

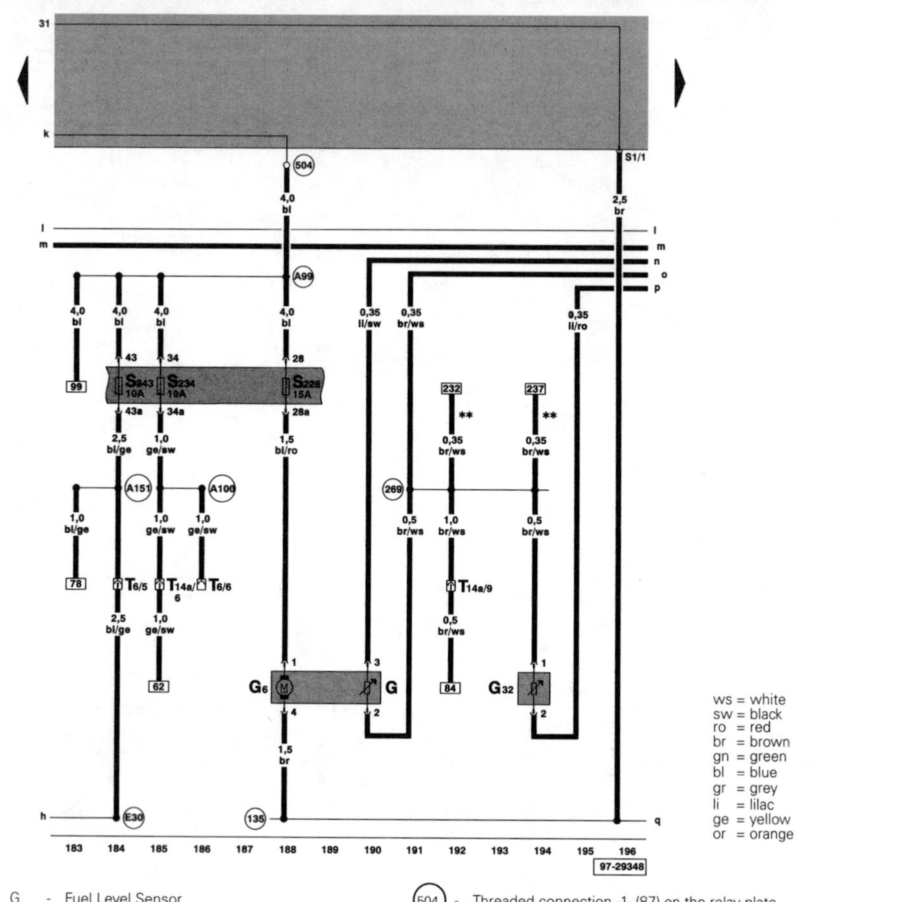

ws = white
sw = black
ro = red
br = brown
gn = green
bl = blue
gr = grey
li = lilac
ge = yellow
or = orange

G - Fuel Level Sensor
G6 - Fuel Pump (FP)
G32 - Engine Coolant Level (ECL) Sensor
S228 - Fuse 28 in fuse holder
S234 - Fuse 34 in fuse holder
S243 - Fuse 43 in fuse holder
T6 - 6-Pin Connector, brown, in protective housing for connectors, in plenum chamber, left
T14a - 14-Pin Connector, in engine compartment, in wiring duct, left

(135) - Ground connection -2-, in instrument panel wiring harnes
(269) - Ground connection (sensor ground) -1-, in instrument panel wiring harness

(504) - Threaded connection -1- (87) on the relay plate
(A99) - Connector -1- (87), in instrument panel wiring harness
(A100) - Connector -2- (87), in instrument panel wiring harness
(A151) - Connector -4- (87), in instrument panel wiring harness
(E30) - Connector (87a), in wiring harness engine

** - Vehicles with Multi-Function Indicator (MFI) only

Fuel pump (FP), fuel level sensor, engine coolant level (ECL) sensor

ws = white
sw = black
ro = red
br = brown
gn = green
bl = blue
gr = grey
li = lilac
ge = yellow
or = orange

F1 - Oil Pressure Switch
G22 - Speedometer Vehicle Speed Sensor (VSS)
J217 - Transmission Control Module (TCM)
J285 - Control module with indicator unit in instrument panel insert
K3 - Oil Pressure Warning Light
K38 - Engine Oil Level Indicator Light
S5 - Fuse 5 in fuse holder
S7 - Fuse 7 in fuse holder
T14a - 14-Pin Connector, in engine compartment, in wiring duct, left
T32 - 32-Pin Connector, blue
T68a - 68-Pin Connector, on Transmission Control Module (TCM)

(42) - Ground connection, beside steering column
(49) - Ground connection, on steering column
(135) - Ground connection -2-, in instrument panel wiring harness
(B163) - Plus connector -1- (15) in wiring harness interior

* - Manual transmission only
--- Automatic transmission only

Instrument cluster, oil pressure switch, speedometer vehicle speed sensor (VSS), oil pressure warning light

ws = white
sw = black
ro = red
br = brown
gn = green
bl = blue
gr = grey
li = lilac
ge = yellow
or = orange

211 212 213 214 215 216 217 218 219 220 221 222 223 224

97-29350

G1 - Fuel gauge
G3 - Engine Coolant Temperature (ECT) Gauge
G5 - Tachometer
G21 - Speedometer
H3 - Warning Buzzer
J285 - Control module with indicator unit in instrument panel insert
K2 - Generator (GEN) Warning Light
K28 - Engine Coolant Level/Temperature (ECL/ECT) Warning Light
K105 - Low Fuel Level Warning Light
T32 - 32-Pin Connector, blue

(A13) - Wire connection (door contact switch), in instrument panel wiring harness
(A27) - Wire Connection (vehicle speed signal), in instrument panel wiring harness

Edition 03/01
USA.5102.10.21

Instrument cluster, engine coolant temperature (ECL/ECT) gauge, fuel gauge, tachometer, speedometer, generator (GEN) warning light, low fuel level warning light

ws = white
sw = black
ro = red
br = brown
gn = green
bl = blue
gr = grey
li = lilac
ge = yellow
or = orange

225 226 227 228 229 230 231 232 233 234 235 236 237 238

97-29351

E86 - Multi-Function Indicator Mode Select Switch
E109 - Multi-Function Indicator Memory Switch
G17 - Outside Air Temperature Sensor
J119 - Multi-function Indicator (MFI)
J285 - Control module with indicator unit in instrument panel insert
J533 - Data Bus On Board Diagnostic Interface
K31 - Cruise Control Indicator Light
K83 - Malfunction Indicator Lamp (MIL)
K132 - Electronic Power Control (EPC) Warning Lamp
T6e - 6-Pin Connector
T16 - Data Link Connector (DLC), below instrument panel, left
T32 - 32-Pin Connector, blue
T32a - 32-Pin Connector, green

(A76) - Connector (K-diagnosis wire), in instrument panel wiring harness

** - Vehicles with Multi-Function Indicator (MFI) only

Instrument cluster, multi-function indicator (MFI), outside air temperature sensor, electronic power control (EPC) warning lamp, cruise control indicator light, malfunction indicator lamp

Edition 03/01
USA.5102.10.21

Automatic transmission, 5 speed automatic with Tiptronic

from June 2001

- **1.8L - Engine - Motronic Multiport Fuel Injection (MFI)/132 kW, code AWP**

Deviate relay location and fuseplacements as well as the locations of multiple connectors see section "component locations".

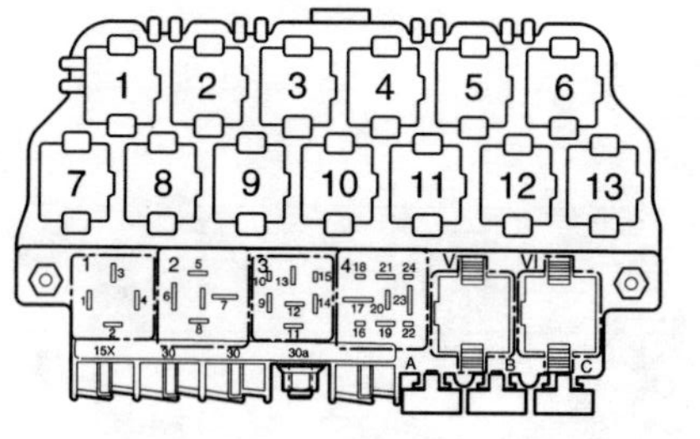

Relay location on the thirteenfold auxiliary relay panel, above relay panel:

11 Park/Neutral Position (PNP) Relay (175)

Relay panel:

4 Fuel Pump (FP) Relay (409)

Note: Number in parentheses indicates production control number stamped on relay housing.

Fuse colors

30 A - green
25 A - white
20 A - yellow
15 A - blue
10 A - red
7,5 A - brown
5 A - beige
3 A - violet

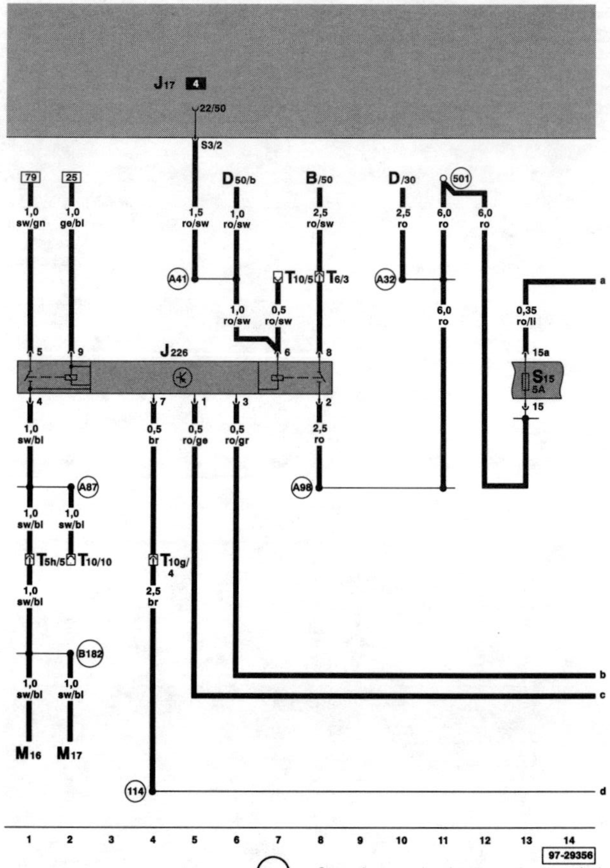

ws = white
sw = black
ro = red
br = brown
gn = green
bl = blue
gr = grey
li = lilac
ge = yellow
or = orange

97-29356

B - Starter
D - Ignition/Starter Switch
J17 - Fuel Pump (FP) Relay
J226 - Park/Neutral Position (PNP) Relay, on the thirteenfold auxiliary relay panel, above relay panel
M16 - Left Back-Up Light
M17 - Right Back-Up Light
S15 - Fuse 15 in fuse holder
T5h - 5-Pin Connector, near left A-pillar, lower part, in harness
T6 - 6-Pin Connector, brown, in protective housing for connectors, in plenum chamber, left
T10 - 10-Pin Connector, orange, in protective housing for connectors, in plenum chamber, left
T10g - 10-Pin Connector, grey, in protective housing for connectors, in plenum chamber, left

(114) - Ground connection, in automatic transmission wiring harness
(501) - Threaded connection -2- (30) on the relay plate
(A32) - Plus connection (30), in instrument panel wiring harness
(A41) - Plus connection (50), in instrument panel wiring harness
(A87) - Connector (RF), in instrument panel wiring harness
(A98) - Plus connector -4- (30), in instrument panel wiring harness
(B182) - Connection (RF), in passenger compartment wiring harness

Park/neutral position (PNP) relay

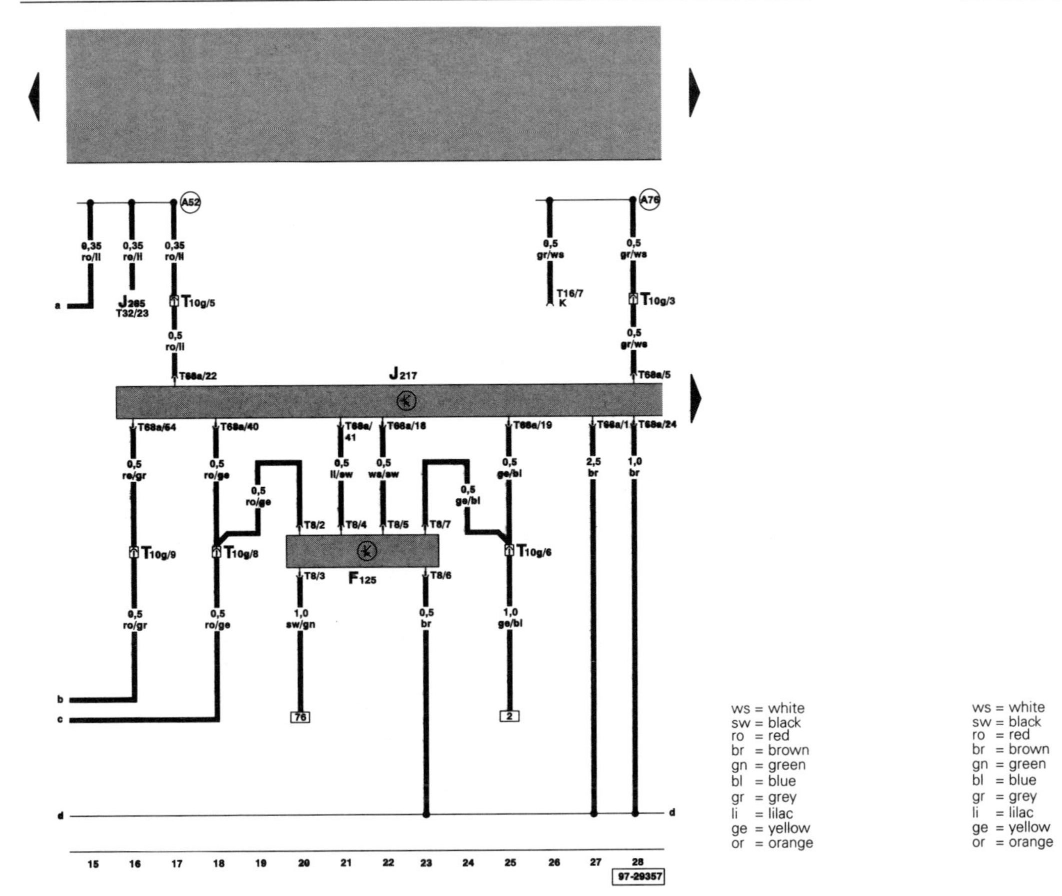

ws = white
sw = black
ro = red
br = brown
gn = green
bl = blue
gr = grey
li = lilac
ge = yellow
or = orange

F125 - Multi-Function Transmission Range (TR) Switch
J217 - Transmission Control Module (TCM), in plenum chamber, center
J285 - Control module with indicator unit in instrument panel insert
T8 - 8-Pin Connector
T10g - 10-Pin Connector, grey, in protective housing for connectors, in plenum chamber, left
T16 - Data Link Connector (DLC), below instrument panel, left
T32 - 32-Pin Connector, blue
T68a - 68-Pin Connector

(A52) - Plus connection (30a), in instrument panel wiring harness

(A76) - Connector (K-diagnosis wire) in instrument panel wiring harness

Transmission control module (TCM), multi-function transmission range (TR) switch

ws = white
sw = black
ro = red
br = brown
gn = green
bl = blue
gr = grey
li = lilac
ge = yellow
or = orange

F270 - Brake Pressure Switch
G93 - Transmission Fluid Temperature Sensor
J217 - Transmission Control Module (TCM), in plenum chamber, center
J220 - Motronic Engine Control Module (ECM), in plenum chamber, center
J285 - Control module with indicator unit in instrument panel insert
N88 - Solenoid Valve 1
N89 - Solenoid Valve 2
N90 - Solenoid Valve 3
N91 - Solenoid Valve 4
N92 - Solenoid Valve 5
N93 - Solenoid Valve 6
N281 - Solenoid Valve 8
N282 - Solenoid Valve 9
N283 - Solenoid Valve 10
T10h - 10-Pin Connector, blue, in protective housing for connectors, in plenum chamber, left
T20b - 20-Pin Connector, on transmission
T32 - 32-Pin Connector, blue
T68a - 68-Pin Connector
T121 - 121-Pin Connector

(114) - Ground connection, in automatic transmission wiring harness
(608) - Ground Connection (in center plenum chamber)

Transmission control module (TCM), solenoid valves, transmission fluid temperature sensor, brake pressure switch

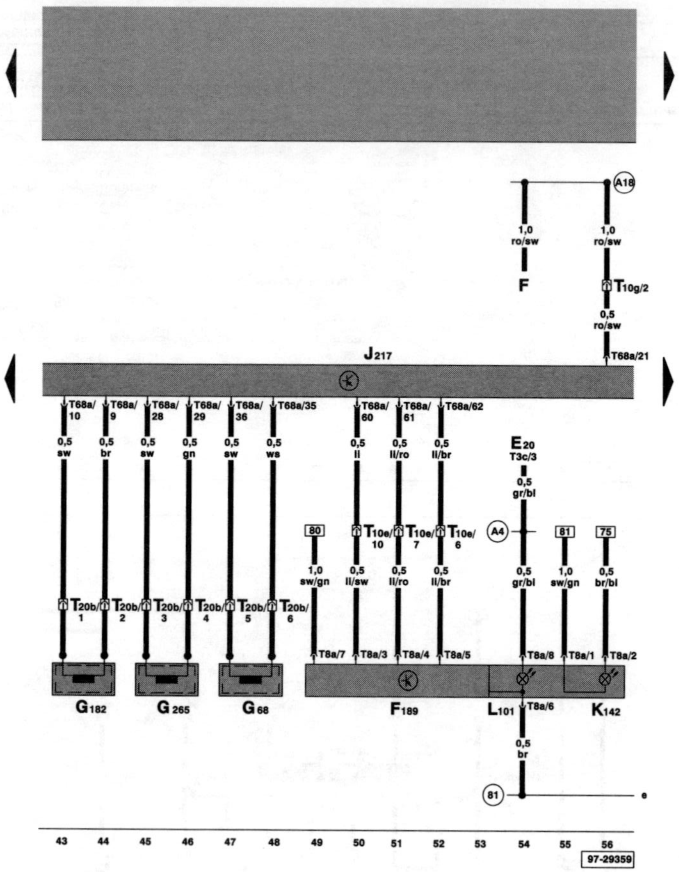

ws = white
sw = black
ro = red
br = brown
gn = green
bl = blue
gr = grey
li = lilac
ge = yellow
or = orange

E20 - Instrument Panel Light Dimmer Switch
F - Brake Light Switch
F189 - Tiptronic Switch
G68 - Vehicle Speed Sensor (VSS)
G182 - Sensor for transmission RPM
G265 - Intermediate Shaft Speed Sensor
J217 - Transmission Control Module (TCM), in plenum chamber, center
K142 - Warning light for selector lever position P/N
L101 - Illumination for selector lever scale
T3c - 3-Pin Connector
T8a - 8-Pin Connector
T10e - 10-Pin Connector, black, in protective housing for connectors, in plenum chamber, left
T10g - 10-Pin Connector, grey, in protective housing for connectors, in plenum chamber, left
T20b - 20-Pin Connector, on transmission
T68a - 68-Pin Connector

(81) - Ground connection -1-, in instrument panel wiring harness
(A4) - Plus connection (58b), in instrument panel wiring harness
(A18) - Wire connection (54), in instrument panel wiring harness

Transmission control module (TCM), vehicle speed sensor (VSS), sensor for transmission RPM, intermediate shaft speed sensor, tiptronic switch

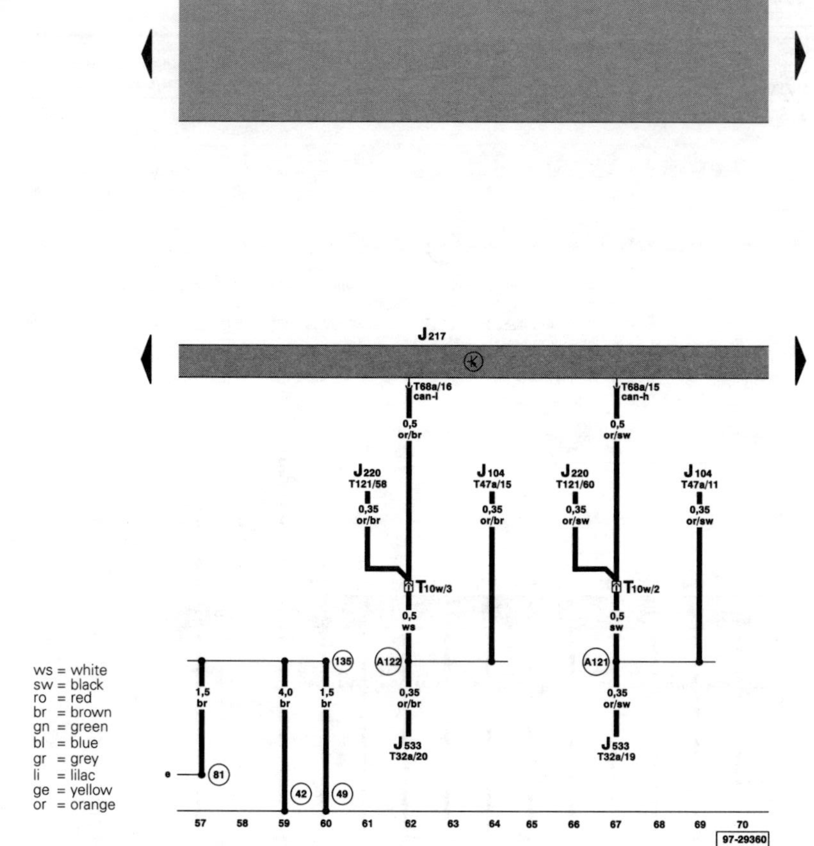

ws = white
sw = black
ro = red
br = brown
gn = green
bl = blue
gr = grey
li = lilac
ge = yellow
or = orange

J104 - ABS Control Module (w/EDL)
J220 - Motronic Engine Control Module (ECM), in plenum chamber, center
J217 - Transmission Control Module (TCM), in plenum chamber, center
J533 - Data Bus On Board Diagnostic Interface
T10w - 10-Pin Connector, white, in protective housing for connectors, in plenum chamber, left
T32a - 32-Pin Connector, green, on Instrument cluster
T47a - 47-Pin Connector, on ABS Control Module
T68a - 68-Pin Connector
T121 - 121-Pin Connector

(42) - Ground connection, beside steering column
(49) - Ground connection, on steering column
(81) - Ground connection -1-, in instrument panel wiring harness
(135) - Ground connection -2-, in instrument panel wiring harness
(A121) - Connection (high bus), in instrument panel wiring harness
(A122) - Connection (low bus), in instrument panel wiring harness

Transmission control module (TCM)

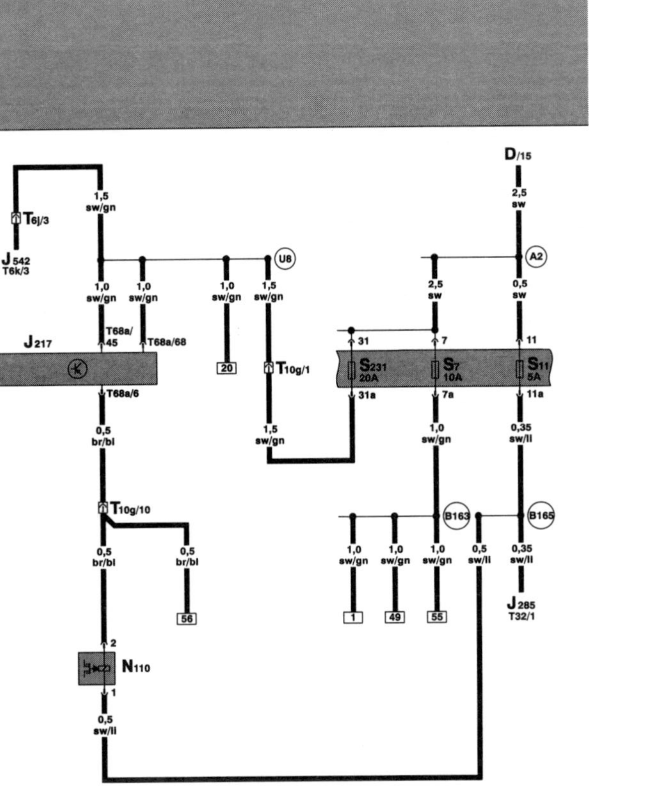

ws = white
sw = black
ro = red
br = brown
gn = green
bl = blue
gr = grey
li = lilac
ge = yellow
or = orange

- D - Ignition/Starter Switch
- J217 - Transmission Control Module (TCM), in plenum chamber, center
- J285 - Control module with indicator unit in instrument panel insert
- J542 - Brake Booster Control Module
- N110 - Shift Lock Solenoid
- S7 - Fuse 7 in fuse holder
- S11 - Fuse 11 in fuse holder
- S231 - Fuse 31 in fuse holder
- T6j - 6-Pin Connector, in engine compartment left
- T6k - 6-Pin Connector
- T10g - 10-Pin Connector, grey, in protective housing for connectors, in plenum chamber, left
- T32 - 32-Pin Connector, blue
- T68a - 68-Pin Connector

- (A2) - Plus connection (15), in instrument panel wiring harness
- (B163) - Plus connector -1- (15) in wiring harness interior
- (B165) - Plus connector -2- (15) in wiring harness interior
- (U8) - Plus connection (15a) in automatic transmission wiring harness

THIS PAGE INTENTIONALLY LEFT

BLANK

ST Scan Tool Codes

GENERAL

All vehicles from model year that are covered by this manual are equipped with the Government required diagnostic system known as On-Board Diagnostics II (OBD II). This system monitors operation and function of all engine management system activity and automatic transmission operation to insure compliance with specified emission levels.

Vehicle emission levels are constantly monitored by the OBD II system and malfunctions are recognized and recorded. A Malfunction Indicator Light (MIL) in the instrument cluster alerts the driver to the fault and the need to have the system checked for fault codes. These codes follow a standard format and are known as Diagnostic Trouble Codes (DTCs).

DTCs are assigned two codes. The first code is a numerical code assigned by the factory. The second code is referred to as a P-code and follows a structure required by law and defined by the Society of Automotive Engineers (SAE). This standard uses a letter to designate the system and four numbers to further identify and detail the malfunction as listed below.

First digit structure is as follows:

- Pxxxx for powertrain
- Bxxxx for body
- Cxxxx for chassis
- Uxxxx for future systems

Second digit structure is:

- P0xxx Government required codes
- P1xxx Manufacturer codes for additional emission system function; not required but reported to the government

Third digit structure is:

- Px1xx measurement of air and fuel
- Px2xx measurement of air and fuel
- Px3xx ignition system
- Px4xx additional emission control
- Px5xx speed and idle regulation
- Px6xx computer and output signals
- Px7xx transmission
- Px8xx transmission
- Px9xx control modules, input and output signals

The fourth and fifth digits designate the individual components and systems.

DTCs and data can be retrieved with Volkswagen Factory Scan Tools such as the VAG 1551, VAG 1552, or the new diagnostic computer VAS 5051 through a Data Link Connector (DLC) located in the center console. See Fig. 1. Several aftermarket scan tools and computer programs are also capable of retrieving this information in this factory mode. The factory mode also allows the scan tool to be used for other system diagnostic functions and information retrieval.

Some DTC information can also be retrieved in a generic mode. The generic mode is not as complete as the factory mode, but allows commercially available scan tools to be used simply to read DTCs. Generic scan tool mode does not have the capability to retrieve the detailed information of a manufacturer-specific scan tool.

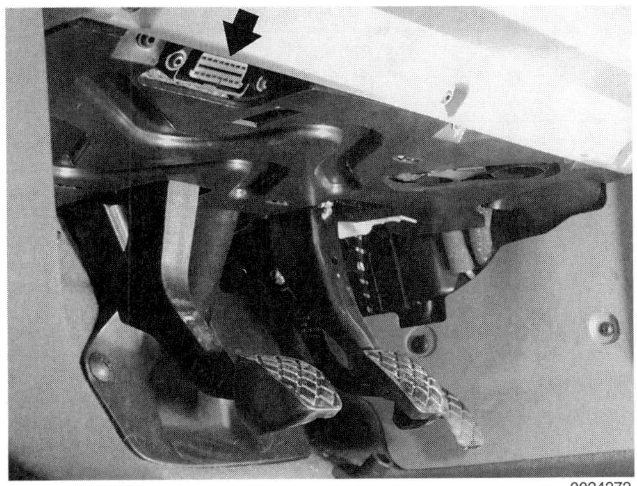

0024272

Fig. 1. Data Link Connector (**arrow**) under left lower side of instrument panel.

ST

SCAN TOOL CODE TABLE

NOTE —
The following table contains a list of available scan tool codes for all Volkswagen and Audi vehicles available at the time of publication. Not all of the codes apply to the vehicles covered by this manual.

Table a. Scan Tool Codes

DTC	P-code	Description
16394	P0010	-A- Camshaft Pos. Actuator Circ. Bank 1 Malfunction
16395	P0020	-A- Camshaft Pos. Actuator Circ. Bank 2 Malfunction
16449	P0065	Air Assisted Injector Control Range/Performance
16450	P0066	Air Assisted Injector Control Low Input/Short to ground
16451	P0067	Air Assisted Injector Control Input/Short to B+
16485	P0101	Mass or Volume Air Flow Circ Range/Performance
16486	P0102	Mass or Volume Air Flow Circ Low Input
16487	P0103	Mass or Volume Air Flow Circ High Input
16489	P0105	Manifold Abs.Pressure or Bar.Pressure Voltage supply
16490	P0106	Manifold Abs.Pressure or Bar.Pressure Range/Performance
16491	P0107	Manifold Abs.Pressure or Bar.Pressure Low Input
16492	P0108	Manifold Abs.Pressure or Bar.Pressure High Input
16496	P0112	Intake Air Temp.Circ Low Input
16497	P0113	Intake Air Temp.Circ High Input
16500	P0116	Engine Coolant Temp.Circ Range/Performance
16501	P0117	Engine Coolant Temp.Circ Low Input
16502	P0118	Engine Coolant Temp.Circ High Input
16504	P0120	Throttle/Pedal Pos.Sensor A Circ Malfunction
16505	P0121	Throttle/Pedal Pos.Sensor A Circ Range/Performance
16506	P0122	Throttle/Pedal Pos.Sensor A Circ Low Input
16507	P0123	Throttle/Pedal Pos.Sensor A Circ High Input
16509	P0125	Insufficient Coolant Temp.for Closed Loop Fuel Control
16512	P0128	Coolant Thermostat/Valve Temperature below control range
16514	P0130	O2 Sensor Circ.,Bank1-Sensor1 Malfunction
16515	P0131	O2 Sensor Circ.,Bank1-Sensor1 Low Voltage
16516	P0132	O2 Sensor Circ.,Bank1-Sensor1 High Voltage
16517	P0133	O2 Sensor Circ.,Bank1-Sensor1 Slow Response
16518	P0134	O2 Sensor Circ.,Bank1-Sensor1 No Activity Detected
16519	P0135	O2 Sensor Heater Circ.,Bank1-Sensor1 Malfunction
16520	P0136	O2 Sensor Circ.,Bank1-Sensor2 Malfunction

Table a. Scan Tool Codes

DTC	P-code	Description
16521	P0137	O2 Sensor Circ.,Bank1-Sensor2 Low Voltage
16522	P0138	O2 Sensor Circ.,Bank1-Sensor2 High Voltage
16523	P0139	O2 Sensor Circ.,Bank1-Sensor2 Slow Response
16524	P0140	O2 Sensor Circ.,Bank1-Sensor2 No Activity Detected
16525	P0141	O2 Sensor Heater Circ.,Bank1-Sensor2 Malfunction
16534	P0150	O2 Sensor Circ.,Bank2-Sensor1 Malfunction
16535	P0151	O2 Sensor Circ.,Bank2-Sensor1 Low Voltage
16536	P0152	O2 Sensor Circ.,Bank2-Sensor1 High Voltage
16537	P0153	O2 Sensor Circ.,Bank2-Sensor1 Slow Response
16538	P0154	O2 Sensor Circ.,Bank2-Sensor1 No Activity Detected
16539	P0155	O2 Sensor Heater Circ.,Bank2-Sensor1 Malfunction
16540	P0156	O2 Sensor Circ.,Bank2-Sensor2 Malfunction
16541	P0157	O2 Sensor Circ.,Bank2-Sensor2 Low Voltage
16542	P0158	O2 Sensor Circ.,Bank2-Sensor2 High Voltage
16543	P0159	O2 Sensor Circ.,Bank2-Sensor2 Slow Response
16544	P0160	O2 Sensor Circ.,Bank2-Sensor2 No Activity Detected
16545	P0161	O2 Sensor Heater Circ.,Bank2-Sensor2 Malfunction
16554	P0170	Fuel Trim,Bank1 Malfunction
16555	P0171	Fuel Trim,Bank1 System too Lean
16556	P0172	Fuel Trim,Bank1 System too Rich
16557	P0173	Fuel Trim,Bank2 Malfunction
16558	P0174	Fuel Trim,Bank2 System too Lean
16559	P0175	Fuel Trim,Bank2 System too Rich
16566	P0182	Fuel temperature sender-G81 Short to ground
16567	P0183	Fuel temperature sender-G81 Interruption/Short to B+
16581	P0197	Engine Oil Temperature Circuit Low Input
16582	P0198	Engine Oil Temperature Circuit High Input
16585	P0201	Cyl.1, Injector Circuit Fault in electrical circuit
16586	P0202	Cyl.2, Injector Circuit Fault in electrical circuit
16587	P0203	Cyl.3, Injector Circuit Fault in electrical circuit
16588	P0204	Cyl.4, Injector Circuit Fault in electrical circuit
16589	P0205	Cyl.5 Injector Circuit Fault in electrical circuit
16590	P0206	Cyl.6 Injector Circuit Fault in electrical circuit
16591	P0207	Cyl.7 Injector Circuit Fault in electrical circuit
16592	P0208	Cyl.8 Injector Circuit Fault in electrical circuit

Table a. Scan Tool Codes

DTC	P-code	Description
16599	P0215	Engine Shut-Off Solenoid Malfunction
16600	P0216	Injector/Injection Timing Control Malfunction
16603	P0219	Engine Overspeed Condition
16605	P0221	Throttle Pos. Sensor -B- Circuit Range/Performance
16606	P0222	Throttle Pos. Sensor -B- Circuit Low Input
16607	P0223	Throttle Pos. Sensor -B- Circuit High Input
16609	P0225	Throttle Pos. Sensor -C- Circuit Voltage supply
16610	P0226	Throttle Pos. Sensor -C- Circuit Range/Performance
16611	P0227	Throttle Pos. Sensor -C- Circuit Low Input
16612	P0228	Throttle Pos. Sensor -C- Circuit Hight Input
16614	P0230	Fuel Pump Primary Circuit Fault in electrical circuit
16618	P0234	Turbocharger Overboost Condition Control limit exceeded
16619	P0235	Turbocharger Boost Sensor (A) Circ Control limit not reached
16620	P0236	Turbocharger Boost Sensor (A) Circ Range/Performance
16621	P0237	Turbocharger Boost Sensor (A) Circ Low Input
16622	P0238	Turbocharger Boost Sensor (A) Circ High Input
16627	P0243	Turbocharger Wastegate Solenoid (A) Open/Short Circuit to Ground
16629	P0245	Turbocharger Wastegate Solenoid (A) Low Input/Short to ground
16630	P0246	Turbocharger Wastegate Solenoid (A) High Input/Short to B+
16636	P0252	Injection Pump Metering Control (A) Range/Performance
16645	P0261	Cyl.1 Injector Circuit Low Input/Short to ground
16646	P0262	Cyl.1 Injector Circuit High Input/Short to B+
16648	P0264	Cyl.2 Injector Circuit Low Input/Short to ground
16649	P0265	Cyl.2 Injector Circuit High Input/Short to B+
16651	P0267	Cyl.3 Injector Circuit Low Input/Short to ground
16652	P0268	Cyl.3 Injector Circuit High Input/Short to B+
16654	P0270	Cyl.4 Injector Circuit Low Input/Short to ground
16655	P0271	Cyl.4 Injector Circuit High Input/Short to B+
16657	P0273	Cyl.5 Injector Circuit Low Input/Short to ground
16658	P0274	Cyl.5 Injector Circuit High Input/Short to B+
16660	P0276	Cyl.6 Injector Circuit Low Input/Short to ground
16661	P0277	Cyl.6 Injector Circuit High Input/Short to B+
16663	P0279	Cyl.7 Injector Circuit Low Input/Short to ground
16664	P0280	Cyl.7 Injector Circuit High Input/Short to B+
16666	P0282	Cyl.8 Injector Circuit Low Input/Short to ground

Table a. Scan Tool Codes

DTC	P-code	Description
16667	P0283	Cyl.8 Injector Circuit High Input/Short to B+
16684	P0300	Random/Multiple Cylinder Misfire Detected
16685	P0301	Cyl.1 Misfire Detected
16686	P0302	Cyl.2 Misfire Detected
16687	P0303	Cyl.3 Misfire Detected
16688	P0304	Cyl.4 Misfire Detected
16689	P0305	Cyl.5 Misfire Detected
16690	P0306	Cyl.6 Misfire Detected
16691	P0307	Cyl.7 Misfire Detected
16692	P0308	Cyl.8 Misfire Detected
16697	P0313	Misfire Detected Low Fuel Level
16698	P0314	Single Cylinder Misfire
16705	P0321	Ign./Distributor Eng.Speed Inp.Circ Range/Performance
16706	P0322	Ign./Distributor Eng.Speed Inp.Circ No Signal
16709	P0325	Knock Sensor 1 Circuit Electrical Fault in Circuit
16710	P0326	Knock Sensor 1 Circuit Range/Performance
16711	P0327	Knock Sensor 1 Circ Low Input
16712	P0328	Knock Sensor 1 Circ High Input
16716	P0332	Knock Sensor 2 Circ Low Input
16717	P0333	Knock Sensor 2 Circ High Input
16719	P0335	Crankshaft Pos. Sensor (A) Circ Malfunction
16720	P0336	Crankshaft Pos. Sensor (A) Circ Range/Performance/Missing tooth
16721	P0337	Crankshaft Pos.Sensor (A) Circ Low Input
16724	P0340	Camshaft Pos. Sensor (A) Circ Incorrect allocation
16725	P0341	Camshaft Pos.Sensor Circ Range/Performance
16726	P0342	Camshaft Pos.Sensor Circ Low Input
16727	P0343	Camshaft Pos.Sensor Circ High Input
16735	P0351	Ignition Coil (A) Cyl.1 Prim./Sec. Circ Malfunction
16736	P0352	Ignition Coil (B) Cyl.2 Prim./Sec. Circ Malfunction
16737	P0353	Ignition Coil (C) Cyl.3 Prim./Sec. Circ Malfunction
16738	P0354	Ignition Coil (D) Cyl.4 Prim./Sec. Circ Malfunction
16739	P0355	Ignition Coil (E) Cyl.5 Prim./Sec. Circ Malfunction
16740	P0356	Ignition Coil (F) Cyl.6 Prim./Sec. Circ Malfunction
16741	P0357	Ignition Coil (G) Cyl.7 Prim./Sec. Circ Malfunction
16742	P0358	Ignition Coil (H) Cyl.8 Prim./Sec. Circ Malfunction

Table a. Scan Tool Codes

DTC	P-code	Description
16764	P0380	Glow Plug/Heater Circuit (A) Electrical Fault in Circuit
16784	P0400	Exhaust Gas Recirc.Flow Malfunction
16785	P0401	Exhaust Gas Recirc.Flow Insufficient Detected
16786	P0402	Exhaust Gas Recirc.Flow Excessive Detected
16787	P0403	Exhaust Gas Recirc. Contr. Circ Malfunction
16788	P0404	Exhaust Gas Recirc. Contr. Circ Range/Performance
16789	P0405	Exhaust Gas Recirc. Sensor (A) Circ Low Input
16790	P0406	Exhaust Gas Recirc. Sensor (A) Circ High Input
16791	P0407	Exhaust Gas Recirc. Sensor (B) Circ Low Input
16792	P0408	Exhaust Gas Recirc. Sensor (B) Circ High Input
16794	P0410	Sec.Air Inj.Sys Malfunction
16795	P0411	Sec.Air Inj.Sys. Incorrect Flow Detected
16796	P0412	Sec.Air Inj.Sys.Switching Valve A Circ Malfunction
16802	P0418	Sec. Air Inj. Sys. Relay (A) Contr. Circ Malfunction
16804	P0420	Catalyst System,Bank1 Efficiency Below Threshold
16806	P0422	Main Catalyst,Bank1 Below Threshold
16811	P0427	Catalyst Temperature Sensor, Bank 1 Low Input/Short to ground
16812	P0428	Catalyst Temperature Sensor, Bank 1 High Input/Open/Short Circuit to B+
16816	P0432	Main Catalyst,Bank2 Efficiency Below Threshold
16820	P0436	Catalyst Temperature Sensor, Bank 2 Range/Performance
16821	P0437	Catalyst Temperature Sensor, Bank 2 Low Input/Short to ground
16822	P0438	Catalyst Temperature Sensor, Bank 2 High Input/Open/Short Circuit to B+
16824	P0440	EVAP Emission Contr.Sys. Malfunction
16825	P0441	EVAP Emission Contr.Sys.Incorrect Purge Flow
16826	P0442	EVAP Emission Contr.Sys.(Small Leak) Leak Detected
16827	P0443	EVAP Emiss. Contr. Sys. Purge Valve Circ Electrical Fault in Circuit
16836	P0452	EVAP Emission Contr.Sys.Press.Sensor Low Input
16837	P0453	EVAP Emission Contr.Sys.Press.Sensor High Input
16839	P0455	EVAP Emission Contr.Sys.(Gross Leak) Leak Detected
16845	P0461	Fuel Level Sensor Circ Range/Performance
16846	P0462	Fuel Level Sensor Circuit Low Input
16847	P0463	Fuel Level Sensor Circuit High Input
16885	P0501	Vehicle Speed Sensor Range/Performance
16887	P0503	Vehicle Speed Sensor Intermittent/Erratic/High Input
16889	P0505	Idle Control System Malfunction

Table a. Scan Tool Codes

DTC	P-code	Description
16890	P0506	Idle Control System RPM Lower than Expected
16891	P0507	Idle Control System Higher than Expected
16894	P0510	Closed Throttle Pos.Switch Malfunction
16915	P0531	A/C Refrigerant Pressure Sensor Circuit Range/Performance
16916	P0532	A/C Refrigerant Pressure Sensor Circuit Low Input
16917	P0533	A/C Refrigerant Pressure Sensor Circuit High Input
16935	P0551	Power Steering Pressure Sensor Circuit Range/Performance
16944	P0560	System Voltage Malfunction
16946	P0562	System Voltage Low Voltage
16947	P0563	System Voltage High Voltage
16952	P0568	Cruise Control Set Signal Incorrect Signal
16955	P0571	Cruise/Brake Switch (A) Circ Malfunction
16984	P0600	Serial Comm. Link (Data Bus) Message Missing
16985	P0601	Internal Contr.Module Memory Check Sum Error
16986	P0602	Control Module Programming Error/Malfunction
16987	P0603	Internal Contr.Module (KAM) Error
16988	P0604	Internal Contr.Module Random Access Memory (RAM) Error
16989	P0605	Internal Contr.Module ROM Test Error
16990	P0606	ECM/PCM Processor
17026	P0642	Knock Control Control Module Malfunction
17029	P0645	A/C Clutch Relay Control Circuit
17034	P0650	MIL Control Circuit Electrical Fault in Circuit
17038	P0654	Engine RPM Output Circuit Electrical Fault in Circuit
17040	P0656	Fuel Level Output Circuit Electrical Fault in Circuit
17084	P0700	Transm.Contr.System Malfunction
17086	P0702	Transm.Contr.System Electrical
17087	P0703	Torque Converter/Brake Switch B Circ Malfunction
17089	P0705	Transm.Range Sensor Circ.(PRNDL Inp.) Malfunction
17090	P0706	Transm.Range Sensor Circ Range/Performance
17091	P0707	Transm.Range Sensor Circ Low Input
17092	P0708	Transm.Range Sensor Circ High Input
17094	P0710	Transm.Fluid Temp.Sensor Circ. Malfunction
17095	P0711	Transm.Fluid Temp.Sensor Circ. Range/Performance
17096	P0712	Transm.Fluid Temp.Sensor Circ. Low Input
17097	P0713	Transm.Fluid Temp.Sensor Circ. High Input

Table a. Scan Tool Codes

DTC	P-code	Description
17099	P0715	Input Turbine/Speed Sensor Circ. Malfunction
17100	P0716	Input Turbine/Speed Sensor Circ. Range/Performance
17101	P0717	Input Turbine/Speed Sensor Circ. No Signal
17105	P0721	Output Speed Sensor Circ Range/Performance
17106	P0722	Output Speed Sensor Circ No Signal
17109	P0725	Engine Speed Inp.Circ. Malfunction
17110	P0726	Engine Speed Inp.Circ. Range/Performance
17111	P0727	Engine Speed Inp.Circ. No Signal
17114	P0730	Gear Incorrect Ratio
17115	P0731	Gear 1 Incorrect Ratio
17116	P0732	Gear 2 Incorrect Ratio
17117	P0733	Gear 3 Incorrect Ratio
17118	P0734	Gear 4 Incorrect Ratio
17119	P0735	Gear 5 Incorrect Ratio
17124	P0740	Torque Converter Clutch Circ Malfunction
17125	P0741	Torque Converter Clutch Circ Performance or Stuck Off
17132	P0748	Pressure Contr.Solenoid Electrical
17134	P0750	Shift Solenoid A malfunction
17135	P0751	Shift Solenoid A Performance or Stuck Off
17136	P0752	Shift Solenoid A Stuck On
17137	P0753	Shift Solenoid A Electrical
17140	P0756	Shift Solenoid B Performance or Stuck Off
17141	P0757	Shift Solenoid B Stuck On
17142	P0758	Shift Solenoid B Electrical
17145	P0761	Shift Solenoid C Performance or Stuck Off
17146	P0762	Shift Solenoid C Stuck On
17147	P0763	Shift Solenoid C Electrical
17152	P0768	Shift Solenoid D Electrical
17157	P0773	Shift Solenoid E Electrical
17174	P0790	Normal/Performance Switch Circ Malfunction
17509	P1101	O2 Sensor Circ.,Bank1-Sensor1Voltage too Low/Air Leak
17510	P1102	O2 Sensor Heating Circ.,Bank1-Sensor1 Short to B+
17511	P1103	O2 Sensor Heating Circ.,Bank1-Sensor1 Output too Low
17512	P1104	Bank1-Sensor2 Voltage too Low/Air Leak
17513	P1105	O2 Sensor Heating Circ.,Bank1-Sensor2 Short to B+

Table a. Scan Tool Codes

DTC	P-code	Description
17514	P1106	O2 Sensor Circ.,Bank2-Sensor1 Voltage too Low/Air Leak
17515	P1107	O2 Sensor Heating Circ.,Bank2-Sensor1 Short to B+
17516	P1108	O2 Sensor Heating Circ.,Bank2-Sensor1 Output too Low
17517	P1109	O2 Sensor Circ.,Bank2-Sensor2 Voltage too Low/Air Leak
17518	P1110	O2 Sensor Heating Circ.,Bank2-Sensor2 Short to B+
17519	P1111	O2 Control (Bank 1) System too lean
17520	P1112	O2 Control (Bank 1) System too rich
17521	P1113	Bank1-Sensor1 Internal Resistance too High
17522	P1114	Bank1-Sensor2 Internal Resistant too High
17523	P1115	O2 Sensor Heater Circ.,Bank1-Sensor1 Short to Ground
17524	P1116	O2 Sensor Heater Circ.,Bank1-Sensor1 Open
17525	P1117	O2 Sensor Heater Circ.,Bank1-Sensor2 Short to Ground
17526	P1118	O2 Sensor Heater Circ.,Bank1-Sensor2 Open
17527	P1119	O2 Sensor Heater Circ.,Bank2-Sensor1 Short to Ground
17528	P1120	O2 Sensor Heater Circ.,Bank2-Sensor1 Open
17529	P1121	O2 Sensor Heater Circ.,Bank2-Sensor2 Short to Ground
17530	P1122	O2 Sensor Heater Circ.,Bank2-Sensor2 Open
17531	P1123	Long Term Fuel Trim Add.Air.,Bank1 System too Rich
17532	P1124	Long Term Fuel Trim Add.Air.,Bank1 System too Lean
17533	P1125	Long Term Fuel Trim Add.Air.,Bank2 System too Rich
17534	P1126	Long Term Fuel Trim Add.Air.,Bank2 System too Lean
17535	P1127	Long Term Fuel Trim mult.,Bank1 System too Rich
17536	P1128	Long Term Fuel Trim mult.,Bank1 System too Lean
17537	P1129	Long Term Fuel Trim mult.,Bank2 System too Rich
17538	P1130	Long Term Fuel Trim mult.,Bank2 System too Lean
17539	P1131	Bank2-Sensor1 Internal Rsistance too High
17540	P1132	O2 Sensor Heating Circ.,Bank1+2-Sensor1 Short to B+
17541	P1133	O2 Sensor Heating Circ.,Bank1+2-Sensor1 Electrical Malfunction
17542	P1134	O2 Sensor Heating Circ.,Bank1+2-Sensor2 Short to B+
17543	P1135	O2 Sensor Heating Circ.,Bank1+2-Sensor2 Electrical Malfunction
17544	P1136	Long Term Fuel Trim Add.Fuel,Bank1 System too Lean
17545	P1137	Long Term Fuel Trim Add.Fuel,Bank1 System too Rich
17546	P1138	Long Term Fuel Trim Add.Fuel,Bank2 System too Lean
17547	P1139	Long Term Fuel Trim Add.Fuel,Bank2 System too Rich
17548	P1140	Bank2-Sensor2 Internal Resistance too High

Table a. Scan Tool Codes

DTC	P-code	Description
17549	P1141	Load Calculation Cross Check Range/Performance
17550	P1142	Load Calculation Cross Check Lower Limit Exceeded
17551	P1143	Load Calculation Cross Check Upper Limit Exceeded
17552	P1144	Mass or Volume Air Flow Circ Open/Short to Ground
17553	P1145	Mass or Volume Air Flow Circ Short to B+
17554	P1146	Mass or Volume Air Flow Circ Supply Malfunction
17555	P1147	O2 Control (Bank 2) System too lean
17556	P1148	O2 Control (Bank 2) System too rich
17557	P1149	O2 Control (Bank 1) Out of range
17558	P1150	O2 Control (Bank 2) Out of range
17559	P1151	Bank1, Long Term Fuel Trim, Range 1 Leanness Lower Limit Exceeded
17560	P1152	Bank1, Long Term Fuel Trim, Range 2 Leanness Lower Limit Exceeded
17562	P1154	Manifold Switch Over Malfunction
17563	P1155	Manifold Abs.Pressure Sensor Circ. Short to B+
17564	P1156	Manifold Abs.Pressure Sensor Circ. Open/Short to Ground
17565	P1157	Manifold Abs.Pressure Sensor Circ. Power Supply Malfunction
17566	P1158	Manifold Abs.Pressure Sensor Circ. Range/Performance
17568	P1160	Manifold Temp.Sensor Circ. Short to Ground
17569	P1161	Manifold Temp.Sensor Circ. Open/Short to B+
17570	P1162	Fuel Temp.Sensor Circ. Short to Ground
17571	P1163	Fuel Temp.Sensor Circ. Open/Short to B+
17572	P1164	Fuel Temperature Sensor Range/Performance/Incorrect Signal
17573	P1165	Bank1, Long Term Fuel Trim, Range 1 Rich Limit Exceeded
17574	P1166	Bank1, Long Term Fuel Trim, Range 2 Rich Limit Exceeded
17579	P1171	Throttle Actuation Potentiometer Sign.2 Range/Performance
17580	P1172	Throttle Actuation Potentiometer Sign.2 Signal too Low
17581	P1173	Throttle Actuation Potentiometer Sign.2 Signal too High
17582	P1174	Fuel Trim, Bank 1 Different injection times
17584	P1176	O2 Correction Behind Catalyst,B1 Limit Attained
17585	P1177	O2 Correction Behind Catalyst,B2 Limit Attained
17586	P1178	Linear 02 Sensor / Pump Current Open Circuit
17587	P1179	Linear 02 Sensor / Pump Current Short to ground
17588	P1180	Linear 02 Sensor / Pump Current Short to B+
17589	P1181	Linear 02 Sensor / Reference Voltage Open Circuit
17590	P1182	Linear 02 Sensor / Reference Voltage Short to ground

SCAN TOOL CODE TABLE

Table a. Scan Tool Codes

DTC	P-code	Description
17591	P1183	Linear 02 Sensor / Reference Voltage Short to B+
17592	P1184	Linear 02 Sensor / Common Ground Wire Open Circuit
17593	P1185	Linear 02 Sensor / Common Ground Wire Short to ground
17594	P1186	Linear 02 Sensor / Common Ground Wire Short to B+
17595	P1187	Linear 02 Sensor / Compens. Resistor Open Circuit
17596	P1188	Linear 02 Sensor / Compens. Resistor Short to ground
17597	P1189	Linear 02 Sensor / Compens. Resistor Short to B+
17598	P1190	Linear 02 Sensor / Reference Voltage Incorrect Signal
17604	P1196	O2 Sensor Heater Circ.,Bank1-Sensor1 Electrical Malfunction
17605	P1197	O2 Sensor Heater Circ.,Bank2-Sensor1 Electrical Malfunction
17606	P1198	O2 Sensor Heater Circ.,Bank1-Sensor2 Electrical Malfunction
17607	P1199	O2 Sensor Heater Circ.,Bank2-Sensor2 Electrical Malfunction
17609	P1201	Cyl.1-Fuel Inj.Circ. Electrical Malfunction
17610	P1202	Cyl.2-Fuel Inj.Circ. Electrical Malfunction
17611	P1203	Cyl.3-Fuel Inj.Circ. Electrical Malfunction
17612	P1204	Cyl.4-Fuel Inj.Circ. Electrical Malfunction
17613	P1205	Cyl.5-Fuel Inj.Circ. Electrical Malfunction
17614	P1206	Cyl.6-Fuel Inj.Circ. Electrical Malfunction
17615	P1207	Cyl.7-Fuel Inj.Circ. Electrical Malfunction
17616	P1208	Cyl.8-Fuel Inj.Circ. Electrical Malfunction
17617	P1209	Intake valves for cylinder shut-off Short circuit to ground
17618	P1210	Intake valves for cylinder shut-off Short to B+
17619	P1211	Intake valves for cylinder shut-off Open circuit
17621	P1213	Cyl.1-Fuel Inj.Circ. Short to B+
17622	P1214	Cyl.2-Fuel Inj.Circ. Short to B+
17623	P1215	Cyl.3-Fuel Inj.Circ. Short to B+
17624	P1216	Cyl.4-Fuel Inj.Circ. Short to B+
17625	P1217	Cyl.5-Fuel Inj.Circ. Short to B+
17626	P1218	Cyl.6-Fuel Inj.Circ. Short to B+
17627	P1219	Cyl.7-Fuel Inj.Circ. Short to B+
17628	P1220	Cyl.8-Fuel Inj.Circ. Short to B+
17629	P1221	Cylinder shut-off exhaust valves Short circuit to ground
17630	P1222	Cylinder shut-off exhaust valves Short to B+
17631	P1223	Cylinder shut-off exhaust valves Open circuit
17633	P1225	Cyl.1-Fuel Inj.Circ. Short to Ground

Table a. Scan Tool Codes

DTC	P-code	Description
17634	P1226	Cyl.2-Fuel Inj.Circ. Short to Ground
17635	P1227	Cyl.3-Fuel Inj.Circ. Short to Ground
17636	P1228	Cyl.4-Fuel Inj.Circ. Short to Ground
17637	P1229	Cyl.5-Fuel Inj.Circ. Short to Ground
17638	P1230	Cyl.6-Fuel Inj.Circ. Short to Ground
17639	P1231	Cyl.7-Fuel Inj.Circ. Short to Ground
17640	P1232	Cyl.8-Fuel Inj.Circ. Short to Ground
17645	P1237	Cyl.1-Fuel Inj.Circ. Open Circ.
17646	P1238	Cyl.2-Fuel Inj.Circ. Open Circ.
17647	P1239	Cyl.3-Fuel Inj.Circ. Open Circ.
17648	P1240	Cyl.4-Fuel Inj.Circ. Open Circ.
17649	P1241	Cyl.5-Fuel Inj.Circ. Open Circ.
17650	P1242	Cyl.6-Fuel Inj.Circ. Open Circ.
17651	P1243	Cyl.7-Fuel Inj.Circ. Open Circ.
17652	P1244	Cyl.8-Fuel Inj.Circ. Open Circ.
17653	P1245	Needle Lift Sensor Circ. Short to Ground
17654	P1246	Needle Lift Sensor Circ. Range/Performance
17655	P1247	Needle Lift Sensor Circ. Open/Short to B+
17656	P1248	Injection Start Control Deviation
17657	P1249	Fuel consumption signal Electrical Fault in Circuit
17658	P1250	Fuel Level Too Low
17659	P1251	Start of Injection Solenoid Circ Short to B+
17660	P1252	Start of Injection Solenoid Circ Open/Short to Ground
17661	P1253	Fuel consumption signal Short to ground
17662	P1254	Fuel consumption signal Short to B+
17663	P1255	Engine Coolant Temp.Circ Short to Ground
17664	P1256	Engine Coolant Temp.Circ Open/Short to B+
17665	P1257	Engine Coolant System Valve Open
17666	P1258	Engine Coolant System Valve Short to B+
17667	P1259	Engine Coolant System Valve Short to Ground
17688	P1280	Fuel Inj.Air Contr.Valve Circ. Flow too Low
17691	P1283	Fuel Inj.Air Contr.Valve Circ. Electrical Malfunction
17692	P1284	Fuel Inj.Air Contr.Valve Circ. Open
17693	P1285	Fuel Inj.Air Contr.Valve Circ. Short to Ground
17694	P1286	Fuel Inj.Air Contr.Valve Circ. Short to B+

Table a. Scan Tool Codes

DTC	P-code	Description
17695	P1287	Turbocharger bypass valve open
17696	P1288	Turbocharger bypass valve short to B+
17697	P1289	Turbocharger bypass valve short to ground
17704	P1296	Cooling system malfunction
17705	P1297	Connection turbocharger - throttle valve pressure hose
17708	P1300	Misfire detected Reason: Fuel level too low
17721	P1319	Knock Sensor 1 Circ. Short to Ground
17728	P1320	Knock Sensor 2 Circ. Short to Ground
17729	P1321	Knock Sensor 3 Circ. Low Input
17730	P1322	Knock Sensor 3 Circ. High Input
17731	P1323	Knock Sensor 4 Circ. Low Input
17732	P1324	Knock Sensor 4 Circ. High Input
17733	P1325	Cyl.1-Knock Contr. Limit Attained
17734	P1326	Cyl.2-Knock Contr. Limit Attained
17735	P1327	Cyl.3-Knock Contr. Limit Attained
17736	P1328	Cyl.4-Knock Contr. Limit Attained
17737	P1329	Cyl.5-Knock Contr. Limit Attained
17738	P1330	Cyl.6-Knock Contr. Limit Attained
17739	P1331	Cyl.7-Knock Contr. Limit Attained
17740	P1332	Cyl.8-Knock Contr. Limit Attained
17743	P1335	Engine Torque Monitoring 2 Control Limint Exceeded
17744	P1336	Engine Torque Monitoring Adaptation at limit
17745	P1337	Camshaft Pos.Sensor,Bank1 Short to Ground
17746	P1338	Camshaft Pos.Sensor,Bank1 Open Circ./Short to B+
17747	P1339	Crankshaft Pos./Engine Speed Sensor Cross Connected
17748	P1340	Crankshaft-/Camshaft Pos.Sens.Signals Out of Sequence
17749	P1341	Ignition Coil Power Output Stage 1 Short to Ground
17750	P1342	Ignition Coil Power Output Stage 1 Short to B+
17751	P1343	Ignition Coil Power Output Stage 2 Short to Ground
17752	P1344	Ignition Coil Power Output Stage 2 Short to B+
17753	P1345	Ignition Coil Power Output Stage 3 Short to Ground
17754	P1346	Ignition Coil Power Output Stage 3 Short to B+
17755	P1347	Bank2,Crankshaft-/Camshaft os.Sens.Sign. Out of Sequence
17756	P1348	Ignition Coil Power Output Stage 1 Open Circuit
17757	P1349	Ignition Coil Power Output Stage 2 Open Circuit

Table a. Scan Tool Codes

DTC	P-code	Description
17758	P1350	Ignition Coil Power Output Stage 3 Open Circuit
17762	P1354	Modulation Piston Displ.Sensor Circ. Malfunction
17763	P1355	Cyl. 1, ignition circuit Open Circuit
17764	P1356	Cyl. 1, ignition circuit Short to B+
17765	P1357	Cyl. 1, ignition circuit Short to ground
17766	P1358	Cyl. 2, ignition circuit Open Circuit
17767	P1359	Cyl. 2, ignition circuit Short Circuit to B+
17768	P1360	Cyl. 2, ignition circuit Short Circuit to Ground
17769	P1361	Cyl. 3, ignition circuit Open Circuit
17770	P1362	Cyl. 3, ignition circuit Short Circuit to B+
17771	P1363	Cyl. 3, ignition circuit Short Circuit to ground
17772	P1364	Cyl. 4 ignition circuit Open Circuit
17773	P1365	Cyl. 4 ignition circuit Short circuit to B+
17774	P1366	Cyl. 4 ignition circuit Short circuit to ground
17775	P1367	Cyl. 5, ignition circuit Open Circuit
17776	P1368	Cyl. 5, ignition circuit Short Circuit to B+
17777	P1369	Cyl. 5, ignition circuit short to ground
17778	P1370	Cyl. 6, ignition circuit Open Circuit
17779	P1371	Cyl. 6, ignition circuit Short Circuit to B+
17780	P1372	Cyl. 6, ignition circuit short to ground
17781	P1373	Cyl. 7, ignition circuit Open Circuit
17782	P1374	Cyl. 7, ignition circuit Short Circuit to B+
17783	P1375	Cyl. 7, ignition circuit short to ground
17784	P1376	Cyl. 8, ignition circuit Open Circuit
17785	P1377	Cyl. 8, ignition circuit Short Circuit to B+
17786	P1378	Cyl. 8, ignition circuit short to ground
17794	P1386	Internal Control Module Knock Control Circ.Error
17795	P1387	Internal Contr. Module altitude sensor error
17796	P1388	Internal Contr. Module drive by wire error
17799	P1391	Camshaft Pos.Sensor,Bank2 Short to Ground
17800	P1392	Camshaft Pos.Sensor,Bank2 Open Circ./Short to B+
17801	P1393	Ignition Coil Power Output Stage 1 Electrical Malfunction
17802	P1394	Ignition Coil Power Output Stage 2 Electrical Malfunction
17803	P1395	Ignition Coil Power Output Stage 3 Electrical Malfunction
17804	P1396	Engine Speed Sensor Missing Tooth

Table a. Scan Tool Codes

DTC	P-code	Description
17805	P1397	Engine speed wheel Adaptation limit reached
17806	P1398	Engine RPM signal, TD Short to ground
17807	P1399	Engine RPM signal, TD Short Circuit to B+
17808	P1400	EGR Valve Circ Electrical Malfunction
17809	P1401	EGR Valve Circ Short to Ground
17810	P1402	EGR Valve Circ Short to B+
17811	P1403	EGR Flow Deviation
17812	P1404	EGR Flow Basic Setting not carried out
17814	P1406	EGR Temp.Sensor Range/Performance
17815	P1407	EGR Temp.Sensor Signal too Low
17816	P1408	EGR Temp.Sensor Signal too High
17817	P1409	Tank Ventilation Valve Circ. Electrical Malfunction
17818	P1410	Tank Ventilation Valve Circ. Short to B+
17819	P1411	Sec.Air Inj.Sys.,Bank2 Flow too Flow
17820	P1412	EGR Different.Pressure Sensor Signal too Low
17821	P1413	EGR Different.Pressure Sensor Signal too High
17822	P1414	Sec.Air Inj.Sys.,Bank2 Leak Detected
17825	P1417	Fuel Level Sensor Circ Signal too Low
17826	P1418	Fuel Level Sensor Circ Signal too High
17828	P1420	Sec.Air Inj.Valve Circ Electrical Malfunction
17829	P1421	Sec.Air Inj.Valve Circ Short to Ground
17830	P1422	Sec.Air Inj.Sys.Contr.Valve Circ Short to B+
17831	P1423	Sec.Air Inj.Sys.,Bank1 Flow too Low
17832	P1424	Sec.Air Inj.Sys.,Bank1 Leak Detected
17833	P1425	Tank Vent.Valve Short to Ground
17834	P1426	Tank Vent.Valve Open
17840	P1432	Sec.Air Inj.Valve Open
17841	P1433	Sec.Air Inj.Sys.Pump Relay Circ. open
17842	P1434	Sec.Air Inj.Sys.Pump Relay Circ. Short to B+
17843	P1435	Sec.Air Inj.Sys.Pump Relay Circ. Short to ground
17844	P1436	Sec.Air Inj.Sys.Pump Relay Circ. Electrical Malfunction
17847	P1439	EGR Potentiometer Error in Basic Seting
17848	P1440	EGR Valve Power Stage Open
17849	P1441	EGR Valve Circ Open/Short to Ground
17850	P1442	EGR Valve Position Sensor Signal too high

Table a. Scan Tool Codes

DTC	P-code	Description
17851	P1443	EGR Valve Position Sensor Signal too low
17852	P1444	EGR Valve Position Sensor range/performance
17853	P1445	Catalyst Temp.Sensor 2 Circ. Range/Performance
17854	P1446	Catalyst Temp.Circ Short to Ground
17855	P1447	Catalyst Temp.Circ Open/Short to B+
17856	P1448	Catalyst Temp.Sensor 2 Circ. Short to Ground
17857	P1449	Catalyst Temp.Sensor 2 Circ. Open/Short to B+
17858	P1450	Sec.Air Inj.Sys.Circ Short to B+
17859	P1451	Sec.Air Inj.Sys.Circ Short to Ground
17860	P1452	Sec.Air Inj.Sys. Open Circ.
17861	P1453	Exhaust gas temperature sensor 1 open/short to B+
17862	P1454	Exhaust gas temperature sensor short 1 to ground
17863	P1455	Exhaust gas temperature sensor 1 range/performance
17864	P1456	Exhaust gas temperature control bank 1 limit attained
17865	P1457	Exhaust gas temperature sensor 2 open/short to B+
17866	P1458	Exhaust gas temperature sensor 2 short to ground
17867	P1459	Exhaust gas temperature sensor 2 range/performance
17868	P1460	Exhaust gas temperature control bank 2 limit attained
17869	P1461	Exhaust gas temperature control bank 1 Range/Performance
17870	P1462	Exhaust gas temperature control bank 2 Range/Performance
17873	P1465	Additive Pump Short Circuit to B+
17874	P1466	Additive Pump Open/Short to Ground
17875	P1467	EVAP Canister Purge Solenoid Valve Short Circuit to B+
17876	P1468	EVAP Canister Purge Solenoid Valve Short Circuit to Ground
17877	P1469	EVAP Canister Purge Solenoid Valve Open Circuit
17878	P1470	EVAP Emission Contr.LDP Circ Electrical Malfunction
17879	P1471	EVAP Emission Contr.LDP Circ Short to B+
17880	P1472	EVAP Emission Contr.LDP Circ Short to Ground
17881	P1473	EVAP Emission Contr.LDP Circ Open Circ.
17882	P1474	EVAP Canister Purge Solenoid Valve electrical malfunction
17883	P1475	EVAP Emission Contr.LDP Circ Malfunction/Signal Circ.Open
17884	P1476	EVAP Emission Contr.LDP Circ Malfunction/Insufficient Vacuum
17885	P1477	EVAP Emission Contr.LDP Circ Malfunction
17886	P1478	EVAP Emission Contr.LDP Circ Clamped Tube Detected
17908	P1500	Fuel Pump Relay Circ. Electrical Malfunction

SCAN TOOL CODE TABLE

Table a. Scan Tool Codes

DTC	P-code	Description
17909	P1501	Fuel Pump Relay Circ. Short to Ground
17910	P1502	Fuel Pump Relay Circ. Short to B+
17911	P1503	Load signal from Alternator Term. DF Range/performance/Incorrect Signal
17912	P1504	Intake Air Sys.Bypass Leak Detected
17913	P1505	Closed Throttle Pos. Does Not Close/Open Circ
17914	P1506	Closed Throttle Pos.Switch Does Not Open/Short to Ground
17915	P1507	Idle Sys.Learned Value Lower Limit Attained
17916	P1508	Idle Sys.Learned Value Upper Limit Attained
17917	P1509	Idle Air Control Circ. Electrical Malfunction
17918	P1510	Idle Air Control Circ. Short to B+
17919	P1511	Intake Manifold Changeover Valve circuit electrical malfunction
17920	P1512	Intake Manifold Changeover Valve circuit Short to B+
17921	P1513	Intake Manifold Changeover Valve2 circuit Short to B+
17922	P1514	Intake Manifold Changeover Valve2 circuit Short to ground
17923	P1515	Intake Manifold Changeover Valve circuit Short to Ground
17924	P1516	Intake Manifold Changeover Valve circuit Open
17925	P1517	Main Relay Circ. Electrical Malfunction
17926	P1518	Main Relay Circ. Short to B+
17927	P1519	Intake Camshaft Contr.,Bank1 Malfunction
17928	P1520	Intake Manifold Changeover Valve2 circuit Open
17929	P1521	Intake Manifold Changeover Valve2 circuit electrical malfunction
17930	P1522	Intake Camshaft Contr.,Bank2 Malfunction
17931	P1523	Crash Signal from Airbag Control Unit range/performance
17933	P1525	Intake Camshaft Contr.Circ.,Bank1 Electrical Malfunction
17934	P1526	Intake Camshaft Contr.Circ.,Bank1 Short to B+
17935	P1527	Intake Camshaft Contr.Circ.,Bank1 Short to Ground
17936	P1528	Intake Camshaft Contr.Circ.,Bank1 Open
17937	P1529	Camshaft Control Circuit Short to B+
17938	P1530	Camshaft Control Circuit Short to ground
17939	P1531	Camshaft Control Circuit open
17941	P1533	Intake Camshaft Contr.Circ.,Bank2 Electrical Malfunction
17942	P1534	Intake Camshaft Contr.Circ.,Bank2 Short to B+
17943	P1535	Intake Camshaft Contr.Circ.,Bank2 Short to Ground
17944	P1536	Intake Camshaft Contr.Circ.,Bank2 Open
17945	P1537	Engine Shutoff Solenoid Malfunction

Table a. Scan Tool Codes

DTC	P-code	Description
17946	P1538	Engine Shutoff Solenoid Open/Short to Ground
17947	P1539	Clutch Vacuum Vent Valve Switch Incorrect signal
17948	P1540	Vehicle Speed Sensor High Input
17949	P1541	Fuel Pump Relay Circ Open
17950	P1542	Throttle Actuation Potentiometer Range/Performance
17951	P1543	Throttle Actuation Potentiometer Signal too Low
17952	P1544	Throttle Actuation Potentiometer Signal too High
17953	P1545	Throttle Pos.Contr Malfunction
17954	P1546	Boost Pressure Contr.Valve Short to B+
17955	P1547	Boost Pressure Contr.Valve Short to Ground
17956	P1548	Boost Pressure Contr.Valve Open
17957	P1549	Boost Pressure Contr.Valve Short to Ground
17958	P1550	Charge Pressure Deviation
17959	P1551	Barometric Pressure Sensor Circ. Short to B+
17960	P1552	Barometric Pressure Sensor Circ. Open/Short to Ground
17961	P1553	Barometric/manifold pressure signal ratio out of range
17962	P1554	Idle Speed Contr.Throttle Pos. Basic Setting Conditions not met
17963	P1555	Charge Pressure Upper Limit exceeded
17964	P1556	Charge Pressure Contr. Negative Deviation
17965	P1557	Charge Pressure Contr. Positive Deviation
17966	P1558	Throttle Actuator Electrical Malfunction
17967	P1559	Idle Speed Contr.Throttle Pos. Adaptation Malfunction
17968	P1560	Maximum Engine Speed Exceeded
17969	P1561	Quantity Adjuster Deviation
17970	P1562	Quantity Adjuster Upper Limit Attained
17971	P1563	Quantity Adjuster Lower Limit Attained
17972	P1564	Idle Speed Contr.Throttle Pos. Low Voltage During Adaptation
17973	P1565	Idle Speed Control Throttle Position lower limit not attained
17974	P1566	Load signal from A/C compressor range/performance
17975	P1567	Load signal from A/C compressor no signal
17976	P1568	Idle Speed Contr.Throttle Pos. mechanical Malfunction
17977	P1569	Cruise control switch Incorrect signal
17978	P1570	Contr.Module Locked
17979	P1571	Left Eng. Mount Solenoid Valve Short to B+
17980	P1572	Left Eng. Mount Solenoid Valve Short to ground

Table a. Scan Tool Codes

DTC	P-code	Description
17981	P1573	Left Eng. Mount Solenoid Valve Open circuit
17982	P1574	Left Eng. Mount Solenoid Valve Electrical fault in circuit
17983	P1575	Right Eng. Mount Solenoid Valve Short to B+
17984	P1576	Right Eng. Mount Solenoid Valve Short to ground
17985	P1577	Right Eng. Mount Solenoid Valve Open circuit
17986	P1578	Right Eng. Mount Solenoid Valve Electrical fault in circuit
17987	P1579	Idle Speed Contr.Throttle Pos. Adaptation not started
17988	P1580	Throttle Actuator B1 Malfunction
17989	P1581	Idle Speed Contr.Throttle Pos. Basic Setting Not Carried Out
17990	P1582	Idle Adaptation at Limit
17991	P1583	Transmission mount valves Short to B+
17992	P1584	Transmission mount valves Short to ground
17993	P1585	Transmission mount valves Open circuit
17994	P1586	Engine mount solenoid valves Short to B+
17995	P1587	Engine mount solenoid valves Short to ground
17996	P1588	Engine mount solenoid valves Open circuit
18008	P1600	Power Supply (B+) Terminal 15 Low Voltage
18010	P1602	Power Supply (B+) Terminal 30 Low Voltage
18011	P1603	Internal Control Module Malfunction
18012	P1604	Internal Control Module Driver Error
18013	P1605	Rough Road/Acceleration Sensor Electrical Malfunction
18014	P1606	Rough Road Spec Engine Torque ABS-ECU Electrical Malfunction
18015	P1607	Vehicle speed signal Error message from instrument cluster
18016	P1608	Steering angle signal Error message from steering angle sensor
18017	P1609	Crash shut-down activated
18019	P1611	MIL Call-up Circ./Transm.Contr.Module Short to Ground
18020	P1612	Electronic Control Module Incorrect Coding
18021	P1613	MIL Call-up Circ Open/Short to B+
18022	P1614	MIL Call-up Circ./Transm.Contr.Module Range/Performance
18023	P1615	Engine Oil Temperature Sensor Circuit range/performance
18024	P1616	Glow Plug/Heater Indicator Circ. Short to B+
18025	P1617	Glow Plug/Heater Indicator Circ. Open/Short to Ground
18026	P1618	Glow Plug/Heater Relay Circ. Short to B+
18027	P1619	Glow Plug/Heater Relay Circ. Open/Short to Ground
18028	P1620	Engine coolant temperature signal open/short to B+

Table a. Scan Tool Codes

DTC	P-code	Description
18029	P1621	Engine coolant temperature signal short to ground
18030	P1622	Engine coolant temperature signal range/performance
18031	P1623	Data Bus Powertrain No Communication
18032	P1624	MIL Request Sign.active
18033	P1625	Data-Bus Powertrain Unplausible Message from Transm.Contr.
18034	P1626	Data-Bus Powertrain Missing Message from Transm.Contr.
18035	P1627	Data-Bus Powertrain missing message from fuel injection pump
18036	P1628	Data-Bus Powertrain missing message from steering sensor
18037	P1629	Data-Bus Powertrain missing message from distance control
18038	P1630	Accelera.Pedal Pos.Sensor 1 Signal too Low
18039	P1631	Accelera.Pedal Pos.Sensor 1 Signal too High
18040	P1632	Accelera.Pedal Pos.Sensor 1 Power Supply Malfunction
18041	P1633	Accelera.Pedal Pos.Sensor 2 Signal too Low
18042	P1634	Accelera.Pedal Pos.Sensor 2 Signal too High
18043	P1635	Data Bus Powertrain missing message f.air condition control
18044	P1636	Data Bus Powertrain missing message from Airbag control
18045	P1637	Data Bus Powertrain missing message f.central electr.control
18046	P1638	Data Bus Powertrain missing message from clutch control
18047	P1639	Accelera.Pedal Pos.Sensor 1+2 Range/Performance
18048	P1640	Internal Contr.Module (EEPROM) Error
18049	P1641	Please check DTC Memory of Air Condition ECU
18050	P1642	Please check DTC Memory of Airbag ECU
18051	P1643	Please check DTC Memory of central electric ECU
18052	P1644	Please check DTC Memory of clutch ECU
18053	P1645	Data Bus Powertrain missing message f.all wheel drive contr.
18054	P1646	Please Check DTC Memory of all wheel drive ECU
18055	P1647	Please check coding of ECUs in Data Bus Powertrain
18056	P1648	Data Bus Powertrain Malfunction
18057	P1649	Data Bus Powertrain Missing message from ABS Control Module
18058	P1650	Data Bus Powertrain Missing message fr.instrument panel ECU
18059	P1651	Data Bus Powertrain missing messages
18060	P1652	Please check DTC Memory of transmission ECU
18061	P1653	Please check DTC Memory of ABS Control Module
18062	P1654	Please check DTC Memory of control panel ECU
18063	P1655	Please check DTC Memory of ADR Control Module

Table a. Scan Tool Codes

DTC	P-code	Description
18064	P1656	A/C clutch relay circuit short to ground
18065	P1657	A/C clutch relay circuit short to B+
18066	P1658	Data Bus Powertrain Incorrect signal from ADR Control Module
18084	P1676	Drive by Wire-MIL Circ. Electrical Malfunction
18085	P1677	Drive by Wire-MIL Circ. Short to B+
18086	P1678	Drive by Wire-MIL Circ. Short to Ground
18087	P1679	Drive by Wire-MIL Circ. Open
18089	P1681	Contr.Unit Programming, Programming not Finished
18092	P1684	Contr.Unit Programming Communication Error
18094	P1686	Contr.Unit Error Programming Error
18098	P1690	Malfunction Indication Light Malfunction
18099	P1691	Malfunction Indication Light Open
18100	P1692	Malfunction Indication Light Short to Ground
18101	P1693	Malfunction Indication Light Short to B+
18102	P1694	Malfunction Indication Light Open/Short to Ground
18112	P1704	Kick Down Switch Malfunction
18113	P1705	Gear/Ratio Monitoring Adaptation limit reached
18119	P1711	Wheel Speed Signal 1 Range/Performance
18124	P1716	Wheel Speed Signal 2 Range/Performance
18129	P1721	Wheel Speed Signal 3 Range/Performance
18131	P1723	Starter Interlock Circ. Open
18132	P1724	Starter Interlock Circ. Short to Ground
18134	P1726	Wheel Speed Signal 4 Range/Performance
18136	P1728	Different Wheel Speed Signals Range/Performance
18137	P1729	Starter Interlock Circ. Short to B+
18141	P1733	Tiptronic Switch Down Circ. Short to Ground
18147	P1739	Tiptronic Switch up Circ. Short to Ground
18148	P1740	Clutch temperature control
18149	P1741	Clutch pressure adaptation at limit
18150	P1742	Clutch torque adaptation at limit
18151	P1743	Clutch slip control signal too high
18152	P1744	Tiptronic Switch Recognition Circ. Short to Ground
18153	P1745	Transm.Contr.Unit Relay Short to B+
18154	P1746	Transm.Contr.Unit Relay Malfunction
18155	P1747	Transm.Contr.Unit Relay Open/Short to Ground

Table a. Scan Tool Codes

DTC	P-code	Description
18156	P1748	Transm.Contr.Unit Self-Check
18157	P1749	Transm.Contr.Unit Incorrect Coded
18158	P1750	Power Supply Voltage Low Voltage
18159	P1751	Power Supply Voltage High Voltage
18160	P1752	Power Supply Malfunction
18168	P1760	Shift Lock Malfunction
18169	P1761	Shift Lock Short to Ground
18170	P1762	Shift Lock Short to B+
18171	P1763	Shift Lock Open
18172	P1764	Transmission temperature control
18173	P1765	Hydraulic Pressure Sensor 2 adaptation at limit
18174	P1766	Throttle Angle Signal Stuck Off
18175	P1767	Throttle Angle Signal Stuck On
18176	P1768	Hydraulic Pressure Sensor 2 Too High
18177	P1769	Hydraulic Pressure Sensor 2 Too Low
18178	P1770	Load Signal Range/Performance
18179	P1771	Load Signal Stuck Off
18180	P1772	Load Signal Stuck On
18181	P1773	Hydraulic Pressure Sensor 1 Too High
18182	P1774	Hydraulic Pressure Sensor 1 Too Low
18183	P1775	Hydraulic Pressure Sensor 1 adaptation at limit
18184	P1776	Hydraulic Pressure Sensor 1 range/performance
18185	P1777	Hydraulic Pressure Sensor 2 range/performance
18186	P1778	Solenoid EV7 Electrical Malfunction
18189	P1781	Engine Torque Reduction Open/Short to Ground
18190	P1782	Engine Torque Reduction Short to B+
18192	P1784	Shift up/down Wire Open/Short to Ground
18193	P1785	Shift up/down Wire Short to B+
18194	P1786	Reversing Light Circ. Open
18195	P1787	Reversing Light Circ. Short to Ground
18196	P1788	Reversing Light Circ. Short to B+
18197	P1789	Idle Speed Intervention Circ. Error Message from Engine Contr.
18198	P1790	Transmission Range Display Circ. Open
18199	P1791	Transmission Range Display Circ. Short to Ground
18200	P1792	Transmission Range Display Circ. Short to B+

SCAN TOOL CODE TABLE

Table a. Scan Tool Codes

DTC	P-code	Description
18201	P1793	Output Speed Sensor 2 Circ. No Signal
18203	P1795	Vehicle Speed Signal Circ. Open
18204	P1796	Vehicle Speed Signal Circ. Short to Ground
18205	P1797	Vehicle Speed Signal Circ. Short to B+
18206	P1798	Output Speed Sensor 2 Circ. Range/Performance
18207	P1799	Output Speed Sensor 2 Circ. Rpm too High
18221	P1813	Pressure Contr.Solenoid 1 Electrical
18222	P1814	Pressure Contr.Solenoid 1 Open/Short to Ground
18223	P1815	Pressure Contr.Solenoid 1 Short to B+
18226	P1818	Pressure Contr.Solenoid 2 Electrical
18227	P1819	Pressure Contr.Solenoid 2 Open/Short to Ground
18228	P1820	Pressure Contr.Solenoid 2 Short to B+
18231	P1823	Pressure Contr.Solenoid 3 Electrical
18232	P1824	Pressure Contr.Solenoid 3 Open/Short to Ground
18233	P1825	Pressure Contr.Solenoid 3 Short to B+
18236	P1828	Pressure Contr.Solenoid 4 Electrical
18237	P1829	Pressure Contr.Solenoid 4 Open/Short to Ground
18238	P1830	Pressure Contr.Solenoid 4 Short to B+
18242	P1834	Pressure Contr.Solenoid 5 Open/Short to Ground
18243	P1835	Pressure Contr.Solenoid 5 Short to B+
18249	P1841	Engine/Transmission Control Modules Versions do not match
18250	P1842	Please check DTC Memory of instrument panel ECU
18251	P1843	Please check DTC Memory of ADR Control Module
18252	P1844	Please check DTC Memory of central electric control ECU
18255	P1847	Please check DTC Memory of brake system ECU
18256	P1848	Please check DTC Memory of engine ECU
18257	P1849	Please check DTC Memory of transmission ECU
18258	P1850	Data-Bus Powertrain Missing Message from Engine Contr.
18259	P1851	Data-Bus Powertrain Missing Message from Brake Contr.
18260	P1852	Data-Bus Powertrain Unplausible Message from Engine Contr.
18261	P1853	Data-Bus Powertrain Unplausible Message from Brake Contr.
18262	P1854	Data-Bus Powertrain Hardware Defective
18263	P1855	Data-Bus Powertrain Software version Contr.
18264	P1856	Throttle/Pedal Pos.Sensor A Circ. Error Message from Engine Contr.
18265	P1857	Load Signal Error Message from Engine Contr.

Table a. Scan Tool Codes

DTC	P-code	Description
18266	P1858	Engine Speed Input Circ. Error Message from Engine Contr.
18267	P1859	Brake Switch Circ. Error Message from Engine Contr.
18268	P1860	Kick Down Switch Error Message from Engine Contr.
18269	P1861	Throttle Position (TP) sensor Error Message from ECM
18270	P1862	Data Bus Powertrain Missing message from instr. panel ECU
18271	P1863	Data Bus Powertrain Missing Message from St. Angle Sensor
18272	P1864	Data Bus Powertrain Missing message from ADR control module
18273	P1865	Data Bus Powertrain Missing message from central electronics
18274	P1866	Data Bus Powertrain Missing messages

AFTERMARKET SUPPLIERS OF DIAGNOSTIC SCAN TOOLS

NOTE —
The following suppliers offer diagnostic scan tools that can be used to retrieve scan tool codes as listed in the table above.

Assenmacher Specialty Tools, Inc.
6440 Odell Place
Boulder, CO 80301
(800)525-2943
www.asttool.com

Baum Tools Unlimited, Inc.
PO Box 5867
Sarasota, FL 34277
(800)848-6657
www.baumtools.com

Mac Tools
4635 Hilton Corporate Drive
Columbus, OH 43232
(800)622-8655
www.mactools.com

Ross-Tech
888 Sumneytown Pike
Lansdale, PA 19446
215-361-8942
www.ross-tech.com

Snap-On Technologies, Inc.
2801 80th St.
Kenosha, WI 53141-1410
(262)656-5200
www.snapon.com

WARNING

Your common sense, good judgement, and general alertness are crucial to safe and successful service work. Before attempting any work on your VW, read the warnings and cautions on page vii and the copyright page at the front of the manual. Review these warnings and cautions each time you prepare to work on your VW. Please also read any warnings and cautions that accompany the procedures in the manual.

A

B

WARNING

Your common sense, good judgement, and general alertness are crucial to safe and successful service work. Before attempting any work on your VW, read the warnings and cautions on page vii and the copyright page at the front of the manual. Review these warnings and cautions each time you prepare to work on your VW. Please also read any warnings and cautions that accompany the procedures in the manual.

WARNING

Your common sense, good judgement, and general alertness are crucial to safe and successful service work. Before attempting any work on your VW, read the warnings and cautions on page vii and the copyright page at the front of the manual. Review these warnings and cautions each time you prepare to work on your VW. Please also read any warnings and cautions that accompany the procedures in the manual.

> **WARNING**
>
> *Your common sense, good judgement, and general alertness are crucial to safe and successful service work. Before attempting any work on your VW, read the warnings and cautions on page vii and the copyright page at the front of the manual. Review these warnings and cautions each time you prepare to work on your VW. Please also read any warnings and cautions that accompany the procedures in the manual.*

WARNING

Your common sense, good judgement, and general alertness are crucial to safe and successful service work. Before attempting any work on your VW, read the warnings and cautions on page vii and the copyright page at the front of the manual. Review these warnings and cautions each time you prepare to work on your VW. Please also read any warnings and cautions that accompany the procedures in the manual.